Merriam-Webster's
Spanish-English
Dictionary

Merriam-Webster's Spanish-English Dictionary

MERRIAM-WEBSTER, INCORPORATED
Springfield, Massachusetts, U.S.A.

A GENUINE MERRIAM-WEBSTER

Copyright © 2016 by Merriam-Webster, Incorporated

ISBN 978-0-87779-824-8

Merriam-Webster's Spanish-English Dictionary, principal copyright 1998

Printed in India

6th Printing Thomson Press India Ltd. Faridabad June 2020 DBS

Contents   Índice

Preface

MERRIAM-WEBSTER'S SPANISH-ENGLISH DICTIONARY is a completely new dictionary designed to meet the needs of English and Spanish speakers in a time of ever-expanding communication among the countries of the Western Hemisphere. It is intended for language learners, teachers, office workers, tourists, business travelers—anyone who needs to communicate effectively in the Spanish and English languages as they are spoken and written in the Americas. This new dictionary provides accurate and up-to-date coverage of current vocabulary in both languages, as well as abundant examples of words used in context to illustrate idiomatic usage. The selection of Spanish words and idioms was based on evidence drawn from a wide variety of modern Latin-American sources and interpreted by trained Merriam-Webster bilingual lexicographers. The English entries were chosen by Merriam-Webster editors from the most recent Merriam-Webster dictionaries, and they represent the current basic vocabulary of American English.

All of this material is presented in a format which is based firmly upon and, in many important ways, is similar to the traditional styling found in the Merriam-Webster monolingual dictionaries. The reader who is familiar with Merriam-Webster dictionaries will immediately recognize this style, with its emphasis on convenience and ease of use, clarity and conciseness of the information presented, precise discrimination of senses, and frequent inclusion of example phrases showing words in actual use. Other features include pronunciations (in the International Phonetic Alphabet) for all English words, full coverage of irregular verbs in both languages, a section on basic Spanish grammar, tables of the most common Spanish and English abbreviations, and a detailed Explanatory Notes section which answers any questions the reader might have concerning the use of this book.

Merriam-Webster's Spanish-English Dictionary represents the combined efforts of many members of the Merriam-Webster Editorial Department, along with advice and assistance from consultants outside the company. The primary defining work was done by Charlene M. Chateauneuf, Seán O'Mannion-Espejo, Karen L. Wilkinson, and Jocelyn Woods; early contributions to the text were also submitted by Cèsar Alegre, Hilton Alers, Marién Díaz, Anne Gatschet, and María D. Guijarro, with Victoria E. Neufeldt, Ph.D., and James L. Rader providing helpful suggestions regarding style. Proofreading was done by Susan L. Brady, Daniel B. Brandon, Charlene M. Chateauneuf, Deanna Stathis Chiasson, Seán O'Mannion-Espejo, James L. Rader, Donna L. Rickerby, Adrienne

M. Scholz, Amy West, Karen L. Wilkinson, and Linda Picard Wood. Brian M. Sietsema, Ph.D., provided the pronunciations. Cross-reference services were provided by Donna L. Rickerby. Karen L. Levister assisted in inputting revisions. Carol Fugiel contributed many hours of clerical assistance and other valuable support. The editorial work relating to typesetting and production was begun by Jennifer S. Goss and continued by Susan L. Brady, who also offered helpful suggestions regarding format. Madeline L. Novak provided guidance on typographic matters. John M. Morse was responsible for the conception of this book as well as for numerous ideas and continued support along the way.

Eileen M. Haraty
Editor
2003

This new revision of *Merriam-Webster's Spanish-English Dictionary* includes more than 4,600 new vocabulary terms, as well as updates to more than 6,000 entries. It also incorporates significantly expanded coverage in more than 700 of the entries for the most essential English and Spanish vocabulary. Included in this expanded coverage are many additional senses, thousands of new examples showing how the words are typically used in context, and more than 2,000 common idioms and phrasal verbs in which these essential words often appear.

Many members of the Merriam-Webster editorial staff contributed to this update. Susan L. Brady assisted with the initial vocabulary selection. Tasha Martino Bigelow did most of the primary defining that laid the project's groundwork. Additional defining and preliminary editing were done by Paul S. Wood. Editors Bigelow and Wood also did much of the proofreading. Joshua S. Guenter, Ph.D., provided the pronunciations. Data file management was performed by Daniel B. Brandon, with advice and assistance from Robert D. Copeland. Mark A. Stevens coordinated with outside consultants, oversaw the book's typesetting and final production, and advised on a variety of related matters. Madeline L. Novak provided editorial guidance and support throughout the course of the project. Company president John M. Morse assisted in planning and scheduling the update, and also provided general guidance and support.

Karen L. Wilkinson
Editor
2016

Prefacio

El DICCIONARIO ESPAÑOL-INGLÉS MERRIAM-WEBSTER es un diccionario completamente nuevo, diseñado con el fin de satisfacer las necesidades de lenguaje de angloparlantes e hispanoparlantes en una era de continuo crecimiento en la comunicación entre los países del hemisferio occidental. El diccionario está destinado a los estudiantes de estos idiomas, así como a los maestros, oficinistas, turistas, viajeros de negocios, o a cualquier persona que necesite expresarse claramente y eficazmente en los idiomas inglés o español tal como se hablan y se escriben en las Américas. Este diccionario provee una cobertura exacta y actualizada del vocabulario corriente en ambos idiomas, así como abundantes ejemplos de palabras empleadas en contexto para ilustrar su uso idiomático. La selección de vocablos y modismos en español se efectuó a base de una vasta gama de fuentes latinoamericanas modernas y fue interpretada por especialistas en lexicografía bilingüe de Merriam-Webster. Las voces inglesas fueron extraídas de los más recientes diccionarios Merriam-Webster por editores de Merriam-Webster, y representan el vocabulario básico actual del inglés americano.

El material se ha organizado en un formato basado en el estilo tradicional característico de los diccionarios monolingües Merriam-Webster. El lector ya familiarizado con los diccionarios Merriam-Webster reconocerá de inmediato este estilo, con su énfasis en la conveniencia y la facilidad de uso, en la claridad y la concisión de la información presentada, en el preciso discernimiento de los sentidos de cada vocablo, y en la frecuente inclusión de frases ejemplares que ilustran el uso de una palabra. Aparecen también pronunciaciones (compuestas en el Alfabeto Fonético Internacional) para todas las voces inglesas, así como una cobertura plena de verbos irregulares en ambos idiomas, una sección de gramática inglesa básica, tablas de abreviaturas comunes, y una sección de Notas explicativas que contesta en detalle cualquier pregunta que pueda tener el lector tocante al uso de este libro.

El *Diccionario Español-Inglés Merriam-Webster* es el fruto del esfuerzo combinado de muchos miembros del departamento editorial de Merriam-Webster, junto con el asesoramiento y la asistencia de consultores exteriores. La obra de definición primaria fue llevada a cabo por Charlene M. Chateauneuf, Seán O'Mannion-Espejo, Karen L. Wilkinson, y Jocelyn Woods; contribuciones textuales preliminares fueron aportadas por Cèsar Alegre, Hilton Alers, Marién Díaz, Anne Gatschet, y María D. Guijarro, y valiosas sugerencias con respecto al estilo del diccionario fueron hechas por Victoria E. Neufeldt, Ph.D., y James L. Rader. La corrección de pruebas fue realizada por Susan L. Brady, Daniel B. Brandon,

Charlene M. Chateauneuf, Deanna Stathis Chiasson, Seán O'Mannion-Espejo, James L. Rader, Donna L. Rickerby, Adrienne M. Scholz, Amy West, Karen L. Wilkinson, y Linda Picard Wood. Las pronunciaciones fueron proporcionadas por Brian M. Sietsema, Ph.D. Los servicios de remisión textual fueron provistos por Donna L. Rickerby. Karen L. Levister ayudó con la entrada de revisiones. Carol Fugiel contribuyó muchas horas de labor de oficina y otros valiosos apoyos. La labor editorial de composición y producción fue comenzada por Jennifer S. Goss y fue continuada por Susan L. Brady, la cual también ofreció sugerencias importantes con respecto al formato. Madeline L. Novak proveyó orientación en asuntos tipográficos. John M. Morse fue responsable de la concepción de este libro, y contribuyó numerosas ideas y apoyo continuo durante su elaboración.

Eileen M. Haraty
Editor
2003

Esta nueva versión corregida del *Diccionario Español-Inglés Merriam-Webster* incluye más de 4600 vocablos adicionales, además de actualizaciones de más de 6000 entradas. También incorpora cobertura considerablemente ampliada en más de 700 de las entradas que corresponden al vocabulario más esencial del inglés y el español. Esta ampliación abarca muchas acepciones adicionales, miles de ejemplos que muestran el uso típico de las palabras en contexto, y más de dos mil de los modismos y verbos preposicionales en los cuales estas palabras tan esenciales suelen aparecer.

Muchos miembros del departamento editorial de Merriam-Webster contribuyeron a la actualización de este libro. Susan L. Brady ayudó en la selección inicial del vocabulario. La obra de definición primaria que sentó las bases del proyecto fue realizada por Tasha Martino Bigelow. Paul S. Wood también contribuyó a esta obra, y además llevó a cabo la revisión preliminar. La corrección de pruebas fue hecha en gran parte por los redactores Bigelow y Wood. Las pronunciaciones fueron provistas por Joshua S. Guenter, Ph.D. La administración de archivos de datos fue ejecutada por Daniel B. Brandon, con el asesoramiento y apoyo de Robert D. Copeland. Mark A. Stevens se coordinó con los asesores externos, supervisó la composición del libro, y aconsejó en varios asuntos relacionados. Madeline L. Novak proporcionó apoyo y orientación editorial durante todo el proyecto. John M. Morse, presidente de la compañía, ayudó con la planificación y programación del proyecto de actualización, y también proporcionó orientación y apoyo general.

Karen L. Wilkinson
Editor
2016

Explanatory Notes

Entries

1. Headwords

A boldface letter, word, or phrase appearing at the left edge of a column of type is a headword or main entry word. The headword may consist of letters set solid, of letters joined by a hyphen, or of letters separated by a space:

> **cafetalero¹, -ra** *adj* . . .
> **lip–read** . . . *vi* . . .
> **computer science** *n* . . .

The headword, together with the material that follows it on the same line and succeeding indented lines, constitutes a dictionary entry.

2. Order of Entries

Alphabetical order throughout the dictionary follows the order of the English alphabet, with one exception: the Spanish letter *ñ* follows the letter *n* and comes before the letter *o*. The headwords are ordered alphabetically letter by letter without regard to intervening spaces or hyphens; for example, *shake-up* follows *shaker*.

Homographs (words with the same spelling) having different parts of speech are usually given separate dictionary entries. These entries have superscript numerals after the headword:

> **hail¹** . . . *vt* . . .
> **hail²** *n* . . .
> **hail³** *interj* . . .
> **madrileño¹, -ña** *adj* . . .
> **madrileño², -ña** *n* . . .

Headwords in a numbered sequence are listed in this order: verb, adverb, adjective, noun, conjunction, preposition, pronoun, interjection, article.

Homographs having the same part of speech are normally included at the same dictionary entry even if they have different origins. On the English-to-Spanish side, however, separate entries are made if the homographs have different inflected forms or if they have different pronunciations. On the Spanish-to-English side, separate entries are made if the homographs differ in gender.

3. Guide Words

A pair of guide words is printed at the top of each page, indicating the first and last main entries that appear on that page:

balero · barbaridad

4. Variants

When a headword is followed by the word *or* and another spelling, the two spellings are variants. Both are standard, and you may choose to use either one:

> **jailer** *or* **jailor** . . . *n* . . .
> **quizá** *or* **quizás** *adv* . . .

Occasionally, a variant spelling is used only for a particular sense of a word. In these cases, the variant spelling is listed after the sense number of the sense to which it pertains:

> **electric** . . . *adj* **1** *or* **electrical** . . .

Sometimes the headword is used interchangeably with a longer phrase containing the headword. For the purposes of this dictionary, such phrases are considered variants of the headword:

> **bunk²** *n* **1** *or* **bunk bed** . . .
> **angina** *nf* **1** *or* **angina de pecho** . . .

Variant wordings of boldface phrases may also be shown:

> **madera** *nf* . . . **3 madera dura** *or*
> **madera noble** . . .
> **atención¹** *nf* . . . **2 poner atención** *or*
> **prestar atención** . . .
> **gasto** *nm* . . . **3 gastos fijos/generales/indirectos** . . .

5. Run-On Entries

A main entry may be followed by one or more derivatives or by a homograph with a different functional label. These are run-on entries. Each is introduced by a boldface dash and each has a functional label. They are not defined, however, since their equivalents can be readily derived by adding the corresponding foreign-language suffix to the terms used to define the main entry word or, in the case of homographs, simply substituting the appropriate part of speech:

> **illegal** . . . *adj* : ilegal — **illegally** *adv*
> [the Spanish adverb is *ilegalmente*]
> **transferir** . . . *vt* TRASLADAR : to
> transfer — **transferible** *adj*
> [the English adjective is *transferable*]
> **Bosnian** . . . *n* : bosnio *m*, -nia *f* —
> **Bosnian** *adj*
> [the Spanish adjective is *bosnio, -nia*]

On the Spanish-to-English side of the dictionary, reflexive verbs are sometimes run on undefined:

> **enrollar** *vt* : to roll up, to coil —
> **enrollarse** *vr*

The absence of a definition means that *enrollarse* has the simple reflexive meaning "to become rolled up or coiled," "to roll itself up."

6. Boldface phrases

A main entry may be followed by one or more phrases in dark, boldface type that contain the main entry word or an inflected form of it. Each boldface phrase is defined at its own numbered sense:

> **álamo** *nm* **1** : poplar **2 álamo temblón** : aspen
>
> **hold¹** . . . *v* . . . — *vi* . . . **3** to hold **forth** : . . . **4** to hold off WAIT : . . .

If the boldface phrase consists only of the entry word and a single preposition, the entry word is represented by a boldface swung dash ~ :

> **pegar** . . . *vt* . . . — *vi* . . . **3** ~ **con** : . . .

The same boldface phrase may appear at two or more senses if it has more than one distinct meaning:

> **wear¹** . . . *v* . . . *vt* . . . **8** to wear out : gastar . . . **9** to wear out EXHAUST : agotar, fatigar . . .
>
> **estar** . . . *v aux* . . . *vi* . . . **16** ~ **por** : to be in favor of **17** ~ **por** : to be about to . . .

A slash / is used between words in a boldface phrase when either of the words separated by the slash can be used in that part of the phrase:

> **casa** *nf* . . . **11 echar/tirar/botar la casa por la ventana** . . .
>
> **same²** *pron* . . . **4 all/just the same** . . .

Words separated by slashes in boldface phrases do not always have the same meaning.

When a boldface phrase contains a slash, a corresponding slash may or may not be included in the definition that follows the phrase:

> **agua** *nf* . . . **4 agua dulce/salada** : fresh/salt water . . .
>
> **go¹** . . . *v* . . . *vi* . . . **59** to go down **well/badly** : caer bien/mal, tener una buena/mala acogida . . .
>
> **pedir** . . . *vt* . . . **3 pedir disculpas/perdón** : to apologize . . .
>
> **break¹** . . . *v* . . . *vt* . . . — *vi* . . . **17 to break free/loose** : soltarse . . .

When no corresponding slash is included in the definition, all wordings shown for the boldface phrase have the same meaning.

If a word in a boldface phrase is followed by "(etc.)", other words similar to the one that precedes the "(etc.)" may be used in that place in the phrase:

> **part²** *n* . . . **6 for my/his (etc.) part** : por mi/su (etc.) parte . . .

> **hablar** . . . — **hablarse** *vr* . . . **2 se**
> **habla inglés (etc.)** : English (etc.)
> spoken

A corresponding "(etc.)" is included in the definition unless a verbal illustration is shown instead of a definition, or the definition is worded in a way that makes the inclusion of "(etc.)" unnecessary:

> **ser¹** . . . *vi* . . . **17 sea cual/quien**
> **(etc.) sea** <sean cuales sean las circunstancias : whatever the circumstances might be> . . .
> **hell** . . . *n* . . . **8 like hell I did/will**
> **(etc.)!** *fam* : ¡y un cuerno! . . .

If the use of the entry word is commonly restricted to one particular phrase, then only the phrase will be defined:

> **ward¹** . . . *vt* **to ward off** : desviar,
> protegerse contra

Pronunciation

1. Pronunciation of English Entry Words

The text between a pair of brackets [ ] following the entry word of an English-to-Spanish entry indicates the pronunciation. The symbols used are explained in the Pronunciation Symbols chart on page 85a.

When more than one pronunciation is shown for a word, different educated speakers of English pronounce that word in different ways. The pronunciation shown second may be just as common as the one shown first. All pronunciations shown are common and acceptable:

> **tomato** [tə'meɪt̬o, -'mɑ-] . . .

When less than a full pronunciation is shown for a compound word, the rest of the pronunciation can be found at the separate entry for that individual part of the compound:

> **gamma ray** ['gæmə] . . .
> **ray** ['reɪ] . . .
> **smoke¹** ['smo:k] . . .
> **smoke detector** [dɪ'tɛktər] . . .

In general, no pronunciation is given for open compounds consisting of two or more English words that are main entries at their own alphabetical place:

> **water lily** *n* : nenúfar *m*

Only the first headword in a series of numbered homographs is given a pronunciation if their pronunciations are the same:

> **dab¹** ['dæb] *vt* . . .
> **dab²** *n* . . .

No pronunciation is shown for principal parts of verbs that are formed regularly by adding a suffix or for other derivative words formed by common suffixes.

2. Pronunciation of Spanish Entry Words

Spanish pronunciation is highly regular, so no pronunciations are given in most Spanish-to-English entries. Exceptions have been made for certain words (such as foreign borrowings) whose Spanish pronunciations are not evident from their spellings:

> **pizza** ['pitsa, 'pisa] ...
> **footing** ['fu,tɪŋ] ...

Functional Labels

An italic label indicating a part of speech or some other functional classification follows the pronunciation or, if no pronunciation is given, the headword. The eight traditional parts of speech—adjective, adverb, conjunction, interjection, noun, preposition, pronoun, and verb—are indicated as follows:

> **daily²** *adj* ...
> **vagamente** *adv* ...
> **and** ... *conj* ...
> **huy** *interj* ...
> **jackal** ... *n* ...
> **para** *prep* ...
> **neither³** *pron* ...
> **leer** ... *v* ...

Verbs that are intransitive are labeled *vi,* and verbs that are transitive are labeled *vt*:

> **deliberar** *vi* : to deliberate ...
> **necessitate** ... *vt* **-tated; -tating**
> : necesitar, requerir

Verbs that are both transitive and intransitive are labeled *v* if all listed senses are both transitive and intransitive. If some senses are only transitive or only intransitive, the entry is subdivided into transitive and intransitive sections, each with its own *vt* or *vi* label, respectively:

> **scrawl¹** ... *v* : garabatear
> **crack¹** ... *vt* ... — *vi* ...
> **esperar** *vt* ... — *vi* ...

If a subdivided verb entry includes irregular verb inflections, it is labeled *v* immediately before the inflections, with the labels *vt* and *vi* serving to introduce the transitive and intransitive subdivisions:

> **satisfy** ... *v* **-fied; -fying** *vt* ... —
> *vi* ...

Spanish reflexive verbs are labeled *vr*:

> **jactarse** *vr* . . .
>
> **abandonar** *vt* . . . — **abando-**
>   **narse** . . . *vr* . . .

Two other labels are used to indicate functional classifications of verbs: *v aux* (auxiliary verb) and *v impers* (impersonal verb).

> **may** . . . *v aux, past* **might** . . .
>
> **hacer** . . . *vt* . . . — *vi* . . . *v impers*
>   **1** *(referring to weather)* <hace frío
>   : it's cold> . . .

Entries for prefixes are labeled *pref*:

> **ciber-** *pref* . . .
>
> **e-** *pref* . . .

Entries for suffixes are labeled *suf*:

> **-less** . . . *suf* . . .
>
> **-ísimo, -ma** *suf* . . .

Entries for English-language and Spanish-language trademarks are labeled *trademark* and *marca registrada*, respectively:

> **Q–tips** . . . *trademark* — se usa para
>   hisopos
>
> **Kleenex** . . . *marca registrada, m* —
>   used for a paper tissue

Entries for English-language service marks (words or names that organizations use to identify their services) are labeled *service mark*:

> **Realtor** . . . *service mark* . . .

Gender Labels

In Spanish-to-English noun entries and trademark entries, the gender of the headword is indicated by an italic *m* (masculine), *f* (feminine), or *mf* (masculine or feminine). In noun entries, the gender label immediately follows the functional label:

> **magnesio** *nm* . . .
>
> **galaxia** *nf* . . .
>
> **turista** *nmf* . . .

In trademark entries, the gender label follows the functional label and is preceded by a comma and a space:

> **Ping–Pong** *marca registrada, m* . . .

If both the masculine and feminine forms are shown for a noun referring to a person, the label is simply *n:*

> **director, -tora** *n* . . .

Spanish noun equivalents of English headwords are also labeled for gender:

> **amnesia** ... *n* : amnesia *f*
> **earache** ... *n* : dolor *m* de oído(s)
> **gamekeeper** ... *n* : guardabosque
>   *mf*

Inflected Forms

1. Nouns

The plurals of nouns are shown in this dictionary when they are irregular, if the root word changes in spelling or accentuation when a plural suffix is added, when an English noun ends in a consonant plus *-o* or in *-ey*, when an English noun ends in *-oo*, when an English noun is a compound that pluralizes the first element instead of the last, when a noun has variant plurals, or whenever the dictionary user might have reasonable doubts regarding the spelling of a plural:

> **tooth** ... *n*, *pl* **teeth** ...
> **garrafón** *nm*, *pl* **-fones** ...
> **potato** ... *n*, *pl* **-toes** ...
> **abbey** ... *n*, *pl* **-beys** ...
> **cuckoo²** *n*, *pl* **-oos** ...
> **brother–in–law** ... *n*, *pl* **brothers–
>   in–law** ...
> **fish²** *n*, *pl* **fish** *or* **fishes** ...
> **hábitat** *nm*, *pl* **-tats** ...
> **tahúr** *nm*, *pl* **tahúres** ...

Cutback (partial) inflected forms are shown for most nouns on the English-to-Spanish side, regardless of the number of syllables in the word. On the Spanish-to-English side, cutback inflections are given for nouns that have three or more syllables; plurals for shorter words are written out in full:

> **shampoo²** *n*, *pl* **-poos** ...
> **calamity** ... *n*, *pl* **-ties** ...
> **mouse** ... *n*, *pl* **mice** ...
> **sartén** *nmf*, *pl* **sartenes** ...
> **hámster** ... *nm*, *pl* **hámsters** ...
> **federación** *nf*, *pl* **-ciones** ...

If only one gender form has a plural which is irregular, that plural form will be given with the appropriate label:

> **campeón, -peona** *n*, *mpl* **-peones**
>   : champion

The plurals of nouns are usually not shown when the base word is unchanged by the addition of the regular plural suffix or when the noun is unlikely to occur in the plural:

> **apple** ... *n* : manzana *f*
> **inglés³** *nm* : English (language)

Nouns that are always plural in form and occur in plural constructions are labeled *npl* for English nouns, *nmpl* for Spanish masculine nouns, *nfpl* for Spanish feminine nouns, or *nmfpl* for Spanish nouns that can be masculine or feminine:

> knickers . . . *npl* . . .
>
> enseres *nmpl* . . .
>
> mancuernas *nfpl* . . .
>
> panties . . . *nmfpl* . . .

Entry words that are unchanged in the plural are labeled *ns & pl* for English nouns, *nms & pl* for Spanish masculine nouns, *nfs & pl* for Spanish feminine nouns, or *nmfs & pl* for Spanish nouns that can be masculine or feminine:

> deer . . . *ns & pl* . . .
>
> lavaplatos *nms & pl* . . .
>
> tesis *nfs & pl* . . .
>
> rompehuelgas *nmfs & pl* . . .

2. Verbs

ENGLISH VERBS

The principal parts of verbs are shown in English-to-Spanish entries when they are irregular, if the spelling of the root word changes when the verb suffix is added, when the verb ends in *-ey*, when there are variant inflected forms, or whenever the dictionary user might have reasonable doubts about the spelling of an inflected form:

> break[1] . . . *v* broke . . . ; broken . . . ;
>   breaking . . .
>
> drag[1] . . . *v* dragged; dragging . . .
>
> monkey[1] . . . *vi* -keyed; -keying . . .
>
> label[1] . . . *vt* -beled *or* -belled; -beling
>   *or* -belling . . .
>
> imagine . . . *vt* -ined; -ining . . .

Cutback inflected forms are usually shown when the verb has two or more syllables:

> multiply . . . *v* -plied; -plying . . .
>
> bevel[1] . . . *v* -eled *or* -elled; -eling *or*
>   -elling . . .
>
> forgo *or* forego . . . *vt* -went; -gone;
>   -going . . .
>
> commit . . . *vt* -mitted; -mitting . . .

The principal parts of an English verb are not shown if the base word does not change when *-s*, *-ed*, and *-ing* are added:

> delay[1] . . . *vt*
>
> pitch[1] . . . *vt*

SPANISH VERBS

Entries for irregular Spanish verbs are cross-referenced by number to the model conjugations appearing in the Conjugation of Spanish Verbs section on pages 72a–78a:

> **abnegarse** {49} *vr* . . .
>
> **volver** {89} *vi* . . .

Entries for Spanish verbs with regular conjugations are not cross-referenced; however, model conjugations for regular Spanish verbs are included on pages 68a–69a in the Conjugation of Spanish Verbs section.

3. Adverbs and Adjectives

The comparative and superlative forms of English adjective and adverb main entries are shown if the spelling of the root word changes when the suffix is added, if the inflection is irregular, or if there are variant inflected forms:

> **wet²** *adj* **wetter; wettest** . . .
>
> **good²** *adj* **better** . . . ; **best** . . .
>
> **evil¹** . . . *adj* **eviler** *or* **eviller; evilest** *or* **evillest** . . .

For adjectives and adverbs that have more than one syllable, only the shortened form *-est* is usually shown for the superlative:

> **early¹** . . . *adv* **earlier; -est** . . .
>
> **gaudy** . . . *adj* **gaudier; -est** . . .
>
> **secure²** *adj* **securer; -est** . . .

At a few entries only the superlative form is shown because there is no evidence that the comparative form is used:

> **mere** . . . *adj, superlative* **merest** . . .

The comparative and superlative forms of adjectives and adverbs are usually not shown if the base word does not change when the suffix is added:

> **quiet³** *adj* **1** . . .

Usage

1. Usage Labels

Two types of usage labels are used in this dictionary—regional and stylistic. Spanish words that are limited in use to a specific area or areas of Latin America, or to Spain, are given labels indicating the countries in which they are most commonly used:

> **guarachear** *vi Cuba, PRi fam* . . .
>
> **bucket** . . . *n* : . . . cubeta *f Mex*

The following regional labels are used in this dictionary: *Arg* (Argentina), *Bol* (Bolivia), *CA* (Central America), *Car* (Caribbean), *Chile* (Chile), *Col* (Colombia), *CoRi* (Costa Rica), *Cuba* (Cuba), *DomRep* (Dominican Republic), *Ecua* (Ecuador), *Sal* (El Salvador), *Guat* (Guatemala), *Hond* (Honduras), *Mex* (Mexico), *Nic* (Nicaragua), *Pan* (Panama), *Par* (Paraguay), *Peru* (Peru), *PRi* (Puerto Rico), *Spain* (Spain), *Uru* (Uruguay), *Ven* (Venezuela).

Since this dictionary focuses on the Spanish spoken in Latin America, only the most common regionalisms from Spain have been included.

A number of Spanish words are given a *fam* (familiar) label as well, indicating that these words are suitable for informal contexts but would not normally be used in formal writing or speaking. The stylistic labels *usu vulgar*, *sometimes offensive*, *often offensive*, and *usu offensive* indicate that a word is usually considered vulgar, or is sometimes, often, or usually considered offensive; such words are entered and defined in this dictionary only if they are very commonly used. The labels are intended to warn the reader that the word in question may be inappropriate in polite conversation.

2. Usage Notes

Usage notes that give information about meaning or grammar may appear in parentheses before the definition:

> **not** ... *adv* **1** (*used to form a negative*)
> : no ...
>
> **within**[2] *prep* ... **2** (*in expressions of distance*) : ... **3** (*in expressions of time*) : ...
>
> **e**[2] *conj* (*used instead of y before words beginning with i- or hi-*) : ...
>
> **poder**[1] ... *v aux* ... **2** (*expressing possibility*) : ... **3** (*expressing permission*) : ...

Orientation about meaning is also sometimes given in parentheses within the definition:

> **calibrate** ... *vt* ... : calibrar (armas), graduar (termómetros)
>
> **palco** *nm* : box (in a theater or stadium)

Occasionally a usage note is used in place of a definition. This is usually done when the entry word has no simple equivalent in the other language. This type of usage note is accompanied by examples of common use:

> **shall** ... *v aux* ... **1** (*used formally to express a command*) <you shall do as I say : harás lo que te digo> ...

3. Illustrations of Usage

Definitions are sometimes followed by verbal illustrations that show a typical use of the word in context or a common idiomatic usage. These verbal illustrations include a translation and are enclosed in angle brackets:

> **lejos** *adv* **1** : far away, distant <a lo lejos : in the distance, far off> ...
>
> **make¹** ... *v* ... *vt* ... **15** ... : hacer (dinero, amigos) <to make a living : ganarse la vida> ...

A slash / is used between words in a verbal illustration when either of the words separated by the slash can occur in that position in the phrase:

> **tener** ... *vt* ... **2** : to have (available) <tener dinero/tiempo para : to have money/time for> ...
>
> **money** ... *n* ... **1** : dinero *m*, plata *f* <to make/lose money : ganar/perder dinero> ...

Words separated by slashes in verbal illustrations do not always have the same meaning.

When a word in a verbal illustration is followed by "(etc.)," other words similar to the one before the "(etc.)" can occur in that position in the phrase:

> **dar** ... *vt* ... **16** CAUSAR : to cause <darle miedo/sed (etc.) a alguien : to make someone frightened/thirsty (etc.)> ...
>
> **turn²** *n* ... **3** INTERSECTION : boca-calle *f* <we took a wrong turn : nos equivocamos de calle/salida (etc.), ...> ...

Occasionally verbal illustrations are used in place of a definition. This is usually done when a boldface phrase has no single-phrase equivalent in the other language, or when its use is more easily understood in context:

> **saber¹** ... *vt* ... **6 qué sé yo** <diamantes, perlas, y qué sé yo : diamonds, pearls, and whatnot> <y qué sé yo dónde : and who knows where (else)> ...
>
> **all¹** ... *adv* ... **8 ~ over** *fam* <to be all over someone for something : criticar duramente a alguien por algo> ...

Definitions

A definition in this dictionary consists of one or more translations for a single sense of a main entry word, a run-on entry word, or a boldface phrase. A boldface colon is used to introduce a definition:

> **fable** ... *n* : fábula *f*
>
> **sonrojar** ... — **sonrojarse** *vr* : to blush

> **aback** . . . *adv* . . . **2 to be taken**
> **aback** : quedarse desconcertado

If more than one translation word or phrase is included in the same definition, the translations are usually separated by commas:

> **as of** *prep* : desde, a partir de

When commas are used within a definition for other reasons, the translations are separated by semicolons instead of commas:

> **love²** *n* . . . **3** BELOVED : amor *m;*
> amado *m,* -da *f;* enamorado *m,* -da
> *f* . . .

A slash / is used between words in a translation phrase when either of the words separated by the slash can be used in that position in the phrase:

> **bajar** *vt* . . . **2** : to bring/take/carry
> down, to get/lift down . . .

Words separated by slashes in translations do not always have the same meaning.

Sense Division

When a word has more than one sense, each sense begins with a boldface numeral:

> **laguna** *nf* **1** : lagoon **2** : gap

Whenever some information (such as a synonym, a boldface word or phrase, a usage note, a cross-reference, or a label) follows a sense number, it applies to that specific sense:

> **abanico** *nm* . . . **2** GAMA : . . .
>
> **tonic²** *n* . . . **2** *or* **tonic water** : . . .
>
> **grillo** *nm* . . . **2 grillos** *nmpl* : . . .
>
> **fairy** . . . *n, pl* **fairies** . . . **2 fairy tale**
> : . . .
>
> **myself** . . . *pron* **1** (*used reflexively*)
> : . . .
>
> **pike** . . . *n* . . . **3** → **turnpike**
>
> **atado²** *nm* . . . **2** *Arg* : . . .

Cross-References

An arrow in an entry means that information about the word you have looked up is available at the separate entry for the word that appears after the arrow. If the word you have looked up is an inflected form, the cross-reference after the arrow will point you to the base form of the word:

> **fue, etc.** → **ir, ser**
>
> **mice** → **mouse**

In other cases, the cross-reference will point you to the entry for a word that has the same meaning as the word you have looked up:

> scapula ... → shoulder blade
> amuck ... → amok

Synonyms

A synonym in small capital letters is often provided before the boldface colon that precedes a definition:

> **seleccionar** *vt* ELEGIR : ...
> **turn**[1] *vt* ... — *vi* ... **1** ROTATE, SPIN
> : ...
> **carta** *nf* ... **2** NAIPE : ...

These synonyms are all main entries or boldface phrases elsewhere in the dictionary. They serve as a helpful guide to the meaning of the entry or sense and also give you an additional term that might be substituted in a similar context.

Notas explicativas

Entradas

1. Lemas

Toda letra, palabra o frase en negrita que aparece al margen izquierdo de una columna de texto de la que forma parte es un lema, o entrada principal. La composición del lema puede constar de letras continuas, de letras unidas por un guión, o bien de letras separadas por un espacio:

> **cafetalero¹, -ra** *adj* . . .
> **lip–read** . . . *vi* . . .
> **computer science** *n* . . .

El lema, junto con el texto que lo sigue tanto en la misma línea como en las líneas sangradas subsiguientes, constituye una entrada del diccionario.

2. Orden de los lemas

El orden alfabético del diccionario concuerda con el orden alfabético latino universal, en el que la letra *ñ* aparece después de la *n* y antes de la *o*, y la *ch* y la *ll* no se consideran letras independientes. Los lemas se suceden alfabéticamente, letra por letra, sin tener en cuenta guiones o espacios intermediarios; por ejemplo, *shake-up* aparece después de *shaker*.

Los homógrafos (palabras que se escriben igual) que pertenecen a distintas categorías gramaticales por lo general aparecen en entradas individuales. Estas entradas tienen un número volado:

> **hail¹** . . . *vt* . . .
> **hail²** *n* . . .
> **hail³** *interj* . . .
> **madrileño¹, -ña** *adj* . . .
> **madrileño², -ña** *n* . . .

Las entradas que siguen una secuencia numerada se listan en el siguiente orden: verbo, adverbio, adjetivo, sustantivo, conjunción, preposición, pronombre, interjección, y por último, artículo.

Los homógrafos que se clasifican bajo una misma categoría gramatical son normalmente incluidos dentro de la misma entrada del diccionario, sin tener en cuenta diferencias de origen semántico. Sin embargo, en la sección Inglés-Español se les asigna a cada uno de estos homógrafos una entrada individual si entre ellos existe alguna diferencia ya sea en la inflexión o en la pronunciación. En la sección Español-Inglés, se les asigna una entrada individual si existe una diferencia de género.

3. Palabras guía

En el margen superior de cada página aparecen dos palabras guía, que indican la primera y última entrada de la página correspondiente:

balero · barbaridad

4. Variantes

Cuando un lema aparece seguido de la palabra *or* y otra ortografía, las dos ortografías se consideran como variantes. Ambas ortografías son estándares, y cualquiera de las dos puede usarse:

> **jailer** *or* **jailor** . . . *n* . . .
> **quizá** *or* **quizás** *adv* . . .

Hay ocasiones en las que una variante ortográfica se emplea únicamente para una de las acepciones de una palabra. En tales casos, la variante ortográfica aparece después del número de la acepción a la cual corresponde:

> **electric** . . . *adj* **1** *or* **electrical** . . .

En otros casos, el lema puede usarse intercambiablemente con una frase de la que forma parte. Para los fines de este diccionario, tales frases se consideran como variantes del lema:

> **bunk²** *n* **1** *or* **bunk bed** . . .
> **angina** *nf* **1** *or* **angina de pecho** . . .

Las frases en negrita también pueden, a su vez, presentar variantes:

> **madera** *nf* . . . **3 madera dura** *or*
> **madera noble** . . .
> **atención¹** *nf* . . . **2 poner atención** *or*
> **prestar atención** . . .
> **gasto** *nm* . . . **3 gastos fijos/genera-**
> **les/indirectos** . . .

5. Entradas secundarias

Una entrada principal puede ser seguida de uno o más derivados del lema, o de un homógrafo de distinta categoría gramatical. Éstas son entradas secundarias. Cada una de estas entradas aparece después de un guión en negrita, y cada una posee su propio calificativo. Tales entradas aparecen sin definición, ya que sus equivalentes en el idioma extranjero pueden derivarse fácilmente al combinar la definición del lema con el sufijo correspondiente, o como sucede con los homógrafos, al sustituir la categoría gramatical por otra. Véase por ejemplo:

> **illegal** . . . *adj* : ilegal — **illegally** *adv*
> [el adverbio español es *ilegalmente*]
> **transferir** . . . *vt* TRASLADAR : to
> transfer — **transferible** *adj*
> [el adjetivo inglés es *transferable*]
> **Bosnian** . . . *n* : bosnio *m*, -nia *f* —
> **Bosnian** *adj*
> [el adjetivo español es *bosnio, -nia*]

En la sección Español-Inglés, los verbos pronominales aparecen en ocasiones como entradas secundarias, sin definición:

> **enrollar** *vt* : to roll up, to coil —
> **enrollarse** *vr*

La ausencia de la definición en este caso comunica al lector que el verbo *enrollarse* tiene una función expresamente reflexiva. Esto elimina la necesidad de agregar una definición que resultaría super-flua como "to become rolled up or coiled," o "to roll itself up."

6. Frases en negrita

Un lema puede aparecer acompañado de una o varias frases en negrita que contienen ya sea el lema, o una inflexión de éste. Cada una de estas frases se presenta como una de las acepciones nume-radas del lema:

> **álamo** *nm* **1** : poplar **2 álamo tem-**
> **blón** : aspen
>
> **hold**[1] . . . *v* . . . — *vi* . . . **3 to hold**
> **forth** : . . . **4 to hold off** WAIT : . . .

Cuando la frase en negrita consta únicamente de una combinación del lema con una preposición, el lema se representa entonces por medio de una tilde en negrita ~ :

> **pegar** . . . *vt* . . . — *vi* . . . **3 ~ con**
> : . . .

Si la frase en cuestión tiene más de un sentido, entonces puede aparecer en dos o más acepciones del mismo lema:

> **wear**[1] . . . *v* . . . *vt* . . . **8 to wear out**
> : gastar . . . **9 to wear out** EXHAUST
> : agotar, fatigar . . .
>
> **estar** . . . *v aux* . . . *vi* . . . **16 ~ por**
> : to be in favor of **17 ~ por** : to be
> about to . . .

Se utiliza una barra inclinada / entre las palabras de una frase en negrita para indicar que cualquiera de las palabras así separadas puede usarse en esa posición dentro de la frase:

> **casa** *nf* . . . **11 echar/tirar/botar la**
> **casa por la ventana** . . .
>
> **same**[2] *pron* . . . **4 all/just the**
> **same** . . .

Las palabras separadas por barras no siempre tienen el mismo sig-nificado.

Cuando una frase en negrita contiene una barra, la definición que sigue puede o no contener una barra correspondiente:

> **agua** *nf* . . . **4 agua dulce/salada**
> : fresh/salt water . . .
>
> **go**[1] . . . *v* . . . *vi* . . . **59 to go down**
> **well/badly** : caer bien/mal, tener
> una buena/mala acogida . . .
>
> **pedir** . . . *vt* . . . **3 pedir disculpas/**
> **perdón** : to apologize . . .
>
> **break**[1] . . . *v* . . . *vt* . . . — *vi* . . . **17**
> **to break free/loose** : soltarse . . .

Si la definición no incluye una barra correspondiente, esto indica que todas las versiones de la frase en negrita tienen el mismo sig-nificado.

Cuando una de las palabras de una frase en negrita aparece seguida de "(etc.)", esto indica que hay otras palabras parecidas a la que precede al "(etc.)" que pueden usarse en esa posición dentro de la frase:

> **part²** *n* ... **6 for my/his (etc.) part**
>   : por mi/su (etc.) parte ...
>
> **hablar** ... **— hablarse** *vr* ... **2 se habla inglés (etc.)** :   English (etc.) spoken

Un "(etc.)" correspondiente se incluye en la definición que sigue a no ser que ésta o se sustituya por un ejemplo de uso o esté construída de tal manera que el "(etc.)" no haga falta:

> **ser¹** ... *vi* ... **17 sea cual/quien (etc.) sea** <sean cuales sean las circunstancias :   whatever the circumstances might be> ...
>
> **hell** ... *n* ... **8 like hell I did/will (etc.)!** *fam* :   ¡y un cuerno! ...

Si el uso común de una palabra es generalmente limitado a una frase determinada, la frase es presentada como la única acepción del lema:

> **ward¹** ... *vt* **to ward off** :   desviar, protegerse contra

Pronunciación

1. Pronunciación de los lemas ingleses

El texto que aparece entre corchetes [ ] inmediatamente después de un lema en la sección Inglés-Español indica la pronunciación del lema. Para una explicación de los símbolos empleados, véase la tabla titulada Símbolos de pronunciación que aparece en la página 85a.

Cuando se incluyen dos o más pronunciaciones que corresponden a la misma palabra, esto indica que diferentes hablantes educados del idioma pronuncian esta palabra de distintas maneras. La segunda variante puede ser tan común como la primera. Todas las pronunciaciones incluidas son comunes y aceptables:

> **tomato** [tə'meɪʈo, -'mɑ-] ...

Cuando un término compuesto aparece con sólo una pronunciación parcial, el resto de la pronunciación puede obtenerse bajo la entrada que corresponde a la parte del término cuya pronunciación se ha omitido:

> **gamma ray** ['gæmə] ...
>
> **ray** ['reɪ] ...
>
> **smoke¹** ['smo:k] ...
>
> **smoke detector** [dɪ'tɛktər] ...

En general, no se indica la pronunciación de términos compuestos cuando éstos están formados de dos o más palabras inglesas que aparecen en el diccionario como lemas:

> **water lily** *n* :   nenúfar *m*

Solamente la primera entrada en una serie de homógrafos nume-
rados incluye la pronunciación si ésta es la misma para todos los
otros homógrafos:

>**dab**[1] [ˈdæb] *vt* . . .
>**dab**[2] *n* . . .

No se indica la pronunciación de las partes principales de los
verbos formados regularmente por añadir un sufijo, ni por otros
derivados formados por sufijos comunes.

2. Pronunciación de los lemas españoles

Dada la alta regularidad de la pronunciación del español, no se
indica la pronunciación de la mayor parte de las entradas que aparecen en la sección Español-Inglés. Sin embargo, se han hecho
excepciones para ciertas palabras (tales como aquéllas que se han
adaptado de otras lenguas) cuya pronunciación en español no
puede derivarse naturalmente de su ortografía:

>**pizza** [ˈpitsa, ˈpisa] . . .
>**footing** [ˈfu,tiŋ] . . .

Calificativos funcionales

Un calificativo en itálicas que indica la categoría gramatical u
otra clasificación funcional del lema aparece inmediatamente después de la pronunciación, o si la pronunciación se ha omitido,
después del lema. Las ocho categorías gramaticales tradiciona-
les—el adjetivo, el adverbio, la conjunción, la interjección, el sustantivo, la preposición, el pronombre, y el verbo—se indican como
sigue:

>**daily**[2] *adj* . . .
>**vagamente** *adv* . . .
>**and** . . . *conj* . . .
>**huy** *interj* . . .
>**jackal** . . . *n* . . .
>**para** *prep* . . .
>**neither**[3] *pron* . . .
>**leer** . . . *v* . . .

Los verbos intransitivos se identifican con el calificativo *vi*, y los
transitivos, *vt*:

>**deliberar** *vi* : to deliberate . . .
>**necessitate** . . . *vt* **-tated; -tating**
>   : necesitar, requerir

Los verbos que son a la vez transitivos e intransitivos llevan el
calificativo *v* si todas las acepciones que aparecen en la entrada son
tanto transitivas como intransitivas; si algunas son o únicamente
transitivas o únicamente intransitivas, la entrada se subdivide en

dos secciones, y cada una de éstas es introducida con el calificativo *vt* o *vi*, respectivamente:

> **scrawl**[1] . . . *v* : garabatear
>
> **crack**[1] . . . *vt* . . . — *vi* . . .
>
> **esperar** *vt* . . . — *vi* . . .

Si una entrada así subdividida incluye inflexiones irregulares, el calificativo *v* aparece inmediatamente delante de las inflexiones, y las acepciones transitivas e intransitivas son introducidas con los calificativos *vt* y *vi*, respectivamente:

> **satisfy** . . . *v* **-fied; -fying** *vt* . . . —
> *vi* . . .

Los verbos pronominales españoles se identifican con el calificativo *vr*:

> **jactarse** *vr* . . .
>
> **abandonar** *vt* . . . — **abando-**
> **narse** . . . *vr* . . .

Por último, dos otros calificativos se emplean para indicar la clasificación funcional de los verbos: *v aux* (auxiliary verb) y *v impers* (impersonal verb).

> **may** . . . *v aux, past* **might** . . .
>
> **hacer** . . . *vt* . . . — *vi* . . . — *v impers*
> **1** *(referring to weather)* <hace frío
> : it's cold> . . .

Los prefijos se identifican con el calificativo *pref*:

> **ciber-** *pref* . . .
>
> **e-** *pref* . . .

Los sufijos se identifican con el calificativo *suf*:

> **-less** . . . *suf* . . .
>
> **-ísimo, -ma** *suf* . . .

Los lemas ingleses y españoles que son marcas registradas se indican con los calificativos *trademark* y *marca registrada*, respectivamente:

> **Q–tips** . . . *trademark* — se usa para
> hisopos
>
> **Kleenex** . . . *marca registrada, m* —
> used for a paper tissue

Los lemas ingleses que son marcas de servicio (palabras o nombres utilizados por una organización para identificar sus servicios) se indican con el calificativo *service mark*:

> **Realtor** . . . *service mark* . . .

Calificativos de género

En toda entrada de la sección Español-Inglés cuyo lema es un sustantivo o una marca registrada, el género del lema se indica con los calificativos *m* (masculino), *f* (femenino), o *mf* (masculino o femenino). Si el lema es un sustantivo, el calificativo de género aparece inmediatamente después del calificativo funcional:

> **magnesio** *nm* ...
>
> **galaxia** *nf* ...
>
> **turista** *nmf* ...

Si el lema es una marca registrada, el calificativo de género aparece después del calificativo funcional y va precedido por una coma y un espacio:

> **Ping–Pong** *marca registrada, m* ...

Si se dan las formas tanto masculina como femenina de un sustantivo que denota a una persona, se aplica el calificativo *n*:

> **director, -tora** *n* ...

Todo sustantivo español que aparece como definición de un lema inglés es acompañado de un calificativo de género:

> **amnesia** ... *n* : amnesia *f*
>
> **earache** ... *n* : dolor *m* de oído(s)
>
> **gamekeeper** ... *n* : guardabosque
> *mf*

Inflexiones

1. Sustantivos

En este diccionario se indica el plural de un sustantivo en los siguientes casos: cuando el plural es irregular, cuando la acentuación o la ortografía del vocablo raíz cambia al añadir el sufijo del plural, cuando un sustantivo inglés termina en una consonante seguida de *-o* o de *-ey*, cuando un sustantivo inglés termina en *-oo*, cuando un sustantivo inglés es un término compuesto del cual el elemento a pluralizar es el primero y no el último, cuando un sustantivo tiene variantes en el plural, o cuando podría suscitarse una duda razonable en cuanto a la ortografía del plural:

> **tooth** ... *n*, *pl* **teeth** ...
>
> **garrafón** *nm*, *pl* **-fones** ...
>
> **potato** ... *n*, *pl* **-toes** ...
>
> **abbey** ... *n*, *pl* **-beys** ...
>
> **cuckoo**[2] *n*, *pl* **-oos** ...
>
> **brother–in–law** ... *n*, *pl* **brothers– in–law** ...
>
> **fish**[2] *n*, *pl* **fish** *or* **fishes** ...
>
> **hábitat** *nm*, *pl* **-tats** ...
>
> **tahúr** *nm*, *pl* **tahúres** ...

En la sección Inglés-Español, la forma plural de la mayor parte de los sustantivos se indica por medio de una inflexión reducida, sin tener en cuenta el número de sílabas que el lema contenga. En la sección Español-Inglés, se dan inflexiones reducidas sólo para aquellos sustantivos que contengan tres o más sílabas, mientras que las formas plurales de sustantivos más breves se presentan enteras:

> **shampoo**[2] *n, pl* -poos ...
> **calamity** ... *n, pl* -ties ...
> **mouse** ... *n, pl* mice ...
> **sartén** *nmf, pl* sartenes ...
> **hámster** ... *nm, pl* hámsters ...
> **federación** *nf, pl* -ciones ...

Si se produce un plural irregular en sólo uno de los géneros, la forma plural se da con el calificativo correspondiente:

> **campeón, -peona** *n, mpl* -peones
> : champion

La forma plural de un sustantivo generalmente no aparece si el vocablo raíz permanece inalterado por la adición del sufijo plural regular, o cuando no es probable que el sustantivo se use en el plural:

> **apple** ... *n* : manzana *f*
> **inglés**[3] *nm* : English (language)

Aquellos sustantivos que siempre son plurales en forma y que ocurren en construcciones plurales son clasificados *npl* si son sustantivos ingleses, *nmpl* si son sustantivos masculinos españoles, *nfpl* si son sustantivos femeninos españoles, o *nmfpl* si son sustantivos españoles que pueden ser o masculino o femenino:

> **knickers** ... *npl* ...
> **enseres** *nmpl* ...
> **mancuernas** *nfpl* ...
> **panties** ... *nmfpl* ...

Toda entrada que permanece inalterada en el plural es clasificada *ns & pl* si es un sustantivo inglés, *nms & pl* si es un sustantivo masculino español, *nfs & pl* si es un sustantivo femenino español, y *nmfs & pl* si es un sustantivo español que puede ser o masculino o femenino:

> **deer** ... *ns & pl* ...
> **lavaplatos** *nms & pl* ...
> **tesis** *nfs & pl* ...
> **rompehuelgas** *nmfs & pl* ...

2. Verbos

VERBOS INGLESES

En la sección Inglés-Español, las partes principales de los verbos se indican en los siguientes casos: cuando el verbo es irregular, cuando la ortografía del vocablo raíz cambia al añadir un sufijo verbal, cuando el verbo termina en *-ey*, cuando una inflexión tiene variantes, o cuando puede suscitarse una duda razonable en cuanto a la ortografía de una inflexión:

> **break**[1] . . . *v* **broke** . . . ; **broken** . . . ;
>   **breaking** . . .
>
> **drag**[1] . . . *v* **dragged; dragging** . . .
>
> **monkey**[1] . . . *vi* **-keyed; -keying** . . .
>
> **label**[1] . . . *vt* **-beled** *or* **-belled; -beling**
>   *or* **-belling** . . .
>
> **imagine** . . . *vt* **-ined; -ining** . . .

Si el verbo consta de dos o más sílabas, se da generalmente una forma reducida de la inflexión:

> **multiply** . . . *v* **-plied; -plying** . . .
>
> **bevel**[1] . . . *v* **-eled** *or* **-elled; -eling** *or*
>   **-elling** . . .
>
> **forgo** *or* **forego** . . . *vt* **-went; -gone;**
>   **-going** . . .
>
> **commit** . . . *vt* **-mitted; -mitting** . . .

Las partes principales de un verbo inglés no aparecen cuando el vocablo raíz no cambia al añadir *-s, -ed,* y *-ing*:

> **delay**[1] . . . *vt*
>
> **pitch**[1] . . . *vt*

VERBOS ESPAÑOLES

En cada entrada correspondiente a un verbo irregular español aparece un número entre llaves que remite al lector a los modelos de conjugación que aparecen en las páginas 72a a 78a de la sección titulada Conjugation of Spanish Verbs:

> **abnegarse** {49} *vr* . . .
>
> **volver** {89} *vi* . . .

Aunque estas remisiones no aparecen en las entradas que corresponden a los verbos regulares españoles, los modelos de conjugación de estas formas pueden consultarse en la susodicha sección, que comienza en la página 68a.

3. Adverbios y adjetivos

ADVERBIOS Y ADJETIVOS INGLESES

Los lemas de adjetivos y adverbios ingleses incluyen las formas comparativas y superlativas cuando la ortografía del vocablo raíz cambia al añadir un sufijo, cuando la inflexión es de forma irregular, o cuando existen variantes de la inflexión:

> **wet**[2] *adj* **wetter; wettest** . . .
>
> **good**[2] *adj* **better** . . . ; **best** . . .
>
> **evil**[1] . . . *adj* **eviler** *or* **eviller; evilest**
>   *or* **evillest** . . .

Las formas superlativas de adjetivos y adverbios ingleses de más de una sola sílaba son representadas generalmente por la forma reducida *-est*:

> **early**[1] . . . *adv* **earlier; -est** . . .
> **gaudy** . . . *adj* **gaudier; -est** . . .
> **secure**[2] *adj* **securer; -est** . . .

En algunas entradas aparece únicamente la forma superlativa porque no existe evidencia del uso de la forma comparativa:

> **mere** . . . *adj, superlative* **merest** . . .

Las formas comparativas y superlativas de los adjetivos y adverbios generalmente no se muestran si el vocablo raíz no cambia al añadir el sufijo:

> **quiet**[3] *adj* **1** . . .

Uso

1. Calificativos de uso

En este diccionario se emplean dos tipos de calificativo de uso: regional y estilístico. Las palabras españolas cuyo uso se limita a ciertas regiones de Latinoamérica o a España reciben calificativos que indican los países en que suelen usarse con más frecuencia:

> **guarachear** *vi Cuba, PRi fam* . . .
> **bucket** . . . *n* : . . . cubeta *f Mex*

Los siguientes calificativos regionales se han empleado en la redacción de este libro: *Arg* (Argentina), *Bol* (Bolivia), *CA* (Centroamérica), *Car* (el Caribe), *Chile* (Chile), *Col* (Colombia), *CoRi* (Costa Rica), *Cuba* (Cuba), *DomRep* (República Dominicana), *Ecua* (Ecuador), *Sal* (El Salvador), *Guat* (Guatemala), *Hond* (Honduras), *Mex* (México), *Nic* (Nicaragua), *Pan* (Panamá), *Par* (Paraguay), *Peru* (Perú), *PRi* (Puerto Rico), *Spain* (España), *Uru* (Uruguay), *Ven* (Venezuela).

Dado el foco primordialmente latinoamericano de este diccionario, la mayoría de los regionalismos que contiene provienen de América Latina. Sin embargo, se han incluido también algunos regionalismos comunes de España.

Varios vocablos en español reciben un calificativo de *fam* (familiar), lo cual indica que el uso de tales palabras es apropiado solamente en contextos informales. Los calificativos estilísticos *usu vulgar*, *sometimes offensive*, *often offensive*, y *usu offensive* indican que el uso de la palabra indicada normalmente se considera como vulgar, o que su uso a veces, normalmente, o frecuentemente se considera como ofensivo. Tales voces aparecen definidas en este diccionario solamente si su uso es muy común. El propósito de estos calificativos es, pues, de servir de advertencia al lector.

2. Notas de uso

En algunos casos, una acepción puede venir precedida de una nota entre paréntesis que proporciona al lector información semántica o gramatical:

> **not** ... *adv* **1** (*used to form a negative*)
> : no ...
>
> **within²** *prep* ... **2** (*in expressions of distance*) : ... **3** (*in expressions of time*) : ...
>
> **e²** *conj* (*used instead of* y *before words beginning with* i- *or* hi-) : ...
>
> **poder¹** ... *v aux* ... **2** (*expressing possibility*) : ... **3** (*expressing permission*) : ...

Este tipo de orientación semántica puede aparecer también entre paréntesis como parte de la definición:

> **calibrate** ... *vt* ... : calibrar (armas), graduar (termómetros)
>
> **palco** *nm* : box (in a theater or stadium)

En algunas ocasiones, una nota de uso aparece en lugar de una definición. Esto ocurre generalmente cuando el lema carece de un equivalente sencillo en el otro idioma. Estas notas de uso aparecen acompañadas de ejemplos que ilustran el uso común del lema:

> **shall** ... *v aux* ... **1** (*used formally to express a command*) <you shall do as I say : harás lo que te digo> ...

3. Ejemplos de uso

Varias definiciones vienen acompañadas de ejemplos de uso. Estos ejemplos sirven para ilustrar un empleo típico del lema en un contexto dado, o un uso idiomático común de la palabra. Los ejemplos de uso incluyen una traducción, y aparecen entre paréntesis angulares:

> **lejos** *adv* **1** : far away, distant <a lo lejos : in the distance, far off> ...
>
> **make¹** ... *v* ... *vt* ... **15** ... : hacer (dinero, amigos) <to make a living : ganarse la vida> ...

Se utiliza una barra inclinada / entre las palabras de un ejemplo de uso para indicar que cualquiera de las palabras así separadas puede usarse en esa posición dentro de la frase:

> **tener** ... *vt* ... **2** : to have (available) <tener dinero/tiempo para : to have money/time for> ...
>
> **money** ... *n* ... **1** : dinero *m*, plata *f* <to make/lose money : ganar/perder dinero> ...

Las palabras separadas por barras no siempre tienen el mismo significado.

Cuando una de las palabras de un ejemplo de uso aparece seguida de "(etc.)", esto indica que hay otras palabras parecidas a la que precede al "(etc.)" que pueden usarse en esa posición dentro de la frase:

> **dar** . . . *vt* . . . **16** CAUSAR : to cause
> \<darle miedo/sed (etc.) a alguien : to
> make someone frightened/thirsty
> (etc.)> . . .

> **turn²** *n* . . . **3** INTERSECTION : boca-
> calle *f* \<we took a wrong turn : nos
> equivocamos de calle/salida (etc.),
> . . .> . . .

En algunas ocasiones, un ejemplo de uso aparece en lugar de una definición. Esto ocurre generalmente cuando una frase en negrita carece de un equivalente en el otro idioma de una sola frase, o cuando su uso se entiende mejor en contexto:

> **saber¹** . . . *vt* . . . **6 qué sé yo** \<dia-
> mantes, perlas, y qué sé yo : dia-
> monds, pearls, and whatnot> \<y qué
> sé yo dónde : and who knows where
> (else)> . . .

> **all¹** . . . *adv* . . . **8 ~ over** *fam* \<to be
> all over someone for something : cri-
> ticar duramente a alguien por
> algo> . . .

Definiciones

En este diccionario, una definición consta de una o más traducciones que corresponden a una sola acepción de un lema, una entrada secundaria, o una frase en negrita. Se introduce una acepción o definición por medio de dos puntos en negrita:

> **fable** . . . *n* : fábula *f*

> **sonrojar** . . . — **sonrojarse** *vr* : to
> blush

> **aback** . . . *adv* . . . **2 to be taken**
> **aback** : quedarse desconcertado

Si se incluye más de una traducción dentro de la misma definición, las traducciones generalmente se separan por comas:

> **as of** *prep* : desde, a partir de

Cuando las comas aparecen en una definición por otras razones, las traducciones se separan por un punto y coma en lugar de una coma:

> **love²** *n* . . . **3** BELOVED : amor *m;*
> amado *m*, -da *f;* enamorado *m*, -da
> *f* . . .

Se utiliza una barra inclinada / entre las palabras de una traducción para indicar que cualquiera de las palabras así separadas puede usarse en esa posición dentro de la frase:

> **bajar** *vt* . . . **2** : to bring/take/carry
> down, to get/lift down . . .

Las palabras separadas por barras no siempre tienen el mismo significado.

División de las acepciones

Cuando una entrada principal tiene varias acepciones, éstas se indican con un número arábigo, compuesto también en negrita:

> **laguna** *nf* **1** : lagoon **2** : gap

Cuando alguna información (como un sinónimo, una palabra o frase en negrita, una nota de uso, una remisión, o un calificativo) aparece después de un número de acepción, ésta se aplica específicamente a dicha acepción:

> **abanico** *nm* . . . **2** GAMA : . . .
>
> **tonic**[2] *n* . . . **2** *or* **tonic water** : . . .
>
> **grillo** *nm* . . . **2 grillos** *nmpl* : . . .
>
> **fairy** . . . *n, pl* **fairies** . . . **2 fairy tale**
> : . . .
>
> **myself** . . . *pron* **1** (*used reflexively*)
> : . . .
>
> **pike** . . . *n* . . . **3** → **turnpike**
>
> **atado**[2] *nm* . . . **2** *Arg* : . . .

Remisiones

Una flecha indica que información correspondiente al lema que precede a la flecha puede encontrarse en la entrada que corresponde a la palabra que la sigue. Si el lema es una inflexión, la remisión que viene después de la flecha dirige al lector a la forma raíz de la palabra:

> **fue, etc.** → **ir, ser**
>
> **mice** → **mouse**

En otros casos, la remisión señala otro lema que tiene el mismo significado que la palabra buscada:

> **scapula** . . . → **shoulder blade**
>
> **amuck** . . . → **amok**

Sinónimos

Frecuentemente se provee un sinónimo compuesto en mayúsculas pequeñas antes de los dos puntos en negrita que preceden a una definición:

> **seleccionar** *vt* ELEGIR : . . .
>
> **turn**[1] *vt* . . . — *vi* . . . **1** ROTATE, SPIN
> : . . .
>
> **carta** *nf* . . . **2** NAIPE : . . .

Toda palabra empleada como sinónimo tiene su propia entrada en el diccionario, ya sea como lema o como frase en negrita. El propósito de estos sinónimos es de orientar al lector y ayudarlo a elegir la acepción correcta, así como de proveer un término que podría usarse alternativamente en el mismo contexto.

Spanish Grammar

Accentuation

Spanish word stress is generally determined according to the following rules:

- Words ending in a vowel, or in *-n* or *-s*, are stressed on the next-to-last syllable (*zapato, llaman*).

- Words ending in a consonant other than *-n* or *-s* are stressed on the last syllable (*perdiz, curiosidad*).

Exceptions to these rules have a written accent mark over the stressed vowel (*fácil, hablará, último*).

There are also a few words which take accent marks in order to distinguish them from homonyms (*si, sí; que, qué; el, él;* etc.)*.

Adverbs ending in *-mente* have two stressed syllables since they retain both the stress of the root word and of the *-mente* suffix (*lentamente, difícilmente*). Many compounds also have two stressed syllables (*limpiaparabrisas*).

Punctuation and Capitalization

Questions and exclamations in Spanish are preceded by an inverted question mark ¿ and an inverted exclamation mark ¡, respectively:

¿Cuándo llamó Ana?
Y tú, ¿qué piensas?

¡No hagas eso!
Pero, ¡qué lástima!

In Spanish, unlike English, the following words are not capitalized:

- Names of days, months, and languages (*jueves, octubre, español*).

- Spanish adjectives or nouns derived from proper nouns (*los nicaragüenses, una teoría marxista*).

---

*The Real Academia Española (Royal Spanish Academy) now recommends always omitting the accent marks from the adverb *solo*, which was previously written as *sólo* to distinguish it from the adjective *solo*; and from all demonstrative pronouns (see Demonstrative Pronouns on page 51a for more information about the latter). Nevertheless, the accented variants of these words are still commonly encountered as of this writing.

Articles

1. Definite Article

Spanish has five forms of the definite article: *el* (masculine singular), *la* (feminine singular), *los* (masculine plural), *las* (feminine plural), and *lo* (neuter). The first four agree in gender and number with the nouns they limit (*el carro*, the car; *las tijeras*, the scissors), although the form *el* is used with feminine singular nouns beginning with a stressed *a-* or *ha-* (*el águila*, *el hambre*).

The neuter article *lo* is used with the masculine singular form of an adjective to express an abstract concept (*lo mejor de este método*, the best thing about this method; *lo meticuloso de su trabajo*, the meticulousness of her work; *lo mismo para mí*, the same for me).

Whenever the masculine article *el* immediately follows the words *de* or *a*, it combines with them to form the contractions *del* and *al*, respectively (*viene del campo*, *vi al hermano de Roberto*).

The use of *el, la, los,* and *las* in Spanish corresponds largely to the use of *the* in English; some exceptions are noted below.

The definite article is used:

- When referring to something as a class (*los gatos son ágiles*, cats are agile; *me gusta el café*, I like coffee).

- In references to meals and in most expressions of time (*¿comiste el almuerzo?*, did you eat lunch?; *vino el año pasado*, he came last year; *son las dos*, it's two o'clock; *prefiero el verano*, I prefer summer; *la reunión es el lunes*, the meeting is on Monday; but: *hoy es lunes*, today is Monday).

- Before titles (except *don, doña, san, santo, santa, fray,* and *sor*) in third-person references to people (*la señora Rivera llamó*, Mrs. Rivera called; but: *hola, señora Rivera*, hello, Mrs. Rivera).

- In references to body parts and personal possessions (*me duele la cabeza*, my head hurts; *dejó el sombrero*, he left his hat).

- To mean "the one" or "the ones" when the subject is already understood (*la de plástico*, the plastic one; *los que vi ayer*, the ones I saw yesterday).

The definite article is omitted:

- Before a noun in apposition, if the noun is not modified (*Caracas, capital de Venezuela;* but: *Pico Bolívar, la montaña más alta de Venezuela*).

- Before a number in a royal title (*Carlos Quinto*, Charles the Fifth).

2. Indefinite Article

The forms of the indefinite article in Spanish are *un* (masculine singular), *una* (feminine singular), *unos* (masculine plural), and *unas* (feminine plural). They agree in number and gender with the nouns they limit (*una mesa,* a table; *unos platos,* some plates), although the form *un* is used with feminine singular nouns beginning with a stressed *a-* or *ha-* (*un ala, un hacha*).

The use of *un, una, unos,* and *unas* in Spanish corresponds largely to the use of *a, an,* and *some* in English, with some exceptions:

- Indefinite articles are generally omitted before nouns identifying someone or something as a member of a class or category (*Paco es profesor/católico,* Paco is a professor/Catholic; *se llama páncreas,* it's called a pancreas).

- They are also often omitted in instances where quantity is understood from context (*vine sin chaqueta,* I came without a jacket; *no tengo carro,* I don't have a car).

Nouns

1. Gender

Nouns in Spanish are either masculine or feminine. A noun's gender can often be determined according to the following guidelines:

- Nouns ending in *-aje, -o,* or *-or* are usually masculine (*el traje, el libro, el sabor*), with some exceptions (*la mano, la foto, la labor,* etc.).

- Nouns ending in *-a, -dad, -ión, -tud,* or *-umbre* are usually feminine (*la alfombra, la capacidad, la excepción, la juventud, la certidumbre*). Exceptions include: *el día, el mapa,* and many learned borrowings ending in *-ma* (*el idioma, el tema*).

Most nouns referring to people or animals agree in gender with the subject (*el hombre, la mujer; el hermano, la hermana; el perro, la perra*). However, some nouns referring to people, including those ending in *-ista,* use the same form for both sexes (*el artista, la artista; el modelo, la modelo;* etc.).

A few names of animals exist in only one gender form (*la jirafa, el sapo,* etc.). In these instances, the adjectives *macho* and *hembra* are sometimes used to distinguish males and females (*una jirafa macho,* a male giraffe).

2. Pluralization

Plurals of Spanish nouns are formed as follows:

- Nouns ending in an unstressed vowel or an accented *-é* are pluralized by adding *-s* (*la vaca, las vacas; el café, los cafés*).

- Nouns ending in a consonant other than -*s*, or in a stressed vowel other than -*é*, are generally pluralized by adding -*es* (*el papel, los papeles; el rubí, los rubíes*). Exceptions include *papá* (*papás*) and *mamá* (*mamás*).

- Nouns with an unstressed final syllable ending in -*s* usually have a zero plural (*la crisis, las crisis; el jueves, los jueves*). Other nouns ending in -*s* add -*es* to form the plural (*el mes, los meses; el país, los países*).

- Nouns ending in -*z* are pluralized by changing the -*z* to -*c* and adding -*es* (*el lápiz, los lápices; la vez, las veces*).

- Many compound nouns have a zero plural (*el paraguas, los paraguas; el aguafiestas, los aguafiestas*).

- The plurals of *cualquiera* and *quienquiera* are *cualesquiera* and *quienesquiera*, respectively.

Adjectives

1. Gender and Number

Most adjectives agree in gender and number with the nouns they modify (*un chico alto, una chica alta, unos chicos altos, unas chicas altas*). Some adjectives, including those ending in -*e* and -*ista* (*fuerte, altruista*) and comparative adjectives ending in -*or* (*mayor, mejor*), vary only for number.

Adjectives whose masculine singular forms end in -*o* generally change the -*o* to -*a* to form the feminine (*pequeño → pequeña*). Masculine adjectives ending in -*án, -ón,* or -*dor,* and masculine adjectives of nationality which end in a consonant, usually add -*a* to form the feminine (*holgazán → holgazana; llorón → llorona; trabajador → trabajadora; irlandés → irlandesa*).

Adjectives are pluralized in much the same manner as nouns:

- The plurals of adjectives ending in an unstressed vowel or an accented -*é* are formed by adding an -*s* (*un postre rico,* unos postres *ricos;* una camisa *café,* unas camisas *cafés*).

- Adjectives ending in a consonant, or in a stressed vowel other than -*é*, are generally pluralized by adding -*es* (*un niño cortés,* unos niños *corteses;* una persona *iraní,* unas personas *iraníes*).

- Adjectives ending in -*z* are pluralized by changing the -*z* to -*c* and adding -*es* (*una respuesta sagaz,* unas respuestas *sagaces*).

2. Shortening

- The following masculine singular adjectives drop their final -*o* when they occur before a masculine singular noun: *bueno* (*buen*), *malo* (*mal*), *uno* (*un*), *alguno* (*algún*), *ninguno* (*ningún*), *primero* (*primer*), *tercero* (*tercer*).

- *Grande* shortens to *gran* before any singular noun.

- *Ciento* shortens to *cien* before any noun.

- *Cualquiera* shortens to *cualquier* before any noun.

- The title *Santo* shortens to *San* before all masculine names except those beginning with *To-* or *Do-* (*San Juan, Santo Tomás*).

3. Position

Descriptive adjectives generally follow the nouns they modify (*una cosa útil, un actor famoso*). However, adjectives that express an inherent quality often precede the noun (*la blanca nieve*).

Some adjectives change meaning depending on whether they occur before or after the noun: *un pobre niño,* a poor (pitiable) child; *un niño pobre,* a poor (not rich) child; *un gran hombre,* a great man; *un hombre grande,* a big man; *el único libro,* the only book; *el libro único,* the unique book; etc.

4. Comparative and Superlative Forms

The comparative of Spanish adjectives is generally rendered as *más . . . que* (more . . . than) or *menos . . . que* (less . . . than): *soy más alta que él,* I'm taller than he (is), I'm taller than him *fam; son menos inteligentes que tú,* they're less intelligent than you.

The superlative of Spanish adjectives usually follows the formula *definite article + (noun +) más/menos + adjective: ella es la estudiante más trabajadora,* she is the hardest-working student; *él es el menos conocido,* he's the least known.

A few Spanish adjectives have irregular comparative and superlative forms:

Adjective	Comparative/Superlative
bueno (good)	**mejor** (better, best)
malo (bad)	**peor** (worse, worst)
grande[1] (big, great), **viejo** (old)	**mayor** (greater, older; greatest, oldest)
pequeño[1] (little), **joven** (young)	**menor** (lesser, younger; least, youngest)
mucho (much), **muchos** (many)	**más** (more, most)
poco (little), **pocos** (few)	**menos** (less, least)

[1] These words have regular comparative and superlative forms when used in reference to physical size: *él es más grande que yo; nuestra casa es la más pequeña.*

ABSOLUTE SUPERLATIVE

The absolute superlative is formed by placing *muy* before the adjective, or by adding the suffix *-ísimo* (*ella es muy simpática* or *ella es simpatiquísima,* she is very nice). The absolute superlative using *-ísimo* is formed according to the following rules:

- Adjectives ending in a consonant other than *-z* simply add the *-ísimo* ending (*fácil → facilísimo*).

- Adjectives ending in *-z* change this consonant to *-c* and add *-ísimo* (*feliz → felicísimo*).

- Adjectives ending in a vowel or diphthong drop the vowel or diphthong and add *-ísimo* (*claro → clarísimo; amplio → amplísimo*).

- Adjectives ending in *-co* or *-go* change these endings to *-qu* and *-gu,* respectively, and add *-ísimo* (*rico → riquísimo; largo → larguísimo*).

- Adjectives ending in *-ble* change this ending to *-bil* and add *-ísimo* (*notable → notabilísimo*).

- Adjectives containing the stressed diphthong *ie* or *ue* will sometimes change these to *e* and *o,* respectively (*ferviente → fervientísimo* or *ferventísimo; bueno → buenísimo* or *bonísimo*).

Adverbs

Adverbs can be formed by adding the adverbial suffix *-mente* to virtually any adjective (*fácil → fácilmente*). If the adjective varies for gender, the feminine form is used as the basis for forming the adverb (*rápido → rápidamente*).

Pronouns

1. Personal Pronouns

The personal pronouns in Spanish are:

Person	Singular		Plural	
FIRST	**yo**	I	**nosotros, -tras**	we
SECOND	**tú**	you (familiar)	**vosotros[2], -tras[2]**	you, all of you
	vos[1]	you		
	usted	you (formal)	**ustedes[3]**	you, all of you
THIRD	**él**	he	**ellos, ellas**	they
	ella	she		
	ello	it (neuter)		

[1] Familiar form used in addition to *tú* in South and Central America.
[2] Familiar form used in Spain.
[3] Formal form used in Spain; familiar and formal form used in Latin America.

FAMILIAR VS. FORMAL

The second-person personal pronouns exist in both familiar and formal forms. The familiar forms are generally used when addressing relatives, friends, and children, although usage varies considerably from region to region; the formal forms are used in other contexts to show courtesy, respect, or emotional distance.

In Spain and in the Caribbean, *tú* is used exclusively as the familiar singular "you." In South and Central America, however, *vos* either competes with *tú* to varying degrees or replaces it entirely. (For a more detailed explanation of *vos* and its corresponding verb forms, refer to the Conjugation of Spanish Verbs section.)

The plural familiar form *vosotros, -tras* is used only in Spain, where *ustedes* is reserved for formal contexts. In Latin America, *vosotros, -tras* is not used, and *ustedes* serves as the all-purpose plural "you."

It should be noted that while *usted* and *ustedes* are regarded as second-person pronouns, they take the third-person form of the verb.

USAGE

In Spanish, personal pronouns are generally omitted (*voy al cine*, I'm going to the movies; *¿llamaron?*, did they call?), although they are sometimes used for purposes of emphasis or clarity (*se lo diré yo*, I will tell them; *vino ella, pero él se quedó*, she came, but he stayed behind). The forms *usted* and *ustedes* are usually included out of courtesy (*¿cómo está usted?*, how are you?).

Personal pronouns are not generally used in reference to inanimate objects or living creatures other than humans; in these instances, the pronoun is most often omitted (*¿es nuevo? no, es viejo*, is it new? no, it's old).

The neuter third-person pronoun *ello* is reserved for indefinite subjects (such as abstract concepts): *todo ello implica* . . . , all of this implies . . . ; *por si ello fuera poco* . . . , as if that weren't enough . . . . It most commonly appears in formal writing and speech. In less formal contexts, *ello* is often either omitted or replaced with *esto, eso,* or *aquello*.

2. Prepositional Pronouns

Prepositional pronouns are used as the objects of prepositions (*¿es para mí?*, is it for me?; *se lo dio a ellos*, he gave it to them).

The prepositional pronouns in Spanish are:

Singular		Plural	
mí	me	**nosotros, -tras**	us
ti	you	**vosotros[1], -tras**[1]	you
usted	you (formal)	**ustedes**	you
él	him	**ellos, ellas**	them
ella	her		
ello	it (neuter)		
sí	yourself, himself, herself, itself, oneself	**sí**	yourselves, themselves

[1] Used primarily in Spain.

When the preposition *con* is followed by *mí*, *ti*, or *sí*, both words are replaced by *conmigo*, *contigo*, and *consigo*, respectively (*¿vienes conmigo?*, are you coming with me?; *habló contigo*, he spoke with you; *no lo trajo consigo*, she didn't bring it with her).

3. Object Pronouns

DIRECT OBJECT PRONOUNS

Direct object pronouns indicate the person or thing that receives the action of a verb. The direct object pronouns in Spanish are:

Singular		Plural	
me	me	**nos**	us
te	you	**os**[1]	you
le[2]	you, him	**les**[2]	you[3], them
lo	you (formal), him, it	**los**	you[3], them
la	you (formal), her, it	**las**	you[3], them

[1] Used only in Spain.
[2] Used mainly in Spain.
[3] See explanation below.

Agreement

The third-person forms agree in both gender and number with the nouns they replace or the people they refer to (*pintó las paredes*, she painted the walls → *las pintó*, she painted them; *visitaron al señor Juárez*, they visited Mr. Juárez → *lo visitaron*, they visited him). The remaining forms vary only for number.

Position

Direct object pronouns are normally affixed to the end of an affirmative command, a simple infinitive, or a present participle (*¡hazlo!*, do it!; *es difícil hacerlo*, it's difficult to do it; *haciéndolo, aprenderás*, you'll learn by doing it). With constructions involving an auxiliary verb and an infinitive or present participle, the pronoun may occur either immediately before the construction or suffixed to it (*lo voy a hacer* or *voy a hacerlo*, I'm going to do it; *estoy haciéndolo* or *lo estoy haciendo*, I'm doing it). In all other cases, the pronoun immediately precedes the conjugated verb (*no lo haré*, I won't do it).

Regional Variation

The second-person ("you") familiar plural form *os* is restricted to Spain. In most parts of Latin America, *los* and *las* are used as both the familiar and formal second-person plural forms.

In Spain and in a few areas of Latin America, *le* and *les* are used in place of *lo* and *los*, respectively, when referring to or addressing people (*le vieron*, they saw him; *les vistió*, she dressed them; *encantado de conocerle*, pleased to meet you).

INDIRECT OBJECT PRONOUNS

Indirect object pronouns represent the secondary goal of the action of a verb (*me dio el regalo*, he gave me the gift; *les dije que no*, I told them no). The indirect object pronouns in Spanish are:

Singular		Plural	
me	(to, for, from) me	**nos**	(to, for, from) us
te	(to, for, from) you	**os**[1]	(to, for, from) you
le	(to, for, from) you, him, her, it	**les**	(to, for, from) you, them
se[2]		**se**[2]	

[1] Used only in Spain.
[2] See explanation below.

Position

Indirect object pronouns follow the same rules as direct object pronouns with regard to their position in relation to verbs. When they occur with direct object pronouns, the indirect object pronoun always precedes (*nos lo dio*, she gave it to us; *estoy trayéndotela*, I'm bringing it to you).

Use of *Se*

When the indirect object pronouns *le* or *les* occur before any direct object pronoun beginning with an *l-*, the indirect object pronouns *le* and *les* convert to *se* (*les mandé la carta*, I sent them the letter → *se la mandé,* I sent it to them; *vamos a comprarle los aretes,* let's buy her the earrings → *vamos a comprárselos,* let's buy them for her).

4. Reflexive Pronouns

Reflexive pronouns are used to refer back to the subject of the verb (*me hice daño,* I hurt myself; *se vistieron,* they got dressed, they dressed themselves; *nos lo compramos,* we bought it for ourselves).

The reflexive pronouns in Spanish are:

Singular		Plural	
me	myself	**nos**	ourselves
te	yourself	**os**[1]	yourselves
se	yourself, himself, herself, itself	**se**	yourselves, themselves

[1] Used only in Spain.

Reflexive pronouns are also used:

- When the verb describes an action performed to one's own body, clothing, etc. (*me quité los zapatos,* I took off my shoes; *se arregló el pelo,* he fixed his hair).

- In the plural, to indicate reciprocal action (*se hablan con frecuencia,* they speak with each other frequently).

- In the third-person singular and plural, as an indefinite subject reference (*se dice que es verdad,* they say it's true; *nunca se sabe,* one never knows; *se escribieron miles de páginas,* thousands of pages were written).

It should be noted that many verbs which take reflexive pronouns in Spanish have intransitive equivalents in English (*ducharse,* to shower; *quejarse,* to complain; etc.).

5. Relative Pronouns

Relative pronouns introduce subordinate clauses acting as nouns or modifiers (*el libro que escribió* . . . , the book that he wrote . . . ; *las chicas a quienes conociste* . . . , the girls whom you met . . .). In Spanish, the relative pronouns are:

que (that, which, who, whom)

quien, quienes (who, whom, that, whoever, whomever)

el cual, la cual, los cuales, las cuales (which, who)

el que, la que, los que, las que (which, who, whoever)

lo cual (which)

lo que (what, which, whatever)

cuanto, cuanta, cuantos, cuantas (all those that, all that, whatever, whoever, as much as, as many as)

Relative pronouns are not omitted in Spanish as they often are in English: *el carro que vi ayer,* the car (that) I saw yesterday. When relative pronouns are used with prepositions, the preposition precedes the clause (*la película sobre la cual le hablé,* the film I spoke to you about).

The relative pronoun *que* can be used in reference to both people and things. Unlike other relative pronouns, *que* does not take the personal *a** when used as a direct object referring to a person (*el hombre que llamé,* the man that I called; but: *el hombre a quien llamé,* the man whom I called).

Quien is used only in reference to people. It varies in number with the explicit or implied antecedent (*las mujeres con quienes charlamos . . . ,* the women we chatted with; *quien lo hizo pagará,* whoever did it will pay).

El cual and *el que* vary for both number and gender, and are therefore often used in situations where *que* or *quien(es)* might create ambiguity: *nos contó algunas cosas sobre los libros, las cuales eran interesantes,* he told us some things about the books which (the things) were interesting.

Lo cual and *lo que* are used to refer back to a whole clause, or to something indefinite (*dijo que iría, lo cual me alegró,* he said he would go, which made me happy; *pide lo que quieras,* ask for whatever you want).

Cuanto varies for both number and gender with the implied antecedent: *conté a cuantas (personas) pude,* I counted as many (people) as I could. If an indefinite mass quantity is referred to, the masculine singular form is used (*anoté cuanto decía,* I jotted down whatever he said).

*The personal *a* is generally used: 1) before direct objects (except direct object pronouns or reflexive pronouns) that refer to people or to something that is personified: *cuida a los niños,* he takes care of the children; *amar a la patria,* to love one's country; and 2) before indirect object pronouns or reflexive pronouns): *permiten a los pasajeros usar sus teléfonos,* they allow passengers to use their phones; *a mí no me importa,* it doesn't matter to me.

Possessives

1. Possessive Adjectives

UNSTRESSED FORMS

Singular		Plural	
mi(s)	my	**nuestro(s), nuestra(s)**	our
tu(s)	your	**vuestro(s)[1], vuestra(s)[1]**	your
su(s)	your, his, her, its	**su(s)**	your, their

[1] Used only in Spain.

STRESSED FORMS

Singular		Plural	
mío(s), mía(s)	my, mine, of mine	**nuestro(s), nuestra(s)**	our, ours, of ours
tuyo(s), tuya(s)	your, yours, of yours	**vuestro(s)[1], vuestra(s)[1]**	your, yours, of yours
suyo(s), suya(s)	your, yours, of yours; his, of his; her, hers, of hers; its, of its	**suyo(s), suya(s)**	your, yours, of yours; their, theirs, of theirs

[1] Used only in Spain.

The unstressed forms of possessive adjectives precede the nouns they modify (*mis zapatos,* my shoes; *nuestra escuela,* our school).

The stressed forms occur after the noun and are often used for purposes of emphasis (*el carro tuyo,* your car; *la pluma es mía,* the pen is mine; *unos amigos nuestros,* some friends of ours).

All possessive adjectives agree with the noun in number. The stressed forms, as well as the unstressed forms *nuestro* and *vuestro,* also vary for gender.

2. Possessive Pronouns

The possessive pronouns have the same forms as the stressed possessive adjectives (see table above). They are always preceded by the definite article, and they agree in number and gender with the nouns they replace (*las llaves mías,* my keys → *las mías,* mine; *los guantes nuestros,* our gloves → *los nuestros,* ours).

Demonstratives

1. Demonstrative Adjectives

The demonstrative adjectives in Spanish are:

Singular		Plural	
este, esta	this	**estos, estas**	these
ese, esa	that	**esos, esas**	those
aquel, aquella	that	**aquellos, aquellas**	those

Demonstrative adjectives agree in gender and number with the nouns they modify (*esta chica, aquellos árboles*). They normally precede the noun, but may occasionally occur after for purposes of emphasis or to express contempt: *en la época **aquella** de cambio*, in that era of change; *el perro **ese** ha ladrado toda la noche*, that (awful, annoying, etc.) dog barked all night long.

The forms *aquel, aquella, aquellos,* and *aquellas* are generally used in reference to people and things that are relatively distant from the speaker in space or time: *ese libro,* that book (a few feet away); *aquel libro,* that book (way over there).

2. Demonstrative Pronouns

The demonstrative pronouns in Spanish are orthographically identical to the demonstrative adjectives. Formerly, Spanish rules of orthography required that the demonstrative pronouns include an accent mark over the stressed vowel (*éste, ése, aquél,* etc.) to distinguish them from the corresponding demonstrative adjectives. However, the Real Academia Española (Royal Spanish Academy) now recommends the omission of the accent mark from these pronouns. This supersedes a previous recommendation calling for the inclusion of the accent mark only when needed to resolve cases of ambiguity. Nevertheless, both the accented and unaccented variants are in common use as of this writing, and are reflected in this dictionary.

In addition, there are three neuter forms—*esto, eso,* and *aquello*—which are used when referring to abstract ideas or unidentified things (*¿te dijo eso?,* he said that to you?; *¿qué es esto?,* what is this?; *tráeme todo aquello,* bring me all that stuff).

Except for the neuter forms, demonstrative pronouns agree in gender and number with the nouns they replace (*esta silla,* this chair → *esta/ésta,* this one; *aquellos vasos,* those glasses → *aquellos/ aquéllos,* those ones).

Gramática inglesa

El adjetivo

El adjetivo inglés es invariable en cuanto a número o género, y suele preceder al sustantivo que modifica:

the *tall* woman
(la mujer *alta*)

the *tall* women
(las mujeres *altas*)

a *happy* child
(un niño *contento*)

happy children
(niños *contentos*)

1. Adjetivos positivos, comparativos, y superlativos

Las formas comparativas y superlativas del adjetivo inglés se pueden construir de tres maneras. Cuando el adjetivo positivo consta de una sola sílaba, la construcción más común es de añadir los sufijos *-er* o *-est* al vocablo raíz; si el adjetivo positivo consta de más de dos sílabas, suele entonces combinarse con los adverbios *more*, *most*, *less* o *least;* al adjetivo positivo de dos sílabas puede aplicarse cualquiera de las dos fórmulas; y por último, existen los adjetivos irregulares cuyas formas comparativas y superlativas son únicas:

Positivo	Comparativo	Superlativo
clean (limpio)	**cleaner** (más limpio)	**cleanest** (el más limpio)
narrow (angosto)	**narrower** (más angosto)	**narrowest** (el más angosto)
meaningful (significativo)	**more meaningful** (más significativo)	**most meaningful** (el más significativo)
less meaningful (menos significativo)	**least meaningful** (el menos significativo)	
good (bueno)	**better** (mejor)	**best** (el mejor)
bad (malo)	**worse** (peor)	**worst** (el peor)

2. Adjetivos demostrativos

Los adjetivos demostrativos *this* y *that* corresponden a los adjetivos españoles *este* y *ese*, respectivamente, y sirven esencialmente la misma función. Debe notarse que este tipo de adjetivo es el único que tiene forma plural:

Singular		Plural	
this	este, esta	**these**	estos, estas
that	ese, esa	**those**	esos, esas

3. Adjetivos descriptivos

Un adjetivo descriptivo describe o indica una cualidad, clase o condición (*a fascinating conversation,* una conversación fascinante; *a positive attitude,* una actitud positiva; *a fast computer,* una computadora rápida).

4. Adjetivos indefinidos

Un adjetivo indefinido se usa para designar personas o cosas no identificadas (*some children,* unos niños o algunos niños; *other hotels,* otros hoteles).

5. Adjetivos interrogativos

El adjetivo interrogativo se usa para formular preguntas:

Whose office is this?
(*¿De quién* es esta oficina?)

Which book do you want?
(*¿Cuál* libro quieres?)

6. El sustantivo empleado como adjetivo

Un sustantivo puede usarse para modificar otro sustantivo. De esta manera el sustantivo funciona igual que un adjetivo (*the Vietnam War,* la Guerra de Vietnam; *word processing,* procesamiento de textos).

7. Adjetivos posesivos

Llámase adjetivo posesivo a la forma posesiva del pronombre personal. A continuación se listan los adjetivos posesivos ingleses y algunos ejemplos de su uso:

Singular	Plural
my	our
your	your
his/her/its	their

Where's *my* watch?
(¿Dónde está *mi* reloj?)

Your cab's here.
(Ha llegado *su/tu* taxi.)

It was *her* idea.
(Fue *su* idea.)

They read *his* book.
(Leyeron *su* libro.)

the box and *its* contents
(la caja y *su* contenido)

We paid for *their* ticket.
(Pagamos por *su* boleto.)

Your tables are ready.
(*Sus* mesas están listas.)

8. Adjetivos predicativos

Un adjetivo predicativo modifica el sujeto de un verbo copulativo (como *be, become, feel, taste, smell,* o *seem*):

She is *happy* with the outcome.
(Está *contenta* con el resultado.)

The milk tastes *sour*.
(La leche sabe *agria*.)

The student seems *puzzled*.
(El estudiante parece estar *desconcertado*.)

9. Adjetivos propios

Un adjetivo propio es derivado de un nombre propio y suele escribirse con mayúscula:

Victorian furniture
(muebles *victorianos*)

a *Puerto Rican* product
(un producto *puertorriqueño*)

10. Adjetivos relativos

Un adjetivo relativo (tal como *which, that, who, whom, whose, where*) se emplea para introducir una cláusula adjetival o sustantiva:

toward late April, by *which* time the report should be finished
(para fines de abril, fecha para *la cual* deberá estar listo el reporte)

a person *whose* identity is unknown
(una persona *cuya* identidad se desconoce)

El adverbio

La mayor parte de los adverbios ingleses se forman a partir de un adjetivo al que se le agrega el sufijo -*ly*:

mad*ly*
(loca*mente*)

wonderful*ly*
(maravillosa*mente*)

Para formar un adverbio de un adjetivo que termina en -*y*, suele cambiarse primero esta terminación a una -*i*, y luego se añade el sufijo -*ly*:

happ*ily*
(feliz*mente*)

daint*ily*
(delicada*mente*)

La forma adverbial que corresponde a varios adjetivos que terminan en -*ic* recibe el sufijo -*ally*:

basic*ally*
(básica*mente*)

numeric*ally*
(numérica*mente*)

Si un adjetivo termina en -*ly*, el adverbio que le corresponde suele escribirse de la misma manera:

she called her mother *daily*
(llamaba a su madre *todos los días*)

the show started *early*
(la función empezó *temprano*)

Por último, hay adverbios que no terminan en -*ly*, por ejemplo:

again (otra vez)
now (ahora)

too (demasiado)
too (también)

1. Adverbios positivos, comparativos, y superlativos

Al igual que el adjetivo, la mayoría de los adverbios ingleses poseen tres grados de comparación: positivo, comparativo, y superlativo. Como regla general, a un adverbio monosilábico se le añade el sufijo -*er* cuando es comparativo, y -*est* cuando es superlativo. Si el adverbio consta de tres o más sílabas, las formas comparativas y superlativas se forman al combinarlo con los adverbios *more/most* o *less/least*. Las formas comparativas y superlativas de un adverbio de dos sílabas pueden obtenerse empleando uno u otro de los dos métodos:

Positivo	Comparativo	Superlativo
fast	fast*er*	fast*est*
easy	easi*er*	easi*est*
madly	more mad*ly*	most mad*ly*
happily	more happi*ly*	most happi*ly*

Finalmente, hay algunos adverbios, tales como *quite* y *very*, que no poseen comparativo.

2. Adverbios de énfasis

Adverbios tales como *just* y *only* suelen usarse para poner el énfasis en otras palabras. El énfasis producido puede cambiar según la posición del adverbio en la oración:

He *just* nodded to me as he passed.
(*Sólo* me saludó con la cabeza al pasar.)

He nodded to me *just* as he passed.
(Me saludó con la cabeza *justamente* cuando me pasó.)

3. Adverbios relativos

Los adverbios relativos (tales como *when, where,* y *why*) se utilizan principalmente para introducir preguntas:

When will he return?
(¿*Cuándo* volverá?)

Where have the children gone?
(¿*A dónde* fueron los niños?)

Why did you do it?
(¿*Por qué* lo hiciste?)

El artículo

1. El artículo definido

En inglés existe solamente una forma del artículo definido, *the.* Este artículo es invariable en cuanto a género o número:

The boys were expelled.
(*Los* chicos fueron expulsados.)

The First Lady dined with *the* ambássador.
(*La* Primera Dama cenó con *el* embajador.)

2. El artículo indefinido

El artículo indefinido *a* se usa con cualquier sustantivo o abreviatura que comience ya sea con una consonante, o con un *sonido* consonántico:

a door   *a* hat

a B.A. degree   *a* one-way street

a union   *a* U.S. Senator

El artículo *a* se emplea también antes de un sustantivo cuya primera sílaba comienza con *h-*, y esta sílaba o no es acentuada, o tiene solamente una acentuación moderada (*a historian, a heroic attempt, a hilarious performance*). Sin embargo, en el inglés hablado, suele más usarse el artículo *an* en estos casos (*an historian, an heroic attempt, an hilarious performance*). Ambas formas son perfectamente aceptables.

El artículo indefinido *an* se usa con cualquier sustantivo o abreviatura que comience con un *sonido* vocal, sin tener en cuenta si la primera letra del sustantivo es vocal o consonante (*an icicle, an nth degree, an honor, an FBI investigation*).

La conjunción

Existen tres tipos principales de conjunciones: la conjunción coordinante, la correlativa, y la subordinante.

1. Conjunciones coordinantes

Las conjunciones coordinantes, tales como *and, because, but, or, nor, since, so,* y *yet*, se emplean para unir elementos gramaticales de igual valor. Estos elementos pueden ser palabras, frases, cláusulas subordinadas, cláusulas principales, u oraciones completas. Las conjunciones coordinantes se emplean para unir elementos similares, para excluir o contrastar, para indicar una alternativa, para indicar una razón, o para precisar un resultado:

unión de elementos similares:
She ordered pencils, pens, *and* erasers.

exclusión o contraste:
He is a brilliant *but* arrogant man.
They offered a promising plan, *but* it had not yet been tested.

alternativa:
She can wait here *or* go on ahead.

razón:
The report is useless, *since* its information is no longer current.

resultado:

His diction is excellent, *so* every word is clear.

2. Conjunciones correlativas

Las conjunciones correlativas se usan en pares, y sirven para unir alternativas y elementos de igual valor gramatical:

Either you go *or* you stay.
(*O* te vas *o* te quedas.)

He had *neither* looks *nor* wit.
(No tenía *ni* atractivo físico *ni* inteligencia.)

3. Conjunciones subordinantes

Las conjunciones subordinantes se usan para unir una cláusula subordinada a una cláusula principal. Estas conjunciones pueden emplearse para expresar la causa, la condición o concesión, el modo, el propósito o resultado, el tiempo, el lugar o la circunstancia, así como las condiciones o posibilidades alternativas:

causa:
Because she learns quickly, she is doing well in her new job.

condición o concesión:
Don't call *unless* you are coming.

modo:
We'll do it *however* you tell us to.

propósito o resultado:
He distributes the mail early *so that* they can read it.

tiempo:
She kept meetings to a minimum *when* she was president.

El sustantivo

A diferencia del sustantivo español, el sustantivo inglés generalmente carece de género. En algunos sustantivos, el género femenino se identifica por la presencia del sufijo *-ess* (*empress, hostess*); existen también aquellos sustantivos que sólo se aplican a miembros de uno u otro sexo, por ejemplo: *husband, wife; father, mother; brother, sister;* así como nombres de ciertos animales: *bull, cow; buck, doe;* etc. Sin embargo, la mayoría de los sustantivos ingleses son neutros. Cuando es preciso atribuirle un género a un sustantivo neutro, suele combinarse éste con palabras como *male, female, man, woman,* etc., por ejemplo:

a *male* parrot
(un loro *macho*)

women writers
(escritoras)

1. Usos básicos

Los sustantivos ingleses suelen usarse como sujetos, objetos directos, objetos de una preposición, objetos indirectos, objetos retenidos, nominativos predicativos, complementos objetivos, construcciones apositivas, y en trato directo:

sujeto:
The *office* was quiet.

objeto directo:
He locked the *office*.

objeto de una preposición:
The file is in the *office*.

objeto indirecto:
He gave his *client* the papers.

objeto retenido:
His client was given the *papers*.

nominativo predicativo:
Mrs. Adams is the managing *partner*.

complemento objetivo:
They made Mrs. Adams managing *partner*.

construcción apositiva:
Mrs. Adams, the managing *partner*, wrote that memo.

trato directo:
Mrs. Adams, may I present Mr. Bonkowski.

2. El sustantivo empleado como adjetivo

Los sustantivos desempeñan una función adjetival cuando preceden a otros sustantivos:

olive oil
(aceite *de oliva*)

business management
(administración *de empresas*)

emergency room
(sala *de emergencias*)

3. La formación del plural

La mayoría de los sustantivos ingleses se pluralizan añadiendo *-s* al final del singular (*book, books; cat, cats; dog, dogs; tree, trees*).

Cuando el sustantivo singular termina en *-s, -x, -z, -ch,* o *-sh,* su forma plural se obtiene añadiendo *-es* al final (*cross, crosses; fox, foxes; witch, witches; wish, wishes; fez, fezes*).

Si el sustantivo singular termina en *-y* precedida de una consonante, la *-y* es convertida en *-i* y se le añade la terminación *-es* (*fairy, fairies; pony, ponies; guppy, guppies*).

No todos los sustantivos ingleses obedecen estas normas. Hay algunos sustantivos (generalmente nombres de animales) que no siempre cambian en el plural (*fish, fish* o *fishes; caribou, caribou* o *caribous*). Por último, hay algunos sustantivos que poseen una forma plural única (*foot, feet; mouse, mice; knife, knives*).

4. El posesivo

La forma posesiva del sustantivo singular generalmente se obtiene al añadir un apóstrofe seguido de una *-s* al final:

> *Jackie's* passport
> (el pasaporte *de Jackie*)

> this hat is *Billy's*
> (este sombrero es *de Billy*)

Cuando el sustantivo termina en *-s,* suele añadirse únicamente el apóstrofe, como sigue:

> the *neighbors'* dog
> (el perro *de los vecinos*)

> *Mr. Collins'* briefcase
> (el portafolios *del Sr. Collins*)

La preposición

La preposición inglesa se combina generalmente con un sustantivo, un pronombre, o el equivalente de un sustantivo (como una frase o cláusula) para formar una frase con función adjetival, adverbial, o sustantiva. Suele distinguirse dos tipos de preposiciones: la preposición simple, es decir, aquélla que consta de una sola palabra (p. ej., *against, from, near, of, on, out,* o *without*), y la compuesta, que consta de más de un elemento (como *according to, by means of,* o *in spite of*).

1. Usos básicos

La preposición se emplea generalmente para unir un sustantivo, un pronombre, o el equivalente de un sustantivo al resto de la oración. Una frase preposicional suele emplearse como adverbio o adjetivo:

> She expected resistance *on his part*.
> He sat down *beside her*.

2. La conjunción vs. la preposición

Las palabras inglesas *after, before, but, for*,* y *since* pueden funcionar como preposiciones así como conjunciones. El papel que

---

*La conjunción for se emplea principalmente en el lenguaje formal y literario.

desempeñan estas palabras suele determinarse según su posición dentro de la oración. Las conjunciones generalmente sirven para unir dos elementos de igual valor gramatical, mientras que las preposiciones suelen preceder a un sustantivo, un pronombre, o una frase sustantiva:

conjunción:
I was a bit concerned *but* not panicky. (*but* vincula dos adjetivos)

preposición:
I was left with nothing *but* hope. (*but* precede a un sustantivo)

conjunción:
The device conserves fuel, *for* it is battery-powered. (*for* vincula dos cláusulas)

preposición:
The device conserves fuel *for* residual heating. (*for* precede a una frase sustantiva)

3. Posición

Una preposición puede aparecer antes de un sustantivo o un pronombre (*below the desk, beside them*), después de un adjetivo (*antagonistic to, insufficient in, symbolic of*), o después de un elemento verbal con el cual combina para formar una frase con función verbal (*take for, take over, come across*).

A diferencia de la preposición española, la preposición inglesa puede aparecer al final de una oración, lo cual sucede frecuentemente en el uso común, especialmente si la preposición forma parte de una frase con función verbal:

After Rourke left, Joyce took *over*.
What does this all add up *to*?

El pronombre

Los pronombres pueden poseer las características siguientes: caso (nominativo, posesivo, u objetivo); número (singular o plural); persona (primera, segunda, o tercera), y género (masculino, femenino, o neutro). Los pronombres ingleses se clasifican en siete categorías principales, de las cuales cada una juega un papel específico.

1. Pronombres demostrativos

Las palabras *this, that, these* y *those* se consideran como pronombres cuando funcionan como sustantivos. (Se les clasifica como adjetivos demostrativos cuando modifican un sustantivo.) El pronombre demostrativo indica a una persona o cosa para distinguirla de otras:

> *These* are the best designs we've seen to date.
> *Those* are strong words.

El pronombre demostrativo también se usa para distinguir a una persona o cosa cercana de otra que se encuentre a mayor distancia (*this is my desk; that is yours*).

2. Pronombres indefinidos

El pronombre indefinido se emplea para designar a una persona o cosa cuya identidad se desconoce o no se puede establecer de inmediato. Estos pronombres se usan generalmente como referencias en la tercera persona, y no se distinguen en cuanto a género. A continuación se listan ejemplos de pronombres indefinidos:

all	either	none
another	everybody	no one
any	everyone	one
anybody	everything	other
anyone	few	several
anything	many	some
both	much	somebody
each	neither	someone
each one	nobody	something

Los pronombres indefinidos deben concordar en cuanto a número con los verbos que les corresponden. Los siguientes pronombres son singulares y deben usarse con un verbo conjugado en singular: *another, anything, each, each one, everything, much, nobody, no one, one, other, someone, something*.

> *Much is* being done.
> *No one wants* to go.

Los pronombres indefinidos *both, few, many, several* entre otros son plurales, y por lo tanto deben emplearse con verbos conjugados en plural:

> *Many were* called; *few were* chosen.

Algunos pronombres, tales como *all, any, none,* y *some,* pueden presentar un problema ya que pueden usarse tanto con verbos singulares como plurales. Como regla general, los pronombres que se usan con sustantivos no numerables emplean verbos singulares, mientras que aquéllos que se usan con sustantivos numerables suelen tomar un verbo plural:

con sustantivo no numerable:
> *All* of the property *is* affected.
> *None* of the soup *was* spilled.
> *Some* of the money *was* spent.

con sustantivo numerable:
All of my shoes *are* black.
None of the clerks *were* available.
Some of your friends *were* there.

3. Pronombres interrogativos

Los pronombres interrogativos *what, which, who, whom,* y *whose,* así como las combinaciones de estos con el sufijo *-ever (whatever, whichever,* etc.) se usan para introducir una pregunta:

Who is she?
He asked me *who* she was.

Whoever can that be?
We wondered *whoever* that could be.

4. Pronombres personales

El pronombre personal refleja la persona, el número, y el género del ser u objeto que representa. La mayoría de los pronombres personales toman una forma distinta para cada uno de estos tres casos:

Persona	Nominativo	Posesivo	Objetivo
PRIMERA			
SINGULAR:	I	my, mine	me
PLURAL:	we	our, ours	us
SEGUNDA			
SINGULAR:	you	your, yours	you
PLURAL:	you	your, yours	you
TERCERA			
SINGULAR:	he	his, his	him
	she	her, hers	her
	it	its, its	it
PLURAL:	they	their, theirs	them

Nótese que los pronombres personales en el caso posesivo no llevan apóstrofe, y no deben confundirse con los homófonos *you're, they're, there's, it's.*

5. Pronombres recíprocos

Los pronombres recíprocos *each other* y *one another* se emplean para indicar una acción o relación mutua:

They do not quarrel with *one another*.
(No se pelean (el uno con el otro).)

Lou and Andy saw *each other* at the party.
(Lou y Andy se vieron en la fiesta.)

Un pronombre recíproco puede usarse también en el caso posesivo:

They always borrowed *one another's* money.
(Siempre se prestaban dinero.)

The two companies depend on *each other's* success.
(Cada una de las dos compañías depende del éxito de la otra.)

6. Pronombres reflexivos

Los pronombres reflexivos se forman al combinar los pronombres personales *him, her, it, my, our, them* y *your* con *-self* o *-selves*. El pronombre reflexivo se usa generalmente para expresar una acción reflexiva, o bien para recalcar el sujeto de una oración, cláusula, o frase:

She dressed *herself.*
He asked *himself* if it was worth it.
I *myself* am not concerned.

7. Pronombres relativos

Los pronombres relativos son *that, what, which, who, whom,* y *whose,* así como las combinaciones de éstos con la terminación *-ever.* Estos pronombres se emplean para introducir oraciones subordinadas con función sustantiva o adjetival.

El pronombre relativo *who* se usa para referirse a personas y, en ciertas ocasiones, algunos animales. *Which* suele usarse para referirse a animales o cosas, y *that* puede usarse para personas, animales, o cosas:

a man *who* sought success
a woman *whom* we trust
Kentucky Firebolt, *who* won yesterday's horse race
a movie *which* was a big hit
a dog *which* kept barking
a boy *that* behaves well
a movie *that* was a big hit
a dog *that* kept barking

En ciertas ocasiones el pronombre relativo puede omitirse:

The man (*whom*) I was talking to is the senator.

El verbo

El verbo inglés posee típicamente las siguientes características: inflexión (p. ej., *help, helps, helping, helped*), persona (primera, segunda, o tercera), número (singular o plural), tiempo (presente, pasado, futuro), aspecto (categorías temporales distintas a los tiempos simples de presente, pasado y futuro), voz (activa o pasiva), y modo (indicativo, subjuntivo e imperativo).

1. La inflexión

Los verbos regulares ingleses tienen cuatro inflexiones diferentes, las cuales se producen al añadir los sufijos *-s* o *-es*, *-ed*, e *-ing*. La mayoría de los verbos irregulares poseen cuatro o cinco inflexiones (p. ej., *see, sees, seeing, saw, seen*); y el verbo *be* tiene ocho (*be, is, am, are, being, was, were, been*).

Los verbos que terminan en una *-e* muda conservan por lo general la *-e* al añadírsele un sufijo que comienza con una consonante (como *-s*), pero esta *-e* desaparece si el sufijo comienza con una vocal (como sucede con *-ed* o *-ing*):

arrange; arranges; arranged; arranging
hope; hopes; hoped; hoping

Sin embargo, algunos de estos verbos conservan la *-e* final para no ser confundidos con otras palabras de ortografía igual, por ejemplo:

dye; dyes; dyed; dyeing
(vs. *dying*, del verbo *die*)
singe; singes; singed; singeing
(vs. *singing*, del verbo *sing*)

Si un verbo consta de una sílaba y termina en una sola consonante a la cual precede una sola vocal, la consonante final se repite al añadir el sufijo *-ed* o *-ing*:

brag; brags; bragged; bragging
grip; grips; gripped; gripping

Cuando un verbo posee esta misma terminación, pero consta de dos o más sílabas, y la última de éstas es acentuada, se repite también al añadir el sufijo *-ed* o *-ing*:

commit; commits; committed; committing
occur; occurs; occurred; occurring

Los verbos que terminan en *-y*, precedida de una consonante, suelen cambiar esta *-y* en *-i* en toda inflexión excepto cuando el sufijo correspondiente es *-ing*:

carry; carries; carried; carrying
study; studies; studied; studying

Cuando un verbo termina en *-c*, se le añade una *-k* en inflexiones cuyos sufijos comienzan con *-e* o *-i*:

mimic; mimics; mimicked; mimicking
traffic; traffics; trafficked; trafficking

2. El tiempo y el aspecto

Los verbos ingleses exhiben generalmente su presente simple o pasado simple en una sola palabra, por ejemplo:

I *do*, I *did*
we *write*, we *wrote*

El tiempo futuro suele expresarse al combinar el verbo auxiliar *shall* o *will* con la forma presente simple o presente progresiva del verbo:

I *shall do* it.
(Lo *haré*.)

We *will come* tomorrow.
(*Vendremos* mañana.)

He *will be arriving* later.
(*Llegará* más tarde.)

Llámase aspecto de un verbo a aquellos tiempos que difieren del presente simple, pasado simple, o futuro simple. A continuación se presentan cuatro de estos tiempos o aspectos: el progresivo, el presente perfecto, el pasado perfecto, y el futuro perfecto.

El tiempo progresivo expresa una acción en progreso:

He *is reading* the paper.
(*Está leyendo* el periódico.)

I *was working* when she called.
(*Estaba trabajando* cuando llamó.)

El presente perfecto se emplea para expresar una acción que ha comenzado en el pasado y que continúa en el presente, o también para expresar una acción que haya tenido lugar en un momento indefinido del pasado:

She *has written* a book.
(*Ha escrito* un libro.)

El pasado perfecto expresa una acción que fue llevada a cabo antes de otra acción o evento en el pasado:

She *had written* many books previously.
(*Había escrito* muchos libros anteriormente.)

El futuro perfecto indica una acción que será llevada a cabo antes de una acción o evento en el futuro:

We *will have finished* the project by then.
(A esas alturas *habremos terminado* el proyecto.)

3. La voz

La voz (activa o pasiva) indica si el sujeto de la oración es el que desempeña la acción del verbo o si es el objeto de esta acción:

Voz activa:
He *respected* his colleagues.
(*Respetaba* a sus colegas.)

Voz pasiva:
He *was respected* by his colleagues.
(*Era respetado* por sus colegas.)

4. El modo

En inglés existen tres modos: indicativo, imperativo, y subjuntivo.

El modo indicativo se emplea ya sea para indicar un hecho, o para hacer una pregunta:

He *is* here.
(*Está* aquí.)

Is he here?
(¿*Está* aquí?)

El modo imperativo se usa para expresar una orden o una petición:

Come here.
(*Ven* aquí.)

Please *come* here.
(*Ven* aquí, por favor.)

El modo subjuntivo expresa una condición contraria a los hechos. El modo subjuntivo en inglés ha caído en desuso, pero suele aparecer en cláusulas introducidas por *if*, y después del verbo *wish*:

I wish he *were* here.
(Quisiera que *estuviera* él aquí.)

If she *were* there, she could have answered that.
(Si *estuviera* ella allá, podría haberlo contestado.)

5. Verbos transitivos e intransitivos

Como en español, el verbo inglés puede ser transitivo o intransitivo. El verbo transitivo es el que puede llevar un complemento directo:

She *sold* her car.
(*Vendió* su coche.)

El verbo intransitivo no lleva un complemento directo:

He *talked* all day.
(*Habló* todo el día.)

Conjugation of Spanish Verbs

Simple Tenses

Tense	Regular Verbs Ending in -AR hablar	
PRESENT INDICATIVE	hablo	hablamos
	hablas	habláis
	habla	hablan
PRESENT SUBJUNCTIVE	hable	hablemos
	hables	habléis
	hable	hablen
PRETERIT INDICATIVE	hablé	hablamos
	hablaste	hablasteis
	habló	hablaron
IMPERFECT INDICATIVE	hablaba	hablábamos
	hablabas	hablabais
	hablaba	hablaban
IMPERFECT SUBJUNCTIVE	hablara	habláramos
	hablaras	hablarais
	hablara	hablaran
	or	
	hablase	hablásemos
	hablases	hablaseis
	hablase	hablasen
FUTURE INDICATIVE	hablaré	hablaremos
	hablarás	hablaréis
	hablará	hablarán
FUTURE SUBJUNCTIVE	hablare	habláremos
	hablares	hablareis
	hablare	hablaren
CONDITIONAL	hablaría	hablaríamos
	hablarías	hablaríais
	hablaría	hablarían
IMPERATIVE		hablemos
	habla	hablad
	hable	hablen
PRESENT PARTICIPLE (GERUND)	hablando	
PAST PARTICIPLE	hablado	

Regular Verbs Ending in -ER		Regular Verbs Ending in -IR	
comer		vivir	
como	comemos	vivo	vivimos
comes	coméis	vives	vivís
come	comen	vive	viven
coma	comamos	viva	vivamos
comas	comáis	vivas	viváis
coma	coman	viva	vivan
comí	comimos	viví	vivimos
comiste	comisteis	viviste	vivisteis
comió	comieron	vivió	vivieron
comía	comíamos	vivía	vivíamos
comías	comíais	vivías	vivíais
comía	comían	vivía	vivían
comiera	comiéramos	viviera	viviéramos
comieras	comierais	vivieras	vivierais
comiera	comieran	viviera	vivieran
or		*or*	
comiese	comiésemos	viviese	viviésemos
comieses	comieseis	vivieses	vivieseis
comiese	comiesen	viviese	viviesen
comeré	comeremos	viviré	viviremos
comerás	comeréis	vivirás	viviréis
comerá	comerán	vivirá	vivirán
comiere	comiéremos	viviere	viviéremos
comieres	comiereis	vivieres	viviereis
comiere	comieren	viviere	vivieren
comería	comeríamos	viviría	viviríamos
comerías	comeríais	vivirías	viviríais
comería	comerían	viviría	vivirían
	comamos		vivamos
come	comed	vive	vivid
coma	coman	viva	vivan
comiendo		viviendo	
comido		vivido	

Compound Tenses

1. Perfect Tenses

The perfect tenses are formed with *haber* and the past participle:

PRESENT PERFECT

> he hablado, etc. (*indicative*)
> haya hablado, etc. (*subjunctive*)

PAST PERFECT

> había hablado, etc. (*indicative*)
> hubiera hablado, etc. (*subjunctive*)
> *or*
> hubiese hablado, etc. (*subjunctive*)

PRETERIT PERFECT

> hube hablado, etc. (*indicative*)

FUTURE PERFECT

> habré hablado, etc. (*indicative*)

CONDITIONAL PERFECT

> habría hablado, etc. (*indicative*)

2. Progressive Tenses

The progressive tenses are formed with *estar* and the present participle:

PRESENT PROGRESSIVE

> estoy llamando, etc. (*indicative*)
> esté llamando, etc. (*subjunctive*)

IMPERFECT PROGRESSIVE

> estaba llamando, etc. (*indicative*)
> estuviera llamando, etc. (*subjunctive*)
> *or*
> estuviese llamando, etc. (*subjunctive*)

PRETERIT PROGRESSIVE

> estuve llamando, etc. (*indicative*)

FUTURE PROGRESSIVE

> estaré llamando, etc. (*indicative*)

CONDITIONAL PROGRESSIVE

> estaría llamando, etc. (*indicative*)

PRESENT PERFECT PROGRESSIVE

      he estado llamando, etc. (*indicative*)

      haya estado llamando, etc. (*subjunctive*)

PAST PERFECT PROGRESSIVE

      había estado llamando, etc. (*indicative*)

      hubiera estado llamando, etc. (*subjunctive*)

      or

      hubiese estado llamando, etc. (*subjunctive*)

Use of *Vos*

In parts of South and Central America, *vos* often replaces or competes with *tú* as the second-person familiar personal pronoun. It is particularly well established in the Río de la Plata region and much of Central America.

The pronoun *vos* often takes a distinct set of verb forms, usually in the present tense and the imperative. These vary widely from region to region; examples of the most common forms are shown below:

INFINITIVE FORM	hablar	comer	vivir
PRESENT INDICATIVE	vos hablás	vos comés	vos vivís
PRESENT SUBJUNCTIVE	vos hablés	vos comás	vos vivás
IMPERATIVE	hablá	comé	viví

In some areas, *vos* may take the *tú* or *vosotros* forms of the verb, while in others (such as Uruguay), *tú* is combined with the *vos* verb forms.

Irregular Verbs

The *imperfect subjunctive*, the *future subjunctive*, the *conditional*, and most forms of the *imperative* are not included in the model conjugations list, but can be derived as follows:

The *imperfect subjunctive* and the *future subjunctive* are formed from the third-person plural form of the preterit tense by removing the last syllable (*-ron*) and adding the appropriate suffix:

PRETERIT INDICATIVE, THIRD-PERSON PLURAL (querer)	quisieron
IMPERFECT SUBJUNCTIVE (querer)	quisiera, quisieras, etc.
	or
	quisiese, quisieses, etc.
FUTURE SUBJUNCTIVE (querer)	quisiere, quisieres, etc.

The conditional uses the same stem as the future indicative:

FUTURE INDICATIVE (poner)   pondré, pondrás, etc.
CONDITIONAL (poner)   pondría, pondrías, etc.

The third-person singular, first-person plural, and third-person plural forms of the *imperative* are the same as the corresponding forms of the present subjunctive.

The second-person plural *(vosotros)* form of the *imperative* is formed by removing the final *-r* of the infinitive form and adding a *-d* (ex.: *oír* → *oíd*).

Model Conjugations of Irregular Verbs

The model conjugations below include the following simple tenses: the *present indicative* (IND), the *present subjunctive* (SUBJ), the *preterit indicative* (PRET), the *imperfect indicative* (IMPF), the *future indicative* (FUT), the second-person singular form of the *imperative* (IMPER), the *present participle* or *gerund* (PRP), and the *past participle* (PP). Each set of conjugations is preceded by the corresponding infinitive form of the verb, shown in bold type. Only tenses containing irregularities are listed, and the irregular verb forms within each tense are displayed in bold type.

Each irregular verb entry in the Spanish-English section of this dictionary is cross-referred by number to one of the following model conjugations. These cross-reference numbers are shown in curly braces { } immediately following the entry's functional label.

1 **abolir** *(defective verb)* : IND abolimos, abolís *(other forms not used)*; SUBJ *(not used)*; IMPER *(only second-person plural is used)*

2 **abrir** : PP abierto

3 **actuar** : IND **actúo, actúas, actúa,** actuamos, actuáis, **actúan;** SUBJ **actúe, actúes, actúe,** actuemos, actuéis, **actúen;** IMPER **actúa**

4 **adquirir** : IND **adquiero, adquieres, adquiere,** adquirimos, adquirís, **adquieren;** SUBJ **adquiera, adquieras, adquiera,** adquiramos, adquiráis, **adquieran;** IMPER **adquiere**

5 **airar** : IND **aíro, aíras, aíra,** airamos, airáis, **aíran;** SUBJ **aíre, aíres, aíre,** airemos, airéis, **aíren;** IMPER **aíra**

6 **andar** : PRET **anduve, anduviste, anduvo, anduvimos, anduvisteis, anduvieron**

7 **asir** : IND **asgo,** ases, ase, asimos, asís, asen; SUBJ **asga, asgas, asga, asgamos, asgáis, asgan**

8 **aunar** : IND **aúno, aúnas, aúna,** aunamos, aunáis, **aúnan;** SUBJ **aúne, aúnes, aúne,** aunemos, aunéis, **aúnen;** IMPER **aúna**

9 **avergonzar** : *IND* **avergüenzo, avergüenzas, avergüenza,** aver-
gonzamos, avergonzáis, **avergüenzan;** *SUBJ* **avergüence,
avergüences, avergüence, avergoncemos, avergoncéis,
avergüencen;** *PRET* **avergoncé;** *IMPER* **avergüenza**

10 **averiguar** : *SUBJ* **averigüe, averigües, averigüe, averigüemos,
averigüéis, averigüen;** *PRET* **averigüé,** averiguaste, averiguó,
averiguamos, averiguasteis, averiguaron

11 **bendecir** : *IND* **bendigo, bendices, bendice,** bendecimos, bende-
cís, **bendicen;** *SUBJ* **bendiga, bendigas, bendiga, bendigamos,
bendigáis, bendigan;** *PRET* **bendije, bendijiste, bendijo, bendi-
jimos, bendijisteis, bendijeron;** *IMPER* **bendice**

12 **caber** : *IND* **quepo,** cabes, cabe, cabemos, cabéis, caben; *SUBJ*
quepa, quepas, quepa, quepamos, quepáis, quepan; *PRET* **cupe,
cupiste, cupo, cupimos, cupisteis, cupieron;** *FUT* **cabré, cabrás,
cabrá, cabremos, cabréis, cabrán**

13 **caer** : *IND* **caigo,** caes, cae, caemos, caéis, caen; *SUBJ* **caiga, cai-
gas, caiga, caigamos, caigáis, caigan;** *PRET* caí, **caíste, cayó,
caímos,** caísteis, **cayeron;** *PRP* **cayendo;** *PP* **caído**

14 **cocer** : *IND* **cuezo, cueces, cuece,** cocemos, cocéis, **cuecen;** *SUBJ*
cueza, cuezas, cueza, cozamos, cozáis, cuezan; *IMPER* **cuece**

15 **coger** : *IND* **cojo,** coges, coge, cogemos, cogéis, cogen; *SUBJ* **coja,
cojas, coja, cojamos, cojáis, cojan**

16 **colgar** : *IND* **cuelgo, cuelgas, cuelga,** colgamos, colgáis, **cuelgan;**
SUBJ **cuelgue, cuelgues, cuelgue, colguemos, colguéis, cuel-
guen;** *PRET* **colgué,** colgaste, colgó, colgamos, colgasteis, col-
garon; *IMPER* **cuelga**

17 **concernir** *(defective verb; used only in the third-person singular
and plural of the present indicative, present subjunctive, and
imperfect subjunctive)* see **25 discernir**

18 **conocer** : *IND* **conozco,** conoces, conoce, conocemos, conocéis,
conocen; *SUBJ* **conozca, conozcas, conozca, conozcamos,
conozcáis, conozcan**

19 **contar** : *IND* **cuento, cuentas, cuenta,** contamos, contáis, **cuen-
tan;** *SUBJ* **cuente, cuentes, cuente,** contemos, contéis, **cuenten;**
IMPER **cuenta**

20 **creer** : *PRET* creí, **creíste, creyó, creímos,** creísteis, **creyeron;** *PRP*
creyendo; *PP* **creído**

21 **cruzar** : *SUBJ* **cruce, cruces, cruce, crucemos, crucéis, crucen;**
PRET **crucé,** cruzaste, cruzó, cruzamos, cruzasteis, cruzaron

22 **dar** : *IND* **doy,** das, da, damos, **dais,** dan; *SUBJ* **dé,** des, **dé,** demos,
deis, den; *PRET* **di,** diste, **dio, dimos,** disteis, **dieron**

23 **decir** : *IND* **digo, dices, dice,** decimos, decís, **dicen;** *SUBJ* **diga,
digas, diga, digamos, digáis, digan;** *PRET* **dije, dijiste, dijo,
dijimos, dijisteis, dijeron;** *FUT* **diré, dirás, dirá, diremos,
diréis, dirán;** *IMPER* **di;** *PRP* **diciendo;** *PP* **dicho**

24 **delinquir** : *IND* **delinco**, delinques, delinque, delinquimos, delin-
quís, delinquen; *SUBJ* **delinca, delincas, delinca, delincamos,
delincáis, delincan**

25 **discernir** : *IND* **discierno, disciernes, discierne**, discernimos, dis-
cernís, **disciernen**; *SUBJ* **discierna, disciernas, discierna**, dis-
cernamos, discernáis, **disciernan**; *IMPER* **discierne**

26 **distinguir** : *IND* **distingo**, distingues, distingue, distinguimos, dis-
tinguís, distinguen; *SUBJ* **distinga, distingas, distinga, distinga-
mos, distingáis, distingan**

27 **dormir** : *IND* **duermo, duermes, duerme**, dormimos, dormís,
duermen; *SUBJ* **duerma, duermas, duerma, durmamos,
durmáis, duerman**; *PRET* dormí, dormiste, **durmió**, dormimos,
dormisteis, **durmieron**; *IMPER* **duerme**; *PRP* **durmiendo**

28 **elegir** : *IND* **elijo, eliges, elige**, elegimos, elegís, **eligen**; *SUBJ* **elija,
elijas, elija, elijamos, elijáis, elijan**; *PRET* elegí, elegiste, **eligió**,
elegimos, elegisteis, **eligieron**; *IMPER* **elige**; *PRP* **eligiendo**

29 **empezar** : *IND* **empiezo, empiezas, empieza**, empezamos,
empezáis, **empiezan**; *SUBJ* **empiece, empieces, empiece, empecemos, empecéis, empiecen**; *PRET* **empecé**, empezaste, empezó,
empezamos, empezasteis, empezaron; *IMPER* **empieza**

30 **enraizar** : *IND* **enraízo, enraízas, enraíza**, enraizamos, enraizáis,
enraízan; *SUBJ* **enraíce, enraíces, enraíce, enraicemos, enrai-
céis, enraícen**; *PRET* **enraicé**, enraizaste, enraizó, enraizamos,
enraizasteis, enraizaron; *IMPER* **enraíza**

31 **erguir** : *IND* **irgo** *or* **yergo, irgues** *or* **yergues, irgue** *or* **yergue**,
erguimos, erguís, **irguen** *or* **yerguen**; *SUBJ* **irga** *or* **yerga, irgas**
or **yergas, irga** *or* **yerga, irgamos, irgáis, irgan** *or* **yergan**;
PRET erguí, erguiste, **irguió**, erguimos, erguisteis, **irguieron**;
IMPER **irgue** *or* **yergue**; *PRP* **irguiendo**

32 **errar** : *IND* **yerro, yerras, yerra**, erramos, erráis, **yerran**; *SUBJ*
yerre, yerres, yerre, erremos, erréis, **yerren**; *IMPER* **yerra**

33 **escribir** : *PP* **escrito**

34 **estar** : *IND* **estoy, estás, está**, estamos, estáis, **están**; *SUBJ* **esté,
estés, esté**, estemos, estéis, **estén**; *PRET* **estuve, estuviste,
estuvo, estuvimos, estuvisteis, estuvieron**; *IMPER* **está**

35 **exigir** : *IND* **exijo**, exiges, exige, exigimos, exigís, exigen; *SUBJ*
exija, exijas, exija, exijamos, exijáis, exijan

36 **forzar** : *IND* **fuerzo, fuerzas, fuerza**, forzamos, forzáis, **fuerzan**;
SUBJ **fuerce, fuerces, fuerce**, forcemos, forcéis, **fuercen**; *PRET*
forcé, forzaste, forzó, forzamos, forzasteis, forzaron; *IMPER*
fuerza

37 **freír** : *IND* **frío, fríes, fríe**, freímos, freís, **fríen**; *SUBJ* **fría, frías,
fría, friamos, friáis, frían**; *PRET* freí, **freíste, frió, freímos,
freísteis, frieron**; *IMPER* **fríe**; *PRP* **friendo**; *PP* **frito**

38 **gruñir** : *PRET* gruñí, gruñiste, **gruñó**, gruñimos, gruñisteis,
gruñeron; *PRP* **gruñendo**

39 **haber** : *IND* **he, has, ha, hemos,** habéis, **han;** *SUBJ* **haya, hayas, haya, hayamos,** hayáis, **hayan;** *PRET* **hube,** hubiste, **hubo,** hubimos, hubisteis, hubieron; *FUT* habré, habrás, habrá, habremos, habréis, habrán; *IMPER* **he**

40 **hacer** : *IND* **hago,** haces, hace, hacemos, hacéis, hacen; *SUBJ* **haga, hagas, haga, hagamos, hagáis, hagan;** *PRET* **hice, hiciste, hizo, hicimos,** hicisteis, **hicieron;** *FUT* haré, harás, hará, haremos, haréis, harán; *IMPER* **haz;** *PP* **hecho**

41 **huir** : *IND* **huyo, huyes, huye,** huimos, huís, **huyen;** *SUBJ* **huya, huyas, huya, huyamos,** huyáis, **huyan;** *PRET* huí, huiste, **huyó,** huimos, huisteis, **huyeron;** *IMPER* **huye;** *PRP* **huyendo**

42 **imprimir** : *PP* **impreso**

43 **ir** : *IND* **voy, vas, va, vamos,** vais, **van;** *SUBJ* **vaya, vayas, vaya, vayamos,** vayáis, **vayan;** *PRET* fui, fuiste, fue, fuimos, fuisteis, fueron; *IMPF* iba, ibas, iba, íbamos, ibais, iban; *IMPER* **ve;** *PRP* **yendo;** *PP* **ido**

44 **jugar** : *IND* **juego, juegas, juega,** jugamos, jugáis, **juegan;** *SUBJ* **juegue, juegues, juegue, juguemos, juguéis, jueguen;** *PRET* **jugué,** jugaste, jugó, jugamos, jugasteis, jugaron; *IMPER* **juega**

45 **lucir** : *IND* **luzco,** luces, luce, lucimos, lucís, lucen; *SUBJ* **luzca, luzcas, luzca, luzcamos, luzcáis, luzcan**

46 **morir** : *IND* **muero, mueres, muere,** morimos, morís, **mueren;** *SUBJ* **muera, mueras, muera, muramos, muráis, mueran;** *PRET* morí, moriste, **murió,** morimos, moristeis, **murieron;** *IMPER* **muere;** *PRP* **muriendo;** *PP* **muerto**

47 **mover** : *IND* **muevo, mueves, mueve,** movemos, movéis, **mueven;** *SUBJ* **mueva, muevas, mueva,** movamos, mováis, **muevan;** *IMPER* **mueve**

48 **nacer** : *IND* **nazco,** naces, nace, nacemos, nacéis, nacen; *SUBJ* **nazca, nazcas, nazca, nazcamos, nazcáis, nazcan**

49 **negar** : *IND* **niego, niegas, niega,** negamos, negáis, **niegan;** *SUBJ* **niegue, niegues, niegue, neguemos, neguéis, nieguen;** *PRET* **negué,** negaste, negó, negamos, negasteis, negaron; *IMPER* **niega**

50 **oír** : *IND* **oigo, oyes, oye,** oímos, oís, **oyen;** *SUBJ* **oiga, oigas, oiga, oigamos, oigáis, oigan;** *PRET* oí, **oíste, oyó,** oímos, **oísteis, oyeron;** *IMPER* **oye;** *PRP* **oyendo;** *PP* **oído**

51 **oler** : *IND* **huelo, hueles, huele,** olemos, oléis, **huelen;** *SUBJ* **huela, huelas, huela,** olamos, oláis, **huelan;** *IMPER* **huele**

52 **pagar** : *SUBJ* **pague, pagues, pague, paguemos, paguéis, paguen;** *PRET* **pagué,** pagaste, pagó, pagamos, pagasteis, pagaron

53 **parecer** : *IND* **parezco,** pareces, parece, parecemos, parecéis, parecen; *SUBJ* **parezca, parezcas, parezca, parezcamos, parezcáis, parezcan**

54 **pedir** : *IND* **pido, pides, pide,** pedimos, pedís, **piden;** *SUBJ* **pida, pidas, pida, pidamos, pidáis, pidan;** *PRET* pedí, pediste, **pidió,** pedimos, pedisteis, **pidieron;** *IMPER* **pide;** *PRP* **pidiendo**

55 **pensar** : *IND* **pienso, piensas, piensa**, pensamos, pensáis, **pien-san**; *SUBJ* **piense, pienses, piense**, pensemos, penséis, **piensen**; *IMPER* **piensa**

56 **perder** : *IND* **pierdo, pierdes, pierde**, perdemos, perdéis, **pierden**; *SUBJ* **pierda, pierdas, pierda**, perdamos, perdáis, **pierdan**; *IMPER* **pierde**

57 **placer** : *IND* **plazco**, places, place, placemos, placéis, placen; *SUBJ* **plazca, plazcas, plazca, plazcamos, plazcáis, plazcan**; *PRET* plací, placiste, plació *or* **plugo**, placimos, placisteis, placieron *or* **pluguieron**

58 **poder** : *IND* **puedo, puedes, puede**, podemos, podéis, **pueden**; *SUBJ* **pueda, puedas, pueda**, podamos, podáis, **puedan**; *PRET* **pude, pudiste, pudo, pudimos, pudisteis, pudieron**; *FUT* **podré, podrás, podrá, podremos, podréis, podrán**; *IMPER* **puede**; *PRP* **pudiendo**

59 **podrir** *or* **pudrir** : *PP* **podrido** *(all other forms based on* pudrir*)*

60 **poner** : *IND* **pongo**, pones, pone, ponemos, ponéis, ponen; *SUBJ* **ponga, pongas, ponga, pongamos, pongáis, pongan**; *PRET* **puse, pusiste, puso, pusimos, pusisteis, pusieron**; *FUT* **pondré, pondrás, pondrá, pondremos, pondréis, pondrán**; *IMPER* **pon**; *PP* **puesto**

61 **producir** : *IND* **produzco**, produces, produce, producimos, producís, producen; *SUBJ* **produzca, produzcas, produzca, produzcamos, produzcáis, produzcan**; *PRET* **produje, produjiste, produjo, produjimos, produjisteis, produjeron**

62 **prohibir** : *IND* **prohíbo, prohíbes, prohíbe**, prohibimos, prohibís, **prohíben**; *SUBJ* **prohíba, prohíbas, prohíba**, prohibamos, prohibáis, **prohíban**; *IMPER* **prohíbe**

63 **proveer** : *PRET* proveí, **proveíste, proveyó, proveímos, proveísteis, proveyeron**; *PRP* **proveyendo**; *PP* **provisto**

64 **querer** : *IND* **quiero, quieres, quiere**, queremos, queréis, **quieren**; *SUBJ* **quiera, quieras, quiera**, queramos, queráis, **quieran**; *PRET* **quise, quisiste, quiso, quisimos, quisisteis, quisieron**; *FUT* **querré, querrás, querrá, querremos, querréis, querrán**; *IMPER* **quiere**

65 **raer** : *IND* **rao** *or* **raigo** *or* **rayo**, raes, rae, raemos, raéis, raen; *SUBJ* **raiga** *or* **raya, raigas** *or* **rayas, raiga** *or* **raya, raigamos** *or* **rayamos, raigáis** *or* **rayáis, raigan** *or* **rayan**; *PRET* **raí, raíste, rayó, raímos, raísteis, rayeron**; *PRP* **rayendo**; *PP* **raído**

66 **reír** : *IND* **río, ríes, ríe, reímos**, reís, **ríen**; *SUBJ* **ría, rías, ría, riamos, riáis, rían**; *PRET* reí, **reíste, rió, reímos, reísteis**, rieron; *IMPER* **ríe**; *PRP* **riendo**; *PP* **reído**

67 **reñir** : *IND* **riño, riñes, riñe**, reñimos, reñís, **riñen**; *SUBJ* **riña, riñas, riña, riñamos, riñáis, riñan**; *PRET* reñí, reñiste, **riñó**, reñimos, reñisteis, **riñeron**; *IMPER* **riñe**; *PRP* **riñendo**

68 reunir : *IND* **reúno, reúnes, reúne,** reunimos, reunís, **reúnen;** *SUBJ* **reúna, reúnas, reúna,** reunamos, reunáis, **reúnan;** *IMPER* **reúne**

69 roer : *IND* roo *or* **roigo** *or* **royo,** roes, roe, roemos, roéis, roen; *SUBJ* roa *or* **roiga** *or* **roya,** roas *or* **roigas** *or* **royas,** roa *or* **roiga** *or* **roya,** roamos *or* **roigamos** *or* **royamos,** roáis *or* **roigáis** *or* **royáis,** roan *or* **roigan** *or* **royan;** *PRET* roí, **roíste, royó, roímos, roísteis, royeron;** *PRP* **royendo;** *PP* **roído**

70 romper : *PP* **roto**

71 saber : *IND* **sé,** sabes, sabe, sabemos, sabéis, saben; *SUBJ* **sepa, sepas, sepa, sepamos, sepáis, sepan;** *PRET* **supe, supiste, supo, supimos, supisteis, supieron;** *FUT* **sabré, sabrás, sabrá, sabremos, sabréis, sabrán**

72 sacar : *SUBJ* **saque, saques, saque, saquemos, saquéis, saquen;** *PRET* **saqué,** sacaste, sacó, sacamos, sacasteis, sacaron

73 salir : *IND* **salgo,** sales, sale, salimos, salís, salen; *SUBJ* **salga, salgas, salga, salgamos, salgáis, salgan;** *FUT* **saldré, saldrás, saldrá, saldremos, saldréis, saldrán;** *IMPER* **sal**

74 satisfacer : *IND* **satisfago,** satisfaces, satisface, satisfacemos, satisfacéis, satisfacen; *SUBJ* **satisfaga, satisfagas, satisfaga, satisfagamos, satisfagáis, satisfagan;** *PRET* **satisfice, satisficiste, satisfizo, satisficimos, satisficisteis, satisficieron;** *FUT* **satisfaré, satisfarás, satisfará, satisfaremos, satisfaréis, satisfarán;** *IMPER* **satisfaz** *or* satisface; *PP* **satisfecho**

75 seguir : *IND* **sigo, sigues, sigue,** seguimos, seguís, **siguen;** *SUBJ* **siga, sigas, siga, sigamos, sigáis, sigan;** *PRET* seguí, seguiste, **siguió,** seguimos, seguisteis, **siguieron;** *IMPER* **sigue;** *PRP* **siguiendo**

76 sentir : *IND* **siento, sientes, siente,** sentimos, sentís, **sienten;** *SUBJ* **sienta, sientas, sienta, sintamos, sintáis, sientan;** *PRET* sentí, sentiste, **sintió,** sentimos, sentisteis, **sintieron;** *IMPER* **siente;** *PRP* **sintiendo**

77 ser : *IND* **soy, eres, es, somos, sois, son;** *SUBJ* **sea, seas, sea, seamos, seáis, sean;** *PRET* **fui, fuiste, fue, fuimos, fuisteis, fueron;** *IMPF* **era, eras, era, éramos, erais, eran;** *IMPER* **sé;** *PRP* **siendo;** *PP* **sido**

78 soler *(defective verb; used only in the present, preterit, and imperfect indicative, and the present and imperfect subjunctive)* see **47 mover**

79 tañer : *PRET* tañí, tañiste, **tañó,** tañimos, tañisteis, **tañeron;** *PRP* **tañendo**

80 tener : *IND* **tengo, tienes, tiene,** tenemos, tenéis, **tienen;** *SUBJ* **tenga, tengas, tenga, tengamos, tengáis, tengan;** *PRET* **tuve, tuviste, tuvo, tuvimos, tuvisteis, tuvieron;** *FUT* **tendré, tendrás, tendrá, tendremos, tendréis, tendrán;** *IMPER* **ten**

81 **traer** : *IND* **traigo**, traes, trae, traemos, traéis, traen; *SUBJ* **traiga, traigas, traiga, traigamos, traigáis, traigan**; *PRET* **traje, trajiste, trajo, trajimos, trajisteis, trajeron**; *PRP* **trayendo**; *PP* **traído**

82 **trocar** : *IND* **trueco, truecas, trueca**, trocamos, trocáis, **truecan**; *SUBJ* **trueque, trueques, trueque, troquemos, troquéis, truequen**; *PRET* **troqué**, trocaste, trocó, trocamos, trocasteis, trocaron; *IMPER* **trueca**

83 **uncir** : *IND* **unzo**, unces, unce, uncimos, uncís, uncen; *SUBJ* **unza, unzas, unza, unzamos, unzáis, unzan**

84 **valer** : *IND* **valgo**, vales, vale, valemos, valéis, valen; *SUBJ* **valga, valgas, valga, valgamos, valgáis, valgan**; *FUT* **valdré, valdrás, valdrá, valdremos, valdréis, valdrán**

85 **variar** : *IND* **varío, varías, varía**, variamos, variáis, **varían**; *SUBJ* **varíe, varíes, varíe**, variemos, variéis, **varíen**; *IMPER* **varía**

86 **vencer** : *IND* **venzo**, vences, vence, vencemos, vencéis, vencen; *SUBJ* **venza, venzas, venza, venzamos, venzáis, venzan**

87 **venir** : *IND* **vengo, vienes, viene**, venimos, venís, **vienen**; *SUBJ* **venga, vengas, venga, vengamos, vengáis, vengan**; *PRET* **vine, viniste, vino, vinimos, vinisteis, vinieron**; *FUT* **vendré, vendrás, vendrá, vendremos, vendréis, vendrán**; *IMPER* **ven**; *PRP* **viniendo**

88 **ver** : *IND* **veo, ves, ve, vemos, veis, ven**; *PRET* **vi**, viste, vio, vimos, visteis, vieron; *IMPER* **ve**; *PRP* **viendo**; *PP* **visto**

89 **volver** : *IND* **vuelvo, vuelves, vuelve**, volvemos, volvéis, **vuelven**; *SUBJ* **vuelva, vuelvas, vuelva**, volvamos, volváis, **vuelvan**; *IMPER* **vuelve**; *PP* **vuelto**

90 **yacer** : *IND* **yazco** *or* **yazgo** *or* **yago**, yaces, yace, yacemos, yacéis, yacen; *SUBJ* **yazca** *or* **yazga** *or* **yaga, yazcas** *or* **yazgas** *or* **yagas, yazca** *or* **yazga** *or* **yaga, yazcamos** *or* **yazgamos** *or* **yagamos, yazcáis** *or* **yazgáis** *or* **yagáis, yazcan** *or* **yazgan** *or* **yagan**; *IMPER* **yace** *or* **yaz**

Verbos irregulares en inglés

INFINITIVO	PRETÉRITO	PARTICIPIO PASADO
arise	arose	arisen
awake	awoke	awoken *o* awaked
be	was, were	been
bear	bore	borne
beat	beat	beaten *o* beat
become	became	become
befall	befell	befallen
begin	began	begun
behold	beheld	beheld
bend	bent	bent
beseech	beseeched *o* besought	beseeched *o* besought
beset	beset	beset
bet	bet	bet
bid	bade *o* bid	bidden *o* bid
bind	bound	bound
bite	bit	bitten
bleed	bled	bled
blow	blew	blown
break	broke	broken
breed	bred	bred
bring	brought	brought
build	built	built
burn	burned *o* burnt	burned *o* burnt
burst	burst	burst
buy	bought	bought
can	could	—
cast	cast	cast
catch	caught	caught
choose	chose	chosen
cling	clung	clung
come	came	come
cost	cost	cost
creep	crept	crept
cut	cut	cut
deal	dealt	dealt
dig	dug	dug
dive	dived *o* dove	dived
do	did	done
draw	drew	drawn
dream	dreamed *o* dreamt	dreamed *o* dreamt
drink	drank	drunk *o* drank
drive	drove	driven
dwell	dwelled *o* dwelt	dwelled *o* dwelt
eat	ate	eaten
fall	fell	fallen
feed	fed	fed
feel	felt	felt
fight	fought	fought
find	found	found
flee	fled	fled

INFINITIVO	PRETÉRITO	PARTICIPIO PASADO
fling	flung	flung
fly	flew	flown
forbid	forbade	forbidden
forecast	forecast	forecast
forego	forewent	foregone
foresee	foresaw	foreseen
foretell	foretold	foretold
forget	forgot	forgotten o forgot
forgive	forgave	forgiven
forsake	forsook	forsaken
freeze	froze	frozen
get	got	got o gotten
give	gave	given
go	went	gone
grind	ground	ground
grow	grew	grown
hang	hung	hung
have	had	had
hear	heard	heard
hide	hid	hidden o hid
hit	hit	hit
hold	held	held
hurt	hurt	hurt
keep	kept	kept
kneel	knelt o kneeled	knelt o kneeled
know	knew	known
lay	laid	laid
lead	led	led
leap	leaped o leapt	leaped o leapt
leave	left	left
lend	lent	lent
let	let	let
lie	lay	lain
light	lit o lighted	lit o lighted
lose	lost	lost
make	made	made
may	might	—
mean	meant	meant
meet	met	met
mow	mowed	mowed o mown
overcome	overcame	overcome
pay	paid	paid
put	put	put
quit	quit	quit
read	read	read
rend	rent	rent
rid	rid	rid
ride	rode	ridden
ring	rang	rung
rise	rose	risen
run	ran	run
saw	sawed	sawed o sawn

INFINITIVO	PRETÉRITO	PARTICIPIO PASADO
say	said	said
see	saw	seen
seek	sought	sought
sell	sold	sold
send	sent	sent
set	set	set
sew	sewed	sewn *o* sewed
shake	shook	shaken
shall	should	—
shear	sheared	sheared *o* shorn
shed	shed	shed
shine	shone *o* shined	shone *o* shined
shoot	shot	shot
show	showed	shown *o* showed
shrink	shrank *o* shrunk	shrunk *o* shrunken
shut	shut	shut
sing	sang *o* sung	sung
sink	sank *o* sunk	sunk
sit	sat	sat
slay	slew	slain
sleep	slept	slept
slide	slid	slid
sling	slung	slung
smell	smelled *o* smelt	smelled *o* smelt
sow	sowed	sown *o* sowed
speak	spoke	spoken
speed	sped *o* speeded	sped *o* speeded
spend	spent	spent
spin	spun	spun
spit	spit *o* spat	spit *o* spat
split	split	split
spread	spread	spread
spring	sprang *o* sprung	sprung
stand	stood	stood
steal	stole	stolen
stick	stuck	stuck
sting	stung	stung
stink	stank *o* stunk	stunk
stride	strode	stridden
strike	struck	struck
swear	swore	sworn
sweep	swept	swept
swell	swelled	swelled *o* swollen
swim	swam	swum
swing	swung	swung
take	took	taken
teach	taught	taught
tear	tore	torn
tell	told	told
think	thought	thought
throw	threw	thrown
thrust	thrust	thrust

INFINITIVO	PRETÉRITO	PARTICIPIO PASADO
tread	trod	trodden *o* trod
undergo	underwent	undergone
understand	understood	understood
undo	undid	undone
wake	woke	woken *o* waked
waylay	waylaid	waylaid
wear	wore	worn
weave	wove *o* weaved	woven *o* weaved
weep	wept	wept
will	would	—
win	won	won
wind	wound	wound
withdraw	withdrew	withdrawn
withhold	withheld	withheld
withstand	withstood	withstood
wring	wrung	wrung
write	wrote	written

Abbreviations in This Work (Abreviaturas empleadas en este libro)

Abbreviation (Abreviatura)	English Expansion (Expansión en inglés)	Spanish Meaning (Significado en español)
adj	adjective	adjetivo
adv	adverb	adverbio
Arg	Argentina	Argentina
Bol	Bolivia	Bolivia
Brit	British	británico
CA	Central America	Centroamérica
Car	Caribbean region	Región del Caribe
Col	Colombia	Colombia
conj	conjunction	conjunción
CoRi	Costa Rica	Costa Rica
DomRep	Dominican Republic	República Dominicana
Ecua	Ecuador	Ecuador
esp	especially	especialmente
f	feminine	femenino
fam	familiar or colloquial	familiar o coloquial
fpl	feminine plural	femenino plural
Guat	Guatemala	Guatemala
Hond	Honduras	Honduras
interj	interjection	interjección
m	masculine	masculino
Mex	Mexico	México
mf	masculine or feminine	masculino o femenino
mfpl	masculine or feminine plural	plural masculino o femenino
mpl	masculine plural	plural masculino
n	noun	sustantivo
nf	feminine noun	sustantivo femenino
nfpl	feminine plural noun	sustantivo plural femenino
nfs & pl	invariable singular or plural feminine noun	sustantivo femenino, invariable en cuanto a número
Nic	Nicaragua	Nicaragua
nm	masculine noun	sustantivo masculino
nmf	masculine or feminine noun	sustantivo masculino o femenino
nmfpl	plural noun invariable for gender	sustantivo plural, invariable en cuanto a género

Abbreviation (Abreviatura)	English Expansion (Expansión en inglés)	Spanish Meaning (Significado en español)
nmfs & pl	noun invariable for both gender and number	sustantivo invariable en cuanto a género y número
nmpl	masculine plural noun	sustantivo plural masculino
nms & pl	invariable singular or plural masculine noun	sustantivo masculino, invariable en cuanto a número
npl	plural noun	sustantivo plural
ns & pl	noun invariable for plural	sustantivo invariable en cuanto a número
Pan	Panama	Panamá
Par	Paraguay	Paraguay
pl	plural	plural
pp	past participle	participio pasado
pref	prefix	prefijo
prep	preposition	preposición
PRi	Puerto Rico	Puerto Rico
pron	pronoun	pronombre
s	singular	singular
Sal	El Salvador	El Salvador
suf	suffix	sufijo
Uru	Uruguay	Uruguay
usu	usually	generalmente
v	verb	verbo
v aux	auxiliary verb	verbo auxiliar
Ven	Venezuela	Venezuela
vi	intransitive verb	verbo intransitivo
v impers	impersonal verb	verbo impersonal
vr	reflexive verb	verbo pronominal
vt	transitive verb	verbo transitivo

Pronunciation Symbols
(Símbolos de pronunciación)

VOWELS (VOCALES)

æ	ask, bat, glad	ask, bat, glad
ɑ	cot, bomb	cot, bomb
a	*New England* **au**nt, *British* ask, glass, *Spanish* c**a**sa	*Nueva Inglaterra* **au**nt, *inglés británico* ask, glass, *español* c**a**sa
e	*Spanish* p**e**so, j**e**fe	*español* p**e**so, j**e**fe
ɛ	**e**gg, b**e**t, f**e**d	**e**gg, b**e**t, f**e**d
ə	**a**bout, jav**e**lin, Alab**a**ma	**a**bout, jav**e**lin, Alab**a**ma
ə	indicates a syllabic pronunciation of the consonant as in bott**le**, pris**m**	denota una pronunciación silábica del consonante, como en bott**le**, pris**m**
i	v**e**ry, **a**ny, thirt**y**, *Spanish* pi**ñ**a	v**e**ry, **a**ny, thirt**y**, *español* pi**ñ**a
i:	**ea**t, b**ea**d, b**ee**	**ea**t, b**ea**d, b**ee**
ɪ	**i**d, b**i**d, p**i**t	**i**d, b**i**d, p**i**t
o	**O**hio, yell**o**wer, potat**o**, *Spanish* **ó**valo	**O**hio, yell**o**wer, potat**o**, *español* **ó**valo
o:	**oa**ts, **o**wn, z**o**ne, bl**o**w	**oa**ts, **o**wn, z**o**ne, bl**o**w
ɔ	**a**wl, m**au**l, c**au**ght, p**a**w	**a**wl, m**au**l, c**au**ght, p**a**w
ʊ	sh**ou**ld, c**ou**ld	sh**ou**ld, c**ou**ld
u	*Spanish* **u**va, c**u**lpa	*español* **u**va, c**u**lpa
u:	b**oo**t, f**ew**, c**oo**	b**oo**t, f**ew**, c**oo**
ʌ	**u**nder, p**u**tt, b**u**d	**u**nder, p**u**tt, b**u**d
eɪ	**eigh**t, w**a**de, b**ay**	**eigh**t, w**a**de, b**ay**
aɪ	**i**ce, b**i**te, t**ie**	**i**ce, b**i**te, t**ie**
aʊ	**ou**t, g**ow**n, pl**ow**	**ou**t, g**ow**n, pl**ow**
ɔɪ	**oy**ster, c**oi**l, b**oy**	**oy**ster, c**oi**l, b**oy**
ər	f**ur**ther, st**ir**	f**ur**ther, st**ir**
ø	*French* d**eu**x, *German* H**ö**hle	*francés* d**eu**x, *alemán* H**ö**hle
~	(tilde as in õ) *French* b**o**n	(tilde como en õ) *francés* b**o**n
:	indicates that the preceding vowel is long	indica que la vocal precedente es larga

CONSONANTS (CONSONANTES)

b	**b**a**b**y, la**b**or, ca**b**	**b**a**b**y, la**b**or, ca**b**
d	**d**ay, rea**d**y, ki**d**	**d**ay, rea**d**y, ki**d**
ʤ	**j**ust, ba**dg**er, fu**dg**e	**j**ust, ba**dg**er, fu**dg**e
ð	**th**en, ei**th**er, ba**th**e	**th**en, ei**th**er, ba**th**e
f	**f**oe, tou**gh**, bu**ff**	**f**oe, tou**gh**, bu**ff**
g	**g**o, bi**gg**er, ba**g**	**g**o, bi**gg**er, ba**g**
h	**h**ot, a**h**a	**h**ot, a**h**a
j	**y**es, vine**y**ard	**y**es, vine**y**ard
k	**c**at, **k**eep, la**cq**uer, flo**ck**	**c**at, **k**eep, la**cq**uer, flo**ck**
l	**l**aw, ho**ll**ow, boi**l**	**l**aw, ho**ll**ow, boi**l**
m	**m**at, he**m**p, ha**mm**er, ri**m**	**m**at, he**m**p, ha**mm**er, ri**m**
n	**n**ew, te**n**t, te**n**or, ru**n**	**n**ew, te**n**t, te**n**or, ru**n**
ŋ	ru**ng**, ha**ng**, swi**ng**er	ru**ng**, ha**ng**, swi**ng**er
p	**p**ay, la**p**se, to**p**	**p**ay, la**p**se, to**p**

r	rope, burn, tar	rope, burn, tar
s	sad, mist, kiss	sad, mist, kiss
ʃ	**sh**oe, mi**ss**ion, slu**sh**	**sh**oe, mi**ss**ion, slu**sh**
t	toe, button, mat	toe, button, mat
t̬	indicates a voiced alveolar flap [ɾ], as in later, catty, battle	indica un flap alveolar sonoro [ɾ], como en later, catty, battle
ʧ	**ch**oose, bat**ch**	**ch**oose, bat**ch**
θ	**th**in, e**th**er, ba**th**	**th**in, e**th**er, ba**th**
v	vat, never, cave	vat, never, cave
w	wet, software	wet, software
x	*German* Ba**ch**, *Scots* lo**ch**, *Spanish* **g**ente, **j**efe	*alemán* Ba**ch**, *escocés* lo**ch**, *español* **g**ente, **j**efe
z	zoo, easy, buzz	zoo, easy, buzz
ʒ	**j**aborandi, a**z**ure, bei**g**e	**j**aborandi, a**z**ure, bei**g**e
h, k,	indicate sounds which are	denotan sonidos presentes en la
p, t	present in the pronunciation of some speakers of English but absent in that of others	forma de pronunciar de algunos angloparlantes pero ausentes en el habla de otros angloparlantes

STRESS MARKS (MARCAS DE ACENTUACIÓN)

ˈ	[high stress] **pen**manship	[acento alto] **pen**manship
ˌ	[low stress] penman**ship**	[acento bajo] penman**ship**

Spelling-to-Sound Correspondences in Spanish

For example words for the phonetic symbols below, see Pronunciation Symbols on page 85a.

VOWELS

a   [a]

e   [e] in open syllables (syllables ending with a vowel); [ɛ] in closed syllables (syllables ending with a consonant)

i   [i]; before another vowel in the same syllable pronounced as [j] ([ʒ] or [ʃ] in Argentina and Uruguay; [ʤ] when at the beginning of a word in the Caribbean)

o   [o] in open syllables (syllables ending with a vowel); [ɔ] in closed syllables (syllables ending with a consonant)

u   [u]; before another vowel in the same syllable pronounced as [w]

y   [i]; before another vowel in the same syllable pronounced as [j] ([ʒ] or [ʃ] in Argentina and Uruguay; [ʤ] when at the beginning of a word in the Caribbean)

CONSONANTS

b   [b] at the beginning of a word or after *m* or *n*; [β] elsewhere

c   [s] before *i* or *e* in Latin America and parts of southern Spain; [θ] in northern Spain; [k] elsewhere

ch   [ʧ]; frequently [ʃ] in Chile and Panama; sometimes [ts] in Chile

d   [d] at the beginning of a word or after *n* or *l*; [ð] elsewhere, frequently silent between vowels

f   [f]; [Φ] in Honduras (no English equivalent for this sound; like [f] but made with both lips)

g   [x] before *i* or *e* ([h] in the Caribbean and Central America); [g] at the beginning of a word or after *n* and not before *i* or *e*; [ɣ] elsewhere, frequently silent between vowels

gu   [gw] at the beginning of a word before *a, o*; [ɣw] elsewhere before *a, o*; frequently just [w] between vowels; [g] at the beginning of a word before *i, e*; [ɣ] elsewhere before *i, e*; frequently silent between vowels

gü   [gw] at the beginning of a word, [ɣw] elsewhere; frequently just [w] between vowels

h   silent

j   [x] ([h] in the Caribbean and Central America)

k   [k]

l   [l]

ll   [j]; [ʒ] or [ʃ] in Argentina and Uruguay; [ʤ] when at the beginning of a word in the Caribbean; [lʲ] in Bolivia, Paraguay, Peru, and parts of northern Spain (no English equivalent; like "lli" in *million*)

m   [m]

n   [n]; frequently [ŋ] at the end of a word when next word begins with a vowel

ñ   [n]

p   [p]

qu   [k]

r   [r] (no English equivalent; a trilled sound) at the beginning of words; [t̬]/[ɾ] elsewhere

rr [r] (no English equivalent; a trilled sound)

s   [s]; frequently [z] before *b*, *d*, *g*, *m*, *n*, *l*, *r*; at the end of a word [h] or silent in many parts of Latin America and some parts of Spain

t   [t]

v   [b] at the beginning of a word or after *m* or *n*; [β] elsewhere

x   [ks] or [gz] between vowels; [s] before consonants

z   [s] in Latin America and parts of southern Spain, [θ] in northern Spain; at the end of a word [h] or silent in many parts of Latin America and some parts of Spain

Spanish-English
Dictionary

A

a¹ *nf* : first letter of the Spanish alphabet

a² *prep* **1** (*indicating direction*) : to ⟨vamos a México : we're going to Mexico⟩ ⟨fui a casa : I went home⟩ ⟨gira a la derecha : turn to the right⟩ **2** (*indicating location*) : at ⟨llegué al hotel : I arrived at the hotel⟩ ⟨al fondo del pasillo : at the end of the hall⟩ ⟨a mi lado : beside me⟩ ⟨vivo a cinco minutos de aquí : I live five minutes from here⟩ **3** (*used before direct objects referring to persons*) ⟨¿llamaste a tu papá? : did you call your dad?⟩ **4** (*used before indirect objects*) ⟨como a usted le guste : as you wish⟩ ⟨le echó un vistazo a la página : she glanced over the page⟩ **5** : in the manner of ⟨papas a la francesa : french fries⟩ ⟨una boda a lo Hollywood : a Hollywood-style wedding⟩ **6** : on, by means of ⟨a pie : on foot⟩ ⟨a mano : by hand⟩ **7** : per, each ⟨tres pastillas al día : three pills per day⟩ **8** (*indicating rate or measure*) ⟨lo venden a 50 pesos el kilo : they sell it for 50 pesos a kilo⟩ ⟨a una velocidad de . . . : at a speed of . . .⟩ **9** (*indicating comparison*) : to ⟨prefiero el vino a la cerveza : I prefer wine to beer⟩ ⟨un margen de dos a uno : a two-to-one margin⟩ **10** (*indicating time*) : at, on ⟨a las dos : at two o'clock⟩ ⟨al principio : at first⟩ ⟨al salir : on/upon leaving⟩ ⟨al día siguiente : on the following day⟩ **11** (*with infinitive*) ⟨enséñales a leer : teach them to read⟩ ⟨problemas a resolver : problems to be solved⟩

a- *pref* : a-

ábaco *nm* : abacus

abad *nm* : abbot

abadesa *nf* : abbess

abadía *nf* : abbey

abajo *adv* **1** : down ⟨póngalo más abajo : put it lower (down)⟩ ⟨arriba y abajo : up and down⟩ ⟨cuesta/río abajo : downhill/downstream⟩ **2** : downstairs ⟨los vecinos de abajo : the downstairs neighbors⟩ **3** : under, beneath ⟨el abajo firmante : the undersigned⟩ **4** : down with ⟨¡abajo la violencia! : down with violence!⟩ **5** ~ **de** : under, beneath **6** **de** ~ : bottom ⟨el cajón de abajo : the bottom drawer⟩ **7** **hacia** ~ *or* **para** ~ : downwards

abalanzarse {21} *vr* : to hurl oneself, to rush

abalorio *nm* : glass bead

abanderado, -da *n* : standard-bearer

abandonado, -da *adj* **1** : abandoned, deserted **2** : neglected **3** : slovenly, unkempt

abandonar *vt* **1** DEJAR : to abandon, to leave **2** : to give up, to quit ⟨abandonaron la búsqueda : they gave up the search⟩ — **abandonarse** *vr* **1** ~ **a** : to succumb to, to neglect oneself **2** ~ **a** : to give oneself over to

abandono *nm* **1** : abandonment **2** : neglect **3** : withdrawal ⟨ganar por abandono : to win by default⟩

abanicar {72} *vt* : to fan — **abanicarse** *vr*

abanico *nm* **1** : fan **2** GAMA : range, gamut

abaratamiento *nm* : price reduction

abaratar *vt* : to lower the price of — **abaratarse** *vr* : to go down in price

abarcar {72} *vt* **1** : to cover, to include, to embrace **2** : to undertake **3** : to monopolize

abaritonado, -da *adj* : baritone

abarrotado, -da *adj* : packed, crammed

abarrotar *vt* : to fill up, to pack

abarrotería *nf CA, Mex* : grocery store

abarrotero, -ra *n Col, Mex* : grocer

abarrotes *nmpl* **1** : groceries, supplies **2** **tienda de abarrotes** : general store, grocery store

abastecedor, -dora *n* : supplier

abastecer {53} *vt* : to supply, to stock — **abastecerse** *vr* : to stock up

abastecimiento → **abasto**

abasto *nm* : supply, supplying ⟨no da abasto : there isn't enough for all⟩

abatible *adj* **1** : reclining (of a chair) **2** : folding

abatido, -da *adj* : dejected, depressed

abatimiento *nm* **1** : drop, reduction **2** : dejection, depression

abatir *vt* **1** DERRIBAR : to demolish, to knock down **2** : to shoot down **3** DEPRIMIR : to depress, to bring low — **abatirse** *vr* **1** DEPRIMIRSE : to get depressed **2** ~ **sobre** : to swoop down on

abdicación *nf, pl* **-ciones** : abdication

abdicar {72} *vt* : to relinquish, to abdicate

abdomen *nm, pl* **-dómenes** : abdomen

abdominal *adj* : abdominal

abecé *nm* : ABC's *pl*

abecedario *nm* ALFABETO : alphabet

abedul *nm* : birch (tree)

abeja *nf* : bee

abejorro *nm* : bumblebee

aberración *nf, pl* **-ciones** : aberration

aberrante *adj* : aberrant, perverse

abertura *nf* **1** : aperture, opening **2** AGUJERO : hole **3** : slit (in a skirt, etc.) **4** GRIETA : crack

abeto *nm* : fir (tree)

abierto¹ *pp* → **abrir**

abierto², -ta *adj* **1** : open ⟨una puerta/boca/caja abierta : an open door/mouth/box⟩ ⟨heridas abiertas : open wounds⟩ ⟨con los brazos abiertos : with open arms⟩ **2** : open (for business, traffic, etc.) **3** DESABROCHADO : open, undone **4** : unlocked, open **5** : on, running (of a faucet) **6** : open, overt ⟨guerra abierta : open warfare⟩ **7** FRANCO : open, frank **8** RECEPTIVO : open, receptive — **abiertamente** *adv*

abigarrado, -da *adj* : multicolored, variegated

abigeato *nm* : rustling (of livestock)

abismal *adj* : abysmal, vast

abismo *nm* : abyss, chasm ⟨al borde del abismo : on the brink of ruin⟩

abjurar *vi* ~ **de** : to abjure — **abjuración** *nf*

ablandamiento *nm* : softening, moderation

ablandar *vt* **1** SUAVIZAR : to soften **2** CALMAR : to soothe, to appease — *vi* : to moderate, to get milder — **ablandarse** *vr* **1** : to become soft, to soften **2** CEDER : to yield, to relent

-able *suf* : -able

ablución *nf, pl* **-ciones** : ablution

abnegación *nf, pl* **-ciones** : self-denial

abnegado, -da *adj* : self-sacrificing, selfless

abnegarse {49} *vr* : to deny oneself

abobado, -da *adj* **1** : silly, stupid **2** : bewildered

abocado, -da *adj* ~ **a 1** : headed for **2** : committed to

abocarse {72} *vr* **1** DIRIGIRSE : to head, to direct oneself **2** DEDICARSE : to dedicate oneself

abochornar *vt* AVERGONZAR : to embarrass, to shame — **abochornarse** *vr*

abofetear *vt* : to slap

abogacía *nf* : law, legal profession

abogado, -da *n* : lawyer, attorney

abogar {52} *vi* ~ **por** : to plead for, to defend, to advocate

abolengo *nm* LINAJE : lineage, ancestry

abolición *nf, pl* **-ciones** : abolition

abolir {1} *vt* DEROGAR : to abolish, to repeal

abolladura *nf* : dent

abollar *vt* : to dent

abombar *vt* : to warp, to cause to bulge — **abombarse** *vr* : to decompose, to go bad

abominable *adj* ABORRECIBLE : abominable

abominación *nf, pl* **-ciones** : abomination

abominar *vt* ABORRECER : to abominate, to abhor

abonado, -da *n* : subscriber

abonar *vt* **1** : to pay **2** FERTILIZAR : to fertilize — **abonarse** *vr* : to subscribe

abono *nm* **1** : payment, installment **2** FERTILIZANTE : fertilizer **3** : season ticket

abordaje *nm* : boarding

abordar *vt* **1** : to address, to broach **2** : to accost, to waylay **3** : to come on board

aborigen[1] *adj, pl* **-rígenes** : aboriginal, native

aborigen[2] *nmf, pl* **-rígenes** : aborigine, indigenous inhabitant

aborrecer {53} *vt* ABOMINAR, ODIAR : to abhor, to detest, to hate

aborrecible *adj* ABOMINABLE, ODIOSO : abominable, detestable

aborrecimiento *nm* : abhorrence, loathing

abortar *vi* : to have an abortion — *vt* **1** : to abort **2** : to quash, to suppress

abortivo, -va *adj* : abortive

aborto *nm* **1** : abortion **2** : miscarriage

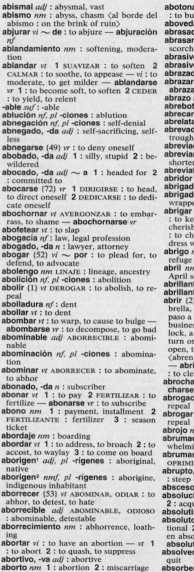

abotonar *vt* : to button — **abotonarse** *vr* : to button up

abovedado, -da *adj* : vaulted

abrasador, -dora *adj* : burning, scorching

abrasar *vt* QUEMAR : to burn, to sear, to scorch

abrasivo[1]**, -va** *adj* : abrasive

abrasivo[2] *nm* : abrasive

abrazadera *nf* : clamp, brace

abrazar {21} *vt* : to hug, to embrace — **abrazarse** *vr*

abrazo *nm* : hug, embrace

abrebotellas *nms & pl* : bottle opener

abrecartas *nms & pl* : letter opener

abrelatas *nms & pl* : can opener

abrevadero *nm* BEBEDERO : watering trough

abreviación *nf, pl* **-ciones** : abbreviation

abreviar *vt* **1** : to abbreviate **2** : to shorten, to cut short

abreviatura → **abreviación**

abridor *nm* : bottle opener, can opener

abrigadero *nm* : shelter, windbreak

abrigado, -da *adj* **1** : sheltered **2** : warm, wrapped up (with clothing)

abrigar {52} *vt* **1** : to shelter, to protect **2** : to keep warm, to dress warmly **3** : to cherish, to harbor ⟨abrigar esperanzas : to cherish hopes⟩ — **abrigarse** *vr* : to dress warmly

abrigo *nm* **1** : coat, overcoat **2** : shelter, refuge

abril *nm* : April ⟨el dos de abril : (on) April second⟩

abrillantador *nm* : polish

abrillantar *vt* : to polish, to shine

abrir {2} *vt* **1** : to open (a door, an umbrella, etc.) **2** : to open, to clear ⟨abrir paso a : to make way for⟩ **3** : to open (a business, an account) **4** : to unlock (a lock, a house), to undo (clothing) **5** : to turn on (a tap or faucet) **6** INICIAR : to open, to start — *vi* : to open, to open up ⟨abren a las nueve : they open at nine⟩ — **abrirse** *vr* **1** : to open, to open up **2** : to clear (of the skies)

abrochar *vt* : to button, to fasten — **abrocharse** *vr* : to fasten, to hook up

abrogación *nf, pl* **-ciones** : annulment, repeal

abrogar {52} *vt* : to abrogate, to annul, to repeal

abrojo *nm* : bur (of a plant)

abrumador, -dora *adj* : crushing, overwhelming

abrumar *vt* **1** AGOBIAR : to overwhelm **2** OPRIMIR : to oppress, to burden

abrupto, -ta *adj* **1** : abrupt **2** ESCARPADO : steep — **abruptamente** *adv*

absceso *nm* : abscess

absolución *nf, pl* **-ciones** **1** : absolution **2** : acquittal

absolutismo *nm* : absolutism

absoluto, -ta *adj* **1** : absolute, unconditional **2 en** ~ : at all ⟨no me gustó en absoluto : I did not like it at all⟩ — **absolutamente** *adv*

absolver {89} *vt* **1** : to absolve **2** : to acquit

absorbencia *nf* : absorbency

absorbente *adj* **1** : absorbent **2** : absorbing, engrossing

absorber *vt* **1** : to absorb, to soak up **2** : to occupy, to take up, to engross

absorción *nf*, *pl* **-ciones** : absorption

absorto, -ta *adj* : absorbed, engrossed

abstemio¹, -mia *adj* : abstemious, teetotal

abstemio², -mia *n* : teetotaler

abstención *nf*, *pl* **-ciones** : abstention — **abstencionismo** *nm*

abstenerse {80} *vr* : to abstain, to refrain

abstinencia *nf* : abstinence

abstracción *nf*, *pl* **-ciones** : abstraction

abstracto, -ta *adj* : abstract

abstraer {81} *vt* : to abstract — **abstraerse** *vr* : to lose oneself in thought

abstraído, -da *adj* : preoccupied, withdrawn

abstruso, -sa *adj* : abstruse

abstuvo, etc. → **abstenerse**

absuelto *pp* → **absolver**

absurdo¹, -da *adj* DISPARATADO, RIDÍCULO : absurd, ridiculous — **absurdamente** *adv*

absurdo² *nm* : absurdity

abuchear *vt* : to boo, to jeer

abucheo *nm* : booing, jeering

abuela *nf* **1** : grandmother **2** : old woman **3** ¡tu abuela! *fam* : no way!, forget about it!

abuelita *nf fam* : grandma *fam*

abuelito *nm fam* : grandpa *fam*

abuelo *nm* **1** : grandfather **2** : old man **3 abuelos** *nmpl* : grandparents, ancestors

abulia *nf* : apathy, lethargy

abúlico, -ca *adj* : lethargic, apathetic

abultado, -da *adj* : bulging, bulky

abultar *vi* : to bulge — *vt* : to enlarge, to expand

abundancia *nf* : abundance

abundante *adj* : abundant, plentiful — **abundantemente** *adv*

abundar *vi* **1** : to abound, to be plentiful **2** ~ **en** : to be in agreement with

aburrido, -da *adj* **1** : bored, tired, fed up **2** TEDIOSO : boring, tedious

aburrimiento *nm* : boredom, weariness

aburrir *vt* : to bore, to tire — **aburrirse** *vr* : to get bored

abusado, -da *adj Mex fam* : sharp, on the ball

abusador, -dora *n* : abuser

abusar *vi* **1** : to go too far, to do something to excess **2** ~ **de** : to abuse (as drugs) **3** ~ **de** : to take unfair advantage of

abusivo, -va *adj* **1** : abusive **2** : outrageous, excessive

abuso *nm* **1** : abuse **2** : injustice, outrage

abyecto, -ta *adj* : despicable, contemptible

acá *adv* **1** AQUÍ : here, over here ⟨¡ven acá! : come here!⟩ ⟨de acá para allá : back and forth⟩ **2** (*in expressions of time*) ⟨de 2010 (para) acá : from 2010 to now, since 2010⟩

acabado¹, -da *adj* **1** : finished, done, completed **2** : old, worn-out

acabado² *nm* : finish ⟨un acabado brillante : a glossy finish⟩

acabar *vi* **1** TERMINAR : to finish, to end ⟨ya acabo : I'm almost done⟩ **2** ~ **de** : to have just ⟨acabo de ver a tu hermano : I just saw your brother⟩ **3** ~ **con** : to put an end to, to stamp out **4 acabar por hacer algo** *or* **acabar haciendo algo** : to end up doing something — *vt* TERMINAR : to finish — **acabarse** *vr* TERMINARSE : to come to an end, to run out ⟨se me acabó el dinero : I ran out of money⟩ ⟨¡se acabó! : that's it!⟩

acabose *or* **acabóse** *nm fam* COLMO : extreme, limit ⟨¡esto es el acabóse! : this is the limit!⟩

acacia *nf* : acacia

academia *nf* : academy

académico¹, -ca *adj* : academic, scholastic — **académicamente** *adv*

académico², -ca *n* : academic, academician

acaecer {53} *vt* (*3rd person only*) : to happen, to take place

acalambrarse *vr* : to cramp up, to get a cramp

acallar *vt* : to quiet, to silence

acalorado, -da *adj* : emotional, heated

acaloramiento *nm* **1** : heat **2** : ardor, passion

acalorar *vt* : to heat up, to inflame — **acalorarse** *vr* : to get upset, to get worked up

acampada *nf* : camp, camping ⟨ir de acampada : to go camping⟩

acampar *vi* : to camp

acanalar *vt* **1** : to groove, to furrow **2** : to corrugate

acantilado *nm* : cliff

acanto *nm* : acanthus

acantonar *vt* : to station, to quarter

acaparador, -dora *adj* : greedy, selfish

acaparar *vt* **1** : to stockpile, to hoard **2** : to monopolize

acápite *nm* : paragraph

acaramelado, -da *adj* **1** : caramel-coated **2** : caramel-colored **3** : sugary **4** : very affectionate (of a couple)

acariciar *vt* : to caress, to stroke, to pet

ácaro *nm* : mite

acarrear *vt* **1** : to haul, to carry **2** : to bring, to give rise to ⟨los problemas que acarrea : the problems that come along with it⟩

acarreo *nm* : transport, haulage

acartonarse *vr* **1** : to stiffen **2** : to become wizened

acaso *adv* **1** : perhaps, by any chance **2 por si acaso** : just in case

acatamiento *nm* : compliance, observance

acatar *vt* : to comply with, to respect

acatarrarse *vr* : to catch a cold

acaudalado, -da *adj* RICO : wealthy, rich

acaudillar *vt* : to lead, to command

acceder *vi* ~ **a** **1** : to accede to, to agree to **2** : to assume (a position) **3** : to gain access to

accesar *vt* : to access (on a computer)

accesibilidad *nf* : accessibility

accesible *adj* ASEQUIBLE : accessible, attainable

acceso *nm* 1 : access 2 : admittance, entrance

accesorio¹, -ria *adj* 1 : accessory 2 : incidental

accesorio² *nm* 1 : accessory 2 : prop (in the theater)

accidentado¹, -da *adj* 1 : eventful, turbulent 2 : rough, uneven 3 : injured

accidentado², -da *n* : accident victim

accidental *adj* : accidental, unintentional — **accidentalmente** *adv*

accidentarse *vr* : to have an accident

accidente *nm* 1 : accident 2 : unevenness 3 **accidente geográfico** : geographical feature

acción *nf, pl* **acciones** 1 : action 2 ACTO : act, deed 3 : share, stock

accionamiento *nm* : activation

accionar *vt* : to put into motion, to activate — *vi* : to gesticulate

accionario, -ria *adj* : stock ⟨mercado accionario : stock market⟩

accionista *nmf* : stockholder, shareholder

acebo *nm* : holly

acechar *vt* : to watch, to spy on 2 : to stalk, to lie in wait for

acecho *nm* **al acecho** : lying in wait

acedera *nf* : sorrel (herb)

aceitar *vt* : to oil

aceite *nm* 1 : oil 2 **aceite de ricino** : castor oil 3 **aceite de oliva** : olive oil

aceitera *nf* 1 : cruet (for oil) 2 : oilcan 3 *Mex* : oil refinery

aceitoso, -sa *adj* : oily

aceituna *nf* OLIVA : olive

aceituno *nm* OLIVO : olive tree

aceleración *nf, pl* **-ciones** : acceleration, speeding up

acelerado, -da *adj* : accelerated, speedy

acelerador *nm* : accelerator

aceleramiento *nm* → **aceleración**

acelerar *vt* 1 : to accelerate, to speed up 2 AGILIZAR : to expedite — *vi* : to accelerate (of an automobile) — **acelerarse** *vr* : to hasten, to hurry up

acelga *nf* : chard, Swiss chard

acendrar *vt* : to purify, to refine

acento *nm* 1 : accent 2 : stress, emphasis

acentuado, -da *adj* : marked, pronounced

acentuar {3} *vt* 1 : to accent 2 : to emphasize, to stress — **acentuarse** *vr* : to become more pronounced

acepción *nf, pl* **-ciones** SIGNIFICADO : sense, meaning

aceptabilidad *nf* : acceptability

aceptable *adj* : acceptable

aceptación *nf, pl* **-ciones** 1 : acceptance 2 APROBACIÓN : approval

aceptar *vt* 1 : to accept 2 : to approve

acequia *nf* 1 : irrigation ditch 2 *Mex* : sewer

acera *nf* : sidewalk

acerado, -da *adj* 1 : made of steel 2 : steely, tough

acerbo, -ba *adj* 1 : harsh, cutting ⟨comentarios acerbos : cutting remarks⟩ 2 : bitter — **acerbamente** *adv*

acerca *prep* ~ **de** : about, concerning

acercamiento *nm* : rapprochement, reconciliation

acercar {72} *vt* APROXIMAR, ARRIMAR : to bring near, to bring closer — **acercarse** *vr* APROXIMARSE, ARRIMARSE : to approach, to draw near

acería *nf* : steel mill

acerico *nm* : pincushion

acero *nm* : steel ⟨acero inoxidable : stainless steel⟩

acérrimo, -ma *adj* 1 : staunch, steadfast 2 : bitter ⟨un acérrimo enemigo : a bitter enemy⟩

acertado, -da *adj* CORRECTO : accurate, correct, on target — **acertadamente** *adv*

acertante¹ *adj* : winning

acertante² *nmf* : winner

acertar {55} *vt* 1 : to guess correctly — *vi* 1 ATINAR : to be correct, to be on target 2 ~ **a** : to manage to

acertijo *nm* ADIVINANZA : riddle

acervo *nm* 1 : pile, heap 2 : wealth, heritage ⟨el acervo artístico del instituto : the artistic treasures of the institute⟩

acetato *nm* : acetate

acetileno *nm* : acetylene

acetona *nf* 1 : acetone 2 : nail-polish remover

achacar {72} *vt* : to attribute, to impute ⟨te achaca todos sus problemas : he blames all his problems on you⟩

achacoso, -sa *adj* : frail, sickly

achaparrado, -da *adj* : stunted, scrubby ⟨árboles achaparrados : scrubby trees⟩

achaque *nm* : ailment

achaques *nmpl* : aches and pains

achatar *vt* : to flatten

achicar {72} *vt* 1 REDUCIR : to make smaller, to reduce 2 : to intimidate 3 : to bail out (water) — **achicarse** *vr* : to become intimidated

achicharrar *vt* : to scorch, to burn to a crisp

achicoria *nf* : chicory

achiote *or* **achote** *nm* : annatto

achispado, -da *adj fam* : tipsy

achuchón *nm, pl* **-chones** 1 : push, shove 2 *fam* : squeeze, hug 3 *fam* : mild illness

aciago, -ga *adj* : fateful, unlucky

acicalar *vt* 1 PULIR : to polish 2 : to dress up, to adorn — **acicalarse** *vr* : to get dressed up

acicate *nm* 1 : spur 2 INCENTIVO : incentive, stimulus

acidez *nf, pl* **-deces** 1 : acidity 2 : sourness 3 **acidez estomacal** : heartburn

ácido¹, -da *adj* AGRIO : acid, sour

ácido² *nm* 1 : acid 2 **ácido clorhídrico** : hydrochloric acid 3 **ácido nítrico** : nitric acid 4 **ácido sulfúrico** : sulfuric acid

acierto *nm* 1 : correct answer, right choice 2 : accuracy, skill

acimut *nm* : azimuth

acitronar *vt Mex* : to fry until crisp

aclamación *nf, pl* **-ciones** : acclaim, acclamation

aclamar *vt* : to acclaim, to cheer, to applaud

aclaración *nf, pl* **-ciones** CLARIFICACIÓN : clarification, explanation

aclarar *vt* 1 CLARIFICAR : to clarify, to explain, to resolve 2 : to lighten 3

aclarar la voz : to clear one's throat — *vi*
1 : to get light, to dawn 2 : to clear up
— **aclararse** *vr* : to become clear

aclaratorio, -ria *adj* : explanatory

aclimatar *vt* : to acclimatize — **aclimatarse** *vr* ~ **a** : to get used to — **aclimatación** *nf*

acné *nm* : acne

acobardar *vt* INTIMIDAR : to frighten, to intimidate — **acobardarse** *vr* 1 : to get frightened, to chicken out 2 : to cower

acodarse *vr* ~ **en** : to lean (one's elbows) on

acogedor, -dora *adj* : cozy, warm, friendly

acoger {15} *vt* 1 REFUGIAR : to take in, to shelter 2 : to receive, to welcome — **acogerse** *vr* 1 REFUGIARSE : to take refuge 2 ~ **a** : to resort to, to avail oneself of

acogida *nf* 1 AMPARO, REFUGIO : refuge, protection 2 RECIBIMIENTO : reception, welcome

acolchar *vt* 1 : to pad (a wall, etc.) 2 : to quilt

acólito *nm* 1 MONAGUILLO : altar boy 2 : follower, helper, acolyte

acomedido, -da *adj* : helpful, obliging

acometer *vt* 1 ATACAR : to attack, to assail 2 EMPRENDER : to undertake, to begin — *vi* ~ **contra** : to rush against

acometida *nf* ATAQUE : attack, assault

acomodado, -da *adj* 1 : suitable, appropriate 2 : well-to-do, prosperous

acomodador, -dora *n* : usher, usherette *f*

acomodar *vt* 1 : to accommodate, to make room for 2 : to adjust, to adapt — **acomodarse** *vr* 1 : to settle in 2 ~ **a** : to adapt to

acomodo *nm* 1 : job, position 2 : arrangement, placement 3 : accommodation, lodging

acompañamiento *nm* : accompaniment

acompañante *nmf* 1 COMPAÑERO : companion 2 : accompanist

acompañar *vt* : to accompany, to go with

acompasado, -da *adj* : rhythmic, regular, measured

acompasar *vt* : to synchronize

acomplejado, -da *adj* : full of complexes, neurotic

acomplejar *vt* : to give a complex, to make neurotic

acondicionado, -da *adj* 1 : equipped 2 **bien acondicionado** : in good shape, in a fit state

acondicionador *nm* 1 : conditioner 2 **acondicionador de aire** : air conditioner

acondicionar *vt* 1 : to condition 2 : to fit out, to furnish

acongojado, -da *adj* : distressed, upset

acongojarse *vr* : to grieve, to become distressed

aconsejable *adj* : advisable

aconsejar *vt* : to advise, to counsel

acontecer {53} *vt (3rd person only)* : to occur, to happen

acontecimiento *nm* SUCESO : event

acopiar *vt* : to gather, to collect, to stockpile

acopio *nm* : collection, stock

acoplamiento *nm* : connection, coupling

acoplar *vt* 1 : to couple, to connect — **acoplarse** *vr* : to fit together

acoquinar *vt* : to intimidate

acorazado[1], -da *adj* BLINDADO : armored

acorazado[2] *nm* : battleship

acordado, -da *adj* : agreed upon

acordar {19} *vt* 1 : to agree on 2 OTORGAR : to award, to bestow — **acordarse** *vr* RECORDAR : to remember, to recall

acorde[1] *adj* 1 : in agreement, in accordance 2 ~ **con** : in keeping with

acorde[2] *nm* : chord

acordeón *nm, pl* -**deones** : accordion — **acordeonista** *nmf*

acordonar *vt* 1 : to cordon off 2 : to lace up 3 : to mill (coins)

acorralar *vt* ARRINCONAR : to corner, to hem in, to corral

acortar *vt* : to shorten, to cut short — **acortarse** *vr* 1 : to become shorter 2 : to end early

acosar *vt* PERSEGUIR : to pursue, to hound, to harass

acoso *nm* ASEDIO : harassment ⟨acoso sexual : sexual harassment⟩

acostar {19} *vt* 1 : to lay (something) down 2 : to put to bed — **acostarse** *vr* 1 : to lie down 2 : to go to bed

acostumbrado, -da *adj* 1 HABITUADO : accustomed 2 HABITUAL : usual, customary

acostumbrar *vt* : to accustom — *vi* : to be accustomed, to be in the habit — **acostumbrarse** *vr*

acotación *nf, pl* -**ciones** 1 : marginal note 2 : stage direction

acotado, -da *adj* : enclosed

acotamiento *nm Mex* : shoulder (of a road)

acotar *vt* 1 ANOTAR : to note, to annotate 2 DELIMITAR : to mark off (land), to demarcate

acre[1] *adj* 1 : acrid, pungent 2 MORDAZ : caustic, biting

acre[2] *nm* : acre

acrecentamiento *nm* : growth, increase

acrecentar {55} *vt* AUMENTAR : to increase, to augment

acreditación *nf, pl* -**ciones** : accreditation

acreditado, -da *adj* 1 : accredited, authorized 2 : reputable

acreditar *vt* 1 : to accredit, to authorize 2 : to credit 3 : to prove, to verify — **acreditarse** *vr* : to gain a reputation

acreedor[1], -dora *adj* : deserving, worthy

acreedor[2], -dora *n* : creditor

acribillar *vt* 1 : to riddle, to pepper (with bullets, etc.) 2 : to hound, to harass

acrílico *nm* : acrylic

acrimonia *nf* 1 : pungency 2 : acrimony

acrimonioso, -sa *adj* : acrimonious

acriollarse *vr* : to adopt local customs, to go native

acristalamiento *nm Spain* : glazing, windows *pl*

acritud *nf* 1 : pungency, bitterness 2 : intensity, sharpness 3 : harshness, asperity

acrobacia *nf* : acrobatics
acróbata *nmf* : acrobat
acrobático, -ca *adj* : acrobatic
acrónimo *nm* : acronym
acta *nf* **1** : document, certificate ⟨acta de nacimiento/defunción : birth/death certificate⟩ **2 actas** *nfpl* : minutes (of a meeting)
actitud *nf* **1** : attitude **2** : posture, position
activación *nf, pl* **-ciones 1** : activation, stimulation **2** ACELERACIÓN : acceleration, speeding up
activar *vt* **1** : to activate **2** : to stimulate, to energize **3** : to speed up
actividad *nf* : activity
activista *nmf* : activist — **activismo** *nm*
activo¹, -va *adj* : active — **activamente** *adv*
activo² *nm* : assets *pl* ⟨activo y pasivo : assets and liabilities⟩
acto *nm* **1** ACCIÓN : act, deed **2** : act (in a play) **3 el acto sexual** : sexual intercourse **4 en el acto** : right away, on the spot **5 acto seguido** : immediately after
actor *nm* ARTISTA : actor
actriz *nf, pl* **actrices** ARTISTA : actress
actuación *nf, pl* **-ciones 1** : performance **2 actuaciones** *nfpl* DILIGENCIAS : proceedings
actual *adj* PRESENTE : present, current
actualidad *nf* **1** : present time ⟨en la actualidad : at present⟩ **2 actualidades** *nfpl* : current affairs
actualización *nf, pl* **-ciones** : updating, modernization
actualizar {21} *vt* : to modernize, to bring up to date
actualmente *adv* : at present, nowadays
actuar {3} *vi* : to act, to perform
actuarial *adj* : actuarial
actuario, -ria *n* : actuary
acuarela *nf* : watercolor
acuario *nm* : aquarium
Acuario¹ *nm* : Aquarius (sign or constellation)
Acuario² *nmf* : Aquarius (person)
acuartelar *vt* : to quarter (troops)
acuático, -ca *adj* : aquatic, water
acuchillar *vt* APUÑALAR : to knife, to stab
acuciante *adj* : pressing, urgent
acucioso, -sa → **acuciante**
acudir *vi* **1** : to go, to come (someplace for a specific purpose) ⟨acudió a la puerta : he went to the door⟩ ⟨acudimos en su ayuda : we came to her aid⟩ **2** : to be present, to show up ⟨acudí a la cita : I showed up for the appointment⟩ **3** ~ **a** : to turn to, to have recourse to ⟨hay que acudir al médico : you must consult the doctor⟩
acueducto *nm* : aqueduct
acuerdo *nm* **1** : agreement **2 estar de acuerdo** : to agree **3 de acuerdo con** : in accordance with **4 de ~** : OK, all right
acullá *adv* : yonder, over there
acumulación *nf, pl* **-ciones** : accumulation
acumulador *nm* : storage battery

acumular *vt* : to accumulate, to amass — **acumularse** *vr* : to build up, to pile up
acumulativo, -va *adj* : cumulative — **acumulativamente** *adv*
acunar *vt* : to rock, to cradle
acuñar *vt* : to coin, to mint
acupuntura *nf* : acupuncture
acurrucarse {72} *vr* : to cuddle, to nestle, to curl up
acusación *nf, pl* **-ciones 1** : accusation, charge **2 la acusación** : the prosecution
acusado¹, -da *adj* : prominent, marked
acusado², -da *n* : defendant ⟨el acusado : the defendant, the accused⟩
acusador, -dora *n* **1** : accuser **2** FISCAL : prosecutor
acusar *vt* **1** : to accuse, to charge **2** : to reveal, to betray ⟨sus ojos acusaban la desconfianza : his eyes revealed distrust⟩ — **acusarse** *vr* : to confess
acusativo *nm* : objective (in grammar)
acusatorio, -ria *adj* : accusatory
acuse *nm* **acuse de recibo** : acknowledgment of receipt
acústica *nf* : acoustics
acústico, -ca *adj* : acoustic
adagio *nm* REFRÁN : adage, proverb
adalid *nm* : leader, champion
adaptable *adj* : adaptable — **adaptabilidad** *nf*
adaptación *nf, pl* **-ciones** : adaptation, adjustment
adaptado, -da *adj* : suited, adapted
adaptador *nm* : adapter (in electricity)
adaptar *vt* **1** MODIFICAR : to adapt **2** : to adjust, to fit — **adaptarse** *vr* : to adapt oneself, to conform
adecentar *vt* : to tidy up
adecuación *nf, pl* **-ciones** ADAPTACIÓN : adaptation
adecuadamente *adv* : adequately
adecuado, -da *adj* **1** IDÓNEO : suitable, appropriate **2** : adequate
adecuar {8} *vt* : to adapt, to make suitable — **adecuarse** *vr* ~ **a** : to be appropriate for, to fit in with
adefesio *nm* : eyesore, monstrosity
adelantado, -da *adj* **1** : advanced, ahead **2** : fast (of a clock or watch) **3 por ~** : in advance
adelantamiento *nm* **1** : advancement **2** : speeding up
adelantar *vt* **1** : to advance, to move forward ⟨adelantar el reloj : to set one's watch/clock ahead⟩ ⟨adelantar una fecha : to move up a date⟩ **2** : to pass, to overtake **3** : to reveal (information) in advance **4** : to advance, to lend (money) — **adelantarse** *vr* **1** : to go ahead ⟨se adelantó para recibirlos : she went ahead to meet them⟩ **2** : to run fast (of a watch or clock) **3** : to get ahead ⟨alguien se me adelantó : someone beat me to it⟩ ⟨no nos adelantemos : let's not get ahead of ourselves⟩ **4 adelantarse a su tiempo** : to be ahead of one's time
adelante *adv* **1** : forward, ahead, in front ⟨dar un paso adelante : to take a step forward⟩ ⟨seguimos adelante con el pro-

yecto : we went ahead with the project⟩
2 de ahora/ahí en adelante : from now/
then on **3 hacia/para** ~ : forward, toward the front **4 más adelante** : further
on, later on **5 ¡adelante!** : come in!

adelanto *nm* **1** : advance, progress **2**
: advance payment **3** : earliness ⟨lleva-
mos una hora de adelanto : we're running an hour ahead of time⟩

adelfa *nf* : oleander

adelgazar {21} *vt* : to thin, to reduce — *vi*
: to lose weight

ademán *nm, pl* **-manes 1** GESTO : gesture
2 ademanes *nmpl* : manners

además *adv* **1** : besides, furthermore **2**
~ **de** : in addition to, as well as

adenoides *nfpl* : adenoids

adentrarse *vr* ~ **en** : to go into, to penetrate

adentro *adv* **1** : in, inside ⟨fuimos adentro : we went inside⟩ ⟨estoy aquí adentro
: I'm in here⟩ **2 mar adentro** : out to sea
3 tierra adentro : inland

adentros *nmpl* **decirse para sus adentros** : to say to oneself ⟨me dije para mis
adentros que nunca regresaría : I told
myself that I'd never go back⟩

adepto¹, -ta *adj* : supportive ⟨ser adepto a
: to be a follower of⟩

adepto², -ta *n* PARTIDARIO : follower,
supporter

aderezar {21} *vt* **1** SAZONAR : to season,
to dress (salad) **2** : to embellish, to
adorn

aderezo *nm* **1** : dressing, seasoning **2**
: adornment, embellishment

adeudar *vt* **1** : to debit **2** DEBER : to owe

adeudo *nm* **1** DÉBITO : debit **2** *Mex*
: debt, indebtedness

adherencia *nf* **1** : adherence (to a rule,
etc.) **2** : adhesion

adherente *adj* : adhesive, sticky

adherir {76} *vt* : to stick to — **adherirse**
vr : to adhere, to stick

adhesión *nf, pl* **-siones 1** : adhesion **2**
: attachment, commitment (to a cause,
etc.)

adhesivo¹, -va *adj* : adhesive

adhesivo² *nm* : adhesive

adicción *nf, pl* **-ciones** : addiction

adición *nf, pl* **-ciones** : addition

adicional *adj* : additional — **adicionalmente** *adv*

adicionar *vt* : to add

adictivo, -va *adj* : addictive

adicto¹, -ta *adj* **1** : addicted **2** : devoted,
dedicated

adicto², -ta *n* **1** : addict **2** PARTIDARIO
: supporter, advocate

adiestrador, -dora *n* : trainer

adiestramiento *nm* : training

adiestrar *vt* : to train

adinerado, -da *adj* : moneyed, wealthy

adiós *nm, pl* **adioses 1** DESPEDIDA
: farewell, good-bye **2 ¡adiós!** : good-
bye!

aditamento *nm* : attachment, accessory

aditivo *nm* : additive

adivinación *nf, pl* **-ciones 1** : guess **2**
: divination, prediction

adivinanza *nf* ACERTIJO : riddle

adivinar *vt* **1** : to guess **2** : to foretell, to
predict

adivino, -na *n* : fortune-teller

adjetivo¹, -va *adj* : adjectival

adjetivo² *nm* : adjective

adjudicación *nf, pl* **-ciones 1** : adjudication **2** : allocation, awarding, granting

adjudicar {72} *vt* **1** : to judge, to adjudicate **2** : to assign, to allocate ⟨adjudicar
la culpa : to assign the blame⟩ **3** : to
award, to grant

adjuntar *vt* : to enclose, to attach

adjunto¹, -ta *adj* : enclosed, attached

adjunto², -ta *n* : deputy, assistant

adjunto³ *nm* : adjunct

administración *nf, pl* **-ciones 1** : administration, management **2 administración de empresas** : business administration

administrador, -dora *n* : administrator,
manager

administrar *vt* : to administer, to manage,
to run

administrativo, -va *adj* : administrative
— **administrativamente** *adv*

admirable *adj* : admirable, impressive —
admirablemente *adv*

admiración *nf, pl* **-ciones** : admiration

admirador, -dora *n* : admirer

admirar *vt* **1** : to admire **2** : to amaze, to
astonish — **admirarse** *vr* : to be amazed

admirativo, -va *adj* : admiring

admisible *adj* : admissible, allowable

admisión *nf, pl* **-siones** : admission, admittance

admitir *vt* **1** : to admit, to let in **2** : to acknowledge, to concede **3** : to allow, to
make room for ⟨la ley no admite cambios
: the law doesn't allow for changes⟩

admonición *nf, pl* **-ciones** : admonition,
warning

admonitorio, -ria *adj* : admonishing

ADN *nm* (*ácido desoxirribonucleico*)
: DNA

adobar *vt* : to marinate

adobe *nm* : adobe

adobo *nm* **1** : marinade, seasoning **2** *Mex*
: spicy marinade used for cooking pork

adoctrinamiento *nm* : indoctrination

adoctrinar *vt* : to indoctrinate

adolecer {53} *vi* PADECER : to suffer
⟨adolece de timidez : he suffers from
shyness⟩

adolescencia *nf* : adolescence

adolescente¹ *adj* : adolescent, teenage

adolescente² *nmf* : adolescent, teenager

adonde *conj* : where ⟨el lugar adonde
vamos es bello : the place where we're
going is beautiful⟩

adónde *adv* : where ⟨¿adónde vamos?
: where are we going?⟩

adondequiera *adv* : wherever, anywhere
⟨adondequiera que vayas : anywhere
you go⟩

adopción *nf, pl* **-ciones** : adoption

adoptar *vt* **1** : to adopt (a measure), to
take (a decision) **2** : to adopt (children)

adoptivo, -va *adj* **1** : adopted (children,
country) **2** : adoptive (parents)

adoquín *nm, pl* **-quines** : paving stone, cobblestone

-ador, -adora *suf* ;**-er** ⟨trabajador, trabajadora : worker⟩

adorable *adj* : adorable, lovable

adoración *nf, pl* **-ciones** : adoration, worship

adorador¹, -dora *adj* : adoring, worshipping

adorador², -dora *n* : worshipper

adorar *vt* : to adore, to worship

adormecer {53} *vt* **1** : to make sleepy, to lull to sleep **2** : to numb — **adormecerse** *vr* **1** : to doze off **2** : to go numb

adormecimiento *nm* **1** SUEÑO : drowsiness, sleepiness **2** INSENSIBILIDAD : numbness

adormilarse *vr* : to doze, to drowse

adornar *vt* DECORAR : to decorate, to adorn

adorno *nm* : ornament, decoration

adosado, -da *adj* : attached (of a structure) ⟨casa adosada : duplex, row house⟩

adosar *vt* **1** : to place against, to affix **2** : to enclose, to attach (to a letter)

adquirido, -da *adj* **1** : acquired **2 mal adquirido** : ill-gotten

adquirir {4} *vt* **1** : to acquire, to gain 2 COMPRAR : to purchase

adquisición *nf, pl* **-ciones 1** : acquisition **2** COMPRA : purchase

adquisitivo, -va *adj* **poder adquisitivo** : purchasing power

adrede *adv* : intentionally, on purpose

adrenalina *nf* : adrenaline

adscribir {33} *vt* : to assign, to appoint — **adscribirse** *vr* ~ **a** : to become a member of

adscripción *nf, pl* **-ciones** : assignment, appointment

adscrito *pp* → **adscribir**

aduana *nf* : customs, customs office

aduanero¹, -ra *adj* : customs

aduanero², -ra *n* : customs officer

aducir {61} *vt* : to adduce, to offer as proof

adueñarse *vr* ~ **de** : to take possession of, to take over

adulación *nf, pl* **-ciones** : adulation, flattery

adulador¹, -dora *adj* : flattering

adulador², -dora *n* : flatterer, toady

adular *vt* LISONJEAR : to flatter

adulteración *nf, pl* **-ciones** : adulteration

adulterar *vt* : to adulterate

adulterio *nm* : adultery

adúltero¹, -ra *adj* : adulterous

adúltero², -ra *n* : adulterer

adultez *nf* : adulthood

adulto, -ta *adj & n* : adult

adusto, -ta *adj* : harsh, severe

advenedizo, -za *n* **1** : upstart, parvenu **2** : newcomer

advenimiento *nm* : advent

adverbio *nm* : adverb — **adverbial** *adj*

adversario¹, -ria *adj* : opposing, contrary

adversario², -ria *n* OPOSITOR : adversary, opponent

adversidad *nf* : adversity

adverso, -sa *adj* DESFAVORABLE : adverse, unfavorable — **adversamente** *adv*

advertencia *nf* AVISO : warning

advertir {76} *vt* **1** : to warn **2** : to notice, to tell ⟨no advertí que estuviera enojada : I couldn't tell she was angry⟩

Adviento *nm* : Advent

adyacente *adj* : adjacent

aéreo, -rea *adj* **1** : aerial, air **2 correo aéreo** : airmail

aeróbic *nm* : aerobics

aeróbico, -ca *adj* : aerobic

aerobio, -bia *adj* : aerobic

aerodeslizador *nm* : hovercraft

aerodinámica *nf* : aerodynamics

aerodinámico, -ca *adj* : aerodynamic, streamlined

aeródromo *nm* : airfield

aeroespacial *adj* : aerospace

aerogenerador *nm* : wind-powered generator

aerolínea *nf* : airline

aeromozo, -za *n* : flight attendant, steward *m*, stewardess *f*

aeronáutica *nf* : aeronautics

aeronáutico, -ca *adj* : aeronautical

aeronave *nf* : aircraft

aeropostal *adj* : airmail

aeropuerto *nm* : airport

aerosol *nm* : aerosol, aerosol spray

aeróstata *nmf* : balloonist

aerotransportado, -da *adj* : airborne

aerotransportar *vt* : to airlift

afabilidad *nf* : affability

afable *adj* : affable — **afablemente** *adv*

afamado, -da *adj* : well-known, famous

afán *nm, pl* **afanes 1** ANHELO : eagerness, desire **2** EMPEÑO : effort, determination

afanador, -dora *n* *Mex* : cleaning person, cleaner

afanarse *vr* : to toil, to strive

afanosamente *adv* : zealously, industriously, busily

afanoso, -sa *adj* **1** : eager, industrious **2** : arduous, hard

afear *vt* : to make ugly, to disfigure

afección *nf, pl* **-ciones 1** : fondness, affection **2** : illness, complaint

afectación *nf, pl* **-ciones** : affectation

afectado, -da *adj* **1** : affected, mannered **2** : influenced **3** : afflicted **4** : feigned

afectar *vt* **1** : to affect **2** : to upset **3** : to feign, to pretend

afectísimo, -ma *adj* **suyo afectísimo** : yours truly

afectivo, -va *adj* : emotional

afecto¹, -ta *adj* **1** : affected, afflicted **2** : fond, affectionate

afecto² *nm* CARIÑO : affection

afectuoso, -sa *adj* CARIÑOSO : affectionate — **afectuosamente** *adv*

afeitadora *nf* : shaver, electric razor

afeitar *vt* RASURAR : to shave — **afeitarse** *vr*

afelpado, -da *adj* : plush

afeminado, -da *adj* : effeminate

aferrado, -da *adj* : obstinate, stubborn

aferrarse {55} *vr* : to cling, to hold on
affidávit *nm, pl* **-dávits** : affidavit
afgano, -na *adj & n* : Afghan
AFI *nm* (Alfabeto Fonético Internacional) : IPA
afianzar {21} *vt* **1** : to secure, to strengthen **2** : to guarantee, to vouch for — **afianzarse** *vr* ESTABLECERSE : to establish oneself — **afianzamiento** *nm*
afiche *nm* : poster
afición *nf, pl* **-ciones 1** : enthusiasm, penchant, fondness ⟨afición al deporte : love of sports⟩ **2** PASATIEMPO : hobby
aficionado[1], -da *adj* ENTUSIASTA : enthusiastic, keen
aficionado[2], -da *n* **1** ENTUSIASTA : enthusiast, fan **2** : amateur
aficionar *vt* : to interest ⟨aficionar a alguien a algo : to get someone interested in something⟩ — **aficionarse** *vr*
áfido *nm* : aphid
afiebrado, -da *adj* : feverish
afilado, -da *adj* **1** : sharp **2** : long, pointed ⟨una nariz afilada : a sharp nose⟩
afilador *nm* : sharpener
afilalápices *nms & pl* : pencil sharpener
afilar *vt* : to sharpen
afiliación *nf, pl* **-ciones** : affiliation
afiliado[1], -da *adj* : affiliated
afiliado[2], -da *n* : member
afiliarse *vr* ~ **a** : to become a member of, to join
afín *adj, pl* **afines 1** PARECIDO : related, similar ⟨la biología y disciplinas afines : biology and related disciplines⟩ **2** PRÓXIMO : adjacent, nearby
afinación *nf, pl* **-ciones 1** : tune-up **2** : tuning (of an instrument)
afinador, -dora *n* : tuner (of musical instruments)
afinar *vt* **1** : to perfect, to refine **2** : to tune (an instrument) — *vi* : to sing or play in tune
afincarse {72} *vr* : to establish oneself, to settle in
afinidad *nf* : affinity, similarity
afirmación *nf, pl* **-ciones 1** : statement **2** : affirmation
afirmar *vt* **1** : to state, to affirm **2** REFORZAR : to make firm, to strengthen
afirmativo, -va *adj* : affirmative — **afirmativamente** *adj*
aflicción *nf, pl* **-ciones** DESCONSUELO, PESAR : grief, sorrow
afligido, -da *adj* : grief-stricken, sorrowful
afligir {35} *vt* **1** : to distress, to upset **2** : to afflict — **afligirse** *vr* : to grieve
aflojar *vt* **1** : to loosen, to slacken **2** *fam* : to pay up, to fork over — *vi* **1** : to slacken, to ease up — **aflojarse** *vr* : to become loose, to slacken
aflorar *vi* : to come to the surface, to emerge
afluencia *nf* **1** : flow, influx **2** : abundance, plenty
afluente *nm* : tributary
afluir {41} *vi* **1** : to flock ⟨la gente afluía a la frontera : people were flocking to the border⟩ **2** : to flow

afónico, -ca *adj* **quedarse afónico** : to lose one's voice, to get laryngitis
aforismo *nm* : aphorism
aforo *nm* **1** : appraisal, assessment **2** : maximum capacity (of a theater, highway, etc.)
afortunado, -da *adj* : fortunate, lucky — **afortunadamente** *adv*
afrecho *nm* : bran, mash
afrenta *nf* : affront, insult
afrentar *vt* : to affront, to dishonor, to insult
africano, -na *adj & n* : African
afroamericano, -na *adj & n* : Afro-American
afrodisiaco *or* **afrodisíaco** *nm* : aphrodisiac
afrontamiento *nm* : confrontation
afrontar *vt* : to confront, to face up to
afrutado, -da *adj* : fruity
aftershave ['aftərʃeif] *nm* : aftershave
afuera *adv* **1** (*indicating direction*) : out, outside ⟨¡afuera! : get out!⟩ **2** (*indicating location*) FUERA : out, outside ⟨estoy aquí afuera : I'm out here, I'm outside⟩ **3 afuera de** : out of, outside
afueras *nfpl* ALEDAÑOS : outskirts
agachadiza *nf* : snipe (bird)
agachar *vt* : to lower (a part of the body) ⟨agachar la cabeza : to bow one's head⟩ — **agacharse** *vr* : to crouch, to stoop, to bend down
agalla *nf* **1** BRANQUIA : gill **2 tener agallas** *fam* : to have guts, to have courage
agarradera *nf* ASA, ASIDERO : handle, grip
agarrado, -da *adj fam* : cheap, stingy
agarrar *vt* **1** : to grab, to grasp **2** : to catch, to take — *vi* agarrar y *fam* : to do (something) abruptly ⟨el día siguiente agarró y se fue : the next day he up and left⟩ — **agarrarse** *vr* **1** : to hold on, to cling **2** *fam* : to get into a fight ⟨se agarraron a golpes : they came to blows⟩
agarre *nm* : grip, grasp
agarrotarse *vr* **1** : to stiffen up **2** : to seize up
agasajar *vt* : to fête, to wine and dine
agasajo *nm* : lavish attention
ágata *nf* : agate
agazaparse *vr* **1** AGACHARSE : to crouch **2** : to hide
agencia *nf* : agency, office
agenciar *vt* : to obtain, to procure — **agenciarse** *vr* : to manage, to get by
agenda *nf* **1** : agenda **2** : appointment book
agente *nmf* **1** : agent **2 agente de viajes** : travel agent **3 agente de bolsa** : stockbroker **4 agente de tráfico** : traffic officer
agigantado, -da *adj* GIGANTESCO : gigantic
agigantar *vt* **1** : to increase greatly, to enlarge **2** : to exaggerate
ágil *adj* **1** : agile, nimble **2** : sharp, lively (of a response, etc.) — **ágilmente** *adv*
agilidad *nf* : agility, nimbleness
agilizar {21} *vt* ACELERAR : to expedite, to speed up
agitación *nf, pl* **-ciones 1** : agitation **2** NERVIOSISMO : nervousness

agitado, -da adj 1 : agitated, excited 2 : choppy, rough, turbulent

agitador, -dora n PROVOCADOR : agitator

agitar vt 1 : to agitate, to shake 2 : to wave, to flap 3 : to stir up — **agitarse** vr 1 : to move back and forth, to flap around 2 : to get upset

aglomeración nf, pl **-ciones** 1 : conglomeration, mass 2 GENTÍO : crowd

aglomerar vt : to cluster, to amass — **aglomerarse** vr : to crowd together

aglutinar vt : to bring together, to bind

agnóstico, -ca adj & n : agnostic

agobiado, -da adj : weary, worn-out, weighted down

agobiante adj 1 : exhausting, overwhelming 2 : stifling, oppressive

agobiar vt 1 OPRIMIR : to oppress, to burden 2 ABRUMAR : to overwhelm 3 : to wear out, to exhaust

agobio nm Spain fam : burden, pressure

agolparse vr : to crowd together

agonía nf : agony, death throes

agonizante adj : dying

agonizar {21} vi 1 : to be dying 2 : to be in agony 3 : to dim, to fade

agorero, -ra adj : ominous

agostar vt 1 : to parch 2 : to wither — **agostarse** vr

agosto nm 1 : August ⟨el cinco de agosto : (on) August fifth⟩ 2 hacer uno su agosto : to make a fortune, to make a killing

agotado, -da adj 1 : exhausted, used up 2 : sold out 3 FATIGADO : worn-out, tired

agotador, -dora adj : exhausting

agotamiento nm FATIGA : exhaustion

agotar vt 1 : to exhaust, to use up 2 : to weary, to wear out — **agotarse** vr

agraciado[1], -da adj 1 : attractive 2 : fortunate

agraciado[2], -da n : winner

agradable adj 1 GRATO, PLACENTERO : pleasant, agreeable 2 ser agradable a la vista : to be easy on the eye(s) — **agradablemente** adv

agradar vi : to be pleasing ⟨nos agradó mucho el resultado : we were very pleased with the result⟩

agradecer {53} vt 1 : to be grateful for 2 : to thank

agradecido, -da adj : grateful, thankful

agradecimiento nm : gratitude, thankfulness

agrado nm 1 GUSTO : taste, liking ⟨no es de su agrado : it's not to his liking⟩ 2 : graciousness, helpfulness 3 con ~ : with pleasure, willingly ⟨lo haré con agrado : I will be happy to do it⟩

agrandar vt 1 : to exaggerate 2 : to enlarge — **agrandarse** vr

agrario, -ria adj : agrarian, agricultural

agravación nf, pl **-ciones** : aggravation, worsening

agravante adj : aggravating

agravar vt 1 : to increase (weight), to make heavier 2 EMPEORAR : to aggravate, to worsen — **agravarse** vr

agraviar vt INJURIAR, OFENDER : to offend, to insult

agravio nm INJURIA : affront, offense, insult

agredir {1} vt : to assail, to attack

agregado[1], -da n 1 : attaché 2 : assistant professor

agregado[2] nm 1 : aggregate 2 AÑADIDURA : addition, something added

agregar {52} vt 1 AÑADIR : to add, to attach 2 : to appoint — **agregarse** vr : to join

agresión nf, pl **-siones** 1 : aggression 2 ATAQUE : attack

agresividad nf : aggressiveness, aggression

agresivo, -va adj : aggressive — **agresivamente** adv

agresor[1], -sora adj : hostile, attacking

agresor[2], -sora n 1 : aggressor 2 : assailant, attacker

agreste adj 1 CAMPESTRE : rural 2 : wild, untamed

agriar vt 1 : to sour, to make sour 2 : to embitter — **agriarse** vr : to turn sour

agrícola adj : agricultural

agricultor, -tora n : farmer, grower

agricultura nf : agriculture, farming

agridulce adj 1 : bittersweet 2 : sweet-and-sour

agrietar vt : to crack — **agrietarse** vr 1 : to crack 2 : to become chapped

agrimensor, -sora n : surveyor

agrimensura nf : surveying

agrio, agria adj 1 ÁCIDO : sour 2 : caustic, acrimonious

agriparse vr : to catch the flu

agroindustria nf : agribusiness

agropecuario, -ria adj : pertaining to livestock and agriculture

agrupación nf, pl **-ciones** GRUPO : group, association

agrupamiento nm : grouping, concentration

agrupar vt : to group together

agua nf 1 : water 2 agua bendita : holy water 3 agua corriente : running water 4 agua dulce/salada : fresh/salt water 5 agua mineral : mineral water 6 agua oxigenada : hydrogen peroxide 7 agua potable : drinking water 8 aguas nfpl : waters ⟨en aguas internacionales : in international waters⟩ 9 aguas negras/residuales : sewage 10 como agua para chocolate Mex fam : furious 11 echar aguas Mex fam : to keep an eye out, to be on the lookout 12 ¡aguas! Mex fam : look out!

aguacate nm : avocado

aguacero nm : shower, downpour

aguado, -da adj 1 DILUIDO : diluted 2 CA, Col, Mex fam : soft, flabby 3 Mex, Peru fam : dull, boring

aguafiestas nmfs & pl : killjoy, stick-in-the-mud, spoilsport

aguafuerte nm : etching

aguamarina nf 1 : aquamarine 2 color aguamarina : aqua

aguanieve nf : sleet ⟨caer aguanieve : to be sleeting⟩

aguantar vt 1 SOPORTAR : to bear, to tolerate 2 : to hold ⟨aguántame la puerta : hold the door for me⟩ 3 : to take, to withstand (weight, etc.) **4** DURAR : to last **5** **aguantar las ganas (de hacer algo)** : to resist the urge (to do something) — vi **1** : to tolerate ⟨no aguanto más : I can't take it anymore⟩ **2** : to hold out, to last **3** : to hold (under pressure, etc.) — **aguantarse** vr **1** : to resign oneself **2** : to restrain oneself

aguante nm **1** TOLERANCIA : tolerance, patience **2** RESISTENCIA : endurance, strength

aguar {10} vt **1** : to water down, to dilute **2 aguar la fiesta** fam : to spoil the party

aguardar vt ESPERAR : to wait for, to await — vi : to be in store

aguardiente nm : clear brandy

aguarrás nm : turpentine

agudeza nf **1** : keenness, sharpness **2** : sharpness (of a sound) **3** : witticism

agudizar {21} vt : to intensify, to heighten

agudo, -da adj **1** : sharp (of a point, etc.) **2** : acute (of an angle), sharp (of an increase) **3** : acute (of an illness), severe (of a crisis) ⟨un dolor agudo : a sharp pain⟩ **4** ESTRIDENTE : shrill **5** : sharp (of eyes or ears) **6** PERSPICAZ : clever, shrewd **7** : acute (of an accent) — **agudamente** adv

agüero nm AUGURIO, PRESAGIO : augury, omen

aguijón nm, pl **-jones 1** : stinger (of a bee, etc.) **2** : goad

aguijonear vt : to goad

águila nf **1** : eagle **2 águila o sol** Mex : heads or tails

aguileño, -ña adj : aquiline

aguilera nf : aerie, eagle's nest

aguilón nm, pl **-lones** : gable

aguinaldo nm **1** : Christmas bonus, year-end bonus **2** PRi, Ven : Christmas carol

agüitarse vr Mex fam : to have the blues, to feel discouraged

aguja nf **1** : needle **2** : steeple, spire

agujerear vt : to make a hole in, to pierce

agujero nm **1** : hole **2 agujero negro** : black hole (in astronomy)

agujeta nf **1** Mex : shoelace **2 agujetas** nfpl : muscular soreness or stiffness

agusanado, -da adj : wormy

aguzar {21} vt : to sharpen ⟨aguzar el ingenio : to sharpen one's wits⟩ **2 aguzar el oído** : to prick up one's ears

ah interj : oh!

ahí adv **1** : there ⟨ahí está : there it is⟩ ⟨pasé por ahí : I went by/through there⟩ ⟨ahí está el problema : therein lies the problem⟩ **2** : then ⟨desde ahí : since then⟩ **3 por ~** : (around) there ⟨lo he visto por ahí : I've seen him around there⟩ ⟨debe estar por ahí : it must be there somewhere⟩ ⟨en 1950 o por ahí : in 1950 or thereabouts⟩ **4 de ahí** : hence **5 de ahí que** : with the result that, so that

ahijado, -da n : godchild, godson m, goddaughter f

ahijar {5} vt : to adopt (a child)

ahínco nm : eagerness, zeal

ahogar {52} vt **1** : to drown **2** : to smother **3** : to choke back, to stifle — **ahogarse** vr

ahogo nm : breathlessness, suffocation

ahondar vt : to deepen — vi : to elaborate, to go into detail

ahora adv **1** : now ⟨ahora voy : I'm coming now⟩ **2** : just (now) ⟨como te decía ahora . . . : as I was just telling you (now) . . .⟩ **3 ahora bien** : however **4 ahora mismo** : right now **5 hasta ~** : so far **6 por ~** : for the time being

ahorcar {72} vt : to hang, to kill by hanging — **ahorcarse** vr

ahorita adv fam : right now, right away

ahorquillado, -da adj : forked

ahorrador, -dora adj : thrifty

ahorrante nmf Chile, CoRi, DomRep, Hon AHORRISTA : investor (in savings)

ahorrar vt **1** : to save (money) **2** : to spare, to conserve — vi : to save up — **ahorrarse** vr : to spare oneself

ahorrativo, -va adj : thrifty, frugal

ahorrista nmf Arg, Uru, Ven AHORRANTE : investor (in savings)

ahorro nm : saving ⟨cuenta de ahorro(s) : savings account⟩

ahuecar {72} vt **1** : to hollow out **2** : to cup (one's hands) **3** : to plump up, to fluff up

ahuizote nm Mex fam : annoying person, pain in the neck

ahumado, -da adj : smoked

ahumar {8} vt : to smoke, to cure

ahuyentar vt **1** : to scare away, to chase away **2** : to banish, to dispel ⟨ahuyentar las dudas : to dispel doubts⟩

airado, -da adj FURIOSO : angry, irate

airar {5} vt : to make angry, to anger

aire nm **1** : air ⟨aire frío : cold air⟩ ⟨un aire caliente : a hot breeze⟩ **2** : air ⟨un aire de autoridad : an air of authority⟩ **3 aire acondicionado** : air-conditioning **4 al aire libre** : in the open air **5 darse aires** : to give oneself airs **6 en el aire** : on the air, broadcasting **7 en el aire** : up in the air, unresolved

airear vt : to air, to air out — **airearse** vr : to get some fresh air

airoso, -sa adj **1** : elegant, graceful **2 salir airoso** : to come out winning

aislado, -da adj : isolated, alone

aislador nm : insulator (part)

aislamiento nm **1** : isolation **2** : insulation

aislante nm : insulator, nonconductor

aislar {5} vt **1** : to isolate **2** : to insulate

ajado, -da adj **1** : worn, shabby **2** : wrinkled, crumpled

ajar vt : to wear out, to spoil

ajardinar vt : to landscape

ajedrecista nmf : chess player

ajedrez nm, pl **-dreces 1** : chess **2** : chess set

ajeno, -na adj **1** : alien **2** : of another, of others ⟨propiedad ajena : somebody else's property⟩ **3 ~ a** : foreign to **4 ~ de** : devoid of, free from

ajetreado, -da adj : hectic, busy

ajetrearse vr : to bustle about, to rush around

ajetreo *nm* : hustle and bustle, fuss

ají *nm, pl* **ajíes** : chili pepper

ajillo *nm* **al ajillo** : in a garlic sauce

ajo *nm* : garlic

ajonjolí *nm, pl* **-líes** : sesame

ajuar *nm* : trousseau

ajustable *adj* : adjustable

ajustado, -da *adj* **1** CEÑIDO : tight, tight-fitting **2** : close, tight ⟨una ajustada victoria : a close victory⟩

ajustar *vt* **1** : to adjust (wages, settings, etc.) **2** ADECUAR : to adapt **3** : to tighten (a bolt, etc.) **4** : to fit (a part) **5** : to take in (clothing) **6** : to fix, to set (a price) **7** SALDAR : to settle — *vi* : to fit — **ajustarse** *vr* : to fit, to conform

ajuste *nm* **1** : adjustment **2** : tightening

ajusticiar *vt* EJECUTAR : to execute, to put to death

al *prep, contraction of* A *and* EL → a²

ala *nf* **1** : wing **2** : brim (of a hat) **3** : end (in football) ⟨ala cerrada : tight end⟩

Alá *nm* : Allah

alabanza *nf* ELOGIO : praise

alabar *vt* : to praise — **alabarse** *vr* : to boast

alabastro *nm* : alabaster

alabear *vt* : to warp — **alabearse** *vr*

alabeo *nm* : warp, warping

alacena *nf* : cupboard, larder

alacrán *nm, pl* **-cranes** ESCORPIÓN : scorpion

ala delta *nf* **1** : hang glider **2** → **aladeltismo**

aladeltismo *nm* : hang gliding

alado, -da *adj* : winged

alambique *nm* : still (to distill alcohol)

alambrada *nf* : wire fence

alambre *nm* **1** : wire **2 alambre de púas** : barbed wire

alameda *nf* **1** : poplar grove **2** : tree-lined avenue

álamo *nm* **1** : poplar **2 álamo temblón** : aspen

alar *nm* : eaves *pl*

alarde *nm* **1** : show, display **2 hacer alarde de** : to make show of, to boast about

alardear *vi* PRESUMIR : to boast, to brag

alargado, -da *adj* : elongated, slender

alargador *nm* : extension cord

alargamiento *nm* : lengthening, extension, elongation

alargar {52} *vt* **1** : to extend, to lengthen **2** PROLONGAR : to prolong — **alargarse** *vr*

alargue *nm* **1** *Arg* → **alargador 2** *Arg, Chile, Uru* : overtime (in sports)

alarido *nm* : howl, shriek

alarma *nf* : alarm

alarmante *adj* : alarming — **alarmantemente** *adv*

alarmar *vt* : to alarm

alazán *nm, pl* **-zanes** : sorrel (color or animal)

alba *nf* AMANECER : dawn, daybreak

albacea *nmf* TESTAMENTARIO : executor, executrix *f*

albahaca *nf* : basil

albanés, -nesa *adj & n, mpl* **-neses** : Albanian

albañil *nmf* : bricklayer, mason

albañilería *nf* : bricklaying, masonry

albaricoque *nm* : apricot

albatros *nm* : albatross

albedrío *nm* : will ⟨libre albedrío : free will⟩

alberca *nf* **1** : reservoir, tank **2** *Mex* : swimming pool

albergar {52} *vt* ALOJAR : to house, to lodge, to shelter

albergue *nm* **1** : shelter, refuge **2** : hostel

albino, -na *adj & n* : albino — **albinismo** *nm*

albóndiga *nf* : meatball

albor *nm* **1** : dawning, beginning **2** BLANCURA : whiteness

alborada *nf* : dawn

alborear *v impers* : to dawn

alborotado, -da *adj* **1** : excited, agitated **2** : rowdy, unruly

alborotador¹, -dora *adj* **1** : noisy, boisterous **2** : rowdy, unruly

alborotador², -dora *n* : agitator, troublemaker, rioter

alborotar *vt* **1** : to excite, to agitate **2** : to incite, to stir up — **alborotarse** *vr* **1** : to get excited **2** : to riot

alboroto *nm* **1** : disturbance, ruckus **2** MOTÍN : riot

alborozado, -da *adj* : jubilant

alborozar {21} *vt* : to gladden, to cheer

alborozo *nm* : joy, elation

álbum *nm* : album ⟨álbum de fotos : photo album⟩ ⟨álbum de recortes : scrapbook⟩

albúmina *nf* : albumin

albur *nm* **1** : chance, risk **2** *Mex* : pun

alca *nf* : auk

alcachofa *nf* : artichoke

alcahuete, -ta *n* CHISMOSO : gossip

alcaide *nm* : warden (in a prison)

alcalde, -desa *n* : mayor

alcaldía *nf* **1** : mayor's office (job) **2** AYUNTAMIENTO : city hall

álcali *nm* : alkali

alcalino, -na *adj* : alkaline — **alcalinidad** *nf*

alcance *nm* **1** : reach **2** : range, scope

alcancía *nf* **1** : piggy bank, money box **2** : collection box (for alms, etc.)

alcanfor *nm* : camphor

alcantarilla *nf* CLOACA : sewer, drain

alcantarillado *nm* : sewer system

alcanzar {21} *vt* **1** : to reach **2** : to catch up with **3** LOGRAR : to achieve, to attain — *vi* **1** DAR : to suffice, to be enough **2** ~ **a** : to manage to

alcaparra *nf* : caper

alcapurria *nf* *PRi* : stuffed fritter made with taro and green banana

alcaravea *nf* : caraway

alcayata *nf* : hook

alcázar *nm* : fortress, castle

alce¹, etc. → **alzar**

alce² *nm* : moose, European elk

alcista *adj* : upward (of a trend), bullish (of markets)

alcoba *nf* : bedroom

alcohol *nm* : alcohol

alcoholemia *nf* **prueba de alcoholemia** : sobriety test

alcohólico, -ca *adj & n* : alcoholic
alcoholismo *nm* : alcoholism
alcoholizarse {21} *vr* : to become an alcoholic
alcornoque *nm* **1** : cork oak **2** *fam* : idiot, fool
alcurnia *nf* : ancestry, lineage
aldaba *nf* : door knocker
aldea *nf* : village
aldeano¹, -na *adj* : village, rustic
aldeano², -na *n* : villager
aleación *nf, pl* **-ciones** : alloy
alear *vt* : to alloy
aleatorio, -ria *adj* : random, fortuitous — **aleatoriamente** *adv*
alebrestar *vt* : to excite, to make nervous — **alebrestarse** *vr*
aleccionar *vt* : to lecture, to teach
aledaño, -ña *adj* : bordering, neighboring
aledaños *nmpl* AFUERAS : outskirts, surrounding area
alegación *nf, pl* **-ciones** **1** *CA, Car* : allegation **2** : statement (in law)
alegar {52} *vt* : to assert, to allege — *vi* DISCUTIR : to argue
alegato *nm* **1** : allegation, claim **2** *Mex* : argument, summation (in law) **3** : argument, dispute
alegoría *nf* : allegory
alegórico, -ca *adj* : allegorical
alegrar *vt* : to make happy, to cheer up ⟨me alegra mucho que . . . : I'm very happy that . . .⟩ — **alegrarse** *vr* : to be glad, to be happy ⟨me alegro de (ver) que . . . : I'm glad (to see) that . . .⟩ ⟨me alegro por ti : I'm happy for you⟩
alegre *adj* **1** : glad, cheerful **2** : colorful, bright **3** *fam* : tipsy
alegremente *adv* : happily, cheerfully
alegría *nf* : joy, cheer, happiness
alejado, -da *adj* : remote
alejamiento *nm* **1** : removal, separation **2** : estrangement
alejar *vt* **1** : to remove, to move away **2** : to estrange, to alienate — **alejarse** *vr* **1** : to move away, to stray **2** : to drift apart
alelado, -da *adj* **1** : bewildered, stupefied **2** : foolish, stupid
aleluya *interj* : hallelujah!, alleluia!
alemán¹, -mana *adj & n, mpl* **-manes** : German
alemán² *nm* : German (language)
alentador, -dora *adj* : encouraging
alentar {55} *vt* : to encourage, to inspire — *vi* : to breathe
alerce *nm* : larch
alérgeno *nm* : allergen
alergia *nf* : allergy
alérgico, -ca *adj* : allergic
alero *nm* **1** : eaves *pl* **2** : forward (in basketball)
alerón *nm, pl* **-rones** : aileron
alerta¹ *adv* : on the alert
alerta² *adj & nf* : alert
alertar *vt* : to alert
aleta *nf* **1** : fin **2** : flipper **3** : small wing
aletargado, -da *adj* : lethargic, sluggish, torpid
aletargarse {52} *vr* : to feel drowsy, to become lethargic

aletear *vi* : to flutter, to flap one's wings
aleteo *nm* : flapping, flutter
alevín *nm, pl* **-vines** **1** : fry, young fish **2** PRINCIPIANTE : beginner
alevosía *nf* **1** : treachery **2** : premeditation
alevoso, -sa *adj* : treacherous
alfabético, -ca *adj* : alphabetical — **alfabéticamente** *adv*
alfabetismo *nm* : literacy
alfabetizado, -da *adj* : literate
alfabetizar {21} *vt* : to alphabetize — **alfabetización** *nf*
alfabeto *nm* : alphabet
alfalfa *nf* : alfalfa
alfanje *nm* : cutlass
alfarería *nf* : pottery
alfarero, -ra *n* : potter
alféizar *nm* : sill, windowsill
alfeñique *nm fam* : wimp, weakling
alférez *nmf, pl* **-reces** **1** : second lieutenant **2** : ensign
alfil *nm* : bishop (in chess)
alfiler *nm* **1** : pin **2** BROCHE : brooch
alfiletero *nm* : pincushion
alfombra *nf* : carpet, rug
alfombrado *nm* : carpeting
alfombrar *vt* : to carpet
alfombrilla *nf* **1** : small rug, mat **2** **alfombrilla de/para ratón** : mouse pad
alforfón *nm, pl* **-fones** : buckwheat
alforja *nf* : saddlebag
alforza *nf* : pleat, tuck
alga *nf* **1** : aquatic plant, alga **2** : seaweed
algarabía *nf* **1** : gibberish, babble **2** : hubbub, uproar
álgebra *nf* : algebra
algebraico, -ca *adj* : algebraic
álgido, -da *adj* **1** : critical, decisive **2** : icy cold
algo¹ *adv* : somewhat, rather ⟨estaba algo nervioso : he was a little nervous⟩
algo² *pron* **1** : something, anything ⟨¿pasa algo? : is something wrong?⟩ ⟨¿dijo algo más? : did he say anything else?⟩ ⟨por algo lo escogió : she chose him for a reason⟩ ⟨algo para/de comer : something to eat⟩ **2** ~ **de** : some, a little ⟨tengo algo de dinero : I've got some money⟩ **3 (o) algo así** : (or) something like that
algodón *nm, pl* **-dones** : cotton
algodoncillo *nm* : milkweed
algodón de azúcar *nm* : cotton candy
algodonero¹, -ra *adj* : cotton
algodonero², -ra *n* : cotton farmer
algoritmo *nm* : algorithm
alguacil *nm* : constable
alguien *pron* **1** : somebody, someone ⟨alguien gritó : someone shouted⟩ ⟨hablaba con alguien : he was talking to somebody⟩ **2** : anybody, anyone ⟨¿hay alguien en casa? : is there anybody home?⟩
alguno¹, -na *adj* (**algún** before masculine singular nouns) **1** : some, any ⟨en algunos casos : in some cases⟩ ⟨algún día : someday, one day⟩ ⟨algunas semanas después : a few weeks later⟩ ⟨¿alguna pregunta? : any questions?⟩ **2** (*in negative constructions*) : not any, not at all

⟨no tengo noticia alguna : I have no news at all⟩ **3 algún que otro, alguna que otra** : the odd, the occasional

alguno², -na *pron* **1** : one, any ⟨alguno de los libros/niños : one of the books/children⟩ ⟨alguno se ofendió : someone got offended⟩ ⟨¿falta alguno? : are there any missing?⟩ **2 algunos, -nas** *pl* : some, a few, any ⟨algunos de los libros/niños : some of the books/children⟩ ⟨algunos dicen que . . . : some (people) say that . . .⟩ ⟨¿hay algunos que te gusten? : are there any that you like?⟩

alhaja *nf* : jewel, gem

alhajar *vt* : to adorn with jewels

alhajero *nm* : jewelry box

alharaca *nf* : fuss

alhelí *nm, pl* **alhelíes** : wallflower

aliado¹, -da *adj* : allied

aliado², -da *n* : ally

alianza *nf* : alliance

aliar {85} *vt* : to ally — **aliarse** *vr* : to form an alliance, to ally oneself

alias *adv & nm* : alias

alicaído, -da *adj* : depressed, discouraged

alicates *nmpl* PINZAS : pliers

aliciente *nm* **1** INCENTIVO : incentive **2** ATRACCIÓN : attraction

alienación *nf, pl* **-ciones** : alienation, derangement

alienar *vt* ENAJENAR : to alienate

aliento *nm* **1** : breath **2** : courage, strength **3 dar aliento a** : to encourage

aligerar *vt* **1** : to lighten **2** ACELERAR : to hasten, to quicken

alijo *nm* : cache, consignment (of contraband)

alimaña *nf* : pest, vermin

alimentación *nf, pl* **-ciones** NUTRICIÓN : nutrition, nourishment

alimentar *vt* **1** NUTRIR : to feed, to nourish **2** MANTENER : to support (a family) **3** FOMENTAR : to nurture, to foster — **alimentarse** *vr* ~ **con** : to live on

alimentario, -ria → **alimenticio**

alimenticio, -cia *adj* **1** : nutritional, food, dietary **2** : nutritious, nourishing

alimento *nm* : food, nourishment

alineación *nf, pl* **-ciones** **1** : alignment **2** : lineup (in sports)

alineamiento *nm* : alignment

alinear *vt* **1** : to align **2** : to line up — **alinearse** *vr* **1** : to fall in, to line up **2** ~ **con** : to align oneself with

aliñar *vt* **1** : to dress (salad) **2** CONDIMENTAR : to season

aliño *nm* : seasoning, dressing

alipús *nm, pl* **-puses** *Mex fam* : booze, drink

alisar *vt* : to smooth

aliscafo *or* **alíscafo** *nm* : hydrofoil

alistamiento *nm* : enlistment, recruitment

alistar *vt* **1** : to recruit **2** : to make ready — **alistarse** *vr* : to join up, to enlist

aliteración *nf, pl* **-ciones** : alliteration

aliviar *vt* MITIGAR : to relieve, to alleviate, to soothe — **aliviarse** *vr* : to recover, to get better

alivio *nm* : relief

aljaba *nf* : quiver (for arrows)

aljibe *nm* : cistern, well

allá *adv* **1** : there, over there ⟨allá arriba : up there⟩ ⟨allá en Cuba : over (there) in Cuba⟩ **2** ~ **por** : back in ⟨allá por los años 80 : back in the 80's⟩ **3 allá tú** : that's up to you **4 ¡allá voy!** : here I come!, here I go! **5 más allá** : farther away **6 más allá de** : beyond

allanamiento *nm* **1** : (police) raid **2 allanamiento de morada** : breaking and entering

allanar *vt* **1** : to raid, to search **2** : to resolve, to solve **3** : to smooth, to level off/out — **allanarse** *vr* : to even out, to level off/out

allegado¹, -da *adj* : close, intimate

allegado², -da *n* : close friend, relation ⟨parientes y allegados : friends and relations⟩

allegar {52} *vt* : to gather, to collect

allende¹ *adv* : beyond, on the other side

allende² *prep* : beyond ⟨allende las montañas : beyond the mountains⟩

allí *adv* **1** : there, over there ⟨todos están allí : everyone's there⟩ ⟨allí mismo : right there⟩ ⟨hasta allí : up to that point⟩

alma *nf* **1** : soul **2** : person, human being **3 no tener alma** : to be pitiless **4 tener el alma en un hilo** : to have one's heart in one's mouth

almacén *nm, pl* **-cenes** **1** BODEGA : warehouse, storehouse **2** TIENDA : shop, store **3 gran almacén** *Spain* : department store

almacenaje → **almacenamiento**

almacenamiento *nm* : storage ⟨almacenamiento de datos : data storage⟩

almacenar *vt* : to store, to put into storage

almacenero, -ra *n* : shopkeeper

almacenista *nmf* MAYORISTA : wholesaler

almádena *nf* : sledgehammer

almanaque *nm* : almanac

almeja *nf* : clam

almendra *nf* **1** : almond **2** : kernel

almendro *nm* : almond tree

almiar *nm* : haystack

almíbar *nm* : syrup

almidón *nm, pl* **-dones** : starch

almidonar *vt* : to starch

aminar *nm* MINARETE : minaret

almirantazgo *nm* : admiralty

almirante *nm* : admiral

almizcle *nm* : musk

almohada *nf* : pillow

almohadilla *nf* **1** : small pillow, cushion **2** : bag, base (in baseball) **3 almohadilla de/para ratón** : mouse pad

almohadón *nm, pl* **-dones** : bolster, cushion

almohazar {21} *vt* : to curry (a horse)

almoneda *nf* SUBASTA : auction

almorranas *nfpl* HEMORROIDES : hemorrhoids, piles

almorzar {36} *vi* : to have lunch — *vt* : to have for lunch

almuerzo *nm* : lunch

alocado, -da *adj* **1** : crazy **2** : wild, reckless **3** : silly, scatterbrained

alocución *nf, pl* **-ciones** : speech, address

áloe *or* **aloe** *nm* : aloe

alojamiento *nm* : lodging, accommodations *pl*

alojar *vt* ALBERGAR : to house, to lodge — **alojarse** *vr* : to lodge, to room

alondra *nf* : lark, skylark

alpaca *nf* : alpaca

alpargata *nf* *Arg, Spain, Uru, Ven* : espadrille

alpinismo *nm* : mountain climbing, mountaineering

alpinista *nmf* : mountain climber

alpino, -na *adj* : Alpine, alpine

alpiste *nm* : birdseed

alquilar *vt* ARRENDAR : to rent, to lease

alquiler *nm* ARRENDAMIENTO : rent, rental

alquimia *nf* : alchemy

alquimista *nmf* : alchemist

alquitrán *nm, pl* **-tranes** BREA : tar

alquitranar *vt* : to tar, to cover with tar

alrededor *adv* 1 : around ⟨lo que sucede alrededor : the things happening around us/you (etc.)⟩ 2 ~ **de** : around ⟨la Tierra gira alrededor del sol : the Earth revolves around the sun⟩ 3 ~ **de** : about, around ⟨alrededor de quince personas : about fifteen people⟩ ⟨alrededor de diciembre : around December⟩ 4 **a mi/tu** (etc.) **alrededor** : around me/you (etc.)

alrededores *nmpl* ALEDAÑOS : surroundings, outskirts

alta *nf* 1 : admission, entry, enrollment 2 **dar de alta** : to release, to discharge (a patient)

altanería *nf* ALTIVEZ, ARROGANCIA : arrogance, haughtiness

altanero, -ra *adj* ALTIVO, ARROGANTE : arrogant, haughty — **altaneramente** *adv*

altar *nm* : altar

altavoz *nm, pl* **-voces** ALTOPARLANTE : loudspeaker

alteración *nf, pl* **-ciones** 1 MODIFICACIÓN : alteration, modification 2 PERTURBACIÓN : disturbance, disruption

alterado, -da *adj* : upset

alterar *vt* 1 MODIFICAR : to alter, to modify 2 PERTURBAR : to disturb, to disrupt — **alterarse** *vr* : to get upset, to get worked up

altercado *nm* DISCUSIÓN, DISPUTA : altercation, argument, dispute

altercar {72} *vi* : to argue

alternador *nm* : alternator

alternancia *nf* : alternation, rotation

alternar *vi* 1 : to alternate 2 : to mix, to socialize — *vt* : to alternate — **alternarse** *vr* : to take turns

alternativa *nf* OPCIÓN : alternative, option

alternativo, -va *adj* 1 : alternating 2 : alternative — **alternativamente** *adv*

alterno, -na *adj* : alternate ⟨corriente alterna : alternating current⟩

alteza *nf* 1 : loftiness, lofty height 2 **Alteza** : Highness

altibajos *nmpl* 1 : unevenness (of terrain) 2 : ups and downs

altiplanicie *nf* → altiplano

altiplano *nm* : high plateau, upland

altisonante *adj* 1 : pompous, affected (of language) 2 *Mex* : rude, obscene (of language)

altitud *nf* : altitude

altivez *nf, pl* **-veces** ALTANERÍA, ARROGANCIA : arrogance, haughtiness

altivo, -va *adj* ALTANERO, ARROGANTE : arrogant, haughty

alto¹ *adv* 1 : high 2 : loud, loudly — **altamente** *adv*

alto², -ta *adj* 1 : tall, high ⟨un hombre/edificio alto : a tall man/building⟩ ⟨altas montañas : high mountains⟩ 2 : high ⟨altas temperaturas : high temperatures⟩ ⟨de alta calidad : of high quality⟩ 3 : high ⟨la alta sociedad : high society⟩ ⟨un alto funcionario : a high-ranking official⟩ 4 : upper ⟨el Alto Nilo : the Upper Nile⟩ 5 : loud ⟨en voz alta : aloud, out loud⟩ 6 **en alta mar** : on the high seas 7 **en alto** : in the air ⟨con la cabeza en alto : with her head held high⟩ 8 **en lo alto de** : high up on/in 9 **por todo lo alto** : in high style

alto³ *nm* 1 ALTURA : height, elevation ⟨tiene un metro de alto : it's one meter tall/high⟩ 2 : stop, halt 3 **altos** *nmpl* : upper floors

alto⁴ *interj* : halt!, stop!

alto el fuego *nm, pl* **altos el fuego** : cease-fire

altoparlante *nm* ALTAVOZ : loudspeaker

altozano *nm* : hillock

altruismo *nm* : altruism

altruista *adj* : altruistic

altura *nf* 1 : height ⟨una altura de dos metros : a height of two meters⟩ ⟨a la altura del pecho : at chest height⟩ ⟨no estuvo a la altura de las expectativas : it didn't meet our expectations⟩ 2 : altitude 3 : loftiness, nobleness 4 **a la altura de** : (up) by, (up) near ⟨en la avenida San Antonio a la altura de la calle Tres : on San Antonio Avenue up by Third Street⟩ 5 **a estas alturas** : at this point, at this stage

alubia *nf* : kidney bean

alucinación *nf, pl* **-ciones** : hallucination

alucinante *adj* : hallucinatory

alucinar *vi* : to hallucinate

alucinógeno¹, -na *adj* : hallucinogenic

alucinógeno² *nm* : hallucinogen

alud *nm* AVALANCHA : avalanche, landslide

aludido, -da *n* 1 : person in question ⟨el aludido : the aforesaid⟩ 2 **darse por aludido** : to take it personally

aludir *vi* : to allude, to refer

alumbrado *nm* ILUMINACIÓN : lighting

alumbramiento *nm* 1 : lighting 2 : childbirth

alumbrar *vt* 1 ILUMINAR : to light, to illuminate 2 : to give birth to

alumbre *nm* : alum

aluminio *nm* : aluminum

alumnado *nm* : student body

alumno, -na *n* : pupil, student ⟨ex-alumno, ex-alumna : alumnus, alumna⟩ ⟨ex-alumnos, ex-alumnas : alumni, alumnae⟩

alusión *nf, pl* **-siones** : allusion, reference
alusivo, -va *adj* ~ **a** : in reference to, regarding
aluvión *nm, pl* **-viones** : flood, barrage
alza *nf* SUBIDA : rise ⟨precios en alza : rising prices⟩
alzacuello *nm* : clerical collar
alzamiento *nm* LEVANTAMIENTO : uprising, insurrection
alzar {21} *vt* 1 ELEVAR, LEVANTAR : to lift, to raise 2 : to erect — **alzarse** *vr* LEVANTARSE : to rise up ⟨alzarse en armas : to rise up in arms⟩
ama *nf* → **amo**
amabilidad *nf* : kindness
amable *adj* : kind, nice — **amablemente** *adv*
amado¹, -da *adj* : beloved, darling
amado², -da *n* : sweetheart, loved one
amaestrar *vt* : to train (animals)
amafiarse *vr Mex fam* : to conspire, to be in cahoots *fam*
amagar {52} *vt* 1 : to show signs of (an illness, etc.) 2 : to threaten — *vi* 1 : to be imminent, to threaten 2 : to feint, to dissemble
amago *nm* 1 AMENAZA : threat 2 : sign, hint
amainar *vi* : to abate, to ease up, to die down
amalgama *nf* : amalgam
amalgamar *vt* : to amalgamate, to unite
amamantar *v* : to breast-feed, to nurse, to suckle
amanecer¹ {53} *v impers* 1 : to dawn 2 : to begin to show, to appear 3 : to wake up (in the morning)
amanecer² *nm* ALBA : dawn, daybreak
amanerado, -da *adj* : affected, mannered
amansar *vt* 1 : to tame 2 : to soothe, to calm down — **amansarse** *vr*
amante¹ *adj* : loving, fond
amante² *nmf* : lover
amañar *vt* : to rig, to fix, to tamper with — **amañarse** *vr* **amañárselas** : to manage
amaño *nm* 1 : skill, dexterity 2 : trick, ruse
amapola *nf* : poppy
amar *vt* : to love — **amarse** *vr*
amargado, -da *adj* : embittered, bitter
amargar {52} *vt* : to make bitter, to embitter — *vi* : to taste bitter
amargo¹, -ga *adj* : bitter — **amargamente** *adv*
amargo² *nm* : bitterness, tartness
amargura *nf* 1 : bitterness 2 : grief, sorrow
amarilis *nf* : amaryllis
amarillear *vi* : to yellow, to turn yellow
amarillento, -ta *adj* : yellowish
amarillismo *nm* : sensationalism
amarillo¹, -lla *adj* : yellow
amarillo² *nm* : yellow
amarra *nf* 1 : mooring, mooring line 2 **soltar las amarras de** : to loosen one's grip on
amarrar *vt* 1 : to moor (a boat) 2 ATAR : to fasten, to tie up, to tie down
amartillar *vt* : to cock (a gun)

amasar *vt* 1 : to amass 2 : to knead 3 : to mix, to prepare
amasijo *nm* : jumble, hodgepodge
amasio, -sia *n* : lover
amateur *adj & nmf* : amateur — **amateurismo** *nm*
amatista *nf* : amethyst
amazona *nf* 1 : Amazon (in mythology) 2 : horsewoman
amazónico, -ca *adj* : amazonian
ambages *nmpl* **sin** ~ : without hesitation, straight to the point
ámbar *nm* 1 : amber 2 **ámbar gris** : ambergris
ambición *nf, pl* **-ciones** : ambition
ambicionar *vt* : to aspire to, to seek
ambicioso, -sa *adj* : ambitious — **ambiciosamente** *adv*
ambidextro, -tra *adj* : ambidextrous
ambientación *nf, pl* **-ciones** : setting, atmosphere
ambiental *adj* : environmental — **ambientalmente** *adv*
ambientalista *nmf* : environmentalist
ambientar *vt* : to give atmosphere to, to set (in literature and drama) — **ambientarse** *vr* : to adjust, to get one's bearings
ambiente *nm* 1 : atmosphere 2 : environment 3 : surroundings *pl*
ambigüedad *nf* : ambiguity
ambiguo, -gua *adj* : ambiguous
ámbito *nm* : domain, field, area
ambivalencia *nf* : ambivalence
ambivalente *adj* : ambivalent
ambos, -bas *adj & pron* : both
ambulancia *nf* : ambulance
ambulante *adj* 1 : traveling, itinerant 2 **vendedor ambulante** : street vendor
ambulatorio¹, -ria *adj* : outpatient
ambulatorio² *nm Spain, Ven* : clinic
ameba *nf* : amoeba — **amébico** *adj*
amedrentar *vt* : to frighten, to intimidate — **amedrentarse** *vr*
amén *nm, pl* **amenes** 1 : amen 2 ~ **de** : in addition to, besides 3 **en un decir amén** : in an instant
amenaza *nf* : threat ⟨amenazas de muerte/bomba : death/bomb threats⟩
amenazador, -dora *adj* : threatening, menacing
amenazante → **amenazador**
amenazar {21} *vt* : to threaten ⟨me amenazó con demandarme : she threatened to sue me⟩ ⟨fue amenazado de muerte : he received death threats⟩ — *vi* : to threaten ⟨amenazan con sanciones : they're threatening sanctions⟩
amenguar {10} *vt* 1 : to diminish 2 : to belittle, to dishonor
amenidad *nf* : pleasantness, amenity
amenizar {21} *vt* 1 : to make pleasant 2 : to brighten up, to add life to
ameno, -na *adj* : agreeable, pleasant
americano, -na *adj & n* : American
amerindio, -dia *adj & n* → **nativo americano**
ameritar *vt* MERECER : to deserve
ametralladora *nf* : machine gun
amianto *nm* : asbestos
amiba → **ameba**

amigable *adj* : friendly, amicable — **amigablemente** *adv*
amígdala *nf* : tonsil
amigdalitis *nf* : tonsillitis
amigo¹, -ga *adj* **1** : friendly, close ⟨es muy amigo mío : he's a very good friend of mine⟩ **2 hacerse (muy) amigo (de)** : to become (good) friends (with) **3 ser (muy) amigo de algo** : to be (very) fond of something
amigo², -ga *n* **1** : friend ⟨un buen/íntimo amigo : a good/close friend⟩ ⟨es una amiga suya : she's a friend of his⟩ **2 hacer amigos** : to make friends
amigote *nm* : crony, pal
amilanar *vt* **1** : to frighten **2** : to daunt, to discourage — **amilanarse** *vr* : to lose heart
aminoácido *nm* : amino acid
aminorar *vt* : to reduce, to lessen — *vi* : to diminish
amistad *nf* : friendship
amistoso, -sa *adj* : friendly — **amistosamente** *adv*
amnesia *nf* : amnesia
amnésico, -ca *adj & n* : amnesiac
amnistía *nf* : amnesty
amnistiar {85} *vt* : to grant amnesty to
amo, ama *n* **1** : master *m*, mistress *f* **2** : owner, keeper (of an animal) **3 ama de casa** : housewife **4 ama de llaves** : housekeeper
amodorrado, -da *adj* : drowsy
amolar {19} *vt* **1** : to grind, to sharpen **2** : to pester, to annoy
amoldable *adj* : adaptable
amoldar *vt* **1** : to mold **2** : to adapt, to adjust — **amoldarse** *vr*
amonestación *nf, pl* **-ciones 1** APERCIBIMIENTO : admonition, warning **2 amonestaciones** *nfpl* : banns
amonestar *vt* APERCIBIR : to admonish, to warn
amoníaco *or* **amoniaco** *nm* : ammonia
amontonamiento *nm* : accumulation, piling up
amontonar *vt* **1** APILAR : to pile up, to heap up **2** : to collect, to gather **3** : to hoard — **amontonarse** *vr*
amor *nm* **1** : love ⟨un poema de amor : a love poem⟩ ⟨su amor por/a la música : his love of music⟩ **2** : loved one, beloved ⟨sí, mi amor : yes, my love⟩ **3 amor propio** : self-esteem **4 hacer el amor** : to make love **5 por amor al arte** : for the love of it **6 ¡por el amor de Dios!** : for God's sake!
amoral *adj* : amoral
amoratado, -da *adj* : black-and-blue, bruised, livid
amordazar {21} *vt* **1** : to gag, to muzzle **2** : to silence
amorfo, -fa *adj* : shapeless, amorphous
amorío *nm* : love affair, fling
amoroso, -sa *adj* **1** : loving, affectionate **2** : amorous ⟨una mirada amorosa : an amorous glance⟩ **3** : charming, cute — **amorosamente** *adv*
amortiguación *nf* : cushioning, absorption

amortiguador *nm* : shock absorber
amortiguar {10} *vt* : to soften (an impact)
amortizar {21} *vt* : to amortize, to pay off — **amortización** *nf*
amotinado¹, -da *adj* : rebellious, insurgent, mutinous
amotinado², -da *n* : rebel, insurgent, mutineer
amotinamiento *nm* : uprising, rebellion
amotinar *vt* : to incite (to riot), to agitate — **amotinarse** *vr* **1** : to riot, to rebel **2** : to mutiny
amparar *vt* : to safeguard, to protect — **ampararse** *vr* **1 ~ de** : to take shelter from **2 ~ en** : to have recourse to
amparo *nm* ACOGIDA, REFUGIO : protection, refuge
amperímetro *nm* : ammeter
amperio *nm* : ampere
ampliación *nf, pl* **-ciones** : expansion, extension
ampliar {85} *vt* **1** : to expand, to extend **2** : to widen **3** : to enlarge (photographs) **4** : to elaborate on, to develop (ideas)
amplificador *nm* : amplifier
amplificar {72} *vt* : to amplify — **amplificación** *nf*
amplio, -plia *adj* **1** : broad, wide (of a street, etc.), spacious (of a room, etc.) ⟨una amplia gama de : a broad range of⟩ ⟨en el sentido más amplio : in the broadest sense⟩ **2** : full, comprehensive **3** : loose, full (of clothes) — **ampliamente** *adv*
amplitud *nf* **1** : breadth, extent **2** : space, spacious quality
ampolla *nf* **1** : blister **2** : vial
ampollar *vt* : to blister — **ampollarse** *vr*
ampolleta *nf* **1** : small vial **2** : hourglass **3** *Chile* : light bulb
ampulosidad *nf* : pomposity, bombast
ampuloso, -sa *adj* GRANDILOCUENTE : pompous, bombastic — **ampulosamente** *adv*
amputar *vt* : to amputate — **amputación** *nf*
amueblar *vt* : to furnish
amuleto *nm* TALISMÁN : amulet, charm
amurallar *vt* : to wall in, to fortify
anacardo *nm* : cashew nut
anaconda *nf* : anaconda
anacrónico, -ca *adj* : anachronistic
anacronismo *nm* : anachronism
ánade *nmf* **1** : duck **2 ánade real** : mallard
anagrama *nm* : anagram
anal *adj* : anal
anales *nmpl* : annals
analfabetismo *nm* : illiteracy
analfabeto, -ta *adj & n* : illiterate
analgésico¹, -ca *adj* : analgesic
analgésico² *nm* : painkiller, analgesic
análisis *nm* : analysis
analista *nmf* : analyst
analítico, -ca *adj* : analytical, analytic — **analíticamente** *adv*
analizar {21} *vt* : to analyze
analogía *nf* : analogy
analógico, -ca *adj* **1** : analogical **2** : analog ⟨computadora analógica : analog computer⟩

análogo · angular

20

análogo, -ga *adj* : analogous, similar

ananá *or* ananás *nm, pl* -nás : pineapple

anaquel *nm* REPISA : shelf

anaranjado[1], -da *adj* NARANJA : orange-colored

anaranjado[2] *nm* NARANJA : orange (color)

anarquía *nf* : anarchy

anárquico, -ca *adj* : anarchic

anarquismo *nm* : anarchism

anarquista *adj & nmf* : anarchist

anatema *nm* : anathema

anatomía *nf* : anatomy — **anatomista** *nmf*

anatómico, -ca *adj* : anatomical — **anatómicamente** *adv*

ancas *nfpl* 1 : haunches, hindquarters 2 ancas de rana : frogs' legs

ancestral *adj* 1 : ancient, traditional 2 : ancestral

ancestro *nm* ASCENDIENTE : ancestor, forefather *m*

ancho[1], -cha *adj* 1 : wide, broad ⟨calles anchas : wide streets⟩ 2 : full, loose-fitting 3 a lo ancho : across (the width of) 4 a sus anchas : at home, comfortable

ancho[2] *nm* 1 : width, breadth ⟨tiene dos metros de ancho : it's two meters wide⟩ 2 ancho de banda : bandwidth

anchoa *nf* : anchovy

anchura *nf* : width, breadth

ancianidad *nf* SENECTUD : old age

anciano[1], -na *adj* : aged, old, elderly

anciano[2], -na *n* : elderly person

ancla *nf* : anchor

ancladero → anclaje

anclaje *nm* : anchorage

anclar *v* FONDEAR : to anchor

andadas *nfpl* 1 : tracks 2 volver a las andadas : to go back to one's old ways, to backslide

andador[1] *nm* 1 : walker, baby walker 2 *Mex* : walkway

andador[2], -dora *n* : walker, one who walks

andadura *nf* : course, journey ⟨su agotadora andadura al campeonato : his exhausting journey to the championship⟩

ándale → andar

andaluz, -luza *adj & n, mpl* -luces : Andalusian

andamiaje *nm* 1 : scaffolding 2 ESTRUCTURA : structure, framework

andamio *nm* : scaffold

andanada *nf* 1 : volley, broadside 2 soltarle una andanada a alguien : to reprimand someone

andanzas *nfpl* : adventures

andar[1] {6} *vi* 1 CAMINAR : to walk 2 IR : to go, to travel 3 FUNCIONAR : to run, to function ⟨el auto anda bien : the car runs well⟩ 4 : to ride ⟨andar en bicicleta : to ride a bike⟩ ⟨andar a caballo : to ride on horseback⟩ 5 : to be ⟨su madre no anda bien : his mother isn't well⟩ ⟨lo andaban buscando : they were looking for him⟩ 6 ¡anda! *or Mex* ¡ándale! : come on!, go on! 7 ~ con SALIR CON : to go out with, to date 8 ~ con : to associate with 9 ~ con/sin ⟨andaba sin

camisa : he had no shirt on⟩ ⟨siempre anda con su guitarra : she always has her guitar with her⟩ 10 andar detrás de : to be after 11 ~ en : to be involved with 12 ~ en REVOLVER : to rummage through 13 ~ por : to be about ⟨anda por los 25 años : she's about 25 years old⟩ — *vt* : to walk, to travel — **andarse** *vr* : to leave, to go

andar[2] *nm* : walk, gait

andas *nfpl* : stand (for a coffin), bier

andén *nm, pl* andenes 1 : (train) platform 2 *CA, Col* : sidewalk

andino, -na *adj* : Andean

andorrano, -na *adj & n* : Andorran

andrajos *nmpl* : rags, tatters

andrajoso, -sa *adj* : ragged, tattered

andrógino, -na *adj* : androgynous

andurriales *nmpl* : remote place

anea *nf* : cattail

anduvo, etc. → andar

anécdota *nf* : anecdote

anecdótico, -ca *adj* : anecdotal

anegar {52} *vt* 1 INUNDAR : to flood 2 AHOGAR : to drown 3 : to overwhelm — **anegarse** *vr* : to be flooded

anejo *nm* → anexo[2]

anemia *nf* : anemia

anémico, -ca *adj* : anemic

anémona *nf* : anemone

anestesia *nf* : anesthesia

anestesiar *vt* : to anesthetize

anestésico[1], -ca *adj* : anesthetic

anestésico[2] *nm* : anesthetic

anestesista *nmf* : anesthetist

aneurisma *nmf* : aneurysm

anexar *vt* : to annex, to attach

anexión *nf, pl* -xiones : annexation

anexo[1], -xa *adj* : attached, joined, annexed

anexo[2] *nm* 1 : annex 2 : supplement (to a book), appendix

anfetamina *nf* : amphetamine

anfibio[1], -bia *adj* : amphibious

anfibio[2] *nm* : amphibian

anfiteatro *nm* 1 : amphitheater 2 : lecture hall

anfitrión, -triona *n, mpl* -triones : host, hostess *f*

ánfora *nf* 1 : urn, jar (with two handles) 2 *Mex, Peru* : ballot box

ángel *nm* 1 : angel 2 ángel de la guarda : guardian angel 3 ángel exterminador : Angel of Death

angelical *adj* : angelic, angelical

angélico, -ca *adj* : angelical

angina *nf* 1 *or* angina de pecho : angina 2 *Mex* : tonsil

anglicano, -na *adj & n* : Anglican

angloparlante[1] *adj* : English-speaking

angloparlante[2] *nmf* : English speaker

anglosajón, -jona *adj & n, mpl* -jones : Anglo-Saxon

angoleño, -ña *adj & n* : Angolan

angora *nf* : angora

angostar *vt* : to narrow — **angostarse** *vr*

angosto, -ta *adj* : narrow

angostura *nf* : narrowness

anguila *nf* : eel

angular *adj* : angular — **angularidad** *nf*

ángulo *nm* **1** : angle **2** : corner **3 ángulo muerto** : blind spot

anguloso, -sa *adj* : angular, sharp ⟨una cara angulosa : an angular face⟩ — **angulosidad** *nf*

angustia *nf* **1** CONGOJA : anguish, distress **2** : anxiety, worry

angustiar *vt* **1** : to anguish, to distress **2** : to worry — **angustiarse** *vr*

angustioso, -sa *adj* **1** : anguished, distressed **2** : distressing, worrisome

anhelante *adj* : yearning, longing

anhelar *vt* : to yearn for, to crave

anhelo *nm* : longing, yearning

anidar *vi* **1** : to nest **2** : to make one's home, to dwell — *vt* : to shelter

anilla *nf* : ring

anillo *nm* SORTIJA : ring

ánima *n* ALMA : soul

animación *nf, pl* **-ciones 1** : animation **2** VIVEZA : liveliness

animado, -da *adj* **1** : animated, lively **2** : cheerful — **animadamente** *adv*

animador, -dora *n* **1** : (television) host **2** : cheerleader

animadversión *nf, pl* **-siones** ANIMOSIDAD : animosity, antagonism

animal¹ *adj* **1** : animal **2** ESTÚPIDO : stupid, idiotic **3** : rough, brutish

animal² *nm* : animal

animal³ *nmf* **1** IDIOTA : idiot, fool **2** : brute, beastly person

animar *vt* **1** ALENTAR : to encourage, to inspire **2** : to animate, to enliven **3** : to brighten up, to cheer up — **animarse** *vr*

anímico, -ca *adj* : mental ⟨estado anímico : state of mind⟩

ánimo *nm* **1** ALMA : spirit, soul **2** : mood, spirits *pl* **3** : encouragement **4** PROPÓSITO : intention, purpose ⟨sociedad sin ánimo de lucro : nonprofit organization⟩ **5** : energy, vitality

animosidad *nf* ANIMADVERSIÓN : animosity, ill will

animoso, -sa *adj* : brave, spirited — **animosamente** *adv*

aniñado, -da *adj* : childlike

aniquilación *nf* → **aniquilamiento**

aniquilamiento *nm* : annihilation, extermination

aniquilar *vt* **1** : to annihilate, to wipe out **2** : to overwhelm, to bring to one's knees — **aniquilarse** *vr*

anís *nm* **1** : anise **2 semilla de anís** : aniseed

aniversario *nm* : anniversary

ano *nm* : anus

anoche *adv* : last night

anochecer¹ {53} *v impers* : to get dark

anochecer² *nm* : dusk, nightfall

anodino, -na *adj* : insipid, dull

ánodo *nm* : anode

anomalía *nf* : anomaly

anómalo, -la *adj* : anomalous

anonadado, -da *adj* : dumbfounded, speechless

anonadar *vt* : to dumbfound, to stun

anonimato *nm* : anonymity

anónimo, -ma *adj* : anonymous — **anónimamente** *adv*

anorak [ano'rak] *nm, pl* **-raks** : anorak

anorexia *nf* : anorexia

anoréxico, -ca *adj* : anorexic

anormal *adj* : abnormal — **anormalmente** *adv*

anormalidad *nf* : abnormality

anotación *nf, pl* **-ciones 1** : annotation, note **2** : scoring (in sports) ⟨lograron una anotación : they managed to score a goal⟩

anotador, -dora *n* : scorer (in sports) ⟨el máximo anotador : the top scorer, the top-scoring player⟩

anotar *vt* **1** : to annotate **2** APUNTAR, ESCRIBIR : to write down, to jot down **3** : to score (in sports) — *vi* : to score

anquilosado, -da *adj* **1** : stiff (of a joint) **2** : stagnated, stale

anquilosamiento *nm* **1** : stiffness (of joints) **2** : stagnation, paralysis

anquilosarse *vr* **1** : to stagnate **2** : to become stiff or paralyzed

anquilostoma *nm* : hookworm

ánsar *nm* : goose

ansarino *nm* : gosling

ansia *nf* **1** INQUIETUD : anxiety, uneasiness **2** ANGUSTIA : anguish, distress **3** ANHELO : longing, yearning

ansiar {85} *vt* : to long for, to yearn for

ansiedad *nf* : anxiety

ansioso, -sa *adj* **1** : anxious, worried **2** : eager — **ansiosamente** *adv*

antagónico, -ca *adj* : conflicting, opposing

antagonismo *nm* : antagonism

antagonista¹ *adj* : antagonistic

antagonista² *nmf* : antagonist, opponent

antagonizar {21} *vt* : to antagonize

antaño *adv* : yesteryear, long ago

antártico, -ca *adj* **1** : antarctic **2 círculo antártico** : antarctic circle

ante¹ *nm* **1** : elk, moose **2** : suede

ante² *prep* **1** : before, in front of **2** : considering, in view of **3 ante todo** : first and foremost, above all

anteanoche *adv* : the night before last

anteayer *adv* : the day before yesterday

antebrazo *nm* : forearm

antecedente¹ *adj* : previous, prior

antecedente² *nm* **1** : precedent **2 antecedentes** *nmpl* : record, background

anteceder *v* : to precede

antecesor, -sora *n* **1** ANTEPASADO : ancestor **2** PREDECESOR : predecessor

antedicho, -cha *adj* : aforesaid, above

antelación *nf, pl* **-ciones 1** : advance notice **2 con ∼** : in advance, beforehand

antemano *adv* **de ∼** : in advance ⟨se lo agradezco de antemano : I thank you in advance⟩

antena *nf* : antenna ⟨antena parabólica : satellite dish⟩

antenoche → **anteanoche**

anteojera *nf* **1** : glasses case **2 anteojeras** *nfpl* : blinders

anteojos *nmpl* GAFAS : glasses, eyeglasses

antepasado¹, -da *adj* : before last ⟨el domingo antepasado : the Sunday before last⟩

antepasado², **-da** *n* ANTECESOR : ancestor

antepecho *nm* **1** : guardrail **2** : ledge, sill

antepenúltimo, **-ma** *adj* : third from last

anteponer {60} *vt* **1** : to place before ⟨anteponer al interés de la nación el interés de la comunidad : to place the interests of the community before national interest⟩ **2** : to prefer

anteproyecto *nm* **1** : draft, proposal **2 anteproyecto de ley** : bill

antera *nf* : anther

anterior *adj* **1** : previous **2** : earlier ⟨tiempos anteriores : earlier times⟩ **3** : anterior, forward, front

anterioridad *nf* **1** : priority **2 con ~** : beforehand, in advance

anteriormente *adv* : previously, beforehand

antes *adv* **1** : before ⟨no se me ocurrió antes : it didn't occur to me before⟩ ⟨es igual que antes : it's the same as before⟩ ⟨una hora antes : an hour earlier⟩ ⟨antes eran más baratos : they used to be cheaper⟩ **2** : rather, sooner ⟨antes prefiero morir : I'd rather die⟩ **3 ~ de** : before, previous to ⟨antes de hoy : before today⟩ ⟨antes de salir : before leaving⟩ ⟨antes de un mes : within a month⟩ **4 antes que** : before ⟨antes que llegue Luis : before Luis arrives⟩ **5 cuanto antes** *or* **lo antes posible** : as soon as possible **6 antes bien** : on the contrary

antesala *nf* **1** : lobby, waiting room **2** : prelude, prologue

anti- *pref* : anti-, against, opposing

antiaborto, **-ta** *adj* : antiabortion

antiácido *nm* : antacid

antiadherente *adj* : nonstick

antiaéreo, **-rea** *adj* : antiaircraft

antiamericano, **-na** *adj* : anti-American

antibalas *adj* : bulletproof

antibiótico¹, **-ca** *adj* : antibiotic

antibiótico² *nm* : antibiotic

anticipación *nf*, *pl* **-ciones** **1** : expectation, anticipation **2 con ~** : in advance

anticipado, **-da** *adj* **1** : advance, early **2 por ~** : in advance

anticipar *vt* **1** : to anticipate, to forestall, to deal with in advance **2** : to pay in advance — **anticiparse** *vr* **1** : to be early **2** ADELANTARSE : to get ahead

anticipo *nm* **1** : advance (payment) **2** : foretaste, preview

anticlimático, **-ca** : anticlimactic

anticlímax *nm* : anticlimax

anticomunismo *nm* : anticommunism

anticomunista *adj & nmf* : anticommunist

anticoncepción *nf*, *pl* **-ciones** : birth control, contraception

anticonceptivo *nm* : contraceptive — **anticonceptivo**, **-va** *adj*

anticongelante *nm* : antifreeze

anticonstitucional *adj* : not constitutional

anticuado, **-da** *adj* : antiquated, outdated

anticuario¹, **-ria** *adj* : antique, antiquarian

anticuario², **-ria** *n* : antiquarian, antiquary

anticuario³ *nm* : antique shop

anticuerpo *nm* : antibody

antidemocrático, **-ca** *adj* : antidemocratic

antidepresivo *nm* : antidepressant

antidisturbios¹ *adj* : riot ⟨policía antidisturbios : riot police⟩

antidisturbios² *nmpl* : riot police

antídoto *nm* : antidote

antidrogas *adj* : antidrug

antier → anteayer

antiestético, **-ca** *adj* : unsightly, unattractive

antifascista *adj & nmf* : antifascist

antifaz *nm*, *pl* **-faces** : mask

antifeminista *adj & nmf* : antifeminist

antífona *nf* : anthem

antígeno *nm* : antigen

antigualla *nf* **1** : antique **2** : relic, old thing

antiguamente *adv* **1** : formerly, once **2** : long ago

antigüedad *nf* **1** : antiquity **2** : seniority **3** : age ⟨con siglos de antigüedad : centuries-old⟩ **4 antigüedades** *nfpl* : antiques

antiguo, **-gua** *adj* **1** : ancient, old **2** : former **3** : old-fashioned ⟨a la antigua : in the old-fashioned way⟩ **4 Antiguo Testamento** : Old Testament

antihigiénico, **-ca** *adj* INSALUBRE : unhygienic, unsanitary

antihistamínico *nm* : antihistamine

antiimperialismo *nm* : anti-imperialism

antiimperialista *adj & nmf* : anti-imperialist

antiinflacionario, **-ria** *adj* : anti-inflationary

antiinflamatorio, **-ria** *adj* : anti-inflammatory

antillano¹, **-na** *adj* CARIBEÑO : Caribbean, West Indian

antillano², **-na** *n* : West Indian

antílope *nm* : antelope

antimonio *nm* : antimony

antimonopolista *adj* : antitrust

antinatural *adj* : unnatural, perverse

antipatía *nf* : aversion, dislike

antipático, **-ca** *adj* : obnoxious, unpleasant

antipatriótico, **-ca** *adj* : unpatriotic

antirrábico, **-ca** *adj* : rabies ⟨vacuna antirrábica : rabies vaccine⟩

antirreglamentario, **-ria** *adj* **1** : unlawful, illegal **2** : foul (in sports)

antirrevolucionario, **-ria** *adj & n* : antirevolutionary

antirrobo, **-ba** *adj* : antitheft

antisemita *adj* : anti-Semitic

antisemitismo *nm* : anti-Semitism

antiséptico¹, **-ca** *adj* : antiseptic

antiséptico² *nm* : antiseptic

antisocial *adj* : antisocial

antitabaco *adj* : antismoking

antiterrorista *adj* : antiterrorist

antítesis *nf* : antithesis

antitoxina *nf* : antitoxin

antitranspirante *nm* : antiperspirant

antiviral *adj* : antiviral

antivirus *nm*, *pl* **antivirus** : antivirus software

antojadizo, -za *adj* CAPRICHOSO : capricious

antojarse *vr* **1** APETECER : to be appealing, to be desirable ⟨se me antoja un helado : I feel like having ice cream⟩ **2** : to seem, to appear ⟨los árboles se antojaban fantasmas : the trees seemed like ghosts⟩

antojitos *nmpl Mex* : traditional Mexican snack foods

antojo *nm* **1** CAPRICHO : whim **2** : craving

antología *nf* **1** : anthology **2 de ∼** *fam* : fantastic, incredible

antónimo *nm* : antonym

antonomasia *nf* **por ∼** : par excellence

antorcha *nf* : torch

antracita *nf* : anthracite

antro *nm* **1** : cave, den **2** : dive, seedy nightclub

antropofagia *nf* CANIBALISMO : cannibalism

antropófago¹, -ga *adj* : cannibalistic

antropófago², -ga *n* CANÍBAL : cannibal

antropoide *adj & nmf* : anthropoid

antropología *nf* : anthropology

antropológico, -ca *adj* : anthropological

antropólogo, -ga *n* : anthropologist

anual *adj* : annual, yearly — **anualmente** *adv*

anualidad *nf* : annuity

anuario *nm* : yearbook, annual

anudar *vt* : to knot, to tie in a knot — **anudarse** *vr*

anuencia *nf* : consent

anulación *nf, pl* **-ciones** : annulment, cancellation

anular *vt* : to annul, to cancel

anunciador, -dora *n* → **anunciante**

anunciante *nmf* : advertiser

anunciar *vt* **1** : to announce **2** : to advertise

anuncio *nm* **1** : announcement **2** : advertisement, commercial

anzuelo *nm* **1** : fishhook **2 morder el anzuelo** : to take the bait

añadido *nm* : addition

añadidura *nf* **1** : additive, addition **2 por ∼** : in addition, furthermore

añadir *vt* **1** AGREGAR : to add **2** AUMENTAR : to increase

añejar *vr* : to age, to ripen

añejo, -ja *adj* **1** : aged, vintage **2** : ancient, musty, stale

añicos *nmpl* : smithereens, bits ⟨hacer(se) añicos : to shatter⟩

añil *nm* **1** : indigo **2** : bluing

año *nm* **1** : year ⟨el año pasado : last year⟩ ⟨en el año 1990 : in (the year) 1990⟩ ⟨en los años '70 : in the '70's⟩ ⟨tiene diez años : she is ten years old⟩ ⟨cumple hoy 80 años : he turns 80 today⟩ ⟨los menores de 18 años : those under the age of 18⟩ **2** : grade ⟨cuarto año : fourth grade⟩ **3 año bisiesto** : leap year **4 año luz** : light-year **5 Año Nuevo** : New Year

añoranza *nf* : longing, yearning

añorar *vt* **1** DESEAR : to long for **2** : to grieve for, to miss — *vi* : to mourn, to grieve

añoso, -sa *adj* : aged, old

añublo *nm* : blight

aorta *nf* : aorta

apa *interj Mex fam* : wow!

apabullante *adj* : overwhelming, crushing

apabullar *vt* : to overwhelm

apacentar {55} *vt* : to pasture, to put to pasture

apache *adj & nmf* : Apache

apachurrado, -da *adj fam* : depressed, down

apachurrar *vt* : to crush, to squash

apacible *adj* : gentle, mild, calm — **apaciblemente** *adv*

apaciguador, -dora *adj* : calming

apaciguamiento *nm* : appeasement

apaciguar {10} *vt* APLACAR : to appease, to pacify — **apaciguarse** *vr* : to calm down

apadrinar *vt* **1** : to be a godparent to **2** : to sponsor, to support

apagado, -da *adj* **1** : off, out ⟨la luz está apagada : the light is off⟩ **2** : dull, subdued

apagador *nm Mex* : switch

apagar {52} *vt* **1** : to turn off, to shut off **2** : to put out, to extinguish — **apagarse** *vr* **1** : to go out (of a light, flame, etc.) **2** DISMINUIR : to wane, to die down

apagón *nm, pl* **-gones** : blackout (of power), power failure

apalabrar *vt* : to arrange with (someone), to arrange for (something)

apalancamiento *nm* : leverage

apalancar {72} *vt* **1** : to jack up **2** : to pry open

apalear *vt* : to beat up, to thrash

apanar *Col, Ecua, Peru* → **empanar**

apantallar *vt Mex* : to dazzle, to impress

apañar *vt* **1** : to seize, to grasp **2** : to repair, to mend — **apañarse** *vr* : to manage, to get along

apaño *nm fam* **1** : patch **2** HABILIDAD : skill, knack

apapachar *vt Mex fam* : to cuddle, to caress — **apapacharse** *vr*

apapacho *nm Mex fam* : cuddle, caress

aparador *nm* **1** : sideboard, cupboard **2** ESCAPARATE, VITRINA : shop window

aparato *nm* **1** : machine, appliance, apparatus ⟨aparato auditivo : hearing aid⟩ ⟨aparato de televisión : television set⟩ **2** : system ⟨aparato digestivo : digestive system⟩ **3** : display, ostentation ⟨sin aparato : without ceremony⟩ **4 aparatos** *nmpl* : braces (for the teeth) **5** : ride (in an amusement park)

aparatoso, -sa *adj* **1** : ostentatious **2** : spectacular

aparcamiento *nm Spain* **1** : parking **2** : parking lot

aparcar {72} *v Spain* : to park

aparcero, -ra *n* : sharecropper

aparear *vt* **1** : to mate (animals) **2** : to match up — **aparearse** *vr* : to mate

aparecer {53} *vi* **1** : to appear **2** PRESENTARSE : to show up **3** : to turn up, to be found — **aparecerse** *vr* : to appear

aparejado, -da *adj* **1 ir aparejado con** : to go hand in hand with **2 llevar aparejado** : to entail

aparejar vt 1 PREPARAR : to prepare, to make ready 2 : to harness (a horse) 3 : to fit out (a ship)

aparejo nm 1 : equipment, gear 2 : harness, saddle 3 : rig, rigging (of a ship)

aparentar vt 1 : to seem, to appear ‹no aparentas tu edad : you don't look your age› 2 FINGIR : to feign, to pretend

aparente adj 1 : apparent 2 : showy, striking — **aparentemente** adv

aparición nf, pl -ciones 1 : appearance 2 PUBLICACIÓN : publication, release 3 FANTASMA : apparition, vision

apariencia nf 1 ASPECTO : appearance, look 2 en ~ : seemingly, apparently

apartado nm 1 : section, paragraph 2 **apartado postal** : P.O. Box

apartamento nm DEPARTAMENTO : apartment

apartar vt 1 ALEJAR : to move away, to put at a distance 2 : to put aside, to set aside, to separate — **apartarse** vr 1 : to step aside, to move away 2 DESVIARSE : to stray

aparte[1] adv 1 : apart, aside ‹modestia aparte : if I say so myself› 2 : separately 3 ~ de : apart from, besides

aparte[2] adj : separate, special

aparte[3] nm : aside (in theater)

apartheid nm : apartheid

apasionado, -da adj : passionate, enthusiastic — **apasionadamente** adv

apasionante adj : fascinating, exciting

apasionar vt : to enthuse, to excite — **apasionarse** vr

apatía nf : apathy

apático, -ca adj : apathetic

apátrida adj 1 : without nationality 2 Ven : unpatriotic

apearse vr 1 DESMONTAR : to dismount 2 : to get out of or off (a vehicle)

apechugar {52} vi fam : to put up with the situation ‹apechugar con : to put up with, to deal with›

apedrear vt : to stone, to throw stones at

apegado, -da adj : attached, close, devoted ‹es muy apegado a su familia : he is very devoted to his family›

apegarse {52} vr ~ a : to become attached to, to grow fond of

apego nm AFICIÓN : attachment, fondness, inclination

apelación nf, pl -ciones : appeal (in court)

apelar vi 1 : to appeal 2 ~ a : to resort to

apelativo nm APELLIDO : last name, surname

apellidarse vr : to have for a last name ‹¿cómo se apellida? : what is your last name?›

apellido nm : last name, surname

apelotonar vt : to roll into a ball, to bundle up

apenar vt : to sadden — **apenarse** vr 1 : to be saddened 2 : to become embarrassed

apenas[1] adv : hardly, scarcely

apenas[2] conj : as soon as

apéndice nm 1 : appendix 2 : appendage

apendicectomía nf : appendectomy

apendicitis nf : appendicitis

apercibimiento nm 1 : preparation 2 AMONESTACIÓN : warning

apercibir vt 1 DISPONER : to prepare, to make ready 2 AMONESTAR : to warn 3 OBSERVAR : to observe, to perceive — **apercibirse** vr 1 : to get ready 2 ~ de : to notice

aperitivo nm 1 : appetizer 2 : aperitif

apero nm : tool, implement

apersonarse vr 1 : to appear, to show up 2 ~ de Col : to take charge of, to oversee

apertura nf 1 : opening, aperture 2 : commencement, beginning 3 : openness

apesadumbrar vt : to distress, to sadden — **apesadumbrarse** vr : to be weighed down

apestar vt 1 : to infect with the plague 2 : to corrupt — vi : to stink

apestoso, -sa adj : stinking, foul

apetecer {53} vt 1 : to crave, to long for ‹apeteció la fama : he longed for fame› 2 : to appeal to ‹me apetece un bistec : I feel like having a steak› ‹¿cuándo te apetece ir? : when do you want to go?› — vi : to be appealing

apetecible adj : appetizing, appealing

apetito nm : appetite

apetitoso, -sa adj : appetizing

apiadarse vr ~ de : to take pity on

apiario nm : apiary

ápice nm 1 : apex, summit 2 PIZCA : bit, smidgen

apicultor, -tora n : beekeeper

apicultura nf : beekeeping

apilar vt AMONTONAR : to heap up, to pile up — **apilarse** vr

apiñado, -da adj : jammed, crowded

apiñar vt : to pack, to cram — **apiñarse** vr : to crowd together, to huddle

apio nm : celery

apisonadora nf : steamroller

apisonar vt : to pack down, to tamp

aplacamiento nm : appeasement

aplacar {72} vt APACIGUAR : to appease, to placate — **aplacarse** vr : to calm down

aplanadora nf : steamroller

aplanar vt : to flatten, to level

aplastante adj : crushing, overwhelming

aplastar vt : to crush, to squash

aplaudir v : to applaud

aplauso nm 1 : applause, clapping 2 : praise, acclaim

aplazamiento nm : postponement

aplazar {21} vt : to postpone, to defer

aplicable adj : applicable — **aplicabilidad** nf

aplicación nf, pl -ciones 1 : application 2 : diligence, dedication

aplicado, -da adj : diligent, industrious

aplicador nm : applicator

aplicar {72} vt : to apply — **aplicarse** vr : to apply oneself

aplique or **apliqué** nm : appliqué

aplomar vt : to plumb, to make vertical

aplomo nm : aplomb, composure

apocado, -da adj : timid

apocalipsis *nms & pl* : apocalypse ⟨el Libro del Apocalipsis : the Book of Revelation⟩

apocalíptico, -ca *adj* : apocalyptic

apocamiento *nm* : timidity

apocarse {72} *vr* **1** : to shy away, to be intimidated **2** : to humble oneself, to sell oneself short

apócrifo, -fa *adj* : apocryphal

apodar *vt* : to nickname, to call — **apodarse** *vr*

apoderado, -da *n* : proxy, agent

apoderar *vt* : to authorize, to empower — **apoderarse** *vr* ~ **de** : to seize, to take over

apodo *nm* SOBRENOMBRE : nickname

apogeo *nm* : acme, peak, zenith

apolillado, -da *adj* **1** : moth-eaten, worm-eaten **2** : old-fashioned

apolítico, -ca *adj* : apolitical

apología *nf* : defense, apology

apoplejía *nf* : apoplexy, stroke

apoplético, -ca *adj* : apoplectic

aporrear *vt* : to bang on, to beat, to bludgeon

aportación *nf, pl* **-ciones** : contribution

aportar *vt* CONTRIBUIR : to contribute, to provide

aporte *nm* → **aportación**

aposento *nm* : chamber, room ⟨los aposentos reales : the royal chambers⟩

apósito *nm* : dressing (for a wound)

apostador, -dora *n* : bettor, better

apostar {19} *v* : to bet, to wager ⟨apuesto que no viene : I bet he's not coming⟩

apostasía *nf* : apostasy

apóstata *nmf* : apostate

apostilla *nf* : note

apostillar *vt* : to annotate

apóstol *nm* : apostle

apostólico, -ca *adj* : apostolic

apóstrofe *nmf* → **apóstrofo**

apóstrofo *nm* : apostrophe

apostura *nf* : elegance, gracefulness

apoteósico, -ca *adj* : tremendous

apoyabrazos *nms & pl* : armrest

apoyacabezas *nms & pl* : headrest

apoyapiés *nms & pl* : footrest

apoyar *vt* **1** : to support, to back **2** : to lean, to rest — **apoyarse** *vr* **1** ~ **en** : to lean on **2** ~ **en** : to be based on, to rest on

apoyo *nm* : support, backing

apreciable *adj* : appreciable, substantial, considerable

apreciación *nf, pl* **-ciones** **1** : appreciation **2** : appraisal, evaluation

apreciar *vt* **1** ESTIMAR : to appreciate, to value **2** EVALUAR : to appraise, to assess — **apreciarse** *vr* : to appreciate, to increase in value

apreciativo, -va *adj* : appreciative

aprecio *nm* **1** ESTIMO : esteem, appreciation **2** EVALUACIÓN : appraisal, assessment

aprehender *vt* **1** : to apprehend, to capture **2** : to conceive of, to grasp

aprehensión *nf, pl* **-siones** : apprehension, capture, arrest

apremiante *adj* : pressing, urgent

apremiar *vt* INSTAR : to pressure, to urge — *vi* URGIR : to be urgent ⟨el tiempo apremia : time is of the essence⟩

apremio *nm* : pressure, urgency

aprender *v* : to learn — **aprenderse** *vr*

aprendiz, -diza *n, mpl* **-dices** : apprentice, trainee

aprendizaje *nm* **1** : apprenticeship **2** : learning

aprensión *nf, pl* **-siones** : apprehension, dread

aprensivo, -va *adj* : apprehensive, worried

apresamiento *nm* : seizure, capture

apresar *vt* : to capture, to seize

aprestar *vt* : to make ready, to prepare — **aprestarse** *vr* : to get ready

apresuradamente *adv* **1** : hurriedly **2** : hastily, too fast

apresurado, -da *adj* : hurried, in a rush

apresuramiento *nm* : hurry, haste

apresurar *vt* : to quicken, to speed up — **apresurarse** *vr* : to hurry up, to make haste

apretado, -da *adj* **1** : tight **2** *fam* : cheap — **apretadamente** *adv*

apretar {55} *vt* **1** : to press, to push (a button) **2** : to tighten **3** : to squeeze, to clasp ⟨apretar el gatillo : to pull the trigger⟩ **4** : to press together ⟨apretar los dientes : to grit one's teeth⟩ — *vi* **1** : to press, to push **2** : to fit tightly, to be too tight ⟨los zapatos me aprietan : my shoes are too tight⟩ — **apretarse** *vr*

apretón *nm, pl* **-tones** **1** : squeeze **2** **apretón de manos** : handshake

apretujado, -da *adj* : cramped, squeezed together

apretujar *vt* : to squash, to squeeze — **apretujarse** *vr*

aprieto *nm* APURO : predicament, difficulty ⟨estar en un aprieto : to be in a fix⟩

aprisa *adv* : quickly, hurriedly

aprisionar *vt* **1** : to imprison **2** : to trap, to box in

aprobación *nf, pl* **-ciones** : approval, endorsement

aprobar {19} *vt* **1** : to approve of **2** : to pass (a law) **3** : to pass (an exam) **4** : to pass (a student) — *vi* : to pass (in school)

aprobatorio, -ria *adj* : approving

aprontar *vt* *Chile, Uru* : to prepare, to ready — **aprontarse** *vr* : to get ready

apropiación *nf, pl* **-ciones** : appropriation

apropiado, -da *adj* : appropriate, proper, suitable — **apropiadamente** *adv*

apropiarse *vr* ~ **de** : to take possession of, to appropriate

aprovechable *adj* : usable

aprovechado¹ *adj* **1** : diligent, hard-working **2** : pushy, opportunistic

aprovechado², -da *n* : pushy person, opportunist

aprovechamiento *nm* : use, exploitation

aprovechar *vt* : to take advantage of (an opportunity, etc.), to make good use of (time, etc.) — *vi* : to make the most of it — **aprovecharse** *vr* ~ **de** : to take advantage of, to exploit

aprovisionamiento *nm* : provisions *pl*, supplies *pl*

aprovisionar *vt* : to provide, to supply (with provisions)

aproximación *nf, pl* **-ciones** 1 : approximation, estimate 2 : rapprochement

aproximado, -da *adj* : approximate, estimated — **aproximadamente** *adv*

aproximar *vt* ACERCAR, ARRIMAR : to approximate, to bring closer — **aproximarse** *vr* ACERCARSE, ARRIMARSE : to approach, to move closer

aptitud *nf* : aptitude, capability

apto, -ta *adj* 1 : suitable, suited, fit 2 HÁBIL : capable, competent

apuesta *nf* : bet, wager

apuesto *adj* : elegant, good-looking

apuntador, -dora *n* : prompter

apuntalar *vt* : to prop up, to shore up

apuntar *vt* 1 : to point (a finger, etc.) 2 : to point at 3 ANOTAR : to write down 4 INSCRIBIR : to sign up 5 : to point out (a fact, etc.) 6 : to prompt (in the theater) — *vi* 1 : to aim ⟨apuntó al blanco con el revólver : she aimed the gun at the target⟩ 2 ∼ a/hacia : to point to/toward — **apuntarse** *vr* 1 : to sign up, to enroll 2 : to score

apunte *nm* : note

apuñalar *vt* : to stab

apuradamente *adv* 1 : with difficulty 2 : hurriedly, hastily

apurado, -da *adj* 1 APRESURADO : rushed, pressured 2 : poor, needy 3 : difficult, awkward 4 : embarrassed

apurar *vt* 1 APRESURAR : to hurry, to rush 2 : to use up, to exhaust 3 : to trouble — **apurarse** *vr* 1 APRESURARSE : to hurry up 2 PREOCUPARSE : to worry

apuro *nm* 1 : predicament, jam ⟨en apuros : in a bind⟩ ⟨me sacó del apuro : he got me out of a jam⟩ 2 : rush, hurry ⟨tengo apuro : I'm in a hurry⟩ ⟨con/sin apuro : in a hurried/leisurely way⟩ 3 : embarrassment

aquejado, -da *adj* ∼ **de** : suffering from

aquejar *vt* : to afflict

aquel¹, aquella *adj, mpl* **aquellos** : that, those

aquel², aquella *or* **aquél, aquélla** *pron, mpl* **aquellos** *or* **aquéllos** 1 : that (one), those (ones) ⟨aquel/aquél fue un año récord : that was a record year⟩ ⟨aquellos/aquéllos que la conocieron : those who knew her⟩ 2 : the former (of two) 3 **todo aquel/aquél que** : anyone who

aquello *pron* (*neuter*) : that, that matter, that business ⟨aquello fue algo serio : that was something serious⟩

aquí *adv* 1 : here ⟨aquí está : here it is⟩ ⟨ven aquí : come here⟩ ⟨aquí adentro : in here⟩ ⟨aquí mismo : right here⟩ ⟨como dicen (por) aquí . . . : as they say (around) here . . .⟩ ⟨de aquí para allá : back and forth⟩ ⟨de aquí en adelante : from now on⟩

aquiescente *adj* : acquiescent

aquiescencia *nf* : acquiescence, approval

aquietar *vt* : to allay, to calm — **aquietarse** *vr* : to calm down

aquilatar *vt* 1 : to assay 2 : to assess, to size up

ara *nf* 1 : altar 2 **en aras de** : in the interests of, for the sake of

árabe¹ *adj & nmf* : Arab, Arabian

árabe² *nm* : Arabic (language)

arabesco *nm* : arabesque — **arabesco, -ca** *adj*

arábigo, -ga *adj* 1 : Arabic, Arabian 2 **número arábigo** : Arabic numeral

arable *adj* : arable

arado *nm* : plow

aragonés¹, -nesa *adj, mpl* **-neses** : of or from Aragón

aragonés², -nesa *n, mpl* **-neses** : person from Aragón

arancel *nm* : tariff, duty

arancelario, -ria *adj* : tariff, duty ⟨barreras arancelarias : tariff barriers⟩

arándano *nm* : blueberry

arandela *nf* : washer (for a faucet, etc.)

araña *nf* 1 : spider 2 : chandelier

arañar *v* : to scratch, to claw

arañazo *nm* : scratch

arar *v* : to plow

arbitraje *nm* 1 : arbitration 2 : refereeing (in sports)

arbitrar *v* 1 : to arbitrate 2 : to referee, to umpire

arbitrariedad *nf* 1 : arbitrariness 2 INJUSTICIA : injustice, wrong

arbitrario, -ria *adj* 1 : arbitrary 2 : unfair, unjust — **arbitrariamente** *adv*

arbitrio *nm* 1 ALBEDRÍO : will 2 JUICIO : judgment

árbitro, -tra *n* 1 : arbitrator, arbiter 2 : referee, umpire

árbol *nm* 1 : tree 2 **árbol genealógico** : family tree

arbolado¹, -da *adj* : wooded

arbolado² *nm* : woodland

arboleda *nf* : grove, wood

arbóreo, -rea *adj* : arboreal

arbusto *nm* : shrub, bush, hedge

arca *nf* 1 : ark 2 : coffer, chest

arcada *nf* 1 : arcade, series of arches 2 **arcadas** *nfpl* : retching ⟨hacer arcadas : to retch⟩

arcaico, -ca *adj* : archaic

arcángel *nm* : archangel

arcano, -na *adj* : arcane

arce *nm* : maple tree

arcén *nm, pl* **arcenes** : hard shoulder, berm

archiconocido, -da *adj* : well-known, famous

archidiócesis *nfs & pl* → **arquidiócesis**

archipiélago *nm* : archipelago

archivador *nm* : filing cabinet

archivar *vt* 1 : to file 2 : to archive

archivero, -ra *n* : archivist

archivista *nmf* : archivist

archivo *nm* 1 : file 2 : archive, archives *pl*

arcilla *nf* : clay

arco *nm* 1 : arch, archway 2 : bow (in archery) 3 : arc 4 : wicket (in croquet) 5 PORTERÍA : goal, goalposts *pl* 6 **arco iris** : rainbow

arcón *nm, pl* **-cones** : large chest

arder *vi* **1** : to burn ⟨el bosque está ardiendo : the forest is in flames⟩ ⟨arder de ira : to burn with anger, to be seething⟩ **2** : to smart, to sting, to burn ⟨le ardía el estómago : he had heartburn⟩

ardid *nm* : scheme, ruse

ardiente *adj* **1** : burning **2** : ardent, passionate — **ardientemente** *adv*

ardilla *nf* **1** : squirrel **2** *or* **ardilla listada** : chipmunk

ardor *nm* **1** : heat **2** : passion, ardor

ardoroso, -sa *adj* : heated, impassioned

arduo, -dua *adj* : arduous, grueling — **arduamente** *adv*

área *nf* : area

arena *nf* **1** : sand ⟨arena movediza : quicksand⟩ **2** : arena

arenal *nm* : sandy area

arenga *nf* : harangue, lecture

arengar {52} *vt* : to harangue, to lecture

arenilla *nf* **1** : fine sand **2 arenillas** *nfpl* : kidney stones

arenisca *nf* : sandstone

arenoso, -sa *adj* : sandy, gritty

arenque *nm* : herring

arepa *nf* : cornmeal bread

arete *nm* : earring

argamasa *nf* : mortar (cement)

argelino, -na *adj & n* : Algerian

argentino, -na *adj & n* : Argentinian, Argentine

argolla *nf* : hoop, ring

argón *nm* : argon

argot *nm* : slang

argucia *nf* : sophistry, subtlety

argüir {41} *vi* : to argue — *vt* **1** ARGUMENTAR : to contend, to argue **2** INFERIR : to deduce **3** PROBAR : to prove

argumentación *nf, pl* **-ciones** : line of reasoning, argument

argumentar *vt* : to argue, to contend

argumento *nm* **1** : argument, reasoning **2** : plot, story line

aria *nf* : aria

aridez *nf, pl* **-deces** : aridity, dryness

árido, -da *adj* : arid, dry

Aries[1] *nm* : Aries (sign or constellation)

Aries[2] *nmf* : Aries (person)

ariete *nm* : battering ram

arisco, -ca *adj* : surly, sullen, unsociable

arista *nf* **1** : ridge, edge **2** : beard (of a plant) **3 aristas** *nfpl* : rough edges, complications, problems

aristocracia *nf* : aristocracy

aristócrata *nmf* : aristocrat

aristocrático, -ca *adj* : aristocratic

aritmética *nf* : arithmetic

aritmético, -ca *adj* : arithmetic, arithmetical — **aritméticamente** *adv*

arlequín *nm, pl* **-quines** : harlequin

arma *nf* **1** : weapon ⟨arma nuclear : nuclear weapon⟩ ⟨arma química/biológica : chemical/biological weapon⟩ ⟨arma de destrucción masiva : weapon of mass destruction⟩ **2 armas** *nfpl* : armed forces **3 arma blanca** : sharp object (used as a weapon) **4 arma de fuego** : firearm

armada *nf* : navy, fleet

armadillo *nm* : armadillo

armado, -da *adj* **1** : armed **2** : assembled, put together **3** *PRi* : obstinate, stubborn

armador, -dora *n* : owner of a ship

armadura *nf* **1** : armor **2** ARMAZÓN : skeleton, framework

armamento *nm* : armament, arms *pl*, weaponry

armar *vt* **1** : to assemble, to put together **2** : to create, to cause ⟨armar un escándalo : to cause a scene⟩ **3** : to arm (soldiers, etc.) — **armarse** *vr* ~ **de** : to arm oneself with ⟨armarse de valor : to steel oneself⟩

armario *nm* **1** CLÓSET, ROPERO : closet **2** ALACENA : cupboard

armatoste *nm fam* : monstrosity, contraption

armazón *nmf, pl* **-zones** **1** ESQUELETO : framework, skeleton ⟨armazón de acero : steel framework⟩ **2** : frames *pl* (of eyeglasses)

armenio, -nia *adj & n* : Armenian

armería *nf* **1** : armory **2** : arms museum **3** : gunsmith's shop **4** : gunsmith's craft

armero, -ra *n* : gunsmith

armiño *nm* : ermine

armisticio *nm* : armistice

armonía *nf* : harmony

armónica *nf* : harmonica

armónico, -ca *adj* **1** : harmonic **2** : harmonious — **armónicamente** *adv*

armonioso, -sa *adj* : harmonious — **armoniosamente** *adv*

armonizar {21} *vt* **1** : to harmonize **2** : to reconcile — *vi* : to harmonize, to blend together

arnés *nm, pl* **arneses** : harness

aro *nm* **1** : hoop **2** : napkin ring **3** *Arg, Chile, Uru* : earring

aroma *nm* : aroma, scent

aromático, -ca *adj* : aromatic

arpa *nf* : harp

arpillera *nf* : burlap

arpista *nmf* : harpist

arpón *nm, pl* **arpones** : harpoon — **arponear** *vt*

arquear *vt* : to arch, to bend ⟨arquear las cejas : to raise one's eyebrows⟩ — **arquearse** *vr* : to bend, to bow

arqueología *nf* : archaeology

arqueológico, -ca *adj* : archaeological

arqueólogo, -ga *n* : archaeologist

arquero, -ra *n* **1** : archer **2** PORTERO : goalkeeper, goalie

arquetípico, -ca *adj* : archetypal

arquetipo *nm* : archetype

arquidiócesis *nfs & pl* : archdiocese

arquitecto, -ta *n* : architect

arquitectónico, -ca *adj* : architectural — **aquitectónicamente** *adv*

arquitectura *nf* : architecture

arrabal *nm* **1** : slum **2 arrabales** *nmpl* : outskirts, outlying area

arracada *nf* : hoop earring

arracimarse *vr* : to cluster together

arraigado, -da *adj* : deep-seated, ingrained

arraigar {52} *vi* : to take root, to become established — **arraigarse** *vr*

arraigo *nm* : roots *pl* ⟨con mucho arraigo : deep-rooted⟩

arrancar {72} *vt* **1** : to pull out (hair), to tear out (a page), to pull up (a weed), to pull off (a piece) **2** : to pick (a flower) **3** : to draw (applause, tears) **4** : to start (a car, etc.), to boot (a computer) **5** ARREBATAR : to snatch — *vi* **1** : to start, to boot (of a computer) **2** : to get going — **arrancarse** *vr* : to pull out, to pull off

arrancón *nm, pl* **-cones** *Mex* **1** : sudden loud start (of a car) **2** **carrera de arrancones** : drag race

arranque *nm* **1** : starter (of a car) **2** ARREBATO : outburst, fit **3** **punto de arranque** : beginning, starting point

arrasar *vt* **1** : to level, to smooth **2** : to devastate, to destroy **3** : to fill to the brim

arrastrar *vt* **1** : to drag, to tow **2** : to draw, to attract — *vi* : to hang down, to trail — **arrastrarse** *vr* **1** : to crawl **2** : to grovel

arrastre *nm* **1** : dragging **2** : pull, attraction **3** **red de arrastre** : dragnet, trawling net

arrayán *nm, pl* **-yanes** MIRTO : myrtle

arrear : to urge on, to drive — *vi* : to hurry along

arrebatado, -da *adj* **1** PRECIPITADO : impetuous, hotheaded, rash **2** : flushed, blushing

arrebatador, -dora *adj* : breathtaking, impressive

arrebatar *vt* **1** : to snatch, to seize **2** CAUTIVAR : to captivate — **arrebatarse** *vr* : to get carried away (with anger, etc.)

arrebato *nm* ARRANQUE : fit, outburst

arreciar *vi* : to intensify, to worsen

arrecife *nm* : reef

arreglado, -da *adj* **1** : fixed, repaired **2** : settled, sorted out **3** : neat, tidy **4** : smart, dressed-up

arreglar *vt* **1** COMPONER : to repair, to fix **2** : to tidy, to straighten ⟨arregla tu cuarto : pick up your room⟩ ⟨deja que te arregle : let me fix your clothes/hair⟩ **3** : to arrange (flowers, etc.) **4** : to solve (a problem), to work out (plans) ⟨quiero arreglar este asunto : I want to settle this matter⟩ — **arreglarse** *vr* **1** : to get ready, to get dressed (up) **2** : to fix, to do ⟨arreglarse el pelo : to fix/do one's hair⟩ **3** : to have/get done ⟨arreglarse el pelo : to have/get one's hair done⟩ **4** **arreglárselas** *fam* : to get by, to manage

arreglo *nm* **1** : repair **2** : arrangement **3** : agreement, understanding

arrellanarse *vr* : to settle (in a chair)

arremangarse {52} *vr* ; to roll up one's sleeves

arremeter *vi* EMBESTIR : to attack, to charge

arremetida *nf* EMBESTIDA : attack, onslaught

arremolinarse *vr* **1** : to crowd around, to mill about **2** : to swirl (about)

arrendador, -dora *n* **1** : landlord, landlady *f* **2** : tenant, lessee

arrendajo *nm* : jay

arrendamiento *nm* **1** ALQUILER : rental, leasing **2** **contrato de arrendamiento** : lease

arrendar {55} *vt* ALQUILAR : to rent, to lease

arrendatario, -ria *n* : tenant, lessee, renter

arreos *nmpl* GUARNICIONES : tack, harness, trappings

arrepentido, -da *adj* : repentant, remorseful

arrepentimiento *nm* : regret, remorse, repentance

arrepentirse {76} *vr* **1** : to regret, to be sorry **2** : to repent

arrestar *vt* DETENER : to arrest, to detain

arresto *nm* **1** DETENCIÓN : arrest **2** **arrestos** *nmpl* : boldness, daring

arriar {85} *vt* **1** : to lower (a flag, etc.) **2** : to slacken (a rope, etc.)

arriate *nm* *Mex, Spain* : bed (for plants), border

arriba *adv* **1** : up, upwards ⟨póngalo más arriba : put it higher (up)⟩ ⟨arriba y abajo : up and down⟩ ⟨¡manos arriba! : (put your) hands up!⟩ ⟨cuesta/río arriba : uphill/upstream⟩ **2** : above, overhead ⟨desde arriba : from above⟩ ⟨el arriba mencionado : the above-mentioned⟩ **3** : upstairs ⟨los vecinos de arriba : the upstairs neighbors⟩ **4** : up with ⟨¡arriba la democracia! : up with democracy!⟩ **5** **~ de** : above, on top of **6** **~ de** : more than ⟨arriba de cien : more than a hundred⟩ **7** **de ~** : top, upper ⟨el cajón de arriba : the top drawer⟩ **8** **de arriba abajo** : from top to bottom, from head to foot **9** **hacia/para ~** : upwards

arribar *vi* **1** : to arrive **2** : to dock, to put into port

arribista *nmf* : parvenu, upstart

arribo *nm* : arrival

arriendo *nm* ARRENDAMIENTO : rent, rental

arriero, -ra *n* : mule driver

arriesgado, -da *adj* **1** : risky **2** : bold, daring

arriesgar {52} *vt* : to risk, to venture — **arriesgarse** *vr* : to take a chance

arrimado, -da *n* *Mex fam* : sponger, freeloader

arrimar *vt* ACERCAR, APROXIMAR : to bring closer, to draw near — **arrimarse** *vr* ACERCARSE, APROXIMARSE : to approach, to get close

arrinconar *vt* **1** ACORRALAR : to corner, to box in **2** : to push aside, to abandon

arroba *nf* **1** (*used for the symbol* @) : at sign ⟨arroba merriam-webster punto com : at merriam-webster dot com⟩ **2** : former unit of measurement

arrobamiento *nm* : rapture, ecstasy

arrobar *vt* : to enrapture, to enchant — **arrobarse** *vr*

arrocero¹, -ra *adj* : rice

arrocero², -ra *n* : rice grower

arrodillarse *vr* : to kneel (down)

arrogancia *nf* ALTANERÍA, ALTIVEZ : arrogance, haughtiness

arrogante *adj* ALTANERO, ALTIVO : arrogant, haughty

arrogarse {52} *vr* : to usurp, to arrogate

arrojado, -da *adj* : daring, fearless

arrojar *vt* **1** : to hurl, to cast, to throw **2** : to give off, to spew out **3** : to yield, to produce **4** *fam* : to vomit — **arrojarse** *vr* PRECIPITARSE : to throw oneself, to leap

arrojo *nm* : boldness, fearlessness

arrollador, -dora *adj* : sweeping, overwhelming

arrollar *vt* **1** : to sweep away, to carry away **2** : to crush, to overwhelm **3** : to run over (with a vehicle)

arropar *vt* : to clothe, to cover (up) — **arroparse** *vr*

arrostrar *vt* : to confront, to face (up to)

arroyo *nm* **1** RIACHUELO : brook, creek, stream **2** : gutter

arroz *nm, pl* **arroces** : rice

arrozal *nm* : rice field, rice paddy

arruga *nf* : wrinkle, fold, crease

arrugado, -da *adj* : wrinkled, creased, lined

arrugar {52} *vt* : to wrinkle, to crease, to pucker — **arrugarse** *vr*

arruinar *vt* : to ruin, to wreck — **arruinarse** *vr* **1** : to be ruined **2** : to fall into ruin, to go bankrupt

arrullar *vt* : to lull to sleep — *vi* : to coo

arrullo *nm* **1** : lullaby **2** : coo (of a dove)

arrumaco *nm fam* : kissing, cuddling

arrumbar *vt* **1** : to lay aside, to put away **2** : to floor, to leave speechless

arsenal *nm* : arsenal

arsénico *nm* : arsenic

arte *nmf (usually m in singular, f in plural)* **1** : art ⟨artes y oficios : arts and crafts⟩ ⟨bellas artes : fine arts⟩ ⟨obra de arte : work of art⟩ **2** HABILIDAD : art, skill ⟨el arte de hacer amigos : the art of making friends⟩ ⟨tener arte para : to be skilled at⟩ **3 artes** *nfpl* : cunning, guile

artefacto *nm* **1** : artifact **2** DISPOSITIVO : device

artemisa *nf* : sagebrush

arteria *nf* : artery — **arterial** *adj*

arteriosclerosis *nf* : arteriosclerosis, hardening of the arteries

artero, -ra *adj* : wily, crafty

artesanal *adj* : pertaining to crafts or craftsmanship, handmade

artesanía *nf* **1** : craftsmanship **2** : handicrafts *pl*

artesano, -na *n* : artisan, craftsman

ártico, -ca *adj* : arctic

articulación *nf, pl* **-ciones** **1** : articulation, pronunciation **2** COYUNTURA : joint

articular *vt* **1** : to articulate, to utter **2** : to connect with a joint **3** : to coordinate, to orchestrate

articulista *nmf* : columnist

artículo *nm* **1** : article, thing **2** : item, feature, report **3 artículo de comercio** : commodity **4 artículos de primera necesidad** : essentials **5 artículos de tocador** : toiletries

artífice *nmf* **1** ARTESANO : artisan **2** : mastermind, architect

artificial *adj* **1** : artificial, man-made **2** : feigned, false — **artificialmente** *adv*

artificio *nm* **1** HABILIDAD : skill **2** APARATO : device, appliance **3** ARDID : artifice, ruse

artificioso, -sa *adj* **1** : skillful **2** : cunning, deceptive

artillería *nf* : artillery

artillero, -ra *n* : gunner

artilugio *nm* : gadget, contraption

artimaña *nf* : ruse, trick

artista *nmf* **1** : artist **2** ACTOR, ACTRIZ : actor, actress *f*

artístico, -ca *adj* : artistic — **artísticamente** *adv*

artrítico, -ca *adj* : arthritic

artritis *nfs & pl* : arthritis

artrópodo *nm* : arthropod

arveja *nf* GUISANTE : pea

arzobispado *nm* : archbishopric

arzobispo *nm* : archbishop

as *nm* : ace

asa *nf* AGARRADERA, ASIDERO : handle, grip

asado¹, -da *adj* : roasted, grilled, broiled

asado² *nm* **1** : roast **2** : barbecued meat **3** : barbecue, cookout

asador *nm* : spit, rotisserie

asaduras *nfpl* : entrails, offal

asalariado¹, -da *adj* : wage-earning, salaried

asalariado², -da *n* : wage earner

asaltante *nmf* **1** : mugger, robber **2** : assailant

asaltar *vt* **1** : to assault **2** : to mug, to rob **3 asaltar al poder** : to seize power

asalto *nm* **1** : assault **2** : mugging, robbery **3** : round (in boxing) **4 asalto al poder** : coup d'etat

asamblea *nf* : assembly, meeting

asambleísta *nmf* : assemblyman *m*, assemblywoman *f*

asar *vt* : to roast, to grill — **asarse** *vr fam* : to roast, to be dying from heat

asbesto *nm* : asbestos

ascendencia *nf* **1** : ancestry, descent **2** ~ **sobre** : influence over

ascendente *adj* : ascending, upward ⟨un curso ascendente : an upward trend⟩

ascender {56} *vt* **1** : to ascend, to rise up **2** : to be promoted ⟨ascendió a gerente : she was promoted to manager⟩ **3** ~ **a** : to amount to, to reach ⟨las deudas ascienden a 20 millones de pesos : the debt amounts to 20 million pesos⟩ — *vt* : to promote

ascendiente¹ *nmf* ANCESTRO : ancestor

ascendiente² *nm* INFLUENCIA : influence, ascendancy

ascensión *nf, pl* **-siones** **1** : ascent, rise **2 Fiesta de la Ascensión** : Ascension Day

ascenso *nm* **1** : ascent, rise **2** : promotion

ascensor *nm* ELEVADOR : elevator

asceta *nmf* : ascetic

ascético, -ca *adj* : ascetic

ascetismo *nm* : asceticism

asco *nm* **1** : disgust ⟨¡qué asco! : that's disgusting!, how revolting!⟩ **2 darle**

asco a alguien : to disgust someone 3
estar hecho un asco : to be filthy 4
hacerle ascos a algo : to turn up one's nose at something
ascua *nf* 1 BRASA : ember 2 **estar en ascuas** *fam* : to be on edge
aseado, -da *adj* : clean, neat
asear *vt* 1 : to wash, to clean 2 : to tidy up — **asearse** *vr*
asechanza *nf* : snare, trap
asechar *vt* : to set a trap for
asediar *vt* 1 SITIAR : to besiege 2 ACOSAR : to harass
asedio *nm* 1 : siege 2 ACOSO : harassment
asegurador¹, -dora *adj* 1 : insuring, assuring 2 : pertaining to insurance
asegurador², -dora *n* : insurer, underwriter
aseguradora *nf* : insurance company
asegurar *vt* 1 : to assure 2 : to secure 3 : to insure — **asegurarse** *vr* 1 CERCIORARSE : to make sure 2 : to take out insurance, to insure oneself
asemejar *vt* 1 : to make similar ⟨ese bigote te asemeja a tu abuelo : that mustache makes you look like your grandfather⟩ 2 *Mex* : to be similar to, to resemble — **asemejarse** *vr* ~ **a** : to look like, to resemble
asentaderas *nfpl fam* : bottom, buttocks *pl*
asentado, -da *adj* : settled, established
asentamiento *nm* : settlement
asentar {55} *vt* 1 : to lay down, to set down, to place 2 : to settle, to establish 3 *Mex* : to state, to affirm — **asentarse** *vr* 1 : to settle 2 ESTABLECERSE : to settle down, to establish oneself
asentimiento *nm* : assent, consent
asentir {76} *vt* : to consent, to agree
aseo *nm* : cleanliness
aséptico, -ca *adj* : aseptic
asequible *adj* ACCESIBLE : accessible, attainable
aserción *nf, pl* **-ciones** → **aserto**
aserradero *nm* : sawmill
aserrar {55} *vt* : to saw
aserrín *nm, pl* **-rrines** : sawdust
aserto *nm* : assertion, affirmation
asesinar *vt* 1 : to murder 2 : to assassinate
asesinato *nm* 1 : murder 2 : assassination
asesino¹, -na *adj* : murderous, homicidal
asesino², -na *n* 1 : murderer, killer 2 : assassin
asesor, -sora *n* : advisor, consultant
asesoramiento *nm* : advice, counsel
asesorar *vt* : to advise, to counsel — **asesorarse** *vr* ~ **de** : to consult
asesoría *nf* 1 : consulting, advising 2 : consultant's office
asestar {55} *vt* 1 : to aim, to point (a weapon) 2 : to deliver, to deal (a blow)
aseveración *nf, pl* **-ciones** : assertion, statement
aseverar *vt* : to assert, to state
asexual *adj* : asexual — **asexualmente** *adv*

asfaltado¹, -da *adj* : paved (with asphalt)
asfaltado² *nm* PAVIMENTO : pavement, asphalt
asfaltar *vt* : to pave, to blacktop
asfalto *nm* : asphalt
asfixia *nf* : asphyxia, asphyxiation, suffocation
asfixiante *adj* 1 : asphyxiating 2 AGOBIANTE : oppressive
asfixiar *vt* : to asphyxiate, to suffocate, to smother — **asfixiarse** *vr*
asga, etc. → **asir**
así¹ *adv* 1 : like this, like that, so ⟨así se hace : that's how it's done⟩ ⟨no puede seguir así : it can't go on like this⟩ ⟨así sea : so be it⟩ ⟨y así sucesivamente : and so on⟩ 2 **así así** : so-so, fair 3 ~ **como** : as well as 4 **así como así** *or* **así nomás** : just like that 5 ~ **de** : so, about so ⟨una caja así de grande : a box about so big⟩ 6 **así mismo** → **asimismo** 7 **así que** : so, therefore 8 **así y todo** : even so
así² *adj* : such, such a, like that ⟨un talento así : a talent like that⟩ ⟨algo así : something like that⟩ ⟨así es la vida : that's life⟩ ⟨si es así . . . : if that's the case . . .⟩
así³ *conj* AUNQUE : even if, even though ⟨no irá, así le paguen : he won't go, even if they pay him⟩
asiático¹, -ca *adj* : Asian
asiático², -ca *n* : Asian
asidero *nm* 1 AGARRADERA, ASA : grip, handle 2 AGARRE : grip, hold
asiduamente *adv* : regularly, frequently
asiduidad *nf* **con** ~ : regularly, frequently
asiduo, -dua *adj* 1 : assiduous 2 : frequent, regular
asiento *nm* 1 : seat, chair ⟨asiento trasero : back seat⟩ 2 : location, site
asignación *nf, pl* **-ciones** 1 : allocation 2 : appointment, designation 3 : allowance, pay 4 *PRi* : homework, assignment
asignar *vt* 1 : to assign, to allocate 2 : to appoint
asignatura *nf* MATERIA : subject, course
asilado, -da *n* : exile, refugee
asilo *nm* : asylum, refuge, shelter
asimetría *nf* : asymmetry
asimétrico, -ca *adj* : asymmetrical, asymmetric
asimilación *nf, pl* **-ciones** : assimilation
asimilar *vt* : to assimilate — **asimilarse** *vr* ~ **a** : to be similar to, to resemble
asimismo *adv* 1 IGUALMENTE : similarly, likewise 2 TAMBIÉN : as well, also
asir {7} *vt* : to seize, to grasp — **asirse** *vr* ~ **a** : to cling to
asistencia *nf* 1 : attendance 2 : assistance 3 : assist (in sports) 4 **asistencia médica** *or Spain* **asistencia sanitaria** : health care, medical care
asistente¹ *adj* : attending, in attendance
asistente² *nmf* 1 : assistant 2 **los asistentes** : those present, those in attendance
asistido, -da *adj* : assisted
asistir *vi* : to attend, to be present ⟨asistir a clase : to attend class⟩ — *vt* : to aid, to assist

asma *nf* : asthma
asmático, -ca *adj* : asthmatic
asno *nm* BURRO : ass, donkey
asociación *nf*, *pl* **-ciones** 1 : association, relationship 2 : society, group, association
asociado¹, -da *adj* : associate, associated
asociado², -da *n* : associate, partner
asociar *vt* 1 : to associate, to connect 2 : to pool (resources) 3 : to take into partnership — **asociarse** *vr* 1 : to become partners 2 ~ **a** : to join, to become a member of
asolar {19} *vt* : to devastate, to destroy
asoleado, -da *adj* : sunny
asolear *vt* : to put in the sun — **asolearse** *vr* : to sunbathe
asomar *vt* : to show, to stick out — *vi* : to appear, to become visible — **asomarse** *vr* 1 : to show, to appear 2 : to lean out, to look out ⟨se asomó por la ventana : he leaned out the window⟩
asombrar *vt* MARAVILLAR : to amaze, to astonish — **asombrarse** *vr* : to marvel, to be amazed
asombro *nm* : amazement, astonishment
asombroso, -sa *adj* : amazing, astonishing — **asombrosamente** *adv*
asomo *nm* 1 : hint, trace 2 **ni por asomo** : by no means
aspa *nf* : blade (of a fan or propeller)
aspaviento *nm* : exaggerated movement, fuss, flounce
aspecto *nm* 1 : aspect 2 APARIENCIA : appearance, look
aspereza *nf* RUDEZA : roughness, coarseness
áspero, -ra *adj* : rough, coarse, abrasive — **ásperamente** *adv*
aspersión *nf*, *pl* **-siones** : sprinkling
aspersor *nm* : sprinkler
aspiración *nf*, *pl* **-ciones** 1 : inhalation, breathing in 2 ANHELO : aspiration, desire
aspiradora *nf* : vacuum cleaner
aspirante *nmf* : applicant, candidate
aspirar *vi* ~ **a** : to aspire to — *vt* : to inhale, to breathe in
aspirina *nf* : aspirin
asquear *adj* : sickening, disgusting
asquear *vt* : to sicken, to disgust
asquerosidad *nf* : filth, foulness
asqueroso, -sa *adj* : disgusting, sickening, repulsive — **asquerosamente** *adv*
asta *nf* 1 : flagpole ⟨a media asta : at half-mast⟩ 2 : horn, antler 3 : shaft (of a weapon)
ástaco *nm* : crayfish
astado, -da *adj* : horned
aster *nm* : aster
asterisco *nm* : asterisk
asteroide *nm* : asteroid
astigmatismo *nm* : astigmatism
astil *nm* : shaft (of an arrow or feather)
astilla *nf* 1 : splinter, chip 2 **de tal palo, tal astilla** : like father, like son
astillar *vt* : to splinter — **astillarse** *vr*
astillero *nm* : dry dock, shipyard
astral *adj* : astral
astringente *adj* & *nm* : astringent — **astringencia** *nf*

astro *nm* 1 : heavenly body 2 : star
astrología *nf* : astrology
astrológico, -ca *adj* : astrological
astrólogo, -ga *n* : astrologer
astronauta *nmf* : astronaut
astronáutica *nf* : astronautics
astronáutico, -ca *adj* : astronautic, astronautical
astronave *nf* : spaceship
astronomía *nf* : astronomy
astronómico, -ca *adj* : astronomical — **astronómicamente** *adv*
astrónomo, -ma *n* : astronomer
astroso, -sa *adj* DESALIÑADO : slovenly, untidy
astucia *nf* 1 : astuteness, shrewdness 2 : cunning, guile
astuto, -ta *adj* 1 : astute, shrewd 2 : crafty, tricky — **astutamente** *adv*
asueto *nm* : time off, break
asumir *vt* 1 : to assume, to take on ⟨asumir el cargo : to take office⟩ 2 SUPONER : to assume, to suppose
asunción *nf*, *pl* **-ciones** : assumption
asunto *nm* 1 CUESTIÓN, TEMA : affair, matter, subject 2 **asuntos** *nmpl* : affairs, business
asustadizo, -za *adj* : nervous, jumpy, skittish
asustado, -da *adj* : frightened, afraid
asustar *vt* ESPANTAR : to scare, to frighten — **asustarse** *vr*
atacante *nmf* : assailant, attacker
atacar {72} *v* : to attack
atado¹, -da *adj* : shy, inhibited
atado² *nm* 1 : bundle, bunch 2 *Arg* : pack (of cigarettes)
atadura *nf* LIGADURA : tie, bond
atajada *nf* : save (in sports)
atajar *vt* 1 IMPEDIR : to block, to stop 2 INTERRUMPIR : to interrupt, to cut off 3 CONTENER : to hold back, to restrain — *vi* ~ **por** : to take a shortcut through
atajo *nm* : shortcut
atalaya *nf* 1 : watchtower 2 : vantage point
atañer {79} *vt* ~ **a** (*3rd person only*) : to concern, to have to do with ⟨eso no me atañe : that does not concern me⟩
ataque *nm* 1 : attack, assault 2 : fit ⟨ataque de risa : fit of laughter⟩ 3 **ataque de nervios** : nervous breakdown 4 **ataque de pánico/ansiedad** : panic/anxiety attack 5 **ataque cardíaco** *or* **ataque al corazón** : heart attack
atar *vt* AMARRAR : to tie, to tie up, to tie down — **atarse** *vr*
atarantado, -da *adj fam* 1 : restless 2 : dazed, stunned
atarantar *vt fam* : to daze, to stun
atarazana *nf* : shipyard
atardecer¹ {53} *v impers* : to get dark
atardecer² *nm* : late afternoon, dusk
atareado, -da *adj* : busy, overworked
atascar {72} *vt* 1 ATORAR : to block, to clog, to stop up 2 : to hinder — **atascarse** *vr* 1 : to become obstructed 2 : to get bogged down 3 PARARSE : to stall
atasco *nm* 1 : blockage 2 EMBOTELLAMIENTO : traffic jam

ataúd *nm* : coffin, casket

ataviar {85} *vt* : to dress, to clothe — **ataviarse** *vr* : to dress up

atavío *nm* ATUENDO : dress, attire

ateísmo *nm* : atheism

atemorizar {21} *vt* : to frighten, to intimidate — **atemorizarse** *vr*

atemperar *vt* : to temper, to moderate

atención[1] *nf*, *pl* **-ciones** **1** : attention **2 poner atención** *or* **prestar atención** : to pay attention **3 llamar la atención** : to attract attention **4 en atención a** : in view of

atención[2] *interj* **1** : attention! **2** : watch out!

atender {56} *vt* **1** : to help, to wait on **2** : to look after, to take care of **3** : to heed, to listen to — *vi* : to pay attention

atenerse {80} *vr* : to abide ⟨tendrás que atenerte a las reglas : you will have to abide by the rules⟩

atentado *nm* : attack, assault

atentamente *adv* **1** : attentively, carefully **2** (*used in correspondence*) : sincerely, sincerely yours

atentar {55} *vi* ~ **contra** : to make an attempt on, to threaten ⟨atentaron contra su vida : they made an attempt on his life⟩

atento, -ta *adj* **1** : attentive, mindful **2** CORTÉS : courteous

atenuación *nf*, *pl* **-ciones** **1** : lessening **2** : understatement

atenuante[1] *adj* : extenuating, mitigating

atenuante[2] *nmf* : extenuating circumstance, excuse

atenuar {3} *vt* **1** MITIGAR : to extenuate, to mitigate **2** : to dim (light), to tone down (colors) **3** : to minimize, to lessen

ateo[1], **atea** *adj* : atheistic

ateo[2], **atea** *n* : atheist

aterciopelado, -da *adj* : velvety, downy

aterido, -da *adj* : freezing, frozen

aterrador, -dora *adj* : terrifying

aterrar {55} *vt* : to terrify, to frighten

aterrizaje *nm* : landing (of a plane)

aterrizar {21} *vt* : to land, to touch down

aterrorizar {21} *vt* **1** : to terrify **2** : to terrorize — **aterrorizarse** *vr* : to be terrified

atesorar *vt* : to hoard, to amass

atestado, -da *adj* : crowded, packed

atestar {55} *vt* **1** ATIBORRAR : to crowd, to pack **2** : to witness, to testify to — *vi* : to testify

atestiguar {10} *vt* : to testify to, to bear witness to — *vi* DECLARAR : to testify

atiborrar *vt* : to pack, to crowd — **atiborrarse** *vr* : to stuff oneself

ático *nm* **1** : penthouse **2** BUHARDILLA, DESVÁN : attic

atigrado, -da *adj* : tabby (of cats), striped (of fur)

atildado, -da *adj* : smart, neat, dapper

atildar *vt* **1** : to put a tilde over **2** : to clean up, to smarten up — **atildarse** *vr* : to get spruced up

atinar *vi* ACERTAR : to be accurate, to be on target

atingencia *nf* : bearing, relevance

atípico, -ca *adj* : atypical

atiplado, -da *adj* : shrill, high-pitched

atirantar *vt* : to make taut, to tighten

atisbar *vt* **1** : to spy on, to watch **2** : to catch a glimpse of, to make out

atisbo *nm* : glimpse, sign, hint

atizador *nm* : poker (for a fire)

atizar {21} *vt* **1** : to poke, to stir, to stoke (a fire) **2** : to stir up, to rouse **3** *fam* : to give, to land (a blow)

atlántico, -ca *adj* : Atlantic

atlas *nm* : atlas

atleta *nmf* : athlete

atlético, -ca *adj* : athletic

atletismo *nm* : athletics

atmósfera *nf* : atmosphere

atmosférico, -ca *adj* : atmospheric

atole *nm* *Mex* **1** : thick hot beverage prepared with cornmeal **2 darle atole con el dedo a alguien** : to string someone along

atolladero *nm* : predicament, fix

atollarse *vr* : to get stuck, to get bogged down

atolón *nm*, *pl* **-lones** : atoll

atolondrado, -da *adj* **1** ATURDIDO : bewildered, dazed **2** DESPISTADO : scatterbrained, absentminded

atómico, -ca *adj* : atomic

atomizador *nm* : atomizer

atomizar {21} *vt* FRAGMENTAR : to fragment, to break into bits

átomo *nm* : atom

atónito, -ta *adj* : astonished, amazed

atontar *vt* **1** : to stupefy **2** : to bewilder, to confuse

atorar *vt* ATASCAR : to block, to clog — **atorarse** *vr* **1** ATASCARSE : to get stuck **2** ATRAGANTARSE : to choke

atormentador, -dora *n* : tormentor

atormentar *vt* : to torment, to torture — **atormentarse** *vr* : to torment oneself, to agonize

atornillar *vt* : to screw (in, on, down)

atorrante *nmf* *Arg* : bum, loafer

atosigar {52} *vt* : to harass, to annoy

atracadero *nm* : dock, pier

atracador, -dora *n* : robber, mugger

atracar {72} *vt* : to dock, to land — *vt* : to hold up, to rob, to mug — **atracarse** *vr* *fam* ~ **de** : to gorge oneself with

atracción *nf*, *pl* **-ciones** : attraction

atraco *nm* : holdup, robbery

atracón *nm*, *pl* **-cones** *fam* **darse un atracón (de)** : to pig out (on)

atractivo[1], **-va** *adj* : attractive — **atractivamente** *adv*

atractivo[2] *nm* : attraction, appeal, charm

atraer {81} *vt* **1** : to attract — **atraerse** *vr* **1** : to attract (each other) **2** GANARSE : to gain, to win

atragantarse *vr* : to choke (on food)

atrancar {72} *vt* : to block, to bar — **atrancarse** *vr*

atrapada *nf* : catch

atrapar *vt* : to trap, to capture

atrás *adv* **1** DETRÁS : back, behind ⟨la parte de atrás : the back/rear part⟩ ⟨dar un paso atrás : to take a step back⟩ **2** ANTES : ago ⟨mucho tiempo atrás : long ago⟩ **3** ~ **de** : in back of, behind **4**

desde ~ : from behind, from the rear
5 hacia ~/para ~ : backwards, toward
the rear **6 dejar atrás** : to leave (the
past, etc.) behind **7 quedarse atrás** : to
fall behind

atrasado, -da *adj* **1** : late, overdue **2**
: backward **3** : old-fashioned **4** : slow
(of a clock or watch)

atrasar *vt* : to delay, to put off — *vi* : to
lose time — **atrasarse** *vr* : to fall behind

atraso *nm* **1** RETRASO : lateness, delay
⟨llegó con 20 minutos de atraso : he was
20 minutes late⟩ **2** : backwardness

atrasos *nmpl* : arrears

atravesar {55} *vt* **1** CRUZAR : to cross, to
go across **2** : to pierce **3** : to lay across
4 : to go through (a situation or crisis) —
atravesarse *vr* **1** : to be in the way ⟨se
me atravesó : it blocked my path⟩ **2** : to
interfere, to meddle

atrayente *adj* : attractive

atreverse *vr* **1** : to dare **2** : to be insolent

atrevido, -da *adj* **1** : bold, daring **2** : insolent

atrevimiento *nm* **1** : daring, boldness **2**
: insolence

atribución *nf, pl* **-ciones** : attribution

atribuible *adj* IMPUTABLE : attributable,
ascribable

atribuir {41} *vt* **1** : to attribute, to ascribe
2 : to grant, to confer — **atribuirse** *vr*
: to take credit for

atribular *vt* : to afflict, to trouble — **atribularse** *vr*

atributo *nm* : attribute

atril *nm* : lectern, stand

atrincherar *vt* : to entrench — **atrincherarse** *vr* **1** : to dig in, to entrench oneself
2 ~ en : to hide behind

atrio *nm* **1** : atrium **2** : portico

atrocidad *nf* : atrocity

atrofia *nf* : atrophy

atrofiar *v* : to atrophy

atronador, -dora *adj* : thunderous, deafening

atropellado, -da *adj* **1** : rash, hasty **2**
: brusque, abrupt — **atropelladamente**
adv

atropellamiento → atropello

atropellar *vt* **1** : to knock down, to run
over **2** : to violate, to abuse — **atropellarse** *vr* : to rush through (a task), to
trip over one's words

atropello *nm* : abuse, violation, outrage

atroz *adj, pl* **atroces** : atrocious, appalling
— **atrozmente** *adv*

atuendo *nm* ATAVÍO : attire, costume

atufar *vt* : to vex, to irritate — **atufarse** *vr*
1 : to get angry **2** : to smell bad, to stink

atún *nm, pl* **atunes** : tuna fish, tuna

aturdimiento *nm* : bewilderment, confusion

aturdir *vt* **1** : to stun, to shock **2** : to bewilder, to confuse, to stupefy —
aturdido, -da *adj*

atuvo, etc. → atenerse

audacia *nf* OSADÍA : boldness, audacity

audaz *adj, pl* **audaces** : bold, audacious,
daring — **audazmente** *adv*

audible *adj* : audible

audición *nf, pl* **-ciones** **1** : hearing **2**
: audition

audiencia *nf* : audience

audífono *nm* **1** : hearing aid **2 audífonos**
nmpl : headphones, earphones

audio *nm* : audio

audiovisual *adj* : audiovisual

auditar *vt* : to audit

auditivo, -va *adj* : auditory, hearing, aural
⟨aparato auditivo : hearing aid⟩

auditor, -tora *n* : auditor

auditoría *nf* : audit

auditorio *nm* **1** : auditorium **2** : audience

auge *nm* **1** : peak, height **2** : boom, upturn

augur *nm* : augur

augurar *vt* : to predict, to foretell

augurio *nm* AGÜERO, PRESAGIO : augury,
omen

augusto, -ta *adj* : august

aula *nf* : classroom

aullar {8} *vt* : to howl, to wail

aullido *nm* : howl, wail

aumentar *vt* ACRECENTAR : to increase,
to raise — *vi* : to rise, to increase, to
grow

aumento *nm* INCREMENTO : increase, rise

aun *adv* **1** : even ⟨ni aun en coche llegaría
a tiempo : I wouldn't arrive on time even
if I drove⟩ **2 aun así** : even so **3 aun
más** : even more

aún *adv* TODAVÍA : still, yet ⟨aún falta
mucho por hacer : there's still a lot left
to do⟩ ⟨aún no lo sabe : she doesn't
know yet⟩

aunar {8} *vt* : to join, to combine — **aunarse** *vr* : to unite

aunque *conj* **1** : though, although, even
if, even though **2 aunque sea** : at least

aura *nf* **1** : aura **2** : turkey buzzard

áureo, -rea *adj* : golden

aureola *nf* **1** : halo **2** : aura (of power,
fame, etc.)

aurícula *nf* : auricle

auricular *nm* **1** : telephone receiver **2**
auriculares *nmpl* : headphones, earphones

aurora *nf* **1** : dawn **2 aurora boreal** : aurora borealis

ausencia *nf* : absence

ausentarse *vr* **1** : to leave, to go away **2**
~ de : to stay away from

ausente¹ *adj* : absent, missing

ausente² *nmf* **1** : absentee **2** : missing
person

auspiciar *vt* **1** PATROCINAR : to sponsor
2 FOMENTAR : to foster, to promote

auspicios *nmpl* : sponsorship, auspices

austeridad *nf* : austerity

austero, -ra *adj* : austere

austral¹ *adj* : southern

austral² *nm* : former monetary unit of Argentina

australiano, -na *adj & n* : Australian

austriaco *or* **austríaco, -ca** *adj & n* : Austrian

autenticar {72} *vt* : to authenticate — **autenticación** *nf*

autenticidad *nf* : authenticity

auténtico, -ca *adj* : authentic — **auténticamente** *adv*

autentificar {72} *vt* : to authenticate — **autentificación** *nf*

autismo *nm* : autism

autista *adj* : autistic

auto *nm* : auto, car

auto- *pref* : self-

autoabastecerse {18} *vr* : to be self-sufficient

autoayuda *nf* : self-help

autobiografía *nf* : autobiography

autobiográfico, -ca *adj* : autobiographical

autobomba *nf Arg, Spain, Uru* : fire truck

auto bomba *nm Chile* : car bomb

autobús *nm, pl* **-buses** : bus

autocar *Spain* → **autobús**

autocine *nm* : drive-in

autocompasión *nf* : self-pity

autocontrol *nm* : self-control

autocracia *nf* : autocracy

autócrata *nmf* : autocrat

autocrático, -ca *adj* : autocratic

autóctono, -na *adj* : indigenous, native ⟨arte autóctono : indigenous art⟩

autodefensa *nf* : self-defense

autodenominarse *vr* : to call oneself

autodestrucción *nf* : self-destruction — **autodestructivo, -va** *adj*

autodeterminación *nf* : self-determination

autodidacta[1] *adj* : self-taught

autodidacta[2] *nmf* : self-taught person

autodidacto[1]**, -ta** *adj* → **autodidacta**[1]

autodidacto[2]**, -ta** *n* → **autodidacta**[2]

autodisciplina *nf* : self-discipline

autoedición *nf* : desktop publishing

autoescuela *nf Spain* : driving school

autoestima *nf* : self-esteem

autogobierno *nm* : self-government

autografiar *vt* : to autograph

autógrafo *nm* : autograph

autoinfligido, -da *adj* : self-inflicted

automación → **automatización**

autómata *nm* : automaton

automático, -ca *adj* : automatic — **automáticamente** *adv*

automatización *nf* : automation

automatizar {21} *vt* : to automate

automercado *nm Ven* : supermarket

automotor, -tora *adj* 1 : self-propelled 2 : automotive, car

automotriz[1] *adj, pl* **-trices** : automotive, car

automotriz[2] *nf, pl* **-trices** : automaker

automóvil *nm* : automobile

automovilista *nmf* : motorist

automovilístico, -ca *adj* : automobile, car ⟨accidente automovilístico : automobile accident⟩

autonombrado, -da *adj* : self-appointed

autonomía *nf* : autonomy

autonómico, -ca *adj* : autonomous

autónomo, -ma *adj* : autonomous — **autónomamente** *adv*

autopista *nf* : expressway, highway

autoproclamado, -da *adj* : self-proclaimed, self-appointed

autopropulsado, -da *adj* : self-propelled

autopsia *nf* : autopsy

autor, -tora *n* 1 : author 2 : perpetrator

autoría *nf* : authorship

autoridad *nf* : authority

autoritario, -ria *adj* : authoritarian

autorización *nf, pl* **-ciones** : authorization

autorizado, -da *adj* 1 : authorized 2 : authoritative

autorizar {21} *vt* : to authorize, to approve

autorretrato *nm* : self-portrait

autoservicio *nm* 1 : self-service restaurant 2 SUPERMERCADO : supermarket

autostop *nm* 1 : hitchhiking 2 **hacer autostop** : to hitchhike

autostopista *nmf* : hitchhiker

autosuficiencia *nf* : self-sufficiency — **autosuficiente** *adj*

autovía *nf* : divided highway

auxiliar[1] *vt* : to aid, to assist

auxiliar[2] *adj* : assistant, auxiliary

auxiliar[3] *nmf* 1 : assistant, helper 2 **auxiliar de vuelo** : flight attendant

auxilio *nm* 1 : aid, assistance 2 **primeros auxilios** : first aid

aval *nm* : guarantee, endorsement

avalancha *nf* ALUD : avalanche

avalar *vt* : to guarantee, to endorse

avaluar {3} *vt* : to evaluate, to appraise

avalúo *nm* : appraisal, evaluation

avance *nm* ADELANTO : advance

avanzado, -da *adj* 1 : advanced 2 : progressive

avanzar {21} *vi* : to advance, to move forward, to make progress — *vt* 1 : to advance, to move forward 2 : to advance, to put forward

avaricia *nf* CODICIA : greed, avarice

avaricioso, -sa *adj* : avaricious, greedy

avaro[1]**, -ra** *adj* : miserly, greedy

avaro[2]**, -ra** *n* : miser

avasallador, -dora *adj* : overwhelming

avasallamiento *nm* : domination

avasallar *vt* : to overpower, to subjugate

avatar *nm* 1 : avatar 2 **avatares** *nmpl* : vagaries, vicissitudes

ave *nf* 1 : bird 2 **aves de corral** : poultry 3 **ave rapaz** *or* **ave de presa** : bird of prey

avecinarse *vr* : to approach, to come near

avecindarse *vr* : to settle, to take up residence

avellana *nf* : hazelnut, filbert

avellano *nm* : hazel

avena *nf* 1 : oat, oats *pl* 2 : oatmeal

avenencia *nf* : agreement, pact

avenida *nf* : avenue

avenir {87} *vt* : to reconcile, to harmonize — **avenirse** *vr* 1 : to agree, to come to terms 2 : to get along

aventajado, -da *adj* : outstanding

aventajar *vt* 1 : to be ahead of, to lead 2 : to surpass, to outdo

aventar {55} *vt* 1 : to fan 2 : to winnow 3 *Col, Mex* : to throw, to toss — **aventarse** *vr* 1 *Col, Mex* : to hurl oneself 2 *Mex fam* : to dare, to take a chance

aventón *nm, pl* **-tones** *Col, Mex fam* : ride, lift

aventura *nf* 1 : adventure 2 RIESGO : venture, risk 3 : love affair

aventurado, -da *adj* : hazardous, risky

aventurar *vt* : to venture, to risk — **aventurarse** *vr* : to take a risk

aventurero¹, -ra *adj* : adventurous

aventurero², -ra *n* : adventurer

avergonzado, -da *adj* **1** : ashamed **2** : embarrassed

avergonzar {9} *vt* APENAR : to shame, to embarrass — **avergonzarse** *vr* APENARSE : to be ashamed, to be embarrassed

avería *nf* **1** : damage **2** : breakdown, malfunction

averiado, -da *adj* **1** : damaged, faulty **2** : broken down

averiar {85} *vt* : to damage — **averiarse** *vr* : to break down

averiguación *nf, pl* **-ciones** : investigation, inquiry

averiguar {10} *vt* **1** : to find out, to ascertain **2** : to investigate

aversión *nf, pl* **-siones** : aversion, dislike

avestruz *nm, pl* **-truces** : ostrich

avezado, -da *adj* : seasoned, experienced

aviación *nf, pl* **-ciones** : aviation

aviador, -dora *n* : aviator, flyer

aviar {85} *vt* **1** : to prepare, to make ready **2** : to tidy up **3** : to equip, to supply

avícola *adj* : poultry

avicultor, -tora *n* : poultry farmer

avicultura *nf* : poultry farming

avidez *nf, pl* **-deces** : eagerness

ávido, -da *adj* : eager, avid — **ávidamente** *adv*

avieso, -sa *adj* **1** : twisted, distorted **2** : wicked, depraved

avinagrado, -da *adj* : vinegary, sour

avío *nm* **1** : preparation, provision **2** : loan (for agriculture or mining) **3** **avíos** *nmpl* : gear, equipment

avión *nm, pl* **aviones** : plane

avionazo *nm Mex* : plane crash

avioneta *nf* : light airplane

avisar *vt* **1** : to notify, to inform **2** : to advise, to warn

aviso *nm* **1** : notice **2** : advertisement, ad **3** ADVERTENCIA : warning **4 estar sobre aviso** : to be on the alert

avispa *nf* : wasp

avispado, -da *adj fam* : clever, sharp

avispero *nm* : wasps' nest

avispón *nm, pl* **-pones** : hornet

avistamiento *nm* : sighting

avistar *vt* : to sight, to catch sight of

avituallar *vt* : to supply with food, to provision

avivar *vt* **1** : to enliven, to brighten **2** : to strengthen, to intensify

avizorar *vt* **1** ACECHAR : to spy on, to watch **2** : to observe, to perceive ⟨se avizoran dificultades : difficulties are expected⟩

axila *nf* : armpit

axioma *nm* : axiom

axiomático, -ca *adj* : axiomatic

ay *interj* **1** : oh! **2** : ouch!, ow!

ayer¹ *adv* : yesterday ⟨ayer por/en la mañana : yesterday morning⟩ ⟨antes de ayer : the day before yesterday⟩

ayer² *nm* ANTAÑO : yesteryear, days gone by

ayote *nm CA, Mex* : squash, pumpkin

ayuda *nf* **1** : help, assistance **2 ayuda de cámara** : valet

ayudante *nmf* : helper, assistant

ayudar *vt* : to help, to assist ⟨ayúdame a levantar esta caja : help me lift this box⟩ ⟨¿en qué puedo ayudarle? : how can I help you?⟩ ⟨¿te ayudo con tus cosas? : can I help you with your things?⟩ — **ayudarse** *vr* ~ **de** : to make use of

ayunar *vi* : to fast

ayunas *nfpl* **en** ~ : fasting ⟨este medicamento ha de tomarse en ayunas : this medication should be taken on an empty stomach⟩

ayuno *nm* : fast

ayuntamiento *nm* **1** : town hall, city hall **2** : town or city council

azabache *nm* : jet ⟨negro azabache : jet black⟩

azada *nf* : hoe

azafata *nf* **1** : stewardess *f* **2** : hostess *f* (on a TV show)

azafrán *nm, pl* **-franes** **1** : saffron **2** : crocus

azahar *nm* : orange blossom

azalea *nf* : azalea

azar *nm* **1** : chance ⟨juegos de azar : games of chance⟩ **2** : accident, misfortune **3 al azar** : at random, randomly

azaroso, -sa *adj* **1** : perilous, hazardous **2** : turbulent, eventful

azimut *nm* : azimuth

azogue *nm* : mercury

azorado, -da *adj* **1** : embarrassed, flustered **2** : amazed, stunned

azorar *vt* **1** : to alarm, to startle **2** : to fluster, to embarrass — **azorarse** *vr* : to get embarrassed

azotar *vt* **1** : to whip, to flog **2** : to lash, to batter **3** : to devastate, to afflict

azote *nm* **1** LÁTIGO : whip, lash **2** *fam* : spanking, licking **3** : calamity, scourge

azotea *nf* : flat roof, terraced roof

azteca *adj & nmf* : Aztec

azúcar *nmf* : sugar — **azucarar** *vt*

azucarado, -da *adj* : sweetened, sugary

azucarera *nf* : sugar bowl

azucarero, -ra *adj* : sugar ⟨industria azucarera : sugar industry⟩

azucena *nf* : white lily

azuela *nf* : adze

azufre *nm* : sulfur — **azufroso, -sa** *adj*

azul *adj & nm* : blue

azulado, -da *adj* : bluish

azulejo *nm* : ceramic tile, floor tile

azuloso, -sa *adj* : bluish

azulete *nm* : bluing

azur¹ *adj* CELESTE : azure

azur² *n* CELESTE : azure, sky blue

azuzar {21} *vt* : to incite, to egg on

B

b *nf* : second letter of the Spanish alphabet

baba *nf* **1** : spittle, saliva **2** : dribble, drool (of a baby) **3** : slime, ooze

babear *vi* **1** : to drool, to slobber **2** : to ooze

babero *nm* : bib

babor *nm* : port, port side ⟨a babor : to port⟩

babosa *nf* : slug (mollusk)

babosada *nf CA, Mex* : silly act or remark

baboso, -sa *adj* **1** : drooling, slobbering **2** : slimy **3** *CA, Mex fam* : silly, dumb

babucha *nf* : slipper

babuino *nm* : baboon

baca *nf* : luggage/roof rack

bacalao *nm* : cod (fish)

bache *nm* **1** : pothole **2** : air pocket **3** : bad period, rough time, slump

bachiller *nmf* : high school graduate

bachillerato *nm* : high school diploma

bacinica *nf* : chamber pot, potty (for children)

bacon *nm Spain* : bacon

bacteria *nf* : bacterium

bacteriano, -na *adj* : bacterial

báculo *nm* : staff, stick

badajo *nm* : clapper (of a bell)

badén *nm, pl* **badenes** **1** VADO : ford **2** : dip, ditch (in a road) **3** : speed bump

bádminton *nm* : badminton

bafle *or* **baffle** *nm* : speaker, loudspeaker

bagaje *nm* **1** → **equipaje** **2** : background, knowledge ⟨bagaje cultural : cultural heritage⟩

bagre *nm* : catfish

baguette *nf* : baguette

bah *interj (expressing disapproval)* : huh!

bahía *nf* : bay

bailar *vt* : to dance — *vi* **1** : to dance **2** : to spin **3** : to be loose, to be too big

bailarín¹, -rina *adj, mpl* **-rines** **1** : dancing **2** : fond of dancing

bailarín², -rina *n, mpl* **-rines** **1** : dancer **2** : ballet dancer, ballerina *f* ⟨prima bailarina : prima ballerina⟩

baile *nm* **1** : dance **2** : dance party, ball **3 llevarse al baile a** *Mex fam* : to take advantage of

baja *nf* **1** DESCENSO : fall, drop **2** : slump, recession **3** : loss, casualty **4 dar de baja** : to discharge, to dismiss **5 darse de baja** : to withdraw, to drop out, to resign

bajada *nf* **1** : descent **2** : dip, slope **3** : decrease, drop **4 bajada de bandera** *Arg, Spain* : minimum fare

bajar *vt* **1** : to lower (a blind, zipper, etc.), to let down (a hem) **2** : to bring/take/carry down, to get/lift down **3** REDUCIR : to lower (prices, a fever, one's voice, etc.) **4** INCLINAR : to lower (the eyes, etc.), to bow (the head) **5** : to go/come down (stairs) **6** DESCARGAR : to download **7 bajar de categoría** : to downgrade — *vi* **1** DISMINUIR : to drop, to fall, to go down **2** : to come/go down ⟨bajar por la escalera : to come/go down

the stairs⟩ **3** : to ebb (of tides) — **bajarse** *vr* ~ **de** : to get off (a train, etc.), to get out of (a car)

bajeza *nf* **1** : low or despicable act **2** : baseness

bajío *nm* **1** : lowland **2** : shoal, sandbank, shallows

bajista *nmf* : bass player, bassist

bajo¹ *adv* **1** : low **2** : softly, quietly

bajo², -ja *adj* **1** : low **2** : short (of stature) **3** : soft, faint, low ⟨en voz baja : in a low voice⟩ **4** : low, deep (in tone) **5** : lower ⟨el bajo Amazonas : the lower Amazon⟩ ⟨la planta baja : the ground/first floor⟩ **6** : lowered ⟨con la mirada baja : with lowered eyes⟩ **7** : base, vile **8 los bajos fondos** : the underworld

bajo³ *nm* **1** : bass, double bass **2** : bass, bass guitar **3** : first floor, ground floor **4** : hemline

bajo⁴ *prep* : under, beneath, below

bajón *nm, pl* **bajones** : sharp drop, slump

bajorrelieve *nm* : bas-relief

bala *nf* **1** : bullet ⟨a prueba de balas : bulletproof⟩ **2** : bale **3 lanzamiento de bala** : shot put

balacear → **balear**

balacera *nf* → **baleo**

balada *nf* : ballad

balance *nm* **1** : balance **2** : balance sheet **3** : outcome, result **4 hacer balance de** : to take stock of

balancear *vt* **1** : to balance **2** : to swing (one's arms, etc.) **3** : to rock (a boat) — **balancearse** *vr* OSCILAR : to swing, to sway, to rock

balanceo *nm* : swaying, rocking, swinging

balancín *nm, pl* **-cines** **1** : rocking chair **2** SUBIBAJA : seesaw

balandra *nf* : sloop

balanza *nf* : scales *pl*, balance ⟨balanza comercial : balance of trade⟩ ⟨balanza de pagos : balance of payments⟩

balar *vi* : to bleat

balaustrada *nf* : balustrade

balazo *nm* **1** TIRO : shot, gunshot **2** : bullet wound

balboa *nf* : balboa (monetary unit of Panama)

balbucear *vi* **1** : to mutter, to stammer **2** : to babble

balbuceo *nm* **1** : mumbling, stammering **2** : babbling

balbucir → **balbucear**

balcánico, -ca *adj* : Balkan

balcón *nm, pl* **balcones** : balcony

balde *nm* **1** CUBO : bucket, pail **2 en** ~ : in vain, to no avail

baldío¹, -día *adj* **1** : fallow **2** : useless, vain

baldío² *nm* **1** : wasteland **2** *Mex* : vacant lot

baldosa *nf* LOSETA : floor tile, paving tile/stone, paving block

balear *vt* : to shoot, to shoot at

baleo *nm* : shooting, shoot-out

balero *nm* **1** *Mex* : ball bearing **2** *Mex*, *PRi* : cup-and-ball toy
balido *nm* : bleat
balín *nm, pl* **balines** : pellet
balística *nf* : ballistics
balístico, -ca *adj* : ballistic
baliza *nf* **1** : buoy **2** : beacon (for aircraft)
ballena *nf* : whale
ballenero¹, -ra *adj* : whaling
ballenero², -ra *n* : whaler
ballenero³ *nm* : whaleboat, whaler
ballesta *nf* **1** : crossbow **2** : spring (of an automobile)
ballet [ba⁴le] *nm* : ballet
balneario *nm* : spa, bathing resort
balompié *nm* FUTBOL : soccer
balón *nm, pl* **balones 1** : ball **2** TANQUE : tank
baloncelista *PRi* → **basquetbolista**
baloncesto *nm* BASQUETBOL : basketball
balonmano *nm* : handball
balsa *nf* **1** : raft **2** : balsa **3** : pond, pool
balsámico, -ca *adj* : soothing
bálsamo *nm* : balsam, balm
balsero, -ra *n* : boat person, refugee
báltico, -ca *adj* : Baltic
baluarte *nm* : bulwark, bastion
bambalina *nf* tras/entre bambalinas : behind the scenes
bambolear *vi* **1** : to sway, to swing **2** : to wobble — **bambolearse** *vr*
bamboleo *nm* **1** : swaying, swinging **2** : wobbling
bambú *nm, pl* **bambúes** *or* **bambús** : bamboo
banal *adj* : banal — **banalidad** *nf*
banana *nf* : banana
bananero¹, -ra *adj* : banana
bananero² *nm* : banana tree
banano *nm* **1** : banana tree **2** *CA, Col* : banana
banca *nf* **1** : banking, banks **2** : bank (in games) **3** BANCO : bench **4** BANQUILLO : bench (in sports)
bancada *nf* **1** : group, faction **2** : workbench
bancal *nm* **1** : terrace (in agriculture) **2** : plot (of land)
bancario, -ria *adj* : bank, banking
bancarrota *nf* QUIEBRA : bankruptcy ⟨en bancarrota : bankrupt⟩
banco *nm* **1** : bank ⟨banco central : central bank⟩ ⟨banco de datos : data bank⟩ ⟨banco de sangre : blood bank⟩ **2** BARRA : bank, bar ⟨banco de arena : sandbank⟩ **3** BANCA : stool, bench **4** : pew **5** : school (of fish)
banda *nf* **1** : band, strip **2** : band (on arm), sash **3** *Mex* : belt ⟨banda transportadora : conveyor belt⟩ **4** : (frequency) band **5** : band (of musicians) **6** : gang (of persons), flock (of birds) **7** : side (of a ship) **8** : touchline (in soccer) **9 banda ancha** : broadband **10 banda de rodadura** : tread (of a tire) **11 banda sonora** *or* **banda de sonido** : sound track
bandada *nf* : flock (of birds), school (of fish)

bandazo *nm* **dar bandazos** : to move from side to side
bandearse *vr* : to look after oneself, to cope
bandeja *nf* **1** : tray, platter **2 bandeja de entrada** : in-box **3 bandeja de salida** : out-box
bandera *nf* : flag, banner
banderazo *nm* : starting signal (in sports)
banderilla *nf* : dart (in bullfighting)
banderín *nm, pl* **-rines** : pennant, small flag
bandido, -da *n* BANDOLERO : bandit, outlaw
bando *nm* **1** FACCIÓN : faction, side **2** EDICTO : proclamation
bandolero, -ra *n* BANDIDO : bandit, outlaw
banjo *nm* : banjo
banquero, -ra *n* : banker
banqueta *nf* **1** : footstool, stool, bench **2** *Mex* : sidewalk
banquete *nm* : banquet ⟨banquete de bodas : wedding reception⟩
banquetear *v* : to feast
banquillo *nm* **1** BANCA : bench (in sports) **2** : dock, defendant's seat
banquina *nf* *Arg, Uru* : shoulder (of a road)
bañadera *Arg, Uru* → **bañera**
bañador *nm* *Spain* : swimsuit, bathing suit
bañar *vt* **1** : to bathe, to wash **2** : to immerse, to dip **3** : to coat, to cover ⟨bañado en lágrimas : bathed in tears⟩ — **bañarse** *vr* **1** : to take a bath, to bathe **2** : to swim, to go swimming
bañera *nf* **1** TINA : bathtub **2 bañera de hidromasaje** : hot tub, whirlpool, Jacuzzi *trademark*
bañero, -ra *n* *Arg, Uru* : lifeguard
bañista *nmf* : bather
baño *nm* **1** : bath ⟨darse un baño : to take a bath⟩ ⟨baño de espuma/burbujas : bubble bath⟩ **2** : swim, dip **3** : bathroom ⟨baños públicos : public restrooms⟩ **4** BAÑERA : bathtub **5** GLASEADO : icing, frosting **6 baño de sangre** : bloodbath
baptista → **bautista**
baqueta *nf* **1** : ramrod **2 baquetas** *nfpl* : drumsticks
bar *nm* : bar
baraja *nf* : deck of cards
barajar *vt* **1** : to shuffle (cards) **2** : to consider
baranda *nf* → **barandal 1**
barandal *nm* **1** : rail, railing **2** : banister, handrail
barandilla *nf* *Spain* → **barandal**
barata *nf* **1** *Mex* : sale, bargain **2** *Chile* : cockroach
baratija *nf* : bauble, trinket
baratillo *nm* : rummage sale, flea market
barato¹ *adv* : cheap, cheaply ⟨te lo vendo barato : I'll sell it to you cheap⟩
barato², -ta *adj* : cheap, inexpensive
barba *nf* **1** : beard, stubble **2** : chin
barbacoa *nf* **1** PARRILLA : barbecue **2** : barbecued meat
bárbaramente *adv* : barbarously
barbaridad *nf* **1** : barbarity, atrocity **2** BURRADA : stupid act or remark **3** MON-

TÓN : ton, load **4 ¡qué barbaridad!** : that's outrageous!

barbarie *nf* : savagery

bárbaro[1] *adv* **pasarlo bárbaro** *fam* : to have a great time

bárbaro[2], **-ra** *adj* **1** : barbarian (in history) **2** CRUEL : cruel **3** GROSERO : rude, crass **4** *fam* : great, fantastic

bárbaro[3], **-ra** *n* : barbarian

barbecho *nm* : fallow land ⟨dejar en barbecho : to leave fallow⟩

barbería *nf* : barbershop

barbero *nm* : barber

barbilla *nf* MENTÓN : chin

barbitúrico *nm* : barbiturate

barbudo[1], **-da** *adj* : bearded

barbudo[2] *nm* : bearded man

barca *nf* : boat

barcaza *nf* : barge

barcia *nf* : chaff

barco *nm* **1** BARCA : boat ⟨viajar en barco : to travel by boat/ship⟩ ⟨barco de guerra/vapor/vela : warship/steamship/sailboat⟩ ⟨barco pesquero : fishing boat⟩ **2** BUQUE, NAVE : ship

barda *nf* *Mex* **1** MURO : wall **2** CERCO : fence

bardo *nm* : bard

baremo *nm* : scale

barítono *nm* : baritone

barman *nm* : bartender

barniz *nm*, *pl* **barnices** : varnish

barnizar {21} *vt* : to varnish

barómetro *nm* : barometer — **barométrico, -ca** *adj*

barón *nm*, *pl* **barones** : baron

baronesa *nf* : baroness

barquero, -ra : boatman *m*, boatwoman *f*

barquillo *nm* **1** : wafer **2** CONO : ice-cream cone

barra *nf* **1** : bar (of metal), rod (for curtains) **2** : bar (of soap, etc.), block (of ice) **3** MOSTRADOR : bar, counter **4** : gang (of friends) **5** : slash (in punctuation) ⟨barra oblicua : forward slash⟩ ⟨barra invertida/inversa : backslash⟩ **6** BANCO : bar, bank ⟨barra de arena : sandbar⟩ **7** **barra de herramientas** : toolbar **8** **barra de labios** : lipstick **9** **barra de pan** *Mex, Spain* : baguette

barraca *nf* **1** CHOZA : shack **2** PUESTO, CASETA : booth, stall

barracuda *nf* : barracuda

barranca *nf* **1** : hillside, slope **2** → **barranco**

barranco *nm* : ravine, gorge

barredora *nf* : street sweeper (machine)

barrena *nf* **1** TALADRO : drill, auger, gimlet **2** : tailspin

barrenar *vt* : to drill

barrendero, -ra *n* : sweeper, street cleaner

barrer *vt* **1** : to sweep **2** : to sweep away **3** : to crush, to defeat — *vi* **1** : to sweep **2** : to make a clean sweep **3** ~ **con** : to sweep away **4** ~ **con** : to wipe out (an enemy), to crush (a sports opponent) — **barrerse** *vr* : to slide (in sports)

barrera *nf* OBSTÁCULO : barrier, obstacle ⟨barrera de sonido : sound barrier⟩ ⟨barrera comercial : trade barrier⟩

barreta *nf* *Arg, Mex* : crowbar

barriada *nf* **1** : district, quarter **2** : shantytown, slums *pl*

barrica *nf* BARRIL, TONEL : barrel, cask, keg

barricada *nf* : barricade

barrida *nf* **1** : sweep **2** : slide (in sports) **3** : clean sweep (in a competition)

barrido *nm* : sweeping

barriga *nf* : belly

barrigón, -gona *adj*, *mpl* **-gones** *fam* : potbellied

barril *nm* **1** BARRICA : barrel, keg **2** **cerveza de barril** : draft beer

barrio *nm* **1** : neighborhood, district **2** **barrios bajos** : slums *pl* **3** **barrio de invasión** *Col* → **invasión** **4** **barrio de chabolas** *Spain* : shantytown, slums *pl*

barrizal *nm* : quagmire

barro *nm* **1** LODO : mud **2** ARCILLA : clay ⟨vajilla de barro : earthenware dishes⟩ **3** ESPINILLA, GRANO : pimple, blackhead

barroco, -ca *adj* : baroque — **barroco** *nm*

barroso, -sa *adj* ENLODADO : muddy

barrote *nm* : bar (on a window)

bártulos *nmpl* : things, belongings ⟨liar los bártulos : to pack one's things⟩

barullo *nm* **1** BULLA : racket, ruckus **2** CONFUSIÓN : mess, confusion

basa *nf* : base, pedestal

basalto *nm* : basalt

basar *vt* FUNDAR : to base — **basarse** *vr* FUNDARSE **1** ~ **en** : to be based on **2** ~ **en** : to base one's position on

báscula *nf* BALANZA : balance, scales *pl*

base *nf* **1** : base, bottom **2** : base (in baseball) **3** FUNDAMENTO : basis, foundation ⟨sentar las bases de : to lay the foundation for⟩ **4** : base ⟨base naval/aérea : naval/air base⟩ **5** REGLAS : rules *pl* **6** ~ **de maquillaje** : foundation (makeup) **7** **a base de** : based on, by means of **8** **base de datos** : database **9** **en base a** : based on, on the basis of

básico, -ca *adj* FUNDAMENTAL : basic — **básicamente** *adv*

basílica *nf* : basilica

basket *or* **básquet** → **basquetbol**

basquetbol *or* **básquetbol** *nm* BALONCESTO : basketball

basquetbolista *nmf* : basketball player

basset *nm* : basset hound

bastante[1] *adv* **1** : enough, sufficiently ⟨he trabajado bastante : I have worked enough⟩ ⟨lo bastante alto (como) para alcanzar : tall enough to reach⟩ **2** : fairly, rather, quite ⟨llegaron bastante temprano : they arrived quite early⟩ ⟨me gustó bastante : I liked it a lot⟩

bastante[2] *adj* **1** : enough, sufficient ⟨¿hay bastantes sillas? : are there enough chairs?⟩ **2** : plenty of, a lot of ⟨había bastante gente : there were a lot of people⟩

bastante[3] *pron* : enough ⟨hemos visto bastante : we have seen enough⟩ ⟨no hay bastantes : there aren't enough⟩

bastar *vi* : to be enough, to suffice ⟨con uno basta (y sobra) : one is (more than) enough⟩ ⟨¡basta (ya)! : that's enough!⟩ — **bastarse** *vr* : to be able to manage on one's own

bastardilla *nf* CURSIVA : italic type, italics *pl*

bastardo¹, -da *adj* **1** ILEGÍTIMO : bastard **2** VIL : base

bastardo², -da *n* : bastard *usu offensive*

bastidor *nm* **1** : framework, frame **2** : wing (in theater) ⟨entre bastidores : backstage, behind the scenes⟩

bastión *nf, pl* **bastiones** BALUARTE : bastion, bulwark

basto¹, -ta *adj* : coarse, rough

basto² *nm* : club (in the Spanish deck of cards)

bastón *nm, pl* **bastones** **1** : cane, walking stick **2** : baton **3** *or* **bastón de esquí** : ski pole **4 bastón de mando** : staff (of authority)

basura *nf* : garbage, trash ⟨tirar/echar/botar algo a la basura : to throw something in the garbage⟩ ⟨sacar la basura : to take out the garbage⟩

basural → **basurero**

basurero¹, -ra *n* : garbage collector

basurero² *nm* **1** *Mex* : garbage can **2** VERTEDERO, BASURAL : garbage dump

bata *nf* **1** : bathrobe, housecoat **2** : smock, coveralls, lab coat

batacazo *nm* **1** : wallop **2 dar el/un batacazo** *Arg, Uru* : to pull off an unexpected win

batalla *nf* **1** : battle ⟨batalla campal : pitched battle⟩ **2** : fight, struggle **3 de ~** : ordinary, everyday

batallar *vi* LIDIAR, LUCHAR : to battle, to fight

batallón *nm, pl* **-llones** : battalion

batata *nf* : yam, sweet potato

batazo *nm* HIT : hit (in baseball)

bate *nm* : baseball bat

batea *nf* **1** : tray, pan **2** : punt (boat)

bateador, -dora *n* : batter, hitter

batear *vi* : to bat — *vt* : to hit

bateo *nm* : batting (in baseball)

batería *nf* **1** PILA : battery **2** : drum kit, drums *pl* **3 batería de cocina** : kitchen utensils *pl*

baterista *nmf* : drummer

batida *nf* REDADA, ALLANAMIENTO : raid

batido *nm* LICUADO : milk shake

batidor *nm* : eggbeater, whisk, mixer

batidora *nf* : (electric) mixer

batir *vt* **1** GOLPEAR : to beat, to hit **2** VENCER : to defeat **3** : to whisk, to beat (eggs), to whip (cream), to cream (butter and sugar) **4** : to flap, to beat (wings) **5** RASTREAR : to comb, to search **6** : to break (a record) **7 batir palmas** : to clap — **batirse** *vr* : to fight

batuta *nf* **1** : baton **2 llevar la batuta** : to be in charge

baúl *nm* **1** : trunk, chest **2** (*in various countries*) : trunk (of a car)

bautismal *adj* : baptismal

bautismo *nm* : baptism, christening

bautista *adj & nmf* : Baptist

bautizar {21} *vt* : to baptize, to christen

bautizo → **bautismo**

bávaro, -ra *adj & n* : Bavarian

baya *nf* : berry

bayeta *nf* : cleaning cloth

bayoneta *nf* : bayonet

baza *nf* : trick (in card games)

bazar *nm* : bazaar

bazo *nm* : spleen

bazofia *nf* **1** : table scraps *pl* **2** : slop, swill **3** : rubbish

bazuca *nf* : bazooka

be *or* **be larga** *or* **be grande** *nf* : (letter) b

beagle *nm* : beagle

beatífico, -ca *adj* : beatific

beato, -ta *adj* **1** : blessed **2** : devout **3** : overly devout

bebe, -ba *n Arg, Uru* : baby

bebé *nm* : baby

bebedero *nm* **1** ABREVADERO : watering trough **2** *Mex* : drinking fountain

bebedor, -dora *n* : (heavy) drinker

beber *v* TOMAR : to drink

bebida *nf* : drink, beverage

bebido, -da *adj* BORRACHO : drunk

beca *nf* : grant, scholarship

becado, -da *n* : grant recipient, scholarship holder

becar {72} *vt* : to award a grant or scholarship to

becario, -ria → **becado**

becerro, -rra *n* : calf

bedel *nmf* : janitor

begonia *nf* : begonia

beige *adj & nm* : beige

beisbol *or* **béisbol** *nm* : baseball

beisbolista *nmf* : baseball player

beldad *nf* BELLEZA, HERMOSURA : beauty

belén *nf, pl* **belenes** NACIMIENTO : Nativity scene

belga *adj & nmf* : Belgian

belicista¹ *adj* : militaristic

belicista² *nmf* : warmonger

bélico, -ca *adj* GUERRERO : war, fighting, military ⟨conflicto bélico : armed conflict⟩

belicoso, -sa *adj* **1** : warlike, martial **2** : aggressive, belligerent

beligerancia *nf* : belligerence

beligerante *adj & nmf* : belligerent

bellaco¹, -ca *adj* : sly, cunning

bellaco², -ca *n* : rogue, scoundrel

belleza *nf* BELDAD, HERMOSURA : beauty

bello, -lla *adj* **1** HERMOSO : beautiful **2 bellas artes** : fine arts — **bellamente** *adv*

bellota *nf* : acorn

bemol *nm* : flat (in music) — **bemol** *adj*

bencina *nf Chile* GASOLINA : gas, gasoline

bencinera *nf Chile* : gas station

bendecir {11} *vt* **1** : to bless **2 bendecir la mesa** : to say grace

bendición *nf, pl* **-ciones** : benediction, blessing

bendiga, bendijo etc. → **bendecir**

bendito¹, -ta *adj* **1** : blessed, holy **2** : fortunate

bendito², -ta *n* : simple person

benefactor¹, -tora *adj* : charitable

benefactor², -tora *n* : benefactor, benefactress *f*

beneficencia *nf* : charity

beneficiar *vt* : to benefit — **beneficiarse** *vr* : to benefit ⟨beneficiarse con/de : to benefit from⟩

beneficiario, -ria n **1** : beneficiary **2** : payee (of a check)

beneficio nm **1** GANANCIA : profit **2** : benefit **3 en/a beneficio de** : in aid of, to benefit **4 en beneficio de alguien** : in someone's interest

beneficioso, -sa adj : beneficial

benéfico, -ca adj : charitable

benemérito, -ta adj : meritorious, worthy

beneplácito nm : approval, consent

benevolencia nf BONDAD : benevolence, kindness

benevolente → **benévolo**

benévolo, -la adj BONDADOSO : benevolent, kind, good

bengala nf **luz de bengala 1** : flare (signal) **2** : sparkler

benigno, -na adj : benign, mild

benjamín, -mina n, mpl **-mines** : youngest child

beodo, -da adj & n : drunk

berberecho nm : cockle

berenjena nf : eggplant

bergantín nm, pl **-tines** : brig (ship)

berlinés¹, -nesa adj : of or from Berlin

berlinés², -nesa n : person from Berlin

berma nf Chile, Col, Ecua, Peru : shoulder (of a road)

bermudas nfpl : Bermuda shorts

berrear vi **1** : to bellow, to low **2** : to bawl, to howl

berrido nm **1** : bellowing **2** : howl, scream

berrinche nm fam : tantrum ⟨hacer (un) berrinche : to throw a tantrum⟩

berro nm : watercress

besar vt : to kiss — **besarse** vr : to kiss (each other)

beso nm : kiss ⟨tirarle un beso a alguien : to blow someone a kiss⟩

bestia¹ adj **1** : ignorant, stupid **2** : boorish, rude

bestia² nf **1** : beast **2** BRUTO : brute

bestia³ nmf **1** IGNORANTE : ignoramus **2** : brute

bestial adj **1** : bestial, beastly **2** fam : huge, enormous ⟨hace un frío bestial : it's freezing cold⟩ **3** fam : great, fantastic

bestialidad nf **1** BRUTALIDAD : brutality **2** DISPARATE : stupid act or remark **3** MONTÓN : load, ton

best-seller [besˈseler] nm, pl **-sellers** : best seller

beta nf : beta (software)

besuquear vt fam : to cover with kisses — **besuquearse** vr fam : to neck, to smooch

betabel nm Mex : beet

betún nm, pl **betunes 1** : shoe polish **2** Mex : icing

bi- pref : bi-

bianual adj : biannual

biberón nm, pl **-rones** : baby's bottle ⟨le dio el biberón al bebé : she gave the baby his bottle⟩

biblia nf **1** : bible **2 la Biblia** : the Bible

bíblico, -ca adj : biblical

bibliografía nf : bibliography — **bibliográfico, -ca** adj

bibliógrafo, -fa n : bibliographer

biblioteca nf **1** : library **2** ESTANTERÍA : bookcase, bookshelves

bibliotecario, -ria n : librarian

bicameral adj : bicameral

bicarbonato nm **1** : bicarbonate **2 bicarbonato de soda** : sodium bicarbonate, baking soda

bicentenario nm : bicentennial

bíceps nms & pl : biceps

bicho nm **1** : small animal **2** INSECTO : bug **3 bicho raro** : weirdo

bici nf fam : bike

bicicleta nf **1** : bicycle ⟨ir en bicicleta : to cycle, to bicycle⟩ ⟨andar/montar en bicicleta : to ride a bicycle⟩ **2 bicicleta de montaña** : mountain bike

bicolor adj : two-tone

bidé or **bidet** nm : bidet

bidireccional adj : two-way

bidón nm, pl **bidones** : large can, (oil) drum

bien¹ adv **1** : well ⟨¿dormiste bien? : did you sleep well?⟩ ⟨todo va bien : everything's going well⟩ **2** : well, right, properly ⟨nos trata bien : she treats us well⟩ ⟨funcionar bien : to work right⟩ **3** : well, skillfully ⟨canta bien : she sings well⟩ ⟨¡bien dicho! : well said!⟩ **4** : well, thoroughly ⟨piénsalo bien : think it over carefully⟩ ⟨bien documentado : well-documented⟩ **5** : very, quite ⟨era bien divertido : it was very enjoyable⟩ **6** : easily ⟨bien podría decirse que . . . : it could very well be said that . . .⟩ **7 bien que** : willingly, readily ⟨no ayuda pero bien que critica : he doesn't help but he's quick to criticize⟩ **8 más bien** : rather **9 no bien** : as soon as **10 si bien** : although

bien² adj **1** : well, OK, all right ⟨¿te sientes bien? : are you feeling all right?⟩ ⟨estoy bien, gracias : I'm fine, thanks⟩ **2** : good, nice, pleasant ⟨las flores huelen bien : the flowers smell very nice⟩ ⟨se está bien aquí : it's very pleasant here⟩ **3** : fine, OK, all right ⟨me parece bien : it seems fine to me⟩ ⟨está bien, no te preocupes : it's OK — don't worry about it⟩ **4** : right, correct, proper ⟨esta frase no está bien : this sentence isn't right⟩ ⟨no está bien que te hable así : it's not right for him to speak to you like that⟩

bien³ nm **1** : good ⟨el bien y el mal : good and evil⟩ **2** : good, sake ⟨por tu (propio) bien : for your (own) good⟩ **3 bienes** nmpl : property, goods, possessions ⟨bienes de consumo : consumer goods⟩ ⟨bienes muebles : personal property⟩ ⟨bienes raíces/inmuebles : real estate⟩

bien⁴ conj **(o) bien . . . (o) bien . . .** : either . . . or . . .

bien⁵ interj **1** BUENO : well, so ⟨bien, empecemos : well, let's get started⟩ ⟨bien, como iba diciendo . . . : so as I was saying . . .⟩ **2 ¡(muy) bien!** : (very) good!, well done! **3 ¡qué bien!** : great!

bienal adj & nf : biennial — **bienalmente** adv

bienaventurado, -da adj **1** : blessed **2** : fortunate, happy

bienestar *nm* **1** : welfare, well-being **2** CONFORT : comfort
bienintencionado, -da *adj* : well-meaning
bienvenida *nf* **1** : welcome **2 dar la bienvenida a** : to welcome
bienvenido, -da *adj* : welcome
bies *nm* : bias (in sewing)
bife *nm Arg, Chile, Uru* : steak
bífido, -da *adj* : forked
bifocales *nmpl* : bifocals — **bifocal** *adj*
bifurcación *nf, pl* **-ciones** : fork (in a river or road)
bifurcarse {72} *vr* : to fork
bigamia *nf* : bigamy
bígamo, -ma *n* : bigamist
bigote *nm* **1** : mustache **2** : whisker (of an animal)
bigotón, -tona *adj, mpl* **-tones** *CA, Mex* : having a big mustache
bikini *nm* : bikini
bilateral *adj* : bilateral — **bilateralmente** *adv*
biliar *adj* : bile ⟨cálculo biliar : gallstone⟩
bilingüe *adj* : bilingual
bilis *nf* : bile
billar *nm* : pool, billiards
billete *nm* **1** : bill ⟨un billete de cinco dólares : a five-dollar bill⟩ ⟨billete de banco : banknote⟩ **2** *Spain* → **boleto**
billetera *nf* : billfold, wallet
billetero, -ra *n CA, Car* : lottery ticket vendor
billón *nm, pl* **billones** **1** : billion (Great Britain) **2** : trillion (U.S.A.)
bimensual *adj* : bimonthly, semimonthly
bimestral *adj* : bimonthly ⟨una revista bimestral : a bimonthly magazine, a magazine that's published every two months⟩ — **bimestralmente** *adv*
bimestre *nm* : two-month period
bimotor *adj* : twin-engine
binacional *adj* : binational
binario, -ria *adj* : binary
bingo *nm* : bingo
binocular *adj* : binocular
binoculares *nmpl* : binoculars
bio- *pref* : bio-
biodegradable *adj* : biodegradable
biodiversidad *nf* : biodiversity
biografía *nf* : biography
biográfico, -ca *adj* : biographical
biógrafo, -fa *n* : biographer
biología *nf* : biology
biológico, -ca *adj* : biological, biologic — **biológicamente** *adv*
biólogo, -ga *n* : biologist
biombo *nm* MAMPARA : folding screen, room divider
biopsia *nf* : biopsy
bioquímica *nf* : biochemistry
bioquímico¹, -ca *adj* : biochemical
bioquímico², -ca *n* : biochemist
biosfera *or* **biósfera** *nf* : biosphere
biotecnología *nf* : biotechnology — **biotecnológico, -ca** *adj*
bip *nm* PITIDO : beep
bipartidismo *nm* : two-party system
bipartidista *adj* : bipartisan
bípedo *nm* : biped
biquini → **bikini**

birlar *vt fam* : to swipe, to pinch
birmano, -na *adj & n* : Burmese
birrete *nm* **1** : mortarboard **2** : biretta
bis¹ *adv* **1** : twice, again (in music) **2** : a, A ⟨artículo 47 bis : Article 47A⟩ ⟨calle 15, número 70 bis : 15th Street, number 70A⟩
bis² *nm* : encore
bis- *pref* : great ⟨bisnieto : great-grandson⟩
bisabuelo, -la *n* : great-grandfather *m*, great-grandmother *f*, great-grandparent
bisagra *nf* : hinge
bisecar {72} *vt* : bisect
bisel *nm* : bevel
biselar *vt* : to bevel
bisexual *adj* : bisexual — **bisexualidad** *nf*
bisiesto *adj* **año bisiesto** : leap year
bisnieto, -ta *n* : great-grandson *m*, great-granddaughter *f*, great-grandchild
bisonte *nm* : bison, buffalo
bisoñé *nm* : hairpiece, toupee
bisoño¹, -ña *adj* : inexperienced
bisoño², -ña *n* : rookie
bistec *nm* : steak, beefsteak
bisturí *nm, pl* **-ríes** ESCALPELO : scalpel
bisutería *nf* : costume jewelry
bit *nm* : bit (unit of information)
bitácora *nf* **1** : ship's log **2** BLOG : blog
bizco, -ca *adj* : cross-eyed
bizcocho *nm* **1** : sponge cake **2** : biscuit
blanca *nf* : half note (in music)
blanco¹, -ca *adj* **1** : white **2 en blanco** : blank (of a paper, etc.) **3 pasar la noche en blanco** : to have a sleepless night
blanco², -ca *n* : white person
blanco³ *nm* **1** : white (color) **2** : white (of the eye) **3** : target, bull's-eye ⟨dar en el blanco : to hit the target, to hit the nail on the head⟩
blancura *nf* : whiteness
blancuzco, -ca *adj* **1** : whitish, off-white **2** PÁLIDO : pale
blandir {1} *vt* : to wave, to brandish
blando, -da *adj* **1** SUAVE : soft (of a bed, etc.), tender (of meat) **2** : weak (in character) **3** : lenient
blandura *nf* **1** : softness, tenderness **2** : leniency
blanqueador *nm* : bleach, whitener
blanquear *vt* **1** : to bleach (clothes), to whitewash (a wall) **2** : to shut out (in sports) **3** : to launder (money) — *vi* : to turn white
blanqueo *nm* **1** : bleaching, whitewashing **2** : money laundering
blanquillo *nm CA, Mex* : egg
blasfemar *vi* : to blaspheme
blasfemia *nf* : blasphemy
blasfemo, -ma *adj* : blasphemous
blazer *nm* : blazer
bledo *nm* **(no) me importa un bledo** *fam* : I don't give a damn
blindado, -da *adj* ACORAZADO : armored
blindaje *nm* **1** : armor, armor plating **2** : shield (for cables, machinery, etc.)
bloc *nm, pl* **blocs** : notepad, pad (of paper)
blof *nm Col, Mex* : bluff

blofear *vi Col, Mex* : to bluff

blog ['blox] *nm, pl* **blogs** BITÁCORA : blog

blondo, -da *adj* : blond, flaxen

bloque *nm* **1** : block (of wood, etc.) **2** GRUPO : bloc ⟨el bloque comunista : the Communist bloc⟩ **3 en bloque** : en masse

bloquear *vt* **1** OBSTRUIR : to block (a road, etc.) **2** : to blockade (a port) **3** : to jam (a mechanism) **4** : to freeze (an account) — **bloquearse** *vr* : to jam, to stick, to lock

bloqueo *nm* **1** : blocking **2** : blockade (of a port, etc.)

blues ['blus] *nm* : blues (music)

blusa *nf* : blouse

blusón *nm, pl* **blusones** : loose shirt, smock

boa *nf* : boa

boato *nm* : ostentation, show

bobada *nf* **1** : stupid remark or action **2** **decir bobadas** : to talk nonsense

bobalicón, -cona *adj, mpl* **-cones** *fam* : silly, stupid

bobina *nf* **1** : roll, spool (of thread), bobbin (in sewing machine) **2** : (electrical) coil

bobo¹, -ba *adj* : silly, stupid

bobo², -ba *n* : fool

bobsleigh ['bobsle] *nm* : bobsled

boca *nf* **1** : mouth **2** : entrance **3** : mouth (of a jar, etc.), muzzle (of a gun) **4 boca arriba** : face up **5 boca abajo** : face down **6 boca del estómago** : pit of the stomach **7 boca de riego/incendios** : hydrant **8 correr de boca en boca** : to spread by word of mouth **9 el boca a boca** : mouth-to-mouth (resuscitation) ⟨hacerle el boca a boca a alguien : to give someone mouth-to-mouth⟩ **10 en boca de todos** : on everyone's lips **11 por boca de** : according to

bocacalle *nf* : entrance to a street ⟨gire a la última bocacalle : turn onto the last side street⟩

bocadillo *nm Spain* : sandwich

bocado *nm* **1** : bite, mouthful ⟨no probó bocado : he didn't have a bite to eat⟩ **2** FRENO : bit (of a bridle)

bocajarro *nm* **a** ~ : point-blank

bocallave *nf* : keyhole

bocanada *nf* **1** : mouthful (of smoke, etc.) **2** : gust (of air)

boceto *nm* : sketch, outline

bochinche *nm fam* : ruckus, uproar

bochorno *nm* **1** VERGÜENZA : embarrassment **2** : hot and humid weather **3** : hot flash

bochornoso, -sa *adj* **1** EMBARAZOSO : embarrassing **2** : hot and muggy

bocina *nf* **1** : horn, trumpet **2** : automobile horn **3** : mouthpiece (of a telephone) **4** *Mex* : loudspeaker

bocinazo *nm* : honk (of a horn)

bocio *nm* : goiter

bocón, -cona *n, mpl* **bocones** *fam* : blabbermouth, loudmouth

boda *nf* : wedding ⟨bodas de oro/plata : golden/silver anniversary⟩

bodega *nf* **1** : wine cellar **2** : wine shop **3** : wine bar **4** : winery, wine producer

sótano : cellar **6** : (ship's) hold **7** *Chile, Col, Mex* : storeroom, warehouse **8** (in various countries) : grocery store

bodegón *nm, pl* **-gones** : still life

bofetada *nf* CACHETADA : slap on the face

bofetear *vt* CACHETEAR : to slap

bofetón *nm, pl* **-tones** → **bofetada**

boga *nf* : fashion, vogue ⟨estar en boga : to be in style⟩

bogey ['bogi] *nm* : bogey (in golf)

bogotano¹, -na *adj* : of or from Bogotá

bogotano², -na *n* : person from Bogotá

bohemio, -mia *adj & n* : bohemian, Bohemian

bohío *nm* (in various countries) : hut

boicot *nm, pl* **boicots** : boycott

boicotear *vt* : to boycott

bóiler *nm Mex* : water heater

boina *nf* : beret

bol *nm* : bowl

bola *nf* **1** : ball ⟨bola de nieve : snowball⟩ ⟨bola de billar : billiard ball⟩ **2** CANICA : marble **3** : scoop (of ice cream) **4** *fam* : lie, fib *fam* **5** *Mex fam* : bunch ⟨una bola de rateros/mentiras : a bunch of thieves/lies⟩ **6** *Mex* : uproar, tumult **7 hacerse bolas con** *Mex* : to muddle up (facts), to make a mess of

bolchevique *adj & nmf* : Bolshevik

bolear *vt Mex* : to polish (shoes)

bolera *nf* : bowling alley

bolero¹ *nm* : bolero

bolero², -ra *n Mex* : shoeshine boy/man *m*, shoeshine girl/woman *f*

boleta *nf* **1** : receipt, ticket, slip **2** : (traffic/parking) ticket **3** *Arg, Mex* FACTURA : bill **4** *or* **boleta electoral** : ballot **5 boleta de calificaciones** *Mex* : report card

boletaje *nm Mex* : tickets *pl*

boletería *nf* TAQUILLA : box office, ticket office

boletín *nm, pl* **-tines** **1** : bulletin **2** : journal, review **3 boletín informativo** : news bulletin **4 boletín de prensa** : press release

boleto *nm* **1** : ticket, fare ⟨boleto de ida/de ida y vuelta : one-way/round-trip ticket⟩ **2** : ticket (for a lottery, etc.)

boli *nm Spain* → **bolígrafo**

boliche *nm* **1** BOLOS : bowling **2** BOLERA : bowling alley **3** *Arg, Uru* : bar, nightclub **4** *Arg, Chile, Uru* : small store

bólido *nm* **1** : race car **2** METEORO : meteor

bolígrafo *nm* : ballpoint pen

bolillo *nm* **1** : bobbin **2** *Mex* : roll, bun

bolita *nf* CANICA : marble

bolívar *nm* : bolivar (monetary unit of Venezuela)

boliviano¹, -na *adj & n* : Bolivian

boliviano² *nm* : boliviano (monetary unit of Bolivia)

bollo *nm* **1** : bun, sweet roll **2** *Arg, Uru* : ball

bolo *nm* : bowling pin

bolos *nmpl* BOLICHE : bowling

bolsa *nf* **1** : bag, sack ⟨bolsa de basura/plástico : garbage/plastic bag⟩ **2** : pocketbook, purse **3** *Mex* : pocket **4** : pouch (of a marsupial) **5** : pocket (of minerals, etc.) **6** *or* **Bolsa** *or* **bolsa de valores** : stock market, stock exchange **7 bolsa de agua caliente** : hot-water bottle **8 bolsa de trabajo** : job bank

bolsear *vt Mex* : to pick (someone's) pocket

bolsillo *nm* **1** : pocket **2 dinero de bolsillo** : pocket change

bolsita *nf* : small bag ⟨bolsita de té : tea bag⟩

bolso *nm* : pocketbook, handbag

bomba *nf* **1** : bomb ⟨bomba atómica : atomic/atom bomb⟩ ⟨bomba de tiempo, bomba de relojería *Spain* : time bomb⟩ **2** : bubble **3** : pump ⟨bomba de agua : water pump⟩ **4** *or* **bomba destapacaños** : plunger (for toilets, etc.) **5** (*in various countries*) : gas station **6 BOMBAZO** : bombshell, shocker **7 pasarlo bomba** : to have a great time

bombacha *nf Arg, Uru* **1** : panties **2** → **bombachos**

bombachos *nmpl* : baggy pants, bloomers

bombardear *vt* **1** : to bomb **2** : to bombard

bombardeo *nm* **1** : bombing, shelling **2** : bombardment

bombardero *nm* : bomber (airplane)

bombástico, -ca *adj* : bombastic

bombazo *nm* **1** : bombshell, shocker **2** *Mex* : (bomb) explosion

bombear *vt* : to pump

bombero, -ra *n* : firefighter, fireman *m*

bombilla *nf* **1** : lightbulb **2** : tube, straw (for maté)

bombillo *nm CA, Col, Ven* : lightbulb

bombín *nm, pl* **-bines** : derby (hat)

bombita *Arg, Uru* → **bombilla**

bombo *nm* **1** : bass drum **2** *fam* : fanfare, hype ⟨con bombos y platillos : with great fanfare⟩

bombón *nm, pl* **bombones** **1** : bonbon, chocolate **2** *Mex* : marshmallow

bombona *nf Ecua, Spain, Ven* : tank (container)

bonachón¹, -chona *adj, mpl* **-chones** *fam* : good-natured, kindhearted

bonachón², -chona *n, mpl* **-chones** *fam* BUENAZO : kindhearted person

bonaerense¹ *adj* : of or from Buenos Aires

bonaerense² *nmf* : person from Buenos Aires

bonanza *nf* **1** PROSPERIDAD : prosperity **2** : calm weather **3** : rich ore deposit, bonanza

bondad *nf* BENEVOLENCIA : goodness, kindness ⟨tener la bondad de hacer algo : to be kind enough to do something⟩

bondadoso, -sa *adj* BENÉVOLO : kind, kindly, good — **bondadosamente** *adv*

bonete *nm* : cap, mortarboard

bongo *or* **bongó** *nm, pl* **bongos** *or* **bongóes** : bongo

boniato *nm* : sweet potato

bonificación *nf, pl* **-ciones** **1** : discount **2** : bonus, extra

bonito¹ *adv* : nicely, well

bonito², -ta *adj* LINDO : pretty, lovely

bonito³ *nm* : bonito (tuna)

bono *nm* **1** : bond ⟨bono bancario : bank bond⟩ **2** : voucher

boqueada *nf* : gasp ⟨dar la última boqueada : to give one's last gasp⟩

boquear *vi* **1** : to gasp **2** : to be dying

boquerón *nm, pl* **-rones** : anchovy

boquete *nm* : hole, opening

boquiabierto, -ta *adj* : open-mouthed, speechless, agape

boquilla *nf* **1** : mouthpiece (of a musical instrument), stem (of a pipe) **2** : cigarette holder **3** : nozzle

borbotar *or* **borbotear** *vi* : to bubble

borboteo *nm* : bubbling

borbotón *nm, pl* **-tones** **1 hervir a borbotones** : to boil rapidly **2 salir a borbotones** : to gush out

borda *nf* : gunwale ⟨echar/tirar algo por la borda : to throw something overboard⟩

bordado *nm* : embroidery

bordar *v* : to embroider

borde *nm* **1** : edge (of a table, etc.), rim (of a glass, etc.) **2** : side (of a road, etc.) **3 al borde de** : on the verge of

bordear *vt* **1** : to border (a city, etc.), to line (a street) **2** : to skirt, to follow (a coastline, etc.) **3** : to border on ⟨bordea la genialidad : it borders on genius⟩

bordillo *nm* : curb

bordo *nm* **a ~** : aboard, on board

bordón *nm, pl* **-dones** **1** : bass string (of a guitar, etc.), snare (of a drum) **2 BASTÓN** : staff

boreal *adj* : northern

borgoña *nf* : burgundy

boricua *adj & nmf fam* : Puerto Rican

borinqueño, -ña *→* **boricua**

borla *nf* **1** : pom-pom, tassel **2** : powder puff

borrachera *nf* : drunkenness ⟨(se) agarró una borrachera : he got drunk⟩

borrachín, -china *n, mpl* **-chines** *fam* : lush, drunk

borracho¹, -cha *adj* EBRIO : drunk

borracho², -cha *n* : drunk, drunkard

borrador *nm* **1** : rough copy, first draft ⟨en borrador : in the rough⟩ **2 BOSQUEJO** : sketch **3** : (blackboard) eraser

borrar *vt* **1** : to erase (on paper), to delete (on a computer) **2** : to wipe, to erase (a disk, etc.) **3** : to erase, to wipe off (a blackboard) **4** : to erase, to blot out (a memory) — **borrarse** *vr* **1** : to fade, to fade away **2** : to resign, to drop out **3** *Mex fam* : to split, to leave ⟨me borro : I'm out of here⟩

borrasca *nf* **1** : area of low pressure **2** TORMENTA : squall, storm

borrascoso, -sa *adj* : blustery, stormy

borrego, -ga *n* : lamb, sheep

borrico *→* **burro**

borrón *nm, pl* **borrones** : smudge, blot ⟨hacer borrón y cuenta nueva : to start with a clean slate⟩

borronear *vt* : to smudge, to blot

borroso, -sa *adj* : blurry, fuzzy

boscoso, -sa *adj* : wooded

bosnio, -nia *adj & n* : Bosnian

bosque *nm* : woods, forest ⟨bosque tropical : rain forest⟩

bosquecillo *nm* : grove, copse, thicket
bosquejar *vt* ESBOZAR : to outline, to sketch
bosquejo *nm* **1** TRAZADO : outline, sketch **2** : draft
bostezar {21} *vi* : to yawn
bostezo *nm* : yawn
bota *nf* **1** : boot **2** : wineskin (small) **3** botas vaqueras *Mex* : cowboy boots
botadero *nm* : garbage dump
botana *nf Mex* : snack, appetizer
botánica *nf* : botany
botánico[1], **-ca** *adj* : botanical
botánico[2], **-ca** *n* : botanist
botar *vt* **1** ARROJAR : to throw, to fling, to hurl **2** TIRAR : to throw out, to throw away **3** ECHAR : to throw (someone) out **4** : to bounce **5** : to launch (a ship) — *vi* **1** SALTAR : to jump **2** *Spain* REBOTAR : to bounce
bote *nm* **1** : small boat ⟨bote de remos : rowboat⟩ ⟨bote salvavidas : lifeboat⟩ **2** : can, jar **3** : jump, bounce ⟨dar botes : to bounce⟩ **4** *Mex fam* : jail **5** bote de basura *CA, Mex* : garbage can, trash can
botella *nf* : bottle
botica *nf* FARMACIA : drugstore, pharmacy
boticario, -ria *n* FARMACÉUTICO : pharmacist, druggist
botín *nm, pl* **botines 1** : baby's bootee : ankle boot **2** : booty, plunder
botiquín *nm, pl* **-quines 1** : medicine cabinet **2** : first aid kit
botón *nm, pl* **botones 1** : button **2** : bud **3** INSIGNIA : badge
botones *nmfs & pl* : bellhop
botulismo *nm* : botulism
boulevard [‚bule'var] → bulevar
bouquet [bu'ke] *nm, pl* **-quets 1** RAMO : bouquet **2** : bouquet, aroma
bourbon *nm* : bourbon
boutique [bu'tik] *nf* : boutique
bóveda *nf* **1** : vault, dome **2** CRIPTA : crypt
bovino, -na *adj* : bovine
box *nm, pl* **boxes 1** : pit (in auto racing) **2** *CA, Mex* : boxing
boxeador, -dora *n* : boxer
boxear *vi* : to box
boxeo *nm* : boxing
boxers *nmpl* : boxer shorts
boya *nf* : buoy
boyante *adj* : buoyant
bozal *nm* **1** : muzzle **2** : halter (for a horse)
bracear *vi* **1** : to wave one's arms **2** : to make strokes (in swimming)
bracero, -ra *n* : migrant worker, day laborer
bragas *nfpl Spain* : panties
braguero *nm* : truss (in medicine)
bragueta *nf* : fly, pants zipper
braille *adj & nm* : braille
bramante *nm* : twine, string
bramar *vi* **1** RUGIR : to roar, to bellow **2** : to howl (of the wind)
bramido *nm* : bellowing, roar
brandy *nm* : brandy
branquia *nf* AGALLA : gill

brasa *nf* ASCUA : ember ⟨a la brasa : grilled⟩
brasero *nm* : brazier
brasier *or* **brassiere** *nm Col, Mex* : brassiere, bra
brasileño, -ña *adj & n* : Brazilian
brasilero, -ra → **brasileño**
bravata *nf* **1** JACTANCIA : boast **2** AMENAZA : threat
bravío, -vía *adj* : wild, fierce
bravo, -va *adj* **1** FEROZ : ferocious, fierce **2** : angry **3** : rough (of the sea) **4** ¡bravo! : bravo!, well done!
bravucón, -cona *n, mpl* **-cones** : bully
bravuconadas *nfpl* : bravado
bravura *nf* **1** FEROCIDAD : fierceness, ferocity **2** VALENTÍA : bravery
braza *nf* **1** *or* **estilo braza** *Spain* : breaststroke ⟨nadar a braza : to swim the breaststroke⟩ **2** : fathom (unit of length)
brazada *nf* : stroke (in swimming)
brazalete *nm* **1** PULSERA : bracelet, bangle **2** BANDA : armband
brazo *nm* **1** : arm ⟨tomar del brazo : to take by the arm⟩ ⟨con los brazos cruzados : with one's arms crossed⟩ ⟨llevar en brazos : to carry in one's arms⟩ **2** : arm (of an object), limb (of a tree) **3** : branch (of a river), inlet (of the sea) **4** brazo derecho : right-hand man **5** brazos *nmpl* : hands, laborers
brea *nf* ALQUITRÁN : tar, pitch
brebaje *nm* : potion, brew
brecha *nf* **1** : gap, breach, opening **2** : breach (of defenses) **3** DIFERENCIA : gap, difference **4** TAJO : gash
brega *nf* **1** LUCHA : struggle **2** : hard work
bregar {52} *vi* **1** LUCHAR : to struggle **2** : to toil **3** ~ con : to deal with
breve *adj* **1** CORTO : brief, short **2** en ~ : shortly, in short — **brevemente** *adv*
brevedad *nf* **1** : brevity, shortness **2** con la mayor brevedad *or* a la brevedad posible : as soon as possible
brezo *nm* : heather
bribón, -bona *n, mpl* **bribones** : rascal, scamp
bricolaje *or* **bricolage** *nm* : do-it-yourself
brida *nf* : bridle
bridge ['brid͡ʒ, 'brɪʒ, 'brɪt͡ʃ] *nm* : bridge (game)
brigada *nf* **1** : brigade **2** : team, squad
brigadier *nm* : brigadier
brillante[1] *adj* **1** : bright (of color, light, etc.) **2** LUSTROSO : shiny, glossy **3** RELUCIENTE : sparkling **4** GENIAL : brilliant — **brillantemente** *adv*
brillante[2] *nm* DIAMANTE : diamond
brillantez *nf* : brilliance, brightness
brillar *vi* : to shine, to sparkle
brillo *nm* **1** : brilliance **2** : luster, shine, gloss ⟨sacarle/darle brillo a : to polish⟩ **3** ESPLENDOR : splendor
brilloso, -sa *adj* LUSTROSO : lustrous, shiny
brincar {72} *vi* **1** SALTAR : to jump (up and down) ⟨brincar de alegría : to jump for joy⟩ **2** : to hop (of a rabbit, etc.), to gambol

brinco *nm* **1** SALTO : jump, leap, skip **2 dar un brinco** : to jump

brindar *vi* : to drink a toast ⟨brindar por : to toast, to drink to⟩ — *vt* : to offer, to provide — **brindarse** *vr* **brindarse a hacer algo** : to volunteer to do something

brindis *nm* : toast, drink ⟨hacer un brindis : to drink a toast⟩

brinque, etc. → **brincar**

brío *nm* **1** : force, determination **2** : spirit, verve

brioso, -sa *adj* : spirited

brisa *nf* : breeze

británico¹, -ca *adj* : British

británico², -ca *n* **1** : British person **2 los británicos** : the British

brizna *nf* **1** : strand **2** : blade (of grass)

broca *nf* : drill bit

brocado *nm* : brocade

brocha *nf* : paintbrush

broche *nm* **1** ALFILER : brooch **2** : fastener, clasp, clip **3** *Mex* : barrette, hair clip **4** *Arg* GRAPA : staple **5 broche de oro** : finishing touch

brocheta *nf* : skewer

brócoli *nm* : broccoli

broma *nf* **1** : joke, prank ⟨le hizo una broma : she played a joke on him⟩ **2 en ~** : in jest, jokingly

bromear *vi* : to joke

bromista¹ *adj* : joking, playful

bromista² *nmf* : joker, prankster

bromo *nm* : bromine

bronca *nf* **1** *fam* : fight, quarrel, fuss ⟨armar una bronca : to kick up a fuss⟩ **2** *fam* : anger ⟨dar bronca : to piss off⟩ ⟨estar con bronca : to be pissed off⟩ ⟨tener bronca con : to have a beef with⟩ **3** *fam* : scolding ⟨echarle (la) bronca a alguien : to tell someone off⟩

bronce *nm* : bronze

bronceado¹, -da *adj* **1** : tanned, suntanned **2** : bronze

bronceado² *nm* **1** : suntan, tan **2** : bronzing

bronceador *nm* : suntan lotion

broncear *vt* : to tan — **broncearse** *vr* : to get a suntan

bronco, -ca *adj* **1** : harsh, rough **2** : untamed, wild

bronquial *adj* : bronchial

bronquio *nm* : bronchial tube

bronquitis *nf* : bronchitis

broqueta *nf* : skewer

brotar *vi* **1** : to bud, to sprout **2** : to spring up, to stream, to gush forth **3** : to appear (of a rash, etc.)

brote *nm* **1** : outbreak **2** : sprout, bud, shoot

broza *nf* **1** : brushwood **2** MALEZA : scrub, undergrowth

bruces → **de bruces**

brujería *nf* HECHICERÍA : witchcraft, sorcery

brujo¹, -ja *adj* : bewitching

brujo², -ja *n* : witch *f*, sorcerer

brújula *nf* : compass

bruma *nf* : haze, mist

brumoso, -sa *adj* : hazy, misty

bruñir {38} *vt* : to burnish, to polish (metals)

brusco, -ca *adj* **1** SÚBITO : sudden, abrupt **2** : curt, brusque — **bruscamente** *adv*

brusquedad *nf* **1** : abruptness, suddenness **2** : brusqueness

brutal *adj* **1** : brutal **2** *fam* : incredible, terrific — **brutalmente** *adv*

brutalidad *nf* : brutality

brutalizar {21} *vt* : to brutalize, to maltreat

bruto¹, -ta *adj* **1** : gross ⟨peso bruto : gross weight⟩ ⟨ingresos brutos : gross income⟩ **2** : raw, unrefined ⟨petróleo (en) bruto : crude oil⟩ ⟨diamantes en bruto : uncut diamonds⟩ **3** ESTÚPIDO : brutish, stupid

bruto², -ta *n* **1** : brute **2** : dunce, blockhead

bubónico, -ca *adj* : bubonic ⟨peste bubónica : bubonic plague⟩

bucal *adj* : oral

bucanero *nm* : buccaneer

buceador, -dora *n* : diver, scuba diver

bucear *vi* **1** : to dive, to swim underwater **2** : to explore, to delve

buceo *nm* : diving, scuba diving

buche *nm* **1** : crop (of a bird) **2** *fam* : belly **3 hacer buches** : to rinse one's mouth

bucle *nm* **1** : curl, ringlet **2** : loop

bucólico, -ca *adj* : bucolic

budín *nm, pl* **budines** : pudding

budismo *nm* : Buddhism

budista *adj & nmf* : Buddhist

buen *adj* → **bueno¹**

buenamente *adv* **1** : easily **2** : willingly

buenaventura *nf* **1** : good luck **2** : fortune, future ⟨le dijo la buenaventura : she told his fortune⟩

buenazo, -za *n fam* BONACHÓN : kindhearted person

bueno¹, -na *adj* (**buen** *before masculine singular nouns*) **1** : good ⟨una buena idea : a good idea⟩ ⟨en buenas condiciones : in good condition⟩ **2** : good, kind ⟨un buen hombre : a good man⟩ ⟨ser bueno con alguien : to be good to someone⟩ **3** : good, proper ⟨buenos modales : good manners⟩ ⟨es bueno ayudar a la gente : it's good to help people⟩ **4** : good, pleasant ⟨buen tiempo : good weather⟩ **5** : good, tasty ⟨esta sopa está buena : this soup is good⟩ **6** FRESCO : fresh **7** : good, healthy ⟨una buena alimentación : a good diet⟩ ⟨es bueno para el corazón : it's good for your heart⟩ **8** *fam* : sexy, hot *fam* ⟨está bueno : he's a hunk⟩ **9** : good, competent ⟨un buen abogado : a good lawyer⟩ ⟨hiciste un buen trabajo : you did a good job⟩ ⟨ser bueno para/en algo : to be good at something⟩ **10** : considerable, goodly ⟨una buena cantidad : a goodly amount, a lot⟩ **11 buenos días** : hello, good day **12 buenas tardes** : good afternoon **13 buenas noches** : good evening, good night **14 de buenas a primeras** : suddenly **15 ¡qué bueno!** : great! **16 un buen día** : one day

bueno² *interj* **1** : OK!, all right! **2** *Mex* : hello! (on the telephone)

bueno³, -na *n* **1** : good guy (in a story, etc.) **2 el bueno de, la buena de** : good old ⟨el bueno de Carlos : good old Carlos⟩

buey *nm* : ox, steer

búfalo *nm* **1** : buffalo **2 búfalo de agua** : water buffalo

bufanda *nf* : scarf

bufar *vi* : to snort

bufet *or* **bufé** *nm* : buffet (meal)

bufete *nm* : law firm, law office

bufido *nm* : snort

bufo, -fa *adj* : comic

bufón, -fona *n, mpl* **bufones 1** : jester **2** : clown, buffoon

bufonada *nf* : antic ⟨hacer bufonadas : to clown around⟩

buhardilla *nf* **1** ÁTICO, DESVÁN : attic **2** : dormer window

búho *nm* **1** : owl **2** *fam* : hermit, recluse

buhonero, -ra *n* MERCACHIFLE : peddler

buitre *nm* : vulture

bujía *nf* : spark plug

bula *nf* : papal bull

bulbo *nm* : bulb

bulboso, -sa *adj* : bulbous

bulevar *nm* : boulevard

búlgaro, -ra *adj & n* : Bulgarian

bulla *nf* BARULLO : racket, rowdiness

bulldog [bul'dog] *nm, pl* **bulldogs** : bulldog

bulldozer [bul'doser] *nm, pl* **-zers** : bulldozer

bullicio *nm* **1** : ruckus, uproar **2** : hustle and bustle

bullicioso, -sa *adj* : noisy, busy, turbulent

bullir {38} *vi* **1** HERVIR : to boil **2** MOVERSE : to stir, to bustle about

bulto *nm* **1** : package, bundle **2** : piece of luggage, bag **3** : size, bulk, volume **4** : form, shape ⟨pude distinguir unos bultos : I could make out some shapes⟩ **5** : lump (on the body), swelling, bulge

bumerán *nm, pl* **-ranes** : boomerang

búnker *nm, pl* **búnkers** : bunker

búnquer → **búnker**

buñuelo *nm* : doughnut, fried pastry

buque *nm* BARCO : ship, vessel ⟨buque de guerra : warship⟩

burbuja *nf* : bubble

burbujeante *adj* : bubbly

burbujear *vi* **1** : to bubble **2** : to fizz

burdel *nm* : brothel

burdo, -da *adj* **1** : coarse, rough **2** : crude, clumsy ⟨una burda mentira : an obvious lie⟩ — **burdamente** *adv*

burgués, -guesa *adj & n, mpl* **burgueses** : bourgeois

burguesía *nf* : bourgeoisie, middle class

burla *nf* **1** : mockery, ridicule **2** : joke, trick **3 hacer burla de** : to make fun of, to mock

burlar *vt* **1** ENGAÑAR : to trick, to deceive **2** ELUDIR : to evade — **burlarse** *vr* ∼ **de** : to make fun of

burlesco, -ca *adj* : burlesque, comic

burlón¹, -lona *adj, mpl* **burlones** : joking, mocking

burlón², -lona *n, mpl* **burlones** : joker

burocracia *nf* : bureaucracy

burócrata *nmf* : bureaucrat

burocrático, -ca *adj* : bureaucratic

burrada *nf* *fam* : stupid act or remark, nonsense

burrito *nm* : burrito

burro¹, -rra *adj fam* : dumb, stupid

burro², -rra *n* **1** ASNO : donkey, ass **2** *fam* : idiot, dunce

burro³ *nm* **1** : sawhorse **2** *Mex* : ironing board **3** *Mex* : stepladder

bursátil *adj* : stock-market

bus *nm* : bus

busca¹ *nf* : search ⟨en busca de : in search of⟩

busca² *nm* *Spain* → **buscapersonas**

buscador¹ *nm* : search engine

buscador², -dora *n* : hunter (for treasure, etc.), prospector

buscapersonas *nms & pl* : beeper, pager

buscapleitos *nmfs & pl* : troublemaker

buscar {72} *vt* **1** : to look for (a person, an object, etc.), to seek (revenge, etc.) **2** : to fetch, to get ⟨ve a buscar ayuda : go (and) get help⟩ **3** : to look for (trouble, etc.) **4** : to look up (in a book, etc.), to search (on the Web) **5 ir a buscar** RECOGER : to pick up (at a place) — *vi* : to look, to search ⟨buscó en los bolsillos : he searched through his pockets⟩ — **buscarse** *vr* : to ask for, to look for ⟨te la estás buscando : you're asking for it/trouble⟩

buscavidas *nmf & pl* : go-getter

busero, -ra *n* CA : bus driver

buseta *nf* Col, CoRi, Ecua, Ven : minibus

busque, etc. → **buscar**

búsqueda *nf* : search ⟨en búsqueda de : in search of⟩ ⟨la búsqueda de la verdad : the search for the truth⟩

busto *nm* : bust

butaca *nf* **1** SILLÓN : armchair, easy chair **2** : seat (in a theatre) **3** *Mex* : pupil's desk

buzo¹, -za *adj Mex fam* : smart, astute ⟨¡ponte buzo! : get with it!, get on the ball!⟩

buzo² *nm* **1** : diver **2** *Arg, Col* : sweatshirt, hoodie **3** *Uru* : sweater **4** *Chile, Peru* : tracksuit

buzón *nm, pl* **buzones** : mailbox ⟨buzón de voz : voice mail⟩

byte *nm* : byte

C

c *nf* : third letter of the Spanish alphabet
cabal *adj* **1** : exact, correct **2** : complete **3** : upright, honest
cabales *nmpl* **no estar en sus cabales** : not to be in one's right mind
cabalgar {52} *vi* : to ride (on horseback)
cabalgata *nf* : cavalcade, procession
cabalidad *nf* **a ~** : thoroughly, conscientiously
caballa *nf* : mackerel
caballar *adj* EQUINO : horse, equine
caballeresco, -ca *adj* : gallant, chivalrous
caballería *nf* **1** : cavalry **2** : horse, mount **3** : knighthood, chivalry
caballeriza *nf* : stable
caballero¹ → **caballeroso**
caballero² *nm* **1** : gentleman **2** : knight ⟨caballero andante : knight errant⟩
caballerosidad *nf* : chivalry, gallantry
caballeroso, -sa *adj* : gentlemanly, chivalrous
caballete *nm* **1** : ridge **2** : easel **3** : trestle (for a table, etc.) **4** : bridge (of the nose) **5** : sawhorse
caballista *nmf* : horseman *m*, horsewoman *f*
caballito *nm* **1** : rocking horse **2 caballito de mar** : sea horse **3 caballitos** *nmpl* : merry-go-round
caballo *nm* **1** : horse **2** : knight (in chess) **3 caballo de fuerza** *or* **caballo de vapor** : horsepower
cabalmente *adv* : fully, exactly
cabaña *nf* : cabin, hut
cabaret [kaba're] *nm, pl* **-rets** : nightclub, cabaret
cabecear *vt* : to head (in soccer) — *vi* **1** : to nod one's head **2** : to lurch, to pitch
cabeceo *nm* : pitch (of a boat, etc.)
cabecera *nf* **1** : headboard **2** : head ⟨cabecera de la mesa : head of the table⟩ **3** : heading, headline **4** : headwaters *pl* **5 médico de cabecera** : family doctor **6 cabecera municipal** *CA, Mex* : downtown area
cabecilla *nmf* : ringleader
cabellera *nf* : head of hair, mane
cabello *nm* : hair
cabelludo, -da *adj* **1** : hairy **2 cuero cabelludo** : scalp
caber {12} *vi* **1** : to fit, to go ⟨¿cabremos todos? : will we all fit?⟩ **2** : to be possible ⟨no cabe duda alguna : there's no doubt about it⟩ ⟨cabe la posibilidad que llegue mañana : it's possible he'll come tomorrow⟩
cabestrillo *nm* : sling ⟨llevo el brazo en cabestrillo : my arm is in a sling⟩
cabestro *nm* : halter (for an animal)
cabeza *nf* **1** : head ⟨de pies a cabeza : from head to toe⟩ ⟨negar/asentir con la cabeza : to shake/nod one's head⟩ ⟨levantar/bajar/volver la cabeza : to raise/lower/turn one's head⟩ **2** : head, mind ⟨pasar por la cabeza : to cross one's mind⟩ **3** PELO : hair **4** : head, leader **5** : head, front, top **6** : head ⟨por cabeza : each, a head⟩ ⟨500 cabezas de ganado : 500 head of cattle⟩ **7** : head (of cabbage, etc.) **8** : head (measurement) **9 de ~** : headfirst **10 dolor de cabeza** : headache
cabezada *nf* **1** : head butt **2** : nod ⟨echar una cabezada : to take a nap, to doze off⟩ **3** → **cabeceo**
cabezal *nm* : bolster
cabeza rapada *nmf* : skinhead
cabezazo *nm* : head butt
cabezón, -zona *adj, mpl* **-zones** *fam* **1** : having a big head **2** : pigheaded, stubborn
cabida *nf* **1** : room, space, capacity **2 dar cabida a** : to accommodate, to hold
cabildear *vi* : to lobby
cabildeo *nm* : lobbying
cabildero, -ra *n* : lobbyist
cabildo *nm* AYUNTAMIENTO **1** : town or city hall **2** : town or city council
cabina *nf* **1** : cabin **2** : booth **3** : cab (of a truck), cockpit (of an airplane)
cabizbajo, -ja *adj* : dejected, downcast
cable *nm* **1** : cable ⟨cables de arranque, cables pasacorriente *Mex* : jumper cables⟩ **2** : cable television **3 cable tensor** : guy, guy line
cableado *nm* : wiring
cabo *nm* **1** : end ⟨al cabo de dos semanas : at the end of two weeks⟩ **2** : stub, end piece **3** : corporal **4** : cape, headland ⟨el Cabo Cañaveral : Cape Canaveral⟩ **5 al fin y al cabo** : after all, in the end **6 llevar a cabo** : to carry out, to do
cabrá, etc. → **caber**
cabra *nf* : goat
cabrío, -ría *adj* : goat
cabriola *nf* **1** : skip, jump **2 hacer cabriolas** : to prance
cabriolar *vi* : to prance
cabrito *nm* : kid, baby goat
cabro, cabra *n* : kid, youth
cabrón, cabrona *n, mpl* **cabrones** *Spain, Mex offensive* : bastard *m offensive*, bitch *f offensive*
cabús *nm, pl* **cabuses** *Mex* : caboose
caca *nf fam* : poop ⟨hacer caca : to poop⟩ ⟨hacerse caca : to poop one's pants/diaper (etc.)⟩
cacahuate *nm Mex* : peanut
cacahuete *nm Spain* : peanut
cacalote *nm Mex* : crow
cacao *nm* **1** : cacao, cocoa bean **2** : hot chocolate, cocoa (drink)
cacarear *vi* : to crow, to cackle, to cluck — *vt fam* : to boast about, to crow about
cacareo *nm* **1** : clucking (of a hen), crowing (of a rooster) **2** : boasting
cacatúa *nf* : cockatoo
cace, etc. → **cazar**
cacería *nf* **1** CAZA : hunt, hunting **2** : hunting party
cacerola *nf* : pan, saucepan
cacha *nf* : butt (of a gun)
cachalote *nm* : sperm whale
cachar *vt fam* : to catch

cacharro *nm* **1** *fam* : thing, piece of junk **2** *fam* : jalopy **3 cacharros** *nmpl* : pots and pans
cache *nm* : cache, cache memory
caché *nm* : cachet
cachear *vt* : to search, to frisk
cachemir *nm* : cashmere
cachemira *nf* → **cachemir**
cacheo *nm* : frisking, body search
cachetada *nf* BOFETADA : slap on the face
cachete *nm* : cheek
cachetear *vt* BOFETEAR : to slap
cachiporra *nf* : bludgeon, club, blackjack
cachirul *nm* *Mex fam* : cheating ⟨hacer cachirul : to cheat⟩
cachivache *nm fam* : thing, piece of junk ⟨cachivaches : stuff, junk⟩
cacho *nm fam* : piece, bit
cachondo, -da *adj* *Mex & Spain fam* : horny, lustful
cachorro, -rra *n* **1** : cub **2** PERRITO : puppy
cachucha *nf* *Mex* : cap, baseball cap
cacique *nm* **1** : chief (of a tribe) **2** : boss (in politics)
caco *nm fam* : thief
cacofonía *nf* : cacophony
cacto *nm* : cactus
cactus → **cacto**
cada *adj* **1** : each, every ⟨cuestan diez pesos cada una : they cost ten pesos each⟩ ⟨cada vez : each/every time⟩ **2** : every ⟨cada dos semanas : every two weeks, every other week⟩ ⟨cada cinco metros : every five meters⟩ **3** : every ⟨cuatro de cada cinco : four out of (every) five⟩ **4** : such, some ⟨sales con cada historia : you come up with such crazy stories⟩ **5 cada vez más** : more and more, increasingly **6 cada vez menos** : less and less
cadalso *nm* : scaffold, gallows
cadáver *nm* : corpse, cadaver
cadavérico, -ca *adj* **1** : cadaverous **2** : cadaveric (in medicine)
caddie *or* **caddy** *nmf, pl* **caddies** : caddy
cadena *nf* **1** : chain **2** : network, channel **3 cadena de montaje** : assembly line **4 cadena perpetua** : life sentence
cadencia *nf* : cadence, rhythm
cadencioso, -sa *adj* : rhythmic, rhythmical
cadera *nf* : hip
cadete *nmf* : cadet
cadmio *nm* : cadmium
caducar {72} *vi* : to expire
caducidad *nf* : expiration
caduco, -ca *adj* **1** : outdated, obsolete **2** : deciduous
caer {13} *vi* **1** : to fall ⟨cayó al suelo : he fell on the floor/ground⟩ ⟨lo dejó caer : she dropped it⟩ **2** : to drop away, to slope **3** : to fall (of night) **4** : to collapse, to fall **5** : to hang (down) **6** : to realize, to understand ⟨caer (en) que . . . : to realize that . . .⟩ **7 ~ en** : to fall into (a trap, etc.) ⟨caer en el error de : to make the mistake of⟩ ⟨caer en manos de : to fall into the hands of⟩ ⟨caer en la tentación : to give in to

temptation⟩ **8 caer en desgracia** : to fall out of favor **9 caer enfermo** : to fall ill **10 caerle bien/mal a alguien** *fam* : to sit well/poorly with someone ⟨me caes bien : I like you⟩ — **caerse** *vr* : to fall (down) ⟨se cayó de rodillas : she fell to her knees⟩
café[1] *adj* : brown ⟨ojos cafés : brown eyes⟩
café[2] *nm* **1** : coffee **2** : café
cafeína *nf* : caffeine
cafetal *nm* : coffee plantation
cafetalero[1]**, -ra** *adj* : coffee ⟨cosecha cafetalera : coffee harvest⟩
cafetalero[2]**, -ra** *n* : coffee grower
cafetera *nf* : coffeepot, coffeemaker
cafetería *nf* **1** : coffee shop, café **2** : lunchroom, cafeteria
cafetero[1]**, -ra** *adj* : coffee-producing
cafetero[2]**, -ra** *n* : coffee grower
cafeticultura *Mex* → **caficultura**
caficultor, -tora *n* : coffee grower
caficultura *nf* : coffee industry
caguama *nf* **1** : large Caribbean turtle **2** *Mex* : large bottle of beer
caída *nf* **1** BAJA, DESCENSO : fall, drop **2** : collapse, downfall
caído, -da *adj* **1** : fallen **2** : drooping, sagging
caiga, etc. → **caer**
caimán *nm, pl* **caimanes** : alligator
caimito *nm* : star apple
caja *nf* **1** : box, case **2** *or* **caja registradora** : cash register, checkout **3** : bed (of a truck) **4** *fam* : coffin **5 caja de cambios** : gearbox **6 caja fuerte** *or* **caja de caudales** : safe **7 caja de seguridad** : safe-deposit box **8 caja negra** : black box **9 caja torácica** : rib cage
cajero, -ra *n* **1** : cashier **2** : teller **3 cajero automático** : automated teller machine, ATM
cajeta *nf* *Mex* : sweet caramel-flavored spread
cajetilla *nf* : pack (of cigarettes)
cajón *nm, pl* **cajones** **1** : drawer, till **2** : crate, case **3** ATAÚD : coffin, casket **4 cajón de arena** : sandbox **5 cajón de estacionamiento** *Mex* : parking space
cajuela *nf* *Mex* : trunk (of a car)
cal *nf* : lime
cala *nf* : cove, inlet
calabacín *nm, pl* **-cines** : zucchini
calabacita *nf* *Mex* : zucchini
calabaza *nf* **1** : pumpkin, squash **2** : gourd **3 dar calabazas a** : to give the brush-off to, to jilt
calabozo *nm* **1** : prison **2** : jail cell
calado[1]**, -da** *adj* : drenched
calado[2] *nm* : draft (of a ship)
calamar *nm* **1** : squid **2 calamares** *nmpl* : calamari
calambre *nm* **1** ESPASMO : cramp **2** : electric shock, jolt
calamidad *nf* DESASTRE : calamity, disaster
calamina *nf* : calamine
calamitoso, -sa *adj* : calamitous, disastrous
calaña *nf* : ilk, kind, sort ⟨una persona de mala calaña : a bad sort⟩

calar *vt* **1** : to soak through **2** : to pierce, to penetrate — *vi* : to catch on — **calarse** *vr* : to get drenched
calavera[1] *nf* **1** : skull **2** *Mex* : taillight
calavera[2] *nm* : rake, rogue
calcar {72} *vt* **1** : to trace **2** : to copy, to imitate
calce, etc. → **calzar**
calceta *nf* : knee-high stocking
calcetería *nf* : hosiery
calcetín *nm, pl* **-tines** : sock
calcinar *vt* : to char, to burn
calcio *nm* : calcium
calco *nm* **1** : transfer, tracing **2** : copy, image
calcomanía *nf* : decal, transfer
calculador, -dora *adj* : calculating
calculadora *nf* : calculator
calcular *vt* **1** : to calculate, to estimate **2** : to plan, to scheme
cálculo *nm* **1** : calculation, estimation **2** : calculus **3** : plan, scheme **4 cálculo biliar** : gallstone **5 hoja de cálculo** : spreadsheet
caldear *vt* : to heat, to warm — **caldearse** *vr* **1** : to heat up **2** : to become heated, to get tense
caldera *nf* **1** : cauldron **2** : boiler
caldero *nm* : cauldron
caldo *nm* **1** : broth, stock **2 caldo de cultivo** : culture medium, breeding ground
caldoso, -sa *adj* : watery
calefacción *nf, pl* **-ciones** : heating, heat
calefactor *nm* : heater
caleidoscopio → **calidoscopio**
calendario *nm* **1** : calendar **2** : timetable, schedule
caléndula *nf* : marigold
calentador *nm* : heater
calentamiento *nm* **1** : heating, warming ⟨calentamiento global : global warming⟩ **2** : warm-up (in sports)
calentar {55} *vt* **1** : to heat, to warm **2** *fam* : to annoy, to anger **3** *fam* : to excite, to turn on — **calentarse** *vr* **1** : to get warm, to heat up **2** : to warm up (in sports) **3** *fam* : to become sexually aroused **4** *fam* : to get mad
calentura *nf* **1** *FIEBRE* : temperature, fever **2** : cold sore
calesa *nf* : buggy
calibrador *nm* : gauge, calipers *pl*
calibrar *vt* : to calibrate — **calibración** *nf*
calibre *nm* **1** : caliber, gauge **2** : importance, excellence **3** : kind, sort ⟨un problema de grueso calibre : a serious problem⟩
calicó *nm* : calico (cloth)
calidad *nf* **1** : quality, grade **2** : position, status **3 en calidad de** : as, in the capacity of
cálido, -da *adj* **1** : hot ⟨un clima cálido : a hot climate⟩ **2** : warm ⟨una cálida bienvenida : a warm welcome⟩
calidoscopio *nm* : kaleidoscope
caliente *adj* **1** : hot, warm ⟨mantenerse caliente : to stay warm⟩ **2** : heated, fiery ⟨una disputa caliente : a heated argument⟩ **3** *fam* : sexually excited, horny

califa *nm* : caliph
calificación *nf, pl* **-ciones 1** *NOTA* : grade (for a course) **2** : rating, score **3** *CLASIFICACIÓN* : qualification, qualifying ⟨ronda de calificación : qualifying round⟩
calificar {72} *vt* **1** : to grade **2** : to describe, to rate ⟨la calificaron de buena alumna : they described her as a good student⟩ **3** : to qualify, to modify (in grammar)
calificativo[1], **-va** *adj* : qualifying
calificativo[2] *nm* : qualifier, epithet
caligrafía *nf* **1** *LETRA* : handwriting **2** : calligraphy
calipso *nm* : calypso
calistenia *nf* : calisthenics
cáliz *nm, pl* **cálices 1** : chalice, goblet **2** : calyx
caliza *nf* : limestone
calizo, -za *adj* : chalky, limy
callado, -da *adj* : quiet, silent — **calladamente** *adv*
callampa *nf Chile* **1** : mushroom **2 callampas** *pl* : slums, shantytown
callar *vi* : to keep quiet, to be silent — *vt* **1** : to silence, to hush ⟨calla a los niños! : keep the children quiet!⟩ **2** : to keep secret — **callarse** *vr* : to remain silent ⟨¡cállate! : be quiet!, shut up!⟩
calle *nf* **1** : street, road ⟨calle de sentido único : one-way street⟩ ⟨calle sin salida : dead-end street⟩ ⟨salir a la calle : to go out/outside⟩ ⟨salir a la(s) calle(s) : to take to the streets⟩ ⟨la echó a la calle : he kicked her out⟩
callejear *vi* : to wander about the streets, to hang out
callejero, -ra *adj* : street ⟨perro callejero : stray dog⟩
callejón *nm, pl* **-jones 1** : alley **2 callejón sin salida** : dead-end street
callejuela *nf* **1** : alley **2** : narrow street, side street
callo *nm* **1** : callus, corn **2 callos** *nmpl* : tripe
calloso, -sa *adj* : callous
calma *nf* : calm, quiet
calmante[1] *adj* : calming, soothing
calmante[2] *nm* : tranquilizer, sedative
calmar *vt* : to calm, to soothe — **calmarse** *vr* **1** : to calm down **2** : to ease (of pain, etc.)
calmo, -ma *adj* : calm, tranquil
calmoso, -sa *adj* **1** : calm, quiet **2** *LENTO* : slow
caló *nm* : Gypsy slang
calor *nm* **1** : heat ⟨hace calor : it's hot outside⟩ ⟨tener calor : to feel hot⟩ ⟨entrar en calor : to warm up, to get warm⟩ **2** : warmth, affection **3** : ardor, passion
caloría *nf* : calorie
calórico, -ca *adj* : caloric
calorífico, -ca *adj* : caloric
calque, etc. → **calcar**
calumnia *nf* : slander, libel — **calumnioso, -sa** *adj*
calumniar *vt* : to slander, to libel
caluroso, -sa *adj* **1** : hot **2** : warm, enthusiastic — **calurosamente** *adv*

calva *nf* : bald spot, bald head
calvario *nm* : ordeal, misery ⟨vivir un calvario : to go through hell⟩
calvicie *nf* : baldness
calvo¹, -va *adj* : bald
calvo², -va *n* : bald person
calza *nf* : block, wedge
calzada *nf* : roadway, avenue
calzado *nm* : footwear
calzador *nm* : shoehorn
calzar {21} *vt* **1** : to wear (shoes) ⟨¿de cuál calza? : what is your shoe size?⟩ ⟨calzar tenis : to wear sneakers⟩ **2** : to provide with shoes
calzoncillos *nmpl* : underpants, briefs
calzones *nmpl* : underpants, panties
cama *nf* **1** : bed **2 cama elástica** : trampoline
camada *nf* : litter, brood
camafeo *nm* : cameo
camaleón *nm, pl* **-leones** : chameleon
cámara *nf* **1** : camera **2** : chamber, room **3** : house (in government) **4** : inner tube
camarada *nmf* **1** : comrade, companion **2** : colleague
camaradería *nf* : camaraderie
camarero, -ra *n* **1** MESERO : waiter, waitress *f* **2** BARMAN : bartender **3** : bellhop *m*, chambermaid *f* (in a hotel) **4** : steward *m*, stewardess *f* (on a ship, etc.)
camarilla *nf* : political clique
camarín *nm, pl* **-rines** **1** *Chile, Peru, Uru* : locker room **2** *Arg, Uru* : dressing room
camarógrafo, -fa *n* : cameraman *m*, camerawoman *f*
camarón *nm, pl* **-rones** **1** : shrimp **2** : prawn
camarote *nm* : cabin, stateroom
camastro *nm* : small hard bed, pallet
cambalache *nm fam* : swap
cambiable *adj* : changeable
cambiante *adj* **1** : changing **2** VARIABLE : changeable, variable
cambiar *vt* **1** : to change ⟨le cambió la vida : it changed her life⟩ ⟨cambiaron el menú : they changed the menu⟩ ⟨cambiar algo de lugar : to move something⟩ **2** : to exchange, to trade ⟨lo cambió por otro : she exchanged it for another⟩ **3** : to change (money) ⟨cambiar pesos a euros : to change pesos into euros⟩ **4** : to change, to replace ⟨cambió la llanta/contraseña : he changed the tire/password⟩ ⟨le cambié el pañal : I changed her diaper⟩ — *vi* **1** : to change ⟨el tiempo cambió : the weather changed⟩ ⟨cambiar de color : to change color⟩ ⟨cambiar de tema : to change the subject⟩ ⟨cambiar de opinión/idea : to change one's mind⟩ **2 cambiar de velocidad** : to shift gears — **cambiarse** *vr* **1** : to change ⟨se ha cambiado mucho : she's changed a lot⟩ **2** *or* **cambiarse de ropa** : to change (clothes) **3** MUDARSE : to move (to a new address)
cambio *nm* **1** : change, alteration ⟨cambio climático : climate change⟩ ⟨cambio de horario : schedule change⟩ ⟨cambio de domicilio : change of address⟩ **2** : exchange (of goods, etc.) **3** : change

(money) **4** : currency exchange **5** : gear ⟨palanca de cambio : gearshift⟩ ⟨caja de cambios : gearbox⟩ **6 a cambio (de)** : in exchange (for) **7 en ～** : instead **8 en ～** : however, on the other hand
cambista *nmf* : exchange broker, money changer
camboyano, -na *adj & n* : Cambodian
cambur *nm Ven* : banana
camello *nm* **1** : camel **2** *fam* TRAFICANTE : drug dealer, pusher
camellón *nm, pl* **-llones** *Mex* : traffic island
camerino *nm* : dressing room
camilla *nf* : stretcher
camillero, -ra *n* : orderly (in a hospital)
caminante *nmf* : wayfarer, walker
caminar *vi* **1** ANDAR : to walk ⟨prefiero ir caminando : I prefer to walk⟩ **2** : to move, to progress **3** FUNCIONAR : to work, to run — *vt* : to walk, to cover (a distance)
caminata *nf* : hike, long walk
camino *nm* **1** : path, road **2** : journey ⟨ponerse en camino : to set off⟩ **3** : way ⟨a medio camino : halfway there⟩
camión *nm, pl* **camiones** **1** : truck **2** *Mex* : bus
camionero, -ra *n* **1** : truck driver **2** *Mex* : bus driver
camioneta *nf* : light truck, van
camisa *nf* **1** : shirt **2 camisa de fuerza** : straitjacket
camiseta *nf* **1** : T-shirt **2** : undershirt
camisón *nm, pl* **-sones** : nightshirt, nightgown
camomila *nf* MANZANILLA : chamomile
camorra *nf fam* : fight, trouble ⟨buscar camorra : to pick a fight⟩
camote *nm* **1** : root vegetable similar to the sweet potato **2 hacerse camote** *Mex fam* : to get mixed up
campal *adj* : pitched, fierce (of a battle)
campamento *nm* : camp
campana *nf* : bell
campanada *nf* : stroke (of a clock), peal (of bells)
campanario *nm* : bell tower, belfry
campanazo *nm* **1** → **campanada** **2 campanazo inicial** : starting bell
campanilla *nf* **1** : bluebell **2** : uvula **3 campanilla blanca** : snowdrop
campante *adj* : nonchalant, smug ⟨seguir tan campante : to go on as if nothing had happened⟩
campaña *nf* **1** CAMPO : countryside, country **2** : campaign **3 tienda de campaña** : tent
campañol *nm* : vole
campechana *nf Mex* : puff pastry
campechano, -na *adj* : friendly and down-to-earth
campeón, -peona *n, mpl* **-peones** : champion
campeonato *nm* : championship
cámper *nm* : camper (vehicle)
campera *nf* CHAQUETA : jacket
campero, -ra *adj* : country, rural
campesino, -na *n* : peasant, farm laborer
campestre *adj* : rural, rustic

camping *nm* **1** : camping **2** : campsite
campiña *nf* CAMPO : countryside, country
campista *nmf* : camper
campo *nm* **1** CAMPAÑA : countryside, country **2** : field (of crops, ice, etc.) **3** : field (in sports), course (in golf) **4** : field, area ⟨su campo de responsabilidad : her area of responsibility⟩ ⟨el campo tecnológico : the field of technology⟩ **5** : camp ⟨campo de refugiados : refugee camp⟩ ⟨campo de concentración : concentration camp⟩ **6 campo de aviación** : airfield **7 campo de batalla** : battlefield **8 campo magnético** : magnetic field **9 estudio de campo** : field study
camposanto *nm* : graveyard, cemetery
campus *nms & pl* : campus
camuflaje *nm* : camouflage
camuflajear *vt* : to camouflage
camuflar → camuflajear
can *nm* : hound, dog
cana *nf* **1** : gray hair ⟨le salen canas : he's going gray⟩ **2 echar una cana al aire** : to let one's hair down
canadiense *adj & nmf* : Canadian
canal¹ *nm* **1** : canal **2** : channel
canal² *nmf* : gutter, groove
canalé *nm* : rib, ribbing (in fabric)
canaleta *nf* : gutter
canalete *nm* : paddle
canalizar {21} *vt* : to channel
canalla¹ *adj fam* : low, rotten
canalla² *nmf fam* : bastard, swine
canapé *nm* **1** : canapé **2** SOFÁ : couch, sofa
canario¹, -ria *adj* : of or from the Canary Islands
canario², -ria *n* : Canary Islander
canario³ *nm* : canary
canasta *nf* : basket
canasto *nm* : (large) basket
cancel *nm* **1** : sliding door **2** : partition
cancelación *nf, pl* **-ciones** **1** : cancellation **2** : payment in full
cancelar *vt* **1** : to cancel **2** : to pay off, to settle
cáncer *nm* : cancer
Cáncer¹ *nm* : Cancer (sign or constellation)
Cáncer² *nmf* : Cancer (person)
cancerígeno¹, -na *adj* : carcinogenic
cancerígeno² *nm* : carcinogen
canceroso, -sa *adj* : cancerous
cancha *nf* : court, field (for sports) ⟨cancha de golf : golf course⟩
canciller *nm* : chancellor
cancillería *nf* : ministry of foreign affairs
canción *nf, pl* **canciones** **1** : song **2 canción de cuna** : lullaby
cancionero¹ *nm* : songbook
cancionero², -ra *n Mex* : singer
candado *nm* : padlock
candela *nf* **1** : flame, fire **2** : candle
candelabro *nm* : candelabra
candelero *nm* **1** : candlestick **2 estar en el candelero** : to be in the spotlight
candente *adj* : red-hot, white-hot
candidato, -ta *n* : candidate, applicant
candidatura *nf* : candidacy

candidez *nf* **1** : simplicity **2** INGENUIDAD : naïveté, ingenuousness
cándido, -da *adj* **1** : simple, unassuming **2** INGENUO : naive, ingenuous
candil *nm* : oil lamp
candilejas *nfpl* : footlights
candor *nm* : naïveté, innocence
caneca *nf Col* **1** : garbage can **2** PAPELERA : wastebasket **3** BIDÓN : drum
canela *nf* : cinnamon
canelones *nmpl* : cannelloni
cangrejo *nm* JAIBA : crab
canguro¹ *nm* : kangaroo
canguro² *nmf Spain fam* : baby-sitter
caníbal¹ *adj* : cannibalistic
caníbal² *nmf* ANTROPÓFAGO : cannibal
canibalismo *nm* ANTROPOFAGIA : cannibalism
canica *nf* : marble ⟨jugar a las canicas : to play marbles⟩
caniche *nm* : poodle
canijo, -ja *adj* **1** *fam* : puny, weak **2** *Mex fam* DIFÍCIL : tough, hard
canilla *nf* **1** : shin **2** *Arg, Uru* : faucet
canillita *nmf Arg* : newspaper vendor
canino¹, -na *adj* : canine
canino², -na *nm* **1** COLMILLO : canine (tooth) **2** : dog, canine
canje *nm* : exchange, trade
canjeable *adj* : exchangeable
canjear *vt* : to exchange, to trade
cannabis *nm* : cannabis
cano, -na *adj* : gray ⟨un hombre de pelo cano : a gray-haired man⟩
canoa *nf* : canoe
canon *nm, pl* **cánones** : canon
canónico, -ca *adj* : canonical
canónigo *nm* : canon (of a church)
canonizar {21} *vt* : to canonize — **canonización** *nf*
canoso, -sa → cano
cansado, -da *adj* **1** : tired ⟨estar cansado : to be tired⟩ **2** : tiresome ⟨ser cansado : to be tiring⟩
cansancio *nm* : tiredness
cansar *vt* : to tire — *vi* : to be tiresome — **cansarse** *vr* **1** : to tire oneself out **2** : to get bored
cansino, -na *adj* : slow, weary, lethargic
cantaleta *nf fam* : nagging ⟨la misma cantaleta : the same old story⟩
cantalupo *nm* : cantaloupe
cantante¹ *adj* : singing
cantante² *nmf* : singer
cantar¹ *vi* **1** : to sing **2** CACAREAR : to crow **3** CHIRRIAR : to chirp (of insects) — *vt* **1** : to sing **2** : to call out, to recite ⟨cantar victoria : to claim victory⟩
cantar² *nm* : song, ballad
cántaro *nm* **1** : pitcher, jug **2 llover a cántaros** *fam* : to rain cats and dogs
cantata *nf* : cantata
cantautor, -tora *n* : singer-songwriter
cantera *nf* : quarry
cantero *nm* **1** MAMPOSTERO : mason, stonemason **2** ARRIATE : bed (for plants)
cántico *nm* : chant
cantidad¹ *adv fam* : a lot ⟨me gustó cantidad : I liked it a lot⟩ ⟨ese carro me costó cantidad : that car cost me plenty⟩

cantidad² *nf* **1** : quantity **2** : sum, amount (of money) **3** *fam* : a lot, a great many ⟨había cantidad de gente : there were tons of people⟩

cantillos *nmpl* : jacks *pl*

cantimplora *nf* : canteen, water bottle

cantina *nf* **1** : tavern, bar **2** : canteen, mess, dining quarters *pl*

cantinero, -ra *n* : bartender

canto *nm* **1** : singing **2** : chant ⟨canto gregoriano : Gregorian chant⟩ **3** : song (of a bird) **4** : edge, end ⟨de canto : on end, sideways⟩ **5 canto rodado** : boulder

cantón *nm, pl* **cantones 1** : canton **2** *Mex fam* : place, home

cantonés¹, -nesa *adj & n, mpl* **-neses** : Cantonese

cantonés² *nm, pl* **-neses** : Cantonese (language)

cantor¹, -tora *adj* **1** : singing **2 pájaro cantor** : songbird

cantor², -tora *n* **1** : singer **2** : cantor

canturrear *v* : to sing softly

caña *nf* **1** : cane ⟨caña de azúcar : sugarcane⟩ **2** : reed **3 caña de pescar** : fishing rod **4 caña del timón** : tiller (of a boat)

cañada *nf* : ravine, gully

cáñamo *nm* : hemp

cañaveral *nm* : sugarcane field

cañería *nf* TUBERÍA : pipe *pl*, piping

cañero¹, -ra *adj* : sugar cane

cañero², -ra *n* **1** : sugar cane grower **2** : sugar cane worker

caño *nm* **1** : pipe **2** : spout **3** : channel (for navigation)

cañón *nm, pl* **cañones 1** : cannon **2** : barrel (of a gun) **3** : canyon

cañonazo *nm* : firing (of a cannon) ⟨saludo de 21 cañonazos : 21-gun salute⟩

cañonear *vt* : to shell, to bombard

cañonero *nm* : gunboat

caoba *nf* : mahogany

caos *nm* : chaos

caótico, -ca *adj* : chaotic

capa *nf* **1** : cape, cloak **2** : coating **3** : layer, stratum **4** : (social) class, stratum

capacidad *nf* **1** : capacity **2** : capability, ability

capacitación *nf, pl* **-ciones** : training

capacitar *vt* : to train, to qualify

capar *vt* : to castrate

caparazón *nm, pl* **-zones** : shell

capataz¹ *nmf, pl* **-taces** : foreman *m*, forewoman *f*

capataz², -taza *n* → **capataz¹**

capaz *adj, pl* **capaces 1** : capable, able ⟨capaz de trabajar : able to work⟩ ⟨es capaz de cualquier cosa : he's capable of anything⟩ **2** COMPETENTE : competent, capable **3** : spacious ⟨capaz para : with room for⟩

capcioso, -sa *adj* : cunning, deceptive ⟨pregunta capciosa : trick question⟩

capea *nf* : amateur bullfight

capear *vt* **1** : to make a pass with the cape (in bullfighting) **2** : to weather (a storm, crisis, etc.)

capellán *nm, pl* **-llanes** : chaplain

capilar¹ *adj* **1** : capillary **2** : hair

capilar² *nm* : capillary

capilla *nf* : chapel

capirotada *nf Mex* : traditional bread pudding

capirotazo *nm* : flip, flick

capital¹ *adj* **1** : capital **2** : chief, principal

capital² *nm* : capital ⟨capital de riesgo : venture capital⟩

capital³ *nf* : capital, capital city

capitalino¹, -na *adj* : of or from a capital city

capitalino², -na *n* : inhabitant of a capital city

capitalismo *nm* : capitalism

capitalista *adj & nmf* : capitalist

capitalizar {21} *vt* : to capitalize — **capitalización** *nf*

capitán, -tana *n, mpl* **-tanes 1** : captain **2 capitán de corbeta** : lieutenant commander

capitanear *vt* : to captain, to command

capitel *nm* : capital (of a column)

capitolio *nm* : capitol

capitulación *nf, pl* **-ciones** : capitulation

capitular *vi* : to capitulate, to surrender

capítulo *nm* **1** : chapter, section **2** : matter, subject

capo, capa *n* : boss

capó *nm* : hood (of a car)

capón *nm, pl* **capones** : capon

caporal *nm* **1** : chief, leader **2** : foreman (on a ranch)

capot → **capó**

capota *nf* : top (of a convertible)

capote *nm* **1** : cloak, overcoat **2** : bullfighter's cape **3** *Mex* : hood (of a car)

capricho *nm* : whim, caprice

caprichoso, -sa *adj* : capricious, fickle

Capricornio¹ *nm* : Capricorn (sign or constellation)

Capricornio² *nmf* : Capricorn (person)

cápsula *nf* : capsule

captar *vt* **1** : to catch, to grasp **2** : to gain, to attract **3** : to harness, to collect (waters)

captor, -tora *n* : captor

captura *nf* : capture, seizure

capturar *vt* : to capture, to seize

capucha *nf* : hood, cowl

capuchino *nm* : cappuccino

capullo *nm* **1** : cocoon **2** : bud (of a flower)

caqui *adj & nm* : khaki

cara *nf* **1** : face **2** : look, appearance ⟨¡qué buena cara tiene ese pastel! : that cake looks delicious!⟩ **3** *fam* : nerve, gall **4 (de) cara a** : facing **5 de cara a** : in view of, in the light of

carabina *nf* : carbine

carabinero, -ra *n* : police officer

caracol *nm* **1** : snail **2** CONCHA : conch, seashell **3** : ringlet

caracola *nf* : conch

carácter *nm, pl* **caracteres 1** ÍNDOLE : character, kind, nature **2** TEMPERAMENTO : character, temperament **3** : character (in writing)

característica *nf* RASGO : trait, feature, characteristic

característico, -ca *adj* : characteristic — **característicamente** *adv*

caracterizar {21} *vt* : to characterize — **caracterización** *nf*

caradura *adj* DESCARADO : cheeky, impudent

caramba *interj* **1** (*expressing annoyance or anger*) : darn!, heck! **2** (*expressing surprise*) : wow!, good Lord!

carámbano *nm* : icicle

carambola *nf* **1** : carom **2** : ruse, trick ⟨por carambola : by a lucky chance⟩

caramelo *nm* **1** : caramel **2** DULCE : candy

caramillo *nm* **1** : pipe, small flute **2** : heap, pile

caraqueño¹, -ña *adj* : of or from Caracas

caraqueño², -ña *n* : person from Caracas

carátula *nf* **1** : title page **2** : cover, dust jacket **3** CARETA : mask **4** *Mex* : face, dial (of a clock or watch)

caravana *nf* **1** : caravan **2** : convoy **3** REMOLQUE : trailer

caray → **caramba**

carbohidrato *nm* : carbohydrate

carbón *nm, pl* **carbones 1** : coal **2** : charcoal

carbonatado, -da *adj* : carbonated

carboncillo *nm* : charcoal

carbonera *nf* : coal cellar, coal bunker (on a ship)

carbonero, -ra *adj* : coal

carbonizar {21} *vt* : to char — **carbonizarse** *vr*

carbono *nm* : carbon

carburador *nm* : carburetor

carburante *nm* : fuel

carca *nmf fam* : old fogy

carcacha *nf fam* : jalopy, wreck

carcaj *nm* : quiver (for arrows)

carcajada *nf* : loud laugh, guffaw ⟨reírse a carcajadas : to roar with laughter⟩

carcajearse *vr* : to roar with laughter, to be in stitches

cárcel *nf* PRISIÓN : jail, prison

carcelario, -ria *adj* : prison

carcelero, -ra *n* : jailer

carcinogénico, -ca *adj* → **cancerígeno**

carcinógeno *nm* → **cancerígeno**

carcinoma *nm* : carcinoma

carcomer *vt* : to eat away at, to consume

carcomido, -da *adj* **1** : worm-eaten **2** : decayed, rotten

cardar *vt* : to card, to comb

cardenal *nm* **1** : cardinal (in religion) **2** : bruise

cardíaco *or* **cardiaco, -ca** *adj* : cardiac, heart

cárdigan *nm, pl* **-gans** : cardigan

cardinal *adj* : cardinal

cardiología *nf* : cardiology

cardiólogo, -ga *n* : cardiologist

cardiovascular *adj* : cardiovascular

cardo *nm* : thistle

cardumen *nm* : school of fish

carecer {53} *vi* ~ **de** : to lack ⟨el cheque carecía de fondos : the check had insufficient funds⟩

carencia *nf* **1** FALTA : lack **2** ESCASEZ : shortage **3** DEFICIENCIA : deficiency

carente *adj* ~ **de** : lacking (in)

careo *nm* : confrontation, face-off

carero, -ra *adj fam* : pricey

carestía *nf* **1** : rise in cost ⟨la carestía de la vida : the high cost of living⟩ **2** : dearth, scarcity

careta *nf* MÁSCARA : mask

carey *nm* **1** : sea turtle **2** : tortoiseshell

carga *nf* **1** : loading **2** : freight, load, cargo **3** : burden, responsibility **4** : charge ⟨carga eléctrica : electrical charge⟩ **5** : attack, charge

cargada *nf Arg, Uru* : joke

cargado, -da *adj* **1** : loaded **2** : bogged down, weighted down **3** : close, stuffy **4** : full, fraught ⟨cargado de tensión/errores : fraught with tension/errors⟩ **5** FUERTE : strong ⟨café cargado : strong coffee⟩ **6 cargado de hombros** : round-shouldered

cargador¹, -dora *n* : longshoreman *m*, longshorewoman *f*

cargador² *nm* **1** : magazine (for a firearm) **2** : charger (for batteries)

cargamento *nm* : cargo, load

cargar {52} *vt* **1** : to carry **2** : to load, to fill **3** : to charge **4** : to burden ⟨cargado de deudas : burdened with debts⟩ **5** SUBIR : to upload — *vi* **1** : to load **2** : to rest (in architecture) **3** ~ **con** : to shoulder, to take on (a responsibility, etc.) **4** ~ **sobre** : to fall upon

cargo *nm* **1** : burden, load **2** : charge ⟨estar a cargo de : to be in charge of⟩ ⟨correr a cargo de : to be paid by⟩ ⟨hacerse cargo de : to take charge of, to take care of⟩ ⟨tener a su cargo : to be in charge of⟩ **3** : charge, cost **4** : position, office

cargue¹, etc. → **cargar**

cargue² *nm Col* : loading

carguero¹, -ra *adj* : freight, cargo ⟨tren carguero : freight train⟩

carguero² *nm* : freighter, cargo ship

cariarse *vr* : to decay (of teeth)

caribe *adj* : Caribbean ⟨el mar Caribe : the Caribbean Sea⟩

caribeño, -ña *adj* : Caribbean

caribú *nm, pl* **caribúes** : caribou

caricatura *nf* **1** : caricature **2** : cartoon

caricaturista *nmf* : caricaturist, cartoonist

caricaturizar {21} *vt* : to caricature

caricia *nf* **1** : caress **2 hacer caricias** : to pet, to stroke

caridad *nf* : charity

caries *nfs & pl* : cavity (in a tooth)

cariño¹ *nm* AFECTO : affection, love

cariño², -ña *n* : darling, sweetheart

cariñoso, -sa *adj* AFECTUOSO : affectionate, loving — **cariñosamente** *adv*

carioca¹ *adj* : of or from Río de Janeiro

carioca² *nmf* : person from Río de Janeiro

carisma *nm* : charisma

carismático, -ca *adj* : charismatic

carita *adj Mex fam* : cute (said of a man) ⟨se cree muy carita : he thinks he's gorgeous⟩

caritativo, -va *adj* : charitable

cariz *nm, pl* **carices** : appearance, aspect

carmesí *adj & nm* : crimson

carmín *nm, pl* **carmines 1** : carmine **2** : lipstick

carnada *nf* CEBO : bait

carnal *adj* **1** : carnal **2 primo carnal** : first cousin

carnaval *nm* : carnival

carne *nf* **1** : meat ⟨carne molida : ground beef⟩ **2** : flesh ⟨carne de gallina : goose bumps⟩

carné → **carnet**

carnero *nm* **1** : ram, sheep **2** : mutton

carnet *nm* **1** : identification card, ID **2** : membership card **3 carnet de conducir** *Spain* : driver's license

carnicería *nf* **1** : butcher shop **2** MATANZA : slaughter, carnage

carnicero, -ra *n* : butcher

carnitas *nfpl Mex* : small chunks of cooked pork

carnívoro¹, -ra *adj* : carnivorous

carnívoro² *nm* : carnivore

carnoso, -sa *adj* : fleshy, meaty

caro¹ *adv* : a lot ⟨costar/pagar caro : to cost/pay a lot⟩ ⟨vender caro : to sell high, to sell at a high price⟩ ⟨un error que me costó caro : a mistake that cost me dearly⟩

caro², -ra *adj* **1** : expensive, dear ⟨es muy/demasiado caro : it's very/too expensive⟩ **2** QUERIDO : dear, beloved

carpa *nf* **1** : carp **2** : big top (of a circus) **3** : tent

carpeta *nf* : folder, binder, portfolio (of drawings, etc.)

carpetazo *nm* **dar carpetazo a** : to shelve, to defer

carpintería *nf* **1** : carpentry **2** : carpenter's workshop

carpintero, -ra *n* : carpenter

carraspear *vi* : to clear one's throat

carraspera *nf* : hoarseness ⟨tener carraspera : to have a frog in one's throat⟩

carrera *nf* **1** : run, running ⟨a la carrera : at full speed⟩ ⟨de carrera : hastily⟩ **2** : race ⟨carrera de caballos : horse race⟩ **3** : course of study ⟨estudiar la carrera de medicina : to study medicine⟩ **4** : career, profession **5** : run (in baseball)

carreta *nf* : cart, wagon

carrete *nm* **1** : spool (for thread), bobbin (in sewing machine), reel (for film, etc.) ⟨carrete de pesca : fishing reel⟩ **2** : roll of film **3** : (electrical) coil

carretear *vi* : to taxi

carretel → **carrete**

carretera *nf* : highway, road ⟨carretera de peaje : turnpike⟩

carretero, -ra *adj* : highway ⟨el sistema carretero : the highway system⟩

carretilla *nf* **1** : wheelbarrow **2 carretilla elevadora** : forklift

carril *nm* **1** : lane ⟨carretera de doble carril : two-lane highway⟩ **2** : rail (on a railroad track)

carrillo *nm* : cheek, jowl

carrito *nm* : cart ⟨carrito de compras : shopping cart⟩

carrizo *nm* JUNCO : reed

carro *nm* **1** COCHE : car **2** : cart **3** *Chile, Mex* : coach (of a train) **4 carro alegórico** : float (in a parade) **5 carro bomba** : car bomb

carrocería *nf* : bodywork, body (of a vehicle)

carroña *nf* : carrion

carroñero, -ra *n* : scavenger (animal)

carroza *nf* **1** : carriage **2** : float (in a parade)

carruaje *nm* : carriage

carrusel *nm* **1** : merry-go-round **2** : carousel ⟨carrusel de equipaje : luggage carousel⟩

carta *nf* **1** : letter ⟨carta de amor : love letter⟩ ⟨carta de renuncia : letter of resignation⟩ **2** NAIPE : playing card **3** : charter, constitution **4** MENÚ : menu **5** : map, chart **6 tomar cartas en** : to intervene

carta blanca *nf* : carte blanche

carta bomba *nf* : letter bomb

cartearse *vr* : to write to one another, to correspond

cartel *nm* : sign, poster

cártel *or* **cartel** *nm* : cartel

cartelera *nf* **1** : billboard **2** : marquee

cartera *nf* **1** BILLETERA : wallet, billfold **2** BOLSO : pocketbook, purse **3** : portfolio ⟨cartera de acciones : stock portfolio⟩

carterista *nmf* : pickpocket

cartero, -ra *n* : letter carrier, mailman *m*

cartílago *nm* : cartilage

cartilla *nf* **1** : primer, reader **2** : booklet ⟨cartilla de ahorros : bankbook⟩

cartografía *nf* : cartography

cartógrafo, -fa *n* : cartographer

cartón *nm, pl* **cartones 1** : cardboard ⟨cartón madera : fiberboard⟩ **2** : carton

cartucho *nm* : cartridge

cartulina *nf* : poster board, cardboard

casa *nf* **1** : house ⟨una casa de dos pisos : a two-story house⟩ ⟨la casa blanca : the White House⟩ **2** HOGAR : home ⟨en casa : at home⟩ ⟨ir a casa : to go home⟩ **3** : home (in sports) ⟨equipo de casa : home team⟩ ⟨partido en casa : home game⟩ ⟨partido fuera de casa : away game⟩ **4** : household, family **5** : company, firm **6 casa de cambio** : currency exchange **7 casa de empeños** : pawnshop **8 casa de (altos) estudios** : institute of (higher) learning, college, university **9 casa de salud** : clinic **10 casa matriz** : headquarters **11 echar/tirar/botar la casa por la ventana** : to spare no expense

casaca *nf* : jacket

casado¹, -da *adj* : married

casado², -da *n* : married person

casamentero, -ra *n* : matchmaker

casamiento *nm* **1** : marriage **2** BODA : wedding

casar *vt* : to marry ⟨el cura que nos casó : the priest who married us⟩ — *vi* : to go together, to match up — **casarse** *vr* **1** : to get married **2** ~ **con** : to marry

casateniente *nmf Mex* : landlord, landlady *f*

cascabel[1] *nm* : small bell
cascabel[2] *nf* : rattlesnake
cascada *nf* CATARATA, SALTO : waterfall, cascade
cascajo *nm* 1 : pebble, rock fragment 2 *fam* : piece of junk
cascanueces *nms & pl* : nutcracker
cascar {72} *vt* : to crack (a shell) — **cascarse** *vr* : to crack, to chip
cáscara *nf* 1 : skin, peel, rind, husk 2 : shell (of a nut or egg)
cascarón *nm, pl* **-rones** 1 : eggshell 2 *Mex* : shell filled with confetti
cascarrabias *nmfs & pl fam* : grouch, crab
casco *nm* 1 : helmet 2 : hull 3 : hoof 4 : fragment, shard 5 : center (of a town) 6 *Mex* : empty bottle 7 **cascos** *nmpl* : headphones
caserío *nm* 1 : country house 2 : hamlet
casero[1], **-ra** *adj* 1 : domestic, household 2 : homemade
casero[2], **-ra** *n* DUEÑO : landlord *m*, landlady *f*
caseta *nf* 1 : booth, stand, stall ⟨caseta de peaje, caseta de cobro *CA, Mex* : tollbooth⟩ 2 : doghouse 3 : dugout (in sports)
casete → cassette
casi *adv* 1 : almost, nearly ⟨casi un año : almost a year⟩ ⟨casi me desmayo : I almost fainted⟩ 2 (*in negative phrases*) : hardly ⟨casi nunca : hardly ever⟩ ⟨no hace casi nada : he hardly does anything⟩
casilla *nf* 1 : booth 2 : pigeonhole 3 : box (on a form) 4 **casilla de correos** *Arg* : P.O. box
casillero *nm* 1 : pigeonhole 2 : set of pigeonholes
casino *nm* 1 : casino 2 : (social) club
caso *nm* 1 : case ⟨en caso de : in case of⟩ ⟨en caso/ese caso : in this/that case⟩ ⟨en todo/cualquier caso : in any case⟩ ⟨en el mejor/peor de los casos : at best/worst⟩ ⟨el caso es que . . . : the fact/thing is (that) . . .⟩ 2 : case (in law or medicine) 3 **hacer caso** : to pay attention ⟨hacer caso de algo : to pay attention to something, to notice something⟩⟨hacerle caso a alguien : to pay attention to someone, to listen to someone⟩ 4 **hacer caso omiso de** : to ignore, to take no notice of 5 **no hay caso** : it's useless, there's no point 6 **no venir al caso** : to be beside the point
caspa *nf* : dandruff
casque, etc. → cascar
casquete *nm* 1 : skullcap 2 **casquete glaciar** : ice cap 3 **casquete polar** : polar ice cap 4 **casquete corto** *Mex* : crew cut
casquillo *nm* : case, casing (of a bullet)
cassette *nmf* : cassette
casta *nf* 1 : caste 2 : lineage, stock ⟨de casta : thoroughbred, purebred⟩ 3 **sacar la casta** *Mex* : to come out ahead
castaña *nf* : chestnut
castañetear *vi* : to chatter (of teeth)

castañeteo *nm* : chatter, chattering (of teeth)
castaño[1], **-ña** *adj* : chestnut, brown
castaño[2] *nm* 1 : chestnut tree 2 : chestnut, brown
castañuela *nf* : castanet
castellano[1], **-na** *adj & n* : Castilian
castellano[2] *nm* ESPAÑOL : Spanish, Castilian (language)
castidad *nf* : chastity
castigar {52} *vt* : to punish
castigo *nm* : punishment
castillo *nm* 1 : castle 2 **castillo de proa** : forecastle 3 **castillo de arena** : sand castle
castizo, -za *adj* 1 AUTÉNTICO : authentic, genuine, pure 2 TRADICIONAL : traditional
casto, -ta *adj* : chaste, pure — **castamente** *adv*
castor *nm* : beaver
castración *nf, pl* **-ciones** : castration
castrar *vt* 1 : to castrate, to spay, to neuter 2 DEBILITAR : to weaken, to debilitate
castrense *adj* : military
casual *adj* 1 : chance ⟨no es casual : it's no accident⟩ 2 *Mex* : casual (of clothing)
casualidad *nf* 1 : chance 2 **por ∼** or **de ∼** : by chance, by any chance
casualmente *adv* : accidentally, by chance
casucha or **casuca** *nf* : shanty, hovel
cataclismo *nm* : cataclysm
catacumbas *nfpl* : catacombs
catador, -dora *n* : wine taster
catalán[1], **-lana** *adj & n, mpl* **-lanes** : Catalan
catalán[2] *nm* : Catalan (language)
catalizador *nm* 1 : catalyst 2 : catalytic converter
catalogar {52} *vt* : to catalog, to classify
catálogo *nm* : catalog
catamarán *nm, pl* **-ranes** : catamaran
cataplasma *nf* : poultice
catapulta *nf* : catapult
catapultar *vt* : to catapult
catar *vt* 1 : to taste, to sample 2 : to look at, to examine
catarata *nf* 1 CASCADA, SALTO : waterfall 2 : cataract
catarro *nm* RESFRIADO : cold, catarrh
catarsis *nf* : catharsis — **catártico, -ca** *adj*
catastro *nm* : property registry
catástrofe *nf* DESASTRE : catastrophe, disaster
catastrófico, -ca *adj* DESASTROSO : catastrophic, disastrous
catcher *nmf* : catcher (in baseball)
catecismo *nm* : catechism
cátedra *nf* 1 : (tenured) professorship 2 : department chair (at a university) 3 : subject, class 4 **libertad de cátedra** : academic freedom
catedral *nf* : cathedral
catedrático, -ca *n* 1 PROFESOR : (tenured) professor 2 : department chair (at a university)
categoría *nf* 1 CLASE : category 2 RANGO : rank, standing 3 **categoría gramatical**

: part of speech **4 de ~** : first-rate, outstanding

categórico, -ca *adj* : categorical, unequivocal — **categóricamente** *adv*

categorizar {21} *vt* : categorize

cateo *CA, Mex* → **cacheo**

catering *or* **cátering** *nm* : catering, food service

catéter *nm* : catheter

cátodo *nm* : cathode

catolicismo *nm* : Catholicism

católico, -ca *adj & n* : Catholic

catorce *adj & nm* : fourteen — **catorce** *pron*

catorceavo¹, -va *adj* : fourteenth

catorceavo² *nm* : fourteenth

catre *nm* : cot

catsup *nm* : ketchup

caucásico, -ca *adj & n* : Caucasian

cauce *nm* **1** LECHO : riverbed **2** : means *pl*, channel

caucho *nm* **1** GOMA : rubber **2** : rubber tree **3** *Ven* : tire

caución *nf, pl* **cauciones** FIANZA : bail, security

caudal *nm* **1** : volume of water **2** RIQUEZA : capital, wealth **3** ABUNDANCIA : abundance

caudaloso, -sa *adj* **1** : large, mighty (of a river) **2** RICO : rich, wealthy

caudillo *nm* : leader, commander

causa *nf* **1** MOTIVO : cause, reason, motive ⟨a causa de : because of⟩ **2** IDEAL : cause ⟨morir por una causa : to die for a cause⟩ **3** : lawsuit

causal¹ *adj* : causal — **causalidad** *nf*

causal² *nm* : cause, grounds *pl*

causante¹ *adj* **~ de** : causing, responsible for

causante² *nmf Mex* : taxpayer

causar *vt* **1** : to cause **2** : to provoke, to arouse ⟨eso me causa gracia : I find that funny⟩

cáustico, -ca *adj* : caustic

cautela *nf* : caution, prudence

cautelar *adj* : precautionary, preventive

cauteloso, -sa *adj* : cautious, prudent — **cautelosamente** *adv*

cauterizar {21} *vt* : to cauterize

cautivador, -dora *adj* : captivating

cautivar *vt* : to captivate, to charm

cautiverio *nm* : captivity

cautivo, -va *adj & n* : captive

cauto, -ta *adj* : cautious, careful

cava *nm* : a Spanish sparkling wine

cavar *vt* : to dig — *vi* **~ en** : to delve into, to probe

caverna *nf* : cavern, cave

cavernícola *nmf* : caveman *m*, cavewoman *f*

cavernoso, -sa *adj* **1** : cavernous **2** : deep, resounding

caviar *nm* : caviar

cavidad *nf* : cavity

cavilar *vi* : to ponder, to deliberate

cayado *nm* : crook, staff

cayena *nf* : cayenne pepper

cayo *nm* ISLOTE : key, islet

cayó, etc. → **caer**

caza¹ *nf* **1** CACERÍA : hunt, hunting **2** : game

caza² *nm* : fighter plane

cazador, -dora *n* **1** : hunter **2 cazador furtivo** : poacher

cazadora *nf* : jacket, bomber jacket

cazar {21} *vt* **1** : to hunt **2** : to catch, to bag **3** *fam* : to land (a job, a spouse) — *vi* : to go hunting

cazatalentos *nmfs & pl* : talent scout

cazo *nm* **1** : saucepan, pot **2** CUCHARÓN : ladle

cazuela *nf* **1** : pan, saucepan **2** : casserole

cazurro, -ra *adj* : sullen, surly

CD *nm* : CD, compact disk

CD–ROM [sede'rom] *nm* : CD-ROM

ce *nf* : (letter) c

cebada *nf* : barley

cebar *vt* **1** : to bait **2** : to feed, to fatten **3** : to prime (a pump, etc.) — **cebarse** *vr* **~ en** : to take it out on

cebo *nm* **1** CARNADA : bait **2** : feed **3** : primer (for firearms)

cebolla *nf* : onion

cebolleta *nf* : scallion, green onion

cebollino *nm* **1** : chive **2** : scallion

cebra *nf* : zebra

cebú *nm, pl* **cebús** *or* **cebúes** : zebu (cattle)

cecear [θeθe'ar] *vi* **1** : to lisp **2** : to pronounce the Spanish letter *s* as /θ/

ceceo [θe'θeo] *nm* **1** : lisp **2** : pronunciation of the Spanish letter *s* as /θ/

cecina *nf* : dried beef, beef jerky

cedazo *nm* : sieve

ceder *vi* **1** : to yield, to give way **2** : to diminish, to abate **3** : to give in, to relent — *vt* : to cede, to hand over

cedro *nm* : cedar

cédula *nf* : document, certificate

cegador, -dora *adj* : blinding

cegar {49} *vt* **1** : to blind **2** : to block, to stop up — *vi* : to be blinded, to go blind

ceguera *nf* : blindness

ceiba *nf* : silk-cotton tree

ceja *nf* **1** : eyebrow ⟨fruncir las cejas : to knit one's brows⟩ **2** : flange, rim

cejar *vi* : to give in, to back down

celada *nf* : trap, ambush

celador, -dora *n* GUARDIA : guard, warden

celda *nf* : cell (of a jail)

celebración *nf, pl* **-ciones** : celebration

celebrado, -da *adj* → **célebre**

celebrante *nmf* OFICIANTE : celebrant

celebrar *vt* **1** : to celebrate **2** : to hold (a meeting) **3** : to say (Mass) **4** : to welcome, to be happy about — *vi* : to be glad — **celebrarse** *vr* **1** : to be celebrated, to fall **2** : to be held, to take place

célebre *adj* : celebrated, famous

celebridad *nf* **1** : celebrity **2** FAMA : fame, celebrity

celeridad *nf* : swiftness

celeste¹ *adj* **1** : celestial **2** : sky blue, azure

celeste² *nm* : sky blue

celestial *adj* : heavenly, celestial

celibato *nm* : celibacy

célibe *adj & nmf* : celibate

cello [ˈtʃelo] → **chelo**
celo *nm* **1** : zeal, fervor **2** : heat (of females), rut (of males) **3 celos** *nmpl* : jealousy ⟨tenerle celos a alguien : to be jealous of someone⟩
celofán *nm, pl* **-fanes** : cellophane
celosía *nf* **1** : lattice window **2** : lattice, trellis
celoso, -sa *adj* **1** : jealous **2** : zealous — **celosamente** *adv*
celta[1] *adj* : Celtic
celta[2] *nmf* : Celt
célula *nf* : cell ⟨célula madre : stem cell⟩
celular[1] *adj* : cellular
celular[2] *nm* : cell phone
celulitis *nf* : cellulite
celuloide *nm* **1** : celluloid **2** : film, cinema
celulosa *nf* : cellulose
cementar *vt* : to cement
cementerio *nm* : cemetery
cemento *nm* : cement
cena *nf* : supper, dinner
cenador *nm* : arbor, gazebo
cenagal *nm* : bog, quagmire
cenagoso, -sa *adj* : swampy
cenar *vi* : to have dinner, to have supper — *vt* : to have for dinner or supper ⟨cenamos tamales : we had tamales for supper⟩
cencerro *nm* : cowbell
cenicero *nm* : ashtray
ceniciento, -ta *adj* : ashen
cenit *nm* : zenith, peak
ceniza *nf* **1** : ash **2 cenizas** *nfpl* : ashes (of a deceased person)
cenizo *nm* : jinx
cenote *nm Mex* : natural deposit of spring water
censar *vt* : to take a census of
censo *nm* : census
censor, -sora *n* : censor, critic
censura *nf* **1** : censorship **2** : censure, criticism
censurable *adj* : reprehensible, blameworthy
censurar *vt* **1** : to censor **2** : to censure, to criticize
centauro *nm* : centaur
centavo *nm* **1** : cent (in English-speaking countries) **2** : unit of currency in various Latin-American countries
centella *nf* **1** : lightning flash **2** : spark
centellear *vi* **1** : to twinkle **2** : to gleam, to sparkle
centelleo *nm* : twinkling, sparkle
centena *nf* : hundred ⟨una centena de personas : a hundred people⟩
centenar *nm* **1** : hundred **2 a centenares** : by the hundreds
centenario[1], **-ria** *adj & n* : hundred-year-old
centenario[2] *nm* : centennial
centeno *nm* : rye
centésima *nf* : hundredth
centésimo[1], **-ma** *adj* : hundredth
centésimo[2] *nm* : hundredth
centi- *pref* : centi-
centigrado *adj* : centigrade, Celsius
centigramo *nm* : centigram

centímetro *nm* : centimeter
céntimo *nm* : cent
centinela *nmf* : sentinel, sentry
centrado, -da *adj* **1** EQUILIBRADO : stable **2** : centered **3** ~ **en** : focused on
central[1] *adj* **1** : central **2** PRINCIPAL : main, principal
central[2] *nf* **1** : main office, headquarters **2** : power plant, power station **3 central camionera** *Mex* : bus terminal
centralista *adj & nmf* : centralist
centralita *nf* : switchboard
centralizar {21} *vt* : to centralize — **centralización** *nf*
centrar *vt* **1** : to center **2** : to focus — **centrarse** *vr* ~ **en** : to focus on, to concentrate on
céntrico, -ca *adj* : central
centrifugar {52} *vt* : to spin (clothing)
centrista *adj & nmf* : centrist
centro[1] *nmf* : center (in sports)
centro[2] *nm* **1** MEDIO : center ⟨centro de atención/gravedad : center of attention/gravity⟩ **2** : downtown **3 centro comercial** : shopping plaza **4 centro de mesa** : centerpiece **5 centro de votación** : polling place
centroamericano, -na *adj & n* : Central American
centrocampista *nmf* : midfielder
ceñido, -da *adj* AJUSTADO : tight, tight-fitting
ceñir {67} *vt* **1** : to encircle, to surround **2** : to hug, to cling to ⟨me ciñe demasiado : it's too tight on me⟩ — **ceñirse** *vr* ~ **a** : to restrict oneself to, to stick to
ceño *nm* **1** : frown, scowl **2 fruncir el ceño** : to frown, to knit one's brows
cepa *nf* **1** : stump (of a tree) **2** : stock (of a vine) **3** LINAJE : ancestry, stock
cepillar *vt* **1** : to brush **2** : to plane (wood) — **cepillarse** *vr*
cepillo *nm* **1** : brush ⟨cepillo de dientes : toothbrush⟩ **2** : plane (for woodworking)
cepo *nm* : trap (for animals)
cera *nf* **1** : wax ⟨cera de abejas : beeswax⟩ **2** : polish
cerámica *nf* **1** : ceramics *pl* **2** : pottery
cerámico, -ca *adj* : ceramic
ceramista *nmf* ALFARERO : potter
cerca[1] *adv* **1** : nearby, close by ⟨vive cerca : he lives nearby⟩ **2** : close, near ⟨cerca de aquí : near here⟩ ⟨su cumpleaños está cerca : her birthday is almost here⟩ **3** ~ **de** : nearly, almost, close to ⟨cerca de 100 personas : nearly 100 people⟩ **4 de** ~ : close up ⟨seguir de cerca : to follow closely⟩
cerca[2] *nf* **1** : fence **2** : (stone) wall
cercado *nm* : enclosure
cercanía *nf* **1** PROXIMIDAD : proximity, closeness **2 cercanías** *nfpl* : outskirts, suburbs
cercano, -na *adj* : near, close
cercar {72} *vt* **1** : to fence in, to enclose **2** : to surround
cercenar *vt* **1** : to cut off, to amputate, to sever **2** : to diminish, to curtail
cerceta *nf* : teal (duck)

cerciorarse *vr* ASEGURARSE ~ **de** : to make sure of, to verify

cerco *nm* **1** : siege **2** : cordon, circle **3** : fence

cerda *nf* **1** : bristle **2** : sow

cerdo *nm* **1** : pig, hog **2 carne de cerdo** : pork

cereal *nm* : cereal — **cereal** *adj*

cerebelo *nm* : cerebellum

cerebral *adj* : cerebral

cerebro *nm* : brain

ceremonia *nf* : ceremony ⟨sin ceremonias : informal/informally, without ceremony⟩ — **ceremonial** *adj*

ceremonioso, -sa *adj* : ceremonious

cereza *nf* : cherry

cerezo *nm* : cherry tree

cerilla *nf* **1** : match **2** : earwax

cerillo *nm* (*in various countries*) : match

cerner {56} *vt* : to sift — **cernerse** *vr* **1** : to hover **2** ~ **sobre** : to loom over, to threaten

cernidor *nm* : sieve

cernir → **cerner**

cero *nm* : zero

ceroso, -sa *adj* : waxy

cerque, etc. → **cercar**

cerquita *adv fam* : very close, very near

cerrado, -da *adj* **1** : closed, shut **2** : thick, broad (of an accent) **3** : cloudy, overcast **4** : quiet, reserved **5** : dense, stupid

cerradura *nf* : lock

cerrajería *nf* : locksmith's shop

cerrajero, -ra *n* : locksmith

cerrar {55} *vt* **1** : to close, to shut (a door, a book, etc.) ⟨cerrar los ojos : to close one's eyes⟩ ⟨cerrar algo (con llave) : to lock something⟩ **2** : to turn off (a faucet, etc.) **3** : to close, to put the top on (a jar, etc.) **4** : to fasten, to button up (buttons), to zip up (a zipper) **5** CONCLUIR : to bring to an end, to close **6** : to close (a business, an account) **7** : to close, to close off (a street, etc.) — *vi* **1** : to close up, to lock up **2** : to close down — **cerrarse** *vr* **1** : to close **2** : to fasten, to button up, to zip up **3** : to conclude, to end

cerrazón *nf*, *pl* **-zones** : obstinacy, stubbornness

cerro *nm* COLINA, LOMA : hill

cerrojo *nm* PESTILLO : bolt, latch

certamen *nm*, *pl* **-támenes** : competition, contest

certero, -ra *adj* : accurate, precise — **certeramente** *adv*

certeza *nf* : certainty

certidumbre *nf* : certainty

certificable *adj* : certifiable

certificación *nf*, *pl* **-ciones** : certification

certificado¹, -da *adj* **1** : certified **2** : registered (of mail)

certificado² *nm* **1** : certificate ⟨certificado de matrimonio/difunción/nacimiento : marriage/death/birth certificate⟩ ⟨certificado de regalo : gift certificate⟩ **2** : registered letter

certificar {72} *vt* **1** : to certify **2** : to register (mail)

cerumen *nm* : earwax

cervato *nm* : fawn

cervecera *nf* : brewery

cervecero, -ra *n* : brewer

cervecería *nf* **1** : brewery **2** : beer hall, bar

cerveza *nf* : beer ⟨cerveza de barril : draft beer⟩

cervical *adj* : cervical

cerviz *nf*, *pl* **cervices** : nape of the neck

cesación *nf*, *pl* **-ciones** : cessation, suspension

cesante *adj* : laid off, unemployed

cesantía *nf* : unemployment

cesar *vi* : to cease, to stop — *vt* : to dismiss, to lay off

cesárea *nf* : cesarean

cesáreo, -rea *adj* : cesarean

cese *nm* **1** : cessation, stop ⟨cese del fuego : cease-fire⟩ **2** : dismissal

cesio *nm* : cesium

cesión *nf*, *pl* **cesiones** : transfer, assignment (of property, etc.)

césped *nm* : lawn, grass

cesta *nf* **1** : basket **2** : jai alai racket

cesto *nm* **1** : hamper **2** : basket (in basketball) **3 cesto de (la) basura** : wastebasket

cetro *nm* : scepter

ch *nf* : fourth letter of the Spanish alphabet — not usually considered a separate letter in alphabetization

chabacano¹, -na *adj* : tacky, tasteless

chabacano² *nm Mex* : apricot

chabola *nf Spain* **1** : shack, shanty **2 barrio de chabolas** → **barrio**

chacal *nm* : jackal

cháchara *nf fam* **1** : small talk, chatter **2 chácharas** *nfpl* : trinkets, junk

chacharear *vi fam* : to chatter, to gab

chacra *nf Arg, Chile, Peru* : small farm

chal *nm* MANTÓN : shawl

chalado¹, -da *adj fam* : crazy, nuts

chalado², -da *n* : nut, crazy person

chalán *nm*, *pl* **chalanes** *Mex* : barge

chalé → **chalet**

chaleco *nm* : vest

chalet *nm Spain* : house

chalupa *nf* **1** : small boat **2** *Mex* : small stuffed tortilla

chamaco, -ca *n Mex fam* : kid, boy *m*, girl *f*

chamarra *nf* **1** : sheepskin jacket **2** : poncho, blanket

chamba *nf Mex, Peru fam* : job, work

chambear *vi Mex, Peru fam* : to work

chamo, -ma *n Ven fam* **1** : kid, boy *m*, girl *f* **2** : buddy, pal

champaña *or* **champán** *nm* : champagne

champiñón *nm*, *pl* **-ñones** : mushroom

champú *nm*, *pl* **-pus** *or* **-púes** : shampoo

champurrado *nm Mex* : hot chocolate thickened with cornstarch

chamuco *nm Mex fam* : devil

chamuscar {72} *vt* : to singe, to scorch — **chamuscarse** *vr*

chamusquina *nf* : scorch

chance *nm* OPORTUNIDAD : chance, opportunity

chancho¹, -cha *adj fam* : dirty, filthy, gross

chancho², -cha *n* **1** : pig, hog **2** *fam* : slob

chanchullero, -ra *adj fam* : shady, crooked

chanchullo *nm fam* : shady deal, scam

chancla *nf* **1** : thong sandal, slipper **2** : old shoe

chancleta → **chancla**

chanclo *nm* **1** : clog **2 chanclos** *nmpl* : overshoes, galoshes, rubbers

chándal *nm, pl* **chándals** *Spain* : sweatsuit, tracksuit

changarro *nm Mex* : small shop, stall

chango, -ga *n Mex* : monkey

chantaje *nm* : blackmail

chantajear *vt* : to blackmail

chantajista *nmf* : blackmailer

chanza *nf* **1** : joke, jest **2** *Mex fam* : chance, opportunity

chao *interj fam* : bye!

chapa *nf* **1** *Arg, Uru* : license plate **2** : sheet, panel, veneer **3** : lock **4** : badge **5** TAPÓN : cap, bottle cap

chapado, -da *adj* **1** : plated **2 chapado a la antigua** : old-fashioned

chapar *vt* **1** : to add a veneer to **2** : to plate (metals)

chaparro¹, -rra *adj* : short and squat, stocky

chaparro², -rra *n* : short, stocky person

chaparrón *nm, pl* **-rrones** **1** : downpour **2** : great quantity, torrent

chapeado, -da *adj Col, Mex* : flushed

chaperón, -rona *n, mpl* **-rones** : chaperon, chaperone

chapín, chapina *adj & n CA* : Guatemalan

chapopote *nm Mex* : tar, blacktop

chapotear *vi* : to splash about

chapucero¹, -ra *adj* **1** : crude, shoddy **2** *Mex fam* : dishonest

chapucero², -ra *n* **1** : sloppy worker, bungler **2** *Mex fam* : cheat, swindler

chapulín *nm, pl* **-lines** *CA, Mex* : grasshopper, locust

chapurrear *or* **chapurrar** *vt* **chapurrear el inglés/español** (etc.) : to speak broken English/Spanish (etc.)

chapuza *nf* **1** : botched job **2** *Mex fam* : fraud, trick ⟨hacer chapuzas : to cheat⟩

chapuzón *nm, pl* **-zones** : dip, swim ⟨darse un chapuzón : to go for a quick dip⟩

chaqueta *nf* : jacket

chara *nf* : jay

charada *nf* : charades (game)

charango *nm* : traditional Andean stringed instrument

charca *nf* : pond, pool

charco *nm* : puddle, pool

charcutería *nf* : delicatessen

charla *nf* : chat, talk

charlar *vi* : to chat, to talk

charlatán¹, -tana *adj* : talkative, chatty

charlatán², -tana *n, mpl* **-tanes** **1** : chatterbox **2** FARSANTE : charlatan, phony

charol *nm* **1** : lacquer, varnish **2** : patent leather **3** : tray

charola *nf Bol, Mex, Peru* : tray

charqui *nm Chile, Peru* : dried beef, beef jerky

charreada *nf Mex* : rodeo

charretera *nf* : epaulet

charro¹, -rra *adj* **1** : gaudy, tacky **2** *Mex* : pertaining to charros

charro², -rra *n Mex* : charro (Mexican cowboy or cowgirl)

charrúa *adj & nmf* : Uruguayan

chárter *adj* : charter

chascarrillo *nm Mex* : joke, funny story

chasco *nm* **1** BROMA : trick, joke **2** DECEPCIÓN : disappointment

chasis *or* **chasís** *nm* : chassis

chasquear *vt* **1** : to snap (the fingers), to click (the tongue) **2** : to snap (a whip)

chasquido *nm* **1** : snap (of fingers), click (of the tongue) **2** : snap, crack

chat *nm, pl* **chats** : chat room

chatarra *nf* : scrap metal

chato, -ta *adj* **1** : pug-nosed **2** : flat

chauvinismo *nm* : chauvinism

chauvinista¹ *adj* : chauvinistic

chauvinista² *nmf* : chauvinist

chaval, -vala *n fam* : kid, boy *m*, girl *f*

chavalo, -vala *Mex, Nic* → **chaval**

chavo¹, -va *adj Mex fam* : young

chavo², -va *n Mex fam* : kid, boy *m*, girl *f*

chavo³ *nm fam* : cent, buck ⟨no tengo un chavo : I'm broke⟩

che¹ *nf* : (letter) ch

che² *interj Arg, Uru* ⟨che, ¡mirá! : hey, look!⟩ ⟨che, ¡qué mal! : wow, how awful!⟩ ⟨en serio, che : hey, I'm being serious⟩

checar {72} *vt Mex* : to check, to verify

checo¹, -ca *adj & n* : Czech

checo² *nm* : Czech (language)

checoslovaco, -ca *adj & n* : Czechoslovakian

cheddar *nm* : cheddar

chef *nm* : chef

chelín *nm, pl* **chelines** : shilling

chelo *nm* : cello, violoncello

cheque¹, etc. → **checar**

cheque² *nm* **1** : check **2 cheque de viajero** : traveler's check

chequear *vt* **1** : to check, to verify **2** : to check in (baggage)

chequeo *nm* **1** INSPECCIÓN : check, inspection **2** : checkup, examination

chequera *nf* : checkbook

chévere *adj fam* : great, fantastic

chic *adj & nm* : chic

chica → **chico**

chicano, -na *adj & n* : Chicano *m*, Chicana *f*

chicha *nf* : fermented alcoholic beverage made from corn

chícharo *nm* : pea

chicharra *nf* **1** CIGARRA : cicada **2** : buzzer

chicharrón *nm, pl* **-rrones** **1** : pork rind **2 darle chicharrón a algo/alguien** *Mex fam* : to get rid of something/someone

chiche *nm Arg, Uru* JUGUETE : toy

chichón *nm, pl* **chichones** : bump, swelling

chicle *nm* : chewing gum

chicloso *nm Mex* : taffy

chico[1], -ca adj 1 : little, small 2 : young
chico[2], -ca n 1 : child, boy m, girl f 2
: young man m, young woman f
chicote nm LÁTIGO : whip, lash
chiffon → chifón
chiflado[1], -da adj fam : nuts, crazy
chiflado[2], -da n fam : crazy person, lunatic
chiflar vi : to whistle — vt : to whistle at,
to boo — chiflarse vr fam ~ por : to be
crazy about
chiflido nm : whistle, whistling
chiflón nm, pl chiflones : draft (of air)
chifón nm, pl chifones : chiffon
chilango[1], -ga adj Mex fam : of or from
Mexico City
chilango[2], -ga n Mex fam : person from
Mexico City
chilaquiles nmpl Mex : shredded tortillas
in sauce
chile nm : chili pepper
chileno, -na adj & n : Chilean
chillar vi 1 : to squeal, to screech 2 : to
scream, to yell 3 : to be gaudy, to clash
chillido nm 1 : scream, shout 2 : squeal,
screech, cry (of an animal)
chillo nm PRi : red snapper
chillón, -llona adj, mpl chillones 1
: piercing, shrill 2 : loud, gaudy
chilpayate nmf Mex fam : child, little kid
chimbo[1], -ba adj 1 : fake, false ⟨un cheque chimbo : a bad check⟩ 2 Ven
: crummy, lousy
chimbo[2] nm Hond : tank (container)
chimenea nf 1 : chimney 2 : fireplace
chimichurri nm Arg : traditional hot sauce
chimpancé nm : chimpanzee
china nf 1 : pebble, small stone 2 PRi
: orange
chinchar vt Spain fam : to annoy, to pester — chincharse vr Spain fam : to put
up with something
chinche[1] nf 1 : bedbug 2 Ven : ladybug 3
: thumbtack
chinche[2] nmf fam : nuisance, pain in the
neck
chinchilla nf : chinchilla
chino[1], -na adj 1 : Chinese 2 Mex : curly,
kinky
chino[2], -na n : Chinese person
chino[3] nm : Chinese (language)
chintz ['ʧints] or chinz nm : chintz
chip nm, pl chips : chip ⟨chip de memoria : memory chip⟩
chipote nm Mex fam : bump (on the
head)
chipotle nm Mex : chipotle
chiquear vt Mex : to spoil, to indulge
chiquero nm POCILGA : pigpen, pigsty
chiquillada nf : childish prank
chiquillo[1], -lla adj : very young, little
chiquillo[2], -lla n : kid, youngster
chiquito[1], -ta adj : tiny
chiquito[2], -ta n : little one, baby
chiribita nf 1 : spark 2 chiribitas nfpl
: spots before the eyes
chiribitil nm 1 DESVÁN : attic, garret 2
: cubbyhole
chirigota nf fam : joke
chirimía nf : traditional reed pipe

chiripa nf 1 : fluke 2 de ~ : by sheer
luck
chirivía nf : parsnip
chirona nf fam : jail
chirriar {85} vi 1 : to squeak, to creak 2
: to screech — chirriante adj
chirrido nm 1 : squeak, squeaking 2
: screech, screeching
chirrión nm, pl chirriones Mex : whip,
lash
chis or chist interj 1 : sh! 2 : hey!
chisme nm 1 : gossip, tale 2 Spain fam
: gadget, thingamajig
chismear vi : to gossip
chismorrear → chismear
chismoso[1], -sa adj : gossipy, gossiping
chismoso[2], -sa n 1 : gossiper, gossip 2
Mex fam : tattletale
chispa[1] adj 1 Mex fam : lively, vivacious
⟨un perrito chispa : a frisky puppy⟩ 2
Spain fam : tipsy
chispa[2] nf 1 : spark 2 echar chispas : to
be furious
chispeante adj : sparkling, scintillating
chispear vi 1 : to give off sparks 2 : to
sparkle
chisporrotear vi 1 : to crackle, to sizzle
chistar vi sin chistar : without a word (of
complaint)
chiste nm 1 : joke, funny story 2 tener
chiste : to be funny 3 tener su chiste
Mex : to be tricky
chistera nf Spain : top hat
chistoso[1], -sa adj 1 : funny, humorous 2
: witty
chistoso[2], -sa n : wit, joker
chiva nf 1 Col, Ecua, Pan : rural bus 2
chivas nfpl Mex fam : stuff, odds and
ends
chivato, -ta n Cuba, Spain 1 : informant,
snitch 2 : tattletale
chivo[1], -va n 1 : kid, young goat 2 chivo
expiatorio : scapegoat
chivo[2] nm 1 : billy goat 2 : fit of anger
chocante adj 1 : shocking 2 : unpleasant, rude
chocar {72} vi 1 : to crash, to collide 2
: to clash, to conflict 3 : to be shocking
⟨le chocó : he was shocked⟩ 4 Mex, Ven
fam : to be unpleasant or obnoxious ⟨me
choca tu jefe : I can't stand your boss⟩ —
vt 1 : to shake (hands) 2 : to clink glasses
chochear vi 1 : to be senile 2 ~ por : to
dote on, to be soft on
chochín nm, pl -chines : wren
chocho, -cha adj 1 : senile 2 : doting
choclo nm 1 : ear of corn, corncob 2
: corn 3 meter el choclo Mex fam : to
make a mistake
chocolate nm 1 : chocolate ⟨chocolate
con leche : milk chocolate⟩ ⟨chocolate
oscuro/amargo/negro : dark chocolate⟩
⟨chocolate blanco : white chocolate⟩ 2
: hot chocolate, cocoa
chocolatín nm, pl -tines → chocolatina
chocolatina nf : chocolate bar
chofer or chófer nm 1 : chauffeur 2
: driver
choke nm : choke (of an automobile)

chole *interj Mex fam* ¡ya chole! : enough!, cut it out!

cholo, -la *adj & n* : mestizo

cholla *nf fam* : head

chollo *nm Spain fam* : bargain

chongo *nm* **1** *Mex* : bun (chignon) **2 chongos** *nmpl Mex* : dessert made with fried bread

choque¹, etc. → chocar

choque² *nm* **1** : crash, collision **2** : clash, conflict **3** : shock

chorizo *nm* : chorizo, pork sausage

choro *nm* **1** MEJILLÓN : mussel **2** : crook, criminal

chorrear *vi* **1** : to drip **2** : to pour out, to gush out

chorrito *nm* : squirt, splash

chorro *nm* **1** : flow, stream, jet **2** *Mex fam* : heap, ton

choteado, -da *adj Mex fam* : worn-out, stale ⟨esa canción está bien choteada : that song's been played to death⟩

chotear *vt* : to make fun of

choteo *nm* : joking around, kidding

chovinismo, chovinista → chauvinismo, chauvinista

chow–chow [ˈtʃautʃau] *nmf* : chow

choza *nf* : hut, shack

christmas *or* **crismas** *nm Spain* : Christmas card

chubasco *nm* : downpour, storm

chuchería *nf* : knickknack, trinket

chucho, -cha *n fam* **1** *CA, Mex, Spain* : mongrel, mutt **2 chuchos de frío** *Arg, Uru* : shivers

chueco, -ca *adj* **1** : crooked, bent **2** *Chile, Mex fam* : dishonest, shady

chulada *nf Mex, Spain fam* : cute or pretty thing ⟨qué chulada de vestido! : what a lovely dress!⟩

chulear *vt Mex fam* : to compliment

chuleta *nf* : cutlet, chop

chulla *nmf* : person from Quito, Ecuador

chulo¹, -la *adj* **1** *fam* : cute, pretty **2** *Spain fam* : cocky, arrogant

chulo² *nm Spain* : pimp

chupada *nf* **1** : suck, sucking **2** : puff, drag (on a cigarette)

chupado, -da *adj fam* **1** : gaunt, skinny **2** : plastered, drunk

chupaflor *nm* COLIBRÍ : hummingbird

chupamirto *nm Mex* : hummingbird

chupar *vt* **1** : to suck **2** : to absorb **3** : to puff on **4** *fam* : to drink, to guzzle — **chuparse** *vr* **1** : to suckle — **chuparse** *vr* **1** : to waste away **2** *fam* : to put up with **3** ¡chúpate esa! *fam* : take that!

chupete *nm* **1** : pacifier **2** *Chile, Peru* : lollipop

chupetear *vt* : to suck (at)

chupón *nm, pl* **chupones 1** : sucker (of a plant) **2** : baby bottle, pacifier

churrasco *nm* **1** : steak **2** : barbecued meat

churro *nm* **1** : fried dough **2** *fam* : attractive person

chusco, -ca *adj* : funny, amusing

chusma *nf* GENTUZA : riffraff, rabble

chutar *vi* : to shoot (in soccer)

chute *nm* : shot (in soccer)

chutney [ˈʃatni] *nm* : chutney

CI *or* **coeficiente intelectual** *nm* : IQ, intelligence quotient

cianotipo *nm* : blueprint

cianuro *nm* : cyanide

ciber– *pref* : cyber–

cibercafé *nm* : Internet café

cibernético, -ca *adj* : cybernetic, cyber–

cicatriz *nf, pl* **-trices** : scar

cicatrizar {21} *vi* : to form a scar, to heal

cicatrizarse *vr* → cicatrizar

cíclico, -ca *adj* : cyclical

ciclismo *nm* : bicycling

ciclista *nmf* : bicyclist

ciclo *nm* : cycle

ciclomotor *nm* : moped

ciclón *nm, pl* **ciclones** : cyclone

cicuta *nf* : hemlock

ciega, ciegue etc. → cegar

ciego¹, -ga *adj* **1** INVIDENTE : blind **2 a ciegas** : blindly **3 quedarse ciego** : to go blind — **ciegamente** *adv*

ciego², -ga *n* INVIDENTE : blind person

cielo *nm* **1** : sky **2** : heaven **3** : ceiling

ciempiés *nms & pl* : centipede

cien¹ *adj* **1** : a hundred, hundred ⟨las primeras cien páginas : the first hundred pages⟩ **2 cien por cien** *or* **cien por ciento** : a hundred percent, through and through, wholeheartedly — **cien** *pron*

cien² *nm* : one hundred

ciénaga *nf* : swamp, bog

ciencia *nf* **1** : science **2** : learning, knowledge **3 a ciencia cierta** : for a fact, for certain

cieno *nm* : mire, mud, silt

científico¹, -ca *adj* : scientific — **científicamente** *adv*

científico², -ca *n* : scientist

ciento¹ *adj* (*used in compound numbers*) : one hundred ⟨ciento uno : one hundred and one⟩

ciento² *nm* **1** : hundred ⟨cientos de personas/años : hundreds of people/years⟩ **2 por** ~ : percent

cierne, etc. → cerner

cierra, etc. → cerrar

cierre *nm* **1** : closing, closure **2** : fastener, clasp, zipper

cierto, -ta *adj* **1** : true, certain, definite ⟨lo cierto es que . . . : the fact is that . . .⟩ **2** : certain, one ⟨cierto día de verano : one summer day⟩ ⟨bajo ciertas circunstancias : under certain circumstances⟩ **3 por** ~ : in fact, as a matter of fact — **ciertamente** *adv*

ciervo, -va *n* : deer, stag *m*, hind *f*

cifra *nf* **1** : figure, number **2** : quantity, amount **3** CLAVE : code, cipher

cifrar *vt* **1** : to write in code **2** : to place, to pin ⟨cifró su esperanza en la lotería : he pinned his hopes on the lottery⟩ **3** : to encrypt (a file, etc.) — **cifrarse** *vr* : to amount ⟨cifrarse en : to amount to⟩

cigarra *nf* CHICHARRA : cicada

cigarrera *nf* : cigarette case

cigarrillo *nm* : cigarette

cigarro *nm* **1** : cigarette **2** PURO : cigar

cigoto *nm* : zygote

cigüeña *nf* : stork

cilantro nm : cilantro, coriander
cilindrada nf : cubic capacity (of an engine)
cilíndrico, -ca adj : cylindrical
cilindro nm : cylinder
cima nf CUMBRE : peak, summit, top
cimarrón, -rrona adj, mpl **-rrones** : untamed, wild
címbalo nm : cymbal
cimbrar vt : to shake, to rock — **cimbrarse** vr : to sway, to swing
cimentar {55} vt **1** : to lay the foundation of, to establish **2** : to strengthen, to cement
cimientos nmpl : base, foundation(s)
cinc nm : zinc
cincel nm : chisel
cincelar vt **1** : to chisel **2** : to engrave
cincha nf : cinch, girth
cinchar vt : to cinch (a horse)
cinco[1] adj & nm : five ⟨mi hija tiene cinco años : my daughter is five (years old)⟩ ⟨el cinco de junio : (on) the fifth of June, (on) June fifth⟩
cinco[2] pron : five ⟨seremos cinco : there will be five of us⟩ ⟨son las cinco y media : it's five-thirty⟩
cincuenta adj & nm : fifty — **cincuenta** pron
cincuentavo[1], **-va** adj : fiftieth
cincuentavo[2] nm : fiftieth (fraction)
cine nf **1** : cinema, movies pl **2** : movie theater
cineasta nmf : filmmaker
cinéfilo, -la n : cinephile, movie buff
cinematografía nf : cinematography
cinematográfico, -ca adj : movie, film, cinematic ⟨la industria cinematográfica : the film industry⟩
cínico[1], **-ca** adj **1** : cynical **2** : shameless, brazen — **cínicamente** adv
cínico[2], **-ca** n : cynic
cinismo nm : cynicism
cinta nf **1** : ribbon **2** : tape ⟨cinta métrica : tape measure⟩ **3** : strap, belt ⟨cinta transportadora : conveyor belt⟩
cinto nm : strap, belt
cintura nf **1** : waist, waistline **2 meter en cintura** fam : to bring into line, to discipline
cinturilla nf : waistband
cinturón nm, pl **-rones 1** : belt **2 cinturón de seguridad** : seat belt **3 cinturón de miseria** : shantytown, slums pl
ciñe, etc. → **ceñir**
ciprés nm, pl **cipreses** : cypress
circo nm : circus
circuitería nf : circuitry
circuito nm : circuit
circulación nf, pl **-ciones 1** : circulation **2** : movement **3** : traffic
circular[1] vi **1** : to circulate **2** : to move along **3** : to drive
circular[2] adj : circular
circular[3] nf : circular, flier
circulatorio, -ria adj : circulatory
círculo nm **1** : circle **2** : club, group
circuncidar vt : to circumcise
circuncisión nf, pl **-siones** : circumcision

circundar vt : to surround — **circundante** adj
circunferencia nf : circumference
circunflejo, -ja adj **acento circunflejo** : circumflex
circunlocución nf, pl **-ciones** : circumlocution
circunloquio nm → **circunlocución**
circunnavegar {52} vt : to circumnavigate — **circunnavegación** nf
circunscribir {33} vt : to circumscribe, to constrict, to limit — **circunscribirse** vr
circunscripción nf, pl **-ciones 1** : limitation, restriction **2** : constituency
circunscrito pp → **circunscribir**
circunspecto, -ta adj : circumspect, prudent
circunstancia nf : circumstance
circunstancial adj : circumstantial, incidental
circunstante nmf **1** : onlooker, bystander **2 los circunstantes** : those present
circunvalación nf, pl **-ciones** : surrounding, encircling ⟨carretera de circunvalación : bypass, beltway⟩
circunvecino, -na adj : surrounding, neighboring
cirio nm : large candle
cirrosis nf : cirrhosis
ciruela nf **1** : plum **2 ciruela pasa** : prune
cirugía nf : surgery ⟨cirugía cardíaca : heart surgery⟩ ⟨cirugía plástica/estética : plastic/cosmetic surgery⟩
cirujano, -na n : surgeon
cisma nm : schism, rift
cisne nm : swan
cisterna nf : cistern, tank
cita nf **1** : quote, quotation **2** : appointment, date
citable adj : quotable
citación nf, pl **-ciones** EMPLAZAMIENTO : summons, subpoena
citadino[1], **-na** adj : of the city, urban
citadino[2], **-na** n : city dweller
citado, -da adj : said, aforementioned
citar vt **1** : to quote, to cite **2** : to make an appointment with **3** : to summon (to court), to subpoena — **citarse** vr ~ **con** : to arrange to meet (someone)
citatorio nm : subpoena
-cito suf → **-ito**
cítrico nm : citrus
ciudad nf **1** : city, town **2 ciudad deportiva** : sports complex **3 ciudad natal** : native city/town **4 ciudad perdida** Mex : shantytown **5 ciudad universitaria** : college or university campus
ciudadanía nf **1** : citizenship **2** : citizenry, citizens pl
ciudadano[1], **-na** adj : civic, city
ciudadano[2], **-na** n **1** NACIONAL : citizen **2** HABITANTE : resident, city dweller
ciudadela nf : citadel, fortress
cívico, -ca adj **1** : civic **2** : civic-minded
civil[1] adj **1** : civil **2** : civilian **3 de** ~ : in plain/civilian clothes ⟨un policía de civil : a plainclothes policeman⟩
civil[2] nmf : civilian
civilidad nf : civility, courtesy
civilización nf, pl **-ciones** : civilization

civilizado, -da *adj* : civilized

civilizar {21} *vt* : to civilize

civismo *nm* : community spirit, civics

cizaña *nf* **sembrar cizaña** : to sow discord

clamar *vi* : to clamor, to raise a protest — *vt* : to cry out for

clamor *nm* : clamor, outcry

clamoroso, -sa *adj* : clamorous, resounding, thunderous

clan *nm* : clan

clandestinidad *nf* : secrecy ⟨en la clandestinidad : underground⟩

clandestino, -na *adj* : clandestine, secret — **clandestinamente** *adv*

clara *nf* : egg white

claraboya *nf* : skylight

claramente *adv* : clearly

clarear *v impers* **1** : to clear, to clear up **2** : to get light, to dawn — *vi* : to go gray, to turn white

claridad *nf* **1** NITIDEZ : clarity **2** : brightness, light

clarificación *nf, pl* **-ciones** ACLARACIÓN : clarification, explanation

clarificar {72} *vt* ACLARAR : to clarify, to explain

clarín *nm, pl* **clarines** : bugle

clarinete *nm* : clarinet

clarividencia *nf* **1** : clairvoyance **2** : perspicacity, discernment

clarividente[1] *adj* **1** : clairvoyant **2** : perspicacious, discerning

clarividente[2] *nmf* : clairvoyant

claro[1] *adv* **1** : clearly ⟨habla más claro : speak more clearly⟩ **2** : of course, surely ⟨¡claro!, ¡claro que sí! : absolutely!, of course!⟩ ⟨claro que entendió : of course she understood⟩

claro[2], **-ra** *adj* **1** : bright, clear **2** : pale, fair, light **3** : clear, evident

claro[3] *nm* **1** : clearing **2 claro de luna** : moonlight

clase *nf* **1** : class **2** ÍNDOLE, TIPO : sort, kind, type **3 clase alta/baja** : upper/lower class

clasicismo *nm* : classicism

clásico[1], **-ca** *adj* **1** : classic **2** : classical

clásico[2] *nm* : classic

clasificación *nf, pl* **-ciones 1** : classification, sorting out **2** : rating **3** CALIFICACIÓN : qualification (in competitions)

clasificado, -da *adj* : classified ⟨aviso clasificado : classified ad⟩

clasificar {72} *vt* **1** : to classify, to sort out **2** : to rate, to rank — *vi* CALIFICAR : to qualify (in competitions) — **clasificarse** *vr*

clasificatorio, -ria *adj* : qualifying

claudicación *nf, pl* **-ciones** : surrender, abandonment of one's principles

claudicar {72} *vi* **1** : to back down, to abandon one's principles

claustro *nm* : cloister

claustrofobia *nf* : claustrophobia

claustrofóbico, -ca *adj* : claustrophobic

cláusula *nf* : clause

clausura *nf* **1** : closure, closing **2** : closing ceremony **3** : cloister

clausurar *vt* **1** : to close, to bring to a close **2** : to close down

clavada *nf* : slam dunk (in basketball)

clavadista *nmf* : diver

clavado[1], **-da** *adj* **1** : nailed, fixed, stuck **2** *fam* : punctual, on the dot **3** *fam* : identical ⟨es clavado a su padre : he's the image of his father⟩

clavado[2] *nm* : dive

clavar *vt* **1** : to nail, to hammer **2** HINCAR : to plunge, to stick **3** : to fix (one's eyes) on — **clavarse** *vr* : to stick oneself (with a sharp object)

clave[1] *adj* : key, essential

clave[2] *nf* **1** CIFRA : code **2** : key ⟨la clave del misterio : the key to the mystery⟩ **3** : clef ⟨clave de sol/fa : treble/bass clef⟩

clavel *nm* : carnation

clavelito *nm* : pink (flower)

clavicémbalo *nm* : harpsichord

clavícula *nf* : collarbone

clavija *nf* **1** : plug **2** : peg, pin

clavo *nm* **1** : nail ⟨clavo grande : spike⟩ **2** : clove **3 dar en el clavo** : to hit the nail on the head

claxon *nm, pl* **cláxones** : horn (of an automobile)

clemencia *nf* : clemency, mercy

clemente *adj* : merciful

cleptomanía *nf* : kleptomania

cleptómano, -na *n* : kleptomaniac

clerecía *nf* : ministry, ministers *pl*

clerical *adj* : clerical

clérigo, -ga *n* : cleric, member of the clergy

clero *nm* : clergy

clic *nm, pl* **clics** : click ⟨haz clic aquí : click here⟩ ⟨doble clic : double click⟩

cliché *nm* **1** : cliché **2** : stencil **3** : negative (of a photograph)

cliente, -ta *n* : customer, client

clientela *nf* : clientele, customers *pl*

clima *nm* **1** : climate **2** AMBIENTE : atmosphere, ambience

climático, -ca *adj* : climatic

climatización *nf, pl* **-ciones** : air-conditioning

climatizar {21} *vt* : to air-condition — **climatizado, -da** *adj*

clímax *nm* : climax

clinch *nm* : clinch (in boxing)

clínica *nf* : clinic

clínico, -ca *adj* : clinical — **clínicamente** *adv*

clip *nm, pl* **clips 1** : clip **2** : paper clip

clíper *nm* : clipper

clítoris *nms & pl* : clitoris

cloaca *nf* ALCANTARILLA : sewer

clocar {82} *vi* : to cluck

cloche *nm* *CA, Car, Col, Ven* : clutch (of an automobile)

clon *nm* : clone

clonar *vt* : to clone

cloqué, etc. → **clocar**

cloquear *vi* : to cluck

cloqueo *nm* : cluck, clucking

clorar *vt* : to chlorinate — **cloración** *nf*

clorhídrico, -ca *adj* **ácido clorhídrico** → **ácido**[2]

cloro *nm* : chlorine

clorofila *nf* : chlorophyll

cloroformo *nm* : chloroform

cloruro *nm* : chloride
clóset *nm, pl* **clósets** 1 : closet 2 : cupboard
club *nm* : club
clueca, clueque etc. → **clocar**
clutch [ˈklatʃ] *nm* : clutch
coa *nf Mex* : hoe
coacción *nf, pl* **-ciones** : coercion, duress
coaccionar *vt* : to coerce
coactivo, -va *adj* : coercive
coagular *v* : to clot, to coagulate — **coagulación** *nf*
coágulo *nm* : clot
coalición *nf, pl* **-ciones** : coalition
coartada *nf* : alibi
coartar *vt* : to restrict, to limit
coba *nf fam* 1 : flattery ⟨darle coba a alguien : to suck up to someone⟩ 2 *Ven* MENTIRA : lie
cobalto *nm* : cobalt
cobarde¹ *adj* : cowardly
cobarde² *nmf* : coward
cobardía *nf* : cowardice
cobaya *nf* : guinea pig
cobertizo *nm* : shed, shelter
cobertor *nm* COLCHA : bedspread, quilt
cobertura *nf* 1 : coverage 2 : cover, collateral
cobija *nf* FRAZADA, MANTA : blanket
cobijar *vt* : to shelter — **cobijarse** *vr* : to take shelter
cobijo *nm* : shelter
cobra *nf* : cobra
cobrador, -dora *n* 1 : collector 2 : conductor (of a bus or train)
cobrar *vt* 1 : to charge 2 : to collect, to draw, to earn 3 : to acquire, to gain 4 : to recover, to retrieve 5 : to cash (a check) 6 : to claim, to take (a life) 7 : to shoot (game), to bag — *vi* 1 : to be paid 2 **llamar por cobrar** *Mex* : to call collect
cobre *nm* : copper
cobrizo, -za *adj* : coppery
cobro *nm* : collection (of money), cashing (of a check)
coca *nf* 1 : coca 2 *fam* : coke, cocaine
Coca *nf* (Coca-Cola, marca registrada) : Coke™, Coca-Cola™
cocaína *nf* : cocaine
cocal *nm* : coca plantation
cocción *nf, pl* **cocciones** : cooking
cocear *vi* : to kick (of an animal)
cocer {14} *vt* 1 COCINAR : to cook 2 HERVIR : to boil
cochambre *nmf fam* : filth, grime
cochambroso, -sa *adj* : filthy, grimy
coche *nm* 1 : car, automobile 2 : coach, carriage 3 **coche bomba** : car bomb 4 **coche cama** : sleeping car 5 **coche fúnebre** : hearse
cochecito *nm* : baby carriage, stroller
cochera *nf* GARAJE : garage, carport
cochinada *nf fam* 1 : filthy language 2 : disgusting behavior 3 : dirty trick
cochinillo *nm* : suckling pig, piglet
cochino¹, -na *adj* 1 : dirty, filthy, disgusting 2 *fam* : rotten, lousy
cochino², -na *n* : pig, hog
cocido¹, -da *adj* 1 : boiled, cooked 2 **bien cocido** : well-done

cocido² *nm* ESTOFADO, GUISADO : stew
cociente *nm* : quotient
cocimiento *nm* : cooking, baking
cocina *nf* 1 : kitchen 2 : stove 3 : cuisine, cooking
cocinar *v* : to cook
cocinero, -ra *n* : cook, chef
cocineta *nf Mex* : kitchenette
coco *nm* 1 : coconut 2 *fam* : head 3 *fam* : bogeyman
cocoa *nf* : cocoa, hot chocolate
cocodrilo *nm* : crocodile
cocotero *nm* : coconut palm
coctel *or* **cóctel** *nm* 1 : cocktail 2 : cocktail party
coctelera *nf* : cocktail shaker
codazo *nm* 1 **darle un codazo a alguien** : to elbow someone, to nudge someone 2 **abrirse paso a codazos** : to elbow one's way through
codear *vt* : to elbow, to jog, to nudge — **codearse** *vr* : to rub elbows, to hobnob
codeína *nf* : codeine
códice *nm* : codex, manuscript
codicia *nf* AVARICIA : avarice
codiciar *vt* : to covet
codicioso, -sa *adj* : avaricious, covetous
codificar {72} *vt* 1 : to codify 2 : to code, to encode
código *nm* 1 : code 2 **código de barras** : bar code 3 **código postal** : zip code 4 **código morse** : Morse code
codo¹, -da *adj Mex* : cheap, stingy
codo², -da *n Mex* : tightwad, cheapskate
codo³ *nm* : elbow
codorniz *nf, pl* **-nices** : quail
coeficiente *nm* 1 : coefficient 2 **coeficiente intelectual** : IQ, intelligence quotient
coexistir *vi* : to coexist — **coexistencia** *nf*
cofradía *nf* 1 : (religious) brotherhood 2 GREMIO : guild
cofre *nm* 1 BAÚL : trunk, chest 2 *Mex* CAPOTE : hood (of a car)
coger {15} *vt* 1 : to seize, to take hold of 2 : to catch 3 : to pick up 4 : to gather, to pick 5 : to gore — **cogerse** *vr* AGARRARSE : to hold on
cogida *nf* 1 : gathering, harvest 2 : goring
cognición *nf, pl* **-ciones** : cognition
cognitivo, -va *adj* : cognitive
cogollo *nm* 1 : heart (of a vegetable) 2 : bud, bulb 3 : core, crux ⟨el cogollo de la cuestión : the heart of the matter⟩
cogote *nm* : scruff, nape
cohabitar *vi* : to cohabit — **cohabitación** *nf*
cohechar *vt* SOBORNAR : to bribe
cohecho *nm* SOBORNO : bribe, bribery
coherencia *nf* : coherence — **coherente** *adj*
cohesión *nf, pl* **-siones** : cohesion
cohesivo, -va *adj* : cohesive
cohete *nm* : rocket
cohibición *nf, pl* **-ciones** 1 : (legal) restraint 2 INHIBICIÓN : inhibition
cohibido, -da *adj* : inhibited, shy

cohibir {62} *vt* : to inhibit, to make self-conscious — **cohibirse** *vr* : to feel shy or embarrassed

cohorte *nf* : cohort

coima *nf Arg, Chile, Peru* : bribe

coimear *vt Arg, Chile, Peru* : to bribe

coincidencia *nf* 1 CASUALIDAD : coincidence 2 ACUERDO : agreement

coincidente *adj* 1 : coincident 2 ACORDE : coinciding

coincidir *vi* 1 : to coincide 2 : to agree

coito *nm* : sexual intercourse, coitus

coja, etc. → **coger**

cojear *vi* 1 : to limp 2 : to wobble, to rock 3 **cojear del mismo pie** : to be two of a kind

cojera *nf* : limp

cojín *nm, pl* **cojines** : cushion, throw pillow

cojinete *nm* 1 : bearing, bushing 2 **cojinete de bola** : ball bearing

cojo¹, -ja *adj* 1 : limping, lame 2 : wobbly 3 : weak, ineffectual

cojo², -ja *n* : lame person

cojones *nmpl usu vulgar* 1 : balls *pl, usu vulgar*; testicles *pl* 2 : balls *pl, usu vulgar*; guts *pl*; courage

col *nf* 1 REPOLLO : cabbage 2 **col de Bruselas** : Brussels sprout 3 **col rizada** : kale

cola *nf* 1 RABO : tail ⟨cola de caballo : ponytail⟩ 2 FILA : line (of people) ⟨hacer cola : to wait in line⟩ 3 : cola, drink 4 : train (of a dress) 5 : tails *pl* (of a tuxedo) 6 PEGAMENTO : glue 7 *fam* : buttocks *pl*, rear end

colaboracionista *nmf* : collaborator, traitor

colaborador, -dora *n* 1 : contributor (to a periodical) 2 : collaborator

colaborar *vi* : to collaborate — **colaboración** *nf*

colación *nf, pl* **-ciones** 1 : light meal 2 : conferring (of a degree) 3 **traer a colación** : to bring up, to broach

colada *nf Spain* : laundry, wash, washing

coladera *nf Mex* : drain

colador *nm* 1 : colander, strainer 2 *PRi* : small coffeepot

colapsar *vt* 1 : to collapse 2 : to paralyze, to bring to a standstill — *vi* : to collapse

colapso *nm* 1 : collapse 2 : standstill

colar {19} *vt* : to strain, to filter — **colarse** *vr* 1 : to sneak in 2 : to cut in line 3 : to slip up, to make a mistake

colateral¹ *adj* : collateral — **colateralmente** *adv*

colateral² *nm* : collateral

colcha *nf* COBERTOR : bedspread, quilt

colchón *nm, pl* **colchones** 1 : mattress 2 : cushion, padding, buffer

colchoneta *nf* : mat (for gymnastic sports)

colear *vi* 1 : to wag its tail 2 **vivito y coleando** *fam* : alive and kicking

colección *nf, pl* **-ciones** : collection

coleccionable *adj* : collectible

coleccionar *vt* : to collect, to keep a collection of

coleccionista *nmf* : collector

colecta *nf* : collection (of donations)

colectar *vt* : to collect

colectivero, -ra *n* 1 *Arg* : bus driver 2 *Chile* : taxi driver

colectividad *nf* : community, group

colectivo¹, -va *adj* : collective — **colectivamente** *adv*

colectivo² *nm* 1 : collective 2 (*in various countries*) : city bus 3 *Chile* : fixed-route taxi

colector¹, -tora *n* : collector ⟨colector de impuestos : tax collector⟩

colector² *nm* 1 : sewer 2 : manifold (of an engine)

colega *nmf* 1 : colleague 2 HOMÓLOGO : counterpart 3 *fam* : buddy

colegiado, -da *n* 1 ÁRBITRO : referee 2 : member (of a professional association)

colegial¹, -giala *adj* 1 : school 2 *Mex fam* : green, inexperienced

colegial², -giala *n* : schoolboy *m*, schoolgirl *f*

colegiatura *nf Mex* : tuition

colegio *nm* 1 : school 2 : college ⟨colegio electoral : electoral college⟩ 3 : professional association

colegir {28} *vt* 1 JUNTAR : to collect, to gather 2 INFERIR : to infer, to deduce

cólera¹ *nm* : cholera

cólera² *nf* FURIA, IRA : anger, rage

colérico, -ca *adj* 1 FURIOSO : angry 2 IRRITABLE : irritable

colesterol *nm* : cholesterol

coleta *nf* 1 : ponytail 2 : pigtail

coletazo *nm* : lash, flick (of a tail)

colgado, -da *adj* 1 : hanging, hanged 2 : pending 3 **dejar colgado a** : to disappoint, to let down

colgante¹ *adj* : hanging, dangling

colgante² *nm* : pendant, charm (on a bracelet)

colgar {16} *vt* 1 : to hang (up), to put up 2 AHORCAR : to hang (someone) 3 : to hang up (a telephone) 4 *fam* : to fail (an exam) — **colgarse** *vr* 1 : to hang, to be suspended 2 AHORCARSE : to hang oneself 3 : to hang up a telephone

colibrí *nm* CHUPAFLOR : hummingbird

cólico *nm* : colic

coliflor *nf* : cauliflower

colilla *nf* : butt (of a cigarette)

colín *nm, pl* **colines** *Spain* : breadstick

colina *nf* CERRO, LOMA : hill

colindante *adj* CONTIGUO : adjacent, neighboring

colindar *vi* : to adjoin, to be adjacent

colirio *nm* : eyedrops *pl*

coliseo *nm* : coliseum

colisión *nf, pl* **-siones** : collision

colisionar *vi* : to collide

collage *nm* : collage

collar *nm* 1 : collar (for an animal) 2 : necklace

collie ['koli] *nmf* : collie

colmado, -da *adj* : heaping

colmar *vt* 1 : to fill to the brim 2 : to fulfill, to satisfy 3 : to heap, to shower ⟨me colmaron de regalos : they showered me with gifts⟩

colmena *nf* : beehive

colmenar *nm* APIARIO : apiary
colmillo *nm* 1 CANINO : canine (tooth), fang 2 : tusk
colmilludo, -da *adj Mex, PRi* : astute, shrewd, crafty
colmo *nm* : height, extreme, limit ⟨el colmo de la locura : the height of folly⟩ ⟨¡eso es el colmo! : that's the last straw!⟩ ⟨para colmo : to top it all off⟩
colocación *nf, pl* **-ciones** 1 : placement, placing 2 : position, job 3 : investment
colocar {72} *vt* 1 PONER : to place, to put 2 : to find a job for 3 : to invest — **colocarse** *vr* 1 SITUARSE : to position oneself 2 : to get a job
colofonia *nf* : rosin
colombiano, -na *adj & n* : Colombian
colon *nm* : (intestinal) colon
colón *nm, pl* **colones** : Costa Rican and Salvadoran unit of currency
colonia *nf* 1 : colony 2 : cologne 3 *Mex* : residential area, neighborhood
colonial *adj* : colonial
colonización *nf, pl* **-ciones** : colonization
colonizador¹, -dora *adj* : colonizing
colonizador², -dora *n* : colonist
colonizar {21} *vt* : to colonize, to settle
colono, -na *n* 1 : settler, colonist 2 : tenant farmer
coloquial *adj* : colloquial
coloquio *nm* 1 : discussion, talk 2 : conference, symposium
color *nm* 1 : color 2 : paint, dye 3 **colores** *nmpl* : colored pencils
coloración *nf, pl* **-ciones** : coloring, coloration
colorado¹, -da *adj* 1 ROJO : red 2 **ponerse colorado** : to blush 3 **chiste colorado** *Mex* : off-color joke
colorado² *nm* ROJO : red
colorante *nm* : coloring ⟨colorante de alimentos : food coloring⟩
colorear *vt* : to color — *vi* 1 : to redden 2 : to ripen
colorete *nm* : blush, rouge
colorido *nm* : color, coloring
colorín *nm, pl* **-rines** 1 : bright color 2 : goldfinch
colosal *adj* : colossal
coloso *nm* : colossus
coludir *vi* : to conspire
columna *nf* 1 : column 2 **columna vertebral** : spine, backbone
columnata *nf* : colonnade
columnista *nmf* : columnist
columpiar *vt* : to push (on a swing) — **columpiarse** *vr* : to swing
columpio *nm* : swing
colusión *nf, pl* **-siones** : collusion
colza *nf* : rape (plant)
coma¹ *nm* : coma ⟨entrar en coma : to go into a coma⟩
coma² *nf* 1 : comma 2 **coma decimal** : decimal point
comadre *nf* 1 : godmother of one's child 2 : mother of one's godchild 3 *fam* : neighbor, female friend 4 *fam* : gossip
comadrear *vi fam* : to gossip
comadreja *nf* : weasel

comadrona *nf* : midwife
comal *nm CA, Mex* : tortilla griddle
comanche *nmf* : Comanche
comandancia *nf* 1 : command headquarters 2 : command
comandante *nmf* 1 : commander, commanding officer 2 : major
comandar *vt* : to command, to lead
comando *nm* 1 : commando 2 : command (for computers)
comarca *nf* REGIÓN : region
comarcal *adj* REGIONAL : regional, local
comatoso, -sa *adj* : comatose
comba *nf* 1 : bend, sag 2 *Spain* : jump rope
combar *vt* : to bend, to curve — **combarse** *vr* 1 : to bend, to buckle 2 : to warp, to bulge, to sag
combate *nm* 1 : combat 2 : fight, boxing match
combatiente *nmf* : combatant, fighter
combatir *vt* : to combat, to fight against — *vi* : to fight
combatividad *nf* : fighting spirit
combativo, -va *adj* : combative, spirited
combi *nf Arg, Mex, Peru* : minibus
combinación *nf, pl* **-ciones** 1 : combination 2 : connection (in travel)
combinado *nm* 1 COCTEL : cocktail 2 EQUIPO : team
combinar *vt* 1 UNIR : to combine, to mix together 2 : to match, to put together — **combinarse** *vr* : to get together, to conspire
combo *nm* 1 : (musical) band 2 *Chile, Peru* : sledgehammer 3 *Chile, Peru* : punch
combustible¹ *adj* : combustible
combustible² *nm* : fuel
combustión *nf, pl* **-tiones** : combustion
comedero *nm* : trough, feeder
comedia *nf* : comedy
comediante *nmf* 1 : actor, actress *f* 2 FARSANTE : fraud
comedido, -da *adj* MESURADO : moderate, restrained
comediógrafo, -fa *n* : playwright
comedor *nm* : dining room
comején *nm, pl* **-jenes** : termite
comelón¹, -lona *adj, mpl* **-lones** *fam* : gluttonous
comelón², -lona *n, pl* **-lones** *fam* : big eater, glutton
comensal *nmf* : dinner guest
comentador, -dora *n* → **comentarista**
comentar *vt* 1 : to comment on, to discuss 2 : to mention, to remark
comentario *nm* 1 : comment, remark ⟨sin comentarios : no comment⟩ 2 : commentary
comentarista *nmf* : commentator
comenzar {29} *v* EMPEZAR : to begin, to start ⟨comenzó a trabajar : he started to work⟩ ⟨comenzó diciendo que . . . , comenzó por decir que . . . : she started by saying that . . .⟩
comer¹ *vt* 1 : to eat 2 : to consume, to eat up, to eat into — *vi* 1 : to eat 2 CENAR : to have a meal 3 **dar de comer** : to feed — **comerse** *vr* : to eat up

comer[2] *nm* : eating, dining

comercial *adj & nm* : commercial — **comercialmente** *adv*

comercializar {21} *vt* **1** : to commercialize **2** : to market — **comercialización** *nf*

comerciante *nmf* : merchant, dealer

comerciar *vi* : to do business, to trade

comercio *nm* **1** : commerce, trade **2** NEGOCIO : business, place of business **3** **comercio electrónico** : e-commerce

comestible[1] *adj* : edible

comestible[2] *nm* **1** : foodstuff, food **2** **comestibles** *nmpl* VÍVERES : groceries, food

cometa[1] *nm* : comet

cometa[2] *nf* : kite

cometer *vt* **1** : to commit **2** **cometer un error** : to make a mistake

cometido *nm* : assignment, task

comezón *nf, pl* **-zones** PICAZÓN : itchiness, itching

comible *adj fam* : eatable, edible

comic *or* **cómic** *nm* : comic strip, comic book

comicidad *nf* HUMOR : humor, wit

comicios *nmpl* : elections, voting

cómico[1], **-ca** *adj* : comic, comical

cómico[2], **-ca** *n* HUMORISTA : comic, comedian, comedienne *f*

comida *nf* **1** : food **2** : meal **3** CENA : dinner **3** *Mex, Spain* ALMUERZO : lunch **5** **comida basura** : junk food **6** **comida rápida** : fast food

comidilla *nf* : talk, gossip

comienzo *nm* **1** : start, beginning **2** **al comienzo** : at first **3** **dar comienzo** : to begin

comillas *nfpl* : quotation marks ⟨entre comillas : in quotes⟩

comilón, -lona → **comelón, -lona**

comilona *nf fam* : feast

comino *nm* **1** : cumin **2** **me vale un comino** *fam* : not to matter to someone ⟨no me importa un comino : I couldn't care less⟩

comisaría *nf* : police station

comisario, -ria *n* : commissioner

comisión *nf, pl* **-siones** **1** : commission, committing **2** : committee, commission **3** : percentage, commission ⟨comisión sobre las ventas : sales commission⟩ ⟨trabajar a comisión : to work on commission⟩

comisionado[1], **-da** *adj* : commissioned, entrusted

comisionado[2], **-da** *n* → **comisario**

comisionar *vt* : to commission

comisura *nf* **comisura de los labios** : corner of the mouth

comité *nm* : committee

comitiva *nf* : retinue, entourage

como[1] *adv* **1** : around, about ⟨cuesta como 500 pesos : it costs around 500 pesos⟩ **2** : kind of, like ⟨tengo como mareos : I'm kind of dizzy⟩

como[2] *conj* **1** : how, as ⟨hazlo como dijiste que lo harías : do it the way you said you would⟩ **2** : since, given that ⟨como estaba lloviendo, no salí : since it was raining, I didn't go out⟩ **3** : if ⟨como lo

vuelva a hacer lo arrestarán : if he does that again he'll be arrested⟩ **4** **como quiera** : in any way

como[3] *prep* **1** : like, as ⟨ligero como una pluma : light as a feather⟩ **2** **así como** : as well as

cómo *adv* : how ⟨¿cómo estás? : how are you?⟩ ⟨¿a cómo están las peras? : how much are the pears?⟩ ⟨¿cómo? : excuse me?, what was that?⟩ ⟨no sé cómo lo hace : I don't know how she does it⟩ ⟨¿cómo es eso? : how come?⟩ ⟨¿cómo que no hay dinero? : what do you mean there's no money?⟩ ⟨¿se puede? ¡cómo no! : may I? of course!⟩ ⟨¡cómo cambian los tiempos! : how times change!⟩

cómoda *nf* : bureau, chest of drawers

comodidad *nf* **1** : comfort **2** : convenience

comodín *nm, pl* **-dines** **1** : joker, wild card **2** : wildcard (symbol) **3** : all-purpose word or thing **4** : pretext, excuse

cómodo, -da *adj* **1** CONFORTABLE : comfortable **2** : convenient — **cómodamente** *adv*

comodoro *nm* : commodore

comoquiera *adv* **1** : in any way **2** **comoquiera que** : in whatever way, however ⟨comoquiera que sea eso : however that may be⟩

compa *nm fam* : buddy, pal

compactar *vt* : to compact, to compress

compact disc ['kompak'dis, -'disk] *nm, pl* **compact discs** ['kompak'dis, -'disks] : compact disc, CD

compacto, -ta *adj* : compact

compadecer {53} *vt* : to sympathize with, to feel sorry for — **compadecerse** *vr* **1** **~ de** : to take pity on **2** **~ con** : to fit, to accord (with)

compadre *nm* **1** : godfather of one's child **2** : father of one's godchild **3** *fam* : buddy, pal

compaginar *vt* **1** COORDINAR : to combine, to coordinate **2** : to collate

compañerismo *nm* : camaraderie

compañero, -ra *n* : companion, mate, partner ⟨compañero de clase : classmate⟩ ⟨compañero de trabajo : coworker⟩

compañía *nf* **1** : company ⟨en compañía de su madre : accompanied by his mother⟩ ⟨me hacía compañía : she was keeping me company⟩ ⟨andar en/con malas compañías : to keep bad company⟩ **2** EMPRESA, FIRMA : company, firm **3** : company (in theater) **4** : company (in the military)

comparable *adj* : comparable

comparación *nf, pl* **-ciones** : comparison

comparado, -da *adj* : comparative ⟨literatura comparada : comparative literature⟩

comparar *vt* : to compare

comparativo[1], **-va** *adj* : comparative, relative — **comparativamente** *adv*

comparativo[2] *nm* : comparative degree or form

comparecencia *nf* **1** : appearance (in court) **2** **orden de comparecencia** : subpoena, summons

comparecer {53} *vi* : to appear (in court)

comparsa *nmf* : extra (in a film, etc.)

compartimiento *or* **compartimento** *nm* : compartment

compartir *vt* : to share

compás *nm, pl* **-pases 1** : beat, rhythm, time **2** : compass

compasión *nf, pl* **-siones** : compassion, pity

compasivo, -va *adj* : compassionate

compatibilidad *nf* : compatibility

compatible *adj* : compatible

compatriota *nmf* PAISANO : compatriot, fellow countryman

compeler *vt* : to compel

compendiar *vt* : to summarize, to condense

compendio *nm* : summary

compenetración *nf, pl* **-ciones** : rapport, mutual understanding

compenetrarse *vr* **1** : to understand each other **2** ~ **con** : to identify oneself with

compensación *nf, pl* **-ciones** : compensation

compensar *vt* : to compensate for, to make up for — *vi* : to be worth one's while

compensatorio, -ria *adj* : compensatory

competencia *nf* **1** : competition, rivalry **2** : competence

competente *adj* : competent, able — **competentemente** *adv*

competición *nf, pl* **-ciones** : competition

competidor[1]**, -dora** *adj* RIVAL : competing, rival

competidor[2]**, -dora** *n* RIVAL : competitor, rival

competir {54} *vi* : to compete

competitividad *nf* : competitiveness

competitivo, -va *adj* : competitive — **competitivamente** *adv*

compilar *vt* : to compile — **compilación** *nf*

compinche *nmf fam* **1** : buddy, pal **2** : partner in crime, accomplice

complacencia *nf* : pleasure, satisfaction

complacer {57} *vt* : to please — **complacerse** *vr* ~ **en** : to take pleasure in

complaciente *adj* : obliging, eager to please

complejidad *nf* : complexity

complejo[1]**, -ja** *adj* : complex

complejo[2] *nm* : complex

complementar *vt* : to complement, to supplement — **complementarse** *vr*

complementario, -ria *adj* : complementary

complemento *nm* **1** : complement, supplement **2** : supplementary pay, allowance

completamente *adv* : completely, totally

completar *vt* TERMINAR : to complete, to finish

completo, -ta *adj* **1** : complete, full, whole ⟨las obras completas : the complete works⟩ ⟨su nombre completo : his full name⟩ **2** : complete, absolute ⟨por completo : completely⟩ **3** DETALLADO : full, detailed **4** VERSÁTIL : well-rounded, versatile

complexión *nf, pl* **-xiones** : (physical) constitution

complicación *nf, pl* **-ciones** : complication

complicado, -da *adj* : complicated

complicar {72} *vt* **1** : to complicate **2** : to involve — **complicarse** *vr*

cómplice *nmf* : accomplice

complicidad *nf* : complicity

complot *nm, pl* **complots** CONFABULACIÓN, CONSPIRACIÓN : conspiracy, plot

componenda *nf* : shady deal, scam

componente *adj* & *nm* : component, constituent

componer {60} *vt* **1** ARREGLAR : to fix, to repair **2** CONSTITUIR : to make up, to compose **3** : to compose, to write **4** : to set (a bone) — **componerse** *vr* **1** : to improve, to get better **2** ~ **de** : to consist of

comportamiento *nm* CONDUCTA : behavior, conduct

comportarse *vr* : to behave, to conduct oneself

composición *nf, pl* **-ciones** **1** OBRA : composition, work **2** : makeup, arrangement

compositor, -tora *n* : composer, songwriter

compostura *nf* **1** : composure **2** : mending, repair

compota *nf* : compote

compra *nf* **1** : purchase **2 ir de compras** : to go shopping **3 orden de compra** : purchase order

comprador, -dora *n* : buyer, shopper

comprar *vt* : to buy, to purchase

compraventa *nf* : buying and selling

comprender *vt* **1** ENTENDER : to comprehend, to understand **2** ABARCAR : to cover, to include — *vi* : to understand ⟨ya comprendo! : now I understand!⟩

comprensible *adj* : understandable — **comprensiblemente** *adv*

comprensión *nf, pl* **-siones** **1** : comprehension, understanding **2** : understanding, sympathy

comprensivo, -va *adj* : understanding

compresa *nf* **1** : compress **2** *or* **compresa higiénica** : sanitary napkin

compresión *nf, pl* **-siones** : compression

compresor *nm* : compressor

comprimido *nm* PÍLDORA, TABLETA : pill, tablet

comprimir *vt* : to compress

comprobable *adj* : provable

comprobación *nf, pl* **-ciones** : verification, confirmation

comprobante *nm* **1** : proof ⟨comprobante de identidad : proof of identity⟩ **2** : voucher, receipt ⟨comprobante de ventas : sales slip⟩

comprobar {19} *vt* **1** : to verify, to check **2** : to prove

comprometedor, -dora *adj* : compromising

comprometer *vt* **1** : to compromise **2** : to jeopardize **3** : to commit, to put under obligation — **comprometerse** *vr* **1** : to commit oneself **2** ~ **con** : to get engaged to

comprometido, -da *adj* **1** : compromising, awkward **2** : committed, obliged **3** : engaged (to be married)

compromiso *nm* **1** : obligation, commitment **2** : engagement ⟨anillo de compromiso : engagement ring⟩ **3** : agreement **4** : awkward situation, fix

compuerta *nf* : floodgate

compuesto[1] *pp* → **componer**

compuesto[2], **-ta** *adj* **1** : fixed, repaired **2** : compound, composite **3** : decked out, spruced up **4** ~ **de** : made up of, consisting of

compuesto[3] *nm* : compound

compulsión *nf, pl* **-siones** : compulsion

compulsivo, -va *adj* **1** : compelling, urgent **2** : compulsive — **compulsivamente** *adv*

compungido, -da *adj* : contrite, remorseful

compungirse {35} *vr* : to feel remorse

compuso, etc. → **componer**

computable *adj* : countable ⟨años computables : years accrued⟩ ⟨ingresos computables : qualifying income⟩

computación *nf, pl* **-ciones** : computing, computers *pl*

computador *nm* → **computadora**

computadora *nf* **1** : computer **2 computadora portátil** : laptop computer

computar *vt* : to compute, to calculate

computarizar {21} *vt* : to computerize

cómputo *nm* : computation, calculation

comulgar {52} *vi* : to receive Communion

común *adj, pl* **comunes 1** : common **2 común y corriente** : ordinary, regular **3 por lo común** : generally, as a rule

comuna *nf* : commune

comunal *adj* : communal

comunicación *nf, pl* **-ciones 1** : communication **2** : access, link **3** : message, report

comunicado *nm* **1** : communiqué **2 comunicado de prensa** : press release

comunicador, -dora *n* : commentator, analyst

comunicar {72} *vt* **1** : to communicate, to convey **2** : to notify — **comunicarse** ~ **con** *vr* **1** : to contact, to get in touch with **2** : to be connected to

comunicativo, -va *adj* : communicative, talkative

comunidad *nf* : community

comunión *nf, pl* **-niones 1** : communion, sharing **2** : Communion

comunismo *nm* : communism, Communism

comunista *adj & nmf* : communist

comunitario, -ria *adj* : community, communal

comúnmente *adv* : commonly

con *prep* **1** : with ⟨vengo con mi padre : I'm going with my father⟩ ⟨¿con quién hablas? : who are you speaking to?⟩ **2** : in spite of ⟨con todo : in spite of it all⟩ **3** : to, towards ⟨ser amable con : to be kind to⟩ **4** : by ⟨con llegar temprano : by arriving early⟩ **5 con (tal) que** : as/so long as

conato *nm* : attempt, effort ⟨conato de robo : attempted robbery⟩

cóncavo, -va *adj* : concave

concebible *adj* : conceivable

concebir {54} *vt* **1** : to conceive **2** : to conceive of, to imagine — *vi* : to conceive, to become pregnant

conceder *vt* **1** : to grant, to bestow **2** : to concede, to admit

concejal, -jala *n* : councilman *m*, councilwoman *f*; alderman *mf*

concejo *nm* : council ⟨concejo municipal : town council⟩

concentración *nf, pl* **-ciones** : concentration

concentrado *nm* : concentrate

concentrar *vt* : to concentrate — **concentrarse** *vr*

concéntrico, -ca *adj* : concentric

concepción *nf, pl* **-ciones** : conception

concepto *nm* NOCIÓN : concept, idea, opinion

conceptuar {3} *vt* : to regard, to judge

concernir {17} *vi* : to be of concern

concertar {55} *vt* **1** : to arrange, to set up **2** : to agree on, to settle **3** : to harmonize — *vi* : to be in harmony

concesión *nf, pl* **-siones 1** : concession **2** : awarding, granting

concesionario, -ria *n* : franchisee

concha *nf* : conch, seashell

concho *nm DomRep* : fixed-route taxi

conciencia *nf* **1** : conscience **2** : consciousness, awareness

concienciar → **concientizar**

concientización *nf, pl* **-ciones** : awareness, awareness-raising

concientizar {21} *vt* : to make aware — **concientizarse** *vr* ~ **de** : to realize, to become aware of

concienzudo, -da *adj* : conscientious

concierto *nm* **1** : concert **2** : agreement **3** : concerto

conciliador[1], **-dora** *adj* : conciliatory

conciliador[2], **-dora** *n* : arbitrator, peacemaker

conciliar *vt* : to reconcile — **conciliación** *nf*

conciliatorio, -ria *adj* → **conciliador**[1]

concilio *nm* : (church) council

conciso, -sa *adj* : concise — **concisamente** *adv* — **concisión** *nf*

concitar *vt* : to arouse

conciudadano, -na *n* : fellow citizen

cónclave *nm* : conclave, private meeting

concluir {41} *vt* **1** TERMINAR : to conclude, to finish **2** DEDUCIR : to deduce, to conclude — *vi* : to end, to conclude

conclusión *nf, pl* **-siones** : conclusion

concluyente *adj* : conclusive

concomitante *adj* : accompanying, attendant

concordancia *nf* : agreement, accordance

concordar {19} *vi* : to agree, to coincide — *vt* : to reconcile

concordia *nf* : concord, harmony

concretar *vt* **1** : to pinpoint, to specify **2** : to fulfill, to realize — **concretarse** *vr* : to become real, to take shape

concretizar → **concretar**

concreto[1], **-ta** *adj* **1** : concrete, actual **2** : definite, specific ⟨en concreto : specifically⟩ — **concretamente** *adv*

concreto[2] *nm* HORMIGÓN : concrete
concurrencia *nf* 1 : audience, turnout 2 : concurrence
concurrente *adj* : concurrent — **concurrentemente** *adv*
concurrido, -da *adj* : busy, crowded
concurrir *vi* 1 : to converge, to come together 2 : to concur, to agree 3 : to take part, to participate 4 : to attend, to be present ⟨concurrir a una reunión : to attend a meeting⟩ 5 ~ a : to contribute to
concursante *nmf* : contestant, competitor
concursar *vt* : to compete in — *vi* : to compete, to participate
concurso *nm* 1 : contest, competition 2 : concurrence, coincidence 3 : crowd, gathering 4 : cooperation, assistance
condado *nm* 1 : county 2 : earldom
conde, -desa *n* : count *m*, earl *m*, countess *f*
condecoración *nf, pl* **-ciones** : decoration, medal
condecorar *vt* : to decorate, to award (a medal)
condena *nf* 1 : condemnation 2 SENTENCIA : sentence
condenable *adj* : reprehensible
condenación *nf, pl* **-ciones** 1 : condemnation 2 : damnation
condenado[1], **-da** *adj* 1 : fated, doomed 2 : convicted, sentenced 3 *fam* : darn, damned
condenado[2], **-da** *n* : convict
condenar *vt* 1 : to condemn 2 : to sentence 3 : to board up, to wall up — **condenarse** *vr* : to be damned
condenatorio, -ria *adj* : condemning ⟨sentencia condenatoria : conviction⟩
condensación *nf, pl* **-ciones** : condensation
condensar *vt* : to condense
condesa *nf* → conde
condescendencia *nf* : condescension
condescender {56} *vi* 1 : to condescend 2 : to agree, to acquiesce
condescendiente *adj* 1 : condescending 2 : accommodating, obliging
condición *nf, pl* **-ciones** 1 : condition, state ⟨en buenas/malas condiciones : in good/bad condition⟩ ⟨no está en condiciones de trabajar : she's in no shape to work⟩ 2 : capacity, position ⟨estar en condiciones de : to be in a position to⟩ 3 : condition, stipulation ⟨a condición de que, con la condición de que : on the condition that⟩ 4 **condiciones** *nfpl* : conditions, circumstances ⟨condiciones de vida : living conditions⟩ ⟨en igualdad de condiciones : on equal footing⟩
condicional *adj* : conditional — **condicionalmente** *adv*
condicionamiento *nm* : conditioning
condicionar *vt* 1 : to condition, to determine 2 ~ a : to be contingent on, to depend on
condimentar *vt* SAZONAR : to season, to spice
condimento *nm* : condiment, seasoning, spice

condolencia *nf* : condolence, sympathy
condolerse {47} *vr* : to sympathize
condominio *nm* : condominium, condo
condón *nm, pl* **condones** : condom
cóndor *nm* : condor
conducción *nf, pl* **-ciones** 1 : conduction (of electricity, etc.) 2 DIRECCIÓN : management, direction
conducir {61} *vt* 1 DIRIGIR, GUIAR : to direct, to lead 2 MANEJAR : to drive (a vehicle) — *vi* 1 : to drive a vehicle 2 ~ a : to lead to — **conducirse** *vr* PORTARSE : to behave, to conduct oneself
conducta *nf* COMPORTAMIENTO : conduct, behavior
conductividad *nf* : conductivity
conducto *nm* : conduit, channel, duct
conductor[1], **-tora** *adj* : conducting, leading
conductor[2], **-tora** *n* : driver
conductor[3] *nm* : conductor (of electricity, etc.)
conectar *vt* : to connect — *vi* ~ **con** : to link up with, to communicate with
conectivo, -va *adj* : connective — **conectividad** *nf*
conector *nm* : connector
conejera *nf* : rabbit hutch
conejillo *nm* **conejillo de Indias** : guinea pig
conejo, -ja *n* : rabbit
conexión *nf, pl* **-xiones** : connection
confabulación *nf, pl* **-ciones** COMPLOT, CONSPIRACIÓN : plot, conspiracy
confabularse *vr* : to plot, to conspire
confección *nf, pl* **-ciones** 1 : preparation 2 : tailoring, dressmaking
confeccionar *vt* : to make, to produce, to prepare
confederación *nf, pl* **-ciones** : confederation
confederarse *vr* : to confederate, to form a confederation
conferencia *nf* 1 REUNIÓN : conference, meeting 2 : lecture
conferenciante *nmf* : lecturer
conferencista *nmf* → conferenciante
conferir {76} *vt* : to confer, to bestow
confesar {55} *v* : to confess — **confesarse** *vr* : to go to confession
confesión *nf, pl* **-siones** 1 : confession 2 : creed, denomination
confesionario *nm* : confessional
confesor *nm* : confessor
confeti *nm* : confetti
confiable *adj* : trustworthy, reliable
confiado, -da *adj* 1 : confident, self-confident 2 : trusting — **confiadamente** *adv*
confianza *nf* 1 : trust ⟨de poca confianza : untrustworthy⟩ 2 : confidence, self-confidence
confianzudo, -da *adj* : forward, presumptuous
confiar {85} *vt* 1 : to confide 2 : to entrust — *vi* ~ **en** : to trust, to have faith/confidence in — **confiarse** *vr* 1 : to be overconfident 2 ~ a : to confide in
confidencia *nf* : confidence, secret

confidencial *adj* : confidential — **confidencialmente** *adv*

confidencialidad *nf* : confidentiality

confidente *nmf* **1** : confidant, confidante *f* **2** : informer

configuración *nf, pl* **-ciones** : configuration, shape

configurar *vt* **1** : to shape, to form **2** : to configure (a computer, etc.)

confín *nm, pl* **confines** : boundary, limit

confinamiento *nm* : confinement

confinar *vt* **1** : to confine, to limit **2** : to exile — *vi* ~ **con** : to border on

confirmación *nf, pl* **-ciones** : confirmation

confirmar *vt* : to confirm, to substantiate

confiscación *nf, pl* **-ciones** : confiscation

confiscar {72} *vt* DECOMISAR : to confiscate, to seize

confitado, -da *adj* : candied

confite *nm* : sugar-coated candy

confitería *nf* **1** DULCERÍA : candy store, confectionery **2** : tearoom, café

confitero, -ra *n* : confectioner

confitura *nf* : preserves, jam

conflagración *nf, pl* **-ciones** **1** : conflagration, fire **2** : war

conflictivo, -va *adj* **1** : troubled **2** : controversial

conflicto *nm* : conflict

confluencia *nf* : junction, confluence

confluir {41} *vi* **1** : to converge, to join **2** : to gather, to assemble

conformación *nf, pl* **-ciones** : makeup, composition

conformar *vt* **1** : to form, to create **2** : to constitute, to make up — **conformarse** *vr* **1** RESIGNARSE : to resign oneself **2** : to comply, to conform **3** ~ **con** : to be content with

conforme[1] *adj* **1** : content, satisfied **2** ~ **a** : in accordance with

conforme[2] *conj* : as ⟨irá mejorando conforme avance el día : it will improve as the day goes on⟩

conformidad *nf* **1** : agreement, consent **2** : resignation

confort *nm* : comfort

confortable *adj* CÓMODO : comfortable

confortar *vt* CONSOLAR : to comfort, to console

confraternidad *nf* : brotherhood, fraternity

confraternizar {21} *vi* : to fraternize — **confraternización** *nf*

confrontación *nf, pl* **-ciones** : confrontation

confrontar *vt* **1** ENCARAR : to confront **2** : to compare **3** : to bring face-to-face — *vi* : to border — **confrontarse** *vr* ~ **con** : to face up to

confundir *vt* **1** : to confuse, to mix up — **confundirse** *vr* **1** : to make a mistake, to be confused ⟨confundirse de número : to get the wrong number⟩

confusión *nf, pl* **-siones** : confusion

confuso, -sa *adj* **1** DESORDENADO : confused, confusing ⟨ideas confusas : confused ideas⟩ ⟨una situación confusa : a confused/confusing situation⟩ ⟨unas voces confusas : a confusion of voices⟩ **2** ATURDIDO, TURBADO : confused, flustered, embarrassed **3** VAGO : hazy, indistinct

congelación *nf, pl* **-ciones** **1** : freezing **2** : frostbite (on skin), exposure

congelado, -da *adj* HELADO : frozen

congelador *nm* HELADORA : freezer

congelamiento *nm* → **congelación**

congelar *vt* : to freeze — **congelarse** *vr*

congeniar *vi* : to get along (with someone)

congénito, -ta *adj* : congenital

congestión *nf, pl* **-tiones** : congestion

congestionado, -da *adj* : congested

congestionamiento *nm* → **congestión**

congestionarse *vr* **1** : to become flushed **2** : to become congested

conglomerado[1], **-da** *adj* : conglomerate, mixed

conglomerado[2] *nm* : conglomerate, conglomeration

congoja *nf* ANGUSTIA : anguish, grief

congoleño, -ña *adj & n* : Congolese

congraciarse *vr* : to ingratiate oneself

congratular *vt* FELICITAR : to congratulate

congregación *nf, pl* **-ciones** : congregation, gathering

congregar {52} *vt* : to bring together — **congregarse** *vr* : to congregate, to assemble

congresista *nmf* : congressman *m*, congresswoman *f*

congreso *nm* : congress, conference

congruencia *nf* **1** : congruence **2** COHERENCIA : coherence — **congruente** *adj*

cónico, -ca *adj* : conical, conic

conífera *nf* : conifer

conífero, -ra *adj* : coniferous

conjetura *nf* : conjecture, guess

conjeturar *vt* : to guess, to conjecture

conjugación *nf, pl* **-ciones** : conjugation

conjugar {52} *vt* **1** : to conjugate **2** : to combine

conjunción *nf, pl* **-ciones** : conjunction

conjuntivitis *nf* : conjunctivitis

conjuntivo, -va *adj* : connective ⟨tejido conjuntivo : connective tissue⟩

conjunto[1], **-ta** *adj* : joint — **conjuntamente** *adv*

conjunto[2] *nm* **1** : collection, group **2** : ensemble, outfit **3** : ensemble, musical group **4** : whole, entirety ⟨en conjunto : as a whole, altogether⟩

conjurar *vt* **1** : to exorcise **2** : to avert, to ward off — *vi* CONSPIRAR : to conspire, to plot

conjuro *nm* **1** : exorcism **2** : spell

conllevar *vt* **1** : to bear, to suffer **2** IMPLICAR : to entail, to involve

conmemorar *vt* : to commemorate — **conmemoración** *nf*

conmemorativo, -va *adj* : commemorative, memorial

conmigo *pron* : with me ⟨habló conmigo : he talked with me⟩

conminar *vt* AMENAZAR : to threaten, to warn

conmiseración *nf, pl* **-ciones** : pity, commiseration

conmoción *nf, pl* **-ciones 1** : shock, upheaval **2** *or* **conmoción cerebral** : concussion

conmocionar *vt* : to shake, to shock

conmovedor, -dora *adj* EMOCIONANTE : moving, touching

conmover {47} *vt* **1** EMOCIONAR : to move, to touch **2** : to shake up — **conmoverse** *vr*

conmutador *nm* **1** : switch **2** : switchboard

conmutar *vt* **1** : to commute (a sentence) **2** : to switch, to exchange

connivencia *nf* : connivance

connotación *nf, pl* **-ciones** : connotation

connotar *vt* : to connote, to imply

cono *nm* : cone

conocedor¹, -dora *adj* : knowledgeable

conocedor², -dora *n* : connoisseur, expert

conocer {18} *vt* **1** : to know, to be acquainted with ⟨¿lo conoces? : do you know him?⟩ **2** : to meet ⟨ya la conocí : I've already met her⟩ **3** : to know, to be familiar with (a topic, etc.) **4** : to get to know, to experience ⟨me gustaría conocer otros países : I'd like to visit other countries⟩ ⟨conocer de primera mano : to experience firsthand⟩ **5** RECONOCER : to recognize ⟨no lo conocí : I didn't recognize you⟩ **6** **dar a conocer** : to disclose, to announce **7** **darse a conocer** : to make oneself known — **conocerse** *vr* **1** : to know each other **2** : to meet **3** : to know oneself

conocible *adj* : knowable

conocido¹, -da *adj* **1** : familiar **2** : well-known, famous

conocido², -da *n* : acquaintance

conocimiento *nm* **1** : knowledge **2** SENTIDO : consciousness

conque *conj* : so, so then, and so ⟨¡ah, conque esas tenemos! : oh, so that's what's going on!⟩

conquista *nf* : conquest

conquistador¹, -dora *adj* : conquering

conquistador², -dora *n* : conqueror

conquistar *vt* : to conquer

consabido, -da *adj* : usual, typical

consagración *nf, pl* **-ciones** : consecration

consagrar *vt* **1** : to consecrate **2** DEDICAR : to dedicate, to devote

consciencia → **conciencia**

consciente *adj* : conscious, aware — **conscientemente** *adv*

conscripción *nf, pl* **-ciones** : conscription, draft

conscripto, -ta *n* : conscript, inductee

consecución *nf, pl* **-ciones** : attainment

consecuencia *nf* **1** : consequence, result ⟨a consecuencia de : as a result of⟩ **2** **en ~** : accordingly

consecuente *adj* : consistent — **consecuentemente** *adv*

consecutivo, -va *adj* : consecutive, successive — **consecutivamente** *adv*

conseguir {75} *vt* **1** : to get, to obtain **2** : to achieve, to attain (a goal, etc.) **3** : to

manage to ⟨consiguió acabar : she managed to finish⟩ ⟨conseguí que lo aceptara : I got him to accept it⟩

consejero, -ra *n* : adviser, counselor

consejo *nm* **1** : piece of advice ⟨me dio algunos consejos : she gave me some advice⟩ ⟨por consejo de : on the advice of⟩ **2** : council ⟨consejo de guerra : court-martial⟩

consenso *nm* : consensus

consensuar *vt* : to reach a consensus on

consentido, -da *adj* : spoiled, pampered

consentimiento *nm* : consent, permission

consentir {76} *vt* **1** PERMITIR : to consent to, to allow **2** MIMAR : to pamper, to spoil — *vi* **~ en** : to agree to, to approve of

conserje *nmf* : custodian, janitor, caretaker

conserva *nf* **1** : preserve(s), jam **2** **conservas** *nfpl* : canned goods

conservación *nf, pl* **-ciones** : conservation, preservation

conservacionista *nmf* : conservationist

conservador¹, -dora *adj & n* : conservative

conservador² *nm* : preservative

conservadurismo *nm* : conservatism

conservante *nm* : preservative

conservar *vt* **1** : to preserve **2** GUARDAR : to keep, to conserve

conservatorio *nm* : conservatory

considerable *adj* : considerable — **considerablemente** *adv*

consideración *nf, pl* **-ciones 1** : consideration **2** : respect **3** **de ~** : considerable, important

considerado, -da *adj* **1** : considerate, thoughtful **2** : respected

considerar *vt* **1** : to consider, to think about ⟨considerar la posibilidad : to consider the possibility⟩ ⟨considerando su edad : considering his age⟩ **2** : to consider, to regard as ⟨lo considera necesario : she considers it necessary⟩ **3** : to treat with consideration — **considerarse** *vr* : to consider oneself

consigna *nf* **1** ESLOGAN : slogan **2** : assignment, orders *pl* **3** : luggage storage

consignación *nf, pl* **-ciones 1** : consignment **2** ASIGNACIÓN : allocation

consignar *vt* **1** : to consign **2** : to record, to write down **3** : to assign, to allocate

consigo *pron* : with her, with him, with you, with oneself ⟨se llevó las llaves consigo : she took the keys with her⟩

consiguiente *adj* **1** : resulting, consequent **2** **por ~** : consequently, as a result

consistencia *nf* : consistency

consistente *adj* **1** : firm, strong, sound **2** : consistent — **consistentemente** *adv*

consistir *vi* **1** **~ en** : to consist of **2** **~ en** : to lie in, to consist in

consola *nf* : console

consolación *nf, pl* **-ciones** : consolation ⟨premio de consolación : consolation prize⟩

consolar {19} *vt* CONFORTAR : to console, to comfort

consolidar *vt* : to consolidate — **consolidación** *nf*

consomé *nm* CALDO : consommé, clear soup

consonancia *nf* **1** : harmony **2 en consonancia con** : in accordance with

consonante[1] *adj* : consonant, harmonious

consonante[2] *nf* : consonant

consorcio *nm* : consortium

consorte *nmf* : consort, spouse

conspicuo, -cua *adj* : eminent, famous

conspiración *nf, pl* **-ciones** COMPLOT, CONFABULACIÓN : conspiracy, plot

conspirador, -dora *n* : conspirator

conspirar *vi* CONJURAR : to conspire, to plot

constancia *nf* **1** PRUEBA : proof, certainty **2** : record, evidence ⟨que quede constancia : for the record⟩ **3** : perseverance, constancy

constante[1] *adj* : constant — **constantemente** *adv*

constante[2] *nf* : constant

constar *vi* **1** : to be evident, to be on record ⟨que conste : believe me, have no doubt⟩ **2 ~ de** : to consist of

constatación *nf, pl* **-ciones** : confirmation, proof

constatar *vt* **1** : to verify **2** : to state

constelación *nf, pl* **-ciones** : constellation

consternación *nf, pl* **-ciones** : consternation, dismay

consternar *vt* : to dismay, to appall

constipación *nf, pl* **-ciones** : constipation

constipado[1]**, -da** *adj* **estar constipado** : to have a cold

constipado[2] *nm* RESFRIADO : cold

constiparse *vr* : to catch a cold

constitución *nf, pl* **-ciones** : constitution — **constitucional** *adj* — **constitucionalmente** *adv*

constitucionalidad *nf* : constitutionality

constituir {41} *vt* **1** FORMAR : to constitute, to make up, to form **2** FUNDAR : to establish, to set up — **constituirse** *vr* **~ en** : to set oneself up as, to become

constitutivo, -va *adj* : constituent, component

constituyente *adj & nmf* : constituent

constreñir {67} *vt* **1** FORZAR, OBLIGAR : to constrain, to oblige **2** LIMITAR : to restrict, to limit

construcción *nf, pl* **-ciones** : construction, building

constructivo, -va *adj* : constructive — **constructivamente** *adv*

constructor, -tora *n* : builder

constructora *nf* : construction company

construir {41} *vt* : to build, to construct

consuelo *nm* : consolation, comfort

consuetudinario, -ria *adj* **1** : customary, habitual **2 derecho consuetudinario** : common law

cónsul *nmf* : consul — **consular** *adj*

consulado *nm* : consulate

consulta *nf* **1** : consultation **2** : inquiry

consultar *vt* : to consult

consultivo, -va *adj* : advisory

consultor[1]**, -tora** *n* : consulting ⟨firma consultora : consulting firm⟩

consultor[2]**, -tora** *n* : consultant

consultoría *nf* : consultancy

consultorio *nm* **1** : office (of a doctor or dentist) **2 → consultoría**

consumación *nf, pl* **-ciones** : consummation

consumado, -da *adj* : consummate, perfect

consumar *vt* **1** : to consummate, to complete **2** : to commit, to carry out

consumible *adj* : consumable

consumición *nf, pl* **-ciones** **1** : consumption **2** : drink (in a restaurant)

consumido, -da *adj* : thin, emaciated

consumidor, -dora *n* : consumer

consumir *vt* : to consume — **consumirse** *vr* : to waste away

consumismo *nm* : consumerism

consumo *nm* : consumption (of food, fuel, etc.)

contabilidad *nf* **1** : accounting, bookkeeping **2** : accountancy

contabilizar {21} *vt* : to enter, to record (in accounting)

contable[1] *adj* : countable

contable[2] *nmf Spain* : accountant, bookkeeper

contactar *vt* : to contact — *vi* **~ con** : to get in touch with, to contact

contacto *nm* : contact

contado[1]**, -da** *adj* **1** : counted ⟨tenía los días contados : his days were numbered⟩ **2** : rare, scarce ⟨en contadas ocasiones : on rare occasions⟩

contado[2] *nm* **al contado** : cash ⟨pagar al contado : to pay in cash⟩

contador[1]**, -dora** *n* : accountant

contador[2] *nm* : meter ⟨contador de agua : water meter⟩ ⟨contador Geiger : Geiger counter⟩

contaduría *nf* **1** : accounting office **2** CONTABILIDAD : accountancy

contagiar *vt* **1** : to infect **2** : to transmit (a disease) — **contagiarse** *vr* **1** : to be contagious **2** : to become infected

contagio *nm* : contagion, infection

contagioso, -sa *adj* : contagious, catching

contaminación *nf, pl* **-ciones** : contamination, pollution

contaminante *nm* : pollutant, contaminant

contaminar *vt* : to contaminate, to pollute

contante *adj* **dinero contante y sonante** **→ dinero**

contar {19} *vt* **1** : to count ⟨contar el dinero : to count the money⟩ **2** : to tell ⟨cuéntame un cuento : tell me a story⟩ ⟨me lo contó todo : she told me everything⟩ **3** : to include, to count — *vi* **1** : to count (up) ⟨contar de diez en diez : to count by tens⟩ **2** : to count, to matter ⟨eso no cuenta : that doesn't count⟩ **3 ~ con** : to count on, to rely on **4 ~ con** : to expect, to count on ⟨no contaba con que . . . : I didn't count on the fact that . . .⟩ **5 ~ con** : to have (support, resources, etc.) — **contarse** *vr* **~ entre** : to be numbered among

contemplación *nf, pl* **-ciones** : contemplation — **contemplativo, -va** *adj*

contemplar *vt* **1** : to contemplate, to ponder **2** : to gaze at, to look at

contemporáneo, -nea *adj & n* : contemporary

contención *nf, pl* **-ciones** : containment, holding

contencioso, -sa *adj* : contentious

contender {56} *vi* **1** : to contend, to compete **2** : to fight

contendiente *nmf* : contender

contenedor *nm* **1** : container, receptacle **2** : Dumpster™

contener {80} *vt* **1** : to contain, to hold **2** ATAJAR : to restrain, to hold back — **contenerse** *vr* : to restrain oneself

contenido¹, -da *adj* : restrained, reserved

contenido² *nm* : contents *pl*, content

contentar *vt* : to please, to make happy — **contentarse** *vr* : to be satisfied, to be pleased

contento¹, -ta *adj* : contented, glad, happy

contento² *nm* : joy, happiness

conteo *nm* : count

contestación *nf, pl* **-ciones** **1** : answer, reply **2** : protest

contestador *nm or* **contestador automático** : answering machine

contestadora *nf* → contestador

contestar *vt* RESPONDER : to answer — *vi* **1** RESPONDER : to answer, to reply **2** : to talk back, to be disrespectful

contexto *nm* : context

contienda *nf* **1** : dispute, conflict **2** : contest, competition

contigo *pron* : with you ⟨voy contigo : I'm going with you⟩

contiguo, -gua *adj* COLINDANTE : contiguous, adjacent

continente *nm* : continent — **continental** *adj*

contingencia *nf* : contingency, eventuality

contingente *adj & nm* : contingent

continuación *nf, pl* **-ciones** **1** : continuation **2 a ~** : next ⟨más detalles a continuación : more details below⟩ **3 a continuación de** : after, following

continuar {3} *v* : to continue ⟨continuó trabajando : she continued working, she continued to work⟩ ⟨continuar ⟨con⟩ algo : to continue (with) something⟩

continuidad *nf* : continuity

continuo, -nua *adj* : continuous, steady, constant — **continuamente** *adv*

contonearse *vr* : to sway one's hips

contoneo *nm* : swaying, wiggling (of the hips)

contorno *nm* **1** : outline **2** **contornos** *nmpl* : outskirts

contorsión *nf, pl* **-siones** : contortion

contra¹ *nf* **1** *fam* : difficulty, snag **2 llevar la contra a** : to oppose, to contradict

contra² *nm* : con ⟨los pros y los contras : the pros and cons⟩

contra³ *prep* : against ⟨se apoyó contra la pared : he leaned against the wall⟩ ⟨luchar contra : to fight against⟩ **2 en contra** : against ⟨las razones en contra : the reasons against it⟩ ⟨protestas en contra del gobierno : anti-government protests⟩

contra- *pref* : counter- ⟨contraataque : counterattack⟩

contraalmirante *nm* : rear admiral

contraatacar {72} *v* : to counterattack — **contraataque** *nm*

contrabajo *nm* : double bass

contrabalancear *vt* : to counterbalance — **contrabalanza** *nf*

contrabandear *v* : to smuggle

contrabandista *nmf* : smuggler, black market dealer

contrabando *nm* **1** : smuggling **2** : contraband

contracción *nf, pl* **-ciones** : contraction

contracepción *nf, pl* **-ciones** : contraception

contraceptivo *nm* ANTICONCEPTIVO : contraceptive

contrachapado *nm* : plywood

contracorriente *nf* **1** : crosscurrent **2 ir a contracorriente** : to go against the tide

contractual *adj* : contractual

contradecir {11} *vt* DESMENTIR : to contradict — **contradecirse** *vr* DESDECIRSE : to contradict oneself

contradicción *nf, pl* **-ciones** : contradiction

contradictorio, -ria *adj* : contradictory

contraer {81} *vt* **1** : to contract (a disease) **2** : to establish by contract ⟨contraer matrimonio : to get married⟩ **3** : to tighten, to contract — **contraerse** *vr* : to contract, to tighten up

contrafuerte *nm* : buttress

contragolpe *nm* **1** : counterattack **2** : backlash

contrahuella *nf* : riser (of a stair)

contralor, -lora *n* : comptroller

contraloría *nf* : office of the comptroller

contralto *nmf* : contralto

contraluz *nm, pl* **-luces a contraluz** : against the light

contramandar *vt* : to countermand

contramano *nm* **a ~** : the wrong way (on a street)

contramedida *nf* : countermeasure

contraparte *nf* **1** : counterpart **2 en ~** : on the other hand

contrapartida *nf* : compensation

contrapelo *nm* **a ~** : in the wrong direction, against the grain

contrapesar *vt* : to counterbalance

contrapeso *nm* : counterbalance

contraponer {60} *vt* **1** : to counter, to oppose **2** : to contrast, to compare

contraportada *nf* : back cover, back page

contraposición *nf, pl* **-ciones** : comparison

contraproducente *adj* : counterproductive

contrapunto *nm* : counterpoint

contrariar {85} *vt* **1** : to contradict, to oppose **2** : to vex, to annoy

contrariedad *nf* **1** : setback, obstacle **2** : vexation, annoyance

contrario, -ria *adj* **1** : contrary, opposite ⟨al contrario : on the contrary⟩ **2** : conflicting, opposed

contrarreloj *adj* **1** : timed **2 a ~** : against the clock

contrarrestar *vt* : to counteract

contrarrevolución *nf, pl* **-ciones** : counterrevolution — **contrarrevolucionario, -ria** *adj & n*

contrasentido *nm* : contradiction

contraseña *nf* : password

contrastante *adj* : contrasting

contrastar *vt* **1** : to resist **2** : to check, to confirm — *vi* : to contrast

contraste *nm* : contrast

contratar *vt* **1** : to contract for **2** : to hire, to engage

contratiempo *nm* **1** PERCANCE : mishap, accident **2** DIFICULTAD : setback, difficulty

contratista *nmf* : contractor

contrato *nm* : contract

contravenir {87} *vt* : to contravene, to infringe

contraventana *nf* : shutter

contravía *nf* Col **ir en contravía** : to drive the wrong way (down a street)

contribución *nf, pl* **-ciones** : contribution

contribuidor, -dora *n* : contributor

contribuir {41} *vt* **1** APORTAR : to contribute **2** : to pay (in taxes) — *vi* **1** : to contribute, to help out **2** : to pay taxes

contribuyente[1] *adj* : contributing

contribuyente[2] *nmf* : taxpayer

contrición *nf, pl* **-ciones** : contrition

contrincante *nmf* : rival, opponent

contrito, -ta *adj* : contrite, repentant

control *nm* **1** : control ⟨control remoto : remote control⟩ ⟨control de natalidad : birth control⟩ **2** : inspection, check **3** : checkpoint, roadblock

controlable *adj* : controllable

controlador, -dora *n* : controller ⟨controlador aéreo : air traffic controller⟩

controlar *vt* **1** : to control **2** : to monitor, to check

controversia *nf* : controversy

controversial → controvertido

controvertido, -da *adj* : controversial

controvertir {76} *vt* : to dispute, to argue about — *vi* : to argue, to debate

contubernio *nm* : conspiracy

contundencia *nf* **1** : forcefulness, weight **2** : severity

contundente *adj* : blunt ⟨un objeto contundente : a blunt instrument⟩ **2** : forceful, convincing — **contundentemente** *adv*

contusión *nf, pl* **-siones** : bruise, contusion

contusionar *vt* MAGULLAR : to bruise

contuvo, etc. → contener

conurbano *nm* Arg : suburbs *pl*

convalecencia *nf* : convalescence

convalecer {53} *vi* : to convalesce, to recover

convaleciente *adj & nmf* : convalescent

convalidar *vt* : to recognize, to validate

convección *nf, pl* **-ciones** : convection

convencer {86} *vt* **1** : to convince, to persuade — **convencerse** *vr*

convencimiento *nm* : belief, conviction

convención *nf, pl* **-ciones** **1** : convention, conference **2** : pact, agreement **3** : convention, custom

convencional *adj* : conventional — **convencionalmente** *adv*

conveniencia *nf* **1** : convenience **2** : fitness, suitability, advisability

conveniente *adj* **1** : convenient **2** : suitable, advisable

convenio *nm* PACTO : agreement, pact

convenir {87} *vi* **1** : to be suitable, to be advisable **2** : to agree

conventillo *nm* Arg, Uru : tenement

convento *nm* **1** : convent **2** : monastery

convergencia *nf* : convergence

convergente *adj* : convergent, converging

converger {15} *or* **convergir** {35} *vi* **1** : to converge **2** ~ **en** : to concur on

conversación *nf, pl* **-ciones** : conversation

conversador, -dora *n* : conversationalist, talker

conversar *vi* : to converse, to talk

conversatorio *nm* CA, Carib, Mex : talk, discussion

conversión *nf, pl* **-siones** : conversion

converso, -sa *n* : convert

convertible *adj & nm* : convertible

convertidor *nm* : converter ⟨convertidor catalítico : catalytic converter⟩

convertir {76} *vt* **1** : to convert (someone) **2** : to convert (money, etc.) **3** ~ **en** : to turn (someone or something) into (something) — **convertirse** *vr* **1** : to convert **2** ~ **en** : to turn into, to become

convexo, -xa *adj* : convex

convicción *nf, pl* **-ciones** : conviction

convicto, -ta *adj* : convicted

convicto[2], **-ta** *n* : convict, prisoner

convidado, -da *n* : guest

convidar *vt* **1** INVITAR : to invite **2** : to offer

convincente *adj* : convincing — **convincentemente** *adv*

convivir *vi* **1** : to coexist **2** : to live together

convocar {72} *vt* : to convoke, to call together

convocatoria *nf* : summons, call

convoy *nm* : convoy

convulsión *nf, pl* **-siones** **1** : convulsion **2** : agitation, upheaval

convulsionar *vt* : to shake, to convulse — **convulsionarse** *vr*

convulsivo, -va *adj* : convulsive

conyugal *adj* : conjugal

cónyuge *nmf* : spouse, partner

coñac *nm* : cognac, brandy

cooperación *nf, pl* **-ciones** : cooperation

cooperador, -dora *adj* : cooperative

cooperar *vi* : to cooperate

cooperativa *nf* : cooperative, co-op

cooperativo, -va *adj* : cooperative

cooptar *vt* : to co-opt

coordenada *nf* : coordinate

coordinación *nf, pl* **-ciones** : coordination

coordinador, -dora *n* : coordinator

coordinar *vt* COMPAGINAR : to coordinate, to combine

copa *nf* **1** : wineglass, goblet **2** : drink ⟨irse de copas : to go out drinking⟩ **3** : cup, trophy **4** : top, crown (of a tree) **5**

copas *nfpl* : cups (suit in the Spanish deck of cards)

copar *vt* **1** : to take ⟨ya está copado el puesto : the job is already taken⟩ **2** : to fill, to crowd

copartícipe *nmf* : joint partner

copero, -ra *adj* : cup ⟨partido copero : cup game⟩

copete *nm* **1** : tuft (of hair) **2 estar hasta el copete** : to be completely fed up

copia *nf* **1** : copy **2** : imitation, replica

copiadora *nf* : photocopier

copiar *vt* : to copy

copiloto *nmf* : copilot

copión, -piona *n, pl* **copiones** : copycat

copioso, -sa *adj* : copious, abundant

copla *nf* **1** : popular song or ballad **2** : stanza

copo *nm* **1** : snowflake **2 copos de avena** : rolled oats **3 copos de maíz** : cornflakes

coprotagonista *nmf* : co-star

cópula *nf* : copulation

copular *vi* : to copulate

coque *nm* : coke (fuel)

coqueta *nf* : dressing table

coquetear *vi* : to flirt

coqueteo *nm* : flirting

coqueto¹, -ta *adj* : flirtatious

coqueto², -ta *n* : flirt

coraje *nm* **1** VALOR : valor, courage **2** IRA : anger ⟨darle coraje a alguien : to make someone angry⟩

corajudo, -da *adj* : brave

coral¹ *adj* : choral

coral² *nm* **1** : coral **2** : chorale

coral³ *nf* : choir

Corán *nm* **el Corán** : the Koran

coraza *nf* **1** : armor, armor plating **2** : shell (of an animal)

corazón *nm, pl* **-zones 1** : heart ⟨de todo corazón : wholeheartedly⟩ ⟨de buen corazón : kindhearted⟩ **2** : core **3** : darling, sweetheart

corazonada *nf* : hunch, impulse

corbata *nf* : tie, necktie

corcel *nm* : steed, charger

corchete *nm* **1** : hook and eye, clasp **2** : square bracket

corcho *nm* : cork

corcholata *nf Mex* : cap, bottle top

corcovear *vi* : to buck

cordel *nm* : cord, string

cordero *nm* : lamb

cordial¹ *adj* : cordial, affable — **cordialmente** *adv*

cordial² *nm* : cordial (liqueur)

cordialidad *nf* : cordiality, warmth

cordillera *nf* : mountain range

córdoba *nf* : Nicaraguan unit of currency

cordón *nm, pl* **cordones 1** : cord ⟨cordón umbilical : umbilical cord⟩ **2** : cordon

cordoncillo *nm* : piping (of clothing, etc.)

cordura *nf* **1** : sanity **2** : prudence, good judgment

coreano¹, -na *adj* & *n* : Korean

coreano² *nm* : Korean (language)

corear *vt* : to chant, to chorus

coreografía *nf* : choreography

coreografiar {85} *vt* : to choreograph

coreográfico, -ca *adj* : choreographic

coreógrafo, -fa *n* : choreographer

corista *nmf* **1** : chorister **2** : chorus girl *f*

cormorán *nm, pl* **-ranes** : cormorant

cornada *nf* : goring, butt (with the horns)

córnea *nf* : cornea

cornear *vt* : to gore

cornejo *nm* : dogwood (tree)

córner *nm* : corner kick

corneta *nf* : bugle, horn, cornet

cornisa *nf* : cornice

cornucopia *nf* : cornucopia

cornudo, -da *adj* : horned

coro *nm* **1** : choir **2** : chorus

corola *nf* : corolla

corolario *nm* : corollary

corona *nf* **1** : crown **2** : wreath, garland **3** : corona (in astronomy)

coronación *nf, pl* **-ciones** : coronation

coronar *vt* **1** : to crown **2** : to reach the top of, to culminate

coronario, -ria *adj* : coronary

coronel, -nela *n* : colonel

coronilla *nf* **1** : crown (of the head) **2 estar hasta la coronilla** : to be completely fed up

corpiño *nm* **1** : bodice **2** *Arg* : brassiere, bra

corporación *nf, pl* **-ciones** : corporation

corporal *adj* : corporal, bodily

corporativo, -va *adj* : corporate

corpóreo, -rea *adj* : corporeal, physical

corpulencia *nf* : stoutness, sturdiness

corpulento, -ta *adj* : robust, stout, sturdy

corpúsculo *nm* : corpuscle

corral *nm* **1** : farmyard **2** : corral, pen, stockyard **3** *or* **corralito** : playpen

correa *nf* **1** : strap, belt **2** TRAÍLLA : leash

correcaminos *nms* & *pl* : roadrunner

corrección *nf, pl* **-ciones 1** : correction **2** : correctness, propriety **3** : rebuke, reprimand **4 corrección de pruebas** : proofreading

correccional *nm* REFORMATORIO : reform school

correctivo, -va *adj* : corrective ⟨lentes correctivos : corrective lenses⟩

correcto, -ta *adj* **1** : correct, right **2** : courteous, polite — **correctamente** *adv*

corrector, -tora *n* : proofreader

corredizo, -za *adj* : sliding ⟨puerta corrediza : sliding door⟩ ⟨nudo corredizo : slipknot⟩

corredor¹, -dora *n* **1** : runner, racer **2** : agent, broker ⟨corredor de bolsa : stockbroker⟩

corredor² *nm* PASILLO : corridor, hallway

correduría *nf* → **corretaje**

corregir {28} *vt* **1** : to correct, to edit (text), to grade (exams) **2** : to reprimand **3 corregir pruebas** : to proofread — **corregirse** *vr* : to reform, to mend one's ways

correlación *nf, pl* **-ciones** : correlation

correo *nm* **1** : mail ⟨correo aéreo : airmail⟩ **2** : post office

correoso, -sa *adj* : leathery, rough

correr *vi* **1** : to run ⟨corrió a/hacia la puerta : he ran to/towards the door⟩ ⟨salí corriendo : I took off running⟩ **2** : to race (in sports) **3** : to rush ⟨¡corre, que se acaban! : hurry, they're almost gone/done!⟩ **4** : to flow, to run **5 a todo** ~ : at top speed, in a hurry — *vt* **1** : to run, to race in **2** : to move, to slide, to roll, to draw (curtains) **3** ~ **con** : to be responsible for ⟨correr con los gastos : to foot the bill⟩ **4 correr peligro** : to be in danger **5 correr un riesgo** : to run a risk — **correrse** *vr* **1** : to move along **2** : to run, to spill over

correspondencia *nf* **1** : correspondence, mail **2** : equivalence **3** : connection, interchange

corresponder *vi* **1** : to correspond ⟨corresponder a/con : to correspond to/with, to match, to fit⟩ **2** : to belong ⟨el título que le corresponde : the title that is rightfully hers⟩ **3** : to be the responsibility of ⟨no le corresponde intervenir : it's not his place to intervene⟩ **4** : to be appropriate, to be fitting ⟨como corresponde : as is appropriate⟩ **5** : to reciprocate — **corresponderse** *vr* : to write to each other

correspondiente *adj* : corresponding, respective

corresponsal *nmf* : correspondent

corretaje *nm* : brokerage

corretear *vi* **1** VAGAR : to loiter, to wander about **2** : to run around, to scamper about — *vt* : to pursue, to chase

correteo *nm* : running around

corrida *nf* **1** : run, dash **2** : bullfight

corrido¹, -da *adj* **1** : straight, continuous **2** : worldly, experienced

corrido² *nm* : Mexican narrative folk song

corriente¹ *adj* **1** : common, everyday **2** : current, present **3** *Mex* : cheap, trashy **4 perro corriente** *Mex* : mutt

corriente² *nf* **1** : current ⟨corriente alterna : alternating current⟩ ⟨corriente continua : direct current⟩ **2** : draft **3** TENDENCIA : tendency, trend

corrillo *nm* : small group, clique

corro *nm* : ring, circle (of people)

corroboración *nf, pl* **-ciones** : corroboration

corroborar *vt* : to corroborate

corroer {69} *vt* **1** : to corrode **2** : to erode, to wear away

corromper *vt* **1** : to corrupt **2** : to rot — **corromperse** *vr*

corrompido, -da *adj* CORRUPTO : corrupt, rotten

corrosión *nf, pl* **-siones** : corrosion

corrosivo, -va *adj* : corrosive

corrugar {52} *vt* : to corrugate — **corrugación** *nf*

corrupción *nf, pl* **-ciones** **1** : decay **2** : corruption

corruptela *nf* : corruption, abuse of power

corruptible *adj* : corruptible

corrupto, -ta *adj* CORROMPIDO : corrupt

corsé *nm* : corset

cortacésped *nm Spain* : lawn mower

cortada *nf* : cut, gash

cortador, -dora *n* : cutter

cortadora *nf* : cutter, slicer

cortadura *nf* : cut, slash

cortafuegos *nms & pl* **1** : firebreak **2** : firewall (program)

cortante *adj* : cutting, sharp

cortar *vt* **1** : to cut ⟨lo cortó en dos : he cut it in half⟩ ⟨cortar en pedazos : to cut into pieces⟩ ⟨cortar en rebanadas/trozos (etc.) : to slice⟩ ⟨cortar leña : to chop wood⟩ ⟨cortar el pasto : to mow the lawn, to cut the grass⟩ **2** CERCENAR : to cut off, to sever **3** TALAR : to cut down, to chop down **4** RECORTAR : to cut out, to clip (coupons, etc.) **5** EDITAR : to cut, to edit **6** INTERRUMPIR : to cut off, to interrupt **7** BLOQUEAR, CERRAR : to block (off), to close (off) **8** : to curdle (milk) — *vi.* **1** : to cut **2** : to break up ⟨cortar con alguien : to break up with someone⟩ **3** : to hang up (the telephone) — **cortarse** *vr* **1** : to cut oneself ⟨cortarse el pelo : to cut one's hair⟩ **2** : to be cut off **3** : to sour, to separate (of milk)

cortaúñas *nms & pl* : nail clippers

corte¹ *nm* **1** : cut, cutting ⟨corte de pelo : haircut⟩ **2** : cut (of clothes) **3** : cutoff, interruption ⟨corte comercial/publicitario : commercial break⟩ ⟨corte de luz, corte de energía eléctrica : power failure⟩

corte² *nf* **1** : court ⟨corte suprema : supreme court⟩ **2 hacer la corte a** : to court, to woo

cortejar *vt* GALANTEAR : to court, to woo

cortejo *nm* **1** GALANTEO : courtship **2** : retinue, entourage

cortés *adj* : courteous, polite — **cortésmente** *adv*

cortesano¹, -na *adj* : courtly

cortesano², -na *n* : courtier

cortesía *nf* **1** : courtesy, politeness **2 de** ~ : complimentary, free

corteza *nf* **1** : bark **2** : crust **3** : peel, rind **4** : cortex ⟨corteza cerebral : cerebral cortex⟩

cortijo *nm* : farmhouse

cortina *nf* : curtain

cortisona *nf* : cortisone

corto¹, -ta *adj* **1** : short (in length or duration) **2** : scarce **3** : timid, shy **4 corto de vista** : nearsighted

corto² *nm* → **cortometraje**

cortocircuito *nm* : short circuit

cortometraje *nm* : short (film)

corvejón *nm, pl* **-jones** JARRETE : hock

corvo, -va *adj* : curved, bent

cosa *nf* **1** : thing, object **2** : matter, affair **3 otra cosa** : anything else, something else

cosecha *nf* : harvest, crop

cosechador, -dora *n* : harvester, reaper

cosechadora *nf* : harvester (machine)

cosechar *vt* **1** : to harvest, to reap **2** : to win, to earn, to garner — *vi* : to harvest

coser *vt* **1** : to sew **2** : to stitch up — *vi* : to sew

cosmético¹, -ca *adj* : cosmetic

cosmético² *nm* : cosmetic

cósmico, -ca *adj* : cosmic

cosmonauta *nmf* : cosmonaut

cosmopolita *adj & nmf* : cosmopolitan

cosmos *nm* : cosmos

cosquillas *nfpl* 1 : tickling 2 hacer cosquillas : to tickle

cosquilleo *nm* : tickling sensation, tingle

cosquilloso, -sa *adj* : ticklish

costa *nf* 1 : coast, shore 2 : cost ⟨a toda costa : at all costs⟩ ⟨a costa de : at the expense of⟩

costado *nm* 1 : side 2 al costado : alongside

costal *nm* 1 : sack 2 ser harina de otro costal → harina

costanera *nf* : boardwalk, waterfront path

costar {19} *v* : to cost ⟨¿cuánto cuesta? : how much does it cost?⟩

costarricense *adj & nmf* : Costa Rican

costarriqueño, -ña → costarricense

coste → costo

costear *vt* : to pay for, to finance

costero, -ra *adj* : coastal, coast

costilla *nf* 1 : rib 2 : chop, cutlet 3 *fam* : better half, wife

costo *nm* 1 : cost, price 2 costo de vida : cost of living

costoso, -sa *adj* : costly, expensive

costra *nf* 1 : crust 2 POSTILLA : scab

costumbre *nf* 1 : custom 2 HÁBITO : habit

costura *nf* 1 : seam 2 : sewing, dressmaking 3 alta costura : haute couture

costurera *nf* : seamstress *f*

costurero *nm* : sewing box

cota *nf* 1 : altitude 2 : level ⟨su máxima cota : its maximum level⟩

cotejar *vt* : to compare, to collate

cotejo *nm* 1 : comparison 2 : match, game

cotidiano, -na *adj* : daily, everyday ⟨la vida cotidiana : daily life⟩

cotilla *nmf Spain fam* : gossip, gossiper

cotización *nf, pl* -ciones 1 : market price 2 : quote, estimate

cotizado, -da *adj* : in demand, sought after

cotizar {21} *vt* : to quote, to value — cotizarse *vr* : to be worth

coto *nm* 1 : enclosure, reserve 2 poner coto a : to put a stop to

cotonete *nf Mex* : (cotton) swab

cotorra *nf* 1 : small parrot 2 *fam* : chatterbox

cotorrear *vi fam* : to chatter, to gab, to blab

cotorreo *nm fam* : chatter, prattle

cowboy [kaoˈboi] *pl* -boys [kaoˈbois] *nm* : cowboy

coyote *nm* 1 : coyote 2 *Mex fam* : smuggler (of illegal immigrants)

coyuntura *nf* 1 ARTICULACIÓN : joint 2 : occasion, moment

coz *nf, pl* coces : kick (of an animal)

CPU [sepeˈu] *nmf* : CPU

crac *nm, pl* cracs : crash (of the stock market)

crack *nm* : crack (cocaine)

cozamos, etc. → cocer

craneal *adj* : cranial

craneano, -na *adj* : cranial

cráneo *nf* : cranium, skull — craneano, -na *adj*

cráter *nm* : crater

crayón *nm, pl* -yones : crayon

creación *nf, pl* -ciones : creation

creador[1], -dora *adj* : creative, creating

creador[2], -dora *n* : creator

crear *vt* 1 : to create, to cause 2 : to originate

creatividad *nf* : creativity

creativo, -va *adj* : creative — creativamente *adv*

creces *nfpl* con creces ⟨cumple con creces las expectativas : it more than meets expectations⟩ ⟨superar con creces : to greatly exceed⟩ ⟨pagar con creces : to pay dearly (for)⟩

crecer {53} *vi* 1 : to grow 2 : to increase, to grow (in number, etc.)

crecida *nf* : flooding, floodwater

crecido, -da *adj* 1 : grown, grown-up 2 : large (of numbers)

creciente *adj* 1 : growing, increasing 2 luna creciente : waxing moon

crecimiento *nm* 1 : growth 2 : increase

credencial *adj* cartas credenciales : credentials

credenciales *nfpl* : documents, documentation, credentials

credibilidad *nf* : credibility

crediticio, -cia *adj* : credit

crédito *nm* : credit

credo *nm* : creed, credo

credulidad *nf* : credulity

crédulo, -la *adj* : credulous, gullible

creencia *nf* : belief

creer {20} *v* 1 : to believe ⟨creer en : to believe in⟩ 2 : to think, to suppose ⟨creo que sí : I think so⟩ ⟨creo que no : I don't think so⟩ ⟨no creo que sea necesario : I don't think it's necessary⟩ 3 ¡ya lo creo! : of course!, indeed! — creerse *vr* 1 : to believe, to think 2 : to regard oneself as ⟨se cree muy guapo : he thinks he's so handsome⟩

creíble *adj* : believable, credible

creído, -da *adj* 1 *fam* : conceited 2 : confident, sure

crema *nf* 1 : cream ⟨crema batida : whipped cream⟩ 2 la crema y nata : the pick of the crop

cremación *nf, pl* -ciones : cremation

cremallera *nf* : zipper

cremar *vt* : to cremate

crematorio *nm* : crematorium

cremoso, -sa *adj* : creamy

crepa *nf Mex* : crepe (pancake)

crepe *or* crep *nmf* : crepe (pancake)

crepé *nm* 1 → crespón 2 papel crepé : crepe paper

crepúsculo *nm* : twilight

crescendo *nm* : crescendo

crespo, -pa *adj* : curly, frizzy

crespón *nm, pl* crespones : crepe (fabric)

cresta *nf* 1 : crest 2 : comb (of a rooster)

creta *nf* : chalk (mineral)

cretino, -na *n* **1** : cretin *often offensive* **2** : idiot, moron, cretin

creyente[1] *adj* : faithful ⟨personas creyentes : believers⟩

creyente[2] *nmf* : believer

creyó, etc. → **creer**

crezca, etc. → **crecer**

cría *nf* **1** : breeding, rearing **2** : young **3** : litter

criadero *nm* : hatchery

criado[1], **-da** *adj* : raised, brought up **2 bien criado** : well-bred

criado[2], **-da** *n* : servant, maid *f*

criador, -dora *n* : breeder

crianza *nf* : upbringing, rearing

criar {85} *vt* **1** : to breed **2** : to bring up, to raise — **criarse** *vr* : to grow up

criatura *nf* **1** : baby, child **2** : creature

criba *nf* : sieve, screen

cribar *vt* : to sift

cric *nm, pl* **crics** : jack

cricket *nm* : cricket (sport)

crimen *nm, pl* **crímenes** : crime

criminal *adj & nmf* : criminal

criminalidad *nf* : crime ⟨alta criminalidad : high crime rates⟩

crin *nf* **1** : mane **2** : horsehair

crío, cría *n Spain* : kid

criollo[1], **-lla** *adj* **1** : Creole **2** : native, national ⟨comida criolla : native cuisine⟩

criollo[2], **-lla** *n* : Creole

criollo[3] *nm* : Creole (language)

cripta *nf* : crypt

críptico, -ca *adj* **1** : cryptic, coded **2** : enigmatic, cryptic

criptón *nm* : krypton

críquet *nm* : cricket (game)

crisálida *nf* : chrysalis, pupa

crisantemo *nm* : chrysanthemum

crisis *nf* **1** : crisis **2 crisis nerviosa** : nervous breakdown

crisma *nf fam* : head ⟨romperle la crisma a alguien : to knock someone's block off⟩

crismas → **christmas**

crisol *nm* **1** : crucible **2** : melting pot

crispar *vt* **1** : to cause to contract **2** : to irritate, to set on edge ⟨eso me crispa los nervios : that gets on my nerves⟩ — **crisparse** *vr* : to tense up

cristal *nm* **1** VIDRIO : glass, piece of glass **2** : crystal

cristalería *nf* **1** : glassware shop **2** : glassware, crystal

cristalino[1], **-na** *adj* : crystalline, clear

cristalino[2] *nm* : lens (of the eye)

cristalizar {21} *vi* : to crystallize — **cristalización** *nf*

cristiandad *nf* : Christendom

cristianismo *nm* : Christianity

cristiano, -na *adj & n* : Christian

Cristo *nm* : Christ

criterio *nm* **1** : criterion **2** : judgment, sense

crítica *nf* **1** : criticism **2** : review, critique

criticar {72} *vt* : to criticize

crítico[1], **-ca** *adj* : critical — **críticamente** *adv*

crítico[2], **-ca** *n* : critic

criticón[1], **-cona** *adj, mpl* **-cones** *fam* : hypercritical

criticón[2], **-cona** *n, mpl* **-cones** *fam* : faultfinder, critic

croar *vi* : to croak

croata *adj & nmf* : Croatian

crocante *adj* : crunchy

croché *or* **crochet** *nm* : crochet

croissant [krwaˈsan, -ˈzan] *nm, pl* **croissants** [krwaˈsans, -ˈzans] : croissant

crol *nm* : crawl (in swimming)

cromático, -ca *adj* : chromatic

cromo *nm* **1** : chromium, chrome **2** : picture card, sports card

cromosoma *nm* : chromosome

crónica *nf* **1** : news report **2** : chronicle, history

crónico, -ca *adj* : chronic

cronista *nmf* **1** : reporter, newscaster **2** HISTORIADOR : chronicler, historian

cronograma *nm* : schedule, timetable

cronología *nf* : chronology

cronológico, -ca *adj* : chronological — **cronológicamente** *adv*

cronometrador, -dora *n* : timekeeper

cronometrar *vt* : to time, to clock

cronómetro *nm* : chronometer

croquet *nm* : croquet

croqueta *nf* : croquette

croquis *nm* : rough sketch

cruasán *nm, pl* **cruasanes** → **croissant**

cruce[1], **etc.** → **cruzar**

cruce[2] *nm* **1** : crossing, cross **2** : crossroads, intersection ⟨cruce peatonal : crosswalk⟩

crucero *nm* **1** : cruise **2** : cruiser, warship **3** *Mex* : intersection

crucial *adj* : crucial — **crucialmente** *adv*

crucificar {72} *vt* : to crucify

crucifijo *nm* : crucifix

crucifixión *nf, pl* **-fixiones** : crucifixion

crucigrama *nm* : crossword puzzle

cruda *nf Mex fam* : hangover

crudeza *nf* : harshness

crudo[1], **-da** *adj* **1** : raw **2** : crude, harsh

crudo[2] *nm* : crude oil

cruel *adj* : cruel — **cruelmente** *adv*

crueldad *nf* : cruelty ⟨la crueldad del tirano : the tyrant's cruelty⟩ ⟨las crueldades de la guerra : the cruelties of war⟩

cruento, -ta *adj* : bloody

crujido *nm* **1** : rustling **2** : creaking **3** : crackling (of a fire) **4** : crunching

crujiente *adj* : crunchy, crisp

crujir *vi* **1** : to rustle **2** : to creak, to crack **3** : to crunch

crup *nm* : croup

crustáceo *nm* : crustacean

crutón *nm, pl* **crutones** : crouton

cruz *nf, pl* **cruces** : cross

cruza *nf* : cross (hybrid)

cruzada *nf* : crusade

cruzado[1], **-da** *adj* : crossed

cruzado[2] *nm* **1** : crusader **2** : Brazilian unit of currency

cruzar {21} *vt* **1** : to cross ⟨cruzar la calle : to cross the street⟩ ⟨cruzar las piernas : to cross one's legs⟩ **2** : to exchange (words, greetings) **3** : to cross, to interbreed — *vi* : to cross — **cruzarse** *vr* **1**

: to intersect **2** : to meet, to pass each other **3 cruzarse de brazos** : to cross one's arms

cuaderno *nm* LIBRETA : notebook

cuadra *nf* **1** : city block **2** : stable

cuadrado¹, -da *adj* : square

cuadrado² *nm* : square ⟨elevar al cuadrado : to square (a number)⟩

cuadragésimo¹, -ma *adj* : fortieth, forty-

cuadragésimo², -ma *n* : fortieth, forty- (in a series)

cuadrante *nm* **1** : quadrant **2** : dial

cuadrar *vi* : to conform, to agree — *vt* : to square — **cuadrarse** *vr* : to stand at attention

cuadriculado *nm* : grid (on a map, etc.)

cuadrilátero *nm* **1** : quadrilateral **2** : ring (in sports)

cuadrilla *nf* : gang, team, group

cuadro *nm* **1** : square ⟨una blusa a cuadros : a checkered blouse⟩ **2** : painting, picture **3** : baseball diamond, infield **4** : panel, board, cadre

cuádruple *adj* : quadruple

cuadruplicar {72} *vt* : to quadruple — **cuadruplicarse** *vr*

cuajada *nf* : curd

cuajar *vi* **1** : to curdle **2** COAGULAR : to clot, to coagulate **3** : to set, to jell **4** : to be accepted ⟨su idea no cuajó : his idea didn't catch on⟩ — *vt* **1** : to curdle **2** ∼ **de** : to fill with

cual¹ *prep* : like, as

cual² *pron* **1 el cual, la cual, los cuales, las cuales** : who, whom, which ⟨la razón por la cual lo dije : the reason I said it⟩ **2 lo cual** : which ⟨se rió, lo cual me dio rabia : he laughed, which made me mad⟩ **3 cada cual** : everyone, everybody

cuál¹ *adj* : which, what ⟨¿cuáles libros? : which books?⟩

cuál² *pron* **1** (*in questions*) : which (one), what (one) ⟨¿cuál es el mejor? : which one is the best?⟩ ⟨¿cuál es tu apellido? : what is your last name?⟩ **2 cuál más, cuál menos** : some more, some less

cualidad *nf* : quality, trait

cualificado, -da *adj Spain* : qualified, trained

cualitativo, -va *adj* : qualitative — **cualitativamente** *adv*

cualquier *adj* → **cualquiera¹**

cualquiera¹ (*cualquier before nouns*) *adj, pl* **cualesquiera 1** : any, whichever ⟨cualquier persona : any person⟩ **2** : everyday, ordinary ⟨un hombre cualquiera : an ordinary man⟩

cualquiera² *pron, pl* **cualesquiera 1** : anyone, anybody, whoever **2** : whatever, whichever

cuán *adv* : how ⟨¡cuán feliz era! : how happy I was!⟩

cuando¹ *conj* **1** : when ⟨cuando llegó : when he arrived⟩ **2** : since, if ⟨cuando lo dices : if you say so⟩ **3 cuando más/menos** : at the most/least **4 de vez en cuando** : from time to time

cuando² *prep* : during, at the time of ⟨cuando la guerra : during the war⟩

cuándo *adv & conj* **1** : when ⟨¿cuándo llegará? : when will she arrive?⟩ ⟨no sabemos cuándo será : we don't know when it will be⟩ **2 ¿de cuándo acá?** : since when?, how come?

cuantía *nf* **1** : quantity, extent **2** : significance, import

cuántico, -ca *adj* : quantum ⟨teoría cuántica : quantum theory⟩

cuantificar {72} *vt* : to quantify

cuantioso, -sa *adj* **1** : abundant, considerable **2** : heavy, grave ⟨cuantiosos daños : heavy damage⟩

cuantitativo, -va *adj* : quantitative — **cuantitativamente** *adv*

cuanto¹ *adv* **1** : as much as ⟨come cuanto puedas : eat as much as you can⟩ **2 cuanto antes** : as soon as possible **3 en** ∼ : as soon as **4 en cuanto a** : as for, as regards

cuanto², -ta *adj* : as many, whatever ⟨llévate cuantas flores quieras : take as many flowers as you wish⟩

cuanto³, -ta *pron* **1** : as much as, all that, everything ⟨tengo cuanto deseo : I have all that I want⟩ **2 unos cuantos, unas cuantas** : a few

cuánto¹ *adv* : how much, how many ⟨¿a cuánto están las peras? : how much are the pears?⟩ ⟨no sé cuánto desean : I don't know how much they want⟩

cuánto², -ta *adj* : how much, how many ⟨¿cuántos niños tiene? : how many children do you have?⟩

cuánto³, -ta *pron* : how much, how many ⟨¿cuántos quieren participar? : how many want to take part?⟩ ⟨¿cuánto cuesta? : how much does it cost?⟩

cuáquero, -ra *adj & n* : Quaker

cuarenta *adj & nm* : forty — **cuarenta** *pron*

cuarentavo¹, -va *adj* : fortieth

cuarentavo² *adj & nm* : fortieth (fraction)

cuarentena *nf* **1** : group of forty **2** : quarantine

Cuaresma *nf* : Lent

cuarta *nf* : fourth (gear)

cuartear *vt* **1** : to quarter **2** : to divide up — **cuartearse** *vr* AGRIETARSE : to crack, to split

cuartel *nm* **1** : barracks, headquarters **2** : mercy ⟨una guerra sin cuartel : a merciless war⟩

cuartelazo *nm* : coup d'etat

cuarteto *nm* : quartet

cuartilla *nf* : sheet (of paper)

cuarto¹, -ta *adj & n* : fourth ⟨la cuarta (persona) : the fourth (person)⟩ ⟨llegó la cuarta : she came in fourth (place)⟩ ⟨una/la cuarta parte de : a quarter of, a fourth of⟩

cuarto² *nm* **1** : quarter, fourth ⟨un cuarto de galón : a quarter of, a fourth of⟩ ⟨cuarto de galón : quart⟩ **2** HABITACIÓN : room

cuarto oscuro *nm* : darkroom

cuarzo *nm* : quartz

cuasi- *pref* : quasi-

cuate, -ta *n Mex* **1** : twin **2** *fam* : buddy, pal

cuatrero, -ra *n* : rustler

cuatrillizo, -za *n* : quadruplet
cuatro[1] *adj & nm* : four ⟨tiene cuatro años : she's four years old⟩ ⟨el cuatro de agosto : (on) the fourth of August, (on) August fourth⟩
cuatro[2] *pron* : four ⟨son cuatro : there are four of them⟩ ⟨son las cuatro y cuarto : it's four fifteen, it's (a) quarter after four⟩
cuatrocientos, -tas *adj & nm* : four hundred — **cuatrocientos** *pron*
cuba *nf* BARRIL : cask, barrel
cubano, -na *adj & n* : Cuban
cubertería *nf* : flatware, silverware
cubeta *nf* 1 : keg, cask 2 : bulb (of a thermometer) 3 *Mex* : bucket, pail
cúbico, -ca *adj* : cubic, cubed
cubículo *nm* : cubicle
cubierta *nf* 1 : covering 2 FORRO : cover, jacket (of a book) 3 : deck
cubierto[1] *pp* → **cubrir**
cubierto[2] *nm* 1 : cover, shelter ⟨bajo cubierto : under cover⟩ 2 : table setting 3 : utensil, piece of silverware
cubil *nm* : den, lair
cúbito *nm* : ulna
cubo *nm* 1 : cube 2 *Spain* BALDE : pail, bucket, can ⟨cubo de basura : garbage can⟩ 3 : hub (of a wheel)
cubrecama *nm* COLCHA : bedspread
cubrir {2} *vt* 1 : to cover ⟨cubierto de algo : covered in/with something⟩ 2 : to cover (costs, etc.) — **cubrirse** *vr*
cucaracha *nf* : cockroach, roach
cuchara *nf* : spoon
cucharada *nf* : spoonful
cucharadita *nf* : teaspoon, teaspoonful
cucharilla *or* **cucharita** *nf* : teaspoon
cucharón *nm, pl* **-rones** : ladle
cuchichear *vi* : to whisper
cuchicheo *nm* : whisper
cuchilla *nf* 1 : kitchen knife, cleaver 2 : blade ⟨cuchilla de afeitar : razor blade, (safety) razor⟩ 3 : crest, ridge
cuchillada *nf* : stab, knife wound
cuchillo *nm* : knife
cuclillas *nfpl* **en** ~ : squatting, crouching
cuclillo *nm* : cuckoo
cuco[1], **-ca** *adj fam* : pretty, cute
cuco[2] *nm* 1 : cuckoo 2 *Arg, Chile, Peru, Uru fam* COCO : bogeyman
cucurucho *nm* : ice-cream cone
cuece, cueza etc. → **cocer**
cuela, etc. → **colar**
cuelga, cuelgue etc. → **colgar**
cuello *nm* 1 : neck 2 : collar, neck (of a shirt) ⟨cuello en V : V-neck⟩ 3 **cuello del útero** : cervix
cuenca *nf* 1 : river basin 2 : eye socket
cuenco *nm* : bowl, basin
cuenta[1], **etc.** → **contar**
cuenta[2] *nf* 1 : calculation, count 2 : account ⟨cuenta corriente : checking account⟩ ⟨cuenta de ahorro(s) : savings account⟩ ⟨cuenta de correo(s) electrónico(s), cuenta de email : e-mail account⟩ 3 : responsibility, liability ⟨corre por cuenta del gobierno : the government is footing the bill⟩ ⟨trabajar por cuenta propia : to be self-employed⟩ 4

: check, bill 5 **a fin de cuentas** : in the end 6 **darse cuenta** : to realize 7 **en buenas cuentas** *Chile* : in short 8 **por cuenta de** : on account of, because of 9 **rendir cuentas** : to be held accountable 10 **tener en cuenta** : to bear in mind 11 **tomar en cuenta** : to take into account
cuentagotas *nfs & pl* 1 : dropper 2 **con** ~ : little by little
cuentakilómetros *nm* 1 : odometer 2 VELOCÍMETRO : speedometer
cuentista *nmf* 1 : short story writer 2 *fam* : liar, fibber
cuento *nm* 1 : story, tale 2 **cuento chino** : tall tale 3 **cuento de hadas** : fairy tale 4 **sin** ~ : countless
cuerda *nf* 1 : cord, rope, string 2 **cuerdas vocales** : vocal cords 3 **darle cuerda a algo** : to wind something up
cuerdo, -da *adj* : sane, sensible
cuerno *nm* 1 : horn, antler 2 : cusp (of the moon) 3 : horn (musical instrument)
cuero *nm* 1 : leather, hide 2 **cuero cabelludo** : scalp
cuerpo *nm* 1 : body 2 : corps ⟨cuerpo policial : police force⟩
cuervo *nm* : crow, raven
cuesta[1], **etc.** → **costar**
cuesta[2] *nf* 1 : slope ⟨cuesta arriba : uphill⟩ 2 **a cuestas** : on one's back
cuestión *nf, pl* **-tiones** ASUNTO, TEMA : matter, affair
cuestionable *adj* : questionable, dubious
cuestionamiento *nm* 1 : question, doubt ⟨hacer cuestionamientos a/sobre : to raise questions about⟩ 2 : questioning
cuestionar *vt* : to question
cuestionario *nm* 1 : questionnaire 2 : quiz
cueva *nf* : cave
cuidado *nm* 1 : care 2 : worry, concern 3 **tener cuidado** : to be careful 4 **¡cuidado!** : watch out!, be careful!
cuidador, -dora *n* : caretaker
cuidadoso, -sa *adj* : careful, attentive — **cuidadosamente** *adv*
cuidar *vt* 1 : to take care of, to look after 2 : to pay attention to — *vi* 1 ~ **de** : to look after 2 **cuidar de que** : to make sure that — **cuidarse** *vr* : to take care of oneself
culata *nf* : butt (of a gun)
culatazo *nm* : kick, recoil
culebra *nf* SERPIENTE : snake
culebrón *nm, pl* **-brones** : soap, soap opera
culinario, -ria *adj* : culinary
culminante *adj* **punto culminante** : peak, high point, climax
culminar *vi* : to culminate — **culminación** *nf*
culo *nm* 1 *fam* : backside, behind 2 : bottom (of a glass)
culpa *nf* 1 : fault, blame ⟨echarle la culpa a alguien : to blame someone⟩ 2 : sin
culpabilidad *nf* : guilt
culpable[1] *adj* : guilty
culpable[2] *nmf* : culprit, guilty party
culpar *vt* : to blame
culposo, -sa *adj* : culpable, negligent

cultivable *adj* : arable
cultivado, -da *adj* **1** : cultivated, farmed **2** : cultured
cultivador, -dora *n* : grower
cultivar *vt* **1** : to cultivate **2** : to foster
cultivo *nm* **1** : cultivation, farming **2** : crop
culto¹, -ta *adj* : cultured, educated
culto² *nm* **1** : worship **2** : cult
cultura *nf* : culture
cultural *adj* : cultural — **culturalmente** *adv*
culturismo *nm* : bodybuilding
cumbre *nf* CIMA : top, peak, summit
cumpleañero, -ra *n* : birthday boy *m*, birthday girl *f*
cumpleaños *nms & pl* : birthday
cumplido¹, -da *adj* **1** : complete, full **2** : courteous, correct
cumplido² *nm* : compliment, courtesy ⟨por cumplido : out of courtesy⟩ ⟨andarse con cumplidos : to stand on ceremony⟩
cumplidor, -dora *adj* : reliable
cumplimentar *vt* **1** : to congratulate **2** : to carry out, to perform
cumplimiento *nm* **1** : completion, fulfillment **2** : performance
cumplir *vt* **1** : to accomplish, to carry out **2** : to comply with, to fulfill **3** : to attain, to reach ⟨su hermana cumple (los) 20 (años) el viernes : her sister will be 20 on Friday⟩ — *vi* **1** : to expire, to fall due **2** : to fulfill one's obligations ⟨cumplir con su deber : to do one's duty⟩ ⟨cumplir con su palabra : to keep one's word⟩ — **cumplirse** *vr* **1** : to come true, to be fulfilled ⟨se cumplieron sus sueños : her dreams came true⟩ **2** : to run out, to expire
cúmulo *nm* **1** MONTÓN : heap, pile **2** : cumulus
cuna *nf* **1** : cradle **2** : birthplace, origin
cundir *vi* **1** : to spread, to propagate (of panic, etc.) **2** : to progress, to make headway
cuneta *nf* : ditch (in a road), gutter
cuña *nf* : wedge
cuñado, -da *n* : brother-in-law *m*, sister-in-law *f*
cuño *nm* : die (for stamping)
cuota *nf* **1** : fee, dues **2** : quota, share **3** : installment, payment
cupé *nm* : coupe
cupo¹, etc. → caber
cupo² *nm* **1** : quota, share **2** : capacity, room
cupón *nm, pl* **cupones** **1** : coupon, voucher **2** **cupón federal** : food stamp
cúpula *nf* : dome, cupola
cura¹ *nm* : priest
cura² *nf* **1** CURACIÓN, TRATAMIENTO : cure, treatment **2** : dressing, bandage

curación *nf, pl* **-ciones** CURA, TRATAMIENTO : cure, treatment
curador, -dora *n* **1** : healer **2** CONSERVADOR : curator
curandero, -ra *nm* **1** : witch doctor **2** : quack, charlatan
curar *vt* **1** : to cure, to heal **2** : to treat, to dress' **3** CURTIR : to tan **4** : to cure (meat) — *vi* : to get well, to recover — **curarse** *vr*
curativo, -va *adj* : healing
curiosear *vi* **1** : to snoop, to pry **2** : to browse — *vt* : to look over, to check
curiosidad *nf* **1** : curiosity **2** : curio
curioso, -sa *adj* **1** : curious, inquisitive **2** : strange, unusual, odd — **curiosamente** *adv*
curita *nf* (*Curitas*, marca registrada) : bandage, Band-Aid™
currículo → **currículum**
currículum *nm, pl* **-lums** **1** : résumé, curriculum vitae **2** : curriculum, course of study
curruca *nf* : warbler
curry [¹kurri] *nm, pl* **-rries** **1** : curry powder **2** : curry (dish)
cursar *vt* **1** : to attend (school), to take (a course) **2** : to dispatch, to pass on
cursi *adj fam* : affected, pretentious
cursilería *nf* **1** : vulgarity, poor taste **2** : pretentiousness
cursillo *nm* : short course
cursiva *nf* BASTARDILLA : italic type, italics *pl*
cursivo, -va *adj* : italic
curso *nm* **1** : course, direction **2** : school year **3** : course, subject (in school)
cursor *nm* : cursor
curtido, -da *adj* : weather-beaten, leathery (of skin)
curtidor, -dora *n* : tanner
curtiduría *nf* : tannery
curtir *vt* **1** : to tan **2** : to harden, to weather — **curtirse** *vr*
curul *nf* ESCAÑO : seat (in a legislative body)
curva *nf* : curve, bend
curvar *vt* : to bend
curvatura *nf* : curvature
curvilíneo, -nea *adj* : shapely
curvo, -va *adj* : curved, bent
cúspide *nf* : zenith, apex, peak
custodia *nf* : custody
custodiar *vt* : to guard, to look after
custodio, -dia *n* : keeper, guardian
cutáneo, -nea *adj* : skin, cutaneous
cúter *nm* : cutter (boat)
cutícula *nf* : cuticle
cutis *nms & pl* : skin, complexion
cuyo, -ya *adj* **1** : whose, of whom, of which **2** **en cuyo caso** : in which case

D

d *nf* : fifth letter of the Spanish alphabet

dactilar *adj* **huellas dactilares** : fingerprints

dádiva *nf* : gift, handout

dadivoso, -sa *adj* : generous

dado, -da *adj* **1** : given **2 dado que** : given that, since

dados *nmpl* : dice

daga *nf* : dagger

dalia *nf* : dahlia

dálmata *nm* : dalmatian

daltónico, -ca *adj* : color-blind

daltonismo *nm* : color blindness

dama *nf* **1** : lady **2 damas** *nfpl* : checkers

damasco *nm* : damask

damisela *nf* : damsel

damnificado, -da *n* : victim (of a disaster)

dance, etc. → danzar

dandi *nm* : dandy

danés¹, -nesa *adj* : Danish

danés², -nesa *n, mpl* **daneses** : Dane, Danish person

danza *nf* : dance, dancing ⟨danza folklórica : folk dance⟩

danzante, -ta *n* BAILARÍN : dancer

danzar {21} *v* BAILAR : to dance

dañar *vt* **1** : to damage, to spoil **2** : to harm, to hurt — **dañarse** *vr*

dañino, -na *adj* : harmful

daño *nm* **1** : damage **2** : harm, injury ⟨daños colaterales : collateral damages⟩ **3 hacer daño a** : to harm, to damage **4 hacerse daño** : to hurt oneself ⟨me he hecho daño en la mano : I've hurt my hand⟩ **5 daños y perjuicios** : damages

dar {22} *vt* **1** : to give (a gift, a donation, etc.) **2** ENTREGAR : to give, to hand (over) **3** PROPORCIONAR : to give (supplies, support, etc.) ⟨dale una oportunidad : give him a chance⟩ **4** CONCEDER : to give (time, permission, etc.) **5** ADMINISTRAR : to give (medicine, etc.) **6** EXPRESAR : to give, to express ⟨dales recuerdos de mi parte : give them my regards⟩ ⟨darle las gracias a : to thank⟩ ⟨dar su palabra : to give one's word⟩ **7** MOSTRAR : to give (an indication, etc.) **8** OFRECER : to give (a reason, etc.) **9** : to give (an impression, etc.) **10** GOLPEAR : to hit ⟨me dio en la cara : it hit me in the face⟩ **11** : to strike ⟨el reloj dio las doce : the clock struck twelve⟩ **12** PRODUCIR : to yield, to produce **13** : to give (a performance, a party, etc.), to show (a film, etc.) **14** : to do (an action) ⟨dar un grito : to give a shout⟩ ⟨dar un paseo : to go for a walk⟩ ⟨me dio un beso : she gave me a kiss⟩ **15** VENDER : to give, to sell **16** CAUSAR : to cause ⟨darle miedo/sed (etc.) a alguien : to make someone frightened/thirsty (etc.)⟩ ⟨me da risa : it makes me laugh, it's funny⟩ ⟨le da problemas/esperanza : it gives her trouble/hope⟩ **17** APLICAR : to apply ⟨dale una mano de pintura : give it a coat of paint⟩ ⟨dar un impulso a : to give a boost to⟩ **18** CONFERIR : to give, to impart (a quality) **19 dar como/por** : to regard as, to consider ⟨dar por hecho : to take for granted⟩ ⟨dar a alguien por muerto : to give someone up for dead⟩ — *vi* **1** : to provide (enough) ⟨no me da para dos pasajes : I don't have enough for two fares⟩ ⟨no me da tiempo : I don't have time⟩ ⟨esto no da para más : this can't go on⟩ ⟨a todo lo que da : at full speed/power (etc.)⟩ **2** : to hand something over ⟨dame : give it to me⟩ **3** : to deal (in cards) **4** : to hit ⟨dar en el blanco : to hit the target⟩ **5** : to give a result ⟨dio positivo al virus : he tested positive for the virus⟩ **6 dale que dale** *or Spain* **dale que te pego** ⟨están dale que dale con el teléfono : they're constantly on the phone⟩ ⟨y ella dale que te pego con sus problemas : and she was going on and on about her problems⟩ **7 darle a** : to press (a button, etc.), to turn (a dial, etc.) **8** **a/sobre** : to overlook, to look out on **9** ~ **con** : to run into **10** ~ **con** : to hit/upon (an idea) **11 dar de sí** : to give, to stretch (of clothing, etc.) — **darse** *vr* **1** : to consider oneself ⟨se dio por vencido : he gave in⟩ **2** : to occur, to arise **3** : to grow, to come up **4** ~ **con/contra** : to hit oneself against, to bump into **5 dárselas de** : to boast about ⟨se las da de muy listo : he thinks he's very smart⟩ **6 dársele bien algo a uno** : to be good at something ⟨se le dan muy bien las matemáticas : she's very good at math⟩

dardo *nm* : dart

dársena *nf* : dock

data *nf* **1** : byline **2 de larga data** : longstanding

datar *vt* : to date — *vi* ~ **de** : to date from, to date back to

dátil *nm* : date (fruit)

dato *nm* **1** : fact, piece of information **2 datos** *nmpl* : data, information

dé → dar

de¹ *nf* : (letter) d

de² *prep* **1** (*indicating connection or belonging*) : of ⟨la casa de Pepe : Pepe's house⟩ ⟨el cuatro de abril : the fourth of April, April fourth⟩ ⟨la reina de Inglaterra : the Queen of England⟩ ⟨el mejor de todos : the best of all⟩ **2** (*indicating a quality or condition*) : of ⟨un asunto de gran importancia : a matter of great importance⟩ ⟨un niño de tres años : a three-year-old boy⟩ ⟨estoy de vacaciones : I'm on vacation⟩ **3** (*indicating content, material, or quantity*) : of ⟨un vaso de agua : a glass of water⟩ ⟨una casa de ladrillo : a brick house, a house made of brick⟩ ⟨una gran cantidad de lluvia : a large amount of rain⟩ **4** (*indicating a source or starting point*) : from ⟨es de Managua : she's from Managua⟩ ⟨salió del edificio : he left the building⟩ **5** (*with time*) : in, at ⟨a las tres de la mañana : at

three in the morning⟩ ⟨salen de noche
: they go out at night⟩ **6** (*with numbers*)
: than ⟨más de tres : more than three⟩ **7**
(*indicating a particular example*) : of ⟨el
mes de junio : the month of June⟩ **8** (*indicating a cause*) ⟨morirse de hambre
; to be dying of/from starvation⟩ ⟨gritar
de alegría : to shout with/for joy⟩ **9**
: about ⟨libros de historia : history
books, books about history⟩ **10** (*indicating purpose*) : for ⟨ropa de deporte
: sportswear, athletic clothes⟩ ⟨máquina
de coser : sewing machine⟩ **11** : as ⟨ella
trabaja de camionera : she works as a
truck driver⟩ **12** : if ⟨de haberlo sabido
: if I had known⟩ ⟨de continuar esta situación : if this situation continues⟩

deambular *vi* : to wander, to roam
deán *nm, pl* **deanes** : dean (of clergy)
debacle *nf* : debacle
debajo *adv* **1** : underneath, below, on the
bottom **2** ~ **de** : under, underneath **3**
por ~ : below, beneath
debate *nm* : debate
debatir *vt* : to debate, to discuss — **debatirse** *vr* : to struggle
debe *nm* : debit column, debit
deber[1] *vt* — *v aux* **1** : must, have
to ⟨debo ir : I must go⟩ ⟨no debes hacerlo
: you mustn't do it⟩ **2** : should, ought to
⟨deberías buscar trabajo : you should
look for work⟩ ⟨debería darte vergüenza
: you ought to be ashamed of yourself⟩ **3**
(*expressing probability*) : must ⟨debe ser
muy tarde : it must be very late⟩ — **de-
berse** *vr* **1** ~ **a** : to be due to **2** ~ **a** : to
have a responsibility towards
deber[2] *nm* **1** OBLIGACIÓN : duty, obligation **2 deberes** *nmpl Spain* : homework
debidamente *adv* : properly, duly
debido, -da *adj* **1** : right, proper, due **2**
~ **a** : due to, owing to
débil *adj* : weak, feeble — **débilmente**
adv
debilidad *nf* : weakness, debility, feebleness
debilitamiento *nm* : weakening
debilitar *vt* : to debilitate, to weaken —
debilitarse *vr*
debilucho[1]**, -cha** *adj* : weak, frail
debilucho[2]**, -cha** *n* : weakling
debitar *vt* : to debit
débito *nm* **1** DEUDA : debt **2** : debit
de bruces *adv* : facedown, face-first ⟨caer
de bruces : to fall flat on one's face⟩
debut [de'but] *nm, pl* **debuts** : debut
debutante[1] *nmf* : beginner, newcomer
debutante[2] *nf* : debutante *f*
debutar *vi* : to debut, to make a debut
década *nf* DECENIO : decade
decadencia *nf* **1** : decadence **2** : decline
decadente *adj* **1** : decadent **2** : declining
decaer {13} *vi* **1** : to decline, to decay, to
deteriorate **2** FLAQUEAR : to weaken, to
flag
decaído, -da *adj fam* : depressed, sad
decaiga, etc. → **decaer**
decano, -na *n* **1** : dean **2** : senior member
decapitar *vt* : to decapitate, to behead
decayó, etc. → **decaer**

decena *nf* : group of ten
decencia *nf* : decency
decenio *nm* DÉCADA : decade
decente *adj* : decent — **decentemente**
adv
decepción *nf, pl* **-ciones** : disappointment, letdown
decepcionante *adj* : disappointing
decepcionar *vt* : to disappoint, to let
down — **decepcionarse** *vr*
deceso *nm* DEFUNCIÓN : death, passing
dechado *nm* **1** : sampler (of embroidery)
2 : model, paragon
decibelio *or* **decibel** *nm* : decibel
decidido, -da *adj* : decisive, determined,
resolute — **decididamente** *adv*
decidir *vt* **1** : to decide ⟨decidí ir : I decided to go⟩ ⟨no he decidido nada : I
haven't made a decision⟩ **2** : to make
(someone) decide, to persuade (someone) — *vi* : to decide ⟨decidir sobre : to
make a decision about⟩ — **decidirse** *vr*
: to make up one's mind ⟨decidirse por
: to decide on, to choose⟩
décima *nf* : tenth (fraction)
decimal *adj* : decimal
décimo[1]**, -ma** *adj & n* : tenth ⟨la décima
(persona) : the tenth (person)⟩ ⟨una/la
décima parte de : a tenth of, one tenth
of⟩ ⟨en décimo lugar : in tenth place⟩
décimo[2] *nm Spain* → **décima**
decimoctavo[1]**, -va** *adj* : eighteenth
decimoctavo[2]**, -va** *n* : eighteenth (in a series)
decimocuarto[1]**, -ta** *adj* : fourteenth
decimocuarto[2]**, -ta** *n* : fourteenth (in a
series)
decimonoveno[1]**, -na** *or* **decimonono, -na**
adj : nineteenth
decimonoveno[2]**, -na** *or* **decimonono, -na**
n : nineteenth (in a series)
decimoquinto[1]**, -ta** *adj* : fifteenth
decimoquinto[2]**, -ta** *n* : fifteenth (in a series)
decimoséptimo[1]**, -ma** *adj* : seventeenth
decimoséptimo[2]**, -ma** *n* : seventeenth (in
a series)
decimosexto[1]**, -ta** *adj* : sixteenth
decimosexto[2]**, -ta** *n* : sixteenth (in a series)
decimotercero[1]**, -ra** *adj* : thirteenth
decimotercero[2]**, -ra** *n* : thirteenth (in a
series)
decir[1] {23} *vt* **1** : to say ⟨dice que no irá
: she says she won't go⟩ **2** : to tell ⟨dime
lo que estás pensando : tell me what
you're thinking⟩ ⟨ya te lo decía yo : I
told you so⟩ **3** : to tell, to say ⟨haz lo que
te digo : do as I say, do what I tell you⟩
⟨te dije que callaras : I told you to be
quiet⟩ **4** : to speak, to talk ⟨no digas
tonterías : don't talk nonsense⟩ **5** : to
call ⟨me dicen Rosy : they call me Rosy⟩
6 como quien dice : so to speak **7 es
decir** : that is to say **8 dicho y hecho**
: no sooner said than done **9** (o) **mejor
dicho** : (or) rather **10 ¡no me digas!**
: you're kidding!, you don't say! **11 por
así decirlo** : so to speak **12 querer decir**
: to mean ⟨¿qué quiere decir? : what do

you mean?⟩ — **decirse** *vr* 1 : to say to oneself 2 : to be said ⟨¿cómo se dice "lápiz" en francés? : how do you say "pencil" in French?⟩

decir² *nm* DICHO : saying, expression

decisión *nf, pl* **-siones** 1 : decision, choice ⟨tomar una decisión : to make a decision⟩ 2 : decisiveness

decisivo, -va *adj* : decisive, conclusive — **decisivamente** *adv*

declamar *vi* : to declaim *vt* : to recite

declaración *nf, pl* **-ciones** 1 : declaration, statement ⟨hacer una declaración : to issue a statement⟩ 2 TESTIMONIO : deposition, testimony ⟨prestar declaración : to give evidence, to testify⟩ 3 **declaración de derechos** : bill of rights 4 **declaración jurada** : affidavit 5 **declaración de la renta** : income tax return

declarado, -da *adj* : professed, open — **declaradamente** *adv*

declarar *vt* : to declare, to state ⟨declarar culpable : to find guilty⟩ ⟨declarar inocente : to find not guilty⟩ — *vi* ATESTIGUAR : to testify — **declararse** *vr* 1 : to declare oneself (to be) ⟨declararse en huelga : to go on strike⟩ ⟨declararse en bancarrota : to declare bankruptcy⟩ 2 : to confess one's love 3 : to plead (in court) ⟨declararse culpable : to plead guilty⟩ ⟨declararse inocente : to plead not guilty⟩ 4 : to testify 5 : to break out (of a fire, etc.)

declinar *vt* : to decline, to turn down *vi* 1 : to draw to a close 2 : to diminish, to decline

declive *nm* 1 DECADENCIA : decline 2 : slope, incline

decodificador *nm* : decoder

decolar *vi Chile, Col, Ecua* : to take off (of an airplane)

decolorar *vt* : to bleach — **decolorarse** *vr* : to fade

decomisar *vt* CONFISCAR : to seize, to confiscate

decomiso *nm* : seizure, confiscation

decoración *nf, pl* **-ciones** 1 : decoration 2 : decor 3 : stage set, scenery

decorado *nm* : stage set, scenery

decorador, -dora *n* : decorator

decorar *vt* ADORNAR : to decorate, to adorn

decorativo, -va *adj* : decorative, ornamental

decoro *nm* : decorum, propriety

decoroso, -sa *adj* : decent, proper, respectable

decrecer {53} *vi* : to decrease, to wane, to diminish — **decreciente** *adj*

decrecimiento *nm* : decrease, decline

decrépito, -ta *adj* : decrepit

decretar *vt* : to decree, to order

decreto *nm* : decree

decúbito *nm* : horizontal position ⟨en decúbito prono/supino : prone/supine⟩

dedal *nm* : thimble

dedalera *nf* DIGITAL : foxglove

dedicación *nf, pl* **-ciones** : dedication, devotion

dedicar {72} *vt* : to dedicate, to devote — **dedicarse** *vr* ~ **a** : to devote oneself to, to engage in

dedicatoria *nf* : dedication (of a book, song, etc.)

dedillo *nm* **conocer algo al dedillo** : to know something backward and forward

dedo *nm* 1 : finger ⟨dedo meñique : little finger⟩ ⟨no mover un dedo : not to lift a finger⟩ ⟨hacer dedo, ir a dedo : to hitchhike⟩ ⟨poner el dedo en la llaga : to hit a nerve⟩ 2 **dedo del pie** : toe

deducción *nf, pl* **-ciones** : deduction

deducible *adj* : deductible

deducir {61} *vt* 1 INFERIR : to deduce 2 DESCONTAR : to deduct

defecar {72} *vi* : to defecate — **defecación** *nf*

defecto *nm* 1 : defect, flaw, shortcoming 2 **en su defecto** : lacking that, in the absence of that

defectuoso, -sa *adj* : defective, faulty

defender {56} *vt* : to defend, to protect — **defenderse** *vr* 1 : to defend oneself 2 : to get by, to know the basics ⟨su inglés no es perfecto pero se defiende : his English isn't perfect but he gets by⟩

defendible *adj* : tenable

defensa¹ *nf* 1 : defense ⟨salió en nuestra defensa : he came to our defense⟩ ⟨actuar en defensa propia : to act in self-defense⟩ ⟨clase de defensa personal : self-defense class⟩ 2 : defense (in sports)

defensa² *nmf* : defender, back (in sports)

defensiva *nf* : defensive, defense

defensivo, -va *adj* : defensive — **defensivamente** *adv*

defensor¹, -sora *adj* : defending, defense

defensor², -sora *n* 1 : defender, advocate 2 : defense counsel

defeño, -ña *n* : person from the Federal District (Mexico City)

deferencia *nf* : deference

deferir {76} *vi* **deferir a** : to defer to

deficiencia *nf* : deficiency, flaw

deficiente *adj* : deficient

déficit *nm, pl* **-cits** 1 : deficit 2 : shortage, lack

deficitario, -ria *adj* : with a deficit (of a country, etc.), negative (of a balance) ⟨una empresa deficitaria : a business that is losing money⟩

definición *nf, pl* **-ciones** : definition

definido, -da *adj* : definite, well-defined

definir *vt* 1 : to define 2 : to determine

definitivamente *adv* 1 : finally 2 : permanently, for good 3 : definitely, absolutely

definitivo, -va *adj* 1 : definitive, conclusive 2 **en definitiva** : all in all, on the whole 3 **en definitiva** *Mex* : permanently, for good

deflación *nf, pl* **-ciones** : deflation

deforestación *nf, pl* **-ciones** : deforestation

deformación *nf, pl* **-ciones** 1 : deformation 2 : distortion

deformar *vt* 1 : to deform, to disfigure 2 : to distort — **deformarse** *vr*

deforme *adj* : deformed, misshapen
deformidad *nf* : deformity
defraudación *nf, pl* **-ciones** : fraud
defraudar *vt* **1** ESTAFAR : to defraud, to cheat **2** : to disappoint
defunción *nf, pl* **-ciones** DECESO : death, passing
degeneración *nf, pl* **-ciones** **1** : degeneration **2** DEPRAVACIÓN : depravity
degenerado, -da *adj* DEPRAVADO : degenerate
degenerar *vi* : to degenerate
degenerativo, -va *adj* : degenerative
degollar {19} *vt* **1** : to slit the throat of, to slaughter **2** DECAPITAR : to behead **3** : to ruin, to destroy
degradación *nf, pl* **-ciones** **1** : degradation **2** : demotion
degradante *adj* : degrading
degradar *vt* **1** : to degrade, to debase **2** : to demote
degustación *nf, pl* **-ciones** : tasting, sampling
degustador, -dora *n* : taster
degustar *vt* : to taste
dehesa *nf* : meadow
deidad *nf* : deity
deificar {72} *vt* : to idolize, to deify
dejadez *nf* : neglect, slovenliness
dejado, -da *adj* **1** : slovenly **2** : careless, lazy
dejar *vt* **1** : to leave ⟨dejé la cartera en casa : I left my purse at home⟩ ⟨déjalo allí : leave it there⟩ ⟨déjalo conmigo : leave it with me⟩ **2** : to drop (someone) off **3** : to leave (a tip, a package, etc.) **4** LEGAR : to leave, to bequeath **5** ABANDONAR : to leave (a spouse, a job, etc.), to give up (an activity) **6** : to leave alone, to let be **7** : to drop (a subject) ⟨déjalo, no importa : forget it—it's not important⟩ **8** POSPONER : to leave, to put off **9** : to leave ⟨dejé las luces encendidas : I left the lights on⟩ ⟨no me dejes esperando : don't leave me waiting⟩ **10** GUARDAR : to leave, to set aside **11** : to leave (a mark, etc.) **12** PERMITIR : to let, to allow ⟨déjalo hablar : let him speak⟩ ⟨deja que se enfríe : let it cool⟩ *vi* **1** ~ **de** : to stop, to quit ⟨dejar de fumar : to quit smoking⟩ **2 no dejar de** : to be sure to ⟨no dejes de llamar : be sure to call⟩ — **dejarse** *vr* **1** : to let oneself be ⟨se deja insultar : he lets himself be insulted⟩ **2** : to forget, to leave ⟨me dejé las llaves en el carro : I left the keys in the car⟩ **3** : to neglect oneself, to let oneself go **4** : to grow ⟨me estoy dejando el pelo largo : I'm growing my hair long⟩
dejo *nm* **1** : aftertaste **2** : touch, hint **3** : (regional) accent
del *contraction of* DE *and* EL → **de**
delación *nf, pl* **-ciones** : denunciation, betrayal
delantal *nm* **1** : apron **2** : pinafore
delante *adv* **1** ENFRENTE : ahead, in front **2** ~ **de** : before, in front of
delantera *nf* **1** : front, front part, front row ⟨tomar la delantera : to take the lead⟩ **2** : forward line (in sports)

delantero¹, -ra *adj* **1** : front, forward **2** **tracción delantera** : front-wheel drive
delantero², -ra *n* : forward (in sports)
delatar *vt* **1** : to betray, to reveal **2** : to denounce, to inform against
delator, -tora *adj* : incriminating
delegación *nf, pl* **-ciones** : delegation
delegado, -da *n* : delegate, representative
delegar {52} *vt* : to delegate
deleitar *vt* : to delight, to please — **deleitarse** *vr*
deleite *nm* : delight, pleasure
deletrear *vt* : to spell ⟨¿como se deletrea? : how do you spell it?⟩
deleznable *adj* **1** : brittle, crumbly **2** : slippery **3** : weak, fragile ⟨una excusa deleznable : a weak excuse⟩
delfín *nm, pl* **delfines** : dolphin
delgadez *nf* : thinness
delgado, -da *adj* **1** FLACO : thin, skinny **2** ESBELTO : slender, slim **3** DELICADO : delicate, fine **4** AGUDO : sharp, clever
deliberado, -da *adj* : deliberate, intentional — **deliberadamente** *adv*
deliberar *vi* : to deliberate — **deliberación** *nf*
delicadamente *adv* : delicately
delicadeza *nf* **1** : delicacy, fineness **2** : gentleness, softness **3** : tact, discretion, consideration
delicado, -da *adj* **1** : delicate, fine **2** : sensitive, frail **3** : delicate, tricky **4** : fussy **5** : tactful, considerate
delicia *nf* : delight
delicioso, -sa *adj* **1** RICO : delicious **2** : delightful
delictivo, -va *adj* : criminal
delictuoso, -sa → **delictivo**
delimitación *nf, pl* **-ciones** **1** : demarcation **2** : defining, specifying
delimitar *vt* **1** : to demarcate **2** : to define, to specify
delincuencia *nf* : delinquency, crime
delincuente¹ *adj* : delinquent
delincuente² *nmf* CRIMINAL : delinquent, criminal
delineador *nm* : eyeliner
delinear *vt* **1** : to delineate, to outline **2** : to draft, to draw up
delinquir {24} *vi* : to break the law
delirante *adj* : delirious
delirar *vi* **1** DESVARIAR : to be delirious **2** : to rave, to talk nonsense
delirio *nm* **1** : delirium **2** FRENESÍ : mania, frenzy ⟨¡fue el delirio! : it was wild!⟩ **3 delirios** *pl* DISPARATES : nonsense, ravings *pl* ⟨delirios de grandeza : delusions of grandeur⟩
delito *nm* : crime, offense
delta *nm* : delta
demacrado, -da *adj* : emaciated, gaunt
demagogo, -ga *n* : demagogue
demanda *nf* **1** : demand ⟨la oferta y la demanda : supply and demand⟩ ⟨tener mucha demanda : to be in great demand⟩ **2** : petition, request **3** : lawsuit
demandado, -da *n* : defendant
demandante *nmf* : plaintiff

demandar *vt* **1** : to demand **2** REQUERIR : to call for, to require **3** : to sue, to file a lawsuit against

demarcar {72} *vt* : to demarcate — **demarcación** *nf*

demás[1] *adj* : remaining ⟨las demás tareas : the rest of the chores⟩

demás[2] *pron* **1** **lo (la, los, las) demás** : the rest, everyone else, everything else ⟨Pepe, Rosa, y los demás : Pepe, Rosa, and everybody else⟩ **2 estar por demás** : to be of no use, to be pointless ⟨no estaría por demás : it couldn't hurt, it's worth a try⟩ **3 por demás** : extremely **4 por lo demás** : otherwise **5 y demás** : and so on, et cetera

demasía *nf* en ~ : excessively, in excess

demasiado[1] *adv* **1** : too ⟨vas demasiado aprisa : you're going too fast⟩ **2** : too much ⟨comí demasiado : I ate too much⟩

demasiado[2], **-da** *adj* : too much, too many, excessive

demencia *nf* **1** : dementia **2** LOCURA : madness, insanity

demencial *adj fam* : crazy, insane

demente[1] *adj* : insane, mad

demente[2] *nmf* : insane person

demeritar *vt* **1** : to detract from **2** : to discredit

demérito *nm* **1** : fault **2** : discredit, disrepute

demo *nf* **1** : demo, demo product/version (etc.) **2** : demo, demo tape

democracia *nf* : democracy

demócrata[1] *adj* : democratic

demócrata[2] *nmf* : democrat

democrático, -ca *adj* : democratic — **democráticamente** *adv*

democratizar {21} *vt* : to democratize, to make democratic — **democratización** *nf*

demografía *nf* **1** : demography **2** : demographics *pl*

demográfico, -ca *adj* : demographic

demoledor, -dora *adj* : devastating

demoler {47} *vt* DERRIBAR, DERRUMBAR : to demolish, to destroy

demolición *nf, pl* **-ciones** : demolition

demonio *nm* **1** DIABLO : devil, demon **2** ¿qué demonios . . . ? : what on earth . . . ?, what the hell . . . ?

demora *nf* : delay

demorar *vt* **1** RETRASAR : to delay **2** TARDAR : to take, to last ⟨la reparación demorará varios días : the repair will take several days⟩ — *vi* : to delay, to linger ⟨no demores : don't delay, don't take too long⟩ — **demorarse** *vr* **1** : to be slow, to take a long time **2** : to take too long

demostración *nf, pl* **-ciones** : demonstration

demostrar {19} *vt* **1** PROBAR : to demonstrate, to prove **2** MANIFESTAR : to show **3** : to demonstrate (a procedure, etc.)

demostrativo, -va *adj* : demonstrative

demudar *vt* : to change, to alter — **demudarse** *vr* : to change one's expression

denegación *nf, pl* **-ciones** : denial, refusal

denegar {49} *vt* : to deny, to turn down

dengue *nm* : dengue

denigrante *adj* : degrading, humiliating

denigrar *vt* **1** DIFAMAR : to denigrate, to disparage **2** : to degrade, to humiliate

denominación *nf, pl* **-ciones** **1** : name, designation **2** : denomination (of money)

denominador *nm* : denominator

denominar *vt* : to designate, to name, to call

denostar {19} *vt* : to revile

denotar *vt* : to denote, to show

densidad *nf* : density, thickness

denso, -sa *adj* : dense, thick — **densamente** *adv*

dentado, -da *adj* SERRADO : serrated, jagged

dentadura *nf* **1** : teeth *pl* **2 dentadura postiza** : dentures *pl*

dental *adj* : dental

dentellada *nf* **1** : bite **2** : tooth mark

dentera *nf* **1** : envy, jealousy **2 dar dentera** : to set one's teeth on edge

dentífrico *nm* : toothpaste

dentista *nmf* : dentist

dentro *adv* **1** ADENTRO : in, inside ⟨por dentro : on the inside⟩ ⟨estoy aquí dentro : I'm in here⟩ **2** ~ **de** : within, inside, in ⟨dentro de la tienda : inside the store⟩ ⟨dentro de los límites de : within the limits of⟩ **3** ~ **de** : in, within (a time period) ⟨dentro de poco : soon, shortly⟩ **4 dentro de todo** : all in all, all things considered **5 por** ~ : inwardly, inside

denuncia *nf* **1** : denunciation, condemnation **2** : police report

denunciante *nmf* : accuser (of a crime)

denunciar *vt* **1** : to denounce, to condemn **2** : to report (to the authorities)

deparar *vt* : to have in store for, to provide with ⟨no sabemos lo que nos depara el destino : we don't know what fate has in store for us⟩

departamental *adj* **1** : departmental **2 tienda departamental** *Mex* : department store

departamento *nm* **1** : department **2** APARTAMENTO : apartment

departir *vi* : to converse

dependencia *nf* **1** : dependence, dependency ⟨dependencia del alcohol : dependence on alcohol⟩ **2** : agency, branch office

depender *vi* **1** : to depend **2** ~ **de** : to depend on **3** ~ **de** : to be subordinate to

dependiente[1] *adj* : dependent

dependiente[2], **-ta** *n* : clerk, salesperson

depilar *vt* : to wax, to shave

deplorable *adj* : deplorable

deplorar *vt* **1** : to deplore **2** LAMENTAR : to regret

deponer {60} *vt* **1** : to depose, to overthrow **2** : to abandon (an attitude or stance) **3 deponer las armas** : to lay down one's arms — *vi* **1** TESTIFICAR : to testify, to make a statement **2** EVACUAR : to defecate

deportación *nf, pl* **-ciones** : deportation

deportar *vt* : to deport

deporte nm **1** : sport, sports pl ⟨hacer deporte : to engage in sports⟩ ⟨practicar un deporte : to do a sport⟩ ⟨por deporte : for the fun of it, for sport⟩ **2 deporte extremo** : extreme sport **3 deporte de invierno/equipo** : water/team sport

deportista¹ adj **1** : fond of sports **2** : sporty

deportista² nmf **1** : sports fan **2** : athlete, sportsman m, sportswoman f

deportividad nf Spain : sportsmanship

deportivo, -va adj **1** : sports, sporting ⟨artículos deportivos : sporting goods⟩ **2** : sporty

deposición nf, pl **-ciones 1** : statement, testimony **2** : removal from office

depositar vt **1** : to deposit, to place **2** : to store — **depositarse** vr : to settle

depósito nm **1** : deposit ⟨hacer un depósito : to make a deposit⟩ **2** : warehouse, storehouse ⟨depósito de armas : arms depot⟩ **3** : tank ⟨depósito de gasolina : gas tank⟩

depravación nf, pl -**ciones** : depravity

depravado, -da adj DEGENERADO : depraved, degenerate

depravar vt : to deprave, to corrupt

depreciación nf, pl -**ciones** : depreciation

depreciar vt : to depreciate, to reduce the value of — **depreciarse** vr : to lose value

depredador¹, -dora adj : predatory

depredador² nm **1** : predator **2** SAQUEADOR : plunderer

depresión nf, pl -**siones 1** : depression **2** : hollow, recess **3** : drop, fall **4** : slump, recession

depresivo nm : depressant

deprimente adj : depressing

deprimir vt **1** : to depress **2** : to lower — **deprimirse** vr ABATIRSE : to get depressed

deprisa adv : fast

depuesto pp → **deponer**

depuración nf, pl -**ciones 1** PURIFICACIÓN : purification **2** PURGA : purge **3** : refinement, polish

depurar vt **1** PURIFICAR : to purify **2** PURGAR : to purge

depuso, etc. → **deponer**

derby nm, pl **derbies** or **derbys 1** : derby (in horse racing) **2** : derby (hat) **3** Spain : local game

derecha nf **1** : right **2** : right hand, right side **3** : right wing, right (in politics)

derechazo nm **1** : pass with the cape on the right hand (in bullfighting) **2** : right (in boxing) **3** : forehand (in tennis)

derechista¹ adj : rightist, right-wing

derechista² nmf : right-winger, rightist

derecho¹ adv **1** : straight ⟨todo derecho : straight ahead⟩ **2** : upright **3** : directly ⟨ir derecho al tema : to get straight to the point⟩

derecho², -cha adj **1** : right **2** : right-hand ⟨el margen derecho : the right-hand margin⟩ **3** RECTO : straight, upright, erect ⟨siéntate derecho : sit up straight⟩

derecho³ nm **1** : right ⟨derechos humanos : human rights⟩ ⟨el derecho al voto : the right to vote⟩ ⟨derecho de nacimiento : birthright⟩ ⟨tener derecho a : to have a right to⟩ ⟨hacer valer sus derechos : to exercise one's rights⟩ ⟨estás en tu derecho : you're within your rights⟩ ⟨no hay derecho : it's not fair⟩ **2** : law ⟨derecho civil : civil law⟩ ⟨derecho de familia : family law⟩ ⟨un estudiante de derecho : a law student⟩ **3** : right side (of cloth or clothing) ⟨ponlo del derecho : turn it right side up/out⟩

de refilón adv **1** : sidelong, obliquely **2** : briefly

deriva nf **1** : drift **2 a la deriva** : adrift

derivación nf, pl -**ciones 1** : derivation **2** RAMIFICACIÓN : ramification, consequence

derivar vi **1** : to drift **2** ~ **de** : to come from, to derive from **3** ~ **en** : to result in — vt : to steer, to direct ⟨derivó la discusión hacia la política : he steered the discussion over to politics⟩ — **derivarse** vr : to be derived from, to arise from

dermatología nf : dermatology

dermatólogo, -ga n : dermatologist

derogación nf, pl -**ciones** : abolition, repeal

derogar {52} vt ABOLIR : to abolish, to repeal

derramamiento nm **1** : spilling, overflowing **2 derramamiento de sangre** : bloodshed

derramar vt **1** : to spill **2** : to shed (tears, blood) — **derramarse** vr **1** : to spill over **2** : to scatter

derrame nm **1** : spilling, shedding **2** : leakage, overflow **3** : discharge, hemorrhage ⟨derrame cerebral : stroke⟩

derrapar vi : to skid

derrape nm : skid

derredor nm **al derredor** or **en derredor** : around, round about

derrengado, -da adj **1** : bent, twisted **2** : exhausted

derretir {54} vt : to melt, to thaw — **derretirse** vr **1** : to melt, to thaw **2** ~ **por** fam : to be crazy about

derribar vt **1** DEMOLER, DERRUMBAR : to demolish, to knock down **2** : to shoot down, to bring down (an airplane) **3** DERROCAR : to overthrow

derribo nm **1** : demolition, razing **2** : shooting down **3** : overthrow

derrocamiento nm : overthrow

derrocar {72} vt DERRIBAR : to overthrow, to topple

derrochador¹, -dora adj : extravagant, wasteful

derrochador², -dora n : spendthrift

derrochar vt : to waste, to squander

derroche nm : extravagance, waste

derrota nf **1** : defeat, rout **2** : course (at sea)

derrotar vt : to defeat

derrotero nm RUTA : course

derrotista adj & nmf : defeatist

derruir {41} vt : to demolish, to tear down

derrumbamiento nm : collapse

derrumbar *vt* **1** DEMOLER, DERRIBAR : to demolish, to knock down **2** DESPEÑAR : to cast down, to topple — **derrumbarse** *vr* DESPLOMARSE : to collapse, to break down

derrumbe *nm* **1** DESPLOME : collapse, fall ⟨el derrumbe del comunismo : the fall of Communism⟩ **2** : landslide

des- *pref* : de-, dis-, un-

desabastecimiento *nm* : shortage, scarcity

desabasto *nm Mex* : shortage, scarcity

desabotonar *vt* : to unbutton, to undo — **desabotonarse** *vr* : to come undone

desabrido, -da *adj* : tasteless, bland

desabrigar {52} *vt* **1** : to undress **2** : to uncover **3** : to deprive of shelter

desabrochar *vt* : to unbutton, to undo — **desabrocharse** *vr* : to come undone

desacato *nm* **1** : disrespect **2** : contempt (of court)

desacelerar *vi* : to decelerate, to slow down

desacertado, -da *adj* **1** : mistaken **2** : unwise

desacertar {55} *vi* ERRAR : to err, to be mistaken

desacierto *nm* ERROR : error, mistake

desaconsejable *adj* : inadvisable

desaconsejado, -da *adj* : ill-advised, unwise

desaconsejar *vt* : to advise against

desacostumbrado, -da *adj* : unaccustomed, unusual

desacreditar *vt* DESPRESTIGIAR : to discredit, to disgrace

desactivar *vt* : to deactivate, to defuse

desacuerdo *nm* : disagreement

desafiante *adj* : defiant

desafiar {85} *vt* RETAR : to defy, to challenge

desafilado, -da *adj* : blunt

desafilar *vt* : to dull, to blunt

desafinado, -da *adj* : out-of-tune, off-key

desafinar *vi* : to go out of tune

desafío *nm* **1** RETO : challenge **2** RESISTENCIA : defiance

desaforado, -da *adj* : wild, unrestrained

desafortunado, -da *adj* : unfortunate, unlucky — **desafortunadamente** *adv*

desafuero *nm* ABUSO : injustice, outrage

desagradable *adj* : unpleasant, disagreeable — **desagradablemente** *adv*

desagradar *vi* : to be unpleasant, to be disagreeable

desagradecido, -da *adj* : ungrateful

desagrado *nm* **1** : displeasure **2** con ∼ : reluctantly

desagravio *nm* **1** : apology **2** : amends, reparation

desagregarse {52} *vr* : to break up, to disintegrate

desaguar {10} *vi* : to drain, to empty

desagüe *nm* **1** : drain **2** : drainage

desaguisado *nm* : mess

desahogado, -da *adj* **1** : well-off, comfortable **2** : spacious, roomy

desahogar {52} *vt* **1** : to relieve, to ease **2** : to give vent to — **desahogarse** *vr* **1**

: to recover, to feel better **2** : to unburden oneself, to let off steam

desahogo *nm* **1** : relief, outlet **2** con ∼ : comfortably

desahuciar *vt* **1** : to deprive of hope **2** : to evict — **desahuciarse** *vr* : to lose all hope

desahucio *nm* : eviction

desairar {5} *vt* : to snub, to rebuff

desaire *nm* : rebuff, snub, slight

desajustar *vt* **1** : to disarrange, to put out of order **2** : to upset (plans)

desajuste *nm* **1** : maladjustment **2** : imbalance **3** : upset, disruption

desalentador, -dora *adj* : discouraging, disheartening

desalentar {55} *vt* DESANIMAR : to discourage, to dishearten — **desalentarse** *vr*

desaliento *nm* : discouragement

desaliñado, -da *adj* : sloppy, untidy (of a person's appearance) — **desaliñadamente** *adv*

desaliño *nm* : sloppiness, untidiness (of a person's appearance)

desalmado, -da *adj* : heartless, callous

desalojar *vt* **1** : to remove, to clear **2** EVACUAR : to evacuate, to vacate **3** : to evict

desalojo *nm* **1** : removal, expulsion **2** : evacuation **3** : eviction

desamarrar *vt* **1** : to cast off **2** : to untie

desamor *nm* **1** FRIALDAD : indifference **2** ENEMISTAD : dislike, enmity

desamparado, -da *adj* DESVALIDO : helpless, destitute

desamparar *vt* : to abandon, to forsake

desamparo *nm* **1** : abandonment, neglect **2** : helplessness

desamueblado, -da *adj* : unfurnished

desandar {6} *vt* : to go back, to return to the starting point

desangelado, -da *adj* : dull, lifeless

desangrar *vt* : to bleed, to bleed dry — **desangrarse** *vr* **1** : to be bleeding **2** : to bleed to death

desanimar *vt* DESALENTAR : to discourage, to dishearten — **desanimarse** *vr*

desánimo *nm* DESALIENTO : discouragement, dejection

desapacible *adj* : unpleasant, disagreeable

desaparecer {53} *vt* : to cause to disappear *vi* : to disappear, to vanish

desaparecido¹, -da *adj* **1** : late, deceased **2** : missing

desaparecido², -da *n* : missing person

desaparición *nf, pl* **-ciones** : disappearance

desapasionado, -da *adj* : dispassionate, impartial — **desapasionadamente** *adv*

desapego *nm* : coolness, indifference

desapercibido, -da *adj* **1** : unnoticed **2** DESPREVENIDO : unprepared, off guard

desaprobación *nf, pl* **-ciones** : disapproval

desaprobar {19} *vt* REPROBAR : to disapprove of

desaprovechar *vt* MALGASTAR : to waste, to misuse *vi* : to lose ground, to slip back

desarmador *nm Mex* : screwdriver
desarmar *vt* **1** : to disarm **2** DESMONTAR : to disassemble, to take apart
desarme *nm* : disarmament
desarraigado, -da *adj* : rootless
desarraigar {52} *vt* : to uproot, to root out
desarregladamente *adv* : untidily, messily
desarreglado, -da *adj* : untidy, disorganized
desarreglar *vt* **1** : to mess up **2** : to upset, to disrupt
desarreglo *nm* **1** : untidiness **2** : disorder, confusion
desarrollar *vt* **1** : to develop **2** : to carry out (an action, etc.) **3** : to explain (a theory, etc.) — **desarrollarse** *vr* **1** : to develop **2** : to take place, to unfold
desarrollo *nm* : development ⟨países en vías de desarrollo : developing countries⟩
desarticulación *nf, pl* **-ciones 1** : dislocation **2** : breaking up, dismantling
desarticular *vt* **1** DISLOCAR : to dislocate **2** : to break up, to dismantle
desasosiego *nm* : sense of unease
desastre *nm* CATÁSTROFE : disaster
desastroso, -sa *adj* : disastrous, catastrophic — **desastrosamente** *adv*
desatar *vt* **1** : to undo, to untie **2** : to unleash **3** : to trigger, to precipitate — **desatarse** *vr* **1** : to come undone **2** : to break out, to erupt
desatascador *nm* : plunger (for toilets, etc.)
desatascar {72} *vt* : to unblock, to clear
desatención *nf, pl* **-ciones 1** : absentmindedness, distraction **2** : discourtesy
desatender {56} *vt* **1** : to disregard **2** : to neglect **3** : to leave unattended
desatento, -ta *adj* **1** DISTRAÍDO : absentminded **2** GROSERO : discourteous, rude
desatinado, -da *adj* : foolish, silly
desatino *nm* : folly, mistake
desatorador *nm* : plunger (for toilets, etc.) **2** : drain cleaner (liquid)
desatornillar → **destornillar**
desautorizar {21} *vt* : to deprive of authority, to discredit
desavenencia *nf* DISCORDANCIA : disagreement, dispute
desayunar *vi* : to have breakfast *vt* : to have for breakfast
desayuno *nm* : breakfast
desazón *nf, pl* **-zones** INQUIETUD : uneasiness, anxiety
desbalance *nm* : imbalance
desbancar {72} *vt* : to displace, to oust
desbandada *nf* : scattering, dispersal
desbarajuste *nm* DESORDEN : disarray, disorder, mess
desbaratar *vt* **1** ARRUINAR : to destroy, to ruin **2** DESCOMPONER : to break, to break down — **desbaratarse** *vr* : to fall apart
desbloquear *vt* **1** : to open up, to clear, to break through **2** : to free, to release
desbocado, -da *adj* : unbridled, rampant
desbocarse {72} *vr* : to run away, to bolt
desbordamiento *nm* : overflowing

desbordante *adj* : overflowing, bursting ⟨desbordante de energía : bursting with energy⟩
desbordar *vt* **1** : to overflow, to spill over **2** : to surpass, to exceed — **desbordarse** *vr*
descabellado, -da *adj* : outlandish, ridiculous
descafeinado, -da *adj* : decaffeinated
descalabrar *vt* : to hit on the head — **descalabrarse** *vr*
descalabro *nm* : setback, misfortune, loss
descalificación *nf, pl* **-ciones 1** : disqualification **2** : disparaging remark
descalificar {72} *vt* **1** : to disqualify **2** DESACREDITAR : to discredit — **descalificarse** *vr*
descalzarse {21} *vr* : take off one's shoes
descalzo, -za *adj* : barefoot
descampado *nm* : open area
descansado, -da *adj* **1** : rested, refreshed **2** : restful, peaceful
descansar *vi* : to rest, to relax ⟨¡descansen! : at ease!⟩ — *vt* : to rest ⟨descansar la vista : to rest one's eyes⟩
descansillo *nm Spain* DESCANSO : landing (of a staircase)
descanso *nm* **1** : rest, relaxation **2** : break **3** : landing (of a staircase) **4** : intermission (in a show), halftime (in sports)
descapotable *adj & nm* : convertible
descarado, -da *adj* : brazen, impudent — **descaradamente** *adv*
descarga *nf* **1** : discharge **2** : unloading
descargable *adj* : downloadable
descargar {52} *vt* **1** : to discharge **2** : to unload **3** : to release, to free **4** : to take out, to vent (anger, etc.) **5** : to download (a file, etc.) — **descargarse** *vr* **1** : to unburden oneself **2** : to quit **3** : to lose power
descargo *nm* **1** : unloading **2** : defense ⟨testigo de descargo : witness for the defense⟩
descarnado, -da *adj* : scrawny, gaunt
descaro *nm* : audacity, nerve
descarriado, -da *adj* : lost, gone astray
descarriarse *vr* : to go astray
descarrilar *vi* : to derail — **descarrilarse** *vr* — **descarrilamiento** *nm*
descartar *vt* : to rule out, to reject — **descartarse** *vr* : to discard
descascarar *vt* : to peel, to shell, to husk — **descascararse** *vr* : to peel off, to chip
descendencia *nf* **1** : descendants *pl* **2** LINAJE : descent, lineage
descendente *adj* : downward, descending
descender {56} *vt* **1** : to descend, to go down **2** BAJAR : to lower, to take down, to let down *vi* **1** : to descend, to come down **2** : to drop, to fall **3** ~ **de** : to be a descendant of
descendiente *adj & nm* : descendant
descenso *nm* **1** : descent **2** BAJA, CAÍDA : drop, fall
descentralizar {21} *vt* : to decentralize — **descentralizarse** *vr* — **descentralización** *nf*

descifrar *vt* : to decipher, to decode — **descifrable** *adj*

desclasificar {72} *vt* : to declassify

descodificador → **decodificador**

descodificar {72} *vt* : to decode

descolgar {16} *vt* **1** : to take down, to let down **2** : to pick up, to answer (the telephone)

descollar {19} *vi* SOBRESALIR : to stand out, to be outstanding, to excel

descolorido, -da *adj* : discolored, faded

descomponer {60} *vt* **1** : to rot, to decompose **2** DESBARATAR : to break, to break down **3** : to damage **4** : to mess up — **descomponerse** *vr* **1** : to break down **2** : to decompose

descomposición *nf*, *pl* **-ciones 1** : breakdown, decomposition **2** : decay

descompuesto¹ *pp* → **descomponer**

descompuesto², -ta *adj* **1** : broken down, out of order **2** : rotten, decomposed

descomunal *adj* **1** ENORME : enormous, huge **2** EXTRAORDINARIO : extraordinary

desconcertar *vt* DISTRAER : to distract

desconcertante *adj* : disconcerting

desconcertar {55} *vt* : to disconcert — **desconcertarse** *vr*

desconchar *vt* : to chip — **desconcharse** *vr* : to chip off, to peel

desconcierto *nm* : uncertainty, confusion

desconectar *vt* **1** : to disconnect, to switch off **2** : to unplug

desconfiado, -da *adj* : distrustful, suspicious

desconfianza *nf* RECELO : distrust, suspicion

desconfiar {85} *vi* ~ **de** : to distrust, to be suspicious of

descongelar *vt* **1** : to thaw **2** : to defrost (a refrigerator, etc.) **3** : to unfreeze (assets) — **descongelarse** *vr*

descongestionante *adj* & *nm* : decongestant

descongestionar *vt* : to clear, to unclog ⟨descongestionar el tráfico : to reduce traffic congestion⟩

desconocer {18} *vt* **1** IGNORAR : to be unaware of **2** : to fail to recognize

desconocido¹, -da *adj* : unknown, unfamiliar

desconocido², -da *n* EXTRAÑO : stranger

desconocimiento *nm* : ignorance

desconsiderado, -da *adj* : inconsiderate, thoughtless — **desconsideradamente** *adj*

desconsolado, -da *adj* : disconsolate, heartbroken, despondent

desconsuelo *nm* AFLICCIÓN : grief, distress, despair

descontaminar *vt* : to decontaminate — **descontaminación** *nf*

descontar {19} *vt* **1** : to discount, to deduct **2** EXCEPTUAR : to except, to exclude

descontento¹, -ta *adj* : discontented, dissatisfied

descontento² *nm* : discontent, dissatisfaction

descontinuar {3} *vt* : to discontinue (a product, etc.)

descontrol *nm* : lack of control, disorder, chaos

descontrolarse *vr* : to get out of control, to be out of hand

desconvocar {72} *vt* : to cancel

descorazonado, -da *adj* : disheartened, discouraged

descorchar *vt* : to uncork

descorrer *vt* : to draw back

descortés *adj*, *pl* **-teses** : discourteous, rude

descortesía *nf* : discourtesy, rudeness

descrédito *nm* DESPRESTIGIO : discredit

descremado, -da *adj* : nonfat, skim

describir {33} *vt* : to describe

descripción *nf*, *pl* **-ciones** : description

descriptivo, -va *adj* : descriptive

descrito *pp* → **describir**

descuartizar {21} *vt* **1** : to cut up, to quarter **2** : to tear to pieces

descubierto¹ *pp* → **descubrir**

descubierto², -ta *adj* **1** : exposed, revealed **2 al descubierto** : out in the open

descubridor, -dora *n* : discoverer, explorer

descubrimiento *nm* : discovery

descubrir {2} *vt* **1** HALLAR : to discover, to find out **2** REVELAR : to uncover, to reveal **3** DEVELAR : to unveil **4** DELATAR : to give away — **descubrirse** *vr*

descuento *nm* REBAJA : discount

descuidado, -da *adj* **1** : neglectful, careless **2** : neglected, unkempt

descuidar *vt* : to neglect, to overlook — *vi* : to be careless — **descuidarse** *vr* **1** : to be careless, to drop one's guard **2** : to let oneself go

descuido *nm* **1** : carelessness, negligence **2** : slip, oversight

desde *prep* **1** : from ⟨desde arriba : from above⟩ ⟨desde la cabeza hasta los pies : from head to foot/toe⟩ **2** : since, from ⟨desde el lunes : since Monday⟩ ⟨desde el principio : right from the start⟩ ⟨desde la mañana hasta la noche : from morning to/until night⟩ **3 desde ahora** : from now on **4 desde entonces** : since then **5 desde hace** : for, since (a time) ⟨ha estado nevando desde hace dos días : it's been snowing for two days⟩ **6 desde luego** : of course **7 desde que** : since, ever since **8 desde ya** : right now, immediately

desdecir {11} *vi* **1** ~ **de** : to be unworthy of **2** ~ **de** : to clash with — **desdecirse** *vr* **1** CONTRADECIRSE : to contradict oneself **2** RETRACTARSE : to go back on one's word

desdén *nm*, *pl* **desdenes** DESPRECIO : disdain, scorn

desdentado, -da *adj* : toothless

desdeñar *vt* DESPRECIAR : to disdain, to scorn, to despise

desdeñoso, -sa *adj* : disdainful, scornful — **desdeñosamente** *adv*

desdibujar *vt* : to blur — **desdibujarse** *vr*

desdicha *nf* **1** : misery **2** : misfortune

desdichado¹, -da *adj* **1** : unfortunate **2** : miserable, unhappy

desdichado², -da *n* : wretch

desdicho *pp* → **desdecir**

desdiga, desdijo etc. → **desdecir**

desdoblar *vt* DESPLEGAR : to unfold

deseable *adj* : desirable

desear *vt* **1** : to wish ⟨te deseo buena suerte : I wish you good luck⟩ **2** QUERER : to want, to desire ⟨dejar mucho que desear : to leave much to be desired⟩

desecar {72} *vt* : to dry (flowers, etc.)

desechable *adj* : disposable

desechar *vt* **1** : to discard, to throw away **2** RECHAZAR : to reject

desecho *nm* **1** : reject **2 desechos** *nmpl* RESIDUOS : rubbish, waste

desembarazarse {21} *vr* ~ **de** : to get rid of

desembarcar {72} *vi* : to disembark *vt* : to unload

desembarco *nm* **1** : landing, arrival **2** : unloading

desembarque → **desembarco**

desembocadura *nf* **1** : mouth (of a river) **2** : opening, end (of a street)

desembocar {72} *vi* ~ **en** *or* ~ **a 1** : to flow into, to join **2** : to lead to, to result in

desembolsar *vt* PAGAR : to disburse, to pay out

desembolso *nm* PAGO : disbursement, payment

desempacar {72} *v* : to unpack

desempatar *vi* : to break a tie

desempate *nm* : tiebreaker, play-off

desempeñar *vt* **1** : to play (a role) **2** : to fulfill, to carry out **3** : to redeem (from a pawnshop) — **desempeñarse** *vr* : to function, to act

desempeño *nm* **1** : fulfillment, carrying out **2** : performance

desempleado¹, -da *adj* : unemployed

desempleado², -da *n* : unemployed person

desempleo *nm* : unemployment

desempolvar *vt* **1** : to dust off **2** : to resurrect, to revive

desencadenar *vt* **1** : to unchain **2** : to trigger, to unleash — **desencadenarse** *vr*

desencajar *vt* **1** : to dislocate (a bone) **2** : to pop out of place, to disengage — **desencajarse** *vr*

desencantar *vt* : to disenchant, to disillusion — **desencantarse** *vr*

desencanto *nm* : disenchantment, disillusionment

desenchufar *vt* : to disconnect, to unplug

desenfadado, -da *adj* **1** : uninhibited, carefree **2** : confident, self-assured

desenfado *nm* **1** DESENVOLTURA : self-assurance, confidence **2** : naturalness, ease

desenfocado, -da *adj* : unfocused, blurry

desenfrenadamente *adv* : wildly, with abandon

desenfrenado, -da *adj* : unbridled, unrestrained

desenfreno *nm* : abandon, lack of restraint

desenfundar *vt* : to draw (a gun)

desenganchar *vt* : to unhitch, to uncouple

desengañar *vt* : to disillusion, to disenchant — **desengañarse** *vr*

desengaño *nm* : disenchantment, disillusionment

desenlace *nm* : ending, outcome

desenmarañar *vt* : to disentangle, to unravel

desenmascarar *vt* : to unmask, to expose

desenredar *vt* **1** : to untangle, to disentangle **2** : to straighten out, to sort out

desenrollar *vt* : to unroll, to unwind

desenroscar *vt* **1** : to unscrew **2** : to unroll — **desenroscarse** *vr*

desentenderse {56} *vr* **1** ~ **de** : to want nothing to do with, to be uninterested in **2** ~ **de** : to pretend ignorance of

desenterrar {55} *vt* **1** EXHUMAR : to exhume **2** : to unearth, to dig up

desentonar *vi* **1** : to clash, to conflict **2** : to be out of tune, to sing off-key

desentrañar *vt* : to get to the bottom of, to unravel

desenvainar *vt* : to draw, to unsheathe (a sword)

desenvoltura *nf* **1** DESENFADO : confidence, self-assurance **2** ELOCUENCIA : eloquence, fluency

desenvolver {89} *vt* : to unwrap, to open — **desenvolverse** *vr* **1** : to unfold, to develop **2** : to manage, to cope

desenvuelto¹ *pp* → **desenvolver**

desenvuelto², -ta *adj* : confident, relaxed, self-assured

deseo *nm* : wish, desire

deseoso, -sa *adj* : eager, anxious

desequilibrado, -da *adj* **1** : off-balance **2** : insane

desequilibrar *vt* : to unbalance, to throw off balance — **desequilibrarse** *vr*

desequilibrio *nm* : imbalance

deserción *nf, pl* **-ciones** : desertion, defection

desertar *vi* **1** : to desert, to defect **2** ~ **de** : to abandon, to neglect

desértico, -ca *adj* **1** : desert **2** : uninhabited

desertor, -tora *n* : deserter, defector

desesperación *nf, pl* **-ciones** : desperation, despair

desesperado, -da *adj* : desperate, despairing, hopeless — **desesperadamente** *adv*

desesperante *adj* **1** : exasperating **2** : agonizing, excruciating

desesperanza *nf* : despair, hopelessness

desesperar *vt* : to exasperate — *vi* : to despair, to lose hope —, **desesperarse** *vr* : to become exasperated

desestabilizar {21} *vt* : to make unstable

desestimar *vt* **1** : to reject, to disallow **2** : to have a low opinion of

desfachatez *nf, pl* **-teces** : audacity, nerve, cheek

desfalcador, -dora *n* : embezzler

desfalcar {72} *vt* : to embezzle

desfalco *nm* : embezzlement

desfallecer {53} *vi* **1** : to weaken **2** : to faint

desfallecimiento *nm* **1** : weakness **2** : fainting

desfasado, -da *adj* **1** : out of sync **2** : out of step, behind the times

desfase *nm* : gap, lag ⟨desfase (de) horario : jet lag⟩

desfavorable *adj* : unfavorable, adverse — **desfavorablemente** *adv*

desfavorecido, -da *adj* : underprivileged

desfigurar *vt* **1** : to disfigure, to mar **2** : to distort, to misrepresent

desfiladero *nm* : narrow gorge, defile

desfilar *vi* : to parade, to march

desfile *nm* : parade, procession

desfogar {52} *vt* **1** : to vent **2** *Mex* : to unclog, to unblock — **desfogarse** *vr* : to vent one's feelings, to let off steam

desgajar *vt* **1** : to tear off **2** : to break apart — **desgajarse** *vr* : to come apart

desgana *nf* **1** INAPETENCIA : lack of appetite **2** APATÍA : apathy, unwillingness, reluctance

desgano *nm* → desgana

desgarbado, -da *adj* : ungainly

desgarrador, -dora *adj* : heartbreaking

desgarradura *nf* : tear, rip

desgarrar *vt* **1** : to tear, to rip **2** : to break (one's heart) — **desgarrarse** *vr*

desgarre → desgarro

desgarro *nm* : tear

desgarrón *nm, pl* -**rrones** : rip, tear

desgastar *vt* **1** : to use up **2** : to wear away, to wear down

desgaste *nm* : deterioration, wear and tear

desglosar *vt* : to break down, to itemize

desglose *nm* : breakdown, itemization

desgobierno *nm* : anarchy, disorder

desgracia *nf* **1** : misfortune **2** : disgrace **3** por ~ : unfortunately

desgraciadamente *adv* : unfortunately

desgraciado¹, -da *adj* **1** : unfortunate, unlucky **2** : vile, wretched

desgraciado², -da *n* : unfortunate person, wretch

desgranar *vt* : to shuck, to shell

desgravar *vt* : to deduct (from taxes), to exempt — **desgravación** *n*

desguazar {21} *vt* *Spain* : to scrap

deshabitado, -da *adj* : unoccupied, uninhabited

deshacer {40} *vt* **1** : to destroy, to ruin **2** DESATAR : to undo, to untie **3** : to break apart, to crumble **4** : to dissolve, to melt **5** : to break, to cancel — **deshacerse** *vr* **1** : to fall apart, to come undone **2** ~ **de** : to get rid of

deshecho¹ *pp* → deshacer

deshecho², -cha *adj* **1** : destroyed, ruined **2** : devastated, shattered **3** : undone, untied

deshelar {55} *vt* **1** : to thaw **2** : to deice (a plane), to defrost — **deshelarse** *vr* **1** : to thaw **2** : to defrost

desherbar *vt* : to weed

desheredado, -da *adj* MARGINADO : dispossessed, destitute

desheredar *vt* : to disinherit

deshicieron, etc. → deshacer

deshidratar *vt* : to dehydrate — **deshidratación** *nf*

deshielo *nm* : thaw, thawing

deshierbar → desherbar

deshilachar *vt* : to fray — **deshilacharse** *vr*

deshizo → deshacer

deshojar *vt* **1** : to remove petals from **2** : to remove pages from

deshollinador, -dora *n* : chimney sweep

deshonestidad *nf* : dishonesty

deshonesto, -ta *adj* : dishonest

deshonor *nm* : dishonor, disgrace

deshonra *nf* : dishonor, disgrace

deshonrar *vt* : to dishonor, to disgrace

deshonroso, -sa *adj* : dishonorable, disgraceful

deshora *nf* a deshoras : at odd times

deshuesadero *nm Mex* : dump

deshuesar *vt* **1** : to pit (a fruit, etc.) **2** : to bone

desidia *nf* **1** APATÍA : apathy, indolence **2** NEGLIGENCIA : negligence, sloppiness

desierto¹, -ta *adj* : deserted, uninhabited

desierto² *nm* : desert

designación *nf, pl* -**ciones** NOMBRAMIENTO : appointment, naming (to an office, etc.)

designar *vt* NOMBRAR : to designate, to appoint, to name

designio *nm* : plan

desigual *adj* **1** : unequal **2** DISPAREJO : uneven **3** : variable, changeable — **desigualmente** *adv*

desigualdad *nf* **1** : inequality **2** : unevenness

desilusión *nf, pl* -**siones** DESENCANTO, DESENGAÑO : disillusionment, disenchantment

desilusionar *vt* DESENCANTAR, DESENGAÑAR : to disillusion, to disenchant — **desilusionarse** *vr*

desinfectante *adj & nm* : disinfectant

desinfectar *vt* : to disinfect — **desinfección** *nf*

desinflar *vt* : to deflate — **desinflarse** *vr*

desinformar *vt* : to misinform

desinhibido, -da *adj* : uninhibited, unrestrained

desintegración *nf, pl* -**ciones** : disintegration

desintegrar *vt* : to disintegrate, to break up — **desintegrarse** *vr*

desinterés *nm* **1** : lack of interest, indifference **2** : unselfishness

desinteresado, -da *adj* GENEROSO : unselfish

desintoxicación *nf, pl* -**ciones** : detox

desintoxicar {72} *vt* : to detox

desistir *vi* **1** : to desist, to stop **2** ~ **de** : to give up, to relinquish

deslave *nm Mex* : landslide

desleal *adj* INFIEL : disloyal — **deslealmente** *adv*

deslealtad *nf* : disloyalty

desligar {52} *vt* **1** : to separate, to undo **2** : to free (from an obligation) — **desligarse** *vr* ~ **de** : to extricate oneself from

deslindar vt **1** : to mark the limits of, to demarcate **2** : to define, to clarify
deslinde nm : demarcation
desliz nm, pl **deslices** : error, mistake, slip ⟨desliz de la lengua : slip of the tongue⟩
deslizador nm **1** : speedboat **2** Mex : hang glider
deslizamiento nm : slip, slide ⟨deslizamiento de tierras : landslide⟩
deslizar {21} vt **1** : to slide, to slip **2** : to slip in — **deslizarse** vr **1** : to slide, to glide **2** : to slip away
deslomarse vr : to wear oneself out, to work oneself to death
deslucido, -da adj **1** : lackluster, dull **2** : faded, dingy, tarnished
deslucir {45} vt **1** : to spoil **2** : to fade, to dull, to tarnish **3** : to discredit
deslumbrar vt : to dazzle — **deslumbrante** adj
deslustrado, -da adj : dull, lusterless
deslustrar vt : to tarnish, to dull
deslustre nm : tarnish
desmadrarse vr : to get out of hand
desmadre nm fam : chaos
desmán nm, pl **desmanes 1** : outrage, abuse **2** : misfortune
desmandarse vr : to behave badly, to get out of hand
desmantelar vt DESMONTAR : to dismantle
desmañado, -da adj : clumsy, awkward
desmarcarse {72} vr : to distance oneself
desmayado, -da adj **1** : fainting, weak **2** : dull, pale
desmayar vi : to lose heart, to falter — **desmayarse** vr DESVANECERSE : to faint, to swoon
desmayo nm **1** : faint, fainting **2 sufrir un desmayo** : to faint
desmedido, -da adj DESMESURADO : excessive, undue
desmejorar vt : to weaken, to make worse vi : to decline (in health), to get worse
desmembrar {55} vt **1** : to dismember **2** : to break up
desmemoriado, -da adj : absentminded, forgetful
desmentido nm : denial
desmentir {76} vt **1** NEGAR : to deny, to refute **2** CONTRADECIR : to contradict
desmenuzar {21} vt **1** : to break down, to scrutinize **2** : to crumble, to shred — **desmenuzarse** vr
desmerecer {53} vt : to be unworthy of vi **1** : to decline in value **2** ~ **de** : to compare unfavorably with
desmesurado, -da adj DESMEDIDO : excessive, inordinate — **desmesuradamente** adv
desmigajar vt : to crumble — **desmigajarse** vr
desmilitarizar {21} vt : to demilitarize
desmitificar {72} vt : to demystify, to dispel the myths surrounding
desmontable adj : removable
desmontar vt **1** : to clear, to level off **2** DESMANTELAR : to dismantle, to take apart vi : to dismount

desmonte nm : clearing, leveling
desmoralizador, -dora adj : demoralizing
desmoralizar {21} vt DESALENTAR : to demoralize, to discourage
desmoronamiento nm : crumbling, falling apart
desmoronar vt : to wear away, to erode — **desmoronarse** vr : to crumble, to deteriorate, to fall apart
desmovilizar {21} vt : to demobilize — **desmovilización** nf
desnatado, -da Spain → **descremado**
desnaturalizar {21} vt **1** : to denature **2** : to distort, to alter
desnivel nm **1** : disparity, difference **2** : unevenness (of a surface)
desnivelado, -da adj **1** : uneven **2** : unbalanced
desnivelar vt **1** : to make uneven **2** : to tip (the balance)
desnucar {72} vt : to break the neck of — **desnucarse** vr : to break one's neck
desnudar vt **1** : to undress, to strip, to lay bare — **desnudarse** vr : to undress, to strip off one's clothing
desnudez nf, pl **-deces** : nudity, nakedness
desnudo¹, -da adj : nude, naked, bare
desnudo² nm : nude
desnutrición nf, pl **-ciones** MALNUTRICIÓN : malnutrition
desnutrido, -da adj MALNUTRIDO : malnourished, undernourished
desobedecer {53} v : to disobey
desobediencia nf : disobedience — **desobediente** adj
desocupación nf, pl **-ciones** : unemployment
desocupado, -da adj **1** : vacant, empty **2** : free, unoccupied **3** : unemployed
desocupar vt **1** : to empty **2** : to vacate, to move out of — **desocuparse** vr : to leave, to quit (a job)
desodorante adj & nm : deodorant
desolación nf, pl **-ciones** : desolation
desolado, -da adj **1** : desolate **2** : devastated, distressed
desolador, -dora adj **1** : devastating **2** : bleak, desolate
desolar {19} vt : to devastate
desollar vt : to skin, to flay
desorbitado, -da adj **1** : excessive, exorbitant **2 con los ojos desorbitados** : with eyes popping out of one's head
desorden nm, pl **desórdenes 1** DESBARAJUSTE : disorder, mess **2** : disorder, disturbance, upset
desordenadamente adv : messily, in a disorderly way
desordenado, -da adj **1** : untidy, messy **2** : disorderly, unruly
desordenar vt : to mess up — **desordenarse** vr : to get messed up
desorganización nf, pl **-ciones** : disorganization
desorganizar {21} vt : to disrupt, to disorganize
desorientar vt : to disorient, to mislead, to confuse — **desorientarse** vr : to become disoriented, to lose one's way

desovar *vi* : to spawn

despachar *vt* **1** : to complete, to conclude **2** : to deal with, to take care of, to handle **3** : to dispatch, to send off **4** *fam* : to finish off, to kill **5** : to serve — *vi* : to serve — **despacharse** *vr fam* : to gulp down, to polish off

despacho *nm* **1** : dispatch, shipment **2** OFICINA : office, study

despacio *adv* LENTAMENTE, LENTO : slowly, slow ⟨¡despacio! : take it easy!, easy does it!⟩

despampanante *adj fam* : breathtaking, stunning

desparasitar *vt* : to worm (an animal), to rid of fleas/ticks/lice (etc.)

desparpajo *nm fam* **1** : self-confidence, nerve **2** *CA* : confusion, muddle

desparramar *vt* **1** : to spill, to splatter **2** : to spread, to scatter

despatarrarse *vr* : to sprawl (out)

despavorido, -da *adj* : terrified, horrified

despecho *nm* **1** : spite **2 a despecho de** : despite, in spite of

despectivo, -va *adj* **1** : contemptuous, disparaging **2** : derogatory, pejorative — **despectivamente** *adv*

despedazar {21} *vt* : to cut to pieces, to tear apart

despedida *nf* **1** : farewell, good-bye **2 despedida de soltera** : bridal shower

despedir {54} *vt* **1** : to see off, to show out **2** : to dismiss, to fire **3** EMITIR : to give off, to emit ⟨despedir un olor : to give off an odor⟩ — **despedirse** *vr* : to take one's leave, to say good-bye

despegado, -da *adj* **1** : separated, detached **2** : cold, distant

despegar {52} *vt* : to remove, to detach *vi* : to take off, to lift off, to blast off

despegue *nm* : takeoff, liftoff

despeinar *vt* or **despeinar a alguien** : to mess up someone's hair — **despeinarse** *vr* ⟨me despeiné : I messed up my hair, my hair got messed up⟩

despejado, -da *adj* **1** : clear, fair **2** : alert **3** : uncluttered, unobstructed

despejar *vt* **1** : to clear, to free **2** : to clarify *vi* **1** : to clear up **2** : to punt (in sports)

despeje *nm* **1** : clearing **2** : punt (in sports)

despellejar *vt* : to skin (an animal)

despelote *nm* : mess, disaster

despenalizar {21} *vt* : to legalize — **despenalización** *nf*

despensa *nf* **1** : pantry, larder **2** PROVISIONES : provisions *pl*, supplies *pl*

despeñadero *nm* : cliff, precipice

despeñar *vt* : to hurl down

desperdiciar *vt* **1** DESAPROVECHAR, MALGASTAR : to waste **2** : to miss, to miss out on

desperdicio *nm* **1** : waste **2 desperdicios** *nmpl* RESIDUOS : refuse, scraps, rubbish

desperdigar {52} *vt* DISPERSAR : to disperse, to scatter

desperezarse {21} *vr* : to stretch

desperfecto *nm* **1** DEFECTO : flaw, defect **2** : damage

despertador *nm* : alarm clock

despertar {55} *vi* : to awaken, to wake up — *vt* **1** : to arouse, to wake **2** EVOCAR : to elicit, to evoke — **despertarse** *vr* : to wake (oneself) up

despiadado, -da *adj* CRUEL : cruel, merciless, pitiless — **despiadadamente** *adv*

despido *nm* : dismissal, layoff

despierto, -ta *adj* **1** : awake, alert **2** LISTO : clever, sharp ⟨con la mente despierta : with a sharp mind⟩

despilfarrador[1], **-dora** *adj* : extravagant, wasteful

despilfarrador[2], **-dora** *n* : spendthrift, prodigal

despilfarrar *vt* MALGASTAR : to squander, to waste

despilfarro *nm* : extravagance, wastefulness

despintar *vt* : to strip the paint from — **despintarse** *vr* : to fade, to wash off, to peel off

despistado[1], **-da** *adj* **1** DISTRAÍDO : absentminded, forgetful, scatterbrained **2** CONFUSO : confused, bewildered

despistado[2], **-da** *n* : absentminded person

despistar *vt* : to throw off the track, to confuse — **despistarse** *vr*

despiste *nm* **1** : absentmindedness **2** : mistake, slip

desplantador *nm* : garden trowel

desplante *nm* : insolence, rudeness

desplazamiento *nm* **1** : movement, displacement **2** : journey

desplazar {21} *vt* **1** : to replace, to displace **2** TRASLADAR : to move, to shift **3** : to scroll (in computing) — **desplazarse** *vr*

desplegar {49} *vt* **1** : to display, to show, to manifest **2** DESDOBLAR : to unfold, to unfurl **3** : to spread (out) **4** : to deploy

despliegue *nm* **1** : display **2** : deployment

desplomarse *vr* **1** : to plummet, to fall **2** DERRUMBARSE : to collapse, to break down

desplome *nm* **1** : fall, drop **2** : collapse

desplumar *vt* : to pluck (a chicken, etc.)

despoblación *nf, pl* **-ciones** : large population decrease

despoblado[1], **-da** *adj* : uninhabited, deserted

despoblado[2] *nm* : open country, deserted area

despoblar {19} *vt* : to reduce the population of ⟨un lugar despoblado : a deserted place⟩

despojar *vt* **1** : to strip, to clear **2** : to divest, to deprive — **despojarse** *vr* **1** ∼ **de** : to remove (clothing) **2** ∼ **de** : to relinquish, to renounce

despojos *nmpl* **1** : remains, scraps **2** : plunder, spoils

desportillar *vt* : to chip — **desportillarse** *vr*

desposar *vt* : to marry — **desposarse** *vr*

desposeer {20} *vt* : to dispossess

déspota *nmf* : despot, tyrant

despotismo *nm* : despotism — **despótico, -ca** *adj*

despotricar {72} *vi* : to rant and rave, to complain excessively

despreciable *adj* **1** : despicable, contemptible **2** : negligible ⟨nada despreciable : not inconsiderable, significant⟩

despreciar *vt* DESDEÑAR, MENOSPRECIAR : to despise, to scorn, to disdain

despreciativo, -va *adj* : scornful, disdainful

desprecio *nm* DESDÉN, MENOSPRECIO : disdain, contempt, scorn

desprender *vt* **1** SOLTAR : to detach, to loosen, to unfasten **2** EMITIR : to emit, to give off — **desprenderse** *vr* **1** : to come off, to come undone **2** : to be inferred, to follow **3** ~ **de** : to part with, to get rid of

desprendido, -da *adj* : generous, unselfish, disinterested

desprendimiento *nm* **1** : detachment **2** GENEROSIDAD : generosity **3** desprendimiento de tierras : landslide

despreocupación *nf, pl* **-ciones** : indifference, lack of concern

despreocupadamente *adv* : in a carefree, easygoing, or unconcerned way

despreocupado, -da *adj* : carefree, easygoing, unconcerned

desprestigiar *vt* DESACREDITAR : to discredit, to disgrace — **desprestigiarse** *vr* : to lose prestige

desprestigio *nm* DESCRÉDITO : discredit, disrepute

desprevenido, -da *adj* DESAPERCIBIDO : unprepared, off guard, unsuspecting

desprolijo, -ja *adj* : untidy, messy

desproporción *nf, pl* **-ciones** : disproportion, disparity

desproporcionado, -da : out of proportion

despropósito *nm* : piece of nonsense, absurdity

desprotegido, -da *adj* : unprotected, vulnerable

desprovisto, -ta *adj* ~ **de** : devoid of, lacking in

después *adv* **1** : afterward, later ⟨mucho después : much later⟩ ⟨me lo dijo después : she told me about it afterward⟩ **2** : then, next ⟨primero uno y después el otro : first one and then the other⟩ ⟨¿que hago después? : what do I do next?⟩ **3** ~ **de** : after, next after ⟨después de comer : after eating⟩ ⟨después del semáforo : after the stoplight⟩ **4 después (de) que** : after ⟨después que lo acabé : after I finished it⟩ **5 después de todo** : after all **6 poco después** : shortly after, soon thereafter

despuntado, -da *adj* : blunt, dull

despuntar *vt* : to blunt *vi* **1** : to dawn **2** : to sprout **3** : to excel, to stand out

desquiciado, -da *adj* : crazy

desquiciar *vt* **1** : to unhinge (a door) **2** : to drive crazy — **desquiciarse** *vr* : to go crazy

desquitarse *vr* **1** : to get even, to retaliate **2** ~ **con** : to take it out on

desquite *nm* : revenge

desregulación *nf, pl* **-ciones** : deregulation

desregular *vt* : to deregulate

desregularización *nf, pl* **-ciones** → **desregulación**

destacadamente *adv* : outstandingly, prominently

destacado, -da *adj* **1** : outstanding, prominent **2** : stationed, posted

destacamento *nm* : detachment (of troops)

destacar {72} *vt* **1** ENFATIZAR, SUBRAYAR : to emphasize, to highlight, to stress ⟨cabe destacar . . . : it's worth mentioning . . .⟩ **2** REALZAR : to highlight, to bring out **3** : to station, to post — *vi* : to stand out — **destacarse** *vr* : to stand out

destajo *nm* **1** : piecework **2 a** ~ : by the item, by the job

destapacaños *nm Mex* : plunger (for toilets, etc.)

destapador *nm* : bottle opener

destapar *vt* **1** : to open, to take the top off **2** DESCUBRIR : to reveal, to uncover **3** : to unblock, to unclog

destape *nm* : uncovering, revealing

destartalado, -da *adj* : dilapidated, tumbledown

destellar *vi* **1** : to sparkle, to flash, to glint **2** : to twinkle

destello *nm* **1** : flash, sparkle, twinkle **2** : glimmer, hint

destemplado, -da *adj* **1** : out of tune **2** : irritable, out of sorts **3** : unpleasant (of weather)

desteñir {67} *vi* **1** : to run, to fade — **desteñirse** *vr* : to fade

desterrado¹, -da *adj* : banished, exiled

desterrado², -da *n* : exile

desterrar {55} *vt* **1** EXILIAR : to banish, to exile **2** ERRADICAR : to eradicate, to do away with

destetar *vt* : to wean

destiempo *adv* **a** ~ : at the wrong time

destierro *nm* EXILIO : exile

destilación *nf, pl* **-ciones** : distillation

destilador, -dora *n* : distiller

destilar *vt* **1** : to exude **2** : to distill

destilería *nf* : distillery

destinación *nf, pl* **-ciones** DESTINO : destination

destinado, -da *adj* : destined, bound

destinar *vt* **1** : to appoint, to assign **2** ASIGNAR : to earmark, to allot

destinatario, -ria *n* **1** : addressee **2** : payee

destino *nm* **1** : destiny, fate **2** DESTINACIÓN : destination **3** : use **4** : assignment, post

destitución *nf, pl* **-ciones** : dismissal, removal from office

destituir {41} *vt* : to dismiss, to remove from office

destornillador *nm* : screwdriver

destornillar *vt* : to unscrew

destrabar *vt* **1** : to untie, to undo, to ease up **2** : to separate

destreza *nf* HABILIDAD : dexterity, skill

destronar *vt* : to depose, to dethrone

destrozado, -da *adj* **1** : ruined, destroyed **2** : devastated, brokenhearted

destrozar {21} *vt* **1** : to smash, to shatter **2** : to destroy, to wreck — **destrozarse** *vr*

destrozo *nm* **1** DAÑO : damage **2** : havoc, destruction

destrucción *nf, pl* **-ciones** : destruction

destructivo, -va *adj* : destructive

destructor[1], **-tora** *adj* : destructive

destructor[2] *nm* : destroyer (ship)

destruir {41} *vt* : to destroy — **destruirse** *vr*

desubicado, -da *adj* **1** : out of place **2** : confused, disoriented

desunión *nf, pl* **-niones** : lack of unity

desunir *vt* : to split, to divide

desusado, -da *adj* **1** INSÓLITO : unusual **2** OBSOLETO : obsolete, disused, antiquated

desuso *nm* : disuse, obsolescence ⟨caer en desuso : to fall into disuse⟩

desvaído, -da *adj* **1** : pale, washed-out **2** : vague, blurred

desvalido, -da *adj* DESAMPARADO : destitute, helpless

desvalijar *vt* **1** : to ransack **2** : to rob

desvalorización *nf, pl* **-ciones** 1 DEVALUACIÓN : devaluation **2** : depreciation

desvalorizar {21} *vt* : to devalue

desván *nm, pl* **desvanes** ÁTICO, BUHARDILLA : attic

desvanecer {53} *vt* **1** DISIPAR : to make disappear, to dispel **2** : to fade, to blur — **desvanecerse** *vr* **1** : to vanish, to disappear **2** : to fade **3** DESMAYARSE : to faint, to swoon

desvanecimiento *nm* **1** : disappearance **2** DESMAYO : faint **3** : fading

desvariar {85} *vi* **1** DELIRAR : to be delirious **2** : to rave, to talk nonsense

desvarío *nm* **1** DELIRIO : delirium **2** **desvaríos** *nmpl* : ravings *pl*

desvelado, -da *adj* : sleepless

desvelar *vt* **1** : to keep awake **2** REVELAR : to reveal, to disclose — **desvelarse** *vr* **1** : to stay awake **2** : to do one's utmost

desvelo *nm* **1** : insomnia **2** **desvelos** *nmpl* : efforts, pains

desvencijado, -da *adj* : dilapidated, rickety

desventaja *nf* : disadvantage, drawback

desventajoso, -sa *adj* : disadvantageous, unfavorable

desventura *nf* INFORTUNIO : misfortune

desventurado, -da *adj* : unfortunate, ill-fated

desvergonzado, -da *adj* : shameless, impudent

desvergüenza *nf* : audacity, impudence

desvestir {54} *vt* : to undress — **desvestirse** *vr* : to get undressed

desviación *nf, pl* **-ciones** **1** : deviation, departure **2** : detour, diversion

desviar {85} *vt* **1** : to change the course of, to divert **2** : to turn away, to deflect — **desviarse** *vr* **1** : to branch off **2** APARTARSE : to stray

desvinculación *nf, pl* **-ciones** : dissociation

desvincular *vt* **~ de** : to separate from, to dissociate from — **desvincularse** *vr*

desvío *nm* **1** : diversion, detour **2** : deviation

desvirtuar {3} *vt* **1** : to impair, to spoil **2** : to detract from **3** : to distort, to misrepresent

desvivirse *vr* : to be devoted to

detalladamente *adv* : in detail, at great length

detallar *vt* : to detail

detalle *nm* **1** : detail ⟨entrar en detalles : to go into detail⟩ **2 al detalle** : retail **3** : thoughtful gesture ⟨tener un detalle con alguien : to do something nice for someone⟩

detallista[1] *adj* **1** : meticulous **2** : retail

detallista[2] *nmf* **1** : perfectionist **2** : retailer

detección *nf, pl* **-ciones** : detection

detectar *vt* : to detect — **detectable** *adj*

detective *nmf* : detective ⟨detective privado/privada : private detective⟩

detector *nm* : detector ⟨detector de mentiras : lie detector⟩

detención *nf, pl* **-ciones** **1** ARRESTO : detention, arrest **2** : stop, halt **3** : delay, holdup

detener {80} *vt* **1** ARRESTAR : to arrest, to detain **2** PARAR : to stop, to halt **3** : to keep, to hold back — **detenerse** *vr* **1** : to stop **2** : to delay, to linger

detenidamente *adv* : thoroughly, at length

detenimiento *nm* **con ~** : carefully, in detail

detentar *vt* : to hold, to retain

detergente *nm* : detergent

deteriorado, -da *adj* : damaged, worn

deteriorar *vt* ESTROPEAR : to damage, to spoil — **deteriorarse** *vr* **1** : to get damaged, to wear out **2** : to deteriorate, to worsen

deterioro *nm* **1** : deterioration, wear **2** : worsening, decline

determinación *nf, pl* **-ciones** **1** : determination, resolve **2 tomar una determinación** : to make a decision

determinado, -da *adj* **1** : certain, particular **2** : determined, resolute

determinante[1] *adj* : determining, deciding

determinante[2] *nm* : determinant

determinar *vt* **1** : to determine **2** : to cause, to bring about — **determinarse** *vr* : to make up one's mind, to decide

detestar *vt* : to detest — **detestable** *adj*

detonación *nf, pl* **-ciones** : detonation

detonador *nm* : detonator

detonante[1] *adj* : detonating, explosive

detonante[2] *nm* **1** → **detonador 2** : catalyst, cause

detonar *vi* : to detonate, to explode

detractor, -tora *n* : detractor, critic

detrás *adv* **1** : behind ⟨caminábamos detrás : we walked along behind⟩ **2 ~ de** : in back of, behind **3 por ~** : from behind, in/at the back

detrimento *nm* : detriment ⟨en detrimento de : to the detriment of⟩

detuvo, etc. → **detener**

deuda *nf* **1** DÉBITO : debt **2 en deuda con** : indebted to

deudo, -da *n* : relative

deudor¹, -dora *adj* : indebted

deudor², -dora *n* : debtor

devaluación *nf, pl* **-ciones** DESVALORIZACIÓN : devaluation

devaluar {3} *vt* : to devalue — **devaluarse** *vr* : to depreciate

devanarse *vr* **devanarse los sesos** : to rack one's brains

devaneo *nm* **1** : flirtation, fling **2** : idle pursuit

devastador, -dora *adj* : devastating

devastar *vt* : to devastate — **devastación** *nf*

develar *vt* **1** REVELAR : to reveal, to uncover **2** : to unveil

devenir {87} *vi* **1** : to come about **2** ~ **en** : to become, to turn into

devoción *nf, pl* **-ciones** : devotion

devolución *nf, pl* **-ciones** REEMBOLSO : return, refund

devolver {89} *vt* **1** : to return, to give back **2** REEMBOLSAR : to refund, to pay back **3** : to vomit, to bring up — *vi* : to vomit, to throw up — **devolverse** *vr* : to return, to come back, to go back

devorar *vt* **1** : to devour **2** : to consume

devoto¹, -ta *adj* : devout — **devotamente** *adv*

devoto², -ta *n* : devotee, admirer

di → **dar, decir**

día *nm* **1** : day ⟨buenos días : hello, good morning⟩ ⟨todos los días : every day⟩ ⟨todo el día : all day⟩ ⟨un día sí y otro no : every other day⟩ ⟨ocho horas al día : eight hours a day⟩ ⟨día hábil : workday, business day⟩ ⟨día festivo/feriado : public holiday⟩ ⟨día de pago : payday⟩ ⟨¿qué día es hoy? : what day is today?⟩ ⟨el día 21 de abril : the 21st of April, April 21st⟩ ⟨el día anterior : the previous day, the day before⟩ **2** : daytime, daylight ⟨de día : by day, in the daytime⟩ ⟨en pleno día : in broad daylight⟩ ⟨día y noche : day and night⟩ **3 al día** : up-to-date ⟨ponerse al día con : to get up to date with, to catch up on⟩ ⟨poner al día : to bring up to date, to update⟩ **4 en su día** : in due time **5 hoy (en) día** : nowadays, these days

diabetes *nf* : diabetes

diabético, -ca *adj & n* : diabetic

diablillo *nm* : little devil, imp

diablo *nm* **1** DEMONIO : devil **2 ¿qué diablos . . . ?** : what on earth . . . ?, what the hell . . . ?

diablura *nf* **1** : prank **2 diabluras** *nfpl* : mischief

diabólico, -ca *adj* : diabolical, diabolic, devilish

diaconisa *nf* : deaconess

diácono *nm* : deacon

diacrítico, -ca *adj* : diacritic, diacritical

diadema *nf* : diadem, crown

diáfano, -na *adj* **1** CLARO : clear **2** TRASLÚCIDO : sheer (of fabric), translucent **3** : bright (of a light, room, etc.)

diafragma *nm* : diaphragm

diagnosticar {72} *vt* : to diagnose

diagnóstico¹, -ca *adj* : diagnostic

diagnóstico² *nm* : diagnosis

diagonal¹ *adj* : diagonal — **diagonalmente** *adv*

diagonal² *nf* **1** : diagonal **2** : slash (punctuation mark)

diagrama *nm* **1** : diagram **2 diagrama de flujo** ORGANIGRAMA : flow chart

dial *nm* : dial (on a radio, etc.)

dialecto *nm* : dialect

dialogar {52} *vi* : to have a talk, to converse

diálogo *nm* : dialogue

diamante *nm* : diamond

diámetro *nm* : diameter

diana *nf* **1** : target, bull's-eye **2 or toque de diana** : reveille

diapasón *nm, pl* **-sones** : tuning fork

diapositiva *nf* : slide, transparency

diariamente *adv* : daily, every day

diario¹ *adv Mex* : every day, daily

diario², -ria *adj* **1** : daily, everyday ⟨la vida diaria : everyday life⟩ ⟨ocho horas diarias : eight hours a day⟩ **2 a diario** : every day, daily

diario³ *nm* **1** : diary **2** PERIÓDICO : newspaper **3 de** ~ : everyday

diarrea *nf* : diarrhea

diatriba *nf* : diatribe, tirade

dibujante *nmf* **1** : draftsman *m*, draftswoman *f* **2** CARICATURISTA : cartoonist

dibujar *vt* **1** : to draw, to sketch **2** : to portray, to depict

dibujo *nm* **1** : drawing ⟨dibujo lineal : line drawing⟩ ⟨dibujo a lápiz : pencil drawing⟩ ⟨dibujo a pulso, dibujo a mano alzada : freehand sketch⟩ **2** : design, pattern **3 dibujos animados** : (animated) cartoons

dicción *nf, pl* **-ciones** : diction

diccionario *nm* : dictionary

dícese → **decir**

dicha *nf* **1** SUERTE : good luck **2** FELICIDAD : happiness, joy

dicho¹ *pp* → **decir**

dicho², -cha *adj* : said, aforementioned

dicho³ *nm* DECIR : saying, proverb

dichoso, -sa *adj* **1** : blessed **2** FELIZ : happy **3** AFORTUNADO : fortunate, lucky

diciembre *nm* : December ⟨el primero de diciembre : (on) December first⟩

diciendo → **decir**

dictado *nm* : dictation

dictador, -dora *n* : dictator

dictadura *nf* : dictatorship

dictamen *nm, pl* **dictámenes** **1** : report **2** : judgment, opinion

dictaminar *vt* : to report *vi* : to give an opinion, to pass judgment

dictar *vt* **1** : to dictate **2** : to pronounce (a judgment) **3** : to give, to deliver (a lecture, etc.)

dictatorial *adj* : dictatorial

didáctico, -ca *adj* : didactic

diecinueve *adj & nm* : nineteen — **diecinueve** *pron*

diecinueveavo¹, -va *adj* : nineteenth

diecinueveavo² *nm* : nineteenth (fraction)

dieciocho *adj & nm* : eighteen — **dieciocho** *pron*

dieciochavo¹, -va *or* **dieciochavo, -va** *adj* : eighteenth

dieciochavo² *or* **dieciochavo** *nm* : eighteenth (fraction)

dieciséis *adj & nm* : sixteen — **dieciséis** *pron*

dieciseisavo¹, -va *adj* : sixteenth

dieciseisavo² *nm* : sixteenth (fraction)

diecisiete *adj & nm* : seventeen — **diecisiete** *pron*

diecisieteavo¹, -va *adj* : seventeenth

diecisieteavo² *nm* : seventeenth (in a series)

diente *nm* **1** : tooth ⟨diente canino : eyetooth, canine tooth⟩ ⟨cepillarse los dientes : to brush one's teeth⟩ ⟨le están saliendo los dientes : he's teething⟩ **2** : tusk, fang **3** : prong, tine **4** : clove (of garlic) **5 diente de león** : dandelion **6 entre dientes** : under one's breath, quietly ⟨hablar entre dientes : to mutter, to mumble⟩

dieron, etc. → **dar**

diesel [ˈdisɛl] *nm* : diesel

diestra *nf* : right hand

diestro¹, -tra *adj* **1** : right **2** : skillful, accomplished

diestro² *nm* : bullfighter, matador

dieta *nf* : diet

dietético, -ca *adj* : dietary, diet

dietista *nmf* : dietitian

diez¹ *nm, pl* **dieces** : ten ⟨el diez de julio : (on) the tenth of July, (on) July tenth⟩ ⟨un as y dos dieces : an ace and two tens⟩

diez² *adj* : ten ⟨tiene diez años : he's ten (years old)⟩

diez³ *pron* : ten ⟨somos diez : there are ten of us⟩ ⟨son las diez : it's ten o'clock⟩

difamación *nf, pl* **-ciones** : defamation, slander

difamar *vt* : to defame, to slander

difamatorio, -ria *adj* : slanderous, defamatory, libelous

diferencia *nf* **1** : difference ⟨partir la diferencia : to split the difference⟩ **2 a diferencia de** : unlike, in contrast to **3 con ~** : by far

diferenciación *nf, pl* **-ciones** : differentiation

diferencial *adj & nm* : differential

diferenciar *vt* : to differentiate between, to distinguish — **diferenciarse** *vr* : to differ

diferendo *nm* : dispute, conflict

diferente *adj* DISTINTO : different ⟨diferente a/de : different from⟩ — **diferentemente** *adv*

diferido *adj* **en ~** ⟨un programa en diferido : a prerecorded program⟩ ⟨transmitir en diferido : to broadcast later⟩

diferir {76} *vt* DILATAR, POSPONER : to postpone, to put off *vi* : to differ

difícil *adj* : difficult, hard ⟨difícil de describir : hard to describe⟩ ⟨una persona difícil : a difficult person⟩ ⟨lo veo difícil : I think it's unlikely⟩

difícilmente *adv* **1** : with difficulty **2** : hardly

dificultad *nf* : difficulty

dificultar *vt* : to make difficult, to obstruct

dificultoso, -sa *adj* : difficult, hard

difteria *nf* : diphtheria

difuminar *vt* : to blur

difundir *vt* **1** : to diffuse, to spread out **2** : to broadcast, to spread

difunto, -ta *adj & n* FALLECIDO : deceased

difusión *nf, pl* **-siones** **1** : spreading **2** : diffusion (of heat, etc.) **3** : broadcast, broadcasting ⟨los medios de difusión : the media⟩

difuso, -sa *adj* : diffuse, widespread

diga, etc. → **decir**

digerir {76} *vt* : to digest — **digerible** *adj*

digestión *nf, pl* **-tiones** : digestion

digestivo, -va *adj* : digestive

digital¹ *adj* : digital — **digitalmente** *adv*

digital² *nf* DEDALERA : foxglove

digitalizar {21} *vt* : to digitalize

digitaria *nf* : crabgrass

dígito *nm* : digit

dignarse *vr* : to deign, to condescend ⟨no se dignó contestar : he didn't deign to answer⟩

dignatario, -ria *n* : dignitary

dignidad *nf* **1** : dignity **2** : dignitary

dignificar {72} *vt* : to dignify

digno, -na *adj* **1** HONORABLE : honorable **2** : worthy ⟨digno de : worthy of⟩ **3** : decent (of a salary, etc.) — **dignamente** *adv*

digresión *nf, pl* **-siones** : digression

dije *nm* : charm (on a bracelet)

dijo, etc. → **decir**

dilación *nf, pl* **-ciones** : delay

dilapidar *vt* : to waste, to squander

dilatar *vt* **1** : to dilate, to widen, to expand **2** DIFERIR, POSPONER : to put off, to postpone — **dilatarse** *vr* **1** : to expand (of gases, metals, etc.) **2** *Mex* : to take long, to be long

dilatorio, -ria *adj* : delaying

dilema *nm* : dilemma

diletante *nmf* : dilettante

diligencia *nf* **1** : diligence, care **2** : promptness, speed **3** : action, step **4** : task, errand **5** : stagecoach **6 diligencias** *nfpl* : judicial procedures, formalities

diligente *adj* : diligent — **diligentemente** *adv*

dilucidar *vt* : to elucidate, to clarify

dilución *nf, pl* **-ciones** : dilution

diluir {41} *vt* : to dilute

diluviar *v impers* : to pour (with rain), to pour down

diluvio *nm* **1** : flood **2** : downpour

dimensión *nf, pl* **-siones** : dimension — **dimensional** *adj*

dimensionar *vt* : to measure, to gauge

diminutivo¹, -va *adj* : diminutive

diminutivo² *nm* : diminutive

diminuto, -ta *adj* : minute, tiny
división *nf, pl* **-siones** : resignation
dimitir *vi* : to resign, to step down
dimos → **dar**
dinámica *nf* : dynamics
dinámico, -ca *adj* : dynamic — **dinámicamente** *adv*
dinamismo *nm* : energy, vigor
dinamita *nf* : dynamite
dinamitar *vt* : to dynamite
dínamo *or* **dinamo** *nm* : dynamo
dinastía *nf* : dynasty
dineral *nm* : fortune, large sum of money
dinero *nm* **1** : money ⟨hacer/ganar/recaudar dinero : to make/earn/raise money⟩ **2 dinero de bolsillo** : pocket money **3 dinero contante y sonante** : cold cash, hard cash **4 dinero en efectivo** : cash
dinosaurio *nm* : dinosaur
dintel *nm* : lintel
dio, etc. → **dar**
diócesis *nfs & pl* : diocese
dios, diosa *n* : god, goddess *f*
Dios *nm* : God ⟨gracias a Dios : thank God⟩ ⟨si Dios quiere : God willing⟩ ⟨por Dios! : for God's sake!⟩ ⟨¡Dios mío! : good God!⟩ ⟨¡vaya por Dios! : for heaven's sake!⟩ ⟨¡Dios me libre! : God/heaven forbid!⟩ ⟨que Dios te bendiga : God bless you⟩ ⟨como Dios manda : proper, properly⟩
dióxido de carbono *nm* : carbon dioxide
diploma *nm* : diploma
diplomacia *nf* : diplomacy
diplomado¹, -da *adj* : qualified, trained
diplomado² *nm Mex* : seminar
diplomático¹, -ca *adj* : diplomatic — **diplomáticamente** *adv*
diplomático², -ca *n* : diplomat
diptongo *nm* : diphthong
diputación *nf, pl* **-ciones** : deputation, delegation
diputado, -da *n* : delegate, representative
dique *nm* : dike
dirá, etc. → **decir**
dirección *nf, pl* **-ciones 1** : address ⟨dirección particular/electrónica : home/e-mail address⟩ **2** : direction ⟨en dirección a : towards⟩ ⟨en dirección contraria : the opposite direction, the other way⟩ **3** : management, leadership **4** : steering (of an automobile) ⟨dirección asistida : power steering⟩
direccional¹ *adj* : directional
direccional² *nf* : directional, turn signal
directa *nf* : high gear
directamente *adv* : straight, directly
directiva *nf* **1** ORDEN : directive **2** DIRECTORIO, JUNTA : board of directors
directivo¹, -va *adj* : executive, managerial
directivo², -va *n* : executive, director
directo, -ta *adj* **1** : direct, straight, immediate **2 en ∼** : live (in broadcasting)
director, -tora *n* **1** : director, manager, head **2** : conductor (of an orchestra)
directorial → **directivo¹**
directorio *nm* **1** : directory **2** DIRECTIVA, JUNTA : board of directors
directriz *nf, pl* **-trices** : guideline

dirigencia *nf* : leaders *pl,* leadership
dirigente¹ *adj* : directing, leading
dirigente² *nmf* : director, leader
dirigible *nm* : dirigible, blimp
dirigir {35} *vt* **1** : to run, to manage (a business, etc.), to lead (a group, etc.) **2** : to conduct (music), to direct (a film) **3** : to address (a letter, comment, etc.) **4** : to aim, to point ⟨dirigir la mirada a/hacia : to look at/towards⟩ ⟨dirigir la atención hacia : to turn one's attention to⟩ — **dirigirse** *vr* — **a 1** : to go towards **2** : to speak to, to address
dirimir *vt* **1** : to resolve, to settle **2** : to annul, to dissolve (a marriage)
discapacidad *nf* MINUSVALÍA : disability, handicap *sometimes offensive*
discapacitado¹, -da *adj* : disabled, handicapped *sometimes offensive*
discapacitado², -da *n* : disabled person, handicapped person *sometimes offensive*
discar {72} *v* : to dial
discernimiento *nm* : discernment
discernir {25} *v* : to discern, to distinguish
disciplina *nf* : discipline
disciplinar *vt* : to discipline — **disciplinario, -ria** *adj*
discípulo, -la *n* : disciple, follower
disc jockey [ˌdɪskˈʤoke, -ˈʤo-] *nmf* : disc jockey
disco *nm* **1** : record ⟨parecer un disco rayado : to sound like a broken record⟩ **2** : disc, disk ⟨disco compacto : compact disc⟩ ⟨disco volador : Frisbee *trademark*⟩ **3** : discus
discografía *nf* : list of records (by a musician)
díscolo, -la *adj* : unruly, disobedient
disconforme *adj* : in disagreement
discontinuidad *nf* : discontinuity
discontinuo, -nua *adj* : discontinuous
discordancia *nf* DESAVENENCIA : conflict, disagreement
discordante *adj* **1** : discordant **2** : conflicting
discordia *nf* : discord
discoteca *nf* **1** : disco, discotheque **2** *CA, Mex* : record store
discreción *nf, pl* **-ciones** : discretion
discrecional *adj* : discretionary
discrepancia *nf* : discrepancy
discrepar *vi* **1** : to disagree **2** : to differ
discreto, -ta *adj* : discreet — **discretamente** *adv*
discriminación *nf, pl* **-ciones** : discrimination
discriminar *vt* **1** : to discriminate against **2** : to distinguish, to differentiate
discriminatorio, -ria *adj* : discriminatory
disculpa *nf* **1** : apology **2** : excuse
disculpable *adj* : excusable
disculpar *vt* **1** : to excuse, to pardon — **disculparse** *vr* : to apologize
discurrir *vi* **1** : to flow **2** : to pass, to go by **3** : to ponder, to reflect
discurso *nm* **1** ORACIÓN : speech, address **2** : discourse, treatise
discusión *nf, pl* **-siones 1** : discussion **2** ALTERCADO, DISPUTA : argument

discutible *adj* : arguable, debatable
discutidor, -dora *adj* : argumentative
discutir *vt* **1** : to discuss **2** : to dispute — *vi* ALTERCAR : to argue, to quarrel
disecar {72} *vt* **1** : to dissect **2** : to stuff (for preservation)
disección *nf, pl* **-ciones** : dissection
diseminación *nf, pl* **-ciones** : dissemination, spreading
diseminar *vt* : to disseminate, to spread
disensión *nf, pl* **-siones** : dissension, disagreement
disenso *nm* : dissent, disagreement
disentería *nf* : dysentery
disentimiento → **disenso**
disentir {76} *vi* : to dissent, to disagree
diseñador, -dora *n* : designer
diseñar *vt* **1** : to design, to plan **2** : to lay out, to outline
diseño *nm* : design
disertación *nf, pl* **-ciones** **1** : lecture, talk **2** : dissertation
disertar *vi* : to lecture, to give a talk
disfraz *nm, pl* **disfraces** **1** : disguise **2** : costume **3** : front, pretense
disfrazar {21} *vt* **1** : to disguise **2** : to mask, to conceal — **disfrazarse** *vr* : to wear a costume, to be in disguise
disfrutar *vt* : to enjoy *vi* : to enjoy oneself, to have a good time
disfrute *nm* : enjoyment
disfunción *nf, pl* **-ciones** : dysfunction — **disfuncional** *adj*
disgregar {52} *vt* : to break up, to disintegrate — **disgregarse** *vr*
disgustar *vt* : to upset, to displease, to make angry ⟨darle un disgusto a alguien : to upset someone⟩ ⟨llevarse un disgusto : to be upset⟩ — **disgustarse** *vr*
disgusto *nm* **1** : annoyance, displeasure **2** : argument, quarrel **3** : trouble, misfortune
disidencia *nf* : dissent
disidente *adj & nmf* : dissident
disímbolo, -la *adj Mex* : dissimilar
disímil *adj* : dissimilar
disimuladamente *adv* : furtively, slyly
disimulado, -da *adj* **1** : concealed, disguised **2** : furtive, sly
disimular *vi* : to dissemble, to pretend *vt* : to conceal, to hide
disimulo *nm* **1** : dissembling, pretense **2** : slyness, furtiveness **3** : tolerance
disipar *vt* **1** : to dissipate, to dispel **2** : to squander — **disiparse** *vr*
diskette [di'sket] *nm* : floppy disk, diskette
dislexia *nf* : dyslexia — **disléxico, -ca** *adj*
dislocar {72} *vt* : to dislocate — **dislocación** *nf*
disminución *nf, pl* **-ciones** : decrease, drop, fall
disminuir {41} *vt* REDUCIR : to reduce, to decrease, to lower *vi* **1** : to lower **2** : to drop, to fall
disociar *vt* : to dissociate, to separate — **disociación** *nf*
disolución *nf, pl* **-ciones** **1** : dissolution, dissolving **2** : breaking up **3** : dissipation

disoluto, -ta *adj* : dissolute, dissipated
disolvente *nm* : solvent
disolver {89} *vt* **1** : to dissolve **2** : to break up — **disolverse** *vr*
disonancia *nf* : dissonance — **disonante** *adj*
dispar *adj* **1** : different, disparate **2** DIVERSO : diverse **3** DESIGUAL : inconsistent
disparado, -da *adj* salir disparado *fam* : to take off in a hurry, to rush away
disparar *vi* **1** : to shoot, to fire **2** *Mex fam* : to pay — *vt* **1** : to shoot **2** *Mex fam* : to treat to, to buy — **dispararse** *vr* : to shoot up, to skyrocket
disparatado, -da *adj* ABSURDO, RIDÍCULO : absurd, ridiculous, crazy
disparate *nm* : silliness, stupidity ⟨decir disparates : to talk nonsense⟩
disparejo, -ja *adj* DESIGUAL : uneven
disparidad *nf* : disparity
disparo *nm* TIRO : shot
dispendio *nm* : wastefulness, extravagance
dispendioso, -sa *adj* : wasteful, extravagant
dispensa *nf* : dispensation
dispensador *nm* : dispenser
dispensar *vt* **1** : to dispense, to give, to grant **2** EXCUSAR : to excuse, to forgive **3** EXIMIR : to exempt
dispensario *nm* **1** : dispensary, clinic **2** *Mex* : dispenser
dispersar *vt* DESPERDIGAR : to disperse, to scatter
dispersión *nf, pl* **-siones** : dispersion
disperso, -sa *adj* : dispersed, scattered
displicencia *nf* : indifference, coldness, disdain
displicente *adj* : indifferent, cold, disdainful
disponer {60} *vt* **1** : to arrange, to lay out **2** : to stipulate, to order **3** : to prepare — *vi* **~ de** : to have at one's disposal — **disponerse** *vr* **~ a** : to prepare to, to be about to
disponibilidad *nf* : availability
disponible *adj* : available
disposición *nf, pl* **-ciones** **1** : disposition **2** : aptitude, talent **3** : order, arrangement **4** : willingness, readiness **5** última disposición : last will and testament
dispositivo *nm* **1** APARATO, MECANISMO : device, mechanism **2** : force, detachment
dispositivo intrauterino *nm* : intrauterine device, IUD
dispuesto¹ *pp* → **disponer**
dispuesto², -ta *adj* PREPARADO : ready, prepared, disposed
dispuso, etc. → **disponer**
disputa *nf* ALTERCADO, DISCUSIÓN : dispute, argument
disputar *vi* : to argue, to contend, to vie — *vt* : to dispute, to question — **disputarse** *vr* : to compete for
disquera *nf* : record label, recording company
disquete → **diskette**

disquisición *nf, pl* **-ciones 1** : formal discourse **2 disquisiciones** *nfpl* : digressions

distancia *nf* **1** : distance ⟨la distancia entre la Tierra y el Sol : the distance between the Earth and the Sun⟩ ⟨está a dos cuadras de distancia : it's two blocks away⟩ **2** : (emotional) distance ⟨guardar/mantener las distancias : to keep one's distance⟩ **3 a ~** : from/at a distance ⟨mando a distancia : remote control⟩

distanciamiento *nm* **1** : distancing **2** : rift, estrangement

distanciar *vt* **1** : to space out **2** : to draw apart — **distanciarse** *vr* : to grow apart, to become estranged

distante *adj* **1** : distant, far-off **2** : aloof

distar *vi* **~ de** : to be far from ⟨dista de ser perfecto : he is far from perfect⟩

diste → dar

distender {56} *vt* : to distend, to stretch

distendido, -da *adj* : relaxed

distensión *nf, pl* **-siones** : easing of relations

distinción *nf, pl* **-ciones** : distinction

distinguible *adj* : distinguishable

distinguido, -da *adj* : distinguished, refined

distinguir {26} *vt* **1** : to distinguish **2** : to honor **3** : to characterize — **distinguirse** *vr*

distintivo, -va *adj* : distinctive — **distintivamente** *adv*

distinto, -ta *adj* **1** DIFERENTE : different ⟨distinto de/a : different from/than⟩ **2** CLARO : distinct, clear, evident **3 distintos, -tas** *pl* : various

distorsión *nf, pl* **-siones** : distortion

distorsionar *vt* : to distort

distracción *nf, pl* **-ciones 1** : distraction, amusement **2** : forgetfulness **3** : oversight

distraer {81} *vt* **1** : to distract **2** ENTRETENER : to entertain, to amuse — **distraerse** *vr* **1** : to get distracted **2** : to amuse oneself

distraídamente *adv* : absentmindedly

distraído[1] *pp* → **distraer**

distraído[2]**, -da** *adj* **1** : distracted, preoccupied **2** DESPISTADO : absentminded

distribución *nf, pl* **-ciones** : distribution

distribuidor, -dora *n* : distributor

distribuir {41} *vt* : to distribute

distributivo, -va *adj* : distributive

distrital *adj* : district, of the district

distrito *nm* : district

distrofia *nf* : dystrophy ⟨distrofia muscular : muscular dystrophy⟩

disturbio *nm* : disturbance

disuadir *vt* : to dissuade, to discourage

disuasión *nf, pl* **-siones** : deterrence

disuasivo, -va *adj* : deterrent, discouraging

disuasorio, -ria *adj* : discouraging

disuelto *pp* → **disolver**

disyuntiva *nf* : dilemma

DIU [ˈdiu] *nm* (dispositivo intrauterino) : IUD, intrauterine device

diurno, -na *adj* : day, daytime

diva *nf* → **divo**

divagar {52} *vi* : to digress

diván *nm, pl* **divanes** : divan

divergencia *nf* : divergence, difference

divergente *adj* : divergent, differing

divergir {35} *vi* **1** : to diverge **2** : to differ, to disagree

diversidad *nf* : diversity, variety

diversificación *nf, pl* **-ciones** : diversification

diversificar {72} *vt* : to diversify

diversión *nf, pl* **-siones** ENTRETENIMIENTO : fun, amusement, diversion

diverso, -sa *adj* : diverse, various ⟨opiniones diversas : diverse opinions⟩ ⟨de diverso(s) tipo(s) : of various kinds⟩

divertido, -da *adj* **1** : amusing, funny **2** : entertaining, enjoyable

divertir {76} *vt* ENTRETENER : to amuse, to entertain — **divertirse** *vr* : to have fun, to have a good time

dividendo *nm* : dividend

dividir *vt* **1** : to divide, to split **2** : to distribute, to share out — **dividirse** *vr*

divinidad *nf* : divinity

divino, -na *adj* : divine

divisa *nf* **1** : currency **2** LEMA : motto **3** : emblem, insignia

divisar *vt* : to discern, to make out

divisible *adj* : divisible

división *nf, pl* **-siones** : division

divisivo, -va *adj* : divisive

divisor *nm* : denominator

divisorio, -ria *adj* : dividing

divo, -va *n* **1** : prima donna **2** : celebrity, star

divorciado[1]**, -da** *adj* **1** : divorced **2** : split, divided

divorciado[2]**, -da** *n* : divorcé *m*, divorcée *f*

divorciar *vt* : to divorce — **divorciarse** *vr* : to get a divorce

divorcio *nm* : divorce

divulgación *nf, pl* **-ciones 1** : spreading, dissemination **2** : popularizing

divulgar {52} *vt* **1** : to spread, to circulate **2** REVELAR : to divulge, to reveal **3** : to popularize — **divulgarse** *vr*

dizque *adv* : supposedly, apparently

do *nm* **1** : C ⟨do sostenido/bemol : C sharp/flat⟩ **2** : do (in singing)

dobladillo *nm* : hem

doblado, -da *adj* **1** : folded **2** : dubbed

doblaje *nm* : dubbing

doblar *vt* **1** : to double **2** PLEGAR : to fold, to bend **3** : to turn ⟨doblar la esquina : to turn the corner⟩ **4** : to dub — *vi* **1** : to turn **2** : to toll, to ring — **doblarse** *vr* **1** : to fold up, to double over **2** : to give in, to yield

doble[1] *adj* : double ⟨doble el número de : double the number of⟩ ⟨doble sentido : double meaning⟩ — **doblemente** *adv*

doble[2] *nm* **1** : double **2** : toll (of a bell), knell

doble[3] *nmf* : stand-in, double

doblegar {52} *vt* **1** : to fold, to crease **2** : to force to yield — **doblegarse** *vr* : to yield, to bow

doble uve *nf Spain* → **ve doble**

doble ve → **ve doble**

doblez[1] *nm, pl* **dobleces** : fold, crease
doblez[2] *nmf* : duplicity, deceitfulness
doce *adj & nm* : twelve — **doce** *pron*
doceavo[1], **-va** *adj* : twelfth
doceavo[2] *nm* : twelfth (fraction)
docena *nf* **1** : dozen **2 docena de fraile** : baker's dozen
docencia *nf* : teaching
docente[1] *adj* : educational, teaching
docente[2] *n* : teacher, lecturer
dócil *adj* : docile — **dócilmente** *adv*
docilidad *nf* : meekness
docto, -ta *adj* : learned, erudite
doctor, -tora *n* : doctor ⟨doctor en pedagogía : doctor of education⟩
doctorado *nm* : doctorate
doctorarse *vr* : to earn one's doctorate
doctrina *nf* : doctrine — **doctrinal** *adj*
documentación *nf, pl* **-ciones** : documentation
documental *adj & nm* : documentary
documentar *vt* : to document
documento *nm* : document
dogma *nm* : dogma
dogmático, -ca *adj* : dogmatic
dogmatismo *nm* : dogmatism
doguillo *nm* : pug (dog)
dólar *nm* : dollar
dolencia *nf* : ailment, malaise
doler {47} *vi* **1** : to hurt, to ache ⟨me duele la cabeza : my head hurts⟩ ⟨no duele nada : it doesn't hurt at all⟩ **2** : to grieve — **dolerse** *vr* **1** : to be distressed **2** : to complain
doliente *nmf* : mourner, bereaved
dolor *nm* **1** : pain, ache ⟨dolor de cabeza/muelas/espalda : headache/toothache/backache⟩ **2** PENA, TRISTEZA : grief, sorrow
dolorido, -da *adj* **1** : sore, aching **2** : hurt, upset
doloroso, -sa *adj* **1** : painful **2** : distressing — **dolorosamente** *adv*
doloso, -sa *adj* : fraudulent — **dolosamente** *adv*
domador, -dora *n* : tamer
domar *vt* : to tame, to break in
domesticado, -da *adj* : domesticated, tame
domésticamente *adv* : domestically
domesticar {72} *vt* : to domesticate, to tame
doméstico, -ca *adj* : domestic, household
domiciliado, -da *adj* : residing
domiciliario, -ria *adj* **1** : home **2 arresto domiciliario** : house arrest
domiciliarse *vr* RESIDIR : to reside
domicilio *nm* : home, residence ⟨cambio de domicilio : change of address⟩
dominación *nf, pl* **-ciones** : domination
dominante *adj* **1** : dominant **2** : domineering
dominar *vt* **1** : to dominate **2** : to master, to be proficient at **3** : to overlook, to offer a view of — *vi* **1** : to predominate, to prevail — **dominarse** *vr* : to control oneself
domingo *nm* : Sunday ⟨el domingo : on Sunday⟩ ⟨Domingo de Pascua/Resurrección : Easter Sunday⟩

dominical *adj* : Sunday ⟨periódico dominical : Sunday newspaper⟩
dominicano, -na *adj & n* : Dominican
dominico, -ca *adj & n* : Dominican (in religion)
dominio *nm* **1** : dominion, power ⟨dominio de/sobre sí mismo : self-control⟩ **2** : mastery **3** : domain, field
dominó *nm, pl* **-nós 1** : domino (tile) **2** : dominoes *pl* (game)
domo *nm* : dome
don[1] *nm* **1** : gift, present **2** : talent, gift ⟨don de gente(s)/mando : people/leadership skills⟩ ⟨tener el don de la palabra : to have a way with words⟩
don[2] *nm* **1** : title of courtesy preceding a man's first name **2 don nadie** : nobody, insignificant person
dona *nf Mex* : doughnut, donut
donación *nf, pl* **-ciones** : donation
donador, -dora *n* : donor
donaire *nm* **1** GARBO : grace, poise **2** : witticism
donante *nf* → **donador**
donar *vt* : to donate
donativo *nm* : donation
doncella *nf* : maiden, damsel
donde[1] *conj* : where ⟨el pueblo donde vivo : the town where I live⟩ ⟨el lugar de donde viene : the place that/where he comes from⟩ ⟨regresamos por donde venimos : we went back the way we came⟩
donde[2] *prep* : over by ⟨lo encontré donde la silla : I found it over by the chair⟩
dónde *adv* : where ⟨¿dónde está su casa? : where is your house?⟩ ⟨¿de dónde eres? : where are you from?⟩ ⟨no sé por dónde empezar : I don't know where to begin⟩
dondequiera *adv* **1** : anywhere, no matter where **2 dondequiera que** : wherever, everywhere
donqueo *nm* : slam dunk
doña *nf* : title of courtesy preceding a woman's first name
dopado, -da *adj* : drugged
dopar *vt* : to drug, to dope — **doparse** *vr*
doping *nm* : doping (in sports)
doquier *adv* **por ~** : everywhere, all over
dorado[1], **-da** *adj* : gold, golden
dorado[2], **-da** *nm* : gilt
dorar *vt* **1** : to gild **2** : to brown (food)
dormido, -da *adj* **1** : asleep **2** : numb ⟨tiene el pie dormido : her foot's numb, her foot's gone to sleep⟩
dormilón, -lona *n, mpl* **-lones** : late riser
dormir {27} *vi* : to sleep — *vt* **1** : to put to sleep/bed **2** : to put to sleep (from boredom, etc.) **3** ANESTESIAR : to put to sleep, to anesthetize **4 dormir la siesta** : to have a nap — **dormirse** *vr* : to fall asleep
dormitar *vi* : to snooze, to doze
dormitorio *nm* **1** : bedroom **2** : dormitory
dorsal[1] *adj* : dorsal
dorsal[2] *nm* : number (worn in sports)
dorso *nm* **1** : back ⟨el dorso de la mano : the back of the hand⟩ **2** *or* **estilo dorso** *Mex* : backstroke

dos[1] *adj & nm* : two ⟨ella tiene dos años : she's two (years old)⟩ ⟨el dos de junio : (on) the second of June, (on) June second⟩

dos[2] *pron* : two ⟨somos dos : there are two of us⟩ ⟨ya somos dos : that makes two of us⟩ ⟨son las dos de la tarde : it's two o'clock in the afternoon⟩

doscientos[1], **-tas** *adj & pron* : two hundred

doscientos[2] *nms & pl* : two hundred (in a series)

dosel *nm* : canopy

dosificación *nf, pl* **-ciones** : dosage

dosificar {72} *vt* **1** : to dose **2** : to use sparingly

dosis *nfs & pl* **1** : dose **2** : amount, quantity

dossier *nm* : dossier

dotación *nf, pl* **-ciones** **1** : endowment, funding **2** : staff, personnel

dotado, -da *adj* **1** : gifted **2** ∼ **de** : endowed with, equipped with

dotar *vt* **1** : to provide, to equip **2** : to endow

dote *nf* **1** : dowry **2 dotes** *nfpl* : talent, gift

doy → **dar**

draga *nf* : dredge

dragado *nm* : dredging

dragar {52} *vt* : to dredge

dragón *nm, pl* **dragones** **1** : dragon **2** : snapdragon

drague, etc. → **dragar**

drama *nm* : drama

dramático, -ca *adj* : dramatic — **dramáticamente** *adv*

dramatizar {21} *vt* : to dramatize — **dramatización** *nf*

dramaturgo, -ga *n* : dramatist, playwright

drástico, -ca *adj* : drastic — **drásticamente** *adv*

drenaje *nm* : drainage

drenar *vt* : to drain

drene *nm Mex* : drain

driblar *vi* : to dribble (in basketball)

drible *nm* : dribble (in basketball)

droga *nf* : drug

drogadicción *nf, pl* **-ciones** : drug addiction

drogadicto, -ta *n* : drug addict

drogar {52} *vt* : to drug — **drogarse** *vr* : to take drugs

drogodependiente *nmf* : drug addict

drogue, etc. → **drogar**

droguería *nf* FARMACIA : drugstore

dromedario *nm* : dromedary

dual *adj* : dual

dualidad *nf* : duality

dualismo *nm* : dualism

ducha *nf* : shower ⟨darse una ducha : to take a shower⟩

ducharse *vr* : to take a shower

ducho, -cha *adj* : experienced, skilled, expert

ducto *nm* **1** : duct, shaft **2** : pipeline

duda *nf* **1** : doubt ⟨no cabe duda : there's no doubt about it⟩ ⟨no tengo ninguna duda que . . . : I have no doubt that . . .⟩ ⟨si tienes alguna duda . . . : if you have any questions . . .⟩ ⟨poner algo en duda : to call something into question⟩ ⟨salir de dudas : to set one's mind at ease⟩ ⟨sin sombra de duda : beyond the shadow of a doubt⟩ **2 sin** ∼ : undoubtedly, without a doubt, no doubt

dudar *vt* : to doubt ⟨lo dudo mucho : I doubt that very much⟩ — *vi* — **en** : to hesitate to ⟨no dudes en pedirme ayuda : don't hesitate to ask me for help⟩

dudoso, -sa *adj* **1** : doubtful **2** : dubious, questionable — **dudosamente** *adv*

duela *nf Mex* : floorboard

duele, etc. → **doler**

duelo *nm* **1** : duel **2** LUTO : mourning

duende *nm* **1** : elf, goblin **2** ENCANTO : magic, charm ⟨una bailarina que tiene duende : a dancer with a certain magic⟩

dueño, -ña *n* **1** : owner, proprietor **2** : landlord, landlady *f*

duerme, etc. → **dormir**

dueto *nm* : duet

dulce[1] *adv* : sweetly, softly

dulce[2] *adj* **1** : sweet **2** : mild, gentle, mellow — **dulcemente** *adv*

dulce[3] *nm* : candy, sweet

dulcería *nf* : candy store

dulcificar {72} *vt* : to sweeten

dulzura *nf* **1** : sweetness **2** : gentleness, mellowness

duna *nf* : dune

dúo *nm* : duo, duet

duodécimo[1], **-ma** *adj* : twelfth

duodécimo[2], **-ma** *nm* : twelfth (in a series)

dúplex *nms & pl* : duplex apartment

duplicación *nf, pl* **-ciones** : duplication, copying

duplicado *nm* : duplicate, copy

duplicar {72} *vt* **1** : to double **2** : to duplicate, to copy

duplicidad *nf* : duplicity

duque *nm* : duke

duquesa *nf* : duchess

durabilidad *nf* : durability

durable → **duradero**

duración *nf, pl* **-ciones** : duration, length

duradero, -ra *adj* : durable, lasting

duramente *adv* **1** : harshly, severely **2** : hard

durante *prep* : during ⟨durante todo el día : all day long⟩ ⟨trabajó durante tres horas : he worked for three hours⟩

durar *v* : to last

durazno *nm* **1** : peach **2** : peach tree

dureza *nf* **1** : hardness, toughness **2** : severity, harshness

durmiente[1] *adj* : sleeping

durmiente[2] *nmf* : sleeper

durmió, etc. → **dormir**

duro[1] *adv* : hard ⟨trabajé tan duro : I worked so hard⟩

duro[2], **-ra** *adj* **1** FIRME : hard (of a surface, etc.), tough (of meat) **2** DIFÍCIL : hard, tough **3** : harsh, severe ⟨no seas tan duro con él : don't be so hard on him⟩

DVD *nm* : DVD

E

e¹ *nf* : sixth letter of the Spanish alphabet

e² *conj (used instead of* **y** *before words beginning with* i- *or* hi-*)* : and

ebanista *nmf* : cabinetmaker

ébano *nm* : ebony

e-book ['ibuk] *nm, pl* **e-books** : e-book, electronic book

ebriedad *nf* EMBRIAGUEZ : inebriation, drunkenness

ebrio, -bria *adj* EMBRIAGADO : inebriated, drunk

ebullición *nf, pl* **-ciones** : boiling

eccema → eczema

eccéntrico → excéntrico

echar *vt* **1** LANZAR : to throw, to toss (a coin), to cast (an anchor, a net) ⟨lo echó a la basura : she threw it away⟩ ⟨echar la cabeza hacia atrás : to throw one's head back⟩ **2** : to throw out (of a place), to expel (from school) ⟨me echaron de la casa : they threw me out of the house⟩ **3** DESPEDIR : to fire, to dismiss **4** EMITIR : to emit, to give off **5** BROTAR : to sprout **6** : to put in, to add **7** : to take, to have (a look) **8** : to mail **9** : to pour **10** : to give (a blessing, etc.), to put (a curse) on **11** : to turn (a key), to slide (a bolt) ⟨echarle (la) llave (a la puerta) : to lock the door⟩ **12 echar abajo** : to demolish **13 echar a perder** : to spoil, to ruin **14 echar de menos** : to miss ⟨echan de menos a su madre : they miss their mother⟩ — *vi* **1** : to start off **2 ~ a** : to begin to ⟨se echó a llorar : he began to cry⟩ — **echarse** *vr* **1** : to throw oneself ⟨se echó en sus brazos : she threw herself into his arms⟩ **2** : to lie down **3** : to put on **4 ~ a** : to begin to **5 echarse a perder** : to go bad, to spoil **6 echárselas de** : to pose as

ecléctico, -ca *adj* : eclectic

eclesiástico¹, -ca *adj* : ecclesiastical, ecclesiastic

**eclesiástico² *nm* CLÉRIGO : cleric, clergyman

eclipsar *vt* **1** : to eclipse **2** : to outshine, to surpass

eclipse *nm* : eclipse

eco *nm* **1** : echo **2 hacerse eco de** : to echo, to repeat

eco- *pref* : eco-

ecografía *nf* : ultrasound scanning

ecología *nf* : ecology

ecológico, -ca *adj* : ecological — **ecológicamente** *adv*

ecologismo *nm* : environmentalism

ecologista *nmf* : ecologist, environmentalist

ecólogo, -ga *n* : ecologist

economía *nf* **1** : economy **2** : economics

económicamente *adv* : financially

económico, -ca *adj* : economic, economical

economista *nmf* : economist

economizar {21} *vt* : to save, to economize on — *vi* : to save money, to be frugal

ecosistema *nm* : ecosystem

ecoturismo *nm* : ecotourism — **ecoturístico, -ca** *adj*

ecuación *nf, pl* **-ciones** : equation

ecuador *nm* : equator

ecuánime *adj* **1** : even-tempered **2** : impartial

ecuanimidad *nf* **1** : equanimity **2** : impartiality

ecuatorial *adj* : equatorial

ecuatoriano, -na *adj & n* : Ecuadorian

ecuestre *adj* : equestrian

ecuménico, -ca *adj* : ecumenical

eczema *nm* : eczema

edad *nf* **1** : age ⟨¿qué edad tiene? : how old is she?⟩ ⟨tiene 20 años de edad : she is 20 years old⟩ ⟨ser mayor de edad : to be of age⟩ ⟨ser menor de edad : to be a minor, to be underage⟩ ⟨una persona de edad : an elderly person⟩ ⟨desde temprana edad : from an early age⟩ **2** : age, epoch, era ⟨la edad media : the Middle Ages⟩ ⟨la edad de oro/bronce : the Golden/Bronze Age⟩

edecán *nm, pl* **-canes** : aide, assistant

edema *nm* : edema

Edén *nm, pl* **Edenes** : Eden, paradise

edición *nf, pl* **-ciones** **1** : edition **2** : publication, publishing

edicto *nm* : edict, proclamation

edificación *nf, pl* **-ciones** **1** : edification **2** : construction, building

edificar {72} *vt* **1** : to edify **2** CONSTRUIR : to build, to construct

edificio *nm* : building, edifice

edil, edila *n* : councillor, councilman *m*, councilwoman *f*

editar *vt* **1** : to edit **2** PUBLICAR : to publish

editor¹, -tora *adj* : publishing ⟨casa editora : publishing house⟩

editor², -tora *n* **1** : editor **2** : publisher

editor³ *nm* : editor (software)

editora *nf* : publisher, publishing company

editorial¹ *adj* **1** : publishing **2** : editorial

editorial² *nm* : editorial

editorial³ *nf* : publishing house

edredón *nm, pl* **-dones** COBERTOR, COLCHA : comforter, eiderdown, quilt

educación *nf, pl* **-ciones** **1** ENSEÑANZA : education ⟨educación primaria/secundaria/superior : primary/secondary/higher education⟩ **2** : manners *pl* ⟨es de mala educación : it's bad manners⟩ — **educacional** *adj*

educado, -da *adj* : polite, well-mannered

educador, -dora *n* : educator

educando, -da *n* ALUMNO, PUPILO : pupil, student

educar {72} *vt* **1** : to educate **2** CRIAR : to bring up, to raise **3** : to train — **educarse** *vr* : to be educated

educativo, -va *adj* : educational

efe *nf* : (letter) f

efectista *adj* : dramatic, sensational

efectivamente *adv* : really, actually

efectividad *nf* : effectiveness

efectivo¹, -va *adj* 1 : effective 2 : real, actual 3 : permanent, regular (of employment)

efectivo² *nm* : cash

efecto *nm* 1 : effect ⟨tener efecto : to take effect⟩ ⟨surtir efecto, producir un efecto : to have an effect⟩ ⟨bajo los efectos del alcohol : under the influence of alcohol⟩ 2 **en ~** : actually, in fact 3 **efecto dominó**: domino effect 4 **efecto secundario** : side effect 5 **efectos** *nmpl* : goods, property ⟨efectos personales : personal effects⟩ 6 **efectos** *nmpl* : effects ⟨efectos especiales : special effects⟩ ⟨efectos de sonido : sound effects⟩

efeméride *nf* : major event

efectuar {3} *vt* : to carry out, to bring about

efervescencia *nf* : effervescence — **efervescente** *adj*

eficacia *nf* 1 : effectiveness, efficacy 2 : efficiency

eficaz *adj, pl* **-caces** 1 : effective 2 EFICIENTE : efficient — **eficazmente** *adv*

eficiencia *nf* : efficiency

eficiente *adj* EFICAZ : efficient — **eficientemente** *adv*

eficientizar {21} *vt Mex* : to streamline, to make more efficient

efigie *nf* : effigy

efímera *nf* : mayfly

efímero, -ra *adj* : ephemeral

efluentes *nmpl* : effluent(s), (liquid) waste

efusión *nf, pl* **-siones** 1 : warmth, effusiveness 2 **con ~** : effusively

efusivo, -va *adj* : effusive — **efusivamente** *adv*

egipcio, -cia *adj & n* : Egyptian

eglefino *nm* : haddock

ego *nm* : ego

egocéntrico, -ca *adj* : egocentric, self-centered

egoísmo *nm* : selfishness, egoism

egoísta¹ *adj* : selfish, egoistic

egoísta² *nmf* : egoist, selfish person

egotismo *nm* : egotism, conceit

egotista¹ *adj* : egotistic, egotistical, conceited

egotista² *nmf* : egotist, conceited person

egresado, -da *n* : graduate

egresar *vi* : to graduate

egreso *nm* 1 : graduation 2 **ingresos y egresos** : income and expenditure

eh *interj* 1 : hey! 2 : eh?, huh?

eje *nm* 1 : axle 2 : axis

ejecución *nf, pl* **-ciones** : execution

ejecutante *nmf* : performer

ejecutar *vt* 1 : to execute, to put to death 2 : to carry out, to perform

ejecutivo, -va *adj & n* : executive

ejecutor, -tora *n* : executor

ejem *interj* : ahem!

ejemplar¹ *adj* : exemplary, model

ejemplar² *nm* 1 : copy (of a book, magazine, etc.) 2 : specimen, example

ejemplificar {72} *vt* : to exemplify, to illustrate

ejemplo *nm* 1 : example 2 **por ~** : for example 3 **dar ejemplo** : to set an example

ejercer {86} — *vi* **~ de** : to practice as, to work as *vt* 1 : to practice 2 : exercise (a right) 3 : to exert

ejercicio *nm* 1 : exercise 2 : practice

ejercitar *vt* 1 : to exercise 2 ADIESTRAR : to drill, to train

ejército *nm* : army

ejidal *adj Mex* : cooperative

ejidatario, -ria *n Mex* : member of a cooperative

ejido *nm* 1 : common land 2 *Mex* : cooperative

ejote *nm Mex* : green bean

el¹ *pron* (*referring to masculine nouns*) 1 : the one ⟨me gusta el verde : I like the green one⟩ ⟨el de la camisa roja : the one with the red shirt⟩ ⟨mi papá y el tuyo : my dad and yours⟩ ⟨el partido de ayer y el de hoy : yesterday's game and today's⟩ 2 **el que** : the one that/who, whoever, he who ⟨el que vino ayer : the one who came yesterday⟩ ⟨el que compré : the one (that) I bought⟩ ⟨el que gane : whoever wins⟩ ⟨el que trabaja duro estará contento : he who works hard will be happy⟩

el², la *art, pl* **los, las** : the ⟨los niños están en la casa : the boys/children are in the house⟩ ⟨me duele el pie : my foot hurts⟩ ⟨¿te gusta el té? : do you like tea?⟩ ⟨los gatos son inteligentes : cats are intelligent⟩ ⟨el lago Titicaca : Lake Titicaca⟩ ⟨llamó el señor Núñez : Mr. Núñez called⟩ ⟨viene el lunes : he's coming on Monday⟩ ⟨son las dos : it's two o'clock⟩ ⟨el cinco por ciento : five percent⟩ ⟨un dólar la docena : a dollar a dozen⟩

él *pron* : he, him ⟨él es mi amigo : he's my friend⟩ ⟨un amigo de él : a friend of his⟩ ⟨a él no le interesa : it doesn't interest him⟩ ⟨hablaremos con él : we will speak with him⟩

elaboración *nf, pl* **-ciones** 1 PRODUCCIÓN : production, making 2 : preparation, devising

elaborado, -da *adj* : elaborate

elaborar *vt* 1 : to make, to produce 2 : to devise, to draw up

elasticidad *nf* : elasticity

elástico¹, -ca *adj* FLEXIBLE : flexible 2 : elastic

elástico² *nm* 1 : elastic (material) 2 : rubber band

elastizado, -da *adj* : elastic

ele *nf* : (letter) l

elección *nf, pl* **-ciones** 1 SELECCIÓN : choice, selection 2 : election

electivo, -va *adj* : elective

electo, -ta *adj* : elect ⟨el presidente electo : the president-elect⟩

elector, -tora *n* : voter

electorado *nm* : electorate

electoral *adj* : electoral, election

electricidad *nf* : electricity

electricista *nmf* : electrician

eléctrico, -ca *adj* : electric, electrical

electrificar {72} *vt* : to electrify — **electrificación** *nf*

electrizar {21} *vt* : to electrify, to thrill — **electrizante** *adj*
electrocardiógrafo *nm* : electrocardiograph
electrocardiograma *nm* : electrocardiogram
electrocutar *vt* : to electrocute — **electrocución** *nf*
electrodo *nm* : electrode
electrodoméstico *nm* : electric appliance
electroimán *nm, pl* **-manes** : electromagnet
electrólisis *nfs & pl* : electrolysis
electrolito *nm* : electrolyte
electromagnético, -ca *adj* : electromagnetic
electromagnetismo *nm* → electromagnetism
electrón *nm, pl* **-trones** : electron
electrónica *nf* : electronics
electrónico, -ca *adj* : electronic, electronics — **electrónicamente** *adv*
elefante, -ta *n* : elephant
elegancia *nf* : elegance
elegante *adj* : elegant, smart — **elegantemente** *adv*
elegía *nf* : elegy
elegíaco, -ca *adj* : elegiac
elegible *adj* : eligible — **elegibilidad** *nf*
elegido, -da *adj* **1** : chosen, selected **2** : elected
elegir {28} *vt* **1** ESCOGER, SELECCIONAR : to choose, to select **2** : to elect
elemental *adj* **1** : elementary, basic **2** : fundamental, essential
elemento *nm* : element
elenco *nm* : cast (of actors)
elevación *nf, pl* **-ciones** : elevation, height
elevado, -da *adj* **1** : elevated, lofty **2** : high
elevador *nm* ASCENSOR : elevator
elevar *vt* **1** ALZAR : to raise, to lift **2** AUMENTAR : to raise, to increase **3** : to elevate (in a hierarchy), to promote **4** : to present, to submit — **elevarse** *vr* : to rise
elfo *nm* : elf
eliminación *nf, pl* **-ciones** : elimination, removal
eliminar *vt* **1** : to eliminate, to remove **2** : to do in, to kill
eliminatoria *nf* : qualifying round (in a competition)
eliminatorio, -ria *adj* : qualifying
elipse *nf* : ellipse
elipsis *nf* : ellipsis
elíptico, -ca *adj* : elliptical, elliptic
elite *or* **élite** *nf* : elite
elitista *adj & nmf* : elitist
elixir *or* **elíxir** *nm* : elixir
ella *pron* : she, her ⟨ella es mi amiga : she is my friend⟩ ⟨un amigo de ella : a friend of hers⟩ ⟨a ella no le interesa : it doesn't interest her⟩ ⟨nos fuimos con ella : we left with her⟩
ello *pron* : it ⟨es por ello que me voy : that's why I'm going⟩
ellos, ellas *pron pl* **1** : they, them ⟨ellas son mis hermanas : they're my sisters⟩ ⟨un amigo de ellos : a friend of theirs⟩ ⟨a

ellos no les interesa : it doesn't interest them⟩ ⟨fuimos con ellos : we went with them⟩ **2 de ellos, de ellas** : theirs
elocución *nf, pl* **-ciones** : elocution
elocuencia *nf* : eloquence
elocuente *adj* : eloquent — **elocuentemente** *adv*
elogiar *vt* ENCOMIAR : to praise
elogio *nm* : praise
elote *nm* **1** *Mex* : corn, maize **2** *CA, Mex* : corncob
elucidación *nf, pl* **-ciones** ESCLARECIMIENTO : elucidation
elucidar *vt* ESCLARECER : to elucidate
eludir *vt* EVADIR : to evade, to avoid, to elude
em- → **en-**
email *nm, pl* **emails** : e-mail ⟨enviar algo por email : to e-mail something⟩
emanación *nf, pl* **-ciones** : emanation
emanar *vi* ~ **de** : to emanate from — *vt* : to exude
emancipar *vt* : to emancipate — **emancipación** *nf*
embadurnar *vt* EMBARRAR : to smear, to daub
embajada *nf* : embassy
embajador, -dora *n* : ambassador
embalaje *nm* : packing, packaging
embalar *vt* EMPAQUETAR : to pack
embaldosar *vt* : to tile, to pave with tiles
embalsamar *vt* : to embalm
embalse *nm* : dam, reservoir
embarazada¹ *adj* ENCINTA, PREÑADA : pregnant, expecting
embarazada² *nf* : pregnant woman
embarazar {21} *vt* **1** : to obstruct, to hamper **2** PREÑAR : to make pregnant
embarazo *nm* **1** : pregnancy **2** IMPEDIMENTO : obstacle, obstruction **3** VERGÜENZA : embarrassment
embarazoso, -sa *adj* : embarrassing, awkward
embarcación *nf, pl* **-ciones** : boat, craft
embarcadero *nm* : wharf, pier, jetty
embarcar {72} *vi* : to embark, to board — *vt* : to load
embarco *nm* : embarkation
embargar {52} *vt* **1** : to seize, to impound **2** : to overwhelm
embargo *nm* **1** : seizure **2** : embargo **3 sin** ~ : however, nevertheless
embarque *nm* **1** : embarkation **2** : shipment
embarrancar {72} *vi* **1** : to run aground **2** : to get bogged down
embarrar *vt* **1** : to cover with mud **2** EMBADURNAR : to smear
embate *nm* **1** : onslaught **2** : battering (of waves or wind)
embaucador, -dora *n* : swindler, deceiver
embaucar {72} *vt* : to trick, to swindle
embeber *vt* : to absorb, to soak up — *vi* : to shrink
embelesado, -da *adj* : spellbound
embelesar *vt* : to enchant, to captivate
embellecer {53} *vt* : to embellish, to beautify
embellecimiento *nm* : beautification, embellishment

embestida *nf* **1** : charge (of a bull) **2** ARREMETIDA : attack, onslaught

embestir {54} *vt* : to hit, to run into, to charge at — *vi* ARREMETER : to charge, to attack

emblanquecer {53} *vt* BLANQUEAR : to bleach, to whiten — **emblanquecerse** *vr* : to turn white

emblema *nm* : emblem

emblemático, -ca *adj* : emblematic

embobado, -da *adj* **1** : captivated, spellbound **2** : dazed

embolar *vt Col* : to polish (shoes)

embolia *nf* : embolism

émbolo *nm* : piston

embolsarse *vr* **1** : to pocket (money) **2** : to collect (payment)

embonar *vi Mex* ENCAJAR : to fit

emborracharse *vr* EMBRIAGARSE : to get drunk

emborronar *vt* **1** : to blot, to smudge **2** GARABATEAR : to scribble

emboscada *nf* : ambush

emboscar {72} *vt* : to ambush — **emboscarse** *vr* : to lie in ambush

embotar *vt* **1** : to dull, to blunt **2** : to weaken, to enervate

embotellamiento *nm* ATASCO : traffic jam

embotellar *vt* ENVASAR : to bottle — **embotellado, -da** *adj*

embragar {52} *vi* : to engage the clutch

embrague *nm* : clutch

embriagado, -da *adj* : inebriated, drunk

embriagador, -dora *adj* : intoxicating

embriagar {52} *vt* : to intoxicate, to make drunk — **embriagarse** *vr* EMBORRACHARSE : to get drunk

embriaguez *nf* EBRIEDAD : drunkenness, inebriation

embridar *vt* : to bridle (a horse)

embrión *nm, pl* **embriones** : embryo

embrionario, -ria *adj* : embryonic

embrollo *nm* ENREDO : confusion, mess, tangle

embrujado *adj* **1** : bewitched **2** : haunted (of a house, etc.)

embrujar *vt* HECHIZAR : to bewitch

embrujo *nm* : spell, curse

embrutecer {18} *vt* **1** : to make dull **2** ATONTAR : to stupefy

embudo *nm* : funnel

embuste *nm* **1** MENTIRA : lie, fib *fam* **2** ENGAÑO : trick, hoax

embustero¹, -ra *adj* : lying, deceitful

embustero², -ra *n* : liar, cheat

embutido *nm* **1** : sausage **2** : inlaid work

embutir *vt* **1** : to cram, to stuff, to jam **2** : to inlay

eme *nf* : (letter) m

emergencia *nf* **1** : emergency **2** : emergence

emergente *adj* **1** : emergent **2** : consequent, resultant

emerger {15} *vi* : to emerge, to surface

emigración *nf, pl* **-ciones** **1** : emigration **2** : migration

emigrante *adj & nmf* : emigrant

emigrar *vi* **1** : to emigrate **2** : to migrate

eminencia *nf* : eminence

eminente *adj* : eminent, distinguished

eminentemente *adv* : basically, essentially

emisario¹, -ria *n* : emissary

emisario² *nm* : outlet (of a body of water)

emisión *nf, pl* **-siones** **1** : emission **2** : broadcast **3** : issue ⟨emisión de acciones : stock issue⟩

emisor *nm* TRANSMISOR : television or radio transmitter

emisora *nf* : radio station

emitir *vt* **1** : to emit, to give off **2** : to broadcast **3** : to issue **4** : to cast (a vote)

emoción *nf, pl* **-ciones** : emotion — **emocional** *adj* — **emocionalmente** *adv*

emocionado, -da *adj* **1** : moved, affected by emotion **2** ENTUSIASMADO : excited

emocionante *adj* **1** CONMOVEDOR : moving, touching **2** EXCITANTE : exciting, thrilling

emocionar *vt* **1** CONMOVER : to move, to touch **2** : to excite, to thrill — **emocionarse** *vr*

emoticón *or* **emoticono** *nm, pl* **-cones** *or* **-conos** : emoticon

emotivo, -va *adj* : emotional, moving

empacador, -dora *n* : packer

empacar {72} *vt* **1** EMPAQUETAR : to pack **2** : to bale — *vi* : to pack — **empacarse** *vr* **1** : to balk, to refuse to budge **2** *Col, Mex fam* : to eat ravenously, to devour

empachar *vt* **1** ESTORBAR : to obstruct **2** : to give indigestion to **3** DISFRAZAR : to disguise, to mask — **empacharse** *vr* **1** INDIGESTARSE : to get indigestion **2** AVERGONZARSE : to be embarrassed

empacho *nm* **1** INDIGESTIÓN : indigestion **2** VERGÜENZA : embarrassment **3** **no tener empacho en** : to have no qualms about

empadronarse *vr* : to register to vote

empalagar {52} *vt* **1** : to seem cloying ⟨me empalaga : I find it cloying⟩ **2** FASTIDIAR : to annoy, to bother

empalagoso, -sa *adj* MELOSO : cloying

empalar *vt* : to impale

empalizada *nf* : palisade (fence)

empalmar *vt* **1** : to splice, to link **2** : to combine — *vi* : to meet, to converge

empalme *nm* **1** CONEXIÓN : connection, link **2** : junction

empanada *nf* : pie, turnover

empanadilla *nf* : meat or seafood pie

empanar *vt* : to bread

empantanar *vt* **1** INUNDAR : to swamp, to bog down **2** ESTANCAR : to bog down, to delay — **empantanarse** *vr*

empañar *vt* **1** : to steam up **2** : to tarnish, to sully

empapado, -da *adj* : soggy, sodden

empapar *vt* MOJAR : to soak, to drench — **empaparse** *vr* **1** : to get soaking wet **2** ~ **de** : to absorb, to be imbued with

empapelar *vt* : to wallpaper

empaque *nm fam* **1** : presence, bearing **2** : pomposity **3** DESCARO : impudence, nerve

empaquetar *vt* EMBALAR : to pack, to package — **empaquetarse** *vr fam* : to dress up

emparedado *nm* : sandwich

emparedar *vt* : to wall in, to confine
emparejar *vt* **1** : to pair, to match up **2** : to make even, to even out — *vi* : to catch up — **emparejarse** *vr* **1** : to pair up **2** : to become even, to even out
emparentado, -da *adj* : related
emparentar {55} *vi* : to become related by marriage
emparrillado *nm Mex* : gridiron (in football)
empastar *vt* **1** : to fill (a tooth) **2** : to bind (a book)
empaste *nm* : filling (of a tooth)
empatar *vt* : to tie, to connect — *vi* : to result in a draw, to be tied — **empatarse** *vr Ven* : to hook up, to link together
empate *nm* : draw, tie
empatía *nf* : empathy
empecinado, -da *adj* TERCO : stubborn
empecinarse *vr* OBSTINARSE : to be stubborn, to persist
empedernido, -da *adj* INCORREGIBLE : hardened, inveterate
empedrado *nm* : paving, pavement
empedrar {55} *vt* : to pave (with stones)
empeine *nm* : instep
empellón *nm, pl* **-llones** : shove, push
empelotado, -da *adj* **1** *Mex fam* : madly in love **2** *fam* : stark naked
empeñado, -da *adj* : determined, committed
empeñar *vt* **1** : to pawn **2** : to pledge, to give (one's word) — **empeñarse** *vr* **1** : to insist stubbornly **2** : to make an effort
empeño *nm* **1** : pledge, commitment **2** : insistence **3** ESFUERZO : effort, determination ⟨poner mucho empeño : to put in a lot of effort⟩ ⟨trabajar con empeño : to work hard⟩ **4** : pawning ⟨casa de empeños : pawnshop⟩
empeoramiento *nm* : worsening, deterioration
empeorar *vi* : to deteriorate, to get worse — *vt* : to make worse
empequeñecer {53} *vi* : to diminish, to become smaller — *vt* : to minimize, to make smaller
emperador *nm* : emperor
emperatriz *nf, pl* **-trices** : empress
empero *conj* : however, nevertheless
empezar {29} *v* COMENZAR : to start, to begin ⟨empezar a hacer algo : to start to do something, to start doing something⟩ ⟨empezar por algo/alguien : to start with something/someone⟩ ⟨empezar por hacer algo : to start by doing something⟩ ⟨empezó diciendo que . . . : she started out by saying that . . .⟩ ⟨para empezar : to begin with⟩
empinado, -da *adj* : steep
empinar *vt* ELEVAR : to lift, to raise — **empinarse** *vr* : to stand on tiptoe
empírico, -ca *adj* : empirical — **empíricamente** *adv*
emplasto *nm* : poultice, dressing
emplazamiento *nm* **1** : location, site **2** CITACIÓN : summons, subpoena

emplazar {21} *vt* **1** CONVOCAR : to convene, to summon **2** : to subpoena **3** UBICAR : to place, to position
empleado, -da *n* : employee
empleador, -dora *n* PATRÓN : employer
emplear *vt* **1** : to employ **2** USAR : to use — **emplearse** *vr* **1** : to get a job **2** : to occupy oneself
empleo *nm* **1** OCUPACIÓN : employment, occupation, job **2** : use, usage
emplomadura *nf Arg, Uru* : filling (in a tooth)
emplumar *vt* : to feather
empobrecer {53} *vt* : to impoverish — *vi* : to become poor — **empobrecerse** *vr*
empobrecimiento *nm* : impoverishment
empollar *vi* : to brood eggs — *vt* : to incubate
empolvar *vt* **1** : to cover with dust **2** : to powder — **empolvarse** *vr* **1** : to gather dust **2** : to powder one's face
emporio *nm* **1** : center, capital, empire ⟨un emporio cultural : a cultural center⟩ ⟨un emporio financiero : a financial empire⟩ **2** : department store
empotrado, -da *adj* : built-in ⟨armarios empotrados : built-in cabinets⟩
empotrar *vt* : to build into, to embed
emprendedor, -dora *adj* : enterprising
emprender *vt* : to undertake, to begin
empresa *nf* **1** COMPAÑÍA, FIRMA : company, corporation, firm **2** : undertaking, venture
empresariado *nm* **1** : business world **2** : management, managers *pl*
empresarial *adj* : business, managerial, corporate
empresario, -ria *n* **1** : manager **2** : businessman *m*, businesswoman *f* **3** : impresario
empréstito *nm* : loan
empujar *vi* : to push, to shove — *vt* **1** : to push **2** PRESIONAR : to spur on, to press
empuje *nm* : impetus, drive
empujón *nm, pl* **-jones** : push, shove
empuñadura *nf* MANGO : hilt, handle
empuñar *vt* **1** ASIR : to grasp **2 empuñar las armas** : to take up arms
emú *nm, pl* **emúes** or **emús** or **emúes** : emu
emular *vt* IMITAR : to emulate — **emulación** *nf*
emulsión *nf, pl* **-siones** : emulsion
emulsionante *nm* : emulsifier
emulsionar *vt* : to emulsify
en *prep* **1** : in (a box, building, city, etc.) ⟨en el aire : in the air⟩ ⟨en el bolsillo : in one's pocket⟩ **2** : on (a surface, etc.) ⟨está en la mesa : it's on the table⟩ ⟨en la costa : on the coast⟩ ⟨en la planta baja : on the ground floor⟩ ⟨en la calle Sur : on South Street⟩ **3** : at (a place or event) ⟨en casa : at home⟩ ⟨en el trabajo : at work⟩ ⟨en la reunión : at the meeting⟩ ⟨todos en la mesa : everyone at the table⟩ ⟨en el 30 de la calle Sur : at 30 South Street⟩ **4** : in, on, as part of ⟨en la película : in the movie⟩ ⟨en el equipo : on the team⟩ **5** : on (television, etc.) **6** : by (plane, train, etc.) **7** : in, within (a day, week, etc.) **8** : in, during (a period) **9** : on, at ⟨en esa ocasión : on that

occasion⟩ ⟨en ese momento : at that moment⟩ **10** : in (a form) ⟨en francés/metros/pedazos : in French/meters/pieces⟩ **11** (*with numbers*) ⟨se ubica en el 26% : it's at 26%⟩ ⟨aumentó en un 90% : it increased by 90%⟩ ⟨se cifran en millones : they amount to millions⟩ **12** : in, made of (a material) ⟨en una state, manner, circumstance⟩ ⟨en peligro : in danger⟩ ⟨en broma : in jest⟩ ⟨en ese caso : in that case⟩ **14** : on (a subject) ⟨un experto en animales : an animal expert⟩ **15** : in (a field or profession) **16** (*with an infinitive verb*) ⟨el primero en ganar el título : the first to win the title⟩

en- *or* **em-** *pref* : en-, em- ⟨enredar : entangle⟩ ⟨empatía : empathy⟩

enagua *nf* : petticoat, slip

enajenación *nf, pl* **-ciones 1** : transfer (of property) **2** : alienation **3** : absentmindedness

enajenado, -da *adj* : out of one's mind

enajenar *vt* **1** : to transfer (property) **2** : to alienate **3** : to enrapture — **enajenarse** *vr* **1** : to become estranged **2** : to go mad

enaltecer {53} *vt* : to praise, to extol

enamorado¹, -da *adj* : in love

enamorado², -da *n* : lover, sweetheart

enamoramiento *nm* : infatuation, crush

enamorar *vt* : to enamor, to win the love of — **enamorarse** *vr* : to fall in love

enamorizado, -da *adj* : amorous, passionate

enano¹, -na *adj* : tiny, minute

enano², -na *n* **1** : little person, dwarf *sometimes offensive*, midget *often offensive* **2** : dwarf (in stories) **3** : shorty, shrimp

enarbolar *vt* **1** : to hoist, to raise **2** : to brandish

enardecer {53} *vt* **1** : to arouse (anger, passions) **2** : to stir up, to excite — **enardecerse** *vr*

encabezado *nm Mex* : headline

encabezamiento *nm* **1** : heading **2** : salutation, opening

encabezar {21} *vt* **1** : to head, to lead **2** : to put a heading on

encabritarse *vr* **1** : to rear up **2** *fam* : to get angry

encadenar *vt* **1** : to chain **2** : to connect, to link **3** INMOVILIZAR : to immobilize

encajar *vi* : to fit, to fit together, to fit in — *vt* **1** : to insert, to stick **2** : to take, to cope with ⟨encajó el golpe : he withstood the blow⟩

encaje *nm* **1** : lace **2** : financial reserve

encajonar *vt* **1** : to box, to crate **2** : to cram in

encalar *vt* : to whitewash

encallar *vi* **1** : to run aground **2** : to get stuck

encallecido, -da *adj* : callused

encamar *vt* : to confine to a bed

encaminado, -da *adj* **1** : on the right track **2** ~ **a** : aimed at, designed to

encaminar *vt* **1** : to direct, to channel **2** : to head in the right direction — **encaminarse** *vr* ~ **a** : to head for, to aim at

encandilar *vt* : to dazzle

encanecer {53} *vi* : to gray, to go gray

encantado, -da *adj* **1** : charmed, bewitched **2** : delighted **3** : haunted

encantador¹, -dora *adj* : charming, delightful

encantador², -dora *n* : magician

encantamiento *nm* : enchantment, spell

encantar *vt* **1** : to enchant, to bewitch **2** : to charm, to delight ⟨me encanta esta canción : I love this song⟩

encanto *nm* **1** : charm, fascination **2** HECHIZO : spell **3** : delightful person or thing

encañonar *vt* : to point (a gun) at, to hold up

encapotado, -da *adj* : cloudy, overcast

encaprichado, -da *adj* : infatuated

encaprichamiento *nm* : infatuation

encapuchado, -da *adj* : hooded

encarado, -da *adj* **estar mal encarado** *fam* : to be ugly-looking, to look mean

encaramar *vt* : to raise, to lift up — **encaramarse** *vr* : to perch

encarar *vt* CONFRONTAR : to face, to confront

encarcelación *nf, pl* **-ciones** → **encarcelamiento**

encarcelamiento *nm* : incarceration, imprisonment

encarcelar *vt* : to incarcerate, to imprison

encarecer {53} *vt* **1** : to increase, to raise (price, value) **2** : to beseech, to entreat — **encarecerse** *vr* : to become more expensive

encarecidamente *adv* : insistently, urgently

encarecimiento *nm* : increase, rise (in price)

encargado¹, -da *adj* : in charge

encargado², -da *n* : manager, person in charge

encargar {52} *vt* **1** : to put in charge of **2** : to recommend, to advise **3** : to order, to request — **encargarse** *vr* ~ **de** : to take charge of

encargo *nm* **1** : errand **2** : job assignment **3** : order ⟨hecho de encargo : custommade, made to order⟩

encariñarse *vr* ~ **con** : to become fond of, to grow attached to

encarnación *nf, pl* **-ciones** : incarnation, embodiment

encarnado¹, -da *adj* **1** : incarnate **2** : flesh-colored **3** : red **4** : ingrown

encarnado² *nm* : red

encarnar *vt* : to incarnate, to embody — **encarnarse** *vr* **encarnarse una uña** : to have an ingrown nail

encarnizado, -da *adj* **1** : bloodshot, inflamed **2** : fierce, bloody

encarnizar {21} *vt* : to enrage, to infuriate — **encarnizarse** *vr* : to be brutal, to attack viciously

encarrilar *vt* : to guide, to put on the right track

encasillar *vt* CLASIFICAR : to classify, to pigeonhole, to categorize

encausar *vt* : to prosecute, to charge

encauzar {21} *vt* : to channel, to guide — **encauzarse** *vr*

encebollado, -da *adj* : cooked with onions

encefalitis *nms & pl* : encephalitis

enceguecedor, -dora *n* : blinding

encendedor *nm* : lighter

encender {56} *vi* : to light — *vt* **1** : to light, to set fire to **2** PRENDER : to switch on **3** : to start (a motor) **4** : to arouse, to kindle — **encenderse** *vr* **1** : to get excited **2** : to blush

encendido¹, -da *adj* **1** : burning **2** : flushed **3** : fiery, passionate

encendido² *nm* : ignition

encerado *nm* **1** : waxing, polishing **2** : blackboard

encerar *vt* : to wax, to polish

encerrar {55} *vt* **1** : to lock (up), to shut away/up ⟨la encerraron en una celda : they locked her in a cell⟩ ⟨está encerrado en su cuarto : he's shut up in his room⟩ **2** : to contain, to include **3** : to involve, to entail

encerrona *nf* **1** TRAMPA : trap, setup **2 prepararle una encerrona a alguien** : to set a trap for someone, to set someone up

encestar *vi* : to make a basket (in basketball)

enchapado *nm* : plating, coating (of metal)

encharcamiento *nm* : flood, flooding

encharcar {72} *vt* : to flood — **encharcarse** *vr* **1** : to flood, to get flooded **2** : to pool

enchilada *nf* : enchilada

enchilar *vt Mex* : to season with chili

enchuecar {72} *vt Chile, Mex fam* : to make crooked, to twist

enchufar *vt* **1** : to plug in **2** : to connect, to fit together

enchufe *nm* **1** : connection **2** : plug, socket

encía *nf* : gum (tissue)

-encia *suf* : -ence ⟨independencia : independence⟩

enciclopedia *nf* : encyclopedia — **enciclopédico, -ca** *adj*

encierro *nm* **1** : confinement **2** : enclosure

encima *adv* **1** : on, on top (of) ⟨se me cayó encima : it fell on (top of) me⟩ ⟨con queso (por) encima : with cheese on top⟩ ⟨no llevo dinero encima : I don't have any money on me⟩ **2** ADEMÁS : as well, besides ⟨y encima : and on top of that⟩ **3** ~ **de** : on, on top of, over, above ⟨encima de la mesa : on (top of) the table⟩ ⟨encima de las nubes : above the clouds⟩ ⟨viven encima de la librería : they live above the bookstore⟩ ⟨miró por encima del hombro : he looked over his shoulder⟩ **4 por** ~ : superficially **5 por encima de** : above, beyond ⟨por encima de la ley : above the law⟩ ⟨por encima de la media : above average⟩ ⟨por encima de todo : above all⟩ ⟨vive por encima de sus posibilidades : she lives above her means⟩ **6 echarse encima** : to take

upon oneself **7 estar encima de** *fam* : to nag, to criticize **8 quitarse de encima** : to get rid of

encina *nf* : evergreen oak

encinta *adj* EMBARAZADA, PREÑADA : pregnant, expecting

enclaustrado, -da *adj* : cloistered, shut away

enclavado, -da *adj* : buried

enclenque *adj* : weak, sickly

encoger {15} *vt* **1** : to shrink, to make smaller **2** : to intimidate — *vi* : to shrink, to contract — **encogerse** *vr* **1** : to shrink **2** : to be intimidated, to cower, to cringe **3 encogerse de hombros** : to shrug (one's shoulders)

encogido, -da *adj* **1** : shriveled, shrunken **2** TÍMIDO : shy, inhibited

encogimiento *nm* **1** : shrinking, shrinkage **2** : shrug **3** TIMIDEZ : shyness

encolerizar {21} *vt* ENFURECER : to enrage, to infuriate — **encolerizarse** *vr*

encomendar {55} *vt* CONFIAR : to entrust, to commend — **encomendarse** *vr*

encomiable *adj* : commendable, praiseworthy

encomiar *vt* ELOGIAR : to praise, to pay tribute to

encomienda *nf* **1** : charge, mission **2** : royal land grant **3** : parcel

encomio *nm* : praise, eulogy

enconar *vt* **1** : to irritate, to anger **2** : to inflame — **enconarse** *vr* **1** : to become heated **2** : to fester

encono *nm* **1** RENCOR : animosity, rancor **2** : inflammation, infection

encontrado, -da *adj* : contrary, opposing

encontrar {19} *vt* **1** HALLAR : to find ⟨encontré el libro : I found the book⟩ ⟨encontraron al culpable : they found the culprit⟩ **2** : to encounter, to meet **3** : to find ⟨lo encuentro muy interesante : I find it very interesting⟩ — **encontrarse** *vr* **1** : to clash, to conflict **2** : to be, to feel ⟨su padre se encuentra mejor : her father is (feeling/doing) better⟩ **3** ~ **con** : to meet, to bump into

encorvar *vt* : to bend, to curve — **encorvarse** *vr* : to hunch over, to stoop

encrespar *vt* **1** : to curl, to ruffle, to ripple **2** : to annoy, to irritate — **encresparse** *vr* **1** : to curl one's hair **2** : to become choppy **3** : to get annoyed

encriptar *vt* : to encrypt

encrucijada *nf* : crossroads

encuadernación *nf, pl* **-ciones** : binding (of books)

encuadernar *vt* EMPASTAR : to bind (a book) — **encuadernador, -dora** *n*

encuadrar *vt* **1** ENMARCAR : to frame **2** ENCAJAR : to fit, to insert **3** COMPRENDER : to contain, to include

encubierto *pp* → **encubrir**

encubrimiento *nm* : cover-up

encubrir {2} *vt* : to cover up, to conceal

encuentro *nm* **1** : meeting, encounter **2** : conference, congress

encuerado, -da *adj fam* : naked

encuerar *vt fam* : to undress

encuesta *nf* **1** INVESTIGACIÓN, PESQUISA : inquiry, investigation **2** SONDEO : survey

encuestador, -dora *n* : pollster

encuestar *vt* : to poll, to take a survey of

encumbrado, -da *adj* **1** : lofty, high **2** : eminent, distinguished

encumbrar {21} *vt* **1** : to exalt, to elevate **2** : to extol — **encumbrarse** *vr* : to reach the top

encurtir *vt* ESCABECHAR : to pickle

ende *adv* por ∼ : therefore, consequently

endeble *adj* : feeble, weak

endemoniado, -da *adj* : fiendish, diabolical

enderezar {21} *vt* **1** : to straighten (out) **2** : to stand on end, to put upright — **enderezarse** *vr* **1** : to straighten up, to sit/stand (up) straight **2** ARREGLARSE : to straighten out, to improve

endeudado, -da *adj* : in debt, indebted

endeudamiento *nm* : indebtedness, debt

endeudarse *vr* **1** : to go into debt **2** : to feel obliged

endiablado, -da *adj* **1** : devilish, diabolical **2** : complicated, difficult

endibia *or* **endivia** *nf* : endive

endilgar {52} *vt fam* : to spring, to foist ⟨me endilgó la responsabilidad : he saddled me with the responsibility⟩

endocrino, -na *adj* : endocrine

endogamia *nf* : inbreeding

endosar *vt* : to endorse

endoso *nm* : endorsement

endulzante *nm* : sweetener

endulzar {21} *vt* **1** : to sweeten **2** : to soften, to mellow — **endulzarse** *vr*

endurecer {53} *vt* : to harden, to toughen — **endurecerse** *vr*

ene *nf* : (letter) n

enebro *nm* : juniper

eneldo *nm* : dill

enema *nm* : enema

enemigo, -ga *adj & n* : enemy

enemistad *nf* : enmity, hostility

enemistar *vt* : to make enemies of — **enemistarse** *vr* ∼ **con** : to fall out with

energético, -ca *adj* **1** : energy ⟨consumo energético : energy consumption⟩ **2** : lively, spirited

energía *nf* : energy

enérgico, -ca *adj* **1** : energetic, vigorous **2** : forceful, emphatic — **enérgicamente** *adv*

energúmeno, -na *n fam* : lunatic, crazy person

enero *nm* : January ⟨el primero de enero : (on) January first⟩

enervar *vt* **1** : to enervate **2** *fam* : to annoy, to get on one's nerves — **enervante** *adj*

enésimo, -ma *adj* : umpteenth, nth

enfadado, -da *adj* : angry, annoyed

enfadar *vt* **1** : to annoy, to make angry — **enfadarse** *vr* : to get angry, to get annoyed

enfado *nm* : anger, annoyance

enfardar *vt* : to bale

énfasis *nms & pl* : emphasis

enfático, -ca *adj* : emphatic — **enfáticamente** *adv*

enfatizar {21} *vt* DESTACAR, SUBRAYAR : to emphasize

enfermar *vt* : to make sick — *vi* : to fall ill, to get sick — **enfermarse** *vr*

enfermedad *nf* **1** INDISPOSICIÓN : illness, sickness ⟨por enfermedad : due to illness⟩ **2** : illness, disease ⟨contraer una enfermedad : to catch/contract an illness⟩ ⟨enfermedad infecciosa : infectious disease⟩ ⟨enfermedad mental : mental illness⟩

enfermería *nf* : infirmary

enfermero, -ra *n* : nurse

enfermizo, -za *adj* : sickly

enfermo¹, -ma *adj* : sick, ill

enfermo², -ma *n* **1** : sick person, invalid **2** PACIENTE : patient

enfilar *vt* **1** : to take, to go along ⟨enfiló la carretera de Montevideo : she went up the road to Montevideo⟩ **2** : to line up, to put in a row **3** : to string, to thread **4** : to aim, to direct — *vi* : to make one's way

enflaquecer {53} *vi* : to lose weight, to become thin *vt* : to emaciate

enfocar {72} *vt* **1** : to focus (on) **2** : to consider, to look at

enfoque *nm* : focus

enfrascarse {72} *vr* ∼ **en** : to immerse oneself in, to get caught up in

enfrentamiento *nm* : clash, confrontation

enfrentar *vt* : to confront, to face — **enfrentarse** *vr* **1** ∼ **con** : to clash with **2** ∼ **a** : to face up to

enfrente *adv* **1** DELANTE : in front **2** : opposite

enfriamiento *nm* **1** CATARRO : chill, cold **2** : cooling off, damper

enfriar {85} *vt* **1** : to chill, to cool **2** : to cool down, to dampen — *vi* : to get cold — **enfriarse** *vr* : to get chilled, to catch a cold

enfundar *vt* : to sheathe, to encase

enfurecer {53} *vt* ENCOLERIZAR : to infuriate — **enfurecerse** *vr* : to fly into a rage

enfurecido, -da *adj* : furious, raging

enfurruñarse *vr fam* : to sulk

engalanar *vt* : to decorate, to deck out — **engalanarse** *vr* : to dress up

enganchar *vt* **1** : to hook, to snag **2** : to attach, to hitch up — **engancharse** *vr* **1** : to get snagged, to get hooked **2** : to enlist

enganche *nm* **1** : hook **2** : coupling, hitch **3** *Mex* : down payment

engañar *vt* **1** EMBAUCAR : to trick, to deceive, to mislead **2** : to cheat on, to be unfaithful to — **engañarse** *vr* **1** : to be mistaken **2** : to deceive oneself

engaño *nm* **1** : deception, trick **2** : fake, feint (in sports)

engañoso, -sa *adj* **1** : deceitful **2** : misleading, deceptive

engarzar {21} *vt* **1** : to set (a gem) **2** ENSARTAR : to string **3** HILAR : to string together — **engarzarse** *vr* ∼ **en** : to get involved in, to get caught up in

engatusar *vt* : to coax, to cajole

engendrar *vt* **1** : to beget, to father **2** : to give rise to, to engender

engendro *nm* **1** : fetus **2** MONSTRUO : monstrosity, freak

engentarse *vr Mex* : to become confused and overwhelmed

englobar *vt* : to include, to embrace

engomado *nm Mex* : sticker

engomar *vt* : to glue, to coat with glue

engordar *vt* : to fatten, to fatten up — *vi* : to gain weight

engorroso, -sa *adj* : bothersome

engranaje *nm* : gears *pl*, cogs *pl*

engranar *vt* : to mesh, to engage — *vi* : to mesh gears

engrandecer {53} *vt* **1** : to enlarge **2** : to exaggerate **3** : to exalt

engrandecimiento *nm* **1** : enlargement **2** : exaggeration **3** : exaltation

engrane *nm Mex* : cogwheel

engrapadora *nf* : stapler

engrapar *vt* : to staple

engrasar *vt* : to grease, to lubricate

engrase *nm* : greasing, lubrication

engreído, -da *adj* PRESUMIDO, VANIDOSO : vain, conceited, stuck-up

engreimiento *nm* ARROGANCIA : arrogance, conceit

engreír {66} *vt* ENVANECER : to make vain — **engreírse** *vr* : to become conceited

engrosar {19} *vt* : to enlarge, to increase, to swell — *vi* ENGORDAR : to gain weight

engrudo *nm* : paste

engullir {38} *vt* : to gulp down, to gobble up — **engullirse** *vr*

enharinar *vt* : to flour

enhebrar *vt* ENSARTAR : to string, to thread

enhilar *vt* : to thread (a needle, etc.)

enhorabuena *nf* FELICIDADES : congratulations *pl*

enigma *nm* : enigma, mystery

enigmático, -ca *adj* : enigmatic — **enigmáticamente** *adv*

enjabonar *vt* : to soap up, to lather — **enjabonarse** *vr*

enjaezar {21} *vt* : to harness

enjalbegar {52} *vt* : to whitewash

enjambrar *vi* : to swarm

enjambre *nm* **1** : swarm **2** MUCHEDUMBRE : crowd, mob

enjaular *vt* **1** : to cage **2** *fam* : to jail, to lock up

enjuagar {52} *vt* : to rinse — **enjuagarse** *vr* : to rinse out

enjuague *nm* **1** : rinse **2 enjuague bucal** : mouthwash

enjugar {52} *vt* : to wipe away (tears)

enjuiciar *vt* **1** : to indict, to prosecute **2** JUZGAR : to try

enlace *nm* **1** : bond, link, connection **2** : liaison **3** HIPERENLACE : link

enlatar *vt* ENVASAR : to can — **enlatado, -da** *adj*

enlazar {21} *v* : to join, to link, to fit together

enlistar *vt* : to list — **enlistarse** *vr* : to enlist

enlodado, -da *adj* LODOSO : muddy

enlodar *vt* **1** : to cover with mud **2** : to stain, to sully — **enlodarse** *vr*

enlodazar → **enlodar**

enloquecedor, -dora *adj* : maddening

enloquecer {53} *vt* : to drive crazy — **enloquecerse** *vr* : to go crazy

enlutarse *vr* : to go into mourning

enmarañar *vt* **1** : to tangle **2** : to complicate **3** : to confuse, to mix up — **enmarañarse** *vr*

enmarcar {72} *vt* **1** ENCUADRAR : to frame **2** : to provide the setting for

enmascarar *vt* : to mask, to disguise — **enmascarado, -da** *adj*

enmasillar *vt* : to putty, to caulk

enmendar {55} *vt* **1** : to amend **2** CORREGIR : to emend, to correct **3** COMPENSAR : to compensate for — **enmendarse** *vr* : to mend one's ways

enmienda *nf* **1** : amendment **2** : correction, emendation

enmohecerse {53} *vr* **1** : to become moldy **2** OXIDARSE : to rust, to become rusty

enmudecer {53} *vt* : to mute, to silence — *vi* : to fall silent

ennegrecer {53} *vt* : to blacken, to darken — **ennegrecerse** *vr*

ennoblecer {53} *vt* **1** : to ennoble **2** : to embellish

enojadizo, -za *adj* IRRITABLE : irritable, cranky

enojado, -da *adj* **1** : annoyed **2** : angry, mad

enojar *vt* **1** : to anger **2** : to annoy, to upset — **enojarse** *vr*

enojo *nm* **1** CÓLERA : anger **2** : annoyance

enojón, -jona *adj, pl* **-jones** *Chile, Mex fam* : irritable, cranky

enojoso, -sa *adj* FASTIDIOSO, MOLESTOSO : annoying, irritating

enorgullecer {53} *vt* : to make proud — **enorgullecerse** *vr* : to pride oneself

enorme *adj* INMENSO : enormous, huge — **enormemente** *adv*

enormidad *nf* **1** : enormity, seriousness **2** : immensity, hugeness

enraizado, -da *adj* : deep-seated, deeply rooted

enraizar {30} *vi* : to take root

enramada *nf* : arbor, bower

enramar *vt* : to cover with branches

enrarecer {53} *vt* : to rarefy — **enrarecerse** *vr*

enredadera *nf* : climbing plant, vine

enredar *vt* **1** : to tangle up, to entangle **2** : to confuse, to complicate **3** : to involve, to implicate — **enredarse** *vr*

enredo *nm* **1** EMBROLLO : muddle, confusion **2** MARAÑA : tangle

enrejado *nm* **1** : railing **2** : grating, grille **3** : trellis, lattice

enrevesado, -da *adj* : complicated, involved

enriquecer {53} *vt* : to enrich — **enriquecerse** *vr* : to get rich

enriquecido, -da *adj* : enriched

enriquecimiento *nm* : enrichment

enrojecer {53} *vt* : to make red, to redden — **enrojecerse** *vr* : to blush

enrolar *vt* RECLUTAR : to recruit — **enrolarse** *vr* INSCRIBIRSE : to enlist, to sign up

enrollado, -da *adj* **1** : rolled up, coiled **2 estar enrollado** *con Spain* : to be involved with (romantically)

enrollar *vt* : to roll up, to coil — **enrollarse** *vr*

enronquecerse {53} *vr* : to become hoarse

enroscar {72} *vt* TORCER : to twist — **enroscarse** *vr* : to coil, to twine

ensacar {72} *vt* : to bag (up)

ensalada *nf* : salad

ensaladera *nf* : salad bowl

ensalmo *nm* : incantation, spell

ensalzar {21} *vt* **1** : to praise, to extol **2** EXALTAR : to exalt

ensamblaje *nm* : assembly

ensamblar *vt* **1** : to assemble **2** : to join, to fit together

ensanchar *vt* **1** : to widen **2** : to expand, to extend — **ensancharse** *vr*

ensanche *nm* **1** : widening **2** : expansion, development

ensangrentado, -da *adj* : bloody, bloodstained

ensangrentar {55} *vt* : to cover or stain with blood

ensañarse *vr* : to act cruelly, to be merciless

ensartar *vt* **1** ENHEBRAR : to string, to thread **2** : to skewer, to pierce

ensayar *vi* : to rehearse — *vt* **1** : to try out, to test **2** : to assay

ensayista *nmf* : essayist

ensayo *nm* **1** : essay **2** : trial, test **3** : rehearsal **4** : assay (of metals)

enseguida *adv* INMEDIATAMENTE : right away, immediately, at once

ensenada *nf* : cove, inlet

enseña *nf* **1** INSIGNIA : emblem, insignia **2** : standard, banner

enseñanza *nf* **1** EDUCACIÓN : education **2** : teaching

enseñar *vt* **1** : to teach **2** MOSTRAR : to show, to display — **enseñarse** *vr* ~ **a** : to learn to, to get used to

enseres *nmpl* : equipment, furnishings *pl* ⟨enseres domésticos : household goods⟩

ensillar *vt* : to saddle (up)

ensimismado, -da *adj* : absorbed, engrossed

ensimismarse *vr* : to lose oneself in thought

ensombrecer {53} *vt* : to cast a shadow over, to darken — **ensombrecerse** *vr*

ensoñación *nf, pl* **-ciones** : fantasy

ensopar *vt* **1** : to drench **2** : to dunk, to dip

ensordecedor, -dora *adj* : deafening, thunderous

ensordecer {53} *vt* : to deafen — *vi* : to go deaf

ensuciar *vt* : to soil, to dirty — **ensuciarse** *vr*

ensueño *nm* **1** : daydream, reverie **2** FANTASÍA : illusion, fantasy

entablar *vt* **1** : to cover with boards **2** : to initiate, to enter into, to start

entallar *vt* AJUSTAR : to tailor, to fit, to take in — *vi* QUEDAR : to fit

entarimado *nm* : flooring, floorboards *pl*

ente *nm* **1** : being, entity **2** : body, organization ⟨ente rector : ruling body⟩ **3** *fam* : eccentric, crackpot

entenado, -da *n Mex* : stepchild, stepson *m*, stepdaughter *f*

entender¹ {56} *vt* **1** COMPRENDER : to understand ⟨no entiendo por qué : I don't understand why⟩ ⟨me has entendido mal : you've misunderstood me⟩ ⟨mis padres no me entienden : my parents don't understand me⟩ ⟨dar a entender : to imply⟩ **2** : to think, to believe ⟨él no lo entiende así : he doesn't see it that way⟩ **3** : to know, to get ⟨si me entiendes : if you know what I mean⟩ **4** : to infer ⟨dar algo a entender : to imply something⟩ — *vi* **1** : to understand ⟨¡ya entiendo! : now I understand!⟩ **2** ~ **de** : to know about **3** ~ **en** : to be in charge of — **entenderse** *vr* **1** : to be understood **2** : to get along well **3** ~ **con** : to deal with

entender² *nm* **a mi entender** : in my opinion

entendible *adj* : understandable

entendido¹, -da *adj* **1** : skilled, expert, knowledgeable **2 tener entendido** : to understand, to be under the impression ⟨teníamos entendido que vendrías : we were under the impression you would come⟩ **3 darse por entendido** : to go without saying

entendido² *nm* : expert, authority, connoisseur

entendimiento *nm* **1** : intellect, mind **2** : understanding, agreement

enterado, -da *adj* : aware, well-informed ⟨estar enterado de : to be privy to⟩ ⟨darse por enterado : to get the message⟩

enteramente *adv* : entirely, completely

enterar *vt* INFORMAR : to inform — **enterarse** *vr* INFORMARSE : to find out, to learn

entereza *nf* **1** INTEGRIDAD : integrity **2** FORTALEZA : fortitude **3** FIRMEZA : resolve

enternecedor, -dora *adj* CONMOVEDOR : touching, moving

enternecer {53} *vt* CONMOVER : to move, to touch

entero¹, -ra *adj* **1** : entire, whole **2** : complete, absolute **3** : intact — **enteramente** *adv*

entero² *nm* **1** : integer, whole number **2** : point (in finance)

enterramiento *nm* : burial

enterrar {55} *vt* : to bury

entibiar *vt* : to cool (down) — **entibiarse** *vr* : to become lukewarm

entidad *nf* **1** ENTE : entity **2** : body, organization **3** : firm, company **4** : importance, significance

entierro *nm* **1** : burial **2** : funeral

entintar *vt* : to ink

entoldado *nm* : awning

entomología *nf* : entomology

entomólogo, -ga *n* : entomologist

entonación *nf, pl* **-ciones** : intonation

entonar *vi* : to be in tune — *vt* **1** : to intone **2** : to tone up

entonces *adv* **1** : then **2 desde ~** : since then **3 en aquel entonces** : in those days

entonado, -da *adj* ENTREABIERTO : half-closed, ajar

entornar *vt* ENTREABRIR : to leave ajar

entorno *nm* : surroundings *pl*, environment

entorpecer {53} *vt* **1** : to hinder, to obstruct **2** : to dull — **entorpecerse** *vr* : to dull the senses

entrada *nf* **1** : entrance, entry ⟨prohibida la entrada : do not enter⟩ **2** : entrance ⟨entrada principal : main entrance⟩ **3** : ticket, admission ⟨entrada gratuita/libre : free admission⟩ **4** : beginning, onset ⟨de entrada : from the start⟩ **5** : entrée **6** : cue (in music) **7 entradas** *nfpl* : income ⟨entradas y salidas : income and expenditures⟩ **8 tener entradas** : to have a receding hairline

entrado, -da *adj* **entrado en años** : elderly

entramado *nm* : framework

entrampar *vt* **1** ATRAPAR : to entrap, to ensnare **2** ENGAÑAR : to deceive, to trick

entrante *adj* **1** : next, upcoming ⟨el año entrante : next year⟩ **2** : incoming, new ⟨el presidente entrante : the president elect⟩

entraña *nf* **1** MEOLLO : core, heart, crux **2 entrañas** *nfpl* VÍSCERAS : entrails

entrañable *adj* : close, intimate

entrañar *vt* : to entail, to involve

entrar *vi* **1** : to enter, to go in, to come in ⟨entré a la casa : I went in the house⟩ ⟨entrar por : to come/go in (through)⟩ ⟨¿puedo entrar? : can I come in?⟩ ⟨la llave no entra : the key won't go in⟩ **2** : to fit ⟨este vestido no me entra : this dress doesn't fit me⟩ **3** : to begin ⟨entro a trabajar a las ocho : I start work at eight⟩ **4** : to affect ⟨me entra el hambre : I'm getting hungry⟩ **5 ~ en** : to enter (a phase, etc.) **6 ~ en** : to be included/considered in **7 ~ en** : to go into, to discuss (details, etc.) **8 ~ en** : to enter into (negotiations, battle, etc.), to come into (contact, conflict, etc.), to go into (effect) **9 ~ en** : to enter (college), to join (an organization), to enter (a profession) — *vt* **1** : to bring in, to introduce **2** : to access

entre *prep* **1** : between ⟨entre las dos ciudades/fechas : between the two cities/dates⟩ ⟨lo dividimos entre los dos : we divided it between the two of us⟩ ⟨la diferencia entre los dos : the difference between the two⟩ ⟨entre todos lo logramos : between all of us we managed it⟩ ⟨entre tú y yo : between you and me⟩ **2** : among ⟨entre las hojas : among the leaves⟩ ⟨entre amigos : among friends⟩ ⟨lo dividimos entre los cuatro : we divided it among the four of us⟩ ⟨conversaban entre sí : they talked among themselves⟩

entreabierto¹ *pp* → **entreabrir**

entreabierto², -ta *adj* ENTORNADO : half-open, ajar

entreabrir {2} *vt* ENTORNAR : to leave ajar

entreacto *nm* : intermission, interval

entrecano, -na *adj* : grayish, graying

entrecejo *nm* **fruncir el entrecejo** : to knit one's brows

entrecomillar *vt* : to place in quotation marks

entrecortadamente *adv* **1** : breathlessly **2** : falteringly

entrecortado, -da *adj* **1** : labored, difficult ⟨respiración entrecortada : shortness of breath⟩ **2** : faltering, hesitant ⟨con la voz entrecortada : with a catch in his voice⟩

entrecortarse *vr* : to falter (of the voice or breath)

entrecruzar {21} *vt* ENTRELAZAR : to interweave, to intertwine — **entrecruzarse** *vr*

entredicho *nm* **1** DUDA : doubt, question **2** : prohibition

entrega *nf* **1** : delivery **2** : handing over, surrender **3** : installment ⟨entrega inicial : down payment⟩

entregar {52} *vt* **1** : to deliver **2** DAR : to give, to present **3** : to hand in, to hand over — **entregarse** *vr* **1** : to surrender, to give in **2** : to devote oneself

entrelazar {21} *vt* ENTRECRUZAR : to interweave, to intertwine

entremedias *adv* **1** : in between, halfway **2** : in the meantime

entremés *nm*, *pl* **-meses 1** APERITIVO : appetizer, hors d'oeuvre **2** : interlude, short play

entremeterse → **entrometerse**

entremetido *nm* → **entrometido**

entremezclar *vt* : to intermingle

entrenador, -dora *n* : trainer, coach

entrenamiento *nm* : training, drill, practice

entrenar *vt* : to train, to drill, to practice — **entrenarse** *vr* : to train, to spar (in boxing)

entrepierna *nf* **1** : inner thigh **2** : crotch **3** : inseam

entrepiso *nm* : mezzanine

entretanto¹ *adv* : meanwhile

entretanto² *nm* **en el entretanto** : in the meantime

entretejer *vt* : to interweave

entretela *nf* : facing (of a garment)

entretelones *nmpl* : inside details

entretención *nf*, *pl* **-ciones** ENTRETENIMIENTO : entertainment

entretener {80} *vt* **1** DIVERTIR : to entertain, to amuse **2** DISTRAER : to distract **3** DEMORAR : to delay, to hold up — **entretenerse** *vr* **1** : to amuse oneself **2** : to dally

entretenido, -da *adj* DIVERTIDO : entertaining, amusing

entretenimiento *nm* **1** : entertainment, pastime **2** DIVERSIÓN : fun, amusement

entretiempo *nm* **1** → **medio tiempo 2** : period between seasons

entrever {88} *vt* **1** : to catch a glimpse of **2** : to make out, to see indistinctly

entreverar *vr* : to mix, to intermingle

entrevero *nm* : confusion, disorder

entrevista *nf* : interview

entrevistador, -dora *n* : interviewer

entrevistar *vt* : to interview — **entrevistarse** *vr* REUNIRSE ~ **con** : to meet with

entristecer {53} *vt* : to sadden

entrometerse *vr* : to interfere, to meddle

entrometido, -da *n* : meddler, busybody

entroncar {72} *vt* RELACIONAR : to establish a relationship between, to connect — *vi* **1** : to be related **2** : to link up, to be connected

entronque *nm* **1** : kinship **2** VÍNCULO : link, connection

entuerto *nm* : wrong, injustice

entumecer {53} *vt* : to make numb, to be numb — **entumecerse** *vr* : to go numb, to fall asleep

entumecido, -da *adj* **1** : numb **2** : stiff (of muscles, joints, etc.)

entumecimiento *nm* : numbness

enturbiar *vt* **1** : to cloud **2** : to confuse — **enturbiarse** *vr*

entusiasmar *vt* : to excite, to fill with enthusiasm — **entusiasmarse** *vr* : to get excited

entusiasmo *nm* : enthusiasm

entusiasta¹ *adj* : enthusiastic

entusiasta² *nmf* AFICIONADO : enthusiast

enumerar *vt* : to enumerate — **enumeración** *nf*

enunciación *nf, pl* **-ciones** : enunciation, statement

enunciado *nm* : statement

enunciar *vt* : to enunciate, to state

envainar *vt* : to sheathe

envalentonar *vt* : to make bold, to encourage — **envalentonarse** *vr*

envanecer {53} *vt* ENGREÍR : to make vain — **envanecerse** *vr*

envasar *vt* **1** EMBOTELLAR : to bottle **2** ENLATAR : to can **3** : to pack in a container

envase *nm* **1** : packaging, packing **2** : container **3** LATA : can **4** : empty bottle

envejecer {53} *vt* : to age, to make look old — *vi* : to age, to grow old

envejecido, -da *adj* : aged, old-looking

envejecimiento *nm* : aging

envenenamiento *nm* : poisoning

envenenar *vt* **1** : to poison **2** : to embitter

envergadura *nf* **1** : span, breadth, spread **2** : importance, scope

envés *nm, pl* **enveses** : reverse, opposite side

enviado, -da *n* : envoy, correspondent

enviar {85} *vt* **1** : to send **2** : to ship

envidia *nf* : envy, jealousy

envidiar *vt* : to envy — **envidiable** *adj*

envidioso, -sa *adj* : envious, jealous

envilecer {53} *vt* : to degrade, to debase

envío *nm* **1** : shipment **2** : remittance

enviudar *vi* : to be widowed, to become a widower

envoltorio *nm* **1** : bundle, package **2** : wrapping, wrapper

envoltura *nf* : wrapper, wrapping

envolver {89} *vt* **1** : to wrap **2** : to envelop, to surround **3** : to entangle, to involve — **envolverse** *vr* **1** : to become involved **2** : to wrap oneself (up)

envuelto *pp* → **envolver**

enyerbar *vt Mex* : to bewitch

enyesar *vt* **1** : to plaster **2** ESCAYOLAR : to put (a broken limb) in a cast

enzima *nf* : enzyme

eón *nm, pl* **eones** : aeon

eperlano *nm* : smelt (fish)

epicentro *nm* : epicenter

épico, -ca *adj* : epic

epicúreo¹, -rea *adj* : epicurean

epicúreo², -rea *n* : epicure

epidemia *nf* : epidemic

epidémico, -ca *adj* : epidemic

epidemiología *nf* : epidemiology — **epidemiológico, -ca** *adj*

epifanía *nf* : feast of the Epiphany (January 6th)

epigrama *nm* : epigram

epilepsia *nf* : epilepsy

epiléptico, -ca *adj & n* : epileptic

epílogo *nm* : epilogue

episcopal *adj* : episcopal

episcopaliano, -na *adj & n* : Episcopalian

episódico, -ca *adj* : episodic

episodio *nm* : episode

epístola *nf* : epistle

epitafio *nm* : epitaph

epíteto *nm* : epithet, name

epítome *nm* : summary, abstract

época *nf* **1** EDAD, ERA, PERÍODO : epoch, age, period **2** : time of year, season **3** de ~ : vintage, antique

epopeya *nf* : epic poem

equidad *nf* JUSTICIA : equity, justice, fairness

equilátero, -ra *adj* : equilateral

equilibrado, -da *adj* : well-balanced

equilibrar *vt* : to balance — **equilibrarse** *vr*

equilibrio *nm* **1** : balance, equilibrium ⟨perder el equilibrio : to lose one's balance⟩ ⟨equilibrio político : balance of power⟩ **2** : poise, aplomb

equilibrista *nmf* ACRÓBATA : acrobat, tightrope walker

equino, -na *adj* : equine

equinoccio *nm* : equinox

equipaje *nm* BAGAJE : baggage, luggage

equipamiento *nm* : equipping, equipment

equipar *vt* : to equip — **equiparse** *vr*

equiparable *adj* : comparable

equiparar *vt* **1** ~ **a/con** : to put on the same level as/with **2** COMPARAR : to compare

equipo *nm* **1** : team, crew **2** : gear, equipment

equis *nf* : (letter) x

equitación *nf, pl* **-ciones** : horseback riding, horsemanship

equitativo, -va *adj* JUSTO : equitable, fair, just — **equitativamente** *adv*

equivalencia *nf* : equivalence

equivalente *adj & nm* : equivalent

equivaler {84} *vi* : to be equivalent

equivocación *nf, pl* **-ciones** ERROR : error, mistake

equivocado, -da *adj* : mistaken, wrong — **equivocadamente** *adv*

equivocar {72} *vt* **1** : to confuse (someone), to make (someone) mess up **2** : to choose badly — **equivocarse** *vr* : to make a mistake, to be wrong ⟨se equivocó de casa : he got the wrong house⟩

equívoco[1], **-ca** *adj* AMBIGUO : ambiguous, equivocal

equívoco[2] *nm* : misunderstanding

era[1], etc. → **ser**

era[2] *nf* EDAD, ÉPOCA : era, age

erario *nm* : public treasury

ere *nf* : (letter) r

erección *nf, pl* **-ciones** : erection, raising

erecto, -ta *adj* : erect

eremita *nmf* ERMITAÑO : hermit

ergonomía *nf* : ergonomics

erguido, -da *adj* : erect, upright

erguir {35} *vt* : to raise, to lift up — **erguirse** *vr* : to straighten up

erigir {35} *vt* : to build, to erect — **erigirse** *vr* ~ **en** : to set oneself up as

erizado, -da *adj* : bristly

erizar {21} *vt* **1** : to make (hair, etc.) stand on end ⟨me eriza la piel : it gives me goose bumps⟩ **2** : to irritate, to grate on (someone) — **erizarse** *vr* : to stand on end

erizo *nm* **1** : hedgehog **2 erizo de mar** : sea urchin

ermitaño[1], **-ña** *n* EREMITA : hermit, recluse

ermitaño[2] *nm* : hermit crab

erogación *nf, pl* **-ciones** : expenditure

erogar {52} *vt* **1** : to pay out **2** : to distribute

erosión *nf, pl* **-siones** : erosion

erosionar *vt* : to erode

erótico, -ca *adj* : erotic

erotismo *nm* : eroticism

erradicar {72} *vt* : to eradicate — **erradicación** *nf*

errado, -da *adj* : wrong, mistaken

errante *adj* VAGABUNDO : errant, wandering

errar {32} *vt* FALLAR : to miss — *vi* **1** DESACERTAR : to be wrong, to be mistaken **2** VAGAR : to wander

errata *nf* : misprint, error

errático, -ca *adj* : erratic — **erráticamente** *adv*

erre *nf* : (letter) r (especially when trilled)

erróneo, -nea *adj* EQUIVOCADO : erroneous, wrong — **erróneamente** *adv*

error *nm* EQUIVOCACIÓN : error, mistake ⟨cometer un error : to make a mistake⟩ ⟨estar en un error : to be mistaken⟩ ⟨por error : by mistake⟩ ⟨error de cálculo : miscalculation⟩ ⟨error de imprenta : misprint⟩ ⟨error de hecho : factual error⟩

eructar *vi* : to belch, to burp

eructo *nm* : belch, burp

erudición *nf, pl* **-ciones** : erudition, learning

erudito[1], **-ta** *adj* LETRADO : erudite, learned

erudito[2], **-ta** *n* : scholar

erupción *nf, pl* **-ciones** **1** : eruption **2** SARPULLIDO : rash

eruptivo, -va *adj* : eruptive

es → ser

esbelto, -ta *adj* DELGADO : slender, slim

esbirro *nm* : henchman

esbozar {21} *vt* BOSQUEJAR : to sketch, to outline

esbozo *nm* **1** : sketch **2** : rough draft

escabechar *vt* **1** ENCURTIR : to pickle **2** *fam* : to kill, to rub out

escabeche *nm* : brine (for pickling)

escabroso, -sa *adj* **1** : rugged, rough **2** : difficult, tough **3** : risqué

escabullirse {38} *vr* : to slip away, to escape

escafandra *nf* : (protective) suit

escala *nf* **1** : scale ⟨en escala de 1 a 10 : on a scale of 1 to 10⟩ ⟨a escala : to scale⟩ ⟨a escala mundial : on a worldwide scale⟩ ⟨producción a gran escala : large-scale production⟩ **2** : scale (in music) **3** ESCALERA : ladder **4** : stopover, layover ⟨hacer escala : to lay over⟩

escalada *nf* : ascent, climb

escalador, -dora *n* ALPINISTA : mountain climber

escalafón *nm, pl* **-fones** **1** : list of personnel **2** : salary scale, rank

escalar *vt* : to climb, to scale — *vi* **1** : to go climbing **2** : to escalate

escaldar *vt* : to scald

escalera *nf* **1** : ladder ⟨escalera de tijera : stepladder⟩ **2** : stairs *pl*, staircase **3** **escalera mecánica** : escalator

escalfar *vt* : to poach (eggs)

escalinata *nf* : flight of stairs

escalofriante *adj* : horrifying, bloodcurdling

escalofrío *nm* : shiver, chill, shudder

escalón *nm, pl* **-lones** **1** : echelon **2** : step, rung

escalonado, -da *adj* GRADUAL : gradual, staggered

escalonar *vt* **1** : to terrace **2** : to stagger, to alternate

escalpelo *nm* BISTURÍ : scalpel

escama *nf* **1** : scale (of fish or reptiles) **2** : flake (of skin)

escamar *vt* **1** : to scale (fish) **2** : to make suspicious

escamocha *nf Mex* : fruit salad

escamoso, -sa *adj* : scaly

escamotear *vt* **1** : to palm, to conceal **2** *fam* : to lift, to swipe **3** : to hide, to cover up

escampar *v impers* : to stop raining

escandalizar {21} *vt* : to shock, to scandalize — *vi* : to make a fuss — **escandalizarse** *vr* : to be shocked

escándalo *nm* **1** : scandal **2** : scene, commotion

escandaloso, -sa *adj* **1** : shocking, scandalous **2** RUIDOSO : noisy, rowdy **3** : flagrant, outrageous — **escandalosamente** *adv*

escandinavo, -va *adj & n* : Scandinavian

escandir *vt* : to scan (poetry)

escanear *vt* : to scan (documents)

escáner *nm* **1** : scan **2** : scanner
escaño *nm* **1** : seat (in a legislative body) **2** BANCO : bench
escapada *nf* HUIDA : flight, escape
escapar *vi* HUIR : to escape, to flee, to run away — **escaparse** *vr* : to escape notice, to leak out
escaparate *nm* **1** : shop window **2** : showcase
escapatoria *nf* **1** : loophole, excuse, pretext ⟨no tener escapatoria : to have no way out⟩ **2** ESCAPADA : escape, flight
escape *nm* **1** FUGA : escape **2** : exhaust (from a vehicle)
escapismo *nm* : escapism — **escapista** *adj*
escápula *nf* OMÓPLATO : scapula, shoulder blade
escarabajo *nm* : beetle
escaramuza *nf* **1** : skirmish **2** : scrimmage
escaramuzar {21} *vi* : to skirmish
escarapela *nf* : rosette (ornament)
escarbar *vt* **1** : to dig, to scratch up **2** : to poke, to pick **3** ~ **en** : to investigate, to pry into
escarcha *nf* **1** : frost **2** *Mex, PRi* : glitter
escarchar *vt* **1** : to frost, to sugar **2** : to candy (fruit)
escardar *vt* **1** : to weed, to hoe **2** : to weed out
escarlata *adj & nf* : scarlet
escarlatina *nf* : scarlet fever
escarmentar {55} *vt* : to punish, to teach a lesson to — *vi* : to learn one's lesson
escarmiento *nm* **1** : lesson, warning **2** CASTIGO : punishment
escarnio *nm* : ridicule, mockery
escarola *nf* : escarole
escarpa *nf* : escarpment, steep slope
escarpado, -da *adj* : steep, sheer
escasamente *adv* : scarcely, barely
escasear *vi* : to be scarce, to run short
escasez *nf, pl* **-seces** : shortage, scarcity
escaso, -sa *adj* **1** : scarce, scant **2** ~ **de** : short of
escatimar *vt* : to skimp on, to be sparing with ⟨no escatimar esfuerzos : to spare no effort⟩
escayola *nf Spain* **1** : plaster (for casts) **2** : cast (in medicine)
escayolar *vt Spain* : to put (a broken limb) in a cast
escena *nf* **1** : scene **2** : stage
escenario *nm* **1** ESCENA : stage **2** : setting, scene ⟨el escenario del crimen : the scene of the crime⟩
escénico, -ca *adj* **1** : scenic **2** : stage
escenificar {72} *vt* : to stage, to dramatize
escenografía *nf* : set design
escepticismo *nm* : skepticism
escéptico[1], -ca *adj* : skeptical
escéptico[2], -ca *n* : skeptic
escindirse *vr* **1** : to split **2** : to break away
escisión *nf, pl* **-siones** : split, division
esclarecer {53} *vt* **1** ELUCIDAR : to elucidate, to clarify **2** ILUMINAR : to illuminate, to light up
esclarecimiento *nm* ELUCIDACIÓN : elucidation, clarification

esclavitud *nf* : slavery
esclavización *nf, pl* **-ciones** : enslavement
esclavizar {21} *vt* : to enslave
esclavo, -va *n* : slave
esclerosis *nf* esclerosis múltiple : multiple sclerosis
esclusa *nf* : floodgate, lock (of a canal)
escoba *nf* : broom
escobilla *nf* : small broom, brush, whisk broom
escocer {14} *vi* ARDER : to smart, to sting — **escocerse** *vr* : to be sore
escocés[1], -cesa *adj, mpl* **-ceses** **1** : Scottish **2** : tartan, plaid
escocés[2], -cesa *n, mpl* **-ceses** : Scottish person, Scot
escocés[3] *nm* **1** : Scottish, Scots (language) **2** *pl* **-ceses** : Scotch (whiskey)
escofina *nf* : file, rasp
escoger {15} *vt* ELEGIR, SELECCIONAR : to choose, to select
escogido, -da *adj* : choice, select
escolar[1] *adj* : school
escolar[2] *nmf* : student, pupil
escolaridad *nf* : schooling ⟨escolaridad obligatoria : compulsory education⟩
escolarización *nf, pl* **-ciones** : education, schooling
escolarizar {21} *vt* : to educate
escollo *nm* **1** : reef **2** OBSTÁCULO : obstacle
escolta *nmf* : escort
escoltar *vt* : to escort, to accompany
escombro *nm* **1** : debris, rubbish **2** **escombros** *nmpl* : ruins, rubble
esconder *vt* OCULTAR : to hide, to conceal
escondidas *nfpl* **1** : hide-and-seek **2 a** ~ : secretly, in secret
escondite *nm* **1** ESCONDRIJO : hiding place **2** ESCONDIDAS : hide-and-seek
escondrijo *nm* ESCONDITE : hiding place
escopeta *nf* : shotgun
escoplo *nm* : chisel
escorar *vi* : to list, to heel (of a boat)
escorbuto *nm* : scurvy
escoria *nf* **1** : slag, dross **2** HEZ : dregs *pl*, scum ⟨la escoria de la sociedad : the dregs of society⟩
Escorpio[1] *or* **Escorpión** *nm* : Scorpio (sign or constellation)
Escorpio[2] *or* **Escorpión** *nmf* : Scorpio (person)
escorpión *nm, pl* **-piones** ALACRÁN : scorpion
escotado, -da *adj* : low-cut (of clothing)
escote *nm* **1** : (low) neckline ⟨escote en V : V-neck⟩ **2 pagar a escote** : to go dutch
escotilla *nf* : hatch, hatchway
escozor *nm* : smarting, stinging
escriba *nm* : scribe
escribanía *nf CoRi, Arg, Uru* : office of a notary public
escribano, -na *n* **1** : court clerk **2** NOTARIO : notary public
escribir {33} *v* **1** : to write ⟨escribir una novela/palabra : to write a novel/word⟩ ⟨escribir a lápiz : to write in pencil⟩

⟨escribir a mano : to write by hand⟩ ⟨escribir a máquina : to type⟩ **2** : how do you spell ⟨¿cómo se escribe? : how do you spell it?⟩ — **escribirse** *vr* CARTEARSE : to write to one another, to correspond

escrito[1] *pp* → **escribir**

escrito[2], **-ta** *adj* : written

escrito[3] *nm* **1** : written document — **escritos** *nmpl* : writings, works

escritor, -tora *n* : writer

escritorio *nm* : desk

escritorzuelo, -la *n* : hack (writer)

escritura *nf* **1** : writing, handwriting **2** : deed **3 las Escrituras** : the Scriptures

escroto *nm* : scrotum

escrúpulo *nm* : scruple

escrupuloso, -sa *adj* : scrupulous METICULOSO : exact, meticulous — **escrupulosamente** *adv*

escrutador, -dora *adj* : penetrating, searching

escrutar *vt* ESCUDRIÑAR : to scrutinize, to examine closely

escrutinio *nm* : scrutiny

escuadra *nf* **1** : square (instrument) **2** : fleet, squadron

escuadrilla *nf* : squadron, formation, flight

escuadrón *nm, pl* **-drones** : squadron

escuálido, -da *adj* **1** : skinny, scrawny **2** INMUNDO : filthy, squalid

escuchar *vt* **1** : to listen to **2** : to hear — *vi* : to listen — **escucharse** *vr*

escudar *vt* : to shield — **escudarse** *vr* ~ **en** : to hide behind

escudería *nf* : team (in car racing)

escudero *nm* : squire

escudo *nm* **1** : shield **2 escudo de armas** : coat of arms

escudriñar *vt* **1** ESCRUTAR : to scrutinize **2** : to inquire into, to investigate

escuela *nf* **1** : school ⟨escuela privada/pública : private/public school⟩ ⟨escuela nocturna : night school⟩ ⟨escuela de verano : summer school⟩ **2** DEPARTAMENTO : school, department

escueto, -ta *adj* **1** : plain, simple **2** : succinct, concise — **escuetamente** *adv*

escuincle, -cla *n Mex fam* : child, kid

esculcar {72} *vt* : to search

esculpir *vt* **1** : to sculpt **2** : to carve, to engrave — *vi* : to sculpt

escultor, -tora *n* : sculptor

escultórico, -ca *adj* : sculptural

escultura *nf* : sculpture

escultural *adj* : statuesque

escupir *v* : to spit

escupitajo *nm* : spit, gob of spit

escurridizo, -za *adj* : slippery, elusive

escurridor *nm* **1** : dish rack **2** : colander

escurrir *vt* **1** : to wring out **2** : to drain — *vi* **1** : to drain **2** : to drip, to drip-dry — **escurrirse** *vr* : to slip away

ese[1], **esa** *adj, mpl* **esos** : that, those ⟨ese mismo día : that very day⟩ ⟨esos niños : those children⟩ ⟨sale con la chica esa : he's dating that girl⟩

ese[2] *nf* : (letter) s

ese[3], **esa** *or* **ése ésa** *pron, mpl* **esos** *or* **ésos** : that (one), those (ones) *pl* ⟨ese/ése es el mío : that one is mine⟩ ⟨esa/ésa no fue la primera vez : that wasn't the first time⟩ ⟨ese/ése no es el hombre : that's not the man⟩

esencia *nf* : essence

esencial *adj* : essential — **esencialmente** *adv*

esfera *nf* **1** : sphere (object or shape) **2** : sphere ⟨esfera de influencia : sphere of influence⟩ ⟨en las altas esferas : in the highest circles⟩ **3** : face, dial (of a clock)

esférico[1], **-ca** *adj* : spherical

esférico[2] *nm* : ball (in sports)

esfinge *nf* : sphinx

esforzado, -da *adj* **1** : energetic, vigorous **2** VALIENTE : courageous, brave

esforzar {36} *vt* : to strain — **esforzarse** *vr* : to make an effort

esfuerzo *nm* **1** : effort **2** ÁNIMO, VIGOR : spirit, vigor **3 sin** ~ : effortlessly

esfumar *vt* : to tone down, to soften — **esfumarse** *vr* **1** : to fade away, to vanish **2** *fam* : to take off, to leave

esgrima *nf* : fencing (sport)

esgrimir *vt* **1** : to brandish, to wield **2** : to use, to resort to — *vi* : to fence

esgrimista *nmf* : fencer

esguince *nm* : sprain, strain (of a muscle)

eslabón *nm, pl* **-bones** : link

eslavo[1], **-va** *adj* : Slavic

eslavo[2], **-va** *n* : Slav

eslogan *nm, pl* **-lóganes** : slogan

eslora *nf* : length

eslovaco, -ca *adj & n* : Slovakian, Slovak

esloveno, -na *adj & nm* : Slovene, Slovenian

esmaltar *vt* : to enamel

esmalte *nm* **1** : enamel **2 esmalte de uñas** : nail polish

esmerado, -da *adj* : careful, painstaking

esmeralda *nf* : emerald

esmerarse *vr* : to take great pains, to do one's utmost

esmeril *nm* : emery

esmero *nm* : meticulousness, great care

esmoquin *nm, pl* **-quins 1** : tuxedo (suit) **2** : tuxedo jacket, dinner jacket

esnob[1] *adj, pl* **esnobs** : snobbish

esnob[2] *nmf, pl* **esnobs** : snob

esnobismo *nm* : snobbery, snobbishness

esnórquel *nm* : snorkel

eso *pron* (neuter) **1** : that ⟨eso no me gusta : I don't like that⟩ **2 ¡eso es!** : that's it!, that's right! **3 a eso de** : around ⟨a eso de las tres : around three o'clock⟩ **4 en** ~ : at that point, just then **5 por** ~ : for that reason ⟨por eso me voy : that's why I'm leaving⟩

esófago *nm* : esophagus

esos → **ese**

ésos → **ése**

esotérico, -ca *adj* : esoteric — **esotéricamente** *adv*

espabilado, -da *adj* : bright, smart

espabilarse *vr* **1** : to awaken **2** : to get a move on **3** : to get smart, to wise up

espacial *adj* **1** : space **2** : spatial

espaciar *vt* DISTANCIAR : to space out, to spread out

espacio *nm* **1** : space, room ⟨hay mucho espacio : there is plenty of space⟩ ⟨ocupa demasiado espacio : it takes up too much space⟩ ⟨espacios abiertos : open spaces⟩ **2** : space (in printing) ⟨a doble espacio : double-spaced⟩ **3** : period, length (of time) ⟨por espacio de : over a period of⟩ **4** : time slot (in television, etc.) **5** : program ⟨espacio televisivo : television program⟩ **6 espacio exterior** : outer space

espacioso, -sa *adj* : spacious, roomy

espada[1] *nf* **1** : sword **2 espadas** *nfpl* : swords (in the Spanish deck of cards)

espada[2] *nm* MATADOR, TORERO : bull-fighter, matador

espadaña *nf* **1** : belfry **2** : cattail

espagueti *nm or* **espaguetis** *nmpl* : spaghetti

espalda *nf* **1** : back **2 espaldas** *nfpl* : shoulders, back **3** *or* **estilo espalda** : backstroke **4 por la espalda** : from behind

espaldarazo *nm* **1** : recognition, support **2** : slap on the back

espantajo *nm* : scarecrow

espantapájaros *nms & pl* : scarecrow

espantar *vt* ASUSTAR : to scare, to frighten — **espantarse** *vr*

espanto *nm* : fright, fear, horror

espantoso, -sa *adj* **1** : frightening, terrifying **2** : frightful, dreadful — **espantosamente** *adv*

español[1], **-ñola** *adj* : Spanish

español[2], **-ñola** *n* : Spaniard

español[3] *nm* CASTELLANO : Spanish (language)

esparadrapo *nm* : adhesive bandage, Band-Aid™

esparcimiento *nm* **1** DIVERSIÓN, RECREO : entertainment, recreation **2** DESCANSO : relaxation **3** DISEMINACIÓN : dissemination, spreading

esparcir {83} *vt* DISPERSAR : to scatter, to spread — **esparcirse** *vr* **1** : to spread out **2** DESCANSARSE : to take it easy **3** DIVERTIRSE : to amuse oneself

espárrago *nm* : asparagus

espartano, -na *adj* : severe, austere

espasmo *nm* : spasm

espasmódico, -ca *adj* : spasmodic — **espasmódicamente** *adv*

espástico, -ca *adj* : spastic

espátula *nf* : spatula

especia *nf* : spice

especial *adj & nm* : special

especialidad *nf* : specialty

especialista *nmf* : specialist, expert

especialización *nf, pl* **-ciones** : specialization

especializarse {21} *vr* : to specialize

especialmente *adv* : especially, particularly

especie *nf* **1** : species **2** CLASE, TIPO : type, kind, sort

especificación *nf, pl* **-ciones** : specification

especificar {72} *vt* : to specify

específico, -ca *adj* : specific — **específicamente** *adv*

espécimen *nm, pl* **especímenes** : specimen

espectacular *adj* : spectacular — **espectacularmente** *adv*

espectáculo *nm* **1** : spectacle, sight **2** : show, performance

espectador, -dora *n* : spectator, onlooker

espectro *nm* **1** : ghost, specter **2** : spectrum

especulación *nf, pl* **-ciones** : speculation

especulador, -dora *n* : speculator

especular *vi* : to speculate

especulativo, -va *adj* : speculative

espejismo *nm* **1** : mirage **2** : illusion

espejo *nm* : mirror

espejuelos *nmpl* ANTEOJOS : spectacles, glasses

espeluznante *adj* : hair-raising, terrifying

espera *nf* : wait

esperado, -da *adj* : anticipated

esperanza *nf* : hope, expectation ⟨dar esperanzas : to give hope⟩ ⟨perder la esperanza : to lose hope⟩ ⟨esperanza de vida : life expectancy⟩

esperanzado, -da *adj* : hopeful

esperanzador, -dora *adj* : encouraging, promising

esperanzar {21} *vt* : to give hope to

esperar *vt* **1** AGUARDAR : to wait for ⟨espero a un amigo : I'm waiting for a friend⟩ ⟨esperé una hora : I waited for an hour⟩ **2** : to expect ⟨no esperaba visitas : I wasn't expecting visitors⟩ ⟨como era de esperar : as was to be expected⟩ ⟨cuando uno menos lo espera : when you least expect it⟩ **3** : to hope ⟨espero poder trabajar : I hope to be able to work⟩ ⟨espero que sí/no : I hope so/not⟩ ⟨espero que llame : I hope he calls⟩ — *vi* : to wait ⟨espere un momento, por favor : just a moment, please⟩ ⟨hay que esperar a que llueva : we have to wait for it to rain⟩ — **esperarse** *vr* **1** : to expect, to be hoped ⟨como podría esperarse : as would be expected⟩ **2** : to hold on, to hang on ⟨espérate un momento : hold on a minute⟩

esperma *nmf* : sperm

esperpéntico, -ca *adj* GROTESCO : grotesque

esperpento *nm fam* MAMARRACHO : sight, fright ⟨voy hecha un esperpento : I really look a sight⟩

espesante *nm* : thickener

espesar *vt* : to thicken — **espesarse** *vr*

espeso, -sa *adj* : thick, heavy, dense

espesor *nm* : thickness, density

espesura *nf* **1** : thickness **2** : thicket

espetar *vt* **1** : to blurt out **2** : to skewer

espía *nmf* : spy

espiar {85} *vt* : to spy on, to observe *vi* : to spy

espiga *nf* **1** : ear (of wheat) **2** : spike (of flowers)

espigado, -da *adj* : willowy, slender

espigar {52} *vt* : to glean, to gather — **espigarse** *vr* : to grow quickly, to shoot up

espigón *nm, pl* **-gones** : breakwater

espina *nf* **1** : thorn **2** : spine ⟨espina dorsal : spinal column⟩ **3** : fish bone **4**

darle mala espina a alguien : to make someone uneasy

espinaca *nf* **1** : spinach (plant) **2 espinacas** *nfpl* : spinach (food)

espinal *adj* : spinal

espinazo *nm* : backbone

espinilla *nf* **1** BARRO, GRANO : pimple **2** : shin

espino *nm* : hawthorn

espinoso, -sa *adj* **1** : thorny, prickly **2** : bony (of fish) **3** : knotty, difficult

espionaje *nm* : espionage

espiración *nf, pl* **-ciones** : exhalation

espiral *adj & nf* : spiral

espirar *vt* EXHALAR : to breathe out, to give off — *vi* : to exhale

espiritismo *nm* : spiritualism

espiritista *nmf* : spiritualist

espíritu *nm* **1** : spirit **2** ÁNIMO : state of mind, spirits *pl* **3 el Espíritu Santo** : the Holy Ghost

espiritual *adj* : spiritual — **espiritualmente** *adv*

espiritualidad *nf* : spirituality

espita *nf* : spigot, tap

esplendidez *nf, pl* **-deces** ESPLENDOR : magnificence, splendor

espléndido, -da *adj* **1** : splendid, magnificent **2** : generous, lavish — **espléndidamente** *adv*

esplendor *nm* ESPLENDIDEZ : splendor

esplendoroso, -sa *adj* MAGNÍFICO : magnificent, grand

espliego *nm* LAVANDA : lavender

espolear *vt* : to spur on

espoleta *nf* **1** DETONADOR : detonator, fuse **2** : wishbone

espolón *nm, pl* **-lones** : spur (of poultry), fetlock (of a horse)

espolvorear *vt* : to sprinkle, to dust

esponja *nf* **1** : sponge **2 tirar la esponja** : to throw in the towel

esponjado, -da *adj* : spongy

esponjoso, -sa *adj* **1** : spongy **2** : soft, fluffy

esponsales *nmpl* : betrothal, engagement

espontaneidad *nf* : spontaneity

espontáneo, -nea *adj* : spontaneous — **espontáneamente** *adv*

espora *nf* : spore

esporádico, -ca *adj* : sporadic — **esporádicamente** *adv*

esposar *vt* : to handcuff

esposas *nfpl* : handcuffs

esposo, -sa *n* : spouse, wife *f*, husband *m*

espray *nm, pl* **esprays** : spray

esprint *nm* : sprint

esprintar *vi* : to sprint

esprínter *nmf* : sprinter

espuela *nf* : spur

espuma *nf* **1** : foam ⟨espuma de afeitar : shaving cream⟩ ⟨espuma de baño : bubble bath (soap)⟩ ⟨baño de espuma : bubble bath⟩ ⟨crecer/subir como la espuma : to mushroom, to skyrocket⟩ **2** : lather **3** : froth, head (on beer)

espumadera *nf* : slotted spoon

espumar *vi* : to foam, to froth — *vt* : to skim off

espumoso, -sa *adj* : foamy, frothy

espurio, -ria *adj* : spurious

esqueje *nm* : cutting (from a plant)

esquela *nf* **1** : note **2** : notice, announcement

esquelético, -ca *adj* : emaciated, skeletal

esqueleto *nm* **1** : skeleton **2** ARMAZÓN : framework

esquema *nm* BOSQUEJO : outline, sketch, plan

esquemático, -ca *adj* : schematic

esquí *nm, pl* **esquíes 1** : ski **2 esquí acuático** : water ski, waterskiing

esquiador, -dora *n* : skier

esquiar {85} *vi* : to ski

esquilar *vt* TRASQUILAR : to shear

esquimal *adj & nmf* : Eskimo

esquina *nf* : corner

esquinazo *nm* **1** : corner **2 dar esquinazo a** *fam* : to stand up, to give the slip to

esquirla *nf* : splinter (of bone, glass, etc.)

esquirol *nm* ROMPEHUELGAS : strikebreaker, scab

esquisto *nm* : shale

esquivar *vt* **1** EVADIR : to dodge, to evade **2** EVITAR : to avoid

esquivo, -va *adj* **1** HURAÑO : aloof, unsociable **2** : shy **3** : elusive, evasive

esquizofrenia *nf* : schizophrenia

esquizofrénico, -ca *adj & n* : schizophrenic

esta *adj* → **este**[1]

ésta → **éste**

estabilidad *nf* : stability

estabilizar {21} *vt* : to stabilize — **estabilizarse** *vr* — **estabilización** *nf* — **estabilizador** *nm*

estable *adj* : stable, steady

establecer {53} *vt* **1** FUNDAR, INSTITUIR : to establish, to found (a city, etc.), to set up (a system, etc.) **2** : to establish (a law, etc.), to set (a standard, etc.) **3** : to establish (relations, etc.) **4** DEMOSTRAR : to establish, to show, to prove — **establecerse** *vr* **1** INSTALARSE : to settle, to establish oneself **2** : to establish, to show, to prove

establecimiento *nm* **1** : establishing **2** : establishment, institution, office

establo *nm* : stable

estaca *nf* : stake, picket, post

estacada *nf* **1** : picket fence **2** : stockade

estacar {72} *vt* **1** : to stake out **2** : to fasten down with stakes — **estacarse** *vr* : to remain rigid

estación *nf, pl* **-ciones 1** : station ⟨estación de servicio : service station, gas station⟩ **2** : season

estacional *adj* : seasonal

estacionamiento *nm* **1** : parking **2** : parking lot

estacionar *vt* **1** : to place, to station **2** : to park — **estacionarse** *vr* **1** : to park **2** : to remain stationary

estacionario, -ria *adj* **1** : stationary **2** : stable

estada *nf* → **estadía**

estadía *nf* ESTANCIA : stay, sojourn

estadio *nm* **1** : stadium **2** : phase, stage

estadista *nmf* : statesman

estadística *nf* **1** : statistic, figure **2** : statistics

estadístico[1], **-ca** *adj* : statistical — **estadísticamente** *adv*

estadístico[2], **-ca** *n* : statistician

estado *nm* **1** : state, condition ⟨estar en buen/mal estado : to be in good/bad condition⟩ **2** : state (nation or region) ⟨los Estados Unidos : the United States⟩ **3** : state, government **4** : status ⟨estado civil : marital status⟩ **5 estado de ánimo** : state of mind **6 estado de cuenta** : account statement **7 estado de emergencia** : state of emergency **8 estado de la nación** : state of the nation **9 estado de salud** : (state of) health, condition **10 estar en estado** : to be expecting, to be pregnant

estadounidense *adj & nmf* AMERICANO, NORTEAMERICANO : American

estafa *nf* : swindle, fraud

estafador, -dora *n* : cheat, swindler

estafar *vt* DEFRAUDAR : to swindle, to defraud

estafeta *nf* **1** : baton (in a relay race) **2** : post office

estalactita *nf* : stalactite

estalagmita *nf* : stalagmite

estallar *vi* **1** REVENTAR : to burst, to explode, to erupt **2** : to break out

estallido *nm* **1** EXPLOSIÓN : explosion **2** : report (of a gun) **3** : outbreak, outburst

estambre *nm* **1** : worsted (fabric) **2** : stamen

estamento *nm* : stratum, class

estampa *nf* **1** ILUSTRACIÓN, IMAGEN : printed image, illustration **2** ASPECTO : appearance, demeanor

estampado[1], **-da** *adj* : patterned, printed

estampado[2] *nm* : print, pattern

estampar *vt* : to stamp, to print, to engrave

estampida *nf* : stampede

estampido *nm* ESTALLIDO : bang

estampilla *nf* **1** : rubber stamp **2** SELLO, TIMBRE : postage stamp

estancado, -da *adj* : stagnant

estancamiento *nm* : stagnation

estancar {72} *vt* **1** : to dam up, to hold back **2** : to bring to a halt, to deadlock — **estancarse** *vr* **1** : to stagnate **2** : to be brought to a standstill, to be deadlocked

estancia *nf* **1** ESTADÍA : stay, sojourn **2** : ranch, farm

estanciero, -ra *n* : rancher, farmer

estanco, -ca *adj* : watertight

estándar *adj & nm* : standard

estandarización *nf, pl* **-ciones** : standardization

estandarizar {21} *vt* : to standardize

estandarte *nm* : standard, banner

estanque *nm* **1** : pool, pond **2** : tank, reservoir

estanquillo *nm Mex* : general store

estante *nm* REPISA : shelf

estantería *nf* : shelves *pl*, bookcase

estaño *nm* : tin

estaquilla *nf* **1** : peg **2** ESPIGA : spike

estar {34} *v aux* : to be ⟨estoy aprendiendo inglés : I'm learning English⟩ ⟨está terminado : it's finished⟩ — *vi* **1** (*indicating a state or condition*) : to be ⟨está lleno : it's full⟩ ⟨está claro que . . . : it's clear that . . .⟩ ⟨ya estás mejor? : are you feeling better now?⟩ ⟨estoy casado : I'm married⟩ ⟨está sin trabajo : she's out of work, she has no job⟩ ⟨está muy alto : he's so tall, he's gotten very tall⟩ **2** (*indicating location*) : to be ⟨están en la mesa : they're on the table⟩ ⟨estamos en la página 2 : we're on page 2⟩ ⟨ahí está el problema : therein lies the problem⟩ **3** : to be at home ⟨¿está Julia? : is Julia in?⟩ **4** : to be, to remain ⟨estaré aquí 5 días : I'll be here for 5 days⟩ **5** : to be ready, to be done ⟨estará para las diez : it will be ready by ten o'clock⟩ **6** : to agree ⟨¿estamos? : are we in agreement?⟩ ⟨estoy contigo : I'm with you⟩ **7** ¿**cómo estás?** : how are you? **8** ¡**está bien!** : all right!, that's fine! **9** ~ **a** : to cost **10** ~ **a** : to be ⟨¿a qué día estamos? : what day is today?, what's today's date?⟩ ⟨está a 15 kilómetros del centro : it's 15 kilometers from the downtown⟩ **11** ~ **con** : to have ⟨está con fiebre : she has a fever⟩ **12** ~ **de** : to be ⟨estoy de vacaciones : I'm on vacation⟩ ⟨está de director hoy : he's acting as director today⟩ **13 estar bien/mal** : to be well/sick **14** ~ **para** : to be in the mood for **15** ~ **para** : to be for (a purpose) ⟨para eso está : that's what it's here for⟩ **16** ~ **por** : to be in favor of **17** ~ **por** : to be about to ⟨está por cerrar : it's on the verge of closing⟩ **18 estar de más** : to be unnecessary **19 estar que** (*indicating a state or condition*) ⟨está que echa chispas : he's hopping mad⟩ — **estarse** *vr* QUEDARSE : to stay, to remain ⟨¡estáte quieto! : be still!⟩

estarcir {83} *vt* : to stencil

estárter *nm* : choke (of a motor)

estatal *adj* : state, national

estática *nf* : static

estático, -ca *adj* : static

estatizar {21} *vt* : to nationalize — **estatización** *nf*

estatua *nf* : statue

estatuilla *nf* : statuette, figurine

estatura *nf* : height, stature ⟨de mediana estatura : of medium height⟩

estatus *nm* : status, prestige

estatutario, -ria *adj* : statutory

estatuto *nm* : statute

este[1], **esta** *adj, mpl* **estos** : this, these ⟨este año : this year⟩ ⟨estas señoras : these ladies⟩ ⟨es un sinvergüenza el tipo este : this guy is a crook⟩

este[2] *adj* : eastern, east

este[3] *nm* **1** ORIENTE : east **2** : east wind **3 el Este** : the East, the Orient

este[4], **esta** *or* **éste, ésta** *pron, mpl* **estos** *or* **éstos** **1** : this (one), these (ones) *pl* ⟨este/éste es el mío : this one is mine⟩ ⟨esta/ésta no es la primera vez : this isn't the first time⟩ ⟨un día de estos/éstos : one of these days⟩ **2** : the latter ⟨se lo

dijo a su hijo, y este/éste me llamó : he
told his son, who called me⟩

estela *nf* **1** : wake (of a ship) **2** RASTRO
: trail (of dust, smoke, etc.)

estelar *adj* : stellar

estelarizar {21} *vt Mex* : to star in, to be
the star of

esténcil *nm* : stencil

estepa *nf* : steppe

estera *nf* : mat

estéreo *adj & nm* : stereo

estereofónico, -ca *adj* : stereophonic

estereotipado, -da *adj* : stereotyped

estereotipar *vt* : to stereotype

estereotipo *nm* : stereotype

estéril **1** : sterile **2** : infertile, sterile,
barren **3** : futile, vain

esterilidad *nf* **1** : sterility **2** : infertility

esterilizar {21} *vt* **1** : to sterilize, to disinfect **2** : to sterilize (a person), to spay (an
animal) — **esterilización** *nf*

esterlina *adj* : sterling

esternón *nm, pl* **-nones** : sternum

estero *nm* : estuary

esteroide *nm* : steroid

estertor *nm* : death rattle

estética *nf* : aesthetics

esteticista *nmf* : beautician

estético, -ca *adj* : aesthetic — **estética-
mente** *adv*

estetoscopio *nm* : stethoscope

estibador, -dora *n* : longshoreman, stevedore

estiércol *nm* : dung, manure

estigma *nm* : stigma

estigmatizar {21} *vt* : to stigmatize, to
brand

estilarse *vr* : to be in fashion

estilete *nm* : stiletto

estilista *nmf* : stylist

estilizar {21} *vt* : to stylize

estilo *nm* **1** : style ⟨estilo de vida : life-
style⟩ **2** : fashion, manner **3** : stylus

estilográfica *nf* : fountain pen

estima *nf* ESTIMACIÓN : esteem, regard

estimable *adj* **1** : considerable **2** : estimable, esteemed

estimación *nf, pl* **-ciones** **1** ESTIMA : esteem, regard **2** : estimate

estimado, -da *adj* : esteemed, dear ⟨Es-
timado señor Ortiz : Dear Mr. Ortiz⟩

estimar *vt* **1** APRECIAR : to esteem, to respect **2** EVALUAR : to estimate, to appraise **3** OPINAR : to consider, to deem

estimulación *nf, pl* **-ciones** : stimulation

estimulante¹ *adj* : stimulating

estimulante² *nm* : stimulant

estimular *vt* **1** : to stimulate **2** : to encourage

estímulo *nm* **1** : stimulus **2** INCENTIVO
: incentive, encouragement

estío *nm* : summertime

estipendio *nm* **1** : salary **2** : stipend, remuneration

estipular *vt* : to stipulate — **estipulación**
nf

estirado, -da *adj* **1** : stretched, extended **2**
PRESUMIDO : stuck-up, conceited

estiramiento *nm* **1** : stretching **2** estiramiento facial : face-lift

estirar *vt* : to stretch (out), to extend —
estirarse *vr*

estirón *nm, pl* **-rones** **1** : pull, tug **2** dar
un estirón : to grow quickly, to shoot up

estirpe *nf* LINAJE : lineage, stock

estival *adj* VERANIEGO : summer

esto *pron* (*neuter*) **1** : this ⟨¿qué es esto?
: what is this?⟩ **2 en ~** : at this point **3
por ~** : for this reason

estocada *nf* **1** : final thrust (in bullfighting) **2** : thrust, lunge (in fencing)

estofa *nf* CLASE : class, quality ⟨de baja
estofa : low-class, poor-quality⟩

estofado *nm* COCIDO, GUISADO : stew

estofar *vt* GUISAR : to stew

estoicismo *nm* : stoicism

estoico¹, -ca *adj* : stoic, stoical

estoico², -ca *n* : stoic

estola *nf* : stole

estolón *nm, pl* **-lones** : runner (of a plant)

estomacal *adj* GÁSTRICO : stomach, gastric

estómago *nm* : stomach

estoniano, -na *adj & n* : Estonian

estonio, -nia *adj & n* : Estonian

estopa *nf* **1** : tow (yarn or cloth) **2** : burlap

estopilla *nf* : cheesecloth

estoque *nm* : rapier, sword

estorbar *vt* OBSTRUIR : to obstruct, to hinder — *vi* : to get in the way

estorbo *nm* **1** : obstacle, hindrance **2**
: nuisance

estornino *nm* : starling

estornudar *vi* : to sneeze

estornudo *nm* : sneeze

estos *adj* → **este¹**

éstos → **éste¹**

estoy → **estar**

estrabismo *nm* : squint

estrado *nm* **1** : dais, platform **2** : bench
(of a judge) **3** : witness stand **4 estrados**
nmpl : courts of law

estrafalario, -ria *adj* ESTRAMBÓTICO,
EXCÉNTRICO : eccentric, bizarre

estragar {52} *vt* DEVASTAR : to ruin, to
devastate

estragón *nm* : tarragon

estragos *nmpl* **1** : ravages, destruction,
devastation ⟨los estragos de la guerra
: the ravages of war⟩ **2 hacer estragos
en** *or* **causar estragos entre** : to play
havoc with

estrambótico, -ca *adj* ESTRAFALARIO,
EXCÉNTRICO : eccentric, bizarre

estrangulador, -dora *n* : strangler

estrangulamiento *nm* : strangling, strangulation

estrangular *vt* AHOGAR : to strangle —
estrangulación *nf*

estratagema *nf* ARTIMAÑA : stratagem,
ruse

estratega *nmf* : strategist

estrategia *nf* : strategy

estratégico, -ca *adj* : strategic, tactical —
estratégicamente *adv*

estratificado, -da *adj* : stratified

estrato *nm* : stratum, layer

estratosfera *nf* : stratosphere

estratosférico, -ca adj **1** : stratospheric **2** : astronomical, exorbitant

estrechamiento nm **1** : narrowing **2** : narrow point **3** : tightening, strengthening (of relations)

estrechar vt **1** : to narrow **2** : to tighten, to strengthen (a bond) **3** : to hug, to embrace **4 estrechar la mano de** : to shake hands with — **estrecharse** vr

estrechez nf, pl **-checes 1** : tightness, narrowness **2 estrecheces** nfpl : financial problems

estrecho¹, -cha adj **1** : tight, narrow **2** ÍNTIMO : close — **estrechamente** adv

estrecho² nm : strait, narrows

estrella nf **1** ASTRO : star ⟨estrella fugaz : shooting star⟩ **2** : destiny ⟨tener buena estrella : to be born lucky⟩ **3** : movie star **4 estrella de mar** : starfish

estrellado, -da adj **1** : starry **2** : star-shaped **3 huevos estrellados** : fried eggs

estrellamiento nm : crash, collision

estrellar vt **1** : to smash, to crash — **estrellarse** vr : to crash, to collide

estrellato nm : stardom

estremecedor, -dora adj : horrifying

estremecer {53} vt : to cause to shake — vi : to tremble, to shake — **estremecerse** vr : to shudder, to shiver (with emotion)

estremecimiento nm : trembling, shaking, shivering

estrenar vt **1** : to use for the first time **2** : to premiere, to open — **estrenarse** vr : to make one's debut

estreno nm DEBUT : debut, premiere

estreñido, -da adj : constipated

estreñimiento nm : constipation

estreñir {67} vt : to constipate, to make constipated — vi : to cause constipation — **estreñirse** vr to get constipated

estrépito nm ESTRUENDO : clamor, din

estrepitoso, -sa adj : clamorous, noisy — **estrepitosamente** adv

estrés nm, pl **estreses** : stress

estresante adj : stressful

estresar vt : to stress, to stress out — **estresado, -da** adj

estría nf : fluting, groove

estribación nf, pl **-ciones 1** : spur, ridge **2 estribaciones** nfpl : foothills

estribar vi FUNDARSE ~ **en** : to be due to, to stem from

estribillo nm : refrain, chorus

estribo nm **1** : stirrup **2** : abutment, buttress **3 perder los estribos** : to lose one's temper

estribor nm : starboard

estricto, -ta adj SEVERO : strict, severe — **estrictamente** adv

estridente adj : strident, shrill, loud — **estridentemente** adv

estrofa nf : stanza, verse

estrógeno nm : estrogen

estropajo nm : scouring pad

estropear vt **1** ARRUINAR : to ruin, to spoil **2** : to break, to damage — **estropearse** vr **1** : to spoil, to go bad **2** : to break down — **estropeado, -da** adj

estropicio nm DAÑO : damage, breakage

estructura nf : structure, framework

estructuración nf, pl **-ciones** : structuring, structure

estructural adj : structural — **estructuralmente** adv

estructurar vt : to structure, to organize

estruendo nm ESTRÉPITO : racket, din, roar

estruendoso, -sa adj : resounding, thunderous

estrujar vt APRETAR : to press, to squeeze

estuario nm : estuary

estuche nm : kit, case

estuco nm : stucco

estudiado, -da adj : affected, mannered

estudiantado nm : student body, students pl

estudiante nmf : student

estudiantil adj : student ⟨la vida estudiantil : student life⟩

estudiar v : to study

estudio nm **1** : study ⟨estar en estudio : to be under consideration⟩ ⟨un estudio sobre la salud nacional : a study of the nation's health⟩ **2** : studio (room or office) **3** : studio (for filming, etc.) **4** : studio (apartment) **5 estudios** nmpl : studies, education ⟨estudios primarios/secundarios/superiores : primary/secondary/higher education⟩ ⟨tener estudios en/de algo : to have studied something⟩

estudioso, -sa adj : studious

estufa nf **1** : stove, heater **2** Col, Mex : cooking stove, range

estupefacción nf, pl **-ciones** : astonishment

estupefaciente¹ adj : narcotic

estupefaciente² nm DROGA, NARCÓTICO : drug, narcotic

estupefacto, -ta adj : astonished, stunned

estupendo, -da adj MARAVILLOSO : stupendous, marvelous — **estupendamente** adv

estupidez nf, pl **-deces 1** : stupidity **2** : nonsense

estúpido¹, -da adj : stupid — **estúpidamente** adv

estúpido², -da n IDIOTA : idiot, fool

estupor nm **1** : stupor **2** : amazement

esturión nm, pl **-riones** : sturgeon

estuvo, etc. → **estar**

esvástica nf : swastika

etanol nm : ethanol

etapa nf FASE : stage, phase

etcétera¹ : et cetera, and so on

etcétera² nmf : et cetera

éter nm : ether

etéreo, -rea adj : ethereal, heavenly

eternidad nf : eternity

eternizar {21} vt PERPETUAR : to make eternal, to perpetuate — **eternizarse** vr fam : to take forever

eterno, -na adj : eternal, endless — **eternamente** adv

ética nf : ethics

ético, -ca adj : ethical — **éticamente** adv

etílico, -ca adj **1** : alcohol, alcoholic ⟨intoxicación etílica : alcohol poisoning⟩ **2** : inebriated, drunken

etimología *nf* : etymology
etimológico, -ca *adj* : etymological
etíope *adj & nmf* : Ethiopian
etiqueta *nf* **1** : etiquette **2** : tag, label **3 de ~** : formal, dressy
etiquetar *vt* : to label
etnia *nf* : ethnic group
étnico, -ca *adj* : ethnic
eucalipto *nm* : eucalyptus
Eucaristía *nf* : Eucharist, communion
eufemismo *nm* : euphemism
eufemístico, -ca *adj* : euphemistic
euforia *nf* : euphoria, joyousness
eufórico, -ca *adj* : euphoric, exuberant, joyous — **eufóricamente** *adv*
eunuco *nm* : eunuch
euro *nm* : euro
europeo, -pea *adj & n* : European
euskera *nm* : Basque (language)
eutanasia *nf* : euthanasia
evacuación *nf, pl* **-ciones** : evacuation
evacuar *vt* **1** : to evacuate, to vacate **2** : to carry out — *vi* **1** : to have a bowel movement, to move one's bowels
evadir *vt* ELUDIR : to evade, to avoid — **evadirse** *vr* : to escape, to slip away
evaluación *nf, pl* **-ciones** : assessment, evaluation
evaluador, -dora *n* : assessor
evaluar {3} *vt* : to evaluate, to assess, to appraise
evangélico, -ca *adj* : evangelical — **evangélicamente** *adv*
evangelio *nm* : gospel
evangelismo *nm* : evangelism
evangelista *nmf* : evangelist
evangelizador, -dora *n* : evangelist, missionary
evaporación *nf, pl* **-ciones** : evaporation
evaporar *vt* : to evaporate — **evaporarse** *vr* ESFUMARSE : to disappear, to vanish
evasión *nf, pl* **-siones 1** : escape, flight **2** : evasion, dodge
evasiva *nf* : excuse, pretext
evasivo, -va *adj* : evasive
evento *nm* : event
eventual *adj* **1** : possible **2** : temporary ⟨trabajadores eventuales : temporary workers⟩ — **eventualmente** *adv*
eventualidad *nf* : possibility, eventuality
evidencia *nf* **1** : evidence, proof **2 poner en evidencia** : to demonstrate, to make clear
evidenciar *vt* : to demonstrate, to show — **evidenciarse** *vr* : to be evident
evidente *adj* : evident, obvious, clear — **evidentemente** *adv*
eviscerar *vt* : to eviscerate
evitable *adj* : avoidable, preventable
evitar *vt* **1** : to avoid **2** PREVENIR : to prevent **3** ELUDIR : to escape, to elude
evocación *nf, pl* **-ciones** : evocation
evocador, -dora *adj* : evocative
evocar {72} *vt* **1** : to evoke **2** RECORDAR : to recall
evolución *nf, pl* **-ciones 1** : evolution **2** : development, progress
evolucionar *vi* **1** : to evolve **2** : to change, to develop
evolutivo, -va *adj* : evolutionary

ex *nmf* : ex
ex- *or* **ex** *pref* : ex-, former ⟨exmarido, ex marido : ex-husband⟩
exabrupto *nm* : pointed remark
exacerbar *vt* **1** : to exacerbate, to aggravate **2** : to irritate, to exasperate
exactamente *adv* : exactly
exactitud *nf* PRECISIÓN : accuracy, precision, exactitude
exacto, -ta *adj* PRECISO : accurate, precise, exact
exageración *nf, pl* **-ciones** : exaggeration
exagerado, -da *adj* **1** : exaggerated **2** : excessive — **exageradamente** *adv*
exagerar *v* : to exaggerate
exaltación *nf, pl* **-ciones 1** : exaltation **2** : excitement, agitation
exaltado¹, -da *adj* : excitable, hotheaded
exaltado², -da *n* : hothead
exaltar *vt* **1** ENSALZAR : to exalt, to extol **2** : to excite, to agitate — **exaltarse** *vr* ACALORARSE : to get overexcited
ex-alumno → alumno
examen *nm, pl* **exámenes 1** : examination, test ⟨examen final/oral : final/written exam⟩ ⟨examen de manejo/conducir : driving test⟩ ⟨hacer/dar un examen : to take a test⟩ **2** : consideration, investigation ⟨someter algo a examen : to examine something⟩
examinar *vt* **1** : to examine **2** INSPECCIONAR : to inspect — **examinarse** *vr* : to take an exam
exánime *adj* **1** : lifeless **2** : exhausted
exasperante *adj* : exasperating
exasperar *vt* IRRITAR : to exasperate, to irritate — **exasperación** *nf*
excavación *nf, pl* **-ciones** : excavation
excavadora *nf* : excavator
excavar *v* : to excavate, to dig
excedente¹ *adj* **1** : excessive **2** : excess, surplus
excedente² *nm* : surplus, excess
exceder *vt* : to exceed, to surpass — **excederse** *vr* : to go too far
excelencia *nf* **1** : excellence **2** : excellency ⟨Su Excelencia : His Excellency⟩
excelente *adj* : excellent — **excelentemente** *adv*
excelso, -sa *adj* : lofty, sublime
excentricidad *nf* : eccentricity
excéntrico, -ca *adj & n* : eccentric
excepción *nf, pl* **-ciones** : exception ⟨a/con excepción de : with the exception of⟩
excepcional *adj* EXTRAORDINARIO : exceptional, extraordinary, rare — **excepcionalmente** *adv*
excepto *prep* SALVO : except
exceptuar {3} *vt* EXCLUIR : to except, to exclude
excesivo, -va *adj* : excessive — **excesivamente** *adv*
exceso *nm* **1** : excess **2 excesos** *nmpl* : excesses, abuses **3 exceso de velocidad** : speeding
excitabilidad *nf* : excitability
excitación *nf, pl* **-ciones** : excitement
excitante *adj* : exciting

excitar *vt* : to excite, to arouse — **excitarse** *vr*

exclamación *nf, pl* **-ciones** : exclamation

exclamar *v* : to exclaim

excluir {41} *vt* EXCEPTUAR : to exclude, to leave out

exclusión *nf, pl* **-siones** : exclusion

exclusividad *nf* 1 : exclusiveness 2 : exclusive rights *pl*

exclusivo, -va *adj* : exclusive — **exclusivamente** *adv*

excombatiente *nmf* : war veteran

excomulgar {52} *vt* : to excommunicate

excomunión *nf, pl* **-niones** : excommunication

excreción *nf, pl* **-ciones** : excretion

excremento *nm* : excrement

excretar *vt* : to excrete

exculpar *vt* : to exonerate, to exculpate — **exculpación** *nf*

excursión *nf, pl* **-siones** : excursion, outing

excursionista *nmf* 1 : sightseer, tourist 2 : hiker

excusa *nf* 1 PRETEXTO : excuse ⟨poner excusas : to make excuses⟩ 2 DISCULPA : apology

excusado *nm Mex* : toilet

excusar *vt* 1 : to excuse 2 : to exempt — **excusarse** *vr* : to apologize, to send one's regrets

execrable *adj* : detestable, abominable

exención *nf, pl* **-ciones** : exemption

exento, -ta *adj* 1 : exempt, free 2 **exento de impuestos** : tax-exempt

exequias *nfpl* FUNERALES : funeral rites

exesposa *or* **ex esposa** *nf* : ex-wife

exhalación *nf, pl* **-ciones** 1 : exhalation 2 : shooting star ⟨salió como una exhalación : he took off like a shot⟩

exhalar *vt* ESPIRAR : to exhale, to give off

exhaustivo, -va *adj* : exhaustive — **exhaustivamente** *adv*

exhausto, -ta *adj* AGOTADO : exhausted, worn-out

exhibición *nf, pl* **-ciones** 1 : exhibition, show 2 : showing

exhibir *vt* : to exhibit, to show, to display — **exhibirse** *vr*

exhortación *nf, pl* **-ciones** : exhortation

exhortar *vt* : to exhort

exhumar *vt* DESENTERRAR : to exhume — **exhumación** *nf*

exigencia *nf* : demand, requirement

exigente *adj* : demanding, exacting

exigir {35} *vt* 1 : to demand, to require 2 : to exact, to levy

exiguo, -gua *adj* : meager

exiliado[1], -da *adj* : exiled, in exile

exiliado[2], -da *n* : exile

exiliar *vt* DESTERRAR : to exile, to banish — **exiliarse** *vr* : to go into exile

exilio *nm* DESTIERRO : exile

eximio, -mia *adj* : distinguished, eminent

eximir *vt* EXONERAR : to exempt

existencia *nf* 1 : existence 2 **existencias** *nfpl* MERCANCÍA : goods, stock

existente *adj* 1 : existing, in existence 2 : in stock

existir *vi* : to exist

exitazo *nm* : big/huge success, big/huge hit, smash

éxito *nm* 1 TRIUNFO : success, hit 2 **tener éxito** : to be successful

exitoso, -sa *adj* : successful — **exitosamente** *adv*

exmarido *or* **ex marido** *nm* : ex-husband

éxodo *nm* : exodus

exoneración *nf, pl* **-ciones** EXENCIÓN : exoneration, exemption

exonerar *vt* 1 EXIMIR : to exempt, to exonerate 2 DESPEDIR : to dismiss

exorbitante *adj* : exorbitant

exorcismo *nm* : exorcism — **exorcista** *nmf*

exorcizar {21} *vt* : to exorcise

exótico, -ca *adj* : exotic

expandir *vt* EXPANSIONAR : to expand — **expandirse** *vr* : to spread

expansión *nf, pl* **-siones** 1 : expansion, spread 2 DIVERSIÓN : recreation, relaxation

expansionar *vt* EXPANDIR : to expand — **expansionarse** *vr* 1 : to expand 2 DIVERTIRSE : to amuse oneself, to relax

expansivo, -va *adj* : expansive

expatriado, -da *adj & n* : expatriate

expatriar {85} *vt* 1 : to expatriate, to exile — **expatriarse** *vr* 1 EMIGRAR : to emigrate 2 : to go into exile

expectación *nf, pl* **-ciones** : expectation, anticipation

expectante *adj* : expectant

expectativa *nf* 1 : expectation, hope ⟨estar a la expectativa de : to await, to wait for⟩ ⟨expectativa(s) de la vida : life expectancy⟩ 2 **expectativas** *nfpl* : prospects

expedición *nf, pl* **-ciones** : expedition

expediente *nm* 1 : expedient, means 2 ARCHIVO : file, dossier, record

expedir {54} *vt* 1 EMITIR : to issue 2 DESPACHAR : to dispatch, to send

expedito, -ta *adj* 1 : free, clear 2 : quick, easy

expeler *vt* : to expel, to eject

expendedor, -dora *n* : dealer, seller

expendio *nm* TIENDA : store, shop

expensas *nfpl* 1 : expenses, costs 2 **a expensas de** : at the expense of

experiencia *nf* 1 : experience 2 EXPERIMENTO : experiment

experimentación *nf, pl* **-ciones** : experimentation

experimentado, -da *adj* : experienced

experimental *adj* : experimental

experimentar *vi* : to experiment — *vt* 1 : to experiment with, to test out 2 : to experience

experimento *nm* EXPERIENCIA : experiment

experto, -ta *adj & n* : expert

expiación *nf, pl* **-ciones** : expiation, atonement

expiar {85} *vt* : to expiate, to atone for

expiración *nf, pl* **-ciones** VENCIMIENTO : expiration

expirar *vi* 1 FALLECER, MORIR : to pass away, to die 2 : to expire

explanada *nf* **1** TERRAZA : terrace **2** PATIO : courtyard, patio **3** : seaside walk, boardwalk
explayar *vt* : to extend — **explayarse** *vr* : to expound, to speak at length
explicable *adj* : explicable, explainable
explicación *nf, pl* **-ciones** : explanation
explicar {72} *vt* : to explain — **explicarse** *vr* **1** : to understand **2** : to explain oneself
explicativo, -va *adj* : explanatory
explicitar *vt* : to state explicitly, to specify
explícito, -ta *adj* : explicit — **explícitamente** *adv*
exploración *nf, pl* **-ciones** : exploration
explorador, -dora *n* : explorer, scout
explorar *vt* : to explore — **exploratorio, -ria** *adj*
explosión *nf, pl* **-siones** **1** ESTALLIDO : explosion **2** : outburst ⟨una explosión de ira : an outburst of anger⟩
explosionar *vi* : to explode
explosivo, -va *adj* : explosive
explotación *nf, pl* **-ciones** **1** : exploitation **2** : operation, running
explotar *vt* : to exploit **2** : to operate, to run — *vi* ESTALLAR, REVENTAR : to explode — **explotable** *adj*
exponencial *adj* : exponential — **exponencialmente** *adv*
exponente *nm* : exponent
exponer {60} *vt* **1** : to exhibit, to show, to display **2** : to explain, to present, to set forth **3** : to expose, to risk — *vi* : to exhibit
exportación *nf, pl* **-ciones** **1** : exportation **2 exportaciones** *nfpl* : exports
exportador, -dora *n* : exporter
exportar *vt* : to export — **exportable** *adj*
exposición *nf, pl* **-ciones** **1** EXHIBICIÓN : exposition, exhibition **2** : exposure **3** : presentation, statement
expósito, -ta *n* : foundling
expositor, -tora *n* **1** : exhibitor **2** : exponent
exprés¹ *adj* : express
exprés² *nms & pl* **1** : express, express train **2** : espresso
expresamente *adv* : expressly, on purpose
expresar *vt* : to express — **expresarse** *vr*
expresión *nf, pl* **-siones** : expression
expresivo, -va *adj* **1** : expressive **2** CARIÑOSO : affectionate — **expresivamente** *adv*
expreso¹, -sa *adj* **1** : express, specific **2** : express ⟨correo expreso : express mail⟩
expreso² *nm* **1** : express train, express **2** : express mail
express → exprés
exprimidor *nm* : juicer
exprimir *vt* **1** : to squeeze **2** : to exploit
expropiar *vt* : to expropriate, to commandeer — **expropiación** *nf*
expuesto¹ *pp* → **exponer**
expuesto², -ta *adj* **1** : exposed **2** : hazardous, risky
expulsar *vt* : to expel, to eject — **expulsarse** *vr*
expulsión *nf, pl* **-siones** : expulsion
expurgar {52} *vt* : to expurgate

expuso, etc. → exponer
exquisitez *nf, pl* **-teces** **1** : exquisiteness, refinement **2** : delicacy, special dish
exquisito, -ta *adj* **1** : exquisite **2** : delicious
extasiarse {85} *vr* : to be in ecstasy, to be enraptured
éxtasis *nms & pl* **1** : ecstasy, rapture **2** : Ecstasy (drug)
extático, -ca *adj* : ecstatic
extemporáneo, -nea *adj* **1** : unseasonable **2** : untimely
extender {56} *vt* **1** : to spread out, to stretch out **2** : to broaden, to expand ⟨extender la influencia : to broaden one's influence⟩ **3** : to draw up (a document), to write out (a check) — **extenderse** *vr* **1** : to spread **2** : to last
extendido, -da *adj* **1** : outstretched **2** : widespread **3** : extended ⟨garantía extendida : extended warranty⟩
extensamente *adv* : extensively, at length
extensible *adj* : extendable
extensión *nf, pl* **-siones** **1** : extension, stretching **2** : expanse, spread **3** : extent, range **4** : length, duration **5** : extension cord
extensivamente *adv* : widely, broadly
extensivo, -va *adj* **1** : extensive **2 hacer extensivo** : to extend
extenso, -sa *adj* **1** : extensive, detailed **2** : spacious, vast
extenuar {3} *vt* : to exhaust, to tire out — **extenuarse** *vr* — **extenuante** *adj*
exterior¹ *adj* **1** : exterior, external **2** : foreign ⟨asuntos exteriores : foreign affairs⟩
exterior² *nm* **1** : outside **2** : abroad
exteriorizar {21} *vt* : to express, to reveal
exteriormente *adv* : outwardly
exterminador¹, -dora *adj* → **ángel**
exterminador², -dora *n* **exterminador, -dora de plagas** : exterminator
exterminar *vt* : to exterminate — **exterminación** *nf*
exterminio *nm* : extermination
externalización *nf, pl* **-ciones** : outsourcing
externalizar {21} *vt* : to outsource
externar *vt Mex* : to express, to display
externo, -na *adj* : external, outward
extinción *nf, pl* **-ciones** : extinction
extinguidor *nm* : fire extinguisher
extinguir {26} *vt* **1** APAGAR : to extinguish, to put out **2** : to wipe out — **extinguirse** *vr* **1** APAGARSE : to go out, to fade out **2** : to die out, to become extinct
extinto, -ta *adj* : extinct
extintor *nm* : extinguisher
extirpación *n, pl* **-ciones** : removal (of a tumor, etc.)
extirpar *vt* **1** : to eradicate, to remove, to excise — **extirparse** *vr*
extorsión *nf, pl* **-siones** **1** : extortion **2** : harm, trouble
extorsionar *vt* : to extort
extra¹ *adv* : extra
extra² *adj* **1** : additional, extra **2** : superior, top-quality

extra³ *nmf* : extra (in movies)

extra⁴ *nm* : extra expense ⟨paga extra : bonus⟩

extra- *pref* : extra-

extracción *nf, pl* **-ciones** : extraction

extracto *nm* **1** : extract ⟨extracto de vainilla : vanilla extract⟩ **2** : abstract, summary

extractor *nm* : extractor

extracurricular *adj* : extracurricular

extradición *nf, pl* **-ciones** : extradition

extraditar *vt* : to extradite

extraer {81} *vt* : to extract

extraído *pp* → extraer

extrajudicial *adj* : out-of-court

extrajudicialmente *adv* : out of court

extralimitarse *vr* : to go too far, to overstep one's bounds

extramatrimonial *adj* : extramarital

extranjero¹, **-ra** *adj* : foreign

extranjero², **-ra** *n* : foreigner

extranjero³ *nm* : foreign countries *pl* ⟨viajó al extranjero : he traveled abroad⟩ ⟨trabajan en el extranjero : they work overseas⟩

extrañamente *adv* : strangely, oddly

extrañamiento *nm* ASOMBRO : amazement, surprise, wonder

extrañar *vt* : to miss (someone) — **extrañarse** *vr* : to be surprised

extrañeza *nf* **1** : strangeness, oddness **2** : surprise

extraño¹, **-ña** *adj* **1** RARO : strange, odd **2** EXTRANJERO : foreign

extraño², **-ña** *n* DESCONOCIDO : stranger

extraoficial *adj* OFICIOSO : unofficial — **extraoficialmente** *adv*

extraordinario, -ria *adj* EXCEPCIONAL : extraordinary — **extraordinariamente** *adv*

extrapolar *vt* : to extrapolate — **extrapolación** *nf*

extrarradio *nm* : outskirts *pl*

extrasensorial *adj* : extrasensory ⟨percepción extrasensorial : extrasensory perception⟩

extraterrestre *adj & nmf* : extraterrestrial, alien

extravagancia *nf* **1** : extravagance, flamboyance **2** : outrageous or outlandish thing

extravagante *adj* **1** : extravagant, flamboyant **2** : outrageous, outlandish

extraviado, -da *adj* : lost, stray

extraviar {85} *vt* **1** : to mislead, to lead astray **2** : to misplace, to lose — **extraviarse** *vr* : to get lost, to go astray

extravío *nm* **1** PÉRDIDA : loss **2** : misconduct

extremado, -da *adj* : extreme — **extremadamente** *adv*

extremar *vt* : to carry to extremes — **extremarse** *vr* : to do one's utmost

extremidad *nf* **1** : extremity, tip, edge **2** **extremidades** *nfpl* : extremities

extremista *adj & nmf* : extremist

extremo¹, **-ma** *adj* **1** : extreme, great ⟨frío extremo : extreme cold⟩ ⟨extrema pobreza : extreme poverty⟩ **2** : extreme, severe ⟨condiciones extremas : extreme conditions⟩ **3** EXTREMISTA : extreme ⟨opiniones extremas : extreme views⟩ **4** : extreme ⟨deportes extremos : extreme sports⟩ **5 en caso extremo** : as a last resort

extremo² *nm* **1** : extreme ⟨de un extremo a otro : from one extreme to the other⟩ **2** : end ⟨el otro extremo de la calle : the other end of the street⟩ ⟨el extremo sur : the southern end/tip⟩ **3 al extremo de** : to the point of ⟨en ~ : in the extreme⟩

extrovertido¹, **-da** *adj* : extroverted, outgoing

extrovertido², **-da** *n* : extrovert

extrudir *vt* : to extrude

exuberancia *nf* **1** : exuberance **2** : luxuriance, lushness

exuberante *adj* : exuberant, luxuriant — **exuberantemente** *adv*

exudar *vt* : to exude

exultación *nf, pl* **-ciones** : exultation, elation

exultante *adj* : exultant, elated — **exultantemente** *adv*

exultar *vi* : to exult, to rejoice

eyacular *vi* : to ejaculate — **eyaculación** *nf*

eyección *nf, pl* **-ciones** : ejection, expulsion

eyectar *vt* : to eject, to expel — **eyectarse** *vr*

F

f *nf* : seventh letter of the Spanish alphabet

fa *nm* **1** : F ⟨fa sostenido/bemol : F sharp/flat⟩ **2** : fa (in singing)

fábrica *nf* FACTORÍA : factory

fabricación *nf, pl* **-ciones** : manufacture

fabricante *nmf* : manufacturer

fabricar {72} *vt* MANUFACTURAR : to manufacture, to make

fabril *adj* INDUSTRIAL : industrial, manufacturing

fábula *nf* **1** : fable **2** : fabrication, fib *fam*

fabuloso, -sa *adj* **1** : fabulous, fantastic **2** : mythical, fabled

facción *nf, pl* **facciones 1** : faction **2** **facciones** *nfpl* RASGOS : features

faceta *nf* : facet

facha *nf* : appearance, look ⟨estar hecho una facha : to look a sight⟩

fachada *nf* : facade

facial *adj* : facial

fácil *adj* **1** : easy **2** : likely, probable ⟨es fácil que no pase : it probably won't happen⟩

facilidad *nf* **1** : facility, ease ⟨con facilidad : with ease, easily⟩ ⟨tener facilidad para : to have a gift for⟩ **2 facilidades** *nfpl* : facilities, services ⟨facilidades de pago : payment plans⟩ **3 facilidades** *nfpl* : opportunities ⟨tenían todas las facilidades : they had every opportunity⟩

facilitar *vt* **1** : to make easier, to facilitate **2** : to provide, to supply — **facilitador, -dora** *n*

fácilmente *adv* : easily, readily

facsímil *nm* **1** : facsimile, copy **2** : fax

factibilidad *nf* : feasibility

factible *adj* : feasible, practicable

factor¹, -tora *n* **1** : agent, factor **2** : baggage clerk

factor² *nm* ELEMENTO : factor, element

factoría *nf* FÁBRICA : factory

factura *nf* **1** : making, manufacturing **2** : bill, invoice

facturación *nf, pl* **-ciones** **1** : invoicing, billing **2** : check-in

facturar *vt* **1** : to bill, to invoice **2** : to register, to check in

facultad *nf* **1** : faculty, ability ⟨facultades mentales : mental faculties⟩ **2** : authority, power **3** : school (of a university) ⟨facultad de derecho : law school⟩

facultar *vt* : to authorize, to empower

facultativo, -va *adj* **1** OPTATIVO : voluntary, optional **2** : medical ⟨informe facultativo : medical report⟩

faena *nf* : task, job, work ⟨faenas domésticas : housework⟩

faenar *vi* **1** : to work, to labor **2** PESCAR : to fish

fagot *nm* : bassoon

Fahrenheit *adj* : Fahrenheit

faisán *nm, pl* **faisanes** : pheasant

faja *nf* **1** : sash, belt **2** : girdle **3** : strip (of land)

fajar *vt* **1** : to wrap (a sash or girdle) around **2** : to hit, to thrash — **fajarse** *vr* **1** : to put on a sash or girdle **2** : to come to blows

fajín *nm, pl* **-jines** : sash, belt

fajo *nm* : bundle, sheaf ⟨un fajo de billetes : a wad of cash⟩

falacia *nf* : fallacy

falaz, -laza *adj, mpl* **falaces** FALSO : fallacious, false

falda *nf* **1** : skirt ⟨falda escocesa : kilt⟩ ⟨falda de tubo : pencil skirt⟩ **2** REGAZO : lap (of the body) **3** VERTIENTE : side, slope

faldón *nm, pl* **-dones** **1** : tail (of a shirt, etc.) **2** : full skirt **3** : christening gown

falible *adj* : fallible

fálico, -ca *adj* : phallic

falla *nf* **1** : flaw, defect **2** : (geological) fault **3** : fault, failing

fallar *vi* **1** FRACASAR : to fail, to go wrong **2** : to rule (in a court of law) — *vt* **1** ERRAR : to miss (a target) **2** : to pronounce judgment on

fallecer {53} *vi* MORIR : to pass away, to die

fallecido, -da *adj & n* DIFUNTO : deceased

fallecimiento *nm* : demise, death

fallido, -da *adj* : failed, unsuccessful

fallo *nm* **1** SENTENCIA : sentence, judgment, verdict **2** : error, fault

falo *nm* : phallus, penis

falsamente *adv* : falsely

falsear *vt* **1** : to falsify, to fake **2** : to distort — *vi* **1** CEDER : to give way **2** : to be out of tune

falsedad *nf* **1** : falseness, hypocrisy **2** MENTIRA : falsehood, lie

falsete *nm* : falsetto

falsificación *nf, pl* **-ciones** **1** : counterfeit, forgery **2** : falsification

falsificador, -dora *n* : counterfeiter, forger

falsificar {72} *vt* **1** : to counterfeit, to forge **2** : to falsify

falso, -sa *adj* **1** FALAZ : false, untrue **2** : counterfeit, forged

falta *nf* **1** CARENCIA : lack ⟨falta de dinero/interés : lack of money/interest⟩ **2** DEFECTO : defect, fault, error ⟨falta de ortografía : spelling mistake⟩ ⟨falta de educación : bad manners⟩ **3** AUSENCIA : absence **4** : offense, misdemeanor **5** : foul (in basketball), fault (in tennis) **6 a falta de** : in the absence of **7 hacer falta** : to be lacking, to be needed ⟨nos hace falta un líder : we need a leader⟩ ⟨no hace falta : it's not necessary⟩ ⟨me hace mucha falta mi familia : I really miss my family⟩ **8 por falta de** : for lack of **9 sin —** : without fail

faltar *vi* **1** : to be lacking, to be needed ⟨me falta tiempo : I don't have time⟩ ⟨le falta imaginación : he lacks imagination⟩ ⟨le falta sal : it needs salt⟩ ⟨falta algo : something's missing⟩ ⟨al libro le falta una página : the book is missing a page⟩ ⟨nos faltan sillas : we need more chairs⟩ **2** : to be absent, to be missing ⟨faltan Juan y María : Juan and María aren't here⟩ ⟨faltar al trabajo/colegio : to miss work/school⟩ **3** QUEDAR : to remain, to be left ⟨falta un mes para la boda : there's a month to go until the wedding, the wedding is a month away⟩ ⟨falta mucho por hacer : there is still a lot to be done⟩ ⟨¿te falta mucho? : are you almost ready/done?⟩ **4 faltar a su promesa/palabra** : not to keep one's promise/word **5 ¡no faltaba más!** : don't mention it!, you're welcome!

faltante *nm* : shortage

falto, -ta *adj* **— de** : lacking (in), short of

fama *nf* **1** : fame **2** REPUTACIÓN : reputation **3 de mala fama** : disreputable

famélico, -ca *adj* HAMBRIENTO : starving, famished

familia *nf* **1** : family ⟨ser como de la familia : to be like one of the family⟩ ⟨sentir como en familia : to feel at home⟩ ⟨le viene de familia : he inherited it, it runs in the family⟩ **2 en ~** : in private **3 familia nuclear** : nuclear family **4 familia política** : in-laws

familiar¹ *adj* **1** CONOCIDO : familiar **2** : familial, family **3** INFORMAL : informal

familiar² *nmf* PARIENTE : relation, relative

familiaridad *nf* **1** : familiarity **2** : informality

familiarizar {21} *vt* : to familiarize — **familiarizarse** *vr*

famoso[1], **-sa** *adj* CÉLEBRE : famous

famoso[2], **-sa** *n* : celebrity

fan *nmf, pl* **fans** AFICIONADO : fan

fanal *nm* **1** : beacon, signal light **2** *Mex* : headlight

fanático, -ca *adj & n* : fanatic

fanatismo *nm* : fanaticism

fandango *nm* : fandango

fanfarria *nf* **1** : (musical) fanfare **2** : pomp, ceremony

fanfarrón[1], **-rrona** *adj, mpl* **-rrones** *fam* : bragging, boastful

fanfarrón[2], **-rrona** *n, mpl* **-rrones** *fam* : braggart

fanfarronada *nf* : boast, bluster

fanfarronear *vi* : to brag, to boast

fango *nm* LODO : mud, mire

fangoso, -sa *adj* LODOSO : muddy

fantasear *vi* : to fantasize, to daydream

fantasía *nf* **1** : fantasy **2** : imagination

fantasioso, -sa *adj* : fanciful

fantasma *nm* : ghost, phantom

fantasmagórico, -ca *adj* : ghostly, eerie

fantasmal *adj* : ghostly

fantástico, -ca *adj* **1** : fantastic, imaginary, unreal **2** *fam* : great, fantastic

FAQ ['fak] *nm, pl* **FAQs** : FAQ

farándula *nf* : show business, theater

faraón *nm, pl* **faraones** : pharaoh

fardo *nm* **1** : bale **2** : bundle

farfullar *v* : to jabber

faringe *nf* : pharynx

fariña *nf* : coarse manioc flour

farmacéutico[1], **-ca** *adj* : pharmaceutical

farmacéutico[2], **-ca** *n* : pharmacist

farmacia *nf* : drugstore, pharmacy

fármaco *nm* : medicine, drug

farmacología *nf* : pharmacology

faro *nm* **1** : lighthouse **2** : headlight

farol *nm* **1** : streetlight **2** : lantern, lamp **3** *fam* : bluff **4** *Mex* : headlight

farola *nf* **1** : lamppost **2** : streetlight

farra *nf* : spree, revelry

fárrago *nm* REVOLTIJO : hodgepodge, jumble

farsa *nf* **1** : farce **2** : fake, sham

farsante *nmf* CHARLATÁN : charlatan, fraud, phony

fascículo *nm* : part (of a publication)

fascinación *nf, pl* **-ciones** : fascination

fascinante *adj* : fascinating

fascinar *vt* **1** : to fascinate **2** : to charm, to captivate

fascismo *nm* : fascism

fascista *adj & nmf* : fascist

fase *nf* : phase, stage

fastidiar *vt* **1** MOLESTAR : to annoy, to bother, to hassle **2** ABURRIR : to bore — *vi* : to be annoying or bothersome — **fastidiarse** *vr* : to put up with something

fastidio *nm* **1** MOLESTIA : annoyance, nuisance, hassle **2** ABURRIMIENTO : boredom

fastidioso, -sa *adj* **1** MOLESTO : annoying, bothersome **2** ABURRIDO : boring — **fastidiosamente** *adv*

fastuoso, -sa *adj* : lavish, luxurious

fatal *adj* **1** MORTAL : fatal **2** *fam* : awful, terrible **3** : fateful, unavoidable

fatalidad *nf* **1** : fatality **2** DESGRACIA : misfortune, bad luck

fatalismo *nm* : fatalism

fatalista[1] *adj* : fatalistic

fatalista[2] *nmf* : fatalist

fatalmente *adv* **1** : unavoidably **2** : unfortunately

fatídico, -ca *adj* : fateful, momentous

fatiga *nf* CANSANCIO : fatigue

fatigado, -da *adj* AGOTADO : weary, tired

fatigar {52} *vt* CANSAR : to fatigue, to tire — **fatigarse** *vr* : to wear oneself out

fatigoso, -sa *adj* : fatiguing, tiring

fatuo, -tua *adj* **1** : fatuous **2** PRESUMIDO : vain

fauces *nfpl* : jaws *pl*, maw

faul *nm, pl* **fauls** : foul, foul ball

fauna *nf* : fauna

fausto *nm* : splendor, magnificence

favor *nm* **1** : favor ⟨¿me haces un favor? : will you do me a favor?⟩ ⟨quiero pedirle un favor : I want to ask you (for) a favor⟩ **2 a/en favor de** : in favor of **en favor de** : in support of, in the interests of ⟨trabajar en favor de una causa : to work for a cause⟩ **4 por ～** : please

favorable *adj* : favorable — **favorablemente** *adv*

favorecedor, -dora *adj* : becoming, flattering

favorecer {53} *vt* **1** : to favor **2** : to look well on, to suit

favorecido, -da *adj* **1** : flattering **2** : fortunate

favoritismo *nm* : favoritism

favorito, -ta *adj & n* : favorite

fax *nm* : fax, facsimile

fayuca *nf Mex* **1** : contraband **2** : black market

faz *nf* **1** : face, countenance ⟨la faz de la tierra : the face of the earth⟩ **2** : side (of coins, fabric, etc.)

fe *nf* **1** : faith **2** : assurance, testimony ⟨dar fe de : to bear witness to⟩ **3** : intention, will ⟨de buena fe : bona fide, in good faith⟩

fealdad *nf* : ugliness

febrero *nm* : February ⟨el primero de febrero : (on) February first⟩

febril *adj* : feverish — **febrilmente** *adv*

fecal *adj* : fecal

fecha *nf* **1** : date ⟨hasta la fecha : to date⟩ ⟨a partir de esta fecha : from today⟩ ⟨adelantar/atrasar la fecha : to move up/back the date⟩ **2 fecha de caducidad/vencimiento** : expiration date **3 fecha límite** : deadline

fechar *vt* : to date, to put a date on

fechoría *nf* : misdeed

fécula *nf* : starch (food)

fecundar *vt* : to fertilize (an egg) — **fecundación** *nf*

fecundidad *nf* **1** : fecundity, fertility **2** : productivity

fecundo, -da *adj* FÉRTIL : fertile, fecund

federación *nf, pl* **-ciones** : federation

federal *adj* : federal

federalismo *nm* : federalism — **federalista** *adj & nmf*

federar *vt* : to federate

fehaciente *adj* : reliable, irrefutable —
  fehacientemente *adv*
felicidad *nf* **1** : happiness **2** ¡**felicidades!**
  : best wishes!, congratulations!, happy
  birthday!
felicitación *nf, pl* **-ciones 1** : congratulation ⟨¡felicitaciones! : congratulations!⟩
  2 : greeting card
felicitar *vt* CONGRATULAR : to congratulate — **felicitarse** *vr* ~ **de** : to be glad
  about
feligrés, -gresa *n, mpl* **-greses** : parishioner
feligresía *nf* : parish
felino, -na *adj & n* : feline
feliz *adj, pl* **felices 1** : happy **2 Feliz
  Navidad** : Merry Christmas
felizmente *adv* **1** : happily **2** : fortunately, luckily
felonía *nf* : felony
felpa *nf* **1** : terry cloth **2** : plush
felpudo *nm* : doormat
femenil *adj* : women's, girls' ⟨futbol femenil : women's soccer⟩
femenino, -na *adj* **1** : feminine **2** : wom-
  en's ⟨derechos femeninos : women's
  rights⟩ **3** : female
fémina *nf* : woman
feminidad *or* **feminidad** *nf* : femininity
feminismo *nm* : feminism
feminista *adj & nmf* : feminist
femoral *adj* : femoral
fémur *nm* : femur, thighbone
fenecer {53} *vi* **1** : to die, to pass away **2**
  : to come to an end, to cease
fénix *nm* : phoenix
fenomenal *adj* **1** : phenomenal **2** *fam*
  : fantastic, terrific — **fenomenalmente**
  adv
fenómeno *nm* **1** : phenomenon **2**
  : prodigy, genius
feo¹ *adv* : badly, bad
feo², fea *adj* **1** : ugly **2** : unpleasant, nasty
  ⟨un olor feo : a nasty smell⟩ ⟨me dijo
  cosas feas : he said awful things to me⟩
  ⟨la cosa se pone fea : things are getting
  ugly⟩
féretro *nm* ATAÚD : coffin, casket
feria *nf* **1** : fair, market **2** : festival, holiday **3** *Mex* : change (money)
feriado, -da *adj* **día feriado** : public holiday
ferial *nm* : fairground
fermentar *v* : to ferment — **fermentación**
  nf
fermento *nm* : ferment
ferocidad *nf* : ferocity, fierceness
feroz *adj, pl* **feroces** FIERO : ferocious,
  fierce — **ferozmente** *adv*
férreo, -rrea *adj* **1** : iron **2** : strong, steely
  ⟨una voluntad férrea : an iron will⟩ **3**
  : strict, severe **4 vía férrea** : railroad
  track
ferretería *nf* **1** : hardware store **2** : hardware **3** : foundry, ironworks
ferrocarril *nm* : railroad, railway
ferrocarrilero → **ferroviario**
ferroviario, -ria *adj* : rail, railroad
ferry *nm, pl* **ferrys** : ferry
fértil *adj* FECUNDO : fertile, fruitful

fertilidad *nf* : fertility
fertilizante¹ *adj* : fertilizing ⟨droga fertilizante : fertility drug⟩
fertilizante² *nm* ABONO : fertilizer
fertilizar *vt* ABONAR : to fertilize — **fertilización** *nf*
ferviente *adj* FERVOROSO : fervent —
  fervientemente *adv*
fervor *nm* : fervor, zeal
fervoroso, -sa *adj* FERVIENTE : fervent,
  zealous
festejar *vt* **1** CELEBRAR : to celebrate **2**
  AGASAJAR : to entertain, to wine and
  dine **3** *Mex fam* : to thrash, to beat
festejo *nm* : celebration, festivity
festín *nm, pl* **festines** : banquet, feast
festinar *vt* : to hasten, to hurry up
festival *nm* : festival
festividad *nf* **1** : festivity **2** : (religious)
  feast, holiday
festivo, -va *adj* **1** : festive **2 día festivo**
  : holiday — **festivamente** *adv*
festón *nm, pl* **-tones** : scallop (decoration)
fetal *adj* : fetal
fetiche *nm* : fetish
fétido, -da *adj* : fetid, foul
feto *nm* : fetus
feudal *adj* : feudal — **feudalismo** *nm*
fiabilidad *nf* : reliability, trustworthiness
fiable *adj* : trustworthy, reliable
fiado, -da *adj* : on credit
fiador, -dora *n* : bondsman, guarantor
fiambrería *nf* : delicatessen
fiambres *nmpl* : cold cuts
fianza *nf* **1** CAUCIÓN : bail, bond **2**
  : surety, deposit
fiar {85} *vt* **1** : to sell on credit **2** : to guarantee — **fiarse** *vr* ~ **de** : to place trust in
fiasco *nm* FRACASO : fiasco, failure
fibra *nf* **1** : fiber **2 fibra de vidrio** : fiberglass
fibroso, -sa *adj* : fibrous
ficción *nf, pl* **ficciones 1** : fiction **2** : fabrication, lie
ficha *nf* **1** : index card **2** : file, record **3**
  : token **4** : domino, checker, counter,
  poker chip
fichaje *nm* : signing (in sports)
fichar *vt* **1** : to open a file on **2** : to sign
  up — *vi* : to punch in, to punch out
fichero *nm* **1** : card file **2** : filing cabinet
ficticio, -cia *adj* : fictitious
fidedigno, -na *adj* FIABLE : reliable, trustworthy
fideicomisario, -ria *n* : trustee
fideicomiso *nm* : trust ⟨guardar en
  fideicomiso : to hold in trust⟩
fidelidad *nf* : fidelity, faithfulness
fideo *nm* : noodle
fiduciario¹, -ria *adj* : fiduciary
fiduciario², -ria *n* : trustee
fiebre *nf* **1** CALENTURA : fever, temperature ⟨fiebre amarilla : yellow fever⟩ **2**
  : fever, excitement
fiel¹ *adj* **1** : faithful, loyal **2** : accurate —
  fielmente *adv*
fiel² *nm* **1** : pointer (of a scale) **2 los
  fieles** : the faithful
fieltro *nm* : felt

fiera *nf* **1** : wild animal, beast **2** : fiend, demon ⟨una fiera para el trabajo : a demon for work⟩

fiereza *nf* : fierceness, ferocity

fiero, -ra *adj* FEROZ : fierce, ferocious

fierro *nm* HIERRO : iron

fiesta *nf* **1** : party, fiesta ⟨fiesta de cumpleaños : birthday party⟩ ⟨no estoy para fiestas : I am in no mood to celebrate⟩ ⟨aguarle la fiesta a alguien : to rain on someone's parade⟩ **2** : holiday, feast day (in religion) ⟨hoy es (día de) fiesta : today is a holiday⟩

figura *nf* **1** : figure ⟨figura retórica : figure of speech⟩ ⟨figuras políticas : political figures⟩ **2** : shape, form **3** : figure, body shape

figuración *nf, pl* **-ciones** : imagining

figurado, -da *adj* : figurative — **figuradamente** *adv*

figurar *vi* **1** : to figure, to be included ⟨Rivera figura entre los más grandes pintores de México : Rivera is among Mexico's greatest painters⟩ **2** : to be prominent, to stand out — *vt* : to represent ⟨esta línea figura el horizonte : this line represents the horizon⟩ — **figurarse** *vr* : to imagine, to think ⟨¡figúrate el lío en que se metió! : imagine the mess she got into!⟩

fijación *nf, pl* **-ciones** **1** : fixation, obsession **2** : fixing, establishing **3** : fastening, securing

fijador *nm* : hair spray

fijamente *adv* : fixedly

fijar *vt* **1** : to fasten, to affix **2** ESTABLECER : to establish, to set up ⟨fijar su residencia : to take up residence⟩ **3** CONCRETAR : to set, to fix ⟨fijar la fecha : to set the date⟩ ⟨fijar la atención en : to focus one's attention on⟩ ⟨fijar la mirada en : to fix one's gaze on⟩ — **fijarse** *vr* **1** : to settle, to become fixed **2** : to notice ⟨fijarse en algo : to notice something, to pay attention to something⟩ ⟨me he fijado que . . . : I noticed that . . .⟩

fijeza *nf* **1** : firmness (of convictions) **2** : persistence, constancy ⟨mirar con fijeza a : to stare at⟩

fijo, -ja *adj* **1** : fixed, firm, steady **2** PERMANENTE : permanent

fila *nf* **1** HILERA : line, file ⟨ponerse en fila : to get in line⟩ ⟨en fila india : (in) single file⟩ **2** : rank, row **3 filas** *nfpl* : ranks ⟨cerrar filas : to close ranks⟩

filamento *nm* : filament

filantropía *nf* : philanthropy

filantrópico, -ca *adj* : philanthropic

filántropo, -pa *n* : philanthropist

filarmónica *nf* : philharmonic

filatelia *nf* : philately, stamp collecting

fildeador, -dora *n* : fielder

filete *nm* **1** : fillet **2** SOLOMILLO : sirloin **3** : thread (of a screw)

filiación *nf, pl* **-ciones** **1** : affiliation, connection **2** : particulars *pl*, (police) description

filial¹ *adj* : filial

filial² *nf* : affiliate, subsidiary

filigrana *nf* **1** : filigree **2** : watermark (on paper)

filipino, -na *adj & n* : Filipino

filmación *nf, pl* **-ciones** : filming, shooting

filmar *vt* : to film, to shoot

filme *or* **film** *nm* PELÍCULA : film, movie

filmoteca *nf* : film library

filo *nm* **1** : cutting edge, blade **2** : edge ⟨al filo del escritorio : at the edge of the desk⟩ ⟨al filo de la medianoche : at the stroke of midnight⟩

filón *nm, pl* **filones** **1** : seam, vein (of minerals) **2** *fam* : successful business, gold mine

filoso, -sa *adj* : sharp

filosofar *vi* : to philosophize

filosofía *nf* : philosophy

filosófico, -ca *adj* : philosophic, philosophical — **filosóficamente** *adv*

filósofo, -fa *n* : philosopher

filtración *nf, pl* **-ciones** : seeping, leaking

filtrar *v* : to filter — **filtrarse** *vr* : to seep through, to leak

filtro *nm* : filter

fin *nm* **1** : end ⟨dar/poner fin a : to end, to put an end to⟩ ⟨llegar a su fin : to come to an end⟩ **2** : purpose, aim, objective **3 a fin de cuentas** : in the end **4 a fin de que** : in order to **5 a fines de mes/año (etc.)** : at the end of the month/year (etc.) **6 al fin y al cabo** : after all **7 con el fin de** *or* **a fin de** : with the purpose of **8 con este fin** : to this end, with this purpose **9 en ~** : in short **10 fin de semana** : weekend **11 por ~** : finally, at last

finado, -da *adj & n* DIFUNTO : deceased

final¹ *adj* : final, ultimate — **finalmente** *adv*

final² *nm* **1** CONCLUSIÓN : end ⟨al final : at the end⟩ **2 a finales de mes/año (etc.)** : at the end of the month/year (etc.)

final³ *nf* : final, play-off

finalidad *nf* **1** : purpose, aim **2** : finality

finalista *nmf* : finalist

finalización *nf, pl* **-ciones** : completion, end

finalizar {21} *v* : to finish, to end

financiación *nf, pl* **-ciones** : financing, funding

financiamiento *nm* → **financiación**

financiar *vt* : to finance, to fund

financiero¹, -ra *adj* : financial

financiero², -ra *n* : financier

financista *nmf* : financier

finanzas *nfpl* : finances, finance ⟨altas finanzas : high finance⟩

finca *nf* **1** : farm, ranch **2** : country house

fineza *nf* FINURA, REFINAMIENTO : refinement

fingido, -da *adj* : false, feigned

fingimiento *nm* : pretense

fingir {35} *v* : to feign, to pretend

finiquitar *vt* **1** : to settle (an account) **2** : to conclude, to bring to an end

finiquito *nm* : settlement (of an account)

finito, -ta *adj* : finite

finja, etc. → **fingir**

finlandés, -desa adj & n : Finnish

fino¹, -na adj 1 : fine, excellent 2 : delicate, slender 3 REFINADO : refined 4 : sharp, acute ⟨olfato fino : keen sense of smell⟩ 5 : subtle

fino² nm : dry sherry

finta nf : feint

fintar or **fintear** vi : to feint

finura nf 1 : fineness, high quality 2 FINEZA, REFINAMIENTO : refinement

fiordo nm : fjord

firma nf 1 : signature 2 : signing 3 EMPRESA : firm, company

firmamento nm : firmament, sky

firmante nmf : signer, signatory

firmar v : to sign

firme adj 1 : firm, resolute 2 : steady, stable

firmemente adv : firmly

firmeza nf 1 : firmness, stability 2 : strength, resolve

fiscal¹ adj : fiscal — **fiscalmente** adv

fiscal² nmf : district attorney, prosecutor

fiscalizar {21} vt 1 : to audit, to inspect 2 : to oversee 3 : to criticize

fisco nm : Treasury (en EEUU), Exchequer (en Gran Bretaña)

fisgar {52} vt HUSMEAR : to pry into, to snoop on

fisgón, -gona n, mpl **fisgones** : snoop, busybody

fisgonear vi : to snoop, to pry

fisgue, etc. → fisgar

física nf : physics

físico¹, -ca adj : physical — **físicamente** adv

físico², -ca n : physicist

físico³ nm : physique, figure

fisiología nf : physiology

fisiológico, -ca adj : physiological, physiologic

fisiólogo, -ga n : physiologist

fisión nf, pl **fisiones** : fission — **fisionable** adj

fisonomía → fisonomía

fisioterapeuta nmf : physical therapist

fisioterapia nf : physical therapy

fisonomía nf : physiognomy, features pl

fistol nm Mex : tie clip

fisura nf : fissure, crevasse

flaccidez nf : limpness

fláccido, -da or **flácido, -da** adj : flaccid, flabby

flaco, -ca adj 1 DELGADO : thin, skinny 2 : feeble, weak ⟨una flaca excusa : a feeble excuse⟩

flagelo nm 1 : scourge, whip 2 : calamity

flagrante adj : flagrant, glaring, blatant — **flagrantemente** adv

flama nf LLAMA : flame

flamable adj Mex : flammable

flamante adj 1 : bright, brilliant 2 : brand-new

flamear vi 1 LLAMEAR : to flame, to blaze 2 ONDEAR : to flap, to flutter

flamenco¹, -ca adj 1 : flamenco 2 : Flemish

flamenco², -ca n : Fleming, Flemish person

flamenco³ nm 1 : Flemish (language) 2 : flamingo 3 : flamenco (music or dance)

flan nm : flan

flanco nm : flank, side

flanquear vt : to flank

flaquear vi DECAER : to flag, to weaken

flaqueza nf 1 DEBILIDAD : frailty, feebleness 2 : thinness 3 : weakness, failing

flash nm : flash (in photography)

flashback nm, pl **flashbacks** : flashback

flatulento, -ta adj : flatulent — **flatulencia** nf

flauta nf 1 : flute 2 **flauta dulce** : recorder

flautín nm, pl **flautines** : piccolo

flautista nmf : flute player, flutist

flecha nf : arrow

flechazo nm : love at first sight

fleco nm 1 : bangs pl 2 : fringe

flema nf : phlegm

flemático, -ca adj : phlegmatic, stolid, impassive

flequillo nm : bangs pl

fletar vt 1 : to charter, to hire 2 : to load (freight)

flete nm 1 : charter fee 2 : shipping cost 3 : freight, cargo

fletero nm : shipper, carrier

flexibilidad nf : flexibility

flexibilizar {21} vt : to make more flexible

flexible¹ adj : flexible

flexible² nm 1 : flexible electrical cord 2 : soft hat

flexión nf, pl **flexiones** 1 : push-up 2 : squat

flexionar vt : to bend (a limb, etc.)

flirtear vi : to flirt

flojear vi 1 DEBILITARSE : to weaken, to flag 2 : to idle, to loaf around

flojedad nf : weakness

flojera nf fam 1 : lethargy, feeling of weakness 2 : laziness

flojo, -ja adj 1 SUELTO : loose, slack 2 : weak, poor ⟨está flojo en las ciencias : he's weak in science⟩ 3 PEREZOSO : lazy

flor nf 1 : flower 2 **a flor de piel** : easily noticed or affected ⟨con los nervios a flor de piel : with one's nerves on edge⟩ ⟨canta con las emociones a flor de piel : her singing is full of emotion⟩ 3 **en ~** : in bloom 4 **flor de Pascua** : poinsettia

flora nf : flora

floración nf, pl **-ciones** : flowering ⟨en plena floración : in full bloom⟩

floral adj : floral

floreado, -da adj : flowered, flowery

florear vi FLORECER : to flower, to bloom — vt 1 : to adorn with flowers 2 Mex : to flatter, to compliment

florecer {53} vi 1 : to bloom, to blossom 2 : to flourish, to thrive

floreciente adj 1 : flowering 2 PRÓSPERO : flourishing, thriving

florecimiento nm : flowering

floreo nm : flourish

florería nf : flower shop, florist's

florero¹, -ra n : florist

florero² nm JARRÓN : vase

florete nm : foil (in fencing)

florido, -da adj 1 : full of flowers 2 : florid, flowery ⟨escritos floridos : flowery prose⟩
florista nmf : florist
floristería → florería
floritura nf : frill, embellishment
flota nf : fleet
flotabilidad nf : buoyancy
flotación nf, pl -ciones : flotation
flotador nm 1 : float 2 : life preserver
flotante adj : floating, buoyant
flotar vi : to float
flote nm a ~ : afloat
flotilla nf : flotilla, fleet
fluctuar {3} vi 1 : to fluctuate 2 VACILAR : to vacillate — **fluctuación** nf — **fluctuante** adj
fluidez nf 1 : fluency 2 : fluidity
fluido¹, -da adj 1 : flowing 2 : fluent 3 : fluid
fluido² nm : fluid
fluir {41} vi : to flow
flujo nm 1 : flow ⟨el flujo y reflujo : the ebb and flow⟩ 2 : discharge
flúor nm : fluorine
fluorescente nm : fluorescent light — **fluorescente** adj
fluoruro nm : fluoride
fluye, etc. → fluir
fobia nf : phobia
foca nf : seal (animal)
focal adj : focal
foco nm 1 : focus 2 : center, pocket 3 : lightbulb 4 : spotlight 5 : headlight
fofo, -fa adj 1 ESPONJOSO : soft, spongy 2 : flabby
fogata nf : bonfire
fogón nm, pl **fogones** : bonfire
fogonazo nm : flash, explosion
fogoso, -sa adj ARDIENTE : ardent
foguear vt : to inure, to accustom
fogueo nm de ~ ⟨un cartucho de fogueo : a blank, a dummy round⟩
foja nf : sheet (of paper)
folículo nm : follicle
folio nm : folio, leaf
folk ['fok, 'folk] nm : folk (music) — **folk** adj
folklore nm : folklore
folklórico, -ca adj : folk, traditional
follaje nm : foliage
folleto nm : pamphlet, leaflet, circular
follón nm, pl **follones** Spain 1 : commotion, fuss 2 : mess
fomentar vt 1 : to foment, to stir up 2 PROMOVER : to promote, to foster
fomento nm : promotion, encouragement
fonda nf 1 POSADA : inn 2 : small restaurant
fondeado, -da adj fam : rich, in the money
fondear vt 1 : to sound 2 : to sound out, to examine 3 Mex : to fund, to finance — vi ANCLAR : to anchor — **fondearse** vr fam : to get rich
fondeo nm 1 : anchoring 2 Mex : funding, financing
fondillos mpl : seat, bottom (of clothing)
fondista nmf : long-distance runner
fondo nm 1 : bottom ⟨el fondo del océano/barril : the bottom of the ocean/ barrel⟩ ⟨llegar al fondo de algo : to get to the bottom of something⟩ 2 : rear, back, end ⟨al fondo de la casa : at the back of the house⟩ 3 PROFUNDIDAD : depth 4 : background ⟨al fondo : in the background⟩ ⟨música de fondo : background music⟩ 5 CONTENIDO : content 6 Mex : slip, petticoat 7 : fund ⟨fondo de inversiones/pensiones : investment/pension fund⟩ ⟨fondo común : joint fund⟩ 8 **fondos** nmpl : funds, resources ⟨cheque sin fondos : bounced check⟩ ⟨recaudar fondos : to raise funds⟩ ⟨fondos públicos : public funds⟩ ⟨fondos de campaña : campaign funds⟩ 9 a ~ : thoroughly, in depth 10 de ~ : fundamental 11 de ~ : long-distance (in sports) 12 en ~ : abreast 13 en el fondo : deep down, at heart 14 **tocar fondo** : to touch bottom (in the sea, etc.), to hit rock bottom
fondue nf : fondue
fonema nm : phoneme
fonética nf : phonetics
fonético, -ca adj : phonetic
fontanería nf PLOMERÍA : plumbing
fontanero, -ra n PLOMERO : plumber
footing ['fu,tɪŋ] nm : jogging ⟨hacer footing : to jog⟩
forajido, -da n : bandit, fugitive, outlaw
foráneo, -nea adj : foreign, strange
forastero, -ra n : stranger, outsider
forcejear vi : to struggle
forcejeo nm : struggle
fórceps nms & pl : forceps pl
forense¹ adj : forensic, legal
forense² nmf : forensic scientist
forestal adj : forest
forja nf FRAGUA : forge
forjar vt 1 : to forge 2 : to shape, to create ⟨forjar un compromiso : to hammer out a compromise⟩ 3 : to invent, to concoct
forma nf 1 : form, shape ⟨tomar forma : to take shape⟩ ⟨dar forma a : to form, to give shape to⟩ ⟨en forma de corazón : in the shape of a heart⟩ 2 MANERA, MODO : manner, way ⟨su forma de vida : their way of life⟩ ⟨formas de pago : payment methods⟩ ⟨estar en forma : to be fit, to be in shape⟩ ⟨estar en baja forma : to be out of shape⟩ 4 **formas** nfpl : appearances, conventions ⟨guardar las formas : to keep up appearances⟩ 5 **de cualquier forma** or **de todas formas** : anyway, in any case 6 **de forma que** : so that
formación nf, pl -ciones 1 : formation 2 : training ⟨formación profesional : vocational training⟩
formal adj 1 : formal 2 : serious, dignified 3 : dependable, reliable
formaldehído nm : formaldehyde
formalidad nf 1 : formality 2 : seriousness, dignity 3 : reliability
formalizar {21} vt : to formalize, to make official
formalmente adv : formally
formar vt 1 : to form, to make 2 CONSTITUIR : to make up, to constitute 3 : to train, to educate — **formarse** vr

DESARROLLARSE : to develop, to take shape **2** EDUCARSE : to be educated

formatear *vt* : to format

formativo, -va *adj* : formative

formato *nm* : format

formidable *adj* **1** : formidable, tremendous **2** *fam* : fantastic, terrific

formón *nm, pl* **formones** : chisel

fórmula *nf* : formula

formulación *nf, pl* **-ciones** : formulation

formular *vt* **1** : to formulate, to draw up **2** : to make, to lodge (a protest or complaint)

formulario *nm* : form ⟨rellenar un formulario : to fill out a form⟩

fornicar {72} *vi* : to fornicate — **fornicación** *nf*

fornido, -da *adj* : well-built, burly, hefty

foro *nm* **1** : forum **2** : public assembly, open discussion

forraje *nm* **1** : fodder **2** : foraging **3** *fam* : hodgepodge

forrajear *vi* : to forage

forrar *vt* **1** : to line (a garment) **2** : to cover (a book)

forro *nm* **1** : lining **2** CUBIERTA : book cover

forsitia *nf* : forsythia

fortalecer {53} *vt* : to strengthen, to fortify — **fortalecerse** *vr*

fortalecimiento *nm* **1** : strengthening, fortifying **2** : fortifications

fortaleza *nf* **1** : fortress **2** FUERZA : strength **3** : resolution, fortitude

fortificación *nf, pl* **-ciones** : fortification

fortificar {72} *vt* **1** : to fortify **2** : to strengthen

fortín *nm, pl* **fortines** : small fort

fortuito, -ta *adj* : fortuitous

fortuna *nf* **1** SUERTE : fortune, luck **2** RIQUEZA : wealth, fortune

forúnculo *nm* : boil

forzado, -da *adj* : forced (of a smile, etc.)

forzar {36} *vt* **1** OBLIGAR : to force, to compel **2** : to force open **3** : to strain ⟨forzar los ojos : to strain one's eyes⟩

forzosamente *adv* **1** : forcibly, by force **2** : necessarily, inevitably ⟨forzosamente tendrán que pagar : they'll have no choice but to pay⟩

forzoso, -sa *adj* **1** : forced, compulsory **2** : necessary, inevitable

fosa *nf* **1** : ditch, pit ⟨fosa séptica : septic tank⟩ **2** TUMBA : grave **3** : cavity ⟨fosas nasales : nasal cavities, nostrils⟩

fosfato *nm* : phosphate

fosforescencia *nf* : phosphorescence — **fosforescente** *adj*

fósforo *nm* **1** CERILLA : match **2** : phosphorus

fósil¹ *adj* : fossilized, fossil

fósil² *nm* : fossil

fosilizar {21} *vt* : to fossilize — **fosilizarse** *vr*

foso *nm* **1** FOSA, ZANJA : ditch **2** : pit (of a theater) **3** : moat

foto *nf* : photo, picture

fotocopia *nf* : photocopy — **fotocopiar** *vt*

fotocopiadora *nf* COPIADORA : photocopier

fotoeléctrico, -ca *adj* : photoelectric

fotogénico, -ca *adj* : photogenic

fotografía *nf* **1** : photograph **2** : photography

fotografiar {85} *vt* : to photograph

fotográfico, -ca *adj* : photographic — **fotográficamente** *adv*

fotógrafo, -fa *n* : photographer

fotosíntesis *nf* : photosynthesis

foul *nm, pl* **fouls** : foul (in sports)

frac *nm, pl* **fracs** : tailcoat, tails *pl*

fracasado¹, -da *adj* : unsuccessful, failed

fracasado², -da *n* : failure

fracasar *vi* **1** FALLAR : to fail **2** : to fall through

fracaso *nm* FIASCO : failure

fracción *nf, pl* **fracciones 1** : fraction **2** : part, fragment **3** : faction, splinter group

fraccionamiento *nm* **1** : division, breaking up **2** *Mex* : residential area, housing development

fraccionar *vt* : to divide, to break up

fraccionario, -ria *adj* : fractional

fractura *nf* : fracture

fracturar *vt* : to fracture — **fracturarse** *vr*

fragancia *nf* : fragrance, scent

fragante *adj* : fragrant

fragata *nf* : frigate

frágil *adj* **1** : fragile **2** : frail, delicate

fragilidad *nf* **1** : fragility **2** : frailty, delicacy

fragmentar *vt* : to fragment — **fragmentación** *nf*

fragmentario, -ria *adj* : fragmentary, sketchy

fragmento *nm* **1** : fragment, shard **2** : bit, snippet **3** : excerpt, passage

fragor *nm* : clamor, din, roar

fragua *nf* FORJA : forge

fraguar {10} *vt* **1** : to forge **2** : to conceive, to concoct, to hatch — *vi* : to set, to solidify

fraile *nm* : friar, monk

frambuesa *nf* : raspberry

francamente *adv* **1** : frankly, candidly **2** REALMENTE : really ⟨es francamente admirable : it's really impressive⟩

francés¹, -cesa *adj, mpl* **franceses** : French

francés², -cesa *n, mpl* **franceses** : French person, Frenchman *m*, Frenchwoman *f*

francés³ *nm* : French (language)

franciscano, -na *adj & n* : Franciscan

francmasón, -sona *n, mpl* **-sones** : Freemason — **francmasonería** *nf*

franco¹, -ca *adj* **1** CÁNDIDO : frank, candid **2** PATENTE : clear, obvious **3** : free ⟨franco a bordo : free on board⟩

franco² *nm* : franc

francotirador, -dora *n* : sniper

franela *nf* : flannel

franja *nf* **1** : stripe, band **2** : border, fringe

franquear *vt* **1** : to clear **2** ATRAVESAR : to cross, to go through **3** : to pay the postage on

franqueo *nm* : postage

franqueza *nf* : frankness

franquicia *nf* **1** EXENCIÓN : exemption **2** : franchise

frasco *nm* : small bottle, flask, vial

frase *nf* **1** : phrase **2** ORACIÓN : sentence

frasear *vt* : to phrase

fraternal *adj* : fraternal, brotherly

fraternidad *nf* **1** : brotherhood **2** : fraternity

fraternizar {21} *vi* : to fraternize — **fraternización** *nf*

fraterno, -na *adj* : fraternal, brotherly

fraude *nm* : fraud

fraudulento, -ta *adj* : fraudulent — **fraudulentamente** *adv*

fray *nm* : brother (title of a friar) ⟨Fray Bartolomé : Brother Bartholomew⟩

frazada *nf* COBIJA, MANTA : blanket

frecuencia *nf* : frequency

frecuentar *vt* : to frequent, to haunt

frecuente *adj* : frequent — **frecuentemente** *adv*

freelance[1] [fri'lans] *adj, pl* **freelance** : freelance

freelance[2] *nmf* : freelancer

fregadero *nm* : kitchen sink

fregado[1]**, -da** *adj fam* : annoying, bothersome

fregado[2] *nm* **1** : scrubbing, scouring **2** *fam* : mess, muddle

fregar {49} *vt* **1** : to scrub, to scour, to wash ⟨fregar los trastes : to do the dishes⟩ ⟨fregar el suelo : to scrub the floor⟩ **2** *fam* : to annoy — *vi* **1** : to wash the dishes **2** : to clean, to scrub **3** *fam* : to be annoying

fregona *nf Spain* : mop

freidera *nf Mex* : frying pan

freír {37} *vt* : to fry — **freírse** *vr*

fréjol *Ecua* → **frijol**

frenado *nm* : braking (of a vehicle)

frenar *vt* **1** : to brake **2** DETENER : to curb, to check — *vi* : to apply the brakes — **frenarse** *vr* : to restrain oneself

frenazo *nm* : sudden stop (in a vehicle) ⟨dar un frenazo : to brake hard⟩

frenesí *nm, pl* **-síes** : frenzy

frenético, -ca *adj* : frantic, frenzied — **frenéticamente** *adv*

freno *nm* **1** : brake **2** : bit (of a bridle) **3** : check, restraint **4 frenos** *nmpl Mex* : braces (for teeth)

frente[1] *nm* **1** : front ⟨en frente : in front, opposite⟩ **2** : facade **3** : front line, front **4** : front (in politics) **5** : front (in meteorology) ⟨frente frío : cold front⟩ **6 de ~** : head-on ⟨chocar de frente a/con : to run head-on into⟩ **7 de frente a** : facing **8 ~ a** : opposite, in front of **9 ~ a** : in the face of (a crisis, etc.), against (an opponent, etc.) **10 estar al ~ de** : to be at the head of, to lead **11 hacer frente a** : to face up to

frente[2] *nf* **1** : forehead, brow **2 frente a frente** : face to face

fresa *nf* **1** : strawberry **2** : drill (in dentistry)

fresco[1]**, -ca** *adj* **1** : fresh **2** : cool **3** *fam* : insolent, nervy

fresco[2] *nm* **1** : coolness **2** : fresh air ⟨al fresco : in the open air, outdoors⟩ **3** : fresco **4** → **refresco**

frescor *nm* : cool air ⟨el frescor de la noche : the cool of the evening⟩

frescura *nf* **1** : freshness **2** : coolness **3** : calmness **4** DESCARO : nerve, audacity

fresno *nm* : ash (tree)

frialdad *nf* **1** : coldness **2** INDIFERENCIA : coldness, indifference

fríamente *adv* : coldly, indifferently

fricción *nf, pl* **fricciones** **1** : friction **2** : rubbing, massage **3** : discord, disagreement ⟨fricción entre los hermanos : friction between the brothers⟩

friccionar *vt* **1** FROTAR : to rub **2** : to massage

friega[1]**, friegue, etc.** → **fregar**

friega[2] *nf* **1** FRICCIÓN : massage **2** : annoyance, bother

frigidez *nf* : (sexual) frigidity

frigorífico *nm Spain* : refrigerator

frijol *nm* : bean ⟨frijoles refritos : refried beans⟩

frío[1]**, fría** *adj* **1** : cold **2** INDIFERENTE : cool, indifferent ⟨me deja frío : it leaves me cold⟩ **3** ESTUPEFACTO, PASMADO : shocked, stunned

frío[2] *nm* **1** : cold ⟨hace mucho frío esta noche : it's very cold tonight⟩ **2** INDIFERENCIA : coldness, indifference **3 tener frío** : to feel cold ⟨tengo frío : I'm cold⟩ **4 tomar frío** RESFRIARSE : to catch a cold

friolento, -ta *adj* : sensitive to cold

friolera *nf* (*used ironically or humorously*) : trifling amount ⟨una friolera de mil dólares : a mere thousand dollars⟩

friolero, -ra → **friolento**

friso *nm* : frieze

fritar *vt* : to fry

frito[1] *pp* → **freír**

frito[2]**, -ta** *adj* **1** : fried **2** *fam* : worn-out, fed up ⟨tener frito a alguien : to get on someone's nerves⟩ **3** *fam* : fast asleep ⟨se quedó frito en el sofá : she fell asleep on the couch⟩

fritura *nf* **1** : frying **2** : fried food

frivolidad *nf* : frivolity

frívolo, -la *adj* : frivolous — **frívolamente** *adv*

fronda *nf* **1** : frond **2 frondas** *nfpl* : foliage

frondoso, -sa *adj* : leafy, luxuriant

frontal *adj* : frontal, head-on ⟨un choque frontal : a head-on collision⟩

frontalmente *adv* : head-on

frontera *nf* : border, frontier

fronterizo, -za *adj* : border, on the border ⟨estados fronterizos : neighboring states⟩

frontón *nm, pl* **frontones** **1** : jai alai **2** : jai alai court

frotar *vt* **1** : to rub **2** : to strike (a match) — **frotarse** *vr* : to rub (together)

frote *nm* : rubbing, rub

fructífero, -ra *adj* : fruitful, productive

fructificar {72} *vi* **1** : to bear or produce fruit **2** : to be productive

fructuoso, -sa *adj* : fruitful

frugal *adj* : frugal, thrifty — **frugalmente** *adv*

frugalidad *adj* : frugality

fruncido *nm* : gathering (of fabric)
fruncir {83} *vt* **1** : to gather (fabric) **2 fruncir el ceño** : to knit one's brow, to frown **3 fruncir la boca** : to pucker up, to purse one's lips
frunza, etc. → **fruncir**
frustración *nf, pl* **-ciones** : frustration
frustrado, -da *adj* **1** : frustrated **2** : failed, unsuccessful
frustrante *adj* : frustrating
frustrar *vt* : to frustrate, to thwart — **frustrarse** *vr* FRACASAR : to fail, to come to nothing ⟨se frustraron sus esperanzas : his hopes were dashed⟩
fruta *nf* : fruit
frutal[1] *adj* : fruit, fruit-bearing
frutal[2] *nm* : fruit tree
frutería *nf* : fruit store
frutero[1], **-ra** *n* : fruit seller
frutero[2] *nm* : fruit bowl
frutilla *nf* : South American strawberry
fruto *nm* **1** : fruit ⟨los frutos de la tierra : the fruits of the earth⟩ **2** : fruit, result ⟨los frutos de su trabajo : the fruits of his labor⟩
fucsia *adj & nm* : fuchsia
fue, etc. → **ir, ser**
fuego *nm* **1** : fire ⟨prender fuego a algo : to set something on fire⟩ ⟨jugar con fuego : to play with fire⟩ ⟨abrir fuego contra : to open fire on⟩ **2** : light ⟨¿tienes fuego? : have you got a light?⟩ **3** : flame, burner (on a stove) ⟨a fuego lento : on low heat⟩ **4** : ardor, passion **5** : skin eruption, cold sore **6 fuegos artificiales** *nmpl* : fireworks
fuelle *nm* : bellows
fuente *nf* **1** MANANTIAL : spring **2** : fountain **3** ORIGEN : source ⟨fuentes informativas : sources of information⟩ ⟨fuente de alimentación/energía : food/energy source⟩ **4** : platter, serving dish **5 fuente de soda** : soda fountain
fuera *adv* **1** AFUERA : outside, out ⟨por fuera : on the outside⟩ ⟨hacia fuera : out, outside, outwards⟩ **2** : abroad, away **3** ∼ **de** : out of, outside of, beyond ⟨fuera del alcance : out of reach⟩ ⟨fuera de peligro : out of danger⟩ **4** ∼ **de** : besides, in addition to ⟨fuera de eso : aside from that⟩ **5 fuera de lugar** : out of place, amiss
fuerce, fuerza etc. → **forzar**
fuero *nm* **1** JURISDICCIÓN : jurisdiction : privilege, exemption **3 fuero interno** : conscience, heart of hearts
fuerte[1] *adv* **1** : strongly, tightly, hard **2** : loudly **3** : abundantly
fuerte[2] *adj* **1** : strong ⟨brazos fuertes : strong arms⟩ **2** RESISTENTE : strong, sturdy **3** : intense (of pain, etc.), strong (of a drug, odor, etc.) **4** : powerful, strong (of wind), heavy (of rain) ⟨un fuerte golpe : a hard blow⟩ **5** : sharp, marked ⟨un fuerte incremento : a sharp increase⟩ **6** : loud ⟨hablar más fuerte : to speak up⟩ **7** : extreme, excessive **8 hacerse fuerte** : to pull oneself together — **fuertemente** *adv*

fuerte[3] *nm* **1** : fort, stronghold **2** : forte, strong point
fuerza *nf* **1** : strength ⟨tener fuerzas para : to have the strength to⟩ ⟨cobrar fuerza : to gather strength⟩ ⟨recuperar fuerzas : to get one's strength back⟩ ⟨con todas sus fuerzas : with all your might⟩ **2** VIOLENCIA : force ⟨fuerza bruta : brute force⟩ **3** : force, strength, power ⟨la fuerza del impacto : the force of the impact⟩ **4** : force, power ⟨fuerza de costumbre : force of habit⟩ ⟨fuerza de voluntad : willpower⟩ ⟨la fuerza de la razón : the power of reason⟩ **5** : (natural) force ⟨la fuerza de la gravedad : the force of gravity⟩ **6** : force ⟨fuerzas armadas/militares : armed/military forces⟩ ⟨fuerzas de seguridad : security forces⟩ ⟨fuerza pública, fuerzas del orden : police⟩ ⟨fuerza de trabajo : workforce⟩ **7 a fuerza de** : by, by dint of **8 a/por la fuerza** : by force, forcibly **9 con** ∼ : hard, firmly, tightly **10 por** ∼ : necessarily, unavoidably
fuerza centrífuga *nf* : centrifugal force
fuete *nm* : riding crop
fuga *nf* **1** HUIDA : flight, escape **2** : fugue **3** : leak ⟨fuga de gas : gas leak⟩
fugarse {52} *vr* **1** : to escape **2** HUIR : to flee, to run away **3** : to elope
fugaz *adj, pl* **fugaces** : brief, fleeting
fugitivo, -va *adj & n* : fugitive
fulana *nf* : hooker, slut
fulano, -na *n* : so-and-so, what's-his-name, what's-her-name ⟨fulano, mengano, y zutano : Tom, Dick, and Harry⟩ ⟨señora fulana de tal : Mrs. so-and-so⟩
fulcro *nm* : fulcrum
fulgor *nm* : brilliance, splendor
fulminante *adj* : devastating, terrible ⟨una mirada fulminante : a withering look⟩
fulminar *vt* : to strike down ⟨fulminar a alguien con la mirada : to look daggers at someone⟩
fumador, -dora *n* : smoker
fumar *v* : to smoke
fumble *nm* : fumble (in football)
fumblear *vt* : to fumble (in football)
fumigar {52} *vt* : to fumigate — **fumigación** *nf* — **fumigador, -dora** *n*
función *nf, pl* **funciones** **1** : function **2** : duty ⟨el presidente en funciones : the acting president⟩ **3** : performance, show **4 en función de** : according to
funcional *adj* : functional — **funcionalmente** *adv*
funcionamiento *nm* **1** : functioning **2 en** ∼ : in operation
funcionar *vi* **1** : to function **2** : to run, to work
funcionario, -ria *n* : civil servant, official
funda *nf* **1** : case, cover, sheath **2** : pillowcase
fundación *nf, pl* **-ciones** : foundation, establishment
fundado, -da *adj* : well-founded, justified
fundador, -dora *n* : founder
fundamental *adj* BÁSICO : fundamental, basic — **fundamentalmente** *adv*

fundamentalismo *nm* : fundamentalism — **fundamentalista** *nmf*

fundamentar *vt* **1** : to lay the foundations for **2** : to support, to back up **3** : to base, to found

fundamento *nm* : basis, foundation, groundwork

fundar *vt* **1** ESTABLECER, INSTITUIR : to found, to establish **2** BASAR : to base — **fundarse** *vr* ∼ **en** : to be based on, to stem from

fundición *nf, pl* **-ciones** **1** : founding, smelting **2** : foundry

fundir *vt* **1** : to melt down, to smelt **2** : to fuse, to merge **3** : to burn out (a light-bulb) — **fundirse** *vr* **1** : to fuse together, to blend, to merge **2** : to melt, to thaw **3** : to fade (in television or movies)

fúnebre *adj* **1** : funeral, funereal **2** LÚGUBRE : gloomy, mournful

funeral¹ *adj* : funeral

funeral² *nm* **1** : funeral **2 funerales** *nmpl* EXEQUIAS : funeral rites

funeraria *nf* **1** : funeral home, funeral parlor **2 director de funeraria** : funeral director, undertaker

funerario, -ria *adj* : funeral

funesto, -ta *adj* : terrible, disastrous ⟨consecuencias funestas : disastrous consequences⟩

fungicida *nm* : fungicide

fungir {35} *vi* : to act, to function ⟨fungir de asesor : to act as a consultant⟩

funicular *nm* : cable car (on a mountain)

funja, etc. → **fungir**

furgón *nm, pl* **furgones** **1** : van, truck **2** : freight car, boxcar **3 furgón de cola** : caboose

furgoneta *nf* : van

furia *nf* **1** CÓLERA, IRA : fury, rage **2** : violence, fury ⟨la furia de la tormenta : the fury of the storm⟩

furibundo, -da *adj* : furious

furiosamente *adv* : furiously, frantically

furioso, -sa *adj* **1** AIRADO : furious, irate **2** : intense, violent

furor *nm* **1** : fury, rage **2** : violence (of the elements) **3** : passion, frenzy **4** : enthusiasm ⟨hacer furor : to be all the rage⟩

furtivo, -va *adj* : furtive — **furtivamente** *adv*

fuselaje *nm* : fuselage

fusible *nm* : (electrical) fuse

fusil *nm* : rifle

fusilar *vt* **1** : to shoot, to execute (by firing squad) **2** *fam* : to plagiarize, to pirate

fusilería *nf* **1** : rifles *pl*, rifle fire **2 descarga de fusilería** : fusillade

fusión *nf, pl* **fusiones** **1** : fusion **2** : union, merger

fusionar *vt* **1** : to fuse **2** : to merge, to amalgamate — **fusionarse** *vr*

fusta *nf* : riding crop

fuste *nm* **1** : shaft **2 de fuste** : important, significant

fustigar {52} *vt* **1** AZOTAR : to whip, to lash **2** : to upbraid, to berate

futbol *or* **fútbol** *nm* **1** : soccer **2 futbol americano** : football

futbolista *nmf* : soccer player

fútbol sala *nm* : indoor soccer

futesa *nf* **1** : small thing, trifle **2 futesas** *nfpl* : small talk

fútil *adj* : trifling, trivial

futón *nm, pl* **-tones** : futon

futurista *adj* : futuristic

futuro¹, -ra *adj* : future

futuro² *nm* PORVENIR : future

G

g *nf* : eighth letter of the Spanish alphabet

gabán *nm, pl* **gabanes** : topcoat, overcoat

gabardina *nf* **1** : gabardine **2** : trench coat, raincoat

gabarra *nf* : barge

gabinete *nm* **1** : cabinet (in government) **2** : study, office (in the home) **3** : (professional) office

gablete *nm* : gable

gabonés, -nesa *adj & n, mpl* **-neses** : Gabonese

gacela *nf* : gazelle

gaceta *nf* : gazette, newspaper

gachas *nfpl* : porridge

gacho, -cha *adj* **1** : drooping, turned downward **2** *Mex fam* : nasty, awful **3 ir a gachas** *fam* : to go on all fours

gaélico¹, -ca *adj* : Gaelic

gaélico² *nm* : Gaelic (language)

gafas *nfpl* ANTEOJOS : eyeglasses, glasses

gafe *nm Spain fam* : jinx, bad luck

gaita *nf* : bagpipes *pl*

gajes *nmpl* **gajes del oficio** : occupational hazards

gajo *nm* **1** : broken branch (of a tree) **2** : cluster, bunch (of fruit) **3** : segment (of citrus fruit)

gala *nf* **1** : gala ⟨vestido de gala : formal dress⟩ ⟨tener algo a gala : to be proud of something⟩ **2 galas** *nfpl* : finery, attire

galáctico, -ca *adj* : galactic

galán *nm, pl* **galanes** **1** : ladies' man, gallant **2** : leading man, hero **3** : boyfriend, suitor

galano, -na *adj* **1** : elegant **2** *Mex* : mottled

galante *adj* : gallant, attentive — **galantemente** *adv*

galantear *vt* **1** CORTEJAR : to court, to woo **2** : to flirt with

galanteo *nm* **1** CORTEJO : courtship **2** : flirtation, flirting

galantería *nf* **1** : gallantry, attentiveness **2** : compliment

galápago *nm* : aquatic turtle

galardón *nm, pl* **-dones** : award, prize
galardonado, -da *adj* : prizewinning
galardonar *vt* : to give an award to
galaxia *nf* : galaxy
galeno *nm fam* : physician, doctor
galeón *nm, pl* **galeones** : galleon
galera *nf* : galley
galería *nf* **1** : gallery, balcony (in a theater) 〈galería comercial : shopping mall〉 **2** : corridor, passage
galerón *nm, pl* **-rones** *Mex* : large hall
galés¹, -lesa *adj* : Welsh
galés², -lesa *n, mpl* **galeses 1** : Welshman *m*, Welshwoman *f* **2 los galeses** : the Welsh
galés³ *nm* : Welsh (language)
galgo *nm* : greyhound
galimatías *nms & pl* : gibberish, nonsense
galio *nm* : gallium
gallardete *nm* : pennant, streamer
gallardía *nf* **1** VALENTÍA : bravery **2** APOSTURA : elegance, gracefulness
gallardo, -da *adj* **1** VALIENTE : brave **2** APUESTO : elegant, graceful
gallear *vi* : to show off, to strut around
gallego¹, -ga *adj* **1** : Galician **2** *fam* : Spanish
gallego², -ga *n* **1** : Galician **2** *fam* : Spaniard
galleta *nf* **1** : cookie **2** : cracker
gallina *nf* **1** : hen **2 gallina de Guinea** : guinea fowl
gallinazo *nm* : vulture, buzzard
gallinero *nm* : chicken coop
gallito, -ta *adj fam* : cocky, belligerent
gallo *nm* **1** : rooster, cock **2** *fam* : squeak or crack in the voice **3** *Mex* : serenade **4 gallo de pelea** : gamecock
galochas *nfpl* : galoshes
galón *nm, pl* **galones 1** : gallon **2** : stripe (military insignia)
galopada *nf* : gallop
galopante *adj* : galloping 〈inflación galopante : galloping inflation〉
galopar *vi* : to gallop
galope *nm* : gallop
galpón *nm, pl* **galpones** : shed, storehouse
galvanizar {21} *vt* : to galvanize — **galvanización** *nf*
gama *nf* **1** : range, spectrum, gamut **2** → **gamo**
gamba *nf Arg, Spain, Uru* : large shrimp, prawn
gamberrada *nf Spain* **1** : act of vandalism **2** : crude thing (to say or do)
gamberro, -rra *n Spain* : hooligan, troublemaker
gambiano, -na *adj & n* : Gambian
gambito *nm* : gambit (in chess)
gamo, -ma *n* : fallow deer
gamuza *nf* **1** : suede **2** : chamois
gana *nf* **1** : desire, inclination **2 con ~s** : enthusiastically, heartily 〈trabajar con ganas : to work enthusiastically〉 〈llover con ganas : to be pouring rain〉 **3 darle ganas a alguien de hacer algo** : to make someone feel like doing something **4 de buena gana** : willingly, readily, gladly **5 de mala gana** : reluctantly,

halfheartedly **6 tener ganas de hacer algo** : to feel like doing something 〈tengo ganas de bailar : I feel like dancing〉 **7 morirse de ganas de hacer algo** : to be dying to do something **8 ponerle ganas a algo** : to put effort into something **9 quedarse con las ganas (de hacer algo)**: to end up not doing something
ganadería *nf* **1** : cattle raising **2** : cattle ranch **3** GANADO : cattle *pl*, livestock
ganadero¹, -ra *adj* : cattle, ranching
ganadero², -ra *n* : rancher
ganado *nm* **1** : cattle *pl*, livestock **2 ganado ovino** : sheep *pl* **3 ganado porcino** : swine *pl*
ganador¹, -dora *adj* : winning
ganador², -dora *n* : winner
ganancia *nf* **1** : profit **2 ganancias** *nfpl* : winnings, gains
ganancioso, -sa *adj* : profitable
ganar *vt* **1** : to win **2** : to gain 〈ganar tiempo : to buy time〉 **3** : to earn 〈ganar dinero : to make money〉 **4** : to acquire, to obtain — *vi* **1** : to win **2** : to profit 〈salir ganando : to come out ahead〉 — **ganarse** *vr* **1** : to gain, to win 〈ganarse a alguien : to win someone over〉 **2** : to earn 〈ganarse la vida : to make a living〉 **3** : to deserve
ganchillo *nm* : crochet hook
gancho *nm* **1** : hook **2** : clothes hanger **3** : hairpin, bobby pin **4** *Col* : safety pin
gandul¹ *nm CA, Car, Col* : pigeon pea
gandul², -dula *n fam* : idler, lazybones
gandulear *vi* : to idle, to loaf, to lounge about
ganga *nf* : bargain
ganglio *nm* **1** : ganglion **2** : gland
gangrena *nf* : gangrene — **gangrenoso, -sa** *adj*
gángster *nmf, pl* **gángsters** : gangster
gansada *nf* : silly thing, nonsense
ganso, -sa *n* **1** : goose, gander *m* **2** : idiot, fool
gañido *nm* : yelp (of a dog)
gañir {38} *vi* : to yelp
garabatear *v* : to scribble, to scrawl, to doodle
garabato *nm* **1** : doodle **2 garabatos** *nmpl* : scribble, scrawl
garaje *nm* : garage
garante *nmf* : guarantor
garantía *nf* **1** : guarantee, warranty **2** : security 〈garantía de trabajo : job security〉
garantizar {21} *vt* : to guarantee
garapiña *nf* : pineapple drink
garapiñar *vt* : to candy
garbanzo *nm* : chickpea
garbo *nm* **1** DONAIRE : grace, poise **2** : jauntiness
garboso, -sa *adj* **1** : graceful **2** : elegant, stylish
garceta *nf* : egret
gardenia *nf* : gardenia
garfio *nm* : hook, gaff
gargajo *nm fam* : phlegm
garganta *nf* **1** : throat **2** : neck (of a person or a bottle) **3** : ravine, narrow pass

gargantilla *nf* : choker, necklace
gárgara *nf* **1** : gargle, gargling **2 hacer gárgaras** : to gargle
gargarizar *vi* : to gargle
gárgola *nf* : gargoyle
garita *nf* **1** : cabin, hut **2** : sentry box, lookout post
garito *nm* : gambling hall
garoso, -sa *adj Col, Ven* : gluttonous, greedy
garra *nf* **1** : claw **2** : hand, paw **3 garras** *nfpl* : claws, clutches ⟨caer en las garras de alguien : to fall into someone's clutches⟩
garrafa *nf* : decanter, carafe
garrafal *adj* : terrible, monstrous
garrafón *nm, pl* **-fones** : large decanter, large bottle
garrapata *nf* : tick
garrobo *nm CA* : large lizard, iguana
garrocha *nf* **1** PICA : lance, pike **2** : pole ⟨salto con/de garrocha : pole vault⟩
garrotazo *nm* : blow (with a club)
garrote *nm* **1** : club, stick **2** *Mex* : brake
garúa *nf* : drizzle
garuar {3} *v impers* LLOVIZNAR : to drizzle
garza *nf* : heron
garzón, -zona *n, mpl* **-zones** *Chile* : waiter *m*, waitress *f*
gas *nm* : gas, vapor, fumes *pl* ⟨gas lacrimógeno : tear gas⟩
gasa *nf* : gauze
gasear *vt* **1** : to gas **2** : to aerate (a liquid)
gaseosa *nf* REFRESCO : soda, soft drink
gaseoso, -sa *adj* **1** : gaseous **2** : carbonated, fizzy
gasfitería *nf Chile, Peru* : plumbing
gasfitero, -ra *n Chile, Peru* : plumber
gasoducto *nm* : gas pipeline
gasoil *nm* : diesel oil, fuel oil
gasóleo → **gasoil**
gasolina *nf* : gasoline, gas
gasolinera *nf* : gas station, service station
gastado, -da *adj* **1** : spent **2** : worn, worn-out
gastador[1], -dora *adj* : extravagant, spendthrift
gastador[2], -dora *n* : spendthrift
gastar *vt* **1** : to spend **2** CONSUMIR : to consume, to use up **3** : to squander, to waste **4** : to wear ⟨gasta un bigote : he sports a mustache⟩ — **gastarse** *vr* **1** : to spend, to expend **2** : to run down, to wear out
gasto *nm* **1** : expense, expenditure **2** DETERIORO : wear **3 gastos fijos/generales/indirectos** : overhead **4 cubrir gastos** : to cover costs, to break even **5 gastos de seguro** : insurance costs **6 gastos de la casa** : household expenses **7 gastos de viaje** : travel expenses **8 gastos de envío** : shipping and handling **9 gasto público** : public spending
gástrico, -ca *adj* : gastric
gastronomía *nf* : gastronomy
gastronómico, -ca *adj* : gastronomic
gastrónomo, -ma *n* : gourmet
gatas *adv* **andar a gatas** : to crawl, to go on all fours

gatear *vi* **1** : to crawl **2** : to climb, to clamber (up)
gatillero *nm Mex* : gunman
gatillo *nm* : trigger
gatito, -ta *n* : kitten
gato[1], -ta *n* **1** : cat ⟨gato manchado : calico cat⟩ ⟨gato montés : wildcat⟩ **2 (aquí) hay gato encerrado** : there's something fishy going on (here) **3 dar gato por liebre a alguien** : to swindle someone **4 llevarse el gato al agua** : to pull it off, to manage it
gato[2] *nm* : jack (for an automobile)
gauchada *nf Arg, Uru* : favor, kindness
gaucho *nm* : gaucho
gaveta *nf* **1** CAJÓN : drawer **2** : till
gavilán *nm, pl* **-lanes** : sparrow hawk
gavilla *nf* **1** : gang, band **2** : sheaf
gaviota *nf* : gull, seagull
gay [ˈge, ˈgai] *adj* : gay (homosexual)
gaza *nf* : loop
gazapo *nm* **1** : young rabbit **2** : misprint, error
gazmoñería *nf* MOJIGATERÍA : prudery, primness
gazmoño[1], -ña *adj* : prudish, prim
gazmoño[2], -ña *n* MOJIGATO : prude, prig
gaznate *nm* : throat, gullet
gazpacho *nm* : gazpacho
ge *nf* : (letter) g
géiser *or* **géyser** *nm* : geyser
gel *nm* : gel
gelatina *nf* : gelatin
gélido, -da *adj* : icy, freezing cold
gelificarse *vr* : to jell
gema *nf* : gem
gemelo[1], -la *adj & n* MELLIZO : twin
gemelo[2] *nm* **1** : cuff link **2 gemelos** *nmpl* BINOCULARES : binoculars
gemido *nm* : moan, groan, wail
Géminis[1] *nm* : Gemini (sign or constellation)
Géminis[2] *nmf* : Gemini (person)
gemir {54} *vi* : to moan, to groan, to wail
gen *or* **gene** *nm* : gene
gendarme *nmf* POLICÍA : police officer, policeman *m*, policewoman *f*
gendarmería *nf* : police
genealogía *nf* : genealogy
genealógico, -ca *adj* : genealogical
generación *nf, pl* **-ciones** **1** : generation ⟨tercera generación : third generation⟩ **2** : generating, creating **3** : class ⟨la generación del '97 : the class of '97⟩
generacional *adj* : generation, generational
generador *nm* : generator
general[1] *adj* **1** : general **2 en ∼** *or* **por lo general** : in general, generally
general[2] *nmf* **1** : general **2 general de división** : major general
generalidad *nf* **1** : generality, generalization **2** : majority
generalización *nf, pl* **-ciones** **1** : generalization **2** : escalation, spread
generalizado, -da *adj* : generalized, widespread
generalizar {21} *vi* : to generalize — *vt* : to spread, to spread out — **generalizarse** *vr* : to become widespread

generalmente *adv* : usually, generally

generar *vt* : to generate — **generarse** *vr*

genérico, -ca *adj* : generic

género *nm* **1** : genre, class, kind ⟨el género humano : the human race, mankind⟩ **2** : gender (in grammar) **3** **géneros** *nmpl* : goods, commodities

generosidad *nf* : generosity

generoso, -sa **1** : generous, unselfish **2** : ample — **generosamente** *adv*

genética *nf* : genetics

genético, -ca *adj* : genetic — **genéticamente** *adv*

genetista *nmf* : geneticist

genial *adj* **1** AGRADABLE : genial, pleasant **2** : brilliant ⟨una obra genial : a work of genius⟩ **3** *fam* FORMIDABLE : fantastic, terrific

genialidad *nf* **1** : genius **2** : stroke of genius **3** : eccentricity

genio *nm* **1** : genius **2** : temper, disposition ⟨de mal genio : bad-tempered⟩ **3** : genie

genital *adj* : genital

genitales *nmpl* : genitals

genocidio *nm* : genocide

gente *nf* **1** : people **2** : relatives *pl*, folks **3 gente menuda** *fam* : children, kids *pl* **4 ser buena gente** : to be nice, to be kind

gentil[1] *adj* **1** AMABLE : kind **2** : gentile

gentil[2] *nmf* : gentile

gentileza *nf* **1** AMABILIDAD : kindness **2** CORTESÍA : courtesy

gentilicio, -cia *adj* **1** : national, tribal **2** : family

gentilmente *adv* : kindly

gentío *nm* MUCHEDUMBRE, MULTITUD : crowd, mob

gentuza *nf* CHUSMA : riffraff, rabble

genuflexión *nf, pl* **-xiones** **1** : genuflection **2 hacer una genuflexión** : to genuflect

genuino, -na *adj* : genuine — **genuinamente** *adv*

geografía *nf* : geography

geográfico, -ca *adj* : geographic, geographical — **geográficamente** *adv*

geógrafo, -fa *n* : geographer

geología *nf* : geology

geológico, -ca *adj* : geologic, geological — **geológicamente** *adv*

geólogo, -ga *n* : geologist

geometría *nf* : geometry

geométrico, -ca *adj* : geometric, geometrical — **geométricamente** *adv*

geopolítico, -ca *adj* : geopolitical

georgiano, -na *adj & n* : Georgian

geranio *nm* : geranium

gerbo *nm* : gerbil

gerencia *nf* : management, administration

gerencial *adj* : managerial

gerente *nmf* : manager, director

geriatría *nf* : geriatrics

geriátrico, -ca *adj* : geriatric

germanio *nm* : germanium

germano, -na *adj* : Germanic, German

germen *nm, pl* **gérmenes** : germ

germicida *nf* : germicide

germinación *nf, pl* **-ciones** : germination

germinar *vi* : to germinate, to sprout

gerundio *nm* : gerund

gesta *nf* : deed, exploit

gestación *nf, pl* **-ciones** : gestation

gesticular *vi* : to gesticulate — **gesticulación** *nf*

gestión *nf, pl* **gestiones** **1** TRÁMITE : procedure, step **2** ADMINISTRACIÓN : management **3 gestiones** *nfpl* : negotiations **4 gestión de datos** : data management

gestionar *vt* **1** : to negotiate, to work towards **2** ADMINISTRAR : to manage, to handle

gesto *nm* **1** ADEMÁN : gesture **2** : facial expression **3** MUECA : grimace

gestor[1]**, -tora** *adj* : facilitating, negotiating, managing

gestor[2]**, -tora** *n* : facilitator, manager

géyser → géiser

ghanés, -nesa *adj & n, mpl* **ghaneses** : Ghanaian

ghetto → gueto

giba *nf* **1** : hump (of an animal) **2** : person with a hump, hunchback *offensive*, humpback *offensive*

gibón *nm, pl* **gibones** : gibbon

giboso[1]**, -sa** *adj* : hunchbacked, humpbacked

giboso[2]**, -sa** *n* : person with a hump, hunchback *offensive*, humpback *offensive*

giga[1] *nf* : jig

giga[2] *nmf fam* : gig, gigabyte

gigabyte *nm* : gigabyte

gigante[1] *adj* : giant, gigantic

gigante[2]**, -ta** *n* : giant

gigantesco, -ca *adj* : gigantic, huge

gime, etc. → gemir

gimnasia *nf* : gymnastics

gimnasio *nm* : gymnasium, gym

gimnasta *nmf* : gymnast

gimnástico, -ca *adj* : gymnastic

gimotear *vi* LLORIQUEAR : to whine, to whimper

gimoteo *nm* : whimpering

ginebra *nf* : gin

ginecología *nf* : gynecology

ginecológico, -ca *adj* : gynecologic, gynecological

ginecólogo, -ga *n* : gynecologist

ginseng *nm* : ginseng

gira *nf* : tour

giralda *nf* : weather vane

girar *vi* **1** : to turn around, to revolve **2** : to swing around, to swivel — *vt* **1** : to turn, to twist, to rotate **2** : to draft (checks) **3** : to transfer (funds)

girasol *nm* MIRASOL : sunflower

giratorio, -ria *adj* : revolving

giro *nm* **1** VUELTA : turn, rotation **2** : change of direction ⟨giro de 180 grados, giro en U : U-turn, about-face⟩ **3 giro bancario** : bank draft **4 giro postal** : money order

giroscopio *or* **giróscopo** *nm* : gyroscope

gis *nm Mex* : chalk

gitano, -na *adj & n* : Gypsy

glacial *adj* : glacial, icy — **glacialmente** *adv*

glaciar *nm* : glacier

gladiador *nm* : gladiator

gladiolo *or* **gladiolo** *nm* : gladiolus

glándula *nf* : gland — **glandular** *adj*

glaseado *nm* : glaze, icing

glasear *vt* : to glaze

glaucoma *nm* : glaucoma

glena *nf* : socket

glicerina *nf* : glycerin

glicina *nf* : glycerin

glicinia *nf* : wisteria

global *adj* **1** : global, worldwide **2** : full, comprehensive **3** : total, overall

globalizar {21} *vt* **1** ABARCAR : to include, to encompass **2** : to extend worldwide — **globalización** *nf*

globalmente *adv* : globally, as a whole

globo *nm* **1** : globe, sphere **2** : balloon **3** **globo ocular** : eyeball

glóbulo *nm* **1** : globule **2** : blood cell, corpuscle

gloria *nf* **1** : glory **2** : fame, renown **3** : delight, enjoyment **4** : star, legend ⟨las glorias del cine : the great names in motion pictures⟩

glorieta *nf* **1** : rotary, traffic circle **2** : bower, arbor **3** : gazebo

glorificar {72} *vt* ALABAR : to glorify — **glorificación** *nf*

glorioso, -sa *adj* : glorious — **gloriosamente** *adv*

glosa *nf* **1** : gloss **2** : annotation, commentary

glosar *vt* **1** : to gloss **2** : to annotate, to comment on (a text)

glosario *nm* : glossary

glotón¹, -tona *adj, mpl* **glotones** : gluttonous

glotón², -tona *n, mpl* **glotones** : glutton

glotón³ *nm, pl* **glotones** : wolverine

glotonería *nf* GULA : gluttony

glucosa *nf* : glucose

glutinoso, -sa *adj* : glutinous

gnomo [ˈnomo] *nm* : gnome

gobernación *nf, pl* **-ciones** : governing, government

gobernador, -dora *n* : governor

gobernante¹ *adj* : ruling, governing

gobernante² *nmf* : ruler, leader, governor

gobernar {55} *vt* **1** : to govern, to rule **2** : to steer, to sail (a ship) — *vi* **1** : to govern **2** : to steer

gobierno *nm* : government

goce², etc. → **gozar**

goce² *nm* **1** PLACER : enjoyment, pleasure **2** : use, possession

gol *nm* : goal (in soccer)

goleada *nf* : rout, defeat (in sports)

goleador, -dora *n* : scorer (of goals) ⟨el máximo goleador del equipo : the team's top scorer⟩

golear *vt* : to rout, to score many goals against (in soccer)

goleta *nf* : schooner

golf *nm* : golf

golfista *nmf* : golfer

golfo *nm* : gulf, bay

golondrina *nf* **1** : swallow (bird) **2** **golondrina de mar** : tern

golosina *nf* : sweet, snack

goloso, -sa *adj* : fond of sweets ⟨ser goloso : to have a sweet tooth⟩

golpazo *nm* : heavy blow, bang, thump

golpe *nm* **1** : blow ⟨caerle/cogerle a golpes a alguien : to give someone a beating⟩ ⟨darse un golpe en la cabeza : to hit one's head⟩ **2** : knock **3** : job, heist ⟨dar el golpe : to do the job⟩ **4 de ~** : suddenly **5 de un golpe** : all at once, in one fell swoop **6 golpe de estado** : coup, coup d'etat **7 golpe de gracia** : coup de grâce **8 golpe de suerte** : stroke of luck **9 golpe de viento** : gust of wind **10 no dar/pegar (ni) golpe** : not to lift a finger, not to do a bit of work

golpeado, -da *adj* **1** : beaten, hit **2** : bruised (of fruit) **3** : dented

golpear *vt* **1** : to beat (up), to hit **2** : to slam, to bang, to strike — *vi* **1** : to knock (at a door) **2** : to beat ⟨la lluvia golpeaba contra el tejado : the rain beat against the roof⟩ — **golpearse** *vr*

golpetear *v* : to knock, to rattle, to tap

golpeteo *nm* : banging, knocking, tapping

golpista¹ *adj* **1** : coup, coup-related ⟨intentona golpista : attempted coup, coup attempt⟩ **2** : pro-coup

golpista² *mf* **1** : coup supporter **2** : military insurgent

golpiza *nf* : beating, pummeling

goma *nf* **1** : gum ⟨goma de mascar : chewing gum⟩ ⟨goma de pegar : glue⟩ **2** CAUCHO : rubber ⟨goma espuma : foam rubber⟩ **3** PEGAMENTO : glue **4** : rubber band **5** *Arg* : tire **6** *or* **goma de borrar** : eraser **7** *CA fam* : hangover

gomina *nf* : hair gel

gomita *nf* : rubber band

gomoso, -sa *adj* : gummy, sticky

góndola *nf* : gondola

gong *nm* : gong

gonorrea *nf* : gonorrhea

gorda *nf Mex* : thick corn tortilla

gordinflón¹, -flona *adj, mpl* **-flones** *fam* : chubby, pudgy

gordinflón², -flona *n, mpl* **-flones** *fam* : chubby person

gordo¹, -da *adj* **1** : fat **2** : thick **3** : fatty, greasy, oily **4** : unpleasant ⟨me cae gorda tu tía : I can't stand your aunt⟩

gordo², -da *n* : fat person

gordo³ *nm* GRASA : fat **2** : jackpot

gordura *nf* : fatness, flab

gorgojo *nm* : weevil

gorgorito *nm* : trill

gorgotear *vi* : to gurgle, to bubble

gorgoteo *nm* : gurgle

gorila *nm* **1** : gorilla **2** *Spain fam* : bouncer

gorjear *vi* **1** : to chirp, to tweet, to warble **2** : to gurgle

gorjeo *nm* **1** : chirping, warbling **2** : gurgling

gorra *nf* **1** : bonnet **2** : cap **3 de ~** *fam* : for free, at someone else's expense ⟨vivir de gorra : to sponge, to freeload⟩

gorrear *vt fam* : to bum, to scrounge — *vi fam* : to freeload

gorrero, -ra *n fam* : freeloader, sponger

gorrión *nm, pl* **gorriones** : sparrow
gorro *nm* **1** : cap ⟨gorro de ducha : shower cap⟩ **2 estar hasta el gorro** : to be fed up
gorrón, -rrona *n, mpl* **gorrones** *fam* : freeloader, scrounger
gorronear *vt fam* : to bum, to scrounge — *vi fam* : to freeload
gota *nf* **1** : drop ⟨una gota de sudor : a bead of sweat⟩ ⟨como dos gotas de agua : like two peas in a pod⟩ ⟨sudar la gota gorda : to sweat buckets, to work very hard⟩ **2** : gout
gotear *v* **1** : to drip **2** : to leak — *v impers* LLOVIZNAR : to drizzle
goteo *nm* : drip, dripping
gotera *nf* **1** : leak **2** : stain (from dripping water)
gotero *nm* : (medicine) dropper
gótico, -ca *adj* : Gothic
gourmet *nmf* : gourmet
gozar {21} *vi* **1** : to enjoy oneself, to have a good time **2 ~ de** : to enjoy, to have, to possess ⟨gozar de buena salud : to enjoy good health⟩ **3 ~ con** : to take delight in
gozne *nm* BISAGRA : hinge
gozo *nm* **1** : joy **2** PLACER : enjoyment, pleasure
gozoso, -sa *adj* : joyful
GPS [hepe'ese] *nm, pl* **GPS** : GPS
grabación *nf, pl* **-ciones** : recording
grabado *nm* **1** : engraving **2 grabado al aguafuerte** : etching
grabador, -dora *n* **1** : engraver **2 →** **grabadora**
grabadora *nf* : recorder, tape recorder ⟨grabadora de DVD : DVD recorder⟩
grabar *vt* **1** : to engrave **2** : to record, to tape — *vi* **grabar al aguafuerte** : to etch — **grabarse** *vr* **grabársele a alguien en la memoria** : to become engraved on someone's mind
gracia *nf* **1** : grace ⟨lo hizo con gracia : she did it gracefully⟩ ⟨una casa con mucha gracia : a very stylish/elegant house⟩ **2** : favor, kindness ⟨por la gracia de Dios : by the grace of God⟩ **3** : humor, wit ⟨su comentario no me hizo gracia : I wasn't amused by his remark⟩ ⟨tener gracia : to be funny⟩ **4** : grace, respite ⟨una semana de gracia : a week's grace⟩ ⟨período de gracia : grace period⟩ **5 gracias** *nfpl* : thanks ⟨¡gracias! : thank you!⟩ ⟨dar gracias : to give thanks⟩
grácil *adj* **1** : graceful **2** : delicate, slender, fine
gracilidad *nm* : gracefulness
gracioso, -sa *adj* **1** CHISTOSO : funny, amusing **2** : cute, attractive
grada *nf* **1** : harrow **2** PELDAÑO : step, stair **3 gradas** *nfpl* : bleachers, grandstand
gradación *nf, pl* **-ciones** : gradation, scale
gradar *vt* : to harrow, to hoe
gradería *nf* : tiers *pl*, stands *pl*, rows *pl* (in a theater)
gradiente *nf* : gradient, slope

grado *nm* **1** : degree (in meteorology and mathematics) ⟨grado centígrado : degree centigrade⟩ **2** : extent, level, degree ⟨en grado sumo : greatly, to the highest degree⟩ **3** RANGO : rank **4** : year, class (in education) **5 de buen grado** : willingly, readily
graduable *adj* : adjustable
graduación *nf, pl* **-ciones** **1** : graduation (from a school) **2** GRADO : rank **3** : alcohol content, proof
graduado[1], -da *adj* **1** : graduated ⟨2 lentes graduados** : prescription lenses⟩
graduado[2], -da *n* : graduate
gradual *adj* : gradual — **gradualmente** *adv*
graduar {3} *v* **1** : to regulate, to adjust **2** CALIBRAR : to calibrate, to gauge — **graduarse** *vr* : to graduate (from a school)
graffiti *or* **grafiti** *nmpl* : graffiti *pl*
gráfica *nf* **→ gráfico[2]**
gráfico[1], -ca *adj* : graphic — **gráficamente** *adv*
gráfico[2] *nm* **1** : graph, chart **2** : graphic (for a computer, etc.) **3 gráfico de barras** : bar graph
grafismo *nm* : graphics *pl*
grafito *nm* : graphite
gragea *nf* **1** : coated pill or tablet **2 grageas** *nfpl* : sprinkles, jimmies
grajo *nm* : rook (bird)
grama *nf* : grass
gramática *nf* : grammar
gramatical *adj* : grammatical — **gramaticalmente** *adv*
gramilla *f* : crabgrass
gramo *nm* : gram
gran → grande
grana *nf* : scarlet, deep red
granada *nf* **1** : pomegranate **2** : grenade ⟨granada de mano : hand grenade⟩
granaderos *nmpl Mex* : riot squad
granadino, -na *adj & n* : Grenadian
granado, -da *adj* **1** DISTINGUIDO : distinguished **2** : choice, select
granate *nm* **1** : garnet **2** : deep red, maroon
grande *adj* (**gran** *before singular nouns*) **1** : large, big ⟨un libro grande : a big book⟩ ⟨un grupo grande : a large group⟩ ⟨grandes cantidades : large quantities⟩ ⟨grandes corporaciones : big corporations⟩ ⟨esta camisa me queda grande : this shirt's (too) big on me⟩ **2** ALTO : tall ⟨¡qué grande estás! : look how much you've grown!⟩ **3** NOTABLE : great ⟨un gran autor : a great writer⟩ **4** (*indicating significance*) : big ⟨un gran error : a big mistake⟩ ⟨su gran oportunidad : his big chance⟩ **5** (*indicating degree*) : great, big ⟨con gran placer : with great pleasure⟩ ⟨un gran éxito : a big/great success⟩ ⟨a gran velocidad : at great speed⟩ ⟨grandes amigos : great friends⟩ ⟨un gran admirador : a great/big admirer, a big fan⟩ **6** : old, grown-up, big ⟨hijos grandes : grown children⟩ ⟨ya eres (una niña/un niño) grande : you're a big girl/boy now⟩ **7 a lo grande** : in style

grandeza *nf* **1** MAGNITUD : greatness, size **2** : nobility **3** : generosity, graciousness **4** : grandeur, magnificence

grandilocuencia *nf* : bombast

grandilocuente *adj* : bombastic

grandiosidad *nf* : grandeur

grandioso, -sa *adj* **1** MAGNÍFICO : grand, magnificent **2** : grandiose

granel *adv* **1 a ~** : galore, in great quantities **2 a ~** : in bulk ⟨vender a granel : to sell in bulk⟩

granero *nm* : barn, granary

granito *nm* : granite

granizada *nf* : hailstorm

granizado *nm* : drink made with crushed ice

granizar {21} *v impers* : to hail

granizo *nm* : hail

granja *nf* : farm

granjear *vt* : to earn, to win — **granjearse** *vr* : to gain, to earn

granjero, -ra *n* : farmer

grano *nm* **1** PARTÍCULA : grain, particle ⟨un grano de arena : a grain of sand⟩ **2** : grain (of rice, etc.), bean (of coffee), seed **3** : grain (of wood or rock) **4** BARRO, ESPINILLA : pimple **5 apartar el grano de la paja** *fam* : to separate the wheat from the chaff **6 ir al grano** : to get to the point

granoso, -sa *adj* : grainy

granuja *nmf* PILLUELO : rascal, urchin

granular *adj* : granular, grainy

granularse *vr* : to break out in spots

granuloso, -sa → **granular**

granza *nf* : chaff

grapa *nf* : staple **2** : clamp

grapadora *nf* ENGRAPADORA : stapler

grapar *vt* ENGRAPAR : to staple

grasa *nf* **1** : grease **2** : fat **3** *Mex* : shoe polish

grasiento, -ta *adj* : greasy, oily

graso, -sa *adj* **1** : fatty **2** : greasy, oily

grasoso, -sa *adj* GRASIENTO : greasy, oily

gratificación *nf, pl* **-ciones** **1** SATISFACCIÓN : gratification **2** : bonus **3** RECOMPENSA : recompense, reward

gratificante *adj* : satisfying, gratifying

gratificar {72} *vt* **1** SATISFACER : to satisfy, to gratify **2** RECOMPENSAR : to reward **3** : to give a bonus to

gratinado, -da *adj* : au gratin

gratis[1] *adv* GRATUITAMENTE : free, for free, gratis

gratis[2] *adj* GRATUITO : free, gratis

gratitud *nf* : gratitude

grato, -ta *adj* AGRADABLE, PLACENTERO : pleasant, agreeable — **gratamente** *adv*

gratuitamente *adv* **1** : gratuitously **2** GRATIS : free, for free, gratis

gratuito, -ta *adj* **1** : gratuitous, unwarranted **2** GRATIS : free, gratis

grava *nf* : gravel

gravamen *nm, pl* **-vámenes** **1** : burden, obligation **2** : (property) tax

gravar *vt* **1** : to burden, to encumber **2** : to levy (a tax)

grave *adj* **1** : grave, important **2** : serious, somber **3** : serious (of an illness)

gravedad *nf* **1** : gravity ⟨centro de gravedad : center of gravity⟩ **2** : seriousness, severity, gravity

gravemente *adv* : gravely, seriously

gravilla *nf* : (fine) gravel

gravitación *nf, pl* **-ciones** : gravitation

gravitacional *adj* : gravitational

gravitar *vi* **1** : to gravitate **2 ~ sobre** : to rest on **3 ~ sobre** : to loom over

gravoso, -sa *adj* **1** ONEROSO : burdensome, onerous **2** : costly

graznar *vi* : to caw, to honk, to quack, to squawk

graznido *nm* : cawing, honking, quacking, squawking

gregario, -ria *adj* : gregarious

gremial *adj* SINDICAL : union, labor

gremialista *nmf* : union supporter

gremio *nm* SINDICATO : union, guild

greña *nf* **1** : mat, tangle **2 greñas** *nfpl* MELENAS : shaggy hair, mop

greñudo, -da *n* HIPPIE, MELENUDO : hippie

gresca *nf fam* : fight, ruckus

grey *nf* : congregation, flock

griego[1] **, -ga** *adj & n* : Greek

griego[2] *nm* : Greek (language)

grieta *nf* : crack, crevice

grifo *nm* **1** : faucet ⟨agua del grifo : tap water⟩ **2** *Peru* : gas station

grillete *nm* : shackle

grillo *nm* **1** : cricket **2 grillos** *nmpl* : fetters, shackles

grima *nf* **1** : disgust, uneasiness **2 darle grima a alguien** : to get on someone's nerves

gringo, -ga *adj & n* YANQUI : Yankee, gringo

gripa *nf Col, Mex* : flu

gripe *nf* : flu

gris *adj* **1** : gray **2** : overcast, cloudy

grisáceo, -cea *adj* : grayish

grisín *nm, pl* **grisines** *Arg, Uru* : breadstick

gritar *v* : to shout, to scream, to cry

gritería *nf* : shouting, clamor

grito *nm* **1** : shout, scream, cry ⟨a grito pelado : at the top of one's voice⟩ **2 ser el último grito** : to be the latest fashion

groenlandés, -desa *adj & n* : Greenlander

grogui *adj fam* : dazed, groggy

grosella *nf* **1** : currant **2 grosella espinosa** : gooseberry

grosería *nf* **1** : insult, coarse language **2** : rudeness, discourtesy

grosero[1] **, -ra** *adj* **1** : rude, fresh **2** : coarse, vulgar — **groseramente** *adv*

grosero[2] **, -ra** *n* : rude person

grosor *nm* : thickness

grosso *adj* **a grosso modo** : roughly, broadly, approximately

grotesco, -ca *adj* : grotesque, hideous

grúa *nf* **1** : crane (machine) **2** : tow truck

gruesa *nf* : gross

grueso[1] **, -sa** *adj* **1** : thick, bulky **2** : heavy, big **3** : stout

grueso[2] *nm* **1** : thickness **2** : main body, mass **3 en ~** : in bulk

grulla *nf* : crane (bird)

grumo *nm* : lump, glob
gruñido *nm* : growl, grunt
gruñir {38} *vi* **1** : to growl, to grunt **2** : to grumble
gruñón¹, -ñona *adj, mpl* **gruñones** *fam* : grumpy, crabby
gruñón², -ñona *n, mpl* **gruñones** *fam* : grumpy person, nag
grupa *nf* : rump, hindquarters *pl*
grupo *nm* : group
gruta *nf* : grotto, cave
guacal *nm Col, Mex, Ven* : crate
guacamayo *nm* : macaw
guacamole *or* **guacamol** *nm* : guacamole
guacamote *nm Mex* : manioc, cassava
guachimán *nm, pl* **-manes** *fam* : watchman
guachinango → **huachinango**
guacho, -cha *adj* **1** *Arg, Col, Chile, Peru* : orphaned **2** *Chile, Peru* : odd (of a shoe, glove, etc.)
guadaña *nf* : scythe
guagua *nf* **1** *Arg, Col, Chile, Peru* : baby **2** *Cuba, PRi* : bus
guaira *nf* **1** *CA* : traditional flute **2** *Peru* : smelting furnace
guajiro, -ra *n Cuba* : peasant
guajolote *nm Mex* : turkey
guanábana *nf* : soursop (fruit)
guanaco *nm* : guanaco (South American mammal)
guandú *nm, pl* **guandú** *or* **guandúes** *CA, Car, Col* : pigeon pea
guango, -ga *adj Mex* **1** : loose-fitting, baggy **2** : slack, loose
guano *nm* : guano
guante *nm* **1** : glove ⟨guante de boxeo : boxing glove⟩ **2 arrojarle el guante (a alguien)** : to throw down the gauntlet (to someone)
guantelete *nm* : gauntlet
guantera *nf* : glove compartment
guapo, -pa *adj* **1** : handsome, good-looking, attractive **2** : elegant, smart **3** *fam* : bold, dashing
guarache → **huarache**
guarachear *vi Cuba, PRi fam* : to go on a spree, to go out on the town
guarangada *nf Arg, Uru fam* : rude or insulting remark
guaraní¹ *adj & nmf, pl* **-níes** : Guarani
guaraní² *nm* : Guarani (language of Paraguay)
guarda *nmf* **1** GUARDIÁN : security guard **2** : keeper, custodian
guardabarros *nms & pl* : fender, mudguard
guardabosque *nmf* : forest ranger, gamekeeper
guardacostas¹ *nmfs & pl* : member of the coast guard
guardacostas² *nms & pl* : coast guard vessel
guardaespaldas *nmfs & pl* : bodyguard
guardafangos *nms & pl* : fender
guardameta *nmf* ARQUERO, PORTERO : goalkeeper, goalie
guardapelo *nm* : locket
guardapolvo *nm* **1** : dustcover **2** : duster, housecoat

guardar *vt* **1** : to guard **2** : to maintain, to preserve **3** CONSERVAR : to put away **4** RESERVAR : to save **5** : to keep (a secret or promise) — **guardarse** *vr* **1** ~ **de** : to refrain from **2** ~ **de** : to guard against, to be careful not to
guardarropa *nm* **1** : coat check **2** ARMARIO : closet, wardrobe
guardavallas *nmf* : goalkeeper
guardería *nf* : nursery, day-care center
guardia¹ *nf* **1** : guard, defense **2** : guard duty, watch **3 en** ~ : on guard
guardia² *nmf* **1** : sentry, guard **2** : police officer, policeman *m*, policewoman *f*
guardiamarina *nmf* : midshipman
guardián, -diana *n, mpl* **guardianes** **1** GUARDA : security guard, watchman **2** : guardian, keeper **3 perro guardián** : watchdog
guarecer {53} *vt* : to shelter, to protect — **guarecerse** *vr* : to take shelter
guarida *nf* **1** : den, lair **2** : hideout
guarismo *nm* : figure, numeral
guarnecer {53} *vt* **1** : to adorn **2** : to garnish **3** : to garrison
guarnición *nf, pl* **-ciones** **1** : garnish **2** : garrison **3** : decoration, trimming, setting (of a jewel)
guaro *nm CA* : liquor distilled from sugarcane
guarrada *nf Spain fam* **1** : filthy mess **2** : dirty trick **3 decir guarradas** : to say filthy/disgusting things, to be vulgar
guarro¹, -rra *adj Spain fam* : dirty, filthy
guarro², -rra *n Spain fam* : filthy, disgusting, or vulgar person
guarura *nm Mex fam* : bodyguard
guasa *nf fam* **1** : joking, fooling around **2 de** ~ : in jest, as a joke
guasón¹, -sona *adj, mpl* **guasones** *fam* : funny, witty
guasón², -sona *n, mpl* **guasones** *fam* : joker, clown
guatemalteco, -ca *adj & n* : Guatemalan
guau *interj* : wow!
guay *adj Spain fam* : cool, neat, great
guayaba *nf* : guava (fruit)
guayín *nm, pl* **guayines** *Mex* : station wagon
gubernamental *adj* : governmental
gubernativo, -va → **gubernamental**
gubernatura *nf Mex* : governing body
guepardo *nm* : cheetah
güero, -ra *adj Mex* : blond, fair
guerra *nf* **1** : war ⟨declarar la guerra : to declare war⟩ ⟨estar en guerra : to be at war⟩ ⟨guerra sin cuartel : all-out war⟩ ⟨guerra civil/nuclear : civil/nuclear war⟩ ⟨hacer la guerra : to wage war⟩ **2** : warfare ⟨guerra de guerrillas : guerrilla warfare⟩ ⟨guerra biológica : biological warfare⟩ **3** LUCHA : conflict, struggle ⟨guerra a muerte : fight to the death⟩ **4 dar guerra** *fam* : to be annoying, to cause trouble
guerrear *vi* : to wage war
guerrero¹, -ra *adj* **1** : war, fighting **2** : warlike
guerrero², -ra *n* : warrior
guerrilla *nf* : guerrilla warfare

guerrillero, -ra *adj & n* : guerrilla
gueto *nm* : ghetto
guía¹ *nf* **1** : directory, guidebook **2** ORIENTACIÓN : guidance, direction ⟨la conciencia me sirve como guía : conscience is my guide⟩
guía² *nmf* : guide, leader ⟨guía de turismo : tour guide⟩
guiar {85} *vt* **1** : to guide, to lead **2** CONDUCIR : to manage — **guiarse** *vr* : to be guided by, to go by
guija *nf* : pebble
guijarro *nm* : pebble
guillotina *nf* : guillotine — **guillotinar** *vt*
guinda¹ *adj & nm Mex* : maroon (color)
guinda² *nf* : morello (cherry)
guindilla *nf* : chili
guineo *nm Car* : banana
guinga *nf* : gingham
guiñada → **guiño**
guiñar *vi* : to wink
guiño *nm* : wink
guiñol *nm* : puppet theater
guión *nm, pl* **guiones** **1** : script, screenplay **2** : hyphen, dash **3** ESTANDARTE : standard, banner
guionista *nmf* : scriptwriter
guirnalda *nf* : garland
guisa *nf* **1** : manner, fashion **2 a guisa de** : like, by way of **3 de tal guisa** : in such a way
guisado ESTOFADO *nm* : stew
guisante *nm* : pea
guisar *vt* **1** ESTOFAR : to stew **2** *Spain* : to cook
guiso *nm* **1** : stew **2** : casserole
güisqui → **whisky**
guita *nf* : string, twine
guitarra *nf* : guitar

guitarrista *nmf* : guitarist
gula *nf* GLOTONERÍA : gluttony, greed
guppy *nm* : guppy
gusano *nm* **1** LOMBRIZ : worm, earthworm ⟨gusano de seda : silkworm⟩ **2** : caterpillar, maggot, grub
gustar *vt* **1** : to taste **2** : to like ⟨¿gustan pasar? : would you like to come in?⟩ — *vi* **1** : to be pleasing ⟨me gustan los dulces : I like sweets⟩ ⟨a María le gusta Carlos : Maria is attracted to Carlos⟩ ⟨no me gusta que me griten : I don't like to be yelled at⟩ **2** ~ **de** : to like, to enjoy ⟨no gusta de chismes : she doesn't like gossip⟩ **3 como guste** : as you wish, as you like
gustativo, -va *adj* : taste ⟨papilas gustativas : taste buds⟩
gusto *nm* **1** : flavor, taste ⟨tiene gusto a chocolate : it tastes like chocolate⟩ **2** : taste, style ⟨de buen/mal gusto : in good/bad taste⟩ ⟨no es de mi gusto : it's not to my taste⟩ **3** : pleasure, liking ⟨tener el gusto de : to have the pleasure of⟩ ⟨con mucho gusto : gladly, with pleasure⟩ ⟨dar gusto : to be a pleasure⟩ ⟨darse el gusto de : to treat oneself to⟩ **4** : whim, fancy ⟨a gusto : at will⟩ **5 a** ~ : comfortable, at ease **6 al gusto** : to taste, as one likes **7 mucho gusto** : pleased to meet you **8 por** ~ : for pleasure
gustosamente *adv* : gladly
gustoso, -sa *adj* **1** : willing, glad ⟨nuestra empresa participará gustosa : our company will be pleased to participate⟩ **2** : zesty, tasty
gutural *adj* : guttural

H

h *nf* : ninth letter of the Spanish alphabet
ha → **haber**
haba *nf* : broad bean
habanero¹, -ra *adj* : of or from Havana
habanero², -ra *n* : native or resident of Havana
habano, -na *n* **1** → **habanero** **2** : cigar from Havana
haber¹ {39} *v aux* **1** : have, has ⟨no ha llegado el envío : the shipment hasn't arrived⟩ ⟨de haberlo sabido : if I had known⟩ ⟨debería haberlo pensado : I should have thought of it⟩ **2** ~ **de** : must ⟨ha de ser tarde : it must be late⟩ — *v impers* (**hay** *in the present indicative*) **1** : there is, there are ⟨hay dos mensajes : there are two messages⟩ ⟨¿hay postre? : do you have any dessert?⟩ ⟨hubo muchos errores : there were a lot of errors⟩ ⟨ha habido varios casos : there have been various cases⟩ **2 hay que** : it is necessary ⟨hay que trabajar más rápido : you/we (etc.) have to work faster⟩ ⟨habrá que hacerlo : it will have

to be done⟩ ⟨hubo que esperar : we had to wait⟩ **3 no hay de qué** : you're welcome, don't mention it **4 ¿qué hay?** *fam* : what's up?, how are things? **5 ¿qué hay de nuevo?** *fam* : what's new?
haber² *nm* **1** : assets *pl* **2** : credit, credit side **3 haberes** *nmpl* : salary, income, remuneration
habichuela *nf* **1** : bean, kidney bean **2** : green bean
hábil *adj* **1** : able, skillful **2** : work, working ⟨días hábiles : workdays, business days⟩
habilidad *nf* CAPACIDAD : ability, skill
habilidoso, -sa *adj* : skillful, clever
habilitación *nf, pl* **-ciones** **1** : authorization **2** : furnishing, equipping
habilitar *vt* **1** : to enable, to authorize, to empower (someone) **2** : to equip, to furnish
hábilmente *adv* : skillfully, expertly
habiloso, -sa *adj Chile fam* : bright, smart, clever
habitable *adj* : habitable, inhabitable

habitación *nf, pl* **-ciones** **1** CUARTO
: room **2** DORMITORIO : bedroom **3**
: habitation, occupancy
habitante *nmf* : inhabitant, resident
habitar *vt* : to inhabit — *vi* : to reside, to
dwell
hábitat *nm, pl* **-tats** : habitat
hábito *nm* **1** : habit, custom **2** : habit (of
a monk or nun)
habitual *adj* : habitual, customary —
habitualmente *adv*
habituar {3} *vt* : to accustom, to habituate
— **habituarse** *vr* ~ **a** : to get used to, to
grow accustomed to
habla *nf* **1** : speech ⟨dejar a alguien sin
habla : to leave someone speechless⟩
⟨quedarse sin habla : to be left speech-
less⟩ **2** : language, dialect **3** de ~
: speaking ⟨de habla inglesa : English-
speaking⟩
hablado, -da *adj* **1** : spoken **2** mal ha-
blado : foulmouthed
hablador¹, -dora *adj* : talkative
hablador², -dora *n* : chatterbox
habladuría *nf* **1** : rumor **2** habladurías
nfpl : gossip, scandal
hablante *nmf* : speaker
hablar *vi* **1** : to speak, to talk ⟨hablar en
broma : to be joking⟩ ⟨hablar más alto
: to speak up, to speak/talk louder⟩ ⟨ha-
blar más bajo : to lower one's voice, to
speak/talk more quietly⟩ **2** ~ **con** : to
talk to, to speak to/with **3** ~ **de** : to
mention, to talk about ⟨hablar bien/mal
de : to speak well/ill of⟩ **4** dar que ha-
blar : to make people talk ⟨va a dar que
hablar : people will start talking/gossip-
ing about him⟩ **5** ¡ni hablar! : no way!
— *vt* **1** : to speak (a language) **2** : to talk
about, to discuss ⟨háblalo con tu jefe
: discuss it with your boss⟩ — **hablarse**
vr **1** : to speak to each other, to be on
speaking terms **2** se habla inglés (etc.)
: English (etc.) spoken
habrá, etc. → **haber**
hacedor, -dora *n* : creator, maker, doer
hacendado, -da *n* : landowner
hacendoso, -sa *adj* : hardworking, industrious
hacer {40} *vt* **1** CREAR, CONSTRUIR : to
make (a cake, a list, a law, etc.), to build
(a building), to write (a book, a check)
⟨hacer planes : to make plans⟩ ⟨hacer
una película : to make a movie⟩ ⟨hacer
un fuego : to make/build a fire⟩ ⟨lo hizo
de madera : he made it out of wood⟩ **2**
: to do (a task, an activity, etc.), to make
(a gesture, a trip, an agreement, etc.), to
pay (a visit) ⟨hacer mandados : to do/
run errands⟩ ⟨hacer los deberes : to do
one's homework⟩ ⟨¿me haces un favor?
: will you do me a favor?⟩ **3** : to make,
to cause, to produce ⟨hacer ruido : to
make noise⟩ **4** EXPRESAR : to voice (an
objection, etc.), to ask (a question) **5** : to
make, to force, to oblige ⟨los hice esperar : I made them wait⟩ ⟨hizo que todos se callaran : he made everyone be
quiet⟩ **6** : to make, to cause, to provoke
⟨me hizo reír/llorar : it made me laugh/

cry⟩ ⟨¿te hice daño? : did I hurt you?⟩ **7**
: to make, to cause to (be) ⟨la hizo famosa : it made her famous⟩ ⟨te hará (un)
hombre : it will make a man out of you⟩
⟨lo hizo funcionar : she made it work⟩
⟨hace que el color parezca más oscuro
: it makes the color seem darker⟩ **8** : to
make (a bed), to pack (a suitcase) **9** PRE-
PARAR : to make, to fix (a meal, etc.) **10**
ADQUIRIR : to make (money, friends,
etc.) — *vi* **1** : to act ⟨haces bien : you're
doing the right thing⟩ **2** : to serve as, to
function as **3** ~ **de** : to play, to perform
as ⟨hizo de Ofelia en "Hamlet" : she
played Ophelia in "Hamlet"⟩ **4** hacer
como que/si : to act as if **5** hacer por
: to try to ⟨hicieron por entendernos
: they tried to understand us⟩ **6** hacer y
deshacer : to do as one pleases — *v impers* **1** (*referring to weather*) ⟨hace frío
: it's cold⟩ ⟨hacía mucho viento : it was
very windy⟩ **2** (*referring to time*) ⟨eso
pasó hace mucho tiempo : that happened a long time ago⟩ ⟨vivo aquí desde
hace dos años, hace dos años que vivo
aquí : I've lived here for two years⟩ ⟨ha-
cía años que no sabía nada de él : I
hadn't heard from him in years⟩ **3** ha-
cer falta : to be necessary, to be needed
4 no le hace : it doesn't matter, it makes
no difference — **hacerse** *vr* **1** : to become **2** : to pretend, to act, to play ⟨ha-
cerse el tonto : to play dumb⟩ **3** : to
seem ⟨el examen se me hizo difícil : the
exam seemed difficult to me⟩ **4** : to get,
to grow ⟨se hace tarde : it's getting/
growing late⟩
hacha *nf* **1** : hatchet, ax
hachazo *nm* : blow, chop (with an ax)
hache *nf* : (letter) h
hachís *nm* : hashish
hacia *prep* **1** : toward, towards ⟨hacia
abajo : downward⟩ ⟨hacia adelante : for-
ward⟩ **2** : near, around, about ⟨hacia las
seis : about six o'clock⟩
hacienda *nf* **1** : estate, ranch, farm **2**
: property **3** : livestock **4** la Hacienda
: department of revenue, tax office
hacinamiento *nm* : overcrowding
hacinar *vt* **1** : to pile up, to stack **2** : to
crowd, to cram — **hacinarse** *vr* : to
crowd together
hackear *vt fam* : to hack, to hack into (a
system, etc.)
hacker *nmf, pl* **hackers** *fam* : hacker
hada *nf* : fairy
hado *nm* : destiny, fate
haga, etc. → **hacer**
haitiano, -na *adj & n* : Haitian
hala *interj Spain* **1** (*expressing encouragement or disbelief*) : come on! **2** (*expressing surprise*) : wow! **3** (*expressing protest*)
: hey!
halagador¹, -dora *adj* : flattering
halagador², -dora *n* : flatterer
halagar {52} *vt* : to flatter, to compliment
halago *nm* : flattery, praise
halagüeño, -ña *adj* **1** : flattering **2** : encouraging, promising
halar *vt CA, Car* → **jalar**

halcón *nm, pl* **halcones** : hawk, falcon

halibut *nm, pl* **-buts** : halibut

hálito *nm* 1 : breath 2 : gentle breeze

hallar *vt* 1 ENCONTRAR : to find 2 DESCUBRIR : to discover, to find out — **hallarse** *vr* 1 : to be situated, to find oneself 2 : to feel ⟨no se halla bien : he doesn't feel comfortable, he feels out of place⟩

hallazgo *nm* 1 : discovery 2 : find ⟨es un verdadero hallazgo! : it's a real find!⟩

halo *nm* 1 : halo 2 : aura

halterofilia *nf* : weight lifting

hamaca *nf* : hammock

hambre *nf* 1 : hunger 2 : starvation 3 **tener hambre** : to be hungry 4 **dar hambre** : to make hungry

hambriento, -ta *adj* : hungry, starving

hambruna *nf* : famine

hamburguesa *nf* 1 : hamburger, burger 2 : patty, burger ⟨una hamburguesa de pavo : a turkey patty/burger⟩

hampa *nf* : criminal underworld

hampón, -pona *n, mpl* **hampones** : criminal, thug

hámster [ˈxamster] *nm, pl* **hámsters** : hamster

han → **haber**

handicap *or* **hándicap** [ˈhandiˌkap] *nm, pl* **-caps** : handicap (in sports)

hangar *nm* : hangar

Hanukkah → **Janucá**

hará, etc. → **hacer**

haragán¹, -gana *adj, mpl* **-ganes** : lazy, idle

haragán², -gana *n, mpl* **-ganes** HOLGAZÁN : slacker, good-for-nothing

haraganear *vi* : to be lazy, to waste one's time

haraganería *nf* : laziness

harapiento, -ta *adj* : ragged, tattered

harapos *nmpl* ANDRAJOS : rags, tatters

hardware [ˈhardˌwer] *nm* : computer hardware

harén *nm, pl* **harenes** : harem

harina *nf* 1 : flour 2 **harina de maíz** : cornmeal 3 **ser harina de otro costal** : to be a horse of a different color

hartar *vt* 1 : to glut, to satiate 2 FASTIDIAR : to tire, to irritate, to annoy — **hartarse** *vr* 1 : to be weary, to get fed up 2 ~ **de** : to gorge oneself on

harto¹ *adv* : most, extremely, very

harto², -ta *adj* 1 : full, satiated 2 : fed up 3 MUCHO : a lot of, much ⟨tiene harto dinero : he has lots of money⟩

hartura *nf* 1 : surfeit 2 : abundance, plenty

has → **haber**

hasta¹ *adv* : even

hasta² *prep* 1 : until, up until ⟨hasta ahora/entonces : until now/then⟩ ⟨until Friday : hasta el viernes⟩ ⟨¡hasta luego! : see you later!⟩ 2 : as far as ⟨nos fuimos hasta Managua : we went all the way to Managua⟩ 3 : to, up/down to ⟨hasta cierto punto : up to a certain point⟩ ⟨tengo el pelo hasta la cintura : my hair is down to my waist⟩ 4 **hasta que** : until ⟨hasta que lleguen : until they arrive⟩

hastiar {85} *vt* 1 : to make weary, to bore 2 : to disgust, to sicken — **hastiarse** *vr* ~ **de** : to get tired of

hastío *nm* 1 TEDIO : tedium 2 REPUGNANCIA : disgust

hatchback *nm* : hatchback (car)

hatillo *nm* : bundle (of clothes)

hato *nm* 1 : flock, herd 2 : bundle (of possessions)

hawaiano, -na *adj & n* : Hawaiian

hay → **haber¹**

haya¹, etc. → **haber**

haya² *nf* : beech (tree and wood)

hayuco *nm* : beechnut

haz¹ → **hacer**

haz² *nm, pl* **haces** 1 FARDO : bundle 2 : beam (of light)

haz³ *nf, pl* **haces** 1 : face 2 **haz de la tierra** : surface of the earth

hazaña *nf* PROEZA : feat, exploit

hazmerreír *nm fam* : laughingstock

he¹ {39} → **hacer**

he² *v impers* **he aquí** : here is, here are, behold

hebilla *nf* : buckle, clasp

hebra *nf* : strand, thread

hebreo¹, -brea *adj & n* : Hebrew

hebreo² *nm* : Hebrew (language)

hecatombe *nf* 1 MATANZA : massacre 2 : disaster

heces → **hez**

hechicería *nf* 1 BRUJERÍA : sorcery, witchcraft 2 : curse, spell

hechicero¹, -ra *adj* : bewitching, enchanting

hechicero², -ra *n* : sorcerer, sorceress *f*

hechizar {21} *vt* 1 EMBRUJAR : to bewitch 2 CAUTIVAR : to charm

hechizo *nm* 1 SORTILEGIO : spell, enchantment 2 ENCANTO : charm, fascination

hecho¹ *pp* → **hacer**

hecho², -cha *adj* 1 : made, done ⟨hecho a mano : handmade⟩ 2 : complete, finished ⟨hecho y derecho : full-fledged⟩

hecho³ *nm* 1 : fact 2 : event ⟨hechos históricos : historic events⟩ 3 : act, action 4 **de ~** : in fact, in reality

hechura *nf* 1 : style 2 : craftsmanship, workmanship 3 : product, creation

hectárea *nf* : hectare

heder {56} *vi* : to stink, to reek

hediondez *nf, pl* **-deces** : stink, stench

hediondo, -da *adj* MALOLIENTE : foul-smelling, stinking

hedor *nm* : stench, stink

hegemonía *nf* 1 : dominance 2 : hegemony (in politics)

helada *nf* : frost (in meteorology)

heladería *nf* : ice-cream parlor, ice-cream stand

helado¹, -da *adj* 1 GÉLIDO : icy, freezing cold 2 CONGELADO : frozen

helado² *nm* : ice cream

heladora *nf* CONGELADOR : freezer

helar {55} *v* CONGELAR : to freeze — *v impers* : to produce frost ⟨anoche heló : there was frost last night⟩ — **helarse** *vr*

helecho *nm* : fern, bracken

hélice *nf* 1 : spiral, helix 2 : propeller

helicóptero *nm* : helicopter
helio *nm* : helium
helipuerto *nm* : heliport
hematoma *nm* **1** : hematoma **2** MORETÓN : bruise
hembra *adj & nf* : female
hemisférico, -ca *adj* : hemispheric, hemispherical
hemisferio *nm* : hemisphere
hemofilia *nf* : hemophilia
hemofílico, -ca *adj & n* : hemophiliac
hemoglobina *nf* : hemoglobin
hemorragia *nf* **1** : hemorrhage **2 hemorragia nasal** : nosebleed
hemorroides *nfpl* ALMORRANAS : hemorrhoids, piles
hemos → **haber**
henchido, -da *adj* : swollen, bloated
henchir {54} *vt* **1** : to stuff, to fill **2** : to swell, to swell up — **henchirse** *vr* **1** : to stuff oneself **2** LLENARSE : to fill up, to be full
hender {56} *vt* : to cleave, to split
hendidura *nf* : crack, crevice, fissure
heno *nm* : hay
hepatitis *nf* : hepatitis
heráldica *nf* : heraldry
heráldico, -ca *adj* : heraldic
heraldo *nm* : herald
herbario, -ria *adj* : herbal
herbicida *nm* : herbicide, weed killer
herbívoro[1], -ra *adj* : herbivorous
herbívoro[2] *nm* : herbivore
hercio *nm* : hertz
hercúleo, -lea *adj* : herculean
heredar *vt* : to inherit
heredero, -ra *n* : heir, heiress *f*
hereditario, -ria *adj* : hereditary
hereje *nmf* : heretic
herejía *nf* : heresy
herencia *nf* **1** : inheritance **2** : heritage **3** : heredity
herético, -ca *adj* : heretical
herida *nf* : injury, wound
herido[1], -da *adj* **1** : injured, wounded **2** : hurt, offended
herido[2], -da *n* : injured person, casualty
herir {76} *vt* **1** : to injure, to wound **2** : to hurt, to offend
hermafrodita *nmf* : hermaphrodite
hermanar *vt* **1** : to unite, to bring together **2** : to match up, to twin (cities)
hermanastro, -tra *n* **1** : half brother *m*, half sister *f* **2** : stepbrother *m*, stepsister *f*
hermandad *nf* **1** FRATERNIDAD : brotherhood ⟨hermandad de mujeres : sisterhood, sorority⟩ **2** : association
hermano, -na *n* : sibling, brother *m*, sister *f* ⟨hermano mayor/menor : big/little brother⟩ ⟨hermana gemela : twin sister⟩
hermético, -ca *adj* : hermetic, watertight — **herméticamente** *adv*
hermoso, -sa *adj* BELLO : beautiful, lovely — **hermosamente** *adv*
hermosura *nf* BELLEZA : beauty, loveliness
hernia *nf* : hernia
herniarse *vr* : to get a hernia, to rupture oneself

héroe *nm* : hero
heroicidad *nf* : heroism, heroic deed
heroico, -ca *adj* : heroic — **heroicamente** *adv*
heroína *nf* **1** : heroine **2** : heroin
heroinómano, -na *n* : heroin addict
heroísmo *nm* : heroism
herpes *nms & pl* **1** : herpes **2** : shingles
herradura *nf* : horseshoe
herraje *nm* : ironwork
herramienta *nf* : tool
herrar {55} *vt* : to shoe (a horse)
herrería *nf* : blacksmith's shop
herrero, -ra *n* : blacksmith
herrumbre *nf* ORÍN : rust
herrumbroso, -sa *adj* OXIDADO : rusty
hertzio → **hercio**
hervidero *nm* **1** : mass, swarm **2** : hotbed (of crime, etc.)
hervidor *nm* : kettle
hervir {76} *vi* **1** BULLIR : to boil, to bubble **2** ~ **de** : to teem with, to be swarming with — *vt* : to boil
hervor *nm* **1** : boiling **2** : fervor, ardor
heterogéneo, -nea *adj* : heterogeneous
heterosexual *adj & nmf* : heterosexual
heterosexualidad *nf* : heterosexuality
hexágono *nm* : hexagon — **hexagonal** *adj*
hez *nf, pl* **heces** **1** ESCORIA : scum, dregs *pl* **2** : sediment, lees *pl* **3 heces** *nfpl* : feces, excrement
hiato *nm* : hiatus
hibernar *vi* : to hibernate — **hibernación** *nf*
híbrido[1], -da *adj* : hybrid
híbrido[2] *nm* : hybrid
hicieron, etc. → **hacer**
hidalgo, -ga *n* : nobleman *m*, noblewoman *f*
hidrante *nm* CA, Col : hydrant
hidratar *vt* : to moisturize — **hidratante** *adj*
hidrato de carbono *nm* : carbohydrate
hidráulico, -ca *adj* : hydraulic
hidroala *nm* : hydrofoil
hidroavión *nm, pl* **-viones** : seaplane
hidrocarburo *nm* : hydrocarbon
hidroeléctrico, -ca *adj* : hydroelectric
hidrofobia *nf* RABIA : hydrophobia, rabies
hidrófugo, -ga *adj* : water-repellent
hidrógeno *nm* : hydrogen
hidromasaje *nm* **bañera de hidromasaje** → **bañera**
hidroplano *nm* : hydroplane
hiede, etc. → **heder**
hiedra *nf* **1** : ivy **2 hiedra venenosa** : poison ivy
hiel *nf* **1** BILIS : bile **2** : bitterness
hiela, etc. → **helar**
hielo *nm* **1** : ice **2** : coldness, reserve ⟨romper el hielo : to break the ice⟩
hiena *nf* : hyena
hiende, etc. → **hender**
hierba *nf* **1** : herb **2** : grass **3 mala hierba** : weed
hierbabuena *nf* : mint, spearmint
hiere, etc. → **herir**
hierra, etc. → **herrar**

hierro *nm* **1** : iron ⟨hierro fundido : cast iron⟩ **2** : branding iron
hierve, etc. → hervir
hígado *nm* : liver
higiene *nf* : hygiene
higiénico, -ca *adj* : hygienic — **higiénicamente** *adv*
higienista *nmf* : hygienist
higo *nm* **1** : fig **2 higo chumbo** : prickly pear (fruit)
higrómetro *nm* : hygrometer
higuera *nf* : fig tree
hijastro, -tra *n* : stepson *m*, stepdaughter *f*
hijo, -ja *n* : son *m*, daughter *f* ⟨hijo adoptivo : adopted son⟩ ⟨soy hija única : I'm an only child⟩ ⟨tiene dos hijos/hijas : she has two sons/daughters⟩ ⟨nuestros hijos : our children⟩
hijo de puta *nm sometimes offensive* : son of a bitch *sometimes offensive*, bastard *offensive*
híjole *interj Mex* : wow!, good grief!
hilacha *nf* **1** : ravel, loose thread **2 mostrar la hilacha** : to show one's true colors
hilado *nm* **1** : spinning **2** HILO : yarn, thread
hilar *vt* **1** : to spin (thread) **2** : to consider, to string together (ideas) — *vi* **1** : to spin **2 hilar delgado** : to split hairs
hilarante *adj* **1** : humorous, hilarious **2 gas hilarante** : laughing gas
hilaridad *nf* : hilarity
hilera *nf* FILA : file, row, line
hilo *nm* **1** : thread ⟨colgar de un hilo : to hang by a thread⟩ ⟨hilo dental : dental floss⟩ **2** LINO : linen **3** : (electric) wire ⟨conexión sin hilos : wireless connection⟩ **4** : theme, thread (of a discourse) **5** : trickle (of water, etc.)
hilvanar *vt* **1** : to baste, to tack **2** : to piece together
himnario *nm* : hymnal
himno *nm* **1** : hymn **2 himno nacional** : national anthem
hincapié *nm* **hacer hincapié en** : to emphasize, to stress
hincar {72} *vt* CLAVAR : to stick, to plunge — **hincarse** *vr* **hincarse de rodillas** : to kneel down, to fall to one's knees
hincha *nmf fam* : fan, supporter
hinchado, -da *adj* **1** : swollen, inflated **2** : pompous, overblown
hinchar *vt* **1** INFLAR : to inflate **2** : to exaggerate — **hincharse** *vr* **1** : to swell up **2** : to become conceited, to swell with pride
hinchazón *nf, pl* **-zones** : swelling
hinche, etc. → henchir
hindi *nm* : Hindi
hindú *adj & nmf* : Hindu
hinduismo *nm* : Hinduism
hiniesta *nf* : broom (plant)
hinojo *nm* **1** : fennel **2 de hinojos** : on bended knee
hinque, etc. → hincar
hipar *vi* : to hiccup
hiperactividad *nf* : hyperactivity
hiperactivo, -va *adj* : hyperactive, overactive
hipérbole *nf* : hyperbole

hiperbólico, -ca *adj* : hyperbolic, exaggerated
hipercrítico, -ca *adj* : hypercritical
hiperenlace *nm* : hyperlink
hipermercado *nm* : large supermarket, hypermarket
hipermétrope *adj* : farsighted
hipermetropía *nf* : farsightedness
hipersensibilidad *nf* : hypersensitivity
hipertensión *nf, pl* **-siones** : hypertension, high blood pressure
hip–hop [ˌxipˈxop] *nm* : hip-hop (music)
hípico, -ca *adj* : equestrian ⟨concurso hípico : horse show⟩
hipil → huipil
hipnosis *nfs & pl* : hypnosis
hipnótico, -ca *adj* : hypnotic
hipnotismo *nm* : hypnotism
hipnotizador[1], -dora *adj* **1** : hypnotic **2** : spellbinding, mesmerizing
hipnotizador[2], -dora *n* : hypnotist
hipnotizar {21} *vt* : to hypnotize
hipo *nm* **1** : hiccup, hiccups *pl*
hipocampo *nm* : sea horse
hipocondría *nf* : hypochondria
hipocondríaco, -ca *adj & n* : hypochondriac
hipocresía *nf* : hypocrisy
hipócrita[1] *adj* : hypocritical — **hipócritamente** *adv*
hipócrita[2] *nmf* : hypocrite
hipodérmico, -ca *adj* **aguja hipodérmica** : hypodermic needle
hipódromo *nm* : racetrack
hipopótamo *nm* : hippopotamus
hipoteca *nf* : mortgage
hipotecar {72} *vt* **1** : to mortgage **2** : to compromise, to jeopardize
hipotecario, -ria *adj* : mortgage
hipotensión *nf, pl* **-siones** : low blood pressure
hipotenusa *nf* : hypotenuse
hipotermia *nf* : hypothermia
hipótesis *nfs & pl* : hypothesis
hipotético, -ca *adj* : hypothetical — **hipotéticamente** *adv*
hippie *or* **hippy** [ˈhipi] *nmf, pl* **hippies** [-pis] : hippie
hiriente *adj* : hurtful, offensive
hirió, etc. → herir
hirsuto, -ta *adj* **1** : hairy **2** : bristly, wiry
hirviente *adj* : boiling
hirvió, etc. → hervir
hisopo *nm* : cotton swab
hispánico, -ca *adj & n* : Hispanic
hispano[1], -na *adj* : Hispanic ⟨de habla hispana : Spanish-speaking⟩
hispano[2], -na *n* : Hispanic (person)
hispanoamericano[1], -na *adj* LATINOAMERICANO : Latin-American
hispanoamericano[2], -na *n* LATINOAMERICANO : Latin American
hispanohablante[1] *adj* : Spanish-speaking
hispanohablante[2] *nmf* : Spanish speaker
histerectomía *nf* : hysterectomy
histeria *nf* **1** : hysteria **2** : hysterics
histérico, -ca *adj* : hysterical — **histéricamente** *adv*
histerismo *nm* **1** : hysteria **2** : hysterics

historia *nf* **1** : history ⟨historia universal : world history⟩ ⟨pasará a la historia como un gran jugador de béisbol : he'll go down in history as a great baseball player⟩ **2** NARRACIÓN, RELATO : story **3** **dejarse de ∼s** : to say something directly, to stop beating around the bush **4** **hacer ∼** : to make history

historiador, -dora *n* : historian

historial *nm* **1** : record, document **2** CURRÍCULUM : résumé, curriculum vitae

histórico, -ca *adj* **1** : historical **2** : historic, important — **históricamente** *adv*

historieta *nf* : comic strip

histrionismo *nm* : histrionics, acting

hit ['hit] *nm, pl* **hits 1** ÉXITO : hit, popular song **2** : hit (in baseball)

hito *nm* : milestone, landmark

hizo → **hacer**

hobby ['hɔbi] *nm, pl* **hobbies** [-bis] : hobby

hocico *nm* : snout, muzzle

hockey ['hɔke, -ki] *nm* : hockey ⟨hockey sobre césped : field hockey⟩

hogar *nm* **1** : home ⟨labores del hogar : housework⟩ ⟨hogar, dulce hogar : home sweet home⟩ **2** : hearth, fireplace

hogareño, -ña *adj* **1** : domestic, homey **2** **ser muy hogareño** : to be a homebody

hogaza *nf* : large loaf (of bread)

hoguera *nf* **1** FOGATA : bonfire **2** **morir en la hoguera** : to burn at the stake

hoja *nf* **1** : leaf, petal, blade (of grass) **2** : sheet (of paper), page (of a book) ⟨hoja de cálculo : spreadsheet⟩ **3** FORMULARIO : form ⟨hoja de pedido : order form⟩ **4** : blade (of a knife) ⟨hoja de afeitar : razor blade⟩

hojalata *nf* : tinplate

hojaldre *nm* : puff pastry

hojarasca *nf* : fallen leaves *pl*

hojear *vt* : to leaf through (a book or magazine)

hojuela *nf* **1** : leaflet, young leaf **2** : flake

hola *interj* : hello!, hi!

holandés¹, -desa *adj, mpl* **-deses** : Dutch

holandés², -desa *n, mpl* **-deses** : Dutch person ⟨los holandeses : the Dutch⟩

holandés³ *nm* : Dutch (language)

holgadamente *adv* : comfortably, easily ⟨vivir holgadamente : to be well-off⟩

holgado, -da *adj* **1** : loose, baggy **2** : at ease, comfortable

holganza *nf* : leisure, idleness

holgar {16} *vi* : to be unnecessary ⟨huelga decir que . . . : it goes without saying that . . .⟩

holgazán¹, -zana *adj, mpl* **-zanes** : lazy

holgazán², -zana *n, mpl* **-zanes** HARAGÁN : slacker, idler

holgazanear *vi* HARAGANEAR : to laze around, to loaf

holgazanería *nf* PEREZA : idleness, laziness

holgura *nf* **1** : looseness **2** COMODIDAD : comfort, ease

holístico, -ca *adj* : holistic

hollar {19} *vt* : to tread on, to trample

hollín *nm, pl* **hollines** TIZNE : soot

holocausto *nm* : holocaust

holograma *nm* : hologram

hombre¹ *nm* **1** : man ⟨el hombre : man, mankind⟩ ⟨la escuela hizo de él un hombre : the school made a man out of him⟩ **2** **hombre de confianza** : right-hand man **3** **hombre de estado** : statesman **4** **hombre de negocios** : businessman **5** **hombre lobo** : werewolf **6** **el hombre de la calle** : the man in/on the street, the average person

hombre² *interj fam* **1** : well, hey **2** : of course!, you bet! **3** : come on!

hombrera *nf* **1** : shoulder pad **2** : epaulet

hombría *nf* : manliness

hombro *nm* : shoulder ⟨encogerse de hombros : to shrug one's shoulders⟩ ⟨hombro con hombro : shoulder to shoulder⟩ ⟨llevé mi hija en hombros : I carried my daughter on my shoulders⟩ **2** **arrimar el hombro** : to lend a hand, to pull one's weight

hombruno, -na *adj* : mannish

homenaje *nm* : homage, tribute ⟨rendir homenaje a : to pay tribute to⟩

homenajeado, -da *n* : guest of honor

homenajear *vt* : to pay homage to, to honor

homeopatía *nf* : homeopathy — **homeopático, -ca** *adj*

homicida¹ *adj* : homicidal, murderous

homicida² *nmf* ASESINO : murderer

homicidio *nm* ASESINATO : homicide, murder

homilía *nf* : homily, sermon

homófono *nm* : homophone

homogeneidad *nf* : homogeneity

homogeneizar {21} *vt* : to homogenize

homogéneo, -nea *adj* : homogeneous — **homogéneamente** *adv*

homógrafo *nm* : homograph

homologación *nf, pl* **-ciones 1** : sanctioning, approval **2** : parity

homologar {52} *vt* **1** : to sanction **2** : to bring into line

homólogo¹, -ga *adj* : homologous, equivalent

homólogo², -ga *n* : counterpart

homónimo¹, -ma *n* TOCAYO : namesake

homónimo² *nm* : homonym

homosexual *adj & nmf* : homosexual

homosexualidad *nf* : homosexuality

honda *nf* : sling

hondo¹ *adv* : deeply

hondo², -da *adj* PROFUNDO : deep ⟨en lo más hondo de : in the depths of⟩ — **hondamente** *adv*

hondonada *nf* **1** : hollow, depression **2** : ravine, gorge

hondura *nf* : depth

hondureño, -ña *adj & n* : Honduran

honestidad *nf* **1** : decency, modesty **2** : honesty

honesto, -ta *adj* **1** : decent, virtuous **2** : honest, honorable — **honestamente** *adv*

hongo *nm* **1** : fungus **2** : mushroom

honor *nm* **1** : honor ⟨en honor a la verdad : to be quite honest⟩ **2** **honores** *nmpl* : honors ⟨hacer los honores : to do the honors⟩

honorable *adj* HONROSO : honorable — **honorablemente** *adv*

honorario, -ria *adj* : honorary

honorarios *nmpl* : payment, fees (for professional services)

honorífico, -ca *adj* : honorary ⟨mención honorífica : honorable mention⟩

honra *nf* 1 : dignity, self-respect ⟨tener a mucha honra : to take great pride in⟩ 2 : good name, reputation

honradamente *adv* : honestly, decently

honradez *nf, pl* **-deces** : honesty, integrity, probity

honrado, -da *adj* 1 HONESTO : honest, upright 2 : honored

honrar *vt* 1 : to honor 2 : to be a credit to ⟨su generosidad lo honra : his generosity does him credit⟩

honroso, -sa *adj* HONORABLE : honorable — **honrosamente** *adv*

hora *nf* 1 : hour ⟨media hora : half an hour⟩ ⟨se pasa horas viendo televisión : he spends hours watching television⟩ 2 : time ⟨¿qué hora es? : what time is it?⟩ ⟨llegar a la hora : to arrive on time⟩ ⟨a la hora en punto : on the dot⟩ ⟨a la hora de comer : at mealtime⟩ ⟨a la última hora : at the last minute⟩ ⟨a primera hora : first thing⟩ ⟨antes de esa hora : early, ahead of time⟩ ⟨es hora de irnos a casa : it's time to go home⟩ ⟨ya es hora de tomarlo en serio : it's about time we took it seriously⟩ 3 CITA : appointment ⟨pedir/dar/tener hora : to make/give/have an appointment⟩ 4 **hora de cierre** : closing time 5 **hora local** : local time 6 **horas de oficina/trabajo** : office/work hours 7 **hora pico** : rush hour 8 **horas extras** : overtime 9 **las altas horas** : the wee hours 10 **trabajar por horas** : to work by the hour

horadar *vt* : to drill a hole in

horario *nm* : schedule, timetable, hours *pl* ⟨horario de visita : visiting hours⟩

horca *nf* 1 : gallows *pl* 2 : pitchfork

horcajadas *nfpl* **a ~** : astride, astraddle

horchata *nf* : cold sweet drink usually made with a kind of tuber

horcón *nm, pl* **horcones** : wooden post, prop

horda *nf* : horde

horizontal *adj* : horizontal — **horizontalmente** *adv*

horizonte *nm* : horizon, skyline

horma *nf* 1 : shoe tree 2 : shoemaker's last

hormiga *nf* : ant

hormigón *nm, pl* **-gones** CONCRETO : concrete

hormigonera *nf* : cement mixer

hormigueo *nm* 1 : tingling, pins and needles *pl* 2 : uneasiness

hormiguero *nm* 1 : anthill 2 : swarm (of people)

hormona *nf* : hormone — **hormonal** *adj*

hornacina *nf* : niche, recess

hornada *nf* : batch

hornear *vt* : to bake

hornilla *nf* : burner (of a stove)

hornillo *nm* : portable stove

horno *nm* 1 : oven ⟨horno de microondas : microwave oven⟩ 2 : kiln

horóscopo *nm* : horoscope

horqueta *nf* 1 : fork (in a river or road) 2 : crotch (in a tree) 3 : small pitchfork

horquilla *nf* 1 : hairpin, bobby pin 2 : pitchfork

horrendo, -da *adj* : horrendous, horrible

horrible *adj* : horrible, dreadful — **horriblemente** *adv*

horripilante *adj* : horrifying, hair-raising

horripilar *vt* : to horrify, to terrify

horror *nm* : horror, dread

horrorizado, -da *adj* : terrified

horrorizar {21} *vt* : to horrify, to terrify — **horrorizarse** *vr*

horroroso, -sa *adj* 1 : horrifying, terrifying 2 : dreadful, bad

hortaliza *nf* 1 : vegetable 2 **hortalizas** *nfpl* : garden produce

hortera *adj Spain fam* : tacky, gaudy

hortícola *adj* : horticultural

horticultura *nf* : horticulture

hosco, -ca *adj* : sullen, gloomy — **hoscamente** *adv*

hospedaje *nm* : lodging, accommodations *pl*

hospedar *vt* : to provide with lodging, to put up — **hospedarse** *vr* : to stay, to lodge

hospicio *nm* : orphanage

hospital *nm* : hospital

hospitalario, -ria *adj* : hospitable

hospitalidad *nf* : hospitality

hospitalización *nf, pl* **-ciones** : hospitalization

hospitalizar {21} *vt* : to hospitalize — **hospitalizarse** *vr*

hostal *nm* : cheap hotel

hostelería *nf* : the hotel industry

hostería *nf* POSADA : inn

hostia *nf* : host, Eucharist

hostigamiento *nm* : harassment

hostigar {52} *vt* ACOSAR, ASEDIAR : to harass, to pester

hostil *adj* : hostile

hostilidad *nf* 1 : hostility, antagonism 2 **hostilidades** *nfpl* : (military) hostilities

hostilizar {21} *vt* : to harass

hotel *nm* : hotel

hotelero¹, -ra *adj* : hotel ⟨la industria hotelera : the hotel business⟩

hotelero², -ra *n* : hotel manager, hotelier

hoy *adv* 1 : today ⟨hoy mismo : right now, this very day⟩ 2 : now, nowadays ⟨de hoy en adelante : from now on⟩

hoyo *nm* AGUJERO : hole

hoyuelo *nm* : dimple

hoz *nf, pl* **hoces** : sickle

hozar {21} *vi* : to root (of a pig)

huachinango *nm Mex* : red snapper

huarache *nm* : sandal

hubo, etc. → **haber**

hueco¹, -ca *adj* 1 : hollow, empty 2 : soft, spongy 3 : hollow, resonant 4 : proud, conceited 5 : superficial

hueco² *nm* 1 : hole, hollow, cavity 2 : gap, space 3 : recess, alcove

huele, etc. → **oler**

huelga *nf* **1** PARO : strike **2 hacer huelga** : to strike, to go on strike

huelguista *nmf* : striker

huella[1], etc. → **hollar**

huella[2] *nf* **1** : footprint ⟨seguir las huellas de alguien : to follow in someone's footsteps⟩ **2** : mark, impact ⟨dejar huella : to leave one's mark⟩ ⟨sin dejar huella : without a trace⟩ **3 huella digital** *or* **huella dactilar** : fingerprint

huérfano[1], **-na** *adj* **1** : orphan, orphaned **2** : defenseless **3 ~ de** : lacking, devoid of

huérfano[2], **-na** *n* : orphan

huerta *nf* **1** : large vegetable garden, truck farm **2** : orchard **3** : irrigated land

huerto *nm* **1** : vegetable garden **2** : orchard

hueso *nm* **1** : bone **2** : pit, stone (of a fruit)

huésped[1], **-peda** *n* INVITADO : guest

huésped[2] *nm* : host ⟨organismo huésped : host organism⟩

huestes *nfpl* **1** : followers **2** : troops, army

huesudo, -da *adj* : bony

hueva *nf* : roe, spawn

huevo *nm* **1** : egg ⟨huevos revueltos : scrambled eggs⟩ ⟨huevo de Pascua : Easter egg⟩ **2 huevos** *nmpl usu vulgar* : balls *pl, usu vulgar*; testicles *pl*

huida *nf* : flight, escape

huidizo, -za *adj* **1** ESCURRIDIZO : elusive, slippery **2** : shy, evasive

huipil *nm CA, Mex* : traditional sleeveless blouse or dress

huir {41} *vi* **1** ESCAPAR : to escape, to flee **2 ~ de** : to avoid

huiro *nm Chile, Peru* : seaweed

huizache *nm* : acacia

hule *nm* **1** : oilcloth, oilskin **2** *Mex* : rubber **3 hule espuma** *Mex* : foam rubber

hulera *nf Mex* : slingshot

humanidad *nf* **1** : humanity, mankind **2** : humanity, compassion **3 humanidades** *nfpl* : humanities *pl*

humanismo *nm* : humanism

humanista *nmf* : humanist

humanístico, -ca *adj* : humanistic

humanitario, -ria *adj & n* : humanitarian

humano[1], **-na** *adj* **1** : human **2** BENÉVOLO : humane, benevolent — **humanamente** *adv*

humano[2] *nm* : human being, human

humareda *nf* : cloud of smoke

humeante *adj* **1** : smoky **2** : smoking, steaming

humear *vi* **1** : to smoke **2** : to steam

humectante[1] *adj* : moisturizing

humectante[2] *nm* : moisturizer

humedad *nf* **1** : humidity **2** : dampness, moistness

humedecer {53} *vt* **1** : to humidify **2** : to moisten, to dampen

húmedo, -da *adj* **1** : humid **2** : moist, damp

humidificador *nm* : humidifier

humidificar {72} *vt* : to humidify

humildad *nf* **1** : humility **2** : lowliness

humilde *adj* **1** : humble **2** : lowly ⟨gente humilde : poor people⟩

humildemente *adv* : meekly, humbly

humillación *nf, pl* **-ciones** : humiliation

humillante *adj* : humiliating

humillar *vt* : to humiliate — **humillarse** *vr* : to humble oneself ⟨humillarse a hacer algo : to stoop to doing something⟩

humo *nm* **1** : smoke, steam, fumes **2 humos** *nmpl* : airs *pl*, conceit

humor *nm* **1** : humor **2** : mood, temper ⟨está de buen humor : she's in a good mood⟩

humorada *nf* **1** BROMA : joke, witticism **2** : whim, caprice

humorismo *nm* : humor, wit

humorista *nmf* : humorist, comedian, comedienne *f*

humorístico, -ca *adj* : humorous — **humorísticamente** *adv*

humoso, -sa *adj* : smoky, steamy

humus *nm* : humus

hundido, -da *adj* **1** : sunken **2** : depressed

hundimiento *nm* **1** : sinking **2** : collapse, ruin

hundir *vt* **1** : to sink **2** : to destroy, to ruin — **hundirse** *vr* **1** : to sink down **2** : to cave in **3** : to break down, to go to pieces

húngaro[1], **-ra** *adj & n* : Hungarian

húngaro[2] *nm* : Hungarian (language)

huracán *nm, pl* **-canes** : hurricane

huraño, -ña *adj* **1** : unsociable, aloof **2** : timid, skittish (of an animal)

hurgar {52} *vt* : to poke, to jab, to rake (a fire) — *vi* **~ en** : to rummage in, to poke through

hurgue, etc. → **hurgar**

hurón *nm, pl* **hurones** : ferret

huronear *vi* : to pry, to snoop

hurra *interj* : hurrah!, hooray!

hurtadillas *nfpl* **a ~** : stealthily, on the sly

hurtar *vt* ROBAR : to steal

hurto *nm* **1** : theft, robbery **2** : stolen property, loot

husmear *vt* **1** : to follow the scent of, to track **2** : to sniff out, to pry into — *vi* **1** : to pry, to snoop **2** : to sniff around (of an animal)

huso *nm* **1** : spindle **2 huso horario** : time zone

huy *interj* : ow!, ouch!

huye, etc. → **huir**

i *nf* : tenth letter of the Spanish alphabet

i- → **in-**

iba, etc. → **ir**

ibérico, -ca *adj* : Iberian

ibero, -ra *or* **íbero, -ra** *adj & n* : Iberian

iberoamericano, -na *adj* HISPANOAMERICANO, LATINOAMERICANO : Latin-American

-ible *suf* : -ible

ice, etc. → **izar**

iceberg *nm, pl* **icebergs** : iceberg

icono *nm* : icon

iconoclasia *nf* : iconoclasm

iconoclasta *nmf* : iconoclast

ictericia *nf* : jaundice

ictérico, -ca *adj* : jaundiced

id *nm* : id

ida *nf* **1** : going, departure **2 ida y vuelta** : round trip **3 idas y venidas** : comings and goings

idea *nf* **1** : idea, notion ⟨una buena/mala idea : a good/bad idea⟩ ⟨tengo una idea : I have an idea⟩ ⟨no tengo (ni) idea : I have no idea⟩ ⟨me hago una idea de cómo es : I'm getting an/some idea of what he's like⟩ **2** : opinion, belief ⟨siempre puedes cambiar de idea : you can always change your mind⟩ ⟨¿de dónde sacaste esa idea? : where did you get that idea?⟩ **3** PROPÓSITO : intention, idea ⟨la idea era llegar temprano : the idea was to arrive early⟩

ideal *adj & nm* : ideal — **idealmente** *adv*

idealismo *nm* : idealism

idealista[1] *adj* : idealistic

idealista[2] *nmf* : idealist

idealizar {21} *vt* : to idealize — **idealización** *nf*

idear *vt* : to devise, to think up

ideario *nm* : ideology

ídem *nm* : the same, ditto

idéntico, -ca *adj* : identical, alike — **idénticamente** *adv*

identidad *nf* : identity

identificable *adj* : identifiable

identificación *nf, pl* **-ciones 1** : identification, identifying **2** : identification document, ID

identificar {72} *vt* : to identify — **identificarse** *vr* **1** : to identify oneself **2 ~ con** : to identify with

ideología *nf* : ideology — **ideológicamente** *adv*

ideológico, -ca *adj* : ideological

ideólogo, -ga *n* : ideologue

idílico, -ca *adj* : idyllic

idilio *nm* **1** : idyll **2** AMORÍO : love affair, romance

idioma *nm* : language ⟨el idioma inglés : the English language⟩

idiomático, -ca *adj* : idiomatic — **idiomáticamente** *adv*

idiosincrasia *nf* : idiosyncrasy

idiosincrásico, -ca *adj* : idiosyncratic

idiota[1] *adj* : idiotic, stupid, foolish

idiota[2] *nmf* : idiot, foolish person

idiotez *nf, pl* **-teces 1** : idiocy **2** : idiotic act or remark ⟨¡no digas idioteces! : don't talk nonsense!⟩

ido[1], **ida** *adj* : crazy, nutty

ido[2] *pp* → **ir**

idólatra[1] *adj* : idolatrous

idólatra[2] *nmf* : idolater

idolatrar *vt* : to idolize

idolatría *nf* : idolatry

ídolo *nm* : idol

idoneidad *nf* : suitability

idóneo, -nea *adj* ADECUADO : suitable, fitting

iglesia *nf* : church

iglú *nm, pl* **iglús** *or* **iglúes** : igloo

ignición *nf, pl* **-ciones** : ignition

ignífugo, -ga *adj* : fireproof

ignominia *nf* : ignomiy, disgrace

ignominioso, -sa *adj* : ignominious, shameful

ignorancia *nf* : ignorance

ignorante[1] *adj* : ignorant — **ignorantemente** *adv*

ignorante[2] *nmf* : ignorant person, ignoramus

ignorar *vt* **1** : to ignore **2** DESCONOCER : to be unaware of ⟨lo ignoramos por absoluto : we have no idea⟩

ignoto, -ta *adj* : unknown

i griega *nf* : (letter) i

igual[1] *adv* **1** : in the same way ⟨las cosas siguen igual : things are the same as ever⟩ **2** : perhaps ⟨igual llueve : it might rain, it may rain⟩ **3** : anyway ⟨iba a venir igual : I was going to come anyway⟩ **4 al igual que** : as well as **5 igual que** : (just) like, the same as ⟨juega básquetbol, igual que su prima : she plays basketball, just like her cousin⟩ ⟨pienso igual que tú : I agree with you, I think the same thing⟩ **6 por ~** : equally

igual[2] *adj* **1** : equal ⟨ser igual a : to be equal to⟩ **2** IDÉNTICO : the same, alike ⟨son iguales : they're the same⟩ ⟨ser igual a : to be the same as⟩ ⟨me es/da igual : it makes no difference to me⟩ **3** : even, smooth **4** SEMEJANTE : similar **5** CONSTANTE : constant

igual[3] *nmf* : equal, peer ⟨sin igual : without equal, unequaled⟩

igualado, -da *adj* **1** : even (of a score) **2** : level **3** *Mex* : disrespectful

igualar *vt* **1** : to equalize **2** NIVELAR : to level, to flatten, to straighten **3** : to tie ⟨igualar el marcador : to even the score⟩ — **igualarse** *vr* **~ a/con** : to equal, to be equal to, to be a match for

igualdad *nf* **1** : equality **2** UNIFORMIDAD : evenness, uniformity

igualitario, -ria *adj* : egalitarian

igualmente *adv* **1** : equally **2** ASIMISMO : likewise

iguana *nf* : iguana

ijada *nf* : flank, loin, side

ijar *nm* → **ijada**

ilegal[1] *adj* : illegal, unlawful — **ilegalmente** *adv*

ilegal² *nmf CA, Mex* : illegal alien
ilegalidad *nf* : illegality
ilegibilidad *nf* : illegibility
ilegible *adj* : illegible — **ilegiblemente** *adv*
ilegitimidad *nf* : illegitimacy
ilegítimo, -ma *adj* : illegitimate, unlawful
ileso, -sa *adj* : uninjured, unharmed
ilícito, -ta *adj* : illicit — **ilícitamente** *adv*
ilimitado, -da *adj* : unlimited
ilógico, -ca *adj* : illogical — **ilógicamente** *adv*
iluminación *nf, pl* **-ciones 1** : illumination **2** ALUMBRADO : lighting
iluminado, -da *adj* : illuminated, lighted
iluminar *vt* **1** : to illuminate, to light (up) **2** : to enlighten
ilusión *nf, pl* **-siones 1** : illusion, delusion **2** ESPERANZA : hope ⟨hacerse ilusiones : to get one's hopes up⟩ **3** *Spain* : happiness, excitement, enthusiasm ⟨¡me hace mucha ilusión que te haya gustado! : I'm so glad you liked it!⟩ ⟨no me hace ilusión ir : I'm not looking forward to going⟩ **4 ilusión óptica** : optical illusion
ilusionado, -da *adj* ESPERANZADO : hopeful, eager
ilusionar *vt* : to build up hope, to excite — **ilusionarse** *vr* : to get one's hopes up
iluso¹, -sa *adj* : naive, gullible
iluso², -sa *n* SOÑADOR : dreamer, visionary
ilusorio, -ria *adj* ENGAÑOSO : illusory, misleading
ilustración *nf, pl* **-ciones 1** : illustration **2** : erudition, learning ⟨la Ilustración : the Enlightenment⟩
ilustrado, -da *adj* **1** : illustrated **2** DOCTO : learned, erudite
ilustrador, -dora *n* : illustrator
ilustrar *vt* **1** : to illustrate **2** ACLARAR, CLARIFICAR : to explain
ilustrativo, -va *adj* : illustrative
ilustre *adj* : illustrious, eminent
im- → in-
imagen *nf, pl* **imágenes** : image, picture
imaginable *adj* : imaginable, conceivable
imaginación *nf, pl* **-ciones** : imagination
imaginar *vt* : to imagine — **imaginarse** *vr* **1** : to suppose, to imagine **2** : to picture
imaginario, -ria *adj* : imaginary
imaginativo, -va *adj* : imaginative — **imaginativamente** *adv*
imaginería *nf* **1** : imagery **2** : image making (in religion)
imán *nm, pl* **imanes** : magnet
imantar *vt* : to magnetize
imbatible *adj* : unbeatable
imbécil¹ *adj* : stupid, idiotic
imbécil² *nmf* **1** : imbecile **2** *fam* : idiot, dope
imbecilidad *nf* **1** : imbecility **2** IDIOTEZ : stupid thing to say or do
imborrable *adj* : indelible
imbuir {41} *vt* : to imbue — **imbuirse** *vr*
imitación *nf, pl* **-ciones 1** : imitation **2** : mimicry, impersonation
imitador¹, -dora *adj* : imitative
imitador², -dora *n* **1** : imitator **2** : mimic

imitar *vt* **1** : to imitate, to copy **2** : to mimic, to impersonate
imitativo, -va *adj* → **imitador¹**
impaciencia *nf* : impatience
impacientar *vt* : to make impatient, to exasperate — **impacientarse** *vr*
impaciente *adj* : impatient — **impacientemente** *adv*
impactado, -da *adj* : shocked, stunned
impactante *adj* **1** : shocking **2** : impressive, powerful
impactar *vt* **1** GOLPEAR : to hit **2** IMPRESIONAR : to impact, to affect — **impactarse** *vr*
impacto *nm* **1** : impact, effect **2** : shock, collision
impagable *adj* **1** : unpayable **2** : priceless
impago¹ *adj* : outstanding, unpaid
impago² *nm* : nonpayment
impala *nm* : impala
impalpable *adj* INTANGIBLE : impalpable, intangible
impar¹ *adj* : odd ⟨números impares : odd numbers⟩
impar² *nm* : odd number
imparable *adj* : unstoppable
imparcial *adj* : impartial — **imparcialmente** *adv*
imparcialidad *nf* : impartiality
impartir *vt* : to impart, to give
impasible *adj* : impassive, unmoved — **impasiblemente** *adv*
impasse *nm* : impasse
impavidez *nf* : fearlessness
impávido, -da *adj* : undaunted
impecable *adj* INTACHABLE : impeccable, faultless — **impecablemente** *adv*
impedido¹, -da *adj* : disabled, crippled
impedido², -da *n* : disabled person, handicapped person *sometimes offensive*
impedimento *nm* **1** : impediment, obstacle **2** : disability
impedir {54} *vt* **1** : to prevent, to block **2** : to impede, to hinder
impeler *vt* **1** : to drive, to propel **2** : to impel
impenetrable *adj* : impenetrable — **impenetrabilidad** *nf*
impenitente *adj* : unrepentant
impensable *adj* : unthinkable
impensado, -da *adj* : unforeseen, unexpected
imperante *adj* : prevailing
imperar *vi* **1** : to reign, to rule **2** PREDOMINAR : to prevail
imperativo¹, -va *adj* **1** : imperative **2** : authoritative, commanding
imperativo² *nm* : imperative
imperceptible *adj* : imperceptible — **imperceptiblemente** *adv*
imperdible *nm Spain* : safety pin
imperdonable *adj* : unforgivable
imperecedero, -ra *adj* **1** : imperishable **2** INMORTAL : immortal, everlasting
imperfección *nf, pl* **-ciones 1** : imperfection **2** DEFECTO : defect, flaw
imperfecto¹, -ta *adj* **1** : imperfect, flawed
imperfecto² *nm* : imperfect tense
imperial *adj* : imperial
imperialismo *nm* : imperialism

imperialista adj & nmf : imperialist

impericia nf : lack of skill, incompetence

imperio nm **1** : empire **2** : authority, rule ⟨el imperio de la ley : the rule of law⟩

imperioso, -sa adj **1** : imperious **2** : pressing, urgent — **imperiosamente** adv

impermeabilizante nm : water repellent, waterproofing

impermeabilizar {21} vt : to waterproof

impermeable¹ adj **1** : impervious **2** : impermeable, waterproof

impermeable² nm : raincoat

impersonal adj : impersonal — **impersonalmente** adv

impersonar vt Mex : to impersonate

impertinencia nf INSOLENCIA : impertinence, insolence

impertinente adj **1** INSOLENTE : impertinent, insolent **2** INOPORTUNO : inappropriate, uncalled-for **3** IRRELEVANTE : irrelevant

impertinentemente adv : impertinently

imperturbable adj : imperturbable, impassive, stolid

ímpetu nm **1** : impetus, momentum **2** : vigor, energy **3** : force, violence

impetuoso, -sa adj : impetuous, impulsive — **impetuosamente** adv

impiedad nf : impiety

impío, -pía adj : impious, ungodly

implacable adj : implacable, relentless — **implacablemente** adv

implantación nf, pl **-ciones 1** : implantation **2** ESTABLECIMIENTO : establishment, introduction

implantado, -da adj : well-established

implantar vt **1** : to implant **2** ESTABLECER : to establish, to introduce — **implantarse** vr

implante nm : implant

implementar vt : to implement — **implementarse** vr — **implementación** nf

implemento nm : implement, tool

implicación nf, pl **-ciones** : implication

implicancia nf : implication

implicar {72} vt **1** ENREDAR, ENVOLVER : to involve, to implicate **2** : to imply

implícito, -ta adj : implied, implicit — **implícitamente** adv

implorar vt : to implore

implosión nf, pl **-siones** : implosion — **implosivo, -va** adj

implosionar vi : to implode

imponderable adj & nm : imponderable

imponente adj : imposing, impressive

imponer {60} vt **1** : to impose **2** : to confer **3** : to introduce, to establish, to set (a fashion) — vi : to be impressive, to command respect — **imponerse** vr **1** : to take on (a duty) **2** : to assert oneself **3** : to prevail

imponible adj : taxable

impopular adj : unpopular — **impopularidad** nf

importación nf, pl **-ciones 1** : importation **2 importaciones** nfpl : imports

importado, -da adj : imported

importador¹, -dora adj : importing

importador², -dora n : importer

importancia nf : importance

importante adj : important, significant — **importantemente** adv

importar vi **1** : to matter, to be important ⟨no importa : it doesn't matter, it's not important⟩ ⟨lo que importa es el resultado : what matters is the result⟩ ⟨no le importa lo que piensen : she doesn't care what they think⟩ ⟨¿qué importa que no les guste? : who cares if they don't like it?⟩ ⟨(no) me importa un bledo/comino : I don't give a damn, I couldn't care less⟩ ⟨no te importo : you don't care about me⟩ **2** : to bother ⟨no le importa hacerlo : he doesn't mind doing it⟩ ⟨si no te importa : if you don't mind, if it's OK with you⟩ — vt : to import

importe nm **1** : price, cost **2** : sum, amount

importunar vt : to bother, to inconvenience — vi : to be inconvenient

importuno, -na adj **1** : inopportune, inconvenient **2** : bothersome, annoying

imposibilidad nf : impossibility

imposibilitado, -da adj **1** : disabled, crippled **2 verse imposibilitado** : to be unable (to do something)

imposibilitar vt **1** : to make impossible **2** : to disable, to incapacitate — **imposibilitarse** vr : to become disabled

imposible adj : impossible — **imposiblemente** adv

imposición nf, pl **-ciones 1** : imposition **2** EXIGENCIA : demand, requirement **3** : tax **4** : deposit

impositivo, -va adj : tax ⟨tasa impositiva : tax rate⟩

impostor, -tora n : impostor

impostura nf **1** : fraud **2** CALUMNIA : slander

impotencia nf **1** : impotence, helplessness, powerlessness **2** : impotence (in medicine)

impotente adj **1** : helpless, powerless **2** : impotent

impracticable adj : impracticable

imprecisión nf, pl **-siones 1** : imprecision, vagueness **2** : inaccuracy

impreciso, -sa adj **1** : imprecise, vague **2** : inaccurate

impredecible adj : unpredictable

impregnar vt : to impregnate

imprenta nf **1** : printing **2** : printing shop, press **3 letra(s) de imprenta → letra**

imprescindible adj : essential, indispensable

impresión nf, pl **-siones 1** : print, printing **2** : impression, feeling ⟨causar una buena/mala impresión : to make a good/bad impression⟩

impresionable adj : impressionable

impresionante adj : impressive, incredible, amazing, shocking (of video, etc.), horrific (of an accident, etc.) — **impresionantemente** adv

impresionar vt **1** : to impress, to strike **2** : to affect, to move **3** : to shock **4** : to expose (film) to light — vi : to make an impression — **impresionarse** vr : to be affected, to be moved

impresionismo *nm* : impressionism
impresionista[1] *adj* : impressionist
impresionista[2] *nmf* : impressionist
impreso[1] *pp* → **imprimir**
impreso[2], **-sa** *adj* : printed
impreso[3] *nm* **1** PUBLICACIÓN : printed matter, publication　**2** FORMULARIO : form
impresor, -sora *n* : printer
impresora *nf* : (computer) printer
imprevisible *adj* : unforeseeable, unpredictable
imprevisión *nf, pl* **-siones** : lack of foresight, thoughtlessness
imprevisto[1], **-ta** *adj* : unexpected, unforeseen
imprevisto[2] *nm* : unexpected occurrence, contingency
imprimir {42} *vt* **1** : to print　**2** : to imprint, to stamp, to impress
improbabilidad *nf* : improbability
improbable *adj* : improbable, unlikely
improcedente *adj* **1** : inadmissible　**2** : inappropriate, improper
improductivo, -va *adj* : unproductive
impronta *nf* : mark, stamp ⟨dejar su impronta : to leave one's mark⟩
improperio *nm* : affront, insult
impropiedad *nf* : impropriety
impropio, -pia *adj* **1** : improper, incorrect　**2** INADECUADO : unsuitable, inappropriate
improvisación *nf, pl* **-ciones** : improvisation, ad-lib
improvisado, -da *adj* : improvised, ad-lib
improvisar *v* : to improvise, to ad-lib
improviso *adj* de ~ : all of a sudden, unexpectedly
imprudencia *nf* **1** : mistake, indiscretion　**2** : carelessness, recklessness
imprudente *adj* **1** : imprudent, unwise, indiscreet　**2** : careless, reckless — **imprudentemente** *adv*
impúdico, -ca *adj* : shameless, indecent
impuesto[1] *pp* → **imponer**
impuesto[2] *nm* : tax
impugnar *vt* : to challenge, to contest
impulsar *vt* **1** : to propel, to drive　**2** : to boost, to promote
impulsividad *nf* : impulsiveness
impulsivo, -va *adj* : impulsive — **impulsivamente** *adv*
impulso *nm* **1** : drive, thrust　**2** : impulse, urge
impulsor, -sora *n* : force, impetus ⟨el principal impulsor de la iniciativa : the main/driving force behind the initiative⟩
impune *adj* : unpunished
impunemente *adv* : with impunity
impunidad *nf* : impunity
impuntualidad *nf* : lack of punctuality
impureza *nf* : impurity
impuro, -ra *adj* : impure
impuso, etc. → **imponer**
imputable *adj* ATRIBUIBLE : attributable
imputación *nf, pl* **-ciones** **1** : attribution　**2** : accusation
imputar *vt* ATRIBUIR : to impute, to attribute

in- *or* **im-** *or* **i-** *or* **ir- pref** : in-, im-, il-, un- ⟨inexacto : inexact⟩ ⟨imperfecto : imperfect⟩ ⟨ilegal : illegal⟩ ⟨inaceptable : unacceptable⟩
inacabable *adj* : endless
inacabado, -da *adj* INCONCLUSO : unfinished
inaccesibilidad *nf* : inaccessibility
inaccesible *adj* **1** : inaccessible　**2** : unattainable
inacción *nf, pl* **-ciones** : inactivity, inaction
inaceptable *adj* : unacceptable
inactividad *nf* : inactivity, idleness
inactivo, -va *adj* : inactive, idle
inadaptado[1], **-da** *adj* : maladjusted
inadaptado[2], **-da** *n* : misfit
inadecuación *nf, pl* **-ciones** : inadequacy
inadecuado, -da *adj* **1** : inadequate　**2** IMPROPIO : inappropriate — **inadecuadamente** *adv*
inadmisible *adj* **1** : inadmissible　**2** : unacceptable
inadvertencia *nf* : oversight
inadvertidamente *adv* : inadvertently
inadvertido, -da *adj* **1** : unnoticed ⟨pasar inadvertido : to go unnoticed⟩　**2** DESPISTADO, DISTRAÍDO : inattentive, distracted
inagotable *adj* : inexhaustible
inaguantable *adj* INSOPORTABLE : insufferable, unbearable
inalámbrico, -ca *adj* : wireless, cordless ⟨acceso inalámbrico a Internet : wireless Internet access⟩ ⟨un teléfono inalámbrico : a cordless phone⟩
inalcanzable *adj* : unreachable, unattainable
inalienable *adj* : inalienable
inalterable *adj* **1** : unalterable, unchangeable　**2** : impassive　**3** : colorfast
inamovible *adj* : immovable, fixed
inanición *nf, pl* **-ciones** : starvation
inanimado, -da *adj* : inanimate
inapelable *adj* : indisputable
inapetencia *nf* : lack of appetite
inaplicable *adj* : inapplicable
inapreciable *adj* **1** : imperceptible, negligible　**2** : invaluable
inapropiado, -da *adj* : inappropriate, unsuitable — **inapropiadamente** *adv*
inarticulado, -da *adj* : inarticulate, unintelligible — **inarticuladamente** *adv*
inasequible *adj* : unattainable, inaccessible
inasistencia *nf* AUSENCIA : absence
inatacable *adj* : unassailable, indisputable
inaudible *adj* : inaudible
inaudito, -ta *adj* : unheard-of, unprecedented
inauguración *nf, pl* **-ciones** **1** : inauguration, opening　**2** : inauguration, beginning
inaugural *adj* : inaugural, opening
inaugurar *vt* **1** : to inaugurate　**2** : to open
inauténtico, -ca *adj* : counterfeit, inauthentic
inca *adj & nmf* : Inca
incaico, -ca *adj* : Inca, Incan
incalculable *adj* : incalculable

incalificable *adj* : indescribable

incandescencia *nf* : incandescence — **incandescente** *adj*

incansable *adj* INFATIGABLE : tireless — **incansablemente** *adv*

incapacidad *nf* 1 : inability, incapacity 2 : disability, handicap 3 : incompetence 4 *Col, CoRi* : sick leave

incapacitado, -da *adj* 1 : disqualified 2 : disabled, handicapped

incapacitar *vt* 1 : to incapacitate, to disable 2 : to disqualify

incapaz *adj, pl* **-paces** 1 : incapable, unable 2 : incompetent, inept

incautación *nf, pl* **-ciones** : seizure, confiscation

incautar *vt* CONFISCAR : to confiscate, to seize — **incautarse** *vr*

incauto, -ta *adj* : unwary, unsuspecting

incendiar *vt* : to set fire to, to burn (down) — **incendiarse** *vr* : to catch fire, to burn down

incendiario¹, -ria *adj* : incendiary, inflammatory

incendiario², -ria *n* : arsonist

incendio *nm* 1 : fire 2 **incendio provocado** : arson

incensario *nm* : censer

incentivar *vt* : to encourage, to stimulate

incentivo *nm* : incentive

incertidumbre *nf* : uncertainty, suspense

incesante *adj* : incessant — **incesantemente** *adv*

incesto *nm* : incest

incestuoso, -sa *adj* : incestuous

incidencia *nf* 1 : incident 2 : effect, impact 3 **por ~** : by chance, accidentally

incidental *adj* : incidental

incidentalmente *adv* : by chance

incidente *nm* : incident, occurrence

incidir *vi* 1 **~ en** : to fall into, to enter into ⟨incidimos en el mismo error : we fell into the same mistake⟩ 2 **~ en** : to affect, to influence, to have a bearing on

incienso *nm* : incense

incierto, -ta *adj* 1 : uncertain 2 : untrue 3 : unsteady, insecure

incinerador *nm* : incinerator

incinerar *vt* 1 : to incinerate 2 : to cremate

incipiente *adj* : incipient

incisión *nf, pl* **-siones** : incision

incisivo¹, -va *adj* : incisive

incisivo² *nm* : incisor

inciso *nm* 1 : digression, aside 2 : paragraph, subsection

incitación *nf, pl* **-ciones** : incitement

incitador, -dora *n* : instigator, agitator

incitador², -dora *adj* : provocative

incitante *adj* : provocative

incitar *vt* : to incite, to rouse

incivilizado, -da *adj* : uncivilized

inclemencia *nf* : inclemency, severity

inclemente *adj* : inclement

inclinación *nf, pl* **-ciones** 1 PROPENSIÓN : inclination, tendency 2 : incline, slope 3 : bow ⟨inclinación de cabeza : nod⟩

inclinado, -da *adj* 1 : sloping, tilted 2 : inclined, apt

inclinar *vt* : to tilt, to lean, to incline ⟨inclinar la cabeza : to bow one's head⟩

— **inclinarse** *vr* 1 : to lean, to lean over 2 : to bow 3 **~ a** : to be inclined to

incluir {41} *vt* : to include

inclusión *nf, pl* **-siones** : inclusion

inclusive *adv* : inclusive ⟨niños de entre dos y cinco años inclusive : children ages two through five inclusive⟩ ⟨hasta el sábado inclusive : up to and including Saturday, through Saturday⟩

inclusivo, -va *adj* : inclusive, open

incluso *adv* AUN : even, in fact ⟨es importante e incluso crucial : it is important and even crucial⟩

incógnita *nf* 1 : unknown quantity (in mathematics) 2 : mystery

incógnito, -ta *adj* 1 : unknown 2 **de incógnito** : incognito

incoherencia *nf* : incoherence

incoherente *adj* : incoherent — **incoherentemente** *adv*

incoloro, -ra *adj* : colorless

incombustible *adj* : fireproof

incomible *adj* : inedible

incomodar *vt* 1 : to make uncomfortable 2 : to inconvenience — **incomodarse** *vr* : to put oneself out, to take the trouble

incomodidad *nf* 1 : discomfort, awkwardness 2 MOLESTIA : inconvenience, bother

incómodo, -da *adj* 1 : uncomfortable, awkward 2 INCONVENIENTE : inconvenient — **incómodamente** *adv*

incomparable *adj* : incomparable

incompatibilidad *nf* : incompatibility

incompatible *adj* : incompatible

incompetencia *nf* : incompetence

incompetente *adj & nmf* : incompetent

incompleto, -ta *adj* : incomplete

incomprendido, -da *adj* : misunderstood

incomprensible *adj* : incomprehensible

incomprensión *nf, pl* **-siones** : lack of understanding, incomprehension

incomunicación *nf, pl* **-ciones** : lack of communication

incomunicado, -da *adj* 1 : cut off, isolated 2 : in solitary confinement

inconcebible *adj* : inconceivable, unthinkable — **inconcebiblemente** *adv*

inconcluso, -sa *adj* INACABADO : unfinished

incondicional *adj* : unconditional — **incondicionalmente** *adv*

inconexo, -xa *adj* 1 : unrelated, unconnected 2 : disjointed

inconfesable *adj* : unspeakable, shameful

inconforme *adj & nmf* : nonconformist

inconformidad *nf* : nonconformity

inconformista *adj & nmf* : nonconformist

inconfundible *adj* : unmistakable, obvious — **inconfundiblemente** *adv*

incongruencia *nf* : incongruity

incongruente *adj* : incongruous

inconmensurable *adj* : vast, immeasurable

inconquistable *adj* : unyielding

inconsciencia *nf* 1 : unconsciousness, lack of awareness 2 : irresponsibility

inconsciente¹ *adj* 1 : unconscious, unaware 2 : reckless, needless — **inconscientemente** *adv*

inconsciente² *nm* **el inconsciente** : the unconscious
inconsecuente *adj* : inconsistent — **inconsecuencia** *nf*
inconsiderado, -da *adj* : inconsiderate, thoughtless
inconsistencia *nf* : inconsistency
inconsistente *adj* **1** : weak, flimsy **2** : inconsistent, weak (of an argument)
inconsolable *adj* : inconsolable — **inconsolablemente** *adv*
inconstancia *nf* : fickleness
inconstante *adj* : fickle, changeable
inconstitucional *adj* : unconstitutional — **inconstitucionalidad** *nf*
incontable *adj* INNUMERABLE : countless, innumerable
incontenible *adj* : uncontrollable, unstoppable
incontestable *adj* INCUESTIONABLE, INDISCUTIBLE : irrefutable, indisputable
incontinencia *nf* : incontinence — **incontinente** *adj*
incontrolable *adj* : uncontrollable
incontrolado, -da *adj* : uncontrolled, out of control
incontrovertible *adj* : indisputable
inconveniencia *nf* **1** : inconvenience, trouble **2** : inappropriateness **3** : tactless remark
inconveniente¹ *adj* **1** INCÓMODO : inconvenient **2** INAPROPIADO : improper, unsuitable
inconveniente² *nm* **1** : obstacle, problem, snag **2** : objection ⟨no tengo inconveniente en hacerlo : I don't mind doing it⟩ **3** : disadvantage, drawback ⟨las ventajas e inconvenientes : the advantages and disadvantages⟩
incordiar *vt Spain* : to annoy, to pester
incorporación *nf, pl* **-ciones** : incorporation
incorporado *adj* : built-in
incorporar *vt* **1** : to incorporate **2** : to add, to include — **incorporarse** *vr* **1** : to sit up **2** ~ **a** : to join
incorpóreo, -rea *adj* : incorporeal, bodiless
incorrección *n, pl* **-ciones** : impropriety, improper word or action
incorrecto, -ta *adj* **1** : incorrect **2** : impolite, rude — **incorrectamente** *adv*
incorregible *adj* : incorrigible — **incorregibilidad** *nf*
incorruptible *adj* : incorruptible
incredulidad *nf* : incredulity, skepticism
incrédulo¹, -la *adj* : incredulous, skeptical
incrédulo², -la *n* : skeptic
increíble *adj* : incredible, unbelievable — **increíblemente** *adv*
incrementar *vt* : to increase — **incrementarse** *vr*
incremento *nm* AUMENTO : increase
increpar *vt* : to tell off *fam*, to yell at, to rebuke
incriminar *vt* : to incriminate — **incriminación** *nf*
incriminatorio, -ria *adj* : incriminating, incriminatory
incruento, -ta *adj* : bloodless

incrustación *nf, pl* **-ciones** : inlay
incrustar *vt* **1** : to embed **2** : to inlay — **incrustarse** *vr* : to become embedded
incubación *nf, pl* **-ciones** : incubation
incubadora *nf* : incubator
incubar *v* : to incubate
incuestionable *adj* INCONTESTABLE, INDISCUTIBLE : unquestionable, indisputable — **incuestionablemente** *adv*
inculcar {72} *vt* : to inculcate, to instill
inculpado, -da *n* : defendant ⟨el inculpado : the defendant, the accused⟩
inculpar *vt* ACUSAR : to accuse, to charge
inculto, -ta *adj* **1** : uncultured, ignorant **2** : uncultivated, fallow
incultura *adj* : ignorance, lack of culture
incumbencia *nf* : obligation, responsibility
incumbir *vi* (*3rd person only*) ~ **a** : to be incumbent upon, to be of concern to ⟨a mí no me incumbe : it's not my concern⟩
incumplido, -da *adj* : irresponsible, unreliable
incumplimiento *nm* **1** : failure to fulfill (conditions, obligations, etc.) ⟨incumplimiento de la ley : failure to comply with the law⟩ ⟨incumplimiento de pago : failure to make payment, default⟩ **2** **incumplimiento de contrato** : breach of contract **3** **incumplimiento de deberes** : neglect of duty
incumplir *vt* : to fail to carry out, to break (a promise, a contract)
incurable *adj* : incurable
incurrir *vi* **1** ~ **en** : to incur ⟨incurrir en gastos : to incur expenses⟩ **2** ~ **en** : to fall into, to commit ⟨incurrió en un error : he made a mistake⟩
incursión *nf, pl* **-siones** : incursion, raid
incursionar *vi* **1** : to raid **2** ~ **en** : to go into, to enter ⟨el actor incursionó en el baile : the actor worked in dance for a while⟩
indagación *nf, pl* **-ciones** : investigation, inquiry
indagar {52} *vt* : to inquire into, to investigate
indagatoria *nf* **1** : statement, deposition **2** : investigation, inquiry, inquest
indebido, -da *adj* : improper, undue — **indebidamente** *adv*
indecencia *nf* : indecency, obscenity
indecente *adj* : indecent, obscene
indecible *adj* : indescribable, inexpressible
indecisión *nf, pl* **-siones** : indecision
indeciso, -sa *adj* **1** IRRESOLUTO : indecisive **2** : undecided
indeclinable *adj* : unavoidable
indecoro *nm* : impropriety, indecorousness
indecoroso, -sa *adj* : indecorous, unseemly
indefectible *adj* : unfailing, sure
indefendible *adj* : indefensible
indefensión *nf* : defenselessness
indefenso, -sa *adj* : defenseless, helpless
indefinible *adj* : indefinable

indefinido, -da adj 1 : undefined, vague 2 INDETERMINADO : indefinite — **indefinidamente** adv

indeleble adj : indelible — **indeleblemente** adv

indelicado, -da adj : indelicate, tactless

indemne adj : unharmed, unhurt

indemnidad nf : indemnity

indemnización nf, pl **-ciones** 1 : indemnity 2 **indemnización por despido** : severance pay

indemnizar {21} vt : to indemnify, to compensate

independencia nf : independence

independiente adj : independent — **independientemente** adv

independista[1] adj : pro-independence

independista[2] nmf : independence supporter

independizar {21} vt : to make independent — **independizarse** vr

indescifrable adj : indecipherable

indescriptible adj : indescribable — **indescriptiblemente** adv

indeseable adj & nmf : undesirable

indestructible adj : indestructible

indeterminado, -da adj 1 INDEFINIDO : indefinite 2 : indeterminate

indexar vt INDICIAR : to index (wages, prices, etc.)

indicación nf, pl **-ciones** 1 : sign, signal 2 : direction, instruction 3 : suggestion, hint

indicado, -da adj 1 APROPIADO : appropriate, suitable 2 : specified, indicated ⟨al día indicado : on the specified day⟩

indicador nm 1 : gauge, dial, meter 2 : indicator ⟨indicadores económicos : economic indicators⟩

indicar {72} vt 1 SEÑALAR : to indicate 2 ENSEÑAR, MOSTRAR : to show

indicativo[1], **-va** adj : indicative

indicativo[2] nm : indicative (mood)

índice nm 1 : index 2 : contents pl, table of contents 3 : index finger, forefinger 4 INDICIO : indication

indiciar vt : to index (prices, wages, etc.)

indicio nm 1 : indication, sign 2 **indicios** nmpl : evidence

indiferencia nf : indifference

indiferente adj 1 : indifferent, unconcerned 2 **ser indiferente** : to be of no concern ⟨me es indiferente : it doesn't matter to me⟩

indiferentemente adv : indifferently

indígena[1] adj : indigenous, native

indígena[2] nmf : native

indigencia nf MISERIA : poverty, destitution

indigente adj & nmf : indigent

indigestarse vr EMPACHARSE : to have indigestion 2 fam : to nauseate, to disgust ⟨ese tipo se me indigesta : that guy makes me sick⟩

indigestión nf, pl **-tiones** EMPACHO : indigestion

indigesto, -ta adj : indigestible, difficult to digest

indignación nf, pl **-ciones** : indignation

indignado, -da adj : indignant

indignante adj : outrageous, infuriating

indignar vt : to outrage, to infuriate — **indignarse** vr

indignidad nf : indignity

indigno, -na adj 1 : unworthy 2 : contemptible, despicable

índigo nm : indigo

indio, -dia adj & n 1 sometimes offensive : Indian often offensive, Native American 2 : Indian (from India)

indio–americano, india–americana n : nativo americano

indirecta nf 1 : hint, innuendo 2 **echar indirectas** or **lanzar indirectas** : to drop a hint, to insinuate

indirecto, -ta adj : indirect — **indirectamente** adv

indisciplina nf : lack of discipline, unruliness

indisciplinado, -da adj : undisciplined, unruly

indiscreción nf, pl **-ciones** 1 IMPRUDENCIA : indiscretion 2 : tactless remark

indiscreto, -ta adj IMPRUDENTE : indiscreet, imprudent — **indiscretamente** adv

indiscriminado, -da adj : indiscriminate — **indiscriminadamente** adv

indiscutible adj 1 INCONTESTABLE, INCUESTIONABLE : indisputable, unquestionable 2 : undisputed ⟨el campeón indiscutible : the undisputed champion⟩ — **indiscutiblemente** adv

indiscutido, -da adj : undisputed

indispensable adj : indispensable — **indispensablemente** adv

indisponer {60} vt 1 : to spoil, to upset 2 : to make ill — **indisponerse** vr 1 : to become ill 2 ~ **con** : to fall out with

indisposición nf, pl **-ciones** : illness

indispuesto, -ta adj : unwell, indisposed

indistinguible adj : indistinguishable

indistintamente adv 1 : indistinctly 2 : indiscriminately

indistinto, -ta adj : indistinct, vague, faint

individual[1] adj : individual — **individualmente** adv

individual[2] nm 1 : place mat 2 **individuales** nmpl : singles (in sports)

individualidad nf : individuality

individualismo nm : individualism

individualista[1] adj : individualistic

individualista[2] nmf : individualist

individualizar {21} vt : to individualize

individuo nm : individual, person

indivisible adj : indivisible — **indivisibilidad** nf

indocumentado, -da n : illegal immigrant

índole nf 1 : nature, character 2 CLASE, TIPO : sort, kind

indolencia nf : indolence, laziness

indolente adj : indolent, lazy

indoloro, -ra adj : painless

indomable adj 1 : indomitable 2 : unruly, unmanageable

indómito, -ta adj 1 : indomitable 2 : untamed

indonesio, -sia adj & n : Indonesian

inducción nf, pl **-ciones** : induction

inducir {61} *vt* **1** : to induce, to cause **2** : to infer, to deduce

inductivo, -va *adj* : inductive

indudable *adj* : unquestionable, beyond doubt

indudablemente *adv* : undoubtedly, unquestionably

indulgencia *nf* **1** : indulgence, leniency **2** : indulgence (in religion)

indulgente *adj* : indulgent, lenient

indultar *vt* : to pardon, to reprieve

indulto *nm* : pardon, reprieve

indumentaria *nf* : clothing, attire

industria *nf* : industry

industrial *adj* : industrial

industrial² *nmf* : industrialist, manufacturer

industrialización *nf, pl* **-ciones** : industrialization

industrializar {21} *vt* : to industrialize

industrioso, -sa *adj* : industrious

inédito, -ta *adj* **1** : unpublished **2** : unprecedented

inefable *adj* : ineffable

ineficacia *nf* **1** : inefficiency **2** : lack of effectiveness

ineficaz *adj, pl* **-caces** : inefficient **2** : ineffective — **ineficazmente** *adv*

ineficiencia *nf* : inefficiency

ineficiente *adj* : inefficient — **ineficientemente** *adv*

inelegancia *nf* : inelegance — **inelegante** *adj*

inelegible *adj* : ineligible — **inelegibilidad** *nf*

ineludible *adj* : inescapable, unavoidable — **ineludiblemente** *adv*

ineptitud *nf* : ineptitude, incompetence

inepto¹, -ta *adj* : inept, incompetent

inepto², -ta *n* : incompetent

inequidad *nf* : inequity

inequitativo, -va *adj* : inequitable

inequívoco, -ca *adj* : unequivocal, unmistakable — **inequívocamente** *adv*

inercia *nf* **1** : inertia **2** : apathy **3 por ~** : out of habit

inerme *adj* : unarmed, defenseless

inerte *adj* : inert

inescrupuloso, -sa *adj* : unscrupulous

inescrutable *adj* : inscrutable

inesperado, -da *adj* : unexpected — **inesperadamente** *adv*

inestabilidad *nf* : instability, unsteadiness

inestable *adj* **1** : unstable, unsteady **2** : changeable (of weather)

inestimable *adj* : inestimable, invaluable

inevitabilidad *nf* : inevitability

inevitable *adj* : inevitable, unavoidable — **inevitablemente** *adv*

inexactitud *nf* : inaccuracy

inexacto, -ta *adj* **1** : inexact, inaccurate

inexcusable *adj* **1** : inexcusable, unforgivable **2** : unavoidable

inexistencia *nf* : lack, nonexistence

inexistente *adj* : nonexistent

inexorable *adj* : inexorable — **inexorablemente** *adv*

inexperiencia *nf* : inexperience

inexperto, -ta *adj* : inexperienced, unskilled

inexplicable *adj* : inexplicable — **inexplicablemente** *adv*

inexplorado, -da *adj* : unexplored

inexpresable *adj* : inexpressible

inexpresivo, -va *adj* : expressionless

inexpugnable *adj* : impregnable

inextricable *adj* : inextricable — **inextricablemente** *adv*

infalibilidad *nf* : infallibility

infalible *adj* : infallible — **infaliblemente** *adv*

infame *adj* **1** : infamous **2** : loathsome, vile ⟨tiempo infame : terrible weather⟩

infamia *nf* : infamy, disgrace

infancia *nf* **1** NIÑEZ : infancy, childhood **2** : children *pl* **3** : beginnings *pl*

infante¹, -ta *n* : prince *m*, princess *f*

infante² *nm* : infantry soldier

infantería *nf* **1** : infantry **2 infantería de marina** : marines *pl*

infantil *adj* **1** : childish, infantile **2** : child's, children's

infarto *nm* **1** : heart attack **2 infarto cerebral** : stroke

infatigable *adj* : indefatigable, tireless — **infatigablemente** *adv*

infección *nf, pl* **-ciones** : infection

infeccioso, -sa *adj* : infectious

infectar *vt* : to infect — **infectarse** *vr*

infecto, -ta *adj* **1** : infected **2** : repulsive, sickening

infecundidad *nf* : infertility

infecundo, -da *adj* : infertile, barren

infelicidad *nf* : unhappiness

infeliz¹ *adj, pl* **-lices** **1** : unhappy **2** : hapless, unfortunate, wretched

infeliz² *nmf, pl* **-lices** : wretch

inferencia *nf* : inference

inferior¹ *adj* : inferior, lower

inferior² *nmf* : inferior, underling

inferioridad *nf* : inferiority

inferir {76} *vt* **1** DEDUCIR : to infer, to deduce **2** : to cause (harm or injury), to inflict

infernal *adj* : infernal, hellish

infertilidad *nf* : infertility

infestación *n, pl* **-ciones** : infestation

infestar *vt* **1** : to infest ⟨infestar de : to infest with⟩ **2** : to overrun, to invade

infición *nf, pl* **-ciones** *Mex* : pollution

infidelidad *nf* : unfaithfulness, infidelity

infiel¹ *adj* : unfaithful, disloyal

infiel² *nmf* : infidel, heathen *often offensive*

infierno *nm* **1** : hell **2** : bedlam, madness **3** : hellhole, hellish place **4 el quinto infierno** : the middle of nowhere

infiltrado, -da *n* : infiltrator

infiltrar *vt* : to infiltrate — **infiltrarse** *vr* — **infiltración** *nf*

ínfimo, -ma *adj* **1** : minuscule, negligible **2** : lousy, very poor

infinidad *nf* **1** : infinity **2** SINFÍN : great number, huge quantity ⟨una infinidad de veces : countless times⟩

infinitesimal *adj* : infinitesimal

infinitivo *nm* : infinitive

infinito¹ *adv* : infinitely, vastly

infinito², -ta *adj* **1** : infinite **2** : limitless, endless — **infinitamente** *adv*

infinito³ *nm* : infinity
inflable *adj* : inflatable
inflación *nf, pl* **-ciones** : inflation
inflacionario, -ria *adj* : inflationary
inflacionista → **inflacionario**
inflamable *adj* : flammable
inflamación *nf, pl* **-ciones** 1 : inflammation 2 : ignition, combustion
inflamar *vt* 1 : to inflame 2 : to ignite
inflamatorio, -ria *adj* : inflammatory
inflar *vt* 1 HINCHAR : to inflate 2 EXAGERAR : to exaggerate — **inflarse** *vr* 1 : to swell 2 : to become conceited
inflexibilidad *nf* : inflexibility
inflexible *adj* : inflexible, unyielding
inflexión *nf, pl* **-xiones** : inflection
infligir {35} *vt* : to inflict
influencia *nf* 1 INFLUJO : influence 2 **influencias** *nfpl* : contacts *pl*, influence ⟨tráfico de influencias : influence peddling⟩
influenciable *adj* : easily influenced, suggestible
influenciar *vt* : to influence
influenza *nf* : influenza
influir {41} *vt* : to influence — *vi* ∼ **en** *or* ∼ **sobre** : to have an influence on, to affect
influjo *nm* INFLUENCIA : influence
influyente *adj* : influential
infografía *nf* : computer graphics *pl*
información *nf, pl* **-ciones** 1 : information ⟨centro/oficina de información : information center/office⟩ 2 : information, directory assistance 3 INFORME : report, inquiry 4 NOTICIAS : news
informado, -da *adj* : informed ⟨bien informado : well-informed⟩
informador, -dora *n* : informer, informant
informal *adj* 1 : unreliable (of persons) 2 : informal, casual 3 : informal, unofficial (in economics) — **informalmente** *adv*
informalidad *nf* : informality
informante *nmf* : informant
informar *vt* ENTERAR : to inform — *vi* : to report — **informarse** *vr* ENTERARSE : to get information, to find out
informática *nf* : computer science, computing
informático¹, -ca *adj* : computer ⟨sistema informático : computer system⟩
informático², -ca *n* : computer specialist
informativo¹, -va *adj* : informative, informational
informativo² *nm* : news program, news
informatización *nf, pl* **-ciones** : computerization
informatizar {21} *vt* : to computerize
informe¹ *adj* AMORFO : shapeless, formless
informe² *nm* 1 : report 2 : reference (for employment) 3 **informes** *nmpl* : information, data
infortunado, -da *adj* : unfortunate, unlucky
infortunio *nm* 1 DESGRACIA : misfortune 2 CONTRATIEMPO : mishap
infracción *nf, pl* **-ciones** : violation, offense, infraction
infractor, -tora *n* : offender

infraestructura *nf* : infrastructure
in fraganti *adv* : red-handed
infrahumano, -na *adj* : subhuman
infranqueable *adj* 1 : impassable 2 : insurmountable
infrarrojo, -ja *adj* : infrared
infrecuente *adj* : infrequent
infringir {35} *vt* : to infringe, to breach
infructuoso, -sa *adj* : fruitless — **infructuosamente** *adv*
ínfulas *nfpl* 1 : conceit 2 **darse ínfulas** : to put on airs
infundado, -da *adj* : unfounded, baseless
infundio *nm* : false story, lie, tall tale ⟨todo eso son infundios : that's a pack of lies⟩
infundir *vt* 1 : to instill (fear, confidence), to arouse (enthusiasm) 2 **infundir ánimo a** : to encourage
infusión *nf, pl* **-siones** : infusion, tea
ingeniar *vt* : to devise, to think up — **ingeniarse** *vr* : to manage, to find a way
ingeniería *nf* : engineering
ingeniero, -ra *n* : engineer
ingenio *nm* 1 : ingenuity 2 CHISPA : wit, wits 3 : device, apparatus 4 **ingenio azucarero** : sugar refinery
ingenioso, -sa *adj* 1 : ingenious 2 : clever, witty — **ingeniosamente** *adv*
ingente *adj* : huge, enormous
ingenuidad *nf* : naïveté, ingenuousness
ingenuo¹, -nua *adj* CÁNDIDO : naive — **ingenuamente** *adv*
ingenuo², -nua *n* : naive person
ingerencia → **injerencia**
ingerir {76} *vt* : to ingest, to consume
ingesta *nf* : consumption, ingestion
ingestión *nf, pl* **-tiones** : ingestion
ingle *nf* : groin
inglés¹, -glesa *adj, mpl* **ingleses** : English
inglés², -glesa *n, mpl* **ingleses** : Englishman *m*, Englishwoman *f*
inglés³ *nm* : English (language)
inglete *nm* : miter joint
ingobernable *adj* : ungovernable, lawless
ingratitud *nf* : ingratitude
ingrato¹, -ta *adj* 1 : ungrateful 2 : thankless, difficult
ingrato², -ta *n* : ingrate
ingrávido, -da *adj* : weightless
ingrediente *nm* : ingredient
ingresar *vt* 1 : to admit ⟨ingresaron a Luis al hospital : Luis was admitted into the hospital⟩ 2 : to deposit — *vi* 1 : to enter, to go in 2 ∼ **en** : to join, to enroll in
ingreso *nm* 1 : entrance, entry 2 : admission 3 : deposit 4 **ingresos** *nmpl* : income, earnings *pl*
íngrimo, -ma *adj* : all alone, all by oneself
inhábil *adj* : clumsy
inhabilidad *nf* 1 : lack of skill 2 : lack of suitability
inhabilitar *vt* 1 : to disqualify, to bar 2 : to disable
inhabitable *adj* : uninhabitable
inhabitado, -da → **deshabitado**
inhabituado, -da *adj* ∼ **a** : unaccustomed to
inhalador *nm* : inhaler
inhalante *nm* : inhalant

inhalar *vt* : to inhale — **inhalación** *nf*
inherente *adj* : inherent
inhibición *nf, pl* **-ciones** COHIBICIÓN : inhibition
inhibir *vt* : to inhibit — **inhibirse** *vr*
inhóspito, -ta *adj* : inhospitable
inhumación *nf, pl* **-ciones** : interment, burial
inhumanidad *nf* : inhumanity
inhumano, -na *adj* : inhuman, cruel, inhumane
inhumar *vt* : to inter, to bury
iniciación *nf, pl* **-ciones 1** : initiation **2** : introduction
iniciado, -da *n* : initiate
iniciador¹, -dora *adj* : initiatory
iniciador², -dora *n* : originator
inicial¹ *adj* : initial, original — **inicialmente** *adv*
inicial² *nf* : initial (letter)
iniciar *vt* **1** COMENZAR : to initiate, to begin **2** : to initiate (someone) — **iniciarse** *vr*
iniciativa *nf* : initiative
inicio *nm* COMIENZO : beginning
inicuo, -cua *adj* : iniquitous, wicked
inigualable *adj* : incomparable (of a person, view, etc.), unrivaled (of popularity, etc.), unbeatable (of prices, etc.)
inigualado, -da *adj* : unequaled
inimaginable *adj* : unimaginable
inimitable *adj* : inimitable
ininteligible *adj* : unintelligible
ininterrumpido, -da *adj* : uninterrupted, continuous — **ininterrumpidamente** *adv*
iniquidad *nf* : iniquity, wickedness
injerencia *nf* : interference
injerirse {76} *vr* ENTROMETERSE, INMISCUIRSE : to meddle, to interfere
injertar *vt* : to graft
injerto *nm* : graft ⟨injerto de piel : skin graft⟩
injuria *nf* AGRAVIO : affront, insult
injuriar *vt* INSULTAR : to insult, to revile
injurioso, -sa *adj* : insulting, abusive
injusticia *nf* : injustice, unfairness
injustificable *adj* : unjustifiable
injustificadamente *adv* : unjustifiably, unfairly
injustificado, -da *adj* : unjustified, unwarranted
injusto, -ta *adj* : unfair, unjust — **injustamente** *adv*
inmaculado, -da *adj* : immaculate, spotless
inmadurez *nf, pl* **-reces** : immaturity
inmaduro, -ra *adj* **1** : immature **2** : unripe
inmediaciones *nfpl* : environs, surrounding area
inmediatamente *adv* ENSEGUIDA : immediately
inmediatez *nf, pl* **-teces** : immediacy
inmediato, -ta *adj* **1** : immediate **2** CONTIGUO : adjoining **3 de ~** : immediately, right away **4 ~ a** : next to, close to
inmejorable *adj* : excellent, unbeatable

inmemorial *adj* : immemorial ⟨tiempos inmemoriales : time immemorial⟩
inmensidad *nf* : immensity, vastness
inmenso, -sa *adj* ENORME : immense, huge, vast — **inmensamente** *adv*
inmensurable *adj* : boundless, immeasurable
inmerecido, -da *adj* : undeserved — **inmerecidamente** *adv*
inmersión *nf, pl* **-siones** : immersion
inmerso, -sa *adj* **1** : immersed **2** : involved, absorbed
inmigración *nf, pl* **-ciones** : immigration
inmigrado, -da *adj & n* : immigrant
inmigrante *adj & nmf* : immigrant
inmigrar *vi* : to immigrate
inminencia *nf* : imminence
inminente *adj* : imminent — **inminentemente** *adv*
inmiscuirse {41} *vr* ENTROMETERSE, INJERIRSE : to meddle, to interfere
inmobiliaria *nf* **1** : real estate agency **2** : developer
inmobiliario, -ria *adj* : real estate, property
inmoderación *n, pl* **-ciones** : intemperance, lack of moderation
inmoderado, -da *adj* : immoderate, excessive — **inmoderamente** *adv*
inmodestia *nf* : immodesty — **inmodesto, -ta** *adj*
inmoral *adj* : immoral
inmoralidad *nf* : immorality
inmortal *adj & nmf* : immortal
inmortalidad *nf* : immortality
inmortalizar {21} *vt* : to immortalize
inmotivado, -da *adj* **1** : unmotivated **2** : groundless
inmovible *adj* : immovable, fixed
inmóvil *adj* **1** : still, motionless **2** : steadfast
inmovilidad *nf* : immobility
inmovilizar {21} *vt* : to immobilize — **inmovilización** *nf*
inmueble *nm* : building, property
inmundicia *nf* : dirt, filth, trash
inmundo, -da *adj* : dirty, filthy, nasty
inmune *adj* : immune
inmunidad *nf* : immunity
inmunizar {21} *vt* : to immunize — **inmunización** *nf*
inmunología *nf* : immunology
inmunológico, -ca *adj* : immune ⟨sistema inmunológico : immune system⟩
inmutable *adj* : immutable, unchangeable
inmutar *vt* : to upset — **inmutarse** *vr* : to get upset, to look upset ⟨ni se inmutó : he didn't even bat an eyelash⟩
innato, -ta *adj* : innate, inborn
innecesario, -ria *adj* : unnecessary — **innecesariamente** *adv*
innegable *adj* : undeniable
innoble *adj* : ignoble — **innoblemente** *adv*
innovación *nf, pl* **-ciones** : innovation
innovador¹, -dora *adj* : innovative
innovador², -dora *n* : innovator
innovar *vt* : to introduce — *vi* : to innovate
innumerable *adj* INCONTABLE : innumerable, countless

inobjetable *adj* : indisputable, unobjectionable

inocencia *nf* : innocence

inocentada *nf* : practical joke

inocente[1] *adj* **1** : innocent **2** INGENUO : naive — **inocentemente** *adv*

inocente[2] *nmf* : innocent person

inocentón[1], **-tona** *adj, mpl* **-tones** : naive, gullible

inocentón[2], **-tona** *n, mpl* **-tones** : simpleton, dupe

inocuidad *nf* : harmlessness

inocular *vt* : to inoculate, to vaccinate — **inoculación** *nf*

inocuo, -cua *adj* : innocuous, harmless

inodoro[1], **-ra** *adj* : odorless

inodoro[2] *nm* : toilet

inofensivo, -va *adj* : inoffensive, harmless

inolvidable *adj* : unforgettable

inoperable *adj* : inoperable

inoperante *adj* : ineffective, inoperative

inopinado, -da *adj* : unexpected — **inopinadamente** *adv*

inoportuno, -na *adj* : untimely, inopportune, inappropriate

inorgánico, -ca *adj* : inorganic

inoxidable *adj* **1** : rustproof **2 acero inoxidable** : stainless steel

inquebrantable *adj* : unshakable, unwavering

inquietamente *adv* **1** : anxiously, uneasily **2** : restlessly

inquietante *adj* : disturbing, worrisome

inquietar *vt* PREOCUPAR : to disturb, to upset, to worry — **inquietarse** *vr*

inquieto, -ta *adj* **1** : anxious, uneasy, worried **2** : restless

inquietud *nf* **1** : anxiety, uneasiness, worry **2** AGITACIÓN : restlessness

inquilinato *nm* : tenancy

inquilino, -na *n* : tenant, occupant

inquina *nf* **1** : aversion, dislike **2** : ill will ⟨tener inquina a alguien : to have a grudge against someone⟩

inquirir {4} *vi* : to make inquiries — *vt* : to investigate

inquisición *nf, pl* **-ciones** : investigation, inquiry

inquisidor[1], **-dora** *adj* : inquisitive

inquisidor[2] *nm* : inquisitor

inquisitivo, -va *adj* : inquisitive, curious — **inquisitivamente** *adv*

insaciable *adj* : insatiable

insalubre *adj* **1** : unhealthy **2** ANTIHIGIÉNICO : unsanitary

insalvable *adj* : insurmountable

insano, -na *adj* **1** LOCO : insane, mad **2** INSALUBRE : unhealthy

insatisfacción *nf, pl* **-ciones** : dissatisfaction

insatisfactorio *nm* : unsatisfactory

insatisfecho, -cha *adj* **1** : dissatisfied **2** : unsatisfied

inscribir {33} *vt* **1** MATRICULAR : to enroll, to register **2** GRABAR : to engrave — **inscribirse** *vr* : to register, to sign up

inscripción *nf, pl* **-ciones** **1** MATRÍCULA : enrollment, registration **2** : inscription

inscrito *pp* → **inscribir**

insecticida[1] *adj* : insecticidal

insecticida[2] *nm* : insecticide

insecto *nm* : insect

inseguridad *nf* **1** : insecurity **2** : lack of safety **3** : uncertainty

inseguro, -ra *adj* **1** : insecure **2** : unsafe **3** : uncertain — **inseguramente** *adv*

inseminar *vt* : to inseminate — **inseminación** *nf*

insensatez *nf, pl* **-teces** : foolishness, stupidity

insensato[1], **-ta** *adj* : foolish, senseless — **insensatamente** *adv*

insensato[2], **-ta** *n* : fool

insensibilidad *nf* : insensitivity

insensible *adj* : insensitive, unfeeling — **insensiblemente** *adv*

inseparable *adj* : inseparable — **inseparablemente** *adv*

inserción *nf, pl* **-ciones** : insertion

insertar *vt* : to insert

inservible *adj* INÚTIL : useless, unusable

insidia *nf* **1** : snare, trap **2** : malice

insidioso, -sa *adj* : insidious

insigne *adj* : noted, famous

insignia *nf* ENSEÑA : insignia, emblem, badge

insignificancia *nf* **1** : insignificance **2** NIMIEDAD : trifle, triviality

insignificante *adj* : insignificant

insincero, -ra *adj* : insincere — **insinceramente** *adv* — **insinceridad** *nf*

insinuación *nf, pl* **-ciones** : insinuation, hint

insinuante *adj* : suggestive

insinuar {3} *vt* : to insinuate, to hint at — **insinuarse** *vr* **1** ~ **a** : to make advances to **2** ~ **en** : to worm one's way into

insípido, -da *adj* : insipid, bland

insistencia *nf* : insistence

insistente *adj* : insistent — **insistentemente** *adv*

insistir *v* : to insist

insociable *adj* : unsociable

insolación *nf, pl* **-ciones** : sunstroke

insolencia *nf* IMPERTINENCIA : insolence

insolente *adj* IMPERTINENTE : insolent — **insolentemente** *adv*

insólito, -ta *adj* : rare, unusual

insoluble *adj* : insoluble — **insolubilidad** *nf*

insolvencia *nf* : insolvency, bankruptcy

insolvente *adj* : insolvent, bankrupt

insomne *adj & nmf* : insomniac

insomnio *nm* : insomnia

insonorizado, -da *adj* : soundproof

insoportable *adj* INAGUANTABLE : unbearable, intolerable

insoslayable *adj* : unavoidable, inescapable

insospechado, -da *adj* : unexpected, unforeseen

insostenible *adj* **1** : not sustainable (of a rate, etc.) **2** : untenable

inspección *nf, pl* **-ciones** : inspection

inspeccionar *vt* : to inspect

inspector, -tora *n* : inspector

inspiración *nf, pl* **-ciones** **1** : inspiration **2** INHALACIÓN : inhalation

inspirador, -dora *adj* : inspiring

inspirar *vt* : to inspire — *vi* INHALAR : to inhale — **inspirarse** *vr*
instalación *nf, pl* **-ciones** : installation
instalar *vt* **1** : to install (a device, etc.) **2** : to install, to induct — **instalarse** *vr* ESTABLECERSE : to settle, to establish oneself
instancia *nf* **1** : petition, request **2 en última instancia** : as a last resort
instantánea *nf* : snapshot
instantáneo, -nea *adj* **1** : instantaneous **2** : instant ⟨café instantáneo : instant coffee⟩ — **instantáneamente** *adv*
instante *nm* **1** : instant, moment, **2 al instante** : immediately **3 a cada instante** : frequently, all the time **4 por instantes** : constantly, incessantly
instar *vt* APREMIAR : to urge, to press — *vi* URGIR : to be urgent or pressing ⟨insta que vayamos pronto : it is imperative that we leave soon⟩
instauración *nf, pl* **-ciones** : establishment
instaurar *vt* : to establish
instigador, -dora *n* : instigator
instigar {52} *vt* : to instigate, to incite
instintivo, -va *adj* : instinctive — **instintivamente** *adv*
instinto *nm* : instinct
institución *nf, pl* **-ciones** : institution
institucional *adj* : institutional — **institucionalmente** *adv*
institucionalizar {21} *vt* : to institutionalize
instituir {41} *vt* ESTABLECER, FUNDAR : to institute, to establish, to found
instituto *nm* : institute
institutriz *nf, pl* **-trices** : governess *f*
instrucción *nf, pl* **-ciones** **1** EDUCACIÓN : education, training **2 instrucciones** *nfpl* : instructions, directions
instructivo, -va *adj* : instructive, educational
instructor, -tora *n* : instructor
instruir {41} *vt* **1** ADIESTRAR : to instruct, to train **2** ENSEÑAR : to educate, to teach
instrumentación *nf, pl* **-ciones** : orchestration
instrumental[1] *adj* : instrumental
instrumental[2] *nm* : instruments *pl*
instrumentar *vt* : to orchestrate
instrumentista *nmf* : instrumentalist
instrumento *nm* **1** : (musical) instrument **2** : instrument (tool or device) **3** : instrument, means *pl*
insubordinado, -da *adj* : insubordinate — **insubordinación** *nf*
insubordinarse *vr* : to rebel
insuficiencia *nf* **1** : insufficiency, inadequacy **2 insuficiencia cardíaca** : heart failure
insuficiente[1] *adj* **1** : insufficient, inadequate **2** : poor, unsatisfactory — **insuficientemente** *adv*
insuficiente[2] *nm* : F, failing grade
insufrible *adj* : insufferable
insular *adj* : insular
insularidad *nf* : insularity
insulina *nf* : insulin

insulso, -sa *adj* **1** INSÍPIDO : insipid, bland **2** : dull
insultante *adj* : insulting
insultar *vt* : to insult
insulto *nm* : insult
insumos *nmpl* : supplies ⟨insumos agrícolas : agricultural supplies⟩
insuperable *adj* **1** : insurmountable **2** : unbeatable
insurgente *adj & nmf* : insurgent — **insurgencia** *nf*
insurrección *nf, pl* **-ciones** : insurrection, uprising
insustancial *adj* : insubstantial, flimsy
insustituible *adj* : irreplaceable
intachable *adj* : irreproachable, faultless
intacto, -ta *adj* : intact
intangible *adj* IMPALPABLE : intangible, impalpable
integración *nf, pl* **-ciones** : integration
integral *adj* **1** : integral, essential **2 pan integral** : whole grain bread
integrante[1] *adj* : integrating, integral
integrante[2] *nmf* : member
integrar *vt* : to make up, to compose — **integrarse** *vr* : to integrate, to fit in
integridad *nf* **1** RECTITUD : integrity, honesty **2** : integrity, soundness ⟨integridad física : personal safety⟩
integrismo *nm* : fundamentalism
integrista *adj & nmf* : fundamentalist
íntegro, -gra *adj* **1** : honest, upright **2** ENTERO : whole, complete **3** : unabridged
intelecto *nm* : intellect
intelectual *adj & nmf* : intellectual — **intelectualmente** *adv*
intelectualidad *nf* : intelligentsia
inteligencia *nf* : intelligence
inteligente *adj* : intelligent — **inteligentemente** *adv*
inteligible *adj* : intelligible — **inteligibilidad** *nf*
intemperancia *adj* : intemperance, excess
intemperie *nf* **1** : bad weather, elements *pl* **2 a la intemperie** : in the open air, outside
intempestivo, -va *adj* : inopportune, untimely — **intempestivamente** *adv*
intención *nf, pl* **-ciones** **1** : intention, plan ⟨tenías buenas intenciones : you had good intentions, your intentions were good⟩ ⟨tener la intención de hacer algo : to intend to do something⟩ ⟨con/sin intención : intentionally/unintentionally⟩ ⟨con la mejor intención : with the best (of) intentions⟩ **2 segunda intención** : ulterior motive
intencionadamente → **intencionalmente**
intencionado, -da → **intencional**
intencional *adj* : intentional
intencionalmente *adv* : intentionally
intendencia *nf* **1** : management, administration **2** *Arg, Par, Uru* : city council, town council **3** *Chile* : governorship
intendente *nmf* **1** : quartermaster **2** *Arg, Par, Uru* : mayor **3** *Chile* : governor
intensidad *nf* : intensity
intensificación *nf, pl* **-ciones** : intensification

intensificador *nm* : intensifier (in linguistics)

intensificar {72} *vt* : to intensify — **intensificarse** *vr*

intensivo, -va *adj* : intensive — **intensivamente** *adv*

intenso, -sa *adj* : intense — **intensamente** *adv*

intentar *vt* : to attempt, to try

intento *nm* **1** PROPÓSITO : intent, intention **2** TENTATIVA : attempt, try

intentona *nf* : attempt ⟨intentona golpista : attempted coup⟩

inter- *pref* : inter-

interacción *nf, pl* **-ciones** : interaction

interactivo, -va *adj* : interactive

interactuar {3} *vi* : to interact

intercalar *vt* : to intersperse, to insert

intercambiable *adj* : interchangeable

intercambiar *vt* CANJEAR : to exchange, to trade

intercambio *nm* CANJE : exchange, trade

interceder *vi* : to intercede

intercepción → interceptación

interceptación *nf, pl* **-ciones** : interception

interceptar *vt* **1** : to intercept, to block **2** **interceptar las líneas** : to wiretap

intercesión *nf, pl* **-siones** : intercession

interconectar *vt* : to connect, to interconnect

interconfesional *adj* : interdenominational

intercontinental *adj* : intercontinental

interdepartamental *adj* : interdepartmental

interdependencia *nf* : interdependence — **interdependiente** *adj*

interdicción *nf, pl* **-ciones** : prohibition

interdisciplinario, -ria *adj* : interdisciplinary

interés *nm, pl* **-reses** **1** : interest ⟨su interés por la ciencia : her interest in science⟩ ⟨tiene interés en aprender español : he is interested in learning Spanish⟩ ⟨perder interés : to lose interest⟩ **2** BENEFICIO : interest ⟨por su propio interés : for one's own benefit⟩ ⟨por puro interés : purely out of self-interest⟩ ⟨el interés público : the public interest⟩ ⟨conflicto de intereses : conflict of interest⟩ **3** : interest, interest rate **4** **intereses** *nmpl* : interest, stake ⟨tener intereses en : to have an interest in⟩

interesado[1], -da *adj* **1** : interested **2** : selfish, self-seeking

interesado[2], -da *n* **1** : interested party ⟨los interesados deberán rellenar una solicitud : anyone who is interested should fill out an application⟩ **2** : self-centered person

interesante *adj* : interesting

interesar *vt* : to interest — *vi* : to be of interest, to be interesting — **interesarse** *vr*

interestatal *adj* : interstate ⟨autopista interestatal : interstate highway⟩

interestelar *adj* : interstellar

interfase → interfaz

interfaz *nf, pl* **-faces** : interface

interferencia *nf* : interference, static

interferir {76} *vi* : to interfere, to meddle — *vt* : to interfere with, to obstruct

interfón *nm, pl* **-fones** *Mex* : intercom

interfono *nm* *Spain* : intercom

intergaláctico, -ca *adj* : intergalactic

intergubernamental *adj* : intergovernmental

interín[1] *or* **ínterin** *adv* : meanwhile

interín[2] *or* **ínterin** *nm, pl* **-rines** : meantime, interim ⟨en el ínterin : in the meantime⟩

interinamente *adv* : temporarily

interinato *nm* : temporary position

interino[1], -na *adj* : acting, temporary, interim

interino[2], -na *n* : substitute, temp

interior[1] *adj* **1** : interior, inside, inner ⟨parte interior : inside⟩ ⟨bolsillo interior : inside pocket⟩ ⟨patio interior : inner courtyard⟩ **2** : inner ⟨voz interior : inner voice⟩ **3** : domestic, internal

interior[2] *nm* **1** : interior, inside **2** : inland region

interiormente *adv* : inwardly

interjección *nf, pl* **-ciones** : interjection

interlocutor, -tora *n* : speaker

interludio *nm* : interlude

intermediario, -ria *adj & n* : intermediary, go-between

intermedio[1], -dia *adj* : intermediate

intermedio[2] *nm* **1** : intermission **2** **por intermedio de** : by means of

interminable *adj* : interminable, endless — **interminablemente** *adv*

intermisión *nf, pl* **-siones** : intermission, pause

intermitente[1] *adj* **1** : intermittent **2** : flashing, blinking (of a light) — **intermitentemente** *adv*

intermitente[2] *nm* : blinker, turn signal

internacional *adj* : international — **internacionalmente** *adv*

internacionalizar {21} *vt* : to internationalize — **internacionalización** *nf*

internado *nm* : boarding school

internamiento *nm* **1** : internment, confinement **2** : admission

internar *vt* : to admit (to a hospital, etc.), to commit (to an institution) — **internarse** *vr* **1** : to penetrate, to advance into **2** ~ **en** : to go into, to enter **3** ~ **en** : to be admitted to

internauta *nmf* : Internet user

Internet *or* **internet** *nmf* : Internet

internista *nmf* : internist

interno[1], -na *adj* : internal ⟨la política interna : domestic policy⟩ — **internamente** *adv*

interno[2], -na *n* **1** : intern **2** : inmate

interpelación *nf, pl* **-ciones** : appeal, plea

interpelar *vt* : to question (formally)

interpersonal *adj* : interpersonal

interpolar *vt* : to insert, to interpolate

interponer {60} *vt* : to interpose — **interponerse** *vr* : to intervene

interpretación *nf, pl* **-ciones** : interpretation

interpretar *vt* **1** : to interpret **2** : to play, to perform

interpretativo, -va *adj* : interpretive
intérprete *nmf* **1** TRADUCTOR : interpreter **2** : performer
interpuesto *pp* → **interponer**
interracial *adj* : interracial
interrelación *nf, pl* **-ciones** : interrelationship
interrelacionar *vi* : to interrelate
interrogación *nf, pl* **-ciones 1** : interrogation, questioning **2 or signo de interrogación** : question mark
interrogador, -dora *n* : interrogator, questioner
interrogante[1] *adj* : questioning
interrogante[2] *nm* : question mark
interrogante[3] *nmf* : question
interrogar {52} *vt* : to interrogate, to question
interrogativo, -va *adj* : interrogative
interrogatorio *nm* : interrogation, questioning
interrumpir *v* : to interrupt
interrupción *nf, pl* **-ciones** : interruption
interruptor *nm* **1** : (electrical) switch **2** : circuit breaker
intersecarse {72} *vr Spain* → **intersectarse**
intersección *nf, pl* **-ciones** : intersection
intersectarse *vr* : to intersect
intersticio *nm* : interstice — **intersticial** *adj*
interuniversitario, -ria *adj* : intercollegiate
interurbano, -na *adj* **1** : intercity **2** : long-distance ⟨llamadas interurbanas : long-distance calls⟩
intervalo *nm* : interval
intervención *nf, pl* **-ciones 1** : intervention **2** : audit **3** : intercepting (of mail, etc.), tapping (of phones) **4 intervención quirúrgica** : operation
intervenir {87} *vi* **1** : to take part in INTERCEDER : to intervene, to intercede — *vt* **1** : to control, to supervise **2** : to audit **3** : to operate on **4** : to tap, to wiretap (a phone)
interventor, -tora *n* **1** : inspector **2** : auditor, comptroller
intestado, -da *adj* : intestate
intestinal *adj* : intestinal
intestino[1], **-na** *adj* : internal, internecine
intestino[2] *nm* : intestine
intimar *vi* ∼ **con** : to become friendly with — *vt* : to require, to call on
intimidación *nf, pl* **-ciones** : intimidation
intimidad *nf* **1** : intimacy **2** : privacy, private life
intimidante *adj* : intimidating
intimidar *vt* ACOBARDAR : to intimidate
intimidatorio, -ria *adj* : intimidating
íntimo, -ma *adj* **1** : intimate, close **2** PRIVADO : private — **íntimamente** *adv*
intitular *vt* : to entitle, to title
intocable *adj* : untouchable
intolerable *adj* : intolerable, unbearable
intolerancia *nf* : intolerance
intolerante[1] *adj* : intolerant
intolerante[2] *nmf* : intolerant person, bigot
intoxicación *nf, pl* **-ciones** : poisoning
intoxicante *nm* : poison

intoxicar {72} *vt* : to poison
intranquilidad *nf* PREOCUPACIÓN : worry, anxiety
intranquilizar {21} *vt* : to upset, to make uneasy — **intranquilizarse** *vr* : to get worried, to be anxious
intranquilo, -la *adj* PREOCUPADO : uneasy, worried
intransferible *adj* : nontransferable
intransigencia *nf* : intransigence
intransigente *adj* : intransigent, unyielding
intransitable *adj* : impassable
intransitivo, -va *adj* : intransitive
intrascendente *adj* : unimportant, insignificant
intratable *adj* **1** : intractable **2** : awkward **3** : unsociable
intravenoso, -sa *adj* : intravenous
intrepidez *nf* : fearlessness
intrépido, -da *adj* : intrepid, fearless
intriga *nf* : intrigue
intrigante *nmf* : schemer
intrigar {52} *v* : to intrigue — **intrigante** *adj*
intrincado, -da *adj* : intricate, involved
intrínseco, -ca *adj* : intrinsic — **intrínsecamente** *adv*
introducción *nf, pl* **-ciones** : introduction
introducir {61} *vt* **1** : to introduce **2** : to bring in **3** : to insert **4** : to input, to enter — **introducirse** *vr* : to penetrate, to get into
introductorio, -ria *adj* : introductory
intromisión *nf, pl* **-siones** : interference, meddling
introspección *nf, pl* **-ciones** : introspection
introspectivo, -va *adj* : introspective
introvertido[1], **-da** *adj* : introverted
introvertido[2], **-da** *n* : introvert
intrusión *nf, pl* **-siones** : intrusion
intruso[1], **-sa** *adj* : intrusive
intruso[2], **-sa** *n* : intruder
intuición *nf, pl* **-ciones** : intuition
intuir {41} *vt* : to intuit, to sense
intuitivo, -va *adj* : intuitive — **intuitivamente** *adv*
inundación *nf, pl* **-ciones** : flood, inundation
inundar *vt* : to flood, to inundate — **inundarse** *vr*
inusitado, -da *adj* : unusual, uncommon — **inusitadamente** *adv*
inusual *adj* : unusual, uncommon — **inusualmente** *adv*
inútil[1] *adj* INSERVIBLE : useless — **inútilmente** *adv*
inútil[2] *nmf* : good-for-nothing
inutilidad *nf* : uselessness
inutilizar {21} *vt* **1** : to make useless **2** INCAPACITAR : to disable, to put out of commission
invadir *vt* : to invade
invalidar *vt* : to nullify, to invalidate
invalidez *nf, pl* **-deces 1** : invalidity **2** : disability
inválido, -da *adj & n* : invalid
invalorable *adj* : invaluable
invaluable *adj* : invaluable

invariable *adj* : invariable — **invariablemente** *adv*

invasión *nf*, *pl* **-siones 1** : invasion **2 or barrio de invasión** *Col* : shantytown, slums *pl*

invasivo, -va *adj* : invasive

invasor[1], **-sora** *adj* : invading

invasor[2], **-sora** *n* : invader

invectiva *nf* : invective, abuse

invencibilidad *nf* : invincibility

invencible *adj* **1** : invincible **2** : insurmountable

invención *nf*, *pl* **-ciones 1** INVENTO : invention **2** MENTIRA : fabrication, lie

inventar *vt* **1** : to invent **2** : to fabricate, to make up — **inventarse** *vr* : to fabricate, to make up

inventariar {85} *vt* : to inventory

inventario *nm* : inventory

inventiva *nf* : ingenuity, inventiveness

inventivo, -va *adj* : inventive

invento *nm* INVENCIÓN : invention

inventor, -tora *n* : inventor

invernadero *nm* : greenhouse, hothouse

invernal *adj* : winter, wintry

invernar {55} *vi* **1** : to spend the winter **2** HIBERNAR : to hibernate

inverosímil *adj* : unlikely, far-fetched

inverosimilitud *nf* : implausibility, improbability

inversión *nf*, *pl* **-siones 1** : inversion **2** : investment

inversionista *nmf* : investor

inverso[1], **-sa** *adj* **1** : inverse, inverted **2** CONTRARIO : opposite **3 a la inversa** : the other way around, vice versa **4 en orden inverso** : in reverse order — **inversamente** *adv*

inverso[2] *n* : inverse

inversor, -sora *n* : investor

invertebrado[1], **-da** *adj* : invertebrate

invertebrado[2] *nm* : invertebrate

invertir {76} *vt* **1** : to invert, to reverse **2** : to invest — *vi* : to make an investment — **invertirse** *vr* : to be reversed

investidura *nf* : investiture, inauguration

investigación *nf*, *pl* **-ciones 1** ENCUESTA, INDAGACIÓN : investigation, inquiry **2** : research ⟨investigación y desarrollo : research and development⟩

investigador[1], **-dora** *adj* : investigative

investigador[2], **-dora** *n* **1** : investigator ⟨investigador privado, investigadora privada : private investigator⟩ **2** : researcher

investigar {52} *vt* **1** INDAGAR : to investigate **2** : to research — *vi* **sobre** : to do research into

investigativo, -va *adj* : investigative

investir {54} *vt* **1** : to empower **2** : to swear in, to inaugurate

inveterado, -da *adj* : inveterate, deep-seated

inviable *adj* : not viable, not feasible

invicto, -ta *adj* : undefeated

invidente[1] *adj* CIEGO : blind, sightless

invidente[2] *nmf* CIEGO : blind person

invierno *nm* : winter, wintertime

inviolable *adj* : inviolable — **inviolabilidad** *nf*

inviolado, -da *adj* : inviolate, pure

invisibilidad *nf* : invisibility

invisible *adj* : invisible — **invisiblemente** *adv*

invitación *nf*, *pl* **-ciones** : invitation

invitado, -da *n* : guest

invitar *vt* : to invite — *vi* : to pay for ⟨invita la casa : it's on the house⟩ ⟨invito yo : it's on me, it's my treat⟩

invocación *nf*, *pl* **-ciones** : invocation

invocar {72} *vt* : to invoke, to call on

involucramiento *nm* : involvement

involucrar *vt* : to implicate, to involve — **involucrarse** *vr* : to get involved

involuntario, -ria *adj* : involuntary — **involuntariamente** *adv*

invulnerable *adj* : invulnerable

inyección *nf*, *pl* **-ciones** : injection, shot

inyectado, -da *adj* **ojos inyectados** : bloodshot eyes

inyectar *vt* : to inject — **inyectarse** *vr*

ion *nm* : ion

iónico, -ca *adj* : ionic

ionizar {21} *vt* : to ionize — **ionización** *nf*

ionosfera *nf* : ionosphere

ir {43} *vi* **1** : to go ⟨ir a pie : to go on foot, to walk⟩ ⟨ir a caballo : to ride horseback⟩ ⟨ir a casa : to go home⟩ ⟨ir por mar : to go by sea⟩ ⟨iba para el aeropuerto : he was headed for the airport⟩ ⟨fui a ver una película : I went to see a movie⟩ ⟨el ir y venir de la gente : the comings and goings (of the people)⟩ ⟨vamos : let's go⟩ ⟨¡voy! : I'm coming!⟩ **2** : to lead, to extend, to stretch ⟨el camino va de Cali a Bogotá : the road goes from Cali to Bogotá⟩ **3** FUNCIONAR : to work, to function ⟨esta computadora ya no va : this computer doesn't work anymore⟩ **4** : to get on, to get along ⟨¿cómo te va? : how are you?, how's it going?⟩ ⟨el negocio no va bien : the business isn't doing well⟩ ⟨ir a mejor/peor : to get better/worse⟩ ⟨ir de mal en peor : to go from bad to worse⟩ **5** : to suit ⟨ese vestido te va bien : that dress really suits you⟩ ⟨el cambio te irá bien : the change will do you good⟩ **6 ~ a** ASISTIR : to go to, to attend **7 ~ con/en/de** : to wear ⟨voy a ir con/en falda : I'm going to wear a skirt⟩ ⟨iba de azul : she was wearing blue⟩ **8 ~ con** (*with a noun*) : to be ⟨ir con prisa : to be in a hurry⟩ ⟨ir con cuidado : to be cautious⟩ **9 ~ con** : to go with, to complement **10 ~ para** : to be studying to be ⟨va para médico : she's studying to be a doctor⟩ **11 ~ para** : to be going on, to be close to (an age) **12 ~ por** : to be aimed at ⟨también va por ti : that goes for you, too⟩ **13 ~ por** : to follow, to go along ⟨fueron por la costa : they followed the shoreline⟩ **14 ~ por** : to be up to (a point or stage) ⟨voy por la última página : I'm on the last page⟩ **15 ~ por** : to go (and) get, to fetch **16 dejarse ir** : to let oneself go **17 ir a parar** : to end up **18 ¡qué va!** *fam* : hardly! **19 ¡vamos!** : come on! **20 vamos a ver** : let's see — *v aux* **1** (*indicating manner*)

⟨ir caminando : to walk, to go on foot⟩ ⟨¡voy corriendo! : I'll be right there!⟩ **2** (*indicating a process*) ⟨va mejorando : he's getting better⟩ ⟨lo iremos haciendo poco a poco : we'll do it little by little⟩ **3** ~ **a** : to be going to ⟨voy a hacerlo : I'm going to do it⟩ ⟨el avión va a despegar : the plane is about to take off⟩ — **irse** *vr* **1** : to leave, to go ⟨¡vámonos! : let's go!⟩ ⟨todo el mundo se fue : everyone left⟩ **2** ESCAPARSE : to leak **3** GASTARSE : to be used up, to be gone

ira *nf* CÓLERA, FURIA : wrath, anger

iracundo, -da *adj* **1** : irate, angry ⟨estar iracundo : to be angry⟩ **2** : irascible ⟨ser iracundo : to be irascible⟩

iraní *adj & nmf* : Iranian

iraquí *adj & nmf* : Iraqi

irascible *adj* : irascible, irritable — **irascibilidad** *nf*

irga, irgue etc. → **erguir**

iridio *nm* : iridium

iridiscencia *nf* : iridescence — **iridiscente** *adj*

iris *nms & pl* **1** : iris **2** **arco iris** : rainbow

irlandés[1], **-desa** *adj, mpl* **-deses** : Irish

irlandés[2], **-desa** *n, pl* **-deses** : Irish person, Irishman *m*, Irishwoman *f*

irlandés[3] *nm* : Irish (language)

ironía *nf* : irony

irónico, -ca *adj* : ironic, ironical — **irónicamente** *adv*

ironizar {21} *vi* : to speak ironically — *vt* : to say ironically

irracional *adj* : irrational — **irracionalmente** *adv*

irracionalidad *nf* : irrationality

irradiación *nf, pl* **-ciones** : irradiation

irradiar *vt* : to radiate, to irradiate

irrazonable *adj* : unreasonable

irreal *adj* : unreal

irrebatible *adj* : unanswerable, irrefutable

irreconciliable *adj* : irreconcilable

irreconocible *adj* : unrecognizable

irrecuperable *adj* : irrecoverable, irretrievable

irredimible *adj* : irredeemable

irreductible *adj* : unyielding

irreemplazable *adj* : irreplaceable

irreflexión *nf, pl* **-xiones** : thoughtlessness

irreflexivo, -va *adj* : rash, unthinking — **irreflexivamente** *adv*

irrefrenable *adj* : uncontrollable, unstoppable ⟨un impulso irrefrenable : an irresistible urge⟩

irrefutable *adj* : irrefutable

irregular *adj* : irregular — **irregularmente** *adv*

irregularidad *nf* : irregularity

irrelevante *adj* : irrelevant — **irrelevancia** *nf*

irreligioso, -sa *adj* : irreligious

irremediable *adj* : incurable — **irremediablemente** *adv*

irreparable *adj* : irreparable

irrepetible *adj* : unrepeatable, unique

irreprimible *adj* : irrepressible

irreprochable *adj* : irreproachable

irresistible *adj* : irresistible — **irresistiblemente** *adv*

irresolución *nf, pl* **-ciones** : indecision, hesitation

irresoluto, -ta *adj* INDECISO : undecided

irrespetar *vt* CA, Carib : to disrespect, to be disrespectful to

irrespeto *nm* : disrespect

irrespetuoso, -sa *adj* : disrespectful — **irrespetuosamente** *adv*

irrespirable *adj* : unbreathable

irresponsabilidad *nf* : irresponsibility

irresponsable *adj* : irresponsible — **irresponsablemente** *adv*

irrestricto, -ta *adj* : unrestricted, unconditional

irreverencia *nf* : disrespect

irreverente *adj* : irreverent, disrespectful

irreversible *adj* : irreversible

irrevocable *adj* : irrevocable — **irrevocablemente** *adv*

irrigar {52} *vt* : to irrigate — **irrigación** *nf*

irrisible *adj* : laughable

irrisión *nf, pl* **-siones** : derision, ridicule

irrisorio, -ria *adj* RISIBLE : ridiculous, ludicrous

irritabilidad *nf* : irritability

irritable *adj* : irritable

irritación *nf, pl* **-ciones** : irritation

irritante *adj* : irritating

irritar *vt* : to irritate — **irritación** *nf*

irrompible *adj* : unbreakable

irrumpir *vi* ~ **en** : to burst into

irrupción *nf, pl* **-ciones** **1** : emergence **2** : invasion

-ísimo, -ma *suf* : very, extremely

isla *nf* : island

Islam *nm* : Islam

islámico, -ca *adj* : Islamic, Muslim

islamismo *nm* **1** : Islam **2** : Islamism — **islamista** *adj & nmf*

islandés[1], **-desa** *adj, mpl* **-deses** : Icelandic

islandés[2], **-desa** *n, mpl* **-deses** : Icelander

islandés[3] *nm* : Icelandic (language)

isleño[1], **-ña** *adj* : island

isleño[2], **-ña** *n* : islander

islote *nm* : islet

isometría *nfs & pl* : isometrics

isométrico, -ca *adj* : isometric

isósceles *adj* : isosceles ⟨triángulo isósceles : isosceles triangle⟩

isótopo *nm* : isotope

israelí *adj & nmf* : Israeli

istmo *nm* : isthmus

itacate *nm* Mex : pack, provisions *pl*

italiano[1], **-na** *adj & n* : Italian

italiano[2] *nm* : Italian (language)

ítem *nm* : item

itinerante *adj* AMBULANTE : traveling, itinerant

itinerario *nm* : itinerary, route

-ito, -cito *suf* **1** : little ⟨un pedacito : a little piece⟩ ⟨su hermanita : his little/baby sister⟩ ⟨sólo un ratito : just a little while⟩ **2** (*used to show affection*) ⟨mi abuelito : my grandpa⟩ ⟨¡pobrecita! : poor thing!⟩ ⟨dame un besito : give me

a kiss⟩ ⟨¿quieres un cafecito? : do you
want a nice cup of coffee?⟩ **3** (*used for
emphasis*) : nice and hot ⟨bien calentito :
nice and hot⟩ ⟨al verlo se quedó calladita : when she
saw him she went quiet⟩

izar {21} *vt* : to hoist, to raise ⟨izar la
bandera : to raise the flag⟩
izquierda *nf* : left
izquierdista *adj & nmf* : leftist
izquierdo, -da *adj* : left

J

j *nf* : tenth letter of the Spanish alphabet
ja *interj* **1** : ha! **2 ja, ja** : ha-ha!
jaba *nf* **1** *Car* : bag, sack **2** *Mex, CA*
: crate, box
jabalí *nm, pl* **-líes** : wild boar
jabalina *nf* : javelin
jabón *nm, pl* **jabones** : soap
jabonar *vt* ENJABONAR : to soap up, to
lather — **jabonarse** *vr*
jabonera *nf* : soap dish
jabonoso, -sa *adj* : soapy
jaca *nf* **1** : pony **2** YEGUA : mare
jacal *nm Mex* : shack, hut
jacinto *nm* : hyacinth
jactancia *nf* **1** : boastfulness **2** : boasting,
bragging
jactancioso¹, -sa *adj* : boastful
jactancioso², -sa *n* : boaster, braggart
jactarse *vr* : to boast, to brag ⟨jactarse de
algo : to brag about something⟩
Jacuzzi [ja'kuzi, -'kusi] *marca registrada,
m* — used for a whirlpool bath
jade *nm* : jade
jadear *vi* : to pant, to gasp, to puff —
jadeante *adj*
jadeo *nm* : panting, gasping, puffing
jaez *nm, pl* **jaeces 1** : harness **2** : kind,
sort, ilk **3 jaeces** *nmpl* : trappings
jaguar *nm* : jaguar
jai alai *nm* : jai alai
jaiba *nf* CANGREJO : crab
jalapeño *nm Mex* : jalapeño pepper
jalar *vt* **1** : to pull, to tug **2** *fam* : to attract, to draw in ⟨las ideas nuevas lo
jalan : new ideas appeal to him⟩ — *vi* **1**
: to pull, to pull together ⟨jalar de algo
: to pull on something⟩ **2** *fam* : to hurry
up, to get going **3** *Mex fam* : to be in
working order ⟨esta máquina no jala
: this machine doesn't work⟩
jalbegue *nm* : whitewash
jalea *nf* : jelly
jalear *vt* : to encourage, to urge on
jaleo *nm* **1** *fam* : uproar, ruckus, racket
2 *fam* : confusion, mess, hassle **3** : cheer-
ing and clapping (for a dance)
jalón *nm, pl* **jalones 1** : milestone, landmark **2** TIRÓN : pull, tug
jalonar *vt* : to mark, to stake out
jalonear *vt Mex, Peru fam* : to tug at — *vi* **1**
fam : to pull, to tug **2** *CA fam* : to haggle
jamaicano, -na → jamaiquino
jamaiquino, -na *adj & n* : Jamaican
jamás *adv* **1** NUNCA : never ⟨jamás vi tal
cosa : I've never seen such a thing⟩ ⟨no
lo olvidaré jamás : I'll never forget it⟩ **2**
nunca jamás *or* **jamás de los jamases**

: never ever **3 para siempre jamás** : for
ever and ever
jamba *nf* : jamb
jamelgo *nm* : nag (horse)
jamón *nm, pl* **jamones 1** : ham **2 jamón
serrano** : cured Spanish ham
Januká *or* **Januká** *nmf* : Hanukkah
japonés¹, -nesa *adj & n, mpl* **-neses** : Japanese ⟨los japoneses : the Japanese (people)⟩
japonés² *nm, pl* **-neses** : Japanese (language)
jaque *nm* **1** : check (in chess) ⟨jaque
mate : checkmate⟩ ⟨dar jaque mate a
: to checkmate⟩ **2 tener en jaque** : to
intimidate, to bully
jaquear *vi* : to check (in chess)
jaqueca *nf* : headache, migraine
jarabe *nm* **1** : syrup ⟨jarabe para la tos
: cough syrup⟩ **2** : Mexican folk dance
jarana *nf* **1** *fam* : revelry, partying, spree
2 *fam* : joking, fooling around **3** : small
guitar
jaranear *vi fam* : to go on a spree, to party
jarcia *nf* **1** : rigging **2** : fishing tackle
jardín *nm, pl* **jardines 1** : garden **2** : yard
(of a house) **3 jardín de niños** *CA, Mex
or* **jardín infantil** *Chile or* **jardín de
infancia** *Spain* : kindergarten **4 jardín
izquierdo/central/derecho** : left/center/
right field **5 los jardines** : the outfield
jardinera *nf* **1** : planter **2** : plant stand
jardinería *nf* : gardening
jardinero, -ra *n* **1** : gardener **2** : outfielder (in baseball)
jarra *nf* **1** : pitcher, jug **2** : stein, mug **3
de jarras** *or* **en jarras** : akimbo
jarrete *nm* **1** : back of the knee **2** CORVE-
JÓN : hock
jarro *nm* **1** : pitcher, jug **2** : mug
jarrón *nm, pl* **jarrones** FLORERO : vase
jaspe *nm* : jasper
jaspeado, -da *adj* VETEADO : streaked,
veined **2** : speckled, mottled
jaula *nf* : cage
jauría *nf* : pack of hounds
javanés, -nesa *adj & n* : Javanese
jazmín *nm, pl* **jazmines** : jasmine
jazz ['jas, 'dʒas] *nm* : jazz
je *interj* → ja
jeans ['jins, 'dʒins] *nmpl* : jeans
jeep ['jip, 'dʒip] *nm, pl* **jeeps** : jeep (military vehicle)
Jeep *marca registrada, m* — used for a
small truck
jefatura *nf* **1** : leadership **2** : headquarters ⟨jefatura de policía : police head-
quarters⟩
jefe, -fa *n* **1** : chief, head, leader ⟨jefe de
bomberos/policía : fire/police chief⟩

⟨jefe del departamento : department head⟩ ⟨jefe de oficina : office manager⟩ ⟨jefe de Estado/gobierno : head of state/government⟩ ⟨jefe de redacción : editor in chief⟩ **2** : boss

Jehová *nm* : Jehovah

jején *nm, pl* **jejenes** : gnat, small mosquito

jengibre *nm* : ginger

jeque *nm* : sheikh, sheik

jerarca *nmf* : leader, chief

jerarquía *nf* **1** : hierarchy **2** RANGO : rank

jerárquico, -ca *adj* : hierarchical

jerbo *nm* : gerbil

jerez *nm, pl* **jereces** : sherry

jerga *nf* **1** : jargon, slang **2** : coarse cloth

jerigonza *nf* GALIMATÍAS : mumbo jumbo, gibberish

jeringa *nf* : syringe

jeringar {52} *vt* **1** : to inject **2** *fam* JOROBAR : to annoy, to pester — *vi fam* JOROBAR : to be annoying, to be a nuisance

jeringuear → jeringar

jeringuilla → jeringa

jeroglífico *nm* : hieroglyphic

jersey *nm, pl* **jerseys 1** : jersey (fabric) **2** *Spain* : sweater

Jesucristo *nm* : Jesus Christ

jesuita *adj & nm* : Jesuit

Jesús *nm* **1** : Jesus **2** ¡**Jesús!** : goodness!, good heavens! **3** ¡**Jesús!** : bless you! (said to someone who has sneezed)

jet *nm* : jet (airplane)

jeta *nf* **1** : snout **2** *fam* : face, mug

jíbaro, -ra *adj* **1** : Jivaro **2** : rustic, rural

jibia *nf* : cuttlefish

jícama *nf* : jicama

jícara *nf Mex* : calabash

jicotea *nf CA, Car, Mex* : turtle

jihad → yihad

jilguero *nm* : European goldfinch

jinete *nmf* : horseman, horsewoman *f*, rider

jinetear *vt* **1** : to ride, to perform (on horseback) **2** DOMAR : to break in (a horse) — *vi* CABALGAR : to ride horseback

jingoísmo [ˈjɪŋɡoˈizmo, ˌdʒɪŋ-] *nm* : jingoism

jingoísta *adj* : jingoist, jingoistic

jiote *nm Mex* : rash

jira *nf* : outing, picnic

jirafa *nf* **1** : giraffe **2** : boom microphone

jirón *nm, pl* **jirones 1** : shred, rag ⟨hecho jirones : in tatters⟩ **2** *Peru* : street

jitomate *nm Mex* : tomato

jockey [ˈjoki, ˈdʒo-] *nmf, pl* **jockeys** [-kis] : jockey

jocosidad *nf* : humor, jocularity

jocoso, -sa *adj* : playful, jocular — **jocosamente** *adv*

jofaina *nf* : washbowl

jogging [ˈjɔɡɪŋ, ˈdʒɔ-] *nm* **1** : jogging **2** *Arg* : sweatpants **3** *Arg* : sweatsuit, tracksuit

jolgorio *nm* : merrymaking, fun

jonrón *nm, pl* **jonrones** : home run

jordano, -na *adj & n* : Jordanian

jornada *nf* **1** : expedition, day's journey **2** **jornada laboral** *or* **jornada de trabajo**

: workday **3 jornadas** *nfpl* : conference, congress

jornal *nm* **1** : day's pay **2 a ∼** : by the day

jornalero, -ra *n* : day laborer

joroba *nf* **1** GIBA : hump **2** *fam* : nuisance, pain in the neck

jorobado¹, -da *adj* GIBOSO : hunchbacked, humpbacked

jorobado², -da *n* GIBOSO : person with a hump, hunchback *offensive*, humpback *offensive*

jorobar *vt fam* JERINGAR : to bother, to annoy — *vi fam* JERINGAR : to be annoying, to be a nuisance

jorongo *nm Mex* : full-length poncho

jota *nf* **1** : jot, bit ⟨no entiendo ni jota : I don't understand a word of it⟩ ⟨no se ve ni jota : you can't see a thing⟩ **2** : jack (in playing cards) **3** : (letter) j

joven¹ *adj, pl* **jóvenes 1** : young **2** : youthful

joven² *nmf, pl* **jóvenes** : young man *m*, young woman *f*, young person

jovial *adj* : jovial, cheerful — **jovialmente** *adv*

jovialidad *nf* : joviality, cheerfulness

joya *nf* **1** : jewel, piece of jewelry **2** : treasure, gem ⟨la nueva empleada es una joya : the new employee is a real gem⟩

joyería *nf* **1** : jewelry store **2** : jewelry **3 joyería de fantasía** : costume jewelry

joyero, -ra *n* **1** : jeweler **2** : jewelry box

joystick [ˈjoistik] *nm, pl* **joysticks** : joystick

juanete *nm* : bunion

jubilación *nf, pl* **-ciones 1** : retirement ⟨jubilación anticipada : early retirement⟩ **2** PENSIÓN : pension

jubilado¹, -da *adj* : retired, in retirement

jubilado², -da *n* : retired person, retiree

jubilar *vt* **1** : to retire, to pension off **2** *fam* : to get rid of, to discard — **jubilarse** *vr* : to retire

jubileo *nm* : jubilee

júbilo *nm* : jubilation, joy

jubiloso, -sa *adj* : jubilant, joyous

judaico, -ca *adj* : Judaic, Jewish

judaísmo *nm* : Judaism

judía *nf* **1** : bean **2** *or* **judía verde** : green bean, string bean

judicatura *nf* **1** : judiciary, judges *pl* **2** : office of judge

judicial *adj* : judicial — **judicialmente** *adv*

judío¹, -día *adj* : Jewish

judío², -día *n* : Jewish person, Jew

judo [ˈjuðo, ˈdʒu-] *nm* : judo

juega, juegue etc. **→ jugar**

juego *nm* **1** : play, playing ⟨poner/entrar en juego : to bring/come into play⟩ ⟨juego limpio/sucio : fair/foul play⟩ **2** : game, sport ⟨juego de cartas : card game⟩ ⟨juego de mesa : board game⟩ ⟨juego de azar : game of chance⟩ ⟨Juegos Olímpicos : Olympic Games⟩ **3** : gaming, gambling ⟨el juego ilegal : illegal gambling⟩ ⟨estar en juego : to be at stake⟩ **4** : ride (at an amusement park) **5** : set ⟨un juego de herramientas/platos

: a set of tools/dishes⟩ 6 SOLTURA : play, slack 7 **fuera de juego** : offside 8 **hacer juego** : to go together, to match 9 **hacerle el juego a** : to play along with 10 **juego de manos** : trick, sleight of hand 11 **juego de palabras** : play on words, pun

juerga *nf* : partying, binge ⟨irse de juerga : to go on a spree⟩

juerguista *nmf* : reveler, carouser

jueves *nms & pl* : Thursday ⟨el jueves : (on) Thursday⟩ ⟨los jueves : (on) Thursdays⟩ ⟨cada (dos) jueves : every (other) Thursday⟩ ⟨el jueves pasado : last Thursday⟩ ⟨el próximo jueves : next Thursday⟩

juez¹ *nmf, pl* **jueces** 1 : judge 2 ÁRBITRO : umpire, referee 3 **juez de paz** : justice of the peace

juez², **jueza** *n → juez*¹

jugada *nf* 1 : play, move 2 : trick ⟨hacer una mala jugada : to play a dirty trick⟩

jugador, -dora *n* 1 : player 2 : gambler

jugar {44} *vi* 1 : to play ⟨jugar al fútbol : to play soccer⟩ ⟨jugar a la lotería : to play the lottery⟩ ⟨jugar a las muñecas : to play with dolls⟩ ⟨jugar limpio/sucio : to play fair/dirty⟩ 2 APOSTAR : to gamble, to bet ⟨jugar a la Bolsa : to play the stock market⟩ 3 : to joke, to kid 4 **jugar con alguien** : to toy with someone — *vt* 1 : to play ⟨jugar un papel : to play a role⟩ ⟨jugar una carta : to play a card⟩ 2 : to bet ⟨jugarlo todo a : to bet everything on⟩ — **jugarse** *vr* 1 : to risk, to gamble away ⟨jugarse la vida : to risk one's life⟩ 2 **jugarse el todo por el todo** : to risk everything

jugarreta *nf fam* : prank, dirty trick

juglar *nm* : minstrel

jugo *nm* 1 : juice ⟨jugo de naranja : orange juice⟩ 2 : substance, essence ⟨sacarle el jugo a algo : to get the most out of something⟩

jugosidad *nf* : juiciness

jugoso, -sa *adj* 1 : juicy 2 : lucrative, profitable

juguete *nm* 1 : toy 2 **de ~** : toy ⟨un camión de juguete : a toy truck⟩

juguetear *vi* 1 : to play, to cavort, to frolic 2 : to toy, to fiddle

juguetería *nf* : toy store

juguetón, -tona *adj, mpl* **-tones** : playful — **juguetonamente** *adv*

juicio *nm* 1 : good judgment, reason, sense ⟨perder el juicio : to lose one's mind⟩ ⟨en su sano juicio : in one's right mind⟩ 2 : opinion ⟨a mi juicio : in my opinion⟩ 3 : trial ⟨llevar/ir a juicio : to take/go to court⟩ ⟨un juicio civil/criminal : a civil/criminal trial⟩

juicioso, -sa *adj* : judicious, wise — **juiciosamente** *adv*

julio *nm* : July ⟨el primero de julio : (on) July first⟩

jumper ['ʤumper] *nm, pl* **jumpers** ['ʤumpers] : jumper, pinafore

juncia *nf* : sedge

junco *nm* 1 : reed, rush 2 : junk (boat)

jungla *nf* : jungle

junio *nm* : June ⟨el primero de junio : (on) June first⟩

junquillo *nm* : jonquil

junta *nf* 1 : board, committee ⟨junta directiva : board of directors⟩ 2 REUNIÓN : meeting, session 3 : junta 4 : regional government (in Spain) 5 : joint, gasket

juntamente *adv* 1 : jointly, together ⟨juntamente con : together with⟩ 2 : at the same time

juntar *vt* 1 UNIR : to unite, to combine, to put together 2 REUNIR : to collect, to gather together, to assemble 3 : to close partially ⟨juntar la puerta : to leave the door ajar⟩ — **juntarse** *vr* 1 : to join together 2 : to move closer together 3 : to get together ⟨nos juntamos a conversar : we got together to chat⟩ ⟨volvió a juntarse con el grupo : he got back together with the group⟩

junto, -ta *adj* 1 UNIDO : joined, united 2 : close, adjacent ⟨colgaron los dos retratos juntos : they hung the two paintings side by side⟩ 3 (*used adverbially*) : together ⟨llegamos juntos : we arrived together⟩ ⟨sabe más que todos juntos : she knows more than all of us put together⟩ 4 **~ a** : next to, alongside of 5 **~ con** : together with, along with

juntura *nf* : joint, coupling

Júpiter *nm* : Jupiter

jura *nf* : oath, pledge ⟨jura de bandera : pledge of allegiance⟩

jurado¹ *nm* : jury (in a trial), panel of judges (in a contest)

jurado² *nmf* 1 : juror 2 : judge (in a contest)

juramentación *nf, pl* **-ciones** : swearing in

juramentar *vt* : to swear in

juramento *nm* 1 : oath ⟨prestar juramento : to swear, to take an oath⟩ ⟨tomarle juramento a : to swear in (an official), to take (a witness) under oath⟩ 2 : swearword, oath

jurar *vt* 1 : to swear ⟨jurar lealtad : to swear loyalty⟩ ⟨jurar bandera : to pledge allegiance to the flag⟩ ⟨no lo sabía, ¡te lo juro! : I swear I didn't know!⟩ 2 : to take an oath ⟨el alcalde juró su cargo : the mayor took the oath of office⟩ 3 **tenérsela jurada a alguien** : to have it in for someone — *vi* : to curse, to swear

jurídico, -ca *adj* : legal

jurisdicción *nf, pl* **-ciones** : jurisdiction — **jurisdiccional** *adj*

jurisprudencia *nf* : jurisprudence, law

jurista *nmf* : jurist

justa *nf* 1 : joust 2 TORNEO : tournament, competition

justamente *adv* 1 PRECISAMENTE : precisely, exactly 2 : justly, fairly

justar *vi* : to joust

justicia *nf* 1 : justice, fairness ⟨hacerle justicia a : to do justice to⟩ ⟨ser de justicia : to be only fair⟩ ⟨en justicia : in all fairness⟩ ⟨pedir justicia : to demand justice⟩ 2 **la justicia** : the law ⟨tomarse la justicia por su mano : to take the law into one's own hands⟩

justiciero, -ra *adj* : righteous, avenging
justificable *adj* : justifiable
justificación *nf, pl* **-ciones** : justification
justificante *nm* **1** : justification **2** : proof, voucher
justificar {72} *vt* **1** : to justify **2** : to excuse, to vindicate — **justificarse** *vr*
justo¹ *adv* **1** : justly **2** : right, exactly ⟨justo en ese momento : right at that moment⟩ ⟨justo en el centro : right in the center/middle⟩ ⟨justo a tiempo : just in time⟩ **3** : tightly
justo², **-ta** *adj* **1** : just, fair **2** : right, exact ⟨la cantidad justa : the exact amount⟩ ⟨lo justo para vivir : just enough to live on⟩ **3** : tight ⟨estos zapatos me que-

dan muy justos : these shoes are too tight⟩
justo³, **-ta** *n* : just person ⟨los justos : the just⟩
juvenil *adj* **1** : juvenile (of crimes, etc.), youth ⟨una organización juvenil : a youth organization⟩ **2** : young, youthful (in appearance, etc.) **3** ADOLESCENTE : teenage **4** : junior (in sports)
juventud *nf* **1** : youth **2** : young people
juzgado *nm* TRIBUNAL : court, tribunal
juzgar {52} *vt* **1** : to try, to judge (a case in court) **2** : to pass judgment on **3** CONSIDERAR : to consider, to deem ⟨a juzgar por los resultados : judging by the results⟩
juzgue, etc. → **juzgar**

K

k *nf* : twelfth letter of the Spanish alphabet
ka *nf* : (letter) k
káiser *nm* : kaiser
kaki → **caqui**
kaleidoscopio → **caleidoscopio**
kamikaze *adj & nm* : kamikaze
kan *nm* : khan
karaoke *nm* : karaoke
karate *or* **kárate** *nm* : karate
kayac *or* **kayak** *nm, pl* **kayacs** *or* **kayaks** : kayak
kebab [ke'bab] *nm, pl* **kebabs** [ke'babs] : kebab
keniano, -na *adj & n* : Kenyan
kermesse *or* **kermés** [ker'mes] *nf, pl* **kermesses** *or* **kermeses** [-'meses] : charity fair, bazaar
kerosene *or* **kerosén** *or* **keroseno** *nm* : kerosene, paraffin
ketchup ['ketʃap, -'tʃup] *nm* : ketchup, catsup
kibutz *or* **kibbutz** *nms & pl* : kibbutz
kilo *nm* **1** : kilo, kilogram **2** *fam* : large amount
kilobyte [,kilo'bait] *nm* : kilobyte
kilociclo *nm* : kilocycle
kilogramo *nm* : kilogram

kilohertzio *nm* : kilohertz
kilometraje *nm* : distance in kilometers, mileage
kilométrico, -ca *adj fam* : endless, very long
kilómetro *nm* : kilometer
kilovatio *nm* : kilowatt
kimono *nm* : kimono
kinder ['kɪndɛr] → **kindergarten**
kindergarten [,kɪndɛr'gartɛn] *nm, pl* **kindergartens** [-tɛns] **1** : kindergarten **2** : nursery school
kinesiología *nf* : physical therapy
kinesiólogo, -ga *n* : physical therapist
kiosco, kiosko → **quiosco**
kiosquero, -ra → **quiosquero**
kit *nm, pl* **kits** : kit
kiwi ['kiwi] *nm* **1** : kiwi (bird) **2** : kiwifruit
klaxon → **claxon**
Kleenex ['klines, -neks] *marca registrada, m* — used for a paper tissue
knockout [nɔ'kaut] → **nocaut**
koala *nm* : koala bear
kriptón *nm* : krypton
kurdo¹, **-da** *adj* : Kurdish
kurdo², **-da** *n* : Kurd
kuwaití [ku,wai'ti] *adj & nmf* : Kuwaiti

L

l *nf* : thirteenth letter of the Spanish alphabet
la¹ *nm* **1** : A ⟨la sostenido/bemol : A sharp/flat⟩ **2** : la (in singing)
la² *pron (referring to feminine nouns)* **1** : her, it ⟨llámala hoy : call her today⟩ ⟨sacó la botella y la abrió : he took out the bottle and opened it⟩ **2** *(formal)* : you ⟨no la vi a usted, Señora Díaz : I didn't see you, Mrs. Díaz⟩ **3** : the one ⟨me gusta la roja : I like the red one⟩ ⟨la de la camisa azul : the one with the blue

shirt⟩ ⟨mi mamá y la tuya : my mom and yours⟩ ⟨la clase de ayer y la de hoy : yesterday's class and today's⟩ **4 la que** : the one that/who, whoever, she who ⟨la que vino ayer : the one who came yesterday⟩ ⟨la que compré : the one (that) I bought⟩ ⟨la que gane : whoever wins⟩
la³ *art* → **el**²
laberíntico, -ca *adj* : labyrinthine
laberinto *nm* : labyrinth, maze
labia *nf fam* : gift of gab ⟨tu amigo tiene labia : your friend has a way with words⟩

labial *adj* : labial, lip ⟨lápiz labial : lipstick⟩

labio *nm* : lip

labor *nf* : work, labor

laborable *adj* 1 : arable 2 : work, working ⟨día laborable : workday, business day⟩

laboral *adj* : work, labor ⟨costos laborales : labor costs⟩

laborar *vi* : to work

laboratorio *nm* : laboratory, lab

laboriosamente *adv* 1 : laboriously 2 : industriously, diligently

laboriosidad *nf* : industriousness, diligence

laborioso, -sa *adj* 1 : laborious, hard 2 : industrious, hardworking

labrado¹, -da *adj* 1 : cultivated, tilled 2 : carved, wrought

labrado² *nm* : cultivated field

labrador, -dora *n* : farmer

labranza *nf* : farming

labrar *vt* 1 : to carve, to work (metal) 2 : to cultivate, to till 3 : to cause, to bring about

labriego, -ga *n* : farm worker

laburar *vi Arg, Uru* TRABAJAR : to work

laburo *nm Arg, Uru* TRABAJO : work, job

laca *nf* 1 : lacquer, shellac 2 : hair spray 3 **laca de uñas** : nail polish

lacayo *nm* : lackey

lace, etc. → **lazar**

lacear *vt* : to lasso

laceración *nf, pl* **-ciones** : laceration

lacerante *adj* : hurtful, wounding

lacerar *vt* 1 : to lacerate, to cut 2 : to hurt, to wound (one's feelings)

lacio, -cia *adj* 1 : limp, lank 2 **pelo lacio** : straight hair

lacónico, -ca *adj* : laconic — **lacónicamente** *adv*

lacra *nf* 1 : scar, mark (on the skin) 2 : stigma, blemish

lacrar *vt* : to seal (with wax)

lacrimógeno, -na *adj* **gas lacrimógeno** : tear gas

lacrimoso, -sa *adj* : tearful, moving

lacrosse *nm* : lacrosse

lactancia *nf* : breast-feeding

lactante *nmf* : nursing infant, suckling

lactar *v* : to breast-feed

lácteo, -tea *adj* 1 : dairy 2 **Vía Láctea** : Milky Way

ladeado, -da *adj* : crooked, tilted, lopsided

ladear *vt* : to tilt, to tip — **ladearse** *vr* : to bend (over)

ladera *nf* : slope, hillside

ladino¹, -na *adj* 1 : cunning, shrewd 2 *CA, Mex* : mestizo

ladino², -na *n* 1 : trickster 2 *CA, Mex* : Spanish-speaking person of indigenous descent 3 *CA, Mex* : mestizo

lado *nm* 1 : side ⟨el lado izquierdo/derecho : the left/right side⟩ ⟨el otro lado : the other side⟩ ⟨el lado de arriba/abajo : the top/bottom⟩ 2 PARTE : place ⟨miró por todos lados : he looked everywhere⟩ 3 : side (in an argument, etc.) ⟨se puso de mi lado : she took my side⟩ 4 **al ~** ⟨los que viven al lado : the people who live next door⟩ ⟨tenemos una tienda al lado : there's a store beside/near us⟩ 5 **al lado de** : next to, beside ⟨al lado de la calle : on/at the side of the road⟩ ⟨a mi lado : beside me⟩ 6 **de al lado** ⟨los de al lado : the next-door neighbors⟩ ⟨el asiento de al lado : the seat next to mine/yours (etc.)⟩ 7 **de ~** : tilted, sideways ⟨está de lado : it's lying on its side⟩ 8 **de un lado a otro** : to and fro, back and forth 9 **dejar a un lado** : to set aside 10 **hacerse a un lado** : to step aside 11 **lado a lado** : side by side 12 **por un lado . . ., por otro lado . . .** : on the one hand . . ., on the other hand . . .

ladrar *vi* : to bark

ladrido *nm* : bark (of a dog), barking

ladrillo *nm* 1 : brick 2 AZULEJO : tile

ladrón, -drona *n, mpl* **ladrones** : robber, thief, burglar

lagartija *nf* : small lizard

lagarto *nm* 1 : lizard 2 **lagarto de Indias** : alligator

lago *nm* : lake

lágrima *nf* : tear, teardrop

lagrimal *nm* : corner of the eye

lagrimear *vi* 1 : to water (of eyes) 2 : to weep easily

laguna *nf* 1 : lagoon 2 : gap

laicado *nm* : laity

laico¹, -ca *adj* : lay, secular

laico², -ca *n* : layman *m*, laywoman *f*

laja *nf* : slab

lama¹ *nf* : slime, ooze

lama² *nm* : lama

lamber *vt* : to lick

lamentable *adj* 1 : unfortunate, lamentable 2 : pitiful, sad

lamentablemente *adv* : unfortunately, regrettably

lamentación *nf, pl* **-ciones** : lamentation, groaning, moaning

lamentar *vt* 1 : to lament 2 : to regret ⟨lo lamento : I'm sorry⟩ — **lamentarse** *vr* : to grumble, to complain

lamento *nm* : lament, groan, cry

lamer *vt* 1 : to lick 2 : to lap against

lamida *nf* : lick

lámina *nf* 1 PLANCHA : sheet, plate 2 : plate, illustration

laminado¹, -da *adj* : laminated

laminado² *nm* : laminate

laminar *vt* : to laminate — **laminación** *nf*

lámpara *nf* : lamp

lampiño, -ña *adj* : hairless

lamprea *nf* : lamprey

lana *nf* 1 : wool ⟨lana de acero : steel wool⟩ 2 *Mex fam* : money, dough

lance¹, etc. → **lanzar**

lance² *nm* 1 INCIDENTE : event, incident 2 RIÑA : quarrel 3 : throw, cast (of a net, etc.) 4 : move, play (in a game), throw (of dice)

lancear *vt* : to spear

lancha *nf* 1 : small boat, launch 2 **lancha motora** : motorboat, speedboat

langosta *nf* 1 : lobster 2 : locust

langostino *nm* : prawn, crayfish

languidecer {53} *vi* : to languish

languidez *nf, pl* **-deces** : languor, listlessness

lánguido, -da *adj* : languid, listless — **languidamente** *adv*

lanolina *nf* : lanolin

lanudo, -da *adj* : woolly

lanza *nf* : spear, lance

lanzadera *nf* **1** : shuttle (for weaving) **2 lanzadera espacial** : space shuttle

lanzado, -da *adj* **1** : impulsive, brazen **2** : forward, determined ⟨ir lanzado : to hurtle along⟩

lanzador, -dora *n* : thrower, pitcher

lanzallamas *nms & pl* : flamethrower

lanzamiento *nm* **1** : throw **2** : pitch (in baseball) **3** : launching, launch

lanzar {21} *vt* **1** : to throw, to hurl **2** : to pitch **3** : to launch — **lanzarse** *vr* **1** : to throw oneself (at, into) **2** ~ **a** : to embark upon, to undertake

laosiano, -na *adj & n* : Laotian

lapa *nf* : limpet

lapicera *Arg, Uru nf* : pen

lapicero *nm* **1** : mechanical pencil **2** *CA, Peru* : ballpoint pen

lápida *nf* : marker, tombstone

lapidar *vt* APEDREAR : to stone

lápiz *nm, pl* **lápices 1** : pencil **2 lápiz labial** *or* **lápiz de labios** : lipstick

lapón, -pona *adj & n, mpl* **lapones** : Lapp

lapso *nm* : lapse, space (of time)

lapsus *nms & pl* : error, slip

laptop *nm pl* **laptops** : laptop

laquear *vt* : to lacquer, to varnish, to shellac

larga *nf* **1 a la larga** : in the long run **2 darle largas a** : to put off, to stall

largamente *adv* **1** : at length, extensively **2** : easily, comfortably **3** : generously

largar {52} *vt* **1** SOLTAR : to let loose, to release **2** AFLOJAR : to loosen, to slacken **3** *fam* : to give, to hand over **4** *fam* : to hurl, to let fly (insults, etc.) — **largarse** *vr fam* : to scram, to beat it

largo¹, -ga *adj* **1** : long **2 a lo largo** : lengthwise **3 a lo largo de** : along **4 a lo largo y ancho de** : the length and breadth of, all over

largo² *nm* : length ⟨tres metros de largo : three meters long⟩

largometraje *nm* : feature film

largue, etc. → **largar**

largueza *nf* : generosity, largesse

larguirucho, -cha *adj fam* : lanky

largura *nf* : length

laringe *nf* : larynx

laringitis *nfs & pl* : laryngitis

larva *nf* : larva — **larval** *adj*

las → **el²**, **los¹**

lasaña *nf* : lasagna

lasca *nf* : chip, chipping

lascivia *nf* : lasciviousness, lewdness

lascivo, -va *adj* : lascivious, lewd — **lascivamente** *adv*

láser *nm* : laser

lasitud *nf* : weariness

laso, -sa *adj* : languid, weary

lástima *nf* **1** : compassion, pity **2** PENA : shame, pity ⟨qué lástima! : what a shame!⟩ ⟨es una lástima que . . . : it's a shame that . . .⟩ ⟨tener/sentir lástima de : to feel sorry for⟩

lastimadura *nf* : injury, wound

lastimar *vt* **1** DAÑAR, HERIR : to hurt, to injure **2** AGRAVIAR : to offend — **lastimarse** *vr* : to hurt oneself

lastimero, -ra *adj* : pitiful, wretched

lastimoso, -sa *adj* **1** : shameful **2** : pitiful, terrible

lastrar *vt* **1** : to ballast **2** : to burden, to encumber

lastre *nm* **1** : burden **2** : ballast

lata *nf* **1** : tin **2** : tin can **3** *fam* : pest, bother, nuisance **4 dar lata** *fam* : to bother, to annoy

latente *adj* : latent

lateral¹ *adj* **1** : lateral, side **2** : indirect — **lateralmente** *adv*

lateral² *nm* : end piece, side

látex *nms & pl* : latex

latido *nm* : beat, throb ⟨latido del corazón : heartbeat⟩

latifundio *nm* : large estate

latigazo *nm* : lash (with a whip)

látigo *nm* AZOTE : whip

latín *nm* : Latin (language)

latino¹, -na *adj* **1** : Latin **2** *fam* : Latin-American

latino², -na *n fam* : Latin American

latinoamericano¹, -na *adj* HISPANOAMERICANO : Latin American

latinoamericano, -na *n* : Latin American

latir *vi* **1** : to beat, to throb **2 latirle a uno** *Mex fam* : to have a hunch ⟨me late que no va a venir : I have a feeling he's not going to come⟩

latitud *nf* **1** : latitude **2** : breadth

lato, -ta *adj* **1** : extended, lengthy **2** : broad (in meaning)

latón *nm, pl* **latones** : brass

latoso¹, -sa *adj fam* : annoying, bothersome

latoso², -sa *n fam* : pest, nuisance

latrocinio *nm* : larceny

laúd *nm* : lute

laudable *adj* : laudable, praiseworthy

laudo *nm* : findings, decision

laureado, -da *adj & n* : laureate

laurear *vt* : to award, to honor

laurel *nm* **1** : laurel, bay (in cooking) ⟨hoja de laurel : bay leaf⟩ **2 dormirse en sus laureles** : to rest on one's laurels

lava *nf* : lava

lavable *adj* : washable

lavabo *nm* **1** LAVAMANOS : sink, washbowl **2** : lavatory, toilet

lavadero *nm* : laundry room

lavado *nm* **1** : laundry, wash **2** : laundering ⟨lavado de dinero : money laundering⟩

lavadora *nf* : washing machine

lavamanos *nms & pl* LAVABO : sink, washbowl

lavanda *nf* ESPLIEGO : lavender

lavandería *nf* : laundry (service)

lavandero, -ra *n* : launderer, laundress *f*

lavaplatos *nms & pl* **1** : dishwasher **2** *Chile, Col, Mex* : kitchen sink

lavar *vt* **1** : to wash, to clean **2** : to launder (money) **3 lavar en seco** : to dry-clean — **lavarse** *vr* **1** : to wash oneself **2 lavarse las manos de** : to wash one's hands of

lavarropas *nms & pl Arg, Uru* : washing machine

lavativa *nf* : enema

lavatorio *nm* : lavatory, washroom

lavavajillas *nms & pl* : dishwasher

laxante *adj & nm* : laxative

laxitud *nf* : laxity, slackness

laxo, -xa *adj* : lax, slack

lazada *nf* : bow, loop

lazar {21} *vt* : to rope, to lasso

lazo *nm* **1** VÍNCULO : link, bond **2** : bow, ribbon **3** : lasso, lariat

LCD *nm* : LCD, liquid crystal display

le *pron* **1** : to her, to him, to it ⟨¿qué le dijiste? : what did you tell him?⟩ **2** : from her, from him, from it ⟨el ladrón le robó la cartera : the thief stole his wallet⟩ **3** : for her, for him, for it ⟨cómprale flores a tu mamá : buy your mom some flowers⟩ **4** (*formal*) : to you, for you ⟨le traje un regalo : I brought you a gift⟩

leal *adj* : loyal, faithful — **lealmente** *adv*

lealtad *nf* : loyalty, allegiance

lebrel *nm* : hound

lección *nf, pl* **lecciones** : lesson

lechada *nf* **1** : whitewash **2** : grout

lechal *adj* : suckling ⟨cordero lechal : suckling lamb⟩

leche *nf* **1** : milk ⟨leche en polvo : powdered milk⟩ **2** : milk (of a plant) **3 leche de magnesia** : milk of magnesia

lechera *nf* **1** : milk jug **2** : dairymaid *f*

lechería *nf* : dairy store

lechero¹, -ra *adj* : dairy

lechero², -ra *n* : milkman *m*, milk dealer

lecho *nm* **1** : bed ⟨un lecho de rosas : a bed of roses⟩ ⟨lecho de muerte : deathbed⟩ **2** : riverbed **3** : layer, stratum (in geology)

lechón, -chona *n, mpl* **lechones** : suckling pig

lechoso, -sa *adj* : milky

lechuga *nf* : lettuce

lechuza *nf* BÚHO : owl, barn owl

lectivo, -va *adj* : school ⟨año lectivo : school year⟩

lector¹, -tora *adj* : reading ⟨nivel lector : reading level⟩

lector², -tora *n* : reader

lector³ *nm* : scanner, reader ⟨lector óptico : optical scanner⟩

lectura *nf* **1** : reading **2** : reading matter

LED *or* **led** *nm* : LED

leer {20} *v* : to read ⟨leer los labios : to lip-read, to read lips⟩ ⟨leer entre las líneas : to read between the lines⟩

legación *nf, pl* **-ciones** : legation

legado *nm* **1** : legacy, bequest **2** : legate, emissary

legajo *nm* : dossier, file

legal *adj* : legal, lawful — **legalmente** *adv*

legalidad *nf* : legality

legalista *adj* : legalistic

legalizar {21} *vt* : to legalize — **legalización** *nf*

legañas *nfpl* : sleep (in the eyes)

legar {52} *vt* **1** : to bequeath, to hand down **2** DELEGAR : to delegate

legendario, -ria *adj* : legendary

legible *adj* : legible — **legibilidad** *nf*

legión *nf, pl* **legiones** : legion

legionario, -ria *n* : legionnaire

legislación *nf, pl* **-ciones** **1** : legislation (act) **2** : laws *pl*, legislation

legislador¹, -dora *adj* : legislative

legislador², -dora *n* : legislator

legislar *vi* : to legislate

legislativo, -va *adj* : legislative

legislatura *nf* **1** : legislature **2** : term of office

legitimar *vt* **1** : to legitimize **2** : to authenticate — **legitimación** *nf*

legitimidad *nf* : legitimacy

legítimo, -ma *adj* **1** : legitimate **2** : genuine, authentic — **legítimamente** *adv*

lego¹, -ga *adj* **1** : secular, lay **2** : uninformed, ignorant

lego², -ga *n* : layperson, layman *m*, laywoman *f*

legua *nf* **1** : league **2 notarse a leguas** : to be very obvious ⟨se notaba a leguas : you could tell from a mile away⟩

legue, etc. → **legar**

legumbre *nf* **1** HORTALIZA : vegetable **2** : legume

leíble *adj* : readable

leída *nf* : reading, read ⟨de una leída : in one reading, at one go⟩

leído¹ *pp* → **leer**

leído², -da *adj* : well-read

lejanía *nf* : remoteness, distance

lejano, -na *adj* : remote, distant, far away

lejía *nf* **1** : lye **2** : bleach

lejos *adv* **1** : far away, distant ⟨a lo lejos : in the distance, far off⟩ ⟨desde lejos : from a distance⟩ **2** : long ago, a long way off ⟨está lejos de los 50 años : he's a long way from 50 years old⟩ **3 de ~** : by far ⟨esta decisión fue de lejos la más fácil : this decision was by far the easiest⟩ **4 ~ de** : far from ⟨lejos de ser reprobado, recibió una nota de B : far from failing, he got a B⟩ **5 ir demasiado lejos** : to go too far

lelo, -la *adj* : silly, stupid

lema *nm* : motto, slogan

lemming *nm* : lemming

lencería *nf* : lingerie

lengua *nf* **1** : tongue ⟨se me traba la lengua : I have trouble speaking, I get tongue-tied⟩ **2** IDIOMA : language ⟨lengua materna : mother tongue⟩ ⟨lengua nativa : native language⟩ ⟨lengua muerta : dead language⟩ **3** : tongue (of flame) **4** : spit (of land) **5 irse de la lengua** : to let something slip, to blab **6 morderse la lengua** : to bite one's tongue **7 sacarle la lengua a alguien** : to stick one's tongue out at someone

lenguado *nm* : sole, flounder

lenguaje *nm* **1** : language, speech **2 lenguaje gestual** *or* **lenguaje de gestos** : sign language **3 lenguaje de programación** : programming language

lengüeta *nf* **1** : tongue (of a shoe), tab, flap **2** : reed (of a musical instrument) **3** : barb, point

lengüetada *nf* **beber a lengüetadas** : to lap (up)

lenidad *nf* : leniency

lenitivo, -va *adj* : soothing

lente *nmf* **1** : lens ⟨lentes de contacto : contact lenses⟩ **2 lentes** *nmpl* ANTEOJOS ; eyeglasses ⟨lentes de sol : sunglasses⟩

lenteja *nf* : lentil

lentejuela *nf* : sequin, spangle

lentilla *nf Spain* : contact lens

lentitud *nf* : slowness

lento¹ *adv* DESPACIO : slowly

lento², -ta *adj* **1** : slow **2** : slow-witted, dull — **lentamente** *adv*

leña *nf* : wood, firewood

leñador, -dora *n* : lumberjack, woodcutter

leñera *nf* : woodshed

leño *nm* : log

leñoso, -sa *adj* : woody

Leo¹ *nm* : Leo (sign or constellation)

Leo² *nmf* : Leo (person)

león, -ona *n, mpl* **leones 1** : lion, lioness *f* **2** (*in various countries*) : puma, cougar

leonado, -da *adj* : tawny

leonino, -na *adj* **1** : lion-like **2** : one-sided, unfair

leopardo *nm* : leopard

leotardo *nm* MALLA : leotard, tights *pl*

leperada *nf Mex* : obscenity

lépero, -ra *adj Mex* : vulgar, coarse

lepra *nf* : leprosy

leproso¹, -sa *adj* : leprous

leproso², -sa *n* : leper

lerdo, -da *adj* **1** : clumsy **2** : dull, oafish, slow-witted

les *pron* **1** : to them ⟨dales una propina : give them a tip⟩ **2** : from them ⟨se les privó de su herencia : they were deprived of their inheritance⟩ **3** : for them ⟨les hice sus tareas : I did their homework for them⟩ **4** : to you *pl*, for you *pl* ⟨les compré un regalo : I bought you all a present⟩

lesbiana *nf* : lesbian — **lesbiano, -na** *adj*

lesbianismo *nm* : lesbianism

lesera *nf Chile fam* : stupid thing

lesión *nf, pl* **lesiones** HERIDA : lesion, wound, injury ⟨una lesión grave : a serious injury⟩

lesionado, -da *adj* HERIDO : injured, wounded

lesionar *vt* : to injure, to wound — **lesionarse** *vr* : to hurt oneself

lesivo, -va *adj* : harmful, damaging

letal *adj* MORTÍFERO : deadly, lethal — **letalmente** *adv*

letanía *nf* **1** : litany **2** *fam* : spiel, song and dance

letárgico, -ca *adj* : lethargic

letargo *nm* : lethargy, torpor

letón¹, -tona *adj & n, mpl* **letones** : Latvian

letón² *nm* : Latvian (language)

letra *nf* **1** : letter ⟨letra mayúscula/minúscula : capital/lowercase letter⟩ ⟨letra en negrilla/negrita : boldface, bold type⟩ ⟨letra cursiva : italics, italic type⟩ ⟨leer la letra pequeña/chica : to read the small print⟩ ⟨aprender las primeras letras : to learn how to read and write⟩ **2** CALIGRAFÍA : handwriting, lettering **3** : lyrics *pl* **4 al pie de la letra** : word for word, by the book **5 letra(s) de molde** *or* **letra(s) de imprenta** : print ⟨escribió su nombre en/con letra(s) de molde/imprenta : she printed her name⟩ **6 letras** *nfpl* : arts (in education)

letrado¹, -da *adj* ERUDITO : learned, erudite

letrado², -da *n* : attorney, lawyer

letrero *nm* RÓTULO : sign, notice

letrina *nf* : latrine

letrista *nmf* : lyricist, songwriter

leucemia *nf* : leukemia

leva *nf* : cam

levadura *nf* **1** : yeast, leavening **2 levadura en polvo** : baking powder

levantado, -da *adj* : awake, up

levantamiento *nm* **1** ALZAMIENTO : uprising **2** : raising, lifting ⟨levantamiento de pesas : weight lifting⟩

levantar *vt* ALZAR : to lift, to raise ⟨levanté la tapa : I lifted the lid⟩ ⟨levantar pesas : to lift weights⟩ ⟨levantar la mano : to raise one's hand⟩ ⟨levantar la mirada/vista : to look up⟩ ⟨levantar la voz : to raise one's voice⟩ **2** : to put up, to erect (a building, etc.) **3** : to give a boost to ⟨me levantó el ánimo : it lifted my spirits⟩ ⟨un plan para levantar al país : a plan to get the country back on its feet⟩ **4** : to lift (an embargo, etc.), to call off (a strike, etc.), to adjourn (a meeting, etc.) **5** : to give rise to, to arouse ⟨levantar sospechas : to arouse suspicion⟩ ⟨levantar una polémica : to spark controversy⟩ **6 levantar cabeza** : to get back on one's feet, to recover — **levantarse** *vr* **1** : to rise, to stand up **2** : to get out of bed, to get up ⟨se levanta a las seis : he gets up at six⟩

levante *nm* **1** : east (direction) **2** : east wind

levar *vt* **levar anclas** : to weigh anchor

leve *adj* **1** : light, slight **2** : trivial, unimportant — **levemente** *adv*

levedad *nf* : lightness

levemente *adv* LIGERAMENTE : lightly, softly

leviatán *nm, pl* **-tanes** : leviathan

levitar *vi* : to levitate

léxico¹, -ca *adj* : lexical

léxico² *nm* : lexicon, glossary

lexicografía *nf* : lexicography

lexicográfico, -ca *adj* : lexicographical, lexicographic

lexicógrafo, -fa *n* : lexicographer

ley *nf* **1** : law ⟨aprobar/derogar una ley : to pass/repeal a law⟩ ⟨violar la ley : to break the law⟩ ⟨fuera de la ley : outside the law⟩ ⟨proyecto de ley : bill (of law)⟩ ⟨la ley de gravedad : the law of gravity⟩ ⟨es ley de vida : it's a fact of life⟩ ⟨con todas las de la ley : proper, properly⟩ **2**

: purity (of metals) ⟨oro de ley : pure gold⟩

leyenda *nf* **1** : legend **2** : caption, inscription

leyó, etc. → **leer**

liar {85} *vt* **1** ATAR : to bind, to tie (up) **2** : to roll (a cigarette) **3** : to confuse — **liarse** *vr* : to get mixed up

libanés, -nesa *adj & n, mpl* **-neses** : Lebanese

libar *vt* **1** : to suck (nectar) **2** : to sip, to swig (liquor, etc.)

libelo *nm* **1** : libel, lampoon **2** : petition (in court)

libélula *nf* : dragonfly

liberación *nf, pl* **-ciones** : liberation, deliverance ⟨liberación de la mujer : women's liberation⟩

liberado, -da *adj* **1** : liberated ⟨una mujer liberada : a liberated woman⟩ **2** : freed, delivered

liberal *adj & nmf* : liberal

liberalidad *nf* : generosity, liberality

liberalismo *nm* : liberalism

liberalizar {21} *vt* : to liberalize — **liberalización** *nf*

liberar *vt* : to liberate, to free — **liberarse** *vr* : to get free of

liberiano, -na *adj & n* : Liberian

libertad *nf* **1** : freedom, liberty ⟨tomarse la libertad de : to take the liberty of⟩ ⟨poner a alguien en libertad : to set someone free⟩ ⟨libertad de expresión : freedom of speech⟩ **2 libertad bajo fianza** : bail **3 libertad condicional** : parole, probation

libertador¹, -dora *adj* : liberating

libertador², -dora *n* : liberator

libertar *vt* LIBRAR : to set free

libertario, -ria *adj & n* : libertarian

libertinaje *nm* : licentiousness, dissipation

libertino¹, -na *adj* : licentious, dissolute

libertino², -na *n* : libertine

libidinoso, -sa *adj* : lustful, lewd

libido *nm* : libido

libio, -bia *adj & n* : Libyan

libra *nf* **1** : pound **2 libra esterlina** : pound sterling

Libra¹ *nm* : Libra (sign or constellation)

Libra² *nmf* : Libra (person)

libramiento *nm* **1** : liberating, freeing **2** LIBRANZA : order of payment **3** *Mex* : beltway

libranza *nf* : order of payment

librar *vt* **1** LIBERTAR : to free (from punishment, etc.), to save (from death, etc.) ⟨líbranos del mal : deliver us from evil⟩ ⟨librar de culpas : to absolve of guilt⟩ **2** : to wage ⟨librar batalla : to do battle⟩ **3** : to issue ⟨librar una orden : to issue an order⟩ — **librarse** *vr* ~ **de** : to free oneself from, to get out of ⟨se libró de pagar una multa : he got out of paying a fine⟩ ⟨librarse de morir : to escape death⟩

libre¹ *adj* **1** : free ⟨un país libre : a free country⟩ ⟨libre de : free from, exempt from⟩ ⟨libre albedrío : free will⟩ ⟨ratos libres : free/spare time⟩ **2** DESOCUPADO : vacant **3 día libre** : day off

libre² *nm Mex* : taxi

librea *nf* : livery

librecambio *nm* : free trade

libremente *adv* : freely

librería *nf* : bookstore

librero¹, -ra *n* : bookseller

librero² *nm Mex* : bookcase

libresco, -ca *adj* : bookish

libreta *nf* CUADERNO : notebook

libretista *nmf* **1** : librettist **2** : scriptwriter

libreto *nm* : libretto, script

libro *nm* **1** : book ⟨libro de texto/cocina : textbook/cookbook⟩ ⟨libro de consulta : reference book⟩ ⟨libro en rústica, libro de tapa/pasta blanda : paperback⟩ ⟨libro de tapa/pasta dura : hardcover⟩ ⟨libro de instrucciones : instruction manual⟩ **2 libros** *nmpl* : books (in bookkeeping), accounts ⟨llevar los libros : to keep the books⟩

liceal *nmf Uru* : high school student

liceano, -na *n Chile* → **liceal**

liceísta *nmf CoRi, Ven* → **liceal**

licencia *nf* **1** : permission **2** : leave, leave of absence **3** : permit, license ⟨licencia de conducir : driver's license⟩

licenciado, -da *n* **1** : university graduate **2** ABOGADO : lawyer

licenciar *vt* **1** : to license, to permit, to allow **2** : to discharge **3** : to grant a university degree to — **licenciarse** *vr* : to graduate

licenciatura *nf* **1** : college degree **2** : course of study (at a college or university)

licencioso, -sa *adj* : licentious, lewd

liceo *nm* (*in various countries*) : secondary school, high school

licitación *nf, pl* **-ciones** : bid, bidding

licitar *vt* : to bid on

lícito, -ta *adj* **1** : lawful, licit **2** JUSTO : just, fair

licor *nm* **1** : liquor **2** : liqueur

licorera *nf* : decanter

licuado *nm* BATIDO : milk shake

licuadora *nf* : blender

licuar {3} *vt* : to liquefy — **licuarse** *vr*

lid *nf* **1** : fight, combat **2** : argument, dispute **3 lides** *nfpl* : matters, affairs **4 en buena lid** : fair and square

líder¹ *adj* : leading, foremost

líder² *nmf* : leader

liderar *vt* DIRIGIR : to lead, to head

liderato *nm* : leadership, leading

liderazgo → **liderato**

lidia *nf* **1** : bullfighting **2** : bullfight

lidiar *vt* : to fight — *vi* BATALLAR, LUCHAR : to struggle, to battle, to wrestle

liebre *nf* : hare

liendre *nf* : nit

lienzo *nm* **1** : linen **2** : canvas, painting **3** : stretch of wall or fencing

liga *nf* **1** ASOCIACIÓN : league **2** GOMITA : rubber band **3** : garter

ligado, -da *adj* : linked, connected

ligadura *nf* **1** ATADURA : tie, bond **2** : ligature

ligamento *nm* : ligament

ligar {52} *vt* : to bind, to tie (up)

ligeramente *adv* **1** : slightly **2** LEVEMENTE : lightly, gently **3** : casually, lightly

ligereza *nf* **1** : lightness **2** : flippancy **3** : agility

ligero, -ra *adj* **1** : light, lightweight **2** : slight, minor **3** : agile, quick **4** : light-hearted, superficial

light ['lait] *adj* : light, low-calorie

ligue, etc. → **ligar**

liguero, -ra *adj* : league

lija *nf or* **papel de lija** : sandpaper

lijar *vt* : to sand

lila[1] *adj* : lilac, light purple

lila[2] *nf* : lilac

lima *nf* **1** : lime (fruit) **2** : file ⟨lima de uñas : nail file⟩

limar *vt* **1** : to file **2** : to polish, to put the final touch on **3** : to smooth over ⟨limar asperezas : to iron out differences⟩

limbo *nm* **1** : limbo **2** : limb (in botany and astronomy)

limeño, -ña *adj* : of or from Lima, Peru

limeño[2], **-ña** *n* : person from Lima, Peru

limero *nm* : lime tree

limitación *nf, pl* **-ciones** **1** : limitation **2** : limit, restriction ⟨sin limitación : unlimited⟩

limitado, -da *adj* **1** RESTRINGIDO : limited **2** : dull, slow-witted

limitar *vt* RESTRINGIR : to limit, to restrict — *vi* ~ **con** : to border on — **limitarse** *vr* ~ **a** : to limit oneself to

límite *nm* **1** : boundary, border **2** : limit ⟨el límite de mi paciencia : the limit of my patience⟩ ⟨límite de velocidad : speed limit⟩ **3 fecha límite** : deadline

limítrofe *adj* LINDANTE, LINDERO : bordering, adjoining

limo *nm* : slime, mud

limón *nm, pl* **limones** **1** : lemon **2** : lemon tree ⟨limón verde *Mex* : lime⟩

limonada *nf* : lemonade

limonero *nm* : lemon tree

limosna *nf* : alms, charity

limosnear *vi* : to beg (for alms)

limosnero, -ra *n* MENDIGO : beggar

limoso, -sa *adj* : slimy

limpiabotas *nmfs & pl* : shoeshine boy/man *m*, shoeshine girl/woman *f*

limpiacristales *nms & pl Spain* **1** : glass cleaner (fluid) **2** : window washer (person)

limpiador[1], **-dora** *adj* : cleaning

limpiador[2], **-dora** *n* : cleaning person, cleaner

limpiamente *adv* : cleanly, honestly, fairly

limpiaparabrisas *nms & pl* : windshield wiper

limpiar *vt* **1** : to clean, to cleanse **2** : to clean up, to remove defects **3** *fam* : to clean out (in a game) **4** *fam* : to swipe, to pinch — *vi* ~ : to clean — **limpiarse** *vr*

limpiavidrios *nmfs & pl* **1** *Mex* : windshield wiper **2** : glass cleaner (fluid) **3** : window washer (person)

límpido, -da *adj* : limpid

limpieza *nf* **1** : cleanliness, tidiness **2** : cleaning **3** HONRADEZ : integrity, honesty **4** DESTREZA : skill, dexterity

limpio[1] *adv* : fairly

limpio[2], **-pia** *adj* **1** : clean, neat **2** : honest ⟨un juego limpio : a fair game⟩ **3** : free

⟨limpio de impurezas : pure, free from impurities⟩ **4** : clear, net ⟨ganancia limpia : clear profit⟩

limusina *nf* : limousine

linaje *nm* ABOLENGO : lineage, ancestry

lince *nm* : lynx

linchamiento *nm* : lynching

linchar *vt* : to lynch

lindante *adj* LIMÍTROFE, LINDERO : bordering, adjoining

lindar *vi* **1** ~ **con** : to border, to skirt **2** ~ **con** BORDEAR : to border on, to verge on

linde *nmf* : boundary, limit

lindero[1], **-ra** *adj* LIMÍTROFE, LINDANTE : bordering, adjoining

lindero[2] *nm* : boundary, limit

lindeza *nf* **1** : prettiness **2** : clever remark **3 lindezas** *nfpl (used ironically)* : insults

lindo[1] *adv* **1** : beautifully, wonderfully ⟨canta lindo tu mujer : your wife sings beautifully⟩ **2 de lo lindo** : a lot, a great deal ⟨los zancudos nos picaban de lo lindo : the mosquitoes were biting away at us⟩

lindo[2], **-da** *adj* **1** BONITO : pretty, lovely **2** MONO : cute

línea *nf* **1** : line ⟨línea divisoria : dividing line⟩ ⟨línea de banda : sideline⟩ ⟨línea de meta : finish line⟩ ⟨línea de puntos : dotted line⟩ ⟨líneas enemigas : enemy lines⟩ ⟨línea de producción : production line⟩ ⟨leer entre líneas : to read between the lines⟩ **2** : line, course, position ⟨en líneas generales : in general terms, along general lines⟩ ⟨línea de conducta : course of action⟩ ⟨línea de investigación : line of inquiry⟩ ⟨la línea del partido : the party line⟩ **3** : line, range ⟨línea de productos : product line⟩ **4** : line, side ⟨línea de sucesión : line of succession⟩ ⟨un primo suyo por línea materna : a cousin on his mother's side⟩ **5** : line, service ⟨línea aérea : airline⟩ ⟨línea telefónica : telephone line⟩ ⟨en línea : on-line⟩ ⟨fuera de línea : off-line⟩ **6** : figure ⟨guardar la línea : to watch one's figure⟩

línea de crédito *nf* : line of credit

lineal *adj* : linear

lineamientos *nmpl* : guidelines

linfa *nf* : lymph

linfático, -ca *adj* : lymphatic

lingote *nm* : ingot

lingüista *nmf* : linguist

lingüística *nf* : linguistics

lingüístico, -ca *adj* : linguistic

linimento *nm* : liniment

lino *nm* **1** : linen **2** : flax

linóleo *nm* : linoleum

linterna *nf* **1** : lantern **2** : flashlight

lío *nm fam* **1** : confusion, mess **2** : hassle, trouble, jam ⟨meterse en un lío : to get into a jam⟩ **3** : affair, liaison

liofilizar {21} *vt* : to freeze-dry

lioso, -sa *adj fam* : confusing, muddled

liquen *nm* : lichen

liquidación *nf, pl* **-ciones** **1** : liquidation **2** : clearance sale **3** : settlement, payment

liquidar *vt* **1** : to liquefy **2** : to liquidate **3** : to settle, to pay off **4** *fam* : to rub out, to kill

liquidez *nf, pl* **-deces** : liquidity

líquido¹, -da *adj* **1** : liquid, fluid **2** : net ⟨ingresos líquidos : net income⟩

líquido² *nm* **1** : liquid, fluid ⟨líquido de frenos : brake fluid⟩ **2** : ready cash, liquid assets

lira *nf* : lyre

lírica *nf* : lyric poetry

lírico, -ca *adj* : lyric, lyrical

lirio *nm* **1** : iris **2 lirio de los valles** MUGUETE : lily of the valley

lirón *nm, pl* **lirones** : dormouse

lisiado¹, -da *adj* : disabled, crippled

lisiado², -da *n* : disabled person, cripple *offensive*

lisiar *vt* : to cripple, to disable — **lisiarse** *vr*

liso, -sa *adj* **1** : smooth **2** : flat **3** : straight ⟨pelo liso : straight hair⟩ **4** : plain, unadorned ⟨liso y llano : plain and simple⟩

lisonja *nf* : flattery

lisonjear *vt* ADULAR : to flatter

lista *nf* **1** : list ⟨es la primera/última de la lista : she's first/last on the list⟩ **2** : roster, roll ⟨pasar lista : to take attendance⟩ **3** : stripe, strip **4** : menu

listado¹, -da *adj* : striped

listado² *nm* : listing

listar *vt* : to list

listeza *nf* : smartness, alertness

listo, -ta *adj* **1** DISPUESTO, PREPARADO : ready ⟨¿estás listo? : are you ready?⟩ **2** : clever, smart ⟨pasarse de listo : to be too clever⟩

listón *nm, pl* **listones** **1** : ribbon **2** : strip (of wood), lath **3** : high bar (in sports)

lisura *nf* : smoothness

litera *nf* : bunk bed, berth

literal *adj* : literal — **literalmente** *adv*

literario, -ria *adj* : literary

literato, -ta *n* : writer, author

literatura *nf* : literature

litigante *adj & nmf* : litigant

litigar {52} *vi* : to litigate, to be in litigation

litigio *nm* **1** : litigation, lawsuit **2 en ~** : in dispute

litio *nm* : lithium

litografía *nf* **1** : lithography **2** : lithograph

litógrafo, -fa *n* : lithographer

litoral¹ *adj* : coastal

litoral² *nm* : shore, seaboard

litosfera *nf* : lithosphere

litro *nm* : liter

lituano¹, -na *adj & n* : Lithuanian

lituano² *nm* : Lithuanian (language)

liturgia *nf* : liturgy

litúrgico, -ca *adj* : liturgical — **litúrgicamente** *adv*

liviandad *nf* LIGEREZA : lightness

liviano, -na *adj* **1** : light, slight **2** INCONSTANTE : fickle

lividez *nf* PALIDEZ : pallor

lívido, -da *adj* **1** AMORATADO : livid **2** PÁLIDO : pallid, extremely pale

living *nm* : living room

ll *nf* : fourteenth letter of the Spanish alphabet (not usually considered a separate letter in alphabetization)

llaga *nf* : sore, wound

llama *nf* **1** : flame **2** : llama

llamada *nf* : call ⟨llamada a larga distancia : long-distance call⟩ ⟨llamada al orden : call to order⟩

llamado¹, -da *adj* : named, called ⟨una mujer llamada Rosa : a woman called Rosa⟩

llamado² → **llamamiento**

llamador *nm* : door knocker

llamamiento *nm* : call, appeal

llamar *vt* **1** : to call, to name ⟨la llamamos Paulita : we call her Paulita⟩ ⟨lo llamaban loco : they called him crazy⟩ ⟨así lo llamamos en Cuba : that's what we call it in Cuba⟩ **2** : to call, to summon ⟨llamar un taxi : to call a taxi⟩ ⟨me llamó desde abajo : she called up to me (from downstairs)⟩ ⟨fue llamado a declarar : she was called to testify⟩ **3** : to call (up), to phone ⟨me llama todos los días : she calls me every day⟩ — *vi* : to knock (on a door), to ring a doorbell ⟨llaman a la puerta : there's someone at the door⟩ — **llamarse** *vr* : to be called, to be named ⟨¿cómo te llamas? : what's your name?⟩ ⟨me llamo Ana : my name is Ana⟩

llamarada *nf* **1** : flare-up, sudden blaze **2** : flushing (of the face)

llamativo, -va *adj* : flashy, showy, striking

llameante *adj* : flaming, blazing

llamear *vi* : to flame, to blaze

llana *nf* **1** : trowel **2 → llano²**

llanamente *adv* : simply, plainly ⟨es, simple y llanamente, un desastre : it's a disaster, plain and simple⟩

llaneza *nf* : simplicity, naturalness

llano¹, -na *adj* **1** : even, flat **2** : frank, open **3** LISO : plain, simple

llano² *nm* : plain

llanta *nf* **1** NEUMÁTICO : tire **2** : rim

llantén *nm, pl* **llantenes** : plantain (weed)

llanto *nm* : crying, weeping

llanura *nf* : plain, prairie

llave *nf* **1** : key ⟨bajo llave : under lock and key⟩ ⟨llave maestra : master key⟩ ⟨cerrar (algo) con llave : to lock (something)⟩ **2** : faucet **3** : valve (in plumbing) **4** INTERRUPTOR : switch **5** : (curly) brace, curly bracket (punctuation mark) **6** : wrench ⟨llave inglesa : monkey wrench⟩

llavero *nm* : key chain, key ring

llegada *nf* : arrival

llegar {52} *vi* **1** : to arrive ⟨llegar temprano/tarde : to arrive early/late⟩ ⟨llegué a Lisboa : I arrived in Lisbon⟩ ⟨llegué al hotel : I arrived at the hotel⟩ ⟨llegó hasta la frontera : he got as far as the border⟩ ⟨cuando llegue el momento : when the time comes⟩ ⟨va a llegar lejos : she's going to go far⟩ **2** : to be enough ⟨no nos llega el sueldo para todo : we can't afford it all on our salary⟩ **3 ~ hasta** : to reach ⟨llega hasta el techo : it goes (all the way) up to the ceiling⟩ ⟨llegué hasta la página 85 : I got up to page

85, I got as far as page 85⟩ ⟨podría llegar a los 35 grados : it could get up to 35 degrees⟩ **4 ~ a** : to reach (an agreement, etc.) **5 ~ a** : to manage to ⟨llegó a terminar la novela : he managed to finish the novel⟩ **6 llegar a ser** : to become ⟨llegó a ser presidente : he became President⟩

llegue, etc. → llegar

llenar vt **1** : to fill, to fill up, to fill in **2** : to meet, to fulfill ⟨los regalos no llenaron sus expectativas : the gifts did not meet her expectations⟩ — **llenarse** vr : to fill up, to become full

llenito, -ta adj fam REGORDETE : chubby, plump

lleno¹, -na adj **1** : full, filled **2 de ~** : completely, fully **3 estar lleno de sí mismo** : to be full of oneself

lleno² nm **1** fam : plenty, abundance **2** : full house

llevadero, -ra adj : bearable

llevar vt **1** : to carry, to take (away) ⟨le llevé las maletas : I carried her bags⟩ ⟨siempre lo lleva consigo : he always has it with him⟩ ⟨me gusta, me lo llevo : I like it—I'll take it⟩ **2** : to wear ⟨llevaba un vestido azul : she wore a blue dress⟩ ⟨llevar el pelo corto/largo : to wear one's hair short/long⟩ **3** : to take ⟨llevamos a Pedro al cine : we took Pedro to the movies⟩ ⟨la llevaron al hospital : they took her to the hospital⟩ **4** : to lead ⟨nos llevó por un pasillo : he led us down a hallway⟩ ⟨me lleva a pensar que . . . : it leads me to believe that . . .⟩ **5** : to lead ⟨llevar una vida sana : to lead a healthy life⟩ **6** : to run, to be in charge of ⟨lleva la biblioteca : she runs the library⟩ **7** : to keep ⟨llevar el ritmo : to keep time⟩ ⟨llevar un diario : to keep a diary⟩ **8** : to take, to require ⟨le llevó horas hacerlo : it took him hours to do it⟩ **9** : to have . . . more than ⟨nos llevan cinco puntos : they're five points ahead of us⟩ ⟨te llevo tres años : I'm three years older than you⟩ **10 llevar a cabo** : to carry out **11 llevar adelante** : to carry on with, to keep going with — vi : to lead ⟨un problema lleva al otro : one problem leads to another⟩ — v aux : to have ⟨llevo mucho tiempo buscándolo : I've been looking for it for a long time⟩ ⟨lleva leído medio libro : he's halfway through the book⟩ — **llevarse** vr **1** : to take away, to carry off/away ⟨una ola se lo llevó : a wave carried him away⟩ ⟨se llevó el primer premio : she took/won first prize⟩ **2** : to get along ⟨siempre nos llevábamos bien : we always got along well⟩

llorar vi : to cry, to weep — vt : to mourn, to bewail

lloriquear vi : to whimper, to whine

lloriqueo nm : whimpering, whining

lloro nm : crying

llorón, -rona n, mpl **llorones** : crybaby, whiner

lloroso, -sa adj : tearful, sad

llovedizo, -za adj : rain ⟨agua llovediza : rainwater⟩

llover {47} v impers : to rain ⟨está lloviendo : it's raining⟩ ⟨llover a cántaros : to rain cats and dogs⟩ — vi : to rain down, to shower ⟨le llovieron regalos : he was showered with gifts⟩

llovizna nf : drizzle, sprinkle

lloviznar v impers : to drizzle, to sprinkle

llueve, etc. → llover

lluvia nf **1** : rain, rainfall **2** : barrage, shower **3 lluvia ácida** : acid rain

lluvioso, -sa adj : rainy

lo¹ pron (referring to masculine nouns) **1** : him, it ⟨lo vi ayer : I saw him yesterday⟩ ⟨lo entiendo : I understand it⟩ ⟨no lo creo : I don't believe so⟩ **2** (formal) : you ⟨disculpe, señor, no lo oí : excuse me, sir, I didn't hear you⟩ **3 lo que** : what, that which ⟨eso es lo que más le gusta : that's what he likes the most⟩

lo² art **1** : the ⟨lo mejor : the best, the best thing⟩ **2** : how ⟨sé lo bueno que eres : I know how good you are⟩ ⟨lo más rápido posible : as quickly as possible⟩

loa nf : praise

loable adj : laudable, praiseworthy — **loablemente** adv

loar vt : to praise, to laud

lobato, -ta n : wolf cub

lobby nm : lobby, pressure group

lobo, -ba n : wolf

lobotomía nf : lobotomy

lóbrego, -ga adj SOMBRÍO : gloomy, dark

lobulado, -da adj : lobed

lóbulo nm : lobe ⟨lóbulo de la oreja : earlobe⟩

locación nf, pl **-ciones** **1** : location (for filming) **2** Mex : place

local¹ adj : local — **localmente** adv

local² nm : premises pl

localidad nf : town, locality

localización nf, pl **-ciones** **1** : locating, localization **2** : location

localizar {21} vt **1** UBICAR : to locate, to find **2** : to localize — **localizarse** vr UBICARSE : to be located ⟨se localiza en el séptimo piso : it is located on the seventh floor⟩

locamente adv **1** : madly **2** : wildly, recklessly

locatario, -ria n : tenant

loción nf, pl **lociones** : lotion

lócker nm, pl **lóckers** : locker

loco¹, -ca adj **1** DEMENTE : crazy, insane, mad **2 a lo loco** : wildly, recklessly **3 volverse loco** : to go mad

loco², -ca n **1** : crazy person, lunatic **2 hacerse el loco** : to act the fool

locomoción nf, pl **-ciones** : locomotion

locomotor, -tora adj : locomotive

locomotora nf **1** : locomotive **2** : driving force

locuaz adj, pl **locuaces** : loquacious, talkative

locución nf, pl **-ciones** : locution, phrase ⟨locución adverbial : adverbial phrase⟩

locura nf **1** : insanity, madness **2** : crazy thing, folly

locutor, -tora n : announcer

lodazal nm : bog, quagmire

lodo nm BARRO : mud, mire

Iodoso, -sa *adj* : muddy

logaritmo *nm* : logarithm

logia *nf* 1 : lodge ⟨logia masónica : Masonic lodge⟩

lógica *nf* : logic

lógico, -ca *adj* : logical — **lógicamente** *adv*

logística *nf* : logistics *pl*

logístico, -ca *adj* : logistic

logo → logotipo

logotipo *nm* : logo

logrado, -da *adj* : successful, skillfully done ⟨un efecto muy logrado : a very convincing effect⟩

lograr *vt* 1 : to get, to obtain 2 : to achieve, to attain — **lograrse** *vr* : to be successful

logro *nm* : achievement, attainment

loma *nf* : hill, hillock

lombriz *nf, pl* **lombrices** : worm ⟨lombriz de tierra : earthworm, night crawler⟩ ⟨lombriz solitaria : tapeworm⟩ ⟨tener lombrices : to have worms⟩

lomo *nm* 1 : back (of an animal) 2 : loin ⟨lomo de cerdo : pork loin⟩ 3 : spine (of a book) 4 : blunt edge (of a knife)

lona *nf* : canvas

loncha *nf* LONJA, REBANADA : slice

lonche *nm* 1 *Mex* ALMUERZO : lunch 2 *Mex* : submarine sandwich 3 *Peru* MERIENDA : afternoon snack, tea

lonchería *nf Mex* : snack bar

londinense[1] *adj* : of or from London

londinense[2] *nmf* : Londoner

longaniza *nf* : spicy pork sausage

longevidad *nf* : longevity

longevo, -va *adj* : long-lived

longitud *nf* 1 LARGO : length ⟨longitud de onda : wavelength⟩ 2 : longitude

longitudinal *adj* : longitudinal — **longitudinalmente** *adv*

lonja *nf* LONCHA, REBANADA : slice

lontananza *nf* : background ⟨en lontananza : in the distance, far away⟩

lord *nm, pl* **lores** (title in England) : lord

loro *nm* : parrot

los[1], **las** *pron* 1 : them ⟨no los conozco muy bien : I don't know them very well⟩ ⟨hice galletas y se las di a los nuevos vecinos : I made cookies and gave them to the new neighbors⟩ 2 : you ⟨voy a llevarlos a los dos : I am going to take both of you⟩ 3 : the ones ⟨me gustan las rojas : I like the red ones⟩ ⟨los de las camisas azules : the ones in the blue shirts⟩ ⟨mis padres y los tuyos : my parents and yours⟩ ⟨las reuniones de ayer y las de hoy : yesterday's meetings and today's⟩ 4 **los que, las que** : those, who, the ones ⟨los que van a cantar deben venir temprano : those who are singing must come early⟩ 5 (used with **haber**) ⟨los hay en varios colores : they come in various colors⟩

los[2] *art* → **el**[2]

losa *nf* : flagstone, paving stone

loseta *nf* BALDOSA : floor tile

lote *nm* 1 : part, share 2 : batch, lot 3 : plot of land, lot

lotería *nf* : lottery

loto *nm* : lotus

loza *nf* 1 : crockery, earthenware 2 : china

lozanía *nf* 1 : healthiness, robustness 2 : luxuriance, lushness

lozano, -na *adj* 1 : robust, healthy-looking ⟨un rostro lozano : a smooth, fresh face⟩ 2 : lush, luxuriant

LSD *nm* : LSD

lubina *nf* : sea bass

lubricante[1] *adj* : lubricating

lubricante[2] *nm* : lubricant

lubricar {72} *vt* : to lubricate, to oil — **lubricación** *nf*

lucero *nm* : bright star ⟨lucero del alba : morning star⟩

lucha *nf* 1 : struggle, fight 2 : wrestling

luchador, -dora *n* 1 : fighter 2 : wrestler

luchar *vi* 1 : to fight, to struggle 2 : to wrestle

luchón, -chona *adj, mpl* **luchones** *Mex* : industrious, hardworking

lucidez *nf, pl* **-deces** : lucidity, clarity

lucido, -da *adj* MAGNÍFICO : magnificent, splendid

lúcido, -da *adj* : lucid

luciente *adj* : bright, shining

luciérnaga *nf* : firefly, glowworm

lucimiento *nm* 1 : brilliance, splendor, sparkle 2 : triumph, success ⟨salir con lucimiento : to succeed with flying colors⟩

lucio *nm* : pike (fish)

lucir {45} *vi* 1 : to shine 2 : to look good, to stand out 3 : to seem, to appear ⟨ahora luce contento : he looks happy now⟩ — *vt* 1 : to wear, to sport 2 : to flaunt, to show off — **lucirse** *vr* 1 : to distinguish oneself, to excel 2 : to show off

lucrarse *vr* : to make a profit

lucrativo, -va *adj* : lucrative, profitable — **lucrativamente** *adv*

lucro *nm* GANANCIA : profit, gain

luctuoso, -sa *adj* : mournful, tragic

lúdico, -ca *adj* : play, playful

luego[1] *adv* 1 DESPUÉS : then, afterwards 2 : later (on) 3 **desde ~** : of course 4 **¡hasta luego!** : see you later! 5 **luego que** : as soon as 6 **luego luego** *Mex fam* : right away, immediately

luego[2] *conj* : therefore ⟨pienso, luego existo : I think, therefore I am⟩

lugar *nm* 1 : place, position ⟨lugar de nacimiento/trabajo : birthplace/workplace⟩ ⟨en algún lugar : somewhere⟩ ⟨en otro lugar : somewhere else⟩ ⟨cambiar algo de lugar : to move something⟩ ⟨poner las cosas en su lugar : to put things away, to straighten up⟩ ⟨te guardo el lugar : I'll save your spot⟩ ⟨yo en tu lugar : if I were in your place, if I were you⟩ ⟨se llevó el primer lugar : she took first place⟩ 2 ESPACIO : space, room ⟨no hay lugar para todos : there isn't room for everyone⟩ 3 **dar lugar a** : to give rise to, to lead to ⟨puede dar lugar a complicaciones : it can lead to complications⟩ 4 **en lugar de** : instead of, on behalf of 5 **en primer lugar** : in the first place, firstly 6 **en último lugar** : last, lastly 7 **lugar común** : cliché, platitude 8 **sin lugar a dudas** : without a

doubt, undoubtedly **9 tener lugar** : to take place
lugareño[1], **-ña** *adj* : village, rural
lugareño[2], **-ña** *n* : villager
lugarteniente *nmf* : lieutenant, deputy
lúgubre *adj* : gloomy, lugubrious
lujo *nm* **1** : luxury **2 de ~** : deluxe
lujoso, -sa *adj* : luxurious
lujuria *nf* : lust, lechery
lujurioso, -sa *adj* : lustful, lecherous
lumbago *nm* : lumbago
lumbar *adj* : lumbar
lumbre *nf* **1** FUEGO : fire **2** : brilliance, splendor **3 poner en la lumbre** : to put on the stove, to warm up
lumbrera *nf* **1** : skylight **2** : vent, port **3** : brilliant person, luminary
luminaria *nf* **1** : altar lamp **2** LUMBRERA : luminary, celebrity
luminiscencia *nf* : luminescence — **luminiscente** *adj*
luminosidad *nf* : luminosity, brightness
luminoso, -sa *adj* : shining, luminous
luna *nf* **1** : moon **2 luna de miel** : honeymoon
lunar[1] *adj* : lunar
lunar[2] *nm* **1** : mole, beauty spot **2** : defect, blemish **3** : polka dot
lunático, -ca *adj & n* : lunatic
lunes *nms & pl* **1** : Monday ⟨el lunes : (on) Monday⟩ ⟨los lunes : (on) Mondays⟩ ⟨cada (dos) lunes : every (other) Monday⟩ ⟨el lunes pasado : last Monday⟩ ⟨el lunes por la noche : on Monday night⟩ ⟨el próximo lunes : next Monday⟩

luneta *nf* **1** : lens (of eyeglasses) **2** : windshield (of an automobile) **3** : crescent
lupa *nf* : magnifying glass
lúpulo *nm* : hops (plant)
lustrabotas → **limpiabotas**
lustrar *vt* : to shine, to polish
lustre *nm* **1** BRILLO : luster, shine **2** : glory, distinction
lustro *nm* : five-year period
lustroso, -sa *adj* BRILLOSO : lustrous, shiny
luto *nm* : mourning ⟨estar de luto : to be in mourning⟩
luxación *nf, pl* **-ciones** : dislocation
luz *nf, pl* **luces** **1** : light ⟨luz del sol : sunlight⟩ ⟨luz eléctrica/artificial : electric/artificial light⟩ ⟨iluminado con una luz tenue : dimly lit⟩ ⟨a plena luz del día : in full/broad daylight⟩ **2** *fam* : power, electricity ⟨se fue la luz : the power/electricity went out⟩ ⟨cortar la luz : to cut off the power⟩ ⟨pagar la luz : to pay the electricity bill⟩ **3** : light, lamp ⟨apagar la luz : to turn off the light⟩ ⟨encender/prender la luz : to turn on the light⟩ ⟨luz de bengala : flare⟩ ⟨luz neón/LED : neon/LED light⟩ **4** : span, spread (between supports) **5 a la luz de** : in light of **6 a todas luces** : by any measure **7 dar a luz** : to give birth **8 sacar a la luz** : to make known, to bring to light **9 salir a la luz** : to become known, to come to light **10 traje de luces** : matador's costume
luzca, etc. → **lucir**

M

m *nf* : fifteenth letter of the Spanish alphabet
macabro, -bra *adj* : macabre
macadán *nm, pl* **-danes** : macadam
macana *nf* **1** : club, cudgel **2** *fam* : nonsense, silliness **3** *fam* : lie, fib *fam*
macanear *vi Arg, Chile, Uru fam* : to talk nonsense — *vt Mex, PRi fam* : to beat
macanudo, -da *adj fam* : great, fantastic
macarrón *nm, pl* **-rrones** **1** : macaroon **2 macarrones** *nmpl* : macaroni
macerar *vt* : to soak (food)
maceta *nf* **1** : flowerpot **2** : mallet **3** *Mex fam* : head
macetero *nm* **1** : plant stand **2** TIESTO : flowerpot, planter
machacar {72} *vt* **1** : to crush, to grind **2** : to beat, to pound — *vi* : to insist, to go on (about)
machacón, -cona *adj, mpl* **-cones** : insistent, tiresome
machete *nm* : machete
machetear *vt* : to hack with a machete — *vi Mex fam* : to plod, to work tirelessly
machismo *nm* **1** : machismo **2** : male chauvinism
machista *nm* : male chauvinist

macho[1] *adj* **1** : male **2** : macho, virile, tough
macho[2] *nm* **1** : male **2** : he-man
machote *nm* **1** *fam* : tough guy, he-man **2** *CA, Mex* : rough draft, model **3** *Mex* : blank form
machucar {72} *vt* **1** : to pound, to beat, to crush **2** : to bruise
machucón *nm, pl* **-cones** **1** MORETÓN : bruise **2** : smashing, pounding
macilento, -ta *adj* : gaunt, wan
macis *nm* : mace (spice)
macizo, -za *adj* **1** : solid ⟨oro macizo : solid gold⟩ **2** : strong, strapping **3** : massive
mácula *nf* : blemish, stain
macuto *nm Spain* : backpack
madeja *nf* **1** : skein, hank **2** : tangle (of hair)
madera *nf* **1** : wood ⟨de madera : made of wood, wooden⟩ ⟨tener madera de algo : to have the makings of something⟩ **2** : lumber, timber **3 madera dura** *or* **madera noble** : hardwood
maderero, -ra *adj* : timber, lumber
madero *nm* : piece of lumber, plank
madrastra *nf* : stepmother

madrazo *nm Mex fam* : punch, blow ⟨se agarraron a madrazos : they beat each other up⟩

madre *nf* **1** : mother ⟨madre biológica/ adoptiva : biological/adoptive mother⟩ ⟨madre de alquiler : surrogate mother⟩ ⟨madre soltera : single/unwed mother⟩ **2 madre política** : mother-in-law **3 la Madre Patria** : the mother country (said of Spain)

madrear *vt Mex fam* : to beat up

madreperla *nf* NÁCAR : mother-of-pearl

madreselva *nf* : honeysuckle

madriguera *nf* : burrow, den, lair

madrileño¹, -ña *adj* : of or from Madrid

madrileño², -ña *n* : person from Madrid

madrina *nf* **1** : godmother **2** : mother of the groom, matron of honor **3** : sponsor

madrugada *nf* **1** : early morning, wee hours **2** ALBA : dawn, daybreak

madrugador, -dora *n* : early riser

madrugar {52} *vi* **1** : to get up early **2** : to get a head start

madurar *v* **1** : to ripen **2** : to mature

madurez *nf, pl* **-reces** **1** : maturity **2** : ripeness

maduro, -ra *adj* **1** : mature **2** : ripe

maestría *nf* **1** : mastery, skill **2** : master's degree

maestro¹, -tra *adj* **1** : masterly, skilled **2** : chief, main **3** : trained ⟨un elefante maestro : a trained elephant⟩

maestro², -tra *n* **1** : teacher (in elementary and middle school) ⟨no hay mejor maestro que la necesidad : necessity is the mother of invention⟩ **2** : expert, master ⟨maestro de cocina : chef⟩ ⟨maestro de ceremonias : master of ceremonies⟩ **3** : maestro

Mafia *nf* : Mafia

mafioso, -sa *n* : mafioso, gangster

magdalena *nf* : bun, muffin

magenta *adj & n* : magenta

magia *nf* : magic

mágico, -ca *adj* : magic, magical — **mágicamente** *adv*

magisterio *nm* **1** : teaching **2** : teachers *pl*, teaching profession

magistrado, -da *n* : magistrate, judge

magistral *adj* : masterful, skillful

magistralmente *adv* : masterfully, brilliantly

magistratura *nf* : office of judge/magistrate

magma *nm* : magma

magnanimidad *nf* : magnanimity

magnánimo, -ma *adj* GENEROSO : magnanimous — **magnánimamente** *adv*

magnate *nmf* : magnate, tycoon

magnesio *nm* : magnesium

magnético, -ca *adj* : magnetic

magnetismo *nm* : magnetism

magnetizar {21} *vt* : to magnetize

magnetofónico, -ca *adj* **cinta magnetofónica** : magnetic tape

magnificar {72} *vt* **1** : to magnify **2** EXAGERAR : to exaggerate **3** ENSALZAR : to exalt, to extol, to praise highly

magnificencia *nf* : magnificence, splendor

magnífico, -ca *adj* ESPLENDOROSO : magnificent, splendid — **magníficamente** *adv*

magnitud *nf* : magnitude

magnolia *nf* : magnolia (flower)

magnolio *nm* : magnolia (tree)

mago, -ga *n* **1** : magician **2** : wizard (in folk tales, etc.) **3 los Reyes Magos** : the Magi

magro, -gra *adj* **1** : lean (of meat) **2** : meager

maguey *nm* : maguey

magulladura *nf* MORETÓN : bruise

magullar *vt* : to bruise — **magullarse** *vr*

mahometano¹, -na *adj* ISLÁMICO : Islamic, Muslim

mahometano², -na *n* : Muslim

mahonesa → **mayonesa**

maicena *nf* : cornstarch

mainframe ['mein,freim] *nm* : mainframe

maíz *nm* : corn, maize

maizal *nm* : cornfield

maja *nf* : pestle

majadería *nf* **1** TONTERÍA : stupidity, foolishness **2** *Mex* LEPERADA : insult, obscenity

majadero¹, -ra *adj* **1** : foolish, silly **2** *Mex* LÉPERO : crude, vulgar

majadero², -ra *n* **1** TONTO : fool **2** *Mex* : rude person, boor

majar *vt* : to crush, to mash

majestad *nf* : majesty ⟨Su Majestad : Your Majesty⟩

majestuosamente *adv* : majestically

majestuosidad *nf* : majesty, grandeur

majestuoso, -sa *adj* : majestic, stately

majo, -ja *adj Spain* **1** : nice, likeable **2** GUAPO : attractive, good-looking

mal¹ *adv* **1** : badly, poorly ⟨baila muy mal : he dances very badly⟩ ⟨hablar mal de alguien : to speak ill of someone⟩ ⟨hice mal en decirlo : I was wrong to say it⟩ ⟨comió algo que le hizo mal : he ate something that didn't agree with him⟩ ⟨algo anda mal : something's wrong⟩ ⟨todo le salió mal : everything went wrong for her⟩ ⟨el primer día no me fue mal : my first day wasn't bad⟩ **2** : wrong, incorrectly ⟨me entendió mal : she misunderstood me⟩ ⟨no lo tomes a mal : don't take it the wrong way⟩ ⟨esta palabra está mal escrita : this word is spelled wrong⟩ ⟨si mal no recuerdo : if I remember correctly⟩ **3** : hardly, with difficulty ⟨te oigo mal : I can hardly hear you⟩ ⟨mal se pueden comparar : you can hardly compare them⟩ ⟨mal puedo esperar : I can hardly wait⟩ **4 de mal en peor** : from bad to worse **5 menos mal** : it's a good thing, it's just as well ⟨menos mal que reaccioné a tiempo : it's a good thing I reacted in time⟩ ⟨menos mal que no viniste : it's just as well you didn't come⟩

mal² *adj* → **malo**

mal³ *nm* **1** : evil, wrong ⟨un mal necesario : a necessary evil⟩ **2** DAÑO : harm, damage ⟨las acusaciones le hicieron mucho mal : the accusations did him a lot of harm⟩ **3** DESGRACIA : misfortune **4**

ENFERMEDAD : illness, sickness **5 mal de ojo** : evil eye

malabar *adj* **juegos malabares** : juggling

malabares *nmpl* : juggling ⟨hacer malabares : to juggle⟩

malabarismos → **malabares**

malabarista *nmf* : juggler

malaconsejado, -da *adj* : ill-advised

malacostumbrado, -da *adj* CONSENTIDO : spoiled, pampered

malacostumbrar *vt* : to spoil

malagradecido, -da *adj* INGRATO : ungrateful

malaisio → **malasio**

malanga *nf* TARO : taro

malaria *nf* PALUDISMO : malaria

malasio, -sia *adj & n* : Malaysian

malauiano, -na *adj & n* : Malawian

malaventura *nf* : misadventure, misfortune

malaventurado, -da *adj* MALHADADO : ill-fated, unfortunate

malayo, -ya *adj & n* : Malay, Malayan

malbaratar *vt* **1** MALGASTAR : to squander **2** : to undersell

malcriado¹, -da *adj* **1** : ill-bred, ill-mannered **2** : spoiled, pampered

malcriado², -da *n* : spoiled brat

malcriar *vt* : to spoil, to raise badly

maldad *nf* **1** : evil, wickedness **2** : evil deed

maldecir {11} *vt* : to curse, to damn — *vi* **1** : to curse, to swear **2** ~ **de** : to speak ill of, to slander, to defame

maldición *nf, pl* **-ciones** : curse

maldiga, maldijo etc. → **maldecir**

maldito, -ta *adj* **1** : cursed, damned ⟨¡maldita sea! : damn it all!⟩ **2** : wicked

maldoso, -sa *adj Mex* : mischievous

maleable *adj* : malleable

maleante *nmf* : crook, thug

malecón *nm, pl* **-cones** : jetty, breakwater

maleducado, -da *adj* : ill-mannered, rude

maleficio *nm* : curse, hex

maléfico, -ca *adj* : evil, harmful

malentender {56} *vt* : to misunderstand

malentendido *nm* : misunderstanding

malestar *nm* **1** : discomfort **2** IRRITACIÓN : annoyance **3** INQUIETUD : uneasiness, unrest

maleta *nf* : suitcase, bag ⟨haz tus maletas : pack your bags⟩

maletera *nf Peru* → **maletero²**

maletero¹, -ra *n* : porter

maletero² *nm* : trunk (of an automobile)

maletín *nm, pl* **-tines** **1** PORTAFOLIO : briefcase **2** : overnight bag, satchel

malevolencia *nf* : malevolence, wickedness

malévolo, -la *adj* : malevolent, wicked

maleza *nf* **1** : thicket, underbrush **2** : weeds *pl*

malformación *nf, pl* **-ciones** : malformation

malgache *adj & nmf* : Madagascan

malgastar *vt* : to squander (resources), to waste (time, effort)

mal habido, -da *adj* : ill-gotten, dirty

malhablado, -da *adj* : foulmouthed

malhadado, -da *adj* MALAVENTURADO : ill-fated

malhechor, -chora *n* : criminal, delinquent, wrongdoer

malherir {76} *vt* : to injure seriously

malhumor *nm* : bad mood

malhumorado, -da *adj* : bad-tempered, cross

malicia *nf* **1** : wickedness, malice **2** : mischief, naughtiness **3** : cunning, craftiness

malicioso, -sa *adj* **1** : malicious **2** PÍCARO : mischievous

malignidad *nf* **1** : malignancy **2** MALDAD : evil

maligno, -na *adj* **1** : malignant ⟨un tumor maligno : a malignant tumor⟩ **2** : evil, harmful, malign

malinchismo *nm Mex* : preference for foreign goods or people — **malinchista** *adj*

malintencionado, -da *adj* : malicious, spiteful

malinterpretar *vt* : to misinterpret

mall ['mol] *nm, pl* **malls** : (shopping) mall

malla *nf* **1** : mesh **2** LEOTARDO : leotard, tights *pl* **3** : malla de baño *Arg, Uru* : swimsuit, bathing suit

mallorquín, -quina *adj & n* : Majorcan

malnutrición *nf, pl* **-ciones** DESNUTRICIÓN : malnutrition

malnutrido, -da *adj* DESNUTRIDO : malnourished, undernourished

malo¹, -la *adj* (**mal** *before masculine singular nouns*) **1** : bad ⟨mala suerte : bad luck⟩ ⟨malas noticias : bad news⟩ ⟨es mala idea : it's a bad idea⟩ ⟨mal aliento : bad breath⟩ ⟨un mal sabor : a bad taste⟩ ⟨un mal actor : a bad actor⟩ ⟨tener un mal día : to have a bad day⟩ ⟨una situación muy mala : a very bad situation⟩ ⟨recibió muy malas críticas : it got very bad reviews⟩ ⟨ese sombrero te queda mal : that hat doesn't look good on you⟩ ⟨llegaste en mal momento : you arrived at a bad time⟩ **2** : bad, poor ⟨en malas condiciones : in bad condition⟩ ⟨es de mala calidad : it's poor quality⟩ **3** : bad, wicked, naughty ⟨una mala persona : a bad person⟩ ⟨malas intenciones : bad intentions⟩ ⟨fuiste muy malo : you were very bad⟩ **4** : bad, improper ⟨ser de mala educación : to be bad manners⟩ ⟨malas palabras : bad words⟩ **5** : bad, harmful ⟨malo para la salud : bad for one's health⟩ **6** (*using the form* **mal**) : sick, ill, unwell ⟨estar/ponerse mal : to be/fall ill⟩ ⟨me siento/encuentro mal : I feel sick⟩ ⟨ando mal del estómago : my stomach is upset⟩ ⟨estar mal del corazón : to have heart trouble⟩ **7** : bad, spoiled (of food) **8 estar de malas** : to be in a bad mood

malo², -la *n* : villain, bad guy (in novels, movies, etc.)

malogrado, -da *adj* : failed, unsuccessful

malograr *vt* **1** : to spoil, to ruin **2** : to waste (an opportunity, time) — **malograrse** *vr* **1** FRACASAR : to fail **2** : to die young

malogro *nm* **1** : untimely death **2** FRA-CASO : failure

maloliente *adj* HEDIONDO : foul-smelling, smelly

malparado, -da *adj* **salir malparado** *or* **quedar malparado** : to come out of (something) badly, to end up in a bad state

malpensado, -da *adj* : distrustful, suspicious

malquerencia *nf* AVERSIÓN : ill will, dislike

malquerer {64} *vt* : to dislike

malquiso, etc. → **malquerer**

malsano, -na *adj* : unhealthy

malsonante *adj* : rude, offensive ⟨palabras malsonantes : foul language⟩

malta *nf* : malt

malteada *nf* : malted milk ⟨malteada de chocolate : chocolate malt⟩

maltratar *vt* **1** : to mistreat, to abuse **2** : to damage, to spoil

maltrato *nm* : mistreatment, abuse

maltrecho, -cha *adj* : battered, damaged

malucho, -cha *adj fam* : sick, under the weather

malva *adj & nm* : mauve

malvado[1], -da *adj* : evil, wicked

malvado[2], -da *n* : evildoer, wicked person

malvavisco *nm* : marshmallow

malvender *vt* : to sell at a loss

malversación *nf, pl* **-ciones** : misappropriation (of funds), embezzlement

malversador, -dora *n* : embezzler

malversar *vt* : to embezzle

malvivir *vi* : to live badly, to just scrape by

mamá *nf fam* : mom, mama

madadera *nf* : baby bottle

mamar *vi* **1** : to suckle **2 darle de mamar a** : to breast-feed — *vt* **1** : to suckle, to nurse **2** : to learn from childhood, to grow up with — **mamarse** *vr fam* : to get drunk

mamario, -ria *adj* : mammary

mamarracho *nm fam* **1** ESPERPENTO : mess, sight **2** : laughingstock, fool **3** : rubbish, junk

mambo *nm* : mambo

mameluco *nm* : overalls *pl*

mami *nf fam* : mommy

mamífero[1], -ra *adj* : mammalian

mamífero[2] *nm* : mammal

mamila *nf* **1** : nipple **2** *Mex* : baby bottle, pacifier

mamografía *nf* : mammogram

mamola *nf* : pat, chuck under the chin

mamotreto *nm fam* **1** : huge book, tome **2** ARMATOSTE : hulk, monstrosity

mampara *nf* BIOMBO : screen, room divider

mamparo *nm* : bulkhead

mampostería *nf* : masonry, stonemasonry

mampostero *nm* : mason, stonemason

mamut *nm, pl* **mamuts** : mammoth

maná *nm* : manna

manada *nf* **1** : flock, herd, pack **2** *fam* : horde, mob ⟨llegaron en manada : they came in droves⟩

manager *or* **mánager** *nmf, pl* **-gers** : manager

manantial *nm* **1** FUENTE : spring **2** : source

manar *vi* **1** : to flow **2** : to abound

manaza *nf* MANO : hand, mitt

manazas *nmfs & pl* : clumsy person, klutz, oaf

manatí *nm, pl* **-tíes** : manatee

mancha *nf* **1** : stain, spot, mark ⟨mancha de sangre : bloodstain⟩ **2** : blemish, blot ⟨una mancha en su reputación : a blemish on his reputation⟩ **3** : patch

manchado, -da *adj* : stained

manchar *vt* **1** ENSUCIAR : to stain, to soil **2** DESHONRAR : to sully, to tarnish — **mancharse** *vr* : to get dirty

mancillar *vt* : to sully, to besmirch

manco, -ca *adj* : one-armed, with one arm/hand

mancomunar *vt* : to combine, to pool — **mancomunarse** *vr* : to unite, to join together

mancomunidad *nf* **1** : commonwealth **2** : association, confederation

mancuernas *nfpl* : cuff links

mancuernillas *nf Mex* : cuff links

mandadero, -ra *n* : errand boy *m*, errand girl *f*, messenger

mandado *nm* **1** : order, command **2** : errand ⟨hacer los mandados : to run errands, to go shopping⟩

mandamás *nmf, pl* **-mases** *fam* : boss, bigwig, honcho

mandamiento *nm* **1** : commandment **2** : command, order, warrant ⟨mandamiento judicial : warrant, court order⟩

mandar *vt* **1** ORDENAR : to command, to order ⟨los mandó (a) callar, los mandó (a) que callaran : she ordered them to be quiet⟩ ⟨mandó (a) construir un monumento : he had a monument built⟩ **2** ENVIAR : to send ⟨te manda saludos : he sends you his regards⟩ ⟨la mandaron a Buenos Aires : they sent her to Buenos Aires⟩ **3** ECHAR : to hurl, to throw **4** ¿mande? *Mex* : yes?, pardon? **5 mandar algo a arreglar** : to have something fixed **6 mandar (a) decir** : to send word, to send a message **7 mandar (a) llamar** : to send for, to summon — *vi* : to be the boss, to be in charge — **mandarse** *vr Mex* : to take liberties, to take advantage

mandarín *nm* : Mandarin

mandarina *nf* : mandarin orange, tangerine

mandatario, -ria *n* **1** : leader (in politics) ⟨primer mandatario : head of state⟩ **2** : agent (in law)

mandato *nm* **1** : term of office **2** : mandate

mandíbula *nf* **1** : jaw **2** : mandible

mandil *nm* **1** DELANTAL : apron **2** : horse blanket

mandilón *nm, pl* **-lones** *fam* : wimp, coward

mandioca *nf* **1** : manioc, cassava **2** : tapioca

mando *nm* **1** : command, leadership **2** : control (for a device) ⟨mando a distancia : remote control⟩ **3 al mando de** : in charge of   **4 al mando de** : under the command of

mandolina *nf* : mandolin

mandón, -dona *adj, mpl* **mandones** : bossy, domineering

mandonear *vt fam* MANGONEAR : to boss around

manecilla *nf* : hand (of a clock), pointer

manejable *adj* **1** : manageable **2** : docile, easily led

manejar *vt* **1** CONDUCIR : to drive (a car) **2** OPERAR : to handle, to operate **3** : to manage **4** : to manipulate (a person) — *vi* : to drive — **manejarse** *vr* **1** COMPORTARSE : to behave **2** : to get along, to manage

manejo *nm* **1** : handling, operation **2** : management

manera *nf* **1** MODO : way, manner, fashion ⟨cada uno lo hace a su manera : everyone does it their own way⟩ ⟨a mi manera de ver : the way I see it⟩ ⟨de esta/esa manera : in this/that way⟩ ⟨de una manera u otra : one way or another⟩ ⟨de manera inmediata : immediately⟩ ⟨de mala manera : badly, rudely⟩ **2 a manera de** : by way of **3 de alguna manera** : somehow, in some way **4 de cualquier manera** *or* **de todas maneras** : anyway, anyhow ⟨de todas maneras tenía que hacerlo : I had to do it anyway⟩ **5 de manera que** : so, in order that **6 de ninguna manera** : by no means, absolutely not **7 de otra manera** : differently, in another way ⟨para decirlo de otra manera : in other words⟩ ⟨de otra manera no hubiera sobrevivido : otherwise he wouldn't have survived⟩ **8 manera de ser** : personality, demeanor **9 no hay manera** : there's no way, it's not possible ⟨no hay manera de saberlo : there's no way to know⟩ **10 maneras** *nfpl* : manners

manga *nf* **1** : sleeve ⟨en mangas de camisa : in shirt sleeves⟩ ⟨sin mangas : without sleeves, sleeveless⟩ **2** MANGUERA : hose

manganeso *nm* : manganese

manglar *nm* : mangrove swamp

mangle *nm* : mangrove

mango *nm* **1** : hilt, handle **2** : mango

mangonear *vt fam* : to boss around, to bully — *vi* **1** : to be bossy **2** : to loaf, to fool around

mangosta *nf* : mongoose

manguera *nf* : hose

manguito *nm* **1** : muff **2** : sleeve (of a pipe, etc.), hose (of a car)

maní *nm, pl* **maníes** : peanut

manía *nf* **1** OBSESIÓN : mania, obsession **2** : craze, fad **3** : odd habit, peculiarity **4** : dislike, aversion

maníaco¹, -ca *or* **maniaco, -ca** *adj* **1** : manic **2** *fam* CRAZED : maniacal

maníaco², -ca *or* **maniaco, -ca** *n* : maniac

maniatar *vt* : to tie the hands of

maniático¹, -ca *adj* **1** MANÍACO : maniacal **2** : obsessive **3** : fussy, finicky

maniático², -ca *n* **1** MANÍACO : maniac, lunatic **2** : obsessive person, fanatic **3** : eccentric, crank

manicomio *nm* : insane asylum, madhouse

manicura *nf* : manicure

manicuro, -ra *n* : manicurist

manido, -da *adj* : hackneyed, stale, trite

manifestación *nf, pl* **-ciones** **1** : manifestation, sign **2** : demonstration, rally

manifestante *nmf* : demonstrator

manifestar {55} *vt* **1** : to demonstrate, to show **2** : to declare — **manifestarse** *vr* **1** : to be or become evident **2** : to state one's position ⟨se han manifestado a favor del acuerdo : they have declared their support for the agreement⟩ **3** : to demonstrate, to rally

manifiesto¹, -ta *adj* : manifest, evident, clear — **manifiestamente** *adv*

manifiesto² *nm* : manifesto

manija *nf* MANGO : handle

manilla → manecilla

manillar *nm* : handlebars *pl*

maniobra *nf* : maneuver, stratagem

maniobrar *v* : to maneuver

manipulación *nf, pl* **-ciones** : manipulation

manipulador¹, -dora *adj* : manipulating, manipulative

manipulador², -dora *n* : manipulator

manipular *vt* **1** : to manipulate **2** MANEJAR : to handle

maniquí¹ *nmf, pl* **-quíes** : mannequin, model

maniquí² *nm, pl* **-quíes** : mannequin, dummy

manirroto¹, -ta *adj* : extravagant

manirroto², -ta *n* : spendthrift

manitas *nmfs & pl Spain* : handyman *m*, handywoman *f*

manito, -ta → mano²

manivela *nf* : crank

manjar *nm* : delicacy, special dish

mano¹ *nf* **1** : hand ⟨lávate las manos : wash your hands⟩ ⟨agárralo con las dos manos : hold it with both hands⟩ ⟨tenía algo en la mano : she had something in her hand⟩ ⟨con mis propias manos : with my own two hands⟩ **2** : coat (of paint or varnish) **3** : hand (in games) **4 a ~** : by hand **5 a ~** *or* **a la mano** : handy, at hand, nearby ⟨tenía los libros a (la) mano : I kept the books handy⟩ **6 bajo ~** : secretly, on the sly **7 caer en manos de** : to fall into the hands of **8 con las manos en la masa** : red-handed **9 darle la mano a alguien** : to shake someone's hand **10 darse la mano** : to shake hands **11 de la mano** : by the hand, hand in hand ⟨me tomó de la mano : he took me by the hand⟩ ⟨la política y la economía van de la mano : politics and economics go hand in hand⟩ **12 de mano en mano** : from one person to the next ⟨pasar de mano en mano : to be passed along/around⟩ **13 de primera mano** : firsthand, at firsthand ⟨conocer de primera mano : to experience firsthand⟩ **14 de segunda mano** : secondhand, used ⟨ropa de segunda mano : sec-ondhand clothing⟩ **15 echar una mano** : to lend a hand **16 mano a mano** : one-on-one **17 mano de obra** : labor, man-power **18 mano de mortero** : pestle **19 mano negra** *Mex fam* : shady dealings *pl* **20 ¡manos arriba!** *or* **¡arriba las ma-nos!** : stick 'em up!, (put your) hands up! **21 tener (buena) mano para** : to be good at

mano², -na *n fam* : buddy, pal ⟨¡oye, mano! : hey man!⟩

manojo *nm* PUÑADO : handful, bunch ⟨ser un manojo de nervios : to be a bag/bundle of nerves⟩

manómetro *nm* : pressure gauge

manopla *nf* **1** : mitten, mitt **2** : brass knuckles *pl*

manosear *vt* **1** : to handle or touch exces-sively **2** ACARICIAR : to fondle, to caress

manoseo *nm* **1** : touching, handling **2** : groping, fondling

manotazo *nm* : slap, smack, swipe

manotear *vi* : to wave one's hands, to ges-ticulate

mansalva *adv* **a ~** : at close range

mansarda *nf* BUHARDILLA : attic

mansedumbre *nf* : gentleness, meekness

mansión *nf*, *pl* **-siones** : mansion

manso, -sa *adj* **1** : gentle, meek **2** : tame — **mansamente** *adv*

manta *nf* **1** COBIJA, FRAZADA : blanket **2** : poncho **3** *Mex* : coarse cotton fab-ric

manteca *nf* **1** GRASA : lard, fat **2** : butter

mantecado *nm* **1** *PRi* HELADO : ice cream **2** (*in various countries*) : unfla-vored ice cream **3** *Spain* : shortbread (made with lard)

mantecoso, -sa *adj* : buttery

mantel *nm* **1** : tablecloth **2** : altar cloth

mantelería *nf* : table linen

mantener {80} *vt* **1** SUSTENTAR : to sup-port, to feed ⟨mantener uno su familia : to support one's family⟩ **2** CONSERVAR : to keep, to preserve ⟨mantener la caima : to keep one's calm⟩ ⟨mantener la paz : to keep the peace⟩ **3** CONTI-NUAR : to keep up, to sustain ⟨mantener una correspondencia : to keep up a cor-respondence⟩ **4** AFIRMAR : to maintain, to affirm — **mantenerse** *vr* **1** : to sup-port oneself, to subsist **2 mantenerse firme** : to hold one's ground

mantenimiento *nm* **1** : maintenance, up-keep **2** : sustenance, food **3** : preserva-tion

mantequera *nf* **1** : churn **2** : butter dish

mantequería *nf* **1** : creamery, dairy **2** : grocery store

mantequilla *nf* : butter

mantilla *nf* : scarf (worn over the head and shoulders)

mantis *nf* **mantis religiosa** : praying mantis

manto *nm* **1** : cloak **2** : mantle (in geol-ogy)

mantón *nm*, *pl* **-tones** CHAL : shawl

mantuvo, etc. → mantener

manual¹ *adj* **1** : manual ⟨trabajo manual : manual labor⟩ **2** : handy, manageable — **manualmente** *adv*

manual² *nm* : manual, handbook

manualidades *nfpl* : handicrafts (in schools)

manubrio *nm* **1** : handle, crank **2** : han-dlebars *pl*

manufactura *nf* **1** FABRICACIÓN : manu-facture **2** : manufactured item, product **3** FÁBRICA : factory

manufacturar *vt* FABRICAR : to manufac-ture

manufacturero¹, -ra *adj* : manufacturing

manufacturero², -ra *n* FABRICANTE : manufacturer

manuscrito¹, -ta *adj* : handwritten

manuscrito² *nm* : manuscript

manutención *nf*, *pl* **-ciones** : mainte-nance, support

manzana *nf* **1** : apple **2** CUADRA : block (enclosed by streets or buildings) **3** *or* **manzana de Adán** : Adam's apple

manzanal *nm* **1** : apple orchard **2** MAN-ZANO : apple tree

manzanar *nm* : apple orchard

manzanilla *nf* **1** : chamomile **2** : chamo-mile tea

manzano *nm* : apple tree

maña *nf* **1** : dexterity, skill **2** : cunning, guile **3 mañas** *or* **malas mañas** *nfpl* : bad habits, vices

mañana *nf* **1** : morning ⟨a las cuatro de la mañana : at four in the morning⟩ ⟨por la mañana : in the morning⟩ **2** : tomorrow

mañanero, -ra *adj* MATUTINO : morning ⟨rocío mañanero : morning dew⟩

mañanitas *nfpl* *Mex* : birthday serenade

mañoso, -sa *adj* **1** HÁBIL : skillful **2** AS-TUTO : cunning, crafty **3** : fussy, finicky

mapa *nm* CARTA : map

mapache *nm* : raccoon

mapamundi *nm* : map of the world

maqueta *nf* : model

maquila *nf* **1** : production, manufacture (for export) **2** → maquiladora

maquiladora *nf* : foreign-owned factory

maquillador, -dora *n* : makeup artist

maquillaje *nm* : makeup

maquillarse *vr* : to put on makeup, to make oneself up

máquina *nf* **1** : machine ⟨máquina de afeitar : electric razor⟩ ⟨máquina de coser : sewing machine⟩ ⟨máquina de escribir : typewriter⟩ ⟨máquina traga-monedas : slot machine⟩ ⟨máquina del tiempo : time machine⟩ ⟨máquina de votación : voting machine⟩ ⟨máquina expendedora : vending machine⟩ ⟨hecho a máquina : machine-made⟩ ⟨escribir a máquina : to type⟩ **2** LOCOMOTORA : engine, locomotive **3** : machine (in politics) **4** *or* **máquina de fotos** CÁMARA : camera **5 a toda máquina** : at full speed

maquinación *nf*, *pl* **-ciones** : machina-tion, scheme, plot

maquinal *adj* : mechanical, automatic — **maquinalmente** *adv*

maquinar *vt* : to plot, to scheme

maquinaria *nf* **1** : machinery **2** : mechanism, works *pl*

maquinilla *nf* **1** : small machine or device **2** *CA, Car* : typewriter

maquinista *nmf* **1** : machinist **2** : railroad engineer

mar *nmf* **1** : sea ⟨un mar agitado : a rough sea⟩ ⟨hacerse a la mar : to set sail⟩ **2 alta mar** : high seas

maraca *nf* : maraca

maraña *nf* **1** : thicket **2** ENREDO : tangle, mess

marasmo *nm* : paralysis, stagnation

maratón *nm, pl* **-tones** : marathon

maravilla *nf* **1** : wonder, marvel ⟨a las mil maravillas : wonderfully, marvelously⟩ ⟨hacer maravillas : to work wonders⟩ **2** : marigold

maravillar *vt* ASOMBRAR : to astonish, to amaze — **maravillarse** *vr* : to be amazed, to marvel

maravilloso, -sa *adj* ESTUPENDO : wonderful, marvelous — **maravillosamente** *adv*

marbete *nm* **1** ETIQUETA : label, tag **2** *PRi* : registration sticker (of a car)

marca *nf* **1** : mark ⟨marca de nacimiento : birthmark⟩ **2** : brand, make ⟨artículos de marca : brand-name items⟩ **3** : trademark ⟨marca registrada : registered trademark⟩ **4** : record (in sports) ⟨batir la marca : to beat the record⟩

marcado, -da *adj* : marked ⟨un marcado contraste : a marked contrast⟩ — **marcadamente** *adv*

marcador *nm* **1** TANTEADOR : scoreboard **2** : marker, felt-tip pen **3 marcador de libros** : bookmark

marcaje *nm* **1** : scoring (in sports) **2** : guarding (in sports)

marcapasos *nms & pl* : pacemaker

marcar {72} *vt* **1** : to mark **2** : to brand (livestock) **3** : to indicate, to show **4** RESALTAR : to emphasize **5** : to dial (a telephone) **6** : to guard (an opponent) **7** ANOTAR : to score (a goal, a point) — *vi* **1** ANOTAR : to score **2** : to dial

marcha *nf* **1** : march ⟨cerrar la marcha : to bring up the rear⟩ **2** : hike, walk ⟨ir de marcha : to go hiking⟩ **3** : pace, speed ⟨a toda marcha : at top speed⟩ **4** : gear (of an automobile) ⟨marcha atrás : reverse, reverse gear⟩ ⟨dar marcha atrás : to go into reverse⟩ **5** : departure **6** : march (in music) ⟨marcha fúnebre/ nupcial : funeral/wedding march⟩ **7** : course ⟨la marcha de los acontecimientos : the course of events⟩ **8 dar marcha atrás (en algo)** : to backtrack (on something) **9 en ~** : in motion, in gear, under way ⟨poner en marcha : to activate, to start, to set in motion⟩ ⟨ponerse en marcha : to set off⟩

marchar *vi* **1** IR : to go, to travel **2** ANDAR : to walk **3** FUNCIONAR : to work, to go **4** : to march — **marcharse** *vr* : to leave

marchitar *vi* : to make wither, to wilt — **marchitarse** *vr* **1** : to wither, to shrivel up, to wilt **2** : to languish, to fade away

marchito, -ta *adj* : withered, faded

marcial *adj* : martial, military

marciano, -na *adj & n* : Martian

marco *nm* **1** : frame, framework **2** : goalposts *pl* **3** AMBIENTE : setting, atmosphere **4** : mark (unit of currency)

marea *nf* **1** : tide **2 marea negra** : oil slick

mareado, -da *adj* **1** : dizzy, light-headed **2** : queasy, nauseous **3** : seasick, airsick, carsick

marear *vt* **1** : to make sick ⟨los gases me marearon : the fumes made me sick⟩ **2** : to bother, to annoy — **marearse** *vr* **1** : to get sick, to become nauseated **2** : to feel dizzy **3** : to get tipsy

marejada *nf* **1** : surge, swell (of the sea) **2** : undercurrent, ferment, unrest

maremoto *nm* : tidal wave

mareo *nm* **1** : dizzy spell **2** : nausea **3** : seasickness, motion sickness **4** : annoyance, vexation

marfil *nm* : ivory

margarina *nf* : margarine

margarita *nf* **1** : daisy **2** : margarita (cocktail)

margen[1] *nf, pl* **márgenes** : bank (of a river), side (of a street)

margen[2] *nm, pl* **márgenes 1** : edge, border ⟨dejar al margen : to exclude⟩ **2** : margin ⟨margen de ganancia : profit margin⟩ ⟨margen de error : margin of error⟩

marginación *nf, pl* **-ciones** : marginalization, exclusion

marginado[1], **-da** *adj* **1** DESHEREDADO : outcast, alienated, dispossessed **2 clases marginadas** : underclass

marginado[2], **-da** *n* : outcast, misfit

marginal *adj* : marginal, fringe

marginar *vt* : to ostracize, to exclude

mariachi *nm* **1** : mariachi band **2** : mariachi musician **3** : mariachi music

maridaje *nm* : marriage, union

maridar *vt* UNIR : to marry, to unite

marido *nm* ESPOSO : husband

marihuana *or* **mariguana** *or* **marijuana** *nf* : marihuana

marimacho *nmf fam* **1** : mannish woman **2** : tomboy

marimba *nf* : marimba

marina *nf* **1** : coast, coastal area **2** : navy, fleet ⟨marina mercante : merchant marine⟩

marinada *nf* : marinade

marinar *vt* : to marinate

marinero[1], **-ra** *adj* **1** : seaworthy **2** : sea, marine

marinero[2] *nm* : sailor

marino[1], **-na** *adj* : marine, sea

marino[2] *nm* : sailor, seaman

marioneta *nf* TÍTERE : puppet, marionette

mariposa *nf* **1** : butterfly **2 mariposa nocturna** : moth

mariquita[1] *nf* : ladybug

mariquita[2] *nm fam* : sissy, wimp

mariscal *nm* **1** : marshal **2 mariscal de campo** : field marshal (in the military), quarterback (in football)

marisco *nm* **1** : shellfish **2 mariscos** *nmpl* : seafood

marisma *nf* : marsh, salt marsh

marital *adj* : marital, married ⟨la vida marital : married life⟩

marítimo, -ma *adj* : maritime, shipping ⟨la industria marítima : the shipping industry⟩

marketing ['marketin] *nm* : marketing

marmita *nf* : (cooking) pot

mármol *nm* : marble

mármóreo, -rea *adj* : marble

marmota *nf* **1** : marmot **2 marmota de América** : woodchuck, groundhog

maroma *nf* **1** : rope **2** : acrobatic stunt **3** *Mex* : somersault

marque, etc. → **marcar**

marqués, -quesa *n, pl* **marqueses** : marquis *m*, marquess *m*, marquise *f*, marchioness *f*

marquesina *nf* **1** : marquee, canopy **2** : shelter (at a bus stop, etc.)

marqueta *nf Mex* : block (of chocolate), lump (of sugar or salt)

marranada *nf* **1** : disgusting thing **2** : dirty trick

marrano¹, -na *adj* : filthy, disgusting

marrano², -na *n* **1** CERDO : pig, hog **2** *fam* : dirty pig, slob

marrar *vt* : to miss (a target) — *vi* : to fail, to go wrong

marras *adv* **1** : long ago **2 de ~** : said, aforementioned ⟨el individuo de marras : the individual in question⟩

marrasquino *nm* : maraschino

marrón *adj & nm, pl* **marrones** CASTAÑO : brown

marroquí *adj & nmf, pl* **-quíes** : Moroccan

marsopa *nf* : porpoise

marsupial *nm* : marsupial

marta *nf* **1** : marten **2 marta cebellina** : sable (animal)

Marte *nm* : Mars

martes *nms & pl* **1** : Tuesday ⟨el martes : (on) Tuesday⟩ ⟨los martes : (on) Tuesdays⟩ ⟨cada (dos) martes : every (other) Tuesday⟩ ⟨el martes pasado : last Tuesday⟩ ⟨el próximo martes : next Tuesday⟩ **2 martes de Carnaval** : Mardi Gras

martillar *or* **martillear** *v* : to hammer

martillazo *nm* : blow with a hammer

martillo *nm* **1** : hammer **2 martillo neumático** : jackhammer

martín pescador *nm, pl* **martines pescadores** : kingfisher

martinete *nm* **1** : heron **2** : pile driver

mártir *nmf* : martyr

martirio *nm* **1** : martyrdom **2** : ordeal, torment

martirizar {21} *vt* **1** : to martyr **2** ATORMENTAR : to torment

marxismo *nm* : Marxism

marxista *adj & nmf* : Marxist

marzo *nm* : March ⟨el nueve de marzo : (on) the ninth of March, (on) March ninth⟩

mas *conj* PERO : but

más¹ *adv* **1** : more ⟨¿hay algo más grande? : is there anything bigger?⟩ ⟨unos días más tarde : a few days later⟩ ⟨es más complicado de lo que parece : it's more complicated than it seems⟩ ⟨no puedo esperar más : I can't wait any longer⟩ ⟨éste me gusta más que ése : I like this one better than that one⟩ ⟨ahora más que nunca : now more than ever⟩ **2** : most ⟨Luis es el más alto (del grupo) : Luis is the tallest (in the group)⟩ ⟨el que más me gusta : the one I like the most/best⟩ ⟨estudia lo más posible : he studies as much as possible⟩ **3** : rather ⟨más querría andar : I would rather walk⟩ **4 a ~** : besides, in addition **5 más allá** : further, farther ⟨la tienda está más allá : the shop is farther down⟩ **6 más allá de** : beyond, past ⟨está más allá de la iglesia : it's beyond/past the church⟩ ⟨ir más allá de los límites : to go beyond the limits⟩ **7 ~ de** : more than (a number or amount) ⟨más de cien personas : more than a hundred people⟩ ⟨más de una hora : more than an hour⟩ **8 qué . . . más . . .** : what . . . , what a . . . ⟨qué día más bonito! : what a beautiful day!⟩

más² *adj* **1** : more ⟨dáme dos kilos más : give me two more kilos⟩ **2** : most ⟨la que ganó más dinero : the one who earned the most money⟩ **3** : else ⟨¿quién más quiere vino? : who else wants wine?⟩ ⟨nadie más : nobody else⟩

más³ *n* : plus sign

más⁴ *prep* : plus ⟨tres más dos es igual a cinco : three plus two equals five⟩

más⁵ *pron* **1** : more ⟨¿tienes más? : do you have more?⟩ **2 a lo más** : at most **3 de ~** : extra, excess **4 ~ bien** : rather **5 más o menos** : more or less, approximately **6 por más que** : no matter how much ⟨por más que corras no llegarás a tiempo : no matter how fast you run you won't arrive on time⟩

masa *nf* **1** : mass, volume ⟨masa atómica : atomic mass⟩ ⟨producción en masa : mass production⟩ **2** : dough, batter **3 masas** *nfpl* : people, masses ⟨las masas populares : the common people⟩ **4 masa harina** *Mex* : corn flour (for tortillas, etc.) **5 en masa** : en masse

masacrar *vt* : to massacre

masacre *nf* : massacre

masaje *nm* : massage

masajear *vt* : to massage

masajista *nmf* : masseur *m*, masseuse *f*

mascar {72} *v* MASTICAR : to chew

máscara *nf* **1** CARETA : mask **2** : appearance, pretense **3 máscara antigás** : gas mask

mascarada *nf* : masquerade

mascarilla *nf* **1** : mask (in medicine) ⟨mascarilla de oxígeno : oxygen mask⟩ **2** : facial mask (treatment)

mascota *nf* **1** : mascot **2** : pet

masculinidad *nf* : masculinity

masculino, -na *adj* **1** : masculine, male **2** : manly **3** : masculine (in grammar)

mascullar *v* : to mumble, to mutter

masificación *nf, pl* **-ciones** **1** : mass adoption, propagation **2** *Spain* : overcrowding

masificado, -da *adj* : overcrowded

masilla *nf* : putty
masivamente *adv* : en masse
masivo, -va *adj* : mass ⟨comunicación masiva : mass communication⟩
masón *nm, pl* **masones** FRANCMASÓN : Mason, Freemason
masonería *nf* FRANCMASONERÍA : Masonry, Freemasonry
masónico, -ca *adj* : Masonic
masoquismo *nm* : masochism
masoquista¹ *adj* : masochistic
masoquista² *nmf* : masochist
masque, etc. → **mascar**
Máster *nm* : Master's degree
masticar {72} *v* MASCAR : to chew, to masticate
mástil *nm* **1** : mast **2** ASTA : flagpole **3** : neck (of a stringed instrument)
mastín *nm, pl* **mastines** : mastiff
mástique *nm* : putty, filler
mastodonte *nm* : mastodon
masturbación *nf, pl* **-ciones** : masturbation
masturbarse *vr* : to masturbate
mata *nf* **1** ARBUSTO : bush, shrub **2** : plant ⟨mata de tomate : tomato plant⟩ **3** : sprig, tuft **4 mata de pelo** : mop of hair
matadero *nm* : slaughterhouse, abattoir
matado, -da *adj Mex* : strenuous, exhausting
matador *nm* TORERO : matador, bullfighter
matamoscas *nms & pl* : flyswatter
matanza *nf* MASACRE : slaughter, butchering
matar *vt* **1** : to kill **2** : to slaughter, to butcher **3** APAGAR : to extinguish, to put out (fire, light) **4** : to tone down (colors) **5** : to pass, to waste (time) **6** : to trump (in card games) — *vi* **1** : to kill — **matarse** *vr* **1** : to be killed **2** SUICIDARSE : to commit suicide **3** *fam* : to exhaust oneself ⟨se mató tratando de terminarlo : he knocked himself out trying to finish it⟩
matasanos *nms & pl fam* : quack
matasellar *vt* : to cancel (a stamp), to postmark
matasellos *nms & pl* : postmark
matatena *nf Mex* : jacks
mate¹ *adj* : matte, dull
mate² *nm* **1** : maté **2** : slam dunk (in basketball) **3 jaque mate** : checkmate ⟨darle mate a *or* darle jaque mate a : to checkmate⟩
matemática → **matemáticas**
matemáticas *nfpl* : mathematics, math
matemático¹, -ca *adj* : mathematical — **matemáticamente** *adv*
matemático², -ca *n* : mathematician
materia *nf* **1** : matter ⟨materia gris : gray matter⟩ **2** : material ⟨materia prima : raw material⟩ **3** : (academic) subject **4 en materia de** : on the subject of, concerning
material¹ *adj* **1** : material, physical, real **2 daños materiales** : property damage
material² *nm* **1** : material ⟨material de construcción : building material⟩ **2** EQUIPO : equipment, gear

materialismo *nm* : materialism
materialista¹ *adj* : materialistic
materialista² *nmf* **1** : materialist **2** *Mex* : truck driver
materializar {21} *vt* : to bring to fruition, to realize — **materializarse** *vr* : to materialize, to come into being
materialmente *adv* **1** : physically ⟨materialmente imposible : physically impossible⟩ **2** : really, absolutely
maternal *adj* : maternal, motherly
maternidad *nf* **1** : maternity, motherhood **2** : maternity hospital, maternity ward
materno, -na *adj* : maternal
matinal *adj* MATUTINO : morning ⟨la pálida luz matinal : the pale morning light⟩
matinée *or* **matiné** *nf* : matinee
matiz *nm, pl* **matices 1** : hue, shade **2** : nuance
matización *nf, pl* **-ciones 1** : tinting, toning, shading **2** : clarification (of a statement)
matizar {21} *vt* **1** : to tinge, to tint (colors) **2** : to vary, to modulate (sounds) **3** : to qualify (statements)
matón *nm, pl* **matones** : thug, bully
matorral *nm* **1** : thicket **2** : scrub
matraca *nf* **1** : rattle, noisemaker **2 dar la matraca a** : to pester, to nag
matriarca *nf* : matriarch
matriarcado *nm* : matriarchy
matrícula *nf* **1** : list, roll, register **2** INSCRIPCIÓN : registration, enrollment **3** : registration number (of a vehicle) **4** *or* **placa de matrícula** : license plate, tag
matriculación *nf, pl* **-ciones** : matriculation, registration
matricular *vt* **1** INSCRIBIR : to enroll, to register (a person) **2** : to register (a vehicle) — **matricularse** *vr* : to matriculate
matrimonial *adj* : marital, matrimonial ⟨la vida matrimonial : married life⟩
matrimonio *nm* **1** : marriage, matrimony ⟨matrimonio civil/religioso : civil/religious wedding⟩ ⟨nació fuera del matrimonio : he was born out(side) of wedlock⟩ **2** : married couple
matriz *nf, pl* **matrices 1** : uterus, womb **2** : original, master copy **3** : main office, headquarters **4** : stub (of a check) **5** : matrix ⟨matriz de puntos : dot matrix⟩
matrona *nf* : matron
matronal *adj* : matronly
matutino¹, -na *adj* : morning ⟨la edición matutina : the morning edition⟩
matutino² *nm* : morning paper
maullar {8} *vi* : to meow
maullido *nm* : meow
mauritano, -na *adj & n* : Mauritanian
mausoleo *nm* : mausoleum
maxilar *nm* : jaw, jawbone
máxima *nf* : maxim
máxime *adv* ESPECIALMENTE : especially, principally
maximizar {21} *vt* : to maximize
máximo¹, -ma *adj* : maximum, greatest, highest
máximo² *nm* **1** : maximum **2 al máximo** : to the utmost **3 como ~** : at the most, at the latest

maya[1] *adj & nmf* : Mayan

maya[2] *nmf* : Maya, Mayan

mayo *nm* : May ⟨el primero de mayo : (on) the first of May, (on) May first⟩

mayonesa *nf* : mayonnaise

mayor[1] *adj* **1** *comparative of* GRANDE : bigger, larger, greater, elder, older **2** *superlative of* GRANDE : biggest, largest, greatest, eldest, oldest **3** : grown-up, mature ⟨hacerse mayor : to grow up⟩ **4** : main, major **5** : elderly **6** : major ⟨una sonata en re mayor : a sonata in D major⟩ **7 mayor de edad** : of (legal) age **8 al por mayor** *or* **por** — : wholesale

mayor[2] *nmf* **1** : major (in the military) **2** : adult, grown-up ⟨tus mayores : your elders⟩ ⟨las personas mayores : the elderly⟩

mayoral *nm* CAPATAZ : foreman, overseer

mayordomo *nm* : butler

mayoreo *nm* : wholesale

mayoría *nf* **1** : majority ⟨la mayoría de : most of, the majority of⟩ ⟨estar en mayoría : to be in the majority⟩ ⟨mayoría de edad : adulthood, age of majority⟩ **2 en su mayoría** : on the whole

mayorista[1] *adj* ALMACENISTA : wholesale

mayorista[2] *nmf* : wholesaler

mayoritariamente *adv* : primarily, chiefly

mayoritario, -ria *adj & n* : majority ⟨un consenso mayoritario : a majority consensus⟩

mayormente *adv* : primarily, chiefly

mayúscula *nf* : capital letter

mayúsculo, -la *adj* **1** : capital, uppercase **2** : huge, terrible ⟨un problema mayúsculo : a huge problem⟩

maza *nf* **1** : mace (weapon) **2** : drumstick **3** *fam* : bore, pest

mazacote *nm* **1** : concrete **2** : lumpy mess (of food) **3** : eyesore, crude work of art

mazapán *nm, pl* **-panes** : marzipan

mazmorra *nf* CALABOZO : dungeon

mazo *nm* **1** : mallet **2** : pestle **3** MANOJO : handful, bunch

mazorca *nf* **1** CHOCLO : cob, ear of corn **2 pelar la mazorca** *Mex fam* : to smile from ear to ear

me *pron* **1** : me ⟨me vieron : they saw me⟩ **2** : to me, for me, from me ⟨dame el libro : give me the book⟩ ⟨me lo compró : he bought it for me⟩ ⟨me robaron la cartera : they stole my pocketbook⟩ **3** : myself, to myself, for myself, from myself ⟨me preparé una buena comida : I cooked myself a good dinner⟩ ⟨me equivoqué : I made a mistake⟩

meada *nf usu vulgar* : piss *usu vulgar* ⟨echar una meada : to take a piss⟩

meados *nmpl usu vulgar* ORINA : piss *usu vulgar*

mear *vi usu vulgar* : to piss *usu vulgar*, to take a piss *usu vulgar*

mecánica *nf* : mechanics

mecánico[1]**, -ca** *adj* : mechanical — **mecánicamente** *adv*

mecánico[2]**, -ca** *n* **1** : mechanic **2** : technician ⟨mecánico dental : dental technician⟩

mecanismo *nm* : mechanism

mecanización *nf, pl* **-ciones** : mechanization

mecanizar {21} *vt* : to mechanize

mecanografía *nf* : typing

mecanografiar {85} *vt* : to type

mecanógrafo, -fa *n* : typist

mecate *nm* CA, Mex, Ven : rope, twine, cord

mecedor *nm* : glider (seat)

mecedora *nf* : rocking chair

mecenas *nmfs & pl* : patron (of the arts), sponsor

mecenazgo *nm* PATROCINIO : sponsorship, patronage

mecer {86} *vt* **1** : to rock **2** COLUMPIAR : to push (on a swing) — **mecerse** *vr* : to rock, to swing, to sway

mecha *nf* **1** : fuse **2** : wick **3 mechas** *nfpl* : highlights (in hair)

mechero *nm* **1** : burner **2** *Spain* : lighter

mechón *nm, pl* **mechones** : lock (of hair)

medalla *nf* : medal, medallion

medallista *nmf* : medalist

medallón *nm, pl* **-llones** **1** : medallion **2** : locket

media *nf* **1** CALCETÍN : sock **2** : average, mean **3 medias** *nfpl* : stockings, hose, tights **4 a medias** : by halves, half and half, halfway ⟨ir a medias : to go halves⟩ ⟨verdad a medias : half-truth⟩

mediación *nf, pl* **-ciones** : mediation

mediado, -da *adj* **1** : half full, half empty, half over **2** : halfway through ⟨mediada la tarea : halfway through the job⟩

mediador, -dora *n* : mediator

mediados *nmpl* **a mediados de** : halfway through, in the middle of ⟨a mediados del mes : towards the middle of the month, mid-month⟩

medialuna *nf* **1** : crescent **2** : croissant, crescent roll

medianamente *adv* : fairly, moderately

medianero, -ra *adj* **1** : dividing **2** : mediating

medianía *nf* **1** : middle position **2** : mediocre person, mediocrity

mediano, -na *adj* **1** : medium, average ⟨la mediana edad : middle age⟩ **2** : mediocre

medianoche *nf* : midnight

mediante *prep* : through, by means of ⟨Dios mediante : God willing⟩

mediar *vi* **1** : to mediate ⟨mediar en algo : to mediate something⟩ ⟨mediar por : to intercede on behalf of⟩ ⟨mediar con/ante : to intercede with⟩ **2** : to be in the middle, to be halfway through **3** : to elapse, to pass ⟨mediaron cinco años entre el inicio de la guerra y el armisticio : five years passed between the start of the war and the armistice⟩ **4** : to be a consideration ⟨media el hecho de que cuesta mucho : one must take into account that it is costly⟩ **5** : to come up, to happen ⟨medió algo urgente : something pressing came up⟩

mediatizar {21} *vt* : to influence, to interfere with

medicación *nf, pl* **-ciones** : medication, treatment

medicamento *nm* : medication, medicine, drug

medicar {72} *vt* : to medicate — **medicarse** *vr* : to take medicine

medicatura *nf Ven* : first aid clinic

medicina *nf* : medicine

medicinal *adj* **1** : medicinal **2** : medicated

medicinar *vt* : to give medication to, to dose

medición *nf, pl* **-ciones** : measuring, measurement

médico¹, -ca *adj* : medical ⟨una receta médica : a doctor's prescription⟩

médico², -ca *n* DOCTOR : doctor, physician

medida *nf* **1** : measurement, measure ⟨hecho a medida : custom-made⟩ ⟨tomar las medidas de algo : to measure something⟩ ⟨tomarle las medidas a alguien : to measure someone⟩ **2** : measure, step ⟨tomar medidas : to take steps⟩ ⟨medidas cautelares : precautionary measures⟩ ⟨medidas de seguridad : security measures⟩ **3** : moderation, prudence ⟨sin medida : immoderately⟩ **4** : extent, degree ⟨en cierta/gran medida : to a certain/great extent⟩ ⟨en la medida de lo posible : as far as possible, to the extent possible⟩ **5 a medida que** : as ⟨a medida que aumenta : as it increases⟩

medidor *nm* : meter, gauge

medieval *adj* : medieval — **medievalista** *nmf*

medievo → **medioevo**

medio¹ *adv* **1** : half ⟨está medio dormida : she's half asleep⟩ **2** : rather, kind of

medio², -dia *adj* **1** : half ⟨una media hora : half an hour⟩ ⟨medio hermano : half brother⟩ ⟨estar a media luz : to be dimly lit⟩ ⟨son las tres y media : it's half past three, it's three-thirty⟩ **2** : midway, halfway ⟨a medio camino : halfway there⟩ ⟨a media tarde : (in the) mid-afternoon⟩ **3** : middle ⟨la clase media : the middle class⟩ **4** : average ⟨la temperatura media : the average temperature⟩

medio³ *nm* **1** CENTRO : middle, center ⟨en medio de : in the middle of, amid⟩ ⟨estar en medio : to be in the way⟩ ⟨ponerse en medio : to get in the way⟩ **2** AMBIENTE : milieu, environment **3** : medium, spiritualist **4** : means *pl*, way ⟨por medio de : by means of⟩ ⟨los medios de comunicación : the media⟩ ⟨medios sociales : social media⟩ **5 medios** *nmpl* : means, resources

medioambiental *adj* : environmental

medio ambiente *nm* : environment

mediocampista *nmf* : midfielder

mediocre *adj* : mediocre, average

mediocridad *nf* : mediocrity

mediodía *nm* : noon, midday

medioevo *nm* : Middle Ages

medio tiempo *nm* : halftime

medir {54} *vt* **1** : to measure **2** : to weigh, to consider ⟨medir los riesgos : to weigh

the risks⟩ — *vi* : to measure — **medirse** *vr* : to be moderate, to exercise restraint

meditabundo, -da *adj* PENSATIVO : pensive, thoughtful

meditación *nf, pl* **-ciones** : meditation, thought

meditar *vi* : to meditate, to think ⟨meditar sobre la vida : to contemplate life⟩ — *vt* **1** : to think over, to consider **2** : to plan, to work out

meditativo, -va *adj* : pensive

mediterráneo, -nea *adj* : Mediterranean

médium *nmf, pl* **médiums** : medium (person)

medrar *vi* **1** PROSPERAR : to prosper, to thrive **2** AUMENTAR : to increase, to grow

medro *nm* PROSPERIDAD : prosperity, growth

medroso, -sa *adj* : fainthearted, fearful

médula *nf* **1** : marrow, pith **2 médula espinal** : spinal cord

medular *adj* : fundamental, core ⟨el punto medular : the crux of the matter⟩

medusa *nf* : jellyfish

megabyte *nm* : megabyte

megáfono *nm* : megaphone

megahercio *nm* : megahertz

megahertzio *nm* : megahertz

megatón *nm, pl* **-tones** : megaton

megavatio *nm* : megawatt

mejicano → **mexicano**

mejilla *nf* : cheek

mejillón *nm, pl* **-llones** : mussel

mejor *adv* **1** : better ⟨Carla cocina mejor que Ana : Carla cooks better than Ann⟩ **2** : best ⟨ella es la que lo hace mejor : she's the one who does it best⟩ **3** : rather ⟨mejor morir que rendirme : I'd rather die than give up⟩ **4** : it's better that . . . ⟨mejor te vas : you'd better go⟩ **5 a lo mejor** : maybe, perhaps

mejor² *nmf* **1** *comparative of* BUENO : better ⟨a falta de algo mejor : for lack of something better⟩ **2** *comparative of* BIEN : better ⟨está mucho mejor : he's much better⟩ **3** *superlative of* BUENO : best, the better ⟨mi mejor amigo : my best friend⟩ **4** *superlative of* BIEN : best, the better ⟨duermo mejor en un clima seco : I sleep best in a dry climate⟩ **5** PREFERIBLE : preferable, better **6 lo mejor** : the best thing, the best part

mejor³ *nmf (with definite article)* : the better (one), the best (one)

mejora *nf* : improvement

mejoramiento *nm* : improvement

mejorana *nf* : marjoram

mejorar *vt* : to improve, to make better — *vi* : to improve, to get better — **mejorarse** *vr*

mejoría *nf* : improvement, betterment

mejunje *nm* : concoction, brew

melancolía *nf* : melancholy, sadness

melancólico, -ca *adj* : melancholy, sad

melanoma *nm* : melanoma

melaza *nf* : molasses

melena *nf* **1** : mane **2** : long hair **3 melenas** *nfpl* GREÑAS : shaggy hair, mop

melenudo, -da *adj fam* : long-haired

melindroso¹, -sa *adj* **1** : affected **2** : fussy, finicky

melindroso², -sa *n* : finicky person, fussbudget

melisa *nf* : lemon balm

mella *nf* **1** : dent, nick **2 hacer mella en** : to have an effect on, to make an impression on

mellado, -da *adj* **1** : chipped, dented **2** : gap-toothed

mellar *vt* : to dent, to nick

mellizo, -za *adj* & *n* GEMELO : twin

melocotón *nm*, *pl* **-tones** : peach

melodía *nf* : melody, tune

melódico, -ca *adj* : melodic

melodioso, -sa *adj* : melodious

melodrama *nm* : melodrama

melodramático, -ca *adj* : melodramatic

melón *nm*, *pl* **melones** : melon, cantaloupe

meloso, -sa *adj* **1** : sweet **2** EMPALAGOSO : cloying, saccharine

membrana *nf* **1** : membrane **2 membrana interdigital** : web, webbing (of a bird's foot) — **membranoso, -sa** *adj*

membresía *nf* : membership, members *pl*

membrete *nm* : letterhead, heading ⟨papel con membrete : official stationery, letterhead⟩

membrillo *nm* : quince

membrudo, -da *adj* FORNIDO : muscular, well-built

memez *nf*, *pl* **memeces** : stupid thing

memo, -ma *adj* : silly, stupid

memorabilia *nf* : memorabilia

memorable *adj* : memorable

memorándum *or* **memorando** *nm*, *pl* **-dums** *or* **-dos** **1** : memorandum, memo **2** : memo book, appointment book

memoria *nf* **1** : memory ⟨de memoria : by heart⟩ ⟨hacer memoria : to try to remember⟩ ⟨traer a la memoria : to call to mind⟩ **2** RECUERDO : remembrance, memory ⟨su memoria perdurará para siempre : his memory will live forever⟩ **3** : report ⟨memoria anual : annual report⟩ **4 memorias** *nfpl* : memoirs

memoria de acceso aleatorio *nf* : random-access memory, RAM

memorizar {21} *vt* : to memorize — **memorización** *nf*

mena *nf* : ore

menaje *nm* : household goods *pl*, furnishings *pl*

mención *nf*, *pl* **-ciones** : mention

mencionar *vt* : to mention, to refer to

mendaz *adj*, *pl* **mendaces** : false, untruthful, dishonest

mendicidad *nf* : begging

mendigar {52} *vi* : to beg — *vt* : to beg for

mendigo, -ga *n* LIMOSNERO : beggar

mendrugo *nm* : crust (of bread)

menear *vt* **1** : to shake (one's head) **2** : to sway, to wiggle (one's hips) **3** : to wag (a tail) **4** : to stir (a liquid) — **menearse** *vr* **1** : to wiggle one's hips **2** : to fidget

meneo *nm* **1** : movement **2** : shake, toss **3** : swaying, wagging, wiggling **4** : stir, stirring

menester *nm* **1** : activity, occupation, duties *pl* **2 ser menester** : to be necessary ⟨es menester que vengas : you must come⟩

menestra *nf* **1** *Ecuador* : legume stew **2** *Peru* : legume **3** *Spain* : mixed cooked vegetables

mengano, -na → **fulano**

mengua *nf* **1** : decrease, decline **2** : lack, want **3** : discredit, dishonor

menguar *vt* : to diminish, to lessen — *vi* **1** : to decline, to decrease **2** : to wane — **menguante** *adj*

meningitis *nf* : meningitis

menisco *nm* : cartilage

menjurje → **mejunje**

menopausia *nf* : menopause

menopáusico, -ca *nf* : menopausal

menor¹ *adj* **1** *comparative of* PEQUEÑO : smaller, lesser, younger ⟨es menor que su hermana : he's younger than his sister⟩ ⟨en menor medida : to a lesser extent/degree⟩ **2** *superlative of* PEQUEÑO : smallest, least, youngest **3** : minor ⟨un problema menor : a minor problem⟩ **4** : minor (in music) ⟨en tono de mi menor : in the key of E minor⟩ **5 al por menor** : retail **6 ser menor de edad** : to be a minor, to be underage

menor² *nmf* : minor, juvenile

menos¹ *adv* **1** : less ⟨llueve menos en agosto : it rains less in August⟩ ⟨éste me gusta menos que ése : I like this one less than that one⟩ ⟨soy menos alta que mis hermanas : I'm not as tall as my sisters⟩ ⟨es menos difícil de lo que parece : it's less difficult than it looks⟩ **2** : least ⟨el coche menos caro : the least expensive car⟩ ⟨en el momento menos pensado : when you least expect it⟩ ⟨es lo menos que puedo hacer : it's the least I can do⟩ ⟨trabaja lo menos posible : he works as little as possible⟩ ⟨los que menos ganan : those who earn the least⟩ ⟨lo que menos necesitamos es otra crisis : the last thing we need is another crisis⟩ **3** ∼ **de** : less than, fewer than ⟨tienen menos de 50 empleados : they have fewer than 50 employees⟩ ⟨en menos de un minuto : in less than a minute⟩

menos² *adj* **1** : less, fewer ⟨tengo más trabajo y menos tiempo : I have more work and less time⟩ ⟨hay menos sillas que personas : there are fewer chairs than people⟩ **2** : least, fewest ⟨la clase que tiene menos estudiantes : the class that has the fewest students⟩

menos³ *prep* **1** SALVO, EXCEPTO : except **2** : minus ⟨quince menos cuatro son once : fifteen minus four is eleven⟩

menos⁴ *pron* **1** : less, fewer ⟨no deberías aceptar menos : you shouldn't accept less⟩ **2 al menos** *or* **por lo menos** : at least **3 a menos que** : unless **4 lo de menos** : the least important thing

menoscabar *vt* **1** : to lessen, to diminish **2** : to disgrace, to discredit **3** PERJUDICAR : to harm, to damage

menoscabo *nm* **1** : lessening, diminishing **2** : disgrace, discredit **3** : harm, damage

menospreciar *vt* **1** DESPRECIAR : to scorn, to look down on **2** : to underestimate, to undervalue

menosprecio *nm* DESPRECIO : contempt, scorn

mensaje *nm* : message

mensajería instantánea *nf* : instant messaging

mensajero, -ra *n* : messenger

menso, -sa *adj Mex fam* : foolish, stupid

menstrual *adj* : menstrual

menstruar {3} *vi* : to menstruate — **menstruación** *nf*

mensual *adj* : monthly

mensualidad *nf* **1** : monthly payment, installment **2** : monthly salary

mensualmente *adv* : every month, monthly

mensurable *adj* : measurable

menta *nf* **1** : mint, peppermint **2 menta verde** : spearmint

mentado, -da *adj* **1** : aforementioned **2** FAMOSO : renowned, famous

mental *adj* : mental, intellectual — **mentalmente** *adv*

mentalidad *nf* : mentality

mentalizar {21} *vt* : to prepare mentally — **mentalizarse** *vr*

mentar {55} *vt* **1** : to mention, to name **2 mentar la madre a** *fam* : to insult, to swear at

mente *nf* : mind ⟨tener en mente : to have in mind⟩

-mente *suf* : -ly ⟨frecuentemente : frequently⟩

mentecato¹, -ta *adj* : foolish, simple

mentecato², -ta *n* : fool, idiot

mentir {76} *vi* : to lie

mentira *nf* : lie

mentirijillas *nfpl fam* **de ~** : as a joke, in fun

mentiroso¹, -sa *adj* EMBUSTERO : lying, untruthful

mentiroso², -sa *n* EMBUSTERO : liar

mentís *nm, pl* **mentises** : denial, repudiation ⟨dar el mentís a : to deny, to refute⟩

mentol *nm* : menthol — **mentolado, -da** *adj*

mentón *nm, pl* **mentones** BARBILLA : chin

mentor *nm* : mentor, counselor

menú *nm, pl* **menús** : menu

menudear *vi* : to occur frequently — *vt* : to do repeatedly

menudencia *nf* **1** : trifle **2 menudencias** *nfpl* : giblets

menudeo *nm* : retail, retailing

menudillos *nmpl* : giblets

menudo¹, -da *adj* **1** : minute, small **2 a ~** FRECUENTEMENTE : often, frequently

menudo² *nm* **1** *Mex* : tripe stew **2 menudos** *nmpl* : giblets

meñique *nm or* **dedo meñique** : little finger, pinkie

meollo *nm* **1** MÉDULA : marrow **2** SESO : brains *pl* **3** ENTRAÑA : essence, core ⟨el meollo del asunto : the heart of the matter⟩

mequetrefe *nm fam* : good-for-nothing

meramente *adv* : merely, purely

mercachifle *nm* : peddler, hawker

mercadeo *nm* : marketing

mercader *nmf* : merchant

mercadería *nf* : merchandise, goods *pl*

mercadillo *nm Spain* : flea market

mercado *nm* **1** : market **2 mercado de pulgas** *(in various countries)* : flea market **3 mercado de trabajo/valores** : labor market **4 mercado de valores** *or* **mercado bursátil** : stock market

mercadotecnia *nf* : marketing

mercancía *nf* : merchandise, goods *pl*

mercante *nmf* : merchant, dealer

mercantil *adj* COMERCIAL : commercial, mercantile

merced *nf* **1** : favor **2 ~ a** : thanks to, due to **3 a merced de** : at the mercy of

mercenario, -ria *adj & n* : mercenary

mercería *nf* : notions store

Mercosur *nm* : economic community consisting of Argentina, Brazil, Paraguay, and Uruguay

mercurio *nm* : mercury

Mercurio *nm* : Mercury (planet)

merecedor, -dora *adj* : deserving, worthy

merecer {53} *vt* : to deserve, to merit — *vi* : to be worthy

merecidamente *adv* : rightfully, deservedly

merecido *nm* : something merited, due ⟨recibieron su merecido : they got their just deserts⟩

merecimiento *nm* : merit, worth

merendar {55} *vi* : to have an afternoon snack — *vt* : to have as an afternoon snack

merendero *nm* **1** : lunchroom, snack bar **2** : picnic area

merengue *nm* **1** : meringue **2** : merengue (music or dance)

meridiano¹, -na *adj* **1** : midday **2** : crystal clear

meridiano² *nm* : meridian

meridional *adj* SUREÑO : southern

merienda *nf* : afternoon snack, tea

mérito *nm* : merit

meritorio¹, -ria *adj* : deserving, meritorious

meritorio², -ria *n* : intern, trainee

merluza *nf* : hake

merma *nf* **1** : decrease, cut **2** : waste, loss

mermar *vi* : to decrease, to diminish — *vt* : to reduce, to cut down

mermelada *nf* : marmalade, jam

mero¹, -ra *adv Mex fam* **1** : nearly, almost ⟨ya mero me caí : I almost fell⟩ **2** : just, exactly ⟨aquí mero : right here⟩

mero², -ra *adj* **1** : mere, simple **2** *Mex fam* (used as an intensifier) : very ⟨en el mero centro : in the very center of town⟩

mero³ *nm* : grouper

merodeador, -dora *n* **1** : marauder **2** : prowler

merodear *vi* **1** : to maraud, to pillage **2** : to prowl around, to skulk

mes *nm* : month

mesa *nf* **1** : table ⟨mesa de cocina : kitchen table⟩ ⟨mesa de noche : nightstand, night table⟩ **2** : committee, board ⟨mesa directiva : executive board⟩

mesada *nf* : allowance, pocket money
mesarse *vr* : to pull at ⟨mesarse los cabellos : to tear one's hair⟩
mesero, -ra *n* CAMARERO : waiter, waitress *f*
meseta *nf* : plateau
Mesías *nm* : Messiah
mesita *or Spain* **mesilla** *nf* 1 : small table 2 *or* **mesita/mesilla de noche** : nightstand, night table
mesón *nm, pl* **mesones** : inn
mesonero, -ra *nm* : innkeeper
mesteño, -ña *adj* caballo mesteño : wild horse, mustang
mestizo¹, -za *adj* 1 : of mixed ancestry, mestizo 2 HÍBRIDO : hybrid
mestizo², -za *n* : person of mixed ancestry, mestizo
mesura *nf* 1 MODERACIÓN : moderation, discretion 2 CORTESÍA : courtesy 3 GRAVEDAD : seriousness, dignity
mesurado, -da *adj* COMEDIDO : moderate, restrained
mesurar *vt* : to moderate, to restrain, to temper — **mesurarse** *vr* : to restrain oneself
meta *nf* : goal, objective
metabólico, -ca *adj* : metabolic
metabolismo *nm* : metabolism
metabolizar {21} *vt* : to metabolize
metafísica *nf* : metaphysics
metafísico, -ca *adj* : metaphysical
metáfora *nf* : metaphor
metafórico, -ca *adj* : metaphoric, metaphorical
metal *nm* 1 : metal 2 *or* **metales** *nmpl* : brass, brass section (in an orchestra)
metálico, -ca *adj* : metallic, metal
metalistería *nf* : metalworking
metalizado, -da *adj* : metallic
metalurgia *nf* : metallurgy
metalúrgico¹, -ca *adj* : metallurgical
metalúrgico², -ca *n* : metalworker
metamorfosis *nfs & pl* : metamorphosis
metano *nm* : methane
metedura *nf* metedura de pata : blunder, faux pas
meteórico, -ca *adj* : meteoric
meteorito *nm* : meteorite
meteoro *nm* : meteor
meteorología *nf* : meteorology
meteorológico, -ca *adj* : meteorologic, meteorological
meteorólogo, -ga *n* : meteorologist
meter *vt* 1 : to put ⟨lo metió en un cajón : he put it in a drawer⟩ ⟨metieron su dinero en el banco : they put their money in the bank⟩ ⟨se le metió en la cabeza que . . . : he got it in his head that . . .⟩ 2 : to shut (in a place) ⟨la metieron en la cárcel : they put her in jail⟩ ⟨estuve todo el día metida en la casa : I was stuck in the house all day⟩ 3 : to fit, to squeeze ⟨puedes meter dos líneas más en esa página : you can fit two more lines on that page⟩ 4 : to place (in a job) ⟨lo metieron de dependiente : they got him a job as a store clerk⟩ 5 : to involve ⟨lo metió en un buen lío : she got him in an awful mess⟩ 6 : to make, to cause

⟨meten demasiado ruido : they make too much noise⟩ ⟨un cuento que mete miedo : a scary story⟩ 7 : to spread (a rumor) 8 : to strike (a blow) 9 : to score (a goal or point) 10 : to take up, to take in (clothing) 11 **a todo meter** : at top speed — **meterse** *vr* 1 : to get (in), to enter ⟨se metió en la cama : she got in bed⟩ ⟨el ladrón se metió por la ventana : the thief got in through the window⟩ ⟨¿dónde te has metido? : where are you hiding?, where have you gotten to?⟩ 2 : to put, to stick ⟨no te lo metas en la boca : don't put it in your mouth⟩ ⟨se metió la mano en el bolsillo : he stuck his hand in his pocket⟩ 3 *fam* : to meddle ⟨no te metas en lo que no te importa : mind your own business⟩ 4 ~ **con** *fam* : to pick a fight with, to provoke ⟨no te metas conmigo : don't mess with me⟩ 5 ~ **a/de** : to become ⟨se metió a monja : she became a nun⟩
metiche¹ *adj Mex fam* : nosy
metiche² *nmf Mex fam* : busybody
meticulosidad *nf* : thoroughness, meticulousness
meticuloso, -sa *adj* : meticulous, thorough — **meticulosamente** *adv*
metida *nf* metida de pata *fam* : blunder, gaffe, blooper
metódico, -ca *adj* : methodical — **metódicamente** *adv*
metodista *adj & nmf* : Methodist
método *nm* : method
metodología *nf* : methodology
metomentodo *nmf fam* : busybody
metraje *nm* : length (of a film) ⟨de largo metraje : feature-length⟩
metralla *nf* : shrapnel
metralleta *nf* : submachine gun
métrico, -ca *adj* 1 : metric 2 cinta métrica : tape measure
metro *nm* 1 : meter 2 : subway
metrónomo *nm* : metronome
metrópoli *nf or* **metrópolis** nfs & pl : metropolis
metropolitano, -na *adj* : metropolitan
mexicanismo *nm* : Mexican word or expression
mexicano, -na *adj & n* : Mexican
mexicoamericano, -na *adj & n* : Mexican-American
mexiquense¹ *adj Mex* : of or from Mexico City
mexiquense² *nmf Mex* : person from Mexico City
meza, etc. → mecer
mezcla *nf* 1 : mixing 2 : mixture, blend 3 : mortar (masonry material)
mezclar *vt* 1 : to mix, to blend 2 : to mix up, to muddle 3 INVOLUCRAR : to involve — **mezclarse** *vr* 1 : to get mixed up (in) 2 : to mix, to mingle (socially)
mezclilla *nf Chile, Mex* : denim ⟨pantalones de mezclilla : jeans⟩
mezcolanza *nf* : jumble, hodgepodge
mezquindad *nf* 1 : meanness, stinginess 2 : petty deed, mean action
mezquino¹, -na *adj* 1 : mean, petty 2 : stingy 3 : paltry

mezquino² *nm Mex* : wart
mezquita *nf* : mosque
mi¹ *adj* : my
mi² *nm* **1** : E ⟨mi sostenido/bemol : E sharp/flat⟩ **2** : mi (in singing)
mí *pron* **1** : me ⟨es para mí : it's for me⟩ ⟨a mí no me importa : it doesn't matter to me⟩ **2** mí mismo, mí misma : myself
miasma *nm* : miasma
miau *nm* : meow
mica *nf* : mica
mico *nm* : monkey, long-tailed monkey
micro *nm* **1** *Chile, Arg* : minibus **2** : microphone
micro- *pref* : micro-
microbio *nm* : microbe, germ
microbiología *nf* : microbiology
microbús *nm, pl* **-buses** : minibus
microchip *nm, pl* **microchips** : microchip
microcomputadora *nf* : microcomputer
microcosmos *nms & pl* : microcosm
microfilm *nm, pl* **-films** : microfilm
micrófono *nm* : microphone
micrómetro *nm* : micrometer
microonda *nf* : microwave
microondas *nms & pl* : microwave, microwave oven
microordenador *nm Spain* : microcomputer
microorganismo *nm* : microorganism
microprocesador *nm* : microprocessor
microscópico, -ca *adj* : microscopic
microscopio *nm* : microscope
mide, etc. → **medir**
miedo *nm* **1** TEMOR : fear ⟨le tiene miedo al perro : he's scared of the dog⟩ ⟨tenían miedo de hablar : they were afraid to speak⟩ ⟨morirse de miedo : to be scared to death⟩ ⟨temblar de miedo : to tremble with fear⟩ ⟨miedo escénico : stage fright⟩ **2 dar miedo** : to frighten
miedoso, -sa *adj* TEMEROSO : fearful
miel *nf* : honey
miembro *nm* **1** : member **2** EXTREMIDAD : limb, extremity
mienta, etc. → **mentar**
miente, etc. → **mentir**
-miento *suf* : -ment ⟨entretenimiento : entertainment⟩
mientras¹ *adv* **1** *or* **mientras tanto** : meanwhile, in the meantime **2 mientras más** : the more ⟨mientras más como, más quiero : the more I eat, the more I want⟩
mientras² *conj* **1** : while, as ⟨roncaba mientras dormía : he snored while he was sleeping⟩ **2** : as long as ⟨luchará mientras pueda : he will fight as long as he is able⟩ **3 mientras que** : while, whereas ⟨él es alto mientras que ella es muy baja : he is tall, whereas she is very short⟩
miércoles *nms & pl* **1** : Wednesday ⟨el miércoles : (on) Wednesday⟩ ⟨los miércoles : (on) Wednesdays⟩ ⟨cada (dos) miércoles : every (other) Wednesday⟩ ⟨el miércoles pasado : last Wednesday⟩ ⟨el próximo miércoles : next Wednesday⟩ ⟨el miércoles por la noche

: Wednesday night⟩ **2 Miércoles de Ceniza** : Ash Wednesday
miga *nf* **1** : crumb **2 hacer buenas (malas) migas con** : to get along well (poorly) with
migaja *nf* **1** : crumb **2 migajas** *nfpl* SOBRAS : leftovers, scraps
migra *nf Mex fam* **la migra** : the immigration police
migración *nf, pl* **-ciones** : migration
migrante *nmf* : migrant
migraña *nf* : migraine
migrar *vi* : to migrate
migratorio, -ria *adj* : migratory
mijo *nm* : millet
mil¹ *adj & pron* : thousand
mil² *nm* : one thousand, a thousand
milagro *nm* : miracle ⟨de milagro : miraculously⟩
milagroso, -sa *adj* : miraculous, marvelous — **milagrosamente** *adv*
milenario, -ria *adj* : thousand-year-old
milenio *nm* : millennium
milésima *nf* → **milésimo²**
milésimo¹, -ma *adj* : thousandth
milésimo² *nm* : thousandth
mili *nf Spain fam* : military service
milicia *nf* **1** : militia **2** : military service
miligramo *nm* : milligram
mililitro *nm* : milliliter
milímetro *nm* : millimeter
militancia *nf* : militancy
militante¹ *adj* : militant
militante² *nmf* : militant, activist
militar¹ *vi* **1** : to serve (in the military) **2** : to be active (in politics)
militar² *adj* : military
militar³ *nmf* SOLDADO : soldier
militarismo *nm* : militarism
militarista *adj* : militaristic
militarizar {21} *vt* : to militarize
milla *nf* : mile
millar *nm* : thousand
millón *nm, pl* **millones** : million
millonario, -ria *n* : millionaire
millonésima *nf* → **millonésimo²**
millonésimo¹, -ma *adj* : millionth
millonésimo² *nm* **1** : millionth (in a series) **2** : millionth (fraction)
mil millones *nms & pl* : billion
milmillonésimo¹, -ma *adj* : billionth
milmillonésimo² *nm* **1** : billionth (in a series) **2** : billionth (fraction)
milpa *nf CA, Mex* : cornfield
milpiés *nms & pl* : millipede
mimar *vt* CONSENTIR : to pamper, to spoil
mimbre *nm* : wicker
mimeógrafo *nm* : mimeograph
mímica *nf* **1** : mime, sign language **2** IMITACIÓN : mimicry
mimo *nm* **1** : pampering, indulgence ⟨hacerle mimos a alguien : to pamper someone⟩ **2** : mime
mimoso, -sa *adj* **1** : fussy, finicky **2** : affectionate, clinging
mina *nf* **1** : mine **2** : lead (for pencils)
minar *vt* **1** : to mine **2** DEBILITAR : to undermine
minarete *nm* ALMINAR : minaret
mineral *adj & nm* : mineral

mineralogía *nf* : mineralogy
minería *nf* : mining
minero[1], **-ra** *adj* : mining
minero[2], **-ra** *n* : miner, mine worker
mini- *pref* : mini-
miniatura *nf* : miniature
minicomputadora *nf* : minicomputer
minifalda *nf* : miniskirt
minifundio *nm* : small farm
minimizar {21} *vt* : to minimize
mínimo[1], **-ma** *adj* 1 : minimum ⟨salario mínimo : minimum wage⟩ 2 : least, smallest ⟨es lo mínimo que puede hacer : it's the least he can do⟩ 3 : very small, minute ⟨no tengo la más mínima idea : I haven't the slightest idea⟩
mínimo[2] *nm* 1 : minimum, least amount 2 : modicum, small amount 3 como ~ : at least
minino, -na *n fam* : kitty, pussy
miniserie *nf* : miniseries
ministerial *adj* : ministerial
ministerio *nm* : ministry, department
ministro, -tra *n* : minister, secretary ⟨primer ministro, primera ministra : prime minister⟩ ⟨Ministro de Defensa : Secretary of Defense⟩
minivan [ˌminiˈban, -ˈvan] *nf, pl* **-vanes** : minivan
minoría *nf* : minority
minorista[1] *adj* : retail
minorista[2] *nmf* : retailer
minoritario, -ria *adj* : minority
mintió, etc. → **mentir**
minucia *nf* 1 : (minor) detail 2 INSIGNIFICANCIA : trifle, triviality 3 con minucia : in detail
minuciosamente *adv* 1 : minutely 2 : in great detail 3 : thoroughly, meticulously
minucioso, -sa *adj* 1 : minute 2 DETALLADO : detailed 3 : thorough, meticulous
minué *nm* : minuet
minúsculo, -la *adj* DIMINUTO : tiny, miniscule
minusvalía *nf* : disability, handicap *sometimes offensive*
minusválido[1], **-da** *adj* : handicapped, disabled
minusválido[2], **-da** *n* : handicapped person
minuta *nf* 1 BORRADOR : rough draft 2 : bill, fee
minutero *nm* : minute hand
minuto *nm* : minute
mío[1], **mía** *adj* 1 : my, of mine ⟨¡Dios mío! : my God!, good heavens!⟩ ⟨una amiga mía : a friend of mine⟩ 2 : mine ⟨es mío : it's mine⟩
mío[2], **mía** *pron* (*with definite article*) : mine, my own ⟨tus zapatos son iguales a los míos : your shoes are just like mine⟩
miope *adj* : nearsighted, myopic
miopía *nf* : myopia, nearsightedness
mira *nf* 1 : sight (of a firearm or instrument) 2 : aim, objective ⟨con miras a : with the intention of, with a view to⟩ ⟨de amplias miras : broad-minded⟩ ⟨poner la mira en : to aim at, to aspire to⟩

mirada *nf* 1 : look, glance, gaze ⟨apartar la mirada : to look away⟩ ⟨dirigir/lanzar la mirada a : to glance at⟩ ⟨hay miradas que matan : if looks could kill⟩ 2 EXPRESIÓN : look, expression ⟨una mirada de sorpresa : a look of surprise⟩
mirado, -da *adj* 1 : cautious, careful 2 : considerate 3 **bien mirado** : well thought of 4 **mal mirado** : disliked, disapproved of
mirador *nm* : balcony, lookout, vantage point
miramiento *nm* 1 CONSIDERACIÓN : consideration, respect 2 **sin miramientos** : without due consideration, carelessly
mirar *vt* 1 : to look at ⟨miró el reloj : she looked at her watch⟩ ⟨mirar fijamente : to stare at⟩ ⟨mirar algo (muy) por encima : to glance something over⟩ ⟨la miré en los ojos : I looked her straight in the eye⟩ 2 OBSERVAR : to watch ⟨mirar televisión : to watch television⟩ 3 REFLEXIONAR : to consider, to think over ⟨míralo desde su punto de vista : look at it from her point of view⟩ 4 (*used for emphasis*) ⟨¡mira que eres lista! : you're so clever!⟩ ⟨mire que no soy experto, pero . . . : I'm no expert, but . . .⟩ ⟨¡mira qué gracia! : how funny!⟩ — *vi* 1 : to look ⟨miraba por la ventana : I was looking out the window⟩ ⟨mira bien y lo verás : look carefully and you'll see it⟩ ⟨¡mira! ahí está : look! there he is⟩ ⟨mira, a mí no me importa : look, it doesn't matter to me⟩ 2 ~ a : to face, to overlook 3 ~ por : to look after, to look out for — **mirarse** *vr* 1 : to look at oneself 2 : to look at each other
mirasol *nm* GIRASOL : sunflower
miríada *nf* : myriad
mirlo *nm* : blackbird
mirón, rona *n, mpl* **-rones** 1 : gawker, onlooker 2 : voyeur
mirra *nf* : myrrh
mirto *nm* ARRAYÁN : myrtle
misa *nf* : Mass
misantropía *nf* : misanthropy
misantrópico, -ca *adj* : misanthropic
misántropo, -pa *n* : misanthrope
miscelánea *nf* : miscellany
misceláneo, -nea *adj* : miscellaneous
miserable *adj* 1 LASTIMOSO : miserable, wretched 2 : paltry, meager 3 MEZQUINO : stingy, miserly 4 : despicable, vile
miserablemente *adv* 1 : miserably, wretchedly 2 : shamefully, disgracefully
miseria *nf* 1 POBREZA : poverty 2 : misery, suffering 3 : pittance, meager amount
misericordia *nf* COMPASIÓN : mercy, compassion
misericordioso, -sa *adj* : merciful
mísero, -ra *adj* 1 : wretched, miserable 2 : stingy 3 : paltry, meager
misil *nm* : missile
misión *nf, pl* **misiones** : mission
misionero, -ra *adj & n* : missionary
misiva *nf* : missive, letter

mismísimo, -ma *adj* (*used as an intensifier*) : very, selfsame ⟨el mismísimo día : that very same day⟩
mismo[1] *adv* (*used as an intensifier*) : right, exactly ⟨hazlo ahora mismo : do it right now⟩ ⟨te llamará hoy mismo : he'll definitely call you today⟩
mismo[2], -ma *adj* 1 : same ⟨la misma historia de siempre : the same old story⟩ ⟨ya no es el mismo de antes : he's not the same as he was before⟩ 2 (*used as an intensifier*) : very ⟨en ese mismo momento : at that very moment⟩ 3 : oneself ⟨lo hizo ella misma : she made it herself⟩ 4 por lo mismo : for that reason
misoginia *nf* : misogyny
misógino *nm* : misogynist
miss *nf* : miss ⟨Miss Universo : Miss Universe⟩
misterio *nm* : mystery
misterioso, -sa *adj* : mysterious — **misteriosamente** *adv*
misticismo *nm* : mysticism
místico[1], -ca *adj* : mystic, mystical
místico[2], *n* : mystic
mitad *nf* 1 : half ⟨mitad y mitad : half and half⟩ 2 MEDIO : middle ⟨a mitad de : halfway through⟩ ⟨por la mitad : in half⟩
mítico, -ca *adj* : mythical, mythic
mitigar {52} *vt* ALIVIAR : to mitigate, to alleviate — **mitigación** *nf*
mitin *nm, pl* mítines : (political) meeting, rally
mito *nm* LEYENDA : myth, legend
mitología *nf* : mythology
mitológico, -ca *adj* : mythological
mitosis *nfs & pl* : mitosis
mitra *nf* : miter (bishop's hat)
mixto, -ta *adj* 1 : mixed, joint 2 : coeducational
mixtura *nf* : mixture, blend
mnemónico, -ca *adj* : mnemonic
mobiliario *nm* : furniture
mocasín *nm, pl* -sines : moccasin
mocedad *nf* 1 JUVENTUD : youth 2 : youthful prank
mochila *nf* MORRAL : backpack, knapsack
moción *nf, pl* -ciones 1 MOVIMIENTO : motion, movement 2 : motion (to a court or assembly)
moco *nm* 1 : mucus 2 *fam* : snot ⟨limpiarse los mocos : to wipe one's (runny) nose⟩
mocoso, -sa *n* : kid, brat
moda *nf* 1 : fashion, style 2 a la moda *or* de ~ : in style, fashionable 3 moda pasajera : fad
modales *nmpl* : manners
modalidad *nf* 1 CLASE : kind, type 2 MANERA : way, manner
modelaje *nm* (*in various countries*) : modeling
modelar *vt* : to model, to mold — **modelarse** *vr* : to model oneself after, to emulate
modelo[1] *adj* : model ⟨una casa modelo : a model home⟩
modelo[2] *nm* : model, example, pattern

modelo[3] *nmf* : model, mannequin
módem *or* modem ['moðɛm] *nm* : modem
moderación *nf, pl* -ciones MESURA : moderation
moderado, -da *adj & n* : moderate — **moderadamente** *adv*
moderador, -dora *n* : moderator, chair
moderar *vt* 1 TEMPERAR : to temper, to moderate 2 : to curb, to reduce ⟨moderar gastos : to curb spending⟩ 3 PRESIDIR : to chair (a meeting) — **moderarse** *vr* 1 : to restrain oneself 2 : to diminish, to calm down
modernidad *nf* 1 : modernity 2 : modern age
modernismo *nm* : modernism
modernista[1] *adj* : modernist
modernista[2] *nmf* : modernist
modernizar {21} *vt* : to modernize — **modernización** *nf*
moderno, -na *adj* : modern, up-to-date
modestia *nf* : modesty
modesto, -ta *adj* : modest — **modestamente** *adv*
módico, -ca *adj* : modest, reasonable
modificación *nf, pl* -ciones : alteration
modificador[1], -dora *adj* : modifying, moderating
modificador[2] → modificante
modificante *nm* : modifier
modificar {72} *vt* ALTERAR : to modify, to alter, to adapt
modismo *nm* : idiom
modista *nmf* 1 : dressmaker 2 : fashion designer
modisto *nm* : fashion designer
modo *nm* 1 MANERA : way, manner, mode ⟨de un modo u otro : one way or another⟩ ⟨a mi modo de ver : to my way of thinking⟩ ⟨modo de vida : way of life⟩ 2 : mood (in grammar) 3 : mode (in music) 4 a modo de : by way of, in the manner of, like ⟨a modo de ejemplo : by way of example⟩ 5 de este/ese modo : in this/that way 6 de cualquier modo : in any case, anyway 7 de modo que : so, in such a way that 8 de ningún modo : (in) no way 9 de todos modos : in any case, anyway 10 en cierto modo : in a way, to a certain extent
modorra *nf* : drowsiness, lethargy
modular[1] *v* : to modulate — **modulación** *nf*
modular[2] *adj* : modular
módulo *nm* : module, unit
mofa *nf* 1 : mockery, ridicule 2 hacer mofa de : to make fun of, to ridicule
mofarse *vr* ~ de : to scoff at, to make fun of
mofeta *nf* ZORRILLO : skunk
mofle *nm* CA, Mex : muffler (of a car)
moflete *nm fam* : fat cheek
mofletudo, -da *adj fam* : chubby-cheeked, chubby
mohín *nm, pl* mohines : grimace, face
mohíno, -na *adj* : gloomy, melancholy
moho *nm* 1 : mold, mildew 2 : rust
mohoso, -sa *adj* 1 : moldy 2 : rusty

moisés *nm, pl* **moiseses** : bassinet, cradle

mojado¹, -da *adj* : wet

mojado², -da *n Mex fam* : illegal immigrant

mojar *vt* **1** : to wet, to moisten **2** : to dunk — **mojarse** *vr* : to get wet

mojigatería *nf* **1** : hypocrisy **2** GAZMOÑERÍA : primness, prudery

mojigato¹, -ta *adj* : prudish, prim — **mojigatamente** *adv*

mojigato², -ta *n* : prude, prig

mojón *nm, pl* **mojones** : boundary stone, marker

molar *nm* MUELA : molar

molcajete *nm Mex* : mortar

molde *nm* **1** : mold, form **2 letra(s) de molde** → **letra**

moldear *vt* **1** FORMAR : to mold, to shape **2** : to cast

moldura *nf* : molding

mole¹ *nm Mex* **1** : spicy sauce made with chilies and usually chocolate **2** : meat served with mole sauce

mole² *nf* : mass, bulk

molécula *nf* : molecule — **molecular** *adj*

moler {47} *vt* **1** : to grind, to crush **2** CANSAR : to exhaust, to wear out

molestar *vt* **1** FASTIDIAR : to annoy, to bother ⟨no me molesta : it doesn't bother me, I don't mind⟩ **2** : to disturb, to disrupt — *vi* : to be a nuisance — **molestarse** *vr* **1** : to get annoyed, to be offended **2 — en** : to take the trouble to

molestia *nf* **1** FASTIDIO : annoyance, bother, nuisance **2** : trouble ⟨se tomó la molestia de investigar : she took the trouble to investigate⟩ **3** MALESTAR : discomfort

molesto, -ta *adj* **1** ENOJADO : bothered, annoyed **2** FASTIDIOSO : bothersome, annoying

molestoso, -sa *adj* : bothersome, annoying

molido, -da *adj* **1** MACHACADO : ground, crushed **2 estar molido** : to be exhausted

molienda *nf* : milling, grinding

molinero, -ra *n* : miller

molinillo *nm* : grinder, mill ⟨molinillo de café : coffee grinder⟩

molino *nm* **1** : mill **2 molino de viento** : windmill

molla *nf* : soft fleshy part, flesh (of fruit), lean part (of meat)

molleja *nf* : gizzard

molusco *nm* : mollusk

momentáneamente *adv* : momentarily

momentáneo, -nea *adj* **1** : momentary **2** TEMPORARIO : temporary

momento *nm* **1** : moment, instant ⟨espera un momentito : wait just a moment⟩ **2** : time, period of time ⟨momentos difíciles : hard times⟩ **3** : time, moment (in time) ⟨en este momento : right now, at the moment⟩ ⟨llegar en mal momento : to come at a bad time⟩ ⟨momento decisivo : turning point, critical time⟩ **4** : present, moment ⟨los atletas del momento : the athletes of the moment, today's popular athletes⟩ **5** : momentum **6 a cada momento** : constantly **7 al momento** : right away, at once **8 de ~** : at the moment, for the moment **9 de un momento a otro** : any time now **10 en algún momento** : at some point, sometime **11 en cualquier momento** : at any time **12 en ningún momento** : never, at no time **13 en todo momento** : at all times **14 en un primer momento** : at first, initially **15 por el momento** : for the time being **16 por ~s** : at times

momia *nf* : mummy

monada *nf* **1** : attractive person **2** : cute or pretty thing

monaguillo *nm* ACÓLITO : altar boy

monarca *nmf* : monarch

monarquía *nf* : monarchy

monárquico, -ca *n* : monarchist

monasterio *nm* : monastery

monástico, -ca *adj* : monastic

monda *nf* **1** : peel **2 ser la monda** *Spain fam* : to be hilarious

mondadientes *nms & pl* PALILLO : toothpick

mondar *vt* : to peel

mondongo *nm* ENTRAÑAS : innards *pl*, insides *pl*, guts *pl*

moneda *nf* **1** : coin **2** : money, currency

monedero *nm* : change purse

monetario, -ria *adj* : monetary, financial

mongol, -gola *adj & n* : Mongol, Mongolian

monigote *nm* **1** : rag doll **2** : paper doll

monitor¹, -tora *n* : instructor (in sports)

monitor² *nm* : monitor ⟨monitor de televisión : television monitor⟩

monitorear *vt* : to monitor

monja *nf* : nun

monje *nm* : monk

mono¹, -na *adj fam* : lovely, pretty, cute, darling

mono², -na *n* : monkey

monóculo *nm* : monocle

monogamia *nf* : monogamy

monógamo, -ma *adj* : monogamous

monografía *nf* : monograph

monograma *nm* : monogram

monolingüe *adj* : monolingual

monolítico, -ca *adj* : monolithic

monolito *nm* : monolith

monólogo *nm* : monologue

monomanía *nf* : obsession

monopatín *nm, pl* **-tines** **1** : scooter **2** : skateboard

monopatinaje *nm* : skateboarding

monopolio *nm* : monopoly

monopolizar {21} *vt* : to monopolize — **monopolización** *nf*

monosilábico, -ca *adj* : monosyllabic

monosílabo *nm* : monosyllable

monoteísmo *nm* : monotheism

monoteísta¹ *adj* : monotheistic

monoteísta² *nmf* : monotheist

monotonía *nf* **1** : monotony **2** : monotone

monótono, -na *adj* : monotonous — **monótonamente** *adv*

monóxido *nm* **monóxido de carbono** : carbon monoxide

monovolumen *nm, pl* **-lúmenes** *Spain* : minivan

monseñor *nm* : monsignor

monserga *nf* : gibberish, drivel

monstruo *nm* : monster

monstruosidad *nf* : monstrosity

monstruoso, -sa *adj* : monstrous — **monstruosamente** *adv*

monta *nf* **1** : sum, total **2** : importance, value ⟨de poca monta : unimportant, insignificant⟩

montacargas *nms & pl* : freight elevator

montaje *nm* **1** : assembling, assembly **2** : montage

montante *nm* : transom, fanlight

montaña *nf* **1** MONTE : mountain **2** **montaña rusa** : roller coaster

montañero, -ra *n* : mountaineer, mountain climber

montañismo *nm* : mountaineering, (mountain) climbing

montañoso, -sa *adj* : mountainous

montar *vt* **1** : to mount, to get on **2** : to ride (a horse, a bicycle, etc.) **3** ESTABLECER : to set up, to establish **4** ARMAR : to assemble, to put together, to set up **5** : to set, to mount (gems, etc.) **6** : to edit (a film) **7** : to stage, to put on (a show) **8** : to cock (a gun) **9** : to mount (of a male animal) — *vi* **1** : to get on (a bus, etc), to get in (a car, a truck), to mount (a horse) **2 montar en bicicleta** : to ride a bicycle **3 montar a caballo** CABALGAR : to ride horseback — **montarse** *vr* **1** : to get on, to mount ⟨se montó en el avión : she got on the plane⟩ ⟨volvió a montarse : he got back on again⟩

monte *nm* **1** MONTAÑA : mountain, mount **2** : woodland ⟨monte bajo : underbrush⟩ **3** : outskirts (of a town), surrounding country **4 monte de piedad** : pawnshop

montés *adj, pl* **monteses** : wild (of animals or plants)

montículo *nm* **1** : mound, heap **2** : hillock, knoll

monto *nm* : amount, total

montón *nm, pl* **-tones 1** : heap, pile **2** *fam* : ton, load ⟨un montón de preguntas : a ton of questions⟩ ⟨montones de gente : loads of people⟩

montonero, -ra *n* : guerrilla

montura *nf* **1** : mount (horse) **2** : saddle, tack **3** : setting, mounting (of jewelry) **4** : frame (of glasses)

monumental *adj fam* **1** : tremendous, terrific **2** : massive, huge

monumento *nm* : monument

monzón *nm, pl* **monzones** : monsoon

moño *nm* **1** : bun (chignon) **2** LAZO : bow, knot ⟨corbata de moño : bow tie⟩

moquear *vi* : to snivel

moqueta *nf Spain* : wall-to-wall carpet

moquette *nf Arg, Uru* : wall-to-wall carpet

moquillo *nm* : distemper

mora *nf* **1** : blackberry **2** : mulberry

morada *nf* RESIDENCIA : dwelling, abode

morado¹, -da *adj* : purple

morado² *nm* : purple

morador, -dora *n* : dweller, inhabitant

moral¹ *adj* : moral — **moralmente** *adv*

moral² *nf* **1** MORALIDAD : ethics, morality, morals *pl* **2** ÁNIMO : morale, spirits *pl*

moraleja *nf* : moral (of a story)

moralidad *nf* : morality

moralista¹ *adj* : moralistic

moralista² *nmf* : moralist

morar *vi* : to dwell, to reside

moratón *nm, pl* **-tones** : bruise

moratoria *nf* : moratorium

mórbido, -da *adj* : morbid

morbo *nm* : morbid fascination

morboso, -sa *adj* : morbid — **morbosidad** *nf*

morcilla *nf* : blood sausage, blood pudding

mordacidad *nf* : bite, sharpness

mordaz *adj* : caustic, scathing

mordaza *nf* **1** : gag **2** : clamp

mordedura *nf* : bite (of an animal)

morder {47} *v* **1** : to bite — **morderse** *vr* : to bite ⟨morderse la lengua/las uñas : to bite one's tongue/nails⟩

mordida *nf* **1** : bite **2** *CA, Mex* : bribe, payoff

mordisco *nm* : bite, nibble

mordisquear *vt* : to nibble (on), to bite

morena *nf* **1** : moraine **2** : moray (eel)

moreno¹, -na *adj* **1** : brunette **2** : dark, dark-skinned

moreno², -na *n* **1** : brunette **2** : dark-skinned person

morera *nf* : mulberry

moretón *nm, pl* **-tones** : bruise

morfina *nf* : morphine

morfología *nf* : morphology

morgue *nf* : morgue

moribundo¹, -da *adj* : dying, moribund

moribundo², -da *n* : dying person

morillo *nm* : andiron

morir {46} *vi* **1** FALLECER : to die ⟨murió de cáncer : he died of cancer⟩ **2** APAGARSE : to die out, to go out — **morirse** *vr* **1** : to die **2** ~ **de** (*expressing an extreme state*) ⟨¡me muero de frío/hambre! : I'm freezing/starving!⟩ ⟨cuando lo vi casi me muero de vergüenza : when I saw it I nearly died of embarrassment⟩ ⟨morirse de risa : to die laughing⟩ **3** ~ **por** : to be dying for (something), to be dying to (do something) ⟨se muere por jugar : she's dying to play⟩ ⟨se muere por ti : he's crazy about you⟩

mormón, -mona *adj & n, pl* **mormones** : Mormon

moro¹, -ra *adj* : Moorish

moro², -ra *n* **1** : Moor **2** : Muslim

morocho¹, -cha *adj* : dark-haired

morocho², -cha *n* : dark-haired person

morosidad *nf* **1** : delinquency (in payment) **2** : slowness

moroso, -sa *adj* **1** : delinquent, in arrears ⟨cuentas morosas : delinquent accounts⟩ **2** : slow, sluggish

morral *nm* MOCHILA : backpack, knapsack

morralla *nf* 1 : small fish 2 : trash, riffraff 3 *Mex* : small change

morriña *nf* : homesickness

morro *nm* HOCICO : snout

morsa *nf* : walrus

morse *nm* : Morse code

mortadela *nf* : mortadella

mortaja *nf* SUDARIO : shroud

mortal[1] *adj* 1 : mortal 2 FATAL : fatal, deadly — **mortalmente** *adv*

mortal[2] *nmf* : mortal

mortalidad *nf* : mortality

mortandad *nf* 1 : loss of life, death toll 2 : carnage, slaughter

mortero *nm* : mortar (bowl, cannon, or building material)

mortífero, -ra *adj* LETAL : deadly, fatal

mortificación *nf*, *pl* **-ciones** 1 : mortification 2 TORMENTO : anguish, torment

mortificar {72} *vt* 1 : to mortify 2 TORTURAR : to trouble, to torment — **mortificarse** *vr* : to be mortified, to feel embarrassed

mosaico *nm* : mosaic

mosca *nf* 1 : fly 2 **mosca común** : housefly

moscada *adj* **nuez moscada** : nutmeg

mosquearse *vr* 1 : to become suspicious 2 : to take offense

mosquete *nm* : musket

mosquetero *nm* : musketeer

mosquitero *nm* : mosquito net

mosquito *nm* ZANCUDO : mosquito

mostachón *nm*, *pl* **-chones** : macaroon

mostaza *nf* : mustard

mosto *nm* : must (from a grape)

mostrador *nm* : counter (in a store)

mostrar {19} *vt* 1 : to show 2 EXHIBIR : to exhibit, to display — **mostrarse** *vr* : to show oneself, to appear

mota *nf* 1 : fleck, speck 2 : defect, blemish

mote *nm* SOBRENOMBRE : nickname

moteado, -da *adj* : dotted, spotted, dappled

motel *nm* : motel

motín *nm*, *pl* **motines** 1 : riot 2 : rebellion, mutiny

motivación *nf*, *pl* **-ciones** : motivation — **motivacional** *adj*

motivar *vt* 1 CAUSAR : to cause 2 IMPULSAR : to motivate

motivo *nm* 1 MÓVIL : motive ⟨el motivo del crimen : the motive for the crime⟩ 2 CAUSA : cause, reason ⟨da motivos para el optimismo : it's cause for optimism⟩ 3 TEMA : theme, motif

moto *nf* : motorcycle, motorbike

motocicleta *nf* : motorcycle

motociclismo *nm* : motorcycling

motociclista *nmf* : motorcyclist

motoneta *nf* : scooter

motor[1], **-ra** *adj* MOTRIZ : motor

motor[2] *nm* 1 : motor, engine 2 : driving force, cause

motora *nf* : motorboat

motorismo *nm* : motorcycle riding, motorcycling

motorista *nmf* : motorist

motorizado, -da *adj* : motorized

motriz *adj*, *pl* **motrices** : driving

motu proprio *adv* **de motu proprio** [de'motu'proprio] : voluntarily, of one's own accord

mousse ['mus] *nmf* : mousse

movedizo, -za *adj* 1 : movable 2 : moving 3 : restless

mover {47} *vt* 1 TRASLADAR : to move, to shift 2 AGITAR : to shake, to move ⟨mover la cabeza (diciendo que sí) : to nod⟩ ⟨mover la cabeza (diciendo que no) : to shake one's head⟩ 3 ACCIONAR : to power, to drive 4 ~ a : to cause to (do something) ⟨me movió a pensar : it made me think⟩ ⟨lo movió a escribir : it inspired him to write⟩ — **moverse** *vr* 1 : to move 2 : to hurry, to get a move on 3 : to get moving, to make an effort

movible *adj* : movable

movida *nf* : move (in a game)

móvil[1] *adj* : mobile

móvil[2] *nm* 1 MOTIVO : motive 2 : mobile

movilidad *nf* : mobility

movilizar {21} *vt* : to mobilize — **movilización** *nf*

movimiento *nm* : movement, motion ⟨movimiento del cuerpo : bodily movement⟩ ⟨movimiento sindicalista : labor movement⟩

mozo[1], **-za** *adj* : young, youthful

mozo[2], **-za** *n* 1 JOVEN : young man *m*, young woman *f*, youth 2 : helper, servant 3 *Arg, Chile, Col, Peru* : waiter *m*, waitress *f*

MP3 *nm*, *pl* **MP3** : MP3

mucamo, -ma *n* : servant, maid *f*

muchacha *nf* : maid

muchacho, -cha *n* 1 : kid, boy *m*, girl *f* 2 JOVEN : young man *m*, young woman *f*

muchedumbre *nf* MULTITUD : crowd multitude

mucho[1] *adv* : (very) much, a lot ⟨mucho más fácil/rápido/grande : much easier, faster/bigger⟩ ⟨mucho más tarde : much later⟩ ⟨te quiero mucho : I love you very much⟩ ⟨lo siento mucho : I'm very sorry⟩ ⟨le gusta mucho : he likes it a lot⟩ ⟨¿viajas mucho? : do you travel a lot?⟩ ⟨no habla mucho : she doesn't talk (very) much⟩

mucho[2], **-cha** *adj* 1 : a lot of, many, much ⟨mucha gente : a lot of people, many people⟩ ⟨mucho dinero : a lot of money⟩ ⟨¡muchas gracias! : thank you very much!⟩ ⟨no tengo mucha hambre : I'm not very hungry⟩ ⟨hace mucho tiempo que no lo veo : I haven't seen him in ages⟩ 2 **muchas veces** : often

mucho[3], **-cha** *pron* 1 : a lot, many, much ⟨hay mucho que hacer : there is a lot to do⟩ ⟨muchos no vinieron : many didn't come⟩ 2 **mucho** : long, a long time ⟨tardó mucho en venir : he was a long time getting here⟩ ⟨¿te falta mucho? : will you be much longer?⟩ ⟨hace mucho que no te veo : it's been a long time since I've seen you⟩ 3 **cuando/como** ~ : at most 4 **con** ~ : by far 5 **ni mucho menos** : not at all, far from it 6 **por mucho que** : no matter how much, (as much as ⟨por mucho que quiera no puedo : as much as I would like to, I can't⟩

nucílago *nm* : mucilage

nucosidad *nf* : mucus

nucoso, -sa *adj* : mucous, slimy

nuda *nf* **1** : change ⟨muda de ropa : change of clothes⟩ **2** : molt, molting

mudanza *nf* **1** CAMBIO : change **2** TRAS-LADO : move, moving

mudar *v* **1** CAMBIAR : to change **2** : to molt, to shed — **mudarse** *vr* **1** TRASLA-DARSE : to move (one's residence) **2** : to change (clothes)

mudo[1], **-da** *adj* **1** SILENCIOSO : silent ⟨el cine mudo : silent films⟩ **2** : mute, dumb

mudo[2], **-da** *n* : mute *sometimes offensive*

mueble *nm* **1** : piece of furniture **2 mue-bles** *nmpl* : furniture, furnishings

mueblería *nf* : furniture store

mueca *nf* : grimace, face

muela *nf* **1** : tooth, molar ⟨dolor de mue-las : toothache⟩ ⟨muela de juicio : wis-dom tooth⟩ **2** : millstone **3** : whetstone

muele, etc. → **moler**

muelle[1] *adj* : soft, comfortable, easy

muelle[2] *nm* **1** : wharf, dock **2** RESORTE : spring

muérdago *nm* : mistletoe

muerde, etc. → **morder**

muere, etc. → **morir**

muerte *nf* : death ⟨amenaza de muerte : death threat⟩ ⟨dar un susto de muerte : to scare half to death⟩ ⟨morir de muerte natural : to die of natural causes⟩

muerto[1] *pp* → **morir**

muerto[2], **-ta** *adj* **1** : dead ⟨caer muerto : to die, to drop dead⟩ **2** : lifeless, flat, dull **3 ~ de** : dying of ⟨estoy muerto de hambre : I'm dying of hunger⟩ ⟨muerto de miedo : scared to death⟩

muerto[3], **-ta** *nm* DIFUNTO : dead person, deceased

muesca *nf* : nick, notch

muestra[1], **etc.** → **mostrar**

muestra[2] *nf* **1** : sample **2** SEÑAL : sign, show ⟨una muestra de respeto : a show of respect⟩ **3** EXPOSICIÓN : exhibition, exposition **4** : pattern, model

muestreo *nm* : sample

mueve, etc. → **mover**

mugido *nm* : moo, lowing, bellow

mugir {35} *vi* : to moo, to low, to bellow

mugre *nf* SUCIEDAD : grime, filth

mugriento, -ta *adj* : filthy

muguete *nm* : lily of the valley

muja, etc. → **mugir**

mujer *nf* **1** : woman **2** ESPOSA : wife

mújol *nm* : mullet (fish)

mulato, -ta *adj & n* : mulatto

muleta *nf* : crutch

muletilla *nf* : favorite word or phrase

mullido, -da *adj* **1** : soft, fluffy **2** : spongy, springy

mulo, -la *n* : mule

multa *nf* : fine

multar *vt* : to fine

multi- *pref* : multi-

multicine *nm* : multiplex

multicolor *adj* : multicolored

multicultural *adj* : multicultural

multidisciplinario, -ria *adj* : multidisci-plinary

multifacético, -ca *adj* : multifaceted

multifamiliar *adj* : multifamily

multilateral *adj* : multilateral

multimedia *nf* : multimedia

multimillonario, -ria *n* : multimillionaire

multinacional *adj* : multinational

múltiple *adj* : multiple

multiplicación *nf, pl* **-ciones** : multiplica-tion

multiplicar {72} *v* **1** : to multiply **2** : to increase — **multiplicarse** *vr* **1** : to mul-tiply, to reproduce **2** : to increase, to multiply ⟨multiplicarse por cinco : to increase fivefold⟩

multiplicidad *nf* : multiplicity

múltiplo *nm* : multiple

multipropiedad *nf* : time share

multitud *nf* MUCHEDUMBRE : crowd, mul-titude

multitudinario, -ria *adj* : well-attended ⟨manifestaciones multitudinarias : mass protests⟩ ⟨un concierto multitudinario : a concert with a huge turnout⟩

multiuso, -sa *adj* : multipurpose

multivitamínico, -ca *adj* : multivitamin

mundano, -na *adj* : worldly, earthly

mundial *adj* : worldwide

mundialmente *adv* : worldwide, all over the world

mundo *nm* **1** : world ⟨alrededor del mundo : around the world⟩ ⟨el mundo entero : the whole world⟩ ⟨el mundo ac-tual : today's world⟩ ⟨el Tercer Mundo : the Third World⟩ ⟨el mundo de la moda : the world of fashion⟩ **2** VIDA : world, life ⟨su mundo se derrumbó : his world fell apart⟩ **3** PLANETA : world, planet **4 del mundo** : in the world ⟨el mejor del mundo : the best in the world⟩ ⟨por nada del mundo : not for anything in the world⟩ ⟨tener todo el tiempo del mundo : to have all the time in the world⟩ **5 el otro mundo** : the afterlife, the hereafter ⟨no es nada del otro mundo : it's nothing special⟩ **6 en su mundo** *fam* : in one's own world, in a world of one's own **7 por/en/de todo el mundo** : the (whole) world over **8 todo el mundo** : everyone, everybody

municiones *nfpl* : ammunition, munitions

municipal *adj* : municipal

municipio *nm* **1** : municipality **2** AYUNTAMIENTO : town council

muñeca *nf* **1** : doll ⟨muñeca de trapo : rag doll⟩ **2** MANIQUÍ : mannequin **3** : wrist

muñeco *nm* **1** : doll, boy doll **2** MARIO-NETA : puppet

muñequera *nf* : wristband

muñón *nm, pl* **muñones** : stump (of an arm or leg)

mural *adj & nm* : mural

muralla *nf* : rampart, wall

murciélago *nm* : bat (animal)

murga *nf* : band of street musicians

murió, etc. → **morir**

murmullo *nm* **1** : murmur, murmuring **2** : rustling, rustle ⟨el murmullo de las hojas : the rustling of the leaves⟩

murmuraciones *nfpl* : gossip

murmurar *vt* **1** : to murmur, to mutter **2** : to whisper (gossip) — *vi* **1** : to murmur **2** CHISMEAR : to gossip

muro *nm* : wall

musa *nf* : muse

musaraña *nf* : shrew

muscular *adj* : muscular

musculatura *nf* : muscles *pl*, musculature

músculo *nm* : muscle

musculoso, -sa *adj* : muscular, brawny

muselina *nf* : muslin

museo *nm* : museum

musgo *nm* : moss

musgoso, -sa *adj* : mossy

música *nf* : music

musical *adj* : musical — **musicalmente** *adv*

músico¹, -ca *adj* : musical

músico², -ca *n* : musician

musitar *vt* : to mumble, to murmur

muslo *nm* : thigh

mustio, -tia *adj* : withered (of a plant)

musulmán, -mana *adj & n, mpl* **-manes** : Muslim

mutación *nf, pl* **-ciones** : mutation

mutante *adj & nm* : mutant

mutar *v* : to mutate

mutilar *vt* : to mutilate — **mutilación** *nf*

mutis *nm* **1** : exit (in theater) **2** : silence

mutismo *nm* : silence

mutual *adj* : mutual

mutuo, -tua *adj* : mutual, reciprocal — **mutuamente** *adv*

muy *adv* **1** : very, quite ⟨es muy inteligente : she's very intelligent⟩ ⟨muy bien : very well, fine⟩ ⟨eso es muy americano : that's typically American⟩ ⟨muy poca comida : very little food⟩ **2** : too ⟨es muy grande para él : it's too big for him⟩

N

n *nf* : sixteenth letter of the Spanish alphabet

nabo *nm* : turnip

nácar *nm* MADREPERLA : mother-of-pearl

nacarado, -da *adj* : pearly

nacer {48} *vi* **1** : to be born ⟨nací en Guatemala : I was born in Guatemala⟩ ⟨no nació ayer : he wasn't born yesterday⟩ **2** : to hatch **3** : to bud, to sprout **4** : to rise, to originate **5** **nacer para algo** : to be born to be something **6** **volver a nacer** : to have a lucky escape

nacido¹, -da *adj* **1** : born **2** **recién nacido** : newborn

nacido², -da *n* **1 los nacidos** : those born (at a particular time) **2 recién nacido** : newborn baby

naciente *adj* **1** : newfound, growing **2** : rising ⟨el sol naciente : the rising sun⟩

nacimiento *nm* **1** : birth **2** : source (of a river) **3** : beginning, origin **4** BELÉN : Nativity scene, cr⟨egrave⟩che

nación *nf, pl* **naciones** : nation, country, people (of a country)

nacional¹ *adj* : national

nacional² *nmf* CIUDADANO : national, citizen

nacionalidad *nf* : nationality

nacionalismo *nm* : nationalism

nacionalista¹ *adj* : nationalist, nationalistic

nacionalista² *nmf* : nationalist

nacionalización *nf, pl* **-ciones** **1** : nationalization **2** : naturalization

nacionalizar {21} *vt* **1** : to nationalize **2** : to naturalize (as a citizen) — **nacionalizarse** *vr*

naco, -ca *adj Mex* : trashy, vulgar, common

nada¹ *adv* : not at all, not in the least ⟨no estamos nada cansados : we are not at all tired⟩ ⟨no me importa nada : it doesn't matter at all to me⟩

nada² *nf* **1** : nothingness **2** : smidgen, bit ⟨una nada le disgusta : the slightest thing upsets him⟩

nada³ *pron* **1** : nothing ⟨no estoy haciendo nada : I'm not doing anything⟩ ⟨es mejor que nada : it's better than nothing⟩ ⟨empecé sin nada : I started out with nothing⟩ ⟨no tengo nada que decir : I have nothing to say⟩ ⟨no tiene nada de extraño : there's nothing strange about it⟩ ⟨esta pluma no sirve para nada : this pen is useless⟩ ⟨no me interesa para nada : it doesn't interest me at all⟩ ⟨no es nada comparado con . . . : it's nothing compared to . . .⟩ ⟨no hay nada como la comida casera : there's nothing like home cooking⟩ **2 antes que nada** : first of all (in order), above all (in importance) **3 casi nada** : next to nothing **4 de ~** : you're welcome **5 dentro de nada** : very soon, in no time **6 nada de eso** : nothing of the kind, nothing like that **7 nada más** : nothing else, nothing more **8 nada más** : as soon as, no sooner . . . than ⟨nada más comenzar el partido, marcó : as soon as the game started, he scored; no sooner did the game start than he scored⟩ **9 pues nada** *fam* : anyway

nadador, -dora *n* : swimmer

nadar *vi* **1** : to swim **2 ~ en** : to be swimming in, to be rolling in — *vt* : to swim

nadería *nf* : small thing, trifle

nadie *pron* : nobody, no one ⟨no vi a nadie : I didn't see anyone⟩

nadir *nm* : nadir

nado *nm* **1** *Mex* : swimming **2 a ~** : swimming ⟨cruzó el río a nado : he swam across the river⟩

nafta *nf* **1** : naphtha **2** (*in various countries*) : gasoline
naftalina *nf* : mothballs *pl*
náhuatl[1] *adj & nmf, pl* **nahuas** : Nahuatl
náhuatl[2] *nm* : Nahuatl (language)
nailon → **nilón**
naipe *nm* : playing card
nalga *nf* **1** : buttock **2 nalgas** *nfpl* : buttocks, bottom
nalgada *nf* : smack on the bottom, spanking
namibio, -bia *adj & n* : Namibian
nana *nf* **1** : lullaby **2** *fam* : grandma **3** *CA, Col, Mex, Ven* : nanny
nanay *interj fam* : no way!, not likely!
naranja[1] *adj & nm* : orange (color)
naranja[2] *nf* : orange (fruit)
naranjada *nf* : orangeade
naranjal *nm* : orange grove
naranjo *nm* : orange tree
narcisismo *nm* : narcissism
narcisista[1] *adj* : narcissistic
narcisista[2] *nmf* : narcissist
narciso *nm* : narcissus, daffodil
narco *nmf fam* → **narcotraficante**
narcótico[1], **-ca** *adj* : narcotic
narcótico[2] *nm* : narcotic
narcotizar {21} *vt* : to drug, to dope
narcotraficante *nmf* : drug trafficker
narcotráfico *nm* : drug trafficking
narigón, -gona *adj, mpl* **-gones** : big-nosed
narigudo → **narigón**
nariz *nf, pl* **narices 1** : nose ⟨sonar(se) la nariz : to blow one's nose⟩ **2** : sense of smell
narración *nf, pl* **-ciones** : narration, account
narrador, -dora *n* : narrator
narrar *vt* : to narrate, to tell
narrativa *nf* : narrative, story
narrativo, -va *adj* : narrative
nasa *nf* : creel
nasal *adj* : nasal
nata *nf* **1** *Spain* : cream ⟨nata montada : whipped cream⟩ **2** : skin (on boiled milk)
natación *nf, pl* **-ciones** : swimming
natal *adj* : native, natal
natalicio *nm* : birthday ⟨el natalicio de George Washington : George Washington's birthday⟩
natalidad *nf* : birthrate
natillas *nfpl* : custard
natividad *nf* : birth, nativity
nativo, -va *adj & n* : native
nativo americano, nativa americana *adj & n* : Native American
nato, -ta *adj* : born, natural
natural[1] *adj* **1** : natural ⟨como es natural : naturally, as expected⟩ **3 ~ de** : native of, from **4 de tamaño natural** : life-size
natural[2] *nm* **1** CARÁCTER : disposition, temperament **2** : native ⟨un natural de Venezuela : a native of Venezuela⟩
naturaleza *nf* **1** : nature ⟨la madre naturaleza : mother nature⟩ **2** ÍNDOLE : nature, disposition, constitution ⟨la naturaleza humana : human nature⟩ **3 naturaleza muerta** : still life

naturalidad *nf* : simplicity, naturalness
naturalismo *nm* : naturalism
naturalista[1] *adj* : naturalistic
naturalista[2] *nmf* : naturalist
naturalización *nf, pl* **-ciones** : naturalization
naturalizar {21} *vt* : to naturalize — **naturalizarse** *vr* NACIONALIZARSE : to become naturalized
naturalmente *adv* **1** : naturally, inherently **2** : of course
naufragar {52} *vi* **1** : to be shipwrecked **2** FRACASAR : to fail, to collapse
naufragio *nm* **1** : shipwreck **2** FRACASO : failure, collapse
náufrago[1], **-ga** *adj* : shipwrecked, castaway
náufrago[2], **-ga** *n* : shipwrecked person, castaway
náusea *nf* **1** : nausea **2 dar náuseas** : to nauseate, to disgust **3 náuseas matutinas** : morning sickness
nauseabundo, -da *adj* : nauseating, sickening
náutica *nf* : navigation
náutico, -ca *adj* : nautical
nautilo *nm* : nautilus
navaja *nf* **1** : pocketknife, penknife ⟨navaja de muelle : switchblade⟩ **2 navaja de afeitar** : straight razor
navajazo *nm* : knife wound
navajo, -ja *adj & n* : Navajo
naval *adj* : naval
nave *nf* **1** : ship ⟨nave capitana : flagship⟩ ⟨nave espacial : spaceship⟩ **2** : nave ⟨nave lateral : aisle⟩ **3 quemar uno sus naves** : to burn one's bridges
navegabilidad *nf* : navigability
navegable *adj* : navigable
navegación *nf, pl* **-ciones** : navigation
navegador *nm* : browser ⟨navegador web : web browser⟩
navegante[1] *adj* : sailing, seafaring
navegante[2] *nmf* : navigator
navegar {52} *v* : to navigate, to sail
Navidad *nf* : Christmas ⟨Feliz Navidad : Merry Christmas⟩
navideño, -ña *adj* : Christmas
naviero, -ra *adj* : shipping
navío *nm* : (large) ship
nazca, etc. → **nacer**
nazi *adj & nmf* : Nazi
nazismo *nm* : Nazism
neandertal *or* **neanderthal** *nm* **1** Neandertal *or* Neanderthal *or* hombre de Neandertal/Neanderthal : Neanderthal (man) **2** *fam* : Neanderthal
nébeda *nf* : catnip
neblina *nf* : light fog, mist
neblinoso, -sa *adj* : misty, foggy
nebulosa *nf* : nebula
nebulosidad *nf* : mistiness, haziness
nebuloso, -sa *adj* **1** : hazy, misty **2** : nebulous, vague
necedad *nf* : stupidity, foolishness ⟨decir necedades : to talk nonsense⟩
necesariamente *adv* : necessarily
necesario, -ria *adj* **1** : necessary **2 si es necesario** : if need be **3 hacerse necesario** : to be required

neceser *nm* : toilet kit, vanity case

necesidad *nf* 1 : need, necessity ⟨por necesidad : out of necessity⟩ ⟨en caso de necesidad : if necessary, if need be⟩ 2 : poverty, want 3 **necesidades** *nfpl* : hardships 4 **hacer sus necesidades** : to relieve oneself

necesitado, -da *adj* : needy

necesitar *vt* 1 : to need 2 : to necessitate, to require — *vi* ~ **de** : to have need of

necio¹, -cia *adj* 1 : foolish, silly, dumb 2 *fam* : naughty 3 *Mex* : stubborn

necio², -cia *n* 1 ESTÚPIDO : fool, idiot 2 *Mex* : stubborn person

necrología *nf* : obituary

necrópolis *nfs & pl* : cemetery

néctar *nm* : nectar

nectarina *nf* : nectarine

neerlandés¹, -desa *adj, mpl* **-deses** HOLANDÉS : Dutch

neerlandés², -desa *n, mpl* **-deses** HOLANDÉS : Dutch person

nefando, -da *adj* : unspeakable, heinous

nefario, -ria *adj* : nefarious

nefasto, -ta *adj* 1 : ill-fated, unlucky 2 : disastrous, terrible

negación *nf, pl* **-ciones** 1 : negation, denial 2 : negative (in grammar)

negado, -da *adj* : useless

negar {49} *vt* 1 : to deny 2 REHUSAR : to refuse 3 : to disown — **negarse** *vr* 1 : to refuse 2 : to deny oneself

negativa *nf* 1 : denial 2 : refusal

negativo¹, -va *adj* : negative — **negativamente** *adv*

negativo² *nm* : negative (of a photograph)

negligé *nm* : negligee

negligencia *nf* : negligence

negligente *adj* : neglectful, negligent — **negligentemente** *adv*

negociable *adj* : negotiable

negociación *nf, pl* **-ciones** 1 : negotiation 2 **negociación colectiva** : collective bargaining

negociador, -dora *n* : negotiator

negociante *nmf* : businessman *m*, businesswoman *f*

negociar *vt* : to negotiate — *vi* : to deal, to do business

negocio *nm* 1 : business, place of business ⟨el mundo de los negocios : the business world⟩ 2 : deal, transaction 3 **negocios** *nmpl* : commerce, trade, business

negra *nf* : quarter note

negrero, -ra *n* 1 : slave trader 2 *fam* : slave driver, brutal boss

negrita *or* **negrilla** *nf* : boldface (type)

negro¹, -gra *adj* 1 : black, dark 2 BRONCEADO : suntanned 3 : gloomy, awful, desperate ⟨la cosa se está poniendo negra : things are looking bad⟩ 4 **mercado negro** : black market

negro², -gra *n* 1 : dark-skinned person, black person 2 *fam* : darling, dear

negro³ *nm* : black (color)

negrura *nf* : blackness

negruzco, -ca *adj* : blackish

nene, -na *n* : baby, small child

nenúfar *nm* : water lily

neocelandés → **neozelandés**

neófito, -ta *n* : neophyte, novice

neologismo *nm* : neologism

neón *nm, pl* **neones** : neon

neoyorquino¹, -na *adj* : of or from New York

neoyorquino², -na *n* : New Yorker

neozelandés¹, -desa *adj, mpl* **-deses** : of or from New Zealand

neozelandés², -desa *n, mpl* **-deses** : New Zealander

nepalés, -lesa *adj & n, mpl* **-leses** : Nepali

nepotismo *nm* : nepotism

Neptuno *nm* : Neptune

nervio *nm* 1 : nerve 2 : tendon, sinew, gristle (in meat) 3 : energy, drive 4 : rib (of a vault) 5 **nervios** *nmpl* : nerves ⟨estar mal de los nervios : to be a bag/bundle of nerves⟩ ⟨tener los nervios de punta : to be on edge, to have one's nerves on edge⟩ ⟨crisparle los nervios a alguien : to get on someone's nerves⟩ ⟨ataque de nervios : nervous breakdown⟩ ⟨una guerra de nervios : a war of nerves⟩ ⟨nervios de acero : nerves of steel⟩

nerviosamente *adv* : nervously

nerviosidad → **nerviosismo**

nerviosismo *nf* : nervousness, anxiety

nervioso, -sa *adj* 1 : nervous, nerve ⟨sistema nervioso : nervous system⟩ 2 : high-strung, restless, anxious ⟨ponerse nervioso : to get nervous⟩ 3 : vigorous, energetic

nervudo, -da *adj* : sinewy, wiry

neta *nf Mex fam* : truth ⟨la neta es que me cae mal : the truth is, I don't like her⟩

netamente *adv* : clearly, obviously

neto, -ta *adj* 1 : net ⟨peso neto : net weight⟩ 2 : clear, distinct

neumático¹, -ca *adj* : pneumatic

neumático² *nm* LLANTA : tire

neumonía *nf* PULMONÍA : pneumonia

neural *adj* : neural

neuralgia *nf* : neuralgia

neuritis *nf* : neuritis

neurología *nf* : neurology

neurológico, -ca *adj* : neurological, neurologic

neurólogo, -ga *n* : neurologist

neurosis *nfs & pl* : neurosis

neurótico, -ca *adj & n* : neurotic

neutral *adj* : neutral

neutralidad *nf* : neutrality

neutralizar {21} *vt* : to neutralize — **neutralización** *nf*

neutro, -tra *adj* 1 : neutral 2 : neuter

neutrón *nm, pl* **neutrones** : neutron

nevada *nf* : snowfall

nevado, -da *adj* 1 : snowcapped 2 : snow-white

nevar {55} *v impers* : to snow

nevasca *nf* : snowstorm, blizzard

nevera *nf* REFRIGERADOR : refrigerator

nevería *nf Mex* : ice cream parlor

nevisca *nf* : light snowfall, flurry

nevoso, -sa *adj* : snowy

nexo *nm* VÍNCULO : link, connection, nexus

ni *conj* **1** : neither, nor ⟨no es (ni) bueno ni malo : it's neither good nor bad⟩ ⟨ni hoy ni mañana : neither today nor tomorrow⟩ ⟨ni confirma ni niega las acusaciones : he neither confirms nor denies the allegations⟩ ⟨zonas sin agua ni electricidad : areas without water or power, areas with no water or power⟩ ⟨no pagó ni un centavo : he didn't pay a single cent⟩ ⟨él no lo cree, ni yo tampoco : he doesn't believe it, and neither do I⟩ ⟨no le beneficia a ella ni a nadie : it doesn't benefit her or anyone else⟩ **2 ni que** : not even if, not as if ⟨ni que me pagaran : not even if they paid me⟩ ⟨ni que fuera (yo) su madre : it's not as if I were his mother⟩ **3 ni siquiera** : not even ⟨ni siquiera nos llamaron : they didn't even call us⟩

nicaragüense *adj & nmf* : Nicaraguan

nicho *nm* : niche

nicotina *nf* : nicotine

nidada *nf* : brood (of chicks)

nido *nm* **1** : nest **2** : hiding place, den

niebla *nf* : fog, mist

niega, niegue etc. → **negar**

nieto, -ta *n* **1** : grandson *m*, granddaughter *f* **2 nietos** *nmpl* : grandchildren

nieva, etc. → **nevar**

nieve *nf* **1** : snow **2** *Cuba, Mex, PRi* : sherbet

nigeriano, -na *adj & n* : Nigerian

nigua *nf* : sand flea, chigger

nihilismo *nm* : nihilism

nilón *or* **nilon** *nm, pl* **nilones** : nylon

nimbo *nm* : halo

nimiedad *nf* INSIGNIFICANCIA : trifle, triviality

nimio, -mia *adj* INSIGNIFICANTE : insignificant, trivial

ninfa *nf* : nymph

ningunear *vt Mex fam* : to disrespect

ninguno¹, -na (*ningún before masculine singular nouns*) *adj, mpl* **ningunos** : no, none ⟨no es ninguna tonta : she's no fool⟩ ⟨no dieron ninguna razón : they gave no reason, they didn't give a reason⟩ ⟨no debe hacerse en ningún momento : that should never be done⟩ ⟨no tenemos ninguna idea : we have no idea⟩

ninguno², -na *pron* **1** : neither, none ⟨ninguno de los dos ha vuelto aún : neither one has returned yet⟩ ⟨ninguno de ellos : none of them⟩ **2** : no one, no other ⟨te quiero más que a ninguna : I love you more than any other⟩ ⟨ninguno me dice nada : nobody tells me anything⟩

niña *nf* **1** PUPILA : pupil (of the eye) **2 la niña de los ojos** : the apple of one's eye

niñada *nf* **1** : childishness **2** : trifle, silly thing

niñería → **niñada**

niñero, -ra *n* : baby-sitter, nanny

niñez *nf, pl* **niñeces** INFANCIA : childhood

niño, -ña *n* : child, boy *m*, girl *f* ⟨los niños : the children⟩ ⟨esperar un niño : to be pregnant, to be expecting a baby⟩

nipón, -pona *adj & n, mpl* **nipones** JAPONÉS : Japanese

níquel *nm* : nickel

nitidez *nf, pl* **-deces** CLARIDAD : clarity, vividness, sharpness

nítido, -da *adj* CLARO : clear, vivid, sharp

nitrato *nm* : nitrate

nítrico, -ca *adj* **ácido nítrico** → **ácido²**

nitrógeno *nm* : nitrogen

nitroglicerina *nf* : nitroglycerin

nivel *nm* **1** : level, height ⟨nivel del mar : sea level⟩ ⟨al nivel de : level with⟩ ⟨al nivel del suelo : at floor level⟩ **2** : level, standard ⟨nivel de vida : standard of living⟩ ⟨al mismo nivel que : on a level/par with⟩ ⟨de alto nivel : high-level⟩

nivelador, -dora *n* : leveler

nivelar *vt* : to level (off/out), to even (out) — **nivelarse** *vr*

nixtamal *nm Mex* : corn cooked with lime (used for tortillas)

no¹ *adv* **1** (*indicating a negative response*) : no ⟨¿quieres más? no, gracias : do you want more? no, thanks⟩ ⟨¿la conoces? no : do you know her? no⟩ **2** : no, not ⟨no sé : I don't know⟩ ⟨no tengo ni idea : I have no idea⟩ ⟨no hagas eso! : don't do that!⟩ ⟨no le gusta : she doesn't like it⟩ ⟨no es fácil : it's not easy⟩ ⟨creo que no : I don't think so⟩ ⟨no puedo ver nada : I can't see a thing, I can't see anything⟩ ⟨no hay nadie : there's no one there⟩ ⟨es interesante, ¿no? : it's interesting, isn't it?⟩ ⟨se casó! no! : he got married! no way!⟩ **3** : non- ⟨no fumador : nonsmoker⟩ **4 ¡cómo no!** : of course! **5 no bien** : as soon as, no sooner

no² *nm, pl* **noes** : no

noble¹ *adj* : noble — **noblemente** *adv*

noble² *nmf* : nobleman *m*, noblewoman *f*

nobleza *nf* **1** : nobility **2** HONRADEZ : honesty, integrity

nocaut *nm* : knockout, KO

noche *nf* **1** : night, nighttime, evening ⟨esta noche : tonight⟩ ⟨la noche anterior : the night before⟩ ⟨la noche del lunes : (on) Monday night⟩ ⟨todas las noches : every night⟩ ⟨a altas horas de la noche : late at night⟩ ⟨en medio/mitad de la noche : in the middle of the night⟩ ⟨las diez de la noche : ten (o'clock) at night⟩ ⟨al caer la noche : at nightfall⟩ ⟨pasar la noche : to spend the night⟩ **2 buenas noches** : good evening, good night **3 de noche** *or* **en/por/a la noche** : at night ⟨salir de noche : to go out at night⟩ ⟨era de noche : it was nighttime⟩ ⟨mañana en/por/a la noche : tomorrow night⟩ **4 de la noche a la mañana** : overnight, suddenly **5 hacerse de noche** : to get dark

Nochebuena *nf* : Christmas Eve

nochecita *nf* : dusk

Nochevieja *nf* : New Year's Eve

noción *nf, pl* **nociones 1** CONCEPTO : notion, concept **2 nociones** *nfpl* : smattering, rudiments *pl*

nocivo, -va *adj* DAÑINO : harmful, noxious

noctámbulo, -la *n* **1** : sleepwalker **2** : night owl

nocturno¹, -na *adj* : night, nocturnal

nocturno² *nm* : nocturne

nodriza *nf* : wet nurse

nódulo *nm* : nodule

nogal *nm* 1 : walnut tree 2 *Mex* : pecan tree 3 nogal americano : hickory

nómada¹ *adj* : nomadic

nómada² *nmf* : nomad

nomás *adv* : only, just ⟨lo hice nomás porque sí : I did it just because⟩ ⟨nomás de recordarlo me enojo : I get angry just remembering it⟩ ⟨nomás faltan dos semanas para Navidad : there are only two weeks left till Christmas⟩

nombradía *nf* RENOMBRE : fame, renown

nombrado, -da *adj* : famous, well-known

nombramiento *nm* : appointment, nomination

nombrar *vt* 1 : to appoint 2 : to mention, to name

nombre *nm* 1 : name ⟨nombre y apellido : first and last name, full name⟩ ⟨nombre de pila : first name⟩ ⟨nombre de soltera : maiden name⟩ ⟨nombre de usuario : user name⟩ ⟨nombre artístico : stage name⟩ ⟨nombre de pluma : pen name⟩ ⟨nombre comercial : trade name⟩ ⟨en nombre de : on behalf of⟩ ⟨sin nombre : nameless⟩ ⟨sólo de nombre : in name only⟩ ⟨lo cambiaron de nombre : they changed its name⟩ ⟨no lo conozco de nombre : I don't know him by name⟩ ⟨lo que están haciendo no tiene nombre : what they're doing is an outrage⟩ 2 : noun ⟨nombre propio : proper noun⟩ 3 : fame, renown ⟨hacerse un nombre : to make a name for oneself⟩

nomenclatura *nf* : nomenclature

nomeolvides *nmfs & pl* : forget-me-not

nómina *nf* : payroll

nominación *nf, pl* -ciones : nomination

nominal *adj* : nominal — **nominalmente** *adv*

nominar *vt* : to nominate

nominativo¹, -va *adj* : nominative

nominativo² *nm* : nominative (case)

nomo *nm* : gnome

non¹ *adj* IMPAR : odd, not even

non² *nm* : odd number

nonagésimo¹, -ma *adj* : ninetieth, ninety-

nonagésimo², -ma *n* : ninetieth, ninety- (in a series)

nono, -na *adj* : ninth — **nono** *nm*

nopal *nm* : prickly pear

nopalitos *nmpl Mex* : pickled prickly pear leaves

noquear *vt* : to knock out, to KO

norcoreano, -na *adj & n* : North Korean

nordeste¹ or **noreste** *adj* 1 : northeastern 2 : northeasterly

nordeste² or **noreste** *nm* : northeast

nórdico, -ca *adj & n* 1 ESCANDINAVO : Scandinavian 2 : Norse

noreste → nordeste

noria *nf* 1 : waterwheel 2 : Ferris wheel

norirlandés¹, -desa *adj, mpl* -deses : Northern Irish

norirlandés², -desa *n, mpl* -deses : person from Northern Ireland

norma *nf* 1 : rule, regulation 2 : norm, standard

normal *adj* 1 : normal, usual 2 : standard 3 escuela normal : teacher-training college

normalidad *nf* : normality, normalcy

normalización *nf, pl* -ciones *nf* 1 REGULARIZACIÓN : normalization 2 ESTANDARIZACIÓN : standardization

normalizar {21} *vt* 1 REGULARIZAR : to normalize 2 ESTANDARIZAR : to standardize — **normalizarse** *vr* : to return to normal

normalmente *adv* GENERALMENTE : ordinarily, generally

noroeste¹ *adj* 1 : northwestern 2 : northwesterly

noroeste² *nm* : northwest

norte¹ *adj* : north, northern

norte² *nm* 1 : north 2 : north wind 3 META : aim, objective

norteamericano, -na *adj & n* 1 : North American 2 AMERICANO, ESTADOUNIDENSE : American, native or inhabitant of the United States

norteño¹, -ña *adj* : northern

norteño², -ña *n* : Northerner

noruego¹, -ga *adj & n* : Norwegian

noruego² *nm* : Norwegian (language)

nos *pron pl* 1 : us ⟨nos enviaron a la frontera : they sent us to the border⟩ 2 : ourselves ⟨nos divertimos muchísimo : we enjoyed ourselves a great deal⟩ 3 : each other, one another ⟨nos vimos desde lejos : we saw each other from far away⟩ 4 : to us, for us, from us ⟨nos lo dio : he gave it to us⟩ ⟨nos lo compraron : they bought it from us⟩

nosotros, -tras *pron pl* 1 : we ⟨nosotros llegamos ayer : we arrived yesterday⟩ 2 : us ⟨ven con nosotros : come with us⟩ ⟨a nosotros no nos afecta : it doesn't affect us⟩ ⟨ninguna de nosotras : neither of us⟩ ⟨el de nosotros es mejor : ours is better⟩ 3 nosotros mismos : ourselves ⟨lo arreglamos nosotros mismos : we fixed it ourselves⟩

nostalgia *nf* 1 : nostalgia, longing 2 : homesickness

nostálgico, -ca *adj* 1 : nostalgic 2 : homesick

nota *nf* 1 : note, message ⟨tomar notas : to take notes⟩ 2 : announcement ⟨nota de prensa : press release⟩ 3 : grade, mark (in school) 4 : characteristic, feature, touch 5 : note (in music) 6 : bill, check (in a restaurant)

notable *adj* 1 : notable, noteworthy 2 : outstanding

notablemente *adv* 1 : notably, markedly 2 : outstandingly

notación *nf, pl* -ciones : notation

notar *vt* 1 : to notice ⟨hacer notar algo : to point out something⟩ 2 : to tell ⟨la diferencia se nota inmediatamente : you can tell the difference right away⟩ — **notarse** *vr* 1 : to be evident, to show 2 : to feel, to seem

notaría *nf* : notary's office

notario, -ria *n* : notary, notary public

notebook *nf* : notebook (computer)

noticia *nf* **1** : news item, piece of news ⟨noticia bomba : shocking news, bombshell⟩ **2 noticias** *nfpl* : news

noticiero *or* **noticiario** *nm* : news, news program, newscast

noticioso, -sa *adj* : news ⟨agencia noticiosa : news agency⟩

notificación *nf, pl* **-ciones** : notification

notificar {72} *vt* : to notify, to inform

notoriedad *nf* **1** : knowledge **2** : fame, notoriety

notorio, -ria *adj* **1** OBVIO : obvious, evident **2** CONOCIDO : well-known

novato¹, -ta *adj* : inexperienced, new

novato², -ta *n* : beginner, novice

novecientos¹, -tas *adj & pron* : nine hundred

novecientos² *nms & pl* : nine hundred

novedad *nf* **1** : newness, novelty **2** : innovation **3** : news, development ⟨sin ~ : the same as before **5 sin ~** : without incident, safely

novedoso, -sa *adj* : original, novel

novel *adj* NOVATO : inexperienced, new

novela *nf* **1** : novel **2** : soap opera

novelar *vt* : to make a novel out of

novelesco, -ca *adj* **1** : fictional **2** : fantastic, fabulous

novelista *nmf* : novelist

novena *nf* : novena

noveno, -na *adj & n* : ninth ⟨el noveno piso : the ninth floor⟩ ⟨la novena (persona) : the ninth (person)⟩ ⟨un noveno de . . . : one ninth of . . .⟩

noventa *adj & nm* : ninety — **noventavo** *pron*

noventavo¹, -va *adj* : ninetieth

noventavo² *nm* : ninetieth (fraction)

noviar *vi* : to date, to go out ⟨noviar con : to go out with⟩

noviazgo *nm* **1** : courtship, relationship **2** : engagement, betrothal

novicio, -cia *n* **1** : novice (in religion) **2** PRINCIPIANTE : novice, beginner

noviembre *nm* : November ⟨el primero de noviembre : (on) November first⟩

novilla *nf* : heifer

novillada *nf* : bullfight featuring young bulls

novillero, -ra *n* : apprentice bullfighter

novillo *nm* : young bull

novio, -via *n* **1** : boyfriend *m*, girlfriend *f* **2** PROMETIDO : fiancé *m*, fiancée *f* **3** : bridegroom *m*, bride *f*

novocaína *nf* : novocaine

nubarrón *nm, pl* **-rrones** : storm cloud

nube *nf* **1** : cloud ⟨andar en las nubes : to have one's head in the clouds⟩ ⟨por las nubes : sky-high⟩ **2** : cloud (of dust), swarm (of insects, etc.)

nublado¹, -da *adj* **1** NUBOSO : cloudy, overcast **2** : clouded, dim

nublado² *nm* **1** : storm cloud **2** AMENAZA : menace, threat

nublar *vt* **1** : to cloud **2** OSCURECER : to obscure — **nublarse** *vr* : to get cloudy

nubosidad *nf* : cloudiness

nuboso, -sa *adj* NUBLADO : cloudy

nuca *nf* : nape, back of the neck

nuclear *adj* : nuclear

núcleo *nm* **1** : nucleus **2** : center, heart, core

nudillo *nm* : knuckle

nudismo *nm* : nudism

nudista *adj & nmf* : nudist

nudo *nm* **1** : knot ⟨nudo de rizo : square knot⟩ ⟨nudo corredizo : slipknot⟩ ⟨un nudo en la garganta : a lump in one's throat⟩ **2** : node **3** : junction, hub ⟨nudo de comunicaciones : communication center⟩ **4** : crux, heart (of a problem, etc.)

nudoso, -sa *adj* : knotty, gnarled

nuera *nf* : daughter-in-law

nuestro¹, -tra *adj* : our

nuestro², -tra *pron* (*with definite article*) : ours, our own ⟨el nuestro es más grande : ours is bigger⟩ ⟨es de los nuestros : it's one of ours⟩

nuevamente *adv* : again, anew

nuevas *nfpl* : tidings *pl*

nueve¹ *adj & nm* : nine ⟨tengo nueve años : I am nine years old⟩ ⟨el nueve de noviembre : (on) November ninth⟩

nueve² *pron* : nine ⟨somos nueve : there are nine of us⟩ ⟨son las nueve : it's nine o'clock⟩

nuevecito, -ta *adj* : brand-new

nuevo, -va *adj* **1** : new ⟨una casa nueva : a new house⟩ ⟨¿qué hay de nuevo? : what's new?⟩ **2 de ~** : again, once more **3 Nuevo Testamento** : New Testament

nuez *nf, pl* **nueces 1** : nut **2** : walnut **3** *Mex* : pecan **4 nuez de Adán** : Adam's apple **5 nuez de Brasil** : Brazil nut **6 nuez moscada** : nutmeg

nulidad *nf* **1** : nullity **2** : incompetent person ⟨es una nulidad! : he's hopeless!⟩

nulo, -la *adj* **1** : null, null and void **2** INEPTO : useless, inept ⟨es nula para la cocina : she's hopeless at cooking⟩

numen *nm* : poetic muse, inspiration

numerable *adj* : countable

numeración *nf, pl* **-ciones 1** : numbering **2** : numbers *pl*, numerals *pl* ⟨numeración romana : Roman numerals⟩

numerador *nm* : numerator

numeral *adj* : numeral

numerar *vt* : to number

numerario, -ria *adj* : long-standing, permanent ⟨profesor numerario : tenured professor⟩

numérico, -ca *adj* : numerical — **numéricamente** *adv*

número *nm* **1** : number ⟨número impar : odd number⟩ ⟨número primo : prime number⟩ ⟨número ordinal : ordinal number⟩ ⟨número arábigo : Arabic numeral⟩ ⟨número quebrado : fraction⟩ **2** : issue (of a publication) **3** : size ⟨¿qué número calza? : what's his shoe size?⟩ **4** : lottery ticket **5** : act, routine, number **6 sin ~** : countless

numeroso, -sa *adj* : numerous

numismática *nf* : numismatics

nunca *adv* **1** : never, ever ⟨nunca es tarde : it's never too late⟩ ⟨no trabaja casi nunca : he hardly ever works⟩ **2 nunca**

más : never again   **3 nunca jamás** : never ever

nuncio nm : harbinger, herald
nupcial adj : nuptial, wedding
nupcias nfpl : nuptials pl, wedding
nutria nf **1** : otter **2** : nutria
nutrición nf, pl **-ciones** : nutrition, nourishment
nutricionista nmf : nutritionist
nutrido, -da adj **1** : nourished ⟨mal nutrido : undernourished, malnourished⟩ **2** : considerable, abundant ⟨de nutrido : full of, abounding in⟩
nutriente nm : nutrient
nutrimento nm : nutriment

nutrir vt **1** ALIMENTAR : to feed, to nourish **2** : to foster, to provide
nutritivo, -va adj : nourishing, nutritious
nylon → **nilón**
ñ nf : seventeenth letter of the Spanish alphabet
ñame nm : yam
ñandú nm, pl **ñandúes** or **ñandúes** : rhea
ñapa nf : extra amount ⟨de ñapa : for good measure⟩
ñato, -ta adj : snub-nosed
ñoñear vi fam : to whine
ñoñería nf : inanity
ñoño, -ña adj fam : whiny, fussy ⟨no seas tan ñoño : don't be such a wimp⟩
ñu nm : gnu

O

o¹ nf : eighteenth letter of the Spanish alphabet
o² conj (u before words beginning with o- or ho-) **1** : or ⟨¿vienes con nosotros o te quedas? : are you coming with us or staying?⟩ **2** : either ⟨o vienes con nosotros o te quedas : either you come with us or you stay⟩ **3 o sea** : that is to say, in other words
oasis ms & pl : oasis
obcecado, -da adj **1** : blinded ⟨obcecado por la ira : blinded by rage⟩ **2** : stubborn, obstinate
obcecar {72} vt : to blind (by emotions) — **obcecarse** vr : to become stubborn
obedecer {53} vt **1** : to obey ⟨obedecer órdenes : to obey orders⟩ ⟨obedece a tus padres : obey your parents⟩ — vi **1** : to obey **2 ～ a** : to respond to **3 ～ a** : to be due to, to result from
obediencia nf : obedience
obediente adj : obedient — **obedientemente** adv
obelisco nm : obelisk
obertura nf : overture
obesidad nf : obesity
obeso, -sa adj : obese
óbice nm : obstacle, impediment
obispado nm DIÓCESIS : bishopric, diocese
obispo nm : bishop
obituario nm : obituary
objeción nf, pl **-ciones** : objection ⟨ponerle objeciones a algo : to object to something⟩
objetar v : to object ⟨no tengo nada que objetar : I have no objections⟩
objetividad nf : objectivity
objetivo¹, -va adj : objective — **objetivamente** adv
objetivo² nm **1** META : objective, goal, target **2** : lens
objeto nm **1** COSA : object, thing ⟨objetos de valor : valuables⟩ **2** OBJETIVO : objective, purpose ⟨con objeto de : in order to, with the aim of⟩ **3 objeto volador no identificado** : unidentified flying object

objetor, -tora n : objector ⟨objetor de conciencia : conscientious objector⟩
oblea nf **1** : wafer **2 hecho una oblea** fam : skinny as a rail
oblicuo, -cua adj : oblique — **oblicuamente** adv
obligación nf, pl **-ciones** **1** DEBER : obligation, duty **2** : bond
obligado, -da adj **1** : obliged **2** : obligatory, compulsory **3** : customary
obligar {52} vt : to force, to require, to oblige — **obligarse** vr : to commit oneself, to undertake (to do something)
obligatorio, -ria adj : mandatory, required, compulsory
obliterar vt : to obliterate, to destroy — **obliteración** nf
oblongo, -ga adj : oblong
obnubilación nf, pl **-ciones** : bewilderment, confusion
obnubilar vt : to daze, to bewilder
oboe¹ nm : oboe
oboe² nmf : oboist
obra nf **1** : work ⟨obra de arte : work of art⟩ ⟨obra de teatro : play⟩ ⟨obra de consulta : reference work⟩ **2** : deed ⟨una buena obra : a good deed⟩ **3** : construction work ⟨en obra(s) : under construction⟩ ⟨obras viales : roadwork⟩ **4** : construction site, building site **5 obra maestra** : masterpiece **6 obras públicas** : public works **7 poner en obra** : to put into effect **8 por obra de** : thanks to, because of
obrar vt : to work, to produce ⟨obrar milagros : to work miracles⟩ — vi **1** : to act, to behave ⟨obrar con cautela : to act with caution⟩ **2 obrar en poder de** : to be in possession of
obrero¹, -ra adj : working ⟨la clase obrera : the working class⟩
obrero², -ra n : worker, laborer
obscenidad nf : obscenity
obsceno, -na adj : obscene
obscurecer, obscuridad, obscuro → **oscurecer, oscuridad, oscuro**

obsequiar *vt* REGALAR : to give, to present ⟨lo obsequiaron con una placa : they presented him with a plaque⟩
obsequio *nm* REGALO : gift, present
obsequiosidad *nf* : attentiveness, deference
obsequioso, -sa *adj* : obliging, attentive
observable *adj* : observable
observación *nf, pl* **-ciones** 1 : observation, watching ⟨bajo/en observación : under observation⟩ 2 : remark, comment
observador¹, -dora *adj* : observant
observador², -dora *n* : observer, watcher
observancia *nf* : observance
observante *adj* : observant ⟨los judíos observantes : observant Jews⟩
observar *vt* 1 : to observe, to watch ⟨estábamos observando a los niños : we were watching the children⟩ 2 NOTAR : to notice 3 ACATAR : to obey, to abide by 4 COMENTAR : to remark, to comment
observatorio *nm* : observatory
obsesión *nf, pl* **-siones** : obsession
obsesionar *vt* : to obsess, to preoccupy excessively — **obsesionarse** *vr*
obsesivo, -va *adj* : obsessive
obseso, -sa *adj* : obsessed
obsolescencia *nf* DESUSO : obsolescence — **obsolescente** *adj*
obsoleto, -ta *adj* DESUSADO : obsolete
obstaculizar {21} *vt* IMPEDIR : to obstruct, to hinder
obstáculo *nm* IMPEDIMENTO : obstacle
obstante¹ *conj* **no obstante** : nevertheless, however
obstante² *prep* **no obstante** : in spite of, despite ⟨mantuvo su inocencia no obstante la evidencia : he maintained his innocence in spite of the evidence⟩
obstar *v impers* ~ **a** or ~ **para** : to hinder, to prevent ⟨eso no obsta para que me vaya : that doesn't prevent me from leaving⟩
obstetra *nmf* TOCÓLOGO : obstetrician
obstetricia *nf* : obstetrics
obstétrico, -ca *adj* : obstetric, obstetrical
obstinación *nf, pl* **-ciones** 1 TERQUEDAD : obstinacy, stubbornness 2 : perseverance, tenacity
obstinado, -da *adj* 1 TERCO : obstinate, stubborn 2 : persistent — **obstinadamente** *adv*
obstinarse *vr* EMPECINARSE : to be obstinate, to be stubborn
obstrucción *nf, pl* **-ciones** : obstruction, blockage
obstruccionismo *nm* : filibustering (en política)
obstruccionista *adj* : filibustering (en política)
obstructor, -tora *adj* : obstructive
obstruir {41} *vt* BLOQUEAR : to obstruct, to block, to clog — **obstruirse** *vr*
obtención *nf, pl* **-ciones** : obtaining, procurement
obtener {80} *vt* : to obtain, to secure, to get — **obtenible** *adj*
obturador *nm* : shutter (of a camera)

obturar *vt* : to block
obtuso, -sa *adj* : obtuse
obtuvo, etc. → **obtener**
obús *nm, pl* **obuses** 1 : mortar (weapon) 2 : mortar shell
obviar *vt* : to get around (a difficulty), to avoid
obvio, -via *adj* : obvious — **obviamente** *adv*
oca *nf* : goose
ocasión *nf, pl* **-siones** 1 : occasion, time ⟨en alguna ocasión : occasionally, sometimes⟩ 2 : opportunity, chance 3 : bargain 4 **de** ~ : secondhand 5 **aviso de ocasión** *Mex* : classified ad
ocasional *adj* 1 : occasional 2 : chance, fortuitous
ocasionalmente *adv* 1 : occasionally 2 : by chance
ocasionar *vt* CAUSAR : to cause, to occasion
ocaso *nm* 1 ANOCHECER : sunset, sundown 2 DECADENCIA : decline, fall
occidental *adj* : western
occidente *nm* 1 OESTE, PONIENTE : west 2 **el Occidente** : the West
oceánico, -ca *adj* : oceanic
océano *nm* : ocean
oceanografía *nf* : oceanography — **oceanográfico, -ca** *adj*
ocelote *nm* : ocelot
ochenta *adj & nm* : eighty — **ochenta** *pron*
ochentavo¹, -va *adj* : eightieth
ochentavo² *nm* : eightieth (fraction)
ocho¹ *adj & nm* : eight ⟨tiene ocho años : he's eight (years old)⟩ ⟨el ocho de mayo : (on) the eighth of May, (on) May eighth⟩
ocho² *pron* : eight ⟨somos ocho : there are eight of us⟩ ⟨son las ocho : it's eight o'clock⟩
ochocientos¹, -tas *adj & pron* : eight hundred
ochocientos² *ms & pl* : eight hundred
ocio *nm* 1 : free time, leisure 2 : idleness
ociosamente *adv* : idly
ociosidad *nf* : idleness, inactivity
ocioso, -sa *adj* 1 INACTIVO : idle, inactive 2 INÚTIL : pointless, useless
ocre *nm* : ocher
octágono *nm* : octagon — **octagonal** *adj*
octava *nf* : octave
octavilla *nf* : pamphlet
octavo, -va *adj & n* : eighth ⟨el octavo grado : the eighth grade⟩ ⟨la octava (persona) : the eighth (person)⟩ ⟨un octavo de . . . : one eighth of . . .⟩
octeto *nm* : byte
octogésimo¹, -ma *adj* : eightieth, eighty- **octogésimo², -ma** *n* : eightieth, eighty- (in a series)
octubre *nm* : October ⟨el primero de octubre : (on) October first⟩
ocular *adj* 1 : ocular, eye ⟨músculos oculares : eye muscles⟩ 2 **testigo ocular** : eyewitness
oculista *nmf* : oculist, ophthalmologist
ocultación *nf, pl* **-ciones** : concealment

ocultar *vt* ESCONDER : to conceal, to hide — **ocultarse** *vr*

oculto, -ta *adj* **1** ESCONDIDO : hidden, concealed **2** : occult

ocupación *nf, pl* **-ciones 1** : occupation, activity **2** : occupancy **3** EMPLEO : employment, job

ocupacional *adj* : occupational, job-related

ocupado, -da *adj* **1** : busy **2** : taken ⟨este asiento está ocupado : this seat is taken⟩ **3** : occupied ⟨territorios ocupados : occupied territories⟩ **4 señal de ocupado** : busy signal

ocupante *nmf* : occupant

ocupar *vt* **1** : to occupy, to take possession of **2** : to hold (a position) **3** : to employ, to keep busy **4** : to fill (space, time) **5** : to inhabit (a dwelling) **6** : to bother, to concern — **ocuparse** *vr* ~ **de 1** : to be concerned with **2** : to take care of

ocurrencia *nf* **1** : occurrence, event **2** : witticism **3** : bright idea

ocurrente *adj* **1** : witty **2** : clever, sharp

ocurrir *vi* : to occur, to happen — **ocurrirse** *vr* ~ **a** : to occur to, to strike ⟨se me ocurrió una mejor idea : a better idea occurred to me⟩

oda *nf* : ode

odiar *vt* ABOMINAR, ABORRECER : to hate

odio *nm* : hate, hatred

odioso, -sa *adj* ABOMINABLE, ABORRECIBLE : hateful, detestable

odisea *nf* : odyssey

odómetro *nm* : odometer

odontología *nf* : dentistry, dental surgery

odontólogo, -ga *n* : dentist, dental surgeon

odre *nm* : wineskin

oeste[1] *adj* **1** : west, western ⟨la región oeste : the western region⟩ **2** : westerly

oeste[2] *nm* **1** : west, West **2** : west wind

ofender *vt* AGRAVIAR : to offend, to insult — *vi* : to offend, to be insulting — **ofenderse** *vr* : to take offense

ofensa *nf* : offense, insult

ofensiva *nf* : offensive ⟨pasar a la ofensiva : to go on the offensive⟩

ofensivo, -va *adj* : offensive, insulting — **ofensivamente** *adv*

ofensor, -sora *n* : offender

oferente *nmf* **1** : supplier **2** FUENTE : source ⟨un oferente no identificado : an unidentified source⟩

oferta *nf* **1** : offer **2** : sale, bargain ⟨las camisas están en oferta : the shirts are on sale⟩ **3 oferta y demanda** : supply and demand

ofertar *vt* OFRECER : to offer

oficial[1] *adj* : official — **oficialmente** *adv*

oficial[2] *nmf* **1** : officer, police officer, commissioned officer (in the military) **2** : skilled worker

oficializar {21} *vt* : to make official

oficiante *nmf* : celebrant

oficiar *vt* **1** : to inform officially **2** : to officiate at, to celebrate (Mass) — *vi* ~ **de** : to act as

oficina *nf* : office

oficinista *nmf* : office worker

oficio *nm* **1** : trade, profession ⟨es electricista de oficio : he's an electrician by trade⟩ **2** : function, role **3** : official communication **4** : experience ⟨tener oficio : to be experienced⟩ **5** : religious ceremony

oficioso, -sa *adj* **1** EXTRAOFICIAL : unofficial **2** : officious — **oficiosamente** *adv*

ofimática *nf* : office automation, office computing

ofrecer {53} *vt* **1** : to offer **2** : to provide, to give **3** : to present (an appearance, etc.) — **ofrecerse** *vr* **1** : to offer oneself, to volunteer **2** : to open up, to present itself

ofrecimiento *nm* : offer, offering

ofrenda *nf* : offering

oftalmología *nf* : ophthalmology

oftalmólogo, -ga *n* : ophthalmologist

ofuscación *nf, pl* **-ciones** : blindness, confusion

ofuscar {72} *vt* **1** : to blind, to dazzle **2** CONFUNDIR : to bewilder, to confuse — **ofuscarse** *vr* ~ **con** : to be blinded by

ogro *nm* : ogre

oh *interj* : oh ⟨¡oh, no! : oh no!⟩ ⟨oh, ¡qué raro! : oh, how odd!⟩

ohm *nm, pl* **ohms** : ohm

ohmio → **ohm**

oídas *nfpl de* ~ : by hearsay

oído *nm* **1** : ear ⟨oído interno : inner ear⟩ **2** : hearing ⟨duro de oído : hard of hearing⟩ **3 tocar de oído** : to play by ear

oiga, etc. → **oír**

oír {50} *vi* : to hear — *vt* **1** : to hear **2** ESCUCHAR : to listen to **3** : to pay attention to, to heed **4 ¡oye!** *or* **¡oiga!** : listen!, excuse me!, look here!

ojal *nm* : buttonhole

ojalá *interj* **1** : I hope so!, if only!, God willing! **2** : I hope, I wish, hopefully ⟨¡ojalá que le vaya bien! : I hope things go well for her!⟩ ⟨¡ojalá no llueva! : hopefully it won't rain!⟩

ojeada *nf* : glimpse, glance ⟨echar una ojeada : to have a quick look⟩

ojear *vt* : to eye, to have a look at

ojeras *nfpl* : bags/circles under one's eyes

ojeriza *nf fam* : grudge

ojeroso, -sa *adj* : with bags/circles under one's eyes

ojete *nm* : eyelet

ojiva *nf* : warhead

ojo *nm* **1** : eye ⟨un hombre con/de ojos verdes : a man with green eyes⟩ ⟨ojos negros : dark eyes⟩ ⟨la miré a los ojos : I looked her in the eye⟩ ⟨lo vi con mis propios ojos : I saw it with my own two eyes⟩ ⟨apareció ante nuestros ojos : it appeared before our very eyes⟩ ⟨con los ojos abiertos : with one's eyes open⟩ **2** : judgment, sharpness ⟨tener buen ojo para : to be a good judge of, to have a good eye for⟩ **3** : hole (in cheese), eye (in a needle), center (of a storm) ⟨ojo de cerradura : keyhole⟩ **4** : span (of a bridge) **5 a ojos vistas** : obviously, visibly **6 andar con ojo** : to be careful **7 costar un ojo de la cara** : to cost an arm

and a leg **8 en un abrir y cerrar de ojos**
: in the blink of an eye **9 ojo de agua**
Mex : spring, source **10 ¡ojo!** : look out!,
pay attention! **11 tener ojos de águila**
: to have eyes like a hawk

okupa *fam nf* : squatter

ola *nf* **1** : wave **2 ola de calor** : heat wave

oleada *nf* : swell, wave ⟨una oleada de
protestas : a wave of protests⟩

oleaje *nm* : waves *pl*, surf

óleo *nm* **1** : oil **2** : oil painting

oleoducto *nm* : oil pipeline

oleoso, -sa *adj* : oily

oler {51} *vt* **1** : to smell **2** INQUIRIR : to
pry into, to investigate **3** AVERIGUAR
: to smell out, to uncover — *vi* **1** : to
smell ⟨huele mal : it smells bad⟩ ⟨todo
esto huele mal : there's something fishy
about all of this⟩ **2 ~ a** : to smell like,
to smell of ⟨huele a pino : it smells like
pine⟩ — **olerse** *vr* : to have a hunch, to
suspect

olfatear *vt* **1** : to sniff **2** : to sense, to sniff
out

olfativo, -va *adj* : olfactory

olfato *nm* **1** : sense of smell **2** : nose, instinct

oligarquía *nf* : oligarchy

olimpiada *or* **olimpíada** *nf* **1** : Olympiad
2 *or* **olimpiadas** *nfpl* : Olympics *pl*

olímpico, -ca *adj* : Olympic

olisquear *vt* : to sniff at

oliva *nf* ACEITUNA : olive ⟨aceite de oliva
: olive oil⟩

olivar *nm* : olive grove

olivo *nm* : olive tree

olla *nf* **1** : pot ⟨olla de presión : pressure
cooker⟩ **2 olla podrida** : Spanish stew **3
olla vaporera → vaporera**

olmeca *adj & nmf* : Olmec

olmo *nm* : elm

olor *nm* : smell, odor

oloroso, -sa *adj* : scented, fragrant

olote *nm Mex* : cob, corncob

olvidadizo, -za *adj* : forgetful, absentminded

olvidar *vt* **1** : to forget, to forget about
⟨olvida lo que pasó : forget about what
happened⟩ **2** : to leave behind ⟨olvidé
mi chequera en la casa : I left my checkbook at home⟩ — **olvidarse** *vr* **1** : to forget ⟨se me olvidó mi cuaderno : I forgot
my notebook⟩ ⟨se le olvidó llamarme
: he forgot to call me⟩

olvido *nm* **1** : forgetfulness **2** : oblivion **3**
DESCUIDO : oversight

omaní *adj & nmf* : Omani

ombligo *nm* : navel, belly button

ombudsman *nmfs & pl* : ombudsman

omelette *nmf* : omelet

ominoso, -sa *adj* : ominous — **ominosa-
mente** *adv*

omisión *nf, pl* **-siones** : omission, neglect

omiso, -sa *adj* **1** NEGLIGENTE : neglectful **2 hacer caso omiso de → caso**

omitir *vt* **1** : to omit, to leave out **2** : to
fail to ⟨omitió dar su nombre : he failed
to give his name⟩

ómnibus *n, pl* **-bus** *or* **-buses** : bus, coach

omnipotencia *nf* : omnipotence

omnipotente *adj* TODOPODEROSO : omnipotent, almighty

omnipresencia *nf* : omnipresence

omnipresente *adj* : ubiquitous, omnipresent

omnisciente *adj* : omniscient — **omni-
sciencia** *nf*

omnívoro, -ra *adj* : omnivorous

omóplato *or* **omoplato** *nm* : shoulder
blade

once[1] *adj & nm* : eleven ⟨tiene once años
: she's eleven (years old)⟩ ⟨el once de noviembre : (on) the eleventh of November, (on) November eleventh⟩

once[2] *pron* : eleven ⟨son las once : it's
eleven o'clock⟩ ⟨somos once : there are
eleven of us⟩

onceavo[1], **-va** *adj* : eleventh

onceavo[2] *nm* : eleventh (fraction)

onda *nf* **1** : wave, ripple, undulation
⟨onda sonora : sound wave⟩ **2** : wave (in
hair) **3** : scallop (on clothing) **4** *fam*
: wavelength, understanding ⟨agarrar la
onda : to get the point⟩ ⟨en la onda : on
the ball, with it⟩ **5 ¿qué onda?** *fam*
: what's happening?, what's up?

ondear *vi* : to ripple, to undulate, to flutter

ondulación *nf, pl* **-ciones** : undulation

ondulado, -da *adj* **1** : wavy ⟨pelo ondulado : wavy hair⟩ **2** : undulating

ondulante *adj* : undulating

ondular *vt* : to wave (hair) — *vi* : to undulate, to ripple

oneroso, -sa *adj* GRAVOSO : onerous,
burdensome

ónix *nm* : onyx

onza *nf* : ounce

opacar {72} *vt* **1** : to make opaque or dull
2 : to outshine, to overshadow

opacidad *nf* **1** : opacity **2** : dullness

opaco, -ca *adj* **1** : opaque **2** : dull

ópalo *nm* : opal

opción *nf, pl* **opciones 1** ALTERNATIVA
: option, choice **2** : right, chance ⟨tener
opción a : to be eligible for⟩

opcional *adj* : optional — **opcional-
mente** *adv*

ópera *nf* : opera

operación *nf, pl* **-ciones 1** : operation **2**
: transaction, deal

operacional *adj* : operational

operador, -dora *n* **1** : operator **2** : projectionist, camera operator

operante *adj* : operating, working

operar *vt* **1** : to produce, to bring about **2**
INTERVENIR : to operate on ⟨me opera-
ron : I had an operation, I had surgery⟩
⟨me operaron de la rodilla : I had surgery on my knee, I had knee surgery⟩ ⟨la
operaron de cáncer :she had cancer sur-
gery⟩ ⟨fue operado de un tumor : he had
surgery to remove a tumor⟩ **3** *Mex* : to
operate, to run (a machine) — *vi* **1** : to
operate, to function **2** : to deal, to do
business — **operarse** *vr* **1** : to come
about, to take place **2** : to have an operation, to have surgery

operario, -ria *n* : laborer, worker

operático, -ca → operístico

operativo¹, -va *adj* **1** : operating ⟨capacidad operativa : operating capacity⟩ **2** : operative

oper•ativo² *nm* : operation ⟨operativo militar : military operation⟩

opereta *nf* : operetta

operístico, -ca *adj* : operatic

opiato *nm* : opiate

opinable *adj* : arguable

opinar *vi* **1** : to think, to have an opinion **2** : to express an opinion **3 opinar bien de** : to think highly of — *vt* : to think ⟨opinamos lo mismo : we're of the same opinion, we're in agreement⟩

opinión *nf, pl* **-niones** : opinion, belief

opio *nm* : opium

oponente *nmf* : opponent

oponer {60} *vt* **1** CONTRAPONER : to oppose, to place against **2 oponer resistencia** : to resist, to put up a fight — **oponerse** *vr* ~ **a** : to object to, to be against

oporto *nm* : port (wine)

oportunamente *adv* **1** : at the right time, opportunely **2** : appropriately

oportunidad *nf* : opportunity, chance

oportunismo *nm* : opportunism

oportunista¹ *adj* : opportunistic

oportunista² *nmf* : opportunist

oportuno, -na *adj* **1** : opportune, timely **2** : suitable, appropriate

oposición *nf, pl* **-ciones** : opposition

opositor, -tora *n* ADVERSARIO : opponent

oposum *nm* ZARIGÜEYA : opossum

opresión *nf, pl* **-siones** **1** : oppression **opresión de pecho** : tightness in the chest

opresivo, -va *adj* : oppressive

opresor¹, -sora *adj* : oppressive

opresor², -sora *n* : oppressor

oprimir *vt* **1** : to oppress **2** : to press, to squeeze ⟨oprima el botón : push the button⟩

oprobio *nm* : opprobrium, shame

optar *vi* **1** ~ **por** : to opt for, to choose **2** ~ **a** : to aspire to, to apply for ⟨dos candidatos optan a la presidencia : two candidates are running for president⟩

optativo, -va *adj* FACULTATIVO : optional

óptica *nf* **1** : optics **2** : optician's shop **3** : viewpoint

óptico¹, -ca *adj* : optical, optic

óptico², -ca *n* : optician

optimismo *nm* : optimism

optimista¹ *adj* : optimistic

optimista² *nmf* : optimist

óptimo, -ma *adj* : optimum, optimal

optometría *nf* : optometry — **optometrista** *nmf*

opuesto¹ *pp* → **oponer**

opuesto² *adj* **1** : opposite, contrary **2** : opposed

opulencia *nf* : opulence — **opulento, -ta** *adj*

opus *nm* : opus

opuso, etc. → **oponer**

ora *conj* : now ⟨los matices eran variados, ora verdes, ora ocres : the hues were varied, now green, now ocher⟩

oración *nf, pl* **-ciones** **1** DISCURSO : oration, speech **2** PLEGARIA : prayer **3** FRASE : sentence, clause

oráculo *nm* : oracle

orador, -dora *n* : speaker, orator

oral *adj* : oral — **oralmente** *adv*

órale *interj Mex fam* **1** : sure!, OK! ⟨¿los dos por cinco pesos? ¡órale! : both for five pesos? you've got a deal!⟩ **2** : come on! ⟨¡órale, vámonos! : come on, let's go!⟩

orangután *nm, pl* **-tanes** : orangutan

orar *vi* REZAR : to pray

oratoria *nf* : oratory

oratorio *nm* **1** CAPILLA : oratory, chapel **2** : oratorio

orbe *nm* **1** : orb, sphere **2** GLOBO : globe, world

órbita *nf* **1** : orbit **2** : eye socket **3** ÁMBITO : sphere, field

orbital *adj* : orbital

orbitar *v* : to orbit

orca *nf* : orca, killer whale

orden¹ *nm, pl* **órdenes** **1** : order ⟨todo está en orden : everything's in order⟩ ⟨por orden cronológico : in chronological order⟩ **2 orden del día** : agenda (at a meeting) **3 orden público** : law and order

orden² *nf, pl* **órdenes** **1** : order ⟨una orden religiosa : a religious order⟩ ⟨una orden de tacos : an order of tacos⟩ **2 orden de compra** : purchase order **3 estar a la orden del día** : to be the order of the day, to be prevalent

ordenación *nf, pl* **-ciones** **1** : ordination **2** : ordering, organizing

ordenadamente *adv* : in an orderly fashion, neatly

ordenado, -da *adj* : orderly, neat

ordenador *nm Spain* : computer

ordenamiento *nm* **1** : ordering, organizing **2** : code of (laws)

ordenanza¹ *nf* REGLAMENTO : ordinance, regulation

ordenanza² *nm* : orderly (in the armed forces)

ordenar *vt* **1** MANDAR : to order, to command **2** ARREGLAR : to put in order, to arrange **3** : to ordain (a priest) — **ordenarse** *vr* : to be ordained

ordeñar *vt* : to milk

ordeño *nm* : milking

ordinal *nm* : ordinal (number)

ordinariamente *adv* **1** : usually **2** : coarsely

ordinariez *nf* : coarseness, vulgarity

ordinario, -ria *adj* **1** : ordinary **2** : coarse, common, vulgar **3 de** ~ : usually

orear *vt* : to air

orégano *nm* : oregano

oreja *nf* : ear

orfanato *nm* : orphanage

orfanatorio *nm Mex* : orphanage

orfandad *nf* : state of being an orphan

orfebre *nmf* : goldsmith, silversmith

orfebrería *nf* : articles of gold or silver

orfelinato *nm* : orphanage

orgánico, -ca *adj* : organic — **orgánicamente** *adv*

organigrama *nm* : organization chart, flow chart
organismo *nm* **1** : organism **2** : agency, organization
organista *nmf* : organist
organización *nf, pl* **-ciones** : organization
organizador¹, -dora *adj* : organizing
organizador², -dora *n* : organizer ⟨organizador de bodas : wedding planner⟩
organizar {21} *vt* : to organize, to arrange — **organizarse** *vr* : to get organized
organizativo, -va *adj* : organizational
órgano *nm* : organ
orgasmo *nm* : orgasm
orgía *nf* : orgy
orgullo *nm* : pride
orgulloso, -sa *adj* : proud — **orgullosamente** *adv*
orientación *nf, pl* **-ciones** **1** : orientation **2** DIRECCIÓN : direction, course **3** GUÍA : guidance, direction
oriental¹ *adj* **1** : eastern **2** : oriental **3** *Arg, Uru* : Uruguayan
oriental² *nmf* **1** : Easterner **2** : Oriental **3** *Arg, Uru* : Uruguayan
orientar *vt* **1** : to orient, to position **2** : to guide, to direct — **orientarse** *vr* **1** : to orient oneself, to get one's bearings **2** ~ **hacia** : to turn towards, to lean towards
oriente *nm* **1** : east, East **2 el Oriente** : the Orient
orífice *nmf* : goldsmith
orificio *nm* : orifice, opening
origen *nm, pl* **orígenes** **1** : origin **2** : lineage, birth **3 dar origen a** : to give rise to **4 en su origen** : originally
original *adj & nm* : original — **originalmente** *adv*
originalidad *nf* : originality
originar *vt* : to originate, to give rise to — **originarse** *vr* : to originate, to begin
originario, -ria *adj* ~ **de** : native of
originariamente *adv* : originally
orilla *nf* **1** BORDE : border, edge **2** : bank (of a river) **3** : shore
orillar *vt* **1** : to skirt, to go around **2** : to trim, to edge (cloth) **3** : to settle, to wind up **4** *Mex* : to pull over (a vehicle)
orín *nm* **1** HERRUMBRE : rust **2 orines** *nmpl* : urine
orina *nf* : urine
orinación *nf* : urination
orinal *nm* : urinal (vessel)
orinar *vi* : to urinate — **orinarse** *vr* : to wet oneself
oriol *nm* OROPÉNDOLA : oriole
oriundo, -da *adj* ~ **de** : native of
orla *nf* : border, edging
orlar *vt* : to edge, to trim
ornamentación *nf, pl* **-ciones** : ornamentation
ornamental *adj* : ornamental
ornamentar *vt* ADORNAR : to ornament, to adorn
ornamento *nm* : ornament, adornment
ornar *vt* : to adorn, to decorate
ornitología *nf* : ornithology
ornitólogo, -ga *n* : ornithologist
ornitorrinco *nm* : platypus

oro *nm* **1** : gold **2 oros** *nmpl* : gold coins (in the Spanish deck of cards)
orondo, -da *adj* **1** : rounded, potbellied (of a container) **2** *fam* : smug, self-satisfied
oropel *nm* : glitz, glitter, tinsel
oropéndola *nf* : oriole
orquesta *nf* : orchestra ⟨orquesta sinfónica : symphony (orchestra)⟩ — **orquestal** *adj*
orquestar *vt* : to orchestrate — **orquestación** *nf*
orquídea *nf* : orchid
ortiga *nf* : nettle
ortodoncia *nf* : orthodontics
ortodoncista *nmf* : orthodontist
ortodoxia *nf* : orthodoxy
ortodoxo, -xa *adj* : orthodox
ortografía *nf* : orthography, spelling
ortográfico, -ca *adj* : orthographic, spelling
ortopedia *nf* : orthopedics
ortopédico, -ca *adj* : orthopedic
ortopedista *nmf* : orthopedist
oruga *nf* **1** : caterpillar **2** : track (of a tank, etc.)
orzuelo *nm* : sty, stye (in the eye)
os *pron pl objective form of* VOSOTROS **1** *Spain* : you, to you ⟨os veo pronto : I'll see you soon⟩ **2** : yourselves, to yourselves **3** : each other, to each other
osa *nf* → **oso**
osadía *nf* **1** VALOR : boldness, daring **2** AUDACIA : audacity, nerve
osado, -da *adj* **1** : bold, daring **2** : audacious, impudent — **osadamente** *adv*
osamenta *nf* : skeletal remains *pl*, bones *pl*
osar *vi* : to dare
oscilación *nf, pl* **-ciones** **1** : oscillation **2** : fluctuation **3** : vacillation, wavering
oscilar *vi* **1** BALANCEARSE : to swing, to sway, to oscillate **2** FLUCTUAR : to fluctuate **3** : to vacillate, to waver
oscuramente *adv* : obscurely
oscurecer {53} *vt* **1** : to darken **2** : to obscure, to confuse, to cloud **3 al oscurecer** : at dusk, at nightfall — *v impers* : to grow dark, to get dark — **oscurecerse** *vr* : to darken, to dim
oscuridad *nf* **1** : darkness **2** : obscurity
oscuro, -ra *adj* **1** : dark **2** : obscure **3 a oscuras** : in the dark, in darkness
óseo, ósea *adj* : skeletal, bony
ósmosis *or* **osmosis** *nf* : osmosis
oso, osa *n* **1** : bear **2 Osa Mayor** : Big Dipper **3 Osa Menor** : Little Dipper **4 oso blanco** : polar bear **5 oso hormiguero** : anteater **6 oso de peluche** : teddy bear
ostensible *adj* : ostensible, apparent — **ostensiblemente** *adv*
ostentación *nf, pl* **-ciones** : ostentation, display
ostentar *vt* **1** : to display, to flaunt **2** POSEER : to have, to hold ⟨ostenta el récord mundial : he holds the world record⟩
ostentoso, -sa *adj* : ostentatious, showy — **ostentosamente** *adv*

osteópata *nmf* : osteopath
osteopatía *n* : osteopathy
osteoporosis *nf* : osteoporosis
ostión *nm, pl* **ostiones** 1 *Mex* : oyster 2 *Chile* : scallop
ostra *nf* : oyster
ostracismo *nm* : ostracism
otear *vt* : to scan, to survey, to look over
otero *nm* : knoll, hillock
otitis *nf* : otitis, inflammation of the ear
otomana *nf* : ottoman (furniture)
otomano, -na *adj & n* : Ottoman
otoñal *adj* : autumn, autumnal
otoño *nm* : autumn, fall
otorgamiento *nm* : granting, awarding
otorgar {52} *vt* 1 : to grant, to award 2 : to draw up, to frame (a legal document)
otorrino, -na *n* : ear, nose, and throat doctor
otro¹, otra *adj* 1 : other 2 : another ⟨en otro juego, ellos ganaron : in another game, they won⟩ 3 **otra vez** : again 4 **de otra manera** : otherwise 5 **otra parte** : elsewhere 6 **en otro tiempo** : once, formerly
otro², otra *pron* 1 : another one ⟨dame otro : give me another⟩ ⟨¡otra! : encore!⟩ 2 : other one ⟨el uno o el otro : one or the other⟩ 3 **los otros, las otras** : the others, the rest ⟨me dio una y se quedó con las otras : he gave me one and kept the rest⟩
ovación *nf, pl* **-ciones** : ovation

ovacionar *vt* : to cheer, to applaud
oval → ovalado
ovalado, -da *adj* : oval
óvalo *nm* : oval
ovárico, -ca *adj* : ovarian
ovario *nm* : ovary
oveja *nf* 1 : sheep, ewe 2 **oveja negra** : black sheep
overol *nm* : overalls *pl*
ovillar *vt* : to roll into a ball
ovillo *nm* 1 : ball (of yarn) 2 : tangle
ovni *or* **OVNI** *nm* (*objeto volador no identificado*) : UFO
ovoide *adj* : ovoid, ovoidal
ovulación *nf, pl* **-ciones** : ovulation
ovular *vi* : to ovulate
óvulo *nm* : ovum
oxidación *nf, pl* **-ciones** 1 : oxidation 2 : rusting
oxidado, -da *adj* : rusty
oxidar *vt* 1 : to cause to rust 2 : to oxidize — **oxidarse** *vr* : to rust, to become rusty
óxido *nm* 1 HERRUMBRE, ORÍN : rust 2 : oxide
oxigenar *vt* 1 : to oxygenate 2 : to bleach (hair)
oxígeno *nm* : oxygen
oxiuro *nm* : pinworm
oye, etc. → oír
oyente *nmf* 1 : listener 2 : auditor, auditing student
ozono *nm* : ozone

P

p *nf* : nineteenth letter of the Spanish alphabet
pabellón *nm, pl* **-llones** 1 : pavilion (at a fair, etc.) 2 GLORIETA : gazebo, pavilion 3 : building (of a hospital, etc.) 4 : flag (of a vessel)
pabilo *nm* MECHA : wick
paca *nf* FARDO : bale
pacana *nf* : pecan
pacer {48} *v* : to graze, to pasture
paces → paz
pachanga *nf fam* : party, bash
paciencia *nf* : patience ⟨tener paciencia : to be patient⟩ ⟨perder la paciencia : to lose (one's) patience⟩
paciente *adj & nmf* : patient — **pacientemente** *adv*
pacíficamente *adv* : peacefully, peaceably
pacificar {72} *vt* : to pacify, to calm — **pacificarse** *vr* : to calm down, to abate — **pacificación** *nf*
pacífico, -ca *adj* : peaceful, pacific
pacifismo *nm* : pacifism
pacifista *adj & nmf* : pacifist
pacotilla *nf* **de ~** : shoddy, trashy
pactar *vt* : to agree on (terms, etc.) — *vi* : to come to an agreement
pacto *nm* CONVENIO : pact, agreement
paddock ['padok] *nm* : paddock

padecer {53} *vt* : to suffer (hardship, etc.), to suffer from (an illness) — *vi* ADOLECER : to suffer 2 ~ **de** : to suffer from
padecimiento *nm* 1 : suffering 2 : ailment, condition
padrastro *nm* 1 : stepfather 2 : hangnail
padre¹ *adj Mex fam* : fantastic, great
padre² *nm* 1 : father 2 : Father (title of a priest) 3 **padres** *nmpl* : parents
padrenuestro *nm* : Lord's Prayer
padrino *nm* 1 : godfather 2 : father of the bride 3 : sponsor, patron 4 **padrinos** *nmpl* : godparents
padrón *nm, pl* **padrones** : register, roll ⟨padrón municipal : city register⟩ ⟨padrón electoral : electoral/voter roll⟩
paella *nf* : paella
paga *nf* 1 : payment 2 : pay, wages *pl* 3 : allowance (given to a child)
pagadero, -ra *adj* : payable
pagado, -da *adj* 1 : paid 2 **pagado de sí mismo** : self-satisfied, smug
pagador, -dora *n* : payer
paganismo *nm* : paganism
pagano, -na *adj & n* : pagan
pagar {52} *vt* 1 : to pay (a bill), to pay for (a purchase), to pay off (a debt) 2 : to pay for (a crime, etc.) 3 : to repay (a favor) — *vi* : to pay

pagaré *nm* VALE : promissory note, IOU

página *nf* **1** : page ⟨la página seis : page six⟩ **2 página de inicio** : home page **3 página web** : web page

pago *nm* **1** : payment **2 en pago de** : in return for **3 pago al contado** : cash payment **4 pago anticipado** : advance payment **5 pago inicial** : down payment

pagoda *nf* : pagoda

pague, etc. → **pagar**

paila *nf* **1** : large shallow dish or pan **2** *Hond* : cargo area (of a vehicle)

país *nm* **1** NACIÓN : country, nation **2** REGIÓN : region, territory

paisaje *nm* : scenery, landscape

paisajismo *nm* : landscaping

paisajista *nmf* : landscaper

paisano, -na *n* **1** COMPATRIOTA : compatriot, fellow countryman **2 de ~** : in plain/civilian clothes ⟨un policía de paisano : a plainclothes policeman⟩

paja *nf* **1** : straw **2** *fam* : trash, tripe

pajar *nm* : hayloft, haystack

pajarera *nf* : aviary

pajarita *nf Spain* : bow tie

pájaro *nm* : bird ⟨pájaro cantor : songbird⟩ ⟨pájaro bobo : penguin⟩ ⟨pájaro carpintero : woodpecker⟩

paje *nm* : page (person)

pajita *or* **pajilla** *nf* : (drinking) straw

pajote *nm* : straw, mulch

pakistaní *adj & nmf, pl* **-níes** : Pakistani

pala *nf* **1** : shovel, spade **2** : blade (of an oar or a rotor) **3** : paddle, racket **4** : spatula (for serving food)

palabra *nf* **1** VOCABLO : word ⟨en otras palabras : in other words⟩ ⟨no dijo ni una palabra : she didn't say a word⟩ **2** PROMESA : word, promise ⟨un hombre de palabra : a man of his word⟩ ⟨cumplió (con) su palabra : she kept her word⟩ ⟨le di mi palabra : I gave him my word⟩ **3** HABLA : speech ⟨acuerdo de palabra : verbal agreement⟩ **4** : right to speak ⟨tener/tomar la palabra : to have/take the floor⟩ ⟨pidió la palabra : he asked to speak⟩

palabrería *nf* : empty talk

palabrota *nf* : swearword ⟨decir palabrotas : to swear⟩

palacio *nm* **1** : palace, mansion **2 palacio de justicia** : courthouse **3 palacio municipal** : city hall

paladar *nm* **1** : palate **2** GUSTO : taste

paladear *vt* SABOREAR : to savor

paladín *nm, pl* **-dines** : champion, defender

palanca *nf* **1** : lever, crowbar **2** *fam* : leverage, influence **3 palanca de cambios/velocidad** : gearshift **4 palanca de mando** : joystick

palangana *nf* : washbowl

palanqueta *nf* : jimmy, small crowbar

palapa *nf Mex* : shelter (thatched with palms)

palco *nm* : box (in a theater or stadium)

palear *vt* **1** : to shovel **2** : to paddle

palenque *nm* **1** ESTACADA : stockade, palisade **2** : arena, ring

paleontología *nf* : paleontology

paleontólogo, -ga *n* : paleontologist

palestino, -na *adj & n* : Palestinian

palestra *nf* : arena ⟨salir a la palestra : to join the fray⟩

paleta *nf* **1** : palette **2** : trowel **3** : spatula **4** : blade, vane **5** : paddle **6** *CA, Mex* : lollipop, Popsicle

paletilla *nf* : shoulder blade

paliacate *nm Mex* : bandanna, scarf

paliar *vt* MITIGAR : to alleviate

paliativo[1], -va *adj* : palliative ⟨cuidados paliativos : palliative care⟩ ⟨centro de cuidados paliativos : hospice⟩

paliativo[2] *nm* : palliative

palidecer {53} *vi* : to turn pale

palidez *nf, pl* **-deces** : paleness, pallor

pálido, -da *adj* : pale ⟨se puso pálida : she turned pale⟩

palillo *nm* **1** *or* **palillo de dientes** MONDADIENTES : toothpick **2** *or* **palillo de tambor** : drumstick **3 palillos** *nmpl* : chopsticks

paliza *nf* **1** : beating, pummeling ⟨darle una paliza a : to beat, to thrash⟩ **2** DERROTA : rout, defeat

palma *nf* **1** : palm (of the hand) **2** : palm (tree or leaf) **3 batir/dar palmas** : to clap, to applaud **4 llevarse la palma** *fam* : to take the cake

palmada *nf* **1** : pat ⟨le dio unas palmadas en el hombro : she patted him on the shoulder⟩ **2** BOFETADA, CACHETADA : slap **3** : clap ⟨dar palmadas : to clap⟩

palmarés *nm* : record (of achievements)

palmario, -ria *adj* MANIFIESTO : clear, manifest

palmeado, -da *adj* : webbed

palmear *vt* : to slap on the back — *vi* : to clap, to applaud

palmera *nf* : palm tree

palmito *nm* : heart of palm

palmo *nm* **1** : span, small amount **2 palmo a palmo** : bit by bit, inch by inch **3 palmo a palmo** : thoroughly **4 dejar con un palmo de narices** : to disappoint

palmotear *vi* : to applaud

palmoteo *nm* : clapping, applause

palo *nm* **1** : stick, pole, post **2** : shaft, handle ⟨palo de escoba : broomstick⟩ **3** : mast, spar **4** *or* **palo de golf** : golf club **5** : wood **6** : blow (with a stick) **7** : suit (of cards) **8 de tal palo, tal astilla** : he/she (etc.) is a chip off the old block

paloma *nf* **1** : pigeon, dove **2 paloma de la paz** : dove of peace **3 paloma mensajera** : carrier pigeon

palomilla *nf* : moth

palomitas *nfpl* : popcorn

palpable *adj* : palpable, tangible

palpar *vt* : to feel, to touch — **palparse** *vr* ⟨se palpó la cabeza : he felt/touched his head⟩

palpitación *nf, pl* **-ciones** : palpitation

palpitar *vi* : to palpitate, to throb — **palpitante** *adj*

pálpito *nm* : feeling, hunch

palta *nf Arg, Chile, Peru, Uru* : avocado

paludismo *nm* MALARIA : malaria

palurdo, -da *n* : boor, yokel, bumpkin

pampa *nf* : pampas *pl*

pampeano, -na *adj* : pampas

pampero → pampeano

pan *nm* **1** : bread ⟨una rebanada de pan : a slice of bread⟩ ⟨pan rallado : (grated) bread crumbs⟩ **2** : loaf of bread **3** : cake, bar ⟨pan de jabón : bar of soap⟩ **4 pan árabe** *Arg, Ven, Uru* : pita, pita bread **5 pan blanco** : white bread **6 pan de molde** : sandwich bread (baked in a loaf pan) **7 pan dulce** *CA, Mex* : traditional pastry **8 pan integral** : whole wheat bread **9 pan tostado** : toast **10 ser pan comido** *fam* : to be a piece of cake, to be a cinch

pan- *pref* : pan- ⟨panacea : panacea⟩

pana¹ *nf* : corduroy

pana² *nmf PRi, Ven* : buddy, friend

panacea *nf* : panacea

panadería *nf* : bakery, bread shop

panadero, -ra *n* : baker

panal *nm* : honeycomb

panameño, -ña *adj & n* : Panamanian

pancarta *nf* : placard, sign, banner

panceta *nf* : bacon

pancho *nm Arg, Uru* : hot dog

pancita *nf Mex* : tripe

páncreas *nms & pl* : pancreas

panda *nmf* : panda

pandeado, -da *adj* : warped

pandearse *vr* **1** : to warp **2** : to bulge, to sag

pandemonio *or* **pandemónium** *nm* : pandemonium

pandereta *nf* : tambourine

pandero *nm* : tambourine

pandilla *nf* **1** : group, clique **2** : gang

panecillo *Spain* → **panecito**

panecito *nm* : roll, bun

panegírico *nm* : eulogy

panel *nm* **1** : panel ⟨paneles de madera : wood panels⟩ ⟨panel solar : solar panel⟩ **2** TABLERO : board — **panelista** *nmf*

panela *nf Col, Ecua* : unrefined sugar

panera *nf* : bread box (for storage), bread basket (for serving)

panfleto *nm* : pamphlet

pánico *nm* : panic ⟨tener(le) pánico a algo : to be terrified of something⟩ ⟨pánico escénico : stage fright⟩

panificadora *nf* : bakery

panorama *nm* **1** VISTA : panorama, view **2** : scene, situation ⟨el panorama nacional : the national scene⟩ **3** PERSPECTIVA : outlook

panorámico, -ca *adj* : panoramic

panqueque *nm* : pancake

pantaletas *nfpl* : panties

pantalla *nf* **1** : screen, monitor **2** : lampshade **3** : fan

pantalón *nm, pl* **-lones 1** : pants *pl*, trousers *pl* **2 pantalones cortos** : shorts **3 pantalones vaqueros/tejanos** : jeans **4 pantalones de mezclilla** *Chile, Mex* : jeans **5 pantalones de montar** : jodhpurs

pantano *nm* **1** : swamp, marsh, bayou **2** : reservoir **3** : obstacle, difficulty

pantanoso, -sa *adj* **1** : marshy, swampy **2** : difficult, thorny

panteón *nm, pl* **-teones 1** CEMENTERIO : cemetery **2** : pantheon, mausoleum

pantera *nf* : panther

panties *or* **pantys** *or* **pantis** *nmfpl* **1** *CA, Car* : panties *pl* **2** *Spain* : panty hose

pantimedias *nfpl Mex* : panty hose

pantomima *nf* : pantomime

pantorrilla *nf* : calf (of the leg)

pants *nms & pl Mex* **1** : sweatpants **2** : sweatsuit, tracksuit

pantufla *nf* ZAPATILLA : slipper

panty *or* **panti** *nmf, pl* **-tys** *or* **-ties** *or* **-tis** → **panties**

panza *nf* BARRIGA : belly, paunch

panzón, -zona *adj, mpl* **panzones** : pot-bellied

pañal *nm* **1** : diaper ⟨pañal desechable : disposable diaper⟩ **2 estar en pañales** : to be in its infancy (of things), to be a beginner (of people)

pañería *nf* **1** : cloth, material **2** : fabric store

pañito *nm* : doily

paño *nm* **1** : cloth ⟨en paños menores : in one's underwear⟩ **2** : rag, dust cloth **3** *or* **paño de cocina** : dishcloth **4 paño higiénico** : sanitary napkin

pañoleta *nf* **1** : head scarf **2** : kerchief, scarf (for the neck) **3** CHAL : shawl

pañuelo *nm* **1** : handkerchief **2** : head scarf **3** : scarf (for the neck)

papa¹ *nm* : pope ⟨el Papa : the Pope⟩

papa² *nf* **1** : potato **2 papa dulce** : sweet potato **3 papas fritas** : potato chips, french fries **4 papas a la francesa** *Mex* : french fries

papá *nm fam* **1** : dad *fam*, pop *fam* **2 papás** *nmpl* : parents, folks *fam*

papada *nf* **1** : double chin, jowl **2** : dewlap

papagayo *nm* LORO : parrot

papal *adj* : papal

papalote *nm CA, Car, Mex* : kite

Papanicolau *nm* : Pap smear

Papá Noel *nm* : Santa Claus

papaya *nf* : papaya

papel *nm* **1** : paper, piece of paper **2** : role, part ⟨hizo el papel de Romeo : he played the part of Romeo⟩ ⟨jugar un papel importante en algo : to play an important role in something⟩ **3 papel (de) aluminio** : tinfoil, aluminum foil **4 papel de carta** : writing paper **5 papel de empapelar** *or* **papel pintado** : wallpaper **6 papel de envolver** : wrapping paper **7 papel de fumar** : cigarette paper **8 papel de lija** : sandpaper **9 papel de periódico** : newspaper, newsprint **10 papel de seda** : tissue paper **11 papel film** : plastic wrap **12 papel higiénico** : toilet paper **13 papel maché** : papier-mâché **14 papel moneda** : paper money

papeleo *nm* : paperwork, red tape

papelera *nf* **1** : wastebasket (indoors), trash can (on street) **2** : paper mill

papelería *nf* : stationery store

papelero, -ra *adj* : paper

papeleta *nf* **1** : ballot **2** : ticket, slip

paperas *nfpl* : mumps
papi *nm fam* : daddy, papa
papila gustativa *nf* : taste bud
papilla *nf* **1** : pap (for sick people), baby food **2 hacer papilla** : to beat to a pulp
papiro *nm* : papyrus
paprika *nf* : paprika
paquete *nm* **1** BULTO : package, parcel ⟨paquete bomba : mail bomb⟩ **2** : package (of cookies, etc.), pack (of cigarettes) **3** : package, bundle ⟨paquete turístico : tour package⟩ ⟨paquete de software : software bundle⟩
paquistaní *adj & nmf* : Pakistani
par¹ *adj* : even (in number)
par² *nm* **1** : pair, couple ⟨un par de zapatos : a pair of shoes⟩ **2** : equal, peer ⟨sin par : matchless, peerless⟩ **3** : par (in golf) **4** : rafter **5 de par en par** : wide open
par³ *nf* **1** : par ⟨por encima de la par : above par⟩ **2 a la par que** : at the same time as, as well as ⟨interesante a la par que instructivo : both interesting and informative⟩
para *prep* **1** (*indicating a recipient*) : for ⟨un regalo para ti : a present for you⟩ **2** (*indicating a purpose or goal*) : for ⟨la comida es para la fiesta : the food is for the party⟩ ⟨¿para qué? : what for?⟩ **3** (*indicating comparison*) : for ⟨alta para su edad : tall for her age⟩ ⟨es bueno para lo que cuesta : it's good for what it costs⟩ **4** : for (a time) ⟨una cita para el lunes : an appointment for Monday⟩ **5** : to (a time) ⟨faltan cinco para las ocho : it's five (minutes) to eight⟩ **6** : around, by (a time) ⟨para mañana estarán listos : they'll be ready by tomorrow⟩ **7** : to, towards ⟨para adelante/atrás : forwards/backwards⟩ ⟨para la derecha/izquierda : to the right/left⟩ ⟨van para el río : they're heading towards the river⟩ **8** (*used before an infinitive*) : to, in order to ⟨lo hace para molestarte : he does it to annoy you⟩ ⟨para no ser visto : in order not to be seen⟩ **9** (*used before an infinitive*) : to ⟨estoy listo para salir : I'm ready to leave⟩ ⟨demasiado joven para entender : too young to understand⟩ ⟨lo compré para devolverlo el mismo día : I bought it only to return it the same day⟩ **10 para que** : so, so that, in order that ⟨te lo digo para que sepas : I'm telling you so you'll know⟩
parabién *nm, pl* **-bienes** : congratulations *pl*
parábola *nf* **1** : parable **2** : parabola
parabrisas *nms & pl* : windshield
paracaídas *nms & pl* : parachute ⟨saltar/lanzarse en paracaídas : to parachute⟩
paracaidista *nmf* **1** : parachutist **2** : paratrooper
parachoques *nms & pl* : bumper
parada *nf* **1** : stop ⟨parada de autobús : bus stop⟩ **2** : stop (action) **3** : catch, save, parry (in sports) **4** DESFILE : parade
paradero *nm* **1** : whereabouts **2** : bus stop

paradigma *nm* : paradigm
paradisíaco, -ca *or* **paradisiaco, -ca** *adj* : heavenly
parado¹, -da *adj* **1** : motionless, idle, stopped **2** : standing (up) ⟨estar parado : to stand, to be standing⟩ **3** : confused, bewildered **4 bien/mal parado** : in good/bad shape ⟨salió bien parado : it turned out well for him⟩
parado², -da *n Spain* : unemployed person
paradoja *nf* : paradox
paradójico, -ca *adj* : paradoxical
parador *nm* **1** : roadside inn **2** : state-run hotel (in Spain) **3 parador en corto** *Car, Mex, Ven* : shortstop
parafernalia *nf* : paraphernalia
parafina *nf* **1** : paraffin **2** *Chile* : kerosene
parafrasear *vt* : to paraphrase
paráfrasis *nfs & pl* : paraphrase
paragolpes *nms & pl Arg, Par, Uru* : bumper
paraguas *nms & pl* : umbrella
paraguayo, -ya *adj & n* : Paraguayan
paraíso *nm* **1** : paradise, heaven **2** **paraíso fiscal** : tax shelter
paraje *nm* : spot, place
paralelismo *nm* : parallel, similarity
paralelo¹, -la *adj* : parallel
paralelo² *nm* : parallel
paralelogramo *nm* : parallelogram
parálisis *nfs & pl* **1** : paralysis **2** : standstill **3 parálisis cerebral** : cerebral palsy
paralizar {21} *vt* **1** : to paralyze **2** : to paralyze, to bring to a standstill — **paralizarse** *vr*
paramédico, -ca *n* : paramedic
parámetro *nm* : parameter
páramo *nm* : barren plateau, moor
parangón *nm, pl* **-gones** **1** : comparison **2 sin ~** : incomparable
paraninfo *nm* : auditorium, assembly hall
paranoia *nf* : paranoia
paranoico, -ca *adj & n* : paranoid
paranormal *adj* : paranormal
parapente *nm* : paragliding
parapetarse *vr* : to take cover
parapeto *nm* : parapet, rampart
parapléjico, -ca *adj & n* : paraplegic
parar *vt* **1** DETENER : to stop **2** : to stand, to prop ⟨parar la oreja : to perk up one's ears⟩ **3** : to stop, to block (a blow, etc.) — *vi* **1** CESAR : to stop ⟨habla sin parar : she talks nonstop⟩ ⟨no paraba de llorar : he wouldn't stop crying⟩ **2** : to stay, to put up **3** : to go on strike **4 ir a parar** : to end up, to wind up ⟨ir a parar a manos de alguien : to fall into someone's hands⟩ ⟨va a parar al hospital : he's going to end up in the hospital⟩ — **pararse** *vr* **1** : to stop ⟨pararse en seco : to stop dead⟩ **2** ATASCARSE : to stall (out) **3** : to stand up, to get up
pararrayos *nms & pl* : lightning rod
parasitario, -ria *adj* : parasitic
parásito *nm* : parasite
parasol *nm* SOMBRILLA : parasol
parcela *nf* : parcel, tract of land
parcelar *vt* : to parcel (land)

parchar *vt* : to patch, to patch up
parche *nm* : patch
parcial[1] *adj* **1** : partial ⟨un éxito parcial : a partial success⟩ **2** TENDENCIOSO : partial, biased — **parcialmente** *adv*
parcial[2] *nm* : exam (covering a portion of a semester's or trimester's material)
parcialidad *nf* : partiality, bias
parco, -ca *adj* **1** : sparing, frugal **2** : moderate, temperate **3** LACÓNICO : laconic, concise
pardo, -da *adj* : brownish grey
pardusco → **pardo**
parecer[1] {53} *vi* **1** : to seem, to look, to appear to be ⟨parece fácil : it looks easy⟩ ⟨parece que van a ganar : it looks like they're going to win⟩ ⟨así parece : so it seems⟩ ⟨pareces una princesa : you look like a princess⟩ ⟨¿qué te parece? : what do you think?⟩ ⟨me parece que sí : I think so⟩ ⟨me parece bien : that seems fine to me⟩ **3** : to like, to be in agreement ⟨si te parece : if you like, if it's all right with you⟩ — **parecerse** *vr* — **a** : to resemble
parecer[2] *nm* **1** OPINIÓN : opinion ⟨en mi parecer : in my opinion⟩ ⟨es del parecer que . . . : he's of the opinion that . . .⟩ **2** ASPECTO : appearance ⟨al parecer : apparently⟩
parecido[1], **-da** *adj* **1** : similar, alike **2** : bien parecido : good-looking
parecido[2] *nm* : resemblance, similarity ⟨tener un parecido con : to bear a resemblance to⟩
pared *nf* **1** : wall ⟨las paredes oyen : the walls have ears⟩ **2** : face (of a mountain)
paredón *nm, pl* **-dones** **1** : rock face **2** : wall (for executions by firing squad)
pareja *nf* **1** : couple, pair ⟨por parejas : in pairs⟩ ⟨vivir en pareja : to live together⟩ ⟨pareja de hecho : unmarried couple living together⟩ **2** : partner, mate ⟨tu pareja ideal : your ideal mate⟩ **3** : mate (to a glove, etc.)
parejo, -ja *adj* **1** : even, smooth, level **2** : equal, similar **3** al parejo de : on a par with
parentela *nf* : relations *pl*, kinfolk
parentesco *nm* : relationship, kinship
paréntesis *nms & pl* **1** : parenthesis ⟨entre paréntesis : in parentheses⟩ **2** : digression **3** entre ∼ : by the way
parentético, -ca *adj* : parenthetic, parenthetical
pargo *nm* : red snapper
paria *nmf* : pariah, outcast
paridad *nf* : parity, equality
pariente *nmf* : relative, relation
parir *vi* : to give birth — *vt* : to give birth to, to bear
paritario, -ria *adj* : equal, of peers/equals
parka *nf* : parka
parking *nm* : parking lot
parlamentar *vi* : to talk, to parley
parlamentario[1], **-ria** *adj* : parliamentary
parlamentario[2], **-ria** *n* : member of parliament
parlamento *nm* **1** : parliament **2** : negotiations *pl*, talks *pl*

parlanchín[1], **-china** *adj, mpl* **-chines** : chatty, talkative
parlanchín[2], **-china** *n, mpl* **-chines** : chatterbox
parlante *nm* ALTOPARLANTE : loudspeaker
parlotear *vi fam* : to gab, to chat, to prattle
parloteo *nm fam* : prattle, chatter
paro *nm* **1** HUELGA : strike **2** : stoppage, stopping **3** *Spain* : unemployment **4** *Spain* : unemployment benefits **5** paro cardíaco/cardiaco : cardiac arrest **6** paro forzoso : layoff
parodia *nf* : parody
parodiar *vt* : to parody
paroxismo *nm* **1** : fit, paroxysm **2** : peak, height ⟨llevar paroxismo : to carry to the extreme⟩
parpadear *vi* **1** : to blink **2** : to flicker
parpadeo *nm* **1** : blink, blinking **2** : flickering
párpado *nm* : eyelid
parque *nm* **1** : park **2** CORRAL : playpen (for children) **3** parque de diversiones/atracciones : amusement park **4** parque infantil : playground **5** parque natural : nature preserve **6** parque nacional : national park **7** parque temático : theme park
parqueadero *nm Col* : parking lot
parquear *vt* : to park — **parquearse** *vr*
parqueo *nm* : parking
parquet *or* **parqué** *nm* : parquet
parquímetro *nm* : parking meter
parra *nf* : vine, grapevine
párrafo *nm* : paragraph
parranda *nf fam* : party, spree ⟨irse de parranda : to party, to go partying⟩
parrilla *nf* **1** : broiler, grill ⟨a la parrilla : broiled, grilled⟩ **3** : grill (restaurant) **4** : grate **5** BACA : luggage rack, roof rack
parrillada *nf* **1** BARBACOA : barbecue **2** : grill (restaurant)
párroco *nm* : parish priest
parroquia *nf* **1** : parish **2** : parish church **3** : customers *pl*, clientele
parroquial *adj* : parochial
parroquiano, -na *nm* **1** : parishioner **2** : customer, patron
parsimonia *nf* **1** : calm **2** : thrift
parsimonioso, -sa *adj* **1** : calm, unhurried **2** : parsimonious, thrifty
parte[1] *nm* : report, dispatch ⟨parte meteorológico : weather report⟩
parte[2] *nf* **1** : part (of a whole) ⟨la mayor parte de : the majority of⟩ ⟨una quinta parte de : one fifth of⟩ **2** : place, part ⟨en alguna/cualquier parte : somewhere/anywhere⟩ ⟨en ninguna parte : nowhere, not anywhere⟩ ⟨por todas partes : everywhere⟩ ⟨ir a otra parte : to go somewhere else⟩ **3** : party (in negotiations, etc.) **4** de parte de : on behalf of ⟨de mi parte : on my behalf, for me⟩ **5** ¿de parte de quién? : may I ask who's calling? **6** en gran parte : largely, in large part **7** en ∼ : partly, in part **8** la mayor parte de : most of, the majority of **9** por otra parte : on the other hand **10** por

parte de : on the part of ⟨por mi parte : on my part, as far as I'm concerned⟩

11 tomar parte : to take part

partero, -ra *n* : midwife

partición *nf, pl* **-ciones** : division, sharing

participación *nf, pl* **-ciones 1** : participation **2** : share, interest **3** : announcement, notice

participante *nmf* **1** : participant **2** : competitor, entrant

participar *vi* **1** : to participate, to take part ⟨participar en algo : to participate in something⟩ **2** ~ **en** : to have a share in — *vt* : to announce, to notify

partícipe *nmf* : participant

participio *nm* : participle

partícula *nf* : particle

particular¹ *adj* **1** : particular, specific ⟨en particular : in particular⟩ **2** : private ⟨clases particulares : private lessons⟩ ⟨una casa particular : a private home⟩ **3** : special, unique ⟨¿qué tiene de particular? : what's so special about it?⟩ **4 de** ~ *Arg, Uru* : in plain/civilian clothes ⟨un policía de particular : a plainclothes policeman⟩

particular² *nm* **1** : matter, detail **2** : individual

particularidad *nf* : characteristic, peculiarity

particularizar {21} *vt* **1** : to distinguish, to characterize **2** : to specify

particularmente *adv* **1** : particularly, especially **2** : personally

partida *nf* **1** : departure **2** : item, entry **3** : certificate ⟨partida de nacimiento : birth certificate⟩ **4** : game, match, hand **5** : party, group

partidario, -ria *n* : follower, supporter ⟨soy partidario de . . . : I'm in favor of . . . , I support . . .⟩

partido *nm* **1** : (political) party **2** : game, match ⟨partido de futbol : soccer game⟩ ⟨partido amistoso : non-league game, non-championship game⟩ **3** APOYO : support, following **4** PROVECHO : profit, advantage ⟨sacar partido de : to profit from⟩ **5 un buen partido** : a good catch (for marriage)

partir *vt* **1** : to cut, to split **2** : to break, to crack **3** : to share (out), to divide — *vi* **1** : to leave, to depart **2** ~ **de** : to start from **3 a partir de** : as of, from ⟨a partir de hoy : as of today⟩ — **partirse** *vr* **1** : to smash, to split open **2** : to become chapped

partisano, -na *adj & n* : partisan

partitura *nf* : (musical) score

parto *nm* **1** : childbirth, delivery, labor ⟨estar de parto : to be in labor⟩ **2** : product, creation, brainchild

parvulario *nm* **1** : nursery school **2** : kindergarten

párvulo, -la *n* : toddler, preschooler

pasa *nf* **1** : raisin **2 pasa de Corinto** : currant

pasable *adj* : passable, tolerable — **pasablemente** *adv*

pasada *nf* **1** : passage, passing **2** : pass, wipe, coat (of paint) **3 de** ~ : in passing **4 mala pasada** : dirty trick

pasadizo *nm* : passageway, corridor

pasado¹, -da *adj* **1** : past ⟨el año pasado : last year⟩ ⟨pasado mañana : the day after tomorrow⟩ ⟨pasadas las siete : after seven o'clock⟩ **2** : overripe (of fruit), slightly spoiled **3** : well done (of meat), overcooked **4** : past tense (in grammar) **5 or pasado de moda** : old-fashioned, out-of-date

pasado² *nm* : past

pasador *nm* **1** : bolt, latch **2** : barrette **3** *Mex* : bobby pin **4** : quarterback (in American football)

pasaje *nm* **1** : ticket (for travel) **2** TARIFA : fare **3** : passageway **4** : passengers *pl* **5** : passage (from a book, etc.)

pasajero¹, -ra *adj* : passing, fleeting

pasajero², -ra *n* : passenger

pasamanos *nms & pl* : banister (of a staircase), handrail

pasamontañas *nms & pl* : balaclava, ski mask

pasante *nmf* : assistant

pasapalos *nmpl Ven* : snacks, hors d'oeuvres

pasaporte *nm* : passport

pasar *vi* **1** : to pass, to go ⟨la gente que pasa : the people who are passing (by), the people who pass by⟩ ⟨nos dejaron pasar : they let us (go) through⟩ ⟨pasamos por el centro : we went through the downtown⟩ ⟨nunca paso por esa calle : I never go down that street⟩ ⟨pasé por delante de la escuela : I went by/past the school⟩ **2** : to pass (of time) **3** : to pass, to pass down ⟨el trono pasó a su hijo : the throne passed to his son⟩ **4** : to go (on), to move (on) ⟨pasaron a la final : they moved on to the finals⟩ ⟨pasar a ser : to go on to become⟩ ⟨pasar de . . . a . . . : to go from . . . to . . .⟩ **5** : to drop by/in, to stop by ⟨pasamos por su casa : we dropped by his house⟩ **6** : to come in, to enter ⟨¿se puede pasar? : may we come in?⟩ **7** CABER : to go through, to fit **8** : to happen ⟨¿qué pasa? : what's happening?, what's going on?⟩ ⟨lo que pasa es que . . . : what's happening is that . . . , the thing is that . . .⟩ ⟨¿qué le pasa? : what's the matter with him?⟩ ⟨pase lo que pase : come what may⟩ **9** : to manage, to get by ⟨pasar sin algo : to manage without something⟩ **10** : to be acceptable, to pass ⟨puede pasar : it will do⟩ **11** : to pass (in an exam, etc.) **12** TERMINAR : to be over, to end **13** ~ **de** : to exceed, to go beyond **14** ~ **por** : to pass as/for ⟨podría pasar por tu hermana : she could pass as/for your sister⟩ **15** ~ **por** : to go through, to experience (difficulties, etc.) — *vt* **1** : to pass, to give ⟨¿me pasas la sal? : would you pass me the salt?⟩ **2** PEGAR : to give (an illness) **3** : to pass (a test) **4** : to cross (a bridge, river, etc.), to go through (a barrier) **5** : to spend (time) ⟨pasamos una semana en Acapulco : we spent a week in Acapulco⟩ **6** TOLERAR : to tolerate **7** SUFRIR : to go through, to suffer **8** : to show (a movie, etc.)

9 ADELANTAR, SUPERAR : to overtake, to pass, to surpass **10** : to pass (something over something) ⟨le pasó un trapo : he wiped it with a cloth⟩ ⟨pasar la aspiradora (por algo) : to vacuum (something)⟩ **11** ~ **con** : to put (a caller) through to ⟨pásame con el jefe : put me through to the boss⟩ **12 pasar de largo** : to go right past (without stopping) **13 pasarlo/pasarla bien** : to have a good time **14 pasarlo/pasarla mal** : to have a bad time, to have a hard time **15** ~ **por** : to put through ⟨pasa la sopa por un colador : put the soup through a strainer⟩ **16 pasar por alto** : to overlook, to omit — **pasarse** *vr* **1** : to pass, to go away ⟨se me pasó el mareo : the/my nausea has passed⟩ **2** : to stop by **3** : to slip one's mind, to slip by ⟨la fecha se me pasó : the date slipped by me⟩ **4** : to go too far ⟨se pasa de listo : he's too clever for his own good⟩ ⟨no te pases con la sal : go easy with/on the salt⟩ **5** : to go bad, to spoil

pasarela *nf* **1** : gangplank **2** : footbridge **3** : runway, catwalk

pasatiempo *nm* : pastime, hobby

Pascua *nf* **1** : Easter ⟨Domingo de Pascua : Easter Sunday⟩ **2** : Passover **3** : Christmas **4 Pascuas** *nfpl* : Christmas season

pase *nm* **1** PERMISO : pass, permit **2** : pass (in sports) **3 pase de abordar** *Mex* : boarding pass

paseante *nmf* : walker (person)

pasear *vi* **1** : to take a walk, to go for a ride — *vt* **1** : to take for a walk **2** : to parade around, to show off — **pasearse** *vr* **1** : to walk around, to go for a ride

paseo *nm* **1** : walk, stroll ⟨dar un paseo : to go for a walk⟩ **2** : ride **3** EXCURSIÓN : outing, trip **4** : avenue, walk **5** *or* **paseo marítimo** : boardwalk

pasillo *nm* CORREDOR : hallway, corridor, aisle

pasión *nf*, *pl* **pasiones** : passion

pasional *adj* : passionate ⟨crimen pasional : crime of passion⟩

pasionaria → **pasiflora**

pasivo¹, -va *adj* : passive — **pasivamente** *adv*

pasivo² *nm* **1** : liability ⟨activos y pasivos : assets and liabilities⟩ **2** : debit side (of an account)

pasmado, -da *adj* : stunned, flabbergasted

pasmar *vt* : to amaze, to stun — **pasmarse** *vr*

pasmo *nm* **1** : shock, astonishment **2** : wonder, marvel

pasmoso, -sa *adj* : incredible, amazing — **pasmosamente** *adv*

paso¹, -sa *adj* : dried ⟨ciruela pasa : prune⟩

paso² *nm* **1** : passage, passing ⟨de paso : in passing, on the way⟩ ⟨estar de paso : to be passing through⟩ ⟨el paso del tiempo : the passage of time⟩ **2** : way, path ⟨abrir/dejar paso a : to make way for⟩ ⟨ceda el paso : yield⟩ ⟨prohibido el paso : do not enter, no entry⟩ **3** : crossing ⟨paso de peatones : crosswalk⟩ ⟨paso

elevado : overpass⟩ ⟨paso subterráneo : underpass, tunnel⟩ ⟨paso a desnivel : underpass, overpass⟩ ⟨paso a nivel : railroad crossing⟩ **4** : pass (through mountains) ⟨salir del paso : to get out of a jam⟩ **5** : step ⟨dar un paso para adelante/atrás : to take a step forward/back⟩ ⟨estar a un paso de : to be within spitting distance of⟩ ⟨oír pasos : to hear footsteps⟩ **6** : step (in a process) ⟨paso a paso : step by step⟩ ⟨un paso positivo : a step in the right direction⟩ **7** : pace, gait ⟨a buen paso : quickly, at a good rate⟩ ⟨a este paso : at this rate⟩

pasta *nf* **1** : paste ⟨pasta de dientes *or* pasta dental : toothpaste⟩ **2** : pasta **3** : pastry dough **4 libro en pasta dura** : hardcover book **5 tener pasta de** : to have the makings of

pastar *vi* : to graze — *vt* : to put to pasture

pastel¹ *adj* : pastel

pastel² *nm* **1** : cake ⟨pastel de cumpleaños : birthday cake⟩ **2** : pie, turnover **3** : pastel

pastelería *nf* **1** : bakery, pastry shop **2** : baking, pastry making

pasteurización *nf*, *pl* **-ciones** : pasteurization

pasteurizar {21} *vt* : to pasteurize

pastilla *nf* **1** COMPRIMIDO, PÍLDORA : pill, tablet **2** : lozenge ⟨pastilla para la tos : cough drop⟩ **3** : cake (of soap), bar (of chocolate)

pastizal *nm* : pasture, grazing land

pasto *nm* **1** : pasture **2** HIERBA : grass, lawn

pastor, -tora *n* **1** : shepherd, shepherdess *f* **2** : minister, pastor **3 pastor alemán** : German shepherd

pastoral *adj* & *nf* : pastoral

pastorear *vt* : to shepherd, to tend

pastorela *nf* *Mex* : traditional Christmas play

pastoso, -sa *adj* **1** : pasty, doughy **2** : smooth, mellow (of sounds)

pata¹ *nf* **1** : paw, leg (of an animal) **2** *fam* : foot, leg (of a person) **3** : foot, leg (of furniture) **4 mala pata** *fam* : bad luck **5 meter la pata** *fam* : to put one's foot in it, to make a faux pas **6 patas de gallo** : crow's-feet **7 patas (para) arriba** : upside-down

pata² *nm* *Peru* : pal, buddy

patada *nf* **1** PUNTAPIÉ : kick ⟨le dio una patada : she kicked him⟩ **2** : stamp (of the foot)

patalear *vi* **1** : to kick **2** : to stamp one's feet

pataleta *nf* *fam* : tantrum

patán¹ *adj*, *pl* **patanes** : boorish, crude

patán² *nm*, *pl* **patanes** : boor, lout

patata *nf* *Spain* **1** : potato **2 patatas fritas** : potato chips, french fries

paté *nm* : pâté

pateador, -dora *n* : kicker (in sports)

patear *vt* : to kick — *vi* : to stamp one's foot

patentar *vt* : to patent

patente¹ *adj* EVIDENTE : obvious, patent — **patentemente** *adv*

patente² *nf* **1** : patent **2** *Arg, Chile, Uru* : license plate

paternal *adj* : fatherly, paternal

paternidad *nf* **1** : fatherhood, paternity **2** : parenthood **3** : authorship

paterno, -na *adj* : paternal ⟨abuela paterna : paternal grandmother⟩

patético, -ca *adj* : pathetic, moving

patetismo *nm* : pathos

patíbulo *nm* : gallows, scaffold

patilla *nf* **1** : arm (of glasses) **2** *Col* : watermelon **3** **patillas** *nfpl* : sideburns

patín *nm, pl* **patines** : skate ⟨patín de ruedas : roller skate⟩ ⟨patín en línea : in-line skate⟩

pátina *nf* : patina

patinador, -dora *n* : skater

patinaje *nm* : skating ⟨patinaje artístico : figure skating⟩

patinar *vi* **1** : to skate **2** : to skid, to slip **3** *fam* : to slip up, to blunder

patinazo *nm* **1** : skid **2** *fam* : blunder, slipup

patineta *nf* **1** : scooter **2** : skateboard

patinete *nm* : scooter

patio *nm* **1** : courtyard, patio **2** **patio de recreo** : playground

patito, -ta *n* : duckling

patizambo, -ba *adj* : knock-kneed

pato, -ta *n* **1** : duck **2** **pato real** : mallard **3** **pagar el pato** *fam* : to take the blame

patología *nf* : pathology

patológico, -ca *adj* : pathological

patólogo, -ga *n* : pathologist

patoso, -sa *adj* *Spain* : clumsy

patovica *nm* *Arg, Uru fam* : bouncer

patraña *nf* : tall tale, humbug, nonsense

patria *nf* : native land

patriarca *nm* : patriarch — **patriarcal** *adj*

patriarcado *nm* : patriarchy

patrimonio *nm* : patrimony, legacy

patrio, -tria *adj* **1** : native, home ⟨suelo patrio : native soil⟩ **2** : paternal

patriota¹ *adj* : patriotic

patriota² *nmf* : patriot

patriotería *nf* : jingoism, chauvinism

patriotero¹, -ra *adj* : jingoistic, chauvinistic

patriotero², -ra *n* : jingoist, chauvinist

patriótico, -ca *adj* : patriotic

patriotismo *nm* : patriotism

patrocinador, -dora *n* : sponsor, patron

patrocinar *vt* : to sponsor

patrocinio *nm* : sponsorship, patronage

patrón¹, -trona *n, mpl* **patrones** **1** JEFE : boss **2** CAPITÁN : skipper **3** *Spain* CASERO : landlord *m*, landlady *f* **4** : patron saint

patrón² *nm, pl* **patrones** **1** : standard **2** : pattern (in sewing)

patronal *adj* **1** : management, employers' ⟨sindicato patronal : employers' association⟩ **2** : pertaining to a patron saint ⟨fiesta patronal : patron saint's day⟩

patronato *nm* **1** : board, council **2** : foundation, trust

patrono, -na *n* **1** : employer **2** : patron saint

patrulla *nf* **1** : patrol **2** : police car, cruiser

patrullar *v* : to patrol

patrullero *nm* **1** : police car **2** : patrol boat **3** : patrol plane

paulatino, -na *adj* : gradual

paupérrimo, -ma *adj* : destitute, poverty-stricken

pausa *nf* : pause, break ⟨hacer una pausa : to pause, to break⟩ ⟨pausa comercial/publicitaria : commercial break⟩

pausado¹ *adv* : slowly, deliberately ⟨habla más pausado : speak more slowly⟩

pausado², -da *adj* : slow, deliberate — **pausadamente** *adv*

pauta *nf* **1** : rule, guideline **2** : lines *pl* (on paper)

pava *nf* *Arg, Bol, Chile* : kettle

pavimentar *vt* : to pave

pavimento *nm* : pavement

pavo, -va *n* **1** : turkey **2** **pavo real** : peacock **3** **comer pavo** : to be a wallflower

pavón *nm, pl* **pavones** : peacock

pavonearse *vr* **1** : to strut, to swagger **2** **pavonearse de** : to brag about

pavoneo *nm* : strut, swagger

pavor *nm* TERROR : dread, terror

pavoroso, -sa *adj* ATERRADOR : dreadful, terrifying

paya *nf* *Chile* → **payada**

payada *nf* *Arg, Uru* : song with improvised lyrics

payasada *nf* **1** : antic ⟨hacer payasadas : to clown around⟩ **2** TONTERÍA : foolish thing **3** FARSA : joke, farce

payasear *vi* : to clown around

payaso, -sa *n* **1** : clown **2** : clown, funny person

paz *nf, pl* **paces** **1** : peace **2** **descanse en paz** : rest in peace **3** **dejar en paz** : to leave alone **4** **hacer las paces** : to make up, to reconcile

pazca, etc. → **pacer**

PC [ˈpeˈse, piˈsi] *nmf* : PC, personal computer

PDA [pedeˈa, pidiˈe] *nm* : PDA

pe *nf* : (letter) p

peaje *nm* : toll

peatón *nm, pl* **-tones** : pedestrian

peatonal *adj* : pedestrian

peca *nf* : freckle

pecado *nm* : sin

pecador¹, -dora *adj* : sinful, sinning

pecador², -dora *n* : sinner

pecaminoso, -sa *adj* : sinful

pecar {72} *vi* **1** : to sin **2** ~ **de** ⟨pecan de optimistas/optimismo : they're too optimistic⟩

pécari *or* **pecarí** *nm* : peccary

pececillo *nm* : small fish

pecera *nf* : fishbowl, fish tank

pecho *nm* **1** : chest **2** SENO : breast, bosom **3** : heart, courage **4** **dar el pecho** : to breast-feed **5** *or* **estilo (de) pecho** : breaststroke **6** **tomarse algo a pecho** : to take something to heart

pechuga *nf* : breast (of fowl)

pecoso, -sa *adj* : freckled

pectoral *adj* : pectoral

peculado *nm* : embezzlement

peculiar *adj* **1** CARACTERÍSTICO : particular, characteristic **2** RARO : peculiar, uncommon

peculiaridad *nf* : peculiarity

pecuniario, -ria *adj* : pecuniary

pedagogía *nf* : pedagogy

pedagógico, -ca *adj* : pedagogic, pedagogical

pedagogo, -ga *n* : educator

pedal *nm* : pedal ⟨pedal del acelerador : accelerator pedal⟩

pedalear *vi* : to pedal

pedante¹ *adj* : pedantic

pedante² *nmf* : pedant

pedantería *nf* : pedantry

pedazo *nm* TROZO : piece, bit, chunk ⟨caerse a pedazos : to fall to pieces⟩ ⟨hacer pedazos : to tear into shreds, to smash to pieces⟩

pedernal *nm* : flint

pedestal *nm* : pedestal

pedestre *adj* : commonplace, pedestrian

pediatra *nmf* : pediatrician

pediatría *nf* : pediatrics

pediátrico, -ca *adj* : pediatric

pedido *nm* **1** : order (of merchandise) ⟨hacer un pedido : to place an order⟩ **2** : request

pedigrí *nm, pl* **-gríes** : pedigree

pedir {54} *vt* **1** : to ask for, to request ⟨le pedí un préstamo a Claudia : I asked Claudia for a loan⟩ ⟨le pedí que nos llamara : I asked her to call us⟩ ⟨me pidieron ayuda/permiso : they asked me for help/permission⟩ ⟨pide 200 dólares por la bici : he's asking 200 dollars for the bike⟩ **2** : to order (food, merchandise) **3** **pedir disculpas/perdón** : to apologize — *vi* **1** : to order **2** : to beg

pedo *nm fam* : fart *fam*

pedrada *nf* **1** : blow (with a rock or stone) ⟨la ventana se quebró de una pedrada : the window was broken by a rock⟩ **2** *fam* : cutting remark, dig

pedregal *nm* : rocky ground

pedregoso, -sa *adj* : rocky, stony

pedrera *nf* CANTERA : quarry

pedrería *nf* : precious stones *pl*, gems *pl*

pega *nf* Chile : work

pegadizo, -za *adj* : catchy

pegado, -da *adj* **1** : glued, stuck, stuck together **2 ~ a** : right next to

pegajoso, -sa *adj* **1** : sticky, gluey **2** : catchy ⟨una tonada pegajosa : a catchy tune⟩ **3** : clingy (of a person)

pegamento *nm* : adhesive, glue

pegar {52} *vt* **1** : to stick, to glue, to paste **2** : to attach, to sew on **3** : to infect with, to give ⟨me pegó el resfriado : he gave me his cold⟩ **4** : to give (a slap, a kick, etc.), to deal (a blow) ⟨le pegó un tiro/puñetazo : she shot/punched him⟩ ⟨me pegó un susto : he startled me⟩ **5** : to give (a shout, a jump, etc.) ⟨pegó un alarido : she let out a scream⟩ **6** : to put against, to put near — *vi* **1** ADHERIRSE : to stick, to adhere **2** : to hit ⟨pegar en algo : to hit (against) something⟩ ⟨pegarle a alguien : to hit someone⟩ **3 ~ con** : to match, to go with — **pegarse** *vr*

1 : to hit oneself ⟨me pegué en el codo : I hit my elbow⟩ **2** : to hit each other **3** : to stick, to take hold **4** : to be contagious

pegote *nm* **1** : sticky mess **2** *Mex* : sticker, adhesive label

pegue, etc. → **pegar**

peinado *nm* : hairstyle, hairdo

peinador, -dora *n* : hairdresser

peinar *vt* **1** : to comb (hair) **2** : to style, to do (hair) **3** RASTREAR : to comb, to search — **peinarse** *vr* **1** : to comb one's hair **2** : to get one's hair done

peine *nm* : comb

peineta *nf* : ornamental comb

peladez *nf, pl* **-deces** *Mex fam* : obscenity, bad language

pelado, -da *adj* **1** : bald, hairless **2** : peeled **3** : bare, barren **4** : broke, penniless **5** *Mex fam* : coarse, crude

pelador *nm* : peeler

pelagra *nf* : pellagra

pelaje *nm* : coat (of an animal), fur

pelapapas *nms* : (potato) peeler

pelar *vt* **1** : to peel, to shell **2** : to skin **3** : to pluck **4** : to remove hair from **5** *fam* : to clean out (of money) — **pelarse** *vr* **1** : to peel **2** *fam* : to get a haircut **3** *Mex fam* : to split, to leave

peldaño *nm* **1** : step, stair **2** : rung

pelea *nf* **1** LUCHA : fight **2** : quarrel

pelear *vi* **1** LUCHAR : to fight **2** DISPUTAR : to quarrel — **pelearse** *vr*

pelele *nm* : puppet

peleón, -ona *adj, mpl* **-ones** *Spain* : quarrelsome, argumentative

peleonero, -ra *adj Mex* : quarrelsome

peletería *nf* **1** : fur shop **2** : fur trade

peletero, -ra *n* : furrier

peliagudo, -da *adj* : tricky, difficult, ticklish

pelícano *nm* : pelican

película *nf* **1** : movie, film ⟨dar/poner una película : to show a movie⟩ ⟨película de acción/suspenso/terror : action/suspense/horror movie⟩ ⟨película de vaqueros : Western⟩ **2** : (photographic) film **3** : thin covering, layer

peligrar *vi* : to be in danger

peligro *nm* **1** : danger, peril ⟨estar en peligro : to be in danger⟩ ⟨estar fuera de peligro : to be out of danger⟩ ⟨poner en peligro : to put in danger, to endanger⟩ ⟨peligro de incendio : fire hazard⟩ **2** : risk ⟨correr (el) peligro de : to run the risk of⟩

peligroso, -sa *adj* : dangerous, hazardous

pelirrojo¹, -ja *adj* : red-haired, redheaded

pelirrojo², -ja *n* : redhead

pellejo *nm* **1** : hide, skin **2 salvar el pellejo** : to save one's neck

pellizcar {72} *vt* **1** : to pinch **2** : to nibble on

pellizco *nm* : pinch ⟨me dio un pellizco : she gave me a pinch⟩ ⟨un pellizco de : a pinch of⟩

pelmazo¹, -za *adj fam* : boring

pelmazo², -za *n fam* : bore

pelo *nm* **1** : hair **2** : fur **3** : pile, nap **4 a pelo** : bareback **5 con pelos y señales** : in great detail **6 no tener pelos en la**

lengua : not to mince words, to be blunt **7 ponerle los pelos de punta a alguien** : to make someone's hair stand on end **8 por un pelo** : just barely **9 tomarle el pelo a alguien** : to tease someone, to pull someone's leg

pelón¹, -lona *adj, mpl* **pelones 1** : bald **2** *fam* : broke **3** *Mex fam* : tough, difficult

pelón², -lona *n, mpl* **pelones** : bald person

pelota *nf* **1** : ball **2** *fam* : head **3 en pelotas** *fam* : naked **4 jugar a la pelota** : to play ball **5 pasar la pelota** *fam* : to pass the buck **6 pelota vasca** : jai alai

pelotera *nf* **1** : fight **2** : ruckus, row

pelotón *nm, pl* **-tones** : squad, detachment

peltre *nm* : pewter

peluca *nf* : wig

peluche *nm* : plush (fabric) ⟨oso de peluche : teddy bear⟩

peludo, -da *adj* : hairy, shaggy, bushy

peluquería *nf* **1** : hairdresser's, barbershop **2** : hairdressing

peluquero, -ra *n* : barber, hairdresser

peluquín *nm, pl* **-quines** TUPÉ : hairpiece, toupee

pelusa *nf* **1** : down **2** : lint (on clothes)

pélvico, -ca *adj* : pelvic

pelvis *nfs & pl* : pelvis

pena *nf* **1** SENTENCIA : sentence, penalty ⟨pena de muerte, pena capital : death penalty⟩ **2** AFLICCIÓN : sorrow, grief ⟨me da pena : it makes me sad⟩ ⟨morir de pena : to die of a broken heart⟩ ⟨qué pena! : what a shame!, how sad!⟩ **3** VERGÜENZA : shame, embarrassment **4 penas** *nfpl* : problems, troubles ⟨olvidar tus penas : to forget your troubles⟩ **5 penas** *nfpl* : difficulty, trouble ⟨a duras penas : with great difficulty⟩ **6 valer la pena** : to be worthwhile

penacho *nm* **1** : crest, tuft **2** : plume (of feathers)

penal¹ *adj* : criminal, penal

penal² *nm* CÁRCEL : prison, penitentiary

penalidad *nf* **1** : hardship **2** : penalty, punishment

penalizar {21} *vt* : to penalize

penalty *nm* : penalty (in sports)

penar *vt* : to punish, to penalize — *vi* : to suffer, to grieve

pendenciero, -ra *adj* : argumentative, quarrelsome

pender *vi* : to hang **2** : to be pending

pendiente¹ *adj* **1** : pending ⟨asuntos pendientes : unfinished business⟩ ⟨cuentas pendientes : outstanding bills⟩ **2 estar pendiente de** : to pay a lot of attention to **3 estar pendiente de** : to be awaiting

pendiente² *nm Spain* : earring

pendiente³ *nf* : slope, incline

pendón *nm, pl* **pendones** : banner

péndulo *nm* : pendulum

pene *nm* : penis

penetración *nf, pl* **-ciones 1** : penetration **2** : insight

penetrante *adj* **1** : penetrating ⟨una mirada/mente penetrante : a penetrating look/mind⟩ **2** : bitter (of cold or wind), pungent (of smells) **3** ESTRIDENTE : piercing, shrill

penetrar *vi* **1** : to penetrate, to sink in **2** ~ **por** *or* ~ **en** : to pierce, to go in, to enter into ⟨el frío penetra por la ventana : the cold comes right in through the window⟩ — *vt* **1** : to penetrate, to permeate **2** : to pierce ⟨el dolor penetró su corazón : sorrow pierced her heart⟩ **3** : to fathom, to understand

penicilina *nf* : penicillin

península *nf* : peninsula — **peninsular** *adj*

penique *nm* : penny

penitencia *nf* : penance, penitence

penitenciaría *nf* : penitentiary

penitente *adj & n* : penitent

penol *nm* : yardarm

penosamente *adv* : with difficulty

penoso, -sa *adj* **1** : painful, distressing **2** : difficult, arduous **3** : shy, bashful

pensado, -da *adj* **1 bien pensado** : well thought-out **2 en el momento menos pensado** : when least expected **3 poco pensado** : badly thought-out **4 mal pensado** : evil-minded

pensador, -dora *n* : thinker

pensamiento *nm* **1** : thought **2** : thinking **3** : pansy

pensar {55} *vi* **1** : to think ⟨pensar bien/mal de alguien : to think well/poorly of someone⟩ **2** ~ **en** : to think about ⟨pensaba en otra cosa : I was thinking about something else⟩ **3 dar que pensar** : to provide food for thought — *vt* **1** : to think ⟨pienso que es necesario : I think it's necessary⟩ ⟨¿qué piensas de su nueva canción? : what do you think about her new song?⟩ **2** : to think about ⟨está pensando comprar una casa : she's thinking about buying a house⟩ **3** : to intend, to plan on ⟨¿qué piensas hacer? : what do you plan to do?⟩ ⟨no pienso casarme : I don't intend to get married⟩ — **pensarse** *vr* : to think over

pensativo, -va *adj* : pensive, thoughtful

pensión *nf, pl* **pensiones 1** JUBILACIÓN : pension **2** : boarding house **3 pensión alimenticia** : alimony

pensionado, -da *n* → **pensionista**

pensionista *nmf* **1** JUBILADO : pensioner, retiree **2** : boarder, lodger

pentágono *nm* : pentagon — **pentagonal** *adj*

pentagrama *nm* : staff (in music)

penthouse ['pent,haus] *nm* : penthouse

penúltimo, -ma *adj* : next to last, penultimate

penumbra *nf* : partial darkness, shadow

penuria *nf* **1** ESCASEZ : shortage, scarcity **2** : poverty

peña *nf* : rock, crag

peñasco *nm* : crag, large rock

peñascoso, -sa *adj* : craggy

peñón → **peñasco**

peón *nm, pl* **peones 1** : laborer, peon **2** : pawn (in chess)

peonía *nf* : peony
peor[1] *adv* **1** *comparative of* MAL : worse ⟨se llevan peor que antes : they get along worse than before⟩ **2** *superlative of* MAL : worst ⟨me fue peor que a nadie : I did the worst of all⟩ ⟨el secreto peor guardado : the worst-kept secret⟩ **3 cada vez peor** : worse and worse **4 de mal en peor** : from bad to worse
peor[2] *adj* **1** *comparative of* MALO : worse ⟨es peor que el original : it's worse than the original⟩ **2** *superlative of* MALO : worst ⟨la peor parte : the worst part⟩ ⟨el peor de todos : the worst of all⟩
pepa *nf* : seed, pit (of a fruit)
pepenador, -dora *n CA, Mex* : scavenger
pepenar *vt CA, Mex* : to scavenge, to scrounge
pepinillo *nm* : pickle, gherkin
pepino *nm* : cucumber
pepita *nf* **1** : seed, pip **2** : nugget **3** *Mex* : dried pumpkin seed
peque, etc. → **pecar**
pequeñez *nf, pl* **-ñeces 1** : smallness **2** : trifle, triviality **3 pequeñez de espíritu** : pettiness
pequeño, -ña *adj* **1** : small, little ⟨un libro pequeño : a small book⟩ **2** : young, little ⟨su hermana pequeña : his little sister⟩ **3** CORTO : short **4** LIGERO : slight
pequeño[2], **-ña** *n* : child, little one
pera *nf* **1** : pear **2** *Arg, Chile, Uru* BARBILLA, MENTÓN : chin **3** *Arg, Chile, Uru* : goatee **4** : rubber bulb (for suction, etc.) **5 pedirle peras al olmo** : to ask the impossible
peral *nm* : pear tree
peraltar *vt* : to bank (a road)
peralte *nm* : bank (of a road)
perca *nf* : perch (fish)
percal *nm* : percale
percance *nm* : mishap, misfortune
per cápita *adv & adj* : per capita
percatarse *vr* ~ **de** : to notice, to become aware of
percebe *nm* : barnacle
percepción *nf, pl* **-ciones 1** : perception **2** : idea, notion **3** COBRO : receipt (of payment), collection
perceptible *adj* : perceptible, noticeable — **perceptiblemente** *adv*
percha *nf* **1** : perch **2** : coat hanger **3** : coatrack, coat hook
perchero *nm* : coatrack
percibir *vt* **1** : to perceive, to notice, to sense **2** : to earn, to draw (a salary)
percudido, -da *adj* : grimy
percudir *vt* : to make grimy — **percudirse** *vr*
percusión *nf, pl* **-siones** : percussion
percusor *or* **percutor** *nm* : hammer (of a firearm)
perdedor[1], **-dora** *adj* : losing
perdedor[2], **-dora** *n* : loser
perder {56} *vt* **1** : to lose ⟨perdió las llaves : he lost his keys⟩ ⟨perder dinero/peso : to lose money/weight⟩ ⟨perder la paciencia/confianza : to lose patience/confidence⟩ ⟨perder la vida : to lose one's life⟩ **2** : to lose (a game, contest, etc.) **3**

: to miss (a train, an event, etc.) ⟨perdimos la oportunidad : we missed the opportunity⟩ **4** : to waste (time) — *vi* : to lose — **perderse** *vr* **1** EXTRAVIARSE : to get lost **2** : to miss **3** DESAPARECER : to disappear
perdición *nf, pl* **-ciones** : ruin
pérdida *nf* **1** : loss ⟨pérdidas económicas : economic losses⟩ **2** : waste (of time, money, etc.) **3** : leak (of liquid, gas, etc.)
perdidamente *adv* : hopelessly
perdido, -da *adj* **1** : lost ⟨objetos perdidos : lost and found⟩ ⟨una bala perdida : a stray bullet⟩ **2** : inveterate, incorrigible ⟨es un caso perdido : he's a hopeless case⟩ ⟨dar algo por perdido : to give something up as a lost cause⟩ **3 de ~** *Mex fam* : at least **4 estar perdido** : to be in trouble, to be done for
perdigón *nm, pl* **-gones** : shot, pellet
perdiz *nf, pl* **perdices** : partridge
perdón[1] *nm, pl* **perdones** : forgiveness, pardon ⟨me pidió perdón : she apologized to me⟩
perdón[2] *interj* : excuse me!, sorry!
perdonable *adj* : forgivable
perdonar *vt* **1** DISCULPAR : to forgive, to pardon ⟨¿me perdonas? : do you forgive me?⟩ ⟨perdona que te interrumpa : pardon me for interrupting⟩ **2** : to excuse from (a task, etc.), to write off (a debt) ⟨perdonarle la vida a alguien : to spare someone's life⟩ — *vi* : to excuse, to pardon ⟨perdona, pero . . . : excuse/pardon me, but . . .⟩
perdurable *adj* : lasting
perdurar *vi* : to last, to endure, to survive
perecedero, -ra *adj* : perishable
perecer {53} *vi* : to perish, to die
peregrinación *nf, pl* **-ciones** : pilgrimage
peregrinaje *nm* → **peregrinación**
peregrino[1], **-na** *adj* **1** : unusual, odd **2** MIGRATORIO : migratory
peregrino[2], **-na** *n* : pilgrim
perejil *nm* : parsley
perenne *adj* : perennial ⟨árbol de hoja perenne : evergreen tree⟩
perentorio, -ria *adj* **1** : peremptory **2** URGENTE : urgent **3** FIJO : fixed, set
pereza *nf* FLOJERA, HOLGAZANERÍA : laziness, idleness
perezoso[1], **-sa** *adj* FLOJO, HOLGAZÁN : lazy
perezoso[2] *nm* : sloth (animal)
perfección *nf, pl* **-ciones** : perfection ⟨a la perfección : perfectly⟩
perfeccionamiento *nm* : perfecting, refinement
perfeccionar *vt* **1** : to perfect **2** : to improve, to refine
perfeccionismo *nm* : perfectionism
perfeccionista *nmf* : perfectionist
perfecto, -ta *adj* : perfect — **perfectamente** *adv*
perfidia *nf* : treachery
pérfido, -da *adj* : perfidious
perfil *nm* **1** : profile ⟨de perfil : from the side, in profile⟩ **2** CONTORNO : profile, outline **3 perfiles** *nmpl* RASGOS : features, characteristics

perfilar *vt* : to outline, to define — **perfilarse** *vr* **1** : to be outlined, to be silhouetted **2** : to take shape
perforación *nf, pl* **-ciones 1** : perforation **2** : drilling
perforadora *nf* **1** : hole punch (for paper) **2** : drill (in mining, etc.)
perforar *vt* **1** : to perforate, to pierce **2** : to drill, to bore
perfumar *vt* : to perfume, to scent — **perfumarse** *vr* : to put on perfume
perfume *nm* : perfume, scent
perfumería *nf* **1** : perfume shop **2** : perfumes *pl* **3** : perfume industry
pergamino *nm* : parchment
pérgola *nf* : arbor
pericia *nf* : skill, expertise
pericial *adj* : expert ⟨testigo pericial : expert witness⟩
perico *nm* COTORRA : small parrot
periferia *nf* : periphery, outskirts
periférico¹, -ca *adj* : outlying, peripheral
periférico² *nm* **1** *CA, Mex* : beltway **2** : peripheral
perilla *nf* **1** : goatee **2** : pommel (on a saddle) **3** *Col, Mex* : knob, handle **4 perilla de la oreja** : earlobe **5 de perillas** *fam* : handy, just right
perímetro *nm* : perimeter
periódico¹, -ca *adj* : periodic — **periódicamente** *adv*
periódico² *nm* DIARIO : newspaper
periodismo *nm* : journalism
periodista *nmf* : journalist
periodístico, -ca *adj* : journalistic, news
período *or* **periodo** *nm* : period
peripecia *nf* VICISITUD : vicissitude, reversal ⟨las peripecias de su carrera : the ups and downs of her career⟩ ⟨contar las peripecias de : to tell the adventures of⟩
periquera *nf Mex* : high chair (for a baby)
periquito *nm* : parakeet
periscopio *nm* : periscope
perito, -ta *adj & n* : expert
perjudicar {72} *vt* : to harm, to be detrimental to ⟨perjudicar la salud : to be bad for your health⟩
perjudicial *adj* : harmful, detrimental ⟨ser perjudicial para : to be harmful to⟩
perjuicio *nm* **1** : harm, damage ⟨causar perjuicio a : to cause damage to⟩ **2 en perjuicio de** : to the detriment of **3 sin perjuicio de** : without detriment to, without affecting
perjurar *vi* : to perjure oneself
perjurio *nm* : perjury
perla *nf* **1** : pearl **2 de perlas** *fam* : wonderfully ⟨me viene de perlas : it suits me just fine⟩
permanecer {53} *vi* **1** QUEDARSE : to remain, to stay **2** SEGUIR : to remain, to continue to be
permanencia *nf* **1** : permanence, continuance **2** ESTANCIA : stay
permanente¹ *adj* **1** : permanent **2** : constant — **permanentemente** *adv*
permanente² *nf* : perm, permanent (wave) ⟨hacerse la permanente : to get a perm⟩
permeabilidad *nf* : permeability

permeable *adj* : permeable
permisible *adj* : permissible, allowable
permisividad *nf* : permissiveness
permisivo, -va *adv* : permissive
permiso *nm* **1** : permission ⟨dar permiso : to give permission⟩ **2** : permit, license ⟨permiso de conducir : driver's license⟩ ⟨permiso de residencia : green card⟩ ⟨permiso de trabajo : work permit⟩ **3** : leave, furlough **4 con —** : excuse me, pardon me **5 de —** : on leave
permitir *vt* **1** : to permit, to allow ⟨no me permitió pasar : he wouldn't let me through⟩ ⟨¿me permite? : may I?⟩ **2** POSIBILITAR : to enable, to allow — **permitirse** *vr* : to allow oneself ⟨permitirse el lujo de : to allow oneself the luxury of⟩
permuta *nf* : exchange
permutación *nf, pl* **-ciones** : permutation
permutar *vt* INTERCAMBIAR : to exchange
pernera *nf* : leg (of pants, etc.)
pernicioso, -sa *adj* : pernicious, destructive
pernil *nm* **1** : haunch (of an animal) **2** : leg (of meat), ham **3** : trouser leg
perno *nm* : bolt, pin
pernoctar *vi* : to stay overnight, to spend the night
pero¹ *nm* **1** : fault, defect ⟨ponerle peros a : to find fault with⟩ **2** : objection
pero² *conj* **1** : but ⟨lo siento, pero no puedo : I'm sorry, but I can't⟩ **2** (*used for emphasis*) ⟨¿pero qué le ve? : what on earth does she see in him?⟩ ⟨es muy, pero muy caro : it's extremely expensive⟩
perogrullada *nf* : truism, platitude, cliché
peroné *nm* : fibula
perorar *vi* : to deliver a speech
perorata *nf* : oration, long-winded speech
peróxido *nm* : peroxide
perpendicular *adj & nf* : perpendicular
perpetrar *vt* : to perpetrate
perpetuar {3} *vt* ETERNIZAR : to perpetuate
perpetuidad *nf* : perpetuity
perpetuo, -tua *adj* : perpetual — **perpetuamente** *adv*
perplejidad *nf* : perplexity
perplejo, -ja *adj* : perplexed, puzzled
perrada *nf fam* : dirty trick
perrera *nf* : kennel, dog pound
perrero, -ra *n* : dogcatcher
perrito, -ta *n* CACHORRO : puppy, small dog
perro, -rra *n* **1** : dog, bitch *f* **2 perro callejero** : stray dog **3 perro caliente** : hot dog **4 perro cobrador** : retriever **5 perro faldero** : lapdog **6 perro guardián** : guard dog **7 perro guía/lazarillo** : guide dog **8 perro pastor** : sheepdog **9 perro policía** : police dog **10 perro rastreador** : tracking dog **11 perro salchicha** : dachshund
persa¹ *adj & nmf* : Persian
persa² *nm* : Persian (language)
per se *adv* : per se
persecución *nf, pl* **-ciones 1** : pursuit, chase **2** : persecution

perseguible *adj* : chargeable
perseguidor, -dora *n* **1** : pursuer **2** : persecutor
perseguir {75} *vt* **1** : to pursue, to chase **2** : to persecute **3** : to pester, to annoy
perseverancia *nf* : perseverance
perseverante *adj* : persistent
perseverar *vi* : to persevere
persiana *nf* : blind, venetian blind
persignarse *vr* SANTIGUARSE : to cross oneself, to make the sign of the cross
persistir *vi* **1** : to persist **2** ~ **en** : to persist in — **persistencia** *nf* — **persistente** *adj*
persona *nf* **1** : person ⟨miles de personas : thousands of people⟩ **2 en** ~ : in person **3 por** ~ : per person
personaje *nm* **1** : character (in drama or literature) **2** : personage, celebrity
personal[1] *adj* : personal — **personalmente** *adv*
personal[2] *nm* : personnel, staff
personalidad *nf* **1** : personality **2** PERSONAJE : personage, celebrity
personalizar {21} *vt* : to personalize — *vi* : to name names
personero, -ra *n* **1** : representative **2** : spokesperson, spokesman *m*, spokeswoman *f*
personificar {72} *vi* : to personify — **personificación** *nf*
perspectiva *nf* **1** : perspective **2** VISTA : view **3** : prospect, outlook ⟨tener buenas perspectivas : to have good prospects⟩ ⟨en perspectiva : in the offing, in prospect⟩ **4** : perspective, point of view ⟨mirándolo en perspectiva : looking back (at it), (looking at it) in retrospect/hindsight⟩
perspicacia *nf* : shrewdness, perspicacity, insight
perspicaz *adj, pl* **-caces** : shrewd, perspicacious
persuadir *vt* : to persuade ⟨lo persuadí de/para que viniera : I persuaded him to come⟩ — **persuadirse** *vr* : to become convinced
persuasión *nf, pl* **-siones** : persuasion
persuasivo, -va *adj* : persuasive
pertenecer {53} *vi* : to belong ⟨pertenecer a : to belong to⟩
perteneciente *adj* ~ **a** : belonging to
pertenencia *nf* **1** : membership **2** : ownership **3 pertenencias** *nfpl* : belongings, possessions
pértiga *nf* GARROCHA : pole ⟨salto con/de pértiga : pole vault⟩
pertinaz *adj, pl* **-naces** **1** OBSTINADO : obstinate **2** PERSISTENTE : persistent
pertinencia *nf* : pertinence, relevance
pertinente *adj* **1** : pertinent, relevant **2** : appropriate
pertrechos *nmpl* : equipment, gear
perturbación *nf, pl* **-ciones** : disturbance, disruption
perturbador, -dora *adj* **1** INQUIETANTE : disturbing, troubling **2** : disruptive
perturbar *vt* **1** : to disturb, to trouble **2** : to disrupt
peruano, -na *adj & n* : Peruvian

perversidad *nf* : perversity, depravity
perversión *nf, pl* **-siones** : perversion
perverso, -sa *adj* : wicked, depraved
pervertido[1], **-da** *adj* DEPRAVADO : perverted, depraved
pervertido[2], **-da** *n* : pervert
pervertir {76} *vt* : to pervert, to corrupt
pesa *nf* **1** : weight **2 levantamiento de pesas** : weight lifting
pesadamente *adv* **1** : heavily **2** : slowly, clumsily
pesadez *nf, pl* **-deces** **1** : heaviness **2** ABURRIMIENTO : tediousness **3** PLOMO : drag, bore
pesadilla *nf* : nightmare
pesado[1], **-da** *adj* **1** : heavy **2** LENTO : slow **3** MOLESTO : irritating, annoying **4** ABURRIDO : tedious, boring **5** DIFÍCIL : tough, difficult
pesado[2], **-da** *n fam* : bore, pest
pesadumbre *nf* AFLICCIÓN : grief, sorrow, sadness
pésame *nm* : condolences *pl* ⟨darle el pésame a alguien : to give someone one's condolences⟩ ⟨mi más sentido pésame : my heartfelt condolences⟩
pesar[1] *vt* **1** : to weigh ⟨pesa dos kilos : it weighs two kilos⟩ **2** EXAMINAR : to consider, to think over — *vi* **1** : to weigh ⟨¿cuánto pesa? : how much does it weigh?⟩ **2** : to be heavy **3** : to weigh heavily, to be a burden ⟨la responsabilidad le pesa : the responsibility is a burden on him⟩ **4** INFLUIR : to carry weight, to have bearing **5** (with personal pronouns) : to grieve, to sadden ⟨me pesa mucho no haber ido : I really regret not having gone⟩ **6 pese a** : in spite of, despite **7 pese a que** : in spite of the fact that
pesar[2] *nm* **1** AFLICCIÓN, PENA : sorrow, grief **2** REMORDIMIENTO : remorse **3 a pesar de** : in spite of, despite ⟨a pesar de todo : in spite of it all⟩ **4 a pesar de que** : in spite of the fact that
pesaroso, -sa *adj* **1** : sad, mournful **2** ARREPENTIDO : sorry, regretful
pesca *nf* **1** : fishing ⟨ir de pesca : to go fishing⟩ **2** : catch
pescadería *nf* : fish market
pescado *nm* : fish (as food)
pescador, -dora *n* : fisherman *m*, fisherwoman *f*
pescar {72} *vt* **1** : to fish for **2** : to catch **3** *fam* : to get a hold of, to land — *vi* : to fish, to go fishing
pescuezo *nm* : neck
pesebre *nm* **1** : manger **2** : Nativity scene
pesebrera *nf Col* : stable
pesera *nf* → **pesero**
pesero *nm Mex* : minibus
peseta *nf* : peseta (Spanish unit of currency)
pesimismo *nm* : pessimism
pesimista[1] *adj* : pessimistic
pesimista[2] *nmf* : pessimist
pésimo, -ma *adj* : dreadful, abominable
peso *nm* **1** : weight, heaviness ⟨perder/ganar peso : to lose/gain weight⟩ ⟨peso bruto/neto : gross/net weight⟩ **2** : bur-

den, responsibility **3** : weight (in sports)
⟨peso pesado : heavyweight⟩ **4** BÁSCULA
: scale **5** : peso (currency)

pesque, etc. → pescar

pesquería *nf* : fishery

pesquero¹, -ra *adj* : fishing ⟨pueblo
pesquero : fishing village⟩

pesquero² *nm* : fishing boat

pesquisa *nf* INVESTIGACIÓN : inquiry, investigation

pestaña *nf* **1** : eyelash **2** : flange, rim

pestañear *vi* : to blink

pestañeo *nm* : blink

peste *nf* **1** : plague, pestilence **2** : stench,
stink **3** : nuisance, pest

pesticida *nm* : pesticide

pestilencia *nf* **1** : stench, foul odor **2**
: pestilence

pestillo *nm* CERROJO : bolt, latch

petaca *nf* **1** *Mex* : suitcase **2 petacas** *nfpl*
Mex fam : bottom, behind

pétalo *nm* : petal

petardear *vi* : to backfire

petardeo *nm* : backfiring

petardo *nm* : firecracker

petate *nm* *Hond, Mex* : mat

petición *nf, pl* **-ciones** : petition, request
⟨a petición de : at the request of⟩

peticionar *vt* : to petition

peticionario, -ria *n* : petitioner

petirrojo *nm* : robin

petiso, -sa *or* **petizo, -za** *n* : shorty

peto *nm* : bib (of clothing)

pétreo, -trea *adj* : stone, stony

petrificar {72} *vt* : to petrify

petróleo *nm* : oil, petroleum

petrolero¹, -ra *adj* : oil ⟨industria petro-
lera : oil industry⟩

petrolero² *nm* : oil tanker

petrolífero, -ra → petrolero¹

petulancia *nf* INSOLENCIA : insolence,
petulance

petulante *adj* INSOLENTE : insolent, petulant — **petulantemente** *adv*

petunia *nf* : petunia

peyorativo, -va *adj* : pejorative

pez¹ *nm, pl* **peces** **1** : fish **2 pez de colores** : goldfish **3 pez espada** : swordfish
4 pez gordo : big shot

pez² *nf, pl* **peces** : pitch, tar

pezón *nm, pl* **pezones** : nipple

pezuña *nf* : hoof ⟨pezuña hendida : cloven hoof⟩

pH ['pe'atʃe, 'pi'etʃ] *nm* : pH

phylum ['filum] *nm* : phylum

pi *nf* : pi

piadoso, -sa *adj* **1** : compassionate, merciful **2** DEVOTO : pious, devout — **pia-
dosamente** *adv*

pianista *nmf* : pianist, piano player

piano *nm* : piano ⟨piano de cola : grand
piano⟩

piar {85} *vi* : to chirp, to cheep, to tweet

pibe, -ba *n* *Arg, Uru fam* : kid, child

pica *nf* **1** : pike, lance **2** : goad (in bullfighting) **3** : spade (in playing cards)

picada *nf* **1** : bite, sting (of an insect) **2**
: sharp descent

picadero *nm* **1** : exercise ring (for horses)
2 : riding school

picadillo *nm* **1** : minced meat, hash **2
hacer picadillo a** : to beat to a pulp

picado, -da *adj* **1** : perforated **2** : ground
(of meat), chopped **3** : decayed (of
teeth) **4** : choppy, rough **5** *fam* : annoyed, miffed

picador *nm* : picador

picadura *nf* **1** : sting, bite **2** : prick, puncture **3** : decay, cavity

picaflor *nm* **1** COLIBRÍ : hummingbird **2**
: womanizer

picana *nf* : goad, prod

picante¹ *adj* **1** : hot, spicy **2** : sharp, cutting **3** : racy, risqué

picante² *nm* **1** : spiciness **2** : hot spices *pl*,
hot sauce

picaporte *nm* **1** : latch **2** : door handle **3**
ALDABA : door knocker

picar {72} *vt* **1** : to sting (of bees, etc.), to
bite (of fleas, etc.) **2** : to peck at (of
birds) **3** COMER : to nibble on **4** : to
prick (of a needle, etc.), to punch (a
ticket) **5** : to break, to chip (stone, etc.)
6 : to grind, to chop **7** : to goad, to incite
8 : to pique, to provoke — *vi* **1** : to itch
⟨esta camisa me pica : this shirt is itchy⟩
2 : to sting **3** : to be spicy, to be hot **4**
: to nibble **5** : to take the bait **6** ~ **en**
: to dabble in **7 picar muy alto** : to aim
too high — **picarse** *vr* **1** : to get a cavity,
to decay **2** : to go bad (of food) **3** : to get
annoyed, to take offense **4** : to become
choppy (of the sea)

picardía *nf* **1** : cunning, craftiness **2**
: prank, dirty trick

picaresco, -ca *adj* **1** : picaresque **2** : mischievous, naughty

pícaro¹, -ra *adj* **1** : mischievous **2** : cunning, sly **3** : off-color, risqué

pícaro², -ra *n* **1** : rogue, scoundrel **2** : rascal

picazón *nf, pl* **-zones** COMEZÓN : itch

picea *nf* : spruce (tree)

pichel *nm* : pitcher, jug

pichón, -chona *n, mpl* **pichones** **1**
: young pigeon, squab **2** *Mex fam* : novice, greenhorn

picnic *nm* : picnic

pico *nm* **1** : peak **2** : point **3** : corner **4**
: beak, bill **5** *fam* : mouth **6** : pick,
pickax **7 y pico** : and a little, and a bit
⟨las siete y pico : a little after seven⟩
⟨dos metros y pico : a bit over two me-
ters⟩

picor *nm* : itch, irritation

picoso, -sa *adj* *Mex* : very hot, spicy

picota *nf* **1** : pillory, stock **2 poner a
alguien en la picota** : to put someone on
the spot

picotada *nf* → picotazo

picotazo *nm* : peck (of a bird)

picotear *vt* : to peck — *vi* : to nibble, to
pick

pictórico, -ca *adj* : pictorial

picudo, -da *adj* **1** : pointy, sharp **2** ~
para *Mex fam* : clever at, good at

pide, etc. → pedir

pie *nm* **1** : foot **2** : base, bottom, stem,
foot ⟨pie de la cama : foot of the bed⟩
⟨pie de una lámpara : base of a lamp⟩

⟨pie de la escalera : bottom of the stairs⟩
⟨pie de una copa : stem of a glass⟩ ⟨pie
de la página : foot of the page⟩ ⟨pie de
foto : caption⟩ **3** : foot (in measurement) ⟨pie cuadrado : square foot⟩ **4**
: cue (in theater) **5 a** ~ : on foot **6 de**
~ : on one's feet, standing ⟨estar de pie
: to be standing⟩ ⟨ponerse de pie : to
stand up⟩ **7 en** ~ : standing ⟨mante-
nerse en pie : to remain standing⟩ ⟨se-
guir en pie : to remain valid, to stand⟩ **8
al pie de la letra** : word for word **9 con
buen pie** : well ⟨comenzar con buen pie
: to start on the right foot, to get off to a
good start⟩ **10 con pies de plomo** : very
cautiously **11 dar pie a** : to give cause
for, to give rise to **12 de a pie** : average,
ordinary **13 de pies a cabeza** : from
head to toe **14 en pie de guerra** : ready
for war **15 en pie de igualdad** : on equal
footing **16 hacer pie** : to touch bottom
(in water) **17 no tener ni pies ni cabeza**
: to make no sense
piedad *nf* **1** COMPASIÓN : mercy, pity **2**
DEVOCIÓN : piety, devotion
piedra *nf* **1** : stone **2** : flint (of a lighter)
3 : hailstone **4 piedra angular** : cornerstone **5 piedra arenisca** : sandstone **6
piedra caliza** : limestone **7 piedra de
afilar** : whetstone, grindstone **8 piedra
de molino** : millstone **9 piedra de pómez** : pumice stone **10 piedra de toque**
: touchstone **11 piedra imán** : lodestone
12 piedra preciosa : precious stone
piel *nf* **1** : skin **2** CUERO : leather, hide
⟨piel de venado : deerskin⟩ **3** : fur, pelt
4 CÁSCARA : peel, skin **5 piel de gallina**
: goose bumps *pl* ⟨me pone la piel de gallina : it gives me goose bumps⟩
piélago *nm* **el piélago** : the deep, the
ocean
piensa, *etc.* → **pensar**
pienso *nm* : feed, fodder
pierde, *etc.* → **perder**
pierna *nf* : leg ⟨cruzar las piernas : to
cross one's legs⟩
pieza *nf* **1** ELEMENTO : piece, part, component ⟨vestido de dos piezas : two-
piece dress⟩ ⟨pieza de recambio/re-
puesto : spare part⟩ ⟨pieza clave : key
element⟩ **2** : piece (in chess) **3** OBRA
: piece, work ⟨pieza de teatro : play⟩ **4**
: room, bedroom
pífano *nm* : fife
pifia *nf fam* : goof, blunder
pifiar *vt fam* : to mess up, to bungle
pigargo *nm* : osprey
pigmentación *nf, pl* **-ciones** : pigmentation
pigmento *nm* : pigment
pigmeo, -mea *adj & n* : pygmy, Pygmy
pijama *nm* : pajamas *pl*
pila *nf* **1** BATERÍA : battery ⟨pila de linterna : flashlight battery⟩ **2** MONTÓN
: pile, heap **3** : sink, basin, font ⟨pila
bautismal : baptismal font⟩ ⟨pila para
pájaros : birdbath⟩
pilar *nm* **1** : pillar, column **2** : support,
mainstay

píldora *nf* PASTILLA : pill ⟨tomar la
píldora (anticonceptiva) : to be on the
pill⟩
pileta *nf Arg, Uru* **1** FREGADERO, LAVABO
: sink **2** PISCINA : swimming pool
pillaje *nm* : pillage, plunder
pillar *vt* **1** *fam* : to catch ⟨¡cuidado! ¡nos
pillarán! : watch out! they'll catch us!⟩ **2**
fam : to grasp, to catch on ⟨¿no lo pillas?
: don't you get it?⟩ — **pillarse** *vr* : to
catch (one's finger, etc.)
pillo¹, -lla *adj* : cunning, crafty
pillo², -lla *n* **1** : rascal, brat **2** : rogue,
scoundrel
pilluelo, -la *n* : urchin
pilón *nm, pl* **pilones** **1** PILA : basin **2**
: pillar, tower (for cables), pylon (of a
bridge) **3** *Mex* : extra, free gift
pilotar *vt* : to pilot (a plane), to steer (a
ship), to drive (an automobile)
pilote *nm* : pile (stake)
pilotear → **pilotar**
piloto¹ *nm* **1** : pilot light **2** *Arg* : raincoat
3 **piloto automático** : autopilot, automatic pilot
piloto² *nmf* : pilot (of a plane or ship),
driver (of an automobile)
piltrafa *nf* **1** : poor quality meat **2**
: wretch **3 piltrafas** *nfpl* : food scraps
pimentero *nm* : pepper shaker
pimentón *nm, pl* **-tones** **1** : paprika **2**
: cayenne pepper
pimienta *nf* **1** : pepper (condiment)
⟨pimienta blanca/negra : white/black
pepper⟩ **2 pimienta de Jamaica** : allspice
pimiento *nm* : pepper (fruit) ⟨pimiento
verde : green pepper⟩ ⟨pimiento morrón
: pimiento, pimento⟩
pináculo *nm* **1** : pinnacle (of a building)
2 : peak, acme
pinar *nm* : pine forest
pinball [pin'bol] *nm* : pinball
pincel *nm* **1** : paintbrush **2** : makeup
brush
pincelada *nf* **1** : brushstroke **2 últimas
pinceladas** : final touches
pinchar *vt* **1** : to puncture (a tire, balloon, etc.) **2** : to prick, to stick, to jab **3**
PROVOCAR : to goad, to tease, to needle
4 : to give an injection **5** : to click on (a
link, etc.) ⟨pinche aquí : click here⟩ **6**
fam : to tap, to wiretap (a phone) — *vi* **1**
: to be prickly **2** : to get a flat tire **3** *fam*
: to get beaten, to lose out — **pincharse**
vr **1** INYECTARSE : to shoot up **2** : to go
flat (of a tire)
pinchazo *nm* **1** : prick, jab **2** : puncture,
flat tire
pinche¹ *adj Mex* MALDITO : damned
pinche² *nmf* : kitchen assistant
pincho *nm* **1** : thorn, spine (of a plant) **2**
Spain : bar snack
Ping–Pong *marca registrada, m* — used
for table tennis
pingüe *adj* **1** : rich, huge (of profits) **2**
: lucrative
pingüino *nm* : penguin
pininos *or* **pinitos** *nmpl* : first steps
⟨hacer pininos : to take one's first steps,
to toddle⟩
pino *nm* : pine, pine tree

pinta *nf* **1** : dot, spot **2** : pint **3** *fam* : aspect, appearance ⟨las peras tienen buena pinta : the pears look good⟩ ⟨tener pinta de : to look like⟩ **4 pintas** *nfpl Mex* : graffiti

pintadas *nfpl* : graffiti

pintado, -da *adj* : spotted

pintalabios *nms & pl* : lipstick

pintar *vt* **1** : to paint **2** : to draw, to mark **3** : to describe, to depict — *vi* **1** : to paint, to draw **2** : to look ⟨no pinta bien : it doesn't look good⟩ **3** *fam* : to count ⟨aquí no pinta nada : he has no say here⟩ — **pintarse** *vr* **1** MAQUILLARSE : to put on makeup **2 pintárselas solo** *fam* : to manage by oneself, to know it all

pintarrajear *vt* : to daub (with paint)

pinto, -ta *adj* : speckled, spotted

pintor, -tora *n* **1** : painter (artist) **2** *or* **pintor de brocha gorda** : painter (of buildings, etc.)

pintoresco, -ca *adj* : picturesque, quaint

pintura *nf* **1** : paint **2** : painting ⟨pintura al óleo : oil painting⟩ ⟨pintura a la acuarela : watercolor painting⟩

pinza *nf* **1** : clothespin **2** HORQUILLA : bobby pin **3** : claw, pincer (of a crab, etc.) **4** : pleat, dart (in clothing) **5 pinzas** *nfpl* : tweezers **6 pinzas** *or* **pinzas** ALICATES : pliers, pincers **7 pinzas** *nfpl* : tongs (for food)

pinzón *nm, pl* **pinzones** : finch

piña *nf* **1** : pineapple **2** : pine cone

piñata *nf* : piñata

piñón *nm, pl* **piñones** **1** : pine nut **2** : pinion (of a machine), sprocket (of a bicycle)

pío¹, pía *adj* **1** DEVOTO : pious, devout **2** : pied, dappled

pío² *nm* **1** : peep, tweet, cheep **2 no decir ni pío** : not to say a word

piocha *nf* **1** : pickax **2** *Mex* : goatee

piojo *nm* : louse

piojoso, -sa *adj* **1** : lousy **2** : filthy

piola¹ *adj fam* **1** *Arg* : cool *fam*, good **2 pasar piola** *Chile, Peru* : to go unnoticed

piola² *nf* : cord

pionero¹, -ra *adj* : pioneering

pionero², -ra *n* : pioneer

pipa *nf* **1** : pipe (for smoking) **2** *Cuba, Mex* : tanker truck **3** *Spain* : seed

pipí *nm fam* : pee *fam* ⟨hacer pipí : to take a pee⟩

pipián *nm, pl* **pipianes** *Mex* : a spicy sauce or stew

pipiolo, -la *n fam* **1** : greenhorn, novice **2** : kid, youngster

pique¹, etc. → picar

pique² *nm* **1** : pique, resentment **2** : rivalry, competition **3 a pique de** : about to, on the verge of **4 irse a pique** : to sink, to founder

piqueta *nf* : pickax

piquete *nm* **1** : picketers *pl*, picket line **2** : squad, detachment **3** *Mex* : prick, jab **4** *Mex* : insect bite

piquetear *vt* **1** : to picket **2** *Mex* : to prick, to jab

pira *nf* : pyre

piragua *nf* : canoe

piragüismo *nm* : canoeing

piragüista *nmf* : canoeist, canoer

pirámide *nf* : pyramid

piraña *nf* : piranha

pirata¹ *adj* **1** : bootleg, pirated **2** : pirate ⟨un barco pirata : a pirate ship⟩

pirata² *nmf* **1** : pirate **2** : pirate, bootlegger **3 pirata aéreo** : hijacker **4 pirata informático** : hacker

piratear *vt* **1** : to hijack, to commandeer **2** : to bootleg, to pirate

piratería *nf* : piracy, bootlegging

piromanía *nf* : pyromania

pirómano, -na *n* : pyromaniac

piropo *nm* : flirtatious compliment

pirotecnia *nf* : fireworks *pl*, pyrotechnics *pl*

pirotécnico, -ca *adj* : fireworks, pyrotechnic

pírrico, -ca *adj* : Pyrrhic

pirueta *nf* : pirouette

pirulí *nm* : cone-shaped lollipop

pis → pipí

pisada *nf* **1** : footstep **2** HUELLA : footprint

pisapapeles *nms & pl* : paperweight

pisar *vt* **1** : to step on/in ⟨no pises las flores : don't step on the flowers⟩ **2** : to set foot in (a place) **3** : to walk all over, to mistreat — *vi* : to step, to walk, to tread

piscina *nf* **1** : swimming pool **2** : fish pond

Piscis¹ *nm* : Pisces (sign or constellation)

Piscis² *nmf* : Pisces (person)

piso *nm* **1** PLANTA : floor, story **2** SUELO : floor **3** PAVIMENTO : surface (of a road) **4** CAPA : layer **5** *Spain* : apartment

pisotear *vt* **1** : to stamp on, to trample **2** PISAR : to walk all over **3** : to flout, to disregard

pisotón *nm, pl* **-tones** : stamp, step ⟨sufrieron empujones y pisotones : they were pushed and stepped on⟩

pista *nf* **1** RASTRO : trail, track ⟨siguen la pista de los sospechosos : they're on the trail of the suspects⟩ **2** : clue **3** CAMINO : road, trail **4** : track, racetrack **5** *Chile* : lane (of a road) **6** : ring, arena, rink ⟨pista de patinaje/hielo : skating/ice rink⟩ **7** : track (of a recording) **8 pista de aterrizaje** : runway, airstrip **9 pista de baile** : dance floor **10 pista de tenis** *Spain* : tennis court

pistacho *nm* : pistachio

pistilo *nm* : pistil

pistola *nf* **1** : pistol, handgun **2** : spray gun

pistolera *nf* : holster

pistolero *nm* : gunman

pistón *nm, pl* **pistones** **1** : piston **2** : key, valve (of an instrument)

pita *nf* **1** : twine **2** : pita (bread)

pitar *vi* **1** : to blow a whistle **2** : to whistle, to boo **3** : to beep, to honk, to toot — *vt* **1** : to whistle at, to boo **2** : to call, to signal (a foul)

pitido *nm* **1** : whistle, whistling **2** : beep, honk, toot

pitillo *nm* : cigarette

pito *nm* **1** SILBATO : whistle **2** CLAXON, BOCINA : horn **3 no me importa un pito** *fam* : I don't give a damn

pitón *nm, pl* **pitones 1** : python **2** : point of a bull's horn

pitonisa *nf* : fortune-teller

pituitario, -ria *adj* : pituitary

pívot *nmf, pl* **pívots** : center (in basketball)

pivote *nm* : pivot

piyama *nmf* : pajamas *pl*

pizarra *nf* **1** : slate **2** : blackboard **3** : scoreboard

pizarrón *nm, pl* **-rrones** : blackboard, chalkboard

pizca *nf* **1** : pinch ⟨una pizca de canela : a pinch of cinnamon⟩ **2** : speck, trace ⟨ni pizca : not a bit⟩ **3** *Mex* : harvest

pizcar {72} *vt Mex* : to harvest

pizque, etc. → **pizcar**

pizza ['pitsa, 'pisa] *nf* : pizza

pizzería *nf* : pizzeria, pizza parlor

placa *nf* **1** : sheet, plate **2** : plaque **3** : plate (in photography) **4** : badge, insignia **5 placa de circuito(s)** : circuit board **6 placa de matrícula** : license plate, tag **7 placa dental** : plaque, tartar

placard [pla'kar] *nm, pl* **-cards** *Arg, Uru* : built-in closet

placebo *nm* : placebo

placenta *nf* : placenta

placentero, -ra *adj* AGRADABLE, GRATO : pleasant, agreeable — **placenteramente** *adv*

placer¹ {57} *vi* GUSTAR : to be pleasing ⟨hazlo como te plazca : do it however you please⟩

placer² *nm* **1** : pleasure, enjoyment ⟨ha sido un placer : it has been a pleasure⟩ **2 a ∼** : as much as one wants

plácido, -da *adj* TRANQUILO : placid, calm

plaga *nf* **1** : plague, infestation (of insects, etc.), blight (of crops, etc.) **2** CALAMIDAD : disaster, scourge

plagado, -da *adj* **∼ de** : filled with, covered with

plagar {52} *vt* : to plague

plagiar *vt* **1** : to plagiarize **2** SECUESTRAR : to kidnap, to abduct

plagiario, -ria *n* **1** : plagiarist **2** SECUESTRADOR : kidnapper, abductor

plagio *nm* **1** : plagiarism **2** SECUESTRO : kidnapping, abduction

plague, etc. → **plagar**

plan *nm* **1** : plan, strategy, program ⟨plan de inversiones : investment plan⟩ ⟨plan de estudios : curriculum⟩ **2** PLANO : plan, diagram **3** : attitude, intent, purpose ⟨ponte en plan serio : be serious⟩ ⟨estamos en plan de divertirnos : we're looking to have some fun⟩

plana *nf* **1** : page ⟨noticias en primera plana : front-page news⟩ **2 plana mayor** : staff (in the military)

plancha *nf* **1** : iron, ironing **2** : grill, griddle ⟨a la plancha : grilled⟩ **3** : sheet,

plate ⟨plancha para hornear : baking sheet⟩ **4** *fam* : blunder, blooper

planchada *nf* : ironing, pressing

planchado *nm* → **planchada**

planchar *v* : to iron

planchazo *nm fam* : goof, blunder

plancton *nm* : plankton

planeación *nf, pl* **-ciones** *Col, Hon, Mex* → **planeamiento**

planeador *nm* : glider (aircraft)

planeamiento *nm* : plan, planning

planear *vt* : to plan — *vi* : to glide (in the air)

planeo *nm* : gliding, soaring

planeta *nm* : planet

planetario¹, -ria *adj* **1** : planetary **2** : global, worldwide

planetario² *nm* : planetarium

planicie *nf* : plain

planificación *nf, pl* **-ciones** : planning ⟨planificación familiar : family planning⟩

planificador, -dora *n* : planner

planificar {72} *vt* : to plan

planilla *nf* **1** LISTA : list **2** NÓMINA : payroll **3** TABLA : chart, table **4** *Mex* : slate, ticket (of candidates) **5 planilla de cálculo** *Arg, Chile* : spreadsheet

plano¹, -na *adj* : flat, level, plane

plano² *nm* **1** PLAN : map, plan **2** : plane (surface) **3** NIVEL : level ⟨en un plano personal : on a personal level⟩ **4** : shot (in photography) ⟨primer plano : close-up⟩ **5 de ∼** : flatly, outright, directly ⟨se negó de plano : he flatly refused⟩

planta *nf* **1** : plant ⟨planta de interior : houseplant⟩ **2** FÁBRICA : plant, factory **3** PISO : floor, story ⟨planta baja : ground floor, first floor⟩ **4** : staff, employees *pl* **5** : sole (of the foot)

plantación *nf, pl* **-ciones 1** : plantation **2** : planting

plantado, -da *adj* **1** : planted **2 dejar plantado** *fam* : to stand up (a date), to dump (a lover)

plantar *vt* **1** : to sow ⟨plantar de flores : to plant with flowers⟩ **2** : to put in, to place **3** *fam* : to plant, to land ⟨plantar un beso : to plant a kiss⟩ **4** *fam* : to leave, to jilt — **plantarse** *vr* **1** : to stand firm **2** *fam* : to arrive, to show up **3** *fam* : to balk

planteamiento *nm* **1** : approach, position ⟨el planteamiento feminista : the feminist viewpoint⟩ **2** : explanation, exposition **3** : proposal, suggestion, plan

plantear *vt* **1** : to set forth (an argument, etc.), to bring up (a topic, possibility, etc.), to suggest (an idea, etc.) ⟨no lo plantearía así : I wouldn't describe/explain it like that⟩ **2** : to establish, to set up **3** : to create, to pose (a problem) — **plantearse** *vr* **1** : to think about **2** : to arise

plantel *nm* **1** : educational institution **2** : staff, team

planteo → **planteamiento**

plantilla *nf* **1** : insole **2** : pattern, template, stencil **3** *Mex, Spain* : staff, roster of employees

plantío *nm* : field (planted with a crop)
plantón *nm, pl* **plantones 1** : seedling **2** : long wait ⟨darle (un) plantón a alguien : to stand someone up⟩
plañidero¹, -ra *adj* : mournful
plañidero², -ra *nf* : hired mourner
plañir {38} *v* : to mourn, to lament
plasma *nm* : plasma
plasmar *vt* : to express, to give form to — **plasmarse** *vr*
plasta *nf* : soft mass, lump
plástica *nf* : modeling, sculpture
plasticidad *nf* : plasticity
plástico¹, -ca *adj* : plastic
plástico² *nm* : plastic
plastificar {72} *vt* : to laminate
plata *nf* **1** : silver (metal) **2** : silver, silverware **3** : money
plataforma *nf* **1** ESTRADO, TARIMA : platform, dais **2** : platform (in politics) **3** : springboard, stepping stone **4 plataforma continental** : continental shelf **5 plataforma de lanzamiento** : launchpad **6 plataforma petrolífera** : oil rig (at sea)
platal *nm* : large sum of money, fortune
platanal *or* **platanar** *nm* : banana plantation
platanero¹, -ra *adj* : banana, banana-producing
platanero², -ra *n* : banana grower
plátano *nm* **1** : banana (plant, fruit) **2** : plantain (plant, fruit) **3** : plane tree **plátano macho** *Mex* : plantain
platea *nf* : orchestra seats *pl* (in a theater)
plateado, -da *adj* **1** : silver, silvery **2** : silver-plated
platería *nf* **1** : silver, silverware **2** : silver shop
plática *nf* **1** : talk, lecture **2** : chat, conversation
platicar {72} *vi* : to talk, to chat — *vt Mex* : to tell, to say
platija *nf* : flatfish, flounder
platillo *nm* **1** : saucer ⟨platillo volador : flying saucer⟩ **2** : cymbal **3** : pan (of a scale) **4** *Mex* : dish ⟨platillos típicos : local dishes⟩
platino *nm* : platinum
plato *nm* **1** : plate, dish ⟨lavar los platos : to do the dishes⟩ **2** : serving, helping **3** : course (of a meal) ⟨primer/segundo plato : first/second course⟩ ⟨plato fuerte/principal : main course⟩ **4** : dish ⟨plato típico : typical dish⟩ ⟨plato dulce/salado : sweet/savory dish⟩ **5** : home plate (in baseball) **6 plato hondo** : soup bowl **7 plato llano** : dinner plate
plató *nm* : set (in the movies)
platónico, -ca *adj* : platonic
playa *nf* **1** : beach, seashore **2 playa de estacionamiento** : parking lot
playera *nf* **1** : canvas sneaker **2** *CA, Mex* : T-shirt
playboy [plei'boi] *nm, pl* **playboys** : playboy
plaza *nf* **1** : square, plaza **2** : marketplace **3** : space, seat (in a vehicle) **4** EMPLEO, PUESTO : post, position **5** : place, spot (on a team, etc.) **6 plaza fuerte** : strong-

hold, fortified city **7 plaza de toros** : bullring
plazca, etc. → placer
plazo *nm* **1** : period, term ⟨un plazo de cinco días : a period of five days⟩ ⟨préstamos a corto/largo plazo : short-term/long-term loans⟩ ⟨el plazo se cumplió : the deadline has passed⟩ **2** ABONO : installment ⟨pagar a plazos : to pay in installments⟩
plazoleta *nf* : small square
plazuela → plazoleta
pleamar *nf* : high tide
plebe *nf* : common people, masses *pl*
plebeyo¹, -ya *adj* : plebeian
plebeyo², -ya *n* : plebeian, commoner
plegable *adj* : folding, collapsible
plegadizo → plegable
plegar {49} *vt* DOBLAR : to fold, to bend — **plegarse** *vr* : to give in, to yield
plegaria *nf* ORACIÓN : prayer
pleito *nm* **1** : lawsuit **2** : fight, argument, dispute
plenamente *adv* COMPLETAMENTE : fully, completely
plenario, -ria *adj* : full
plenilunio *nm* : full moon
plenitud *nf* : fullness, abundance
pleno, -na *adj* (*often used as an intensifier*) COMPLETO : full, complete ⟨en pleno uso de sus facultades : in full command of his faculties⟩ ⟨en plena noche : in the middle of the night⟩ ⟨a plena luz (del día) : in broad daylight⟩ ⟨en pleno corazón de la ciudad : right in the heart of the city⟩ ⟨en plena cara : right in the face⟩
plétora *nf* : plethora
pleuresía *nf* : pleurisy
pliega, pliegue etc. → plegar
pliego *nm* **1** HOJA : sheet of paper **2** : sealed document
pliegue *nm* **1** DOBLEZ : crease, fold **2** : pleat
plisar *vt* : to pleat
plomada *nf* **1** : plumb line **2** : weight, sinker
plomería *nf* FONTANERÍA : plumbing
plomero, -ra *n* FONTANERO : plumber
plomizo, -za *adj* : leaden
plomo *nm* **1** : lead ⟨sin plomo : unleaded⟩ **2** : plumb line **3** : weight, sinker **4** *Spain* FUSIBLE : fuse **5** *fam* : bore, drag **6 a ~** : plumb, straight
plugo, etc. → placer
pluma *nf* **1** : feather, quill (for writing) **2** : pen **3** LLAVE : faucet **4 pluma fuente** : fountain pen
plumaje *nm* : plumage
plumero *nm* : feather duster
plumilla *nf* : nib
plumón *nm, pl* **plumones 1** : down **2** : marker, felt-tip pen
plumoso, -sa *adj* : feathery, downy
plural *adj* & *nm* : plural
pluralidad *nf* : plurality
pluralizar {21} *vt* **1** : to pluralize **2** : to expand, to multiply
pluriempleado, -da *adj* : holding more than one job

pluriempleo *nm* : moonlighting
plus *nm* : bonus
pluscuamperfecto *nm* : pluperfect —
pluscuamperfecto, -ta *adj*
plusvalía *nf* : appreciation, capital gain
Plutón *nm* : Pluto
plutocracia *nf* : plutocracy
plutonio *nm* : plutonium
población *nf, pl* **-ciones** 1 : population
⟨población activa : working population⟩
2 : city, town, village 3 población callampa *Chile* : shantytown, slums *pl*
poblado¹, -da *adj* 1 : inhabited, populated 2 : full, thick ⟨cejas pobladas
: bushy eyebrows⟩
poblado² *nm* : village, settlement
poblador, -dora *n* : settler
poblar {19} *vt* 1 : to populate, to inhabit
2 : to settle, to colonize 3 ~ **de** : to
stock with, to plant with — **poblarse** *vr*
: to fill up, to become crowded
pobre¹ *adj* 1 : poor, impoverished 2
: poor, unfortunate ⟨¡pobre de mí! : poor
me!⟩ 3 : poor, bad (in quality) ⟨pobres
resultados : poor results⟩ 4 : poor, deficient ⟨una dieta pobre : a poor diet⟩
pobre² *nmf* : poor person ⟨los pobres : the
poor⟩ ⟨¡pobre! : poor thing!⟩
pobremente *adv* : poorly
pobreza *nf* : poverty
pocilga *nf* CHIQUERO : pigsty, pigpen
pocillo *nm* : small coffee cup, demitasse
poción *or* **pócima** *nf, pl* **pociones** *or* **pó-
cimas** : potion
poco¹ *adv* 1 : little, not much ⟨poco probable : not very likely⟩ ⟨come poco : he
doesn't eat much⟩ 2 : a short time, a
while ⟨tardaremos poco : we won't be
very long⟩ 3 **poco antes** : shortly before
4 **poco después** : shortly after
poco², -ca *adj* 1 : little, not much, (a) few
⟨tengo poco dinero : I don't have much
money⟩ ⟨en no pocas ocasiones : on
more than a few occasions⟩ ⟨unos pocos
meses : a few months⟩ ⟨muy poca gente
: very few people⟩ 2 **pocas veces**
: rarely
poco³, -ca *pron* 1 : little, few ⟨le falta
poco para terminar : he's almost fin-
ished⟩ ⟨uno de los pocos que quedan
: one of the remaining few⟩ 2 **un poco**
: a little, a bit ⟨un poco de vino : a little
wine⟩ ⟨un poco extraño : a bit strange⟩
3 **a** ~ *(Mex (used to express disbelief)* ⟨¿a
poco no se te hizo difícil? : you mean
you didn't find it difficult?⟩ 4 **de a poco**
: little by little 5 **dentro de poco**
: shortly, in a little while 6 **hace poco**
: not long ago 7 **poco a poco** : little by
little 8 **por** ~ : nearly, almost
podar *vt* : to prune, to trim
podcast [pod'kast] *nm, pl* **podcasts**
: podcast
poder¹ {58} *v aux* 1 : to be able to, can
⟨no puede hablar : he can't speak⟩ ⟨no
pude acabarlo : I couldn't finish it⟩ 2
(expressing possibility) : might, may
⟨puede llover : it may rain at any mo-
ment⟩ ⟨¿cómo puede ser? : how can that
be?⟩ ⟨se podría/podía haber evitado : it

could have been avoided⟩ 3 *(expressing
permission)* : can, may ⟨¿puedo ir a la
fiesta? : can I go to the party?⟩ ⟨¿se
puede? : may I come in?⟩ 4 *(expressing
a request)* : can ⟨¿me puedes ayudar?
: can you help me?⟩ ⟨¿me lo podrías explicar? : could/would you explain it to
me?⟩ 5 *(expressing annoyance)* : can
⟨¿no puedes estarte quieto? : can't you
sit still?⟩ ⟨¡podrías/podías haberme llamado! : you could have called me!⟩ 6
(expressing moral obligation) : can ⟨no
puedo juzgarlo : I can't judge him⟩ — *vi*
1 : to beat, to defeat ⟨cree que le puede
a cualquiera : he thinks he can beat any-
one⟩ 2 : to be possible ⟨¿crees que
vendrán? — puede (que sí) : do you
think they'll come? — maybe⟩ 3 ~ **con**
: to cope with, to manage ⟨no puedo
con estos niños! : I can't handle these
children!⟩ 4 **a/hasta más no poder** ⟨es
competitivo a más no poder : he's as
competitive as they come⟩ ⟨comimos
hasta más no poder : we ate until we
couldn't eat another bite⟩ 5 **no poder
más** : to have had enough ⟨no puede
más : she can't take anymore⟩ 6 **no poder menos que** : not to be able to help
(doing something) ⟨no pudo menos que
asombrarse : she couldn't help but be
amazed⟩
poder² *nm* 1 : power, control ⟨tener poder sobre alguien : to have power over
someone⟩ 2 : power, influence ⟨el poder
del amor : the power of love⟩ 3 : power,
ability ⟨poderes mágicos : magical pow-
ers⟩ ⟨poder adquisitivo : purchasing
power⟩ 4 : power, control (of a country,
etc.) ⟨llegar al poder : to come to power⟩
⟨estar en el poder : to be in power⟩ 5
: power, authority ⟨el poder de veto
: veto power⟩ ⟨tener el poder para : to
have the authority to⟩ 6 : branch (of
government) ⟨el poder legislativo : the
legislature⟩ ⟨los poderes públicos : the
authorities⟩ 7 : power, force ⟨poder militar : military might⟩ 8 : possession ⟨es-
tar en el poder de : to be in the hands of⟩
9 : power of attorney
poderío *nm* 1 : power 2 : wealth, influence
poderosamente *adv* : powerfully
poderoso, -sa *adj* 1 : powerful 2
: wealthy, influential 3 : effective
podiatría *nf* : podiatry
podio *nm* : podium
pódium → **podio**
podología *nf* : podiatry, chiropody
podólogo, -ga *n* : podiatrist, chiropodist
podrá, etc. → **poder**
podredumbre *nf* 1 : decay, rottenness 2
: corruption
podrido, -da *adj* 1 : rotten, decayed 2
: corrupt 3 *Arg, Chile, Uru* HARTO : fed
up
podrir → **pudrir**
poema *nm* : poem
poesía *nf* 1 : poetry 2 POEMA : poem
poeta *nmf* : poet
poético, -ca *adj* : poetic, poetical

poetisa *nf* : póetess *f*, poet

pogrom *nm* : pogrom

póker *or* **poker** *nm* : poker (card game)

polaco¹, -ca *adj* : Polish

polaco², -ca *n* : Pole, Polish person

polaco³ *nm* : Polish (language)

polar *adj* : polar

polarizar {21} *vt* : to polarize — **polarizarse** *vr* — **polarización** *nf*

Polaroid *marca registrada, f* — used for a camera that produces developed photos or for the photos produced in this way

polea *nf* : pulley

polémica *nf* CONTROVERSIA : controversy, polemics

polémico, -ca *adj* CONTROVERTIDO : controversial, polemical

polemizar {21} *vi* : to argue, to debate

polemonio *nm* : phlox

polen *nm, pl* **pólenes** : pollen

polera *nf Chile* : T-shirt

polerón *nm, pl* **-rones** *Chile* : sweatshirt

policía¹ *nf* : police

policía² *nmf* : police officer, policeman *m*, policewoman *f*

policíaco, -ca *or* **policiaco, -ca** *adj* : police ⟨novela policíaca : detective story⟩

policial *adj* : police

polideportivo *nm* : sports center

poliéster *nm* : polyester

polifacético, -ca *adj* : versatile, multifaceted

poligamia *nf* : polygamy

polígamo¹, -ma *adj* : polygamous

polígamo², -ma *n* : polygamist

poligonal *adj* : polygonal

polígono *nm* **1** : polygon **2** *Spain* : zone

poliinsaturado, -da *adj* : polyunsaturated

polilla *nf* : moth

polímero *nm* : polymer

polinesio, -sia *adj & n* : Polynesian

polinizar {21} *vt* : to pollinate — **polinización** *nf*

polio *nf* : polio

poliomielitis *nf* : poliomyelitis, polio

polisón *nm, pl* **-sones** : bustle (on clothing)

politeísmo *nm* : polytheism — **politeísta** *adj & nmf*

política *nf* **1** : politics **2** : policy ⟨política interior/exterior : domestic/foreign policy⟩

políticamente *adv* : politically

político¹, -ca *adj* **1** : political **2** : tactful, politic **3** : by marriage ⟨padre político : father-in-law⟩

político², -ca *n* : politician

póliza *nf* : policy ⟨póliza de seguros : insurance policy⟩

polizón *nm, pl* **-zones** : stowaway ⟨viajar de polizón : to stow away⟩

polka *nf* : polka

polla *nf* **1** APUESTA : bet **2** *Chile* LOTERÍA : lottery

pollera *nf* **1** : chicken coop **2** : skirt

pollero, -ra *n* **1** : poultry farmer **2** : poultry farm **3** *Mex fam* COYOTE : smuggler of illegal immigrants

pollito, -ta *n* : chick, young bird, fledgling

pollo, -lla *n* **1** : chicken **2** POLLITO : chick **3** JOVEN : young man *m*, young lady *f*

polluelo *nm* → **pollito**

polo *nm* **1** : pole ⟨el Polo Norte : the North Pole⟩ ⟨polo negativo : negative pole⟩ **2** : polo (sport) **3** : polo shirt **4** : focal point, center **5** **polo opuesto** : exact opposite

pololo, -la *n Chile fam* : boyfriend *m*, girlfriend *f*

poltrona *nf* : armchair, easy chair

polución *nf, pl* **-ciones** CONTAMINACIÓN : pollution

polvareda *nf* **1** : cloud of dust **2** : uproar, fuss

polvera *nf* : compact (for face powder)

polvo *nm* **1** : dust ⟨quitar/limpiar el polvo : to dust⟩ **2** : powder ⟨polvo(s) de hornear : baking powder⟩ **3 polvos** *nmpl* : face powder **4 en ~** : powdered, ground **5 estar hecho polvo** *fam* : to be worn out **6 hacer polvo** *fam* : to crush, to shatter

pólvora *nf* **1** : gunpowder **2** : fireworks *pl*

polvoriento, -ta *adj* : dusty, powdery

polvorín *nm, pl* **-rines** : magazine, ammunition dump

pomada *nf* : ointment, cream

pomelo *nm* : grapefruit

pómez *nf or* **piedra pómez** : pumice

pomo *nm* **1** : pommel (on a sword) **2** : knob, handle **3** : perfume bottle

pompa *nf* **1** : bubble **2** : pomp, splendor **3 pompas fúnebres** : funeral

pompón *nm, pl* **pompones** BORLA : pompom

pomposidad *nf* **1** : pomp, splendor **2** : pomposity, ostentation

pomposo, -sa *adj* : pompous — **pomposamente** *adv*

pómulo *nm* : cheekbone

pon → **poner**

ponchadura *nf Mex* : puncture, flat (tire)

ponchar *vt* **1** *Car, CA, Col, Ven* : to strike out (in baseball) **2** *Mex* : to puncture — **poncharse** *vr* **1** *Car, CA, Col, Ven* : to strike out (in baseball) **2** *Mex* : to blow out (of a tire)

ponche *nm* **1** : punch (drink) **2 ponche de huevo** : eggnog

poncho *nm* : poncho

ponderación *nf, pl* **-ciones** **1** : consideration, deliberation **2** : high praise

ponderar *vt* **1** : to weigh, to consider **2** : to speak highly of

pondrá, etc. → **poner**

ponedora *nf* : layer (bird)

ponencia *nf* **1** DISCURSO : paper, presentation, address **2** INFORME : report

ponente *nmf* : speaker, presenter

poner {60} *vt* **1** COLOCAR : to put, to place ⟨pon el libro en la mesa : put the book on the table⟩ **2** AGREGAR, AÑADIR : to put in, to add (an ingredient, etc.) **3** : to put on (clothes) ⟨le puse el suéter : I put her sweater on (her)⟩ **4** CONTRIBUIR : to contribute **5** ESCRIBIR : to put in writing ⟨no le puso su nombre : he didn't put his name on it⟩ **6** : to give (a task, etc.), to impose (a fine) **7** : to prepare, to arrange ⟨poner la mesa : to set the table⟩ **8** : to name ⟨le pusimos Ana : we called her Ana⟩ **9** ESTABLECER : to set up, to establish ⟨puso un restaurante : he opened up a restaurant⟩ **10** INSTALAR : to install, to put in **11** (*with an adjective or adverb*) : to make ⟨me pone nervioso : it makes me nervous⟩ ⟨siempre lo pones de mal humor : you always put him in a bad mood⟩ **12** : to turn on, to switch on **13** : to set (an alarm, etc.) ⟨pon la música más alta/fuerte : turn up the music⟩ **14** SUPONER : to suppose ⟨pongamos que no viene : supposing he doesn't come⟩ **15** : to give (an example) **16** : to raise (objections), to create (problems, etc.) **17** : to lay (eggs) **18** ~ a : to start (someone doing something) ⟨lo puse a trabajar : I put him to work⟩ **19** ~ de : to place as ⟨la pusieron de directora : they made her director⟩ **20** ~ en : to put in (a state or condition) ⟨poner en duda : to call into question⟩ ⟨lo puso en peligro : she put him in danger⟩ — *vi* **1** : to contribute **2** : to lay eggs — **ponerse** *vr* **1** : to move (into a position) ⟨ponerse de pie : to stand up⟩ **2** : to put on, to wear **3** : to become, to turn ⟨se puso colorado : he turned red⟩ **4** : to start ⟨me puse a llorar : I started to cry⟩ **5** : to set (of the sun or moon)

poni *or* **poney** *nm* : pony

ponga, etc. → poner

poniente *nm* **1** OCCIDENTE : west **2** : west wind

ponqué *nm Col, Ven* : cake

pontificar {72} *vi* : to pontificate

pontífice *nm* : pontiff, pope

pontón *nm, pl* **pontones** : pontoon

ponzoña *nf* VENENO : poison — **ponzoñoso, -sa** *adj*

pop ['pop] *adj & nm* : pop (music)

popa *nf* **1** : stern **2 a ~** : astern, abaft, aft

popelín *nm, pl* **-lines** : poplin

popelina *nf* : poplin

popó *nm fam* **1** : poop **2 hacer popó** : to poop, to go poop

popote *nm Mex* : straw, drinking straw

populachero, -ra *adj* : common, popular, vulgar

populacho *nm* : rabble, masses *pl*

popular *adj* **1** : popular **2** : traditional **3** : colloquial — **popularmente** *adv*

popularidad *nf* : popularity

popularizar {21} *vt* : to popularize — **popularizarse** *vr*

populista *adj & nmf* : populist — **populismo** *nm*

populoso, -sa *adj* : populous

popurrí *nm* : potpourri

por *prep* **1** : for, during ⟨se quedaron allí por la semana : they stayed there for the week⟩ ⟨por el momento : for now, at the moment⟩ **2** : around, during ⟨por noviembre empieza a nevar : around November it starts to snow⟩ ⟨por la mañana : in the morning⟩ ⟨por la noche : at night⟩ **3** : around (a place) ⟨debe estar por allí : it must be over there⟩ ⟨por to-

das partes : everywhere⟩ **4** : by, through, along ⟨por la puerta : through the door⟩ ⟨pasamos por el centro : we went through the downtown⟩ ⟨pasé por tu casa : I stopped by your house⟩ ⟨por la costa : along the coast⟩ ⟨caminando por la calle : walking down the street⟩ **5** : for, for the sake of ⟨lo hizo por su madre : he did it for his mother⟩ ⟨¡por Dios! : for heaven's sake!⟩ **6** : because of, on account of ⟨llegué tarde por el tráfico : I arrived late because of the traffic⟩ ⟨dejar por imposible : to give up as impossible⟩ ⟨perdón por la demora : sorry for the delay⟩ **7** : per ⟨60 millas por hora : 60 miles per hour⟩ ⟨por docena : by the dozen⟩ **8** : for, in exchange for, instead of ⟨su hermana habló por él : his sister spoke on his behalf⟩ ⟨lo vendió por cien dólares : he sold it for a hundred dollars⟩ **9** : by means of ⟨hablar por teléfono : to talk on the phone⟩ ⟨por escrito : in writing⟩ ⟨por avión : by plane⟩ **10** : as for ⟨por mí : as far as I'm concerned⟩ **11** : times ⟨tres por dos son seis : three times two is six⟩ **12** SEGÚN : from, according to ⟨por lo que dices : judging from what you're telling me⟩ **13** : as, for ⟨por ejemplo : for example⟩ **14** : by ⟨hecho por mi abuela : made by my grandmother⟩ ⟨por correo : by mail⟩ **15** : for, in order to ⟨lucha por ganar su respeto : he struggles to win her respect⟩ **16 estar por** : to be about to **17 por ciento** : percent **18 por favor** : please **19 por lo tanto** : therefore, consequently **20 ¿por qué?** : why? **21 por que → porque 22 por . . . que** : no matter how ⟨por mucho que intente : no matter how hard I try⟩ **23 por si** *or* **por si acaso** : just in case

porcelana *nf* : china, porcelain

porcentaje *nm* : percentage

porche *nm* : porch

porción *nf, pl* **porciones** **1** : portion **2** PARTE : part, share **3** RACIÓN : serving, helping

pordiosear *vi* MENDIGAR : beg

pordiosero, -ra *n* MENDIGO : beggar

porfiado, -da *adj* OBSTINADO, TERCO : obstinate, stubborn — **porfiadamente** *adv*

porfiar {85} *vi* : to insist, to persist

pormenor *nm* DETALLE : detail

pormenorizar {21} *vi* : to go into detail — *vt* : to tell in detail

pornografía *nf* : pornography

pornográfico, -ca *adj* : pornographic

poro *nm* : pore

poroso, -sa *adj* : porous — **porosidad** *nf*

poroto *nm Arg, Chile, Uru* : bean

porque *conj* **1** : because **2** *or* **por que** : in order that

porqué *nm* : reason, cause ⟨no explicó el porqué : he didn't explain the reason⟩

porquería *nf* **1** SUCIEDAD : dirt, filth **2** : nastiness, vulgarity **3** : worthless thing, trifle **4** : junk food

porra *nf* **1** : nightstick, club **2** *Mex* : fans *pl* **3** *Mex* : cheer, yell ⟨los aficionados le echaban porras : the fans cheered him on⟩ **4 mandar a alguien a la porra** : to tell someone to go to hell

porrazo *nm* **1** : blow, whack **2 de golpe y porrazo** : suddenly

porrista *nmf* **1** : cheerleader **2** : fan, supporter

porro *nm fam* : joint *fam*, marijuana cigarette

portaaviones *nms & pl* : aircraft carrier

portada *nf* **1** : title page **2** : cover **3** : facade, front

portador, -dora *n* : carrier, bearer ⟨cheque al portador : check payable to bearer⟩

portaequipajes *nms & pl* **1** : luggage rack, roof rack **2** : trunk (of a car)

portafolio *or* **portafolios** *nm, pl* **-lios** MALETÍN : briefcase **2** : portfolio (of investments)

portal *nm* **1** : portal, doorway **2** VESTÍBULO : vestibule, hall **3** : portal (on the web)

portar *vt* **1** : to carry, to bear **2** : to wear — **portarse** *vr* CONDUCIRSE : to behave ⟨pórtate bien : behave yourself⟩ ⟨se portó mal con ella : he treated her badly⟩

portátil¹ *adj* : portable

portátil² *nmf* : laptop computer

portaviandas *nms & pl* : lunch box

portaviones *nm* → **portaaviones**

portavoz *nmf, pl* **-voces** : spokesperson, spokesman *m*, spokeswoman *f*

portazo *nm* : slam ⟨dar un portazo : to slam the door⟩

porte *nm* **1** ASPECTO : bearing, demeanor **2** TRANSPORTE : transport, carrying ⟨porte pagado : postage paid⟩ **3** : size ⟨de gran porte : large-sized⟩

portento *nm* MARAVILLA : marvel, wonder

portentoso, -sa *adj* MARAVILLOSO : marvelous, wonderful

porteño, -ña *adj* : of or from Buenos Aires

portería *nf* **1** ARCO : goal, goalposts *pl* **3** : superintendent's office

portero, -ra *n* **1** ARQUERO : goalkeeper, goalie **2** : doorman *m* (at a hotel, etc.), bouncer (at a nightclub, etc.) **3** : janitor, superintendent

pórtico *nm* : portico

portilla *nf* : porthole

portón *nm, pl* **portones** **1** : main door **2** : gate

portorriqueño, -ña → **puertorriqueño**

portugués¹, -guesa *adj & n, mpl* **-gueses** : Portuguese

portugués² *nm* : Portuguese (language)

porvenir *nm* FUTURO : future

pos *adv* **en pos de** : in pursuit of

pos- *or* **post-** *pref* : post-

posada *nf* **1** : inn **2** *Mex* : Advent celebration

posaderas *nfpl* : bottom, backside

posadero, -ra *n* : innkeeper

posar *vi* : to pose — *vt* : to place, to lay — **posarse** *vr* **1** : to land, to light, to perch **2** : to settle, to rest

posavasos *nms & pl* : coaster (for drinks)

posdata → **postdata**

pose *nf* : pose

poseedor, -dora *n* : possessor, holder

poseer {20} *vt* : to possess, to hold, to have

poseído, -da *adj* : possessed

posesión *nf, pl* **-siones** : possession

posesionarse *vr* ~ **de** : to take possession of, to take over

posesivo¹, -va *adj* : possessive

posesivo² *nm* : possessive case

posfechar *vt* : to postdate

posguerra *nf* : postwar period

posibilidad *nf* **1** : possibility ⟨existe la posibilidad de que . . . : the possibility exists that . . .⟩ **2 posibilidades** *nfpl* : means, income

posibilitar *vt* : to make possible, to permit

posible *adj* **1** : possible ⟨es posible que . . . : it's possible that . . .⟩ **2 a/de ser posible** : if possible **3 dentro de lo posible** *or* **en lo posible** : as far as possible **4 hacer todo lo posible** : to do everything possible **5 lo mejor/antes (etc.) posible** : as well/soon (etc.) as possible **6 si es posible** : if possible — **posiblemente** *adv*

posición *nf, pl* **-ciones** **1** : position, place ⟨en posición vertical : in an upright position⟩ **2** : status, standing **3** : attitude, stance

posicionar *vt* **1** : to position, to place **2** : to establish — **posicionarse** *vr*

positivo¹, -va *adj* : positive — **positivamente** *adv*

positivo² *nm* : print (in photography)

posmoderno, -na *adj* : postmodern

poso *nm* **1** : sediment, dregs *pl* **2** : grounds *pl* (of coffee)

posoperatorio, -ria *adj* : postoperative

posparto *adj* : postnatal ⟨depresión posparto : postpartum depression⟩

posponer {60} *vt* **1** : to postpone **2** : to put behind, to subordinate

pospuso, etc. → **posponer**

posta *nf* **1** : relay race **2** : post, station **3** *Chile* : emergency medical center

postal¹ *adj* : postal

postal² *nf* : postcard

postdata *nf* : postscript

poste *nm* **1** : post, pole ⟨poste de teléfonos : telephone pole⟩ **2** : goalpost (in sports)

póster *or* **poster** *nm, pl* **pósters** *or* **posters** : poster, placard

postergación *nf, pl* **-ciones** : postponement, deferring

postergar {52} *vt* **1** : to delay, to postpone **2** : to pass over (an employee)

posteridad *nf* : posterity

posterior *adj* **1** ULTERIOR : later, subsequent **2** TRASERO : back, rear

posterioridad *nf* **con** ~ : subsequently, later

posteriormente *adv* : subsequently

postgrado *nm* : graduate course

postgraduado, -da *n* : graduate student, postgraduate

postguerra → **posguerra**

postigo nm 1 CONTRAVENTANA : shutter 2 : small door, wicket gate

postilla nf : scab

Post—it marca registrada, m — used for a slip of paper with a sticky edge

postizo, -za adj : artificial, false ⟨dentadura postiza : dentures⟩

postnatal adj : postnatal

postor, -tora n : bidder ⟨mejor postor : highest bidder⟩

postración nf, pl **-ciones** 1 : prostration 2 ABATIMIENTO : depression

postrado, -da adj 1 : prostrate 2 **postrado en cama** : bedridden

potranco, -ca n → **potro¹**

postrar vt DEBILITAR : to debilitate, to weaken — **postrarse** vr : to prostrate oneself

postre¹ nm : dessert ⟨de postre comimos helado : we had ice cream for dessert⟩

postre² nf **a la postre** : in the end

postrero, -ra adj (**postrer** before masculine singular nouns) ÚLTIMO : last

postulación nf, pl **-ciones** 1 : collection 2 : nomination (of a candidate)

postulado nm : postulate, assumption

postulante, -ta n : candidate, applicant

postular vt 1 : to postulate 2 : to nominate 3 : to propose — **postularse** vr : to run, to be a candidate

póstumo, -ma adj : posthumous — **póstumamente** adv

postura nf 1 : posture, position (of the body) 2 ACTITUD, POSICIÓN : position, stance

potable adj : drinkable, potable ⟨agua potable : (safe) drinking water⟩

potaje nm : thick vegetable soup

potasa nf : potash

potasio nm : potassium

pote nm 1 OLLA : pot 2 : jar, container

potencia nf 1 : power ⟨potencias extranjeras : foreign powers⟩ ⟨elevado a la tercera potencia : raised to the third power⟩ 2 : capacity, potency 3 **en ~** : in the making ⟨un líder en potencia : a leader in the making⟩

potencial adj & nm : potential

potenciar vt : to promote, to foster

potenciómetro nm : dimmer, dimmer switch

potentado, -da n 1 SOBERANO : sovereign, ruler 2 MAGNATE : tycoon, magnate

potente adj 1 : powerful, strong 2 : potent, virile

potestad nf 1 AUTORIDAD : authority, jurisdiction 2 **patria potestad** : custody, guardianship

potrero nm 1 : field, pasture 2 : cattle ranch

potro¹, -tra n : colt m, filly f

potro² nm 1 : rack (for torture) 2 : horse (in gymnastics)

pozo nm 1 : well ⟨pozo de petróleo, pozo petrolero : oil well⟩ 2 : deep pool (in a river) 3 : mine shaft 4 Arg, Par, Uru : pothole 5 **pozo séptico** : cesspool

pozole nm Mex : spicy stew made with pork and hominy

práctica nf 1 : practice, experience 2 : practice ⟨la práctica de la medicina : the practice of medicine⟩ 3 : practice ⟨en la práctica : in practice⟩ ⟨poner en práctica : to put into practice⟩ 4

prácticas nfpl : practice, training

practicable adj : practicable, feasible

prácticamente adv : practically

practicante¹ adj : practicing ⟨católicos practicantes : practicing Catholics⟩

practicante² nmf : practitioner

practicar {72} vt 1 : to practice 2 : to perform, to carry out 3 : to exercise (a profession), to play (a sport) — vi : to practice

práctico, -ca adj : practical ⟨a efectos prácticos : for all practical purposes⟩

pradera nf : grassland, prairie

prado nm 1 CAMPO : field, meadow 2 : park

pragmático, -ca adj : pragmatic — **pragmáticamente** adv

pragmatismo nm : pragmatism

pre- pref : pre-

preámbulo nm 1 INTRODUCCIÓN : preamble, introduction 2 RODEO : evasion ⟨gastar preámbulos : to beat around the bush⟩

prebélico, -ca adj : antebellum

prebenda nf : privilege

precalentar {55} vt : to preheat

precariedad nf : precariousness

precario, -ria adj : precarious — **precariamente** adv

precaución nf, pl **-ciones** 1 : precaution ⟨medidas de precaución : precautionary measures⟩ 2 PRUDENCIA : caution, care ⟨con precaución : cautiously⟩

precautorio, -ria adj : precautionary

precaver vt PREVENIR : to prevent, to guard against — **precaverse** vr PREVENIRSE : to take precautions, to be on guard

precavido, -da adj CAUTELOSO : cautious, prudent

precedencia nf : precedence, priority

precedente¹ adj : preceding, previous

precedente² nm : precedent

preceder v : to precede

precepto nm : rule, precept

preciado, -da adj : esteemed, prized, valuable

preciarse vr 1 JACTARSE : to boast, to brag 2 **~ de** : to pride oneself on

precintar vt 1 : to seal 2 : to shut down (a business), to seal off (an area)

precinto nm : seal

precio nm 1 : price ⟨¿qué precio tiene? : how much is it?⟩ ⟨no tener precio : to be priceless⟩ 2 : cost, sacrifice ⟨a cualquier precio : at any cost⟩ 3 **precio de salida** : starting price 4 **precio de venta** : retail price

preciosidad nf : beautiful thing ⟨este vestido es una preciosidad : this dress is lovely⟩

precioso,-sa adj 1 HERMOSO : beautiful, exquisite 2 VALIOSO : precious, valuable

precipicio nm 1 : precipice 2 RUINA : ruin

precipitación *nf, pl* **-ciones** **1** PRISA : haste, hurry, rush **2** : precipitation, rain, snow

precipitado, -da *adj* **1** : hasty, sudden **2** : rash — **precipitadamente** *adv*

precipitar *vt* **1** APRESURAR : to hasten, to speed up **2** ARROJAR : to hurl, to throw — **precipitarse** *vr* **1** APRESURARSE : to rush **2** : to act rashly ⟨tal vez me precipito : perhaps I'm being too hasty⟩ **3** ARROJARSE : to throw oneself

precisamente *adv* JUSTAMENTE : precisely, exactly

precisar *vt* **1** : to specify, to determine exactly **2** NECESITAR : to need, to require — *vi* : to be necessary

precisión *nf, pl* **-siones** **1** EXACTITUD : precision, accuracy **2** CLARIDAD : clarity (of style, etc.) **3** NECESIDAD : necessity ⟨tener precisión de : to have need of⟩

preciso, -sa *adj* **1** EXACTO : precise **2** : very, exact ⟨en ese preciso instante : at that very instant⟩ **3** NECESARIO : necessary ⟨es preciso que . . . : it is necessary that . . .⟩

precocidad *nf* : precocity

precocinar *vt* : to precook

preconcebido, -da *adj* : preconceived

precondición *nf, pl* **-ciones** : precondition

preconizar {21} *vt* **1** : to recommend, to advocate **2** : to extol

precoz *adj, pl* **precoces** **1** : precocious **2** : early, premature — **precozmente** *adv*

precursor, -sora *n* : forerunner, precursor

predecesor, -sora *n* ANTECESOR : predecessor

predecir {11} *vt* : to foretell, to predict

predestinado, -da *adj* : predestined, fated

predestinar *vt* : to predestine — **predestinación** *nf*

predeterminar *vt* : to predetermine

prédica *nf* SERMÓN : sermon

predicado *nm* : predicate

predicador, -dora *n* : preacher

predicar {72} *v* : to preach

predicción *nf, pl* **-ciones** **1** : prediction **2** PRONÓSTICO : forecast ⟨predicción del tiempo : weather forecast⟩

prediga, predijo etc. → **predecir**

predilección *nf, pl* **-ciones** : predilection, preference

predilecto, -ta *adj* : favorite

predio *nm* : property, piece of land

predisponer {60} *vt* **1** : to predispose, to incline **2** : to prejudice, to bias

predisposición *nf, pl* **-ciones** **1** : predisposition, tendency **2** : prejudice, bias

predispuesto, -ta *adj* ∼ **a** : prone to

predominante *adj* : predominant — **predominantemente** *adv*

predominar *vi* PREVALECER : to predominate, to prevail

predominio *nm* : predominance, prevalence

preeminente *adj* : preeminent — **preeminencia** *nf*

preescolar *adj & nm* : preschool

preestreno *nm* : preview

prefabricado, -da *adj* : prefabricated

prefacio *nm* : preface

prefecto *nm* : prefect

preferencia *nf* **1** : preference **2** PRIORIDAD : priority **3** : right-of-way (of traffic) **4 de** ∼ : preferably

preferencial *adj* : preferential

preferente *adj* : preferential, special ⟨trato preferente : special treatment⟩

preferentemente *adv* : preferably

preferible *adj* : preferable ⟨es preferible que . . . : it's better that . . .⟩ ⟨ser preferible a : to be preferable to⟩

preferido, -da *adj & n* : favorite

preferir {76} *vt* : to prefer ⟨prefiero ir : I'd rather go⟩ ⟨prefiero que no vayas : I'd rather (that) you didn't go⟩ ⟨prefiero éste a ése : I prefer this one to/over that one⟩

prefigurar *vt* : to foreshadow, prefigure

prefijo *nm* **1** : prefix (in linguistics) **2** *Spain* : area code

pregonar *vt* **1** : to proclaim, to announce **2** : to hawk (merchandise) **3** : to extol **4** : to reveal, to disclose

pregrabado, -da *adj* : prerecorded

pregunta *nf* **1** : question **2 hacer una pregunta** : to ask a question

preguntar *vt* : to ask, to question — *vi* : to ask, to inquire ⟨preguntar por : to ask about⟩ — **preguntarse** *vr* : to wonder

preguntón, -tona *adj, mpl* **-tones** : inquisitive

prehistórico, -ca *adj* : prehistoric

prejuiciado, -da *adj* : prejudiced

prejuicio *nm* : prejudice ⟨tener prejuicios contra : to be prejudiced against⟩

prejuzgar {52} *vt* : to prejudge

prelado *nm* : prelate

preliminar *adj & nm* : preliminary

preludio *nm* : prelude

prematrimonial *adj* : premarital

prematuro, -ra *adj* : premature

premeditación *nf, pl* **-ciones** : premeditation

premeditar *vt* : to premeditate, to plan

premenstrual *adj* : premenstrual

premiado[1], -da *adj* : winning, prizewinning

premiado[2], -da *n* : prizewinner

premiar *vt* **1** : to award a prize to **2** : to reward

premier *nmf* : premier, prime minister

premio *nm* **1** : prize ⟨premio gordo : grand prize, jackpot⟩ ⟨dar/ganar un premio : to give/win a prize⟩ **2** : reward **3** : premium

premisa *nf* : premise, basis

premolar *nm* : bicuspid (tooth)

premonición *nf, pl* **-ciones** : premonition

premura *nf* : haste, urgency

prenatal *adj* : prenatal

prenda *nf* **1** : piece of clothing **2** : security, pledge **3** : forfeit (in a game)

prendar *vt* **1** : to charm, to captivate **2** : to pawn, to pledge — **prendarse** *vr* ∼ **de** : to fall in love with

prendedor *nm* : brooch, pin

prender *vt* **1** SUJETAR : to pin, to fasten **2** APRESAR : to catch, to apprehend **3** : to light (a cigarette, a match) **4** : to turn on ⟨prende la luz : turn on the light⟩ **5** **prender fuego a** : to set fire to — *vi* **1** : to take root **2** : to catch fire **3** : to catch on — **prenderse** *vr* : to catch fire

prensa *nf* **1** : printing press **2** : press ⟨conferencia de prensa : press conference⟩ ⟨la prensa : the press, the newspapers⟩

prensar *vt* : to press

prensil *adj* : prehensile

preñado, -da *adj* **1** : pregnant **2** ~ **de** : filled with

preñar *vt* EMBARAZAR : to make pregnant

preñez *nf, pl* **preñeces** : pregnancy

preocupación *nf, pl* **-ciones** INQUIETUD : worry, concern

preocupado, -da *adj* : worried ⟨preocupado por : worried about⟩

preocupante *adj* : worrisome

preocupar *vt* INQUIETAR : to worry, to concern ⟨eso me preocupa : that worries me⟩ — **preocuparse** *vr* **1** APURARSE : to worry, to be concerned ⟨preocuparse por : to worry about⟩ **2** ~ **de** : to take care of (something) ⟨preocuparse de que . . . : to make sure that . . .⟩

preparación *nf, pl* **-ciones** **1** : preparation, readiness **2** : education, training **3** : (medicinal) preparation

preparado¹, -da *adj* **1** : ready, prepared **2** : trained

preparado² *nm* : preparation, mixture

preparar *vt* **1** : to prepare ⟨preparé el almuerzo : I made lunch, I got lunch ready⟩ ⟨preparar un examen : to prepare for an exam⟩ **2** : to teach, to train, to coach — **prepararse** *vr* : to get ready, to prepare ⟨prepararse para algo : to get ready for something⟩ ⟨se prepara para salir : she's getting ready to leave⟩

preparativos *nmpl* : preparations

preparatoria *nf Mex* : high school

preparatorio, -ria *adj* : preparatory

preponderante *adj* : preponderant, predominant — **preponderancia** *nf* — **preponderantemente** *adv*

preposición *nf, pl* **-ciones** : preposition — **preposicional** *adj*

prepotente *adj* : arrogant, domineering, overbearing — **prepotencia** *nf*

prerrogativa *nf* : prerogative, privilege

presa *nf* **1** : capture, seizure ⟨hacer presa de : to seize⟩ **2** : catch, prey ⟨presa de : prey to, seized with⟩ **3** : claw, fang **4** DIQUE : dam **5** : morsel, piece (of food)

presagiar *vt* : to presage, to portend

presagio *nm* : omen, portent

presbiterio *nm* : sanctuary (of a church)

prescindible *adj* : expendable, dispensable

prescindir *vi* ~ **de 1** : to do without, to dispense with **2** DESATENDER : to ignore, to disregard **3** OMITIR : to omit, to skip

prescribir {33} *vt* : to prescribe

prescripción *nf, pl* **-ciones** : prescription

prescrito *pp* → prescribir

presencia *nf* **1** : presence ⟨en presencia de : in the presence of⟩ **2** ASPECTO : appearance

presenciar *vt* **1** : to witness **2** : to be present at, to attend

presentable *adj* : presentable

presentación *nf, pl* **-ciones** **1** : presentation **2** : introduction **3** : appearance

presentador, -dora *n* : host (of a show), anchor (of a newscast)

presentar *vt* **1** MOSTRAR : to present, to show **2** : to have, to show (a symptom) **3** : to offer, to give (an excuse, etc.) **4** : to submit (a document), to file (a complaint) **5** : to launch (a product) **6** : to introduce (a person) **7** : to host (a show), to anchor (a newscast) — **presentarse** *vr* **1** : to show up, to appear ⟨preséntese en la oficina central : report to the central office⟩ **2** SURGIR : to arise, to come up **3** : to introduce oneself **4** ~ **a** : to enter (a competition), to run in (an election)

presente¹ *adj* **1** : present, in attendance **2** : present, current ⟨del presente mes/año : of the current month/year⟩ **3** **tener presente** : to keep in mind

presente² *nf* **por la presente** : hereby (in a letter)

presente³ *nm* : present (time, tense)

presente⁴ *nmf* : one present ⟨entre los presentes se encontraban . . . : those present included . . .⟩

presentimiento *nm* : premonition, hunch, feeling

presentir {76} *vt* : to sense, to intuit ⟨presentía lo que iba a pasar : he sensed what was going to happen⟩

preservación *nf, pl* **-ciones** : preservation

preservar *vt* **1** : to preserve **2** : to protect

preservativo *nm* CONDÓN : condom

presidencia *nf* **1** : presidency **2** : chairmanship

presidencial *adj* : presidential

presidente¹ *nmf* → presidente²

presidente², -ta *n* **1** : president **2** : chair, chairperson (of a group or event) **3** : presiding judge

presidiario, -ria *n* : convict, prisoner

presidio *nm* : prison, penitentiary

presidir *vt* **1** MODERAR : to preside over, to chair **2** : to dominate, to rule over

presilla *nf* : eye, loop, fastener

presión *nf, pl* **presiones** **1** : pressure **2** **presión arterial** : blood pressure

presionar *vt* **1** : to pressure **2** : to press, to push — *vi* : to put on the pressure

preso¹, -sa *adj* **1** : imprisoned ⟨estar preso : to be imprisoned⟩ **2** **llevarse/tomar preso a** : to imprison, to take prisoner

preso², -sa *n* : prisoner

prestación *nf, pl* **-ciones** **1** : providing, provision **2** : benefit ⟨prestaciones sociales : welfare, government assistance⟩ **3** : feature

prestado, -da *adj* **1** : borrowed, on loan **2** **pedir prestado** : to borrow, to ask to borrow **3** **tomar prestado** : to borrow

prestamista *nmf* : moneylender, pawn-broker

préstamo *nm* **1** : loan **2** : lending, borrowing **3** BARBARISMO : loanword, borrowing

prestar *vt* **1** : to lend, to loan ⟨¿me prestas el paraguas? : can I borrow your umbrella?⟩ **2** : to render (a service), to give (aid) **3 prestar atención** : to pay attention **4 prestar declaración** : to testify **5 prestar juramento** : to take an oath — **prestarse** *vr* ~ **a/para** : **1** : to lend oneself to ⟨se presta a confusiones : it lends itself to confusion⟩ **2** : to agree to **3** : to participate in

prestatario, -ria *n* : borrower

presteza *nf* : promptness, speed

prestidigitación *nf, pl* **-ciones** : sleight of hand

prestidigitador, -dora *n* : conjurer, magician

prestigio *nm* : prestige — **prestigioso, -sa** *adj*

presto[1] *adv* : promptly, at once

presto[2], **-ta** *adj* **1** : quick, prompt **2** DISPUESTO, PREPARADO : ready

presumido, -da *adj* VANIDOSO : conceited, vain

presumir *vt* SUPONER : to presume, to suppose — *vi* **1** ALARDEAR : to boast, to show off **2** ~ **de** : to consider oneself ⟨presume de inteligente : he thinks he's intelligent⟩

presunción *nf, pl* **-ciones** **1** SUPOSICIÓN : presumption, supposition **2** VANIDAD : conceit, vanity

presunto, -ta *adj* : presumed, supposed, alleged — **presuntamente** *adv*

presuntuoso, -sa *adj* : conceited

presuponer {60} *vt* : to presuppose

presupuestal *adj* : budget, budgetary

presupuestar *vi* : to budget — *vt* : to budget for

presupuestario, -ria *adj* : budget, budgetary

presupuesto *nm* **1** : budget, estimate **2** : assumption, supposition

presurizar {21} *vt* : to pressurize

presuroso, -sa *adj* : hasty, quick

pretencioso, -sa *adj* : pretentious — **pretenciosamente** *adv*

pretender *vt* INTENTAR : to attempt, to try ⟨pretendo estudiar : I'm trying to study⟩ **2** AFIRMAR : to claim ⟨pretende ser pobre : he claims he's poor⟩ **3** : to seek, to aspire to ⟨¿qué pretendes tú? : what are you after?⟩ **4** CORTEJAR : to court **5 pretender que** : to expect ⟨¿pretendes que lo crea? : do you expect me to believe you?⟩

pretendido, -da *adj* **1** SUPUESTO : supposed, so-called **2** FALSO : feigned, false

pretendiente[1] *nmf* **1** : candidate, applicant **2** : pretender, claimant (to a throne, etc.)

pretendiente[2] *nm* : suitor

pretensión *nf, pl* **-siones** **1** : intention, hope, plan **2** : claim (to a throne, etc.) **3** : pretension ⟨sin pretensiones : unpretentious⟩

pretérito *nm* : preterit, past (tense)

pretextar *vt* : to claim, to feign

pretexto *nm* EXCUSA : pretext, excuse

pretil *nm* : parapet, railing

prevalecer {53} *vi* : to prevail, to triumph

prevaleciente *adj* : prevailing, prevalent

prevalerse {84} *vr* ~ **de** : to avail oneself of, to take advantage of

prevención *nf, pl* **-ciones** **1** : prevention **2** : preparation, readiness **3** : precautionary measure **4** : prejudice, bias

prevenido, -da *adj* **1** PREPARADO : prepared, ready **2** ADVERTIDO : forewarned **3** CAUTELOSO : cautious

prevenir {87} *vt* **1** : to prevent **2** : to warn — **prevenirse** *vr* ~ **contra** *or* ~ **de** : to take precautions against

preventivo, -va *adj* : preventive, precautionary

prever {88} *vt* **1** ANTICIPAR : to foresee, to anticipate **2** PLANEAR : to plan

previo[1], **-via** *adj* **1** : previous, prior **2** PRELIMINAR : preliminary

previo[2], **-via** *prep* : after, upon ⟨previo pago : after paying, upon payment⟩

previsible *adj* : foreseeable

previsión *nf, pl* **-siones** **1** : foresight **2** : prediction, forecast **3** : precaution **4** **previsión social** : welfare

previsor, -sora *adj* : farsighted, prudent

prieto, -ta *adj* **1** : dark **2** *Car, Mex* : dark-skinned **3** : tight, compressed

prima *nf* **1** : premium **2** : bonus **3** → primo

primacía *nf* **1** : precedence, priority **2** : superiority, supremacy

primado *nm* : primate (bishop)

primario, -ria *adj* : primary

primate *nm* : primate

primavera *nf* **1** : spring (season) **2** PRÍMULA : primrose

primaveral *adj* : spring

primera *nf* **1** : first (gear) **2** : first class

primeramente *adv* : firstly, first of all

primero[1] *adv* **1** : first **2** : rather, sooner

primero[2], **-ra** *adj* (*primer before masculine singular nouns*) **1** : first ⟨el primer paso : the first step⟩ **2** : top, leading ⟨de primera clase : first-class⟩ **3** : main, basic ⟨nuestro primer objetivo : our main objective⟩ ⟨lo primero es no alarmarse : the most important thing is not to panic⟩ **4 de primera** : first-rate

primero[3], **-ra** *n* : first ⟨el primero de enero : (on) the first of January, (on) January first⟩ ⟨el primero en llegar : the first to arrive⟩ ⟨la primera de tres fases : the first of three stages⟩

primicia *nf* **1** : first fruits **2** : scoop, exclusive

primigenio, -nia *adj* : original, primary

primitivo, -va *adj* **1** : primitive **2** ORIGINAL : original

primo[1] *adj* **1** : prime (of a number) **2** : raw ⟨materia prima : raw material⟩

primo[2], **-ma** *n* **1** : cousin ⟨primo hermano : first cousin⟩ **2** *Spain* : sucker

primogénito, -ta *adj & n* : firstborn

primor *nm* **1** : skill, care **2** : beauty, elegance

primordial *adj* **1** : primordial **2** : basic, fundamental

primoroso, -sa *adj* **1** : exquisite, fine, delicate **2** : skillful

prímula *nf* : primrose

princesa *nf* : princess

principado *nm* : principality

principal¹ *adj* **1** : main, principal **2** : foremost, leading

principal² *nm* : capital, principal

principalmente *adv* : mainly, chiefly

príncipe *nm* : prince

principesco, -ca *adj* : princely

principiante¹ *adj* : beginning

principiante² *nmf* : beginner, novice

principiar *vt* EMPEZAR : to begin

principio *nm* **1** COMIENZO : beginning ⟨empieza por el principio : start at the beginning⟩ **2** : principle (theory, law) **3** : principle (moral belief) **4** al principio : at first **5** a principios de : at the beginning of ⟨a principios de agosto : at the beginning of August⟩ **6** en ~ : in principle **7** en un principio : at first **8** por ~ : on principle

pringar {52} *vt* **1** : to dip (in grease) **2** : to soil, to spatter (with grease) — **pringarse** *vr*

pringoso, -sa *adj* : greasy

pringue¹, etc. → pringar

pringue² *nm* : grease, drippings *pl*

prior, priora *n* : prior *m*, prioress *f*

priorato *nm* : priory

prioridad *nf* : priority, precedence

prisa *nf* **1** : hurry, rush **2** a ~ or de ~ : quickly, fast **3** a toda prisa : as fast as possible **4** correr prisa : to be urgent **5** darse prisa : to hurry **6** tener prisa : to be in a hurry

prisión *nf*, *pl* **prisiones 1** CÁRCEL : prison, jail **2** ENCARCELAMIENTO : imprisonment

prisionero, -ra *n* : prisoner

prisma *nm* : prism

prismáticos *nmpl* : binoculars

prístino, -na *adj* : pristine

privacidad *nf* : privacy

privación *nf*, *pl* **-ciones 1** : deprivation ⟨privación de libertad : deprivation of liberty⟩ **2** : privation, want

privado, -da *adj* : private ⟨en privado : in private⟩ — **privadamente** *adv*

privar *vt* **1** DESPOJAR : to deprive ⟨privar a alguien de algo : to deprive someone of something⟩ **2** : to stun, to knock out — **privarse** *vr* : to deprive oneself

privativo, -va *adj* : exclusive, particular

privatizar {21} *vt* : to privatize

privilegiado, -da *adj* **1** : privileged **2** EXCEPCIONAL : exceptional

privilegiar *vt* : to grant a privilege to, to favor

privilegio *nm* : privilege

pro¹ *nm* **1** : pro, advantage ⟨los pros y contras : the pros and cons⟩ **2** en pro de : for, in favor of

pro² *prep* : for, in favor of ⟨grupos pro derechos humanos : groups supporting human rights⟩

pro- *pref* : pro-

proa *nf* : bow, prow

probabilidad *nf* : probability ⟨con toda probabilidad : in all likelihood⟩

probable *adj* : probable, likely ⟨es probable que pierdan : it's likely that they'll lose⟩

probablemente *adv* : probably

probador¹ *nm* : fitting room, dressing room

probador², -dora *n* : tester

probar {19} *vt* **1** : to demonstrate, to prove **2** : to test, to try out **3** : to try on (clothing) **4** : to taste, to sample — *vi* : to try ⟨probar a hacer algo : to try doing something⟩ — **probarse** *vr* : to try on (clothing)

probeta *nf* : test tube

probidad *nf* : probity

problema *nm* : problem ⟨resolver un problema : to solve a problem⟩

problemática *nf* : set of problems ⟨la problemática que debemos enfrentar : the problems we must face⟩

proboscide *nf* : proboscis

problemático, -ca *adj* : problematic

procaz *adj, pl* **procaces 1** : insolent, impudent **2** : indecent

procedencia *nf* : origin, source

procedente *adj* **1** : proper, fitting **2** ~ de : coming from

proceder *vi* **1** AVANZAR : to proceed **2** : to act, to behave **3** : to be appropriate, to be fitting **4** ~ a : to proceed to **5** ~ de : to originate from, to come from

procedimiento *nm* **1** : procedure, process **2** : proceedings *pl* (in law)

prócer *nmf* : eminent person, leader

procesado, -da *n* : accused, defendant

procesador *nm* : processor ⟨procesador de textos : word processor⟩

procesamiento *nm* : processing ⟨procesamiento de datos : data processing⟩

procesar *vt* **1** : to prosecute, to try **2** : to process

procesión *nf, pl* **-siones** : procession

proceso *nm* **1** : process **2** : trial, proceedings *pl* **3** → procesamiento

proclama *nf* : proclamation

proclamación *nf, pl* **-ciones** : proclamation

proclamar *vt* : to proclaim — **proclamarse** *vr*

proclive *adj* ~ a : inclined to, prone to

proclividad *nf* : proclivity, inclination

procrear *vi* : to procreate — **procreación** *nf*

procurador, -dora *n* ABOGADO : attorney

procurar *vt* **1** INTENTAR : to try, to endeavor ⟨procura llegar temprano : try to arrive early⟩ ⟨procura que no se enteren : make sure they don't find out⟩ **2** CONSEGUIR : to obtain, to procure

prodigar {52} *vt* : to lavish, to be generous with

prodigio *nm* : wonder, marvel

prodigioso, -sa *adj* : prodigious, marvelous

pródigo¹, -ga *adj* **1** : generous, lavish **2** : wasteful, prodigal

pródigo², -ga *n* : spendthrift, prodigal

producción *nf, pl* **-ciones 1** : production (action or quantity) **2** : production (in cinema, etc.) **3 producción en serie** : mass production

producir {61} *vt* **1** : to produce, to make, to manufacture **2** : to cause, to bring about **3** : to bear (interest) — **producirse** *vr* : to take place, to occur

productividad *nf* : productivity

productivo, -va *adj* **1** : productive **2** LUCRATIVO : profitable

producto *nm* **1** : product ⟨producto alimenticio : foodstuff⟩ ⟨producto interno bruto : gross domestic product⟩ **2** : proceeds *pl*, yield

productor¹, -tora *adj* : producing

productor², -tora *n* : producer

productora *nf* : production company

proeza *nf* HAZAÑA : feat, exploit

profanar *vt* : to profane, to desecrate — **profanación** *nf*

profano¹, -na *adj* **1** : profane **2** : worldly, secular, lay

profano², -na *n* **1** : layman *mf*, layperson *mf* **2** LAICO : layman *m*, laywoman *f*, layperson *mf* (in religion)

profecía *nf* : prophecy

proferir {76} *vt* **1** : to utter **2** : to hurl (insults)

profesar *vt* **1** : to profess, to declare **2** : to practice, to exercise

profesión *nf, pl* **-siones** : profession, occupation

profesional *adj & nmf* : professional — **profesionalmente** *adv*

profesionalismo *nm* : professionalism

profesionalizar {21} *vt* : to make (more) professional

profesionista *nmf Mex* : professional

profesor, -sora *n* **1** : teacher (of older children) **2** : professor (in a university) **3** : instructor, tutor

profesorado *nm* **1** : faculty **2** : teaching profession

profeta *nm* : prophet

profético, -ca *adj* : prophetic

profetizar {21} *vt* : to prophesy

prófugo, -ga *adj & n* : fugitive

profundidad *nf* **1** : depth, profundity **2** **en ∼** : in depth, thoroughly

profundizar {21} *vt* **1** : to deepen **2** : to study in depth — *vi* **∼ en** : to go deeply into, to study in depth

profundo, -da *adj* **1** HONDO : deep ⟨poco profundo : shallow⟩ **2** : profound — **profundamente** *adv*

profusión *nf, pl* **-siones** : abundance, profusion

profuso, -sa *adj* : profuse, abundant, extensive

progenie *nf* : progeny, offspring

progenitor, -tora *n* **1** : father *m*, mother *f* ⟨sus progenitores : his parents⟩ **2** ANTEPASADO : ancestor, progenitor

progesterona *nf* : progesterone

prognóstico *nm* : prognosis

programa *nm* **1** : program (on television, etc.) **2** : program (pamphlet) **3** : plan, schedule **4** : program (on a computer) **5** *or* **programa de estudios** : curriculum, syllabus

programable *adj* : programmable

programación *nf, pl* **-ciones 1** : programming (on television) **2** : programming (of computers) **3** : planning (of an event)

programador, -dora *n* : programmer

programar *vt* **1** : to schedule (times, shows, etc.), to plan (an event) **2** : to program (a computer, etc.)

progresar *vi* : to progress, to make progress

progresista *adj & nmf* : progressive

progresivo, -va *adj* : progressive, gradual — **progresivamente** *adv*

progreso *nm* : progress ⟨hacer progresos : to make progress⟩

prohibición *nf, pl* **-ciones** : ban, prohibition

prohibir {62} *vt* : to prohibit, to ban, to forbid ⟨prohibido fumar : no smoking⟩ ⟨prohibido el paso : do not enter⟩ ⟨me prohibió ir : she forbade me to go⟩ ⟨se prohibe el uso de pesticidas : the use of pesticides is banned/prohibited⟩

prohibitivo, -va *adj* : prohibitive

prohijar {5} *vt* ADOPTAR : to adopt

prójimo *nm* : neighbor, fellow man

prole *nf* : offspring, progeny

proletariado *nm* : proletariat, working class

proletario, -ria *adj & n* : proletarian

proliferar *vi* : to proliferate — **proliferación** *nf*

prolífico, -ca *adj* : prolific

prolijo, -ja *adj* : wordy, long-winded

prólogo *nm* : prologue, preface, foreword

prolongación *nf, pl* **-ciones** : extension, lengthening

prolongar {52} *vt* **1** : to prolong (a life, a war, etc.), to extend (a visit, etc.) **2** : to extend, to lengthen (in size) — **prolongarse** *vr* CONTINUAR : to last, to continue

promediar *vt* **1** : to average **2** : to divide in half — *vi* : to be half over

promedio *nm* **1** : average ⟨como promedio : on average⟩ **2** : middle, midpoint

promesa *nf* : promise ⟨cumplir (con) una promesa : to keep a promise⟩

prometedor, -dora *adj* : promising, hopeful

prometer *vt* : to promise ⟨¿me lo prometes? : (do you) promise?⟩ — *vi* : to show promise — **prometerse** *vr* COMPROMETERSE : to get engaged

prometido¹, -da *adj* : engaged

prometido², -da *n* NOVIO : fiancé *m*, fiancée *f*

prominente *adj* : prominent — **prominencia** *nf* — **prominentemente** *adv*

promiscuo, -cua *adj* : promiscuous — **promiscuidad** *nf*

promisorio, -ria *adj* **1** : promising **2** : promissory

promoción *nf, pl* **-ciones 1** : promotion **2** : class, year **3** : play-off (in soccer)

promocionar *vt* : to promote — **promocional** *adj*

promontorio *nm* : promontory, headland
promotor, -tora *n* **1** : promoter **2** INSTIGADOR : instigator **3** : developer (of real estate)
promover {47} *vt* **1** FOMENTAR : to promote, to encourage **2** : to promote (in rank, etc.) **3** PROVOCAR : to provoke, to cause
promulgación *nf, pl* **-ciones 1** : enactment **2** : proclamation, enactment
promulgar {52} *vt* **1** : to promulgate, to proclaim **2** : to enact (a law or decree)
prono, -na *adj* : prone
pronombre *nm* : pronoun
pronosticar {72} *vt* : to predict, to forecast
pronóstico *nm* **1** PREDICCIÓN : forecast, prediction ⟨pronóstico del tiempo : weather forecast⟩ **2** : prognosis
prontitud *nf* **1** PRESTEZA : promptness, speed **2** con ~ : promptly, quickly
pronto[1] *adv* **1** : quickly, promptly **2** : soon **3** de ~ : suddenly **4** ¡hasta pronto! : see you soon! **5** lo más pronto posible : as soon as possible **6** por de pronto : for now **7** tan pronto como : as soon as
pronto[2]**, -ta** *adj* **1** RÁPIDO : quick, speedy, prompt **2** PREPARADO : ready
pronunciación *nf, pl* **-ciones** : pronunciation
pronunciado, -da *adj* **1** : pronounced, sharp, steep **2** : marked, noticeable
pronunciamiento *nm* **1** : pronouncement **2** : military uprising
pronunciar *vt* **1** : to pronounce, to say **2** : to give, to deliver (a speech) **3 pronunciar un fallo** : to pronounce sentence — **pronunciarse** *vr* : to declare oneself (for or against), to make a statement
propagación *nf, pl* **-ciones** : propagation, spreading
propaganda *nf* **1** : propaganda **2** PUBLICIDAD : advertising (activity or materials)
propagar {52} *vt* **1** : to propagate **2** : to spread, to disseminate — **propagarse** *vr*
propalar *vt* **1** : to divulge **2** : to spread
propano *nm* : propane
propasarse *vr* **1** : to go too far, to overstep one's bounds **2** ~ con : to make sexual advances towards
propensión *nf, pl* **-siones** INCLINACIÓN : inclination, propensity
propenso, -sa *adj* ~ a : prone to, susceptible to
propiamente *adv* **1** : properly, correctly **2** : exactly, precisely ⟨propiamente dicho : strictly speaking⟩
propiciar *vt* **1** : to propitiate **2** : to favor, to foster
propicio, -cia *adj* : favorable, propitious
propiedad *nf* **1** : property ⟨propiedad privada : private property⟩ ⟨ser propiedad de : to be the property of⟩ **2** : ownership **3** CUALIDAD : property, quality **4** : suitability, appropriateness ⟨con propiedad : appropriately, properly⟩
propietario[1]**, -ria** *adj* : proprietary
propietario[2]**, -ria** *n* DUEÑO : proprietor (of a business), owner

propina *nf* : tip, gratuity ⟨le di una buena propina : I tipped him well⟩
propinar *vt* : to give, to strike ⟨propinar una paliza : to give a beating⟩
propio, -pia *adj* **1** : own ⟨su propia casa : his own house⟩ ⟨tienen recursos propios : they have their own resources⟩ **2** APROPIADO : appropriate, suitable **3** CARACTERÍSTICO : characteristic, typical ⟨es propio de la región : it's typical of the region⟩ **4** MISMO : oneself ⟨el propio director : the director himself⟩
proponer {60} *vt* **1** : to propose, to suggest **2** : to nominate — **proponerse** *vr* : to intend, to plan, to set out ⟨lo que se propone lo cumple : he does what he sets out to do⟩
proporción *nf, pl* **-ciones 1** : proportion ⟨en proporción a : in proportion to⟩ **2** : ratio (in mathematics) **3 proporciones** *nfpl* : proportions, size ⟨de grandes proporciones : very large⟩
proporcionado, -da *adj* **1** : proportionate **2** : proportioned ⟨bien proporcionado : well-proportioned⟩ — **proporcionadamente** *adv*
proporcional *adj* : proportional — **proporcionalmente** *adv*
proporcionar *vt* **1** : to provide, to give ⟨les proporcionó la información : she provided them with the information⟩ **2** : to proportion, to adapt
proposición *nf, pl* **-ciones** : proposal, proposition
propósito *nm* **1** INTENCIÓN : purpose, intention **2** a ~ : by the way **3** a ~ : on purpose, intentionally **4 a propósito de** : on the subject of
propuesta *nf* PROPOSICIÓN : proposal
propulsar *vt* **1** IMPULSAR : to propel, to drive **2** PROMOVER : to promote, to encourage
propulsión *nf, pl* **-siones** : propulsion ⟨propulsión a chorro : jet propulsion⟩
propulsor[1] *nm* : propellant
propulsor[2]**, -sora** *n* : promoter, proponent
propulsor[3]**, -sora** *adj* : propellant
propuso, etc. → **proponer**
prórroga *nf* **1** : extension, deferment **2** : overtime (in sports)
prorrogar {52} *vt* **1** : to extend (a deadline) **2** : to postpone
prorrumpir *vi* **1** : to burst forth, to break out ⟨prorrumpí en lágrimas : I burst into tears⟩
prosa *nf* : prose
prosaico, -ca *adj* : prosaic, mundane
proscribir {33} *v* **1** PROHIBIR : to prohibit, to ban, to proscribe **2** DESTERRAR : to banish, to exile
proscripción *nf, pl* **-ciones 1** PROHIBICIÓN : ban **2** DESTIERRO : banishment
proscrito[1] *pp* → **proscribir**
proscrito[2]**, -ta** *n* **1** DESTERRADO : exile **2** : outlaw
prosecución *nf, pl* **-ciones 1** : continuation **2** : pursuit

proseguir {75} *vt* **1** CONTINUAR : to continue **2** : to pursue (studies, goals) — *vi* : to continue, to go on
prospección *nf, pl* -ciones : prospecting, exploration
prospectar *vi* : to prospect
prospecto *nm* **1** : leaflet, brochure **2** : prospectus (for investors, etc.)
prospector, -tora *n* : prospector
prosperar *vi* : to prosper, to thrive
prosperidad *nf* : prosperity
próspero, -ra *adj* : prosperous, flourishing
próstata *nf* : prostate
prostíbulo *nm* : brothel
prostitución *nf, pl* -ciones : prostitution
prostituir {41} *vt* : to prostitute — **prostituirse** *vr* : to prostitute oneself
prostituto, -ta *n* : prostitute
protagonista *nmf* **1** : protagonist, main character **2** : star (in a film, etc.) **3** : leader, central figure
protagonizar {21} *vt* **1** : to star in **2** : to cause (an accident, etc.), to carry out (an attack, a campaign, etc.)
protección *nf, pl* -ciones : protection
protector¹, -tora *adj* : protective ⟨chaleco protector : chest protector⟩
protector², -tora *n* **1** : protector, guardian **2** : patron
protector³ *nm* : protector, guard ⟨protector de pantallas : screen saver⟩
protectorado *nm* : protectorate
proteger {15} *vt* : to protect, to defend ⟨proteger de/contra algo : to protect against something⟩ — **protegerse** *vr*
protegido, -da *n* : protégé
proteína *nf* : protein
prótesis *nfs & pl* : prosthesis
protesta *nf* **1** : protest **2** *Mex* : promise, oath
protestante *adj & nmf* : Protestant
protestantismo *nm* : Protestantism
protestar *vi* **1** : to protest, to object **2** ~ **por** : to complain about — *vt* : to protest, to object to
protocolo *nm* : protocol
protón *nm, pl* **protones** : proton
protoplasma *nm* : protoplasm
prototipo *nm* : prototype
protuberancia *nf* : protuberance — **protuberante** *adj*
provecho *nm* **1** : benefit, advantage ⟨sacar provecho de : to benefit from⟩ **2** ¡buen provecho! : bon appétit!
provechoso, -sa *adj* BENEFICIOSO : beneficial, profitable, useful — **provechosamente** *adv*
proveedor, -dora *n* : provider, supplier
proveedor de servicios de Internet *or* **PSI** *nm* : Internet service provider, ISP
proveer {63} *vt* : to provide, to supply ⟨proveer a alguien de algo : to provide someone with something⟩ — **proveerse** *vr* ~ **de** : to obtain, to supply oneself with
provenir {87} *vi* ~ **de** : to come from
provenzal¹ *adj* : Provençal
provenzal² *nmf* : Provençal
provenzal³ *nm* : Provençal (language)

proverbio *nm* REFRÁN : proverb — **proverbial** *adj*
providencia *nf* **1** : providence, foresight **2** : Providence, God **3 providencias** *nfpl* : steps, measures
providencial *adj* : providential
provincia *nf* : province — **provincial** *adj*
provinciano, -na *adj* : provincial, unsophisticated
provisión *nf, pl* -siones **1** : provision, providing **2 provisiones** *nfpl* : provisions, supplies
provisional *adj* : provisional, temporary
provisionalmente *adv* : provisionally, tentatively
provisorio, -ria *adj* : provisional, temporary
provisto *pp* → proveer
provocación *nf, pl* -ciones : provocation
provocador¹, -dora *adj* : provocative, provoking
provocador², -dora *n* AGITADOR : agitator
provocar {72} *vt* **1** CAUSAR : to provoke, to cause **2** IRRITAR : to provoke, to pique **3** : to arouse (sexually) **4** *Col, Peru, Ven fam* APETECER : to appeal to ⟨¿qué te provoca comer? : what would you like to eat?⟩
provocativo, -va *adj* : provocative
proxeneta *nmf* : pimp *m*
próximamente *adv* : shortly, soon
proximidad *nf* **1** : nearness, proximity **2 proximidades** *nfpl* : vicinity
próximo, -ma *adj* **1** : near, close ⟨la Navidad está próxima : Christmas is almost here⟩ ⟨las próximas elecciones : the coming election⟩ ⟨en un futuro próximo : in the near future⟩ ⟨próximo a la ciudad : near the city⟩ **2** SIGUIENTE : next, following ⟨la próxima semana : the following week, next week⟩ — **próximo, -ma** *pron*
proyección *nf, pl* -ciones **1** : projection **2** : showing, screening (of a film) **3** : range, influence, diffusion
proyeccionista *nmf* : projectionist
proyectar *vt* **1** : to plan **2** LANZAR : to throw, to hurl **3** : to project, to cast (light or shadow) **4** : to show, to screen (a film)
proyectil *nm* : projectile, missile
proyecto *nm* **1** : plan, project **2 proyecto de ley** : bill
proyector *nm* **1** : projector **2** : spotlight
prudencia *nf* : prudence, care, discretion
prudencial *adj* : prudent, sensible, cautious ⟨a una distancia prudencial : at a safe distance⟩
prudente *adj* : prudent, sensible, cautious
prueba¹, etc. → probar
prueba² *nf* **1** : proof, (piece of) evidence ⟨como prueba de : as proof of⟩ ⟨pruebas científicas : scientific evidence⟩ **2** : trial, test ⟨prueba del embarazo : pregnancy test⟩ ⟨vamos a hacer la prueba : let's try it⟩ **3** : proof (in printing or photography) **4** : event, qualifying round (in

prurito · pujar 246

prurito *nm* **1** : itching **2** : desire, urge
PSI → **proveedor de servicios de Internet**
psicoanálisis *nm* : psychoanalysis — **psicoanalista** *nmf*
psicoanalítico, -ca *adj* : psychoanalytic
psicoanalizar {21} *vt* : to psychoanalyze
psicodélico, -ca *adj* : psychedelic
psicología *nf* : psychology
psicológico, -ca *adj* : psychological — **psicológicamente** *adv*
psicólogo, -ga *n* : psychologist
psicópata *nmf* : psychopath
psicopático, -ca *adj* : psychopathic
psicosis *nfs & pl* : psychosis
psicosomático, -ca *adj* : psychosomatic
psicoterapeuta *nmf* : psychotherapist
psicoterapia *nf* : psychotherapy
psicótico, -ca *adj & n* : psychotic
psique *nf* : psyche
psiquiatra *nmf* : psychiatrist
psiquiatría *nf* : psychiatry
psiquiátrico[1], -ca *adj* : psychiatric
psiquiátrico[2] *nm* : mental hospital
psíquico, -ca *adj* : psychic
psiquis *nfs & pl* : psyche
psoriasis *nf* : psoriasis
púa *nf* **1** : barb ⟨alambre de púas : barbed wire⟩ **2** : tooth (of a comb) **3** : quill, spine (of an animal) **4** : thorn, spine (of a plant) **5** : pick (for a guitar, etc.)
pub [ˈpub, ˈpab] *nm, pl* **pubs** : bar, nightclub
pubertad *nf* : puberty
pubiano → **púbico**
púbico, -ca *adj* : pubic
publicación *nf, pl* **-ciones** : publication
publicar {72} *vt* **1** : to publish **2** DIVULGAR : to divulge, to disclose
publicidad *nf* **1** : publicity **2** : advertising
publicista *nmf* : publicist
publicitar *vt* **1** : to publicize **2** : to advertise
publicitario, -ria *adj* : advertising, publicity ⟨agencia publicitaria : advertising agency⟩
público[1], -ca *adj* : public ⟨hacer público : to make public⟩ — **públicamente** *adv*
público[2] *nm* **1** : public ⟨en público : in public⟩ **2** : audience, spectators *pl*
puchero *nm* **1** : pot **2** : stew **3** : pout ⟨hacer pucheros : to pout⟩
pucho *nm* **1** : waste, residue **2** : cigarette **3** : cigarette butt **4** **a puchos** : little by little, bit by bit
púdico, -ca *adj* : chaste, modest
pudiente *adj* **1** : powerful **2** : rich, wealthy
pudín *nm, pl* **pudines** BUDÍN : pudding
pudo, etc. → **poder**
pudor *nm* : modesty, reserve
pudoroso, -sa *adj* : modest, reserved, shy
pudrir {59} *vt* **1** : to rot **2** *fam* : to annoy, to upset — **pudrirse** *vr* **1** : to rot **2** : to languish
puebla, etc. → **poblar**

pueblerino, -na *adj* : provincial
pueblo *nm* **1** NACIÓN : people **2** : common people **3** ALDEA, POBLADO : town, village **4** **pueblo jóven** *Peru* : shantytown, slums *pl*
puede, etc. → **poder**
puente *nm* **1** : bridge **2** : bridge (in dentistry) **3** **puente aéreo** : airlift (military), air shuttle (commercial) **4** **puente levadizo** : drawbridge
puerco[1], -ca *adj* : dirty, filthy
puerco[2], -ca *n* **1** CERDO, MARRANO : pig, hog **2** : pig, dirty or greedy person **3** **puerco espín** : porcupine
pueril *adj* : childish, puerile
puerro *nm* : leek
puerta *nf* **1** : door (of a house, etc.), entrance (of a hotel, etc.), gate (in a fence, etc.) ⟨llamar a la puerta : to knock at/on the door⟩ ⟨puerta principal : front door, main entrance⟩ ⟨puerta trasera : back door⟩ **2** **a las puertas de** : on the verge of **3** **a puerta cerrada** : behind closed doors **4** **puerta de embarque** : gate (in an airport)
puerto *nm* **1** : port, harbor ⟨puerto pesquero : fishing port⟩ ⟨puerto marítimo : seaport⟩ **2** : mountain pass **3** : port (in a computer)
puertorriqueño, -ña *adj & n* : Puerto Rican
pues *conj* **1** : since, because, for ⟨lo hicieron, pues consideraron que era necesario : they did it because they considered it necessary⟩ **2** (*used interjectionally*) : well, then ⟨¡pues claro que sí! : well, of course!⟩ ⟨¡pues no voy! : well then, I'm not going!⟩
puesta *nf* **1** : setting ⟨puesta de/del sol : sunset⟩ **2** : laying (of eggs) **3** **puesta al día** : updating **4** **puesta a punto** : tune-up **5** **puesta en escena** : production (in theater) **6** **puesta en marcha** : start, starting up
puestero, -ra *n* : seller, vendor
puesto[1] *pp* → **poner**
puesto[2], -ta *adj* **1** : dressed ⟨bien puesto : well-dressed⟩ **2** : set (of a table)
puesto[3] *nm* **1** LUGAR, SITIO : place, position **2** : place (in a ranking) **3** : kiosk, stand, stall **4** : post, station ⟨puesto de policía : police station⟩ ⟨puesto de socorro : first-aid post⟩ **5** *or* **puesto de trabajo** : position, job **6** **puesto que** : since, given that
púgil → **pugilista**
pugilato *nm* BOXEO : boxing
pugilista *nmf* BOXEADOR : boxer (athlete)
pugna *nf* **1** CONFLICTO, LUCHA : conflict, struggle **2** **en** ~ : at odds, in conflict
pugnar *vi* ~ **por** : to strive to (do something), to strive for (something)
pugnaz *adj* : pugnacious
pujante *adj* : mighty, powerful
pujanza *nf* : strength, vigor ⟨pujanza económica : economic strength⟩
pujar *vi* **1** : to push, to strain **2** ~ **por** : to struggle to (do something), to struggle for (something)

pulcritud *nf* **1** : neatness, tidiness **2** ESMERO : meticulousness

pulcro, -cra *adj* **1** : clean, neat **2** : exquisite, delicate, refined

pulga *nf* **1** : flea **2 tener malas pulgas** : to be bad-tempered

pulgada *nf* : inch

pulgar *nm* **1** : thumb **2** : big toe

pulir *vt* **1** : to polish, to shine **2** REFINAR : to refine, to perfect

pulla *nf* **1** : cutting remark, dig, gibe **2** : obscenity

pulmón *nm, pl* **pulmones** : lung

pulmonar *adj* : pulmonary

pulmonía *nf* NEUMONÍA : pneumonia

pulóver *nm, pl* **-veres** : pullover, sweater

pulpa *nf* : pulp, flesh

pulpería *nf* : small grocery store

púlpito *nm* : pulpit

pulpo *nm* : octopus

pulque *nm* : Mexican alcoholic drink made from maguey sap

pulsación *nf, pl* **-ciones** **1** : beat, pulsation, throb **2** : keystroke

pulsar *vt* **1** APRETAR : to press, to push **2** : to strike (a key), to pluck (a string) **3** : to assess — *vi* : to beat, to throb

pulsera *nf* : bracelet

pulso *nm* **1** : pulse ⟨tomarle el pulso a alguien : to take someone's pulse⟩ ⟨tomarle el pulso a la opinión : to sound out opinion⟩ **2** : steady hand ⟨dibujo a pulso : freehand sketch⟩ ⟨a pulso : through effort, through hard work⟩

pulular *vi* ABUNDAR : to abound, to swarm ⟨en el río pululan los peces : the river is teeming with fish⟩

pulverizador *nm* **1** : atomizer, spray **2** : spray gun

pulverizar {21} *vt* **1** : to pulverize, to crush **2** : to spray

pum *interj* : bang!

puma *nf* : cougar, puma

puna *nf* **1** : Andean plateau **2** : altitude sickness

punción *nf, pl* **punciones** : puncture

punible *adj* : punishable

punitivo, -va *adj* : punitive

punce, etc. → **punzar**

punk¹ *adj* : punk

punk² *nm* : punk, punk rock

punk³ *nmf* : punk, punk rocker

punta *nf* **1** : tip, end ⟨punta del dedo : fingertip⟩ ⟨en la punta de la lengua : at the tip of one's tongue⟩ ⟨en la otra punta del país : on the other side of the country⟩ ⟨cortar las puntas : to trim (hair)⟩ **2** : point (of a weapon, pencil, etc.) ⟨punta de lanza : spearhead⟩ ⟨acabar en punta : to be pointed⟩ ⟨sacar punta a : to sharpen⟩ **3** : point, headland **4** : bunch, lot ⟨una punta de ladrones : a bunch of thieves⟩ **5 a punta de** : by, by dint of **6 de ~** : on end

puntada *nf* **1** : stitch (in sewing) **2** PUNZADA : sharp pain, stitch, twinge **3** *Mex* : witticism, quip

puntal *nm* : prop, support

puntapié *nm* PATADA : kick ⟨darle un puntapié a alguien : to kick someone⟩

puntazo *nm* CORNADA : wound (from a goring)

puntear *vt* **1** : to pluck (a guitar) **2** : to lead (in sports)

puntería *nf* : aim, marksmanship

puntero *nm* **1** : pointer **2** : leader

puntiagudo, -da *adj* : sharp, pointed

puntilla *nf* **1** : lace edging **2** : dagger (in bullfighting) **3 de puntillas** : on tiptoe

puntilloso, -sa *adj* : punctilious

punto *nm* **1** : dot, point **2** : period (in punctuation) **3** : point, item, question **4** : spot, place **5** : point, moment, stage **6** : point, extent **7** : point (in a score) **8** : stitch **9 en ~** : on the dot, sharp ⟨a las dos en punto : at two o'clock sharp⟩ **10 al punto** : at once **11 a punto de** : about to, on the verge of ⟨estaba a punto de salir : I was about to leave⟩ ⟨a punto del colapso : on the verge of collapse⟩ **12 a punto fijo** : exactly, certainly **13 dos puntos** : colon **14 en su punto** : just right **15 hasta cierto punto** : up to a point **16 punto decimal** : decimal point **17 punto de partida** : starting point **18 punto de vista** : point of view **19 punto final** : period (in punctuation) ⟨poner punto final a algo : to end something⟩ **20 punto fuerte/débil** : strong/weak point **21 punto muerto** : neutral (in an automobile), deadlock (in talks, etc.) **22 puntos cardinales** : points of the compass **23 puntos suspensivos** : ellipsis (in punctuation) **24 punto y aparte** : (period and) new paragraph **25 punto y coma** : semicolon **26 y punto** : period ⟨es el mejor que hay y punto : it's the best there is, period⟩

puntocom *nm, pl* **puntocom** : dot-com

puntuación *nf, pl* **-ciones** **1** : punctuation **2** : scoring (action), score, grade

puntual *adj* **1** : prompt, punctual **2** : exact, accurate — **puntualmente** *adv*

puntualidad *nf* : promptness, punctuality

puntualizar {21} *vt* **1** : to specify, to state **2** : to point out

puntuar {3} *vt* : to punctuate — *vi* : to score points

punzada *nf* : sharp pain, twinge, stitch

punzante *adj* **1** : sharp **2** CÁUSTICO : biting, caustic

punzar {21} *vt* : to pierce, to puncture

punzón *nm, pl* **punzones** **1** : awl **2** : hole punch

puñado *nm* **1** : handful **2 a puñados** : lots of, by the handful

puñal *nm* DAGA : dagger

puñalada *nf* : stab, stab wound

puñetazo *nm* : punch (with the fist) ⟨le dio un puñetazo en la cara : she punched him in the face⟩

puño *nm* **1** : fist **2** : handful, fistful **3** : cuff (of a shirt) **4** : handle, hilt **5 de su puño y letra** : in one's own handwriting

pupa *nf* CRISÁLIDA : pupa, chrysalis

pupila *nf* : pupil (of the eye)

pupilente *nm* *Mex* : contact lens

pupilo, -la *n* **1** : pupil, student **2** : ward, charge

pupitre *nm* : writing desk

puramente *adv* : purely

puré *nm* : puree ⟨puré de papas : mashed potatoes⟩

pureza *nf* : purity

purga *nf* **1** : laxative **2** : purge

purgante *adj & nm* : laxative, purgative

purgar {52} *vt* **1** : to purge, to cleanse **2** : to liquidate (in politics) **3** : to give a laxative to — **purgarse** *vr* **1** : to take a laxative **2** ~ **de** : to purge oneself of

purgatorio *nm* : purgatory

purgue, etc. → **purgar**

purificador *nm* : purifier

purificar {72} *vt* : to purify — **purificación** *nf*

puritano¹, -na *adj* : puritanical, puritan

puritano², -na *n* **1** : Puritan **2** : puritan

puro¹ *adv* : sheer, much ⟨de puro terco : out of sheer stubbornness⟩

puro², -ra *adj* **1** : pure ⟨aire puro : fresh air⟩ **2** : plain, simple, sheer ⟨por pura curiosidad : from sheer curiosity⟩ **3** : only, just ⟨emplean puras mujeres : they only employ women⟩ **4 pura sangre** : Thoroughbred horse

puro³ *nm* : cigar

púrpura *nf* : purple

purpúreo, -rea *adj* : purple

purpurina *nf* : glitter (for decoration)

pus *nm* : pus

pusilánime *adj* COBARDE : cowardly

puso, etc. → **poner**

pústula *nf* : pustule, pimple

puta *nf offensive* : whore, prostitute

putrefacción *nf, pl* **-ciones** : putrefying, rotting

putrefacto, -ta *adj* **1** PODRIDO : putrid, rotten **2** : decayed

pútrido, -da *adj* : putrid, rotten

puya *nf* **1** : point (of a lance) **2 lanzar una puya** : to gibe, to taunt

Q

q *nf* : twentieth letter of the Spanish alphabet

que¹ *conj* **1** : that ⟨dice que está listo : he says (that) he's ready⟩ ⟨espero que lo haga : I hope (that) she does it⟩ ⟨es posible que vuelva a pasar : it's possible (that) it will happen again⟩ ⟨estaba tan cansado que casi se durmió : he was so tired (that) he almost fell asleep⟩ ⟨me di cuenta de que era ella : I realized (that) it was her⟩ **2** : than ⟨ella es más alta que él : she is taller than he is⟩ ⟨más que nada : more than anything⟩ **3** (*expressing permission or desire*) ⟨¡que entre! : send him in!⟩ ⟨¡que te vaya bien! : I wish you well!⟩ **4** (*used in repeating a statement or question*) ⟨¡que no lo toques! : I told you not to touch it!⟩ ⟨que si quieres más : I asked if you wanted more⟩ ⟨¿cómo que no lo sabes? : what do you mean you don't know?⟩ **5** (*indicating a reason or cause*) ⟨¡cuidado, que te caes! : be careful, you're about to fall!⟩ ⟨no provoques al perro, que te va a morder : don't provoke the dog or (else) he'll bite⟩ **6** (*indicating a continuing or repeated action*) ⟨estaba todo el día corre que (te) corre : I was running around nonstop all day⟩ **7 es que** : the thing is that, I'm afraid that ⟨es que no tengo ganas de ir : the thing is that I don't want to go⟩ **8 yo que tú** : if I were you

que² *pron* **1** : who, that ⟨la niña que viene : the girl who is coming⟩ ⟨todos los chicos que están aquí : all (of) the boys who are here⟩ ⟨es el hombre que llamó ayer : he's the man who called yesterday⟩ ⟨no conozco a nadie que lo crea : I don't know anyone who believes it⟩ **2** : whom, that ⟨los alumnos que enseñé : the students that I taught⟩ ⟨la persona con que habló : the person with whom he spoke⟩ ⟨el hombre al que pertenece : the man to whom it belongs⟩ **3** : that, which ⟨el carro que me gusta : the car that I like⟩ ⟨el asunto al que hizo referencia : the matter to which she referred⟩ ⟨el delito del que fue acusado : the crime of which he was accused⟩ **4 el (la, lo, las, los) que** → **el¹, la¹, lo¹, los¹**

qué¹ *adv* : how, what ⟨¡qué bonito! : how pretty!⟩

qué² *adj* : what, which ⟨¿qué hora es? : what time is it?⟩

qué³ *pron* : what ⟨¿qué quieres? : what do you want?⟩ ⟨¿y qué? : so what?⟩ ⟨¿qué es eso? : what is that?⟩ ⟨¿sabes qué? : you know what?⟩ ⟨qué de . . . : what a lot of . . .⟩

quebracho *nm* : quebracho (tree)

quebrada *nf* DESFILADERO : ravine, gorge

quebradero *nm* **quebradero de cabeza** : headache, problem

quebradizo, -za *adj* FRÁGIL : breakable, delicate, fragile

quebrado¹, -da *adj* **1** : bankrupt **2** : rough, uneven **3** ROTO : broken

quebrado² *nm* : fraction

quebrantamiento *nm* **1** : breaking **2** : deterioration, weakening

quebrantar *vt* **1** : to break, to split, to crack **2** : to weaken **3** : to violate (a law or contract)

quebranto *nm* **1** : break, breaking **2** AFLICCIÓN : affliction, grief **3** PÉRDIDA : loss

quebrar {55} *vt* **1** ROMPER : to break **2** DOBLAR : to bend, to twist — *vi* **1** : to go bankrupt **2** : to fall out, to break up — **quebrarse** *vr*

queda *nf* : curfew

quedar *vi* **1** PERMANECER : to remain, to stay ⟨queda abierto hasta el 31 : it will remain open until the 31st⟩ **2** : to be, to end up being ⟨quedamos contentos con las mejoras : we were pleased with the improvements⟩ ⟨el partido quedó empatado : the game ended in a tie⟩ ⟨el pastel quedó muy rico : the cake came out really well, the cake was delicious⟩ ⟨queda claro que . . . : it's clear that . . .⟩ 3 : to be situated ⟨queda muy lejos : it's very far, it's too far away⟩ 4 : to be left ⟨quedan sólo dos alternativas : there are only two options left⟩ ⟨no me queda mucho dinero : I don't have much money left⟩ ⟨queda mucho por hacer : there's still a lot left to do⟩ 5 : to fit, to suit ⟨estos zapatos no me quedan : these shoes don't fit⟩ ⟨me queda grande : it's big on me⟩ ⟨ese color te queda bien : that color looks good on you⟩ 6 : to agree to meet ⟨a qué hora quedamos? : what time are we meeting?⟩ ⟨quedé con un amigo para cenar : I arranged to have dinner with a friend⟩ 7 **quedar bien/mal con alguien** : to make a good/bad impression on someone 8 ~ **en** : to agree, to arrange ⟨en qué quedamos? : what's the plan?, what are we doing?⟩ — **quedarse** vr 1 : to stay ⟨se quedó en casa : she stayed at home⟩ 2 : to keep on ⟨se quedó esperando : he kept on waiting⟩ 3 **quedarse atrás** : to stay behind, to get left behind ⟨no quedarse atrás : to be no slouch⟩ 4 ~ **con** : to remain ⟨me quedé con hambre después de comer : I was still hungry after I ate⟩

quedo¹ adv : softly, quietly

quedo², **-da** adj : quiet, still

quehacer nm 1 : work 2 **quehaceres** nmpl : chores

queja nf : complaint

quejarse vr 1 : to complain 2 : to groan, to moan

quejica¹ adj fam : whiny

quejica² nmf fam : whiny person

quejido nm 1 : groan, moan 2 : whine, whimper

quejoso, -sa adj : complaining, whining

quema nf 1 FUEGO : fire 2 : burning

quemado, -da adj 1 : burned, burnt 2 : annoyed 3 : burned out 4 : sunburned

quemador nm : burner

quemadura nf : burn

quemar vt 1 : to burn (wood, letters, etc.), to burn down (a building) 2 : to burn (calories, etc.) 3 : to burn, to overcook 4 : to burn (skin, clothes, etc.) ⟨te ha quemado el sol : you have a sunburn⟩ 5 DERROCHAR : to squander 6 : to burn (a DVD, etc.) 7 : to burn out (an engine), to blow (a fuse) — vi 1 : to burn ⟨en el trópico el sol quema mucho : the sun is very strong in the tropics⟩ 2 : to be burning hot — **quemarse** vr 1 : to burn, to burn down 2 : to burn oneself ⟨me quemé la mano : I burned my hand⟩ 3 : to get sunburned 4 : to burn out, to blow

quemarropa nf a ~ : point-blank

quemazón nf, pl **-zones** 1 : burning 2 : intense heat 3 : itch 4 : cutting remark

quena nf : Peruvian reed flute

quepa, etc. → **caber**

querella nf 1 : complaint 2 : lawsuit

querellante nmf : plaintiff

querellarse vr ~ **contra** : to bring suit against, to sue

querer¹ {64} vt 1 DESEAR : to want, to desire ⟨quiere ser profesor : he wants to be a teacher⟩ ⟨cuánto quieres por esta computadora? : how much do you want for this computer?⟩ ⟨qué quieres que haga? : what do you want me to do?⟩ ⟨quiero que ella me ayude : I want her to help me⟩ ⟨quisiera cancelar la cuenta : I'd like to cancel the account⟩ ⟨quisiera que no fuera así : I wish it weren't so⟩ ⟨léelo cuando quieras : read it whenever you like⟩ ⟨no quería decírselo : he didn't want to tell her⟩ ⟨no quiso dar detalles : she wouldn't give any details⟩ 2 : to love, to like, to be fond of ⟨te quiero : I love you⟩ ⟨te quiere bien : he's very fond of you⟩ 3 (indicating a request) ⟨quieres pasarme la leche? : please pass the milk⟩ ⟨quieres decirme qué pasa? : do you mind telling me what's going on?⟩ 4 **querer decir** : to mean ⟨qué quieres decir con eso? : what do you mean by that?⟩ ⟨eso no es lo que quiero decir : that's not what I meant to say⟩ 5 **sin** ~ : unintentionally — vi : like, want ⟨si quieres : if you like⟩ ⟨no quiero! : I don't want to!⟩

querer² nm : love, affection

querido¹, **-da** adj : dear, beloved

querido², **-da** n : dear, sweetheart

queroseno nm : kerosene

querrá, etc. → **querer**

querúbico, -ca adj : cherubic

querubín nm, pl **-bines** : cherub

quesadilla nf : quesadilla

quesería nf : cheese shop

queso nm : cheese

quetzal nm 1 : quetzal (bird) 2 : monetary unit of Guatemala

quiche nf : quiche

quicio nm 1 **estar fuera de quicio** : to be beside oneself 2 **sacar de quicio** : to exasperate, to drive crazy

quid nm : crux, gist ⟨el quid de la cuestión : the crux of the matter⟩

quiebra¹, **etc.** → **quebrar**

quiebra² nf 1 : break, crack 2 BANCARROTA : failure, bankruptcy

quien pron, pl **quienes** 1 : who, whom ⟨no sé quién ganará : I don't know who will win⟩ ⟨las personas con quienes trabajo : the people with whom I work⟩ ⟨su amigo, a quien conoció en México : his friend, whom he met in Mexico⟩ 2 : whoever, whomever ⟨quien quiere salir que salga : whoever wants to can leave⟩ 3 : anyone, some people ⟨hay quienes no están de acuerdo : some people don't agree⟩ ⟨no hay quien lo aguante : there's no one who would tolerate it⟩

quién pron, pl **quiénes** 1 : who, whom ⟨quién sabe? : who knows?⟩ ⟨con quién hablo? : with whom am I speaking?⟩ 2 **de** ~ : whose ⟨de quién es este libro? : whose book is this?⟩

quienquiera *pron, pl* **quienesquiera** : whoever, whomever

quiere, etc. → querer

quieto, -ta *adj* **1** : calm, quiet **2** INMÓVIL : still

quietud *nf* **1** : calm, tranquility **2** INMOVILIDAD : stillness

quijada *nf* : jaw, jawbone

quijotesco, -ca *adj* : quixotic

quilate *nm* : karat

quilla *nf* : keel

quimera *nf* : chimera, illusion

quimérico, -ca *adj* : fanciful

química, -ca *nf* : chemistry

químico¹, -ca *adj* : chemical

químico², -ca *n* : chemist

quimioterapia *nf* : chemotherapy

quimono *nm* : kimono

quincalla *nf* : trinkets *pl*

quince *adj & nm* : fifteen — **quince** *pron*

quinceañero, -ra *n* : fifteen-year-old, teenager

quinceavo¹, -va *adj* : fifteenth

quinceavo² *nm* : fifteenth (fraction)

quincena *nf* : two week period, fortnight

quincenal *adj* : bimonthly, semimonthly

quincuagésimo¹, -ma *adj* : fiftieth, fifty-

quincuagésimo², -ma *n* : fiftieth, fifty- (in a series)

quingombó *nm* : okra

quiniela *nf* : sports lottery

quinientos¹, -tas *adj & pron* : five hundred

quinientos² *nms & pl* : five hundred

quinina *nf* : quinine

quino *nm* : cinchona

quinqué *nm* : oil lamp

quinquenal *adj* : five-year ⟨un plan quinquenal : a five-year plan⟩

quinta *nf* : country house, villa

quintaesencia *nf* : quintessence — **quintaesencial** *adj*

quintal *nm* : hundredweight

quinteto *nm* : quintet

quintillizo, -za *n* : quintuplet

quinto, -ta *adj & n* : fifth ⟨el quinto grado : the fifth grade⟩ ⟨la quinta (persona) : the fifth (person)⟩ ⟨llegó el quinto : he came in fifth (place)⟩ ⟨un quinto de : a fifth of⟩

quíntuplo, -la *adj* : quintuple, five-fold

quiosco *nm* **1** : kiosk **2** : newsstand **3** **quiosco de música** : bandstand

quiosquero, -ra *n* : kiosk vendor

quirófano *nm* : operating room

quiromancia *nf* : palmistry

quiropráctica *nf* : chiropractic

quiropráctico, -ca *n* : chiropractor

quirúrgico, -ca *adj* : surgical — **quirúrgicamente** *adv*

quiso, etc. → querer

quisquilloso¹, -sa *adj* : fastidious, fussy

quisquilloso², -sa *n* : fussy person, fussbudget

quiste *nm* : cyst

quitaesmalte *nm* : nail polish remover

quitamanchas *nms & pl* : stain remover

quitanieves *nms & pl* : snowplow

quitar *vt* **1** : to remove, to take away/off/out ⟨quita la olla del fuego : take the pot off the heat/burner⟩ ⟨quitarle el polvo a algo : to dust something⟩ ⟨quítalo de en medio : get it out of the way⟩ ⟨¡quítame las manos (de encima)! : get your hands off me!⟩ **2** : to take, to take away ⟨le quitó las llaves : she took away his keys⟩ ⟨trataron de quitarle el dinero : they tried to take her money⟩ ⟨le quitaron la vida : they took his life, they killed him⟩ ⟨no me quita el sueño : I'm not losing any sleep over it⟩ **3** : to take off (one's clothes) ⟨le quitó los zapatos al paciente : she took the patient's shoes off⟩ **4** : to get rid of, to relieve ⟨quitar el dolor : to relieve the pain⟩ ⟨nadie le va a quitar esa idea de la cabeza : nobody's going to change his mind⟩ **5** : to take up (time) — **quitarse** *vr* **1** : to withdraw, to leave, to go away ⟨se me quitaron las ganas de salir : I don't feel like going out anymore⟩ **2** : to take off (one's clothes) **3** **~ de** : to give up (a habit) **4 quitarse de encima** : to get rid of ⟨me he quitado un peso de encima : that's a load off my mind⟩

quitasol *nm* : parasol

quiteño¹, -ña *adj* : of or from Quito

quiteño², -ña *n* : person from Quito

quizá *or* **quizás** *adv* : maybe, perhaps

quórum *nm, pl* **quórums** : quorum

R

r *nf* : twenty-first letter of the Spanish alphabet

rábano *nm* **1** : radish **2 rábano picante** : horseradish

rabí *nmf, pl* **rabíes** : rabbi

rabia *nf* **1** HIDROFOBIA : rabies, hydrophobia **2** : rage, anger

rabiar *vi* **1** : to rage, to be furious **2** : to be in great pain **3 a ~** *fam* : like crazy, like mad

rabieta *nf* BERRINCHE : tantrum

rabillo *nm* : corner (of the eye)

rabino, -na *n* : rabbi

rabioso, -sa *adj* **1** : enraged, furious **2** : rabid

rabo *nm* **1** COLA : tail **2 el rabo del ojo** : the corner of one's eye

rácano, -na *adj fam* : stingy

racha *nf* **1** : gust of wind **2** : run, series, string ⟨racha perdedora : losing streak⟩

racheado, -da *adj* : gusty, windy

racial *adj* : racial

racimo *nm* : bunch, cluster ⟨un racimo de uvas : a bunch of grapes⟩

raciocinio *nm* : reason, reasoning

ración *nf, pl* **raciones 1** : share, ration **2**
PORCIÓN : portion, helping
racional *adj* : rational, reasonable — **ra-cionalmente** *adv*
racionalidad *nf* : rationality
racionalización *nf, pl* **-ciones** : rationalization
racionalizar {21} *vt* **1** : to rationalize **2**
: to streamline
racionamiento *nm* : rationing
racionar *vt* : to ration
racismo *nm* : racism
racista *adj & nmf* : racist
radar *nm* : radar
radiación *nf, pl* **-ciones** : radiation, irradiation
radiactividad *nf* : radioactivity
radiactivo, -va *adj* : radioactive
radiador *nm* : radiator
radial *adj* **1** : radial **2** : radio, broadcasting ⟨emisora radial : radio transmitter⟩
radiante *adj* : radiant — **radiantemente**
adv
radiar *vt* **1** : to radiate **2** : to irradiate **3**
: to broadcast (on the radio)
radical¹ *adj* : radical, extreme — **radicalmente** *adv*
radical² *nm* : radical
radicalismo *nm* : radicalism
radicar {72} *vi* **1** : to be found, to lie **2**
ARRAIGAR : to take root — **radicarse** *vr*
: to settle, to establish oneself
radio¹ *nm* **1** : radius **2** : radium
radio² *nmf* : radio
radioactividad *nf* : radioactivity
radioactivo, -va *adj* : radioactive
radioaficionado, -da *n* : ham radio operator
radiodifusión *nf, pl* **-siones** : radio broadcasting
radiodifusora *nf* : radio station
radioemisora *nf* : radio station
radiofaro *nm* : radio beacon
radiofónico, -ca *adj* : radio ⟨estación radiofónica pública : public radio station⟩
radiofrecuencia *nf* : radio frequency
radiografía *nf* : X ray (photograph)
radiografiar {85} *vt* : to x-ray
radiología *nf* : radiology
radiólogo, -ga *n* : radiologist
radionovela *nf* : radio soap opera
radioterapia *nf* : radiation therapy
radioyente *nmf* : radio listener
radón *nm* : radon
raer {65} *vt* RASPAR : to scrape, to scrape
off
ráfaga *nf* **1** : gust (of wind) **2** : flash,
burst ⟨una ráfaga de luz : a flash of
light⟩
rafting *nm* : rafting
ragtime *nm* : ragtime
raid *nm* CA, Mex fam : lift, ride
raído, -da *adj* : worn, shabby
raiga, etc. → **raer**
raíz *nf, pl* **raíces 1** : root **2** : origin,
source **3 a raíz de** : following, as a result
of **4 echar raíces** : to take root
raja *nf* **1** : crack, slit **2** : slice, wedge
rajá *nm* : raja
rajadura *nf* : crack, split

rajar *vt* HENDER : to crack, to split — *vi* **1**
fam : to chatter **2** *fam* : to boast, to brag
— **rajarse** *vr* **1** : to crack, to split open
2 *fam* : to back out
rajatabla *adv* **a ~** : strictly, to the letter
ralea *nf* : kind, sort, ilk ⟨son de la misma
ralea : they're two of a kind⟩
ralentí *nm* **dejar al ralentí** : to leave (a
motor) idling
rallado, -da *adj* **1** : grated **2 pan rallado**
: bread crumbs *pl*
rallador *nm* : grater
rallar *vt* : to grate
ralo, -la *adj* : sparse, thin
RAM *nf* : RAM, random-access memory
rama *nf* : branch
Ramadán *nm, pl* **-danes** : Ramadan
ramaje *nm* : branches *pl*
ramal *nm* **1** : spur (of a railroad line) **2**
: halter, strap
rambla *nf* **1** : avenue, boulevard **2** *Arg,
Uru* : seaside walk, boardwalk
ramera *nf* : harlot, prostitute
ramificación *nf, pl* **-ciones** : ramification
ramificarse {72} *vr* : to branch out, to divide into branches
ramillete *nm* **1** RAMO : bouquet **2** : select
group, cluster
ramo *nm* **1** : branch **2** RAMILLETE : bouquet **3** : division (of science or industry)
4 Domingo de Ramos : Palm Sunday
rampa *nf* : ramp, incline
rana *nf* **1** : frog **2 rana toro** : bullfrog
ranchera *nf Mex* : traditional folk song
ranchería *nf* : settlement
ranchero, -ra *n* : rancher, farmer
rancho *nm* **1** : ranch, farm **2** : hut **3**
: settlement, camp **4** : food, mess (for
soldiers, etc.)
rancio, -cia *adj* **1** : aged, mellow (of wine)
2 : ancient, old **3** : rancid
rango *nm* **1** : rank, status **2** : high social
standing **3** : pomp, splendor
ranúnculo *nm* : buttercup
ranura *nf* : groove, slot
rap *nm* : rap (music)
rapar *vt* **1** : to crop **2** : to shave
rapaz¹ *adj, pl* **rapaces** : rapacious, predatory
rapaz², -paza *n, mpl* **rapaces** : youngster,
child
rape *nm* : close haircut
rapé *nm* : snuff
rapero, -ra *n* : rapper, rap artist
rapidez *nf* : rapidity, speed
rápido¹ *adv* : quickly, fast ⟨¡manejas tan
rápido! : you drive so fast!⟩
rápido², -da *adj* : rapid, quick —
rápidamente *adv*
rápido³ *nm* **1** : express train **2 rápidos**
nmpl : rapids
rapiña *nf* **1** : plunder, pillage **2 ave de
rapiña** : bird of prey
raposa *nf* : vixen (fox)
rapsodia *nf* : rhapsody
raptar *vt* SECUESTRAR : to abduct, to kidnap
rapto *nm* **1** SECUESTRO : kidnapping, abduction **2** ARREBATO : fit, outburst

raptor, -tora *n* SECUESTRADOR : kidnapper

raquero, -ra *n* : beachcomber

raqueta *nf* 1 : racket (in sports) 2 : snowshoe

raquítico, -ca *adj* 1 : scrawny, weak 2 : measly, skimpy

raquitismo *nm* : rickets

raramente *adv* : seldom, rarely

rareza *nf* 1 : rarity 2 : peculiarity, oddity

raro, -ra *adj* 1 EXTRAÑO : odd, strange, peculiar 2 : unusual, rare 3 : exceptional 4 **rara vez** : seldom, rarely

ras *nm* **a ras de** : level with

rasar *vt* 1 : to skim, to graze 2 : to level

rascacielos *nms & pl* : skyscraper

rascar {72} *vt* 1 : to scratch 2 : to scrape — **rascarse** *vr* : to scratch an itch

rasgadura *nf* 1 : tear, rip

rasgar {52} *vt* 1 : to rip, to tear — **rasgarse** *vr*

rasgo *nm* 1 : stroke (of a pen) ⟨a grandes rasgos : in broad outlines⟩ 2 CARACTERÍSTICA : trait, characteristic 3 : gesture, deed 4 **rasgos** *nmpl* FACCIONES : features

rasgón *nm, pl* **rasgones** : rip, tear

rasgue, etc. → **rasgar**

rasguear *vt* : to strum

rasguñar *vt* 1 : to scratch 2 : to sketch, to outline

rasguño *nm* 1 : scratch 2 : sketch

raso¹, -sa *adj* 1 : level, flat 2 **soldado raso** : private (in the army) ⟨los soldados rasos : the ranks⟩

raso² *nm* : satin

raspadura *nf* 1 : scratching, scraping 2 **raspaduras** *nfpl* : scrapings

raspar *vt* 1 : to scrape 2 : to file down, to smooth — *vi* : to be rough

rasposo, -sa *adj* : rough, scratchy

rasque, etc. → **rascar**

rastra *nf* 1 : harrow 2 **a rastras** : by dragging, unwillingly

rastrear *vt* 1 : to track, to trace 2 : to comb, to search 3 : to trawl

rastrero, -ra *adj* 1 : creeping, crawling 2 : vile, despicable

rastrillar *vt* : to rake, to harrow

rastrillo *nm* 1 : rake 2 *Mex* : razor

rastro *nm* 1 PISTA : trail, track 2 VESTIGIO : trace, sign

rastrojo *nm* : stubble (of plants)

rasuradora *nf Mex, CA* : electric razor, shaver

rasurar *vt* AFEITAR : to shave — **rasurarse** *vr*

rata¹ *nm fam* : pickpocket, thief

rata² *nf* 1 : rat 2 *Col, Pan, Peru* : rate, percentage

rata almizclera *nf* : muskrat

ratear *vt* : to pilfer, to steal

ratero, -ra *n* : petty thief

ratificación *nf, pl* **-ciones** : ratification

ratificar {72} *vt* 1 : to ratify 2 : to confirm

rato *nm* 1 : while 2 **pasar el rato** : to pass the time 3 **a cada rato** : all the time, constantly ⟨les sacaba dinero a cada rato : he was always taking money from them⟩ 4 **al poco rato** : later, shortly

after 5 **pasar un mal rato** : to have a bad/hard/tough time

ratón¹, -tona *n, mpl* **ratones** 1 : mouse 2 **ratón de biblioteca** *fam* : bookworm

ratón² *nm, pl* **ratones** 1 : (computer) mouse 2 *CoRi* : biceps

ratonera *nf* : mousetrap

raudal *nm* 1 : torrent 2 **a raudales** : in abundance

ravioli *or* **ravioles** *nmpl* : ravioli

raya¹, etc. → **raer**

raya² *nf* 1 : line ⟨pasarse de la raya : to go over the line, to go too far⟩ 2 : stripe 3 : skate, ray 4 : part (in the hair) ⟨hacerse la raya : to part one's hair⟩ 5 : crease (in clothing)

rayado, -da *adj* : striped, lined

rayar *vt* 1 ARAÑAR : to scratch 2 : to scrawl on, to mark up ⟨rayaron las paredes : they covered the walls with graffiti⟩ — *vi* 1 : to scratch 2 AMANECER : to dawn, to break ⟨al rayar el alba : at break of day⟩ 3 **~ con** : to be adjacent to, to be next to 4 **~ en** : to border on, to verge on ⟨su respuesta raya en lo ridículo : his answer borders on the ridiculous⟩ — **rayarse** *vr*

rayo *nm* 1 : ray, beam ⟨rayo láser : laser beam⟩ ⟨rayo gamma : gamma ray⟩ ⟨rayo de sol : sunbeam⟩ 2 RELÁMPAGO : lightning bolt 3 **rayos X** : X-ray

rayón *nm, pl* **rayones** : rayon

rayuela *nf* : hopscotch

raza *nf* 1 : race ⟨raza humana : human race⟩ 2 : breed, strain 3 **de ~** : thoroughbred (of a horse), purebred, pedigreed

razón *nf, pl* **razones** 1 MOTIVO : reason, motive ⟨en razón de : by reason of, because of⟩ ⟨tuvo sus razones : she had her reasons⟩ ⟨razón de más para hacerlo : all the more reason to do it⟩ 2 : reasoning, sense ⟨perder la razón : to lose one's mind⟩ 3 **con ~** : with good reason ⟨se quejaron, y con razón : they complained, and with good reason⟩ ⟨con razón no tiene novia : no wonder he doesn't have a girlfriend⟩ 4 **con razón o sin ella** : rightly or wrongly 5 **tener razón** : to be right ⟨en algo tiene razón : he's right about one thing⟩ 6 **darle la razón a alguien** : to say/admit that someone is right

razonable *adj* : reasonable — **razonablemente** *adv*

razonado, -da *adj* : itemized, detailed

razonamiento *nm* : reasoning

razonar *v* : to reason, to think

re *nm* 1 : D ⟨re sostenido/bemol : D sharp/flat⟩ 2 : re (in singing)

re- *pref* : re-

reabastecimiento *nm* : replenishment

reabierto *pp* → **reabrir**

reabrir {2} *vt* : to reopen — **reabrirse** *vr*

reacción *nf, pl* **-ciones** 1 : reaction 2 **motor a reacción** : jet engine

reaccionar *vi* : to react, to respond

reaccionario, -ria *adj & n* : reactionary

reacio, -cia *adj* : resistant, opposed

reacondicionar *vt* : to recondition

reactivación *nf, pl* **-ciones** : reactivation, revival

reactivar *vt* : reactivate, revive

reactor *nm* **1** : reactor ⟨reactor nuclear : nuclear reactor⟩ **2** : jet engine **3** : jet airplane, jet

reafirmar *vt* : to reaffirm, to assert, to strengthen

reagruparse *vr* : to regroup

reajustar *vt* : to readjust, to adjust

reajuste *nm* : readjustment ⟨reajuste de precios : price increase⟩

real *adj* **1** : real, true **2** : royal

realce *nm* **1** : embossing, relief **2 dar realce** : to highlight, to bring out

realeza *nf* : royalty

realidad *nf* **1** : reality **2 en ~** : in truth, actually

realinear *vt* : to realign — **realineamiento** *nm*

realismo *nm* **1** : realism **2** : royalism

realista[1] *adj* **1** : realistic **2** : realist **3** : royalist

realista[2] *nmf* **1** : realist **2** : royalist

realizable *adj* : feasible, attainable, workable

realización *nf, pl* **-ciones** : execution, realization

realizador, -dora *n* : (television or movie) producer

realizar {21} *vt* **1** : to carry out, to execute **2** : to produce, to direct (a film or play) **3** : to fulfill, to achieve **4** : to realize (a profit) — **realizarse** *vr* **1** : to come true **2** : to fulfill oneself

realmente *adv* : really, in reality

realzar {21} *vt* **1** : to heighten, to raise **2** : to highlight, to enhance

reanimación *nf, pl* **-ciones** : revival, resuscitation

reanimar *vt* **1** : to revive, to restore **2** : to resuscitate — **reanimarse** *vr* : to come around, to recover

reanudación *nf, pl* **-ciones** : resumption, renewal

reanudar *vt* : to resume, to renew — **reanudarse** *vr* : to resume, to continue

reaparecer {53} *vi* **1** : to reappear **2** : to make a comeback

reaparición *nf, pl* **-ciones** : reappearance

reapertura *nf* : reopening

reata *nf* **1** : rope **2** *Mex* : lasso, lariat **3 de ~** : single file

reavivar *vt* : to revive, to reawaken

rebaja *nf* **1** : reduction **2 DESCUENTO** : discount **3 rebajas** *nfpl* : sale

rebajar *vt* **1** : to reduce, to lower ⟨a precios rebajados : at reduced prices, on sale⟩ **2** : to lessen, to diminish **3** : to humiliate — **rebajarse** *vr* **1** : to humble oneself **2 rebajarse a** : to stoop to

rebanada *nf* : slice

rebanadora *nf* : slicer

rebañar *vt* : to mop up, to sop up

rebaño *nm* **1** : flock **2** : herd

rebasar *vt* **1** : to surpass, to exceed **2** *Mex* : to pass, to overtake

rebatiña *nf* : scramble, fight (over something)

rebatir *vt* **REFUTAR** : to refute

rebato *nm* **1** : surprise attack **2 tocar a rebato** : to sound the alarm

rebeca *nf* *Spain* : cardigan

rebelarse *vr* : to rebel

rebelde[1] *adj* : rebellious, unruly

rebelde[2] *nmf* **1** : rebel **2** : defaulter

rebeldía *nf* **1** : rebelliousness **2 en ~** : in default

rebelión *nf, pl* **-liones** : rebellion

reblandecer {18} *vt* : to soften

rebobinar *vt* : to rewind

reborde *nm* : border, flange, rim

rebosante *adj* : brimming, overflowing ⟨rebosante de salud : brimming with health⟩

rebosar *vi* **1** : to overflow **2 ~ de** : to abound in, to be bursting with — *vt* : to radiate

rebotar *vi* **1** : to bounce **2** : to ricochet, to rebound

rebote *nm* **1** : bounce **2** : rebound, ricochet

rebozar {21} *vt* : to coat in batter

rebozo *nm* **1** : shawl, wrap **2 sin ~** : frankly, openly

rebullir {38} *v* : to move, to stir — **rebullirse** *vr*

rebuscado, -da *adj* : affected, pretentious

rebuscar {72} *vi* : to search thoroughly

rebuznar *vi* : to bray

rebuzno *nm* : bray, braying

recabar *vt* **1** : to gather, to obtain, to collect **2 recabar fondos** : to raise money

recado *nm* **1** : message ⟨mandar recado : to send word⟩ **2** *Spain* : errand

recaer {13} *vi* **1** : to relapse **2 ~ en** *or* **~ sobre** : to fall on, to fall to

recaída *nf* : relapse

recaiga, etc. → recaer

recalar *vi* : to arrive

recalcar {72} *vt* : to emphasize, to stress

recalcitrante *adj* : recalcitrant

recalentar {55} *vt* **1** : to reheat, to warm up **2** : to overheat

recámara *nf* **1** *Col, Mex, Pan* : bedroom **2** : chamber (of a firearm)

recamarera *nf* *Mex* : chambermaid

recambio *nm* **1** : spare part **2** : refill (for a pen, etc.)

recapacitar *vi* **1** : to reconsider **2 ~ en** : to reflect on, to weigh

recapitular *v* : to recapitulate — **recapitulación** *nf*

recargable *adj* : rechargeable

recargado, -da *adj* : overly elaborate or ornate

recargar {52} *vt* **1** : to recharge (a battery), to reload (a gun) **2** : to reload (a web page, etc.) **3** : to overload — **recargarse** *vr* *Mex* **~ contra** : to lean against

recargo *nm* : surcharge

recatado, -da *adj* **MODESTO** : modest, demure

recato *nm* **PUDOR** : modesty

recaudación *nf, pl* **-ciones** **1** : collection **2** : earnings *pl*, takings *pl*

recaudador, -dora *n* **recaudador de impuestos** : tax collector

recaudar *vt* : to collect

recaudo *nm* : safe place ⟨a (buen) recaudo : in safe keeping⟩

recayó, etc. → **recaer**

rece, etc. → **rezar**

recelar *vi* ~ **de** : to distrust, to be suspicious of ⟨recelábamos de ella : we didn't trust her, we were suspicious of her⟩

recelo *nm* : distrust, suspicion

receloso, -sa *adj* : distrustful, suspicious

recepción *nf, pl* **-ciones** : reception

recepcionista *nmf* : receptionist

receptáculo *nm* : receptacle

receptividad *nf* : receptiveness

receptivo, -va *adj* : receptive

receptor¹, -tora *adj* : receiving

receptor², -tora *n* **1** : recipient **2** : catcher (in baseball), receiver (in football)

receptor³ *nm* : receiver ⟨receptor de televisión : television set⟩

recesión *nf, pl* **-siones** : recession

recesivo, -va *adj* : recessive

receso *nm* : recess, adjournment

receta *nf* **1** : recipe **2** : prescription

recetar *vt* : to prescribe (medications)

rechazar {21} *vt* **1** : to reject **2** : to turn down, to refuse

rechazo *nm* : rejection, refusal

rechifla *nf* : booing, jeering

rechinar *vi* **1** : to squeak **2** : to grind, to gnash ⟨hacer rechinar los dientes : to grind one's teeth⟩

rechistar *vi* : to complain, to answer back ⟨trabajó sin rechistar : he worked without complaint⟩

rechoncho, -cha *adj fam* : chubby, squat

rechupete *adj fam* **de** ~ : delicious, scrumptious

recibidor *nm* : vestibule, entrance hall

recibimiento *nm* : reception, welcome

recibir *vt* **1** : to receive, to get **2** : to receive, to greet (visitors) — *vi* : to receive visitors — **recibirse** *vr* **1** : to graduate **2** ~ **de** : to qualify as

recibo *nm* : receipt

reciclable *adj* : recyclable

reciclado → **reciclaje**

reciclaje *nm* **1** : recycling **2** : retraining

reciclar *vt* **1** : to recycle **2** : to retrain

recién *adv* **1** : newly, recently ⟨recién nacido : newborn⟩ ⟨recién casados : newlyweds⟩ ⟨recién llegado : newcomer⟩ **2** : just, only just ⟨recién ahora me acordé : I just now remembered⟩

reciente *adj* : recent — **recientemente** *adv*

recinto *nm* **1** : enclosure **2** : site, premises *pl*

recio¹ *adv* **1** : strongly, hard **2** : loudly, loud

recio², -cia *adj* **1** : severe, harsh **2** : tough, strong

recipiente¹ *nm* : container, receptacle

recipiente² *nmf* : recipient

reciprocar {72} *vi* : to reciprocate

reciprocidad *nf* : reciprocity

recíproco, -ca *adj* : reciprocal, mutual — **recíprocamente** *adv*

recitación *nf, pl* **-ciones** : recitation, recital

recital *nm* : recital

recitar *vt* : to recite

reclamación *nf, pl* **-ciones** **1** : claim, demand **2** QUEJA : complaint

reclamar *vi* **1** EXIGIR : to demand, to require **2** : to claim — *vi* : to complain

reclamo *nm* **1** : bird call, lure **2** : lure, decoy **3** : inducement, attraction **4** : advertisement **5** : complaint

reclinable *adj* : reclining

reclinar *vt* : to rest, to lean — **reclinarse** *vr* : to recline, to lean back

recluir {41} *vt* : to confine, to lock up — **recluirse** *vr* : to shut oneself up, to withdraw

reclusión *nf, pl* **-siones** : imprisonment

recluso, -sa *n* **1** : inmate, prisoner **2** SOLITARIO : recluse

recluta *nmf* : recruit, draftee

reclutamiento *nm* **1** : recruitment, recruiting

reclutar *vt* ENROLAR : to recruit, to enlist

recobrar *vt* : to recover, to regain — **recobrarse** *vr* : to recover, to recuperate

recocer {14} *vt* : to overcook, to cook again

recodo *nm* : bend

recogedor *nm* : dustpan

recogepelotas *nmfs & pl* : ball boy *m*, ball girl *f*

recoger {15} *vt* **1** : to collect, to gather **2** : to get, to pick up, to retrieve **3** : to clean up, to tidy (up)

recogido, -da *adj* : quiet, secluded

recogimiento *nm* **1** : collecting, gathering **2** : withdrawal **3** : absorption, concentration

recolección *nf, pl* **-ciones** **1** : collection ⟨recolección de basura : trash pickup⟩ **2** : harvest

recolectar *vt* **1** : to gather, to collect **2** : to harvest, to pick

recomendable *adj* : advisable, recommended

recomendación *nf, pl* **-ciones** : recommendation

recomendar {55} *vt* **1** : to recommend **2** ACONSEJAR : to advise

recompensa *nf* : reward, recompense

recompensar *vt* **1** PREMIAR : to reward **2** : to compensate

reconciliación *nf, pl* **-ciones** : reconciliation

reconciliar *vt* : to reconcile — **reconciliarse** *vr*

recóndito, -ta *adj* **1** : remote, isolated **2** : hidden **3** **en lo más recóndito de** : in the depths of

reconfortar *vt* : to comfort — **reconfortante** *adj*

reconocer {18} *vt* **1** : to recognize **2** : to admit **3** : to examine

reconocible *adj* : recognizable

reconocido, -da *adj* **1** : recognized, accepted **2** : grateful

reconocimiento *nm* **1** : acknowledgment, recognition, avowal **2** : (medical) examination **3** : reconnaissance

reconquista *nf* : reconquest

reconquistar *vt* **1** : to reconquer, to recapture **2** RECUPERAR : to regain, to recover

reconsiderar *vt* : to reconsider — **reconsideración** *nf*

reconstrucción *nf, pl* **-ciones** : reconstruction

reconstructivo, -va *adj* : reconstructive

reconstruir {41} *vt* : to rebuild, to reconstruct

reconversión *nf, pl* **-siones** : restructuring

reconvertir {76} *vt* **1** : to restructure **2** : to retrain

recopilación *nf, pl* **-ciones** **1** : summary **2** : collection, compilation

recopilar *vt* : to compile, to collect

récord *or* **record** [ˈrɛkɔr] *nm, pl* **récords** *or* **records** [-kɔrs] : record ⟨record mundial : world record⟩ — **récord** *or* **record** *adj*

recordar {19} *vt* **1** : to recall, to remember **2** : to remind — *vi* **1** ACORDARSE : to remember ⟨si mal no recuerdo : if I recall/remember correctly⟩ **2** DESPERTAR : to wake up

recordatorio¹, -ria *adj* : commemorative

recordatorio² *nm* : reminder

recorrer *vt* **1** : to travel through, to tour **2** : to cover (a distance) **3** : to go over, to look over

recorrido *nm* **1** : journey, trip **2** : path, route, course **3** : round (in golf)

recortar *vt* **1** : to cut, to reduce **2** : to cut out **3** : to trim, to cut off **4** : to outline — **recortarse** *vr* : to stand out ⟨los árboles se recortaban en el horizonte : the trees were silhouetted against the horizon⟩

recorte *nm* **1** : cut, reduction **2** : clipping ⟨recortes de periódicos : newspaper clippings⟩

recostar {19} *vt* : to lean, to rest — **recostarse** *vr* : to lie down, recline

recoveco *nm* **1** VUELTA : bend, turn **2** : nook, corner **3 recovecos** *nmpl* : intricacies, ins and outs

recreación *nf, pl* **-ciones** **1** : re-creation **2** DIVERSIÓN : recreation, entertainment

recrear *vt* **1** : to re-create **2** : to entertain, to amuse — **recrearse** *vr* : to enjoy oneself

recreativo, -va *adj* : recreational

recreo *nm* **1** DIVERSIÓN : entertainment, amusement **2** : recess, break

recriminación *nf, pl* **-ciones** : reproach, recrimination

recriminar *vt* : to reproach — **recriminarse** *vr*

recrudecer {53} *v* : to intensify, to worsen — **recrudecerse** *vr*

recta *nf* : straight line

rectal *adj* : rectal

rectangular *adj* : rectangular

rectángulo *nm* : rectangle

rectificación *nf, pl* **-ciones** : rectification, correction

rectificar {72} *vt* **1** : to rectify, to correct **2** : to straighten (out)

rectitud *nf* : honesty, rectitude

recto¹ *adv* : straight

recto², -ta *adj* **1** : straight **2** : upright, honorable **3** : sound

recto³ *nm* : rectum

rector¹, -tora *adj* : governing, managing

rector², -tora *n* : rector

rectoría *nf* : rectory

recuadro *nm* : box (containing text, etc.)

recubierto *pp* → **recubrir**

recubrir {2} *vt* : to cover, to coat

recuento *nm* : recount (de votos, etc.), count

recuerdo *nm* **1** : memory **2** : souvenir, memento **3 recuerdos** *nmpl* : regards

recular *vi* **1** : to back up **2** REPLEGARSE : to retreat, to fall back **3** RETRACTARSE : to back down

recuperación *nf, pl* **-ciones** **1** : recovery, recuperation **2 recuperación de datos** : data retrieval

recuperar *vt* **1** : to recover, to get back, to retrieve **2** : to recuperate **3** : to make up for (lost time, etc.) — **recuperarse** *vr* ~ **de** : to recover from, to get over

recurrente *adj* : recurrent, recurring

recurrir *vi* ~ **a** : to turn to, to appeal to **2** ~ **a** : to resort to **3** : to appeal (in law)

recurso *nm* **1** : recourse ⟨el último recurso : the last resort⟩ **2** : appeal (in law) **3 recursos** *nmpl* : resources, means ⟨recursos naturales : natural resources⟩

red *nf* **1** : net, mesh **2** : network, system, chain ⟨redes sociales : social media⟩ **3** : trap, snare **4 la red/Red** : the Internet, the Web **5 red barredera** : dragnet

redacción *nf, pl* **-ciones** **1** : writing, composition **2** : editing

redactar *vt* **1** : to write, to draft **2** : to edit

redactor, -tora *n* : editor

redada *nf* **1** : raid **2** : catch, haul

redecorar *v* : to redecorate

redefinir *vt* : to redefine — **redefinición** *nf*

redención *nf, pl* **-ciones** : redemption

redentor¹, -tora *adj* : redeeming

redentor², -tora *n* : redeemer

redescubierto *pp* → **redescubrir**

redescubrir {2} *vt* : to rediscover

redicho, -cha *adj fam* : affected, pretentious

redil *nm* **1** : sheepfold **2 volver al redil** : to return to the fold

redimir *vt* : to redeem, to deliver (from sin)

rediseñar *vt* : to redesign

redistribuir {41} *vt* : to redistribute — **redistribución** *nf*

rédito *nm* : return, yield

redituar {3} *vt* : to produce, to yield

redoblar *vt* : to redouble, to strengthen — **redoblado, -da** *adj*

redoble *nm* : drum roll

redomado, -da *adj* **1** : sly, crafty **2** : utter, out-and-out

redonda *nf* **1** : region, surrounding area **2 a la redonda** ALREDEDOR : around ⟨de diez millas a la redonda : for ten miles around⟩ **3** : whole note

redondear *vt* : to round off, to round out

redondel *nm* 1 : ring, circle 2 : bullring, arena

redondez *nf* : roundness

redondo, -da *adj* 1 : round ⟨mesa redonda : round table⟩ 2 : great, perfect ⟨un negocio redondo : an excellent deal⟩ 3 : straightforward, flat ⟨un rechazo redondo : a flat refusal⟩ 4 *Mex* : round-trip 5 en ~ : around

reducción *nf*, *pl* **-ciones** : reduction, decrease

reducido, -da *adj* 1 : reduced, limited 2 : small

reducir {61} *vt* 1 DISMINUIR : to reduce, to decrease, to cut 2 : to subdue 3 : to boil down — **reducirse** *vr* ~ a : to come down to, to be nothing more than

redundancia *nf* : redundancy

redundante *adj* : redundant

reedición *nf*, *pl* **-ciones** : reprint

reeditar *vt* : to reprint

reelegir {28} *vt* : to reelect — **reelección** *nf*

reembolsable *adj* : refundable

reembolsar *vt* 1 : to refund, to reimburse 2 : to repay

reembolso *nm* : refund, reimbursement

reemplazable *adj* : replaceable

reemplazar {21} *vt* : to replace, to substitute

reemplazo *nm* : replacement, substitution

reencarnación *nf*, *pl* **-ciones** : reincarnation

reencuentro *nm* : reunion

reestablecer {53} *vt* : to reestablish

reestructurar *vt* : to restructure

reexaminar *vt* : to reexamine

refacción *nf*, *pl* **-ciones** 1 *Mex* : spare part, replacement part 2 : repair, renovation

refaccionar *vt* : to repair, to renovate

refaccionaria *nf Mex* : repair shop

referencia *nf* : reference 2 **hacer referencia a** : to refer to

referendo → **referéndum**

referente *adj* ~ a : concerning

réferi *or* **referi** [ˈreferi] *nmf* : referee

referir {76} *vt* 1 : to relate, to tell 2 : to refer ⟨nos refirió al diccionario : she referred us to the dictionary⟩ — **referirse** *vr* ~ a 1 : to refer to 2 : to be concerned, to be in reference to ⟨en lo que se refiere a la educación : as far as education is concerned⟩

refilón → **de refilón**

refinado¹, -da *adj* : refined

refinado² *nm* : refining

refinamiento *nm* 1 : refining 2 FINURA : refinement

refinanciar *vt* : to refinance

refinar *vt* : to refine

refinería *nf* : refinery

reflectante *adj* : reflective, reflecting

reflector¹, -tora *adj* : reflecting

reflector² *nm* 1 : spotlight, searchlight 2 : reflector

reflejar *vt* : to reflect — **reflejarse** *vr* : to be reflected ⟨la decepción se refleja en su rostro : the disappointment shows on her face⟩

reflejo *nm* 1 : reflection 2 : reflex 3 **reflejos** *nmpl* : highlights, streaks (in hair)

reflexión *nf*, *pl* **-xiones** : reflection, thought

reflexionar *vi* : to reflect, to think

reflexivo, -va *adj* 1 : reflective, thoughtful 2 : reflexive

reflujo *nm* 1 : ebb, ebb tide 2 **el flujo y reflujo** : the ebb and flow

reforma *nf* 1 : reform 2 : alteration, renovation

reformador, -dora *n* : reformer

reformar *vt* 1 : to reform 2 : to change, to alter 3 : to renovate, to repair — **reformarse** *vr* : to mend one's ways

reformatorio *nm* : reform school

reforzar {36} *vt* 1 : to reinforce, to strengthen 2 : to encourage, to support

refracción *nf*, *pl* **-ciones** : refraction

refractar *vt* : to refract — **refractarse** *vr*

refrán *nm*, *pl* **refranes** ADAGIO : proverb, saying

refregar {49} *vt* : to scrub

refrenar *vt* 1 : to rein in (a horse) 2 : to restrain, to check — **refrenarse** *vr* : to restrain oneself

refrendar *vt* 1 : to countersign, to endorse 2 : to stamp (a passport)

refrescante *adj* : refreshing

refrescar {72} *vt* 1 : to refresh, to cool 2 : to brush up (on) 3 **refrescar la memoria** : to refresh one's memory — *vi* : to turn cooler

refresco *nm* : refreshment, soft drink ⟨refresco de cola : cola⟩

refriega *nf* : skirmish, scuffle

refrigeración *nf*, *pl* **-ciones** 1 : refrigeration 2 : air-conditioning

refrigerador *nmf* NEVERA : refrigerator

refrigeradora *nf Col, Peru* : refrigerator

refrigerante *nm* : coolant

refrigerar *vt* 1 : to refrigerate 2 : to air-condition

refrigerio *nm* : snack, refreshments *pl*

refrito¹, -ta *adj* : refried

refrito² *nm* : fried dish

refuerzo *nm* : reinforcement, support

refugiado, -da *n* : refugee

refugiar *vt* : to shelter — **refugiarse** *vr* ACOGERSE : to take refuge

refugio *nm* : refuge, shelter

refulgencia *nf* : brilliance, splendor

refulgir {35} *vi* : to shine brightly

refundir *vt* 1 : to recast (metals) 2 : to revise, to rewrite

refunfuñar *vi* : to grumble, to groan

refutar *vt* : to refute — **refutación** *nf*

regadera *nf* 1 : watering can 2 : shower head, shower 3 : sprinkler

regaderazo *nm Mex* : shower

regadío *nm* **tierra de** ~ : irrigated land

regalado, -da *adj* 1 : dirt cheap 2 : comfortable, easy

regalar *vt* 1 OBSEQUIAR : to present (as a gift), to give away 2 : to regale, to entertain 3 : to flatter, to make a fuss over — **regalarse** *vr* : to pamper oneself

regalía *nf* : royalty, payment

regaliz *nm*, *pl* **-lices** : licorice

regalo *nm* **1** OBSEQUIO : gift, present **2** : pleasure, comfort **3** : treat

regalón, -lona *adj, mpl* **-lones** *Chile fam* : spoiled (of a person)

regañadientes *mpl* **a** ~ : reluctantly, unwillingly

regañar *vt* : to scold, to give a talking to — *vi* **1** QUEJARSE : to grumble, to complain **2** REÑIR : to quarrel, to argue

regañina *nf fam* : scolding

regaño *nm fam* : scolding

regañón, -ñona *adj, mpl* **-ñones** *fam* : grumpy, irritable

regar {49} *vt* **1** : to irrigate **2** : to water **3** : to wash, to hose down **4** : to spill, to scatter

regata *nf* : regatta, yacht race

regate *nm* : dodge, feint

regatear *vt* **1** : to haggle over **2** ESCATIMAR : to skimp on, to be sparing with — *vi* : to bargain, to haggle

regateo *nm* : bargaining, haggling

regatón *nm, pl* **-tones** : cap, tip

regazo *nm* : lap (of a person)

regencia *nf* : regency

regenerar *vt* : to regenerate — **regenerarse** *vr* : **regeneración** *nf*

regentar *vt* : to run, to manage

regente *nmf* : regent

reggae ['rege, 'rigi] *nm* : reggae

regidor, -dora *n* : town councillor

régimen *nm, pl* **regímenes** **1** : regime **2** : diet **3** : regimen, rules *pl* ⟨régimen de vida : lifestyle⟩

regimiento *nm* : regiment

regio, -gia *adj* **1** : great, magnificent **2** : regal, royal

región *nf, pl* **regiones** : region, area

regional *adj* : regional — **regionalmente** *adv*

regir {28} *vt* **1** : to rule **2** : to manage, to run **3** : to control, to govern ⟨las costumbres que rigen la conducta : the customs which govern behavior⟩ — *vi* : to apply, to be in force ⟨las leyes rigen en los tres países : the laws apply in all three countries⟩ — **regirse** *vr* ~ **por** : to go by, to be guided by

registrador¹, -dora *adj* **caja registradora** : cash register

registrador², -dora *n* : registrar, recorder

registrar *vt* **1** : to register, to record **2** GRABAR : to record, to tape **3** : to search, to examine — **registrarse** *vr* **1** INSCRIBIRSE : to register **2** OCURRIR : to happen, to occur

registro *nm* **1** : register **2** : registration **3** : registry, record office **4** : range (of a voice or musical instrument) **5** : search

regla *nf* **1** NORMA : rule, regulation **2** : ruler ⟨regla de cálculo : slide rule⟩ **3** MENSTRUACIÓN : period, menstruation

reglamentación *nf, pl* **-ciones 1** : regulation **2** : rules *pl*

reglamentar *vt* : to regulate, to set rules for

reglamentario, -ria *adj* : regulation, official ⟨equipo reglamentario : standard equipment⟩

reglamento *nm* : regulations *pl*, rules *pl* ⟨reglamento de tráfico : traffic regulations⟩

regocijar *vt* : to gladden, to delight — **regocijarse** *vr* : to rejoice

regocijo *nm* : delight, rejoicing

regodearse *vr* : to delight, to gloat ⟨regodearse en/con : to delight in, to gloat about/over⟩

regordete, -ta *adj fam* LLENITO : chubby

regresar *vt* DEVOLVER : to give back — *vi* : to return, to come back, to go back

regresión *nf, pl* **-siones** : regression, return

regresivo, -va *adj* : regressive

regreso *nm* **1** : return **2 estar de regreso** : to be back, to be home

reguero *nm* **1** : irrigation ditch **2** : trail, trace **3 propagarse como reguero de pólvora** : to spread like wildfire

regulable *adj* : adjustable

regulación *nf, pl* **-ciones** : regulation, control

regulador¹, -dora *adj* : regulating, regulatory

regulador² *nm* **1** : regulator, governor **2 regulador de tiro** : damper (in a chimney)

regular¹ *vt* : to regulate, to control

regular² *adj* **1** : regular **2** : fair, OK, so-so **3** : medium, average **4 por lo regular** : in general, generally

regularidad *nf* : regularity

regularización *nf, pl* **-ciones** NORMALIZACIÓN : normalization

regularizar {21} *vt* NORMALIZAR : to normalize, to make regular

regularmente *adv* : regularly

regurgitar *vi* : to regurgitate

regusto *nm* : aftertaste

rehabilitar *vt* **1** : to rehabilitate **2** : to reinstate **3** : renovate, to restore — **rehabilitación** *nf*

rehacer {40} *vt* **1** : to redo **2** : to remake, to repair, to renew — **rehacerse** *vr* **1** : to recover **2** ~ **de** : to get over

rehecho *pp* → **rehacer**

rehén *nm, pl* **rehenes** : hostage

rehicieron, etc. → **rehacer**

rehizo → **rehacer**

rehuir {41} *vt* : to avoid, to shun

rehusar {8} *v* : to refuse

reimprimir *vt* : to reprint

reina *nf* : queen

reinado *nm* : reign

reinante *adj* **1** : reigning **2** : prevailing, current

reinar *vi* **1** : to reign **2** : to prevail

reincidencia *nf* : recidivism

reincidente *adj & nmf* : recidivist

reincidir *vi* : to backslide, to relapse

reincorporar *vt* : to reinstate — **reincorporarse** *vr* ~ **a** : to return to, to rejoin

reiniciar *vt* **1** : to resume, to restart **2** : to reboot (a computer)

reino *nm* : kingdom, realm ⟨reino animal : animal kingdom⟩

reinstalar *vt* **1** : to reinstall **2** : to reinstate

reintegración *nf, pl* **-ciones 1** : reinstatement, reintegration **2** : refund, reimbursement

reintegrar *vt* **1** : to reintegrate, reinstate **2** : to refund, to reimburse — **reintegrarse** *vr* ~ **a** : to return to, to rejoin

reintegro *nm* : refund, reimbursement

reintroducir {61} *vt* : to reintroduce

reír {66} *vi* : to laugh — *vt* : to laugh at — **reírse** *vr*

reiteración *nf, pl* **-ciones** : reiteration, repetition

reiterado, -da *adj* : repeated ⟨lo explicó en reiteradas ocasiones : he explained it repeatedly⟩ — **reiteradamente** *adv*

reiterar *vt* : to reiterate, to repeat

reiterativo, -va *adj* : repetitive, repetitious

reivindicación *nf, pl* **-ciones** **1** : demand, claim **2** : vindication

reivindicar {72} *vt* **1** : to vindicate **2** : to demand, to claim **3** : to restore

reja *nf* **1** : grille, grating ⟨entre rejas : behind bars⟩ **2** : plowshare

rejego, -ga *adj Mex fam* : stubborn

rejilla *nf* : grille, grate, screen

rejuvenecer {53} *vt* : to rejuvenate — *vi* : to be rejuvenated — **rejuvenecerse** *vr*

rejuvenecimiento *nm* : rejuvenation

relación *nf, pl* **-ciones** **1** : relation, connection, relevance **2** : relationship **3** RELATO : account **4** LISTA : list **5** : ratio (in mathematics) **6 con relación a** *or* **en relación con** : in relation to, concerning **7 relaciones públicas** : public relations, PR

relacionar *vt* : to relate, to connect — **relacionarse** *vr* ~ **con** : to be connected to, to be linked with

relajación *nf, pl* **-ciones** : relaxation

relajado, -da *adj* **1** : relaxed, loose **2** : dissolute, depraved

relajante *adj* : relaxing

relajar *vt* : to relax, to slacken — *vi* : to be relaxing — **relajarse** *vr*

relajo *nm* **1** : commotion, ruckus **2** : joke, laugh ⟨lo hizo de relajo : he did it for a laugh⟩

relamerse *vr* : to smack one's lips, to lick one's chops

relámpago *nm* : flash of lightning

relampaguear *vi* : to flash

relanzar {21} *vt* : to relaunch

relatar *vt* : to relate, to tell

relatividad *nf* : relativity

relativismo *nm* : relativism

relativo, -va *adj* **1** : relative **2 en lo relativo a** : with regard to, concerning — **relativamente** *adv*

relato *nm* **1** : story, tale **2** : account

relax [re'las] *nm* : relaxation

releer {20} *vt* : to reread

relegar {52} *vt* **1** : to relegate **2 relegar al olvido** : to consign to oblivion

relevante *adj* : outstanding, important

relevar *vt* **1** : to relieve, to take over from **2** ~ **de** : to exempt from — **relevarse** *vr* : to take turns

relevo *nm* **1** : relief, replacement **2** : relay ⟨carrera de relevos : relay race⟩

relicario *nm* **1** : shrine, container (for relics) **2** : locket

relieve *nm* **1** : relief, projection ⟨mapa en relieve : relief map⟩ ⟨letras en relieve : embossed letters⟩ **2** : prominence, importance **3 poner en relieve** : to highlight, to emphasize

religión *nf, pl* **-giones** : religion

religiosamente *adv* : religiously, faithfully

religioso¹, -sa *adj* : religious

religioso², -sa *n* : monk *m*, nun *f*

relinchar *vi* : to neigh, to whinny

relincho *nm* : neigh, whinny

reliquia *nf* **1** : relic **2 reliquia de familia** : family heirloom

rellano *nm* : landing (of a stairway)

rellenar *vt* **1** : to refill **2** : to stuff, to fill **3** : to fill out

relleno¹, -na *adj* : stuffed, filled

relleno² *nm* : stuffing, filling

reloj *nm* **1** : clock **2** : watch **3 reloj de arena** : hourglass **4 reloj de pulsera** : wristwatch **5 como un reloj** : like clockwork

relojería *nf* **1** : watchmaker's shop **2** : watchmaking, clockmaking

relojero, -ra *n* : watchmaker, clockmaker

reluciente *adj* : brilliant, shining

relucir {45} *vi* **1** : to glitter, to shine **2 salir a relucir** : to come to the surface **3 sacar a relucir** : to bring up, to mention

relumbrante *adj* : dazzling

relumbrar *vi* : to shine brightly

relumbrón *nm, pl* **-brones** **1** : flash, glare **2 de** ~ : flashy, showy

remachar *vt* **1** : to rivet **2** : to clinch (a nail) **3** : to stress, to drive home — *vi* : to smash, to spike (a ball)

remache *nm* **1** : rivet **2** : smash, spike (in sports)

remanente *nm* **1** : remainder, balance **2** : surplus

remangar {52} *vt* : to roll up — **remangarse** *vr* : to roll up one's sleeves

remanso *nm* : pool

remar *vi* **1** : to row, to paddle **2** : to struggle, to toil

remarcar {72} *vt* : to emphasize, to stress

rematado, -da *adj* : utter, complete

rematador, -dora *n* : auctioneer

rematar *vt* **1** : to finish off **2** : to auction — *vi* **1** : to shoot **2** : to end

remate *nm* **1** : shot (in sports) ⟨sacar un remate : to take a shot⟩ **2** : auction **3** : end, conclusion **4 como** ~ : to top it off **5 de** ~ : completely, utterly

remecer {86} *vt* : to sway, to swing

remedar *vt* **1** IMITAR : to imitate, to copy **2** : to mimic, to ape

remediar *vt* **1** : to remedy, to repair **2** : to help out, to assist **3** EVITAR : to prevent, to avoid

remedio *nm* **1** : remedy, cure **2** : solution **3** : option ⟨no me quedó más remedio : I had no other choice⟩ ⟨no hay remedio : it can't be helped⟩ **4 poner remedio a** : to put a stop to **5 sin** ~ : unavoidable, inevitable

remedo *nm* : imitation

rememorar *vi* : to recall ⟨rememorar los viejos tiempos : to reminisce⟩

remendar {55} *vt* **1** : to mend, to patch, to darn **2** : to correct

remera *nf Arg, Uru* : T-shirt
remero, -ra *n* : rower
remesa *nf* **1** : remittance **2** : shipment
remezón *nm, pl* **-zones** : mild earthquake, tremor
remiendo *nm* **1** : patch **2** : correction
remilgado, -da *adj* **1** : prim, prudish **2** : affected
remilgo *nm* : primness, affectation
reminiscencia *nf* : reminiscence
remisión *nf, pl* **-siones** **1** ENVÍO : sending, delivery **2** : remission **3** : reference, cross-reference
remiso, -sa *adj* **1** : lax, remiss **2** : reluctant
remite *nm* : return address
remitente[1] *nm* : return address
remitente[2] *nmf* : sender (of a letter, etc.)
remitir *vt* **1** : to send, to remit **2** ~ **a** : to refer to, to direct to ⟨nos remitió al diccionario : he referred us to the dictionary⟩ — *vi* **1** : to subside, to let up — **remitirse** *vr* ~ **a** : to refer to
remo *nm* **1** : paddle, oar **2** : rowing (sport)
remoción *nf, pl* **-ciones** **1** : removal **2** : dismissal
remodelación *nf, pl* **-ciones** **1** : remodeling **2** : reorganization, restructuring
remodelar *vt* **1** : to remodel **2** : to restructure
remojar *vt* **1** : to soak, to steep **2** : to dip, to dunk **3** : to celebrate with a drink
remojo *nm* **1** : soaking, steeping **2 poner en remojo** : to soak, to leave soaking
remolacha *nf* : beet
remolcador *nm* : tugboat
remolcar {72} *vt* : to tow, to haul
remolino *nm* **1** : whirlwind **2** : eddy, whirlpool **3** : crowd, throng **4** : cowlick
remolón, -lona *adj, mpl* **-lones** : lazy
remolque *nm* **1** : towing, tow **2** : trailer **3 a** ~ : in tow
remontar *vt* **1** : to overcome **2** SUBIR : to go up — **remontarse** *vr* **1** : to soar **2** ~ **a** : to date from, to go back to
rémora *nf* : obstacle, hindrance
remorder {47} *vt* INQUIETAR : to trouble, to distress
remordimiento *nm* : remorse
remotamente *adv* : remotely, vaguely
remoto, -ta *adj* **1** : remote, unlikely ⟨hay una posibilidad remota : there is a slim possibility⟩ **2** : distant, far-off
remover {47} *vt* **1** : to stir **2** : to move around, to turn over **3** : to stir up **4** : to remove **5** : to dismiss
removible *adj* : removable
remozamiento *nm* : renovation
remozar {21} *vt* **1** : to renew, to brighten up **2** : to redo, to renovate
remuneración *nf, pl* **-ciones** : remuneration, pay
remunerar *vt* : to pay, to remunerate
renacer {48} *vi* : to be reborn, to revive
renacimiento *nm* **1** : rebirth, revival **2 el Renacimiento** : the Renaissance
renacuajo *nm* : tadpole, pollywog
renal *adj* : renal, kidney
rencilla *nf* : quarrel

renco, -ca *adj* : lame
rencor *nm* **1** : rancor, enmity, hostility **2 guardar rencor** : to hold a grudge ⟨guardarle rencor a alguien por algo : to resent someone for something, to hold a grudge against someone for something⟩
rencoroso, -sa *adj* : resentful, bitter, rancorous
rendición *nf, pl* **-ciones** **1** : surrender, submission **2** : yield, return
rendido, -da *adj* **1** : submissive **2** : worn-out, exhausted **3** : devoted
rendija *nf* GRIETA : crack, split
rendimiento *nm* **1** : performance **2** : yield, efficiency
rendir {54} *vt* **1** : to render, to give ⟨rendir las gracias : to give thanks⟩ ⟨rendir homenaje a : to pay homage to⟩ **2** : to yield **3** CANSAR : to exhaust — *vi* **1** CUNDIR : to progress, to make headway **2** : to last, to go a long way — **rendirse** *vr* : to surrender, to give up
renegado, -da *n* : renegade
renegar {49} *vi* **1** ~ **de** : to renounce, to disown, to give up **2** ~ **de** : to complain about — *vt* **1** : to deny vigorously **2** : to abhor, to hate
renglón *nm, pl* **renglones** **1** : line (of writing) **2** : merchandise, line (of products)
rengo, -ga *adj* : lame
renguear *vi* : to limp
reno *nm* : reindeer
renombrado, -da *adj* : renowned, famous
renombre *nm* NOMBRADÍA : renown, fame
renovable *adj* : renewable
renovación *nf, pl* **-ciones** **1** : renewal ⟨renovación de un contrato : renewal of a contract⟩ **2** : change, renovation
renovar {19} *vt* **1** : to renew, to restore **2** : to renovate
renquear *vi* : to limp, to hobble
renquera *nf* COJERA : limp, lameness
renta *nf* **1** : income **2** : rent **3 impuesto sobre la renta** : income tax
rentable *adj* : profitable — **rentabilidad** *nf*
rentar *vt* **1** : to produce, to yield **2** ALQUILAR : to rent
renuencia *nf* : reluctance, unwillingness
renuente *adj* : reluctant, unwilling
renuncia *nf* **1** : resignation **2** : renunciation **3** : waiver
renunciar *vi* **1** : to resign **2** ~ **a** : to renounce, to relinquish ⟨renunció al título : he relinquished the title⟩
reñido, -da *adj* **1** : tough, hard-fought **2** : at odds, on bad terms
reñir {67} *vi* **1** : to argue **2** ~ **con** : to fall out with, to go up against — *vt* : to scold, to reprimand
reo, rea *n* **1** : accused, defendant **2** : offender, culprit
reojo *nm* **de** ~ : out of the corner of one's eye ⟨una mirada de reojo : a sidelong glance⟩
reorganizar {21} *vt* : to reorganize — **reorganización** *nf*

repantigarse {52} *vr* : to slouch, to loll about

reparación *nf, pl* **-ciones** 1 : reparation, amends 2 : repair

reparador, -dora *adj* : refreshing

reparar *vt* 1 : to repair, to fix, to mend 2 : to make amends for 3 : to correct 4 : to restore, to refresh — *vi* 1 ~ **en** : to observe, to take notice of 2 ~ **en** : to consider, to think about ⟨sin reparar en las consecuencias : without thinking about the consequences⟩ ⟨no repararon en gastos : they spared no expense, money was no object⟩

reparo *nm* 1 : repair, restoration 2 : reservation, qualm ⟨no tuvieron reparos en decírmelo : they didn't hesitate to tell me⟩ 3 **poner reparos a** : to find fault with, to object to

repartición *nf, pl* **-ciones** 1 : distribution 2 : department, division

repartidor¹, -dora *adj* : delivery ⟨camión repartidor : delivery truck⟩

repartidor², -dora *n* : delivery person, distributor

repartimiento *nm* → **repartición**

repartir *vt* 1 : to allocate 2 DISTRIBUIR : to distribute, to hand out 3 : to spread

reparto *nm* 1 : allocation 2 : distribution 3 : cast (of characters)

repasador *nm Arg, Uru* : dish towel

repasar *vt* 1 : to pass by again 2 : to review, to go over 3 : to mend

repaso *nm* 1 : review 2 : mending 3 : checkup, overhaul

repatriar {85} *vt* : to repatriate — **repatriación** *nf*

repavimentar *vt* : to resurface

repelente¹ *adj* : repellent, repulsive

repelente² *nm* : repellent ⟨repelente de insectos : insect repellent⟩

repeler *vt* 1 : to repel, to resist, to repulse 2 : to reject 3 : to disgust ⟨el sabor me repele : I find the taste repulsive⟩

repensar {55} *v* : to rethink, to reconsider

repente *nm* 1 : sudden movement, start ⟨de repente : suddenly⟩ 2 : fit, outburst ⟨un repente de ira : a fit of anger⟩

repentino, -na *adj* : sudden — **repentinamente** *adv*

repercusión *nf, pl* **-siones** : repercussion

repercutir *vi* 1 : to reverberate, to echo 2 ~ **en** : to have effects on, to have repercussions on

repertorio *nm* : repertoire

repetición *nf, pl* **-ciones** 1 : repetition 2 : rerun, repeat

repetidamente *adv* : repeatedly

repetido, -da *adj* 1 : repeated, numerous 2 **repetidas veces** : repeatedly, time and again

repetir {54} *vt* 1 : to repeat 2 : to have a second helping of — *vi* 1 : to repeat a year (in school) 2 : to have a second helping 3 : to give indigestion — **repetirse** *vr* 1 : to repeat oneself 2 : to recur

repetitivo, -va *adj* : repetitive, repetitious

repicar {72} *vt* : to ring — *vi* : to ring out, to peal

repique *nm* : ringing, pealing

repiqueteo *nm* 1 : ringing, pealing 2 : drumming

repisa *nf* : shelf, ledge ⟨repisa de chimenea : mantelpiece⟩ ⟨repisa de ventana : windowsill⟩

replantear *vt* : to redefine, to restate — **replantearse** *vr* : to reconsider

replegar {49} *vt* : to fold — **replegarse** *vr* RETIRARSE : to retreat, to withdraw

repleto, -ta *adj* 1 : replete, full 2 ~ **de** : packed with, crammed with

réplica *nf* 1 : reply 2 : replica, reproduction 3 : aftershock

replicación *nf, pl* **-ciones** : replication

replicar {72} *vt* 1 : to reply, to retort 2 : to argue, to answer back

repliegue *nm* 1 : fold 2 : retreat, withdrawal

repollo *nm* COL : cabbage

reponer {60} *vt* 1 : to replace, to put back 2 : to reinstate 3 : to reply — **reponerse** *vr* : to recover

reportaje *nm* : article, story, report

reportar *vt* 1 : to check, to restrain 2 : to bring, to carry, to yield ⟨me reportó numerosos beneficios : it brought me many benefits⟩ 3 : to report — **reportarse** *vr* 1 CONTENERSE : to control oneself 2 PRESENTARSE : to report, to show up

reporte *nm* : report

reportear *vt* : to report on, to cover

reportero, -ra *n* 1 : reporter 2 **reportero gráfico** : photojournalist

reposado, -da *adj* : calm

reposapiés *nm, pl* **reposapiés** : footrest

reposar *vi* 1 : to rest, to repose 2 : to stand, to settle ⟨deje reposar la masa media hora : let the dough stand for half an hour⟩ 3 : to lie, to be buried — **reposarse** *vr* : to settle

reposición *nf, pl* **-ciones** 1 : replacement 2 : reinstatement 3 : revival

repositorio *nm* : repository

reposo *nm* : repose, rest

repostar *vi* 1 : to stock up 2 : to refuel

repostería *nf* 1 : confectioner's shop 2 : pastry-making

repostero, -ra *n* : confectioner

repreguntar *vt* : to cross-examine

repreguntas *nfpl* : cross-examination

reprender *vt* : to reprimand, to scold

reprensible *adj* : reprehensible

represa *nf* : dam

represalia *nf* 1 : reprisal, retaliation 2 **tomar represalias** : to retaliate

represar *vt* : to dam

representación *nf, pl* **-ciones** 1 : representation 2 : performance 3 **en representación de** : on behalf of

representante *nmf* 1 : representative 2 : performer

representar *vt* 1 : to represent, to act for 2 : to perform 3 : to look, to appear as 4 : to symbolize, to stand for 5 : to signify, to mean — **representarse** *vr* : to imagine, to picture

representativo, -va *adj* : representative

represión *nf, pl* **-siones** : repression

represivo, -va *adj* : repressive

reprimenda *nf* : reprimand

reprimir *vt* **1** : to repress **2** : to suppress, to stifle

reprobable *adj* : reprehensible, culpable

reprobación *nf, pl* **-ciones** : disapproval

reprobar {19} *vt* **1** DESAPROBAR : to condemn, to disapprove of **2** : to fail (a course)

reprobatorio, -ria *adj* : disapproving, admonishing

reprochable *adj* : reprehensible

reprochar *vt* : to reproach — **reprocharse** *vr*

reproche *nm* : reproach

reproducción *nf, pl* **-ciones** : reproduction

reproducir {61} *vt* : to reproduce — **reproducirse** *vr* **1** : to breed, to reproduce **2** : to recur

reproductor¹, -tora *adj* : reproductive

reproductor² *nm* : player ⟨reproductor de DVD : DVD player⟩

reptar *vi* : to crawl, to slither

reptil¹ *adj* : reptilian

reptil² *nm* : reptile

república *nf* : republic

republicano, -na *adj & n* : republican — **republicanismo** *nf*

repudiar *vt* : to repudiate — **repudiación** *nf*

repudio *nm* : repudiation

repuesto¹ *pp* → **reponer**

repuesto² *nm* **1** : spare part **2** de ~ : spare ⟨rueda de repuesto : spare wheel⟩

repugnancia *nf* : repugnance

repugnante *adj* : repulsive, repugnant, revolting

repugnar *vt* : to cause repugnance, to disgust — **repugnarse** *vr*

repujar *vt* : to emboss

repulsa *nf* **1** : rejection **2** : condemnation

repulsivo, -va *adj* : repulsive

repuntar *vt Arg, Chile* : to round up (cattle) — *vi* **1** : to begin to appear — **repuntarse** *vr* : to fall out, to quarrel

repuso, etc. → **reponer**

reputación *nf, pl* **-ciones** : reputation

reputar *vt* : to consider, to deem

requerir {76} *vt* **1** : to require, to call for **2** : to summon, to send for

requesón *nm, pl* **-sones** : curd cheese, cottage cheese

réquiem *nm* : requiem

requisa *nf* **1** : requisition **2** : seizure **3** : inspection

requisar *vt* **1** : to requisition **2** : to seize **3** INSPECCIONAR : to inspect

requisito *nm* **1** : requirement **2 requisito previo** : prerequisite

res *nf* **1** : beast, animal **2** *CA, Mex* : beef **3 reses** *nfpl* : cattle ⟨60 reses : 60 head of cattle⟩

resabio *nm* **1** VICIO : bad habit, vice **2** DEJO : aftertaste

resaca *nf* **1** : undertow **2** : hangover

resaltar *vi* **1** SOBRESALIR : to stand out **2 hacer resaltar** : to bring out, to highlight — *vt* : to stress, to emphasize

resarcimiento *nm* **1** : compensation **2** : reimbursement

resarcir {83} *vt* : to compensate, to indemnify — **resarcirse** *vr* ~ **de** : to make up for

resbalada *nf* : slip

resbaladizo, -za *adj* **1** RESBALOSO : slippery **2** : tricky, ticklish, delicate

resbalar *vi* **1** : to slip, to slide **2** : to slip up, to make a mistake **3** : to skid — **resbalarse** *vr*

resbalón *nm, pl* **-lones** : slip

resbaloso, -sa *adj* : slippery

rescatar *vt* **1** : to rescue, to save **2** : to recover, to get back

rescate *nm* **1** : rescue **2** : recovery **3** : ransom

rescindir *vt* : to rescind, to annul, to cancel

rescisión *nf, pl* **-siones** : annulment, cancellation

rescoldo *nm* : embers *pl*

resecar {72} *vt* : to make dry, to dry up — **resecarse** *vr* : to dry up

reseco, -ca *adj* : dry

resentido, -da *adj* : resentful

resentimiento *nm* : resentment

resentirse {76} *vr* **1** : to suffer, to be weakened **2** OFENDERSE : to be/get upset ⟨se resintió porque la insultaron : she got upset when they insulted her, she resented being insulted⟩ **3** ~ **de** : to feel the effects of — **resentir** *vt* **1** : to feel (effects, etc.) : to resent

reseña *nf* **1** : report, summary, review **2** : description

reseñar *vt* **1** : to review **2** DESCRIBIR : to describe

reserva *nf* **1** : reservation **2** : reserve **3** : confidence, privacy ⟨con la mayor reserva : in strictest confidence⟩ **4** de ~ : spare, in reserve **5 reservas** *nfpl* : reservations, doubts

reservación *nf, pl* **-ciones** : reservation

reservado, -da *adj* **1** : reserved, reticent **2** : confidential

reservar *vt* : to reserve — **reservarse** *vr* **1** : to save oneself **2** : to conceal, to keep to oneself

reservorio *nm* : reservoir, reserve

resfriado *nm* CATARRO : cold

resfriar {85} *vt* : to cool — **resfriarse** *vr* **1** : to cool off **2** : to catch a cold

resfrío *nm* : cold

resguardar *vt* : to safeguard, to protect — **resguardarse** *vr*

resguardo *nm* **1** : safeguard, protection **2** : receipt, voucher **3** : border guard, coast guard

residencia *nf* **1** : residence **2** : boarding house

residencial *adj* : residential

residente *adj & nmf* : resident

residir *vi* **1** VIVIR : to reside, to dwell **2** ~ **en** : to lie in, to consist of

residual *adj* : residual

residuo *nm* **1** : residue **2** : remainder **3 residuos** *nmpl* : waste ⟨residuos nucleares : nuclear waste⟩

resignación *nf, pl* **-ciones** : resignation

resignar *vt* : to resign — **resignarse** *vr* ~ **a** : to resign oneself to

resina *nf* 1 : resin 2 **resina epoxídica** : epoxy

resistencia *nf* 1 : resistance 2 AGUANTE : endurance, strength, stamina 3 : heating element

resistente *adj* 1 : resistant 2 : strong, tough

resistir *vt* 1 TOLERAR : to stand, to bear, to tolerate 2 : to withstand, to resist 3 : to resist (temptation, etc.) — *vi* : to resist ⟨resistió hasta el último minuto : he held out until the last minute⟩ — **resistirse** *vr* ~ **a** : to be resistant to, to be reluctant ⟨se resiste a aceptarlo : she's reluctant to accept it⟩

resma *nf* : ream

resollar {19} *vi* : to breathe heavily, to wheeze

resolución *nf, pl* **-ciones** 1 : resolution, settlement 2 : decision 3 : determination, resolve

resolver {89} *vt* 1 : to resolve, to settle 2 : to decide — **resolverse** *vr* : to make up one's mind

resonancia *nf* 1 : resonance 2 : impact, repercussions *pl*

resonante *adj* 1 : resonant 2 : tremendous, resounding ⟨un éxito resonante : a resounding success⟩

resonar {19} *vi* : to resound, to ring

resoplar *vi* 1 : to puff, to pant 2 : to snort

resoplo *nm* 1 : puffing, panting 2 : snort

resorte *nm* 1 MUELLE : spring 2 : elasticity 3 : influence, means *pl* ⟨tocar resortes : to pull strings⟩

resortera *nf Mex* : slingshot

respaldar *vt* : to back, to support, to endorse — **respaldarse** *vr* : to lean back

respaldo *nm* 1 : back (of an object) 2 : support, backing

respectar *vt* : to concern, to relate to ⟨por lo que a mí respecta : as far as I'm concerned⟩

respectivo, -va *adj* : respective — **respectivamente** *adv*

respecto *nm* 1 ~ **a** : in regard to, concerning 2 **al respecto** : on this matter, in this respect

respetable *adj* : respectable — **respetabilidad** *nf*

respetar *vt* : to respect

respeto *nm* 1 : respect, consideration 2 **respetos** *nmpl* : respects ⟨presentar sus respetos : to pay one's respects⟩

respetuosidad *nf* : respectfulness

respetuoso, -sa *adj* : respectful — **respetuosamente** *adv*

respingado, -da *adj* : snub-nosed

respingo *nm* : start, jump

respiración *nf, pl* **-ciones** 1 : respiration, breathing 2 **respiración boca a boca** : mouth-to-mouth resuscitation

respiradero *nm* : vent, ventilation shaft

respirador *nm* : respirator

respirar *v* : to breathe

respiratorio, -ria *adj* : respiratory

respiro *nm* 1 : breath 2 : respite, break

resplandecer {53} *vi* 1 : to shine 2 : to stand out

resplandeciente *adj* 1 : resplendent, shining 2 : radiant

resplandor *nm* 1 : brightness, brilliance, radiance 2 : flash

responder *vt* : to answer — *vi* 1 : to answer, to reply, to respond 2 ~ **a** : to respond to ⟨responder al tratamiento : to respond to treatment⟩ 3 ~ **de** : to answer for, to vouch for (something) 4 ~ **por** : to vouch for (someone)

respondón, -dona *adj, mpl* **-dones** *fam* : sassy, fresh, impertinent

responsabilidad *nf* : responsibility ⟨tener la responsabilidad de : to be responsible for⟩ ⟨exigen responsabilidades a la compañía : the company is being held responsible/accountable⟩

responsabilizarse {21} *vr* : to accept responsibility ⟨responsabilizarse de : to accept responsibility for⟩

responsable¹ *adj* : responsible — **responsablemente** *adv*

responsable² *nmf* : person responsible ⟨los responsables del proyecto : those in charge of the project⟩ ⟨los responsables del desastre : those responsible for the disaster⟩

respuesta *nf* : answer, response

resquebrajar *vt* : to split, to crack — **resquebrajarse** *vr*

resquemor *nm* : resentment, bitterness

resquicio *nm* 1 : crack 2 : opportunity, chance 3 : trace ⟨sin un resquicio de remordimiento : without a trace of remorse⟩ 4 **resquicio legal** : loophole

resta *nf* SUSTRACCIÓN : subtraction

restablecer {53} *vt* : to reestablish, to restore — **restablecerse** *vr* : to recover

restablecimiento *nm* 1 : reestablishment, restoration 2 : recovery

restallar *vi* : to crack, to crackle, to click

restallido *nm* : crack, crackle

restante *adj* 1 : remaining 2 **lo restante, los restantes** : the rest

restañar *vt* : to stanch

restar *vt* 1 : to deduct, to subtract ⟨restar un punto : to deduct a point⟩ 2 : to minimize, to play down — *vi* : to remain, to be left

restauración *nf, pl* **-ciones** 1 : restoration 2 : catering, food service

restaurante *nm* : restaurant

restaurar *vt* : to restore

restitución *nf, pl* **-ciones** : restitution, return

restituir {41} *vt* : to return, to restore, to reinstate

resto *nm* 1 : rest, remainder 2 **restos** *nmpl* : remains ⟨restos de comida : leftovers⟩ ⟨restos arqueológicos : archeological ruins⟩ 3 **restos mortales** : mortal remains

restorán *nm, pl* **-ranes** : restaurant

restregadura *nf* : scrub, scrubbing

restregar {49} *vt* 1 : to rub 2 : to scrub — **restregarse** *vr*

restricción *nf, pl* **-ciones** : restriction, limitation

restrictivo, -va *adj* : restrictive

restringido, -da *adj* LIMITADO : limited, restricted

restringir {35} vt LIMITAR : to restrict, to limit

restructuración nf, pl **-ciones** : restructuring

restructurar vt : to restructure

resucitación nf, pl **-ciones** : resuscitation ⟨resucitación cardiopulmonar : CPR, cardiopulmonary resuscitation⟩

resucitar vt 1 : to resuscitate, to revive, to resurrect 2 : to revitalize

resuello nm 1 : puffing, heavy breathing, wheezing 2 : break, breather

resueltamente adv : resolutely

resuelto[1] pp → **resolver**

resuelto[2], **-ta** adj : determined, resolved, resolute

resulta nf 1 : consequence, result 2 **a resultas de** or **de resultas de** : as a result of

resultado nm : result, outcome

resultante adj & nf : resultant

resultar vi 1 : to work, to work out ⟨mi idea no resultó : my idea didn't work out⟩ 2 : to be, to turn out to be, to end up being ⟨resultó bien simpático : he turned out to be very nice⟩ ⟨resultó cancelado : it was canceled, it ended up being canceled⟩ ⟨resulta más sencillo/barato : it's simpler/cheaper, it ends up being simpler/cheaper⟩ ⟨me resulta muy interesante : I find it very interesting⟩ ⟨resultó (ser) una falsa alarma : it turned out to be a false alarm⟩ ⟨resulta que ya lo había hecho : it turns out she'd already done it⟩ ⟨resultó con heridas graves : he sustained serious injuries⟩ 3 ~ **en** : to lead to, to result in 4 ~ **de** : to be the result of

resumen nm, pl **-súmenes** 1 : summary, summation 2 **en** ~ : in summary, in short

resumidero nm : drain

resumir v : to summarize, to sum up

resurgimiento nm : resurgence

resurgir {35} vi : to reappear, to revive

resurrección nf, pl **-ciones** : resurrection 2 or **Domingo de Resurrección** : Easter, Easter Sunday

retablo nm : tableau

retador, -dora n : challenger (in sports)

retaguardia nf : rear guard

retahíla nf : string, series ⟨una retahíla de insultos : a volley of insults⟩

retaliación nf, pl **-ciones** : retaliation

retama nf : broom (plant)

retar vt DESAFIAR : to challenge, to defy

retardar vt 1 RETRASAR : to delay, to retard 2 : to postpone

retazo nm 1 : remnant, scrap 2 : fragment, piece ⟨retazos de su obra : bits and pieces from his writings⟩

retén nm, pl **retenes** 1 : squad, patrol ⟨de retén : on call, on duty⟩ 2 CONTROL : checkpoint, roadblock 3 Ven : reform school

retención nf, pl **-ciones** 1 : retention 2 : deduction, withholding

retener {80} vt 1 : to retain, to keep 2 : to withhold 3 : to detain

retentivo, -va adj : retentive

reticencia nf 1 : reluctance, reticence 2 : insinuation

reticente adj 1 : reluctant, reticent 2 : insinuating, misleading

retina nf : retina

retintín nm, pl **-tines** 1 : jingle, jangle 2 **con** ~ : sarcastically

retirada nf 1 : retreat ⟨batirse en retirada : to withdraw, to beat a retreat⟩ 2 : withdrawal (of funds) 3 : retirement 4 : refuge, haven

retirado, -da adj 1 : remote, distant, far off 2 : secluded, quiet

retirar vt 1 : to remove, to take away, to recall 2 : to withdraw, to take out — **retirarse** vr 1 REPLEGARSE : to retreat, to withdraw 2 JUBILARSE : to retire

retiro nm 1 JUBILACIÓN : retirement 2 : withdrawal, retreat 3 : seclusion

reto nm DESAFÍO : challenge, dare

retocar {72} vt : to touch up

retomar vt : to pick up, to resume

retoñar vi : to sprout

retoño nm : sprout, shoot

retoque nm : touch-up, finishing touch

retorcer {14} vt 1 : to twist 2 : to wring — **retorcerse** vr 1 : to get twisted, to get tangled up 2 : to squirm, to writhe, to wiggle about

retorcido, -da adj 1 : twisted 2 : complicated

retorcijón nm, pl **-jones** : cramp, sharp pain

retórica nf : rhetoric

retórico, -ca adj : rhetorical — **retóricamente** adv

retornar v : to return

retorno nm : return

retozar {21} vi : to frolic, to romp

retozo nm : frolicking

retozón, -zona adj, mpl **-zones** : playful

retracción nf, pl **-ciones** : retraction, withdrawal

retractable adj : retractable

retractación nf, pl **-ciones** : retraction (of a statement, etc.)

retractarse vr 1 : to withdraw, to back down 2 ~ **de** : to take back, to retract

retraer {81} vt 1 : to bring back 2 : to dissuade — **retraerse** vr 1 RETIRARSE : to withdraw, to retire 2 REFUGIARSE : to take refuge

retraído, -da adj : withdrawn, retiring, shy

retraimiento nm 1 : shyness, timidity 2 : withdrawal

retransmisión nf, pl **-siones** Spain : broadcast

retransmitir vt Spain : to broadcast

retrasado, -da adj 1 : retarded, mentally slow 2 : behind, in arrears 3 : backward (of a country) 4 : slow (of a watch)

retrasar vt 1 DEMORAR, RETARDAR : to delay, to hold up 2 : to put off, to postpone 3 : to turn back (a clock) — **retrasarse** vr 1 : to be late 2 : to fall behind 3 : to lose time (of a clock)

retraso nm 1 ATRASO : delay, lateness 2 **retraso mental** : mental retardation *sometimes offensive*

retratar *vt* **1** : to portray, to depict **2** : to photograph **3** : to paint a portrait of

retrato *nm* **1** : depiction, portrayal **2** : portrait, photograph

retrete *nm* : restroom, toilet

retribución *nf, pl* **-ciones** **1** : pay, payment **2** : reward

retribuir {41} *vt* **1** : to pay **2** : to reward

retroactivo, -va *adj* : retroactive — **retroactivamente** *adv*

retroalimentación *nf, pl* **-ciones** : feedback

retroceder *vi* **1** : to move back, to turn back **2** : to back off, to back down **3** : to recoil (of a firearm)

retroceso *nm* **1** : backward movement **2** : backing down **3** : setback, relapse **4** : recoil

retrógrado, -da *adj* **1** : reactionary **2** : retrograde

retropropulsión *nf* : jet propulsion

retroproyector *nm* : overhead projector

retrospectiva *nf* : retrospective, hindsight

retrospectivamente *adv* : in retrospect

retrospectivo, -va *adj* **1** : retrospective **2** **mirada retrospectiva** : backward glance

retrovisor *nm* : rearview mirror

retruécano *nm* : pun, play on words

retumbar *vi* **1** : to boom, to thunder **2** : to resound, to reverberate

retumbo *nm* : booming, thundering, roll

retuvo, etc. → **retener**

reubicar {72} *vt* : to relocate — **reubicación** *nf*

reuma *or* **reúma** *nmf* → **reumatismo**

reumático, -ca *adj* : rheumatic

reumatismo *nm* : rheumatism

reunión *nf, pl* **-niones** **1** : meeting **2** : gathering, reunion

reunir {68} *vt* **1** : to unite, to join, to bring together **2** : to have, to possess ⟨reunieron los requisitos necesarios : they fulfilled the necessary requirements⟩ **3** : to gather, to collect, to raise (funds) — **reunirse** *vr* : to meet

reutilizable *adj* : reusable

reutilizar {21} *vt* : to recycle, to reuse

revalidar *vt* **1** : to confirm, to ratify **2** : to defend (a title)

revalorizar {21} *vt* : to reevaluate, to reassess

revaluar {3} *vt* : to reevaluate — **revaluación** *n*

revancha *nf* **1** DESQUITE : revenge **2** : rematch

revelación *nf, pl* **-ciones** : revelation

revelado *nm* : developing (of film)

revelador¹, -dora *adj* : revealing

revelador² *nm* : developer

revelar *vt* **1** : to reveal, to disclose **2** : to develop (film)

revendedor, -dora *n* **1** : scalper **2** DETALLISTA : retailer

revender *vt* **1** : to resell **2** : to scalp

reventa *nf* **1** : resale **2** : scalping

reventar {55} *vi* **1** ESTALLAR, EXPLOTAR : to burst, to blow up **2** ~ **de** : to be bursting with — *vt* **1** : to burst **2** *fam* : to annoy, to rile — **reventarse** *vr* : to burst

reventón *nm, pl* **-tones** **1** : burst, bursting **2** : blowout, flat tire **3** *Mex fam* : bash, party

reverberar *vi* : to reverberate — **reverberación** *nf*

reverdecer {53} *vi* **1** : to grow green again **2** : to revive

reverencia *nf* **1** : reverence **2** : bow, curtsy

reverenciar *vt* : to revere, to venerate

reverendo¹, -da *adj* **1** : reverend **2** *fam* : total, absolute ⟨es un reverendo imbécil : he is a complete idiot⟩

reverendo², -da *n* : reverend

reverente *adj* : reverent

reversa *nf Col, Mex* : reverse (gear)

reversible *adj* : reversible

reversión *nf, pl* **-siones** : reversion

reverso *nm* **1** : back, other side **2 el reverso de la medalla** : the complete opposite

revertir {76} *vi* **1** : to revert, to go back **2** ~ **en** : to result in, to end up as — *vt* : to reverse (a decision, etc.)

revés *nm, pl* **reveses** **1** : back, wrong side **2** : setback, reversal **3** : backhand (in sports) **4 al revés** : the other way around, upside down, inside out **5 al revés de** : contrary to

revestimiento *nm* : covering, facing (of a building)

revestir {54} *vt* **1** : to coat, to cover, to surface **2** : to conceal, to disguise **3** : to take on, to assume ⟨la reunión revistió gravedad : the meeting took on a serious note⟩

revisar *vt* **1** : to examine, to inspect, to check **2** : to check over, to overhaul (machinery) **3** : to revise

revisión *nf, pl* **-siones** **1** : revision **2** : inspection, check ⟨revisión de cuentas : (financial) audit⟩ ⟨revisión médica : checkup⟩

revisor, -sora *n* **1** : inspector **2** : conductor (on a train)

revista *nf* **1** : magazine, journal **2** : revue **3 pasar revista** : to review, to inspect

revistar *vt* : to review, to inspect

revistero *nm* : magazine rack

revitalizar {21} *vt* : to revitalize — **revitalización** *nf*

revivir *vi* : to revive, to come alive again — *vt* : to relive

revocación *nf, pl* **-ciones** **1** : revocation, repeal **2** : reversal

revocar {72} *vt* **1** : to revoke, to repeal **2** : to plaster (a wall)

revolcar {82} *vt* : to knock over, to knock down — **revolcarse** *vr* : to roll around, to wallow

revolcón *nm, pl* **-cones** *fam* : tumble, fall

revolotear *vi* : to flutter around, to flit

revoloteo *nm* : fluttering, flitting

revoltijo *or* **revoltillo** *nm* **1** FÁRRAGO : mess, jumble **2** *Mex* : traditional seafood dish

revoltoso, -sa *adj* : unruly, rebellious

revolución *nf, pl* **-ciones** : revolution

revolucionar *vt* : to revolutionize

revolucionario, -ria *adj & n* : revolutionary

revolver {89} *vt* **1** : to move about, to mix, to shake, to stir **2** : to upset (one's stomach) **3** : to mess up, to rummage through ⟨revolver la casa : to turn the house upside down⟩ — **revolverse** *vr* **1** : to toss and turn **2** VOLVERSE : to turn around

revólver *nm* : revolver

revoque *nm* : plaster

revuelo *nm* **1** : fluttering **2** : commotion, stir

revuelta *nf* : uprising, revolt

revuelto[1] *pp* → **revolver**

revuelto[2], **-ta** *adj* **1** : choppy, rough ⟨mar revuelto : rough sea⟩ **2** : untidy **3** **huevos revueltos** : scrambled eggs

rey *nm* : king

reyerta *nf* : brawl, fight

rezagado, -da *n* : straggler, latecomer

rezagar {52} *vt* **1** : to leave behind **2** : to postpone — **rezagarse** *vr* : to fall behind, to lag

rezar {21} *vi* **1** : to pray **2** : to say ⟨como reza el refrán : as the saying goes⟩ **3** ~ **con** : to concern, to have to do with — *vt* **1** : to say, to recite ⟨rezar un Ave María : to say a Hail Mary⟩

rezo *nm* : prayer, praying

rezongar {52} *vi* : to gripe, to grumble

rezumar *v* : to ooze, to leak

ría, etc. → **reír**

riachuelo *nm* ARROYO : brook, stream

riada *nf* : flood

ribera *nf* : bank, shore

ribete *nm* **1** : border, trim **2** : frill, adornment **3** **ribetes** *nmpl* : hint, touch ⟨tiene sus ribetes de genio : there's a touch of genius in him⟩

ribetear *vt* : to border, to edge, to trim

ricachón[1], **-chona** *adj, mpl* **-chones** *fam* : rich, wealthy

ricachón[2], **-chona** *n, mpl* **-chones** *fam* : rich person

ricamente *adv* : richly, splendidly

rice, etc. → **rizar**

rickshaw ['rikʃo] *nm* : rickshaw

rico[1], **-ca** *adj* **1** : rich, wealthy **2** : fertile **3** : luxurious, valuable **4** : delicious **5** : adorable, lovely **6** : great, wonderful

rico[2], **-ca** *n* : rich person

ridiculez *nf, pl* **-leces** : absurdity

ridiculizar {21} *vt* : to ridicule

ridículo[1], **-la** *adj* ABSURDO, DISPARATADO : ridiculous, ludicrous — **ridículamente** *adv*

ridículo[2], **-la** *n* **1 hacer el ridículo** : to make a fool of oneself **2 poner en ridículo** : to ridicule

ríe, etc. → **reír**

riega, riegue etc. → **regar**

riego *nm* : irrigation

riel *nm* : rail, track

rienda *nf* **1** : rein **2 dar rienda suelta a** : to give free rein to **3 llevar las riendas** : to be in charge **4 tomar las riendas** : to take control

riesgo *nm* : risk

riesgoso, -sa *adj* : risky

rifa *nf* : raffle

rifar *vt* : to raffle — *vi* : to quarrel, to fight

rifle *nm* : rifle

rige, rija etc. → **regir**

rigidez *nf, pl* **-deces** **1** : rigidity, stiffness ⟨rigidez cadavérica : rigor mortis⟩ **2** : inflexibility

rígido, -da *adj* **1** : rigid, stiff **2** : strict — **rígidamente** *adv*

rigor *nm* **1** : rigor, harshness **2** : precision, meticulousness **3 de** ~ : usual ⟨la respuesta de rigor : the standard reply⟩ **4 de** ~ : essential, obligatory **5 en** ~ : strictly speaking, in reality

riguroso, -sa *adj* : rigorous — **rigurosamente** *adv*

rima *nf* **1** : rhyme **2 rimas** *nfpl* : verse, poetry

rimar *vi* : to rhyme

rimbombante *adj* **1** : grandiose, showy **2** : bombastic, pompous

rímel *or* **rimel** *or* **rimmel** *nm* : mascara

rin *nm Col, Mex* : wheel, rim (of a tire)

rincón *nm, pl* **rincones** : corner, nook

rinde, etc. → **rendir**

ring ['rin] *nm, pl* **rings** : (boxing) ring

rinoceronte *nm* : rhinoceros

riña *nf* **1** : fight, brawl **2** : dispute, quarrel

riñe, etc. → **reñir**

riñón *nm, pl* **riñones** : kidney

río[1] → **reír**

río[2] *nm* **1** : river **2** : torrent, stream ⟨un río de lágrimas : a flood of tears⟩

ripio *nm* **1** : debris, rubble **2** : gravel

riqueza *nf* **1** : wealth, riches *pl* **2** : richness **3 riquezas naturales** : natural resources

risa *nf* **1** : laughter, laugh **2 dar risa** : to make laugh ⟨me dio mucha risa : I found it very funny⟩ **3** *fam* **morirse de la risa** : to die laughing, to crack up

risco *nm* : crag, cliff

risible *adj* IRRISORIO : ludicrous, laughable

risita *nf* : giggle, titter, snicker

risotada *nf* : guffaw

ristra *nf* : string, series *pl*

risueño, -ña *adj* **1** : cheerful, pleasant **2** : promising

rítmico, -ca *adj* : rhythmical, rhythmic — **rítmicamente** *adv*

ritmo *nm* **1** : rhythm **2** : pace, tempo ⟨trabajó a ritmo lento : she worked at a slow pace⟩

rito *nm* : rite, ritual

ritual *adj & nm* : ritual — **ritualmente** *adv*

rival *adj & nmf* COMPETIDOR : rival

rivalidad *nf* : rivalry, competition

rivalizar {21} *vi* ~ **con** : to rival, to compete with

rizado, -da *adj* **1** : curly **2** : ridged **3** : rippled, undulating

rizar {21} *vt* **1** : to curl **2** : to ripple, to ruffle (a surface) **3** : to crumple, to fold — **rizarse** *vr* **1** : to frizz **2** : to ripple

rizo *nm* **1** : curl **2** : loop (in aviation)

robalo *or* **róbalo** *nm* : sea bass

robar *vt* **1** : to steal **2** : to rob, to burglarize **3** SECUESTRAR : to abduct, to kidnap **4** : to captivate — *vi* ~ **en** : to break into

roble *nm* : oak

robo *nm* : robbery, theft ⟨robo de identidad : identity theft⟩
robot *nm*, *pl* **robots** : robot — **robótico,
-ca** *adj*
robótica *nf* : robotics
robustecer {53} *vt* : to grow stronger, to
strengthen
robustez *nf* : sturdiness, robustness
robusto, -ta *adj* : robust, sturdy
roca *nf* : rock, boulder
roce¹, etc. → rozar
roce² *nm* **1** : rubbing, chafing **2** : brush,
graze, touch **3** : close contact, familiarity **4** : friction, disagreement
rociador *nm* : sprinkler
rociar {85} *vt* : to spray, to sprinkle
rocío *nm* **1** : dew **2** : shower, light rain
rock *or* **rock and roll** *nm* : rock, rock and
roll
rocola *nf* : jukebox
rocoso, -sa *adj* : rocky
rodada *nf* : track (of a tire), rut
rodado, -da *adj* **1** : wheeled **2** : dappled
(of a horse)
rodadura *nf* : rolling, taxiing
rodaja *nf* : round, slice
rodaje *nm* **1** : filming, shooting **2** : breaking in (of a vehicle)
rodamiento *nm* **1** : bearing ⟨rodamiento
de bolas : ball bearings⟩ **2** : rolling
rodante *adj* : rolling
rodar {19} *vi* **1** : to roll, to roll down, to
roll along ⟨rodé por la escalera : I tum-
bled down the stairs⟩ ⟨todo rodaba bien
: everything was going along well⟩ **2**
GIRAR : to turn, to go around **3** : to
move about, to travel ⟨andábamos ro-
dando por todas partes : we drifted along
from place to place⟩ — *vt* **1** : to film, to
shoot **2** : to break in (a new vehicle)
rodear *vt* **1** : to surround ⟨rodeado de
montañas : surrounded by mountains⟩ **2**
: to round up (cattle) — *vi* **1** : to go
around **2** : to beat around the bush —
rodearse *vr* ~ **de** : to surround oneself
with
rodeo *nm* **1** : rodeo, roundup **2** DESVÍO
: detour **3** : evasion ⟨andar con rodeos
: to beat around the bush⟩ ⟨sin rodeos
: without reservations⟩
rodilla *nf* : knee
rodillera *nf* : knee pad
rodillo *nm* **1** : roller **2** : rolling pin
rododendro *nm* : rhododendron
roedor¹, -dora *adj* : gnawing
roedor² *nm* : rodent
roer {69} *vt* **1** : to gnaw **2** : to eat away at,
to torment
rogar {16} *vt* : to beg, to request — *vi*
1 : to beg, to plead **2** : to pray
roiga, etc. → roer
rojez *nf* : redness
rojizo, -za *adj* : reddish
rojo¹, -ja *adj* **1** : red **2 ponerse rojo** : to
blush
rojo² *nm* : red
rol *nm* **1** : role **2** : list, roll
rollizo, -za *adj* : chubby, plump
rollo *nm* **1** : roll, coil ⟨un rollo de cinta : a
roll of tape⟩ ⟨en rollo : rolled up⟩ **2** *fam*

: roll of fat **3** *fam* : boring speech, lecture
ROM *nf*, *pl* **ROM** *or* **ROMs** : ROM
romance *nm* **1** : Romance language **2**
: ballad **3** : romance **4 en buen romance** : simply stated, simply put
romano, -na *adj & n* : Roman
romanticismo *nm* : romanticism
romántico, -ca *adj* : romantic —
romántico, -ca *n* — **románticamente**
adv
rombo *nm* : rhombus
romería *nf* **1** : pilgrimage, procession **2**
: crowd, gathering
romero¹, -ra *n* PEREGRINO : pilgrim
romero² *nm* : rosemary
romo, -ma *adj* : blunt, dull
rompecabezas *nms & pl* : puzzle, riddle
rompecorazones *nmfs & pl* : heartbreaker
rompehielos *nms & pl* : icebreaker (ship)
rompehuelgas *nmfs & pl* ESQUIROL
: strikebreaker, scab
rompenueces *nms & pl* : nutcracker
rompeolas *ns & pl* : breakwater, jetty
romper {70} *vt* **1** : to break (a glass, a
bone, etc.) **2** : to rip, to tear (cloth, paper) **3** : to break off (relations), to break
(a contract) **4** : to break through/down
(a door, etc.) **5** GASTAR : to wear out **6**
: to break ⟨romper el hielo/silencio : to
break the ice/silence⟩ — *vi* **1** : to break
⟨al romper del día : at the break of day⟩
2 ~ a : to begin to, to burst out with
⟨romper a llorar : to burst into tears⟩ **3**
~ **con** : to break with (tradition, etc.),
to break away from **4** ~ **con alguien**
: to break up with someone — **romperse**
vr
rompope *nm* CA, Mex : drink similar to
eggnog
ron *nm* : rum
roncar {72} *vi* **1** : to snore **2** : to roar
roncha *nf* : rash
ronco, -ca *adj* **1** : hoarse **2** : husky (of the
voice) — **roncamente** *adv*
ronda *nf* **1** : beat, patrol **2** : round (of
drinks, of negotiations, of a game)
rondar *vt* **1** : to patrol **2** : to hang around
⟨siempre está rondando la calle : he's always hanging around the street⟩ **3** : to
be approximately ⟨debe rondar los
cincuenta : he must be about 50⟩ — *vi* **1**
: to be on patrol **2** : to prowl around, to
roam about
ronque, etc. → roncar
ronquera *nf* : hoarseness
ronquido *nm* **1** : snore **2** : roar
ronronear *vi* : to purr
ronroneo *nm* : purr, purring
ronzal *nm* : halter (for an animal)
ronzar {21} *v* : to munch, to crunch
roña *nf* **1** : mange **2** : dirt, filth **3** *fam*
: stinginess
roñoso, -sa *adj* **1** : mangy **2** : dirty **3** *fam*
: stingy
ropa *nf* **1** : clothes *pl*, clothing ⟨ropa sucia : dirty clothes, (dirty) laundry⟩ ⟨ropa
de abrigo : warm clothes⟩ ⟨cambiarse de

ropa : to change one's clothes, to get changed⟩ **2 ropa interior** : underwear

ropaje *nm* : apparel, garments *pl*, regalia

ropero *nm* ARMARIO, CLÓSET : wardrobe, closet

rosa[1] *adj* : rose-colored, pink

rosa[2] *nm* : rose, pink (color)

rosa[3] *nf* : rose (flower)

rosáceo, -cea *adj* : pinkish

rosado[1], **-da** *adj* **1** : pink **2 vino rosado** : rosé

rosado[2] *nm* : pink (color)

rosal *nm* : rosebush

rosario *nm* **1** : rosary **2** : series ⟨un rosario de islas : a string of islands⟩

rosbif *nf* : roast beef

rosca *nf* **1** : thread (of a screw) ⟨una tapa a rosca : a screw top⟩ **2** : ring, coil

roscón *nm*, *pl* **roscones** : ring-shaped cake

roseta *nf* : rosette

rosetón *nm*, *pl* **-tones** : rose window

rosquilla *nf* : ring-shaped pastry, doughnut

rostro *nm* : face, countenance

rotación *nf*, *pl* **-ciones** : rotation

rotar *vt* : to rotate, to turn — *vi* : to turn, to spin

rotativo[1], **-va** *adj* : rotary

rotativo[2] *nm* : newspaper

rotatorio, -ria *adj* → **rotativo**[1]

roto[1] *pp* → **romper**

roto[2], **-ta** *adj* **1** : broken **2** : ripped, torn

rotonda *nf* **1** : traffic circle, rotary **2** : rotunda

rotor *nm* : rotor

rotoso, -sa *adj Arg, Uru, Peru* : ragged, scruffy

rótula *nf* : kneecap

rotulador *nm Spain* **1** : felt-tip pen **2** : highlighter

rotular *vt* **1** : to head, to entitle **2** : to label

rótulo *nm* **1** : heading, title **2** : label, sign

rotundo, -da *adj* **1** REDONDO : round **2** : categorical, absolute ⟨un éxito rotundo : a resounding success⟩ — **rotundamente** *adv*

rotura *nf* : break, tear, fracture

rough [ˈrʌf, ˈraf] *nm* **el rough** : the rough (in golf)

router *nm*, *pl* **routers** : router (in computing)

roya[1] *nf* : plant rust

roya[2], **etc.** → **roer**

rozado, -da *adj* GASTADO : worn

rozadura *nf* **1** : scratch, abrasion **2** : rubbed spot, sore

rozamiento *nf* : rubbing, friction

rozar {21} *vt* **1** : to chafe, to rub against **2** : to border on, to touch on **3** : to graze, to touch lightly — **rozarse** *vr* ~ **con** *fam* : to rub shoulders with

ruandés, -desa *adj & n* : Rwandan

rubéola *nf* : German measles, rubella

rubí *nm*, *pl* **rubíes** : ruby

rubicundo, -da *adj* : ruddy ⟨una cara rubicunda : a ruddy face⟩

rubio, -bia *adj & n* : blond

rublo *nm* : ruble

rubor *nm* **1** : flush, blush **2** : blush, rouge

ruborizarse {21} *vr* : to blush

rúbrica *nf* : title, heading

rubricar {72} *vt* **1** : sign with a flourish ⟨firmado y rubricado : signed and sealed⟩ **2** : to endorse, to sanction

rubro *nm* **1** : heading, title **2** : line, area (in business)

rucio, rucia *adj* : gray

rudeza *nf* ASPEREZA : roughness, coarseness

rudimentario, -ria *adj* : rudimentary — **rudimentariamente** *adv*

rudimento *nm* : rudiment, basics *pl*

rudo, -da *adj* **1** : rough, harsh **2** : coarse, unpolished — **rudamente** *adv*

rueda[1], **etc.** → **rodar**

rueda[2] *nf* **1** : wheel **2** RODAJA : round slice **3** : circle, ring **4 rueda de andar** : treadmill **5 rueda de prensa** : press conference **6 ir sobre ruedas** : to go smoothly

ruedita *nf* : caster (on furniture)

ruedo *nm* **1** : bullring, arena **2** : rotation, turn **3** : hem

ruega, ruegue etc. → **rogar**

ruego *nm* : request, appeal, plea

rufián *nf*, *pl* **rufianes** : villain, scoundrel, ruffian

rugby *nm* : rugby

rugido *nm* : roar

rugir {35} *vi* : to roar

rugoso, -sa *adj* **1** : rough, bumpy **2** : wrinkled

ruibarbo *nm* : rhubarb

ruido *nm* : noise, sound

ruidoso, -sa *adj* : loud, noisy — **ruidosamente** *adv*

ruin *adj* **1** : base, despicable **2** : mean, stingy

ruina *nf* **1** : ruin, destruction ⟨llevar a alguien a la ruina : to ruin someone, to bring someone to ruin⟩ ⟨estar en la ruina : to be ruined⟩ **2** : ruin, downfall ⟨la avaricia será su ruina : greed will be his ruin⟩ **3** : collapse (of a building, etc.) ⟨amenazar ruina : to threaten to collapse⟩ **4 ruinas** *nfpl* : ruins, remains ⟨ruinas romanas : Roman ruins⟩ ⟨estar/quedar en ruinas : to be/lie in ruins⟩

ruinoso, -sa *adj* **1** : run-down, dilapidated **2** : ruinous, disastrous

ruiseñor *nm* : nightingale

ruja, etc. → **rugir**

rulero *nm Arg, Peru, Uru* : curler, roller

ruleta *nf* : roulette

ruletero, -ra *n Mex fam* : taxi driver

rulo *nm* : curler, roller

ruma *nf Chile, Peru, Ven* : pile, heap

rumano, -na *n* : Romanian, Rumanian

rumba *nf* : rumba

rumbo *nm* **1** : direction, course ⟨con rumbo a : bound for, heading for⟩ ⟨perder el rumbo : to go off course, to lose one's bearings⟩ ⟨sin rumbo : aimless, aimlessly⟩ **2** : ostentation, pomp **3** : lavishness, generosity

rumiante *adj & nm* : ruminant

rumiar *vt* **1** : to ponder, to mull over — *vi* **1** : to chew the cud **2** : to ruminate, to ponder

rummy *nm* : rummy (card game)
rumor *nm* **1** : rumor **2** : murmur
rumorearse *or* **rumorarse** *vr* : to be rumored ⟨se rumorea que se va : rumor has it that she's leaving⟩ — **rumoreado, -da** *adj*
rumoroso, -sa *adj* : murmuring, babbling ⟨un arroyo rumoroso : a babbling brook⟩
rupestre *adj* : cave ⟨pinturas rupestres : cave paintings⟩
rupia *nf* : rupee

ruptura *nf* **1** : break **2** : breaking, breach (of a contract) **3** : breaking off, breakup
rural *adj* : rural
ruso¹, -sa *adj & n* : Russian
ruso² *nm* : Russian (language)
rústico¹, -ca *adj* : rural, rustic
rústico², -ca *n* : rustic, country dweller
ruta *nf* : route
rutina *nf* : routine, habit
rutinario, -ria *adj* : routine, ordinary ⟨visita rutinaria : routine visit⟩ — **rutinariamente** *adv*

S

s *nf* : twenty-second letter of the Spanish alphabet
sábado *nm* **1** : Saturday ⟨el sábado : (on) Saturday⟩ ⟨los sábados : (on) Saturdays⟩ ⟨cada (dos) sábados : every (other) Saturday⟩ ⟨el sábado pasado : last Saturday⟩ ⟨el próximo sábado : next Saturday⟩ **2** : Sabbath
sábalo *nm* : shad
sábana *nf* : savanna
sábana *nf* : sheet, bedsheet
sabandija *nf* BICHO : bug, small reptile, pesky creature
sabático, -ca *adj* : sabbatical
sabedor, -dora *adj* : aware, informed
sabelotodo *nmf fam* : know-it-all
saber¹ {71} *vt* **1** : to know ⟨no lo sé : I don't know⟩ ⟨no sé qué decirte : I don't know what to tell you⟩ ⟨no sabes lo que te espera : you don't know what you're in for⟩ ⟨saber la respuesta : to know the answer⟩ ⟨sabe mucho de política : he knows a lot about politics⟩ ⟨¿sabes dónde está? : do you know where it is?⟩ ⟨creo que no, pero ¿qué sé yo? : I don't think so, but what do I know?⟩ ⟨quién sabe qué va a pasar : who knows what will happen⟩ **2** : to know how to, to be able to ⟨sabe tocar el violín : she can play the violin⟩ **3** : to learn, to find out ⟨lo supe ayer : I found out yesterday⟩ ⟨no sé nada de ellos : I haven't heard from them⟩ **4** ~ **a** : to wit, namely **5 que yo sepa** : as far as I know **6 qué sé yo** ⟨diamantes, perlas, y qué sé yo : diamonds, pearls, and whatnot⟩ ⟨y qué sé yo dónde : and who knows where (else)⟩ — *vi* **1** : to know, to suppose ⟨¿quién sabe? : who knows?⟩ ⟨nunca se sabe : you never know, one never knows⟩ **2** : to be informed ⟨supimos del desastre : we heard about the disaster⟩ **3** : to taste ⟨esto no sabe bien : this doesn't taste right⟩ **4** ~ **a** : to taste like ⟨sabe a naranja : it tastes like orange⟩ — **saberse** *vr* : to know ⟨ese chiste no me lo sé : I don't know that joke⟩
saber² *nm* : knowledge, learning
sabiamente *adv* : wisely
sabido, -da *adj* : well-known

sabiduría *nf* **1** : wisdom **2** : learning, knowledge
sabiendas *adv* **1 a** ~ : knowingly **2 a sabiendas de que** : knowing full well that
sabihondo, -da *n fam* : know-it-all
sabio¹, -bia *adj* **1** PRUDENTE : wise, sensible **2** DOCTO : learned
sabio², -bia *n* **1** : wise person **2** : learned person
sable *nm* : saber, cutlass
sablear *vt* **1** : to bum, to scrounge, to sponge **2** : to scrounge off, to sponge off
sabor *nm* **1** : flavor, taste **2 sin** ~ : flavorless
saborear *vt* **1** : to taste, to savor **2** : to enjoy, to relish
saborizante *nm* : flavor, flavoring
sabotaje *nm* : sabotage
saboteador, -dora *n* : saboteur
sabotear *vt* : to sabotage
sabrá, etc. → saber
sabroso, -sa *adj* **1** RICO : delicious, tasty **2** AGRADABLE : pleasant, nice, lovely
sabueso *nm* **1** : bloodhound **2** *fam* : detective, sleuth
sacacorchos *nms & pl* : corkscrew
sacapuntas *nms & pl* : pencil sharpener
sacar {72} *vt* **1** : to pull out, to take out ⟨saca el pollo del congelador : take the chicken out of the freezer⟩ ⟨me sacaron de la cama : they dragged me out of bed⟩ ⟨sacó un as : he drew an ace⟩ ⟨sacar la basura : to take out the garbage⟩ ⟨¡sácalo de la casa! : get it out of the house!⟩ **2** : to get, to obtain ⟨saqué un 100 en el examen : I got 100 on the exam⟩ ⟨sacó cuatro puntos de ventaja : she got a four point lead⟩ **3** : to get out, to extract ⟨le saqué la información : I got the information from him⟩ ⟨sacar sangre : to draw blood⟩ ⟨me sacó de un apuro : she got me out of a jam⟩ ⟨sacar provecho de : to benefit from⟩ **4** : to take (someone) out ⟨lo saqué a comer : I took him out to eat⟩ ⟨la sacó a bailar : he asked her to dance⟩ **5** : to stick out ⟨sacar la lengua : to stick out one's tongue⟩ **6** : to bring out, to introduce ⟨sacar un libro : to publish a book⟩ ⟨sacaron una moda nueva : they introduced

a new style⟩ ⟨sacar algo a la venta : to release something for sale⟩ ⟨sacar a relucir un tema : to bring up a topic⟩ **7** : to take (a photo, a shot) **8** : to make (copies) **9** RETIRAR : to withdraw (money) **10** : to draw, to reach (a conclusion) **11** CALCULAR : to work out, to tally up **12** **sacar adelante** AVANZAR : to get started, to move forward **13** **sacar adelante** MANTENER : to support, to keep afloat **14** **sacar de encima** : to get rid of — *vi* **1** : to kick off (in soccer or football) **2** : to serve (in sports)

sacarina *nf* : saccharin

sacarosa *nf* : sucrose

sacerdocio *nm* : priesthood

sacerdotal *adj* : priestly

sacerdote, -tisa *n* : priest *m*, priestess *f*

saciar *vt* **1** HARTAR : to sate, to satiate **2** SATISFACER : to satisfy

saciedad *nf* **1** : fullness ⟨comer hasta la saciedad : to eat one's fill⟩ **2** hacer algo **hasta la saciedad** : to do something ad nauseam

saco *nm* **1** : bag, sack **2** : sac **3** : jacket, sport coat

sacramento *nm* : sacrament — **sacramental** *adj*

sacrificar {72} *vt* **1** : to sacrifice **2** : to euthanize, to put down — **sacrificarse** *vr* : to sacrifice oneself, to make sacrifices

sacrificio *nm* : sacrifice

sacrilegio *nm* : sacrilege

sacrílego, -ga *adj* : sacrilegious

sacristán *nm, pl* **-tanes** : sexton

sacristía *nf* : vestry

sacro, -cra *adj* SAGRADO : sacred ⟨arte sacro : sacred art⟩

sacrosanto, -ta *adj* : sacrosanct

sacudida *nf* **1** : shaking **2** : jerk, jolt, shock **3** : shake-up, upheaval

sacudir *vt* **1** : to shake, to beat **2** : to jerk, to jolt **3** : to dust off **4** CONMOVER : to shake up, to shock — **sacudirse** *vr* : to shake off

sacudón *nm, pl* **-dones** : intense jolt or shake-up

sádico¹, -ca *adj* : sadistic

sádico², -ca *n* : sadist

sadismo *nm* : sadism

safari *nm* : safari

saga *nf* : saga

sagacidad *nf* : shrewdness

sagaz *adj, pl* **sagaces** PERSPICAZ : shrewd, discerning, sagacious

sagazmente *adv* : shrewdly

Sagitario¹ *nm* : Sagittarius (sign or constellation)

Sagitario² *nmf* : Sagittarius (person)

sagrado, -da *adj* : sacred, holy

sainete *nm* : comedy sketch, one-act farce ⟨este proceso es un sainete : these proceedings are a farce⟩

sajar *vt* : to lance, to cut open

sal¹ → **salir**

sal² *nf* **1** : salt **2** CA, Mex : misfortune, bad luck

sala *nf* **1** : living room **2** : room, hall ⟨sala de conferencias : lecture hall⟩ ⟨sala

de urgencias : emergency room⟩ ⟨sala de baile : ballroom⟩

salado, -da *adj* **1** : salty **2** **agua salada** : salt water

salamandra *nf* : salamander

salami *nm* : salami

salar *vt* **1** : to salt **2** : to spoil, to ruin **3** CoRi, Mex : to jinx, to bring bad luck

salarial *adj* : salary, salary-related

salario *nm* **1** : salary **2** **salario mínimo** : minimum wage

salaz *adj, pl* **salaces** : salacious, lecherous

salchicha *nf* **1** : sausage **2** : frankfurter, wiener

salchichón *nf, pl* **-chones** : a type of deli meat

salchichonería *nf Mex* **1** : delicatessen **2** : cold cuts *pl*

saldar *vt* : to settle, to pay off ⟨saldar una cuenta : to settle an account⟩

saldo *nm* **1** : settlement, payment **2** : balance ⟨saldo de cuenta : account balance⟩ **3** : remainder, leftover merchandise

saldrá, etc. → **salir**

salero *nm* **1** : salt shaker **2** : wit, charm

salga, etc. → **salir**

salida *nf* **1** : exit ⟨salida de emergencia/incendios : emergency/fire exit⟩ ⟨una calle sin salida : a dead-end street⟩ **2** : leaving, departure **3** SOLUCIÓN : way out, solution **4** : start (of a race) **5** OCURRENCIA : wisecrack, joke **6** **salida del sol** : sunrise

salido *adj* : protuding

saliente¹ *adj* **1** : departing, outgoing **2** : projecting **3** DESTACADO : salient, prominent

saliente² *nm* **1** : projection, protrusion **2** **ventana en saliente** : bay window

salinidad *nf* : salinity, saltiness

salino, -na *adj* : saline ⟨solución salina : saline solution⟩

salir {73} *vi* **1** : to go out, to come out, to get out ⟨salió del edificio : she came/went out of the building⟩ ⟨salí a la calle : I went outside⟩ ⟨salimos todas las noches : we go out every night⟩ ⟨salimos a desayunar : we went out for breakfast⟩ ⟨me ayudó a salir del apuro : he helped me out of a jam⟩ ⟨salieron ilesos : they escaped unharmed⟩ ⟨por la tarde salió el sol : in the afternoon the sun came out⟩ **2** PARTIR : to leave, to depart ⟨salí de casa a las seis : I left home at six (o'clock)⟩ ⟨salió del hospital : she's out of the hospital⟩ ⟨salieron para Bogotá : they left for Bogotá⟩ ⟨salió a buscarla : he went to go pick her up⟩ ⟨¿a qué hora sale el vuelo? : what time does the flight leave?⟩ ⟨salió corriendo : she took off running⟩ **3** APARECER : to appear ⟨salió en todos los diarios : it came out in all the papers⟩ ⟨le están saliendo los dientes : she's teething⟩ ⟨me salen canas : I'm going gray, I'm getting gray hairs⟩ ⟨le salen granos : she breaks out, she gets pimples⟩ ⟨le salió un sarpullido : he broke out in a rash⟩ **4** : to come out, to become available ⟨su libro acaba de salir : her book just came out⟩ ⟨salir a la venta : to be released (for sale)⟩ **5** : to rise (of the sun) **6** : to come up (of a topic), to come up (of news) ⟨salir a relucir : to come out, to come to light⟩ **7** : to project, to stick out **8** : to cost, to come to ⟨sale muy caro : it's too expensive⟩ **9** RESULTAR : to turn out, to prove ⟨salir bien/mal : to turn out well/badly⟩ **10** : to come up, to occur ⟨salga lo que salga : whatever happens⟩ ⟨salió una oportunidad : an opportunity came up⟩ **11** ~ **a** : to take after, to look like, to resemble **12 salir adelante** : to overcome difficulties, to advance ⟨salir adelante en la vida : to get ahead in life⟩ ⟨es difícil, pero saldremos adelante : it's difficult, but we'll get through it⟩ ⟨sin ello el país/proyecto no saldrá adelante : without it the country/project won't move forward⟩ **13** ~ **con** : to go out with, to date — **salirse** vr **1** : to escape, to get out, to leak out **2** : to come loose, to come off **3 salirse con la suya** : to get one's own way

saliva nf : saliva

salival adj : salivary ⟨glándula salival : salivary gland⟩

salivar vi : to salivate

salmo nm : psalm

salmodia nf : chant

salmodiar v : to chant

salmón[1] adj : salmon-colored

salmón[2] nm, pl **salmones** : salmon

salmuera nf : brine

salobre adj : brackish, briny

salón nm, pl **salones 1** : hall, large room ⟨salón de clase : classroom⟩ ⟨salón de baile : ballroom⟩ **2** : salon ⟨salón de belleza : beauty salon⟩ **3** : parlor, sitting room

salpicadera nf Mex : fender

salpicadero nm Spain : dashboard

salpicadura nf : spatter, splash

salpicar {72} vt **1** : to spatter, to splash **2** : to sprinkle, to scatter about

salpimentar {55} vt **1** : to season (with salt and pepper) **2** : to spice up

salpullido → sarpullido

salsa nf **1** : sauce ⟨salsa picante : hot sauce⟩ ⟨salsa inglesa : Worcestershire sauce⟩ ⟨salsa tártara : tartar sauce⟩ **2** : gravy **3** : salsa (music) **4 salsa mexicana** : salsa (sauce)

salsero, -ra n : salsa musician

saltador, -dora n : jumper

saltamontes nms & pl : grasshopper

saltar vi **1** BRINCAR : to jump, to leap ⟨saltó de la silla : he jumped out of his chair⟩ ⟨el gato saltó sobre el ratón : the cat pounced on the mouse⟩ ⟨saltó a la fama : she rose to fame⟩ **2** REBOTAR : to bounce **3** : to come off, to pop out ⟨el corcho saltó de la botella : the cork popped out of the bottle⟩ **4** : to shatter, to break **5** : to explode, to blow up **6** : to jump, to increase ⟨saltó de 500.000 a un millón : it jumped from 500,000 to a million⟩ **7 saltar a la vista** : to be glaringly

obvious **8 saltar de alegría** : to jump for joy — vt **1** : to jump, to jump over ⟨saltó la reja : he jumped over the railing⟩ **2** : to skip, to miss — **saltarse** vr **1** OMITIR : to skip, to omit ⟨me salté ese capítulo : I skipped that chapter⟩ **2** : to come off, to fall off

saltarín, -rina adj, mpl **-rines** : leaping, hopping ⟨frijol saltarín : jumping bean⟩

salteado, -da adj **1** : sautéed **2** : jumbled up ⟨los episodios se transmitieron salteados : the episodes were broadcast in random order⟩

salteador nm : highwayman

saltear vt **1** SOFREÍR : to sauté **2** : to skip around, to skip over

saltimbanqui nmf : acrobat

salto nm **1** BRINCO : jump, leap, skip **2** : jump, dive (in sports) ⟨salto de longitud, salto (en) largo : long jump⟩ **3** : gap, omission **4 dar saltos** : to jump up and down **5** or **salto de agua** CATARATA : waterfall

saltón, -tona adj, mpl **saltones** : bulging, protruding

salubre adj : healthful, salubrious

salubridad nf : healthiness, health

salud nf **1** : health ⟨buena salud : good health⟩ **2 ¡salud!** : bless you! (when someone sneezes) **3 ¡salud!** : cheers!, to your health!

saludable adj **1** SALUBRE : healthful **2** SANO : healthy, well

saludar vt **1** : to greet, to say hello to **2** : to salute — **saludarse** vr

saludo nm **1** : greeting, regards pl **2** : salute

salutación nf, pl **-ciones** : salutation

salva nf **1** : salvo, volley **2 salva de aplausos** : round of applause

salvación nf, pl **-ciones 1** : salvation **2** RESCATE : rescue

salvado nm : bran

salvador, -dora n **1** : savior, rescuer **2 el Salvador** : the Savior

salvadoreño, -ña adj & n : Salvadoran, El Salvadoran

salvaguardar vt : to safeguard

salvaguardia or **salvaguarda** nf : safeguard, defense

salvajada nf ATROCIDAD : atrocity, act of savagery

salvaje[1] adj **1** : wild ⟨animales salvajes : wild animals⟩ **2** : savage, cruel **3** : primitive, uncivilized

salvaje[2] nmf : savage

salvajismo nm : savagery

salvamanteles nms & pl : trivet

salvamento nm **1** : rescuing, lifesaving **2** : salvation **3** : refuge

salvapantallas nms & pl : screen saver

salvar vt **1** : to save, to rescue **2** : to cover (a distance) **3** : to get around (an obstacle), to overcome (a difficulty) **4** : to cross, to jump across **5 salvando** : except for, excluding — **salvarse** vr **1** : to survive, to escape **2** : to save one's soul

salvavidas[1] nms & pl **1** : life preserver **2 bote salvavidas** : lifeboat

salvavidas[2] nmf : lifeguard

salvedad *nf* **1** EXCEPCIÓN : exception **2** : proviso, stipulation

salvia *nf* : sage (plant)

salvo[1], **-va** *adj* **1** : unharmed, sound ⟨sano y salvo : safe and sound⟩ **2 a ~** : safe from danger

salvo[2] *prep* **1** EXCEPTO : except (for), save ⟨todos asistirán salvo Jaime : all will attend except for Jaime⟩ **2 salvo que** : unless ⟨salvo que llueva : unless it rains⟩

salvoconducto *nm* : safe-conduct

samba *nf* : samba

San *adj* → **santo**[1]

sanar *vt* : to heal, to cure — *vi* : to get well, to recover

sanatorio *nm* **1** : sanatorium **2** : clinic, private hospital

sanción *nf*, *pl* **sanciones** : sanction

sancionar *vt* **1** : to penalize, to impose a sanction on **2** : to sanction, to approve

sancochar *vt* : to parboil

sandalia *nf* : sandal

sándalo *nm* : sandalwood

sandez *nf*, *pl* **sandeces** ESTUPIDEZ : nonsense, silly thing to say

sandía *nf* : watermelon

sandwich ['sandwit∫, 'saŋgwit∫] *nm*, *pl* **sandwiches** [-dwit∫es, -gwi-] EMPAREDADO : sandwich

saneamiento *nm* **1** : cleaning up, sanitation **2** : reorganizing, streamlining

sanear *vt* **1** : to clean up, to sanitize **2** : to reorganize, to streamline

sangrante *adj* **1** : bleeding **2** : flagrant, blatant

sangrar *vi* : to bleed — *vt* : to indent (a paragraph, etc.)

sangre *nf* **1** : blood **2 a sangre fría** : in cold blood **3 a sangre y fuego** : by violent force **4 pura sangre** : thoroughbred

sangría *nf* **1** : bleeding (in medicine) **2** : sangria (wine punch) **3** : drain, draining ⟨una sangría fiscal : a financial drain⟩ **4** : indentation, indenting

sangriento, -ta *adj* **1** : bloody **2** : cruel

sanguijuela *nf* **1** : leech, bloodsucker **2** : sponger, leech

sanguinario, -ria *adj* : bloodthirsty

sanguíneo, -nea *adj* **1** : blood ⟨vaso sanguíneo : blood vessel⟩ **2** : sanguine, ruddy

sanidad *nf* **1** : health **2** : public health, sanitation

sanitario[1], **-ria** *adj* **1** : sanitary **2** : health ⟨centro sanitario : health center⟩

sanitario[2], **-ria** *n* : sanitation worker

sanitario[3] *nm* Col, Mex, Ven : toilet ⟨los sanitarios : the toilets, the restroom⟩

sano, -na *adj* **1** SALUDABLE : healthy **2** : wholesome **3** : whole, intact

santiaguino, -na *adj* : of or from Santiago, Chile

santiamén *nm* **en un santiamén** : in no time at all

santidad *nf* : holiness, sanctity

santificar {72} *vt* : to sanctify, to consecrate, to hallow

santiguarse {10} *vr* PERSIGNARSE : to cross oneself

santo[1], **-ta** *adj* **1** : holy, saintly ⟨el Santo Padre : the Holy Father⟩ ⟨una vida santa : a saintly life⟩ **2 Santo, Santa** (*San before names of masculine saints except those beginning with D or T*) : Saint ⟨Santa Clara : Saint Claire⟩ ⟨Santo Tomás : Saint Thomas⟩ ⟨San Francisco : Saint Francis⟩

santo[2], **-ta** *n* : saint

santo[3] *nm* **1** : saint's day **2** CUMPLEAÑOS : birthday

santuario *nm* : sanctuary

santurrón, -rrona *adj*, *mpl* **-rrones** : overly pious, sanctimonious — **santurronamente** *adv*

saña *nf* **1** : fury, rage **2** : viciousness ⟨con saña : viciously⟩

sapo *nm* : toad

saque[1], etc. → **sacar**

saque[2] *nm* **1** : kickoff (in soccer or football) **2** : serve, service (in sports)

saqueador, -dora *n* DEPREDADOR : plunderer, looter

saquear *vt* : to sack, to plunder, to loot

saqueo *nm* : sacking, plunder, looting

sarampión *nm* : measles *pl*

sarape *nm* CA, Mex : blanket (worn as a poncho)

sarcasmo *nm* : sarcasm

sarcástico, -ca *adj* : sarcastic

sarcófago *nm* : sarcophagus

sardina *nf* : sardine

sardónico, -ca *adj* : sardonic

sarga *nf* : serge

sargento *nmf* : sergeant

sari *nm* : sari

sarna *nf* : mange

sarnoso, -sa *adj* : mangy

sarpullido *nm* ERUPCIÓN : rash

sarro *nm* **1** : deposit, coating **2** : tartar, plaque

sarta *nf* **1** : string, series (of insults, etc.) **2** : string (of pearls, etc.)

sartén *nmf*, *pl* **sartenes** **1** : frying pan **2 tener la sartén por el mango** : to call the shots, to be in control

sasafrás *nm* : sassafras

sastre, -tra *n* : tailor

sastrería *nf* **1** : tailoring **2** : tailor's shop

Satanás *or* **Satán** *nm* : Satan, the devil

satánico, -ca *adj* : satanic

satélite *nm* : satellite

satín *or* **satén** *nm*, *pl* **satines** *or* **satenes** : satin

satinado, -da *adj* : satin, glossy

sátira *nf* : satire

satírico, -ca *adj* : satirical, satiric

satirizar {21} *vt* : to satirize

sátiro *nm* : satyr

satisfacción *nf*, *pl* **-ciones** : satisfaction

satisfacer {74} *vt* **1** : to satisfy **2** : to fulfill, to meet **3** : to pay, to settle — **satisfacerse** *vr* **1** : to be satisfied **2** : to take revenge

satisfactorio, -ria *adj* : satisfactory — **satisfactoriamente** *adv*

satisfecho, -cha *adj* : satisfied, content, pleased

saturación *nf*, *pl* **-ciones** : saturation

saturar vt 1 : to saturate, to fill up 2 : to satiate, to surfeit

saturnismo nm : lead poisoning

Saturno nm : Saturn

sauce nm : willow

saúco nm : elder (tree)

saudí or **saudita** adj & nmf : Saudi, Saudi Arabian

sauna nmf : sauna

savia nf : sap

saxo¹ nm fam : sax fam, saxophone

saxo² nmf fam : sax player fam, saxophone player

saxofón nm, pl **-fones** : saxophone — **saxofonista** nmf

sazón¹ nf, pl **sazones** 1 : flavor, seasoning 2 : ripeness, maturity ⟨en sazón : in season, ripe⟩ 3 **a la sazón** : at that time, then

sazón² nmf, pl **sazones** Mex : flavor, seasoning

sazonar vt CONDIMENTAR : to season, to spice

scanner [es'kaner] → **escáner**

scout [es'kaut] nmf, pl **scouts** : scout

se pron 1 : to him, to her, to you, to them ⟨se los daré a ella : I'll give them to her⟩ 2 : each other, one another ⟨se abrazaron : they hugged each other⟩ 3 : himself, herself, itself, yourself, yourselves, themselves ⟨se afeitó antes de salir : he shaved before leaving⟩ 4 (used in passive constructions) ⟨se dice que es hermosa : they say she's beautiful⟩ ⟨se habla inglés : English spoken⟩

sé → **saber, ser**

sea, etc. → **ser**

sebo nm 1 : grease, fat 2 : tallow 3 : suet

secado nm : drying

secador nm : hair dryer

secadora nf 1 : dryer, clothes dryer 2 Mex : hair dryer

secamente adv : curtly, brusquely

secante nm : blotting paper, blotter

secar {72} v : to dry — **secarse** vr 1 : to get dry 2 : to dry up

sección nf, pl **secciones** 1 : section ⟨sección transversal : cross section⟩ 2 : department, division

seccionar vt : to section, to divide

seco, -ca adj 1 : dry 2 DISECADO : dried ⟨fruta seca : dried fruit⟩ 3 : thin, lean 4 : curt, brusque 5 : sharp ⟨un golpe seco : a sharp blow⟩ 6 : dry, alcohol-free 7 **a secas** : simply, just ⟨se llama Chico, a secas : he's just called Chico⟩ 8 **en ~** : abruptly, suddenly ⟨frenar en seco : to make a sudden stop⟩

secoya nf : sequoia, redwood

secreción nf, pl **-ciones** : secretion

secretar vt : to secrete

secretaría nf 1 : secretariat, administrative department 2 Mex : ministry, cabinet office

secretariado nm 1 : secretariat 2 : secretarial profession

secretario, -ria n : secretary — **secretarial** adj

secreto¹, -ta adj : secret — **secretamente** adv

secreto² nm 1 : secret 2 : secrecy

secta nf : sect

sectario, -ria adj & n : sectarian

sector nm : sector

secuaz nmf, pl **secuaces** : follower, henchman, underling

secuela nf : consequence, sequel ⟨las secuelas de la guerra : the aftermath of the war⟩

secuencia nf : sequence

secuestrador, -dora n 1 : kidnapper, abductor 2 : hijacker

secuestrar vt 1 RAPTAR : to kidnap, to abduct 2 : to hijack, to commandeer 3 CONFISCAR : to confiscate, to seize

secuestro nm 1 RAPTO : kidnapping, abduction 2 : hijacking 3 : seizure, confiscation

secular adj : secular — **secularismo** nm — **secularización** nf

secundar vt : to support, to second

secundaria nf 1 : secondary education, high school 2 Mex : junior high school, middle school

secundario, -ria adj : secondary

secuoya nf : sequoia

sed nf 1 : thirst ⟨tener sed : to be thirsty⟩ 2 **tener sed de** : to hunger for, to thirst for

seda nf : silk

sedación nf, pl **-ciones** : sedation

sedal nm : fishing line

sedán nm, pl **sedanes** : sedan

sedante adj & nm CALMANTE : sedative

sedar vt : to sedate

sede nf 1 : seat, headquarters 2 : venue, site 3 **la Santa Sede** : the Holy See

sedentario, -ria adj : sedentary

sedición nf, pl **-ciones** : sedition — **sedicioso, -sa** adj

sediento, -ta adj : thirsty, thirsting

sedimento nm : sediment — **sedimentario, -ria** adj — **sedimentación** nf

sedoso, -sa adj : silky, silken

seducción nf, pl **-ciones** : seduction

seducir {61} vt 1 : to seduce 2 : to captivate, to charm

seductivo, -va adj : seductive

seductor¹, -tora adj 1 SEDUCTIVO : seductive 2 ENCANTADOR : charming, alluring

seductor², -tora n : seducer

segador nm : daddy longlegs

segador, -dora n : harvester

segar {49} vt 1 : to reap, to harvest, to cut 2 : to sever abruptly ⟨una vida segada por la enfermedad : a life cut short by illness⟩

seglar¹ adj LAICO : lay, secular

seglar² nmf LAICO : layperson, layman m, laywoman f

segmentado, -da adj : segmented

segmento nm : segment

segregación nf, pl **-ciones** : segregation

segregar {52} vt 1 : to segregate 2 SECRETAR : to secrete

seguida nf **en ~** : right away, immediately ⟨vuelvo en seguida : I'll be right back⟩

seguidamente *adv* **1** : next, immediately after **2** : without a break, continuously

seguido[1] *adv* **1** RECTO : straight, straight ahead **2** : often, frequently

seguido[2]**, -da** *adj* **1** CONSECUTIVO : consecutive, successive ⟨tres días seguidos : three days in a row⟩ **2** : straight, unbroken **3** ~ **por** *or* ~ **de** : followed by

seguidor, -dora *n* : follower, supporter

seguimiento *nm* **1** : following, pursuit **2** : continuation ⟨darle seguimiento a : to follow up on⟩ **3** : tracking, monitoring

seguir {75} *vt* **1** : to follow ⟨el policía los siguió : the policeman followed them⟩ ⟨me siguieron con la mirada : they followed me with their eyes⟩ ⟨seguiré tu consejo : I'll follow your advice⟩ ⟨seguir el ejemplo de : to follow the example of⟩ ⟨me cuesta seguirle el ritmo : I have trouble keeping up with her⟩ ⟨seguir el procedimiento : to follow procedure⟩ ⟨en los meses que siguieron a la tragedia : in the months that followed the tragedy⟩ **2** : to go along, to keep on ⟨seguimos toda la carretera panamericana : we continued along the PanAmerican Highway⟩ ⟨siguió hablando : he kept on talking⟩ ⟨sigue aumentando : it continues to increase⟩ ⟨lo sigue creyendo : he still believes it⟩ ⟨seguir el curso : to stay on course⟩ **3** : to take (a course, a treatment) — *vi* **1** : to go on, to keep going ⟨sigue adelante : keep going, carry on⟩ ⟨sigue derecho : keep going straight⟩ **2** : to remain, to continue to be ⟨¿todavía sigues aquí? : you're still here?⟩ ⟨sigue con vida : she's still alive⟩ ⟨todo sigue igual : everything's still the same⟩ ⟨seguimos a la espera de noticias : we're still awaiting news⟩ **3** : to follow, to come after ⟨la frase que sigue : the following sentence⟩ ⟨¿qué sigue después? : what comes next?⟩

según[1] *adv* : it depends ⟨según y como : it all depends on⟩

según[2] *conj* **1** COMO, CONFORME : as, just as ⟨según lo dejé : just as I left it⟩ ⟨hace anotaciones según va leyendo : she makes notes as she reads⟩ **2** : depending on how ⟨según se vea : depending on how one sees it⟩

según[3] *prep* **1** : according to ⟨según los rumores : according to the rumors⟩ **2** : depending on ⟨según los resultados : depending on the results⟩

segundero *nm* : second hand (on a clock)

segundo[1]**, -da** *adj* : second ⟨el segundo lugar : second place⟩ ⟨el segundo piso : the second floor⟩ ⟨llegó la segunda : she came in second⟩

segundo[2]**, -da** *n* **1** : second (in a series) **2** : second (person), second in command

segundo[3] *nm* : second ⟨sesenta segundos : sixty seconds⟩

seguramente *adv* **1** : for sure, surely **2** : probably

seguridad *nf* **1** : safety (against accidents, etc.), security (against attacks, etc.) ⟨seguridad ciudadana : public safety⟩ ⟨seguridad nacional : national security⟩ ⟨de alta/máxima seguridad : high/maximum security⟩ ⟨medidas de seguridad : safety/security measures⟩ **2** : (financial) security ⟨seguridad social : Social Security⟩ **3** CERTEZA : certainty, assurance ⟨con toda seguridad : with complete certainty⟩ **4** : confidence, self-confidence

seguro[1] *adv* : certainly, definitely ⟨va a llover, seguro : it's going to rain for sure⟩ ⟨¡seguro que sí! : of course!⟩

seguro[2]**, -ra** *adj* **1** : safe, secure **2** : sure, certain ⟨estoy segura que es él : I'm sure that's him⟩ **3** : reliable, trustworthy **4** : self-assured

seguro[3] *nm* **1** : insurance ⟨seguro de vida : life insurance⟩ **2** : fastener, clasp **3** *Mex* : safety pin

seis *adj & nm* : six ⟨tiene seis años : she's six (years old)⟩ ⟨el seis de agosto : (on) the sixth of August, (on) August sixth⟩

seis *pron* : six ⟨somos seis : there are six of us⟩ ⟨son las seis : it's six o'clock⟩

seiscientos[1]**, -tas** *adj & pron* : six hundred

seiscientos[2] *nms & pl* : six hundred

seísmo *nm Spain* : earthquake

selección *nf, pl* **-ciones** **1** ELECCIÓN : selection, choice **2 selección natural** : natural selection

seleccionador, -dora *n* : manager (in sports)

seleccionar *vt* ELEGIR : to select, to choose

selectividad *nf Spain* : entrance examination

selectivo, -va *adj* : selective — **selectivamente** *adv*

selecto, -ta *adj* **1** : choice, select **2** EXCLUSIVO : exclusive

selenio *nm* : selenium

self–service [self'serbis] *nm* : self-service restaurant

sellar *vt* **1** : to seal **2** : to stamp

sello *nm* **1** : seal **2** ESTAMPILLA, TIMBRE : postage stamp **3** : hallmark, characteristic

selva *nf* **1** BOSQUE : woods *pl*, forest ⟨selva húmeda : rain forest⟩ **2** JUNGLA : jungle

selvático, -ca *adj* **1** : forest, jungle ⟨sendero selvático : jungle path⟩ **2** : wild

semáforo *nm* **1** : traffic light **2** : stop signal

semana *nf* : week

semanal *adj* : weekly — **semanalmente** *adv*

semanario *nm* : weekly (publication)

semántica *nf* : semantics

semántico, -ca *adj* : semantic

semblante *nm* **1** : countenance, face **2** : appearance, look

semblanza *nf* : biographical sketch, profile

sembrado *nm* : cultivated field

sembrar {55} *vt* **1** : to plant, to sow **2** : to scatter, to strew ⟨sembrar el pánico : to spread panic⟩

semejante[1] *adj* **1** PARECIDO : similar, alike **2** TAL : such ⟨nunca he visto cosa semejante : I have never seen such a thing〉

semejante² nm PRÓJIMO : fellowman
semejanza nf PARECIDO : similarity, resemblance
semejar vi : to resemble, to look like — **semejarse** vr : to be similar, to look alike
semen nm : semen
semental nm : stud (animal) 〈caballo semental : stallion〉
semestral adj : biannual, semiannual
semestre nm : semester
semi- pref : semi-
semibreve nf : whole note
semicírculo nm : semicircle, half circle
semiconductor nm : semiconductor
semidiós nm, pl **-dioses** : demigod m
semifinal nf : semifinal
semilla nf : seed
semillero nm 1 : bed (for plants), seed tray 2 : hotbed, breeding ground
seminario nm 1 : seminary 2 : seminar, graduate course
semiprecioso, -sa adj : semiprecious
semita nmf : Semite — **semítico, -ca** adj
sémola nf : semolina
sempiterno, -na adj ETERNO : eternal, everlasting
senado nm : senate
senador, -dora n : senator
sencillamente adv : simply, plainly
sencillez nf : simplicity
sencillo¹, -lla adj 1 : simple, easy 2 : plain, unaffected 3 : single
sencillo² nm 1 : single (recording) 2 : small change (coins) 3 : one-way ticket
senda nf CAMINO, SENDERO : path, way
senderismo nm : hiking
sendero nm CAMINO, SENDA : path, way
sendos, -das adj pl : each, both 〈llevaban sendos vestidos nuevos : they were each wearing a new dress〉
senectud nf ANCIANIDAD : old age
senegalés, -lesa adj & n, mpl **-leses** : Senegalese
senil adj : senile — **senilidad** nf
seno nm 1 : breast, bosom 〈los senos : the breasts〉 〈el seno de la familia : the bosom of the family〉 2 : sinus 3 **seno materno** : womb
sensación nf, pl **-ciones** 1 IMPRESIÓN : feeling 〈tener la sensación : to have a feeling〉 2 : sensation 〈causar sensación : to cause a sensation〉
sensacional adj : sensational
sensacionalismo nm : sensationalism — **sensacionalista** adj
sensatez nf 1 : good sense 2 **con ~** : sensibly
sensato, -ta adj : sensible, sound — **sensatamente** adv
sensibilidad nf 1 : sensitivity, sensibility 2 SENSACIÓN : feeling
sensibilizar {21} vt : to sensitize
sensible adj 1 : sensitive 2 APRECIABLE : considerable, significant 3 : sentient, capable of feeling
sensiblemente adv : considerably, significantly

sensiblería nf : sentimentality, mush
sensiblero, -ra adj : mawkish, sentimental, mushy
sensitivo, -va adj 1 : sense 〈órganos sensitivos : sense organs〉 2 : sentient, capable of feeling
sensor nm : sensor
sensorial adj : sensory
sensual adj : sensual, sensuous — **sensualmente** adv
sensualidad nf : sensuality
sentado, -da adj 1 : sitting, seated 2 : established, settled 〈dar por sentado : to take for granted〉 〈dejar sentado : to make clear〉 3 : sensible, steady, judicious
sentar {55} vt 1 : to seat, to sit 2 : to establish, to set — vi 1 : to suit 〈ese color te sienta : that color suits you〉 2 : to agree with (of food or drink) 〈las cebollas no me sientan : onions don't agree with me〉 3 : to please 〈le sentó mal el paseo : she didn't enjoy the trip〉 — **sentarse** vr : to sit, to sit down 〈siéntese, por favor : please have a seat〉
sentencia nf 1 : sentence, judgment 2 : maxim, saying
sentenciar vt : to sentence
sentido¹, -da adj 1 : heartfelt, sincere 〈mi más sentido pésame : my sincérest condolences〉 2 : touchy, sensitive 3 : offended, hurt
sentido² nm 1 : sense 〈sentido común : common sense〉 〈los cinco sentidos : the five senses〉 〈sin sentido : senseless〉 2 CONOCIMIENTO : consciousness 3 SIGNIFICADO : meaning, sense 〈doble sentido : double entendre〉 4 : direction 〈calle de sentido único : one-way street〉
sentimental adj 1 : sentimental 2 : love, romantic 〈vida sentimental : love life〉
sentimentalismo nm : sentimentality
sentimiento nm 1 : feeling, emotion 2 PESAR : regret, sorrow
sentir {76} vt 1 : to feel, to experience 〈no siento nada de dolor : I don't feel any pain〉 〈sentía sed : he was feeling thirsty〉 〈sentir amor : to feel love〉 2 PERCIBIR : to perceive, to sense 〈sentir un ruido : to hear a noise〉 3 LAMENTAR : to regret, to feel sorry for 〈lo siento mucho : I'm very sorry〉 — vi 1 : to have feeling, to feel 2 **sin ~** : without noticing, inadvertently — **sentirse** vr 1 : to feel 〈¿te sientes mejor? : are you feeling better?〉 2 Chile, Mex : to take offense
seña nf 1 : sign, signal 〈hablar por señas : to talk in sign language〉 2 **dar señas de** : to show signs of
señal nf 1 : signal 〈señales de radio/televisión : radio/television signals〉 2 : sign 〈señal de tráfico/tránsito : traffic sign〉 3 : signal (with the hand, etc.) 〈señales de humo : smoke signals〉 4 INDICIO : sign, indication 〈señales de vida : signs of life〉 〈señal de alarma/alerta : warning sign〉 〈no hay señales de violencia : there are no signs of violence〉 〈como señal de protesta : as a sign of protest〉 〈en señal de : as a token of〉 〈sin dejar señal : without

leaving a trace⟩ ⟨una buena señal : a good sign⟩ **5** MARCA : mark

señalado, -da *adj* : distinguished, notable

señalador *nm* : marker ⟨señalador de libros : bookmark⟩

señalar *vt* **1** INDICAR : to indicate, to show **2** : to mark **3** : to point out, to stress **4** : to fix, to set — **señalarse** *vr* : to distinguish oneself

señalización *nf*, *pl* **-ciones 1** : signs *pl*, signage **2** : installing of signs

señalizar {21} *vt* **1** : to mark (with signs or guides) ⟨la ruta está claramente señalizada : the route is clearly marked⟩ **2** : to put up signs on/in

señor, -ñora *n* **1** : gentleman *m*, man *m*, lady *f*, woman *f*, wife *f* ⟨señoras y señores : ladies and gentlemen⟩ ⟨un señor de setenta años : a 70-year-old man⟩ ⟨la señora de la casa : the lady of the house⟩ ⟨mi señora : my wife⟩ **2** : Mr. *m*, Mrs. *f* ⟨buenos días, señor López : good morning, Mr. López⟩ ⟨¿conoces a la señora Ortega? : do you know Mrs. Ortega?⟩ **3** : Sir *m*, Madam *f* ⟨Estimados señores : Dear Sirs⟩ **4** : Mr. *m*, Madam *f* ⟨Señora presidenta : . . . : Madam President : . . .⟩ ⟨Señor presidente : . . . : Mr. President : . . .⟩ ⟨habló con el señor embajador : she spoke with the ambassador⟩ **5** : lord *m*, lady *f* ⟨el Señor : the Lord⟩

señoría *nf* **1** : lordship **2** Su Señoría : Your Honor

señorial *adj* : stately, regal

señorío *nm* **1** : manor, estate **2** : dominion, power **3** : elegance, class

señorita *nf* **1** : young lady, young woman **2** : Miss

señuelo *nm* **1** : decoy **2** : bait

sepa, etc. → saber

separación *nf*, *pl* **-ciones 1** : separation, division **2** : gap, space

separadamente *adv* : separately, apart

separado¹, -da *adj* **1** : separated **2** : separate ⟨vidas separadas : separate lives⟩ **3** por ~ : separately

separado², -da *n* : person who is separated ⟨separados y divorciados : separated and divorced people⟩

separador *nm* : divider

separar *vt* **1** : to separate, to divide **2** : to split up, to pull apart **3** : to put aside, to set aside — **separarse** *vr* **1** : to separate, to split up ⟨sus padres se separaron : his parents separated⟩ ⟨separarse de alguien : to separate from someone⟩ **2** : to split up (of a group, etc.)

separo *nm Mex* : cell (in a jail or prison)

sepelio *nm* : interment, burial

sepia¹ *adj & nm* : sepia

sepia² *nf* : cuttlefish

septentrional *adj* : northern

séptico, -ca *adj* : septic

septiembre *nm* : September ⟨el cinco de septiembre : (on) the fifth of September⟩

séptimo, -ma *adj & n* : seventh ⟨el séptimo piso : the seventh floor⟩ ⟨llegó en la séptima : she came in seventh (place)⟩ ⟨un séptimo de : a seventh of⟩

septuagésimo¹, -ma *adj* : seventieth

septuagésimo² *nm* : seventieth

sepulcral *adj* **1** : deathly **2** : dismal, gloomy

sepulcro *nm* TUMBA : tomb, sepulchre

sepultar *vt* ENTERRAR : to bury

sepultura *nf* **1** : burial **2** TUMBA : grave, tomb

seque, etc. → secar

sequedad *nf* **1** : dryness **2** : brusqueness, curtness

sequía *nf* : drought

séquito *nm* : retinue, entourage

ser¹ {77} *vi* **1** (*expressing identity*) : to be ⟨él es mi hermano : he is my brother⟩ ⟨¿quién es? : who is it?⟩ ⟨soy yo : it's me⟩ **2** (*expressing a quality*) : to be ⟨Camila es linda : Camila is pretty⟩ ⟨no seas tonto : don't be silly⟩ ⟨éste es el mejor : this one is the best⟩ ⟨es mío : it's mine⟩ ⟨es para ti : it's for you⟩ ⟨es para abrir latas : it's for opening cans⟩ ⟨son de Juan : they're Juan's⟩ ⟨somos de Managua : we're from Managua⟩ ⟨no creo que sea necesario : I don't think it's necessary⟩ ⟨quiero que seas feliz : I want you to be happy⟩ **3** (*indicating group, category, etc.*) : to be ⟨soy abogada : I'm a lawyer⟩ ⟨es un mamífero : it's a mammal⟩ **4** : to be, to exist, to live ⟨ser, o no ser : to be or not to be⟩ **5** : to be, to take place, to occur ⟨el concierto es el domingo : the concert is on Sunday⟩ ⟨la reunión fue en la escuela : the meeting was at the school⟩ **6** (*expressing time, date, season*) : to be ⟨son las diez : it's ten o'clock⟩ ⟨hoy es el 9 : today's the 9th⟩ **7** : to be (a price), to cost, to come to ⟨¿cuánto es? : how much is it?⟩ **8** : to be, to equal ⟨dos más dos son cuatro : two plus two is four⟩ **9** (*with the future tense*) ⟨¿será posible? : can it be possible?⟩ ⟨serán las ocho : it must be eight o'clock⟩ **10** a no ser que : unless **11** como sea *or* sea como sea : one way or another, somehow ⟨hay que terminarlo como sea; hay que terminarlo, sea como sea : one way or another, we have to finish it⟩ **12** cuando sea : anytime, whenever **13** donde sea : anywhere, wherever **14** es que : the thing is that ⟨es que no lo conozco : it's just that I don't know him⟩ **15** o sea : in other words **16** ¡sea! : agreed!, all right! **17** sea cual/quien (etc.) sea ⟨sean cuales sean las circunstancias : whatever the circumstances might be⟩ ⟨sea quien sea, no lo van a permitir : no matter who he is, they're not going to allow it⟩ **18** sea . . . sea : either . . . or — *v aux* (*used in passive constructions*) : to be ⟨la cuenta ha sido pagada : the bill has been paid⟩ ⟨él fue asesinado : he was murdered⟩

ser² *nm* : being ⟨ser humano : human being⟩

seráfico, -ca *adj* : angelic

serbio¹, -bia *adj & n* : Serb, Serbian

serbio² *nm* : Serbian (language)

serbocroata¹ *adj* : Serbo-Croatian

serbocroata² *nm* : Serbo-Croatian (language)

serenar *vt* : to calm, to soothe — **serenarse** *vr* CALMARSE : to calm down
serenata *nf* : serenade
serenidad *nf* : serenity, calmness
sereno¹, -na *adj* 1 SOSEGADO : serene, calm, composed 2 : fair, clear (of weather) 3 : calm, still (of the sea) — **serenamente** *adv*
sereno² *nm* : night watchman
seriado, -da *adj* : serial
serial *nm* : serial (on radio or television)
seriamente *adv* : seriously
serie *nf* 1 : series 2 SERIAL : serial 3 fabricación en serie : mass production 4 fuera de serie : extraordinary, amazing
seriedad *nf* 1 : seriousness, earnestness 2 : gravity, importance
serio, -ria *adj* 1 : serious, earnest 2 : reliable, responsible 3 : important 4 en ~ : seriously, in earnest — **seriamente** *adv*
sermón *nm, pl* **sermones** 1 : sermon 2 *fam* : harangue, lecture
sermonear *vt fam* : to harangue, to lecture
seropositivo *adj* 1 : positive (in blood testing) ⟨es seropositivo : he's positive, he tested positive⟩ 2 : HIV positive
serpentear *vi* : to twist, to wind — **serpenteante** *adj*
serpentina *nf* : paper streamer
serpiente *nf* : serpent, snake
serrado, -da *adj* DENTADO : serrated
serranía *nf* : mountainous area
serrano, -na *adj* : from the mountains
serrar {55} *vt* : to saw
serrín *nm, pl* **serrines** : sawdust
serruchar *vt* : to saw up
serrucho *nm* : saw, handsaw
servicentro *nm Peru* : gas station
servicial *adj* : obliging, helpful
servicio *nm* 1 : service ⟨servicio postal : postal service⟩ ⟨servicios sociales : social services⟩ ⟨servicio público : public service⟩ 2 SAQUE : serve (in sports) 3 : help, servants *pl* 4 **servicios** *nmpl* : restrooms 5 **fuera de servicio** : out of service
servidor, -dora *n* 1 : servant 2 su seguro servidor : yours truly (in correspondence)
servidumbre *nf* 1 : servitude 2 : help, servants *pl*
servil *adj* 1 : servile, subservient 2 : menial
servilismo *nm* : servility
servilleta *nf* : napkin
servir {54} *vi* : to work, to be useful ⟨esta máquina no sirve para nada : this machine is completely useless⟩ ⟨esa excusa no sirve : that excuse doesn't work⟩ ⟨su talento no le sirvió de mucho : his talent didn't do him much good⟩ ⟨deshazte de lo que no te sirve : get rid of what you don't need⟩ ⟨¿para qué sirve? : what's it for?⟩ 2 : to serve ⟨¿en qué puedo servirle? : how may I help you?⟩ 3 : to serve (in sports) 4 : to serve (in the military, etc.) 5 ~ de : to serve as ⟨servir de ejemplo : to serve as an example⟩ — *vt* 1 : to serve ⟨¿en qué puedo servirlo?

: how may I help you?⟩ ⟨¿te sirvo más café? : would you like more coffee?⟩ 2 SURTIR : to fill (an order) — **servirse** *vr* 1 : to help oneself to 2 : to be kind enough ⟨sírvase enviarnos un catálogo : please send us a catalog⟩
sésamo *nm* AJONJOLÍ : sesame, sesame seeds *pl*
sesear *vi* : to pronounce the Spanish letter *c* before *i* or *e* or the Spanish letter *z* as /s/
sesenta *adj & nm* : sixty — **sesenta** *pron*
sesentavo¹, -va *adj* : sixtieth
sesentavo² *n* : sixtieth (fraction)
seseo *nm* : pronunciation of the Spanish letter *c* before *i* or *e* or the Spanish letter *z* as /s/
sesgado, -da *adj* 1 : inclined, tilted 2 : slanted, biased
sesgar {52} *vt* 1 : to cut on the bias 2 : to tilt 3 : to bias, to slant
sesgo *nm* : bias
sesgue, etc. → **sesgar**
sesión *nf, pl* **sesiones** 1 : session (of a legislature, etc.), meeting 2 : showing, performance ⟨sesión de tarde : afternoon showing⟩
sesionar *vi* REUNIRSE : to meet, to be in session
seso *nm* 1 : brains, intelligence 2 **sesos** *nmpl* : brains (as food)
sesudo, -da *adj* 1 : prudent, sensible 2 : brainy
set *nm, pl* **sets** : set (in tennis)
seta *nf* : mushroom
setecientos¹, -tas *adj & pron* : seven hundred
setecientos² *nms & pl* : seven hundred
setenta *adj & nm* : seventy — **setenta** *pron*
setentavo¹, -va *adj* : seventieth
setentavo² *nm* : seventieth
setiembre → **septiembre**
seto *nm* 1 : fence, enclosure 2 seto vivo : hedge
setter *nm, pl* **setter** *or* **setters** : setter (dog)
seudónimo *nm* : pseudonym
severidad *nf* 1 : harshness, severity 2 : strictness
severo, -ra *adj* 1 : harsh, severe 2 ESTRICTO : strict — **severamente** *adv*
sexagésimo¹, -ma *adj* : sixtieth, sixty-
sexagésimo², -ma *n* : sixtieth, sixty- (in a series)
sexismo *nm* : sexism — **sexista** *adj & nmf*
sexo *nm* : sex
sextante *nm* : sextant
sexteto *nm* : sextet
sexto, -ta *adj & n* : sixth ⟨el sexto lugar : sixth place⟩ ⟨llegó la sexta : she came in sixth (place)⟩ ⟨un sexto de : a sixth of⟩
sexual *adj* : sexual, sex ⟨educación sexual : sex education⟩ — **sexualmente** *adv*
sexualidad *nf* : sexuality
sexy *adj, pl* **sexy** *or* **sexys** : sexy
sheriff *nmf, pl* **sheriffs** : sheriff
shock [ˈʃɔk, ˈtʃɔk] *nm* : shock ⟨estado de shock : state of shock⟩

short *nm, pl* **shorts** : shorts *pl*

show *nm, pl* **shows** : show

si[1] *nm* **1** : B ⟨si sostenido/bemol : B sharp/flat⟩ **2** : ti (in singing)

si[2] *conj* **1** : if ⟨lo haré si me pagan : I'll do it if they pay me⟩ ⟨si lo supiera te lo diría : if I knew it I would tell you⟩ **2** : whether, if ⟨no importa si funciona o no : it doesn't matter whether it works (or not)⟩ **3** (*expressing desire, protest, or surprise*) ⟨si supiera la verdad : if only I knew the truth⟩ ⟨¡si no quiero! : but I don't want to!⟩ **4 si bien** : although ⟨si bien se ha progresado : although progress has been made⟩ **5 si no** : otherwise, or else ⟨si no, no voy : otherwise I won't go⟩

sí[1] *adv* **1** : yes ⟨sí, gracias : yes, please⟩ ⟨creo que sí : I think so⟩ **2 sí que** : indeed, absolutely ⟨esta vez sí que ganaré : this time I'm sure to win⟩ **3 porque sí** *fam* : because, just because ⟨lo hizo porque sí : he did it just because⟩

sí[2] *nm, pl* **síes** : yes ⟨dar el sí : to say yes, to express consent⟩

sí[3] *pron* **1** : oneself, yourself, yourselves *pl*, itself, himself, herself, themselves *pl* ⟨puede decidir por sí mismo : he can decide for himself⟩ ⟨los hechos hablan por sí solos : the facts speak for themselves⟩ ⟨se culpa a sí misma : she blames herself⟩ ⟨dio lo mejor de sí : he gave it his all⟩ **2 de por sí** or **en sí** : by itself, in itself, per se **3 fuera de sí** : beside oneself/ yourself (etc.) **4 para sí (mismo)** : to oneself/yourself (etc.), for oneself/yourself (etc.) ⟨¿qué quiere decir?—dijo para sí : "what does it mean?" she said to herself⟩ ⟨lo hicieron para sí mismos : they did it for themselves⟩ **5 entre ~** : among themselves

siamés, -mesa *adj & n, mpl* **siameses** : Siamese

sicario, -ria *n* : hired killer, hit man

siciliano, -na *adj & n* : Sicilian

sico- → **psico-**

sicomoro *or* **sicómoro** *nm* : sycamore

SIDA *or* **sida** *nm* (*síndrome de inmunodeficiencia adquirida*) : AIDS

siderurgia *nf* : iron and steel industry

siderúrgico, -ca *adj* : steel, iron ⟨la industria siderúrgica : the steel industry⟩

sidra *nf* : hard cider

siega[1], **siegue, etc.** → **segar**

siega[2] *nf* **1** : harvesting **2** : harvest time **3** : harvested crop

siembra[1], **etc.** → **sembrar**

siembra[2] *nf* **1** : sowing ⟨sowing season **3** SEMBRADO : cultivated field

siempre *adv* **1** : always ⟨siempre tienes hambre : you're always hungry⟩ **2** : still ⟨¿siempre te vas? : are you still going?⟩ **3** *Mex* : after all ⟨siempre no fui : I didn't go after all⟩ **4 siempre que** : whenever, every time ⟨siempre que pasa : every time he walks by⟩ **5 para ~** : forever, for good **6 siempre y cuando** : provided that

sien *nf* : temple (on the forehead)

sienta, etc. → **sentar**

siente, etc. → **sentir**

sierpe *nf* : serpent, snake

sierra[1], **etc.** → **serrar**

sierra[2] *nf* **1** : saw ⟨sierra de vaivén : jigsaw⟩ **2** CORDILLERA : mountain range **3** : mountains *pl* ⟨viven en la sierra : they live in the mountains⟩

siervo, -va *n* **1** : slave **2** : serf

siesta *nf* : nap, siesta

siete[1] *adj & nm* : seven ⟨tiene siete años : she's seven (years old)⟩ ⟨la página siete : page seven⟩ ⟨el siete de junio : (on) the seventh of June, (on) June seventh⟩

siete[2] *pron* : seven ⟨somos siete : there are seven of us⟩ ⟨son las siete : it's seven o'clock⟩

sífilis *nf* : syphilis

sifón *nm, pl* **sifones** : siphon

siga, sigue etc. → **seguir**

sigilo *nm* : secrecy, stealth

sigiloso, -sa *adj* FURTIVO : furtive, stealthy — **sigilosamente** *adv*

sigla *nf* : acronym, abbreviation

siglo *nm* **1** : century **2** : age ⟨el Siglo de Oro : the Golden Age⟩ ⟨hace siglos que no te veo : I haven't seen you in ages⟩ **3** : world, secular life

signar *vt* : to sign (a treaty or agreement)

signatario, -ria *n* : signatory

significación *nf, pl* **-ciones** **1** : significance, importance **2** : meaning

significado *nm* **1** : sense, meaning **2** : significance

significante *adj* : significant

significar {72} *vt* **1** : to mean, to signify **2** : to express, to make known — **significarse** *vr* **1** : to draw attention, to become known **2** : to take a stance

significativo, -va *adj* **1** : significant, important **2** : meaningful — **significativamente** *adv*

signo *nm* **1** : sign ⟨signo de igual : equal sign⟩ ⟨un signo de alegría : a sign of happiness⟩ **2** : (punctuation) mark ⟨signo de interrogación : question mark⟩ ⟨signo de admiración : exclamation point⟩ ⟨signo de intercalación : caret⟩

siguiente *adj* : next, following

sílaba *nf* : syllable

silábico, -ca *adj* : syllabic

silbar *v* : to whistle

silbato *nm* PITO : whistle

silbido *nm* : whistle, whistling

silenciador *nm* **1** : muffler (of an automobile) **2** : silencer

silenciar *vt* **1** : to silence **2** : to muffle

silencio *nm* **1** : silence, quiet ⟨silencio! : be quiet!⟩ **2** : rest (in music)

silencioso, -sa *adj* : silent, quiet — **silenciosamente** *adv*

sílice *nf* : silica

silicio *nm* : silicon

silla *nf* **1** : chair **2 silla alta** : high chair (for a baby) **3 silla de ruedas** : wheelchair

sillín *nm, pl* **sillines** : saddle

sillón *nm, pl* **sillones** : armchair, easy chair

silo *nm* : silo

silueta *nf* **1** : silhouette **2** : figure, shape

silvestre *adj* : wild ⟨flor silvestre : wildflower⟩
silvicultor, -tora *n* : forester
silvicultura *nf* : forestry
sima *nf* ABISMO : chasm, abyss
simbólico, -ca *adj* : symbolic — **simbólicamente** *adv*
simbolismo *nm* : symbolism
simbolizar {21} *vt* : to symbolize
símbolo *nm* : symbol
simetría *nf* : symmetry
simétrico, -ca *adj* : symmetrical, symmetric
simiente *nf* : seed
símil *nm* **1** : simile **2** : analogy, comparison
similar *adj* SEMEJANTE : similar, alike
similitud *nf* : similarity, resemblance
simio *nm* : ape
simpatía *nf* **1** : liking, affection ⟨tomarle simpatía a : to take a liking to⟩ **2** : warmth, friendliness **3** : support, solidarity
simpático, -ca *adj* : nice, friendly, likeable
simpatizante *nf* : sympathizer, supporter
simpatizar {21} *vi* **1** : to get along, to hit it off ⟨simpaticé mucho con él : I really liked him⟩ **2** ~ **con** : to sympathize with, to support
simple¹ *adj* **1** SENCILLO : plain, simple, easy **2** : pure, mere ⟨por simple vanidad : out of pure vanity⟩ **3** : simpleminded, foolish
simple² *n* : fool, simpleton
simplemente *adv* : simply, merely, just
simpleza *nf* **1** : foolishness **2** NECEDAD : nonsense
simplicidad *nf* : simplicity
simplificar {72} *vt* : to simplify — **simplificación** *nf*
simplista *adj* : simplistic
simposio *or* **simposium** *nm* : symposium
simulación *nf, pl* **-ciones** : simulation
simulacro *nm* : imitation, sham ⟨simulacro de juicio : mock trial⟩
simular *vt* **1** : to simulate **2** : to feign, to pretend
simultáneo, -nea *adj* : simultaneous — **simultáneamente** *adv*
sin *prep* **1** : without ⟨sin querer : unintentionally⟩ ⟨sin refinar : unrefined⟩ ⟨café sin leche : coffee without milk⟩ ⟨un vuelo sin escalas : a nonstop flight⟩ **2** **sin que** : without ⟨lo hicimos sin que él se diera cuenta : we did it without him noticing⟩
sinagoga *nf* : synagogue
sinceridad *nf* : sincerity
sincero, -ra *adj* : sincere, honest, true — **sinceramente** *adv*
síncopa *nf* : syncopation
sincopar *vt* : to syncopate
sincronizar {21} *vt* : to synchronize — **sincronización** *nf*
sindical *adj* GREMIAL : union, labor ⟨representante sindical : union representative⟩
sindicalismo *nm* : unionism — **sindicalista** *nmf*

sindicalizar {21} *vt* : to unionize — **sindicalizarse** *vr* **1** : to form a union **2** : to join a union
sindicar → **sindicalizar**
sindicato *nm* GREMIO : union, guild
síndrome *nm* : syndrome ⟨síndrome de Down : Down's syndrome⟩ ⟨síndrome tóxico : poisoning⟩
síndrome premenstrual *nm* : premenstrual syndrome, PMS
sinfín *nm* : endless number ⟨un sinfín de problemas : no end of problems⟩
sinfonía *nf* : symphony
sinfónica *nf* : symphony orchestra
sinfónico, -ca *adj* : symphonic, symphony
singular¹ *adj* **1** : singular, unique **2** PARTICULAR : peculiar, odd **3** : singular (in grammar) — **singularmente** *adv*
singular² *nm* : singular
singularidad *nf* **1** : uniqueness **2** : strangeness, peculiarity
singularizar {21} *vt* : to make unique or distinct — **singularizarse** *vr* : to stand out, to distinguish oneself
siniestrado, -da *adj* : damaged, wrecked ⟨zona siniestrada : disaster zone⟩
siniestro¹, -tra *adj* **1** IZQUIERDO : left, left-hand **2** MALVADO : sinister, evil
siniestro² *nm* : accident, disaster
sinnúmero *nm* → **sinfín**
sino *conj* **1** : but, rather ⟨no será hoy, sino mañana : it won't be today, but tomorrow⟩ **2** EXCEPTO : but, except ⟨no hace sino despertar suspicacias : it does nothing but arouse suspicion⟩
sinónimo¹, -ma *adj* : synonymous
sinónimo² *nm* : synonym
sinopsis *nfs & pl* RESUMEN : synopsis, summary
sinrazón *nf, pl* **-zones** : wrong, injustice
sinsabores *nmpl* : woes, troubles
sinsonte *nm* : mockingbird
sintáctico, -ca *adj* : syntactic
sintaxis *nfs & pl* : syntax
síntesis *nfs & pl* **1** : synthesis, fusion **2** SINOPSIS : synopsis, summary
sintético, -ca *adj* : synthetic — **sintéticamente** *adv*
sintetizador *nm* : synthesizer
sintetizar {21} *vt* **1** : to synthesize **2** RESUMIR : to summarize
sintió, etc. → **sentir**
síntoma *nm* : symptom
sintomático, -ca *adj* : symptomatic
sintonía *nf* **1** : tuning in (of a radio) **2** **en sintonía con** : in tune with, attuned to
sintonizador *nm* : tuner, knob for tuning (of a radio, etc.)
sintonizar {21} *vt* : to tune (in) to — *vi* **1** : to tune in **2** ~ **con** : to be in tune with, to empathize with
sinuoso, -sa *adj* **1** : winding, sinuous **2** : devious
sinvergüenza¹ *adj* **1** DESCARADO : shameless, brazen, impudent **2** TRAVIESO : naughty
sinvergüenza² *nmf* **1** : rogue, scoundrel **2** : brat, rascal

sionista *adj & nmf* : Zionist — **sionismo** *nm*

siqui- → psiqui-

siquiera *adv* **1** : at least ⟨dame siquiera un poquito : at least give me a little bit⟩ **2** (*in negative constructions*) : not even ⟨ni siquiera nos saludaron : they didn't even say hello to us⟩

sir *nm* : sir (in titles)

sirena *nf* **1** : mermaid **2** : siren ⟨sirena de niebla : foghorn⟩

sirio, -ria *adj & n* : Syrian

sirope *nm* : syrup

sirve, etc. → servir

sirviente, -ta *n* : servant, maid *f*

sisear *vi* : to hiss

siseo *nm* : hiss

sísmico, -ca *adj* : seismic

sismo *nm* **1** TERREMOTO : earthquake **2** TEMBLOR : tremor

sismógrafo *nm* : seismograph

sistema *nm* **1** : system ⟨sistema nervioso : nervous system⟩ ⟨el sistema métrico : the metric system⟩ ⟨sistema solar : solar system⟩ ⟨entrar al sistema : to log in⟩ ⟨salir del sistema : to log out⟩ **2** : method ⟨trabajar con sistema : to work methodically⟩

sistemático, -ca *adj* : systematic — **sistemáticamente** *adv*

sistematizar {21} *vt* : to systematize

sistémico, -ca *adj* : systemic

sitiar *vt* ASEDIAR : to besiege

sitio *nm* **1** LUGAR : place, site ⟨vámonos a otro sitio : let's go somewhere else⟩ **2** ESPACIO : room, space ⟨hacer sitio a : to make room for⟩ **3** : siege ⟨estado de sitio : state of siege⟩ **4** *Mex* : taxi stand **5** *or* **sitio web** : site, Web site

situación *nf, pl* **-ciones** : situation

situado, -da *adj* : situated, placed

situar {3} *vt* UBICAR : to place, to locate — **situarse** *vr* **1** : to be placed, to be located **2** : to make a place for oneself, to do well

skateboard [es'keitbor] *nm, pl* **skateboards** : skateboard

skateboarding [es'keitbordin] *nm* : skateboarding

sketch *nm* : sketch, skit

slip *nm* : briefs *pl*, underpants *pl*

smog *nm* : smog

smoking → esmoquin

SMS ['ese'eme'ese, 'es'em'es] *nm, pl* **SMS** : text message

snob → esnob

snorkel → esnórquel

snowboard *nm, pl* **snowboards** **1** : snowboard **2** : snowboarding

so *prep* : under ⟨so pena de : under penalty of⟩

sobaco *nm* : armpit

sobado, -da *adj* **1** : worn, shabby **2** : well-worn, hackneyed

sobar *vt* **1** : to finger, to handle **2** : to knead **3** : to rub, to massage **4** *fam* : to beat, to pummel

soberanía *nf* : sovereignty

soberano, -na *adj & n* : sovereign

soberbia *nf* **1** ORGULLO : pride, arrogance **2** MAGNIFICENCIA : magnificence

soberbio, -bia *adj* **1** : proud, arrogant **2** : grand, magnificent

sobornar *vt* : to bribe

soborno *nm* **1** : bribery **2** : bribe

sobra *nf* **1** : excess, surplus **2 de ∼** : extra, to spare **3 sobras** *nfpl* : leftovers, scraps

sobrado, -da *adj* : abundant, excessive, more than enough

sobrante¹ *adj* : remaining, superfluous

sobrante² *nm* : remainder, surplus

sobrar *vi* : to be in excess, to be superfluous ⟨más vale que sobre a que falte : it's better to have too much than not enough⟩

sobre¹ *nm* **1** : envelope **2** : packet ⟨un sobre de sazón : a packet of seasoning⟩

sobre² *prep* **1** : on, on top of ⟨sobre la mesa : on the table⟩ ⟨apilados uno sobre otro : piled one on top of another⟩ **2** : over, above ⟨hay montañas sobre la ciudad : there are mountains above the city⟩ ⟨se inclinó sobre mí : she leaned over me⟩ ⟨temperaturas sobre los 30 grados : temperatures above 30 degrees⟩ **3** : about ⟨¿tiene libros sobre Bolivia? : do you have books on Bolivia?⟩ **4 sobre todo** : especially, above all

sobrealimentar *vt* : to overfeed

sobrecalentar {55} *vt* : to overheat — **sobrecalentarse** *vr*

sobrecama *nmf* : bedspread

sobrecarga *nf* **1** : excess weight **2** : overload

sobrecargar {52} *vt* : to overload, to overburden, to weigh down

sobrecargo *nm* : purser

sobrecogedor, -dora *adj* : shocking

sobrecoger {15} *vt* **1** : to surprise, to startle **2** : to scare — **sobrecogerse** *vr*

sobrecubierta *nf* : dust jacket

sobredosis *nfs & pl* : overdose

sobreentender {56} *vt* : to infer, to understand

sobreestimar *vt* : to overestimate, to overrate

sobreexcitado, -da *adj* : overexcited

sobreexponer {60} *vt* : to overexpose

sobregirar *vt* : to overdraw

sobregiro *nm* : overdraft

sobrehumano, -na *adj* : superhuman

sobrellevar *vt* : to endure, to bear

sobremanera *adv* : exceedingly

sobremesa *nf* : after-dinner conversation

sobrenatural *adj* : supernatural

sobrenombre *nm* APODO : nickname

sobrentender → sobreentender

sobrepasar *vt* : to exceed, to surpass — **sobrepasarse** *vr* PASARSE : to go too far

sobrepeso *nm* **1** : excess weight **2** : overweight, obesity

sobrepoblación, sobrepoblado → superpoblación, superpoblado

sobreponer {60} *vt* **1** SUPERPONER : to superimpose **2** ANTEPONER : to put first, to give priority to — **sobreponerse** *vr* **1** : to pull oneself together **2 ∼ a** : to overcome

sobreprecio *nm* : surcharge

sobreprotector, -tora *adj* : overprotective

sobresaliente[1] *adj* **1** : protruding, projecting **2** : outstanding, noteworthy **3** : significant, salient

sobresaliente[2] *nmf* : understudy

sobresalir {73} *vi* **1** : to protrude, to jut out, to project **2** : to stand out, to excel

sobresaltar *vt* : to startle, to frighten — **sobresaltarse** *vr*

sobresalto *nm* : start, fright

sobresueldo *nm* : bonus, additional pay

sobretasa *nf* : surcharge ⟨sobretasa a la gasolina : gas tax⟩

sobretodo *nm* : overcoat

sobrevalorar *or* **sobrevaluar** {3} *vt* : to overrate

sobrevender *vt* : to oversell

sobrevenir {87} *vi* ACAECER : to take place, to come about ⟨podrían sobrevenir complicaciones : complications could occur⟩

sobrevivencia → **supervivencia**

sobreviviente → **superviviente**

sobrevivir *vi* : to survive — *vt* : to outlive, to outlast

sobrevolar {19} *vt* : to fly over, to overfly

sobriedad *nf* : sobriety, moderation

sobrino, -na *n* : nephew *m*, niece *f*

sobrio, -bria *adj* : sober — **sobriamente** *adv*

socarrón, -rrona *adj, mpl* **-rrones 1** : sly, cunning **2** : sarcastic

socavar *vt* : to undermine

socavón *nm, pl* **-vones** : pothole

sociabilidad *nf* : sociability

sociable *adj* : sociable

social *adj* : social — **socialmente** *adv*

socialista *adj & nmf* : socialist — **socialismo** *nm*

socializar {21} *vt* **1** : to nationalize **2** : to socialize — *vi* : to socialize

sociedad *nf* **1** : society ⟨sociedad democrática : democratic society⟩ ⟨una sociedad secreta : a secret society⟩ **2** : company, enterprise **3 sociedad anónima** : incorporated company

socio, -cia *n* **1** : member **2** : partner

socioeconómico, -ca *adj* : socioeconomic

sociología *nf* : sociology

sociológico, -ca *adj* : sociological — **sociológicamente** *adv*

sociólogo, -ga *n* : sociologist

socorrer *vt* : to assist, to come to the aid of

socorrido, -da *adj* ÚTIL : handy, practical

socorrismo *nm* : lifesaving

socorrista *nmf* **1** : rescue worker **2** : lifeguard

socorro *nm* AUXILIO **1** : aid, help ⟨equipo de socorro : rescue team⟩ **2 ¡socorro!** : help!

soda *nf* **1** : soda, soda water **2** *CA, Car* REFRESCO : soda, soda pop

sodio *nf* : sodium

soez *adj, pl* **soeces** GROSERO : rude, vulgar — **soezmente** *adv*

sofá *nm* : couch, sofa

sofistería *nf* : sophistry — **sofista** *nmf*

sofisticación *nf, pl* **-ciones** : sophistication

sofisticado, -da *adj* : sophisticated

sofocante *adj* : suffocating, stifling

sofocar {72} *vt* **1** AHOGAR : to suffocate, to smother **2** EXTINGUIR : to extinguish, to put out (a fire) **3** APLASTAR : to crush, to put down ⟨sofocar una rebelión : to crush a rebellion⟩ — **sofocarse** *vr* **1** : to suffocate **2** *fam* : to get upset, to get mad

sofoco *nm* : hot flash

sofreír {66} *vt* : to sauté

sofrito[1], **-ta** *adj* : sautéed

sofrito[2] *nm* : seasoning sauce

softbol *nm* : softball

software *nm* : software

soga *nf* : rope

soja → **soya**

sojuzgar *vt* : to subdue, to conquer, to subjugate

sol[1] *nm* **1** : G ⟨sol sostenido/bemol : G sharp/flat⟩ **2** : so, sol (in singing)

sol[2] *nm* **1** : sun ⟨a pleno sol : in the sun⟩ ⟨tomar el sol : to sunbathe⟩ **2** : Peruvian unit of currency

solamente *adv* SÓLO : only, just

solapa *nf* **1** : lapel (of a jacket) **2** : flap (of an envelope)

solapado, -da *adj* : secret, underhanded

solapar *vt* : to cover up, to keep secret — **solaparse** *vr* : to overlap

solar[1] {19} *vt* : to floor, to tile

solar[2] *adj* : solar, sun

solar[3] *nm* **1** TERRENO : lot, piece of land, site **2** *Cuba, Peru* : tenement building

solariego, -ga *adj* : ancestral

solaz *nm, pl* **solaces 1** CONSUELO : solace, comfort **2** DESCANSO : relaxation, recreation

solazarse {21} *vr* : to relax, to enjoy oneself

soldado *nm* **1** : soldier **2 soldado raso** : private, enlisted man

soldador[1], **-dora** *n* : welder

soldador[2] *nm* : soldering iron

soldadura *nf* **1** : welding **2** : soldering, solder

soldar {19} *vt* **1** : to weld **2** : to solder

soleado, -da *adj* : sunny

soledad *nf* : loneliness, solitude

solemne *adj* : solemn — **solemnemente** *adv*

solemnidad *nf* : solemnity

soler {78} *vi* : to be in the habit of, to tend to ⟨solía tomar café por la tarde : she usually drank coffee in the afternoon⟩ ⟨eso suele ocurrir : that frequently happens⟩

solera *nf* **1** : prop, support **2** : tradition

solfeo *nm* : sol-fa

solicitante *nmf* : applicant

solicitar *vt* **1** : to request, to solicit **2** : to apply for ⟨solicitar empleo : to apply for employment⟩

solícito, -ta *adj* : solicitous, attentive, obliging

solicitud *nf* **1** : solicitude, concern **2** : request **3** : application

solidaridad *nf* : solidarity

solidario, -ria *adj* : supportive, united in support ⟨se declararon solidarios con la nueva ley : they declared their support for the new law⟩ ⟨espíritu solidario : spirit of solidarity⟩

solidarizar {21} *vi* : to be in solidarity ⟨solidarizamos con la huelga : we support the strike⟩

solidez *nf* 1 : solidity, firmness 2 : soundness (of an argument, etc.)

solidificar {72} *vt* : to solidify, to make solid — **solidificarse** *vr* — **solidificación** *nf*

sólido¹, -da *adj* 1 : solid, firm 2 : sturdy, well-made 3 : sound, well-founded — **sólidamente** *adv*

sólido² *nm* : solid

soliloquio *nm* : soliloquy

solista *nmf* : soloist

solitaria *nf* TENIA : tapeworm

solitario¹, -ria *adj* 1 : lonely 2 : solitary 3 DESIERTO : deserted, lonely ⟨una calle solitaria : a deserted street⟩

solitario², -ria *n* : recluse, loner

solitario³ *nm* : solitaire

sollozar {21} *vi* : to sob

sollozo *nm* : sob

solo¹, -la *adj* 1 : alone, by oneself ⟨me dejaron solo : they left me on my own⟩ ⟨lo hizo ella sola : she did it all by herself⟩ 2 : lonely 3 ÚNICO : only, sole, unique ⟨hay un solo problema : there's only one problem⟩ 4 **a solas** : alone

solo² *nm* : solo

solo³ *or* **sólo** *adv* SOLAMENTE : just, only ⟨solo quieren comer : they just want to eat⟩

solomillo *nm* : sirloin, loin

solsticio *nm* : solstice

soltar {19} *vt* 1 : to let go of, to drop ⟨¡suéltame el brazo! : let go of my arm!⟩ ⟨soltó las riendas : he dropped the reins⟩ 2 : to release, to set free 3 : to pay out (a rope, etc.) 4 AFLOJAR : to loosen, to slacken 5 : to undo, to untie (a knot, etc.) 6 : to give, to let out (a shout, etc.) 7 : to come out with (a swearword, etc.) — **soltarse** *vr* 1 : to get loose, to break free 2 : to come undone

soltería *nf* : state of being single

soltero¹, -ra *adj* : single, unmarried

soltero², -ra *n* 1 : bachelor *m*, single man *m*, single woman *f* 2 **apellido de soltera** : maiden name

soltura *nf* 1 : looseness, slackness 2 : fluency (of language) 3 : agility, ease of movement

soluble *adj* : soluble — **solubilidad** *nf*

solución *nf*, *pl* **-ciones** 1 : solution (in a liquid) 2 : answer, solution

solucionar *vt* RESOLVER : to solve, to resolve — **solucionarse** *vr*

solvencia *nf* 1 : solvency 2 : settling, payment (of debts) 3 : reliability ⟨solvencia moral : trustworthiness⟩

solvente¹ *adj* 1 : solvent 2 : reliable, trustworthy

solvente² *nm* : solvent

sombra *nf* 1 : shadow 2 : shade 3 **sombras** *nfpl* : darkness, shadows *pl* 4 **sin**

sombra de duda : without a shadow of a doubt 5 **sombra de ojos** : eye shadow

sombreado, -da *adj* 1 : shady 2 : shaded, darkened

sombrear *vt* : to shade

sombrerero, -ra *n* : milliner, hatter

sombrero *nm* 1 : hat 2 **sin ~** : bareheaded 3 **sombrero hongo** : derby

sombrilla *nf* : parasol, umbrella

sombrío, -bría *adj* LÓBREGO : dark, somber, gloomy — **sombríamente** *adv*

somero, -ra *adj* : superficial, cursory, shallow

someter *vt* 1 : to subjugate, to conquer 2 : to subordinate 3 : to subject (to treatment or testing) 4 : to submit, to present ⟨lo someterán a votación : they will put it to a vote⟩ ⟨someter a la justicia : to bring to justice⟩ — **someterse** *vr* 1 : to submit, to yield 2 : to undergo

sometimiento *nm* 1 : submission, subjection 2 : presentation

somier *nm*, *pl* **somieres** *or* **somiers** : box spring

somnífero¹, -ra *adj* : soporific

somnífero² *nm* : sleeping pill

somnolencia *nf* : drowsiness, sleepiness

somnoliento, -ta *adj* : drowsy, sleepy

somorgujo *or* **somormujo** *nm* : loon, grebe

somos → ser¹

son¹ → ser

son² *nm* 1 : sound ⟨al son de la trompeta : at the sound of the trumpet⟩ 2 : news, rumor 3 **en son de** : as, in the manner of, by way of ⟨en son de broma : as a joke⟩ ⟨en son de paz : in peace⟩

sonado, -da *adj* : celebrated, famous, much-discussed

sonaja *nf* : rattle

sonajero *nm* : rattle (toy)

sonambulismo *nm* : sleepwalking

sonámbulo, -la *n* : sleepwalker

sonante *adj* **dinero contante y sonante → dinero**

sonar¹ {19} *vi* 1 : to sound ⟨suena bien : it sounds good⟩ ⟨sonaba contenta : she sounded happy⟩ 2 : to sound, to ring (of bells, a phone, etc.), to go off (of an alarm), to ring out (of shots), to play (of music) 3 : to be pronounced (of a letter) 4 : to look or sound familiar ⟨me suena ese nombre : that name rings a bell⟩ 5 : to fly (of rumors), to be talked about ⟨suena para reemplazar a Díaz : there is talk that he might replace Díaz⟩ 6 **~ a** : to sound like — *vt* 1 : to ring 2 : to blow (a trumpet, a nose) — **sonarse** *vr* : to blow one's nose

sonar² *nm* : sonar

sonata *nf* : sonata

sonda *nf* 1 : sounding line 2 : probe 3 CATÉTER : catheter

sondar *vt* 1 : to sound, to probe (in medicine, drilling, etc.) 2 : to probe, to explore (outer space)

sondear *vt* 1 : to sound 2 : to probe 3 : to sound out, to test (opinions, markets)

sondeo *nm* 1 : sounding, probing 2 : drilling 3 ENCUESTA : survey, poll

soneto *nm* : sonnet
sónico, -ca *adj* : sonic
sonido *nm* : sound
sonoridad *nf* : resonance
sonoro, -ra *adj* **1** : resonant, sonorous, voiced (in linguistics) **2** : resounding, loud **3 banda sonora** : soundtrack
sonreír {66} *vi* : to smile
sonriente *adj* : smiling
sonrisa *nf* : smile
sonrojar *vt* : to cause to blush — **sonrojarse** *vr* : to blush
sonrojo *nm* RUBOR : blush
sonrosado, -da *adj* : rosy, pink
sonsacar {72} *vt* : to wheedle, to extract
sonsonete *nm* **1** : tapping **2** : drone **3** : mocking tone
soñador¹, -dora *adj* : dreamy
soñador², -dora *n* : dreamer
soñar {19} *v* **1** : to dream **2** ∼ **con** : to dream about **3 soñar despierto** : to daydream
soñoliento, -ta *adj* : sleepy, drowsy
sopa *nf* **1** : soup **2 estar hecho una sopa** : to be soaked to the bone
sopapa *nm Arg* : plunger (for toilets, etc.)
sopapo *nm fam* : slap
sopera *nf* : soup tureen
sopesar *vt* : to weigh, to evaluate
soplar *vi* : to blow — *vt* : to blow on, to blow out, to blow off
soplete *nm* : blowtorch
soplido *nm* : puff
soplo *nm* : puff, gust
soplón, -plona *n, mpl* **soplones** *fam* : tattletale, sneak
soponcio *nm fam* **1** : fainting spell ⟨sufrió un soponcio : he fainted⟩ **2** : shock, fit ⟨cuando se enteró le dio un/el soponcio : when he found out, he was horrified⟩
sopor *nm* SOMNOLENCIA : drowsiness, sleepiness
soporífero, -ra *adj* : soporific
soportable *adj* : bearable, tolerable
soportar *vt* **1** SOSTENER : to support, to hold up **2** RESISTIR : to withstand, to resist **3** AGUANTAR : to bear, to tolerate
soporte *nm* : base, stand, support
soprano *nmf* : soprano
sor *nf* : Sister (religious title)
sorber *vt* **1** : to sip, to suck in **2** : to absorb, to soak up
sorbete *nm* : sherbet
sorbo *nm* **1** : sip, gulp, swallow **2 beber a sorbos** : to sip
sordera *nf* : deafness
sórdido, -da *adj* : sordid, dirty, squalid
sordina *nf* : mute (for a musical instrument)
sordo, -da *adj* **1** : deaf **2** : muted, muffled
sordomudo, -da *n* : deaf-mute
sorgo *nm* : sorghum
soriasis *nfs & pl* : psoriasis
sorna *nf* : sarcasm, mocking tone
soroche *nm Peru* : altitude sickness
sorprendente *adj* : surprising — **sorprendentemente** *adv*
sorprender *vt* : to surprise — **sorprenderse** *vr*

sorpresa *nf* : surprise
sorpresivo, -va *adj* **1** : surprising, surprise **2** IMPREVISTO : sudden, unexpected
sortear *vt* **1** RIFAR : to raffle, to draw lots for **2** : to dodge, to avoid
sorteo *nm* : drawing, raffle
sortija *nf* **1** ANILLO : ring **2** : curl, ringlet
sortilegio *nm* **1** HECHIZO : spell, charm **2** HECHICERÍA : sorcery
SOS *nm* : SOS
sosegado, -da *adj* SERENO : calm, tranquil, serene
sosegar {49} *vt* : to calm, to pacify — **sosegarse** *vr*
sosiego *nm* : tranquillity, serenity, calm
soslayar *vt* ESQUIVAR : to dodge, to evade
soslayo *nm* **de** ∼ : obliquely, sideways ⟨mirar de soslayo : to look askance⟩
soso, -sa *adj* **1** INSÍPIDO : bland, flavorless **2** ABURRIDO : dull, boring
sospecha *nf* : suspicion
sospechar *vt* : to suspect — *vi* : to be suspicious
sospechosamente *adv* : suspiciously
sospechoso¹, -sa *adj* : suspicious, suspect
sospechoso², -sa *n* : suspect
sostén *nm, pl* **sostenes 1** APOYO : support **2** : sustenance **3** : brassiere, bra
sostener {80} *vt* **1** : to support, to hold up **2** : to hold ⟨sostenme la puerta : hold the door for me⟩ ⟨sostener una conversación : to hold a conversation⟩ **3** : to sustain, to maintain — **sostenerse** *vr* **1** : to stand, to hold oneself up **2** : to continue, to remain
sostenible *adj* : sustainable, tenable — **sostenibilidad** *nf*
sostenido¹, -da *adj* **1** : sustained, prolonged **2** : sharp (in music)
**sostenido² *nm* : sharp (in music)
sostuvo, etc. → **sostener**
sota *nf* : jack (in the Spanish deck of cards)
sotana *nf* : cassock
sótano *nm* : basement
sotavento *nm* : lee ⟨a sotavento : leeward⟩
soterrar {55} *vt* **1** : to bury **2** : to conceal, to hide away
soto *nm* : grove, copse
souvenir *nm, pl* **-nirs** RECUERDO : souvenir, memento
soviético, -ca *adj* : Soviet
soy → **ser**
soya *nf* : soy, soybean
spaghetti → **espagueti**
spam *nm, pl* **spams** : spam (e-mail)
spaniel *nm, pl* **spaniels** : spaniel
SPM → **síndrome premenstrual**
sport [ɛˈspor] *adj* : sport, casual
sprint [ɛˈsprin, -ˈsprint] *nm* : sprint — **sprinter** *nmf*
squash [ɛˈskwaʃ, -ˈskwatʃ] *nm* : squash (sport)
Sr. *nm* : Mr.
Sra. *nf* : Mrs., Ms.
Srta. *or* **Srita.** *nf* : Miss, Ms.
staccato *adj* : staccato

stand *nm, pl* **stands** : stand, kiosk

standard → **estándar**

statu quo *nm* : status quo

stop [es'top] *nm* : stop sign

stress → **estrés**

su *adj* 1 : his, her, its, their, one's ⟨su libro : her book⟩ ⟨sus consecuencias : its consequences⟩ 2 (*formal*) : your ⟨tómese su medicina, señor : take your medicine, sir⟩

suave *adj* 1 BLANDO : soft 2 LISO : smooth 3 : gentle, mild 4 *Mex fam* : great, fantastic

suavemente *adv* : smoothly, gently, softly

suavidad *nf* : softness, smoothness, mellowness

suavizante *nm* : softener, fabric softener

suavizar {21} *vt* 1 : to soften, to smooth out 2 : to tone down — **suavizarse** *vr*

sub- *pref* : sub-

subacuático, -ca *adj* : underwater

subalterno¹, -na *adj* 1 SUBORDINADO : subordinate 2 SECUNDARIO : secondary

subalterno², -na *n* SUBORDINADO : subordinate

subarrendar {55} *vt* : to sublet

subasta *nf* : auction

subastador, -dora *n* : auctioneer

subastar *vt* : to auction, to auction off

subcampeón, -peona *n, mpl* **-peones** : runner-up

subcomisión *nf, pl* **-siones** : subcommittee

subcomité *nm* : subcommittee

subconsciente *adj & nm* : subconscious — **subconscientemente** *adv*

subcontratar *vt* : to subcontract

subcontratista *nmf* : subcontractor

subcultura *nf* : subculture

subdesarrollado, -da *adj* : underdeveloped

subdesarrollo *nm* : underdevelopment

subdirector, -tora *n* : assistant manager

súbdito, -ta *n* : subject (of a monarch)

subdividir *vt* : to subdivide

subdivisión *nf, pl* **-siones** : subdivision

subestimar *vt* : to underestimate, to undervalue

subexponer {60} *vt* : to underexpose

subexposición *nf, pl* **-ciones** : underexposure

subgrupo *nm* : subgroup

subibaja *nm* : seesaw

subida *nf* 1 : ascent, climb 2 : rise, increase 3 : slope, hill ⟨ir de subida : to go uphill⟩

subido, -da *adj* 1 : intense, strong ⟨amarillo subido : bright yellow⟩ 2 **subido de tono** : risqué

subir *vt* 1 : to bring/take/carry up, to lift up 2 : to climb, to go/come up (stairs, etc.) 3 : to raise (a blind, etc.), to pull up (a zipper, etc.), to take up (a hem) 4 AUMENTAR : to raise (prices, etc.) ⟨subir el volumen : to turn up the volume⟩ 5 CARGAR : to upload — *vi* 1 : to go/come up 2 AUMENTAR : to rise, to increase 3 : to be promoted 4 ~ **a** : to get on, to mount ⟨subir a un tren : to get on a train⟩ — **subirse** *vr* 1 : to climb (up) 2 : to pull up (clothing) 3 **subirse a la cabeza** : to go to one's head

súbito, -ta *adj* 1 REPENTINO : sudden 2 **de** ~ : all of a sudden, suddenly — **súbitamente** *adv*

subjetivo, -va *adj* : subjective — **subjetivamente** *adv* — **subjetividad** *nf*

subjuntivo¹, -va *adj* : subjunctive

subjuntivo² *nm* : subjunctive

sublevación *nf, pl* **-ciones** ALZAMIENTO : uprising, rebellion

sublevar *vt* : to incite to rebellion — **sublevarse** *vr* : to rebel, to rise up

sublimar *vt* : to sublimate — **sublimación** *nf*

sublime *adj* : sublime

submarinismo *nm* : scuba diving

submarinista *nmf* : scuba diver

submarino¹, -na *adj* : submarine, undersea

submarino² *nm* : submarine

subnormal¹ *adj* 1 *usu offensive* : mentally handicapped *sometimes offensive* 2 : idiotic

subnormal² *nmf* 1 *usu offensive* : mentally handicapped person 2 : moron, idiot

suboficial *nmf* : noncommissioned officer, petty officer

subordinado, -da *adj & n* : subordinate

subordinar *vt* : to subordinate — **subordinarse** *vr* — **subordinación** *nf*

subproducto *nm* : by-product

subrayar *vt* 1 : to underline, to underscore 2 ENFATIZAR : to highlight, to emphasize

subrepticio, -cia *adj* : surreptitious — **subrepticiamente** *adv*

subsanar *vt* 1 RECTIFICAR : to rectify, to correct 2 : to overlook, to excuse 3 : to make up for

subscribir → **suscribir**

subsecretario, -ria *n* : undersecretary

subsecuente *adj* : subsequent — **subsecuentemente** *adv*

subsidiar *vt* : to subsidize

subsidiaria *nf* : subsidiary

subsidio *nm* : subsidy

subsiguiente *adj* : subsequent

subsistencia *nf* 1 : subsistence 2 : sustenance

subsistir *vi* 1 : to subsist, to live 2 : to endure, to survive

substancia → **sustancia**

subte *nm Arg, Uru* : subway

subteniente *nmf* : second lieutenant

subterfugio *nm* : subterfuge

subterráneo¹, -nea *adj* : underground, subterranean

subterráneo² *nm* 1 : underground passage, tunnel 2 *Arg, Uru* : subway

subtitular *vt* : to subtitle

subtítulo *nm* : subtitle, subheading

subtotal *nm* : subtotal

suburbano, -na *adj* : suburban

suburbio *nm* 1 : suburb 2 : slum (outside a city)

subvención *nf, pl* **-ciones** : subsidy, grant

subvencionar *vt* : to subsidize

subversivo, -va *adj & n* : subversive — **subversión** *nf*

subvertir {76} *vt* : to subvert

subyacente *adj* : underlying

subyacer *vi* ~ **en/a** : to underlie

subyugar {52} *vt* : to subjugate — **subyugación** *nf*

succión *nf*, *pl* **succiones** : suction

succionar *vt* : to suck up, to draw in

sucedáneo *nm* : substitute ⟨sucedáneo de azúcar : sugar substitute⟩

suceder *vi* **1** OCURRIR : to happen, to occur ⟨¿qué sucede? : what's going on?⟩ ⟨suceda lo que suceda : come what may⟩ **2** ~ **a** : to follow, to succeed ⟨a la primavera sucede el verano : summer follows spring⟩ — *vt* : to succeed ⟨suceder a alguien : to succeed someone⟩

sucesión *nf*, *pl* **-siones 1** : succession **2** : sequence, series **3** : issue, heirs *pl* **4** : estate, inheritance

sucesivamente *adv* : successively, consecutively ⟨y así sucesivamente : and so on⟩

sucesivo, -va *adj* : successive, following

suceso *nm* **1** : event, happening, occurrence **2** : incident, crime

sucesor, -sora *n* : successor

suciedad *nf* **1** : dirtiness, filthiness **2** MUGRE : dirt, filth

sucinto, -ta *adj* CONCISO : succinct, concise — **sucintamente** *adv*

sucio, -cia *adj* : dirty, filthy

sucre *nm* : Ecuadoran unit of currency

suculento, -ta *adj* : succulent

sucumbir *vi* : to succumb

sucursal *nf* : branch (of a business)

sudadera *nf* **1** : sweatshirt **2** : sweatsuit, tracksuit

sudado, -da → **sudoroso**

sudafricano, -na *adj & n* : South African

sudamericano, -na *adj & n* : South American

sudanés, -nesa *adj & n*, *mpl* **-neses** : Sudanese

sudar *vi* TRANSPIRAR : to sweat, to perspire

sudario *nm* : shroud

sudeste → **sureste**

sudoeste → **suroeste**

sudor *nm* TRANSPIRACIÓN : sweat, perspiration

sudoroso, -sa *adj* : sweaty

sueco[1], -ca *adj* : Swedish

sueco[2], -ca *n* : Swede

sueco[3] *nm* : Swedish (language)

suegro, -gra *n* **1** : father-in-law *m*, mother-in-law *f* **2** **suegros** *nmpl* : in-laws

suela *nf* : sole (of a shoe)

suelda, etc. → **soldar**

sueldo *nm* : salary, wage

suele, etc. → **soler**

suelo *nm* **1** : ground ⟨caerse al suelo : to fall down, to hit the ground⟩ **2** : floor, flooring **3** TIERRA : soil, land

suelta, etc. → **soltar**

suelto[1], -ta *adj* **1** : loose, free, unattached ⟨dinero suelto : loose change⟩ ⟨una camisa suelta : a loose shirt⟩ ⟨cabos sueltos : loose ends⟩ ⟨el perro estaba suelto : the dog was loose⟩ ⟨un papelito suelto : a scrap of paper⟩ ⟨con el pelo suelto : with one's hair down⟩ **2** : individual, separate, odd ⟨¿las venden sueltas? : do they sell them individually?⟩ **3** : fluent, fluid

suelto[2] *nm* : loose change

suena, etc. → **sonar**

sueña, etc. → **soñar**

sueño *nm* **1** : dream **2** : sleep ⟨perder el sueño : to lose sleep⟩ **3** : sleepiness ⟨tener sueño : to be sleepy⟩

suero *nm* **1** : serum **2** : whey **3 suero de mantequilla/manteca** : buttermilk

suerte *nf* **1** FORTUNA : luck, fortune ⟨tener suerte : to be lucky⟩ ⟨estar de suerte : to be in luck⟩ ⟨le deseo suerte : I wish him luck⟩ ⟨¡buena suerte! : good luck!⟩ ⟨por suerte : luckily⟩ ⟨con suerte : with any luck⟩ ⟨traer mala suerte : to be/bring bad luck⟩ ⟨fue una suerte que . . . : it's a lucky thing that . . .⟩ **2** DESTINO : fate, destiny, lot ⟨tentar a la suerte : to tempt fate⟩ ⟨la dejaron a su suerte : they left her to her fate⟩ ⟨correr la misma suerte : to meet the same fate⟩ **3** CLASE, GÉNERO : sort, kind ⟨toda suerte de cosas : all kinds of things⟩

suertudo[1], -da *adj fam* : lucky

suertudo[2], -da *n fam* : lucky person

suéter *nm* : sweater

suficiencia *nf* **1** : adequacy **2** : competence, fitness **3** : self-satisfaction

suficiente *adj* **1** BASTANTE : enough, sufficient ⟨tener suficiente : to have enough⟩ **2** : suitable, fit **3** : smug, complacent

suficientemente *adv* : sufficiently, enough

sufijo *nm* : suffix

suflé *nm* : soufflé

sufragar {52} *vt* **1** AYUDAR : to help out, to support **2** : to defray (costs) — *vi* : to vote

sufragio *nm* : suffrage, vote

sufrido, -da *adj* **1** : long-suffering, patient **2** : sturdy, serviceable (of clothing)

sufrimiento *nm* : suffering

sufrir *vt* **1** : to suffer ⟨sufrir una pérdida : to suffer a loss⟩ **2** : to tolerate, to put up with ⟨ella no lo puede sufrir : she can't stand him⟩ — *vi* : to suffer

sugerencia *nf* : suggestion

sugerente *adj* **1** : suggestive (of words, etc.), revealing (of clothes) **2** : intriguing, provocative

sugerir {76} *vt* **1** PROPONER, RECOMENDAR : to suggest, to recommend, to propose **2** : to suggest, to bring to mind

sugestión *nf*, *pl* **-tiones** : suggestion, prompting ⟨poder de sugestión : power of suggestion⟩

sugestionable *adj* : suggestible, impressionable

sugestionar *vt* : to influence, to sway — **sugestionarse** *vr* ~ **con** : to talk oneself into, to become convinced of

sugestivo, -va *adj* **1** : suggestive **2** : interesting, stimulating

suicida[1] *adj* : suicidal

suicida[2] *nmf* : suicide victim, suicide

suicidarse *vr* : to commit suicide
suicidio *nm* : suicide
suite *nf* : suite
suizo, -za *adj & n* : Swiss
sujeción *nf, pl* **-ciones** 1 : holding, fastening 2 : subjection
sujetador *nm* 1 : fastener 2 : holder ⟨sujetador de tazas : cup holder⟩
sujetalibros *nms & pl* : bookend
sujetapapeles *nms & pl* CLIP : paper clip
sujetar *vt* 1 : to hold on to, to steady, to hold down 2 FIJAR : to fasten, to attach 3 DOMINAR : to subdue, to conquer —
sujetarse *vr* 1 : to hold on, to hang on 2 ~ a : to abide by
sujeto¹, -ta *adj* 1 : secure, fastened 2 ~ a : subject to
**sujeto² ** *nm* 1 INDIVIDUO : individual, character 2 : subject (in grammar)
sulfúrico, -ca *adj* ácido sulfúrico → ácido²
sulfuro *nm* : sulfur
sultán *nm, pl* **sultanes** : sultan
suma *nf* 1 CANTIDAD : sum, quantity 2 : addition
sumamente *adv* : extremely, exceedingly
sumar *vt* 1 : to add, to add up 2 : to add up to, to total — *vi* : to add up —
sumarse *vr* ~ a : to join
sumariamente *adv* : summarily
sumario¹, -ria *adj* SUCINTO : succinct, summary
**sumario² ** *nm* : summary
sumergible *adj* : waterproof
sumergir {35} *vt* : to submerge, to immerse, to plunge — **sumergirse** *vr*
sumersión *nf, pl* **-siones** : submerging, immersion
sumidero *nm* : drain, sewer
suministrar *vt* : to supply, to provide
suministro *nm* : supply, provision
sumir *vt* SUMERGIR : to plunge, to immerse, to sink — **sumirse** *vr*
sumisión *nf, pl* **-siones** 1 : submission 2 : submissiveness
sumiso, -sa *adj* : submissive, acquiescent, docile
sumo, -ma *adj* 1 : extreme, great, high ⟨la suma autoridad : the highest authority⟩ 2 **a lo sumo** : at the most — **sumamente** *adv*
sunita *nmf* : Sunni
suntuoso, -sa *adj* : sumptuous, lavish — **suntuosamente** *adv*
supeditar *vt* SUBORDINAR : to subordinate — **supeditación** *nf*
super¹ or súper *adj fam* : super, great
**super² ** *nm* SUPERMERCADO : market, supermarket
super- *pref* : super-
superabundancia *nf* : overabundance — **superabundante** *adj*
superación *nf, pl* **-ciones** : surpassing, overcoming
superar *vt* 1 : to surpass, to exceed 2 : to overcome, to surmount — **superarse** *vr* : to improve oneself
superávit *nm, pl* **-vit** *or* **-vits** : surplus
superchería *nf* : trickery, fraud
supercomputadora *nf* : supercomputer

superdotado, -da *n* : a very talented person
superestrella *nf* : superstar
superestructura *nf* : superstructure
superficial *adj* : superficial — **superficialmente** *adv*
superficialidad *nf* : superficiality
superficie *nf* 1 : surface 2 : area ⟨la superficie de un triángulo : the area of a triangle⟩
superfluo, -flua *adj* : superfluous — **superfluidad** *nf*
superintendente *nmf* : supervisor, superintendent
**superior¹ ** *adj* 1 : superior 2 : upper ⟨nivel superior : upper level⟩ 3 : higher ⟨educación superior : higher education⟩ 4 ~ a : above, higher than, in excess of
**superior² ** *nm* : superior
superioridad *nf* : superiority
superlativo¹, -va *adj* : superlative
**superlativo² ** *nm* : superlative
supermercado *nm* : supermarket
superpoblación *nf, pl* **-ciones** : overpopulation
superpoblado, -da *adj* : overpopulated
superponer {60} *vt* : to superimpose
superpotencia *nf* : superpower
superproducción → **sobreproducción**
supersónico, -ca *adj* : supersonic
superstición *nf, pl* **-ciones** : superstition
supersticioso, -sa *adj* : superstitious
supervisar *vt* : to supervise, to oversee
supervisión *nf, pl* **-siones** : supervision
supervisor, -sora *n* : supervisor, overseer
supervivencia *nf* : survival
superviviente *nmf* : survivor
supino, -na *adj* : supine
suplantación *nf, pl* **-ciones** : supplanting, replacement ⟨suplantación de identidad : identity theft⟩
suplantar *vt* : to supplant, to replace
suplemental → **suplementario**
suplementario, -ria *adj* : supplementary, additional, extra
suplemento *nm* : supplement
suplencia *nf* : substitution, replacement
suplente *adj & nmf* : substitute ⟨equipo suplente : replacement team⟩
supletorio, -ria *adj* : extra, additional ⟨teléfono supletorio : extension phone⟩ ⟨cama supletoria : spare bed⟩
súplica *nf* : plea, entreaty
suplicar {72} *vt* IMPLORAR, ROGAR : to entreat, to implore, to supplicate
suplicio *nm* TORMENTO : ordeal, torture
suplir *vt* 1 COMPENSAR : to make up for, to compensate for 2 REEMPLAZAR : to replace, to substitute
supo, etc. → **saber**
suponer {60} *vt* 1 PRESUMIR : to suppose, to assume ⟨supongo que sí : I guess so, I suppose so⟩ ⟨se supone que van a llegar mañana : they're supposed to arrive tomorrow⟩ 2 : to imply, to suggest 3 : to involve, to entail ⟨el éxito supone mucho trabajo : success involves a lot of work⟩

suposición *nf, pl* **-ciones** PRESUNCIÓN : supposition, assumption

supositorio *nm* : suppository

supremacía *nf* : supremacy

supremo, -ma *adj* : supreme

supresión *nf, pl* **-siones** 1 : suppression, elimination 2 : deletion

suprimir *vt* 1 : to suppress, to eliminate 2 : to delete

supuestamente *adv* : supposedly, allegedly

supuesto, -ta *adj* 1 : supposed, alleged ⟨los supuestos expertos : the supposed experts⟩ ⟨un nombre supuesto : an assumed name⟩ 2 **por ~** : of course, absolutely

supurar *vi* : to ooze, to discharge

supuso, etc. → suponer

sur[1] *adj* : southern, southerly, south

sur[2] *nm* 1 : south, South 2 : south wind

surafricano, -na → sudafricano

suramericano, -na → sudamericano

surcar {72} *vt* 1 : to plow (through) 2 : to groove, to score, to furrow

surco *nm* : groove, furrow, rut

sureño[1], **-ña** *adj* : southern, Southern

sureño[2], **-ña** *n* : Southerner

sureste[1] *adj* 1 : southeast, southeastern 2 : southeasterly

sureste[2] *nm* : southeast, Southeast

surf *nm* : surfing

surfear *vi* : to surf

surfing → surf

surfista *nmf* : surfer

surgimiento *nm* : rise, emergence

surgir {35} *vi* : to rise, to arise, to emerge

suroeste[1] *adj* 1 : southwest, southwestern 2 : southwesterly

suroeste[2] *nm* : southwest, Southwest

surrealismo *nm* : surrealism

surrealista[1] *adj* : surreal, surrealistic

surrealista[2] *nmf* : surrealist

surtido[1], **-da** *adj* 1 : assorted, varied 2 : stocked, provisioned

surtido[2] *nm* : assortment, selection

surtidor *nm* 1 : jet, spout 2 *Arg, Chile, Spain* : gas pump

surtir *vt* 1 : to supply, to provide ⟨surtir un pedido : to fill an order⟩ 2 **surtir efecto** : to have an effect — *vi* : to spout, to spurt up — **surtirse** *vr* : to stock up

susceptible *adj* : susceptible, sensitive — **susceptibilidad** *nf*

suscitar *vt* : to provoke, to give rise to

suscribir {33} *vt* 1 : to sign (a formal document) 2 : to endorse, to sanction — **suscribirse** *vr* ~ **a** : to subscribe to

suscripción *nf, pl* **-ciones** 1 : subscription 2 : endorsement, sanction 3 : signing

suscriptor, -tora *n* : subscriber

susodicho, -cha *adj* : aforementioned, aforesaid

suspender *vt* 1 COLGAR : to suspend, to hang 2 : to suspend, to discontinue 3 : to suspend, to dismiss

suspense *nm Spain → suspenso*

suspensión *nf, pl* **-siones** : suspension

suspenso *nm* : suspense

suspensores *nmpl Chile* : suspenders

suspicacia *nf* : suspicion, mistrust

suspicaz *adj, pl* **-caces** DESCONFIADO : suspicious, wary

suspirar *vi* : to sigh

suspiro *nm* : sigh

surque, etc. → surcar

suscrito *pp → suscribir*

sustancia *nf* 1 : substance 2 **sin ~** : shallow, lacking substance

sustancial *adj* 1 : substantial 2 ESENCIAL, FUNDAMENTAL : essential, fundamental — **sustancialmente** *adv*

sustancioso, -sa *adj* 1 NUTRITIVO : hearty, nutritious 2 : substantial, solid

sustantivo *nm* : noun

sustentación *nf, pl* **-ciones** SOSTÉN : support

sustentar *vt* 1 : to support, to hold up 2 : to sustain, to nourish 3 : to maintain, to hold (an opinion) — **sustentarse** *vr* : to support oneself

sustento *nm* 1 : means of support, livelihood 2 : sustenance, food

sustitución *nf, pl* **-ciones** : replacement, substitution

sustituir {41} *vt* 1 : to replace, to substitute for 2 : to stand in for

sustituto, -ta *n* : substitute, stand-in

susto *nm* : fright, scare

sustracción *nf, pl* **-ciones** 1 RESTA : subtraction 2 : theft

sustraer {81} *vt* 1 : to remove, to take away 2 RESTAR : to subtract 3 : to steal — **sustraerse** *vr* ~ **a** : to avoid, to evade

susurrar *vi* 1 : to whisper 2 : to murmur 3 : to rustle (leaves, etc.) — *vt* : to whisper

susurro *nm* 1 : whisper 2 : murmur 3 : rustle, rustling

sutil *adj* 1 : delicate, thin, fine 2 : subtle — **sutilmente** *adv*

sutileza *nf* 1 : delicacy 2 : subtlety

sutura *nf* : suture, stitch

SUV [esu'bi, esju-] *nm, pl* **SUV** *or* **SUVs** [esu'bis, esju-] : SUV

suyo[1], **-ya** *adj* 1 : his, her, its, theirs ⟨los libros suyos : his books⟩ ⟨un amigo suyo : a friend of hers⟩ ⟨esta casa es suya : this house is theirs⟩ 2 (*formal*) : yours ⟨¿este abrigo es suyo, señor? : is this your coat, sir?⟩

suyo[2], **-ya** *pron* 1 : his, hers, theirs ⟨mi guitarra y la suya : my guitar and hers⟩ ⟨ellos trajeron las suyas : they brought theirs, they brought their own⟩ 2 (*formal*) : yours ⟨usted olvidó la suya : you forgot yours⟩

switch *nm* : switch

T

t *nf* : twenty-third letter of the Spanish alphabet

taba *nf* : anklebone

tabacalero[1], -ra *adj* : tobacco ⟨industria tabacalera : tobacco industry⟩

tabacalero[2], -ra *n* : tobacco grower

tabaco *nm* : tobacco

tábano *nm* : horsefly

tabaquería *nf* : tobacco shop

tabaquismo *nm* **tabaquismo pasivo** : passive smoking

taberna *nf* : tavern, bar

tabernáculo *nm* : tabernacle

tabernero, -ra *n* **1** : bar owner **2** : bartender

tabicar {72} *vt* : to wall up

tabique *nm* : thin wall, partition

tabla *nf* **1** : table, list ⟨tabla de multiplicar : multiplication table⟩ **2** : board, plank, slab ⟨tabla de planchar : ironing board⟩ **3** : plot, strip (of land) **4** : box pleat **5 tablas** *nfpl* : stage, boards *pl*

tablado *nm* **1** : floor **2** : platform, scaffold **3** : stage

tablao *nm* : flamenco bar

tablero *nm* **1** : bulletin board **2** : board (in games) ⟨tablero de damas : checkerboard⟩ ⟨tablero de circuitos : circuit board⟩ **3** PIZARRA : blackboard **4** : switchboard **5 tablero de instrumentos** : dashboard, instrument panel

tablet → **tableta 3**

tableta *nf* **1** : tablet, pill **2** : bar (of chocolate) **3** : tablet (computer)

tabletear *vi* : to rattle, to clack

tableteo *nm* : clack, rattling

tablilla *nf* **1** : small board or tablet **2** : bulletin board **3** : splint

tabloide *nm* : tabloid

tablón *nm*, *pl* **tablones 1** : plank, beam **2 tablón de anuncios** : bulletin board

tabú[1] *adj* : taboo

tabú[2] *nm*, *pl* **tabúes** *or* **tabús** : taboo

tabulador *nm* : tabulator

tabular[1] *vt* : to tabulate

tabular[2] *adj* : tabular

taburete *nm* : footstool, stool

tacañería *nf* : stinginess

tacaño[1], -ña *adj* MEZQUINO : stingy, miserly

tacaño[2], -ña *n* : miser, tightwad

tacha *nf* **1** : flaw, blemish, defect **2 poner tacha a** : to find fault with **3 sin ~** : flawless

tachadura *nf* : erasure, correction

tachar *vt* **1** : to cross out, to delete **2 ~ de** : to accuse of, to label as ⟨lo tacharon de mentiroso : they accused him of being a liar⟩

tacho *nm* *Arg, Chile, Ecua, Peru, Uru* **1** : wastebasket **2 ~ de (la) basura** : garbage can

tachón *nm*, *pl* **tachones** : stud, hobnail

tachonar *vt* : to stud

tachuela *nf* : tack, hobnail, stud

tácito, -ta *adj* : tacit, implicit — **tácitamente** *adv*

taciturno, -na *adj* **1** : taciturn **2** : sullen, gloomy

tacle *nm* : tackle

tacleada *nf* : tackle (in football)

taclear *vt* : to tackle (in football)

taco *nm* **1** : wad, stopper, plug **2** : pad (of paper) **3** : cleat **4** : heel (of a shoe) **5** : cue (in billiards) **6** : light snack, bite **7** : taco

tacón *nm*, *pl* **tacones** : heel (of a shoe) ⟨de tacón alto : high-heeled⟩

taconazo *nm* **1** PATADA : (heel) kick **2** : stamp, heel tap ⟨dar un taconazo : to click one's heels⟩

táctica *nf* : tactic, tactics *pl*

táctico, -ca *adj* : tactical

táctil *adj* : tactile

tacto *nm* **1** : touch, touching, feel **2** DELICADEZA : tact

tafeta *nf* *Arg, Mex, Uru* : taffeta

tafetán *nm*, *pl* **-tanes** : taffeta

tahúr *nm* : tahúres : gambler

tailandés[1], -desa *adj & n*, *pl* **-deses** : Thai

tailandés[2] *nm* : Thai (language)

taimado, -da *adj* **1** : crafty, sly **2** *Chile* : sullen, sulky

tajada *nf* **1** : slice **2 sacar tajada** *fam* : to get one's share

tajante *adj* **1** : cutting, sharp **2** : decisive, categorical

tajantemente *adj* : emphatically, categorically

tajar *vt* : to cut, to slice

tajear *vt* **1** : to cut **2** : to hack, to slash

tajo *nm* **1** : cut, slash, gash **2** ESCARPA : steep cliff

tal[1] *adv* **1** : so, in such a way **2 tal como** : just as ⟨tal como lo hice : just the way I did it⟩ **3 con tal que** : provided that, as long as **4 ¿qué tal?** : how are you?, how's it going?

tal[2] *adj* **1** : such, such a ⟨a tal grado : to such a degree⟩ ⟨de tal manera que : such that, in such a way that⟩ ⟨¡yo no dije tal cosa! : I said no such thing!⟩ **2** (*indicating an unspecified person or thing*) ⟨en tal día, a tal hora : on such and such a day at such and such a time⟩ ⟨un tal Pérez : a Mr. Pérez, some guy named Pérez⟩ **3 tal vez** : maybe, perhaps

tal[3] *pron* **1** : such a one, someone **2** : such a thing, something **3 tal para cual** : two of a kind

tala *nf* : felling (of trees)

taladradora *nf* : jackhammer

taladrar *vt* : to drill

taladro *nm* : drill, auger ⟨taladro eléctrico : power drill⟩

talante *nm* **1** HUMOR : mood, disposition **2** VOLUNTAD : will, willingness

talar *vt* **1** : to cut down, to fell **2** DEVASTAR : to devastate, to destroy

talco *nm* **1** : talc **2** : talcum powder

talego *nm* : sack

talento *nm* : talent, ability

talentoso, -sa *adj* : talented, gifted

talismán *nm, pl* **-manes** AMULETO : talisman, charm

talla *nf* **1** ESTATURA : height **2** : size (in clothing) **3** : stature, status **4** : sculpture, carving

tallar *vt* **1** : to sculpt, to carve **2** : to measure (someone's height) **3** : to deal (cards)

tallarín *nf, pl* **-rines** : noodle

talle *nm* **1** : size **2** : waist, waistline **3** : figure, shape

taller *nm* **1** : shop, workshop **2** : studio (of an artist)

tallo *nm* **1** : stalk, stem ⟨tallo de maíz : cornstalk⟩

talón *nm, pl* **talones** **1** : heel (of the foot) **2** : stub (of a check) **3** **talón de Aquiles** : Achilles' heel

talonario *nm* : checkbook

taltuza *nf* : gopher

talud *nm* **1** : slope, incline

tamal *nm* : tamale

tamaño¹, -ña *adj* : such a big ⟨¿crees tamaña mentira? : do you believe such a lie?⟩

tamaño² *nm* **1** : size **2** **de tamaño natural** : life-size

tamarindo *nm* : tamarind

tambaleante *adj* **1** : wobbly, unsteady, teetering **2** : staggering, swaying, tottering

tambalear *vi* ~ **tambalearse**

tambalearse *vr* **1** : to teeter **2** : to stagger, to sway, to totter

tambaleo *nm* : staggering, lurching, swaying

también *adv* : too, as well, also

tambor *nm* : drum

tamborilear *vi* : to drum, to tap

tamborileo *nm* : tapping, drumming

tamiz *nm* : sieve

tamizar {21} *vt* : to sift

tampoco *adv* : neither, not either ⟨ni yo tampoco : me neither⟩

tampón *nm, pl* **tampones** **1** : ink pad **2** : tampon

tam–tam *nm* : tom-tom

tan¹ *adv* **1** : so, so very ⟨no es tan difícil : it is not that difficult⟩ **2** : as ⟨tan pronto como : as soon as⟩ **3** **tan siquiera** : at least, at the least **4** **tan sólo** : only, merely

tan² *pron* **tan es así** : so much so

tanda *nf* **1** : turn, shift **2** : batch, lot, series

tándem *nm* **1** : tandem (bicycle) **2** : duo, pair

tangente *adj & nf* : tangent — **tangencial** *adj*

tangerina *nf* : tangerine

tangible *adj* : tangible

tango *nm* : tango

tanino *nm* : tannin

tanque *nm* **1** : tank ⟨buque tanque : tanker (ship)⟩ **2** : tank (vehicle)

tanteador *nm* MARCADOR : scoreboard

tantear *vt* **1** : to feel, to grope **2** : to size up, to weigh — *vi* **3** : to keep score **3** : to feel one's way

tanteo *nm* **1** : estimate, rough calculation **2** : testing, sizing up **3** : scoring

tanto¹ *adv* **1** : so much ⟨te quiero tanto : I love you so much⟩ ⟨ha cambiado tanto que no lo reconocí : he has changed so much that I didn't recognize him⟩ ⟨tanto mejor : so much the better⟩ **2** : so long ⟨¿por qué te tardaste tanto? : why did you take so long?⟩ **3** **tanto como** : as much as ⟨trabajo tanto como ella : I work as much as she does⟩ ⟨¿te gustó tanto como a mí? : did you like it as much as I did?⟩

tanto², -ta *adj* **1** : so much, so many, such ⟨no hagas tantas preguntas : don't ask so many questions⟩ ⟨tiene tanto encanto : he has such charm, he's so charming⟩ **2** : as much, as many ⟨come tantos dulces como yo : she eats as many sweets as I do⟩ **3** : odd, however many ⟨cuarenta y tantos años : forty-odd years⟩

tanto³ *nm* **1** : certain amount **2** : goal, point (in sports) **3** **al tanto** : abreast, in the picture **4** **un tanto** : somewhat, rather ⟨un tanto cansado : rather tired⟩

tanto⁴, -ta *pron* **1** : so much, so many ⟨tiene tanto que hacer : she has so much to do⟩ ⟨¡no me des tantos! : don't give me so many!⟩ **2** **en** ~ : while **3** **entre** ~ : meanwhile **4** **otro tanto** : again as much, again as many ⟨tiene un metro de ancho y otro tanto de altura : it's a meter wide and a meter high⟩ ⟨otro tanto podría decirse de . . .⟩ : the same can be said of . . .⟩ **5** **por lo tanto** : therefore **6** **tanto es así** : so much so

tañer {79} *vt* **1** : to ring (a bell) **2** : to play (a musical instrument)

tañido *nm* **1** CAMPANADA : ring, peal, toll **2** : sound (of an instrument)

tapa *nf* **1** : cover, top, lid **2** *Spain* : bar snack

tapacubos *nms & pl* : hubcap

tapadera *nf* **1** : cover, lid **2** : front, cover (for an organization or person)

tapar *vt* **1** CUBRIR : to cover, to cover up **2** OBSTRUIR : to block, to obstruct — **taparse** *vr*

taparrabos *nms & pl* : loincloth

tapete *nm* **1** : small rug, mat **2** : table cover **3** **poner sobre el tapete** : to bring up for discussion

tapia *nf* : (adobe) wall, garden wall

tapiar *vt* **1** : to wall in **2** : to enclose, to block off

tapicería *nf* **1** : upholstery **2** TAPIZ : tapestry

tapicero, -ra *n* : upholsterer

tapioca *nf* : tapioca

tapir *nm* : tapir

tapiz *nm, pl* **tapices** : tapestry

tapizado *nm* : upholstery

tapizar {21} *vt* **1** : to upholster **2** : to cover, to carpet

tapón *nm, pl* **tapones** **1** : cork **2** : bottle cap **3** : plug, stopper **4** *fam* : traffic jam **5** *Arg* : fuse

taponar *vt* : to block, to stop up

tapujo *nm* **1** : deceit, pretension **2** **sin tapujos** : openly, frankly

taquigrafía *nf* : stenography, shorthand
taquigráfico, -ca *adj* : stenographic
taquígrafo, -fa *n* : stenographer
taquilla *nf* **1** : box office, ticket office **2** : earnings *pl*, take
taquillero, -ra *adj* : box-office, popular ⟨un éxito taquillero : a box-office success⟩
tara *nf* : defect
tarántula *nf* : tarantula
tararear *vt* : to hum
tardanza *nf* : lateness, delay
tardar *vi* **1** : to take time, to delay ⟨tardaron en responder : they took a while to respond⟩ ⟨no tardes : don't take too long⟩ **2 a más tardar** : at the latest — *vt* DEMORAR **1** : to take (time) ⟨tarda una hora : it takes an hour⟩ ⟨tardar mucho : to take a long time⟩ ⟨tardar el doble : to take twice as long⟩ — **tardarse** *vr*
tarde¹ *adv* **1** : late **2 tarde o temprano** : sooner or later
tarde² *nf* **1** : afternoon, evening **2 ¡buenas tardes!** : good afternoon!, good evening! **3 en la tarde** *or* **por la tarde** : in the afternoon, in the evening
tardío, -día *adj* : late, tardy
tardo, -da *adj* : slow
tarea *nf* **1** : task, job **2** : homework
tarifa *nf* **1** : rate ⟨tarifas postales : postal rates⟩ **2** : fare (for transportation) **3** : price list **4** ARANCEL : duty
tarima *nf* PLATAFORMA : dais, platform, stage
tarjeta *nf* : card ⟨tarjeta de crédito/débito : credit/debit card⟩ ⟨tarjeta postal : postcard⟩ ⟨tarjeta de felicitación : greeting card⟩ ⟨tarjeta navideña, tarjeta de Navidad : Christmas card⟩ ⟨tarjeta de video/memoria : video/memory card⟩ ⟨tarjeta de visita : business card, calling card⟩
taro *nm* : taro
tarrina *nf* : tub
tarro *nm* **1** : jar, pot **2** *Arg, Chile, CoRi, Uru* : can, tin
tarta *nf* **1** : tart **2** *Spain* : cake
tartaleta *nf* : tart
tartamudear *vi* : to stammer, to stutter
tartamudeo *nm* : stutter, stammer
tartamudo¹, -da *adj* : stuttering, stammering
tartamudo², -da *n* : person who stutters or stammers
tartán *nm, pl* **tartanes** : tartan, plaid
tártaro *nm* : tartar
tartera *nf* *Spain* : lunch box
tasa *nf* **1** : rate ⟨tasa de desempleo : unemployment rate⟩ **2** : tax, fee **3** : appraisal, valuation
tasación *nf, pl* **-ciones** : appraisal, assessment
tasador, -dora *n* : assessor, appraiser
tasajo *nm* : dried beef, beef jerky
tasar *vt* **1** VALORAR : to appraise, to value **2** : to set the price of **3** : to ration, to limit
tasca *nf* : cheap bar, dive
tatarabuela *nf* : great-great-grandmother
tatarabuelo *nm* : great-great-grandfather
tatuaje *nm* : tattoo, tattooing

tatuar {3} *vt* : to tattoo
taurino, -na *adj* : bull, bullfighting
Tauro¹ *nm* : Taurus (sign or constellation)
Tauro² *nmf* : Taurus (person)
tauromaquia *nf* : (art of) bullfighting
taxi *nm, pl* **taxis** : taxi, taxicab
taxidermia *nf* : taxidermy
taxidermista *nmf* : taxidermist
taxista *nmf* : taxi driver
taza *nf* **1** : cup **2** : cupful **3** : (toilet) bowl **4** : basin (of a fountain)
tazón *nm, pl* **tazones** **1** : bowl **2** : large cup, mug
te¹ *nf* : (letter) t
te² *pron* **1** : you ⟨te quiero : I love you⟩ **2** : for you, to you, from you ⟨me gustaría dártelo : I would like to give it to you⟩ **3** : yourself, for yourself, to yourself, from yourself ¡cálmate! : calm yourself!⟩ ⟨¿te guardaste uno? : did you keep one for yourself?⟩ **4** : thee
té *nm* **1** : tea **2** : tea party
tea *nf* : torch
teatral *adj* : theatrical — **teatralmente** *adv*
teatro *nm* **1** : theater **2 hacer teatro** : to put on an act, to exaggerate
teca *nf* : teak
techado *nm* **1** : roof **2 bajo techado** : under cover, indoors
techar *vt* : to roof, to shingle
techo *nm* **1** TEJADO : roof **2** : ceiling **3** : upper limit, ceiling
techumbre *nf* : roofing
tecla *nf* **1** : key (of a musical instrument or a machine) **2 dar en la tecla** : to hit the nail on the head
teclado *nm* **1** : keyboard **2 teclado numérico** : (number) keypad
teclear *vt* : to type in, to enter
técnica *nf* **1** : technique, skill **2** : technology
técnico¹, -ca *adj* : technical — **técnicamente** *adv*
técnico², -ca *n* : technician, expert, engineer
tecnología *nf* : technology
tecnológico, -ca *adj* : technological — **tecnológicamente** *adv*
tecolote *nm* *Mex* : owl
tedio *nm* : tedium, boredom
tedioso, -sa *adj* : tedious, boring — **tediosamente** *adv*
tee ['ti] *nm* : tee (in golf)
teja *nf* : tile
tejado *nm* TECHO : roof
tejanos *nmpl* : jeans
tejar *vt* : to tile
tejedor, -dora *n* : weaver
tejemaneje *nm* **1** : intrigue, machination **2** : fuss, commotion
tejer *vt* **1** : to knit, to crochet **2** : to weave **3** FABRICAR : to concoct, to make up, to fabricate
tejido *nm* **1** TELA : fabric, cloth **2** : weave, texture **3** : tissue ⟨tejido muscular : muscle tissue⟩
tejo *nm* **1** : yew **2** : hopscotch (children's game)
tejón *nm, pl* **tejones** : badger

tela *nf* **1** : fabric, cloth, material **2 tela de araña** : spiderweb **3 poner en tela de juicio** : to call into question, to doubt
telar *nm* : loom
telaraña *nf* : spiderweb, cobweb
tele *nf fam* : TV, television
telecomunicación *nf, pl* **-ciones** : telecommunication
teleconferencia *nf* : teleconference
telediario *nm Spain* : news, news program
teledifusión *nf, pl* **-siones** : television broadcasting
teledirigido, -da *adj* : remote-controlled
teleférico *nm* : cable car
telefonazo *nm fam* : (telephone) call
telefonear *v* : to telephone, to call
telefónico, -ca *adj* : phone, telephone ⟨llamada telefónica : phone call⟩
telefonista *nmf* : telephone operator
teléfono *nm* **1** : telephone ⟨contestar el teléfono : to answer the phone⟩ ⟨número de teléfono : phone number⟩ ⟨teléfono celular : cell phone, mobile phone⟩ **2 llamar por teléfono** : to telephone, to make a phone call
telegrafiar {85} *v* : to telegraph
telégrafo *nm* : telegraph
telegrama *nm* : telegram
telemárketing *nm* : telemarketing
telenovela *nf* : soap opera
telepatía *nf* : telepathy
telepático, -ca *adj* : telepathic — **telepáticamente** *adv*
telerrealidad *nf* : reality TV, reality television
telescópico, -ca *adj* : telescopic
telescopio *nm* : telescope
telesilla *nmf* : ski lift
telespectador, -dora *n* : (television) viewer
telesquí *nm, pl* **-squís** : ski lift
televidente *nmf* : (television) viewer
televisar *vt* : to televise
televisión *nf, pl* **-siones** : television, TV ⟨televisión de alta definición : high definition television⟩ ⟨hay un programa de ciencia en la televisión : there's a science program on TV⟩
televisivo, -va *adj* : television ⟨serie televisiva : television series⟩
televisor *nm* : television set
telón *nm, pl* **telones 1** : curtain (in the theater) **2 telón de fondo** : backdrop, background
tema *nm* **1** ASUNTO : theme, topic, subject **2** MOTIVO : motif, central theme
temario *nm* **1** : set of topics (for study) **2** : agenda
temática *nf* : subject matter
temático, -ca *adj* : thematic
temblar {55} *vi* **1** : to tremble, to shake, to shiver ⟨le temblaban las rodillas : his knees were shaking⟩ **2** : to shudder, to be afraid ⟨tiemblo con sólo pensarlo : I shudder to think of it⟩
temblor *nm* **1** : shaking, trembling **2** : tremor, earthquake
temblorosamente *adv* : shakily
tembloroso, -sa *adj* : tremulous, trembling, shaking ⟨con la voz temblorosa : with a shaky voice⟩

temer *vt* : to fear, to dread ⟨temíamos lo peor : we feared the worst⟩ — *vi* : to be afraid ⟨temer por alguien/algo : to fear for someone/something⟩ — **temerse** *vr*
temerario, -ria *adj* : reckless, rash — **temerariamente** *adv*
temeridad *nf* **1** : temerity, recklessness, rashness **2** : rash act
temeroso, -sa *adj* MIEDOSO : fearful, frightened
temible *adj* : fearsome, dreadful
temor *nm* MIEDO : fear, dread
témpano *nm* : ice floe
temperamento *nm* : temperament — **temperamental** *adj*
temperancia *nf* : temperance
temperar *vt* MODERAR : to temper, to moderate — *vi* : to have a change of air
temperatura *nf* : temperature
tempestad *nf* **1** : storm, tempest **2 tempestad de arena** : sandstorm
tempestuoso, -sa *adj* : tempestuous, stormy
templado, -da *adj* **1** : temperate, mild **2** : moderate, restrained **3** : warm, warm **4** VALIENTE : courageous, bold
templanza *nf* **1** : temperance, moderation **2** : mildness (of weather)
templar *vt* **1** : to temper (steel) **2** : to restrain, to moderate **3** : to tune (a musical instrument) **4** : to warm up, to cool down — **templarse** *vr* **1** : to be moderate **2** : to warm up, to cool down
temple *nm* **1** : temper (of steel, etc.) **2** HUMOR : mood ⟨de buen temple : in a good mood⟩ **3** : tuning **4** VALOR : courage
templo *nm* **1** : temple **2** : church, chapel
tempo *nm* : tempo (in music)
temporada *nf* **1** : season, time ⟨temporada de béisbol : baseball season⟩ **2** : period, spell ⟨por temporadas : on and off⟩
temporal[1] *adj* **1** : temporal **2** : temporary
temporal[2] *nm* **1** : storm **2 capear el temporal** : to weather the storm
temporalmente *adv* : temporarily
temporario, -ria *adj* : temporary — **temporariamente** *adv*
temporero[1] **, -ra** *adj* : temporary, seasonal
temporero[2] **, -ra** *n* : temporary or seasonal worker
temporizador *nm* : timer
tempranero, -ra *adj* : early
temprano[1] *adv* : early ⟨lo más temprano posible : as soon as possible⟩ ⟨por la mañana temprano : early in the morning⟩
temprano[2] **, -na** *adj* : early ⟨la parte temprana del siglo : the early part of the century⟩
ten → **tener**
tenacidad *nf* : tenacity, perseverance
tenacillas *nfpl* **1** : tongs **2** : curling iron (for hair)
tenaz *adj, pl* **tenaces 1** : tenacious, persistent **2** : strong, tough
tenaza *nf, or* **tenazas** *nfpl* **1** : pliers, pincers **2** : tongs **3** : claw (of a crustacean)
tenazmente *adv* : tenaciously
tendedero *nm* : clothesline

tendencia *nf* **1** PROPENSIÓN : tendency, inclination **2** : trend

tendencioso, -sa *adj* : biased

tendente → tendiente

tender {56} *vt* **1** EXTENDER : to spread out, to lay out **2** EXTENDER : to extend, to hold out (one's hand) **3** : to hang out (clothes) **4** : to run (cables, etc.) **5** : to set (a trap) **6** : to set (a table), to make (a bed) — *vi* ~ **a** : to tend to, to have a tendency towards — **tenderse** *vr* : to stretch out, to lie down

tenderete *nm* : (market) stall

tendero, -ra *n* : shopkeeper, storekeeper

tendido *nm* **1** : laying (of cables, etc.) **2** : seats *pl*, section (at a bullfight)

tendiente *adj* ~ **a** : aimed at, designed to

tendón *nm, pl* **tendones** : tendon

tendrá, etc. → tener

tenebrosidad *nf* : darkness, gloom

tenebroso, -sa *adj* **1** OSCURO : gloomy, dark **2** SINIESTRO : sinister

tenedor[1], -dora *n* : holder **2 tenedor de libros, tenedora de libros** : bookkeeper

tenedor[2] *nm* : table fork

teneduría *nf* **teneduría de libros** : book-keeping

tenencia *nf* **1** : possession, holding **2** : tenancy **3** : tenure

tener {80} *vt* **1** : to have ⟨tiene un coche azul : he has a blue car⟩ ⟨¿lo tienes contigo? : do you have it with you?⟩ ⟨tienen tres hijos : they have three children⟩ ⟨tiene ojos verdes : she has green eyes⟩ ⟨tiene mucha experiencia : he has a lot of experience⟩ ⟨¿tiene hora? : do you have the time?, can you tell me what time it is?⟩ **2** : to have (available) ⟨tener dinero/tiempo para : to have money/time for⟩ ⟨no tuve más remedio : I had no choice⟩ **3** : to have (plans, etc.) ⟨tengo mucho que hacer : I have a lot to do⟩ ⟨hoy tiene clase : he has class today⟩ **4** : to have, to cause (consequences, etc.) **5** (*indicating age*) ⟨tiene veinte años : he's twenty years old⟩ **6** (*indicating dimensions*) ⟨tiene un metro de largo : it's one meter long⟩ **7** (*expressing thoughts, feelings, or sensations*) ⟨tengo frío/hambre/miedo : I'm cold/hungry/scared⟩ ⟨no tengo ni idea : I have no idea⟩ ⟨tengo confianza en ti : I have confidence in you⟩ ⟨eso nos tiene contentos : that makes us happy⟩ **8** : to have (an illness or injury) **9** : to have, to experience (problems, etc.) ⟨tuve un buen día : I had a good day⟩ **10** : to have, to receive (news, etc.) **11** : to have, to show (a quality) ⟨tienes razón : you're right⟩ ⟨eso no tiene sentido : that doesn't make sense⟩ ⟨no tiene nada de malo/raro : there's nothing bad/strange about it⟩ **12** : to have, to include ⟨el libro tiene 500 páginas : the book has 500 pages⟩ **13** : to use, to exercise ⟨tener cuidado : to be careful⟩ **14** (*indicating condition*) ⟨tenía la camisa manchada : his shirt was stained⟩ **15** (*indicating position*) ⟨tenía las manos en los bolsillos : she had her hands in her pockets⟩ **16** : to hold ⟨ten

esto : hold this⟩ **17** : to have, to give birth to **18** ~ **por** : to think, to consider ⟨me tienes por loco : you think I'm crazy⟩ — *v aux* **1 tener que** : to have to ⟨tengo que salir : I have to leave⟩ ⟨tiene que estar aquí : it has to be here, it must be here⟩ **2** (*with past participle*) ⟨tenía pensado escribirte : I've been thinking of writing to you⟩ **3** (*in expressions of time*) ⟨tengo diez años haciendo esto : I have been doing this for ten years⟩ ⟨tiene años de estar aquí : it's been here for years⟩ — **tenerse** *vr* **1** : to stand up **2** ~ **por** : to consider oneself ⟨me tengo por afortunado : I consider myself lucky⟩

tenería *nf* CURTIDURÍA : tannery

tenga, etc. → tener

tenia *nf* SOLITARIA : tapeworm

teniente *nmf* **1** : lieutenant **2 teniente coronel** : lieutenant colonel

tenis *nms & pl* **1** : tennis **2 tenis** *nmpl* : sneakers *pl*

tenista *nmf* : tennis player

tenor *nm* **1** : tenor **2** : tone, sense

tensar *vt* **1** : to tense, to make taut **2** : to draw (a bow) — **tensarse** *vr* : to become tense

tensión *nf, pl* **tensiones** **1** : tension, tautness **2** : stress, strain **3 tensión arterial** : blood pressure **4** : voltage, tension ⟨de alta tensión : high-tension⟩

tenso, -sa *adj* : tense — **tensamente** *adv*

tentación *nf, pl* **-ciones** : temptation ⟨caer en la tentación : to give in to temptation⟩ ⟨caer en la tentación de : to be tempted into⟩ ⟨resistir la tentación de : to resist the temptation to⟩

tentáculo *nm* : tentacle, feeler

tentador[1], -dora *adj* : tempting

tentador[2], -dora *n* : tempter, temptress *f*

tentar {55} *vt* **1** TOCAR : to feel, to touch **2** PROBAR : to test, to try **3** ATRAER : to tempt, to entice

tentativa *nf* : attempt, try

tentempié *nm fam* : snack, bite

tenue *adj* **1** : tenuous **2** : faint, weak, dim **3** : light, fine **4** : thin, slender

teñir {67} *vt* **1** : to dye **2** : to stain

teología *nf* : theology

teológico, -ca *adj* : theological

teólogo, -ga *n* : theologian

teorema *nm* : theorem

teoría *nf* : theory

teórico[1], -ca *adj* : theoretical — **teóricamente** *adv*

teórico[2], -ca *n* : theorist

teorizar {21} *vi* : to theorize

tepe *nm* : sod, turf

teponaztle *nm Mex* : traditional drum

tequila *nm* : tequila

terapeuta *nmf* : therapist

terapéutica *nf* : therapeutics

terapéutico, -ca *adj* : therapeutic

terapia *nf* **1** : therapy **2 terapia intensiva** : intensive care

tercer → tercero

tercermundista *adj* : third-world

tercero[1], -ra *adj* (**tercer** *before masculine singular nouns*) **1** : third ⟨el tercer piso/grado : the third floor/grade⟩ ⟨una/la

tercera parte de : a third of, one third of⟩
2 el Tercer Mundo : the Third World
tercero², -ra n : third (in a series)
terceto nm 1 : triplet (in literature) 2 : trio (in music)
terciar vt 1 : to place diagonally 2 : to divide into three parts — vi 1 : to mediate 2 ~ en : to take part in
terciario, -ria adj : tertiary
tercio¹, -cia → tercero
tercio² nm : third ⟨dos tercios : two thirds⟩
terciopelo nm : velvet
terco, -ca adj OBSTINADO : obstinate, stubborn
tergiversación nf, pl -ciones : distortion
tergiversar vt : to distort, to twist
termal adj : thermal, hot
termas nfpl : hot springs
térmico, -ca adj : thermal, heat ⟨energía térmica : thermal energy⟩
terminación nf, pl -ciones : termination, conclusion
terminal¹ adj : terminal — terminalmente adv
terminal² nm (in some regions f) : (electric or electronic) terminal
terminal³ nf (in some regions m) : terminal, station
terminante adj : final, definitive, categorical — terminantemente adv
terminar vt 1 CONCLUIR : to end, to conclude 2 ACABAR : to complete, to finish off — vi 1 : to finish 2 : to stop, to end — terminarse vr 1 : to run out 2 : to come to an end
término nm 1 CONCLUSIÓN : end, conclusion 2 : term, expression 3 : period, term of office 4 : place, position ⟨en primer término : first of all⟩ 5 término medio : happy medium 6 por término medio : on average 7 términos nmpl : terms, specifications ⟨los términos del acuerdo : the terms of the agreement⟩
terminología nf : terminology
termita nf : termite
termo nm : thermos
termodinámica nf : thermodynamics
termómetro nm : thermometer
termostato nm : thermostat
ternera nf : veal
ternero, -ra n : calf
terno nm 1 : set of three 2 : three-piece suit
ternura nf : tenderness
terquedad nf OBSTINACIÓN : obstinacy, stubbornness
terracota nf : terra-cotta
terraplén nm, pl -plenes : terrace, embankment
terráqueo, -quea adj 1 : earth 2 globo terráqueo : the earth, globe (of the earth)
terrateniente nmf : landowner
terraza nf 1 : terrace, veranda 2 : balcony (in a theater) 3 : terrace (in agriculture)
terremoto nm : earthquake
terrenal adj : worldly, earthly
terreno nm 1 : terrain 2 SUELO : earth, ground 3 : plot, tract of land 4 perder

terreno : to lose ground 5 preparar el terreno : to pave the way
terrestre adj : terrestrial
terrible adj : terrible, horrible — terriblemente adv
terrier nmf : terrier
territorial adj : territorial
territorio nm : territory
terrón nm, pl terrones 1 : clod (of earth) 2 terrón de azúcar : lump of sugar
terror nm : terror
terrorífico, -ca adj : horrific, terrifying
terrorismo nm : terrorism
terrorista adj & nmf : terrorist
terroso, -sa adj : earthy ⟨colores terrosos : earthy colors⟩
terruño nm : native land, homeland
terso, -sa adj 1 : smooth 2 : glossy, shiny 3 : polished, flowing (of a style)
tersura nf 1 : smoothness 2 : shine
tertulia nf : gathering, group ⟨tertulia literaria : literary circle⟩
tesauro nm : thesaurus
tesis nfs & pl : thesis
tesón nm : persistence, tenacity
tesonero, -ra adj : persistent, tenacious
tesorería nf : treasurer's office
tesorero, -ra n : treasurer
tesoro nm 1 : treasure 2 : thesaurus 3 : treasury
test nm : test
testaferro nm : figurehead
testamentario, -ria n ALBACEA : executor
testamento nm : testament, will
testar vi : to draw up a will
testarudo, -da adj : stubborn, pigheaded
testículo nm : testicle
testificar {72} v : to testify
testigo nmf 1 : witness 2 testigo presencial : eyewitness
testimonial adj 1 : testimonial 2 : token
testimoniar vi : to testify
testimonio nm : testimony, statement
teta nf : teat
tétano or tétanos nm : tetanus, lockjaw
tetera nf 1 : teapot 2 : teakettle
tetilla nf 1 : teat 2 : nipple
tetina : nipple (on a bottle)
tétrico, -ca adj : somber, gloomy
textil adj & nm : textile
texto nm : text
textual adj : literal, exact — textualmente adv
textura nf : texture
tez nf, pl teces : complexion, coloring
ti pron 1 : you ⟨es para ti : it's for you⟩ 2 ti mismo, ti misma : yourself 3 : thee
tía → tío
tiamina nf : thiamine
tianguis nm Mex : open-air market
tibetano¹, -na adj & n : Tibetan
tibetano² nm : Tibetan (language)
tibia nf : tibia
tibieza nf 1 : warmth, mildness 2 : lack of enthusiasm, coolness, indifference
tibio, -bia adj 1 : lukewarm, tepid 2 : cool, unenthusiastic
tiburón nm, pl -rones 1 : shark 2 : raider (in finance)
tic nm 1 : click, tick 2 tic nervioso : tic

tico, -ca adj & n fam : Costa Rican
tictac nm **1** : ticking, tick-tock **2 hacer tictac** : to tick
tiembla, etc. → **temblar**
tiempo nm **1** : time ⟨justo a tiempo : just in time⟩ ⟨ahorrar/matar/perder tiempo : to save/kill/waste time⟩ ⟨ganar tiempo : to buy time⟩ ⟨tiempo libre : spare time⟩ ⟨al poco tiempo : soon after⟩ ⟨al tiempo que : (while) at the same time⟩ ⟨con tiempo : in good time, in advance⟩ ⟨con el tiempo : in/with/over time⟩ ⟨no tengo tiempo, no me da tiempo : I don't have time⟩ ⟨hace tiempo que vive aquí : she has lived here for a while⟩ ⟨desde hace mucho tiempo : for quite a while⟩ **2** : period of time ⟨un tiempo de : a period of⟩ ⟨esperamos un tiempo : we waited a while⟩ ⟨cada cierto tiempo : every so often⟩ ⟨en los tiempos que corren : nowadays⟩ **3** : season, moment ⟨antes de tiempo : prematurely⟩ ⟨fuera de tiempo : at the wrong time⟩ ⟨hace buen tiempo : the weather is fine, it's nice outside⟩ **4** : weather **5 tierra firme** : dry/solid ground **6** : tempo (in music) **6** : tempo (in music) **7** : tense (in grammar) **8** : half (in sports) ⟨medio tiempo : half-time⟩ **9 medio tiempo** or **tiempo parcial** ⟨un empleo de medio tiempo, un empleo a tiempo parcial : a part-time job⟩ ⟨trabajar medio tiempo, trabajar a tiempo parcial : to work part-time⟩ **10 tiempo compartido** : timeshare **11 tiempo completo** : full-time ⟨un empleo de tiempo completo : a full-time job⟩ ⟨trabajar a/de tiempo completo : to work full-time⟩
tienda nf **1** : store, shop **2** or **tienda de campaña** : tent
tiende, etc. → **tender**
tiene, etc. → **tener**
tienta¹, etc. → **tentar**
tienta² nf **andar a tientas** : to feel one's way, to grope around
tiernamente adv : tenderly
tierno, -na adj **1** : affectionate, tender **2** : tender, young
tierra nf **1** : land ⟨vender tierra : to sell land⟩ **2** SUELO : ground, earth ⟨camino de tierra : dirt road⟩ ⟨tomar tierra : to land⟩ ⟨caer a tierra : to fall to earth⟩ **3** : country, homeland, soil **4 tierra adentro** : inland **5 tierra firme** : dry/solid ground **6 tierra natal** : native land **7 tierras altas** : highlands **8 tierras bajas** : lowlands **9 la Tierra** : the Earth
tieso, -sa adj **1** : stiff, rigid **2** : upright, erect
tiesto nm MACETA : flowerpot
tiesura nf : stiffness, rigidity
tifoideo, -dea adj : typhoid ⟨fiebre tifoidea : typhoid fever⟩
tifón nm, pl **tifones** : typhoon
tifus nm : typhus
tigre, -gresa n **1** : tiger, tigress f **2** : jaguar
tijera nf **1** or **tijeras** nfpl : scissors **2 de ~** : folding ⟨escalera de tijera : stepladder⟩
tijereta nf : earwig

tijeretada nf or **tijeretazo** nm : cut, snip
tila nf : lime blossom tea
tildar vt **~ de** : to brand as, to call ⟨lo tildaron de traidor : they branded him as a traitor⟩
tilde nf **1** : accent mark **2** : tilde (accent over ñ)
tilín nm, pl **tilines** : tinkle
tilo nm : linden (tree)
timador, -dora n : swindler
timar vt : to swindle, to cheat
timbal nm **1** : kettledrum **2 timbales** nmpl : timpani
timbre nm **1** : bell ⟨tocar el timbre : to ring the doorbell⟩ **2** : tone, timbre **3** SELLO : seal, stamp **4** CA, Mex : postage stamp
timidez nf : timidity, shyness
tímido, -da adj : timid, shy — **tímidamente** adv
timo nm fam : swindle, trick, hoax
timón nm, pl **timones** : rudder ⟨estar al timón : to beat the helm⟩
timonel nm : coxswain
timorato, -ta adj **1** : timorous **2** : sanctimonious
tímpano nm **1** : eardrum **2 tímpanos** nmpl : timpani, kettledrums
tina nf **1** BAÑERA : tub, bathtub **2** : vat
tinaco nm Mex : water tank
tinaja nf : large clay pot/jar
tinieblas nfpl **1** OSCURIDAD : darkness **2** : ignorance
tino nm **1** : good judgment, sense **2** : tact, sensitivity, insight
tinta nf : ink
tinte nm **1** : dye, coloring **2** : overtone ⟨tintes raciales : racial overtones⟩
tintero nm **1** : inkwell **2 quedarse en el tintero** : to remain unsaid
tintinear vt : to jingle, to clink, to tinkle
tintineo nm : clink, jingle, tinkle
tinto, -ta adj **1** : dyed, stained ⟨tinto en sangre : bloodstained⟩ **2** : red (of wine)
tintorería nf : dry cleaner (service)
tintura nf **1** : dye, tint **2** : tincture ⟨tintura de yodo : tincture of iodine⟩
tiña, etc. → **teñir**
tiña nf : ringworm
tío, tía n : uncle m, aunt f
tiovivo nm : merry-go-round
tipear vt (in various countries) : to type
tipi nm : tepee
típico, -ca adj : typical — **típicamente** adv
tipificar {72} vt **1** : to classify, to categorize **2** : to typify
tiple nm : soprano
tipo¹ nm **1** CLASE : type, kind, sort **2** : figure, build, appearance **3** : rate ⟨tipo de interés : interest rate⟩ **4** : (printing) type, typeface **5** : style, model ⟨un vestido tipo 60's : a 60's-style dress⟩
tipo², -pa n fam : guy m, gal f, character
tipografía nf : typography, printing
tipográfico, -ca adj : typographic, typographical
tipógrafo, -fa n : printer, typographer
tique or **tiquet** nm **1** : ticket **2** : receipt

tira *nf* **1** : strip, strap **2 tira cómica** : comic, comic strip

tirabuzón *nf, pl* **-zones** : corkscrew

tirachinas *nms & pl* : slingshot

tirada *nf* **1** : throw **2** : distance, stretch **3** IMPRESIÓN : printing, issue

tiradero *nm Mex* **1** : dump **2** : mess, clutter

tirado, -da *adj Spain fam* **1** : dirt cheap **2** : very easy

tirador[1] *nm* : handle, knob

tirador[2], **-dora** *n* : marksman *m*, markswoman *f*

tiragomas *nms & pl* : slingshot

tiranía *nf* : tyranny

tiránico, -ca *adj* : tyrannical

tiranizar {21} *vt* : to tyrannize

tirano[1], **-na** *adj* : tyrannical, despotic

tirano[2], **-na** *n* : tyrant

tirante[1] *adj* **1** : tense, strained **2 tirantes** *nmpl* : suspenders

tirante[2] *nm* **1** : shoulder strap **2 tirantes** *nmpl* : suspenders

tirantez *nf* **1** : tautness **2** : tension, friction, strain

tirar *vt* **1** : to throw, to hurl, to toss ⟨tírame la pelota : throw/toss me the ball⟩ **2** BOTAR : to throw away/out (garbage), to waste (money, etc.) **3** DERRIBAR : to knock down **4** : to shoot, to fire, to launch (a rocket), to drop (a bomb) **5** : to shoot (in sports) **6** *Car, Spain* : to take (a photo) **7** : to print, to run off **8** *Arg, Chile, Uru* : to pull — *vi* **1** : to pull, to draw **2** : to shoot ⟨tirar a matar : to shoot to kill⟩ **3** : to shoot (in sports) **4** : to attract **5** : to get by, to manage ⟨va tirando : he's managing along, he's managing⟩ **6** ~ **a** : to tend towards, to be rather ⟨tira a picante : it's a bit spicy⟩ — **tirarse** *vr* **1** : to throw oneself **2** *fam* : to spend (time)

tiritar *vi* : to shiver, to tremble

tiro *nm* **1** BALAZO, DISPARO : shot, gunshot ⟨pegarle un tiro a alguien : to shoot someone⟩ ⟨matar a alguien a tiros : to shoot someone dead⟩ ⟨errar el tiro : to miss the mark⟩ **2** : shot, kick (in sports) ⟨tiro libre : free shot/throw/kick⟩ ⟨tiro penal : penalty shot/kick⟩ **3** : flue **4** : team (of horses, etc.) **5 a ~** : within range ⟨ponerse a tiro : to come within range⟩ ⟨estar a tiro : to be within range, to be within reach⟩ **6 al tiro** : right away **7 tiro de gracia** : coup de grâce, death blow

tiroideo, -dea *adj* : thyroid

tiroides *nmf* : thyroid, thyroid gland — **tiroides** *adj*

tirolés, -lesa *adj* : Tyrolean

tirón *nm, pl* **tirones 1** : pull, tug, yank **2 de un tirón** : all at once, in one go **3 tirón de orejas** : slap on the wrist, minor punishment

tiroteo *nm* **1** : shooting **2** : gunfight, shoot-out

tirria *nf* **tener tirria a** *fam* : to have a grudge against

titánico, -ca *adj* : titanic, huge

titanio *nm* : titanium

títere *nm* : puppet

tití *nm, pl* **tití** *or* **titíes** *or* **titís** : marmoset

titilar *vi* : to twinkle, to flicker

titileo *nm* : twinkle, flickering

titiritero, -ra *n* **1** : puppeteer **2** : acrobat

tito, tita *n fam* : uncle *m*, auntie *f*

titubear *vi* **1** : to hesitate **2** : to stutter, to stammer — **titubeante** *adj*

titubeo *nm* **1** : hesitation **2** : stammering

titulado, -da *adj* **1** : titled, entitled **2** : qualified

titular[1] *vt* : to title, to entitle — **titularse** *vr* **1** : to be called, to be entitled **2** : to receive a degree

titular[2] *adj* : titular, official

titular[3] *nm* : headline

titular[4] *nmf* **1** : owner, holder **2** : office-holder, incumbent

titularidad *nf* **1** : ownership, title **2** : position, office (with a title) **3** : starting position (in sports)

título *nm* **1** : title **2** : degree, qualification **3** : security, bond **4 a título de** : by way of, in the capacity of

tiza *nf* : chalk

tiznar *vt* : to blacken (with soot, etc.)

tizne *nm* HOLLÍN : soot

tiznón *nm, pl* **tiznones** : stain, smudge

tlapalería *nf Mex* : hardware store

TNT *nm* (trinitrotolueno) : TNT

toalla *nf* **1** : towel **2 tirar la toalla** : to throw in the towel

toallita *nf* : washcloth

tobillo *nm* : ankle

tobogán *nm, pl* **-ganes 1** : toboggan, sled **2** : slide, chute

tocadiscos *nms & pl* : record player

tocado[1], **-da** *adj* **1** : bad, bruised (of fruit) **2** *fam* : touched, not all there

tocado[2] *nm* : headdress

tocador[1] *nm* **1** : dressing table, vanity table **2 artículos de tocador** : toiletries

tocador[2], **-dora** *n* : player (of music)

tocante *adj* ~ **a** : with regard to, regarding

tocar {72} *vt* **1** : to touch, to feel, to handle **2** : to touch on, to refer to **3** : to concern, to affect **4** : to play (a musical instrument) **5** : to ring (a bell), to sound **6 tocar fondo** : to hit/reach rock bottom — *vi* **1** : to knock ⟨tocar a la puerta : to knock on the door⟩ **2** : to sound, to ring ⟨tocó el timbre : the doorbell rang⟩ **3** : to fall to, to be up to, to be one's turn ⟨¿a quién le toca manejar? : whose turn is it to drive?⟩ ⟨a él le toca decidir : it's up to him to decide⟩ ⟨nos toca el 50 por ciento : we get 50 percent⟩ **4** : to come by chance ⟨les tocó la lotería : they won the lottery⟩ ⟨nos tocas vivir en tiempos difíciles : it's our fate to live in difficult times⟩ **5** ~ **en** : to touch on, to border on ⟨eso toca en lo ridículo : that's almost ludicrous⟩ — **tocarse** *vr* **1** : to touch ⟨se tocó la frente : he touched his forehead⟩ **2** : to touch (each other)

tocayo, -ya *n* : namesake

tocineta *nf Col, Ven* : bacon

tocino *nm* **1** : bacon **2** : salt pork

tocología *nf* OBSTETRICIA : obstetrics

tocólogo, -ga *n* OBSTETRA : obstetrician

tocón *nm*, *pl* **tocones** CEPA : stump (of a tree)

todavía *adv* **1** AÚN : still, yet ⟨todavía puedes verlo : you can still see it⟩ **2** : even ⟨todavía más rápido : even faster⟩ **3 todavía no** : not yet

todo¹, -da *adj* **1** : all, whole, entire ⟨toda la comunidad : the whole community⟩ ⟨toda la noche : all night, the whole night⟩ ⟨todo tipo de : all kinds of⟩ ⟨con toda sinceridad : with all sincerity⟩ **2** : every, each, any ⟨a todo nivel : at every level⟩ ⟨todos los días : every day⟩ ⟨toda persona menor de 18 años : anyone under the age of 18⟩ **3** : maximum ⟨a toda velocidad : at top speed⟩ **4 todo el mundo** : everyone, everybody

todo² *nm* : whole

todo³, -da *pron* **1** : everything, all, every bit ⟨lo sabe todo : he knows it all⟩ ⟨tienen de todo : they have some of everything⟩ ⟨hizo todo lo que pudo : she did everything she could⟩ ⟨no los encontré todos : I didn't find all of them⟩ ⟨es todo un soldado : he's a soldier through and through⟩ ⟨fue todo un éxito : it was quite a success⟩ **2 todos, -das** *pl* : everybody, everyone, all ⟨todos estamos de acuerdo : everybody agrees, we all agree⟩ ⟨¿estamos todos? : are we all here?⟩ ⟨es mejor para todos : it's better for everyone⟩ ⟨agradeció a todos : he thanked everyone⟩ ⟨es la más famosa de todos : she's the most famous of them all⟩ **3 ante ~** : above all, first and foremost **4 con todo (y eso)** : even so, nevertheless **5 del todo** : completely **6 sobre ~** : above all

todopoderoso, -sa *adj* OMNIPOTENTE : almighty

todoterreno *nm* : all-terrain vehicle

toga *nf* **1** : toga **2** : gown, robe (for magistrates, etc.)

toldo *nm* : awning, canopy

tolerable *adj* : tolerable — **tolerablemente** *adv*

tolerancia *nf* : tolerance, toleration

tolerante *adj* : tolerant — **tolerantemente** *adv*

tolerar *vt* : to tolerate

tolete *nm* : oarlock

tolva *nf* : hopper (container)

toma *nf* **1** : taking, seizure, capture **2** DOSIS : dose **3** : take, shot **4 toma de corriente** : wall socket, outlet **5 toma y daca** : give-and-take

tomado *adj* : drunk

tomar *vt* **1** : to take ⟨tomé el libro : I took the book⟩ ⟨tomar un taxi : to take a taxi⟩ ⟨tomar una foto : to take a photo⟩ ⟨toma dos años : it takes two years⟩ ⟨tomaron medidas drásticas : they took drastic measures⟩ **2** : to make (a decision) **3** BEBER : to drink **4** CONSUMIR : to have (food), to take (medicine) **5** CAPTURAR : to capture, to seize **6** : to take, to interpret ⟨no lo tomes a mal : don't take it the wrong way⟩ **7** : to take for, to mistake for **8 tomar el sol** : to sunbathe **9 tomar prestado** : to

borrow **10 tomar tierra** : to land — *vi* **1** : to take something ⟨toma, te lo presto : here, I'll lend it to you⟩ **2** : to drink (alcohol) — **tomarse** *vr* **1** : to take ⟨tomarse la molestia de : to take the trouble to⟩ **2** : to drink, to eat, to have

tomate *nm* : tomato

tomillo *nm* : thyme

tomo *nm* : volume, tome

ton *nm* **sin ton ni son** : without rhyme or reason

tonada *nf* **1** : tune, song **2** : accent

tonalidad *nf* : tones *pl*, color scheme

tonel *nm* BARRICA : barrel, cask

tonelada *nf* : ton

tonelaje *nm* : tonnage

tónica *nf* **1** : tonic (water) **2** : tonic (in music) **3** : trend, tone ⟨dar la tónica : to set the tone⟩

tónico¹, -ca *adj* : tonic

tónico² *nm* : tonic ⟨tónico capilar : hair tonic⟩

tonificar {72} *vt* : to tone, to tone up

tono *nm* **1** : tone ⟨tono muscular : muscle tone⟩ **2** : shade (of colors) **3** : key (in music)

tontamente *adv* : foolishly, stupidly

tontear *vi* **1** : to fool around, to play the fool **2** : to flirt

tontería *nf* **1** : foolishness **2** : stupid remark or action **3 decir tonterías** : to talk nonsense

tonto¹, -ta *adj* **1** : dumb, stupid **2** : silly **3 a tontas y a locas** : without thinking, haphazardly

tonto², -ta *n* : fool, idiot

topacio *nm* : topaz

toparse *vr* **~ con** : to bump into, to run into, to come across ⟨me topé con algunas dificultades : I ran into some problems⟩

tope *nm* **1** : limit, end ⟨hasta el tope : to the limit, to the brim⟩ **2** : stop, check, buffer ⟨tope de puerta : doorstop⟩ **3** : bump, collision **4** *Mex* : speed bump

tópico¹, -ca *adj* **1** : topical, external **2** : trite, commonplace

tópico² *nm* **1** : topic, subject **2** : cliché, trite expression

topo *nm* **1** : mole (animal) **2** *fam* : clumsy person

topografía *nf* : topography

topográfico, -ca *adj* : topographic, topographical

toque¹, etc. → tocar

toque² *nm* **1** : touch ⟨el último toque : the finishing touch⟩ ⟨un toque de color : a touch of color⟩ **2** : ringing, peal, chime **3** *Mex* : shock, jolt **4 toque de queda** : curfew **5 toque de diana** : reveille

toquetear *vt* : to touch, to handle, to finger

toquilla *nf* : shawl

tórax *nm* : thorax

torbellino *nm* : whirlwind

torcedura *nf* **1** : twisting, buckling **2** : sprain

torcer {14} *vt* **1** : to bend, to twist **2** : to sprain **3** : to turn (a corner) **4** : to wring,

to wring out **5** : to distort — *vi* : to turn
— **torcerse** *vr*
torcido, -da *adj* **1** : twisted, crooked **2**
: devious
tordo *nm* ZORZAL : thrush
torear *vt* **1** : to fight (bulls) **2** : to dodge,
to sidestep
toreo *nm* : bullfighting
torero, -ra *n* MATADOR : bullfighter, matador
tormenta *nf* **1** : storm ⟨tormenta de nieve
: snowstorm⟩ **2** : turmoil, frenzy
tormento *nm* **1** : torment, anguish **2**
: torture
tormentoso, -sa *adj* : stormy, turbulent
— **tormentosamente** *adv*
tornado *nm* : tornado
tornamesa *nmf* : turntable
tornar *vt* **1** : to return, to give back **2** : to
make, to render — *vi* : to go back —
tornarse *vr* : to become, to turn into
tornasol *nm* **1** : reflected light **2** : sunflower **3** : litmus
tornear *vt* : to turn (in carpentry)
torneo *nm* : tournament
tornillo *nm* **1** : screw **2 tornillo de banco**
: vise
torniquete *nm* **1** : tourniquet **2** : turnstile
torno *nm* **1** : lathe **2** : winch **3 torno de
banco** : vise **4 en torno a** : around,
about ⟨en torno a este asunto : about
this issue⟩ ⟨en torno suyo : around him⟩
toro *nm* : bull
toronja *nf* : grapefruit
toronjil *nm* : balm, lemon balm
torpe *adj* **1** DESMAÑADO : clumsy, awkward **2** : stupid, dull — **torpemente** *adv*
torpedear *vt* : to torpedo
torpedero, -ra *n* : shortstop
torpedo *nm* : torpedo
torpeza *nf* **1** : clumsiness, awkwardness **2**
: stupidity **3** : blunder
torre *nf* **1** : tower ⟨torre de perforación
: oil rig⟩ **2** : turret **3** : rook, castle (in
chess)
torreja *nf* : French toast
torrencial *adj* : torrential — **torrencial-
mente** *adv*
torrente *nm* **1** : torrent **2 torrente sanguíneo** : bloodstream
torreón *nm, pl* **-rreones** : tower (of a castle)
torreta *nf* : turret (of a tank, ship, etc.)
tórrido, -da *adj* : torrid
torrija *nf Spain* → **torreja**
torso *nm* : torso, trunk
torta *nf* **1** (*in various countries*) : cake **2**
: pie, tart **3** *Mex* : sandwich
tortazo *nm fam* : blow, wallop
tortícolis *nf* : stiff neck
tortilla *nf* **1** : tortilla **2** *or* **tortilla de
huevo** : omelet
tórtola *nf* : turtledove
tortuga *nf* **1** : turtle, tortoise **2 tortuga de
agua dulce** : terrapin **3 tortuga boba**
: loggerhead
tortuoso, -sa *adj* : tortuous, winding
tortura *nf* : torture
torturador, -dora *n* : torturer
torturar *vt* : to torture, to torment

torvo, -va *adj* : grim, stern, baleful
torzamos, etc. → **torcer**
tos *nf* **1** : cough **2 tos ferina** : whooping
cough
tosco, -ca *adj* : rough, coarse
toser *vi* : to cough
tosquedad *nf* : coarseness, roughness
tostada *nf* **1** : piece of toast **2** *Mex* : fried
tortilla
tostador *nm* **1** : toaster **2** : roaster (for
coffee)
tostadora *nf* **1** : toaster **2** : roaster (for
coffee)
tostar {19} *vt* **1** : to toast **2** : to roast (coffee) **3** : to tan — **tostarse** *vr* : to get a
tan
tostón *nm, pl* **tostones** *Car* : fried plantain chip
total[1] *adv* : in the end, so ⟨total, que no fui
: in short, I didn't go⟩
total[2] *adj & n* : total — **totalmente** *adv*
totalidad *nf* : totality, whole
totalitario, -ria *adj & n* : totalitarian
totalitarismo *nm* : totalitarianism
totalizar {21} *vt* : to total, to add up to
tótem *nm, pl* **tótems** : totem
totopo *nm* CA, Mex : tortilla chip
totuma *nf* : calabash
touchdown *nm* : touchdown (in football)
tour [ˈtur] *nm, pl* **tours** : tour, excursion
toxicidad *nf* : toxicity
tóxico[1], **-ca** *adj* : toxic, poisonous
tóxico[2] *nm* : poison
toxicomanía *nf* : drug addiction
toxicómano, -na *n* : drug addict
toxina *nf* : toxin
tozudez *nf* : stubbornness, obstinacy
tozudo, -da *adj* : stubborn, obstinate —
tozudamente *adv*
traba *nf* **1** : tie, bond **2** : obstacle, hindrance
trabajador[1], **-dora** *adj* : hardworking
trabajador[2], **-dora** *n* : worker
trabajar *vi* **1** : to work ⟨trabaja mucho
: he works hard⟩ ⟨trabajo de secretaria
: I work as a secretary⟩ **2** : to strive
⟨trabajan por mejores oportunidades
: they're striving for better opportuni-
ties⟩ **3** : to act, to perform ⟨trabajar en
una película : to be in a movie⟩ — *vt* **1**
: to work (metal) **2** : to knead **3** : to till
4 : to work on ⟨tienes que trabajar el
español : you need to work on your
Spanish⟩
trabajo *nm* **1** : work, job **2** LABOR : labor, work ⟨tengo mucho trabajo : I have
a lot of work to do⟩ ⟨¡buen trabajo!
: good job!, good work!⟩ **3** TAREA : task
4 ESFUERZO : effort **5** : piece of writing,
essay, paper **6 costar trabajo** : to be difficult **7 tomarse el trabajo** : to take the
trouble **8 trabajo en equipo** : teamwork
9 trabajos *nmpl* : hardships, difficulties
trabajoso, -sa *adj* LABORIOSO : laborious
— **trabajosamente** *adv*
trabalenguas *nms & pl* : tongue twister
trabar *vt* **1** : to join, to connect **2** : to
impede, to hold back **3** : to strike up (a
conversation), to form (a friendship) **4**
: to thicken (sauces) — **trabarse** *vr* **1** : to

jam **2** : to become entangled **3** : to be tongue-tied, to stammer

trabucar {72} *vt* : to confuse, to mix up

trabuco *nm* : blunderbuss

tracalero, -ra *adj Mex* : dishonest, tricky

tracción *nf* : traction

trace, etc. → **trazar**

tracto *nm* : tract

tractor *nm* : tractor

tradición *nf, pl* **-ciones** : tradition

tradicional *adj* : traditional — **tradicionalmente** *adv*

traducción *nf, pl* **-ciones** : translation

traducible *adj* : translatable

traducir {61} *vt* **1** : to translate **2** : to convey, to express — **traducirse** *vr* ~ **en** : to result in

traductor, -tora *n* : translator

traer {81} *vt* **1** : to bring ⟨trae una ensalada : bring a salad⟩ **2** CAUSAR : to cause, to bring about ⟨el problema puede traer graves consecuencias : the problem could have serious consequences⟩ **3** : to carry, to have ⟨todos los periódicos traían las mismas noticias : all of the newspapers carried the same news⟩ **4** LLEVAR : to wear — **traerse** *vr* **1** : to bring along **2 traérselas** : to be difficult

traficante *nmf* : dealer, trafficker

traficar {72} *vi* **1** : to trade, to deal **2** ~ **con** : to traffic in

tráfico *nm* **1** : trade **2** : traffic

tragaluz *nf, pl* **-luces** : skylight, fanlight

tragamonedas *nmfs & pl* : slot machine

tragaperras *nmfs & pl Spain* → **tragamonedas**

tragar {52} *v* : to swallow — **tragarse** *vr*

tragedia *nf* : tragedy

trágico, -ca *adj* : tragic — **trágicamente** *adv*

trago *nm* **1** : swallow, swig **2** : drink, liquor **3 trago amargo** : hard time

trague, etc. → **tragar**

traición *nf, pl* **traiciones** **1** : treason **2** : betrayal, treachery

traicionar *vt* : to betray

traicionero, -ra → **traidor**

traidor¹, -dora *adj* : traitorous, treacherous

traidor², -dora *n* : traitor

traiga, etc. → **traer**

tráiler [ˈtreɪlər] *or* **trailer** [ˈtreɪlər, ˈtreɪlər] *nm* : trailer

traílla *nf* **1** : leash **2** : harrow

traje *nm* **1** : suit **2** : dress **3** : costume **4 traje de baño** : swimsuit, bathing suit **5 traje de luces** : matador's outfit **6 traje de neopreno/buzo** : wet suit

trajín *nm, pl* **trajines** **1** : transport **2** *fam* : hustle and bustle

trajinar *vt* : to transport, to carry — *vi* : to rush around

trajo, etc. → **traer**

trama *nf* **1** : plot **2** : weave, weft (fabric)

tramar *vt* **1** : to plot, to plan **2** : to weave

tramitación *nf, pl* **-ciones** : processing

tramitar *vt* : to transact, to negotiate, to handle

trámite *nm* : procedure, step

tramo *nm* **1** : stretch, section **2** : flight (of stairs)

trampa *nf* **1** : trap ⟨trampa mortal : death trap⟩ **2 hacer trampas** : to cheat

trampear *vt* : to cheat

trampero, -ra *n* : trapper

trampilla *nf* : trapdoor

trampolín *nm, pl* **-lines** **1** : diving board **2** : trampoline **3** : springboard ⟨un trampolín al éxito : a springboard to success⟩ **4** : ski jump

tramposo¹, -sa *adj* : crooked, cheating

tramposo², -sa *n* : cheat, swindler

tranca *nf* **1** : stick, club **2** : bar, crossbar

trancar {72} *vt* : to bar (a door or window)

trancazo *nm* GOLPE : blow, hit

trance *nm* **1** : critical juncture, tough time **2** : trance **3 en trance de** : in the process of ⟨en trance de extinción : on the verge of extinction⟩

tranco *nm* **1** : stride **2** UMBRAL : threshold

tranque, etc. → **trancar**

tranquilidad *nf* : tranquility, peace

tranquilizador, -dora *adj* **1** : soothing **2** : reassuring

tranquilizante¹ *adj* **1** : reassuring **2** : tranquilizing

tranquilizante² *nm* : tranquilizer

tranquilizar {21} *vt* CALMAR : to calm down, to soothe ⟨tranquilizar la conciencia : to ease the conscience⟩ — **tranquilizarse** *vr*

tranquilo, -la *adj* CALMO : calm, tranquil ⟨una vida tranquila : a quiet life⟩ — **tranquilamente** *adv*

transacción *nf, pl* **-ciones** : transaction

transar *vi* TRANSIGIR : to give way, to compromise — *vt* : to buy and sell

transatlántico¹, -ca *adj* : transatlantic

transatlántico² *nm* : ocean liner

transbordador *nm* **1** : ferry **2 transbordador espacial** : space shuttle

transbordar *v* : to transfer

transbordo *nm* : transfer

transcendencia → **trascendencia**

transcender → **trascender**

transcribir {33} *vt* : to transcribe

transcrito *pp* → **transcribir**

transcripción *nf, pl* **-ciones** : transcription

transcurrir *vi* : to elapse, to pass

transcurso *nm* : course, progression ⟨en el transcurso de cien años : over the course of a hundred years⟩

transeúnte *nmf* **1** : passerby **2** : transient

transexual *adj & nmf* : transsexual

transferencia *nf* : transfer, transference

transferir {76} *vt* TRASLADAR : to transfer — **transferible** *adj*

transfigurar *vt* : to transfigure, to transform — **transfiguración** *nf*

transformación *nf, pl* **-ciones** : transformation, conversion

transformador *nm* : transformer

transformar *vt* **1** CONVERTIR : to convert **2** : to transform, to change, to alter — **transformarse** *vr*

tránsfuga *nmf* : defector, turncoat

transfusión *nf, pl* **-siones** : transfusion

transgénico[1], **-ca** *adj* : genetically modified

transgénico[2] *nm* : genetically modified plant or animal

transgredir {1} *vt* : to transgress — **transgresión** *nf* — **transgresor, -sora** *n*

transición *nf*, *pl* **-ciones** : transition ⟨período de transición : transition period⟩

transido, -da *adj* : overcome, beset ⟨transido de dolor : racked with pain⟩

transigir {35} *vi* **1** : to give in, to compromise **2** ~ **con** : to tolerate, to put up with

transistor *nm* : transistor

transitable *adj* : passable

transitar *vi* : to go, to pass, to travel ⟨transitar por la ciudad : to travel through the city⟩

transitivo, -va *adj* : transitive

tránsito *nm* **1** TRÁFICO : traffic ⟨hora de máximo tránsito : rush hour⟩ **2** : transit, passage, movement **3** : death, passing

transitorio, -ria *adj* **1** : transitory **2** : provisional, temporary — **transitoriamente** *adv*

translúcido, -da *adj* : translucent

translucir → **traslucir**

transmisible *adj* : transmissible

transmisión *nf*, *pl* **-siones** **1** : transmission, broadcast **2** : transfer **3** : transmission (of an automobile)

transmisor *nm* : transmitter

transmitir *vt* **1** : to transmit, to broadcast **2** : to pass on, to transfer — *vi* : to transmit, to broadcast

transparencia *nf* : transparency

transparentar *vt* : to reveal, to betray — **transparentarse** *vr* **1** : to be transparent **2** : to show through

transparente[1] *adj* : transparent — **transparentemente** *adv*

transparente[2] *nm* : shade, blind

transpiración *nf*, *pl* **-ciones** SUDOR : perspiration, sweat

transpirado, -da *adj* : sweaty

transpirar *vi* **1** SUDAR : to perspire, to sweat **2** : to transpire

transplantar, transplante → **trasplantar, trasplante**

transponer {60} *vt* **1** : to transpose, to move about **2** TRASPLANTAR : to transplant — **transponerse** *vr* **1** OCULTARSE : to hide **2** PONERSE : to set, to go down (of the sun or moon) **3** DORMITAR : to doze off

transportación *nf*, *pl* **-ciones** : transportation

transportador *nm* **1** : protractor **2** : conveyor

transportar *vt* **1** : to transport, to carry **2** : to transmit **3** : to transpose (music) — **transportarse** *vr* : to get carried away

transporte *nm* : transport, transportation ⟨transporte público : public transit, mass transit⟩

transportista *nmf* : hauler, carrier, trucker

transpuso, etc. → **transponer**

transversal *adj* : transverse, cross ⟨corte transversal : cross section⟩

transversalmente *adv* : obliquely

transverso, -sa *adj* : transverse

tranvía *nm* : streetcar, trolley

trapeador *nm* : mop

trapear *vt* : to mop

trapecio *nm* **1** : trapezoid **2** : trapeze

trapecista *nmf* : trapeze artist

trapezoide *nm* : trapezoid

trapo *nm* **1** : cloth, rag ⟨trapo de polvo : dust cloth⟩ **2 soltar el trapo** : to burst into tears **3 trapos** *nmpl fam* : clothes

tráquea *nf* : trachea, windpipe

traquetear *vi* : to clatter, to jolt

traqueteo *nm* **1** : jolting **2** : clattering, clatter

tras *prep* **1** : after ⟨día tras día : day after day⟩ ⟨uno tras otro : one after another⟩ **2** : behind ⟨tras la puerta : behind the door⟩

trasbordar, trasbordo → **transbordar, transbordo**

trascendencia *nf* **1** : importance, significance **2** : transcendence

trascendental *adj* **1** : transcendental **2** : important, momentous

trascendente *adj* **1** : important, significant **2** : transcendent

trascender {56} *vi* **1** : to leak out, to become known **2** : to spread, to have a wide effect **3** ~ **a** : to smell of ⟨la casa trascendía a flores : the house smelled of flowers⟩ **4** ~ **de** : to transcend, to go beyond — *vt* : to transcend

trasero[1], **-ra** *adj* POSTERIOR : rear, back

trasero[2] *nm* : buttocks

trasfondo *nm* **1** : background, backdrop **2** : undertone, undercurrent

trasformación → **transformación**

trasgo *nm* : goblin, imp

trasgredir → **transgredir**

trashumante *adj* : seasonally migratory

trasiego *nm* **1** : coming and going **2** : transfer

trasladar *vt* **1** TRANSFERIR : to transfer, to move **2** POSPONER : to postpone **3** TRADUCIR : to translate **4** COPIAR : to copy, to transcribe — **trasladarse** *vr* MUDARSE : to move, to relocate

traslado *nm* **1** : transfer, move **2** : copy

traslapar *vt* : to overlap — **traslaparse** *vr*

traslapo *nm* : overlap

traslúcido, -da → **translúcido**

traslucir {45} *vi* : to reveal, to show — **traslucirse** *vr* : to show through

trasluz *nm*, *pl* **-luces al trasluz** : against the light

trasmano *nm* **a** ~ : out of the way, out of reach

trasmisión, trasmitir → **transmisión, transmitir**

trasnochar *vi* : to stay up all night

traspapelar *vt* : to misplace, to mislay (papers, etc.)

trasparencia, trasparente → **transparencia, transparente**

traspasar *vt* **1** PERFORAR : to pierce, to go through **2** : to go beyond ⟨traspasar los límites : to overstep the limits⟩ **3**

ATRAVESAR : to cross, to go across **4** : to sell, to transfer

traspaso *nm* : transfer, sale

traspié *nm* **1** : stumble **2** : blunder

traspiración → **transpiración**

trasplantar *vt* : to transplant

trasplante *nm* : transplant

trasponer → **transponer**

trasportar → **transportar**

trasquilar *vt* ESQUILAR : to shear

trastada *nf fam* : dirty trick

traste *nm* **1** : fret (on a guitar) **2** *CA, Mex, PRi* : kitchen utensil ⟨lavar los trastes : to do the dishes⟩ **3 dar al traste con** : to ruin, to destroy **4 irse al traste** : to fall through

trastero *nm* : junk room

trastienda *nf* : back room

trastornar *vt* : to disturb, to upset, to disrupt — **trastornarse** *vr*

trastorno *nm* **1** : disorder ⟨trastorno mental : mental disorder⟩ **2** : disturbance, upset

trastos *nmpl* **1** : implements, utensils **2** *fam* : pieces of junk, stuff

trasunto *nm* : image, likeness

tratable *adj* **1** : friendly, sociable **2** : treatable

tratado *nm* **1** : treatise **2** : treaty

tratamiento *nm* : treatment

tratante *nmf* : dealer, trader

tratar *vi* **1** ~ **con** : to deal with, to have contact with ⟨no trato mucho con los clientes : I don't have much contact with customers⟩ **2** ~ **de** : to try to ⟨estoy tratando de comer : I am trying to eat⟩ **3** ~ **de/sobre** : to be about, to concern ⟨el libro trata de las plantas : the book is about plants⟩ **4** ~ **en** : to deal in ⟨trata en herramientas : he deals in tools⟩ — *vt* **1** : to treat ⟨tratan bien a sus empleados : they treat their employees well⟩ **2** : to treat (a patient, a condition) **3** : to handle ⟨trató el tema con delicadeza : he handled the subject tactfully⟩ **4** : to treat (wood, etc.) — **tratarse** *vr* **1** : to socialize with **2** ~ **de** : to be about, to concern

trato *nm* **1** : deal, agreement **2** : relationship, dealings *pl* **3** : treatment ⟨malos tratos : ill-treatment⟩

trauma *nm* : trauma

traumático, -ca *adj* : traumatic — **traumáticamente** *adv*

traumatismo *nm* : injury ⟨traumatismo cervical : whiplash⟩

través *nm* **1 a través de** : across, through **2 al través** : crosswise, across **3 de través** : sideways

travesaño *nm* **1** : crossbar **2** : transom (of a window), crosspiece

travesía *nf* : voyage, crossing (of the sea)

travesti *or* **travestí** *adj & nmf, pl* **-tis** *or* **-tíes** : transvestite

travesura *nf* **1** : prank, mischievous act **2 travesuras** *nfpl* : mischief

travieso, -sa *adj* : mischievous, naughty — **traviesamente** *adv*

trayecto *nm* **1** : journey **2** : route **3** : trajectory, path

trayectoria *nf* **1** : course, path, trajectory **2** : history (of a company, etc.), career (of a person)

trayendo → **traer**

traza *nf* **1** DISEÑO : design, plan **2** : appearance

trazado *nm* **1** BOSQUEJO : outline, sketch **2** PLAN : plan, layout

trazar {21} *vt* **1** : to trace **2** : to draw up, to devise **3** : to outline, to sketch

trazo *nm* **1** : stroke, line **2** : sketch, outline

trébol *nm* **1** : clover, shamrock **2** : club (playing card)

trece *adj & nm* : thirteen — **trece** *pron*

treceavo¹, -va *adj* : thirteenth

treceavo² *nm* : thirteenth (fraction)

trecho *nm* **1** : stretch, period ⟨de trecho en trecho : at intervals⟩ **2** : distance, space

tregua *nf* **1** : truce **2** : lull, respite **3 sin** ~ : relentless, unrelenting

treinta *adj & nm* : thirty — **treinta** *pron*

treintavo¹, -va *adj* : thirtieth

treintavo² *nm* : thirtieth (fraction)

tremendamente *adv* : tremendously

tremendo, -da *adj* **1** : tremendous, enormous **2** : terrible, dreadful **3** *fam* : great, super

trementina *nf* AGUARRÁS : turpentine

trémulo, -la *adj* **1** : trembling, shaky **2** : flickering

tren *nm* **1** : train **2** : set, assembly ⟨tren de aterrizaje : landing gear⟩ ⟨tren motriz : drive train⟩ **3** : speed, pace ⟨a todo tren : at top speed⟩

trenca *nf Spain* : duffle coat

trence, etc. → **trenzar**

trenza *nf* : braid, pigtail

trenzar {21} *vt* : to braid — **trenzarse** *vr* : to get involved

trepador, -dora *adj* : climbing ⟨rosal trepador : rambling rose⟩

trepadora *nf* **1** : climbing plant, climber **2** : nuthatch

trepar *vi* **1** : to climb ⟨trepar a un árbol : to climb up a tree⟩ **2** : to creep, to spread (of a plant)

trepidación *nf, pl* **-ciones** : vibration

trepidante *adj* **1** : vibrating **2** : fast, frantic

trepidar *vi* **1** : to shake, to vibrate **2** : to hesitate, to waver

tres¹ *adj & nm* : three ⟨tiene tres años : she's three years old⟩ ⟨el tres de mayo : (on) the third of May, (on) May third⟩ ⟨el siglo tres : the third century⟩

tres² *pron* : three ⟨somos tres : there are three of us⟩ ⟨son las tres : it's three (o'clock)⟩

trescientos¹, -tas *adj & pron* : three hundred

trescientos² *nms & pl* : three hundred

tresillo *nm* **1** : three-piece suit **2** *Spain* : three-piece furniture set **3** *Spain* : three-seat sofa

treta *nf* : trick, ruse

tri- *pref* : tri-

tríada *nf* : triad

triángulo *nm* : triangle — **triangular** *adj*

tribal *adj* : tribal

tribu *nf* : tribe

tribulación *nf, pl* **-ciones** : tribulation

tribuna *nf* **1** : dais, platform **2** : stands *pl*, bleachers *pl*, grandstand

tribunal *nm* : court, tribunal

tributar *vt* : to pay, to render — *vi* : to pay taxes'

tributario¹, -ria *adj* : tax ⟨evasión tributaria : tax evasion⟩

tributario² *nm* : tributary

tributo *nm* **1** : tax **2** : tribute

triciclo *nm* : tricycle

tricolor *adj* : tricolor

tricotar *vt Spain* : to knit

tridente *nm* : trident

tridimensional *adj* : three-dimensional, 3-D

trienal *adj* : triennial

trifulca *nf fam* : row, ruckus

trigal *nm* : wheat field

trigésimo¹, -ma *adj* : thirtieth, thirty-

trigésimo², -ma *n* : thirtieth, thirty- (in a series)

trigo *nm* **1** : wheat **2 trigo sarraceno** : buckwheat

trigonometría *nf* : trigonometry

trigueño, -ña *adj* **1** : light brown (of hair) **2 MORENO** : dark, olive-skinned

trillado, -da *adj* : trite, hackneyed

trilladora *nf* : thresher, threshing machine

trillar *vt* : to thresh

trillizo, -za *n* : triplet

trilogía *nf* : trilogy

trimestral *adj* : quarterly — **trimestralmente** *adv*

trimestre *nm* : trimester

trinar *vi* **1** : to thrill **2** : to warble

trinchar *vt* : to carve, to cut up

trinchera *nf* **1** : trench, ditch **2** : trench coat

trineo *nm* : sled, sleigh

trinidad *nf* **la Trinidad** : the Trinity

trino *nm* : trill, warble

trinquete *nm* : ratchet

trío *nm* : trio

tripa *nf* **1 INTESTINO** : gut, intestine **2 tripas** *nfpl fam* : belly, tummy, insides *pl* ⟨dolerle a uno las tripas : to have a stomach ache⟩

tripartito, -ta *adj* : tripartite

triple *adj & nm* : triple

triplicado *nm* : triplicate

triplicar {72} *vt* : to triple, to treble

trípode *nm* : tripod

tripulación *nf, pl* **-ciones** : crew

tripulante *nmf* : crew member

tripular *vt* : to man

triquiñuela *nf* : trick

tris *nm* **estar en un tris de** : to be within an inch of, to be very close to

triste *adj* **1** : sad, gloomy ⟨ponerse triste : to become sad⟩ **2** : desolate, dismal ⟨una perspectiva triste : a dismal outlook⟩ **3** : sorry, sorry-looking ⟨la triste verdad : the sorry truth⟩

tristemente *adv* : sadly

tristeza *nf DOLOR* : sadness, grief

tristón, -tona *adj, mpl* **-tones** : melancholy, downhearted

tritón *nm, pl* **tritones** : newt

triturador *nm* → **trituradora**

trituradora *nf* **1** : grinder **2 trituradora de papel** : paper shredder **3 trituradora de basura** : garbage disposal

triturar *vt* : to crush, to grind

triunfador¹, -dora *adj* : triumphal, triumphant

triunfador², -dora *n* : winner

triunfal *adj* : triumphal, triumphant — **triunfalmente** *adv*

triunfante *adj* : triumphant, victorious

triunfar *vi* : to triumph, to win

triunfo *nm* **1** : triumph, victory **2 ÉXITO** : success **3** : trump (in card games)

triunvirato *nm* : triumvirate

trivial *adj* **1** : trivial **2** : trite, commonplace

trivialidad *nf* : triviality

triza *nf* **1** : shred, bit **2 hacer trizas** : to tear into shreds, to smash to pieces

trocar {82} *vt* **1 CAMBIAR** : to exchange, to trade **2 CAMBIAR** : to change, to alter, to transform **3 CONFUNDIR** : to confuse, to mix up

trocear *vt* : to carve, to cut up

trocha *nf* : path, trail

troce, etc. → **trozar**

trofeo *nm* : trophy

tromba *nf* **1** : whirlwind **2 tromba de agua** : downpour, cloudburst

trombón *nm, pl* **trombones 1** : trombone **2** : trombonist — **trombonista** *nmf*

trombosis *nf* : thrombosis

trompa *nf* **1** : trunk (of an elephant), proboscis (of an insect) **2** : horn ⟨trompa de caza : hunting horn⟩ **3** : tube, duct (in the body)

trompada *nf fam* **1** : punch, blow **2** : bump, collision (of persons)

trompazo *nm fam* : bang, bump, smack

trompear *vt fam* : to punch

trompeta *nf* : trumpet

trompetista *nmf* : trumpet player, trumpeter

trompicón *nm, pl* **-cones 1** : stumble, lurch **2 a trompicones** : in fits and starts

trompo *nm* : spinning top

trona *nf Spain* : high chair (for a baby)

tronada *nf* : thunderstorm

tronado, -da *adj fam* : nuts, crazy

tronar {19} *vi* **1** : to thunder, to roar **2** : to be furious, to rage **3 CA, Mex fam** : to shoot — *v impers* : to thunder ⟨está tronando : it's thundering⟩

tronchar *vt* **1** : to snap, to break off **2** : to cut off (relations)

tronco *nm* **1** : trunk (of a tree) **2** : log **3** : torso

trono *nm* **1** : throne **2 fam** : toilet

tropa *nf* **1** : troop, soldiers *pl* **2** : crowd, mob **3** : herd (of livestock)

tropel *nm* : mob, swarm

tropezar {29} *vi* **1** : to trip, to stumble **2** : to slip up, to blunder **3 ~ con** : to run into, to bump into **4 ~ con** : to come up against (a problem) — **tropezarse** *vr* **~ con** : to run into, to bump into

tropezón *nm, pl* **-zones 1** : stumble **2** : mistake, slip

tropical *adj* : tropical

trópico *nm* **1** : tropic ⟨trópico de Cáncer : tropic of Cancer⟩ **2 el trópico** : the tropics

tropiezo *nm* **1** CONTRATIEMPO : snag, setback **2** EQUIVOCACIÓN : mistake, slip

troqué, etc. → **trocar**

troquel *nm* : die (for stamping)

trotamundos *nmf* : globe-trotter

trotar *vi* **1** : to trot **2** : to jog **3** *fam* : to rush about

trote *nm* **1** : trot **2** *fam* : rush, bustle **3 de ~** : durable, for everyday use

troupe *nf* : troupe

trovador, -dora *n* : troubadour

trozar {21} *vt* : to cut up, to dice

trozo *nm* **1** PEDAZO : piece, bit, chunk **2** : passage, extract

trucha *nf* : trout

truco *nm* **1** : trick **2** : knack

truculento, -ta *adj* : horrifying, gruesome

trueca, trueque etc. → **trocar**

truena, etc. → **tronar**

trueno *nm* : thunder

trueque *nm* : barter, exchange

trufa *nf* : truffle

truhán, truhana *n*, *pl* **truhanes** : rogue, scoundrel

truncar {72} *vt* **1** : to truncate, to cut short **2** : to thwart, to frustrate ⟨truncó sus esperanzas : she shattered her hopes⟩

trunco, -ca *adj* **1** : truncated **2** : unfinished, incomplete

trunque, etc. → **truncar**

trust *nm* : trust (business group)

tu *adj* **1** : your ⟨tu vestido : your dress⟩ ⟨toma tus vitaminas : take your vitamins⟩ **2** : thy

tú *pron* **1** : you ⟨tú eres mi hijo : you are my son⟩ **2** : thou

tuba *nf* : tuba

tubérculo *nm* : tuber

tuberculosis *nf* : tuberculosis

tuberculoso, -sa *adj* : tuberculous, tubercular

tubería *nf* : pipes *pl*, tubing

tuberoso, -sa *adj* : tuberous

tubo *nm* **1** : tube ⟨tubo de ensayo : test tube⟩ **2** : pipe ⟨tubo de desagüe : drainpipe⟩ **3 tubo digestivo** : alimentary canal

tubular *adj* : tubular

tuerca *nf* : nut ⟨tuercas y tornillos : nuts and bolts⟩

tuerce, etc. → **torcer**

tuerto, -ta *adj* : one-eyed, blind in one eye

tuerza, etc. → **torcer**

tuesta, etc. → **tostar**

tuétano *nm* : marrow

tufo *nm* **1** : fume, vapor **2** *fam* : stench, stink

tugurio *nm* : hovel

tul *nm* : tulle

tulipán *nm*, *pl* **-panes** : tulip

tullido¹, -da *adj* : disabled, crippled

tullido², -da *n* : disabled person

tumba *nf* **1** SEPULCRO : tomb **2** FOSA : grave **3** : felling of trees

tumbar *vt* **1** : to knock down **2** : to fell, to cut down — *vi* : to fall down — **tumbarse** *vr* ACOSTARSE : to lie down

tumbo *nm* **1** : tumble, fall **2 dar tumbos** : to jolt, to bump around

tumbona *nf* *Spain* : deck chair

tumor *nm* : tumor

túmulo *nm* : burial mound

tumulto *nm* **1** ALBOROTO : commotion, tumult **2** MOTÍN : riot **3** MULTITUD : crowd

tumultuoso, -sa *adj* : tumultuous

tuna *nf* : prickly pear (fruit)

tunante, -ta *n* : crook, scoundrel

tundra *nf* : tundra

tunecino, -na *adj & n* : Tunisian

túnel *nm* : tunnel

tungsteno *nm* : tungsten

túnica *nf* : tunic

tupé *nm* PELUQUÍN : toupee

tupido, -da *adj* **1** DENSO : dense, thick **2** OBSTRUIDO : obstructed, blocked up

turba *nf* **1** : peat **2** : mob, throng

turbación *nf*, *pl* **-ciones** **1** : disturbance **2** : alarm, concern **3** : confusion

turbante *nm* : turban

turbar *vt* **1** : to disturb, to disrupt **2** : to worry, to upset **3** : to confuse

turbina *nf* : turbine

turbio, -bia *adj* **1** : cloudy, murky, turbid **2** : dim, blurred **3** : shady, crooked

turbulencia *nf* : turbulence

turbulento, -ta *adj* : turbulent

turco¹, -ca *adj* : Turkish

turco², -ca *n* : Turk

turco³ *nm* : Turkish (language)

turgente *adj* : turgid, swollen

turismo *nm* : tourism, tourist industry

turista *nmf* : tourist, vacationer

turístico, -ca *adj* : tourist, travel

turnar *vi* : to take turns, to alternate

turno *nm* **1** : turn ⟨ya te tocará tu turno : you'll get your turn⟩ **2** : shift, duty ⟨turno de noche : night shift⟩ **3 por turno** : alternately

turón *nm*, *pl* **turones** : polecat

turquesa *nf* : turquoise

turrón *nm*, *pl* **turrones** : nougat

tusa *nf* : corn husk

tutear *vt* : to address as *tú*

tutela *nf* **1** : guardianship **2** : tutelage, protection

tuteo *nm* : addressing as *tú*

tutor, -tora *n* **1** : tutor **2** : guardian

tutoría *nf* : guardianship

tutorial *nm* : tutorial

tuvo, etc. → **tener**

tuyo¹, -ya *adj* : yours, of yours ⟨un amigo tuyo : a friend of yours⟩ ⟨¿es tuya esta casa? : is this house yours?⟩

tuyo², -ya *pron* **1** : yours ⟨ése es el tuyo : that one is yours⟩ ⟨trae la tuya : bring your own⟩ **2 los tuyos** : your relations, your friends ⟨¿vendrán los tuyos? : are your folks coming?⟩

tweed [ˈtwið] *nm* : tweed

U

u¹ *nf* : twenty-fourth letter of the Spanish alphabet

u² *conj* (*used instead of* **o** *before words beginning with* o- *or* ho-) : or

uapiti *nm, pl* **-ties** *or* **-tís** *or* **-tí** : American elk, wapiti

ubicación *nf, pl* **-ciones** : location, position

ubicar {72} *vt* **1** SITUAR : to place, to put, to position **2** LOCALIZAR : to locate, to find — **ubicarse** *vr* **1** LOCALIZARSE : to be placed, to be located **2** SITUARSE : to position oneself

ubicuo, -cua *adj* : ubiquitous

ubre *nf* : udder

UCP [use'pe] (*unidad central de procesamiento* → CPU

ucraniano¹, -na *adj & n* : Ukrainian

ucraniano² *nm* : Ukrainian (language)

Ud., Uds. → **usted**

uf *interj* : phew!

ufanarse *vr* ~ **de** : to boast about

ufano, -na *adj* **1** ORGULLOSO : proud **2** : self-satisfied, smug

ugandés, -desa *adj & n, mpl* **-deses** : Ugandan

ukelele *nm* : ukulele

úlcera *nf* : ulcer — **ulceroso, -sa** *adj*

ulcerar *vt* : to ulcerate — **ulcerarse** *vr*

ulterior *adj* : later, subsequent — **ulteriormente** *adv*

últimamente *adv* : lately, recently

ultimar *vt* **1** : to complete, to finish, to finalize **2** MATAR : to kill

ultimátum *nm, pl* **-tums** : ultimatum

último, -ma *adj* **1** : last, final (la última galleta : the last cookie) (en último caso : as a last resort) (estar en último lugar : to be in last place) **2** : last, latest, most recent (su último viaje a España : her last trip to Spain) (en los últimos años : in recent years) (las últimas noticias : the latest news) (a última hora : at the last moment) **3** : last, farthest (el último piso : the top floor) **4 por ~** : finally

último², -ma *n* : last one

ultra- *pref* : ultra-

ultrajar *vt* : to offend, to outrage, to insult

ultraje *nm* : outrage, insult

ultramar *nm* **de** ~ *or* **en** ~ : overseas, abroad

ultranza *nf* **1 a** ~ : to the extreme (defender a ultranza : to defend fiercely) **2 a** ~ : extreme, out-and-out (perfeccionismo a ultranza : rabid perfectionism)

ultrarrojo, -ja *adj* : infrared

ultrasecreto, -ta *adj* : top secret

ultrasónico, -ca *adj* : ultrasonic

ultrasonido *nm* : ultrasound

ultravioleta *adj* : ultraviolet

ulular *vi* **1** : to hoot **2** : to howl, to wail

ululato *nm* : hoot (of an owl), wail (of a person)

umbilical *adj* : umbilical (cordón umbilical : umbilical cord)

umbral *nm* : threshold, doorstep

un¹ *adj* → **uno¹**

un², **una** *art, mpl* **unos 1** : a, an (un año : a year) (una persona : a person) **2 unos** *or* **unas** *pl* : some, a few (hace unas semanas : a few weeks ago) **3 unos** *or* **unas** *pl* : about, approximately (unos veinte años antes : about twenty years before)

unánime *adj* : unanimous — **unánimemente** *adv*

unanimidad *nf* **1** : unanimity **2 por** ~ : unanimously

uncir {83} *vt* : to yoke

undécimo¹, -ma *adj* : eleventh

undécimo², -ma *n* : eleventh (in a series)

ungir {35} *vt* : to anoint

ungüento *nm* : ointment, salve

ungulado, -da *adj* : hoofed

únicamente *adv* : only, solely

único¹, -ca *adj* **1** : only, sole (lo único que necesito : the only thing I need) (es hijo único : he's an only child) **2** : unique, extraordinary

único², -ca *n* : only one (los únicos que vinieron : the only ones who showed up)

unicornio *nm* : unicorn

unidad *nf* **1** : unity **2** : unit (of army, currency, etc.) **3** : drive, unit (unidad (de memoria) flash : flash drive)

unido, -da *adj* **1** : joined, united **2** : close (of friends, etc.)

unificar {72} *vt* : to unify — **unificación** *nf*

uniformado, -da *adj* : uniformed

uniformar *vt* : to standardize, to make uniform

uniforme¹ *adj* : uniform — **uniformemente** *adv*

uniforme² *nm* : uniform

uniformidad *nf* : uniformity

unilateral *adj* : unilateral — **unilateralmente** *adv*

unión *nf, pl* **uniones 1** : union (partnership) (Unión Europea : European Union) **2** : union, joining **3** JUNTURA : joint, coupling

unir *vt* **1** JUNTAR : to unite, to join **2** CONECTAR : to link, to connect **3** COMBINAR : to combine, to blend — **unirse** *vr* **1** : to join together **2** : to combine, to mix together **3** ~ **a** : to join (a group, etc.)

unísono *nm* : unison (al unísono : in unison)

unitario, -ria *adj* : unitary, unit (precio unitario : unit price)

universal *adj* : universal — **universalidad** *nf* — **universalmente** *adv*

universidad *nf* : university

universitario¹, -ria *adj* : university, college

universitario², -ria *n* : university student, college student

universo *nm* : universe

unja, etc. → **ungir**

uno¹, una *adj* (*un before masculine singular nouns*) : one (una cosa más : one more thing) (tiene treinta y un años : he's thirty-one years old) (el tomo uno : volume one)

uno² *nm* : one, number one

uno³, una *pron* **1** : one (number) ⟨uno por uno : one by one⟩ ⟨es la una : it's one o'clock⟩ **2** : one (person or thing) ⟨una es mejor que las otras : one (of them) is better than the others⟩ ⟨hacerlo uno mismo : to do it oneself⟩ ⟨uno no puede vivir así : you/one can't live like that⟩ **3 unos, unas** *pl* : some (ones), some people **4 uno y otro** : both **5 unos y otros** : all of them **6 el uno al otro** : one another, each other ⟨se enseñaron los unos a los otros : they taught each other⟩

untar *vt* **1** : to anoint **2** : to smear, to grease **3** : to bribe

unza, etc. → **uncir**

uña *nf* **1** : fingernail, toenail **2** : claw, hoof, stinger

UPC [upe'se] *nm* (*unidad de procesamiento central*) → **CPU**

uranio *nm* : uranium

Urano *nm* : Uranus

urbanismo *nm* : city planning

urbanización *nf, pl* **-ciones** : housing development, residential area

urbanizar {21} *vt* : to develop (an area) — **urbanizado, -da** *adj* — **urbanizadora** *nf*

urbano, -na *adj* **1** : urban **2** CORTÉS : urbane, polite

urbe *nf* : large city, metropolis

urdimbre *nf* : warp (in a loom)

urdir *vt* : to engineer, to devise

uretra *nf* : urethra

urgencia *nf* **1** : urgency ⟨con urgencia : urgently⟩ **2** EMERGENCIA : emergency ⟨sala de urgencias : emergency room⟩ ⟨fue intervenido de urgencia : he had emergency surgery⟩

urgente *adj* **1** : urgent **2** : express (mail) — **urgentemente** *adv*

urgido, -da *adj* **estar urgido de** : to be in urgent need of

urgir {35} *v impers* : to be urgent, to be pressing ⟨me urge localizarlo : I urgently need to find him⟩ ⟨el tiempo urge : time is running out⟩

urinario, -ria *adj* : urinary

urja, etc. → **urgir**

urna *nf* **1** : urn **2** : ballot box ⟨acudir a las urnas : to go to the polls⟩

urogallo *nm* : grouse (bird)

urraca *nf* **1** : magpie **2 urraca de América** : blue jay

urticaria *nf* : hives

uruguayo, -ya *adj & n* : Uruguayan

usado, -da *adj* **1** : used, secondhand **2** : worn, worn-out

usanza *nf* : custom, usage

usar *vt* **1** : to use, to make use of ⟨lo usó de martillo : he used it as a hammer⟩ **2** CONSUMIR : to consume, to use (up) **3** LLEVAR : to wear **4 de usar y tirar** : disposable — **usarse** *vr* **1** : to be used **2** : to be in fashion

usina *nf* : power plant

uso *nm* **1** : use ⟨hacer uso de : to make use of⟩ ⟨objetos de uso personal : personal items⟩ **2** : wear ⟨uso y desgaste : wear and tear⟩ **3** COSTUMBRE : custom **4 al uso** : typical, standard ⟨una casa al uso : a typical house⟩

usted *pron* **1** (*formal form of address in most countries; often written as Ud. or Vd.*) : you ⟨usted la conoce : you know her⟩ ⟨¿a usted le gusta el café? : do you like coffee?⟩ ⟨con/para usted : with/for you⟩ **2 ustedes** *pl* (*often written as Uds. or Vds.*) : you, all of you ⟨muchos de ustedes : many of you⟩

usual *adj* : usual, common, normal ⟨poco usual : not very common⟩ — **usualmente** *adv*

usuario, -ria *n* : user

usura *nf* : usury

usurpador, -dora *n* : usurper

usurpar *vt* : to usurp — **usurpación** *nf*

utensilio *nm* : utensil, tool

uterino, -na *adj* : uterine

útero *nm* : uterus, womb

útil *adj* : useful, handy, helpful

utilería *nf* : props *pl*

útiles *nmpl* : implements, tools

utilidad *nf* **1** : utility, usefulness **2 utilidades** *nfpl* : profits

utilitario, -ria *adj* : utilitarian

utilizable *adj* : usable, fit for use

utilización *nf, pl* **-ciones** : utilization, use

utilizar {21} *vt* : to use, to utilize

útilmente *adv* : usefully

utopía *nf* : utopia

utópico, -ca *adj* : utopian

uva *nf* : grape

uve *nf Spain* → **ve²**

uve doble *nf Spain* → **ve doble**

úvula *nf* : uvula

uy *interj* **1** : oh! **2** : ow!

V

v *nf* : twenty-fifth letter of the Spanish alphabet

va → **ir**

vaca *nf* : cow

vacación *nf, pl* **-ciones** **1** : vacation ⟨dos semanas de vacaciones : two weeks of vacation⟩ **2 estar de vacaciones** : to be on vacation **3 irse de vacaciones** : to go on vacation

vacacionar *vi Mex* : to vacation

vacacionista *nmf CA, Mex* : vacationer

vacante¹ *adj* : vacant, empty

vacante² *nf* : vacancy (for a job)

vaciar {85} *vt* **1** : to empty, to empty out, to drain **2** AHUECAR : to hollow out **3** : to cast (in a mold) — *vi* **~ en** : to flow into, to empty into

vacilación *nf, pl* **-ciones** : hesitation, vacillation

vacilante *adj* **1** : hesitant, unsure **2** : shaky, unsteady **3** : flickering

vacilar *vi* **1** : to hesitate, to vacillate, to waver **2** : to be unsteady, to wobble **3** : to flicker **4** *fam* : to joke, to fool around

vacío¹, -cía *adj* **1** : vacant **2** : empty **3** : meaningless

vacío² *nm* **1** : emptiness, void **2** : space, gap **3** : vacuum **4 hacerle el vacío a alguien** : to ostracize someone, to give someone the cold shoulder

vacuidad *nf* : vacuousness

vacuna *nf* : vaccine

vacunación *nf, pl* **-ciones** INOCULACIÓN : vaccination, inoculation

vacunar *vt* INOCULAR : to vaccinate, to inoculate

vacuno¹, -na *adj* : bovine ⟨ganado vacuno : cattle⟩

vacuno² *nm* : bovine

vacuo, -cua *adj* : empty, shallow, inane

vadear *vt* : to ford, to wade across

vado *nm* : ford

vagabundear *vi* : to wander, to roam about

vagabundo¹, -da *adj* **1** ERRANTE : wandering **2** : stray

vagabundo², -da *n* : vagrant, bum, vagabond

vagamente *adv* : vaguely

vagancia *nf* **1** : vagrancy **2** PEREZA : laziness, idleness

vagar {52} *vi* ERRAR : to roam, to wander

vagina *nf* : vagina — **vaginal** *adj*

vago¹, -ga *adj* **1** : vague **2** PEREZOSO : lazy, idle

vago², -ga *n* **1** : idler, loafer **2** VAGABUNDO : vagrant, bum

vagón *nm, pl* **vagones** : car (of a train)

vagoneta *nf* : station wagon

vague, etc. → **vagar**

vaguedad *nf* : vagueness

vahído *nm* : dizzy spell

vaho *nm* **1** : breath **2** : vapor, steam (on glass, etc.)

vaina *nf* **1** : sheath, scabbard **2** : pod (of a pea or bean) **3** *fam* MOLESTIA : nuisance, bother **4** *fam* COSA : thing

vainilla *nf* : vanilla

vaivén *nm, pl* **vaivenes** **1** : swinging, swaying, rocking **2** : change, fluctuation ⟨los vaivenes de la vida : life's ups and downs⟩

vajilla *nf* : dishes *pl*, set of dishes

valdrá, etc. → **valer**

vale *nm* **1** : voucher **2** PAGARÉ : promissory note, IOU

valedero, -ra *adj* : valid

valentía *nf* : courage, valor

valer {84} *vt* **1** : to be worth ⟨valen una fortuna : they're worth a fortune⟩ ⟨no vale protestar : there's no point in protesting⟩ ⟨valer la pena : to be worth the trouble⟩ **2** : to cost ⟨¿cuánto vale? : how much does it cost?⟩ **3** : to earn, to gain ⟨le valió una reprimenda : it earned him a reprimand⟩ **4** : to protect, to aid

⟨¡válgame Dios! : God help me!⟩ **5** : to be equal to — *vi* **1** : to have value ⟨sus consejos no valen para nada : his advice is worthless⟩ **2** : to be valid, to count ⟨¡eso no vale! : that doesn't count!⟩ **3 hacerse valer** : to assert oneself **4 más vale** : it's better ⟨más vale que te vayas : you'd better go⟩ — **valerse** *vr* **1** ~ **de** : to take advantage of **2 valerse solo** *or* **valerse por sí mismo** : to look after oneself **3** *Mex* : to be fair ⟨no se vale : it's not fair⟩

valeroso, -sa *adj* : brave, valiant

valet [ˈbalet, -ˈle] *nm* : jack (in playing cards)

valga, etc. → **valer**

valía *nf* : value, worth

validar *vt* : to validate — **validación** *nf*

validez *nf* : validity

válido, -da *adj* : valid

valiente *adj* **1** : brave, valiant **2** (*used ironically*) : fine, great ⟨¡valiente amiga! : what a fine friend!⟩ — **valientemente** *adv*

valija *nf* : suitcase, valise

valioso, -sa *adj* PRECIOSO : valuable, precious

Valium *marca registrada, m* — used for a drug that reduces anxiety and stress

valla *nf* **1** : fence, barricade **2** : hurdle (in sports) **3** : obstacle, hindrance

vallar *vt* : to fence, to put a fence around

valle *nm* : valley, vale

valor *nm* **1** : value, worth, importance **2** CORAJE : courage, valor **3 valores** *nmpl* : values, principles **4 valores** *nmpl* : securities, bonds **5 sin** ~ : worthless

valoración *nf, pl* **-ciones** **1** EVALUACIÓN : valuation, appraisal, assessment **2** APRECIACIÓN : appreciation

valorar *vt* **1** EVALUAR : to evaluate, to appraise, to assess **2** APRECIAR : to value, to appreciate

valorizarse {21} *vr* : to appreciate, to increase in value — **valorización** *nf*

vals *nm* : waltz

valuación *nf, pl* **-ciones** : valuation, appraisal

valuar {3} *vt* : to value, to appraise, to assess

válvula *nf* **1** : valve **2 válvula reguladora** : throttle

vamos → **ir**

vampiro *nm* : vampire

van → **ir**

vanagloriarse *vr* : to boast, to brag

vandalismo : vandalism

vándalo *nm* : vandal — **vandalismo** *nm*

vanguardia *nf* **1** : vanguard **2** : avant-garde **3 a la vanguardia** : at the forefront

vanguardista¹ *adj* : avant-garde

vanguardista² *nmf* : avant-gardist

vanidad *nf* : vanity

vanidoso, -sa *adj* PRESUMIDO : vain, conceited

vano, -na *adj* **1** INÚTIL : vain, useless **2** : vain, worthless ⟨vanas promesas : empty promises⟩ **3 en** ~ : in vain, of no avail — **vanamente** *adv*

vapor *nm* **1** : vapor, steam **2** : steamer, steamship **3 al vapor** : steamed

vaporera *nf* : steamer (for cooking)

vaporizador *nm* : vaporizer

vaporizar {21} *vt* : to vaporize — **vaporizarse** *vr* — **vaporización** *nf*

vaporoso, -sa *adj* : sheer, airy

vapulear *vt* : to beat, to thrash

vaquero¹, -ra *adj* : cowboy ⟨pantalón vaquero : jeans⟩

vaquero², -ra *n* : cowboy *m*, cowgirl *f*

vaqueros *nmpl* JEANS : jeans

vaquilla *nf* : heifer

vara *nf* **1** : pole, stick, rod **2** : staff (of office) **3** : lance, pike (in bullfighting) **4** : yardstick **5 vara de oro** : goldenrod

varado, -da *adj* **1** : beached, aground **2** : stranded

varar *vt* : to beach (a ship), to strand — *vi* : to run aground

variable *adj & nf* : variable — **variabilidad** *nf*

variación *nf*, *pl* **-ciones** : variation

variado, -da *adj* : varied, diverse

variante *adj & nf* : variant

varianza *nf* : variance

variar {85} *vt* **1** : to change, to alter **2** : to diversify — *vi* **1** : to vary, to change **2 variar de opinión** : to change one's mind

varicela *nf* : chicken pox

várices *or* **varices** *nfpl* : varicose veins

varicoso, -sa *adj* : varicose

variedad *nf* DIVERSIDAD : variety, diversity

varilla *nf* **1** : rod, bar **2** : spoke (of a wheel) **3** : rib (of an umbrella)

vario, -ria *adj* **1** : varied, diverse **2** : variegated, motley **3** : changeable **4 varios, varias** *pl* : various, several

variopinto, -ta *adj* : diverse, assorted, motley

varita *nf* : wand ⟨varita mágica : magic wand⟩

varón *nm*, *pl* **varones** **1** HOMBRE : man, male **2** NIÑO : boy

varonil *adj* **1** : masculine, manly **2** : mannish

vas → **ir**

vasallo, -lla *n* : vassal — **vasallaje** *nm*

vasco¹, -ca *adj & n* : Basque

vasco² *nm* : Basque (language)

vascular *adj* : vascular

vaselina *nf* : petroleum jelly

vasija *nf* : container, vessel

vaso *nm* **1** : glass, tumbler **2** : glassful **3** : vessel ⟨vaso sanguíneo : blood vessel⟩ **4 ahogarse en un vaso de agua** : to make a mountain out of a molehill **5 una tormenta en un vaso de agua** : a tempest in a teapot

vástago *nm* **1** : offspring, descendant **2** : shoot (of a plant)

vastedad *nf* : vastness, immensity

vasto, -ta *adj* : vast, immense

vataje *nm* : wattage

váter *nm* **1** : toilet **2** : bathroom

vaticinar *vt* : to predict, to foretell

vaticinio *nm* : prediction, prophecy

vatio *nm* : watt

vaya, etc. → **ir**

Vd., Vds. → **usted**

ve¹, etc. → **ir, ver**

ve² or ve corta *or* **ve pequña** *or* **ve chica** *nf* : (letter) v

vea, etc. → **ver**

vecinal *adj* : local

vecindad *nf* **1** : neighborhood, vicinity **2 casa de vecindad** : tenement

vecindario *nm* **1** : neighborhood, area **2** : residents *pl*

vecino¹, -na *adj* : neighboring

vecino², -na *n* **1** : neighbor **2** : resident, inhabitant

veda *nf* **1** PROHIBICIÓN : prohibition **2** : closed season (for hunting or fishing)

vedar *vt* **1** : to prohibit, to ban **2** IMPEDIR : to impede, to prevent

ve doble *or* **doble ve** *nf* : (letter) w

vegetación *nf*, *pl* **-ciones** **1** : vegetation **2 vegetaciones** *nfpl* : adenoids

vegetal *adj & nm* : vegetable, plant

vegetar *vi* : to vegetate

vegetariano, -na *adj & n* : vegetarian — **vegetarianismo** *nm*

vegetativo, -va *adj* : vegetative

vehemente *adj* : vehement — **vehemencia** *nf* — **vehementemente** *adv*

vehículo *nm* : vehicle ⟨vehículo deportivo utilitario : sport-utility vehicle⟩ — **vehicular** *adj*

veía, etc. → **ver**

veinte *adj & nm* : twenty — **veinte** *pron*

veinteavo, -va *adj* : twentieth

veinteavo² *nm* : twentieth (fraction)

veintena *nf* : group of twenty, score ⟨una veintena de participantes : about twenty participants⟩

vejación *nf*, *pl* **-ciones** : ill-treatment, humiliation

vejete *nm* : old fellow, codger

vejez *nf* : old age

vejiga *nf* **1** : bladder **2** AMPOLLA : blister

vela *nf* **1** : watch, vigil, wake **2** : candle **3** : sail **4** : sailing **5 pasar la noche en vela** : to be up all night

velada *nf* : evening party

velado, -da *adj* **1** : veiled, hidden **2** : blurred **3** : muffled

velador¹, -dora *n* : guard, night watchman

velador² *nm* **1** : candlestick **2** : night table

velar *vt* **1** : to hold a wake over **2** : to watch over, to sit up with **3** : to blur, to expose (a photo) **4** : to veil, to conceal — *vi* **1** : to stay awake **2 ~ por** : to watch over, to look after

velatorio *nm* VELORIO : wake (for the dead)

velcro *marca registrada, m* — used for a type of nylon fastener

veleidad *nf* **1** : fickleness **2** : whim, caprice

veleidoso, -sa *adj* : fickle, capricious

velero *nm* **1** : sailing ship **2** : sailboat

veleta *nf* : weather vane

vello *nm* **1** : body hair **2** : down, fuzz

vellón *nm*, *pl* **vellones** **1** : fleece, sheepskin **2** PRi : nickel (coin)

vellosidad *nf* : fuzziness, hairiness

velloso, -sa *adj* : downy, fuzzy, hairy

velludo, -da adj : hairy
velo nm : veil
velocidad nf 1 : speed, velocity ⟨límite de velocidad : speed limit⟩ ⟨exceso de velocidad : speeding⟩ ⟨a gran velocidad : at high speed⟩ ⟨de alta velocidad : high-speed⟩ 2 MARCHA : gear (of an automobile)
velocímetro nm : speedometer
velocista nmf : sprinter
velorio nm VELATORIO : wake (for the dead)
velour nm : velour, velours
veloz adj, pl **veloces** : fast, quick, swift — **velozmente** adv
ven → **venir**
vena nf 1 : vein ⟨vena yugular : jugular vein⟩ 2 : vein, seam, lode 3 : grain (of wood) 4 : style ⟨en vena lírica : in a lyrical vein⟩ 5 : strain, touch ⟨una vena de humor : a touch of humor⟩ 6 : mood
venado nm 1 : deer 2 : venison
venal adj : venal
vencedor, -dora n : winner, victor
vencejo nm : swift (bird)
vencer {86} vt 1 DERROTAR : to vanquish, to defeat 2 SUPERAR : to overcome, to surmount — vi 1 GANAR : to win, to triumph 2 CADUCAR : to expire ⟨el plazo vence el jueves : the deadline is Thursday⟩ 3 : to be due, to mature — **vencerse** vr 1 DOMINARSE : to control oneself 2 : to break, to collapse
vencido, -da adj 1 : defeated 2 : expired 3 : due, payable 4 **darse por vencido** : to give up
vencimiento nm 1 : defeat 2 : expiration 3 : maturity (of a loan)
venda nf : bandage
vendaje nm : bandage, dressing
vendar vt 1 : to bandage 2 **vendar los ojos** : to blindfold
vendaval nm : gale, strong wind
vendedor, -dora n : salesperson, salesman m, saleswoman f
vender vt 1 : to sell 2 : to sell out, to betray — **venderse** vr 1 : to be sold ⟨se vende : for sale⟩ 2 : to sell out
vendetta nf : vendetta
vendible adj : salable, marketable
vendimia nf : grape harvest
vendrá, etc. → **venir**
veneno nm 1 : poison 2 : venom
venenoso, -sa adj : poisonous, venomous
venerable adj : venerable
veneración nf, pl **-ciones** : veneration, reverence
venerar vt : to venerate, to revere
venéreo, -rea adj : venereal ⟨enfermedad venérea : venereal disease⟩
venero nm 1 VENA : seam, lode, vein 2 MANANTIAL : spring 3 FUENTE : origin, source
venezolano, -na adj & n : Venezuelan
venga, etc. → **venir**
venganza nf : vengeance, revenge
vengar {52} vt : to avenge — **vengarse** vr : to get even, to revenge oneself
vengativo, -va adj : vindictive, vengeful
vengue, etc. → **vengar**

venia nf 1 PERMISO : permission, leave 2 PERDÓN : pardon 3 : bow (of the head)
venial adj : venial
venida nf 1 LLEGADA : arrival, coming 2 REGRESO : return 3 **idas y venidas** : comings and goings
venidero, -ra adj : coming, future
venir {87} vi 1 : to come ⟨lo vi venir : I saw him coming⟩ ⟨vino a verte : she came to see you⟩ ⟨vino a/de la oficina : he came to/from the office⟩ ⟨¡no me vengas con cuentos! : I don't want to hear your excuses!⟩ ⟨¡venga! : come on!⟩ 2 : to arrive ⟨vinieron en coche : they came by car⟩ 3 : to come, to originate ⟨sus zapatos vienen de Italia : her shoes are from Italy⟩ 4 : to come, to be available ⟨viene envuelto en plástico : it comes wrapped in plastic⟩ 5 : to come back, to return ⟨no vengas tarde : don't come back late⟩ 6 : to affect, to overcome ⟨me vino un vahído : a dizzy spell came over me⟩ 7 : to fit ⟨te viene un poco grande : it's a little big for you⟩ 8 (with the present participle) : to have been ⟨viene entrenando diariamente : he's been training daily⟩ 9 ~ a (with the infinitive) : to end up, to turn out ⟨viene a ser lo mismo : it comes out the same⟩ 10 **que viene** : coming, next ⟨el año que viene : next year⟩ 11 **venir bien** : to be suitable, to be just right — **venirse** vr 1 : to come, to arrive ⟨¿te vienes conmigo? : are you coming with me?⟩ 2 : to come back 3 **venirse abajo** : to fall apart, to collapse
venta nf 1 : sale 2 **venta al por menor** or **venta al detalle** : retail 3 **venta al por mayor** : wholesale 4 **venta por correo** : mail order
ventaja nf 1 : advantage 2 : lead, head start ⟨llevar (la) ventaja : to be in the lead⟩ 3 **ventajas** nfpl : perks, extras
ventajoso, -sa adj 1 : advantageous 2 : profitable — **ventajosamente** adv
ventana nf 1 : window (of a building) 2 **ventana de la nariz** : nostril
ventanal nm : large window
ventanilla nf 1 : window (of a vehicle or airplane) 2 : ticket window, box office
ventero, -ra n : innkeeper
ventilación nf, pl **-ciones** : ventilation
ventilador nm 1 : ventilator 2 : fan
ventilar vt 1 : to ventilate, to air out 2 : to air, to discuss 3 : to make public, to reveal — **ventilarse** vr : to get some air
ventisca nf : snowstorm, blizzard
ventisquero nm : snowdrift
ventolera nf : gust of wind
ventosa nf : sucker
ventosear vi : to break wind
ventosidad nf : wind, flatulence
ventoso, -sa adj : windy
ventrículo nm : ventricle
ventrílocuo, -cua n : ventriloquist
ventriloquia nf : ventriloquism
ventura nf 1 : fortune, luck, chance 2 : happiness 3 **a la ventura** : at random, as it comes

venturoso, -sa adj **1** AFORTUNADO : fortunate, lucky **2** : successful

Venus nm : Venus

venza, etc. → **vencer**

ver[1] {88} vt **1** : to see ⟨no veo nada : I can't see anything⟩ ⟨lo vi con mis propios ojos : I saw it with my own eyes⟩ ⟨vimos una película : we saw a movie⟩ **2** ENTENDER : to understand, to see ⟨ya lo veo : now I get it⟩ ⟨no veo por qué : I don't see why ⟨¿ves lo que quiero decir? : do you see what I mean?⟩ **3** EXAMINAR : to examine, to look into ⟨lo veré : I'll take a look at it⟩ **4** JUZGAR : to see, to judge ⟨otra forma de verlo : another way of looking at it⟩ ⟨lo veo bien : I think it's good/fine⟩ **5** VISITAR : to see, to meet, to visit ⟨vino a verte : she came to see you⟩ **6** AVERIGUAR : to see, to find out ⟨vino a ver cómo estabas : she came to see how you were⟩ — vi **1** : to see **2** ENTERARSE : to learn, to find out **3** ENTENDER : to understand ⟨ya veo : (so) I see⟩ ⟨a mi modo de ver : to my way of thinking, the way I see it⟩ **4 (vamos) a ver** : let's see — **verse** vr **1** HALLARSE : to find oneself **2** PARECER : to look, to appear **3** ENCONTRARSE : to see each other, to meet

ver[2] nm **1** : looks pl, appearance **2** : opinion ⟨a mi ver : in my view⟩

vera nf : side ⟨a la vera del camino : alongside the road⟩

veracidad nf : truthfulness, veracity

veranda nf : veranda

veraneante nmf : summer vacationer

veranear vi : to spend the summer

veraneo nm : summer vacation

veraniego, -ga adj **1** ESTIVAL : summer ⟨el sol veraniego : the summer sun⟩ **2** : summery

verano nm : summer

veras nfpl **de ~** : really, truly

veraz adj, pl **veraces** : truthful

verbal adj : verbal — **verbalmente** adv

verbalizar {21} vt : to verbalize, to express

verbena nf FIESTA : festival, fair

verbigracia adv : for example

verbo nm : verb

verbosidad nf : wordiness

verboso, -sa adj : verbose, wordy

verdad nf **1** : truth ⟨es verdad : it's true⟩ ⟨a decir verdad : to tell the truth⟩ **2 de ~** : really, truly **3 de ~** : real ⟨un amigo de verdad : a true friend⟩ **4 ¿verdad?** : right?, isn't that so?

verdaderamente adv : really, truly

verdadero, -dera adj **1** REAL, VERÍDICO : true, real **2** AUTÉNTICO : genuine

verde[1] adj **1** : green (in color) **2** : green, unripe **3** : inexperienced, green **4** : dirty, risqué

verde[2] nm : green

verdeante adj : verdant

verdín nm, pl **verdines** : slime, scum

verdor nm : greenness

verdoso, -sa adj : greenish

verdugo nm **1** : executioner, hangman **2** : tyrant

verdugón nm, pl **-gones** : welt (on the body)

verdulería nf : greengrocer's store

verdulero, -ra n : greengrocer

verdura nf : vegetable(s), green(s)

vereda nf **1** SENDA : path, trail **2** : sidewalk, pavement

veredicto nm : verdict

verga nf : spar, yard (of a ship)

vergonzoso, -sa adj **1** : disgraceful, shameful **2** : bashful, shy — **vergonzosamente** adv

vergüenza nf **1** : embarrassment ⟨me hiciste pasar vergüenza : you embarrassed me⟩ ⟨me da vergüenza : I'm embarrassed (about it)⟩ ⟨¡qué vergüenza! : how embarrassing!⟩ **2** : disgrace, shame ⟨ser una vergüenza para : to be a disgrace to⟩ **3** : bashfulness, shyness

vericueto nm : rough terrain

verídico, -ca adj **1** REAL, VERDADERO : true, real **2** VERAZ : truthful

verificación nf, pl **-ciones** : verification **2** : testing, checking

verificador, -dora n : inspector, tester

verificar {72} vt **1** : to verify, to confirm **2** : to test, to check **3** : to carry out, to conduct — **verificarse** vr **1** : to take place, to occur **2** : to come true

verja nf **1** : rails pl (of a fence) **2** : grating, grille **3** : gate

vermut nm, pl **vermuts** : vermouth

vernáculo, -la adj : vernacular

vernal adj : vernal, spring

verosímil adj **1** : probable, likely **2** : credible, realistic

verosimilitud nf **1** : probability, plausibility **2** : realism

verraco nm : boar

verruga nf : wart

versado, -da adj **~ en** : versed in, knowledgeable about

versar vi **~ sobre** : to deal with, to be about

versátil adj **1** : versatile **2** : fickle

versatilidad nf **1** : versatility **2** : fickleness

versículo nm : verse (in the Bible)

versión nf, pl **versiones 1** : version **2** : translation

verso nm : verse

versus prep : versus, against

vértebra nf : vertebra — **vertebral** adj

vertebrado[1], **-da** adj : vertebrate

vertebrado[2] nm : vertebrate

vertedero nm **1** : garbage dump **2** DESAGÜE : drain, outlet

verter {56} vt **1** : to pour (liquid), to dump (waste) **2** DERRAMAR : to spill, to shed **3** VACIAR : to empty out **4** EXPRESAR : to express, to voice **5** TRADUCIR : to translate, to render — vi : to flow

vertical adj & nf : vertical — **verticalmente** adv

vértice nm : vertex, apex

vertido nm : spilling, spill

vertiente nf **1** : slope **2** : aspect, side, element

vertiginoso, -sa adj : dizzying — **vertiginosamente** adv

vértigo nm : vertigo, dizziness

vesícula *nf* **1** : vesicle **2 vesícula biliar** : gallbladder

vespertino, -na *adj* : evening

vestíbulo *nm* : vestibule, hall, lobby, foyer

vestido *nm* **1** : dress, costume, clothes *pl* **2** : dress (garment)

vestidor *nm* : dressing room

vestiduras *nfpl* **1** : clothing, raiment, regalia **2** : vestments (of a priest)

vestigio *nm* : vestige, sign, trace

vestimenta *nf* ROPA : clothing, clothes *pl*

vestir {54} *vt* **1** : to dress, to clothe **2** LLEVAR : to wear ⟨vestir de blanco : to wear white⟩ **3** ADORNAR : to decorate, to dress up — *vi* : to dress ⟨vestir bien : to dress well⟩ **2** : to look good, to suit the occasion — **vestirse** *vr* **1** : to get dressed **2** ~ **con** : to wear, to dress in **3** ~ **de** : to dress up as ⟨se vistieron de soldados : they dressed up as soldiers⟩ **4** ~ **de** : to wear, to dress in

vestuario *nm* **1** : wardrobe **2** : dressing room, locker room

veta *nf* **1** : grain (in wood) **2** : vein, seam, lode **3** : trace, streak ⟨una veta de terco : a stubborn streak⟩

vetar *vt* : to veto

veteado, -da *adj* : streaked, veined

veteranía *nf* **1** EXPERIENCIA : experience **2** ANTIGÜEDAD : seniority

veterano, -na *adj & n* : veteran

veterinaria *nf* : veterinary medicine

veterinario¹, -ria *adj* : veterinary

veterinario², -ria *n* : veterinarian

veto *nm* : veto

vetusto, -ta *adj* ANTIGUO : ancient, very old

vez *nf, pl* **veces 1** : time, occasion ⟨a la vez : at the same time⟩ ⟨a veces : at times, occasionally⟩ ⟨algunas veces : sometimes⟩ ⟨cada vez : each/every time⟩ ⟨cada vez más : more and more⟩ ⟨cada vez menos : less and less⟩ ⟨de vez en cuando : from time to time⟩ **2** (*with numbers*) : time ⟨una vez : once⟩ ⟨dos veces : twice⟩ ⟨de una vez : all at once⟩ ⟨de una vez para siempre : once and for all⟩ ⟨una y otra vez : time after time, again and again⟩ **3** : turn ⟨a su vez : in turn⟩ ⟨en vez de : instead of⟩ ⟨hacer las veces de : to act as, to stand in for⟩ **4 alguna vez** : sometime (in the future), on occasion (in the past) ⟨¿has viajado alguna vez? : have you ever traveled?⟩

vía¹ *nf* **1** RUTA, CAMINO : road, route, way ⟨vía pública : public thoroughfare⟩ ⟨Vía Láctea : Milky Way⟩ **2** MEDIO : means, way ⟨por la vía diplomática : through diplomatic channels⟩ ⟨por vía aérea : by air, airmail⟩ ⟨por vía oral : orally⟩ **3** : track, line (of a railroad) **4** : tract ⟨vía urinaria : urinary tract⟩ **5 en vías de** : in the process of ⟨en vías de solución : on the road to a solution⟩ ⟨países en vías de desarrollo : developing countries⟩ ⟨animales en vías de extinción : endangered animals⟩

vía² *prep* : via

viable *adj* : viable, feasible — **viabilidad** *nf*

viaducto *nm* : viaduct

viajante *mf* : traveling salesman, traveling saleswoman

viajar *vi* : to travel, to journey

viaje *nm* : trip, journey ⟨ir de viaje : to go on a trip⟩ ⟨estar de viaje : to be away⟩ ⟨¡buen viaje! : have a good trip!⟩ ⟨viaje de ida : one-way trip⟩ ⟨viaje de ida y vuelta/regreso : round trip⟩ ⟨viaje de regreso/vuelta : return trip⟩ ⟨viaje de negocios : business trip⟩ ⟨viaje en tren : train trip⟩

viajero¹, -ra *adj* : traveling

viajero², -ra *n* **1** : traveler **2** PASAJERO : passenger

vial *adj* : road, traffic

viático *nm* : travel allowance, travel expenses *pl*

víbora *nf* : viper

vibración *nf, pl* **-ciones** : vibration

vibrador *nm* : vibrator

vibrante *adj* **1** : vibrant **2** : vibrating

vibrar *vi* : to vibrate

vicario, -ria *n* : vicar

vice- *pref* : vice-

vicealmirante *nmf* : vice admiral

vicepresidente, -ta *n* : vice president — **vicepresidencia** *nf*

viceversa *adv* : vice versa, conversely

viciado, -da *adj* : stuffy, close

viciar *vt* **1** : to corrupt **2** : to invalidate **3** FALSEAR : to distort **4** : to pollute, to adulterate

vicio *nm* **1** : vice, depravity **2** : bad habit **3** : defect, blemish

vicioso, -sa *adj* : depraved, corrupt

vicisitud *nf* : vicissitude

víctima *nf* : victim

victimario, -ria *n* ASESINO : killer, murderer

victimizar {21} *vt Arg, Mex* : to victimize

victoria *nf* : victory — **victorioso, -sa** *adj* — **victoriosamente** *adv*

victoriano, -na *adj* : Victorian

vid *nf* : vine, grapevine

vida *nf* **1** : life ⟨con vida : alive⟩ ⟨sin vida : lifeless, dead⟩ ⟨perder/quitarse la vida : to lose/take one's life⟩ **2** : life ⟨la vida cotidiana : everyday life⟩ ⟨vida nocturna : nightlife⟩ ⟨estilo de vida : lifestyle, way of life⟩ ⟨así es la vida : that's life⟩ **3** : life, lifetime ⟨nunca en mi/la vida : never in my life⟩ ⟨de por vida : for life⟩ **4** : life ⟨vida animal/vegetal : animal/plant life⟩ **5** BIOGRAFÍA : life, biography **6** : living, livelihood ⟨ganarse la vida : to earn one's living⟩ **7** VIVEZA : life, liveliness **8 media vida** : half-life

vidente *nmf* **1** : psychic, clairvoyant **2** : sighted person

video *or* **vídeo** *nm* : video

videocámara *nf* : video camera

videocasete *or* **videocassette** *nm* : videocassette

videocasetera *or* **videocassettera** *nf* : videocassette recorder, video recorder, VCR

videocinta *nf* : videotape

videoclip *nm, pl* **-clips** : video
videoclub *nm* : video store
videograbar *vt Mex* : to videotape
videojuego *nm* : video game
vidriado *nm* : glaze
vidriar *vt* : to glaze (pottery, tile, etc.)
vidriera *nf* 1 : stained-glass window 2 : glass door or window 3 : store window
vidriero, -ra *n* : glazier
vidrio *nm* 1 : glass, piece of glass 2 : windowpane
vidrioso, -sa *adj* 1 : brittle, fragile 2 : slippery 3 : glassy, glazed (of eyes) 4 : touchy, delicate
vieira *nf* 1 : scallop 2 : scallop shell
viejo¹, -ja *adj* 1 ANCIANO : old, elderly 2 ANTIGUO : former, long-standing ⟨viejas tradiciones : old traditions⟩ ⟨viejos amigos : old friends⟩ 3 GASTADO : old, worn, worn-out 4 **hacerse viejo** : to get old
viejo², -ja *n* ANCIANO : old man *m*, old woman *f*
viene, etc. → **venir**
viento *nm* 1 : wind 2 **hacer viento** : to be windy 3 **contra viento y marea** : against all odds 4 **viento en popa** : splendidly, successfully
vientre *nm* 1 : abdomen, belly 2 : womb 3 : bowels *pl*
viernes *nms & pl* : Friday ⟨el viernes : (on) Friday⟩ ⟨los viernes : (on) Fridays⟩ ⟨cada (dos) viernes : every (other) Friday⟩ ⟨el viernes pasado : last Friday⟩ ⟨el próximo viernes : next Friday⟩
vierte, etc. → **verter**
vietnamita¹ *adj & nmf* : Vietnamese
vietnamita² *nm* : Vietnamese (language)
viga *nf* 1 : beam, rafter, girder 2 **viga voladiza** : cantilever
vigencia *nf* 1 : validity 2 : force, effect ⟨entrar en vigencia : to go into effect⟩
vigente *adj* : valid, in force
vigésimo¹, -ma *adj* : twentieth, twenty- ⟨la vigésima segunda edición : the twenty-second edition⟩
vigésimo², -ma *n* : twentieth, twenty- (in a series)
vigía *nmf* : lookout
vigilancia *nf* : vigilance, watchfulness ⟨bajo vigilancia : under surveillance⟩
vigilante¹ *adj* : vigilant, watchful
vigilante² *nmf* : watchman, guard
vigilar *vt* 1 CUIDAR : to look after, to keep an eye on 2 GUARDAR : to watch over, to guard — *vi* 1 : to be watchful 2 : to keep watch
vigilia *nf* 1 VELA : wakefulness 2 : night work 3 : vigil (in religion)
vigor *nm* 1 : vigor, energy, strength 2 VIGENCIA : force, effect ⟨entrar en vigor : to take effect⟩
vigorizante *adj* : invigorating
vigorizar {21} *vt* : to strengthen, to invigorate
vigoroso, -sa *adj* : vigorous — **vigorosamente** *adv*
VIH *nm* (virus de inmunodeficiencia humana) : HIV
vikingo, -ga *adj & n* : Viking

vil *adj* : vile, despicable, base
vileza *nf* 1 : vileness 2 : despicable action, villainy
vilipendiar *vt* : to vilify, to revile
villa *nf* 1 : town, village 2 : villa 3 **villa miseria** *or* **villa de emergencia** *Arg* : shantytown, slums *pl*
villancico *nm* : carol, Christmas carol
villano, -na *n* 1 : villain 2 : peasant
vilmente *adv* : basely
vilo *nm* 1 **en ~** : in the air 2 **en ~** : uncertain, in suspense
vinagre *nm* : vinegar
vinagrera *nf* : cruet (for vinegar)
vinagreta *nf* : vinaigrette
vinatería *nf* : wine shop
vinculación *nf, pl* **-ciones** 1 : linking RELACIÓN : bond, link, connection
vincular *vt* CONECTAR, RELACIONAR : to tie, to link, to connect
vínculo *nm* 1 LAZO : tie, link, bond 2 HIPERENLACE : link
vindicación *nf, pl* **-ciones** : vindication
vindicar *vt* 1 : to vindicate 2 : to avenge
vinilo *nm* : vinyl
vino¹, etc. → **venir**
vino² *nm* : wine
viña *nf* : vineyard
viñedo *nm* : vineyard
viñeta *nf* : cartoon
vio, etc. → **ver**
viola¹ *nf* : viola
violación *nf, pl* **-ciones** 1 : violation, offense 2 : rape
violador¹, -dora *n* : violator, offender
violador² *nm* : rapist
violar *vt* 1 : to rape 2 : to violate (a law or right) 3 PROFANAR : to desecrate
violencia *nf* : violence
violentamente *adv* : by force, violently
violentar *vt* 1 FORZAR : to break open, to force 2 : to distort (words or ideas) — **violentarse** *vr* : to force oneself
violento, -ta *adj* 1 : violent 2 EMBARAZOSO, INCÓMODO : awkward, embarrassing
violeta¹ *adj & nm* : violet (color)
violeta² *nf* : violet (flower)
violín *nm, pl* **-lines** : violin
violinista *nmf* : violinist
violonchelista *nmf* : cellist
violonchelo *nm* : cello, violoncello
VIP *nmf, pl* **VIPs** : VIP
viraje *nm* 1 : turn, swerve 2 : change
viral *adj* : viral
virar *vi* : to tack, to turn, to veer
virgen¹ *adj* : virgin ⟨lana virgen : virgin wool⟩
virgen² *nmf, pl* **vírgenes** : virgin ⟨la Santísima Virgen : the Blessed Virgin⟩
virginal *adj* : virginal, chaste
virginidad *nf* : virginity
Virgo¹ *nm* : Virgo (sign or constellation)
Virgo² *nmf* : Virgo (person)
vírico, -ca *adj Spain* : viral
viril *adj* : virile — **virilidad** *nf*
virrey, -rreina *n* : viceroy *m*
virtual *adj* : virtual — **virtualmente** *adv*
virtud *nf* 1 : virtue 2 **en virtud de** : by virtue of

virtuosismo *nm* : virtuosity
virtuoso[1], **-sa** *adj* : virtuous
virtuoso[2], **-sa** *n* : virtuoso
viruela *nf* 1 : smallpox 2 : pockmark
virulencia *nf* : virulence
virulento, -ta *adj* : virulent
virus *nm* : virus
viruta *nf* : shaving
visa *nf* : visa
visado *nm Spain* : visa
visceral *adj* : visceral
vísceras *nfpl* : viscera, entrails
viscosidad *nf* : viscosity
viscoso, -sa *adj* : viscous
visera *nf* : visor
visibilidad *nf* : visibility
visible *adj* : visible — **visiblemente** *adv*
visillo *nm* : sheer curtain, lace curtain
visión *nf, pl* **visiones** 1 : vision, eyesight 2 : view, perspective 3 : vision, illusion ⟨ver visiones : to be seeing things⟩
visionario, -ria *adj & n* : visionary
visita *nf* 1 : visit, call ⟨hacer una visita : to pay a visit⟩ ⟨ir de visita : to go visiting⟩ 2 : visitor ⟨tener visita(s) : to have company⟩
visitador, -dora *n* : visitor, frequent caller
visitante[1] *adj* : visiting
visitante[2] *nmf* : visitor
visitar *vt* : to visit
vislumbrar *vt* 1 : to discern, to make out 2 : to begin to see, to have an inkling of
vislumbre *nf* : glimmer, gleam
viso *nm* 1 APARIENCIA : appearance ⟨tener visos de : to seem, to show signs of⟩ 2 DESTELLO : glint, gleam 3 : sheen, iridescence
visón *nm, pl* **visones** : mink
visor *nm* 1 : viewfinder (of a camera), sight (of a gun) 2 : scout (in sports)
víspera *nf* 1 : eve, day before 2 **vísperas** *nfpl* : vespers
vista *nf* 1 VISIÓN : vision, eyesight ⟨perder la vista : to lose one's eyesight⟩ 2 MIRADA : look, gaze, glance ⟨bajó la vista : he looked down⟩ ⟨fijar la vista en : to fix one's gaze on⟩ 3 PANORAMA : view, vista, panorama 4 : hearing (in court) 5 **a la vista** : in sight, in view 6 **a primera vista** : at first sight 7 **con vistas a** : with a view to 8 **en vista de** : in view of 9 **hacer la vista gorda** : to turn a blind eye 10 **¡hasta la vista!** : so long!, see you! 11 **perder de vista** : to lose sight of 12 **punto de vista** : point of view 13 **saltar a la vista** : to be obvious, to stand out
vistazo *nm* : glance, look
viste, etc. → **ver**[1], **vestir**
visto[1] *pp* → **ver**
visto[2], **-ta** *adj* 1 : obvious, clear 2 : in view of, considering 3 **estar bien visto** : to be approved of 4 **estar mal visto** : to be frowned upon 5 **por lo visto** : apparently 6 **nunca visto** : unheard-of 7 **visto que** : since, given that
visto[3] *nm* **visto bueno** : approval
vistoso, -sa *adj* : colorful, bright
visual *adj* : visual — **visualmente** *adv*
visualizador *nm* : display (of a device)

visualizar {21} *vt* 1 : to visualize 2 : to display (on a screen)
vital *adj* 1 : vital 2 : lively, dynamic
vitalicio, -cia *adj* : life, lifetime
vitalidad *nf* : vitality
vitamina *nf* : vitamin
vitamínico, -ca *adj* : vitamin ⟨complejos vitamínicos : vitamin compounds⟩
viticultor, -ra *n* : wine producer
viticultura *nf* : wine producing
vítor *nm* : cheer
vitorear *vt* : to cheer
vitral *nm* : stained-glass window
vítreo, -rea *adj* : glass, glassy
vitrina *nf* 1 : showcase, display case 2 : store window
vitriolo *nm* : vitriol
vituperar *vt* : to condemn, to lambaste
viudez *nf* : state of being widowed ⟨su primer año de viudez : his first year as a widower⟩
viudo, -da *n* : widower *m*, widow *f*
viva *nm* : cheer
vivacidad *nf* VIVEZA : vivacity, liveliness
vivamente *adv* 1 : in a lively manner 2 : vividly 3 : strongly, acutely ⟨lo recomendamos vivamente : we strongly recommend it⟩
vivar *vi* : to cheer
vivaracho, -cha *adj* 1 : lively, vivacious 2 : bright, sparkling
vivaz *adj, pl* **vivaces** 1 : lively, vivacious 2 : clever, sharp 3 : perennial
vivencia *nf* : experience
víveres *nmpl* : provisions, supplies, food
vivero *nm* 1 : nursery (for plants) 2 : hatchery, fish farm
viveza *nf* 1 VIVACIDAD : liveliness 2 BRILLO : vividness, brightness 3 ASTUCIA : cleverness, sharpness
vívidamente *adv* : vividly
vívido, -da *adj* : vivid, lively
vividor, -dora *n* : sponger, parasite
vivienda *nf* 1 : housing 2 MORADA : dwelling, home
viviente *adj* : living
vivificar {72} *vt* : to revitalize, to give life to
vivir[1] *vi* 1 : to live, to be alive ⟨¡viva la democracia! : long live democracy!⟩ 2 SUBSISTIR : to subsist, to make a living 3 RESIDIR : to reside 4 : to spend one's life ⟨vive para trabajar : she lives to work⟩ 5 ~ **de** : to live on — *vt* 1 : to live ⟨vivir su vida : to live one's life⟩ 2 EXPERIMENTAR : to go through, to experience
vivir[2] *nm* 1 : life, lifestyle 2 **de mal vivir** : disreputable
vivisección *nf, pl* **-ciones** : vivisection
vivo, -va *adj* 1 : alive 2 INTENSO : vivid, bright, intense 3 ANIMADO : lively, vivacious 4 ASTUTO : sharp, clever 5 **en** ~ : live ⟨transmisión en vivo : live broadcast⟩ 6 **al rojo vivo** : red-hot
vocablo *nm* PALABRA : word
vocabulario *nm* : vocabulary
vocación *nf, pl* **-ciones** : vocation
vocacional *adj* : vocational
vocal[1] *adj* : vocal

vocal² *nmf* : member (of a committee, board, etc.)

vocal³ *nf* : vowel

vocalista *nmf* CANTANTE : singer, vocalist

vocalizar {21} *vi* : to vocalize

vocear *v* : to shout

vocerío *nm* : clamor, shouting

vocero, -ra *n* PORTAVOZ : spokesperson, spokesman *m*, spokeswoman *f*

vociferante *adj* : vociferous

vociferar *vi* GRITAR : to shout, to yell

vodevil *nm* : vaudeville

vodka *nm* : vodka

voladizo¹, -za *adj* : projecting

voladizo² *nm* : projection

volador, -dora *adj* : flying

volando *adv* : quickly, in a hurry

volante¹ *adj* : flying

volante² *nm* **1** : steering wheel **2** FOLLETO : flier, circular **3** : shuttlecock **4** : flywheel **5** : balance wheel (of a watch) **6** : ruffle, flounce

volantín *nm, pl* **-tines** : kite

volar {19} *vi* **1** : to fly **2** CORRER : to go quickly, to rush ⟨el tiempo vuela : time flies⟩ ⟨pasar volando : to fly past⟩ **3** DESAPARECER : to disappear ⟨el dinero ya voló : the money's already gone⟩ — *vt* **1** : to blow up, to demolish **2** : to irritate

volátil *adj* : volatile — **volatilidad** *nf*

volcán *nm, pl* **volcanes** : volcano

volcánico, -ca *adj* : volcanic

volcar {82} *vt* **1** : to upset, to knock over, to turn over **2** : to empty out **3** : to make dizzy **4** : to cause a change of mind in **5** : to irritate — *vi* **1** : to overturn, to tip over **2** : to capsize — **volcarse** *vr* **1** : to overturn **2** : to do one's utmost

volea *nf* : volley (in sports)

volear *vi* : to volley (in sports)

voleibol *nm* : volleyball

voleo *nm* **al voleo** : haphazardly, at random

volframio *nm* : wolfram, tungsten

volibol *Car, Hond, Mex* → **voleibol**

volición *nf, pl* **-ciones** : volition

volqué, etc. → **volcar**

voltaje *nm* : voltage ⟨de alto voltaje : high-voltage⟩

voltear *vt* **1** : to turn over, to turn upside down **2** : to reverse, to turn inside out **3** : to turn ⟨voltear la cara : to turn one's head⟩ **4** : to knock down — *vi* **1** : to roll over, to do somersaults **2** : to turn ⟨volteó a la izquierda : he turned left⟩ — **voltearse** *vr* **1** : to turn around **2** : to change one's allegiance

voltereta *nf* : somersault, tumble

voltio *nm* : volt

volubilidad *nf* : fickleness

voluble *adj* : fickle, changeable

volumen *nm, pl* **-lúmenes 1** TOMO : volume, book **2** : capacity, size, bulk **3** CANTIDAD : amount ⟨el volumen de ventas : the volume of sales⟩ **4** : volume, loudness

voluminoso, -sa *adj* : voluminous, massive, bulky

voluntad *nf* **1** : will, volition ⟨por propia voluntad : of one's own free will⟩ **2** DE-

SEO : desire, wish **3** INTENCIÓN : intention **4 a voluntad** : at will **5 buena voluntad** : good will **6 mala voluntad** : ill will **7 fuerza de voluntad** : willpower

voluntariado *nm* : volunteer service ⟨programa de voluntariado : volunteer program⟩

voluntario¹, -ria *adj* : voluntary — **voluntariamente** *adv*

voluntario², -ria *n* : volunteer

voluntarioso, -sa *adj* **1** : stubborn **2** : willing, eager

voluptuosidad *nf* : voluptuousness

voluptuoso, -sa *adj* : voluptuous — **voluptuosamente** *adv*

voluta *nf* : spiral, column (of smoke)

volver {89} *vi* **1** : to return, to come/go back ⟨volver a casa : to return home⟩ ⟨volver de vacaciones : to get back from vacation⟩ ⟨no vuelvas por aquí : don't come back here⟩ ⟨volver atrás : to turn back⟩ **2** ~ **a** : to return to ⟨volver al tema : to get back to the subject⟩ ⟨volver a la normalidad : to get back to normal⟩ **3** ~ **a** : to do again ⟨volvieron a llamar : they called again⟩ ⟨volver a pasar/ocurrir/suceder : to happen again⟩ **4 volver en sí** : to come to, to regain consciousness — *vt* **1** : to turn, to turn over, to turn inside out **2** : to return, to repay, to restore **3** : to cause, to make ⟨la volvía loca : it was driving her crazy⟩ — **volverse** *vr* **1** : to become ⟨se volvió deprimido : he became depressed⟩ **2** : to turn around

vomitar *vi* : to vomit — *vt* **1** : to vomit **2** : to spew out (lava, etc.)

vómito *nm* **1** : vomiting **2** : vomit

voracidad *nf* : voracity

vorágine *nf* : whirlpool, maelstrom

voraz *adj, pl* **voraces** : voracious — **vorazmente** *adv*

vórtice *nm* **1** : whirlpool, vortex **2** TORBELLINO : whirlwind

vos *pron* (*in some regions of Latin America*) : you ⟨para vos : for you⟩ ⟨¿vos sos José? : are you José?⟩

vosear *vt* : to address as vos

vosotros, -tras *pron pl Spain* **1** : you, yourselves **2** : ye

votación *nf, pl* **-ciones** : vote, voting ⟨someter a votación : to put to a vote, to vote on⟩

votante *nmf* : voter

votar *vi* : to vote ⟨votar por : to vote for⟩ ⟨votar a favor de : to vote in favor of⟩ ⟨votar en contra de : to vote against⟩ — *vt* : to vote for

voto *nm* **1** : vote **2** : vow (in religion) **3 votos** *nmpl* : good wishes

voy → **ir**

voz *nf, pl* **voces 1** : voice ⟨alzar la voz : to raise one's voice⟩ **2** : opinion, say **3** GRITO : shout, yell **4** : sound **5** VOCABLO : word, term **6** : rumor **7 a voces** : loudly, in a loud voice **8 a voz en cuello** : at the top of one's lungs **9 dar voces** : to shout **10 en voz alta** : aloud, in a loud voice **11 en voz baja** : softly, in a low voice

vudú *nm* : voodoo

vuela, etc. → volar

vuelca, vuelque etc. → volcar

vuelco *nm* **1** : upset, overturning ⟨dar un vuelco : to overturn⟩ ⟨me dio un vuelco el corazón : my heart skipped a beat⟩ **2** : drastic change, reversal ⟨dar un vuelco inesperado : to take an unexpected turn⟩

vuelo *nm* **1** : flight, flying ⟨alzar el vuelo : to take flight⟩ ⟨remontar el vuelo : to climb, to fly up⟩ **2** : flight (of an aircraft) ⟨un vuelo directo : a direct flight⟩ **3** : flare, fullness (of clothing) **4 al vuelo** : on the wing

vuelta *nf* **1** GIRO : turn ⟨se dio la vuelta : he turned around⟩ ⟨vuelta en U : U-turn, about-face⟩ **2** REVOLUCIÓN : circle, revolution ⟨dio la vuelta al mundo : she went around the world⟩ ⟨las ruedas daban vueltas : the wheels were spinning⟩ **3** : flip, turn ⟨le dio la vuelta : she flipped it over⟩ **4** : bend, curve ⟨a la vuelta de la esquina : around the corner⟩ **5** REGRESO : return ⟨de ida y vuelta : round-trip⟩ ⟨a vuelta de correo : by return mail⟩ **6** : round, lap (in sports or games) **7** PASEO : walk, drive, ride ⟨dio una vuelta : he went for a walk⟩ **8**

DORSO, REVÉS : back, other side ⟨a la vuelta : on the back⟩ **9** : cuff (of pants) **10 darle vueltas a algo** : to think something over **11 darle vuelta a la página** : to move on, to begin a new phase **12 dar una vuelta de campana** : to roll over (completely) **13 estar de vuelta** : to be back

vuelto *pp* → volver

vuelve, etc. → volver

vuestro¹, -stra *adj Spain* : your, of yours ⟨vuestros coches : your cars⟩ ⟨una amiga vuestra : a friend of yours⟩

vuestro², -stra *pron Spain (with definite article)* : yours ⟨la vuestra es más grande : yours is bigger⟩ ⟨esos son los vuestros : those are yours⟩

vulgar *adj* **1** : common **2** : vulgar

vulgaridad *nf* : vulgarity

vulgarmente *adv* : vulgarly, popularly

vulgo *nm* **el vulgo** : the masses, common people

vulnerable *adj* : vulnerable — **vulnerabilidad** *nf*

vulnerar *vt* **1** : to injure, to damage (one's reputation or honor) **2** : to violate, to break (a law or contract)

W

w *nf* : twenty-sixth letter of the Spanish alphabet

wafle *nm* : waffle

waflera *nf* : waffle iron

wapití *nm, pl* **-ties** *or* **-tís** *or* **-tí** : wapiti, elk

wáter → váter

web *nmf* : web, World Wide Web

webcam *nf, pl* **webcams** : webcam

webmaster *nmf, pl* **-ters** : Webmaster

western *nm, pl* **westerns** : western

whisky *nm, pl* **whiskys** *or* **whiskies** : whiskey

wigwam *nm* : wigwam

windsurf [ˈwinsurf] *nm* : windsurfing

X

x *nf* : twenty-seventh letter of the Spanish alphabet

xenofobia *nf* : xenophobia

xenófobo¹, -ba *adj* : xenophobic

xenófobo², -ba *n* : xenophobe

xenón *nm* : xenon

xerografiar *vt* : to photocopy, to xerox

Xerox *marca registrada, f* — used for a photocopier

xilófono *nm* : xylophone

Y

y¹ *nf* : twenty-eighth letter of the Spanish alphabet

y² *conj* (**e** *before words beginning with i- or hi-*) **1** : and ⟨mi hermano y yo : my brother and I⟩ ⟨más y más : more and more⟩ ⟨¿y los demás? : and (what about) the others?⟩ **2** (*used in numbers*) ⟨cincuenta y cinco : fifty-five⟩ **3** *fam* : well ⟨y por supuesto : well, of course⟩ **4 ¿y qué?** : so what?

ya¹ *adv* **1** : already ⟨ya terminó : she's finished already⟩ ⟨ya en los años sesenta : as early as the 1960's⟩ **2** : now, right now ⟨¡hazlo ya! : do it now!⟩ ⟨ya mismo : right away⟩ ⟨desde ya : as of now, immediately⟩ **3** : later, soon ⟨ya iremos : we'll go later on⟩ **4** : no longer, anymore ⟨ya no fuma : he no longer smokes⟩ **5** : yes, right ⟨ya, pero . . . : yes, I know, but . . .⟩ **6** (*used for emphasis*)

⟨¡ya lo sé! : I know!⟩ ⟨ya lo creo : of course⟩ **7 no ya** : not only ⟨no ya lloran sino gritan : they're not only crying but screaming⟩ **8 ya que** : now that, since ⟨ya que sabe la verdad : now that she knows the truth⟩

ya² *conj* **ya . . . ya** : whether . . . or, first . . . then ⟨ya le gusta, ya no : first he likes it, then he doesn't⟩

yac *nm* : yak

yacer {90} *vi* : to lie ⟨en esta tumba yacen sus abuelos : his grandparents lie in this grave⟩

yacimiento *nm* : bed, deposit ⟨yacimiento petrolífero : oil field⟩

yaga, etc. → yacer

yang *nm* : yang ⟨el yin y el yang : (the) yin and yang⟩

yanqui *adj & nmf* : Yankee

yarda *nf* : yard

yate *nm* : yacht

yayo, yaya *n fam* : grandpa *m*, grandma *f*

yaz, yazca, yazga etc. → yacer

yedra *nf* : ivy

yegua *nf* : mare

yelmo *nm* : helmet

yema *nf* **1** : bud, shoot **2** : yolk (of an egg) **3 yema del dedo** : fingertip

yen *nm* : yen (currency)

yendo → ir

yerba *nf* **1 or yerba mate** : maté **2** → hierba

yerga, yergue etc. → erguir

yermo¹, -ma *adj* : barren, deserted

yermo² *nm* : wasteland

yerno *nm* : son-in-law

yerra, etc. → errar

yerro *nm* : blunder, mistake

yesca *nf* : tinder

yeso *nm* **1** : plaster (material) **2** : cast (for a limb) **3** : gypsum

yídish *nm* : Yiddish

yihad *nmf* : jihad

yin *nm* : yin ⟨el yin y el yang : (the) yin and yang⟩

yo¹ *nm* : ego, self

yo² *pron* **1** : I ⟨yo la vi : I saw her⟩ ⟨¿quién lo hizo? yo : who did it? I did⟩ **2** : me ⟨todos menos yo : everyone except me⟩ ⟨tan bajo como yo : as short as me⟩ **3 soy yo** : it's me

yodo *nm* : iodine

yoga *nm* : yoga

yogurt *or* **yogur** *nm* : yogurt

Yom Kippur *n* : Yom Kippur

yoyo *or* **yoyó** *nm* : yo-yo

yuca *nf* **1** : yucca (plant) **2** : cassava, manioc

yucateco¹, -ca *adj* : of or from the Yucatán

yucateco², -ca *n* : person from the Yucatán

yudo → judo

yugo *nm* : yoke

yugoslavo, -va *adj & n* : Yugoslavian

yugular *adj* : jugular ⟨vena yugular : jugular vein⟩

yungas *nfpl Bol, Chile, Peru* : warm tropical valleys

yunque *nm* : anvil

yunta *nf* : yoke, team (of oxen)

yuppy *nmf, pl* **yuppies** : yuppie

yute *nm* : jute

yuxtaponer {60} *vt* : to juxtapose — **yuxtaposición** *nf*

yuyo *nm* (*in various countries*) **1** : weed **2** : herb

Z

z *nf* : twenty-ninth letter of the Spanish alphabet

zacate *nm CA, Mex* **1** : grass, fodder **2** : hay

zafacón *nm, pl* **-cones** *Car* : wastebasket

zafar *vt* : to loosen, to untie — **zafarse** *vr* **1** : to loosen up, to come undone **2** : to get free of

zafio, -fia *adj* : coarse, crude

zafiro *nm* : sapphire

zaga *nf* **1** : defense (in sports) **2 a la zaga** *or* **en ~** : behind, in the rear

zagual *nm* : paddle (of a canoe)

zaguán *nm, pl* **zaguanes** : front hall, vestibule

zaherir {76} *vt* **1** : to criticize sharply **2** : to wound, to mortify

zahones *nmpl* : chaps

zaino, -na *adj* : chestnut (color)

zalamería *nf* : flattery, sweet talk

zalamero¹, -ra *adj* : flattering, fawning

zalamero², -ra *n* : flatterer

zambullida *nf* : dive, plunge

zambullir {38} *vt* : to dip, to submerge — **zambullirse** *vr* : to dive, to plunge

zamparse *vr* : to gobble, to wolf down (food)

zanahoria *nf* : carrot

zancada *nf* : stride, step

zancadilla *nf* **1** : trip, stumble **2** *fam* : trick, ruse

zanco *nm* : stilt

zancuda *nf* : wading bird

zancudo *nm* MOSQUITO : mosquito

zángano *nm* : drone, male bee

zanja *nf* : ditch, trench

zanjar *vt ACLARAR* : to settle, to clear up, to resolve

zapallo *nm Arg, Chile, Peru, Uru* : pumpkin

zapapico *nm* : pickax

zapata *nf* : brake shoe

zapatear *vi* : to stamp one's feet

zapatería *nf* **1** : shoemaker's, shoe factory **2** : shoe store

zapatero¹, -ra *adj* : dry, tough, poorly cooked

zapatero², **-ra** *n* : shoemaker, cobbler

zapatilla *nf* **1** PANTUFLA : slipper **2** *Mex* : women's shoe **3** *or* **zapatilla de deporte** : sneaker

zapato *nm* : shoe

zapping ['sapin, 'θapin] *nm* : channel surfing

zar, zarina *n* : czar *m*, czarina *f*

zarandear *vt* **1** : to sift, to sieve **2** : to shake, to jostle, to jiggle

zarapito *nm* : curlew

zarcillo *nm* **1** : earring **2** : tendril (of a plant)

zarigüeya *nf* : opossum

zarpa *nf* : paw

zarpar *vi* : to set sail, to raise anchor

zarpazo *nm* : swipe (with a paw)

zarza *nf* : bramble, blackberry bush

zarzamora *nf* **1** : blackberry **2** : bramble, blackberry bush

zarzaparrilla *nf* : sarsaparilla

zarzuela *nf* : Spanish operetta

zas *interj* : bam!, wham!

zepelín *nm*, *pl* **-lines** : zeppelin

zeta *nf* : (letter) z

zigoto *nm* : zygote

zigzag *nm*, *pl* **zigzags** *or* **zigzagues** : zigzag

zigzaguear *vi* : to zigzag

zimbabuense *adj* & *nmf* : Zimbabwean

zinc *nm* : zinc

zinnia *nf* : zinnia

zíper *nm* *CA*, *Mex* : zipper

zócalo *nm* *Mex* : main square

zodíaco *or* **zodiaco** *nm* : zodiac — **zodíacal** *adj*

zombi *or* **zombie** *nmf* : zombie

zona *nf* : zone, district, area ⟨zona comercial : business district⟩ ⟨zonas rurales/urbanas : rural/urban areas⟩ ⟨zona de conflicto : conflict zone⟩

zonzo¹, **-za** *adj* : stupid, silly

zonzo², **-za** *n* : idiot, nitwit

zoo *nm* : zoo

zoología *nf* : zoology

zoológico¹, **-ca** *adj* : zoological

zoológico² *nm* : zoo

zoólogo, **-ga** *n* : zoologist

zoom *nm* : zoom lens

zopilote *nm* *CA*, *Mex* : buzzard

zoquete *nmf* *fam* : oaf, blockhead

zorrillo *nm* MOFETA : skunk

zorro¹, **-rra** *adj* : sly, crafty

zorro², **-rra** *n* **1** : fox, vixen **2** : sly crafty person

zorzal *nm* : thrush

zozobra *nf* : anxiety, worry

zozobrar *vi* : to capsize

zueco *nm* : clog (shoe)

zulú¹ *adj* & *nmf*, *pl* **zulúes** *or* **zulús** *or* **zulú** : Zulu

zulú² *nm* : Zulu (language)

zumaque *nm* : sumac

zumbar *vi* : to buzz, to hum ⟨le zumbaban los oídos : her ears were ringing⟩ — *vt fam* **1** : to hit, to thrash **2** : to make fun of

zumbido *nm* : buzzing, humming

zumo *nf* JUGO : juice

zurcir {83} *vt* : to darn, to mend

zurdo¹, **-da** *adj* : left-handed

zurdo², **-da** *n* : left-handed person

zurrón *nm*, *pl* **zurrones** : leather bag

zurza, etc. → **zurcir**

zutano, **-na** → **fulano**

English-Spanish
Dictionary

A

a¹ ['eɪ] *n, pl* **a's** *or* **as** ['eɪz] **1** : primera letra del alfabeto inglés **2 A** : la *m* ⟨a sharp/flat : la sostenido/bemol⟩

a² [ə, 'eɪ] *art* (**an** [ən, 'æn] *before vowel or silent h*) **1** : un *m*, una *f* ⟨a house : una casa⟩ ⟨a little more : un poco más⟩ ⟨half an hour : media hora⟩ ⟨what a surprise! : ¡qué sorpresa!⟩ ⟨she's a lawyer : es abogada⟩ ⟨it's a Rembrandt : es un Rembrandt⟩ ⟨a Mr. Jones called : llamó un tal señor Jones⟩ **2** PER : por, a la, al ⟨30 kilometers an hour : 30 kilómetros por hora⟩ ⟨twice a month : dos veces al mes⟩

a- [ə] *pref* : a-

aardvark ['ɑrd₁vɑrk] *n* : oso *m* hormiguero

aback [ə'bæk] *adv* **1** : por sorpresa **2 to be taken aback** : quedarse desconcertado

abacus ['æbəkəs] *n, pl* **abaci** ['æbə₁saɪ, -₁ki:] *or* **abacuses** : ábaco *m*

abaft [ə'bæft] *adv* : a popa

abandon¹ [ə'bændən] *vt* **1** DESERT, FORSAKE : abandonar, desamparar (a alguien), desertar de (algo) **2** GIVE UP, SUSPEND : renunciar a, suspender ⟨he abandoned the search : suspendió la búsqueda⟩ **3** EVACUATE, LEAVE : abandonar, evacuar, dejar ⟨to abandon ship : abandonar el buque⟩ **4 to abandon oneself** : entregarse, abandonarse

abandon² *n* : desenfreno *m* ⟨with wild abandon : desenfrenadamente⟩

abandoned [ə'bændənd] *adj* **1** DESERTED : abandonado **2** UNRESTRAINED : desenfrenado, desinhibido

abandonment [ə'bændənmənt] *n* : abandono *m*, desamparo *m*

abase [ə'beɪs] *vt* **abased; abasing** : degradar, humillar, rebajar

abash [ə'bæʃ] *vt* : avergonzar, abochornar

abashed [ə'bæʃt] *adj* : avergonzado

abate [ə'beɪt] *vi* **abated; abating** : amainar, menguar, disminuir

abattoir ['æbə₁twɑr] *n* : matadero *m*

abbess ['æbɪs, -₁bes, -bəs] *n* : abadesa *f*

abbey ['æbi] *n, pl* **-beys** : abadía *f*

abbot ['æbət] *n* : abad *m*

abbreviate [ə'bri:vi₁eɪt] *vt* **-ated; -ating** : abreviar

abbreviation [ə₁bri:vi'eɪʃən] *n* : abreviación *f*, abreviatura *f*

ABC's [₁eɪ₁bi:'si:z] *npl* : abecé *m*

abdicate ['æbdɪ₁keɪt] *v* **-cated; -cating** : abdicar

abdication [₁æbdɪ'keɪʃən] *n* : abdicación *f*

abdomen ['æbdəmən, æb'do:mən] *n* : abdomen *m*, vientre *m*

abdominal [æb'dɑmənəl] *adj* : abdominal — **abdominally** *adv*

abduct [æb'dʌkt] *vt* : raptar, secuestrar

abduction [æb'dʌkʃən] *n* : rapto *m*, secuestro *m*

abductor [æb'dʌktər] *n* : raptor *m*, -tora *f*; secuestrador *m*, -dora *f*

abed [ə'bed] *adv & adj* : en cama

aberrant [æ'berənt, 'æbərənt] *adj* **1** ABNORMAL : anormal, aberrante **2** ATYPICAL : anómalo, atípico

aberration [₁æbə'reɪʃən] *n* **1** : aberración *f* **2** DERANGEMENT : perturbación *f* mental

abet [ə'bet] *vt* **abetted; abetting** ASSIST : ayudar ⟨to aid and abet : ser cómplice de⟩

abeyance [ə'beɪənts] *n* : desuso *m*, suspensión *f*

abhor [əb'hɔr, æb-] *vt* **-horred; -horring** : abominar, aborrecer

abhorrence [əb'hɔrənts, æb-] *n* : aborrecimiento *m*, odio *m*

abhorrent [əb'hɔrənt, æb-] *adj* : abominable, aborrecible, odioso

abide [ə'baɪd] *v* **abode** [ə'bo:d] *or* **abided; abiding** *vt* STAND : soportar, tolerar ⟨I can't abide them : no los puedo ver⟩ — *vi* **1** ENDURE : quedar, permanecer **2** DWELL : morar, residir **3 to abide by** : atenerse a

ability [ə'bɪləti] *n, pl* **-ties 1** CAPABILITY : aptitud *f*, capacidad *f*, facultad *f* **2** COMPETENCE : competencia *f* **3** TALENT : talento *m*, don *m*, habilidad *f*

abject ['æb₁dʒekt, æb'-] *adj* **1** WRETCHED : miserable, desdichado **2** HOPELESS : abatido, desesperado **3** SERVILE : servil ⟨abject flattery : halagos serviles⟩ — **abjectly** *adv*

abjure [æb'dʒʊr] *vt* **-jured; -juring** : abjurar de

ablaze [ə'bleɪz] *adj* **1** BURNING : ardiendo, en llamas **2** RADIANT : resplandeciente, radiante

able ['eɪbəl] *adj* **abler; ablest 1** CAPABLE : capaz, hábil **2** COMPETENT : competente

-able *suf* : -able

ablution [ə'blu:ʃən] *n* : ablución *f* ⟨to perform one's ablutions : lavarse⟩

ably ['eɪbəli] *adv* : hábilmente, eficientemente

abnormal [æb'nɔrməl] *adj* : anormal — **abnormally** *adv*

abnormality [₁æbnər'mæləti, -nɔr-] *n, pl* **-ties** : anormalidad *f*

aboard¹ [ə'bord] *adv* : a bordo

aboard² *prep* : a bordo de

abode¹ → **abide**

abode² [ə'bo:d] *n* : morada *f*, residencia *f*, vivienda *f*

abolish [ə'bɑlɪʃ] *vt* : abolir, suprimir

abolition [₁æbə'lɪʃən] *n* : abolición *f*, supresión *f*

abominable [ə'bɑmənəbəl] *adj* DETESTABLE : abominable, aborrecible, espantoso

abominate [ə'bɑmə₁neɪt] *vt* **-nated; -nating** : abominar, aborrecer

abomination [ə₁bɑmə'neɪʃən] *n* : abominación *f*

aboriginal [₁æbə'rɪdʒənəl] *adj* : aborigen, indígena

aborigine [ˌæbəˈrɪʤəni] n NATIVE : aborigen mf, indígena mf
abort [əˈbɔrt] vt 1 : abortar (en medicina) 2 CALL OFF : suspender, abandonar — vi : abortar, hacerse un aborto
abortion [əˈbɔrʃən] n : aborto m
abortive [əˈbɔrtɪv] adj UNSUCCESSFUL : fracasado, frustrado, malogrado
abound [əˈbaʊnd] vi to abound in : abundar en, estar lleno de
about¹ [əˈbaʊt] adv 1 APPROXIMATELY : aproximadamente, casi, más o menos ⟨about a hundred dollars : unos cien dólares⟩ 2 AROUND : por todas partes, alrededor ⟨the children are running about : los niños están corriendo por todas partes⟩ 3 to be about to : estar a punto de 4 to be out and about → out³ 5 to be up and about → up³
about² prep 1 AROUND : alrededor de (un lugar, una persona, etc.) 2 CONCERNING : de, acerca de, sobre ⟨he always talks about politics : siempre habla de política⟩ ⟨she's worried about him : está preocupada por él⟩ ⟨you need to do something about it : tienes que hacer algo⟩ 3 (indicating a quality) ⟨there's something weird about it : hay algo raro (en el asunto)⟩ ⟨there's something about her : tiene algo, tiene un no sé qué⟩ 4 (indicating manner) ⟨be quick about it : date prisa, apúrate⟩ 5 to be (all) about : tratarse de (dícese de un asunto), ser muy partidario de (dícese de una persona)
about–face [əˈbaʊtˈfeɪs] n 1 : media vuelta f 2 : cambio m total (de opinión, etc.), giro m de 180 grados
above¹ [əˈbʌv] adv 1 OVERHEAD : por encima, arriba ⟨the floor above : el piso de arriba⟩ ⟨I looked at the sky above : alcé la vista hacia el cielo⟩ 2 : más arriba ⟨as stated above : como se indica más arriba⟩ 3 OVER, MORE : más ⟨groups of six and above : grupos de seis o más⟩ ⟨children age 10 and above : niños a partir de los 10 años⟩ 4 : sobre cero (dícese de temperaturas) 5 from above : de arriba, desde arriba ⟨looking down from above : mirando desde arriba⟩ ⟨orders from above : órdenes de arriba⟩
above² adj 1 : anterior, antedicho ⟨for the above reasons : por las razones antedichas⟩ 2 the above : lo anterior
above³ prep 1 OVER : encima de, arriba de, sobre 2 : superior a, por encima de ⟨he's above those things : él está por encima de esas cosas⟩ 3 : más de, superior a ⟨he earns above $50,000 : gana más de $50,000⟩ ⟨a number above 10 : un número superior a 10⟩ 4 above all : sobre todo
aboveboard¹ [əˈbʌvˈbord, -ˌbord] adv open and aboveboard : sin tapujos
aboveboard² adj : legítimo, sincero
aboveground adj : sobre el nivel del suelo
abrade [əˈbreɪd] vt abraded; abrading 1 ERODE : erosionar, corroer 2 SCRAPE : raspar

abrasion [əˈbreɪʒən] n 1 SCRAPE, SCRATCH : raspadura f, rasguño m 2 EROSION : erosión f
abrasive¹ [əˈbreɪsɪv] adj 1 ROUGH : abrasivo, áspero 2 BRUSQUE, IRRITATING : brusco, irritante
abrasive² n : abrasivo m
abreast [əˈbrɛst] adv 1 : en fondo, al lado ⟨to march three abreast : marchar de tres en fondo⟩ 2 to keep abreast : mantenerse al día
abridge [əˈbrɪʤ] vt abridged; abridging : compendiar, resumir
abridgment or **abridgement** [əˈbrɪʤmənt] n : compendio m, resumen m
abroad [əˈbrɔd] adv 1 ABOUT, WIDELY : por todas partes, en todas direcciones ⟨the news spread abroad : la noticia corrió por todas partes⟩ 2 OVERSEAS : en el extranjero, en el exterior
abrogate [ˈæbrəˌgeɪt] vt -gated; -gating : abrogar
abrupt [əˈbrʌpt] adj 1 SUDDEN : abrupto, repentino, súbito 2 BRUSQUE, CURT : brusco, cortante — **abruptly** adv
abruptness [əˈbrʌptnəs] n 1 SUDDENNESS : lo repentino 2 BRUSQUENESS : brusquedad f
abscess [ˈæbˌsɛs] n : absceso m
abscond [æbˈskɑnd] vi : huir, fugarse
absence [ˈæbsənts] n 1 : ausencia f (de una persona) 2 LACK : falta f, carencia f
absent¹ [ˈæbˈsɛnt] vt to absent oneself : ausentarse
absent² [ˈæbsənt] adj : ausente
absentee [ˌæbsənˈtiː] n : ausente mf
absentminded [ˌæbsəntˈmaɪndəd] adj : distraído, despistado
absentmindedly [ˌæbsəntˈmaɪndədli] adv : distraídamente
absentmindedness [ˌæbsəntˈmaɪndədnəs] n : distracción f, despiste m
absolute [ˈæbsəˌluːt, ˌæbsəˈluːt] adj 1 COMPLETE, PERFECT : completo, pleno, perfecto 2 UNCONDITIONAL : absoluto, incondicional 3 DEFINITE : categórico, definitivo
absolutely [ˈæbsəˌluːtli, ˌæbsəˈluːtli] adv 1 COMPLETELY : completamente, absolutamente 2 CERTAINLY : desde luego ⟨do you agree? absolutely! : ¿estás de acuerdo? ¡desde luego!⟩
absolution [ˌæbsəˈluːʃən] n : absolución f
absolutism [ˈæbsəˌluːˌtɪzəm] n : absolutismo m
absolve [əbˈzɑlv, æb-, -ˈsɑlv] vt -solved; -solving : absolver, perdonar
absorb [əbˈzɔrb, æb-, -ˈsɔrb] vt 1 : absorber, embeber (un líquido), amortiguar (un golpe, la luz) 2 ENGROSS : absorber 3 ASSIMILATE : asimilar
absorbed [əbˈzɔrbd, æb-, -ˈsɔrbd] adj ENGROSSED : absorto, ensimismado
absorbency [əbˈzɔrbəntsi, æb-, -ˈsɔr-] n : absorbencia f
absorbent [əbˈzɔrbənt, æb-, -ˈsɔr-] adj : absorbente
absorbing [əbˈzɔrbɪŋ, æb-, -ˈsɔr-] adj : absorbente, fascinante

absorption [əbˈzɔrpʃən, æb-, -ˈsɔrp-] *n*
1 : absorción *f* **2** CONCENTRATION
: concentración *f*

abstain [əbˈsteɪn, æb-] *vi* : abstenerse

abstainer [əbˈsteɪnər, æb-] *n* : abstemio
m, -mia *f*

abstemious [æbˈstiːmiəs] *adj* : abstemio,
sobrio — **abstemiously** *adv*

abstention [əbˈstɛntʃən, æb-] *n* : abstención *f*

abstinence [ˈæbstənənts] *n* : abstinencia *f*

abstract¹ [æbˈstrækt, ˈæb,-] *vt* **1** EXTRACT
: abstraer, extraer **2** SUMMARIZE
: compendiar, resumir

abstract² *adj* : abstracto — **abstractly**
[æbˈstræktli, ˈæb,-] *adv*

abstract³ [ˈæb,strækt] *n* : resumen *m*,
compendio *m*, sumario *m*

abstraction [æbˈstrækʃən] *n* **1** : abstracción *f*, idea *f* abstracta **2** ABSENT-
MINDEDNESS : distracción *f*

abstruse [əbˈstruːs, æb-] *adj* : abstruso,
recóndito — **abstrusely** *adv*

absurd [əbˈsərd, -ˈzərd] *adj* : absurdo,
ridículo, disparatado — **absurdly** *adv*

absurdity [əbˈsərdəti, -ˈzər-] *n, pl* -**ties** **1**
: absurdo *m* **2** NONSENSE : disparate *m*,
despropósito *m*

abundance [əˈbʌndənts] *n* : abundancia *f*

abundant [əˈbʌndənt] *adj* : abundante,
cuantioso, copioso

abundantly [əˈbʌndəntli] *adv* : abundantemente, en abundancia

abuse¹ [əˈbjuːz] *vt* **abused; abusing** **1**
MISUSE : abusar de **2** MISTREAT : maltratar **3** REVILE : insultar, injuriar,
denostar

abuse² [əˈbjuːs] *n* **1** MISUSE : abuso *m* **2**
MISTREATMENT : abuso *m*, maltrato *m* **3**
INSULTS : insultos *mpl*, improperios *mpl*
⟨a string of abuse : una serie de imprope-
rios⟩

abuser [əˈbjuːzər] *n* : abusador *m*, -dora *f*

abusive [əˈbjuːsɪv] *adj* **1** ABUSING : abusivo **2** INSULTING : ofensivo, injurioso,
insultante — **abusively** *adv*

abut [əˈbʌt] *v* **abutted; abutting** *vt* : bordear — *vi* **to abut on** : colindar con

abutment [əˈbʌtmənt] *n* BUTTRESS
: contrafuerte *m*, estribo *m*

abysmal [əˈbɪzməl] *adj* TERRIBLE : atroz,
desastroso

abysmally [əˈbɪzməli] *adv* : desastrosamente, terriblemente

abyss [əˈbɪs, ˈæbɪs] *n* : abismo *m*, sima *f*

acacia [əˈkeɪʃə] *n* : acacia *f*

academic [ˌækəˈdɛmɪk] *adj* **1** : académico **2** THEORETICAL : teórico — **ac-
ademically** [-mɪkli] *adv*

academic² *n* : académico *m*, -ca *f*

academician [ˌækədəˈmɪʃən] *n* → **academic**

academy [əˈkædəmi] *n, pl* -**mies** : academia *f*

acanthus [əˈkænθəs] *n* : acanto *m*

accede [ækˈsiːd] *vi* -**ceded; -ceding** **1**
AGREE : acceder, consentir **2** ASCEND
: subir, acceder ⟨he acceded to the
throne : subió al trono⟩

accelerate [ɪkˈsɛləˌreɪt, æk-] *v* -**ated;
-ating** *vt* : acelerar, apresurar — *vi* : acelerar (dícese de un carro)

acceleration [ɪkˌsɛləˈreɪʃən, æk-] *n* : aceleración *f*

accelerator [ɪkˈsɛləˌreɪtər, æk-] *n* : acelerador *m*

accent¹ [ˈæk,sɛnt, ækˈsɛnt] *vt* : acentuar

accent² [ˈæk,sɛnt, -sənt] *n* **1** : acento *m* **2**
EMPHASIS, STRESS : énfasis *m*, acento *m*

accentuate [ɪkˈsɛntʃuˌeɪt, æk-] *vt* -**ated;
-ating** : acentuar, poner énfasis en

accept [ɪkˈsɛpt, æk-] *vt* **1** : aceptar AC-
KNOWLEDGE : admitir, reconocer

acceptability [ɪkˌsɛptəˈbɪləti, æk-] *n*
:ˈaceptabilidad *f*

acceptable [ɪkˈsɛptəbəl, æk-] *adj* : aceptable, admisible — **acceptably** [-bli] *adv*

acceptance [ɪkˈsɛptənts, æk-] *n* : aceptación *f*, aprobación *f*

access¹ [ˈæk,sɛs] *vt* : obtener acceso a, entrar a

access² *n* : acceso *m*

accessibility [ɪkˌsɛsəˈbɪləti] *n, pl* -**ties**
: accesibilidad *f*

accessible [ɪkˈsɛsəbəl, æk-] *adj* : accesible, asequible

accession [ɪkˈsɛʃən, æk-] *n* **1** : ascenso *f*,
subida *f* (al trono, etc.) **2** ACQUISITION
: adquisición *f*

accessory¹ [ɪkˈsɛsəri, æk-] *adj* : auxiliar

accessory² *n, pl* -**ries** **1** : accesorio *m*,
complemento *m* **2** ACCOMPLICE : cóm-
plice *mf*

accident [ˈæksədənt] *n* **1** MISHAP : accidente *m* **2** CHANCE : casualidad *f*

accidental [ˌæksəˈdɛntəl] *adj* : accidental,
casual, imprevisto, fortuito

accidentally [ˌæksəˈdɛntəli, -ˈdɛntli] *adv*
1 BY CHANCE : por casualidad **2** UNIN-
TENTIONALLY : sin querer, involuntariamente

acclaim¹ [əˈkleɪm] *vt* : aclamar, elogiar

acclaim² *n* : aclamación *f*, elogio *m*

acclamation [ˌækləˈmeɪʃən] *n* : aclamación *f*

acclimate [ˈækləˌmeɪt, əˈklaɪmət] → **acclimatize**

acclimatize [əˈklaɪməˌtaɪz] *v* -**tized; -tiz-
ing** *vt* **1** : aclimatar **2** **to acclimatize
oneself** : aclimatarse

accolade [ˈækəˌleɪd, -ˌlɑd] *n* **1** PRAISE
: elogio *m* **2** AWARD : galardón *m*

accommodate [əˈkɑməˌdeɪt] *vt* -**dated;
-dating** **1** ADAPT : acomodar, adaptar **2**
SATISFY : tener en cuenta, satisfacer **3**
HOLD : dar cabida a, tener cabida para

accommodation [əˌkɑməˈdeɪʃən] *n* **1**
: adaptación *f*, adecuación *f* **2** **accommodations** *npl* LODGING : alojamiento
m, hospedaje *m*

accompaniment [əˈkʌmpənəmənt, -ˈkɑm-]
: acompañamiento *m*

accompanist [əˈkʌmpənɪst, -ˈkɑm-] *n*
: acompañante *mf*

accompany [əˈkʌmpəni, -ˈkɑm-] *vt* -**nied;
-nying** : acompañar

accomplice [əˈkɑmpləs, -ˈkʌm-] *n* : cómplice *mf*

accomplish [ə'kamplıʃ, -'kʌm-] vt : efectuar, realizar, lograr, llevar a cabo

accomplished [ə'kamplıʃt, -'kʌm-] adj : consumado, logrado

accomplishment [ə'kamplıʃmənt, -'kʌm-] n 1 ACHIEVEMENT : logro m, éxito m 2 SKILL : destreza f, habilidad f

accord[1] [ə'kɔrd] vt GRANT : conceder, otorgar — vi **to accord with** : concordar con, conformarse con

accord[2] n 1 AGREEMENT : acuerdo m, convenio m 2 VOLITION : voluntad f ⟨of one's own accord : voluntariamente, de motu proprio⟩

accordance [ə'kɔrdənts] n 1 ACCORD : acuerdo m, conformidad f 2 **in accordance with** : conforme a, según, de acuerdo con

accordingly [ə'kɔrdıŋli] adv 1 CORRESPONDINGLY : en consecuencia 2 CONSEQUENTLY : por consiguiente, por lo tanto

according to [ə'kɔrdıŋ] prep : según, de acuerdo con, conforme a

accordion [ə'kɔrdiən] n : acordeón m

accordionist [ə'kɔrdiənist] n : acordeonista mf

accost [ə'kɔst] vt : abordar, dirigirse a

account[1] [ə'kaʊnt] vt : considerar, estimar ⟨he accounts himself lucky : se considera afortunado⟩ — vi **to account for** : dar cuenta de, explicar

account[2] n 1 : cuenta f ⟨bank/checking account : cuenta bancaria/corriente⟩ ⟨savings account : cuenta de ahorro(s)⟩ ⟨e-mail account : cuenta de email, cuenta de correo(s) electrónico(s)⟩ 2 EXPLANATION : versión f, explicación f 3 REPORT : relato m, informe m 4 IMPORTANCE : importancia f ⟨to be of no account : no tener importancia⟩ 5 **accounts** npl : contabilidad f 6 **by all accounts** : a decir de todos 7 **by one's own account** ⟨by her own account : según ella misma⟩ 8 **on account of** BECAUSE OF : a causa de, debido a, por 9 **on no account** : de ninguna manera 10 **on someone's account** : por alguien 11 **to take into account** : tener en cuenta

accountability [ə,kaʊntə'bıləti] n : responsabilidad f

accountable [ə'kaʊntəbəl] adj : responsable

accountancy [ə'kaʊntəntsi] n : contabilidad f

accountant [ə'kaʊntənt] n : contador m, -dora f; contable mf Spain

accounting [ə'kaʊntıŋ] n : contabilidad f

accoutrements or **accouterments** [ə'ku:trəmənts, -'ku:tər-] npl 1 EQUIPMENT : equipo m, avíos mpl 2 ACCESSORIES : accesorios mpl 3 TRAPPINGS : símbolos mpl ⟨the accoutrements of power : los símbolos del poder⟩

accredit [ə'krɛdət] vt : acreditar, autorizar

accreditation [ə,krɛdə'teɪʃən] n : acreditación f, homologación f

accrual [ə'kru:əl] n : incremento m, acumulación f

accrue [ə'kru:] vi **-crued; -cruing** : acumularse, aumentarse

accumulate [ə'kju:mjə,leɪt] v **-lated; -lating** vt : acumular, amontonar — vi : acumularse, amontonarse

accumulation [ə,kju:mjə'leɪʃən] n : acumulación f, amontonamiento m

accuracy ['ækjərəsi] n : exactitud f, precisión f

accurate ['ækjərət] adj : exacto, correcto, fiel, preciso — **accurately** adv

accusation [,ækjə'zeɪʃən] n : acusación f

accusatory [ə'kju:zə,tori] adj : acusatorio

accuse [ə'kju:z] vt **-cused; -cusing** : acusar, delatar, denunciar

accused [ə'kju:zd] ns & pl DEFENDANT : acusado m, -da f

accuser [ə'kju:zər] n : acusador m, -dora f

accustom [ə'kʌstəm] vt : acostumbrar, habituar

ace ['eɪs] n : as m

acerbic [ə'sərbık, æ-] adj : acerbo, mordaz

acetate ['æsə,teɪt] n : acetato m

acetone ['æsə,to:n] n : acetona f

acetylene [ə'sɛtə,li:n, -tə,lɪn] n : acetileno m

ache[1] ['eɪk] vi **ached; aching** 1 : doler 2 **to ache for** : anhelar, ansiar

ache[2] n : dolor m

achieve [ə'tʃi:v] vt **achieved; achieving** : lograr, alcanzar, conseguir, realizar

achievement [ə'tʃi:vmənt] n : logro m, éxito m, realización f

Achilles' heel [ə'kɪlɪz-] n : talón m de Aquiles

acid[1] ['æsəd] adj 1 SOUR : ácido, agrio 2 CAUSTIC, SHARP : acerbo, mordaz — **acidly** adv

acid[2] n : ácido m

acidic [ə'sɪdık, æ-] adj : ácido

acidity [ə'sɪdəti, æ-] n, pl **-ties** : acidez f

acid rain n : lluvia f ácida

acid test n : prueba f de fuego

acknowledge [ɪk'nɑlıdʒ, æk-] vt **-edged; -edging** 1 ADMIT : reconocer, admitir 2 RECOGNIZE : reconocer 3 **to acknowledge receipt of** : acusar recibo de

acknowledgment [ɪk'nɑlıdʒmənt, æk-] n 1 RECOGNITION : reconocimiento m 2 THANKS : agradecimiento m

acme ['ækmi] n : colmo m, apogeo m, cúspide f

acne ['ækni] n : acné m

acolyte ['ækə,laɪt] n : acólito m

acorn ['eɪ,kɔrn, -kərn] n : bellota f

acoustic [ə'ku:stık] or **acoustical** [-stıkəl] adj : acústico — **acoustically** adv

acoustics [ə'ku:stıks] ns & pl : acústica f

acquaint [ə'kweɪnt] vt 1 INFORM : enterar, informar 2 FAMILIARIZE : familiarizar 3 **to be acquainted with** : conocer a (una persona), estar al tanto de (un hecho)

acquaintance [ə'kweɪntənts] n 1 KNOWLEDGE : conocimiento m 2 : conocido m, -da f ⟨friends and acquaintances : amigos y conocidos⟩

acquiesce [,ækwi'ɛs] vi **-esced; -escing** : consentir, conformarse

acquiescence [ˌækwiˈɛsənts] *n* : consentimiento *m*, aquiescencia *f*

acquiescent [ˌækwiˈɛsənt] *adj* : acquiescente

acquire [əˈkwaɪr] *vt* **-quired; -quiring** : adquirir, obtener

acquisition [ˌækwəˈzɪʃən] *n* : adquisición *f*

acquisitive [əˈkwɪzətɪv] *adj* : adquisitivo, codicioso

acquit [əˈkwɪt] *vt* **-quitted; -quitting** **1** : absolver, exculpar **2 to acquit oneself** : comportarse, defenderse

acquittal [əˈkwɪtəl] *n* : absolución *f*, exculpación *f*

acre [ˈeɪkər] *n* : acre *m*

acreage [ˈeɪkərɪdʒ] *n* : superficie *f* en acres

acrid [ˈækrəd] *adj* **1** BITTER : acre **2** CAUSTIC : acre, mordaz — **acridly** *adv*

acrimonious [ˌækrəˈmoʊniəs] *adj* : áspero, cáustico, sarcástico

acrimony [ˈækrəˌmoʊni] *n, pl* **-nies** : acrimonia *f*

acrobat [ˈækrəˌbæt] *n* : acróbata *mf*, saltimbanqui *mf*

acrobatic [ˌækrəˈbætɪk] *adj* : acrobático

acrobatics [ˌækrəˈbætɪks] *ns & pl* : acrobacia *f*

acronym [ˈækrəˌnɪm] *n* : acrónimo *m*

across[1] [əˈkrɔs] *adv* **1** CROSSWISE : al través **2** : a través, del otro lado ⟨he's already across : ya está del otro lado⟩ **3** : de ancho ⟨40 feet across : 40 pies de ancho⟩

across[2] *prep* **1** : al otro lado de ⟨across the street : al otro lado de la calle⟩ **2** : a través de ⟨a log across the road : un tronco a través del camino⟩

across–the–board *adj* : general, para todos

acrylic [əˈkrɪlɪk] *n* : acrílico *m*

act[1] [ˈækt] *vi* **1** : actuar ⟨he acted alone : actuó solo⟩ ⟨she acted courageously : actuó con coraje⟩ ⟨to act in one's own interests : actuar uno en su propio interés⟩ **2** : tomar medidas ⟨he acted to save the business : tomó medidas para salvar el negocio⟩ **3** BEHAVE : comportarse ⟨to act like children : actuar como niños⟩ **4** PERFORM : actuar, interpretar **5** : fingir, simular ⟨to act dumb : hacerse el tonto⟩ ⟨he acted as if nothing had happened : actuó como si no hubiera pasado nada⟩ **6** FUNCTION : actuar, servir, funcionar **7 to act as** : servir de, hacer de **8 to act on** : seguir (un consejo, etc.), actuar respecto a **9 to act on** AFFECT : actuar sobre **10 to act out** MISBEHAVE : portarse mal (para hacerse notar) **11 to act out** PERFORM : representar **12 to act up** MISBEHAVE : portarse mal **13 to act up** MALFUNCTION : funcionar mal **14 to act up** WORSEN : agravarse

act[2] *n* **1** DEED : acto *m*, hecho *m*, acción *f* **2** DECREE : ley *f*, decreto *m* **3** : acto *m* (en una obra de teatro), número *m* (en un espectáculo) **4** PRETENSE : fingimiento *m*

acting[1] [ˈæktɪŋ] *adj* INTERIM : interino, en funciones

acting[2] *n* : interpretación *f*, actuación *f*

action [ˈækʃən] *n* **1** DEED : acción *f*, acto *m*, hecho *m* ⟨to take action : tomar medidas⟩ **2** BEHAVIOR : actuación *f*, comportamiento *m* **3** LAWSUIT : demanda *f* **4** MOVEMENT : movimiento *m* **5** COMBAT : combate *m* **6** PLOT : acción *f*, trama *f* **7** MECHANISM : mecanismo *m* **8 in** ∼ : en acción **9 to go into action** : entrar en acción

activate [ˈæktəˌveɪt] *vt* **-vated; -vating** : activar

activation [ˌæktəˈveɪʃən] *n* : activación *f*

active [ˈæktɪv] *adj* **1** MOVING : activo, en movimiento **2** LIVELY : vigoroso, enérgico **3** : en actividad ⟨an active volcano : un volcán en actividad⟩ **4** OPERATIVE : vigente

actively [ˈæktɪvli] *adv* : activamente, enérgicamente

activist [ˈæktɪvɪst] *n* : activista *mf* — **activism** [-ˌvɪzəm] *n* — **activist** *adj*

activity [ækˈtɪvəti] *n, pl* **-ties** **1** MOVEMENT : actividad *f*, movimiento *m* **2** VIGOR : vigor *m*, energía *f* **3** OCCUPATION : actividad *f*, ocupación *f*

actor [ˈæktər] *n* : actor *m*, artista *mf*

actress [ˈæktrəs] *n* : actriz *f*

actual [ˈæktʃuəl] *adj* : real, verdadero

actuality [ˌæktʃuˈæləti] *n, pl* **-ties** : realidad *f*

actually [ˈæktʃuəli, -ʃəli] *adv* : realmente, en realidad

actuary [ˈæktʃuˌeri] *n, pl* **-aries** : actuario *m*, -ria *f* de seguros — **actuarial** [ˌæktʃuˈeriəl] *adj*

acumen [əˈkjuːmən] *n* : perspicacia *f*

acupuncture [ˈækjuˌpʌŋktʃər] *n* : acupuntura *f*

acute [əˈkjuːt] *adj* **acuter; acutest** **1** SHARP : agudo **2** PERCEPTIVE : perspicaz, sagaz **3** KEEN : fino, muy desarrollado, agudo ⟨an acute sense of smell : un fino olfato⟩ **4** SEVERE : grave **5** : agudo

acute angle : ángulo *m* agudo

acutely [əˈkjuːtli] *adv* : intensamente ⟨to be acutely aware : estar perfectamente consciente⟩

acuteness [əˈkjuːtnəs] *n* : agudeza *f*

ad [ˈæd] → **advertisement**

adage [ˈædɪdʒ] *n* : adagio *m*, refrán *m*, dicho *m*

adamant [ˈædəmənt, -ˌmænt] *adj* : firme, categórico, inflexible — **adamantly** *adv*

Adam's apple [ˈædəmz] *n* : nuez *f* de Adán

adapt [əˈdæpt] *vt* : adaptar, ajustar — *vi* : adaptarse

adaptability [əˌdæptəˈbɪləti] *n* : adaptabilidad *f*, flexibilidad *f*

adaptable [əˈdæptəbəl] *adj* : adaptable, amoldable

adaptation [ˌæˌdæpˈteɪʃən, -dəp-] *n* **1** : adaptación *f*, modificación *f* **2** VERSION : versión *f*

adapter [əˈdæptər] *n* : adaptador *m*

add [ˈæd] *vt* **1** : añadir, agregar ⟨add the flour : añadir la harina⟩ **2** : agregar, añadir ⟨to add a comment : añadir una observación⟩ **3** : sumar (números) **4** IN-

CLUDE : incluir **5 to add up** : sumar ⟨add up the costs : suma los gastos⟩ — *vi* **1** : sumar **2 to add to** INCREASE : aumentar ⟨to add to the confusion : para aumentar la confusión⟩ **3 to add up** SQUARE : cuadrar **4 to add up to** : sumar en total

adder ['ædər] *n* : víbora *f*

addict¹ [ə'dɪkt] *vt* : causar adicción en

addict² ['ædɪkt] *n* **1** : adicto *m*, -ta *f* **2 drug addict** : drogadicto *m*, -ta *f*; toxicómano *m*, -na *f*

addicted [ə'dɪktəd] *adj* : adicto

addiction [ə'dɪkʃən] *n* **1** : adicción *f*, dependencia *f* **2 drug addiction** : drogadicción *f*

addictive [ə'dɪktɪv] *adj* : adictivo

addition [ə'dɪʃən] *n* **1** : adición *f*, añadidura *f* **2 in ~** : además, también

additional [ə'dɪʃənəl] *adj* : extra, adicional, de más

additionally [ə'dɪʃənəli] *adv* : además, adicionalmente

additive ['ædətɪv] *n* : aditivo *m*

addle ['ædəl] *vt* **-dled; -dling** : confundir, enturbiar

address¹ [ə'drɛs] *vt* **1** : dirigirse a, pronunciar un discurso ante ⟨to address a jury : dirigirse a un jurado⟩ **2** : dirigir, ponerle la dirección a ⟨to address a letter : dirigir una carta⟩

address² [ə'drɛs, 'æ,drɛs] *n* **1** SPEECH : discurso *m*, alocución *f* **2** : dirección *f* (de una residencia, etc.)

addressee [,æ,drɛ'si:, ə-] *n* : destinatario *m*, -ria *f*

adduce [ə-'du:s, 'dju:s] *vt* **-duced; -ducing** : aducir

adenoids ['æd,nɔɪd, -dən,ɔɪd] *npl* : adenoides *fpl*

adept [ə'dɛpt] *adj* : experto, hábil — **adeptly** *adv*

adequacy ['ædɪkwəsi] *n, pl* **-cies** : lo adecuado, lo suficiente

adequate ['ædɪkwət] *adj* **1** SUFFICIENT : adecuado, suficiente **2** ACCEPTABLE, PASSABLE : adecuado, aceptable

adequately ['ædɪkwətli] *adv* : suficientemente, apropiadamente

adhere [æd'hɪr, əd-] *vi* **-hered; -hering 1** STICK : pegarse, adherirse **2 to adhere to** : adherirse a (una política, etc.), cumplir con (una promesa)

adherence [æd'hɪrənts, əd-] *n* : adhesión *f*, adherencia *f*, observancia *f* (de una ley, etc.)

adherent¹ [æd'hɪrənt, əd-] *adj* : adherente, adhesivo, pegajoso

adherent² *n* : adepto *m*, -ta *f*; partidario *m*, -ria *f*

adhesion [æd'hi:ʒən, əd-] *n* : adhesión *f*, adherencia *f*

adhesive¹ [æd'hi:sɪv, əd-, -zɪv] *adj* : adhesivo

adhesive² *n* : adhesivo *m*, pegamento *m*

adjacent [ə'dʒeɪsənt] *adj* : adyacente, colindante, contiguo

adjective ['ædʒɪktɪv] *n* : adjetivo *m* — **adjectival** [,ædʒɪk'taɪvəl] *adj*

adjoin [ə'dʒɔɪn] *vt* : lindar con, colindar con

adjoining [ə'dʒɔɪnɪŋ] *adj* : contiguo, colindante

adjourn [ə'dʒərn] *vt* : levantar, suspender ⟨the meeting is adjourned : se levanta la sesión⟩ — *vi* : aplazarse

adjournment [ə'dʒərnmənt] *n* : suspensión *f*, aplazamiento *m*

adjudicate [ə'dʒu:dɪ,keɪt] *vt* **-cated; -cating** : juzgar, arbitrar

adjudication [ə,dʒu:dɪ'keɪʃən] *n* **1** JUDGING : arbitrio *m* (judicial) **2** JUDGMENT : fallo *m*

adjunct ['æ,dʒʌŋkt] *n* : adjunto *m*, complemento *m*

adjust [ə'dʒʌst] *vt* : ajustar, arreglar, regular — *vi* **to adjust to** : adaptarse a

adjustable [ə'dʒʌstəbəl] *adj* : ajustable, regulable, graduable

adjustment [ə'dʒʌstmənt] *n* : ajuste *m*, modificación *f*

ad–lib¹ ['æd'lɪb] *v* **-libbed; -libbing** : improvisar

ad–lib² *adj* : improvisado

administer [æd'mɪnəstər, əd-] *vt* : administrar

administration [æd,mɪnə'streɪʃən, əd-] *n* **1** MANAGING : administración *f*, dirección *f* **2** GOVERNMENT, MANAGEMENT : administración *f*, gobierno *m*

administrative [æd'mɪnə,streɪtɪv, əd-] *adj* : administrativo — **administratively** *adv*

administrator [æd'mɪnə,streɪtər, əd-] *n* : administrador *m*, -dora *f*

admirable ['ædmərəbəl] *adj* : admirable, loable — **admirably** *adv*

admiral ['ædmərəl] *n* : almirante *mf*

admiralty ['ædmərəlti] *n* : almirantazgo *m*

admiration [,ædmə'reɪʃən] *n* : admiración *f*

admire [æd'maɪr] *vt* **-mired; -miring** : admirar

admirer [æd'maɪrər] *n* : admirador *m*, -dora *f*

admiring [æd'maɪrɪŋ] *adj* : admirativo, de admiración

admiringly [æd'maɪrɪŋli] *adv* : con admiración

admissible [æd'mɪsəbəl] *adj* : admisible, aceptable

admission [æd'mɪʃən] *n* **1** ADMITTANCE : entrada *f*, admisión *f* **2** ACKNOWLEDGMENT : reconocimiento *m*, admisión *f*

admit [æd'mɪt, əd-] *vt* **-mitted; -mitting 1** : admitir, dejar entrar ⟨the museum admits children : el museo deja entrar a los niños⟩ **2** ACKNOWLEDGE : reconocer, admitir

admittance [æd'mɪtənts, əd-] *n* : admisión *f*, entrada *f*, acceso *m*

admittedly [æd'mɪtədli, əd-] *adv* : la verdad es que, lo cierto es que ⟨admittedly we went too fast : la verdad es que fuimos demasiado de prisa⟩

admonish [æd'mɑnɪʃ, əd-] *vt* : amonestar, reprender

admonition [,ædmə'nɪʃən] *n* : admonición *f*

ad nauseam [ˌæd'nɔziəm] *adv* : hasta la saciedad

ado [ə'du:] *n* 1 FUSS : ruido *m*, alboroto *m* 2 TROUBLE : dificultad *f*, lío *m* 3 **without further ado** : sin más preámbulos

adobe [ə'do:bi] *n* : adobe *m*

adolescence [ˌædəl'ɛsənts] *n* : adolescencia *f*

adolescent[1] [ˌædəl'ɛsənt] *adj* : adolescente, de adolescencia

adolescent[2] *n* : adolescente *mf*

adopt [ə'dɑpt] *vt* : adoptar

adopted [ə'dɑptəd] *adj* : adoptivo

adoption [ə'dɑpʃən] *n* : adopción *f*

adoptive [ə'dɑptɪv] *adj* : adoptivo

adorable [ə'dorəbəl] *adj* : adorable, encantador

adorably [ə'dorəbli] *adv* : de manera adorable

adoration [ˌædə'reɪʃən] *n* : adoración *f*

adore [ə'dor] *vt* adored; adoring 1 WORSHIP : adorar 2 LOVE : querer, adorar 3 LIKE : encantarle (algo a uno), gustarle mucho (algo a uno) ⟨I adore your new dress : me encanta tu vestido nuevo⟩

adorn [ə'dorn] *vt* : adornar, ornar, engalanar

adornment [ə'dornmənt] *n* : adorno *m*, decoración *f*

adrenaline [ə'drɛnələn] *n* : adrenalina *f*

adrift [ə'drɪft] *adj & adv* : a la deriva

adroit [ə'drɔɪt] *adj* : diestro, hábil — **adroitly** *adv*

adroitness [ə'drɔɪtnəs] *n* : destreza *f*, habilidad *f*

adulation [ˌædʒəleɪʃən] *n* : adulación *f*

adult[1] [ə'dʌlt, 'æˌdʌlt] *adj* : adulto

adult[2] *n* : adulto *m*, -ta *f*

adulterate [ə'dʌltəˌreɪt] *vt* -ated; -ating : adulterar — **adulteration** [əˌdʌltə'reɪʃən] *n*

adulterer [ə'dʌltərər] *n* : adúltero *m*, -ra *f*

adulterous [ə'dʌltərəs] *adj* : adúltero

adultery [ə'dʌltəri] *n, pl* -teries : adulterio *m*

adulthood [ə'dʌltˌhʊd] *n* : adultez *f*, edad *f* adulta

advance[1] [æd'vænts, əd-] *v* -vanced; -vancing *vt* 1 : avanzar, adelantar ⟨to advance troops : avanzar las tropas⟩ 2 PROMOTE : ascender, promover 3 PROPOSE : proponer, presentar 4 : adelantar, anticipar ⟨they advanced me next month's salary : me adelantaron el sueldo del próximo mes⟩ — *vi* 1 PROCEED : avanzar, adelantarse 2 PROGRESS : progresar

advance[2] *adj* : anticipado ⟨advance notice : previo aviso⟩

advance[3] *n* 1 PROGRESSION : avance *m* 2 PROGRESS : adelanto *m*, mejora *f*, progreso *m* 3 RISE : aumento *m*, alza *f* 4 LOAN : anticipo *m*, préstamo *m* 5 in ~ : por adelantado

advanced [æd'vænst, əd-] *adj* 1 DEVELOPED : avanzado, desarrollado 2 PRECOCIOUS : adelantado, precoz 3 HIGHER : superior

advancement [æd'vænsmənt, əd-] *n* 1 FURTHERANCE : fomento *m*, adelanta-

miento *m*, progreso *m* 2 PROMOTION : ascenso *m*

advantage [əd'væntɪʤ, æd-] *n* 1 SUPERIORITY : ventaja *f*, superioridad *f* ⟨to have the/an advantage : tener ventaja⟩ 2 GAIN : provecho *m*, partido *m* 3 to take **advantage of** : aprovecharse de

advantageous [ˌædˌvæn'teɪʤəs, -vən-] *adj* : ventajoso, provechoso — **advantageously** *adv*

advent ['ædˌvɛnt] *n* 1 **Advent** : Adviento *m* 2 ARRIVAL : advenimiento *m*, venida *f*

adventure [æd'vɛntʃər, əd-] *n* : aventura *f*

adventurer [æd'vɛntʃərər, əd-] *n* : aventurero *m*, -ra *f*

adventurous [æd'vɛntʃərəs, əd-] *adj* 1 : intrépido, aventurero ⟨an adventurous traveler : un viajero intrépido⟩ 2 RISKY : arriesgado, aventurado

adverb ['ædˌvərb] *n* : adverbio *m* — **adverbial** [æd'vərbiəl] *adj*

adversary ['ædvərˌsɛri] *n, pl* -saries : adversario *m*, -ria *f*

adverse [æd'vərs, 'ædˌ] *adj* 1 OPPOSING : opuesto, contrario 2 UNFAVORABLE : adverso, desfavorable — **adversely** *adv*

adversity [æd'vərsəti, əd-] *n, pl* -ties : adversidad *f*

advertise ['ædvərˌtaɪz] *v* -tised; -tising *vt* : anunciar, hacerle publicidad a — *vi* : hacer publicidad, hacer propaganda

advertisement ['ædvərˌtaɪzmənt; ædˈvərtəzmənt] *n* : anuncio *m*, aviso *m*

advertiser ['ædvərˌtaɪzər] *n* : anunciante *mf*

advertising ['ædvərˌtaɪzɪŋ] *n* : publicidad *f*, propaganda *f*

advice [æd'vaɪs] *n* : consejo *m*, recomendación *f* ⟨take my advice : sigue mis consejos⟩

advisability [ædˌvaɪzə'bɪləti, əd-] *n* : conveniencia *f*

advisable [æd'vaɪzəbəl, əd-] *adj* : aconsejable, recomendable, conveniente

advise [æd'vaɪz, əd-] *v* -vised; -vising *vt* 1 COUNSEL : aconsejar, asesorar ⟨I advise that you wait : le aconsejo que espere⟩ ⟨I advise you to wait : le aconsejo esperar⟩ ⟨she advised us against buying it : nos aconsejó que no lo compráramos⟩ 2 RECOMMEND : recomendar ⟨I advise that you wait, I advise waiting : les aconsejo que esperen⟩ ⟨he advised caution : aconsejó actuar con cautela⟩ 3 INFORM : informar, notificar ⟨they advised him of his rights : le informaron de sus derechos⟩ — *vi* : dar consejo ⟨to advise against : desaconsejar⟩

adviser *or* **advisor** [æd'vaɪzər, əd-] *n* : consejero *m*, -ra *f*; asesor *m*, -sora *f*

advisory [æd'vaɪzəri, əd-] *adj* 1 : consultivo 2 **in an advisory capacity** : como asesor

advocacy ['ædvəkəsi] *n* : promoción *f*, apoyo *m*

advocate[1] ['ædvəˌkeɪt] *vt* -cated; -cating : recomendar, abogar por, ser partidario de

advocate[2] ['ædvəkət] *n* : defensor *m*, -sora *f*; partidario *m*, -ria *f*

adze ['ædz] *n* : azuela *f*

aeon ['i:ən, 'i:,ɑn] *n* : eón *m*, siglo *m*, eternidad *f*

aerate ['ær,eɪt] *vt* -ated; -ating : gasear (un líquido), oxigenar (la sangre)

aerial[1] ['æriəl] *adj* : aéreo

aerial[2] *n* : antena *f*

aerie ['æri, 'ɪri, 'eɪəri] *n* : aguilera *f*

aerobic [,ær'o:bɪk] *adj* : aerobio, aeróbico ⟨aerobic exercises : ejercicios aeróbicos⟩

aerobics [,ær'o:bɪks] *ns & pl* : aeróbic *m*

aerodynamic [,æro:daɪ'næmɪk] *adj* : aerodinámico — **aerodynamically** [-mɪkli] *adv*

aerodynamics [,æro:daɪ'næmɪks] *n* : aerodinámica *f*

aeronautical [,ærə'nɔtɪkəl] *adj* : aeronáutico

aeronautics [,ærə'nɔtɪks] *n* : aeronáutica *f*

aerosol ['ærə,sɔl] *n* : aerosol *m*

aerospace[1] ['æro:,speɪs] *adj* : aeroespacial

aerospace[2] *n* : espacio *m*

aesthetic [ɛs'θɛtɪk] *adj* : estético — **aesthetically** [-tɪkli] *adv*

aesthetics [ɛs'θɛtɪks] *n* : estética *f*

afar [ə'fɑr] *adv* : lejos, a lo lejos

affability [,æfə'bɪləti] *n* : afabilidad *f*

affable ['æfəbəl] *adj* : afable — **affably** *adv*

affair [ə'fær] *n* **1** MATTER : asunto *m*, cuestión *f*, caso *m* **2** EVENT : ocasión *f*, acontecimiento *m* **3** LIAISON : amorío *m*, aventura *f* **4** business affairs : negocios *mpl* **5** current affairs : actualidades *fpl*

affect [ə'fɛkt, æ-] *vt* **1** INFLUENCE, TOUCH : afectar, tocar **2** FEIGN : fingir

affectation [,æ,fɛk'teɪʃən] *n* : afectación *f*

affected [ə'fɛktəd, æ-] *adj* **1** FEIGNED : afectado, fingido **2** MOVED : conmovido

affecting [ə'fɛktɪŋ, æ-] *adj* : conmovedor

affection [ə'fɛkʃən] *n* : afecto *m*, cariño *m*

affectionate [ə'fɛkʃənət] *adj* : afectuoso, cariñoso — **affectionately** *adv*

affidavit [,æfə'deɪvət, 'æfə,-] *n* : declaración *f* jurada, afidávit *m*

affiliate[1] [ə'fɪli,eɪt] *v* -ated; -ating *vt* to be affiliated with : estar afiliado a

affiliate[2] [ə'fɪliət] *n* : afiliado *m*, -da *f* (persona), filial *f* (organización)

affiliation [ə,fɪli'eɪʃən] *n* : afiliación *f*, filiación *f*

affinity [ə'fɪnəti] *n, pl* -ties : afinidad *f*

affirm [ə'fərm] *vt* : afirmar, aseverar, declarar

affirmation [,æfər'meɪʃən] *n* : afirmación *f*, aserto *m*, declaración *f*

affirmative[1] [ə'fərmətɪv] *adj* : afirmativo ⟨affirmative action : acción afirmativa⟩

affirmative[2] *n* **1** : afirmativa *f* **2** to answer in the affirmative : responder afirmativamente, dar una respuesta afirmativa

affix [ə'fɪks] *vt* : fijar, poner, pegar

afflict [ə'flɪkt] *vt* **1** : afligir, aquejar **2** to be afflicted with : padecer de, sufrir de

affliction [ə'flɪkʃən] *n* **1** TRIBULATION : tribulación *f* **2** AILMENT : enfermedad *f*, padecimiento *m*

affluence ['æ,flu:ənts; æ'flu:-, ə-] *n* : afluencia *f*, abundancia *f*, prosperidad *f*

affluent ['æ,flu:ənt; æ'flu:-, ə-] *adj* : próspero, adinerado

afford [ə'ford] *vt* **1** : tener los recursos para, permitirse el lujo de ⟨I can afford it : puedo permitírmelo⟩ **2** PROVIDE : ofrecer, proporcionar, dar

affordable [ə'fordəbəl] *adj* : asequible (dícese de precios)

affront[1] [ə'frʌnt] *vt* : afrentar, ofender

affront[2] *n* : afrenta *f*, insulto *m*, ofensa *f*

Afghan ['æf,gæn, -gən] *n* : afgano *m*, -na *f* — **Afghan** *adj*

afield [ə'fi:ld] *adv* farther afield : más lejos

afire [ə'faɪr] *adj* : ardiendo, en llamas

aflame [ə'fleɪm] *adj* : llameante, en llamas

afloat [ə'flo:t] *adv & adj* : a flote

afoot [ə'fut] *adj* **1** WALKING : a pie, andando **2** UNDER WAY : en marcha ⟨something suspicious is afoot : algo sospechoso se está tramando⟩

aforementioned [ə'for'mɛntʃənd] *adj* : antedicho, susodicho

aforesaid [ə'for,sɛd] *adj* : antes mencionado, antedicho

afraid [ə'freɪd] *adj* **1** to be afraid : tener miedo ⟨she's afraid of the dark : le tiene miedo a la oscuridad⟩ ⟨I was afraid to look down : me daba miedo mirar para abajo⟩ **2** to be afraid that : temerse que ⟨I'm afraid not : me temo que no⟩

afresh [ə'frɛʃ] *adv* **1** : de nuevo, otra vez **2** to start afresh : volver a empezar

African ['æfrɪkən] *n* : africano *m*, -na *f* — **African** *adj*

African–American[1] [,æfrɪkənə'mɛrɪkən] *adj* : afroamericano

African–American[2] *n* : afroamericano *m*, -na *f*

Afro–American[1] [,æfroə'mɛrɪkən] *adj* → **African–American**[1]

Afro–American[2] *n* → **African–American**[2]

aft ['æft] *adv* : a popa

after[1] ['æftər] *adv* **1** AFTERWARD : después **2** BEHIND : detrás, atrás

after[2] *adj* : posterior, siguiente ⟨in after years : en los años posteriores⟩

after[3] *conj* : después, después de que ⟨after we ate : después de que comimos, después de comer⟩

after[4] *prep* **1** FOLLOWING : después de, tras ⟨after Saturday/lunch : después del sábado/almuerzo⟩ ⟨after a year : después de un año⟩ ⟨day after day : día tras día⟩ ⟨the day after tomorrow : pasado mañana⟩ ⟨it's ten (minutes) after six : son las seis y diez⟩ ⟨I shouted after him : le grité (mientras se alejaba)⟩ ⟨I'm not cleaning up after you : no voy a limpiar lo que tú ensucias⟩ **2** BEHIND : tras, detrás de ⟨she ran after the dog : corrió tras el perro⟩ **3** CONCERNING : por ⟨they asked after you : preguntaron por ti⟩ **4** CONSIDERING : después de **5** PURSUING : tras ⟨to be after someone : andar tras alguien⟩ **6** : al estilo de ⟨to be named after : llevar el nombre de⟩ ⟨to take after : parecerse a) **7 after all** : después de todo

aftereffect ['æftərɪ,fɛkt] *n* : efecto *m* secundario

afterlife ['æftər,laɪf] *n* : vida *f* venidera, vida *f* después de la muerte

aftermath ['æftər,mæθ] *n* : consecuencias *fpl*, resultados *mpl*

afternoon [,æftər'nu:n] *n* : tarde *f*

aftershave ['æftər,ʃeɪv] *n* : aftershave *m*, loción *f* para después de afeitarse

aftershock ['æftər,ʃak] *n* : réplica *f* (de un terremoto)

aftertaste ['æftər,teɪst] *n* : resabio *m*, regusto *m*

afterthought ['æftər,θɔt] *n* : ocurrencia *f* tardía, idea *f* tardía

afterward ['æftərwərd] *or* **afterwards** [-wərdz] *adv* : después, luego ⟨soon afterward : poco después⟩

again [ə'gɛn, -'gɪn] *adv* **1** ANEW, OVER : de nuevo, otra vez ⟨all over again : otra vez desde el principio⟩ ⟨never again : nunca más⟩ ⟨again and again : una y otra vez⟩ **2** BESIDES : además **3 then again** : por otra parte

against [ə'gɛnst, -'gɪnst] *prep* **1** TOUCHING : contra ⟨against the wall : contra la pared⟩ **2** OPPOSING : contra, en contra de ⟨to vote against : votar en contra de⟩ ⟨he acted against my advice : no siguió mi consejo⟩ ⟨against her wishes/will : en contra de su voluntad⟩

agape [ə'geɪp] *adj* : boquiabierto

agate ['ægət] *n* : ágata *f*

age¹ ['eɪdʒ] *vi* **aged; aging** : envejecer, madurar

age² *n* **1** : edad *f* ⟨ten years of age : diez años de edad⟩ ⟨at the age of 35 : a los 35 años, a la edad de 35⟩ ⟨at your age : a tu edad⟩ ⟨people of all ages : personas de todas las edades⟩ ⟨those under age 18 : los menores de 18 años⟩ ⟨from an early age : desde pequeño⟩ ⟨to be of age : ser mayor de edad⟩ ⟨to come of age : cumplir la mayoría de edad⟩ ⟨he came of age as a writer : alcanzó su madurez como escritor⟩ ⟨to act one's age : actuar con madurez⟩ **2** PERIOD : era *f*, siglo *m*, época *f* **3** **old age** : vejez *f* **4 ages** *npl* : siglos *mpl*, eternidad *f* ⟨it's been ages since I've seen her : hace mucho tiempo que no la veo⟩

aged *adj* **1** ['eɪdʒəd, 'eɪdʒd] OLD : anciano, viejo, vetusto **2** ['eɪdʒd] (*indicating a specified age*) ⟨a girl aged 10 : una niña de 10 años de edad⟩

ageless ['eɪdʒləs] *adj* **1** : eternamente joven **2** TIMELESS : eterno, perenne

agency ['eɪdʒənsi] *n, pl* **-cies** **1** : agencia *f*, oficina *f* ⟨travel agency : agencia de viajes⟩ **2 through the agency of** : a través de, por medio de

agenda [ə'dʒɛndə] *n* : agenda *f*, orden *m* del día

agent ['eɪdʒənt] *n* **1** MEANS : agente *m*, medio *m*, instrumento *m* **2** REPRESENTATIVE : agente *mf*, representante *mf*

aggravate ['ægrə,veɪt] *vt* **-vated; -vating** **1** WORSEN : agravar, empeorar **2** ANNOY : irritar, exasperar

aggravation [,ægrə'veɪʃən] *n* **1** WORSENING : empeoramiento *m* **2** ANNOYANCE : molestia *f*, irritación *f*, exasperación *f*

aggregate¹ ['ægrɪ,geɪt] *vt* **-gated; -gating** : juntar, sumar

aggregate² ['ægrɪgət] *adj* : total, global, conjunto

aggregate³ ['ægrɪgət] *n* **1** CONGLOMERATE : agregado *m*, conglomerado *m* **2** WHOLE : total *m*, conjunto *m*

aggression [ə'grɛʃən] *n* **1** ATTACK : agresión *f* **2** AGGRESSIVENESS : agresividad *f*

aggressive [ə'grɛsɪv] *adj* : agresivo — **aggressively** *adv*

aggressiveness [ə'grɛsɪvnəs] *n* : agresividad *f*

aggressor [ə'grɛsər] *n* : agresor *m*, -sora *f*

aggrieved [ə'gri:vd] *adj* : ofendido, herido

aghast [ə'gæst] *adj* : espantado, aterrado, horrorizado

agile ['ædʒəl] *adj* : ágil

agility [ə'dʒɪləti] *n, pl* **-ties** : agilidad *f*

aging¹ ['eɪdʒɪŋ] *adj* **1** : envejecido **2** : anticuado

aging² *n* : envejecimiento

agitate ['ædʒə,teɪt] *v* **-tated; -tating** *vt* **1** SHAKE : agitar **2** UPSET : inquietar, perturbar — *vi* **to agitate against** : hacer campaña en contra de

agitated ['ædʒə,teɪtəd] *adj* : agitado, inquieto

agitation [,ædʒə'teɪʃən] *n* : agitación *f*, inquietud *f*

agitator ['ædʒə,teɪtər] *n* : agitador *m*, -dora *f*

agnostic [æg'nastɪk] *n* : agnóstico *m*, -ca *f*

ago [ə'go:] *adv* : hace ⟨two years ago : hace dos años⟩ ⟨long ago : hace tiempo, hace mucho tiempo⟩

agog [ə'gag] *adj* : ansioso, curioso

agonize ['ægə,naɪz] *vi* **-nized; -nizing** **1** : atormentarse, angustiarse **2 to agonize over** : preocuparse mucho por

agonizing ['ægə,naɪzɪŋ] *adj* : angustioso, terrible — **agonizingly** [-zɪŋli] *adv*

agony ['ægəni] *n, pl* **-nies** **1** PAIN : dolor *m* **2** ANGUISH : angustia *f*

agrarian [ə'grɛriən] *adj* : agrario

agree [ə'gri:] *v* **agreed; agreeing** *vt* **1** : estar de acuerdo ⟨we all agree that . . . : todos estamos de acuerdo que . . .⟩ **2** ADMIT, CONCEDE : reconocer, admitir **3** : acceder a, consentir en ⟨she agreed to come : accedió a venir⟩ ⟨he agreed that she could come : consintió en que viniera⟩ ⟨she agreed to be interviewed : concedió una entrevista⟩ — *vi* **1** CONCUR : estar de acuerdo ⟨to agree with someone/something : estar de acuerdo con alguien/algo⟩ ⟨we agree on/about . . . : estamos de acuerdo en . . .⟩ ⟨we can't agree on a date : no nos ponemos de acuerdo en la fecha⟩ **2** TALLY, SQUARE : concordar **3** : concordar (en gramática) **4 to agree on** : ponerse de acuerdo en **5 to agree to** : acceder a ⟨he

agreed to the plan : accedió al plan⟩ 6
to agree with SUIT : sentarle bien (a alguien)

agreeable [əˈgriːəbəl] *adj* 1 PLEASANT : agradable, simpático 2 WILLING : dispuesto 3 ACCEPTABLE : aceptable ⟨is it agreeable to you? : ¿te parece bien?⟩

agreeableness [əˈgriːəbəlnəs] *n* 1 PLEASANTNESS : simpatía *f* 2 WILLINGNESS : disposición *f*, buena voluntad *f* 3 ACCEPTABILITY : aceptabilidad *f*

agreeably [əˈgriːəbli] *adv* : agradablemente

agreement [əˈgriːmənt] *n* 1 : acuerdo *m*, conformidad *f* ⟨in agreement with : de acuerdo con⟩ 2 CONTRACT, PACT : acuerdo *m*, pacto *m*, convenio *m* 3 CONCORD, HARMONY : concordia *f*

agribusiness [ˈægrɪˌbɪznəs, -nəz] *n* : agroindustria *f*

agriculture [ˈægrɪˌkʌltʃər] *n* : agricultura *f*

agricultural [ˌægrɪˈkʌltʃərəl] *adj* : agrícola

aground [əˈgraʊnd] *adj* : encallado, varado

ahead [əˈhɛd] *adv* 1 : al frente, delante, adelante ⟨he walked ahead : caminó delante⟩ ⟨to go straight ahead : ir todo recto⟩ 2 BEFOREHAND : por adelantado, con antelación 3 LEADING : a la delantera 4 **to get ahead** : adelantar, progresar 5 **to look/think ahead** : mirar hacia el futuro

ahead of *prep* 1 : al frente de, delante de, antes de 2 **to get ahead of** : adelantarse a

ahem [əˈhɛm] *interj* : ¡ejem!

ahoy [əˈhɔɪ] *interj* **ship ahoy!** : ¡barco a la vista!

aid¹ [ˈeɪd] *vt* : ayudar, auxiliar

aid² *n* 1 HELP : ayuda *f*, asistencia *f* 2 ASSISTANT : asistente *mf*

aide [ˈeɪd] *n* : ayudante *mf*

AIDS [ˈeɪdz] *n* : SIDA *m*, sida *m*

ail [ˈeɪl] *vt* : molestar, afligir — *vi* : sufrir, estar enfermo

aileron [ˈeɪləˌrɑn] *n* : alerón *m*

ailment [ˈeɪlmənt] *n* : enfermedad *f*, dolencia *f*, achaque *m*

aim¹ [ˈeɪm] *vt* 1 POINT : apuntar (un arma, una cámara, etc.) 2 DIRECT : dirigir ⟨he aimed the stone at the window : arrojó la piedra hacia la ventana⟩ ⟨a well-aimed blow : un golpe certero⟩ 3 INTEND : proponerse, querer (hacer algo) ⟨we aim to please : nuestro objetivo es complacer⟩ 4 **to be aimed at** ⟨his criticism wasn't aimed at her : sus críticas no iban dirigidas a ella⟩ ⟨it's aimed at reducing costs : tiene como objetivo la reducción de gastos⟩ — *vi* 1 POINT : apuntar ⟨she aimed at the target : le apuntó al blanco⟩ 2 ASPIRE : aspirar ⟨to aim high/low : aspirar a mucho/poco⟩ 3 **to aim at/for** ⟨it aims at reducing costs : tiene como objetivo la reducción de gastos⟩ ⟨to aim for a goal : proponerse como meta⟩

aim² *n* 1 MARKSMANSHIP : puntería *f* 2 GOAL : propósito *m*, objetivo *m*, fin *m*

aimless [ˈeɪmləs] *adj* : sin rumbo, sin objeto

aimlessly [ˈeɪmləsli] *adv* : sin rumbo, sin objeto

ain't [ˈeɪnt] *fam* contraction of **am not** or **are not** or **is not** or **have not** or **had not** → **be**, **have**

air¹ [ˈær] *vt* 1 or **to air out** : airear, ventilar 2 EXPRESS : airear, manifestar, comunicar 3 BROADCAST : transmitir, emitir

air² *n* 1 : aire *m* ⟨in the open air : al aire libre⟩ ⟨to vanish into thin air : desaparecerse⟩ 2 MELODY : aire *m* 3 APPEARANCE : aire *m*, aspecto *m* 4 → **air-conditioning** 5 **airs** *npl* : aires *mpl*, afectación *f* 6 **by ~** : por avión (dícese de una carta), en avión (dícese de una persona) 7 **to be on the air** : estar en el aire, estar emitiendo 8 **to be up in the air** : estar en el aire, no estar resuelto

airbase [ˈærˌbeɪs] *n* : base *f* aérea

airborne [ˈærˌborn] *adj* 1 : aerotransportado ⟨airborne troops : tropas aerotransportadas⟩ 2 FLYING : volando, en el aire

air-condition [ˌærkənˈdɪʃən] *vt* : climatizar, condicionar con el aire

air-conditioned [-ʃənd] *adj* : climatizado, con aire acondicionado

air conditioner [ˌærkənˈdɪʃənər] *n* : acondicionador *m* de aire

air-conditioning [ˌærkənˈdɪʃənɪŋ] *n* : aire *m* acondicionado

aircraft [ˈærˌkræft] *ns & pl* : avión *m*, aeronave *f* 2 **aircraft carrier** : portaaviones *m*

airfield [ˈærˌfiːld] *n* : aeródromo *m*, campo *m* de aviación

air force *n* : fuerza *f* aérea

airlift [ˈærˌlɪft] *n* : puente *m* aéreo, transporte *m* aéreo

airline [ˈærˌlaɪn] *n* : aerolínea *f*, línea *f* aérea

airliner [ˈærˌlaɪnər] *n* : avión *m* de pasajeros

airmail¹ [ˈærˌmeɪl] *vt* : enviar por vía aérea

airmail² *n* : correo *m* aéreo

airman [ˈærmən] *n*, *pl* **-men** [-mən, -ˌmɛn] 1 AVIATOR : aviador *m*, -dora *f* 2 : soldado *m* de la fuerza aérea

airplane [ˈærˌpleɪn] *n* : avión *m*

airport [ˈærˌport] *n* : aeropuerto *m*

airship [ˈærˌʃɪp] *n* : dirigible *m*, zepelín *m*

airsick [ˈærˌsɪk] *adj* : mareado (al viajar en avión)

airstrip [ˈærˌstrɪp] *n* : pista *f* de aterrizaje

airtight [ˈærˈtaɪt] *adj* : hermético, herméticamente cerrado

air vent → **vent²**

airwaves [ˈærˌweɪvz] *npl* : radio *m*, televisión *f*

airy [ˈæri] *adj* **airier** [-iər]; **-est** 1 DELICATE, LIGHT : delicado, ligero 2 BREEZY : aireado, bien ventilado

aisle [ˈaɪl] *n* : pasillo *m*, nave *f* lateral (de una iglesia)

ajar [əˈdʒɑr] *adj* : entreabierto, entornado

akimbo [əˈkɪmbo] *adj & adv* : en jarras

akin [əˈkɪn] *adj* 1 RELATED : emparentado 2 SIMILAR : semejante, parecido

alabaster [ˈæləˌbæstər] *n* : alabastro *m*

alacrity [ə'lækrəṭi] *n* : presteza *f*, prontitud *f*

alarm[1] [ə'lɑrm] *vt* **1** WARN : alarmar, alertar **2** FRIGHTEN : asustar

alarm[2] *n* **1** WARNING : alarma *f*, alerta *f* **2** APPREHENSION, FEAR : aprensión *f*, inquietud *f*, temor *m* **3 alarm clock** : despertador *m*

alarming [ə'lɑrmɪŋ] *adj* : alarmante

alas [ə'læs] *interj* : ¡ay!

Albanian [æl'beɪniən] *n* : albanés *m*, -nesa *f* — **Albanian** *adj*

albatross ['ælbə,trɔs] *n, pl* **-tross** *or* **-trosses** : albatros *m*

albeit [ɔl'bi:ət, æl-] *conj* : aunque

albino [æl'baɪno] *n, pl* **-nos** : albino *m*, -na *f*

album ['ælbəm] *n* : álbum *m* ⟨photo album : álbum de fotos⟩

albumen [æl'bju:mən] *n* **1** : clara *f* de huevo **2** → albumin

albumin [æl'bju:mən] *n* : albúmina *f*

alchemist ['ælkəmɪst] *n* : alquimista *mf*

alchemy ['ælkəmi] *n, pl* **-mies** : alquimia *f*

alcohol ['ælkə,hɔl] *n* **1** ETHANOL : alcohol *m*, etanol *m* **2** LIQUOR : alcohol *m*, bebidas *fpl* alcohólicas

alcohol–free *adj* : sin alcohol

alcoholic[1] [,ælkə'hɔlɪk] *adj* : alcohólico

alcoholic[2] *n* : alcohólico *m*, -ca *f*

alcoholism ['ælkəhɔ,lɪzəm] *n* : alcoholismo *m*

alcove ['æl,koːv] *n* : nicho *m*, hueco *m*

alderman ['ɔldərmən] *n, pl* **-men** [-mən, -,mɛn] : concejal *mf*

ale ['eɪl] *n* : cerveza *f*

alert[2] *adj* **1** WATCHFUL : alerta, vigilante **2** QUICK : listo, vivo

alert[3] *n* : alerta *f*, alarma *f*

alertly [ə'lɜrtli] *adv* : con listeza

alertness [ə'lɜrtnəs] *n* **1** WATCHFULNESS : vigilancia *f* **2** ASTUTENESS : listeza *f*, viveza *f*

alfalfa [æl'fælfə] *n* : alfalfa *f*

alga ['ælgə] *n, pl* **-gae** ['æl,dʒi:] : alga *f*

algebra ['ældʒəbrə] *n* : álgebra *m*

algebraic [ˌældʒə'breɪɪk] *adj* : algebraico — **algebraically** [-ɪkli] *adv*

Algerian [æl'dʒɪriən] *n* : argelino *m*, -na *f* — **Algerian** *adj*

algorithm ['ælgə,rɪðəm] *n* : algoritmo *m*

alias[1] ['eɪliəs] *adv* : alias

alias[2] *n* : alias *m*

alibi[1] ['ælə,baɪ] *vi* : ofrecer una coartada

alibi[2] *n* **1** : coartada *f* **2** EXCUSE : pretexto *m*, excusa *f*

alien[1] ['eɪliən] *adj* **1** STRANGE : ajeno, extraño **2** FOREIGN : extranjero, foráneo **3** EXTRATERRESTRIAL : extraterrestre

alien[2] *n* **1** FOREIGNER : extranjero *m*, -ra *f*; forastero *m*, -ra *f* **2** EXTRATERRESTRIAL : extraterrestre *mf*

alienate ['eɪliə,neɪt] *vt* **-ated; -ating 1** ESTRANGE : alienar, enajenar **2 to alienate oneself** : alejarse, distanciarse

alienation [ˌeɪliə'neɪʃən] *n* : alienación *f*, enajenación *f*

alight [ə'laɪt] *vi* **1** DISMOUNT : bajarse, apearse **2** LAND : posarse, aterrizar

align [ə'laɪn] *vt* : alinear

alignment [ə'laɪnmənt] *n* : alineación *f*, alineamiento *m*

alike[1] [ə'laɪk] *adv* : igual, del mismo modo

alike[2] *adj* : igual, semejante, parecido

alimentary [ˌælə'mɛntəri] *adj* **1** : alimenticio **2 alimentary canal** : tubo *m* digestivo

alimony ['ælə,moːni] *n, pl* **-nies** : pensión *f* alimenticia

alive [ə'laɪv] *adj* **1** LIVING : vivo, viviente ⟨alive and kicking : vivito y coleando⟩ **2** LIVELY : animado, activo **3** ACTIVE : vigente, en uso **4** AWARE : consciente ⟨alive to the danger : consciente del peligro⟩

alkali ['ælkə,laɪ] *n, pl* **-lies** [-,laɪz] *or* **-lis** [-,laɪz] : álcali *m*

alkaline ['ælkələn, -,laɪn] *adj* : alcalino

all[1] ['ɔl] *adv* **1** COMPLETELY : todo, completamente ⟨all wet : todo mojado⟩ ⟨all alone : completamente solo⟩ ⟨all too often : con demasiada frecuencia⟩ ⟨it's all yours : es todo para ti⟩ ⟨I'm all for it : estoy totalmente a su favor⟩ ⟨she forgot all about it : lo olvidó por completo⟩ **2** : igual ⟨the score is 14 all : están 14 iguales, están empatados a 14⟩ **3 all around** : para todos **4 all but** ALMOST : casi **5 ~ of** ONLY : sólo, solamente **6 ~ of** AT LEAST : por lo menos **7 ~ over** EVERYWHERE : por todas partes **8 ~ over** *fam* ⟨to be all over someone for something : criticar duramente a alguien por algo⟩ **9 ~ over** : aglomerados alrededor de ⟨to be all over each other : estar muy acaramelados⟩ **10 all that** : tan ⟨it hasn't changed all that much : no ha cambiado tanto/demasiado⟩ ⟨it's not all that bad : no es para tanto⟩ **11 all the better** : tanto mejor **12 all the more** : aún más, todavía más

all[2] *adj* : todo ⟨all the children : todos los niños⟩ ⟨in all likelihood : con toda probabilidad, con la mayor probabilidad⟩ ⟨all night : toda la noche⟩ ⟨people of all kinds : gente de todo tipo⟩

all[3] *pron* **1** : todo ⟨they ate it all : lo comieron todo⟩ ⟨that's all : eso es todo⟩ ⟨enough for all : suficiente para todos⟩ ⟨the best of all : el mejor de todos⟩ ⟨some of the girls, but not all : algunas de las muchachas, pero no todas⟩ ⟨all I know is that . . . : lo único que sé es que . . ., todo lo que sé es que . . .⟩ ⟨for all I know : que yo sepa⟩ **2 all in all** : en general **3 all told** *or* **in all** : en total **4 and all** : y todo eso **5 at all** (*in questions*) ⟨did you find out anything at all? : ¿supiste algo?⟩ **6 (not) at all** (*in negative constructions*) : en absoluto, para nada ⟨he did nothing at all, he didn't do anything at all : no hizo nada en absoluto⟩ ⟨I don't like it at all : no me gusta para nada⟩ **7 to give it one's all** : dar todo de sí **8 when all is said and done** : a fin de cuentas

Allah ['ɑlə, 'ɑlə] *n* : Alá *m*

all–around [ˌɔlə'raund] *adj* : completo, amplio

allay [əˈleɪ] vt **1** ALLEVIATE : aliviar, mitigar **2** CALM : aquietar, calmar

allegation [ˌælɪˈɡeɪʃən] n : alegato m, acusación f

allege [əˈlɛdʒ] vt -leged; -leging **1** : alegar, afirmar **2 to be alleged** : decirse, pretenderse ⟨she is alleged to be wealthy : se dice que es adinerada⟩

alleged [əˈlɛdʒd, əˈlɛdʒəd] adj : presunto, supuesto

allegedly [əˈlɛdʒədli] adv : supuestamente, según se alega

allegiance [əˈliːdʒənts] n : lealtad f, fidelidad f ⟨to pledge allegiance to : jurar lealtad a⟩

allegorical [ˌæləˈɡɔrɪkəl] adj : alegórico

allegory [ˈæləˌɡori] n, pl -ries : alegoría f

alleluia [ˌæləˈluːjə, -æ-] → **hallelujah**

allergen [ˈælərdʒən] n : alérgeno m

allergic [əˈlərdʒɪk] adj : alérgico

allergy [ˈælərdʒi] n, pl -gies : alergia f

alleviate [əˈliːviˌeɪt] vt -ated; -ating : aliviar, mitigar, paliar

alleviation [əˌliːviˈeɪʃən] n : alivio m

alley [ˈæli] n, pl -leys **1** : callejón m **2 bowling alley** : bolera f

alliance [əˈlaɪənts] n : alianza f, coalición f

alligator [ˈæləˌɡeɪtər] n : caimán m

all-important [ˌɔlɪmˈpɔrtənt] adj : crucial, de fundamental importancia

alliteration [əˌlɪtəˈreɪʃən] n : aliteración f

all-night [ˈɔlˈnaɪt] adj **1** : que dura toda la noche (dícese de una fiesta, etc.) **2** : que está abierto toda la noche (dícese de un restaurante, etc.)

all-nighter [ˈɔlˈnaɪtər] n fam **to pull an all-nighter** : trasnochar (estudiando, etc.)

allocate [ˈæləˌkeɪt] vt -cated; -cating : asignar, adjudicar

allocation [ˌæləˈkeɪʃən] n : asignación f, reparto m, distribución f

allot [əˈlɑt] vt -lotted; -lotting : repartir, distribuir, asignar

allotment [əˈlɑtmənt] n : reparto m, asignación f, distribución f

all-out [ˈɔlˈaʊt] adj : total, con todo ⟨all-out war : guerra sin cuartel⟩

allow [əˈlaʊ] vt **1** PERMIT : permitir, dejar ⟨she allowed him to leave : le permitió irse, le permitió que se fuera⟩ ⟨we won't allow that to happen : no permitiremos que eso pase⟩ ⟨it allows you to create web pages : permite crear páginas web⟩ ⟨no dogs allowed : no se admiten perros⟩ **2** ALLOT : conceder, dar (tiempo, etc.) **3** ADMIT, CONCEDE : admitir, conceder **4** : admitir (pruebas) — vi **to allow for** : tener en cuenta

allowable [əˈlaʊəbəl] adj **1** PERMISSIBLE : permisible, lícito **2** : deducible ⟨allowable expenditure : gasto deducible⟩

allowance [əˈlaʊənts] n **1** : complemento m (para gastos, etc.), mesada f (para niños) **2 to make allowance(s)** : tener en cuenta, disculpar

alloy [ˈæˌlɔɪ] n : aleación f

all-purpose [ˈɔlˈpərpəs] adj : multiuso ⟨all-purpose flour : harina común⟩

all right¹ adv **1** YES : sí, por supuesto **2** WELL : bien ⟨I did all right : me fue bien⟩ **3** DEFINITELY : bien, ciertamente, sin duda ⟨he's sick all right : está bien enfermo⟩

all right² adj **1** OK : bien ⟨are you all right? : ¿estás bien?⟩ **2** SATISFACTORY : bien, bueno ⟨your work is all right : tu trabajo es bueno⟩

all-round [ˈɔlˈraʊnd] → **all-around**

allspice [ˈɔlspaɪs] n : pimienta f de Jamaica

all-terrain vehicle [ˈɔltəˈreɪn-] n : todoterreno m, vehículo m todoterreno

all-time [ˈɔlˌtaɪm] adj : de todos los tiempos, histórico ⟨my all-time favorite : mi favorito de todos los tiempos⟩ ⟨an all-time record/high/low : un récord/máximo/mínimo histórico⟩

allude [əˈluːd] vi -luded; -luding : aludir, referirse

allure¹ [əˈlʊr] vt -lured; -luring : cautivar, atraer

allure² n : atractivo m, encanto m

allusion [əˈluːʒən] n : alusión f

ally¹ [əˈlaɪ, ˈæˌlaɪ] vi -lied; -lying : aliarse

ally² [ˈæˌlaɪ, əˈlaɪ] n : aliado m, -da f

almanac [ˈɔlməˌnæk, ˈæl-] n : almanaque m

almighty [ɔlˈmaɪti] adj : omnipotente, todopoderoso

almond [ˈɑmənd, ˈɑl-, ˈæ-, ˈæl-] n : almendra f

almost [ˈɔlˌmoːst, ɔlˈmoːst] adv : casi, prácticamente

alms [ˈɑmz, ˈɑlmz, ˈælmz] ns & pl : limosna f, caridad f

aloe [ˈæloː] n : áloe m

aloft [əˈlɔft] adv : en alto, en el aire

alone¹ [əˈloːn] adv : sólo, solamente, únicamente

alone² adj : solo ⟨they're alone in the house : están solos en la casa⟩

along¹ [əˈlɔŋ] adv **1** FORWARD : adelante ⟨farther along : más adelante⟩ ⟨move along! : ¡circulen, por favor!⟩ **2 to bring along** : traer **3 ~ with** : con, junto con **4 all along** : desde el principio

along² prep **1** : por, a lo largo de ⟨along the coast : a lo largo de la costa⟩ **2** : en, en el curso de, por ⟨along the way : en el curso del viaje⟩

alongside¹ [əˌlɔŋˈsaɪd] adv : al costado, al lado

alongside² or **alongside of** prep : junto a, al lado de

aloof [əˈluːf] adj : distante, reservado

aloofness [əˈluːfnəs] n : reserva f, actitud f distante

aloud [əˈlaʊd] adv : en voz alta

alpaca [ælˈpækə] n : alpaca f

alphabet [ˈælfəˌbɛt] n : alfabeto m

alphabetical [ˌælfəˈbɛtɪkəl] or **alphabetic** [-ˈbɛtɪk] adj : alfabético — **alphabetically** [-tɪkli] adv

alphabetize [ˈælfəbəˌtaɪz] vt -ized; -izing : alfabetizar, poner en orden alfabético

alpine [ˈælˌpaɪn] adj : alpino

already [ɔlˈrɛdi] adv : ya

also [ˈɔlˌsoː] adv : también, además

altar ['ɔltər] *n* : altar *m*

alter ['ɔltər] *vt* : alterar, cambiar, modificar

alteration [ˌɔltəˈreɪʃən] *n* : alteración *f*, cambio *m*, modificación *f*

altercation [ˌɔltərˈkeɪʃən] *n* : altercado *m*, disputa *f*

alternate¹ ['ɔltərˌneɪt] *v* **-nated; -nating** : alternar

alternate² ['ɔltərnət] *adj* **1** : alterno ⟨alternate cycles of inflation and depression : ciclos alternos de inflación y depresión⟩ **2** : uno sí y otro no ⟨he cooks on alternate days : cocina un día sí y otro no⟩

alternate³ ['ɔltərnət] *n* : suplente *mf*; sustituto *m*, -ta *f*

alternately ['ɔltərnətli] *adv* : alternativamente, por turno

alternating current ['ɔltərˌneɪtɪŋ] *n* : corriente *f* alterna

alternation [ˌɔltərˈneɪʃən] *n* : alternancia *f*, rotación *f*

alternative¹ [ɔlˈtərnətɪv] *adj* : alternativo

alternative² *n* : alternativa *f*

alternatively [ɔlˈtərnətɪvli] *adv* (*indicating another option*) ⟨(or,) you could come here (, o,) si prefieres, podrías venir aquí⟩

alternator ['ɔltərˌneɪtər] *n* : alternador *m*

although [ɔlˈðoː] *conj* : aunque, a pesar de que

altitude ['æltəˌtuːd, -ˌtjuːd] *n* : altitud *f*, altura *f*

alto ['ælˌtoː] *n*, *pl* **-tos** : alto *mf*, contralto *mf*

altogether [ˌɔltəˈgɛðər] *adv* **1** COMPLETELY : completamente, totalmente, del todo **2** ON THE WHOLE : en suma, en general

altruism ['æltruˌɪzəm] *n* : altruismo *m*

altruistic [ˌæltruˈɪstɪk] *adj* : altruista — **altruistically** [-tɪkli] *adv*

alum ['æləm] *n* : alumbre *m*

aluminum [əˈluːmənəm] *n* : aluminio *m*

alumna [əˈlʌmnə] *n*, *pl* **-nae** [-ˌniː] : exalumna *f*

alumnus [əˈlʌmnəs] *n*, *pl* **-ni** [-ˌnaɪ] : exalumno *m*

always ['ɔlwiz, -ˌweɪz] *adv* **1** INVARIABLY : siempre, invariablemente **2** FOREVER : para siempre

am → **be**

amalgam [əˈmælgəm] *n* : amalgama *f*

amalgamate [əˈmælgəˌmeɪt] *vt* **-ated; -ating** : amalgamar, unir, fusionar

amalgamation [əˌmælgəˈmeɪʃən] *n* : fusión *f*, unión *f*

amaryllis [ˌæməˈrɪləs] *n* : amarilis *f*

amass [əˈmæs] *vt* : amasar, acumular

amateur ['æməˌfər, -tər, -ˌtur, -ˌtjur] *n* **1** : amateur *mf* **2** BEGINNER : principiante *mf*; aficionado *m*, -da *f*

amateurish ['æməˌfərɪʃ, -ˌtər-, -ˌtur-, -ˌtjur-] *adj* : amateur, inexperto

amaze [əˈmeɪz] *vt* **amazed; amazing** : asombrar, maravillar, pasmar

amazement [əˈmeɪzmənt] *n* : asombro *m*, sorpresa *f*

amazing [əˈmeɪzɪŋ] *adj* : asombroso, sorprendente — **amazingly** [-zɪŋli] *adv*

Amazon ['æməˌzɑn] *n* : amazona *f* (en mitología)

Amazonian [ˌæməˈzoːniən] *adj* : amazónico

ambassador [æmˈbæsədər] *n* : embajador *m*, -dora *f*

amber ['æmbər] *n* : ámbar *m*

ambergris ['æmbərˌgrɪs, -ˌgriːs] *n* : ámbar *m* gris

ambidextrous [ˌæmbɪˈdɛkstrəs] *adj* : ambidextro — **ambidextrously** *adv*

ambience *or* **ambiance** ['æmbiənts, 'ambiˌɑnts] *n* : ambiente *m*, atmósfera *f*

ambiguity [ˌæmbəˈgjuːəti] *n*, *pl* **-ties** : ambigüedad *f*

ambiguous [æmˈbɪgjuəs] *adj* : ambiguo

ambition [æmˈbɪʃən] *n* : ambición *f*

ambitious [æmˈbɪʃəs] *adj* : ambicioso — **ambitiously** *adv*

ambivalence [æmˈbɪvələnts] *n* : ambivalencia *f*

ambivalent [æmˈbɪvələnt] *adj* : ambivalente

amble¹ ['æmbəl] *vi* **-bled; -bling** : ir tranquilamente, pasearse despreocupadamente

amble² *n* : paseo *m* tranquilo

ambulance ['æmbjələnts] *n* : ambulancia *f*

ambush¹ ['æmˌbuʃ] *vt* : emboscar

ambush² *n* : emboscada *f*, celada *f*

ameliorate [əˈmiːljəˌreɪt] *v* **-rated; -rating** IMPROVE : mejorar

amelioration [əˌmiːljəˈreɪʃən] *n* : mejora *f*

amen ['eɪˈmɛn, 'ɑ-] *interj* : amén

amenable [əˈmiːnəbəl, -ˈmɛ-] *adj* RESPONSIVE : susceptible, receptivo, sensible

amend [əˈmɛnd] *vt* **1** IMPROVE : mejorar, enmendar **2** CORRECT : enmendar, corregir

amendment [əˈmɛndmənt] *n* : enmienda *f*

amends [əˈmɛndz] *ns & pl* : compensación *f*, reparación *f*, desagravio *m*

amenity [əˈmɛnəti, -ˈmiː-] *n*, *pl* **-ties** **1** PLEASANTNESS : lo agradable, amenidad *f* **2 amenities** *npl* : servicios *mpl*, comodidades *fpl*

American [əˈmɛrɪkən] *n* : americano *m*, -na *f* — **American** *adj*

American Indian *n sometimes offensive* → **Native American**

amethyst ['æməθəst] *n* : amatista *f*

amiability [ˌeɪmiːəˈbɪləti] *n* : amabilidad *f*, afabilidad *f*

amiable ['eɪmiəbəl] *adj* : amable, afable — **amiably** [-bli] *adv*

amicable ['æmɪkəbəl] *adj* : amigable, amistoso, cordial — **amicably** [-bli] *adv*

amid [əˈmɪd] *or* **amidst** [əˈmɪdst] *prep* : en medio de, entre

amino acid [əˈmiːno] *n* : aminoácido *m*

amiss¹ [əˈmɪs] *adv* : mal, fuera de lugar ⟨to take amiss : tomar a mal, llevar a mal⟩

amiss² *adj* **1** WRONG : malo, inoportuno **2 there's something amiss** : pasa algo, algo anda mal

ammeter ['æˌmiːtər] *n* : amperímetro *m*

ammonia [əˈmoːnjə] *n* : amoníaco *m*

ammunition [ˌæmjəˈnɪʃən] *n* 1 : municiones *fpl* 2 ARGUMENTS : argumentos *mpl*

amnesia [æmˈniːʒə] *n* : amnesia *f*

amnesiac [æmˈniːʒiˌæk] *n* : amnésico *m*, -ca *f* — **amnesiac** *adj*

amnesty [ˈæmnəsti] *n, pl* **-ties** : amnistía *f*

amoeba [əˈmiːbə] *n, pl* **-bas** *or* **-bae** [-ˌbiː] : ameba *f* — **amoebic** [əˈmiːbɪk] *adj*

amok [əˈmʌk, -ˈmɑk] *adv* **to run amok** : correr a ciegas, enloquecerse, desbocarse (dícese de la economía, etc.)

among [əˈmʌŋ] *or* **amongst** [əˈmʌŋkst] *prep* : entre

amoral [eɪˈmɔrəl] *adj* : amoral

amorous [ˈæmərəs] *adj* 1 PASSIONATE : apasionado 2 ENAMORED : enamorado 3 LOVING : amoroso, cariñoso

amorously [ˈæmərəsli] *adv* : con cariño

amorphous [əˈmɔrfəs] *adj* : amorfo, informe

amortize [ˈæmərˌtaɪz, əˈmɔr-] *vt* **-tized;** **-tizing** : amortizar

amount[1] [əˈmaʊnt] *vi* **to amount to** 1 : equivaler a, significar ⟨that amounts to treason : eso equivale a la traición⟩ 2 : ascender (a) ⟨my debts amount to $2000 : mis deudas ascienden a $2000⟩

amount[2] *n* : cantidad *f*, suma *f*

ampere [ˈæmˌpɪr] *n* : amperio *m*

ampersand [ˈæmpərˌsænd] *n* : el signo &

amphetamine [æmˈfɛtəˌmiːn] *n* : anfetamina *f*

amphibian [æmˈfɪbiən] *n* : anfibio *m*

amphibious [æmˈfɪbiəs] *adj* : anfibio

amphitheater [ˈæmfəˌθiːətər] *n* : anfiteatro *m*

ample [ˈæmpəl] *adj* **ampler; amplest** 1 LARGE, SPACIOUS : amplio, extenso, grande 2 ABUNDANT : abundante, generoso

amplifier [ˈæmpləˌfaɪər] *n* : amplificador *m*

amplify [ˈæmpləˌfaɪ] *vt* **-fied; -fying** : amplificar

amply [ˈæmpli] *adv* : ampliamente, abundantemente, suficientemente

amputate [ˈæmpjəˌteɪt] *vt* **-tated; -tating** : amputar

amputation [ˌæmpjəˈteɪʃən] *n* : amputación *f*

amuck [əˈmʌk] → **amok**

amulet [ˈæmjələt] *n* : amuleto *m*, talismán *m*

amuse [əˈmjuːz] *vt* **amused; amusing** 1 ENTERTAIN : entretener, distraer 2 : hacer reír, divertir ⟨the joke amused us : la broma nos hizo reír⟩

amusement [əˈmjuːzmənt] *n* 1 ENTERTAINMENT : diversión *f*, entretenimiento *m*, pasatiempo *m* 2 LAUGHTER : risa *f*

amusement park *n* : parque *m* de diversiones

an *art* → **a**[2]

anachronism [əˈnækrəˌnɪzəm] *n* : anacronismo *m*

anachronistic [əˌnækrəˈnɪstɪk] *adj* : anacrónico

anaconda [ˌænəˈkɑndə] *n* : anaconda *f*

anagram [ˈænəˌgræm] *n* : anagrama *m*

anal [ˈeɪnəl] *adj* : anal

analgesic [ˌænəlˈdʒiːzɪk, -sɪk] *n* : analgésico *m*

analog [ˈænəˌlɔg] *adj* : analógico

analogical [ˌænəˈlɑdʒɪkəl] *adj* : analógico — **analogically** [-kli] *adv*

analogous [əˈnæləgəs] *adj* : análogo

analogy [əˈnælədʒi] *n, pl* **-gies** : analogía *f*

analysis [əˈnæləsəs] *n, pl* **-yses** [-ˌsiːz] 1 : análisis *m* 2 PSYCHOANALYSIS : psicoanálisis *m*

analyst [ˈænəlɪst] *n* 1 : analista *mf* 2 PSYCHOANALYST : psicoanalista *mf*

analytic [ˌænəˈlɪtɪk] *or* **analytical** [-tɪkəl] *adj* : analítico — **analytically** [-tɪkli] *adv*

analyze [ˈænəˌlaɪz] *vt* **-lyzed; -lyzing** : analizar

anarchic [æˈnɑrkɪk] *adj* : anárquico — **anarchically** [-kɪkli] *adv*

anarchism [ˈænərˌkɪzəm, -nɑr-] *n* : anarquismo *m*

anarchist [ˈænərkɪst, -nɑr-] *n* : anarquista *mf*

anarchy [ˈænərki, -nɑr-] *n* : anarquía *f*

anathema [əˈnæθəmə] *n* : anatema *m*

anatomic [ˌænəˈtɑmɪk] *or* **anatomical** [-mɪkəl] *adj* : anatómico — **anatomically** [-mɪkli] *adv*

anatomy [əˈnætəmi] *n, pl* **-mies** : anatomía *f*

ancestor [ˈænˌsɛstər] *n* : antepasado *m*, -da *f*; antecesor *m*, -sora *f*

ancestral [ænˈsɛstrəl] *adj* : ancestral, de los antepasados

ancestry [ˈænˌsɛstri] *n* 1 DESCENT : ascendencia *f*, linaje *m*, abolengo *m* 2 ANCESTORS : antepasados *mpl*, -das *fpl*

anchor[1] [ˈæŋkər] *vt* 1 MOOR : anclar, fondear 2 FASTEN : sujetar, asegurar, fijar

anchor[2] *n* 1 : ancla *f* 2 → **anchorman** 3 → **anchorwoman**

anchorage [ˈæŋkərɪdʒ] *n* : anclaje *m*

anchorman [ˈæŋkərˌmæn] *n, pl* **-men** [-mən, -ˌmɛn] : presentador *m* (de televisión)

anchorwoman [ˈæŋkərˌwʊmən] *n, pl* **-women** [-ˌwɪmən] : presentadora *f* (de televisión)

anchovy [ˈænˌtʃoːvi, ænˈtʃoː-] *n, pl* **-vies** *or* **-vy** : anchoa *f*, boquerón *m*

ancient [ˈeɪntʃənt] *adj* 1 : antiguo ⟨ancient history : historia antigua⟩ 2 OLD : viejo

ancients [ˈeɪntʃənts] *npl* : los antiguos *mpl*

and [ˈænd] *conj* 1 : y (*e before words beginning with* i- *or* hi-) ⟨books and papers : libros y papeles⟩ ⟨six and a half : seis y medio⟩ ⟨a hundred and ten : ciento diez⟩ ⟨2 and 2 equal 4 : 2 más 2 es igual a 4⟩ ⟨at (the corner of) First and Main : en la esquina de First y Main⟩ 2 : con ⟨ham and eggs : huevos con jamón⟩ 3 IN ORDER TO : a, de ⟨go and see : ve a ver⟩ ⟨try and finish it : trata de terminarlo⟩ 4 (*indicating continuation*) ⟨she cried and cried : no dejaba de llorar⟩ 5 (*used for emphasis*) ⟨hundreds and hundreds of people : cientos de personas⟩ ⟨more and more difficult : cada vez más difícil⟩

Andalusian [ˌændəˈluːʒən] *adj* : andaluz *m*, -luza *f* — **Andalusian** *adj*

Andean ['ændiən] *adj* : andino
andiron ['æn,daıərn] *n* : morillo *m*
Andorran [æn'dɔrən] *n* : andorrano *m*, -na *f* — **Andorran** *adj*
androgynous [æn'drɑdʒənəs] *adj* : andrógino
anecdotal [,ænık'do:t̬əl] *adj* : anecdótico
anecdote ['ænık,do:t] *n* : anécdota *f*
anemia [ə'ni:miə] *n* : anemia *f*
anemic [ə'ni:mık] *adj* : anémico
anemone [ə'nɛməni] *n* : anémona *f*
anesthesia [,ænəs'θi:ʒə] *n* : anestesia *f*
anesthetic[1] [,ænəs'θɛt̬ık] *adj* : anestésico
anesthetic[2] *n* : anestésico *m*
anesthetist [ə'nɛsθət̬ıst] *n* : anestesista *mf*
anesthetize [ə'nɛsθə,taız] *vt* **-tize; -tized** : anestesiar
aneurysm ['ænjə,rızəm] *n* : aneurisma *mf*
anew [ə'nu:, -'nju:] *adv* : de nuevo, otra vez, nuevamente
angel ['eındʒəl] *n* : ángel *m* ⟨the Angel of Death : el ángel exterminador⟩
angelic [æn'dʒɛlık] *or* **angelical** [-lıkəl] *adj* : angélico, angelical — **angelically** [-lıkli] *adv*
anger[1] ['æŋgər] *vt* : enojar, enfadar
anger[2] *n* : enojo *m*, enfado *m*, ira *f*, cólera *f*, rabia *f*
angina [æn'dʒaınə] *n* : angina *f*
angle[1] ['æŋgəl] *v* **angled; angling** *vt* DIRECT, SLANT : orientar, dirigir — *vi* FISH : pescar (con caña)
angle[2] *n* **1** : ángulo *m* **2** POINT OF VIEW : perspectiva *f*, punto *m* de vista
angler ['æŋglər] *n* : pescador *m*, -dora *f*
Anglican ['æŋglıkən] *n* : anglicano *m*, -na *f* — **Anglican** *adj*
angling ['æŋglıŋ] *n* : pesca *f* con caña
Anglo-Saxon[1] [æŋglo'sæksən] *adj* : anglosajón
Anglo-Saxon[2] *n* : anglosajón *m*, -jona *f*
Angolan [æŋ'go:lən, æn-] *n* : angoleño *m*, -ña *f* — **Angolan** *adj*
angora [æŋ'gorə, æn-] *n* : angora *f*
angrily ['æŋgrəli] *adv* : furiosamente, con ira
angry ['æŋgri] *adj* **angrier; -est** : enojado, enfadado, furioso
anguish ['æŋgwıʃ] *n* : angustia *f*, congoja *f*
anguished ['æŋgwıʃt] *adj* : angustiado, acongojado
angular ['æŋgjələr] *adj* : angular (dícese de las formas), anguloso (dícese de las caras)
animal ['ænəməl] *n* **1** : animal *m* **2** BRUTE : bruto *m*, -ta *f*
animate[1] ['ænə,meıt] *vt* **-mated; -mating** : animar
animate[2] ['ænəmət] *adj* : animado
animated ['ænə,meıt̬əd] *adj* **1** LIVELY : animado, vivo, vivaz **2** animated cartoon : dibujos *mpl* animados
animation [,ænə'meıʃən] *n* : animación *f*
animosity [,ænə'mɑsət̬i] *n, pl* **-ties** : animosidad *f*, animadversión *f*
anise ['ænəs] *n* : anís *m*
aniseed ['ænəs,si:d] *n* : anís *m*, semilla *f* de anís
ankle ['æŋkəl] *n* : tobillo *m*

anklebone ['æŋkəl,bo:n] *n* : taba *f*
annals ['ænəlz] *npl* : anales *mpl*, crónica *f*
anneal [ə'ni:l] *vt* **1** TEMPER : templar **2** STRENGTHEN : fortalecer
annatto [ə'nɑt̬o] *n* : achiote *m*
annex[1] [ə'nɛks, 'æ,nɛks] *vt* : anexar
annex[2] ['æ,nɛks, -nıks] *n* : anexo *m*, anejo *m*
annexation [,æ,nɛk'seıʃən] *n* : anexión *f*
annihilate [ə'naıə,leıt] *vt* **-lated; -lating** : aniquilar
annihilation [ə,naıə'leıʃən] *n* : aniquilación *f*, aniquilamiento *m*
anniversary [,ænə'vərsəri] *n, pl* **-ries** : aniversario *m*
annotate ['ænə,teıt] *vt* **-tated; -tating** : anotar
annotation [,ænə'teıʃən] *n* : anotación *f*
announce [ə'nauns] *vt* **-nounced; -nouncing** : anunciar
announcement [ə'naunsmənt] *n* : anuncio *m*
announcer [ə'naunsər] *n* : anunciador *m*, -dora *f*; comentarista *mf*; locutor *m*, -tora *f*
annoy [ə'nɔı] *vt* : molestar, fastidiar, irritar
annoyance [ə'nɔıəns] *n* **1** IRRITATION : irritación *f*, fastidio *m* **2** NUISANCE : molestia *f*, fastidio *m*
annoying [ə'nɔıın] *adj* : molesto, fastidioso, engorroso — **annoyingly** [-ıŋli] *adv*
annual[1] ['ænjuəl] *adj* : anual — **annually** *adv*
annual[2] *n* **1** : planta *f* anual **2** YEARBOOK : anuario *m*
annuity [ə'nu:ət̬i] *n, pl* **-ties** : anualidad *f*
annul [ə'nʌl] *vt* **anulled; anulling** : anular, invalidar
annulment [ə'nʌlmənt] *n* : anulación *f*
anode ['æ,no:d] *n* : ánodo *m*
anoint [ə'nɔınt] *vt* : ungir
anomalous [ə'nɑmələs] *adj* : anómalo
anomaly [ə'nɑməli] *n, pl* **-lies** : anomalía *f*
anonymity [,ænə'nımət̬i] *n* : anonimato *m*
anonymous [ə'nɑnəməs] *adj* : anónimo — **anonymously** *adv*
anorak ['ænə,ræk] *n* : anorak *m*
anorexia [,ænə'rɛksiə] *n* : anorexia *f*
anorexic [,ænə'rɛksık] *adj* : anoréxico
another[1] [ə'nʌðər] *adj* **1** : otro ⟨another drink : otra copa⟩ ⟨another two days : dos días más, otros dos días⟩ ⟨yet another example : otro ejemplo más⟩ ⟨it was just another day : fue un día como cualquier otro⟩ **2** : otro ⟨at another time : en otro momento, en otra ocasión⟩ ⟨that's another matter : eso es otra cuestión⟩ **3** (*indicating similarity*) : otro ⟨another Great Depression : otra Gran Depresión⟩
another[2] *pron* : otro ⟨one after another : uno tras otro, una tras otra⟩ ⟨at one time or another : en algún momento⟩ ⟨for one reason or another : por alguna razón⟩ ⟨one way or another : de una u otra forma/manera⟩
answer[1] ['ænsər] *vt* **1** : contestar (a) ⟨to answer the telephone : contestar el teléfono⟩ ⟨to answer a question : contes-

tar (a) una pregunta⟩ ⟨he didn't answer me : no me contestó⟩ **2** FULFILL : satisfacer **3** : responder a (acusaciones, etc.) — *vi* **1** : contestar, responder **2 to answer back** TALK BACK : contestar (con impertinencia) **3 to answer for someone** : contestar por alguien **4 to answer for something** : responder de algo, pagar por algo ⟨she'll answer for that mistake : pagará por ese error⟩ **5 to answer to** : responder a

answer² *n* **1** REPLY : respuesta *f*, contestación *f* ⟨a straight answer : una respuesta clara⟩ ⟨there's no answer : no contestan (el teléfono)⟩ ⟨I never got an answer : nunca me dieron respuesta⟩ ⟨in answer to your question : en respuesta a su pregunta⟩ **2** : respuesta *f*, solución *f* (en un examen, etc.) **3** SOLUTION : solución *f* ⟨there's no easy answer : no tiene una solución fácil⟩

answerable ['ænsərəbəl] *adj* : responsable

answering machine *n* : contestador *m* (automático)

ant ['ænt] *n* : hormiga *f*

antacid [ænt'æsəd, 'æn,tæ-] *n* : antiácido *m*

antagonism [æn'tægə,nɪzəm] *n* : antagonismo *m*, hostilidad *f*

antagonist [æn'tægənɪst] *n* : antagonista *mf*

antagonistic [æn,tægə'nɪstɪk] *adj* : antagonista, hostil

antagonize [æn'tægə,naɪz] *vt* -nized; -nizing : antagonizar

antarctic [ænt'ɑrktɪk, -'ɑrtɪk] *adj* : antártico

antarctic circle *n* : círculo *m* antártico

anteater ['ænt,iːt̬ər] *n* : oso *m* hormiguero

antebellum [,ænti'beləm] *adj* : prebélico

antecedent¹ [,æntə'siːdənt] *adj* : antecedente, precedente

antecedent² *n* : antecedente *mf*; precursor *m*, -sora *f*

antelope ['æntəl,oːp] *n*, *pl* -lope *or* -lopes : antílope *m*

antenatal [,ænti'neɪt̬əl] → prenatal

antenna [æn'tenə] *n*, *pl* -nae [-,niː, -,naɪ] *or* -nas : antena *f*

anterior [æn'tɪriər] *adj* : anterior

anthem ['ænθəm] *n* : himno *m* ⟨national anthem : himno nacional⟩

anther ['ænθər] *n* : antera *f*

anthill ['ænt,hɪl] *n* : hormiguero *m*

anthology [æn'θɑlədʒi] *n*, *pl* -gies : antología *f*

anthracite ['ænθrə,saɪt] *n* : antracita *f*

anthropoid¹ ['ænθrə,pɔɪd] *adj* : antropoide

anthropoid² *n* : antropoide *mf*

anthropological [,ænθrəpə'lɑdʒɪkəl] *adj* : antropológico

anthropologist [,ænθrə'pɑlədʒɪst] *n* : antropólogo *m*, -ga *f*

anthropology [,ænθrə'pɑlədʒi] *n* : antropología *f*

anti- [,ænti, æntaɪ] *pref* : anti-

antiabortion [,ænti̯ə'bɔrʃən, ,æntaɪ-] *adj* : antiaborto

antiaircraft [,ænti'ær,kræft, ,æntaɪ-] *adj* : antiaéreo

anti–American [,ænti̯ə'mɛrɪkən, ,æntaɪ-] *adj* : antiamericano

antibiotic¹ [,æntibaɪ'ɑt̬ɪk, ,æntaɪ-, -bi-] *adj* : antibiótico

antibiotic² *n* : antibiótico *m*

antibody ['ænti,bɑdi] *n*, *pl* -bodies : anticuerpo *m*

antic¹ ['æntɪk] *adj* : extravagante, juguetón

antic² *n* : payasada *f*, travesura *f*

anticipate [æn'tɪsə,peɪt] *vt* -pated; -pating **1** FORESEE : anticipar, prever **2** EXPECT : esperar, contar con

anticipation [æn,tɪsə'peɪʃən] *n* **1** FORESIGHT : previsión *f* **2** EXPECTATION : anticipación *f*, expectación *f*, esperanza *f*

anticipatory [æn'tɪsəpə,tori] *adj* : en anticipación, en previsión

anticlimactic [,æntiklaɪ'mæktɪk] *adj* : anticlimático, decepcionante

anticlimax [,ænti'klaɪ,mæks] *n* : anticlímax *m*

anticommunism [,ænti'kɑmjə,nɪzəm, ,æntaɪ-] *n* : anticomunismo *m*

anticommunist¹ [,ænti'kɑmjənɪst, ,æntaɪ-] *adj* : anticomunista

anticommunist² *n* : anticomunista *mf*

antidemocratic [,ænti,dɛmə'krætɪk, ,æntaɪ-] *adj* : antidemocrático

antidepressant [,ænti'dɪ'prɛsənt] *n* : antidepresivo *m* — **antidepressant** *adj*

antidote ['ænti,doːt] *n* : antídoto *m*

antidrug [,ænti'drʌg, ,æntaɪ-; 'ænti,drʌg, 'æntaɪ-] *adj* : antidrogas

antifascist [,ænti'fæʃɪst, ,æntaɪ-] *adj* : antifascista

antifeminist [,ænti'fɛmənɪst, ,æntaɪ-] *adj* : antifeminista

antifreeze ['ænti,friːz] *n* : anticongelante *m*

antigen ['æntɪdʒən, -,dʒɛn] *n* : antígeno *m*

antihistamine [,ænti'hɪstə,miːn, -mən] *n* : antihistamínico *m*

anti–imperialism [,ænti'ɪm'pɪri̯ə,lɪzəm, ,æntaɪ-] *n* : antiimperialismo *m*

anti–imperialist [,ænti'ɪm'pɪri̯əlɪst, ,æntaɪ-] *adj* : antiimperialista

anti–inflammatory [,æntiɪm'flæmə,tori] *adj* : antiinflamatorio

anti–inflationary [,æntiɪm'fleɪʃə,nɛri, ,æntaɪ-] *adj* : antiinflacionario

antimony ['æntə,moːni] *n* : antimonio *m*

antipathy [æn'tɪpəθi] *n*, *pl* -thies : antipatía *f*, aversión *f*

antiperspirant [,ænti'pərspərənt, ,æntaɪ-] *n* : antitranspirante *m*

antiquarian¹ [,æntə'kweriən] *adj* : antiguo, anticuario ⟨an antiquarian book : un libro antiguo⟩

antiquarian² *n* : anticuario *m*, -ria *f*

antiquary ['æntə,kweri] *n* : → **antiquarian**

antiquated ['æntə,kweɪt̬əd] *adj* : anticuado, pasado de moda

antique¹ [æn'tiːk] *adj* **1** OLD : antiguo, de época ⟨an antique mirror : un espejo antiguo⟩ **2** OLD–FASHIONED : anticuado, pasado de moda

antique² *n* : antigüedad *f*

antiquity [æn'tıkwəṭi] *n, pl* **-ties** : antigüedad

antirevolutionary [ˌænti̞ˌrevəˈluːʃəˌneri, ˌæntaı-] *adj* : antirrevolucionario

anti–Semitic [ˌæntisəˈmıṭık, ˌæntaı-] *adj* : antisemita

anti–Semitism [ˌæntiˈseməˌtızəm, ˌæntaı-] *n* : antisemitismo *m*

antiseptic[1] [ˌæntəˈseptık] *adj* : antiséptico — **antiseptically** [-tıkli] *adv*

antiseptic[2] *n* : antiséptico *m*

antismoking [ˌænti̞ˈsmoːkıŋ, ˌæntaı-] *adj* : antitabaco

antisocial [ˌæntiˈsoːʃəl, ˌæntaı-] *adj* **1** : antisocial **2** UNSOCIABLE : poco sociable

antiterrorist [ˌæntiˈterərıst, ˌæntaı-] *adj* : antiterrorista

antitheft [ˌæntiˈθeft, ˌæntaı-] *adj* : antirrobo

antithesis [ænˈtıθəsıs] *n, pl* **-eses** [-ˌsiːz] : antítesis *f*

antitoxin [ˌæntiˈtaksən, ˌæntaı-] *n* : antitoxina *f*

antitrust [ˌæntiˈtrʌst, ˌæntaı-] *adj* : antimonopolista

antiviral [ˌæntiˈvaırəl, ˌæntaı-] *adj* : antiviral

antivirus [ˌæntiˈvaırəs, ˌæntaı-] *adj* → antiviral

antivirus software *n* : antivirus *m*

antler [ˈæntlər] *n* : asta *f*, cuerno *m*

antonym [ˈæntəˌnım] *n* : antónimo *m*

anus [ˈeınəs] *n* : ano *m*

anvil [ˈænvəl, -vıl] *n* : yunque *m*

anxiety [æŋˈkˈzaıəṭi] *n, pl* **-eties** **1** UNEASINESS : inquietud *f*, preocupación *f*, ansiedad *f* **2** APPREHENSION : ansiedad *f*, angustia *f*

anxious [ˈæŋkʃəs] *adj* **1** WORRIED : inquieto, preocupado, ansioso **2** WORRISOME : preocupante, inquietante **3** EAGER : ansioso, deseoso

anxiously [ˈæŋkʃəsli] *adv* : con inquietud, con ansiedad

any[1] [ˈeni] *adv* **1** : algo ⟨is it any better? : ¿está (algo) mejor?⟩ ⟨I can't stand it any more : no lo soporto más⟩ ⟨do you want any more? : ¿quiere más?⟩ **2** : para nada ⟨it is not any good : no sirve para nada⟩

any[2] *adj* **1** : alguno ⟨is there any doubt? : ¿hay alguna duda?⟩ ⟨call me if you have any questions : llámeme si tiene alguna pregunta⟩ **2** : cualquier ⟨I can answer any question : puedo responder a cualquier pregunta⟩ **3** : todo ⟨in any case : en todo caso⟩ **4** : ningún ⟨he would not accept it under any circumstances : no lo aceptaría bajo ninguna circunstancia⟩

any[3] *pron* **1** : alguno ⟨are there any left? : ¿queda alguno?⟩ ⟨did you see any of the girls? : ¿viste a alguna de las chicas?⟩ **2** : ninguno ⟨I don't want any : no quiero ninguno⟩ ⟨I couldn't attend any of the meetings : no pude asistir a ninguna de las reuniones⟩

anybody [ˈeniˌbʌdi, -ˌba-] → anyone

anyhow [ˈeniˌhau] *adv* **1** HAPHAZARDLY : de cualquier manera **2** IN ANY CASE : de todos modos, en todo caso

anymore [ˌeniˈmor] *adv* **1** : ya, ya más ⟨he doesn't dance anymore : ya no baila más⟩ **2** : todavía ⟨do they sing anymore? : ¿cantan todavía?⟩

anyone [ˈeniˌwʌn] *pron* **1** : alguien ⟨is anyone here? : ¿hay alguien aquí?⟩ ⟨if anyone wants to come : si alguno quiere venir⟩ **2** : cualquiera ⟨anyone can play : cualquiera puede jugar⟩ **3** : nadie ⟨I don't want anyone here : no quiero a nadie aquí⟩

anyplace [ˈeniˌpleıs] → anywhere

anything [ˈeniˌθıŋ] *pron* **1** : algo, alguna cosa ⟨do you want anything (else)? : ¿quieres algo (más)?, ¿quieres alguna cosa (más)?⟩ **2** : nada ⟨hardly anything : casi nada⟩ **3** : cualquier cosa ⟨I eat anything : como de todo⟩ **4** ~ **but** : no . . .ni mucho menos ⟨he was anything but pleased : no estaba contento, ni mucho menos⟩ **5** **anything goes** : todo vale **6** ~ **like** ⟨it wasn't anything like what I expected : no fue en absoluto lo que esperaba⟩ ⟨we don't have anything like enough : no tenemos suficiente, ni mucho menos⟩

anytime [ˈeniˌtaım] *adv* : en cualquier momento, a cualquier hora, cuando sea

anyway [ˈeniˌweı] *or* **anyways** [-ˌweız] → anyhow

anywhere [ˈeniˌhwer] *adv* **1** : en algún sitio, en alguna parte ⟨do you see it anywhere? : ¿lo ves en alguna parte?⟩ **2** : en ningún sitio, por ninguna parte ⟨I can't find it anywhere : no puedo encontrarlo por ninguna parte⟩ **3** : en cualquier parte, dondequiera, donde sea ⟨put it anywhere : ponlo dondequiera⟩

aorta [eıˈɔrtə] *n, pl* **-tas** *or* **-tae** [-ˌti, -ˌtaı] : aorta *f*

Apache [əˈpætʃi] *n, pl* **Apache** *or* **Apaches** : apache *mf*

apart [əˈpart] *adv* **1** SEPARATELY : aparte, separadamente **2** ASIDE : aparte, a un lado **3 to fall apart** : deshacerse, hacerse pedazos **4 to take apart** : desmontar, desmantelar

apartheid [əˈpar,teıt, -ˌtaıt] *n* : apartheid *m*

apartment [əˈpartmənt] *n* : apartamento *m*, departamento *m*, piso *m* Spain

apartment building *n* : bloque *m* de apartamentos/departamentos, bloque *m* de pisos Spain

apathetic [ˌæpəˈθeṭık] *adj* : apático, indiferente — **apathetically** [-tıkli] *adv*

apathy [ˈæpəθi] *n* : apatía *f*, indiferencia *f*

ape[1] [ˈeıp] *vt* **aped; aping** : imitar, remedar

ape[2] *n* : simio *m*; mono *m*, -na *f*

aperitif [əˌperəˈtiːf] *n* : aperitivo *m*

aperture [ˈæpərˌtʃər, -ˌtʃur] *n* : abertura *f*, rendija *f*, apertura *f* (en fotografía)

apex [ˈeıˌpeks] *n, pl* **apexes** *or* **apices** [ˈeıpəˌsiːz, ˈæ-] : ápice *m*, cúspide *f*, cima *f*

aphid [ˈeıfıd, ˈæ-] *n* : áfido *m*

aphorism ['æfə,rɪzəm] n : aforismo m

aphrodisiac [,æfrə'di:zi,æk, -'dɪ-] n : afro-disíaco m

apiary ['eɪpi,ɛri] n, pl -aries : apiario m, colmenar m

apiece [ə'pi:s] adv : cada uno

aplenty [ə'plɛnti] adj : en abundancia

aplomb [ə'plɑm, -'plʌm] n : aplomo m

apocalypse [ə'pɑkə,lɪps] n : apocalipsis m

apocalyptic [ə,pɑkə'lɪptɪk] adj : apoca-líptico

apocrypha [ə'pɑkrəfə] n : textos mpl apó-crifos

apocryphal [ə'pɑkrəfəl] adj : apócrifo

apolitical [,eɪpə'lɪtɪkəl] adj : apolítico

apologetic [ə,pɑlə'dʒɛtɪk] adj : lleno de disculpas

apologetically [ə,pɑlə'dʒɛtɪkli] adv : disculpándose, con aire de disculpas

apologize [ə'pɑlə,dʒaɪz] vi -gized; -gizing : disculparse, pedir perdón

apology [ə'pɑlədʒi] n, pl -gies : disculpa f, excusa f

apoplectic [,æpə'plɛktɪk] adj : apoplético

apoplexy ['æpə,plɛksi] n : apoplejía f

apostasy [ə'pɑstəsi] n, pl -sies : apostasía f

apostate [ə'pɑs,teɪt] n : apóstata mf

apostle [ə'pɑsəl] n : apóstol m

apostolic [,æpə'stɑlɪk] adj : apostólico

apostrophe [ə'pɑstrə,fi:] n : apóstrofo m (ortográfico)

apothecary [ə'pɑθə,kɛri] n, pl -caries : boticario m, -ria f

appall [ə'pɔl] vt : consternar, horrorizar

appalling [ə'pɔlɪŋ] adj : atroz, horroroso

apparatus [,æpə'ræt̬əs, -'reɪ-] n, pl -tuses or -tus : aparato m, equipo m

apparel [ə'pærəl] n : atavío m, ropa f

apparent [ə'pærənt] adj 1 VISIBLE : visi-ble 2 OBVIOUS : claro, evidente, mani-fiesto 3 SEEMING : aparente, ostensible

apparently [ə'pærəntli] adv : aparente-mente, al parecer

apparition [,æpə'rɪʃən] n : aparición f, vi-sión f

appeal[1] [ə'pi:l] vt : apelar ⟨to appeal a de-cision : apelar contra una decisión⟩ — vi 1 to appeal for : pedir, solicitar 2 to ap-peal to : atraer a ⟨that doesn't appeal to me : eso no me atrae⟩

appeal[2] n 1 : apelación f (en derecho) 2 PLEA : ruego m, súplica f 3 ATTRACTION : atracción f, atractivo m, interés m

appear [ə'pɪr] vi 1 : aparecer, aparecerse, presentarse ⟨he suddenly appeared : apareció de repente⟩ 2 COME OUT : aparecer, salir, publicarse 3 : compare-cer (ante el tribunal), actuar (en el tea-tro) 4 SEEM : parecer

appearance [ə'pɪrənts] n 1 APPEARING : aparición f, presentación f, compare-cencia f (ante una tribunal), publicación f (de un libro) 2 LOOK : apariencia f, aspecto m 3 by all appearances : según parece 4 to keep up appearances : guardar las apariencias 5 to make an appearance : hacer acto de presencia

appease [ə'pi:z] vt -peased; -peasing 1 CALM, PACIFY : aplacar, apaciguar, sose-gar 2 SATISFY : satisfacer, mitigar

appeasement [ə'pi:zmənt] n : aplaca-miento m, apaciguamiento m

append [ə'pɛnd] vt : agregar, añadir, ad-juntar

appendage [ə'pɛndɪdʒ] n 1 ADDITION : apéndice m, añadidura f 2 LIMB : miembro m, extremidad f

appendectomy [,æpən'dɛktəmi] n, pl -mies : apendicectomía f

appendicitis [ə,pɛndə'saɪt̬əs] n : apendici-tis f

appendix [ə'pɛndɪks] n, pl -dixes or -dices [-də,si:z] : apéndice m

appetite ['æpə,taɪt] n 1 CRAVING : apetito m, deseo m, ganas fpl 2 PREFERENCE : gusto m, preferencia f ⟨the cultural appetites of today : los gustos culturales de hoy⟩

appetizer ['æpə,taɪzər] n : aperitivo m, entremés m, botana f Mex, tapa f Spain

appetizing ['æpə,taɪzɪŋ] adj : apetecible, apetitoso — appetizingly [-zɪŋli] adv

applaud [ə'plɔd] v : aplaudir

applause [ə'plɔz] n : aplauso m

apple ['æpəl] n : manzana f

apple tree n : manzano m

appliance [ə'plaɪənts] n 1 : aparato m 2 household appliance : electrodomés-tico m, aparato m electrodoméstico

applicability [,æplɪkə'bɪləti, ə,plɪkə-] n : aplicabilidad f

applicable ['æplɪkəbəl, ə'plɪkə-] adj : apli-cable, pertinente

applicant ['æplɪkənt] n : solicitante mf, aspirante mf, postulante mf; candidato m, -ta f

application [,æplə'keɪʃən] n 1 USE : apli-cación f, empleo m, uso m 2 DILIGENCE : aplicación f, diligencia f, dedicación f 3 REQUEST : solicitud f, petición f, demanda f

applicator ['æplə,keɪt̬ər] n : aplicador m

appliqué[1] [,æplə'keɪ] vt : decorar con apli-ques

appliqué[2] n : aplique m

apply [ə'plaɪ] v -plied; -plying vt 1 : apli-car (una sustancia, los frenos, el conoci-miento) 2 to apply oneself : dedicarse, aplicarse — vi 1 : aplicarse, referirse ⟨the rules apply to everyone : las reglas se aplican a todos⟩ 2 to apply for : soli-citar, pedir

appoint [ə'pɔɪnt] vt 1 NAME : nombrar, designar 2 FIX, SET : fijar, señalar, desig-nar ⟨to appoint a date : fijar una fecha⟩ 3 EQUIP : equipar ⟨a well-appointed of-fice : una oficina bien equipada⟩

appointee [ə,pɔɪn'ti:, ,æ-] n : persona f de-signada

appointment [ə'pɔɪntmənt] n 1 APPOINT-ING : nombramiento m, designación f 2 ENGAGEMENT : cita f, hora f ⟨to have/make an appointment : tener/concertar una cita⟩ 3 POST : puesto m

apportion [ə'pɔrʃən] vt : distribuir, re-partir

apportionment [ə'pɔrʃənmənt] n : distribución f, repartición f, reparto m

apposite ['æpəzət] adj : apropiado, oportuno, pertinente — **appositely** adv

appraisal [ə'preɪzəl] n : evaluación f, valoración f, tasación f, apreciación f

appraise [ə'preɪz] vt -praised; -praising : evaluar, valuar, tasar, apreciar

appraiser [ə'preɪzər] n : tasador m, -dora f

appreciable [ə'priːʃəbəl, -'prɪʃiə-] adj : apreciable, sensible, considerable — **appreciably** [-bli] adv

appreciate [ə'priːʃiˌeɪt, -'prɪ-] v -ated; -ating vt 1 VALUE : apreciar, valorar 2 : agradecer ⟨we appreciate his frankness : agradecemos su franqueza⟩ 3 UNDERSTAND : darse cuenta de, entender — vi : apreciarse, valorizarse

appreciation [əˌpriːʃiˈeɪʃən, -ˌprɪ-] n 1 GRATITUDE : agradecimiento m, reconocimiento m 2 VALUING : apreciación f, valoración f, estimación f ⟨art appreciation : apreciación artística⟩ 3 UNDERSTANDING : comprensión f, entendimiento m

appreciative [ə'priːʃətɪv, -'prɪ-; ə'priːʃiˌeɪ-] adj 1 : apreciativo ⟨an appreciative audience : un público apreciativo⟩ 2 GRATEFUL : agradecido 3 ADMIRING : de admiración

apprehend [ˌæpri'hɛnd] vt 1 ARREST : aprehender, detener, arrestar 2 DREAD : temer 3 COMPREHEND : comprender, entender

apprehension [ˌæpri'hɛnʃən] n 1 ARREST : arresto m, detención f, aprehensión f 2 ANXIETY : aprensión f, ansiedad f, temor m 3 UNDERSTANDING : comprensión f, percepción f

apprehensive [ˌæpri'hɛntsɪv] adj : aprensivo, inquieto — **apprehensively** adv

apprentice¹ [ə'prɛntɪs] vt -ticed; -ticing : colocar de aprendiz

apprentice² n : aprendiz m, -diza f

apprenticeship [ə'prɛntɪsˌʃɪp] n : aprendizaje f

apprise [ə'praɪz] vt -prised; -prising : informar, avisar

approach¹ [ə'proːtʃ] vt 1 NEAR : acercarse a 2 APPROXIMATE : aproximarse a 3 : abordar, dirigirse a ⟨I approached my boss with the proposal : me dirigí a mi jefe con la propuesta⟩ 4 TACKLE : abordar, enfocar, considerar — vi : acercarse, aproximarse

approach² n 1 NEARING : acercamiento m, aproximación f 2 POSITION : enfoque m, planteamiento m 3 OFFER : propuesta f, oferta f 4 ACCESS : acceso m, vía f de acceso

approachable [ə'proːtʃəbəl] adj : accesible, asequible

approbation [ˌæprə'beɪʃən] n : aprobación f

appropriate¹ [ə'proːpriˌeɪt] vt -ated; -ating 1 SEIZE : apropiarse de 2 ALLOCATE : destinar, asignar

appropriate² [ə'proːpriət] adj : apropiado, adecuado, idóneo — **appropriately** adv

appropriateness [ə'proːpriətnəs] n : idoneidad f, propiedad f

appropriation [əˌproːpri'eɪʃən] n 1 SEIZURE : apropiación f 2 ALLOCATION : asignación f

approval [ə'pruːvəl] n 1 : aprobación f, visto m bueno 2 **on approval** : a prueba

approve [ə'pruːv] vt -proved; -proving 1 : aprobar, sancionar, darle el visto bueno a 2 **to approve of** : consentir en, aprobar ⟨he doesn't approve of smoking : está en contra del tabaco⟩

approximate¹ [ə'prɑksəˌmeɪt] vt -mated; -mating : aproximarse a, acercarse a

approximate² [ə'prɑksəmət] adj : aproximado

approximately [ə'prɑksəmətli] adv : aproximadamente, más o menos

approximation [əˌprɑksə'meɪʃən] n : aproximación f

appurtenance [ə'pərtənənts] n : accesorio m

apricot ['æprəˌkɑt, 'eɪ-] n : albaricoque m, chabacano m Mex

April ['eɪprəl] n : abril m ⟨they arrived on the 23rd of April, they arrived on April 23rd : llegaron el 23 de abril⟩

apron ['eɪprən] n : delantal m, mandil m

apropos¹ [ˌæprə'poː, 'æprəˌpoː] adv : a propósito

apropos² adj : pertinente, oportuno, acertado

apropos of prep : a propósito de

apt ['æpt] adj 1 FITTING : apto, apropiado, acertado, oportuno 2 LIABLE : propenso, inclinado 3 CLEVER, QUICK : listo, despierto

aptitude ['æptəˌtuːd, -ˌtjuːd] n 1 : aptitud f, capacidad f ⟨aptitude test : prueba de aptitud⟩ 2 TALENT : talento m, facilidad f

aptly ['æptli] adv : acertadamente

aqua ['ækwə, 'ɑ-] n : color m aguamarina

aquamarine [ˌɑkwəmə'riːn, ˌæ-] n 1 : aguamarina f 2 → **aqua**

Aquarius [ə'kwæriəs] n 1 : Acuario m (signo o constelación) 2 : Acuario mf (persona)

aquatic [ə'kwɑtɪk, -'kwæ-] adj : acuático

aqueduct ['ækwəˌdʌkt] n : acueducto m

aqueous ['eɪkwiəs, 'æ-] adj : acuoso

aquiline ['ækwəˌlaɪn, -lən] adj : aguileño

Arab¹ ['ærəb] adj : árabe

Arab² n : árabe mf

arabesque [ˌærə'bɛsk] n : arabesco m

Arabian¹ [ə'reɪbiən] adj : árabe

Arabian² n → **Arab²**

Arabic¹ ['ærəbɪk] adj : árabe

Arabic² n : árabe m (idioma)

arable ['ærəbəl] adj : arable, cultivable

arbiter ['ɑrbətər] n : árbitro m, -tra f

arbitrariness ['ɑrbəˌtrerinəs] n : arbitrariedad f

arbitrary ['ɑrbəˌtreri] adj : arbitrario — **arbitrarily** [ˌɑrbə'trerəli] adv

arbitrate ['ɑrbəˌtreɪt] v -trated; -trating : arbitrar

arbitration [ˌɑrbə'treɪʃən] n : arbitraje m

arbitrator ['ɑrbə,treɪtər] n : árbitro m, -tra f

arbor ['ɑrbər] n : cenador m, pérgola f

arboreal [ɑr'boriəl] adj : arbóreo

arc¹ ['ɑrk] vi **arced; arcing** : formar un arco

arc² n : arco m

arcade [ɑr'keɪd] n **1** ARCHES : arcada f **2** MALL : galería f comercial

arcane [ɑr'keɪn] adj : arcano, secreto, misterioso

arch¹ ['ɑrtʃ] vt : arquear — vi : formar un arco, arquearse

arch² adj **1** CHIEF : principal **2** MISCHIE-VOUS : malicioso, pícaro

arch³ n : arco m

archaeological or **archeological** [,ɑrkiə'lɑdʒɪkəl] adj : arqueológico

archaeologist or **archeologist** [,ɑrki'ɑlədʒɪst] n : arqueólogo m, -ga f

archaeology or **archeology** [,ɑrki'ɑlədʒi] n : arqueología f

archaic [ɑr'keɪɪk] adj : arcaico — **archaically** [-ɪkli] adv

archangel ['ɑrk,eɪndʒəl] n : arcángel m

archbishop [ɑrtʃ'bɪʃəp] n : arzobispo m

archbishopric [ɑrtʃ'bɪʃəprɪk] n : arzobispado m

archdiocese [ɑrtʃ'daɪəsəs, -,si:z, -,si:s] n : arquidiócesis f, archidiócesis f

archer ['ɑrtʃər] n : arquero m, -ra f

archery ['ɑrtʃəri] n : tiro m al arco

archetypal [,ɑrki'taɪpəl] adj : arquetípico

archetype ['ɑrki,taɪp] n : arquetipo m

archipelago [,ɑrkə'pelə,go:, ,ɑrtʃə-] n, pl **-goes** or **-gos** [-go:z] : archipiélago m

architect ['ɑrkə,tekt] n : arquitecto m, -ta f

architectural [,ɑrkə'tektʃərəl] adj : arquitectónico — **architecturally** adv

architecture ['ɑrkə,tektʃər] n : arquitectura f

archive¹ ['ɑr,kaɪv] vt **archived; archiving** : archivar

archive² n or **archives** ['ɑr,kaɪvz] npl : archivo m

archivist ['ɑrkəvɪst, -,kaɪ-] n : archivero m, -ra f; archivista mf

archway ['ɑrtʃ,weɪ] n : arco m, pasadizo m abovedado

arctic ['ɑrktɪk, 'ɑrt-] adj **1** : ártico ⟨arctic regions : zonas árticas⟩ **2** FRIGID : glacial

arctic circle n : círculo m ártico

ardent ['ɑrdənt] adj **1** PASSIONATE : ardiente, fogoso, apasionado **2** FERVENT : ferviente, fervoroso — **ardently** adv

ardor ['ɑrdər] n : ardor m, pasión f, fervor m

arduous ['ɑrdʒuəs] adj : arduo, duro, riguroso — **arduously** adv

arduousness ['ɑrdʒuəsnəs] n : dureza f, rigor m

are → be

area ['æriə] n **1** SURFACE : área f, superficie f **2** REGION : área f, región f, zona f **3** FIELD : área f, terreno m, campo m (de conocimiento)

area code n : código m de la zona, prefijo m Spain

arena [ə'ri:nə] n **1** : arena f, estadio m ⟨sports arena : estadio deportivo⟩ **2** : arena f, ruedo m ⟨the political arena : el ruedo político⟩

aren't ['ɑrənt] contraction of **are not → be**

Argentine ['ɑrdʒən,taɪn, -,ti:n] or **Argentinean** or **Argentinian** [,ɑrdʒən'tɪniən] n : argentino m, -na f — **Argentine** or **Argentinean** or **Argentinian** adj

argon ['ɑr,gɑn] n : argón m

argot ['ɑrgət, -,go:] n : argot m

arguable ['ɑrgjuəbəl] adj : discutible — **arguably** [-bli] adv

argue ['ɑr,gju:] v **-gued; -guing** vi **1** REASON : argumentar, argüir, razonar ⟨to argue for something : abogar por algo, argumentar a favor de algo⟩ ⟨to argue against something : argumentar en contra de algo⟩ **2** DISPUTE : discutir, pelear(se), alegar ⟨to argue about something : discutir por algo, pelear(se) por algo⟩ — vt **1** SUGGEST : sugerir **2** MAINTAIN : alegar, argüir, sostener **3** DISCUSS : discutir, debatir

argument ['ɑrgjəmənt] n **1** REASONING : argumento m, razonamiento m **2** DISCUSSION : discusión f, debate m **3** QUARREL : pelea f, riña f, disputa f

argumentative [,ɑrgjə'mentətɪv] adj : discutidor

argyle ['ɑr,gaɪl] n : diseño m de rombos

aria ['ɑriə] n : aria f

arid ['ærəd] adj : árido

aridity [ə'rɪdəti, æ-] n : aridez f

Aries ['eri:z, -i,i:z] n **1** : Aries m (signo o constelación) **2** : Aries mf (persona)

arise [ə'raɪz] vi **arose** [ə'ro:z]; **arisen** [ə'rɪzən]; **arising 1** ASCEND : ascender, subir, elevarse **2** ORIGINATE : originarse, surgir, presentarse **3** GET UP : levantarse

aristocracy [,ærə'stɑkrəsi] n, pl **-cies** : aristocracia f

aristocrat [ə'rɪstə,kræt] n : aristócrata mf

aristocratic [ə,rɪstə'krætɪk] adj : aristocrático, noble

arithmetic¹ [,ærɪθ'metɪk] or **arithmetical** [-tɪkəl] adj : aritmético

arithmetic² [ə'rɪθmə,tɪk] n : aritmética

ark ['ɑrk] n : arca f

arm¹ ['ɑrm] vt : armar — vi : armarse

arm² n **1** : brazo m (del cuerpo, de un sillón, de una máquina), manga f (de una prenda) ⟨he took her (by the) arm : la tomó del brazo⟩ **2** BRANCH : rama f, sección f **3** WEAPON : arma f ⟨to take up arms : tomar las armas⟩ **4** ~ **in** ~: del brazo **5** → **coat of arms**

armada [ɑr'mɑdə, -'meɪ-] n : armada f, flota f

armadillo [,ɑrmə'dɪlo] n, pl **-los** : armadillo m

armament ['ɑrməmənt] n : armamento m

armband ['ɑrm,bænd] n : brazalete m

armchair ['ɑrm,tʃer] n : butaca f, sillón m

armed ['ɑrmd] adj **1** : armado ⟨armed robbery : robo a mano armada⟩ **2** armed forces : fuerzas fpl armadas **3** (used in combination) : de brazos ⟨long-armed : de brazos largos⟩ ⟨one-armed : manco⟩

Armenian [ɑrˈmiːniən] *n* : armenio *m*, -nia *f* — **Armenian** *adj*

armistice [ˈɑrməstɪs] *n* : armisticio *m*

armor [ˈɑrmər] *n* : armadura *f*, coraza *f*

armored [ˈɑrmərd] *adj* : blindado, acorazado

armory [ˈɑrməri] *n, pl* **-mories** : arsenal *m* (almacén), armería *f* (museo), fábrica *f* de armas

armpit [ˈɑrmˌpɪt] *n* : axila *f*, sobaco *m*

armrest [ˈɑrmˌrɛst] *n* : apoyabrazos *m*

army [ˈɑrmi] *n, pl* **-mies** **1** : ejército *m* (militar) **2** MULTITUDE : legión *f*, multitud *f*, ejército *m*

aroma [əˈroːmə] *n* : aroma *f*

aromatic [ˌærəˈmætɪk] *adj* : aromático

around¹ [əˈraʊnd] *adv* **1** : en un círculo ⟨to go around (and around) : dar vueltas⟩ ⟨to turn around : darse la vuelta, voltearse⟩ ⟨the road goes around the lake : la carretera bordea el lago⟩ **2** : de circunferencia ⟨a tree three feet around : un árbol de tres pies de circunferencia⟩ **3** : alrededor ⟨for miles around : por millas a la redonda⟩ ⟨all around : por todos lados, todo alrededor⟩ ⟨he looked around : miró a su alrededor⟩ ⟨they crowded around to watch : se aglomeraron para observar⟩ **4** : por ahí ⟨they're around somewhere : deben estar por ahí⟩ ⟨there was no one around : no había nadie⟩ ⟨is your mother around? : ¿está tu madre?⟩ ⟨I'll see you around! : ¡nos vemos!⟩ **5** : por/en muchas partes ⟨to wander around : deambular⟩ ⟨scattered around : esparcidos⟩ **6** APPROXIMATELY : más o menos, aproximadamente ⟨around 5 o'clock : a eso de las 5⟩ ⟨it's around 50 dollars : cuesta unos 50 dólares⟩ **7 the wrong way around** : al revés

around² *prep* **1** SURROUNDING : alrededor de, en torno a **2** THROUGH : por, en ⟨he traveled around Mexico : viajó por México⟩ ⟨around the house : en casa⟩ **3** : a la vuelta de ⟨around the corner : a la vuelta de la esquina⟩ **4** NEAR : alrededor de, cerca de

arousal [əˈraʊzəl] *n* : excitación *f*

arouse [əˈraʊz] *vt* **aroused; arousing 1** AWAKE : despertar **2** EXCITE : despertar, suscitar, excitar

arraign [əˈreɪn] *vt* : hacer comparecer (ante un tribunal)

arraignment [əˈreɪnmənt] *n* : orden *m* de comparecencia, acusación *f*

arrange [əˈreɪndʒ] *vt* **-ranged; -ranging 1** ORDER : arreglar, poner en orden, disponer **2** SETTLE : arreglar, fijar, concertar **3** ADAPT : arreglar, adaptar

arrangement [əˈreɪndʒmənt] *n* **1** ORDER : arreglo *m*, orden *m* **2** ARRANGING : disposición *f* ⟨floral arrangement : arreglo floral⟩ **3** AGREEMENT : arreglo *m*, acuerdo *m*, convenio *m* **4 arrangements** *npl* : preparativos *mpl*, planes *mpl*

array¹ [əˈreɪ] *vt* **1** ORDER : poner en orden, presentar, formar **2** GARB : vestir, ataviar, engalanar

array² *n* **1** ORDER : orden *m*, formación *f* **2** ATTIRE : atavío *m*, galas *mpl* **3** RANGE, SELECTION : selección *f*, serie *f*, gama *f* ⟨an array of problems : una serie de problemas⟩

arrears [əˈrɪrz] *npl* : atrasos *mpl* ⟨to be in arrears : estar atrasado en los pagos⟩

arrest¹ [əˈrɛst] *vt* **1** APPREHEND : arrestar, detener **2** CHECK, STOP : detener, parar

arrest² *n* **1** APPREHENSION : arresto *m*, detención *f* ⟨under arrest : detenido⟩ **2** STOPPING : paro *m*

arrival [əˈraɪvəl] *n* : llegada *f*, venida *f*, arribo *m*

arrive [əˈraɪv] *vi* **-rived; -riving 1** COME : llegar, arribar **2** SUCCEED : triunfar, tener éxito

arrogance [ˈærəgəns] *n* : arrogancia *f*, soberbia *f*, altanería *f*, altivez *f*

arrogant [ˈærəgənt] *adj* : arrogante, soberbio, altanero, altivo — **arrogantly** *adv*

arrogate [ˈærəˌgeɪt] *vt* **-gated; -gating** to **arrogate to oneself** : arrogarse

arrow [ˈæro] *n* : flecha *f*

arrowhead [ˈærəˌhed] *n* : punta *f* de flecha

arroyo [əˈroɪo] *n* : arroyo *m*

arsenal [ˈɑrsənəl] *n* : arsenal *m*

arsenic [ˈɑrsənɪk] *n* : arsénico *m*

arson [ˈɑrsən] *n* : incendio *m* premeditado

arsonist [ˈɑrsənɪst] *n* : incendiario *m*, -ria *f*; pirómano *m*, -na *f*

art [ˈɑrt] *n* **1** : arte *m* **2** SKILL : destreza *f*, habilidad *f*, maña *f* **3 arts** *npl* : letras *fpl* (en la educación) **4 arts and crafts** : artes y oficios **5 fine arts** : bellas artes *fpl*

arterial [ɑrˈtɪriəl] *adj* : arterial

arteriosclerosis [ɑrˌtɪrioskləˈroːsɪs] *n* : arteriosclerosis *f*

artery [ˈɑrtəri] *n, pl* **-teries 1** : arteria *f* **2** THOROUGHFARE : carretera *f* principal, arteria *f*

artful [ˈɑrtfəl] *adj* **1** INGENIOUS : ingenioso, diestro **2** CRAFTY : astuto, taimado, ladino, artero — **artfully** *adv*

art gallery → gallery

arthritic [ɑrˈθrɪtɪk] *adj* : artrítico

arthritis [ɑrˈθraɪtəs] *n, pl* **-tides** [ɑrˈθrɪtəˌdiːz] : artritis *f*

arthropod [ˈɑrθrəˌpɑd] *n* : artrópodo *m*

artichoke [ˈɑrtəˌtʃoːk] *n* : alcachofa *f*

article [ˈɑrtɪkəl] *n* **1** ITEM : artículo *m*, objeto *m* **2** ESSAY : artículo *m* **3** CLAUSE : artículo *m*, cláusula *f* **4** : artículo *m* ⟨definite article : artículo determinado⟩

articulate¹ [ɑrˈtɪkjəˌleɪt] *vt* **-lated; -lating 1** UTTER : articular, enunciar, expresar **2** CONNECT : articular (en anatomía)

articulate² [ɑrˈtɪkjələt] *adj* to **be articulate** : poder articular palabras, expresarse bien

articulately [ɑrˈtɪkjələtli] *adv* : elocuentemente, con fluidez

articulateness [ɑrˈtɪkjələtnəs] *n* : elocuencia *f*, fluidez *f*

articulation [ɑrˌtɪkjəˈleɪʃən] *n* **1** JOINT : articulación *f* **2** UTTERANCE : articulación *f*, declaración *f* **3** ENUNCIATION : articulación *f*, pronunciación *f*

artifact ['ɑrtə,fækt] *n* : artefacto *m*

artifice ['ɑrtəfəs] *n* : artificio *m*

artificial [,ɑrtə'fɪʃəl] *adj* **1** SYNTHETIC : artificial, sintético **2** FEIGNED : artificial, falso, afectado

artificially [,ɑrtə'fɪʃəli] *adv* : artificialmente, con afectación

artillery [ɑr'tɪləri] *n, pl* **-leries** : artillería *f*

artisan ['ɑrtəzən, -sən] *n* : artesano *m*, -na *f*

artist ['ɑrtɪst] *n* : artista *mf*

artistic [ɑr'tɪstɪk] *adj* : artístico — **artistically** [-tɪkli] *adv*

artistry ['ɑrtəstri] *n* : maestría *f*, arte *m*

artless ['ɑrtləs] *adj* : sencillo, natural, ingenuo, cándido — **artlessly** *adv*

artlessness ['ɑrtləsnəs] *n* : ingenuidad *f*, candidez *f*

arty ['ɑrti] *or* **artsy** ['ɑrtsi] *adj* **artier; -est** : pretenciosamente artístico

as¹ ['æz] *adv* **1** : tan, tanto ⟨this one's not as difficult : éste no es tan difícil⟩ ⟨he has a lot of time, but I don't have as much : él tiene mucho tiempo, pero yo no tengo tanto⟩ ⟨he was angry, but she was just as angry : él estaba enojado, pero ella estaba tan enojada como él⟩ **2** SUCH AS : como ⟨some trees, as oak and pine : algunos árboles, como el roble y el pino⟩

as² *conj* **1** LIKE : como, igual que ⟨(as) white as snow : blanca como la nieve⟩ ⟨she's as smart/guilty as he is : ella es tan inteligente/culpable como él⟩ ⟨she's Italian, as am I : es italiana, igual que yo⟩ ⟨she believes it, as do I : ella lo cree, y yo también⟩ ⟨twice as big as : el doble de grande que⟩ ⟨as soon as possible : lo más pronto posible⟩ **2** : como ⟨do (it) as I do : haz como yo⟩ ⟨knowing him as I do : conociéndolo como lo conozco⟩ ⟨as it happens . . . : da la casualidad de que . . .⟩ ⟨as is often/usually the case : como suele ocurrir⟩ ⟨as was to be expected : como era de esperar⟩ **3** WHEN, WHILE : cuando, mientras, a la vez que ⟨I saw it as I was leaving : lo vi cuando salía⟩ **4** BECAUSE : porque ⟨as I was tired, I stayed home : porque estaba cansada, me quedé en casa⟩ **5** THOUGH : aunque, por más que ⟨strange as it may appear : por extraño que parezca⟩ ⟨much as it pains me to say so : aunque me da pena decirlo⟩ ⟨try as he might : por más que trataba⟩ **6** as for CONCERNING : en cuanto a **7** as if : como si ⟨it looks as if : parece que⟩ ⟨as if I weren't there : como si no estuviera ahí⟩ **8** as is : tal (y) como está ⟨it's being sold as is : se vende tal como está⟩ **9** as it is : tal (y) como está ⟨leave it as it is : déjalo tal como está⟩ **10** as it is ALREADY : ya ⟨we have too much to do as it is : ya tenemos demasiado que hacer⟩ **11** as of : a partir de **12** as to CONCERNING : en cuanto a ⟨I'm at a loss as to how to explain it : no sé como explicarlo⟩ **13** so as to IN ORDER TO : para

as³ *prep* **1** : de ⟨I met her as a child : la conocí de pequeña⟩ ⟨he works as a secretary : trabaja de secretario⟩ **2** LIKE : como ⟨behave as a man : compórtate como un hombre⟩ ⟨I'm telling you this as a friend : te lo digo como amigo⟩

as⁴ *pron* : que ⟨in the same building as my brother : en el mismo edificio que mi hermano⟩

asbestos [æz'bɛstəs, æs-] *n* : asbesto *m*, amianto *m*

ascend [ə'sɛnd] *vi* : ascender, subir — *vt* : subir, subir a, escalar

ascendancy [ə'sɛndənsi] *n* : ascendiente *m*, predominio *m*

ascendant¹ [ə'sɛndənt] *adj* **1** RISING : ascendente **2** DOMINANT : superior, dominante

ascendant² *n* **to be in the ascendant** : estar en alza, ir ganando predominio

ascension [ə'sɛntʃən] *n* : ascensión *f*

ascent [ə'sɛnt] *n* **1** RISE : ascensión *f*, subida *f*, ascenso *m* **2** SLOPE : cuesta *f*, pendiente *f*

ascertain [,æsər'teɪn] *vt* : determinar, establecer, averiguar

ascetic¹ [ə'sɛtɪk] *adj* : ascético

ascetic² *n* : asceta *mf*

asceticism [ə'sɛtə,sɪzəm] *n* : ascetismo *m*

ascribable [ə'skraɪbəbəl] *adj* : atribuible, imputable

ascribe [ə'skraɪb] *vt* **-cribed; -cribing** : atribuir, imputar

aseptic [eɪ'sɛptɪk] *adj* : aséptico

asexual [,eɪ'sɛkʃʊəl] *adj* : asexual

as for *prep* CONCERNING : en cuanto a, respecto a, para

ash ['æʃ] *n* **1** : ceniza *f* ⟨to reduce to ashes : reducir a cenizas⟩ **2** : fresno *m* (árbol)

ashamed [ə'ʃeɪmd] *adj* : avergonzado, abochornado, apenado — **ashamedly** [ə'ʃeɪmədli] *adv*

ashen ['æʃən] *adj* : lívido, ceniciento, pálido

ashore [ə'ʃor] *adv* **1** : en tierra **2 to go ashore** : desembarcar

ashtray ['æʃ,treɪ] *n* : cenicero *m*

Ash Wednesday *n* : Miércoles *m* de Ceniza

Asian¹ ['eɪʒən, -ʃən] *adj* : asiático

Asian² *n* : asiático *m*, -ca *f*

aside [ə'saɪd] *adv* **1** : a un lado ⟨to step aside : hacerse a un lado⟩ **2** : de lado, aparte ⟨jesting aside : bromas aparte⟩ **3 to set aside** : guardar, apartar, reservar

aside from *prep* **1** BESIDES : además de **2** EXCEPT : aparte de, menos

as if *conj* : como si

asinine ['æsən,aɪn] *adj* : necio, estúpido

ask ['æsk] *vt* **1** : preguntar ⟨to ask a question : hacer una pregunta⟩ ⟨ask him if he's coming : pregúntale si viene⟩ **2** REQUEST : pedir, solicitar ⟨to ask someone (for) a favor, to ask a favor of someone : pedirle un favor a alguien⟩ **3** INVITE : invitar ⟨she asked us to the party : nos invitó a la fiesta⟩ ⟨we asked them over for dinner : los invitamos a cenar⟩ ⟨he asked her out : la invitó a salir⟩ — *vi* **1** INQUIRE : preguntar ⟨I asked about/after her children : pregunté por sus niños⟩ **2** REQUEST : pedir ⟨we asked for help : pedimos ayuda⟩ ⟨if you need help, ask : si necesitas ayuda, pídela⟩ **3 to ask for it/trouble** : buscársela

askance [əˈskæns] *adv* **1** SIDELONG : de reojo, de soslayo **2** SUSPICIOUSLY : con recelo, con desconfianza

askew [əˈskju:] *adj* : torcido, ladeado

asleep [əˈsli:p] *adj* **1** : dormido, durmiendo **2 to fall asleep** : quedarse dormido

as of *prep* : desde, a partir de

asparagus [əˈspærəgəs] *n* : espárrago *m*

aspect [ˈæˌspɛkt] *n* : aspecto *m*

aspen [ˈæspən] *n* : álamo *m* temblón

asperity [æˈspɛrəṭi, ə-] *n, pl* **-ties** : aspereza *f*

aspersion [əˈspərʒən] *n* : difamación *f*, calumnia *f*

asphalt [ˈæsˌfɔlt] *n* : asfalto *m*

asphyxia [æˈsfɪksiə, ə-] *n* : asfixia *f*

asphyxiate [æˈsfɪksiˌeɪt] *v* **-ated; -ating** *vt* : asfixiar — *vi* : asfixiarse

asphyxiation [æˌsfɪksiˈeɪʃən] *n* : asfixia *f*

aspirant [ˈæspərənt, əˈspaɪrənt] *n* : aspirante *mf*, pretendiente *mf*

aspiration [ˌæspəˈreɪʃən] *n* **1** DESIRE : aspiración *f*, anhelo *m*, ambición *f* **2** BREATHING : aspiración *f*

aspire [əˈspaɪr] *vi* **-pired; -piring** : aspirar

aspirin [ˈæspərən, ˈæspə-] *n, pl* **aspirin** *or* **aspirins** : aspirina *f*

ass [ˈæs] *n* **1** : asno *m* **2** IDIOT : imbécil *mf*, idiota *mf*

assail [əˈseɪl] *vt* : atacar, asaltar

assailant [əˈseɪlənt] *n* : asaltante *mf*, atacante *mf*

assassin [əˈsæsən] *n* : asesino *m*, -na *f*

assassinate [əˈsæsənˌeɪt] *vt* **-nated; -nating** : asesinar

assassination [əˌsæsənˈeɪʃən] *n* : asesinato *m*

assault[1] [əˈsɔlt] *vt* : atacar, asaltar, agredir

assault[2] *n* : ataque *m*, asalto *m*, agresión *f*

assay[1] [ˈæˌseɪ, æˈseɪ] *vt* : ensayar

assay[2] [ˈæˌseɪ, æˈseɪ] *n* : ensayo *m*

assemble [əˈsɛmbəl] *v* **-bled; -bling** *vt* **1** GATHER : reunir, recoger, juntar **2** CONSTRUCT : ensamblar, montar, construir — *vi* : reunirse, congregarse

assembly [əˈsɛmbli] *n, pl* **-blies** **1** MEETING : reunión *f* **2** CONSTRUCTING : ensamblaje *m*, montaje *m*

assembly line *n* : cadena *f* de montaje

assemblyman [əˈsɛmblimən] *n, pl* **-men** [-mən, -ˌmɛn] : asambleísta *m*

assemblywoman [əˈsɛmbliˌwʊmən] *n, pl* **-women** [-ˌwɪmən] : asambleísta *f*

assent[1] [əˈsɛnt] *vi* : asentir, consentir

assent[2] *n* : asentimiento *m*, aprobación *f*

assert [əˈsərt] *vt* **1** AFFIRM : afirmar, aseverar, mantener **2 to assert oneself** : imponerse, hacerse valer

assertion [əˈsərʃən] *n* : afirmación *f*, aseveración *f*, aserto *m*

assertive [əˈsərṭɪv] *adj* : firme, enérgico

assertiveness [əˈsərṭɪvnəs] *n* : confianza *f* en sí mismo

assess [əˈsɛs] *vt* **1** IMPOSE : gravar (un impuesto), imponer **2** EVALUATE : evaluar, valorar, aquilatar

assessment [əˈsɛsmənt] *n* : evaluación *f*, valoración *f*

assessor [əˈsɛsər] *n* : evaluador *m*, -dora *f*; tasador *m*, -dora *f*

asset [ˈæˌsɛt] *n* **1** : ventaja *f*, recurso *m* **2** **assets** *npl* : bienes *mpl*, activo *m* ⟨assets and liabilities : activo y pasivo⟩

assiduous [əˈsɪdʒuəs] *adj* : diligente, aplicado, asiduo — **assiduously** *adv*

assign [əˈsaɪn] *vt* **1** APPOINT : designar, nombrar **2** ALLOT : asignar, señalar **3** ATTRIBUTE : atribuir, dar, conceder

assignment [əˈsaɪnmənt] *n* **1** TASK : función *f*, tarea *f*, misión *f* **2** HOMEWORK : tarea *f*, asignación *f* PRi, deberes *mpl* Spain **3** APPOINTMENT : nombramiento *m* **4** ALLOCATION : asignación *f*

assimilate [əˈsɪməˌleɪt] *v* **-lated; -lating** *vt* : asimilar — *vi* : adaptarse, integrarse

assimilation [əˌsɪməˈleɪʃən] *n* : asimilación *f*

assist[1] [əˈsɪst] *vt* : asistir, ayudar

assist[2] *n* : asistencia *f*, contribución *f*

assistance [əˈsɪstənts] *n* : asistencia *f*, ayuda *f*, auxilio *m*

assistant [əˈsɪstənt] *n* : ayudante *mf*, asistente *mf*

associate[1] [əˈsoːʃiˌeɪt, -si-] *v* **-ated; -ating** *vt* **1** CONNECT, RELATE : asociar, relacionar **2 to be associated with** : estar relacionado con, estar vinculado a — *vi* **to associate with** : relacionarse con, frecuentar

associate[2] [əˈsoːʃiət, -siət] *n* : asociado *m*, -da *f*; colega *mf*; socio *m*, -cia *f*

association [əˌsoːʃiˈeɪʃən, -si-] *n* **1** ORGANIZATION : asociación *f*, sociedad *f* **2** RELATIONSHIP : asociación *f*, relación *f*

as soon as *conj* : en cuanto, tan pronto como

assorted [əˈsɔrṭəd] *adj* : surtido

assortment [əˈsɔrtmənt] *n* : surtido *m*, variedad *f*, colección *f*

assuage [əˈsweɪʤ] *vt* **-suaged; -suaging** **1** EASE : aliviar, mitigar **2** CALM : calmar, aplacar **3** SATISFY : saciar, satisfacer

assume [əˈsuːm] *vt* **-sumed; -suming** **1** SUPPOSE : suponer, asumir **2** UNDERTAKE : asumir, encargarse de **3** TAKE ON : adquirir, adoptar, tomar ⟨to assume importance : tomar importancia⟩ **4** FEIGN : adoptar, afectar, simular

assumed [əˈsuːmd] *adj* : fingido, falso ⟨an assumed air of confidence : un aire de falsa confianza⟩ ⟨an assumed name : un nombre falso/ficticio/supuesto, un seudónimo⟩

assumption [əˈsʌmpʃən] *n* : asunción *f*, presunción *f*

assurance [əˈʃʊrənts] *n* **1** CERTAINTY : certidumbre *f*, certeza *f* **2** CONFIDENCE : confianza *f*, aplomo *m*, seguridad *f*

assure [əˈʃʊr] *vt* **-sured; -suring** : asegurar, garantizar ⟨I assure you that I'll do it : te aseguro que lo haré⟩

assured [əˈʃʊrd] *adj* **1** CERTAIN : seguro, asegurado **2** CONFIDENT : confiado, seguro de sí mismo

aster [ˈæstər] *n* : aster *m*

asterisk [ˈæstəˌrɪsk] *n* : asterisco *m*

astern [ə'stərn] *adv* **1** BEHIND : detrás, a popa **2** BACKWARDS : hacia atrás

asteroid ['æstə,rɔɪd] *n* : asteroide *m*

asthma ['æzmə] *n* : asma *m*

asthmatic [æz'mætɪk] *adj* : asmático

as though → as if

astigmatism [ə'stɪgmə,tɪzəm] *n* : astigmatismo *m*

as to *prep* **1** ABOUT : sobre, acerca de **2** → according to

astonish [ə'stanɪʃ] *vt* : asombrar, sorprender, pasmar

astonishing [ə'stanɪʃɪŋ] *adj* : asombroso, sorprendente, increíble — **astonishingly** *adv*

astonishment [ə'stanɪʃmənt] *n* : asombro *m*, estupefacción *f*, sorpresa *f*

astound [ə'staʊnd] *vt* : asombrar, pasmar, dejar estupefacto

astounding [ə'staʊndɪŋ] *adj* : asombroso, pasmoso — **astoundingly** *adv*

astraddle [ə'strædəl] *adv* : a horcajadas

astral ['æstrəl] *adj* : astral

astray [ə'streɪ] *adv & adj* : perdido, extraviado, descarriado

astride [ə'straɪd] *adv* : a horcajadas

astringency [ə'strɪndʒənsi] *n* : astringencia *f*

astringent¹ [ə'strɪndʒənt] *adj* : astringente

astringent² *n* : astringente *m*

astrologer [ə'stralədʒər] *n* : astrólogo *m*, -ga *f*

astrological [ˌæstrə'ladʒɪkəl] *adj* : astrológico

astrology [ə'stralədʒi] *n* : astrología *f*

astronaut ['æstrə,nɔt] *n* : astronauta *mf*

astronautic [ˌæstrə'nɔtɪk] *or* **astronautical** [-tɪkəl] *adj* : astronáutico

astronautics [ˌæstrə'nɔtɪks] *ns & pl* : astronáutica *f*

astronomer [ə'stranəmər] *n* : astrónomo *m*, -ma *f*

astronomical [ˌæstrə'namɪkəl] *adj* **1** : astronómico **2** ENORMOUS : astronómico, enorme, gigantesco

astronomy [ə'stranəmi] *n, pl* **-mies** : astronomía *f*

astute [ə'stuːt, -'stjuːt] *adj* : astuto, sagaz, perspicaz — **astutely** *adv*

astuteness [ə'stuːtnəs, -'stjuːt-] *n* : astucia *f*, sagacidad *f*, perspicacia *f*

asunder [ə'sʌndər] *adv* : en dos, en pedazos ⟨to tear asunder : hacer pedazos⟩

as well as¹ *conj* : tanto como

as well as² *prep* BESIDES : además de, aparte de

as yet *adv* : aún, todavía

asylum [ə'saɪləm] *n* **1** REFUGE : refugio *m*, santuario *m*, asilo *m* **2 insane asylum** : manicomio *m*

asymmetrical [ˌeɪsə'metrɪkəl] *or* **asymmetric** [-'metrɪk] *adj* : asimétrico

asymmetry [ˌeɪ'sɪmətri] *n* : asimetría *f*

at ['æt] *prep* **1** (*indicating location*) : en, a ⟨at the top : en lo alto⟩ ⟨at the rear : al fondo⟩ ⟨at Ann's house : en casa de Ana⟩ ⟨is she at home? : ¿está en casa?⟩ ⟨he was sitting at the table : estaba sentado a la mesa⟩ ⟨someone is knocking at the door : llaman a la puerta⟩ **2** (*indica-*

ting the recipient of an action, motion, or feeling) ⟨she shouted at me : me gritó⟩ ⟨don't look at me! : ¡a mí no me mires!⟩ ⟨he's laughing at you : está riéndose de ti⟩ ⟨to be angry at someone : estar enojado con alguien⟩ **3** (*indicating a reaction or cause*) ⟨he laughed at the joke : se rió con el chiste⟩ ⟨to be surprised at something : sorprenderse por algo⟩ ⟨at the invitation of : por invitación de⟩ **4** (*indicating an activity or state*) ⟨children who are at play : niños que están jugando⟩ ⟨you're good at this : eres bueno para esto⟩ ⟨he's at peace now : ahora descansa en paz⟩ ⟨at peace/war : en paz/guerra⟩ ⟨to be at risk : peligrar⟩ **5** (*used for the symbol* @) : arroba ⟨at merriam-webster dot com : arroba merriam-webster punto com⟩ **6** (*indicating a rate or measure*) ⟨a ⟨at 80 miles an hour : a 80 millas por hora⟩ ⟨they sell at a dollar each : se venden a un dólar cada uno⟩ **7** (*indicating an age or time*) ⟨a ⟨at ten o'clock : a las diez⟩ ⟨at age 65 : a los 65 años (de edad)⟩ ⟨at last : por fin⟩ **8 at it** ⟨while we're at it : ya que estamos (en ello)⟩ ⟨they're at it again! : ¡ya empezaron otra vez!⟩

at all *adv* : en absoluto, para nada

ate → eat

atheism ['eɪθi,ɪzəm] *n* : ateísmo *m*

atheist ['eɪθiɪst] *n* : ateo *m*, atea *f*

atheistic [ˌeɪθi'ɪstɪk] *adj* : ateo

athlete ['æθ,liːt] *n* : atleta *mf*

athletic [æθ'lɛtɪk] *adj* : atlético

athletics [æθ'lɛtɪks] *ns & pl* : atletismo *m*

Atlantic [ət'læntɪk, æt-] *adj* : atlántico

atlas ['ætləs] *n* : atlas *m*

ATM [ˌeɪ,tiː'ɛm] *n* : cajero *m* automático

atmosphere ['ætmə,sfɪr] *n* **1** AIR : atmósfera *f*, aire *m* **2** AMBIENCE : ambiente *m*, atmósfera *f*, clima *m*

atmospheric [ˌætmə'sfɪrɪk, -'sfɛr-] *adj* : atmosférico — **atmospherically** [-ɪkli] *adv*

atoll ['æ,tɔl, 'eɪ-, -,tɑl] *n* : atolón *m*

atom ['ætəm] *n* **1** : átomo *m* **2** SPECK : ápice *m*, pizca *f*

atomic [ə'tamɪk] *adj* : atómico

atomic bomb *n* : bomba *f* atómica

atomizer ['ætə,maɪzər] *n* : atomizador *m*, pulverizador *m*

atone [ə'toːn] *vi* **atoned; atoning to atone for** : expiar

atonement [ə'toːnmənt] *n* : expiación *f*, desagravio *m*

atop¹ [ə'tap] *adv* : encima

atop² *prep* : encima de, sobre

atrium ['eɪtriəm] *n, pl* **atria** [-triə] *or* **atriums** **1** : atrio *m* **2** : aurícula *f* (del corazón)

atrocious [ə'troːʃəs] *adj* : atroz — **atrociously** *adv*

atrocity [ə'trasəti] *n, pl* **-ties** : atrocidad *f*

atrophy¹ ['ætrəfi] *vt* **-phied; -phying** : atrofiar

atrophy² *n, pl* **-phies** : atrofia *f*

at sign *n* (*used for the symbol* @) : arroba *f*

attach [ə'tætʃ] vt 1 FASTEN : sujetar, atar, amarrar, pegar 2 JOIN : juntar, adjuntar 3 ATTRIBUTE : dar, atribuir ⟨I attached little importance to it : le di poca importancia⟩ 4 SEIZE : embargar 5 to become attached to someone : encariñarse con alguien

attaché [ˌætəˈʃeɪ, ˌætæ-, ə'tæ-] n : agregado m, -da f

attaché case n : maletín m

attachment [ə'tætʃmənt] n 1 ACCESSORY : accesorio m 2 CONNECTION : conexión f, acoplamiento m 3 FONDNESS : apego m, cariño m, afición f

attack¹ [ə'tæk] vt 1 ASSAULT : atacar, asaltar, agredir 2 TACKLE : acometer, combatir, enfrentarse con

attack² n 1 : ataque m ⟨an attack on/against : un ataque a/contra⟩ ⟨to launch an attack : lanzar un ataque⟩ 2 : ataque m ⟨heart attack : ataque cardíaco, infarto⟩ ⟨panic/anxiety attack : ataque de pánico/ansiedad⟩

attacker [ə'tækər] n : asaltante mf

attain [ə'teɪn] vt 1 ACHIEVE : lograr, conseguir, alcanzar, realizar 2 REACH : alcanzar, llegar a

attainable [ə'teɪnəbəl] adj : realizable, asequible

attainment [ə'teɪnmənt] n : logro m, consecución f, realización f

attempt¹ [ə'tempt] vt : intentar, tratar de

attempt² n : intento m, tentativa f

attend [ə'tend] vt 1 : asistir a ⟨to attend a meeting : asistir a una reunión⟩ 2 : atender, ocuparse de, cuidar ⟨to attend a patient : atender a un paciente⟩ 3 HEED : atender a, hacer caso de 4 ACCOMPANY : acompañar

attendance [ə'tendənts] n 1 ATTENDING : asistencia f 2 TURNOUT : concurrencia f

attendant¹ [ə'tendənt] adj : concomitante, inherente

attendant² n : asistente mf, acompañante mf, guarda mf

attention [ə'tentʃən] n 1 : atención f ⟨I brought the problem to his attention : le informé del problema⟩ ⟨it has come to our attention that . . . : se nos ha informado que . . .⟩ ⟨to attract someone's attention : atraer la atención de alguien⟩ 2 to pay attention : prestar atención, hacer caso ⟨to pay attention to someone/something : prestarle atención a algo/alguien⟩ ⟨don't pay any attention to him : no le hagas caso⟩ ⟨she didn't pay attention to the rumors : no hizo caso de los rumores⟩ 3 to stand at attention : estar firme

attentive [ə'tentɪv] adj : atento — **attentively** adv

attentiveness [ə'tentɪvnəs] n 1 THOUGHTFULNESS : cortesía f, consideración f 2 CONCENTRATION : atención f, concentración f

attest [ə'test] vt : atestiguar, dar fe de

attestation [ˌæˌtsˈteɪʃən] n : testimonio m

attic [ˈætɪk] n : ático m, desván m, buhardilla f

attire¹ [ə'taɪr] vt -tired; -tiring : ataviar

attire² n : atuendo m, atavío m

attitude [ˈæt̬ɪˌtuːd, -ˌtjuːd] n 1 FEELING : actitud f 2 POSTURE : postura f

attorney [ə'tərni] n, pl -neys : abogado m, -da f

attract [ə'trækt] vt 1 : atraer 2 to attract attention : llamar la atención

attraction [ə'trækʃən] n : atracción f, atractivo m

attractive [ə'træktɪv] adj : atractivo, atrayente

attractively [ə'træktɪvli] adv : de manera atractiva, de buen gusto, hermosamente

attractiveness [ə'træktɪvnəs] n : atractivo m

attributable [ə'trɪbjut̬əbəl] adj : atribuible, imputable

attribute¹ [ə'trɪˌbjuːt] vt -tributed; -tributing : atribuir

attribute² [ˈætrəˌbjuːt] n : atributo m, cualidad f

attribution [ˌætrəˈbjuːʃən] n : atribución f

attrition [ə'trɪʃən] n : desgaste m ⟨war of attrition : guerra de desgaste⟩

attune [ə'tuːn, -'tjuːn] vt -tuned; -tuning 1 ADAPT : adaptar, adecuar 2 to be attuned to : estar en armonía con

ATV [ˌeɪˌtiːˈviː] → all-terrain vehicle

atypical [ˌeɪ'tɪpɪkəl] adj : atípico

aubergine [ˈoʊbərˌʒiːn] → eggplant

auburn [ˈɔbərn] adj : castaño rojizo

auction¹ [ˈɔkʃən] vt : subastar, rematar

auction² n : subasta f, remate m

auctioneer [ˌɔkʃəˈnɪr] n : subastador m, -dora f; rematador m, -dora f

audacious [ə'deɪʃəs] adj : audaz, atrevido

audacity [ə'dæsət̬i] n, pl -ties : audacia f, atrevimiento m, descaro m

audible [ˈɔdəbəl] adj : audible — **audibly** [-bli] adv

audience [ˈɔdiənts] n 1 INTERVIEW : audiencia f 2 PUBLIC : audiencia f, público m, auditorio m, espectadores mpl

audio¹ [ˈɔdiˌoː] adj : de sonido, de audio

audio² n : audio m

audiovisual [ˌɔdioˈvɪʒuəl] adj : audiovisual

audit¹ [ˈɔdət] vt 1 : auditar (finanzas) 2 : asistir como oyente a (una clase o un curso)

audit² n : auditoría f

audition¹ [ɔ'dɪʃən] vi : hacer una audición

audition² n : audición f

auditor [ˈɔdət̬ər] n 1 : auditor m, -tora f (de finanzas) 2 STUDENT : oyente mf

auditorium [ˌɔdəˈtoriəm] n, pl -riums or -ria [-riə] : auditorio m, sala f

auditory [ˈɔdəˌtori] adj : auditivo

auger [ˈɔgər] n : taladro m, barrena f

augment [ɔg'mɛnt] vt : aumentar, incrementar

augmentation [ˌɔgmənˈteɪʃən] n : aumento m, incremento m

au gratin [ˌoːˈgrɑtən, -ˈgræ-] adj : gratinado

augur¹ [ˈɔgər] vt : augurar, presagiar — vi to augur well : ser de buen agüero

augur² n : augur m

augury [ˈɔgjuri, -gər-] *n, pl* **-ries** : augurio *m*, presagio *m*, agüero *m*

august [ɔˈgʌst] *adj* : augusto

August [ˈɔgəst] *n* : agosto *m* ⟨they arrived on the 20th of August, they arrived on August 20th : llegaron el 20 de agosto⟩

auk [ˈɔk] *n* : alca *f*

aunt [ˈænt, ˈɑnt] *n* : tía *f*

auntie [ˈænti, ˈɑnti] *n* : tita *f*

aura [ˈɔrə] *n* : aura *f*

aural [ˈɔrəl] *adj* : auditivo

auricle [ˈɔrɪkəl] *n* : aurícula *f*

aurora borealis [əˈrorəˌboriˈæləs] *n* : aurora *f* boreal

auspices [ˈɔspəsəz, -ˌsiːz] *npl* : auspicios *mpl*

auspicious [ɔˈspɪʃəs] *adj* : prometedor, propicio, de buen augurio

austere [ɔˈstɪr] *adj* : austero, severo, adusto — **austerely** *adv*

austerity [ɔˈsterəti] *n, pl* **-ties** : austeridad *f*

Australian [ɔˈstreɪljən] *n* : australiano *m*, -na *f* — **Australian** *adj*

Austrian [ˈɔstriən] *n* : austriaco *m*, -ca *f* — **Austrian** *adj*

authentic [əˈθɛntɪk, ɔ-] *adj* : auténtico, genuino — **authentically** [-tɪkli] *adv*

authenticate [əˈθɛntɪˌkeɪt, ɔ-] *vt* **-cated; -cating** : autenticar, autentificar

authenticity [ˌɔˌθɛnˈtɪsəti] *n* : autenticidad *f*

author [ˈɔθər] *n* **1** WRITER : escritor *m*, -tora *f*; autor *m*, -tora *f* **2** CREATOR : autor *m*, -tora *f*; creador *m*, -dora *f*; artífice *mf*

authoritarian [ɔˌθɔrəˈtɛriən, ə-] *adj* : autoritario

authoritative [əˈθɔrəˌteɪtɪv, ɔ-] *adj* **1** RELIABLE : fidedigno, autorizado **2** DICTATORIAL : autoritario, dictatorial, imperioso

authoritatively [əˈθɔrəˌteɪtɪvli, ɔ-] *adv* **1** RELIABLY : con autoridad **2** DICTATORIALLY : de manera autoritaria

authority [əˈθɔrəti, ɔ-] *n, pl* **-ties** **1** EXPERT : autoridad *f* **2** POWER : autoridad *f* **3** AUTHORIZATION : autorización *f* **4 the authorities** : las autoridades **5 on good authority** : de buena fuente ⟨he has it on good authority that . . . : sabe de buena fuente que . . .⟩

authorization [ˌɔθərəˈzeɪʃən] *n* : autorización *f*

authorize [ˈɔθəˌraɪz] *vt* **-rized; -rizing** : autorizar, facultar

authorship [ˈɔθərˌʃɪp] *n* : autoría *f*

autism [ˈɔˌtɪzəm] *n* : autismo *m*

autistic [ɔˈtɪstɪk] *adj* : autista

auto [ˈɔto] → **automobile**

auto- [ˈɔto] *pref* **1** SELF- : auto- **2** : automático

autobiographical [ˌɔtoˌbaɪəˈgræfɪkəl] *adj* : autobiográfico

autobiography [ˌɔtobaɪˈɑgrəfi] *n, pl* **-phies** : autobiografía *f*

autocracy [ɔˈtɑkrəsi] *n, pl* **-cies** : autocracia *f*

autocrat [ˈɔtəˌkræt] *n* : autócrata *mf*

autocratic [ˌɔtəˈkrætɪk] *adj* : autocrático — **autocratically** [-tɪkli] *adv*

autograph¹ [ˈɔtəˌgræf] *vt* : autografiar

autograph² *n* : autógrafo *m*

automaker [ˈɔtoˌmeɪkər] *n* : fabricante *mf* de autos, automotriz *f*

automate [ˈɔtəˌmeɪt] *vt* **-mated; -mating** : automatizar

automatic [ˌɔtəˈmætɪk] *adj* : automático — **automatically** [-tɪkli] *adv*

automatic pilot → **autopilot**

automation [ˌɔtəˈmeɪʃən] *n* : automatización *f*

automaton [ɔˈtɑməˌtɑn] *n, pl* **-atons** or **-ata** [-tə, -ˌtɑ] : autómata *m*

automobile [ˌɔtəmoˈbiːl, -ˈmoˌbiːl] *n* : automóvil *m*, auto *m*, carro *m*, coche *m*

automotive [ˌɔtəˈmotɪv] *adj* : automotor

autonomous [ɔˈtɑnəməs] *adj* : autónomo — **autonomously** *adv*

autonomy [ɔˈtɑnəmi] *n, pl* **-mies** : autonomía *f*

autopilot [ˈɔtoˌpaɪlət] *n* : piloto *m* automático

autopsy [ˈɔˌtɑpsi, -təp-] *n, pl* **-sies** : autopsia *f*

autumn [ˈɔtəm] *n* : otoño *m*

autumnal [ɔˈtʌmnəl] *adj* : otoñal

auxiliary¹ [ɔgˈzɪljəri, -ˈzɪləri] *adj* : auxiliar

auxiliary² *n, pl* **-ries** : auxiliar *mf*, ayudante *mf*

avail¹ [əˈveɪl] *vt* **to avail oneself** : aprovecharse, valerse

avail² *n* **1** : provecho *m*, utilidad *f* **2 to no avail** : en vano **3 to be of no avail** : no servir de nada, ser inútil

availability [əˌveɪləˈbɪləti] *n, pl* **-ties** : disponibilidad *f*

available [əˈveɪləbəl] *adj* : disponible

avalanche [ˈævəˌlæntʃ] *n* : avalancha *f*, alud *m*

avant–garde¹ [ˌɑˌvɑntˈgɑrd] *adj* : vanguardista

avant–garde² *n* : vanguardia *f* — **avant–gardist** [ˌɑˌvɑntˈgɑrdɪst] *n*

avarice [ˈævərəs] *n* : avaricia *f*, codicia *f*

avaricious [ˌævəˈrɪʃəs] *adj* : avaricioso, codicioso

avatar [ˈævəˌtɑr] *n* : avatar *m*

avenge [əˈvɛndʒ] *vt* **avenged; avenging** : vengar

avenue [ˈævəˌnuː, -ˌnjuː] *n* **1** : avenida *f* **2** MEANS : vía *f*, camino *m*

average¹ [ˈævrɪdʒ, ˈævə-] *vt* **-aged; -aging** **1** : hacer un promedio de ⟨he averages 8 hours a day : hace un promedio de 8 horas diarias⟩ **2** : calcular el promedio de, promediar (en matemáticas)

average² *adj* **1** MEAN : medio ⟨the average temperature : la temperatura media⟩ **2** ORDINARY : común, ordinario ⟨the average man : el hombre común⟩

average³ *n* : promedio *m*

averse [əˈvərs] *adj* : reacio, opuesto

aversion [əˈvərʒən] *n* : aversión *f*

avert [əˈvərt] *vt* **1** : apartar, desviar ⟨he averted his eyes from the scene : apartó los ojos de la escena⟩ **2** AVOID, PREVENT : evitar, prevenir

aviary [ˈeɪviˌɛri] *n, pl* **-aries** : pajarera *f*

aviation [ˌeɪviˈeɪʃən] *n* : aviación *f*

aviator [ˈeɪviˌeɪtər] *n* : aviador *m*, -dora *f*

avid ['ævɪd] *adj* **1** GREEDY : ávido, codicioso **2** ENTHUSIASTIC : ávido, entusiasta, ferviente — **avidly** *adv*

avocado [ˌævəˈkɑdo, ˌʌvə-] *n, pl* **-dos** : aguacate *m*, palta *f*

avocation [ˌævəˈkeɪʃən] *n* : pasatiempo *m*, afición *f*

avoid [əˈvɔɪd] *vt* **1** SHUN : evitar, eludir **2** FORGO : evitar, abstenerse de ⟨I always avoided gossip : siempre evitaba los chismes⟩ **3** EVADE : evitar ⟨if I can avoid it : si puedo evitarlo⟩

avoidable [əˈvɔɪdəbəl] *adj* : evitable

avoidance [əˈvɔɪdənts] *n* : el evitar

avoirdupois [ˌævərdəˈpɔɪz] *n* : sistema *m* inglés de pesos y medidas

avow [əˈvaʊ] *vt* : reconocer, confesar

avowal [əˈvaʊəl] *n* : reconocimiento *m*, confesión *f*

await [əˈweɪt] *vt* : esperar

awake[1] [əˈweɪk] *v* **awoke** [əˈwoːk]; **awoken** [əˈwoːkən] *or* **awaked**; **awaking** : despertar

awake[2] *adj* : despierto

awaken [əˈweɪkən] → **awake**[1]

award[1] [əˈwɔrd] *vt* : otorgar, conceder, conferir

award[2] *n* **1** PRIZE : premio *m*, galardón *m* **2** MEDAL : condecoración *f*

aware [əˈwær] *adj* : consciente ⟨to be aware of : darse cuenta de, estar consciente de⟩

awareness [əˈwærnəs] *n* : conciencia *f*, conocimiento *m*

awash [əˈwɔʃ] *adj* : inundado

away[1] [əˈweɪ] *adv* **1** : de aquí, de allí ⟨it's 10 miles away (from here) : queda/está a 10 millas (de aquí)⟩ ⟨she's away from the office : está fuera de la oficina⟩ ⟨far away from home : lejos de casa⟩ ⟨go away! : ¡fuera de aquí!, ¡vete!⟩ ⟨he walked away : se alejó (caminando)⟩ ⟨she looked away : desvió la mirada⟩ ⟨stay away from the dog : no te acerques al perro⟩ **2** : en un lugar seguro ⟨she tucked it away in a drawer : lo guardó en un cajón⟩ ⟨the files are locked away : los archivos están guardados bajo llave⟩ **3** (*indicating a gradual diminishing*) ⟨to fade away : desvanecerse, apagarse⟩ ⟨to waste away (from illness) : consumirse (por enfermedad)⟩ **4** NONSTOP,

STEADILY : sin parar, a un ritmo constante ⟨she was typing away at the computer : estaba tecleando en la computadora⟩ **5** : fuera de casa (en deportes) ⟨they played at home and away : jugaron en casa y fuera de casa⟩

away[2] *adj* **1** ABSENT : ausente ⟨away for the week : ausente por la semana⟩ **2**

away game : partido *m* fuera de casa

awe[1] ['ɔ] *vt* **awed; awing** : abrumar, asombrar, impresionar

awe[2] *n* : asombro *m*

awesome ['ɔsəm] *adj* **1** IMPOSING : imponente, formidable **2** AMAZING : asombroso

awestruck ['ɔˌstrʌk] *adj* : asombrado

awful ['ɔfəl] *adj* **1** AWESOME : asombroso **2** DREADFUL : horrible, terrible, atroz **3** ENORMOUS : enorme, tremendo ⟨an awful lot of people : muchísima gente, la mar de gente⟩

awfully ['ɔfəli] *adv* **1** EXTREMELY : terriblemente, extremadamente **2** BADLY : muy mal, espantosamente

awhile [əˈhwaɪl] *adv* : un rato, algún tiempo

awkward ['ɔkwərd] *adj* **1** CLUMSY : torpe, desmañado **2** EMBARRASSING : embarazoso, delicado ⟨an awkward position : una situación embarazosa⟩ — **awkwardly** *adv*

awkwardness ['ɔkwərdnəs] *n* **1** CLUMSINESS : torpeza *f* **2** INCONVENIENCE : incomodidad *f*

awl ['ɔl] *n* : punzón *m*

awning ['ɔnɪŋ] *n* : toldo *m*

awry [əˈraɪ] *adj* **1** ASKEW : torcido **2 to go awry** : salir mal, fracasar

ax *or* **axe** ['æks] *n* : hacha *f*

axiom ['æksiəm] *n* : axioma *m*

axiomatic [ˌæksiəˈmætɪk] *adj* : axiomático

axis ['æksɪs] *n, pl* **axes** [-ˌsiːz] : eje *m*

axle ['æksəl] *n* : eje *m*

aye[1] ['aɪ] *adv* : sí

aye[2] *n* : sí *m*

azalea [əˈzeɪljə] *n* : azalea *f*

azimuth ['æzəməθ] *n* : azimut *m*, acimut *m*

Aztec ['æzˌtɛk] *n* : azteca *mf*

azure[1] ['æʒər] *adj* : azur, celeste

azure[2] *n* : azur *m*

B

b ['biː] *n, pl* **b's** *or* **bs** ['biːz] **1** : segunda letra del alfabeto inglés **2 B** : si *m* ⟨B sharp/flat : si sostenido/bemol⟩

babble[1] ['bæbəl] *vi* **-bled; -bling 1** PRATTLE : balbucear **2** CHATTER : parlotear *fam* **3** MURMUR : murmurar

babble[2] *n* : balbuceo *m* (de bebé), parloteo *m* (de adultos), murmullo *m* (de voces, de un arroyo)

babe ['beɪb] *n* → **baby**[3]

baboon [bæˈbuːn] *n* : babuino *m*

baby[1] ['beɪbi] *vt* **-bied; -bying** : mimar, consentir

baby[2] *adj* **1** : de niño ⟨a baby carriage : un cochecito⟩ ⟨baby talk : habla infantil⟩ **2** TINY : pequeño, minúsculo

baby[3] *n, pl* **-bies** : bebé *m*; niño *m*, -ña *f*; bebe *m*, -ba *f* *Arg, Uru*

babyhood ['beɪbiˌhʊd] *n* : niñez *f*, primera infancia *f*

babyish ['beɪbiɪʃ] *adj* : infantil, pueril

baby–sit [ˈbeɪbiˌsɪt] *vi* **-sat** [-ˌsæt]; **-sitting** : cuidar niños, hacer de canguro *Spain*

baby–sitter [ˈbeɪbiˌsɪtər] *n* : niñero *m*, -ra *f*; canguro *mf Spain*

baccalaureate [ˌbækəˈlɔriət] *n* : licenciatura *f*

bachelor [ˈbætʃələr] *n* **1** : soltero *m* **2** : licenciado *m*, -da *f* ⟨bachelor of arts degree : licenciatura en filosofía y letras⟩

back¹ [ˈbæk] *vt* **1** *or* **to back up** SUPPORT : apoyar, respaldar **2** *or* **to back up** REVERSE : dar marcha atrás a, dar reversa a *Col, Mex* (un vehículo) **3** : estar detrás de, formar el fondo de ⟨trees back the garden : detrás del jardín hay unos árboles⟩ **4** : apostar por (un caballo, etc.) **5** *or* **to back up** : acompañar (en música) **6 to back up** : hacer una copia de seguridad de (archivos, etc.) **7 to back up** BLOCK : atascar — *vi* **1** *or* **to back away/up** : echarse atrás **2** *or* **to back up** : dar marcha atrás, dar reversa *Col, Mex* (en un vehículo) **3 to back off** : dejar a alguien en paz **4 to back off/down** : volverse atrás, echarse para atrás **5 to back off/out** RENEGE : volverse atrás, echarse para atrás, rajarse *fam* **6 to back up** : hacer copias de seguridad

back² *adv* **1** : atrás, hacia atrás, detrás ⟨to move back : moverse atrás⟩ ⟨to step back : dar un paso atrás⟩ ⟨to lean back : reclinarse⟩ ⟨it's two miles back : queda dos millas atrás⟩ ⟨back and forth : de acá para allá⟩ **2** AGO : atrás, antes, ya ⟨some years back : unos años atrás, ya unos años⟩ ⟨10 months back : hace diez meses⟩ **3** : de vuelta, de regreso ⟨we're back : estamos de vuelta⟩ ⟨I'll be back soon : vuelvo enseguida⟩ ⟨she ran back : volvió corriendo⟩ ⟨he never went back : nunca regresó⟩ ⟨I forgot to put it back : me olvidé de devolverlo a su lugar⟩ **4** : como respuesta, en cambio ⟨to call back : llamar de nuevo⟩ ⟨he smiled back at me : me devolvió la sonrisa⟩ ⟨she gave the money back : devolvió el dinero⟩

back³ *adj* **1** REAR : de atrás, posterior, trasero **2** OVERDUE : atrasado **3 back pay** : atrasos *mpl*

back⁴ *n* **1** : espalda *f* (de un ser humano), lomo *m* (de un animal) **2** : respaldo *m* (de una silla), espalda *f* (de ropa) **3** REVERSE : reverso *m*, dorso *m*, revés *m* ⟨the back of an envelope : el reverso de un sobre⟩ **4** REAR : fondo *m*, parte *f* de atrás **5** : defensa *mf* (en deportes) **6 back to back** : espalda con espalda **7 back to back** CONSECUTIVE : seguido **8 back to front** BACKWARD : al revés **9 behind someone's back** : a espaldas de alguien ⟨behind my back : a mis espaldas⟩ **10 in ~**: en la parte de atrás, al fondo **11 in back of** : detrás de ⟨12 out ~**: detrás de la casa (etc.) **13 to turn one's back on someone** : volverle la espalda a alguien

backache [ˈbækˌeɪk] *n* : dolor *m* de espalda

backbite [ˈbækˌbaɪt] *v* **-bit** [-ˌbɪt]; **-bitten** [-ˌbɪtən]; **-biting** *vt* : calumniar, hablar mal de — *vi* : murmurar

backbone [ˈbækˌboːn] *n* **1** : columna *f* vertebral **2** FIRMNESS : firmeza *f*, carácter *m*

backdrop [ˈbækˌdrɑp] *n* : telón *m* de fondo

backer [ˈbækər] *n* **1** SUPPORTER : partidario *m*, -ria *f* **2** SPONSOR : patrocinador *m*, -dora *f*

backfire¹ [ˈbækˌfaɪr] *vi* **-fired; -firing 1** : petardear (dícese de un automóvil) **2** FAIL : fallar, salir el tiro por la culata

backfire² *n* : petardeo *m*, explosión *f*

background [ˈbækˌɡraʊnd] *n* **1** : fondo *m* (de un cuadro, etc.) ⟨background color : color de fondo⟩ ⟨background noise/music : ruido/música de fondo⟩ **2** : segundo plano *m* ⟨a shy person who stays in the background : una persona tímida que permanece en (un) segundo plano⟩ ⟨the program runs in the background : el programa se ejecuta en segundo plano⟩ **3** *or* **background information** : antecedentes *mpl* (de una situación) **4** : historial *m*, antecedentes *mpl* (de una persona) ⟨family background : historial familiar⟩ ⟨professional background : experiencia profesional⟩ ⟨background check : verificación de antecedentes⟩

backhand¹ [ˈbækˌhænd] *adv* : de revés, con el revés

backhand² *n* : revés *m*

backhanded [ˈbækˌhændəd] *adj* **1** : dado con el revés, de revés **2** INDIRECT : indirecto, ambiguo

backing [ˈbækɪŋ] *n* **1** SUPPORT : apoyo *m*, respaldo *m* **2** REINFORCEMENT : refuerzo *m* **3** SUPPORTERS : partidarios *mpl*, -rias *fpl*

backlash [ˈbækˌlæʃ] *n* : reacción *f* violenta

backlog [ˈbækˌlɔɡ] *n* : atraso *m*, trabajo *m* acumulado

backpack¹ [ˈbækˌpæk] *vi* : viajar con mochila

backpack² *n* : mochila *f*

backrest [ˈbækˌrest] *n* : respaldo *m*

backside [ˈbækˌsaɪd] *n* : trasero *m*

backslash [ˈbækˌslæʃ] *n* : barra *f* invertida, barra *f* inversa

backslide [ˈbækˌslaɪd] *vi* **-slid** [-ˌslɪd]; **-slid** *or* **-slidden** [-ˌslɪdən]; **-sliding** : recaer, reincidir

backstage [ˌbækˈsteɪdʒ, ˈbækˌ-] *adv & adj* : entre bastidores

backstroke [ˈbækˌstroːk] *n* : estilo *m* espalda, estilo *m* dorso *Mex*

backtrack [ˈbækˌtræk] *vi* : dar marcha atrás, volverse atrás

backup [ˈbækˌʌp] *n* **1** SUPPORT : respaldo *m*, apoyo *m* **2** : copia *f* de seguridad (de un archivo, etc.)

backward¹ [ˈbækwərd] *or* **backwards** [-wərdz] *adv* **1** : hacia atrás **2** : de espaldas ⟨he fell backwards : se cayó de espaldas⟩ **3** : al revés ⟨you're doing it backwards : lo estás haciendo al revés⟩ **4 to bend over backwards** : hacer todo lo posible

backward² *adj* **1** : hacia atrás ⟨a backward glance : una mirada hacia atrás⟩

RETARDED : retrasado **3** SHY : tímido **4** UNDERDEVELOPED : atrasado

backwardness ['bækwərdnəs] *n* : atraso *m* (dícese de una región), retraso *m* (dícese de una persona)

backwoods [,bæk'wʊdz] *npl* : monte *m*, región *f* alejada

backyard [,bæk'jɑrd] *n* : jardín *m* trasero

bacon ['beɪkən] *n* : tocino *m*, tocineta *f* Col, Ven, bacon *m* Spain

bacterial [bæk'tɪriəl] *adj* : bacteriano

bacterium [bæk'tɪriəm] *n, pl* **-ria** [-iə] : bacteria *f*

bad¹ ['bæd] *adv* → **badly**

bad² *adj* **1** POOR : malo ⟨a bad example : un mal ejemplo⟩ ⟨a bad idea : una mala idea⟩ ⟨in bad shape : en malas condiciones⟩ ⟨it smells/tastes bad : huele/sabe mal⟩ **2** UNPLEASANT, UNFAVORABLE : malo ⟨bad news : malas noticias⟩ ⟨bad luck : mala suerte⟩ ⟨bad reviews : mala crítica⟩ ⟨a bad dream : una pesadilla⟩ ⟨it smells/tastes bad : huele/sabe mal⟩ **3** UNSUITABLE : malo ⟨bad lighting : mala iluminación⟩ ⟨you've come at a bad time : llegas en mal momento⟩ **4** INCORRECT, FAULTY : malo ⟨bad spelling : mala ortografía⟩ ⟨a bad check : un cheque sin fondos⟩ **5** ROTTEN : podrido ⟨to go bad : echarse a perder⟩ **6** UNHEALTHY, SERIOUS : malo, grave ⟨to have bad eyesight : tener mala vista⟩ ⟨a bad injury : una herida grave⟩ ⟨he's in bad health, his health is bad : está mal de salud⟩ **7** HARMFUL : malo, perjudicial **8** CORRUPT, EVIL : malo, corrupto ⟨the bad guys : los malos⟩ **9** NAUGHTY : malo, travieso **10 from bad to worse** : de mal en peor **11 to be bad about something** : ser malo para algo **12 to be in a bad way** : estar mal **13 too bad!** : ¡qué lástima!

bad³ *n* : lo malo ⟨the good and the bad : lo bueno y lo malo⟩

bade → **bid**

badge ['bæʤ] *n* : insignia *f*, botón *m*, chapa *f*

badger¹ ['bæʤər] *vt* : fastidiar, acosar, importunar

badger² *n* : tejón *m*

badly ['bædli] *adv* **1** : mal **2** URGENTLY : mucho, con urgencia **3** SEVERELY : gravemente

bad–mannered ['bæd'mænərd] *adj* : maleducado

badminton ['bæd,mɪntən, -,mɪt-] *n* : bádminton *m*

badness ['bædnəs] *n* : maldad *f*

bad–tempered ['bæd'tɛmpərd] *adj* : malhumorado

baffle ['bæfəl] *vi* **-fled; -fling 1** PERPLEX : desconcertar, confundir **2** FRUSTRATE : frustrar

bafflement ['bæfəlmənt] *n* : desconcierto *m*, confusión *f*

bag¹ ['bæg] *v* **bagged; bagging** *vi* SAG : formar bolsas — *vt* **1** : ensacar, poner en una bolsa **2** : cobrar (en la caza), cazar

bag² *n* **1** : bolsa *f*, saco *m* **2** HANDBAG : cartera *f*, bolso *m*, bolsa *f* Mex **3** SUITCASE : maleta *f*, valija *f* **4 to have bags under one's eyes** : tener ojeras

bagel ['beɪgəl] *n* : rosquilla *f* de pan

baggage ['bægɪʤ] *n* : equipaje *m*

baggy ['bægi] *adj* **baggier; -est** : holgado, ancho

bagpipe ['bæg,paɪp] *n or* **bagpipes** ['bæg,paɪps] *npl* : gaita *f*

baguette [bæ'gɛt] *n* : baguette *f*, barra *f* de pan Mex, Spain

bail¹ ['beɪl] *vt* **1** : achicar (agua de un bote) **2 to bail out** : poner en libertad (de una cárcel) bajo fianza **3 to bail out** EXTRICATE : sacar de apuros — *vi* **1** *or* **to bail out** *fam* : largarse *fam*, rajarse *fam* ⟨when things got difficult, she bailed (out on us) : cuando las cosas se pusieron difíciles, nos dejó colgados⟩ **2 to bail out** : tirarse en paracaídas (de un avión)

bail² *n* : fianza *f*, caución *f*

bailiff ['beɪləf] *n* : alguacil *mf*

bailiwick ['beɪli,wɪk] *n* : dominio *m*

bailout ['beɪl,aʊt] *n* : rescate *m* (financiero)

bait¹ ['beɪt] *vt* **1** : cebar (un anzuelo o cepo) **2** HARASS : acosar

bait² *n* : cebo *m*, carnada *f*

bake¹ ['beɪk] *vt* **baked; baking** : hornear, hacer al horno

bake² *n* : fiesta con platos hechos al horno

baker ['beɪkər] *n* : panadero *m*, -ra *f*

baker's dozen *n* : docena *f* de fraile

bakery ['beɪkəri] *n, pl* **-ries** : panadería *f*

bakeshop ['beɪk,ʃɑp] *n* : pastelería *f*, panadería *f*

baking powder *n* : levadura *f* en polvo

baking soda → **sodium bicarbonate**

balaclava [,bælə'klɑvə, -'klæ-] *n* : pasamontañas *m*

balance¹ ['bæləns] *v* **-anced; -ancing** *vt* **1** : hacer el balance de (una cuenta) ⟨to balance the books : cuadrar las cuentas⟩ **2** EQUALIZE : balancear, equilibrar **3** HARMONIZE : armonizar — *vi* : balancearse

balance² *n* **1** SCALES : balanza *f*, báscula *f* **2** COUNTERBALANCE : contrapeso *m* **3** EQUILIBRIUM : equilibrio *m* ⟨to keep/lose one's balance : mantener/perder el equilibrio⟩ **4** REMAINDER : balance *m*, resto *m* **5 balance of trade** : balanza comercial **6 balance of payments** : balanza de pagos **7 to be/hang in the balance** : estar en el aire

balanced ['bælənst] *adj* : equilibrado, balanceado

balboa [bæl'boːə] *n* : balboa *f* (unidad monetaria)

balcony ['bælkəni] *n, pl* **-nies 1** : balcón *m*, terraza *f* (de un edificio) **2** : galería *f* (de un teatro)

bald ['bɔld] *adj* **1** : calvo, pelado, pelón **2** PLAIN : simple, puro ⟨the bald truth : la pura verdad⟩

balding ['bɔldɪŋ] *adj* : quedándose calvo

baldly ['bɔldli] *adv* : sin reparos, sin rodeos, francamente

baldness ['bɔldnəs] n : calvicie f

bale[1] ['beɪl] vt **baled; baling** : empacar, hacer balas de

bale[2] n : bala f, fardo m, paca f

baleful ['beɪlfəl] adj 1 DEADLY : mortífero 2 SINISTER : siniestro, funesto, torvo ⟨a baleful glance : una mirada torva⟩

balk[1] ['bɔk] vt : obstaculizar, impedir — vi 1 : plantarse fam (dícese de un caballo, etc.) 2 **to balk at** : resistirse a, mostrarse reacio a

balk[2] n : obstáculo m

Balkan ['bɔlkən] adj : balcánico

balky ['bɔki] adj **balkier; -est** : reacio, obstinado, terco

ball[1] ['bɔl] vt : apelotonar, ovillar

ball[2] n 1 : pelota f, bola f, balón m, bollo m Arg, Uru ⟨ball of yarn : ovillo de lana⟩ 2 DANCE : baile m (de etiqueta) 3 : bola f, bola f mala (en béisbol) 4 : parte anterior de la planta (de un pie) 5 **balls** npl usu vulgar : cojones mpl, usu vulgar; huevos mpl, usu vulgar; testículos mpl 6 **balls** npl GUTS : cojones mpl, usu vulgar; agallas fpl fam 7 **on the ball** : espabilado, alerta 8 **the ball is in your/his** (etc.) **court** ⟨the ball is in your court : ahora te corresponde a ti⟩ 9 **to drop the ball** : cometer un gran error 10 **to get/set/start the ball rolling** : poner las cosas en marcha 11 **to keep the ball rolling** : mantener el impulso 12 **to play ball** : jugar al béisbol/baloncesto (etc.) 13 **to play ball** COOPERATE : cooperar

ballad ['bæləd] n : romance m, balada f

balladeer [,bælə'dɪr] n : cantante mf de baladas

ballast[1] ['bæləst] vt : lastrar

ballast[2] n : lastre m

ball bearing n : cojinete m de bola

ballerina [,bælə'ri:nə] n : bailarina f ⟨prima ballerina : primera bailarina⟩

ballet [bæ'leɪ, 'bæ,leɪ] n : ballet m

ballet dancer n : bailarín m, -rina f

ball game n : partido m de beisbol

ballistic [bə'lɪstɪk] adj : balístico

ballistics [bə'lɪstɪks] ns & pl : balística f

balloon[1] [bə'lu:n] vi 1 : viajar en globo 2 SWELL : hincharse, inflarse

balloon[2] n : globo m

balloonist [bə'lu:nɪst] n : aeróstata mf

ballot[1] ['bælət] vi : votar

ballot[2] n 1 : papeleta f (de voto), boleta f electoral 2 BALLOTING : votación f 3 VOTE : voto m

ballot box n : urna f

ballpoint pen ['bɔl,pɔɪnt] n : bolígrafo m

ballroom ['bɔl,ru:m, -,rum] n : sala f de baile

ballyhoo ['bæli,hu:] n : propaganda f, publicidad f, bombo m fam

balm ['bɑm, 'bɑlm] n : bálsamo m, ungüento m

balmy ['bɑmi, 'bɑl-] adj **balmier; -est** 1 MILD : templado, agradable 2 SOOTHING : balsámico 3 CRAZY : chiflado fam, chalado fam

baloney [bə'lo:ni] n NONSENSE : tonterías fpl, estupideces fpl

balsa ['bɔlsə] n : balsa f

balsam ['bɔlsəm] n or **balsam fir** : abeto m balsámico

Baltic ['bɔltɪk] adj : báltico

balustrade ['bælə,streɪd] n : balaustrada f

bam[1] ['bæm] n BANG : explosión f, estallido m, estampido m

bam[2] interj : ¡zas!

bamboo [bæm'bu:] n : bambú m

bamboozle [bæm'bu:zəl] vt **-zled; -zling** : engañar, embaucar

ban[1] ['bæn] vt **banned; banning** : prohibir, proscribir

ban[2] n : prohibición f, proscripción f

banal [bə'nɑl, bə'næl, 'beɪnəl] adj : banal, trivial

banality [bə'næləṭi] n, pl **-ties** : banalidad f, trivialidad f

banana [bə'nænə] n : banano m, plátano m, banana f, cambur m Ven, guineo m Car

band[1] ['bænd] vt 1 BIND : fajar, atar 2 **to band together** : unirse, juntarse

band[2] n 1 STRIP : banda f, cinta f (de un sombrero, etc.) 2 STRIPE : franja f 3 : banda f (de radiofrecuencia) 4 RING : anillo m 5 GROUP : banda f, grupo m, conjunto m ⟨jazz band : conjunto de jazz⟩

bandage[1] ['bændɪdʒ] vt **-daged; -daging** : vendar

bandage[2] n : vendaje m, venda f

Band–Aid ['bænd'eɪd] trademark se usa para una venda adhesiva

bandanna or **bandana** [bæn'dænə] n : pañuelo m (de colores)

bandit ['bændət] n : bandido m, -da f; bandolero m, -ra f

bandstand ['bænd,stænd] n : quiosco m de música

bandwagon ['bænd,wægən] n 1 : carroza f de músicos 2 **to jump on the bandwagon** : subirse al carro, seguir la moda

bandwidth ['bænd,wɪdθ] n : ancho m de banda

bandy ['bændi] vt **-died; -dying** 1 EXCHANGE : intercambiar 2 **to bandy about** : circular, propagar

bane ['beɪn] n 1 POISON : veneno m 2 RUIN : ruina f, pesadilla f

baneful ['beɪnfəl] adj : nefasto, funesto

bang[1] ['bæŋ] vt 1 STRIKE : golpear, darse ⟨he banged his elbow against the door : se dio con el codo en la puerta⟩ 2 SLAM : cerrar (la puerta) con/de un portazo 3 **to bang up** : rayar o abollar (algo), dejar (a alguien) con moretones — vi 1 SLAM : cerrarse con un golpe 2 **to bang on** : aporrear, golpear ⟨she was banging on the table : aporreaba la mesa⟩

bang[2] adv : directamente, exactamente

bang[3] n 1 BLOW : golpe m, porrazo m, trancazo m 2 EXPLOSION : explosión f, estallido m, estampido m 3 SLAM : portazo m 4 **bangs** npl : flequillo m, fleco m

bang[4] interj : ¡pum!

bangle ['bæŋgəl] n : brazalete m, pulsera f

banish ['bænɪʃ] vt 1 EXILE : desterrar, exiliar 2 EXPEL : expulsar

banishment ['bænɪʃmənt] *n* **1** EXILE : destierro *m*, exilio *m* **2** EXPULSION : expulsión *f*

banister ['bænəstər] *n* HANDRAIL : pasamanos *m*, barandilla *f*, barandal *m*

banjo ['bæn‚dʒoː] *n*, *pl* **-jos** : banjo *m*

bank¹ ['bæŋk] *vt* **1** TILT : peraltar (una carretera), ladear (un avión) **2** HEAP : amontonar **3** : cubrir (un fuego) **4** : depositar (dinero en un banco) — *vi* **1** : ladearse (dícese de un avión) **2** : tener una cuenta (en un banco) **3 to bank on** : contar con

bank² *n* **1** MASS : montón *m*, montículo *m*, masa *f* **2** : orilla *f*, ribera *f* (de un río) **3** : peralte *m* (de una carretera) **4** : banco *m* ⟨World Bank : Banco Mundial⟩ ⟨blood bank : banco de sangre⟩ **5** : banca *f* (en juegos)

bankbook ['bæŋk‚bʊk] *n* : libreta *f* bancaria, libreta *f* de ahorros

banker ['bæŋkər] *n* : banquero *m*, -ra *f*

banking ['bæŋkɪŋ] *n* : banca *f*

banknote *n* : billete *m* de banco

bankrupt¹ ['bæŋ‚krʌpt] *vt* : hacer quebrar, llevar a la quiebra, arruinar

bankrupt² *adj* **1** : en bancarrota, en quiebra **2 ~ of** LACKING : carente de, falto de

bankrupt³ *n* : fallido *m*, -da *f*; quebrado *m*, -da *f*

bankruptcy ['bæŋ‚krʌptsi] *n*, *pl* **-cies** : ruina *f*, quiebra *f*, bancarrota *f*

bank statement → statement

bank teller → teller

banner¹ ['bænər] *adj* : excelente

banner² *n* : estandarte *m*, bandera *f*

banns ['bænz] *npl* : amonestaciones *fpl*

banquet¹ ['bæŋkwət] *vi* : celebrar un banquete

banquet² *n* : banquete *m*

banter¹ ['bæntər] *vi* : bromear, hacer bromas

banter² *n* : bromas *fpl*

baptism ['bæp‚tɪzəm] *n* : bautismo *m*

baptismal [bæp'tɪzməl] *adj* : bautismal

baptismal font → font

Baptist ['bæptɪst] *n* : bautista *mf*, baptista *mf* — **Baptist** *adj*

baptize [bæp'taɪz, 'bæp‚taɪz] *vt* **-tized; -tizing** : bautizar

bar¹ ['bar] *vt* **barred; barring 1** OBSTRUCT : obstruir, bloquear **2** EXCLUDE : excluir **3** PROHIBIT : prohibir **4** SECURE : atrancar, asegurar ⟨bar the door! : ¡atranca la puerta!⟩

bar² *n* **1** : barra *f*, barrote *m* (de una ventana), tranca *f* (de una puerta) ⟨behind bars : entre rejas⟩ **2** BARRIER : barrera *f*, obstáculo *m* **3** LAW : abogacía *f* **4** STRIPE : franja *f* **5** COUNTER : mostrador *m*, barra *f* **6** TAVERN : bar *m*, taberna *f* **7** MEASURE : compás *m* (en música)

bar³ *prep* : excepto, con excepción de **2 bar none** : sin excepción

barb ['barb] *n* **1** POINT : púa *f*, lengüeta *f* **2** GIBE : pulla *f*

barbarian¹ [bar'bæriən] *adj* **1** : bárbaro **2** CRUDE : tosco, bruto

barbarian² *n* : bárbaro *m*, -ra *f*

barbaric [bar'bærɪk] *adj* **1** PRIMITIVE : primitivo **2** CRUEL : brutal, cruel

barbarity [bar'bærəṭi] *n*, *pl* **-ties** : barbaridad *f*

barbarous ['barbərəs] *adj* **1** UNCIVILIZED : bárbaro **2** MERCILESS : despiadado, cruel

barbarously ['barbərəsli] *adv* : bárbaramente

barbecue¹ ['barbɪ‚kjuː] *vt* **-cued; -cuing** : asar a la parrilla

barbecue² *n* : barbacoa *f*, parrillada *f*

barbed ['barbd] *adj* **1** : con púas ⟨barbed wire : alambre de púas⟩ **2** BITING : mordaz

barber ['barbər] *n* : barbero *m*, -ra *f*

barbershop ['barbər‚ʃap] *n* : peluquería *f*, barbería *f*

barbiturate [bar'bɪtʃərət] *n* : barbitúrico *m*

bar code *n* : código *m* de barras

bard ['bard] *n* : bardo *m*

bare¹ ['bær] *vt* **bared; baring** : desnudar

bare² *adj* **1** NAKED : desnudo **2** EXPOSED : descubierto, sin protección **3** EMPTY : desprovisto, vacío **4** MINIMUM : mero, mínimo ⟨the bare necessities : las necesidades mínimas⟩ **5** PLAIN : puro, sencillo

bareback ['bær‚bæk] *or* **barebacked** [-‚bækt] *adv & adj* : a pelo

barefaced ['bær‚feɪst] *adj* : descarado

barefoot ['bær‚fʊt] *or* **barefooted** [-‚fʊṭəd] *adv & adj* : descalzo

bareheaded ['bær‚hɛdəd] *adv & adj* : sin sombrero, con la cabeza descubierta

barely ['bærli] *adv* : apenas, por poco

bareness ['bærnəs] *n* : desnudez *f*

bargain¹ ['bargən] *vi* HAGGLE : regatear, negociar — *vt* BARTER : trocar, cambiar

bargain² *n* **1** AGREEMENT : acuerdo *m*, convenio *m* ⟨to strike a bargain : cerrar un trato⟩ ⟨into the bargain : además, encima⟩ **2** : ganga *f* ⟨bargain price : precio de ganga⟩

bargaining *n* : regateo *m*, negociación *f*

barge¹ ['bardʒ] *vi* **barged; barging 1** : mover con torpeza **2 to barge in** : entrometerse, interrumpir

barge² *n* : barcaza *f*, gabarra *f*

bar graph *n* : gráfico *m* de barras

baritone ['bærə‚toːn] *n* : barítono *m*

bark¹ ['bark] *vi* : ladrar — *vt* **or to bark out** : gritar ⟨to bark out an order : dar una orden a gritos⟩

bark² *n* **1** : ladrido *m* (de un perro) **2** : corteza *f* (de un árbol) **3** *or* **barque** : tipo de embarcación con velas de proa y popa

barley ['barli] *n* : cebada *f*

barmaid ['bar‚meɪd] *n* : camarera *f*

barman ['bar‚mæn] *n*, *pl* **-men** [-mən, -‚mɛn] → **bartender**

barn ['barn] *n* : granero *m* (para cosechas), establo *m* (para ganado)

barnacle ['barnɪkəl] *n* : percebe *m*

barnyard ['barn‚jard] *n* : corral *m*

barometer [bə'ramətər] *n* : barómetro *m*

barometric [‚bærə'mɛtrɪk] *adj* : barométrico

baron ['bærən] n 1 : barón m 2 TYCOON : magnate mf

baroness ['bærənıs, -nəs, -ˌnɛs] n : baronesa f

baronial [bə'ro:niəl] adj 1 : de barón 2 STATELY : señorial, majestuoso

baroque [bə'ro:k, -'rɑk] adj : barroco

barracks ['bærəks] ns & pl : cuartel m

barracuda [ˌbærə'ku:də] n, pl **-da** or **-das** : barracuda f

barrage [bə'rɑʒ, -'rɑdʒ] n 1 : descarga f (de artillería) 2 DELUGE : aluvión m ⟨a barrage of questions : un aluvión de preguntas⟩

barred ['bɑrd] adj : excluido, prohibido

barrel[1] ['bærəl] v **-reled** or **-relled; -reling** or **-relling** vi : ir disparado

barrel[2] n 1 : barril m, tonel m 2 : cañón m (de un arma de fuego), cilindro m (de una cerradura)

barren ['bærən] adj 1 STERILE : estéril (dícese de las plantas o la mujer), árido (dícese del suelo) 2 DESERTED : yermo, desierto

barrette [bɑ'rɛt, bə-] n : pasador m, broche m para el cabello

barricade[1] ['bærəˌkeɪd, ˌbærə'-] vt **-caded; -cading** : cerrar con barricadas

barricade[2] n : barricada f

barrier ['bæriər] n 1 : barrera f 2 OBSTACLE : obstáculo m, impedimento m

barring ['bɑrıŋ] prep : excepto, salvo, a excepción de

barrio ['bɑrio, 'bær-] n : barrio m

barroom ['bɑrˌru:m, -ˌrum] n : bar m

barrow ['bærˌo:] → **wheelbarrow**

bartender ['bɑrˌtɛndər] n : camarero m, -ra f; barman m

barter[1] ['bɑrtər] vt : cambiar, trocar

barter[2] n : trueque m, permuta f

basalt [bə'sɔlt, 'bæˌl-] n : basalto m

base[1] ['beıs] vt **based; basing** : basar, fundamentar, establecer

base[2] adj **baser; basest** 1 : de baja ley (dícese de un metal) 2 CONTEMPTIBLE : vil, despreciable

base[3] n, pl **bases** 1 : base f 2 : pie m (de una montaña, una estatua, etc.)

baseball ['beısˌbɔl] n : beisbol m, béisbol m

baseball cap n : gorra f de visera, gorra f de beisbol

baseless ['beısləs] adj : infundado

basely ['beısli] adv : vilmente

basement ['beısmənt] n : sótano m

baseness ['beısnəs] n : vileza f, bajeza f

bash[1] ['bæʃ] vt : golpear violentamente

bash[2] n 1 BLOW : golpe m, porrazo m, madrazo m Mex fam 2 PARTY : fiesta f, juerga f fam

bashful ['bæʃfəl] adj : tímido, vergonzoso, penoso

bashfulness ['bæʃfəlnəs] n : timidez f

basic[1] ['beısık] adj 1 FUNDAMENTAL : básico, fundamental 2 RUDIMENTARY : básico, elemental 3 : básico (en química)

basic[2] n : fundamento m, rudimento m

basically ['beısıkli] adv : fundamentalmente

basil ['beızəl, 'bæzəl] n : albahaca f

basilica [bə'sılıkə] n : basílica f

basin ['beısən] n 1 WASHBOWL : palangana f, lavamanos m, lavabo m 2 : cuenca f (de un río)

basis ['beısəs] n, pl **bases** [-ˌsi:z] 1 BASE : base f, pilar m 2 FOUNDATION : fundamento m, base f 3 on a weekly basis : semanalmente

bask ['bæsk] vi : disfrutar, deleitarse ⟨to bask in the sun : disfrutar del sol⟩

basket ['bæskət] n : cesta f, cesto m, canasta f

basketball ['bæskətˌbɔl] n : baloncesto m, basquetbol m, basket m

Basque ['bæsk, 'bɑsk] n : Basque mf — **Basque** adj

bas-relief [ˌbɑrı'li:f] n : bajorrelieve m

bass[1] ['beıs] adj : de bajo (dícese de una voz, etc.) ⟨bass clef : clave de fa⟩ ⟨bass string : bordón⟩

bass[2] ['bæs] n, pl **bass** or **basses** : róbalo m (pesca)

bass[3] ['beıs] n 1 : bajo m (tono, voz, cantante) 2 → **bass guitar** 3 → **double bass**

bass drum n : bombo m

basset hound ['bæsət,haund] n : basset m

bass guitar n : bajo m (guitarra)

bassinet [ˌbæsə'nɛt] n : moisés m, cuna f

bassist ['beısıst] n : bajista f

bassoon [bə'su:n, bæ-] n : fagot m

bass viol ['beıs'vaıəl, -ˌo:l] → **double bass**

bastard[1] ['bæstərd] adj : bastardo

bastard[2] n 1 usu offensive : bastardo m, -da f 2 offensive : hijo m de puta sometimes offensive; cabrón m Mex, Spain offensive 3 sometimes offensive : tipo m ⟨the poor bastard : el pobre diablo⟩ ⟨what a lucky bastard! : ¡qué suertudo!⟩

bastardize ['bæstərˌdaız] vt **-ized; -izing** DEBASE : degradar, envilecer

baste ['beıst] vt **basted; basting** 1 STITCH : hilvanar 2 : bañar (con su jugo durante la cocción)

bastion ['bæstʃən] n : bastión m, baluarte m

bat[1] ['bæt] vt **batted; batting** 1 HIT : batear 2 without batting an eye : sin pestañear

bat[2] n 1 : murciélago m (animal) 2 : bate m ⟨baseball bat : bate de beisbol⟩

batch ['bætʃ] n : hornada f, tanda f, grupo m, cantidad f

bate ['beıt] vt **bated; bating** 1 : aminorar, reducir 2 with bated breath : con ansiedad, aguantando la respiración

bath ['bæθ, 'bɑθ] n, pl **baths** ['bæðz, 'bæθs, 'bɑðz, 'bɑθs] 1 BATHING : baño m ⟨to take a bath : bañarse⟩ 2 : baño m (en fotografía, etc.) 3 BATHROOM : baño m, cuarto m de baño 4 SPA : balneario m 5 LOSS : pérdida f

bathe ['beıð] v **bathed; bathing** vt 1 WASH : bañar, lavar 2 SOAK : poner en remojo 3 FLOOD : inundar ⟨to bathe with light : inundar de luz⟩ — vi : bañarse, ducharse

bather ['beıðər] n : bañista mf

bathing suit → **swimsuit**

bathrobe ['bæθˌro:b] n : bata f (de baño)

bathroom ['bæθ,ru:m, -,rʊm] n : baño m, cuarto m de baño

bathtub ['bæθ,tʌb] n : bañera f, tina f (de baño)

baton [bə'tɑn] n : batuta f, bastón m

battalion [bə'tæljən] n : batallón m

batten ['bætən] vt **to batten down the hatches** : cerrar las escotillas

batter[1] ['bæṭər] vt **1** BEAT : aporrear, golpear **2** MISTREAT : maltratar

batter[2] n **1** : masa f para rebozar **2** HITTER : bateador m, -dora f

battered ['bæṭərd] adj **1** ABUSED : maltratado **2** DAMAGED : maltrecho **3** INJURED : apaleado, aporreado

battering ram n : ariete m

battery ['bæṭəri] n, pl **-teries 1** : lesiones fpl ⟨assault and battery : agresión con lesiones⟩ **2** ARTILLERY : batería f **3** : batería f, pila f (de electricidad) **4** SERIES : serie f

batting ['bæṭɪŋ] n **1** or **cotton batting** : algodón m en láminas **2** : bateo m (en beisbol)

battle[1] ['bæṭəl] vi **-tled; -tling** : luchar, pelear

battle[2] n : batalla f, lucha f, pelea f

battle–ax ['bæṭəl,æks] n : hacha f de guerra

battlefield ['bæṭəl,fi:ld] n : campo m de batalla

battleship ['bæṭəl,ʃɪp] n : acorazado m

batty ['bæṭi] adj **battier; -est** : chiflado fam, chalado fam

bauble ['bɔbəl] n : chuchería f, baratija f

Bavarian [bə'veriən] n : bávaro m, -ra f — **Bavarian** adj

bawdiness ['bɔdinəs] n : picardía f

bawdy ['bɔdi] adj **bawdier; -est** : subido de tono, verde, colorado Mex

bawl[1] ['bɔl] vi : llorar a gritos

bawl[2] n : grito m, alarido m

bawl out vt SCOLD : regañar

bay[1] ['beɪ] vi HOWL : aullar

bay[2] adj : castaño, zaino (dícese de los caballos)

bay[3] n **1** : bahía f ⟨Bay of Campeche : Bahía de Campeche⟩ **2** or **bay horse** : caballo m castaño **3** LAUREL : laurel m (en cocina) ⟨bay leaf : hoja de laurel⟩ **4** HOWL : aullido m **5** : saliente m ⟨bay window : ventana en saliente⟩ **6** COMPARTMENT : área f, compartimento m **7 at —** : acorralado

bayonet[1] [,beɪə'nɛt, 'beɪə,nɛt] vt **-neted; -neting** : herir o matar con bayoneta

bayonet[2] n : bayoneta f

bayou ['baɪ,u:, -,o:] n : pantano m

bazaar [bə'zɑr] n **1** : bazar m **2** SALE : venta f benéfica

bazooka [bə'zu:kə] n : bazuca f

BB ['bi:bi] n : balín m

be ['bi:] vi **was** ['wɑz, 'wʌz], **were** ['wər], **been** ['bɪn]; **being; am** ['æm]; **is** ['ɪz]; **are** ['ɑr] vi **1** (expressing identity or category) : ser ⟨José is a doctor : José es doctor⟩ ⟨I'm Ann's sister : soy la hermana de Ann⟩ ⟨who is it? : ¿quién es? soy yo⟩ ⟨apes are mammals : los simios son mamíferos⟩ ⟨if I were

you : yo en tu lugar, yo que tú⟩ **2** (expressing a quality) : ser ⟨the dress is red : el vestido es rojo⟩ ⟨she's very intelligent : ella es muy inteligente⟩ ⟨she's 10 years old : tiene 10 años⟩ ⟨you're so silly! : ¡qué tonto eres!⟩ ⟨I want you to be happy : quiero que seas feliz⟩ **3** (expressing origin or possession) : ser ⟨she's from Managua : es de Managua⟩ ⟨it's mine : es mío⟩ **4** (expressing location) : estar, quedar ⟨he's not at home : no está en casa⟩ ⟨the cups are on the table : las tazas están en la mesa⟩ ⟨it's ten miles away : está/queda diez millas de aquí⟩ **5** EXIST : ser, existir ⟨to be or not to be : ser, o no ser⟩ ⟨I think, therefore I am : pienso, luego existo⟩ **6** COME, GO : estar, ir, venir ⟨have you been to Paris? : ¿has estado en París?, ¿has ido a París?⟩ ⟨she's been and gone : llegó y se fue⟩ **7** (expressing a state of being) : estar, tener ⟨how are you? : ¿cómo estás?⟩ ⟨I'm cold/hungry : tengo frío/hambre⟩ ⟨they're sick : están enfermos⟩ ⟨she's angry : está enojada⟩ ⟨to be frank : para serte franco⟩ **8** COST : ser, costar ⟨it's $5 : cuesta $5⟩ **9** EQUAL : ser (igual a) ⟨two plus two is four : dos más dos son cuatro⟩ **10** OCCUR : ser ⟨the concert is (on) Sunday : el concierto es el domingo⟩ — v impers **1** (indicating time) : ser ⟨it's eight o'clock : son las ocho⟩ ⟨it's Friday : hoy es viernes⟩ **2** (indicating a condition) : hacer, estar ⟨it's sunny : hace sol⟩ ⟨it's very dark in here : está muy oscuro aquí dentro⟩ **3** (used with there) : haber ⟨there's a book on the table : hay un libro en la mesa⟩ ⟨there was an accident : hubo un accidente⟩ ⟨there's someone at the door : llaman a la puerta⟩ — v aux **1** (expressing progression) : estar ⟨I'm working : estoy trabajando⟩ ⟨what were you saying? : ¿qué estabas diciendo?⟩ ⟨it's snowing : está nevando⟩ ⟨we've been waiting : hemos estado esperando⟩ **2** (expressing future action) ⟨I'm seeing him tonight : voy a verlo esta noche⟩ ⟨are you coming tomorrow? : ¿vienes mañana?⟩ ⟨she was never/not to see him again : nunca volvería a verlo⟩ ⟨the best is yet to come : lo mejor está por venir⟩ **3** (used in passive constructions) : ser ⟨it was finished yesterday : fue acabado ayer, se acabó ayer⟩ **4** (expressing possibility) : poderse ⟨can she be trusted? : ¿se puede confiar en ella?⟩ ⟨it was nowhere to be found : no se pudo encontrar por ninguna parte⟩ ⟨you're not to blame : no tienes la culpa⟩ **5** (expressing obligation) : deber ⟨you are to stay here : debes quedarte aquí⟩ ⟨he was to come yesterday : se esperaba que viniese ayer⟩ **6 to be oneself** : ser uno mismo ⟨be yourself : sé tú mismo⟩

beach[1] ['bi:tʃ] vt : hacer varar, hacer encallar

beach[2] n : playa f

beachcomber ['bi:tʃ,ko:mər] n : raquero m, -ra f

beachhead ['biːtʃˌhɛd] n : cabeza f de playa

beacon ['biːkən] n : faro m

bead¹ ['biːd] vi : formarse en gotas

bead² n 1 : cuenta f 2 DROP : gota f 3 **beads** npl NECKLACE : collar m

beady ['biːdi] adj **beadier; -est** 1 : de forma de cuenta 2 **beady eyes** : ojos mpl pequeños y brillantes

beagle ['biːgəl] n : beagle m

beak ['biːk] n : pico m

beaker ['biːkər] n 1 CUP : taza f alta 2 : vaso m de precipitados (en un laboratorio)

beam¹ ['biːm] vi 1 SHINE : brillar 2 SMILE : sonreír radiantemente — vt BROADCAST : transmitir, emitir

beam² n 1 : viga f, barra f 2 RAY : rayo m, haz m de luz 3 : haz m de radiofaro (para guiar pilotos, etc.)

bean ['biːn] n 1 : habichuela f, frijol m 2 **broad bean** : haba f 3 **string bean** : judía f

bear¹ ['bær] v **bore** ['bor]; **borne** ['born] : bearing vt 1 CARRY : llevar, portar 2 : dar a luz a (un niño) 3 PRODUCE : dar (frutas, cosechas) 4 ENDURE, SUPPORT : soportar, resistir, aguantar 5 SHOW : llevar, tener ⟨to bear a resemblance to : tener una similitud con (algo), tener un parecido con (alguien)⟩ 6 **to bear out** : corroborar — vi 1 TURN : doblar, dar la vuelta, girar ⟨bear right : doble a la derecha⟩ 2 **to bear up** : resistir 3 **to bear with** : tener paciencia con

bear² n, pl **bears** or **bear** : oso m, osa f

bearable ['bærəbəl] adj : soportable

beard ['bɪrd] n 1 : barba f 2 : arista f (de plantas)

bearded ['bɪrdəd] adj : barbudo, de barba

bearer ['bærər] n : portador m, -dora f

bearing ['bærɪŋ] n 1 CONDUCT, MANNERS : comportamiento, modales mpl 2 SUPPORT : soporte f 3 SIGNIFICANCE : relación f, importancia f ⟨to have no bearing on : no tener nada que ver con⟩ 4 : cojinete m, rodamiento m (de una máquina) 5 COURSE, DIRECTION : dirección f, rumbo m ⟨to get one's bearings : orientarse⟩

beast ['biːst] n 1 : bestia f, fiera f ⟨beast of burden : animal de carga⟩ 2 BRUTE : bruto m, -ta f; bestia mf

beastly ['biːstli] adj : detestable, repugnante

beat¹ ['biːt] v **beat; beaten** ['biːtən] or **beat; beating** vt 1 STRIKE : golpear, pegar, darle una paliza (a alguien) 2 DEFEAT : vencer, derrotar (a un rival, etc.), batir (un récord) 3 : superar, ser mejor que ⟨nothing beats a nice, hot bath : no hay nada mejor que un baño caliente⟩ 4 AVOID : anticiparse a, evitar ⟨to beat the crowd : evitar el gentío⟩ 5 STIR, WHIP : batir 6 : batir (alas) 7 **beat it!** fam : ¡lárgate! 8 **it beats me** : no sé 9 **to beat down** : echar abajo (una puerta) 10 **to beat out** DEFEAT : vencer, derrotar 11 **to beat up** : darle una paliza (a alguien)

12 **to beat up on** : darle frecuentes palizas (a alguien) — vi 1 : batir 2 THROB : palpitar, latir 3 **to beat down** : pegar fuerte, caer a plomo (dícese del sol)

beat² adj EXHAUSTED : derrengado, muy cansado ⟨I'm beat! : ¡estoy molido!⟩

beat³ n 1 : golpe m, redoble m (de un tambor), latido m (del corazón) 2 RHYTHM : ritmo m, tiempo m

beater ['biːtər] n 1 : batidor m, -dora f 2 EGGBEATER : batidor m

beatific [ˌbiːəˈtɪfɪk] adj : beatífico

beating ['biːtɪŋ] n 1 : paliza f 2 DEFEAT : derrota f

beau ['boː] n, pl **beaux** or **beaus** : pretendiente m, galán m

beautician [bjuːˈtɪʃən] n : esteticista mf

beautification [ˌbjuːtəfəˈkeɪʃən] n : embellecimiento m

beautiful ['bjuːtɪfəl] adj : hermoso, bello, lindo, precioso

beautifully ['bjuːtɪfli] adv 1 ATTRACTIVELY : hermosamente 2 EXCELLENTLY : maravillosamente, excelentemente

beautify ['bjuːtəˌfaɪ] -**fied; -fying** vt : embellecer

beauty ['bjuːti] n, pl -**ties** : belleza f, hermosura f, beldad f

beauty shop or **beauty parlor** or **beauty salon** n : salón m de belleza

beauty spot n : lunar m

beaver ['biːvər] n : castor m

because [bɪˈkʌz, -ˈkɔz] conj : porque

because of prep : por, a causa de, debido a

beck ['bɛk] n **to be at the beck and call of** : estar a la entera disposición de, estar sometido a la voluntad de

beckon ['bɛkən] vi **to beckon to someone** : hacerle señas a alguien

become [bɪˈkʌm] v -**came** [-ˈkeɪm]; -**come; -coming** vi : hacerse, volverse, ponerse ⟨he became famous : se hizo famoso⟩ ⟨to become sad : ponerse triste⟩ ⟨to become accustomed to : acostumbrarse a⟩ — vt 1 BEFIT : ser apropiado para 2 SUIT : favorecer, quedarle bien (a alguien) ⟨that dress becomes you : ese vestido te favorece⟩

becoming [bɪˈkʌmɪŋ] adj 1 SUITABLE : apropiado 2 FLATTERING : favorecedor

bed¹ ['bɛd] v **bedded; bedding** vt : acostar — vi : acostarse

bed² n 1 : cama f, lecho m ⟨to make the bed : hacer la cama⟩ ⟨to go to bed : acostarse⟩ ⟨to be time for bed : ser hora de acostarse⟩ 2 : cauce m (de un río), fondo m (del mar) 3 : arriate m (para plantas) 4 LAYER, STRATUM : capa f, estrato m 5 : caja f (de una camioneta)

bed and breakfast n : pensión f con desayuno

bedbug ['bɛdˌbʌg] n : chinche f

bedclothes ['bɛdˌkloːðz, -ˌkloːz] npl : ropa f de cama, sábanas fpl

bedding ['bɛdɪŋ] n 1 → **bedclothes** 2 : cama f (para animales)

bedeck [bɪˈdɛk] vt : adornar, engalanar

bedevil [bɪ'dɛvəl] *vt* **-iled** *or* **-illed**; **-iling** *or* **-illing** : acosar, plagar

bedlam ['bɛdləm] *n* : locura *f*, caos *m*, alboroto *m*

bedraggled [bɪ'drægəld] *adj* : desaliñado, despeinado

bedridden ['bɛd,rɪdən] *adj* : postrado en cama

bedrock ['bɛd,rak] *n* : lecho *m* de roca

bedroom ['bɛd,ru:m, -,rʊm] *n* : dormitorio *m*, habitación *f*, pieza *f*, recámara *f* *Col, Mex, Pan*

bedsheet → sheet

bedside table ['bɛd,saɪd-] *n* : mesita *f* de noche

bedspread ['bɛd,sprɛd] *n* : cubrecama *m*, colcha *f*, cobertor *m*

bedtime ['bɛd,taɪm] *n* : hora *f* de acostarse

bee ['bi:] *n* **1** : abeja *f* (insecto) **2** GATHERING : círculo *m*, reunión *f*

beech ['bi:tʃ] *n*, *pl* **beeches** *or* **beech** : haya *f*

beechnut ['bi:tʃ,nʌt] *n* : hayuco *m*

beef¹ ['bi:f] *vt* **to beef up** : fortalecer, reforzar — *vi* COMPLAIN : quejarse

beef² *n*, *pl* **beefs** ['bi:fs] *or* **beeves** ['bi:vz] : carne *f* de vaca, carne *f* de res *CA, Mex*

beefsteak ['bi:f,steɪk] *n* : filete *m*, bistec *m*

beehive ['bi:,haɪv] *n* : colmena *f*

beekeeper ['bi:,ki:pər] *n* : apicultor *m*, -tora *f*

beekeeping ['bi:,ki:pɪŋ] *n* : apicultura *f*

beeline ['bi:,laɪn] *n* **to make a beeline for** : ir derecho a, ir directo hacia

been → be

beep¹ ['bi:p] *v* : pitar

beep² *n* : pitido *m*

beeper ['bi:pər] *n* : buscapersonas *m*, busca *f* *Spain*

beer ['bɪr] *n* : cerveza *f*

beeswax ['bi:z,wæks] *n* : cera *f* de abejas

beet ['bi:t] *n* : remolacha *f*, betabel *m* *Mex*

beetle ['bi:təl] *n* : escarabajo *m*

befall [bɪ'fɔl] *v* **-fell** [-'fɛl]; **-fallen** [-'fɔlən] *vt* : sucederle a, acontecerle a — *vi* : acontecer

befit [bɪ'fɪt] *vt* **-fitted**; **-fitting** : convenir a, ser apropiado para

before¹ [bɪ'for] *adv* **1** : antes ⟨before and after : antes y después⟩ **2** : anterior ⟨the month before : el mes anterior⟩

before² *conj* : antes que ⟨he would die before surrendering : moriría antes que rendirse⟩

before³ *prep* **1** : antes de ⟨before eating : antes de comer⟩ **2** : delante de, ante ⟨I stood before the house : estaba parada delante de la casa⟩ ⟨before the judge : ante el juez⟩

beforehand [bɪ'for,hænd] *adv* : antes, por adelantado, de antemano, con anticipación

befriend [bɪ'frɛnd] *vt* : hacerse amigo de

befuddle [bɪ'fʌdəl] *vt* **-dled**; **-dling** : aturdir, ofuscar, confundir

beg ['bɛg] *v* **begged**; **begging** *vt* **1** : mendigar, pedir (dinero, etc.) **2** : pedir, suplicar ⟨I begged him to go : le supliqué que fuera⟩ — *vi* **1** : mendigar, pedir limosna **2 to beg for** : implorar, suplicar

⟨she begged for mercy : imploró clemencia⟩

beget [bɪ'gɛt] *vt* **-got** [-'gat]; **-gotten** [-'gatən] *or* **-got**; **-getting** : engendrar

beggar ['bɛgər] *n* : mendigo *m*, -ga *f*; pordiosero *m*, -ra *f*

begin [bɪ'gɪn] *v* **-gan** [-'gæn]; **-gun** [-'gʌn]; **-ginning** *vt* : empezar, comenzar, iniciar ⟨she began to work, she began working : empezó a trabajar⟩ — *vi* **1** START : empezar, comenzar, iniciarse **2** ORIGINATE : nacer, originarse **3 to begin with** : en primer lugar, para empezar

beginner [bɪ'gɪnər] *n* : principiante *mf*

beginning [bɪ'gɪnɪŋ] *n* : principio *m*, comienzo *m* ⟨at the beginning of the week : a principios de la semana⟩

begone [bɪ'gɔn] *interj* : ¡fuera de aquí!

begonia [bɪ'go:njə] *n* : begonia *f*

begrudge [bɪ'grʌdʒ] *vt* **-grudged**; **-grudging 1** : dar/hacer (etc.) de mala gana ⟨he did the work, but he begrudged every moment of it : hizo el trabajo, pero de muy mala gana⟩ ⟨I don't begrudge the money I spent : no me molesta el dinero que gasté⟩ **2** (*indicating disapproval*) ⟨he begrudges (her) her success : a él le molesta que ella tenga éxito⟩

beguile [bɪ'gaɪl] *vt* **-guiled**; **-guiling 1** DECEIVE : engañar **2** AMUSE : divertir, entretener

behalf [bɪ'hæf, -'haf] *n* **1** : favor *m*, beneficio *m*, parte *f* **2 on behalf of** *or* **in behalf of** : de parte de, en nombre de

behave [bɪ'heɪv] *vi* **-haved**; **-having** : comportarse, portarse

behavior [bɪ'heɪvjər] *n* : comportamiento *m*, conducta *f*

behead [bɪ'hɛd] *vt* : decapitar

behest [bɪ'hɛst] *n* **1** : mandato *m*, orden *f* **2 at the behest of** : a instancia de

behind¹ [bɪ'haɪnd] *adv* : atrás, detrás ⟨to fall behind : quedarse atrás⟩

behind² *prep* **1** : atrás de, detrás de, tras ⟨behind the house : detrás de la casa⟩ ⟨one behind another : uno tras otro⟩ **2** : atrasado con, después de ⟨behind schedule : atrasado con el trabajo⟩ ⟨I arrived behind the others : llegué después de los otros⟩ **3** SUPPORTING : en apoyo de, detrás ⟨we're behind you all the way! : ¡tienes todo nuestro apoyo!⟩

behind³ [bɪ'haɪnd, 'bɪ,haɪnd] *n* : trasero *m*

behold [bɪ'ho:ld] *vt* **-held**; **-holding** : contemplar

beholder [bɪ'ho:ldər] *n* : observador *m*, -dora *f*

behoove [bɪ'hu:v] *vt* **-hooved**; **-hooving** : convenirle a, corresponderle a ⟨it behooves us to help him : nos conviene ayudarlo⟩

beige¹ ['beɪʒ] *adj* : beige

beige² *n* : beige *m*

being ['bi:ɪŋ] *n* **1** EXISTENCE : ser *m*, existencia *f* **2** CREATURE : ser *m*, ente *m*

belabor [bɪ'leɪbər] *vt* **to belabor the point** : extenderse sobre el tema

belated [bɪ'leɪtəd] *adj* : tardío, retrasado

belch¹ ['bɛltʃ] *vi* **1** BURP : eructar **2** EXPEL : expulsar, arrojar

belch[2] *n* : eructo *m*

beleaguer [bɪ'li:gər] *vt* **1** BESIEGE : asediar, sitiar **2** HARASS : fastidiar, molestar

belfry ['belfri] *n*, *pl* **-fries** : campanario *m*

Belgian ['beldʒən] *n* : belga *mf* — **Belgian** *adj*

belie [bɪ'laɪ] *vt* **-lied; -lying 1** MISREPRESENT : falsear, ocultar **2** CONTRADICT : contradecir, desmentir

belief [bə'li:f] *n* **1** TRUST : confianza *f* **2** CONVICTION : creencia *f*, convicción *f* **3** FAITH : fe *f*

believable [bə'li:vəbəl] *adj* : verosímil, creíble

believe [bə'li:v] *v* **-lieved; -lieving** *vt* : creer ⟨I don't believe it! : ¡no puedo creerlo!⟩ ⟨believe it or not : aunque no lo creas, lo creas o no⟩ ⟨I can't believe my eyes : si no lo veo, no lo creo⟩ ⟨you'd better believe it! : ¡ya lo creo!, ¡por supuesto!⟩ — *vi* : creer

believer [bə'li:vər] *n* **1** : creyente *mf* **2** : partidario *m*, -ria *f*; entusiasta *mf* ⟨she's a great believer in vitamins : ella es una gran partidaria de las vitaminas⟩

belittle [bɪ'lɪtəl] *vt* **-littled; -littling 1** DISPARAGE : menospreciar, denigrar, rebajar **2** MINIMIZE : minimizar, quitar importancia a

bell[1] ['bel] *vt* : ponerle un cascabel a

bell[2] *n* : campana *f*, cencerro *m* (para una vaca o cabra), cascabel *m* (para un gato), timbre *m* (de teléfono, de la puerta)

belle ['bel] *n* : belleza *f*, beldad *f*

bellhop ['bel,hɑp] *n* : botones *m*

bellicose ['belɪ,ko:s] *adj* : belicoso *m*

belligerence [bə'lɪdʒərənts] *n* : agresividad *f*, beligerancia *f*

belligerent[1] [bə'lɪdʒərənt] *adj* : agresivo, beligerante

belligerent[2] *n* : beligerante *mf*

bellow[1] ['bɛ,lo:] *vi* : bramar, mugir — *vt* : gritar

bellow[2] *n* : bramido *m*, grito *m*

bellows ['bɛ,lo:z] *ns & pl* : fuelle *m*

bellwether ['bel,wɛðər] *n* : líder *mf*

belly[1] ['beli] *vi* **-lied; -lying** SWELL : hincharse, inflarse

belly[2] *n*, *pl* **-lies** : abdomen *m*, vientre *m*, barriga *f*, panza *f*

belly button *n* : ombligo *m*

belong [bɪ'lɔŋ] *vi* **1** : pertenecer (a), ser propiedad (de) ⟨it belongs to her : pertenece a ella, es suyo, es de ella⟩ **2** : ser parte (de), ser miembro (de) ⟨he belongs to the club : es miembro del club⟩ **3** : deber estar, ir ⟨your coat belongs in the closet : tu abrigo va en el ropero⟩

belongings [bɪ'lɔŋɪŋz] *npl* : pertenencias *fpl*, efectos *mpl* personales

beloved[1] [bɪ'lʌvəd, -'lʌvd] *adj* : querido, amado

beloved[2] *n* : amado *m*, -da *f*; enamorado *m*, -da *f*; amor *m*

below[1] [bɪ'lo:] *adv* **1** : abajo ⟨the floor below : el piso de abajo⟩ ⟨the pilot looked at the ground below : el piloto miraba el suelo allá abajo⟩ ⟨from below : desde abajo⟩ **2** : más abajo ⟨as stated below : como se indica más abajo⟩ **3**

UNDER, LOWER : más bajo ⟨children age 10 and below : niños menores de los 11 años⟩ **4** : abajo (en un navío) **5** : bajo cero (dícese de temperaturas)

below[2] *prep* **1** : abajo de, debajo de ⟨below the window : debajo de la ventana⟩ **2** : por debajo de, bajo ⟨below average : por debajo del promedio⟩ ⟨5 degrees below zero : 5 grados bajo cero⟩

belt[1] ['belt] *vt* **1** : ceñir con un cinturón, ponerle un cinturón a **2** THRASH : darle una paliza a, darle un trancazo a

belt[2] *n* **1** : cinturón *m*, cinto *m* (para el talle) **2** BAND, STRAP : cinta *f*, correa *f*, banda *f Mex* **3** AREA : frente *m*, zona *f*

beltway ['belt,weɪ] *n* : carretera *f* de circunvalación; periférico *m CA, Mex*; libramiento *m Mex*

bemoan [bɪ'mo:n] *vt* : lamentarse de

bemuse [bɪ'mju:z] *vt* **-mused; -musing 1** BEWILDER : confundir, desconcertar **2** ENGROSS : absorber

bench ['bentʃ] *n* **1** SEAT : banco *m*, escaño *m*, banca *f* **2** : estrado *m* (de un juez) **3** COURT : tribunal *m* **4** : banca *f* (en deportes)

bend[1] ['bend] *v* **bent** ['bent]; **bending** *vt* : torcer, doblar, curvar, flexionar — *vi* **1** : torcerse, agacharse ⟨to bend over : inclinarse⟩ **2** TURN : torcer, hacer una curva **3 on bended knee** : de rodillas, de hinojos

bend[2] *n* **1** TURN : vuelta *f*, recodo *m* **2** CURVE : curva *f*, ángulo *m*, codo *m*

beneath[1] [bɪ'ni:θ] *adv* : bajo, abajo, debajo

beneath[2] *prep* : bajo de, abajo de, por debajo de

benediction [,benə'dɪkʃən] *n* : bendición *f*

benefactor ['benə,fæktər] *n* : benefactor *m*, -tora *f*

benefactress ['benə,fæktrɪs] *n* : benefactora *f*

beneficial [,benə'fɪʃəl] *adj* : beneficioso, provechoso — **beneficially** *adv*

beneficiary [,benə'fɪʃi,eri, -'fɪʃəri] *n*, *pl* **-ries** : beneficiario *m*, -ria *f*

benefit[1] ['benəfɪt] *vt* : beneficiar — *vi* : beneficiarse

benefit[2] *n* **1** ADVANTAGE : beneficio *m*, ventaja *f*, provecho *m* **2** AID : asistencia *f*, beneficio *m* **3** : función *f* benéfica (para recaudar fondos)

benevolence [bə'nevələnts] *n* : bondad *f*, benevolencia *f*

benevolent [bə'nevələnt] *adj* : benévolo, bondadoso — **benevolently** *adv*

benign [bɪ'naɪn] *adj* **1** GENTLE, KIND : benévolo, amable **2** FAVORABLE : propicio, favorable **3** MILD : benigno ⟨a benign tumor : un tumor benigno⟩

bent ['bent] *n* : aptitud *f*, inclinación *f*

benumb [bɪ'nʌm] *vt* : entumecer

bequeath [bɪ'kwi:θ, -'kwi:ð] *vt* : legar, dejar en testamento

bequest [bɪ'kwest] *n* : legado *m*

berate [bɪ'reɪt] *vt* **-rated; -rating** : reprender, regañar

bereaved[1] [bɪ'ri:vd] *adj* : que está de luto, afligido (por la muerte de alguien)

bereaved² *n* **the bereaved** : los deudos del difunto (o de la difunta)

bereavement [bɪˈriːvmənt] *n* **1** SORROW : dolor *m*, pesar *m* **2** LOSS : pérdida *f*

bereft [bɪˈrɛft] *adj* : privado, desprovisto

beret [bəˈreɪ] *n* : boina *f*

berm [ˈbərm] *n* : arcén *m*

Bermuda shorts [bərˈmjuːdə-] *npl* : bermudas *fpl*

berry¹ [ˈbɛri] *n, pl* **-ries** : baya *f*

berserk [bərˈsərk, -ˈzərk] *adj* **1** : enloquecido **2 to go beserk** : volverse loco

berth¹ [ˈbərθ] *vi* : atracar

berth² *n* **1** DOCK : atracadero *m* **2** ACCOMMODATION : litera *f*, camarote *m* **3** POSITION : trabajo *m*, puesto *m*

beseech [bɪˈsiːtʃ] *vt* **-seeched** *or* **-sought** [-ˈsɔt]; **-seeching** : suplicar, implorar, rogar

beset [bɪˈsɛt] *vt* **-set; -setting 1** HARASS : acosar **2** SURROUND : rodear

beside [bɪˈsaɪd] *prep* : al lado de, junto a ⟨the car beside mine : el coche al lado del mío⟩ ⟨that's beside the point : eso no tiene nada que ver, eso no viene al caso⟩

besides¹ [bɪˈsaɪdz] *adv* **1** ALSO : además, también, aparte **2** MOREOVER : además, por otra parte

besides² *prep* **1** : además de, aparte de ⟨six others besides you : seis otros además de ti⟩ **2** EXCEPT : excepto, fuera de, aparte de

besiege [bɪˈsiːdʒ] *vt* **-sieged; -sieging** : asediar, sitiar, cercar

besmirch [bɪˈsmərtʃ] *vt* : ensuciar, mancillar

besotted [bɪˈsɑtəd] *adj* : enamorado

best¹ [ˈbɛst] *vt* : superar, ganar a

best² *adv* (*superlative of* **well**) : mejor ⟨as best I can : lo mejor que puedo⟩

best³ *adj* (*superlative of* **good**) : mejor ⟨my best friend : mi mejor amigo⟩

best⁴ *n* **1 the best** : lo mejor, el mejor, la mejor, los mejores, las mejores **2 at** ∼ : a lo más **3 to do one's best** : hacer todo lo posible **4 to make the best of** it ⟨I'll just have to make the best of it : tendré que arreglármelas como pueda⟩

best–case *adj* **a/the best-case scenario** : el mejor de los casos

bestial [ˈbɛstʃəl, ˈbiːs-] *adj* **1** : bestial **2** BRUTISH : brutal, salvaje

best man *n* : padrino *m*

bestow [bɪˈstoː] *vt* : conferir, otorgar, conceder

bestowal [bɪˈstoːəl] *n* : concesión *f*, otorgamiento *m*

best seller *n* : best-seller *m*

bet¹ [ˈbɛt] *v* **bet; betting** *vt* : apostar — *vi* **1 to bet on** : apostarle a **2 you bet!** : ¡ya lo creo!, ¡por supuesto!

bet² *n* : apuesta *f*

beta [ˈbeɪtə] *n* : beta *f* (software)

betoken [bɪˈtoːkən] *vt* : denotar, ser indicio de

betray [bɪˈtreɪ] *vt* **1** : traicionar ⟨to betray one's country : traicionar uno a su patria⟩ **2** DIVULGE, REVEAL : delatar, revelar ⟨to betray a secret : revelar un secreto⟩

betrayal [bɪˈtreɪəl] *n* : traición *f*, delación *f*, revelación *f* ⟨betrayal of trust : abuso de confianza⟩

betrothal [bɪˈtroːðəl, -ˈtrɔ-] *n* : esponsales *mpl*, compromiso *m*

betrothed [bɪˈtroːðd, -ˈtrɔθt] *n* FIANCÉ : prometido *m*, -da *f*

better¹ [ˈbɛtər] *vt* **1** IMPROVE : mejorar **2** SURPASS : superar

better² *adv* (*comparative of* **well**) **1** : mejor **2** MORE : más ⟨better than 50 miles : más de 50 millas⟩

better³ *adj* (*comparative of* **good**) **1** : mejor ⟨the weather is better today : hace mejor tiempo hoy⟩ ⟨I was sick, but now I'm better : estuve enfermo, pero ahora estoy mejor⟩ **2** : mayor ⟨the better part of a month : la mayor parte de un mes⟩

better⁴ *n* **1** : el mejor, la mejor ⟨the better of the two : el mejor de los dos⟩ **2 to get the better of** : vencer a, quedar por encima de, superar

betterment [ˈbɛtərmənt] *n* : mejoramiento *m*, mejora *f*

better off *adj* (*comparative of* **well off**) **1** : mejor ⟨to be better off : salir ganando, venirle mejor a uno⟩ **2** WEALTHIER : más adinerado

betting [ˈbɛtɪŋ] *n* : apuestas *fpl*

bettor *or* **better** [ˈbɛtər] *n* : apostador *m*, -dora *f*

between¹ [bɪˈtwiːn] *adv* **1** : en medio, por lo medio **2 in** ∼ : intermedio

between² *prep* : entre ⟨between the chair and the wall : entre la silla y la pared⟩ ⟨between now and then : de aquí a entonces⟩ ⟨between nine and ten o'clock : entre las nueve y las diez⟩ ⟨between five and ten people : entre cinco y diez personas⟩ ⟨between you and me : entre nosotros⟩ ⟨they divided it between them : se lo dividieron entre ellos/sí⟩ ⟨the difference between the two brands : la diferencia entre las dos marcas⟩ ⟨to choose between two options : escoger entre dos opciones⟩

bevel¹ [ˈbɛvəl] *v* **-eled** *or* **-elled; -eling** *or* **-elling** *vt* : biselar — *vi* INCLINE : inclinarse

bevel² *n* : bisel *m*

beverage [ˈbɛvrɪdʒ, ˈbɛvə-] *n* : bebida *f*

bevy [ˈbɛvi] *n, pl* **bevies** : grupo *m* (de personas), bandada *f* (de pájaros)

bewail [bɪˈweɪl] *vt* : lamentarse de, llorar

beware [bɪˈwær] *vi* **to beware of** : tener cuidado con ⟨beware of the dog! : ¡cuidado con el perro!⟩ — *vt* : guardarse de, cuidarse de

bewilder [bɪˈwɪldər] *vt* : desconcertar, dejar perplejo

bewilderment [bɪˈwɪldərmənt] *n* : desconcierto *m*, perplejidad *f*

bewitch [bɪˈwɪtʃ] *vt* **1** : hechizar, embrujar **2** CHARM : cautivar, encantar

bewitchment [bɪˈwɪtʃmənt] *n* : hechizo *m*

beyond¹ [biˈjɑnd] *adv* **1** FARTHER, LATER : más allá, más lejos (en el espacio), más adelante (en el tiempo) **2** MORE : más ⟨$50 and beyond : $50 o más⟩

beyond² *n* **the beyond** : el más allá, lo desconocido

beyond³ *prep* **1** : más allá de ⟨beyond the frontier : más allá de la frontera⟩ **2** : fuera de ⟨beyond one's reach : fuera de su alcance⟩ **3** BESIDES : además de

bi- *pref* : bi-

biannual [ˌbaɪˈænjuəl] *adj* : bianual — **biannually** *adv*

bias¹ [ˈbaɪəs] *vt* **-ased** *or* **-assed; -asing** *or* **-assing 1** : predisponer, sesgar, influir en, afectar **2 to be biased against** : tener prejuicio contra

bias² *n* **1** : sesgo *m*, bies *m* (en la costura) **2** PREJUDICE : prejuicio *m* **3** TENDENCY : inclinación *f*, tendencia *f*

biased [ˈbaɪəst] *adj* : tendencioso, parcial

bib [ˈbɪb] *n* **1** : peto *m* **2** : babero *m* (para niños)

Bible [ˈbaɪbəl] *n* : Biblia *f*

biblical [ˈbɪblɪkəl] *adj* : bíblico

bibliographer [ˌbɪbliˈɑɡrəfər] *n* : bibliógrafo *m*, -fa *f*

bibliography [ˌbɪbliˈɑɡrəfi] *n*, *pl* **-phies** : bibliografía *f* — **bibliographic** [ˌbɪbliəˈɡræfɪk] *adj*

bicameral [ˌbaɪˈkæmərəl] *adj* : bicameral

bicarbonate [ˌbaɪˈkɑrbənət, -ˌneɪt] *n* : bicarbonato *m*

bicentennial [ˌbaɪsɛnˈtɛniəl] *n* : bicentenario *m*

biceps [ˈbaɪˌsɛps] *ns & pl* : bíceps *m*

bicker¹ [ˈbɪkər] *vi* : pelear, discutir, reñir

bicker² *n* : pelea *f*, riña *f*, discusión *f*

bicuspid [baɪˈkʌspɪd] *n* : premolar *m*

bicycle¹ [ˈbaɪsɪkəl, -ˌsɪ-] *vi* **-cled; -cling** : ir en bicicleta

bicycle² *n* : bicicleta *f*

bicycling [ˈbaɪsɪklɪŋ] *n* : ciclismo *m*

bicyclist [ˈbaɪsɪkəlɪst] *n* : ciclista *mf*

bid¹ [ˈbɪd] *v* **bade** [ˈbæd, ˈbeɪd] *or* **bid; bidden** [ˈbɪdən] *or* **bid; bidding 1** ORDER : pedir, mandar **2** INVITE : invitar **3** SAY : dar, decir ⟨to bid good evening : dar las buenas noches⟩ ⟨to bid farewell to : decir adiós a⟩ **4** : ofrecer (en una subasta), declarar (en juegos de cartas)

bid² *n* **1** OFFER : oferta *f* (en una subasta), declaración *f* (en juegos de cartas) **2** INVITATION : invitación *f* **3** ATTEMPT : intento *m*, tentativa *f*

bidder [ˈbɪdər] *n* : postor *m*, -tora *f*

bide [ˈbaɪd] *v* **bode** [ˈboːd] *or* **bided; bided; biding** *vt* : esperar, aguardar ⟨to bide one's time : esperar el momento oportuno⟩ — *vi* DWELL : morar, vivir

bidet [bɪˈdeɪ] *n* : bidé *m*, bidet *m*

biennial [baɪˈɛniəl] *adj* : bienal — **biennially** *adv*

bier [ˈbɪr] *n* **1** STAND : andas *fpl* **2** COFFIN : ataúd *m*, féretro *m*

bifocals [ˈbaɪˌfoːkəlz] *npl* : lentes *mpl* bifocales, bifocales *mpl* — **bifocal** [ˈbaɪˌfoːkəl] *adj*

big [ˈbɪg] *adj* **bigger; biggest 1** LARGE : grande ⟨a big guy : un tipo grande⟩ ⟨a great big house : una casa grandísima⟩ ⟨a big group : un grupo grande/numeroso⟩ ⟨big words : palabras difíciles⟩ **2** (*indicating degree*) ⟨to be a big eater : ser un comelón⟩ ⟨to be a big believer in something : ser un gran partidario de algo⟩ **3** IMPORTANT, MAJOR : importante, grande ⟨a big decision : una gran decisión⟩ **4** POPULAR : popular, famoso, conocido ⟨the next big thing : el próximo exitazo⟩ **5** KIND : generoso ⟨it was very big of him : fue muy generoso de su parte⟩ **6 to be big on** : ser entusiasta de

bigamist [ˈbɪgəmɪst] *n* : bígamo *m*, -ma *f*

bigamous [ˈbɪgəməs] *adj* : bígamo

bigamy [ˈbɪgəmi] *n* : bigamia *f*

Big Dipper → **dipper**

big–headed [ˈbɪgˈhɛdəd] *adj fam* : creído

bighorn [ˈbɪgˌhɔrn] *n*, *pl* **-horn** *or* **-horns** *or* **bighorn sheep** : oveja *f* salvaje de las montañas

bight [ˈbaɪt] *n* : bahía *f*, ensenada *f*, golfo *m*

bigot [ˈbɪgət] *n* : intolerante *mf*

bigoted [ˈbɪgətəd] *adj* : intolerante, prejuiciado, fanático

bigotry [ˈbɪgətri] *n*, *pl* **-tries** : intolerancia *f*

big picture *n* **to look at the big picture** : ver las cosas desde una perspectiva global

big shot *n* : pez *m* gordo *fam*, mandamás *mf*

big toe *n* : dedo *m* gordo (del pie)

bigwig [ˈbɪgˌwɪg] → **big shot**

bike [ˈbaɪk] *n* **1** : bicicleta *f*, bici *f fam* **2** : motocicleta *f*, moto *f*

bike lane *or* **bicycle lane** *n* : carril *m* para bicicletas

bikini [bəˈkiːni] *n* : bikini *m*

bilateral [baɪˈlætərəl] *adj* : bilateral — **bilaterally** *adv*

bile [ˈbaɪl] *n* **1** : bilis *f* **2** IRRITABILITY : mal genio *m*

bilingual [baɪˈlɪŋgwəl] *adj* : bilingüe

bilk [ˈbɪlk] *vt* : burlar, estafar, defraudar

bill¹ [ˈbɪl] *vt* : pasarle la cuenta a — *vi* : acariciar ⟨to bill and coo : acariciarse⟩

bill² *n* **1** LAW : proyecto *m* de ley, ley *f* **2** INVOICE : cuenta *f*, factura *f* **3** POSTER : cartel *m* **4** PROGRAM : programa *m* (del teatro) **5** : billete *m* ⟨a five-dollar bill : un billete de cinco dólares⟩ **6** BEAK : pico *m*

billboard [ˈbɪlˌbɔrd] *n* : cartelera *f*

billet¹ [ˈbɪlət] *vt* : acuartelar, alojar

billet² *n* : alojamiento *m*

billfold [ˈbɪlˌfoːld] *n* : billetera *f*, cartera *f*

billiard [ˈbɪljərd] *adj* : de billar ⟨billiard ball : bola de billar⟩

billiards [ˈbɪljərdz] *n* : billar *m*

billion [ˈbɪljən] *n*, *pl* **billions** *or* **billion** : mil millones *mpl*

billionth [ˈbɪljənθ] *n* : milmillonésimo *m* — **billionth** *adj*

billow¹ [ˈbɪloː] *vi* : hincharse, inflarse

billow² *n* **1** WAVE : ola *f* **2** CLOUD : nube *f* ⟨a billow of smoke : un nube de humo⟩

billowy [ˈbɪlowi] *adj* : ondulante

billy goat [ˈbɪlˌgoːt] *n* : macho *m* cabrío

bimonthly [baɪˈmʌnθli] *adj* **1** SEMIMONTHLY : bimensual, quincenal **2** : bimestral

bin · bitter

bin ['bɪn] n : cubo m, cajón m
binary ['baɪnəri, -,neri] adj : binario m
binational [baɪ'næʃənəl] adj : binacional
bind ['baɪnd] vt **bound** ['baʊnd]; **binding**
  1 TIE : atar, amarrar **2** OBLIGATE : obligar **3** UNITE : aglutinar, ligar, unir **4** BANDAGE : vendar **5** : encuadernar (un libro)
binder ['baɪndər] n **1** FOLDER : carpeta f **2** : encuadernador m, -dora f (de libros)
binding ['baɪndɪŋ] n **1** : encuadernación f (de libros) **2** COVER : cubierta f, forro m
binge ['bɪndʒ] n : juerga f, parranda f fam
bingo ['bɪŋ,goː] n, pl **-gos** : bingo m
binocular [baɪ'nɑkjələr, bə-] adj : binocular
binoculars [bə'nɑkjələrz, baɪ-] npl : binoculares mpl
bio- pref : bio- ⟨biochemistry : bioquímica⟩
biochemical[1] [,baɪoˈkɛmɪkəl] adj : bioquímico
biochemical[2] n : bioquímico m
biochemist [,baɪoˈkɛmɪst] n : bioquímico m, -ca f
biochemistry [,baɪoˈkɛməstri] n : bioquímica f
biodegradable [,baɪodɪˈgreɪdəbəl] adj : biodegradable
biodiversity [,baɪodəˈvərsəti, -daɪ-] n, pl **-ties** : biodiversidad f
biographer [baɪˈɑgrəfər] n : biógrafo m, -fa f
biographical [,baɪoˈgræfɪkəl] adj : biográfico
biography [baɪˈɑgrəfi, biː-] n, pl **-phies** : biografía f
biologic [,baɪoˈlɑdʒɪk] or **biological** [-dʒɪkəl] adj : biológico
biological weapon n : arma f biológica
biologist [baɪˈɑlədʒɪst] n : biólogo m, -ga f
biology [baɪˈɑlədʒi] n : biología f
biopsy ['baɪ,ɑpsi] n, pl **-sies** : biopsia f
biosphere ['baɪə,sfɪr] n : biosfera f, biósfera f
biotechnology [,baɪotɛkˈnɑlədʒi] n : biotecnología f — **biotechnological** [,baɪo,tɛknəˈlɑdʒɪkəl] adj
bipartisan [baɪˈpɑrtəzən, -sən] adj : bipartidista, de dos partidas
biped ['baɪ,pɛd] n : bípedo m
birch ['bərtʃ] n : abedul m
bird ['bərd] n : pájaro m (pequeño), ave f (grande)
birdbath ['bərd,bæθ, -,baθ] n : pila f para pájaros
bird dog n : perro m, -rra f de caza
bird of prey n : ave f rapaz, ave f de presa
birdseed ['bərd,siːd] n : alpiste m
bird's-eye ['bərdz,aɪ] adj **1** : visto desde arriba ⟨bird's-eye view : vista aérea⟩ **2** CURSORY : rápido, somero
birdwatching ['bərd,watʃɪŋ] n : observación f de aves
biretta [bəˈrɛtə] n : birrete m
birth ['bərθ] n **1** : nacimiento m, parto m **2** ORIGIN : origen m, nacimiento m
birth certificate n : partida f de nacimiento, acta f de nacimiento, certificado m de nacimiento

birth control n : control m de natalidad
birthday ['bərθ,deɪ] n : cumpleaños m, aniversario m ⟨birthday boy/girl : cumpleañero/cumpleañera⟩
birthmark ['bərθ,mɑrk] n : mancha f de nacimiento
birthplace ['bərθ,pleɪs] n : lugar m de nacimiento
birthrate ['bərθ,reɪt] n : índice m de natalidad
birthright ['bərθ,raɪt] n : derecho m de nacimiento
biscuit ['bɪskət] n : bizcocho m
bisect ['baɪ,sɛkt, ,baɪ-] vt : bisecar
bisexual [,baɪˈsɛkʃuəl] adj : bisexual — **bisexuality** [,baɪ,sɛkʃuˈæləti] n
bishop ['bɪʃəp] n **1** : obispo m **2** : alfil m (en ajedrez)
bishopric ['bɪʃəprɪk] n : obispado m
bison ['baɪzən, -sən] ns & adj : bisonte m
bistro ['biː,stroː, 'bɪs-] n, pl **-tros** : bar m, restaurante m pequeño
bit ['bɪt] n **1** FRAGMENT, PIECE : pedazo m, trozo m ⟨he smashed it to bits : lo hizo pedazos⟩ **2** : freno m, bocado m (de una brida) **3** : broca f (de un taladro) **4** : bit m (de información) **5** : rato m, momento m ⟨stay a bit (longer) : quédate un ratito⟩ **6** SKETCH : sketch m (en teatro, etc.) **7** a bit SOMEWHAT : un poco **8** a bit of : un poco de **9** bit by bit : poco a poco **10** every bit as ... as : tan ..., como **11** quite a bit : bastante
bitch[1] ['bɪtʃ] vi COMPLAIN : quejarse, reclamar
bitch[2] n **1** : perra f **2** offensive : bruja f, cabrona f Spain, Mex offensive **3** fam : cosa f difícil ⟨the exam was a bitch : el examen fue dificilísimo⟩ ⟨life's a bitch : la vida es dura⟩
bite[1] ['baɪt] v **bit** ['bɪt]; **bitten** ['bɪtən]; **biting** vt **1** : morder **2** STING : picar **3** PUNCTURE : punzar, pinchar **4** GRIP : agarrar **5** to bite one's tongue : morderse la lengua **6** to bite someone's head off : explotar, perder los estribos (sin provocación) **7** to bite the bullet : hacer de tripas corazón **8** to bite the dust : morder el polvo (dícese de una persona), pasar a mejor vida (dícese de una cosa) — vi **1** : morder ⟨that dog bites : ese perro muerde⟩ **2** STING : picar (dícese de un insecto), cortar (dícese del viento) **3** : picar ⟨the fish are biting now : ya están picando los peces⟩ **4** GRAB : agarrarse
bite[2] n **1** BITING : mordisco m, dentellada f **2** SNACK : bocado m ⟨a bite to eat : algo de comer⟩ **3** : picadura f (de un insecto), mordedura f (de un animal) **4** SHARPNESS : mordacidad f, penetración f
biting ['baɪtɪŋ] adj **1** PENETRATING : cortante, penetrante **2** CAUSTIC : mordaz, sarcástico
bit part n : papel m secundario
bitter ['bɪtər] adj **1** ACRID : amargo, acre **2** PENETRATING : cortante, penetrante ⟨bitter cold : frío glacial⟩ **3** HARSH : duro, amargo ⟨to the bitter end : hasta el final⟩ **4** INTENSE, RELENTLESS : in-

tenso, extremo, implacable ⟨bitter hatred : odio implacable⟩

bitterly [ˈbɪt̬ərli] adv : amargamente

bitterness [ˈbɪt̬ərnəs] n : amargura f

bittersweet [ˈbɪt̬ər₁swiːt] adj : agridulce

bizarre [bəˈzɑr] adj : extraño, singular, estrafalario, estrambótico — **bizarrely** adv

blab [ˈblæb] vi **blabbed; blabbing** : parlotear fam, cotorrear fam

blabbermouth [ˈblæbər₁maʊθ] n fam : bocón m, -cona f fam

black¹ [ˈblæk] vt : ennegrecer

black² adj **1** : negro (color, raza) **2** SOILED : sucio **3** DARK : oscuro, negro **4** WICKED : malvado, perverso, malo **5** GLOOMY : negro, sombrío, deprimente

black³ n **1** : negro m (color) **2** : negro m, -gra f (persona)

black–and–blue [₁blækənˈbluː] adj : amoratado

blackball [ˈblæk₁bɔl] vt **1** OSTRACIZE : hacerle el vacío a, aislar **2** BOYCOTT : boicotear

blackberry [ˈblæk₁beri] n, pl -ries : mora f

blackbird [ˈblæk₁bərd] n : mirlo m

blackboard [ˈblæk₁bɔrd] n : pizarra f, pizarrón m

black box n : caja f negra

blacken [ˈblækən] vt **1** BLACK : ennegrecer **2** DEFAME : deshonrar, difamar, manchar

black eye n : ojo m morado

blackhead [ˈblæk₁hɛd] n : espinilla f, punto m negro

black hole n : agujero m negro

blackish [ˈblækɪʃ] adj : negruzco

blackjack [ˈblæk₁dʒæk] n **1** : cachiporra f (arma) **2** : veintiuna f (juego de cartas)

blacklist¹ [ˈblæk₁lɪst] vt : poner en la lista negra

blacklist² n : lista f negra

blackmail¹ [ˈblæk₁meɪl] vt : chantajear, hacer chantaje a

blackmail² n : chantaje m

blackmailer [ˈblæk₁meɪlər] n : chantajista mf

blackness [ˈblæknəs] n : negrura f

blackout [ˈblæk₁aʊt] n **1** : apagón m (de poder eléctrico) **2** FAINT : desmayo m, desvanecimiento m

black out vt : dejar sin luz — vi FAINT : perder el conocimiento, desmayarse

black sheep n : oveja f negra

blacksmith [ˈblæk₁smɪθ] n : herrero m

blacktop [ˈblæk₁tɑp] n : asfalto m

bladder [ˈblædər] n : vejiga f

blade [ˈbleɪd] n : hoja f (de un cuchillo), cuchilla f (de un patín), pala f (de un remo o una hélice), brizna f (de hierba)

blamable [ˈbleɪməbəl] adj : culpable

blame¹ [ˈbleɪm] vt **blamed; blaming** : culpar, echar la culpa a

blame² n : culpa f

blameless [ˈbleɪmləs] adj : intachable, sin culpa, inocente — **blamelessly** adv

blameworthiness [ˈbleɪm₁wərðinəs] n : culpa f, culpabilidad f

blameworthy [ˈbleɪm₁wərði] adj : culpable, reprochable, censurable

blanch [ˈblæntʃ] vt WHITEN : blanquear — vi PALE : palidecer

bland [ˈblænd] adj : soso, insulso, desabrido ⟨a bland smile : una sonrisa insulsa⟩ ⟨a bland diet : una dieta fácil de digerir⟩

blandishments [ˈblændɪʃmənts] npl : lisonjas fpl, halagos mpl

blandly [ˈblændli] adv : de manera insulsa

blandness [ˈblændnəs] n : lo insulso, lo desabrido

blank¹ [ˈblæŋk] vt OBLITERATE : borrar

blank² adj **1** DAZED : perplejo, desconcertado **2** EXPRESSIONLESS : sin expresión, inexpresivo **3** : en blanco (dícese de un papel), liso (dícese de una pared) **4** EMPTY : vacío, en blanco ⟨a blank stare : una mirada vacía⟩ ⟨his mind went blank : se quedó en blanco⟩

blank³ n **1** SPACE : espacio m en blanco **2** FORM : formulario m **3** CARTRIDGE : cartucho m de fogueo **4** or **blank key** : llave f ciega

blank check n **1** : cheque m en blanco **2** CARTE BLANCHE : carta f blanca

blanket¹ [ˈblæŋkət] vt : cubrir

blanket² adj : global

blanket³ n : manta f, cobija f, frazada f

blankly [ˈblæŋkli] adv : sin comprender

blankness [ˈblæŋknəs] n **1** PERPLEXITY : desconcierto m, perplejidad f **2** EMPTINESS : vacío m, vacuidad f

blare¹ [ˈblær] vi **blared; blaring** : resonar

blare² n : estruendo m

blarney [ˈblɑrni] n : labia f fam

blasé [blɑˈzeɪ] adj : displicente, indiferente

blaspheme [blæsˈfiːm, ˈblæs₁-] vi -phemed; -pheming : blasfemar

blasphemer [blæsˈfiːmər, ˈblæs₁-] n : blasfemo m, -ma f

blasphemous [ˈblæsfəməs] adj : blasfemo

blasphemy [ˈblæsfəmi] n, pl -mies : blasfemia f

blast¹ [ˈblæst] vt **1** BLOW UP : volar, hacer volar **2** ATTACK : atacar, arremeter contra

blast² n **1** GUST : ráfaga f **2** EXPLOSION : explosión f

blast–off [ˈblæst₁ɔf] n : despegue m

blast off vi : despegar

blatant [ˈbleɪtənt] adj : descarado — **blatantly** [ˈbleɪtəntli] adv

blaze¹ [ˈbleɪz] v **blazed; blazing** vi SHINE : arder, brillar, resplandecer — vt MARK : marcar, señalar ⟨to blaze a trail : abrir un camino⟩

blaze² n **1** FIRE : fuego m **2** BRIGHTNESS : resplandor m, brillantez f **3** OUTBURST : arranque m ⟨a blaze of anger : un arranque de cólera⟩ **4** DISPLAY : alarde m, llamarada f ⟨a blaze of color : un derroche de color⟩

blazer [ˈbleɪzər] n : chaqueta f deportiva, blazer m

bleach¹ [ˈbliːtʃ] vt : blanquear, decolorar

bleach² n : lejía f, blanqueador m

bleachers [ˈbliːtʃərz] ns & pl : gradas fpl, tribuna f descubierta

bleak ['bliːk] *adj* **1** DESOLATE : inhóspito, sombrío, desolado **2** DEPRESSING : deprimente, triste, sombrío

bleakly ['bliːkli] *adv* : sombríamente

bleakness ['bliːknəs] *n* : lo inhóspito, lo sombrío

blear ['blɪr] *adj* : empañado, nublado

bleary ['blɪri] *adj* **1** : adormilado, fatigado **2 bleary–eyed** : con los ojos nublados

bleat¹ ['bliːt] *vi* : balar

bleat² *n* : balido *m*

bleed ['bliːd] *v* **bled** ['blɛd]; **bleeding** *vi* **1** : sangrar **2** GRIEVE : sufrir, afligirse **3** EXUDE : exudar (dícese de una planta), correrse (dícese de los colores) — *vt* **1** : sangrar (a una persona), purgar (frenos) **2 to bleed someone dry** : sacarle todo el dinero a alguien

blemish¹ ['blɛmɪʃ] *vt* : manchar, marcar

blemish² *n* : imperfección *f*, mancha *f*, marca *f*

blend¹ ['blɛnd] *vt* **1** MIX : mezclar **2** COMBINE : combinar, aunar

blend² *n* : mezcla *f*, combinación *f*

blender ['blɛndər] *n* : licuadora *f*

bless ['blɛs] *vt* **blessed** ['blɛst]; **blessing 1** : bendecir ⟨God bless you! : ¡que Dios te bendiga!⟩ ⟨you did the dishes? bless you! : ¿lavaste los trastes? ¡mil gracias!⟩ ⟨he's a little forgetful, bless his heart : es un poco olvidadizo, el pobre⟩. **2 bless you!** (*said to someone who has sneezed*) : ¡salud! **3 to bless with** : dotar de **4 to bless oneself** : santiguarse

blessed ['blɛsəd] *or* **blest** ['blɛst] *adj* : bienaventurado, bendito, dichoso

blessedly ['blɛsədli] *adv* : felizmente, alegremente, afortunadamente

blessing ['blɛsɪŋ] *n* **1** : bendición *f* **2** APPROVAL : aprobación *f*, consentimiento *m*

blew → **blow**

blight¹ ['blaɪt] *vt* : arruinar, infestar

blight² *n* **1** : añublo *m* **2** PLAGUE : peste *f*, plaga *f* **3** DECAY : deterioro *m*, ruina *f*

blimp ['blɪmp] *n* : dirigible *m*

blind¹ ['blaɪnd] *vt* **1** : cegar, dejar ciego **2** DAZZLE : deslumbrar

blind² *adj* **1** SIGHTLESS : ciego ⟨to go blind : quedarse ciego⟩ **2** INSENSITIVE : ciego, insensible, sin razón **3** CLOSED : sin salida ⟨blind alley : callejón sin salida⟩

blind³ *n* **1** : persiana *f* (para una ventana) **2** COVER : escondite *m*, escondrijo *m*

blind date *n* : cita *f* a ciegas

blinders ['blaɪndərz] *npl* : anteojeras *fpl*

blindfold¹ ['blaɪnd,foːld] *vt* : vendar los ojos

blindfold² *n* : venda *f* (para los ojos)

blinding ['blaɪndɪŋ] *adj* : enceguecedor, cegador ⟨with blinding speed : con una rapidez inusitada⟩

blindly ['blaɪndli] *adv* : a ciegas, ciegamente

blindness ['blaɪndnəs] *n* : ceguera *f*

blind spot *n* **1** : ángulo *m* muerto (de un vehículo) **2** WEAKNESS : punto *m* débil

blink¹ ['blɪŋk] *vi* **1** WINK : pestañear, parpadear **2** : brillar intermitentemente

blink² *n* : pestañeo *m*, parpadeo *m*

blinker ['blɪŋkər] *n* : intermitente *m*, direccional *f*

bliss ['blɪs] *n* **1** HAPPINESS : dicha *f*, felicidad *f* absoluta **2** PARADISE : paraíso *m*

blissful ['blɪsfəl] *adj* : dichoso, feliz — **blissfully** *adv*

blister¹ ['blɪstər] *vi* : ampollarse

blister² *n* : ampolla *f* (en la piel o una superficie), burbuja *f* (en una superficie)

blithe ['blaɪθ, 'blaɪð] *adj* **blither; blithest 1** CAREFREE : despreocupado **2** CHEERFUL : alegre, risueño — **blithely** *adv*

blitz¹ ['blɪts] *vt* **1** BOMBARD : bombardear **2** : atacar con rapidez

blitz² *n* **1** : bombardeo *m* aéreo **2** CAMPAIGN : ataque *m*, acometida *f*

blizzard ['blɪzərd] *n* : tormenta *f* de nieve, ventisca *f*

bloat ['bloːt] *vi* : hincharse, inflarse

blob ['blɑb] *n* : gota *f*, mancha *f*, borrón *m*

bloc ['blɑk] *n* : bloque *m*

block¹ ['blɑk] *vt* **1** OBSTRUCT : bloquear (una calle, una arteria, etc.) ⟨you're blocking my light : me estás tapando la luz⟩ **2** *or* **to block up** CLOG : obstruir, atascar, atorar (una tubería, etc.) **3** IMPEDE : bloquear, impedir **4** : bloquear (en deportes) **5 to block in** : cerrarle el paso a (un vehículo) **6 to block off** BARRICADE : cortar (una calle) **7 to block out** : tapar (el sol, etc.) **8 to block out** FORGET, IGNORE : borrar de la mente

block² *n* **1** PIECE : bloque *m* ⟨building blocks : cubos de construcción⟩ ⟨auction block : plataforma de subastas⟩ ⟨starting block : taco de salida⟩ **2** OBSTRUCTION : obstrucción *f*, bloqueo *m* ⟨mental block : bloqueo mental⟩ **3** : cuadra *f*, manzana *f* (de edificios) ⟨to go around the block : dar la vuelta a la cuadra⟩ **4** BUILDING : edificio *m* (de apartamentos, oficinas, etc.) **5** SERIES, GROUP : serie *f*, grupo *m* ⟨a block of tickets : una serie de entradas⟩ **6 block and tackle** : aparejo *m* de poleas

blockade¹ [blɑ'keɪd] *vt* **-aded; -ading** : bloquear

blockade² *n* : bloqueo *m*

blockage ['blɑkɪʤ] *n* : bloqueo *m*, obstrucción *f*

blockbuster ['blɑk,bʌstər] *n* : gran éxito *m* (de taquilla)

blockhead ['blɑk,hɛd] *n* : bruto *m*, -ta *f*; estúpido *m*, -da *f*

block letters *npl* : letras *fpl* de molde/imprenta (mayúsculas)

blog ['blɔg, 'blɑg] *n* : blog *m*, bitácora *f*

blond¹ *or* **blonde** ['blɑnd] *adj* : rubio, güero *Mex*, claro (dícese de la madera)

blond² *or* **blonde** *n* : rubio *m*, -bia *f*; güero *m*, -ra *f Mex*

blood ['blʌd] *n* **1** : sangre *f* ⟨to draw blood : sacar sangre⟩ **2** LIFEBLOOD : vida *f*, alma *f* **3** LINEAGE : linaje *m*, sangre *f* ⟨blood relatives : parientes consanguíneos⟩ **4 in cold blood** : a sangre fría

blood bank *n* : banco *m* de sangre

bloodbath ['blʌd,bæθ, -,baθ] *n* : masacre *f*, baño *m* de sangre

bloodcurdling ['blʌd,kərdəlɪŋ] *adj* : espeluznante, aterrador

blood donor *n* : donador *m*, -dora *f* de sangre; donante *mf* de sangre

blooded ['blʌdəd] *adj* : de sangre ⟨cold-blooded animal : animal de sangre fría⟩

blood group *n* : grupo *m* sanguíneo

bloodhound ['blʌd,haund] *n* : sabueso *m*

bloodless ['blʌdləs] *adj* 1 : incruento, sin derramamiento de sangre 2 LIFELESS : desanimado, insípido, sin vida

bloodmobile ['blʌdmo,bi:l] *n* : unidad *f* móvil para donantes de sangre

blood pressure *n* : tensión *f*, presión *f* (arterial)

bloodshed ['blʌd,ʃed] *n* : derramamiento *m* de sangre

bloodshot ['blʌd,ʃat] *adj* : inyectado de sangre

bloodstain ['blʌd,steɪn] *n* : mancha *f* de sangre

bloodstained ['blʌd,steɪnd] *adj* : manchado de sangre

bloodstream ['blʌd,stri:m] *n* : torrente *m* sanguíneo, corriente *f* sanguínea

bloodsucker ['blʌd,sʌkər] *n* : sanguijuela *f*

blood test *n* : análisis *m* de sangre

bloodthirsty ['blʌd,θərsti] *adj* : sanguinario

blood transfusion *n* : transfusión *f* de sangre

blood vessel *n* : vaso *m* sanguíneo

bloody ['blʌdi] *adj* **bloodier; -est** : ensangrentado, sangriento

bloom¹ ['blu:m] *vi* 1 FLOWER : florecer 2 MATURE : madurar

bloom² *n* 1 FLOWER : flor *f* ⟨to be in bloom : estar en flor⟩ 2 FLOWERING : floración *f* ⟨in full bloom : en plena floración⟩ 3 : rubor *m* (de la tez) ⟨in the bloom of youth : en plena juventud, en la flor de la vida⟩

bloomers ['blu:mərz] *npl* : bombachos *mpl*

blooper ['blu:pər] *n* : metedura *f* de pata *fam*

blossom¹ ['blɑsəm] *vi* : florecer, dar flor

blossom² *n* : flor *f*

blot¹ ['blat] *vt* **blotted; blotting** 1 SPOT : emborronar, borronear 2 DRY : secar

blot² *n* 1 STAIN : mancha *f*, borrón *m* 2 BLEMISH : mancha *f*, tacha *f*

blotch¹ ['blatʃ] *vt* : emborronar, borronear

blotch² *n* : mancha *f*, borrón *m*

blotchy ['blatʃi] *adj* **blotchier; -est** : lleno de manchas

blotter ['blatər] *n* : hoja *f* de papel secante, secante *m*

blouse ['blaus, 'blauz] *n* : blusa *f*

blow¹ ['blo:] *v* **blew** ['blu:]; **blown** ['blo:n]; **blowing** *vi* 1 : soplar (dícese del viento) 2 : agitarse (etc.) con el viento ⟨to blow open/shut : abrirse/cerrarse⟩⟨to blow off/away : volar⟩ 3 SOUND : sonar (dícese de un silbato, etc.) 4 to blow off *fam* : dejar plantado a (alguien) *fam*, no ir a (una cita, etc.) 5 to blow out : fundirse (dícese de un fusible eléctrico), re-

ventarse (dícese de una llanta) 6 to blow over : pasar, dispersarse (dícese de una tormenta) 7 to blow over : pasar, calmarse, caer en el olvido (dícese de una situación) — *vt* 1 : soplar, echar ⟨to blow smoke : echar humo⟩ 2 SOUND : tocar, sonar 3 SHAPE : soplar, dar forma a (vidrio, etc.) 4 BUNGLE : echar a perder 5 to blow one's nose : sonarse la nariz

blow² *n* 1 PUFF : soplo *m*, soplido *m* 2 GALE : vendaval *f* 3 HIT, STROKE : golpe *m* 4 CALAMITY : golpe *m*, desastre *m* 5 to come to blows : llegar a las manos

blow–dry ['blo:,draɪ] *n*, *pl* **-dries** : secado *m* (de pelo)

blower ['blo:ər] *n* FAN : ventilador *m*

blowout ['blo:,aut] *n* : reventón *m*

blowtorch ['blo:,tɔrtʃ] *n* : soplete *m*

blow up *vi* EXPLODE : estallar, hacer explosión — *vt* BLAST : volar, hacer volar

blubber¹ ['blʌbər] *vi* : lloriquear

blubber² *n* : esperma *f* de ballena

bludgeon ['blʌdʒən] *vt* : aporrear

blue¹ ['blu:] *adj* **bluer; bluest** 1 : azul 2 MELANCHOLY : melancólico, triste

blue² *n* : azul *m*

bluebell ['blu:,bel] *n* : campanilla *f*

blueberry ['blu:,beri] *n*, *pl* **-ries** : arándano *m*

bluebird ['blu:,bərd] *n* : azulejo *m*

blue cheese *n* : queso *m* azul

blue–collar ['blu:'kalər] *adj* : obrero

blueprint ['blu:,prɪnt] *n* 1 : plano *m*, proyecto *m*, cianotipo *m* 2 PLAN : anteproyecto *m*, programa *m*

blues ['blu:z] *npl* 1 DEPRESSION : depresión *f*, melancolía *f* 2 : blues *m* ⟨to sing the blues : cantar blues⟩

bluff¹ ['blʌf] *vi* : hacer un farol, blofear *Col, Mex*

bluff² *adj* 1 STEEP : escarpado 2 FRANK : campechano, franco, directo

bluff³ *n* 1 : farol *m*; blof *m Col, Mex* 2 CLIFF : acantilado *m*, risco *m*

bluing *or* **blueing** ['blu:ɪŋ] *n* : añil *m*, azulete *m*

bluish ['blu:ɪʃ] *adj* : azulado

blunder¹ ['blʌndər] *vi* 1 STUMBLE : tropezar, dar traspiés 2 ERR : cometer un error, tropezar, meter la pata *fam*

blunder² *n* : error *m*, fallo *m* garrafal, metedura *f* de pata *fam*

blunderbuss ['blʌndər,bʌs] *n* : trabuco *m*

blunt¹ ['blʌnt] *vt* 1 : despuntar (un lápiz, etc.), desafilar (un cuchillo, etc.) 2 : embotar (la mente, etc.), suavizar (críticas)

blunt² *adj* 1 DULL : desafilado, despuntado 2 DIRECT : directo, franco, categórico

bluntly ['blʌntli] *adv* : sin rodeos, francamente, bruscamente

bluntness ['blʌntnəs] *n* 1 DULLNESS : falta *f* de filo 2 FRANKNESS : franqueza *f*

blur¹ ['blər] *vt* **blurred; blurring** : desdibujar, hacer borroso

blur² *n* 1 SMEAR : mancha *f*, borrón *m* 2 : aspecto *m* borroso ⟨everything was just a blur : todo se volvió borroso⟩

blurb ['blərb] *n* : propaganda *f*, nota *f* publicitaria

blurred ['blərd] *adj* : borroso

blurry ['bləri] *adj* : borroso

blurt ['blərt] *vt* : espetar, decir impulsivamente

blush[1] ['blʌʃ] *vi* : ruborizarse, sonrojarse, hacerse colorado

blush[2] *n* : rubor *m*, sonrojo *m*

bluster[1] ['blʌstər] *vi* 1 BLOW : soplar con fuerza 2 BOAST : fanfarronear, echar bravatas

bluster[2] *n* : fanfarronada *f*, bravatas *fpl*

blustery ['blʌstəri] *adj* : borrascoso, tempestuoso

boa ['boːə] *n* : boa *f*

boar ['bor] *n* : cerdo *m* macho, verraco *m*

board[1] ['bord] *vt* 1 : embarcarse en, subir a bordo de (una nave o un avión), subir a (un tren o carro) 2 LODGE : hospedar, dar hospedaje con comidas a 3 to board up : cerrar con tablas

board[2] *n* 1 PLANK : tabla *f*, tablón *m* 2 : tablero *m* ⟨chessboard : tablero de ajedrez⟩ 3 → cardboard 4 → bulletin board 5 → blackboard 6 → surfboard 7 MEALS : comida *f* ⟨board and lodging : comida y alojamiento⟩ 8 COMMITTEE, COUNCIL : junta *f*, consejo *m* 9 across the board : en general, para todos 10 on ~ → aboard 11 on ~⟨to get someone on board : conseguir el apoyo de alguien⟩ ⟨to be on board : apoyar algo, apoyar a alguien⟩

boarder ['bordər] *n* LODGER : huésped *m*, -peda *f*

board game *n* : juego *m* de mesa

boardinghouse ['bordɪŋˌhaʊs] *n* : casa *f* de huéspedes

boarding school *n* : internado *m*

boardroom ['bordˌruːm, -ˌrʊm] *n* : sala *f* de juntas

boardwalk ['bordˌwɔk] *n* : paseo *m* marítimo

boast[1] ['boːst] *vi* : alardear, presumir, jactarse

boast[2] *n* : jactancia *f*, alarde *m*

boaster ['boːstər] *n* : presumido *m*, -da *f*; fanfarrón *m*, -rrona *f fam*

boastful ['boːstfəl] *adj* : jactancioso, fanfarrón *fam*

boastfully ['boːstfəli] *adv* : de manera jactanciosa

boastfulness ['boːstfəlnəs] *n* : jactancia *f*

boat[1] ['boːt] *vt* : transportar en barco, poner a bordo

boat[2] *n* : barco *m*, embarcación *f*, bote *m*, barca *f*

boatman ['boːtmən] *n*, *pl* **-men** [-mən, -ˌmɛn] : barquero *m*

boat person *n* : balsero *m*, -ra *f*

boatwoman ['boːtˌwʊmən] *n*, *pl* **-women** [-ˌwɪmən] : barquera *f*

bob[1] ['bab] *v* **bobbed**; **bobbing** *vi* 1 : balancearse, mecerse ⟨to bob up and down : subir y bajar⟩ 2 *or* to bob up APPEAR : presentarse, surgir — *vt* 1 : inclinar (la cabeza o el cuerpo) 2 CUT : cortar, recortar ⟨she bobbed her hair : se cortó el pelo⟩

bob[2] *n* 1 : inclinación *f* (de la cabeza, del cuerpo), sacudida *f* 2 FLOAT : flotador *m*, corcho *m* (de pesca) 3 : pelo *m* corto

bobbin ['babən] *n* : bobina *f*, carrete *m* (de una máquina de coser)

bobby pin ['babiˌpɪn] *n* : horquilla *f*

bobcat ['babˌkæt] *n* : lince *m* rojo

bobolink ['babəˌlɪŋk] *n* : tordo *m* arrocero

bobsled ['babˌsled] *n* : bobsleigh *m*

bobwhite ['babˌʰwaɪt] *n* : codorniz *m* (del Nuevo Mundo)

bode[1] ['boːd] *v* **boded**; **boding** *vt* : presagiar, augurar — *vi* to bode well : ser de buen agüero

bode[2] → **bide**

bodice ['badəs] *n* : corpiño *m*

bodied ['badid] *adj* : de cuerpo ⟨lean-bodied : de cuerpo delgado⟩ ⟨able-bodied : no discapacitado⟩

bodiless ['badiləs, 'badələs] *adj* : incorpóreo

bodily[1] ['badəli] *adv* : en peso ⟨to lift someone bodily : levantar a alguien en peso⟩

bodily[2] *adj* : corporal, del cuerpo ⟨bodily harm : daños corporales⟩

body ['badi] *n*, *pl* **bodies** 1 : cuerpo *m*, organismo *m* 2 CORPSE : cadáver *m* 3 PERSON : persona *f*, ser *m* humano 4 : nave *f* (de una iglesia), carrocería (de un automóvil), fuselaje *m* (de un avión), casco *m* (de una nave) 5 COLLECTION, MASS : conjunto *m*, grupo *m*, masa *f* ⟨in a body : todos juntos, en masa⟩ 6 ORGANIZATION : organismo *m*, organización *f*

bodybuilding ['badiˌbɪldɪŋ] *n* : culturismo *m*

bodyguard ['badiˌgard] *n* : guardaespaldas *mf*

bodywork ['badiˌwərk] *n* : carrocería *f*

bog[1] ['bag, 'bɔg] *v* **bogged**; **bogging** *vt* to bog down 1 SWAMP : empantanar, inundar ⟨to get bogged down : quedar empantanado⟩ 2 STALL : estancar, paralizar — *vi* to bog down 1 STICK : embarrancar, empantanarse 2 STALL : estancarse, empantanarse

bog[2] *n* : lodazal *m*, ciénaga *f*, cenagal *m*

bogey ['bʊgi, 'boː-] *n* 1 : bogey *m* (en golf) 2 → bugaboo

bogeyman ['bʊgiˌmæn, 'boː-] *n*, *pl* **-men** [-mən] : coco *m fam*; cuco *m* ⟨*Arg, Chile, Peru, Uru fam*⟩ ⟨the bogeyman will get you! : ¡viene el coco!⟩ ⟨he's the bogeyman of conservatives : es el coco de los conservativos⟩

boggle ['bagəl] *vi* **-gled**; **-gling** : quedarse atónito, quedarse pasmado ⟨the mind boggles! : ¡es increíble!⟩

boggy ['bagi, 'bɔ-] *adj* **boggier**; **-est** : cenagoso

bogus ['boːgəs] *adj* : falso, fingido, falaz

bohemian [boːˈhiːmiən] *n* : bohemio *m*, -mia *f* — **bohemian** *adj*

boil[1] ['bɔɪl] *vi* 1 : hervir 2 to boil down to : reducirse a 3 to make one's blood boil : hervirle la sangre a uno — *vt* 1 : hervir, hacer hervir ⟨to boil water : hervir agua⟩ 2 : cocer, hervir ⟨to boil potatoes : cocer papas⟩ **3 to boil something down to** : reducir algo a

boil² *n* **1** BOILING : hervor *m* **2** : forúnculo *m* (en medicina)

boiler ['bɔɪlər] *n* : caldera *f*

boiling ['bɔɪlɪŋ] *adj* **1** : hirviendo **2** HOT : caliente ⟨I'm boiling : me muero de calor⟩

boiling point *n* : punto *m* de ebullición

boisterous ['bɔɪstərəs] *adj* : bullicioso, escandaloso — **boisterously** *adv*

bold¹ ['boːld] *adj* **1** COURAGEOUS : valiente **2** INSOLENT : insolente, descarado **3** DARING : atrevido, audaz — **boldly** *adv*

bold² → **boldface**

boldface ['boːld,feɪs] *or* **boldface type** *n* : negrita *f*

boldness ['boːldnəs] *n* **1** COURAGE : valor *m*, coraje *m* **2** INSOLENCE : atrevimiento *m*, insolencia *f*, descaro *m* **3** DARING : audacia *f*

bolero [bə'lero] *n, pl* **-ros** : bolero *m*

bolivar [bə'liː,var, 'bɑləvər] *n* : bolívar *m* (unidad monetaria)

Bolivian [bə'lɪviən] *n* : boliviano *m*, -na *f* — **Bolivian** *adj*

boliviano [bə,lɪvi'ano] *n* : boliviano *m* (unidad monetaria)

boll ['boːl] *n* : cápsula *f* (del algodón)

boll weevil *n* : gorgojo *m* del algodón

bologna [bə'loːni] *n* : salchicha *f* ahumada

Bolshevik ['boːlʃə,vɪk, 'bɑl-] *n* : bolchevique *nmf* — **Bolshevik** *adj*

bolster¹ ['boːlstər] *vt* **-stered; -stering** : reforzar, reafirmar ⟨to bolster morale : levantar la moral⟩

bolster² *n* : cabezal *m*, almohadón *m*

bolt¹ ['boːlt] *vt* **1** : atornillar, sujetar con pernos ⟨bolted to the floor : sujetado con pernos al suelo⟩ **2** : cerrar con pestillo, echar el cerrojo a ⟨to bolt the door : echar el cerrojo a la puerta⟩ **3 to bolt down** : engullir ⟨she bolted down her dinner : engulló su comida⟩ — *vi* : echar a correr, salir corriendo ⟨he bolted from the room : salió corriendo de la sala⟩

bolt² *n* **1** LATCH : pestillo *m*, cerrojo *m* **2** : tornillo *m*, perno *m* ⟨nuts and bolts : tuercas y tornillos⟩ **3** : rollo *m* ⟨a bolt of cloth : un rollo de tela⟩ **4 lightning bolt** : relámpago *m*, rayo *m*

bomb¹ ['bɑm] *vt* : bombardear

bomb² *n* **1** : bomba *f* **2** FAILURE : desastre *m*

bombard [bɑm'bard, bəm-] *vt* : bombardear

bombardment [bɑm'bardmənt] *n* : bombardeo *m*

bombast ['bɑm,bæst] *n* : grandilocuencia *f*, ampulosidad *f*

bombastic [bɑm'bæstɪk] *adj* : grandilocuente, ampuloso, bombástico

bomber ['bɑmər] *n* : bombardero *m*

bombing ['bɑmɪŋ] *n* : bombardeo *m*

bombproof ['bɑm,pruːf] *adj* : a prueba de bombas

bombshell ['bɑm,ʃɛl] *n* : bomba *f* ⟨a political bombshell : una bomba política⟩

bona fide ['boːnə,faɪd, 'bɑ-; ,boːnə'faɪdi] *adj* **1** : de buena fe ⟨a bona fide offer : una oferta de buena fe⟩ **2** GENUINE : genuino, auténtico

bonanza [bə'nænzə] *n* : bonanza *f*

bonbon ['bɑn,bɑn] *n* : bombón *m*

bond¹ ['bɑnd] *vt* **1** INSURE : dar fianza a, asegurar **2** STICK : adherir, pegar — *vi* : adherirse, pegarse

bond² *n* **1** LINK, TIE : vínculo *m*, lazo *m* **2** BAIL : fianza *f*, caución *f* **3** : bono *m* ⟨stocks and bonds : acciones y bonos⟩ **4 bonds** *npl* FETTERS : cadenas *fpl*

bondage ['bɑndɪdʒ] *n* : esclavitud *f*

bondholder ['bɑnd,hoːldər] *n* : tenedor *m*, -dora *f* de bonos

bondsman ['bɑndzmən] *n, pl* **-men** [-mən, -,mɪn] **1** SLAVE : esclavo *m* **2** SURETY : fiador *m*, -dora *f*

bone¹ ['boːn] *vt* **boned; boning 1** : deshuesar **2 to bone up on** *fam* : estudiar

bone² *n* **1** : hueso *m* **2 to feel it in one's bones** : tener un presentimiento **3 to have a bone to pick with someone** : tener que arreglar cuentas con alguien **4 to the bone** : muchísimo ⟨it chilled me to the bone : se me heló la sangre⟩ **5 to throw someone a bone** : hacerle una pequeña concesión a alguien

boneless ['boːnləs] *adj* : sin huesos, sin espinas

boner ['boːnər] *n* : metedura *f* de pata, metida *f* de pata

bonfire ['bɑn,faɪr] *n* : hoguera *f*, fogata *f*, fogón *m*

bongo ['bɑŋgo, 'bɔŋ-] *n* : bongó *m*, bongo *m*

bonito [bə'niː,to] *n, pl* **-tos** *or* **-to** : bonito *m*

bonnet ['bɑnət] *n* : sombrero *m* (de mujer), gorra *f* (de niño)

bonus ['boːnəs] *n* **1** : prima *f*, bonificación *f* (pagado al empleado) **2** ADVANTAGE, BENEFIT : beneficio *m*, provecho *m*

bony ['boːni] *adj* **bonier; -est** : huesudo

boo¹ ['buː] *vt* : abuchear

boo² *n, pl* **boos** : abucheo *m*

booby ['buːbi] *n, pl* **-bies** : bobo *m*, -ba *f*; tonto *m*, -ta *f*

boogeyman ['bugi,mæn] *n, pl* **-men** [-mən, -,mɛn] → **bogeyman**

book¹ ['bʊk] *vt* : reservar ⟨to book a flight : reservar un vuelo⟩ — *vi* : hacer una reservación

book² *n* **1** : libro *m* **2 the Book** : la Biblia **3 by the book** : según las reglas

bookcase ['bʊk,keɪs] *n* : estantería *f*, librero *m* *Mex*, biblioteca *f*

bookend ['bʊk,ɛnd] *n* : sujetalibros *m*

bookie ['bʊki] → **bookmaker**

bookish ['bʊkɪʃ] *adj* : libresco

bookkeeper ['bʊk,kiːpər] *n* : tenedor *m*, -dora *f* de libros; contable *mf* *Spain*

bookkeeping ['bʊk,kiːpɪŋ] *n* : contabilidad *f*, teneduría *f* de libros

booklet ['bʊklət] *n* : folleto *m*

bookmaker ['bʊk,meɪkər] n : corredor m, -dora f de apuestas

bookmark[1] ['bʊk,mark] n   **1** : señalador m de libros, marcador m de libros   **2** : marcador m (de Internet)

bookmark[2] vt : marcar (una página web)

bookseller ['bʊk,slər] n : librero m, -ra f

bookshelf ['bʊk,ʃelf] n, pl **-shelves**   **1** : estante m   **2 bookshelves** npl : estantería f

bookstore ['bʊk,stor] n : librería f

bookworm ['bʊk,wərm] n : ratón m de biblioteca fam

boom[1] ['bu:m] vi   **1** THUNDER : tronar, resonar   **2** FLOURISH, PROSPER : estar en auge, prosperar

boom[2] n   **1** BOOMING : bramido m, estruendo m   **2** FLOURISHING : augé m ⟨population boom : auge de población⟩

boomerang ['bu:mə,ræŋ] n : bumerán m

boon[1] ['bu:n] adj **boon companion** : amigo m, -ga f del alma

boon[2] n : ayuda f, beneficio m, adelanto m

boondocks ['bu:n,dɑks] npl : área f rural remota, región f alejada

boor ['bʊr] n : grosero m, -ra f

boorish ['bʊrɪʃ] adj : grosero

boost[1] ['bu:st] vt   **1** LIFT : levantar, alzar   **2** INCREASE : aumentar, incrementar   **3** PROMOTE : promover, fomentar, hacer publicidad por

boost[2] n   **1** THRUST : impulso m, empujón m   **2** ENCOURAGEMENT : estímulo m, aliento m   **3** INCREASE : aumento m, incremento m

booster ['bu:stər] n   **1** SUPPORTER : partidario m, -ria f   **2 booster rocket** : cohete m propulsor   **3 booster shot** : vacuna f de refuerzo

boot[1] ['bu:t] vt KICK : dar una patada a, patear

boot[2] n   **1** : bota f, botín m   **2** KICK : puntapié m, patada f

bootee or **bootie** ['bu:ti] n : botita f, botín m

booth ['bu:θ] n, pl **booths** ['bu:ðz, 'bu:θs] : cabina f (de teléfono, de votar), caseta f (de información), barraca f (a una feria)

bootleg[1] ['bu:t,leg] adj : pirata ⟨bootleg software : software pirata⟩

bootleg[2] vt : piratear (un video, etc.)

bootlegger ['bu:t,legər] n : contrabandista mf del alcohol

bootlegging ['bu:t,legɪŋ] n : piratería f

booty ['bu:ti] n, pl **-ties** : botín m

booze ['bu:z] n fam : alcohol m

border[1] ['bordər] vt   **1** EDGE : ribetear, bordear   **2** BOUND : limitar con, lindar con — vi VERGE : rayar, lindar ⟨that borders on absurdity : eso raya en el absurdo⟩

border[2] n   **1** EDGE : borde m, orilla f   **2** TRIM : ribete m   **3** FRONTIER : frontera f

borderline[1] ['bordər,laɪn] adj : dudoso

borderline[2] n : límite m

bore[1] ['bor] vt **bored; boring**   **1** PIERCE : taladrar, perforar ⟨to bore metals : taladrar metales⟩   **2** OPEN : hacer, abrir

⟨to bore a tunnel : abrir un túnel⟩   **3** WEARY : aburrir

bore[2] → **bear**[1]

bore[3] n   **1** : pesado m, -da f (persona aburrida)   **2** TEDIOUSNESS : pesadez f, lo aburrido   **3** DIAMETER : calibre m

bored ['bord] adj : aburrido ⟨to be bored stiff, to be bored to tears/death : aburrirse como una ostra⟩

boredom ['bordəm] n : aburrimiento m

boring ['borɪŋ] adj : aburrido, pesado

born ['born] adj   **1** : nacido   **2** : nato ⟨she's a born singer : es una cantante nata⟩ ⟨he's a born leader : nació para mandar⟩

borne pp → **bear**[1]

borough ['bəro] n : distrito m municipal

borrow ['bɑro] vt   **1** : pedir prestado, tomar prestado   **2** APPROPRIATE : apropiarse de, adoptar

borrower ['bɑrəwər] n : prestatario m, -ria f

borrowing ['bɑrəwɪŋ] n : préstamo m (en lingüística)

Bosnian ['bɑzniən, 'bɔz-] n : bosnio m, -nia f — **Bosnian** adj

bosom[1] ['bʊzəm, 'bu:-] adj : íntimo

bosom[2] n   **1** CHEST : pecho m   **2** BREAST : pecho m, seno m   **3** CLOSENESS : seno m ⟨in the bosom of her family : en el seno de su familia⟩

bosomed ['bʊzəmd, 'bu:-] adj : con busto ⟨big-bosomed : con mucho busto⟩

boss[1] ['bɔs] vt   **1** SUPERVISE : dirigir, supervisar   **2 to boss around** : mandonear fam, mangonear fam

boss[2] n : jefe m, -fa f; patrón m, -trona f

bossy ['bɔsi] adj **bossier; -est** : mandón fam, autoritario, dominante

botanist ['bɑtənɪst] n : botánico m, -ca f

botany ['bɑtəni] n : botánica f — **botanical** [bə'tænɪkəl] adj

botch[1] ['bɑtʃ] vt : hacer una chapuza de, estropear

botch[2] n : chapuza f

both[1] ['boθ] adj : ambos, ambas; los dos, las dos ⟨both classes : ambas clases, las dos clases⟩

both[2] conj : tanto como ⟨both Ann and her mother are tall : tanto Ana como su madre son altas⟩

both[3] pron : ambos ambas; los dos, las dos ⟨both of the women laughed : ambas mujeres rieron, las dos mujeres rieron⟩ ⟨we both went : fuimos los dos⟩ ⟨he knows both of my sisters : conoce a mis dos hermanas⟩

bother[1] ['bɑðər] vt   **1** IRK : preocupar ⟨nothing's bothering me : nada me preocupa⟩ ⟨what's bothering him? : ¿qué le pasa?⟩   **2** PESTER : molestar, fastidiar — vi **to bother to** : molestarse en, tomar la molestia de

bother[2] n   **1** TROUBLE : molestia f, problemas mpl   **2** ANNOYANCE : molestia f, fastidio m

bothersome ['bɑðərsəm] adj : molesto, fastidioso

bottle[1] ['bɑtəl] vt **bottled; bottling** : embotellar, envasar

bottle[2] n : botella f, frasco m

bottleneck ['bɑtəl,nɛk] *n* 1 : cuello *m* de botella (en un camino) 2 : embotellamiento *m*, atasco *m* (de tráfico) 3 OBSTACLE : obstáculo *m*

bottle opener *n* : abrebotellas *m*

bottom[1] ['bɑtəm] *adj* : más bajo, inferior, de abajo

bottom[2] *n* 1 : fondo *m* (de una caja, de una taza, del mar), pie *m* (de una escalera, una página, una montaña), asiento *m* (de una silla), parte *f* de abajo (de una pila) 2 CAUSE : origen *m*, causa *f* ⟨to get to the bottom of : llegar al fondo de⟩ 3 BUTTOCKS : trasero *m*, nalgas *fpl*

bottomless ['bɑtəmləs] *adj* : sin fondo, sin límites

bottom line *n* 1 : balance *m* final (en contabilidad) 2 **the bottom line** : lo esencial, lo más importante 3 **the bottom line** : el resultado final

botulism ['bɑtʃə,lɪzəm] *n* : botulismo *m*

boudoir [bə'dwar, bu-; 'bu:,-, 'bu-] *n* : tocador *m*

bough ['baʊ] *n* : rama *f*

bought → **buy**[1]

bouillon ['bu:,jɑn; 'bʊl,jɑn, -jən] *n* : caldo *m*

boulder ['boːldər] *n* : canto rodado, roca *f* grande

boulevard ['bʊlə,vard, 'bu:-] *n* : bulevar *m*, boulevard *m*

bounce[1] ['baʊnts] *v* **bounced; bouncing** *vt* 1 : hacer rebotar 2 **to bounce a check** : emitir un cheque sin fondos — *vi* 1 : rebotar 2 : ser devuelto (dícese de un cheque)

bounce[2] *n* : rebote *m*

bouncer ['baʊntsər] *n* : portero *m*; patovica *m Arg, Uru fam*; gorila *m Spain fam*

bouncy ['baʊntsi] *adj* **bouncier; -est** 1 LIVELY : vivo, exuberante, animado 2 RESILIENT : elástico, flexible 3 : que rebota (dícese de una pelota)

bound[1] ['baʊnd] *vt* : delimitar, rodear — *vi* LEAP : saltar, dar brincos

bound[2] *adj* 1 OBLIGED : obligado 2 : encuadernado, empastado ⟨a book bound in leather : un libro encuadernado en cuero⟩ 3 DETERMINED : decidido, empeñado 4 **to be bound to** : ser seguro que, tener que, no caber duda que ⟨it was bound to happen : tenía que suceder⟩ 5 **bound for** : con rumbo a ⟨bound for Chicago : con rumbo a Chicago⟩ ⟨to be homeward bound : ir camino a casa⟩

bound[3] *n* 1 LIMIT : límite *m* 2 LEAP : salto *m*, brinco *m*

boundary ['baʊndri, -dəri] *n, pl* **-aries** : límite *m*, línea *f* divisoria, linde *mf*

boundless ['baʊndləs] *adj* : sin límites, infinito

bounteous ['baʊntiəs] *adj* 1 GENEROUS : generoso 2 ABUNDANT : copioso, abundante — **bounteously** *adv*

bountiful ['baʊntɪfəl] *adj* 1 GENEROUS, LIBERAL : pródigo, generoso 2 ABUNDANT : copioso, abundante

bounty ['baʊnti] *n, pl* **-ties** 1 GENEROSITY : generosidad *f* 2 REWARD : recompensa *f*

bouquet [boː'keɪ, bu:-] *n* 1 : ramo *m*, ramillete *m* 2 FRAGRANCE : bouquet *m*, aroma *m*

bourbon ['bərbən, 'bʊr-] *n* : bourbon *m*, whisky *m* americano

bourgeois[1] ['bʊrʒ,wa, bʊrʒ'wa] *adj* : burgués

bourgeois[2] *n* : burgués *m*, -guesa *f*

bourgeoisie [,bʊrʒ,wa'zi] *n* : burguesía *f*

bout ['baʊt] *n* 1 : encuentro *m*, combate *m* (en deportes) 2 ATTACK : ataque *m* (de una enfermedad) 3 PERIOD, SPELL : período *m* (de actividad)

boutique [bu:'ti:k] *n* : boutique *f*

bovine[1] ['boː,vaɪn, -,vi:n] *adj* : bovino, vacuno

bovine[2] *n* : bovino *m*

bow[1] ['baʊ] *vi* 1 : hacer una reverencia, inclinarse 2 SUBMIT : ceder, resignarse, someterse — *vt* 1 LOWER : inclinar, bajar 2 BEND : doblar

bow[2] ['baʊ] *n* 1 BOWING : reverencia *f*, inclinación *f* 2 : proa *f* (de un barco)

bow[3] ['boː] *vi* CURVE : arquearse, doblarse

bow[4] ['boː] *n* 1 ARCH, CURVE : arco *m*, curva *f* 2 : arco *m* (arma o vara para tocar varios instrumentos de música) 3 : lazo *m*, moño *m* ⟨to tie a bow : hacer un moño⟩

bowel ['baʊəl] *n* 1 INTESTINE : intestino *m* ⟨to move one's bowels, to have a bowel movement : evacuar (el vientre)⟩ 2 **the bowels** : las entrañas ⟨in the bowels of the earth : en las entrañas de la tierra⟩

bower ['baʊər] *n* : enramada *f*

bowl[1] ['boːl] *vi* : jugar a los bolos

bowl[2] *n* : tazón *m*, cuenco *m*, bol *m* ⟨salad bowl : ensaladera⟩

bowler ['boːlər] *n* : jugador *m*, -dora *f* de bolos

bowling ['boːlɪŋ] *n* : bolos *mpl*

bowling alley *n* : bolera *f*, boliche *m*

bowling pin *n* : bolo *m*

bow tie *n* : corbata *f* de moño, pajarita *f Spain*

box[1] ['bɑks] *vt* 1 PACK : empaquetar, embalar, encajonar 2 SLAP : bofetear, cachetear — *vi* : boxear

box[2] *n* 1 CONTAINER : caja *f*, cajón *m* 2 COMPARTMENT : compartimento *m*, palco *m* (en el teatro) 3 SLAP : bofetada *f*, cachetada *f*

boxcar ['bɑks,kar] *n* : vagón *m* de carga, furgón *m*

boxer ['bɑksər] *n* 1 : boxeador *m*, -dora *f* 2 **boxers** *pl* → **boxer shorts**

boxer shorts *n* : boxers *mpl*, calzoncillos *mpl*, calzones *mpl*

boxing ['bɑksɪŋ] *n* : boxeo *m*

box office *n* : taquilla *f*, boletería *f*

box-office ['bɑks'ɔfəs] *adj* : taquillero

box spring *n* : somier *m*

boy ['bɔɪ] *n* 1 : chico *m*, muchacho *m* 2 **or little boy** : niño *m*, chico *m* 3 SON : hijo *m*

boycott[1] ['bɔɪ,kɑt] *vt* : boicotear

boycott[2] *n* : boicot *m*

boyfriend ['bɔɪ,frɛnd] *n* 1 FRIEND : amigo *m* 2 SWEETHEART : novio *m*

boyhood ['bɔɪ,hʊd] *n* : niñez *f*

boyish ['bɔɪʃ] *adj* : de niño, juvenil

bra ['brɑ] → **brassiere**

brace[1] ['breɪs] *v* **braced; bracing** *vt* **1** PROP UP, SUPPORT : apuntalar, sostener **2** INVIGORATE : vigorizar **3** REINFORCE : reforzar — *vi* **to brace oneself** PREPARE : prepararse

brace[2] *n* **1** CLAMP, REINFORCEMENT : abrazadera *f*, refuerzo *m* **2** → **curly brace** **3 braces** *npl* : aparatos *mpl* (de ortodoncia), frenos *mpl Mex*

bracelet ['breɪslət] *n* : brazalete *m*, pulsera *f*

bracken ['brækən] *n* : helecho *m*

bracket[1] ['brækət] *vt* **1** SUPPORT : asegurar, apuntalar **2** : poner entre corchetes **3** CATEGORIZE, GROUP : catalogar, agrupar

bracket[2] *n* **1** SUPPORT : soporte *m* **2** : corchete *m* (marca de puntuación) **3** CATEGORY, CLASS : clase *f*, categoría *f*

brackish ['brækɪʃ] *adj* : salobre

brad ['bræd] *n* : clavo *m* con cabeza pequeña, clavito *m*

brag[1] ['bræg] *vi* **bragged; bragging** : alardear, fanfarronear, jactarse

brag[2] *n* : alarde *m*, jactancia *f*, fanfarronada *f*

braggart ['brægərt] *n* : fanfarrón *m*, -rrona *f fam*; jactancioso *m*, -sa *f*

braid[1] ['breɪd] *vt* : trenzar

braid[2] *n* : trenza *f*

braille ['breɪl] *n* : braille *m*

brain[1] ['breɪn] *vt* : romper la crisma a, aplastar el cráneo a

brain[2] *n* **1** : cerebro *m* **2 brains** *npl* INTELLECT : inteligencia *f*, sesos *mpl*

brainchild ['breɪn,tʃaɪld] *n* IDEA : creación *f*, invento *m*

brainless ['breɪnləs] *adj* : estúpido, tonto

brainstorm ['breɪn,stɔrm] *n* : idea *f* brillante, idea *f* genial

brainy ['breɪni] *adj* **brainier; -est** : inteligente, listo

braise ['breɪz] *vt* **braised; braising** : cocer a fuego lento, estofar

brake[1] ['breɪk] *v* **braked; braking** : frenar

brake[2] *n* : freno *m*

bramble ['bræmbəl] *n* : zarza *f*, zarzamora *f*

bran ['bræn] *n* : salvado *m*

branch[1] ['bræntʃ] *vi* **1** : echar ramas (dicese de una planta) **2** *or* **to branch off** DIVERGE : ramificarse, separarse **3** **to branch out** : diversificarse

branch[2] *n* **1** : rama *f* (de una planta) **2** EXTENSION : ramal *m* (de un camino, un ferrocarril, un río), brazo *m* (de un río), rama *f* (de una familia o un campo de estudio), sucursal *f* (de una empresa), agencia *f* (del gobierno)

brand[1] ['brænd] *vt* **1** : marcar (ganado) **2** LABEL : tachar, tildar ⟨they branded him as a liar : lo tacharon de mentiroso⟩

brand[2] *n* **1** : marca *f* (de ganado) **2** STIGMA : estigma *m* **3** MAKE : marca *f*

brandish ['brændɪʃ] *vt* : blandir

brand–name ['brænd'neɪm] *adj* : de marca

brand name *n* : marca *f*

brand–new ['brænd'nu:, -'nju:] *adj* : nuevo, flamante

brandy ['brændi] *n, pl* **-dies** : brandy *m*

brash ['bræʃ] *adj* **1** IMPULSIVE : impulsivo, impetuoso **2** BRAZEN : excesivamente desenvuelto, descarado

brass ['bræs] *n* **1** : latón *m* **2** GALL, NERVE : descaro *m*, cara *f fam* **3** OFFICERS : mandamases *mpl fam* **4** : metal *m*, metales *mpl* (de una orquesta)

brass band *n* : banda *f* de metales

brassiere ['bræzɪr, brɑ-] *n* : sostén *m*, brasier *m Col, Mex*

brassy ['bræsi] *adj* **brassier; -est** : dorado

brat ['bræt] *n* : mocoso *m*, -sa *f*; niño *m* mimado, niña *f* mimada

bravado [brə'vɑdo] *n, pl* **-does** *or* **-dos** : bravuconadas *fpl*, bravatas *fpl*

brave[1] ['breɪv] *vt* **braved; braving** : afrontar, hacer frente a

brave[2] *adj* **braver; bravest** : valiente, valeroso — **bravely** *adv*

brave[3] *n* : guerrero *m* (nativo americano)

bravery ['breɪvəri] *n* : valor *m*, valentía *f*

bravo ['brɑ,vo:] *n, pl* **-vos** : bravo *m*

brawl[1] ['brɔl] *vi* : pelearse, pegarse

brawl[2] *n* : pelea *f*, reyerta *f*

brawn ['brɔn] *n* : fuerza *f* muscular

brawny ['brɔni] *adj* **brawnier; -est** : musculoso

bray[1] ['breɪ] *vi* : rebuznar

bray[2] *n* : rebuzno *m*

brazen ['breɪzən] *adj* **1** : de latón **2** BOLD : descarado, directo

brazenly ['breɪzənli] *adv* : descaradamente, insolentemente

brazenness ['breɪzənnəs] *n* : descaro *m*, atrevimiento *m*

brazier ['breɪʒər] *n* : brasero *m*

Brazilian [brə'zɪljən] *n* : brasileño *m*, -ña *f* — **Brazilian** *adj*

Brazil nut [brə'zɪl,nʌt] *n* : nuez *f* de Brasil

breach[1] ['britʃ] *vt* **1** PENETRATE : abrir una brecha en, penetrar **2** VIOLATE : infringir, violar

breach[2] *n* **1** VIOLATION : infracción *f*, violación *f* ⟨breach of trust : abuso de confianza⟩ ⟨breach of contract : incumplimiento de contrato⟩ **2** GAP, OPENING : brecha *f*

bread[1] ['bred] *vt* : empanar

bread[2] *n* : pan *m*

bread box *n* : panera *f*

breadstick ['bred,stɪk] *n* : palito *m* de pan; grisín *m Arg, Uru*; colín *m Spain*

breadth ['bretθ] *n* : ancho *m*, anchura *f*

breadwinner ['bred,wɪnər] *n* : sostén *m* de la familia

break[1] ['breɪk] *v* **broke** ['bro:k]; **broken** ['bro:kən]; **breaking** *vt* **1** : romper, quebrar (cristales, un hueso, etc.) ⟨break something in two : partir algo en dos⟩ **2** : descomponer, romper (un aparato, etc.) **3** *or* **to break up** DIVIDE, SPLIT : dividir, separar **4** : abrir (la piel), salir a (la superficie) **5** : romper (el vacío) **6** VIOLATE : infringir, violar (la ley, etc.), romper (un contrato), faltar a (una promesa)

⟨to break the speed limit : exceder el límite de velocidad⟩ **7** SURPASS : batir (un récord), superar **8** CRUSH, RUIN : arruinar, deshacer, destrozar ⟨to break someone's spirit : quebrantar el espíritu de alguien⟩ **9** *or* **to break in** TAME : domar **10** : dar, comunicar ⟨to break the news to someone : darle la noticia a alguien⟩ **11** INTERRUPT, END : interrumpir, cortar (un circuito), romper (el silencio), hacer perder (la concentración), perder (una mala costumbre), superar (un punto muerto) **12** *or* **to break up** DISRUPT : romper (la monotonía, etc.) **13** SLOW : amortiguar (una caída) ⟨without breaking (one's) stride : sin cambiar el paso⟩ **14** SOLVE : esclarecer (un caso), descifrar (un código) **15** : cambiar ⟨to break a twenty : cambiar un billete de veinte dólares⟩ **16** **to break down** KNOCK DOWN : derribar, romper **17** **to break down** DIVIDE : desglosar (gastos, etc.), dividir **18** **to break in** : ablandar (zapatos) **19** **to break in** TRAIN : capacitar (a un nuevo empleado, etc.) **20** **to break off** : partir, romper, separar (un pedazo) **21** **to break open** : forzar (una puerta, etc.) **22** **to break someone of something** : quitarle a alguien la costumbre de hacer algo **23** **to break up** STOP : poner fin a, disolver (una manifestación, etc.), detener (una pelea) **24** **to break up** : hacer pedazos (algo), deshacer (grumos, etc.) — *vi* **1** : romperse, quebrarse ⟨my computer broke : se me rompió la computadora⟩ **2** DISSIPATE : disparse **3** DIVIDE, SPLIT : dividirse **4** : desatarse (dícese de una tormenta), romper (dícese del día) **5** : romper (dícese de olas) **6** CHANGE : cambiar (dícese de la voz), acabarse (dícese del calor, etc.) **7** FALTER : entrecortarse (dícese de la voz) **8** : no poder resistir ⟨he broke under the strain : no pudo con el estrés⟩ **9** DECREASE : bajar ⟨my fever broke : me bajó la fiebre⟩ **10** PAUSE : parar, hacer una pausa **11** : divulgarse, revelarse ⟨the news broke : la noticia se divulgó⟩ **12** **to break away** : separarse **13** **to break down** SEPARATE : descomponerse **14** **to break down** MALFUNCTION : averiarse, descomponerse, estropearse **15** **to break down** : perder el control ⟨she broke down in tears : rompió a llorar⟩ **16** **to break even** : alcanzar su punto de equilibrio (financiero) **17** **to break free/loose** : soltarse **18** **to break in** : entrar (por la fuerza) **19** **to break into** : entrar a (una casa, etc.) para robar **20** **to break off** DETACH : romperse, desprenderse **21** **to break off** END : romper (relaciones, etc.) ⟨she broke off in the middle of a sentence : se detuvo en la mitad de una frase⟩ **22** **to break out** ERUPT : desencadenarse **23** **to break out in** : salirle a uno (un sarpullido, etc.) **24** **to break out of** : escaparse de **25** **to break through** : penetrar **26** **to break up** FRAGMENT : hacerse pedazos **27** **to break up** DISPERSE : disolverse **28** **to**

break up : separarse ⟨they broke up : se separaron⟩ ⟨she broke up with him : rompió con él⟩

break[2] *n* **1** : ruptura *f*, rotura *f*, fractura *f* (de un hueso), claro *m* (entre las nubes), cambio *m* (del tiempo) **2** CHANCE : oportunidad *f* ⟨a lucky break : un golpe de suerte⟩ **3** REST : descanso *m* ⟨to take a break : tomar(se) un descanso⟩ **4** : corte *m*, pausa *f* ⟨commercial break : corte comercial/publicitario, pausa publicitaria/comercial⟩

breakable [ˈbreɪkəbəl] *adj* : quebradizo, frágil

breakage [ˈbreɪkɪdʒ] *n* **1** BREAKING : rotura *f* **2** DAMAGE : destrozos *mpl*, daños *mpl*

breakdown [ˈbreɪkˌdaʊn] *n* **1** : avería *f* (de máquinas), interrupción *f* (de comunicaciones), fracaso *m* (de negociaciones) **2** ANALYSIS : análisis *m*, desglose *m* **3** *or* **nervous breakdown** : crisis *f* nerviosa

break down *vi* **1** : estropearse, descomponerse ⟨the machine broke down : la máquina se descompuso⟩ **2** FAIL : fracasar **3** CRY : echarse a llorar — *vt* **1** DESTROY : derribar, echar abajo **2** OVERCOME : vencer (la resistencia), disipar (sospechas) **3** ANALYZE : analizar, descomponer

breaker [ˈbreɪkər] *n* **1** WAVE : ola *f* grande **2** : interruptor *m* automático (de electricidad)

breakfast[1] [ˈbrɛkfəst] *vi* : desayunar

breakfast[2] *n* : desayuno *m*

break–in [ˈbreɪkˌɪn] *n* : robo *m*

breakneck [ˈbreɪkˌnɛk] *adj* **at breakneck speed** : a una velocidad vertiginosa

break out *vi* **1** : salirse ⟨she broke out in spots : le salieron granos⟩ **2** ERUPT : estallar (dícese de una guerra, la violencia, etc.) **3** ESCAPE : fugarse, escaparse

breakthrough [ˈbreɪkˌθruː] *n* : avance *m* (importante)

breakup [ˈbreɪkˌəp] *n* **1** DIVISION : desintegración *f* **2** : ruptura *f*

break up *vt* **1** DIVIDE : dividir **2** : disolver (una muchedumbre, una pelea, etc.) — *vi* **1** BREAK : romperse **2** SEPARATE : deshacerse, separarse ⟨I broke up with him : terminé con él⟩

breakwater [ˈbreɪkˌwɔtər, -ˌwɑ-] *n* : rompeolas *m*, malecón *m*, espigón *m*

breast [ˈbrɛst] *n* **1** : pecho *m*, seno *m* (de una mujer) **2** CHEST : pecho *m*

breastbone [ˈbrɛstˌboːn] *n* : esternón *m*

breast–feed [ˈbrɛstˌfiːd] *vt* **-fed** [-ˌfɛd] : **-feeding** : amamantar, darle de mamar (a un niño)

breaststroke [ˈbrɛstˌstroːk] *adj* : estilo *m* (de) pecho, estilo *m* braza *Spain*

breath [ˈbrɛθ] *n* **1** BREATHING : aliento *m* ⟨to hold one's breath : aguantar la respiración⟩ ⟨she was short of breath : le faltaba el aire⟩ **2** BREEZE : soplo *m* ⟨a breath of fresh air : un soplo de aire fresco⟩ **3** **under one's breath** : entre dientes, en voz baja

breathe [ˈbriːð] *v* **breathed; breathing** *vi* **1** : respirar **2** LIVE : vivir, respirar **3** **to**

breathe in : aspirar **4 to breathe out** : espirar — *vt* **1** : respirar, aspirar ⟨to breathe fresh air : respirar el aire fresco⟩ ⟨to breathe a sigh of relief : suspirar aliviado⟩ **2** UTTER : decir ⟨I won't breathe a word of this : no diré nada de esto⟩ **3 to breathe in** : aspirar (aire, etc.) **4 to breathe out** : espirar (aire, etc.)

breather ['bri:ðər] *n* : respiro *m*, resuello *m*

breathing ['bri:ðɪŋ] *n* : respiración *f*

breathless ['brɛθləs] *adj* : sin aliento, jadeante

breathlessly ['brɛθləsli] *adv* : entrecortadamente, jadeando

breathlessness ['brɛθləsnəs] *n* : dificultad *f* al respirar

breathtaking ['brɛθ,teɪkɪŋ] *adj* IMPRESSIVE : impresionante, imponente

breeches ['brɪtʃəz, 'bri:-] *npl* : pantalones *mpl*, calzones *mpl*, bombachos *mpl*

breed[1] ['bri:d] *v* **bred** ['brɛd]; **breeding** *vt* **1** : criar (animales) **2** ENGENDER : engendrar, producir ⟨familiarity breeds contempt : la confianza hace perder el respeto⟩ **3** RAISE, REAR : criar, educar — *vi* REPRODUCE : reproducirse

breed[2] *n* **1** : variedad *f* (de plantas), raza *f* (de animales) **2** CLASS : clase *f*, tipo *m*

breeder ['bri:dər] *n* : criador *m*, -dora *f* (de animales); cultivador *m*, -dora *f* (de plantas)

breeze[1] ['bri:z] *vi* **breezed**; **breezing** : pasar con ligereza ⟨to breeze in : entrar como si nada⟩

breeze[2] *n* : brisa *f*, soplo *m* (de aire)

breezy ['bri:zi] *adj* **breezier**; **-est** **1** AIRY, WINDY : aireado, ventoso **2** LIVELY : animado, alegre **3** NONCHALANT : despreocupado

brethren → **brother**

brevity ['brɛvəti] *n*, *pl* **-ties** : brevedad *f*, concisión *f*

brew[1] ['bru:] *vt* **1** : fabricar, elaborar (cerveza) **2** FOMENT : tramar, maquinar, fomentar — *vi* **1** : fabricar cerveza **2** : amenazar ⟨a storm is brewing : una tormenta amenaza⟩

brew[2] *n* **1** BEER : cerveza *f* **2** POTION : brebaje *m*

brewer ['bru:ər] *n* : cervecero *m*, -ra *f*

brewery ['bru:əri, 'bruri] *n*, *pl* **-eries** : cervecería *f*

briar ['braɪər] → **brier**

bribe[1] ['braɪb] *vt* **bribed**; **bribing** : sobornar, cohechar, coimear *Arg, Chile, Peru*

bribe[2] *n* : soborno *m*, cohecho *m*, coima *f Arg, Chile, Peru*, mordida *f CA, Mex*

bribery ['braɪbəri] *n*, *pl* **-eries** : soborno *m*, cohecho *m*, coima *f*, mordida *f CA, Mex*

bric-a-brac ['brɪkə,bræk] *npl* : baratijas *fpl*, chucherías *fpl*

brick[1] ['brɪk] *vt* **to brick up** : tabicar, tapiar

brick[2] *n* : ladrillo *m*

bricklayer ['brɪk,leɪər] *n* : albañil *mf*

bricklaying ['brɪk,leɪɪŋ] *n* : albañilería *f*

bridal ['braɪdəl] *adj* : nupcial, de novia

bride ['braɪd] *n* : novia *f*

bridegroom ['braɪd,gru:m] *n* : novio *m*

bridesmaid ['braɪdz,meɪd] *n* : dama *f* de honor

bridge[1] ['brɪdʒ] *vt* **bridged**; **bridging** **1** : tender un puente sobre **2 to bridge the gap** : salvar las diferencias

bridge[2] *n* **1** : puente *m* **2** : caballete *m* (de la nariz) **3** : puente *m* de mando (de un barco) **4** : puente *m* (dental) **5** : bridge *m* (juego de naipes)

bridle[1] ['braɪdəl] *v* **-dled**; **-dling** *vt* **1** : embridar (un caballo) **2** RESTRAIN : refrenar, dominar, contener — *vi* **to bridle at** : molestarse por, picarse por

bridle[2] *n* : brida *f*

brief[1] ['bri:f] *vt* : dar órdenes a, instruir

brief[2] *adj* : breve, sucinto, conciso

brief[3] *n* **1** : resumen *m*, sumario *m* **2 briefs** *npl* : calzoncillos *mpl*

briefcase ['bri:f,keɪs] *n* : portafolio *m*, maletín *m*

briefing ['bri:fɪŋ] *n* : reunión *f* informativa

briefly ['bri:fli] *adv* : brevemente, por poco tiempo

brier ['braɪər] *n* **1** BRAMBLE : zarza *f*, rosal *m* silvestre **2** HEATH : brezo *m* veteado

brig ['brɪg] *n* **1** : bergantín *m* (barco) **2** : calabozo *m* (en un barco)

brigade [brɪ'geɪd] *n* : brigada *f*

brigadier [,brɪgə'dɪr] *n* : brigadier *m*

brigadier general [,brɪgə'dɪr] *n* : general *m* de brigada

brigand ['brɪgənd] *n* : bandolero *m*, -ra *f*; forajido *m*, -da *f*

bright ['braɪt] *adj* **1** : brillante (dícese del sol, de los ojos), vivo (dícese de un color), claro, fuerte **2** CHEERFUL : alegre, animado ⟨bright and early : muy temprano⟩ **3** INTELLIGENT : listo, inteligente ⟨a bright idea : una idea luminosa⟩

brighten ['braɪtən] *vt* **1** ILLUMINATE : iluminar **2** ENLIVEN : alegrar, animar — *vi* **1** : hacerse más brillante **2 to brighten up** : animarse, alegrarse, mejorar

brightly ['braɪtli] *adv* : vivamente, intensamente, alegremente

brightness ['braɪtnəs] *n* **1** LUMINOSITY : luminosidad *f*, brillantez *f*, resplandor *m*, brillo *m* **2** CHEERFULNESS : alegría *f*, ánimo *m*

brilliance ['brɪljənts] *n* **1** BRIGHTNESS : resplandor *m*, fulgor *m*, brillo *m*, brillantez *f* **2** INTELLIGENCE : inteligencia *f*, brillantez *f*

brilliancy ['brɪljəntsi] → **brilliance**

brilliant ['brɪljənt] *adj* : brillante

brilliantly ['brɪljəntli] *adv* : brillantemente, con brillantez

brim[1] ['brɪm] *vi* **brimmed**; **brimming** **1** *or* **to brim over** : desbordarse, rebosar **2 to brim with tears** : llenarse de lágrimas

brim[2] *n* **1** : ala *f* (de un sombrero) **2** : borde *m* (de una taza o un vaso)

brimful ['brɪm'fʊl] *adj* : lleno hasta el borde, repleto, rebosante

brimless ['brɪmləs] *adj* : sin ala

brimstone ['brɪm,sto:n] *n* : azufre *m*

brindled ['brɪndəld] *adj* : manchado, pinto

brine ['braɪn] *n* **1** : salmuera *f*, escabeche *m* (para encurtir) **2** OCEAN : océano *m*, mar *m*

bring ['brɪŋ] *vt* **brought** ['brɔt]; **bringing 1** : traer, llevar ⟨bring me some coffee : tráigame un café⟩ **2** ATTRACT : traer, atraer **3** : traer (problemas), conseguir (la paz), dar (alegría), obtener (ganancias) ⟨it brought him fame : lo lanzó a la fama⟩ ⟨it brought a smile to her face : la hizo sonreír⟩ **4** : llevar (a un estado) ⟨bring it to a boil : dejarlo hervir⟩ **5** YIELD : rendir, alcanzar ⟨to bring a good price : alcanzar un precio alto⟩ **6** : aportar (experiencia, etc.) **7** : presentar (cargos, etc.) **8** : llevar (a un tema) **9 to bring about** : ocasionar, provocar **10 to bring around** CONVINCE : convencer **11 to bring back** RETURN : devolver **12 to bring back** REINSTATE, REINTRODUCE : restablecer, reintroducir **13 to bring back** : traer (de otro lugar) **14 to bring back** : recordar, traer (recuerdos) **15 to bring down** LOWER : hacer bajar **16 to bring down** OVERTHROW : derrocar **17 to bring down** : derribar (a balazos, etc.) **18 to bring forth** PRODUCE : producir **19 to bring in** : invitar (a expertos), atraer (clientes) **20 to bring in** : ganar (dinero), obtener (ganancias) **21 to bring on** : provocar ⟨you brought this on yourself : te la buscaste⟩ **22 to bring oneself to** : animarse a (hacer algo) **23 to bring out** : sacar, publicar (un libro, etc.) **24 to bring out** EMPHASIZE : hacer resaltar **25 to bring to** REVIVE : resucitar **26 to bring up** REAR : criar **27 to bring up** MENTION : sacar, mencionar

brininess ['braɪninəs] *n* : salinidad *f*

brink ['brɪŋk] *n* : borde *m*

briny ['braɪni] *adj* **brinier; -est** : salobre

brisk ['brɪsk] *adj* **1** LIVELY : rápido, enérgico, brioso **2** INVIGORATING : fresco, estimulante

brisket ['brɪskət] *n* : falda *f*

briskly ['brɪskli] *adv* : rápidamente, enérgicamente, con brío

briskness ['brɪsknəs] *n* : brío *m*, rapidez *f*

bristle¹ ['brɪsəl] *vi* **-tled; -tling 1** : erizarse, ponerse de punta **2** : enfurecerse, enojarse ⟨she bristled at the suggestion : se enfureció ante tal sugerencia⟩ **3** : estar plagado, estar repleto ⟨a city bristling with tourists : una ciudad repleta de turistas⟩

bristle² *n* : cerda *f* (de un animal), pelo *m* (de una planta)

bristly ['brɪsəli] *adj* **bristlier; -est** : áspero y erizado

British¹ ['brɪtɪʃ] *adj* : británico

British² *n* **the British** (*used with a plural verb*) : los británicos

brittle ['brɪtəl] *adj* **brittler; brittlest** : frágil, quebradizo

brittleness ['brɪtəlnəs] *n* : fragilidad *f*

broach ['broːtʃ] *vt* BRING UP : mencionar, abordar, sacar

broad ['brɔd] *adj* **1** WIDE : ancho **2** SPACIOUS : amplio, extenso **3** FULL : pleno ⟨in broad daylight : en pleno día⟩ **4** OB-

VIOUS : claro, evidente **5** TOLERANT : tolerante, liberal **6** GENERAL : general **7** ESSENTIAL : principal, esencial ⟨the broad outline : los rasgos esenciales⟩

broadband¹ ['brɔd,bænd] *adj* : de banda ancha

broadband² *n* : banda *f* ancha

broad bean *n* : haba *f*

broadcast¹ ['brɔd,kæst] *vt* **-cast; -casting 1** SCATTER : esparcir, diseminar **2** CIRCULATE, SPREAD : divulgar, difundir, propagar **3** TRANSMIT : transmitir, emitir

broadcast² *n* **1** TRANSMISSION : transmisión *f*, emisión *f* **2** PROGRAM : programa *m*, emisión *f*

broadcaster ['brɔd,kæstər] *n* : presentador *m*, -dora *f*; locutor *m*, -tora *f*

broadcloth ['brɔd,klɔθ] *n* : paño *m* fino

broaden ['brɔdən] *vt* : ampliar, ensanchar — *vi* : ampliarse, ensancharse

broadloom ['brɔd,luːm] *adj* : tejido en telar ancho

broadly ['brɔdli] *adv* **1** GENERALLY : en general, aproximadamente **2** WIDELY : extensivamente

broad-minded ['brɔd'maɪndəd] *adj* : tolerante, de amplias miras

broad-mindedness [brɔd'maɪndədnəs] *n* : tolerancia *f*

broadside ['brɔd,saɪd] *n* **1** VOLLEY : andanada *f* **2** ATTACK : ataque *m*, invectiva *f*, andanada *f*

brocade [bro'keɪd] *n* : brocado *m*

broccoli ['brɑkəli] *n* : brócoli *m*

brochure [bro'ʃʊr] *n* : folleto *m*

brogue ['broːg] *n* : acento *m* irlandés

broil ['brɔɪl] *vt* : asar a la parrilla

broil² *n* : asado *m*

broiler ['brɔɪlər] *n* **1** GRILL : parrilla *f* **2** : pollo *m* para asar

broke¹ ['broːk] → **break¹**

broke² *adj* : pelado, arruinado ⟨to go broke : arruinarse, quebrar⟩

broken ['broːkən] *adj* **1** DAMAGED, SHATTERED : roto, quebrado, fracturado **2** IRREGULAR, UNEVEN : accidentado, irregular, recortado **3** VIOLATED : roto, quebrantado **4** INTERRUPTED : interrumpido, discontinuo **5** CRUSHED : abatido, quebrantado ⟨a broken man : un hombre destrozado⟩ **6** IMPERFECT : mal ⟨to speak broken English : hablar el inglés con dificultad⟩

brokenhearted [ˌbroːkən'hɑrtəd] *adj* : descorazonado, desconsolado

broker¹ ['broːkər] *vt* : hacer corretaje de

broker² *n* **1** : agente *mf*; corredor *m*, -dora *f* **2** → **stockbroker**

brokerage ['broːkərɪʤ] *n* : corretaje *m*, agencia *f* de corredores

bromine ['broː,miːn] *n* : bromo *m*

bronchial ['brɑŋkiəl] *adj* : bronquial

bronchitis [brɑn'kaɪtəs, brɑŋ-] *n* : bronquitis *f*

bronze¹ ['brɑnz] *vt* **bronzed; bronzing** : broncear

bronze² *n* : bronce *m*

brooch ['broːtʃ, 'bruːtʃ] *n* : broche *m*, prendedor *m*

brood[1] ['bru:d] vt 1 INCUBATE : empollar, incubar 2 PONDER : sopesar, considerar — vi 1 INCUBATE : empollar 2 REFLECT : rumiar, reflexionar 3 WORRY : ponerse melancólico, inquietarse

brood[2] adj : de cría

brood[3] n : nidada f (de pájaros), camada f (de mamíferos)

brooder ['bru:dər] n 1 THINKER : pensador m, -dora f 2 INCUBATOR : incubadora f

brook[1] ['brʊk] vt TOLERATE : tolerar, admitir

brook[2] n : arroyo m

broom ['bru:m, 'brʊm] n 1 : retama f, hiniesta f 2 : escoba f (para barrer)

broomstick ['bru:mˌstɪk, 'brʊm-] n : palo m de escoba

broth ['brɔθ] n, pl **broths** ['brɔθs, 'brɔðz] : caldo m

brothel ['brɑðəl, 'brɔ-] n : burdel m

brother ['brʌðər] n, pl **brothers** also **brethren** ['brðrən, -ðərn] 1 : hermano m 2 KINSMAN : pariente m, familiar m

brotherhood ['brʌðərˌhʊd] n 1 FELLOWSHIP : fraternidad f 2 ASSOCIATION : hermandad f

brother-in-law ['brʌðərɪnˌlɔ] n, pl **brothers-in-law** : cuñado m

brotherly ['brʌðərli] adj : fraternal

brought → bring

brow ['braʊ] n 1 EYEBROW : ceja f 2 FOREHEAD : frente f 3 : cima f ⟨the brow of a hill : la cima de una colina⟩

browbeat ['braʊˌbi:t] vt -beat; -beaten [-ˌbi:tən] or -beat; -beating : intimidar

brown[1] ['braʊn] vt 1 : dorar (en cocina) 2 TAN : broncear — vi 1 : dorarse (en cocina) 2 TAN : broncearse

brown[2] adj : marrón, café, castaño (dícese del pelo), moreno (dícese de la piel)

brown[3] n : marrón m, café m

brown bread n 1 : pan m integral 2 : pan m negro (dulce)

brownie ['braʊni] n : bizcocho m de chocolate y nueces

brownish ['braʊnɪʃ] adj : pardo

brown rice n : arroz m integral

browse ['braʊz] v **browsed; browsing** vt 1 LOOK : mirar 2 : explorar (la Internet) — vi 1 GRAZE : pacer 2 LOOK : mirar, echar un vistazo 3 : navegar (en/por Internet)

browser ['braʊzər] or **Web browser** n : navegador m (de Internet)

bruin ['bru:ɪn] n BEAR : oso m

bruise[1] ['bru:z] vt **bruised; bruising** 1 : contusionar, machucar, magullar (a una persona) 2 DAMAGE : magullar, dañar (frutas) 3 CRUSH : majar 4 HURT : herir (los sentimientos)

bruise[2] n : moretón m, cardenal m, magulladura f (dícese de frutas)

brunch ['brʌntʃ] n : combinación f de desayuno y almuerzo

brunet[1] or **brunette** [bru:'nɛt] adj : moreno

brunet[2] or **brunette** n : moreno m, -na f

brunt ['brʌnt] n **to bear the brunt of** : llevar el peso de, aguantar el mayor impacto de

brush[1] ['brʌʃ] vt 1 : cepillar ⟨I brushed my teeth : me cepillé los dientes⟩ 2 SWEEP : quitar, sacudir ⟨he brushed the dirt off his pants : se sacudió el polvo de los pantalones⟩ 3 PAINT, APPLY : pintar 4 GRAZE : rozar 5 **to brush off** DISREGARD : hacer caso omiso de (algo), no hacerle caso (a alguien) — vi **to brush up (on)** : repasar, refrescar, dar un repaso a

brush[2] n 1 or **brushwood** ['brʌʃˌwʊd] : broza f 2 SCRUB, UNDERBRUSH : maleza f 3 : cepillo m, pincel m (de artista), brocha f 4 TOUCH : roce m 5 SKIRMISH : escaramuza f

brush-off ['brʌʃˌɔf] n **to give the brush-off to** : dar calabazas a

brushstroke ['brʌʃˌstro:k] n : pincelada f

brusque ['brʌsk] adj : brusco — **brusquely** adv

brusqueness ['brʌsknəs] n : brusquedad f

brussels sprout ['brʌsəlzˌspraʊt] n : col f de Bruselas

brutal ['bru:təl] adj : brutal, cruel, salvaje — **brutally** adv

brutality [bru:'tæləti] n, pl **-ties** : brutalidad f

brutalize ['bru:təlˌaɪz] vt **-ized; -izing** : brutalizar, maltratar

brute[1] ['bru:t] adj : bruto ⟨brute force : fuerza bruta⟩

brute[2] n 1 BEAST : bestia f, animal m 2 : bruto m, -ta f; bestia mf (persona)

brutish ['bru:tɪʃ] adj 1 : de animal 2 CRUEL : brutal, salvaje 3 STUPID : bruto, estúpido

bubble[1] ['bʌbəl] vi **-bled; -bling** : burbujear ⟨to bubble over with joy : rebosar de alegría⟩

bubble[2] n : burbuja f

bubble bath n 1 : baño m de espuma/burbujas 2 : espuma f de baño (jabón)

bubble gum n : chicle m (de) globo, chicle m (de) bomba

bubbly ['bʌbəli] adj **bubblier; -est** 1 BUBBLING : burbujeante 2 LIVELY : vivaz, lleno de vida

bubonic plague [bu:'bɑnɪk-, 'bju:-] n : peste f bubónica

buccaneer [ˌbʌkə'nɪr] n : bucanero m

buck[1] ['bʌk] vi 1 : corcovear (dícese de un caballo o un burro) 2 JOLT : dar sacudidas 3 **to buck against** : resistirse a, rebelarse contra 4 **to buck up** : animarse, levantar el ánimo — vt OPPOSE : oponerse a, ir en contra de

buck[2] n, pl **buck** or **bucks** 1 : animal m macho, ciervo m (macho) 2 DOLLAR : dólar m 3 **to pass the buck** fam : pasar la pelota fam

bucket ['bʌkət] n : balde m, cubo m, cubeta f Mex

bucketful ['bʌkətˌfʊl] n : balde m lleno

buckle[1] ['bʌkəl] v **-led; -ling** vt 1 FASTEN : abrochar 2 BEND, TWIST : combar, torcer — vi 1 BEND, TWIST : combarse, torcerse, doblarse (dícese de las rodillas) 2

to buckle down : ponerse a trabajar con esmero **3 to buckle up** : abrocharse

buckle² n **1** : hebilla f **2** TWISTING : torcedura f

buckshot ['bʌkˌʃɑt] n : perdigón m

buckskin ['bʌkˌskɪn] n : gamuza f

buck tooth n : diente m saliente, diente m salido

bucktoothed ['bʌkˌtu:θt] adj : de dientes salientes, de dientes salidos

buckwheat ['bʌkˌʰwi:t] n : alforfón m, trigo m sarraceno

bucolic [bju'kɑlɪk] adj : bucólico

bud¹ ['bʌd] v budded; budding vt GRAFT : injertar — vi : brotar, hacer brotes

bud² n : brote m, yema f, capullo m (de una flor)

Buddhism ['bu:ˌdɪzəm, 'bʊ-] n : budismo m

Buddhist ['bu:dɪst, 'bʊ-] n : budista mf — **Buddhist** adj

budding ['bʌdɪŋ] adj : en ciernes

buddy ['bʌdi] n, pl -dies fam : amigo m, -ga f; compinche mf fam; cuate m, -ta f Mex fam

budge ['bʌdʒ] vi budged; budging **1** MOVE : moverse, desplazarse **2** YIELD : ceder

budget¹ ['bʌdʒət] vt : presupuestar (gastos), asignar (dinero) — vi : presupuestar, planear el presupuesto

budget² n : presupuesto

budgetary ['bʌdʒəˌtɛri] adj : presupuestario

buff¹ ['bʌf] vt POLISH : pulir, sacar brillo a, lustrar

buff² adj : beige, amarillento

buff³ n **1** : beige m, amarillento m **2** ENTHUSIAST : aficionado m, -da f; entusiasta mf

buffalo ['bʌfəˌlo:] n, pl -lo or -loes **1** : búfalo m **2** BISON : bisonte m

buffer ['bʌfər] n **1** BARRIER : barrera f ⟨buffer state : estado tapón⟩ **2** SHOCK ABSORBER : amortiguador m

buffet¹ ['bʌfət] vt : golpear, zarandear, sacudir

buffet² n BLOW : golpe m

buffet³ [ˌbʌ'feɪ, ˌbu-] n **1** : bufete m, bufé m (comida) **2** SIDEBOARD : aparador m

buffoon [ˌbʌ'fu:n] n : bufón m, -fona f; payaso m, -sa f

bug¹ ['bʌg] vt bugged; bugging **1** PESTER : fastidiar, molestar **2** : ocultar micrófonos en

bug² n **1** INSECT : bicho m, insecto m **2** DEFECT : defecto m, falla f, problema m **3** GERM : microbio m, virus m **4** MICROPHONE : micrófono m

bugaboo ['bʌgəˌbu:] n : pesadilla f, terror m, coco m

bugbear ['bʌgˌbær] n : problema m, obstáculo m

buggy ['bʌgi] n, pl -gies **1** : calesa f (tirada por caballos) **2** : cochecito m (para niños)

bugle ['bju:gəl] n : clarín m, corneta f

bugler ['bju:gələr] n : corneta mf

build¹ ['bɪld] v built ['bɪlt]; building vt **1** CONSTRUCT : construir, edificar, ensamblar, levantar **2** DEVELOP : desarrollar, elaborar, forjar **3** INCREASE : incrementar, aumentar — vi **1 to build on** : ampliar (conocimientos, etc.) **2 to build up** : aumentar, intensificar

build² n PHYSIQUE : físico m, complexión f

builder ['bɪldər] n : constructor m, -tora f; contratista mf

building ['bɪldɪŋ] n **1** EDIFICE : edificio m **2** CONSTRUCTION : construcción f

buildup ['bɪldˌʌp] n : acumulación f

built-in ['bɪlt'ɪn] adj **1** : empotrado ⟨built-in cabinets : armarios empotrados⟩ **2** INHERENT : incorporado, intrínseco

built-up ['bɪlt'ʌp] adj : urbanizado

bulb ['bʌlb] n **1** : bulbo m (de una planta), cabeza f (de ajo), cubeta f (de un termómetro) **2** LIGHTBULB : bombilla f, foco m, bombillo m CA, Col, Ven

bulbous ['bʌlbəs] adj : bulboso

Bulgarian [bʌl'gæriən, bʊl-] n **1** : búlgaro m, -ra f **2** : búlgaro m (idioma) — **Bulgarian** adj

bulge¹ ['bʌldʒ] vi bulged; bulging : abultar, sobresalir

bulge² n : bulto m, protuberancia f

bulk¹ ['bʌlk] vi — vi hinchar — vi EXPAND, SWELL : ampliarse, hincharse

bulk² n **1** SIZE, VOLUME : volumen m, tamaño m **2** FIBER : fibra f **3** MASS : mole f **4 the bulk of** : la mayor parte de **5 in ~** : en grandes cantidades

bulkhead ['bʌlkˌhɛd] n : mamparo m

bulky ['bʌlki] adj bulkier; -est : voluminoso, grande

bull¹ ['bʊl] adj : macho

bull² n **1** : toro m, macho m (de ciertas especies) **2** : bula f (papal) **3** DECREE : decreto m, edicto m

bulldog ['bʊlˌdɔg] n : bulldog m

bulldoze ['bʊlˌdo:z] vt -dozed; -dozing **1** LEVEL : nivelar (el terreno), derribar (un edificio) **2** FORCE : forzar ⟨he bulldozed his way through : se abrió paso a codazos⟩

bulldozer ['bʊlˌdo:zər] n : bulldozer m

bullet ['bʊlət] n : bala f

bulletin ['bʊlətən, -lətən] n **1** or **news bulletin** : boletín m informativo, boletín m de noticias **2** NEWSLETTER : boletín m

bulletin board n : tablón m de anuncios

bulletproof ['bʊlətˌpru:f] adj : antibalas, a prueba de balas

bullfight ['bʊlˌfaɪt] n : corrida f (de toros)

bullfighter ['bʊlˌfaɪtər] n : torero m, -ra f; matador m

bullfighting ['bʊlˌfaɪtɪŋ] n : lidia f, toreo m

bullfrog ['bʊlˌfrɔg] n : rana f toro

bullheaded ['bʊl'hɛdəd] adj : testarudo

bullion ['bʊljən] n : oro m en lingotes, plata f en lingotes

bullish ['bʊlɪʃ] adj : alcista

bullock ['bʊlək] n **1** STEER : buey m, toro m castrado **2** : toro m joven, novillo m

bullring ['bʊlˌrɪŋ] n : plaza f de toros, redondel m, ruedo m

bull's-eye ['bʊlzˌaɪ] n, pl **bull's-eyes** : diana f, blanco m

bully¹ ['bʊli] vt **-lied; -lying** : intimidar, amedrentar, mangonear

bully² n, pl **-lies** : matón m; bravucón m, -na f

bulrush ['bʊlˌrʌʃ] n : especie f de junco

bulwark ['bʊlˌwərk, -ˌwɔrk; 'bʌlˌwərk] n : baluarte m, bastión f

bum¹ ['bʌm] v **bummed; bumming** vi **to bum around** : vagabundear, vagar — vt : gorronear fam, sablear fam

bum² adj : inútil, malo ⟨a bum rap : una acusación falsa⟩

bum³ n **1** LOAFER : vago m, -ga f **2** HOBO, TRAMP : vagabundo m, -da f

bumblebee ['bʌmbəlˌbi:] n : abejorro m

bump¹ ['bʌmp] vt : chocar contra, golpear contra, dar ⟨to bump one's head : darse (un golpe) en la cabeza⟩ — vi **to bump into** MEET : encontrarse con, tropezarse con

bump² n **1** BULGE : bulto m, protuberancia f **2** IMPACT : golpe m, choque m **3** JOLT : sacudida f

bumper¹ ['bʌmpər] adj : extraordinario, récord ⟨a bumper crop : una cosecha abundante⟩

bumper² n : parachoques mpl

bumpkin ['bʌmpkən] n : palurdo m, -da f

bumpy ['bʌmpi] adj **bumpier; -est** : desigual, lleno de baches (dícese de un camino), agitado (dícese de un vuelo en avión)

bun ['bʌn] n **1** : bollo m (dulce) **2** ROLL : panecito m **3** CHIGNON : moño m, chongo m Mex

bunch¹ ['bʌntʃ] vt : agrupar, amontonar — vi **to bunch up** : amontonarse, agruparse, fruncirse (dícese de una tela)

bunch² n : grupo m, montón m, ramo m (de flores)

bundle¹ ['bʌndəl] vt **-dled; -dling** : liar, atar

bundle² n **1** : fardo m, atado m, bulto m, haz m (de palos) **2** PARCEL : paquete m **3** LOAD : montón m ⟨a bundle of money : un montón de dinero⟩

bungalow ['bʌŋgəˌlo:] n : tipo de casa de un solo piso

bungle¹ ['bʌŋgəl] vt **-gled; -gling** : echar a perder, malograr

bungle² n : chapuza f, desatino m

bungler ['bʌŋgələr] n : chapucero m, -ra f; inepto m, -ta f

bunion ['bʌnjən] n : juanete m

bunk¹ ['bʌŋk] vi : dormir (en una litera)

bunk² n **1** or **bunk bed** : litera f **2** NONSENSE : tonterías fpl, bobadas fpl

bunker ['bʌŋkər] n **1** : carbonera f (en un barco) **2** SHELTER : búnker m

bunny ['bʌni] n, pl **-nies** : conejo m, -ja f

buoy¹ ['bu:i, 'bɔɪ] vt **to buoy up 1** : mantener a flote **2** CHEER, HEARTEN : animar, levantar el ánimo a

buoy² n : boya f

buoyancy ['bɔɪənsi, 'bu:jən-] n **1** : flotabilidad f **2** OPTIMISM : confianza f, optimismo m

buoyant ['bɔɪənt, 'bu:jənt] adj : boyante, flotante

bur or **burr** ['bər] n : abrojo m (de una planta)

burden¹ ['bərdən] vt : cargar, oprimir

burden² n : carga f, peso m

burdensome ['bərdənsəm] adj : oneroso

bureau ['bjʊro] n **1** CHEST OF DRAWERS : cómoda f **2** DEPARTMENT : departamento m (del gobierno) **3** AGENCY : agencia f ⟨travel bureau : agencia de viajes⟩

bureaucracy [bjʊ'rɑkrəsi] n, pl **-cies** : burocracia f

bureaucrat ['bjʊrəˌkræt] n : burócrata mf

bureaucratic [ˌbjʊrə'krætɪk] adj : burocrático

burgeon ['bərdʒən] vi : florecer, retoñar, crecer

burger ['bərgər] n **1** → hamburger **2** PATTY : hamburguesa f ⟨a turkey burger : una hamburguesa de pavo⟩

burglar ['bərglər] n : ladrón m, -drona f

burglar alarm n : alarma f antirrobo

burglarize ['bərgləˌraɪz] vt **-ized; -izing** : robar

burglary ['bərgləri] n, pl **-glaries** : robo m

burgle ['bərgəl] vt **-gled; -gling** : robar

burgundy ['bərgəndi] n, pl **-dies** : borgoña m, vino m de Borgoña

burial ['bɛriəl] n : entierro m, sepelio m

burlap ['bərlæp] n : arpillera f

burlesque¹ [bər'lɛsk] vt **-lesqued; -lesquing** : parodiar

burlesque² n **1** PARODY : parodia f **2** REVUE : revista f (musical)

burly ['bərli] adj **burlier; -est** : fornido, corpulento, musculoso

Burmese [ˌbərˈmiːz, -ˈmiːs] n : birmano m, -na f — **Burmese** adj

burn¹ ['bərn] v **burned** or **burnt** ['bərnt]; **burning** vt **1** : quemar (leña, etc.) ⟨to burn a candle : encender una vela⟩ **2** : quemar (piel, ropa, etc.) ⟨I burned my hand : me quemé la mano⟩ ⟨to burn a hole in something : quemar algo (haciendo un agujero)⟩ **3** STING : hacer escocer **4** OVERCOOK : quemar **5** CONSUME : usar, gastar ⟨a gas-burning engine : un motor que funciona con gas⟩ ⟨to burn (up) calories : quemar calorías⟩ **6** CHEAT : estafar, timar **7** RECORD, WRITE : quemar (un DVD, etc.) **8** or **to burn down** : quemar, incendiar (un edificio) **9 to burn out** : quemar (un motor, etc.) **10 to burn up** : quemar, incendiar ⟨the fire burned up homes and forests : el incendio arrasó con casas y bosques⟩ — vi **1** : arder (dícese de un fuego o un edificio), quemarse ⟨I smell something burning : huele a quemado⟩ ⟨the house burned to the ground : la casa fue arrasada por el incendio⟩ **2** : estar prendido, estar encendido ⟨we left the lights burning : dejamos las luces encendidas⟩ **3** STING : arder **4** : quemarse (dícese de la comida) **5** or **to burn up** : tener fiebre ⟨you're burning (up)! : ¡estás hirviendo!⟩ **6** : arder (dícese de las mejillas, etc.) **7 to burn down** : incendiarse, quemarse **8 to burn off** : disiparse (dícese de la niebla, etc.) **9 to burn out** : consumirse, apagarse **10 to burn out** : quemarse (dícese de un motor, etc.) **11 to burn out** : quemarse, agotarse (dícese de una persona) **12 to burn to death** : morir quemado **13 to burn up** : desintegrarse (dícese de un asteroide, etc.) **14 to burn with** : arder de ⟨he was burning with jealousy : ardía de celos⟩

burn² n : quemadura f

burned out or **burnt out** adj **1** : con el interior destruido (dícese de un edificio) **2** : quemado, agotado (dícese de una persona)

burner [ˈbərnər] n : quemador m

burnish [ˈbərnɪʃ] vt : bruñir

burp¹ [ˈbərp] vi : eructar — vt : hacer eructar

burp² n : eructo m

burr → bur

burrito [bəˈriːt̬o] n, pl **-tos** : burrito m

burro [ˈbəro, ˈbʊr-] n, pl **-os** : burro m

burrow¹ [ˈbəro] vi **1** : cavar, hacer una madriguera **2 to burrow into** : hurgar en — vt : cavar, excavar

burrow² n : madriguera f, conejera f (de un conejo)

bursar [ˈbərsər] n : administrador m, -dora f

burst¹ [ˈbərst] v **burst; bursting** vi **1** : reventarse (dícese de una llanta o un globo), estallar (dícese de obuses o fuegos artificiales), romperse (dícese de un dique) **2 to burst in** : irrumpir en **3 to burst into (something)** or **to burst out in (something)** : empezar a (hacer algo), echar a (hacer algo) ⟨to burst into tears : echarse a llorar⟩ — vt : reventar

burst² n **1** EXPLOSION : estallido m, explosión f, reventón m (de una llanta) **2** OUTBURST : arranque m (de actividad, de velocidad), arrebato m (de ira), salva f (de aplausos)

bury [ˈberi] vt **buried; burying 1** INTER : enterrar, sepultar **2** HIDE : esconder, ocultar **3 to bury oneself in** : enfrascarse en

bus¹ [ˈbʌs] v **bused** or **bussed** [ˈbʌst] : **busing** or **bussing** [ˈbʌsɪŋ] vt : transportar en autobús — vi : viajar en autobús

bus² n : autobús m, bus m, camión m Mex, colectivo m Arg, Bol, Peru

busboy [ˈbʌsˌbɔɪ] n : ayudante mf de camarero

bus driver n : chofer mf (de autobús); conductor m, -tora f (de autobús); busero m, -ra f CA; camionero m, -ra f Mex; colectivero m, -ra f Arg

bush [ˈbʊʃ] n **1** SHRUB : arbusto m, mata f **2** THICKET : maleza f, matorral m

bushel [ˈbʊʃəl] n : medida de áridos igual a 35.24 litros

bushing [ˈbʊʃɪŋ] n : cojinete m

bushy [ˈbʊʃi] adj **bushier; -est** : espeso, poblado ⟨bushy eyebrows : cejas pobladas⟩

busily [ˈbɪzəli] adv : afanosamente, diligentemente

business [ˈbɪznəs, -nəz-] n **1** OCCUPATION : ocupación f, oficio m **2** DUTY, MISSION : misión f, deber m, responsabilidad f **3** ESTABLISHMENT, FIRM : empresa f, firma f, negocio m, comercio m **4** COMMERCE : negocios mpl, comercio m ⟨to go out of business : cerrar⟩ ⟨to open for business : abrir al público⟩ ⟨business hours : horas de atención al público⟩ ⟨business meeting/trip : reunión/viaje de negocios⟩ **5** AFFAIR, MATTER : asunto m, cuestión f, cosa f ⟨it's none of your business : no es asunto tuyo⟩ ⟨to have no business doing something : no tener derecho a hacer algo⟩

business class n : clase f ejecutiva, clase f preferente Spain

business day n : día m hábil, día m laborable

businesslike [ˈbɪznəsˌlaɪk, -nəz-] n : profesional

businessman [ˈbɪznəsˌmæn, -nəz-] n, pl **-men** [-mən, -ˌmen] : empresario m, hombre m de negocios

businesswoman [ˈbɪznəsˌwʊmən, -nəz-] n, pl **-women** [-ˌwɪmən] : empresaria f, mujer f de negocios

bus shelter n : marquesina f

bus station n : estación f de autobús, terminal f de autobús

bus stop n : parada f de autobús

bust¹ [ˈbʌst] vt **1** BREAK, SMASH : romper, estropear, destrozar **2** TAME : domar, amansar (un caballo) — vi : romperse, estropearse

bust² n **1** : busto m (en la escultura) **2** BREASTS : pecho m, senos mpl, busto m

bustle¹ [ˈbʌsəl] vi **-tled; -tling to bustle about** : ir y venir, trajinar, ajetrearse

bustle² n **1** or **hustle and bustle** : bullicio m, ajetreo m **2** : polisón m (en la ropa femenina)

busy¹ [ˈbɪzi] vt **busied; busying to busy oneself with** : ocuparse con, ponerse a, entretenerse con

busy² adj **busier; -est 1** OCCUPIED : ocupado, atareado ⟨he's busy working : está ocupado en su trabajo⟩ ⟨the telephone was busy : el teléfono estaba ocupado⟩ **2** BUSTLING : concurrido, animado ⟨a busy street : una calle concurrida, una calle con mucho tránsito⟩

busybody [ˈbɪziˌbɑdi] n, pl **-bodies** : entrometido m, -da f; metiche mf fam; metomentodo mf

busy signal n : tono m de ocupado, señal f de comunicando Spain

but¹ [ˈbʌt] conj **1** NEVERTHELESS : pero, no obstante, sin embargo ⟨I called her but she didn't answer : la llamé pero no contestó⟩ **2** EXCEPT : pero ⟨I'd do it, but I don't have time : lo haría pero no me da tiempo⟩ ⟨I had no choice but to leave : no tuve más remedio que irme⟩ ⟨they do nothing but argue : no hacen más que discutir⟩ **3** (used for emphasis) : pero ⟨but it's not fair! : ¡pero no es justo!⟩ **4** THAT : que ⟨there is no doubt but he is lazy : no cabe duda que es perezoso⟩ **5** WITHOUT : sin que **6** YET : pero ⟨he was poor but proud : era pobre pero orgulloso⟩ **7 but then** HOWEVER : pero

but · bygone

but² *prep* **1** EXCEPT : excepto, menos ⟨everyone but Charles : todos menos Charles⟩ ⟨no one but you would think that : sólo a ti te ocurriría eso⟩ ⟨we've had nothing but rain : no hace más que llover⟩ ⟨the last but one : el penúltimo⟩ **2 but for** : si no fuera por

butcher¹ ['buʧər] *vt* **1** SLAUGHTER : matar (animales) **2** KILL : matar, asesinar, masacrar **3** BOTCH : estropear, hacer una chapuza

butcher² *n* **1** : carnicero *m*, -ra *f* **2** KILLER : asesino *m*, -na *f* **3** BUNGLER : chapucero *m*, -ra *f*

butcher shop *n* : carnicería *f*

butler ['bʌtlər] *n* : mayordomo *m*

butt¹ ['bʌt] *vt* **1** : embestir (con los cuernos), darle un cabezazo a **2** ABUT : colindar con, bordear — *vi* **to butt in 1** INTERRUPT : interrumpir **2** MEDDLE : entrometerse, meterse

butt² *n* **1** BUTTING : embestida *f* (de cuernos), cabezazo *m* **2** TARGET : blanco *m* ⟨the butt of their jokes : el blanco de sus bromas⟩ **3** BOTTOM, END : extremo *m*, culata *f* (de un rifle), colilla *f* (de un cigarrillo)

butte ['bju:t] *n* : colina *f* empinada y aislada

butter¹ ['bʌtər] *vt* **1** : untar con mantequilla **2 to butter up** : halagar

butter² *n* : mantequilla *f*

buttercup ['bʌtər,kʌp] *n* : ranúnculo *m*

butterfat ['bʌtər,fæt] *n* : grasa *f* de la leche

butterfly ['bʌtər,flaɪ] *n*, *pl* **-flies** : mariposa *f*

buttermilk ['bʌtər,mɪlk] *n* : suero *m* de manteca/mantequilla

butternut ['bʌtər,nʌt] *n* : nogal *m* ceniciento (árbol)

butterscotch ['bʌtər,skɑʧ] *n* : caramelo *m* duro hecho con mantequilla

buttery ['bʌtəri] *adj* : mantecoso

buttock ['bʌtək, -tɑk] *n* : nalga *f*

button¹ ['bʌtən] *vt* : abrochar, abotonar — *vi* : abrocharse, abotonarse

button² *n* : botón *m*

buttonhole¹ ['bʌtən,ho:l] *vt* **-holed; -holing** : acorralar

buttonhole² *n* : ojal *m*

buttress¹ ['bʌtrəs] *vt* : apoyar, reforzar

buttress² *n* **1** : contrafuerte *m* (en la arquitectura) **2** SUPPORT : apoyo *m*, sostén *m*

buxom ['bʌksəm] *adj* : con mucho busto, con mucho pecho

buy¹ ['baɪ] *v* **bought** ['bɔt]; **buying** *vt* **1** : comprar **2** BELIEVE : tragarse **3** BRIBE : comprar **4 to buy into** : comprar acciones de **5 to buy into** BELIEVE : tragarse **6 to buy off** BRIBE : comprar **7 to buy out** : comprar la parte de **8 to buy time** : ganar tiempo **9 to buy up** : comprar (en grandes cantidades) — *vi* : comprar

buy² *n* BARGAIN : compra *f*, ganga *f*

buyer ['baɪər] *n* : comprador *m*, -dora *f*

buzz¹ ['bʌz] *vi* : zumbar (dícese de un insecto), sonar (dícese de un teléfono o un despertador)

buzz² *n* **1** : zumbido *m* (de insectos) **2** : murmullo *m*, rumor *m* (de voces)

buzzard ['bʌzərd] *n* VULTURE : buitre *m*, zopilote *m* CA, Mex

buzzer ['bʌzər] *n* : timbre *m*, chicharra *f*

buzzword ['bʌz,wərd] *n* : palabra *f* de moda

by¹ ['baɪ] *adv* **1** NEAR : cerca ⟨he lives close by : vive muy cerca⟩ **2** PAST : pasando ⟨the train went by : pasó el tren⟩ ⟨they rushed by : pasaron corriendo⟩ ⟨as time goes by : con el paso del tiempo⟩ **3 by and by** : poco después, dentro de poco **4 by and large** : en general **5 to put by** : reservar, poner a un lado, apartar **6 to stop by** : pasar por casa, hacer una visita

by² *prep* **1** NEAR : cerca de, al lado de, junto a ⟨she was standing by the window : estaba parada al lado de la ventana⟩ **2** PAST : por, por delante de ⟨they walked by him : pasaron por delante de él⟩ **3** VIA : por ⟨she left by the back door : salió por la puerta trasera⟩ **4** (*indicating manner*) ⟨made by hand : hecho a mano⟩ ⟨he took her by the hand : la tomó de la mano⟩ ⟨you learn by making mistakes : uno aprende equivocándose⟩ ⟨I know her by sight/name : la conozco de vista/nombre⟩ ⟨she read by candlelight : leía a la luz de una vela⟩ ⟨to travel by train : viajar en tren⟩ ⟨to pay by credit card : pagar con tarjeta de crédito⟩ **5** (*indicating cause or agent*) : por ⟨built by the Romans : construido por los romanos⟩ ⟨a book by Borges : un libro de Borges⟩ ⟨I was surprised by the result : el resultado me sorprendió⟩ **6** AT : por ⟨stop/come by my house tonight : pásate por casa esta noche⟩ **7** DURING : de, durante ⟨by night : de noche⟩ **8** (*in expressions of time*) : para ⟨we'll be there by ten : estaremos allí para las diez⟩ ⟨by then : para entonces⟩ **9** : por ⟨I swear by all that's sacred : te lo juro por todo lo sagrado⟩ ⟨he said he'd do it, and by God, he did it! : dijo que lo haría y, efectivamente, lo hizo⟩ **10** : con ⟨what do you mean by that? : ¿qué quieres decir con eso?⟩ **11** (*with numbers, rates, and amounts*) : por ⟨to pay by the hour : pagar por hora⟩ ⟨it was reduced by 10 percent : se redujo (en) un 10 por ciento⟩ ⟨by a narrow margin : por un estrecho margen⟩ ⟨10 feet by 20 feet : 10 pies por 20 pies⟩ ⟨divide 100 by 10 : dividir 100 por/entre 10⟩ **12** : según ⟨by my watch, it's ten o'clock : según mi reloj, son las diez⟩ ⟨that's fine by me : por mí no hay problema⟩ ⟨to play by the rules : respetar las reglas⟩ **13** : a ⟨little by little : poco a poco⟩ **14** : por ⟨one by one : uno por uno⟩ ⟨two by two : de dos en dos⟩ **15 by oneself** : solo

by and by *adv* : dentro de poco

bye ['baɪ] *interj* *fam* : ¡adiós!, ¡chao!, ¡hasta luego!

bygone¹ ['baɪ,gɔn] *adj* : pasado

bygone² *n* **let bygones be bygones** : lo pasado, pasado está

bylaw *or* **byelaw** ['baɪ,lɔ] *n* : norma *f*, reglamento *m*

byline ['baɪ,laɪn] *n* : data *f*

bypass¹ ['baɪ,pæs] *vt* : evitar

bypass² *n* **1** BELTWAY : carretera *f* de circunvalación **2** DETOUR : desvío *m*

by-product ['baɪ,prɑdəkt] *n* : subproducto *m*, producto *m* derivado

bystander ['baɪ,stændər] *n* : espectador *m*, -dora *f*

byte ['baɪt] *n* : byte *m*

byway ['baɪ,weɪ] *n* : camino *m* (apartado), carretera *f* secundaria

byword ['baɪ,wərd] *n* **1** PROVERB : proverbio *m*, refrán *m* **2 to be a byword for** : ser sinónimo de

C

c ['si:] *n*, *pl* **c's** *or* **cs** **1** : tercera letra del alfabeto inglés **2 C** : do *m* ⟨C sharp/flat : do sostenido/bemol⟩

cab ['kæb] *n* **1** TAXI : taxi *m* **2** : cabina *f* (de un camión o una locomotora) **3** CARRIAGE : coche *m* de caballos

cabal [kə'bɑl, -'bæl] *n* **1** INTRIGUE, PLOT : conspiración *f*, complot *m*, intriga *f* **2** : grupo *m* de conspiradores

cabaret [,kæbə'reɪ] *n* : cabaret *m*

cabbage ['kæbɪʤ] *n* : col *f*, repollo *m*

cabbie *or* **cabby** ['kæbi] *n* : taxista *mf*

cabin ['kæbən] *n* **1** HUT : cabaña *f*, choza *f*, barraca *f* **2** STATEROOM : camarote *m* **3** : cabina *f* (de un automóvil o avión)

cabinet ['kæbnət] *n* **1** CUPBOARD : armario *m* **2** : gabinete *m*, consejo *m* de ministros **3 medicine cabinet** : botiquín *m*

cabinetmaker ['kæbnət,meɪkər] *n* : ebanista *m*

cable¹ ['keɪbəl] *vt* **-bled; -bling** : enviar un cable, telegrafiar

cable² *n* **1** : cable *m* (para colgar o sostener algo) **2** : cable *m* eléctrico **3** → **cable television**

cable car *n* → **streetcar 2** : funicular *m* (en una montaña), teleférico *m*

cable television *n* : cable *m*, televisión *f* por cable

caboose [kə'bu:s] *n* : furgón *m* de cola, cabús *m* Mex

cabstand ['kæb,stænd] *n* : parada *f* de taxis

cacao [kə'kaʊ, -'keɪo] *n*, *pl* **cacaos** : cacao *m*

cache¹ ['kæʃ] *vt* **cached; caching** : esconder, guardar en un escondrijo

cache² *n* **1** : escondite *m*, escondrijo *m* ⟨cache of weapons : escondrijo de armas⟩ **2** : cache *m* ⟨cache memory : memoria cache⟩

cachet [kæ'ʃeɪ] *n* : caché *m*, prestigio *m*

cackle¹ ['kækəl] *vi* **-led; -ling 1** CLUCK : cacarear **2** : reírse o carcajearse estridentemente ⟨he was cackling with delight : estaba carcajeándose de gusto⟩

cackle² *n* **1** : cacareo *m* (de una polla) **2** LAUGH : risa *f* estridente

cacophony [kæ'kɑfəni, -'kɔ-] *n*, *pl* **-nies** : cacofonía *f*

cactus ['kæktəs] *n*, *pl* **cacti** [-,taɪ] *or* **-tuses** : cacto *m*, cactus *m*

cadaver [kə'dævər] *n* : cadáver *m*

cadaveric [kə'dævərɪk] *adj* : cadavérico (en medicina)

cadaverous [kə'dævərəs] *adj* : cadavérico

caddie¹ *or* **caddy** ['kædi] *vi* **caddied; caddying** : trabajar de caddie, hacer de caddie

caddie² *or* **caddy** *n*, *pl* **-dies** : caddie *m*

caddy ['kædi] *n*, *pl* **-dies** : cajita *f* para té

cadence ['keɪdənts] *n* : cadencia *f*, ritmo *m*

cadenced ['keɪdəntst] *adj* : cadencioso, rítmico

cadet [kə'dɛt] *n* : cadete *mf*

cadmium ['kædmiəm] *n* : cadmio *m*

cadre ['kæ,dreɪ, 'kɑ-, -,dri:] *n* : cuadro *m* (de expertos)

café [kæ'feɪ, kə-] *n* : café *m*, cafetería *f*

cafeteria [,kæfə'tɪriə] *n* : cafetería *f*, restaurante *m* de autoservicio

caffeine [kæ'fi:n] *n* : cafeína *f*

cage¹ ['keɪʤ] *vt* **caged; caging** : enjaular

cage² *n* : jaula *f*

cagey ['keɪʤi] *adj* **cagier; -est 1** CAUTIOUS : cauteloso, reservado **2** SHREWD : astuto, vivo — **cagily** [-ʤəli] *adv*

cahoots [kə'hu:ts] *n* **to be in cahoots** *fam* : estar confabulado

caisson ['keɪ,sɑn, -sən] *n* **1** : cajón *m* de municiones **2** : cajón *m* hidráulico

cajole [kə'ʤo:l] *vt* **-joled; -joling** : engatusar

cake¹ ['keɪk] *v* **caked; caking** *vt* : cubrir ⟨caked with mud : cubierto de barro⟩ — *vi* : endurecerse

cake² *n* **1** : torta *f*, bizcocho *m*, pastel *m* **2** : pastilla *f* (de jabón) **3 to take the cake** : llevarse la palma, ser el colmo

calabash ['kælə,bæʃ] *n* : calabaza *f*

calamari [,kɑlə'mɑri] *ns & pl* : calamares *mpl*

calamine ['kælə,maɪn] *n* : calamina *f* ⟨calamine lotion : loción de calamina⟩

calamitous [kə'læmətəs] *adj* : desastroso, catastrófico, calamitoso — **calamitously** *adv*

calamity [kə'læməti] *n*, *pl* **-ties** : desastre *m*, desgracia *f*, calamidad *f*

calcium ['kælsiəm] *n* : calcio *m*

calculate ['kælkjə,leɪt] *v* **-lated; -lating** *vt* **1** COMPUTE : calcular, computar **2** ESTIMATE : calcular, creer **3** INTEND : planear, tener la intención de ⟨I calculated on spending $100 : planeaba gastar $100⟩ — *vi* : calcular, hacer cálculos

calculated ['kælkjə,leɪtəd] *adj* **1** ESTIMATED : calculado **2** DELIBERATE : intencional, premeditado, deliberado

calculating [ˈkælkjəˌleɪtɪŋ] *adj* SHREWD : calculador, astuto

calculation [ˌkælkjəˈleɪʃən] *n* : cálculo *m*

calculator [ˈkælkjəˌleɪtər] *n* : calculadora *f*

calculus [ˈkælkjələs] *n*, *pl* **-li** [-ˌlaɪ] **1** : cálculo *m* ⟨differential calculus : cálculo diferencial⟩ **2** TARTAR : sarro *m* (dental)

caldron [ˈkɔldrən] → **cauldron**

calendar [ˈkæləndər] *n* **1** : calendario *m* **2** SCHEDULE : calendario *m*, programa *m*, agenda *f*

calf [ˈkæf, ˈkaf] *n*, *pl* **calves** [ˈkævz, ˈkavz] **1** : becerro *m*, -rra *f*; ternero *m*, -ra *f* (de vacunos) **2** : cría *f* (de otros mamíferos) **3** : pantorrilla *f* (de la pierna)

calfskin [ˈkæfˌskɪn] *n* : piel *f* de becerro

caliber or **calibre** [ˈkæləbər] *n* **1** : calibre *m* ⟨a .38 caliber gun : una pistola de calibre .38⟩ **2** ABILITY : calibre *m*, valor *m*, capacidad *f*

calibrate [ˈkæləˌbreɪt] *vt* **-brated; -brating** : calibrar (armas), graduar (termómetros)

calibration [ˌkæləˈbreɪʃən] *n* : calibrado *m*, calibración *f*

calico [ˈkælɪˌko] *n*, *pl* **-coes** or **-cos 1** : calicó *m*, percal *m* (estampado) **2** or **calico cat** : gato *m* manchado

calipers [ˈkæləpərz] *npl* : calibrador *m*

caliph or **calif** [ˈkeɪləf, ˈkæ-] *n* : califa *m*

calisthenics [ˌkæləsˈθɛnɪks] *ns* & *pl* : calistenia *f*

calk [ˈkɔk] → **caulk**

call¹ [ˈkɔl] *vi* **1** CRY, SHOUT : llamar, gritar ⟨she called to me from upstairs : me llamó desde arriba⟩ **2** VISIT : hacer (una) visita, visitar **3** SING : cantar (dícese de las aves) **4 to call back** : volver a llamar (por teléfono) **5 to call for** : exigir, requerir, necesitar ⟨it calls for patience : requiere mucha paciencia⟩ **6 to call for** SUMMON : llamar **7 to call for** DEMAND : pedir **8 to call in** : llamar ⟨to call in sick : reportarse enfermo⟩ **9 to call on** VISIT : visitar **10 to call on** IMPLORE : intimar, apelar — *vt* **1** SUMMON : llamar (un perro, un taxi, a una persona, etc.) ⟨he called her name : la llamó⟩ ⟨I was called away : tuve que ausentarme⟩ **2** or **to call up** TELEPHONE : llamar (por teléfono), telefonear ⟨he called 911 : llamó al 911⟩ **3** NAME : llamar ⟨what do you call this? : ¿cómo se llama esto?⟩ ⟨call me Kathy : llámeme Kathy⟩ ⟨to call someone names : insultar a alguien⟩ **4** ANNOUNCE, READ : anunciar, leer ⟨to call roll : pasar lista⟩ **5** CONSIDER : considerar ⟨call me crazy, but . . . : quizá esté loco, pero . . .⟩ ⟨give me a dollar and we'll call it even : dame un dólar y estamos en paz⟩ ⟨let's call it a day : basta por hoy⟩ **6** PREDICT : pronosticar **7** : convocar (elecciones, etc.) **8** CANCEL : cancelar (un partido) **9** : cobrar (un penal, etc.) **10 to call down** REPRIMAND : reprender, reñir **11 to call in a favor** : cobrar un favor **12 to call in**

an order : llamar para hacer un pedido **13 to call into question/doubt** : poner en duda **14 to call off** CANCEL : cancelar **15 to call off** : llamar (un perro) **16 to call someone on something** *fam* ⟨he's rude, but no one calls him on it : es maleducado, pero nadie le dice nada⟩ **17 to call up** DRAFT : llamar a filas

call² *n* **1** SHOUT : grito *m*, llamada *f* **2** : grito *m* (de un animal), reclamo *m* (de un pájaro) **3** SUMMONS : llamada *f* ⟨call to action : llamada a la acción⟩ **4** DEMAND : llamado *m*, petición *f* **5** VISIT : visita *f* ⟨to pay a call on someone : hacerle una visita a alguien⟩ **6** DECISION : decisión *f* (en deportes) **7** ANNOUNCEMENT : llamada *f*, aviso *m* (para pasajeros, etc.) **8** or **telephone call** or **phone call** : llamada *f* (telefónica) ⟨to return someone's call : devolverle la llamada a alguien⟩ **9 to be on call** : estar de guardia

call center *n* : centro *m* de atención (telefónica), centro *m* de llamadas

caller [ˈkɔlər] *n* **1** VISITOR : visita *f* **2** : persona *f* que llama (por teléfono)

calligraphy [kəˈlɪgrəfi] *n*, *pl* **-phies** : caligrafía *f*

calling [ˈkɔlɪŋ] *n* : vocación *f*, profesión *f*

calliope [kəˈlaɪəˌpi, ˈkæliˌo:p] *n* : órgano *m* de vapor

callous [ˈkæləs] *adj* **1** CALLUSED : calloso, encallecido **2** UNFEELING : insensible, desalmado, cruel

callously [ˈkæləsli] *adv* : cruelmente, insensiblemente

callousness [ˈkæləsnəs] *n* : insensibilidad *f*, crueldad *f*

callow [ˈkælo] *adj* : inexperto, inmaduro

callus [ˈkæləs] *n* : callo *m*

callused [ˈkæləst] *adj* : encallecido, calloso

calm¹ [ˈkam, ˈkalm] *vt* : tranquilizar, calmar, sosegar — *vi* or **to calm down** : tranquilizarse, calmarse ⟨calm down! : ¡tranquilízate!⟩

calm² *adj* **1** TRANQUIL : calmo, tranquilo, sereno, ecuánime **2** STILL : en calma (dícese del mar), sin viento (dícese del aire)

calm³ *n* : tranquilidad *f*, calma *f*

calmly [ˈkamli, ˈkalm-] *adv* : con calma, tranquilamente

calmness [ˈkamnəs, ˈkalm-] *n* : calma *f*, tranquilidad *f*

caloric [kəˈlɔrɪk] *adj* : calórico (dícese de los alimentos), calorífico (dícese de la energía)

calorie [ˈkæləri] *n* : caloría *f*

calumniate [kəˈlʌmniˌeɪt] *vt* **-ated; -ating** : calumniar, difamar

calumny [ˈkæləmni] *n*, *pl* **-nies** : calumnia *f*, difamación *f*

calve [ˈkæv, ˈkav] *vi* **calved; calving** : parir (dícese de los mamíferos)

calves → **calf**

calypso [kəˈlɪpˌso:] *n*, *pl* **-sos** : calipso *m*

calyx [ˈkeɪlɪks, ˈkæ-] *n*, *pl* **-lyxes** or **-lyces** [-ləˌsiːz] : cáliz *m*

cam [ˈkæm] *n* : leva *f*

camaraderie [ˌkɑmˈrɑdəri, ˌkæm-; ˌkɑm-əˈrɑ-] *n* : compañerismo *m*, camaradería *f*

Cambodian [kæmˈboːdiən] *n* : camboyano *m*, -na *f* — **Cambodian** *adj*

camcorder [ˈkæmˌkɔrdər] *n* : videocámara *f*

came → **come**

camel [ˈkæməl] *n* : camello *m*

cameo [ˈkæmiˌoː] *n, pl* **-eos** 1 : camafeo *m* 2 *or* **cameo performance** : actuación *f* especial

camera [ˈkæmrə, ˈkæmərə] *n* : cámara *f*, máquina *f* fotográfica

cameraman [ˈkæmrəˌmæn, ˈkæmərə-] *n, pl* **-men** [-mən, -ˌmɛn] : cámara *m*

camerawoman [ˈkæmrəˌwʊmən, ˈkæmərə-] *n, pl* **-women** [-ˌwɪmən] : cámara *f*

camouflage¹ [ˈkæməˌflɑʒ, -ˌflɑʤ] *vt* **-flaged; -flaging** : camuflajear, camuflar

camouflage² *n* : camuflaje *m*

camp¹ [ˈkæmp] *vi* : acampar, ir de camping

camp² *n* 1 : campamento *m* 2 FACTION : campo *m*, bando *m* ⟨in the same camp : del mismo bando⟩ 3 **to pitch camp** : acampar, poner el campamento 4 **to break camp** : levantar el campamento

campaign¹ [kæmˈpeɪn] *vi* : hacer (una) campaña

campaign² *n* : campaña *f*

campaigner [kæmˈpeɪnər] *n* : defensor *m*, -sora *f* ⟨civil rights campaigners : defensores de los derechos civiles⟩

campanile [ˌkæmpəˈniːˌli, -ˈniːl] *n, pl* **-niles** *or* **-nili** [-ˈniːˌli] : campanario *m*

camp bed *n* : cama *f* plegable

camper [ˈkæmpər] *n* 1 : campista *mf* (persona) 2 : cámper *m* (vehículo)

campground [ˈkæmpˌgraʊnd] *n* : campamento *m*, camping *m*

camphor [ˈkæmfər] *n* : alcanfor *m*

camping [ˈkæmpɪŋ] *n* : camping *m*

campsite [ˈkæmpˌsaɪt] *n* : campamento *m*, camping *m*

campus [ˈkæmpəs] *n* : campus *m*, recinto *m* universitario

can¹ [ˈkæn] *v aux, past* **could** [ˈkʊd]; *present s & pl* **can** 1 (*referring to ability*) : poder ⟨I can't hear you : no te oigo⟩ ⟨I can do it myself : puedo hacerlo yo mismo⟩ ⟨I can't decide : no me decido⟩ ⟨it can withstand high temperatures : puede soportar altas temperaturas⟩ 2 (*referring to knowledge*) : saber ⟨he can already read and write : ya sabe leer y escribir⟩ 3 MAY : poder ⟨can I sit down? : ¿puedo sentarme?⟩ 4 (*expressing possibility*) : poder ⟨can/could you help me? : ¿podría ayudarme?⟩ ⟨sorry, I can't : lo siento pero no puedo⟩ ⟨I'll do what I can : haré lo que pueda⟩ ⟨he can't come : no puede venir⟩ ⟨he can be annoying : a veces es pesado⟩ ⟨it can get crowded : a veces se llena de gente⟩ ⟨it can't be! : ¡no puede ser!⟩ ⟨you can't be serious! : ¡no lo dirás en serio!⟩ ⟨where can they be? : ¿dónde estarán?⟩ ⟨we were as happy as can be : estábamos contentísimos⟩ 5 (*used to suggest or demand*) : po

der ⟨why can't you be more romantic? : ¿por qué no puedes ser más romántico?⟩ ⟨you can always ask for help : siempre puedes pedir ayuda⟩ ⟨you can't leave so soon! : ¡no te vayas tan pronto!⟩ 6 **no can do** *fam* : ni pongo

can² [ˈkæn] *vt* **canned; canning** 1 : enlatar, envasar ⟨to can tomatoes : enlatar tomates⟩ 2 DISMISS, FIRE : despedir, echar

can³ *n* : lata *f*, envase *m*, cubo *m* ⟨a can of beer : una lata de cerveza⟩ ⟨garbage can : cubo de basura⟩

Canadian [kəˈneɪdiən] *n* : canadiense *mf* — **Canadian** *adj*

canal [kəˈnæl] *n* 1 : canal *m*, tubo *m* ⟨alimentary canal : tubo digestivo⟩ 2 : canal *m* ⟨Panama Canal : Canal de Panamá⟩

canapé [ˈkænəpi, -ˌpeɪ] *n* : canapé *m*

canary [kəˈnɛri] *n, pl* **-naries** : canario *m*

cancel [ˈkæntsəl] *vt* **-celed** *or* **-celled; -celing** *or* **-celling** 1 : cancelar 2 **to cancel out** : anular

cancellation [ˌkæntsəˈleɪʃən] *n* : cancelación *f*

cancer [ˈkæntsər] *n* : cáncer *m*

Cancer *n* 1 : Cáncer *m* (signo o constelación) 2 : Cáncer *mf* (persona)

cancerous [ˈkæntsərəs] *adj* : canceroso

candelabrum [ˌkændəˈlɑbrəm, -ˈlæ-] *or* **candelabra** [-brə] *n, pl* **-bra** *or* **-bras** : candelabro *m*

candid [ˈkændɪd] *adj* 1 FRANK : franco, sincero, abierto 2 : natural, espontáneo (en la fotografía)

candidacy [ˈkændədəsi] *n, pl* **-cies** : candidatura *f*

candidate [ˈkændəˌdeɪt, -dət] *n* : candidato *m*, -ta *f*

candidly [ˈkændɪdli] *adv* : con franqueza

candied [ˈkændid] *adj* : confitado

candle [ˈkændəl] *n* : vela *f*, candela *f*, cirio *m* (ceremonial)

candlelight [ˈkændəlˌlaɪt] *n* **by ~** : a la luz de una vela

candlestick [ˈkændəlˌstɪk] *n* : candelero *m*

candor [ˈkændər] *n* : franqueza *f*

candy [ˈkændi] *n, pl* **-dies** : dulce *m*, caramelo *m*

cane¹ [ˈkeɪn] *vt* **caned; caning** 1 : tapizar (muebles) con mimbre 2 FLOG : azotar con una vara

cane² *n* 1 : bastón *m* (para andar), vara *f* (para castigar) 2 REED : caña *f*, mimbre *m* (para muebles)

canine¹ [ˈkeɪˌnaɪn] *adj* : canino

canine² *n* 1 DOG : canino *m*; perro *m*, -rra *f* 2 *or* **canine tooth** : colmillo *m*, diente *m* canino

canister [ˈkænəstər] *n* : lata *f*, bote *m*

canker [ˈkæŋkər] *n* : úlcera *f* bucal

cannabis [ˈkænəbɪs] *n* : cannabis *m*

cannelloni [ˌkænəˈloːni] *n* : canelones *mpl*

cannery [ˈkænəri] *n, pl* **-ries** : fábrica *f* de conservas

cannibal [ˈkænɪbəl] *n* : caníbal *mf*; antropófago *m*, -ga *f*

cannibalism [ˈkænəbəˌlɪzəm] *n* : canibalismo *m*, antropofagia *f*

cannibalistic [ˌkænəbəˈlɪstɪk] *adj* : antropófago, caníbal

cannily [ˈkænəli] *adv* : astutamente, sagazmente

cannon [ˈkænən] *n, pl* **-nons** *or* **-non** : cañón *m*

cannot (can not) [ˈkænˌɑt, kəˈnɑt] → **can**[1]

canny [ˈkæni] *adj* **-nier; -est** SHREWD : astuto, sagaz

canoe[1] [kəˈnuː] *vt* **-noed; -noeing** : ir en canoa

canoe[2] *n* : canoa *f*, piragua *f*

canoeing [kəˈnuːɪŋ] *n* : piragüismo *m*

canoeist [kəˈnuːɪst] *or* **canoer** [kəˈnuːər] *n* : piragüista *mf*

canon [ˈkænən] *n* **1** : canon *m* ⟨canon law : derecho canónico⟩ **2** WORKS : canon *m* ⟨the canon of American literature : el canon de la literatura americana⟩ **3** : canónigo *m* (de una catedral) **4** STANDARD : canon *m*, norma *f*

canonical [kəˈnɑnɪkəl] *adj* : canónico

canonize [ˈkænəˌnaɪz] *vt* **-ized; -izing** : canonizar

can opener *n* : abrelatas *m*

canopy [ˈkænəpi] *n, pl* **-pies** : dosel *m*, toldo *m*

cant[1] [ˈkænt] *vt* TILT : ladear, inclinar — *vi* **1** SLANT : ladearse, inclinarse, escorar (dícese de un barco) **2** : hablar insinceramente

cant[2] *n* **1** SLANT : plano *m* inclinado **2** JARGON : jerga *f* **3** : palabras *fpl* insinceras

can't [ˈkænt, ˈkant] *contraction of* **can not** → **can**[1]

cantaloupe [ˈkæntəlˌoːp] *n* : melón *m*, cantalupo *m*

cantankerous [kænˈtæŋkərəs] *adj* : irritable, irascible — **cantankerously** *adv*

cantankerousness [kænˈtæŋkərəsnəs] *n* : irritabilidad *f*, irascibilidad *f*

cantata [kənˈtɑtə] *n* : cantata *f*

canteen [kænˈtiːn] *n* **1** FLASK : cantimplora *f* **2** CAFETERIA : cantina *f*, comedor *m* **3** : club *m* para actividades sociales y recreativas

canter[1] [ˈkæntər] *vi* : ir a medio galope

canter[2] *n* : medio galope *m*

cantilever [ˈkæntəˌliːvər, -ˌlevər] *n* **1** : viga *f* voladiza **2 cantilever bridge** : puente *m* voladizo

canto [ˈkænˌtoː] *n, pl* **-tos** : canto *m*

canton [ˈkæntən, -ˌtɑn] *n* : cantón *m*

Cantonese [ˌkæntənˈiːz, -ˈiːs] *n* **1** : cantonés *m*, -nesa *f* **2** : cantonés *m* (idioma) — **Cantonese** *adj*

cantor [ˈkæntər] *n* : solista *mf*

canvas [ˈkænvəs] *n* **1** : lona *f* **2** SAILS : velas *fpl* (de un barco) **3** : lienzo *m*, tela *f* (de pintar) **4** PAINTING : pintura *f*, óleo *m*, cuadro *m*

canvass[1] [ˈkænvəs] *vt* **1** SOLICIT : solicitar votos o pedidos de, hacer campaña entre **2** SOUND OUT : sondear (opiniones, etc.)

canvass[2] *n* SURVEY : sondeo *m*, encuesta *f*

canyon [ˈkænjən] *n* : cañón *m*

cap[1] [ˈkæp] *vt* **capped; capping 1** COVER : tapar (un recipiente), enfundar (un diente), cubrir (una montaña) **2** CLIMAX : coronar, ser el punto culminante de ⟨to cap it all off : para colmo⟩ **3** LIMIT : limitar, poner a tope a

cap[2] *n* **1** : gorra *f*, gorro *m*, cachucha *f* *Mex* ⟨baseball cap : gorra de béisbol⟩ **2** COVER, TOP : tapa *f*, tapón *m* (de botellas), corcholata *f Mex* **3** LIMIT : tope *m*, límite *m*

capability [ˌkeɪpəˈbɪləti] *n, pl* **-ties** : capacidad *f*, habilidad *f*, competencia *f*

capable [ˈkeɪpəbəl] *adj* : competente, capaz, hábil — **capably** [-bli] *adv*

capacious [kəˈpeɪʃəs] *adj* : amplio, espacioso, de gran capacidad

capacity[1] [kəˈpæsəti] *adj* : completo, total ⟨a capacity crowd : un lleno completo⟩

capacity[2] *n, pl* **-ties 1** ROOM, SPACE : capacidad *f*, cabida *f*, espacio *m* **2** CAPABILITY : habilidad *f*, competencia *f* **3** FUNCTION, ROLE : calidad *f*, función *f* ⟨in his capacity as ambassador : en su calidad de embajador⟩

cape [ˈkeɪp] *n* **1** : capa *f* **2** : cabo *m* ⟨Cape Horn : el Cabo de Hornos⟩

caper[1] [ˈkeɪpər] *vi* : dar saltos, correr y brincar

caper[2] *n* **1** : alcaparra *f* ⟨olives and capers : aceitunas y alcaparras⟩ **2** ANTIC, PRANK : broma *f*, travesura *f* **3** LEAP : brinco *m*, salto *m*

capful [ˈkæpˌful] *n* : tapa *f*, tapita *f*

capillary[1] [ˈkæpəˌleri] *adj* : capilar

capillary[2] *n, pl* **-ries** : capilar *m*

capital[1] [ˈkæpətəl] *adj* **1** : capital ⟨capital punishment : pena capital⟩ **2** : mayúsculo (dícese de las letras) **3** : de capital ⟨capital assets : activo fijo⟩ ⟨capital gain : ganancia de capital, plusvalía⟩ **4** EXCELLENT : excelente, estupendo

capital[2] *n* **1** *or* **capital city** : capital *f*, sede *f* del gobierno **2** WEALTH : capital *m* **3** *or* **capital letter** : mayúscula *f* **4** : capitel *m* (de una columna)

capitalism [ˈkæpətəlˌɪzəm] *n* : capitalismo *m*

capitalist[1] [ˈkæpətəlɪst] *or* **capitalistic** [ˌkæpətəlˈɪstɪk] *adj* : capitalista

capitalist[2] *n* : capitalista *mf*

capitalization [ˌkæpətələˈzeɪʃən] *n* : capitalización *f*

capitalize [ˈkæpətəlˌaɪz] *v* **-ized; -izing** *vt* **1** FINANCE : capitalizar, financiar **2** : escribir con mayúscula — *vi* **to capitalize on** : sacar partido de, aprovechar

capitol [ˈkæpətəl] *n* : capitolio *m*

capitulate [kəˈpɪtʃəˌleɪt] *vi* **-lated; -lating** : capitular

capitulation [kəˌpɪtʃəˈleɪʃən] *n* : capitulación *f*

capon [ˈkeɪˌpɑn, -pən] *n* : capón *m*

cappuccino [ˌkɑpəˈtʃiːnoː] *n* : capuchino *m* (café)

caprice [kəˈpriːs] *n* : capricho *m*, antojo *m*

capricious [kəˈprɪʃəs, -ˈpriː-] *adj* : caprichoso — **capriciously** *adv*

Capricorn [ˈkæprɪˌkɔrn] *n* **1** : Capricornio *m* (signo o constelación) **2** : Capricornio *mf* (persona)

capsize [ˈkæpˌsaɪz, kæpˈsaɪz] v **-sized;
-sizing** vi : volcar, volcarse — vt : hacer
volcar

capsule [ˈkæpsəl, -ˌsuːl] n **1** : cápsula f (en
la farmacéutica y botánica) **2 space
capsule** : cápsula f espacial

captain¹ [ˈkæptən] n¹ : capitanear

captain² n **1** : capitán m, -tana f **2** HEAD-
WAITER : jefe m, -fa f de comedor **3 captain of industry** : magnate mf

caption¹ [ˈkæpʃən] vt : ponerle una leyenda a (una ilustración), titular (un
artículo), subtitular (una película)

caption² n **1** HEADING : titular m, encabezamiento m **2** : leyenda f (al pie de
una ilustración) **3** SUBTITLE : subtítulo
m

captivate [ˈkæptəˌveɪt] vt **-vated; -vating**
CHARM : cautivar, hechizar, encantar

captivating [ˈkæptəˌveɪtɪŋ] adj : cautivador, hechicero, encantador

captive¹ [ˈkæptɪv] adj : cautivo

captive² n : cautivo m, -va f

captivity [kæpˈtɪvəti] n : cautiverio m

captor [ˈkæptər] n : captor m, -tora f

capture¹ [ˈkæpʃər] vt **-tured; -turing 1**
SEIZE : capturar, apresar **2** CATCH
: captar ⟨to capture one's interest
: captar el interés de uno⟩

capture² n : captura f, apresamiento m

car [ˈkɑr] n **1** AUTOMOBILE : automóvil
m, carro m, coche m **2** : vagón m, coche
m (de un tren) **3** : cabina f (de un
ascensor)

carafe [kəˈræf, -ˈrɑf] n : garrafa f

caramel [ˈkɑrməl; ˈkærəməl, -ˌmɛl] n **1**
: caramelo m, azúcar f quemada **2 or
caramel candy** : caramelo m, dulce m de
leche

carat [ˈkærət] n : quilate m

caravan [ˈkærəˌvæn] n : caravana f

caraway [ˈkærəˌweɪ] n : alcaravea f

carbine [ˈkɑrˌbaɪn, -ˌbiːn] n : carabina f

carbohydrate [ˌkɑrboˈhaɪˌdreɪt, -drət] n
: carbohidrato m, hidrato m de carbono

car bomb n : carro m bomba, coche m
bomba, auto m bomba Chile

carbon [ˈkɑrbən] n **1** : carbono m **2** →
carbon paper 3 → **carbon copy**

carbonated [ˈkɑrbəˌneɪtəd] adj : carbonatado (dícese del agua), gaseoso (dícese de
las bebidas)

carbon copy n **1** : copia f al carbón **2**
DUPLICATE : duplicado m, copia f exacta

carbon dioxide [-daɪˈɑkˌsaɪd] n : dióxido
m de carbono

carbon footprint n : huella f de carbono

carbon monoxide [-məˈnɑkˌsaɪd] n
: monóxido m de carbono

carbon paper n : papel m carbón

carburetor [ˈkɑrbəˌreɪtər, -bjə-] n : carburador m

carcass [ˈkɑrkəs] n : cuerpo m (de un animal muerto)

carcinogen [kɑrˈsɪnədʒən, ˈkɑrsənəˌdʒen]
n : carcinógeno m, cancerígeno m

carcinogenic [ˌkɑrsənoˈdʒɛnɪk] adj
: carcinogénico

carcinoma [ˌkɑrsəˈnoːmə] n : carcinoma
m

card¹ [ˈkɑrd] vt : cardar (fibras)

card² n **1** : carta f, naipe m ⟨to play cards
: jugar a las cartas⟩ ⟨a deck of cards
: una baraja⟩ **2** : tarjeta f ⟨birthday card
: tarjeta de cumpleaños⟩ ⟨business card
: tarjeta (de visita)⟩ **3** : tarjeta f (bancaria) ⟨credit/debit card : tarjeta de cré-
dito/débito⟩ **4** : tarjeta f (de memoria,
etc.) **5 to be in the cards** : estar escrito
⟨it just wasn't in the cards : estaba
escrito que no iba a pasar⟩

cardboard [ˈkɑrdˌbord] n : cartón m,
cartulina f

cardiac [ˈkɑrdiˌæk] adj : cardíaco, cardiaco

cardigan [ˈkɑrdɪgən] n : cárdigan m,
chaqueta f de punto

cardinal¹ [ˈkɑrdənəl] adj FUNDAMENTAL
: cardinal, fundamental

cardinal² n : cardenal m

cardinal number n : número m cardinal

cardinal point n : punto m cardinal

cardiologist [ˌkɑrdiˈɑlədʒɪst] n : cardiólogo m, -ga f

cardiology [ˌkɑrdiˈɑlədʒi] n : cardiología f

cardiopulmonary resuscitation [ˌkɑrdio
ˈpʊlmənˌeri-, -ˈpʌl-] n → CPR

cardiovascular [ˌkɑrdioˈvæskjələr] adj
: cardiovascular

care¹ [ˈkær] v **cared; caring** vi **1** : importarle a uno ⟨they don't care : no les im-
porta⟩ ⟨I could/couldn't care less : (no)
me importa un bledo/comino⟩ ⟨see if I
care! : ¡me tiene sin cuidado!⟩ ⟨who
cares? : ¿y qué?, ¿qué importa?⟩ **2** LOVE
: querer ⟨show her that you care (about
her) : demuéstrale que la quieres⟩ **3**
: preocuparse, inquietarse ⟨she cares
about the poor : se preocupa por los
pobres⟩ **4 to care for** TEND : cuidar (de),
atender, encargarse de **5 to care for**
LOVE : querer, sentir cariño por **6 to
care for** LIKE : gustarle (algo a uno) ⟨I
don't care for your attitude : tu actitud
no me agrada⟩ — vt **1** WISH : desear,
querer ⟨if you care to go : si deseas ir⟩ **2**
: importarle a uno ⟨I don't care what
happens to her : a mí no me importa lo
que le pase⟩ ⟨for all I care, he can quit
right now : por mí, puede renunciarse
ahora mismo⟩ ⟨what does she care? : ¿a
ella qué le importa?⟩

care² n **1** ANXIETY : inquietud f, preocupación f ⟨to be without a care in the
world : no tener ninguna preocupación⟩
2 CAREFULNESS : cuidado m, atención f
⟨handle with care : manejar con cui-
dado⟩ **3** : cargo m, cuidado m ⟨medical
care : asistencia médica⟩ ⟨hair care : el
cuidado del cabello/pelo⟩ ⟨the children
are in my care : los niños están a mi cui-
dado/cargo⟩ **4 care of** : a casa de (en
una carta) **5 take care!** : ¡cuídate! **6 to
take care** : tener cuidado **7 to take care
of** CARE FOR : cuidar (de), atender **8 to
take care of** DEAL WITH : encargarse de

careen [kəˈriːn] vi **1** SWAY : oscilar, balancearse **2** CAREER : ir a toda velocidad

career¹ [kəˈrɪr] vi : ir a toda velocidad

career² *n* VOCATION : vocación *f*, profesión *f*, carrera *f*

carefree ['kær‚fri:, ‚kær¹-] *adj* : despreocupado

careful ['kærfəl] *adj* **1** CAUTIOUS : cuidadoso, cauteloso ⟨you can't be too careful : toda prudencia es poca⟩ **2** PAINSTAKING : cuidadoso, esmerado, meticuloso ⟨after careful consideration : después de considerarlo detenidamente⟩

carefully ['kærfəli] *adv* : con cuidado, cuidadosamente

carefulness ['kærfəlnəs] *n* **1** CAUTION : cuidado *m*, cautela *f* **2** METICULOUSNESS : esmero *m*, meticulosidad *f*

caregiver ['kær‚gɪvər] *n* : persona *f* que cuida a niños o enfermos

careless ['kærləs] *adj* : descuidado, negligente — **carelessly** *adv*

carelessness ['kærləsnəs] *n* : descuido *m*, negligencia *f*

caress¹ [kə'rɛs] *vt* : acariciar

caress² *n* : caricia *f*

caret ['kærət] *n* : signo *m* de intercalación

caretaker ['kɛr‚teɪkər] *n* : conserje *mf*; velador *m*, -dora *f*

cargo ['kar‚go:] *n, pl* **-goes** *or* **-gos** : cargamento *m*, carga *f*

Caribbean [kærə'bi:ən, kə'rɪbiən] *adj* : caribeño ⟨the Caribbean Sea : el mar Caribe⟩

caribou ['kærə‚bu:] *n, pl* **-bou** *or* **-bous** : caribú *m*

caricature¹ ['kærɪkə‚tʃʊr] *vt* **-tured; -turing** : caricaturizar

caricature² *n* : caricatura *f*

caricaturist ['kærɪkə‚tʃʊrɪst] *n* : caricaturista *mf*

caries ['kær‚i:z] *ns & pl* : caries *f*

caring ['kærɪŋ] *n* **1** AFFECTIONATE : cariñoso, solícito **2** KIND : bondadoso

carjacking ['kar‚dʒækɪŋ] *n* : robo *m* de un vehículo (por asalto)

carmine ['karmən, -‚maɪn] *n* : carmín *m*

carnage ['karnɪdʒ] *n* : matanza *f*, carnicería *f*

carnal ['karnəl] *adj* : carnal

carnation [kar'neɪʃən] *n* : clavel *m*

carnival ['karnəvəl] *n* : carnaval *m*, feria *f*

carnivore ['karnə‚vor] *n* : carnívoro *m*

carnivorous [kar'nɪvərəs] *adj* : carnívoro

carol¹ ['kærəl] *vi* **-oled** *or* **-olled; -oling** *or* **-olling** : cantar villancicos

carol² *n* : villancico *m*

caroler *or* **caroller** ['kærələr] *n* : persona *f* que canta villancicos

carom¹ ['kærəm] *vi* **1** REBOUND : rebotar ⟨the bullet caromed off the wall : la bala rebotó contra el muro⟩ **2** : hacer carambola (en billar)

carom² *n* : carambola *f*

carouse [kə'rauz] *vi* **-roused; -rousing** : irse de parranda, irse de juerga

carousel *or* **carrousel** [‚kærə'sɛl, 'kærə‚-] *n* : carrusel *m*, tiovivo *m*

carouser [kə'rauzər] *n* : juerguista *mf*

carp¹ ['karp] *vi* **1** COMPLAIN : quejarse **2 to carp at** : criticar

carp² *n, pl* **carp** *or* **carps** : carpa *f*

carpenter ['karpəntər] *n* : carpintero *m*, -ra *f*

carpentry ['karpəntri] *n* : carpintería *f*

carpet¹ ['karpət] *vt* : alfombrar

carpet² *n* : alfombra *f*

carpeting ['karpətɪŋ] *n* : alfombrado *m*

carport ['kar‚port] *n* : cochera *f*, garaje *m* abierto

carriage ['kærɪdʒ] *n* **1** TRANSPORT : transporte *m* **2** POSTURE : porte *m*, postura *f* **3** *or* **horse–drawn carriage** : carruaje *m*, coche *m* **4** *or* **baby carriage** : cochecito *m*

carrier ['kæriər] *n* **1** : transportista *mf*, empresa *f* de transportes **2** : portador *m*, -dora *f* (de una enfermedad) **3 aircraft carrier** : portaaviones *m*

carrier pigeon : paloma *f* mensajera

carrion ['kæriən] *n* : carroña *f*

carrot ['kærət] *n* : zanahoria *f*

carry ['kæri] *v* **-ried; -rying** *vt* **1** : llevar, cargar, transportar (cargamento) ⟨to carry a bag : cargar una bolsa⟩ ⟨to carry money : llevar dinero encima, traer dinero consigo⟩ **2** : llevar (sangre, agua, etc.) **3** HAVE : tener (una garantía, etc.), llevar (una advertencia) **4** BEAR : soportar, aguantar, resistir (peso) **5** STOCK : vender, tener en abasto **6** ENTAIL : llevar, implicar, acarrear **7** WIN, PASS : ganar (una elección o competición), aprobar (una moción) **8** : estar embarazada de (un hijo) **9** : portar, ser portador de (un virus, etc.) **10** : llevar (en matemáticas) **11 to be/get carried away** : pasarse, excederse ⟨to be/get carried away by something : dejarse llevar por algo⟩ **12 to carry a tune** : cantar bien **13 to carry off** ACHIEVE : conseguir, lograr **14 to carry off** TAKE : llevarse **15 to carry on** CONTINUE : seguir con, continuar con **16 to carry on** CONDUCT : realizar, ejercer, mantener ⟨to carry on research : realizar investigaciones⟩ ⟨to carry on a correspondence : mantener una correspondencia⟩ **17 to carry oneself** : portarse, comportarse ⟨he carried himself honorably : se comportó dignamente⟩ **18 to carry out** COMPLETE : llevar a cabo, realizar, efectuar **19 to carry out** FULFILL : cumplir (una orden, etc.) **20 to carry through** SUSTAIN : sustentar, sostener — *vi* **1** : oírse, proyectarse ⟨her voice carries well : su voz se puede oír desde lejos⟩ **2 to carry on** CONTINUE : seguir, continuar **3 to carry on** : portarse de manera escandalosa o inapropiada ⟨it's embarrassing how he carries on : su manera de comportarse da vergüenza⟩

carryall ['kæri‚ɔl] *n* : bolsa *f* de viaje

carsick ['kar‚sɪk] *adj* : mareado (de ir en coche)

cart¹ ['kart] *vt* : acarrear, llevar

cart² *n* : carreta *f*, carro *m*

carte blanche ['kart'blanʃ] *n* : carta *f* blanca

cartel [kar'tɛl] *n* : cártel *m*

cartilage ['kartəlɪdʒ] *n* : cartílago *m*

cartographer [kɑr'tɑgrəfər] n : cartógrafo m, -fa f

cartography [kɑr'tɑgrəfi] n : cartografía f

carton ['kɑrtən] n : caja f de cartón

cartoon [kɑr'tu:n] n 1 : chiste m (gráfico), caricatura f ⟨a political cartoon : un chiste político⟩ 2 COMIC STRIP : tira f cómica, historieta f 3 : dibujo m animado ⟨to watch cartoons : mirar dibujos animados⟩

cartoonist [kɑr'tu:nɪst] n : caricaturista mf, dibujante mf (de chistes)

cartridge ['kɑrtrɪdʒ] n : cartucho m

cartwheel ['kɑrt,hwi:l] n : voltereta f lateral

carve ['kɑrv] vt **carved; carving 1** : tallar (madera), esculpir (piedra), grabar ⟨he carved his name in the bark : grabó su nombre en la corteza⟩ **2** SLICE : cortar, trinchar (carne) **3 to carve out** : hacerse, conquistar

carving ['kɑrvɪŋ] n : talla f, escultura f (de madera, piedra, etc.)

cascade[1] [kæs'keɪd] vi **-caded; -cading** : caer en cascada

cascade[2] n : cascada f, salto m de agua

case[1] ['keɪs] vt **cased; casing 1** BOX, PACK : embalar, encajonar **2** INSPECT : observar, inspeccionar (antes de cometer un delito)

case[2] n **1** : caso m ⟨an unusual case : un caso insólito⟩ ⟨a case of the flu : un caso de gripe⟩ ⟨a murder case : un caso de asesinato⟩ **2** BOX : caja f **3** CONTAINER : funda f, estuche m **4** SUITCASE : maleta f, valija f **5** ARGUMENT : argumento m ⟨to make a case for : presentar argumentos a favor de⟩ **6** : caso m (en gramática) **7 in any case** : de todos modos, en cualquier caso **8 in ~** : como precaución ⟨just in case : por si acaso⟩ **9 in case of** : en caso de **10 in that case** : en ese caso

casement ['keɪsmənt] n : ventana f con bisagras

cash[1] ['kæʃ] vt : convertir en efectivo, cobrar, cambiar (un cheque) — vi **to cash in on** : sacar partido de

cash[2] n : efectivo m, dinero m en efectivo ⟨cash on delivery : entrega contra reembolso⟩ ⟨hard/cold cash : dinero contante y sonante⟩

cashew ['kæ,ʃu:, kə'ʃu:] n : anacardo m

cashier[1] [kæ'ʃɪr] vt : destituir, despedir

cashier[2] n : cajero m, -ra f

cashmere ['kæʒ,mɪr, 'kæʃ-] n : cachemir m

cash register n : caja f registradora

casing ['keɪsɪŋ] n **1** : caja f, cubierta f **2** : casquillo m (de una bala, etc.) **3** FRAME : marco m (de una puerta o ventana)

casino [kə'si:,no:] n, pl **-nos** : casino m

cask ['kæsk] n : tonel m, barrica f, barril m

casket ['kæskət] n COFFIN : ataúd m, féretro m

cassava [kə'sɑvə] n : mandioca f, yuca f

casserole ['kæsə,ro:l] n **1** : cazuela f **2** : guiso m, guisado m ⟨tuna casserole : guiso de atún⟩

cassette [kə'sɛt, kæ-] n : cassette m

cassock ['kæsək] n : sotana f

cast[1] ['kæst] vt **cast; casting 1** THROW : tirar, echar, arrojar ⟨the die is cast : la suerte está echada⟩ **2** DIRECT : echar ⟨he cast a glance at the door : echó una mirada a la puerta⟩ **3** : depositar (un voto) **4** : asignar ⟨to cast a role : asignar un papel⟩ ⟨to cast someone as : asignarle a alguien el papel de⟩ **5** MOLD : moldear, fundir, vaciar **6** : proyectar (luz, etc.) ⟨to cast a shadow : proyectar una sombra⟩ ⟨to cast a shadow/pall on : ensombrecer⟩ **7 to be cast away** : quedarse varado (en un lugar remoto tras naufragar) **8 to cast adrift** : dejar a la deriva **9 to cast aside** : desechar (las preocupaciones, etc.) **10 to cast a spell on** : hechizar **11 to cast off** GET RID OF : deshacerse de **12 to cast out** EXPEL : expulsar — vi **1 to cast about/around for** : tratar de encontrar **2 to cast off** : desamarrar, soltar (las) amarras **3 to cast off** : cerrar (puntos) **4 to cast on** : montar puntos

cast[2] n **1** THROW : lance m, lanzamiento m **2** APPEARANCE : aspecto m, forma f **3** : elenco m, reparto m (de una obra de teatro) **4** MOLD : molde m **5** : yeso m, escayola f Spain (en medicina)

castanet [,kæstə'nɛt] n : castañuela f

castaway[1] ['kæstə,weɪ] adj : náufrago

castaway[2] n : náufrago m, -ga f

caste ['kæst] n : casta f

caster ['kæstər] n : ruedita f (de un mueble)

castigate ['kæstə,geɪt] vt **-gated; -gating** : castigar severamente, censurar, reprobar

Castilian [kæ'stɪljən] n **1** : castellano m, -na f **2** : castellano m (idioma) — **Castilian** adj

cast iron n : hierro m fundido

castle ['kæsəl] n **1** : castillo m **2** : torre f (en ajedrez)

cast–off ['kæst,ɔf] adj : desechado

castoff ['kæst,ɔf] n : desecho m

castor oil ['kæstər-] n : aceite m de ricino

castrate ['kæs,treɪt] vt **-trated; -trating** : castrar

castration [kæ'streɪʃən] n : castración f

casual ['kæʒʊəl] adj **1** FORTUITOUS : casual, fortuito **2** INDIFFERENT : indiferente, despreocupado **3** INFORMAL : informal **4** IRREGULAR, OCCASIONAL : eventual, ocasional — **casually** ['kæʒʊəli, 'kæʒəli] adv

casualness ['kæʒʊəlnəs] n **1** INDIFFERENCE : indiferencia f, despreocupación f **2** INFORMALITY : informalidad f

casualty ['kæʒʊəlti, 'kæʒəl-] n, pl **-ties 1** ACCIDENT : accidente m serio, desastre m **2** VICTIM : víctima f, baja f; herido m, -da f

cat ['kæt] n : gato m, -ta f

cataclysm ['kætə,klɪzəm] n : cataclismo m

cataclysmal [,kætə'klɪzməl] or **cataclysmic** [,kætə'klɪzmɪk] adj : catastrófico

catacombs ['kætə,ko:mz] *npl* : catacumbas *fpl*

Catalan ['kætələn, -,læn] *n* **1** : catalán *m*, catalana *f* **2** : catalán *m* (idioma) — **Catalan** *adj*

catalog[1] *or* **catalogue** ['kætə,log] *vt* **-loged** *or* **-logued; -loging** *or* **-loguing** : catalogar

catalog[2] *n* : catálogo *m*

catalyst ['kætələst] *n* : catalizador *m*

catalytic converter [,kætəl'ıtık-] *n* : catalizador *m*, convertidor *m* catalítico

catamaran [,kætəmə'ræn, 'kætəmə-,ræn] *n* : catamarán *m*

catapult[1] ['kætə,pʌlt, -,pʊlt] *vt* : catapultar

catapult[2] *n* : catapulta *f*

cataract ['kætə,rækt] *n* : catarata *f*

catarrh [kə'tar] *n* : catarro *m*

catastrophe [kə'tæstrə,fi:] *n* : catástrofe *f*

catastrophic [,kætə'strafık] *adj* : catastrófico — **catastrophically** [-fıkli] *adv*

catcall ['kæt,kol] *n* : rechifla *f*, abucheo *m*

catch[1] ['kætʃ, 'kɛtʃ] *v* **caught** ['kot]; **catching** *vt* **1** GRASP : agarrar, coger *Spain* **2** CAPTURE, TRAP : capturar, agarrar, atrapar, coger *Spain* **3** SURPRISE, INTERRUPT : agarrar, pillar *fam*, coger *Spain* ⟨they caught him red-handed : lo pillaron con las manos en la masa⟩ ⟨to catch by surprise : tomar por sorpresa⟩ ⟨we got caught in the rain : nos agarró la lluvia⟩ ⟨you've caught me at a bad time : llegas en mal momento⟩ ⟨I caught her just as she was leaving : llegué justo cuando ella salía⟩ **4** ENTANGLE : enganchar, enredar ⟨to get caught up in something : quedarse enredado en algo⟩ **5** MAKE : alcanzar (un tren, etc.) **6** TAKE : tomar (un tren, etc.) **7** : contagiarse de ⟨to catch a cold : contagiarse de un resfriado, resfriarse⟩ **8** ATTRACT : llamar (la atención), captar (el interés) **9** UNDERSTAND : captar ⟨if you catch my drift : si me entiendes⟩ **10** PERCEIVE : percibir ⟨to catch a glimpse of : alcanzar a ver⟩ **11** NOTICE, DETECT : darse cuenta de, detectar ⟨to catch (una película), ir a (un concierto, etc.) — *vi* **1** GRASP : agarrar **2** HOOK : engancharse **3** IGNITE : prender, agarrar **4** to catch on : hacerse popular **5** to catch on LEARN : agarrarle la onda **6** to catch on UNDERSTAND : entender, darse cuenta **7** to catch up : ponerse al día ⟨to catch up on the news : ponerse al día con las noticias⟩ **8** to catch up to/with : alcanzar

catch[2] *n* **1** CATCHING : captura *f*, atrapada *f*, parada *f* (de una pelota) **2** : redada *f* (de pescado), presa *f* (de caza) ⟨he's a good catch : es un buen partido⟩ **3** LATCH : pestillo *m*, pasador *m* **4** DIFFICULTY, TRICK : problema *m*, trampa *f*, truco *m*

catcher ['kætʃər, 'kɛ-] *n* : catcher *mf*; receptor *m*, -tora *f* (en béisbol)

catching ['kætʃıŋ, 'kɛ-] *adj* : contagioso

catchphrase ['kætʃ,freız, 'kɛtʃ-] *n* : eslogan *m*, lema *m*

catchup ['kætʃəp, 'kɛ-] → **ketchup**

catchword ['kætʃ,wərd, 'kɛtʃ-] *n* : eslogan *m*, lema *m*

catchy ['kætʃi, 'kɛ-] *adj* **catchier; -est** : pegajoso ⟨a catchy song : una canción pegajosa⟩

catechism ['kætə,kızəm] *n* : catecismo *m*

categorical [,kætə'gorıkəl] *adj* : categórico, absoluto, rotundo — **categorically** [-kli] *adv*

categorize ['kætıgə,raız] *vt* **-rized; -rizing** : clasificar, catalogar

category ['kætə,gori] *n, pl* **-ries** : categoría *f*, género *m*, clase *f*

cater ['keıtər] *vi* **1** : proveer servicio de alimentos (para fiestas, bodas, etc.) **2** to cater to : atender a ⟨to cater to all tastes : atender a todos los gustos⟩ — *vt* : proveer servicio de alimentos para

catercorner[1] ['kæti,kornər, 'kætə-, 'kıti-] *or* **cater-cornered** [-,kornərd] *adv* : diagonalmente, en diagonal

catercorner[2] *or* **cater-cornered** *adj* : diagonal

caterer ['keıtərər] *n* : proveedor *m*, -dora *f* de comida

catering ['keıtərıŋ] *n* : servicio *m* de alimentos, catering *m*

caterpillar ['kætər,pılər] *n* : oruga *f*

catfish ['kæt,fıʃ] *n* : bagre *m*

catgut ['kæt,gʌt] *n* : cuerda *f* de tripa

catharsis [kə'θarsıs] *n, pl* **catharses** [-,si:z] : catarsis *f*

cathartic[1] [kə'θartık] *adj* : catártico

cathartic[2] *n* : purgante *m*

cathedral [kə'θi:drəl] *n* : catedral *f*

catheter ['kæθətər] *n* : catéter *m*, sonda *f*

cathode ['kæ,θo:d] *n* : cátodo *m*

catholic ['kæθəlık] *adj* **1** BROAD, UNIVERSAL : liberal, universal **2** Catholic : católico

Catholic *n* : católico *m*, -ca *f*

Catholicism [kə'θalə,sızəm] *n* : catolicismo *m*

catlike ['kæt,laık] *adj* : felino

catnap[1] ['kæt,næp] *vi* **-napped; -napping** : tomarse una siestecita

catnap[2] *n* : siesta *f* breve, siestecita *f*

catnip ['kæt,nıp] *n* : nébeda *f*

catsup ['kɛtʃəp, 'kætsəp] → **ketchup**

cattail ['kæt,teıl] *n* : espadaña *f*, anea *f*

cattiness ['kætinəs] *n* : malicia *f*

cattle ['kætəl] *npl* : ganado *m*, reses *fpl*

cattleman ['kætəlmən, -,mæn] *n, pl* **-men** [-mən, -,men] : ganadero *m*

catty ['kæti] *adj* **cattier; -est** : malicioso, malintencionado

catwalk ['kæt,wok] *n* : pasarela *f*

Caucasian[1] [ko'keızən] *adj* : caucásico

Caucasian[2] *n* : caucásico *m*, -ca *f*

caucus ['kokəs] *n* : junta *f* de políticos

caught → **catch**

cauldron ['koldrən] *n* : caldera *f*

cauliflower ['kalı,flauər, 'ko-] *n* : coliflor *f*

caulk[1] ['kok] *vt* : enmasillar (una grieta)

caulk[2] *n* : masilla *f*

causal ['kozəl] *adj* : causal — **causality** [ko'zæləti] *n*

cause[1] ['koz] *vt* **caused; causing** : causar, provocar, ocasionar

cause[2] *n* **1** ORIGIN : causa *f*, origen *m* **2** REASON : causa *f*, razón *f*, motivo *m* **3** LAWSUIT : litigio *m*, pleito *m* **4** MOVEMENT : causa *f*, movimiento *m*

causeless ['kɔzləs] *adj* : sin causa

causeway ['kɔz‚weɪ] *n* : camino *m* elevado

caustic ['kɔstɪk] *adj* **1** CORROSIVE : cáustico, corrosivo **2** BITING : mordaz, sarcástico

cauterize ['kɔtə‚raɪz] *vt* -ized; -izing : cauterizar

caution[1] ['kɔʃən] *vt* : advertir

caution[2] *n* **1** WARNING : advertencia *f*, aviso *m* **2** CARE, PRUDENCE : precaución *f*, cuidado *m*, cautela *f*

cautionary ['kɔʃə‚neri] *adj* : admonitorio ⟨cautionary tale : cuento moral⟩

cautious ['kɔʃəs] *adj* : cauteloso, cuidadoso, precavido

cautiously ['kɔʃəsli] *adv* : cautelosamente, con precaución

cautiousness ['kɔʃəsnəs] *n* : cautela *f*, precaución *f*

cavalcade [‚kævəl'keɪd, 'kævəl‚-] *n* **1** : cabalgata *f* **2** SERIES : serie *f*

cavalier[1] [‚kævə'lɪr] *adj* : altivo, desdeñoso — **cavalierly** *adv*

cavalier[2] *n* : caballero *m*

cavalry ['kævəlri] *n*, *pl* -ries : caballería *f*

cave[1] ['keɪv] *vi* caved; caving *or* to cave in : derrumbarse

cave[2] *n* : cueva *f*

caveman ['keɪv‚mæn] *n*, *pl* -men [-mən, -‚mɛn] : cavernícola *m*

cavern ['kævərn] *n* : caverna *f*

cavernous ['kævərnəs] *adj* : cavernoso — **cavernously** *adv*

cavewoman ['keɪv‚wʊmən] *n*, *pl* -women [-‚wɪmən] : cavernícola *f*

caviar *or* **caviare** ['kævi‚ɑr, 'kɑ-] *n* : caviar *m*

cavity ['kævəti] *n*, *pl* -ties **1** HOLE : cavidad *f*, hueco *m* **2** CARIES : caries *f*

cavort [kə'vɔrt] *vi* : brincar, hacer cabriolas

caw[1] ['kɔ] *vi* : graznar

caw[2] *n* : graznido *m*

cayenne pepper [‚kaɪ'ɛn, ‚keɪ-] *n* : pimienta *f* cayena, pimentón *m*

CD [‚si'di:] *n* : CD *m*, disco *m* compacto

CD–ROM [‚si‚di'ram] *n* : CD-ROM *m*

cease ['si:s] *v* ceased; ceasing *vt* : dejar de ⟨they ceased bickering : dejaron de discutir⟩ — *vi* : cesar, pasarse

cease–fire ['si:s‚'faɪr] *n* : alto *m* el fuego, cese *m* del fuego

ceaseless ['si:sləs] *adj* : incesante, continuo

cedar ['si:dər] *n* : cedro *m*

cede ['si:d] *vt* ceded; ceding : ceder, conceder

ceiling ['si:lɪŋ] *n* **1** : techo *m*, cielo *m* raso **2** LIMIT : límite *m*, tope *m*

celebrant ['sɛləbrənt] *n* : celebrante *mf*, oficiante *mf*

celebrate ['sɛlə‚breɪt] *v* -brated; -brating *vt* **1** : celebrar, oficiar ⟨to celebrate Mass : celebrar la misa⟩ **2** : celebrar, festejar ⟨we're celebrating our anniversary : estamos celebrando nuestro aniversario⟩ **3** EXTOL : alabar, ensalzar, exaltar — *vi* : estar de fiesta, divertirse

celebrated ['sɛlə‚breɪtəd] *adj* : célebre, famoso, renombrado

celebration [‚sɛlə'breɪʃən] *n* : celebración *f*, festejos *mpl*

celebrity [sə'lɛbrəti] *n*, *pl* -ties **1** RENOWN : fama *f*, renombre *m*, celebridad *f* **2** PERSONALITY : celebridad *f*, personaje *m*

celery ['sɛləri] *n*, *pl* -eries : apio *m*

celestial [sə'lɛstʃəl, -'lɪstiəl] *adj* **1** : celeste **2** HEAVENLY : celestial, paradisíaco

celibacy ['sɛləbəsi] *n* : celibato *m*

celibate[1] ['sɛləbət] *adj* : célibe

celibate[2] *n* : célibe *mf*

cell ['sɛl] *n* **1** : célula *f* (de un organismo) **2** : celda *f* (en una cárcel, etc.) **3** : elemento *m* (de una pila)

cellar ['sɛlər] *n* **1** BASEMENT : sótano *m* **2** : bodega *f* (de vinos)

cellist ['tʃɛlɪst] *n* : violonchelista *mf*

cello ['tʃɛ‚lo] *n*, *pl* -los : chelo *m*, violonchelo *m*

cellophane ['sɛlə‚feɪn] *n* : celofán *m*

cell phone *n* : teléfono *m* celular

cellular ['sɛljələr] *adj* : celular

cellulite ['sɛljə‚laɪt] *n* : celulitis *f*

celluloid ['sɛljə‚lɔɪd] *n* : celuloide *m*

cellulose ['sɛljə‚lo:s] *n* : celulosa *f*

Celsius ['sɛlsiəs] *adj* : centígrado ⟨100 degrees Celsius : 100 grados centígrados⟩

Celt ['kɛlt, 'sɛlt] *n* : celta *mf*

Celtic[1] ['kɛltɪk, 'sɛl-] *adj* : celta

Celtic[2] *n* : celta *m*

cement[1] [sɪ'mɛnt] *vi* : unir o cubrir algo con cemento, cementar

cement[2] *n* **1** : cemento *m* **2** GLUE : pegamento *m*

cement mixer *n* : hormigonera *f*

cemetery ['sɛmə‚teri] *n*, *pl* -teries : cementerio *m*, panteón *m*

censer ['sɛntsər] *n* : incensario *m*

censor[1] ['sɛntsər] *vt* : censurar

censor[2] *n* : censor *m*, -sora *f*

censorious [sɛn'soriəs] *adj* : de censura, crítico

censorship ['sɛntsər‚ʃɪp] *n* : censura *f*

censure[1] ['sɛntʃər] *vt* -sured; -suring : censurar, criticar, reprobar — **censurable** [-tʃərəbəl] *adj*

censure[2] *n* : censura *f*, reproche *m* oficial

census ['sɛntsəs] *n* : censo *m*

cent ['sɛnt] *n* : centavo *m*

centaur ['sɛn‚tɔr] *n* : centauro *m*

centennial[1] [sɛn'tɛniəl] *adj* : del centenario

centennial[2] *n* : centenario *m*

center[1] ['sɛntər] *vt* **1** : centrar **2** CONCENTRATE : concentrar, fijar, enfocar — *vi* : centrarse, enfocarse

center[2] *n* **1** : centro *m* ⟨center of gravity : centro de gravedad⟩ **2** : centro *m* (en futbol americano), pívot *mf* (en basquetbol)

centerpiece ['sɛntər‚pi:s] *n* : centro *m* de mesa

centi- ['sɛntə] *pref* : centi-

centigrade ['sɛntə‚greɪd, 'san-] *adj* : centígrado

centigram ['sɛntə,græm, 'sɑn-] n : centigramo m

centimeter ['sɛntə,miːtər, 'sɑn-] n : centímetro m

centipede ['sɛntə,piːd] n : ciempiés m

central ['sɛntrəl] adj 1 : céntrico, central ⟨in a central location : en un lugar céntrico⟩ 2 MAIN, PRINCIPAL : central, fundamental, principal

Central American[1] : centroamericano

Central American[2] n : centroamericano m, -na f

centralist ['sɛntrəlɪst] n : centralista mf — **centralist** adj

centralization [,sɛntrələ'zeɪʃən] n : centralización f

centralize ['sɛntrə,laɪz] vt -ized; -izing : centralizar

centre ['sɛntər] → **center**

centrifugal force [sɛn'trɪfjəgəl-, -'trɪfɪ-] : fuerza f centrífuga

centrist ['sɛntrɪst] n : centrista mf — **centrist** adj

century ['sɛntʃəri] n, pl -ries : siglo m

CEO [,siː,iː'oː] n (chief executive officer) : director m, -tora f general (de una compañía)

ceramic[1] [sə'ræmɪk] adj : de cerámica

ceramic[2] n 1 : objeto m de cerámica, cerámica f 2 **ceramics** npl : cerámica f

cereal[1] ['sɪriəl] adj : cereal

cereal[2] n : cereal m

cerebellum [,sɛrə'bɛləm] n, pl -**bellums** or -**bella** [-'bɛlə] : cerebelo m

cerebral [sə'riːbrəl, 'sɛrə-] adj : cerebral

cerebral palsy n : parálisis f cerebral

cerebrum [sə'riːbrəm, 'sɛrə-] n, pl -**brums** or -**bra** [-brə] : cerebro m

ceremonial[1] [,sɛrə'moːniəl] adj : ceremonial

ceremonial[2] n : ceremonial m

ceremonious [,sɛrə'moːniəs] adj 1 FORMAL : ceremonioso, formal 2 CEREMONIAL : ceremonial

ceremony ['sɛrə,moːni] n, pl -nies : ceremonia f ⟨without ceremony : sin ceremonias⟩ ⟨not to stand on ceremony : dejarse de ceremonias⟩

cerise [sə'riːs] n : rojo m cereza

certain[1] ['sərtən] adj 1 DEFINITE : cierto, determinado ⟨a certain percentage : un porcentaje determinado⟩ 2 TRUE : cierto, con certeza ⟨I don't know for certain : no sé exactamente⟩ 3 : cierto, alguno ⟨it has a certain charm : tiene cierta gracia⟩ 4 INEVITABLE : seguro, inevitable 5 ASSURED : seguro, asegurado ⟨she's certain to do well : seguro que le irá bien⟩

certain[2] pron SOME : ciertos, algunos ⟨certain of my friends : algunos de mis amigos⟩

certainly ['sərtənli] adv 1 DEFINITELY : ciertamente, seguramente 2 OF COURSE : por supuesto

certainty ['sərtənti] n, pl -ties : certeza f, certidumbre f, seguridad f

certifiable [,sərtə'faɪəbəl] adj : certificable

certificate [sər'tɪfɪkət] n : certificado m, acta f ⟨birth certificate : partida/acta/certificación de nacimiento⟩

certification [,sərtəfə'keɪʃən] n : certificación f

certified ['sərtə,faɪd] adj 1 ACCREDITED : acreditado, certificado, diplomado, titulado 2 VERIFIED : certificado 3 fam REAL : verdadero, auténtico

certify ['sərtə,faɪ] vt -fied; -fying 1 VERIFY : certificar, verificar, confirmar, constatar 2 ENDORSE : endosar, aprobar oficialmente 3 ACCREDIT, LICENSE : acreditar, autorizar

certitude ['sərtə,tuːd, -,tjuːd] n : certeza f, certidumbre f

cervical ['sərvɪkəl] adj 1 : cervical (dícese del cuello) 2 : del cuello del útero

cervix ['sərvɪks] n, pl -**vices** [-və-,siːz] or -**vixes** : cuello m del útero

cesarean[1] [sɪ'zæriən] adj : cesáreo

cesarean[2] or **cesarean section** n : cesárea f

cesium ['siːziəm] n : cesio m

cessation [sɛ'seɪʃən] n : cesación f, cese m

cesspool ['sɛs,puːl] n : pozo m séptico

chafe ['tʃeɪf] v **chafed**; **chafing** vi : enojarse, irritarse — vt : rozar

chaff ['tʃæf] n 1 : barcia f, granzas fpl 2 to separate the wheat from the chaff : separar el grano de la paja

chagrin[1] [ʃə'grɪn] vt : desilusionar, avergonzar

chagrin[2] n : desilusión f, disgusto m

chain[1] ['tʃeɪn] vt : encadenar

chain[2] n 1 : cadena f ⟨steel chain : cadena de acero⟩ ⟨restaurant chain : cadena de restaurantes⟩ 2 SERIES : serie f ⟨chain of events : serie de eventos⟩ 3 **chains** npl FETTERS : grillos mpl

chain-smoke ['tʃeɪn'smoːk] n : fumar un cigarrillo tras otro

chair[1] ['tʃɛr] vt : presidir, moderar

chair[2] n 1 : silla f 2 CHAIRMANSHIP : presidencia f 3 → **chairman, chairwoman, chairperson** 4 or **department chair** : catedrático m, -ca f (de una universidad)

chairlift ['tʃɛr,lɪft] n : telesilla mf

chairman ['tʃɛrmən] n, pl -**men** [-mən, -,mɛn] : presidente m

chairmanship ['tʃɛrmən,ʃɪp] n : presidencia f

chairperson ['tʃɛr,pərsən] n : presidente mf, presidenta f

chairwoman ['tʃɛr,wʊmən] n, pl -**women** [-,wɪmən] : presidenta f

chalet [ʃæ'leɪ] n : chalet m, chalé m

chalice ['tʃælɪs] n : cáliz m

chalk[1] ['tʃɔk] vt : escribir con tiza

chalk[2] n 1 LIMESTONE : caliza f, caliza f 2 : tiza f, gis m Mex (para escribir)

chalkboard ['tʃɔk,bord] → **blackboard**

chalk up vt 1 ASCRIBE : atribuir, adscribir 2 SCORE : apuntarse, anotarse (una victoria, etc.)

chalky ['tʃɔki] adj **chalkier**; -**est** 1 PALE : pálido 2 POWDERY : polvoriento

challenge[1] ['tʃælɪndʒ] vt **-lenged; -lenging**
1 DISPUTE : disputar, cuestionar, poner
en duda **2** DARE : desafiar, retar **3** STIM-
ULATE : estimular, incentivar

challenge[2] n : reto m, desafío m

challenger ['tʃælɪndʒər] n : retador m,
-dora f; contendiente mf

challenging ['tʃælɪndʒɪŋ] adj **1** DEMAND-
ING : exigente **2** DEFIANT : desafiante,
de desafío **3** STIMULATING : estimulante,
provocador

chamber ['tʃeɪmbər] n **1** ROOM : cámara f,
sala f ⟨the senate chamber : la cámara
del senado⟩ **2** : recámara f ⟨de un arma
de fuego⟩, cámara f ⟨de combustión⟩ **3**
: cámara f ⟨chamber of commerce
: cámara de comercio⟩ **4 chambers** npl
or **judge's chambers** : despacho m del
juez

chambermaid ['tʃeɪmbər,meɪd] n : camarera f

chamber music n : música f de cámara

chamber pot n : bacinica f

chameleon [kə'miːljən, -liən] n : camaleón m

chamois ['ʃæmi] n, pl **chamois** [-mi, -miz]
: gamuza f

chamomile ['kæmə,maɪl, -,miːl] n **1**
: manzanilla f, camomila f **2 chamomile
tea** : manzanilla f

champ[1] ['tʃæmp, 'tʃɑmp] vi **1** : masticar
ruidosamente **2 to champ at the bit**
: impacientarse, comerle a uno la impaciencia

champ[2] ['tʃæmp] n : campeón m, -peona f

champagne [ʃæm'peɪn] n : champaña m,
champán m

champion[1] ['tʃæmpiən] vt : defender, luchar por (una causa)

champion[2] n **1** ADVOCATE, DEFENDER
: paladín m; campeón m, -peona f; defensor
m, -sora f **2** WINNER : campeón m, -peona
f ⟨world champion : campeón mundial⟩

championship ['tʃæmpiən,ʃɪp] n : campeonato m

chance[1] ['tʃænts] v **chanced; chancing** vi
1 HAPPEN : ocurrir por casualidad **2 to
chance upon** : encontrar por casualidad
— vt RISK : arriesgarse a (hacer algo)
⟨we can't chance it : no podemos arries-
garnos⟩

chance[2] adj : fortuito, casual ⟨a chance
encounter : un encuentro casual⟩

chance[3] n **1** FATE, LUCK : azar m, suerte
f, fortuna f **2** OPPORTUNITY : oportunidad f, ocasión f **3** PROBABILITY : probabilidad f, posibilidad f **4** RISK : riesgo m
5 : boleto m (de una rifa o lotería) **6 by
chance** : por casualidad

chancellor ['tʃæntsələr] n **1** : canciller m
2 : rector m, -tora f (de una universidad)

chancy ['tʃæntsi] adj **chancier, -est** : riesgoso, arriesgado

chandelier [,ʃændə'lɪr] n : araña f de luces

change[1] ['tʃeɪndʒ] v **changed; changing** vt
1 ALTER : cambiar ⟨to change one's
mind : cambiar de idea/opinión⟩ ⟨to
change direction : cambiar de dirección⟩
2 EXCHANGE, REPLACE : cambiar (pilas,
etc.), cambiar de ⟨he changed the sub-

ject : cambió de tema⟩ ⟨to change jobs
: cambiar de trabajo⟩ ⟨to change places
: cambiar de sitio⟩ ⟨to change (dinero)
⟨can you change a twenty? : ¿me puedes
cambiar un billete de veinte dólares?⟩
⟨to change dollars into yen : cambiar
dólares a yen⟩ **4** : cambiar ⟨I changed
the baby, I changed the baby's diaper : le
cambié el pañal al bebé⟩ ⟨to change the
bed/sheets : cambiar las sábanas⟩ ⟨to
change one's clothes : cambiarse (de
ropa)⟩ **5 to change hands** : cambiar de
manos/dueño — vi **1** : cambiar ⟨you
haven't changed : no has cambiado⟩ **2**
: cambiarse (de ropa) **3 to change over
to** : cambiar a (otro sistema, etc.)

change[2] n **1** ALTERATION : cambio m ⟨a
change for the better/worse : un cambio
para mejor/peor⟩ ⟨for a change : para
variar⟩ ⟨to make changes to : hacerle
cambios a⟩ **2** REPLACEMENT, EXCHANGE
: cambio m ⟨an oil change : un cambio de
aceite⟩ ⟨a change of address : un cambio
de dirección⟩ ⟨a change of scenery : un
cambio de aire(s)⟩ ⟨a change of clothes
: una muda (de ropa)⟩ **3** : cambio m,
vuelto m ⟨two dollars change : dos dólares de vuelto⟩ ⟨do you have change for a
twenty? : ¿tienes cambio de veinte dólares?⟩ **4** COINS : cambio m, monedas fpl
⟨loose change : dinero suelto⟩

changeable ['tʃeɪndʒəbəl] adj : cambiante,
variable

changeless ['tʃeɪndʒləs] adj : invariable,
constante

changeover ['tʃeɪndʒ,oːvər] n : cambio m

changing ['tʃeɪndʒɪŋ] adj : cambiante,
variable

changing room n FITTING ROOM : probador m

changing table n : cambiador m

channel[1] ['tʃænəl] vt **-neled** or **-nelled;
-neling** or **-nelling** : encauzar, canalizar

channel[2] n **1** RIVERBED : cauce m **2**
STRAIT : canal m, estrecho m ⟨English
Channel : Canal de la Mancha⟩ **3**
COURSE, MEANS : vía f, conducto m ⟨the
usual channels : las vías normales⟩ **4**
: canal m (de televisión)

channel surfing n : zapping m

chant[1] ['tʃænt] v : salmodiar, cantar

chant[2] n **1** : salmodia f **2 Gregorian
chant** : canto m gregoriano

Chanukah ['xɑnəkə, 'hɑ-] → **Hanukkah**

chaos ['keɪˌɑs] n : caos m

chaotic [keɪ'ɑtɪk] adj : caótico — **chaoti-
cally** [-tɪkli] adv

chap n FELLOW : tipo m, hombre m

chapel ['tʃæpəl] n : capilla f

chaperon[1] or **chaperone** ['ʃæpə,roːn] vt
-oned; -oning : ir de chaperón, acompañar

chaperon[2] or **chaperone** n : chaperón m,
-rona f; acompañante mf

chaplain ['tʃæplɪn] n : capellán m

chapped ['tʃæpt] adj : agrietado ⟨chapped
lips : labios agrietados⟩

chapter ['tʃæptər] n **1** : capítulo m (de un
libro) **2** BRANCH : sección f, división f
(de una organización)

char [ˈtʃɑr] *v* **charred; charring** *vt* **1**
BURN : carbonizar **2** SCORCH : cha-
muscar — *vi* **1** : carbonizarse **2** : chamuscarse

character [ˈkærɪktər] *n* **1** LETTER, SYM-
BOL : carácter *m* ⟨Chinese characters
: caracteres chinos⟩ **2** DISPOSITION
: carácter *m*, personalidad *f* ⟨of good
character : de buena reputación⟩ ⟨to
build character : forjar el carácter⟩ **3**
REPUTATION : carácter *m*, reputación *f*
⟨character attacks : ataques personales⟩
4 NATURE, QUALITIES : carácter *m* ⟨the
national character : el carácter nacio-
nal⟩ ⟨the character of the wine : el
carácter del vino⟩ ⟨the room has no
character : la habitación no tiene
carácter⟩ **5** : tipo *m*, personaje *m* peculiar ⟨he's quite a character! : ¡él es algo
serio!⟩ **6** : personaje *m* (ficticio) **7 to be
in character** : ser típico de alguien **8 to
be out of character** : no ser típico de alguien

characteristic[1] [ˌkærɪktəˈrɪstɪk] *adj* : característico, típico — **characteristically**
[-tɪkli] *adv*

characteristic[2] *n* : característica *f*

characterization [ˌkærɪktərəˈzeɪʃən] *n*
: caracterización *f*

characterize [ˈkærɪktəˌraɪz] *vt* **-ized;
-izing** : caracterizar

charades [ʃəˈreɪdz] *ns & pl* : charada *f*

charcoal [ˈtʃɑrˌkoːl] *n* : carbón *m*

chard [ˈtʃɑrd] → **Swiss chard**

charge[1] [ˈtʃɑrdʒ] *v* **charged; charging** *vt* **1**
: cargar ⟨to charge the batteries : cargar
las pilas⟩ **2** ENTRUST : encomendar, encargar **3** COMMAND : ordenar, mandar **4**
ACCUSE : acusar ⟨charged with robbery
: acusado de robo⟩ **5** : cargar a una
cuenta, comprar a crédito — *vi* **1** : cargar (contra el enemigo) ⟨charge! : ¡a la
carga!⟩ **2** : cobrar ⟨they charge too
much : cobran demasiado⟩

charge[2] *n* **1** : carga *f* (eléctrica) **2** : carga
f (de dinamita, etc.) **3** BURDEN : carga *f*,
peso *m* **4** RESPONSIBILITY : cargo *m*, responsabilidad *f* ⟨to take charge of : hacerse cargo de⟩ ⟨to be in charge : ser el
responsable⟩ ⟨to be in charge of : tener a
su cargo⟩ **5** : persona *f* al cuidado de
alguien ⟨her young charges : los niños
que están a su cargo⟩ **6** ACCUSATION
: cargo *m*, acusación *f* ⟨to press charges
: presentar cargos⟩ **7** COST : costo *m*,
cargo *m*, precio *m* ⟨free of charge : gra-
tis⟩ ⟨they gave it to us free of charge
: nos lo regalaron gratuitamente⟩ **8** AT-
TACK : carga *f*, ataque *m* **9 to get a
charge out of** ENJOY : disfrutar de, deleitarse con

chargeable [ˈtʃɑrdʒəbəl] *adj* **1** : perseguible (dícese de un delito) **2** ~ **to** : a cargo
de (una cuenta)

charge card → **credit card**

charger [ˈtʃɑrdʒər] *n* : corcel *m*, caballo *m*
(de guerra)

chariot [ˈtʃæriət] *n* : carro *m* (de guerra)

charisma [kəˈrɪzmə] *n* : carisma *m*

charismatic [ˌkærəzˈmætɪk] *adj* : carismático

charitable [ˈtʃærətəbəl] *adj* **1** GENEROUS
: caritativo ⟨a charitable organization
: una organización benéfica⟩ **2** KIND,
UNDERSTANDING : generoso, benévolo,
comprensivo — **charitably** [-bli] *adv*

charitableness [ˈtʃærətəbəlnəs] *n* : caridad *f*

charity [ˈtʃærəti] *n, pl* **-ties 1** GENEROSITY
: caridad *f* **2** ALMS : caridad *f*, limosna *f*
3 : organización *f* benéfica, obra *f* de
beneficencia

charlatan [ˈʃɑrlətən] *n* : charlatán *m*,
-tana *f*; farsante *mf*

charley horse [ˈtʃɑrliˌhɔrs] *n* : calambre *m*

charm[1] [ˈtʃɑrm] *vt* : encantar, cautivar,
fascinar

charm[2] *n* **1** AMULET : amuleto *m*,
talismán *m* **2** ATTRACTION : encanto *m*,
atractivo *m* ⟨it has a certain charm
: tiene cierto atractivo⟩ **3** : dije *m*, colgante *m* ⟨charm bracelet : pulsera de di-
jes⟩

charmer [ˈtʃɑrmər] *n* : persona *f* encantadora

charming [ˈtʃɑrmɪŋ] *adj* : encantador, fascinante

chart[1] [ˈtʃɑrt] *vt* **1** : trazar un mapa de,
hacer un gráfico de **2** PLAN : trazar, planear ⟨to chart a course : trazar un derro-
tero⟩

chart[2] *n* **1** MAP : carta *f*, mapa *m* **2** DIA-
GRAM : gráfico *m*, cuadro *m*, tabla *f*

charter[1] [ˈtʃɑrtər] *vt* **1** : establecer los
estatutos de (una organización) **2** RENT
: alquilar, fletar

charter[2] *adj* : chárter ⟨a charter flight
: un vuelo chárter⟩

charter[3] *n* **1** STATUTES : estatutos *mpl* **2**
CONSTITUTION : carta *f*, constitución *f*

chartreuse [ʃɑrˈtruːz, -ˈtruːs] *n* : color *m*
verde-amarillo intenso

chary [ˈtʃæri] *adj* **charier; -est 1** WARY
: cauteloso, precavido **2** SPARING : parco

chase[1] [ˈtʃeɪs] *vt* **chased; chasing 1** PUR-
SUE : perseguir, ir a la caza de **2** DRIVE
: ahuyentar, echar ⟨he chased the dog
from the garden : ahuyentó al perro del
jardín⟩ **3** : grabar (metales)

chase[2] *n* **1** PURSUIT : persecución *f*, caza
f **2 the chase** HUNTING : caza *f*

chaser [ˈtʃeɪsər] *n* **1** PURSUER : perseguidor *m*, -dora *f* **2** : bebida *f* que se toma
después de un trago de licor

chasm [ˈkæzəm] *n* : abismo *m*, sima *f*

chassis [ˈtʃæsi, ˈʃæsi] *n, pl* **chassis** [-siz]
: chasis *m*, armazón *m*

chaste [ˈtʃeɪst] *adj* **chaster; -est 1** : casto
2 MODEST : modesto, puro **3** AUSTERE
: austero, sobrio

chastely [ˈtʃeɪstli] *adv* : castamente

chasten [ˈtʃeɪsən] *vt* : castigar, sancionar

chasteness [ˈtʃeɪstnəs] *n* **1** MODESTY
: modestia *f*, castidad *f* **2** AUSTERITY
: sobriedad *f*, austeridad *f*

chastise [ˈtʃæsˌtaɪz, tʃæsˈ-] *vt* **-tised; -tis-
ing 1** REPRIMAND : reprender, corregir,
reprobar **2** PUNISH : castigar

chastisement ['tʃæs,taɪzmənt, tʃæs'taɪz-, 'tʃæstəz-] n : castigo m, corrección f

chastity ['tʃæstəti] n : castidad f, decencia f, modestia f

chat[1] ['tʃæt] vi **chatted; chatting** : charlar, platicar

chat[2] n : charla f, plática f

château [ʃæ'to:] n, pl **-teaus** [-'to:z] or **-teaux** [-'to:, -'to:z] : mansión f campestre

chat room n : chat m, sala f de chat

chattel ['tʃætəl] n : bienes fpl muebles, enseres mpl

chatter[1] ['tʃætər] vi **1** : castañetear (dícese de los dientes) **2** GAB : parlotear fam, cotorrear fam

chatter[2] n **1** CHATTERING : castañeteo m (de dientes) **2** GABBING : parloteo m fam, cotorreo m fam, cháchara f fam

chatterbox ['tʃætər,bɑks] n : parlanchín m, -china f; charlatán m, -tana f; hablador m, -dora f

chatty ['tʃæti] adj **chattier; -est 1** TALKATIVE : parlanchín, charlatán **2** CONVERSATIONAL : familiar, conversador ⟨a chatty letter : una carta llena de noticias⟩

chauffeur[1] ['ʃo:fər, ʃo'fər] vi : trabajar de chofer privado — vt : hacer de chofer para

chauffeur[2] n : chofer m privado

chauvinism ['ʃo:və,nɪzəm] n : chauvinismo m, patriotería f

chauvinist ['ʃo:vənɪst] n : chauvinista mf; patriotero m, -ra f

chauvinistic [,ʃo:və'nɪstɪk] adj : chauvinista, patriotero

cheap[1] ['tʃi:p] adv : barato ⟨to sell cheap : vender barato⟩

cheap[2] adj **1** INEXPENSIVE : barato, económico **2** SHODDY : barato, mal hecho **3** STINGY : tacaño, agarrado fam, codo Mex

cheapen ['tʃi:pən] vt : degradar, rebajar

cheaply ['tʃi:pli] adv : barato, a precio bajo

cheapness ['tʃi:pnəs] n **1** : precio m bajo **2** STINGINESS : tacañería f

cheapskate ['tʃi:p,skeɪt] n : tacaño m, -ña f; codo m, -da f Mex

cheat[1] ['tʃi:t] vt **1** : defraudar, estafar, engañar **2 to cheat on** : engañar (a un/una amante) — vi : hacer trampa

cheat[2] n **1** CHEATING : engaño m, fraude m, trampa f **2** → **cheater**

cheater ['tʃi:tər] n : estafador m, -dora f; tramposo m, -sa f

check[1] ['tʃek] vt **1** VERIFY : verificar, comprobar (la ortografía, etc.) **2** INSPECT : revisar, chequear, inspeccionar **3** CONSULT : consultar, chequear ⟨let me check the files : déjame chequear los archivos⟩ **4** HALT : frenar, parar, detener **5** RESTRAIN : refrenar, contener, reprimir **6** MARK : marcar, señalar **7** or **to check in** : chequear, facturar (maletas, equipaje) **8** CHECKER : marcar con cuadros **9 to check off** : marcar (algo en una lista) **10 to check out** INVESTIGATE : investigar **11 to check out** fam LOOK AT : mirar

12 to check out SIGN OUT : sacar (libros) **13 to check out** RING UP : cobrar (en una tienda) — vi **1** VERIFY : comprobar, verificar **2 to check back with** fam : volver a contactar ⟨I'll check back with you later : te llamaré/hablaré (etc.) más tarde⟩ **3 to check in** : registrarse (en un hotel) **4 to check into** INVESTIGATE : investigar **5 to check off on** APPROVE : aprobar **6 to check on** : ir a ver, visitar, llamar ⟨she checks on the patients regularly : visita a los pacientes regularmente⟩ **7 to check out** : pagar e irse (de un hotel) **8 to check out** SQUARE : cuadrar **9 to check up on** : vigilar, controlar **10 to check with** : consultar

check[2] n **1** HALT : detención f súbita, parada f **2** RESTRAINT : control m, freno m **3** INSPECTION : verificación f, comprobación f, inspección f, chequeo m ⟨she gave the list a quick check : le echó una ojeada a la lista⟩ ⟨security/background check : verificación de identidad/antecedentes⟩ ⟨system check : comprobación del sistema⟩ ⟨sound check : prueba de sonido⟩ **4** : cheque m ⟨to pay by check : pagar con cheque⟩ **5** VOUCHER : resguardo m, comprobante m **6** BILL : cuenta f (en un restaurante) **7** : jaque m (en ajedrez) **8** or **check mark** : marca f **9** or **check pattern** : dibujo m a/de cuadros

checkbook ['tʃek,bʊk] n : chequera f

checked adj : a/de cuadros

checker[1] ['tʃekər] vt : marcar con cuadros

checker[2] n **1** : pieza f (en el juego de damas) **2** : verificador m, -dora f **3** CASHIER : cajero m, -ra f

checkerboard ['tʃekər,bord] n : tablero m de damas

checkered adj **1** → **checked** **2** TROUBLED : accidentado

checkers ['tʃekərz] n : damas fpl

check–in ['tʃek,ɪn] n **1** : facturación f **2** or **check-in desk/counter** : mostrador m de facturación

checking account n : cuenta f corriente

checklist ['tʃek,lɪst] n : lista f de control

checkmate[1] ['tʃek,meɪt] vt **-mated; -mating 1** : dar jaque mate a (en ajedrez) **2** THWART : frustrar, arruinar

checkmate[2] n : jaque mate m

checkout ['tʃek,aʊt] n or **checkout counter** : caja f

checkpoint ['tʃek,pɔɪnt] n : puesto m de control

checkroom ['tʃek,ru:m, -,rʊm] n : guardarropa m

checkup ['tʃek,ʌp] n : examen m médico, chequeo m

cheddar ['tʃedər] n : queso m Cheddar

cheek ['tʃi:k] n **1** : mejilla f, cachete m **2** IMPUDENCE : insolencia f, descaro m

cheekbone ['tʃi:k,bo:n] n : pómulo m

cheeked ['tʃi:kt] adj used in combination : de mejillas ⟨rosy-cheeked : de mejillas sonrosadas⟩

cheeky ['tʃi:ki] adj **cheekier; -est** : descarado, insolente, atrevido

cheep[1] ['tʃi:p] vi : piar

cheep[2] *n* : pío *m*

cheer[1] ['tʃɪr] *vt* **1** ENCOURAGE : alentar, animar **2** GLADDEN : alegrar, levantar el ánimo a **3** ACCLAIM : aclamar, vitorear, echar porras a

cheer[2] *n* **1** CHEERFULNESS : alegría *f*, buen humor *m*, jovialidad *f* **2** APPLAUSE : aclamación *f*, ovación *f*, aplausos *mpl* ⟨three cheers for the chief! : ¡viva el jefe!⟩ **3** cheers! : ¡salud!

cheerful ['tʃɪrfəl] *adj* : alegre, de buen humor

cheerfully ['tʃɪrfəli] *adv* : alegremente, jovialmente

cheerfulness ['tʃɪrfəlnəs] *n* : buen humor *m*, alegría *f*

cheerily ['tʃɪrəli] *adv* : alegremente

cheeriness ['tʃɪrinəs] *n* : buen humor *m*, alegría *f*

cheerleader ['tʃɪr,li:dər] *n* : porrista *mf*

cheerless ['tʃɪrləs] *adj* BLEAK : triste, sombrío

cheery ['tʃɪri] *adj* **cheerier; -est** : alegre, de buen humor

cheese ['tʃi:z] *n* : queso *m*

cheeseburger ['tʃi:z,bərgər] *n* : hamburguesa *f* con queso

cheesecake ['tʃi:z,keɪk] *n* : tarta *f* de queso

cheesecloth ['tʃi:z,klɔθ] *n* : estopilla *f*

cheesy ['tʃi:zi] *adj* **cheesier; -est 1** : a queso **2** : que contiene queso **3** CHEAP : barato, de mala calidad

cheetah ['tʃi:tə] *n* : guepardo *m*

chef ['ʃɛf] *n* : chef *m*

chemical[1] ['kɛmɪkəl] *adj* : químico — **chemically** [-mɪkli] *adv*

chemical[2] *n* : sustancia *f* química

chemical weapon *n* : arma *f* química

chemise [ʃə'mi:z] *n* **1** : camiseta *f*, prenda *f* interior de una pieza **2** : vestido *m* holgado

chemist ['kɛmɪst] *n* : químico *m*, -ca *f*

chemistry ['kɛmɪstri] *n*, *pl* **-tries** : química *f*

chemotherapy [,ki:mo'θɛrəpi, ,kɛmo-] *n*, *pl* **-pies** : quimioterapia *f*

cherish ['tʃɛrɪʃ] *vt* **1** VALUE : apreciar, valorar **2** HARBOR : abrigar, albergar

cherry ['tʃɛri] *n*, *pl* **-ries 1** : cereza *f* (fruta) **2** : cerezo *m* (árbol)

cherub ['tʃɛrəb] *n* **1** *pl* **-ubim** ['tʃɛrə,bɪm, 'tʃɛrjə-] ANGEL : ángel *m*, querubín *m* **2** *pl* **-ubs** : niño *m* regordete, niña *f* regordeta

cherubic [tʃə'ru:bɪk] *adj* : querúbico, angelical

chess ['tʃɛs] *n* : ajedrez *m*

chessboard ['tʃɛs,bord] *n* : tablero *m* de ajedrez

chessman ['tʃɛsmən, -,mæn] *n*, *pl* **-men** [-mən, -,mæn] : pieza *f* de ajedrez

chest ['tʃɛst] *n* **1** : cofre *m*, baúl *m* **2** : pecho *m* ⟨chest pains : dolores de pecho⟩

chestnut ['tʃɛst,nʌt] *n* **1** : castaña *f* (fruto) **2** : castaño *m* (árbol)

chest of drawers *n* : cómoda *f*

chevron ['ʃɛvrən] *n* : galón *m* (de un oficial militar)

chew[1] ['tʃu:] *vt* **1** : masticar, mascar **2 to chew out** SCOLD : regañar **3 to chew the fat** CHAT : charlar, platicar **4 to chew up** : destrozar a mordiscos **5 to chew up** DESTROY : destrozar — *vi* **to chew on/over** THINK OVER : pensar

chew[2] *n* : algo que se masca (como tabaco)

chewing gum *n* : goma *f* de mascar, chicle *m*

chewy ['tʃu:i] *adj* **chewier; -est 1** : fibroso (dícese de las carnes o los vegetales) **2** : pegajoso, chicloso (dícese de los dulces)

chic[1] ['ʃi:k] *adj* : chic, elegante, de moda

chic[2] *n* : chic *m*, elegancia *f*

Chicana [tʃɪ'kɑnə] *n* : chicana *f*

Chicano [tʃɪ'kɑno] *n* : chicano *m*, -na *f* — **Chicano** *adj*

chick ['tʃɪk] *n* : pollito *m*, -ta *f*; polluelo *m*

chicken[1] ['tʃɪkən] *adj* : miedoso, cobarde

chicken[2] *n* **1** FOWL : pollo *m* **2** COWARD : cobarde *mf*

chickenhearted ['tʃɪkən,hɑrtəd] *adj* : miedoso, cobarde

chicken out *vi* *fam* : acobardarse, rajarse

chicken pox *n* : varicela *f*

chickpea ['tʃɪk,pi:] *n* : garbanzo *m*

chicle ['tʃɪkəl] *n* : chicle *m* (resina)

chicory ['tʃɪkəri] *n*, *pl* **-ries 1** : endibia *f* (para ensaladas) **2** : achicoria *f* (aditivo de café)

chide ['tʃaɪd] *vt* **chid** ['tʃɪd] *or* **chided; chid** *or* **chidden** ['tʃɪdən] *or* **chided; chiding** ['tʃaɪdɪŋ] : regañar, reprender

chief[1] ['tʃi:f] *adj* : principal, capital ⟨chief negotiator : negociador en jefe⟩ — **chiefly** *adv*

chief[2] *n* : jefe *m*, -fa *f* ⟨fire/police chief : jefe de bomberos/policía⟩

chief executive officer *n* → CEO

chieftain ['tʃi:ftən] *n* : jefe *m*, -fa *f* (de una tribu)

chiffon [ʃɪ'fɑn, 'ʃɪ,-] *n* : chifón *m*

chigger ['tʃɪgər] *n* : nigua *f*

chignon ['ʃi:n,jɑn, -,jɔn] *n* : moño *m*, chongo *m* *Mex*

child ['tʃaɪld] *n*, *pl* **children** ['tʃɪldrən] **1** BABY, YOUNGSTER : niño *m*, -ña *f*; criatura *f* **2 children** *npl* OFFSPRING : hijo *m*, -ja *f*; progenie *f*

childbearing[1] ['tʃaɪld,bɛrɪŋ] *adj* : relativo al parto ⟨of childbearing age : en edad fértil⟩

childbearing[2] → **childbirth**

childbirth ['tʃaɪld,bərθ] *n* : parto *m*

childhood ['tʃaɪld,hʊd] *n* : infancia *f*, niñez *f*

childish ['tʃaɪldɪʃ] *adj* : infantil, inmaduro — **childishly** *adv*

childishness ['tʃaɪldɪʃnəs] *n* : inmadurez *f*

childless ['tʃaɪldləs] *adj* : sin hijos

childlike ['tʃaɪld,laɪk] *adj* : infantil, inocente ⟨a childlike imagination : una imaginación infantil⟩

childproof ['tʃaɪld,pru:f] *adj* : a prueba de niños

Chilean ['tʃɪliən, tʃɪ'leɪən] *n* : chileno *m*, -na *f* — **Chilean** *adj*

chili or **chile** or **chilli** [ˈtʃɪli] n, pl **chilies** or **chiles** or **chillies** **1** or **chili pepper** : chile m, ají m **2** : chile m con carne

chill¹ [ˈtʃɪl] v : enfriar

chill² adj : frío, gélido ⟨a chill wind : un viento frío⟩

chill³ n **1** CHILLINESS : fresco m, frío m **2** SHIVER : escalofrío m **3** DAMPER : enfriamiento m, frío m ⟨to cast a chill over : enfriar⟩

chilliness [ˈtʃɪlinəs] n : frío m, fresco m

chilly [ˈtʃɪli] adj **chillier; -est** : frío ⟨it's chilly tonight : hace frío esta noche⟩

chime¹ [ˈtʃaɪm] v **chimed; chiming** vt : hacer sonar (una campana) — vi : sonar una campana, dar campanadas

chime² n **1** BELLS : juego m de campanitas sintonizadas, carillón m **2** PEAL : tañido m, campanada f

chime in vi : meterse en una conversación

chimera or **chimaera** [kaɪˈmɪrə, kə-] n : quimera f

chimney [ˈtʃɪmni] n, pl **-neys** : chimenea f

chimney sweep n : deshollinador m, -dora f

chimp [ˈtʃɪmp, ˈʃɪmp] → chimpanzee

chimpanzee [ˌtʃɪmˌpænˈziː, ˌʃɪm-; tʃɪmˈpænzi, ʃɪm-] n : chimpancé m

chin [ˈtʃɪn] n : barbilla f, mentón m, barba f, pera f Arg, Chile, Uru

china [ˈtʃaɪnə] n **1** PORCELAIN : porcelana f, loza f **2** CROCKERY, TABLEWARE : loza f, vajilla f

chinchilla [tʃɪnˈtʃɪlə] n : chinchilla f

Chinese¹ [ˈtʃaɪˈniːz, -ˈniːs] adj : chino

Chinese² n **1** : chino m (idioma) **2 the Chinese** (used with a plural verb) : los chinos

chink [ˈtʃɪŋk] n : grieta f, abertura f

chintz [ˈtʃɪnts] n : chintz m, chinz m

chip¹ [ˈtʃɪp] v **chipped; chipping** vt : desportillar, desconchar, astillar (madera) — vi : desportillarse, desconcharse, descascararse (dícese de la pintura, etc.)

chip² n **1** : astilla f (de madera o vidrio), lasca f (de piedra) ⟨he's a chip off the old block : de tal palo, tal astilla⟩ **2** : bocado m pequeño (en rodajas o rebanadas) ⟨tortilla chips : totopos, tortillitas tostadas⟩ **3** : ficha f (de póker, etc.) **4** NICK : mella f **5** : chip m ⟨memory chip : chip de memoria⟩

chip in v CONTRIBUTE : contribuir

chipmunk [ˈtʃɪpˌmʌŋk] n : ardilla f listada

chipotle [tʃəˈpoːtleɪ, tʃi-] n : chipotle m

chipper [ˈtʃɪpər] adj : alegre y vivaz

chiropodist [kəˈrɑpədɪst, ʃə-] n : podólogo m, -ga f

chiropody [kəˈrɑpədi, ʃə-] n : podología f

chiropractic [ˈkaɪrəˌpræktɪk] n : quiropráctica f

chiropractor [ˈkaɪrəˌpræktər] n : quiropráctico m, -ca f

chirp¹ [ˈtʃərp] vi : gorjear (dícese de los pájaros), chirriar (dícese de los grillos)

chirp² n : gorjeo m (de un pájaro), chirrido m (de un grillo)

chisel¹ [ˈtʃɪzəl] vt **-eled** or **-elled; -eling** or **-elling** **1** : cincelar, tallar, labrar **2** CHEAT : estafar, defraudar

chisel² n : cincel m (para piedras y metales), escoplo m (para madera), formón m

chiseler [ˈtʃɪzələr] n SWINDLER : estafador m, -dora f; fraude mf

chit [ˈtʃɪt] n : resguardo m, recibo m

chitchat [ˈtʃɪtˌtʃæt] n : cotorreo m, charla f

chivalric [ʃəˈvælrɪk] → chivalrous

chivalrous [ˈʃɪvəlrəs] adj **1** KNIGHTLY : caballeresco, relativo a la caballería **2** GENTLEMANLY : caballeroso, honesto, cortés

chivalrousness [ˈʃɪvəlrəsnəs] n : caballerosidad f, cortesía f

chivalry [ˈʃɪvəlri] n, pl **-ries** **1** KNIGHTHOOD : caballería f **2** CHIVALROUSNESS : caballerosidad f, nobleza f, cortesía f

chive [ˈtʃaɪv] n : cebollino m

chloride [ˈklorˌaɪd] n : cloruro m

chlorinate [ˈklorəˌneɪt] vt **-nated; -nating** : clorar

chlorination [ˌklorəˈneɪʃən] n : cloración f

chlorine [ˈklorˌiːn] n : cloro m

chloroform [ˈklorəˌfɔrm] n : cloroformo m

chlorophyll [ˈklorəˌfɪl] n : clorofila f

chock–full [ˈtʃɑkˈfʊl, ˈtʃʌk-] adj : colmado, repleto

chocolate [ˈtʃɑkələt, ˈtʃɔk-] n **1** : chocolate m **2** BONBON : bombón m **3** : color m chocolate, marrón m

choice¹ [ˈtʃɔɪs] adj **choicer; choicest** : selecto, escogido, de primera calidad

choice² n **1** CHOOSING : elección f, selección f **2** OPTION : elección f, opción f ⟨I have no choice : no tengo alternativa⟩ **3** PREFERENCE : preferencia f, elección f **4** VARIETY : surtido m, selección f ⟨a wide choice : un gran surtido⟩

choir [ˈkwaɪr] n : coro m

choirboy [ˈkwaɪrˌbɔɪ] n : niño m de coro

choke¹ [ˈtʃoːk] v **choked; choking** vt **1** ASPHYXIATE, STRANGLE : sofocar, asfixiar, ahogar, estrangular **2** BLOCK : tapar, obstruir — vi **1** SUFFOCATE : asfixiarse, sofocarse, ahogarse ⟨to choke on food : atragantarse con comida⟩ **2** CLOG : taparse, obstruirse

choke² n **1** CHOKING : estrangulación f **2** : choke m, estárter m (de un motor)

choker [ˈtʃoːkər] n : gargantilla f

cholera [ˈkɑlərə] n : cólera m

cholesterol [kəˈlɛstəˌrɔl] n : colesterol m

choose [ˈtʃuːz] v **chose** [ˈtʃoːz]; **chosen** [ˈtʃoːzən]; **choosing** vt **1** SELECT : escoger, elegir ⟨choose only one : escoja sólo uno⟩ **2** DECIDE : decidir ⟨he chose to leave : decidió irse⟩ **3** PREFER : preferir ⟨which one do you choose? : ¿cuál prefiere?⟩ — vi : escoger ⟨much to choose from : mucho de donde escoger⟩

choosy or **choosey** [ˈtʃuːzi] adj **choosier; -est** : exigente, remilgado

chop¹ [ˈtʃɑp] vt **chopped; chopping** **1** MINCE : picar, cortar, moler (carne) **2 to chop down** : cortar, talar (un árbol)

chop² n **1** CUT : hachazo m (con una hacha), tajo m (con una cuchilla) **2** BLOW : golpe m (penetrante) ⟨karate chop

: golpe de karate⟩ **3** : chuleta *f* ⟨pork chops : chuletas de cerdo⟩

chopper ['tʃɑpər] → **helicopter**

choppy ['tʃɑpi] *adj* **choppier; -est 1** : agitado, picado (dícese del mar) **2** DISCONNECTED : incoherente, inconexo

chops ['tʃɑps] *npl* **1** : quijada *f*, mandíbula *f*, boca *f* (de una persona) **2 to lick one's chops** : relamerse

chopsticks ['tʃɑp,stɪks] *npl* : palillos *mpl*

choral ['kɔrəl] *adj* : coral

chorale [kə'ræl, -'rɑl] *n* **1** : coral *f* (composición musical vocal) **2** CHOIR, CHORUS : coral *f*, coro *m*

chord ['kɔrd] *n* **1** : acorde *m* (en música) **2** : cuerda *f* (en anatomía o geometría)

chore ['tʃɔr] *n* **1** TASK : tarea *f* rutinaria **2** BOTHER, NUISANCE : lata *f fam*, fastidio *m* **3 chores** *npl* WORK : quehaceres *mpl*, faenas *fpl*

choreograph ['kɔriə,græf] *vt* : coreografiar

choreographer [,kɔri'ɑgrəfər] *n* : coreógrafo *m*, -fa *f*

choreographic [,kɔriə'græfɪk] *adj* : coreográfico

choreography [,kɔri'ɑgrəfi] *n, pl* **-phies** : coreografía *f*

chorister ['kɔrəstər] *n* : corista *mf*

chorizo [tʃə'riːzo, -so] *n* : chorizo *m*

chortle[1] ['tʃɔrtəl] *vi* **-tled; -tling** : reírse (con satisfacción o júbilo)

chortle[2] *n* : risa *f* (de satisfacción o júbilo)

chorus[1] ['kɔrəs] *vt* : corear

chorus[2] *n* **1** : coro *m* (grupo o composición musical) **2** REFRAIN : coro *m*, estribillo *m*

chose → **choose**

chosen ['tʃoːzən] *adj* : elegido, selecto

chow ['tʃau] *n* **1** FOOD : comida *f* **2** : chow-chow *mf* (perro)

chowder ['tʃaudər] *n* : sopa *f* de pescado

Christ ['kraɪst] *n* **1** : Cristo *m* **2 for Christ's sake** : ¡por Dios!

christen ['krɪsən] *vt* **1** BAPTIZE : bautizar **2** NAME : bautizar con el nombre de

Christendom ['krɪsəndəm] *n* : cristiandad *f*

christening ['krɪsənɪŋ] *n* : bautismo *m*, bautizo *m*

Christian[1] ['krɪstʃən] *adj* : cristiano

Christian[2] *n* : cristiano *m*, -na *f*

Christianity [,krɪstʃi'ænəţi, ,krɪs'tʃæ-] *n* : cristianismo *m*

Christian name *n* : nombre *m* de pila

Christmas ['krɪsməs] *n* : Navidad *f* ⟨Christmas season : las Navidades⟩

Christmas carol *n* → **carol**[2]

Christmas eve *n* : Nochebuena *f*

chromatic [kro'mæţɪk] *adj* : cromático ⟨chromatic scale : escala cromática⟩

chrome ['kro:m] *n* : cromo *m* (metal)

chromium ['kro:miəm] *n* : cromo *m* (elemento)

chromosome ['kro:mə,so:m, -,zo:m] *n* : cromosoma *m*

chronic ['krɑnɪk] *adj* : crónico — **chronically** [-nɪkli] *adv*

chronicle[1] ['krɑnɪkəl] *vt* **-cled; -cling** : escribir (una crónica o historia)

chronicle[2] *n* : crónica *f*, historia *f*

chronicler ['krɑnɪklər] *n* : historiador *m*, -dora *f*; cronista *mf*

chronological [,krɑnəl'ɑdʒɪkəl] *adj* : cronológico — **chronologically** [-kli] *adv*

chronology [krə'nɑlədʒi] *n, pl* **-gies** : cronología *f*

chronometer [krə'nɑmətər] *n* : cronómetro *m*

chrysalis ['krɪsələs] *n, pl* **chrysalides** [krɪ'sælə,diːz] *or* **chrysalises** : crisálida *f*

chrysanthemum [krɪ'sænθəməm] *n* : crisantemo *m*

chubbiness ['tʃʌbinəs] *n* : gordura *f*

chubby ['tʃʌbi] *adj* **chubbier; -est** : gordito, regordete, rechoncho

chuck[1] ['tʃʌk] *vt* **1** TOSS : tirar, lanzar, aventar *Col, Mex* **2 to chuck under the chin** : hacer la mamola

chuck[2] *n* **1** PAT : mamola *f*, palmada *f* **2** TOSS : lanzamiento *m* **3** *or* **chuck steak** : corte *m* de carne de res

chuckle[1] ['tʃʌkəl] *vi* **-led; -ling** : reírse entre dientes

chuckle[2] *n* : risita *f*, risa *f* ahogada

chug ['tʃʌg] *vi* **chugged; chugging** : resoplar, traquetear

chum[1] ['tʃʌm] *vi* **chummed; chumming** : ser camaradas, ser cuates *Mex fam*

chum[2] *n* : amigo *m*, -ga *f*; camarada *mf*; compinche *mf fam*

chummy ['tʃʌmi] *adj* **chummier; -est** : amistoso ⟨they're very chummy : son muy amigos⟩

chump ['tʃʌmp] *n* : tonto *m*, -ta *f*; idiota *mf*

chunk ['tʃʌŋk] *n* **1** PIECE : cacho *m*, pedazo *m*, trozo *m* **2** : cantidad *f* grande ⟨a chunk of money : mucho dinero⟩

chunky ['tʃʌŋki] *adj* **chunkier; -est 1** STOCKY : fornido, robusto **2** : que contiene pedazos

church ['tʃərtʃ] *n* **1** : iglesia *f* ⟨to go to church : ir a la iglesia⟩ **2** CHRISTIANS : iglesia *f*, conjunto *m* de fieles cristianos **3** DENOMINATION : confesión *f*, secta *f* **4** CONGREGATION : feligreses *mpl*, fieles *mpl*

churchgoer ['tʃərtʃ,go:ər] *n* : practicante *mf*

churchyard ['tʃərtʃ,jɑrd] *n* : cementerio *m* (junto a una iglesia)

churn[1] ['tʃərn] *vt* **1** : batir (crema), hacer (mantequilla) **2** : agitar con fuerza, revolver **3 to churn out** : producir en masa — *vi* : agitarse, arremolinarse

churn[2] *n* : mantequera *f*

chute ['ʃuːt] *n* : conducto *m* inclinado, vertedero *m* (para basuras)

chutney ['tʃʌtni] *n, pl* **-neys** : chutney *m*

chutzpah ['hutspə, 'xut-, -,spɑ] *n* : descaro *m*, frescura *f*, cara *f fam*

cicada [sə'keɪdə, -'kɑ-] *n* : cigarra *f*, chicharra *f*

cider ['saɪdər] *n* **1** : jugo *m* (de manzana, etc.) **2 hard cider** : sidra *f*

cigar [sɪ'gɑr] *n* : puro *m*, cigarro *m*

cigarette [,sɪgə'rɛt, 'sɪgə,rɛt] *n* : cigarrillo *m*, cigarro *m*

cilantro [sɪ'lɑntro:, -'læn-] *n* : cilantro *m*

cinch[1] ['sɪntʃ] vt 1 : cinchar (un caballo) 2 ASSURE : asegurar

cinch[2] n 1 : cincha f (para caballos) 2 : algo fácil o seguro ⟨it's a cinch : es bien fácil, es pan comido⟩

cinchona [sɪŋ'koːnə] n : quino m

cinder ['sɪndər] n 1 EMBER : brasa f, ascua f 2 **cinders** npl ASHES : cenizas fpl

cinema ['sɪnəmə] n : cine m

cinematic [ˌsɪnə'mætɪk] adj : cinematográfico

cinematography [ˌsɪnəmə'tɑgrəfi] n : cinematografía f

cinephile ['sɪnə'faɪl] n : cinéfilo m, -fila f

cinnamon ['sɪnəmən] n : canela f

cipher ['saɪfər] n 1 ZERO : cero m 2 CODE : cifra f, clave f

circa ['sərkə] prep : alrededor de, hacia ⟨circa 1800 : hacia el año 1800⟩

circle[1] ['sərkəl] v **-cled; -cling** vt 1 : encerrar en un círculo, poner un círculo alrededor de 2 : girar alrededor de, dar vueltas a ⟨we circled the building twice : le dimos vueltas al edificio dos veces⟩ — vi : dar vueltas

circle[2] n 1 : círculo m 2 CYCLE : ciclo m ⟨to come full circle : volver al punto de partida⟩ 3 GROUP : círculo m, grupo m (social) 4 **to have (dark) circles under one's eyes** : tener ojeras

circuit ['sərkət] n 1 BOUNDARY : circuito m, perímetro m (de una zona o un territorio) 2 TOUR : circuito m, recorrido m, tour m 3 : circuito m (eléctrico) ⟨a short circuit : un cortocircuito⟩

circuitous [ˌsər'kjuːətəs] adj : sinuoso, tortuoso

circuitry ['sərkətri] n, pl **-ries** : sistema m de circuitos

circular[1] ['sərkjələr] adj ROUND : circular, redondo

circular[2] n : circular f

circulate ['sərkjə,leɪt] v **-lated; -lating** vi : circular — vt 1 : circular (noticias, etc.) 2 DISSEMINATE : hacer circular, divulgar

circulation [ˌsərkjə'leɪʃən] n : circulación f

circulatory ['sərkjələ,tori] adj : circulatorio

circumcise ['sərkəm,saɪz] vt **-cised; -cising** : circuncidar

circumcision [ˌsərkəm'sɪʒən, 'sərkəm,-] n : circuncisión f

circumference [sər'kʌmfrənts] n : circunferencia f

circumflex ['sərkəm,flɛks] n : acento m circunflejo

circumlocution [ˌsərkəmlo'kjuːʃən] n : circunlocución f

circumnavigate [ˌsərkəm'nævə,geɪt] vt **-gated; -gating** : circunnavegar

circumscribe ['sərkəm,skraɪb] vt **-scribed; -scribing** 1 : circunscribir, trazar una figura alrededor de 2 LIMIT : circunscribir, limitar

circumspect ['sərkəm,spɛkt] adj : circunspecto, prudente, cauto

circumstance ['sərkəm,stænts] n 1 EVENT : circunstancia f, acontecimiento m 2 **circumstances** npl SITUATION : circunstancias fpl, situación f ⟨under the circumstances : dadas las circunstancias⟩ ⟨under no circumstances : de ninguna manera, bajo ningún concepto⟩ 3 **circumstances** npl : situación f económica

circumstantial [ˌsərkəm'stænʃəl] adj : circunstancial

circumvent [ˌsərkəm'vɛnt] vt : evadir, burlar (una ley o regla), sortear (una responsabilidad o dificultad)

circumvention [ˌsərkəm'vɛntʃən] n : evasión f

circus ['sərkəs] n : circo m

cirrhosis [sə'roːsɪs] n, pl **-rhoses** [-'roːˌsiːz] : cirrosis f

cistern ['sɪstərn] n : cisterna f, aljibe m

citadel ['sɪtədəl, -ˌdɛl] n FORTRESS : ciudadela f, fortaleza f

citation [saɪ'teɪʃən] n 1 SUMMONS : emplazamiento m, citación f, convocatoria f (judicial) 2 QUOTATION : cita f 3 COMMENDATION : elogio m, mención f (de honor)

cite ['saɪt] vt **cited; citing** 1 ARRAIGN, SUBPOENA : emplazar, citar, hacer comparecer (ante un tribunal) 2 QUOTE : citar 3 COMMEND : elogiar, honrar (oficialmente)

citizen ['sɪtəzən] n : ciudadano m, -na f

citizenry ['sɪtəzənri] n, pl **-ries** : ciudadanía f, conjunto m de ciudadanos

citizenship ['sɪtəzənˌʃɪp] n : ciudadanía f ⟨Nicaraguan citizenship : ciudadanía nicaragüense⟩

citrus ['sɪtrəs] n, pl **-rus** or **-ruses** : cítrico m

city ['sɪti] n, pl **cities** : ciudad f

civic ['sɪvɪk] adj : cívico

civic-minded [ˌsɪvɪk'maɪndəd] adj : cívico

civics ['sɪvɪks] ns & pl : civismo m

civil ['sɪvəl] adj 1 : civil ⟨civil law : derecho civil⟩ 2 POLITE : civil, cortés

civilian [sə'vɪljən] n : civil mf ⟨soldiers and civilians : soldados y civiles⟩

civility [sə'vɪləti] n, pl **-ties** : cortesía f, educación f

civilization [ˌsɪvələ'zeɪʃən] n : civilización f

civilize ['sɪvəˌlaɪz] vt **-lized; -lizing** : civilizar — **civilized** adj

civil liberties npl : derechos mpl civiles

civilly ['sɪvəli] adv : cortésmente

civil rights npl : derechos mpl civiles

civil servant n : funcionario m, -ria f

civil service n : administración f pública

civil war n : guerra f civil

clack[1] ['klæk] vi : tabletear

clack[2] n : tableteo m

clad ['klæd] adj 1 CLOTHED : vestido 2 COVERED : cubierto

claim[1] ['kleɪm] vt 1 DEMAND : reclamar, reivindicar ⟨she claimed her rights : reclamó sus derechos⟩ 2 MAINTAIN : afirmar, sostener ⟨they claim it's theirs : sostienen que es suyo⟩

claim[2] n 1 DEMAND : demanda f, reclamación f 2 DECLARATION : declaración f, afirmación f 3 **to stake a claim** : reclamar, reivindicar

claimant [ˈkleɪmənt] *n* : demandante *mf* (ante un juez), pretendiente *mf* (al trono, etc.)

clairvoyance [klærˈvɔɪənts] *n* : clarividencia *f*

clairvoyant¹ [klærˈvɔɪənt] *adj* : clarividente

clairvoyant² *n* : clarividente *mf*

clam [ˈklæm] *n* : almeja *f*

clamber [ˈklæmbər] *vi* : trepar o subirse torpemente

clammy [ˈklæmi] *adj* **clammier; -est** : húmedo y algo frío

clamor¹ [ˈklæmər] *vi* : gritar, clamar

clamor² *n* : clamor *m*

clamorous [ˈklæmərəs] *adj* : clamoroso, ruidoso, estrepitoso

clamp¹ [ˈklæmp] *vt* : sujetar con abrazaderas

clamp² *n* : abrazadera *f*

clam up *vi fam* : callarse, negarse a hablar

clan [ˈklæn] *n* : clan *m*

clandestine [klænˈdɛstɪn] *adj* : clandestino, secreto

clang¹ [ˈklæŋ] *vi* : hacer resonar (dícese de un objeto metálico)

clang² *n* : ruido *m* metálico fuerte

clangor [ˈklæŋər, -gər] *n* : estruendo *m* metálico

clank¹ [ˈklæŋk] *vi* : producir un ruido metálico seco

clank² *n* : ruido *m* metálico seco

clap¹ [ˈklæp] *v* **clapped; clapping** *vt* 1 SLAP, STRIKE : golpear ruidosamente, dar una palmada ⟨to clap one's hands : batir palmas, dar palmadas⟩ 2 APPLAUD : aplaudir — *vi* APPLAUD : aplaudir

clap² *n* 1 SLAP : palmada *f*, golpecito *m* 2 NOISE : ruido *m* seco ⟨a clap of thunder : un trueno⟩

clapboard [ˈklæbərd, ˈklæpˌbord] *n* : tabla *f* de madera (para revestir muros)

clapper [ˈklæpər] *n* : badajo *m* (de una campana)

clapping [ˈklæpɪŋ] *n* : aplausos *mpl*

clarification [ˌklærəfəˈkeɪʃən] *n* : clarificación *f*

clarify [ˈklærəˌfaɪ] *vt* **-fied; -fying** 1 EXPLAIN : aclarar 2 : clarificar (un líquido)

clarinet [ˌklærəˈnɛt] *n* : clarinete *m*

clarion [ˈklæriən] *adj* : claro y sonoro

clarity [ˈklærəti] *n* : claridad *f*, nitidez *f*

clash¹ [ˈklæʃ] *vi* 1 : sonar, chocarse ⟨the cymbals clashed : los platillos sonaron⟩ 2 : chocar, enfrentarse ⟨the students clashed with the police : los estudiantes se enfrentaron con la policía⟩ 3 CONFLICT : estar en conflicto, oponerse 4 : desentonar (dícese de los colores), coincidir (dícese de los datos)

clash² *n* 1 : ruido *m* (producido por un choque) 2 CONFLICT, CONFRONTATION : enfrentamiento *m*, conflicto *m*, choque *m*

clasp¹ [ˈklæsp] *vt* 1 FASTEN : sujetar, abrochar 2 EMBRACE, GRASP : agarrar, sujetar, abrazar

clasp² *n* 1 FASTENING : broche *m*, cierre *m* 2 EMBRACE, SQUEEZE : apretón *m*, abrazo *m*

class¹ [ˈklæs] *vt* : clasificar, catalogar

class² *n* 1 KIND, TYPE : clase *f*, tipo *m*, especie *f* 2 : clase *f*, rango *m* social ⟨the working class : la clase obrera⟩ 3 LESSON : clase *f*, curso *m* ⟨English class : clase de inglés⟩ ⟨to take a class : tomar/hacer un curso⟩ 4 : clase *f* ⟨she told the whole class : se lo dijo a toda la clase⟩ ⟨the class of '97 : la promoción del 97⟩ 5 STYLE : clase *f*, estilo *m* 6 : clase *f* (en un vuelo) ⟨business class : clase ejecutiva⟩

classic¹ [ˈklæsɪk] *adj* : clásico

classic² *n* : clásico *m*, obra *f* clásica

classical [ˈklæsɪkəl] *adj* : clásico — **classically** [-kli] *adv*

classicism [ˈklæsəˌsɪzəm] *n* : clasicismo *m*

classification [ˌklæsəfəˈkeɪʃən] *n* : clasificación *f*

classified [ˈklæsəˌfaɪd] *adj* 1 : clasificado ⟨classified ads : avisos clasificados⟩ 2 RESTRICTED : confidencial, secreto ⟨classified documents : documentos secretos⟩

classify [ˈklæsəˌfaɪ] *vt* **-fied; -fying** : clasificar, catalogar

classless [ˈklæsləs] *adj* : sin clases

classmate [ˈklæsˌmeɪt] *n* : compañero *m*, -ra *f* de clase

classroom [ˈklæsˌruːm] *n* : aula *f*, salón *m* de clase

classy [ˈklæsi] *adj* **classier; -est** : con clase

clatter¹ [ˈklætər] *vi* : traquetear, hacer ruido

clatter² *n* : traqueteo *m*, ruido *m*, estrépito *m*

clause [ˈklɔz] *n* : cláusula *f*

claustrophobia [ˌklɔstrəˈfoːbiə] *n* : claustrofobia *f*

claustrophobic [ˌklɔstrəˈfoːbɪk] *adj* : claustrofóbico

clavicle [ˈklævɪkəl] *n* : clavícula *f*

claw¹ [ˈklɔ] *v* : arañar

claw² *n* : garra *f*, uña *f* (de un gato), pinza *f* (de un crustáceo)

clay [ˈkleɪ] *n* : arcilla *f*, barro *m*

clean¹ [ˈkliːn] *vt* 1 *or* **to clean up** : limpiar ⟨to clean oneself up : lavarse⟩ 2 : limpiar (pescado, etc.) 3 **to clean one's plate** : comérselo todo 4 **to clean out** : limpiar y ordenar (un lugar) 5 **to clean out** : dejar pelado, limpiar, robarle todo — *vi* 1 *or* **to clean up** : limpiar ⟨to clean up after dinner : lavar los platos/trastes⟩ ⟨I'm not cleaning up after you : no voy a limpiar lo que tú ensucias⟩ 2 **to clean up** : hacerse su agosto, enriquecerse

clean² *adv* : limpio, limpiamente ⟨to play clean : jugar limpio⟩

clean³ *adj* 1 : limpio 2 UNADULTERATED : puro ⟨clean water : agua pura⟩ 3 IRREPROACHABLE : intachable, sin mancha ⟨to have a clean record : no tener antecedentes penales⟩ 4 GREEN : limpio ⟨clean energy : energía limpia⟩ 5 CLEAR, SHARP : claro, nítido ⟨clean lines : líneas sencillas/puras⟩ 6 DECENT : decente 7 COMPLETE : completo, absoluto ⟨a clean break with the past : un corte radical con el pasado⟩

cleaner ['kli:nər] *n* **1** : limpiador *m*, -dora *f* **2** : producto *m* de limpieza ⟨glass/window cleaner : limpiavidrios⟩ **3** DRY CLEANER : tintorería *f* ⟨the cleaner/cleaner's/cleaners : la tintorería⟩

cleaning ['kli:nɪŋ] *n* : limpieza *f*

cleanliness ['klɛnlinəs] *n* : limpieza *f*, aseo *m*

cleanly¹ ['kli:nli] *adv* : limpiamente, con limpieza

cleanly² ['klɛnli] *adj* **cleanlier; -est** : limpio, pulcro

cleanness ['kli:nnəs] *n* : limpieza *f*

cleanse ['klɛnz] *vt* **cleansed; cleansing** : limpiar, purificar

cleanser ['klɛnzər] *n* : limpiador *m*, purificador *m*

clean sweep *n* : barrida *f* (en una competencia)

clear¹ ['klɪr] *vt* **1** CLARIFY : aclarar, clarificar (un líquido) **2** : despejar (una superficie), desatascar (un tubo), desmontar (una selva) ⟨to clear the table : levantar la mesa⟩ ⟨to clear a path : abrir un camino⟩ ⟨to clear a space for : hacer lugar para⟩ ⟨to clear one's throat : carraspear, aclararse la voz⟩ **3** EMPTY, EVACUATE : vaciar, evacuar **4** EXONERATE : absolver, limpiar el nombre de **5** EARN : ganar, sacar (una ganancia de) **6** : pasar sin tocar ⟨he cleared the hurdle : saltó por encima de la valla⟩ **7** AUTHORIZE : autorizar **8** to clear away : poner en su sitio **9** to clear off : quitar de ⟨let me clear (the papers) off the table : déjame quitar los papeles de la mesa⟩ **10** to clear out : ordenar **11** to clear up RESOLVE : aclarar, resolver, esclarecer — *vi* **1** DISPERSE : irse, despejarse, disiparse **2** : ser compensado (dícese de un cheque) **3** to clear up : despejar (dícese del tiempo), mejorarse (dícese de una enfermedad)

clear² *adv* : claro, claramente

clear³ *adj* **1** BRIGHT : claro, lúcido **2** FAIR : claro, despejado **3** TRANSPARENT : transparente, translúcido **4** EVIDENT, UNMISTAKABLE : claro, evidente, obvio ⟨a clear explanation : una explicación clara⟩ ⟨is that clear?, do I make myself clear? : ¿está claro?⟩ ⟨I want to be clear : (quiero) que quede claro⟩ **5** SHARP : claro, nítido **6** CERTAIN : seguro ⟨to be clear on something : entender algo⟩ **7** ALERT : despejado, lúcido ⟨to have a clear head : estar despejado⟩ **8** : despejado (dícese de las vías, etc.) ⟨keep the area clear of clutter : mantener la zona libre de objetos⟩

clear⁴ *n* **1** in the clear : inocente, libre de toda sospecha **2** in the clear SAFE : fuera de peligro

clearance ['klɪrənts] *n* **1** CLEARING : despeje *m* **2** SPACE : espacio *m* (libre), margen *m* **3** AUTHORIZATION : autorización *f*, despacho *m* (de la aduana)

clear–cut ['klɪr'kʌt] *adj* : bien definido

clearing ['klɪrɪŋ] *n* : claro *m* (de un bosque)

clearly ['klɪrli] *adv* **1** DISTINCTLY : claramente, directamente **2** OBVIOUSLY : obviamente, evidentemente

cleat ['kli:t] *n* **1** : taco *m* **2 cleats** *npl* : zapatos *mpl* deportivos (con tacos)

cleavage ['kli:vɪdʒ] *n* **1** CLEFT : hendidura *f*, raja *f* **2** : escote *m* (del busto)

cleave¹ ['kli:v] *vi* **cleaved** ['kli:vd] *or* **clove** ['klo:v]; **cleaving** ADHERE : adherirse, unirse

cleave² *vt* **cleaved; cleaving** SPLIT : hender, dividir, partir

cleaver ['kli:vər] *n* : cuchilla *f* de carnicero

clef ['klɛf] *n* : clave *f*

cleft ['klɛft] *n* : hendidura *f*, raja *f*, grieta *f*

clemency ['klɛməntsi] *n* : clemencia *f*

clement ['klɛmənt] *adj* **1** MERCIFUL : clemente, piadoso **2** MILD : clemente, apacible

clench ['klɛntʃ] *vt* **1** CLUTCH : agarrar **2** TIGHTEN : apretar (el puño, los dientes)

clergy ['klərdʒi] *n, pl* **-gies** : clero *m*

clergyman ['klərdʒimən] *n, pl* **-men** [-mən, -ˌmɛn] : clérigo *m*

cleric ['klɛrɪk] *n* : clérigo *m*, -ga *f*

clerical ['klɛrɪkəl] *adj* **1** : clerical ⟨a clerical collar : un alzacuello⟩ **2** : de oficina ⟨clerical staff : personal de oficina⟩

clerk¹ ['klərk, *Brit* 'klɑrk] *vi* : trabajar de oficinista, trabajar de dependiente

clerk² *n* **1** : funcionario *m*, -ria *f* (de una oficina gubernamental) **2** : oficinista *mf*, empleado *m*, -da *f* de oficina **3** SALESPERSON : dependiente *m*, -ta *f*

clever ['klɛvər] *adj* **1** SKILLFUL : ingenioso, hábil **2** SMART : listo, inteligente, astuto

cleverly ['klɛvərli] *adv* **1** SKILLFULLY : ingeniosamente, hábilmente **2** INTELLIGENTLY : inteligentemente

cleverness ['klɛvərnəs] *n* **1** SKILL : ingenio *m*, habilidad *f* **2** INTELLIGENCE : inteligencia *f*

clew ['klu:] → **clue**

cliché [kli'ʃeɪ] *n* : cliché *m*, tópico *m*

click¹ ['klɪk] *vt* **1** : chasquear (los dedos, etc.) ⟨to click one's heels : dar un taconazo⟩ **2** : hacer clic en (un botón, etc.) — *vi* **1** : hacer clic **2** SNAP : chasquear **3** SUCCEED : tener éxito **4** GET ALONG : congeniar, llevarse bien

click² *n* : chasquido *m* (de los dedos, etc.), clic *m* (de un botón, etc.)

client ['klaɪənt] *n* : cliente *m*, -ta *f*

clientele [ˌklaɪən'tɛl, ˌkli:-] *n* : clientela *f*

cliff ['klɪf] *n* : acantilado *m*, precipicio *m*, risco *m*

climate ['klaɪmət] *n* : clima *m*

climatic [klaɪ'mætɪk, klə-] *adj* : climático

climax¹ ['klaɪˌmæks] *vi* : llegar al punto culminante, culminar — *vt* : ser el punto culminante de

climax² *n* : clímax *m*, punto *m* culminante

climb¹ ['klaɪm] *vt* : escalar, trepar a, subir a ⟨to climb a mountain : escalar una montaña⟩ — *vi* **1** RISE : subir, ascender ⟨prices are climbing : los precios están subiendo⟩ **2** : subirse, treparse ⟨to climb up a tree : treparse a un árbol⟩

climb² *n* : ascenso *m*, subida *f*

climber [ˈklaɪmər] *n* **1** : escalador *m*, -dora *f* ⟨a mountain climber : un alpinista⟩ **2** : trepadora *f* (planta)

climbing [ˈklaɪmɪŋ] *n* MOUNTAINEERING : montañismo *m*, alpinismo *m*

clinch¹ [ˈklɪntʃ] *vt* **1** FASTEN, SECURE : remachar (un clavo), afianzar, abrochar **2** SETTLE : decidir, cerrar ⟨to clinch the title : ganar el título⟩

clinch² *n* : abrazo *m*, clinch *m* (en el boxeo)

clincher [ˈklɪntʃər] *n* : argumento *m* decisivo

cling [ˈklɪŋ] *vi* **clung** [ˈklʌŋ]; **clinging 1** STICK : adherirse, pegarse **2** : aferrarse, agarrarse ⟨he clung to the railing : se aferró a la barandilla⟩

clingy [ˈklɪŋi] *adj* **clingier; -est 1** : ajustado, ceñido (dícese de la ropa) **2** : pegajoso (dícese de una persona)

clinic [ˈklɪnɪk] *n* : clínica *f*

clinical [ˈklɪnɪkəl] *adj* : clínico — **clinically** [-kli] *adv*

clink¹ [ˈklɪŋk] *vi* : tintinear

clink² *n* : tintineo *m*

clip¹ [ˈklɪp] *v* **clipped; clipping 1** CUT : cortar, recortar **2** HIT : golpear, dar un puñetazo a **3** FASTEN : sujetar (con un clip)

clip² *n* **1** → **clippers 2** BLOW : golpe *m*, puñetazo *m* **3** PACE : paso *m* rápido **4** FASTENER : clip *m* ⟨a paper clip : un sujetapapeles⟩

clipper [ˈklɪpər] *n* **1** : clíper *m* (buque de vela) **2 clippers** *npl* : tijeras *fpl* ⟨nail clippers : cortaúñas⟩

clipping [ˈklɪpɪŋ] *n* **1** : recorte *m* (de un periódico) **2** BIT : pedazo *m*, trozo *m* (de uña, etc.), recorte *m* (de pasto, etc.)

clique [ˈklik, ˈklɪk] *n* : grupo *m* exclusivo, camarilla *f* (de políticos)

clitoris [ˈklɪtərəs, klɪˈtɔrəs] *n, pl* **clitorides** [-ˈtɔrəˌdiːz] : clítoris *m*

cloak¹ [ˈkloːk] *vt* : encubrir, envolver (en un manto de)

cloak² *n* : capa *f*, capote *m*, manto *m* ⟨under the cloak of darkness : al amparo de la oscuridad⟩

cloakroom [ˈkloːkˌruːm, -ˌrʊm] *n* : guardarropa *m*

clobber [ˈklɑbər] *vt* : dar una paliza a

clock¹ [ˈklɑk] *vt* **1** : cronometrar **2 to clock in/out** : fichar (al entrar/salir)

clock² *n* **1** : reloj *m* (de pared), cronómetro *m* (en deportes o competencias) **2 around the clock** : las veinticuatro horas

clockmaker [ˈklɑkˌmeɪkər] *n* : relojero *m*, -ra *f*

clockmaking [ˈklɑkˌmeɪkɪŋ] *n* : relojería *f*

clockwise [ˈklɑkˌwaɪz] *adv & adj* : en la dirección de las manecillas del reloj

clockwork [ˈklɑkˌwərk] *n* : mecanismo *m* de relojería

clod [ˈklɑd] *n* **1** : terrón *m* **2** OAF : zoquete *mf*

clog¹ [ˈklɑg] *v* **clogged; clogging** *vt* **1** HINDER : estorbar, impedir **2** BLOCK : atascar, tapar — *vi* : atascarse, taparse

clog² *n* **1** OBSTACLE : traba *f*, impedimento *m*, estorbo *m* **2** : zueco *m* (zapato)

cloister [ˈklɔɪstər] *n* : claustro *m*

clone¹ [ˈkloːn] *vt* : clonar

clone² *n* **1** : clon *m* (de un organismo) **2** COPY : copia *f*, reproducción *f*

close¹ [ˈkloːz] *v* **closed; closing** *vt* **1** : cerrar (una puerta, un libro, un archivo, etc.) ⟨to close one's eyes : cerrar los ojos⟩ **2** *or* **to close up** : cerrar (una empresa, etc.) ⟨they close the store at five o'clock : cierran la tienda a las cinco⟩ **3** *or* **to close down** : cerrar (una empresa, etc.) ⟨they had to close the restaurant : tuvieron que cerrar el restaurante⟩ **4** *or* **to close off** : cerrar (una calle) **5** *or* **to close out** : cerrar (una cuenta) **6** *or* **to close out** END : concluir, terminar **7** : hacer, cerrar (un trato) **8** REDUCE : cerrar, reducir (una distancia) **9 to close up** : cerrar (una casa, etc.) — *vi* **1** : cerrarse, cerrar ⟨the door closed behind her : la puerta se cerró tras ella⟩ ⟨they close on Sundays : cierran los domingos⟩ **2** TERMINATE : concluirse, terminar **3 to close at (a price)** : cotizar (a un precio) al cierre **4 to close down** : cerrar (dícese de una empresa, etc.) **5 to close in** APPROACH : acercarse, aproximarse **6 to close on** : cerrar (un trato), cerrar la compra/ venta de (una casa)

close² [ˈkloːs] *adv* : cerca, de cerca

close³ *adj* **closer; closest 1** NEAR : cercano, próximo ⟨stay close to me : no te separes de mi lado⟩ ⟨don't get too close to the fire : no te acerques al fuego⟩ ⟨we must be getting close by now : ya estaremos muy cerca⟩ ⟨Christmas is getting close : se acerca la Navidad⟩ ⟨at close range/quarters : de cerca⟩ ⟨to live in close quarters : vivir muy apretados⟩ **2** SIMILAR : parecido, similar ⟨they're close in age : tienen casi la misma edad⟩ ⟨close in size : de tamaño parecido⟩ ⟨to bear a close resemblance to : tener un gran parecido con/a⟩ **3** (*indicating approximation*) ⟨did I guess right?—no, but you're close : ¿acerté?—no, pero casi⟩ ⟨not even close : ni por asomo⟩ ⟨close, but no cigar : casi, pero no⟩ **4** (*indicating that something nearly did or didn't happen*) ⟨that was close!, that was a close one/call/shave! : ¡nos salvamos por los pelos!⟩ ⟨we won, but it was close : ganamos por los pelos⟩ **5** STRICT : estricto, detallado ⟨keep a close eye/watch on him : vigílalo bien⟩ ⟨to pay close attention to : prestar mucha atención a⟩ **6** STUFFY : de aire viciado o sofocante (dícese de un lugar) **7** TIGHT : apretado, entallado, ceñido ⟨it's a close fit : es muy apretado⟩ **8** : cercano ⟨close relatives : parientes cercanos⟩ **9** INTIMATE : íntimo ⟨close friends : amigos íntimos⟩ ⟨those close to the president : los allegados del presidente⟩ **10** ACCURATE : fiel, exacto **11** : reñido ⟨a close election : una elección muy reñida⟩ ⟨she came in a close second : quedó en segundo lugar por una diferencia mínima⟩ **12 to be close to** : estar a punto de, estar al borde de ⟨he was close to crying/tears : estaba a punto de llorar, estaba a punto de las lágrimas⟩ ⟨to be close to death : estar al borde de la muerte⟩

close⁴ ['kloːz] n : fin m, final m, conclusión f

close-knit ['kloːsˈnɪt] adj : unido, íntimo

closely ['kloːsli] adv : cerca, de cerca

closeness ['kloːsnəs] n **1** NEARNESS : cercanía f, proximidad f **2** INTIMACY : intimidad f

closet¹ ['klɑzət] vt **to be closeted with** : estar encerrado con

closet² n : armario m, guardarropa f, clóset m

close-up ['kloːsˌʌp] n : primer plano m

closure ['kloːʒər] n **1** CLOSING, END : cierre m, clausura f, fin m **2** FASTENER : cierre m

clot¹ ['klɑt] v **clotted; clotting** vt : coagular, cuajar — vi : cuajarse, coagularse

clot² n : coágulo m

cloth ['klɔθ] n, pl **cloths** ['klɔðz, 'klɔθs] **1** FABRIC : tela f **2** RAG : trapo m **3** TABLECLOTH : mantel m

clothe ['kloːð] vt **clothed** or **clad** ['klæd]; **clothing** DRESS : vestir, arropar, ataviar

clothes ['kloːz, 'kloːðz] npl **1** CLOTHING : ropa f **2** BEDCLOTHES : ropa f de cama

clothesline ['kloːzˌlaɪn] n : tendedero m

clothespin ['kloːzˌpɪn] n : pinza f (para la ropa)

clothing ['kloːðɪŋ] n : ropa f, indumentaria f

cloud¹ ['klaʊd] vt : nublar, oscurecer — vi **to cloud over** : nublarse

cloud² n : nube f

cloudburst ['klaʊdˌbərst] n : chaparrón m, aguacero m

cloudiness ['klaʊdinəs] n : nubosidad f

cloudless ['klaʊdləs] adj : despejado, claro

cloudy ['klaʊdi] adj **cloudier; -est** : nublado, nuboso

clout¹ ['klaʊt] vt : bofetear, dar un tortazo a

clout² n **1** BLOW : golpe m, tortazo m fam **2** INFLUENCE : influencia f, palanca f fam

clove¹ ['kloːv] n **1** : diente m (de ajo) **2** : clavo m (especia)

clove² → **cleave**

cloven hoof ['kloːvən] n : pezuña f hendida

clover ['kloːvər] n : trébol m

cloverleaf ['kloːvərˌliːf] n, pl **-leafs** or **-leaves** [-ˌliːvz] : intersección f en trébol

clown¹ ['klaʊn] vi : payasear, bromear ⟨stop clowning around : déjate de payasadas⟩

clown² n : payaso m, -sa f

clownish ['klaʊnɪʃ] adj **1** : de payaso **2** BOORISH : grosero — **clownishly** adv

cloying ['klɔɪɪŋ] adj : empalagoso, meloso

club¹ ['klʌb] vt **clubbed; clubbing** : aporrear, dar garrotazos a

club² n **1** CUDGEL : garrote m, porra f **2** : palo m ⟨golf club : palo de golf⟩ **3** : trébol m, basto m (en la baraja española) **4** ASSOCIATION : club m

clubfoot ['klʌbˌfʊt] n, pl **-feet** : pie m deforme

clubhouse ['klʌbˌhaʊs] n : sede f de un club

cluck¹ ['klʌk] vi : cloquear, cacarear

cluck² n : cloqueo m, cacareo m

clue¹ ['kluː] vt **clued; clueing** or **cluing** or **to clue in** : dar una pista a, informar

clue² n : pista f, indicio m

clump¹ ['klʌmp] vi **1** : caminar con pisadas fuertes **2** LUMP : agruparse, aglutinarse — vt : amontonar

clump² n **1** : grupo m (de arbustos o árboles), terrón m (de tierra) **2** : pisada f fuerte

clumsily ['klʌmzəli] adv : torpemente, sin gracia

clumsiness ['klʌmzinəs] n : torpeza f

clumsy ['klʌmzi] adj **clumsier; -est 1** AWKWARD : torpe, desmañado **2** TACTLESS : carente de tacto, poco delicado

clung → **cling**

clunky ['klʌŋki] adj : torpe, poco elegante

cluster¹ ['klʌstər] vt : agrupar, juntar — vi : agruparse, apiñarse, arracimarse

cluster² n : grupo m, conjunto m, racimo m (de uvas)

clutch¹ ['klʌtʃ] vt : agarrar, asir — vi **to clutch at** : tratar de agarrar

clutch² n **1** GRASP, GRIP : agarre m, apretón m **2** : embrague m, clutch m (de una máquina) **3 clutches** npl : garras fpl ⟨he fell into their clutches : cayó en sus garras⟩

clutter¹ ['klʌtər] vt : atiborrar o atestar de cosas, llenar desordenadamente

clutter² n : desorden m, revoltijo m

coach¹ ['koːtʃ] vt : entrenar (atletas, artistas), preparar (alumnos)

coach² n **1** CARRIAGE : coche m, carruaje m, carroza f **2** : vagón m de pasajeros (de un tren) **3** BUS : autobús m, ómnibus m **4** : pasaje m aéreo de segunda clase **5** TRAINER : entrenador m, -dora f

coagulate [koˈægjəˌleɪt] v **-lated; -lating** vt : coagular, cuajar — vi : coagularse, cuajarse

coal ['koːl] n **1** EMBER : ascua f, brasa f **2** : carbón m ⟨a coal mine : una mina de carbón⟩

coalesce [ˌkoːəˈlɛs] vi **-alesced; -alescing** : unirse

coalition [ˌkoːəˈlɪʃən] n : coalición f

coarse ['kors] adj **coarser; coarsest 1** : grueso (dícese de la arena o la sal), basto (dícese de las telas), áspero (dícese de la piel) **2** CRUDE, ROUGH : basto, tosco, ordinario **3** VULGAR : grosero — **coarsely** adv

coarsen ['korsən] vt : hacer áspero o basto — vi : volverse áspero o basto

coarseness ['korsnəs] n : aspereza f, tosquedad f

coast¹ ['koːst] vi : deslizarse, rodar sin impulso

coast² n : costa f, litoral m

coastal [ˈkoːstəl] *adj* : costero
coaster [ˈkoːstər] *n* : posavasos *m*
coast guard *n* : guardia *f* costera, guarda-costas *mpl*
coastline [ˈkoːstˌlaɪn] *n* : costa *f*
coat [ˈkoːt] *vt* : cubrir, revestir, bañar (en un líquido)
coat [ˈkoːt] *n* **1** : abrigo *m* ⟨a sport coat : una chaqueta, un saco⟩ **2** : pelaje *m* (de animales) **3** LAYER : capa *f*, mano *f* (de pintura)
coat check *n* : guardarropa *m*
coat hanger *n* : percha *f*, gancho *m*
coating [ˈkoːtɪŋ] *n* : capa *f*
coat of arms *n* : escudo *m* de armas
coatrack [ˈkoːtˌræk] *n* : percha *f*, perchero *m*
coax [ˈkoːks] *vt* : engatusar, persuadir
cob [ˈkɑb] → **corncob**
cobalt [ˈkoːˌbɔlt] *n* : cobalto *m*
cobble [ˈkɑbəl] *vt* **cobbled; cobbling 1** : fabricar o remendar (zapatos) **2 to cobble together** : improvisar, hacer apresuradamente
cobbler [ˈkɑblər] *n* **1** SHOEMAKER : zapatero *m*, -ra *f* **2 fruit cobbler** : tarta *f* de fruta
cobblestone [ˈkɑbəlˌstoːn] *n* : adoquín *m*
cobra [ˈkoːbrə] *n* : cobra *f*
cobweb [ˈkɑbˌwɛb] *n* : telaraña *f*
coca [ˈkoːkə] *n* : coca *f*
cocaine [koːˈkeɪn, ˈkoːˌkeɪn] *n* : cocaína *f*
cock[1] [ˈkɑk] *vt* **1** : ladear ⟨to cock one's head : ladear la cabeza⟩ **2** : montar, amartillar (un arma de fuego)
cock[2] *n* **1** ROOSTER : gallo *m* **2** FAUCET : grifo *m*, llave *f* **3** : martillo *m* (de un arma de fuego)
cockatoo [ˈkɑkəˌtuː] *n, pl* **-toos** : cacatúa *f*
cockeyed [ˈkɑkˌaɪd] *adj* **1** ASKEW : ladeado, torcido, chueco **2** ABSURD : disparatado, absurdo
cockfight [ˈkɑkˌfaɪt] *n* : pelea *f* de gallos
cockiness [ˈkɑkinəs] *n* : arrogancia *f*
cockle [ˈkɑkəl] *n* : berberecho *m*
cockpit [ˈkɑkˌpɪt] *n* : cabina *f*
cockroach [ˈkɑkˌroːtʃ] *n* : cucaracha *f*
cocktail [ˈkɑkˌteɪl] *n* **1** : coctel *m*, cóctel *m* **2** APPETIZER : aperitivo *m*
cocky [ˈkɑki] *adj* **cockier; -est** : creído, engreído
cocoa [ˈkoːˌkoː] *n* **1** CACAO : cacao *m* **2** : cocoa *f*, chocolate *m* (bebida)
coconut [ˈkoːkəˌnʌt] *n* : coco *m*
cocoon [kəˈkuːn] *n* : capullo *m*
cod [ˈkɑd] *n, pl* **cod** : bacalao *m*
coddle [ˈkɑdəl] *vt* **-dled; -dling** : mimar, consentir
code[1] [ˈkoːd] *vt* **coded; coding 1** ENCODE : cifrar (mensajes, etc.) **2** ENCODE : codificar (datos, etc.) **3** MARK : codificar
code[2] *n* **1** : código *m* ⟨civil code : código civil⟩ **2** : código *m*, clave *f* ⟨secret code : clave secreta⟩
codeine [ˈkoːˌdiːn] *n* : codeína *f*
codex [ˈkoːˌdɛks] *n, pl* **-dexes** [-ˌdɛksəz] *or* **-dices** [-dəˌsiːz] : códice *m*
codger [ˈkɑdʒər] *n* : viejo *m*, vejete *m*

codify [ˈkɑdəˌfaɪ, ˈkoː-] *vt* **-fied; -fying** : codificar
coeducational [ˌkoːˌɛdʒəˈkeɪʃənəl] *adj* : mixto
coefficient [ˌkoːəˈfɪʃənt] *n* : coeficiente *m*
coerce [koːˈərs] *vt* **-erced; -ercing** : coaccionar, forzar, obligar
coercion [koːˈərʒən, -ʃən] *n* : coacción *f*
coercive [koːˈərsɪv] *adj* : coactivo
coexist [ˌkoːɪgˈzɪst] *vi* : coexistir
coexistence [ˌkoːɪgˈzɪstənts] *n* : coexistencia *f*
coffee [ˈkɔfi] *n* : café *m*
coffeemaker [ˈkɔfiˌmeɪkər] *n* : cafetera *f*
coffeepot [ˈkɔfiˌpɑt] *n* : cafetera *f*
coffee table *n* : mesa *f* de centro
coffer [ˈkɔfər] *n* : cofre *m*
coffin [ˈkɔfən] *n* : ataúd *m*, féretro *m*
cog [ˈkɑg] *n* : diente *m* (de una rueda dentada)
cogent [ˈkoːdʒənt] *adj* : convincente, persuasivo
cogitate [ˈkɑdʒəˌteɪt] *vi* **-tated; -tating** : reflexionar, meditar, discurrir
cogitation [ˌkɑdʒəˈteɪʃən] *n* : reflexión *f*, meditación *f*
cognac [ˈkoːnˌjæk] *n* : coñac *m*
cognate [ˈkɑgˌneɪt] *adj* : relacionado, afín
cognition [kɑgˈnɪʃən] *n* : cognición *f*
cognitive [ˈkɑgnətɪv] *adj* : cognitivo
cogwheel [ˈkɑgˌʍiːl] *n* : rueda *f* dentada
cohabit [ˌkoːˈhæbət] *vi* : cohabitar — **cohabitation** [ˌkoːˌhæbəˈteɪʃən] *n*
cohere [koːˈhɪr] *vi* **-hered; -hering 1** ADHERE : adherirse, pegarse **2** : ser coherente o congruente
coherence [koːˈhɪrənts] *n* : coherencia *f*, congruencia *f*
coherent [koːˈhɪrənt] *adj* : coherente, congruente — **coherently** *adv*
cohesion [koːˈhiːʒən] *n* : cohesión *f*
cohesive [koːˈhiːsɪv, -zɪv] *adj* : cohesivo
cohort [ˈkoːˌhɔrt] *n* **1** : cohorte *f* (de soldados) **2** COMPANION : compañero *m*, -ra *f*; colega *mf*
coiffure [kwɑˈfjʊr] *n* : peinado *m*
coil[1] [ˈkɔɪl] *vt* : enrollar — *vi* : enrollarse, enroscarse
coil[2] *n* **1** : rollo *m* (de cuerda, etc.), espiral *f* (de humo) **2** : bobina *f* (eléctrica)
coin[1] [ˈkɔɪn] *vt* **1** MINT : acuñar (moneda) **2** INVENT : acuñar, crear, inventar ⟨to coin a phrase : como se suele decir⟩
coin[2] *n* : moneda *f*
coincide [ˌkoːɪnˈsaɪd, ˈkoːɪnˌsaɪd] *vi* **-cided; -ciding** : coincidir
coincidence [koːˈɪntsədənts] *n* : coincidencia *f*, casualidad *f* ⟨what a coincidence! : ¡qué casualidad!⟩
coincident [koːˈɪntsədənt] *adj* : coincidente, concurrente
coincidental [koːˌɪntsəˈdɛntəl] *adj* : casual, accidental, fortuito
coitus [ˈkoːətəs] *n* : coito *m*
coke [ˈkoːk] *n* : coque *m*
Coke [ˈkoːk] *trademark* se usa para un refresco de cola
cola [ˈkoːlə] *n* : refresco *m* de cola
colander [ˈkɑləndər, ˈkʌ-] *n* : colador *m*

cold¹ [ˈkoːld] *adj* : frío ⟨it's cold out : hace frío⟩ ⟨a cold reception : una fría recepción⟩ ⟨in cold blood : a sangre fría⟩

cold² *n* **1** : frío *m* ⟨to feel the cold : sentir frío⟩ **2** : resfriado *m*, catarro *m* ⟨to catch a cold : resfriarse⟩

cold–blooded [ˈkoːldˈbləˌdəd] *adj* **1** CRUEL : cruel, despiadado **2** : de sangre fría (dícese de los reptiles, etc.)

cold cuts *npl* : fiambres *mpl*

coldly [ˈkoːldli] *adv* : fríamente, con frialdad

coldness [ˈkoːldnəs] *n* : frialdad *f* (de una persona o una actitud), frío *m* (de la temperatura)

cold sore *n* : fuego *m*, calentura *f*

coleslaw [ˈkoːlˌslɔ] *n* : ensalada *f* de col

colic [ˈkɑlɪk] *n* : cólico *m*

coliseum [ˌkɑləˈsiːəm] *n* : coliseo *m*, arena *f*

collaborate [kəˈlæbəˌreɪt] *vi* **-rated; -rating** : colaborar

collaboration [kəˌlæbəˈreɪʃə n] *n* : colaboración *f*

collaborator [kəˈlæbəˌreɪtər] *n* **1** COLLEAGUE : colaborador *m*, -dora *f* **2** TRAITOR : colaboracionista *mf*

collage [kəˈlɑʒ] *n* : collage *m*

collapse¹ [kəˈlæps] *vi* **-lapsed; -lapsing 1** : derrumbarse, desplomarse, hundirse ⟨the building collapsed : el edificio se derrumbó⟩ **2** FALL : desplomarse, caerse ⟨he collapsed on the bed : se desplomó en la cama⟩ ⟨to collapse with laughter : morirse de risa⟩ **3** FAIL : fracasar, quebrar, arruinarse **4** FOLD : plegarse

collapse² *n* **1** FALL : derrumbe *m*, desplome *m* **2** BREAKDOWN, FAILURE : fracaso *m*, colapso *m* (físico), quiebra *f* (económica)

collapsible [kəˈlæpsəbəl] *adj* : plegable

collar¹ [ˈkɑlər] *vt* : agarrar, atrapar

collar² *n* **1** : cuello *m* **2** : collar *m* (para un animal)

collarbone [ˈkɑlərˌboːn] *n* : clavícula *f*

collate [kəˈleɪt; ˈkɑˌleɪt, ˈkoː-] *vt* **-lated; -lating 1** COMPARE : cotejar, comparar **2** : ordenar, recopilar (páginas)

collateral¹ [kəˈlætərəl] *adj* : colateral

collateral² *n* : garantía *f*, fianza *f*, prenda *f*

colleague [ˈkɑˌliːg] *n* : colega *mf*; compañero *m*, -ra *f*

collect¹ [kəˈlɛkt] *vt* **1** GATHER : recopilar, reunir, recoger ⟨she collected her thoughts : puso en orden sus ideas⟩ **2** : coleccionar, juntar ⟨to collect stamps : coleccionar timbres⟩ **3** : cobrar (una deuda), recaudar (un impuesto) **4** PICK UP : recoger, ir a buscar **5** DRAW : cobrar, percibir (un sueldo, etc.) — *vi* **1** ACCUMULATE : acumularse, juntarse **2** CONGREGATE : congregarse, reunirse

collect² *adv & adj* : por cobrar, a cobro revertido

collectible *or* **collectable** [kəˈlɛktəbəl] *adj* : coleccionable

collection [kəˈlɛkʃ ə n] *n* **1** COLLECTING : colecta *f* (de contribuciones), cobro *m* (de deudas), recaudación *f* (de impuestos) **2** GROUP : colección *f* (de objetos), grupo *m* (de personas)

collective¹ [kəˈlɛktɪv] *adj* : colectivo — **collectively** *adv*

collective² *n* : colectivo *m*

collector [kəˈlɛktər] *n* **1** : coleccionista *mf* (de objetos) **2** : cobrador *m*, -dora *f* (de deudas)

college [ˈkɑlɪʤ] *n* **1** : universidad *f* **2** : colegio *m* (de electores o profesionales)

collegiate [kəˈliːʤət] *adj* : universitario

collide [kəˈlaɪd] *vi* **-lided; -liding** : chocar, colisionar, estrellarse

collie [ˈkɑli] *n* : collie *mf*

collision [kəˈlɪʒən] *n* : choque *m*, colisión *f*

colloquial [kəˈloːkwiəl] *adj* : coloquial

colloquialism [kəˈloːkwiəˌlɪzəm] *n* : expresión *f* coloquial

collusion [kəˈluːʒən] *n* : colusión *f*

cologne [kəˈloːn] *n* : colonia *f*

Colombian [kəˈlɑmbiən] *n* : colombiano *m*, -na *f* — **Colombian** *adj*

colon¹ [ˈkoːlən] *n*, *pl* **colons** *or* **cola** [-lə] : colon *m* (de los intestinos)

colon² *n*, *pl* **colons** : dos puntos *mpl* (signo ortográfico)

colonel [ˈkərnəl] *n* : coronel *m*

colonial¹ [kəˈloːniəl] *adj* : colonial

colonial² *n* : colono *m*, -na *f*

colonist [ˈkɑlənɪst] *n* : colono *m*, -na *f*; colonizador *m*, -dora *f*

colonization [ˌkɑlənəˈzeɪʃ ə n] *n* : colonización *f*

colonize [ˈkɑləˌnaɪz] *vt* **-nized; -nizing 1** : establecer una colonia en **2** SETTLE : colonizar

colonnade [ˌkɑləˈneɪd] *n* : columnata *f*

colony [ˈkɑləni] *n*, *pl* **-nies** : colonia *f*

color¹ [ˈkʌlər] *vt* **1** : colorear, pintar **2** INFLUENCE : influir en, influenciar — *vi* BLUSH : sonrojarse, ruborizarse

color² *n* **1** : color *m* ⟨primary colors : colores primarios⟩ **2** INTEREST, VIVIDNESS : color *m*, colorido *m* ⟨local color : color local⟩

coloration [kʌləˈreɪʃ ə n] *n* : coloración *f*

color–blind [ˈkʌlərˌblaɪnd] *adj* : daltónico

color blindness *n* : daltonismo *m*

colored [ˈkʌlərd] *adj* **1** : de color (dícese de los objetos) **2** *sometimes offensive* : de color, negro (dícese de las personas)

colorfast [ˈkʌlərˌfæst] *adj* : que no se destiñe

colorful [ˈkʌlərfəl] *adj* **1** : lleno de colorido, de colores vivos **2** PICTURESQUE, STRIKING : pintoresco, llamativo

coloring [ˈkʌlərɪŋ] *n* **1** : color *m*, colorido *m* **2** **food coloring** : colorante *m*

colorless [ˈkʌlərləs] *adj* **1** : incoloro, sin color **2** DULL : soso, aburrido

color scheme *n* : combinación *f* de colores, tonalidad *f*

colossal [kəˈlɑsəl] *adj* : colosal

colossus [kəˈlɑsəs] *n*, *pl* **-si** [-ˌsaɪ] : coloso *m*

colt [ˈkoːlt] *n* : potro *m*, potranco *m*

column [ˈkɑləm] *n* : columna *f*

columnist [ˈkɑləmnɪst, -ləmɪst] *n* : columnista *mf*

coma [ˈkoːmə] *n* : coma *m*, estado *m* de coma

Comanche [kəˈmænt͡ʃi] *n* : comanche *mf* — **Comanche** *adj*

comatose [ˈkoːməˌtoːs, ˈkɑ-] *adj* : comatoso, en estado de coma

comb[1] [ˈkoːm] *vt* 1 : peinar (el pelo) 2 SEARCH : peinar, rastrear, registrar a fondo

comb[2] *n* 1 : peine *m* 2 : cresta *f* (de un gallo)

combat[1] [kəmˈbæt, ˈkɑmˌbæt] *vt* **-bated** *or* **-batted; -bating** *or* **-batting** : combatir, luchar contra

combat[2] [ˈkɑmˌbæt] *n* : combate *m*, lucha *f*

combatant [kəmˈbætənt] *n* : combatiente *mf*

combative [kəmˈbætɪv] *adj* : combativo

combination [ˌkɑmbəˈneɪʃən] *n* : combinación *f*

combine[1] [kəmˈbaɪn] *v* **-bined; -bining** *vt* : combinar, aunar — *vi* : combinarse, mezclarse

combine[2] [ˈkɑmˌbaɪn] *n* 1 ALLIANCE : alianza *f* comercial o política 2 HARVESTER : cosechadora *f*

combustible [kəmˈbʌstəbəl] *adj* : inflamable, combustible

combustion [kəmˈbʌst͡ʃən] *n* : combustión *f*

come [ˈkʌm] *vi* **came** [ˈkeɪm]; **come; coming** 1 APPROACH : venir, aproximarse ⟨here he comes : acá viene⟩ 2 ARRIVE : venir, llegar ⟨she came yesterday : vino ayer⟩ ⟨did the mail come? : ¿llegó el correo?⟩ 3 : venir (a un lugar, una reunión, etc.) ⟨come with me : ven conmigo⟩ ⟨are you coming to the wedding? : ¿vienes a la boda?⟩ ⟨come (and) visit us! : ¡ven a visitarnos!⟩ ⟨I'm coming! : ¡voy!⟩ 4 HAPPEN : ocurrir, pasar ⟨to come at a bad time : llegar en mal momento⟩ 5 : venir ⟨it comes in three colors : viene en tres colores⟩ 6 : estar, ir (en una serie) ⟨B comes after A : la B va después de la A⟩ 7 **come again?** : ¿cómo? 8 **come on!** (*used to encourage or urge*) : ¡vamos! 9 **come on!** (*expressing surprise, disbelief, etc.*) : ¡anda! 10 **come to think of it** : ahora que lo pienso 11 **come what may** : pase lo que pase 12 **if it comes to that** : si es necesario 13 **to be coming up** : acercarse (dícese de una fecha, etc.) ⟨her birthday is coming up : falta poco para su cumpleaños⟩ 14 **to come about** HAPPEN : ocurrir, pasar 15 **to come across** FIND : tropezarse con, dar con 16 **to come across as** : dar la impresión de, parecer ser 17 **to come along** APPEAR, ARRIVE : aparecer, llegar 18 **to come along** : venir con alguien ⟨would you like to come along? : ¿quieres venir conmigo?⟩ 19 **to come along** PROGRESS : ir ⟨how's the project coming along? : ¿qué tal va el proyecto?⟩ 20 **to come apart** : deshacerse 21 **to come around** : convencerse al final 22 **to come around** : venir, pasar ⟨why don't you come around to my

place tonight? : ¿por qué no pasas por casa esta noche?⟩ 23 **to come back** RETURN : volver ⟨come back here! : ¡vuelve acá!⟩ ⟨that style's coming back : ese estilo está volviendo⟩ 24 **to come back** RETORT : replicar, contestar 25 **to come between** : interponerse entre 26 **to come by** STOP BY : pasar por casa 27 **to come by** GET, OBTAIN : conseguir 28 **to come clean** : confesar, desahogar la conciencia 29 **to come down** : caer (dícese de la lluvia, etc.), bajar (dícese de los precios, etc.) 30 **to come down hard on** : ser duro con 31 **to come down to** : reducirse a 32 **to come down with** : caer enfermo de 33 **to come forward** : presentarse 34 **to come from** : venir de (un lugar, etc.) 35 **to come in** ENTER : entrar, pasar 36 **to come in** ARRIVE : llegar 37 **to come in** : desempeñar una función ⟨that's where you come in : ahí es donde entras tú⟩ ⟨come in handy : venir bien, ser útil⟩ 38 **to come into** ACQUIRE : adquirir ⟨come into a fortune : heredar una fortuna⟩ 39 **to come of** : resultar de 40 **to come off** DETACH : soltarse, desprenderse 41 **to come off** SUCCEED : tener éxito, ser un éxito 42 **to come off as** : dar la impresión de, parecer ser 43 **to come off well/poorly** : irle bien/mal a uno ⟨he came off poorly in the debate : le fue mal en el debate⟩ 44 **to come on** TURN ON : encenderse 45 **to come on** BEGIN : empezar 46 **to come on to someone** : insinuársele a alguien 47 **to come out** : salir, aparecer, publicarse 48 **to come out** : declararse ⟨to come out in favor of : declararse a favor de⟩ 49 **to come out** : declararse homosexual 50 **to come out and say** : decir sin rodeos 51 **to come over** STOP BY : pasar por casa 52 **to come over someone** : sobrevenirle (una emoción) a alguien ⟨I don't know what came over her : no sé qué le pasó⟩ 53 **to come through** : pasar por, sobrevivir a 54 **to come through** SHOW : ser evidente 55 **to come through** : recibirse (dícese de una señal, etc.), llegar 56 **to come to** REVIVE : recobrar el conocimiento, volver en sí 57 **to come to** : llegar a (un lugar) 58 **to come to** : llegar a, ascender a (una cantidad) 59 **to come to** REACH : llegar a, alcanzar (un acuerdo, etc.) ⟨to come to an end : llegar a su fin⟩ ⟨to come to a boil : empezar a hervir⟩ 60 **to come to** : ocurrírsele (a alguien) ⟨the answer came to me : la respuesta me vino, se me ocurrió la respuesta⟩ 61 **to come to believe (etc.)** : llegar a ser/creer (etc.) 62 **to come to pass** HAPPEN : acontecer 63 **to come to terms** : llegar a un acuerdo 64 **to come under** ⟨to come under attack/criticism : ser atacado/criticado⟩ ⟨to come under the control of : quedar bajo el control de⟩ 65 **to come under** : ir bajo (una categoría, etc.) 66 **to come undone** : desatarse, desabrocharse 67 **to come up** ARISE : surgir 68 **to come up** RISE, APPEAR

: salir **69 to come up** : resultar, salir, quedar ⟨the shot came up short : el tiro se quedó corto⟩ ⟨to come up heads/tails : salir cara/cruz⟩ **70 to come up against** : enfrentarse a, tropezar con **71 to come up to someone** : acercarse a alguien **72 to come up with** : encontrar (una solución), idear (un plan), conseguir (dinero) ⟨we couldn't come up with a better idea : no se nos ocurrió una mejor⟩ **73 to have it coming** : tenerlo merecido **74 what's coming to someone** ⟨one day he'll get what's coming to him : algún día recibirá su merecido⟩ **75 when it comes to** : en cuanto a, cuando se trata de ⟨when it comes to chess, he's the best : cuando se trata de ajedrez, él es el mejor⟩

comeback ['kʌm,bæk] *n* **1** RETORT : réplica *f*, respuesta *f* **2** RETURN : retorno *m*, regreso *m* ⟨the champion announced his comeback : el campeón anunció su regreso⟩

comedian [kə'miːdiən] *n* : cómico *m*, -ca *f*; humorista *mf*

comedienne [kə,miːdi'ɛn] *n* : cómica *f*, humorista *f*

comedy ['kɑmədi] *n, pl* **-dies** : comedia *f*

comely ['kʌmli] *adj* comelier; -est : bello, bonito

comet ['kɑmət] *n* : cometa *m*

comfort[1] ['kʌmpfərt] *vt* **1** CHEER : confortar, alentar **2** CONSOLE : consolar

comfort[2] *n* **1** CONSOLATION : consuelo *m* **2** WELL-BEING : confort *m*, bienestar *m* **3** CONVENIENCE : comodidad *f* ⟨the comforts of home : las comodidades del hogar⟩

comfortable ['kʌmpfərtəbəl, 'kʌmpftə-] *adj* : cómodo, confortable — **comfortably** ['kʌmpfərtəbli, 'kʌmpftə-] *adv*

comforter ['kʌmpfərtər] *n* QUILT : edredón *m*, cobertor *m*

comic[1] ['kɑmɪk] *adj* : cómico, humorístico

comic[2] *n* **1** COMEDIAN : cómico *m*, -ca *f*; humorista *mf* **2** *or* **comic book** : historieta *f*, cómic *m*

comical ['kɑmɪkəl] *adj* : cómico, gracioso, chistoso

comic strip *n* : tira *f* cómica, historieta *f*

coming[1] ['kʌmɪŋ] *adj* : siguiente, próximo, que viene

coming[2] *n* **1** ARRIVAL : llegada *f* **2** comings and goings** : idas y venidas *fpl*

comma ['kɑmə] *n* : coma *f*

command[1] [kə'mænd] *vt* **1** ORDER : ordenar, mandar **2** CONTROL, DIRECT : comandar, tener el mando de — *vi* **1** : dar órdenes **2** GOVERN : estar al mando *m*, gobernar

command[2] *n* **1** CONTROL, LEADERSHIP : mando *m*, control *m*, dirección *f* **2** ORDER : orden *f*, mandato *m* **3** MASTERY : maestría *f*, destreza *f*, dominio *m* **4** : tropa *f* asignada a un comandante

commandant ['kɑmən,dɑnt, -,dænt] *n* : comandante *mf*

commandeer [,kɑmən'dɪr] *vt* : piratear, secuestrar (un vehículo, etc.)

commander [kə'mændər] *n* : comandante *mf*

commanding [kə'mændɪŋ] *adj* AUTHORITATIVE : autoritario, imperativo, imperioso

commandment [kə'mændmənt] *n* : mandamiento *m*, orden *f* ⟨the Ten Commandments : los diez mandamientos⟩

commando [kə'mændoː] *n* : comando *m*

commemorate [kə'mɛmə,reɪt] *vt* **-rated; -rating** : conmemorar

commemoration [kə,mɛmə'reɪʃən] *n* : conmemoración *f*

commemorative [kə'mɛmrətɪv, -'mɛmə,reɪtɪv] *adj* : conmemorativo

commence [kə'mɛns] *v* **-menced; -mencing** *vt* : iniciar, comenzar — *vi* : iniciarse, comenzar

commencement [kə'mɛnsmənt] *n* **1** BEGINNING : inicio *m*, comienzo *m* **2** : ceremonia *f* de graduación

commend [kə'mɛnd] *vt* **1** ENTRUST : encomendar **2** RECOMMEND : recomendar **3** PRAISE : elogiar, alabar

commendable [kə'mɛndəbəl] *adj* : loable, meritorio, encomiable

commendation [,kɑmən'deɪʃən, -,mɛn-] *n* : elogio *m*, encomio *m*

commensurate [kə'mɛnsərət, -'mɛntʃʊrət] *adj* : proporcionado ⟨commensurate with : en proporción a⟩

comment[1] ['kɑ,mɛnt] *vi* **1** : hacer comentarios **2 to comment on** : comentar, hacer observaciones sobre

comment[2] *n* : comentario *m*, observación *f*

commentary ['kɑmən,tɛri] *n, pl* **-taries** : comentario *m*, crónica *f* (deportiva)

commentator ['kɑmən,teɪtər] *n* **1** HOST, ANCHOR : comentarista *mf*, cronista *mf* (de deportes) **2** : comentarista *mf* ⟨political commentators : comentaristas políticos⟩

commerce ['kɑmərs] *n* : comercio *m*

commercial[1] [kə'mərʃəl] *adj* : comercial — **commercially** *adv*

commercial[2] *n* : comercial *m*

commercialize [kə'mərʃə,laɪz] *vt* **-ized; -izing** : comercializar

commiserate [kə'mɪzə,reɪt] *vi* **-ated; -ating** : compadecerse, consolarse

commiseration [kə,mɪzə'reɪʃən] *n* : conmiseración *f*

commission[1] [kə'mɪʃən] *vt* **1** : nombrar (un oficial) **2** : comisionar, encargar ⟨to commission a painting : encargar una pintura⟩

commission[2] *n* **1** : nombramiento *m* (al grado de oficial) **2** COMMITTEE : comisión *f*, comité *m* **3** COMMITTING : comisión *f*, realización *f* (de un acto) **4** PERCENTAGE : comisión *f* ⟨sales commissions : comisiones de venta⟩

commissioned officer *n* : oficial *mf*

commissioner [kə'mɪʃənər] *n* **1** : comisionado *m*, -da *f*; miembro *m* de una comisión **2** : comisario *m*, -ria *f* (de policía, etc.)

commit [kə'mɪt] *vt* **-mitted; -mitting** **1** ENTRUST : encomendar, confiar **2** CON-

FINE : internar (en un hospital), encarcelar (en una prisión) **3** PERPETRATE : cometer ⟨to commit a crime : cometer un crimen⟩ **4 to commit oneself** : comprometerse

commitment [kə'mɪtmənt] *n* **1** RESPONSIBILITY : compromiso *m*, responsabilidad *f* **2** DEDICATION : dedicación *f*, devoción *f* ⟨commitment to the cause : devoción a la causa⟩

committee [kə'mɪti] *n* : comité *m*

commodious [kə'mo:diəs] *adj* SPACIOUS : amplio, espacioso

commodity [kə'mɑdəti] *n, pl* **-ties** : artículo *m* de comercio, mercancía *f*, mercadería *f*

commodore ['kɑmə,dor] *n* : comodoro *m*

common[1] ['kɑmən] *adj* **1** PUBLIC : común, público ⟨the common good : el bien común⟩ **2** SHARED : común ⟨a common interest : un interés común⟩ **3** GENERAL : común, general ⟨it's common knowledge : todo el mundo lo sabe⟩ **4** ORDINARY : ordinario, común y corriente ⟨the common man : el hombre medio, el hombre de la calle⟩

common[2] *n* **1** : tierra *f* comunal **2 in ∼** : en común

common cold *n* : resfriado *m* común

common denominator *n* : denominador *m* común

commoner ['kɑmənər] *n* : plebeyo *m*, -ya *f*

common law *n* : derecho *m* consuetudinario

commonly ['kɑmənli] *adv* **1** FREQUENTLY : comúnmente, frecuentemente **2** USUALLY : normalmente

common noun *n* : nombre *m* común

commonplace[1] ['kɑmən,pleɪs] *adj* : común, ordinario

commonplace[2] *n* : cliché *m*, tópico *m*

common sense *n* : sentido *m* común

commonwealth ['kɑmən,welθ] *n* : entidad *f* política ⟨the British Commonwealth : la Mancomunidad Británica⟩

commotion [kə'mo:ʃən] *n* **1** RUCKUS : alboroto *m*, jaleo *m*, escándalo *m* **2** STIR, UPSET : revuelo *m*, conmoción *f*

communal [kə'mju:nəl] *adj* : comunal

commune[1] [kə'mju:n] *vi* **-muned; -muning** : estar en comunión

commune[2] [kɑ,mju:n, kə'mju:n] *n* : comuna *f*

communicable [kə'mju:nɪkəbəl] *adj* CONTAGIOUS : transmisible, contagioso

communicate [kə'mju:nə,keɪt] *v* **-cated; -cating** *vt* **1** CONVEY : comunicar, expresar, hacer saber **2** TRANSMIT : transmitir (una enfermedad), contagiar — *vi* : comunicarse, expresarse

communication [kə,mju:nə'keɪʃən] *n* : comunicación *f*

communicative [kə'mju:nɪ,keɪtɪv, -kətɪv] *adj* : comunicativo

communion [kə'mju:njən] *n* **1** SHARING : comunión *f* **2 Communion** : comunión *f*, eucaristía *f*

communiqué [kə'mju:nə,keɪ, -,mju:nə'keɪ] *n* : comunicado *m*

communism *or* **Communism** ['kɑmjə,nɪzəm] *n* : comunismo *m*

communist[1] *or* **Communist** ['kɑmjə,nɪst] *adj* : comunista ⟨the Communist Party : el Partido Comunista⟩

communist[2] *or* **Communist** *n* : comunista *mf*

communistic *or* **Communistic** [,kɑmjə'nɪstɪk] *adj* : comunista

community[1] [kə'mju:nəti] *n, pl* **-ties** : comunidad *f*

community[2] *adj* : comunitario

commute [kə'mju:t] *v* **-muted; -muting** *vt* REDUCE : conmutar, reducir (una sentencia) — *vi* : viajar de la residencia al trabajo

commuter [kə'mju:tər] *n* : persona *f* que viaja diariamente al trabajo

compact[1] [kəm'pækt, 'kɑm,pækt] *vt* : compactar, consolidar, comprimir

compact[2] [kəm'pækt, 'kɑm,pækt] *adj* **1** DENSE, SOLID : compacto, macizo, denso **2** CONCISE : breve, conciso

compact[3] ['kɑm,pækt] *n* **1** AGREEMENT : acuerdo *m*, pacto *m* **2** : polvera *f*, estuche *m* de maquillaje **3** *or* **compact car** : auto *m* compacto

compact disc ['kɑm,pækt'dɪsk] *n* : disco *m* compacto, compact disc *m*

compactly [kəm'pæktli, 'kɑm,pækt-] *adv* **1** DENSELY : densamente **2** CONCISELY : concisamente, brevemente

companion [kəm'pænjən] *n* **1** COMRADE : compañero *m*, -ra *f*; acompañante *mf* **2** MATE : pareja *f* (de un zapato, etc.)

companionable [kəm'pænjənəbəl] *adj* : sociable, amigable

companionship [kəm'pænjən,ʃɪp] *n* : compañerismo *m*, camaradería *f*

company ['kʌmpəni] *n, pl* **-nies** **1** FIRM : compañía *f*, empresa *f* **2** GROUP : compañía *f* (de actores o soldados) **3** GUESTS : visita *f* ⟨we have company : tenemos visita⟩ **4** COMPANIONSHIP : compañía *f* ⟨to keep someone company : hacerle compañía a alguien⟩ ⟨I enjoy her company : me gusta estar con ella⟩ **5 to be in good company** : no ser el único

comparable ['kɑmpərəbəl] *adj* : comparable, parecido

comparative[1] [kəm'pærətɪv] *adj* RELATIVE : comparativo, relativo — **comparatively** *adv*

comparative[2] *n* : comparativo *m*

compare[1] [kəm'pær] *v* **-pared; -paring** *vt* : comparar — *vi* **to compare with** : poder comparar con, tener comparación con

compare[2] *n* : comparación *f* ⟨beyond compare : sin igual, sin par⟩

comparison [kəm'pærəsən] *n* : comparación *f*

compartment [kəm'pɑrtmənt] *n* : compartimento *m*, compartimiento *m*

compass ['kʌmpəs, 'kɑm-] *n* **1** RANGE, SCOPE : alcance *m*, extensión *f*, límites *mpl* **2** : compás *m* (para trazar circunferencias) **3** : compás *m*, brújula *f* ⟨the points of the compass : los puntos cardinales⟩

compassion [kəm'pæʃən] n : compasión f, piedad f, misericordia f

compassionate [kəm'pæʃənət] adj : compasivo

compatibility [kəm,pætə'bıləti] n : compatibilidad f

compatible [kəm'pætəbəl] adj : compatible, afín

compatriot [kəm'peıtriət, -'pæ-] n : compatriota mf; paisano m, -na f

compel [kəm'pɛl] vt **-pelled; -pelling** : obligar, compeler

compelling [kəm'pɛlıŋ] adj **1** FORCEFUL : fuerte **2** ENGAGING : absorbente **3** PERSUASIVE : persuasivo, convincente

compendium [kəm'pɛndiəm] n, pl **-diums** or **-dia** [-diə] : compendio m

compensate ['kampən,seıt] v **-sated; -sating** vi to compensate for : compensar — vt : indemnizar, compensar

compensation [,kampən'seıʃən] n : compensación f, indemnización f

compensatory [kəm'pɛnʃsə,tori] adj : compensatorio

compete [kəm'pi:t] vi **-peted; -peting** : competir, contender, rivalizar

competence ['kampətənts] n : competencia f, aptitud f

competency ['kampətənʃi] → **competence**

competent ['kampətənt] adj : competente, capaz

competition [,kampə'tıʃən] n : competencia f, concurso m

competitive [kəm'pɛtətıv] adj : competitivo

competitively [kəm'pɛtətıvli] adv : competitivamente ⟨competitively priced : a precios competitivos⟩

competitiveness [kəm'pɛtətıvnəs] n : competitividad f

competitor [kəm'pɛtətər] n : competidor m, -dora f

compilation [,kampə'leıʃən] n : recopilación f, compilación f

compile [kəm'paıl] vt **-piled; -piling** : compilar, recopilar

complacency [kəm'pleısənsi] n : satisfacción f consigo mismo, suficiencia f

complacent [kəm'pleısənt] adj : satisfecho de sí mismo, suficiente

complain [kəm'pleın] vi **1** GRIPE : quejarse, regañar, rezongar **2** PROTEST : reclamar, protestar

complaint [kəm'pleınt] n **1** GRIPE : queja f **2** AILMENT : afección f, dolencia f **3** ACCUSATION : reclamo m, acusación f

complement¹ ['kamplə,mɛnt] vt : complementar

complement² ['kampləmənt] n : complemento m

complementary [,kamplə'mɛntəri] adj : complementario

complete¹ [kəm'pli:t] vt **-pleted; -pleting** **1** : completar, hacer entero ⟨this piece completes the collection : esta pieza completa la colección⟩ **2** FINISH : completar, acabar, terminar ⟨she completed her studies : completó sus estudios⟩

complete² adj **completer; -est** **1** WHOLE : completo, entero, íntegro **2** FINISHED : terminado, acabado **3** TOTAL : completo, total, absoluto

completely [kəm'pli:tli] adv : completamente, totalmente

completion [kəm'pli:ʃən] n : finalización f, cumplimiento m

complex¹ [kam'plɛks, kəm-; 'kam-,plɛks] adj : complejo, complicado

complex² ['kam,plɛks] n : complejo m

complexion [kəm'plɛkʃən] n : cutis m, tez f ⟨of dark complexion : de tez morena⟩

complexity [kəm'plɛksəti, kam-] n, pl **-ties** : complejidad f

compliance [kəm'plaıənts] n : conformidad f ⟨in compliance with the law : conforme a la ley⟩

compliant [kəm'plaıənt] adj : dócil, sumiso

complicate ['kamplə,keıt] vt **-cated; -cating** : complicar

complicated ['kamplə,keıtəd] adj : complicado

complication [,kamplə'keıʃən] n : complicación f

complicity [kəm'plısəti] n, pl **-ties** : complicidad f

compliment¹ ['kamplə,mɛnt] vt : halagar, florear Mex

compliment² ['kampləmənt] n **1** : halago m, cumplido m **2** compliments npl : saludos mpl ⟨give them my compliments : déles saludos de mi parte⟩

complimentary [,kamplə'mɛntəri] adj **1** FLATTERING : halagador, halagüeño **2** FREE : de cortesía, gratis

comply [kəm'plaı] vi **-plied; -plying** : cumplir, acceder, obedecer

component¹ [kəm'po:nənt, 'kam-,po:-] adj : componente

component² n : componente m, elemento m, pieza f

compose [kəm'po:z] vt **-posed; -posing** **1** : componer, crear ⟨to compose a melody : componer una melodía⟩ **2** CALM : calmar, serenar ⟨to compose oneself : serenarse⟩ **3** CONSTITUTE : constar, componer ⟨to be composed of : constar de⟩ **4** : componer (un texto a imprimirse)

composed [kəm'po:zd] adj : tranquilo

composer [kəm'po:zər] n : compositor m, -tora f

composite¹ [kəm'pazət, kam-; 'kampəzət] adj : compuesto (de varias partes)

composite² n : compuesto m, mezcla f

composition [,kampə'zıʃən] n **1** MAKEUP : composición f **2** ESSAY : ensayo m, trabajo m

compost ['kam,po:st] n : abono m vegetal

composure [kəm'po:ʒər] n : compostura f, serenidad f

compote ['kam,po:t] n : compota f

compound¹ ['kam'paund, kəm-; 'kam,paund] vt **1** COMBINE, COMPOSE : combinar, componer **2** AUGMENT : agravar, aumentar ⟨to compound a problem : agravar un problema⟩

compound² [ˈkɑmˌpaʊnd; kɑmˈpaʊnd, kəm-] *adj* : compuesto ⟨compound interest : interés compuesto⟩

compound³ [ˈkɑmˌpaʊnd] *n* **1** MIXTURE : compuesto *m*, mezcla *f* **2** ENCLOSURE : recinto *m* (de residencias, etc.)

comprehend [ˌkɑmprɪˈhend] *vt* **1** UNDERSTAND : comprender, entender **2** INCLUDE : comprender, incluir, abarcar

comprehensible [ˌkɑmprɪˈhentsəbəl] *adj* : comprensible

comprehension [ˌkɑmprɪˈhentʃən] *n* : comprensión *f*

comprehensive [ˌkɑmprɪˈhentsɪv] *adj* **1** INCLUSIVE : inclusivo, exhaustivo **2** BROAD : extenso, amplio

compress¹ [kəmˈpres] *vt* : comprimir

compress² [ˈkɑmˌpres] *n* : compresa *f*

compression [kəmˈpreʃən] *n* : compresión *f*

compressor [kəmˈpresər] *n* : compresor *m*

comprise [kəmˈpraɪz] *vt* **-prised; -prising** **1** INCLUDE : comprender, incluir **2** : componerse de, constar de ⟨the installation comprises several buildings : la instalación está compuesta de varios edificios⟩

compromise¹ [ˈkɑmprəˌmaɪz] *v* **-mised; -mising** *vi* : transigir, avenirse — *vt* JEOPARDIZE : comprometer, poner en peligro

compromise² *n* : acuerdo *m* mutuo, compromiso *m*

comptroller [kənˈtroʊlər, ˈkɑmpˌtroʊ-] : contralor *m*, -lora *f*; interventor *m*, -tora *f*

compulsion [kəmˈpʌlʃən] *n* **1** COERCION : coacción *f* **2** URGE : compulsión *f*, impulso *m*

compulsive [kəmˈpʌlsɪv] *adj* : compulsivo

compulsory [kəmˈpʌlsəri] *adj* : obligatorio

compunction [kəmˈpʌŋkʃən] *n* **1** QUALM : reparo *m*, escrúpulo *m* **2** REMORSE : remordimiento *m*

computation [ˌkɑmpjuˈteɪʃən] *n* : cálculo *m*, cómputo *m*

compute [kəmˈpjuːt] *vt* **-puted; -puting** : computar, calcular

computer [kəmˈpjuːtər] *n* : computadora *f*, computador *m*, ordenador *m Spain*

computerization [kəmˌpjuːtərəˈzeɪʃən] *n* : informatización *f*

computerize [kəmˈpjuːtəˌraɪz] *vt* **-ized; -izing** : computarizar, informatizar

computer programmer → programmer

computer programming → programming

computer science *n* : informática *f*

computing [kəmˈpjuːtɪŋ] *n* : informática *f*

comrade [ˈkɑmˌræd] *n* : camarada *mf*; compañero *m*, -ra *f*

con¹ [ˈkɑn] *vt* **conned; conning** SWINDLE : estafar, timar

con² *adv* : contra

con³ *n* : contra *m* ⟨the pros and cons : los pros y los contras⟩

concave [kɑnˈkeɪv, ˈkɑnˌkeɪv] *adj* : cóncavo

conceal [kənˈsiːl] *vt* : esconder, ocultar, disimular

concealment [kənˈsiːlmənt] *n* : ocultación *f*

concede [kənˈsiːd] *vt* **-ceded; -ceding** **1** ALLOW, GRANT : conceder **2** ADMIT : conceder, reconocer ⟨to concede defeat : reconocer la derrota⟩

conceit [kənˈsiːt] *n* : engreimiento *m*, presunción *f*

conceited [kənˈsiːtəd] *adj* : presumido, engreído, presuntuoso

conceivable [kənˈsiːvəbəl] *adj* : concebible, imaginable

conceivably [kənˈsiːvəbli] *adv* : posiblemente, de manera concebible

conceive [kənˈsiːv] *v* **-ceived; -ceiving** *vi* : concebir, embarazarse — *vt* IMAGINE : concebir, imaginar

concentrate¹ [ˈkɑntsənˌtreɪt] *v* **-trated; -trating** *vt* : concentrar — *vi* : concentrarse

concentrate² *n* : concentrado *m*

concentration [ˌkɑntsənˈtreɪʃən] *n* : concentración *f*

concentration camp *n* : campo *m* de concentración

concentric [kənˈsentrɪk] *adj* : concéntrico

concept [ˈkɑnˌsept] *n* : concepto *m*, idea *f*

conception [kənˈsepʃən] *n* **1** : concepción *f* (de un bebé) **2** IDEA : concepto *m*, idea *f*

concern¹ [kənˈsərn] *vt* **1** : tratarse de, tener que ver con ⟨the novel concerns a sailor : la novela se trata de un marinero⟩ **2** INVOLVE : concernir, incumbir a, afectar ⟨that does not concern me : eso no me incumbe⟩

concern² *n* **1** AFFAIR : asunto *m* **2** WORRY : inquietud *f*, preocupación *f* **3** BUSINESS : negocio *m*

concerned [kənˈsərnd] *adj* **1** ANXIOUS : preocupado, ansioso **2** INTERESTED, INVOLVED : interesado, afectado

concerning [kənˈsərnɪŋ] *prep* REGARDING : con respecto a, acerca de, sobre

concert [ˈkɑnˌsərt] *n* **1** AGREEMENT : concierto *m*, acuerdo *m* **2** : concierto *m* (musical)

concerted [kənˈsərtəd] *adj* : concertado, coordinado ⟨to make a concerted effort : coordinar los esfuerzos⟩

concerto [kənˈʧertoː] *n, pl* **-ti** [-ˌti, -ˌti] *or* **-tos** : concierto *m* ⟨violin concerto : concierto para violín⟩

concession [kənˈseʃən] *n* : concesión *f*

conch [ˈkɑŋk, ˈkɑnʧ] *n, pl* **conchs** [ˈkɑŋks] *or* **conches** [ˈkɑnʧəz] : caracol *m* (animal), caracola *f* (concha)

conciliatory [kənˈsɪliəˌtori] *adj* : conciliador, conciliatorio

concise [kənˈsaɪs] *adj* : conciso, breve — **concisely** *adv*

conclave [ˈkɑnˌkleɪv] *n* : cónclave *m*

conclude [kənˈkluːd] *v* **-cluded; -cluding** *vt* **1** END : concluir, finalizar ⟨to conclude a meeting : concluir una reunión⟩ **2** DECIDE : concluir, llegar a la conclusión de — *vi* END : concluir, terminar

conclusion [kən'klu:ʒən] *n* **1** INFERENCE : conclusión *f* **2** END : fin *m*, final *m*

conclusive [kən'klu:sɪv] *adj* : concluyente, decisivo — **conclusively** *adv*

concoct [kən'kɑkt, kɑn-] *vt* **1** PREPARE : preparar, confeccionar **2** DEVISE : inventar, tramar

concoction [kən'kɑkʃən] *n* : invención *f*, mejunje *m*, brebaje *m*

concord [ˈkɑn₁kɔrd, ˈkɑŋ-] *n* **1** HARMONY : concordia *f*, armonía *f* **2** AGREEMENT : acuerdo *m*

concordance [kən'kɔrdənts] *n* : concordancia *f*

concourse [ˈkɑn₁kors] *n* : explanada *f*, salón *m* (para pasajeros)

concrete¹ [kɑn'kri:t, ˈkɑn₁kri:t] *adj* **1** REAL : concreto ⟨concrete objects : objetos concretos⟩ **2** SPECIFIC : determinado, específico **3** : de concreto, de hormigón ⟨concrete walls : paredes de concreto⟩

concrete² [ˈkɑn₁kri:t, kɑn'kri:t] *n* : concreto *m*, hormigón *m*

concur [kən'kər] *vi* **concurred; concurring 1** COINCIDE : concurrir, coincidir **2** AGREE : concurrir, estar de acuerdo

concurrence [kən'kərənts] *n* **1** AGREEMENT : coincidencia *f* **2** COINCIDENCE : concurrencia *f*, concurso *m*, coincidencia *f*

concurrent [kən'kərənt] *adj* : concurrente, simultáneo

concussion [kən'kʌʃən] *n* : conmoción *f* cerebral

condemn [kən'dɛm] *vt* **1** CENSURE : condenar, reprobar, censurar **2** : declarar insalubre (alimentos), declarar ruinoso (un edificio) **3** SENTENCE : condenar ⟨condemned to death : condenado a muerte⟩

condemnation [₁kɑn₁dɛm'neɪʃən] *n* : condena *f*, reprobación *f*

condensation [₁kɑn₁dɛn'seɪʃən, -dən-] *n* : condensación *f*

condense [kən'dɛnts] *v* **-densed; -densing** *vt* **1** ABRIDGE : condensar, resumir **2** : condensar (vapor, etc.) — *vi* : condensarse

condescend [₁kɑndɪ'sɛnd] *vi* **1** DEIGN : condescender, dignarse **2** to **condescend to someone** : tratar a alguien con condescendencia

condescending [₁kɑndɪ'sɛndɪŋ] *adj* : condescendiente

condescension [₁kɑndɪ'sɛntʃən] *n* : condescendencia *f*

condiment [ˈkɑndəmənt] *n* : condimento *m*

condition¹ [kən'dɪʃən] *vt* **1** DETERMINE : condicionar, determinar **2** : acondicionar (el pelo o el aire), poner en forma (el cuerpo)

condition² *n* **1** STIPULATION : condición *f*, estipulación *f* ⟨on the condition that : a condición de que⟩ **2** STATE : condición *f*, estado *m* ⟨in good/poor condition : en buenas/malas condiciones⟩ ⟨he's in good condition : está en buena forma⟩ ⟨he's out of condition : no está en

forma⟩ **3 conditions** *npl* : condiciones *fpl*, situación *f* ⟨working conditions : condiciones del trabajo⟩

conditional [kən'dɪʃənəl] *adj* : condicional — **conditionally** *adv*

conditioner [kən'dɪʃənər] *n* : acondicionador *m*

condo [ˈkɑndo:] → **condominium**

condolence [kən'do:lənts] *n* **1** SYMPATHY : condolencia *f* **2 condolences** *npl* : pésame *m*

condom [ˈkɑndəm] *n* : condón *m*

condominium [₁kɑndə'mɪniəm] *n*, *pl* **-ums** : condominio *m*

condone [kən'do:n] *vt* **-doned; -doning** : aprobar, perdonar, tolerar

condor [ˈkɑndər, -₁dɔr] *n* : cóndor *m*

conducive [kən'du:sɪv, -'dju:-] *adj* : propicio, favorable

conduct¹ [kən'dʌkt] *vt* **1** GUIDE : guiar, conducir ⟨to conduct a tour : guiar una visita⟩ **2** DIRECT : conducir, dirigir ⟨to conduct an orchestra : dirigir una orquesta⟩ **3** CARRY OUT : realizar, llevar a cabo ⟨to conduct an investigation : llevar a cabo una investigación⟩ **4** TRANSMIT : conducir, transmitir (calor, electricidad, etc.) **5** to **conduct oneself** BEHAVE : conducirse, comportarse

conduct² [ˈkɑn₁dʌkt] *n* **1** MANAGEMENT : conducción *f*, dirección *f*, manejo *m* ⟨the conduct of foreign affairs : la conducción de asuntos exteriores⟩ **2** BEHAVIOR : conducta *f*, comportamiento *m*

conduction [kən'dʌkʃən] *n* : conducción *f*

conductivity [₁kɑn₁dʌk'tɪvəṭi] *n*, *pl* **-ties** : conductividad *f*

conductor [kən'dʌktər] *n* **1** : conductor *m*, -tora *f*; revisor *m*, -sora *f* (en un tren); cobrador *m*, -dora *f* (en un bus); director *m*, -tora *f* (de una orquesta) **2** : conductor *m* (de electricidad, etc.)

conduit [ˈkɑn₁du:ət, -₁dju:-] *n* : conducto *m*, canal *m*, vía *f*

cone [ˈko:n] *n* **1** : piña *f* (fruto de las coníferas) **2** : cono *m* (en geometría) **3 ice-cream cone** : cono *m*, barquillo *m*, cucurucho *m*

confection [kən'fɛkʃən] *n* : dulce *m*

confectioner [kən'fɛkʃənər] *n* : confitero *m*, -ra *f*

confectionery [kən'fɛkʃə₁nɛri] *n*, *pl* **-eries 1** : dulces *mpl*, golosinas *fpl* **2 or confectionery shop** : confitería *f* (tienda)

confederacy [kən'fɛdərəsi] *n*, *pl* **-cies** : confederación *f*

confederate¹ [kən'fɛdə₁reɪt] *v* **-ated; -ating** *vt* : unir, confederar — *vi* : confederarse, aliarse

confederate² [kən'fɛdərət] *adj* : confederado

confederate³ *n* : cómplice *mf*; aliado *m*, -da *f*

confederation [kən'fɛdə'reɪʃən] *n* : confederación *f*, alianza *f*

confer [kən'fər] *v* **-ferred; -ferring** *vt* : conferir, otorgar — *vi* to **confer with** : consultar

conference [ˈkɑnfrənts, -fərənts] *n* : conferencia *f* ⟨press conference : conferencia de prensa⟩

confess [kən'fɛs] vt : confesar — vi 1 : confesar ⟨the prisoner confessed : el detenido confesó⟩ 2 : confesarse (en religión)

confession [kən'fɛʃən] n : confesión f

confessional [kən'fɛʃənəl] n : confesionario m

confessor [kən'fɛsər] n : confesor m

confetti [kən'fɛt̬i] n : confeti m

confidant ['kɑnfə,dɑnt, -,dænt] n : confidente mf

confidante ['kɑnfə,dɑnt, -,dænt] n : confidente f

confide [kən'faɪd] v **-fided; -fiding** : confiar

confidence ['kɑnfədənts] n 1 TRUST : confianza f 2 SELF-ASSURANCE : confianza f en sí mismo, seguridad f en sí mismo 3 SECRET : confidencia f, secreto m

confident ['kɑnfədənt] adj 1 SURE : seguro 2 SELF-ASSURED : confiado, seguro de sí mismo

confidential [,kɑnfə'dɛntʃəl] adj : confidencial — **confidentially** [,kɑnfə'dɛntʃəli] adv

confidentiality [,kɑnfə,dɛntʃi'æləti] n : confidencialidad f

confidently ['kɑnfədəntli] adv : con seguridad, con confianza

configuration [kən,fɪgjə'reɪʃən] n : configuración f

configure [kən'fɪgjər] vt : configurar (un sistema, etc.)

confine [kən'faɪn] vt **-fined; -fining** 1 LIMIT : confinar, restringir, limitar 2 IMPRISON : recluir, encarcelar, encerrar

confined [kən'faɪnd] adj SMALL : limitado ⟨confined spaces : espacios limitados⟩

confinement [kən'faɪnmənt] n : confinamiento m, reclusión f, encierro m

confines ['kɑn,faɪnz] npl : límites mpl, confines mpl

confirm [kən'fərm] vt 1 RATIFY : ratificar 2 VERIFY : confirmar, verificar 3 : confirmar (en religión)

confirmation [,kɑnfər'meɪʃən] n : confirmación f

confiscate ['kɑnfə,skeɪt] vt **-cated; -cating** : confiscar, incautar, decomisar

confiscation [,kɑnfə'skeɪʃən] n : confiscación f, incautación f, decomiso m

conflagration [,kɑnflə'greɪʃən] n : conflagración f

conflict¹ [kən'flɪkt] vi : estar en conflicto, oponerse

conflict² ['kɑn,flɪkt] n : conflicto m ⟨to be in conflict : estar en desacuerdo⟩

confluence ['kɑn,flu:ənts, kən'flu:ənts] n : confluencia f

conform [kən'fɔrm] vi 1 ACCORD, COMPLY : ajustarse, adaptarse, conformarse ⟨it conforms with our standards : se ajusta a nuestras normas⟩ 2 CORRESPOND : corresponder, encajar ⟨to conform to the truth : corresponder a la verdad⟩

conformity [kən'fɔrmət̬i] n, pl **-ties** : conformidad f

confound [kən'faʊnd, kɑn-] vt : confundir, desconcertar

confront [kən'frʌnt] vt : afrontar, enfrentarse a, encarar

confrontation [,kɑnfrən'teɪʃən] n : enfrentamiento m, confrontación f

confuse [kən'fju:z] vt **-fused; -fusing** 1 PUZZLE : confundir, enturbiar 2 COMPLICATE : confundir, enredar, complicar ⟨to confuse the issue : complicar las cosas⟩

confused [kən'fju:zd] adj 1 : confundido (dícese de una persona) 2 : confuso (dícese de una explicación, etc.)

confusing [kən'fju:zɪŋ] adj : complicado, que confunde

confusion [kən'fju:ʒən] n 1 PERPLEXITY : confusión f 2 MESS, TURMOIL : confusión f, embrollo m, lío m fam

congeal [kən'dʒi:l] vi 1 FREEZE : congelarse 2 COAGULATE, CURDLE : coagularse, cuajarse

congenial [kən'dʒi:niəl] adj : agradable, simpático

congenital [kən'dʒɛnət̬əl] adj : congénito

congest [kən'dʒɛst] vt 1 : congestionar (en la medicina) 2 CROWD : abarrotar, atestar, congestionar (el tráfico) — vi : congestionarse

congested [kən'dʒɛstəd] adj : congestionado

congestion [kən'dʒɛstʃən] n : congestión f

conglomerate¹ [kən'glamərət] adj : conglomerado

conglomerate² [kən'glamərət] n : conglomerado m

conglomeration [kən,glamə'reɪʃən] n : conglomerado m, acumulación f

Congolese [,kɑŋgə'li:z, -'li:s] n : congoleño m, -ña f — **Congolese** adj

congratulate [kən'grædʒə,leɪt, -'grætʃə-] vt **-lated; -lating** : felicitar

congratulation [kən,grædʒə'leɪʃən, -,grætʃə-] n : felicitación f ⟨congratulations! : ¡felicidades!, ¡enhorabuena!⟩

congregate ['kɑŋgrɪ,geɪt] v **-gated; -gating** vt : congregar, reunir — vi : congregarse, reunirse

congregation [,kɑŋgrɪ'geɪʃən] n 1 GATHERING : congregación f, fieles mpl (a un servicio religioso) 2 PARISHIONERS : feligreses mpl

congress ['kɑŋgrəs] n : congreso m

congressional [kən'grɛʃənəl, kɑn-] adj : del congreso

congressman ['kɑŋgrəsmən] n, pl **-men** [-mən, -,mɛn] : congresista m, diputado m

congresswoman ['kɑŋgrəs,wʊmən] n, pl **-women** [-,wɪmən] : congresista f, diputada f

congruence [kən'gru:ənts, 'kɑŋgru-ənts] n : congruencia f

congruent [kən'gru:ənt, 'kɑŋgruənt] adj : congruente

conic ['kɑnɪk] → **conical**

conical ['kɑnɪkəl] adj : cónico

conifer ['kɑnəfər, 'ko:-] n : conífera f

coniferous [ko:'nɪfərəs, kə-] adj : conífero

conjecture[1] [kən'dʒɛktʃər] v **-tured; -tur-ing** : conjeturar

conjecture[2] n : conjetura f, presunción f

conjugal ['kandʒɪgəl, kən'dʒu:-] adj : conyugal

conjugate ['kandʒə,geɪt] vt **-gated; -gat-ing** : conjugar

conjugation [,kandʒə'geɪʃən] n : conjugación f

conjunction [kən'dʒʌŋkʃən] n : conjunción f ⟨in conjunction with : en combinación con⟩

conjunctivitis [kən,dʒʌŋkti'vaɪtəs] n : conjuntivitis f

conjure ['kandʒər, 'kʌn-] v **-jured; -juring** vt **1** ENTREAT : rogar, suplicar **2 to conjure up** : hacer aparecer (apariciones), evocar (memorias, etc.) — vi : practicar la magia

conjurer or **conjuror** ['kandʒərər, 'kʌn-] n : mago m, -ga f; prestidigitador m, -dora f

con man n : timador m

connect [kə'nɛkt] vt **1** JOIN, LINK : conectar (cables, etc.), comunicar (habitaciones) **2** RELATE : relacionar, asociar (ideas) ⟨evidence that connects him with the crime : evidencias que lo vinculan con el crimen⟩ — vi **1** : conectar, comunicarse ⟨to connect to the Internet : conectar a la Internet⟩ **2 to connect with someone** : sintonizar con alguien

connection [kə'nɛkʃən] n : conexión f, enlace m ⟨professional connections : relaciones profesionales⟩

connective [kə'nɛktɪv] adj : conectivo, conjuntivo ⟨connective tissue : tejido conjuntivo⟩ — **connectivity** n

connector [kə'nɛktər] n : conector m

connivance [kə'naɪvənts] n : connivencia f, complicidad f

connive [kə'naɪv] vi **-nived; -niving** CONSPIRE, PLOT : actuar en connivencia, confabularse, conspirar

connoisseur [,kanə'sər, -'sʊr] n : conocedor m, -dora f; entendido m, -da f

connotation [,kanə'teɪʃən] n : connotación f

connote [kə'no:t] vt **-noted; -noting** : connotar

conquer ['kaŋkər] vt : conquistar, vencer

conqueror ['kaŋkərər] n : conquistador m, -dora f

conquest ['kan,kwɛst, 'kaŋ-] n : conquista f

conscience ['kantʃənts] n : conciencia f, consciencia f ⟨to have a clear conscience : tener la conciencia limpia⟩

conscientious [,kantʃi'ɛntʃəs] adj : concienzudo — **conscientiously** adv

conscious ['kantʃəs] adj **1** AWARE : consciente ⟨to become conscious of : darse cuenta de⟩ **2** ALERT, AWAKE : consciente **3** INTENTIONAL : intencional, deliberado

consciously ['kantʃəsli] adv INTENTIONALLY : intencionalmente, deliberadamente, a propósito

consciousness ['kantʃəsnəs] n **1** AWARENESS : conciencia f, consciencia f **2** conocimiento m ⟨to lose consciousness : perder el conocimiento⟩

conscript[1] [kən'skrɪpt] vt : reclutar, alistar, enrolar

conscript[2] ['kan,skrɪpt] n : conscripto m, -ta f; recluta mf

conscription [kən'skrɪpʃən] n : conscripción f

consecrate ['kantsə,kreɪt] vt **-crated; -crating** : consagrar

consecration [,kantsə'kreɪʃən] n : consagración f, dedicación f

consecutive [kən'sɛkjətɪv] adj : consecutivo, seguido ⟨on five consecutive days : cinco días seguidos⟩

consecutively [kən'sɛkjətɪvli] adv : consecutivamente

consensus [kən'sɛntsəs] n : consenso m

consent[1] [kən'sɛnt] vi **1** AGREE : acceder, ponerse de acuerdo **2 to consent to do something** : consentir en hacer algo

consent[2] n : consentimiento m, permiso m ⟨by common consent : de común acuerdo⟩

consequence ['kantsə,kwɛnts, -kwənts] n **1** RESULT : consecuencia f, secuela f **2** IMPORTANCE : importancia f, trascendencia f

consequent ['kantsə,kwənt, -,kwɛnt] adj : consiguiente

consequential [,kantsə'kwɛntʃəl] adj **1** CONSEQUENT : consiguiente **2** IMPORTANT : importante, trascendente, trascendental

consequently ['kantsə,kwəntli, -,kwɛnt-] adv : por consiguiente, por ende, por lo tanto

conservation [,kantsər'veɪʃən] n : conservación f, protección f

conservationist [,kantsər'veɪʃənɪst] n : conservacionista mf

conservatism [kən'sərvə,tɪzəm] n : conservadurismo m

conservative[1] [kən'sərvətɪv] adj **1** : conservador **2** CAUTIOUS : moderado, cauteloso ⟨a conservative estimate : un cálculo moderado⟩

conservative[2] n : conservador m, -dora f

conservatory [kən'sərvə,tori] n, pl **-ries** : conservatorio m

conserve[1] [kən'sərv] vt **-served; -serving** : conservar, preservar

conserve[2] ['kan,sərv] n PRESERVES : confitura f

consider [kən'sɪdər] vt **1** CONTEMPLATE : considerar, pensar en ⟨we'd considered attending : habíamos pensado en asistir⟩ **2** : considerar, tener en cuenta ⟨consider the consequences : considera las consecuencias⟩ **3** JUDGE, REGARD : considerar, estimar

considerable [kən'sɪdərəbəl] adj : considerable — **considerably** [-bli] adv

considerate [kən'sɪdərət] adj : considerado, atento

consideration [kən,sɪdə'reɪʃən] n : consideración f ⟨to take into consideration : tener en cuenta⟩

considering [kən'sɪdərɪŋ] prep : teniendo en cuenta, visto

consign [kənˈsaɪn] *vt* **1** COMMIT, EN-
TRUST : confiar, encomendar **2** TRANS-
FER : consignar, transferir **3** SEND : consignar, enviar (mercancía)
consignment [kənˈsaɪnmənt] *n* **1** : envío
m, remesa *f* **2 on** ~ : en consignación
consist [kənˈsɪst] *vi* **1** LIE : consistir ⟨suc-
cess consists in hard work : el éxito consiste en trabajar duro⟩ **2** : constar, componerse ⟨the set consists of 5 pieces : el
juego se compone de 5 piezas⟩
consistency [kənˈsɪstəntsi] *n, pl* **-cies 1**
: consistencia *f* (de una mezcla o sustancia) **2** COHERENCE : coherencia *f* **3** UNI-
FORMITY : regularidad *f*, uniformidad *f*
consistent [kənˈsɪstənt] *adj* **1** COMPATI-
BLE : compatible, coincidente ⟨consis-
tent with policy : coincidente con la po-
lítica⟩ **2** UNIFORM : uniforme, constante,
regular — **consistently** [kənˈsɪstəntli]
adv
consolation [ˌkɑntsəˈleɪʃən] *n* **1** : consuelo *m* **2 consolation prize** : premio *m*
de consolación
console[1] [kənˈsoːl] *vt* **-soled; -soling**
: consolar
console[2] [ˈkɑntsoːl] *n* : consola *f*
consolidate [kənˈsɑləˌdeɪt] *vt* **-dated;
-dating** : consolidar, unir
consolidation [kənˌsɑləˈdeɪʃən] *n* : consolidación *f*
consommé [ˌkɑntsəˈmeɪ] *n* : consomé *m*
consonant [ˈkɑntsənənt] *n* : consonante
m
consort[1] [kənˈsɔrt] *vi* : asociarse, relacionarse, tener trato ⟨to consort with criminals : tener trato con criminales⟩
consort[2] [ˈkɑntsɔrt] *n* : consorte *mf*
consortium [kənˈsɔrʃəm] *n, pl* **-tia** [-ʃə] *or*
-tiums [-ʃəmz] : consorcio *m*
conspicuous [kənˈspɪkjuəs] *adj* **1** OBVI-
OUS : visible, evidente **2** STRIKING : llamativo
conspicuously [kənˈspɪkjuəsli] *adv* : de
manera llamativa
conspiracy [kənˈspɪrəsi] *n, pl* **-cies** : conspiración *f*, complot *m*, confabulación *f*
conspirator [kənˈspɪrətər] *n* : conspirador
m, -dora *f*
conspire [kənˈspaɪr] *vi* **-spired; -spiring**
: conspirar, confabularse
constable [ˈkɑntstəbəl, ˈkɑntstə-] *n*
: agente *mf* de policía (en un pueblo)
constancy [ˈkɑntstəntsi] *n, pl* **-cies**
: constancia *f*
constant[1] [ˈkɑntstənt] *adj* **1** FAITHFUL
: leal, fiel **2** INVARIABLE : constante, invariable **3** CONTINUAL : constante, continuo
constant[2] *n* : constante *f*
constantly [ˈkɑntstəntli] *adv* : constantemente, continuamente
constellation [ˌkɑntstəˈleɪʃən] *n* : constelación *f*
consternation [ˌkɑntstərˈneɪʃən] *n* : consternación *f*
constipate [ˈkɑntstəˌpeɪt] *vt* **-pated; -pat-
ing** : estreñir
constipated [ˈkɑntstəˌpeɪtəd] *adj* : estreñido

constipation [ˌkɑntstəˈpeɪʃən] *n* : estreñimiento *m*, constipación *f* (de vientre)
constituency [kənˈstɪtʃuəntsi] *n, pl* **-cies
1** : distrito *m* electoral **2** : residentes *mpl*
de un distrito electoral
constituent[1] [kənˈstɪtʃuənt] *adj* **1** COMPO-
NENT : constituyente, componente **2**
: constituyente, constitutivo ⟨a constituent assembly : una asamblea constitu-
yente⟩
constituent[2] *n* **1** COMPONENT : componente *m* **2** VOTER : elector *m*, -tora *f*;
votante *mf*
constitute [ˈkɑntstəˌtuːt, -ˌtjuːt] *vt* **-tuted;
-tuting 1** ESTABLISH : constituir, establecer **2** COMPOSE, FORM : constituir, componer
constitution [ˌkɑntstəˈtuːʃən, -ˈtjuː-] *n*
: constitución *f*
constitutional [ˌkɑntstəˈtuːʃənəl, -ˈtjuː-]
adj : constitucional
constitutionality [ˌkɑntstəˌtuːʃəˈnæ-ləti,
-ˌtjuː-] *n* : constitucionalidad *f*
constrain [kənˈstreɪn] *vt* **1** COMPEL
: constreñir, obligar **2** CONFINE : constreñir, limitar, restringir **3** RESTRAIN
: contener, refrenar
constraint [kənˈstreɪnt] *n* : restricción *f*,
limitación *f*
constrict [kənˈstrɪkt] *vt* : estrechar, apretar, comprimir
constriction [kənˈstrɪkʃən] *n* : estrechamiento *m*, compresión *f*
construct [kənˈstrʌkt] *vt* : construir
construction [kənˈstrʌkʃən] *n* : construcción *f*
constructive [kənˈstrʌktɪv] *adj* : constructivo
construe [kənˈstruː] *vt* **-strued; -struing**
: interpretar
consul [ˈkɑntsəl] *n* : cónsul *mf*
consular [ˈkɑntsələr] *adj* : consular
consulate [ˈkɑntsələt] *n* : consulado *m*
consult [kənˈsʌlt] *vt* : consultar — *vi* **to
consult with** : consultar con, solicitar la
opinión de
consultancy [kənˈsʌltəntsi] *n, pl* **-cies**
: consultoría *f*
consultant [kənˈsʌltənt] *n* : consultor *m*,
-tora *f*; asesor *m*, -sora *f*
consultation [ˌkɑntsəlˈteɪʃən] *n* : consulta
f
consumable [kənˈsuːməbəl] *adj* : consumible
consume [kənˈsuːm] *vt* **-sumed; -suming**
: consumir, usar, gastar
consumer [kənˈsuːmər] *n* : consumidor
m, -dora *f*
consumerism [kənˈsuːməˌrɪzəm] *n* : consumismo *m*
consummate[1] [ˈkɑntsəˌmeɪt] *vt* **-mated;
-mating** : consumar
consummate[2] [kənˈsʌmət, ˈkɑntsə-mət]
adj : consumado, perfecto
consummation [ˌkɑntsəˈmeɪʃən] *n* : consumación *f*
consumption [kənˈsʌmpʃən] *n* USE : consumo *m*, uso *m* ⟨consumption of electricity : consumo de electricidad⟩

contact¹ ['kɑn,tækt, kən'-] *vt* : ponerse en contacto con, contactar (con)

contact² ['kɑn,tækt] *n* 1 TOUCHING : contacto *m* ‹to come into contact with : entrar en contacto con› 2 TOUCH : contacto *m*, comunicación *f* ‹to lose contact with : perder contacto con› 3 CONNECTION : contacto *m* (en negocios) 4 → contact lens

contact lens ['kɑn,tækt'lɛnz] *n* : lente *mf* de contacto, pupilente *m* Mex

contagion [kən'teɪdʒən] *n* : contagio *m*

contagious [kən'teɪdʒəs] *adj* : contagioso

contain [kən'teɪn] *vt* 1 : contener 2 to contain oneself : contenerse

container [kən'teɪnər] *n* : recipiente *m*, envase *m*

containment [kən'teɪnmənt] *n* : contención *f*

contaminant [kən'tæmənənt] *n* : contaminante *m*

contaminate [kən'tæmə,neɪt] *vt* -nated; -nating : contaminar

contamination [kən,tæmə'neɪʃən] *n* : contaminación *f*

contemplate ['kɑntəm,pleɪt] *v* -plated; -plating *vt* 1 VIEW : contemplar 2 PONDER : contemplar, considerar 3 CONSIDER, PROPOSE : proponerse, proyectar, pensar en ‹to contemplate a trip : pensar en viajar› — *vi* MEDITATE : meditar

contemplation [,kɑntəm'pleɪʃən] *n* : contemplación *f*

contemplative [kən'templətɪv, 'kɑntəm,pleɪtɪv] *adj* : contemplativo

contemporaneous [kən,tempə'reɪniəs] *adj* → contemporary¹

contemporary¹ [kən'tempə,reri] *adj* : contemporáneo

contemporary² *n, pl* -raries : contemporáneo *m*, -nea *f*

contempt [kən'tempt] *n* 1 DISDAIN : desprecio *m*, desdén *m* ‹to hold in contempt : despreciar› 2 : desacato *m* (ante un tribunal)

contemptible [kən'temptəbəl] *adj* : despreciable, vil

contemptuous [kən'temptʃuəs] *adj* : despectivo, despreciativo, desdeñoso

contemptuously [kən'temptʃuəsli] *adv* : despectivamente, con desprecio

contend [kən'tend] *vi* 1 STRUGGLE : luchar, lidiar, contender ‹to contend with a problem : lidiar con un problema› 2 COMPETE : competir ‹to contend for a position : competir por un puesto› — *vt* 1 ARGUE, MAINTAIN : argüir, sostener, afirmar ‹he contended that he was right : afirmó que tenía razón› 2 CONTEST : protestar contra (una decisión, etc.), disputar

contender [kən'tendər] *n* : contendiente *mf*; aspirante *mf*; competidor *m*, -dora *f*

content¹ [kən'tent] *vt* SATISFY : contentar, satisfacer

content² *adj* : conforme, contento, satisfecho

content³ *n* CONTENTMENT : contento *m*, satisfacción *f* ‹to one's heart's content

: hasta quedar satisfecho, a más no poder›

content⁴ ['kɑn,tent] *n* 1 MEANING : contenido *m*, significado *m* 2 PROPORTION : contenido *m*, proporción *f* ‹fat content : contenido de grasa› 3 contents *npl* : contenido *m*, sumario *m* (de un libro) ‹table of contents : índice de materias›

contented [kən'tentəd] *adj* : conforme, satisfecho ‹a contented smile : una sonrisa de satisfacción›

contentedly [kən'tentədli] *adv* : con satisfacción

contention [kən'tenʃən] *n* 1 DISPUTE : disputa *f*, discusión *f* 2 COMPETITION : competencia *f*, contienda *f* 3 OPINION : argumento *m*, opinión *f*

contentious [kən'tenʃəs] *adj* 1 CONTROVERSIAL : controvertido 2 DEBATED : discutido 3 ARGUMENTATIVE : discutidor

contentment [kən'tentmənt] *n* : satisfacción *f*, contento *m*

contest¹ [kən'test] *vt* : disputar, cuestionar, impugnar ‹to contest a will : impugnar un testamento›

contest² ['kɑn,test] *n* 1 STRUGGLE : lucha *f*, contienda *f* 2 GAME : concurso *m*, competencia *f*

contestable [kən'testəbəl] *adj* : discutible, cuestionable

contestant [kən'testənt] *n* : concursante *mf*; competidor *m*, -dora *f*

context ['kɑn,tekst] *n* : contexto *m*

contiguous [kən'tɪgjuəs] *adj* : contiguo

continent¹ ['kɑntənənt] *adj* : continente

continent² *n* : continente *m* — **continental** [,kɑntən'entəl] *adj*

contingency [kən'tɪndʒəntsi] *n, pl* -cies : contingencia *f*, eventualidad *f* ‹contingency plan : plan de emergencia›

contingent¹ [kən'tɪndʒənt] *adj* 1 POSSIBLE : contingente, eventual 2 ACCIDENTAL : fortuito, accidental 3 to be contingent on : depender de, estar sujeto a

contingent² *n* : contingente *m*

continual [kən'tɪnjuəl] *adj* : continuo, constante — **continually** [kən'tɪnjuəli, -'tɪnjəli] *adv*

continuance [kən'tɪnjuəns] *n* 1 CONTINUATION : continuación *f* 2 DURATION : duración *f* 3 : aplazamiento *m* (de un proceso)

continuation [kən,tɪnju'eɪʃən] *n* : continuación *f*, prolongación *f*

continue [kən'tɪnju:] *v* -tinued; -tinuing *vi* 1 CARRY ON : continuar, seguir, proseguir ‹please continue : continúe, por favor› 2 ENDURE, LAST : continuar, prolongarse, durar 3 RESUME : continuar, reanudarse — *vt* 1 : continuar, seguir ‹she continued writing : continuó escribiendo› 2 RESUME : continuar, reanudar 3 EXTEND, PROLONG : continuar, prolongar

continuity [,kɑntə'nu:əti, -'nju:-] *n, pl* -ties : continuidad *f*

continuous [kən'tɪnjuəs] *adj* : continuo — **continuously** *adv*

contort [kən'tɔrt] vt : torcer, retorcer, contraer (el rostro) — vi : contraerse, demudarse

contortion [kən'tɔrʃən] n : contorsión f

contour [ˈkɑnˌtur] n 1 OUTLINE : contorno m 2 **contours** npl SHAPE : forma f, curvas fpl 3 **contour map** : mapa m topográfico

contraband [ˈkɑntrəˌbænd] n : contrabando m

contraception [ˌkɑntrəˈsɛpʃən] n : anticoncepción f, contracepción f

contraceptive[1] [ˌkɑntrəˈsɛptɪv] adj : anticonceptivo, contraceptivo

contraceptive[2] n : anticonceptivo m, contraceptivo m

contract[1] [kən'trækt, 1 usu ˈkɑnˌtrækt] vt 1 : contratar (servicios profesionales) 2 : contraer (una enfermedad, una deuda) 3 TIGHTEN : contraer (un músculo) 4 SHORTEN : contraer (una palabra) — vi : contraerse, reducirse

contract[2] [ˈkɑnˌtrækt] n : contrato m

contraction [kən'trækʃən] n : contracción f

contractor [ˈkɑnˌtræktər, kən'træk-] n : contratista mf

contractual [kən'træktʃuəl] adj : contractual — **contractually** adv

contradict [ˌkɑntrəˈdɪkt] vt : contradecir, desmentir

contradiction [ˌkɑntrəˈdɪkʃən] n : contradicción f

contradictory [ˌkɑntrəˈdɪktəri] adj : contradictorio

contralto [kən'trælˌtoː] n, pl **-tos** : contralto m (voz), contralto mf (vocalista)

contraption [kən'træpʃən] n DEVICE : aparato m, artefacto m

contrary[1] [ˈkɑnˌtreri, 2 often kən-'treri] adj 1 OPPOSITE : contrario, opuesto 2 BALKY, STUBBORN : terco, testarudo 3 **contrary to** : al contrario de, en contra de ⟨contrary to the facts : en contra de los hechos⟩

contrary[2] [ˈkɑnˌtreri] n, pl **-traries** 1 OPPOSITE : lo contrario, lo opuesto 2 **on the contrary** : al contrario, todo lo contrario

contrast[1] [kən'træst] vi DIFFER : contrastar, diferir — vt COMPARE : contrastar, comparar

contrast[2] [ˈkɑnˌtræst] n : contraste m

contravene [ˌkɑntrəˈviːn] vt **-vened; -vening** : contravenir, infringir

contribute [kən'trɪbjət] v **-uted; -uting** vt : contribuir, aportar (dinero, bienes, etc.) — vi : contribuir

contribution [ˌkɑntrəˈbjuːʃən] n : contribución f

contributor [kən'trɪbjətər] n : contribuidor m, -dora f; colaborador m, -dora f (en periodismo)

contrite [ˈkɑnˌtrait, kən'trait] adj REPENTANT : contrito, arrepentido

contrition [kən'trɪʃən] n : contrición f, arrepentimiento m

contrivance [kən'traivənts] n 1 DEVICE : aparato m, artefacto m 2 SCHEME : artimaña f, treta f, ardid m

contrive [kən'traiv] vt **-trived; -triving** 1 DEVISE : idear, ingeniar, maquinar 2 MANAGE : lograr, ingeniárselas para ⟨she contrived a way out of the mess : se las ingenió para salir del enredo⟩

control[1] [kən'troːl] vt **-trolled; -trolling** : controlar — **controllable** [kən'troːləbəl] adj

control[2] n 1 : control m, dominio m, mando m ⟨to be under control : estar bajo control⟩ ⟨to be out of control : estar fuera de control⟩ ⟨he likes to be in control : le gusta mandar⟩ ⟨to be in control of : controlar⟩ ⟨to lose control : perder el control⟩ ⟨it's beyond my control : no está en mis manos⟩ ⟨for reasons beyond our control : por causas ajenas a nuestra voluntad⟩ 2 RESTRAINT : control m, limitación f ⟨birth control : control natal⟩ ⟨gun control : control de armas⟩ 3 : control m, dispositivo m de mando ⟨remote control : control remoto⟩

controller [kən'troːlər, ˈkɑnˌ-] n 1 → comptroller 2 : controlador m, -dora f ⟨air traffic controller : controlador aéreo⟩

controversial [ˌkɑntrəˈvərʃəl, -siəl] adj : controvertido ⟨a controversial decision : una decisión controvertida⟩

controversy [ˈkɑntrəˌvərsi] n, pl **-sies** : controversia f

controvert [ˈkɑntrəˌvərt, ˌkɑntrə'-] vt : controvertir, contradecir

contusion [kən'tuːʒən, -tjuː-] n BRUISE : contusión f, moretón m

conundrum [kə'nʌndrəm] n RIDDLE : acertijo m, adivinanza f

convalesce [ˌkɑnvə'lɛs] vi **-lesced; -lescing** : convalecer

convalescence [ˌkɑnvə'lɛsənts] n : convalecencia f

convalescent[1] [ˌkɑnvə'lɛsənt] adj : convaleciente

convalescent[2] n : convaleciente mf

convection [kən'vɛkʃən] n : convección f

convene [kən'viːn] v **-vened; -vening** vt : convocar — vi : reunirse

convenience [kən'viːnjənts] n 1 : conveniencia f ⟨at your convenience : cuando le resulte conveniente⟩ 2 AMENITY : comodidad f ⟨modern conveniences : comodidades modernas⟩

convenience store n : tienda f de conveniencia

convenient [kən'viːnjənt] adj : conveniente, cómodo — **conveniently** adv

convent [ˈkɑnvənt, -ˌvɛnt] n : convento m

convention [kən'vɛnʃən] n 1 PACT : convención f, convenio m, pacto m ⟨the Geneva Convention : la Convención de Ginebra⟩ 2 MEETING : convención f, congreso m 3 CUSTOM : convención f

conventional [kən'vɛnʃənəl] adj : convencional — **conventionally** adv

converge [kən'vərdʒ] vi **-verged; -verging** : converger, convergir

convergence [kən'vərdʒənts] n : convergencia f

convergent [kən'vərdʒənt] *adj* : convergente

conversant [kən'vərsənt] *adj* **conversant with** : versado con, experto en

conversation [ˌkɑnvər'seɪʃən] *n* : conversación *f*

conversational [ˌkɑnvər'seɪʃənəl] *adj* : familiar ⟨a conversational style : un estilo familiar⟩

conversationalist [ˌkɑnvər'seɪʃənəlɪst] *noun* : conversador *m*, -dora *f*

converse¹ [kən'vərs] *vi* **-versed; -versing** : conversar

converse² [kən'vərs, 'kɑn,vərs] *adj* : contrario, opuesto, inverso

conversely [kən'vərsli, 'kɑn,vərs-] *adv* : a la inversa

conversion [kən'vərʒən] *n* **1** CHANGE : conversión *f*, transformación *f*, cambio *m* **2** : conversión *f* (a una religión)

convert¹ [kən'vərt] *vt* **1** : convertir (a una religión o un partido) **2** CHANGE : convertir, cambiar — *vi* : convertirse

convert² ['kɑn,vərt] *n* : converso *m*, -sa *f*

converter *or* **convertor** [kən'vərtər] *n* : convertidor *m*

convertible¹ [kən'vərtəbəl] *adj* : convertible

convertible² *n* : convertible *m*, descapotable *m*

convex [kɑn'vɛks, 'kɑn,-, kɑn'-] *adj* : convexo

convey [kən'veɪ] *vt* **1** TRANSPORT : transportar, conducir **2** TRANSMIT : transmitir, comunicar, expresar (noticias, ideas, etc.)

conveyance [kən'veɪəns] *n* **1** TRANSPORT : transporte *m*, transportación *f* **2** COMMUNICATION : transmisión *f*, comunicación *f* **3** TRANSFER : transferencia *f*, traspaso *m* (de una propiedad)

conveyor [kən'veɪər] *n* : transportador *m*, -dora *f* ⟨conveyor belt : cinta transportadora⟩

convict¹ [kən'vɪkt] *vt* : declarar culpable

convict² ['kɑn,vɪkt] *n* : preso *m*, -sa *f*; presidiario *m*, -ria *f*; recluso *m*, -sa *f*

conviction [kən'vɪkʃən] *n* **1** : condena *f* (de un acusado) **2** BELIEF : convicción *f*, creencia *f*

convince [kən'vɪns] *vt* **-vinced; -vincing** : convencer

convincing [kən'vɪntsɪŋ] *adj* : convincente, persuasivo

convincingly [kən'vɪntsɪŋli] *adv* : de forma convincente

convivial [kən'vɪvjəl, -'vɪviəl] *adj* : jovial, festivo, alegre

conviviality [kən,vɪvi'æləti] *n, pl* **-ties** : jovialidad *f*

convoke [kən'vo:k] *vt* **-voked; -voking** : convocar

convoluted ['kɑnvə,lu:təd] *adj* : intrincado, complicado

convoy ['kɑn,vɔɪ] *n* : convoy *m*

convulse [kən'vʌls] *v* **-vulsed; -vulsing** *vt* : convulsionar ⟨convulsed with laughter : muerto de risa⟩ — *vi* : sufrir convulsiones

convulsion [kən'vʌlʃən] *n* : convulsión *f*

convulsive [kən'vʌlsɪv] *adj* : convulsivo — **convulsively** *adv*

coo¹ ['ku:] *vi* : arrullar

coo² *n* : arrullo *m* (de una paloma)

cook¹ ['kʊk] *vi* : cocinar — *vt* **1** : preparar (comida) **2 to cook up** CONCOCT : inventar, tramar

cook² *n* : cocinero *m*, -ra *f*

cookbook ['kʊk,bʊk] *n* : libro *m* de cocina

cookery ['kʊkəri] *n, pl* **-eries** : cocina *f*

cookie *or* **cooky** ['kʊki] *n, pl* **-ies** : galleta *f* (dulce)

cooking ['kʊkɪŋ] *n* **1** COOKERY : cocina *f* **2** : cocción *f*, cocimiento *m* ⟨cooking time : tiempo de cocción⟩

cookout ['kʊk,aʊt] *n* : comida *f* al aire libre

cool¹ ['ku:l] *vt* : refrescar, enfriar — *vi* **1** : refrescarse, enfriarse ⟨the pie is cooling : el pastel se está enfriando⟩ **2** : calmarse, tranquilizarse ⟨his anger cooled : su ira se calmó⟩

cool² *adj* **1** : fresco, frío ⟨cool weather : tiempo fresco⟩ **2** CALM : tranquilo, sereno **3** ALOOF : frío, distante **4** *fam* EXCELLENT, TRENDY : muy en la onda *fam*, piola *Arg fam*, guay *Spain fam*

cool³ *n* **1** : fresco *m* ⟨the cool of the evening : el fresco de la tarde⟩ **2** COMPOSURE : calma *f*, serenidad *f*

coolant ['ku:lənt] *n* : refrigerante *m*

cooler ['ku:lər] *n* : nevera *f* portátil

coolly ['ku:lli] *adv* **1** CALMLY : con calma, tranquilamente **2** COLDLY : fríamente, con frialdad

coolness ['ku:lnəs] *n* **1** : frescura *f*, frescor *m* ⟨the coolness of the evening : el frescor de la noche⟩ **2** CALMNESS : tranquilidad *f*, serenidad *f* **3** COLDNESS, INDIFFERENCE : frialdad *f*, indiferencia *f*

coop¹ ['ku:p, 'kʊp] *vt or* **to coop up** : encerrar ⟨cooped up in the house : encerrado en la casa⟩

coop² *n* : gallinero *m*

co–op ['ko:,ɑp] *n* → **cooperative²**

cooperate [ko'ɑpə,reɪt] *vi* **-ated; -ating** : cooperar, colaborar

cooperation [ko,ɑpə'reɪʃən] *n* : cooperación *f*, colaboración *f*

cooperative¹ [ko'ɑpərətɪv, -'ɑpə,reɪtɪv] *adj* : cooperativo

cooperative² [ko'ɑpərətɪv] *n* : cooperativa *f*

co–opt [ko'ɑpt] *vt* **1** : nombrar como miembro, cooptar **2** APPROPRIATE : apropiarse

coordinate¹ [ko'ɔrdən,eɪt] *v* **-nated; -nating** *vt* : coordinar — *vi* : coordinarse, combinar, acordar

coordinate² [ko'ɔrdənət] *adj* **1** COORDINATED : coordinado **2** EQUAL : igual, semejante

coordinate³ [ko'ɔrdənət] *n* : coordenada *f*

coordination [ko,ɔrdən'eɪʃən] *n* : coordinación *f*

coordinator [ko'ɔrdən,eɪtər] *n* : coordinador *m*, -dora *f*

cop ['kɑp] → **police officer**

cope [ˈkoːp] *vi* **coped; coping 1**
: arreglárselas **2 to cope with** : hacer
frente a, poder con ⟨I can't cope with all
this! : ¡no puedo con todo esto!⟩
copier [ˈkɑpiər] *n* : copiadora *f*, fotocopiadora *f*
copilot [ˈkoːˌpaɪlət] *n* : copiloto *m*
copious [ˈkoːpiəs] *adj* : copioso, abundante — **copiously** *adv*
copiousness [ˈkoːpiəsnəs] *n* : abundancia
f
copper [ˈkɑpər] *n* : cobre *m*
coppery [ˈkɑpəri] *adj* : cobrizo
copse [ˈkɑps] *n* THICKET : soto *m*, matorral *m*
copulate [ˈkɑpjəˌleɪt] *vi* **-lated; -lating**
: copular
copulation [ˌkɑpjəˈleɪʃən] *n* : cópula *f*, relaciones *fpl* sexuales
copy¹ [ˈkɑpi] *v* **copied; copying 1** DU-
PLICATE : hacer una copia de, duplicar,
reproducir **2** IMITATE : copiar, imitar
copy² *n, pl* **copies 1** : copia *f*, duplicado
m (de un documento), reproducción *f*
(de una obra de arte) **2** : ejemplar *m* (de
un libro), número *m* (de una revista) **3**
TEXT : manuscrito *m*, texto *m*
copycat [ˈkɑpiˌkæt] *n* : copión *m*, -piona *f*
copyright¹ [ˈkɑpiˌraɪt] *vt* : registrar los
derechos de
copyright² *n* : derechos *mpl* de autor
coral¹ [ˈkɔrəl] *adj* : de coral ⟨a coral reef
: un arrecife de coral⟩
coral² *n* : coral *m*
coral snake *n* : serpiente *f* de coral
cord [ˈkɔrd] *n* **1** ROPE, STRING : cuerda *f*,
cordón *m*, cordel *m* **2** : cuerda *f*, cordón
m, médula *f* (en la anatomía) ⟨vocal
cords : cuerdas vocales⟩ **3** : cuerda *f* ⟨a
cord of firewood : una cuerda de leña⟩ **4**
or **electric cord** : cable *m* eléctrico
cordial¹ [ˈkɔrdʒəl] *adj* : cordial — **cordi-
ally** *adv*
cordial² *n* : cordial *m*
cordiality [ˌkɔrdʒiˈæləti] *n* : cordialidad *f*
cordless [ˈkɔrdləs] *adj* : inalámbrico
cordon¹ [ˈkɔrdən] *vt* **to cordon off**
: acordonar
cordon² *n* : cordón *m*
corduroy [ˈkɔrdəˌrɔɪ] *n* **1** : pana *f* **2 cor-
duroys** *npl* : pantalones *mpl* de pana
core¹ [ˈkor] *vt* **cored; coring** : quitar el
corazón a (una fruta)
core² *n* **1** : corazón *m*, centro *m* (de
algunas frutas) **2** CENTER : núcleo *m*,
centro *m* **3** ESSENCE : núcleo *m*, meollo
m ⟨to the core : hasta la médula⟩
coriander [ˈkɔriˌændər] *n* : cilantro *m*
cork¹ [ˈkɔrk] *vt* : ponerle un corcho a
cork² *n* : corcho *m*
corkscrew [ˈkɔrkˌskruː] *n* : tirabuzón *m*,
sacacorchos *m*
cormorant [ˈkɔrmərənt, -ˌrænt] *n* : cormorán *m*
corn¹ [ˈkɔrn] *vt* : conservar en salmuera
⟨corned beef : carne en conserva⟩
corn² *n* **1** GRAIN : grano *m* **2** : maíz *m*,
choclo *m*, elote *m Mex* ⟨corn tortillas
: tortillas de maíz⟩ **3** : callo *m* ⟨corn
plaster : emplasto para callos⟩

corncob [ˈkɔrnˌkɑb] *n* : mazorca *f* (de
maíz), choclo *m*, elote *m CA, Mex*
cornea [ˈkɔrniə] *n* : córnea *f*
corner¹ [ˈkɔrnər] *vt* **1** TRAP : acorralar,
arrinconar **2** MONOPOLIZE : monopolizar, acaparar (un mercado) — *vi* : tomar
una curva, doblar una esquina (en un
automóvil)
corner² *n* **1** ANGLE : rincón *m*, esquina *f*
(de una mesa, etc.), ángulo *m* (de una
página) ⟨the corner of a room : el rincón
de una habitación⟩ ⟨all corners of the
world : todos los rincones del mundo⟩ **2**
INTERSECTION : esquina *f* **3** BEND
: curva *f* (en una carretera) **4** PREDICA-
MENT, IMPASSE : aprieto *m*, impasse *m*
⟨to be backed into a corner : estar aco-
rralado⟩ **5 corner of the eye** : lagrimal
m, rabillo *m* **6 corner of the mouth** : comisura *f* de los labios **7 to cut corners**
: economizar esfuerzos
corner kick *n* : córner *m*
cornerstone [ˈkɔrnərˌstoːn] *n* : piedra *f*
angular
cornet [kɔrˈnet] *n* : corneta *f*
cornfield [ˈkɔrnˌfiːld] *n* : maizal *m*; milpa *f*
CA, Mex
cornflakes [ˈkɔrnˌfleɪks] *npl* : copos *mpl*
de maíz
cornice [ˈkɔrnɪs] *n* : cornisa *f*
cornmeal [ˈkɔrnˌmiːl] *n* : harina *f* de maíz
cornstalk [ˈkɔrnˌstɔk] *n* : tallo *m* del maíz
cornstarch [ˈkɔrnˌstɑrtʃ] *n* : maicena *f*,
almidón *m* de maíz
cornucopia [ˌkɔrnəˈkoːpiə, -njə-] *n*
: cornucopia *f*
corny [ˈkɔrni] *adj* **cornier; -est 1** SENTI-
MENTAL : sentimental, cursi **2** SILLY
: tonto (dícese de un chiste, etc.)
corolla [kəˈrɑlə] *n* : corola *f*
corollary [ˈkɔrəˌleri] *n, pl* **-laries** : corolario *m*
corona [kəˈroːnə] *n* : corona *f* (del sol)
coronary¹ [ˈkɔrəˌneri] *adj* : coronario
coronary² *n, pl* **-naries 1** : trombosis *f*
coronaria **2** HEART ATTACK : infarto *m*,
ataque *m* al corazón
coronation [ˌkɔrəˈneɪʃən] *n* : coronación *f*
coroner [ˈkɔrənər] *n* : médico *m* forense
corporal¹ [ˈkɔrpərəl] *adj* : corporal ⟨cor-
poral punishment : castigos corporales⟩
corporal² *n* : cabo *m*
corporate [ˈkɔrpərət] *adj* : corporativo,
empresarial
corporation [ˌkɔrpəˈreɪʃən] *n* : sociedad *f*
anónima, corporación *f*, empresa *f*
corporeal [kɔrˈporiəl] *adj* **1** PHYSICAL
: corpóreo **2** MATERIAL : material,
tangible — **corporeally** *adv*
corps [ˈkor] *n, pl* **corps** [ˈkorz] : cuerpo *m*
⟨medical corps : cuerpo médico⟩ ⟨diplo-
matic corps : cuerpo diplomático⟩
corpse [ˈkɔrps] *n* : cadáver *m*
corpulence [ˈkɔrpjələnts] *n* : obesidad *f*,
gordura *f*
corpulent [ˈkɔrpjələnt] *adj* : obeso, gordo
corpuscle [ˈkɔrˌpʌsəl] *n* : corpúsculo *m*,
glóbulo *m* (sanguíneo)
corral¹ [kəˈræl] *vt* **-ralled; -ralling** : acorralar (ganado)

corral² *n* : corral *m*
correct¹ [kə'rɛkt] *vt* **1** RECTIFY : corregir, rectificar **2** REPRIMAND : corregir, reprender
correct² *adj* **1** ACCURATE, RIGHT : correcto, exacto ⟨to be correct : estar en lo cierto⟩ **2** PROPER : correcto, apropiado
correction [kə'rɛkʃən] *n* : corrección *f*
corrective [kə'rɛktɪv] *adj* : correctivo
correctly [kə'rɛktli] *adv* : correctamente
correctness [kə'rɛk(t)nəs] *n* **1** ACCURACY : exactitud *f* **2** PROPRIETY : corrección *f*
correlate ['kɔrə,leɪt] *vt* -**lated**; -**lating** : relacionar, poner en correlación
correlation [,kɔrə'leɪʃən] *n* : correlación *f*
correspond [,kɔrə'spand] *vi* **1** MATCH : corresponder, concordar, coincidir **2** WRITE : corresponderse, escribirse
correspondence [,kɔrə'spandənts] *n* : correspondencia *f*
correspondent [,kɔrə'spandənt] *n* : corresponsal *mf*
corresponding [kɔrə'spandɪŋ, kar-] *adj* : correspondiente
correspondingly [kɔrə'spandɪŋli] *adv* : en consecuencia, de la misma manera
corridor ['kɔrədər, -,dɔr] *n* : corredor *m*, pasillo *m*
corroborate [kə'rabə,reɪt] *vt* -**rated**; -**rating** : corroborar
corroboration [kə,rabə'reɪʃən] *n* : corroboración *f*
corrode [kə'ro:d] *v* -**roded**; -**roding** *vt* : corroer — *vi* : corroerse
corrosion [kə'ro:ʒən] *n* : corrosión *f*
corrosive [kə'ro:sɪv] *adj* : corrosivo
corrugate ['kɔrə,geɪt] *vt* -**gated**; -**gating** : ondular, acanalar, corrugar
corrugated ['kɔrə,geɪtəd] *adj* : ondulado, acanalado ⟨corrugated cardboard : cartón ondulado⟩
corrupt¹ [kə'rʌpt] *vt* **1** PERVERT : corromper, pervertir, degradar (información) **2** BRIBE : sobornar
corrupt² *adj* : corrupto, corrompido
corruptible [kə'rʌptəbəl] *adj* : corruptible
corruption [kə'rʌpʃən] *n* : corrupción *f*
corsage [kɔr'saʒ, -'sadʒ] *n* : ramillete *m* que se lleva como adorno
corset ['kɔrsət] *n* : corsé *m*
cortex ['kɔr,tɛks] *n*, *pl* -**tices** ['kɔrtə,si:z] *or* -**texes** : corteza *f* ⟨cerebral cortex : corteza cerebral⟩
cortisone ['kɔrtə,so:n, -zo:n] *n* : cortisona *f*
cosmetic¹ [kaz'mɛtɪk] *adj* : cosmético ⟨cosmetic surgery : cirugía estética⟩
cosmetic² *n* : cosmético *m*
cosmic ['kazmɪk] *adj* **1** : cósmico ⟨cosmic ray : rayo cósmico⟩ **2** VAST : grandioso, inmenso, vasto
cosmonaut ['kazmə,nɔt] *n* : cosmonauta *mf*
cosmopolitan¹ [,kazmə'palətən] *adj* : cosmopolita
cosmopolitan² *n* : cosmopolita *mf*
cosmos ['kazməs, -,mo:s, -,mas] *n* : cosmos *m*, universo *m*

cost¹ ['kɔst] *v* **cost**; **costing** *vt* : costar ⟨how much does it cost? : ¿cuánto cuesta?, ¿cuánto vale?⟩ — *vi* : costar ⟨these cost more : éstos cuestan más⟩
cost² *n* : costo *m*, precio *m*, coste *m* ⟨cost of living : costo de vida⟩ ⟨victory at all costs : victoria a toda costa⟩
co–star ['ko:,star] *n* : coprotagonista *mf*
Costa Rican¹ [,kostə'ri:kən] *adj* : costarricense
Costa Rican² *n* : costarricense *mf*
costly ['kɔstli] *adj* : costoso, caro
costume ['kas,tu:m, -,tju:m] *n* **1** : traje *m* ⟨national costume : traje típico⟩ **2** : disfraz *m* ⟨costume party : fiesta de disfraces⟩ **3** OUTFIT : vestimenta *f*, traje *m*, conjunto *m*
costume jewelry *n* : bisutería *f*
cosy ['ko:zi] → **cozy**
cot ['kat] *n* : catre *m*
coterie ['ko:tə,ri, ,ko:tə'-] *n* : tertulia *f*, círculo *m* (social)
cottage ['katɪdʒ] *n* : casita *f* (de campo)
cottage cheese *n* : requesón *m*
cotton ['katən] *n* : algodón *m*
cotton batting → **batting**
cotton candy *n* : algodón *m* de azúcar
cottonmouth ['katən,mauθ] → **moccasin**
cottonseed ['katən,si:d] *n* : semilla *f* de algodón
cotton swab → **swab**
cottontail ['katən,teɪl] *n* : conejo *m* de cola blanca
couch¹ ['kautʃ] *vt* : expresar, formular ⟨couched in strong language : expresado en lenguaje enérgico⟩
couch² SOFA : sofá *m*
couch potato *n* : haragán *m*, -gana *f*; vago *m*, -ga *f*
cougar ['ku:gər] *n* : puma *m*
cough¹ ['kɔf] *vi* : toser
cough² *n* : tos *f*
could ['kud] → **can**
council ['kauntsəl] *n* **1** : concejo *m* ⟨city council : concejo municipal, ayuntamiento⟩ **2** MEETING : concejo *m*, junta *f* **3** BOARD : consejo *m* **4** : concilio *m* (eclesiástico)
councillor *or* **councilor** ['kauntsələr] *n* : concejal *m*, -jala *f*
councilman ['kauntsəlmən] *n*, *pl* -**men** [-mən, -,mɛn] : concejal *m*
councilwoman ['kauntsəl,wumən] *n*, *pl* -**women** [-,wɪmən] : concejala *f*
counsel¹ ['kauntsəl] *v* -**seled** *or* -**selled**; -**seling** *or* -**selling** *vt* ADVISE : aconsejar, asesorar, recomendar — *vi* CONSULT : consultar
counsel² *n* **1** ADVICE : consejo *m*, recomendación *f* **2** CONSULTATION : consulta *f* **3** *counsel* *ns* & *pl* LAWYER : abogado *m*, -da *f*
counselor *or* **counsellor** ['kauntsələr] *n* : consejero *m*, -ra *f*; consultor *m*, -tora *f*; asesor *m*, -sora *f*
count¹ ['kaunt] *vt* **1** : contar **2** INCLUDE : contar **3** CONSIDER : considerar ⟨count yourself (as) lucky : considérate afortunado⟩ **4 to count down** : contar los días (etc.) que faltan **5 to count in/**

out ⟨count me in : cuenta conmigo, yo me apunto⟩ ⟨count me out : no cuentes conmigo⟩ — vi 1 : contar ⟨to count out loud : contar en voz alta⟩ 2 MATTER : contar, valer, importar ⟨that's what counts : eso es lo que cuenta⟩ 3 to count on : contar con 4 to count towards : contar para

count² n 1 COMPUTATION : cómputo m, recuento m, cuenta f ⟨to lose count : perder la cuenta⟩ 2 CHARGE : cargo m ⟨two counts of robbery : dos cargos de robo⟩ 3 POINT : punto m, aspecto m ⟨you're wrong on all counts : se equivoca en todo lo que dice⟩ 4 : conde m, -a f (noble)

countable ['kaʊntəbəl] adj : numerable

countdown ['kaʊnt,daʊn] n : cuenta f atrás

countenance¹ ['kaʊntənənts] vt -nanced; -nancing : permitir, tolerar

countenance² n FACE : semblante m, rostro m

counter¹ ['kaʊntər] vt 1 → counteract 2 OPPOSE : oponerse a, resistir — vi RETALIATE : responder, contraatacar

counter² adv counter to : contrario a, en contra de

counter³ adj : contrario, opuesto

counter⁴ n 1 PIECE : ficha f (de un juego) 2 : mostrador m (de un negocio), ventanilla f (en un banco) 3 : contador m (aparato) 4 COUNTERBALANCE : fuerza f opuesta, contrapeso m

counter- pref : contra- ⟨counterattack : contraataque⟩

counteract [,kaʊntər'ækt] vt : contrarrestar

counterattack ['kaʊntərə,tæk] n : contraataque m

counterbalance¹ [,kaʊntər'bælənts] vt -anced; -ancing : contrapesar

counterbalance² ['kaʊntər,bælənts] n : contrapeso m

counterclockwise [,kaʊntər'klɑk-,waɪz] adv & adj : en el sentido opuesto al de las manecillas del reloj

counterfeit¹ ['kaʊntər,fɪt] vt 1 : falsificar (dinero) 2 PRETEND : fingir, aparentar

counterfeit² adj : falso, inauténtico

counterfeit³ n : falsificación f

counterfeiter ['kaʊntər,fɪtər] n : falsificador m, -dora f

countermand ['kaʊntər,mænd, ,kaʊntər'-] vt : contramandar

countermeasure ['kaʊntər,mɛʒər] n : contramedida f

counterpart ['kaʊntər,pɑrt] n : homólogo m, contraparte f Mex

counterpoint ['kaʊntər,pɔɪnt] n : contrapunto m

counterproductive [,kaʊntərprə'dʌktɪv] adj : contraproducente

counterrevolution [,kaʊntər,rɛvə-'luːʃən] n : contrarrevolución f

counterrevolutionary¹ [,kaʊntər,rɛvə-'luːʃən,ɛri] adj : contrarrevolucionario

counterrevolutionary² n, pl -ries : contrarrevolucionario m, -ria f

countersign ['kaʊntər,saɪn] n : contraseña f

countess ['kaʊntɪs] n : condesa f

countless ['kaʊntləs] adj : incontable, innumerable

country¹ ['kʌntri] adj : campestre, rural

country² n, pl -tries 1 NATION : país m, nación f, patria f ⟨country of origin : país de origen⟩ ⟨love of one's country : amor a la patria⟩ 2 : campo m ⟨they left the city for the country : se fueron de la ciudad al campo⟩

countryman ['kʌntrimən] n, pl -men [-mən, -,mɛn] : compatriota mf; paisano m, -na f

countryside ['kʌntri,saɪd] n : campo m, campiña f

county ['kaʊnti] n, pl -ties : condado m

coup ['kuː] n, pl coups ['kuːz] 1 : golpe m maestro 2 → coup d'état

coup de grâce or coup de grace [,kuː:də'grɑs] ns & pl : tiro m de gracia, golpe m de gracia

coup d'état or coup d'etat [,kuːdeɪ'tɑ] n, pl coups d'état or coups d'etat [,kuːdeɪ'tɑ] : golpe m (de estado), cuartelazo m

coupe ['kuːp] n : cupé m

couple¹ ['kʌpəl] vt -pled; -pling : acoplar, enganchar, conectar

couple² n 1 PAIR : par m ⟨a couple of hours : un par de horas, unas dos horas⟩ 2 : pareja f ⟨a young couple : una pareja joven⟩

coupling ['kʌplɪŋ] n : acoplamiento m

coupon ['kuː,pɑn, 'kjuː-] n : cupón m

courage ['kərɪdʒ] n : valor m, valentía f, coraje m

courageous [kə'reɪdʒəs] adj : valiente, valeroso

courageously [kə'reɪdʒəsli] adv : con valor, con coraje

courier ['kʊriər, 'kəriər] n : mensajero m, -ra f

course¹ ['kors] vi coursed; coursing : correr (a toda velocidad)

course² n 1 PROGRESS : curso m, transcurso m ⟨to run its course : seguir su curso⟩ ⟨to follow the normal course : seguir su curso normal⟩ ⟨in due course : a su debido tiempo⟩ ⟨in/during the course of : en/durante el transcurso de⟩ 2 DIRECTION : rumbo m (de un avión), derrota f, derrotero m (de un barco) ⟨to stay on course : mantener el rumbo⟩ ⟨to go off course : desviarse de su rumbo⟩ 3 PATH, WAY : camino m, vía f 4 : plato m (de una cena) ⟨the main course : el plato principal⟩ 5 : curso m (académico) 6 : pista f (de carreras, de esquí, de obstáculos), campo m (de golf) 7 course of action : línea f de conducta 8 of course : desde luego, por supuesto ⟨yes, of course! : ¡claro que sí!⟩

court¹ ['kort] vt WOO : cortejar, galantear

court² n 1 PALACE : palacio m 2 RETINUE : corte f, séquito m 3 COURTYARD : patio m 4 : cancha f (de tenis, baloncesto, etc.) 5 TRIBUNAL : corte f, tribunal *m* ⟨the Supreme Court : la Corte Suprema⟩

courteous ['kərt̮iəs] *adj* : cortés, atento, educado — **courteously** *adv*

courtesan ['kərt̮əzən, 'kər-] *n* : cortesana *f*

courtesy ['kərt̮əsi] *n, pl* **-sies** : cortesía *f*

courthouse ['kort,haʊs] *n* : palacio *m* de justicia, juzgado *m*

courtier ['kort̮iər, 'kortʃər] *n* : cortesano *m*, -na *f*

courtly ['kortli] *adj* **courtlier; -est** : distinguido, elegante, cortés

court–martial[1] ['kort,marʃəl] *vt* : someter a consejo de guerra

court-martial[2] *n, pl* **courts–martial** ['korts,marʃəl] : consejo *m* de guerra

court order *n* : mandamiento *m* judicial

courtroom ['kort,ru:m] *n* : tribunal *m*, corte *f*

courtship ['kort,ʃɪp] *n* : cortejo *m*, noviazgo *m*

courtyard ['kort,jard] *n* : patio *m*

cousin ['kʌzən] *n* : primo *m*, -ma *f*

couture [ku:'tur] *n* : industria *f* de la moda ⟨haute couture : alta costura⟩

cove ['ko:v] *n* : ensenada *f*, cala *f*

covenant ['kʌvənənt] *n* : pacto *m*, contrato *m*

cover[1] ['kʌvər] *vt* 1 : cubrir, tapar ⟨cover your head : cúbrete la cabeza⟩ ⟨cover your eyes : tápate los ojos⟩ ⟨cover the pot : tapa la olla, ponle la tapa a la olla⟩ ⟨covered with mud : cubierto de lodo⟩ 2 : tratar (un tema), cubrir (noticias) 3 INSURE : cubrir, asegurar 4 GUARD, PROTECT : cubrir 5 : cubrir (gastos) 6 TRAVEL : recorrer, cubrir 7 to cover one's ass/butt : cubrirse las espaldas 8 to cover up : cubrir, tapar 9 to cover up HIDE : ocultar — *vi* 1 to cover for REPLACE : sustituir a 2 to cover for PROTECT : encubrir a

cover[2] *n* 1 SHELTER : cubierta *f*, abrigo *m*, refugio *m* ⟨to take cover : ponerse a cubierto⟩ ⟨under cover of darkness : al amparo de la oscuridad⟩ 2 LID, TOP : cubierta *f*, tapa *f* 3 : cubierta *f* (de un libro), portada *f* (de una revista) ⟨to read from cover to cover : leer de principio a fin⟩ 4 : funda *f* (protectora) 5 FRONT, FACADE : fachada *f* 6 **covers** *npl* BEDCLOTHES : ropa *f* de cama, cobijas *fpl*, mantas *fpl*

coverage ['kʌvəridʒ] *n* : cobertura *f*

coveralls ['kʌvər,ɔlz] *npl* : overol *m* (con mangas)

covering ['kʌvərɪŋ] *n* : cubierta *f*

coverlet ['kʌvərlət] *n* : cobertor *m*

cover letter *n* : carta *f* de presentación

covert[1] ['ko:,vərt, 'kʌvərt] *adj* : encubierto, secreto ⟨covert operations : operaciones encubiertas⟩

covert[2] ['kʌvərt, 'ko:-] *n* THICKET : espesura *f*, maleza *f*

cover–up ['kʌvər,ʌp] *n* : encubrimiento *m* (de algo ilícito)

covet ['kʌvət] *vt* : codiciar

covetous ['kʌvət̮əs] *adj* : codicioso

covey ['kʌvi] *n, pl* **-eys** 1 : bandada *f* pequeña (de codornices, etc.) 2 GROUP : grupo *m*

cow[1] ['kaʊ] *vt* : intimidar, acobardar

cow[2] *n* : vaca *f*, hembra *f* (de ciertas especies)

coward ['kaʊərd] *n* : cobarde *mf*

cowardice ['kaʊərdɪs] *n* : cobardía *f*

cowardly ['kaʊərdli] *adj* : cobarde

cowbell ['kaʊ,bɛl] *n* : cencerro *m*, esquila *f*

cowboy ['kaʊ,bɔɪ] *n* : vaquero *m*, cowboy *m*

cower ['kaʊər] *vi* : encogerse (de miedo), acobardarse

cowgirl ['kaʊ,gərl] *n* : vaquera *f*

cowherd ['kaʊ,hərd] *n* : vaquero *m*, -ra *f*

cowhide ['kaʊ,haɪd] *n* : cuero *m*, piel *f* de vaca

cowl ['kaʊl] *n* : capucha *f* (de un monje)

cowlick ['kaʊ,lɪk] *n* : remolino *m*

coworker ['ko:,wərkər] *n* : colega *mf*; compañero *m*, -ra *f* de trabajo

cowpuncher ['kaʊ,pʌntʃər] → cowboy

cowslip ['kaʊ,slɪp] *n* : prímula *f*, primavera *f*

coxswain ['kaksən, -,sweɪn] *n* : timonel *m*

coy ['kɔɪ] *adj* 1 SHY : tímido, cohibido 2 FLIRTATIOUS : coqueto

coyote [kaɪ'o:t̮i, 'kaɪ,o:t] *n, pl* **coyotes** or **coyote** : coyote *m*

cozy ['ko:zi] *adj* **cozier; -est** : acogedor, cómodo

CPR [,si:,pi:'ar] *n* (cardiopulmonary resuscitation) : resucitación *f* cardiopulmonar

CPU [,si:,pi:'ju:] *n* (central processing unit) : CPU *mf*, UPC *mf*, UCP *mf*

crab ['kræb] *n* : cangrejo *m*, jaiba *f*

crabby ['kræbi] *adj* **crabbier; -est** : gruñón, malhumorado

crabgrass ['kræb,græs] *n* : digitaria *f*, gramilla *f*

crack[1] ['kræk] *vt* 1 : chasquear, hacer restallar (un látigo, etc.) ⟨to crack one's knuckles : hacer crujir los nudillos⟩ 2 SPLIT : rajar, agrietar, resquebrajar 3 BREAK : romper (un huevo), cascar (nueces), forzar (una caja fuerte) 4 OPEN : abrir (un libro), dejar entreabierta (una puerta, etc.) 5 SOLVE : resolver, descifrar (un código) 6 to crack a smile : sonreír — *vi* 1 : restallar ⟨the whip cracked : el látigo restalló⟩ 2 SPLIT : rajarse, resquebrajarse, agrietarse 3 : quebrarse (dícese de la voz) 4 : dejar de resistirse (en un interrogatorio, etc.) ⟨he cracked under the strain : sufrió una crisis nerviosa⟩ 5 to crack down on : tomar medidas severas contra 6 to crack up : echarse a reír 7 to get cracking : ponerse manos a la obra

crack[2] *adj* FIRST-RATE : buenísimo, de primera

crack[3] *n* 1 : chasquido *m*, restallido *m*, estallido *m* (de un arma de fuego), crujido *m* (de huesos) ⟨a crack of thunder : un trueno⟩ 2 WISECRACK : chiste *m*, ocurrencia *f*, salida *f* 3 CREVICE : raja *f*, grieta *f*, fisura *f* **4** BLOW : golpe *m* **5** ATTEMPT : intento *m*

crackdown [ˈkræk,daʊn] *n* : medidas *fpl* enérgicas

crack down *vt* : tomar medidas enérgicas

cracker [ˈkrækər] *n* : galleta *f* (de soda, etc.)

crackle[1] [ˈkrækəl] *vi* -**led**; -**ling** : chisporrotear, crujir

crackle[2] *n* : crujido *m*

crackpot [ˈkræk,pɑt] *n* : excéntrico *m*, -ca *f*; chiflado *m*, -da *f*

crack–up [ˈkræk,ʌp] *n* **1** CRASH : choque *m*, estrellamiento *m* **2** BREAKDOWN : crisis *f* nerviosa

crack up *vt* **1** : estrellar (un vehículo) **2** : hacer reír **3** : elogiar ⟨it isn't all that it's cracked up to be : no es tan bueno como se dice⟩ — *vi* **1** : estrellarse **2** LAUGH : echarse a reír

cradle[1] [ˈkreɪdəl] *vt* -**dled**; -**dling** : acunar, mecer (a un niño)

cradle[2] *n* : cuna *f*

craft [ˈkræft] *n* **1** TRADE : oficio *m* ⟨the craft of carpentry : el oficio de carpintero⟩ **2** CRAFTSMANSHIP, SKILL : arte *m*, artesanía *f*, destreza *f* **3** CRAFTINESS : astucia *f*, maña *f* **4** *pl usually* **craft** BOAT : barco *m*, embarcación *f* **5** *pl usually* **craft** AIRCRAFT : avión *m*, aeronave *f*

craftiness [ˈkræftinəs] *n* : astucia *f*, maña *f*

craftsman [ˈkræftsmən] *n, pl* -**men** [-mən, -ˌmɛn] : artesano *m*, -na *f*

craftsmanship [ˈkræftsmənˌʃɪp] *n* : artesanía *f*, destreza *f*

crafty [ˈkræfti] *adj* **craftier**; -**est** : astuto, taimado

crag [ˈkræg] *n* : peñasco *m*

craggy [ˈkrægi] *adj* **craggier**; -**est** : peñascoso

cram [ˈkræm] *v* **crammed**; **cramming** *vt* **1** JAM : embutir, meter **2** STUFF : atiborrar, abarrotar ⟨crammed with people : atiborrado de gente⟩ — *vi* : estudiar a última hora, memorizar (para un examen)

cramp[1] [ˈkræmp] *vt* **1** : dar calambre en **2** RESTRICT : limitar, restringir, entorpecer ⟨to cramp someone's style : cortarle el vuelo a alguien⟩ — *vi or* **to cramp up** : acalambrarse

cramp[2] *n* **1** SPASM : calambre *m*, espasmo *m* (de los músculos) **2** **cramps** *npl* : retorcijones *mpl* ⟨stomach cramps : retorcijones de estómago⟩

cranberry [ˈkrænˌbɛri] *n, pl* -**berries** : arándano *m* (rojo y agrio)

crane[1] [ˈkreɪn] *vt* **craned**; **craning** : estirar ⟨to crane one's neck : estirar el cuello⟩

crane[2] *n* **1** : grulla *f* (ave) **2** : grúa *f* (máquina)

cranial [ˈkreɪniəl] *adj* : craneal, craneano

cranium [ˈkreɪniəm] *n, pl* -**niums** *or* -**nia** [-niə] : cráneo *m*

crank[1] [ˈkræŋk] *vt or* **to crank up** : arrancar (con una manivela)

crank[2] *n* **1** : manivela *f*, manubrio *m* **2** ECCENTRIC : excéntrico *m*, -ca *f*

cranky [ˈkræŋki] *adj* **crankier**; -**est** : irritable, malhumorado

cranny [ˈkræni] *n, pl* -**nies** : grieta *f* ⟨every nook and cranny : todos los rincones⟩

crash[1] [ˈkræʃ] *vi* **1** SMASH : caerse con estrépito, estrellarse **2** COLLIDE : estrellarse, chocar **3** BOOM, RESOUND : retumbar, resonar — *vt* **1** SMASH : estrellar **2 to crash a party** : colarse en una fiesta **3 to crash one's car** : tener un accidente

crash[2] *n* **1** DIN : estrépito *m* **2** COLLISION : choque *m*, colisión *f* ⟨car crash : accidente automovilístico⟩ **3** FAILURE : quiebra *f* (de un negocio), crac *m* (de la bolsa)

crash course *n* : curso *m* intensivo

crash helmet *n* : casco *m*

crass [ˈkræs] *adj* : grosero, de mal gusto

crate[1] [ˈkreɪt] *vt* **crated**; **crating** : empacar en un cajón

crate[2] *n* : cajón *m* (de madera)

crater [ˈkreɪtər] *n* : cráter *m*

cravat [krəˈvæt] *n* : corbata *f*

crave [ˈkreɪv] *vt* **craved**; **craving** : ansiar, apetecer, tener muchas ganas de

craven [ˈkreɪvən] *adj* : cobarde, pusilánime

craving [ˈkreɪvɪŋ] *n* : ansia *f*, antojo *m*, deseo *m*

crawfish [ˈkrɔˌfɪʃ] → **crayfish**

crawl[1] [ˈkrɔl] *vi* **1** CREEP : arrastrarse, gatear (dícese de un bebé) **2** TEEM : estar plagado

crawl[2] *n* **1** : paso *m* lento **2** : crol *m* (en natación)

crayfish [ˈkreɪˌfɪʃ] *n* **1** : ástaco *m* (de agua dulce) **2** : langostino *m* (de mar)

crayon [ˈkreɪˌɑn, -ən] *n* : crayón *m*

craze [ˈkreɪz] *n* : moda *f* pasajera, manía *f*

crazed [ˈkreɪzd] *adj* : enloquecido

crazily [ˈkreɪzəli] *adv* : locamente, erráticamente, insensatamente

craziness [ˈkreɪzinəs] *n* : locura *f*, demencia *f*

crazy [ˈkreɪzi] *adj* **crazier**; -**est** **1** *usu offensive* INSANE : loco, demente ⟨to go crazy : volverse loco⟩ **2** ABSURD, FOOLISH : loco, insensato, absurdo **3** WEIRD, OUTLANDISH : extraño, raro **4** WILD : loco ⟨the team won and the crowd went crazy : el equipo ganó y el público se enloqueció⟩ **5 like crazy** : como loco **6 to be crazy** : estar loco por **7 to drive/make someone crazy** : sacar a alguien de quicio

creak[1] [ˈkriːk] *vi* : chirriar, rechinar, crujir

creak[2] *n* : chirrido *m*, crujido *m*

creaky [ˈkriːki] *adj* **creakier**; -**est** : chirriante, que cruje

cream[1] [ˈkriːm] *vt* **1** BEAT, MIX : batir, mezclar (azúcar y mantequilla, etc.) **2** : preparar (alimentos) con crema

cream[2] *n* **1** : crema *f*, nata *f* *Spain* (de leche) ⟨whipped cream : crema batida, nata montada⟩ **2** LOTION : crema *f*, loción *f* **3** ELITE : crema *f*, elite *f* ⟨the cream of the crop : la crema y nata, lo mejor⟩

cream cheese *n* : queso *m* crema

creamery [ˈkriːməri] *n, pl* **-eries** : fábrica *f* de productos lácteos

creamy [ˈkriːmi] *adj* **creamier; -est** : cremoso

crease[1] [ˈkriːs] *vt* **creased; creasing** 1 : plegar, poner una raya en (pantalones) 2 WRINKLE : arrugar

crease[2] *n* : pliegue *m*, doblez *m*, raya *f* (de pantalones)

create [kriˈeɪt] *vt* **-ated; -ating** : crear, hacer

creation [kriˈeɪʃən] *n* : creación *f*

creative [kriˈeɪtɪv] *adj* : creativo, original ⟨creative people : personas creativas⟩ ⟨a creative work : un obra original⟩

creatively [kriˈeɪtɪvli] *adv* : creativamente, con originalidad

creativity [ˌkriːeɪˈtɪvəti] *n* : creatividad *f*

creator [kriˈeɪtər] *n* : creador *m*, -dora *f*

creature [ˈkriːtʃər] *n* : ser *m* viviente, criatura *f*, animal *m*

crèche [ˈkrɛʃ, ˈkreɪʃ] *n* : nacimiento *m*

credence [ˈkriːdənts] *n* : crédito *m*

credentials [krɪˈdɛntʃəlz] *npl* : referencias *fpl* oficiales, cartas *fpl* credenciales

credibility [ˌkrɛdəˈbɪləti] *n* : credibilidad *f*

credible [ˈkrɛdəbəl] *adj* : creíble

credit[1] [ˈkrɛdɪt] *vt* 1 BELIEVE : creer, dar crédito a 2 : ingresar, abonar ⟨to credit $100 to an account : ingresar $100 en (una) cuenta⟩ 3 ATTRIBUTE : atribuir ⟨they credit the invention to him : a él se le atribuye el invento⟩

credit[2] *n* 1 : saldo *m* positivo, saldo *m* a favor (de una cuenta) 2 : crédito *m* ⟨to buy on credit : comprar a crédito⟩ ⟨credit card : tarjeta de crédito⟩ ⟨credit limit : límite de crédito⟩ ⟨credit history : historial crediticio⟩ 3 CREDENCE : crédito *m* ⟨I gave credit to everything he said : di crédito a todo lo que dijo⟩ 4 RECOGNITION : reconocimiento *m* ⟨he deserves all the credit : todo el mérito es suyo⟩ ⟨to get/take the credit for : llevarse/atribuírse el mérito de⟩ 5 : orgullo *m*, honor *m* ⟨she's a credit to the school : ella es el orgullo de la escuela⟩ 6 : crédito *m* ⟨a course worth three credits : un curso de tres créditos⟩ ⟨extra credit : puntos extras⟩ 7 **credits** *npl* : créditos *mpl* (de una película)

creditable [ˈkrɛdɪtəbəl] *adj* : encomiable, loable — **creditably** [-bli] *adv*

credit card *n* : tarjeta de crédito

creditor [ˈkrɛdɪtər] *n* : acreedor *m*, -dora *f*

credo [ˈkriːdoː, ˈkreɪ-] *n* : credo *m*

credulity [krɪˈduːləti, -ˈdjuː-] *n* : credulidad *f*

credulous [ˈkrɛdʒələs] *adj* : crédulo

creed [ˈkriːd] *n* : credo *m*

creek [ˈkriːk, ˈkrɪk] *n* : arroyo *m*, riachuelo *m*

creel [ˈkriːl] *n* : nasa *f*, cesta *f* (de pescador)

creep[1] [ˈkriːp] *vi* **crept** [ˈkrɛpt]; **creeping** 1 CRAWL : arrastrarse, gatear 2 : moverse lentamente o sigilosamente ⟨he crept out of the house : salió sigilosamente de la casa⟩ 3 SPREAD : trepar (dícese de una planta)

creep[2] *n* 1 CRAWL : paso *m* lento 2 : asqueroso *m*, -sa *f* 3 **creeps** *npl* : calofríos *mpl* ⟨that gives me the creeps : eso me da escalofríos⟩

creeper [ˈkriːpər] *n* : planta *f* trepadora, trepadora *f*

creepy [ˈkriːpi] *adj* 1 SPOOKY : que da miedo, espeluznante 2 UNPLEASANT : asqueroso

cremate [ˈkriːˌmeɪt] *vt* **-mated; -mating** : cremar

cremation [krɪˈmeɪʃən] *n* : cremación *f*

crematorium [ˌkriːməˈtoːriəm, ˌkrɛ-] *n* : crematorio *m*

Creole [ˈkriːˌoːl] *n* 1 : criollo *m*, criolla *f* 2 : criollo *m* (idioma) — **Creole** *adj*

crepe *or* **crêpe** [ˈkreɪp] *n* 1 : crespón *m* (tela) 2 PANCAKE : crepe *mf*, crepa *f Mex*

crepe paper *n* : papel *m* crepé

crescendo [krɪˈʃɛnˌdoː] *n, pl* **-dos** *or* **-does** : crescendo *m*

crescent [ˈkrɛsənt] *n* : creciente *m*

crest [ˈkrɛst] *n* 1 : cresta *f*, penacho *m* (de un ave) 2 PEAK, TOP : cresta *f* (de una ola), cima *f* (de una colina) 3 : emblema *m* (sobre un escudo de armas)

crestfallen [ˈkrɛstˌfɔlən] *adj* : alicaído, abatido

cretin [ˈkriːtən] *n* 1 *often offensive* : cretino *m*, -na *f* (en medicina) 2 : cretino *m*, -na *f*; imbécil *mf*

crevasse [krɪˈvæs] *n* : grieta *f*, fisura *f*

crevice [ˈkrɛvɪs] *n* : grieta *f*, hendidura *f*

crew [ˈkruː] *n* 1 : tripulación *f* (de una nave) 2 TEAM : equipo *m* (de trabajadores o atletas)

crew cut *n* : pelo *m* al rape, casquete *m* corto *Mex*

crib [ˈkrɪb] *n* 1 MANGER : pesebre *m* 2 GRANARY : granero *m* 3 : cuna *f* (de un bebé)

crick [ˈkrɪk] *n* : calambre *m*, espasmo *m* muscular

cricket [ˈkrɪkət] *n* 1 : grillo *m* (insecto) 2 : críquet *m* (juego)

crime [ˈkraɪm] *n* 1 : crimen *m*, delito *m* ⟨to commit a crime : cometer un delito⟩ 2 : crimen *m*, delincuencia *f* ⟨organized crime : crimen organizado⟩

criminal[1] [ˈkrɪmənəl] *adj* : criminal

criminal[2] *n* : criminal *mf*, delincuente *mf*

crimp [ˈkrɪmp] *vt* : ondular, rizar (el pelo), arrugar (una tela, etc.)

crimson [ˈkrɪmzən] *n* : carmesí *m*

cringe [ˈkrɪndʒ] *vi* **cringed; cringing** : encogerse

crinkle[1] [ˈkrɪŋkəl] *v* **-kled; -kling** : arrugar — *vi* : arrugarse

crinkle[2] *n* : arruga *f*

crinkly [ˈkrɪŋkəli] *adj* : arrugado

cripple[1] [ˈkrɪpəl] *vt* **-pled; -pling** 1 DISABLE : lisiar, dejar inválido 2 INCAPACITATE : inutilizar, incapacitar

cripple[2] *n offensive* : lisiado *m*, -da *f*

crisis [ˈkraɪsɪs] *n, pl* **crises** [-ˌsiːz] : crisis *f*

crisp[1] [ˈkrɪsp] *vt* : tostar, hacer crujiente

crisp[2] *adj* 1 CRUNCHY : crujiente, crocante 2 FIRM, FRESH : firme, fresco ⟨crisp lettuce : lechuga fresca⟩ 3 LIVELY : vivaz, alegre ⟨a crisp tempo : un ritmo alegre⟩ **4** INVIGORATING : fresco, vigorizante ⟨the crisp autumn air : el fresco aire otoñal⟩ — **crisply** adv

crisp[3] n : postre m de fruta (con pedacitos de masa dulce por encima)

crispy ['krɪspi] adj **crispier; -est** : crujiente ⟨crispy potato chips : papitas crujientes⟩

crisscross ['krɪsˌkrɔs] vt : entrecruzar

criterion [kraɪ'tɪriən] n, pl **-ria** [-iə] : criterio m

critic ['krɪtɪk] n **1** : crítico m, -ca f (de las artes) **2** FAULTFINDER : detractor m, -tora f; criticón m, -cona f

critical ['krɪtɪkəl] adj : crítico

critically ['krɪtɪkli] adv : críticamente ⟨critically ill : gravemente enfermo⟩

criticism ['krɪtəˌsɪzəm] n : crítica f

criticize ['krɪtəˌsaɪz] vt **-cized; -cizing 1** EVALUATE, JUDGE : criticar, analizar, evaluar **2** CENSURE : criticar, reprobar

critique [krɪ'tiːk] n : crítica f, evaluación f

croak[1] ['kroːk] vi : croar

croak[2] n : croar m, canto m (de la rana)

Croatian [kro'eɪʃən] n : croata mf — **Croatian** adj

crochet[1] [kro'ʃeɪ] v : tejer al croché

crochet[2] n : croché m, crochet m

crock ['krɑk] n : vasija f de barro

crockery ['krɑkəri] n : vajilla f (de barro)

crocodile ['krɑkəˌdaɪl] n : cocodrilo m

crocus ['kroːkəs] n, pl **-cuses** : azafrán m

croissant [krə'sɑnt] n : croissant m

crone ['kroːn] n : vieja f bruja

crony ['kroːni] n, pl **-nies** : amigote m fam; compinche mf fam

crook[1] ['krʊk] vt : doblar (el brazo o el dedo)

crook[2] n **1** STAFF : cayado m (de pastor), báculo m (de obispo) **2** THIEF : ratero m, -ra f; ladrón m, -drona f

crooked ['krʊkəd] adj **1** BENT : chueco, torcido **2** DISHONEST : deshonesto

crookedness ['krʊkədnəs] n **1** : lo torcido, lo chueco **2** DISHONESTY : falta f de honradez

croon ['kruːn] v : cantar suavemente

crop[1] ['krɑp] vt **cropped; cropping** vt TRIM : recortar, cortar — vi **to crop up** : aparecer, surgir ⟨these problems keep cropping up : estos problemas no cesan de surgir⟩

crop[2] n **1** : buche m (de un ave o insecto) **2** WHIP : fusta f (de jinete) **3** HARVEST : cosecha f, cultivo m

croquet [ˌkroː'keɪ] n : croquet m

croquette [ˌkroː'kɛt] n : croqueta f

cross[1] ['krɔs] vt **1** : cruzar, atravesar ⟨to cross the street : cruzar la calle⟩ ⟨several canals cross the city : varios canales atraviesan la ciudad⟩ **2** : cruzar (los brazos, los dedos, las piernas) **3** INTERBREED : cruzar (en genética) **4 cross my heart** : te lo juro **5 to cross off/out** : tachar ⟨he crossed his name off the list : tachó su nombre de la planilla⟩ ⟨he crossed off/out his name : tachó su nombre⟩ **6 to cross one's mind** : ocurrírsele a uno **7 to cross paths** : cruzarse con alguien

⟨I crossed paths with him, we crossed paths : me crucé con él⟩

cross[2] adj **1** : que atraviesa ⟨cross ventilation : ventilación que atraviesa un cuarto⟩ **2** CONTRARY : contrario, opuesto ⟨cross purposes : objetivos opuestos⟩ **3** ANGRY : enojado, de mal humor

cross[3] n **1** : cruz f ⟨the sign of the cross : la señal de la cruz⟩ **2** : cruza f (en biología)

crossbar ['krɔsˌbɑr] n : travesaño m, tranca f

crossbones ['krɔsˌboːnz] npl **1** : huesos mpl cruzados **2** → **skull**

crossbow ['krɔsˌboː] n : ballesta f

crossbreed ['krɔsˌbriːd] vt **-bred** [-ˌbrɛd] : -**breeding** : cruzar

cross–country ['krɔs'kʌntri] n : cross m

crosscurrent ['krɔsˌkərənt] n : contracorriente f

cross–examination [ˌkrɔsɪgˌzæmə'neɪʃən] n : repreguntas fpl, interrogatorio m

cross–examine [ˌkrɔsɪg'zæmən] vt **-ined; -ining** : repreguntar

cross–eyed ['krɔsˌaɪd] adj : bizco

crossfire ['krɔsˌfaɪr] n : fuego m cruzado

crossing ['krɔsɪŋ] n **1** INTERSECTION : cruce m, paso m ⟨pedestrian crossing : paso de peatones⟩ **2** VOYAGE : travesía f (del mar)

cross–legged ['krɔsˌlɛgəd] adv : con las piernas cruzadas

crossly ['krɔsli] adv : con enojo, con enfado

crosspiece ['krɔsˌpiːs] n : travesaño m

cross–reference [ˌkrɔs'rɛfərəns, -'rɛfərənts] n : referencia f, remisión f

crossroads ['krɔsˌroːdz] n : cruce m, encrucijada f, crucero m Mex

cross section n **1** SECTION : corte m transversal **2** SAMPLE : muestra f representativa ⟨a cross section of the population : una muestra representativa de la población⟩

crosswalk ['krɔsˌwɔk] n : cruce m peatonal, paso m de peatones

crossways ['krɔsˌweɪz] → **crosswise**

crosswise[1] ['krɔsˌwaɪz] adv : transversalmente, diagonalmente

crosswise[2] adj : transversal, diagonal

crossword ['krɔsˌwərd] or **crossword puzzle** n : crucigrama m

crotch ['krɑtʃ] n : entrepierna f

crotchety ['krɑtʃəti] adj CRANKY : malhumorado, irritable, enojadizo

crouch ['kraʊtʃ] vi : agacharse, ponerse de cuclillas

croup ['kruːp] n : crup m

crouton ['kruːˌtɑn] n : crutón m

crow[1] ['kroː] vi **1** : cacarear, cantar (como un cuervo) **2** BRAG : alardear, presumir

crow[2] n **1** : cuervo m (ave) **2** : cantar m (del gallo)

crowbar ['kroːˌbɑr] n : palanca f

crowd[1] ['kraʊd] vi : aglomerarse, amontonarse — vt : atestar, atiborrar, llenar

crowd[2] n : multitud f, muchedumbre f, gentío m

crowded [ˈkraʊdəd] *adj* : repleto, atestado, abarrotado

crown¹ [ˈkraʊn] *vt* : coronar

crown² *n* : corona *f*

crow's–feet *npl* : patas *fpl* de gallo

crucial [ˈkruːʃəl] *adj* : crucial, decisivo

crucible [ˈkruːsəbəl] *n* : crisol *m*

crucifix [ˈkruːsəˌfɪks] *n* : crucifijo *m*

crucifixion [ˌkruːsəˈfɪkʃən] *n* : crucifixión *f*

crucify [ˈkruːsəˌfaɪ] *vt* **-fied; -fying** : crucificar

crude [ˈkruːd] *adj* **cruder; -est** **1** RAW, UNREFINED : crudo, sin refinar ⟨crude oil : petróleo crudo⟩ **2** VULGAR : grosero, de mal gusto **3** ROUGH : tosco, burdo, rudo

crudely [ˈkruːdli] *adv* **1** VULGARLY : groseramente **2** ROUGHLY : burdamente, de manera rudimentaria

crudity [ˈkruːdəti] *n, pl* **-ties** **1** VULGARITY : grosería *f* **2** COARSENESS, ROUGHNESS : tosquedad *f*, rudeza *f*

cruel [ˈkruːəl] *adj* **crueler** *or* **crueller; cruelest** *or* **cruellest** : cruel

cruelly [ˈkruːəli] *adv* : cruelmente

cruelty [ˈkruːəlti] *n, pl* **-ties** : crueldad *f* ⟨the tyrant's cruelty : la crueldad del tirano⟩ ⟨the cruelties of war : las crueldades de la guerra⟩

cruet [ˈkruːɪt] *n* : vinagrera *f*, aceitera *f*

cruise¹ [ˈkruːz] *vi* **cruised; cruising** **1** : hacer un crucero **2** : navegar o conducir a una velocidad constante ⟨cruising speed : velocidad de crucero⟩

cruise² *n* : crucero *m*

cruiser [ˈkruːzər] *n* **1** WARSHIP : crucero *m*, buque *m* de guerra **2** : patrulla *f* (de policía)

crumb [ˈkrʌm] *n* : miga *f*, migaja *f* ⟨bread crumbs : migas de pan, pan rallado⟩

crumble [ˈkrʌmbəl] *v* **-bled; -bling** *vt* : desmigajar, desmenuzar — *vi* : desmigajarse, desmoronarse, desmenuzarse

crumbly [ˈkrʌmbli] *adj* : que se desmenuza fácilmente

crummy [ˈkrʌmi] *adj* **crummier; -est** *fam* : malo

crumple [ˈkrʌmpəl] *v* **-pled; -pling** *vt* RUMPLE : arrugar — *vi* **1** WRINKLE : arrugarse **2** COLLAPSE : desplomarse

crunch¹ [ˈkrʌntʃ] *vt* **1** : ronzar (con los dientes) **2** : hacer crujir (con los pies, etc.) — *vi* : crujir

crunch² *n* : crujido *m*

crunchy [ˈkrʌntʃi] *adj* **crunchier; -est** : crujiente

crusade¹ [kruːˈseɪd] *vi* **-saded; -sading** : hacer una campaña (a favor de o contra algo)

crusade² *n* **1** : campaña *f* (de reforma, etc.) **2** Crusade : cruzada *f*

crusader [kruːˈseɪdər] *n* **1** : cruzado *m* (en la Edad Media) **2** : campeón *m*, -peona *f* (de una causa)

crush¹ [ˈkrʌʃ] *vt* **1** SQUASH : aplastar, apachurrar **2** GRIND, PULVERIZE : triturar, machacar **3** SUPPRESS : aplastar, suprimir **4** DEFEAT : darle una paliza a

crush² *n* **1** CROWD, MOB : gentío *m*, multitud *f*, aglomeración *f* **2** INFATUATION : enamoramiento *m*

crushing [ˈkrʌʃɪŋ] *adj* : aplastante, abrumador

crust [ˈkrʌst] *n* **1** : corteza *f*, costra *f* (de pan) **2** : tapa *f* de masa, pasta *f* (de un pastel) **3** LAYER : capa *f*, corteza *f* ⟨the earth's crust : la corteza terrestre⟩

crustacean [ˌkrʌsˈteɪʃən] *n* : crustáceo *m*

crusty [ˈkrʌsti] *adj* **crustier; -est** **1** : de corteza dura **2** CROSS, GRUMPY : enojado, malhumorado

crutch [ˈkrʌtʃ] *n* : muleta *f*

crux [ˈkrʌks, ˈkrʊks] *n, pl* **cruxes** : quid *m*, esencia *f*, meollo *m* ⟨the crux of the problem : el quid del problema⟩

cry¹ [ˈkraɪ] *vi* **cried; crying** **1** SHOUT : gritar **2** WEEP : llorar **3 to cry for** DEMAND : pedir a gritos, clamar por **4 to cry out** : gritar (de dolor, etc.) **5 to cry out against** : clamar contra **6 to cry over** : llorar por

cry² *n, pl* **cries** **1** SHOUT : grito *m* **2** WEEPING : llanto *m* **3** : chillido *m* (de un animal)

crybaby [ˈkraɪˌbeɪbi] *n, pl* **-bies** : llorón *m*, -rona *f*

crypt [ˈkrɪpt] *n* : cripta *f*

cryptic [ˈkrɪptɪk] *adj* : enigmático, críptico

crystal [ˈkrɪstəl] *n* : cristal *m*

crystalline [ˈkrɪstəlɪn] *adj* : cristalino

crystallize [ˈkrɪstəˌlaɪz] *v* **-lized; -lizing** *vt* : cristalizar, materializar ⟨to crystallize one's thoughts : cristalizar uno sus pensamientos⟩ — *vi* : cristalizarse

C–section [ˈsiːˌsɛkʃən] → **cesarean²**

cub [ˈkʌb] *n* : cachorro *m*

Cuban [ˈkjuːbən] *n* : cubano *m*, -na *f* — **Cuban** *adj*

cubbyhole [ˈkʌbiˌhoːl] *n* : chiribitil *m*

cube¹ [ˈkjuːb] *vt* **cubed; cubing** **1** : elevar (un número) al cubo **2** : cortar en cubos

cube² *n* **1** : cubo *m* **2 ice cube** : cubito *m* de hielo **3 sugar cube** : terrón *m* de azúcar

cubic [ˈkjuːbɪk] *adj* : cúbico

cubicle [ˈkjuːbɪkəl] *n* : cubículo *m*

cuckoo¹ [ˈkuːˌkuː, ˈkʊ-] *adj* : loco, chiflado

cuckoo² *n, pl* **-oos** : cuco *m*, cuclillo *m*

cucumber [ˈkjuːˌkʌmbər] *n* : pepino *m*

cud [ˈkʌd] *n* **to chew the cud** : rumiar

cuddle¹ [ˈkʌdəl] *v* **-dled; -dling** *vi* : abrazarse tiernamente, acurrucarse — *vt* : abrazar

cuddle² *n* : abrazo *m*

cudgel¹ [ˈkʌdʒəl] *vt* **-geled** *or* **-gelled; -geling** *or* **-gelling** : apalear, aporrear

cudgel² *n* : garrote *m*, porra *f*

cue¹ [ˈkjuː] *vt* **cued; cuing** *or* **cueing** : darle el pie a, darle la señal a

cue² *n* **1** SIGNAL : señal *f*, pie *m* (en teatro), entrada *f* (en música) **2** : taco *m* (de billar)

cuff¹ [ˈkʌf] *vt* : bofetear, cachetear

cuff² *n* **1** : puño *m* (de una camisa), vuelta *f* (de pantalones) **2** SLAP : bofetada *f*, cachetada *f* **3 cuffs** *npl* HANDCUFFS : esposas *fpl*

cuff link n : gemelo m
cuisine [kwɪˈziːn] n : cocina f ⟨Mexican cuisine : la cocina mexicana⟩
cul–de–sac [ˈkʌldɪˌsæk] n : calle f sin salida
culinary [ˈkʌləˌneri, ˈkjuːləˌ] adj : culinario
cull [ˈkʌl] vt : seleccionar
culminate [ˈkʌlməˌneɪt] vi -nated; -nating : culminar
culmination [ˌkʌlməˈneɪʃən] n : culminación f, punto m culminante
culpable [ˈkʌlpəbəl] adj : culpable
culprit [ˈkʌlprɪt] n : culpable mf
cult [ˈkʌlt] n : culto m
cultivate [ˈkʌltəˌveɪt] vt -vated; -vating 1 TILL : cultivar, labrar 2 FOSTER : cultivar, fomentar 3 REFINE : cultivar, refinar ⟨to cultivate the mind : cultivar la mente⟩
cultivation [ˌkʌltəˈveɪʃən] n 1 : cultivo m ⟨under cultivation : en cultivo⟩ 2 CULTURE, REFINEMENT : cultura f, refinamiento m
cultural [ˈkʌltʃərəl] adj : cultural — **culturally** adv
culture [ˈkʌltʃər] n 1 CULTIVATION : cultivo m 2 REFINEMENT : cultura f, educación f, refinamiento m 3 CIVILIZATION : cultura f, civilización f ⟨the Incan culture : la cultura inca⟩
cultured [ˈkʌltʃərd] adj 1 EDUCATED, REFINED : culto, educado, refinado 2 : de cultivo, cultivado ⟨cultured pearls : perlas de cultivo⟩
culvert [ˈkʌlvərt] n : alcantarilla f
cumbersome [ˈkʌmbərsəm] adj : torpe y pesado, difícil de manejar
cumin [ˈkʌmən] n : comino m
cumulative [ˈkjuːmjələtɪv, -ˌleɪtɪv] adj : acumulativo
cumulus [ˈkjuːmjələs] n, pl -li [-ˌlaɪ, -ˌliː] : cúmulo m
cunning[1] [ˈkʌnɪŋ] adj 1 CRAFTY : astuto, taimado 2 CLEVER : ingenioso, hábil 3 CUTE : mono, gracioso, lindo
cunning[2] n 1 SKILL : habilidad f 2 CRAFTINESS : astucia f, maña f
cup[1] [ˈkʌp] vt cupped; cupping : ahuecar (las manos)
cup[2] n 1 : taza f ⟨a cup of coffee : una taza de café⟩ 2 CUPFUL : taza f 3 : media pinta f (unidad de medida) 4 GOBLET : copa f 5 TROPHY : copa f, trofeo m
cupboard [ˈkʌbərd] n : alacena f, armario m
cupcake [ˈkʌpˌkeɪk] n : pastelito m
cupful [ˈkʌpˌful] n : taza f
cupola [ˈkjuːpələ, -ˌloː] n : cúpula f
cur [ˈkər] n : perro m callejero, perro m corriente Mex
curate [ˈkjʊrət] n : cura m, párroco m
curator [ˈkjʊrˌeɪtər, kjʊˈreɪtər] n : conservador m, -dora f (de un museo); director m, -tora f (de un zoológico)
curb[1] [ˈkərb] vt : refrenar, restringir, controlar
curb[2] n 1 RESTRAINT : freno m, control m 2 : borde m de la acera
curd [ˈkərd] n : cuajada f

curdle [ˈkərdəl] v -dled; -dling vi : cuajarse — vt : cuajar ⟨to curdle one's blood : helarle la sangre a uno⟩
curdled [ˈkərdəld] adj : cortado (dícese de la leche, etc.)
cure[1] [ˈkjʊr] vt cured; curing 1 HEAL : curar, sanar 2 REMEDY : remediar 3 PROCESS : curar (alimentos, etc.)
cure[2] n 1 RECOVERY : curación f, recuperación f 2 REMEDY : cura f, remedio m
curfew [ˈkərˌfjuː] n : toque m de queda
curio [ˈkjʊriˌoː] n, pl -rios : curiosidad f, objeto m curioso
curiosity [ˌkjʊriˈɑsəti] n, pl -ties : curiosidad f
curious [ˈkjʊriəs] adj 1 INQUISITIVE : curioso 2 STRANGE : curioso, raro
curl[1] [ˈkərl] vt 1 : rizar, ondular (el pelo) 2 COIL : enrollar 3 TWIST : torcer ⟨to curl one's lip : hacer una mueca⟩ — vi 1 : rizarse, ondularse 2 to curl up : acurrucarse (con un libro, etc.)
curl[2] n 1 RINGLET : rizo m, bucle m 2 COIL : espiral f, rosca f
curler [ˈkərlər] n : rulo m
curlew [ˈkərˌluː, ˈkərlˌjuː] n, pl -lews or -lew : zarapito m
curly [ˈkərli] adj curlier; -est : rizado, crespo
curly brace or **curly bracket** n : llave f (signo de puntuación)
currant [ˈkərənt] n 1 : grosella f (fruta) ⟨black currant : grosella negra⟩ ⟨red currant : grosella roja⟩ 2 RAISIN : pasa f de Corinto
currency [ˈkərəntsi] n, pl -cies 1 PREVALENCE, USE : uso m, aceptación f, difusión f ⟨to be in currency : estar en uso⟩ 2 MONEY : moneda f, dinero m
current[1] [ˈkərənt] adj 1 PRESENT : actual ⟨current events : actualidades⟩ 2 PREVALENT : corriente, común — **currently** adv
current[2] n : corriente f
curriculum [kəˈrɪkjələm] n, pl -la [-lə] : currículum m, currículo m, programa m de estudio
curriculum vitae [ˈviːˌtaɪ, ˈvaɪtiː] n, pl curricula vitae : currículum m, currículo m
curry[1] [ˈkəri] vt -ried; -rying 1 GROOM : almohazar (un caballo) 2 : condimentar con curry 3 to curry favor : congraciarse (con alguien)
curry[2] n, pl -ries : curry m
curse[1] [ˈkərs] v cursed; cursing vt 1 DAMN : maldecir 2 INSULT : injuriar, insultar, decir malas palabras a 3 AFFLICT : afligir — vi : maldecir, decir malas palabras
curse[2] n 1 : maldición f ⟨to put a curse on someone : echarle una maldición a alguien⟩ 2 AFFLICTION : maldición f, aflicción f, cruz f
cursor [ˈkərsər] n : cursor m
cursory [ˈkərsəri] adj : rápido, superficial, somero
curt [ˈkərt] adj : cortante, brusco, seco — **curtly** adv

curtail [kər'teɪl] vt : acortar, limitar, restringir

curtailment [kər'teɪlmənt] n : restricción f, limitación f

curtain ['kərtən] n : cortina f (de una ventana), telón m (en un teatro)

curtness ['kərtnəs] n : brusquedad f, sequedad f

curtsy¹ or **curtsey** ['kərtsi] vt **-sied** or **-seyed; -sying** or **-seying** : hacer una reverencia

curtsy² or **curtsey** n, pl **-sies** or **-seys** : reverencia f

curvature ['kərvə,tʃur] n : curvatura f

curve¹ ['kərv] v **curved; curving** vi : torcerse, describir una curva — vt : encorvar

curve² n : curva f

cushion¹ ['kuʃən] vt **1** : poner cojines o almohadones a **2** SOFTEN : amortiguar, mitigar, suavizar ⟨to cushion a blow : amortiguar un golpe⟩

cushion² n **1** : cojín m, almohadón m **2** PROTECTION : colchón m, protección f

cusp ['kʌsp] n : cúspide f (de un diente), cuerno m (de la luna)

cuspid ['kʌspɪd] n : diente m canino, colmillo m

custard ['kʌstərd] n : natillas fpl

custodian [,kʌs'toːdiən] n : custodio m, -dia f; guardián, -diana f

custody ['kʌstədi] n, pl **-dies** : custodia f, cuidado m ⟨to be in custody : estar detenido⟩

custom¹ ['kʌstəm] adj : a la medida, a la orden

custom² n **1** : costumbre f, tradición f **2 customs** npl : aduana f ⟨customs officer : agente de aduanas⟩

customarily [,kʌstə'merəli] adv : habitualmente, normalmente, de costumbre

customary ['kʌstə,meri] adj **1** TRADITIONAL : tradicional **2** USUAL : habitual, de costumbre

customer ['kʌstəmər] n : cliente m, -ta f

custom–made ['kʌstəm'meɪd] adj : hecho a la medida

cut¹ ['kʌt] v **cut; cutting** vt **1** : cortar ⟨to cut paper : cortar papel⟩ ⟨cut the meat into strips : cortar la carne en tiras⟩ ⟨cut the apple in half : cortar la manzana por la mitad⟩ ⟨to cut a hole in : hacer un agujero en⟩ ⟨to cut (off) a piece : cortar un trozo⟩ **2** : cortarse ⟨to cut one's finger : cortarse uno el dedo⟩ **3** TRIM : cortar, recortar ⟨to have one's hair cut : cortarse el pelo⟩ **4** INTERSECT : cruzar, atravesar **5** SHORTEN : acortar, abreviar **6** REDUCE : reducir, rebajar ⟨to cut prices : rebajar los precios⟩ **7** : cortar (en informática) ⟨to cut and paste : cortar y pegar⟩ **8** : cortar (una baraja) **9** : sacar (de un equipo, etc.) **10** SKIP : faltar a (clase) **11** TURN OFF : apagar **12** DILUTE : cortar (drogas) **13 cut it out!** : ¡basta ya! **14 not to cut it** : no ser lo suficientemente bueno **15 to cut a deal** : hacer/cerrar un trato **16 to cut away** : cortar **17 to cut back** PRUNE : podar **18 to cut back** REDUCE : reducir (gastos, etc.) **19 to cut down** FELL : cortar, talar **20 to cut down** REDUCE : reducir **21 to cut down** KILL : matar **22 to cut in** : cortar y mezclar (mantequilla, etc.) **23 to cut off** : cortar (una rama, una pierna, etc.) **24 to cut off** : cortar (el acceso, etc.) **25 to cut off** INTERRUPT : interrumpir **26 to cut off** ISOLATE : aislar **27 to cut off** : cortarle el paso a un vehículo, etc.) **28 to cut one's teeth** : salirle los dientes a uno **29 to cut out** CLIP : recortar **30 to cut out** EXCLUDE : excluir **31 to cut up** : cortar en pedazos — vi **1** : cortar, cortarse **2 to cut back** : hacer economías **3 to cut down** : moderarse **4 to cut in** : entrometerse **5 to cut in line** : colarse **6 to cut up** CLOWN AROUND : hacer payasadas

cut² n **1** : corte m ⟨a cut of meat : un corte de carne⟩ **2** SLASH : tajo m, corte m, cortadura f **3** REDUCTION : rebaja f, reducción f ⟨a cut in the rates : una rebaja en las tarifas⟩

cutaneous [kju'teɪniəs] adj : cutáneo

cutback ['kʌt,bæk] n : recorte m, reducción f

cute ['kjuːt] adj **cuter; cutest** : mono fam, lindo

cuticle ['kjuːtɪkəl] n : cutícula f

cutlass ['kʌtləs] n : alfanje m

cutlery ['kʌtləri] n : cubiertos mpl

cutlet ['kʌtlət] n : chuleta f

cutoff ['kʌt,ɔf] n **1** INTERRUPTION : corte m, interrupción f **2** DEADLINE : fecha límite, fecha f tope **3 cutoffs** npl : shorts mpl de mezclilla

cut–rate ['kʌt,reɪt] adj : a precio rebajado

cutter ['kʌtər] n **1** : cortadora f (implemento) **2** : cortador m, -dora f (persona) **3** : cúter m (embarcación)

cutthroat ['kʌt,θroːt] adj : despiadado, desalmado ⟨cutthroat competition : competencia feroz⟩

cutting¹ ['kʌtɪŋ] adj **1** : cortante ⟨a cutting wind : un viento cortante⟩ **2** CAUSTIC : mordaz

cutting² n : esqueje m (de una planta)

cuttlefish ['kʌtəl,fɪʃ] n, pl **-fish** or **-fishes** : jibia f, sepia f

cyanide ['saɪə,naɪd, -nɪd] n : cianuro m

cyber- ['saɪbər-] pref : ciber- m

cybernetic [,saɪbər'netɪk] adj : cibernético

cycle¹ ['saɪkəl] vi **-cled; -cling** : andar en bicicleta, ir en bicicleta

cycle² n **1** : ciclo m ⟨life cycle : ciclo de vida, ciclo vital⟩ **2** BICYCLE : bicicleta f **3** MOTORCYCLE : motocicleta f

cyclic ['saɪklɪk, 'sɪ-] or **cyclical** [-klɪkəl] adj : cíclico

cycling ['saɪklɪŋ] n : ciclismo m

cyclist ['saɪklɪst] n : ciclista mf

cyclone ['saɪ,kloːn] n **1** : ciclón m **2** TORNADO : tornado m

cyclopedia or **cyclopaedia** [,saɪklə-'piːdiə] → encyclopedia

cylinder ['sɪləndər] n : cilindro m

cylindrical [sə'lɪndrɪkəl] adj : cilíndrico

cymbal ['sɪmbəl] n : platillo m, címbalo m

cynic ['sɪnɪk] n : cínico m, -ca f

cynical ['sınıkəl] *adj* : cínico

cynicism ['sınə,sızəm] *n* : cinismo *m*

cypress ['saıprəs] *n* : ciprés *m*

cyst ['sıst] *n* : quiste *m*

czar ['zar, 'sar] *n* : zar *m*

czarina [za'ri:nə, sa-] *n* : zarina *f*

Czech ['tʃɛk] *n* **1** : checo *m*, -ca *f* **2** : checo *m* (idioma) — **Czech** *adj*

Czechoslovak [,tʃɛko'slo:,vak, -,væk] *or* **Czechoslovakian** [-slo'vakiən, -'væ-] *n* : checoslovaco *m*, -ca *f* — **Czechoslovak** *or* **Czechoslovakian** *adj*

D

d ['di:] *n*, *pl* **d's** *or* **ds** ['di:z] **1** : cuarta letra del alfabeto inglés **2** : re *m* ⟨D sharp/flat : re sostenido/bemol⟩

dab¹ ['dæb] *vt* **dabbed; dabbing** : darle toques ligeros a, aplicar suavemente

dab² *n* **1** BIT : toque *m*, pizca *f*, poco *m* ⟨a dab of ointment : un toque de ungüento⟩ **2** PAT : toque *m* ligero, golpecito *m*

dabble ['dæbəl] *v* **-bled; -bling** *vt* SPATTER : salpicar — *vi* **1** SPLASH : chapotear **2** TRIFLE : jugar, interesarse superficialmente

dabbler ['dæbələr] *n* : diletante *mf*

dachshund ['daks,hunt, -,hund; 'daksənt, -sənd] *n* : perro *m* salchicha

dad ['dæd] *n* : papá *m* *fam*

daddy ['dædi] *n*, *pl* **-dies** : papi *m* *fam*

daddy longlegs ['lɔŋ,lɛgz] *n*, *pl* **daddy longlegs** : segador *m* (insecto)

daffodil ['dæfə,dıl] *n* : narciso *m*

daft ['dæft] *adj* : tonto, bobo

dagger ['dægər] *n* : daga *f*, puñal *m*

dahlia ['dæljə, 'dal-, 'deıl-] *n* : dalia *f*

daily¹ ['deıli] *adv* : a diario, diariamente

daily² *adj* : diario, cotidiano

daily³ *n*, *pl* **-lies** : diario *m*, periódico *m*

daintily ['deıntəli] *adv* : delicadamente, con delicadeza

daintiness ['deıntinəs] *n* : delicadeza *f*, finura *f*

dainty¹ ['deınti] *adj* **daintier; -est 1** DELICATE : delicado **2** FASTIDIOUS : remilgado, melindroso **3** DELICIOUS : exquisito, sabroso

dainty² *n*, *pl* **-ties** DELICACY : exquisitez *f*, manjar *m*

dairy¹ ['dæri] *adj* : lácteo ⟨dairy products : productos lácteos⟩

dairy² *n*, *pl* **-ries 1** *or* **dairy store** : lechería *f* **2** *or* **dairy farm** : granja *f* lechera

dairymaid ['dæri,meıd] *n* : lechera *f*

dairyman ['dærimən, -,mæn] *n*, *pl* **-men** [-mən, -,mɛn] : lechero *m*

dais ['deıəs] *n* : tarima *f*, estrado *m*

daisy ['deızi] *n*, *pl* **-sies** : margarita *f*

dale ['deıl] *n* : valle *m*

dally ['dæli] *vi* **-lied; -lying 1** TRIFLE : juguetear **2** DAWDLE : entretenerse, perder tiempo

dalmatian [dæl'meıʃən, dɔl-] *n* : dálmata *m*

dam¹ ['dæm] *vt* **dammed; damming** : represar

dam² *n* **1** : represa *f*, dique *m* **2** : madre *f* (de animales domésticos)

damage¹ ['dæmıdʒ] *vt* **-aged; -aging** : dañar (un objeto o una máquina), perjudicar (la salud o una reputación)

damage² *n* **1** : daño *m*, perjuicio *m* ⟨to cause damage to : ocasionar daños a⟩ **2** **damages** *npl* : daños y perjuicios *mpl*

damaging ['dæmıdʒıŋ] *adj* : perjudicial

damask ['dæməsk] *n* : damasco *m*

dame ['deım] *n* LADY : dama *f*, señora *f*

damn¹ ['dæm] *vt* **1** CONDEMN : condenar **2** CURSE : maldecir

damn² *or* **damned** ['dæmd] *adj* : condenado *fam*, maldito *fam*

damn³ *n* : pito *m*, bledo *m*, comino *m* ⟨it's not worth a damn : no vale un pito⟩ ⟨I don't give a damn : me importa un comino⟩

damnable ['dæmnəbəl] *adj* : condenable, detestable

damnation [dæm'neıʃən] *n* : condenación *f*

damned¹ ['dæmd] *adv* VERY : muy

damned² *adj* **1** → **damnable 2** REMARKABLE : extraordinario

damning ['dæmıŋ] *adj* : condenatorio

damp¹ ['dæmp] *vt* → **dampen**

damp² *adj* : húmedo

damp³ *n* MOISTURE : humedad *f*

dampen ['dæmpən] *vt* **1** MOISTEN : humedecer **2** DISCOURAGE : desalentar, desanimar

damper ['dæmpər] *n* **1** : regulador *m* de tiro (de una chimenea) **2** : sordina *f* (de un piano) **3 to put a damper on** : desanimar, apagar (el entusiasmo), enfriar

dampness ['dæmpnəs] *n* : humedad *f*

damsel ['dæmzəl] *n* : damisela *f*

dance¹ ['dænts] *v* **danced; dancing** : bailar

dance² *n* : baile *m*

dancer ['dæntsər] *n* : bailarín *m*, -rina *f*

dandelion ['dændə,laıən] *n* : diente *m* de león

dandruff ['dændrəf] *n* : caspa *f*

dandy¹ ['dændi] *adj* **dandier; -est** : excelente, magnífico, macanudo *fam*

dandy² *n*, *pl* **-dies 1** : dandi *m* **2** : algo *m* excelente ⟨this new program is a dandy : este programa nuevo es algo excelente⟩

Dane ['deın] *n* : danés *m*, -nesa *f*

danger ['deındʒər] *n* : peligro *m*

dangerous ['deındʒərəs] *adj* : peligroso

dangle ['dæŋgəl] *v* **-gled; -gling** *vi* HANG : colgar, pender — *vt* **1** SWING : hacer oscilar **2** PROFFER : ofrecer (como incentivo) **3 to keep someone dangling** : dejar a alguien en suspenso

Danish[1] [ˈdeɪnɪʃ] *adj* : danés
Danish[2] *n* : danés *m* (idioma)
dank [ˈdæŋk] *adj* : frío y húmedo
dapper [ˈdæpər] *adj* : pulcro, atildado
dappled [ˈdæpəld] *adj* : moteado ⟨a dappled horse : un caballo rodado⟩
dare[1] [ˈdær] *v* **dared; daring** *vi* : osar, atreverse ⟨how dare you! : ¡cómo te atreves!⟩ — *vt* **1** CHALLENGE : desafiar, retar **2 to dare to do** something : atreverse a hacer algo, osar hacer algo
dare[2] *n* : desafío *m*, reto *m*
daredevil [ˈdær.dɛvəl] *n* : persona *f* temeraria
daring[1] [ˈdærɪŋ] *adj* : osado, atrevido, audaz
daring[2] *n* : arrojo *m*, coraje *m*, audacia *f*
dark[1] [ˈdɑrk] *adj* **1** : oscuro (dícese del ambiente o de los colores), moreno (dícese del pelo o de la piel) ⟨it's getting dark : está oscureciendo⟩ **2** SOMBER : sombrío, triste
dark[2] *n* **1** : oscuridad *f*, tinieblas *f* ⟨to be afraid of the dark : tenerle miedo a la oscuridad⟩ **2** NIGHT : noche ⟨before dark : antes del anochecer⟩
dark chocolate *n* : chocolate *m* oscuro, chocolate *m* amargo, chocolate *m* negro
darken [ˈdɑrkən] *vt* **1** DIM : oscurecer **2** SADDEN : entristecer — *vi* : ensombrecerse, nublarse
darkly [ˈdɑrkli] *adv* **1** DIMLY : oscuramente **2** GLOOMILY : tristemente **3** MYSTERIOUSLY : misteriosamente, enigmáticamente
darkness [ˈdɑrknəs] *n* : oscuridad *f*, tinieblas *f*
darkroom [ˈdɑrk.ruːm, -.rʊm] *n* : cuarto *m* oscuro
darling[1] [ˈdɑrlɪŋ] *adj* **1** BELOVED : querido, amado **2** CHARMING : encantador, mono *fam*
darling[2] *n* **1** BELOVED : querido *m*, -da *f*; amado *m*, -da *f*; cariño *m*, -ña *f* **2** FAVORITE : preferido *m*, -da *f*; favorito *m*, -ta *f*
darn[1] [ˈdɑrn] *vt* : zurcir
darn[2] *n* : zurcido *m* **2** → **damn**[3]
dart[1] [ˈdɑrt] *vt* THROW : lanzar, tirar — *vi* DASH : lanzarse, precipitarse
dart[2] *n* **1** : dardo *m* **2 darts** *npl* : juego *m* de dardos
dash[1] [ˈdæʃ] *vt* **1** SMASH : romper, estrellar **2** HURL : arrojar, lanzar **3** SPLASH : salpicar **4** FRUSTRATE : frustrar **5 to dash off** : hacer (algo) rápidamente — *vi* **1** SMASH : romperse, estrellarse **2** DART : lanzarse, irse apresuradamente
dash[2] *n* **1** BURST, SPLASH : arranque *m*, salpicadura *f* (de aguas) **2** : guión *m* largo (signo de puntuación) **3** DROP : gota *f*, pizca *f* **4** VERVE : brío *m* **5** RACE : carrera *f* ⟨a 100-meter dash : una carrera de 100 metros⟩ **6 to make a dash for it** : precipitarse (hacia), echarse a correr **7** → **dashboard**
dashboard [ˈdæʃ.bord] *n* : tablero *m* de instrumentos
dashing [ˈdæʃɪŋ] *adj* : gallardo, apuesto
data [ˈdeɪtə, ˈdæ-, ˈdɑ-] *ns & pl* : datos *mpl*, información *f*

data bank *n* : banco *m* de datos
database [ˈdeɪtə.beɪs, ˈdæ-, ˈdɑ-] *n* : base *f* de datos
data processing *n* : procesamiento *m* de datos
date[1] [ˈdeɪt] *v* **dated; dating** *vt* **1** : fechar (una carta, etc.), datar (un objeto) ⟨it was dated June 9 : estaba fechada el 9 de junio⟩ **2** : salir con ⟨she's dating my brother : sale con mi hermano⟩ — *vi* : datar
date[2] *n* **1** : fecha *f* ⟨to date : hasta la fecha⟩ **2** EPOCH, PERIOD : época *f*, período *m* **3** APPOINTMENT : cita *f* **4** COMPANION : acompañante *mf* **5** : dátil *m* (fruta)
dated [ˈdeɪtəd] *adj* OUT-OF-DATE : anticuado, pasado de moda
datum [ˈdeɪtəm, ˈdæ-, ˈdɑ-] *n, pl* **-ta** [-tə] *or* **-tums** : dato *m*
daub[1] [ˈdɔb] *vt* : embadurnar
daub[2] *n* : mancha *f*
daughter [ˈdɔtər] *n* : hija *f*
daughter–in–law [ˈdɔtərɪn.lɔ] *n, pl* **daughters–in–law** : nuera *f*, hija *f* política
daunt [ˈdɔnt] *vt* : amilanar, acobardar, intimidar
daunting [ˈdɔntɪŋ] *adj* : desalentador
dauntless [ˈdɔntləs] *adj* : intrépido, impávido
dawdle [ˈdɔdəl] *vi* **-dled; -dling 1** DALLY : demorarse, entretenerse, perder tiempo **2** LOITER : vagar, holgazanear, haraganear
dawn[1] [ˈdɔn] *vi* **1** : amanecer, alborear, despuntar ⟨Saturday dawned clear and bright : el sábado amaneció claro y luminoso⟩ **2 to dawn on** : hacerse obvio ⟨it dawned on me that she was right : me di cuenta de que tenía razón⟩
dawn[2] *n* **1** DAYBREAK : amanecer *m*, alba *f* **2** BEGINNING : albor *m*, comienzo *m* ⟨the dawn of history : los albores de la historia⟩ **3 from dawn to dusk** : de sol a sol
day [ˈdeɪ] *n* **1** : día *m* ⟨the day after tomorrow : pasado mañana⟩ ⟨the day before yesterday : anteayer⟩ ⟨the other day : el otro día⟩ ⟨twice a day, two times a day : dos veces al día⟩ ⟨every day : todos los días⟩ ⟨all day : todo el día⟩ **2** DATE : fecha *f* ⟨what day is (it) today? : ¿qué día es hoy?⟩ **3** TIME : día *m*, tiempo *m* ⟨in those days : en aquellos tiempos⟩ ⟨in my day : en mis tiempos⟩ ⟨to the present day : hasta nuestros días⟩ ⟨to this day : hasta el día de hoy⟩ **4** WORKDAY : jornada *f* laboral **5 any day now** SOON : cualquier día de estos **6 in this day and age** : hoy (en) día **7 one day** SOMEDAY : algún día **8 the good old days** : los viejos tiempos **9 these days** : hoy (en) día **10 to make someone's day** : alegrarle el día a alguien
daybreak [ˈdeɪ.breɪk] *n* : alba *f*, amanecer *m*
day care *n* : servicio *m* de guardería infantil
daydream[1] [ˈdeɪ.driːm] *vi* : soñar despierto, fantasear

daydream[2] *n* : ensueño *m*, ensoñación *f*, fantasía *f*

daylight ['deɪ,laɪt] *n* **1** : luz *f* del día ⟨in broad daylight : a plena luz del día⟩ **2 →** **daybreak 3 → daytime**

daylight saving time *n* : hora *f* de verano

daytime ['deɪ,taɪm] *n* : horas *fpl* diurnas, día *m*

day–to–day *adj* : diario, cotidiano

daze[1] ['deɪz] *vt* **dazed; dazing 1** STUN : aturdir **2** DAZZLE : deslumbrar, ofuscar

daze[2] *n* **1** : aturdimiento *m* **2 in a daze** : aturdido, atontado

dazzle[1] ['dæzəl] *vt* **-zled; -zling** : deslumbrar, ofuscar

dazzle[2] *n* : resplandor *m*, brillo *m*

dazzling ['dæzəlɪŋ] *adj* : deslumbrante

de– *pref* : des-

deacon ['di:kən] *n* : diácono *m*

deaconess ['di:kənəs] *n* : diaconisa *f*

deactivate [di'æktə,veɪt] **-vated; -vating** *vt* : desactivar

dead[1] ['dɛd] *adv* **1** ABRUPTLY : repentinamente, súbitamente ⟨to stop dead : parar en seco⟩ **2** ABSOLUTELY : absolutamente ⟨I'm dead certain : estoy absolutamente seguro⟩ **3** DIRECTLY : justo ⟨dead ahead : justo adelante⟩

dead[2] *adj* **1** LIFELESS : muerto ⟨to drop dead : caerse muerto⟩ **2** NUMB : entumecido, dormido **3** INDIFFERENT : indiferente, frío **4** INACTIVE : inactivo ⟨a dead volcano : un volcán inactivo⟩ **5** : desconectado (dícese de un teléfono), descargado (dícese de una batería) **6** EXHAUSTED : agotado, derrengado, muerto **7** OBSOLETE : obsoleto, muerto ⟨a dead language : una lengua muerta⟩ **8** EXACT : exacto ⟨(in the) dead center : justo en el blanco⟩ **9** QUIET, SLOW : muerto (dícese de una fiesta, etc.), de poco movimiento (comercial) **10** : perdido ⟨if she catches you, you're dead : si te agarra, te mata⟩ **11 drop dead!** : ¡vete al infierno! **12 to be caught dead in** ⟨I wouldn't be caught dead in that outfit : no me pondría ese conjunto ni muerta⟩

dead[3] *n* **1 the dead** : los muertos **2 in the dead of night** : a las altas horas de la noche **3 in the dead of winter** : en pleno invierno

deadbeat ['dɛd,bi:t] *n* **1** LOAFER : vago *m*, -ga *f*; holgazán *m*, -zana *f* **2** FREELOADER : gorrón *m*, -rrona *f fam*; gorrero *m*, -ra *f fam*

deaden ['dɛdən] *vt* **1** : atenuar (un dolor), entorpecer (sensaciones) **2** DULL : deslustrar **3** DISPIRIT : desanimar **4** MUFFLE : amortiguar, reducir (sonidos)

dead–end ['dɛd'ɛnd] *adj* **1** : sin salida ⟨dead-end street : calle sin salida⟩ **2** : sin futuro ⟨a dead-end job : un trabajo sin porvenir⟩

dead end *n* : callejón *m* sin salida

dead heat *n* : empate *m*

deadline ['dɛd,laɪn] *n* : fecha *f* límite, fecha *f* tope, plazo *m* (determinado)

deadlock[1] ['dɛd,lɑk] *vt* : estancar — *vi* : estancarse, llegar a punto muerto

deadlock[2] *n* : punto *m* muerto, impasse *m*

deadly[1] ['dɛdli] *adv* : extremadamente, sumamente ⟨deadly serious : muy en serio⟩

deadly[2] *adj* **deadlier; -est 1** LETHAL : mortal, letal, mortífero **2** ACCURATE : certero, preciso ⟨with deadly aim : con puntería infalible⟩ **3** CAPITAL : capital ⟨the seven deadly sins : los siete pecados capitales⟩ **4** DULL : funesto, aburrido **5** EXTREME : extremo, absoluto ⟨a deadly calm : una calma absoluta⟩

deadpan[1] ['dɛd,pæn] *adv* : de manera inexpresiva, sin expresión

deadpan[2] *adj* : inexpresivo, impasible

deaf ['dɛf] *adj* : sordo

deafen ['dɛfən] *vt* **-ened; -ening** : ensordecer

deafening ['dɛfənɪŋ] *adj* : ensordecedor

deaf–mute ['dɛf'mju:t] *n* : sordomudo *m*, -da *f*

deafness ['dɛfnəs] *n* : sordera *f*

deal[1] ['di:l] *v* **dealt; dealing** *vt* **1** *or* **to deal out** APPORTION : repartir ⟨to deal justice : repartir la justicia⟩ **2** DISTRIBUTE : repartir, dar (naipes) **3** DELIVER : asestar, propinar ⟨to deal a blow : asestar un golpe⟩ — *vi* **1** : dar, repartir (en juegos de naipes) **2 to deal in** : comerciar en, traficar con (drogas) **3 to deal with** CONCERN : tratar de, tener que ver con ⟨the book deals with poverty : el libro trata de la pobreza⟩ **4 to deal with** HANDLE : tratar (con), encargarse de **5 to deal with** TREAT : tratar ⟨the judge dealt with him severely : el juez lo trató con severidad⟩ **6 to deal with** ACCEPT : aceptar (una situación o desgracia)

deal[2] *n* **1** : reparto *m* (de naipes) **2** AGREEMENT, TRANSACTION : trato *m*, acuerdo *m*, transacción *f* ⟨to cut/make/strike a deal : hacer un trato⟩ **3** TREATMENT : trato *m* ⟨he got a raw deal : le hicieron una injusticia⟩ **4** BARGAIN : ganga *f*, oferta *f* ⟨she got a good deal on the car : consiguió el coche a un precio barato⟩ **5 a good/great deal** : mucho, una gran cantidad **6 big deal** : cosa *f* importante ⟨don't worry, it's no big deal : no te preocupes, no tiene importancia⟩ ⟨so what? big deal! : ¿a quién le importa?⟩ **7 the real deal** ⟨to be the real deal : ser auténtico, ser de verdad⟩

dealer ['di:lər] *n* : comerciante *mf*, traficante *mf*

dealership ['di:lər,ʃɪp] *n* : concesión *f*

dealings ['di:lɪŋz] *npl* **1** : relaciones *fpl* (personales) **2** TRANSACTIONS : negocios *mpl*, transacciones *fpl*

dean ['di:n] *n* **1** : deán *m* (del clero) **2** : decano *m*, -na *f* (de una facultad o profesión)

dear[1] ['dɪr] *adj* **1** ESTEEMED, LOVED : querido, estimado ⟨a dear friend : un amigo querido⟩ ⟨Dear Sir : Estimado Señor⟩ **2** COSTLY : caro, costoso

dear[2] *n* : querido *m*, -da *f*; amado *m*, -da *f*

dearly ['dɪrli] *adv* **1** : mucho ⟨I love them dearly : los quiero mucho⟩ **2** : caro ⟨to pay dearly : pagar caro⟩

dearth ['dərθ] *n* : escasez *f*, carestía *f*

death ['dɛθ] *n* 1 : muerte *f*, fallecimiento *m* ⟨to be the death of : matar⟩ 2 FATALITY : víctima *f* (mortal); muerto *m*, -ta *f* 3 END : fin *m* ⟨the death of civilization : el fin de la civilización⟩

deathbed ['dɛθ,bɛd] *n* : lecho *m* de muerte

deathblow ['dɛθ,blo:] *n* : golpe *m* mortal

death certificate *n* : certificado *m* de defunción, acta *f* de defunción

deathless ['dɛθləs] *adj* : eterno, inmortal

deathly ['dɛθli] *adj* : de muerte, sepulcral (dícese del silencio), cadavérico (dícese de la palidez)

death penalty *n* : pena *f* de muerte

death trap *n* : trampa *f* mortal, vehículo *m* (o edificio *m*, etc.) peligroso

debacle [dɪ'bakəl, -'bæ-] *n* : desastre *m*, debacle *m*, fiasco *m*

debar [dɪ'bɑr] *vt* **-barred; -barring** : excluir, prohibir

debase [dɪ'beɪs] *vt* **-based; -basing** : degradar, envilecer

debatable [dɪ'beɪtəbəl] *adj* : discutible

debate¹ [dɪ'beɪt] *vt* **-bated; -bating** : debatir, discutir

debate² *n* : debate *m*, discusión *f*

debauch [dɪ'bɔtʃ] *vt* : pervertir, corromper

debauchery [dɪ'bɔtʃəri] *n, pl* **-eries** : libertinaje *m*, intemperancia *f*

debilitate [dɪ'bɪlə,teɪt] *vt* **-tated; -tating** : debilitar

debility [dɪ'bɪləti] *n, pl* **-ties** : debilidad *f*

debit¹ ['dɛbɪt] *vt* : adeudar, cargar, debitar

debit² *n* : débito *m*, cargo *m*, debe *m*

debit card *n* : tarjeta *f* de débito

debonair [,dɛbə'nær] *adj* : elegante y desenvuelto, apuesto

debris [də'bri:, deɪ-; 'deɪ,bri:] *n, pl* **-bris** [-'bri:z, -,bri:z] 1 RUBBLE, RUINS : escombros *mpl*, ruinas *fpl*, restos *mpl* 2 RUBBISH : basura *f*, desechos *mpl*

debt ['dɛt] *n* 1 : deuda *f* ⟨to pay a debt : saldar una deuda⟩ 2 INDEBTEDNESS : endeudamiento *m*

debtor ['dɛtər] *n* : deudor *m*, -dora *f*

debunk [dɪ'bʌŋk] *vt* DISCREDIT : desacreditar, desprestigiar

debut¹ [deɪ'bju:, 'deɪ,bju:] *vi* : debutar

debut² *n* 1 : debut *m* (de un actor), estreno *m* (de una obra) 2 : debut *m*, presentación *f* (en sociedad)

debutante ['dɛbju,tɑnt] *n* : debutante *f*

decade ['dɛ,keɪd, dɛ'keɪd] *n* : década *f*

decadence ['dɛkədənts] *n* : decadencia *f*

decadent ['dɛkədənt] *adj* : decadente

decaf¹ ['di:,kæf] → **decaffeinated**

decaf² *n* : café *m* descafeinado

decaffeinated [di'kæfə,neɪtəd] *adj* : descafeinado

decal ['di:,kæl, di'kæl] *n* : calcomanía *f*

decamp [dɪ'kæmp] *vi* : irse, largarse *fam*

decanter [dɪ'kæntər] *n* : licorera *f*, garrafa *f*

decapitate [dɪ'kæpə,teɪt] *vt* **-tated; -tating** : decapitar

decay¹ [dɪ'keɪ] *vi* 1 DECOMPOSE : descomponerse, pudrirse 2 DETERIORATE : deteriorarse 3 : cariarse (dícese de los dientes)

decay² *n* 1 DECOMPOSITION : descomposición *f* 2 DECLINE, DETERIORATION : decadencia *f*, deterioro *m* 3 : caries *f* (de los dientes)

decease¹ [dɪ'si:s] *vi* **-ceased; -ceasing** : morir, fallecer

decease² *n* : fallecimiento *m*, defunción *f*, deceso *m*

deceased *n* : difunto *m*, -ta *f*

deceit [dɪ'si:t] *n* 1 DECEPTION : engaño *m* 2 DISHONESTY : deshonestidad *f*

deceitful [dɪ'si:tfəl] *adj* : falso, embustero, engañoso, mentiroso

deceitfully [dɪ'si:tfəli] *adv* : con engaño, con falsedad

deceitfulness [dɪ'si:tfəlnəs] *n* : falsedad *f*, engaño *m*

deceive [dɪ'si:v] *vt* **-ceived; -ceiving** : engañar, burlar

deceiver [dɪ'si:vər] *n* : impostor *m*, -tora *f*

decelerate [dɪ'sɛlə,reɪt] *vi* **-ated; -ating** : reducir la velocidad, desacelerar

December [dɪ'sɛmbər] *n* : diciembre *m* ⟨they arrived on the 18th of December, they arrived on December 18th : llegaron el 18 de diciembre⟩

decency ['di:sənsi] *n, pl* **-cies** : decencia *f*, decoro *m*

decent ['di:sənt] *adj* 1 CORRECT, PROPER : decente, decoroso, correcto 2 CLOTHED : vestido, presentable 3 MODEST : púdico, modesto 4 ADEQUATE : decente, adecuado ⟨decent wages : paga adecuada⟩

decently ['di:səntli] *adv* : decentemente

decentralize [di'sɛntrə,laɪz] *v* **-lized** [-,laɪzd]; **-lizing** [-,laɪzɪŋ] *vt* : descentralizar — *vi* : descentralizarse

deception [dɪ'sɛpʃən] *n* : engaño *m*

deceptive [dɪ'sɛptɪv] *adj* : engañoso, falaz — **deceptively** *adv*

decibel ['dɛsəbəl, -,bɛl] *n* : decibelio *m*

decide [dɪ'saɪd] *v* **-cided; -ciding** *vt* 1 CONCLUDE : decidir, llegar a la conclusión de ⟨he decided what to do : decidió qué iba a hacer⟩ 2 DETERMINE : decidir, determinar ⟨one blow decided the fight : un solo golpe determinó la pelea⟩ 3 CONVINCE : decidir ⟨her pleas decided me to help : sus súplicas me decidieron a ayudarla⟩ 4 RESOLVE : resolver — *vi* : decidirse

decided [dɪ'saɪdəd] *adj* 1 UNQUESTIONABLE : indudable 2 RESOLUTE : decidido, resuelto — **decidedly** *adv*

deciduous [dɪ'sɪdʒuəs] *adj* : caduco, de hoja caduca

decimal¹ ['dɛsəməl] *adj* : decimal

decimal² *n* : número decimal

decimal point *n* : punto *m* decimal, coma *f* decimal

decipher [dɪ'saɪfər] *vt* : descifrar — **decipherable** [-əbəl] *adj*

decision [dɪ'sɪʒən] *n* : decisión *f*, determinación *f* ⟨to make a decision : tomar una decisión⟩

decisive [dɪ'saɪsɪv] *adj* 1 DECIDING : decisivo ⟨the decisive vote : el voto decisivo⟩ 2 CONCLUSIVE : decisivo, concluyente, contundente ⟨a decisive

victory : una victoria contundente⟩ **3**
RESOLUTE : decidido, resuelto, firme

decisively [dɪ'saɪsɪvli] *adv* : con decisión, de manera decisiva

decisiveness [dɪ'saɪsɪvnəs] *n* **1** FORCEFULNESS : contundencia *f* **2** RESOLUTION : firmeza *f*, decisión *f*, determinación *f*

deck¹ ['dɛk] *vt* **1** FLOOR : tumbar, derribar ⟨she decked him with one blow : lo tumbó de un solo golpe⟩ **2 to deck out** : adornar, engalanar

deck² *n* **1** : cubierta *f* (de un barco) **2** *or* **deck of cards** : baraja *f* (de naipes)

deck chair *n* : silla *f* de playa

declaim [dɪ'kleɪm] *v* : declamar

declaration [ˌdɛklə'reɪʃən] *n* : declaración *f*, pronunciamiento *m* (oficial)

declare [dɪ'klær] *vt* **-clared; -claring** : declarar, manifestar ⟨to declare war : declarar la guerra⟩ ⟨they declared their support : manifestaron su apoyo⟩

declassify [di'klæsə,faɪ] *vt* **-fied; -fying** : desclasificar

decline¹ [dɪ'klaɪn] *v* **-clined; -clining** *vi* **1** DESCEND : descender **2** DETERIORATE : deteriorarse, decaer ⟨her health is declining : su salud se está deteriorando⟩ **3** DECREASE : disminuir, decrecer, decaer **4** REFUSE : rehusar — *vt* **1** INFLECT : declinar **2** REFUSE, TURN DOWN : declinar, rehusar

decline² *n* **1** DETERIORATION : decadencia *f*, deterioro *m* **2** DECREASE : disminución *f*, descenso *m* **3** SLOPE : declive *m*, pendiente *f*

decode [dɪ'koːd] *vt* **-coded; -coding** : descifrar (un mensaje), descodificar (una señal)

decoder [dɪ'koːdər] *n* : decodificador *m*

decompose [ˌdiːkəm'poːz] *v* **-posed; -posing** *vt* **1** BREAK DOWN : descomponer **2** ROT : descomponer, pudrir — *vi* : descomponerse, pudrirse

decomposition [ˌdiːˌkɑmpə'zɪʃən] *n* : descomposición *f*

decongestant [ˌdiːkən'dʒɛstənt] *n* : descongestionante *m*

decontaminate [ˌdiːkən'tæmə,neɪt] *vt* **-nated; -nating** : descontaminar — **decontamination** [ˌdiːkənˌtæmə'neɪʃən] *n*

decor *or* **décor** [deɪ'kɔr, 'deɪ,kɔr] *n* : decoración *f*

decorate ['dɛkə,reɪt] *vt* **-rated; -rating 1** ADORN : decorar, adornar **2** : condecorar ⟨he was decorated for bravery : lo condecoraron por valor⟩

decoration [ˌdɛkə'reɪʃən] *n* **1** ADORNMENT : decoración *f*, adorno *m* **2** : condecoración *f* (de honor)

decorative ['dɛkərətɪv, -ˌreɪ-] *adj* : decorativo, ornamental, de adorno

decorator ['dɛkə,reɪtər] *n* : decorador *m*, -dora *f*

decorum [dɪ'korəm] *n* : decoro *m*

decoy¹ ['di:,kɔɪ, dɪ'-] *vt* : atraer (con señuelo)

decoy² *n* : señuelo *m*, reclamo *m*

decrease¹ [dɪ'kri:s] *v* **-creased; -creasing** *vi* : decrecer, disminuir, bajar — *vt* : reducir, disminuir

decrease² ['di:,kri:s] *n* : disminución *f*, descenso *m*, bajada *f*

decree¹ [dɪ'kri:] *vt* **-creed; -creeing** : decretar

decree² *n* : decreto *m*

decrepit [dɪ'krɛpɪt] *adj* **1** FEEBLE : decrépito, débil **2** DILAPIDATED : deteriorado, ruinoso

decry [dɪ'kraɪ] *vt* **-cried; -crying** : censurar, criticar

dedicate ['dɛdɪ,keɪt] *vt* **-cated; -cating 1** : dedicar ⟨she dedicated the book to Carlos : le dedicó el libro a Carlos⟩ **2** : consagrar, dedicar ⟨to dedicate one's life : consagrar uno su vida⟩

dedication [ˌdɛdɪ'keɪʃən] *n* **1** DEVOTION : dedicación *f*, devoción *f* **2** : dedicatoria *f* (de un libro, una canción, etc.) **3** CONSECRATION : dedicación *f*

deduce [dɪ'du:s, -'dju:s] *vt* **-duced; -ducing** : deducir, inferir

deduct [dɪ'dʌkt] *vt* : deducir, descontar, restar

deductible [dɪ'dʌktəbəl] *adj* : deducible

deduction [dɪ'dʌkʃən] *n* : deducción *f*

deed¹ ['di:d] *vt* : ceder, transferir

deed² *n* **1** ACT : acto *m*, acción *f*, hecho *m* ⟨a good deed : una buena acción⟩ **2** FEAT : hazaña *f*, proeza *f* **3** TITLE : escritura *f*, título *m*

deem ['di:m] *vt* : considerar, juzgar

deep¹ ['di:p] *adv* : hondo, profundamente ⟨to dig deep : cavar hondo⟩

deep² *adj* **1** : hondo, profundo ⟨the deep end : la parte honda⟩ ⟨a deep wound : una herida profunda⟩ ⟨take a deep breath : respire hondo⟩ **2** : de fondo, de profundidad ⟨the shelf is six inches deep : el estante mide seis pulgadas de fondo⟩ ⟨the lake is 50 meters deep : el lago tiene 50 metros de profundidad⟩ **3** INTENSE : profundo, intenso ⟨with deep regret : con profundo pesar⟩ **4** SERIOUS : grave, serio ⟨to be in deep trouble : estar en serios aprietos⟩ **5** DARK : intenso, subido ⟨deep red : rojo subido⟩ **6** LOW : profundo ⟨a deep tone : un tono profundo⟩ **7** ABSORBED : absorto ⟨deep in thought : absorto en la meditación⟩

deep³ *n* **1 the deep** : lo profundo, el piélago **2 the deep of night** : lo más profundo de la noche

deepen ['di:pən] *vt* **1** : ahondar, profundizar **2** INTENSIFY : intensificar — *vi* **1** : hacerse más profundo **2** INTENSIFY : intensificarse

deeply ['di:pli] *adv* : hondo, profundamente ⟨I'm deeply sorry : lo siento sinceramente⟩

deep–rooted ['di:p'ru:təd, -'ru-] *adj* : profundamente arraigado, enraizado

deep–seated ['di:p'si:təd] *adj* **1** → **deep–rooted 2** : profundo (dícese de un miedo, etc.)

deer ['dɪr] *ns & pl* : ciervo *m*, venado *m*

deerskin ['dɪr,skɪn] *n* : piel *f* de venado

deface [dɪ'feɪs] *vt* **-faced; -facing** MAR : desfigurar

defamation [ˌdɛfə'meɪʃən] *n* : difamación *f*

defamatory [dɪ'fæmə,tori] *adj* : difamatorio

defame [dɪ'feɪm] *vt* **-famed; -faming** : difamar, calumniar

default[1] [dɪ'fɔlt, 'dɪ:,fɔlt] *vi* **1** : no cumplir (con una obligación), no pagar **2** : no presentarse (en un tribunal)

default[2] *n* **1** NEGLECT : omisión *f*, negligencia *f* **2** NONPAYMENT : impago *m*, falta *f* de pago **3 to win by default** : ganar por abandono

defaulter [dɪ'fɔltər] *n* : moroso *m*, -sa *f*; rebelde *mf* (en un tribunal)

defeat[1] [dɪ'fiːt] *vt* **1** FRUSTRATE : frustrar **2** BEAT : vencer, derrotar

defeat[2] *n* : derrota *f*, rechazo *m* (de legislación), fracaso *m* (de planes, etc.)

defeatist [dɪ'fiːtɪst] *n* : derrotista *mf* — **defeatist** *adj*

defecate ['dɛfɪ,keɪt] *vi* **-cated; -cating** : defecar

defect[1] [dɪ'fɛkt] *vi* : desertar

defect[2] ['dɪ:,fɛkt, dɪ'fɛkt] *n* : defecto *m*

defection [dɪ'fɛkʃən] *n* : deserción *f*

defective [dɪ'fɛktɪv] *adj* **1** FAULTY : defectuoso **2** DEFICIENT : deficiente

defector [dɪ'fɛktər] *n* : desertor *m*, -tora *f*

defend [dɪ'fɛnd] *vt* : defender

defendant [dɪ'fɛndənt] *n* : acusado *m*, -da *f*; demandado *m*, -da *f*

defender [dɪ'fɛndər] *n* **1** ADVOCATE : defensor *m*, -sora *f* **2** : defensa *mf* (en deportes)

defense [dɪ'fɛns, 'dɪ:,fɛns] *n* : defensa *f*

defenseless [dɪ'fɛnsləs] *adj* : indefenso

defenselessness [dɪ'fɛnsləsnəs] *n* : indefensión *f*

defensive[1] [dɪ'fɛnsɪv] *adj* : defensivo

defensive[2] *n* **on the defensive** : a la defensiva

defer [dɪ'fər] *v* **-ferred; -ferring** *vt* POSTPONE : diferir, aplazar, posponer — *vi* **to defer to** : deferir a

deference ['dɛfərənts] *n* : deferencia *f*

deferential [,dɛfə'rɛntʃəl] *adj* : respetuoso

deferment [dɪ'fərmənt] *n* : aplazamiento *m*

defiance [dɪ'faɪənts] *n* : desafío *m*

defiant [dɪ'faɪənt] *adj* : desafiante, insolente

deficiency [dɪ'fɪʃəntsi] *n, pl* **-cies** : deficiencia *f*, carencia *f*

deficient [dɪ'fɪʃənt] *adj* : deficiente, carente

deficit ['dɛfəsɪt] *n* : déficit *m*

defile [dɪ'faɪl] *vt* **-filed; -filing 1** DIRTY : ensuciar, manchar **2** CORRUPT : corromper **3** DESECRATE, PROFANE : profanar **4** DISHONOR : deshonrar

defilement [dɪ'faɪlmənt] *n* **1** DESECRATION : profanación *f* **2** CORRUPTION : corrupción *f* **3** CONTAMINATION : contaminación *f*

define [dɪ'faɪn] *vt* **-fined; -fining 1** BOUND : delimitar, demarcar **2** CLARIFY : aclarar, definir **3** : definir ⟨to define a word : definir una palabra⟩

definite ['dɛfənɪt] *adj* **1** CERTAIN : definido, determinado **2** CLEAR : claro, explícito **3** UNQUESTIONABLE : seguro, incuestionable

definite article *n* : artículo *m* definido

definitely ['dɛfənɪtli] *adv* **1** DOUBTLESSLY : indudablemente, sin duda **2** DEFINITIVELY : definitivamente, seguramente

definition [,dɛfə'nɪʃən] *n* : definición *f*

definitive [dɪ'fɪnətɪv] *adj* **1** CONCLUSIVE : definitivo, decisivo **2** AUTHORITATIVE : de autoridad, autorizado — **definitively** *adv*

deflate [dɪ'fleɪt] *vt* **-flated; -flating 1** : desinflar (una llanta, etc.) **2** REDUCE : rebajar ⟨to deflate one's ego : bajarle los humos a uno⟩ — *vi* : desinflarse

deflation [dɪ'fleɪʃən] *n* : deflación *f* (económica)

deflect [dɪ'flɛkt] *vt* : desviar — *vi* : desviarse

deforestation [di,fɔrə'steɪʃən] *n* : deforestación *f*

deform [dɪ'fɔrm] *vt* : deformar

deformation [,di:,fɔr'meɪʃən] *n* : deformación *f*

deformed [dɪ'fɔrmd] *adj* : deforme

deformity [dɪ'fɔrməti] *n, pl* **-ties** : deformidad *f*

defraud [dɪ'frɔd] *vt* : estafar, defraudar

defray [dɪ'freɪ] *vt* : sufragar, costear

defrost [dɪ'frɔst] *vt* : descongelar, deshelar — *vi* : descongelarse, deshelarse

deft ['dɛft] *adj* : hábil, diestro — **deftly** *adv*

defunct [dɪ'fʌŋkt] *adj* **1** DECEASED : difunto, fallecido **2** EXTINCT : extinto, fenecido

defuse [dɪ'fjuːz] *vt* : desactivar ⟨to defuse the situation : reducir las tensiones⟩

defy [dɪ'faɪ] *vt* **-fied; -fying 1** CHALLENGE : desafiar, retar **2** DISOBEY : desobedecer **3** RESIST : resistir, hacer imposible, hacer inútil ⟨to defy understanding/explanation : ser incomprensible/inexplicable⟩ ⟨to defy all reason : ir en contra de toda lógica⟩

degenerate[1] [dɪ'dʒɛnə,reɪt] *vi* **-ated; -ating** : degenerar

degenerate[2] [dɪ'dʒɛnərət] *adj* : degenerado

degeneration [di,dʒɛnə'reɪʃən] *n* : degeneración *f*

degenerative [dɪ'dʒɛnərətɪv] *adj* : degenerativo

degradation [,dɛgrə'deɪʃən] *n* : degradación *f*

degrade [dɪ'greɪd] *vt* **-graded; -grading 1** : degradar, envilecer **2 to degrade oneself** : rebajarse

degrading [dɪ'greɪdɪŋ] *adj* : degradante

degree [dɪ'griː] *n* **1** EXTENT : grado *m* ⟨a third degree burn : una quemadura de tercer grado⟩ **2** : título *m* (de enseñanza superior) **3** : grado *m* (de un círculo, de la temperatura) **4 by degrees** : gradualmente, poco a poco

dehydrate [dɪ'haɪ,dreɪt] *v* **-drated; -drating** *vt* : deshidratar — *vi* : deshidratarse

dehydration [,di:haɪ'dreɪʃən] *n* : deshidratación *f*

deice [ˌdiːˈaɪs] *vt* **-iced; -icing** : deshelar, descongelar

deify [ˈdiːəˌfaɪ, ˈdeɪ-] *vt* **-fied; -fying** : deificar

deign [ˈdeɪn] *vi* : dignarse, condescender

deity [ˈdiːəˌti, ˈdeɪ-] *n, pl* **-ties 1 the Deity** : Dios *m* **2** GOD, GODDESS : deidad *f*; dios *m*, diosa *f*

dejected [dɪˈdʒɛktəd] *adj* : abatido, desalentado, desanimado

dejection [dɪˈdʒɛkʃən] *n* : abatimiento *m*, desaliento *m*, desánimo *m*

delay¹ [dɪˈleɪ] *vt* **1** POSTPONE : posponer, postergar **2** HOLD UP : retrasar, demorar — *vi* : tardar, demorar

delay² *n* **1** LATENESS : tardanza *f* **2** HOLDUP : demora *f*, retraso *m*

delectable [dɪˈlɛktəbəl] *adj* **1** DELICIOUS : delicioso, exquisito **2** DELIGHTFUL : encantador

delegate¹ [ˈdɛlɪˌgeɪt] *v* **-gated; -gating** : delegar

delegate² [ˈdɛlɪgət, -ˌgeɪt] *n* : delegado *m*, -da *f*

delegation [ˌdɛlɪˈgeɪʃən] *n* : delegación *f*

delete [dɪˈliːt] *vt* **-leted; -leting 1** : suprimir, tachar, eliminar **2** : borrar (en informática)

delete key *n* : tecla *f* de borrar, tecla *f* de borrado

deletion [dɪˈliːʃən] *n* : supresión *f*, tachadura *f*, eliminación *f*

deli [ˈdɛli] → **delicatessen**

deliberate¹ [dɪˈlɪbəˌreɪt] *v* **-ated; -ating** *vt* : deliberar sobre, reflexionar sobre, considerar — *vi* : deliberar

deliberate² [dɪˈlɪbərət] *adj* **1** CONSIDERED : reflexionado, premeditado **2** INTENTIONAL : deliberado, intencional **3** SLOW : lento, pausado

deliberately [dɪˈlɪbərətli] *adv* **1** INTENTIONALLY : adrede, a propósito **2** SLOWLY : pausadamente, lentamente

deliberation [dɪˌlɪbəˈreɪʃən] *n* **1** CONSIDERATION : deliberación *f*, consideración *f* **2** SLOWNESS : lentitud *f*

delicacy [ˈdɛlɪkəsi] *n, pl* **-cies 1** : manjar *m*, exquisitez *f* ⟨caviar is a real delicacy : el caviar es un verdadero manjar⟩ **2** FINENESS : delicadeza *f* **3** FRAGILITY : fragilidad *f*

delicate [ˈdɛlɪkət] *adj* **1** SUBTLE : delicado ⟨a delicate fragrance : una fragancia delicada⟩ **2** DAINTY : delicado, primoroso, fino **3** FRAGILE : frágil **4** SENSITIVE : delicado ⟨a delicate matter : un asunto delicado⟩

delicately [ˈdɛlɪkətli] *adv* : delicadamente, con delicadeza

delicatessen [ˌdɛlɪkəˈtɛsən] *n* : charcutería *f*, fiambrería *f*, salchichonería *f Mex*

delicious [dɪˈlɪʃəs] *adj* : delicioso, exquisito, rico — **deliciously** *adv*

delight¹ [dɪˈlaɪt] *vt* : deleitar, encantar — **to delight in** : deleitarse con, complacerse en

delight² *n* **1** JOY : placer *m*, deleite *m*, gozo *m* **2** : encanto *m* ⟨your garden is a delight : su jardín es un encanto⟩

delighted [dɪˈlaɪtəd] *adj* : encantado ⟨I'm delighted to meet you : estoy encantada de conocerlo⟩

delightful [dɪˈlaɪtfəl] *adj* : delicioso, encantador

delightfully [dɪˈlaɪtfəli] *adv* : de manera encantadora, de maravilla

delineate [dɪˈlɪniˌeɪt] *vt* **-eated; -eating** : delinear, trazar, bosquejar

delinquency [dɪˈlɪŋkwənsi] *n, pl* **-cies** : delincuencia *f*

delinquent¹ [dɪˈlɪŋkwənt] *adj* **1** : delincuente **2** OVERDUE : vencido y sin pagar, moroso

delinquent² *n* : delincuente *mf* ⟨juvenile delinquent : delincuente juvenil⟩

delirious [dɪˈlɪriəs] *adj* : delirante ⟨delirious with joy : loco de alegría⟩

delirium [dɪˈlɪriəm] *n* : delirio *m*, desvarío *m*

deliver [dɪˈlɪvər] *vt* **1** FREE : liberar, librar **2** DISTRIBUTE : entregar, repartir (periódicos, etc.) **3** : asistir en el parto de (un niño) **4** : pronunciar ⟨to deliver a speech : pronunciar un discurso⟩ **5** PROJECT : despachar, lanzar ⟨he delivered a fast ball : lanzó una pelota rápida⟩ **6** DEAL : propinar, asestar ⟨to deliver a blow : asestar un golpe⟩ — *vi* **1** : hacer entregas **2** : cumplir ⟨to deliver on one's promise : cumplir (con) su promesa⟩

deliverance [dɪˈlɪvərənts] *n* : liberación *f*, rescate *m*, salvación *f*

deliverer [dɪˈlɪvərər] *n* RESCUER : libertador *m*, -dora *f*; salvador *m*, -dora *f*

delivery [dɪˈlɪvəri] *n, pl* **-eries 1** LIBERATION : liberación *f* **2** : entrega *f*, reparto *m* ⟨cash on delivery : entrega contra reembolso⟩ ⟨home delivery : servicio a domicilio⟩ **3** CHILDBIRTH : parto *m*, alumbramiento *m* **4** SPEECH : expresión *f* oral, modo *m* de hablar **5** THROW : lanzamiento *m*

dell [ˈdɛl] *n* : hondonada *f*, valle *m* pequeño

delta [ˈdɛltə] *n* : delta *m*

delude [dɪˈluːd] *vt* **-luded; -luding 1** : engañar **2 to delude oneself** : engañarse

deluge¹ [ˈdɛlˌjuːdʒ, -ˌjuːʒ] *vt* **-uged; -uging 1** FLOOD : inundar **2** OVERWHELM : abrumar ⟨deluged with requests : abrumado de pedidos⟩

deluge² *n* **1** FLOOD : inundación *f* **2** DOWNPOUR : aguacero *m* **3** BARRAGE : aluvión *m*

delusion [dɪˈluːʒən] *n* **1** : ilusión *f* (falsa) **2 delusions of grandeur** : delirios *mpl* de grandeza

deluxe [dɪˈlʌks, -ˈlʊks] *adj* : de lujo

delve [ˈdɛlv] *vi* **delved; delving 1** DIG : escarbar **2 to delve into** PROBE : cavar en, ahondar en

demagogue [ˈdɛməˌgɑg] *n* : demagogo *m*, demagoga *f*

demand¹ [dɪˈmænd] *vt* : demandar, exigir, reclamar

demand² *n* **1** REQUEST : petición *f*, pedido *m*, demanda *f* ⟨by popular demand : a petición del público⟩ **2** CLAIM : reclamación *f*, exigencia *f* **3** MARKET : demanda *f* ⟨supply and demand : la oferta y la demanda⟩

demanding [dɪ'mændɪŋ] *adj* : exigente

demarcate [dɪ'mɑr,keɪt, 'di:,mɑr-] *vt* **-cated; -cating** : demarcar, delimitar

demarcation [,di:,mɑr'keɪʃən] *n* : demarcación *f*, deslinde *m*

demean [dɪ'mi:n] *vt* : degradar, rebajar

demeaning [dɪ'mi:nɪŋ] *adj* : degradante

demeanor [dɪ'mi:nər] *n* : comportamiento *m*, conducta *f*

demented [dɪ'mɛntəd] *adj* : demente, loco

dementia [dɪ'mɛntʃə] *n* : demencia *f*

demerit [dɪ'mɛrət] *n* : demérito *m*

demigod ['dɛmi,ɡɑd, -,ɡɔd] *n* : semidiós *m*

demilitarize [dɪ'mɪlətə,raɪz] *vt* **-rized; -rizing** : desmilitarizar

demise [dɪ'maɪz] *n* **1** DEATH : fallecimiento *m*, deceso *m* **2** END : hundimiento *m*, desaparición *f* (de una institución, etc.)

demitasse ['dɛmi,tæs, -,tɑs] *n* : taza *f* pequeña (de café)

demo ['dɛmo] *n* **1** DEMONSTRATION : mostración *f* (de productos, etc.) **2** *or* **demo product/version** (etc.) : demo *f*, producto *m* (o versión *f*, etc.) de demostración **3** *or* **demo tape** : demo *f*, cinta *f* de demostración

demobilization [di,mo:bələ'zeɪʃən] *n* : desmovilización *f*

demobilize [di'mo:bə,laɪz] *vt* **-lized; -lizing** : desmovilizar

democracy [dɪ'mɑkrəsi] *n, pl* **-cies** : democracia *f*

democrat ['dɛmə,kræt] *n* : demócrata *mf*

democratic [,dɛmə'krætɪk] *adj* : democrático — **democratically** [-tɪkli] *adv*

democratize [dɪ'mɑkrə,taɪz] *vt* **-tized; -tizing** : democratizar — **democratization** [dɪ'mɑkrətə'zeɪʃən] *n*

demographic[1] [,dɛmə'ɡræfɪk] *adj* : demográfico

demographic[2] *n* **1** : perfil *m* demográfico **2** **demographics** *npl* : estadísticas *fpl* demográficas, demografía *f*

demography [dɪ'mɑɡrəfi] *n* : demografía *f*

demolish [dɪ'mɑlɪʃ] *vt* **1** RAZE : demoler, derribar, arrasar **2** DESTROY : destruir, destrozar

demolition [,dɛmə'lɪʃən, ,di:-] *n* : demolición *f*, derribo *m*

demon ['di:mən] *n* : demonio *m*, diablo *m*

demonstrably [dɪ'mɑnstrəbli] *adv* : manifiestamente, claramente

demonstrate ['dɛmən,streɪt] *vt* **-strated; -strating** **1** SHOW : demostrar **2** PROVE : probar, demostrar **3** EXPLAIN : explicar, ilustrar — *vi* : manifestarse ⟨to demonstrate for something : manifestarse a favor de algo⟩ ⟨to demonstrate against something : manifestarse en contra de algo⟩

demonstration [,dɛmən'streɪʃən] *n* **1** SHOW : muestra *f*, demostración *f* **2** RALLY : manifestación *f*

demonstrative [dɪ'mɑnstrətɪv] *adj* **1** EFFUSIVE : efusivo, expresivo, demostrativo **2** : demostrativo (en lingüística)

⟨demonstrative pronoun : pronombre demostrativo⟩

demonstrator ['dɛmən,streɪtər] *n* PROTESTER : manifestante *mf*

demoralize [dɪ'mɔrə,laɪz] *vt* **-ized; -izing** : desmoralizar

demote [dɪ'mo:t] *vt* **-moted; -moting** : degradar, bajar de categoría

demotion [dɪ'mo:ʃən] *n* : degradación *f*, descenso *m* de categoría

demur [dɪ'mər] *vi* **-murred; -murring** **1** OBJECT : oponerse **2** **to demur at** : ponerle objeciones a (algo)

demure [dɪ'mjʊr] *adj* : recatado, modesto — **demurely** *adv*

demystify [dɪ'mɪstə,faɪ] *vi* **-fied; -fying** : desmitificar

den ['dɛn] *n* **1** LAIR : cubil *m*, madriguera *f* **2** HIDEOUT : guarida *f* **3** STUDY : estudio *m*, gabinete *m*

denature [dɪ'neɪtʃər] *vt* **-tured; -turing** : desnaturalizar

dengue ['dɛnɡi, -,ɡeɪ] *n* : dengue *m*

denial [dɪ'naɪəl] *n* **1** REFUSAL : rechazo *m*, denegación *f*, negativa *f* **2** REPUDIATION : negación *f* (de una creencia, etc.), rechazo *m*

denigrate ['dɛnɪ,ɡreɪt] *vt* **-grated; -grating** : denigrar

denim ['dɛnəm] *n* **1** : tela *f* vaquera, mezclilla *f* *Chile, Mex* **2** **denims** *npl* → **jeans**

denizen ['dɛnəzən] *n* : habitante *mf*; morador *m*, -dora *f*

denomination [dɪ,nɑmə'neɪʃən] *n* **1** FAITH : confesión *f*, fe *f* **2** VALUE : denominación *f*, valor *m* (de una moneda)

denominator [dɪ'nɑmə,neɪtər] *n* : denominador *m*

denote [dɪ'no:t] *vt* **-noted; -noting** **1** INDICATE, MARK : indicar, denotar, señalar **2** MEAN : significar

denouement [,deɪnu:'mɑ] *n* : desenlace *m*

denounce [dɪ'naʊnts] *vt* **-nounced; -nouncing** **1** CENSURE : denunciar, censurar **2** ACCUSE : denunciar, acusar, delatar

dense ['dɛnts] *adj* **denser; -est** **1** THICK : espeso, denso ⟨dense vegetation : vegetación densa⟩ ⟨a dense fog : una niebla espesa⟩ **2** STUPID : estúpido, burro *fam*

densely ['dɛntsli] *adv* **1** THICKLY : densamente **2** STUPIDLY : torpemente

denseness ['dɛntsnəs] *n* **1** → **density** **2** STUPIDITY : estupidez *f*

density ['dɛntsəṭi] *n, pl* **-ties** : densidad *f*

dent[1] ['dɛnt] *vt* : abollar, mellar

dent[2] *n* : abolladura *f*, mella *f*

dental ['dɛntəl] *adj* : dental

dental floss *n* : hilo *m* dental

dental surgeon *n* : odontólogo *m*, -ga *f*

dentifrice ['dɛntəfrɪs] *n* : dentífrico *m*, pasta *f* de dientes

dentist ['dɛntɪst] *n* : dentista *mf*

dentistry ['dɛntɪstri] *n* : odontología *f*

dentures ['dɛntʃərz] *npl* : dentadura *f* postiza

denude [dɪ'nu:d, -'nju:d] *vt* **-nuded; -nuding** STRIP : desnudar, despojar

denunciation [dɪ,nʌntsi'eɪʃən] *n* : denuncia *f*, acusación *f*

deny [di'naɪ] vt **-nied; -nying 1** REFUTE : desmentir, negar **2** DISOWN, REPUDIATE : negar, renegar de **3** REFUSE : denegar **4 to deny oneself** : privarse, sacrificarse

deodorant [di'o:dərənt] n : desodorante m

deodorize [di'o:də,raɪz] vt **-ized; -izing** : eliminar los malos olores

depart [di'pɑrt] vt : salirse de — vi **1** LEAVE : salir, partir, irse **2** DIE : morir

department [di'pɑrtmənt] n **1** DIVISION : sección f (de una tienda, una organización, etc.), departamento m (de una empresa, una universidad, etc.), ministerio m (del gobierno) **2** PROVINCE, SPHERE : esfera f, campo m, competencia f

departmental [di,pɑrt'mɛntəl, ,di:-] adj : departamental

department chair → chair²

department store n : grandes almacenes mpl

departure [di'pɑrtʃər] n **1** LEAVING : salida f, partida f **2** DEVIATION : desviación f

depend [di'pɛnd] vi **1** RELY : contar (con), confiar (en) ⟨depend on me! : ¡cuenta conmigo!⟩ **2 to depend on** : depender de ⟨success depends on hard work : el éxito depende de trabajar duro⟩ **3 that depends** : según, eso depende

dependable [di'pɛndəbəl] adj : responsable, digno de confianza, fiable

dependence [di'pɛndən̩s] n : dependencia f

dependency [di'pɛndən̩si] n, pl **-cies 1 → dependence 2** : posesión f (de una unidad política)

dependent¹ [di'pɛndənt] adj : dependiente

dependent² n : persona f a cargo de alguien

depict [di'pɪkt] vt **1** PORTRAY : representar **2** DESCRIBE : describir

depiction [di'pɪkʃən] n : representación f, descripción f

deplete [di'pli:t] vt **-pleted; -pleting 1** EXHAUST : agotar **2** REDUCE : reducir

depletion [di'pli:ʃən] n **1** EXHAUSTION : agotamiento m **2** REDUCTION : reducción f, disminución f

deplorable [di'plorəbəl] adj **1** CONTEMPTIBLE : deplorable, despreciable **2** LAMENTABLE : lamentable

deplore [di'plor] vt **-plored; -ploring 1** REGRET : deplorar, lamentar **2** CONDEMN : condenar, deplorar

deploy [di'plɔɪ] vt : desplegar

deployment [di'plɔɪmənt] n : despliegue m

deport [di'port] vt **1** EXPEL : deportar, expulsar (de un país) **2 to deport oneself** BEHAVE : comportarse

deportation [,di:,por'teɪʃən] n : deportación f

depose [di'po:z] vt **-posed; -posing** : deponer

deposit¹ [di'pɑzət] vt **-ited; -iting** : depositar

deposit² n **1** : depósito m (en el banco) **2** DOWN PAYMENT : entrega f inicial **3** : depósito m, yacimiento m (en geología)

deposition [,dɛpə'zɪʃən] n TESTIMONY : deposición f

depository [di'pɑzə,tori] n, pl **-ries** : almacén m, depósito m

depot [in sense 1 usu 'di:,po:, 2 usu 'di:-] n **1** STOREHOUSE : almacén m, depósito m **2** STATION, TERMINAL : terminal mf, estación f (de autobuses, ferrocarriles, etc.)

deprave [di'preɪv] vt **-praved; -praving** : depravar, pervertir

depraved [di'preɪvd] adj : depravado, degenerado

depravity [di'prævəti] n, pl **-ties** : depravación f

depreciate [di'pri:ʃi,eɪt] v **-ated; -ating** vt **1** DEPRECIATE : depreciar, devaluar **2** DISPARAGE : menospreciar, despreciar — vi : depreciarse, devaluarse

depreciation [di,pri:ʃi'eɪʃən] n : depreciación f, devaluación f

depress [di'prɛs] vt **1** PRESS, PUSH : apretar, presionar, pulsar **2** REDUCE : reducir, hacer bajar (precios, ventas, etc.) **3** SADDEN : deprimir, abatir, entristecer **4** DEVALUE : depreciar

depressant n : depresivo m

depressed [di'prɛst] adj **1** DEJECTED : deprimido, abatido **2** : deprimido, en crisis (dícese de la economía)

depressing [di'prɛsɪŋ] adj : deprimente, triste

depression [di'prɛʃən] n **1** DESPONDENCY : depresión f, abatimiento m **2** : depresión (en una superficie) **3** RECESSION : depresión f económica, crisis f

deprivation [,dɛprə'veɪʃən] n : privación f

deprive [di'praɪv] vt **-prived; -priving** : privar

depth ['dɛpθ] n, pl **depths** ['dɛpθs, 'dɛps] **1** : profundidad f **2 depths** npl ⟨in the depths of winter : en pleno invierno⟩ ⟨in the depths of despair : en la más profunda desesperación⟩ **3 in depth** : a fondo **4 out of one's depth** : perdido ⟨I'm out of my depth : esto es demasiado difícil/especializado (etc.) para mí⟩

deputation [,dɛpjə'teɪʃən] n : diputación f

deputize ['dɛpju,taɪz] vt **-tized; -tizing** : nombrar como segundo

deputy ['dɛpjuti] n, pl **-ties** : suplente mf, sustituto m, -ta f

derail [di'reɪl] v : descarrilar

derailment [di'reɪlmənt] n : descarrilamiento m

derange [di'reɪndʒ] vt **-ranged; -ranging 1** DISARRANGE : desarreglar, desordenar **2** DISTURB, UPSET : trastornar, perturbar **3** MADDEN : enloquecer, volver loco

deranged [di'reɪndʒd] adj DISTURBED, INSANE : trastornado, perturbado

derangement [di'reɪndʒmənt] n **1** DISTURBANCE, UPSET : trastorno m **2** INSANITY : locura f, perturbación f mental

derby ['dɑrbi] n, pl **-bies 1** : derby m ⟨the Kentucky Derby : el Derby de Kentucky〉 **2** : sombrero *m* hongo, bombín *m*

deregulate [di'rɛgjʊ,leɪt] *vt* -lated; -lating : desregular

deregulation [di,rɛgjʊ'leɪʃən] *n* : desregulación *f*

derelict¹ ['dɛrə,lɪkt] *adj* **1** ABANDONED : abandonado, en ruinas **2** REMISS : negligente, remiso

derelict² *n* **1** : propiedad *f* abandonada **2** VAGRANT : vagabundo *m*, -da *f*

deride [di'raɪd] *vt* -rided; -riding : ridiculizar, burlarse de

derision [di'rɪʒən] *n* : escarnio *m*, irrisión *f*, mofa *f*

derisive [di'raɪsɪv] *adj* : burlón

derisory [di'raɪsəri, -zə-] *adj* **1** → **derisive 2** PALTRY, MEAGER : irrisorio, mísero 〈a derisory price : un precio irrisorio〉

derivation [,dɛrə'veɪʃən] *n* : derivación *f*

derivative¹ [di'rɪvətɪv] *adj* **1** DERIVED : derivado **2** BANAL : carente de originalidad, banal

derivative² *n* : derivado *m*

derive [di'raɪv] *v* -rived; -riving *vt* **1** OBTAIN : obtener, sacar **2** DEDUCE : deducir, inferir — *vi* : provenir, derivar, proceder

dermatologist [,dərmə'tɑlədʒɪst] *n* : dermatólogo *m*, -ga *f*

dermatology [,dərmə'tɑlədʒi] *n* : dermatología *f*

derogatory [di'rɑgə,tori] *adj* : despectivo, despreciativo

derrick ['dɛrɪk] *n* **1** CRANE : grúa *f* **2** : torre *f* de perforación (sobre un pozo de petróleo)

descend [di'sɛnd] *vt* : descender, bajar — *vi* **1** : descender, bajar 〈he descended from the platform : descendió del estrado〉 **2** DERIVE : descender, provenir **3** STOOP : rebajarse 〈I descended to his level : me rebajé a su nivel〉 **4 to descend upon** : caer sobre, invadir

descendant¹ [di'sɛndənt] *adj* : descendente

descendant² *n* : descendiente *mf*

descent [di'sɛnt] *n* **1** : bajada *f*, descenso *m* 〈the descent from the mountain : el descenso de la montaña〉 **2** ANCESTRY : ascendencia *f*, linaje *m* **3** SLOPE : pendiente *f*, cuesta *f* **4** FALL : caída *f* **5** ATTACK : incursión *f*, ataque *m*

describe [di'skraɪb] *vt* -scribed; -scribing : describir

description [di'skrɪpʃən] *n* : descripción *f*

descriptive [di'skrɪptɪv] *adj* : descriptivo 〈descriptive adjective : adjetivo calificativo〉

desecrate ['dɛsi,kreɪt] *vt* -crated; -crating : profanar

desecration [,dɛsi'kreɪʃən] *n* : profanación *f*

desegregate [di'sɛgrə,geɪt] *vt* -gated; -gating : eliminar la segregación racial de

desegregation [di,sɛgrə'geɪʃən] *n* : eliminación *f* de la segregación racial

desert¹ [di'zərt] *vt* : abandonar (una persona o un lugar), desertar de (una causa, etc.) — *vi* : desertar

desert² ['dɛzərt] *adj* : desierto 〈a desert island : una isla desierta〉

desert³ *n* **1** ['dɛzərt] : desierto *m* (en geografía) **2** [di'zərt] → **deserts**

deserted [di'zərtəd] *adj* : desierto

deserter [di'zərtər] *n* : desertor *m*, -tora *f*

desertion [di'zərʃən] *n* : abandono *m*, deserción *f* (militar)

deserts [di'zərts] *npl* : merecido *m* 〈to get one's just deserts : llevarse uno su merecido〉

deserve [di'zərv] *vt* -served; -serving : merecer

deservedly [di'zərvədli] *adv* : merecidamente

deserving [di'zərvɪŋ] *adj* : meritorio 〈deserving of : digno de〉

desiccate ['dɛsi,keɪt] *vt* -cated; -cating : desecar, deshidratar

design¹ [di'zaɪn] *vt* **1** DEVISE : diseñar, concebir, idear **2** PLAN : proyectar **3** SKETCH : trazar, bosquejar

design² *n* **1** PLAN, SCHEME : plan *m*, proyecto *m* 〈by design : a propósito, intencionalmente〉 **2** SKETCH : diseño *m*, bosquejo *m* **3** PATTERN, STYLE : diseño *m*, estilo *m* **4 designs** *npl* INTENTIONS : propósitos *mpl*, designios *mpl*

designate ['dɛzɪg,neɪt] *vt* -nated; -nating **1** INDICATE, SPECIFY : indicar, especificar **2** APPOINT : nombrar, designar

designation [,dɛzɪg'neɪʃən] *n* **1** NAMING : designación *f* **2** NAME : denominación *f*, nombre *m* **3** APPOINTMENT : designación *f*, nombramiento *m*

designer¹ [di'zaɪnər] *adj* : de diseño, de marca

designer² *n* : diseñador *m*, -dora *f*

desirability [di,zaɪrə'bɪləti] *n*, *pl* -ties **1** ADVISABILITY : conveniencia *f* **2** ATTRACTIVENESS : atractivo *m*

desirable [di'zaɪrəbəl] *adj* **1** ADVISABLE : conveniente, aconsejable **2** ATTRACTIVE : deseable, atractivo

desire¹ [di'zaɪr] *vt* -sired; -siring **1** WANT : desear **2** REQUEST : rogar, solicitar

desire² *n* : deseo *m*, anhelo *m*, ansia *m*

desist [di'sɪst, -'zɪst] *vi* **to desist from** : desistir de, abstenerse de

desk ['dɛsk] *n* : escritorio *m*, pupitre *m* (en la escuela)

desktop¹ ['dɛsk,tɑp] *adj* : de escritorio

desktop² *or* **desktop computer** *n* : computadora *f*, computador *m*, ordenador *m* *Spain* (no portátil)

desktop publishing *n* : autoedición *f*

desolate¹ ['dɛsə,leɪt, -zə-] *vt* -lated; -lating : devastar, desolar

desolate² ['dɛsələt, -zə-] *adj* **1** BARREN : desolado, desierto, yermo **2** DISCONSOLATE : desconsolado, desolado

desolation [,dɛsə'leɪʃən, -zə-] *n* : desolación *f*

despair¹ [di'spær] *vi* : desesperar, perder las esperanzas

despair² *n* : desesperación *f*, desesperanza *f*

despairing *adj* : desesperado

desperate ['dɛspərət] *adj* **1** HOPELESS : desesperado, sin esperanzas **2** RASH

: desesperado, precipitado **3** SERIOUS,
URGENT : grave, urgente, apremiante ⟨a
desperate need : una necesidad apre-
miante⟩

desperately ['dɛspərətli] *adv* : desesperadamente, urgentemente

desperation [‚dɛspə'reɪʃən] *n* : desesperación *f*

despicable [dɪ'spɪkəbəl, 'dɛspɪ-] *adj* : vil,
despreciable, infame

despise [dɪ'spaɪz] *vt* **-spised; -spising**
: despreciar

despite [də'spaɪt] *prep* : a pesar de, aún
con

despoil [dɪ'spɔɪl] *vt* : saquear

despondency [dɪ'spandənsi] *n* : desaliento *m*, desánimo *m*, depresión *f*

despondent [dɪ'spandənt] *adj* : desalentado, desanimado

despot ['dɛspət, -‚pat] *n* : déspota *mf*;
tirano *m*, -na *f*

despotic [des'patɪk] *adj* : despótico

despotism ['dɛspə‚tɪzəm] *n* : despotismo
m

dessert [dɪ'zərt] *n* : postre *m*

dessertspoon [dɪ'zərt‚spu:n] *n* : cuchara *f*
de postre

destination [‚dɛstə'neɪʃən] *n* : destino *m*,
destinación *f*

destined ['dɛstənd] *adj* **1** FATED : predestinado **2** BOUND : destinado, con destino
(a), con rumbo (a)

destiny ['dɛstəni] *n, pl* **-nies** : destino *m*

destitute ['dɛstə‚tu:t, -‚tju:t] *adj* **1** LACK-
ING : carente, desprovisto **2** POOR : indigente, en miseria

destitution [‚dɛstə'tu:ʃən, -'tju:-] *n* : indigencia *f*, miseria *f*

destroy [dɪ'strɔɪ] *vt* **1** KILL : matar **2** DE-
MOLISH : destruir, destrozar

destroyer [dɪ'strɔɪər] *n* : destructor *m*
(buque)

destruction [dɪ'strʌkʃən] *n* : destrucción
f, ruina *f*

destructive [dɪ'strʌktɪv] *adj* : destructor,
destructivo

desultory ['dɛsəl‚tori] *adj* **1** AIMLESS : sin
rumbo, sin objeto **2** DISCONNECTED
: inconexo

detach [dɪ'tætʃ] *vt* : separar, quitar, desprender

detached [dɪ'tætʃt] *adj* **1** SEPARATE : separado, suelto **2** ALOOF : distante, indiferente **3** IMPARTIAL : imparcial, objetivo

detachment [dɪ'tætʃmənt] *n* **1** SEPARA-
TION : separación *f* **2** DETAIL : destacamento *m* (de tropas) **3** ALOOFNESS : reserva *f*, indiferencia *f* **4** IMPARTIALITY
: imparcialidad *f*

detail¹ [dɪ'teɪl, 'di:‚teɪl] *vt* : detallar, exponer en detalle

detail² *n* **1** : detalle *m*, pormenor *m* ⟨to go
into detail : entrar en detalles⟩ ⟨in detail
: con/en detalle, detalladamente⟩ **2**
: destacamento *m* (de tropas)

detailed [dɪ'teɪld, 'di:‚teɪld] *adj* : detallado,
minucioso

detain [dɪ'teɪn] *vt* **1** HOLD : detener **2** DE-
LAY : entretener, demorar, retrasar

detect [dɪ'tɛkt] *vt* : detectar, descubrir

detection [dɪ'tɛkʃən] *n* : descubrimiento
m

detective [dɪ'tɛktɪv] *n* : detective *mf* ⟨pri-
vate detective : detective privado⟩ ⟨de-
tective novel : novela policial/policíaca⟩
⟨detective work : investigación⟩

detector [dɪ'tɛktər] *n* : detector *m*

detention [dɪ'tɛnʃən] *n* : detención *m*

deter [dɪ'tər] *vt* **-terred; -terring** : disuadir,
impedir

detergent [dɪ'tərdʒənt] *n* : detergente *m*

deteriorate [dɪ'tɪriə‚reɪt] *vi* **-rated; -rating**
: deteriorarse, empeorar

deterioration [dɪ‚tɪriə'reɪʃən] *n* : deterioro
m, empeoramiento *m*

determinant¹ [dɪ'tərmənənt] *adj* : determinante

determinant² *n* **1** : factor *m* determinante
2 : determinante *m* (en matemáticas)

determination [dɪ‚tərmə'neɪʃən] *n* **1** DE-
CISION : determinación *f*, decisión *f* **2**
RESOLUTION : resolución *f*, determinación *f* ⟨with grim determination : con
una firme resolución⟩

determine [dɪ'tərmən] *vt* **-mined; -mining**
1 ESTABLISH : determinar, establecer **2**
SETTLE : decidir **3** FIND OUT : averiguar
4 BRING ABOUT : determinar

determined [dɪ'tərmənd] *adj* RESOLUTE
: decidido, resuelto

deterrence [dɪ'tərəns] *n* : disuasión *f*

deterrent [dɪ'tərənt] *n* : medida *f* disuasiva

detest [dɪ'tɛst] *vt* : detestar, odiar, aborrecer

detestable [dɪ'tɛstəbəl] *adj* : detestable,
odioso, aborrecible

dethrone [dɪ'θro:n] *vt* **-throned; -throning**
: destronar

detonate ['dɛtən‚eɪt] *v* **-nated; -nating** *vt*
: hacer detonar — *vi* : detonar, estallar

detonation [‚dɛtən'eɪʃən] *n* : detonación *f*

detonator ['dɛtən‚eɪtər] *n* : detonador *m*

detour¹ ['di:‚tur, di'tur] *vi* : desviarse

detour² *n* : desvío *m*, rodeo *m*

detox¹ ['di:‚taks, di'taks] *vt fam* : desintoxicar

detox² *n fam* : desintoxicación *f*

detract [dɪ'trækt] *vi* **to detract from**
: restarle valor a, quitarle méritos a

detractor [dɪ'træktər] *n* : detractor *m*,
-tora *f*

detriment ['dɛtrəmənt] *n* : detrimento *m*,
perjuicio *m*

detrimental [‚dɛtrə'mɛntəl] *adj* : perjudicial — **detrimentally** *adv*

devaluation [di‚vælju'eɪʃən] *n* : devaluación *f*

devalue [di'vælju:] *vt* **-ued; -uing** : devaluar, depreciar

devastate ['dɛvə‚steɪt] *vt* **-tated; -tating**
: devastar, arrasar, asolar

devastating ['dɛvə‚steɪtɪŋ] *adj* **1** DE-
STRUCTIVE, PAINFUL : devastador **2**
CUTTING, POWERFUL : demoledor, aplas-
tante, arrollador

devastation [‚dɛvə'steɪʃən] *n* : devastación *f*, estragos *mpl*

develop [dɪ'vɛləp] *vt* **1** FORM, MAKE : desarrollar, elaborar, formar **2** : revelar
(en fotografía) **3** FOSTER : desarrollar,

fomentar **4** EXPLOIT : explotar (recursos), urbanizar (un área) **5** ACQUIRE : adquirir ⟨to develop an interest : adquirir un interés⟩ **6** CONTRACT : contraer (una enfermedad) — *vi* **1** GROW : desarrollarse **2** ARISE : aparecer, surgir

developed [dɪ'vɛləpt] *adj* : avanzado, desarrollado

developer [dɪ'vɛləpər] *n* **1** : inmobiliaria *f*, urbanizadora *f* **2** : revelador *m* (en fotografía)

developing [dɪ'vɛləpɪŋ] *adj* : en vías de desarrollo ⟨dícese de países⟩

development [dɪ'vɛləpmənt] *n* **1** : desarrollo *m* ⟨physical development : desarrollo físico⟩ **2** : urbanización *f* (de un área), explotación *f* (de recursos), creación *f* (de inventos) **3** EVENT : acontecimiento *m*, suceso *m* ⟨to await developments : esperar acontecimientos⟩

deviant ['di:viənt] *adj* : desviado, anormal

deviate ['di:vi,eɪt] *v* -ated; -ating *vi* : desviarse, apartarse — *vt* : desviar

deviation [,di:vi'eɪʃən] *n* : desviación *f*

device [dɪ'vaɪs] *n* **1** MECHANISM : dispositivo *m*, aparato *m*, mecanismo *m* **2** EMBLEM : emblema *m*

devil¹ ['dɛvəl] *vt* -iled *or* -illed; -iling *or* -illing **1** : sazonar con picante y especias **2** PESTER : molestar

devil² *n* **1** SATAN : el diablo, Satanás *m* **2** DEMON : diablo *m*, demonio *m* **3** FIEND : persona *f* diabólica; malvado *m*, -da *f* **4** FELLOW : persona *f* ⟨you lucky devil! : ¡vaya suerte que tienes!⟩ ⟨poor devil : pobre diablo⟩

devilish ['dɛvəlɪʃ] *adj* : diabólico

devilry ['dɛvəlri] *n*, *pl* -ries : diabluras *fpl*, travesuras *fpl*

devious ['di:viəs] *adj* **1** CRAFTY : taimado, artero **2** WINDING : tortuoso, sinuoso

devise [dɪ'vaɪz] *vt* -vised; -vising **1** INVENT : idear, concebir, inventar **2** PLOT : tramar

devoid [dɪ'vɔɪd] *adj* ∼ of : carente de, desprovisto de

devote [dɪ'vo:t] *vt* -voted; -voting **1** DEDICATE : consagrar, dedicar ⟨to devote one's life : dedicar uno su vida⟩ **2 to devote oneself** : dedicarse

devoted [dɪ'vo:təd] *adj* **1** FAITHFUL : leal, fiel **2 to be devoted to someone** : tenerle mucho cariño a alguien

devotee [,dɛvə'ti:, -'teɪ] *n* : devoto *m*, -ta *f*

devotion [dɪ'vo:ʃən] *n* **1** DEDICATION : dedicación *f*, devoción *f* **2 devotions** PRAYERS : oraciones *fpl*, devociones *fpl*

devour [dɪ'vaʊər] *vt* : devorar

devout [dɪ'vaʊt] *adj* **1** PIOUS : devoto, piadoso **2** EARNEST, SINCERE : sincero, ferviente — **devoutly** *adv*

devoutness [dɪ'vaʊtnəs] *n* : devoción *f*, piedad *f*

dew ['du:, 'dju:] *n* : rocío *m*

dewlap ['du:,læp, 'dju:-] *n* : papada *f*

dew point : punto *m* de condensación

dewy ['du:i, 'dju:i] *adj* **dewier; -est** : cubierto de rocío

dexterity [dɛk'stɛrəti] *n*, *pl* -ties : destreza *f*, habilidad *f*

dexterous ['dɛkstrəs] *adj* : diestro, hábil

dexterously ['dɛkstrəsli] *adv* : con destreza, con habilidad, hábilmente

diabetes [,daɪə'bi:,ti:z] *n* : diabetes *f*

diabetic¹ [,daɪə'bɛtɪk] *adj* : diabético

diabetic² *n* : diabético *m*, -ca *f*

diabolic [,daɪə'bɑlɪk] *or* **diabolical** [-lɪkəl] *adj* : diabólico, satánico

diacritic [,daɪə'krɪtɪk] *n* : diacrítico *m*

diacritical [,daɪə'krɪtɪkəl] *or* **diacritic** *adj* : diacrítico

diadem ['daɪə,dɛm, -dəm] *n* : diadema *f*

diagnose ['daɪɪg,no:s, ,daɪɪg'no:s] *vt* -nosed; -nosing : diagnosticar

diagnosis [,daɪɪg'no:sɪs] *n*, *pl* -noses [-'no:,si:z] : diagnóstico *m*

diagnostic [,daɪɪg'nɑstɪk] *adj* : diagnóstico

diagonal¹ [daɪ'ægənəl] *adj* : diagonal, en diagonal

diagonal² *n* : diagonal *f*

diagonally [daɪ'ægənəli] *adv* : diagonalmente, en diagonal

diagram¹ ['daɪə,græm] *vt* -gramed *or* -grammed; -graming *or* -gramming : hacer un diagrama de

diagram² *n* : diagrama *m*, gráfico *m*, esquema *m*

dial¹ ['daɪl] *v* **dialed** *or* **dialled; dialing** *or* **dialling** : marcar, díscar

dial² *n* **1** : esfera *f* (de un reloj), dial *m* (de un radio), disco *m* (de un teléfono)

dialect ['daɪə,lɛkt] *n* : dialecto *m*

dialogue ['daɪə,lɔg] *n* : diálogo *m*

dial tone *n* : tono *m* (de marcar/marcado/discar)

diameter [daɪ'æmətər] *n* : diámetro *m*

diamond ['daɪmənd, 'daɪə-] *n* **1** : diamante *m*, brillante *m* ⟨a diamond necklace : un collar de brillantes⟩ **2** : rombo *m*, forma *f* de rombo **3** : diamante *m* (naipe) **4** INFIELD : cuadro *m*, diamante *m* (en béisbol)

diaper ['daɪpər, 'daɪə-] *n* : pañal *m*

diaphragm ['daɪə,fræm] *n* : diafragma *m*

diarrhea ['daɪə'ri:ə] *n* : diarrea *f*

diary ['daɪəri] *n*, *pl* -ries : diario *m*

diatribe ['daɪə,traɪb] *n* : diatriba *f*

dice¹ ['daɪs] *v* **diced; dicing** : cortar en cubos

dice² *ns* & *pl* **1** → **die²** **2** : dados *mpl* (juego)

dicker ['dɪkər] *vt* : regatear

dictate¹ ['dɪk,teɪt, dɪk'teɪt] *v* -tated; -tating *vt* **1** : dictar ⟨to dictate a letter : dictar una carta⟩ **2** ORDER : mandar, ordenar — *vi* : dar órdenes

dictate² ['dɪk,teɪt] *n* **1** : mandato *m*, orden *f* **2 dictates** *npl* : dictados *mpl* ⟨the dictates of conscience : los dictados de la conciencia⟩

dictation [dɪk'teɪʃən] *n* : dictado *m*

dictator ['dɪk,teɪtər] *n* : dictador *m*, -dora *f*

dictatorial [,dɪktə'toriəl] *adj* : dictatorial — **dictatorially** *adv*

dictatorship [dɪk'teɪtər,ʃɪp, 'dɪk,-] *n* : dictadura *f*

diction ['dɪkʃən] *n* **1** : lenguaje *m*, estilo *m* **2** ENUNCIATION : dicción *f*, articulación *f*

dictionary ['dɪkʃə,nɛri] n, pl **-naries** : diccionario m

did → do

didactic [daɪ'dæktɪk] adj : didáctico

die¹ ['daɪ] vi **died** ['daɪd]; **dying** ['daɪɪŋ] 1 : morir, morirse 2 CEASE : morir, morirse ⟨a dying civilization : una civilización moribunda⟩ 3 STOP : apagarse, dejar de funcionar ⟨the motor died : el motor se apagó⟩ 4 **to be dying for/to** : morirse por ⟨I'm dying for a coffee : me muero por un café⟩ ⟨I'm dying to leave : me muero por irme⟩ 5 **to die away** FADE : irse apagando, disminuir (dícese de un sonido) 6 **to die down** SUBSIDE : disminuir, amainar (dícese del viento, etc.), irse apagando (dícese de los aplausos, las llamas, etc.), calmarse (dícese de un escándalo, etc.) 7 **to die laughing** : morirse de risa 8 **to die of** : morir de, morirse de ⟨he died of old age : murió de viejo⟩ 9 **to die out** : extinguirse

die² ['daɪ] n, pl **dice** ['daɪs] : dado m

die³ n, pl **dies** ['daɪz] 1 STAMP : troquel m, cuño m 2 MOLD : matriz f, molde m

diehard ['daɪ,hɑrd] adj : fanático

diesel ['diːzəl, -səl] n : diesel m

diet¹ ['daɪət] vi : ponerse a régimen, hacer dieta

diet² n : régimen m, dieta f

dietary ['daɪə,tɛri] adj : alimenticio, dietético

dietitian or **dietician** [,daɪə'tɪʃən] n : dietista mf

differ ['dɪfər] vi **-fered**; **-fering** 1 : diferir, diferenciarse 2 VARY : variar 3 DISAGREE : discrepar, diferir, no estar de acuerdo

difference ['dɪfrənts, 'dɪfərənts] n 1 : diferencia f ⟨to tell/notice the difference : notar/ver la diferencia⟩ 2 DISCREPANCY : diferencia f ⟨to split the difference : dividirse la diferencia (en partes iguales)⟩ 3 DISAGREEMENT : diferencia f, desacuerdo m ⟨to resolve/settle one's differences : resolver/saldar sus diferencias⟩ 4 **same difference!** : ¡es casi lo mismo! 5 **to make a difference** MATTER : importar ⟨what difference does it make? : ¿qué importa?⟩ ⟨it makes no difference to me : me da igual⟩ 6 **to make a difference in** AFFECT : afectar, influir en

different ['dɪfrənt, 'dɪfərənt] adj : distinto, diferente

differential¹ [,dɪfə'rɛntʃəl] adj : diferencial

differential² n : diferencial m

differentiate [,dɪfə'rɛntʃi,eɪt] v **-ated**; **-ating** vt 1 : hacer diferente 2 DISTINGUISH : distinguir, diferenciar — vi : distinguir

differentiation [,dɪfə,rɛntʃi'eɪʃən] n : diferenciación f

differently ['dɪfrəntli, 'dɪfərənt-] adv : de otra manera, de otro modo, distintamente

difficult ['dɪfɪ,kʌlt] adj : difícil

difficulty ['dɪfɪ,kʌlti] n, pl **-ties** 1 : dificultad f 2 PROBLEM : problema f, dificultad f

diffidence ['dɪfədənts] n 1 SHYNESS : retraimiento m, timidez f, apocamiento m 2 RETICENCE : reticencia f

diffident ['dɪfədənt] adj 1 SHY : tímido, apocado, inseguro 2 RESERVED : reservado

diffuse¹ [dɪ'fjuːz] v **-fused**; **-fusing** vt : difundir, esparcir — vi : difundirse, esparcirse

diffuse² [dɪ'fjuːs] adj 1 WORDY : prolijo, verboso 2 WIDESPREAD : difuso

diffusion [dɪ'fjuːʒən] n : difusión f

dig¹ ['dɪg] v **dug** ['dʌg], **digging** vt 1 : cavar, excavar ⟨to dig a hole : cavar un hoyo⟩ 2 EXTRACT : sacar ⟨to dig up potatoes : sacar papas del suelo⟩ 3 POKE, THRUST : clavar, hincar ⟨he dug me in the ribs : me dio un codazo en las costillas⟩ 4 **to dig out** RETRIEVE, EXTRACT : descubrir, sacar a luz — vi 1 : cavar, excavar 2 or **to dig around** RUMMAGE : hurgar (en los bolsillos, etc.) ⟨I dug (around) in my purse for my keys : hurgué en el bolso buscando las llaves⟩ 3 **to dig for** : buscar ⟨to dig for gold : buscar oro (cavando en el suelo)⟩ ⟨to dig for clues : buscar pistas, investigar⟩ 4 **to dig in** : atrincherarse 5 **to dig in** : empezar a comer ⟨dig in! : ¡a comer!⟩ 6 **to dig into** POKE : clavarse en 7 **to dig into** INVESTIGATE : investigar

dig² n 1 POKE : codazo m 2 GIBE : pulla f 3 EXCAVATION : excavación f

digest¹ ['daɪ,dʒɛst, dɪ-] vt 1 ASSIMILATE : digerir, asimilar 2 : digerir (comida) 3 SUMMARIZE : compendiar, resumir

digest² ['daɪ,dʒɛst] n : compendio m, resumen m

digestible [daɪ'dʒɛstəbəl, dɪ-] adj : digerible

digestion [daɪ'dʒɛstʃən, dɪ-] n : digestión f

digestive [daɪ'dʒɛstɪv, dɪ-] adj : digestivo ⟨the digestive system : el sistema digestivo⟩

digit ['dɪdʒət] n 1 NUMERAL : dígito m, número m 2 FINGER, TOE : dedo m

digital ['dɪdʒətəl] adj : digital ⟨digital camera : cámara digital⟩ — **digitally** adv

digitalize ['dɪdʒətə,laɪz] vt **-ized**; **-izing** : digitalizar

dignified ['dɪgnə,faɪd] adj : digno, decoroso

dignify ['dɪgnə,faɪ] vt **-fied**; **-fying** : dignificar, honrar

dignitary ['dɪgnə,tɛri] n, pl **-taries** : dignatario m, -ria f

dignity ['dɪgnəti] n, pl **-ties** : dignidad f

digress [daɪ'grɛs, də-] vi : desviarse del tema, divagar

digression [daɪ'grɛʃən, də-] n : digresión f

dike or **dyke** ['daɪk] n : dique m

dilapidated [də'læpə,deɪtəd] adj : ruinoso, desvencijado, destartalado

dilapidation [də,læpə'deɪʃən] n : deterioro m, estado m ruinoso

dilate [daɪ'leɪt, 'daɪ,leɪt] v **-lated**; **-lating** vt : dilatar — vi : dilatarse

dilemma [dɪ'lɛmə] n : dilema m

dilettante [ˈdɪlə,tɑnt, -ˌtænt] n, pl **-tantes** [-ˌtɑnts, -ˌtænts] or **-tanti** [ˌdɪləˈtɑnti, -ˈtæn-] : diletante mf

diligence [ˈdɪləʤənts] n : diligencia f, aplicación f

diligent [ˈdɪləʤənt] adj : diligente ⟨a diligent search : una búsqueda minuciosa⟩ — **diligently** adv

dill [ˈdɪl] n : eneldo m

dillydally [ˈdɪliˌdæli] vi **-lied; -lying** : demorarse, perder tiempo

dilute [daɪˈluːt, də-] vt **-luted; -luting** : diluir, aguar

dilution [daɪˈluːʃən, də-] n : dilución f

dim¹ [ˈdɪm] v **dimmed; dimming** vt : atenuar (la luz), nublar (la vista), borrar (la memoria), opacar (una superficie) — vi : oscurecerse, apagarse

dim² adj **dimmer; dimmest 1** FAINT : oscuro, tenue (dícese de la luz), nublado (dícese de la vista), borrado (dícese de la memoria) **2** STUPID : tonto, torpe **3 to take a dim view of** : ver con malos ojos

dime [ˈdaɪm] n : moneda f de diez centavos

dimension [dəˈmɛntʃən, daɪ-] n **1** : dimensión f **2 dimensions** npl EXTENT, SCOPE : dimensiones fpl, extensión f, medida f

diminish [dəˈmɪnɪʃ] vt LESSEN : disminuir, reducir, amainar — vi DWINDLE, WANE : menguar, reducirse

diminutive [dəˈmɪnjʊtɪv] adj : diminutivo, minúsculo

dimly [ˈdɪmli] adv : indistintamente, débilmente

dimmer [ˈdɪmər] n : potenciómetro m, conmutador m de luces (en automóviles)

dimness [ˈdɪmnəs] n : oscuridad f, debilidad f (de la vista), imprecisión f (de la memoria)

dimple [ˈdɪmpəl] n : hoyuelo m

din [ˈdɪn] n : estrépito m, estruendo m

dine [ˈdaɪn] vi **dined; dining** : cenar

diner [ˈdaɪnər] n **1** : comensal mf (persona) **2** : vagón m restaurante (en un tren) **3** : cafetería f, restaurante m barato

dinghy [ˈdɪŋi, ˈdɪŋgi, ˈdɪŋki] n, pl **-ghies** : bote m

dinginess [ˈdɪnʤənəs] n **1** DIRTINESS : suciedad f **2** SHABBINESS : lo gastado, lo deslucido

dingy [ˈdɪnʤi] adj **dingier; -est 1** DIRTY : sucio **2** SHABBY : gastado, deslucido

dining car n : coche m comedor (de un tren)

dining room n : comedor m

dinner [ˈdɪnər] n **1** : cena f, comida f **2** BANQUET : cena f, banquete m

dinner jacket n : esmoquin m (chaqueta)

dinosaur [ˈdaɪnəˌsɔr] n : dinosaurio m

dint [ˈdɪnt] n **by dint of** : a fuerza de

diocese [ˈdaɪəsəs, -siˌz, -ˌsiːs] n, pl **-ceses** [ˈdaɪəsəsəz] : diócesis f

dip¹ [ˈdɪp] v **dipped; dipping** vt **1** DUNK, PLUNGE : sumergir, mojar, meter **2** LADLE : servir con cucharón **3** LOWER : bajar, arriar (una bandera) — vi **1** DE-

SCEND, DROP : bajar en picada, descender **2** SLOPE : bajar, inclinarse

dip² n **1** SWIM : chapuzón m **2** DROP : descenso m, caída f **3** SLOPE : cuesta f, declive m **4** SAUCE : salsa f

diphtheria [dɪfˈθɪriə] n : difteria f

diphthong [ˈdɪfˌθɔŋ] n : diptongo m

diploma [dəˈploːmə] n, pl **-mas** : diploma m

diplomacy [dəˈploːməsi] n **1** : diplomacia f **2** TACT : tacto m, discreción f

diplomat [ˈdɪpləˌmæt] n **1** : diplomático m, -ca f (en relaciones internacionales) **2** : persona f diplomática

diplomatic [ˌdɪploˈmætɪk] adj : diplomático ⟨diplomatic immunity : inmunidad diplomática⟩

dipper [ˈdɪpər] n **1** LADLE : cucharón m, cazo m **2 Big Dipper** : Osa f Mayor **3 Little Dipper** : Osa f Menor

dipstick [ˈdɪpˌstɪk] n : varilla f de medición (del aceite)

dire [ˈdaɪr] adj **direr; direst 1** HORRIBLE : espantoso, terrible, horrendo **2** EXTREME : extremo ⟨dire poverty : pobreza extrema⟩

direct¹ [dəˈrɛkt, daɪ-] vt **1** ADDRESS : dirigir, mandar **2** AIM, POINT : dirigir **3** GUIDE : indicarle el camino (a alguien), orientar **4** MANAGE : dirigir ⟨to direct a film : dirigir una película⟩ **5** COMMAND : ordenar, mandar

direct² adv : directamente

direct³ adj **1** STRAIGHT : directo **2** FRANK : franco

direct debit n : débito m automático

direct current n : corriente f continua

direction [dəˈrɛkʃən, daɪ-] n **1** SUPERVISION : dirección f **2** INSTRUCTION, ORDER : instrucción f, orden f **3** COURSE : dirección f, rumbo m ⟨to change direction : cambiar de dirección⟩ **4 to ask directions** : pedir indicaciones

directional [dəˈrɛkʃənəl, daɪ-] adj : direccional

directive [dəˈrɛktɪv, daɪ-] n : directiva f

directly [dəˈrɛktli, daɪ-] adv **1** STRAIGHT : directamente ⟨directly north : directamente al norte⟩ **2** FRANKLY : francamente **3** EXACTLY : exactamente, justo ⟨directly opposite : justo enfrente⟩ **4** IMMEDIATELY : en seguida, inmediatamente

directness [dəˈrɛktnəs, daɪ-] n : franqueza f

director [dəˈrɛktər, daɪ-] n **1** : director m, -tora f **2 board of directors** : junta f directiva, directorio m

directory [dəˈrɛktəri, daɪ-] n, pl **-ries** : guía f, directorio m ⟨telephone directory : directorio telefónico⟩ ⟨directory assistance : servicio de información (telefónica)⟩

dirge [ˈdərʤ] n : canto m fúnebre

dirigible [ˈdɪrəʤəbəl, dəˈrɪʤə-] n : dirigible m, zepelín m

dirt [ˈdərt] n **1** FILTH : suciedad f, mugre f, porquería f **2** SOIL : tierra f

dirt cheap adj : baratísimo, regalado

dirtiness [ˈdərtinəs] n : suciedad f

dirty¹ [ˈdərtʃi] vt **dirtied; dirtying** : ensuciar, manchar

dirty² adj **dirtier; -est 1** SOILED, STAINED : sucio, manchado **2** DISHONEST : sucio, deshonesto ⟨a dirty player : un jugador tramposo⟩ ⟨a dirty trick : una mala pasada⟩ **3** INDECENT : indecente, cochino ⟨a dirty joke : un chiste verde⟩

dis- pref : des-

disability [ˌdɪsəˈbiləṭi] n, pl **-ties** : minusvalía f, discapacidad f, invalidez f

disable [dɪsˈeɪbəl] vt **-abled; -abling** : dejar inválido, inutilizar, incapacitar

disabled [dɪsˈeɪbəld] adj : minusválido, discapacitado

disabuse [ˌdɪsəˈbjuːz] vt **-bused; -busing** : desengañar, sacar del error

disadvantage [ˌdɪsədˈvæntɪdʒ] n : desventaja f

disadvantageous [ˌdɪsˌædˌvænˈteɪ-dʒəs] adj : desventajoso, desfavorable

disagree [ˌdɪsəˈgriː] vi **1** DIFFER : discrepar, no coincidir **2** DISSENT : disentir, discrepar, no estar de acuerdo ⟨I disagree (with you) : no estoy de acuerdo (contigo)⟩ **3 to disagree with someone** : sentarle mal a alguien (dícese de comida, etc.)

disagreeable [ˌdɪsəˈgriːəbəl] adj : desagradable

disagreement [ˌdɪsəˈgriːmənt] n **1** : desacuerdo m **2** DISCREPANCY : discrepancia f **3** ARGUMENT : discusión f, altercado m, disputa f

disallow [ˌdɪsəˈlaʊ] vt **1** : rechazar, desestimar **2** : anular (en deportes)

disappear [ˌdɪsəˈpɪr] vi : desaparecer, desvanecerse ⟨to disappear from view : perderse de vista⟩

disappearance [ˌdɪsəˈpɪrənts] n : desaparición f

disappoint [ˌdɪsəˈpɔɪnt] vt : decepcionar, defraudar, fallar

disappointing [ˌdɪsəˈpɔɪntɪŋ] adj : decepcionante

disappointment [ˌdɪsəˈpɔɪntmənt] n : decepción f, desilusión f, chasco m

disapproval [ˌdɪsəˈpruːvəl] n : desaprobación f

disapprove [ˌdɪsəˈpruːv] vi **-proved; -proving** : desaprobar, estar en contra

disapprovingly [ˌdɪsəˈpruːvɪŋli] adv : con desaprobación

disarm [dɪsˈɑrm] vt : desarmar

disarmament [dɪsˈɑrməmənt] n : desarme m ⟨nuclear disarmament : desarme nuclear⟩

disarrange [ˌdɪsəˈreɪndʒ] vt **-ranged; -ranging** : desarreglar, desordenar

disarray [ˌdɪsəˈreɪ] n : desorden m, confusión f, desorganización f

disassemble [ˌdɪsəˈsɛmbəl] v **-bled; -bling** vt : desarmar, desmontar — vi : desarmarse, desmontarse

disassociate → dissociate

disaster [dɪˈzæstər] n : desastre m, catástrofe f

disastrous [dɪˈzæstrəs] adj : desastroso

disband [dɪsˈbænd] vt : disolver — vi : disolverse, dispersarse

disbar [dɪsˈbɑr] vt **-barred; -barring** : prohibir de ejercer la abogacía

disbelief [ˌdɪsbɪˈliːf] n : incredulidad f

disbelieve [ˌdɪsbɪˈliːv] v **-lieved; -lieving** : no creer, dudar

disburse [dɪsˈbərs] vt **-bursed; -bursing** : desembolsar

disbursement [dɪsˈbərsmənt] n : desembolso m

disc → disk

discard [dɪsˈkɑrd, ˈdɪsˌkɑrd] vt : desechar, deshacerse de, botar — vi : descartarse (en juegos de naipes)

discern [dɪˈsərn, -ˈzərn] vt : discernir, distinguir, percibir

discernible [dɪˈsərnəbəl, -ˈzər-] adj : perceptible, visible

discerning [dɪˈsərnɪŋ, -ˈzər-] adj : refinado (dícese del gusto), perspicaz, sagaz

discernment [dɪˈsərnmənt, -ˈzərn-] n : discernimiento m, criterio m

discharge¹ [dɪsˈtʃɑrdʒ, ˈdɪsˌ-] v **-charged; -charging 1** UNLOAD : descargar (carga), desembarcar (pasajeros) **2** SHOOT : descargar, disparar **3** FREE : liberar, poner en libertad **4** DISMISS : despedir **5** EMIT : despedir (humo, etc.), descargar (electricidad) **6** : cumplir con (una obligación), saldar (una deuda) — vi **1** : descargarse (dícese de una batería) **2** OOZE : supurar

discharge² [ˈdɪsˌtʃɑrdʒ, dɪsˈ-] n **1** EMISSION : descarga f (de electricidad), emisión f (de gases) **2** DISMISSAL : despido m (del empleo), baja f (del ejército) **3** SECRETION : secreción f

disciple [dɪˈsaɪpəl] n : discípulo m, -la f

discipline¹ [ˈdɪsəplən] vt **-plined; -plining 1** PUNISH : castigar, sancionar (a los empleados) **2** CONTROL : disciplinar **3 to discipline oneself** : disciplinarse

discipline² n **1** FIELD : disciplina f, campo m **2** TRAINING : disciplina f **3** PUNISHMENT : castigo m **4** SELF-CONTROL : dominio m de sí mismo

disc jockey n : disc jockey mf

disclaim [dɪsˈkleɪm] vt DENY : negar

disclose [dɪsˈkloːz] vt **-closed; -closing** : revelar, poner en evidencia

disclosure [dɪsˈkloːʒər] n : revelación f

disco [ˈdɪsko] n **1** → **discotheque 2** or **disco music** : disco f, música f disco

discolor [dɪsˈkʌlər] vt **1** BLEACH : decolorar **2** FADE : desteñir **3** STAIN : manchar — vi : decolorarse, desteñirse

discoloration [dɪsˌkʌləˈreɪʃən] n STAIN : mancha f

discomfort [dɪsˈkʌmfərt] n **1** PAIN : molestia f, malestar m **2** UNEASINESS : inquietud f

disconcert [ˌdɪskənˈsərt] vt : desconcertar

disconcerting [ˌdɪskənˈsərtɪŋ] adj : desconcertante

disconnect [ˌdɪskəˈnɛkt] vt : desconectar

disconnected [ˌdɪskəˈnɛktəd] adj : inconexo

disconsolate [dɪsˈkɑntsələt] adj : desconsolado

discontent [ˌdɪskənˈtɛnt] n : descontento m

discontented [ˌdɪskən'tɛntəd] *adj* : descontento

discontinue [ˌdɪskən'tɪnjuː] *vt* **-ued; -uing** : suspender, descontinuar

discontinuity [dɪsˌkɑntə'nuːəti, -'njuː-] *n, pl* **-ties** : discontinuidad *f*

discontinuous [ˌdɪskən'tɪnjəwəs] *adj* : discontinuo

discord ['dɪsˌkɔrd] *n* **1** STRIFE : discordia *f*, discordancia *f* **2** : disonancia *f* (en música)

discordant [dɪs'kɔrdənt] *adj* : discordante — **discordantly** *adv*

discotheque ['dɪskəˌtɛk, ˌdɪskə'tɛk] *n* : discoteca *f*

discount¹ ['dɪsˌkaʊnt, dɪs'-] *vt* **1** REDUCE : descontar, rebajar (precios) **2** DISREGARD : descartar, ignorar

discount² ['dɪsˌkaʊnt] *n* : descuento *m*, rebaja *f*

discourage [dɪs'kərɪʤ] *vt* **-aged; -aging 1** DISHEARTEN : desalentar, desanimar **2** DISSUADE : disuadir **3** DETER : impedir

discouragement [dɪs'kərɪʤmənt] *n* : desánimo *m*, desaliento *m*

discouraging [dɪs'kərəʤɪŋ] *adj* : desalentador

discourse¹ [dɪs'kors] *vi* **-coursed; -coursing** : disertar, conversar

discourse² ['dɪsˌkors] *n* **1** TALK : conversación *f* **2** SPEECH, TREATISE : discurso *m*, tratado *m*

discourteous [dɪs'kərtiəs] *adj* : descortés — **discourteously** *adv*

discourtesy [dɪs'kərtəsi] *n, pl* **-sies** : descortesía *f*

discover [dɪs'kʌvər] *vt* : descubrir

discoverer [dɪs'kʌvərər] *n* : descubridor *m*, -dora *f*

discovery [dɪs'kʌvəri] *n, pl* **-ries** : descubrimiento *m*

discredit¹ [dɪs'krɛdət] *vt* **1** DISBELIEVE : no creer, dudar **2** : desacreditar, desprestigiar, poner en duda ⟨they discredited his research : desacreditaron sus investigaciones⟩

discredit² *n* **1** DISREPUTE : descrédito *m*, desprestigio *m* **2** DOUBT : duda *f*

discreet [dɪs'kriːt] *adj* : discreto — **discreetly** *adv*

discrepancy [dɪs'krɛpənsi] *n, pl* **-cies** : discrepancia *f*

discretion [dɪs'krɛʃən] *n* **1** : discreción *f* **2** JUDGMENT : discernimiento *m*, criterio *m*

discretionary [dɪs'krɛʃəˌnɛri] *adj* : discrecional

discriminate [dɪs'krɪməˌneɪt] *v* **-nated; -nating** *vt* DISTINGUISH : distinguir, discriminar, diferenciar — *vi* : discriminar ⟨to discriminate against women : discriminar a las mujeres⟩

discriminating [dɪs'krɪməˌneɪtɪŋ] *adj* : refinado (dícese del gusto), entendido (dícese de personas)

discrimination [dɪsˌkrɪmə'neɪʃən] *n* **1** PREJUDICE : discriminación *f* **2** DISCERNMENT : discernimiento *m*

discriminatory [dɪs'krɪmənəˌtori] *adj* : discriminatorio

discus ['dɪskəs] *n, pl* **-cuses** [-kəsəz] : disco *m*

discuss [dɪs'kʌs] *vt* : hablar de, discutir, tratar (de)

discussion [dɪs'kʌʃən] *n* : discusión *f*, debate *m*, conversación *f*

disdain¹ [dɪs'deɪn] *vt* : desdeñar, despreciar ⟨they disdained to reply : no se dignaron a responder⟩

disdain² *n* : desdén *m*

disdainful [dɪs'deɪnfəl] *adj* : desdeñoso — **disdainfully** *adv*

disease [dɪ'ziːz] *n* : enfermedad *f*, mal *m*, dolencia *f*

diseased [dɪ'ziːzd] *adj* : enfermo

disembark [ˌdɪsɪm'bɑrk] *v* : desembarcar

disembarkation [dɪsˌɛmˌbɑr'keɪʃən] *n* : desembarco *m*, desembarque *m*

disembodied [ˌdɪsɪm'bɑdid] *adj* : incorpóreo

disenchant [ˌdɪsɪn'tʃænt] *vt* : desilusionar, desencantar, desengañar

disenchanted [ˌdɪsɪn'tʃæntəd] *adj* : desilusionado, desencantado

disenchantment [ˌdɪsɪn'tʃæntmənt] *n* : desencanto *m*, desilusión *f*

disenfranchise [ˌdɪsɪn'frænˌtʃaɪz] *vt* **-chised; -chising** : privar del derecho a votar

disengage [ˌdɪsɪn'geɪʤ] *vt* **-gaged; -gaging** : soltar, desconectar (un mecanismo)

disentangle [ˌdɪsɪn'tæŋgəl] *vt* **-gled; -gling** UNTANGLE : desenredar, desenmarañar

disfavor [dɪs'feɪvər] *n* : desaprobación *f*

disfigure [dɪs'fɪgjər] *vt* **-ured; -uring** : desfigurar (a una persona), afear (un edificio, un área)

disgrace¹ [dɪs'greɪs] *vt* **-graced; -gracing** : deshonrar

disgrace² *n* **1** DISHONOR : desgracia *f*, deshonra *f* **2** SHAME : vergüenza *f* ⟨he's a disgrace to his family : es una vergüenza para su familia⟩

disgraceful [dɪs'greɪsfəl] *adj* : vergonzoso, deshonroso, ignominioso

disgracefully [dɪs'greɪsfəli] *adv* : vergonzosamente

disgruntle [dɪs'grʌntəl] *vt* **-tled; -tling** : enfadar, contrariar

disgruntled [dɪs'grʌntəld] *adj* : descontento, contrariado

disguise¹ [dɪs'kaɪz] *vt* **-guised; -guising 1** : disfrazar, enmascarar (el aspecto) **2** CONCEAL : encubrir, disimular

disguise² *n* : disfraz *m*

disgust¹ [dɪs'kʌst] *vt* : darle asco (a alguien), asquear, repugnar ⟨that disgusts me : eso me da asco⟩

disgust² *n* : asco *m*, repugnancia *f*

disgusting [dɪs'kʌstɪŋ] *adj* : asqueroso, repugnante — **disgustingly** *adv*

dish¹ ['dɪʃ] *vt* **1** *or* **to dish out/up** SERVE : servir **2** *or* **to dish out** DISPENSE : repartir (dinero, etc.), dar (consejos) **3** **to dish it out** : criticar

dish² *n* **1** : plato *m* ⟨the national dish : el plato nacional⟩ **2** PLATE : plato *m* ⟨to wash the dishes : lavar los platos⟩ **3 serving dish** : fuente *f*

dishcloth ['dɪʃ,klɔθ] *n* : paño *m* de cocina (para secar), trapo *m* de fregar (para lavar)

dishearten [dɪs'hɑrtən] *vt* : desanimar, desalentar

dishevel [dɪ'ʃɛvəl] *vt* **-eled** *or* **-elled; -eling** *or* **-elling** : desarreglar, despeinar (el pelo)

disheveled *or* **dishevelled** [dɪ'ʃɛvəld] *adj* : despeinado (dícese del pelo), desarreglado, desaliñado

dishonest [dɪ'sɑnəst] *adj* : deshonesto, fraudulento — **dishonestly** *adv*

dishonesty [dɪ'sɑnəsti] *n, pl* **-ties** : deshonestidad *f*, falta *f* de honradez

dishonor[1] [dɪ'sɑnər] *vt* : deshonrar

dishonor[2] *n* : deshonra *f*

dishonorable [dɪ'sɑnərəbəl] *adj* : deshonroso — **dishonorably** [-bli] *adv*

dishrag ['dɪʃ,ræg] → **dishcloth**

dishtowel ['dɪʃ,tauəl] → **dishcloth**

dishwasher ['dɪʃ,wɔʃər] *n* : lavaplatos *m*, lavavajillas *m*

disillusion [,dɪsə'lu:ʒən] *vt* : desilusionar, desencantar, desengañar

disillusionment [,dɪsə'lu:ʒənmənt] *n* : desilusión *f*, desencanto *m*

disinclination [dɪs,ɪnklə'neɪʃən, -,ɪŋ-] *n* : aversión *f*

disinclined [,dɪsɪn'klaɪnd] *adv* : poco dispuesto

disinfect [,dɪsɪn'fɛkt] *vt* : desinfectar

disinfectant[1] [,dɪsɪn'fɛktənt] *adj* : desinfectante

disinfectant[2] *n* : desinfectante *m*

disinherit [,dɪsɪn'hɛrət] *vt* : desheredar

disintegrate [dɪs'ɪntə,greɪt] *v* **-grated; -grating** *vt* : desintegrar, deshacer — *vi* : desintegrarse, deshacerse

disintegration [dɪs,ɪntə'greɪʃən] *n* : desintegración *f*

disinterested [dɪs'ɪntərəstəd, -,rɛs-] *adj* **1** INDIFFERENT : indiferente **2** IMPARTIAL : imparcial, desinteresado

disinterestedness [dɪs'ɪntərəstədnəs, -,rɛs-] *n* : desinterés *m*

disjointed [dɪs'dʒɔɪntəd] *adj* : inconexo, incoherente

disk *or* **disc** ['dɪsk] *n* : disco *m*

diskette [dɪs'kɛt] *n* : diskette *m*, disquete *m*

dislike[1] [dɪs'laɪk] *vt* **-liked; -liking** : tenerle aversión a (algo), tenerle antipatía (a alguien), no gustarle (algo a uno)

dislike[2] *n* : aversión *f*, antipatía *f* ⟨to take a dislike to : tomarle antipatía a⟩

dislocate ['dɪslo,keɪt, dɪs'lo:-] *vt* **-cated; -cating** : dislocar

dislocation [,dɪslo'keɪʃən] *n* : dislocación *f*

dislodge [dɪs'lɑdʒ] *vt* **-lodged; -lodging** : sacar, desalojar, desplazar

disloyal [dɪs'lɔɪəl] *adj* : desleal

disloyalty [dɪs'lɔɪəlti] *n, pl* **-ties** : deslealtad *f*

dismal ['dɪzməl] *adj* **1** GLOOMY : sombrío, lúgubre, tétrico **2** DEPRESSING : deprimente, triste

dismantle [dɪs'mæntəl] *vt* **-tled; -tling** : desmantelar, desmontar, desarmar

dismay[1] [dɪs'meɪ] *vt* : consternar

dismay[2] *n* : consternación *f*

dismember [dɪs'mɛmbər] *vt* : desmembrar

dismiss [dɪs'mɪs] *vt* **1** : dejar salir, darle permiso (a alguien) para retirarse **2** DISCHARGE : despedir, destituir **3** REJECT : descartar, desechar, rechazar

dismissal [dɪs'mɪsəl] *n* **1** : permiso *m* para retirarse **2** DISCHARGE : despido *m* (de un empleado), destitución *f* (de un funcionario) **3** REJECTION : rechazo *m*

dismount [dɪs'maunt] *vi* : desmontar, bajarse, apearse

disobedience [,dɪsə'bi:diənts] *n* : desobediencia *f* — **disobedient** [-ənt] *adj*

disobey [,dɪsə'beɪ] *v* : desobedecer

disorder[1] [dɪs'ɔrdər] *vt* : desordenar, desarreglar

disorder[2] *n* **1** DISARRAY : desorden *m* **2** UNREST : disturbios *mpl*, desórdenes *mpl* **3** AILMENT : afección *f*, indisposición *f*, dolencia *f*

disorderly [dɪs'ɔrdərli] *adj* **1** UNTIDY : desordenado, desarreglado **2** UNRULY : indisciplinado, alborotado **3** disorderly conduct : conducta *f* escandalosa

disorganization [dɪs,ɔrgənə'zeɪʃən] *n* : desorganización *f*

disorganize [dɪs'ɔrgə,naɪz] *vt* **-nized; -nizing** : desorganizar

disorient [dɪs'ɔri,ɛnt] *vt* : desorientar

disown [dɪs'o:n] *vt* : renegar de, repudiar

disparage [dɪs'pærɪdʒ] *vt* **-aged; -aging** : menospreciar, denigrar

disparagement [dɪs'pærɪdʒmənt] *n* : menosprecio *m*

disparate ['dɪspərət, dɪs'pærət] *adj* : dispar, diferente

disparity [dɪs'pærəti] *n, pl* **-ties** : disparidad *f*

dispassionate [dɪs'pæʃənət] *adj* : desapasionado, imparcial — **dispassionately** *adv*

dispatch[1] [dɪs'pætʃ] *vt* **1** SEND : despachar, enviar **2** KILL : despachar, matar **3** HANDLE : despachar

dispatch[2] *n* **1** SENDING : envío *m*, despacho *m* **2** MESSAGE : despacho *m*, reportaje *m* (de un periodista), parte *m* (en el ejército) **3** PROMPTNESS : prontitud *f*, rapidez *f*

dispel [dɪs'pɛl] *vt* **-pelled; -pelling** : disipar, desvanecer

dispensable [dɪ'spɛntsəbəl] *adj* : prescindible

dispensary [dɪ'spɛntsəri] *n, pl* **-ries** : dispensario *m*

dispensation [,dɪspən'seɪʃən] *n* EXEMPTION : exención *m*, dispensa *f*

dispense [dɪ'spɛnts] *v* **-pensed; -pensing** *vt* **1** DISTRIBUTE : repartir, distribuir, dar **2** ADMINISTER, BESTOW : administrar (justicia), conceder (favores, etc.) **3** : preparar y despachar (medicamentos) — *vi* **to dispense with** : prescindir de

dispenser [dɪs'pɛntsər] *n* : dispensador *m*, distribuidor *m* automático

dispersal [dɪs'pərsəl] n : dispersión f
disperse [dɪs'pərs] v **-persed; -persing** vt : dispersar, diseminar — vi : dispersarse
dispersion [dɪ'spərʒən] n : dispersión f
dispirit [dɪ'spɪrət] vt : desalentar, desanimar
dispirited [dɪ'spɪrətəd] adj : desanimado
displace [dɪs'pleɪs] vt **-placed; -placing 1** : desplazar (un líquido, etc.) **2** REPLACE : reemplazar
displacement [dɪs'pleɪsmənt] n **1** : desplazamiento m (de personas) **2** REPLACEMENT : sustitución f, reemplazo m
display[1] [dɪs'pleɪ] vt : exponer, exhibir, mostrar
display[2] n **1** : muestra f, exposición f, alarde m **2** : visualizador m (de un aparato)
displease [dɪs'pliːz] v **-pleased; -pleasing** : desagradar a, disgustar, contrariar
displeasure [dɪs'plɛʒər] n : desagrado m
disposable [dɪs'poːzəbəl] adj **1** : desechable ⟨disposable diapers : pañales desechables⟩ **2** AVAILABLE : disponible
disposal [dɪs'poːzəl] n **1** PLACEMENT : disposición f, colocación f **2** REMOVAL : eliminación f **3** → garbage disposal **4** to have at one's disposal : disponer de, tener a su disposición
dispose [dɪs'poːz] v **-posed; -posing** vt **1** ARRANGE : disponer, colocar **2** INCLINE : predisponer — vi **1** to dispose of DISCARD : desechar, deshacerse de **2** to dispose of HANDLE : despachar **3** to be disposed to do something : estar dispuesto a hacer algo
disposition [ˌdɪspə'zɪʃən] n **1** ARRANGEMENT : disposición f **2** TENDENCY : predisposición f, inclinación f **3** TEMPERAMENT : temperamento m, carácter m
dispossess [ˌdɪspə'zɛs] vt : desposeer
disproportion [ˌdɪsprə'porʃən] n : desproporción f
disproportionate [ˌdɪsprə'porʃənət] adj : desproporcionado — **disproportionately** adv
disprove [dɪs'pruːv] vt **-proved; -proving** : rebatir, refutar
disputable [dɪs'pjuːtəbəl, 'dɪspjutəbəl] adj : discutible
dispute[1] [dɪs'pjuːt] v **-puted; -puting** vt **1** QUESTION : discutir, cuestionar **2** OPPOSE : combatir, resistir — vi ARGUE, DEBATE : discutir
dispute[2] n **1** DEBATE : debate m, discusión f **2** QUARREL : disputa f, discusión f
disqualification [dɪsˌkwɑləfə'keɪʃən] n : descalificación f
disqualify [dɪs'kwɑləˌfaɪ] vt **-fied; -fying** : descalificar, inhabilitar
disquiet[1] [dɪs'kwaɪət] vt : inquietar
disquiet[2] n : ansiedad f, inquietud f
disregard[1] [ˌdɪsrɪ'gɑrd] vt : ignorar, no prestar atención a
disregard[2] n : indiferencia f
disrepair [ˌdɪsrɪ'pær] n : mal estado m
disreputable [dɪs'rɛpjutəbəl] adj : de mala fama (dícese de una persona o un lugar), vergonzoso (dícese de la conducta)

disreputably [dɪs'rɛpjutəbli] adv : vergonzosamente
disrepute [ˌdɪsrɪ'pjuːt] n : descrédito m, mala fama f, deshonra f
disrespect [ˌdɪsrɪ'spɛkt] n : falta f de respeto
disrespectful [ˌdɪsrɪ'spɛktfəl] adj : irrespetuoso — **disrespectfully** adv
disrobe [dɪs'roːb] v **-robed; -robing** vt : desvestir, desnudar — vi : desvestirse, desnudarse
disrupt [dɪs'rʌpt] vt : trastornar, perturbar
disruption [dɪs'rʌpʃən] n : trastorno m
disruptive [dɪs'rʌptɪv] adj : perjudicial, perturbador — **disruptively** adv
dissatisfaction [dɪsˌsætəs'fækʃən] n : descontento m, insatisfacción f
dissatisfied [dɪs'sætəsˌfaɪd] adj : descontento, insatisfecho
dissatisfy [dɪs'sætəsˌfaɪ] vt **-fied; -fying** : no contentar, no satisfacer
dissect [dɪ'sɛkt] vt : disecar
dissection [dɪ'sɛkʃən] n : disección f
dissemble [dɪ'sɛmbəl] v **-bled; -bling** vt HIDE : ocultar, disimular — vi PRETEND : fingir, disimular
disseminate [dɪ'sɛməˌneɪt] vt **-nated; -nating** : diseminar, difundir, divulgar
dissemination [dɪˌsɛmə'neɪʃən] n : diseminación f, difusión f
dissension [dɪ'sɛntʃən] n : disensión f, desacuerdo m
dissent[1] [dɪ'sɛnt] vi : disentir
dissent[2] n : disentimiento m, disensión f, disenso m
dissertation [ˌdɪsər'teɪʃən] n **1** DISCOURSE : disertación f, discurso m **2** THESIS : tesis f
disservice [dɪs'sərvɪs] n : perjuicio m
dissident[1] [dɪsədənt] adj : disidente
dissident[2] n : disidente mf
dissimilar [dɪ'sɪmələr] adj : distinto, diferente, disímil
dissipate ['dɪsəˌpeɪt] vt **-pated; -pating 1** DISPERSE : disipar, dispersar **2** SQUANDER : malgastar, desperdiciar, derrochar, disipar
dissipation [ˌdɪsə'peɪʃən] n : libertinaje m
dissociate [dɪ'soːʃiˌeɪt, -si-] or **disassociate** [ˌdɪsə'soːʃiˌeɪt, -si-] v **-ated** [-ˌeɪtəd]; **-ating** [-ˌeɪtɪŋ] vt : disociar ⟨to dissociate oneself : disociarse⟩ — vi : disociarse
dissociation [dɪˌsoːʃi'eɪʃən, -si-] n : disociación f
dissolute ['dɪsəˌluːt] adj : disoluto
dissolution [ˌdɪsə'luːʃən] n : disolución f
dissolve [dɪ'zɑlv] v **-solved; -solving** vt : disolver — vi : disolverse
dissonance ['dɪsənənts] n : disonancia f
dissuade [dɪ'sweɪd] vt **-suaded; -suading** : disuadir
distance[1] ['dɪstənts] vt **-tanced** [-təntst]; **-tancing** [-təntsɪŋ] **to distance oneself** : distanciarse
distance[2] n **1** : distancia f ⟨the distance between two points : la distancia entre dos puntos⟩ ⟨in the distance : a lo lejos⟩ **2** RESERVE : actitud f distante, reserva f

⟨to keep one's distance : guardar las distancias⟩

distant ['dɪstənt] *adj* **1** FAR : distante, lejano **2** REMOTE : distante, lejano, remoto **3** ALOOF : distante, frío

distantly ['dɪstəntli] *adv* **1** LOOSELY : aproximadamente, vagamente **2** COLDLY : fríamente, con frialdad

distaste [dɪs'teɪst] *n* : desagrado *m*, aversión *f*

distasteful [dɪs'teɪstfəl] *adj* : desagradable, de mal gusto

distemper [dɪs'tɛmpər] *n* : moquillo *m*

distend [dɪs'tɛnd] *vt* : dilatar, hinchar — *vi* : dilatarse, hincharse

distill [dɪs'tɪl] *vt* : destilar

distillation [ˌdɪstə'leɪʃən] *n* : destilación *f*

distiller [dɪs'tɪlər] *n* : destilador *m*, -dora *f*

distillery [dɪs'tɪləri] *n*, *pl* **-ries** [-riz] : destilería *f*

distinct [dɪs'tɪŋkt] *adj* **1** DIFFERENT : distinto, diferente **2** CLEAR, UNMISTAKABLE : marcado, claro, evidente ⟨a distinct possibility : una clara posibilidad⟩

distinction [dɪs'tɪŋkʃən] *n* **1** DIFFERENTIATION : distinción *f* **2** DIFFERENCE : diferencia *f* **3** EXCELLENCE : distinción *f*, excelencia *f* ⟨a writer of distinction : un escritor destacado⟩

distinctive [dɪs'tɪŋktɪv] *adj* : distintivo, característico — **distinctively** *adv*

distinctiveness [dɪs'tɪŋktɪvnəs] *n* : peculiaridad *f*

distinctly [dɪs'tɪŋktli] *adv* : claramente, con claridad

distinguish [dɪs'tɪŋgwɪʃ] *vt* **1** DIFFERENTIATE : distinguir, diferenciar **2** DISCERN : distinguir ⟨he distinguished the sound of the piano : distinguió el sonido del piano⟩ **3** to distinguish oneself : señalarse, distinguirse — *vi* DISCRIMINATE : distinguir

distinguishable [dɪs'tɪŋgwɪʃəbəl] *adj* : distinguible

distinguished [dɪs'tɪŋgwɪʃt] *adj* : distinguido

distinguishing [dɪs'tɪŋgwɪʃɪŋ] *adj* : distintivo

distort [dɪs'tɔrt] *vt* **1** MISREPRESENT : distorsionar, tergiversar **2** DEFORM : distorsionar, deformar

distortion [dɪs'tɔrʃən] *n* : distorsión *f*, deformación *f*, tergiversación *f*

distract [dɪs'trækt] *vt* : distraer, entretener

distracted [dɪs'træktəd] *adj* : distraído

distraction [dɪs'trækʃən] *n* **1** INTERRUPTION : distracción *f*, interrupción *f* **2** CONFUSION : confusión *f* **3** AMUSEMENT : diversión *f*, entretenimiento *m*, distracción *f*

distraught [dɪs'trɔt] *adj* : afligido, turbado

distress[1] [dɪs'tɛrs] *vt* : afligir, darle pena (a alguien), hacer sufrir

distress[2] *n* **1** SORROW : dolor *m*, angustia *f*, aflicción *f* **2** PAIN : dolor *m* **3** in ∼ : en peligro

distressful [dɪs'trɛsfəl] *adj* : doloroso, penoso

distressing [dɪs'trɛsɪŋ] *adj* : angustioso

distribute [dɪs'trɪˌbjuːt, -bjʊt] *vt* **-uted; -uting** : distribuir, repartir

distribution [ˌdɪstrə'bjuːʃən] *n* : distribución *f*, reparto *m*

distributive [dɪs'trɪbjʊtɪv] *adj* : distributivo

distributor [dɪs'trɪbjʊtər] *n* : distribuidor *m*, -dora *f*

district ['dɪsˌtrɪkt] *n* **1** REGION : región *f*, zona *f*, barrio *m* (de una ciudad) **2** : distrito *m* (zona política)

district attorney *n* : fiscal *mf* (del distrito)

distrust[1] [dɪs'trʌst] *vt* : desconfiar de

distrust[2] *n* : desconfianza *f*, recelo *m*

distrustful [dɪs'trʌstfəl] *adj* : desconfiado, receloso, suspicaz

disturb [dɪs'tərb] *vt* **1** BOTHER : molestar, perturbar ⟨sorry to disturb you : perdone la molestia⟩ **2** DISARRANGE : desordenar **3** WORRY : inquietar, preocupar **4** to disturb the peace : alterar el orden público

disturbance [dɪs'tərbənts] *n* **1** COMMOTION : alboroto *m*, disturbio *m* **2** INTERRUPTION : interrupción *f*

disturbed [dɪs'tərbd] *adj* **1** : trastornado ⟨mentally/emotionally disturbed : con trastornos mentales/emocionales⟩ **2** WORRIED, UNSETTLED : inquieto, agitado

disturbing [dɪs'tərbɪŋ] *adj* : inquietante

disuse [dɪs'juːs] *n* : desuso *m*

disused [dɪs'juːzd] *adj* **1** ABANDONED : abandonado **2** ANTIQUATED : desusado

ditch[1] ['dɪtʃ] *vt* **1** : cavar zanjas en **2** DISCARD : deshacerse de, botar

ditch[2] *n* : zanja *f*, fosa *f*, cuneta *f* (en una carretera)

dither ['dɪðər] *n* **to be in a dither** : estar nervioso, ponerse como loco

ditto ['dɪtˌoː] *n*, *pl* **-tos** **1** : lo mismo, ídem *m* **2 ditto marks** : comillas *fpl*

ditty ['dɪti] *n*, *pl* **-ties** : canción *f* corta y simple

diurnal [daɪ'ərnəl] *adj* **1** DAILY : diario, cotidiano **2** : diurno ⟨a diurnal animal : un animal diurno⟩

diva ['diːvə] *n* : diva *f*

divan ['daɪˌvæn, dɪ'-] *n* : diván *m*

dive[1] ['daɪv] *vi* **dived** *or* **dove** ['doːv]; **dived; diving** **1** PLUNGE : tirarse al agua, zambullirse, dar un clavado **2** SUBMERGE : sumergirse **3** DROP : bajar en picada (dícese de un avión), caer en picada **4** : bucear, hacer submarinismo ⟨to dive for pearls : bucear buscando perlas⟩

dive[2] *n* **1** PLUNGE : zambullida *f*, clavado *m* (en el agua) **2** DESCENT : descenso *m* en picada **3** BAR, JOINT : antro *m*

diver ['daɪvər] *n* **1** : saltador *m*, -dora *f*; clavadista *mf* **2** : buceador *m*, -dora *f*; buzo *mf*; submarinista *mf*

diverge [də'vərdʒ, daɪ-] *vi* **-verged; -verging** **1** SEPARATE : divergir, separarse **2** DIFFER : divergir, discrepar

divergence [də'vərdʒənts, daɪ-] *n* : divergencia *f* — **divergent** [-ənt] *adj*

diverse [daɪ'vərs, də-, 'daɪˌvərs] *adj* : diverso, variado

diversification [daɪ,vərsəfə'keɪʃən, də-] *n*
: diversificación *f*

diversify [daɪ'vərsə,faɪ, də-] *vt* **-fied; -fying**
: diversificar, variar

diversion [daɪ'vərʒən, də-] *n* **1** DEVIA-
TION : desviación *f* **2** AMUSEMENT, DIS-
TRACTION : diversión *f*, distracción *f*,
entretenimiento *m*

diversity [daɪ'vərsəti, də-] *n, pl* **-ties** : diversidad *f*

divert [də'vərt, daɪ-] *vt* **1** DEFLECT : desviar **2** DISTRACT : distraer **3** AMUSE : divertir, entretener

divest [daɪ'vest, də-] *vt* **1** UNDRESS : desnudar, desvestir **2** to divest of : despojar
de

divide [də'vaɪd] *v* **-vided; -viding** *vt* **1**
HALVE : dividir, partir por la mitad **2**
SHARE : repartir, dividir ⟨to divide be-
tween/among : dividir entre⟩ **3** : dividir
(números) ⟨to divide by : dividir por⟩ —
vi : dividirse, dividir (en matemáticas)

dividend ['dɪvə,dɛnd, -dənd] *n* **1** : dividendo *m* (en finanzas) **2** ADVANTAGE,
BENEFIT : beneficio *m*, provecho *m* ⟨to
pay dividends : reportar beneficios⟩ **3**
: dividendo *m* (en matemáticas)

divider [dɪ'vaɪdər] *n* **1** : separador *m*
(para ficheros, etc.) **2** *or* **room divider**
: mampara *f*, biombo *m*

divination [,dɪvə'neɪʃən] *n* : adivinación *f*

divine[1] [də'vaɪn] *adj* **diviner; -est 1** : divino **2** SUPERB : divino, espléndido —
divinely *adv*

divine[2] *n* : clérigo *m*, eclesiástico *m*

diving ['daɪvɪŋ] *n* **1** : clavados *mpl* **2**
: buceo *m*, submarinismo *m*

diving board *n* : trampolín *m*

divinity [dɪ'vɪnəti] *n, pl* **-ties** : divinidad *f*

divisible [dɪ'vɪzəbəl] *adj* : divisible

division [dɪ'vɪʒən] *n* **1** DISTRIBUTION : división *f*, reparto *m* ⟨division of labor
: distribución del trabajo⟩ **2** PART : división *f*, sección *f* **3** : división *f* (en
matemáticas)

divisive [dɪ'vaɪsɪv] *adj* : divisivo

divisor [dɪ'vaɪzər] *n* : divisor *m*

divorce[1] [də'vors] *v* **-vorced; -vorcing** *vt*
: divorciar — *vi* : divorciarse

divorce[2] *n* : divorcio *m*

divorcé [dɪ,vor'seɪ, -'si:; -'vor,-] *n* : divorciado *m*

divorced *adj* : divorciado

divorcée [dɪ,vor'seɪ, -'si:; -'vor,-] *n* : di-
vorciada *f*

divulge [də'vʌldʒ, daɪ-] *vt* **-vulged; -vulg-
ing** : revelar, divulgar

dizzily ['dɪzəli] *adv* : vertiginosamente

dizziness ['dɪzinəs] *n* : mareo *m*, vahído
m, vértigo *m*

dizzy ['dɪzi] *adj* **dizzier; -est 1** : mareado
⟨I feel dizzy : estoy mareado⟩ **2** DIZZY-
ING : vertiginoso ⟨a dizzy speed : una
velocidad vertiginosa⟩

dizzying ['dɪzɪŋ] *adj* : vertiginoso

DNA [,di:,ɛn'eɪ] *n* (deoxyribonucleic acid)
: ADN *m*

do[1] ['du:] *v* **did** ['dɪd]; **done** ['dʌn]; **doing;
does** ['dʌz] *vt* **1** CARRY OUT, PERFORM
: hacer, realizar, llevar a cabo ⟨she did

her best : hizo todo lo posible⟩ ⟨I didn't
do it! : ¡no fui yo!⟩ ⟨do something! : ¡haz
algo!⟩ ⟨I did something to my knee : me
lastimé la rodilla⟩ ⟨she did nothing to
help : no hizo nada para ayudar⟩ ⟨I have
nothing to do : no tengo nada que hacer⟩
⟨are you doing anything tonight? : ¿haces algo esta noche?⟩ ⟨what can I do for
you? : ¿en qué puedo servirle?⟩ ⟨to do
the chores : hacer los quehaceres⟩ ⟨to do
the right thing : hacer lo correcto⟩ ⟨to
do someone a favor : hacerle un favor a
alguien⟩ **2** : dedicarse a, trabajar en
⟨what do you do (for a living)? : ¿a qué
te dedicas?⟩ **3** COMPLETE : hacer ⟨did
you do your homework? : ¿hiciste la tarea?⟩ **4** PREPARE : hacer, preparar (comida) **5** ARRANGE : arreglar, peinar (el
pelo) ⟨to do one's hair : peinarse⟩ ⟨to do
one's makeup/face : maquillarse⟩ **6** GO
: ir a (una velocidad) ⟨he was doing 90
(miles per hour) : iba a 90 millas por
hora⟩ **7** VISIT : visitar (un lugar) **8** : hacer ⟨the change will do you good : el
cambio te hará bien⟩ ⟨that color does
nothing for you : ese color no te queda
bien⟩ ⟨that song does nothing for me
: esa canción no me dice nada⟩ **9** CRE-
ATE, PRODUCE : hacer ⟨to do laundry : lavar la
ropa⟩ **10** WASH, CLEAN
: lavar, limpiar ⟨to do laundry : lavar la
ropa⟩ **11** DECORATE : pintar, decorar
12 to do in RUIN : estropear, arruinar **13
to do in** KILL : matar, liquidar *fam* **14 to
do in** TIRE, EXHAUST : agotar **15 to do
lunch/dinner (etc.)** : juntarse a almor-
zar/cenar (etc.) **16 to do over** : volver a
hacer **17 to do up** FASTEN : atar, abrochar **18 what is/are . . . doing . . .?**
(*expressing surprise or annoyance*) ⟨what
are you doing here? : ¿qué haces aquí?⟩
⟨what is my coat doing on the floor?
: ¿qué hace mi abrigo en el suelo?⟩ — *vi*
1 : hacer ⟨you did well : hiciste bien⟩ **2**
FARE : estar, ir, andar ⟨how are you
doing? : ¿cómo estás?, ¿cómo te va?⟩ **3**
SERVE : servir, ser suficiente, alcanzar
⟨this will do for now : esto servirá por el
momento⟩ **4 could do with** ⟨I could do
with a cup of coffee : un café no me
vendría mal⟩ **5 to do away with** ABOLISH
: abolir, suprimir **6 to do away with**
KILL : eliminar, matar **7 to do by** TREAT
: tratar ⟨he does well by her : él la trata
bien⟩ **8 to do well** : hacer bien en **9
to do without** MANAGE : arreglárselas
10 to do without something : pasar sin
algo, prescindir de algo **11 to have to do
with** : tener que ver con ⟨that has nothing to do with it : eso no tiene nada que
ver (con el asunto)⟩ ⟨I didn't have
anything to do with it : no tuve nada que
ver con eso⟩ **12 to want nothing to do
with** : hacerle la cruz a — *v aux* **1** (*used
in questions and negative statements*) ⟨do
you know her? : ¿la conoces?⟩ ⟨I don't
like that : a mí no me gusta eso⟩ ⟨I don't
know : no sé⟩ ⟨do not touch : no
tocar⟩ **2** (*used for emphasis*) ⟨I do hope
you'll come : espero que vengas⟩
3 (*used as a substitute verb to avoid*

repetition) ⟨do you speak English?—yes, I do : ¿habla inglés?—sí⟩ ⟨so do I : yo también⟩

do² ['do:] *n* : do *m* (en el canto)

docile ['dɑsəl] *adj* : dócil, sumiso

dock¹ ['dɑk] *vt* **1** CUT : cortar **2** : descontar dinero de (un sueldo) — *vi* ANCHOR, LAND : fondear, atracar

dock² *n* **1** PIER : atracadero *m* **2** WHARF : muelle *m* **3** : banquillo *m* de los acusados (en un tribunal)

dockworker ['dɑkˌwərkər] *n* : estibador *m*, -dora *f*

dockyard ['dɑkˌjɑrd] *n* : astillero *m*

doctor¹ *vt* **1** TREAT : tratar, curar **2** ALTER : adulterar, alterar, falsificar (un documento)

doctor² *n* **1** : doctor *m*, -tora *f* ⟨Doctor of Philosophy : doctor en filosofía⟩ **2** PHYSICIAN : médico *m*, -ca *f*; doctor *m*, -tora *f*

doctorate ['dɑktərət] *n* : doctorado *m*

doctrine ['dɑktrɪn] *n* : doctrina *f*

document¹ ['dɑkjuˌment] *vt* : documentar

document² ['dɑkjumənt] *n* : documento *m*

documentary¹ [ˌdɑkjuˈmentəri] *adj* : documental

documentary² *n, pl* **-ries** : documental *m*

documentation [ˌdɑkjumənˈteɪʃən] *n* : documentación *f*

dodge¹ ['dɑdʒ] *v* **dodged; dodging** *vt* : esquivar, eludir, evadir (impuestos) — *vi* : echarse a un lado

dodge² *n* **1** RUSE : truco *m*, treta *f*, artimaña *f* **2** EVASION : regate *m*, evasión *f*

doe ['do:] *n, pl* **does** *or* **doe** : gama *f*, cierva *f*

doer ['du:ər] *n* : hacedor *m*, -dora *f*

does → **do**

doesn't ['dʌzənt] *contraction of* **does not** → **do**

doff ['dɑf, 'dɔf] *vt* : quitarse ⟨to doff one's hat : quitarse el sombrero⟩

dog¹ ['dɔg, 'dɑg] *vt* **dogged; dogging** : seguir de cerca, perseguir, acosar ⟨to dog someone's footsteps : seguir los pasos de alguien⟩ ⟨dogged by bad luck : perseguido por la mala suerte⟩

dog² *n* **1** : perro *m*, -rra *f* **2** → **hot dog** **3** *offensive* : mujer *f* fea **4** sick as a dog : muy enfermo **5** to let sleeping dogs lie : no remover el avispero

dogcatcher ['dɔgˌkætʃər] *n* : perrero *m*, -ra *f*

dog–eared ['dɔgˌɪrd] *adj* : con las esquinas dobladas

dogged ['dɔgəd] *adj* : tenaz, terco, obstinado

doggy ['dɔgi] *n, pl* **doggies** : perrito *m*, -ta *f*

doghouse ['dɔgˌhaʊs] *n* : casita *f* de perro

dogma ['dɔgmə] *n* : dogma *m*

dogmatic [dɔgˈmætɪk] *adj* : dogmático

dogmatism ['dɔgməˌtɪzəm] *n* : dogmatismo *m*

dogwood ['dɔgˌwʊd] *n* : cornejo *m*

doily ['dɔɪli] *n, pl* **-lies** : pañito *m*

doings ['du:ɪŋz] *npl* : eventos *mpl*, actividades *fpl*

do–it–yourself *n* : bricolaje *m*

doldrums ['do:ldrəmz, 'dɑl-] *npl* **1** : zona *f* de las calmas ecuatoriales **2** to be in the doldrums : estar abatido (dícese de una persona), estar estancado (dícese de una empresa)

dole ['do:l] *n* **1** ALMS : distribución *f* a los necesitados, limosna *f* **2** : subsidios *mpl* de desempleo

doleful ['do:lfəl] *adj* : triste, lúgubre

dolefully ['do:lfəli] *adv* : con pesar, de manera triste

dole out *vt* **doled out; doling out** : repartir

doll ['dɑl, 'dɔl] *n* : muñeco *m*, -ca *f*

dollar ['dɑlər] *n* : dólar *m*

dolly ['dɑli] *n, pl* **-lies** **1** → **doll** **2** : plataforma *f* rodante

dolphin ['dɑlfən, 'dɔl-] *n* : delfín *m*

dolt ['do:lt] *n* : imbécil *mf*; tonto *m*, -ta *f*

domain [do'meɪn, də-] *n* **1** TERRITORY : dominio *m*, territorio *m* **2** FIELD : campo *m*, esfera *f*, ámbito *m* ⟨the domain of art : el ámbito de las artes⟩

dome ['do:m] *n* : cúpula *f*, bóveda *f*

domestic¹ [də'mestɪk] *adj* **1** HOUSEHOLD : doméstico, casero **2** : nacional, interno ⟨domestic policy : política interna⟩ **3** TAME : domesticado

domestic² *n* : empleado *m* doméstico, empleada *f* doméstica

domestically [də'mestɪkli] *adv* : domésticamente

domesticate [də'mestɪˌkeɪt] *vt* **-cated; -cating** : domesticar

domicile ['dɑməˌsaɪl, 'do:-; 'dɑməsɪl] *n* : domicilio *m*

dominance ['dɑmənənts] *n* : dominio *m*, dominación *f*

dominant ['dɑmənənt] *adj* : dominante

dominate ['dɑməˌneɪt] *v* **-nated; -nating** : dominar

domination [ˌdɑməˈneɪʃən] *n* : dominación *f*

domineer [ˌdɑməˈnɪr] *vt* : dominar sobre, avasallar, tiranizar

domineering [ˌdɑməˈnɪrɪŋ] *adj* : dominante

Dominican¹ [də'mɪnɪkən] *adj* **1** : dominicano **2** : dominico (en religión)

Dominican² *n* **1** : dominicano *m*, -na *f* **2** : dominico *m*, -ca *f* (en religión)

dominion [də'mɪnjən] *n* **1** POWER : dominio *m* **2** DOMAIN, TERRITORY : dominio *m*, territorio *m*

domino ['dɑməˌno:] *n, pl* **-noes** *or* **-nos** **1** : dominó *m* **2 dominoes** *npl* : dominó *m* (juego)

don ['dɑn] *vt* **donned; donning** : ponerse

donate ['do:ˌneɪt, do:'-] *vt* **-nated; -nating** : donar, hacer un donativo de

donation [do:'neɪʃən] *n* : donación *f*, donativo *m*

done¹ ['dʌn] → **do**

done² *adj* **1** FINISHED : terminado, acabado, concluido ⟨now I'm done : ya terminé⟩ **2** COOKED : cocinado

donkey ['dɑŋki, 'dʌŋ-] *n, pl* **-keys** : burro *m*, asno *m*

donor ['do:nər] *n* : donante *mf*; donador *m*, -dora *f*

don't ['do:nt] *contraction of* do not → do

donut → doughnut

doodle[1] ['du:dəl] *v* -dled; -dling : garabatear

doodle[2] *n* : garabato *m*

doom[1] ['du:m] *vt* : condenar ⟨to be doomed (to failure) : estar condenado al fracaso⟩

doom[2] *n* 1 JUDGMENT : sentencia *f*, condena *f* 2 DEATH : muerte *f* 3 FATE : destino *m* 4 RUIN : perdición *f*, ruina *f*

door ['dor] *n* 1 : puerta *f* ⟨there's someone at the door : llaman a la puerta⟩ ⟨to answer the door : abrir la puerta⟩ ⟨can you get the door for me? : ¿me abres/cierras la puerta?⟩ ⟨garage/refrigerator door : puerta del garaje/refrigerador⟩ 2 ENTRANCE : entrada *f*

doorbell ['dor,bɛl] *n* : timbre *m*

doorknob ['dor,nɑb] *n* : pomo *m*, perilla *f*

doorman ['dorman] *n, pl* -men [-mən, -,mɛn] : portero *m*

doormat ['dor,mæt] : felpudo *m*

doorstep ['dor,stɛp] *n* : umbral *m*

doorstop ['dor,stɑp] *n* : tope *m* de puerta

doorway ['dor,weɪ] *n* : entrada *f*, portal *m*

dope[1] ['do:p] *vt* doped; doping : drogar, narcotizar

dope[2] *n* 1 DRUG : droga *f*, estupefaciente *m*, narcótico *m* 2 IDIOT : idiota *mf*; tonto *m*, -ta *f* 3 INFORMATION : información *f*

dopey ['do:pi] *adj* 1 GROGGY : atontado, grogui *fam* 2 FOOLISH : tonto 3 DRUGGED : drogado

doping *n* : doping *m* (en deportes)

dormant ['dormənt] *adj* : inactivo, latente

dormer ['dormər] *n* : buhardilla *f*

dormitory ['dormə,tori] *n, pl* -ries : dormitorio *m*, residencia *f* de estudiantes

dormouse ['dor,maʊs] *n* : lirón *m*

dorsal ['dorsəl] *adj* : dorsal — **dorsally** *adv*

dory ['dori] *n, pl* -ries : bote *m* de fondo plano

dosage ['do:sɪʤ] *n* : dosis *f*

dose[1] ['do:s] *vt* dosed; dosing : medicinar

dose[2] *n* : dosis *f*

dossier ['dɑs,jeɪ, 'dɑs-] *n* : dossier *m*

dot[1] ['dɑt] *vt* dotted; dotting 1 : poner el punto sobre (una letra) 2 SCATTER : esparcir, salpicar

dot[2] *n* : punto *m* ⟨at six on the dot : a las seis en punto⟩ ⟨dots and dashes : puntos y rayas⟩

dot–com ['dɑt,kɑm] *n* : puntocom *f*

dote ['do:t] *vi* doted; doting : chochear

double[1] ['dʌbəl] *v* -bled; -bling *vt* 1 : doblar, duplicar (una cantidad), redoblar (esfuerzos) 2 FOLD : doblar, plegar 3 to double one's fist : apretar el puño — *vi* 1 : doblarse, duplicarse 2 to double over : retorcerse

double[2] *adj* : doble — **doubly** *adv*

double[3] *n* : doble *mf*

double–barreled *or* **double–barrelled** [,dʌbəl'bærəld] *adj* 1 : de dos cañones

(dícese de un arma de fuego) 2 TWO-FOLD : doble

double bass *n* : contrabajo *m*

double bed *n* : cama *f* de matrimonio

double–breasted [,dʌbəl'brɛstəd] *adj* : cruzado

double–check [,dʌbəl'tʃɛk] *vt* : verificar dos veces

double chin *n* : papada *f*

double–click [,dʌbəl'klɪk] *vi* : hacer doble clic

double–cross [,dʌbəl'krɔs] *vt* : traicionar

double–crosser [,dʌbəl'krɔsər] *n* : traidor *m*, -dora *f*

double entendre ['dʌbələn'tɑndrə] *n* : doble sentido *m*

double–glazed [,dʌbəl'gleɪzd] *n* : con doble acristalamiento

double–jointed [,dʌbəl'ʤɔintəd] *adj* : con articulaciones dobles

double–spaced [,dʌbəl'speɪst] *n* : a doble espacio

double–talk ['dʌbəl,tɔk] *n* : ambigüedades *fpl*, lenguaje *m* con doble sentido

doubt[1] ['daʊt] *vt* 1 QUESTION : dudar de, cuestionar 2 DISTRUST : desconfiar de 3 : dudar, creer poco probable ⟨I doubt it very much : lo dudo mucho⟩

doubt[2] *n* 1 UNCERTAINTY : duda *f*, incertidumbre *f* ⟨to cast/throw doubt on, to cast/throw/call into doubt, to raise doubts about : poner en duda/cuestión⟩ 2 DISTRUST : desconfianza *f* 3 SKEPTICISM : duda *f*, escepticismo *m* 4 beyond doubt : sin lugar a duda ⟨beyond any/all doubt : fuera de toda duda⟩ ⟨beyond a reasonable doubt : más allá de toda duda razonable⟩ 5 in doubt : en duda ⟨if/when in doubt : en/ante la duda⟩ ⟨the outcome remains in doubt : aún no se conoce el resultado⟩ 6 no doubt DOUBTLESS : sin duda ⟨there's no doubt about it : no hay/cabe duda⟩ 7 without (a) doubt : sin duda ⟨without a shadow of a doubt : sin el menor asomo de duda⟩

doubtful ['daʊtfəl] *adj* 1 QUESTIONABLE : dudoso 2 UNCERTAIN : dudoso, incierto

doubtfully ['daʊtfəli] *adv* : dudosamente, sin estar convencido

doubtless ['daʊtləs] *or* **doubtlessly** *adv* : sin duda

douche[1] ['du:ʃ] *vt* douched; douching : irrigar

douche[2] *n* : ducha *f*, irrigación *f*

dough ['do:] *n* : masa *f*

doughnut *or* **donut** ['do:,nʌt] *n* : rosquilla *f*, dona *f Mex*

doughty ['daʊti] *adj* **doughtier; -est** : fuerte, valiente

doughy ['do:i] *adj* **doughier; -est** 1 : pastoso 2 PALE : pálido

dour ['daʊər, 'dʊr] *adj* 1 STERN : severo, adusto 2 SULLEN : hosco, taciturno — **dourly** *adv*

douse ['daʊs, 'daʊz] *vt* doused; dousing 1 DRENCH : empapar, mojar 2 EXTINGUISH : extinguir, apagar

dove[1] ['do:v] → dive

dove[2] ['dʌv] *n* : paloma *f*

dovetail ['dʌv,teɪl] *vi* : encajar, enlazar

dowdy ['daʊdi] *adj* **dowdier; -est** : sin gracia, poco elegante

dowel ['daʊəl] *n* : clavija *f*

down¹ ['daʊn] *vt* **1** FELL : tumbar, derribar, abatir **2** DEFEAT : derrotar

down² *adv* **1** DOWNWARD : hacia abajo ⟨to bend down : agacharse⟩ ⟨to fall down : caer, caerse⟩ ⟨to look down : mirar (hacia) abajo⟩ ⟨she came down to say hello : bajó a saludarnos⟩ ⟨put it down on the table : ponlo en la mesa⟩ ⟨they knocked the wall down : tiraron abajo la pared⟩ **2** BELOW : abajo ⟨we keep it down in the basement : lo guardamos abajo en el sótano⟩ ⟨what's going on down there? : ¿qué pasa allí abajo?⟩ **3** LOWERED : bajado ⟨keep down! : ¡no te levantes!⟩ **4** : a, hacia ⟨he went down to the store : fue a la tienda⟩ ⟨come down and see us! : ¡ven a visitarnos!⟩ **5** : hacia el sur ⟨we went down to Florida : fuimos a Florida⟩ **6** AWAY, OVER : hacia el fondo/lado (etc.) ⟨move down so I can sit : córrete un poco para que pueda sentarme⟩ **7** (*indicating reduction*) ⟨she turned the volume down : bajó el volumen⟩ **8** THOROUGHLY : bien, completamente ⟨to hose down : lavar (con manguera)⟩ **9** (*indicating restriction of motion*) ⟨tie it down : átalo⟩ **10** (*indicating following to a place or source*) ⟨were you able to track her down? : ¿pudiste localizarla?⟩ ⟨they couldn't pin down the cause : no pudieron averiguar la causa⟩ **11** (*indicating lesser importance in a series, etc.*) ⟨it's pretty far/low down on my list : no es muy importante para mí⟩ **12** : en el estómago ⟨to keep food down : retener comida⟩ **13 down to** INCLUDING : hasta ⟨down to the last detail : hasta el último detalle⟩ **14 down with . . .!** : abajo . . .! ⟨down with racism! : ¡abajo el racismo!⟩ **15 to hand/pass down** : transmitir (cuentos, etc.), pasar ⟨it was handed down to me by my grandmother : lo heredé de mi abuela⟩ **16 to lie down** : acostarse, echarse **17 to put down** ⟨to put down money, to put down a deposit : pagar un depósito⟩ **18 to sit down** : sentarse **19 to take/write down** : apuntar, anotar

down³ *adj* **1** DESCENDING : de bajada ⟨the down elevator : el ascensor de bajada⟩ **2** : abajo ⟨it's down on the bottom shelf : está en el estante de abajo⟩ ⟨it's further down : está más abajo⟩ ⟨I'm down here : estoy aquí abajo⟩ **3** LOWERED : bajado **4** REDUCED : reducido, rebajado ⟨attendance is down : la concurrencia ha disminuido⟩ ⟨to keep prices down : mantener los precios bajos⟩ **5** DOWNCAST : abatido, deprimido ⟨to feel down : andar deprimido⟩ **6** INOPERATIVE : inoperante ⟨the system is down : el sistema no funciona⟩ **7** BEHIND : perdiendo ⟨they're down (by) ten points : van perdiendo por diez puntos⟩ **8** COMPLETED : hecho, acabado ⟨two down, one to go : dos menos, falta uno⟩

down⁴ *n* **1** : plumón *m* **2 ups and downs** : altibajos *mpl*

down⁵ *prep* **1** : (hacia) abajo ⟨down the mountain : montaña abajo⟩ ⟨I walked down the stairs : bajé por la escalera⟩ **2** ALONG : por, a lo largo de ⟨we ran down the beach : corrimos por la playa⟩ **3** : a través de ⟨down the years : a través de los años⟩

down–and–out *adj* : indigente

downcast ['daʊn,kæst] *adj* **1** SAD : triste, abatido **2 with downcast eyes** : con los ojos bajos, con los ojos mirando al suelo

downfall ['daʊn,fɔl] *n* : ruina *f*, perdición *f*

downgrade¹ ['daʊn,greɪd] *vt* **-graded; -grading** : bajar de categoría

downgrade² *n* : bajada *f*

downhearted ['daʊn'hɑrtəd] *adj* : desanimado, descorazonado

downhill ['daʊn'hɪl] *adv & adj* : cuesta abajo

download¹ ['daʊn,loːd] *vt* : descargar, bajar (en informática)

download² *n* : descarga *f* (de archivos, etc.)

downloadable *adj* : descargable

down payment *n* : entrega *f* inicial

downplay ['daʊn,pleɪ] *vt* : minimizar

downpour ['daʊn,por] *n* : aguacero *m*, chaparrón *m*

downright¹ ['daʊn,raɪt] *adv* THOROUGHLY : absolutamente, completamente

downright² *adj* : patente, manifiesto, absoluto ⟨a downright refusal : un rechazo categórico⟩

downside ['daʊn,saɪd] *n* : desventaja *f*

downsize ['daʊn,saɪz] *vt* **-sized -sizing** : recortar, reducir

downstairs¹ ['daʊn'stærz] *adv* : abajo

downstairs² ['daʊn'stærz] *adj* : del piso de abajo

downstairs³ ['daʊn'stærz, -,stærz] *n* : planta *f* baja

downstream ['daʊn'striːm] *adv* : río abajo

Down syndrome *or* **Down's syndrome** *n* : síndrome *m* de Down

down–to–earth [,daʊntu'ərth] *adj* : práctico, realista

downtown¹ [,daʊn'taʊn] *adv* : hacia el centro, al centro, en el centro (de la ciudad)

downtown² *adj* : del centro (de la ciudad) ⟨downtown Chicago : el centro de Chicago⟩

downtown³ [,daʊn'taʊn, 'daʊn,taʊn] *n* : centro *m* (de la ciudad)

downtrodden ['daʊn,trɑdən] *adj* : oprimido

downward ['daʊnwərd] *or* **downwards** [-wərdz] *adv & adj* : hacia abajo

downwind ['daʊn'wɪnd] *adv & adj* : en la dirección del viento

downy ['daʊni] *adj* **downier; -est 1** : cubierto de plumón, plumoso **2** VELVETY : aterciopelado, velloso

dowry ['daʊri] *n, pl* **-ries** : dote *f*

doze¹ ['doːz] *vi* **dozed; dozing** : dormitar

doze² *n* : sueño *m* ligero, cabezada *f*

dozen ['dʌzən] *n, pl* **dozens** *or* **dozen** : docena *f* ⟨a dozen eggs : una docena de

huevos〉 〈ten dozen : diez docenas〉
〈dozens (and dozens) : decenas, monto-
nes〉

drab ['dræb] *adj* **drabber; drabbest** 1
BROWNISH : pardo 2 DULL, LACKLUS-
TER : monótono, gris, deslustrado

draft¹ ['dræft, 'drɑft] *vt* 1 CONSCRIPT : reclutar 2 COMPOSE, SKETCH : hacer un
borrador de, redactar

draft² *adj* 1 : de barril 〈draft beer : cerveza de barril〉 2 : de tiro 〈draft horses
: caballos de tiro〉

draft³ *n* 1 HAULAGE : tiro *m* 2 DRINK,
GULP : trago *m* 3 OUTLINE, SKETCH
: bosquejo *m*, borrador *m*, versión *f* 4
: corriente *f* de aire, chiflón *m*, tiro *m*
(de una chimenea) 5 CONSCRIPTION
: conscripción *f* 6 bank draft : giro *m*
bancario, letra *f* de cambio

draftee [dræf'ti:] *n* : recluta *mf*

draftsman ['dræftsmən] *n, pl* **-men**
[-mən, -ˌmɛn] : dibujante *m*

draftswoman ['dræfts,wʊmən] *n, pl*
-women [-ˌwɪmən] : dibujante *f*

drafty ['dræfti] *adj* **draftier; -est** : con co-
rrientes de aire

drag¹ ['dræg] *v* **dragged; dragging** *vt* 1
HAUL, TRAIL : arrastrar 〈I could barely
drag myself out of bed : me costó levan-
tarme de la cama〉 2 DREDGE : dragar 3
INVOLVE : meter, involucrar 〈don't drag
me into this : no me metas en esto〉 4 to
drag one's feet/heels : dar largas a algo
〈they're still dragging their feet (on the
issue) : siguen dando largas al asunto〉 5
to drag out PROLONG : alargar, dilatar —
vi 1 TRAIL : arrastrarse 2 LAG : rezagarse 3 : hacerse pesado/largo 〈the day
dragged on : el día se hizo largo〉

drag² *n* 1 RESISTANCE : resistencia *f*
(aerodinámica) 2 HINDRANCE : traba *f*,
estorbo *m* 3 BORE : pesadez *f*, plomo *m*
fam 4 : chupada *f* (de un cigarrillo)

dragnet ['dræg,nɛt] *n* 1 : red *f* barredera
(en pesca) 2 : operativo *m* policial de
captura

dragon ['drægən] *n* : dragón *m*

dragonfly ['drægən,flaɪ] *n, pl* **-flies** : libélula *f*

drain¹ ['dreɪn] *vt* 1 EMPTY : vaciar, drenar
2 EXHAUST : agotar, consumir — *vi* 1
: escurrir, escurrirse 〈the dishes are
draining : los platos están escurriéndose〉
2 EMPTY : desaguar 3 to **drain away**
: irse agotando

drain² *n* 1 : desagüe *m* 2 SEWER : alcantarilla *f* 3 GRATING : sumidero *m*, resumidero *m*, rejilla *f* 4 EXHAUSTION : agotamiento *m*, disminución *f* (de energía,
etc.) 〈to be a drain on : agotar, consu-
mir〉 5 to **throw down the drain** : tirar
por la ventana

drainage ['dreɪnɪdʒ] *n* : desagüe *m*, drenaje *m*

drainpipe ['dreɪn,paɪp] *n* : tubo *m* de
desagüe, caño *m*

drake ['dreɪk] *n* : pato *m* (macho)

drama ['drɑmə, 'dræ-] *n* 1 THEATER
: drama *m*, teatro *m* 2 PLAY : obra *f* de
teatro, drama *m*

dramatic [drə'mætɪk] *adj* : dramático —
dramatically [-tɪkli] *adv*

dramatist ['dræmətɪst, 'drɑ-] *n* : dramaturgo *m*, -ga *f*

dramatization [ˌdræmətə'zeɪʃən, ˌdrɑ-] *n*
: dramatización *f*

dramatize ['dræmə,taɪz, 'drɑ-] *vt* **-tized;
-tizing** : dramatizar

drank → drink

drape¹ ['dreɪp] *vt* **draped; draping** 1
COVER : cubrir (con tela) 2 HANG
: disponer los pliegues de

drape² *n* 1 HANG : caída *f* 2 **drapes** *npl*
: cortinas *fpl*

drapery ['dreɪpəri] *n, pl* **-eries** 1 CLOTH
: pañería *f*, tela *f* para cortinas 2 **drap-
eries** *npl* : cortinas *fpl*

drastic ['dræstɪk] *adj* 1 HARSH, SEVERE
: drástico, severo 2 EXTREME : radical,
excepcional — **drastically** [-tɪkli] *adv*

draught ['dræft, 'drɑft] *n* → **draft³**

draughty ['dræfti] → **drafty**

draw¹ ['drɔ] *v* **drew** ['dru:], **drawn**
['drɔn]; **drawing** *vt* 1 PULL : tirar de, jalar,
correr (cortinas) 2 ATTRACT : atraer 〈to
feel drawn to : sentirse atraído por〉 〈to
draw attention : llamar la atención〉
3 PROVOKE, ELICIT : provocar, suscitar
(críticas, etc.) 〈to draw cheers/applause
: arrancar vítores/aplausos〉 4 INHALE
: aspirar 〈to draw breath : respirar〉 5
EXTRACT : sacar (agua, sangre, etc.) 〈to
draw a gun : sacar una pistola〉 6 TAKE
: sacar 〈to draw a number : sacar un
número〉 7 WITHDRAW : retirar, sacar
(dinero) 〈he drew a hundred dollars
from his account : sacó cien dólares de
su cuenta〉 8 WRITE : hacer, extender
(un cheque) 9 COLLECT : cobrar, percibir
(un sueldo, etc.) 10 BEND : tensar (un
arco) 11 SKETCH : dibujar, trazar 〈to
draw a picture : dibujar algo, hacer un
dibujo〉 12 FORMULATE : sacar, formular,
llegar a 〈to draw a conclusion : llegar a
una conclusión〉 13 MAKE : hacer (una
distinción, una comparación) 14 to **draw
oneself up** : erguirse 15 to **draw out** : hacer hablar (sobre algo), hacer salir de sí
mismo 16 to **draw out** PROLONG : prolongar, alargar, extender 17 to **draw up**
DRAFT : redactar — *vi* 1 SKETCH : dibujar 2 TUG : tirar, jalar 3 to **draw away**
: alejarse 4 to **draw near** : acercarse 5 to
draw on/upon USE : hacer uso de (información, etc.) 6 to **draw to a close** : terminar, finalizar 7 to **draw up** STOP : parar

draw² *n* 1 DRAWING, RAFFLE : sorteo *m*
2 TIE : empate *m* 3 ATTRACTION : atracción *f* 4 PUFF : chupada *f* (de un cigarrillo, etc.)

drawback ['drɔ,bæk] *n* : desventaja *f*,
inconveniente *m*

drawbridge ['drɔ,brɪdʒ] *n* : puente *m* levadizo

drawer ['drɔr, 'drɔər] *n* 1 ILLUSTRATOR
: dibujante *mf* 2 : gaveta *f*, cajón *m* (en
un mueble) 3 **drawers** *npl* UNDERPANTS
: calzones *mpl*

drawing ['drɔɪŋ] *n* **1** LOTTERY : sorteo *m*, lotería *f* **2** SKETCH : dibujo *m*, bosquejo *m*

drawing room *n* : salón *m*

drawl¹ ['drɔl] *vi* : hablar arrastrando las palabras

drawl² *n* : habla *f* lenta y con vocales prolongadas

dread¹ ['dred] *vt* : tenerle pavor a, temer

dread² *adj* : pavoroso, aterrado

dread³ *n* : pavor *m*, temor *m*

dreadful ['dredfəl] *adj* **1** DREAD : pavoroso **2** TERRIBLE : espantoso, atroz, terrible — **dreadfully** *adv*

dream¹ ['dri:m] *v* **dreamed** ['drempt, 'dri:md] *or* **dreamt** ['drempt]; **dreaming** *vi* **1** ⟨to dream about : soñar con⟩ **2** FANTASIZE : fantasear — *vt* **1** : soñar **2** IMAGINE : imaginarse **3 to dream up** : inventar, idear

dream² *n* **1** : sueño *m*, ensueño *m* **2 bad dream** NIGHTMARE : pesadilla *f*

dreamer ['dri:mər] *n* : soñador *m*, -dora *f*

dreamlike ['dri:m,laɪk] *adj* : de ensueño

dreamy ['dri:mi] *adj* **dreamier; -est 1** DISTRACTED : soñador, distraído **2** DREAMLIKE : de ensueño **3** MARVELOUS : maravilloso

drearily ['drɪrəli] *adv* : sombríamente

dreary ['drɪri] *adj* **drearier; -est** : deprimente, lóbrego, sombrío

dredge¹ ['drɛdʒ] *vt* **dredged; dredging 1** DIG : dragar **2** COAT : espolvorear, enharinar

dredge² *n* : draga *f*

dredger ['drɛdʒər] *n* : draga *f*

dregs ['drɛgz] *npl* **1** LEES : posos *mpl*, heces *fpl* (de un líquido) **2** : heces *fpl*, escoria *f* ⟨the dregs of society : la escoria de la sociedad⟩

drench ['drɛntʃ] *vt* : empapar, mojar, calar

dress¹ ['drɛs] *vt* **1** CLOTHE : vestir ⟨she was dressed in red : iba (vestida) de rojo⟩ **2** DECORATE : decorar, adornar **3** : preparar (pollo o pescado), aliñar (ensalada) **4** : curar, vendar (una herida) **5** FERTILIZE : abonar (la tierra) **6 to dress down** SCOLD : regañar **7 to dress up** EMBELLISH : adornar, engalanar **8 to dress up** DISGUISE : disfrazar — *vi* **1** : vestirse ⟨to dress well/badly : vestir bien/mal⟩ **2 to dress down** : vestirse informalmente **3 to dress up** : ataviarse, engalanarse, ponerse de etiqueta **4 to dress up** : disfrazarse, vestirse ⟨we dressed up as ghosts : nos disfrazamos de fantasmas⟩

dress² *n* **1** APPAREL : indumentaria *f*, ropa *f* **2** : vestido *m*, traje *m* (de mujer)

dresser ['drɛsər] *n* : cómoda *f* con espejo

dressing ['drɛsɪŋ] *n* **1** : vestirse *m* **2** *or* **salad dressing** : aderezo *m*, aliño *m* **3** STUFFING : relleno *m* (de pollo, etc.) **4** : apósito *m*, vendaje *m*, gasa *f* (para una herida)

dressing gown *n* : bata *f*

dressing room *n* **1** FITTING ROOM : probador *m* **2** : camerino *m* (en un teatro)

dressing table *n* : tocador *m*

dressmaker ['drɛs,meɪkər] *n* : modista *mf*

dressmaking ['drɛs,meɪkɪŋ] *n* : costura *f*

dress rehearsal *n* : ensayo *m* general

dressy ['drɛsi] *adj* **dressier; -est** : de mucho vestir, elegante

drew → **draw**

dribble¹ ['drɪbəl] *vi* **-bled; -bling 1** DRIP : gotear **2** DROOL : babear **3** : driblar (en basquetbol)

dribble² *n* **1** TRICKLE : goteo *m*, hilo *m* **2** DROOL : baba *f* **3** : drible *m* (en basquetbol)

drier → **dry²**, **dryer**

driest *adj* → **dry²**

drift¹ ['drɪft] *vi* **1** : dejarse llevar por la corriente, ir a la deriva (dícese de un bote), ir sin rumbo (dícese de una persona) **2** ACCUMULATE : amontonarse, acumularse, apilarse

drift² *n* **1** DRIFTING : deriva *f* **2** HEAP, MASS : montón *m* (de arena, etc.), ventisquero *m* (de nieve) **3** MEANING : sentido *m*

drifter ['drɪftər] *n* : vagabundo *m*, -da *f*

driftwood ['drɪft,wʊd] *n* : madera *f* flotante

drill¹ ['drɪl] *vt* **1** BORE : perforar, taladrar **2** INSTRUCT : instruir por repetición — *vi* **1** TRAIN : entrenarse **2 to drill for oil** : perforar en busca de petróleo

drill² *n* **1** : taladro *m*, barrena *f* **2** EXERCISE, PRACTICE : ejercicio *m*, instrucción *f*

drily → **dryly**

drink¹ ['drɪŋk] *v* **drank** ['dræŋk]; **drunk** ['drʌŋk] *or* **drank; drinking** *vt* **1** IMBIBE : beber, tomar **2 to drink up** ABSORB : absorber — *vi* **1** : beber **2** : beber alcohol, tomar

drink² *n* **1** : bebida *f* ⟨food and drink : comida y bebida⟩ **2** : bebida *f* alcohólica ⟨to drive someone to drink : llevar a alguien a la bebida⟩

drinkable ['drɪŋkəbəl] *adj* : potable

drinker ['drɪŋkər] *n* : bebedor *m*, -dora *f*

drinking water *n* : agua *f* potable

drinking straw → **straw**

drip¹ ['drɪp] *vi* **dripped; dripping** : gotear, chorrear

drip² *n* **1** DROP : gota *f* **2** DRIPPING : goteo *m*

drip-dry ['drɪp,draɪ] *adj* : de lavar y poner

drippings *npl* : pringue *m*, jugo *m*

drive¹ ['draɪv] *v* **drove** ['dro:v]; **driven** ['drɪvən]; **driving** *vt* **1** : manejar, conducir (un vehículo) **2** : llevar (en un automóvil) ⟨she drove me home : me llevó a casa⟩ **3** IMPEL : llevar, impulsar, impeler ⟨to drive someone to do something : llevar a alguien a hacer algo⟩ **4** COMPEL : obligar, forzar **5** : arrear (ganado) **6** POWER : hacer funcionar **7** PROPEL : impeler, impulsar **8** : clavar, hincar ⟨to drive a stake into : clavar una estaca en⟩ **9** : hacer trabajar mucho, exigir mucho ⟨he drives himself too hard : se exige demasiado⟩ **10** : lanzar (una pelota) **11 to drive away/off/out** : ahuyentar, echar, expulsar **12 to drive back** REPEL : hacer retroceder **13 to drive crazy** : volver loco **14 to drive up/down**

: hacer subir/bajar (dícese de precios, etc.) — *vi* 1 : manejar, conducir ⟨do you know how to drive? : ¿sabes manejar?⟩ 2 : viajar (en auto) 3 **to drive at** : querer decir, insinuar 4 **to drive away/off** : alejarse (en un auto) ⟨they drove off : su auto se alejó⟩

drive² *n* 1 RIDE : viaje *m*, paseo *m* (en un automóvil) ⟨a two-hour drive : un viaje de dos horas⟩ 2 CAMPAIGN : campaña *f* ⟨fund-raising drive : campaña para recaudar fondos⟩ 3 DRIVEWAY : camino *m* de entrada, entrada *f* 4 TRANSMISSION : transmisión *f* ⟨front-wheel drive : tracción delantera⟩ 5 ENERGY : dinamismo *m*, energía *f* 6 INSTINCT, NEED : instinto *m*, necesidad *f* básica 7 AMBITION, INITIATIVE : empuje *m*, iniciativa *f* 8 : disparo *m* fuerte, tiro *m* fuerte (en deportes) 9 : ofensiva *f* (militar) 10 STREET : calle *f* ⟨she lives on Oak Drive : vive en la calle Oak⟩ 11 : marcha *f* ⟨to put a car in/into drive : poner en marcha un auto⟩ 12 : unidad *f* ⟨flash drive : unidad (de memoria) flash⟩

drive–in *n* : autocine *m*

drivel¹ ['drɪvəl] *n* : tontería *f*, estupidez *f*

driver ['draɪvər] *n* : conductor *m*, -tora *f*; chofer *m*

driveway ['draɪv,weɪ] *n* : camino *m* de entrada, entrada *f* (para coches)

driving ['draɪvɪŋ] *adj* : torrencial (dícese de la lluvia), que azota (dícese del viento) ⟨the driving force behind the reform : el principal impulsor de la reforma⟩

drizzle¹ ['drɪzəl] *vi* -zled; -zling : lloviznar, garuar

drizzle² *n* : llovizna *f*, garúa *f*

droll ['droːl] *adj* : cómico, gracioso, chistoso — **drolly** *adv*

dromedary ['drɑmə,deri] *n*, *pl* -daries : dromedario *m*

drone¹ ['droːn] *vi* **droned; droning** 1 BUZZ : zumbar 2 MURMUR : hablar con monotonía, murmurar

drone² *n* 1 : zángano *m* (abeja) 2 BUZZ, HUM : zumbido *m*, murmullo *m*

drool¹ ['druːl] *vi* : babear

drool² *n* : baba *f*

droop¹ ['druːp] *vi* 1 HANG : inclinarse (dícese de la cabeza), encorvarse (dícese de los escombros), marchitarse (dícese de las flores) 2 FLAG : decaer, flaquear ⟨his spirits drooped : se desanimó⟩

droop² *n* : inclinación *f*, caída *f*

drop¹ ['drɑp] *v* **dropped; dropping** *vt* 1 : dejar caer, soltar ⟨she dropped the glass : se le cayó el vaso⟩ 2 SEND : mandar ⟨drop me a line : mándame unas líneas⟩ 3 ABANDON : abandonar, dejar ⟨to drop the subject : cambiar de tema⟩ 4 LOWER : bajar ⟨he dropped his voice : bajó la voz⟩ 5 OMIT : omitir 6 REDUCE : reducir, rebajar (precios, etc.) 7 *fam* : perder (peso) 8 *fam* SPEND : gastar 9 : dejar caer (una noticia, etc.) ⟨to drop a hint : lanzar una indirecta⟩ 10 **to drop off** : dejar ⟨I dropped her off at the store : la dejé en la tienda⟩ — *vi* 1 DRIP : gotear 2

FALL : caer(se) ⟨to drop to the ground : caer al suelo⟩ ⟨to drop out of sight : perderse de vista⟩ 3 *or* **to drop off** DECREASE, DESCEND : bajar, descender ⟨the wind dropped in : amainó el viento⟩ 4 **to drop back/behind** : rezagarse, quedarse atrás 5 **to drop by/in** : pasar ⟨he dropped by for a visit : pasó a visitarnos⟩ 6 **to drop off** : quedarse dormido 7 **to drop out (of something)** : abandonar algo ⟨he dropped out (of school) : abandonó los estudios⟩

drop² *n* 1 : gota *f* (de líquido) 2 DECLINE : caída *f*, bajada *f*, descenso *m* 3 INCLINE : caída *f*, pendiente *f* ⟨a 20-foot drop : una caída de 20 pies⟩ 4 SWEET : pastilla *f*, dulce *m* 5 **drops** *npl* : gotas *fpl* (de medicina)

droplet ['drɑplət] *n* : gotita *f*

dropper ['drɑpər] *n* : gotero *m*, cuentagotas *m*

dross ['drɑs, 'drɔs] *n* : escoria *f*

drought ['draʊt] *n* : sequía *f*

drove¹ → **drive**

drove² ['droːv] *n* : multitud *f*, gentío *m*, manada *f* (de ganado) ⟨in droves : en manada⟩

drown ['draʊn] *vt* 1 : ahogar 2 INUNDATE : anegar, inundar 3 **to drown out** : ahogar — *vi* : ahogarse

drowse¹ ['draʊz] *vi* **drowsed; drowsing** DOZE : dormitar

drowse² *n* : sueño *m* ligero, cabezada *f*

drowsiness ['draʊzinəs] *n* : somnolencia *f*, adormecimiento *m*

drowsy ['draʊzi] *adj* **drowsier; -est** : somnoliento, soñoliento

drub ['drʌb] *vt* **drubbed; drubbing** 1 BEAT, THRASH : golpear, apalear 2 DEFEAT : derrotar por completo

drudge¹ ['drʌdʒ] *vi* **drudged; drudging** : trabajar como esclavo, trabajar duro

drudge² *n* : esclavo *m*, -va *f* del trabajo

drudgery ['drʌdʒəri] *n*, *pl* -eries : trabajo *m* pesado

drug¹ ['drʌg] *vt* **drugged; drugging** : drogar, narcotizar

drug² *n* 1 MEDICATION : droga *f*, medicina *f*, medicamento *m* 2 NARCOTIC : narcótico *m*, estupefaciente *m*, droga *f*

drug addict → **addict**

druggist ['drʌgɪst] *n* : farmacéutico *m*, -ca *f*

drug pusher → **pusher**

drugstore ['drʌg,stor] *n* : farmacia *f*, botica *f*, droguería *f*

drum¹ ['drʌm] *v* **drummed; drumming** *vt* 1 : meter a fuerza ⟨he drummed it into my head : me lo metió en la cabeza a fuerza⟩ 2 **to drum up** : conseguir, obtener (apoyo, etc.) — *vi* : tocar el tambor

drum² *n* 1 : tambor *m* 2 : bidón *m* ⟨oil drum : bidón de petróleo⟩

drummer ['drʌmər] *n* : baterista *mf*

drumstick ['drʌm,stɪk] *n* 1 : palillo *m* (de tambor), baqueta *f* 2 : muslo *m* de pollo

drunk¹ *pp* → **drink¹**

drunk² ['drʌŋk] *adj* : borracho, embriagado, ebrio

drunk³ *n* : borracho *m*, -cha *f*

drunkard ['drʌŋkərd] n : borracho m, -cha f

drunken ['drʌŋkən] adj : borracho, ebrio ⟨drunken driver : conductor ebrio⟩ ⟨drunken brawl : pleito de borrachos⟩

drunkenly ['drʌŋkənli] adv : como un borracho

drunkenness ['drʌŋkənnəs] n : borrachera f, embriaguez f, ebriedad f

dry[1] ['draɪ] v **dried; drying** vt : secar ⟨to dry the dishes : secar los platos⟩ ⟨to dry one's eyes : secarse las lágrimas⟩ — vi 1 or **to dry out/up** : secarse **2 to dry up** RUN OUT : agotarse

dry[2] adj **drier; driest 1** : seco ⟨the well went dry : el pozo se secó⟩ ⟨to have a dry mouth : tener la boca seca⟩ ⟨there was not a dry eye in the house : no hubo quien no llorara⟩ **2** THIRSTY : sediento **3** : donde la venta de bebidas alcohólicas está prohibida ⟨a dry county : un condado seco⟩ **4** : seco, sin alcohol ⟨a dry party : una fiesta seca⟩ **5** DULL : aburrido, árido ⟨a dry class : una clase aburrida⟩ **6** : sutil e irónico (dícese de un sentido de humor)

dry–clean ['draɪ,kli:n] v : limpiar en seco

dry cleaner n : tintorería f (servicio) ⟨the dry cleaner/cleaner's/cleaners : la tintorería⟩

dry cleaning n : limpieza f en seco

dryer ['draɪər] n 1 or **hair dryer** : secador m, secadora f Mex **2** or **clothes dryer** : secadora f

dry goods npl : artículos mpl de confección

dry ice n : hielo m seco

dryly ['draɪli] adv : secamente

dryness ['draɪnəs] n : sequedad f, aridez f

dual ['du:əl, 'dju:-] adj : doble

dualism ['du:ə,lɪzəm] n : dualismo m

duality [du:'æləti] n, pl **-ties** : dualidad f

dub ['dʌb] vt **dubbed; dubbing 1** CALL : apodar **2** : doblar (una película), mezclar (una grabación)

dubious ['du:biəs, 'dju:-] adj **1** UNCERTAIN : dudoso, indeciso **2** QUESTIONABLE : sospechoso, dudoso, discutible

dubiously ['du:biəsli, 'dju:-] adv **1** UNCERTAINLY : dudosamente, con desconfianza **2** SUSPICIOUSLY : de modo sospechoso, con recelo

duchess ['dʌtʃəs] n : duquesa f

duck[1] ['dʌk] vt **1** LOWER : agachar, bajar (la cabeza) **2** PLUNGE : zambullir **3** EVADE : eludir, evadir — vi **to duck down** : agacharse

duck[2] n, pl **duck** or **ducks** : pato m, -ta f

duckling ['dʌklɪŋ] n : patito m, -ta f

duct ['dʌkt] n : conducto m

dud[1] ['dʌd] adj : que fracasa, que no funciona ⟨a dud movie : un fracaso de taquilla⟩ ⟨a dud grenade : una granada que no estalla⟩

dud[2] n **1** : fracaso m ⟨a box-office dud : un fracaso de taquilla⟩ **2** : cosa f que no funciona ⟨this match is a dud : este fósforo no prende⟩ **3 duds** npl fam : trapos mpl fam, ropa f

dude ['du:d, 'dju:d] n GUY : tipo m

due[1] ['du:, 'dju:] adv : justo a, derecho hacia ⟨due north : derecho hacia el norte⟩

due[2] adj **1** PAYABLE : pagadero, sin pagar ⟨the rent is due : hay que pagar el alquiler⟩ **2** APPROPRIATE : debido, apropiado ⟨after due consideration : con las debidas consideraciones⟩ ⟨with all due respect : con el debido respeto⟩ **3** EXPECTED : esperado ⟨the train is due soon : esperamos el tren muy pronto, el tren debe llegar pronto⟩ ⟨the movie is due out in April : la película sale en abril⟩ **4** due to : debido a, por

due to : debido a, por

due[3] n **1 to give someone his (her) due** : darle a alguien su merecido **2 dues** npl : cuota f

duel[1] ['du:əl, 'dju:-] vi : batirse en duelo

duel[2] n : duelo m

duet [du'ɛt, dju-] n : dúo m

due to prep : debido a

duffel bag or **duffle bag** n : bolso m (deportivo)

duffle coat or **duffel coat** n : chaqueta f de lana (con capucha), trenca f Spain

dug → **dig**

dugout ['dʌg,aut] n **1** CANOE : piragua f **2** SHELTER : refugio m subterráneo

duke ['du:k, 'dju:k] n : duque m

dull[1] ['dʌl] vt **1** DIM : opacar, quitarle el brillo a, deslustrar **2** BLUNT : desafilar (un filo), despuntar (un lápiz, etc.) **3** BLUNT : entorpecer (los sentidos), embotar (la mente), aliviar (el dolor), amortiguar (sonidos)

dull[2] adj **1** STUPID : torpe, lerdo, lento **2** BLUNT : desafilado, despuntado **3** LACKLUSTER : sin brillo, deslustrado **4** BORING : aburrido, soso, pesado — **dully** adv

dullness ['dʌlnəs] n **1** STUPIDITY : estupidez f **2** MONOTONY : monotonía f, lo aburrido **3** : falta f de brillo **4** BLUNTNESS : falta f de filo

duly ['du:li, 'dju:-] adv PROPERLY : debidamente, a su debido tiempo

dumb ['dʌm] adj **1** often offensive MUTE : mudo **2** STUPID : estúpido, tonto, bobo — **dumbly** adv

dumbbell ['dʌm,bɛl] n **1** WEIGHT : pesa f **2** : estúpido m, -da f

dumbfound or **dumfound** [,dʌm'faund] vt : dejar atónito, dejar sin habla

dummy[1] ['dʌmi] adj : falso, de imitación, artificial

dummy[2] n, pl **-mies 1** SHAM : imitación f, sustituto m **2** PUPPET : muñeco m **3** MANNEQUIN : maniquí m **4** IDIOT : tonto m, -ta f; idiota mf

dump[1] ['dʌmp] vt : descargar, verter

dump[2] n **1** : vertedero m, basural m, basurero m, botadero m, tiradero m Mex **2** down in the dumps : triste, deprimido

dumpling ['dʌmplɪŋ] n : bola f de masa hervida

Dumpster trademark se usa para un contenedor de basura

dumpy ['dʌmpi] adj **dumpier; -est** : rechoncho, regordete

dun[1] ['dʌn] vt **dunned; dunning** : apremiar (a un deudor)

dun[2] adj : pardo (color)

dunce ['dʌnts] *n* : estúpido *m*, -da *f*; burro *m*, -rra *f fam*

dune ['du:n, 'dju:n] *n* : duna *f* (de arena)

dung ['dʌŋ] *n* **1** FECES : excrementos *mpl* **2** MANURE : estiércol *m*

dungarees [ˌdʌŋgə'ri:z] *n* **1** → jeans **2** → overalls

dungeon ['dʌndʒən] *n* : mazmorra *f*, calabozo *m*

dunk ['dʌŋk] *vt* : mojar, ensopar

duo ['du:o:, 'dju:-] *n, pl* **duos** : dúo *m*, par *m*

dupe¹ ['du:p, 'dju:-] *vt* **duped; duping** : engañar, embaucar

dupe² *n* : inocentón *m*, -tona *f*; simple *mf*

duplex¹ ['du:ˌplɛks, 'dju:-] *adj* : doble

duplex² *n* : casa *f* de dos viviendas, dúplex *m*

duplicate¹ ['du:plɪˌkeɪt, 'dju:-] *vt* **-cated; -cating 1** COPY : duplicar, hacer copias de **2** REPEAT : repetir, reproducir

duplicate² ['du:plɪkət, 'dju:-] *adj* : duplicado ⟨a duplicate invoice : una factura por duplicado⟩

duplicate³ ['du:plɪkət, 'dju:-] *n* : duplicado *m*, copia *f*

duplication [ˌdu:plɪ'keɪʃən, ˌdju:-] *n* **1** DUPLICATING : duplicación *f*, repetición *f* (de esfuerzos) **2** DUPLICATE : copia *f*, duplicado *m*

duplicity [du'plɪsəti, ˌdju:-] *n, pl* **-ties** : duplicidad *f*

durability [ˌdurə'bɪləti, ˌdjur-] *n* : durabilidad *f* (de un producto), permanencia *f*

durable ['durəbəl, 'djur-] *adj* : duradero

duration [du'reɪʃən, dju-] *n* : duración *f*

duress [du'rɛs, dju-] *n* : coacción *f*

during ['durɪŋ, 'djur-] *prep* : durante

dusk ['dʌsk] *n* : anochecer *m*, crepúsculo *m*

dusky ['dʌski] *adj* **duskier; -est** : oscuro (dícese de los colores)

dust¹ ['dʌst] *vt* **1** : quitar el polvo de **2** SPRINKLE : espolvorear

dust² *n* : polvo *m*

dustcover ['dʌstˌkʌvər] *n* **1** : guardapolvo *m*, funda *f* **2** → dust jacket

duster ['dʌstər] *n* **1** *or* dust cloth : trapo *m* de polvo **2** HOUSECOAT : guardapolvo *m* **3** feather duster : plumero *m*

dust jacket *n* : sobrecubierta *f*

dustpan ['dʌstˌpæn] *n* : recogedor *m*

dusty ['dʌsti] *adj* **dustier; -est** : cubierto de polvo, polvoriento

Dutch¹ ['dʌtʃ] *adj* : holandés

Dutch² *n* **1** : holandés *m* (idioma) **2** the Dutch (*used with a plural verb*) : los holandeses

Dutchman ['dʌtʃmən] *n, pl* **-men** [-mən, -ˌmɛn] : holandés *m* (persona)

Dutch treat *n* : invitación o pago a escote

Dutchwoman ['dʌtʃˌwumən] *n, pl* **-women** [-ˌwɪmən] : holandesa *f* (persona)

dutiful ['du:tɪfəl, 'dju:-] *adj* : motivado por sus deberes, responsable

duty ['du:ti, 'dju:-] *n, pl* **-ties 1** OBLIGATION : deber *m*, obligación *f*, responsabilidad *f* **2** TAX : impuesto *m*, arancel *m*

duty–free [ˌdu:ti'fri:, ˌdju:-] *adj* : libre de impuestos

duvet [du'veɪ, 'du:ˌveɪ] *n* : edredón *m*, cobertor *m*

DVD [ˌdi:ˌvi:'di:] *n* : DVD *m* ⟨DVD player/recorder : reproductor/grabador de DVD⟩

dwarf¹ ['dwɔrf] *vt* **1** STUNT : arrestar el crecimiento de **2** : hacer parecer pequeño

dwarf² *n, pl* **dwarfs** ['dwɔrfs] *or* **dwarves** ['dwɔrvz] **1** : enano *m*, -na *f* (en cuentos) **2** *sometimes offensive* : enano *m*, -na *f*

dwell ['dwɛl] *vi* **dwelled** *or* **dwelt** ['dwɛlt]; **dwelling 1** RESIDE : residir, morar, vivir **2 to dwell on** : pensar demasiado en, insistir en

dweller ['dwɛlər] *n* : habitante *mf*

dwelling ['dwɛlɪŋ] *n* : morada *f*, vivienda *f*, residencia *f*

dwindle ['dwɪndəl] *vi* **-dled; -dling** : menguar, reducirse, disminuir

dye¹ ['daɪ] *vt* **dyed; dyeing** : teñir

dye² *n* : tintura *f*, tinte *m*

dying → die

dyke → dike

dynamic [daɪ'næmɪk] *adj* : dinámico

dynamics [daɪ'næmɪks] *npl* : dinámica *f*

dynamite¹ ['daɪnəˌmaɪt] *vt* **-mited; -miting** : dinamitar

dynamite² *n* : dinamita *f*

dynamo ['daɪnəˌmo:] *n, pl* **-mos** : dínamo *m*, generador *m* de electricidad

dynasty ['daɪnəsti, -ˌnæs-] *n, pl* **-ties** : dinastía *f*

dysentery ['dɪsənˌtɛri] *n, pl* **-teries** : disentería *f*

dysfunction [dɪs'fʌŋkʃən] *n* : disfunción *f* — **dysfunctional** [dɪs'fʌŋkʃənəl] *adj*

dyslexia [dɪs'lɛksiə] *n* : dislexia *f* — **dyslexic** [dɪs'lɛksɪk] *adj*

dystrophy ['dɪstrəfi] *n, pl* **-phies 1** : distrofia *f* **2** → muscular dystrophy

E

e ['i:] *n, pl* **e's** *or* **es** ['i:z] **1** : quinta letra del alfabeto inglés **2 E** : mi *m* ⟨E sharp/flat : mi sostenido/bemol⟩

e- *pref* : electrónico ⟨e-mail : email, correo electrónico⟩

each¹ ['i:tʃ] *adv* : cada uno ⟨they cost $10 each : cuestan $10 cada uno⟩

each² *adj* : cada ⟨each student : cada estudiante⟩ ⟨each and every one : todos sin excepción⟩

each³ *pron* **1** : cada uno, cada una ⟨each of us : cada uno de nosotros⟩ ⟨each of the cities : cada una de las ciudades⟩ **2 each other** : el uno al otro ⟨we are helping each other : nos ayudamos el uno al otro⟩ ⟨they all looked at each other : todos se miraron unos a otros⟩ ⟨they love each other : se quieren⟩

eager ['i:gər] *adj* **1** ENTHUSIASTIC : entusiasta, ávido, deseoso **2** ANXIOUS : ansioso, impaciente ⟨she's eager to meet you : está ansiosa de/por conocerte⟩ ⟨to be eager for change : tener deseos de cambio⟩

eagerly ['i:gərli] *adv* : con entusiasmo, ansiosamente

eagerness ['i:gərnəs] *n* : entusiasmo *m*, deseo *m*, impaciencia *f*

eagle ['i:gəl] *n* : águila *f*

ear ['ɪr] *n* **1** : oído *m*, oreja *f* ⟨inner ear : oído interno⟩ ⟨big ears : orejas grandes⟩ **2 ear of corn** : mazorca *f*, choclo *m* **3 to play by ear** : tocar de oído **4 to play it by ear** : improvisar

earache ['ɪr,eɪk] *n* : dolor *m* de oído(s)

eardrum ['ɪr,drʌm] *n* : tímpano *m*

earl ['ərl] *n* : conde *m*

earldom ['ərldəm] *n* : condado *m*

earliest ['ərlɪəst] *n* **at the earliest** ⟨it won't happen until next year at the earliest : lo más pronto que podría ocurrir sería el año que viene⟩

earliness ['ərlinəs] *n* : lo temprano

earlobe ['ɪr,lo:b] *n* : lóbulo *m* de la oreja, perilla *f* de la oreja

early¹ ['ərli] *adv* **earlier; -est 1** : temprano ⟨he arrived early : llegó temprano, llegó antes de la hora⟩ ⟨she bought the tickets a month early : compró las entradas con un mes de antelación⟩ **2** SOON : pronto ⟨why didn't you tell me earlier? : ¿por qué no me lo dijiste antes?⟩ ⟨as early as possible : lo más pronto posible, cuanto antes⟩ **3** (*long ago*) ⟨as early as the 1960's : ya en los años sesenta⟩ **4** *or* ~ **on** : al principio ⟨early (on) in his career : al principio de su carrera⟩

early² *adj* **earlier; -est 1** (*referring to a beginning*) : primero ⟨the early stages/ hours : las primeras etapas/horas⟩ ⟨the earliest example : el primer ejemplo⟩ ⟨in early May : a principios de mayo⟩ ⟨early in the morning : por la mañana temprano⟩ **2** (*referring to antiquity*) : primitivo, antiguo ⟨early man : el hombre primitivo⟩ ⟨early painting : la pintura antigua⟩ ⟨in earlier times : antiguamente, en épocas anteriores⟩ **3** (*referring to a designated time*) : temprano, antes de la hora, prematuro ⟨he was early : llegó temprano⟩ ⟨early fruit : frutas tempraneras⟩ ⟨an early death : una muerte prematura⟩ ⟨early retirement : jubilación anticipada⟩ ⟨an earlier version : una versión anterior⟩

earmark ['ɪr,mɑrk] *vt* : destinar ⟨funds earmarked for education : fondos destinados a la educación⟩

earn ['ərn] *vt* **1** : ganar ⟨to earn money : ganar dinero⟩ **2** DESERVE : ganarse

earner ['ərnər] *n or* **wage earner** : asalariado *m*, -da *f*

earnest¹ ['ərnəst] *adj* : serio, sincero

earnest² *n* **in** ~ : en serio, de verdad ⟨we began in earnest : empezamos de verdad⟩

earnestly ['ərnəstli] *adv* **1** SERIOUSLY : con seriedad, en serio **2** FERVENTLY : de todo corazón

earnestness ['ərnəstnəs] *n* : seriedad *f*, sinceridad *f*

earnings ['ərnɪŋz] *npl* : ingresos *mpl*, ganancias *fpl*, utilidades *fpl*

earphone ['ɪr,fo:n] *n* : audífono *m*, auricular *m*

earplug ['ɪr,plʌg] *n* : tapón *m* para el oído

earring ['ɪr,rɪŋ] *n* : zarcillo *m*, arete *m*, aro *m Arg, Chile, Uru*, pendiente *m Spain*

earshot ['ɪr,ʃɑt] *n* : alcance *m* del oído ⟨out of earshot : demasiado lejos para oír⟩

earth ['ərθ] *n* **1** LAND, SOIL : tierra *f*, suelo *m* **2 the Earth** : la Tierra **3 on** ~ : en el mundo ⟨what on earth . . .? : ¿qué demonios/diablos . . .?⟩

earthen ['ərθən, -ðən] *adj* : de tierra, de barro

earthenware ['ərθən,wær, -ðən-] *n* : loza *f*, vajilla *f* de barro

earthly ['ərθli] *adj* : terrenal, mundano

earthquake ['ərθ,kweɪk] *n* : terremoto *m*, sismo *m*

earthworm ['ərθ,wərm] *n* : lombriz *f* (de tierra)

earthy ['ərθi] *adj* **earthier; -est 1** : terroso ⟨earthy colors : colores terrosos⟩ **2** DOWN-TO-EARTH : realista, práctico, llano **3** COARSE, CRUDE : basto, grosero, tosco ⟨earthy jokes : chistes groseros⟩

earwax ['ɪr,wæks] *n* → **wax²**

earwig ['ɪr,wɪg] *n* : tijereta *f*

ease¹ ['i:z] *v* **eased; easing** *vt* **1** ALLEVIATE : aliviar, calmar ⟨it eased her mind : la tranquilizó⟩ **2** REDUCE : paliar (un problema), reducir (tensiones), aligerar (una carga) **3** LOOSEN, RELAX : aflojar (una cuerda), relajar (restricciones) **4** : mover con cuidado ⟨I eased myself into the chair : me senté con cuidado en la silla⟩ — *vi* **1** : moverse con cuidado **2 to ease off/up** : calmarse (dícese del dolor), amainar (dícese del viento) **3 to ease up on** : aflojar (una cuerda), moderarse con (la comida, etc.), no ser tan duro con (alguien)

ease² *n* **1** CALM, RELIEF : tranquilidad *f*, comodidad *f*, desahogo *m* **2** FACILITY : facilidad *f* ⟨with ease : con facilidad⟩ **3 at** ~ : relajado, cómodo ⟨to put someone at ease : tranquilizar a alguien⟩ ⟨at ease! : ¡descansen!⟩

easel ['i:zəl] *n* : caballete *m*

easily ['i:zəli] *adv* **1** : fácilmente, con facilidad **2** UNQUESTIONABLY : con mucho, de lejos

easiness ['i:zinəs] *n* : facilidad *f*, soltura *f*

east¹ ['i:st] *adv* : al este ⟨to travel east : viajar hacia el este⟩

east² *adj* : del este, oriental ⟨east winds : vientos del este⟩

east³ *n* **1** : este *m* **2 the East** : el Oriente

eastbound ['i:st,baʊnd] *adj* : que va hacia el este

Easter ['iːstər] n 1 : Pascua f (de Resurrección) 2 or **Easter Sunday** : Domingo m de Pascua, Domingo m de Resurrección

Easter egg n : huevo m de Pascua (pintado)

easterly ['iːstərli] adv & adj : del este

eastern ['iːstərn] adj 1 : Oriental, del Este ⟨Eastern Europe : Europa del Este⟩ 2 : oriental, este

Easterner ['iːstərnər] n : habitante mf del este

eastward ['iːstwərd] adv & adj : hacia el este

easy[1] ['iːzi] adj easier; -est 1 : fácil ⟨easy to use : fácil de usar⟩ ⟨it's easy to see why : es fácil ver por qué⟩ ⟨to make something easier : facilitar algo⟩ 2 COMFORTABLE : fácil, cómodo 3 RELAXED : relajado 4 to be easy on the eye(s): ser agradable a la vista

easy[2] adv easier; -est 1 to come easy : ser fácil de conseguir 2 to go easy on : no ser muy duro con (alguien), no pasarse con (algo) 3 to take it easy RELAX : relajarse 4 to take it easy CALM DOWN : tranquilizarse, calmarse

easy chair n : sillón m, butaca f

easygoing [ˌiːziˈgoːɪŋ] adj : tolerante, poco exigente

eat ['iːt] v ate ['eɪt], eaten ['iːtən]; eating vt 1 : comer ⟨eat it up! : ¡cómetelo!⟩ 2 CORRODE : corroer 3 or to eat up CONSUME : comerse (comida, ganancias), consumir (tiempo, recursos), gastar (combustible) — vi 1 : comer 2 to eat away at or to eat into : comerse, consumir, corroer 3 to eat out : comer fuera

eatable[1] ['iːtəbəl] adj : comestible, comible fam

eatable[2] n 1 : algo para comer 2 eatables npl : comestibles mpl, alimentos mpl

eater ['iːtər] n : persona f o animal m que come ⟨a big eater : un comelón⟩ ⟨meat/plant eaters : carnívoros/herbívoros⟩

eaves ['iːvz] npl : alero m

eavesdrop ['iːvzˌdrɑp] vi -dropped; -dropping : escuchar a escondidas ⟨he was eavesdropping on us : nos escuchaba a escondidas⟩

eavesdropper ['iːvzˌdrɑpər] n : persona f que escucha a escondidas

ebb[1] ['ɛb] vi 1 : bajar (dícese de la marea) 2 DECLINE : menguar, decaer, disminuir

ebb[2] n 1 : reflujo m (de la marea) 2 DECLINE : decadencia f, declive m, disminución f ⟨to be at a low ebb : tocar fondo⟩ 3 the ebb and flow : el flujo y reflujo

ebony[1] ['ɛbəni] adj 1 : de ébano 2 BLACK : de color negro, negro

ebony[2] n, pl -nies : ébano m

e-book ['iːˌbʊk] n : libro m electrónico, e-book m

ebullience [ɪˈbʊljənts, -ˈbʌl-] n : efervescencia f, vivacidad f

ebullient [ɪˈbʊljənt, -ˈbʌl-] adj : efervescente, vivaz

eccentric[1] [ɪkˈsɛntrɪk] adj 1 : excéntrico ⟨an eccentric wheel : una rueda excéntrica⟩ 2 ODD, SINGULAR : excéntrico, extraño, raro — **eccentrically** [-trɪkli] adv

eccentric[2] n : excéntrico m, -ca f

eccentricity [ˌɛkˌsɛnˈtrɪsəti] n, pl -ties : excentricidad f

ecclesiastic [ɪˌkliːziˈæstɪk] n : eclesiástico m, clérigo m

ecclesiastical [ɪˌkliːziˈæstɪkəl] or **ecclesiastic** adj : eclesiástico — **ecclesiastically** adv

echelon ['ɛʃəˌlɑn] n 1 : escalón m (de tropas o aviones) 2 LEVEL : nivel m, esfera f, estrato m

echo[1] ['ɛˌkoː] v echoed; echoing vi : hacer eco, resonar — vt : repetir, hacerse eco de

echo[2] n, pl echoes : eco m

éclair [eɪˈklær, i-] n : pastel m relleno de crema

eclectic [ɛˈklɛktɪk, ɪ-] adj : ecléctico

eclipse[1] [ɪˈklɪps] vt eclipsed; eclipsing : eclipsar

eclipse[2] n : eclipse m

eco- ['iko] pref : eco-, ecológico, ecológicamente

eco-friendly ['ikoˈfrɛndli] adj : ecológico

ecological [ˌiːkəˈlɑdʒɪkəl, ˌɛkə-] adj : ecológico — **ecologically** adv

ecologist [iˈkɑlədʒɪst, ɛ-] n : ecólogo m, -ga f

ecology [iˈkɑlədʒi, ɛ-] n, pl -gies : ecología f

e-commerce ['iːˌkɑmərs] n : comercio m electrónico

economic [ˌiːkəˈnɑmɪk, ˌɛkə-] adj : económico

economical [ˌiːkəˈnɑmɪkəl, ˌɛkə-] adj : económico — **economically** adv

economics [ˌiːkəˈnɑmɪks, ˌɛkə-] n 1 : economía f 2 the economics of : el aspecto m económico de

economist [iˈkɑnəmɪst] n : economista mf

economize [iˈkɑnəˌmaɪz] v -mized; -mizing : economizar, ahorrar ⟨to economize on something : economizar algo⟩

economy [iˈkɑnəmi] n, pl -mies 1 : economía f, sistema m económico 2 THRIFT : economía f, ahorro m

ecosystem ['iːkoˌsɪstəm] n : ecosistema m

ecotourism [ˌiːkoˈtʊrˌɪzəm] n : ecoturismo m

ecru ['ɛˌkruː, 'eɪ-] n : color m crudo

ecstasy ['ɛkstəsi] n, pl -sies 1 : éxtasis m 2 Ecstasy : éxtasis m (droga)

ecstatic [ɛkˈstætɪk, ɪk-] adj : extático ⟨to be ecstatic about : estar muy entusiasmado con⟩

ecstatically [ɛkˈstætɪkli, ɪk-] adv : con éxtasis, con gran entusiasmo

Ecuadoran [ˌɛkwəˈdorən] or **Ecuadorean** or **Ecuadorian** [-ˈdoriən] n, -na f — **Ecuadorean** or **Ecuadorian** adj

ecumenical [ˌɛkjuˈmɛnɪkəl] adj : ecuménico

eczema [ɪgˈziːmə, ˈɛgzəmə, ˈɛksə-] n : eczema m

eddy¹ [ˈɛdi] *vi* **eddied; eddying** : arremolinarse, formar remolinos

eddy² *n, pl* **-dies** : remolino *m*

edema [ɪˈdiːmə] *n* : edema *m*

Eden [ˈiːdən] *n* : Edén *m*

edge¹ [ˈɛdʒ] *v* **edged; edging** *vt* **1** BORDER : bordear, ribetear, orlar ⟨edged with lace : con borde de encaje⟩ **2** SHARPEN : afilar, aguzar **3** *or* **to edge one's way** : avanzar poco a poco **3** **to edge away/closer** : alejarse/acercarse poco a poco **4 to edge out** : derrotar por muy poco — *vi* ADVANCE : ir avanzando (poco a poco)

edge² *n* **1** : borde *m* (de una cama, etc.), filo *m* (de un cuchillo), margen *m* (de una página) **2** BORDER : borde *m*, orilla *f*, margen *f* ⟨at the water's edge : a la orilla del agua⟩ **3** ADVANTAGE : ventaja *f* **4 to be on edge** : tener los nervios de punta **5 to be on the edge of** : estar al borde (de la guerra, etc.)

edgewise [ˈɛdʒˌwaɪz] *adv* SIDEWAYS : de lado, de canto

edginess [ˈɛdʒinəs] *n* : tensión *f*, nerviosismo *m*

edging [ˈɛdʒiŋ] *n* : borde *m*

edgy [ˈɛdʒi] *adj* **edgier; -est** : tenso, nervioso

edible [ˈɛdəbəl] *adj* : comestible, comible *fam*

edict [ˈiːˌdɪkt] *n* : edicto *m*, mandato *m*, orden *f*

edification [ˌɛdəfəˈkeɪʃən] *n* : edificación *f*, instrucción *f*

edifice [ˈɛdəfɪs] *n* : edificio *m*

edify [ˈɛdəˌfaɪ] *vt* **-fied; -fying** : edificar

edit [ˈɛdɪt] *vt* **1** : editar (un texto, una película, etc.), corregir (un texto) **2** MANAGE : dirigir (un periódico, etc.) **3** *or* **edit out** DELETE : recortar, cortar

edition [ɪˈdɪʃən] *n* : edición *f*

editor [ˈɛdɪtər] *n* **1** : editor *m*, -tora *f* (de libros, artículos, etc.); redactor *m*, -tora *f* (de artículos) **2** : director *m*, -tora *f* (de un periódico, etc.) **3** : editor *m*, -tora *f* (de una película, etc.) **4** : editor *m* (software)

editorial¹ [ˌɛdɪˈtoriəl] *adj* **1** : de redacción **2** : editorial ⟨an editorial comment : un comentario editorial⟩

editorial² *n* : editorial *m*

editorship [ˈɛdətərˌʃɪp] *n* : dirección *f*

educate [ˈɛdʒəˌkeɪt] *vt* **-cated; -cating 1** TEACH : educar, enseñar **2** INSTRUCT : formar, educar, instruir **3** INFORM : informar, concientizar

educated [ˈɛdʒəˌkeɪtəd] *adj* : culto

education [ˌɛdʒəˈkeɪʃən] *n* : educación *f*

educational [ˌɛdʒəˈkeɪʃənəl] *adj* **1** : docente, de enseñanza ⟨an educational institution : una institución docente⟩ **2** PEDAGOGICAL : pedagógico **3** INSTRUCTIONAL : educativo, instructivo ⟨an educational film : una película educativa⟩

educator [ˈɛdʒəˌkeɪtər] *n* : educador *m*, -dora *f*

eel [ˈiːl] *n* : anguila *f*

eerie [ˈɪri] *adj* **eerier; -est 1** SPOOKY : que da miedo, espeluznante **2** GHOSTLY : fantasmagórico

eerily [ˈɪrəli] *adv* : de manera extraña y misteriosa

efface [ɪˈfeɪs, ɛ-] *vt* **-faced; -facing** : borrar

effect¹ [ɪˈfɛkt] *vt* **1** CARRY OUT : efectuar, llevar a cabo **2** ACHIEVE : lograr, realizar

effect² *n* **1** RESULT : efecto *m*, resultado *m*, consecuencia *f* ⟨to no effect : sin resultado⟩ ⟨to have an effect : producir/surtir efecto⟩ **2** MEANING : sentido *m* ⟨something to that effect : algo por el estilo⟩ **3** INFLUENCE : efecto *m*, influencia *f* **4 effects** *npl* : efectos *mpl* ⟨sound effects : efectos de sonido⟩ **5 effects** *npl* BELONGINGS : efectos *mpl*, pertenencias *fpl* **6 to come/go into effect** *or* **to take effect** : entrar en vigor **7 for ~** : para impresionar ⟨he paused for effect : hizo una pausa dramática⟩ **8 in ~** REALLY : en realidad, de hecho

effective [ɪˈfɛktɪv] *adj* **1** EFFECTUAL : efectivo, eficaz **2** OPERATIVE : vigente **3** REAL : efectivo

effectively [ɪˈfɛktɪvli] **1** : eficazmente, con eficacia **2** IN EFFECT : en realidad, de hecho

effectiveness [ɪˈfɛktɪvnəs] *n* : eficacia *f*, efectividad *f*

effectual [ɪˈfɛktʃuəl] *adj* : eficaz, efectivo — **effectually** *adv*

effeminate [əˈfɛmənət] *adj* : afeminado

effervesce [ˌɛfərˈvɛs] *vi* **-vesced; -vescing 1** : estar en efervescencia, burbujear (dícese de líquidos) **2** : estar eufórico, estar muy animado (dícese de las personas)

effervescence [ˌɛfərˈvɛsənts] *n* : efervescencia *f* — **effervescent** [ˌɛfərˈvɛsənt] *adj*

effete [ɛˈfiːt, ɪ-] *adj* **1** WORN-OUT : desgastado, agotado **2** DECADENT : decadente **3** EFFEMINATE : afeminado

efficacious [ˌɛfəˈkeɪʃəs] *adj* : eficaz, efectivo

efficacy [ˈɛfɪkəsi] *n, pl* **-cies** : eficacia *f*

efficiency [ɪˈfɪʃəntsi] *n, pl* **-cies 1** : eficiencia *f* **2** YIELD : rendimiento *m*

efficient [ɪˈfɪʃənt] *adj* **1** : eficiente **2** : de alto rendimiento (dícese de una máquina) — **efficiently** *adv*

effigy [ˈɛfədʒi] *n, pl* **-gies** : efigie *f*

effluent [ˈɛˌfluːənt, ɛˈfluː-] *n* : efluentes *mpl*

effort [ˈɛfərt] *n* **1** EXERTION : esfuerzo *m* **2** ATTEMPT : tentativa *f*, intento *m* ⟨it's not worth the effort : no vale la pena⟩ ⟨to make an/the effort to do something : hacer un/el esfuerzo para hacer algo⟩ ⟨to make no effort to do something : no molestarse en hacer algo⟩

effortless [ˈɛfərtləs] *adj* : sin esfuerzo, natural

effortlessly [ˈɛfərtləsli] *adv* : sin esfuerzo

effrontery [ɪˈfrʌntəri] *n, pl* **-teries** : insolencia *f*, desfachatez *f*, descaro *m*

effusive [ɛˈfjuːsɪv, ɪ-] *adj* : efusivo — **effusively** *adv*

effusiveness [ɪˈfjuːsɪvnəs, ɛ-] *n* : efusión *f*

EFL [ˌiː'ɛf'ɛl] n (English as a foreign language) : inglés m como lengua extranjera

egalitarian [ɪˌgælə'tæriən] adj : igualitario

egg¹ ['ɛg] vt **to egg on** : incitar, azuzar

egg² n **1** : huevo m ⟨egg white/yolk : clara/yema de huevo⟩ **2** OVUM : óvulo m

eggbeater ['ɛgˌbiːtər] n : batidor m (de huevos)

eggnog ['ɛgˌnɑg] n : ponche m de huevo, rompope m CA, Mex

eggplant ['ɛgˌplænt] n : berenjena f

eggshell ['ɛgˌʃɛl] n : cascarón m

ego ['iːˌgoː] n, pl **egos** **1** SELF-ESTEEM : amor m propio, ego m **2** SELF : ego m, yo m

egocentric [ˌiːgoʊ'sɛntrɪk] adj : egocéntrico

egoism ['iːgoʊˌwɪzəm] n : egoísmo m

egoist ['iːgoʊwɪst] n : egoísta mf

egoistic [ˌiːgoʊ'wɪstɪk] adj : egoísta

egotism ['iːgəˌtɪzəm] n : egotismo m

egotist ['iːgətɪst] n : egotista mf

egotistic [ˌiːgə'tɪstɪk] or **egotistical** [-'tɪstɪkəl] adj : egotista — **egotistically** adv

egregious [ɪ'griːdʒəs] adj : atroz, flagrante, mayúsculo — **egregiously** adv

egress ['iːˌgrɛs] n : salida f

egret ['iːgrət, -ˌgrɛt] n : garceta f

Egyptian [ɪ'dʒɪpʃən] n **1** : egipcio m, -cia f **2** : egipcio m (idioma) — **Egyptian** adj

eh ['eɪ, 'ɛ] interj **1** WHAT : ¿qué? **2** : ¿eh?, ¿no? ⟨pretty clever, eh? : qué listo, ¿no?⟩

eiderdown ['aɪdərˌdaʊn] n **1** : plumón m **2** COMFORTER : edredón m

eight¹ ['eɪt] adj : ocho ⟨she's eight (years old) : tiene ocho años⟩

eight² n : ocho m ⟨the eight of hearts : el ocho de corazones⟩

eight³ pron : ocho ⟨there are eight of us : somos ocho⟩ ⟨it's eight (o'clock) : son las ocho⟩

eighteen¹ [eɪt'tiːn] adj & pron : dieciocho

eighteen² n : dieciocho m

eighteenth¹ [eɪt'tiːnθ] adj : decimoctavo

eighteenth² n **1** : decimoctavo m, -va f (en una serie) **2** : dieciochoavo m, dieciochoava parte f

eighth¹ ['eɪtθ] adv : en octavo lugar

eighth² adj : octavo

eighth³ n **1** : octavo m, -va f (en una serie) ⟨(on) the eighth of May : el ocho de mayo⟩ **2** : octavo m, octava parte f

eight hundred¹ adj & pron : ochocientos

eight hundred² n : ochocientos m

eightieth¹ ['eɪtiəθ] adj : octogésimo

eightieth² n **1** : octogésimo m, -ma f (en una serie) **2** : ochentavo m, ochentava parte f

eighty¹ ['eɪti] adj & pron : ochenta

eighty² n, pl **eighties** **1** : ochenta m **2 the eighties** : los ochenta

either¹ ['iːðər, 'aɪ-] adv : tampoco ⟨she doesn't believe it and he doesn't, either : ella no lo cree y él tampoco⟩ ⟨me either! : ¡yo tampoco!⟩

either² adj **1** : cualquiera (de los dos) ⟨we can watch either movie : podemos ver cualquiera de las dos películas⟩ **2** : nin-

guno de los dos ⟨she wasn't in either room : no estaba en ninguna de las dos salas⟩ **3** EACH : cada ⟨on either side of : a cada lado de, a ambos lados de⟩

either³ pron **1** : cualquiera (de los dos) ⟨either of the answers is correct : cualquiera de las dos respuestas es correcta⟩ **2** : ninguno (de los dos) ⟨which of the two do you want? I don't like either : ¿cuál de las dos quieres? no me gusta ninguna⟩ **3** : ¿alguno ⟨is either of you interested? : ¿está alguno de ustedes (dos) interesado?⟩

either⁴ conj **1** : o, u ⟨either David or Daniel could go : puede ir o David o Daniel⟩ **2** : ni ⟨he didn't call either yesterday or today : no llamó ni ayer ni hoy⟩

ejaculate [ɪ'dʒækjəˌleɪt] v **-lated; -lating** vt **1** : eyacular **2** EXCLAIM : exclamar — vi : eyacular

ejaculation [ɪˌdʒækjə'leɪʃən] n **1** : eyaculación f (en fisiología) **2** EXCLAMATION : exclamación f

eject [ɪ'dʒɛkt] vt **1** : expulsar (a alguien) **2** : expulsar (un CD, etc.), expeler (un gas) — vi : expulsarse

ejection [ɪ'dʒɛkʃən] n : expulsión f

eke out ['iːk-] vt **eked out; eking out** **1** STRETCH : estirar (provisiones, etc.) **2 to eke out a living** : ganarse la vida a duras penas

EKG [ˌiːˌkeɪ'dʒiː] n, pl **EKGs** **1** → electrocardiogram **2** → electrocardiograph

elaborate¹ [ɪ'læbəˌreɪt] v **-rated; -rating** vt : elaborar (una teoría, etc.) — vi **to elaborate on** : ampliar, entrar en detalles sobre

elaborate² [ɪ'læbərət] adj **1** DETAILED : detallado, minucioso, muy elaborado **2** COMPLICATED : complicado, muy elaborado — **elaborately** adv

elaboration [ɪˌlæbə'reɪʃən] n : elaboración f

elapse [ɪ'læps] vi **elapsed; elapsing** : transcurrir, pasar

elastic¹ [ɪ'læstɪk] adj **1** : elástico **2** : (de) elástico, elastizado (dícese de cintura, etc.)

elastic² n **1** : elástico m **2 or elastic band** → rubber band

elasticity [ɪˌlæs'tɪsəti, ˌiːˌlæs-] n, pl **-ties** : elasticidad f

elated [ɪ'leɪtəd] adj : eufórico

elation [ɪ'leɪʃən] n : euforia f, júbilo m, alborozo m

elbow¹ ['ɛlˌboː] vt : darle un codazo a

elbow² n : codo m

elder¹ ['ɛldər] adj : mayor

elder² n **1** : anciano m, -na f ⟨the tribal elders : los ancianos de la tribu⟩ **2** : miembro m del consejo (en varias religiones) **3** : mayor mf ⟨she's my elder by one year : es un año mayor que yo⟩

elderberry ['ɛldərˌbɛri] n, pl **-berries** : baya f de saúco (fruta), saúco m (árbol)

elderly ['ɛldərli] adj : mayor, de edad, anciano ⟨the elderly : las personas mayores, los ancianos⟩

eldest ['ɛldəst] adj : mayor ⟨the eldest : el/la mayor, el/la de más edad⟩

elect[1] [i'lɛkt] *vt* **1** : elegir ⟨she was elected President : la eligieron Presidenta⟩ **2** : elegir (hacer algo)

elect[2] *adj* : electo ⟨the president-elect : el presidente electo⟩

elect[3] *npl* **the elect** : los elegidos *mpl*

election [i'lɛkʃən] *n* : elección *f* ⟨an election campaign : una campaña electoral⟩

elective[1] [i'lɛktɪv] *adj* **1** : electivo **2** OPTIONAL : facultativo, optativo

elective[2] *n* : asignatura *f* electiva

electoral [i'lɛktərəl] *adj* : electoral

electorate [i'lɛktərət] *n* : electorado *m*

electric [i'lɛktrɪk] *adj* **1** *or* **electrical** [-trɪkəl] : eléctrico **2** THRILLING : electrizante, emocionante

electric cord → **cord**

electrician [i,lɛk'trɪʃən] *n* : electricista *mf*

electricity [i,lɛk'trɪsəti] *n, pl* **-ties 1** : electricidad *f* **2** CURRENT : corriente *m* eléctrica

electric razor → **razor**

electric shock → **shock**[2]

electric socket → **socket**

electrification [i,lɛktrəfə'keɪʃən] *n* : electrificación *f*

electrify [i'lɛktrə,faɪ] *vt* **-fied; -fying 1** : electrificar **2** THRILL : electrizar, emocionar

electrocardiogram [i,lɛktro'kɑrdiə,græm] *n* : electrocardiograma *m*

electrocardiograph [i,lɛktro'kɑrdiə,græf] *n* : electrocardiógrafo *m*

electrocute [i'lɛktrə,kju:t] *vt* **-cuted; -cuting** : electrocutar

electrocution [i,lɛktrə'kju:ʃən] *n* : electrocución *f*

electrode [i'lɛk,tro:d] *n* : electrodo *m*

electrolysis [i,lɛk'trɑləsəs] *n* : electrólisis *f*

electrolyte [i'lɛktrə,laɪt] *n* : electrolito *m*

electromagnet [i,lɛktro'mægnət] *n* : electroimán *m*

electromagnetic [i,lɛktromæg'nɛtɪk] *adj* : electromagnético — **electromagnetically** [-tɪkli] *adv*

electromagnetism [i,lɛktro'mægnə,tɪzəm] *n* : electromagnetismo *m*

electron [i'lɛk,trɑn] *n* : electrón *m*

electronic [i,lɛk'trɑnɪk] *adj* : electrónico ⟨electronic devices : aparatos electrónicos⟩ — **electronically** [-nɪkli] *adv*

electronic mail *n* : correo *m* electrónico

electronics [i,lɛk'trɑnɪks] *n* **1** : electrónica *f* **2** : sistema *m* electrónico (de un aparato)

electroplate [i'lɛktrə,pleɪt] *vt* **-plated; -plating** : galvanizar mediante electrólisis

elegance ['ɛlɪgənts] *n* : elegancia *f*

elegant ['ɛlɪgənt] *adj* : elegante — **elegantly** *adv*

elegiac [,ɛlə'dʒaɪək] *adj* : elegíaco

elegy ['ɛlədʒi] *n, pl* **-gies** : elegía *f*

element ['ɛləmənt] *n* **1** COMPONENT : elemento *m*, factor *m* ⟨the element of surprise : el factor sorpresa⟩ ⟨an element of risk : un factor de riesgo⟩ **2** : elemento *m* (en la química) **3** MILIEU : elemento *m*, medio *m* ⟨to be in one's element : estar en su elemento⟩ **4** GROUP : elemento *m*, grupo *m* ⟨criminal elements : elementos criminales⟩ **5 elements** *npl* RUDIMENTS : elementos *mpl* (básicos), rudimentos *mpl* **6 the elements** WEATHER : los elementos *mpl* **7** *or* **heating element** : resistencia *f*

elemental [,ɛlə'mɛntəl] *adj* **1** BASIC : elemental, primario **2** : elemental (dícese de los elementos químicos)

elementary [,ɛlə'mɛntri] *adj* **1** SIMPLE : elemental **2** : de enseñanza primaria ⟨elementary (school) teachers : maestros de enseñanza primaria⟩ ⟨elementary school/education : escuela/educación primaria⟩

elephant ['ɛləfənt] *n* : elefante *m*, -ta *f*

elevate ['ɛlə,veɪt] *vt* **-vated; -vating 1** RAISE : elevar, levantar, alzar **2** PROMOTE : elevar, ascender **3** UPLIFT : elevar, levantar (el espíritu, etc.) **4** INCREASE : aumentar, elevar (niveles, etc.)

elevation [,ɛlə'veɪʃən] *n* **1** : elevación *f* **2** ALTITUDE : altura *f*, altitud *f* **3** PROMOTION : ascenso *m*

elevator ['ɛlə,veɪtər] *n* **1** : ascensor *m*, elevador *m* **2** *or* **freight elevator** : montacargas *m*

eleven[1] [ɪ'lɛvən] *adj & pron* : once

eleven[2] *n* : once *m*

eleventh[1] [ɪ'lɛvənθ] *adj* : undécimo

eleventh[2] *n* **1** : undécimo *m*, -ma *f* (en una serie) **2** : onceavo *m*, onceava parte *f*

elf ['ɛlf] *n, pl* **elves** ['ɛlvz] : elfo *m*, duende *m*

elfin ['ɛlfən] *adj* **1** : de elfo, menudo **2** ENCHANTING, MAGIC : mágico, encantador

elfish ['ɛlfɪʃ] *adj* **1** : de elfo **2** MISCHIEVOUS : travieso

elicit [ɪ'lɪsət] *vt* : provocar (una reacción), obtener (una respuesta)

eligibility [,ɛlədʒə'bɪləti] *n, pl* **-ties** : elegibilidad *f*

eligible ['ɛlədʒəbəl] *adj* **1** QUALIFIED : que reúne los requisitos, elegible ⟨to be eligible for benefits : tener derecho a recibir prestaciones⟩ ⟨eligible voters : votantes habilitados⟩ **2** SUITABLE : idóneo ⟨an eligible bachelor : un buen partido⟩

eliminate [ɪ'lɪmə,neɪt] *vt* **-nated; -nating 1** : eliminar **2** RULE OUT : eliminar, descartar

elimination [ɪ,lɪmə'neɪʃən] *n* : eliminación *f*

elite[1] [eɪ'li:t, i-] *n* : elite *f*, élite *f*

elite[2] *n* : de elite, de élite

elitist [eɪ'li:tɪst, i-] *n* : elitista *mf* — **elitist** *adj*

elixir [i'lɪksər] *n* : elixir *m*

elk ['ɛlk] *n* : alce *m* (de Europa), uapití *m* (de América)

ellipse [ɪ'lɪps, ɛ-] *n* : elipse *f*

ellipsis [ɪ'lɪpsəs, ɛ-] *n, pl* **-lipses** [-,si:z] **1** : elipsis *f* **2** : puntos *mpl* suspensivos (en la puntuación)

elliptical [ɪ'lɪptɪkəl, ɛ-] *or* **elliptic** [-tɪk] *adj* : elíptico

elm ['ɛlm] *n* : olmo *m*

elocution [,ɛlə'kju:ʃən] *n* : elocución *f*

elongate [i'lɔŋˌgeɪt] *vt* **-gated; -gating** : alargar

elongation [ˌiːˌlɔŋ'geɪʃən] *n* : alargamiento *m*

elope [i'loːp] *vi* **eloped; eloping** : fugarse

elopement [i'loːpmənt] *n* : fuga *f*

eloquence ['ɛləkwənts] *n* : elocuencia *f*

eloquent ['ɛləkwənt] *adj* : elocuente — **eloquently** *adv*

El Salvadoran [ˌɛlˌsælvə'dɔrən] *n* : salvadoreño *m*, -ña *f* — **El Salvadoran** *adj*

else¹ ['ɛls] *adv* **1** (*indicating an alternative or addition*) ⟨how else? : ¿de qué otro modo?⟩ ⟨when else? : ¿a qué otra hora?, ¿en qué otro día? (etc.)⟩ ⟨where else? : ¿en qué otro lugar?⟩ ⟨to go someplace else : ir a otro sitio⟩ **2 or else** OTHERWISE : de otro modo, de lo contrario

else² *adj* **1** OTHER : otro ⟨anyone else : cualquier otro⟩ ⟨someone else : otro, otra persona⟩ ⟨everyone else : todos los demás⟩ ⟨everything else : todo lo demás⟩ ⟨nobody else : ningún otro, nadie más⟩ ⟨somebody else : otra persona⟩ **2** MORE : más ⟨nothing else : nada más⟩ ⟨anything else? : ¿algo más?⟩ ⟨what else? : ¿qué más?⟩

elsewhere ['ɛlsˌʰwɛr] *adv* : en/a otra parte, en/a otro sitio/lugar ⟨to go elsewhere : ir a otro lugar⟩ ⟨elsewhere in the book : en otra parte del libro⟩

elucidate [i'luːsəˌdeɪt] *vt* **-dated; -dating** : dilucidar, elucidar, esclarecer

elucidation [iˌluːsə'deɪʃən] *n* : elucidación *f*, esclarecimiento *m*

elude [i'luːd] *vt* **eluded; eluding** : eludir, evadir

elusive [i'luːsɪv] *adj* **1** : esquivo, escurridizo (dícese de una presa, etc.) ⟨an elusive goal : una meta difícil de alcanzar⟩ **2** : difícil de precisar (dícese de una cualidad, etc.)

elusively [i'luːsɪvli] *adv* : de manera esquiva

elves → **elf**

em- → **en-**

'em [əm] → **them**

emaciate [i'meɪʃiˌeɪt] *vt* **-ated; -ating** : enflaquecer

e-mail¹ ['iːˌmeɪl] *vt* : enviarle/mandarle un email a (alguien), enviarle/mandarle un correo electrónico a (alguien), enviar/mandar (algo) por email, enviar/mandar (algo) por correo electrónico — *vi* : enviar/mandar un email, enviar/mandar un correo electrónico

e-mail² ['iːˌmeɪl] *n* : email *m*, correo *m* electrónico ⟨e-mail address : dirección de correo electrónico, dirección de email⟩

emanate ['ɛməˌneɪt] *v* **-nated; -nating** *vi* : emanar, provenir, proceder — *vt* : emanar

emanation [ˌɛmə'neɪʃən] *n* : emanación *f*

emancipate [i'mæntsəˌpeɪt] *vt* **-pated; -pating** : emancipar

emancipation [iˌmæntsə'peɪʃən] *n* : emancipación *f*

embalm [ɪm'bɑm, ɛm-, -'bɑlm] *vt* : embalsamar

embankment [ɪm'bæŋkmənt, ɛm-] *n* : terraplén *m*, muro *m* de contención

embargo¹ [ɪm'bɑrgo, ɛm-] *vt* **-goed; -going** : imponer un embargo sobre

embargo² *n, pl* **-goes** : embargo *m*

embark [ɪm'bɑrk, ɛm-] *vt* : embarcar — *vi* **1** : embarcarse **2 to embark on** START : emprender, comenzar

embarkation [ˌɛmˌbɑr'keɪʃən] *n* : embarque *m*, embarco *m*

embarrass [ɪm'bærəs, ɛm-] *vt* : avergonzar, abochornar ⟨you embarrassed me : me hiciste pasar vergüenza⟩

embarrassed [ɪm'bærəst ɛm-] *adj* : embarazoso, violento ⟨I'm embarrassed (about it) : me da vergüenza⟩ ⟨an embarrassed silence : un silencio embarazoso⟩

embarrassing [ɪm'bærəsɪŋ, ɛm-] *adj* : embarazoso, violento ⟨how embarrassing! : ¡qué vergüenza!⟩

embarrassment [ɪm'bærəsmənt, ɛm-] *n* : vergüenza *f*, bochorno *m*, pena *f* ⟨to be an embarrassment to someone : ser una vergüenza para alguien⟩

embassy ['ɛmbəsi] *n, pl* **-sies** : embajada *f*

embed [ɪm'bɛd, ɛm-] *vt* **-bedded; -bedding** : incrustar, empotrar (en una pared, etc.), grabar (en la memoria) ⟨a firmly embedded belief : una creencia arraigada⟩

embellish [ɪm'bɛlɪʃ, ɛm-] *vt* : adornar, embellecer

embellishment [ɪm'bɛlɪʃmənt, ɛm-] *n* : adorno *m*

ember ['ɛmbər] *n* : ascua *f*, brasa *f*

embezzle [ɪm'bɛzəl, ɛm-] *vt* **-zled; -zling** : desfalcar, malversar

embezzlement [ɪm'bɛzəlmənt, ɛm-] *n* : desfalco *m*, malversación *f*

embezzler [ɪm'bɛzələr, ɛm-] *n* : desfalcador *m*, -dora *f*; malversador *m*, -dora *f*

embitter [ɪm'bɪtər, ɛm-] *vt* : amargar

emblem ['ɛmbləm] *n* : emblema *m*, símbolo *m*

emblematic [ˌɛmblə'mætɪk] *adj* : emblemático, simbólico

embodiment [ɪm'bɑdimənt, ɛm-] *n* : encarnación *f*, personificación *f*

embody [ɪm'bɑdi, ɛm-] *vt* **-bodied; -bodying** **1** PERSONIFY : encarnar, personificar **2** INCLUDE : incorporar

embolism ['ɛmbəˌlɪzəm] *n* : embolia *f*

emboss [ɪm'bɑs, ɛm-, -'bɔs] *vt* : repujar (metal o cuero), grabar en relieve ⟨embossed lettering : caracteres en relieve⟩

embrace¹ [ɪm'breɪs, ɛm-] *v* **-braced; -bracing** *vt* **1** HUG : abrazar **2** ADOPT : adoptar, abrazar (una causa), aceptar (un cambio) **3** WELCOME : aprovechar (una oportunidad) **4** INCLUDE : abarcar — *vi* : abrazarse

embrace² *n* : abrazo *m*

embroider [ɪm'brɔɪdər, ɛm-] *vt* : bordar (una tela), adornar (una historia)

embroidery [ɪm'brɔɪdəri, ɛm-] *n, pl* **-ies** : bordado *m*

embroil [ɪm'brɔɪl, ɛm-] *vt* : enredar ⟨to become embroiled in something : enredarse en algo⟩

embryo ['ɛmbri,o:] *n, pl* **embryos** : embrión *m*

embryonic [,ɛmbri'ɑnɪk] *adj* : embrionario

emend [i'mɛnd] *vt* : enmendar, corregir

emendation [,i:,mɛn'deɪʃən] *n* : enmienda *f*

emerald[1] ['ɛmrəld, 'ɛmə-] *adj* : verde esmeralda

emerald[2] *n* : esmeralda *f*

emerge [i'mərdʒ] *vi* **emerged; emerging** **1** : salir, emerger ⟨to emerge from : salir de⟩ **2** ARISE, DEVELOP : surgir **3** : revelarse (dícese de la verdad, etc.) **4 to emerge victorious** : salir victorioso

emergence [i'mərdʒənts] *n* : aparición *f*, surgimiento *m*

emergency [i'mərdʒəntsi] *n, pl* **-cies** **1** : emergencia *f* ⟨in case of emergency : en caso de emergencia⟩ ⟨emergency exit/landing/vehicle : salida/aterrizaje/vehículo de emergencia⟩ **2** : urgencia *f*, emergencia *f* (en medicina)

emergency room *n* : sala *f* de urgencia(s), sala *f* de emergencia(s)

emergent [i'mərdʒənt] *adj* : emergente

emery ['ɛməri] *n, pl* **-eries** : esmeril *m*

emery board *n* : lima *f* de uñas (de esmeril)

emigrant ['ɛmɪgrənt] *n* : emigrante *mf*

emigrate ['ɛmə,greɪt] *vi* **-grated; -grating** : emigrar

emigration [,ɛmə'greɪʃən] *n* : emigración *f*

eminence ['ɛmənənts] *n* **1** PROMINENCE : eminencia *f*, prestigio *m*, renombre *m* **2** DIGNITARY : eminencia *f*; dignatario *m*, -ria *f* ⟨Your Eminence : Su Eminencia⟩

eminent ['ɛmənənt] *adj* : eminente, ilustre

eminently ['ɛmənəntli] *adv* : sumamente

emissary ['ɛmə,sɛri] *n, pl* **-saries** : emisario *m*, -ria *f*

emission [i'mɪʃən] *n* : emisión *f*

emit [i'mɪt] *vt* **emitted; emitting** : emitir, despedir, producir

emote [i'mo:t] *vi* **emoted; emoting** : exteriorizar las emociones

emoticon [i'moti,kɑn] *n* : emoticono *m*, emoticón *m*

emotion [i'mo:ʃən] *n* : emoción *f*, sentimiento *m*

emotional [i'mo:ʃənəl] *adj* **1** : emocional, afectivo ⟨an emotional reaction : una reacción emocional⟩ **2** SENSITIVE : emotivo, sensible **3** MOVING : emotivo, conmovedor, emocionante **4 to get emotional** : emocionarse

emotionally [i'mo:ʃənəli] *adv* : emocionalmente

empathize ['ɛmpə,θaɪz] *vi* **-thized; -thizing** : sentir empatía ⟨to empathize with : identificarse con⟩

empathy ['ɛmpəθi] *n* : empatía *f*

emperor ['ɛmpərər] *n* : emperador *m*

emphasis ['ɛmfəsɪs] *n, pl* **-phases** [-,si:z] **1** : énfasis *m*, hincapié *m* ⟨to put/place/lay emphasis on : poner énfasis en, hacer hincapié en⟩ **2** : acento, énfasis *m* (en lingüística)

emphasize ['ɛmfə,saɪz] *vt* **-sized; -sizing** **1** : enfatizar, subrayar, recalcar **2** : acen-

tuar, enfatizar (en lingüística) **3** ACCENTUATE : acentuar, (hacer) resaltar

emphatic [ɪm'fætɪk, ɛm-] *adj* **1** : enfático, enérgico, categórico ⟨an emphatic "no" : un "no" rotundo⟩ ⟨an emphatic victory : una victoria aplastante⟩ **2 to be emphatic about** : poner mucho énfasis en — **emphatically** [-ɪkli] *adv*

empire ['ɛm,paɪr] *n* : imperio *m*

empirical [ɪm'pɪrɪkəl, ɛm-] *adj* : empírico — **empirically** [-ɪkli] *adv*

employ[1] [ɪm'plɔɪ, ɛm-] *vt* **1** USE : usar, utilizar, emplear **2** HIRE : contratar, emplear **3** : emplear, dar empleo a ⟨they employ 20 people : emplean a 20 personas⟩ **4** OCCUPY : ocupar, dedicar, emplear

employ[2] [ɪm'plɔɪ, ɛm-; 'ɪm,-, 'ɛm,-] *n* **1** : puesto *m*, cargo *m*, ocupación *f* **2 to be in the employ of** : estar al servicio de, trabajar para

employee [ɪm,plɔɪ'i:, ɛm-, -'plɔɪ,i:] *n* : empleado *m*, -da *f*

employer [ɪm'plɔɪər, ɛm-] *n* : patrón *m*, -trona *f*; empleador *m*, -dora *f*

employment [ɪm'plɔɪmənt, ɛm-] *n* : trabajo *m*, empleo *m*

employment agency *n* : agencia *f* de colocación, agencia *f* de trabajo

empower [ɪm'paʊər, ɛm-] *vt* : facultar, autorizar, conferirle poder a

empowerment [ɪm'paʊərmənt, ɛm-] *n* : autorización *f*

empress ['ɛmprəs] *n* : emperatriz *f*

emptiness ['ɛmptinəs] *n* : vacío *m*, vacuidad *f*

empty[1] ['ɛmpti] *v* **-tied; -tying** *vt* : vaciar ⟨to empty (out) your pockets : vaciar sus bolsillos⟩ — *vi* **1** *or* **to empty out** : vaciarse (dícese de un lugar) **2 to empty into** : desaguar en, (dícese de un río)

empty[2] *adj* **emptier; -est** **1** : vacío **2** VACANT : desocupado, libre **3** MEANINGLESS : vacío, hueco, vano

empty[3] *n, pl* **-ties** : envase *m* vacío

empty–handed [,ɛmpti'hændəd] *adj* : con las manos vacías

empty–headed [,ɛmpti'hɛdəd] *adj* : cabeza hueca, tonto

emu ['i:,mju:] *n* : emú *m*

emulate ['ɛmjə,leɪt] *vt* **-lated; -lating** : emular

emulation [,ɛmjə'leɪʃən] *n* : emulación *f*

emulsifier [i'mʌlsə,faɪər] *n* : emulsionante *m*

emulsify [i'mʌlsə,faɪ] *vt* **-fied; -fying** : emulsionar

emulsion [i'mʌlʃən] *n* : emulsión *f*

en– *or* **em–** *pref* : en-, em- ⟨entangle : enredar⟩ ⟨empathy : empatía⟩

enable [i'neɪbəl, ɛ-] *vt* **-abled; -abling** **1** PERMIT : permitir, hacer posible, posibilitar ⟨to enable someone to do something : permitirle a alguien hacer algo⟩ **2** ACTIVATE : activar, habilitar

enact [i'nækt, ɛ-] *vt* **1** : promulgar (un ley o decreto) **2** : representar (un papel en el teatro)

enactment [i'næktmənt, ɛ-] *n* : promulgación *f*

enamel[1] [ɪˈnæməl] *vt* **-eled** *or* **-elled; -eling** *or* **-elling** : esmaltar

enamel[2] *n* : esmalte *m*

enamor [ɪˈnæmər] *vt* **1** : enamorar **2 to be enamored of** : estar enamorado de (una persona), estar entusiasmado con (algo)

encamp [ɪnˈkæmp, ɛn-] *vi* : acampar

encampment [ɪnˈkæmpmənt, ɛn-] *n* : campamento *m*

encase [ɪnˈkeɪs, ɛn-] *vt* **-cased; -casing** : encerrar, revestir

-ence *suf* : -encia ⟨independence : independencia⟩

encephalitis [ɪnˌsɛfəˈlaɪtəs, ɛn-] *n, pl* **-litides** [ˈlɪtəˌdiːz] : encefalitis *f*

enchant [ɪnˈtʃænt, ɛn-] *vt* **1** BEWITCH : hechizar, encantar, embrujar **2** CHARM, FASCINATE : cautivar, fascinar, encantar

enchanting [ɪnˈtʃæntɪŋ, ɛn-] *adj* : encantador

enchanter [ɪnˈtʃæntər, ɛn-] *n* SORCERER : mago *m*, encantador *m*

enchantment [ɪnˈtʃæntmənt, ɛn-] *n* **1** SPELL : encanto *m*, hechizo *m* **2** CHARM : encanto *m*

enchantress [ɪnˈtʃæntrəs, ɛn-] *n* **1** SORCERESS : maga *f*, hechicera *f* **2** CHARMER : mujer *f* cautivadora

enchilada [ˌɛntʃəˈlɑːdə] *n* : enchilada *f*

encircle [ɪnˈsərkəl, ɛn-] *vt* **-cled; -cling** : rodear, ceñir, cercar

enclose [ɪnˈkloːz, ɛn-] *vt* **-closed; -closing 1** SURROUND : encerrar, cercar, rodear **2** INCLUDE : incluir, adjuntar, acompañar ⟨please find enclosed : le(s) envío adjunto⟩

enclosure [ɪnˈkloːʒər, ɛn-] *n* **1** ENCLOSING : encierro *m* **2** : cercado *m* (de terreno), recinto *m* ⟨an enclosure for the press : un recinto para la prensa⟩ **3** : anexo *m* (de una carta), documento *m* adjunto

encode [ɪnˈkoːd, ɛn-] *vt* **1** : cifrar (mensajes, etc.) **2** : codificar (datos, etc.) **3** : codificar (tarjetas de crédito, etc.)

encompass [ɪnˈkʌmpəs, ɛn-, -ˈkɑm-] *vt* **1** SURROUND : circundar, rodear **2** INCLUDE : abarcar, comprender

encore[1] [ˈɑnˌkor] *vt* **1** : bis *m* ⟨encore! : ¡otra!⟩

encounter[1] [ɪnˈkaʊntər, ɛn-] *vt* **1** MEET : encontrar, encontrarse con, toparse con, tropezar con **2** FIGHT : combatir, luchar contra

encounter[2] *n* : encuentro *m*

encourage [ɪnˈkʌrɪdʒ, ɛn-] *vt* **-aged; -aging 1** : animar, alentar ⟨she encouraged me to participate : me animó a participar⟩ **2** FOSTER : fomentar, promover

encouragement [ɪnˈkʌrɪdʒmənt, ɛn-] *n* : ánimo *m*, aliento *m*

encouraging [ɪnˈkʌrədʒɪŋ, ɛn-] *adj* : alentador, esperanzador

encroach [ɪnˈkroːtʃ, ɛn-] *vi* **to encroach on/upon** : invadir (territorio), abusar (derechos), quitar (tiempo)

encroachment [ɪnˈkroːtʃmənt, ɛn-] *n* : invasión *f*, usurpación *f*

encrust [ɪnˈkrʌst, ɛn-] *vt* **1** : recubrir con una costra **2** INLAY : incrustar ⟨encrusted with gems : incrustado de gemas⟩

encrypt [ɪnˈkrɪpt, ɛn-] *vt* : cifrar, encriptar (datos, etc.)

encumber [ɪnˈkʌmbər, ɛn-] *vt* **1** BLOCK : obstruir, estorbar **2** BURDEN : cargar, gravar

encumbrance [ɪnˈkʌmbrənts, ɛn-] *n* : estorbo *m*, carga *f*, gravamen *m*

encyclopedia [ɪnˌsaɪkləˈpiːdiə, ɛn-] *n* : enciclopedia *f*

encyclopedic [ɪnˌsaɪkləˈpiːdɪk, ɛn-] *adj* : enciclopédico

end[1] [ˈɛnd] *vt* **1** STOP : terminar, poner fin a, acabar con **2** CONCLUDE : concluir, terminar — *vi* **1** : terminar(se), acabar, concluir(se) **2 to end up doing something** : acabar/terminar haciendo algo, acabar/terminar por hacer algo

end[2] *n* **1** : extremo *m* (de una cuerda, etc.), punta *f* (de un lápiz, etc.), final *m* (de una calle, etc.) ⟨I'm at the end of my rope : no puedo aguantar más⟩ **2** CONCLUSION : fin *m*, final *m* ⟨to bring something to an end : terminar algo, poner fin a algo⟩ ⟨to come to an end : llegar a su fin⟩ ⟨to put an end to : acabar con, poner fin a⟩ **3** AIM : fin *m*, objetivo *m* **4** : ala *f* (en fútbol americano) ⟨tight end : ala cerrada⟩ **5 at the end** : al fin, al final ⟨at the end of April : a fines/finales de abril⟩ **6 end to end** : juntados por los extremos **7 in the end** : al final **8 on end** : parado, (en posición) vertical ⟨my hair stood on end : se me pusieron los pelos de punta⟩ **9 on end** : sin parar ⟨he read for hours on end : pasaba horas enteras leyendo⟩

endanger [ɪnˈdeɪndʒər, ɛn-] *vt* : poner en peligro

endangered [ɪnˈdeɪndʒərd, ɛn-] *adj* : en peligro

endear [ɪnˈdɪr, ɛn-] *vt* **to endear oneself to** : ganarse la simpatía de, granjearse el cariño de

endearing [ɪnˈdɪrɪŋ, ɛn-] *adj* : encantador

endearment [ɪnˈdɪrmənt, ɛn-] *n* : expresión *f* de cariño

endeavor[1] [ɪnˈdɛvər, ɛn-] *vt* : intentar, esforzarse por ⟨he endeavored to improve his work : intentó mejorar su trabajo⟩

endeavor[2] *n* : intento *m*, esfuerzo *m*

ending [ˈɛndɪŋ] *n* **1** CONCLUSION : final *m*, desenlace *m* **2** SUFFIX : sufijo *m*, terminación *f*

endive [ˈɛnˌdaɪv, ˌɑnˈdiːv] *n* : endibia *f*, endivia *f*

endless [ˈɛndləs] *adj* **1** INTERMINABLE : interminable, inacabable, sin fin ⟨endless hours : horas interminables⟩ ⟨endless prairie : praderas interminables⟩ ⟨an endless source of : ·una fuente inagotable de⟩ ⟨with endless patience : con paciencia infinita⟩ **2** COUNTLESS : innumerable, incontable ⟨endless possibilities : posibilidades infinitas⟩ ⟨endless questions : preguntas incesantes⟩

endlessly [ˈɛndləsli] *adv* : interminable-mente, eternamente, sin parar

endocrine [ˈɛndəkrən, -ˌkraɪn, -ˌkriːn] *adj* : endocrino

endorse [ɪnˈdɔrs, ɛn-] *vt* **-dorsed; -dorsing 1** SIGN : endosar, firmar **2** APPROVE, SUPPORT : aprobar, respaldar **3** PROMOTE : promocionar

endorsement [ɪnˈdɔrsmənt, ɛn-] *n* **1** SIGNATURE : endoso *m*, firma *f* **2** APPROVAL, SUPPORT : aprobación *f*, aval *m*

endow [ɪnˈdaʊ, ɛn-] *vt* : dotar ⟨to be endowed with : estar dotado de⟩

endowment [ɪnˈdaʊmənt, ɛn-] *n* **1** FUNDING : dotación *f* **2** DONATION : donación *f*, legado *m* **3** ATTRIBUTE, GIFT : atributo *m*, dones *fpl*

endurable [ɪnˈdʊrəbəl, ɛn-, -ˈdjʊr-] *adj* : tolerable, soportable

endurance [ɪnˈdʊrəns, ɛn-, -ˈdjʊr-] *n* : resistencia *f*, aguante *m*

endure [ɪnˈdʊr, ɛn-, -ˈdjʊr] *v* **-dured; -during** *vt* **1** BEAR : resistir, soportar, aguantar **2** TOLERATE : tolerar, soportar — *vi* LAST : durar, perdurar

enema [ˈɛnəmə] *n* : enema *m*, lavativa *f*

enemy [ˈɛnəmi] *n*, *pl* **-mies** : enemigo *m*, -ga *f*

energetic [ˌɛnərˈdʒɛtɪk] *adj* : enérgico, vigoroso — **energetically** [-ʈɪkli] *adv*

energize [ˈɛnərˌdʒaɪz] *vt* **-gized; -gizing 1** ACTIVATE : activar **2** INVIGORATE : vigorizar

energy [ˈɛnərdʒi] *n*, *pl* **-gies 1** : energía *f* **2** EFFORT : energías *fpl*, esfuerzo *m*

enervate [ˈɛnərˌveɪt] *vt* **-vated; -vating** : enervar, debilitar

enfold [ɪnˈfoːld, ɛn-] *vt* : envolver

enforce [ɪnˈfɔrs, ɛn-] *vt* **-forced; -forcing 1** : hacer respetar, hacer cumplir (una ley, etc.) **2** IMPOSE : imponer ⟨to enforce one's will : imponer su voluntad⟩

enforcement [ɪnˈfɔrsmənt, ɛn-] *n* : imposición *f*

enfranchise [ɪnˈfræn,tʃaɪz, ɛn-] *vt* **-chised; -chising** : conceder el voto a

enfranchisement [ɪnˈfræn,tʃaɪzmənt, ɛn-] *n* : concesión *f* del voto

engage [ɪnˈgeɪdʒ, ɛn-] *v* **-gaged; -gaging** *vt* **1** ABSORB : captar (la atención, etc.) ⟨to engage someone in conversation : entablar conversación con alguien⟩ **2** : engranar ⟨to engage the clutch : embragar⟩ **3** HIRE : contratar **4** : entablar combate con (un enemigo) — *vi* **1** MESH, INTERLOCK : engranar **2 to engage in** PURSUE : dedicarse a (una actividad) **3 to engage in** INITIATE : entablar

engaged [ɪnˈgeɪdʒd, ɛn-] *adj* **1** BETROTHED : comprometido, prometido ⟨to get engaged (to someone) : comprometerse (con alguien), prometerse (a alguien)⟩ **2 to be engaged in** : dedicarse a (una actividad)

engagement [ɪnˈgeɪdʒmənt, ɛn-] *n* **1** APPOINTMENT : compromiso *m*, cita *f* **2** BETROTHAL : compromiso *m* (acto), noviazgo *m* (período) ⟨engagement ring : anillo de compromiso⟩

engaging [ɪnˈgeɪdʒɪŋ, ɛn-] *adj* : atractivo, encantador, interesante

engender [ɪnˈdʒɛndər, ɛn-] *vt* **-dered; -dering** : engendrar

engine [ˈɛndʒən] *n* **1** MOTOR : motor *m* **2** LOCOMOTIVE : locomotora *f*, máquina *f*

engineer[1] [ˌɛndʒəˈnɪr] *vt* **1** : diseñar, construir (un sistema, un mecanismo, etc.) **2** CONTRIVE : maquinar, tramar, fraguar

engineer[2] *n* **1** : ingeniero *m*, -ra *f* **2** : maquinista *mf* (de locomotoras)

engineering [ˌɛndʒəˈnɪrɪŋ] *n* : ingeniería *f*

English[1] [ˈɪŋglɪʃ, ˈɪŋlɪʃ] *adj* : inglés ⟨the English language : la lengua inglesa⟩ ⟨an English teacher : un profesor de inglés⟩

English[2] *n* **1** : inglés *m* (idioma) **2 the English** (*used with a plural verb*) : los ingleses

Englishman [ˈɪŋglɪʃmən, ˈɪŋlɪʃ-] *n*, *pl* **-men** [-mən, -ˌmɛn] : inglés *m*

English muffin *n* : panecillo *m* (que se parte en dos y se come tostado)

Englishwoman [ˈɪŋglɪʃ,wʊmən, ˈɪŋlɪʃ-] *n*, *pl* **-women** [-ˌwɪmən] : inglesa *f*

engrave [ɪnˈgreɪv, ɛn-] *vt* **-graved; -graving** : grabar

engraver [ɪnˈgreɪvər, ɛn-] *n* : grabador *m*, -dora *f*

engraving [ɪnˈgreɪvɪŋ, ɛn-] *n* : grabado *m*

engross [ɪnˈgroːs, ɛn-] *vt* : absorber ⟨to be engrossed in something : estar absorto en algo⟩

engrossed [ɪnˈgroːst, ɛn-] *adj* : absorto

engrossing [ɪnˈgroːsɪŋ, ɛn-] *adj* : fascinante, absorbente

engulf [ɪnˈgʌlf, ɛn-] *vt* : envolver, sepultar

enhance [ɪnˈhænts, ɛn-] *vt* **-hanced; -hancing** : realzar, aumentar, mejorar

enhancement [ɪnˈhæntsmənt, ɛn-] *n* : mejora *f*, realce *m*, aumento *m*

enigma [ɪˈnɪgmə] *n* : enigma *m*

enigmatic [ˌɛnɪgˈmætɪk, ˌiːnɪg-] *adj* : enigmático — **enigmatically** [-ʈɪkli] *adv*

enjoin [ɪnˈdʒɔɪn, ɛn-] *vt* **1** COMMAND : ordenar, imponer **2** FORBID : prohibir, vedar

enjoy [ɪnˈdʒɔɪ, ɛn-] *vt* **1** : disfrutar, gozar de ⟨did you enjoy the book? : ¿te gustó el libro?⟩ ⟨to enjoy good health : gozar de buena salud⟩ **2 to enjoy oneself** : divertirse, pasarlo bien

enjoyable [ɪnˈdʒɔɪəbəl, ɛn-] *adj* : agradable, placentero, divertido

enjoyment [ɪnˈdʒɔɪmənt, ɛn-] *n* : placer *m*, goce *m*, disfrute *m*, deleite *m*

enlarge [ɪnˈlɑrdʒ, ɛn-] *v* **-larged; -larging** *vt* : ampliar (una foto, etc.), agrandar (un espacio) — *vi* **1** : ampliarse **2 to enlarge upon** : extenderse sobre, entrar en detalles sobre

enlargement [ɪnˈlɑrdʒmənt, ɛn-] *n* : expansión *f*, ampliación *f* (dícese de fotografías)

enlighten [ɪnˈlaɪtən, ɛn-] *vt* **1** INSTRUCT : ilustrar **2** : iluminar (en religión)

enlightenment [ɪnˈlaɪtənmənt, ɛn-] *n* **1** : ilustración *f* ⟨the Enlightenment : la Ilustración⟩ **2** CLARIFICATION : aclaración *f*

enlist [ɪnˈlɪst, ɛn-] *vt* **1** ENROLL : alistar, reclutar **2** SECURE : conseguir ⟨to enlist the support of : conseguir el apoyo de⟩ — *vi* : alistarse

enlisted man [ɪnˈlɪstəd, ɛn-] *n* : soldado *m* raso

enlistment [ɪnˈlɪstmənt, ɛn-] *n* : alistamiento *m*, reclutamiento *m*

enliven [ɪnˈlaɪvən, ɛn-] *vt* : animar, alegrar, darle vida a

en masse [ɑnˈmæs, -ˈmɑs, ɛn-] *adv* : en masa, masivamente

enmity [ˈɛnməti] *n, pl* **-ties** : enemistad *f*, animadversión *f*

ennoble [ɪˈnoːbəl, ɛ-] *vt* **-bled; -bling** : ennoblecer

ennui [ˌɑnˈwiː] *n* : hastío *m*, tedio *m*, fastidio *m*, aburrimiento *m*

enormity [ɪˈnɔrməti] *n, pl* **-ties 1** ATROCITY : atrocidad *f*, barbaridad *f* **2** IMMENSITY : enormidad *f*, inmensidad *f*

enormous [ɪˈnɔrməs] *adj* : enorme, inmenso, tremendo — **enormously** *adv*

enough[1] [ɪˈnʌf] *adv* **1** : bastante, suficientemente ⟨it's small enough to fit in a briefcase : es lo bastante pequeño como para caber en un maletín⟩ **2** QUITE : bastante ⟨it seems simple enough : parece bastante sencillo⟩ **3 fair enough!** : ¡está bien!, ¡de acuerdo! **4 strangely/oddly enough** : por extraño que parezca **5 sure enough** : en efecto, sin duda alguna **6 well enough** : muy bien, bastante bien

enough[2] *adj* : bastante, suficiente ⟨do we have enough chairs? : ¿tenemos suficientes sillas?⟩

enough[3] *pron* : (lo) suficiente, (lo) bastante ⟨enough to eat : lo suficiente para comer⟩ ⟨it's more than enough : basta y sobra, es más que suficiente⟩ ⟨it's not enough : no basta⟩ ⟨I've had enough! : ¡estoy harto!, ¡está bueno ya!⟩ ⟨(that's enough! : ¡basta ya!⟩

enquire [ɪnˈkwaɪr, ɛn-] **enquiry** [ˈɪnˌkwaɪri, ˈɛn-, -kwəri; ɪnˈkwaɪri, ɛn-] → **inquire, inquiry**

enrage [ɪnˈreɪdʒ, ɛn-] *vt* **-raged; -raging** : enfurecer, encolerizar

enraged [ɪnˈreɪdʒd, ɛn-] *adj* : enfurecido, furioso

enrapture [ɪnˈræptʃər, ɛn-] *vt* **-tured; -turing** : cautivar, arrobar

enrich [ɪnˈrɪtʃ, ɛn-] *vt* : enriquecer

enrichment [ɪnˈrɪtʃmənt, ɛn-] *n* : enriquecimiento *m*

enroll *or* **enrol** [ɪnˈroːl, ɛn-] *v* **-rolled; -rolling** *vt* : matricular, inscribir — *vi* : matricularse, inscribirse

enrollment [ɪnˈroːlmənt, ɛn-] *n* : matrícula *f*, inscripción *f*

en route [ɑnˈruːt, ɛnˈraʊt] *adv* : de camino, por el camino

ensconce [ɪnˈskɑnts, ɛn-] *vt* **-sconced; -sconcing** : acomodar, instalar, establecer cómodamente

ensemble [ɑnˈsɑmbəl] *n* : conjunto *m*

enshrine [ɪnˈʃraɪn, ɛn-] *vt* **-shrined; -shrining** : conservar religiosamente, preservar

ensign [ˈɛnsən, ˈɛnˌsaɪn] *n* **1** FLAG : enseña *f*, pabellón *m* **2** : alférez *mf* (de fragata)

enslave [ɪnˈsleɪv, ɛn-] *vt* **-slaved; -slaving** : esclavizar

enslavement [ɪnˈsleɪvmənt, ɛn-] *n* : esclavización *f*

ensnare [ɪnˈsnær, ɛn-] *vt* **-snared; -snaring** : atrapar

ensue [ɪnˈsuː, ɛn-] *vi* **-sued; -suing** : seguir, resultar ⟨in the ensuing weeks : en las semanas siguientes⟩

ensure [ɪnˈʃʊr, ɛn-] *vt* **-sured; -suring** : asegurar, garantizar

entail [ɪnˈteɪl, ɛn-] *vt* : implicar, suponer, conllevar

entangle [ɪnˈtæŋɡəl, ɛn-] *vt* **-gled; -gling** : enredar

entanglement [ɪnˈtæŋɡəlmənt, ɛn-] *n* : enredo *m*

enter [ˈɛntər] *vt* **1** : entrar en/a **2** JOIN : entrar en/a, incorporarse a, ingresar a **3** : entrar en/a (un debate, una profesión, etc.) **4** BEGIN : entrar en (una etapa, etc.) **5** RECORD : anotar, inscribir **6** INPUT : introducir, dar entrada a **7** : presentar (una queja, etc.) ⟨she entered a guilty plea : se declaró culpable⟩ **8** : presentarse a (un concurso, etc.), inscribirse en (una carrera, etc.) — *vi* **1** : entrar **2 to enter into** : entrar en, establecer (un acuerdo), entablar (negociaciones, etc.) **3 to enter into** AFFECT, INFLUENCE : incidir en, influir en

enterprise [ˈɛntərˌpraɪz] *n* **1** UNDERTAKING : empresa *f* **2** BUSINESS : empresa *f*, firma *f* **3** INITIATIVE : iniciativa *f*, empuje *m*

enterprising [ˈɛntərˌpraɪzɪŋ] *adj* : emprendedor

entertain [ˌɛntərˈteɪn] *vt* **1** : recibir, agasajar ⟨to entertain guests : tener invitados⟩ **2** CONSIDER : considerar, contemplar **3** AMUSE : entretener, divertir — *vi* : tener invitados

entertainer [ˌɛntərˈteɪnər] *n* : artista *mf*

entertaining [ˌɛntərˈteɪnɪŋ] *adj* : entretenido, divertido

entertainment [ˌɛntərˈteɪnmənt] *n* **1** : entretenimiento *m*, diversión *f* **2** SHOW : espectáculo *m*

enthrall *or* **enthral** [ɪnˈθrɔl, ɛn-] *vt* **-thralled; -thralling** : cautivar, embelesar

enthuse [ɪnˈθuːz, ɛn-] *v* **-thused; -thusing** *vt* **1** EXCITE : entusiasmar **2** : decir con entusiasmo — *vi* **to enthuse over** : hablar con entusiasmo sobre

enthusiasm [ɪnˈθuːziˌæzəm, ɛn-, -ˈθjuː-] *n* : entusiasmo *m*

enthusiast [ɪnˈθuːziˌæst, ɛn-, -ˈθjuː-, -əst] *n* : entusiasta *mf*; aficionado *m*, -da *f*

enthusiastic [ɪnˌθuːziˈæstɪk, ɛn-, -ˌθjuː-] *adj* : entusiasta, aficionado

enthusiastically [ɪnˌθuːziˈæstɪkli, ɛn-, -ˌθjuː-] *adv* : con entusiasmo

entice [ɪnˈtaɪs, ɛn-] *vt* **-ticed; -ticing** : atraer, tentar

enticement [ɪnˈtaɪsmənt, ɛn-] *n* : tentación *f*, atracción *f*, señuelo *m*

entire [ɪnˈtaɪr, ɛn-] *adj* : entero, completo ⟨the entire family : toda la familia⟩

entirely [ɪn'taɪrli, ɛn-] *adv* : completamente, totalmente

entirety [ɪn'taɪrti, ɛn-, -'taɪrəti] *n, pl* **-ties** : totalidad *f* ⟨in its entirety : en su totalidad⟩

entitle [ɪn'taɪtəl, ɛn-] *vt* **-tled; -tling 1** : titular, intitular ⟨a book entitled "My Life" : un libro titulado "Mi vida"⟩ **2** : dar derecho a ⟨it entitles you to participate : le da derecho a participar⟩ **3 to be entitled to** : tener derecho a

entitlement [ɪn'taɪtəlmənt, ɛn-] *n* RIGHT : derecho *m*

entity ['ɛntəti] *n, pl* **-ties** : entidad *f*, ente *m*

entomologist [ˌɛntə'malədʒɪst] *n* : entomólogo *m*, -ga *f*

entomology [ˌɛntə'malədʒi] *n* : entomología *f*

entourage [ˌɑntu'raʒ] *n* : séquito *m*

entrails ['ɛn,treɪlz, -trəlz] *npl* : entrañas *fpl*, vísceras *fpl*

entrance¹ [ɪn'trænts, ɛn-] *vt* **-tranced; -trancing** : encantar, embelesar, fascinar

entrance² ['ɛntrənts] *n* **1** ENTERING : entrada *f* ⟨to make an entrance : entrar en escena⟩ **2** ENTRY : entrada *f* ⟨the main entrance : la entrada principal⟩ **3** ADMISSION : entrada *f*, ingreso *m* ⟨entrance examination : examen de ingreso⟩

entrant ['ɛntrənt] *n* : candidato *m*, -ta *f* (en un examen); participante *mf* (en un concurso)

entrap [ɪn'træp, ɛn-] *vt* **-trapped; -trapping** : atrapar, entrampar, hacer caer en una trampa

entrapment [ɪn'træpmənt, ɛn-] *n* : captura *f*

entreat [ɪn'tri:t, ɛn-] *vt* : suplicar, rogar

entreaty [ɪn'tri:ti, ɛn-] *n, pl* **-treaties** : ruego *m*, súplica *f*

entrée or **entree** ['ɑn,treɪ, 'ɑn'-] *n* : plato *m* principal

entrench [ɪn'trɛntʃ, ɛn-] *vt* **1** FORTIFY : atrincherar ⟨a posición militar⟩ **2** : consolidar, afianzar ⟨firmly entrenched in his job : afianzado en su puesto⟩

entrepreneur [ˌɑntrəprə'nər, -'njʊr] *n* : empresario *m*, -ria *f*

entrust [ɪn'trʌst, ɛn-] *vt* **to entrust something to someone** *or* **to entrust someone with something** : confiarle/encomendarle algo a alguien

entry ['ɛntri] *n, pl* **-tries 1** ENTRANCE : entrada *f* ⟨a side entry : una entrada lateral⟩ **2** ENTERING : entrada *f* ⟨after her entry into politics : después de su entrada en política⟩ **3** ADMISSION : entrada *f*, ingreso *m* **4** : entrada *f* (en un diccionario, etc.), anotación *f* (en un diario), partida *f* (en contabilidad) **5** PARTICIPANT : participante *mf*

entwine [ɪn'twaɪn, ɛn-] *vt* **-twined; -twining** : entrelazar, entretejer, entrecruzar

enumerate [ɪ'nu:mə,reɪt, ɛ-, -'nju:-] *vt* **-ated; -ating 1** LIST : enumerar **2** COUNT : contar, enumerar

enumeration [ɪ,nu:mə'reɪʃən, ɛ-, -,nju:-] *n* : enumeración *f*, lista *f*

enunciate [i'nʌntsi,eɪt, ɛ-] *vt* **-ated; -ating 1** STATE : enunciar, decir **2** PRONOUNCE : articular, pronunciar

enunciation [i,nʌntsi'eɪʃən, ɛ-] *n* **1** STATEMENT : enunciación *f*, declaración *f* **2** ARTICULATION : articulación *f*, pronunciación *f*, dicción *f*

envelop [ɪn'vləp, ɛn-] *vt* : envolver, cubrir

envelope ['ɛnvə,lo:p, 'ɑn-] *n* : sobre *m*

enviable ['ɛnviəbəl] *adj* : envidiable

envious ['ɛnviəs] *adj* : envidioso ⟨an envious look : una mirada de envidia⟩ ⟨to be envious of : envidiar⟩ — **enviously** *adv*

environment [ɪn'vaɪrənmənt, ɛn-, -'vaɪ-ərn-] *n* **1** : ambiente *m*, entorno *m* ⟨her home environment : su ambiente/entorno familiar⟩ **2 the environment** : el medio *m* ambiente

environmental [ɪn,vaɪrən'mɛntəl, ɛn-, -,vaɪərn-] *adj* : ambiental, medioambiental ⟨environmental protection : protección del medio ambiente⟩

environmentalism [-,lɪzəm] *n* : ecologismo *m*

environmentalist [ɪn,vaɪrən'mɛntəlɪst, ɛn-, -,vaɪərn-] *n* : ecologista *mf*

environmentally [ɪn,vaɪrən'mɛntəli, ɛn-, -,vaɪərn-] *adv* : ecológicamente ⟨environmentally friendly : verde, ecológico⟩

environs [ɪn'vaɪrənz, ɛn-, -'vaɪərnz] *npl* : alrededores *mpl*, entorno *m*, inmediaciones *fpl*

envisage [ɪn'vɪzɪdʒ, ɛn-] *vt* **-aged; -aging 1** IMAGINE : imaginarse, concebir **2** FORESEE : prever

envision [ɪn'vɪʒən, ɛn-] *vt* : imaginar

envoy ['ɛn,vɔɪ, 'ɑn-] *n* : enviado *m*, -da *f*

envy¹ ['ɛnvi] *vt* **-vied; -vying** : envidiar

envy² *n, pl* **envies** : envidia *f*

enzyme ['ɛn,zaɪm] *n* : enzima *f*

eon ['i:ən, i:,ɑn] → **aeon**

epaulet [ˌpə'lɛt] *n* : charretera *f*

ephemeral [ɪ'fɛmərəl, -'fi:-] *adj* : efímero, fugaz

epic¹ ['ɛpɪk] *adj* : épico ⟨an epic film : una (película) épica⟩

epic² *n* : poema *m* épico, epopeya *f*

epicenter ['ɛpɪ,sɛntər] *n* : epicentro *m*

epicure ['ɛpɪ,kjʊr] *n* : epicúreo *m*, -rea *f*; gastrónomo *m*, -ma *f*

epicurean [ˌɛpɪkjʊ'ri:ən, -'kjʊriən] *adj* : epicúreo

epidemic¹ [ˌɛpə'dɛmɪk] *adj* : epidémico

epidemic² *n* : epidemia *f*

epidemiology [ˌɛpəˌdi:mi'alədʒi] *n* : epidemiología *f* — **epidemiologic** [ˌɛpə-ˌdi:miə'ladʒɪk] *or* **epidemiological** [-'ladʒɪkəl] *adj*

epigram ['ɛpə,græm] *n* : epigrama *m*

epilepsy ['ɛpə,lɛpsi] *n, pl* **-sies** : epilepsia *f*

epileptic¹ [ˌɛpə'lɛptɪk] *adj* : epiléptico

epileptic² *n* : epiléptico *m*, -ca *f*

epilogue ['ɛpə,lɔg, -,lɑg] *n* : epílogo *m*

epiphany [ɪ'pɪfəni] *n, pl* **-nies 1 Epiphany** : Epifanía *f* **2 to have an epiphany** : tener una revelación

episcopal [ɪ'pɪskəpəl] *adj* : episcopal

Episcopalian [ɪ,pɪskə'peɪljən] *n* : episcopaliano *m*, -na *f*

episode ['ɛpə,soːd] *n* : episodio *m*

episodic [,ɛpə'sɑdɪk] *adj* : episódico

epistle [ɪ'pɪsəl] *n* : epístola *f*, carta *f*

epitaph ['ɛpə,tæf] *n* : epitafio *m*

epithet ['ɛpə,θɛt, -θət] *n* : epíteto *m*

epitome [ɪ'pɪtəmi] *n* **1** SUMMARY : epítome *m*, resumen *m* **2** EMBODIMENT : personificación *f*

epitomize [ɪ'pɪtə,maɪz] *vt* **-mized; -mizing 1** SUMMARIZE : resumir **2** EMBODY : ser la personificación de (dícese de una persona), ser representativo de

epoch ['ɛpək, 'ɛ,pɑk, 'iː,pɑk] *n* : época *f*, era *f*

epoxy [ɪ'pɑksi] *n, pl* **epoxies** : resina *f* epoxídica

equable ['ɛkwəbəl, 'iː-] *adj* **1** CALM, STEADY : ecuánime **2** UNIFORM : estable (dícese de la temperatura), constante (dícese del clima), uniforme

equably ['ɛkwəbli, 'iː-] *adv* : con ecuanimidad

equal¹ ['iːkwəl] *vt* **equaled** *or* **equalled; equaling** *or* **equalling 1** : ser igual a ⟨two plus three equals five : dos más tres es igual a cinco⟩ **2** MATCH : igualar

equal² *adj* **1** SAME : igual **2** ADEQUATE : adecuado, capaz ⟨she's equal to the task : es capaz de hacerlo⟩

equal³ *n* : igual *mf*

equality [ɪ'kwɑləti] *n, pl* **-ties** : igualdad *f*

equalize ['iːkwə,laɪz] *v* **-ized; -izing** *vt* **1** : igualar (oportunidades), equiparar (salarios) **2** : igualar (la presión) — *vi* **1** : igualar **2** (*Brit*) TIE : empatar (en deportes)

equalizer ['iːkwə,laɪzər] *n* : gol *m* del empate

equally ['iːkwəli] *adv* **1** : igualmente, por igual ⟨to treat everyone equally : tratar a todos (por) igual⟩ ⟨equally quickly : con la misma rapidez⟩ **2** EVENLY : por igual ⟨to divide equally : dividir en/a partes iguales⟩

equal opportunity employer *n* : empresa *f* con una política de igualdad de oportunidades

equal sign *n* : signo *m* de igual

equanimity [,iːkwə'nɪməti, ,ɛ-] *n, pl* **-ties** : ecuanimidad *f*

equate [ɪ'kweɪt] *vt* **equated; equating 1** : equiparar, identificar **2 to equate to** : equivaler a, ser igual a

equation [ɪ'kweɪʒən] *n* : ecuación *f*

equator [ɪ'kweɪtər] *n* **the Equator** : el ecuador

equatorial [,iːkwə'toriəl, ,ɛ-] *adj* : ecuatorial

equestrian¹ [ɪ'kwɛstriən, ɛ-] *adj* : ecuestre

equestrian² *n* : jinete *mf*, caballista *mf*

equilateral [,iːkwə'lætərəl, ,ɛ-] *adj* : equilátero

equilibrium [,iːkwə'lɪbriəm, ,ɛ-] *n, pl* **-riums** *or* **-ria** [-riə] : equilibrio *m*

equine ['iː,kwaɪn, 'ɛ-] *adj* : equino, hípico

equinox ['iːkwə,nɑks, 'ɛ-] *n* : equinoccio *m*

equip [ɪ'kwɪp] *vt* **equipped; equipping 1** FURNISH : equipar ⟨to equip someone

with something : proveer a alguien de algo⟩ **2** PREPARE : preparar

equipment [ɪ'kwɪpmənt] *n* : equipo *m* ⟨sports equipment : artículos deportivos⟩

equitable ['ɛkwətəbəl] *adj* : equitativo, justo, imparcial

equity ['ɛkwəti] *n, pl* **-ties 1** FAIRNESS : equidad *f*, imparcialidad *f* **2** VALUE : valor *m* líquido

equivalence [ɪ'kwɪvələnts] *n* : equivalencia *f*

equivalent¹ [ɪ'kwɪvələnt] *adj* : equivalente ⟨to be equivalent to : equivaler a⟩

equivalent² *n* : equivalente *m*

equivocal [ɪ'kwɪvəkəl] *adj* **1** AMBIGUOUS : equívoco, ambiguo **2** QUESTIONABLE : incierto, dudoso, sospechoso

equivocate [ɪ'kwɪvə,keɪt] *vi* **-cated; -cating** : usar lenguaje equívoco, contestar con evasivas

equivocation [ɪ,kwɪvə'keɪʃən] *n* : evasiva *f*, subterfugio *m*

-er *suf* **1** : -ador *m*, -adora *f* ⟨worker : trabajador(a)⟩ ⟨adapter : adaptador⟩ **2** : más ⟨hotter : más caliente⟩

era ['ɪrə, 'ɛrə, 'iːrə] *n* : era *f*, época *f*

eradicate [ɪ'rædə,keɪt] *vt* **-cated; -cating** : erradicar

erase [ɪ'reɪs] *vt* **erased; erasing** : borrar

eraser [ɪ'reɪsər] *n* : goma *f* de borrar, borrador *m*

erasure [ɪ'reɪʃər] *n* : tachadura *f*

ere¹ ['ɛr] *conj* : antes de que

ere² *prep* **1** : antes de **2 ere long** : dentro de poco

erect¹ [ɪ'rɛkt] *vt* **1** CONSTRUCT : levantar, erigir (un monumento, etc.) **2** RAISE : levantar, armar

erect² *adj* : erguido, derecho, erecto

erection [ɪ'rɛkʃən] *n* **1** : erección *f* (en fisiología) **2** BUILDING : construcción *f*

ergonomics [,ərgə'nɑmɪks] *npl* : ergonomía *f*

ermine ['ərmən] *n* : armiño *m*

erode [ɪ'roːd] *v* **eroded; eroding** *vt* : erosionar (el suelo), corroer (metales) ⟨to erode someone's confidence : minar la confianza de alguien⟩ — *vi* : erosionarse, corroerse ⟨his popular support eroded : perdió el apoyo popular⟩

erosion [ɪ'roːʒən] *n* **1** : erosión *f*, corrosión *f* **2** DETERIORATION : deterioro *m*

erotic [ɪ'rɑtɪk] *adj* : erótico — **erotically** [-tɪkli] *adv*

eroticism [ɪ'rɑtə,sɪzəm] *n* : erotismo *m*

err ['ɛr, 'ər] *vi* : equivocarse, errar

errand ['ɛrənd] *n* : mandado *m*, encargo *m*, recado *m* *Spain* ⟨to run an errand (for somebody) : hacer(le) un mandado (a alguien)⟩

errant ['ɛrənt] *adj* **1** WANDERING : errante **2** ASTRAY : descarriado

erratic [ɪ'rætɪk] *adj* **1** INCONSISTENT : errático, irregular, inconsistente **2** ECCENTRIC : excéntrico, raro

erratically [ɪ'rætɪkli] *adv* : erráticamente, de manera irregular

erroneous [ɪˈroːniəs, ɛ-] *adj* : erróneo — **erroneously** *adv*

error [ˈɛrər] *n* : error *m*, equivocación *f* ⟨to be in error : estar en un error⟩ ⟨to do something in error : hacer algo por equivocación⟩ ⟨to make an error : cometer un error⟩ ⟨spelling error : falta de ortografía⟩

ersatz [ˈɛr,sɑts, ˈərˌsæts] *adj* : artificial, sustituto

erstwhile [ˈərstˌʍwaɪl] *adj* : antiguo

erudite [ˈɛrəˌdaɪt, ˈɛrjʊ-] *adj* : erudito, letrado

erudition [ˌɛrəˈdɪʃən, ˌɛrjʊ-] *n* : erudición *f*

erupt [ɪˈrʌpt] *vi* 1 : hacer erupción, entrar en erupción (dícese de un volcán) 2 : estallar (dícese de la violencia, etc.)

eruption [ɪˈrʌpʃən] *n* 1 : erupción *f* 2 OUTBREAK : estallido *m*, brote *m*

eruptive [ɪˈrʌptɪv] *adj* : eruptivo

escalate [ˈɛskəˌleɪt] *v* -lated; -lating *vt* 1 : intensificar (un conflicto), aumentar (precios) — *vi* : intensificarse, aumentarse

escalation [ˌɛskəˈleɪʃən] *n* : intensificación *f*, escalada *f*, aumento *m*, subida *f*

escalator [ˈɛskəˌleɪtər] *n* : escalera *f* mecánica

escapade [ˈɛskəˌpeɪd] *n* : aventura *f*

escape[1] [ɪˈskeɪp, ɛ-] *v* -caped; -caping *vt* 1 : escaparse de (la policía, etc.) ⟨the name escapes me : el nombre se me escapa⟩ ⟨nothing escapes her (notice) : nada se le escapa⟩ 2 AVOID : escapar a, librarse de (un castigo), salvarse de (la muerte) — *vi* 1 : escaparse 2 SURVIVE : salvarse

escape[2] *n* 1 FLIGHT : fuga *f*, huida *f*, escapada *f* 2 LEAKAGE : escape *m*, fuga *f* 3 : escapatoria *f*, evasión *f* ⟨to have no escape : no tener escapatoria⟩ ⟨escape from reality : evasión de la realidad⟩

escapee [ˌɪˌskeɪˈpiː, ˌɛ-] *n* : fugitivo *m*, -va *f*

escapism [ɪˈskeɪpˌɪzəm] *n* : escapismo *m* — **escapist** [ɪˈskeɪpɪst] *adj*

escarole [ˈɛskəˌroːl] *n* : escarola *f*

escarpment [ɪsˈkɑrpmənt, ɛs-] *n* : escarpa *f*

eschew [ɛˈʃuː, ɪsˈʧuː] *vt* : evitar, rehuir, abstenerse de

escort[1] [ˈɛsˌkɔrt, ɛ-] *vt* 1 : escoltar 2 : llevar (a un prisionero) 3 ACCOMPANY : acompañar

escort[2] [ˈɛsˌkɔrt] *n* 1 : escolta *f* ⟨under armed/police escort : con escolta armada/policial⟩ 2 COMPANION : acompañante *mf*

escrow [ˈɛsˌkroː] *n* **in escrow** : en depósito, en custodia de un tercero

Eskimo [ˈɛskəˌmoː] *n* 1 : esquimal *mf* 2 : esquimal *m* (idioma) — **Eskimo** *adj*

ESL [ˌiː,ɛsˈɛl] *n* (English as a second language) : inglés *m* como lengua extranjera

esophagus [ɪˈsɑfəgəs, iː-] *n, pl* **-gi** [-ˌgaɪ, -ˌʤaɪ] : esófago *m*

esoteric [ˌɛsəˈtɛrɪk] *adj* : esotérico, hermético

espadrille [ˈɛspəˌdrɪl] *n* : alpargata *f Arg, Spain, Uru, Ven*; sandalia *f*

especially [ɪˈspɛʃəli] *adv* 1 : especialmente, particularmente 2 SPECIFICALLY : expresamente, especialmente

espionage [ˈɛspɪəˌnɑʒ, -ˌnɑʤ] *n* : espionaje *m*

espouse [ɪˈspaʊz, ɛ-] *vt* **espoused; espousing** 1 MARRY : casarse con 2 ADOPT, ADVOCATE : apoyar, adherirse a, adoptar

espresso [ɛˈsprɛˌsoː] *n, pl* **-sos** : café *m* exprés

essay[1] [ˈɛseɪ, ˈɛˌseɪ] *vt* : intentar, tratar

essay[2] [ˈɛˌseɪ] *n* 1 : ensayo *m* (publicado) 2 COMPOSITION, PAPER : redacción *f*, trabajo *m* 3 ATTEMPT : intento *m*

essayist [ˈɛˌseɪɪst] *n* : ensayista *mf*

essence [ˈɛsənts] *n* 1 CORE : esencia *f*, núcleo *m*, meollo *m* ⟨in essence : esencialmente⟩ 2 EXTRACT : esencia *f*, extracto *m* 3 PERFUME : esencia *f*, perfume *m*

essential[1] [ɪˈsɛntʃəl] *adj* : esencial ⟨to be essential to : ser esencial para⟩ — **essentially** *adv*

essential[2] *n* : elemento *m* esencial ⟨the (bare) essentials : lo imprescindible⟩

-est *suf* : (el/los/la/las) más ⟨the biggest : el/la más grande, los/las más grandes⟩

establish [ɪˈstæblɪʃ, ɛ-] *vt* 1 FOUND : establecer, fundar 2 SET UP : establecer, instaurar, instituir 3 PROVE : establecer, demostrar

established [ɪˈstæblɪʃt, ɛ-] *adj* 1 ACCEPTED : establecido 2 : de amplia trayectoria (dícese de una empresa, etc.) 3 OFFICIAL : oficial

establishment [ɪˈstæblɪʃmənt, ɛ-] *n* 1 ESTABLISHING : establecimiento *m*, fundación *f*, instauración *f* 2 BUSINESS : negocio *m*, establecimiento *m* 3 **the Establishment** : la clase dirigente

estate [ɪˈsteɪt, ɛ-] *n* 1 POSSESSIONS : bienes *mpl*, propiedad *f*, patrimonio *m* ⟨the estate of the deceased : la sucesión del difunto⟩ 2 PROPERTY : hacienda *f*, finca *f*, propiedad *f*

esteem[1] [ɪˈstiːm, ɛ-] *vt* : estimar, apreciar

esteem[2] *n* : estima *f*, aprecio *m*

esthetic [ɛsˈθɛtɪk] → **aesthetic**

estimable [ˈɛstəməbəl] *adj* : estimable

estimate[1] [ˈɛstəˌmeɪt] *vt* **-mated; -mating** : calcular, estimar

estimate[2] [ˈɛstəmət] *n* 1 : cálculo *m* aproximado ⟨to make an estimate : hacer un cálculo⟩ 2 ASSESSMENT : valoración *f*, estimación *f* 3 QUOTE : presupuesto *m*

estimation [ˌɛstəˈmeɪʃən] *n* 1 JUDGMENT : juicio *m*, opinión *f* ⟨in my estimation : en mi opinión, a mi juicio⟩ 2 ESTIMATE : cálculo *m* aproximado

estimator [ˈɛstəˌmeɪtər] *n* : tasador *m*, -dora *f*

Estonian [ɛˈstoːniən] *n* : estonio *m*, -nia *f* — **Estonian** *adj*

estrange [ɪˈstreɪnʤ, ɛ-] *vt* **-tranged; -tranging** : enajenar, apartar, alejar ⟨he is estranged from his wife : está separado de su mujer⟩

estrangement [ɪ'streɪndʒmənt, ɛ-] n : alejamiento m, distanciamiento m

estrogen ['ɛstrədʒən] n : estrógeno m

estrus ['ɛstrəs] n : celo m

estuary ['ɛstʃʊˌwɛri] n, pl **-aries** : estuario m

et cetera [ɛt'sɛtərə, -'sɛtrə] : etcétera

etch ['ɛtʃ] v : grabar al aguafuerte

etching ['ɛtʃɪŋ] n : aguafuerte m, grabado m al aguafuerte

eternal [ɪ'tərnəl, i:-] adj **1** EVERLASTING : eterno **2** INTERMINABLE : constante, incesante

eternally [ɪ'tərnəli, i:-] adv : eternamente, para siempre

eternity [ɪ'tərnəti, i:-] n, pl **-ties** : eternidad f

ethanol ['ɛθəˌnɔl, -ˌnoːl] n : etanol m

ether ['i:θər] n : éter m

ethereal [ɪ'θɪriəl, i:-] adj **1,** CELESTIAL : etéreo, celeste **2** DELICATE : delicado

ethical ['ɛθɪkəl] adj : ético ⟨ethical code/question : código/cuestión de ética⟩ — **ethically** adv

ethics ['ɛθɪks] ns & pl **1** : ética f **2** MORALITY : ética f, moralidad f

Ethiopian [ˌi:θi'o:piən] n : etíope mf — **Ethiopian** adj

ethnic ['ɛθnɪk] adj : étnico ⟨ethnic group : etnia, grupo étnico⟩ ⟨ethnic cleansing : limpieza étnica⟩

etiquette ['ɛtɪkət, -ˌkɛt] n : etiqueta f, protocolo m

etymological [ˌɛtəmə'lɑdʒɪkəl] adj : etimológico

etymology [ˌɛtə'mɑlədʒi] n, pl **-gies** : etimología f

eucalyptus [ˌju:kə'lɪptəs] n, pl **-ti** [-ˌtaɪ] or **-tuses** [-təsəz] : eucalipto m

Eucharist ['ju:kərɪst] n : Eucaristía f

eulogize ['ju:ləˌdʒaɪz] vt **-gized; -gizing** : elogiar, encomiar

eulogy ['ju:lədʒi] n, pl **-gies** : panegírico m (pronunciado en los funerales)

eunuch ['ju:nək] n : eunuco m

euphemism ['ju:fəˌmɪzəm] n : eufemismo m

euphemistic [ˌju:fə'mɪstɪk] adj : eufemístico

euphoria [jʊ'foriə] n : euforia f

euphoric [jʊ'forɪk] adj : eufórico

euro ['jʊrˌo:] n, pl **euros** or **euro** : euro m

European[1] [ˌjʊrə'pi:ən] adj : europeo ⟨European Union : Unión Europea⟩

European[2] n : europeo m, -pea f

euthanasia [ˌju:θə'neɪʒə, -ʒiə] n : eutanasia f

euthanize ['ju:θəˌnaɪz] **-nized; -nizing** n : sacrificar (un perro, etc.)

evacuate [ɪ'vækjuˌeɪt] v **-ated; -ating** vt VACATE : evacuar, desalojar — vi WITHDRAW : retirarse

evacuation [ɪˌvækjʊ'eɪʃən] n : evacuación f, desalojo m

evade [ɪ'veɪd] vt **evaded; evading** : eludir ⟨to evade taxes : evadir impuestos⟩

evaluate [ɪ'væljuˌeɪt] vt **-ated; -ating** : evaluar, valorar, tasar

evaluation [ɪˌvæljʊ'eɪʃən] n : evaluación f, valoración f, tasación f

evangelical [ˌi:ˌvæn'dʒɛlɪkəl, ˌɛvən-] adj : evangélico

evangelism [ɪ'vændʒəˌlɪzəm] n : evangelismo m

evangelist [ɪ'vændʒəlɪst] n **1** : evangelista m **2** PREACHER : predicador m, -dora f

evaporate [ɪ'væpəˌreɪt] vi **-rated; -rating 1** VAPORIZE : evaporarse **2** VANISH : evaporarse, desvanecerse, esfumarse

evaporated milk n : leche f evaporada

evaporation [ɪˌvæpə'reɪʃən] n : evaporación f

evasion [ɪ'veɪʒən] n : evasión f

evasive [ɪ'veɪsɪv] adj : evasivo

evasiveness [ɪ'veɪsɪvnəs] n : carácter m evasivo

eve ['i:v] n **1** : víspera f ⟨on the eve of the festivities : en vísperas de las festividades⟩ **2** → **evening**

even[1] ['i:vən] vt **1** LEVEL : allanar, nivelar, emparejar **2** EQUALIZE : igualar, equilibrar **3 to even out** : nivelar, emparejar — vi **to even out** : nivelarse, emparejarse

even[2] adv **1** : hasta, incluso ⟨even a child can do it : hasta un niño puede hacerlo⟩ ⟨he looked content, even happy : se le veía satisfecho, incluso feliz⟩ **2** (in negative constructions) : ni siquiera ⟨he didn't even try : ni siquiera lo intentó⟩ **3** (in comparisons) : aún, todavía ⟨even better : aún mejor, todavía mejor⟩ **4 even if** : aunque **5 even so** : aun así **6 even though** : aun cuando, a pesar de que, aunque

even[3] adj **1** SMOOTH : uniforme, liso, parejo **2** FLAT : plano, llano **3** EQUAL : igual, igualado ⟨an even score : un marcador igualado⟩ **4** REGULAR : regular, constante ⟨an even pace : un ritmo constante⟩ **5** EXACT : exacto, justo **6** : par ⟨even number : número par⟩ **7 to be even** : estar en paz, estar a mano **8 to get even** : desquitarse, vengarse

evening ['i:vnɪŋ] n **1** : tarde f, noche f ⟨good evening : buenas tardes/noches⟩ ⟨in the evening : por la noche⟩ ⟨evening class : clase nocturna⟩ **2** : velada f ⟨an evening of music : una velada musical⟩

evening gown or **evening dress** n : traje m de noche

evenings ['i:vnɪŋz] adv : por las noches

evenly ['i:vənli] adv **1** UNIFORMLY : de modo uniforme, de manera constante **2** FAIRLY : igualmente, equitativamente

evenness ['i:vənnəs] n : uniformidad f, igualdad f, regularidad f

event [ɪ'vɛnt] n **1** : acontecimiento m, suceso m, prueba f (en deportes) **2 in any event** or **at all events** : de cualquier modo **3 in the event that** : en caso de que

even–tempered ['i:vən'tɛmpərd] adj : ecuánime

eventful [ɪ'vɛntfəl] adj : lleno de incidentes, memorable

eventual [ɪ'vɛntʃuəl] adj : final, consiguiente

eventuality [ɪˌvɛntʃʊ'æləti] n, pl **-ties** : eventualidad f

eventually [ɪ'vɛntʃuəli] *adv* : finalmente, al fin, con el tiempo

ever ['ɛvər] *adv* **1** ALWAYS : siempre ⟨as ever : como siempre⟩ ⟨ever since (then) : desde entonces⟩ ⟨ever since we met : desde que nos conocimos⟩ **2** (*in questions*) : alguna vez, algún día ⟨have you ever been to Mexico? : ¿has estado en México alguna vez?⟩ ⟨do you ever plan to go back? : ¿piensas volver algún día?⟩ **3** (*in negative constructions*) : nunca ⟨doesn't he ever work? : ¿es que nunca trabaja?⟩ ⟨nobody ever helps me : nadie nunca me ayuda⟩ ⟨we hardly ever speak : casi nunca hablamos⟩ **4** (*in comparisons*) : nunca ⟨better than ever : mejor que nunca⟩ ⟨the best song I ever heard : la mejor canción que he oído nunca⟩ **5** (*as intensifier*) ⟨I'm ever so happy! : ¡estoy tan y tan feliz!⟩ ⟨he looks ever so angry : parece estar muy enojado⟩

evergreen[1] ['ɛvər,griːn] *adj* : de hoja perenne

evergreen[2] *n* : planta *f* de hoja perenne

everlasting [,ɛvər'læstɪŋ] *adj* : eterno, perpetuo, imperecedero

evermore [,ɛvər'mor] *adv* : eternamente

every ['ɛvri] *adj* **1** EACH : cada ⟨every time : cada vez⟩ ⟨every other house : cada dos casas⟩ **2** ALL : todo ⟨every month : todos los meses⟩ ⟨every other year : un año sí y otro no, cada dos años⟩ ⟨every woman : toda mujer, todas las mujeres⟩ **3** COMPLETE : pleno, entero ⟨to have every confidence : tener plena confianza⟩ **4 every now and then** *or* **every once in a while** *or* **every so often** : de vez en cuando

everybody ['ɛvri,bʌdi, -,bʌ-] *pron* : todos, todo el mundo

everyday [,ɛvri'deɪ, 'ɛvri,-] *adj* : cotidiano, diario, corriente ⟨everyday clothes : ropa de todos los días⟩

everyone ['ɛvri,wʌn] → **everybody**

everything ['ɛvri,θɪŋ] *pron* : todo

everywhere ['ɛvri,ʍɛr] *adv* : en todas partes, por todas partes, dondequiera ⟨I looked everywhere : busqué en/por todas partes⟩ ⟨everywhere we go : dondequiera que vayamos⟩

evict [ɪ'vɪkt] *vt* : desalojar, desahuciar

eviction [ɪ'vɪkʃən] *n* : desalojo *m*, desahucio *m*

evidence ['ɛvədənts] *n* **1** INDICATIONS : indicios *mpl*, señales *mpl* ⟨to be in evidence : estar a la vista⟩ **2** PROOF : evidencia *f*, prueba *f* **3** TESTIMONY : testimonio *m*, declaración *f* ⟨to give evidence : declarar como testigo, prestar declaración⟩

evident ['ɛvɪdənt] *adj* : evidente, patente, manifiesto

evidently ['ɛvɪdəntli, ,ɛvɪ'dɛntli] *adv* **1** CLEARLY : claramente, obviamente **2** APPARENTLY : aparentemente, evidentemente, al parecer

evil[1] ['iːvəl, -vɪl] *adj* **eviler** *or* **eviller**; **evilest** *or* **evillest** : malvado (dícese de las personas), maligno (dícese de los espíritus), maléfico (dícese de las influencias)

⟨evil deeds : malas acciones, maldades⟩ ⟨an evil spell : una maldición⟩

evil[2] *n* **1** WICKEDNESS : mal *m*, maldad *f* **2** MISFORTUNE : desgracia *f*, mal *m*

evildoer [,iːvəl'duːər, ,iːvɪl-] *n* : malhechor *m*, -chora *f*; malvado *m*, -da *f*

evil eye *n* **the evil eye** : el mal de ojo

evince [ɪ'vɪnts] *vt* **evinced; evincing** : mostrar, manifestar, revelar

eviscerate [ɪ'vɪsə,reɪt] *vt* **-ated; -ating** : eviscerar

evocation [,iːvo'keɪʃən, ,ɛ-] *n* : evocación *f*

evocative [ɪ'vɑkətɪv] *adj* : evocador

evoke [ɪ'voːk] *vt* **evoked; evoking** : evocar, provocar

evolution [,ɛvə'luːʃən, ,iː-] *n* : evolución *f*, desarrollo *m*

evolutionary [,ɛvə'luːʃə,nɛri, ,iː-] *adj* : evolucionario, desarrollarse

evolve [i'vɑlv] *vi* **evolved; evolving** : evolucionar, desarrollarse

ewe ['juː] *n* : oveja *f* (hembra)

ex ['ɛks] *n* : ex *mf*

ex- ['ɛks] *pref* : ex-, ex ⟨ex-wife : exesposa, ex esposa⟩

exacerbate [ɪg'zæsər,beɪt] *vt* **-bated; -bating** : exacerbar

exact[1] [ɪg'zækt, ɛ-] *vt* : exigir, imponer, arrancar

exact[2] *adj* : exacto, preciso

exacting [ɪg'zæktɪŋ, ɛg-] *adj* : exigente, riguroso

exactitude [ɪg'zæktə,tuːd, ɛg-, -,tjuːd] *n* : exactitud *f*, precisión *f*

exactly [ɪg'zæktli, ɛ-] *adv* : exactamente ⟨it's exactly six o'clock : son las seis en punto⟩ ⟨exactly! : ¡exacto!⟩

exaggerate [ɪg'zædʒə,reɪt, ɛg-] *v* **-ated; -ating** : exagerar

exaggerated [ɪg'zædʒə,reɪtəd, ɛg-] *adj* : exagerado — **exaggeratedly** *adv*

exaggeration [ɪg,zædʒə'reɪʃən, ɛg-] *n* : exageración *f*

exalt [ɪg'zɔlt, ɛg-] *vt* : exaltar, ensalzar, glorificar

exaltation [,ɛg,zɔl'teɪʃən, ,ɛk,sɔl-] *n* : exaltación *f*

exam [ɪg'zæm, ɛg-] → **examination**

examination [ɪg,zæmə'neɪʃən, ɛg-] *n* **1** TEST : examen *m* **2** INSPECTION : inspección *f*, revisión *f* **3** : reconocimiento *m*, examen *m* (en medicina) **4** INVESTIGATION : examen *m*, estudio *m*

examine [ɪg'zæmən, ɛg-] *vt* **-ined; -ining** **1** TEST : examinar **2** INSPECT : inspeccionar, revisar **3** : examinar, revisar (en medicina) **4** STUDY : examinar

example [ɪg'zæmpəl, ɛg-] *n* : ejemplo *m* ⟨for example : por ejemplo⟩ ⟨to set an example : dar ejemplo⟩ ⟨to make an example of someone : darle un castigo ejemplar a alguien⟩

exasperate [ɪg'zæspə,reɪt, ɛg-] *vt* **-ated; -ating** : exasperar, sacar de quicio

exasperation [ɪg,zæspə'reɪʃən, ɛg-] *n* : exasperación *f*

excavate ['ɛkskə,veɪt] *vt* **-vated; -vating** : excavar

excavation [ˌɛkskəˈveɪʃən] n : excavación f

excavator [ˈɛkskəˌveɪtər] n : excavadora f

exceed [ɪkˈsiːd, ɛk-] vt 1 : exceder de, sobrepasar (un límite, etc.) 2 **to exceed expectations** : superar las expectativas 3 **to exceed one's authority** : excederse en sus facultades

exceedingly [ɪkˈsiːdɪŋli, ɛk-] adv : extremadamente, sumamente

excel [ɪkˈsɛl, ɛk-] v **-celled; -celling** vi : destacar, sobresalir (to excel at/in something : destacar(se) en algo) — vt : superar

excellence [ˈɛksələnts] n : excelencia f

excellency [ˈɛksələntsi] n, pl **-cies** : excelencia f (His Excellency : Su Excelencia)

excellent [ˈɛksələnt] adj : excelente, sobresaliente — **excellently** adv

except¹ [ɪkˈsɛpt] vt : exceptuar, excluir

except² conj : pero, si no fuera por

except³ prep : excepto, menos, salvo (everyone except Carlos : todos menos Carlos)

except for → **except³**

exception [ɪkˈsɛpʃən] n 1 : excepción f 2 **to take exception to** : ofenderse por, objetar a 3 **with the exeption of** : a/con excepción de

exceptional [ɪkˈsɛpʃənəl] adj : excepcional, extraordinario — **exceptionally** adv

excerpt¹ [ɛkˈsərpt, ɛgˈzərpt, ˈɛkˌ-, ˈgˌ-] vt : escoger, seleccionar

excerpt² [ˈɛkˌsərpt, ˈɛgˌzərpt] n : pasaje m, selección f

excess¹ [ˈɛkˌsɛs, ɪkˈsɛs] adj 1 : excesivo, de sobra 2 **excess baggage** : exceso m de equipaje

excess² [ɪkˈsɛs, ˈɛkˌsɛs] n 1 SUPERFLUITY : exceso m, superfluidad f (an excess of energy : un exceso de energía) 2 SURPLUS : excedente m, sobrante m (in excess of : superior a)

excessive [ɪkˈsɛsɪv, ɛk-] adj : excesivo, exagerado, desmesurado — **excessively** adv

exchange¹ [ɪksˈtʃeɪndʒ, ɛks-; ˈɛks-ˌtʃeɪndʒ] vt **-changed; -changing** : cambiar, intercambiar, canjear (to exchange something for something : cambiar algo por algo)

exchange² n 1 : cambio m, intercambio m, canje m (in exchange for : a cambio de) 2 **stock exchange** : bolsa f (de valores) 3 **or telephone exchange** : central f telefónica

exchangeable [ɪksˈtʃeɪndʒəbəl, ɛks-] adj : canjeable

exchange rate n : tasa f de cambio

exchequer [ˈɛksˌtʃɛkər, ɪksˈtʃɛkər] n TREASURY : erario m, tesoro m, fisco m

excise¹ [ɪkˈsaɪz, ɛk-] vt **-cised; -cising** : extirpar

excise² [ˈɛkˌsaɪz] n **excise tax** : impuesto m interno, impuesto m sobre el consumo

excitability [ɪkˌsaɪtəˈbɪləti, ɛk-] n : excitabilidad f

excitable [ɪkˈsaɪtəbəl, ɛk-] adj : nervioso

excitation [ˌɛkˌsaɪˈteɪʃən] n : excitación f

excite [ɪkˈsaɪt, ɛk-] vt **-cited; -citing** 1 AROUSE, STIMULATE : excitar, mover, estimular 2 ANIMATE : entusiasmar, animar 3 EVOKE, PROVOKE : provocar, despertar, suscitar (to excite curiosity : despertar la curiosidad)

excited [ɪkˈsaɪtəd, ɛk-] adj 1 STIMULATED : excitado 2 ENTHUSIASTIC : entusiasmado, emocionado

excitedly [ɪkˈsaɪtədli, ɛk-] adv : con excitación, con entusiasmo

excitement [ɪkˈsaɪtmənt, ɛk-] n 1 ENTHUSIASM : entusiasmo m, emoción f 2 AGITATION : agitación f, alboroto m, conmoción f 3 AROUSAL : excitación f

exciting [ɪkˈsaɪtɪŋ, ɛk-] adj 1 : emocionante 2 AROUSING : excitante

exclaim [ɪksˈkleɪm, ɛk-] v : exclamar

exclamation [ˌɛkskləˈmeɪʃən] n : exclamación f

exclamation point n : signo m de admiración

exclude [ɪksˈkluːd, ɛks-] vt **-cluded; -cluding** 1 LEAVE OUT : excluir 2 RULE OUT : excluir, descartar 3 BAR : no admitir

excluding [ɪksˈkluːdɪŋ, ɛks-] prep : excluyendo, sin incluir

exclusion [ɪksˈkluːʒən, ɛks-] n : exclusión f

exclusive¹ [ɪksˈkluːsɪv, ɛks-] adj 1 SOLE : exclusivo, único 2 SELECT : exclusivo, selecto 3 **exclusive of** → **excluding**

exclusive² n : exclusiva f

exclusively [ɪksˈkluːsɪvli, ɛks-] adv : exclusivamente, únicamente

exclusiveness [ɪksˈkluːsɪvnəs, ɛks-] n : exclusividad f

excommunicate [ˌɛkskəˈmjuːnəˌkeɪt] vt **-cated; -cating** : excomulgar

excommunication [ˌɛkskəˌmjuːnəˈkeɪʃən] n : excomunión f

excrement [ˈɛkskrəmənt] n : excremento m

excrete [ɪkˈskriːt, ɛk-] vt **-creted; -creting** : excretar

excretion [ɪkˈskriːʃən, ɛk-] n : excreción f

excruciating [ɪkˈskruːʃiˌeɪtɪŋ, ɛk-] adj : insoportable, atroz, terrible — **excruciatingly** adv

exculpate [ˈɛkskəlˌpeɪt] vt **-pated; -pating** : exculpar

excursion [ɪkˈskərʒən, ɛk-] n 1 OUTING : excursión f, paseo m 2 DIGRESSION : digresión f

excusable [ɪkˈskjuːzəbəl, ɛk-] adj : disculpable

excuse¹ [ɪkˈskjuːz, ɛk-] vt **-cused; -cusing** 1 PARDON : disculpar, perdonar (excuse me : con permiso, perdóneme, perdón) 2 DISMISS : dejar salir (may I be excused? : ¿puedo ir?) 3 EXEMPT : disculpar, eximir 4 JUSTIFY : excusar, justificar 5 **to excuse yourself** : excusarse

excuse² [ɪkˈskjuːs, ɛk-] n 1 JUSTIFICATION : excusa f, justificación f 2 PRETEXT : pretexto m 3 **to make excuses** : poner excusas 4 **to make one's excuses to someone** : pedirle disculpas a alguien

execute [ˈɛksɪˌkjuːt] *vt* **-cuted; -cuting 1** CARRY OUT : ejecutar, llevar a cabo, desempeñar **2** ENFORCE : ejecutar, cumplir (un testamento, etc.) **3** KILL : ejecutar, ajusticiar

execution [ˌɛksɪˈkjuːʃən] *n* **1** PERFORMANCE : ejecución *f*, desempeño *m* **2** IMPLEMENTATION : cumplimiento *m* **3** : ejecución *f* (por un delito)

executioner [ˌɛksɪˈkjuːʃənər] *n* : verdugo *m*

executive¹ [ɪɡˈzɛkjətɪv, ɛɡ-] *adj* : ejecutivo

executive² *n* : ejecutivo *m*, -va *f*

executor [ɪɡˈzɛkjətər, ɛɡ-] *n* : albacea *mf*, testamentario *m*, -ria *f*

executrix [ɪɡˈzɛkjəˌtrɪks, ɛɡ-] *n, pl* **executrices** [-ˌzɛkjəˈtraɪˌsiːz] *or* **executrixes** [-ˈzɛkjəˌtrɪksəz] : albacea *f*, testamentaria *f*

exemplary [ɪɡˈzɛmpləri, ɛɡ-] *adj* : ejemplar

exemplify [ɪɡˈzɛmpləˌfaɪ, ɛɡ-] *vt* **-fied; -fying** : ejemplificar, ilustrar, demostrar

exempt¹ [ɪɡˈzɛmpt, ɛɡ-] *vt* : eximir ⟨to exempt someone from something : eximir a alguien de algo⟩

exempt² *adj* : exento ⟨to be exempt from : estar exento de⟩

exemption [ɪɡˈzɛmpʃən, ɛɡ-] *n* : exención *f*

exercise¹ [ˈɛksərˌsaɪz] *v* **-cised; -cising** *vt* **1** : ejercitar (el cuerpo) **2** : ejercitar (un caballo), sacar a pasear (un perro) **3** USE : ejercer, hacer uso de ⟨to exercise caution/restraint : obrar con cautela/moderación⟩ — *vi* **1** : hacer ejercicio

exercise² *n* **1** : ejercicio *m* ⟨to get exercise : hacer ejercicio⟩ ⟨arm exercises : ejercicios para los brazos⟩ **2** : ejercicio *m* ⟨math exercises : ejercicios de matemáticas⟩ **3** MANEUVER : ejercicio *m*, maniobra *f* **4** USE : ejercicio *m* **5 exercises** *npl* CEREMONY : ceremonia *f*

exert [ɪɡˈzərt, ɛɡ-] *vt* : ejercer, emplear **2 to exert oneself** : esforzarse

exertion [ɪɡˈzərʃən, ɛɡ-] *n* **1** USE : ejercicio *m* (de autoridad, etc.), uso *m* (de fuerza, etc.) **2** EFFORT : esfuerzo *m*, empeño *m*

exhalation [ˌɛksəˈleɪʃən, ˌɛkshə-] *n* : exhalación *f*

exhale [ɛksˈheɪl] *v* **-haled; -haling** *vt* **1** : exhalar, espirar **2** EMIT : exhalar, despedir, emitir — *vi* : espirar

exhaust¹ [ɪɡˈzɔst, ɛɡ-] *vt* **1** DEPLETE : agotar **2** TIRE : cansar, fatigar, agotar **3** EMPTY : vaciar

exhaust² *n* **1** *or* **exhaust fumes** : gases *mpl* de escape **2** *or* **exhaust pipe** : tubo *m* de escape, caño *m* de escape *Arg, Uru* **3** *or* **exhaust system** : sistema *m* de escape

exhausted [ɪɡˈzɔstəd, ɛɡ-] *adj* : agotado, derrengado

exhausting [ɪɡˈzɔstɪŋ, ɛɡ-] *adj* : extenuante, agotador

exhaustion [ɪɡˈzɔstʃən, ɛɡ-] *n* : agotamiento *m*

exhaustive [ɪɡˈzɔstɪv, ɛɡ-] *adj* : exhaustivo

exhibit¹ [ɪɡˈzɪbət, ɛɡ-] *vt* **1** DISPLAY : exhibir, exponer **2** PRODUCE, SHOW : mostrar, presentar

exhibit² *n* **1** OBJECT : objeto *m* expuesto **2** EXHIBITION : exposición *f*, exhibición *f* **3** EVIDENCE : prueba *f* instrumental **4 to be on exhibit** : estar expuesto

exhibition [ˌɛksəˈbɪʃən] *n* **1** : exposición *f*, exhibición *f* **2 to make an exhibition of oneself** : dar el espectáculo, hacer el ridículo

exhibitor [ɪɡˈzɪbətər] *n* : expositor *m*, -tora *f*

exhilarate [ɪɡˈzɪləˌreɪt, ɛɡ-] *vt* **-rated; -rating 1** : animar mucho, llenar de alegría **2** STIMULATE : estimular

exhilaration [ɪɡˌzɪləˈreɪʃən, ɛɡ-] *n* : alegría *f*, regocijo *m*, júbilo *m*

exhort [ɪɡˈzɔrt, ɛɡ-] *vt* : exhortar

exhortation [ˌɛkˌsɔrˈteɪʃən, -sər-; ˌɛɡˌzɔr-] *n* : exhortación *f*

exhumation [ˌɛkskjuˈmeɪʃən, -hju-; ˌɛɡzu-, -zju-] *n* : exhumación *f*

exhume [ɪɡˈzuːm, -ˈzjuːm; ɪksˈjuːm, -ˈhjuːm] *vt* **-humed; -huming** : exhumar, desenterrar

ex–husband [ˈɛksˈhʌzbənd] *n* : ex marido *m*

exigencies [ˈɛksɪdʒənsiz, ɪɡˈzɪdʒənˌsiːz] *npl* : exigencias *fpl*

exile¹ [ˈɛɡˌzaɪl, ˈɛkˌsaɪl] *vt* **exiled; exiling** : exiliar, desterrar

exile² *n* **1** BANISHMENT : exilio *m*, destierro *m* **2** OUTCAST : exiliado *m*, -da *f*; desterrado *m*, -da *f*

exist [ɪɡˈzɪst, ɛɡ-] *vi* **1** BE : existir **2** LIVE : subsistir, vivir

existence [ɪɡˈzɪstənts, ɛɡ-] *n* : existencia *f*

existent [ɪɡˈzɪstənt, ɛɡ-] *adj* : existente

existing [ɪɡˈzɪstɪŋ] *adj* : existente

exit¹ [ˈɛɡzət, ˈɛksət] *vi* : salir, hacer mutis (en el teatro) — *vt* : salir de ⟨to exit the building : salir del edificio⟩ ⟨to exit a program : salir de un programa⟩

exit² *n* **1** DEPARTURE : salida *f*, partida *f* **2** EGRESS : salida *f* ⟨emergency exit : salida de emergencia⟩

exodus [ˈɛksədəs] *n* : éxodo *m*

exonerate [ɪɡˈzɑnəˌreɪt, ɛɡ-] *vt* **-ated; -ating** : exonerar, disculpar, absolver

exoneration [ɪɡˌzɑnəˈreɪʃən, ɛɡ-] *n* : exoneración *f*

exorbitant [ɪɡˈzɔrbətənt, ɛɡ-] *adj* : exorbitante, excesivo

exorcise [ˈɛkˌsɔrˌsaɪz, -sər-] *vt* **-cised; -cising** : exorcizar

exorcism [ˈɛksərˌsɪzəm] *n* : exorcismo *m*

exotic¹ [ɪɡˈzɑtɪk, ɛɡ-] *adj* : exótico — **exotically** [-ɪkli] *adv*

exotic² *n* : planta *f* exótica

expand [ɪkˈspænd, ɛk-] *vt* **1** ENLARGE : expandir, ampliar **2** BROADEN, EXTEND : ampliar, extender — *vi* **1** ENLARGE : ampliarse, extenderse **2** : expandirse, dilatarse (dícese de los metales, gases, etc.) **3 to expand on/upon** : extenderse en/sobre, explayarse en/sobre

expanse [ɪkˈspænts, ɛk-] *n* : extensión *f*

expansion [ɪkˈspænʃən, ɛk-] *n* **1** ENLARGEMENT : expansión *f*, ampliación *f* **2** EXPANSE : extensión *f*

expansive [ɪk'spæntsɪv, ɛk-] *adj* 1 : expansivo 2 OUTGOING : expansivo, comunicativo 3 AMPLE : ancho, amplio — **expansively** *adv*

expatriate[1] [ɛks'peɪtri,eɪt] *vt* -ated; -ating : expatriar

expatriate[2] [ɛks'peɪtriət, -,eɪt] *adj* : expatriado

expatriate[3] [ɛks'peɪtriət, -,eɪt] *n* : expatriado *m*, -da *f*

expect [ɪk'spkt, ɛk-] *vt* 1 SUPPOSE : suponer, imaginarse ⟨I expect so : supongo que sí⟩ 2 ANTICIPATE : esperar ⟨we're expecting company : esperamos visita⟩ ⟨rain is expected : se pronostican lluvias⟩ ⟨I expect to win : espero ganar⟩ 3 COUNT ON, REQUIRE : contar con, esperar ⟨I expect you to come : cuento con que vengas⟩ ⟨we expected more of/from you : esperábamos otra cosa de ti⟩ — *vi* **to be expecting** : estar embarazada

expectancy [ɪk'spɛktəntsi, ɛk-] *n, pl* **-cies** 1 : expectación *f*, expectativa *f* 2 → **life expectancy**

expectant [ɪk'spɛktənt, ɛk-] *adj* 1 ANTICIPATING : expectante 2 EXPECTING : futuro ⟨expectant mother : futura madre⟩

expectantly [ɪk'spɛktəntli, ɛk-] *adv* : con expectación

expectation [,ɛk,spɛk'teɪʃən] *n* 1 ANTICIPATION : expectación *f* ⟨to have every expectation of : tener muchas esperanzas de⟩ 2 EXPECTANCY : expectativa *f* ⟨it didn't live up to expectations : no estaba a la altura de las expectativas⟩

expedient[1] [ɪk'spiːdiənt, ɛk-] *adj* : conveniente, oportuno

expedient[2] *n* : expediente *m*, recurso *m*

expedite ['ɛkspə,daɪt] *vt* -dited; -diting 1 FACILITATE : facilitar, dar curso a 2 HASTEN : acelerar

expedition [,ɛkspə'dɪʃən] *n* : expedición *f*

expeditious [,ɛkspə'dɪʃəs] *adj* : pronto, rápido

expel [ɪk'spɛl, ɛk-] *vt* **-pelled; -pelling** 1 : expulsar (a alguien) 2 : expulsar, expeler (aire, etc.)

expend [ɪk'spɛnd, ɛk-] *vt* 1 DISBURSE : gastar, desembolsar 2 CONSUME : consumir, agotar

expendable [ɪk'spɛndəbəl, ɛk-] *adj* : prescindible

expenditure [ɪk'spɛndɪtʃər, ɛk-, -,tʃʊr] *n* : gasto *m*

expense [ɪk'spɛnts, ɛk-] *n* 1 COST : gasto *m* 2 **expenses** *npl* : gastos *mpl*, expensas *fpl* 3 **at the expense of** : a costa de, a expensas de

expensive [ɪk'spɛntsɪv, ɛk-] *adj* : costoso, caro — **expensively** *adv*

experience[1] [ɪk'spɪriəns, ɛk-] *vt* **-enced; -encing** : experimentar (sentimientos), tener (dificultades), sufrir (una pérdida)

experience[2] *n* : experiencia *f*

experienced [ɪk'spɪriənst, ɛk-] *adj* : con experiencia, experimentado

experiment[1] [ɪk'spɛrəmənt, ɛk-, -'spɪr-] *vi* **to experiment on/with** : experimentar con, hacer experimentos con

experiment[2] *n* : experimento *m*

experimental [ɪk,spɛrə'mntəl, ɛk-, -,spɪr-] *adj* : experimental — **experimentally** *adv*

experimentation [ɪk,spɛrəmən'teɪʃən, ɛk-, -,spɪr-] *n* : experimentación *f*

expert[1] ['ɛk,spərt, ɪk'spərt] *adj* : experto, de experto ⟨expert testimony : testimonio pericial⟩ ⟨expert at (doing) something : experto en (hacer) algo⟩ — **expertly** *adv*

expert[2] ['ɛk,spərt] *n* : experto *m*, -ta *f*; perito *m*, -ta *f*

expertise [,ɛkspər'tiːz] *n* : pericia *f*, competencia *f*

expiate ['ɛkspi,eɪt] *vt* -ated; -ating : expiar

expiation [,ɛkspi'eɪʃən] *n* : expiación *f*

expiration [,ɛkspə'reɪʃən] *n* 1 EXHALATION : exhalación *f*, espiración *f* 2 DEATH : muerte *f* 3 TERMINATION : vencimiento *m*, caducidad *f*

expire [ɪk'spaɪr, ɛk-] *vi* **-pired; -piring** 1 EXHALE : espirar 2 DIE : expirar, morir 3 TERMINATE : caducar, vencer

explain [ɪk'spleɪn, ɛk-] *vt* 1 : explicar 2 **to explain yourself** : excusarse — **explainable** [ɪk'spleɪnəbəl, ɛk-] *adj*

explanation [,ɛksplə'neɪʃən] *n* : explicación *f*

explanatory [ɪk'splænə,tori, ɛk-] *adj* : explicativo, aclaratorio

expletive ['ɛksplətɪv] *n* : improperio *m*, palabrota *f fam*, grosería *f*

explicable [ɛk'splɪkəbəl, 'ɛkspli-] *adj* : explicable

explicit [ɪk'splɪsət, ɛk-] *adj* : explícito, claro, categórico, rotundo — **explicitly** *adv*

explicitness [ɪk'splɪsətnəs, ɛk-] *n* : claridad *f*, carácter *m* explícito

explode [ɪk'sploːd, ɛk-] *v* **-ploded; -ploding** *vt* 1 BURST : hacer explosionar, hacer explotar 2 REFUTE : rebatir, refutar, desmentir — *vi* 1 BURST : explotar, estallar, reventar 2 SKYROCKET : dispararse

exploit[1] [ɪk'splɔɪt, ɛk-] *vt* : explotar, aprovecharse de

exploit[2] ['ɛk,splɔɪt] *n* : hazaña *f*, proeza *f*

exploitation [,ɛk,splɔɪ'teɪʃən] *n* : explotación *f*

exploration [,ɛksplə'reɪʃən] *n* : exploración *f*

exploratory [ɪk'splorə,tori, ɛk-] *adj* : exploratorio

explore [ɪk'splor, ɛk-] *vt* **-plored; -ploring** : explorar, investigar, examinar

explorer [ɪk'splorər, ɛk-] *n* : explorador *m*, -dora *f*

explosion [ɪk'sploːʒən, ɛk-] *n* : explosión *f*, estallido *m*

explosive[1] [ɪk'sploːsɪv, ɛk-] *adj* : explosivo, fulminante — **explosively** *adv*

explosive[2] *n* : explosivo *m*

exponent [ɪk'sponənt, 'ɛk,spo:-] *n* 1 : exponente *m* 2 ADVOCATE : defensor *m*, -sora *f*; partidario *m*, -ria *f*

exponential [,ɛkspə'nɛntʃəl] *adj* : exponencial — **exponentially** *adv*

export[1] [ɛk'spoːr, 'ɛk,spoːr] vt : exportar
export[2] ['ɛk,spoːr] n 1 : artículo m de exportación 2 → **exportation**
exportation [,ɛk,spoːr'teɪʃən] n : exportación f
exporter [ɛk'spoːrtər, 'ɛk,spoːr-] n : exportador m, -dora f
expose [ɪk'spoːz, ɛk-] vt -**posed; -posing**
1 : exponer (al peligro, a los elementos, a una enfermedad) 2 : exponer (una película a la luz) 3 DISCLOSE : revelar, develar, sacar a la luz 4 UNMASK : desenmascarar ⟨to expose someone as a fraud : demostrar que alguien es un farsante⟩
exposé [,ɛkspoʊ'zeɪ] n : exposición f (de hechos), revelación f (de un escándalo)
exposed [ɪk'spoːzd, ɛk-] adj : expuesto, al descubierto ⟨exposed brick : ladrillo a la vista⟩
exposition [,ɛkspə'zɪʃən] n : exposición f
exposure [ɪk'spoːʒər, ɛk-] n 1 : exposición f (a la luz, a enfermedades, etc.) 2 : congelación f (en medicina) 3 DISCLOSURE : revelación f 4 PUBLICITY : publicidad f 5 ORIENTATION : orientación f ⟨a room with a northern exposure : una sala orientada al norte⟩ 6 : exposición f (en fotografía)
expound [ɪk'spaʊnd, ɛk-] vt : exponer, explicar — vi : hacer comentarios detallados
express[1] [ɪk'sprɛs, ɛk-] vt 1 : expresar ⟨to express oneself : expresarse⟩ 2 : mandar/enviar (una carta, etc.) por correo expreso
express[2] adv : por correo expreso, por correo urgente
express[3] adj 1 EXPLICIT : expreso, explícito 2 SPECIFIC : específico ⟨for that express purpose : con ese fin específico⟩ 3 RAPID : expreso, rápido — **expressly** adv
express[4] n 1 or **express mail** : expreso m, correo m expreso/urgente 2 : expreso m, tren m expreso
expression [ɪk'sprɛʃən, ɛk-] n 1 UTTERANCE : expresión f ⟨freedom of expression : libertad de expresión⟩ 2 : expresión f (en la matemática) 3 PHRASE : frase, expresión f 4 LOOK : expresión f, cara f, gesto m ⟨with a sad expression : con un gesto de tristeza⟩
expressionless [ɪk'sprɛʃənləs, ɛk-] adj : inexpresivo
expressive [ɪk'sprɛsɪv, ɛk-] adj : expresivo
expressway [ɪk'sprɛs,weɪ, ɛk-] n : autopista f
expropriate [ɛk'sproʊpri,eɪt] vt -**ated; -ating** : expropiar
expulsion [ɪk'spʌlʃən, ɛk-] n : expulsión f
expurgate ['ɛkspər,geɪt] vt -**gated; -gating** : expurgar
exquisite [ɛk'skwɪzət, 'ɛk,skwɪ-] adj 1 FINE : exquisito, primoroso ⟨in exquisite detail : con todo lujo de detalles⟩ 2 EXTREME : intenso (dícese del dolor, etc.), exquisito

exquisiteness [ɛk'skwɪzətnəs, 'ɛk,skwɪ-] n : exquisitez f
extant ['ɛkstənt, ɛk'stænt] adj : existente
extemporaneous [ɛk,stɛmpə'reɪniəs] adj : improvisado — **extemporaneously** adv
extend [ɪk'stɛnd, ɛk-] vt 1 STRETCH : extender, tender 2 PROLONG : prolongar (una visita, etc.), prorrogar (un plazo) 3 ENLARGE : agrandar, ampliar 4 PROFFER : dar (una bienvenida), presentar (disculpas) ⟨to extend an invitation : invitar⟩ — vi : extenderse
extendable adj : extensible
extended [ɪk'stɛndəd, ɛk-] adj LENGTHY : prolongado, largo ⟨extended warranty : garantía extendida⟩
extension [ɪk'stɛnʃən, ɛk-] n 1 EXTENDING : extensión f, ampliación f (de un edificio), prórroga f (de un plazo), prolongación f (de una visita) 2 ADDITION, ANNEX : ampliación f, anexo m 3 LINE : extensión f, interno m
extension cord n : extensión f; alargador m; alargue m Arg, Uru
extensive [ɪk'stɛnsɪv, ɛk-] adj 1 BROAD : extenso, amplio ⟨extensive damage : cuantiosos daños⟩ 2 THOROUGH : exhaustivo — **extensively** adv
extent [ɪk'stɛnt, ɛk-] n 1 SIZE : extensión f, magnitud f 2 DEGREE, SCOPE : alcance m, grado m ⟨to a certain extent : hasta cierto punto⟩ ⟨to a great extent : en gran parte⟩
extenuate [ɪk'stɛnjə,weɪt, ɛk-] vt -**ated; -ating** : atenuar, aminorar, mitigar ⟨extenuating circumstances : (circunstancias) atenuantes⟩
exterior[1] [ɛk'stɪriər] adj : exterior
exterior[2] n : exterior m
exterminate [ɪk'stərmə,neɪt, ɛk-] vt -**nated; -nating** : exterminar
extermination [ɪk,stərmə'neɪʃən, ɛk-] n : exterminación f, exterminio m
exterminator [ɪk'stərmə,neɪtər, ɛk-] n : exterminador m, -dora f de plagas; fumigador m, -dora f
external [ɪk'stərnəl, ɛk-] adj : externo, exterior — **externally** adv
extinct [ɪk'stɪŋkt, ɛk-] adj : extinto
extinction [ɪk'stɪŋkʃən, ɛk-] n : extinción f
extinguish [ɪk'stɪŋgwɪʃ, ɛk-] vt : extinguir, apagar
extinguisher [ɪk'stɪŋgwɪʃər, ɛk-] n : extinguidor m, extintor m
extirpate ['ɛkstər,peɪt] vt -**pated; -pating** : extirpar, exterminar
extol [ɪk'stoːl, ɛk-] vt -**tolled; -tolling** : exaltar, ensalzar, alabar
extort [ɪk'stɔrt, ɛk-] vt : extorsionar
extortion [ɪk'stɔrʃən, ɛk-] n : extorsión f
extra[1] ['ɛkstrə] adv 1 : extra, más, super ⟨extra special : super especial⟩ ⟨to pay extra for : pagar más/extra por⟩ 2 : excepcionalmente ⟨to be extra careful : tener especial cuidado⟩
extra[2] adj 1 ADDITIONAL : adicional, suplementario, de más ⟨to be/cost extra : no estar incluido en el precio⟩ ⟨at no

extra charge : sin costo adicional⟩ 2 SU-
PERIOR : superior

extra³ *n* 1 : extra *m* 2 : extra *mf* (en
películas)

extra- *pref* : extra-

extract¹ [ık'strækt, ɛk-] *vt* : extraer, sacar

extract² ['ɛk,strækt] *n* 1 EXCERPT : pasaje
m, selección *f*, trozo *m* 2 : extracto *m*
⟨vanilla extract : extracto de vainilla⟩

extraction [ık'strækʃən, ɛk-] *n* : extracción *f*

extractor [ık'stræktər, ɛk-] *n* : extractor *m*

extracurricular [,ɛkstrəkə'rıkjələr] *adj* :
extracurricular

extradite ['ɛkstrə,daıt] *vt* -dited; -diting :
extraditar

extradition [,ɛkstrə'dıʃən] *n* : extradición *f*

extramarital [,ɛkstrə'mærətəl] *adj* : extramatrimonial

extraneous [ɛk'streıniəs] *adj* 1 OUTSIDE
: externo 2 SUPERFLUOUS : superfluo,
ajeno — **extraneously** *adv*

extraordinary [ık'strɔrdən,ɛri, ,ɛkstrə'ɔrd-]
adj : extraordinario, excepcional — **ex-
traordinarily** [ık,strɔrdən'ɛrəli, ,kstrə,ɔrd-]
adv

extrapolate [ık'stræpə,leıt] *v* -lated; -lat-
ing : extrapolar — *vi* : hacer una extrapolación — **extrapolation**
[ık,stræpə'leıʃən] *n*

extrasensory [,ɛkstrə'sɛntsəri] *adj* : extrasensorial

extraterrestrial¹ [,ɛkstrətə'rɛstriəl] *adj*
: extraterrestre

extraterrestrial² *n* : extraterrestre *mf*

extravagance [ık'strævıgənts, ɛk-] *n* 1
EXCESS : exceso *m*, extravagancia *f* 2
WASTEFULNESS : derroche *m*, despilfa-
rro *m* 3 LUXURY : lujo *m*

extravagant [ık'strævıgənt, ɛk-] *adj* 1 EX-
CESSIVE : excesivo, exagerado, extravagante 2 WASTEFUL : despilfarrador, derrochador, gastador 3 EXORBITANT
: costoso, exorbitante

extravagantly [ık'strævıgəntli, ɛk-] *adv* 1
LAVISHLY : a lo grande 2 EXCESSIVELY
: exageradamente, desmesuradamente

extravaganza [ık,strævə'gænzə, ɛk-] *n*
: gran espectáculo *m*

extreme¹ [ık'stri:m, ɛk-] *adj* 1 : extremo
⟨extreme cold : frío extremo⟩ ⟨of extreme importance : de suma importan-
cia⟩ 2 : extremo, extremista ⟨extreme
views : opiniones extremas⟩ 3 SEVERE,
DRASTIC : extremo ⟨extreme conditions
: condiciones extremas⟩ ⟨extreme measures : medidas excepcionales, medidas
drásticas⟩ 4 : más lejos ⟨the extreme
north : el extremo norte/septentrional⟩
5 : extremo ⟨extreme sports : deportes
extremos⟩

extreme² *n* 1 : extremo *m* 2 in the extreme : en extremo, en sumo grado

extremely [ık'stri:mli, ɛk-] *adv* : sumamente, extremadamente, terriblemente
⟨extremely large : grandísimo⟩

extremist [ık'stri:mıst, ɛk-] *n* : extremista
mf — **extremist** *adj*

extremity [ık'strɛməti, ɛk-] *n*, *pl* -ties 1
EXTREME : extremo *m* 2 **extremities** *npl*
LIMBS : extremidades *fpl*

extricate ['ɛkstrə,keıt] *vt* -cated; -cating
: librar, sacar

extrovert ['ɛkstrə,vərt] *n* : extrovertido *m*,
-da *f*

extroverted ['ɛkstrə,vərtəd] *adj* : extrovertido

extrude [ık'stru:d, ɛk-] *vt* -truded; -trud-
ing : extruir, expulsar

exuberance [ıg'zu:bərənts, ɛg-] *n* 1 JOY-
OUSNESS : euforia *f*, exaltación *f* 2
VIGOR : exuberancia *f*, vigor *m*

exuberant [ıg'zu:bərənt, ɛg-] *adj* 1 JOY-
OUS : eufórico 2 LUSH : exuberante —
exuberantly *adv*

exude [ıg'zu:d, ɛg-] *vt* -uded; -uding 1
OOZE : rezumar, exudar 2 EMANATE
: emanar, irradiar

exult [ıg'zʌlt, ɛg-] *vi* : exultar, regocijarse

exultant [ıg'zʌltənt, ɛg-] *adj* : exultante,
jubiloso — **exultantly** *adv*

exultation [,ɛksəl'teıʃən, ,ɛgzəl-] *n* : exultación *f*, júbilo *m*, alborozo *m*

ex–wife ['ɛks'waıf] *n* : ex esposa *f*

eye¹ ['aı] *vt* eyed; eyeing *or* eying : mirar,
observar

eye² *n* 1 : ojo *m* 2 VISION : visión *f*, vista
f, ojo *m* ⟨to have a good eye for bargains
: tener un buen ojo para las gangas⟩ 3
GAZE : mirada *f*, ojeada *f* ⟨before my
(very) eyes : ante mis propios ojos⟩
⟨keep an eye on him : vigílalo⟩ ⟨keep an
eye out for her : fíjate a ver si la ves⟩
⟨don't take your eyes off the road : no
apartes la vista de la carretera⟩ 4 AT-
TENTION : atención *f* ⟨to catch one's eye
: llamar la atención⟩ 5 POINT OF VIEW
: punto *m* de vista ⟨in the eyes of the law
: según la ley⟩ 6 : ojo *m* (de una aguja,
una papa, una tormenta)

eyeball ['aı,bɔl] *n* : globo *m* ocular

eyebrow ['aı,brau] *n* : ceja *f* ⟨to raise an
eyebrow at : asombrarse ante⟩

eye–catching ['aı,kætʃıŋ, -,kɛ-] *adj* : llamativo

eyed ['aıd] *adj used in combination* : de
ojos ⟨blue-eyed : de ojos azules⟩ ⟨wide-
eyed : con los ojos muy abiertos⟩ ⟨cross-
eyed : bizco⟩ ⟨one-eyed : tuerto⟩

eyedropper ['aı,drɑpər] *n* : cuentagotas *f*

eyedrops ['aı,drɑps] *npl* : colirio *m*

eyeglasses ['aı,glæsəz] *npl* : anteojos
mpl, lentes *mpl*, espejuelos *mpl*, gafas *fpl*

eyelash ['aı,læʃ] *n* : pestaña *f*

eyelet ['aılət] *n* : ojete *m*

eyelid ['aı,lıd] *n* : párpado *m*

eyeliner ['aı,laınər] *n* : delineador *m* (de ojos)

eye–opener ['aı,o:pənər] *n* : revelación *f*,
sorpresa *f*

eye–opening ['aı,o:pənıŋ] *adj* : revelador

eyepiece ['aı,pi:s] *n* : ocular *m*

eye shadow *n* : sombra *f* de ojos

eyesight ['aı,saıt] *n* : vista *f*, visión *f*

eyesore ['aı,sor] *n* : monstruosidad *f*, adefesio *m*

eyestrain ['aı,streın] *n* : fatiga *f* visual,
vista *f* cansada

eyetooth ['aı,tu:θ] *n* : colmillo *m*

eyewitness ['aı'wıtnəs] *n* : testigo *mf* ocular, testigo *mf* presencial

eyrie ['aıri] → aerie

F

f ['ɛf] *n*, *pl* **f's** *or* **fs** ['ɛfs] 1 : sexta letra del alfabeto inglés 2 **F** : fa *m* (en el canto) 2 **F** : fa *m* ⟨F sharp/flat : fa sostenido/bemol⟩ 3 **F** : insuficiente *m* (calificación)

fa ['fɑ] *n* : fa *m* (en el canto)

fable ['feɪbəl] *n* : fábula *f*

fabled ['feɪbəld] *adj* : legendario, fabuloso

fabric ['fæbrɪk] *n* 1 MATERIAL : tela *f*, tejido *m* 2 STRUCTURE : estructura *f* ⟨the fabric of society : la estructura de la sociedad⟩

fabricate ['fæbrɪˌkeɪt] *vt* **-cated; -cating** 1 CONSTRUCT, MANUFACTURE : construir, fabricar 2 INVENT : inventar (excusas o mentiras)

fabrication [ˌfæbrɪˈkeɪʃən] *n* 1 LIE : mentira *f*, invención *f* 2 MANUFACTURE : fabricación *f*

fabulous ['fæbjələs] *adj* 1 LEGENDARY : fabuloso, legendario 2 INCREDIBLE : increíble, fabuloso ⟨fabulous wealth : riqueza fabulosa⟩ 3 WONDERFUL : magnífico, estupendo, fabuloso — **fabulously** *adv*

facade [fəˈsɑd] *n* : fachada *f*

face¹ ['feɪs] *v* **faced; facing** *vt* 1 LINE : recubrir (una superficie), forrar (ropa) 2 CONFRONT : enfrentarse a, afrontar, hacer frente a ⟨to face the music : afrontar las consecuencias⟩ ⟨to face the facts : aceptar la realidad⟩ 3 : estar de cara a, estar enfrente de ⟨she's facing her brother : está de cara a su hermano⟩ 4 OVERLOOK : dar a — *vi* : mirar (hacia), estar orientado (a) **5 to face up to** CONFRONT : hacer frente a

face² *n* 1 : cara *f*, rostro *m* ⟨he told me to my face : me lo dijo a la cara⟩ ⟨face to face : cara a cara⟩ 2 EXPRESSION : cara *f*, expresión *f* ⟨to make a face : poner mala cara⟩ ⟨he couldn't keep a straight face : no pudo aguantarse la risa⟩ ⟨to put on a brave face : no demostrar que uno tiene⟩ 3 GRIMACE : mueca *f* ⟨to make faces : hacer muecas⟩ 4 APPEARANCE : fisonomía *f*, aspecto *m* ⟨the face of society : la fisonomía de la sociedad⟩ ⟨on the face of it : aparentemente, a primera vista⟩ 5 PERSON : cara *f* 6 PRESTIGE : prestigio *m* ⟨to lose face : desprestigiarse⟩ ⟨to save face : salvar las apariencias⟩ 7 FRONT, SIDE : cara *f* (de una moneda), esfera *f* (de un reloj), fachada *f* (de un edificio), pared *f* (de una montaña) 8 SURFACE : superficie *f*, faz *f* (de la tierra), cara *f* (de la luna) **9 in the face of** DESPITE : en medio de, en visto de, ante **10 to be/get in someone's face** *fam* : gritarle a alguien, regañarle a alguien **11 to fly in the face of** : hacer caso omiso de algo

facedown ['feɪsˌdaʊn] *adv* : boca abajo

face–first [ˌfeɪsˈfərst] *adv* : de bruces

faceless ['feɪsləs] *adj* ANONYMOUS : anónimo

face–lift ['feɪsˌlɪft] *n* 1 : estiramiento *m* facial 2 RENOVATION : renovación *f*, remozamiento *m*

face–off ['feɪsˌɔf] *n* : confrontación *f*, careo *m*

facet ['fæsət] *n* 1 : faceta *f* (de una piedra) 2 ASPECT : faceta *f*, aspecto *m*

facetious [fəˈsiːʃəs] *adj* : gracioso, burlón, bromista

facetiously [fəˈsiːʃəsli] *adv* : en tono de burla

facetiousness [fəˈsiːʃəsnəs] *n* : jocosidad *f*

face–to–face *adv & adj* : cara a cara

faceup ['feɪsˌʌp] *adv* : boca arriba

face value *n* : valor *m* nominal

facial¹ ['feɪʃəl] *adj* : de la cara, facial

facial² *n* : tratamiento *m* facial, limpieza *f* de cutis

facile ['fæsəl] *adj* SUPERFICIAL : superficial, simplista

facilitate [fəˈsɪləˌteɪt] *vt* **-tated; -tating** : facilitar — **facilitator** [fəˈsɪləˌteɪtər] *n*

facility [fəˈsɪləti] *n*, *pl* **-ties** 1 EASE : facilidad *f* 2 CENTER, COMPLEX : centro *m*, complejo *m* 3 **facilities** *npl* AMENITIES : comodidades *fpl*, servicios *mpl*

facing ['feɪsɪŋ] *n* 1 LINING : entretela *f* (de una prenda) 2 : revestimiento *m* (de un edificio)

facsimile [fækˈsɪməli] *n* : facsímil *m*

fact ['fækt] *n* 1 : hecho *m* ⟨as a matter of fact : de hecho⟩ 2 INFORMATION : información *f*, datos *mpl* ⟨facts and figures : datos y cifras⟩ 3 REALITY : realidad *f* ⟨in fact : en realidad⟩

faction ['fækʃən] *n* : facción *m*, bando *m*

factional ['fækʃənəl] *adj* : entre facciones

factor ['fæktər] *n* : factor *m*

factory ['fæktəri] *n*, *pl* **-ries** : fábrica *f*

factual ['fæktʃuəl] *adj* : basado en hechos, objetivo

factually ['fæktʃuəli] *adv* : en cuanto a los hechos

faculty ['fækəlti] *n*, *pl* **-ties** 1 : facultad *f* ⟨the faculty of sight : las facultades visuales, el sentido de la vista⟩ 2 APTITUDE : aptitud *f*, facilidad *f* 3 TEACHERS : cuerpo *m* docente

fad ['fæd] *n* : moda *f* pasajera, manía *f*

fade ['feɪd] *v* **faded; fading** *vi* 1 WITHER : debilitarse (dícese de las personas), marchitarse (dícese de las flores y las plantas) 2 DISCOLOR : desteñirse, decolorarse 3 DIM : apagarse (dícese de la luz), perderse (dícese de los sonidos), fundirse (dícese de las imágenes) 4 VANISH : desvanecerse, decaer — *vt* DISCOLOR : desteñir

fag ['fæg] *vt* **fagged; fagging** EXHAUST : cansar, fatigar

fagot *or* **faggot** ['fægət] *n* : haz *m* de leña

Fahrenheit ['færənˌhaɪt] *adj* : Fahrenheit

fail¹ ['feɪl] *vi* 1 WEAKEN : fallar, deteriorarse 2 STOP : fallar, detenerse ⟨his heart failed : le falló el corazón⟩ 3 : fracasar, fallar ⟨her plan failed : su plan fracasó⟩ ⟨the crops failed : se perdió la cosecha⟩

⟨if all else fails : como último recurso⟩ **4** : quebrar ⟨a business about to fail : una empresa a punto de quebrar⟩ **5 to fail in** : faltar a, no cumplir con ⟨to fail in one's duties : faltar a sus deberes⟩ — *vt* **1** FLUNK : reprobar (un examen) **2** : fallar ⟨words fail me : las palabras me fallan, no encuentro palabras⟩ **3** DISAPPOINT : fallar, decepcionar ⟨don't fail me! : ¡no me falles!⟩

fail² *n* : fracaso *m*

failing ['feɪlɪŋ] *n* : defecto *m*

failure ['feɪljər] *n* **1** : fracaso *m*, malogro *m* ⟨crop failure : pérdida de la cosecha⟩ ⟨heart failure : insuficiencia cardíaca⟩ ⟨engine failure : falla mecánica⟩ **2** BANKRUPTCY : bancarrota *f*, quiebra *f* **3** : fracaso *m* (persona) ⟨he was a failure as a manager : como gerente, fue un fracaso⟩

faint¹ ['feɪnt] *vi* : desmayarse

faint² *adj* **1** COWARDLY, TIMID : cobarde, tímido **2** DIZZY : mareado ⟨faint with hunger : desfallecido de hambre⟩ **3** SLIGHT : leve, ligero, vago ⟨I haven't the faintest idea : no tengo la más mínima idea⟩ **4** INDISTINCT : tenue, indistinto, apenas perceptible

faint³ *n* : desmayo *m*

fainthearted ['feɪnt'hɑrṭəd] *adj* : cobarde, pusilánime

faintly ['feɪntli] *adv* : débilmente, ligeramente, levemente

faintness ['feɪntnəs] *n* **1** INDISTINCTNESS : lo débil, falta *f* de claridad **2** FAINTING : desmayo *m*, desfallecimiento *m*

fair¹ ['fær] *adj* **1** ATTRACTIVE, BEAUTIFUL : bello, hermoso, atractivo **2** (*relating to weather*) : bueno, despejado **3** JUST : justo (dícese de personas, precios, etc.) ⟨fair elections : elecciones limpias⟩ ⟨one's fair share : lo que a uno le corresponde⟩ ⟨give her a fair chance : dale una oportunidad⟩ ⟨to be fair, . . . : en honor a la verdad, . . .⟩ **4** ADEQUATE : adecuado, aceptable ⟨fair to middling : mediano, regular⟩ ⟨he's in fair condition : se encuentra en estado estable⟩ ⟨a fair number : un buen número⟩ ⟨I have a fair idea of how it works : tengo una idea de como funciona⟩ ⟨they have a fair chance of winning : tienen (bastantes) posibilidades de ganar⟩ **5** BLOND, LIGHT : rubio (dícese del pelo), blanco (dícese de la tez) **6** all's fair in love and war : en el amor y en la guerra todo vale **7 fair and square** : con todas las de la ley, en buena ley **8 fair enough** : de acuerdo, me parece razonable **9 fair's fair** : lo justo es justo **10 fair game** : presa *f* fácil **11 to play fair** : jugar limpio

fair² *n* : feria *f*

fairground ['fær,graʊnd] *n* : parque *m* de diversiones

fair-haired ['fær'hærd] *adj* : rubio

fairly ['færli] *adv* **1** IMPARTIALLY : imparcialmente, limpiamente, equitativamente **2** QUITE : bastante **3** MODERATELY : medianamente

fairness ['færnəs] *n* **1** IMPARTIALITY : imparcialidad *f*, justicia *f* **2** LIGHTNESS : blancura *f* (de la piel), lo rubio (del pelo)

fairy ['færi] *n, pl* **fairies 1** : hada *f* **2 fairy tale** : cuento *m* de hadas

fairyland ['færi,lænd] *n* **1** : país *m* de las hadas **2** : lugar *m* encantador

faith ['feɪθ] *n, pl* **faiths** ['feɪθs, 'feɪðz] **1** BELIEF : fe *f* **2** ALLEGIANCE : lealtad *f* **3** CONFIDENCE, TRUST : confianza *f*, fe *f* **4** RELIGION : religión *f*

faithful ['feɪθfəl] *adj* : fiel — **faithfully** *adv*

faithfulness ['feɪθfəlnəs] *n* : fidelidad *f*

faithless ['feɪθləs] *adj* **1** DISLOYAL : desleal **2** : infiel (en la religión) — **faithlessly** *adv*

faithlessness ['feɪθləsnəs] *n* : deslealtad *f*

fake¹ ['feɪk] *v* **faked; faking** *vt* **1** FALSIFY : falsificar, falsear **2** FEIGN : fingir — *vi* **1** PRETEND : fingir **2** : hacer un engaño, hacer una finta (en deportes)

fake² *adj* : falso, fingido, postizo

fake³ *n* **1** IMITATION : imitación *f*, falsificación *f* **2** IMPOSTOR : impostor *m*, -tora *f*; charlatán *m*, -tana *f*; farsante *mf* **3** FEINT : engaño *m*, finta *f* (en deportes)

faker ['feɪkər] *n* : impostor *m*, -tora *f*; charlatán *m*, -tana *f*; farsante *mf*

falcon ['fælkən, 'fɔl-] *n* : halcón *m*

fall¹ ['fɔl] *vi* **fell** ['fɛl]; **fallen** ['fɔlən]; **falling 1** : caer, caerse ⟨the rain was falling : caía la lluvia⟩ ⟨a vase fell off the shelf : un jarrón se cayó del estante⟩ **2** : caerse, caer ⟨she tripped and fell down the stairs : tropezó y se cayó por las escaleras⟩ **3** HANG : caer **4** : caer (dícese de la noche) **5** DROP, LOWER : caer (dícese de los ingresos, etc.), bajar (dícese de los precios, las temperaturas, etc.), reducirse (dícese de la voz) ⟨her face fell : se le descompuso la cara⟩ **6** BECOME : volverse, quedarse ⟨to fall silent : callarse, quedarse callado⟩ ⟨to fall in love : enamorarse⟩ **7** : caer (ante un enemigo), rendirse ⟨the city fell : la ciudad se rindió⟩ **8** : caer ⟨to fall in battle : caer en combate⟩ **9** OCCUR : caer ⟨Christmas falls on a Friday : la Navidad cae en viernes⟩ **10 to fall (all) over oneself to** : desvivirse por **11 to fall apart** : deshacerse **12 to fall asleep** : dormirse, quedarse dormido **13 to fall away** : decaer, disminuir **14 to fall back** RETREAT : retirarse **15 to fall behind** : quedarse atrás **16 to fall behind on/with** : atrasarse en, retrasarse en **17 to fall down** : caerse **18 to fall down on the job** : no cumplir con su deber **19 to fall flat** : no ser bien recibido (dícese de un chiste, etc.), no dar resultado **20 to fall for** : enamorarse de **21 to fall for** BELIEVE : tragarse **22 to fall in** COLLAPSE : hundirse **23 to fall in** : formar filas **24 to fall into place** : ir bien, aclararse **25 to fall into the hands of** : caer en manos de **26 to fall in with** : juntarse con **27 to fall off** LESSEN : disminuir **28 to fall off** DETACH : desprenderse, caerse **29 to fall on** ATTACK : atacar, caer sobre **30 to fall out** : caerse (dícese del pelo, etc.) **31 to fall out** AR-GUE : pelearse **32 to fall out** : romper filas **33 to fall out of favor** : caer en desgracia **34 to fall out of use** : caer en desuso **35 to fall over** : caerse **36 to fall sick** : caer enfermo, enfermarse **37 to fall through** : fracasar, caer en la nada **38 to fall to** : tocar a, corresponder a ⟨the task fell to him : le tocó a él hacerlo⟩

fall² *n* **1** TUMBLE : caída *f* ⟨to break one's fall : frenar una su caída⟩ ⟨a fall of three feet : una caída de tres pies⟩ **2** FALLING : derrumbe *m* (de rocas), aguacero *m* (de lluvia), nevada *f* (de nieve), bajada *f* (de precios), disminución *f* (de cantidades) **3** AUTUMN : otoño *m* **4** DOWNFALL : caída *f*, ruina *f* **5 falls** *npl* WATERFALL : cascada *f*, catarata *f*

fallacious [fə'leɪʃəs] *adj* : erróneo, engañoso, falaz

fallacy ['fæləsi] *n, pl* **-cies** : falacia *f*

fall back *vi* **1** RETREAT : retirarse, replegarse **2 to fall back on** : recurrir a

fall guy *n* SCAPEGOAT : chivo *m* expiatorio

fallible ['fæləbəl] *adj* : falible

fallout ['fɔl,aʊt] *n* **1** : lluvia *f* radioactiva **2** CONSEQUENCES : secuelas *fpl*, consecuencias *fpl*

fallow¹ ['fælo] *adj* **to lie fallow** : estar en barbecho

fallow² *n* : barbecho *m*

false ['fɔls] *adj* **falser; falsest 1** UNTRUE : falso ⟨true or false? : ¿verdadero o falso?⟩ ⟨a false name : un nombre falso/ficticio⟩ **2** ERRONEOUS, MISTAKEN : erróneo, equivocado ⟨false hopes : falsas expectativas⟩ ⟨false alarm : falsa alarma⟩ **3** FAKE : falso, postizo ⟨false teeth : dentadura postiza⟩ **4** UNFAITH-FUL : infiel **5** INSINCERE, FEIGNED : falso **6** FRAUDULENT : fraudulento ⟨under false pretenses : por fraude⟩ **7 false move** : movimiento *m* en falso

falsehood ['fɔls,hʊd] *n* : mentira *f*, falsedad *f*

falsely ['fɔlsli] *adv* : falsamente, con falsedad

falseness ['fɔlsnəs] *n* : falsedad *f*

falsetto [fɔl'sɛto] *n, pl* **-tos** : falsete *m*

falsification [,fɔlsəfə'keɪʃən] *n* : falsificación *f*

falsify ['fɔlsə,faɪ] *vt* **-fied; fying** : falsificar, falsear

falsity ['fɔlsəti] *n, pl* **-ties** : falsedad *f*

falter ['fɔltər] *vi* **-tered; -tering 1** TOT-TER : tambalearse **2** STAMMER : titubear, tartamudear **3** WAVER : vacilar

faltering ['fɔltərɪŋ] *adj* : titubeante, vacilante — **falteringly** *adv*

fame ['feɪm] *n* : fama *f*

famed ['feɪmd] *adj* : famoso, célebre, afamado

familial [fə'mɪljəl, -liəl] *adj* : familiar

familiar¹ [fə'mɪljər] *adj* **1** KNOWN : familiar, conocido ⟨to be familiar with : estar familiarizado con⟩ **2** INFORMAL : familiar, informal **3** INTIMATE : íntimo, de

confianza **4** FORWARD : confianzudo, atrevido — **familiarly** *adv*

familiar² *n* : espíritu *m* guardián

familiarity [fə,mɪli'ærəti, -,mɪl'jær-] *n, pl* **-ties 1** KNOWLEDGE : conocimiento *m*, familiaridad *f* **2** INFORMALITY, INTI-MACY : confianza *f*, familiaridad *f* **3** FORWARDNESS : exceso *m* de confianza, descaro *m*

familiarize [fə'mɪljə,raɪz] *vt* **-ized; -izing 1** : familiarizar **2 to familiarize oneself** : familiarizarse

family ['fæmli, 'fæmə-] *n, pl* **-lies** : familia *f*

family name *n* SURNAME : apellido *m*

family room *n* : living *m*, sala *f* (informal)

family tree *n* : árbol *m* genealógico

famine ['fæmən] *n* : hambre *f*, hambruna *f*

famish ['fæmɪʃ] *vi* **to be famished** : estar famélico, estar hambriento, morir de hambre *fam*

famous ['feɪməs] *adj* : famoso

famously ['feɪməsli] *adv* **to get on famously** : llevarse de maravilla

fan¹ ['fæn] *vt* **fanned; fanning 1** : abanicar (a una persona), avivar (un fuego) **2** STIMULATE : avivar, estimular

fan² *n* **1** : ventilador *m*, abanico *m* **2** AD-MIRER, ENTHUSIAST : aficionado *m*, -da *f*; entusiasta *mf*; admirador *m*, -dora *f*

fanatic¹ [fə'nætɪk] *or* **fanatical** [-tɪ-kəl] *adj* : fanático

fanatic² *n* : fanático *m*, -ca *f*

fanaticism [fə'nætə,sɪzəm] *n* : fanatismo *m*

fan belt *n* : correa *f* del ventilador

fanciful ['fæntsɪfəl] *adj* **1** CAPRICIOUS : caprichoso, fantástico, extravagante **2** IMAGINATIVE : imaginativo — **fancifully** *adv*

fancy¹ ['fæntsi] *vt* **-cied; -cying 1** IMAG-INE : imaginarse, figurarse ⟨fancy that! : ¡figúrate!, ¡imagínate!⟩ **2** CRAVE : apetecer, tener ganas de

fancy² *adj* **fancier; -est 1** ELABORATE : elaborado **2** LUXURIOUS : lujoso, elegante — **fancily** ['fæntsəli] *adv*

fancy³ *n, pl* **-cies 1** LIKING : gusto *m*, afición *f* **2** WHIM : antojo *m*, capricho *m* **3** IMAGINATION : fantasía *f*, imaginación *f*

fandango [fæn'dæŋgo] *n, pl* **-gos** : fandango *m*

fanfare ['fæn,fær] *n* : fanfarria *f*

fang ['fæŋ] *n* : colmillo *m* (de un animal), diente *m* (de una serpiente)

fanlight ['fæn,laɪt] *n* : tragaluz *m*

fantasia [fæn'teɪʒə, -ziə; ,fæntə-'zi:ə] *n* : fantasía *f*

fantasize ['fæntə,saɪz] *vi* **-sized; -sizing** : fantasear

fantastic [fæn'tæstɪk] *adj* **1** UNBELIEV-ABLE : fantástico, increíble, extraño **2** ENORMOUS : fabuloso, inmenso ⟨fantastic sums : sumas fabulosas⟩ **3** WON-DERFUL : estupendo, fantástico, bárbaro *fam*, macanudo *fam* — **fantastically** [-tɪkli] *adv*

fantasy ['fæntəsi] *n, pl* **-sies** : fantasía *f*

FAQ ['fæk, ˌɛf‚eɪ'kjuː] n, pl **FAQs** (frequently asked question, frequently asked questions) : FAQ m (lista de preguntas)

far[1] ['fɑr] adv **farther** ['fɑrðər] or **further** ['fər-]; **farthest** or **furthest** [-ðəst] **1** : lejos ⟨far from here : lejos de aquí⟩ ⟨to go far : llegar lejos⟩ ⟨far away : a lo lejos⟩ ⟨in the far distant future : en un futuro lejano⟩ ⟨her birthday isn't far off/away : falta poco para su cumpleaños⟩ **2** MUCH : muy, mucho ⟨far bigger : mucho más grande⟩ ⟨far better : mucho mejor⟩ ⟨far different : muy distinto/diferente⟩ ⟨far too expensive : demasiado caro⟩ **3** (indicating a particular point, degree, or extent) ⟨we got as far as Chicago : llegamos hasta Chicago⟩ ⟨as far north as Toronto : tan al norte como Toronto⟩ ⟨to go so far as to say : decir tanto como⟩ ⟨as far as I know : que yo sepa⟩ **4** (indicating an advanced point or extent) : lejos ⟨to go far (in life) : llegar lejos (en la vida)⟩ ⟨not to go far enough : quedarse corto⟩ ⟨we've come too far to quit now : hemos llegado demasiado lejos para dejarlo ahora⟩ ⟨we still have far to go : aún nos queda un largo camino por recorrer⟩ ⟨to take something too far : llevar algo demasiado lejos⟩ **5** as/so far as WITH REGARD TO : en lo que respecta a **6** as/so far as (expressing an opinion) : en lo que a mí respecta, por mí⟩ **7** by far : con mucho, de lejos ⟨it's by far the best : es con mucho el mejor⟩ **8** far and wide : por todas partes **9** far from it! : ¡todo lo contrario! **10** far off : muy errado **11** so far : hasta ahora, todavía

far[2] adj **farther** or **further**; **farthest** or **furthest** **1** DISTANT, REMOTE : lejano, remoto ⟨the far horizon : el horizonte lejano⟩ ⟨the far reaches of outer space : los confines del espacio exterior⟩ ⟨the Far East : el Lejano Oriente, el Extremo Oriente⟩ ⟨in the far future : en el/un futuro lejano/remoto⟩ **2** : más lejano ⟨on the far side of the lake : en el otro lado del lago⟩ ⟨at the far end of the room : en el otro extremo de la sala⟩ **3** the far left/right : la extrema izquierda/derecha (en la política)

faraway ['fɑrəˌweɪ] adj : remoto, lejano

farce ['fɑrs] n : farsa f

farcical ['fɑrsɪkəl] adj : absurdo, ridículo

fare[1] ['fær] vi **fared; faring** : ir, salir ⟨how did you fare? : ¿cómo te fue?⟩

fare[2] n **1** : pasaje m, billete m, boleto m ⟨half fare : medio pasaje⟩ **2** FOOD : comida f

farewell[1] ['fær'wɛl] adj : de despedida

farewell[2] n : despedida f

far–fetched ['fɑr'fɛtʃt] adj : improbable, exagerado

farina [fə'riːnə] n : harina f

farm[1] ['fɑrm] vt **1** : cultivar, labrar **2** : criar (animales) — vi : ser agricultor

farm[2] n : granja f, hacienda f, finca f, estancia f

farmer ['fɑrmər] n : agricultor m, granjero m

farmhand ['fɑrmˌhænd] n : peón m

farmhouse ['fɑrmˌhaʊs] n : granja f, vivienda f (del granjero, casa f de hacienda

farming ['fɑrmɪŋ] n : labranza f, cultivo m, crianza f (de animales)

farmland ['fɑrmˌlænd] n : tierras fpl de labranza

farmyard ['fɑrmˌjɑrd] n : corral m

far–off ['fɑrˌɔf, -ˈɔf] adj : remoto, distante, lejano

far–reaching ['fɑr'riːtʃɪŋ] adj : de gran alcance

farsighted ['fɑrˌsaɪtəd] adj **1** : hipermétrope **2** JUDICIOUS : con visión de futuro, previsor, precavido

farsightedness ['fɑrˌsaɪtədnəs] n **1** : hipermetropía f **2** PRUDENCE : previsión f

fart[1] ['fɑrt] vi usu vulgar : tirarse un pedo fam

fart[2] n usu vulgar **1** : pedo m fam **2** old fart : viejo m, -ja f

farther[1] ['fɑrðər] adv **1** AHEAD : más lejos (en el espacio), más adelante (en el tiempo) **2** MORE : más

farther[2] adj : más lejano, más remoto

farthermost ['fɑrðərˌmoːst] adj : (el) más lejano

farthest[1] ['fɑrðəst] adv **1** : lo más lejos ⟨I jumped farthest : salté lo más lejos⟩ **2** : lo más avanzado ⟨he progressed farthest : progresó al punto más avanzado⟩ **3** : más ⟨the farthest developed plan : el plan más desarrollado⟩

farthest[2] adj : más lejano

fascinate ['fæsənˌeɪt] vt **-nated; -nating** : fascinar, cautivar

fascinating ['fæsənˌeɪtɪŋ] adj : fascinante

fascination [ˌfæsən'eɪʃən] n : fascinación f

fascism ['fæʃˌɪzəm] n : fascismo m

fascist[1] ['fæʃɪst] adj : fascista

fascist[2] n : fascista mf

fashion[1] ['fæʃən] vt : formar, moldear

fashion[2] n **1** MANNER : manera f, modo m **2** CUSTOM : costumbre f **3** STYLE : moda f

fashionable ['fæʃənəbəl] adj : de moda, chic

fashionably ['fæʃənəbli] adv : a la moda

fashion show n : desfile m de modelos

fast[1] ['fæst] vi : ayunar

fast[2] adv **1** SECURELY : firmemente, seguramente ⟨to hold fast : agarrarse duro⟩ **2** RAPIDLY : rápidamente, rápido, de prisa **3** to run fast : ir adelantado (dícese de un reloj) **4** SOUNDLY : profundamente ⟨fast asleep : profundamente dormido⟩

fast[3] adj **1** SECURE : firme, seguro ⟨to make fast : amarrar (un barco)⟩ **2** FAITHFUL : leal ⟨fast friends : amigos leales⟩ **3** RAPID : rápido, veloz **4** : adelantado ⟨my watch is fast : tengo el reloj adelantado⟩ **5** DEEP : profundo ⟨a fast sleep : un sueño profundo⟩ **6** COLORFAST : inalterable, que no destiñe **7** DISSOLUTE : extravagante, disipado, disoluto

fast[4] n : ayuno m

fasten ['fæsən] *vt* **1** ATTACH : sujetar, atar **2** FIX : fijar ⟨to fasten one's eyes on : fijar los ojos en⟩ **3** SECURE : abrochar (ropa o cinturones), atar (cordones), cerrar (una maleta) — *vi* : abrocharse, cerrar

fastener ['fæsənər] *n* : cierre *m*, sujetador *m*

fastening ['fæsənɪŋ] *n* : cierre *m*, sujetador *m*

fast food *n* : comida *f* rápida

fastidious [fæs'tɪdiəs] *adj* : quisquilloso, exigente — **fastidiously** *adv*

fat¹ ['fæt] *adj* **fatter; fattest 1** OBESE : gordo, obeso **2** THICK : grueso

fat² *n* : grasa *f*

fatal ['feɪtəl] *adj* **1** DEADLY : mortal **2** ILL-FATED : malhadado, fatal **3** MOMENTOUS : fatídico

fatalism ['feɪtəl,ɪzəm] *n* : fatalismo *m*

fatalist ['feɪtəlɪst] *n* : fatalista *mf*

fatalistic [,feɪtəl'ɪstɪk] *adj* : fatalista

fatality [feɪ'tæləti, fə-] *n*, *pl* **-ties** : víctima *f* mortal

fatally ['feɪtəli] *adv* : mortalmente

fate ['feɪt] *n* **1** DESTINY : destino *m* **2** END, LOT : final *m*, suerte *f*

fated ['feɪtəd] *adj* : predestinado

fateful ['feɪtfəl] *adj* **1** MOMENTOUS : fatídico, aciago **2** PROPHETIC : profético — **fatefully** *adv*

father¹ ['faðər] *vt* : engendrar

father² *n* **1** : padre *m* ⟨my father and my mother : mi padre y mi madre⟩ ⟨Father Smith : el padre Smith⟩ **2 the Father** GOD : el Padre, Dios *m*

fatherhood ['faðər,hʊd] *n* : paternidad *f*

father-in-law ['faðərɪn,lɔ] *n*, *pl* **fathers-in-law** : suegro *m*

fatherland ['faðər,lænd] *n* : patria *f*

fatherless ['faðərləs] *adj* : huérfano de padre, sin padre

fatherly ['faðərli] *adj* : paternal

fathom¹ ['fæðəm] *vt* UNDERSTAND : entender, comprender

fathom² *n* : braza *f*

fatigue¹ [fə'ti:g] *vt* **-tigued; -tiguing** : fatigar, cansar

fatigue² *n* : fatiga *f*

fatness ['fætnəs] *n* : gordura *f* (de una persona o un animal), grosor *m* (de un objeto)

fatten ['fætən] *vt* : engordar, cebar

fattening ['fætnɪŋ] *adj* : que engorda

fatty ['fæti] *adj* **fattier; -est** : graso, grasoso

fatuous ['fætʃʊəs] *adj* : necio, fatuo — **fatuously** *adv*

faucet ['fɔsət] *n* : llave *f*, canilla *f* *Arg, Uru*, grifo *m*

fault¹ ['fɔlt] *vt* : encontrar defectos a

fault² *n* **1** SHORTCOMING : defecto *m*, falta *f* **2** DEFECT : falta *f*, defecto *m*, falla *f* ⟨to find fault with : encontrarle defectos a, criticar⟩ **3** BLAME : culpa *f* ⟨to be at fault : tener la culpa⟩ **4** FRACTURE : falla *f* (geológica)

faultfinder ['fɔlt,faɪndər] *n* : criticón *m*, -cona *f*

faultfinding ['fɔlt,faɪndɪŋ] *n* : crítica *f*

faultless ['fɔltləs] *adj* : sin culpa, sin imperfecciones, impecable

faultlessly ['fɔltləsli] *adv* : impecablemente, perfectamente

faulty ['fɔlti] *adj* **faultier; -est** : defectuoso, imperfecto — **faultily** ['fɔltəli] *adv*

fauna ['fɔnə] *n* : fauna *f*

faux ['fo:] *adj* : de imitación

faux pas [,fo:'pɑ] *n*, *pl* **faux pas** [*same or* -'pɑz] : metedura *f* de pata *fam*

favor¹ ['feɪvər] *vt* **1** SUPPORT : estar a favor de, ser partidario de, apoyar **2** OBLIGE : hacerle un favor a **3** PREFER : preferir **4** RESEMBLE : parecerse a, salir a

favor² *n* : favor *m* ⟨in favor of : a favor de⟩ ⟨an error in his favor : un error a su favor⟩

favorable ['feɪvərəbəl] *adj* : favorable, propicio

favorably ['feɪvərəbli] *adv* : favorablemente, bien

favorite¹ ['feɪvərət] *adj* : favorito, preferido

favorite² *n* : favorito *m*, -ta *f*; preferido *m*, -da *f*

favoritism ['feɪvərə,tɪzəm] *n* : favoritismo *m*

fawn¹ ['fɔn] *vi* : adular, lisonjear

fawn² *n* : cervato *m*

fax¹ ['fæks] *n* : facsímil *m*, facsímile *m*

fax² *vt* **1** : mandarle un fax a **2** : enviar por fax

faze ['feɪz] *vt* **fazed; fazing** : desconcertar, perturbar

fear¹ ['fɪr] *vt* : temer, tener miedo de — *vi* : temer

fear² *n* : miedo *m*, temor *m* ⟨for fear of : por temor a⟩

fearful ['fɪrfəl] *adj* **1** FRIGHTENING : espantoso, aterrador, horrible **2** FRIGHTENED : temeroso, miedoso

fearfully ['fɪrfəli] *adv* **1** EXTREMELY : extremadamente, terriblemente **2** TIMIDLY : con temor

fearless ['fɪrləs] *adj* : intrépido, impávido

fearlessly ['fɪrləsli] *adv* : sin temor

fearlessness ['fɪrləsnəs] *n* : intrepidez *f*, impavidez *f*

fearsome ['fɪrsəm] *adj* : aterrador

feasibility [,fi:zə'bɪləti] *n* : viabilidad *f*, factibilidad *f*

feasible ['fi:zəbəl] *adj* : viable, factible, realizable

feast¹ ['fi:st] *vi* : banquetear — *vt* **1** : agasajar, festejar **2 to feast one's eyes on** : regalarse la vista con

feast² *n* **1** BANQUET : banquete *m*, festín *m* **2** FESTIVAL : fiesta *f*

feat ['fi:t] *n* : proeza *f*, hazaña *f*

feather¹ ['feðər] *vt* **to feather one's nest** : hacer su agosto

feather² *n* **1** : pluma *f* **2 a feather in one's cap** : un triunfo personal

feathered ['feðərd] *adj* : con plumas

feathery ['feðəri] *adj* **1** DOWNY : plumoso **2** LIGHT : liviano

feature¹ ['fi:tʃər] *v* **-tured; -turing** *vt* **1** IMAGINE : imaginarse **2** PRESENT : presentar — *vi* : figurar

feature² *n* **1** CHARACTERISTIC : característica *f*, rasgo *m* **2** : largometraje *m* (en el cine), artículo *m* (en un periódico), documental *m* (en la televisión) **3 features** *npl* : rasgos *mpl*, facciones *fpl* ⟨delicate features : facciones delicadas⟩

February ['fɛbjʊ,ri, 'fɛbʊ-, 'fɛbrʊ-] *n* : febrero *m* ⟨they arrived on the 21st of February, they arrived on February 21st : llegaron el 21 de febrero⟩

fecal ['fi:kəl] *adj* : fecal

feces ['fi:,si:z] *npl* : heces *fpl*, excrementos *mpl*

feckless ['fɛkləs] *adj* : irresponsable

fecund ['fɛkənd, 'fi:-] *adj* : fecundo

fecundity [fɪ'kʌndəṭi, fe-] *n* : fecundidad *f*

federal ['fɛdrəl, -dərəl] *adj* : federal

federalism ['fɛdrə,lɪzəm, -dərə-] *n* : federalismo *m*

federalist¹ ['fɛdrəlɪst, -dərə-] *adj* : federalista

federalist² *n* : federalista *mf*

federate ['fɛdə,reɪt] *vt* -ated; -ating : federar

federation [,fɛdə'reɪʃən] *n* : federación *f*

fedora [fɪ'dorə] *n* : sombrero *m* flexible de fieltro

fed up *adj* : harto

fee ['fi:] *n* **1** : honorarios *mpl* (a un médico, un abogado, etc.) **2 entrance fee** : entrada *f*

feeble ['fi:bəl] *adj* **feebler; feeblest 1** WEAK : débil, endeble **2** INEFFECTIVE : flojo, pobre, poco convincente

feebleminded [,fi:bəl'maɪndəd] *adj* **1** *often offensive* : débil mental **2** FOOLISH, STUPID : imbécil, tonto

feebleness ['fi:bəlnəs] *n* : debilidad *f*

feebly ['fi:bli] *adv* : débilmente

feed¹ ['fi:d] *v* **fed** ['fɛd]; **feeding** *vt* **1** : dar de comer a, nutrir, alimentar (a una persona) **2** : alimentar (un fuego o una máquina), proveer (información), introducir (datos) — *vi* : comer, alimentarse

feed² *n* **1** NOURISHMENT : alimento *m* **2** FODDER : pienso *m*

feedback ['fi:d,bæk] *n* **1** : retroalimentación *f* (electrónica) **2** RESPONSE : reacción *f*

feeder ['fi:dər] *n* : comedero *m* (para animales)

feel¹ ['fi:l] *v* **felt** ['fɛlt]; **feeling** *vi* **1** : sentirse, encontrarse ⟨I feel tired : me siento cansada⟩ ⟨he feels hungry/cold : tiene hambre/frío⟩ ⟨she feels like a fool : se siente como una idiota⟩ ⟨to feel like doing something : tener ganas de hacer algo⟩ **2** SEEM : parecer ⟨it feels like spring : parece primavera⟩ ⟨it feels like rain : parece que va a llover⟩ ⟨it feels smooth : es suave al tacto⟩ **3** THINK : parecerse, opinar, pensar ⟨how does he feel about that? : ¿qué opina él de eso?⟩ **4 to feel (around) for** : buscar a tientas **5 to feel for** PITY : compadecer — *vt* **1** TOUCH : tocar, palpar ⟨to feel one's way : tantear, ir a tientas⟩ **2** SENSE : sentir ⟨to feel the cold : sentir el frío⟩ **3** CONSIDER : sentir, creer, considerar ⟨I didn't feel it necessary to inform him : no creí

necesario informarle⟩ **4 to feel out** : tantear **5 to feel up** *fam* : manosear, meterle mano a *fam*

feel² *n* **1** SENSATION, TOUCH : sensación *f*, tacto *m* **2** ATMOSPHERE : ambiente *m*, atmósfera *f* **3 to have a feel for** : tener un talento especial para

feeler ['fi:lər] *n* : antena *f*, tentáculo *m*

feeling ['fi:lɪŋ] *n* **1** SENSATION : sensación *f*, sensibilidad *f* **2** EMOTION : sentimiento *m* **3** HUNCH, INTUITION : sensación *f* **4** OPINION : opinión *f* **5 feelings** *npl* SENSIBILITIES : sentimientos *mpl* ⟨to hurt/spare someone's feelings : herir/no herir los sentimientos de alguien⟩ ⟨no hard feelings, right? : no me guardas rencor, ¿verdad?⟩ ⟨to have feelings for someone : tener sentimientos por alguien⟩

feet → foot

feign ['feɪn] *vt* : simular, aparentar, fingir

feint¹ ['feɪnt] *vi* : fintar, fintear

feint² ['feɪnt] *n* : finta *f*

felicitate [fɪ'lɪsə,teɪt] *vt* -tated; -tating : felicitar, congratular

felicitation [fɪ,lɪsə'teɪʃən] *n* : felicitación *f*

felicitous [fɪ'lɪsəṭəs] *adj* : acertado, oportuno

feline¹ ['fi:,laɪn] *adj* : felino

feline² *n* : felino *m*, -na *f*

fell¹ ['fɛl] *vt* : talar (un árbol), derribar (a una persona)

fell² → fall

fellow¹ ['fɛ,lo:] *adj* ⟨his fellow students : sus compañeros de estudios⟩ ⟨fellow citizen : conciudadano, paisano⟩

fellow² *n* **1** COMPANION : compañero *m*, -ra *f*; camarada *mf* **2** ASSOCIATE : socio *m*, -cia *f* **3** MAN : tipo *m*, hombre *m*

fellowman [,fɛlo'mæn] *n*, *pl* **-men** : prójimo *m*, semejante *m*

fellowship ['fɛlo,ʃɪp] *n* **1** COMPANIONSHIP : camaradería *f*, compañerismo *m* **2** ASSOCIATION : fraternidad *f* **3** GRANT : beca *f* (de investigación)

felon ['fɛlən] *n* : malhechor *m*, -chora *f*; criminal *mf*

felonious [fə'lo:niəs] *adj* : criminal

felony ['fɛləni] *n*, *pl* **-nies** : delito *m* grave

felt¹ ['fɛlt] *n* : fieltro *m*

felt² → feel

felt–tip ['fɛlt,tɪp] *or* **felt–tip pen** *n* : marcador *m*, rotulador *m* Spain

female¹ ['fi:,meɪl] *adj* : femenino

female² *n* **1** : hembra *f* (de animal) **2** WOMAN : mujer *f*

feminine ['fɛmənən] *adj* : femenino

femininity [,fɛmə'nɪnəṭi] *n* : feminidad *f*, femineidad *f*

feminism ['fɛmə,nɪzəm] *n* : feminismo *m*

feminist¹ ['fɛmənɪst] *adj* : feminista

feminist² *n* : feminista *mf*

femoral ['fɛmərəl] *adj* : femoral

femur ['fi:mər] *n*, *pl* **femurs** *or* **femora** ['fɛmərə] : fémur *m*

fence¹ ['fɛnts] *v* **fenced; fencing** *vt* : vallar, cercar — *vi* : hacer esgrima

fence² *n* : cerca *f*, valla *f*, cerco *m*, barda *f* Mex

fencer ['fɛntsər] *n* : esgrimista *mf*

fencing ['fɛntsɪŋ] n 1 : esgrima m (deporte) 2 : materiales mpl para cercas 3 ENCLOSURE : cercado m

fend ['fɛnd] vt **to fend off** : rechazar (un enemigo), parar (un golpe), eludir (una pregunta) — vi **to fend for oneself** : arreglárselas sólo, valerse por sí mismo

fender ['fɛndər] n : guardabarros mpl, salpicadera f Mex

fennel ['fɛnəl] n : hinojo m

ferment¹ [fər'mɛnt] v : fermentar

ferment² ['fər,mɛnt] n 1 : fermento m (en la química) 2 TURMOIL : agitación f, conmoción f

fermentation [,fərmən'teɪʃən, -,mɛn-] n : fermentación f

fern ['fərn] n : helecho m

ferocious [fə'roːʃəs] adj : feroz — **ferociously** adv

ferociousness [fə'roːʃəsnəs] n : ferocidad f

ferocity [fə'rɑsəṭi] n : ferocidad f

ferret¹ ['fɛrət] vi SNOOP : hurgar, husmear — vt **to ferret out** : descubrir

ferret² n : hurón m

Ferris wheel ['fɛrɪs] n : noria f

ferry¹ ['fɛri] vt **-ried; -rying** : llevar, transportar

ferry² n, pl **-ries** : transbordador m, ferry m

ferryboat ['fɛri,boːt] n : transbordador m, ferry m

fertile ['fərṭəl] adj : fértil, fecundo

fertility [fər'tɪləṭi] n : fertilidad f

fertilization [,fərṭələ'zeɪʃən] n : fertilización f (del suelo), fecundación (de un huevo)

fertilize ['fərṭəl,aɪz] vt **-ized; -izing** 1 : fecundar (un huevo) 2 : fertilizar, abonar (el suelo)

fertilizer ['fərṭəl,aɪzər] n : fertilizante m, abono m

fervent ['fərvənt] adj : ferviente, fervoroso, ardiente — **fervently** adv

fervid ['fərvɪd] adj : ardiente, apasionado — **fervidly** adv

fervor ['fərvər] n : fervor m, ardor m

fester ['fɛstər] vi : enconarse, supurar

festival ['fɛstəvəl] n : fiesta f, festividad f, festival m

festive ['fɛstɪv] adj : festivo — **festively** adv

festivity [fɛs'tɪvəṭi] n, pl **-ties** : festividad f, celebración f

festoon¹ [fɛs'tuːn] vt : adornar, engalanar

festoon² n GARLAND : guirnalda f

fetal ['fiːṭəl] adj : fetal

fetch ['fɛtʃ] vt 1 BRING : traer, recoger, ir a buscar 2 REALIZE : realizar, venderse por ⟨the jewelry fetched $10,000 : las joyas se vendieron por $10,000⟩

fetching ['fɛtʃɪŋ] adj : atractivo, encantador

fête¹ ['feɪt, 'fɛt] vt **fêted; fêting** : festejar, agasajar

fête² n : fiesta f

fetid ['fɛṭəd] adj : fétido

fetish ['fɛṭɪʃ] n : fetiche m

fetlock ['fɛt,lɑk] n : espolón m

fetter ['fɛṭər] vt : encadenar, poner grillos a

fetters ['fɛṭərz] npl : grillos mpl, grilletes mpl, cadenas fpl

fettle ['fɛṭəl] n **in fine fettle** : en buena forma, en plena forma

fetus ['fiːṭəs] n : feto m

feud¹ ['fjuːd] vi : pelear, contender

feud² n : contienda f, enemistad f (heredada)

feudal ['fjuːdəl] adj : feudal

feudalism ['fjuːdəl,ɪzəm] n : feudalismo m

fever ['fiːvər] n : fiebre f, calentura f

feverish ['fiːvərɪʃ] adj 1 : afiebrado, con fiebre, febril 2 FRANTIC : febril, frenético

few¹ ['fjuː] adj **fewer; fewest** : pocos ⟨with few exceptions : con pocas excepciones⟩ ⟨a few times : varias veces⟩ ⟨fewer people : menos gente⟩ ⟨the fewest (number of) points : el menor número de puntos⟩

few² pron **fewer; fewest** 1 : pocos ⟨few (of them) were ready : pocos estaban listos⟩ ⟨the fewer, the better : cuantos menos mejor⟩ ⟨our group is the fewest in number : nuestro grupo tiene el menor número de personas⟩ 2 **a few** : algunos, unos cuantos ⟨a few of the women came : algunas de las mujeres vinieron⟩ ⟨I read a few (of them) : leí algunos, leí unos cuantos⟩ 3 **few and far between** : contados

fiancé [,fiː,ɑn'seɪ, ,fiː'ɑn,seɪ] n : prometido m, novio m

fiancée [,fiː,ɑn'seɪ, ,fiː'ɑn,seɪ] n : prometida f, novia f

fiasco [fiː'æs,koː] n, pl **-coes** : fiasco m, fracaso m

fiat ['fiː,ɑt, -,æt, -ət; 'faɪət, -,æt] n : decreto m, orden m

fib¹ ['fɪb] vi **fibbed; fibbing** fam : decir bolas

fib² n fam : bola f fam, mentira f

fibber ['fɪbər] n : mentirosillo m, -lla f; cuentista mf fam

fiber or **fibre** ['faɪbər] n : fibra f

fiberboard ['faɪbər,boɪd] n : cartón m madera

fiberglass ['faɪbər,glæs] n : fibra f de vidrio

fibrous ['faɪbrəs] adj : fibroso

fibula ['fɪbjələ] n, pl **-lae** [-,liː, -,laɪ] or **-las** : peroné m

fickle ['fɪkəl] adj : inconstante, voluble, veleidoso

fickleness ['fɪkəlnəs] n : volubilidad f, inconstancia f, veleidad f

fiction ['fɪkʃən] n : ficción f

fictional ['fɪkʃənəl] adj : ficticio

fictitious [fɪk'tɪʃəs] adj 1 IMAGINARY : ficticio, imaginario 2 FALSE : falso, ficticio

fiddle¹ ['fɪdəl] vi **-dled; -dling** 1 : tocar el violín 2 **to fiddle with** : juguetear con, toquetear

fiddle² n : violín m

fiddler ['fɪdlər, 'fɪdələr] n : violinista mf

fiddlesticks ['fɪdəl,stɪks] interj : ¡tonterías!

fidelity [fəˈdɛləṭi, fai-] *n, pl* **-ties** : fidelidad *f*

fidget[1] [ˈfɪdʒət] *vi* **1** : moverse, estarse inquieto **2 to fidget with** : juguetear con

fidget[2] *n* **1** : persona *f* inquieta **2 fidgets** *npl* RESTLESSNESS : inquietud *f*

fidgety [ˈfɪdʒəṭi] *adj* : inquieto

fiduciary[1] [fəˈduːʃiˌɛri, -ˈdjuː-, -ʃəri] *adj* : fiduciario

fiduciary[2] *n, pl* **-ries** : fiduciario *m*, -ria *f*

field[1] [ˈfiːld] *vt* : interceptar y devolver (una pelota), presentar (un candidato), sortear (una pregunta)

field[2] *adj* : de campaña, de campo ⟨field hospital : hospital de campaña⟩ ⟨field goal : gol de campo⟩ ⟨field trip : viaje de estudio⟩

field[3] *n* **1** : campo *m* (de cosechas, de batalla, de magnetismo) **2** : campo *m*, cancha *f* (en deportes) ⟨baseball field : campo de beisbol⟩ ⟨left/right/center field : jardín izquierdo/derecho/central⟩ **3** : campo *m* (de trabajo), esfera *f* (de actividades) ⟨the field of economics : el campo de la economía⟩

fielder [ˈfiːldər] *n* : jugador *m*, -dora *f* de campo; fildeador *m*, -dora *f*

field glasses *n* : binoculares *mpl*, gemelos *mpl*

field hockey *n* : hockey *m* sobre césped

fiend [ˈfiːnd] *n* **1** DEMON : demonio *m* **2** EVILDOER : persona *f* maligna; malvado *m*, -da *f* **3** FANATIC : fanático *m*, -ca *f*

fiendish [ˈfiːndɪʃ] *adj* : diabólico — **fiendishly** *adv*

fierce [ˈfɪrs] *adj* **fiercer; -est** **1** FEROCIOUS : fiero, feroz **2** HEATED : acalorado **3** INTENSE : intenso, violento, fuerte — **fiercely** *adv*

fierceness [ˈfɪrsnəs] *n* **1** FEROCITY : ferocidad *f*, fiereza *f* **2** INTENSITY : intensidad *f*, violencia *f*

fieriness [ˈfaɪərinəs] *n* : pasión *f*, ardor *m*

fiery [ˈfaɪəri] *adj* **fierier; -est** **1** BURNING : ardiente, llameante **2** GLOWING : encendido **3** PASSIONATE : acalorado, ardiente, fogoso

fiesta [fiˈɛstə] *n* : fiesta *f*

fife [ˈfaɪf] *n* : pífano *m*

fifteen[1] [fɪfˈtiːn] *adj & pron* : quince

fifteen[2] *n* : quince *m*

fifteenth[1] [fɪfˈtiːnθ] *adj* : decimoquinto

fifteenth[2] *n* **1** : decimoquinto *m*, -ta *f* (en una serie) **2** : quinceavo *m*, quinceava parte *f*

fifth[1] [ˈfɪfθ] *adv* : en quinto lugar

fifth[2] *adj* : quinto ⟨(on) the fifth of June : el cinco de junio⟩

fifth[3] *n* **1** : quinto *m*, -ta *f* (en una serie) **2** : quinto *m*, quinta parte *f* **3** : quinta *f* (en la música) **4** *or* **fifth gear** : quinta *f*

fiftieth[1] [ˈfɪftiəθ] *adj* : quincuagésimo

fiftieth[2] *n* **1** : quincuagésimo *m*, -ma *f* (en una serie) **2** : cincuentavo *m*, cincuentava parte *f*

fifty[1] [ˈfɪfti] *adj & pron* : cincuenta

fifty[2] *n, pl* **-ties** : cincuenta *m*

fifty–fifty[1] [ˌfɪftiˈfɪfti] *adv* : a medias, mitad y mitad

fifty–fifty[2] *adj* **to have a fifty–fifty chance** : tener un cincuenta por ciento de posibilidades

fig [ˈfɪg] *n* : higo *m*

fight[1] [ˈfaɪt] *v* **fought** [ˈfɔt]; **fighting** *vi* **1** : luchar, combatir, pelear ⟨to fight to the death : pelear a muerte⟩ ⟨to fight for one's life : debatirse entre la vida y la muerte⟩ **2 to fight back** : defenderse **3 to fight about/over** : discutir por **4 to fight on** : seguir luchando — *vt* **1** : luchar contra, combatir contra **2 to fight back** SUPPRESS : reprimir, contener **3 to fight off** : rechazar, combatir

fight[2] *n* **1** COMBAT : lucha *f*, pelea *f*, combate *m* **2** MATCH : pelea *f*, combate *m* (en boxeo) **3** QUARREL : disputa *f*, pelea *f*, pleito *m*

fighter [ˈfaɪṭər] *n* **1** COMBATANT : luchador *m*, -dora *f*; combatiente *mf* **2** BOXER : boxeador *m*, -dora *f*

figment [ˈfɪgmənt] *n* **figment of the imagination** : producto *m* de la imaginación

figurative [ˈfɪgjərəṭɪv, -gjə-] *adj* : figurado, metafórico

figuratively [ˈfɪgjərəṭɪvli, -gjə-] *adv* : en sentido figurado, de manera metafórica

figure[1] [ˈfɪgjər, -gər] *v* **-ured; -uring** *vt* **1** CALCULATE : calcular **2** ESTIMATE : figurarse, calcular ⟨he figured it was possible : se figuró que era posible⟩ **3 to figure in** : incluir en los cálculos **4 to figure out** : entender — *vi* **1** FEATURE, STAND OUT : figurar, destacar **2 that figures!** : ¡obvio!, ¡no me extraña nada! **3 to figure on** : contar con, tener en cuenta **4 to figure on doing something** : pensar hacer algo

figure[2] *n* **1** DIGIT : número *m*, cifra *f* **2** PRICE : precio *m*, cifra *f* **3** PERSONAGE : figura *f*, personaje *m* **4** : figura *f*, tipo *m*, físico *m* ⟨to have a good figure : tener buen tipo, tener un buen físico⟩ **5** DESIGN, OUTLINE : figura *f* **6 figures** *npl* : aritmética *f*

figurehead [ˈfɪgjərˌhɛd, -gər-] *n* : testaferro *m*, líder *mf* sin poder

figure of speech *n* : figura *f* retórica, figura *f* de hablar

figure out *vt* **1** UNDERSTAND : entender **2** RESOLVE : resolver (un problema, etc.)

figurine [ˌfɪgjəˈriːn] *n* : estatuilla *f*

filament [ˈfɪləmənt] *n* : filamento *m*

filbert [ˈfɪlbərt] *n* : avellana *f*

filch [ˈfɪltʃ] *vt* : hurtar, birlar *fam*

file[1] [ˈfaɪl] *v* **filed; filing** *vt* **1** CLASSIFY : clasificar **2** : archivar (documentos) **3** SUBMIT : presentar ⟨to file charges : presentar cargos⟩ **4** SMOOTH : limar — *vi* : desfilar, entrar (o salir) en fila

file[2] *n* **1** : lima *f* ⟨nail file : lima de uñas⟩ **2** DOCUMENTS : archivo *m* **3** LINE : fila *f* **4** : archivo *m* (de una computadora)

filial [ˈfɪliəl, ˈfɪljəl] *adj* : filial

filibuster[1] [ˈfɪləˌbʌstər] *vi* : practicar el obstruccionismo

filibuster[2] *n* : obstruccionismo *m*

filibusterer [ˈfɪləˌbʌstərər] *n* : obstruccionista *mf*

filigree [ˈfɪləˌgriː] *n* : filigrana *f*

filing cabinet n : archivador m
Filipino [ˌfɪləˈpiːnoː] n : filipino m, -na f —
 Filipino adj
fill¹ [ˈfɪl] vt 1 : llenar, ocupar ⟨to fill a cup
 : llenar una taza⟩ ⟨to fill a room : ocupar
 una sala⟩ 2 STUFF : rellenar 3 PLUG : tapar, rellenar, empastar (un diente) 4
 SATISFY : cumplir con, satisfacer 5 or to
 fill in/out : rellenar, llenar ⟨fill (in) the
 blanks : rellene los espacios⟩ ⟨to fill out
 a form : rellenar un formulario⟩ 6 **to fill**
 someone in on : poner a alguien al corriente de 7 **to fill up** : llenar (hasta
 arriba) — vi or **to fill up** : llenarse ⟨her
 eyes filled with tears : se le llenaron los
 ojos de lágrimas⟩
fill² n 1 FILLING, STUFFING : relleno m 2
 to eat one's fill : comer lo suficiente 3
 to have one's fill of : estar harto de
filler [ˈfɪlər] n : relleno m
fillet¹ [ˈfɪlət, fɪˈleɪ, ˈfɪˌleɪ] vt : cortar en file-
 tes
fillet² n : filete m
fill in vt INFORM : informar, poner al corriente — vi **to fill in for** : reemplazar a
filling [ˈfɪlɪŋ] n 1 : relleno m 2 : empaste
 m (de un diente)
filling station → gas station
filly [ˈfɪli] n, pl -lies : potra f, potranca f
film¹ [ˈfɪlm] vt : filmar — vi : rodar
film² n 1 COATING : capa f, película f 2
 : película f (fotográfica) 3 MOVIE : película f, filme m
filmmaker [ˈfɪlmˌmeɪkər] n : cineasta mf
filmy [ˈfɪlmi] adj filmier; -est 1 GAUZY
 : diáfano, vaporoso 2 : cubierto de una
 película
filter¹ [ˈfɪltər] vt : filtrar
filter² n : filtro m
filth [ˈfɪlθ] n : mugre f, porquería f, roña f
filthiness [ˈfɪlθinəs] n : suciedad f
filthy [ˈfɪlθi] adj filthier; -est 1 DIRTY
 : mugriento, sucio 2 OBSCENE : obsceno,
 indecente
filtration [fɪlˈtreɪʃən] n : filtración f
fin [ˈfɪn] n 1 : aleta f 2 : alerón m (de un
 automóvil o un avión)
finagle [fəˈneɪɡəl] vt -gled; -gling
 : arreglárselas para conseguir
final¹ [ˈfaɪnəl] adj 1 DEFINITIVE : definitivo, final, inapelable 2 ULTIMATE : final
 3 LAST : último, final
final² n 1 : final f (en deportes) 2 **finals**
 npl : exámenes mpl finales
finale [fɪˈnæli, -ˈnɑ-] n : final m ⟨grand
 finale : final triunfal⟩
finalist [ˈfaɪnəlɪst] n : finalista mf
finality [faɪˈnæləti, fə-] n, pl -ties : finalidad f
finalize [ˈfaɪnəlˌaɪz] vt -ized; -izing : finalizar
finally [ˈfaɪnəli] adv 1 LASTLY : por
 último, finalmente 2 EVENTUALLY : por
 fin, al final 3 DEFINITIVELY : definitivamente
finance¹ [fəˈnænts, ˈfaɪˌnænts] vt -nanced;
 -nancing : financiar
finance² n 1 : finanzas fpl 2 **finances** npl
 RESOURCES : recursos mpl financieros

financial [fəˈnæntʃəl, faɪ-] adj : financiero,
 económico
financially [fəˈnæntʃəli, faɪ-] adv : económicamente
financier [ˌfɪnənˈsɪr, ˌfaɪˌnæn-] n : financiero m, -ra f; financista mf
financing [fəˈnæn[t]sɪŋ, ˈfaɪˌnæntsɪŋ] n : financiación f, financiamiento m
finch [ˈfɪntʃ] n : pinzón m
find¹ [ˈfaɪnd] vt found [ˈfaʊnd]; **finding** 1
 LOCATE : encontrar ⟨I can't find it : no lo
 encuentro⟩ ⟨he was nowhere to be
 found : no se lo encontraba por ninguna
 parte⟩ 2 CHANCE UPON : encontrar (por
 casualidad) ⟨I found a dollar : encontré
 un dólar⟩ 3 LEARN : encontrar, descubrir ⟨to find the answer : encontrar la
 solución⟩ ⟨we found that . . . : descubri-
 mos que . . .⟩ 4 GET : encontrar, obtener
 ⟨to find the time to do something : encontrar el tiempo para hacer algo⟩ ⟨to
 find satisfaction in : obtener satisfacción
 de⟩ 5 PERCEIVE : encontrar ⟨I find it
 strange/difficult : lo encuentro raro/difí-
 cil, me resulta raro/difícil⟩ 6 DECLARE
 : declarar, hallar ⟨they found him guilty
 : lo declararon culpable⟩ 7 **to find fault**
 : criticar 8 **to find favor/approval** : ser
 bien recibido 9 **to find oneself** ⟨she
 found herself in an unfamiliar place : se
 encontró en un lugar desconocido⟩ ⟨he
 found himself in a bad situation : se vio
 en apuros⟩ ⟨I found myself thinking
 about her : me di cuenta de que estaba
 pensando en ella⟩ 10 **to find oneself**
 ⟨he left to find himself : se fue para
 encontrarse a sí mismo⟩ 11 **to find one's**
 way : encontrar el camino, orientarse 12
 to find out : descubrir, averiguar
find² n : hallazgo m
finder [ˈfaɪndər] n : descubridor m, -dora f
finding [ˈfaɪndɪŋ] n 1 FIND : hallazgo m 2
 findings npl : conclusiones fpl
find out vt DISCOVER : descubrir, averiguar — vi LEARN : enterarse
fine¹ [ˈfaɪn] vt fined; fining : multar
fine² adj finer; finest 1 PURE : puro (dícese del oro y de la plata) 2 THIN : fino,
 delgado 3 : fino ⟨fine sand : arena fina⟩
 4 SMALL : pequeño, minúsculo ⟨fine
 print : letras minúsculas⟩ 5 SUBTLE : sutil, delicado 6 EXCELLENT : excelente,
 magnífico, selecto 7 FAIR : bueno ⟨it's a
 fine day : hace buen tiempo⟩ 8 EXQUI-
 SITE : exquisito, delicado, fino 9 **fine**
 arts : bellas artes fpl
fine³ n : multa f
finely [ˈfaɪnli] adv 1 EXCELLENTLY : con
 arte 2 ELEGANTLY : elegantemente 3
 PRECISELY : con precisión 4 **to chop**
 finely : picar muy fino, picar en trozos
 pequeños
fineness [ˈfaɪnnəs] n 1 EXCELLENCE
 : excelencia f 2 ELEGANCE : elegancia f,
 refinamiento m 3 DELICACY : delicadeza f, lo fino 4 PRECISION : precisión f
 5 SUBTLETY : sutileza f 6 PURITY : ley f
 (de oro y plata)
finery [ˈfaɪnəri] n : galas fpl, adornos mpl

finesse¹ [fə'nɛs] vt **-nessed; -nessing** : ingeniar

finesse² n **1** REFINEMENT : refinamiento m, finura f **2** TACT : delicadeza f, tacto m, diplomacia f **3** CRAFTINESS : astucia f

fine–tune ['fain'tu:n] vt **1** : poner a punto (un motor), ajustar **2** REFINE : afinar, ajustar

finger¹ ['fɪŋgər] vt **1** HANDLE : tocar, toquetear **2** ACCUSE : acusar, delatar

finger² n : dedo m ⟨to lay a finger on someone : ponerle a alguien la mano encima⟩ ⟨not to lift a finger : no mover un dedo, no hacer nada⟩ ⟨to point a finger at someone : culpar a alguien⟩ ⟨to put one's finger on it : dar en el clavo⟩ ⟨to work one's fingers to the bone : deslomarse trabajando⟩

fingerling ['fɪŋgərlɪŋ] n : pez m pequeño y joven

fingernail ['fɪŋgər,neɪl] n : uña f

fingerprint¹ ['fɪŋgər,prɪnt] vt : tomar las huellas digitales a

fingerprint² n : huella f digital

fingertip ['fɪŋgər,tɪp] n : punta f del dedo, yema f del dedo

finicky ['fɪnɪki] adj : maniático, melindroso, mañoso

finish¹ ['fɪnɪʃ] vt **1** COMPLETE : acabar, terminar **2** : aplicar un acabado a (muebles, etc.) **3** RUIN, DESTROY : acabar con **4 to finish off** : terminar **5 to finish up** : terminar — vi **1** : terminar **2 to finish up** : terminar, acabar

finish² n **1** END : fin m, final m **2** REFINEMENT : refinamiento m **3** : acabado m ⟨a glossy finish : un acabado brillante⟩

finish line n : línea f de meta

finite ['faɪ,naɪt] adj : finito

fink¹ vi fam **to fink on someone** : delatar a alguien

fink² ['fɪŋk] n fam : mequetrefe mf fam

Finn ['fɪn] n : finlandés m, -desa f

Finnish¹ ['fɪnɪʃ] adj : finlandés

Finnish² n : finlandés m (idioma)

fiord [fi'ɔrd] → **fjord**

fir ['fər] n : abeto m

fire¹ ['faɪr] vt **fired; firing 1** IGNITE, KINDLE : encender **2** ENLIVEN : animar, avivar **3** DISMISS : despedir ⟨I was fired : me despidieron⟩ **4** SHOOT : disparar ⟨to fire a gun at someone : dispararle a alguien (con un arma de fuego)⟩ **5** BAKE : cocer (cerámica) **6 to fire off** : disparar (un arma, etc.) **7 to fire off** : lanzar (preguntas) **8 to fire up** ENERGIZE, MOTIVATE : entusiasmar **9 to fire up** START : arrancar, poner en marcha (un motor, etc.) — vi SHOOT : disparar ⟨to fire at someone : dispararle a alguien, disparar contra alguien⟩

fire² n **1** : fuego m **2** BURNING : incendio m ⟨forest fire : incendio forestal⟩ ⟨fire alarm : alarma contra incendios⟩ ⟨to be on fire : estar en llamas⟩ ⟨to catch (on) fire : prender fuego⟩ ⟨to set fire to : prenderle fuego a⟩ **3** ENTHUSIASM : ardor m, entusiasmo m **4** SHOOTING : fuego m, disparos mpl ⟨to open fire : abrir fuego⟩ ⟨to hold one's fire : hacer

alto el fuego⟩ ⟨to come under enemy fire : ser sometido al fuego enemigo⟩ **5 to come under fire** : ser blanco de críticas

firearm ['faɪr,ɑrm] n : arma f de fuego

fireball ['faɪr,bɔl] n **1** : bola f de fuego **2** METEOR : bólido m

firebreak ['faɪr,breɪk] n : cortafuegos m

firebug ['faɪr,bʌg] n : pirómano m, -na f; incendiario m, -ria f

firecracker ['faɪr,krækər] n : petardo m

fire door n : puerta f cortafuegos

fire engine n : coche m de bomberos, autobomba f

fire escape n : escalera f de incendios

fire exit n : salida f de incendios

fire extinguisher n : extinguidor m de incendios

firefighter ['faɪr,faɪtər] n : bombero m, -ra f

firefly ['faɪr,flaɪ] n, pl **-flies** : luciérnaga f

fireman ['faɪrmən] n, pl **-men** [-mən, -,mɛn] FIREFIGHTER : bombero m

fireplace ['faɪr,pleɪs] n : hogar m, chimenea f

fireproof¹ ['faɪr,pru:f] vt : hacer incombustible

fireproof² adj : incombustible, ignífugo

fireside¹ ['faɪr,saɪd] adj : informal ⟨fireside chat : charla informal⟩

fireside² n **1** HEARTH : chimenea f, hogar m **2** HOME : hogar m, casa f

fire station n : estación f de bomberos

fire truck n → **fire engine**

firewall ['faɪr,wɔl] n : cortafuegos m

firewood ['faɪr,wʊd] n : leña f

fireworks ['faɪr,wərks] npl : fuegos mpl artificiales, pirotecnia f

firing squad n : pelotón m de ejecución

firm¹ ['fərm] vt or **to firm up** : endurecer

firm² adj **1** VIGOROUS : fuerte, vigoroso **2** SOLID, UNYIELDING : firme, duro, sólido **3** UNCHANGING : firme, inalterable **4** RESOLUTE : firme, resuelto

firm³ n : empresa f, firma f, compañía f

firmament ['fərməmənt] n : firmamento m

firmly ['fərmli] adv : firmemente

firmness ['fərmnəs] n : firmeza f

first¹ ['fərst] adv **1** : primero ⟨finish your homework first : primero termina tu tarea⟩ ⟨first and foremost : ante todo⟩ ⟨first of all : en primer lugar⟩ **2** : por primera vez ⟨I saw it first in Boston : lo vi por primera vez en Boston⟩

first² adj & pron **1** : primero ⟨the first time : la primera vez⟩ ⟨the first of many : el primero de muchos, la primera de muchas⟩ ⟨at first sight : a primera vista⟩ ⟨in the first place : en primer lugar⟩ ⟨the first ten applicants : los diez primeros candidatos⟩ ⟨that's the first I've heard of it! : ¡(es la) primera noticia (que tengo)!, ¡ahora me entero!⟩ **2** FOREMOST : principal, primero ⟨first tenor : tenor principal⟩

first³ n **1** : primero m, -ra f ⟨the first of April : el primero/uno de abril⟩ **2 first base** : primera base f **3** or **first gear** : primera f **4 at ~** : al principio

first aid n : primeros auxilios mpl ⟨first aid kit : botiquín⟩

firstborn n : primogénito m, -ta f — **firstborn** adj

first-class¹ ['fərst'klæs] adv : en primera ⟨to travel first-class : viajar en primera⟩

first-class² adj : de primera

first class n : primera clase f

firsthand¹ ['fərst'hænd] adv : directamente

firsthand² adj : de primera mano

first lady n : primera dama f

first lieutenant n : teniente mf; teniente primero m, teniente primera f

firstly ['fərstli] adv : primeramente, principalmente, en primer lugar

first name n : nombre m de pila

first-rate¹ ['fərst'reɪt] adv : muy bien

first-rate² adj : de primera, de primera clase

first sergeant n : sargento mf

firth ['fərθ] n : estuario m

fiscal ['fɪskəl] adj : fiscal — **fiscally** adv

fish¹ ['fɪʃ] vi 1 : pescar 2 to fish for SEEK : buscar, rebuscar ⟨to fish for compliments : andar a la caza de cumplidos⟩ — vt : pescar

fish² n, pl fish or fishes : pez m (vivo), pescado m (para comer)

fishbowl ['fɪʃ,bo:l] n : pecera f

fisherman ['fɪʃərmən] n, pl -men [-mən, -,mɛn] : pescador m

fisherwoman ['fɪʃər,wʊmən] n, pl -women [-,wɪmən] : pescadora f

fishery ['fɪʃəri] n, pl -eries 1 → fishing 2 : zona f pesquera, pesquería f

fishhook ['fɪʃ,hʊk] n : anzuelo m

fishing ['fɪʃɪŋ] n : pesca f, industria f pesquera

fishing pole or **fishing rod** n : caña f de pescar

fish market n : pescadería f

fish sticks npl : palitos mpl de pescado

fishy ['fɪʃi] adj fishier; -est 1 : a pescado ⟨a fishy taste : un sabor a pescado⟩ 2 QUESTIONABLE : dudoso, sospechoso ⟨there's something fishy going on : aquí hay gato encerrado⟩

fission ['fɪʃən, -ʒən] n : fisión f

fissure ['fɪʃər] n : fisura f, hendidura f

fist ['fɪst] n : puño m

fistful ['fɪst,fʊl] n : puñado m

fisticuffs ['fɪstɪ,kʌfs] npl : lucha f a puñetazos

fit¹ ['fɪt] v fitted; fitting vt 1 MATCH : corresponder a, coincidir con ⟨the punishment fits the crime : el castigo corresponde al crimen⟩ 2 : quedar ⟨the dress doesn't fit me : el vestido no me queda⟩ 3 GO : caber, encajar en ⟨her key fits the lock : su llave encaja en la cerradura⟩ 4 INSERT, INSTALL : poner, colocar 5 ADAPT : adecuar, ajustar, adaptar 6 or to fit out EQUIP : equipar 7 to fit in : acomodar — vi 1 : quedar, entallar ⟨these pants don't fit : estos pantalones no me quedan⟩ 2 CONFORM : encajar, cuadrar 3 to fit in : encajar, estar integrado 4 to fit in : adaptarse (dícese de una persona)

fit² adj fitter; fittest 1 SUITABLE : adecuado, apropiado, conveniente ⟨do as you see/think fit : haz lo que creas conveniente⟩ ⟨she didn't see fit to mention it : no juzgó necesario mencionarlo⟩ 2 QUALIFIED : calificado, competente 3 HEALTHY : sano, en forma ⟨to get/keep fit : ponerse/mantenerse en forma⟩

fit³ n 1 ATTACK : ataque m, acceso m, arranque m 2 to be a good fit : quedar bien 3 to be a tight fit : ser muy entallado (de ropa), estar apretado (de espacios)

fitful ['fɪtfəl] adj : irregular, intermitente — **fitfully** adv

fitness ['fɪtnəs] n 1 HEALTH : salud f, buena forma f (física) 2 SUITABILITY : idoneidad f

fitting¹ ['fɪtɪŋ] adj : adecuado, apropiado

fitting² n : accesorio m

fitting room n : probador m

five¹ ['faɪv] adj : cinco ⟨the child is five (years old) : el niño tiene cinco años⟩

five² n : cinco m ⟨the five of hearts : el cinco de corazones⟩ ⟨it's five (o'clock) : son las cinco⟩

five³ pron : cinco ⟨there are five of us : somos cinco⟩

five hundred¹ adj & pron : quinientos

five hundred² n : quinientos m

fiver ['faɪvər] n fam : billete m de cinco dólares

fix¹ ['fɪks] vt 1 ATTACH, SECURE : sujetar, asegurar, fijar 2 ESTABLISH, SET : fijar (precios, fechas, etc.), concretar (planes, etc.) 3 : fijar (los ojos, la mirada, etc.) 4 REPAIR : arreglar, reparar 5 SOLVE : resolver, solucionar 6 PREPARE : preparar ⟨to fix dinner : preparar la cena⟩ 7 RIG : arreglar, amañar ⟨to fix a race : arreglar una carrera⟩ 8 ARRANGE : arreglar ⟨to fix one's hair/face : peinarse/maquillarse⟩ ⟨she fixed it so we won't have to pay : lo arregló para que no tengamos que pagar⟩ 9 PUNISH : castigar ⟨I'll fix him! : ¡se las verá conmigo!⟩ 10 to fix oneself up : arreglarse 11 to fix someone up : arreglarle una cita a alguien 12 to fix someone up ⟨I'll fix you up : te lo arreglaré todo⟩ ⟨they fixed us up with a rental car : nos consiguió un auto/carro/coche de alquiler⟩ 13 to fix up : arreglar (una casa, etc.)

fix² n 1 PREDICAMENT : aprieto m, apuro m 2 : posición f ⟨to get a fix on : establecer la posición de⟩

fixate ['fɪk,seɪt] vi -ated; -ating : obsesionarse

fixation [fɪk'seɪʃən] n : fijación f, obsesión f

fixed ['fɪkst] adj 1 STATIONARY : estacionario, inmóvil 2 UNCHANGING : fijo, inalterable 3 INTENT : fijo ⟨a fixed stare : una mirada fija⟩ 4 to be comfortably fixed : estar en posición acomodada

fixedly ['fɪksədli] adv : fijamente

fixedness ['fɪksədnəs, 'fɪkst-] n : rigidez f

fixture ['fɪkstʃər] n 1 : parte f integrante, elemento m fijo 2 fixtures npl : instalaciones fpl (de una casa)

fizz[1] ['fiz] vi : burbujear

fizz[2] n : efervescencia f

fizzle[1] ['fizəl] vi -zled; -zling 1 FIZZ : burbujear 2 FAIL : fracasar

fizzle[2] n : fracaso m, fiasco m

fizzy ['fizi] adj **fizzier; -est** : gaseoso, efervescente

fjord [fi'ɔrd] n : fiordo m

flab ['flæb] n : gordura f

flabbergast ['flæbər,gæst] vt : asombrar, pasmar, dejar atónito

flabby ['flæbi] adj **flabbier; -est** : blando, fofo, aguado CA, Col, Mex

flaccid ['flæksəd, 'flæsəd] adj : fláccido

flag[1] ['flæg] vi **flagged; flagging** 1 : hacer señales con banderas 2 WEAKEN : flaquear, desfallecer

flag[2] n : bandera f, pabellón m, estandarte m

flagon ['flægən] n : jarra f grande

flagpole ['flæg,po:l] n : asta f, mástil m

flagrant ['fleigrənt] adj : flagrante — **flagrantly** adv

flagship ['flæg,ʃɪp] n : buque m insignia

flagstaff ['flæg,stæf] → flagpole

flagstone ['flæg,sto:n] n : losa f, piedra f

flail ['fleil] vt 1 : trillar (grano) 2 : sacudir, agitar (los brazos)

flair ['flær] n : don m, facilidad f

flak ['flæk] ns & pl 1 : fuego m antiaéreo 2 CRITICISM : críticas fpl

flake[1] ['fleik] vi **flaked; flaking** : desmenuzarse, pelarse (dícese de la piel)

flake[2] n : copo m (de nieve), escama f (de la piel), astilla f (de madera)

flamboyance [flæm'bɔiənts] n : extravagancia f

flamboyant [flæm'bɔiənt] adj : exuberante, extravagante, rimbombante

flame[1] ['fleim] vi **flamed; flaming** 1 BLAZE : arder, llamear 2 GLOW : brillar, encenderse

flame[2] n BLAZE : llama f ⟨to burst into flames : estallar en llamas⟩ ⟨to go up in flame : incendiarse⟩

flamenco [flə'mɛŋko] n : flamenco m (música o baile) — **flamenco** adj

flamethrower ['fleim,θro:ər] n : lanzallamas m

flamingo [flə'mɪŋgo] n, pl **-gos** : flamenco m

flammable ['flæməbəl] adj : inflamable, flamable

flan ['flæn, 'flɑn] n : flan m

flange ['flændʒ] n : reborde m, pestaña f

flank[1] ['flæŋk] vt 1 : flanquear (para defender o atacar) 2 BORDER, LINE : bordear

flank[2] n : ijada f (de un animal), costado m (de una persona), falda f (de una colina), flanco m (de un cuerpo de soldados)

flannel ['flænəl] n : franela f

flap[1] ['flæp] v **flapped; flapping** vi 1 : aletear ⟨the bird was flapping (its wings) : el pájaro aleteaba⟩ 2 FLUTTER : ondear, agitarse — vt : batir, agitar

flap[2] n 1 FLAPPING : aleteo m 2 : soplada f (de un sobre), hoja f (de una mesa), faldón m (de una chaqueta)

flapjack ['flæp,dʒæk] → pancake

flare[1] ['flær] vi **flared; flaring** 1 FLAME, SHINE : llamear, brillar 2 or **to flare up** : estallar, explotar (de cólera) ⟨tempers flared : se encendieron los ánimos⟩ 3 **to flare up** : recrudecerse (dícese de una enfermedad)

flare[2] n 1 FLASH : destello m 2 SIGNAL : (luz f de) bengala f 3 **solar flare** : erupción f solar

flare-up ['flær,ʌp] n 1 : llamarada f 2 OUTBREAK : estallido m, brote m 3 : empeoramiento m (de una enfermedad)

flash[1] ['flæʃ] vi 1 SHINE, SPARKLE : destellar, brillar, relampaguear 2 : pasar como un relámpago ⟨an idea flashed through my mind : una idea me cruzó la mente como un relámpago⟩ — vt : despedir, lanzar (una luz), transmitir (un mensaje)

flash[2] adj SUDDEN : repentino

flash[3] n 1 : destello m (de luz), fogonazo m (de una explosión) 2 **flash of lightning** : relámpago m 3 **in a flash** : de repente, de un abrir y cerrar los ojos

flashback ['flæʃ,bæk] n : flashback m

flashiness ['flæʃinəs] n : ostentación f

flashlight ['flæʃ,lait] n : linterna f

flashy ['flæʃi] adj **flashier; -est** : llamativo, ostentoso

flask ['flæsk] n : frasco m

flat[1] ['flæt] vt **flatted; flatting** 1 FLATTEN : aplanar, achatar 2 : bajar de tono (en música)

flat[2] adv 1 EXACTLY : exactamente ⟨in ten minutes flat : en diez minutos exactos⟩ 2 : desafinado, demasiado bajo (en la música) ⟨to sing flat : cantar desafinado⟩ 3 HORIZONTALLY ⟨she fell flat on her back/face : cayó de espaldas/bruces⟩ ⟨lay the map flat on the desk : extiende el mapa sobre el escritorio⟩ 4 COMPLETELY : completamente ⟨I'm flat broke : estoy pelado⟩

flat[3] adj **flatter; flattest** 1 EVEN, LEVEL : plano, llano 2 SMOOTH : liso 3 LOW : bajo (dícese de los zapatos, etc.) 4 SPREAD : tendido (dícese de una persona), extendido (dícese de una cosa) 5 DEFINITE : categórico, rotundo, explícito ⟨a flat refusal : una negativa categórica⟩ 6 : plano ⟨flat rate : tarifa plana⟩ 7 DULL : aburrido, soso, monótono (dícese de la voz) 8 DEFLATED : desinflado, pinchado, ponchado Mex 9 : bemol (en música) 10 : sin efervescencia 11 MATTE : mate

flat[4] n 1 PLAIN : llano m, terreno m llano 2 : bemol m (en la música) 3 APARTMENT : apartamento m, departamento m 4 or **flat tire** : pinchazo m, ponchadura f Mex 5 **flats** npl : zapatos mpl bajos

flatbed ['flæt,bɛd] n : camión m de plataforma

flatcar ['flæt,kɑr] n : vagón m abierto

flatfish ['flæt,fɪʃ] n : platija f

flat-footed ['flæt,fʊtəd, ,flæt'-] adj : de pies planos

flatly ['flætli] adv DEFINITELY : categóricamente, rotundamente

flatness ['flætnəs] *n* **1** EVENNESS : lo llano, lisura *f*, uniformidad *f* **2** DULLNESS : monotonía *f*

flat–out ['flæt'aʊt] *adj* **1** : frenético, a toda máquina ⟨a flat-out effort : un esfuerzo frenético⟩ **2** CATEGORICAL : descarado, rotundo, categórico

flatten ['flætən] *vt* : aplanar, achatar

flatter ['flætər] *vt* **1** OVERPRAISE : adular **2** COMPLIMENT : halagar **3** : favorecer ⟨the photo flatters you : la foto te favorece⟩

flatterer ['flætərər] *n* : adulador *m*, -dora *f*

flattering ['flætərɪŋ] *adj* **1** COMPLIMENTARY : halagador **2** BECOMING : favorecedor

flattery ['flætəri] *n, pl* **-ries** : halagos *mpl*

flatulence ['flætʃələns] *n* : flatulencia *f*, ventosidad *f*

flatulent ['flætʃələnt] *adj* : flatulento

flatware ['flæt,wær] *n* : cubertería *f*, cubiertos *mpl*

flaunt[1] ['flɔnt] *vt* : alardear, hacer alarde de

flaunt[2] *n* : alarde *m*, ostentación *f*

flavor[1] ['fleɪvər] *vt* : dar sabor a, sazonar

flavor[2] *n* : gusto *m*, sabor *m* **2** → **flavoring**

flavored ['fleɪvərd] *adj* : con sabor

flavorful ['fleɪvərfəl] *adj* : sabroso

flavoring ['fleɪvərɪŋ] *n* : condimento *m*, sazón *f* ⟨artificial flavoring : saborizante artificial⟩

flavorless ['fleɪvərləs] *adj* : sin sabor

flaw ['flɔ] *n* : falla *f*, defecto *m*, imperfección *f*

flawed ['flɔd] *adj* : imperfecto, con defectos

flawless ['flɔləs] *adj* : impecable, perfecto — **flawlessly** *adv*

flax ['flæks] *n* : lino *m*

flaxen ['flæksən] *adj* : rubio, blondo (dícese del pelo)

flay ['fleɪ] *vt* **1** SKIN : desollar, despellejar **2** VILIFY : criticar con dureza, vilipendiar

flea ['fli:] *n* : pulga *f*

flea market *n* : mercado *m* de pulgas, tianguis *m Mex*, mercadillo *m Spain*

fleck[1] ['flɛk] *vt* : salpicar

fleck[2] *n* : mota *f*, pinta *f*

fledgling ['flɛdʒlɪŋ] *n* : polluelo *m*, pollito *m*

flee ['fli:] *v* **fled** ['flɛd]; **fleeing** *vi* : huir, escapar(se) — *vt* : huir de

fleece[1] ['fli:s] *vt* **fleeced; fleecing** **1** SHEAR : esquilar, trasquilar **2** SWINDLE : estafar, defraudar

fleece[2] *n* : lana *f*, vellón *m*

fleet[1] ['fli:t] *vi* : moverse con rapidez

fleet[2] *adj* SWIFT : rápido, veloz

fleet[3] *n* : flota *f*

fleet admiral *n* : almirante *mf*

fleeting ['fli:tɪŋ] *adj* : fugaz, breve

Fleming ['flɛmɪŋ] *n* : flamenco *m*, -ca *f*

Flemish ['flɛmɪʃ] *n* **1 the Flemish** (*used with a plural verb*) : los flamencos *mpl* **2** : flamenco *m* (idioma) — **Flemish** *adj*

flesh ['flɛʃ] *n* **1** : carne *f* (de seres humanos y animales) **2** : pulpa *f* (de frutas)

flesh out *vt* : desarrollar, darle cuerpo a

fleshy ['flɛʃi] *adj* **fleshier; -est** : gordo (dícese de las personas), carnoso (dícese de la fruta)

flew → **fly**

flex ['flɛks] *vt* : doblar, flexionar

flexibility [,flɛksə'bɪləti] *n, pl* **-ties** : flexibilidad *f*, elasticidad *f*

flexible ['flɛksəbəl] *adj* : flexible — **flexibly** [-bli] *adv*

flextime ['flɛks,taɪm] *n* : horario *m* flexible

flick[1] ['flɪk] *vt* : dar un capirotazo a (con el dedo) ⟨to flick a switch : darle al interruptor⟩ — *vi* **1** FLIT : revolotear **2 to flick through** : hojear (un libro)

flick[2] *n* : coletazo *m* (de una cola), capirotazo *m* (de un dedo)

flicker[1] ['flɪkər] *vi* **1** FLUTTER : revolotear, aletear **2** BLINK, TWINKLE : parpadear, titilar

flicker[2] *n* **1** : parpadeo *m*, titileo *m* **2** HINT, TRACE : indicio *m*, rastro *m* ⟨a flicker of hope : un rayo de esperanza⟩

flier ['flaɪər] *n* **1** AVIATOR : aviador *m*, -dora *f* **2** CIRCULAR : folleto *m* publicitario, circular *f*

flight ['flaɪt] *n* **1** : vuelo *m* (de aves o aviones), trayectoria *f* (de proyectiles) **2** TRIP : vuelo *m* **3** FLOCK, SQUADRON : bandada *f* (de pájaros), escuadrilla *f* (de aviones) **4** ESCAPE : huida *f*, fuga *f* **5 flight of fancy** : ilusiones *fpl*, fantasía *f* **6 flight of stairs** : tramo *m*

flight attendant *n* : auxiliar *mf* de vuelo

flightless ['flaɪtləs] *adj* : no volador

flighty ['flaɪti] *adj* **flightier; -est** : caprichoso, frívolo

flimsy ['flɪmzi] *adj* **flimsier; -est 1** LIGHT, THIN : ligero, fino **2** WEAK : endeble, poco sólido **3** IMPLAUSIBLE : pobre, flojo, poco convincente ⟨a flimsy excuse : una excusa floja⟩

flinch ['flɪntʃ] *vi* **1** WINCE : estremecerse **2** RECOIL : recular, retroceder

fling[1] ['flɪŋ] *vt* **flung** ['flʌŋ]; **flinging 1** THROW : lanzar, tirar, arrojar **2 to fling oneself** : lanzarse, tirarse, precipitarse

fling[2] *n* **1** THROW : lanzamiento *m* **2** ATTEMPT : intento *m* **3** AFFAIR : aventura *f* **4** BINGE : juerga *f*

flint ['flɪnt] *n* : pedernal *m*

flinty ['flɪnti] *adj* **flintier; -est 1** : de pedernal **2** STERN, UNYIELDING : severo, inflexible

flip[1] ['flɪp] *v* **flipped; flipping** *vt* **1** TOSS : tirar ⟨to flip a coin : echar a cara o cruz⟩ **2** OVERTURN : dar la vuelta a, voltear — *vi* **1** : moverse bruscamente **2 to flip through** : hojear (un libro)

flip[2] *adj* : insolente, descarado

flip[3] *n* **1** FLICK : capirotazo *m*, golpe *m* ligero **2** SOMERSAULT : voltereta *f*

flip–flop ['flɪp,flɑp] *n* **1** REVERSAL : giro *m* radical **2** THONG : chancla *f*, chancleta *f*

flippancy ['flɪpəntsi] *n, pl* **-cies** : ligereza *f*, falta *f* de seriedad

flippant ['flɪpənt] *adj* : ligero, frívolo, poco serio

flipper ['flɪpər] *n* : aleta *f*

flirt¹ ['flərt] *vi* **1** : coquetear, flirtear **2** TRIFLE : jugar ⟨to flirt with death : jugar con la muerte⟩

flirt² *n* : coqueto *m*, -ta *f*

flirtation [,flər'teɪʃən] *n* : devaneo *m*, coqueteo *m*

flirtatious [,flər'teɪʃəs] *adj* : insinuante, coqueto

flit ['flɪt] *vi* **flitted; flitting 1** : revolotear **2 to flit about** : ir y venir rápidamente

float¹ ['floːt] *vi* **1** : flotar **2** WANDER : vagar, errar — *vt* **1** : poner a flote, hacer flotar (un barco) **2** LAUNCH : hacer flotar (una empresa) **3** ISSUE : emitir (acciones en la bolsa)

float² *n* **1** : flotador *m*, corcho *m* (para pescar) **2** BUOY : boya *f* **3** : carroza *f* (en un desfile)

floating ['floːtɪŋ] *adj* : flotante

flock¹ ['flɑk] *vi* **1** : moverse en rebaño **2** CONGREGATE : congregarse, reunirse

flock² *n* : rebaño *m* (de ovejas), bandada *f* (de pájaros)

floe ['floː] *n* : témpano *m* de hielo

flog ['flɑg] *vt* **flogged; flogging** : azotar, fustigar

flood¹ ['flʌd] *vt* : inundar, anegar

flood² *n* **1** INUNDATION : inundación *f* **2** TORRENT : avalancha *f*, diluvio *m*, torrente *m* ⟨a flood of tears : un mar de lágrimas⟩

floodgate ['flʌd,geɪt] *n* : compuerta *f*, esclusa *f* ⟨to open the floodgates for/to : abrirle las puertas a, desatar una ola de⟩

flooding ['flʌdɪŋ] *n* : inundación *f*

floodlight ['flʌd,laɪt] *n* : foco *m*

floodwater ['flʌd,wɔtər] *n* : crecida *f*, creciente *f*

floor¹ ['floːr] *vt* **1** : solar, poner suelo a (una casa o una sala) **2** KNOCK DOWN : derribar, echar al suelo **3** NONPLUS : desconcertar, confundir, dejar perplejo

floor² *n* **1** : suelo *m*, piso *m* ⟨dance floor : pista de baile⟩ **2** STORY : piso *m*, planta *f* ⟨ground floor : planta baja⟩ ⟨second floor : primer piso⟩ **3** : mínimo *m* (de sueldos, precios, etc.)

floorboard ['floːr,bord] *n* : tabla *f* del suelo, suelo *m*, piso *m*

flooring ['floːrɪŋ] *n* : entarimado *m*

floor show *n* : espectáculo *m* (en un cabaret, etc.)

floor tile → tile²

flop¹ ['flɑp] *vi* **flopped; flopping 1** FLAP : golpearse, agitarse **2** COLLAPSE : dejarse caer, desplomarse **3** FAIL : fracasar

flop² *n* **1** FAILURE : fracaso *m* **2 to take a flop** : caerse

floppy ['flɑpi] *adj* **floppier; -est 1** : blando, flexible **2 floppy disk** : diskette *m*, disquete *m*

flora ['florə] *n* : flora *f*

floral ['florəl] *adj* : floral, floreado

florid ['florɪd] *adj* **1** FLOWERY : florido **2** REDDISH : rojizo

florist ['florɪst] *n* : florista *mf*

floss¹ ['flɔs] *vi* : limpiarse los dientes con hilo dental

floss² *n* **1** : hilo *m* de seda (de bordar) **2 → dental floss**

flotation [flo'teɪʃən] *n* : flotación *f*

flotilla [flo'tɪlə] *n* : flotilla *f*

flotsam ['flɑtsəm] *n* **1** : restos *mpl* flotantes (en el mar) **2 flotsam and jetsam** : desechos *mpl*, restos *mpl*

flounce¹ ['flaʊnts] *vi* **flounced; flouncing** : moverse haciendo aspavientos ⟨she flounced into the room : entró en la sala haciendo aspavientos⟩

flounce² *n* **1** RUFFLE : volante *m* **2** FLOURISH : aspaviento *m*

flounder¹ ['flaʊndər] *vi* **1** STRUGGLE : forcejear **2** STUMBLE : no saber qué hacer o decir, perder el hilo (en un discurso)

flounder² *n, pl* **flounder** *or* **flounders** : platija *f*

flour¹ ['flaʊər] *vt* : enharinar

flour² *n* : harina *f*

flourish¹ ['flərɪʃ] *vi* THRIVE : florecer, prosperar, crecer (dícese de las plantas) — *vt* BRANDISH : blandir

flourish² *n* : floritura *f*, floreo *m*

flourishing ['flərɪʃɪŋ] *adj* : floreciente, próspero

flout ['flaʊt] *vt* : desobedecer (una regla, etc.) descaradamente

flow¹ ['floː] *vi* **1** COURSE : fluir, manar, correr **2** CIRCULATE : circular, correr ⟨traffic is flowing smoothly : el tránsito está circulando con fluidez⟩

flow² *n* **1** FLOWING : flujo *m*, circulación *f* **2** STREAM : corriente *f*, chorro *m*

flow chart *n* : diagrama *m*, organigrama *m*

flower¹ ['flaʊər] *vi* : florecer, florear

flower² *n* : flor *f*

flowerbed ['flaʊər,bɛd] *n* : arriate *m Mex, Spain*; cantero *m*

flowered ['flaʊərd] *adj* : florido, floreado

floweriness ['flaʊərinəs] *n* : floritura *f*

flowering¹ ['flaʊərɪŋ] *adj* : floreciente

flowering² *n* : floración *f*, florecimiento *m*

flowerpot ['flaʊər,pɑt] *n* : maceta *f*, tiesto *m*, macetero *m*

flowery ['flaʊəri] *adj* **1** : florido **2** FLOWERED : floreado, de flores

flowing ['floːɪŋ] *adj* : fluido, corriente

flown → fly

flu ['fluː] *n* : gripe *f*, gripa *f Col, Mex*

fluctuate ['flʌktʃʊ,eɪt] *vi* **-ated; -ating** : fluctuar

fluctuation [,flʌktʃʊ'eɪʃən] *n* : fluctuación *f*

flue ['fluː] *n* : tiro *m*, salida *f* de humos

fluency ['fluːəntsi] *n* : fluidez *f*, soltura *f*

fluent ['fluːənt] *adj* : fluido

fluently ['fluːəntli] *adv* : con soltura, con fluidez

fluff¹ ['flʌf] *vt* **1** : ahuecar (una almohada, etc.) **2** BUNGLE : echar a perder, equivocarse

fluff² *n* **1** FUZZ : pelusa *f* **2** DOWN : plumón *m*

fluffy ['flʌfi] *adj* **fluffier; -est 1** DOWNY : lleno de pelusa, velloso **2** SPONGY : esponjoso

fluid¹ ['fluːɪd] *adj* : fluido

fluid² n : fluido m, líquido m
fluidity [flu'ɪdəʈi] n : fluidez f
fluid ounce n : onza f líquida (29.57 mililitros)
fluke ['flu:k] n : golpe m de suerte, chiripa f, casualidad f
flummox ['flʌməks] vt CONFUSE : desconcertar
flung → **fling**
flunk ['flʌŋk] vt FAIL : reprobar — vi : salir reprobando
fluorescent [,flur'esənt, ,flɔr-] adj : fluorescente
fluoride ['flɔr,aɪd, 'flur-] n : fluoruro m
fluorine ['flɔr,i:n] n : flúor m
flurry ['fləri] n, pl **-ries** 1 GUST : ráfaga f 2 SNOWFALL : nevisca f 3 BUSTLE : frenesí m, bullicio m 4 BARRAGE : aluvión m, oleada f ⟨a flurry of questions : un aluvión de preguntas⟩
flush¹ ['flʌʃ] vt 1 : limpiar con agua ⟨to flush the toilet : jalar la cadena⟩ 2 RAISE : hacer salir, levantar (en la caza) — vi BLUSH : ruborizarse, sonrojarse
flush² adv : al mismo nivel, a ras
flush³ adj 1 or **flushed** ['flʌʃt] : colorado, rojo, encendido (dícese de la cara) 2 FILLED : lleno a rebosar 3 ABUNDANT : copioso, abundante 4 AFFLUENT : adinerado 5 ALIGNED, SMOOTH : alineado, liso 6 **flush against** : pegado a, contra
flush⁴ n 1 FLOW, JET : chorro m, flujo m rápido 2 SURGE : arrebato m, arranque m ⟨a flush of anger : un arrebato de cólera⟩ 3 BLUSH : rubor m, sonrojo m 4 GLOW : resplandor m, flor f ⟨the flush of youth : la flor de la juventud⟩ ⟨in the flush of victory : en la euforia del triunfo⟩
fluster¹ ['flʌstər] vt : poner nervioso, aturdir
fluster² n : agitación f, confusión f
flute ['flu:t] n : flauta f
fluted ['flu:ʈəd] adj 1 GROOVED : acanalado 2 WAVY : ondulado
fluting ['flu:ʈɪŋ] n : estrías fpl
flutist ['flu:ʈɪst] n : flautista mf
flutter¹ ['flʌʈər] vi 1 : revolotear (dícese de un pájaro), ondear (dícese de una bandera), palpitar con fuerza (dícese del corazón) 2 **to flutter about** : ir y venir, revolotear — vt : sacudir, batir
flutter² n 1 FLUTTERING : revoloteo m, aleteo m 2 COMMOTION, STIR : revuelo m, agitación f
flux ['flʌks] n 1 : flujo m (en física y medicina) 2 CHANGE : cambio m ⟨to be in a state of flux : estar cambiando continuamente⟩
fly¹ ['flaɪ] v **flew** ['flu:]; **flown** ['flo:n]; **flying** vi 1 : volar ⟨the birds flew off/away : los pájaros se echaron a volar⟩ 2 TRAVEL : volar ⟨we flew to Europe : volamos a Europa, fuimos en avión a Europa⟩ 3 SOAR, SAIL : volar ⟨he tripped and went flying : se tropezó y salió volando⟩ ⟨clouds flew across the sky : las nubes pasaban rápido por el cielo⟩ ⟨bullets were flying in all directions : las ba-

las silbaban en todas direcciones⟩ 4 : ondear (dícese de una bandera, etc.) 5 FLEE : huir, escapar 6 RUSH : correr, irse volando 7 : correr (dícese de rumores), lanzarse (dícese de insultos) 8 PASS : pasar (volando) ⟨how time flies! : ¡cómo pasa el tiempo!⟩ ⟨our vacation flew by : las vacaciones se nos pasaron volando⟩ 9 **to fly open** : abrir de golpe — vt 1 : pilotar (un avión), hacer volar (una cometa) 2 : transportar, llevar (en avión)
fly² n, pl **flies** 1 : mosca f ⟨to drop like flies : caer como moscas⟩ 2 : bragueta f (de pantalones, etc.)
flyer → **flier**
flying saucer n : platillo m volador
flypaper ['flaɪ,peɪpər] n : papel m matamoscas
flyswatter ['flaɪ,swɑʈər] n : matamoscas m
flywheel ['flaɪ,hwi:l] n : volante m
foal¹ ['fo:l] vi : parir
foal² n : potro m, -tra f
foam¹ ['fo:m] vi : hacer espuma
foam² n : espuma f
foam rubber n : goma f espuma, hule m espuma Mex
foamy ['fo:mi] adj **foamier; -est** : espumoso
focal ['fo:kəl] adj 1 : focal, central 2 **focal point** : foco m, punto m de referencia
fo'c'sle ['fo:ksəl] → **forecastle**
focus¹ ['fo:kəs] v **-cused** or **-cussed; -cusing** or **-cussing** vt 1 : enfocar (un instrumento) 2 CONCENTRATE : concentrar, centrar — vi : enfocar, fijar la vista
focus² n, pl **-ci** ['fo:,saɪ, -,kaɪ] 1 : foco m ⟨to be in focus : estar enfocado⟩ 2 FOCUSING : enfoque m 3 CENTER : centro m, foco m
fodder ['fɑdər] n : pienso m, forraje m
foe ['fo:] n : enemigo m, -ga f
fog¹ ['fɔg, 'fɑg] v **fogged; fogging** vt : empañar — vi **to fog up** : empañarse
fog² n : niebla f, neblina f
foggy ['fɔgi, 'fɑ-] adj **foggier; -est** : nebuloso, brumoso
foghorn ['fɔg,hɔrn, 'fɑg-] n : sirena f de niebla
fogy ['fo:gi] n, pl **-gies** : carca mf fam, persona f chapada a la antigua
foible ['fɔɪbəl] n : flaqueza f, debilidad f
foil¹ ['fɔɪl] vt : frustrar, hacer fracasar
foil² n 1 : lámina f de metal, papel m de aluminio 2 CONTRAST : contraste m, complemento m 3 SWORD : florete m (en esgrima)
foist ['fɔɪst] vt : encajar, endilgar fam, colocar
fold¹ ['fo:ld] vt 1 BEND : doblar, plegar 2 CLASP : cruzar (brazos), enlazar (manos), plegar (alas) 3 EMBRACE : estrechar, abrazar 4 **to fold in** : incorporar ⟨fold in the cream : incorpore la crema⟩ 5 **to fold up** : doblar, plegar — vi 1 FAIL : fracasar, venirse abajo 2 **to fold up** : doblarse, plegarse
fold² n 1 SHEEPFOLD : redil m (para ovejas) 2 FLOCK : rebaño m ⟨to return to

the fold : volver al redil⟩ 3 CREASE : pliegue *m*, doblez *m*

-fold [ˌfoːld] *suf* 1 : (multiplicado) por ⟨to increase fourfold : multiplicarse por cuatro, cuadruplicarse⟩ ⟨there's been a tenfold increase in thefts : el número de robos se ha multiplicado por diez⟩ 2 (*indicating a number of parts*) ⟨a threefold problem : un problema que tiene tres aspectos⟩

folder [ˈfoːldər] *n* 1 CIRCULAR : circular *f*, folleto *m* 2 BINDER : carpeta *f* 3 : carpeta *f*, directorio *m* (en informática)

foliage [ˈfoːliːʤ, -liʤ] *n* : follaje *m*

folio [ˈfoːliˌoː] *n*, *pl* **-lios** : folio *m*

folk¹ [ˈfoːk] *adj* : popular, folklórico ⟨folk customs : costumbres populares⟩ ⟨folk dance : danza folklórica⟩ ⟨folk music : (música) folk⟩

folk² *n*, *pl* **folk** *or* **folks** 1 PEOPLE : gente *f* 2 : folk *m*, música *f* folk 3 **folks** *npl* : familia *f*, padres *mpl*

folklore [ˈfoːkˌlor] *n* : folklore *m*

folksy [ˈfoːksi] *adj* **folksier; -est** : campechano

follicle [ˈfɑlɪkəl] *n* : folículo *m*

follow [ˈfɑloː] *vt* 1 : seguir (un camino, a una persona, etc.) 2 PURSUE : seguir, perseguir 3 : venir después de, seguir a (en una serie, etc.) 4 OBEY : seguir (instrucciones, etc.), cumplir (la ley, etc.) 5 MONITOR : seguir 6 UNDERSTAND : entender ⟨I don't follow you : no (te) entiendo⟩ 7 **to follow suit** : hacer lo mismo 8 **to follow up** : darle seguimiento a (un caso, etc.), seguir (una pista) — *vi* 1 : seguir 2 UNDERSTAND : entender 3 **as follows** ⟨it reads as follows . . . : dice lo siguiente . . ., dice así . . .⟩ 4 **it follows that . . .** : se deduce que . . . 5 **to follow through** : continuar con algo 6 **to follow through on/with** : continuar con (un plan, etc.), cumplir (una promesa, etc.) 7 **to follow up** : dar seguimiento ⟨to follow up (on) a lead : seguir una pista⟩ ⟨he followed up with us later : nos contactó después⟩ ⟨she followed up with another best seller : después sacó otro best-seller⟩

follower [ˈfɑloʊər] *n* : seguidor *m*, -dora *f*

following¹ [ˈfɑloʊɪŋ] *adj* NEXT : siguiente

following² *n* FOLLOWERS : seguidores *mpl*

following³ *prep* AFTER : después de

follow–up [ˈfɑloʊˌʌp] *n* : continuación *f*, seguimiento *m*

folly [ˈfɑli] *n*, *pl* **-lies** : locura *f*, desatino *m*

foment [foˈment] *vt* : fomentar

fond [ˈfɑnd] *adj* 1 LOVING : cariñoso, tierno 2 PARTIAL : aficionado 3 FERVENT : ferviente, fervoroso

fondle [ˈfɑndəl] *vt* **-dled; -dling** : acariciar

fondly [ˈfɑndli] *adv* : cariñosamente, afectuosamente

fondness [ˈfɑndnəs] *n* 1 LOVE : cariño *m* 2 LIKING : afición *f*

fondue [fɑnˈduː, -ˈdjuː] *n* : fondue *f*

font [ˈfɑnt] *n* 1 *or* **baptismal font** : pila *f* bautismal 2 FOUNTAIN : fuente *f*

food [ˈfuːd] *n* : comida *f*, alimento *m*

food chain *n* : cadena *f* alimenticia

food poisoning *n* : intoxicación *f* alimenticia

food processor *n* : robot *m* de cocina

foodstuff [ˈfuːdˌstʌf] *n* : comestible *m*, producto *m* alimenticio

fool¹ [ˈfuːl] *vi* 1 JOKE : bromear, hacer el tonto ⟨I was only fooling : sólo estaba bromeando⟩ 2 *or* **to fool around** TOY : jugar, juguetear ⟨don't fool (around) with the computer : no juegues con la computadora⟩ 3 **to fool around** : perder el tiempo ⟨he fools around instead of working : pierde el tiempo en vez de trabajar⟩ 4 **to fool around** : tener líos (amorosos) — *vt* DECEIVE : engañar, burlar ⟨he had me fooled : me tenía convencido⟩ ⟨he fooled me into thinking that . . . : me hizo creer que . . .⟩ ⟨stop fooling yourself! : ¡desengáñate!⟩

fool² *n* 1 IDIOT : idiota *mf*; tonto *m*, -ta *f*; bobo *m*, -ba *f* 2 JESTER : bufón *m*, -fona *f* 3 **to make a fool of** : poner/dejar en ridículo, hacer quedar en ridículo ⟨to make a fool of oneself : hacer el ridículo, quedar en ridículo⟩

foolhardiness [ˈfuːlˌhɑrdinəs] *n* : imprudencia *f*

foolhardy [ˈfuːlˌhɑrdi] *adj* RASH : imprudente, temerario, precipitado

foolish [ˈfuːlɪʃ] *adj* 1 STUPID : insensato, estúpido 2 SILLY : idiota, tonto

foolishly [ˈfuːlɪʃli] *adv* : tontamente

foolishness [ˈfuːlɪʃnəs] *n* : insensatez *f*, estupidez *f*, tontería *f*

foolproof [ˈfuːlˌpruːf] *adj* : infalible

foot [ˈfʊt] *n*, *pl* **feet** [ˈfiːt] 1 : pie *m* ⟨to go on foot : ir a pie⟩ ⟨to be on one's feet : estar de pie⟩ 2 **to get/start off on the wrong foot** : empezar con mal pie 3 **to put one's best foot forward** : tratar de dejar una buena impresión 4 **to put one's foot down** : no ceder 5 **to put one's foot in one's mouth** : meter la pata 6 **to stand on one's own two feet** : valerse por sí mismo 7 **to think on one's feet** : pensar con rapidez

footage [ˈfʊtɪʤ] *n* : medida *f* en pies, metraje *m* (en el cine)

football [ˈfʊtˌbɔl] *n* : futbol *m* americano, fútbol *m* americano

footbridge [ˈfʊtˌbrɪʤ] *n* : pasarela *f*, puente *m* peatonal

foothills [ˈfʊtˌhɪlz] *npl* : estribaciones *fpl*

foothold [ˈfʊtˌhoːld] *n* 1 : punto *m* de apoyo 2 **to gain a foothold** : afianzarse en una posición

footing [ˈfʊtɪŋ] *n* 1 BALANCE : equilibrio *m* 2 FOOTHOLD : punto *m* de apoyo 3 BASIS : base *f* ⟨on an equal footing : en igualdad⟩

footlights [ˈfʊtˌlaɪts] *npl* : candilejas *fpl*

footlocker [ˈfʊtˌlɑkər] *n* : baúl *m* pequeño, cofre *m*

footloose [ˈfʊtˌluːs] *adj* : libre y sin compromiso

footman [ˈfʊtmən] *n*, *pl* **-men** [-mən, -ˌmɛn] : lacayo *m*

footnote [ˈfʊtˌnoːt] *n* : nota *f* al pie de la página

footpath ['fʊtˌpæθ] n : sendero m, senda f, vereda f

footprint ['fʊtˌprɪnt] n : huella f

footrace ['fʊtˌreɪs] n : carrera f pedestre

footrest ['fʊtˌrɛst] n : apoyapiés m, reposapiés m

footstep ['fʊtˌstɛp] n 1 STEP : paso m 2 FOOTPRINT : huella f

footstool ['fʊtˌstuːl] n : taburete m, escabel m

footwear ['fʊtˌwær] n : calzado m

footwork ['fʊtˌwərk] n : juego m de piernas, juego m de pies

for¹ ['fɔr] conj : puesto que, porque

for² prep 1 (indicating purpose) : para, de, por ⟨the food for the party : la comida para la fiesta⟩ ⟨clothes for children : ropa para niños⟩ ⟨it's time for dinner : es la hora de comer⟩ ⟨to travel for pleasure : viajar por placer⟩ ⟨what's that for? : ¿para qué es/sirve eso?⟩ 2 (indicating a recipient) : para ⟨a gift for you : un regalo para ti⟩ 3 (indicating an object of thoughts or feelings) : por ⟨his admiration for her : su admiración por ella⟩ ⟨I feel sorry for him : le tengo lástima⟩ 4 BECAUSE OF : por ⟨for fear of : por miedo de⟩ ⟨to jump for joy : saltar de alegría⟩ 5 : por, en beneficio de ⟨he fought for his country : luchó por su patria⟩ ⟨I did it for you : lo hice por ti⟩ ⟨for your own good : por tu propio bien⟩ 6 (indicating to whom a statement applies) : para ⟨it's difficult for me : me es difícil, es difícil para mí⟩ ⟨it's time for us to go : es hora de irnos⟩ ⟨I'd hate for you to miss it : sería una lástima que te lo perdieras⟩ 7 IN FAVOR OF : a favor de 8 (indicating a goal) : para ⟨to study for a test : estudiar para un examen⟩ ⟨a cure for cancer : una cura para el cáncer⟩ ⟨for more information, call . . . : para más información, llame al . . .⟩ ⟨they ran for safety : corrieron para ponerse a salvo⟩ 9 TOWARDS, TO : para ⟨he left for the office : salió para la oficina⟩ ⟨the train for London : el tren para Londres⟩ 10 (indicating correspondence or exchange) : por, para ⟨I bought it for $5 : lo compré por $5⟩ ⟨a lot of trouble for nothing : mucha molestia para nada⟩ 11 AS FOR : para, con respecto a 12 (indicating duration) : por, durante ⟨he's going for two years : se va por dos años⟩ ⟨I spoke for ten minutes : hablé (durante) diez minutos⟩ ⟨she has known it for three months : lo sabe desde hace tres meses⟩ ⟨they won't arrive for hours yet : tardarán horas en llegar⟩ ⟨he drove for 100 miles : hizo 100 millas⟩ 13 (indicating a particular time) : para, por ⟨the wedding is planned for April : la boda está prevista para abril⟩ ⟨that's enough for now : basta por ahora⟩ 14 INSTEAD OF, ON BEHALF OF : por ⟨to speak for someone : hablar por alguien⟩ ⟨say hello for me : dales saludos de mi parte⟩ 15 (indicating association) : para ⟨he works for the university : trabaja para la universidad⟩ 16 (used in listing items) : para ⟨for one thing . . .

: para empezar . . .⟩ 17 : para (una enfermedad) ⟨for colds and flu : para resfriados y gripe⟩ 18 (indicating amount or value) : por, de ⟨a check for $100 : un cheque por/de $100⟩ 19 (indicating meaning) ⟨The French word for "good" is "bon" : en francés la palabra "bon" significa "bueno"⟩ ⟨what's the word for "taxi" in Japanese? : ¿como se dice "taxi" en japonés?⟩ 20 (used in comparisons) : para ⟨he's tall for his age : es alto para su edad⟩ 21 (used in comparing numbers or amounts) : por ⟨for every dollar invested, there's a return of five dollars : por cada dólar invertido, hay un retorno de cinco dólares⟩ 22 (used for emphasis) : por ⟨for crying out loud! : ¡por el amor de Dios!⟩ 23 : para, con ocasión de ⟨a gift for his birthday : un regalo para su cumpleaños⟩ 24 for all IN SPITE OF : a pesar de 25 for all : por ⟨she can go now for all I care : por mí que se vaya ahora⟩ ⟨for all I know : que yo sepa⟩ 26 for breakfast/lunch/dinner (etc.)⟨we had eggs for breakfast : desayunamos huevos⟩ ⟨what's for dinner/dessert? : ¿qué hay de comer/postre?⟩ 27 in for (to be) for a surprise : se va a llevar una sorpresa⟩ 28 in for it ⟨if mom finds out, you're in for it : si mamá se entera, te mata⟩ 29 not for ⟨it's not for you to say she can't go : no te corresponde a ti decir que no vaya⟩

forage ['fɔrɪdʒ] v -aged; -aging vi : hurgar (en busca de alimento) — vt : buscar (provisiones)

foray ['fɔrˌeɪ] n : incursión f

forbear¹ [fɔr'bær] vi -bore [-'bor]; -borne [-'born]; -bearing 1 ABSTAIN : abstenerse 2 : tener paciencia

forbear² → forebear

forbearance [fɔr'bærənts] n 1 ABSTAINING : abstención f 2 PATIENCE : paciencia f

forbid [fɔr'bɪd] vt -bade [-'bæd, -'beɪd]; -bidden [-'bɪdən]; -bidding 1 PROHIBIT : prohibir 2 PREVENT : impedir

forbidden [fɔr'bɪdən] adj : prohibido

forbidding [fɔr'bɪdɪŋ] adj 1 IMPOSING : imponente 2 DISAGREEABLE : desagradable, ingrato 3 GRIM : severo

force¹ ['fɔrs] vt forced; forcing 1 COMPEL : obligar, forzar 2 : forzar ⟨to force open the window : forzar la ventana⟩ ⟨to force a lock : forzar una cerradura⟩ 3 IMPOSE : imponer, obligar

force² n 1 : fuerza f ⟨brute force : fuerza bruta⟩ ⟨the force of gravity : la fuerza de la gravedad⟩ ⟨force of habit : la fuerza de la costumbre⟩ ⟨security forces : fuerzas de seguridad⟩ 2 by force : por la fuerza 3 in force : en vigor/vigencia

forced ['fɔrst] adj : forzado, forzoso

forceful ['fɔrsfəl] adj : fuerte, enérgico, contundente

forcefully ['fɔrsfəli] adv : con energía, con fuerza

forcefulness ['fɔrsfəlnəs] n : contundencia f, fuerza f

forceps ['forsəps, -ˌseps] *ns & pl* : fórceps *m*

forcible ['forsəbəl] *adj* **1** FORCED : forzoso **2** CONVINCING : contundente, convincente — **forcibly** [-bli] *adv*

ford[1] ['ford] *vt* : vadear

ford[2] *n* : vado *m*

fore[1] ['for] *adv* **1** FORWARD : hacia adelante **2 fore and aft** : de popa a proa

fore[2] *adj* **1** FORWARD : delantero, de adelante **2** FORMER : anterior

fore[3] *n* **1** : frente *m*, delantera *f* **2 to come to the fore** : empezar a destacar, saltar a primera plana

fore–and–aft ['forənˌæft, -ənd-] *adj* : longitudinal

forearm ['forˌɑrm] *n* : antebrazo *m*

forebear ['forˌbær] *n* : antepasado *m*, -da *f*

foreboding [for'boːdɪŋ] *n* : premonición *f*, presentimiento *m*

forecast[1] ['forˌkæst] *vt* **-cast; -casting** : pronosticar, predecir

forecast[2] *n* : predicción *f*, pronóstico *m* ⟨weather forecast : pronóstico del tiempo, parte meteorológico⟩

forecastle ['foːksəl] *n* : castillo *m* de proa

foreclose [for'kloːz] *vt* **-closed; -closing** : ejecutar (una hipoteca)

forefather ['forˌfɑðər] *n* : antepasado *m*, ancestro *m*

forefinger ['forˌfɪŋgər] *n* : índice *m*, dedo *m* índice

forefoot ['forˌfʊt] *n* : pata *f* delantera

forefront ['forˌfrʌnt] *n* : frente *m*, vanguardia *f* ⟨in the forefront : a la vanguardia⟩

forego [for'goː] *vt* **-went; -gone; -going 1** PRECEDE : preceder **2 → forgo**

foregoing [for'goːɪŋ] *adj* : precedente, anterior

foregone [for'gɔn] *adj* : previsto ⟨a foregone conclusion : un resultado inevitable⟩

foreground ['forˌgraʊnd] *n* : primer plano *m*

forehand[1] ['forˌhænd] *adj* : directo, derecho

forehand[2] *n* : golpe *m* del derecho

forehead ['forəd, 'forˌhed] *n* : frente *f*

foreign ['forən] *adj* **1** : extranjero, exterior ⟨foreign countries : países extranjeros⟩ ⟨foreign trade : comercio exterior⟩ **2** ALIEN : ajeno, extraño ⟨foreign to their nature : ajeno a su carácter⟩ ⟨a foreign body : un cuerpo extraño⟩

foreigner ['forənər] *n* : extranjero *m*, -ra *f*

foreknowledge [for'nɑlɪdʒ] *n* : conocimiento *m* previo

foreleg ['forˌleg] *n* : pata *f* delantera

foreman ['formən] *n, pl* **-men** [-mən, -ˌmen] : capataz *mf* ⟨foreman of the jury : presidente del jurado⟩

foremost[1] ['forˌmoːst] *adv* : en primer lugar

foremost[2] *adj* : más importante, principal, grande

forenoon ['forˌnuːn] *n* : mañana *m*

forensic [fə'rensɪk] *adj* **1** RHETORICAL : retórico, de argumentación **2** : forense ⟨forensic medicine : medicina forense⟩

foreordain [ˌforor'deɪn] *vt* : predestinar, predeterminar

forequarter ['forˌkwortər] *n* : cuarto *m* delantero

forerunner ['forˌrʌnər] *n* : precursor *m*, -sora *f*

foresee [for'siː] *vt* **-saw; -seen; -seeing** : prever

foreseeable [for'siːəbəl] *adj* : previsible ⟨in the foreseeable future : en el futuro inmediato⟩

foreshadow [for'ʃædoː] *vt* : anunciar, prefigurar

foresight ['forˌsaɪt] *n* : previsión *f*

foresighted ['forˌsaɪtəd] *adj* : previsto

forest ['forəst] *n* : bosque *m* (en zonas templadas), selva *f* (en zonas tropicales)

forestall [for'stɔl] *vt* **1** PREVENT : prevenir, impedir **2** PREEMPT : adelantarse a

forested ['forəstəd] *adj* : arbolado

forester ['forəstər] *n* : silvicultor *m*, -tora *f*

forestland ['forəstˌlænd] *n* : zona *f* boscosa

forest ranger → ranger

forestry ['forəstri] *n* : silvicultura *f*, ingeniería *f* forestal

foreswear → forswear

foretaste[1] ['forˌteɪst] *vt* **-tasted; -tasting** : anticipar

foretaste[2] *n* : anticipo *m*

foretell [for'tel] *vt* **-told; -telling** : predecir, pronosticar, profetizar

forethought ['forˌθɔt] *n* : previsión *f*, reflexión *f* previa

forever [fər'evər] *adv* **1** PERPETUALLY : para siempre, eternamente **2** CONTINUALLY : siempre, constantemente

forevermore [forˌevər'mor] *adv* : por siempre jamás

forewarn [for'worn] *vt* : prevenir, advertir

forewoman ['forˌwʊmən] *n, pl* **-women** [-ˌwɪmən] : capataz *f*, jefa *f* ⟨forewoman of the jury : presidente/presidenta del jurado⟩

foreword ['forwərd] *n* : prólogo *m*

forfeit[1] ['forfət] *vt* : perder el derecho a

forfeit[2] *n* **1** FINE, PENALTY : multa *f* **2** : prenda *f* (en un juego)

forge[1] ['fordʒ] *v* **forged; forging** *vt* **1** : forjar (metal o un plan) **2** COUNTERFEIT : falsificar — *vi* **to forge ahead** : avanzar, seguir adelante

forge[2] *n* : forja *f*

forger ['fordʒər] *n* : falsificador *m*, -dora *f*

forgery ['fordʒəri] *n, pl* **-eries** : falsificación *f*

forget [fər'get] *v* **-got** [-'gɑt]; **-gotten** [-'gɑtən] *or* **-got; -getting** *vt* : olvidar — *vi* **to forget about** : olvidarse de, no acordarse de

forgetful [fər'getfəl] *adj* : olvidadizo

forgetfulness [fər'getfəlnəs] *n* : olvido *m*, mala memoria *f*

forget–me–not [fər'getmiˌnɑt] *n* : nomeolvides *mf*

forgettable [fər'getəbəl] *adj* : poco memorable

forgivable [fər'gɪvəbəl] *adj* : perdonable

forgive [fər'gɪv] *vt* **-gave** [-'geɪv]; **-given** [-'gɪvən]; **-giving** : perdonar

forgiveness [fərˈgɪvnəs] *n* : perdón *m*

forgiving [fərˈgɪvɪŋ] *adj* : indulgente, comprensivo, clemente

forgo *or* **forego** [forˈgoː] *vt* **-went; -gone; -going** : privarse de, renunciar a

fork[1] [ˈfork] *vi* : ramificarse, bifurcarse — *vt* **1** : levantar (con un tenedor, una horca, etc.) **2 to fork out/over** : desembolsar

fork[2] *n* **1** : tenedor *m* (utensilio de cocina) **2** PITCHFORK : horca *f*, horquilla *f* **3** : bifurcación *f* (de un río o camino), horqueta *f* (de un árbol)

forked [ˈforkt, ˈforkəd] *adj* : bífido, ahorquillado

forklift [ˈfork,lɪft] *n* : carretilla *f* elevadora

forlorn [fərˈlorn] *adj* **1** DESOLATE : abandonado, desolado, desamparado **2** SAD : triste **3** DESPERATE : desesperado

forlornly [fərˈlornli] *adv* **1** SADLY : con tristeza **2** HALFHEARTEDLY : sin ánimo

form[1] [ˈform] *vt* **1** FASHION, MAKE : formar **2** DEVELOP : moldear, desarrollar **3** CONSTITUTE : constituir, formar **4** ACQUIRE : adquirir (un hábito), formar (una idea) — *vi* : tomar forma, formarse

form[2] *n* **1** SHAPE : forma *f*, figura *f* ⟨in the form of : en forma de⟩ **2** MANNER : manera *f*, forma *f* **3** DOCUMENT : formulario *m* ⟨tax form : formulario de declaración de renta⟩ ⟨to fill out a form : rellenar/llenar un formulario⟩ **4** : forma *f* ⟨in good form : en buena forma⟩ ⟨true to form : fiel a su costumbre⟩ **5** MOLD : molde *m* **6** KIND, VARIETY : clase *f*, tipo *m* ⟨some form of : algún tipo de⟩ **7** : forma *f* (en gramática) ⟨plural forms : formas plurales⟩

formal[1] [ˈforməl] *adj* **1** CEREMONIOUS : formal, de etiqueta, ceremonioso **2** OFFICIAL : formal, oficial, de forma

formal[2] *n* **1** BALL : baile *m* formal, baile *m* de etiqueta **2** *or* **formal dress** : traje *m* de etiqueta

formaldehyde [fərˈmældə,haɪd] *n* : formaldehído *m*

formality [fərˈmæləti] *n*, *pl* **-ties** : formalidad *f*

formalize [ˈformə,laɪz] *vt* **-ized; -izing** : formalizar

formally [ˈforməli] *adv* : formalmente

format[1] [ˈfor,mæt] *vt* **-matted; -matting** : formatear

format[2] *n* : formato *m*

formation [forˈmeɪʃən] *n* **1** FORMING : formación *f* **2** SHAPE : forma *f* **3 in formation** : en formación

formative [ˈformətɪv] *adj* : formativo

former [ˈformər] *adj* **1** PREVIOUS : antiguo, anterior ⟨the former president : el antiguo presidente⟩ **2** : primero (de dos)

formerly [ˈformərli] *adv* : anteriormente, antes

formidable [ˈformədəbəl, forˈmɪdə-] *adj* : formidable — **formidably** *adv*

formless [ˈformləs] *adj* : informe, amorfo

formula [ˈformjələ] *n*, *pl* **-las** *or* **-lae** [-ˌliː, -ˌlaɪ] **1** : fórmula *f* **2 baby formula** : preparado *m* para biberón

formulate [ˈformjə,leɪt] *vt* **-lated; -lating** : formular, hacer

formulation [ˌformjəˈleɪʃən] *n* : formulación *f*

fornicate [ˈfornə,keɪt] *vi* **-cated; -cating** : fornicar

fornication [ˌfornəˈkeɪʃən] *n* : fornicación *f*

forsake [fərˈseɪk] *vt* **-sook** [-ˈsʊk]; **-saken** [-ˈseɪkən]; **-saking 1** ABANDON : abandonar, desamparar **2** RELINQUISH : renunciar a

forswear [forˈswær] *v* **-swore; -sworn; -swearing** *vt* RENOUNCE : renunciar a — *vi* : perjurar

forsythia [fərˈsɪθiə] *n* : forsitia *f*

fort [ˈfort] *n* **1** STRONGHOLD : fuerte *m*, fortaleza *f*, fortín *m* **2** BASE : base *f* militar

forte [ˈfort, ˈforˌteɪ] *n* : fuerte *m*

forth [ˈforθ] *adv* **1** : adelante ⟨from this day forth : de hoy en adelante⟩ **2 and so forth** : etcétera

forthcoming [forθˈkʌmɪŋ, ˈforθˌ-] *adj* **1** COMING : próximo **2** DIRECT, OPEN : directo, franco, comunicativo

forthright [ˈforθ,raɪt] *adj* : directo, franco — **forthrightly** *adv*

forthrightness [ˈforθ,raɪtnəs] *n* : franqueza *f*

forthwith [forθˈwɪθ, -ˈwɪð] *adv* : inmediatamente, en el acto, enseguida

fortieth[1] [ˈfortiəθ] *adj* : cuadragésimo

fortieth[2] *n* **1** : cuadragésimo *m*, -ma *f* (en una serie) **2** : cuarentavo *m*, cuarentava parte *f*

fortification [ˌfortəfəˈkeɪʃən] *n* : fortificación *f*

fortify [ˈfortə,faɪ] *vt* **-fied; -fying** : fortificar

fortitude [ˈfortə,tuːd, -ˌtjuːd] *n* : fortaleza *f*, valor *m*

fortnight [ˈfort,naɪt] *n* : quince días *mpl*, dos semanas *fpl*

fortnightly[1] [ˈfort,naɪtli] *adv* : cada quince días

fortnightly[2] *adj* : quincenal

fortress [ˈfortrəs] *n* : fortaleza *f*

fortuitous [forˈtuːətəs, -ˈtjuː-] *adj* : fortuito, accidental

fortunate [ˈfortʃənət] *adj* : afortunado

fortunately [ˈfortʃənətli] *adv* : afortunadamente, con suerte

fortune [ˈfortʃən] *n* **1** : fortuna *f* ⟨to seek one's fortune : buscar uno su fortuna⟩ **2** LUCK : suerte *f*, fortuna *f* **3** DESTINY, FUTURE : destino *m*, buenaventura *f* **4** : dineral *m*, platal *m* ⟨she spent a fortune : se gastó un dineral⟩

fortune–teller [ˈfortʃən,tɛlər] *n* : adivino *m*, -na *f*

fortune–telling [ˈfortʃən,tɛlɪŋ] *n* : adivinación *f*

forty[1] [ˈforti] *adj & pron* : cuarenta

forty[2] *n*, *pl* **forties** : cuarenta *m*

forum [ˈforəm] *n*, *pl* **-rums** : foro *m*

forward[1] [ˈforwərd] *vt* **1** PROMOTE : promover, adelantar, fomentar **2** SEND : remitir, enviar

forward² *adv* **1** : adelante, hacia adelante ⟨to go forward : irse adelante⟩ **2 from this day forward** : de aquí en adelante

forward³ *adj* **1** : hacia adelante, delantero **2** BRASH : atrevido, descarado

forward⁴ *n* : delantero *m*, -ra *f* (en deportes)

forwardness ['fɔrwərdnəs] *n* : atrevimiento *m*, descaro *m*

forwards ['fɔrwərdz] *adv* → **forward²**

fossil¹ ['fɑsəl] *adj* : fósil

fossil² *n* : fósil *m*

fossilize ['fɑsə,laɪz] *vt* -ized; -izing : fosilizar — *vi* : fosilizarse

foster¹ ['fɔstər] *vt* : promover, fomentar

foster² *adj* : adoptivo ⟨foster child : niño adoptivo⟩

fought → **fight**

foul¹ ['faʊl] *vi* : cometer faltas (en deportes) — *vt* **1** DIRTY, POLLUTE : contaminar, ensuciar **2** TANGLE : enredar

foul² *adv* **1** → **foully 2** : contra las reglas

foul³ *adj* **1** REPULSIVE : asqueroso, repugnante **2** CLOGGED : atascado, obstruido **3** TANGLED : enredado **4** OBSCENE : obsceno **5** BAD : malo ⟨foul weather : mal tiempo⟩ **6** : antirreglamentario (en deportes)

foul⁴ *n* : falta *f*, faul *m*

foully ['faʊli] *adv* : asquerosamente

foulmouthed ['faʊl,mæʊðd, -,maʊθt] *adj* : malhablado

foulness ['faʊlnəs] *n* **1** DIRTINESS : suciedad *f* **2** INCLEMENCY : inclemencia *f* **3** OBSCENITY : obscenidad *f*, grosería *f*

foul play *n* : actos *mpl* criminales

foul shot *n* → **free throw**

foul–up ['faʊl,ʌp] *n* : lío *m*, confusión *f*, desastre *m*

foul up *vt* SPOIL : estropear, arruinar — *vi* BUNGLE : echar todo a perder

found¹ → **find**

found² ['faʊnd] *vt* : fundar, establecer

foundation [faʊn'deɪʃən] *n* **1** FOUNDING : fundación *f* **2** BASIS : fundamento *m*, base *f* **3** INSTITUTION : fundación *f* **4** : cimientos *mpl* (de un edificio) **5 or foundation makeup** : base *f* de maquillaje

founder¹ ['faʊndər] *vi* SINK : hundirse, irse a pique

founder² *n* : fundador *m*, -dora *f*

founding ['faʊndɪŋ] *adj* : fundador ⟨the founding fathers : los fundadores⟩

foundling ['faʊndlɪŋ] *n* : expósito *m*, -ta *f*

foundry ['faʊndri] *n, pl* -dries : fundición *f*

fount ['faʊnt] *n* SOURCE : fuente *f*, origen *m*

fountain ['faʊntən] *n* **1** SPRING : fuente *f*, manantial *m* **2** SOURCE : fuente *f*, origen *m* **3** JET : chorro *m* (de agua), surtidor *m*

fountain pen *n* : pluma *f* fuente, estilográfica *f*

four¹ ['fɔr] *adj* : cuatro ⟨the child is four (years old) : la niña tiene cinco años⟩

four² *n* **1** : cuatro *m* ⟨the four of hearts : el cuatro de corazones⟩ ⟨it's four o'clock : son las cuatro⟩ **2 on all fours** : a gatas

four³ *pron* : cuatro ⟨there are four of us : somos cuatro⟩

four hundred¹ *adj & pron* : cuatrocientos

four hundred² *n* : cuatrocientos *m*

four–poster [,fɔr'postər] *n* : cama *f* de (cuatro) columnas

fourscore ['fɔr'skor] *adj* EIGHTY : ochenta

fourteen¹ [for'ti:n] *adj & pron* : catorce

fourteen² *n* : catorce *m*

fourteenth¹ [for'ti:nθ] *adj* : decimocuarto

fourteenth² *n* **1** : decimocuarto *m*, -ta *f* (en una serie) **2** : catorceavo *m*, catorceava parte *f*

fourth¹ ['forθ] *adv* : en cuarto lugar

fourth² *adj* : cuarto

fourth³ *n* **1** : cuarto *m*, -ta *f* (en una serie) ⟨(on) the fourth of August : el cuatro de agosto⟩ **2** : cuarto *m*, cuarta parte *f* **3 or fourth gear** : cuarta *f*

fowl ['faʊl] *n, pl* **fowl** *or* **fowls 1** BIRD : ave *f* **2** CHICKEN : pollo *m*

fox¹ ['fɑks] *vt* TRICK : engañar **2** BAFFLE : confundir

fox² *n, pl* **foxes** : zorro *m*, -ra *f*

foxglove ['fɑks,glʌv] *n* : dedalera *f*, digital *f*

foxhole ['fɑks,ho:l] *n* : hoyo *m* para atrincherarse, trinchera *f* individual

foxy ['fɑksi] *adj* **foxier; -est** SHREWD : astuto

foyer ['fɔɪər, 'fɔɪ,jeɪ] *n* : vestíbulo *m*

fracas ['freɪkəs, 'fræ-] *n, pl* **-cases** [-kəsəz] : altercado *m*, pelea *f*, reyerta *f*

fraction ['frækʃən] *n* **1** : fracción *f*, quebrado *m* **2** PORTION : porción *f*, parte *f*

fractional ['frækʃənəl] *adj* **1** : fraccionario **2** TINY : minúsculo, mínimo, insignificante

fractious ['frækʃəs] *adj* **1** UNRULY : rebelde **2** IRRITABLE : malhumorado, irritable

fracture¹ ['fræktʃər] *vt* **-tured; -turing** : fracturar

fracture² *n* **1** : fractura *f* (de un hueso) **2** CRACK : fisura *f*, grieta *f*, falla *f* (geológica)

fragile ['frædʒəl, -,dʒaɪl] *adj* : frágil

fragility [frə'dʒɪləti] *n, pl* **-ties** : fragilidad *f*

fragment¹ ['fræg,mɛnt] *vt* : fragmentar — *vi* : fragmentarse, hacerse añicos

fragment² ['frægmənt] *n* : fragmento *m*, trozo *m*, pedazo *m*

fragmentary ['frægmən,tɛri] *adj* : fragmentario, incompleto

fragmentation [,frægmən'teɪʃən, -,mn-] *n* : fragmentación *f*

fragrance ['freɪgrənts] *n* : fragancia *f*, aroma *m*

fragrant ['freɪgrənt] *adj* : fragante, aromático — **fragrantly** *adv*

frail ['freɪl] *adj* : débil, delicado

frailty ['freɪlti] *n, pl* **-ties** : debilidad *f*, flaqueza *f*

frame¹ ['freɪm] *vt* **framed; framing 1** FORMULATE : formular, elaborar **2** BORDER : enmarcar, encuadrar **3** INCRIMINATE : incriminar

frame² *n* **1** BODY : cuerpo *m* **2** : armazón *f* (de un edificio, un barco, o un avión), bastidor *m* (de un automóvil), cuadro *m* (de una bicicleta), marco *m* (de un cuadro, una ventana, una puerta, etc.) **3 frames** *npl* : armazón *mf*, montura *f* (para anteojos) **4 frame of mind** : estado *m* de ánimo

framework ['freɪm,wərk] *n* **1** SKELETON, STRUCTURE : armazón *f*, estructura *f* **2** BASIS : marco *m*

franc ['fræŋk] *n* : franco *m*

franchise ['fræn,tʃaɪz] *n* **1** LICENSE : licencia *f* exclusiva, concesión *f* (en comercio) **2** SUFFRAGE : sufragio *m*

franchisee [,fræn,tʃaɪˈziː, -tʃə-] *n* : concesionario *m*, -ria *f*

Franciscan [frænˈsɪskən] *n* : franciscano *m*, -na *f* — **Franciscan** *adj*

frank[1] ['fræŋk] *vt* : franquear

frank[2] *adj* : franco, sincero, cándido — **frankly** *adv*

frank[3] *n* : franqueo *m* (de correo)

frankfurter ['fræŋkfərtər, -,fər-] *or* **frankfurt** [-fərt] *n* : salchicha *f* (de Frankfurt, de Viena), perro *m* caliente

frankincense ['fræŋkən,sɛnts] *n* : incienso *m*

frankness ['fræŋknəs] *n* : franqueza *f*, sinceridad *f*, candidez *f*

frantic ['fræntɪk] *adj* : frenético, desesperado — **frantically** *adv*

fraternal [frəˈtərnəl] *adj* : fraterno, fraternal

fraternity [frəˈtərnəṭi] *n, pl* **-ties** : fraternidad *f*

fraternization [,frætərnəˈzeɪʃən] *n* : fraternización *f*, confraternización *f*

fraternize ['frætər,naɪz] *vi* **-nized; -nizing** : fraternizar, confraternizar

fraud ['frɔd] *n* **1** DECEPTION, SWINDLE : fraude *m*, estafa *f*, engaño *m* **2** IMPOSTOR : impostor *m*, -tora *f*; farsante *mf*

fraudulent ['frɔdʒələnt] *adj* : fraudulento — **fraudulently** *adv*

fraught ['frɔt] *adj* **fraught with** : lleno de, cargado de

fray[1] ['freɪ] *vt* **1** WEAR : desgastar, deshilachar **2** IRRITATE : crispar, irritar (los nervios) — *vi* : desgastarse, deshilacharse

fray[2] *n* : pelea *f* ⟨to join the fray : salir a la palestra⟩ ⟨to return to the fray : volver a la carga⟩

frazzle[1] ['fræzəl] *vt* **-zled; -zling 1** FRAY : desgastar, deshilachar **2** EXHAUST : agotar, fatigar

frazzle[2] *n* EXHAUSTION : agotamiento *m*

freak ['friːk] *n* **1** ODDITY : ejemplar *m* anormal, fenómeno *m*, rareza *f* **2** ENTHUSIAST : entusiasta *mf*

freakish ['friːkɪʃ] *adj* : extraño, estrafalario, raro

freak out *vt* : ponerse como loco — *vt* : darle un ataque (a alguien)

freckle[1] ['frɛkəl] *vi* **-led; -ling** : cubrirse de pecas

freckle[2] *n* : peca *f*

free[1] ['friː] *vt* **freed; freeing 1** LIBERATE : libertar, liberar, poner en libertad **2** RELIEVE, RID : librar, eximir **3** RE-

LEASE, UNTIE : desatar, soltar **4** UN-CLOG : desatascar, destapar

free[2] *adv* **1** FREELY : libremente **2** GRATIS : gratuitamente, gratis

free[3] *adj* **freer; freest 1** : gratuito, gratis ⟨free tickets : entradas gratuitas⟩ ⟨it's free : es gratis⟩ **2** : libre ⟨to set free : liberar, dejar/poner en libertad⟩ ⟨to get free : escaparse⟩ **3** PERMITTED : libre ⟨to be free to do something : ser libre de hacer algo⟩ **4** : libre (dícese de un país, etc.) ⟨free speech : libertad de expresión⟩ ⟨free trade : libre comercio⟩ **5** EXEMPT : libre ⟨tax-free : libre de impuestos⟩ **6** VOLUNTARY : espontáneo, voluntario, libre **7** UNOCCUPIED : libre, desocupado ⟨I'm free tomorrow : mañana estoy libre⟩ ⟨a free seat : un asiento libre⟩ ⟨he waved with his free hand : nos saludó con su mano libre⟩ **8** LOOSE : suelto **9** : generoso ⟨they were very free with their money : fueron muy generosos con su dinero⟩ **10 for free** : gratis **11 free from/of** : libre de

freeborn ['friːˈbɔrn] *adj* : nacido libre

freedom ['friːdəm] *n* : libertad *f*

free enterprise *n* : libre empresa *f*

free-for-all ['friːfərˌɔl] *n* : pelea *f*, batalla *f* campal

free gift *n* : obsequio *m*

freehand ['friːˌhænd] *adj* : a pulso, a mano alzada

free kick *n* : tiro *m* libre

freelance[1] ['friːˌlænts] *vi* **-lanced; -lancing** : trabajar por cuenta propia

freelance[2] *adj* : por cuenta propia, freelance

freelancer ['friːˌlæntsər] *n* : trabajador *m*, -dora *f* por cuenta propia; freelance *mf*

freeload ['friːˌloːd] *vi* : gorronear *fam*, gorrear *fam*

freeloader ['friːˌloːdər] *n* : gorrón *m*, -rrona *f*; gorrero *m*, -ra *f*; vividor *m*, -dora *f*

freely ['friːli] *adv* **1** FREE : libremente **2** GRATIS : gratis, gratuitamente

Freemason ['friːˈmeɪsən] *n* : francmasón *m*, masón *m*

Freemasonry ['friːˈmeɪsənri] *n* : francmasonería *f*, masonería *f*

free-range ['friːˌreɪŋg] *adj* : de granja

freestanding ['friːˈstændɪŋ] *adj* : de pie, no empotrado, independiente

free throw *n* : tiro *m* libre (en baloncesto)

freeway ['friːˌweɪ] *n* : autopista *f*

freewill ['friːˌwɪl] *adj* : de propia voluntad

free will *n* : libre albedrío *m*, propia voluntad *f*

freeze[1] ['friːz] *v* **froze** ['froːz]; **frozen** ['froːzən]; **freezing** *vi* **1** : congelarse, helarse ⟨the water froze in the lake : el agua se congeló en el lago⟩ ⟨my blood froze : se me heló la sangre⟩ ⟨I'm freezing : me estoy helando⟩ **2** STOP : quedarse inmóvil **3** : bloquearse (dícese de una computadora) — *vt* : helar, congelar (líquidos), congelar (alimentos, precios, activos), bloquear (cuentas, etc.)

freeze[2] *n* **1** FROST : helada *f* **2** FREEZING : congelación *f*, congelamiento *m*

freeze–dried ['fri:z'draɪd] *adj* : liofilizado

freeze–dry ['fri:z'draɪ] *vt* **-dried; -drying** : liofilizar

freezer ['fri:zər] *n* : congelador *m*

freezing ['fri:zɪŋ] *adj* : helando ⟨it's freezing! : ¡hace un frío espantoso!⟩

freezing point *n* : punto *m* de congelación

freight¹ ['freɪt] *vt* : enviar como carga

freight² *n* **1** SHIPPING, TRANSPORT : transporte *m*, porte *m*, flete *m* **2** GOODS : mercancías *fpl*, carga *f*

freighter ['freɪtər] *n* : carguero *m*, buque *m* de carga

freight train *n* : tren *m* de carga, tren *m* de mercancías

French¹ ['frɛntʃ] *adj* : francés

French² *n* **1** : francés *m* (idioma) **2 the French** (*used with a plural verb*) : los franceses

French doors *npl* : puerta *f* ventana

French dressing *n* **1** : aderezo *m* cremoso con sabor a tomate **2** (*Brit*) VINAIGRETTE : vinagreta *f*

french fries ['frɛntʃˌfraɪz] *npl* : papas *fpl* fritas

Frenchman ['frɛntʃmən] *n, pl* **-men** [-mən, -ˌmɛn] : francés *m*

French toast *n* : torreja *f*, torrija *f Spain*

French windows *npl* → **French doors**

Frenchwoman ['frɛntʃˌwumən] *n, pl* **-women** [-ˌwɪmən] : francesa *f*

frenetic [frɪ'nɛtɪk] *adj* : frenético — **frenetically** [-tɪkli] *adv*

frenzied ['frɛnzid] *adj* : frenético

frenzy ['frɛnzi] *n, pl* **-zies** : frenesí *m*

frequency ['fri:kwənsi] *n, pl* **-cies** : frecuencia *f*

frequent¹ [fri'kwɛnt, 'fri:kwənt] *vt* : frecuentar

frequent² ['fri:kwənt] *adj* : frecuente — **frequently** *adv*

fresco ['frɛsˌko:] *n, pl* **-coes** : fresco *m*

fresh ['frɛʃ] *adj* **1** : dulce ⟨freshwater : agua dulce⟩ **2** PURE : puro **3** : fresco ⟨fresh fruits : frutas frescas⟩ **4** CLEAN, NEW : limpio, nuevo ⟨fresh clothes : ropa limpia⟩ ⟨fresh evidence : evidencia nueva⟩ **5** REFRESHED : fresco, descansado **6** IMPERTINENT : descarado, impertinente

freshen ['frɛʃən] *vt* : refrescar, arreglar — *vi* **to freshen up** : arreglarse, lavarse

freshet ['frɛʃət] *n* : arroyo *m* desbordado

freshly ['frɛʃli] *adv* : recientemente, recién

freshman ['frɛʃmən] *n, pl* **-men** [-mən, -ˌmɛn] : estudiante *mf* de primer año universitario

freshness ['frɛʃnəs] *n* : frescura *f*

freshwater ['frɛʃˌwɔtər] *n* : agua *f* dulce

fret¹ ['frɛt] *vi* **fretted; fretting** : preocuparse, inquietarse

fret² *n* **1** VEXATION : irritación *f*, molestia *f* **2** WORRY : preocupación *f* **3** : traste *m* (de un instrumento musical)

fretful ['frɛtfəl] *adj* : fastidioso, quejoso, neurótico

fretfully ['frɛtfəli] *adv* : ansiosamente, fastidiosamente, inquieto

fretfulness ['frɛtfəlnəs] *n* : inquietud *f*, irritabilidad *f*

friar ['fraɪər] *n* : fraile *m*

friction ['frɪkʃən] *n* **1** RUBBING : fricción *f* **2** CONFLICT : fricción *f*, roce *m*

Friday ['fraɪˌdeɪ, -di] *n* : viernes *m* ⟨today is Friday : hoy es viernes⟩ ⟨(on) Friday : el viernes⟩ ⟨(on) Fridays : los viernes⟩ ⟨last Friday : el viernes pasado⟩ ⟨next Friday : el viernes que viene⟩ ⟨every other Friday : cada dos viernes⟩ ⟨Friday afternoon/morning : viernes por la tarde/mañana⟩

fridge ['frɪdʒ] → **refrigerator**

fried ['fraɪd] *adj* : frito

friend ['frɛnd] *n* : amigo *m*, -ga *f* ⟨to be/make friends with : ser/hacerse amigo de⟩

friendless ['frɛndləs] *adj* : sin amigos

friendliness ['frɛndlinəs] *n* : simpatía *f*, amabilidad *f*

friendly ['frɛndli] *adj* **friendlier; -est 1** : simpático, amable, de amigo ⟨a friendly child : un niño simpático⟩ ⟨friendly advice : consejo de amigo⟩ **2** : agradable, acogedor ⟨a friendly atmosphere : un ambiente agradable⟩ **3** GOOD-NATURED : amigable, amistoso ⟨friendly competition : competencia amistosa⟩

friendship ['frɛndˌʃɪp] *n* : amistad *f*

frieze ['fri:z] *n* : friso *m*

frigate ['frɪɡət] *n* : fragata *f*

fright ['fraɪt] *n* : miedo *m*, susto *m*

frighten ['fraɪtən] *vt* : asustar, espantar

frightened ['fraɪtənd] *adj* : asustado, temeroso

frightening ['fraɪtənɪŋ] *adj* : espantoso, aterrador

frightful ['fraɪtfəl] *adj* **1** → **frightening 2** TREMENDOUS : espantoso, tremendo

frightfully ['fraɪtfəli] *adv* : terriblemente, tremendamente

frigid ['frɪdʒɪd] *adj* : glacial, extremadamente frío

frigidity [frɪ'dʒɪdəti] *n* **1** COLDNESS : frialdad *f* **2** : frigidez *f* (sexual)

frill ['frɪl] *n* **1** RUFFLE : volante *m* **2** EMBELLISHMENT : floritura *f*, adorno *m*

frilly ['frɪli] *adj* **frillier; -est 1** RUFFLY : con volantes **2** OVERDONE : recargado

fringe¹ ['frɪndʒ] *vt* **fringed; fringing** : orlar, bordear

fringe² *n* **1** BORDER : fleco *m*, orla *f* **2** EDGE : periferia *f*, margen *m* **3 fringe benefits** : incentivos *mpl*, extras *mpl*

Frisbee ['frɪzbi] *trademark* se usa para un disco volador que se lanza de un jugador a otro

frisk ['frɪsk] *vi* FROLIC : retozar, juguetear — *vt* SEARCH : cachear, registrar

friskiness ['frɪskinəs] *n* : vivacidad *f*

frisky ['frɪski] *adj* **friskier; -est** : retozón, juguetón

fritter¹ ['frɪtər] *vt* : desperdiciar, malgastar ⟨I frittered away the money : malgasté el dinero⟩

fritter² *n* : buñuelo *m*

frivolity [frɪ'vɑləti] *n, pl* **-ties** : frivolidad *f*

frivolous ['frɪvələs] *adj* : frívolo, de poca importancia

frivolously ['frɪvələsli] *adv* : frívolamente, a la ligera

frizz[1] ['frɪz] *vi* : rizarse, encresparse, ponerse chino *Mex*

frizz[2] *n* : rizos *mpl* muy apretados

frizzy ['frɪzi] *adj* **frizzier; -est** : rizado, crespo, chino *Mex*

fro ['froː] *adv* **to and fro** : de aquí para allá, de un lado para otro

frock ['frɑk] *n* DRESS : vestido *m*

frog ['frɔg, 'frɑg] *n* **1** : rana *f* **2 to have a frog in one's throat** : tener carraspera

frogman ['frɔg,mæn, 'frɑg-, -mən] *n, pl* **-men** [-mən, -,mɛn] : hombre *m* rana, submarinista *mf*

frolic[1] ['frɑlɪk] *vi* **-icked; -icking** : retozar, juguetear

frolic[2] *n* FUN : diversión *f*

frolicsome ['frɑlɪksəm] *adj* : juguetón

from ['frʌm, 'frəm] *prep* **1** (*indicating a starting, central, or lowest point*) : desde, de, a partir de ⟨from Cali to Bogota : de Cali a Bogotá⟩ ⟨where are you from? : ¿de dónde eres?⟩ ⟨he watched us from above : nos miraba desde arriba⟩ ⟨from that time onward : desde entonces⟩ ⟨from January to March : de enero a marzo, desde enero hasta marzo⟩ ⟨from tomorrow : a partir de mañana⟩ ⟨they cost from 5 to 10 dollars : cuestan entre 5 y 10 dólares⟩ ⟨to speak from the heart : hablar con el corazón⟩ **2** OFF, OUT OF : de ⟨she took it from the drawer : lo sacó del cajón⟩ **3** (*indicating a source or sender*) : de ⟨a letter from my friend : una carta de mi amiga⟩ ⟨a quote from Shakespeare : una cita de Shakespeare⟩ **4** (*indicating distance*) : de ⟨10 feet from the entrance : a 10 pies de la entrada⟩ ⟨we got separated from the group : nos vimos separados del grupo⟩ **5** (*indicating a cause*) : de ⟨red from crying : rojos de llorar⟩ ⟨he died from the cold : murió del frío⟩ **6** (*indicating material*) : de ⟨made from wood : (hecho) de madera⟩ **7** (*indicating blocking, removal, etc.*) : de ⟨to protect from : proteger de⟩ ⟨to provide relief from : aliviar⟩ ⟨to refrain from : abstenerse de⟩ ⟨to omit from : omitir de⟩ ⟨she was excluded from the club : no la admitieron en el club⟩ **8** (*indicating a change*) : de ⟨from bad to worse : de mal en peor⟩ **9** (*in mathematics*) : de ⟨to subtract 10 from 30 : restarle 10 a 30, restar 10 de 30⟩ **10** (*indicating alternatives*) : de ⟨to choose from (among) : elegir de (entre)⟩

frond ['frɑnd] *n* : fronda *f*, hoja *f*

front[1] ['frʌnt] *vi* **1** FACE : dar, estar orientado ⟨the house fronts north : la casa da al norte⟩ **2** : servir de pantalla ⟨he fronts for his boss : sirve de pantalla para su jefe⟩

front[2] *adj* : delantero, de adelante, primero ⟨the front row : la primera fila⟩ ⟨the front door : la puerta principal⟩ ⟨it appeared on the front page : salió en primera plana⟩

front[3] *n* **1** : frente *m*, parte *f* de adelante, delantera *f* ⟨the front of the class : el frente de la clase⟩ ⟨at the front of the train : en la parte delantera del tren⟩ **2** AREA, ZONE : frente *m*, zona *f* ⟨the Eastern front : el frente oriental⟩ ⟨on the educational front : en el frente de la enseñanza⟩ **3** FACADE : fachada *f* (de un edificio o una persona) **4** : frente *m* (en meteorología)

frontage ['frʌntɪʤ] *n* : fachada *f*, frente *m*

frontal ['frʌntəl] *adj* : frontal, de frente

frontier [,frʌn'tɪr] *n* : frontera *f*

frontiersman [,frʌn'tɪrzmən] *n, pl* **-men** [-mən, -,mɛn] : hombre *m* de la frontera

front–wheel drive ['frʌnt'hwiːl-] *n* : tracción *f* delantera

frost[1] ['frɔst] *vt* **1** FREEZE : helar **2** ICE : bañar (pasteles)

frost[2] *n* **1** : helada *f* (en meteorología) **2** : escarcha *f* ⟨frost on the window : escarcha en la ventana⟩

frostbite ['frɔst,baɪt] *n* : congelación *f*

frostbitten ['frɔst,bɪtən] *adj* : congelado (dícese de una persona), quemado (dícese de una planta)

frosting ['frɔstɪŋ] *n* ICING : baño *m*, glaseado *m*, betún *m* *Mex*

frosty ['frɔsti] *adj* **frostier; -est** **1** CHILLY : helado, frío **2** COOL, UNFRIENDLY : frío, glacial

froth ['frɔθ] *n, pl* **froths** ['frɔθs, 'frɔðz] : espuma *f*

frothy ['frɔθi] *adj* **frothier; -est** : espumoso

frown[1] ['fraʊn] *vi* **1** : fruncir el ceño, fruncir el entrecejo **2 to frown at** : mirar (algo) con ceño, mirar (a alguien) con ceño **2 to frown on/upon** : desaprobar

frown[2] *n* : ceño *m* (fruncido)

froze → **freeze**

frozen → **freeze**

frugal ['fruːgəl] *adj* : frugal, ahorrativo, parco — **frugally** *adv*

frugality [fruː'gæləti] *n* : frugalidad *f*

fruit[1] ['fruːt] *vi* : dar fruto

fruit[2] *n* **1** : fruta *f* (término genérico), fruto *m* (término particular) **2 fruits** *npl* REWARDS : frutos *mpl* ⟨the fruits of his labor : los frutos de su trabajo⟩

fruitcake ['fruːt,keɪk] *n* : pastel *m* de frutas

fruitful ['fruːtfəl] *adj* : fructífero, provechoso

fruition [fruː'ɪʃən] *n* **1** : cumplimiento *m*, realización *f* **2 to bring to fruition** : realizar

fruitless ['fruːtləs] *adj* : infructuoso, inútil — **fruitlessly** *adv*

fruit salad *n* : ensalada *f* de frutas

fruity ['fruːti] *adj* **fruitier; -est** : (con sabor) a fruta

frumpy ['frʌmpi] *adj* **frumpier; -est** : anticuado y sin atractivo

frustrate ['frʌs,treɪt] *vt* **-trated; -trating** : frustrar

frustrating ['frʌs,treɪtɪŋ] *adj* : frustrante — **frustratingly** *adv*

frustration [,frʌs'treɪʃən] *n* : frustración *f*

fry[1] ['fraɪ] *vt* **fried; frying** : freír

fry² *n, pl* **fries 1** : fritura *f*, plato *m* frito **2** : fiesta *f* en que se sirven frituras **3** *pl* **fry** : alevín *m* (pez) **4 fries** *npl* → **French fries**

frying pan *n* : sartén *mf*

fuchsia ['fju:ʃə] *n* **1** : fucsia *f* (planta) **2** : fucsia *m* (color)

fuddle ['fʌdəl] *vt* **-dled; -dling** : confundir, atontar

fuddy–duddy ['fʌdi,dʌdi] *n, pl* **-dies** : persona *f* chapada a la antigua, carca *mf*

fudge¹ ['fʌʤ] *vt* **fudged; fudging 1** FALSIFY : amañar, falsificar **2** DODGE : esquivar

fudge² *n* : dulce *m* blando de chocolate y leche

fuel¹ ['fju:əl] *vt* **-eled** *or* **-elled; -eling** *or* **-elling 1** : abastecer de combustible **2** STIMULATE : estimular

fuel² *n* : combustible *m*, carburante *m* (para motores)

fugitive¹ ['fju:ʤəɾɪv] *adj* **1** RUNAWAY : fugitivo **2** FLEETING : efímero, pasajero, fugaz

fugitive² *n* : fugitivo *m*, -va *f*

fugue ['fju:g] *n* : fuga *f*

fulcrum ['fʊlkrəm, 'fʌl-] *n, pl* **-crums** *or* **-cra** [-krə] : fulcro *m*

fulfill *or* **fulfil** [fʊl'fɪl] *vt* **-filled; -filling 1** PERFORM : cumplir con, realizar, llevar a cabo **2** SATISFY : satisfacer

fulfillment [fʊl'fɪlmənt] *n* **1** PERFORMANCE : cumplimiento *m*, ejecución *f* **2** SATISFACTION : satisfacción *f*, realización *f*

full¹ ['fʊl, 'fʌl] *adv* **1** VERY : muy ⟨full well : muy bien, perfectamente⟩ **2** ENTIRELY : completamente ⟨she swung full around : giró completamente⟩ **3** DIRECTLY : de lleno, directamente ⟨he looked me full in the face : me miró directamente a la cara⟩

full² *adj* **1** FILLED : lleno ⟨a full glass : un vaso lleno⟩ ⟨I'm full : estoy lleno⟩ ⟨full of holes : lleno de agujeros⟩ **2** COMPLETE : completo, detallado ⟨two full weeks : dos semanas completas⟩ ⟨a full report : un informe detallado⟩ **3** MAXIMUM : todo, pleno ⟨at full speed : a toda velocidad⟩ ⟨in full bloom : en plena flor⟩ **4** PLUMP : redondo, llenito *fam*, regordete *fam* ⟨a full face : una cara redonda⟩ ⟨a full figure : un cuerpo llenito⟩ **5** AMPLE : amplio ⟨a full skirt : una falda amplia⟩

full³ *n* **1 to pay in full** : pagar en su totalidad **2 to the full** : al máximo

full–fledged ['fʊl'flɛʤd] *adj* : hecho y derecho

full–length ['fʊl,lɛŋθ] *adj* **1** : de cuerpo entero (dícese de un espejo, etc.) **2** : largo (dícese de un vestido, etc.) **3** : de extensión normal ⟨full-length film : largometraje⟩

full moon *n* : luna *f* llena

fullness ['fʊlnəs] *n* **1** ABUNDANCE : plenitud *f*, abundancia *f* **2** : amplitud *f* (de una falda)

full–scale ['fʊl'skeɪl] *adj* **1** : a escala natural **2** COMPLETE : total ⟨full-scale war : guerra total⟩ ⟨a full-scale investigation : una investigación rigurosa⟩

full–time¹ ['fʊl,taɪm] *adv* : a/de tiempo completo

full–time² *adj* : de tiempo completo

fully ['fʊli] *adv* **1** COMPLETELY : completamente, totalmente **2** : al menos, por lo menos ⟨fully half of them : al menos la mitad de ellos⟩

fulsome ['fʊlsəm] *adj* : excesivo, exagerado, efusivo

fumble¹ ['fʌmbəl] *v* **-bled; -bling** *vt* **1** : dejar caer, fumblear **2 to fumble one's way** : ir a tientas — *vi* **1** GROPE : hurgar, tantear **2 to fumble with** : manejar con torpeza

fumble² *n* : fumble *m* (en futbol americano)

fume¹ ['fju:m] *vi* **fumed; fuming 1** SMOKE : echar humo, humear **2** : estar furioso

fume² *n* : gas *m*, humo *m*, vapor *m*

fumigate ['fju:mə,geɪt] *vt* **-gated; -gating** : fumigar

fumigation [,fju:mə'geɪʃən] *n* : fumigación *m*

fun¹ ['fʌn] *adj* : divertido, entretenido

fun² *n* **1** AMUSEMENT : diversión *f*, entretenimiento *m* ⟨the party was really fun : la fiesta fue muy divertida⟩ ⟨for fun : por diversión⟩ **2** ENJOYMENT : disfrute *m* **3 to have fun** : divertirse **4 to make fun of** : reírse de, burlarse de

function¹ ['fʌŋkʃən] *vi* : funcionar, desempeñarse, servir

function² *n* **1** PURPOSE : función *f* **2** GATHERING : reunión *f* social, recepción *f* **3** CEREMONY : ceremonia *f*, acto *m*

functional ['fʌŋkʃənəl] *adj* : funcional — **functionally** *adv*

functionary ['fʌŋkʃə,neri] *n, pl* **-aries** : funcionario *m*, -ria *f*

fund¹ ['fʌnd] *vt* : financiar

fund² *n* **1** SUPPLY : reserva *f*, cúmulo *m* **2** : fondo *m* ⟨investment fund : fondo de inversiones⟩ **3 funds** *npl* RESOURCES : fondos *mpl*

fundamental¹ [,fʌndə'mentəl] *adj* **1** BASIC : fundamental, básico **2** PRINCIPAL : esencial, principal **3** INNATE : innato, intrínseco

fundamental² *n* : fundamento *m*

fundamentalism [,fʌndə'mentəl,izəm] *n* : integrismo *m*, fundamentalismo *m*

fundamentalist [,fʌndə'mentəlist] *n* : integrista *mf*, fundamentalista *mf* — **fundamentalist** *adj*

fundamentally [,fʌndə'mentəli] *adv* : fundamentalmente, básicamente

funding ['fʌndɪŋ] *n* : financiación *f*

fund–raiser ['fʌnd,reɪzər] *n* : función *f* para recaudar fondos

funeral¹ ['fju:nərəl] *adj* **1** : funeral, funerario, fúnebre ⟨funeral procession : cortejo fúnebre⟩ **2 funeral home/parlor** : funeraria *f*

funeral² *n* : funeral *m*, funerales *mpl*

funereal [fju:'nɪriəl] *adj* : fúnebre

fungicide ['fʌnʤə,saɪd, 'fʌŋgə-] *n* : fungicida *m*

fungus [ˈfʌŋgəs] *n, pl* **fungi** [ˈfʌnˌdʒaɪ, ˈfʌŋˌgaɪ] : hongo *m*

funk [ˈfʌŋk] *n* **1** FEAR : miedo *m* **2** DEPRESSION : depresión *f*

funky [ˈfʌŋki] *adj* **funkier; -est** ODD, QUAINT : raro, extraño, original

funnel[1] [ˈfʌnəl] *vt* **-neled; -neling** CHANNEL : canalizar, encauzar

funnel[2] *n* **1** : embudo *m* **2** SMOKESTACK : chimenea *f* (de un barco o vapor)

funnies [ˈfʌniz] *npl* : tiras *fpl* cómicas

funny [ˈfʌni] *adj* **funnier; -est** **1** AMUSING : divertido, cómico **2** STRANGE : extraño, raro

fur[1] [ˈfər] *adj* : de piel

fur[2] *n* **1** : pelaje *m*, piel *f* **2** : prenda *f* de piel

furbish [ˈfərbɪʃ] *vt* : pulir, limpiar

furious [ˈfjuriəs] *adj* : furioso *f* FRANTIC : violento, frenético, vertiginoso (dícese de la velocidad)

furiously [ˈfjuriəsli] *adv* **1** ANGRILY : furiosamente **2** FRANTICALLY : frenéticamente

furlong [ˈfərˌlɔŋ] *n* : estadio *m* (201.2 m)

furlough[1] [ˈfərˌloː] *vt* : dar permiso a, dar licencia a

furlough[2] *n* LEAVE : permiso *m*, licencia *f*

furnace [ˈfərnəs] *n* : horno *m*

furnish [ˈfərnɪʃ] *vt* **1** SUPPLY : proveer, suministrar **2** : amueblar ⟨furnished apartment : departamento amueblado⟩

furnishings [ˈfərnɪʃɪŋz] *npl* **1** ACCESSORIES : accesorios *mpl* **2** FURNITURE : muebles *mpl*, mobiliario *m*

furniture [ˈfərnɪtʃər] *n* : muebles *mpl*, mobiliario *m*

furor [ˈfjurˌɔr, -ər] *n* **1** RAGE : furia *f*, rabia *f* **2** UPROAR : escándalo *m*, jaleo *m*, alboroto *m*

furrier [ˈfəriər] *n* : peletero *m*, -ra *f*

furrow[1] [ˈfərˌoː] *vt* **1** : surcar **2 to furrow one's brow** : fruncir el ceño

furrow[2] *n* **1** GROOVE : surco *m* **2** WRINKLE : arruga *f*, surco *m*

furry [ˈfəri] *adj* **furrier; -est** : peludo (dícese de un animal), peluche (dícese de un objeto)

further[1] [ˈfərðər] *vt* : promover, fomentar

further[2] *adv* **1** FARTHER : más lejos, más adelante **2** MOREOVER : además **3** MORE : más ⟨I'll consider it further in the morning : lo consideraré más en la mañana⟩

further[3] *adj* **1** FARTHER : más lejano **2** ADDITIONAL : adicional, más

furtherance [ˈfərðərənʃ] *n* : promoción *f*, fomento *m*, adelantamiento *m*

furthermore [ˈfərðərˌmor] *adv* : además

furthermost [ˈfərðərˌmoːst] *adj* : más lejano, más distante

furthest [ˈfərðəst] → **farthest**[1], **farthest**[2]

furtive [ˈfərtɪv] *adj* : furtivo, sigiloso — **furtively** *adv*

furtiveness [ˈfərtɪvnəs] *n* STEALTH : sigilo *m*

fury [ˈfjuri] *n, pl* **-ries** **1** RAGE : furia *f*, ira *f* **2** VIOLENCE : furia *f*, furor *m*

fuse[1] [ˈfjuːz] *or* **fuze** *vt* **fused** *or* **fuzed; fusing** *or* **fuzing** : equipar con un fusible

fuse[2] *v* **fused; fusing** *vt* **1** SMELT : fundir **2** MERGE : fusionar, fundir — *vi* : fundirse, fusionarse

fuse[3] *n* : fusible *m*

fuselage [ˈfjuːsəˌlɑʒ, -zə-] *n* : fuselaje *m*

fusillade [ˈfjuːsəˌlɑd, -ˌleɪd, ˌfjuːsəˈ-, -zə-] *n* : descarga *f* de fusilería

fusion [ˈfjuːʒən] *n* : fusión *f*

fuss[1] [ˈfʌs] *vi* **1** WORRY : preocuparse **2 to fuss with** : juguetear con, toquetear **3 to fuss over** : mimar

fuss[2] *n* **1** COMMOTION : alboroto *m*, escándalo *m* **2** ATTENTION : atenciones *fpl* **3** COMPLAINT : quejas *fpl*

fussbudget [ˈfʌsˌbʌdʒət] *n* : quisquilloso *m*, -sa *f*; melindroso *m*, -ra *f*

fussiness [ˈfʌsinəs] *n* **1** IRRITABILITY : irritabilidad *f* **2** : lo recargado (dícese de la decoración, etc.) **3** METICULOUSNESS : meticulosidad *f*

fussy [ˈfʌsi] *adj* **fussier; -est** **1** IRRITABLE : irritable, nervioso **2** OVERELABORATE : recargado **3** METICULOUS : meticuloso **4** FASTIDIOUS : quisquilloso, exigente

futile [ˈfjuːtəl, ˈfjuːˌtaɪl] *adj* : inútil, vano

futility [fjuˈtɪləti] *n, pl* **-ties** : inutilidad *f*

futon [ˈfuːˌtɑn] *n* : futón *m*

future[1] [ˈfjuːtʃər] *adj* : futuro

future[2] *n* : futuro *m* ⟨in the future : en el futuro⟩ ⟨a job with a future : un trabajo con futuro⟩

futuristic [ˌfjuːtʃəˈrɪstɪk] *adj* : futurista

fuze → **fuse**[1]

fuzz [ˈfʌz] *n* : pelusa *f*

fuzziness [ˈfʌzinəs] *n* **1** : vellosidad *f* **2** INDISTINCTNESS : falta *f* de claridad

fuzzy [ˈfʌzi] *adj* **fuzzier; -est** **1** FLUFFY, FURRY : con pelusa, peludo **2** INDISTINCT : indistinto, borroso ⟨a fuzzy image : una imagen borrosa⟩

G

g [ˈdʒiː] *n, pl* **g's** *or* **gs** [ˈdʒiːz] **1** : séptima letra del alfabeto inglés **2** : sol *m* ⟨G sharp/flat : sol sostenido/bemol⟩

gab[1] [ˈgæb] *vi* **gabbed; gabbing** : charlar, cotorrear *fam*, parlotear *fam*

gab[2] *n* CHATTER : cotorreo *m fam*, parloteo *m fam*

gabardine [ˈgæbərˌdiːn] *n* : gabardina *f*

gabby [ˈgæbi] *adj* **gabbier; -est** : hablador, parlanchín

gable [ˈgeɪbəl] *n* : gablete *m*, aguilón *m*

Gabonese [ˌgæbəˈniːz, -ˈniːs] *n* : gabonés *m*, -nesa *f* — **Gabonese** *adj*

gad ['gæd] *vi* **gadded; gadding** WANDER : deambular, vagar, callejear

gadfly ['gæd,flaɪ] *n, pl* **-flies 1** : tábano *m* (insecto) **2** FAULTFINDER : criticón *m*, -cona *f fam*

gadget ['gæʤət] *n* : artilugio *m*, aparato *m*

gadgetry ['gæʤətri] *n* : artilugios *mpl*, aparatos *mpl*

Gaelic ['geɪlɪk, 'gæ] *n* : gaélico *m* (idioma) — **Gaelic** *adj*

gaff ['gæf] *n* **1** : garfio *m* **2** → **gaffe**

gaffe ['gæf] *n* : metedura *f* de pata *fam*

gag¹ ['gæg] *v* **gagged; gagging** *vt* : amordazar ⟨to tie up and gag : atar y amordazar⟩ — *vi* **1** CHOKE : atragantarse **2** RETCH : hacer arcadas

gag² *n* **1** : mordaza *f* (para la boca) **2** JOKE : chiste *m*

gage → **gauge**

gaggle ['gægəl] *n* : bandada *f*, manada *f* (de gansos)

gaiety ['geɪəti] *n, pl* **-eties 1** MERRYMAKING : juerga *f* **2** MERRIMENT : alegría *f*, regocijo *m*

gaily ['geɪli] *adv* : alegremente

gain¹ ['geɪn] *vt* **1** ACQUIRE, OBTAIN : ganar, obtener, adquirir, conseguir ⟨to gain knowledge : adquirir conocimientos⟩ ⟨to gain a victory : obtener una victoria⟩ **2** REACH : alcanzar, llegar a **3** INCREASE : ganar, aumentar ⟨to gain weight : aumentar de peso⟩ **4** : adelantarse, ganar ⟨the watch gains two minutes a day : el reloj se adelanta dos minutos por día⟩ **5 to gain on someone** : ganarle terreno a alguien — *vi* **1** PROFIT : beneficiarse **2** INCREASE : aumentar

gain² *n* **1** PROFIT : beneficio *m*, ganancia *f*, lucro *m*, provecho *m* **2** INCREASE : aumento *m*

gainful ['geɪnfəl] *adj* : lucrativo, beneficioso, provechoso ⟨gainful employment : trabajo remunerado⟩

gait ['geɪt] *n* : paso *m*, andar *m*, manera *f* de caminar

gal ['gæl] *n* : muchacha *f*

gala¹ ['geɪlə, 'gæ-, 'gɑ-] *adj* : de gala

gala² *n* : gala *f*, fiesta *f*

galactic [gə'læktɪk] *adj* : galáctico

galaxy ['gæləksi] *n, pl* **-axies** : galaxia *f*

gale ['geɪl] *n* **1** WIND : vendaval *f*, viento *m* fuerte **2 gales of laughter** : carcajadas *fpl*

Galician [gə'lɪʃən] *n* : gallego *m*, -ga *f* — **Galician** *adj*

gall¹ ['gɔl] *vt* **1** CHAFE : rozar **2** IRRITATE, VEX : irritar, molestar

gall² *n* **1** BILE : bilis *f*, hiel *f* **2** INSOLENCE : audacia *f*, insolencia *f*, descaro *m* **3** SORE : rozadura *f* (de un caballo) **4** : agalla *f* (de una planta)

gallant ['gælənt] *adj* **1** BRAVE : valiente, gallardo **2** CHIVALROUS, POLITE : galante, cortés

gallantry ['gæləntri] *n, pl* **-ries** : galantería *f*, caballerosidad *f*

gallbladder ['gɔl,blædər] *n* : vesícula *f* biliar

galleon ['gæljən] *n* : galeón *m*

gallery ['gæləri] *n, pl* **-leries 1** BALCONY : galería *f* (para espectadores) **2** CORRIDOR : pasillo *m*, galería *f*, corredor *m* **3** *or* **art gallery** : galería *f* (para exposiciones)

galley ['gæli] *n, pl* **-leys** : galera *f*

gallium ['gæliəm] *n* : galio *m*

gallivant ['gælə,vænt] *vi* : callejear

gallon ['gælən] *n* : galón *m*

gallop¹ ['gæləp] *vi* : galopar

gallop² *n* : galope *m*

gallows ['gæ,loːz] *n, pl* **-lows** *or* **-lowses** [-,loːzəz] : horca *f*

gallstone ['gɔl,stoːn] *n* : cálculo *m* biliar

galore [gə'lor] *adj* : en abundancia ⟨bargains galore : muchísimas gangas⟩

galoshes [gə'lɑʃəz] *npl* : galochas *fpl*, chanclos *mpl*

galvanize ['gælvən,aɪz] *vt* **-nized; -nizing 1** STIMULATE : estimular, excitar, impulsar **2** : galvanizar (metales)

Gambian ['gæmbiən] *n* : gambiano *m*, -na *f* — **Gambian** *adj*

gambit ['gæmbɪt] *n* **1** : gambito *m* (en ajedrez) **2** STRATAGEM : estratagema *f*, táctica *f*

gamble¹ ['gæmbəl] *v* **-bled; -bling** *vi* : jugar, arriesgarse — *vt* **1** BET, WAGER : apostar, jugarse **2** RISK : arriesgar

gamble² *n* **1** BET : apuesta *f* **2** RISK : riesgo *m*

gambler ['gæmblər] *n* : jugador *m*, -dora *f*

gambling ['gæmbəlɪŋ] *n* : juego *m*

gambol ['gæmbəl] *vi* **-boled** *or* **-bolled; -boling** *or* **-bolling** FROLIC : retozar, juguetear

game¹ ['geɪm] *adj* **1** READY : listo, dispuesto ⟨we're game for anything : estamos listos para lo que sea⟩ **2** LAME : cojo

game² *n* **1** : juego *m* ⟨card game : juego de cartas/naipes⟩ ⟨board game : juego de mesa⟩ ⟨video game : videojuego⟩ **2** MATCH : partido *m* (de fútbol, ajedrez, etc.), partida *f* (de ajedrez, etc.) **3** ROUND : juego *m* **4** : caza *f* ⟨big game : caza mayor⟩ **5 early in the game** : al principio **6 late in the game** : tarde ⟨it's a little late in the game for that : ya es tarde para eso⟩ **7 to be ahead of the game** : llevar la delantera **8 to beat someone at their own game** : vencer a alguien con sus propias armas **9 to be on/off one's game** : estar/no estar en forma **10 to play games (with someone)** : jugar con alguien, manipular a alguien

gamecock ['geɪm,kɑk] *n* : gallo *m* de pelea

gamekeeper ['geɪm,ki:pər] *n* : guardabosque *mf*

gamely ['geɪmli] *adv* : animosamente

gaming ['geɪmɪŋ] *n* **1** GAMBLING : juego *m* **2** : juegos *mpl* ⟨online gaming : juegos en línea⟩

gamma ray ['gæmə] *n* : rayo *m* gamma

gamut ['gæmət] *n* : gama *f*, espectro *m* ⟨to run the gamut : pasar por toda la gama⟩

gamy or **gamey** ['geɪmi] adj **gamier; -est**
: con sabor de animal de caza, fuerte
gander ['gændər] n 1 : ganso m (animal)
2 GLANCE : mirada f, vistazo m, ojeada f
gang¹ ['gæŋ] vi **to gang up** : agruparse,
unirse
gang² n : banda f, pandilla f
gangland ['gæŋ,lænd] n : hampa f
gangling ['gæŋglɪŋ] adj LANKY : larguirucho fam
ganglion ['gæŋgliən] n, pl **-glia** [-gliə]
: ganglio m
gangplank ['gæŋ,plæŋk] n : pasarela f
gangrene ['gæŋ,griːn, 'gæŋ-; gæŋ'-, gæŋ'-]
n : gangrena f
gangster ['gæŋstər] n : gángster mf
gangway ['gæŋ,weɪ] n 1 : pasarela f 2
gangway! : ¡abran paso!
gap ['gæp] n 1 BREACH, OPENING : espacio m, brecha f, abertura f 2 GORGE
: desfiladero m, barranco m 3 : laguna f
⟨a gap in my education : una laguna en
mi educación⟩ 4 INTERVAL : pausa f,
intervalo m 5 DISPARITY : brecha f, disparidad f
gape¹ ['geɪp] vi **gaped; gaping** 1 OPEN
: abrirse, estar abierto 2 STARE : mirar
fijamente con la boca abierta, mirar boquiabierto
gape² n 1 OPENING : abertura f, brecha f
2 STARE : mirada f boquiabierta
garage¹ [gə'rɑːʒ, -'rɑːdʒ] vt **-raged; -raging**
: dejar en un garaje
garage² n : garaje m, cochera f
garb¹ ['gɑrb] vt : vestir, ataviar
garb² n : vestimenta f, atuendo f
garbage ['gɑrbɪdʒ] n : basura f, desechos
mpl
garbage can n : bote m de basura CA,
Mex; basurero m Mex; caneca f Col;
cubo m de (la) basura Spain; tacho m de
basura Arg, Chile, Ecua, Peru, Uru; tarro
m de (la) basura Arg, Chile, CoRi, Uru
garbage disposal n : trituradora f de basura
garbageman ['gɑrbɪdʒmən] n, pl **-men**
[-mən, -ˌmɛn] : basurero m
garbage truck n : camión m de la basura
garble ['gɑrbəl] vt **-bled; -bling** : tergiversar, distorsionar
garbled ['gɑrbəld] adj : incoherente, incomprensible
garden¹ ['gɑrdən] vi : trabajar en el jardín
garden² n : jardín m ⟨vegetable garden
: huerto⟩
garden center n : centro m de jardinería
gardener ['gɑrdənər] n : jardinero m, -ra f
gardenia [gɑr'diːnjə] n : gardenia f
gardening ['gɑrdənɪŋ] n : jardinería f
gargantuan [gɑr'gæntʃuən] adj : gigantesco, colosal
gargle¹ ['gɑrgəl] vi **-gled; -gling** : hacer
gárgaras, gargarizar
gargle² n : gárgara f
gargoyle ['gɑr,gɔɪl] n : gárgola f
garish ['gærɪʃ] adj GAUDY : llamativo,
chillón, charro — **garishly** adv
garland¹ ['gɑrlənd] vt : adornar con
guirnaldas
garland² n : guirnalda f

garlic ['gɑrlɪk] n : ajo m
garment ['gɑrmənt] n : prenda f
garner ['gɑrnər] vt : recoger, cosechar
garnet ['gɑrnət] n : granate m
garnish¹ ['gɑrnɪʃ] vt : aderezar, guarnecer
garnish² n : aderezo m, guarnición f
garret ['gærət] n : buhardilla f, desván m
garrison¹ ['gærəsən] vt 1 QUARTER
: acuartelar (tropas) 2 OCCUPY : guarnecer, ocupar (con tropas)
garrison² n 1 : guarnición f (ciudad) 2
FORT : fortaleza f, poste m militar
garrulous ['gærələs] adj : charlatán,
parlanchín
garter ['gɑrtər] n : liga f
gas¹ ['gæs] v **gassed; gassing** vt : gasear
— vi **to gas up** : llenar el tanque con
gasolina
gas² n, pl **gases** ['gæsəz] 1 : gas m ⟨tear
gas : gas lacrimógeno⟩ 2 → **gasoline**
gaseous ['gæʃəs, 'gæsiəs] adj : gaseoso
gash¹ ['gæʃ] vt : hacer un tajo en, cortar
gash² n : cuchillada f, tajo m
gasket ['gæskət] n : junta f
gas mask n : máscara f antigás
gasoline ['gæsə,liːn, ˌgæsə'-] n : gasolina f,
nafta f, bencina f Chile
gasp¹ ['gæsp] vi 1 : boquear ⟨to gasp with
surprise : gritar de asombro⟩ 2 PANT
: jadear, respirar con dificultad
gasp² n 1 : boqueada f ⟨a gasp of surprise
: un grito sofocado⟩ 2 PANTING : jadeo
m
gas pedal n : acelerador m
gas station n : estación f de servicio; gasolinera f; bencinera f Chile; bomba f
Chile, CoRi, Ven
gas tank n : tanque m, depósito m (de ga-
solina/bencina/nafta)
gastric ['gæstrɪk] adj : gástrico ⟨gastric
juice : jugo gástrico⟩
gastronomic [ˌgæstrə'nɑmɪk] adj : gastronómico
gastronomy [gæs'trɑnəmi] n : gastronomía f
gate ['geɪt] n : portón m, verja f, puerta f
gatekeeper ['geɪt,kiːpər] n : guarda mf;
guardián m, -diana f
gateway ['geɪt,weɪ] n : puerta f (de acceso), entrada f
gather ['gæðər] vt 1 ASSEMBLE, COLLECT
: juntar, recoger, reunir ⟨to gather dust
: acumular polvo⟩ 2 HARVEST : recoger,
cosechar 3 : fruncir (una tela) 4 INFER
: deducir, suponer — vi : reunirse, congregarse, acumularse
gathering ['gæðərɪŋ] n : reunión f
gauche ['goʊʃ] adj : torpe, falto de tacto
gaucho ['gaʊtʃo] n : gaucho m
gaudy ['gɔdi] adj **gaudier; -est** : chillón,
llamativo
gauge¹ ['geɪdʒ] vt **gauged; gauging** 1
MEASURE : medir 2 ESTIMATE, JUDGE
: estimar, evaluar, juzgar
gauge² n 1 : indicador m ⟨pressure gauge
: indicador de presión⟩ 2 CALIBER : calibre m 3 INDICATION : indicio m, muestra f
gaunt ['gɔnt] adj : demacrado, descarnado

gauntlet ['gɔntlət] n : guante m ⟨to run the gauntlet of : exponerse a⟩

gauze ['gɔz] n : gasa f

gauzy ['gɔzi] adj **gauzier; -est** : diáfano, vaporoso

gave → **give**

gavel ['gævəl] n : martillo m (de un juez, un subastador, etc.)

gawk ['gɔk] vi GAPE : mirar boquiabierto

gawker ['gɔkər] n : mirón m, -rona f

gawky ['gɔki] adj **gawkier; -est** : desmañado, torpe, desgarbado

gay[1] ['geɪ] adj **1** MERRY : alegre **2** BRIGHT, COLORFUL : vistoso, vivo **3** HOMOSEXUAL : homosexual

gay[2] n HOMOSEXUAL : homosexual mf

gaze[1] ['geɪz] vi **gazed; gazing** : mirar (fijamente)

gaze[2] n : mirada f (fija)

gazebo [gə'ziːbo] n : pabellón m, cenador m, glorieta f

gazelle [gə'zɛl] n : gacela f

gazette [gə'zɛt] n : gaceta f

gazetteer [,gæzə'tɪr] n : diccionario m geográfico

gazpacho [gɔz'pɑtʃo, gə'spɑ-] n : gazpacho m

gear[1] ['gɪr] vt ADAPT, ORIENT : adaptar, ajustar, orientar ⟨a book geared to children : un libro adaptado a los niños⟩ — vi **to gear up** : prepararse

gear[2] n **1** CLOTHING : ropa f **2** BELONGINGS : efectos mpl personales **3** EQUIPMENT, TOOLS : equipo m, aparejo m, herramientas fpl ⟨fishing gear : aparejo de pescar⟩ ⟨landing gear : tren de aterrizaje⟩ **4** COGWHEEL : rueda f dentada **5** : marcha f, velocidad f (de un vehículo) ⟨to put in gear : poner en marcha⟩ ⟨to change gear(s) : cambiar de velocidad⟩

gearbox ['gɪr,bɑks] n : caja f de cambios

gearshift ['gɪr,ʃɪft] n TRANSMISSION : palanca f de cambio, palanca f de velocidad

geek ['giːk] n fam **1** : intelectual mf (en general); fanático m -ca f (de algo específico) ⟨a computer geek : un genio informático⟩ **2** MISFIT : inadaptado m, -da f

geese → **goose**

Geiger counter ['gaɪgər,kauntər] n : contador m Geiger

gel ['dʒɛl] n : gel m

gelatin ['dʒɛlətən] n : gelatina f

gem ['dʒɛm] n : joya f, gema f, alhaja f

Gemini ['dʒɛmə,naɪ] n **1** : Géminis m (signo o constelación) **2** : Géminis mf (persona)

gemstone ['dʒɛm,stoːn] n : piedra f (semipreciosa o preciosa), gema f

gender ['dʒɛndər] n **1** SEX : sexo m **2** : género m (en la gramática)

gene ['dʒiːn] n : gen m, gene m

genealogical [,dʒiːniə'lɑdʒɪkəl] adj : genealógico

genealogy [,dʒiːni'ɑlədʒi, ,dʒɛ-, -'æ-] n, pl **-gies** : genealogía f

genera → **genus**

general[1] ['dʒɛnrəl, 'dʒɛnə-] adj : general ⟨in general : en general, por lo general⟩

⟨general election : elecciones generales⟩ ⟨general knowledge : cultura general⟩

general[2] n : general mf

generality [,dʒɛnə'rælətɪ] n, pl **-ties** : generalidad f

generalization [,dʒɛnrələ'zeɪʃən, ,dʒɛnərə-] n : generalización f

generalize ['dʒɛnrə,laɪz, 'dʒɛnərə-] v **-ized; -izing** : generalizar

generally ['dʒɛnrəli, 'dʒɛnərə-] adv : generalmente, por lo general, en general

general practitioner n : médico m, -ca f de cabecera

generate ['dʒɛnə,reɪt] vt **-ated; -ating** : generar, producir

generation [,dʒɛnə'reɪʃən] n : generación f — **generational** [,dʒɛnə'reɪʃənəl] adj

generator ['dʒɛnə,reɪtər] n : generador m

generic [dʒə'nɛrɪk] adj : genérico

generosity [,dʒɛnə'rɑsəti] n, pl **-ties** : generosidad f

generous ['dʒɛnərəs] adj **1** OPENHANDED : generoso, dadivoso, desprendido **2** ABUNDANT, AMPLE : abundante, amplio, generoso — **generously** adv

genetic [dʒə'nɛtɪk] adj : genético — **genetically** [-tɪkli] adv

genetically modified adj : transgénico

geneticist [dʒə'nɛtəsɪst] n : genetista mf

genetics [dʒə'nɛtɪks] n : genética f

genial ['dʒiːniəl] adj GRACIOUS : simpático, cordial, afable — **genially** adv

geniality [,dʒiːni'ælətɪ] n : simpatía f, afabilidad f

genie ['dʒiːni] n : genio m

genital ['dʒɛnətəl] adj : genital

genitals ['dʒɛnətəlz] npl : genitales mpl

genius ['dʒiːnjəs] n : genio m

genocide ['dʒɛnə,saɪd] n : genocidio m

genre ['ʒɑnrə, 'ʒɑr] n : género m

genteel [dʒɛn'tiːl] adj : cortés, fino, refinado

gentile[1] ['dʒɛn,taɪl] adj : gentil

gentile[2] n : gentil mf

gentility [dʒɛn'tɪlətɪ] n, pl **-ties** **1** : nobleza f (de nacimiento) **2** POLITENESS, REFINEMENT : cortesía f, refinamiento m

gentle ['dʒɛntəl] adj **gentler; gentlest** **1** NOBLE : bien nacido, noble **2** DOCILE : dócil, manso **3** KINDLY : bondadoso, amable **4** MILD : suave, apacible ⟨a gentle breeze : una brisa suave⟩ **5** SOFT : suave (dícese de un sonido), ligero (dícese del tacto) **6** MODERATE : moderado, gradual ⟨a gentle slope : una cuesta gradual⟩

gentleman ['dʒɛntəlmən] n, pl **-men** [-mən, -,mɛn] : caballero m, señor m

gentlemanly ['dʒɛntəlmənli] adj : caballeroso

gentleness ['dʒɛntəlnəs] n : delicadeza f, suavidad f, ternura f

gentlewoman ['dʒɛntəl,wʊmən] n, pl **-women** [-,wɪmən] : dama f, señora f

gently ['dʒɛntli] adv **1** CAREFULLY, SOFTLY : con cuidado, suavemente, ligeramente **2** KINDLY : amablemente, con delicadeza

gentry ['dʒɛntri] n, pl **-tries** : aristocracia f

genuflect ['dʒɛnjʊ,flɛkt] vi : doblar la rodilla, hacer una genuflexión

genuflection [,dʒɛnjʊ'flɛkʃən] n : genuflexión f

genuine ['dʒɛnjuwən] adj 1 AUTHENTIC, REAL : genuino, verdadero, auténtico 2 SINCERE : sincero — **genuinely** adv

genus ['dʒiːnəs] n, pl **genera** ['dʒɛnərə] : género m

geographer [dʒi'ɑgrəfər] n : geógrafo m, -fa f

geographical [,dʒiːə'græfɪkəl] or **geographic** [-fɪk] adj : geográfico — **geographically** [-fɪkli] adv

geography [dʒi'ɑgrəfi] n, pl **-phies** : geografía f

geologic [,dʒiːə'lɑdʒɪk] or **geological** [-dʒɪkəl] adj : geológico — **geologically** [-dʒɪkli] adv

geologist [dʒi'ɑlədʒɪst] n : geólogo m, -ga f

geology [dʒi'ɑlədʒi] n : geología f

geometric [,dʒiːə'mɛtrɪk] or **geometrical** [-trɪkəl] adj : geométrico

geometry [dʒi'ɑmətri] n, pl **-tries** : geometría f

geopolitical [,dʒiːoːpə'lɪtɪkəl] adj : geopolítico

Georgian ['dʒɔrdʒən] n 1 : georgiano m (idioma) 2 : georgiano m, -na f — **Georgian** adj

geranium [dʒə'reɪniəm] n : geranio m

gerbil ['dʒərbəl] n : jerbo m, gerbo m

geriatric [,dʒɛri'ætrɪk] adj : geriátrico

geriatrics [,dʒɛri'ætrɪks] n : geriatría f

germ ['dʒərm] n 1 MICROORGANISM : microbio m, germen m 2 BEGINNING : germen m, principio m ⟨the germ of a plan : el germen de un plan⟩

German ['dʒərmən] n 1 : alemán m, -mana f 2 : alemán m (idioma) — **German** adj

germane [dʒər'meɪn] adj : relevante, pertinente

Germanic [dʒər'mænɪk] adj : germano

germanium [dʒər'meɪniəm] n : germanio m

German measles n : rubéola f

German shepherd n : pastor m alemán

germ cell n : célula f germen

germicide ['dʒərmə,saɪd] n : germicida m

germinate ['dʒərmə,neɪt] v **-nated; -nating** vi : germinar — vt : hacer germinar

germination [,dʒərmə'neɪʃən] n : germinación f

gerund ['dʒɛrənd] n : gerundio m

gestation [dʒɛ'steɪʃən] n : gestación f

gesticulate [dʒɛ'stɪkjə,leɪt] vi **-lated; -lating** : gesticular — **gesticulation** [dʒɛ,stɪkjə'leɪʃən] n

gesture[1] ['dʒɛstʃər] vi **-tured; -turing** : gesticular, hacer gestos

gesture[2] n 1 : gesto m, ademán m 2 SIGN, TOKEN : gesto m, señal f ⟨a gesture of friendship : una señal de amistad⟩

get ['gɛt] v **got** ['gɑt]; **got** or **gotten** ['gɑtən]; **getting** vt 1 OBTAIN : conseguir, obtener, adquirir ⟨to get a job : conseguir trabajo⟩ ⟨she got the dress on sale : compró el vestido rebajado⟩ ⟨to get someone's attention : atraer la atención de alguien⟩ ⟨to get a good night's sleep : dormir bien⟩ 2 RECEIVE : recibir ⟨to get a letter : recibir una carta⟩ ⟨we've been getting a lot of rain : ha llovido mucho⟩ 3 EARN : ganar ⟨he gets $10 an hour : gana $10 por hora⟩ 4 FETCH : traer ⟨get me my book : tráeme el libro⟩ ⟨go (and) get your coat : vete a buscar tu abrigo⟩ 5 CATCH : tomar (un tren, etc.), agarrar (una pelota, etc.) 6 SEIZE, GRASP : agarrar ⟨he got me by the arm : me agarró del brazo⟩ 7 CAPTURE : agarrar, capturar 8 SEND : mandar, hacer llegar ⟨we got a message to her : le hicimos llegar un mensaje⟩ 9 TAKE : llevar ⟨we got him to the hospital : lo llevamos al hospital⟩ 10 : hacer ir/mover (etc.) ⟨he got them out of bed : los sacó de la cama⟩ ⟨we got ourselves through customs : pasamos por la aduana⟩ 11 : hacer progresar ⟨flattery will get you nowhere : con halagos no conseguirás nada⟩ 12 FIT : hacer entrar/pasar (etc.) ⟨can you get it into this box : ¿puedes meterlo en esta caja?⟩ ⟨I can't get the key into the lock : la llave no entra en la cerradura⟩ ⟨can you get it through the door? : ¿va a pasar por la puerta?⟩ 13 CONTRACT : contagiarse de, contraer ⟨she got the measles from him : (a ella) le dio el sarampión⟩ 14 SUFFER, SUSTAIN : sufrir (una herida, etc.) 15 PREPARE : preparar (una comida, etc.) 16 : tener (una impresión, etc.) ⟨where did you get that idea? : ¿de dónde sacaste esa idea?⟩ 17 CAUSE, ELICIT : causar, provocar ⟨to get a laugh : hacer reír⟩ 18 (to cause to do something) ⟨I can't get them to behave : no puedo hacer que se porten bien⟩ ⟨I got him to agree : logré convencerlo⟩ ⟨she got the computer working, she got the computer to work : hizo funcionar la computadora⟩ 19 (to cause to be) ⟨I got my feet wet : me mojé los pies⟩ ⟨to get one's hair cut : cortarse el pelo⟩ ⟨he got himself ready to go : se preparó para ir⟩ ⟨let me get this straight : a ver si te entiendo⟩ 20 ANSWER : contestar (el teléfono), abrir (la puerta) 21 fam BOTHER : molestar, irritar ⟨what really gets me is . . . : lo que más me molesta es . . .⟩ 22 UNDERSTAND : entender ⟨now I get it! : ¡ya entiendo!⟩ ⟨I didn't get your name : no oí su nombre⟩ 23 NOTICE : notar, ver 24 STUMP : agarrar, pillar 25 TRICK : engañar 26 MOVE, SADDEN : conmover 27 RECEIVE : captar, recibir (un canal, etc.) 28 HIT : dar ⟨it got him in the leg : le dio en la pierna⟩ 29 KILL : matar, acabar con 30 **to get across** : comunicar, hacer entender 31 **to get back** : recuperar (dinero, etc.) 32 **to get someone back** : vengarse de alguien 33 **to get down** : bajar (de un estante, etc.) 34 **to get down** SWALLOW : tragar 35 **to get down** DEPRESS, SADDEN : deprimir 36 **to get down** WRITE DOWN : anotar 37 **to get in** SUBMIT, DELIVER : entregar 38 **to get in** : hacer (un comentario, etc.), dar (un golpe, etc.) ⟨to get a word in edgewise

: meter baza⟩ **39 to get in** : arreglárselas para hacer ⟨we got in a visit to the museum : pudimos visitar el museo⟩ **40 to get into** : meter (a alguien) en (un asunto) ⟨to get oneself into trouble : meterse en un lío⟩ **41 to get off** REMOVE : quitar **42 to get off** : librar de, salvar de (un castigo) **43 to get off** SEND : mandar, enviar **44 to get out** EXTRACT, REMOVE : sacar, quitar **45 to get something out of someone** : sacarle algo a alguien **46 to get something over with** : quitarse algo de encima **47 to get through** : hacer llegar (un mensaje, etc.) **48 to get through** SUSTAIN : mantener, sustentar **49 to get through** LAST : alcanzar **50 to get together** COLLECT : juntar, reunir ⟨to get oneself together : organizarse⟩ **51 to get up** RAISE, LIFT : subir **52 to get up** MUSTER : armarse de (valor), cobrar (fuerzas) **53 to get up** : organizar (una petición, etc.) **54 to have got** : tener ⟨I've got a headache : tengo un dolor de cabeza⟩ **55 to have got to** : tener que ⟨you've got to come : tienes que venir⟩ — *vi* **1** BECOME : ponerse, volverse, hacerse ⟨to get angry : ponerse furioso, enojarse⟩ ⟨to get wet/dirty : mojarse/ensuciarse⟩ ⟨to get dressed : vestirse⟩ ⟨to get used to something : acostumbrarse a algo⟩ ⟨to get lost : perderse⟩ ⟨it's getting late : se hace tarde⟩ **2** GO, MOVE : ir, avanzar ⟨he didn't get far : no avanzó mucho⟩ **3** PROGRESS : progresar, avanzar ⟨now we're getting somewhere! : ¡ahora sí que estamos progresando!⟩ **4** ARRIVE : llegar ⟨to get home : llegar a casa⟩ ⟨she got to the last page : llegó a la última página⟩ **5 get out (of here)!** (*expressing surprise or disbelief*) : ¡anda!, ¡qué va! **6 to get across** COMMUNICATE : comunicarse, hacerse entender **7 to get after** *fam* NAG : estar encima de/a **8 to get ahead** : adelantarse, progresar **9 to get along** : llevarse bien (con alguien), congeniar **10 to get along** MANAGE : arreglárselas **11 to get along** PROGRESS : marchar, progresar **12 to get around** SPREAD, CIRCULATE : difundirse ⟨word got around that . . . : se corrió la voz de que . . .⟩ **13 to get around** CIRCUMVENT : evitar, vencer **14 to get around** WALK : caminar, andar **15 to get around** TRAVEL : viajar **16 to get around to doing something** : encontrar el tiempo para hacer algo **17 to get at** REACH : llegar a, alcanzar **18 to get at** DISCOVER : descubrir **19 to get at** IMPLY : insinuar **20 to get away** : salir ⟨I can't get away until later : no puedo salir hasta más tarde⟩ **21 to get away** ESCAPE : escaparse **22 to get away** MANAGE : arreglárselas (con/sin algo) **24 to get away with** ⟨to get away with a crime : salir impune de un delito⟩ ⟨how does he get away with being so rude? : ¿cómo se le permite ser tan grosero?⟩ **25 to get back** RETURN : volver **26 to get back** RETREAT

: echarse atrás **27 to get back at someone** : vengarse de alguien **28 to get back to** : volver a, reanudar (una actividad) **29 to get back to** : volver a contactar **30 to get behind** : atrasarse **31 to get behind** SUPPORT : apoyar **32 to get by** MANAGE : arreglárselas **33 to get down to something** : ponerse a hacer algo **34 to get going** LEAVE : irse **35 to get going** : ponerse a hacer algo **36 to get going on something** : ponerse a hacer algo **37 to get in** ENTER : entrar ⟨it got in through the window : entró por la ventana⟩ **38 to get in** ARRIVE : llegar **39 to get in** : entrar, ser aceptado **40 to get into** : entrar en/a (una universidad, etc) **41 to get into** : meterse en (una situación) ⟨to get into trouble : meterse en un lío⟩ ⟨to get into an argument : empezar a discutir⟩ **42 to get into** : entusiasmarse con, interesarse en **43 to get into** : afectar a ⟨what's gotten into him? : ¿qué le pasa?⟩ **44 to get into** : llegar a (un lugar) **45 to get into** : ponerse ⟨I can't get into these jeans : estos jeans no me entran⟩ **46 to get in/into** BOARD : subir (a) **47 to get it** ⟨when mom finds out, you're going to get it! : cuando mamá se entere, ¡te mata!⟩ **48 to get off** : quedar impune ⟨to get off with a warning : librarse con sólo una amonestación⟩ **49 to get off** : salir (del trabajo) **50 to get off** : salirse de (un tema, etc.) **51 to get off (of)** EXIT : bajarse (de) **52 to get on** ⟨how are you getting on? : ¿qué tal te va?⟩ **54 to get on** SUCCEED : tener éxito **55 to get on** : ocuparse de ⟨I'll get right on it : lo haré ahora mismo⟩ **56 to get on/onto** MOUNT : montarse (a) **57 to get on/onto** BOARD : subirse (a) **58 to get onto** : empezar a hablar de (un tema) **59 to get on with** : seguir con (una actividad) **60 to get out** LEAVE : salir **61 to get out** LEAK : difundirse, filtrarse **62 to get out (of)** EXIT : bajarse (de) **63 to get out of** : escapar de **64 to get out of** : salvarse de **65 to get over** : recuperarse de (una enfermedad, etc.), superar (el miedo, etc.), aceptar (una situación), no guardar (rencor), olvidar a (un amante), consolarse de (una pérdida) **66 to get through** : sobrevivir (el invierno), superar (una crisis, etc.) **67 to get through** : aprobar (un examen) **68 to get through** : comunicar (por teléfono) **69 to get through** : hacer entender ⟨I think I finally got through (to him) : creo que por fin lo hice entender⟩ **70 to get through (with)** FINISH : terminar, acabar **71 to get to** BOTHER : molestar, irritar **72 to get to be** BECOME : llegar a ser **73 to get together** MEET : reunirse **74 to get together** UNITE : unirse, juntarse **75 to get up** : levantarse **76 to get up on** : subirse a **77 to get up to** : hacer (travesuras, etc.) **78 to get up to** REACH : alcanzar, llegar hasta — *v aux* ⟨I got paid : me pagaron⟩ ⟨they got married : se casaron⟩

getaway ['gɛtə,weɪ] *n* ESCAPE : fuga *f*, huida *f*, escapada *f*

get–go ['gɪt,goː, 'gɛt–] *n* **from the get-go** : desde el primer momento

get–together ['gɛtə,gɛðər] *n* : reunión *f* (informal)

geyser ['gaɪzər] *n* : géiser *m*

Ghanaian ['gɑniən, 'gæ–] *n* : ghanés *m*, -nesa — **Ghanaian** *adj*

ghastly ['gæstli] *adj* **ghastlier; -est** 1 HORRIBLE : horrible, espantoso 2 PALE : pálido, cadavérico

gherkin ['gərkən] *n* : pepinillo *m*

ghetto ['gɛtoː] *n*, *pl* **-tos** *or* **-toes** : gueto *m*

ghost ['goːst] *n* 1 : fantasma *m*, espectro *m* 2 **the Holy Ghost** : el Espíritu Santo

ghostly ['goːstli] *adv* : fantasmal

ghoul ['guːl] *n* 1 : demonio *m* (que come cadáveres) 2 : persona *f* de gustos macabros

GI [,ʤiː'aɪ] *n*, *pl* **GI's** *or* **GIs** : soldado *m* estadounidense

giant[1] ['ʤaɪənt] *adj* : gigante, gigantesco, enorme

giant[2] *n* : gigante *m*, -ta *f*

gibberish ['ʤɪbərɪʃ] *n* : galimatías *m*, jerigonza *f*

gibbon ['gɪbən] *n* : gibón *m*

gibe[1] ['ʤaɪb] *vi* **gibed; gibing** : mofarse, burlarse

gibe[2] *n* : pulla *f*, burla *f*, mofa *f*

giblets ['ʤɪbləts] *npl* : menudos *mpl*, menudencias *fpl*

giddiness ['gɪdinəs] *n* 1 DIZZINESS : vértigo *m*, mareo *m* 2 SILLINESS : frivolidad *f*, estupidez *f*

giddy ['gɪdi] *adj* **giddier; -est** 1 DIZZY : mareado, vertiginoso 2 FRIVOLOUS, SILLY : frívolo, tonto

gift ['gɪft] *n* 1 TALENT : don *m*, talento *m*, dotes *fpl* 2 PRESENT : regalo *m*, obsequio *m*

gift certificate *n* : certificado *m* de regalo

gifted ['gɪftəd] *adj* TALENTED : talentoso

gig[1] ['gɪg] *n* : trabajo *m* (de duración limitada) ⟨to play a gig : tocar en un concierto⟩

gig[2] *n fam* : giga *mf fam*, gigabyte *m*

gigabyte ['ʤɪgə,baɪt, 'gɪ–] *n* : gigabyte *m*

gigantic [ʤaɪ'gæntɪk] *adj* : gigantesco, enorme, colosal

giggle[1] ['gɪgəl] *vi* **-gled; -gling** : reírse tontamente

giggle[2] *n* : risita *f*, risa *f* tonta

gild ['gɪld] *vt* **gilded** *or* **gilt** ['gɪlt]; **gilding** : dorar

gill ['gɪl] *n* : agalla *f*, branquia *f*

gilt[1] ['gɪlt] *adj* : dorado

gilt[2] *n* : dorado *m*

gimlet ['gɪmlət] *n* 1 : barrena *f* (herramienta) 2 : bebida *f* de vodka o ginebra y limón

gimmick ['gɪmɪk] *n* 1 GADGET : artilugio *m* 2 CATCH : engaño *m*, trampa *f* 3 SCHEME, TRICK : ardid *m*, truco *m*

gin ['ʤɪn] *n* : ginebra *f* (bebida alcohólica)

ginger ['ʤɪnʤər] *n* : jengibre *m*

ginger ale *n* : gaseosa *f* de jengibre

gingerbread ['ʤɪnʤər,brɛd] *n* : pan *m* de jengibre

gingerly ['ʤɪnʤərli] *adv* : con cuidado, cautelosamente

gingham ['gɪnəm] *n* : guinga *f*

ginseng ['ʤɪn,sɪn, –,sɛn] *n* : ginseng *m*

giraffe [ʤə'ræf] *n* : jirafa *f*

gird ['gərd] *vt* **girded** *or* **girt** ['gərt]; **girding** 1 BIND : ceñir, atar 2 ENCIRCLE : rodear 3 **to gird oneself** : prepararse

girder ['gərdər] *n* : viga *f*

girdle[1] ['gərdəl] *vt* **-dled; -dling** 1 GIRD : ceñir, atar 2 SURROUND : rodear, circundar

girdle[2] *n* : faja *f*

girl ['gərl] *n* 1 : chica *f*, muchacha *f* 2 *or* **little girl** : niña *f*, chica *f* 3 SWEETHEART : novia *f* 4 DAUGHTER : hija *f*

girlfriend ['gərl,frɛnd] *n* : novia *f*, amiga *f*

girlhood ['gərl,hʊd] *n* : niñez *f*, juventud *f* (de una muchacha)

girlish ['gərlɪʃ] *adj* : de niña

girth ['gərθ] *n* 1 : circunferencia *f* (de un árbol, etc.), cintura *f* (de una persona) 2 CINCH : cincha *f* (para caballos, etc.)

gist ['ʤɪst] *n* : quid *m*, meollo *m*

give[1] ['gɪv] *v* **gave** ['geɪv]; **given** ['gɪvən]; **giving** *vt* 1 HAND : dar, entregar ⟨give it to me : dámelo⟩ 2 PRESENT : dar, regalar ⟨they gave him a gold watch : le regalaron un reloj de oro⟩ 3 DONATE : dar, donar ⟨to give blood : dar sangre⟩ ⟨to give money to charity : dar dinero a organizaciones benéficas⟩ 4 PAY : dar, pagar ⟨I'll give you $10 for the blue one : te daré $10 por el azul⟩ 5 : dar (un grito, un salto, etc.) ⟨she gave me a kiss : me dio un beso⟩ ⟨he gave us the signal : nos dio la señal⟩ 6 ADMINISTER : dar (un castigo, una inyección, etc.) 7 OFFER : dar ⟨he gave me his hand : me dio la mano⟩ ⟨she didn't give a reason : no dijo por qué⟩ 8 PROVIDE : dar ⟨to give one's word : dar uno su palabra⟩ ⟨she gave me a ride to work : me llevó a la oficina⟩ ⟨cows give milk : las vacas dan leche⟩ 9 ATTRIBUTE : dar ⟨to give credit to someone : darle el mérito a alguien⟩ 10 PRONOUNCE : dictar (una sentencia) 11 CAUSE : dar, causar, ocasionar ⟨to give trouble : causar problemas⟩ ⟨to give someone to understand : darle a entender a alguien⟩ 12 GRANT : dar, otorgar ⟨to give permission : dar permiso⟩ 13 **to give away** : regalar 14 **to give away** REVEAL : revelar 15 **to give away** : llevar (a una novia) al altar 16 **to give away** BETRAY : delatar 17 **to give back** RETURN : devolver 18 **to give in (to)** : ceder (a) 19 **to give off** EMIT : despedir 20 **to give oneself (over) to** : entregarse a 21 **to give out** DISTRIBUTE : distribuir 22 **to give up** : dejar, renunciar a, abandonar ⟨to give up smoking : dejar de fumar⟩ — *vi* 1 : hacer regalos 2 *or* **to give way** YIELD : ceder, romperse ⟨it gave under the weight of the crowd : cedió bajo el peso de la muchedumbre⟩ 3 **to give in/up** SURRENDER : rendirse, entregarse 4 **to give out** : agotarse, acabarse ⟨the supplies gave out : las provisiones se agotaron⟩

give² *n* FLEXIBILITY : flexibilidad *f*, elasticidad *f*

give–and–take *n* : toma y daca *m*

giveaway ['gɪvəˌweɪ] *n* **1** : revelación *f* involuntaria **2** GIFT : regalo *m*, obsequio *m*

given ['gɪvən] *adj* **1** INCLINED : dado, inclinado ⟨he's given to quarreling : es muy dado a discutir⟩ **2** SPECIFIC : dado, determinado ⟨at a given time : en un momento dado⟩

given name *n* : nombre *m* de pila

give or take APPROXIMATELY : más o menos

gizzard ['gɪzərd] *n* : molleja *f*

glacial ['gleɪʃəl] *adj* : glacial — **glacially** *adv*

glacier ['gleɪʃər] *n* : glaciar *m*

glad ['glæd] *adj* **gladder; gladdest 1** PLEASED : alegre, contento ⟨she was glad I came : se alegró de que haya venido⟩ ⟨glad to meet you! : ¡mucho gusto!⟩ **2** HAPPY, PLEASING : feliz, agradable ⟨glad tidings : buenas nuevas⟩ **3** WILLING : dispuesto, gustoso ⟨I'll be glad to do it : lo haré con mucho gusto⟩

gladden ['glædən] *vt* : alegrar

glade ['gleɪd] *n* : claro *m*

gladiator ['glædiˌeɪtər] *n* : gladiador *m*

gladiolus [ˌglædi'oːləs] *n, pl* **-li** [-li, -ˌlaɪ] : gladiolo *m*, gladíolo *m*

gladly ['glædli] *adv* : con mucho gusto

gladness ['glædnəs] *n* : alegría *f*, gozo *m*

glamor *or* **glamour** ['glæmər] *n* : atractivo *m*, hechizo *m*, encanto *m*

glamorous ['glæmərəs] *adj* : atractivo, encantador

glance¹ ['glænts] *vi* **glanced; glancing 1** RICOCHET : rebotar ⟨it glanced off the wall : rebotó en la pared⟩ **2 to glance at** : mirar, echar un vistazo a **3 to glance away** : apartar los ojos

glance² *n* : mirada *f*, vistazo *m*, ojeada *f*

gland ['glænd] *n* : glándula *f*

glandular ['glændʒʊlər] *adj* : glandular

glare¹ ['glær] *vi* **glared; glaring 1** SHINE : brillar, relumbrar **2** STARE : mirar con ira, lanzar una mirada feroz

glare² *n* **1** BRIGHTNESS : resplandor *m*, luz *f* deslumbrante **2** : mirada *f* feroz

glaring ['glærɪŋ] *adj* **1** BRIGHT : deslumbrante, brillante **2** FLAGRANT, OBVIOUS : flagrante, manifiesto ⟨a glaring error : un error que salta a la vista⟩

glaringly ['glærɪŋli] *adv* ⟨to be glaringly obvious : saltar a la vista⟩

glass ['glæs] *n* **1** : vidrio *m*, cristal *m* ⟨stained glass : vidrio de color⟩ **2** : vaso *m* ⟨a glass of milk : un vaso de leche⟩ **3 glasses** *npl* SPECTACLES : gafas *fpl*, anteojos *mpl*, lentes *mpl*, espejuelos *mpl*

glassblowing ['glæsˌbloːɪŋ] *n* : soplado *m* del vidrio

glassful ['glæsˌfʊl] *n* : vaso *m*, copa *f*

glassware ['glæsˌwær] *n* : cristalería *f*

glassy ['glæsi] *adj* **glassier; -est 1** : vítreo **2** : vidrioso ⟨glassy eyes : ojos vidriosos⟩

glaucoma [glaʊ'koːmə, glɔ-] *n* : glaucoma *m*

glaze¹ ['gleɪz] *vt* **glazed; glazing 1** : ponerle vidrios a (una ventana, etc.) **2** : vidriar (cerámica) **3** : glasear (papel, verduras, etc.)

glaze² *n* : vidriado *m*, glaseado *m*, barniz *m*

glazier ['gleɪʒər] *n* : vidriero *m*, -ra *f*

glazing ['gleɪzɪŋ] *n* : vidrios *mpl*, acristalamiento *m* Spain ⟨double-glazing : doble vidrio, doble acristalamiento⟩

gleam¹ ['gliːm] *vi* : brillar, destellar, relucir

gleam² *n* **1** LIGHT : luz *f* (oscura) **2** GLINT : destello *m*, rayo *m*, vislumbre *f* ⟨a gleam of hope : un rayo de esperanza⟩

glean ['gliːn] *vt* : recoger, espigar

glee ['gliː] *n* : alegría *f*, júbilo *m*, regocijo *m*

gleeful ['gliːfəl] *adj* : lleno de alegría

glen ['glɛn] *n* : cañada *f*

glib ['glɪb] *adj* **glibber; glibbest 1** : simplista ⟨a glib reply : una respuesta simplista⟩ **2** : con mucha labia (dícese de una persona)

glibly ['glɪbli] *adv* : con mucha labia

glide¹ ['glaɪd] *vi* **glided; gliding** : deslizarse (en una superficie), planear (en el aire)

glide² *n* : planeo *m*

glider ['glaɪdər] *n* **1** : planeador *m* (aeronave) **2** : mecedor *m* (tipo de columpio)

glimmer¹ ['glɪmər] *vi* : brillar con luz trémula

glimmer² *n* **1** : luz *f* trémula, luz *f* tenue **2** GLEAM : rayo *m*, vislumbre *f* ⟨a glimmer of understanding : un rayo de entendimiento⟩

glimpse¹ ['glɪmps] *vt* **glimpsed; glimpsing** : vislumbrar, entrever

glimpse² *n* : mirada *f* breve ⟨to catch a glimpse of : alcanzar a ver, vislumbrar⟩

glint¹ ['glɪnt] *vi* GLEAM, SPARKLE : destellar

glint² *n* **1** SPARKLE : destello *m*, centelleo *m* **2 to have a glint in one's eye** : chispearle los ojos a uno

glisten¹ ['glɪsən] *vi* : brillar, centellear

glisten² *n* : brillo *m*, centelleo *m*

glitch ['glɪtʃ] *n* **1** MALFUNCTION : mal funcionamiento *m* **2** SNAG : problema *m*, complicación *f*

glitter¹ ['glɪtər] *vi* **1** SPARKLE : destellar, relucir, brillar **2** FLASH : relampaguear ⟨his eyes glittered in anger : le relampagueaban los ojos de ira⟩

glitter² *n* **1** BRIGHTNESS : brillo *m* **2** : purpurina *f* (para decoración)

glitz ['glɪts] *n* : oropel *m*

gloat ['gloːt] *vi* **to gloat over** : regodearse en

glob ['glɑb] *n* : plasta *f*, masa *f*, grumo *m*

global ['gloːbəl] *adj* **1** FULL, COMPREHENSIVE : global **2** WORLDWIDE : global, mundial — **globally** *adv* — **globalization** [ˌgloːbələ'zeɪʃən] *n*

global warming *n* : calentamiento *m* global

globe ['gloːb] *n* **1** SPHERE : esfera *f*, globo *m* **2** EARTH : globo *m*, Tierra *f* **3** : globo *m* terráqueo (modelo de la Tierra)

globe–trotter ['glo:b,trɑtər] n : trota-mundos mf

globule ['glɑ,bju:l] n : glóbulo m

gloom ['glu:m] n 1 DARKNESS : penum-bra f, oscuridad f 2 MELANCHOLY : melancolía f, tristeza f

gloomily ['glu:məli] adv : tristemente

gloomy ['glu:mi] adj **gloomier; -est** 1 DARK : oscuro, tenebroso ⟨gloomy weather : tiempo gris⟩ 2 MELANCHOLY : melancólico 3 PESSIMISTIC : pesimista 4 DEPRESSING : deprimente, lúgubre

glorification [,glorəfə'keɪʃən] n : glorifi-cación f

glorify ['glorə,faɪ] vt **-fied; -fying** : glorifi-car

glorious ['gloriəs] adj 1 ILLUSTRIOUS : glorioso, ilustre 2 MAGNIFICENT : magnífico, espléndido, maravilloso — **gloriously** adv

glory[1] ['glori] vi **-ried; -rying** EXULT : exultar, regocijarse

glory[2] n, pl **-ries** 1 RENOWN : gloria f, fama f, honor m 2 PRAISE : gloria f ⟨glory to God : gloria a Dios⟩ 3 MAG-NIFICENCE : magnificencia f, esplendor m, gloria f 4 to be in one's glory : estar uno en su gloria

gloss[1] ['glɔs, 'glɑs] vt 1 EXPLAIN : glosar, explicar 2 POLISH : lustrar, pulir 3 to **gloss over** : quitarle importancia a, mi-nimizar

gloss[2] n 1 SHINE : lustre m, brillo m 2 EXPLANATION : glosa f, explicación f breve 3 → glossary

glossary ['glɔsəri, 'glɑ-] n, pl **-ries** : glosa-rio m

glossy ['glɔsi, 'glɑ-] adj **glossier; -est** : brillante, lustroso, satinado (dícese del papel)

glove ['glʌv] n : guante m ⟨boxing glove : guante de boxeo⟩

glove compartment n : guantera f

glow[1] ['glo:] vi 1 SHINE : brillar, res-plandecer 2 BRIM : rebosar ⟨to glow with health : rebosar de salud⟩

glow[2] n 1 BRIGHTNESS : resplandor m, brillo m, luminosidad f 2 FEELING : sensación f (de bienestar), oleada f (de sentimiento) 3 INCANDESCENCE : incandescencia f

glower ['glaʊər] vi : fruncir el ceño

glowworm ['glo:,wərm] n : luciérnaga f

glucose ['glu:,ko:s] n : glucosa f

glue[1] ['glu:] vt **glued; gluing** or **glueing** : pegar con cola

glue[2] n : pegamento m, cola f

gluey ['glu:i] adj **gluier; -est** : pegajoso

glum ['glʌm] adj **glummer; glummest** 1 SULLEN : hosco, sombrío 2 DREARY, GLOOMY : sombrío, triste, melancólico

glut[1] ['glʌt] vt **glutted; glutting** 1 SATIATE : saciar, hartar 2 INUNDAR : inundar (el mercado)

glut[2] n : exceso m, superabundancia f

glutinous ['glu:tənəs] adj STICKY : pega-joso, glutinoso

glutton ['glʌtən] n : glotón m, -tona f

gluttonous ['glʌtənəs] adj : glotón

gluttony ['glʌtəni] n, pl **-tonies** : gloto-nería f, gula f

glycerin or **glycerine** ['glɪsrən, 'glɪ-] n : glicerina f

gnarled ['nɑrld] adj 1 KNOTTY : nudoso 2 TWISTED : retorcido

gnash ['næʃ] vt : hacer rechinar (los dientes)

gnat ['næt] n : jején m

gnaw ['nɔ] vt : roer

gnome ['no:m] n : gnomo m

gnu ['nu:, 'nju:] n, pl **gnu** or **gnus** : ñu m

go[1] ['go:] v **went** ['wɛnt]; **gone** ['gɔn 'gɑn]; **going; goes** ['go:z] vi 1 : ir ⟨to go slow : ir despacio⟩ ⟨to go shopping : ir de compras⟩ ⟨to go to work : ir a trabajar⟩ ⟨to go to school : ir a la escuela⟩ ⟨we went to Spain : fuimos a España⟩ ⟨we went to see a movie : fuimos a ver una película⟩ ⟨you should go (to/and) see her : deberías ir a verla⟩ ⟨we went up/down to the mountains : fuimos a las montañas, fuimos al norte/sur a ver las montañas⟩ ⟨to go for a drive : ir a dar una vuelta en coche⟩ ⟨to go on foot : ir a pie⟩ 2 (used figuratively) : ir ⟨she'll go far : llegará lejos⟩ ⟨I wouldn't go so far as to say that . . . : no diría tanto como que . . .⟩ ⟨this time he's gone too far : esta vez se ha pasado⟩ ⟨to go a long way towards : ayudar en gran medida a⟩ 3 LEAVE : irse, marcharse, salir ⟨let's go! : ¡vámonos!⟩ ⟨the train went on time : el tren salió a tiempo⟩ 4 DISAPPEAR : pa-sarse, irse ⟨her fear is gone : se le ha pa-sado el miedo⟩ ⟨those days have gone : esos días ya pasaron⟩ 5 DIE : morir 6 EXTEND : ir, extenderse, llegar ⟨this road goes to the river : este camino se ex-tiende hasta el río⟩ ⟨to go from top to bottom : ir de arriba abajo⟩ 7 LEAD, CONNECT : dar ⟨that door goes to the cellar : esa puerta da al sótano⟩ 8 FUNC-TION : funcionar, marchar ⟨the car won't go : el coche no funciona⟩ ⟨to get something going : poner algo en mar-cha⟩ 9 SELL : venderse ⟨it goes for $15 : se vende por $15⟩ 10 (to be disposed of) ⟨that one can go : podemos deshacernos de ése⟩ 11 FAIL : fallarse (dícese de la vista, etc.), gastarse (dícese de pilas, etc.), estropearse (dícese de un motor, etc.) 12 GIVE WAY : ceder, romperse (dí-cese de un dique, etc.) 13 PROGRESS : ir, andar, seguir ⟨my exam went well : me fue bien en el examen⟩ ⟨how did the meeting go? : ¿qué tal la reunión?⟩ 14 BECOME : volverse, quedarse ⟨to go crazy : volverse loco⟩ ⟨he's going bald : se está quedando calvo⟩ ⟨the tire went flat : la llanta se desinfló⟩ 15 (describing a condition) ⟨to go hungry : pasar ham-bre⟩ ⟨to go barefoot : ir descalzo⟩ ⟨to go unnoticed : pasar desapercibido⟩ 16 (describing a story, song, etc.) ⟨how does the story go? : ¿qué pasa en el cuento?⟩ ⟨how does the song go? : it goes like this: . . . : ¿cómo es la canción?—es así: . . .⟩ ⟨the legend goes that . . . : cuenta la leyenda que . . ., según (dice) la leyenda . . .⟩ 17 FIT : caber ⟨it will go through the door : cabe por la puerta⟩

18 : pasar (dícese del tiempo) ⟨the time went quickly : el tiempo pasó rápidamente⟩ **19** SOUND : sonar **20 anything goes!** : ¡todo vale! **21 to be good/ready to go** : estar listo **22 to go** : faltar ⟨only 10 days to go : faltan sólo 10 días⟩ ⟨we still have a long way to go : aún nos queda mucho camino por recorrer⟩ **23 to go** : para llevar (dícese de comida, etc.) **24 to go about** DO : hacer **25 to go about** APPROACH, TACKLE : abordar, emprender **26 to go after** PURSUE : perseguir **27 to go against** : ir en contra de **28 to go against** : jugar contra (en deportes) **29 to go ahead** (*to proceed without delay or hesitation*) ⟨go ahead and start without me : empiecen sin mí⟩ ⟨I went ahead and bought it : me decidí y lo compré⟩ ⟨sure, go (right) ahead! : ¡por supuesto!⟩ **30 to go ahead (with)** : seguir adelante (con) **31 to go all out** : hacer lo máximo ⟨he went all out for his wife's birthday : en el cumpleaños de su esposa tiró la casa por la ventana⟩ **32 to go along** PROCEED : ir, marchar **33 to go along** ACQUIESCE : acceder ⟨to go along with something : acceder a algo, aceptar algo⟩ ⟨to go along with someone : cooperar con alguien⟩ **34 to go along with** ⟨the stress that goes along with the job : el estrés que conlleva el trabajo⟩ **35 to go around** : correr (dícese de un rumor, etc.), circular ⟨there's a bug going around : hay un virus dando vueltas por ahí⟩ **36 to go around** ⟨there's enough/plenty to go around : hay para todos⟩ **37 to go at** ATTACK : atacar **38 to go at** : atacar, abordar (un problema, etc.) **39 to go at it** ARGUE, FIGHT : discutir, pelearse **40 to go away** LEAVE : irse **41 to go away** DISAPPEAR : desaparecer **42 to go back** RETURN : volver (a un lugar, un tema, etc.) ⟨he never went back : nunca volvió⟩ ⟨to go back to school : volver a la escuela⟩ **43 to go back** : remontarse ⟨the records go back to 1900 : los registros se remontan a 1900⟩ ⟨we go back a long way : nos conocemos desde hace muchos años⟩ **44 to go back on** : faltar uno a (su promesa) **45 to go back to (doing) something** : volver a hacer algo, reanudar algo ⟨to go back to sleep : volver a dormir⟩ ⟨she went back to work : reanudó el trabajo⟩ ⟨afterwards he went back to reading : después siguió leyendo⟩ **46 to go bad** SPOIL : estropearse, echarse a perder **47 to go beyond** : ir más allá de **48 to go by** PASS : pasar **49 to go by** : guiarse por (una regla, etc.), juzgar por (las apariencias, etc.) **50 to go by** : hacerse llamar ⟨he goes by "Ed" : se hace llamar "Ed"⟩ **51 to go by** STOP BY : pasar por **52 to go down** : hundirse (dícese de un barco), caer (dícese de un avión), caerse (dícese de una persona) **53 to go down** DECREASE : bajar, disminuir **54 to go down** : dejar de funcionar (dícese de un sistema, etc.) **55 to go down** : caer (dícese de un gobierno, etc.) **56 to go**

down SET : ponerse (dícese del sol) **57 to go down** : pasar (dícese de comida) ⟨it went down the wrong way : se me atragantó, se me fue por mal camino⟩ **58 to go down in history** → history **59 to go down well/badly** : caer bien/mal, tener una buena/mala acogida **60 to go for** : interesarse uno en, gustarle a uno (algo, alguien) ⟨I don't go for that : eso no me interesa⟩ **61 to go for** SELECT : decidirse por **62 to go for** ACCEPT : aceptar **63 to go for** ATTACK : atacar **64 to go for** PURSUE : ir tras, ir a por *Spain* **65 to go for** : ir por ⟨that goes for you, too! : ¡también va por ti!⟩ **66 to go in** : esconderse (dícese del sol o de la luna) **67 to go in on** ⟨we both/all went in on the gift together : el regalo lo compramos a medias/entre todos⟩ **68 to go in for** LIKE : interesarse uno, gustarle a uno (algo) **69 to go into** : entrar en ⟨to go into action/effect : entrar en acción/vigor⟩ ⟨to go into hiding : esconderse⟩ **70 to go into** DISCUSS : entrar en **71 to go into** LOOK INTO : investigar **72 to go into** : dedicarse a (una profesión) **73 to go off** : estallar, explotar (dícese de una bomba, etc.), dispararse (dícese de una pistola, etc.) **74 to go off** SOUND : sonar **75 to go off** : echarse a perder (dícese de la comida, etc.) **76 to go off** TURN OFF : apagarse **77 to go off on** *fam* SCOLD : regañar **78 to go on** CONTINUE : seguir, continuar ⟨life goes on : la vida sigue⟩ ⟨we can't go on like this : no podemos seguir así⟩ ⟨we went on to Chicago : seguimos el viaje a Chicago, continuamos nuestro camino a Chicago⟩ ⟨she went on working : siguió trabajando⟩ ⟨she went on to say that . . . : pasó a decir que . . .⟩ ⟨to go on to become : llegar/pasar a ser⟩ **79 to go on** LAST : durar **80 to go on** HAPPEN : pasar, ocurrir ⟨what's going on? : ¿qué pasa?⟩ **81 to go on** RAMBLE : no parar de hablar **82 to go on** : guiarse por (pruebas, etc.) **83 to go on (ahead)** : ir adelante, adelantarse **84 to go out** LEAVE : salir **85 to go out** : apagarse ⟨the power went out : se fue la electricidad⟩ **86 to go out** : bajar (dícese de la marea) **87 to go out** : emitirse (dícese de un anuncio, etc.) **88 to go out with** DATE : salir con **89 to go over** EXAMINE, REVIEW : examinar, repasar **90 to go over to** : pasarse a (la competencia, etc.) **91 to go over to** APPROACH : acercarse a **92 to go over well/badly** : caer bien/mal, tener una buena/mala acogida **93 to go there** *fam* ⟨let's not go there : no quiero hablar/pensar de eso⟩ **94 to go through** : penetrar, atravesar **95 to go through** USE UP : gastar, agotar **96 to go through** SEARCH : registrar, revolver en **97 to go through** : pasar por (dificultades, etapas, etc.) **98 to go through** PERFORM : hacer **99 to go through** : ser aprobado (dícese de un proyecto de ley, etc.) **100 to go through someone's head/mind** : pasársele por la cabeza/mente a alguien

101 to go through with : llevar a cabo **102 to go to** : otorgarse a, transmitirse a ⟨the prize went to . . . : el premio se lo llevó . . .⟩ **103 to go to** (*to begin to be in*) ⟨to go to sleep : dormirse⟩ ⟨to go to war : entrar en guerra⟩ **104 to go together** MATCH : combinar, hacer juego, armonizar **105 to go to show/prove** : demostrar **106 to go to trouble/expense** (etc.) ⟨he went to a lot of trouble : se esmeró mucho⟩ ⟨they went to great expense : gastaron mucho⟩ **107 to go towards** : contribuir a **108 to go under** FOUNDER : hundirse **109 to go up** RISE, INCREASE : subir **110 to go up** : levantarse ⟨dícese de un edificio⟩ **111 to go with** MATCH : armonizar con, hacer juego con, ir bien con **112 to go with** CHOOSE : elegir, decidirse por **113 to go without** MAKE DO : arreglárselas (sin algo) **114 to go without something** : prescindir de algo — *v aux* **to be going to** : ir a ⟨I'm going to write a letter : voy a escribir una carta⟩ ⟨it's not going to last : no va a durar⟩

go² *n, pl* **goes 1** ATTEMPT : intento *m* ⟨to have a go at : intentar, probar⟩ **2** SUCCESS : éxito *m* **3** ENERGY : energía *f*, empuje *m* ⟨to be on the go : no parar, no descansar⟩

goad¹ ['goːd] *vt* : aguijonear (un animal), incitar (a una persona)

goad² *n* : aguijón *m*

go–ahead *n* APPROVAL : luz *f* verde

goal ['goːl] *n* **1** : portería *f*, arco *m*, marco *m* (en deportes) **2** : gol *m* (en deportes) ⟨to score a goal : anotar un gol⟩ **3** AIM, OBJECTIVE : meta *m*; objetivo *m*

goalie ['goːli] → **goalkeeper**

goalkeeper ['goːlˌkiːpər] *n* : portero *m*, -ra *f*; guardameta *mf*; arquero *m*, -ra *f*

goalpost ['goːlˌpoːst] *n* : poste *m* (de la portería)

goaltender ['goːlˌtɛndər] → **goalkeeper**

goat ['goːt] *n* **1** : cabra *f* (hembra) **2 billy goat** : macho *m* cabrío, chivo *m*

goatee [goːˈtiː] *n* : barbita *f* de chivo; perilla *f*; pera *f Arg, Chile, Uru*; piocha *f Mex*

goatskin ['goːtˌskɪn] *n* : piel *f* de cabra

gob ['gɑb] *n* : masa *f*, grumo *m*

gobble ['gɑbəl] *v* **-bled; -bling** *vt* **to gobble up/down** : tragar, engullir — *vi* : hacer ruidos de pavo

gobbledygook ['gɑbəldiˌgʊk, -ˌguːk] *n* GIBBERISH : jerigonza *f*

go–between ['goːbɪˌtwiːn] *n* : intermediario *m*, -ria *f*; mediador *m*, -dora *f*

goblet ['gɑblət] *n* : copa *f*

goblin ['gɑblən] *n* : duende *m*, trasgo *m*

god ['gɑd, 'gɔd] *n* **1** : dios *m* **2 God** : Dios *m*

godchild ['gɑd,ʧaɪld, 'gɔd-] *n, pl* **-children** : ahijado *m*, -da *f*

goddaughter ['gɑd,dɔtər, 'gɔd-] *n* : ahijada *f*

goddess ['gɑdəs, 'gɔ-] *n* : diosa *f*

godfather ['gɑd,fɑðər, 'gɔd-] *n* : padrino *m*

godless ['gɑdləs, 'gɔd-] *adj* : ateo

godlike ['gɑd,laɪk, 'gɔd-] *adj* : divino

godly ['gɑdli, 'gɔd-] *adj* **godlier; -est 1** DIVINE : divino **2** DEVOUT, PIOUS : piadoso, devoto, beato

godmother ['gɑd,mʌðər, 'gɔd-] *n* : madrina *f*

godparent ['gɑd,pærənt, 'gɔd-] *n* : padrino *m*, madrina *f* ⟨her godparents : sus padrinos⟩

godsend ['gɑd,sɛnd, 'gɔd-] *n* : bendición *f*, regalo *m* divino

godson ['gɑd,sʌn, 'gɔd-] *n* : ahijado *m*

goes → **go**

go–getter ['goːˌgɛtər] *n* : persona *f* ambiciosa, buscavidas *mf fam*

goggle ['gɑgəl] *vi* **-gled; -gling** : mirar con ojos desorbitados

goggles ['gɑgəlz] *npl* : gafas *fpl* (protectoras), anteojos *mpl*

going [ˌgoːɪŋ] *n* **1** DEPARTURE : salida *f*, partida *f* **2** (*describing progress*) ⟨it's been slow going : las cosas van despacio⟩ ⟨it's going to be tough going : va a ser difícil⟩ **3 comings and goings** → **coming²**

goings–on [ˌgoːɪŋzˈɑn, -ˈɔn] *npl* : sucesos *mpl*, ocurrencias *fpl*

goiter ['gɔɪtər] *n* : bocio *m*

gold¹ ['goːld] *adj* **1** : (hecho) de oro **2** : dorado, de color oro

gold² *n* : oro *m*

golden ['goːldən] *adj* **1** : (hecho) de oro **2** : dorado, de color oro ⟨golden hair : pelo rubio⟩ **3** FLOURISHING, PROSPEROUS : dorado, próspero ⟨golden years : años dorados⟩ **4** FAVORABLE : favorable, excelente ⟨a golden opportunity : una excelente oportunidad⟩

goldenrod ['goːldən,rɑd] *n* : vara *f* de oro

golden rule *n* : regla *f* de oro

goldfinch ['goːld,fɪnʧ] *n* : jilguero *m*

goldfish ['goːld,fɪʃ] *n* : pez *m* de colores

gold mine *n* : mina *f* de oro

goldsmith ['goːld,smɪθ] *n* : orífice *mf*, orfebre *mf*

golf¹ ['gɑlf, 'gɔlf] *vi* : jugar (al) golf

golf² *n* : golf *m*

golf ball *n* : pelota *f* de golf

golf cart *n* : carrito *m* de golf

golf club *n* **1** : palo *m* de golf (implemento) **2** : club *m* de golf (organización)

golf course *n* : campo *m* de golf, cancha *f* de golf

golfer ['gɑlfər, 'gɔl-] *n* : golfista *mf*

gondola ['gɑndələ, gɑnˈdoːlə] *n* : góndola *f*

gone ['gɔn] *adj* **1** DEAD : muerto **2** PAST : pasado, ido ⟨those days are gone : esos días ya pasaron⟩ ⟨her fear is gone : se le ha pasado el miedo⟩ **3** LOST : perdido, desaparecido ⟨my car is gone! : ¡mi coche no está!⟩ **4 to be far gone** : estar muy avanzado **5 to be gone on** : estar loco por

goner ['gɔnər] *n* **to be a goner** : estar en las últimas

gong ['gɔŋ, 'gɑŋ] *n* : gong *m*

gonorrhea [ˌgɑnəˈriːə] *n* : gonorrea *f*

good[1] ['gʊd] adv 1 (used as an intensifier)
: bien ⟨a good strong rope : una cuerda
bien fuerte⟩ 2 WELL : bien

good[2] adj **better** ['bɛt̬ər]; **best** ['bɛst] 1
(of high quality) : bueno ⟨a good restau-
rant : un buen restaurante⟩ ⟨the book is
no good : el libro es malísimo⟩ ⟨in good
condition : en buenas condiciones⟩
⟨keep up the good work! : ¡buen trabajo!
sigue así⟩ 2 ACCEPTABLE : aceptable 3
PLEASANT : bueno, agradable ⟨good
weather : buen tiempo⟩ ⟨the sauce is
good : la salsa está buena⟩ ⟨that dress
looks good on you : se ve vestido te queda
bien⟩ ⟨to have a good time : divertirse⟩
⟨have a good day! : ¡qué te vaya bien!⟩ 4
FORTUNATE : bueno ⟨good news : buenas noticias⟩ ⟨good luck : buena suerte⟩
⟨it's a good thing that . . . : menos mal
que . . .⟩ 5 SUITABLE : bueno ⟨a good
day for a picnic : un buen día para ir de
picnic⟩ ⟨these tires are no good : estas
llantas no sirven⟩ 6 SOUND : bueno, sensato ⟨good advice : buenos consejos⟩
⟨with good reason : con razón⟩ 7 PROM-
ISING : bueno ⟨a good deal : un buen
negocio⟩ ⟨a good bet : una apuesta se-
gura⟩ 8 HEALTHY : bueno ⟨good for a
cold : bueno para los resfriados⟩ ⟨it's
good for you : es bueno para uno⟩ ⟨a
good diet : una buena alimentación⟩ ⟨to
be in good health : estar bien de salud⟩
⟨I'm not feeling very good : no me siento
bien⟩ 9 FULL : completo, entero ⟨a good
hour : una hora entera⟩ ⟨to get a good
night's sleep : dormir por la noche⟩ 10
THOROUGH : bueno ⟨a good kick : una
buena patada⟩ ⟨take a good look at it
: míralo bien⟩ ⟨we had a good laugh
: nos reímos mucho⟩ 11 CONSIDERABLE
: bueno, bastante ⟨a good many people
: muchísima gente, un buen número de
gente⟩ 12 ATTRACTIVE, DESIRABLE
: bueno ⟨a good salary/price : un buen
sueldo/precio⟩ 13 (referring to status)
: bueno ⟨a good family : una buena fami-
lia⟩ 14 APPROVING : bueno ⟨good reviews : buena crítica⟩ 15 KIND, VIRTU-
OUS : bueno, amable ⟨she's a good
person : es buena gente⟩ ⟨that's good of
you! : ¡qué amable!⟩ ⟨good deeds : buenas obras⟩ ⟨the good guys : los buenos⟩
16 CLOSE : íntimo ⟨we're good friends
: somos muy amigos⟩ 17 WELL-BE-
HAVED : bueno ⟨be good : sé bueno⟩ 18
LOYAL, FAITHFUL : bueno, fiel 19
(within bounds) : bueno (en deportes) 20
SKILLED : bueno, hábil ⟨to be good at
: tener facilidad para⟩ ⟨a good cook : un
buen cocinero⟩ ⟨he's good with children
: es bueno con los niños⟩ 21 PLEASED,
CHEERFUL : bueno ⟨in a good mood : de
buen humor⟩ ⟨helping others makes me
feel good : me siento bien ayudando a los
demás⟩ 22 SATISFIED : satisfecho ⟨no
thanks—I'm good : no, gracias—estoy
bien⟩ 23 FRESH : fresco 24 FUNNY
: gracioso ⟨she's always good for a laugh
: es muy divertida⟩ ⟨he said he didn't
know? that's a good one : ¿dijo que no lo

sabía? no me hagas reír⟩ 25 (in greetings) : bueno ⟨good morning : buenos
días⟩ ⟨good afternoon/evening : buenas
tardes⟩ ⟨good night : buenas noches⟩ 26
(used as a response) ⟨I'm ready—good,
let's go : estoy listo—bueno, vamos⟩ 27
as good as NEARLY : casi 28 **as good
as it gets** fam ⟨this is as good as it gets
: mejor imposible, no hay mejor⟩ 29
good and (used for emphasis) ⟨good and
hot : muy caliente⟩ ⟨I hit him good and
hard : le pegué bien duro⟩ ⟨when I'm
good and ready : cuando me dé la gana⟩
30 **good God/heavens!** : ¡Dios mío! 31
good old : el bueno de, la buena de
⟨good old Carl : el bueno de Carl⟩ 32 **to
be good about** ⟨she's very good about
calling us : nunca se olvida de llamar-
nos⟩ ⟨I'm trying to be better about exer-
cising : estoy tratando de hacer más ejer-
cicio⟩ 33 **to be good for** fam ⟨he's
good for the money : seguro que te pa-
gará⟩ 34 **to be good (for/until)** : valer
(por/hasta) ⟨good for one free meal
: vale por una comida gratis⟩ ⟨the car is
good for a few more years : al carro le
quedan unos años más⟩ 35 **to be good
to go** fam : estar listo 36 **too good to
be true** : demasiado bueno para ser
cierto 37 **to make good** : tener éxito 38
to make good on : cumplir con

good[3] n 1 RIGHT : bien m ⟨to do good
: hacer el bien⟩ ⟨to be up to no good
: estar tramando algo⟩ 2 GOODNESS
: bondad f 3 BENEFIT : bien m, provecho
m ⟨it's for your own good : es por tu propio bien⟩ ⟨for the common good : por el
bien común⟩ 4 **goods** npl PROPERTY
: efectos mpl personales, posesiones fpl 5
goods npl WARES : mercancía f, mercadería f, artículos mpl ⟨consumer goods
: bienes de consumo⟩ 6 **for ~** : para
siempre 7 **the good** : los buenos 8 **to be
in good with someone** fam : estar a
bien con alguien 9 **to be no good** : no
servir (para nada) 10 **to deliver the
goods** fam : cumplir con lo prometido
11 **to get/have the goods on** fam
: obtener/tener pruebas contra

good-bye or **good-by** ['gʊd'baɪ] n : adiós
m

good-for-nothing ['gʊdfər,nʌθɪŋ]   n
: inútil mf; haragán m, -gana f; holgazán
m, -zana f

Good Friday n : Viernes m Santo

good-hearted ['gʊd'hɑrt̬əd] adj : bondadoso, benévolo, de buen corazón

good-looking ['gʊd'lʊkɪŋ] adj : bello,
bonito, guapo

goodly ['gʊdli] adj **goodlier; -est** : considerable, importante ⟨a goodly number
: un número considerable⟩

good-natured ['gʊd'neɪtʃərd] adj : amigable, amistoso, bonachón fam

goodness ['gʊdnəs] n 1 : bondad f 2
thank goodness! : ¡gracias a Dios!,
¡menos mal!

good-tempered ['gʊd'tɛmpərd] adj : de
buen genio

goodwill [ˌgʊdˈwɪl] n **1** BENEVOLENCE : benevolencia f, buena voluntad f **2** : buen nombre m (de comercios), renombre m comercial

goody [ˈgʊdi] n, pl **goodies** : cosa f rica para comer, golosina f

gooey [ˈguːi] adj **gooier; gooiest** : pegajoso

goof¹ [ˈguːf] vi fam **1** or **to goof up** BLUNDER : cometer un error, equivocarse **2 to goof off** : holgazanear **3 to goof around** : hacer tonterías

goof² n **1** fam : bobo m, -ba f; tonto m, -ta f **2** BLUNDER : error m, planchazo m fam

goofy [ˈguːfi] adj **goofier; -est** SILLY : tonto, bobo

goose [ˈguːs] n, pl **geese** [ˈgiːs] : ganso m, -sa f; ánsar m; oca f

gooseberry [ˈguːsˌbɛri, ˈguːz-] n, pl **-berries** : grosella f espinosa

goose bumps npl : carne f de gallina

gooseflesh [ˈguːsˌflɛʃ] → **goose bumps**

goose pimples → **goose bumps**

gopher [ˈgoːfər] n : taltuza f

gore¹ [ˈgor] vt **gored; goring** : cornear

gore² n BLOOD : sangre f

gorge¹ [ˈgorʤ] vt **gorged; gorging** **1** SATIATE : saciar, hartar **2 to gorge oneself** : hartarse, atiborrarse, atracarse fam

gorge² n RAVINE : desfiladero m

gorgeous [ˈgorʤəs] adj : hermoso, espléndido, magnífico

gorilla [gəˈrɪlə] n : gorila m

gory [ˈgori] adj **gorier; -est** BLOODY : sangriento

gosh [ˈgɑʃ, ˈgɔʃ] interj : ¡caramba!

gosling [ˈgɑzlɪŋ, ˈgɔz-] n : ansarino m

gospel [ˈgɑspəl] n **1** or **Gospel** : evangelio m ⟨the four Gospels : los cuatro evangelios⟩ **2 the gospel truth** : el evangelio, la pura verdad

gossamer [ˈgɑsəmər, ˈgɑzə-] adj : tenue, sutil ⟨gossamer wings : alas tenues⟩

gossip¹ [ˈgɑsɪp] vi : chismear, contar chismes

gossip² n **1** fam : chismoso m, -sa f; cotilla mf Spain fam (persona) **2** RUMOR : chisme m, rumor m

gossiper [ˈgɑsɪpər] n GOSSIP : chismoso m, -sa f; cotilla mf Spain fam

gossipy [ˈgɑsɪpi] adj : chismoso

got → **get**

Gothic [ˈgɑθɪk] adj : gótico

gotten → **get**

gouge¹ [ˈgauʤ] vt **gouged; gouging** **1** : excavar **2** SWINDLE : estafar, extorsionar

gouge² n **1** CHISEL : formón m **2** GROOVE : ranura f, hoyo m (hecho por un formón)

goulash [ˈguːˌlɑʃ, -ˌlæʃ] n : estofado m, guiso m al estilo húngaro

gourd [ˈgord, ˈgʊrd] n : calabaza f

gourmand [ˈgʊrˌmɑnd] n **1** GLUTTON : glotón m, -tona f **2** → **gourmet**

gourmet [ˈgʊrˌmeɪ, gʊrˈmeɪ] n : gourmet mf; gastrónomo m, -ma f

gout [ˈgaʊt] n : gota f

govern [ˈgʌvərn] vt **1** RULE : gobernar **2** CONTROL, DETERMINE : determinar, controlar, guiar **3** RESTRAIN : dominar (las emociones, etc.) — vi : gobernar

governess [ˈgʌvərnəs] n : institutriz f

government [ˈgʌvərmənt] n : gobierno m

governmental [ˌgʌvərˈmɛntəl] adj : gubernamental, gubernativo

governor [ˈgʌvənər, ˈgʌvərnər] n **1** : gobernador m, -dora f (de un estado, etc.) **2** : regulador m (de una máquina)

governorship [ˈgʌvənərˌʃɪp, ˈgʌvərnər-] n : cargo m de gobernador

gown [ˈgaʊn] n **1** : vestido m ⟨evening gown : traje de fiesta⟩ **2** : toga f (de magistrados, clérigos, etc.)

GPS [ˌdʒiːˈpiːˈɛs] n (Global Positioning System) : GPS m

grab¹ [ˈgræb] v **grabbed; grabbing** vt SNATCH : agarrar, arrebatar — vi : agarrarse

grab² npl **1 to make a grab for** : tratar de agarrar **2 up for grabs** : disponible, libre

grace¹ [ˈgreɪs] vt **graced; gracing** **1** HONOR : honrar **2** ADORN : adornar, embellecer

grace² n **1** : gracia f ⟨by the grace of God : por la gracia de Dios⟩ **2** BLESSING : bendición f (de la mesa) **3** RESPITE : plazo m, gracia f ⟨a five days' grace (period) : un plazo de cinco días, un período de gracia de cinco días⟩ **4** GRACIOUSNESS : gentileza f, cortesía f **5** ELEGANCE : elegancia f, gracia f **6 to be in the good graces of** : estar en buenas relaciones con **7 with good grace** : de buena gana

graceful [ˈgreɪsfəl] adj : lleno de gracia, garboso, grácil

gracefully [ˈgreɪsfəli] adv : con gracia, con garbo

gracefulness [ˈgreɪsfəlnəs] n : gracilidad f, apostura f, gallardía f

graceless [ˈgreɪsləs] adj **1** DISCOURTEOUS : descortés **2** CLUMSY, INELEGANT : torpe, desgarbado, poco elegante

gracious [ˈgreɪʃəs] adj : cortés, gentil, cordial

graciously [ˈgreɪʃəsli] adv : gentilmente

graciousness [ˈgreɪʃəsnəs] n : gentileza f

gradation [greɪˈdeɪʃən, grə-] n : gradación f

grade¹ [ˈgreɪd] vt **graded; grading** **1** SORT : clasificar **2** LEVEL : nivelar **3** : calificar (exámenes, alumnos)

grade² n **1** QUALITY : categoría f, calidad f **2** RANK : grado m, rango m (militar) **3** YEAR : grado m, curso m, año m ⟨sixth grade : el sexto grado⟩ **4** MARK : nota f, calificación f (en educación) **5** SLOPE : cuesta f, pendiente f, gradiente f

grade school → **elementary school**

gradient [ˈgreɪdiənt] n : gradiente f

gradual [ˈgræʤʊəl] adj : gradual, paulatino

gradually [ˈgræʤʊəli, ˈgræʤəli] adv : gradualmente, poco a poco

graduate¹ [ˈgræʤʊˌeɪt] v **-ated; -ating** vi : graduarse, licenciarse — vt : graduar ⟨a graduated thermometer : un termómetro graduado⟩

graduate² ['grædʒʊət] *adj* : de postgrado ⟨graduate course : curso de postgrado⟩

graduate³ *n* 1 : licenciado *m*, -da *f*; graduado *m*, -da *f* (de la universidad) 2 : bachiller *mf* (de la escuela secundaria)

graduate student *n* : postgraduado *m*, -da *f*

graduation [ˌgrædʒʊ'eɪʃən] *n* : graduación *f*

graffiti [grə'fiːti, græ-] *npl* : pintadas *fpl*, graffiti *mpl*

graft¹ ['græft] *vt* : injertar

graft² *n* 1 : injerto *m* ⟨skin graft : injerto cutáneo⟩ 2 CORRUPTION : soborno *m* (político), ganancia *f* ilegal

grain ['greɪn] *n* 1 : grano *m* ⟨a grain of corn : un grano de maíz⟩ ⟨like a grain of sand : como grano de arena⟩ 2 CEREALS : cereales *mpl* 3 : veta *f*, vena *f*, grano *m* (de madera) 4 SPECK, TRACE : pizca *f*, ápice *m* ⟨a grain of truth : una pizca de verdad⟩ 5 grano *m* (unidad de peso) 6 **to go against the grain** : ir a contrapelo

grainy ['greɪni] *adj* **grainier; -est** : granuloso, granulado, granular

gram ['græm] *n* : gramo *m*

grammar ['græmər] *n* : gramática *f*

grammar school → elementary school

grammatical [grə'mætɪkəl] *adj* : gramatical — **grammatically** [-kli] *adv*

gran ['græn] → **grandma**

granary ['greɪnəri, 'græ-] *n*, *pl* **-ries** : granero *m*

grand ['grænd] *adj* 1 FOREMOST : grande 2 IMPRESSIVE : impresionante, magnífico ⟨a grand view : una vista magnífica⟩ 3 LAVISH : grandioso, suntuoso, lujoso ⟨to live in a grand manner : vivir a lo grande⟩ 4 FABULOUS : fabuloso, magnífico ⟨to have a grand time : pasarlo estupendamente, pasarlo en grande⟩ 5 **grand total** : total *m*, suma *f* total

grandchild ['grænd,tʃaɪld] *n*, *pl* **-children** : nieto *m*, -ta *f*

granddad ['grænd,dæd] → **grandpa**

granddaughter ['grænd,dɔtər] *n* : nieta *f*

grandeur ['grændʒər] *n* : grandiosidad *f*, esplendor *m*

grandfather ['grænd,fɑðər] *n* : abuelo *m*

grandiose ['grændi,oːs, ˌgrændi'-] *adj* 1 IMPOSING : imponente, grandioso 2 POMPOUS : pomposo, presuntuoso

grandma ['græn,mɑ, -,mɔ] *n fam* : abuelita *f fam*, nana *f fam*, yaya *f fam*

grandmother ['grænd,mʌðər] *n* : abuela *f*

grandpa ['græm,pɑ, -,pɔ] *n fam* : abuelito *m fam*, yayo *m fam*

grandparents ['grænd,pærənts] *npl* : abuelos *mpl*

grand piano *n* : piano *m* de cola

grandson ['grænd,sʌn] *n* : nieto *m*

grandstand ['grænd,stænd] *n* : tribuna *f*

granite ['grænɪt] *n* : granito *m*

granny ['græni] *n*, *pl* **-nies** → **grandma**

grant¹ ['grænt] *vt* 1 ALLOW : conceder ⟨to grant a request : conceder una petición⟩ 2 BESTOW : conceder, dar, otorgar ⟨to grant a favor : otorgar un favor⟩ 3 ADMIT : reconocer, admitir ⟨I'll grant that

he's clever : reconozco que es listo⟩ 4 **to take for granted** : dar (algo) por sentado

grant² *n* 1 GRANTING : concesión *f*, otorgamiento *m* 2 SCHOLARSHIP : beca *f* 3 SUBSIDY : subvención *f*

granular ['grænjʊlər] *adj* : granular

granulated ['grænjʊˌleɪtəd] *adj* : granulado

grape ['greɪp] *n* : uva *f*

grapefruit ['greɪp,fruːt] *n* : toronja *f*, pomelo *m*

grapevine ['greɪp,vaɪn] *n* 1 : vid *f*, parra *f* 2 **through the grapevine** : por vías secretas ⟨I heard it through the grapevine : me lo contaron⟩

graph ['græf] *n* : gráfica *f*, gráfico *m*

graphic¹ ['græfɪk] *adj* VIVID : vívido, gráfico

graphic² *n* 1 GRAPH, CHART : gráfica *f*, gráfico *m* 2 **graphics** *npl* : gráficos *mpl*, infografía *f*

graphically ['græfɪkli] *adv* : gráficamente

graphic arts *npl* : artes *fpl* gráficas

graphite ['græ,faɪt] *n* : grafito *m*

grapple ['græpəl] *v* **-pled; -pling** *vt* GRIP : agarrar (con un garfio) — *vi* STRUGGLE : forcejear, luchar (con un problema, etc.)

grasp¹ ['græsp] *vt* 1 GRIP, SEIZE : agarrar, asir 2 COMPREHEND : entender, comprender — *vi* **to grasp at** : aprovechar

grasp² *n* 1 GRIP : agarre *m* 2 CONTROL : control *m*, garras *fpl* 3 REACH : alcance *m* ⟨within your grasp : a su alcance⟩ 4 UNDERSTANDING : comprensión *f*, entendimiento *m*

grasping ['græspɪŋ] *adj* : avaricioso

grass ['græs] *n* 1 : hierba *f* (planta) 2 PASTURE : pasto *m*, zacate *m CA, Mex* 3 LAWN : césped *m*, pasto *m*

grasshopper ['græs,hɑpər] *n* : saltamontes *m*

grassland ['græs,lænd] *n* : pradera *f*

grassroots ['græs,ruːts, -,rʊts] *adj* : de base ⟨at the grassroots level : a nivel de base⟩ ⟨a grassroots movement : un movimiento de base⟩

grass roots *npl* : las bases ⟨the party's grass roots : las bases del partido⟩

grassy ['græsi] *adj* **grassier; -est** : cubierto de hierba

grate¹ ['greɪt] *v* **grated; -ing** *vt* 1 : rallar (en cocina) 2 SCRAPE : rascar 3 **to grate one's teeth** : hacer rechinar los dientes — *vi* 1 RASP, SQUEAK : chirriar 2 IRRITATE : irritar ⟨it grates on me : me crispa⟩ ⟨to grate on one's nerves : crisparle los nervios a uno⟩

grate² *n* 1 : parrilla *f* (para cocinar) 2 GRATING : reja *f*, rejilla *f*, verja *f* (en una ventana)

grateful ['greɪtfəl] *adj* : agradecido

gratefully ['greɪtfəli] *adv* : con agradecimiento

gratefulness ['greɪtfəlnəs] *n* : gratitud *f*, agradecimiento *m*

grater ['greɪtər] *n* : rallador *m*

gratification [ˌgrætəfə'keɪʃən] *n* : gratificación *f*

gratify ['græɟə,faɪ] vt **-fied; -fying** 1 PLEASE : complacer 2 SATISFY : satisfacer, gratificar

grating ['greɪtɪŋ] n : reja f, rejilla f

gratis[1] ['græṭəs, 'greɪ-] adv : gratis, gratuitamente

gratis[2] adj : gratis, gratuito

gratitude ['græṭə,tu:d, -,tju:d] n : gratitud f, agradecimiento m

gratuitous [grə'tu:əṭəs] adj UNWARRANTED : gratuito, injustificado — **gratuitously** [grə'tu:əṭəsli] adv

gratuity [grə'tu:əṭi] n, pl **-ities** TIP : propina f

grave[1] ['greɪv] adj **graver; gravest** 1 IMPORTANT : grave, de mucha gravedad 2 SERIOUS, SOLEMN : grave, serio

grave[2] n : tumba f, sepultura f

gravel ['grævəl] n : grava f, gravilla f

gravelly ['grævəli] adj 1 : de grava 2 HARSH : áspero (dícese de la voz)

gravely ['greɪvli] adv : gravemente

gravestone ['greɪv,sto:n] n : lápida f

graveyard ['greɪv,jɑrd] n CEMETERY : cementerio m, panteón m, camposanto m

gravitate ['grævə,teɪt] vi **-tated; -tating** : gravitar

gravitation [,grævə'teɪʃən] n : gravitación f

gravitational [,grævə'teɪʃənəl] adj : gravitacional

gravity ['grævəṭi] n, pl **-ties** 1 SERIOUSNESS : gravedad f, seriedad f 2 : gravedad f ⟨the law of gravity : la ley de la gravedad⟩

gravy ['greɪvi] n, pl **-vies** : salsa f (preparada con el jugo de la carne asada)

gray[1] ['greɪ] vt : hacer gris — vi : encanecer, ponerse gris

gray[2] adj 1 : gris (dícese del color) 2 : cano, canoso ⟨gray hair : pelo canoso⟩ ⟨to go gray : volverse cano⟩ 3 DISMAL, GLOOMY : gris, triste

gray[3] n : gris m

grayish ['greɪɪʃ] adj : grisáceo

graze ['greɪz] v **grazed; grazing** vi : pastar, pacer — vt 1 : pastorear (ganado) 2 BRUSH : rozar 3 SCRATCH : raspar

grease[1] ['gri:s, 'gri:z] vt **greased; greasing** : engrasar, lubricar

grease[2] n : grasa f

greasy ['gri:si, -zi] adj **greasier; -est** 1 : grasiento 2 OILY : graso, grasoso

great ['greɪt] adj 1 LARGE : grande ⟨a great mountain : una montaña grande⟩ ⟨a great crowd : una gran muchedumbre⟩ ⟨a great big house : una casa grandísima⟩ ⟨a great success : un gran éxito⟩ 2 EXTREME, INTENSE : grande, intenso, fuerte ⟨with great care/difficulty : con gran cuidado/dificultad⟩ ⟨in great pain : muy dolorido⟩ ⟨there's no great hurry : no hay prisa⟩ ⟨a great admirer of : un gran admirador de⟩ 3 IMPORTANT : grande ⟨a great poet : un gran poeta⟩ ⟨great works of art : grandes obras de arte⟩ 4 EXCELLENT, TERRIFIC : excelente, estupendo, fabuloso ⟨to have a great time : pasarlo en grande⟩ ⟨a great movie : una película estupenda⟩ ⟨he's

great at soccer : juega muy bien al fútbol⟩ ⟨you look great! : ¡te ves muy bien!⟩ 5 : bis- ⟨great-grandson : bisabuelo/bisnieto⟩ ⟨great niece : sobrina nieta⟩ ⟨great-great-grandmother : tatarabuela⟩ 6 **a great deal (of)** : mucho, un montón (de) 7 **a great while** : mucho tiempo 8 **great!** : ¡qué bien!

great–aunt [,greɪt'ænt, -'ant] n : tía f abuela

greater ['greɪṭər] (*comparative of* **great**) : mayor

greatest ['greɪṭəst] (*superlative of* **great**) : el mayor, la mayor

great–grandchild [,greɪt'grænd-,ʧaɪld] n, pl **-children** [-,ʧɪldrən] : bisnieto m, -ta f

great–grandfather [,greɪt'grænd-,fɑðər] n : bisabuelo m

great–grandmother [,greɪt'grænd-,mʌðər] n : bisabuela f

greatly ['greɪtli] adv 1 MUCH : mucho, sumamente ⟨to be greatly improved : haber mejorado mucho⟩ 2 VERY : muy ⟨greatly superior : muy superior⟩

greatness ['greɪtnəs] n : grandeza f

great–uncle [,greɪt'ʌŋkəl] n : tío m abuelo

grebe ['gri:b] n : somorgujo m

greed ['gri:d] n 1 AVARICE : avaricia f, codicia f 2 GLUTTONY : glotonería f, gula f

greedily ['gri:dəli] adv : con avaricia, con gula

greediness ['gri:dinəs] → **greed**

greedy ['gri:di] adj **greedier; -est** 1 AVARICIOUS : codicioso, avaricioso 2 GLUTTONOUS : glotón

Greek ['gri:k] n 1 : griego m, -ga f 2 : griego m (idioma) — **Greek** adj

green[1] ['gri:n] adj 1 : verde (dícese del color) 2 UNRIPE : verde, inmaduro 3 INEXPERIENCED : verde, novato

green[2] n 1 : verde m 2 **greens** npl VEGETABLES : verduras fpl

greenback ['gri:n,bæk] n fam : billete m (dinero)

green card n : permiso m de residencia y trabajo

greenery ['gri:nəri] n, pl **-eries** : plantas fpl verdes, vegetación f

greengrocer ['gri:n,gro:sər] n : verdulero m, -ra f

greenhorn ['gri:n,hɔrn] n : novato m, -ta f

greenhouse ['gri:n,haʊs] n : invernadero m

greenhouse effect : efecto m invernadero

greenish ['gri:nɪʃ] adj : verdoso

Greenlander ['gri:n,ləndər, -,læn-] n : groenlandés m, -desa f

greenness ['gri:nnəs] n 1 : verdor m 2 INEXPERIENCE : inexperiencia f

green thumb n **to have a green thumb** : tener buena mano para las plantas

greet ['gri:t] vt 1 : saludar ⟨to greet a friend : saludar a un amigo⟩ 2 : acoger, recibir ⟨they greeted him with boos : lo recibieron con abucheos⟩

greeting ['gri:tɪŋ] n 1 : saludo m 2 **greetings** npl REGARDS : saludos mpl, recuerdos mpl

greeting card *n* : tarjeta *f* de felicitación

gregarious [grɪˈgæriəs] *adj* : gregario (dícese de los animales), sociable (dícese de las personas) — **gregariously** *adv*

gregariousness [grɪˈgæriəsnəs] *n* : sociabilidad *f*

gremlin [ˈgrɛmlən] *n* : duende *m*

grenade [grəˈneɪd] *n* : granada *f*

Grenadian [grəˈneɪdiən] *n* : granadino *m*, -na *f* — **Grenadian** *adj*

grew → **grow**

grey → **gray**

greyhound [ˈgreɪˌhaʊnd] *n* : galgo *m*

grid [ˈgrɪd] *n* **1** GRATING : rejilla *f* **2** NETWORK : red *f* (de electricidad, etc.) **3** : cuadriculado *m* (de un mapa)

griddle [ˈgrɪdəl] *n* : plancha *f*

griddle cake → **pancake**

gridiron [ˈgrɪdˌaɪərn] *n* **1** GRILL : parrilla *f* **2** : campo *m* de futbol americano

gridlock [ˈgrɪdˌlɑk] *n* : atasco *m* completo (de una red de calles)

grief [ˈgriːf] *n* **1** SORROW : dolor *m*, pena *f* **2** ANNOYANCE, TROUBLE : problemas *mpl*, molestia *f*

grief–stricken *adj* : afligido, desconsolado

grievance [ˈgriːvənts] *n* COMPLAINT : queja *f*

grieve [ˈgriːv] *v* **grieved; grieving** *vt* DISTRESS : afligir, entristecer, apenar — *vi* **1** : sufrir, afligirse **2 to grieve for** *or* **to grieve over** : llorar, lamentar

grievous [ˈgriːvəs] *adj* **1** OPPRESSIVE : gravoso, opresivo, severo **2** GRAVE, SERIOUS : grave, severo, doloroso

grievously [ˈgriːvəsli] *adv* : gravemente, de gravedad

grill¹ [ˈgrɪl] *vt* **1** : asar (a la parrilla) **2** INTERROGATE : interrogar

grill² *n* **1** : parrilla *f* (para cocinar) **2** : parrillada *f* (comida) **3** : parrilla *f* (restaurante)

grille *or* **grill** [ˈgrɪl] *n* : reja *f*, enrejado *m*

grim [ˈgrɪm] *adj* **grimmer; grimmest 1** CRUEL : cruel, feroz **2** STERN : adusto, severo ⟨a grim expression : un gesto severo⟩ **3** GLOOMY : sombrío, deprimente **4** SINISTER : macabro, siniestro **5** UNYIELDING : inflexible, persistente ⟨with grim determination : con una voluntad de hierro⟩

grimace¹ [ˈgrɪməs, grɪˈmeɪs] *vi* **-maced; -macing** : hacer muecas

grimace² *n* : mueca *f*

grime [ˈgraɪm] *n* : mugre *f*, suciedad *f*

grimly [ˈgrɪmli] *adv* **1** STERNLY : severamente **2** RESOLUTELY : inexorablemente

grimy [ˈgraɪmi] *adj* **grimier; -est** : mugriento, sucio

grin¹ [ˈgrɪn] *vi* **grinned; grinning** : sonreír abiertamente

grin² *n* : sonrisa *f* abierta

grind¹ [ˈgraɪnd] *v* **ground** [ˈgraʊnd]; **grinding** *vt* **1** CRUSH : moler, machacar, triturar **2** SHARPEN : afilar **3** POLISH : pulir **4 to grind one's teeth** : rechinarle los dientes a uno **5 to grind down** OPPRESS : oprimir, agobiar — *vi* **1**

: funcionar con dificultad, rechinar ⟨to grind to a halt : pararse poco a poco, llegar a un punto muerto⟩ **2** STUDY : estudiar mucho

grind² *n* : trabajo *m* pesado ⟨the daily grind : la rutina diaria⟩

grinder [ˈgraɪndər] *n* : molinillo *m* ⟨coffee grinder : molinillo de café⟩

grindstone [ˈgraɪndˌstoːn] *n* : piedra *m* de afilar

gringo [ˈgrɪŋgo] *n* : gringo *m*, -ga *f*

grip¹ [ˈgrɪp] *vt* **gripped; gripping 1** GRASP : agarrar, asir **2** HOLD, INTEREST : captar el interés de

grip² *n* **1** GRASP : agarre *m*, asidero *m* ⟨to have a firm grip on something : agarrarse bien de algo⟩ **2** CONTROL, HOLD : control *m*, dominio *m* ⟨to lose one's grip on : perder el control de⟩ ⟨inflation tightened its grip on the economy : la inflación se afianzó en su dominio de la economía⟩ ⟨to get a grip on oneself : controlarse, calmarse⟩ **3** UNDERSTANDING : comprensión *f*, entendimiento *m* ⟨to come to grips with : llegar a entender⟩ **4** HANDLE : asidero *m*, empuñadura *f* (de un arma)

gripe¹ [ˈgraɪp] *v* **griped; griping** *vt* IRRITATE, VEX : irritar, fastidiar, molestar — *vi* COMPLAIN : quejarse, rezongar

gripe² *n* : queja *f*

grippe [ˈgrɪp] *n* : influenza *f*, gripe *f*, gripa *f* Col, Mex

gripping [ˈgrɪpɪŋ] *adj* : apasionante

grisly [ˈgrɪzli] *adj* **grislier; -est** : horripilante, horroroso, truculento

grist [ˈgrɪst] *n* : molienda *f* ⟨it's all grist for the mill : todo ayuda, todo es provechoso⟩

gristle [ˈgrɪsəl] *n* : cartílago *m*

gristly [ˈgrɪsli] *adj* **gristlier; -est** : duro, con mucho cartílago

grit¹ [ˈgrɪt] *vt* **gritted; gritting** : hacer rechinar (los dientes, etc.)

grit² *n* **1** SAND : arena *f* **2** GRAVEL : grava *f* **3** COURAGE : valor *m*, coraje *m* **4 grits** *npl* : sémola *f* de maíz

gritty [ˈgrɪti] *adj* **grittier; -est 1** : arenoso ⟨a gritty surface : una superficie arenosa⟩ **2** PLUCKY : valiente

grizzled [ˈgrɪzəld] *adj* : entrecano

grizzly bear [ˈgrɪzli] *n* : oso *m* pardo

groan¹ [ˈgroːn] *vi* **1** MOAN : gemir, quejarse **2** CREAK : crujir

groan² *n* **1** MOAN : gemido *m*, quejido *m* **2** CREAK : crujido *m*

grocer [ˈgroːsər] *n* : tendero *m*, -ra *f*

grocery [ˈgroːsəri, -ʃəri] *n, pl* **-ceries 1** *or* **grocery store** : tienda *f* de comestibles, tienda *f* de abarrotes **2 groceries** *npl* : comestibles *mpl*, abarrotes *mpl*

groggy [ˈgrɑgi] *adj* **groggier; -est** : atontado, grogui, tambaleante

groin [ˈgrɔɪn] *n* : ingle *f*

grommet [ˈgrɑmət, ˈgrʌ-] *n* : arandela *f*

groom¹ [ˈgruːm, ˈgrʊm] *vt* **1** : cepillar, almohazar (un animal) **2** : arreglar, cuidar ⟨well-groomed : bien arreglado⟩ **3** PREPARE : preparar

groom² *n* **1** : mozo *m*, -za *f* de cuadra **2** BRIDEGROOM : novio *m*

groove¹ ['gru:v] *vt* **grooved; grooving** : acanalar, hacer ranuras en, surcar

groove² *n* **1** FURROW, SLOT : ranura *f*, surco *m* **2** RUT : rutina *f*

grope ['gro:p] *v* **groped; groping** *vi* : andar a tientas, tantear ⟨he groped for the switch : buscó el interruptor a tientas⟩ — *vt* **to grope one's way** : avanzar a tientas

gross¹ ['gro:s] *vt* : tener entrada bruta de, recaudar en bruto

gross² *adj* **1** FLAGRANT : flagrante, grave ⟨a gross error : un error flagrante⟩ ⟨a gross injustice : una injusticia grave⟩ **2** FAT : muy gordo, obeso **3** : bruto ⟨gross national product : producto nacional bruto⟩ **4** COARSE, VULGAR : grosero, basto **5** *fam* DISGUSTING : asqueroso

gross³ *n* **1** *pl* **gross** : gruesa *f* (12 docenas) **2** *or* **gross income** : ingresos *mpl* brutos

grossly ['gro:sli] *adv* **1** EXTREMELY : extremadamente ⟨grossly unfair : totalmente injusto⟩ **2** CRUDELY : groseramente

grotesque [gro:'tɛsk] *adj* : grotesco

grotesquely [gro:'tɛskli] *adv* : de forma grotesca

grotto ['grɑto] *n*, *pl* **-toes** : gruta *f*

grouch¹ ['grɑʊtʃ] *vi* : refunfuñar, rezongar

grouch² *n* **1** COMPLAINT : queja *f* **2** GRUMBLER : gruñón *m*, -ñona *f*; cascarrabias *mf fam*

grouchy ['grɑʊtʃi] *adj* **grouchier; -est** : malhumorado, gruñón

ground¹ ['grɑʊnd] *vt* **1** BASE : fundar, basar **2** INSTRUCT : enseñar los conocimientos básicos a ⟨to be well grounded in : ser muy entendido en⟩ **3** : conectar a tierra (un aparato eléctrico) **4** : varar, hacer encallar (un barco) **5** : restringir (un avión o un piloto) a la tierra **6** *fam* : no dejar salir (como castigo)

ground² *n* **1** EARTH, SOIL : suelo *m*, tierra *f* ⟨to dig (in) the ground : cavar la tierra⟩ ⟨to fall to the ground : caerse al suelo⟩ **2** LAND, TERRAIN : terreno *m* ⟨high ground : terreno alto⟩ ⟨to be on solid/firm ground : pisar terreno firme⟩ **3** BASIS, REASON : razón *f*, motivo *m* ⟨grounds for complaint : motivos de queja⟩ **4** INFORMATION : información *f* ⟨we've covered a lot of ground : hemos abarcado muchos temas/puntos⟩ **5** VIEWS : terreno *m* ⟨to find a common/middle ground : encontrar un terreno común⟩ **6** BACKGROUND : fondo *m* **7** FIELD : campo *m*, plaza *f* ⟨parade ground : plaza de armas⟩ **8** : tierra *f* (para electricidad) **9** **grounds** *npl* PREMISES : recinto *m*, terreno *m* **10** **grounds** *npl* DREGS : posos *mpl* (de café) **11** **from the ground up** COMPLETELY : completamente, radicalmente **12** **from the ground up** FRESH : de cero ⟨to build/start from the ground up : construir/empezar de cero⟩ **13** **into the ground** ⟨he ran the business into the

ground : llevó la empresa a la ruina⟩ ⟨she's working herself into the ground : se mata trabajando⟩ **14** **to break new ground** : abrir nuevos caminos **15** **to gain/lose ground** : ganar/perder terreno **16** **to get off the ground** : llegar a concretarse **17** **to hold/stand one's ground** : no ceder terreno

ground³ → **grind**

groundhog ['grɑʊnd,hɔg] *n* : marmota *f* (de América)

grounding ['grɑʊndɪŋ] *n* : conocimientos *mpl* básicos

groundless ['grɑʊndləs] *adj* : infundado

groundwork ['grɑʊnd,wərk] *n* **1** FOUNDATION : fundamento *m*, base *f* **2** PREPARATION : trabajo *m* preparatorio

group¹ ['gru:p] *vt* : agrupar

group² *n* : grupo *m*, agrupación *f*, conjunto *m*, compañía *f*

grouper ['gru:pər] *n* : mero *m*

grouse¹ ['grɑʊs] *vi* **groused; grousing** : quejarse, rezongar, refunfuñar

grouse² *n*, *pl* **grouse** *or* **grouses** : urogallo *m* (ave)

grout ['grɑʊt] *n* : lechada *f*

grove ['gro:v] *n* : bosquecillo *m*, arboleda *f*, soto *m*

grovel ['grɑvəl, 'grʌ-] *vi* **-eled** *or* **-elled; -eling** *or* **-elling** **1** CRAWL : arrastrarse **2** : humillarse, postrarse ⟨to grovel before someone : postrarse ante alguien⟩

grow ['gro:] *v* **grew** ['gru:]; **grown** ['gro:n]; **growing** *vi* **1** : crecer ⟨palm trees grow on the islands : en las islas crecen palmas⟩ ⟨my hair grows very fast : mi pelo crece muy rápido⟩ **2** DEVELOP, MATURE : desarrollarse, madurar **3** INCREASE : crecer, aumentar **4** BECOME : hacerse, volverse, ponerse ⟨she was growing angry : se estaba poniendo furiosa⟩ ⟨to grow dark : oscurecerse⟩ **5** **to grow apart** : distanciarse **6** **to grow from** : nacer de **7** **to grow into** BECOME : convertirse en **8** **to grow on someone** : empezar a gustarle a alguien **9** **to grow out of** : dejar atrás (las cosas de la niñez) **10** **to grow to** : llegar a ⟨I grew to love the city : aprendí a amar la ciudad⟩ **11** **to grow up** : hacerse mayor ⟨grow up! : ¡no seas niño!⟩ — *vt* **1** CULTIVATE, RAISE : cultivar **2** : dejar crecer ⟨to grow one's hair : dejarse crecer el pelo⟩ **3** EXPAND, DEVELOP : expansionar, desarrollar (una empresa, etc.)

grower ['gro:ər] *n* : cultivador *m*, -dora *f*

growl¹ ['grɑʊl] *vi* : gruñir (dícese de un animal), refunfuñar (dícese de una persona)

growl² *n* : gruñido *m*

grown ['gro:n] → **grown–up¹**

grown–up¹ ['gro:n,əp] *adj* : adulto, mayor

grown–up² *n* : adulto *m*, -ta *f*; persona *f* mayor

growth ['gro:θ] *n* **1** : crecimiento *m* ⟨to stunt one's growth : detener el crecimiento⟩ **2** INCREASE : aumento *m*, crecimiento *m*, expansión *f* **3** DEVELOPMENT : desarrollo *m* ⟨economic growth : desarrollo económico⟩ ⟨a five days' growth of beard : una barba de cinco días⟩ **4** LUMP, TUMOR : bulto *m*, tumor *m*

grub¹ [ˈgrʌb] *vi* **grubbed; grubbing 1** DIG : escarbar **2** RUMMAGE : hurgar, buscar **3** DRUDGE : trabajar duro

grub² *n* **1** : larva *f* ⟨beetle grub : larva del escarabajo⟩ **2** DRUDGE : esclavo *m*, -va *f* del trabajo **3** FOOD : comida *f*

grubby [ˈgrʌbi] *adj* **grubbier, -est** : mugriento, sucio

grudge¹ [ˈgrʌʤ] *vt* **grudged; grudging** : dar/hacer (etc.) de mala gana ⟨I don't grudge the money I spent : no me molesta el dinero que gasté⟩

grudge² *n* **1** : rencor *m*, resentimiento *m* ⟨to hold a grudge : guardar rencor⟩ ⟨to hold a grudge against someone for something : guardarle rencor a alguien por algo⟩

grueling *or* **gruelling** [ˈgruːlɪŋ, ˈgruːə-] *adj* : extenuante, agotador, duro

gruesome [ˈgruːsəm] *adj* : horripilante, truculento, horroroso

gruff [ˈgrʌf] *adj* **1** BRUSQUE : brusco ⟨a gruff reply : una respuesta brusca⟩ **2** HOARSE : ronco — **gruffly** *adv*

grumble¹ [ˈgrʌmbəl] *vi* **-bled; -bling 1** COMPLAIN : refunfuñar, rezongar, quejarse **2** RUMBLE : hacer un ruido sordo, retumbar ⟨dícese del trueno⟩

grumble² *n* **1** COMPLAINT : queja *f* **2** RUMBLE : ruido *m* sordo, estruendo *m*

grumbler [ˈgrʌmbələr] *n* : gruñón *m*, -ñona *f*

grumpy [ˈgrʌmpi] *adj* **grumpier, -est** : malhumorado, gruñón

grungy [ˈgrʌnʤi] *adj* : sucio

grunt¹ [ˈgrʌnt] *vi* : gruñir

grunt² *n* : gruñido *m*

guacamole [ˌgwɑkəˈmoːli] *n* : guacamole *m*, guacamol *m*

guanaco [gwɑˈnɑko] *n* : guanaco *m*

guano [ˈgwɑno] *n* : guano *m*

guarantee¹ [ˌgærənˈtiː] *vt* **-teed; -teeing 1** PROMISE : asegurar, prometer **2** : poner bajo garantía, garantizar (un producto o servicio)

guarantee² *n* **1** PROMISE : garantía *f*, promesa *f* ⟨lifetime guarantee : garantía de por vida⟩ **2** → **guarantor**

guarantor [ˌgærənˈtɔr] *n* : garante *mf*; fiador *m*, -dora *f*

guaranty [ˈgærənˌtiː] → **guarantee**

guard¹ [ˈgɑrd] *vt* **1** DEFEND, PROTECT : defender, proteger **2** : guardar, vigilar, custodiar ⟨to guard the frontier : vigilar la frontera⟩ ⟨she guarded my secret well : guardó bien mi secreto⟩ — *vi* **to guard against** : protegerse contra, evitar

guard² *n* **1** WATCHMAN : guarda *mf* ⟨security guard : guarda de seguridad⟩ **2** SOLDIERS : guardia *f* **3** VIGILANCE : guardia *f*, vigilancia *f* ⟨to be on guard : estar en guardia⟩ ⟨to let one's guard down : bajar la guardia⟩ ⟨to catch someone off guard : agarrar a alguien desprevenido⟩ ⟨to keep under guard : vigilar⟩ **4** SAFEGUARD : salvaguardia *f*, dispositivo *m* de seguridad (en una máquina) **5**

PRECAUTION : precaución *f*, protección *f* **6** : guardia *mf* (en deportes)

guard dog *n* : perro *m* guardián

guarded [ˈgɑrdəd] *adj* : cauteloso

guardhouse [ˈgɑrdˌhaʊs] *n* : cuartel *m* de la guardia

guardian [ˈgɑrdiən] *n* **1** PROTECTOR : guardián *m*, -diana *f*; custodio *m*, -dia *f* ⟨guardian angel : ángel de la guarda⟩ **2** : tutor *m*, -tora *f* (de un niño)

guardianship [ˈgɑrdiənˌʃɪp] *n* : custodia *f*, tutela *f*

guardrail [ˈgɑrdˌreɪl] *n* **1** : antepecho *m* (de un puente, etc.) **2** : barrera *f* de contención (de una carretera)

Guatemalan [ˌgwɑtəˈmɑlən] *n* : guatemalteco *m*, -ca *f* — **Guatemalan** *adj*

guava [ˈgwɑvə] *n* : guayaba *f*

gubernatorial [ˌguːbənəˈtɔriːəl, ˌgjuː-] *adj* : del gobernador

guerrilla *or* **guerilla** [gəˈrɪlə] *n* : guerrillero *m*, -ra *f*

guess¹ [ˈgɛs] *vt* **1** CONJECTURE : adivinar, conjeturar ⟨guess what happened! : ¡adivina lo que pasó!⟩ **2** SUPPOSE : pensar, creer, suponer ⟨I guess so : supongo que sí⟩ **3** : adivinar correctamente, acertar ⟨to guess the answer : acertar la respuesta⟩ — *vi* : adivinar

guess² *n* : conjetura *f*, suposición *f*

guesswork [ˈgɛsˌwərk] *n* : suposiciones *fpl*, conjeturas *fpl*

guest [ˈgɛst] *n* : huésped *mf*; invitado *m*, -da *f*

guffaw¹ [gəˈfɔ] *vi* : reírse a carcajadas, carcajearse *fam*

guffaw² [gəˈfɔ, ˈgʌˌfɔ] *n* : carcajada *f*, risotada *f*

guidance [ˈgaɪdənts] *n* : orientación *f*, consejos *mpl*

guide¹ [ˈgaɪd] *vt* **guided; guiding 1** DIRECT, LEAD : guiar, dirigir, conducir **2** ADVISE, COUNSEL : aconsejar, orientar

guide² *n* : guía *f*

guidebook [ˈgaɪdˌbʊk] *n* : guía *f* (para viajeros)

guide dog *n* : perro *m* guía, perro *m* lazarillo

guideline [ˈgaɪdˌlaɪn] *n* : pauta *f*, directriz *f*

guild [ˈgɪld] *n* : gremio *m*, sindicato *m*, asociación *f*

guile [ˈgaɪl] *n* : astucia *f*, engaño *m*

guileless [ˈgaɪlləs] *adj* : inocente, cándido, sin malicia

guillotine¹ [ˈgɪləˌtiːn, ˈgiːjəˌ-] *vt* **-tined; -tining** : guillotinar

guillotine² *n* : guillotina *f*

guilt [ˈgɪlt] *n* : culpa *f*, culpabilidad *f*

guilty [ˈgɪlti] *adj* **guiltier, -est** : culpable

guinea fowl *n* : gallina *f* de Guinea

guinea pig *n* : conejillo *m* de Indias, cobaya *f*

guise [ˈgaɪz] *n* : apariencia *f*, aspecto *m*, forma *f*

guitar [gəˈtɑr, gɪ-] *n* : guitarra *f*

guitarist [gəˈtɑrɪst, gɪ-] *n* : guitarrista *mf*

gulch [ˈgʌlʧ] *n* : barranco *m*, quebrada *f*

gulf [ˈgʌlf] *n* **1** : golfo *m* ⟨the Gulf of Mexico : el Golfo de México⟩ **2** GAP

: brecha f ⟨the gulf between generations : la brecha entre las generaciones⟩ **3** CHASM : abismo m

gull [ˈɡʌl] n : gaviota f

gullet [ˈɡʌlət] n : garganta f

gullible [ˈɡʌlɪbəl] adj : crédulo

gully [ˈɡʌli] n, pl **-lies** : barranco m, hondonada f

gulp¹ [ˈɡʌlp] vt **1** : engullir, tragar ⟨he gulped down the whiskey : engulló el whisky⟩ **2** SUPPRESS : suprimir, reprimir, tragar ⟨to gulp down a sob : reprimir un sollozo⟩ — vi : tragar saliva, tener un nudo en la garganta

gulp² n : trago m

gum [ˈɡʌm] n **1** CHEWING GUM : goma f de mascar, chicle m **2 gums** npl : encías fpl

gumbo [ˈɡʌm‚bo:] n : sopa f de quingombó

gumdrop [ˈɡʌm‚drɑp] n : pastilla f de goma

gummy [ˈɡʌmi] adj **gummier; -est** : gomoso

gumption [ˈɡʌmpʃən] n : iniciativa f, agallas fpl fam

gun¹ [ˈɡʌn] vt **gunned; gunning** 1 or to **gun down** : matar a tiros, asesinar **2** : acelerar (rápidamente) ⟨to gun the engine : acelerar el motor⟩

gun² n **1** CANNON : cañón m **2** FIREARM : arma f de fuego **3** SPRAY GUN : pistola f **4** to jump the gun : adelantarse, salir antes de tiempo

gunboat [ˈɡʌn‚bo:t] n : cañonero m

gunfight [ˈɡʌn‚faɪt] n : tiroteo m, balacera f

gunfire [ˈɡʌn‚faɪr] n : disparos mpl

gunman [ˈɡʌnmən] n, pl **-men** [-mən, -‚mɛn] : pistolero m, gatillero m Mex

gunner [ˈɡʌnər] n : artillero m, -ra f

gunnysack [ˈɡʌni‚sæk] n : saco m de yute

gunpoint [ˈɡʌn‚pɔɪnt] n **at ~** : a punta de pistola

gunpowder [ˈɡʌn‚paʊdər] n : pólvora f

gunshot [ˈɡʌn‚ʃɑt] n : disparo m, tiro m, balazo m

gunsmith [ˈɡʌn‚smɪθ] n : armero m, -ra f

gunwale [ˈɡʌnəl] n : borda f

guppy [ˈɡʌpi] n, pl **-pies** : guppy m

gurgle¹ [ˈɡərɡəl] vi **-gled; -gling** 1 : borbotar, gorgotear (dícese de un líquido) **2** : gorjear (dícese de un niño)

gurgle² n **1** : borboteo m, gorgoteo m (de un líquido) **2** : gorjeo m (de un niño)

gush [ˈɡʌʃ] vi **1** SPOUT : surgir, salir a chorros, chorrear **2** : hablar con entusiasmo efusivo ⟨she gushed with praise : se deshizo en elogios⟩

gust [ˈɡʌst] n : ráfaga f, racha f

gusto [ˈɡʌs‚to:] n, pl **gustoes** : entusiasmo m ⟨with gusto : con deleite, con ganas⟩

gusty [ˈɡʌsti] adj **gustier; -est** : racheado

gut¹ [ˈɡʌt] vt **gutted; gutting 1** EVISCERATE : limpiar (un pollo, un pescado, etc.) **2** : destruir el interior de (un edificio)

gut² n **1** INTESTINE : intestino m **2 guts** npl INNARDS : tripas fpl fam, entrañas fpl **3 guts** npl COURAGE : valentía f, agallas fpl

gutter [ˈɡʌtər] n **1** : canal mf, canaleta f (de un techo) **2** : cuneta f, arroyo m (de una calle)

guttural [ˈɡʌtərəl] adj : gutural

guy [ˈɡaɪ] n **1** → **guyline** **2** FELLOW : tipo m, hombre m

guyline [ˈɡaɪ‚laɪn] n : cable m tensor

guzzle [ˈɡʌzəl] vt **-zled; -zling** : chupar, tragarse

gym [ˈdʒɪm] → **gymnasium**

gymnasium [dʒɪmˈneɪziəm, -ʒəm] n, pl **-siums** or **-sia** [-ziːə, -ʒə] : gimnasio m

gymnast [ˈdʒɪmnəst, -‚næst] n : gimnasta mf

gymnastic [dʒɪmˈnæstɪk] adj : gimnástico

gymnastics [dʒɪmˈnæstɪks] ns & pl : gimnasia f

gynecologic [‚ɡaɪnəkəˈlɑdʒɪk, ‚dʒɪnə-] or **gynecological** [‚ɡaɪnəkəˈlɑdʒɪkəl, ‚dʒɪnə-] adj : ginecológico

gynecologist [‚ɡaɪnəˈkɑlədʒɪst, ‚dʒɪnə-] n : ginecólogo m, -ga f

gynecology [‚ɡaɪnəˈkɑlədʒi, ‚dʒɪnə-] n : ginecología f

gyp¹ [ˈdʒɪp] vt **gypped; gypping** : estafar, timar

gyp² n **1** SWINDLER : estafador m, -dora f **2** FRAUD, SWINDLE : estafa f, timo m fam

gypsum [ˈdʒɪpsəm] n : yeso m

Gypsy [ˈdʒɪpsi] n, pl **-sies** : gitano m, -na f

gyrate [ˈdʒaɪ‚reɪt] vi **-rated; -rating** : girar, rotar

gyration [dʒaɪˈreɪʃən] n : giro m, rotación f

gyroscope [ˈdʒaɪrə‚sko:p] n : giroscopio m, giróscopo m

H

h [ˈeɪtʃ] n, pl **h's** or **hs** [ˈeɪtʃəz] : octava letra del alfabeto inglés

ha [ˈhɑ] interj : ¡ja!

haberdashery [ˈhæbər‚dæʃəri] n, pl **-eries** : tienda f de ropa para caballeros

habit [ˈhæbɪt] n **1** CUSTOM : hábito m, costumbre f ⟨to break/kick a bad habit : perder una mala costumbre⟩ ⟨to be in the habit of doing something : acostumbrar/soler hacer algo, tener la costumbre de hacer algo⟩ ⟨she got into the habit of sleeping in : se le hizo costumbre dormir hasta tarde⟩ ⟨to make a habit of doing something : tomar el costumbre de hacer algo⟩ ⟨don't make a habit of it : que no se repita⟩ **2** : hábito m (de un monje o una religiosa) **3** ADDICTION : dependencia f, adicción f ⟨to have a drug habit : ser drogadicto⟩ ⟨to kick the habit : dejar el vicio⟩

habitable ['hæbɪtəbəl] *adj* : habitable

habitat ['hæbɪ,tæt] *n* : hábitat *m*

habitation [,hæbɪ'teɪʃən] *n* 1 OCCUPANCY : habitación *f* 2 RESIDENCE : residencia *f*, morada *f*

habit-forming ['hæbɪt,fɔrmɪŋ] *adj* : que crea dependencia

habitual [hə'bɪtʃʊəl] *adj* 1 CUSTOMARY : habitual, acostumbrado 2 INVETERATE : incorregible, empedernido — **habitually** *adv*

habituate [hə'bɪtʃu,eɪt] *vt* -**ated; -ating** : habituar, acostumbrar

hack¹ ['hæk] *vt* 1 : cortar, tajar (a hachazos, etc.) ⟨to hack one's way : abrirse paso⟩ 2 : entrar en, hackear *fam* (un sistema, etc.) — *vi* 1 : hacer tajos 2 COUGH : toser 3 to hack into : entrar en, hackear *fam*

hack² *n* 1 CHOP : hachazo *m*, tajo *m* 2 HORSE : caballo *m* de alquiler 3 WRITER : escritor *m*, -tora *f* a sueldo; escritorzuelo *m*, -la *f* 4 COUGH : tos *f* seca

hacker ['hækər] *n* : pirata *m* informático, pirata *f* informática; hacker *mf fam*

hackles ['hækəlz] *npl* 1 : pluma *f* erizada (de un ave), pelo *m* erizado (de un perro, etc.) 2 to get one's hackles up : ponerse furioso

hackney ['hækni] *n, pl* -**neys** : caballo *m* de silla, caballo *m* de tiro

hackneyed ['hæknid] *adj* TRITE : trillado, gastado

hacksaw ['hæk,sɔ] *n* : sierra *f* para metales

had → **have**

haddock ['hædək] *ns & pl* : eglefino *m*

hadn't ['hædənt] *contraction of* **had not** → **have**

hag ['hæg] *n offensive* : bruja *f*, vieja *f* fea

haggard ['hægərd] *adj* : demacrado, macilento — **haggardly** *adv*

haggle ['hægəl] *vi* -**gled; -gling** : regatear

ha-ha *or* **ha ha** [,hɑ'hɑ, 'hɑ'hɑ] *interj* : ¡ja, ja!

hail¹ ['heɪl] *vt* 1 GREET : saludar 2 SUMMON : llamar ⟨to hail a taxi : llamar un taxi⟩ 3 WELCOME : aclamar — *vi* : granizar (en meteorología)

hail² *n* 1 : granizo *m* 2 BARRAGE : aluvión *m*, lluvia *f*

hail³ *interj* : ¡salve!

hailstone ['heɪl,stoːn] *n* : granizo *m*, piedra *f* de granizo

hailstorm ['heɪl,stɔrm] *n* : granizada *f*

hair ['hær] *n* 1 : pelo *m*, cabello *m* ⟨to get one's hair cut : cortarse el pelo⟩ 2 : vello *m* (en las piernas, etc.)

hairbreadth ['hær,bredθ] *or* **hairsbreadth** ['hærz-] *n* **by a hairbreadth** : por un pelo

hairbrush ['hær,brʌʃ] *n* : cepillo *m* (para el pelo)

haircut ['hær,kʌt] *n* : corte *m* de pelo

hairdo ['hær,du] *n, pl* -**dos** : peinado *m*

hairdresser ['hær,drɛsər] *n* 1 : peluquero *m*, -ra *f* 2 the hairdresser's : la peluquería

hairdressing ['hær,drɛsɪŋ] *n* : peluquería *f* (profesión o actividad)

haired ['hærd] *adj used in combination* : de pelo ⟨long-haired : de pelo largo⟩ ⟨red-haired : pelirrojo⟩

hairiness ['hærinəs] *n* : vellosidad *f*

hairless ['hærləs] *adj* : sin pelo, calvo, pelón

hairline ['hær,laɪn] *n* 1 : línea *f* delgada 2 : nacimiento *m* del pelo ⟨to have a receding hairline : tener entradas⟩

hairpiece ['hær,piːs] *n* : bisoñé *m*, peluquín *m*

hairpin ['hær,pɪn] *n* : horquilla *f*

hair-raising ['hær,reɪzɪŋ] *adj* : espeluznante

hair spray *n* : laca *f*, fijador *m* (para el pelo)

hairstyle ['hær,staɪl] *n* : peinado *m*

hairy ['hæri] *adj* **hairier; -est** : peludo, velludo

Haitian ['heɪʃən, 'heɪʃiən] *n* : haitiano *m*, -na *f* — **Haitian** *adj*

hake ['heɪk] *n* : merluza *f*

hale¹ ['heɪl] *vt* **haled; haling** : arrastrar, halar ⟨to hale to court : arrastrar al tribunal⟩

hale² *adj* : saludable, robusto

half¹ ['hæf, 'hɑf] *adv* 1 PARTIALLY : medio, a medias ⟨half cooked : medio cocido⟩ ⟨half closed/open : entreabierto⟩ ⟨she was half asleep : estaba medio dormida⟩ 2 : medio ⟨half full : medio lleno⟩ ⟨it's half past eleven (o'clock) : son las once y media⟩ ⟨she's half Mexican : es medio mexicana⟩ 3 half off : a mitad de precio

half² *adj* : medio, a medias ⟨a half hour : una media hora⟩ ⟨a half truth : una verdad a medias⟩

half³ *n, pl* **halves** ['hævz, 'hɑvz] 1 : mitad *f* ⟨to cut in half, to cut into halves : cortar por la mitad⟩ 2 : tiempo *m* (en deportes)

half⁴ *pron* : la mitad ⟨half of my friends : la mitad de mis amigos⟩ ⟨do you want half? : ¿quieres la mitad?⟩ ⟨half a million people : medio millón de personas⟩

half brother *n* : medio hermano *m*, hermanastro *m*

halfhearted ['hæf'hɑrtəd] *adj* : sin ánimo, poco entusiasta

halfheartedly ['hæf'hɑrtədli] *adv* : con poco entusiasmo, sin ánimo

half-life ['hæf,laɪf] *n, pl* **half-lives** : media vida *f*

half-mast ['hæf'mæst] *n* **at ~** : a media asta

half-moon ['hæf'muːn] *n, pl* **half-moons** : media luna *f*

half note *n* : blanca *f* (en música)

half-price ['hæf,praɪs] *adj & adv* : a mitad de precio ⟨a half-price sale : rebajas de 50 por ciento⟩

half price *n* : mitad *f* de precio ⟨to buy at half price, to pay half price for : comprar a mitad de precio⟩

half sister *n* : media hermana *f*, hermanastra *f*

halftime ['hæf,taɪm] *n* : descanso *m*, medio tiempo *m* (en deportes)

half–truth ['hæf,tru:θ] *n* : verdad *f* a medias

halfway[1] ['hæf'weɪ] *adv* : a medio camino, a mitad de camino

halfway[2] *adj* : medio, intermedio ⟨a halfway point : un punto intermedio⟩

half-wit ['hæf,wɪt] *n* : tonto *m*, -ta *f*; imbécil *mf*

half-witted ['hæf'wɪtəd] *adj* : estúpido

halibut ['hælɪbət] *ns & pl* : halibut *m*

hall ['hɔl] *n* **1** BUILDING : residencia *f* estudiantil, facultad *f* (de una universidad) **2** VESTIBULE : entrada *f*, vestíbulo *m*, zaguán *m* **3** CORRIDOR : corredor *m*, pasillo *m* **4** AUDITORIUM : sala *f*, salón *m* ⟨concert hall : sala de conciertos⟩ **5** city hall : ayuntamiento *m*

hallelujah [,hælə'lu:jə, ,hɑ-] *interj* : ¡aleluya!

hallmark ['hɔl,mɑrk] *n* : sello *m* (distintivo)

hallow ['hæ,lo:] *vt* : santificar, consagrar

hallowed ['hæ,lo:d, 'hæ,lo:əd, 'hɑ,lo:d] *adj* : sagrado

Halloween [,hælə'wi:n, ,hɑ-] *n* : víspera *f* de Todos los Santos

hallucinate [hæ'lu:sən,eɪt] *vi* **-nated; -nating** : alucinar

hallucination [hə,lu:sən'eɪʃən] *n* : alucinación *f*

hallucinatory [hə'lu:sənə,tori] *adj* : alucinante

hallucinogen [hə'lu:sənədʒən] *n* : alucinógeno *m*

hallucinogenic [hə,lu:sənə'dʒɛnɪk] *adj* : alucinógeno

hallway ['hɔl,weɪ] *n* **1** ENTRANCE : entrada *f* **2** CORRIDOR : corredor *m*, pasillo *m*

halo ['heɪ,lo:] *n, pl* **-los** *or* **-loes** : aureola *f*, halo *m*

halt[1] ['hɔlt] *vi* : detenerse, pararse — *vt* **1** STOP : detener, parar (a una persona) **2** INTERRUPT : interrumpir (una actividad)

halt[2] *n* **1** : alto *m*, parada *f* **2 to come to a halt** : pararse, detenerse

halter ['hɔltər] *n* **1** : cabestro *m*, ronzal *m* (para un animal) **2** : blusa *f* sin espalda

halting ['hɔltɪŋ] *adj* HESITANT : vacilante, titubeante — **haltingly** *adv*

halve ['hæv, 'hɑv] *vt* **halved; halving 1** DIVIDE : partir por la mitad **2** REDUCE : reducir a la mitad

halves → half

ham ['hæm] *n* **1** : jamón *m* **2** : payaso *m*, -sa *f*; persona *f* graciosa **3** *or* ham radio operator : radioaficionado *m*, -da *f* **4 hams** *npl* HAUNCHES : ancas *fpl*

hamburger ['hæm,bərgər] *or* **hamburg** [-,bərg] *n* **1** : carne *f* molida **2** : hamburguesa *f* (emparedado)

hamlet ['hæmlət] *n* VILLAGE : aldea *f*, poblado *m*

hammer[1] ['hæmər] *vt* **1** STRIKE : clavar, golpear **2** NAIL : clavar, martillar **3** DEFEAT : darle una paliza a **4 to hammer out** NEGOTIATE : elaborar, negociar, llegar a — *vi* : martillar, golpear

hammer[2] *n* **1** : martillo *m* **2** : percusor *m*, percutor *m* (de un arma de fuego)

hammock ['hæmək] *n* : hamaca *f*

hamper[1] ['hæmpər] *vt* : obstaculizar, dificultar

hamper[2] *n* : cesto *m*, canasta *f*

hamster ['hæmpstər] *n* : hámster *m*

hamstring ['hæm,strɪŋ] *vt* **-strung** [-,strʌŋ]; **-stringing 1** : cortarle el tendón del corvejón a (un animal) **2** INCAPACITATE : incapacitar, inutilizar

hand[1] ['hænd] *vt* **1** : pasar, dar, entregar **2 to hand back** RETURN : devolver **3 to hand down** : dejar en herencia **4 to hand in** SUBMIT : entregar, presentar **5 to hand it to** *fam* : aplaudir, felicitar ⟨I've got to hand it to you—you did a great job! : ¡tengo que reconocer que hiciste muy bien!⟩ **6 to hand out** DISTRIBUTE : distribuir **7 to hand over** SURRENDER : entregar

hand[2] *n* **1** : mano *f* ⟨made by hand : hecho a mano⟩ ⟨hand in hand : tomados de la mano⟩ ⟨to hold hands : ir tomados de la mano⟩ ⟨to raise one's hand : levantar la mano⟩ ⟨to join hands : darse las manos⟩ **2** POINTER : manecilla *f*, aguja *f* (de un reloj o instrumento) **3** SIDE : lado *m* ⟨on the one hand . . .on the other hand . . . : por un lado . . .por otro lado . . .⟩ **4** HANDWRITING : letra *f*, escritura *f* **5** APPLAUSE : aplauso *m* ⟨let's give them all a hand! : ¡aplausos para todos!⟩ **6** : mano *f*, cartas *fpl* (en juegos de naipes) **7** WORKER : obrero *m*, -ra *f*; trabajador *m*, -dora *f* **8 hands** *npl* CONTROL : manos *fpl* ⟨to fall into the hands of : caer en manos de⟩ ⟨it's out of my hands : no está en mis manos⟩ **9 at hand** NEAR : a mano ⟨to keep close at hand : tener a mano⟩ ⟨the problem at hand : el problema más acuciante⟩ **10 on hand** AVAILABLE : a mano, disponible **11 on hand** PRESENT, NEAR : presente, cerca **12 on one's hands** ⟨I had some time on my hands : tenía un rato libre⟩ ⟨she has all that work on her hands : tiene tanto trabajo que hacer⟩ **13 on one's hands and knees** : a gatas **14 out of hand** : descontrolado ⟨the situation is getting out of hand : la situación se les/nos (etc.) va de las manos⟩ **15 out of hand** IMMEDIATELY : sin miramientos **16 to ask for someone's hand (in marriage)** : pedir la mano de alguien **17 to give/lend a hand** : echar una mano **18 to go hand in hand** : ir de la mano **19 to have a hand in** : tener parte en **20 to have one's hands full** : estar muy ocupado **21 to have one's hands tied** : tener las manos atadas **22 to live from hand to mouth** : vivir al día **23 to try one's hand at** : probar a hacer **24 to wait on someone hand and foot** : hacerle de sirviente/sirvienta a alguien

handbag ['hænd,bæg] *n* : cartera *f*, bolso *m*, bolsa *f Mex*

handball ['hænd,bɔl] *n* : frontón *m*, pelota *f*

handbill ['hænd,bɪl] *n* : folleto *m*, volante *m*

handbook ['hænd,bʊk] *n* : manual *m*

handbrake ['hænd,breɪk] n : freno m de mano

handcuff ['hænd,kʌf] vt : esposar, ponerle esposas (a alguien)

handcuffs ['hænd,kʌfs] npl : esposas fpl

handful ['hænd,fʊl] n : puñado m

handgun ['hænd,gʌn] n : pistola f, revólver m

handheld ['hænd,hɛld] adj : de mano

handicap¹ ['hændi,kæp] vt -capped; -capping 1 : asignar un handicap a (en deportes) 2 HAMPER : obstaculizar, poner en desventaja

handicap² n 1 sometimes offensive DISABILITY : minusvalía f, discapacidad f 2 DISADVANTAGE : desventaja f, handicap m (en deportes)

handicapped ['hændi,kæpt] adj sometimes offensive DISABLED : minusválido, discapacitado

handicraft ['hændi,kræft] n : artesanía f

handily ['hændəli] adv EASILY : fácilmente, con facilidad

handiwork ['hændi,wərk] n 1 WORK : trabajo m 2 CRAFTS : artesanías fpl

handkerchief ['hæŋkərtʃəf, -,tʃi:f] n, pl -chiefs : pañuelo m

handle¹ ['hændəl] v -dled; -dling vt 1 TOUCH : tocar 2 MANAGE : tratar, manejar, despachar 3 SELL : comerciar con, vender — vi : responder, conducirse (dícese de un vehículo)

handle² n : asa m, asidero m, mango m (de un cuchillo, etc.), pomo m (de una puerta), tirador m (de un cajón)

handlebars ['hændəl,bɑrz] npl : manubrio m, manillar m

handler ['hændlər] n : cuidador m, -dora f

handling ['hændəlɪŋ] n 1 MANAGEMENT : manejo m 2 TOUCHING : manoseo m 3 shipping and handling : porte m, transporte m

handmade ['hænd,meɪd] adj : hecho a mano

hand—me—downs ['hændmi,daʊnz] npl : ropa f usada

handout ['hænd,aʊt] n 1 AID : dádiva f, limosna f 2 LEAFLET : folleto m

handpick ['hænd,pɪk] vt : seleccionar con cuidado

handrail ['hænd,reɪl] n : pasamanos m, barandilla f, barandal m

handsaw ['hænd,sɔ] n : serrucho m

hands down adv 1 EASILY : con facilidad 2 UNQUESTIONABLY : con mucho, de lejos

hands—free ['hændz'fri:] adj : (de) manos libres

handshake ['hænd,ʃeɪk] n : apretón m de manos

handsome ['hæntsəm] adj handsomer; -est 1 ATTRACTIVE : apuesto, guapo, atractivo 2 GENEROUS : generoso 3 SIZABLE : considerable

handsomely ['hæntsəmli] adv 1 ELEGANTLY : elegantemente 2 GENEROUSLY : con generosidad

handspring ['hænd,sprɪŋ] n : voltereta f

handstand ['hænd,stænd] n to do a handstand : pararse de manos

hand—to—hand ['hændtə'hænd] adj : cuerpo a cuerpo

hand truck → truck²

handwriting ['hænd,raɪtɪŋ] n : letra f, escritura f

handwritten ['hænd,rɪtən] adj : escrito a mano

handy ['hændi] adj handier; -est 1 NEARBY : a mano, cercano 2 USEFUL : útil, práctico 3 DEXTEROUS : hábil

handyman ['hændi,mæn] n, pl -men [-mən, -,mɛn] : hombre m que hace pequeños arreglos del hogar, manitas m Spain

handywoman ['hændi,wʊmən] n, pl -women [-,wɪmən] : mujer f que hace pequeños arreglos del hogar, manitas f Spain

hang¹ ['hæŋ] v hung ['hʌŋ]; hanging vt 1 SUSPEND : colgar, tender (ropa lavada), colocar (una pintura, etc.) 2 past tense often hanged EXECUTE : colgar, ahorcar 3 to hang one's head : bajar la cabeza — vi 1 FALL : caer (dícese de las telas y la ropa) 2 DANGLE : colgar 3 HOVER : flotar, sostenerse en el aire 4 : ser ahorcado 5 DROOP : inclinarse 6 to hang around fam : pasar el rato 7 to hang back : quedar atrás 8 to hang in there : seguir adelante 9 to hang on : WAIT esperar 10 to hang on (to) : agarrarse (a) 6 to hang out fam : pasar el rato 11 to hang out with someone : andar con alguien 12 to be hanging over one or to be hanging over one's head : tener pendiente, quedarle a alguien por resolver/terminar (etc.) ⟨I can't relax with this test hanging over me : no puedo relajarme hasta que me quite de encima este examen⟩ 13 to hang tight : seguir adelante 14 to hang tough : mantenerse firme 15 to hang up : colgar ⟨he hung up on me : me colgó⟩

hang² n 1 DRAPE : caída f 2 to get the hang of something : agarrarle la onda a algo

hangar ['hæŋər, 'hæŋ,gər] n : hangar m

hanger ['hæŋər] n : percha f, gancho m (para ropa)

hang glider ['hæŋ,glaɪdər] n : ala f delta (vehículo), deslizador m Mex

hang gliding ['hæŋ,glaɪdɪŋ] n : ala f delta (deporte), aladeltismo m

hangman ['hæŋmən] n, pl -men [-mən, -,mɛn] : verdugo m

hangnail ['hæŋ,neɪl] n : padrastro m

hangout ['hæŋ,aʊt] n : lugar m popular, sitio m muy frecuentado

hangover ['hæŋ,o:vər] n : resaca f

hank ['hæŋk] n : madeja f

hanker ['hæŋkər] vi to hanker for : tener ansias de, tener ganas de

hankering ['hæŋkərɪŋ] n : ansia f, anhelo m

hankie or **hanky** ['hæŋki] n, pl -kies : pañuelo m

Hanukkah ['xɑnəkə, 'hɑ-] n : Janucá, Januká, Hanukkah

haphazard [hæp'hæzərd] *adj* : casual, fortuito, al azar — **haphazardly** *adv*

hapless ['hæpləs] *adj* UNFORTUNATE : desafortunado, desventurado — **haplessly** *adv*

happen ['hæpən] *vi* 1 OCCUR : pasar, ocurrir, suceder, tener lugar 2 BEFALL : pasar, acontecer ⟨what happened to her? : ¿qué le ha pasado?⟩ 3 CHANCE : resultar, ocurrir por casualidad ⟨it happened that I wasn't home : resulta que estaba fuera de casa⟩ ⟨he happens to be right : da la casualidad de que tiene razón⟩

happening ['hæpənɪŋ] *n* : suceso *m*, acontecimiento *m*

happiness ['hæpinəs] *n* : felicidad *f*, dicha *f*

happy ['hæpi] *adj* **happier; -est** 1 JOYFUL : feliz, contento, alegre ⟨I'm happy for you : me alegro por ti⟩ ⟨a happy smile : una sonrisa de alegría⟩ 2 FORTUNATE : afortunado, feliz — **happily** [-pəli] *adv*

happy–go–lucky ['hæpigo:'lʌki] *adj* : despreocupado

harangue[1] [hə'ræŋ] *vt* **-rangued; -ranguing** : arengar

harangue[2] *n* : arenga *f*

harass [hə'ræs, 'hærəs] *vt* 1 BESIEGE, HOUND : acosar, asediar, hostigar 2 ANNOY : molestar

harassment [hə'ræsmənt, 'hærəsmənt] *n* : acoso *m*, hostigamiento *m* ⟨sexual harassment : acoso sexual⟩

harbinger ['harbindʒər] *n* 1 HERALD : heraldo *m*, precursor *m* 2 OMEN : presagio *m*

harbor[1] ['harbər] *vt* 1 SHELTER : dar refugio a, albergar 2 CHERISH, KEEP : abrigar, guardar, albergar ⟨to harbor doubts : guardar dudas⟩

harbor[2] *n* 1 REFUGE : refugio *m* 2 PORT : puerto *m*

hard[1] ['hard] *adv* 1 FORCEFULLY : fuerte, con fuerza ⟨the wind blew hard : el viento sopló fuerte⟩ 2 STRENUOUSLY : duro, mucho ⟨to work hard : trabajar duro⟩ 3 **to take something hard** : tomarse algo muy mal, estar muy afectado por algo

hard[2] *adj* 1 FIRM, SOLID : duro, firme, sólido 2 DIFFICULT : difícil, arduo 3 SEVERE : severo, duro ⟨a hard winter : un invierno severo⟩ 4 UNFEELING : insensible, duro 5 DILIGENT : diligente ⟨to be a hard worker : ser muy trabajador⟩ 6 FORCEFUL : fuerte ⟨dice de un golpe, etc.⟩ 7 HARSH : fuerte ⟨dícese de una luz⟩, definido ⟨dícese de una línea⟩ 8 **hard liquor** : bebidas *fpl* fuertes 9 **hard water** : agua *f* dura 10 **to be hard on** *fam* CRITICIZE, PUNISH : ser duro con 11 **to be hard on** *fam* HARM : ser malo para 12 **to be hard on** *fam* STRESS : ser difícil para 13 **to be hard up** *fam* : estar/andar mal de dinero 14 **to be hard up for** *fam* : andar escaso de 15 **to have a hard time** *fam* : pasarlo mal 16 **to have a hard time with/doing**

something *fam* : costarle a uno hacer algo 17 **to learn the hard way** *fam* : aprender a las malas 18 **to do something the hard way** *fam* : complicar las cosas

hardback ['hard,bæk] *n* : libro *m* de tapa dura

hardball ['hard,bɔl] *n* 1 → **baseball** 2 **to play hardball** : ser agresivo, jugar sucio

hard–boiled ['hard,bɔɪld] *adj* : duro (dícese de un huevo)

hard copy *n* : copia *f* impresa

hardcover[1] ['hard,kʌvər] *adj* : de pasta dura, de tapa dura

hardcover[2] *n* : libro *m* de pasta/tapa dura

hard disk *n* : disco *m* duro

hard drive → **hard disk**

harden ['hardən] *vt* 1 SOLIDIFY, CONGEAL : endurecer 2 : endurecer, hacer duro (a una persona) ⟨to harden someone's heart : endurecerle el corazón a alguien⟩ 3 : reforzar, fortalecer (la determinación, etc.) — *vi* 1 SOLIDIFY, CONGEAL : endurecerse 2 : reforzarse, fortalecerse 3 : endurecerse, hacerse duro (dícese de la voz, etc.)

hard–fought ['hard'fɔt] *adj* : muy reñido

hardheaded [,hard'hedəd] *adj* 1 STUBBORN : testarudo, terco 2 REALISTIC : realista, práctico — **hardheadedly** *adv*

hard–hearted [,hard'hartəd] *adj* : despiadado, insensible — **hard–heartedly** *adv*

hard–heartedness [,hard'hartədnəs] *n* : dureza *f* de corazón

hardly ['hardli] *adv* 1 SCARCELY : apenas, casi ⟨I hardly knew her : apenas la conocía⟩ ⟨hardly ever : casi nunca⟩ 2 NOT : difícilmente, poco, no ⟨they can hardly blame me! : ¡difícilmente pueden echarme la culpa!⟩ ⟨it's hardly likely : es poco probable⟩

hardness ['hardnəs] *n* 1 FIRMNESS : dureza *f* 2 DIFFICULTY : dificultad *f* 3 SEVERITY : severidad *f*

hardship ['hard,ʃɪp] *n* : dificultad *f*, privación *f*

hardware ['hard,wær] *n* 1 TOOLS : ferretería *f* 2 : hardware *m* (de una computadora)

hardware store *n* : ferretería *f*

hardwood ['hard,wʊd] *n* : madera *f* dura, madera *f* noble

hardworking ['hard'wərkɪŋ] *adj* : trabajador

hardy ['hardi] *adj* **hardier; -est** : fuerte, robusto, resistente (dícese de las plantas) — **hardily** [-dəli] *adv*

hare ['hær] *n, pl* **hare** *or* **hares** : liebre *f*

harebrained ['hær,breɪnd] *adj* : estúpido, absurdo, disparatado

harem ['hærəm] *n* : harén *m*

hark ['hark] *vi* 1 (*used only in the imperative*) LISTEN : escuchar 2 **hark back** RETURN : volver 3 **hark back** RECALL : recordar

harlequin ['harlɪkən, -kwən] *n* : arlequín *m*

harlot ['harlət] *n* : ramera *f*

harm[1] ['harm] *vt* : hacerle daño a, perjudicar

harm² *n* **1** : daño *m*, perjuicio *m* ⟨I meant no harm : no lo dije/hice (etc.) con mala intención⟩ ⟨to do more harm than good : hacer más mal/daño que bien⟩ ⟨there's no harm in asking : con preguntar no se pierde nada⟩ **2 in harm's way** : en peligro **3 no harm done** *fam* : no fue nada, no pasó nada

harmful ['hɑrmfəl] *adj* : dañino, perjudicial — **harmfully** *adv*

harmless ['hɑrmləs] *adj* : inofensivo, inocuo — **harmlessly** *adv*

harmlessness ['hɑrmləsnəs] *n* : inocuidad *f*

harmonic [hɑr'mɑnɪk] *adj* : armónico — **harmonically** [-nɪkli] *adv*

harmonica [hɑr'mɑnɪkə] *n* : armónica *f*

harmonious [hɑr'mo:niəs] *adj* : armonioso — **harmoniously** *adv*

harmonize ['hɑrmə,naɪz] *v* **-nized; -nizing** : armonizar

harmony ['hɑrməni] *n, pl* **-nies** : armonía *f*

harness¹ ['hɑrnəs] *vt* **1** : enjaezar (un animal) **2** UTILIZE : utilizar, aprovechar

harness² *n* : arreos *mpl*, guarniciones *fpl*, arnés *m*

harp¹ ['hɑrp] *vi* **to harp on** : insistir sobre, machacar sobre

harp² *n* : arpa *f*

harpist ['hɑrpɪst] *n* : arpista *mf*

harpoon¹ [hɑr'pu:n] *vt* : arponear

harpoon² *n* : arpón *m*

harpsichord ['hɑrpsɪ,kɔrd] *n* : clavicémbalo *m*

harrow¹ ['hær,o:] *vt* **1** CULTIVATE : gradar, labrar (la tierra) **2** TORMENT : atormentar

harrow² *n* : grada *f*, rastra *f*

harry ['hæri] *vt* **-ried; -rying** HARASS : acosar, hostigar

harsh ['hɑrʃ] *adj* **1** ROUGH : áspero **2** SEVERE : duro, severo **3** : discordante (dícese de los sonidos) — **harshly** *adv*

harshness ['hɑrʃnəs] *n* **1** ROUGHNESS : aspereza *f* **2** SEVERITY : dureza *f*, severidad *f*

harvest¹ ['hɑrvəst] *v* : cosechar

harvest² *n* **1** HARVESTING : siega *f*, recolección *f* **2** CROP : cosecha *f*

harvester ['hɑrvəstər] *n* : segador *m*, -dora *f*; cosechadora *f* (máquina)

has → have

has–been ['hæz,bɪn, -,bɛn] *n* : vieja gloria *f*

hash¹ ['hæʃ] *vt* **1** MINCE : picar **2 to hash over** DISCUSS : discutir, repasar

hash² *n* **1** : picadillo *m* (comida) **2** JUMBLE : revoltijo *m*, fárrago *m*

hashish ['hæ,ʃi:ʃ, hæ'ʃi:ʃ] *n* : hachís *m*

hasn't ['hæzənt] *contraction of* **has not → has**

hasp ['hæsp] *n* : picaporte *m*, pestillo *m*

hassle¹ ['hæsəl] *vt* **-sled; -sling** : fastidiar, molestar

hassle² *n* **1** ARGUMENT : discusión *f*, disputa *f*, bronca *f* **2** FIGHT : pelea *f*, riña *f* **3** BOTHER, TROUBLE : problemas *mpl*, lío *m*

hassock ['hæsək] *n* **1** CUSHION : almohadón *m*, cojín *m* **2** FOOTSTOOL : escabel *m*

haste ['heɪst] *n* **1** : prisa *f*, apuro *m* **2 to make haste** : darse prisa, apurarse

hasten ['heɪsən] *vt* : acelerar, precipitar — *vi* : apresurarse, apurarse

hasty ['heɪsti] *adj* **hastier; -est 1** HURRIED, QUICK : rápido, apresurado, apurado **2** RASH : precipitado — **hastily** [-təli] *adv*

hat ['hæt] *n* : sombrero *m*

hatch¹ ['hæʧ] *vt* **1** : incubar, empollar (huevos) **2** DEVISE : idear, tramar — *vi* : salir del cascarón

hatch² *n* : escotilla *f*

hatchback ['hæʧ,bæk] *n* **1** : hatchback *m* (automóvil) **2** : puerta *f* trasera

hatchery ['hæʧəri] *n, pl* **-ries** : criadero *m*

hatchet ['hæʧət] *n* : hacha *f*

hatchway ['hæʧ,weɪ] *n* : escotilla *f*

hate¹ ['heɪt] *vt* **hated; hating** : odiar, aborrecer, detestar

hate² *n* : odio *m*

hateful ['heɪtfəl] *adj* : odioso, aborrecible, detestable — **hatefully** *adv*

hatred ['heɪtrəd] *n* : odio *m*

hatter ['hætər] *n* : sombrerero *m*, -ra *f*

haughtiness ['hɔtinəs] *n* : altanería *f*, altivez *f*

haughty ['hɔti] *adj* **haughtier; -est** : altanero, altivo — **haughtily** [-təli] *adv*

haul¹ ['hɔl] *vt* **1** DRAG, PULL : arrastrar, jalar **2** TRANSPORT : transportar

haul² *n* **1** PULL : tirón *m*, jalón *m* **2** CATCH : redada *f* **3** JOURNEY : viaje *m*, trayecto *m* ⟨it's a long haul : es un trayecto largo⟩

haulage ['hɔlɪʤ] *n* : transporte *m*, tiro *m*

hauler ['hɔlər] *n* : transportista *mf*

haunch ['hɔnʧ] *n* **1** HIP : cadera *f* **2 haunches** *npl* HINDQUARTERS : ancas *fpl*, cuartos *mpl* traseros

haunt¹ ['hɔnt] *vt* **1** : rondar, habitar (dícese de un fantasma) **2** FREQUENT : frecuentar, rondar **3** PREOCCUPY : perseguir, obsesionar

haunt² *n* : guarida *f* (de animales o ladrones), lugar *m* predilecto

haunted ['hɔntəd] *adj* : embrujado, encantado (dícese de una casa, etc.)

haunting ['hɔntɪŋ] *adj* : inolvidable (por ser hermoso o triste) — **hauntingly** *adv*

haute ['o:t] *adj* **1** : de moda, de categoría **2 haute couture** [,o:tku'tur] : alta costura *f* **3 haute cuisine** [,o:tkwɪ'zi:n] : alta cocina *f*

have ['hæv, *in sense 7 as an auxiliary verb usu* 'hæf] *v* **had** ['hæd]; **having; has** ['hæz, *in sense 7 as an auxiliary verb usu* 'hæs] *vt* **1** POSSESS : tener ⟨she has long hair : tiene el pelo largo⟩ ⟨they have three children : tienen tres hijos⟩ ⟨do you have change? : ¿tienes cambio?⟩ ⟨you can have it : te lo doy⟩ **2** OBTAIN : conseguir ⟨I must have it! : ¡no puedo sin ello!⟩ **3** (*indicating availability*) : tener ⟨when you have a minute : cuando tengas un momento⟩ **4** : tener (en casa) ⟨we have guests : tenemos visita⟩ **5**

EXPERIENCE, UNDERGO : tener ⟨I have a toothache : tengo un dolor de muelas⟩ ⟨to have surgery : operarse⟩ ⟨to have a good time : pasarlo bien⟩ **6** : tener (una idea, una opinión, etc.) **7** INCLUDE : tener, incluir ⟨April has 30 days : abril tiene 30 días⟩ **8** CONSUME : comer, tomar **9** RECEIVE : tener, recibir ⟨he had my permission : tenía mi permiso⟩ **10** ALLOW : permitir, tolerar ⟨I won't have it! : ¡no lo permitiré!⟩ **11** HOLD : hacer ⟨to have a party : dar una fiesta⟩ ⟨to have a meeting : celebrar una reunión⟩ **12** DO : hacer ⟨to have a nap : echarse una siesta⟩ ⟨to have a look at : mirar⟩ ⟨I'll have a talk with him : hablaré con él⟩ **13** HOLD : tener ⟨he had me in his power : me tenía en su poder⟩ ⟨she had me by the arm : me tenía agarrado del brazo⟩ **14** BEAR : tener (niños) **15** (*indicating causation*) ⟨she had a dress made : mandó hacer un vestido⟩ ⟨to have one's hair cut : cortarse el pelo⟩ ⟨have her call me : dile que me llame⟩ ⟨he had it ready : lo tenía listo⟩ **16** (*indicating loss, damage, etc.*) ⟨she had her car stolen : le robaron el auto⟩ **17** to be had : ser engañado ⟨I've been had! : ¡me han engañado!⟩ **18** to be had ⟨there were none to be had : no había disponibles⟩ **19** to have back ⟨can I have my book back? : ¿me puedes devolver el libro?⟩ **20** to have back : volver a invitar ⟨we must have you back : tienes que volver a visitarnos⟩ **21** to have back ⟨it's good to have you back! : ¡qué gusto volver a verte por aquí!⟩ **22** to have it easy/rough (etc.) : tenerlo todo muy fácil/difícil (etc.) **23** to have it in for : tenerle manía a **24** to have it in one : ser capaz ⟨she doesn't have it in her to be cruel : no es capaz de ser cruel⟩ **25** to have it out (with) : aclarar(le) las cosas (a) **26** to have off : tener (un día, etc.) libre **27** to have on WEAR : llevar **28** to have over : invitar (a casa) **29** to have on one : tener/llevar encima ⟨I don't have it on me : no lo tengo encima⟩ **30** to have with one : traer (a alguien), tener/llevar (algo) encima — *v aux* **1** : haber ⟨she has been very busy : ha estado muy ocupada⟩ ⟨I've lived here three years : hace tres años que vivo aquí⟩ **2** (*used in tags*) ⟨you've finished, haven't you? : ha terminado, ¿no?⟩ **3** to have got (*used in the present tense*) *fam* : tener ⟨I've got an idea : tengo una idea⟩ ⟨we've got to leave : tenemos que salir⟩ **4** you've got me! : ¡no sé!, ¡ni idea! **5** to have had it : no dar para más (dícese de una cosa) **6** to have had it (with someone/something) : estar harto (de alguien/algo) **7** to have to : deber, tener que ⟨we have to leave : tenemos que salir⟩

haven ['heɪvən] *n* : refugio *m*

havoc ['hævək] *n* **1** DESTRUCTION : estragos *mpl*, destrucción *f* **2** CHAOS, DISORDER : desorden *m*, caos *m*

Hawaiian[1] ['hə'waɪən] *adj* : hawaiano

Hawaiian[2] *n* : hawaiano *m*, -na *f*

hawk[1] ['hɔk] *vt* : pregonar, vender (mercancías) en la calle

hawk[2] *n* : halcón *m*

hawker ['hɔkər] *n* : vendedor *m*, -dora *f* ambulante

hawthorn ['hɔ,θɔrn] *n* : espino *m*

hay ['heɪ] *n* : heno *m*

hay fever *n* : fiebre *f* del heno

hayloft ['heɪ,lɔft] *n* : pajar *m*

hayseed ['heɪ,sid] *n* : palurdo *m*, -da *f*

haystack ['heɪ,stæk] *n* : almiar *m*

haywire ['heɪ,waɪr] *adj* : descompuesto, desbaratado ⟨to go haywire : estropearse⟩

hazard[1] ['hæzərd] *vt* : arriesgar, aventurar

hazard[2] *n* **1** DANGER : peligro *m*, riesgo *m* **2** CHANCE : azar *m*

hazardous ['hæzərdəs] *adj* : arriesgado, peligroso

haze[1] ['heɪz] *vt* **hazed; hazing** : abrumar, acosar

haze[2] *n* : bruma *f*, neblina *f*

hazel ['heɪzəl] *n* **1** : avellano *m* (árbol) **2** : color *m* avellana

hazelnut ['heɪzəl,nʌt] *n* : avellana *f*

haziness ['heɪzinəs] *n* **1** MISTINESS : nebulosidad *f* **2** VAGUENESS : vaguedad *f*

hazy ['heɪzi] *adj* **hazier; -est** **1** MISTY : brumoso, neblinoso, nebuloso **2** VAGUE : vago, confuso

he ['hi:] *pron* : él

head[1] ['hɛd] *vt* **1** LEAD : encabezar **2** DIRECT : dirigir — *vi* : dirigirse

head[2] *adj* MAIN : principal ⟨the head office : la oficina central, la sede⟩ ⟨head of state/government : jefe de estado/gobierno⟩

head[3] *n* **1** : cabeza *f* ⟨from head to foot : de pies a cabeza⟩ ⟨to stand on one's head : pararse de cabeza⟩ ⟨to nod one's head : asentir con la cabeza⟩ **2** MIND : mente *f*, cabeza *f* ⟨use your head! : ¡usa la cabeza!⟩ ⟨to add in one's head : sumar mentalmente⟩ ⟨it's all in your head : es pura imaginación tuya⟩ ⟨to come into one's head : venirle a la cabeza⟩ ⟨to enter one's head : pasársele por la cabeza⟩ ⟨to put something out of your head : sacarse algo de la cabeza⟩ ⟨don't put ideas in his head! : ¡no le metas ideas a la cabeza!⟩ ⟨she's gotten it into her head that . . . : se le ha metido en la cabeza que . . .⟩ **3** TIP, TOP : cabeza *f* (de un clavo, un martillo, etc.), cabecera *f* (de una mesa o un río), punta *f* (de una flecha), flor *m* (en un repollo, etc.), encabezamiento *m* (de una carta, etc.), espuma *f* (de cerveza) **4** DIRECTOR, LEADER : director *m*, -tora *f*; jefe *m*, -fa *f*; cabeza *f* (de una familia) ⟨head of state/government : jefe de Estado/gobierno⟩ **5** : cara *f* (de una moneda) ⟨heads or tails : cara o cruz⟩ **6** : cabeza *f* ⟨500 head of cattle : 500 cabezas de ganado⟩ ⟨$10 a head : $10 por cabeza⟩ **7** to come to a head : llegar a un punto crítico **8** heads or/not tails ⟨I can't make heads nor tails of it : para mí no tiene ni pies ni cabeza⟩ **9** heads will roll : van a rodar cabezas

10 over one's head ⟨it's over my head : no alcanzo a entenderlo⟩ ⟨the joke went over his head : no entendió el chiste⟩ **11 to be head over heels (in love)** : estar perdidamente enamorado **12 to be out of one's head** : estar como una cabra **13 to go to someone's head** : subírsele a la cabeza a alguien **14 to have a good head on one's shoulders** : tener cabeza **15 to hold one's head high** : ir con la cabeza bien alta **16 to keep/lose one's head** : mantener/perder la calma **17 to keep one's head above water** : mantenerse a flote **18 to keep one's head down** : mantenerse al margen **19 to rear its (ugly) head** : aparecer

headache ['hɛd,eɪk] n : dolor m de cabeza, jaqueca f

headband ['hɛd,bænd] n : cinta f del pelo

headboard ['hɛd,bɔrd] n : cabecera f

headdress ['hɛd,drɛs] n : tocado m

headfirst ['hɛd'fərst] adv : de cabeza

headgear ['hɛd,gɪr] n : gorro m, casco m, sombrero m

heading ['hɛdɪŋ] n **1** DIRECTION : dirección f **2** TITLE : encabezamiento m, título m **3** : membrete m (de una carta)

headland ['hɛdlənd, -,lænd] n : cabo m

headlight ['hɛd,laɪt] n : faro m, foco m, farol m Mex

headline ['hɛd,laɪn] n : titular m

headlong¹ ['hɛd'lɔŋ] adv **1** HEADFIRST : de cabeza **2** HASTILY : precipitadamente

headlong² ['hɛd,lɔŋ] adj : precipitado

headmaster ['hɛd,mæstər] n : director m

headmistress ['hɛd,mɪstrəs, -'mɪs-] n : directora f

head–on ['hɛd'ɑn, -'ɔn] adv & adj : de frente

headphones ['hɛd,foːnz] npl : audífonos mpl, cascos mpl

headquarters ['hɛd,kwɔrtərz] ns & pl **1** SEAT : oficina f central, sede f **2** : cuartel m general (de los militares)

headrest ['hɛd,rɛst] n : apoyacabezas m

headroom ['hɛd,ruːm, -,rʊm] n : espacio m libre entre la cabeza y el techo (de un coche, etc.)

headset ['hɛd,sɛt] n : audífonos mpl, cascos mpl

headship ['hɛd,ʃɪp] n : dirección f

head start n : ventaja f

headstone ['hɛd,stoːn] n : lápida f

headstrong ['hɛd'strɔŋ] adj : testarudo, obstinado, empecinado

heads–up ['hɛdz'ʌp] n fam WARNING : aviso m ⟨to give someone a heads-up : avisarle/advertirle a alguien⟩

headwaiter ['hɛd'weɪtər] n : jefe m, -fa f de comedor

headwaters ['hɛd,wɔtərz, -,wɑ-] npl : cabecera f

headway ['hɛd,weɪ] n : progreso m ⟨to make headway against : avanzar contra⟩

heady ['hɛdi] adj **headier; -est 1** INTOXICATING : embriagador, excitante **2** SHREWD : astuto, sagaz

heal ['hiːl] vt : curar, sanar — vi **1** : sanar, curarse **2 to heal up** : cicatrizarse

healer ['hiːlər] n **1** : curandero m, -dera f **2** : curador m, -dora f (cosa)

health ['hɛlθ] n : salud f ⟨health care : asistencia médica⟩ ⟨health center : centro sanitario⟩ ⟨health food : alimentos naturales⟩

healthful ['hɛlθfəl] adj : saludable, salubre — **healthfully** adv

healthiness ['hɛlθinəs] n : lozanía f

healthy ['hɛlθi] adj **healthier; -est** : sano, bien — **healthily** [-θəli] adv

heap¹ ['hiːp] vt **1** PILE : amontonar, apilar **2** SHOWER : colmar

heap² n : montón m, pila f

hear ['hɪr] v **heard** ['hərd]; **hearing** vt **1** : oír ⟨do you hear me? : ¿me oyes?⟩ ⟨I can't hear myself think : no puedo pensar con tanto ruido⟩ **2** HEED : oír, prestar atención a **3** LEARN : oír, enterarse de **4 to hear out** : escuchar hasta el final — vi **1** : oír ⟨to hear about : oír hablar de⟩ **2 to hear from** : tener noticias de **3 to hear of** : oír hablar de ⟨I've heard of him : lo conozco de oídas⟩ **4 not to hear of** : no permitir ⟨I won't hear of it! : ¡no lo permitiré!, ¡ni hablar!⟩ **5 not/never to hear the end of** ⟨I'll never hear the end of it, she'll never let me hear the end of it : nunca me lo dejará olvidar⟩

hearing ['hɪrɪŋ] n **1** : oído m ⟨hard of hearing : duro de oído⟩ **2** : vista f (en un tribunal) **3** ATTENTION : consideración f, oportunidad f de expresarse **4** EARSHOT : alcance m del oído

hearing aid n : audífono m

hearken ['hɑrkən] vt : escuchar

hearsay ['hɪr,seɪ] n : rumores mpl

hearse ['hərs] n : coche m fúnebre

heart ['hɑrt] n **1** : corazón m ⟨heart rate : ritmo cardíaco⟩ ⟨heart disease : enfermedades cardíacas⟩ ⟨heart surgery : cirugía cardíaca⟩ ⟨heart murmur : soplo en el corazón⟩ **2** CENTER, CORE : corazón m, centro m ⟨the heart of the matter : el meollo del asunto⟩ **3** FEELINGS : corazón m, sentimientos mpl ⟨a broken heart : un corazón destrozado⟩ ⟨to have a good heart : tener buen corazón⟩ ⟨to take something to heart : tomarse algo a pecho⟩ ⟨from the heart : con toda sinceridad⟩ ⟨to be close to one's heart : significar mucho a alguien⟩ ⟨with a light heart : con el corazón alegre⟩ ⟨with a heavy heart : deprimido, acongojado⟩ ⟨my heart sank : se me cayó el alma a los pies⟩ **4** COURAGE : valor m, corazón m ⟨to take heart : animarse, cobrar ánimos⟩ **5** : corazón m (naipe) **6 at heart** : en el fondo **7 by heart** : de memoria **8 to one's heart's content** : a voluntad, todo lo que quiere

heartache ['hɑrt,eɪk] n : pena f, angustia f

heart attack n : infarto m, ataque m al corazón

heartbeat ['hɑrt,biːt] n : latido m (del corazón)

heartbreak ['hɑrt,breɪk] n : congoja f, angustia f

heartbreaker [ˈhɑrtˌbreɪkər] n : rompecorazones mf

heartbreaking [ˈhɑrtˌbreɪkɪŋ] adj : desgarrador, que parte el corazón

heartbroken [ˈhɑrtˌbroːkən] adj : desconsolado, destrozado

heartburn [ˈhɑrtˌbərn] n : acidez f estomacal

hearten [ˈhɑrtən] vt : alentar, animar

heartfelt [ˈhɑrtˌfɛlt] adj : sentido

hearth [ˈhɑrθ] n : hogar m, chimenea f

heartily [ˈhɑrtəli] adv 1 ENTHUSIASTICALLY : de buena gana, con entusiasmo 2 TOTALLY : totalmente, completamente

heartless [ˈhɑrtləs] adj : desalmado, despiadado, cruel

heart of palm n : palmito m

heartsick [ˈhɑrtˌsɪk] adj : abatido, desconsolado

heartstrings [ˈhɑrtˌstrɪŋz] npl : fibras fpl del corazón

heartwarming [ˈhɑrtˌwɔrmɪŋ] adj : conmovedor, emocionante

hearty [ˈhɑrti] adj **heartier; -est** 1 CORDIAL, WARM : cordial, caluroso 2 STRONG : fuerte ⟨to have a hearty appetite : ser de buen comer⟩ 3 SUBSTANTIAL : abundante, sustancioso ⟨a hearty breakfast : un desayuno abundante⟩

heat[1] [ˈhiːt] vt : calentar

heat[2] n 1 WARMTH : calor m 2 HEATING : calefacción f 3 EXCITEMENT : calor m, entusiasmo m ⟨in the heat of the moment : en el calor del momento⟩ 4 ESTRUS : celo m

heated [ˈhiːtəd] adj 1 WARMED : calentado 2 IMPASSIONED : acalorado, apasionado

heater [ˈhiːtər] n : calentador m, estufa f, calefactor m

heath [ˈhiːθ] n 1 MOOR : páramo m 2 HEATHER : brezo m

heathen[1] [ˈhiːðən] adj often offensive : pagano

heathen[2] n, pl **-thens** or **-then** often offensive : pagano m, -na f; infiel mf

heather [ˈhɛðər] n : brezo m

heating [ˈhiːtɪŋ] n : calefacción f

heat wave n : ola f de calor

heave[1] [ˈhiːv] v **heaved** or **hove** [ˈhoːv]; **heaving** vt 1 LIFT, RAISE : levantar con esfuerzo 2 HURL : lanzar, tirar 3 to heave a sigh : echar un suspiro, suspirar — vi 1 : subir y bajar, palpitar (dícese del pecho) 2 to heave up RISE : levantarse

heave[2] n 1 EFFORT : gran esfuerzo m (para levantar algo) 2 THROW : lanzamiento m

heaven [ˈhɛvən] n 1 : cielo m ⟨for heaven's sake : por Dios⟩ 2 **heavens** npl SKY : cielo m ⟨the heavens opened up : empezó a llover a cántaros⟩

heavenly [ˈhɛvənli] adj 1 : celestial, celeste 2 DELIGHTFUL : divino, encantador

heavily [ˈhɛvəli] adv 1 : mucho, muy ⟨heavily salted foods : comidas muy saladas⟩ ⟨he relies heavily on her : depende mucho de ella⟩ ⟨to smoke/drink

heavily : fumar/beber mucho⟩ 2 LABORIOUSLY : pesadamente

heaviness [ˈhɛvinəs] n : peso m, pesadez f

heavy [ˈhɛvi] adj **heavier; -est** 1 WEIGHTY : pesado ⟨to be heavy : pesar mucho, ser pesado⟩ ⟨how heavy is it? : ¿cuánto pesa?⟩ 2 DENSE, THICK : denso, espeso, grueso ⟨a heavy coat : un grueso abrigo⟩ ⟨a heavy beard : una barba poblada⟩ 3 LARGE, HIGH : grande, alto ⟨heavy turnout : alta concurrencia⟩ 4 INTENSE : intenso ⟨heavy traffic : denso tráfico⟩ ⟨heavy trading : mucha actividad (en la bolsa, etc.)⟩ 5 FORCEFUL : fuerte 6 SEVERE : severo ⟨heavy losses : grandes pérdidas⟩ 7 SERIOUS, IMPORTANT : serio, importante 8 PROFOUND : profundo ⟨to be a heavy sleeper : tener el sueño pesado⟩ 9 FILLING : pesado, fuerte 10 SLUGGISH : lento, tardo 11 STOUT : corpulento

heavy-duty [ˈhɛviˈduːˌti, -ˈdjuː-] adj : muy resistente, fuerte

heavyweight [ˈhɛviˌweɪt] n : peso m pesado (en deportes)

Hebrew[1] [ˈhiːˌbruː] adj : hebreo

Hebrew[2] n 1 : hebreo m, -brea f 2 : hebreo m (idioma)

heck [ˈhɛk] n : ¡caramba!, ¡caray! ⟨a heck of a lot : un montón⟩ ⟨what the heck is . . .? : ¿que diablos es . . .?⟩

heckle [ˈhɛkəl] vt **-led; -ling** : interrumpir (a un orador)

hectare [ˈhɛkˌtær] n : hectárea f

hectic [ˈhɛktɪk] adj : agitado, ajetreado — **hectically** [-tɪkli] adv

he'd [ˈhiːd] contraction of **he had** or **he would** → **have, would**

hedge[1] [ˈhɛdʒ] v **hedged; hedging** vt 1 : cercar con un seto 2 to hedge one's bet : cubrirse — vi 1 : dar rodeos, contestar con evasivas 2 to hedge against : cubrirse contra, protegerse contra

hedge[2] n 1 : seto m vivo 2 SAFEGUARD : salvaguardia f, protección f

hedgehog [ˈhɛdʒˌhɔɡ, -ˌhɑɡ] n : erizo m

heed[1] [ˈhiːd] vt : prestar atención a, hacer caso de

heed[2] n : atención f

heedless [ˈhiːdləs] adj : descuidado, despreocupado, inconsciente ⟨to be heedless of : hacer caso omiso de⟩ — **heedlessly** adv

heel[1] [ˈhiːl] vi : inclinarse

heel[2] n 1 : talón m (del pie), tacón m (de calzado) 2 to be close/hard/hot on the heels of : ir pisándole los talones (a alguien), seguir (algo) inmediatamente 3 to cool one's heels fam : esperar 4 to dig one's heels in : no ceder

heft [ˈhɛft] vt : sopesar

hefty [ˈhɛfti] adj **heftier; -est** : robusto, fornido, pesado

hegemony [hɪˈdʒɛməni] n, pl **-nies** : hegemonía f

heifer [ˈhɛfər] n : novilla f

height [ˈhaɪt] n 1 PEAK : cumbre f, cima f, punto m alto ⟨at the height of her career : en la cumbre de su carrera⟩ ⟨the height of stupidity : el colmo de la estupidez⟩ 2

: estatura f (de una persona), altura f (de un objeto) **3** ALTITUDE : altura f

heighten ['haɪtən] vt **1** : hacer más alto **2** INTENSIFY : aumentar, intensificar — vi : aumentarse, intensificarse

heinous ['heɪnəs] adj : atroz, abominable, nefando

heir ['ær] n : heredero m, -ra f

heiress ['ærəs] n : heredera f

heirloom ['ær,lu:m] n : reliquia f de familia

heist ['haɪst] n : golpe m, asalto m, atraco m ⟨to pull a heist : dar un golpe⟩

held → **hold**

helicopter ['hɛlə,kɑptər] n : helicóptero m

heliport ['hɛlə,pɔrt] n : helipuerto m

helium ['hi:liəm] n : helio m

helix ['hi:lɪks] n, pl **helices** ['hɛlə,si:z, 'hi:-] or **helixes** ['hi:lɪksəz] : hélice f

hell ['hɛl] n **1** : infierno m **2** (referring to a bad situation) ⟨a living hell : un auténtico infierno⟩ ⟨to go through hell : vivir un infierno, pasar las de Caín⟩ ⟨all hell broke loose : se armó la gorda⟩ **3** fam (used for emphasis) ⟨she was mad as hell : estaba que echaba chispas⟩ ⟨a/one hell of a (nice) guy : un tipo genial⟩ ⟨it hurts like hell : duele muchísimo⟩ ⟨to run like hell : correr como loco⟩ ⟨what (in) the hell . . .? : ¿que diablos/demonios . . .?⟩ ⟨you scared the hell out of me! : ¡qué susto me pegaste!⟩ **4 come hell or high water** fam : sea como sea, pase lo que pase **5 go to hell!** fam : ¡vete al infierno! **6 (just) for the hell of it** fam : sólo por divertirse **7 like hell** fam : malísimo ⟨you look like hell : tienes muy mala cara⟩ **8 like hell I did/will (etc.)!** fam : ¡y un cuerno! **9 there will be hell to pay** fam : se va a armar la gorda **10 to catch hell** fam ⟨she caught hell from the boss : el jefe le echó la bronca⟩ **11 to give someone hell** fam : echarle la bronca a alguien **12 to raise hell** fam : armar un buen lío, armar jarana

he'll ['hi:l, 'hɪl] contraction of **he shall** or **he will** → **shall, will**

hellhole ['hɛl,ho:l] n : infierno m

hellish ['hɛlɪʃ] adj : horroroso, infernal

hello [hə'lo:, hɛ-] interj : ¡hola!

helm ['hɛlm] n **1** : timón m **2 to take the helm** : tomar el mando

helmet ['hɛlmət] n : casco m

help¹ ['hɛlp] vt **1** : ayudar ⟨can I help you? : ¿en qué puedo servirle?⟩ **2** ALLEVIATE : aliviar **3** SERVE : servir ⟨help yourself! : ¡sírvete!⟩ **4** AVOID : evitar ⟨it can't be helped : no lo podemos evitar, no hay más remedio⟩ ⟨I couldn't help smiling : no pude menos que sonreír⟩ **5 to help out** : echarle una mano a — vi **1** : ayudar ⟨I was only trying to help : sólo quería ayudar⟩ **2 to help out** : echar una mano

help² n **1** ASSISTANCE : ayuda f ⟨help! : ¡socorro!, ¡auxilio!⟩ ⟨to call for help : pedir ayuda⟩ ⟨to go for help : ir a buscar ayuda⟩ ⟨she was a big help : me ayudó mucho⟩ ⟨she's no help : no me

ayuda en absoluto⟩ ⟨thanks for your help : gracias por ayudarme⟩ ⟨help menu/screen : menú/pantalla de ayuda⟩ **2** STAFF : personal m (en una oficina), servicio m doméstico ⟨help wanted : se necesita personal⟩

help desk n : servicio m de asistencia (técnica), soporte m técnico

helper ['hɛlpər] n : ayudante mf

helpful ['hɛlpfəl] adj **1** OBLIGING : servicial, amable, atento **2** USEFUL : útil, práctico — **helpfully** adv

helpfulness ['hɛlpfəlnəs] n **1** KINDNESS : bondad f, amabilidad f **2** USEFULNESS : utilidad f

helping ['hɛlpɪŋ] n : porción f

helpless ['hɛlpləs] adj **1** POWERLESS : incapaz, impotente **2** DEFENSELESS : indefenso

helplessly ['hɛlpləsli] adv : en vano, inútilmente

helplessness ['hɛlpləsnəs] n POWERLESSNESS : incapacidad f, impotencia f

helter–skelter [,hɛltər'skɛltər] adv : atropelladamente, precipitadamente

hem¹ ['hɛm] vt **hemmed; hemming 1** : hacerle el dobladillo a **2 to hem in** : encerrar

hem² n : dobladillo m

he–man ['hi:,mæn] n, pl **-men** [-mən, -,mɛn] : macho m, machote m

hematoma [,hi:mə'to:mə] n : hematoma m

hemisphere ['hɛmə,sfɪr] n : hemisferio m

hemispheric [,hɛmə'sfɪrɪk, -'sfɪr-] or **hemispherical** [-ɪkəl] adj : hemisférico

hemline ['hɛm,laɪn] n : bajo m (de un vestido, etc.)

hemlock ['hɛm,lɑk] n : cicuta f

hemoglobin ['hi:mə,glo:bən] n : hemoglobina f

hemophilia [,hi:mə'fɪliə] n : hemofilia f

hemophiliac [,hi:mə'fɪli,æk] n : hemofílico m, -ca f — **hemophiliac** adj

hemorrhage¹ ['hɛmərɪdʒ] vi **-rhaged; -rhaging** : sufrir una hemorragia

hemorrhage² n : hemorragia f

hemorrhoids ['hɛmə,rɔɪdz, 'hɛm-,rɔɪdz] npl : hemorroides fpl, almorranas fpl

hemp ['hɛmp] n : cáñamo m

hen ['hɛn] n : gallina f

hence ['hɛnts] adv **1** : de aquí, de ahí ⟨10 years hence : de aquí a 10 años⟩ ⟨a dog bit me, hence my dislike of animals : un perro me mordió, de ahí mi aversión a los animales⟩ **2** THEREFORE : por lo tanto, por consiguiente

henceforth ['hɛnts,fɔrθ, ,hɛnts'-] adv : de ahora en adelante

henchman ['hɛntʃmən] n, pl **-men** [-mən, -,mɛn] : secuaz m f, esbirro m

henpeck ['hɛn,pɛk] vt : dominar (al marido)

hepatitis [,hɛpə'taɪtəs] n, pl **-titides** [-'tɪtə,di:z] : hepatitis f

her¹ ['hər] adj : su, sus, de ella ⟨her house : su casa, la casa de ella⟩

her² ['hər, ər] pron **1** (used as direct object) : la ⟨I saw her yesterday : la vi ayer⟩ ⟨I like her : me gusta⟩ **2** (used as indirect *object*) : le, se ⟨he gave her the book : le dio el libro⟩ ⟨he sent it to her : se lo mandó⟩ **3** (*used as object of a preposition*) : ella ⟨we did it for her : lo hicimos por ella⟩ ⟨taller than her : más alto que ella⟩

herald[1] [ˈhɛrəld] *vt* ANNOUNCE : anunciar, proclamar

herald[2] *n* **1** MESSENGER : heraldo *m* **2** HARBINGER : precursor *m*

heraldic [hɛˈrældɪk, hə-] *adj* : heráldico

heraldry [ˈhɛrəldri] *n, pl* **-ries** : heráldica *f*

herb [ˈərb, ˈhərb] *n* : hierba *f*

herbal [ˈərbəl, ˈhər-] *adj* : herbario

herbicide [ˈərbə,saɪd, ˈhər-] *n* : herbicida *m*

herbivore [ˈərbə,vor, ˈhər-] *n* : herbívoro *m*

herbivorous [ˌərˈbɪvərəs, ˌhər-] *adj* : herbívoro

herculean [ˌhərkjəˈliːən, ˌhərˈkjuː-liən] *adj* : hercúleo, sobrehumano

herd[1] [ˈhərd] *vt* : reunir en manada, conducir en manada — *vi* : ir en manada (dícese de los animales), apiñarse (dícese de la gente)

herd[2] *n* : manada *f*

herder [ˈhərdər] → **herdsman**

herdsman [ˈhərdzmən] *n, pl* **-men** [-mən, -ˌmɛn] : vaquero *m* (de ganado), pastor *m* (de ovejas)

here[1] [ˈhɪr] *adv* **1** : aquí, acá ⟨come here! : ¡ven acá!⟩ ⟨right here : aquí mismo⟩ ⟨she's not here : no está⟩ **2** NOW : en este momento, ahora, ya ⟨here he comes : ya viene⟩ ⟨here it's three o'clock (already) : ahora son las tres⟩ **3** : en este punto ⟨here we agree : estamos de acuerdo en este punto⟩ **4 here and now** : ahora mismo, en este mismo momento **5 here and there** : aquí y allá **6 here (you are/go)!** : ¡toma! **7 the here and now** : el presente, el momento **8 to be neither here nor there** : no venir al caso

hereabouts [ˈhɪrə,bauts] *or* **hereabout** [-ˌbaut] *adv* : por aquí (cerca)

hereafter[1] [hɪrˈæftər] *adv* **1** : de aquí en adelante, a continuación **2** : en el futuro

hereafter[2] *n* **the hereafter** : el más allá

hereby [hɪrˈbaɪ] *adv* : por este medio

hereditary [həˈrɛdə,tɛri] *adj* : hereditario

heredity [həˈrɛdəṭi] *n* : herencia *f*

herein [hɪrˈɪn] *adv* : aquí

hereof [hɪrˈʌv] *adv* : de aquí

hereon [hɪrˈɑn, -ˈɔn] *adv* : sobre esto

heresy [ˈhɛrəsi] *n, pl* **-sies** : herejía *f*

heretic [ˈhɛrə,tɪk] *n* : hereje *mf*

heretical [hɪˈrɛṭɪkəl] *adj* : herético

hereto [hɪrˈtuː] *adv* : a esto

heretofore [ˈhɪrṭə,for] *adv* HITHERTO : hasta ahora

hereunder [hɪrˈʌndər] *adv* : a continuación, abajo

hereupon [hɪrə,pɑn, -ˈpɔn] *adv* : con esto, en ese momento

herewith [hɪrˈwɪθ] *adv* : adjunto

heritage [ˈhɛrəṭɪʤ] *n* : patrimonio *m* (nacional)

hermaphrodite [hərˈmæfrə,daɪt] *n* : hermafrodita *mf*

hermetic [hərˈmɛṭɪk] *adj* : hermético — **hermetically** [-ṭɪkli] *adv*

hermit [ˈhərmət] *n* : ermitaño *m*, -ña *f*; eremita *mf*

hernia [ˈhərniə] *n, pl* **-nias** *or* **-niae** [-niˌi:, -niˌaɪ] : hernia *f*

hero [ˈhiː,roː, ˈhɪr,oː] *n, pl* **-roes 1** : héroe *m* **2** PROTAGONIST : protagonista *m*

heroic [hɪˈroːɪk] *adj* : heroico — **heroically** [-ɪkli] *adv*

heroics [hɪˈroːɪks] *npl* : actos *mpl* heroicos

heroin [ˈhɛroən] *n* : heroína *f*

heroine [ˈhɛroən] *n* **1** : heroína *f* **2** PROTAGONIST : protagonista *f*

heroism [ˈhɛro,ɪzəm] *n* : heroísmo *m*

heron [ˈhɛrən] *n* : garza *f*

herpes [ˈhər,piːz] *n* : herpes *m*

herring [ˈhɛrɪŋ] *n, pl* **-ring** *or* **-rings** : arenque *m*

hers [ˈhərz] *pron* : suyo, de ella ⟨these suitcases are hers : estas maletas son suyas⟩ ⟨hers are bigger : los de ella son más grandes⟩

herself [hərˈsɪlf] *pron* **1** (*used reflexively*) : se ⟨she dressed herself : se vistió⟩ **2** (*used emphatically*) : ella misma ⟨she fixed it herself : lo arregló ella misma, lo arregló por sí sola⟩

hertz [ˈhərts, ˈhrts] *ns & pl* : hercio *m*

he's [ˈhiːz] *contraction of* **he is** *or* **he has** → **be, have**

hesitancy [ˈhɛzəṭənsi] *n, pl* **-cies** : vacilación *f*, titubeo *m*, indecisión *f*

hesitant [ˈhɛzəṭənt] *adj* : titubeante, vacilante — **hesitantly** *adv*

hesitate [ˈhɛzə,teɪt] *vi* **-tated; -tating** : vacilar, titubear

hesitation [ˌhɛzəˈteɪʃən] *n* : vacilación *f*, indecisión *f*, titubeo *m*

heterogeneous [ˌhɛṭərəˈʤiːniəs, -njəs] *adj* : heterogéneo

heterosexual[1] [ˌhɛṭəroˈskʃuəl] *adj* : heterosexual

heterosexual[2] *n* : heterosexual *mf*

heterosexuality [ˌhɛṭəro,skʃuˈæləṭi] *n* : heterosexualidad *f*

hew [ˈhjuː] *v* **hewed;** **hewed** *or* **hewn** [ˈhjuːn]; **hewing** *vt* **1** CUT : cortar, talar (árboles) **2** SHAPE : labrar, tallar — *vi* CONFORM : conformarse, ceñirse

hex[1] [ˈhɛks] *vt* : hacerle un maleficio (a alguien)

hex[2] *n* : maleficio *m*

hexagon [ˈhɛksə,gɑn] *n* : hexágono *m*

hexagonal [hɛkˈsægənəl] *adj* : hexagonal

hey [ˈheɪ] *interj* : ¡eh!, ¡oye!

heyday [ˈheɪ,deɪ] *n* : auge *m*, apogeo *m*

hi [ˈhaɪ] *interj* : ¡hola!

hiatus [haɪˈeɪṭəs] *n* **1** : hiato *m* **2** PAUSE : pausa *f*

hibernate [ˈhaɪbər,neɪt] *vi* **-nated; -nating** : hibernar, invernar

hibernation [ˌhaɪbərˈneɪʃən] *n* : hibernación *f*

hiccup[1] [ˈhɪkəp] *vi* **-cuped; -cuping** : hipar, tener hipo

hiccup[2] *n* : hipo *m* ⟨to have the hiccups : tener hipo⟩

hick [ˈhɪk] *n* BUMPKIN : palurdo *m*, -da *f*

hickory ['hɪkəri] n, pl **-ries** : nogal m americano

hidden ['hɪdən] adj : oculto

hide¹ ['haɪd] v hid ['hɪd]; **hidden** ['hɪdən] or hid; **hiding** vt 1 CONCEAL : esconder ‹to be in hiding : estar escondido› 2 : ocultar ‹to hide one's motives : ocultar uno sus motivos› 3 SCREEN : tapar, no dejar ver — vi : esconderse

hide² n : piel f, cuero m ‹to save one's hide : salvar el pellejo›

hide–and–seek ['haɪdənd'si:k] n to play **hide–and–seek** : jugar a las escondidas

hidebound ['haɪd,baʊnd] adj : rígido, conservador

hideous ['hɪdiəs] adj : horrible, horroroso, espantoso — **hideously** adv

hideout ['haɪd,aʊt] n : guarida f, escondrijo m

hierarchical [,haɪə'rɑrkɪkəl] adj : jerárquico

hierarchy ['haɪə,rɑrki] n, pl **-chies** : jerarquía f

hieroglyphic [,haɪərə'glɪfɪk] n : jeroglífico m

hi–fi ['haɪ'faɪ] n 1 → **high fidelity** 2 : equipo m de alta fidelidad

high¹ ['haɪ] adv 1 : alto ‹to aim high : apuntar alto› 2 **high and low** : por todas partes 3 **to leave high and dry** : dejar tirado

high² adj 1 TALL : alto ‹a high wall : un muro alto› ‹it's two feet high : tiene dos pies de altura› ‹waist-high : que llega hasta la cintura› ‹the highest mountain : la montaña más alta› 2 ELEVATED : alto, elevado ‹high ground : terreno elevado› ‹high prices : precios elevados› ‹high blood pressure : presión alta› ‹at a high rate of speed : a gran velocidad› 3 GREAT : grande ‹a high number : un número grande› ‹high hopes : grandes esperanzas› 4 GOOD, FAVORABLE : bueno, favorable ‹in high esteem : en gran estima› ‹on a high note : con una nota de optimismo› ‹the high point of the trip : el mejor momento del viaje› 5 STRONG : fuerte ‹high winds : fuertes vientos› 6 : alto ‹high society : alta sociedad› ‹high-ranking : alto, de alto rango› ‹the high life : la gran vida› 7 : alto (en música) 8 : pleno ‹in high summer : en pleno verano› 9 INTOXICATED : borracho, drogado

high³ n 1 : récord m, punto m máximo ‹to reach an all-time high : batir el récord› 2 : zona f de alta presión (en meteorología) 3 or **high gear** : directa f 4 **on high** : en las alturas

highbrow ['haɪ,braʊ] n : intelectual mf

high chair n : silla f alta (para bebé), periquera f Mex, trona f Spain

higher ['haɪər] adj : superior ‹higher education : enseñanza superior›

high fidelity n : alta fidelidad f

high–flown ['haɪ'flo:n] adj : altisonante

high–handed ['haɪ'hændəd] adj : arbitrario

high–heeled ['haɪ'hi:ld] adj : de tacón alto

highlands ['haɪləndz] npl : tierras fpl altas, altiplano m

high–level ['haɪ'lɛvəl] adj : de alto nivel

highlight¹ ['haɪ,laɪt] vt 1 EMPHASIZE : destacar, poner en relieve, subrayar 2 : ser el punto culminante de

highlight² n : punto m culminante

highlighter ['haɪ,laɪtər] n : marcador m, rotulador m Spain

highly ['haɪli] adv 1 VERY : muy, sumamente 2 FAVORABLY : muy bien ‹to speak highly of ; hablar muy bien de› ‹to think highly of : tener en mucho a›

highness ['haɪnəs] n 1 HEIGHT : altura f 2 **Highness** : Alteza f ‹Your Royal Highness : Su Alteza Real›

high–pitched ['haɪ'pɪtʃt] adj : agudo

high–rise ['haɪ,raɪz] adj : alto, de muchas plantas

high school n : escuela f superior, escuela f secundaria

high seas npl : alta mar f

high–speed ['haɪ'spi:d] adj : de alta velocidad

high–spirited ['haɪ'spɪrətəd] adj : vivaz, muy animado, brioso

high–strung [,haɪ'strʌŋ] adj : nervioso

high–tech ['haɪ'tɛk] adj : de alta tecnología

high–tension ['haɪ'tɛntʃən] adj : de alta tensión

high–voltage ['haɪ'vo:ltɪdʒ] adj : de alto voltaje

highway ['haɪ,weɪ] n : carretera f

highwayman ['haɪ,weɪmən] n, pl **-men** [-mən, -,mɛn] : salteador m (de caminos), bandido m

hijack¹ ['haɪ,dʒæk] vt : secuestrar

hijack² n : secuestro m

hijacker ['haɪ,dʒækər] n : secuestrador m, -dora f

hike¹ ['haɪk] v hiked; hiking vi : hacer una caminata — vt RAISE : subir

hike² n 1 : caminata f, excursión f 2 INCREASE : subida f (de precios)

hiker ['haɪkər] n : excursionista mf

hilarious [hɪ'læriəs, haɪ-] adj : muy divertido, hilarante

hilarity [hɪ'lærəti, haɪ-] n : hilaridad f

hill ['hɪl] n 1 : colina f, cerro m 2 SLOPE : cuesta f, pendiente f

hillbilly ['hɪl,bɪli] n, pl **-lies** : palurdo m, -da f (de las montañas)

hillock ['hɪlək] n 1 : loma f, altozano m, otero m

hillside ['hɪl,saɪd] n : ladera f, cuesta f

hilltop ['hɪl,tɑp] n : cima f, cumbre f

hilly ['hɪli] adj **hillier; -est** : montañoso, accidentado

hilt ['hɪlt] n : puño m, empuñadura f

him ['hɪm, əm] pron 1 (used as direct object) : lo ‹I found him : lo encontré› 2 (used as indirect object) : le, se ‹we gave him a present : le dimos un regalo› ‹I sent it to him : se lo mandé› 3 (used as object of a preposition) : él ‹she was thinking of him : pensaba en él› ‹younger than him : más joven que él›

himself [hɪm'sɛlf] pron 1 (used reflexively) : se ‹he washed himself : se lavó› 2 (used *emphatically*) : él mismo ⟨he did it himself : lo hizo él mismo, lo hizo por sí solo⟩

hind[1] [ˈhaɪnd] *adj* : trasero, posterior ⟨hind legs : patas traseras⟩

hind[2] *n* : cierva *f*

hinder [ˈhɪndər] *vt* : dificultar, impedir, estorbar

Hindi [ˈhɪndi:] *n* : hindi *m*

hindquarters [ˈhaɪndˌkwɔrtərz] *npl* : cuartos *mpl* traseros

hindrance [ˈhɪndrənts] *n* : estorbo *m*, obstáculo *m*, impedimento *m*

hindsight [ˈhaɪndˌsaɪt] *n* : retrospectiva *f* ⟨with the benefit of hindsight : en retrospectiva, con la perspectiva que da la experiencia⟩

Hindu[1] [ˈhɪnˌdu:] *adj* : hindú

Hindu[2] *n* : hindú *mf*

Hinduism [ˈhɪnduˌɪzəm] *n* : hinduismo *m*

hinge[1] [ˈhɪnʤ] *v* **hinged; hinging** *vt* : unir con bisagras — *vi* **to hinge on/upon** : depender of

hinge[2] *n* : bisagra *f*, gozne *m*

hint[1] [ˈhɪnt] *vt* : insinuar, dar a entender — *vi* : soltar indirectas

hint[2] *n* **1** INSINUATION : insinuación *f*, indirecta *f* **2** TIP : consejo *m*, sugerencia *f* **3** TRACE : pizca *f*, indicio *m*

hinterland [ˈhɪntərˌlænd, -lənd] *n* : interior *m* (de un país)

hip[1] [ˈhɪp] *n* : cadera *f*

hip–hop [ˈhɪpˌhɑp] *n* : hip-hop *m*

hippie [ˈhɪpi] *n* : hippie *mf*, hippy *mf*

hippo [ˈhɪpo:] *n, pl* **hippos** → **hippopotamus**

hippopotamus [ˌhɪpəˈpɑtəməs] *n, pl* **-muses** *or* **-mi** [-ˌmaɪ] : hipopótamo *m*

hire[1] [ˈhaɪr] *vt* **hired; hiring 1** EMPLOY : contratar, emplear **2** RENT : alquilar, arrendar

hire[2] *n* **1** RENT : alquiler *m* ⟨for hire : se alquila⟩ **2** WAGES : paga *f*, sueldo *m* **3** EMPLOYEE : empleado *m*, -da *f*

his[1] [ˈhɪz, ɪz] *adj* : su, sus, de él ⟨his hat : su sombrero, el sombrero de él⟩

his[2] *pron* : suyo, de él ⟨the decision is his : la decisión es suya⟩ ⟨it's his, not hers : es de él, no de ella⟩

Hispanic[1] [hɪˈspænɪk] *adj* : hispano, hispánico

Hispanic[2] *n* : hispano *m*, -na *f*; hispánico *m*, -ca *f*

hiss[1] [ˈhɪs] *vi* : sisear, silbar — *vt* : decir entre dientes

hiss[2] *n* : siseo *m*, silbido *m*

historian [hɪˈstoriən] *n* : historiador *m*, -dora *f*

historic [hɪˈstorɪk] *or* **historical** [-ɪkəl] *adj* : histórico — **historically** [-ɪkli] *adv*

history [ˈhɪstəri] *n, pl* **-ries 1** : historia *f* **2** RECORD : historial *m* ⟨family history : historial personal⟩ **3 to go down in history** : pasar a la historia **4 to go down in history** : hacer historia

histrionics [ˌhɪstriˈɑnɪks] *ns & pl* : histrionismo *m*

hit[1] [ˈhɪt] *v* **hit; hitting** *vt* **1** STRIKE : golpear (algo), pegarle a (alguien), batear (una pelota) ⟨he hit the dog : le pegó al

perro⟩ **2** : chocar contra, dar con, dar en (el blanco) ⟨the car hit a tree : el coche chocó contra un árbol⟩ ⟨it hit me in the face : me dio en la cara⟩ ⟨he hit his head against the door : se dio con la cabeza contra la puerta⟩ **3** *fam* OPERATE : apretar (un botón), darle a (un freno, un interruptor, etc.) **4** ATTACK : atacar **5** AFFECT : afectar ⟨the news hit us hard : la noticia nos afectó mucho⟩ **6** ENCOUNTER : tropezar con, toparse con ⟨to hit a snag : tropezar con un obstáculo⟩ **7** : ocurrírsele a uno ⟨it hit me that . . . : se me ocurrió que . . ., me di cuenta de que . . .⟩ **8** REACH : llegar a, alcanzar ⟨the price hit $10 a pound : el precio alcanzó los $10 dólares por libra⟩ ⟨to hit the headlines : ser noticia⟩ **9** ARRIVE AT : llegar a ⟨to hit town : llegar a la ciudad⟩ ⟨let's hit the beach! : ¡vamos a la playa!⟩ **10** MAKE : hacer ⟨to hit a home run : hacer un jonrón⟩ **11 to hit it off (with)** : congeniar (con) **12 to hit someone up for something** : pedirle algo a alguien **13 to hit the ceiling/roof** *fam* : poner el grito en el cielo **14 to hit the hay/sack** *fam* : irse al catre, acostarse **15 to hit the nail on the head** *fam* : dar en el clavo **16 to hit the road** *fam* : ponerse en marcha — *vi* **1** : golpear **2 to hit back** : devolver el golpe **3 to hit on** *fam* : tratar de ligarse a **4 to hit on/upon** : dar con (una solución, etc.)

hit[2] *n* **1** BLOW : golpe *m* **2** : impacto *m* (de un arma) **3** SUCCESS : éxito *m* **4** : visita *f* (a un sitio Web)

hit–and–run [ˌhɪtændˈrʌn] *adj* **1** : en que el conductor culpable se da a la fuga (dícese del accidente de tránsito) **2** : fugitivo (dícese de un conductor)

hitch[1] [ˈhɪʧ] *vt* **1** : mover con sacudidas **2** ATTACH : enganchar, atar, amarrar **3 to hitch up** : subirse (los pantalones, etc.) — *vi* → **hitchhike**

hitch[2] *n* **1** JERK : tirón *m*, jalón *m* **2** OBSTACLE : obstáculo *m*, impedimento *m*, tropiezo *m*

hitchhike [ˈhɪʧˌhaɪk] *vi* **-hiked; -hiking** : hacer autostop, ir de aventón *Col, Mex fam*

hitchhiker [ˈhɪʧˌhaɪkər] *n* : autostopista *mf*

hither [ˈhɪðər] *adv* : acá, por aquí

hitherto [ˈhɪðərˌtu:, ˌhɪðərˈ-] *adv* : hasta ahora

hit man *n* : sicario *m*, -ria *f*; asesino *m*, -na *f*

hitter [ˈhɪtər] *n* BATTER : bateador *m*, -dora *f*

HIV [ˌeɪʧˌaɪˈvi:] *n* (*human immunodeficiency virus*) : VIH *m*, virus *m* del sida ⟨HIV negative/positive : VIH negativo/positivo⟩

hive [ˈhaɪv] *n* **1** : colmena *f* **2** SWARM : enjambre *m* **3** : lugar *m* muy activo ⟨a hive of activity : un hervidero de actividad⟩

hives [ˈhaɪvz] *ns & pl* : urticaria *f*

hoard[1] [ˈhord] *vt* : acumular, atesorar

hoard[2] *n* : tesoro *m*, reserva *f*, provisión *f*

hoarfrost ['hor,frɔst] *n* : escarcha *f*
hoarse ['hors] *adj* **hoarser; hoarsest**
: ronco — **hoarsely** *adv*
hoarseness ['horsnəs] *n* : ronquera *f*
hoary ['hori] *adj* **hoarier; -est** 1 : cano,
canoso 2 OLD : vetusto, antiguo
hoax¹ ['ho:ks] *vt* : engañar, embaucar,
bromear
hoax² *n* : engaño *m*, broma *f*
hobble¹ ['habəl] *v* **-bled; -bling** *vi* LIMP
: cojear, renguear
hobble² *n* LIMP : cojera *f*, rengo *m*
hobby ['habi] *n, pl* **-bies** : pasatiempo *m*,
afición *f*
hobgoblin ['hab,gablən] *n* : duende *m*
hobnail ['hab,neɪl] *n* : tachuela *f*
hobnob ['hab,nab] *vi* **-nobbed; -nobbing**
: codearse
hobo ['ho:,bo:] *n, pl* **-boes** : vagabundo *m*,
-da *f*
hock¹ ['hak] *vt* PAWN : empeñar
hock² *n* **in hock** : empeñado
hockey ['haki] *n* : hockey *m*
hodgepodge ['hadʒ,padʒ] *n* : mezcolanza
f
hoe¹ ['ho:] *vt* **hoed; hoeing** : remover con
una azada
hoe² *n* : azada *f*
hog¹ ['hɔg, 'hag] *vt* **hogged; hogging**
: acaparar, monopolizar
hog² *n* 1 PIG : cerdo *m*, -da *f* 2 GLUTTON
: glotón *m*, -tona *f*
hogshead ['hɔgz,hed, 'hagz-] *n* : tonel *m*
hoist¹ ['hɔɪst] *vt* : levantar, alzar, izar (una
bandera, una vela)
hoist² *n* : grúa *f*
hold¹ ['ho:ld] *v* **held** ['held]; **holding** *vt* 1
POSSESS : tener ⟨to hold office : ocupar
un puesto⟩ 2 RESTRAIN : detener, controlar ⟨to hold one's temper : controlar
su mal genio⟩ 3 CLASP, GRASP : agarrar,
coger ⟨to hold hands : agarrarse de la
mano⟩ ⟨hold it tightly : agárralo fuerte⟩
4 CARRY : llevar, tener (en la mano o las
manos) 5 : sujetar, mantener fijo ⟨hold
this nail for me : sujétame este clavo⟩
⟨hold it upright : mantenlo derecho⟩
⟨hold the door : sostén la puerta⟩ 6
CONTAIN : dar cabida a, tener capacidad
para (personas, etc.), tener una capacidad de (litros, etc.) 7 *or* to hold in store
: deparar 8 SUPPORT : aguantar, sostener
9 REGARD : considerar, estimar ⟨he held
me responsible : me consideró responsa-
ble⟩ 10 CONDUCT : celebrar (una reunión, una elección), realizar (un evento),
mantener (una conversación) 11 KEEP,
RESERVE : guardar 12 MAINTAIN : mantener 13 DETAIN : detener 14 to hold
against : tomar en cuenta, guardar rencor por 15 to hold back REPRESS, CON-
TAIN : reprimir, contener 16 to hold
back WITHHOLD : retener, ocultar (información) 17 to hold down : conservar
(un trabajo) 18 to hold in CONTAIN
: contener 19 to hold off RESIST : resistir
20 to hold one's liquor : ser de buen beber 21 to hold one's tongue : callarse
22 to hold out : extender, tender (la
mano, etc.), dar (esperanzas) 23 to hold

over POSTPONE : postergar, aplazar 24
to hold up DELAY : retrasar 25 to hold
up LIFT : levantar 26 to hold up *fam*
ROB : robarle (a alguien), atracar, asaltar
— *vi* 1 : aguantar, resistir ⟨the rope will
hold : la cuerda resistirá⟩ 2 : ser válido,
valer ⟨my offer still holds : mi oferta todavía es válida⟩ 3 to hold forth : perorar, arengar 4 to hold off WAIT : esperar,
aguantar 5 to hold off (on) DELAY : retrasar 6 to hold on WAIT : esperar,
aguantar 7 to hold on to : agarrarse a 8
to hold out LAST : aguantar, durar 9 to
hold out RESIST : resistir 10 to hold out
for AWAIT : esperar (algo mejor) 11 to
hold to : mantenerse firme en 12 to
hold together : mantenerse unidos 13
to hold up : aguantar ⟨how are you
holding up? : ¿cómo estás?, ¿cómo lo
estás llevando?⟩ 14 to hold with : estar
de acuerdo con
hold² *n* 1 GRIP : agarre *m*, llave *f* (en deportes) 2 CONTROL : control *m*, dominio
m ⟨to get hold of oneself : controlarse⟩
3 DELAY : demora *f* 4 : bodega *f* (en un
barco o un avión) 5 on hold DELAYED
: suspendido ⟨to put on hold : suspender
temporalmente⟩ 6 on hold : en espera
(en el teléfono) ⟨to be/put on hold
: estar/poner en espera⟩ 7 no holds
barred : sin restricciones 8 to get hold
of : conseguir, localizar 9 to take hold
: establecerse 10 to take hold of GRASP
: agarrar
holder ['ho:ldər] *n* : poseedor *m*, -dora *f*;
titular *mf*
holdings ['ho:ldɪŋz] *npl* : propiedades *fpl*
holdup ['ho:ld,ʌp] *n* 1 ROBBERY : atraco
m 2 DELAY : retraso *m*, demora *f*
hole ['ho:l] *n* : agujero *m*, hoyo *m*
holiday ['halə,deɪ] *n* 1 : día *m* feriado,
fiesta *f* ⟨happy holidays : felices fiestas⟩
2 VACATION : vacaciones *fpl*
holiness ['ho:linəs] *n* 1 : santidad *f* 2 **His
Holiness** : Su Santidad
holistic [ho:'lɪstɪk] *adj* : holístico
holler¹ ['halər] *vi* : gritar, chillar
holler² *n* : grito *m*, chillido *m*
hollow¹ ['ha,lo:] *vt or* to hollow out
: ahuecar
hollow² *adj* **hollower; -est** 1 : hueco,
hundido (dícese de las mejillas, etc.), cavernoso (dícese de un sonido) 2 EMPTY,
FALSE : vacío, falso
hollow³ *n* 1 CAVITY : hueco *m*, depresión
f, cavidad *f* 2 VALLEY : hondonada *f*, valle *m*
hollowness ['ha,lo:nəs] *n* 1 HOLLOW
: hueco *m*, cavidad *f* 2 FALSENESS
: falsedad *f* 3 EMPTINESS : vacuidad *f*
holly ['hali] *n, pl* **-lies** : acebo *m*
holocaust ['halə,kɔst, 'ho:-, 'hɔ-] *n* : holocausto *m*
hologram ['ho:lə,græm, 'ha-] *n* : holograma *m*
holster ['ho:lstər] *n* : pistolera *f*
holy ['ho:li] *adj* **holier; -est** : santo, sagrado
Holy Ghost → Holy Spirit
holy orders → order²

Holy Spirit n the Holy Spirit : el Espíritu Santo

homage [ˈɑmɪʤ, ˈhɑ-] n : homenaje m

home [ˈhoːm] n **1** : hogar m, casa f ⟨home sweet home : hogar dulce hogar⟩ ⟨there's no place like home : como en casa no se está en ningún sitio⟩ ⟨to leave home : irse de casa⟩ ⟨to hit close to home : tocar muy de cerca⟩ **2** HOUSE, RESIDENCE : casa f, domicilio m ⟨to own one's own home : tener casa propia⟩ ⟨a home away from home : una segunda casa⟩ **3** SEAT : sede f **4** HABITAT : hábitat m **5** INSTITUTION : residencia f, asilo m **6** → home plate **7 at home** : en casa ⟨is Julia at home? : ¿está Julia (en casa)?⟩ **8 at home** : cómodo ⟨make yourself at home : estás en tu casa⟩ **9 to play at home** : jugar en casa

homebody [ˈhoːmˌbɑdi] n, pl **-dies** : persona f hogareña

homecoming [ˈhoːmˌkʌmɪŋ] n : regreso m (a casa)

home game n : partido m en casa

homegrown [ˈhoːmˈgroːn] adj **1** : de cosecha propia **2** LOCAL : local

homeland [ˈhoːmˌlænd] n : patria f, tierra f natal, terruño m

homeless [ˈhoːmləs] adj : sin hogar, sin techo

homely [ˈhoːmli] adj **homelier; -est 1** DOMESTIC : casero, hogareño **2** UGLY : feo, poco atractivo

homemade [ˈhoːmˈmeɪd] adj : casero, hecho en casa

homemaker [ˈhoːmˌmeɪkər] n : ama f de casa, persona f que se ocupa de la casa

homeopathy [ˌhoːmiˈɑpəθi] n : homeopatía f — **homeopathic** adj

home page n : página f de inicio

home plate n : base f del bateador

home run n : jonrón m

homesick [ˈhoːmˌsɪk] adj : nostálgico ⟨to be homesick : echar de menos a la familia⟩

homesickness [ˈhoːmˌsɪknəs] n : nostalgia f, morriña f

homespun [ˈhoːmˌspʌn] adj : simple, sencillo

homestead [ˈhoːmˌsted] n : estancia f, hacienda f

hometown [ˈhoːmˌtaʊn] n : ciudad f natal, pueblo m natal

homeward[1] [ˈhoːmwərd] or **homewards** [-wərdz] adv : de vuelta a casa, hacia casa

homeward[2] adj : de vuelta, de regreso

homework [ˈhoːmˌwərk] n : tarea f, deberes mpl Spain, asignación f PRi

homey [ˈhoːmi] adj **homier; -est** : hogareño

homicidal [ˌhɑməˈsaɪdəl, ˌhoː-] adj : homicida

homicide [ˈhɑməˌsaɪd, ˈhoː-] n : homicidio m

homily [ˈhɑməli] n, pl **-lies** : homilía f

hominy [ˈhɑməni] n : maíz m descascarado

homogeneity [ˌhoːməʤəˈniːəti, -ˈneɪ-] n, pl **-ties** : homogeneidad f

homogeneous [ˌhoːməˈʤiːniəs, -njəs] adj : homogéneo — **homogeneously** adv

homogenize [hoːˈmɑʤəˌnaɪz, hə-] vt **-nized; -nizing** : homogeneizar

homograph [ˈhɑməˌgræf, ˈhoː-] n : homógrafo m

homologous [hoːˈmɑləgəs, hə-] adj : homólogo

homonym [ˈhɑməˌnɪm, ˈhoː-] n : homónimo m

homophone [ˈhɑməˌfoːn, ˈhoː-] n : homófono m

homosexual[1] [ˌhoːməˈsɛkʃʊəl] adj : homosexual

homosexual[2] n : homosexual mf

homosexuality [ˌhoːməˌsɛkʃʊˈæləti] n : homosexualidad f

honcho [ˈhɑnˌʧoː] n : pez m gordo ⟨the head honcho : el jefe⟩

Honduran [hɑnˈdʊrən, -ˈdjʊr-] n : hondureño m, -ña f — **Honduran** adj

hone [ˈhoːn] vt **honed; honing** : afilar

honest [ˈɑnəst] adj : honesto, honrado — **honestly** adv

honesty [ˈɑnəsti] n, pl **-ties** : honestidad f, honradez f

honey [ˈhʌni] n, pl **-eys** : miel f

honeybee [ˈhʌniˌbiː] n : abeja f

honeycomb [ˈhʌniˌkoːm] n : panal m

honeymoon[1] [ˈhʌniˌmuːn] vi : pasar la luna de miel

honeymoon[2] n : luna f de miel

honeysuckle [ˈhʌniˌsʌkəl] n : madreselva f

honk[1] [ˈhɑŋk, ˈhɔŋk] vi **1** : graznar (dícese del ganso) **2** : tocar la bocina (dícese de un vehículo), pitar

honk[2] n : graznido m (del ganso), bocinazo m (de un vehículo)

honor[1] [ˈɑnər] vt **1** RESPECT : honrar **2** : cumplir con ⟨to cumplir con one's word : cumplir con su palabra⟩ **3** : aceptar (un cheque, etc.)

honor[2] n **1** : honor m ⟨in honor of : en honor de⟩ ⟨a man of honor : un hombre de honor/palabra⟩ ⟨guest of honor : invitado de honor⟩ **2 honors** npl AWARDS : honores mpl, condecoraciones fpl **3 on my honor** : juro por mi honor **4 to do someone the honor of** : hacerle a alguien el honor de **5 to do the honors** : hacer los honores **6 Your Honor** : Su Señoría

honorable [ˈɑnərəbəl] adj : honorable, honroso — **honorably** [-bli] adv

honorary [ˈɑnəˌreri] adj : honorario

hood [ˈhʊd] n **1** : capucha f **2** : capó m, bonete m Car (de un automóvil)

hooded [ˈhʊdəd] adj : encapuchado

hoodie [ˈhʊdi] n : sudadera f (con capucha); buzo m Arg, Col

hoodlum [ˈhʊdləm, ˈhuːd-] n THUG : maleante mf, matón m

hoodwink [ˈhʊdˌwɪŋk] vt : engañar

hoof [ˈhʊf, ˈhuːf] n, pl **hooves** [ˈhʊvz, ˈhuːvz] or **hoofs** : pezuña f, casco m

hoofed [ˈhʊft, ˈhuːft] adj : ungulado

hook[1] [ˈhʊk] n **1** : gancho m **2** CATCH : pescar **3 to hook up** CONNECT : conectar (algo a algo) **4 to hook up** fam

⟨don't worry—I'll hook you up : no te preocupes, te lo arreglaré todo⟩ — *vi* **1** : abrocharse, engancharse **2 to hook up** *fam* MEET : reunirse **3 to hook up** *fam* JOIN, UNITE : juntarse, unirse

hook² *n* **1** : gancho *m*, percha *f* **2 to let someone off the hook** : dejar a alguien ir sin castigo

hooked ['hʊkt] *adj* **1** : en forma de gancho **2 to be hooked on** : estar enganchado a

hooker ['hʊkər] *n* : prostituta *f*, fulana *f* *fam*

hookworm ['hʊk,wərm] *n* : anquilostoma *m*

hooligan ['hu:lɪgən] *n* : gamberro *m*, -rra *f*

hoop ['hu:p] *n* : aro *m*

hooray [hʊ'reɪ] → **hurrah**

hoot¹ ['hu:t] *vi* **1** SHOUT : gritar ⟨to hoot with laughter : morirse de risa, reírse a carcajadas⟩ **2** : ulular (dícese de un búho), tocar la bocina (dícese de un vehículo), silbar (dícese de un tren o de un barco)

hoot² *n* **1** : ululato *m* (de un búho), silbido *m* (de un tren), bocinazo *m* (de un vehículo) **2** GUFFAW : carcajada *f*, risotada *f* **3 I don't give a hoot** : me vale un comino, me importa un pito

hop¹ ['hɑp] *vi* **hopped; hopping** : brincar, saltar

hop² *n* **1** LEAP : salto *m*, brinco *m* **2** FLIGHT : vuelo *m* corto **3** : lúpulo *m* (planta)

hope¹ ['ho:p] *v* **hoped; hoping** : esperar — *vt* : esperar que ⟨we hope she comes : esperamos que venga⟩ ⟨I hope so/not : espero que sí/no⟩

hope² *n* : esperanza *f* ⟨to have high hopes of : tener muchas esperanzas de⟩ ⟨to get one's hopes up : hacerse ilusiones⟩ ⟨in the hope of : con la esperanza de⟩ ⟨in the hope that : con la esperanza de que⟩

hopeful ['ho:pfəl] *adj* : esperanzado

hopefully ['ho:pfəli] *adv* **1** : con esperanza ⟨"it's a good sign," she said hopefully : "es buena señal," dijo esperanzada⟩ **2** ⟨hopefully, it won't rain : ojalá no llueva, espero que no llueva⟩ ⟨the rain will hopefully continue : se espera que las lluvias continúen⟩

hopeless ['ho:pləs] *adj* **1** DESPAIRING : desesperado **2** IMPOSSIBLE : imposible ⟨a hopeless case : un caso perdido⟩

hopelessly ['ho:pləsli] *adv* **1** : sin esperanzas, desesperadamente **2** COMPLETELY : totalmente, completamente **3** IMPOSSIBLY : imposiblemente

hopelessness ['ho:pləsnəs] *n* : desesperanza *f*

hopper ['hɑpər] *n* : tolva *f*

hopping¹ *adv* **to be hopping mad** : estar furioso

hopping² *adj* BUSY : animado, concurrido

hopscotch ['hɑp,skɑtʃ] *n* : tejo *m*

horde ['hɔrd] *n* : horda *f*, multitud *f*

horizon [hə'raɪzən] *n* : horizonte *m*

horizontal [,hɔrə'zɑntəl] *adj* : horizontal — **horizontally** *adv*

hormone ['hɔr,mo:n] *n* : hormona *f* — **hormonal** [hɔr'mo:nəl] *adj*

horn ['hɔrn] *n* **1** : cuerno *m* (de un toro, una vaca, etc.) **2** : cuerno *m*, trompa *f* (instrumento musical) **3** : bocina *f*, claxon *m* (de un vehículo)

horned ['hɔrnd, 'hɔrnəd] *adj* : cornudo, astado, con cuernos

hornet ['hɔrnət] *n* : avispón *m*

horny ['hɔrni] *adj* **hornier; -est 1** CALLOUS : calloso **2** LUSTFUL *fam* : caliente *fam*

horoscope ['hɔrə,sko:p] *n* : horóscopo *m*

horrendous [hɔ'rɛndəs] *adj* : horrendo, horroroso

horrible ['hɔrəbəl] *adj* : horrible, espantoso, horroroso — **horribly** [-bli] *adv*

horrid ['hɔrɪd] *adj* : horroroso, horrible — **horridly** *adv*

horrific [hɔ'rɪfɪk] *adj* : terrorífico, horroroso

horrify ['hɔrə,faɪ] *vt* **-fied; -fying** : horrorizar

horrifying ['hɔrə,faɪɪŋ] *adj* : horripilante, horroroso

horror ['hɔrər] *n* : horror *m*

hors d'oeuvre [ɔr'dərv] *n*, *pl* **hors d'oeuvres** [-'dərvz] : entremés *m*

horse ['hɔrs] *n* **1** : caballo *m* **2 a horse of a different color** : harina de otro costal **3 from the horse's mouth** ⟨I heard it straight from the horse's mouth : me lo dijo él mismo, me lo dijo ella misma⟩ **4 hold your horses** : un momentito

horseback ['hɔrs,bæk] *n* **on** ~ : a caballo

horseback riding *n* : equitación *f*

horse chestnut *n* : castaña *f* de Indias

horsefly ['hɔrs,flaɪ] *n*, *pl* **-flies** : tábano *m*

horsehair ['hɔrs,hær] *n* : crin *f*

horseman ['hɔrsmən] *n*, *pl* **-men** [-mən, -,mɛn] : jinete *m*, caballista *m*

horsemanship ['hɔrsmən,ʃɪp] *n* : equitación *f*

horseplay ['hɔrs,pleɪ] *n* : payasadas *fpl*

horsepower ['hɔrs,paʊər] *n* : caballo *m* de fuerza

horse racing *n* : carreras *fpl* de caballos

horseradish ['hɔrs,rædɪʃ] *n* : rábano *m* picante

horseshoe ['hɔrs,ʃu:] *n* : herradura *f*

horsewhip ['hɔrs,hwɪp] *vt* **-whipped; -whipping** : azotar

horsewoman ['hɔrs,wʊmən] *n*, *pl* **-women** [-,wɪmən] : amazona *f*, jinete *f*, caballista *f*

horsey *or* **horsy** ['hɔrsi] *adj* **horsier; -est** : relacionado a los caballos, caballar

horticultural [,hɔrtə'kʌltʃərəl] *adj* : hortícola

horticulture ['hɔrtə,kʌltʃər] *n* : horticultura *f*

hose¹ ['ho:z] *vt* **hosed; hosing** : regar o lavar con manguera

hose² *n* **1** *pl* **hose** SOCKS : calcetines *mpl*, medias *fpl* **2** *pl* **hose** STOCKINGS : medias *fpl* **3** *pl* **hoses** : manguera *f*, manga *f*

hosiery ['ho:ʒəri, 'ho:zə-] *n* : calcetería *f*, medias *fpl*

hospice ['hɑspəs] *n* : centro *m* de cuidados paliativos

hospitable [hɑ'spɪt̬əbəl, 'hɑs̩pɪ-] *adj* : hospitalario — **hospitably** [-bli] *adv*

hospital ['hɑs̩pɪt̬əl] *n* : hospital *m*

hospitality [ˌhɑspə'tæləti] *n, pl* **-ties** : hospitalidad *f*

hospitalization [ˌhɑs̩pɪt̬ələ'zeɪʃən] *n* : hospitalización *f*

hospitalize ['hɑs̩pɪt̬əˌlaɪz] *vt* **-ized; -izing** : hospitalizar

host¹ ['hoːst] *vt* : presentar (un programa de televisión, etc.)

host² *n* **1** : anfitrión *m*, -triona *f* (en la casa, a un evento); presentador *m*, -dora *f* (de un programa de televisión, etc.) **2** *or* **host organism** : huésped *m* **3** TROOPS : huestes *fpl* **4** MULTITUDE : multitud *f* ⟨for a host of reasons : por muchas razones⟩ **5** EUCHARIST : hostia *f*, Eucaristía *f*

hostage ['hɑstɪʤ] *n* : rehén *m*

hostel ['hɑstəl] *n* : albergue *m* juvenil

hostess ['hoːstɪs] *n* : anfitriona *f* (en la casa), presentadora *f* (de un programa)

hostile ['hɑstəl, -ˌtaɪl] *adj* : hostil — **hostilely** *adv*

hostility [hɑs'tɪləti] *n, pl* **-ties** : hostilidad *f*

hot ['hɑt] *adj* **hotter; hottest 1** : caliente, cálido, caluroso ⟨hot water : agua caliente⟩ ⟨a hot climate : un clima cálido⟩ ⟨a hot day : un día caluroso⟩ ⟨it's hot in here : hace calor aquí dentro⟩ **2** ARDENT, FIERY : ardiente, acalorado ⟨to have a hot temper : tener mal genio⟩ **3** SPICY : picante **4** FRESH : reciente, nuevo ⟨hot news : noticias de última hora⟩ ⟨hot off the press : de último momento⟩ **5** EAGER : ávido **6** STOLEN : robado **7** *fam* SEXY : guapo, bueno *fam* **8 hot and bothered** *or* **hot under the collar** : enojado — **hotly** *adv*

hot air *n* : palabrería *f*

hotbed ['hɑtˌbɛd] *n* **1** : semillero *m* (de plantas) **2** : hervidero *m*, semillero *m* (de crimen, etc.)

hot chocolate *n* COCOA : chocolate *m*, cocoa *f*, cacao *m* (bebida)

hot dog *n* : perro *m* caliente; pancho *m* *Arg, Uru*

hotel [hoː'tɛl] *n* : hotel *m*

hotelier [hoː'tɛljər, ˌoːtəl'jeɪ] *n* : hotelero *m*, -ra *f*

hot flash *n* : bochorno *m*, sofoco *m* (de la menopausia)

hothead ['hɑtˌhɛd] *n* : exaltado *m*, -da *f*

hotheaded ['hɑt'hɛdəd] *adj* : exaltado

hothouse ['hɑtˌhaʊs] *n* : invernadero *m*

hot plate *n* : placa *f* (de cocina)

hot rod *n* : coche *m* con motor modificado

hot tub *n* : bañera *f* de hidromasaje

hot water *n* **to get into hot water** : meterse en un lío

hot-water bottle *n* : bolsa *f* de agua caliente

hound¹ ['haʊnd] *vt* : acosar, perseguir

hound² *n* : perro *m* (de caza)

hour ['aʊər] *n* **1** : hora *f* ⟨on the hour : a la hora en punto⟩ ⟨60 miles an/per hour

: 60 millas por hora⟩ ⟨by the hour : por hora(s)⟩ ⟨at all hours : a todas horas⟩ ⟨until all hours : hasta las tantas, hasta muy tarde⟩ ⟨open 24 hours (a day) : abierto 24 horas (al día)⟩ **2 hours** *npl* : horas *pl*, horario *m* (de una empresa, etc.) **3 the wee hours** ⟨in/until the wee hours (of the morning/night) : a/hasta las altas horas de la madrugada/noche⟩

hourglass ['aʊərˌglæs] *n* : reloj *m* de arena

hourly ['aʊərli] *adv & adj* : cada hora, por hora

house¹ ['haʊz] *vt* **housed; housing** : albergar, alojar, hospedar

house² ['haʊs] *n, pl* **houses** ['haʊzəz, -səz] **1** HOME : casa *f* ⟨come (over) to my house : ven a mi casa⟩ ⟨house pet : animal doméstico⟩ ⟨house painter : pintor de casas⟩ **2** : cámara *f* (del gobierno) **3** BUSINESS : casa *f*, empresa *f* **4 on the house** : gratis ⟨it's on the house : invita la casa⟩ **5 to bring the house down** : ser muy aplaudido **6 to clean house** : limpiar la casa **7 to get/put/set one's house in order** : poner sus asuntos en orden, ordenar sus asuntos **8 to keep house** : ocuparse de la casa **9 to play house** : jugar a las casitas **10 to set up house** : poner casa

houseboat ['haʊsˌboːt] *n* : casa *f* flotante

housebroken ['haʊsˌbroːkən] *adj* : enseñado

housecoat ['haʊsˌkoːt] *n* : bata *f*, guardapolvo *m*

housefly ['haʊsˌflaɪ] *n, pl* **-flies** : mosca *f* común

household¹ ['haʊsˌhoːld] *adj* **1** DOMESTIC : doméstico, de la casa **2** FAMILIAR : conocido por todos

household² *n* : casa *f*, familia *f*

householder ['haʊsˌhoːldər] *n* : dueño *m*, -ña *f* de casa

housekeeper ['haʊsˌkiːpər] *n* : ama *f* de llaves

housekeeping ['haʊsˌkiːpɪŋ] *n* : gobierno *m* de la casa, quehaceres *mpl* domésticos

housemaid ['haʊsˌmeɪd] *n* : criada *f*, mucama *f*, muchacha *f*, sirvienta *f*

houseplant ['haʊsˌplænt] *n* : planta *f* de interior

housewarming ['haʊsˌwɔrmɪŋ] *n* : fiesta *f* de estreno de una casa

housewife ['haʊsˌwaɪf] *n, pl* **-wives** : ama *f* de casa

housework ['haʊsˌwərk] *n* : faenas *fpl* domésticas, quehaceres *mpl* domésticos

housing ['haʊzɪŋ] *n* **1** HOUSES : vivienda *f* **2** COVERING : caja *f* protectora

hove → heave

hovel ['hʌvəl, 'hɑ-] *n* : casucha *f*, tugurio *m*

hover ['hʌvər, 'hɑ-] *vi* **1** : cernerse, sostenerse en el aire **2 to hover about** : rondar

hovercraft ['hʌvərˌkræft] *n* : aerodeslizador *m*

how ['haʊ] *adv* **1** : cómo ⟨how are you? : ¿cómo estás?⟩ ⟨I don't know how to fix it : no sé cómo arreglarlo⟩ ⟨how do I look? : ¿cómo estoy?⟩ ⟨how big is it?

: ¿cómo es de grande?, ¿qué tan grande es? ⟨how bad is it? : ¿de qué gravedad es?, ¿qué tan grave es?⟩ ⟨how do you do : mucho gusto⟩ **2** (*used for emphasis*) : qué ⟨how beautiful! : ¡qué bonito!⟩ ⟨how right you are! : ¡cuánta razón tiene!⟩ ⟨I can't tell you how grateful I am : no puedo decirte lo agradecida que estoy⟩ **3** : cuánto ⟨how old are you? : ¿cuántos años tienes?⟩ ⟨how many people are here? : ¿cuánta gente está aquí?⟩ **4 and how!** : ¡y cómo! **5 how about . . .?** : ¿qué te parece . . .? **6 how come?** *fam* : ¿cómo es eso?, ¿por qué? **7 how come . . .?** : ¿cómo es que . . .?, ¿por qué . . .? **8 how much** : cuánto **9 how so?** : ¿por qué dice(s) eso? **10 how's that?** *fam* : ¿qué?, ¿cómo?

however¹ [hau'evər] *adv* **1** : por mucho que, por más que ⟨however hot it is : por mucho calor que haga⟩ **2** NEVERTHELESS : sin embargo, no obstante

however² *conj* : comoquiera que, de cualquier manera que

howl¹ ['haul] *vi* : aullar

howl² *n* : aullido *m*, alarido *m*

hub ['hʌb] *n* **1** CENTER : centro *m* **2** : cubo *m* (de una rueda)

hubbub ['hʌ,bʌb] *n* : algarabía *f*, alboroto *m*, jaleo *m*

hubcap ['hʌb,kæp] *n* : tapacubos *m*

huckster ['hʌkstər] *n* : buhonero *m*, -ra *f*; vendedor *m*, -dora *f* ambulante

huddle¹ ['hʌdəl] *vi* -dled; -dling **1** : apiñarse, amontonarse **2 to huddle together** : acurrucarse

huddle² *n* : grupo *m* (cerrado) ⟨to go into a huddle : discutir en secreto⟩

hue ['hju:] *n* : color *m*, tono *m*

huff ['hʌf] *n* : enojo *m*, enfado *m* ⟨to be in a huff : estar enojado⟩

huffy ['hʌfi] *adj* huffier; -est : enojado, enfadado

hug¹ ['hʌg] *vt* hugged; hugging **1** EMBRACE : abrazar **2** : ir pegado a ⟨the road hugs the river : el camino está pegado al río⟩

hug² *n* : abrazo *m*

huge ['hju:dʒ] *adj* huger; hugest : inmenso, enorme — **hugely** *adv*

hugeness ['hju:dʒnəs] *n* : lo grande

huh ['hʌ] *interj* **1** WHAT : ¿eh?, ¿qué? **2** : ¿eh?, ¿no? ⟨not bad, huh? : no está mal, ¿eh?⟩ **3** (*expressing surprise or disbelief*) : ¡vaya!, ¡anda! **4** (*expressing disapproval*) : ¡bah!

hulk ['hʌlk] *n* **1** : persona *f* fornida **2** : casco *m* (barco), armatoste *m* (edificio, etc.)

hulking ['hʌlkɪŋ] *adj* : grande, pesado

hull¹ ['hʌl] *vt* : pelar

hull² *n* **1** HUSK : cáscara *f* **2** : casco *m* (de un barco, un avión, etc.)

hullabaloo ['hʌləbə,lu:] *n*, *pl* -loos : alboroto *m*, jaleo *m*

hum¹ ['hʌm] *v* hummed; humming *vi* **1** BUZZ : zumbar **2** : estar muy activo, moverse ⟨to hum with activity : bullir de actividad⟩ — *vt* : tararear (una melodía)

hum² *n* : zumbido *m*, murmullo *m*

human¹ ['hju:mən, 'ju:-] *adj* : humano ⟨human rights : derechos humanos⟩ — **humanly** *adv*

human² *n* : humano *m*

human being *n* : ser *m* humano

humane [hju:'meɪn, ju:-] *adj* : humano, humanitario — **humanely** *adv*

humanism ['hju:mə,nɪzəm, 'ju:-] *n* : humanismo *m*

humanist¹ ['hju:mənɪst, 'ju:-] *n* : humanista *mf*

humanist² *or* **humanistic** [,hju:mə'nɪstɪk, ,ju:-] *adj* : humanístico

humanitarian¹ [hju:,mænə'triən, ju:-] *adj* : humanitario

humanitarian² *n* : humanitario *m*, -ria *f*

humanity [hju:'mænəti, ju:-] *n*, *pl* -ties : humanidad *f*

humankind [hju:mən'kaɪnd, 'ju:-] *n* : género *m* humano

humble¹ ['hʌmbəl] *vt* -bled; -bling **1** : humillar **2 to humble oneself** : humillarse

humble² *adj* humbler; humblest : humilde, modesto — **humbly** ['hʌmbli] *adv*

humbug ['hʌm,bʌg] *n* **1** FRAUD : charlatán *m*, -tana *f*; farsante *m* **2** NONSENSE : patrañas *fpl*, tonterías *fpl*

humdrum ['hʌm,drʌm] *adj* : monótono, rutinario

humid ['hju:məd, 'ju:-] *adj* : húmedo

humidifier [hju:'mɪdə,faɪər, ju:-] *n* : humidificador *m*

humidify [hju:'mɪdə,faɪ, ju:-] *vt* -fied; -fying : humidificar

humidity [hju:'mɪdəti, ju:-] *n*, *pl* -ties : humedad *f*

humiliate [hju:'mɪli,eɪt, ju:-] *vt* -ated; -ating : humillar

humiliating [hju:'mɪli,eɪtɪŋ, ju:-] *adj* : humillante

humiliation [hju:,mɪli'eɪʃən, ju:-] *n* : humillación *f*

humility [hju:'mɪləti, ju:-] *n* : humildad *f*

hummingbird ['hʌmɪŋ,bərd] *n* : colibrí *m*, picaflor *m*

hummock ['hʌmək] *n* : montículo *m*

humor¹ ['hju:mər, 'ju:-] *vt* : seguir el humor a, complacer

humor² *n* : humor *m*

humorist ['hju:mərɪst, 'ju:-] *n* : humorista *mf*

humorless ['hju:mərləs, 'ju:-] *adj* : sin sentido del humor ⟨a humorless smile : una sonrisa forzada⟩

humorous ['hju:mərəs, 'ju:-] *adj* : humorístico, cómico — **humorously** *adv*

hump ['hʌmp] *n* : joroba *f*, giba *f*

humpback ['hʌmp,bæk] *n* **1** HUMP, HUNCHBACK : joroba *f*, giba *f* **2** *offensive* HUNCHBACK : jorobado *m*, -da *f*; giboso *m*, -sa *f* (persona) **3** *or* **humpback whale** : ballena *f* jorobada, yubarta *f*

humpbacked ['hʌmp,bækt] *adj* : jorobado, giboso

humus ['hju:məs, 'ju:-] *n* : humus *m*

hunch¹ ['hʌnʧ] *vt* : encorvar — *vi or* **to hunch up** : encorvarse

hunch² *n* PREMONITION : presentimiento *m*

hunchback ['hʌntʃ,bæk] *n* **1** HUMP, HUMPBACK : joroba *f*, giba *f* **2** *offensive* HUMPBACK : jorobado *m*, -da *f*; giboso *m*, -sa *f* (persona)

hunchbacked ['hʌntʃ,bækt] *adj* : jorobado, giboso

hundred[1] ['hʌndrəd] *adj* : cien, ciento

hundred[2] *n, pl* **-dreds** *or* **-dred 1** : cien *m*, ciento *m* ⟨a/one hundred : cien⟩ ⟨a/one hundred (and) one : ciento uno⟩ ⟨hundreds of people : cientos de personas⟩ ⟨hundreds of times : cientos de veces⟩ **2** : billete *m* de cien dólares

hundredth[1] ['hʌndrədθ] *adv* : en centésimo lugar

hundredth[2] *adj* : centésimo

hundredth[3] *n* **1** : centésimo *m*, -ma *f* (en una serie) **2** : centésimo *m*, centésima parte *f*

hundredweight ['hʌndrəd,weɪt] *n* : quintal *m*

hung → **hang**

Hungarian [hʌŋ'gæriən] *n* **1** : húngaro *m*, -ra *f* **2** : húngaro *m* (idioma) — **Hungarian** *adj*

hunger[1] ['hʌŋgər] *vi* **1** : tener hambre **2 to hunger after/for** : ansiar, anhelar

hunger[2] *n* : hambre *m*

hungrily ['hʌŋgrəli] *adv* : ávidamente

hungry ['hʌŋgri] *adj* **hungrier; -est 1** : hambriento **2 to be hungry** : tener hambre

hunk ['hʌŋk] *n* : trozo *m*, pedazo *m*

hunt[1] ['hʌnt] *vt* **1** PURSUE : cazar **2 to hunt for** : buscar

hunt[2] *n* **1** PURSUIT : caza *f*, cacería *f* **2** SEARCH : búsqueda *f*, busca *f*

hunter ['hʌntər] *n* : cazador *m*, -dora *f*

hunting ['hʌntɪŋ] *n* : caza *f* ⟨to go hunting : ir de caza⟩

hurdle[1] ['hərdəl] *vt* **-dled; -dling** : saltar, salvar (un obstáculo)

hurdle[2] *n* : valla *f* (en deportes), obstáculo *m*

hurl ['hərl] *vt* : arrojar, tirar, lanzar

hurrah [hʊ'rɑ, -'rɔ] *interj* : ¡hurra!

hurricane ['hərə,keɪn] *n* : huracán *m*

hurried ['hərid] *adj* : apresurado, precipitado

hurriedly ['hərədli] *adv* : apresuradamente, de prisa

hurry[1] ['həri] *v* **-ried; -rying** *vi* : apurarse, darse prisa, apresurarse — *vt* : apurar, darle prisa (a alguien)

hurry[2] *n* : prisa *f*, apuro *f*

hurt[1] ['hərt] *v* **hurt; hurting** *vt* **1** INJURE : hacer daño a, herir, lastimar ⟨to hurt oneself : hacerse daño⟩ **2** DISTRESS, OFFEND : hacer sufrir, ofender, herir — *vi* : doler ⟨my foot hurts : me duele el pie⟩

hurt[2] *n* **1** INJURY : herida *f* **2** DISTRESS, PAIN : dolor *m*, pena *f*

hurtful ['hərtfəl] *adj* : hiriente, doloroso

hurtle ['hərtəl] *vi* **-tled; -tling** : lanzarse, precipitarse

husband[1] ['hʌzbənd] *vt* : economizar, bien administrar

husband[2] *n* : esposo *m*, marido *m*

husbandry ['hʌzbəndri] *n* **1** MANAGEMENT, THRIFT : economía *f*, buena administración *f* **2** AGRICULTURE : agricultura *f* ⟨animal husbandry : cría de animales⟩

hush[1] ['hʌʃ] *vt* **1** SILENCE : hacer callar, acallar **2** CALM : calmar, apaciguar

hush[2] *n* : silencio *m*

hush-hush ['hʌʃ,hʌʃ, ,hʌʃ'hʌʃ] *adj* : muy secreto, confidencial

husk[1] ['hʌsk] *vt* : descascarar

husk[2] *n* : cáscara *f*

huskily ['hʌskəli] *adv* : con voz ronca

husky[1] ['hʌski] *adj* **huskier; -est 1** HOARSE : ronco **2** BURLY : fornido

husky[2] *n, pl* **-kies** : perro *m*, -rra *f* esquimal

hustle[1] ['hʌsəl] *v* **-tled; -tling** *vt* : darle prisa (a alguien), apurar ⟨they hustled me in : me hicieron entrar a empujones⟩ — *vi* : apurarse, ajetrearse

hustle[2] *n or* **hustle and bustle** : bullicio *m*, ajetreo *m*

hut ['hʌt] *n* : cabaña *f*, choza *f*, barraca *f*, bohío *m*

hutch ['hʌtʃ] *n* **1** CUPBOARD : alacena *f* **2 rabbit hutch** : conejera *f*

hyacinth ['haɪə,sɪnθ] *n* : jacinto *m*

hybrid[1] ['haɪbrəd] *adj* : híbrido

hybrid[2] *n* : híbrido *m*

hydrant ['haɪdrənt] *n* : boca *f* de riego, hidrante *m* CA, Col ⟨fire hydrant : boca de incendios⟩

hydraulic [haɪ'drɔlɪk] *adj* : hidráulico — **hydraulically** *adv*

hydrocarbon [,haɪdro'karbən] *n* : hidrocarburo *m*

hydrochloric acid [,haɪdro'klɔrɪk] *n* : ácido *m* clorhídrico

hydroelectric [,haɪdroɪ'lɛktrɪk] *adj* : hidroeléctrico

hydrofoil ['haɪdrə,fɔɪl] *n* : hidroala *m*, aliscafo *m*

hydrogen ['haɪdrədʒən] *n* : hidrógeno *m*

hydrogen bomb *n* : bomba *f* de hidrógeno

hydrogen peroxide *n* : agua *f* oxigenada, peróxido *m* de hidrógeno

hydrophobia [,haɪdrə'fo:biə] *n* : hidrofobia *f*, rabia *f*

hydroplane ['haɪdrə,pleɪn] *n* : hidroplano *m*

hyena [haɪ'i:nə] *n* : hiena *f*

hygiene ['haɪ,dʒi:n] *n* : higiene *f*

hygienic [haɪ'dʒɛnɪk, -'dʒi:-; ,haɪ-dʒi'nɪk] *adj* : higiénico — **hygienically** [-nɪkli] *adv*

hygienist [haɪ'dʒi:nɪst, -'dʒɛ-; 'haɪ-,dʒi:-] *n* : higienista *mf*

hygrometer [haɪ'grɑmətər] *n* : higrómetro *m*

hymn ['hɪm] *n* : himno *m*

hymnal ['hɪmnəl] *n* : himnario *m*

hype[1] ['haɪp] *n* : bombo *m* publicitario

hype[2] *vt* **hyped; hyping** : promocionar con bombos y platillos

hyperactive [,haɪpər'æktɪv] *adj* : hiperactivo

hyperactivity [,haɪpər,æk'tɪvət̬i] *n, pl* **-ties** : hiperactividad *f*

hyperbole [haɪ'pərbəli] *n* : hipérbole *f*

hyperbolic [,haɪpər'balɪk] *adj* : hiperbólico

hypercritical [ˌhaɪpərˈkrɪt̬əkəl] *adj* : hipercrítico

hyperlink [ˈhaɪpərˌlɪŋk] *n* : hiperenlace *m*

hypermarket [ˈhaɪpərˌmɑrkət] *n* : hipermercado *m*

hypersensitivity [ˌhaɪpərˌsɛnsəˈtɪ-vət̬i] *n* : hipersensibilidad *f*

hypertension [ˈhaɪpərˌtɛntʃən] *n* : hipertensión *f*

hyphen [ˈhaɪfən] *n* : guión *m*

hyphenate [ˈhaɪfənˌeɪt] *vt* **-ated; -ating** : escribir con guión

hypnosis [hɪpˈnoːsɪs] *n, pl* **-noses** [-ˌsiːz] : hipnosis *f*

hypnotic [hɪpˈnɑtɪk] *adj* : hipnótico, hipnotizador

hypnotism [ˈhɪpnəˌtɪzəm] *n* : hipnotismo *m*

hypnotist [ˈhɪpnəˌtɪst] *n* : hipnotizador *m*, -dora *f*

hypnotize [ˈhɪpnəˌtaɪz] *vt* **-tized; -tizing** : hipnotizar

hypochondria [ˌhaɪpəˈkɑndriə] *n* : hipocondría *f*

hypochondriac [ˌhaɪpəˈkɑndriˌæk] *n* : hipocondríaco *m*, -ca *f*

hypocrisy [hɪpˈɑkrəsi] *n, pl* **-sies** : hipocresía *f*

hypocrite [ˈhɪpəˌkrɪt] *n* : hipócrita *mf*

hypocritical [ˌhɪpəˈkrɪt̬əkəl] *adj* : hipócrita

hypodermic[1] [ˌhaɪpəˈdərmɪk] *adj* : hipodérmico

hypodermic[2] *n* : aguja *f* hipodérmica

hypotenuse [haɪˈpɑtənˌuːs, -ˌuːz, -ˌjuːs, -ˌjuːz] *n* : hipotenusa *f*

hypothermia [ˌhaɪpoˈθərmiə] *n* : hipotermia *f*

hypothesis [haɪˈpɑθəsɪs] *n, pl* **-eses** [-ˌsiːz] : hipótesis *f*

hypothetical [ˌhaɪpəˈθɛt̬ɪkəl] *adj* : hipotético — **hypothetically** [-t̬ɪkli] *adv*

hysterectomy [ˌhɪstəˈrɛktəmi] *n, pl* **-mies** : histerectomía *f*

hysteria [hɪsˈtɛriə, -tɪr-] *n* : histeria *f*, histerismo *m*

hysterical [hɪsˈtɛrɪkəl] *adj* : histérico — **hysterically** [-ɪkli] *adv*

hysterics [hɪsˈtɛrɪks] *n* : histeria *f*, histerismo *m*

I

i [ˈaɪ] *n, pl* **i's** *or* **is** [ˈaɪz] : novena letra del alfabeto inglés

I [ˈaɪ] *pron* : yo

Iberian [aɪˈbɪriən] *adj* : ibérico

-ible *suf* : -ible

ice[1] [ˈaɪs] *v* **iced; icing** *vt* **1** FREEZE : congelar, helar **2** CHILL : enfriar **3** to **ice a cake** : bañar un pastel — *vi* : helarse, congelarse

ice[2] *n* **1** : hielo *m* ⟨ice cube : cubito de hielo⟩ **2** SHERBET : sorbete *m*; nieve *f* *Cuba, Mex, PRi*

iceberg [ˈaɪsˌbərg] *n* : iceberg *m*

icebox [ˈaɪsˌbɑks] → **refrigerator**

icebreaker [ˈaɪsˌbreɪkər] *n* : rompehielos *m*

ice cap *n* : casquete *m* glaciar ⟨polar ice cap : casquete polar⟩

ice-cold [ˈaɪsˈkoːld] *adj* : helado

ice cream *n* : helado *m*, mantecado *m* PRi

ice-cream soda → **soda**

ice hockey *n* : hockey *m* sobre hielo

Icelander [ˈaɪsˌlændər, -lən-] *n* : islandés *m*, -desa *f*

Icelandic[1] [aɪsˈlændɪk] *adj* : islandés

Icelandic[2] *n* : islandés *m* (idioma)

ice-skate [ˈaɪsˌskeɪt] *vi* **-skated; -skating** : patinar

ice skater *n* : patinador *m*, -dora *f*

icicle [ˈaɪˌsɪkəl] *n* : carámbano *m*

icily [ˈaɪsəli] *adv* : fríamente, con frialdad ⟨he stared at me icily : me fijó la mirada con mucha frialdad⟩

icing [ˈaɪsɪŋ] *n* : baño *m*, glaseado *m*, betún *m* Mex

icon [ˈaɪˌkɑn, -kən] *n* : icono *m*

iconoclasm [aɪˈkɑnəˌklæzəm] *n* : iconoclasia *f*

iconoclast [aɪˈkɑnəˌklæst] *n* : iconoclasta *mf*

icy [ˈaɪsi] *adj* **icier; -est** **1** : cubierto de hielo ⟨an icy road : una carretera cubierta de hielo⟩ **2** FREEZING : helado, gélido, glacial **3** ALOOF : frío, distante

id [ˈɪd] *n* : id *m*

I'd [ˈaɪd] *contraction of* **I should** *or* **I had** *or* **I would** → **should, have, would**

ID [ˈaɪˈdiː] *n, pl* **ID's** *or* **IDs** → **identification**

ID card → **identification card**

idea [aɪˈdiːə] *n* : idea *f* ⟨to have an idea about something : tener idea de algo⟩ ⟨to have no idea : no tener (ni) idea⟩ ⟨to get the idea : captar la idea⟩ ⟨that's not a bad idea : no es mala idea⟩

ideal[1] [aɪˈdiːəl] *adj* : ideal

ideal[2] *n* : ideal *m*

idealism [aɪˈdiːəˌlɪzəm] *n* : idealismo *m*

idealist [aɪˈdiːəlɪst] *n* : idealista *mf*

idealistic [aɪˌdiːəˈlɪstɪk] *adj* : idealista

idealistically [aɪˌdiːəˈlɪstɪkli] *adv* : con idealismo

idealization [aɪˌdiːələˈzeɪʃən] *n* : idealización *f*

idealize [aɪˈdiːəˌlaɪz] *vt* **-ized; -izing** : idealizar

ideally [aɪˈdiːəli] *adv* : perfectamente

identical [aɪˈdɛntɪkəl] *adj* : idéntico — **identically** [-tɪkli] *adv*

identifiable [aɪˌdɛntəˈfaɪəbəl] *adj* : identificable

identification [aɪˌdɛntəfəˈkeɪʃən] *n* : identificación *f*

identification card *n* : carnet *m* (de identidad), cédula *f* de identidad, tarjeta *f* de identificación/identidad

identify [aɪˈdɛntəˌfaɪ] v **-fied; -fying** vt : identificar — vi **to identify with** : identificarse con

identity [aɪˈdɛntəti] n, pl **-ties** : identidad f

identity card → **identification card**

identity theft n : robo m de identidad, suplantación f de identidad

ideological [ˌaɪdiəˈlɑdʒɪkəl, ˌɪ-] adj : ideológico — **ideologically** [-dʒɪkli] adv

ideologue [ˈaɪdiəˌlɔg, -ˌlɑg] n : ideólogo m, -ga f

ideology [ˌaɪdiˈɑlədʒi, ˌɪ-] n, pl **-gies** : ideología f

idiocy [ˈɪdiəsi] n, pl **-cies** 1 : idiotez f 2 NONSENSE : estupidez f, tontería f

idiom [ˈɪdiəm] n 1 LANGUAGE : lenguaje m 2 EXPRESSION : modismo m, expresión f idiomática

idiomatic [ˌɪdiəˈmætɪk] adj : idiomático

idiosyncrasy [ˌɪdioˈsɪŋkrəsi] n, pl **-sies** : idiosincrasia f

idiosyncratic [ˌɪdiosɪŋˈkrætɪk] adj : idiosincrásico — **idiosyncratically** [-tɪkli] adv

idiot [ˈɪdiət] n 1 usu offensive : idiota mf (en medicina) 2 FOOL : idiota mf; tonto m, -ta f; imbécil mf fam

idiotic [ˌɪdiˈɑtɪk] adj : estúpido, idiota — **idiotically** [ˌɪdiˈɑtɪkli] adv : estúpidamente

idle¹ [ˈaɪdəl] v **idled; idling** vi 1 LOAF : holgazanear, flojear, haraganear 2 : andar al ralentí (dícese de un automóvil), marchar en vacío (dícese de una máquina) — vt : dejar sin trabajo

idle² adj **idler; idlest** 1 VAIN : frívolo, vano, infundado ⟨idle curiosity : pura curiosidad⟩ 2 INACTIVE : inactivo, parado, desocupado 3 LAZY : holgazán, haragán, perezoso

idleness [ˈaɪdəlnəs] n 1 INACTIVITY : inactividad f, ociosidad f 2 LAZINESS : holgazanería f, flojera f, pereza f

idler [ˈaɪdələr] n : haragán m, -gana f; holgazán m, -zana f

idly [ˈaɪdəli] adv : ociosamente

idol [ˈaɪdəl] n : ídolo m

idolater or **idolator** [aɪˈdɑlətər] n : idólatra mf

idolatrous [aɪˈdɑlətrəs] adj : idólatra

idolatry [aɪˈdɑlətri] n, pl **-tries** : idolatría f

idolize [ˈaɪdəˌlaɪz] vt **-ized; -izing** : idolatrar

idyll [ˈaɪdəl] n : idilio m

idyllic [aɪˈdɪlɪk] adj : idílico

if [ˈɪf] conj 1 : si ⟨I would do it if I could : lo haría si pudiera⟩ ⟨if so : si es así⟩ ⟨as if : como si⟩ ⟨if I were you : yo que tú⟩ ⟨if not : si no, de lo contrario⟩ ⟨if only it were true! : ¡si fuera verdad!⟩ 2 WHETHER : si ⟨I don't know if they're ready : no sé si están listos⟩ 3 THOUGH : aunque, si bien ⟨it's pretty, if somewhat old-fashioned : es lindo aunque algo anticuado⟩

igloo [ˈɪˌglu:] n, pl **-loos** : iglú m

ignite [ɪgˈnaɪt] v **-nited; -niting** vt : prenderle fuego a, encender — vi : prender, encenderse

ignition [ɪgˈnɪʃən] n 1 IGNITING : ignición f, encendido m 2 or **ignition switch** : encendido m, arranque m ⟨to turn on the ignition : arrancar el motor⟩

ignoble [ɪgˈno:bəl] adj : innoble — **ignobly** adv

ignominious [ˌɪgnəˈmɪniəs] adj : ignominioso, deshonroso — **ignominiously** adv

ignominy [ˈɪgnəˌmɪni] n, pl **-nies** : ignominia f

ignoramus [ˌɪgnəˈreɪməs] n : ignorante mf; bestia mf; bruto m, -ta f

ignorance [ˈɪgnərənts] n : ignorancia f

ignorant [ˈɪgnərənt] adj 1 : ignorante 2 **to be ignorant of** : no ser consciente de, desconocer, ignorar

ignorantly [ˈɪgnərəntli] adv : ignorantemente, con ignorancia

ignore [ɪgˈnor] vt **-nored; -noring** : ignorar, hacer caso omiso de (algo), no hacer caso de (algo), no hacerle caso (a alguien)

iguana [ɪˈgwanə] n : iguana f, garrobo f CA

il- → **in-**

ill¹ [ˈɪl] adv **worse** [ˈwərs]; **worst** [ˈwərst] : mal ⟨to speak ill of : hablar mal de⟩ ⟨he can ill afford to fail : mal puede permitirse el lujo de fracasar⟩

ill² adj **worse; worst** 1 SICK : enfermo 2 BAD : malo ⟨ill luck : mala suerte⟩

ill³ n 1 EVIL : mal m 2 MISFORTUNE : mal m, desgracia f 3 AILMENT : enfermedad f

I'll [ˈaɪl] contraction of **I shall** or **I will** → **shall, will**

ill–advised [ˈɪləd'vaɪzd] adj : poco aconsejable, imprudente

ill at ease adj : incómodo

ill–bred [ˈɪl'brɛd] adj : malcriado

illegal [ɪˈli:gəl] adj : ilegal — **illegally** adv

illegality [ˌɪli'gæləti] n : ilegalidad f

illegibility [ɪˌlɛdʒə'bɪləti] n, pl **-ties** : ilegibilidad f

illegible [ɪˈlɛdʒəbəl] adj : ilegible — **illegibly** [-bli] adv

illegitimacy [ˌɪlɪ'dʒɪtəməsi] n : ilegitimidad f

illegitimate [ˌɪlɪ'dʒɪtəmət] adj 1 BASTARD : ilegítimo, bastardo 2 UNLAWFUL : ilegítimo, ilegal — **illegitimately** adv

ill–fated [ˈɪl'feɪtəd] adj : malhadado, infortunado, desventurado

ill–gotten [ˈɪl'gatən] adj : mal habido

illicit [ɪˈlɪsət] adj : ilícito — **illicitly** adv

illiteracy [ɪˈlɪtərəsi] n, pl **-cies** : analfabetismo m

illiterate¹ [ɪˈlɪtərət] adj : analfabeto

illiterate² n : analfabeto m, -ta f

ill–mannered [ˌɪl'mænərd] adj : descortés, maleducado

ill–natured [ˌɪl'neɪtʃərd] adj : desagradable, de mal genio

ill–naturedly [ˌɪl'neɪtʃərdli] adv : desagradablemente

illness [ˈɪlnəs] n : enfermedad f

illogical [ɪˈlɑdʒɪkəl] adj : ilógico — **illogically** [-kli] adv

ill–tempered [ˌɪl'tɛmpərd] adj → **ill–natured**

ill–treat [ˌɪl'tri:t] vt : maltratar

ill–treatment [ˌɪl'tri:tmənt] n : maltrato m

illuminate [ɪ'lu:məˌneɪt] vt -nated; -nating 1 : iluminar, alumbrar 2 ELUCIDATE : esclarecer, elucidar

illumination [ɪˌlu:mə'neɪʃən] n 1 LIGHTING : iluminación f, luz f 2 ELUCIDATION : esclarecimiento m, elucidación f

ill-use ['ɪl'ju:z] → **ill-treat**

illusion [ɪ'lu:ʒən] n : ilusión f

illusory [ɪ'lu:səri, -zəri] adj : engañoso, ilusorio

illustrate ['ɪləsˌtreɪt] v -trated; -trating : ilustrar

illustration [ˌɪlə'streɪʃən] n 1 PICTURE : ilustración f 2 EXAMPLE : ejemplo m, ilustración f

illustrative [ɪ'lʌstrətɪv, 'ɪləˌstreɪtɪv] adj : ilustrativo — **illustratively** adv

illustrator ['ɪləˌstreɪtər] n : ilustrador m, -dora f; dibujante mf

illustrious [ɪ'lʌstriəs] adj : ilustre, eminente, glorioso

illustriousness [ɪ'lʌstriəsnəs] n : eminencia f, prestigio m

ill will n : animosidad f, malquerencia f, mala voluntad f

I'm ['aɪm] contraction of **I am → be**

im- → **in-**

image¹ ['ɪmɪdʒ] vt -aged; -aging : imaginar, crear una imagen de

image² n : imagen f

imagery ['ɪmɪdʒri] n, pl -eries 1 IMAGES : imágenes fpl 2 : imaginería f (en el arte)

imaginable [ɪ'mædʒənəbəl] adj : imaginable — **imaginably** [-bli] adv

imaginary [ɪ'mædʒəˌneri] adj : imaginario

imagination [ɪˌmædʒə'neɪʃən] n : imaginación f

imaginative [ɪ'mædʒənətɪv, -əˌneɪtɪv] adj : imaginativo — **imaginatively** adv

imagine [ɪ'mædʒən] vt -ined; -ining 1 : imaginar(se) ⟨try to imagine it : trata de imaginarlo⟩ ⟨just imagine that! : ¡imagínate!⟩ ⟨I can't imagine why : no me imagino por qué⟩ 2 : imaginar, creer (equivocadamente) ⟨she imagines herself to be charming : se cree encantadora⟩ ⟨you're imagining things : son imaginaciones tuyas⟩ 3 BELIEVE : imaginarse, creer ⟨I imagine so : me imagino que sí⟩

imbalance [ɪm'bæləns] n : desajuste m, desbalance m, desequilibrio m

imbecile¹ ['ɪmbəsəl, -ˌsɪl] or **imbecilic** [ˌɪmbə'sɪlɪk] adj : imbécil, estúpido

imbecile² n 1 : imbécil mf (en medicina) 2 FOOL : idiota mf; imbécil mf fam; estúpido m, -da f

imbecility [ˌɪmbə'sɪləti] n, pl -ties : imbecilidad f

imbibe [ɪm'baɪb] v -bibed; -bibing vt 1 DRINK : beber 2 ABSORB : absorber, embeber — vi : beber

imbue [ɪm'bju:] vt -bued; -buing : imbuir

imitate ['ɪməˌteɪt] vt -tated; -tating : imitar, remedar

imitation¹ [ˌɪmə'teɪʃən] adj : de imitación, artificial

imitation² n : imitación f

imitative ['ɪməˌteɪtɪv] adj : imitativo, imitador, poco original

imitator ['ɪməˌteɪtər] n : imitador m, -dora f

immaculate [ɪ'mækjələt] adj 1 PURE : inmaculado, puro 2 FLAWLESS : impecable, intachable — **immaculately** adv

immaterial [ˌɪmə'tɪriəl] adj 1 INCORPOREAL : incorpóreo 2 UNIMPORTANT : irrelevante, sin importancia

immature [ˌɪmə'tʃʊr, -'tjʊr, -'tʊr] adj : inmaduro, verde (dícese de la fruta)

immaturity [ˌɪmə'tʃʊrəti, -'tjʊr-, -'tʊr-] n, pl -ties : inmadurez f, falta f de madurez

immeasurable [ɪ'meʒərəbəl] adj : inconmensurable, incalculable — **immeasurably** [-bli] adv

immediacy [ɪ'mi:diəsi] n : inmediatez f

immediate [ɪ'mi:diət] adj 1 INSTANT : inmediato, instantáneo ⟨immediate relief : alivio instantáneo⟩ 2 DIRECT : inmediato, directo ⟨the immediate cause of death : la causa directa de la muerte⟩ 3 URGENT : urgente, apremiante 4 CLOSE : cercano, próximo, inmediato ⟨her immediate family : sus familiares más cercanos⟩ ⟨in the immediate vicinity : en los alrededores, en las inmediaciones⟩

immediately [ɪ'mi:diətli] adv : inmediatamente, enseguida

immemorial [ˌɪmə'moriəl] adj : inmemorial

immense [ɪ'mɛnts] adj : inmenso, enorme — **immensely** adv

immensity [ɪ'mɛntsəti] n, pl -ties : inmensidad f

immerse [ɪ'mərs] vt -mersed; -mersing 1 SUBMERGE : sumergir 2 **to immerse oneself in** : enfrascarse en

immersion [ɪ'mərʒən] n 1 : inmersión f (en un líquido) 2 : absorción f (en una actividad)

immigrant ['ɪmɪgrənt] n : inmigrante mf

immigrate ['ɪməˌgreɪt] vi -grated; -grating : inmigrar

immigration [ˌɪmə'greɪʃən] n : inmigración f

imminence ['ɪmənənts] n : inminencia f

imminent ['ɪmənənt] adj : inminente — **imminently** adv

immobile [ɪ'mo:bəl] adj 1 FIXED, IMMOVABLE : inmovible, fijo 2 MOTIONLESS : inmóvil

immobility [ˌɪmo'bɪləti] n, pl -ties : inmovilidad f

immobilize [ɪ'mo:bəˌlaɪz] vt -lized; -lizing : inmovilizar, paralizar — **immobilization** n

immoderate [ɪ'mɑdərət] adj : inmoderado, desmesurado, desmedido, excesivo — **immoderately** adv

immodest [ɪ'mɑdəst] adj 1 INDECENT : inmodesto, indecente, impúdico 2 CONCEITED : inmodesto, presuntuoso, engreído — **immodestly** adv

immodesty [ɪ'mɑdəsti] n : inmodestia f

immoral [ɪ'mɔrəl] adj : inmoral

immorality [ˌɪmo'ræləti, ˌɪmə-] n, pl -ties : inmoralidad f

immorally [ɪ'mɔrəli] adv : de manera inmoral

immortal¹ [ɪ'mɔrtəl] adj : inmortal

immortal² n : inmortal mf
immortality [ˌɪ.ˌmɔrˈtæləti] n : inmortalidad f
immortalize [ɪˈmɔrtəlˌaɪz] vt -ized; -izing
: inmortalizar
immovable [ɪˈmuːvəbəl] adj. 1 FIXED
: fijo, inmovible 2 UNYIELDING : inflexible
immune [ɪˈmjuːn] adj 1 : inmune ⟨im-
mune to smallpox : inmune a la viruela⟩
2 EXEMPT : exento, inmune
immune system n : sistema m inmunológico
immunity [ɪˈmjuːnəti] n, pl -ties 1 : inmunidad f 2 EXEMPTION : exención f
immunization [ˌɪmjunəˈzeɪʃən] n : inmunización f
immunize [ˈɪmjuˌnaɪz] vt -nized; -nizing
: inmunizar
immunology [ˌɪmjuˈnɑlədʒi] n : inmunología f
immutable [ɪˈmjuːtəbəl] adj : inmutable
imp [ˈɪmp] n RASCAL : diablillo m; pillo m,
-lla f
impact¹ [ɪmˈpækt] vt 1 STRIKE : chocar
con, impactar 2 AFFECT : afectar, impactar, impresionar — vi 1 STRIKE
: hacer impacto, golpear 2 to impact on
: tener un impacto sobre
impact² [ˈɪmˌpækt] n 1 COLLISION : impacto m, choque m, colisión f 2 EFFECT
: efecto m, impacto m, consecuencias fpl
impacted [ɪmˈpæktəd] adj : impactado,
incrustado (dícese de los dientes)
impair [ɪmˈpær] vt : perjudicar, dañar,
afectar
impairment [ɪmˈpærmənt] n : perjuicio m,
daño m
impala [ɪmˈpɑlə, -ˈpæ-] n, pl impalas or
impala : impala m
impale [ɪmˈpeɪl] vt -paled; -paling : empalar
impalpable [ɪmˈpælpəbəl] adj : impalpable, intangible
impanel [ɪmˈpænəl] vt -eled or -elled;
-eling or -elling : elegir (un jurado)
impart [ɪmˈpɑrt] vt 1 CONVEY : impartir,
dar, conferir 2 DISCLOSE : revelar, divulgar
impartial [ɪmˈpɑrʃəl] adj : imparcial —
impartially adv
impartiality [ɪmˌpɑrʃiˈæləti] n, pl -ties
: imparcialidad f
impassable [ɪmˈpæsəbəl] adj : infranqueable, intransitable — impassably
[-bli] adv
impasse [ˈɪmˌpæs] n 1 DEADLOCK : impasse m, punto m muerto 2 DEAD END
: callejón m sin salida
impassioned [ɪmˈpæʃənd] adj : apasionado, vehemente
impassive [ɪmˈpæsɪv] adj : impasible,
indiferente
impassively [ɪmˈpæsɪvli] adv : impasiblemente, sin emoción
impatience [ɪmˈpeɪʃənts] n : impaciencia f
impatient [ɪmˈpeɪʃənt] adj : impaciente —
impatiently adv
impeach [ɪmˈpiːtʃ] vt : destituir (a un
funcionario) de su cargo

impeachment [ɪmˈpiːtʃmənt] n 1 ACCUSA-
TION : acusación f 2 DISMISSAL : destitución f
impeccable [ɪmˈpekəbəl] adj : impecable
— impeccably [-bli] adv
impecunious [ˌɪmpɪˈkjuːniəs] adj : falto
de dinero
impede [ɪmˈpiːd] vt -peded; -peding
: impedir, dificultar, obstaculizar
impediment [ɪmˈpedəmənt] n 1 HIN-
DRANCE : impedimento m, obstáculo m
2 speech impediment : defecto m del
habla
impel [ɪmˈpel] vt -pelled; -pelling : impeler
impending [ɪmˈpendɪŋ] adj : inminente
impenetrable [ɪmˈpenətrəbəl] adj 1 : impenetrable ⟨an impenetrable forest : una
selva impenetrable⟩ 2 INSCRUTABLE
: incomprensible, inescrutable, impenetrable — impenetrably [-bli] adv
imperative¹ [ɪmˈperətɪv] adj 1 AUTHORI-
TATIVE : imperativo, imperioso 2 NEC-
ESSARY : imprescindible — imperatively
adv
imperative² n : imperativo m
imperceptible [ˌɪmpərˈseptəbəl] adj
: imperceptible — imperceptibly [-bli] adv
imperfect [ɪmˈpɑrfɪkt] adj : imperfecto,
defectuoso — imperfectly adv
imperfection [ˌɪmpərˈfɪkʃən] n : imperfección f, defecto m
imperial [ɪmˈpɪriəl] adj 1 : imperial 2
SOVEREIGN : soberano 3 IMPERIOUS
: imperioso, señorial
imperialism [ɪmˈpɪriəˌlɪzəm] n : imperialismo m
imperialist¹ [ɪmˈpɪriəlɪst] adj : imperialista
imperialist² n : imperialista mf
imperialistic [ɪmˌpɪriəˈlɪstɪk] adj : imperialista
imperil [ɪmˈperəl] vt -iled or -illed; -iling
or -illing : poner en peligro
imperious [ɪmˈpɪriəs] adj : imperioso —
imperiously adv
imperishable [ɪmˈperɪʃəbəl] adj : imperecedero
impermanent [ɪmˈpɑrmənənt] adj : pasajero, inestable, efímero — imperma-
nently adv
impermeable [ɪmˈpərmiəbəl] adj : impermeable
impersonal [ɪmˈpərsənəl] adj : impersonal
— impersonally adv
impersonate [ɪmˈpərsənˌeɪt] vt -ated;
-ating : hacerse pasar por, imitar
impersonation [ɪmˌpərsənˈeɪʃən] n : imitación f
impersonator [ɪmˈpərsənˌeɪtər] n : imitador m, -dora f
impertinence [ɪmˈpərtənənts] n : impertinencia f
impertinent [ɪmˈpərtənənt] adj 1 IRREL-
EVANT : impertinente, irrelevante 2 IN-
SOLENT : impertinente, insolente
impertinently [ɪmˈpərtənəntli] adv : con
impertinencia, impertinentemente
imperturbable [ˌɪmpərˈtərbəbəl] adj
: imperturbable

impervious [ɪmˈpərviəs] *adj* **1** IMPENE-
TRABLE : impermeable **2** INSENSITIVE
: insensible ⟨impervious to criticism
: insensible a la crítica⟩

impetuous [ɪmˈpɛtʃuəs] *adj* : impetuoso,
impulsivo

impetuously [ɪmˈpɛtʃuəsli] *adv* : de manera impulsiva, impetuosamente

impetus [ˈɪmpətəs] *n* : ímpetu *m*, impulso
m

impiety [ɪmˈpaɪəti] *n, pl* **-ties** : impiedad *f*

impinge [ɪmˈpɪndʒ] *vi* **-pinged; -pinging 1
to impinge on** AFFECT : afectar a, incidir
en **2 to impinge on** VIOLATE : violar,
vulnerar

impious [ˈɪmpiəs, ɪmˈpaɪəs] *adj* : impío,
irreverente

impish [ˈɪmpɪʃ] *adj* MISCHIEVOUS : pícaro, travieso

impishly [ˈɪmpɪʃli] *adv* : con picardía

implacable [ɪmˈplækəbəl] *adj* : implacable — **implacably** [-bli] *adv*

implant¹ [ɪmˈplænt] *vt* **1** INCULCATE, IN-
STILL : inculcar, implantar **2** INSERT
: implantar, insertar

implant² [ˈɪmˌplænt] *n* : implante *m* (de
pelo), injerto *m* (de piel)

implantation [ˌɪmˌplænˈteɪʃən] *n* : implantación *f*

implausibility [ɪmˌplɔzəˈbɪləti] *n, pl* **-ties**
: inverosimilitud *f*

implausible [ɪmˈplɔzəbəl] *adj* : inverosímil, poco convincente

implement¹ [ˈɪmpləˌmɛnt] *vt* : poner en
práctica, implementar

implement² [ˈɪmpləmənt] *n* : utensilio *m*,
instrumento *m*, implemento *m*

implementation [ˌɪmpləmənˈteɪʃən] *n*
: implementación *f*, ejecución *f*, cumplimiento *m*

implicate [ˈɪmpləˌkeɪt] *vt* **-cated; -cating**
: implicar, involucrar

implication [ˌɪmpləˈkeɪʃən] *n* **1** CONSE-
QUENCE : implicación *f*, consecuencia *f*
2 INFERENCE : insinuación *f*, inferencia *f*

implicit [ɪmˈplɪsət] *adj* **1** IMPLIED : implícito, tácito **2** ABSOLUTE : absoluto,
completo ⟨implicit faith : fe ciega⟩ —
implicitly *adv*

implied [ɪmˈplaɪd] *adj* : implícito, tácito

implode [ɪmˈploːd] *vi* **-ploded; -ploding**
: implosionar

implore [ɪmˈplor] *vt* **-plored; -ploring**
: implorar, suplicar

implosion [ɪmˈploːʒən] *n* : implosión *f*

imply [ɪmˈplaɪ] *vt* **-plied; -plying 1** SUG-
GEST : insinuar, dar a entender **2** IN-
VOLVE : implicar, suponer ⟨rights imply
obligations : los derechos implican unas
obligaciones⟩

impolite [ˌɪmpəˈlaɪt] *adj* : descortés, maleducado

impoliteness [ˌɪmpəˈlaɪtnəs] *n* : descortesía *f*, falta *f* de educación

impolitic [ɪmˈpɑləˌtɪk] *adj* : imprudente,
poco político

imponderable¹ [ɪmˈpɑndərəbəl] *adj*
: imponderable

imponderable² *n* : imponderable *m*

import¹ [ɪmˈport] *vt* **1** SIGNIFY : significar
2 : importar ⟨to import foreign cars
: importar autos extranjeros⟩

import² [ˈɪmˌport] *n* **1** SIGNIFICANCE
: importancia *f*, significación *f* **2** → **importation**

importance [ɪmˈportənts] *n* : importancia
f

important [ɪmˈportənt] *adj* : importante

importantly [ɪmˈportəntli] *adv* **1** : con
importancia **2 more importantly** : lo
que es más importante

importation [ˌɪmˌporˈteɪʃən] *n* : importación *f*

importer [ɪmˈportər] *n* : importador *m*,
-dora *f*

importune [ˌɪmpərˈtuːn, -ˈtjuːn;
ɪmˈportʃən] *vt* **-tuned; -tuning** : importunar, importunar

impose [ɪmˈpoːz] *v* **-posed; -posing** *vt*
: imponer ⟨to impose a tax : imponer un
impuesto⟩ — *vi* **to impose on** : abusar
de, molestar ⟨to impose on her kindness
: abusar de su bondad⟩

imposing [ɪmˈpoːzɪŋ] *adj* : imponente,
impresionante

imposition [ˌɪmpəˈzɪʃən] *n* : imposición *f*

impossibility [ɪmˌpɑsəˈbɪləti] *n, pl* **-ties**
: imposibilidad *f*

impossible [ɪmˈpɑsəbəl] *adj* **1** : imposible
⟨an impossible task : una tarea imposi-
ble⟩ ⟨to make life impossible for : hacerle la vida imposible a⟩ **2** UNACCEPT-
ABLE : inaceptable

impossibly [ɪmˈpɑsəbli] *adv* : imposiblemente, increíblemente

impostor *or* **imposter** [ɪmˈpɑstər] *n*
: impostor *m*, -tora *f*

impotence [ˈɪmpətənts] *n* : impotencia *f*

impotency [ˈɪmpətəntsi] → **impotence**

impotent [ˈɪmpətənt] *adj* : impotente

impound [ɪmˈpaʊnd] *vt* : incautar, embargar, confiscar

impoverish [ɪmˈpɑvərɪʃ] *vt* : empobrecer

impoverished [ɪmˈpɑvərɪʃt] *adj* : empo-
brecido

impoverishment [ɪmˈpɑvərɪʃmənt] *n*
: empobrecimiento *m*

impracticable [ɪmˈpræktɪkəbəl] *adj* : impracticable

impractical [ɪmˈpræktɪkəl] *adj* : poco
práctico

imprecise [ˌɪmprɪˈsaɪs] *adj* : impreciso

imprecisely [ˌɪmprɪˈsaɪsli] *adv* : con imprecisión

impreciseness [ˌɪmprɪˈsaɪsnəs] → **imprecision**

imprecision [ˌɪmprɪˈsɪʒən] *n* : imprecisión
f, falta de precisión *f*

impregnable [ɪmˈprɛgnəbəl] *adj* : inexpugnable, impenetrable, inconquistable

impregnate [ɪmˈprɛgˌneɪt] *vt* **-nated; -nat-
ing 1** FERTILIZE : fecundar **2** PERME-
ATE, SATURATE : impregnar, empapar,
saturar

impresario [ˌɪmprəˈsɑriˌo, -ˈsær-] *n, pl*
-rios : empresario *m*, -ria *f*

impress [ɪmˈprɛs] *vt* **1** IMPRINT : imprimir, estampar **2** : impresionar, causar
impresión a ⟨I was not impressed : no

me hizo buena impresión⟩ **3 to impress (something) on someone** : recalcarle (algo) a alguien — *vi* : impresionar, hacer una impresión

impression [ɪmˈprɛʃən] *n* **1** IMPRINT : marca *f*, huella *f*, molde *m* (de los dientes) **2** EFFECT : impresión *f*, efecto *m*, impacto *m* ⟨to make a good/bad impression on someone : causarle (una) buena/mala impresión a alguien⟩ **3** PRINTING : impresión *f* **4** NOTION : impresión *f*, noción *f* ⟨to give the impression that : dar la impresión de que⟩ ⟨to have the impression that, to be under the impression that : tener la impresión de que⟩

impressionable [ɪmˈprɛʃənəbəl] *adj* : impresionable

impressionism [ɪmˈprɛʃəˌnɪzəm] *n* : impresionismo *m*

impressionist [ɪmˈprɛʃənɪst] *n* : impresionista *mf* — **impressionist** *adj*

impressive [ɪmˈprɛsɪv] *adj* : impresionante — **impressively** *adv*

impressiveness [ɪmˈprɛsɪvnəs] *n* : calidad de ser impresionante

imprint[1] [ɪmˈprɪnt, ˈɪmˌ-] *vt* **1** : imprimir, estampar

imprint[2] [ˈɪmˌprɪnt] *n* : marca *f*, huella *f*

imprison [ɪmˈprɪzən] *vt* **1** JAIL : encarcelar, aprisionar **2** CONFINE : recluir, encerrar

imprisonment [ɪmˈprɪzənmənt] *n* : encarcelamiento *m*

improbability [ɪmˌprɑbəˈbɪləti] *n, pl* **-ties** : improbabilidad *f*, inverosimilitud *f*

improbable [ɪmˈprɑbəbəl] *adj* : improbable, inverosímil

impromptu[1] [ɪmˈprɑmpˌtuː, -ˌtjuː] *adv* : sin preparación, espontáneamente

impromptu[2] *adj* : espontáneo, improvisado

impromptu[3] *n* : improvisación *f*

improper [ɪmˈprɑpər] *adj* **1** INCORRECT : incorrecto, impropio **2** INDECOROUS : indecoroso

improperly [ɪmˈprɑpərli] *adv* : incorrectamente, indebidamente

impropriety [ˌɪmprəˈpraɪəti] *n, pl* **-eties 1** INDECOROUSNESS : indecoro *m*, falta *f* de decoro **2** ERROR : impropiedad *f*, incorrección *f*

improve [ɪmˈpruːv] *v* **-proved; -proving** : mejorar

improvement [ɪmˈpruːvmənt] *n* : mejoramiento *m*, mejora *f*

improvidence [ɪmˈprɑvədənts] *n* : imprevisión *f*

improvisation [ɪmˌprɑvəˈzeɪʃən, ˌɪmprəvə-] *n* : improvisación *f*

improvise [ˈɪmprəˌvaɪz] *v* **-vised; -vising** : improvisar

imprudence [ɪmˈpruːdənts] *n* : imprudencia *f*, indiscreción *f*

imprudent [ɪmˈpruːdənt] *adj* : imprudente, indiscreto

impudence [ˈɪmpjədənts] *n* : insolencia *f*, descaro *m*

impudent [ˈɪmpjədənt] *adj* : insolente, descarado — **impudently** *adv*

impugn [ɪmˈpjuːn] *vt* : impugnar

impulse [ˈɪmˌpʌls] *n* **1** : impulso *m* **2 on impulse** : sin reflexionar

impulsive [ɪmˈpʌlsɪv] *adj* : impulsivo — **impulsively** *adv*

impulsiveness [ɪmˈpʌlsɪvnəs] *n* : impulsividad *f*

impunity [ɪmˈpjuːnəti] *n* **1** : impunidad *f* **2 with impunity** : impunemente

impure [ɪmˈpjʊr] *adj* **1** : impuro ⟨impure thoughts : pensamientos impuros⟩ **2** CONTAMINATED : con impurezas, impuro

impurity [ɪmˈpjʊrəti] *n, pl* **-ties** : impureza *f*

impute [ɪmˈpjuːt] *vt* **-puted; -puting** ATTRIBUTE : imputar, atribuir

in[1] [ˈɪn] *adv* **1** INSIDE : dentro, adentro ⟨let's go in : vamos adentro⟩ ⟨the burglars broke in through the window : los ladrones entraron por la ventana⟩ **2** (*to or towards a place*) ⟨they flew in yesterday : llegaron ayer (en avión)⟩ ⟨she leaned farther in : se inclinó más (hacia adelante)⟩ **3** (*indicating a union*) ⟨mix the flour in : añade la harina⟩ **4** (*indicating containment*) ⟨to shut in : encerrar⟩ **5** PARTICIPATING ⟨count me in : yo me apunto⟩ **6** (*to a job or position*) ⟨she was voted in : fue elegida, ganó las elecciones⟩ **7** COLLECTED ⟨the crops are in : las cosechas ya están recogidas⟩ ⟨are all the votes in? : ¿tenemos todos los votos?⟩ ⟨the results are in : se conocen los resultados⟩ **8** (*within bounds*) : dentro (en deportes) **9 in that** : en el sentido de que **10 to be in** : estar ⟨is Linda in? : ¿está Linda?⟩ ⟨is the train in? : ¿ha llegado el tren?⟩ **11 to be in** : estar en poder (the Democrats are in : los demócratas están en el poder) **12 to be in for** ⟨they're in for a treat : les va a encantar⟩ ⟨he's in for a surprise : se va a llevar una sorpresa⟩ **13 to be in on** : participar en, tomar parte en **14 to be in with someone** : ser muy amigo de alguien **15 to get in good/bad with someone** : quedar bien/mal con alguien

in[2] *adj* **1** INSIDE ⟨the in part : la parte interior⟩ **2** FASHIONABLE : de moda

in[3] *prep* **1** (*indicating location or position*) ⟨in the lake : en el lago⟩ ⟨a pain in the leg : un dolor en la pierna⟩ ⟨in the sun : al sol⟩ ⟨in the rain : bajo la lluvia⟩ **2** (*with superlatives*) : de ⟨the best in the world : el mejor del mundo⟩ **3** INTO : en, a ⟨he broke it in pieces : lo rompió en pedazos⟩ ⟨she went in the house : se metió a la casa⟩ **4** DURING : por, en, durante ⟨in the afternoon : por la tarde⟩ **5** WITHIN : dentro de ⟨I'll be back in a week : vuelvo dentro de una semana⟩ **6** (*indicating belonging*) : en, de ⟨she plays in a band : toca en una banda⟩ ⟨the first scene in the movie : la primera escena de la película⟩ **7** (*indicating manner or form*) : en, con, de ⟨in Spanish : en español⟩ ⟨written in pencil : escrito con lápiz⟩ ⟨in this way : de esta manera⟩ ⟨in some respects : en algún sentido⟩ ⟨in a circle : en un círculo⟩ ⟨in height : de altura⟩ ⟨in theory : en teoría⟩ ⟨she was in uniform : llevaba uniforme⟩ ⟨she was (dressed) in blue : iba (vestido) de azul⟩ **8** (*indicating states or circumstances*) ⟨to be in luck : tener suerte⟩ ⟨to be in love : estar enamorado⟩ ⟨to be in a hurry : tener prisa⟩ ⟨to be/get in trouble : estar/ meterse en un lío⟩ **9** (*indicating purpose*) : en ⟨in reply : en respuesta, como réplica⟩ **10** (*with regard to*) : en ⟨do you believe in ghosts? : ¿crees en los fantasmas?⟩ **11** : en (un campo) ⟨he works in insurance : trabaja en seguros⟩ **12** (*in approximations*) ⟨she's in her thirties : tiene treinta y tantos años⟩ ⟨in the 1940's : en los años cuarenta⟩ **13** (*indicating a ratio*) : de ⟨one in five : uno de cada cinco⟩

in⁴ *n* **ins and outs** : pormenores *mpl*

in- *or* **im-** *or* **il-** *pref* : in-, im-, i- ⟨inexact : inexacto⟩ ⟨imperfect : imperfecto⟩ ⟨illegal : ilegal⟩

inability [ˌɪnəˈbɪləti] *n, pl* **-ties** : incapacidad *f*

inaccessibility [ˌɪnɪkˌsɛsəˈbɪləti] *n, pl* **-ties** : inaccesibilidad *f*

inaccessible [ˌɪnɪkˈsɛsəbəl] *adj* : inaccesible

inaccuracy [ɪnˈækjərəsi] *n, pl* **-cies 1** : inexactitud *f* **2** MISTAKE : error *m*

inaccurate [ɪnˈækjərət] *n* : inexacto, erróneo, incorrecto

inaccurately [ɪnˈækjərətli] *adv* : incorrectamente, con inexactitud

inaction [ɪnˈækʃən] *n* : inactividad *f*, inacción *f*

inactive [ɪnˈæktɪv] *adj* : inactivo

inactivity [ˌɪnˌækˈtɪvəti] *n, pl* **-ties** : inactividad *f*, ociosidad *f*

inadequacy [ɪnˈædɪkwəsi] *n, pl* **-cies 1** INSUFFICIENCY : insuficiencia *f* **2** INCOMPETENCE : ineptitud *f*, incompetencia *f*

inadequate [ɪnˈædɪkwət] *adj* **1** INSUFFICIENT : insuficiente, inadecuado **2** INCOMPETENT : inepto, incompetente

inadmissible [ˌɪnædˈmɪsəbəl] *adj* : inadmisible

inadvertent [ˌɪnədˈvərtənt] *adj* : inadvertido, involuntario — **inadvertently** *adv*

inadvisable [ˌɪnædˈvaɪzəbəl] *adj* : desaconsejable

inalienable [ɪnˈeɪljənəbəl, -ˈeɪliənə-] *adj* : inalienable

inane [ɪˈneɪn] *adj* **inaner; -est** : estúpido, idiota, necio

inanimate [ɪnˈænəmət] *adj* : inanimado, exánime

inanity [ɪˈnænəti] *n, pl* **-ties 1** STUPIDITY : estupidez *f* **2** NONSENSE : idiotez *f*, disparate *m*

inapplicable [ɪnˈæplɪkəbəl, ˌɪnəˈplɪkəbəl] *adj* IRRELEVANT : inaplicable, irrelevante

inappropriate [ˌɪnəˈproʊpriət] *adj* : inapropiado, inadecuado, impropio

inappropriateness [ˌɪnəˈproʊpriətnəs] *n* : lo inapropiado, impropiedad *f*

inapt [ɪnˈæpt] *adj* **1** UNSUITABLE : inadecuado, inapropiado **2** INEPT : inepto

inarticulate [ˌɪnɑrˈtɪkjələt] *adj* : inarticulado, incapaz de expresarse

inarticulately [ˌɪnɑrˈtɪkjələtli] *adv* : inarticuladamente

inasmuch as [ˌɪnæzˈmʌtʃæz] *conj* : ya que, dado que, puesto que

inattention [ˌɪnəˈtɛntʃən] *n* : falta *f* de atención, distracción *f*

inattentive [ˌɪnəˈtɛntɪv] *adj* : distraído, despistado

inattentively [ˌɪnəˈtɛntɪvli] *adv* : distraídamente, sin prestar atención

inaudible [ɪnˈɔdəbəl] *adj* : inaudible

inaudibly [ɪnˈɔdəbli] *adv* : de forma inaudible

inaugural¹ [ɪˈnɔɡjərəl, -ɡərəl] *adj* : inaugural, de investidura

inaugural² *n* **1** *or* **inaugural address** : discurso *m* de investidura **2** INAUGURATION : investidura *f* (de una persona)

inaugurate [ɪˈnɔɡjəˌreɪt, -ɡə-] *vt* **-rated; -rating 1** BEGIN : inaugurar **2** INDUCT : investir ⟨to inaugurate the president : investir al presidente⟩

inauguration [ɪˌnɔɡjəˈreɪʃən, -ɡə-] *n* **1** : inauguración *f* (de un edificio, un sistema, etc.) **2** : investidura *f* (de una persona)

inauspicious [ˌɪnɔˈspɪʃəs] *adj* : desfavorable, poco propicio

inauthentic [ˌɪnɔˈθɛntɪk] *adj* : inauténtico

inborn [ˈɪnˌbɔrn] *adj* **1** CONGENITAL, INNATE : innato, congénito **2** HEREDITARY : hereditario

inbound [ˈɪnˌbaʊnd] *adj* : que llega, de llegada

in-box [ˈɪnˌbɑks] *n* : bandeja *f* de entrada

inbred [ˈɪnˌbrɛd] *adj* **1** : engendrado por endogamia **2** INNATE : innato

inbreed [ˈɪnˌbriːd] *vt* **-bred; -breeding** : engendrar por endogamia

inbreeding [ˈɪnˌbriːdɪŋ] *n* : endogamia *f*

Inca [ˈɪŋkə] *n* : inca *mf*

incalculable [ɪnˈkælkjələbəl] *adj* : incalculable — **incalculably** [-bli] *adv*

Incan [ˈɪŋkən] *adj* : incaico

incandescence [ˌɪnkənˈdɛsənts] *n* : incandescencia *f*

incandescent [ˌɪnkənˈdɛsənt] *adj* **1** : incandescente **2** BRILLIANT : brillante

incantation [ˌɪnˌkænˈteɪʃən] *n* : conjuro *m*, ensalmo *m*

incapable [ɪnˈkeɪpəbəl] *adj* : incapaz

incapacitate [ˌɪnkəˈpæsəˌteɪt] *vt* **-tated; -tating** : incapacitar

incapacity [ˌɪnkəˈpæsəti] *n, pl* **-ties** : incapacidad *f*

incarcerate [ɪnˈkɑrsəˌreɪt] *vt* **-ated; -ating** : encarcelar

incarceration [ɪnˌkɑrsəˈreɪʃən] *n* : encarcelamiento *m*, encarcelación *f*

incarnate¹ [ɪnˈkɑrˌneɪt] *vt* **-nated; -nating** : encarnar

incarnate² [ɪnˈkɑrnət, -ˌneɪt] *adj* : encarnado

incarnation [ˌɪnˌkɑrˈneɪʃən] *n* : encarnación *f*

incendiary¹ [ɪnˈsɛndiˌri] *adj* : incendiario

incendiary² *n, pl* **-aries** : incendiario *m*, -ria *f*; pirómano *m*, -na *f*

incense¹ [ɪnˈsɛnts] *vt* **-censed; -censing** : indignar, enfadar, enfurecer

incense² [ˈɪnˌsɛnts] *n* : incienso *m*

incentive [ɪnˈsɛntɪv] *n* : incentivo *m*, aliciente *m*, motivación *f*, acicate *m*

inception [ɪnˈsɛpʃən] *n* : comienzo *m*, principio *m*

incessant [ɪnˈsɛsənt] *adj* : incesante, continuo — **incessantly** *adv*

incest [ˈɪnˌsɛst] *n* : incesto *m*

incestuous [ɪnˈsɛstʃuəs] *adj* : incestuoso

inch¹ [ˈɪntʃ] *v* : avanzar poco a poco

inch² *n* 1 : pulgada *f* 2 **every inch** : absoluto, seguro ⟨every inch a winner : un seguro ganador⟩ 3 **within an inch of** : a punto de

incidence [ˈɪnsədənts] *n* 1 FREQUENCY : frecuencia *f*, índice *m* ⟨a high incidence of crime : un alto índice de crímenes⟩ 2 **angle of incidence** : ángulo *m* de incidencia

incident¹ [ˈɪnsədənt] *adj* : incidente

incident² *n* : incidente *m*, incidencia *f*, episodio *m* (en una obra de ficción)

incidental¹ [ˌɪnsəˈdɛntəl] *adj* 1 SECONDARY : incidental, secundario 2 ACCIDENTAL : casual, fortuito

incidental² *n* 1 : algo incidental 2 **incidentals** *npl* : imprevistos *mpl*

incidentally [ˌɪntsəˈdɛntəli, -ˈdɛntli] *adv* 1 BY CHANCE : incidentalmente, casualmente 2 BY THE WAY : a propósito, por cierto

incinerate [ɪnˈsɪnəˌreɪt] *vt* **-ated; -ating** : incinerar

incinerator [ɪnˈsɪnəˌreɪtər] *n* : incinerador *m*

incipient [ɪnˈsɪpiənt] *adj* : incipiente, naciente

incise [ɪnˈsaɪz] *vt* **-cised; -cising** 1 ENGRAVE : grabar, cincelar, inscribir 2 : hacer una incisión en

incision [ɪnˈsɪʒən] *n* : incisión *f*

incisive [ɪnˈsaɪsɪv] *adj* : incisivo, penetrante

incisively [ɪnˈsaɪsɪvli] *adv* : con agudeza

incisor [ɪnˈsaɪzər] *n* : incisivo *m*

incite [ɪnˈsaɪt] *vt* **-cited; -citing** : incitar, instigar

incitement [ɪnˈsaɪtmənt] *n* : incitación *f*

inclemency [ɪnˈklɛməntsi] *n, pl* **-cies** : inclemencia *f*

inclement [ɪnˈklɛmənt] *adj* : inclemente, tormentoso

inclination [ˌɪnkləˈneɪʃən] *n* 1 PROPENSITY : inclinación *f*, tendencia *f* 2 DESIRE : deseo *m*, ganas *fpl* 3 BOW : inclinación *f*

incline¹ [ɪnˈklaɪn] *v* **-clined; -clining** *vi* 1 SLOPE : inclinarse 2 TEND : inclinarse, tender ⟨he is inclined to be late : tiende a llegar tarde⟩ — *vt* 1 LOWER : inclinar, bajar ⟨to incline one's head : bajar la cabeza⟩ 2 SLANT : inclinar 3 PREDISPOSE : predisponer

incline² [ˈɪnˌklaɪn] *n* : inclinación *f*, pendiente *f*

inclined [ɪnˈklaɪnd] *adj* 1 SLOPING : inclinado 2 PRONE : prono, dispuesto, dado

inclose, inclosure → **enclose, enclosure**

include [ɪnˈkluːd] *vt* **-cluded; -cluding** : incluir, comprender

including [ɪnˈkluːdɪŋ] *prep* : incluyendo ⟨including tax : (con) impuestos incluidos⟩ ⟨without including expenses : sin incluir los gastos⟩ ⟨up to and including . . . : hasta . . . inclusive⟩

inclusion [ɪnˈkluːʒən] *n* : inclusión *f*

inclusive [ɪnˈkluːsɪv] *adj* : inclusivo

incognito [ˌɪnkɑɡˈniːˌto, ɪnˈkɑɡnəˌtoː] *adv & adj* : de incógnito

incoherence [ˌɪnkoˈhɪrənts, -ˈhɛr-] *n* : incoherencia *f*

incoherent [ˌɪnkoˈhɪrənt, -ˈhɛr-] *adj* : incoherente — **incoherently** *adv*

incombustible [ˌɪnkəmˈbʌstəbəl] *adj* : incombustible

income [ˈɪnˌkʌm] *n* : ingresos *mpl*, entradas *fpl*

income tax *n* : impuesto *m* sobre la renta

incoming [ˈɪnˌkʌmɪŋ] *adj* 1 ARRIVING : que se recibe (dícese del correo), que llega (dícese de las personas), ascendente (dícese de la marea) 2 NEW : nuevo, entrante ⟨the incoming president : el nuevo presidente⟩ ⟨the incoming year : el año entrante⟩

incommunicado [ˌɪnkəˌmjuːnəˈkɑdo] *adj* : incomunicado

incomparable [ɪnˈkɑmpərəbəl] *adj* : incomparable, sin igual

incompatibility [ˌɪnkəmˌpætəˈbɪləti] *n, pl* **-ties** : incompatibilidad *f*

incompatible [ˌɪnkəmˈpætəbəl] *adj* : incompatible

incompetence [ɪnˈkɑmpətənts] *n* : incompetencia *f*, impericia *f*, ineptitud *f*

incompetent [ɪnˈkɑmpətənt] *adj* : incompetente *mf*; inepto *m*, -ta *f* — **incompetent** *adj*

incomplete [ˌɪnkəmˈpliːt] *adj* : incompleto — **incompletely** *adv*

incomprehensible [ˌɪnˌkɑmpriˈhɛntsəbəl] *adj* : incomprensible

incomprehension [ˌɪnˌkɑmpriˈhɛntʃən] *n* : incomprensión *f*

inconceivable [ˌɪnkənˈsiːvəbəl] *adj* 1 INCOMPREHENSIBLE : incomprensible 2 UNBELIEVABLE : inconcebible, increíble

inconceivably [ˌɪnkənˈsiːvəbli] *adv* : inconcebiblemente, increíblemente

inconclusive [ˌɪnkənˈkluːsɪv] *adj* : no concluyente, no decisivo

incongruity [ˌɪnkənˈɡruːəti, -ˌkɑn-] *n, pl* **-ties** : incongruencia *f*

incongruous [ɪnˈkɑŋɡruəs] *adj* : incongruente, inapropiado, fuera de lugar

incongruously [ɪnˈkɑŋɡruəsli] *adv* : de manera incongruente, inapropiadamente

inconsequential [ˌɪnˌkɑnsəˈkwɛntʃəl] *adj* : intrascendente, de poco importancia

inconsiderable [ˌɪnkənˈsɪdərəbəl] *adj* : insignificante

inconsiderate [ˌɪnkənˈsɪdərət] *adj* : desconsiderado, sin consideración — **inconsiderately** *adv*

inconsistency [ˌɪnkən'sɪstənʦi] *n, pl* **-cies** : inconsecuencia *f*, inconsistencia *f*

inconsistent [ˌɪnkən'sɪstənt] *adj* : inconsecuente, inconsistente

inconsolable [ˌɪnkən'soːləbəl] *adj* : inconsolable — **inconsolably** [-bli] *adv*

inconspicuous [ˌɪnkən'spɪkjuəs] *adj* : discreto, no conspicuo, que no llama la atención

inconspicuously [ˌɪnkən'spɪkjuəsli] *adv* : discretamente, sin llamar la atención

incontestable [ˌɪnkən'tɛstəbəl] *adj* : incontestable, indiscutible — **incontestably** [-bli] *adv*

incontinence [ɪn'kantənənʦ] *n* : incontinencia *f*

incontinent [ɪn'kantənənt] *adj* : incontinente

inconvenience[1] [ˌɪnkən'viːnjənʦ] *vt* **-nienced; -niencing** : importunar, incomodar, molestar

inconvenience[2] *n* : incomodidad *f*, molestia *f*

inconvenient [ˌɪnkən'viːnjənt] *adj* : inconveniente, importuno, incómodo — **inconveniently** *adv*

incorporate [ɪn'kɔrpə,reɪt] *vt* **-rated; -rating** 1 INCLUDE : incorporar, incluir 2 : incorporar, constituir en sociedad (dícese de un negocio)

incorporation [ɪn,kɔrpə'reɪʃən] *n* : incorporación *f*

incorporeal [ˌɪn,kɔr'poriəl] *adj* : incorpóreo

incorrect [ˌɪnkə'rɛkt] *adj* 1 INACCURATE : incorrecto 2 WRONG : equivocado, erróneo 3 IMPROPER : impropio — **incorrectly** *adv*

incorrigible [ɪn'kɔrəʤəbəl] *adj* : incorregible

incorruptible [ˌɪnkə'rʌptəbəl] *adj* : incorruptible

increase[1] [ɪn'kris, 'ɪn,kris] *v* **-creased; -creasing** *vi* GROW : aumentar, crecer, subir (dícese de los precios) — *vt* AUGMENT : aumentar, acrecentar

increase[2] ['ɪn,kris, ɪn'kris] *n* : aumento *m*, incremento *m*, subida *f* (de precios)

increasing [ɪn'krisɪŋ, 'ɪn,krisɪŋ] *adj* : creciente

increasingly [ɪn'krisɪŋli] *adv* : cada vez más

incredible [ɪn'krɛdəbəl] *adj* : increíble — **incredibly** [-bli] *adv*

incredulity [ˌɪnkrɪ'duː,ləʈi, -'dju:-] *n* : incredulidad *f*

incredulous [ɪn'krɛʤələs] *adj* : incrédulo, escéptico

incredulously [ɪn'krɛʤələsli] *adv* : con incredulidad

increment ['ɪŋkrəmənt, 'ɪn-] *n* : incremento *m*, aumento *m*

incremental [ˌɪŋkrə'mɛntəl, ˌɪn-] *adj* : de incremento

incriminate [ɪn'krɪmə,neɪt] *vt* **-nated; -nating** : incriminar

incrimination [ɪn,krɪmə'neɪʃən] *n* : incriminación *f*

incriminatory [ɪn'krɪmənə,tori] *adj* : incriminatorio

incubate ['ɪŋkjuˌbeɪt, 'ɪn-] *v* **-bated; -bating** *vt* : incubar, empollar — *vi* : incubar(se), empollar

incubation [ˌɪŋkju'beɪʃən, ˌɪn-] *n* : incubación *f*

incubator ['ɪŋkjuˌbeɪtər, 'ɪn-] *n* : incubadora *f*

inculcate [ɪn'kʌlˌkeɪt, 'ɪnˌkʌl-] *vt* **-cated; -cating** : inculcar

incumbency [ɪn'kʌmbənʦi] *n, pl* **-cies** 1 OBLIGATION : incumbencia *f* 2 : mandato *m* (en la política)

incumbent[1] [ɪn'kʌmbənt] *adj* : obligatorio

incumbent[2] *n* : titular *mf*

incur [ɪn'kər] *vt* **incurred; incurring** : provocar (al enojo), incurrir en (gastos, obligaciones)

incurable [ɪn'kjurəbəl] *adj* : incurable, sin remedio

incursion [ɪn'kərʒən] *n* : incursión *f*

indebted [ɪn'dɛʈəd] *adj* 1 : endeudado 2 **to be indebted to** : estar en deuda con, estarle agradecido a

indebtedness [ɪn'dɛʈədnəs] *n* : endeudamiento *m*

indecency [ɪn'di:sənʦi] *n, pl* **-cies** : indecencia *f*

indecent [ɪn'di:sənt] *adj* : indecente — **indecently** *adv*

indecipherable [ˌɪndɪ'saɪfərəbəl] *adj* : indescifrable

indecision [ˌɪndɪ'sɪʒən] *n* : indecisión *f*, irresolución *f*

indecisive [ˌɪndɪ'saɪsɪv] *adj* 1 INCONCLUSIVE : indeciso, que no es decisivo 2 IRRESOLUTE : indeciso, irresoluto, vacilante 3 INDEFINITE : indefinido — **indecisively** *adv*

indecorous [ɪn'dɛkərəs, ˌɪndɪ'korəs] *adj* : indecoroso — **indecorously** *adv*

indecorousness [ɪn'dɛkərəsnəs, ˌɪndɪ'korəs-] *n* : indecoro *m*

indeed [ɪn'di:d] *adv* 1 (*emphasizing the truth of a statement*) : efectivamente ⟨yes, indeed : sí, efectivamente⟩ ⟨it's a very serious problem indeed : esto sí que es un problema muy grave⟩ ⟨thank you very much indeed : muchísimas gracias⟩ 2 (*expressing surprise or doubt*) ⟨indeed? : ¿ah, sí?, ¿de veras?, ¡no me digas!⟩ 3 (*strengthening a previous statement*) ⟨it is possible—indeed, probable—that . . . : es posible, e incluso probable, que . . .⟩ 4 (*emphasizing that one does not know the answer*) ⟨how can we help them? how, indeed! : ¿cómo podemos ayudarlos? ¡buena pregunta!⟩

indefatigable [ˌɪndɪ'fæʈɪgəbəl] *adj* : incansable, infatigable — **indefatigably** [-bli] *adv*

indefensible [ˌɪndɪ'fɛnʦəbəl] *adj* 1 VULNERABLE : indefendible, vulnerable 2 INEXCUSABLE : inexcusable

indefinable [ˌɪndɪ'faɪnəbəl] *adj* : indefinible

indefinite [ɪn'dɛfənət] *adj* 1 : indefinido, indeterminado 2 : indefinido (en lingüística) ⟨indefinite pronouns/articles : pronombres/artículos indefinidos⟩ 3 VAGUE : vago, impreciso

indefinitely [ɪn'dɛfənətli] *adv* : indefinidamente, por un tiempo indefinido
indelible [ɪn'dɛləbəl] *adj* : indeleble, imborrable — **indelibly** [-bli] *adv*
indelicacy [ɪn'dɛləkəsi] *n* : falta *f* de delicadeza
indelicate [ɪn'dɛlɪkət] *adj* **1** IMPROPER
: indelicado, indecoroso **2** TACTLESS
: indiscreto, falto de tacto
indemnify [ɪn'dɛmnə,faɪ] *vt* **-fied; -fying 1**
INSURE : asegurar **2** COMPENSATE : indemnizar, compensar
indemnity [ɪn'dɛmnəti] *n, pl* **-ties 1** IN-
SURANCE : indemnidad *f* **2** COMPENSA-
TION : indemnización *f*
indent [ɪn'dɛnt] *vt* : sangrar (un párrafo)
indentation [,ɪn,dɛn'teɪʃən] *n* **1** NOTCH
: muesca *f*, mella *f* **2** INDENTING : sangría *f* (de un párrafo)
indenture[1] [ɪn'dɛntʃər] *vt* **-tured; -turing**
: ligar por contrato
indenture[2] *n* : contrato de aprendizaje
independence [,ɪndə'pɛndənts] *n* : independencia *f*
Independence Day *n* : día *m* de la Independencia (4 de julio en los EE.UU.)
independent[1] [,ɪndə'pɛndənt] *adj* : independiente — **independently** *adv*
independent[2] *n* : independiente *mf*
in–depth *adj* : a fondo, exhaustivo
indescribable [,ɪndɪ'skraɪbəbəl] *adj* : indescriptible, incalificable — **indescrib-
ably** [-bli] *adv*
indestructible [,ɪndɪ'strʌktəbəl] *adj* : indestructible
indeterminate [,ɪndɪ'tərmənət] *adj* **1**
VAGUE : vago, impreciso, indeterminado
2 INDEFINITE : indeterminado, indefinido
index[1] ['ɪn,dɛks] *vt* **1** : ponerle un índice a
(un libro o una revista) **2** : incluir en un
índice ⟨all proper names are indexed
: todos los nombres propios están incluidos en el índice⟩ **3** INDICATE : indicar,
señalar **4** REGULATE : indexar, indiciar
⟨to index prices : indiciar los precios⟩
index[2] *n, pl* **-dexes** *or* **-dices** ['ɪndə,si:z]
1 : índice *m* (de un libro, de precios) **2**
INDICATION : indicio *m*, índice *m*, señal *f*
⟨an index of her character : una señal de
su carácter⟩
index finger *n* FOREFINGER : dedo *m* índice
Indian ['ɪndiən] *n* **1** : indio *m*, -dia *f* **2**
often offensive → **Native American** —
Indian *adj*
indicate ['ɪndə,keɪt] *vt* **-cated; -cating 1**
POINT OUT : indicar, señalar **2** SHOW,
SUGGEST : ser indicio de, ser señal de **3**
EXPRESS : expresar, señalar **4** REGISTER
: marcar, poner (una medida, etc.)
indication [,ɪndə'keɪʃən] *n* : indicio *m*,
señal *f*
indicative [ɪn'dɪkətɪv] *adj* : indicativo
indicator ['ɪndə,keɪtər] *n* : indicador *m*
indict [ɪn'daɪt] *vt* : acusar, procesar (por
un crimen)
indictment [ɪn'daɪtmənt] *n* : acusación *f*
indifference [ɪn'dɪfrənts, -'dɪfə-] *n* : indiferencia *f*

indifferent [ɪn'dɪfrənt, -'dɪfə-] *adj* **1** UN-
CONCERNED : indiferente **2** MEDIOCRE
: mediocre
indifferently [ɪn'dɪfrəntli, -'dɪfə-] *adv* **1**
: con indiferencia, indiferentemente **2**
SO-SO : de modo regular, más o menos
indigence ['ɪndɪdʒənts] *n* : indigencia *f*
indigenous [ɪn'dɪdʒənəs] *adj* : indígena,
nativo
indigent ['ɪndɪdʒənt] *adj* : indigente, pobre
indigestible [,ɪndaɪ'dʒɛstəbəl, -dɪ-] *adj*
: difícil de digerir
indigestion [,ɪndaɪ'dʒɛstʃən, -dɪ-] *n* : indigestión *f*, empacho *m*
indignant [ɪn'dɪgnənt] *adj* : indignado
indignantly [ɪn'dɪgnəntli] *adv* : con indignación
indignation [,ɪndɪg'neɪʃən] *n* : indignación *f*
indignity [ɪn'dɪgnəti] *n, pl* **-ties** : indignidad *f*
indigo ['ɪndɪ,go:] *n, pl* **-gos** *or* **-goes** : añil
m, índigo *m*
indirect [,ɪndə'rɛkt, -daɪ-] *adj* : indirecto
— **indirectly** *adv*
indiscernible [,ɪndɪ'sərnəbəl, -'zər-] *adj*
: imperceptible
indiscreet [,ɪndɪ'skri:t] *adj* : indiscreto —
indiscreetly *adv*
indiscretion [,ɪndɪ'skrɛʃən] *n* : indiscreción *f*
indiscriminate [,ɪndɪ'skrɪmənət] *adj*
: indiscriminado
indiscriminately [,ɪndɪ'skrɪmənətli] *adv*
: sin discriminación, sin discernimiento
indispensable [,ɪndɪ'spɛntsəbəl] *adj*
: indispensable, necesario, imprescindible — **indispensably** [-bli] *adv*
indisposed [,ɪndɪ'spo:zd] *adj* **1** ILL : indispuesto, enfermo **2** AVERSE, DISIN-
CLINED : opuesto, reacio ⟨to be indisposed toward working : no tener ganas
de trabajar⟩
indisputable [,ɪndɪ'spju:təbəl, ɪn'dɪs-
pju:tə-] *adj* : indiscutible, incuestionable,
incontestable — **indisputably** [-bli] *adv*
indistinct [,ɪndɪ'stɪŋkt] *adj* : indistinto —
indistinctly *adv*
indistinctness [,ɪndɪ'stɪŋktnəs] *n* : falta *f*
de claridad
indistinguishable [,ɪndɪ'stɪŋgwɪʃəbəl] *adj*
: indistinguible
individual[1] [,ɪndə'vɪdʒuəl] *adj* **1** PER-
SONAL : individual, personal ⟨individual
traits : características personales⟩ **2**
SEPARATE : individual, separado **3** PAR-
TICULAR : particular, propio
individual[2] *n* : individuo *m*
individualism [,ɪndə'vɪdʒəwə,lɪzəm] *n*
: individualismo *m*
individualist [,ɪndə'vɪdʒuəlɪst] *n* : individualista *mf*
individualistic [,ɪndə,vɪdʒuə'lɪstɪk] *adj*
: individualista
individuality [,ɪndə,vɪdʒu'æləti] *n, pl* **-ties**
: individualidad *f*
individualize [,ɪndə'vɪdʒuə,laɪz] *vt* **-ized;
-izing** : individualizar
individually [,ɪndə'vɪdʒuəli, -dʒəli] *adv*
: individualmente

indivisible [ˌɪndɪˈvɪzəbəl] *adj* : indivisible

indoctrinate [ɪnˈdɑktrəˌneɪt] *vt* **-nated;
-nating 1** TEACH : enseñar, instruir **2**
PROPAGANDIZE : adoctrinar

indoctrination [ɪnˌdɑktrəˈneɪʃən] *n*
: adoctrinamiento *m*

indolence [ˈɪndələns] *n* : indolencia *f*

indolent [ˈɪndələnt] *adj* : indolente

indomitable [ɪnˈdɑmətəbəl] *adj* : invencible, indomable, indomito — **indomitably** [-bli] *adv*

Indonesian [ˌɪndoˈniːʒən, -ʃən] *n* : indonesio *m*, -sia *f* — **Indonesian** *adj*

indoor [ˈɪnˌdor] *adj* : interior (dícese de las plantas), para estar en casa (dícese de la ropa), cubierto (dícese de las piscinas, etc.), bajo techo (dícese de los deportes)

indoors [ˈɪnˈdorz] *adv* : adentro, dentro

indubitable [ɪnˈduːbətəbəl, -ˈdjuː-] *adj*
: indudable, incuestionable, indiscutible

indubitably [ɪnˈduːbətəbli, -ˈdjuː-] *adv* : indudablemente

induce [ɪnˈduːs, -ˈdjuːs] *vt* **-duced; -ducing 1** PERSUADE : persuadir, inducir **2**
CAUSE : inducir, provocar ⟨to induce labor : provocar un parto⟩

inducement [ɪnˈduːsmənt, -ˈdjuːs-] *n* **1** INCENTIVE : incentivo *m*, aliciente *m* **2**
: inducción *f*, provocación *f* (de un parto)

induct [ɪnˈdʌkt] *vt* **1** INSTALL : instalar, investir **2** ADMIT : admitir (como miembro) **3** CONSCRIPT : reclutar (al servicio militar)

inductee [ˌɪnˌdʌkˈtiː] *n* : recluta *mf*, conscripto *m*, -ta *f*

induction [ɪnˈdʌkʃən] *n* **1** INTRODUCTION : iniciación *f*, introducción *f* **2** : inducción *f* (en la lógica o la electricidad)

inductive [ɪnˈdʌktɪv] *adj* : inductivo

indulge [ɪnˈdʌldʒ] *v* **-dulged; -dulging** *vt* **1**
GRATIFY : gratificar, satisfacer **2** SPOIL
: consentir, mimar — *vi* **to indulge in**
: permitirse

indulgence [ɪnˈdʌldʒəns] *n* **1** SATISFYING
: satisfacción *f*, gratificación *f* **2** HUMORING : complacencia *f*, indulgencia *f* **3**
SPOILING : consentimiento *m* **4** : indulgencia *f* (en la religión)

indulgent [ɪnˈdʌldʒənt] *adj* : indulgente, consentido — **indulgently** *adv*

industrial [ɪnˈdʌstriəl] *adj* : industrial — **industrially** *adv*

industrialist [ɪnˈdʌstriəlɪst] *n* : industrial *mf*

industrialization [ɪnˌdʌstriələˈzeɪʃən] *n*
: industrialización *f*

industrialize [ɪnˈdʌstriəˌlaɪz] *vt* **-ized; -izing** : industrializar

industrious [ɪnˈdʌstriəs] *adj* : diligente, industrioso, trabajador

industriously [ɪnˈdʌstriəsli] *adv* : con diligencia, con aplicación

industriousness [ɪnˈdʌstriəsnəs] *n* : diligencia *f*, aplicación *f*

industry [ˈɪndəstri] *n*, *pl* **-tries 1** DILIGENCE : diligencia *f*, aplicación *f* **2**
: industria *f* ⟨the steel industry : la industria siderúrgica⟩

inebriated [ɪˈniːbriˌeɪtəd] *adj* : ebrio, embriagado

inebriation [ɪˌniːbriˈeɪʃən] *n* : ebriedad *f*, embriaguez *f*

inedible [ɪnˈɛdəbəl] *adj* : incomible

ineffable [ɪnˈɛfəbəl] *adj* : inefable — **ineffably** [-bli] *adv*

ineffective [ˌɪnɪˈfɛktɪv] *adj* **1** INEFFECTUAL : ineficaz, inútil **2** INCAPABLE
: incompetente, ineficiente, incapaz

ineffectively [ˌɪnɪˈfɛktɪvli] *adv* : ineficazmente, infructuosamente

ineffectual [ˌɪnɪˈfɛktʃuəl] *adj* : inútil, ineficaz — **ineffectually** *adv*

inefficiency [ˌɪnɪˈfɪʃəntsi] *n*, *pl* **-cies**
: ineficiencia *f*, ineficacia *f*

inefficient [ˌɪnɪˈfɪʃənt] *adj* **1** : ineficiente, ineficaz **2** INCAPABLE, INCOMPETENT
: incompetente, incapaz — **inefficiently** *adv*

inelegance [ɪnˈɛləgənts] *n* : inelegancia *f*

inelegant [ɪnˈɛləgənt] *adj* : inelegante, poco elegante

ineligibility [ɪnˌɛlədʒəˈbɪləti] *n* : inelegibilidad *f*

ineligible [ɪnˈɛlədʒəbəl] *adj* : inelegible

inept [ɪˈnɛpt] *adj* : inepto ⟨inept at : incapaz para⟩

ineptitude [ɪˈnɛptəˌtuːd, -ˌtjuːd] *n* : ineptitud *f*, incompetencia *f*, incapacidad *f*

inequality [ˌɪnɪˈkwɑləti] *n*, *pl* **-ties** : desigualdad *f*

inequitable [ɪnˈɛkwətəbəl] *adj* : inequitativo

inequity [ɪnˈɛkwəti] *n*, *pl* **-ties** : inequidad *f*

inert [ɪˈnərt] *adj* **1** INACTIVE : inerte, inactivo **2** SLUGGISH : lento

inertia [ɪˈnərʃə] *n* : inercia *f*

inescapable [ˌɪnɪˈskeɪpəbəl] *adj* : inevitable, ineludible — **inescapably** [-bli] *adv*

inessential [ˌɪnɪˈsɛntʃəl] *adj* : que no es esencial, innecesario

inestimable [ɪnˈɛstəməbəl] *adj* : inestimable, inapreciable

inevitability [ɪnˌɛvətəˈbɪləti] *n*, *pl* **-ties**
: inevitabilidad *f*

inevitable [ɪnˈɛvətəbəl] *adj* : inevitable — **inevitably** [-bli] *adv*

inexact [ˌɪnɪgˈzækt] *adj* : inexacto

inexactly [ˌɪnɪgˈzæktli] *adv* : sin exactitud

inexcusable [ˌɪnɪkˈskjuːzəbəl] *adj* : inexcusable, imperdonable — **inexcusably** [-bli] *adv*

inexhaustible [ˌɪnɪgˈzɔstəbəl] *adj* **1** INDEFATIGABLE : infatigable, incansable **2**
ENDLESS : inagotable — **inexhaustibly** [-bli] *adv*

inexorable [ɪnˈɛksərəbəl] *adj* : inexorable — **inexorably** [-bli] *adv*

inexpensive [ˌɪnɪkˈspɛntsɪv] *adj* : barato, económico

inexperience [ˌɪnɪkˈspɪriənts] *n* : inexperiencia *f*

inexperienced [ˌɪnɪkˈspɪriəntst] *adj*
: inexperto, novato

inexplicable [ˌɪnɪkˈsplɪkəbəl] *adj* : inexplicable — **inexplicably** [-bli] *adv*

inexpressible [ˌɪnɪkˈsprɛsəbəl] *adj*
: inexpresable, inefable

inextricable [ˌɪnɪkˈstrɪkəbəl, ɪˈnɛk-ˌstrɪ-] adj : inextricable — **inextricably** [-bli] adv

infallibility [ɪnˌfæləˈbɪləti] n : infalibilidad f

infallible [ɪnˈfæləbəl] adj : infalible — **infallibly** [-bli] adv

infamous [ˈɪnfəməs] adj : infame — **infamously** adv

infamy [ˈɪnfəmi] n, pl **-mies** : infamia f

infancy [ˈɪnfəntsi] n, pl **-cies** : infancia f

infant [ˈɪnfənt] n : bebé m; niño m, -ña f

infantile [ˈɪnfənˌtaɪl, -təl, -ˌtiːl] adj : infantil, pueril

infantile paralysis → **poliomyelitis**

infantry [ˈɪnfəntri] n, pl **-tries** : infantería f

infatuated [ɪnˈfætʃuˌeɪtəd] adj **to be infatuated with** : estar encaprichado con

infatuation [ɪnˌfætʃuˈeɪʃən] n : encaprichamiento m, enamoramiento m

infect [ɪnˈfɛkt] vt : infectar, contagiar

infection [ɪnˈfɛkʃən] n : infección f, contagio m

infectious [ɪnˈfɛkʃəs] adj : infeccioso, contagioso

infer [ɪnˈfər] vt **inferred; inferring** 1 DEDUCE : deducir, inferir 2 SURMISE : concluir, suponer, tener entendido 3 IMPLY : sugerir, insinuar

inference [ˈɪnfərəns] n : deducción f, inferencia f, conclusión f

inferior[1] [ɪnˈfɪriər] adj : inferior, malo

inferior[2] n : inferior mf

inferiority [ɪnˌfɪriˈɔrəti] n, pl **-ties** : inferioridad f ⟨**inferiority complex** : complejo de inferioridad⟩

infernal [ɪnˈfərnəl] adj 1 : infernal ⟨infernal fires : fuegos infernales⟩ 2 DIABOLICAL : infernal, diabólico 3 DAMNABLE : maldito, condenado

inferno [ɪnˈfərˌnoː] n, pl **-nos** : infierno m

infertile [ɪnˈfərtəl, -ˌtaɪl] adj : estéril, infecundo

infertility [ˌɪnfərˈtɪləti] n : esterilidad f, infecundidad f

infest [ɪnˈfɛst] vt : infestar, plagar

infestation [ˌɪnˌfɛsˈteɪʃən] n : infestación f, plaga f

infidel [ˈɪnfədəl, -ˌdɛl] n : infiel mf

infidelity [ˌɪnfəˈdɛləti, -faɪ-] n, pl **-ties** 1 UNFAITHFULNESS : infidelidad f 2 DISLOYALTY : deslealtad f

infield [ˈɪnˌfiːld] n : cuadro m, diamante m

infighting [ˈɪnˌfaɪtɪŋ] n : disputas fpl internas, luchas fpl internas

infiltrate [ɪnˈfɪlˌtreɪt, ˈɪnfɪl-] v **-trated; -trating** vt : infiltrar — vi : infiltrarse

infiltration [ˌɪnˌfɪlˈtreɪʃən] n : infiltración f

infiltrator [ɪnˈfɪlˌtreɪtər, ˈɪnfɪl-] n : infiltrado m, -da f

infinite [ˈɪnfənət] adj 1 LIMITLESS : infinito, sin límites 2 VAST : infinito, vasto, extenso

infinitely [ˈɪnfənətli] adv : infinitamente

infinitesimal [ˌɪnˌfɪnəˈtɛsəməl] adj : infinitesimal — **infinitesimally** adv

infinitive [ɪnˈfɪnətɪv] n : infinitivo m

infinity [ɪnˈfɪnəti] n, pl **-ties** 1 : infinito m (en matemáticas, etc.) 2 : infinidad f

⟨an infinity of stars : una infinidad de estrellas⟩

infirm [ɪnˈfərm] adj 1 FEEBLE : enfermizo, endeble 2 INSECURE : inseguro

infirmary [ɪnˈfərməri] n, pl **-ries** : enfermería f, hospital m

infirmity [ɪnˈfərməti] n, pl **-ties** 1 FRAILTY : debilidad f 2 AILMENT : enfermedad f, dolencia f ⟨the infirmities of age : los achaques de la vejez⟩

inflame [ɪnˈfleɪm] v **-flamed; -flaming** vt 1 KINDLE : inflamar, encender 2 : inflamar (una herida) 3 STIR UP : encender, provocar, inflamar — vi : inflamarse

inflammable [ɪnˈflæməbəl] adj 1 FLAMMABLE : inflamable 2 IRASCIBLE : irascible, explosivo

inflammation [ˌɪnfləˈmeɪʃən] n : inflamación f

inflammatory [ɪnˈflæməˌtori] adj : inflamatorio, incendiario

inflatable [ɪnˈfleɪtəbəl] adj : inflable

inflate [ɪnˈfleɪt] vt **-flated; -flating** : inflar, hinchar

inflation [ɪnˈfleɪʃən] n : inflación f

inflationary [ɪnˈfleɪʃəˌnɛri] adj : inflacionario, inflacionista

inflect [ɪnˈflɛkt] vt 1 CONJUGATE, DECLINE : conjugar, declinar 2 MODULATE : modular (la voz)

inflection [ɪnˈflɛkʃən] n : inflexión f

inflexibility [ɪnˌflɛksəˈbɪləti] n, pl **-ties** : inflexibilidad f

inflexible [ɪnˈflɛksɪbəl] adj : inflexible

inflict [ɪnˈflɪkt] vt 1 : infligir, causar, imponer 2 **to inflict oneself on** : imponer uno su presencia (a alguien)

infliction [ɪnˈflɪkʃən] n : imposición f

influence[1] [ˈɪnˌfluˌənts, ɪnˈfluːənts] vt **-enced; -encing** : influenciar, influir en

influence[2] n 1 : influencia f, influjo m ⟨to exert influence over : ejercer influencia sobre⟩ ⟨the influence of gravity : el influjo de la gravedad⟩ 2 **under the influence** : bajo la influencia del alcohol, embriagado

influential [ˌɪnfluˈɛntʃəl] adj : influyente

influenza [ˌɪnfluˈɛnzə] n : gripe f, influenza f, gripa f Col, Mex

influx [ˈɪnˌflʌks] n : afluencia f (de gente), entrada f (de mercancías), llegada f (de ideas)

inform [ɪnˈfərm] vt : informar, notificar, avisar — vi **to inform on** : delatar, denunciar

informal [ɪnˈfərməl] adj 1 UNCEREMONIOUS : sin ceremonia, sin etiqueta 2 CASUAL : informal, familiar (dícese del lenguaje) 3 UNOFFICIAL : informal, extraoficial

informality [ˌɪnfərˈmæləti, -fər-] n, pl **-ties** : informalidad f, familiaridad f, falta f de ceremonia

informally [ɪnˈfərməli] adv : sin ceremonias, de manera informal, informalmente

informant [ɪnˈfərmənt] n : informante mf; informador m, -dora f

information [ˌɪnfərˈmeɪʃən] n : información f

informational [ˌɪnfərˈmeɪʃənəl] *adj* : informativo

information technology *n* : informática *f*

informative [ɪnˈfɔrmətɪv] *adj* : informativo, instructivo

informer [ɪnˈfɔrmər] *n* : informante *mf*; informador *m*, -dora *f*

infraction [ɪnˈfrækʃən] *n* : infracción *f*, violación *f*, transgresión *f*

infrared [ˌɪnfrəˈred] *adj* : infrarrojo

infrastructure [ˈɪnfrəˌstrʌktʃər] *n* : infraestructura *f*

infrequent [ɪnˈfri:kwənt] *adj* : infrecuente, raro

infrequently [ɪnˈfri:kwəntli] *adv* : raramente, con poca frecuencia

infringe [ɪnˈfrɪndʒ] *v* **-fringed; -fringing** *vt* : infringir, violar — *vi* **to infringe on** : abusar de, violar

infringement [ɪnˈfrɪndʒmənt] *n* **1** VIOLATION : violación *f* (de la ley), incumplimiento *m* (de un contrato) **2** ENCROACHMENT : usurpación *f* (de derechos, etc.)

infuriate [ɪnˈfjʊriˌeɪt] *vt* **-ated; -ating** : enfurecer, poner furioso

infuriating [ɪnˈfjʊriˌeɪtɪŋ] *adj* : indignante, exasperante

infuse [ɪnˈfju:z] *vt* **-fused; -fusing 1** INSTILL : infundir **2** STEEP : hacer una infusión de

infusion [ɪnˈfju:ʒən] *n* : infusión *f*

ingenious [ɪnˈdʒi:njəs] *adj* : ingenioso — **ingeniously** *adv*

ingenue *or* **ingénue** [ˈɑndʒəˌnu:, ˈæn-; ˈæʒə-, ˈɑ-] *n* : ingenua *f*

ingenuity [ˌɪndʒəˈnu:əti, -ˈnju:-] *n, pl* **-ities** : ingenio

ingenuous [ɪnˈdʒɛnjʊəs] *adj* **1** FRANK : cándido, franco **2** NAIVE : ingenuo — **ingenuously** *adv*

ingenuousness [ɪnˈdʒɛnjʊəsnəs] *n* **1** FRANKNESS : candidez *f*, candor *m* **2** NAÏVETÉ : ingenuidad *f*

ingest [ɪnˈdʒɛst] *vt* : ingerir

ingestion [ɪnˈdʒɛstʃən] *n* : ingestión *f*

inglorious [ɪnˈglɔriəs] *adj* : deshonroso, ignominioso

ingot [ˈɪŋgət] *n* : lingote *m*

ingrained [ɪnˈgreɪnd] *adj* : arraigado

ingrate [ˈɪnˌgreɪt] *n* : ingrato *m*, -ta *f*

ingratiate [ɪnˈgreɪʃiˌeɪt] *vt* **-ated; -ating** : conseguir la benevolencia de ⟨to ingratiate oneself with someone : congraciarse con alguien⟩

ingratiating [ɪnˈgreɪʃiˌeɪtɪŋ] *adj* : halagador, zalamero, obsequioso

ingratitude [ɪnˈgrætəˌtu:d, -ˌtju:d] *n* : ingratitud *f*

ingredient [ɪnˈgri:diənt] *n* : ingrediente *m*, componente *m*

ingrown [ˈɪnˌgro:n] *adj* **1** : crecido hacia adentro **2 ingrown toenail** : uña *f* encarnada

inhabit [ɪnˈhæbət] *vt* : vivir en, habitar, ocupar

inhabitable [ɪnˈhæbətəbəl] *adj* : habitable

inhabitant [ɪnˈhæbətənt] *n* : habitante *mf*

inhalant [ɪnˈheɪlənt] *n* : inhalante *m*

inhalation [ˌɪnhəˈleɪʃən, ˌɪnə-] *n* : inhalación *f*

inhale [ɪnˈheɪl] *v* **-haled; -haling** *vt* : inhalar, aspirar — *vi* : inspirar

inhaler [ɪnˈheɪlər] *n* : inhalador *m*

inhere [ɪnˈhɪr] *vi* **-hered; -hering** : ser inherente

inherent [ɪnˈhɪrənt, -ˈhɛr-] *adj* : inherente, intrínseco — **inherently** *adv*

inherit [ɪnˈhɛrət] *vt* : heredar

inheritance [ɪnˈhɛrətən̯s] *n* : herencia *f*

inheritor [ɪnˈhɛrətər] *n* : heredero *m*, -ra *f*

inhibit [ɪnˈhɪbət] *vt* IMPEDE : inhibir, impedir

inhibition [ˌɪnhəˈbɪʃən, ˌɪnə-] *n* : inhibición *f*, cohibición *f*

inhospitable [ˌɪnhɑˈspɪtəbəl, -ˈhɑs‚pɪ-] *adj* : inhóspito

inhuman [ɪnˈhju:mən, -ˈju:-] *adj* : inhumano, cruel — **inhumanly** *adv*

inhumane [ˌɪnhju:ˈmeɪn, -ju-] *adj* INHUMAN : inhumano, cruel

inhumanity [ˌɪnhju:ˈmænəti, -ju-] *n, pl* **-ties** : inhumanidad *f*, crueldad *f*

inimical [ɪˈnɪmɪkəl] *adj* **1** UNFAVORABLE : adverso, desfavorable **2** HOSTILE : hostil — **inimically** *adv*

inimitable [ɪˈnɪmətəbəl] *adj* : inimitable

iniquitous [ɪˈnɪkwətəs] *adj* : inicuo, malvado

iniquity [ɪˈnɪkwəti] *n, pl* **-ties** : iniquidad *f*

initial[1] [ɪˈnɪʃəl] *vt* **-tialed** *or* **-tialled; -tialing** *or* **-tialling** : poner las iniciales a, firmar con las iniciales

initial[2] *adj* : inicial, primero — **initially** *adv*

initial[3] *n* : inicial *f*

initiate[1] [ɪˈnɪʃiˌeɪt] *vt* **-ated; -ating 1** BEGIN : comenzar, iniciar **2** INDUCT : instruir **3** INTRODUCE : introducir, instruir

initiate[2] [ɪˈnɪʃiət] *n* : iniciado *m*, -da *f*

initiation [ɪˌnɪʃiˈeɪʃən] *n* : iniciación *f*

initiative [ɪˈnɪʃətɪv] *n* : iniciativa *f*

initiatory [ɪˈnɪʃiəˌtori] *adj* **1** INTRODUCTORY : introductorio **2** : de iniciación ⟨initiatory rites : ritos de iniciación⟩

inject [ɪnˈdʒɛkt] *vt* : inyectar

injection [ɪnˈdʒɛkʃən] *n* : inyección *f*

injudicious [ˌɪndʒʊˈdɪʃəs] *adj* : imprudente, indiscreto, poco juicioso

injunction [ɪnˈdʒʌŋkʃən] *n* **1** ORDER : orden *f*, mandato *m* **2** COURT ORDER : mandamiento *m* judicial

injure [ˈɪndʒər] *vt* **-jured; -juring** WOUND : herir, lesionar **2** HURT : lastimar, dañar, herir **3 to injure oneself** : hacerse daño

injurious [ɪnˈdʒʊriəs] *adj* : perjudicial ⟨injurious to one's health : perjudicial a la salud⟩

injury [ˈɪndʒəri] *n, pl* **-ries 1** WRONG : mal *m*, injusticia *f* **2** DAMAGE, HARM : herida *f*, daño *m*, perjuicio *m*

injustice [ɪnˈdʒʌstəs] *n* : injusticia *f*

ink[1] [ˈɪŋk] *vt* : entintar

ink[2] *n* : tinta *f*

inkling [ˈɪŋklɪŋ] *n* : presentimiento *m*, indicio *m*, sospecha *f*

ink pad *n* : tampón *m* (para entintar)

inkwell ['ɪŋk,wel] *n* : tintero *m*

inky ['ɪŋki] *adj* **1** : manchado de tinta **2** BLACK : negro, impenetrable ⟨inky darkness : negra oscuridad⟩

inland[1] ['ɪn,lænd, -lənd] *adv* : hacia el interior, tierra adentro

inland[2] *adj* : interior

inland[3] *n* : interior *m*

in-law ['ɪn,lɔ] *n* **1** : pariente *m* político **2 in-laws** *pl* : suegros *mpl*

inlay[1] [ɪn'leɪ, 'ɪn,leɪ] *vt* **-laid** [-'leɪd, -,leɪd]; **-laying** : incrustar

inlay[2] ['ɪn,leɪ] *n* **1** : incrustación *f* **2** : empaste *m* (de un diente)

inlet ['ɪn,let, -lət] *n* : cala *f*, ensenada *f*, brazo *m* del mar

in-line skate ['ɪn,laɪn-] *n* : patín *m* en línea

inmate ['ɪn,meɪt] *n* : paciente *mf* (en un hospital); preso *m*, -sa *f* (en una prisión); interno *m*, -na *f* (en un asilo)

in memoriam [,ɪnmə'moriəm] *prep* : en memoria de

inmost ['ɪn,mo:st] → **innermost**

inn ['ɪn] *n* **1** : posada *f*, hostería *f*, fonda *f* **2** TAVERN : taberna *f*

innards ['ɪnərdz] *npl* : entrañas *fpl*, tripas *fpl fam*

innate [ɪ'neɪt] *adj* **1** INBORN : innato **2** INHERENT : inherente

inner ['ɪnər] *adj* : interior, interno

inner city *n* : barrios *mpl* pobres (en el centro de una ciudad)

innermost ['ɪnər,mo:st] *adj* : más íntimo, más profundo

innersole ['ɪnər'so:l] → **insole**

inner tube → **tube**

inning ['ɪnɪŋ] *n* : entrada *f*

innkeeper ['ɪn,ki:pər] *n* : posadero *m*, -ra *f*

innocence ['ɪnəsənts] *n* : inocencia *f*

innocent[1] ['ɪnəsənt] *adj* : inocente — **innocently** *adv*

innocent[2] *n* : inocente *mf*

innocuous [ɪ'nɑkjəwəs] *adj* **1** HARMLESS : inocuo **2** INOFFENSIVE : inofensivo

innovate ['ɪnə,veɪt] *vi* **-vated; -vating** : innovar

innovation [,ɪnə'veɪʃən] *n* : innovación *f*, novedad *f*

innovative ['ɪnə,veɪtɪv] *adj* : innovador

innovator ['ɪnə,veɪtər] *n* : innovador *m*, -dora *f*

innuendo [,ɪnju'endo] *n, pl* **-dos** *or* **-does** : insinuación *f*, indirecta *f*

innumerable [ɪ'nu:mərəbəl, -'nju:-] *adj* : innumerable

inoculate [ɪ'nɑkjə,leɪt] *vt* **-lated; -lating** : inocular

inoculation [ɪ,nɑkjə'leɪʃən] *n* : inoculación *f*

inoffensive [,ɪnə'fɛntsɪv] *adj* : inofensivo

inoperable [ɪn'ɑpərəbəl] *adj* : inoperable

inoperative [ɪn'ɑpərətɪv, -,reɪ-] *adj* : inoperante

inopportune [ɪn,ɑpər'tu:n, -'tju:n] *adj* : inoportuno — **inopportunely** *adv*

inordinate [ɪn'ɔrdənət] *adj* : excesivo, inmoderado, desmesurado — **inordinately** *adv*

inorganic [,ɪn,ɔr'gænɪk] *adj* : inorgánico

inpatient ['ɪn,peɪʃənt] *n* : paciente *mf* hospitalizado

input[1] ['ɪn,pʊt] *vt* **inputted** *or* **input; inputting** : entrar (datos, información)

input[2] *n* **1** CONTRIBUTION : aportación *f*, contribución *f* **2** ENTRY : entrada *f* (de datos) **3** ADVICE, OPINION : consejos *mpl*, opinión *f*

inquest ['ɪn,kwest] *n* INQUIRY, INVESTIGATION : investigación *f*, pesquisa *f* (judicial), indagatoria *f*

inquire [ɪn'kwaɪr] *v* **-quired; -quiring** *vt* : preguntar, informarse de, inquirir ⟨he inquired how to get in : preguntó como entrar⟩ — *vi* **1** ASK : preguntar, informarse ⟨to inquire about : informarse sobre⟩ ⟨to inquire after (someone) : preguntar por (alguien)⟩ **2 to inquire into** INVESTIGATE : investigar, inquirir sobre

inquiringly [ɪn'kwaɪrɪŋli] *adv* : inquisitivamente

inquiry ['ɪn,kwaɪri, ɪn'kwaɪri; 'ɪnkwəri, 'ɪn-] *n, pl* **-ries 1** QUESTION : pregunta *f* ⟨to make inquiries about : pedir información sobre⟩ **2** INVESTIGATION : investigación *f*, inquisición *f*, pesquisa *f*

inquisition [,ɪnkwə'zɪʃən, ,ɪŋ-] *n* **1** : inquisición *f*, interrogatorio *m*, investigación *f* **2 the Inquisition** : la Inquisición *f*

inquisitive [ɪn'kwɪzətɪv] *adj* : inquisidor, inquisitivo, curioso — **inquisitively** *adv*

inquisitiveness [ɪn'kwɪzətɪvnəs] *n* : curiosidad *f*

inquisitor [ɪn'kwɪzətər] *n* : inquisidor *m*, -dora *f*; interrogador *m*, -dora *f*

inroad ['ɪn,ro:d] *n* **1** ENCROACHMENT, INVASION : invasión *f*, incursión *f* **2 to make inroads into** : ocupar parte de (un tiempo), agotar parte de (ahorros, recursos), invadir (un territorio)

insane [ɪn'seɪn] *adj* **1** MAD : loco, demente ⟨to go insane : volverse loco⟩ ⟨to drive someone insane : volver loco a alguien⟩ **2** ABSURD : absurdo, insensato ⟨an insane scheme : un proyecto insensato⟩

insanely [ɪn'seɪnli] *adv* : como un loco ⟨insanely suspicious : loco de recelo⟩

insanity [ɪn'sænəti] *n, pl* **-ties 1** MADNESS : locura *f* **2** FOLLY : locura *f*, insensatez *f*

insatiable [ɪn'seɪʃəbəl] *adj* : insaciable — **insatiably** [-bli] *adv*

inscribe [ɪn'skraɪb] *vt* **-scribed; -scribing 1** ENGRAVE : inscribir, grabar **2** ENROLL : inscribir **3** DEDICATE : dedicar (un libro)

inscription [ɪn'skrɪpʃən] *n* : inscripción *f* (en un monumento), dedicación *f* (en un libro), leyenda *f* (de una ilustración, etc.)

inscrutable [ɪn'skru:təbəl] *adj* : inescrutable, misterioso — **inscrutably** [-bli] *adv*

inseam ['ɪn,si:m] *n* : entrepierna *f*

insect ['ɪn,sɛkt] *n* : insecto *m*

insecticidal [ɪn,sɛktə'saɪdəl] *adj* : insecticida

insecticide [ɪn'sɛktə,saɪd] *n* : insecticida *m*

insecure [ˌɪnsɪˈkjʊr] *adj* : inseguro, poco seguro

insecurely [ˌɪnsɪˈkjʊrli] *adv* : inseguramente

insecurity [ˌɪnsɪˈkjʊrəti] *n, pl* **-ties** : inseguridad *f*

inseminate [ɪnˈsɛməˌneɪt] *vt* **-nated; -nating** : inseminar

insemination [ɪnˌsɛməˈneɪʃən] *n* : inseminación *f*

insensibility [ɪnˌsɛnsəˈbɪləti] *n, pl* **-ties** : insensibilidad *f*

insensible [ɪnˈsɛnsəbəl] *adj* **1** UNCONSCIOUS : inconsciente, sin conocimiento **2** NUMB : insensible, entumecido **3** UNAWARE : inconsciente

insensitive [ɪnˈsɛnsətɪv] *adj* : insensible

insensitivity [ɪnˌsɛnsəˈtɪvəti] *n, pl* **-ties** : insensibilidad *f*

inseparable [ɪnˈsɛpərəbəl] *adj* : inseparable

insert¹ [ɪnˈsərt] *vt* **1** : insertar, introducir, poner, meter ⟨insert your key in the lock : mete tu llave en la cerradura⟩ **2** INTERPOLATE : interpolar, intercalar

insert² [ˈɪnˌsərt] *n* : inserción *f*, hoja *f* insertada (en una revista, etc.)

insertion [ɪnˈsərʃən] *n* : inserción *f*

inshore¹ [ˈɪnˈʃor] *adv* : hacia la costa

inshore² *adj* : cercano a la costa, costero ⟨inshore fishing : pesca costera⟩

inside¹ [ɪnˈsaɪd, ˈɪnˌsaɪd] *adv* : adentro, dentro ⟨to run inside : correr para adentro⟩ ⟨inside and out : por dentro y por fuera⟩

inside² *adj* **1** : interior, de adentro, de dentro ⟨the inside lane : el carril interior⟩ **2** : confidencial ⟨inside information : información confidencial⟩

inside³ *n* **1** : interior *m*, parte *f* de adentro ⟨the inside of the house : el interior de la casa⟩ **2 insides** *npl* BELLY, GUTS : tripas *fpl fam* **3 inside out** : al/del revés ⟨to turn something inside out : darle la vuelta a algo, volver/poner algo al/del revés, voltear algo⟩

inside⁴ *prep* **1** INTO : al interior de **2** WITHIN : dentro de **3** *(referring to time)* : en menos de ⟨inside an hour : en menos de una hora⟩

inside of *prep* INSIDE : dentro de

insider [ɪnˈsaɪdər] *n* : persona *f* enterada

insidious [ɪnˈsɪdiəs] *adj* : insidioso — **insidiously** *adv*

insidiousness [ɪnˈsɪdiəsnəs] *n* : insidia *f*

insight [ˈɪnˌsaɪt] *n* : perspicacia *f*, penetración *f*

insightful [ɪnˈsaɪtfəl] *adj* : perspicaz

insignia [ɪnˈsɪgniə] *or* **insigne** [-ˌniː] *n, pl* **-nia** *or* **-nias** : insignia *f*, enseña *f*

insignificance [ˌɪnsɪgˈnɪfɪkənts] *n* : insignificancia *f*

insignificant [ˌɪnsɪgˈnɪfɪkənt] *adj* : insignificante

insincere [ˌɪnsɪnˈsɪr] *adj* : insincero, poco sincero

insincerely [ˌɪnsɪnˈsɪrli] *adv* : con poca sinceridad

insincerity [ˌɪnsɪnˈsɛrəti, -ˈsɪr-] *n, pl* **-ties** : insinceridad *f*

insinuate [ɪnˈsɪnjuˌeɪt] *vt* **-ated; -ating** : insinuar

insinuation [ɪnˌsɪnjuˈeɪʃən] *n* : insinuación *f*

insipid [ɪnˈsɪpəd] *adj* : insípido

insist [ɪnˈsɪst] *v* : insistir

insistence [ɪnˈsɪstənts] *n* : insistencia *f*

insistent [ɪnˈsɪstənt] *adj* : insistente — **insistently** *adv*

insofar as [ˌɪnsoˈfæræz] *conj* : en la medida en que, en tanto que, en cuanto a

insole [ˈɪnˌsol] *n* : plantilla *f*

insolence [ˈɪnsələnts] *n* : insolencia *f*

insolent [ˈɪnsələnt] *adj* : insolente

insolubility [ɪnˌsaljuˈbɪləti] *n* : insolubilidad *f*

insoluble [ɪnˈsaljəbəl] *adj* : insoluble

insolvency [ɪnˈsalvəntsi] *n, pl* **-cies** : insolvencia *f*

insolvent [ɪnˈsalvənt] *adj* : insolvente

insomnia [ɪnˈsamniə] *n* : insomnio *m*

insomniac [ɪnˈsamniˌæk] *n* : insomne *mf* — **insomniac** *adj*

insomuch as [ˌɪnsoˈmʌtʃæz] → **inasmuch as**

insomuch that *conj* SO : así que, de manera que

inspect [ɪnˈspɛkt] *vt* : inspeccionar, examinar, revisar

inspection [ɪnˈspɛkʃən] *n* : inspección *f*, examen *m*, revisión *f*, revista *f* (de tropas)

inspector [ɪnˈspɛktər] *n* : inspector *m*, -tora *f*

inspiration [ˌɪntspəˈreɪʃən] *n* : inspiración *f*

inspirational [ˌɪntspəˈreɪʃənəl] *adj* : inspirador

inspire [ɪnˈspaɪr] *v* **-spired; -spiring** *vt* **1** INHALE : inhalar, aspirar **2** STIMULATE : estimular, animar, inspirar **3** INSTILL : inspirar, infundir — *vi* : inspirar

instability [ˌɪntstəˈbɪləti] *n, pl* **-ties** : inestabilidad *f*

install [ɪnˈstɔl] *vt* **-stalled; -stalling 1** : instalar ⟨to install a fan : montar un abanico⟩ **2** INDUCT : instalar, investir ⟨to install the new president : instalar el presidente nuevo⟩ **3 to install oneself** : instalarse

installation [ˌɪntstəˈleɪʃən] *n* : instalación *f*

installment [ɪnˈstɔlmənt] *n* **1** : plazo *m*, cuota *f* ⟨to pay in four installments : pagar a cuatro plazos⟩ **2** : entrega *f* (de una publicación o telenovela) **3** INSTALLATION : instalación *f*

instance [ˈɪntstənts] *n* **1** INSTIGATION : instancia *f* **2** EXAMPLE : ejemplo *m* ⟨for instance : por ejemplo⟩ **3** OCCASION : instancia *f*, caso *m*, ocasión *f* ⟨he prefers, in this instance, to remain anonymous : en este caso prefiere quedarse anónimo⟩

instant¹ [ˈɪntstənt] *adj* **1** IMMEDIATE : inmediato, instantáneo ⟨an instant reply ; una respuesta inmediata⟩ **2** : instantáneo ⟨instant coffee : café instantáneo⟩

instant² *n* : momento *m*, instante *m*

instantaneous [ˌɪnstən'teɪnɪəs] *adj* : instantáneo

instantaneously [ˌɪnstən'teɪnɪəsli] *adv* : instantáneamente, al instante

instantly ['ɪnstəntli] *adv* : al instante, instantáneamente

instant messaging *n* : mensajería *f* instantánea

instead [ɪn'sted] *adv* **1** : en cambio, en lugar de eso, en su lugar ⟨Dad was going, but Mom went instead : papá iba a ir, pero mamá fue en su lugar⟩ **2** RATHER : al contrario

instead of *prep* : en vez de, en lugar de

instep ['ɪnˌstep] *n* : empeine *m*

instigate ['ɪnstəˌɡeɪt] *vt* -**gated**; -**gating** INCITE, PROVOKE : instigar, incitar, provocar, fomentar

instigation [ˌɪnstə'ɡeɪʃən] *n* : instancia *f*, incitación *f*

instigator ['ɪnstəˌɡeɪtər] *n* : instigador *m*, -dora *f*; incitador *m*, -dora *f*

instill [ɪn'stɪl] *vt* -**stilled**; -**stilling** : inculcar, infundir

instinct ['ɪnˌstɪŋkt] *n* **1** TALENT : instinto *m*, don *m* ⟨an instinct for the right word : un don para escoger la palabra apropiada⟩ **2** : instinto *m* ⟨maternal instincts : instintos maternales⟩

instinctive [ɪn'stɪŋktɪv] *adj* : instintivo

instinctively [ɪn'stɪŋktɪvli] *adv* : instintivamente, por instinto

instinctual [ɪn'stɪŋkʧʊəl] *adj* : instintivo

institute[1] ['ɪnstəˌtuːt, -ˌtjuːt] *vt* -**tuted**; -**tuting** **1** ESTABLISH : establecer, instituir, fundar **2** INITIATE : iniciar, empezar, entablar

institute[2] *n* : instituto *m*

institution [ˌɪnstə'tuːʃən, -'tjuː-] *n* **1** ESTABLISHING : institución *f*, establecimiento *m* **2** CUSTOM : institución *f*, tradición *f* ⟨the institution of marriage : la institución del matrimonio⟩ **3** ORGANIZATION : institución *f*, organismo *m* **4** ASYLUM : asilo *m*

institutional [ˌɪnstə'tuːʃənəl, -'tjuː-] *adj* : institucional

institutionalize [ˌɪnstə'tuːʃənəˌlaɪz, -'tjuː-] *vt* -**ized**; -**izing** **1** : institucionalizar ⟨institutionalized values : valores institucionalizados⟩ **2** : internar ⟨institutionalized orphans : huérfanos internados⟩

instruct [ɪn'strʌkt] *vt* **1** TEACH, TRAIN : instruir, adiestrar, enseñar **2** COMMAND : mandar, ordenar, dar instrucciones a

instruction [ɪn'strʌkʃən] *n* **1** TEACHING : instrucción *f*, enseñanza *f* **2** COMMAND : orden *f*, instrucción *f* **3 instructions** *npl* DIRECTIONS : 'instrucciones *fpl*, modo *m* de empleo

instructional [ɪn'strʌkʃənəl] *adj* : instructivo, educativo

instructive [ɪn'strʌktɪv] *adj* : instructivo

instructor [ɪn'strʌktər] *n* : instructor *m*, -tora *f*

instrument ['ɪnstrəmənt] *n* **1** : instrumento *m* (musical) **2** TOOL, DEVICE : instrumento *m* **3** MEANS : instrumento *m*

instrumental [ˌɪnstrə'mentəl] *adj* : instrumental

instrumentalist [ˌɪnstrə'mentəlɪst] *n* : instrumentista *mf*

insubordinate [ˌɪnsə'bɔrdənət] *adj* : insubordinado

insubordination [ˌɪnsəˌbɔrdən'eɪʃən] *n* : insubordinación *f*

insubstantial [ˌɪnsəb'stænʧəl] *adj* : insustancial, poco nutritivo (dícese de una comida), poco sólido (dícese de una estructura o un argumento)

insufferable [ɪn'sʌfərəbəl] *adj* UNBEARABLE : insufrible, intolerable, inaguantable, insoportable — **insufferably** [-bli] *adv*

insufficiency [ˌɪnsə'fɪʃəntsi] *n*, *pl* -**cies** : insuficiencia *f*

insufficient [ˌɪnsə'fɪʃənt] *adj* : insuficiente — **insufficiently** *adv*

insular ['ɪnsʊlər, -sjʊ-] *adj* **1** : isleño (dícese de la gente), insular (dícese del clima) ⟨insular residents : residentes de la isla⟩ **2** NARROW-MINDED : de miras estrechas

insularity [ˌɪnsʊ'lærəti, -sjʊ-] *n* : insularidad *f*

insulate ['ɪnsəˌleɪt] *vt* -**lated**; -**lating** : aislar

insulation [ˌɪnsə'leɪʃən] *n* : aislamiento *m*

insulator ['ɪnsəˌleɪtər] *n* : aislador *m* (pieza), aislante *m* (material)

insulin ['ɪnsələn] *n* : insulina *f*

insult[1] [ɪn'sʌlt] *vt* : insultar, ofender, injuriar

insult[2] ['ɪnˌsʌlt] *n* : insulto *m*, injuria *f*, agravio *m*

insulting [ɪn'sʌltɪŋ] *adj* : ofensivo, injurioso, insultante

insultingly [ɪn'sʌltɪŋli] *adv* : ofensivamente, de manera insultante

insurance [ɪn'ʃʊrənts, 'ɪnˌʃʊr-] *n* : seguro *m* ⟨life insurance : seguro de vida⟩ ⟨insurance company/policy : compañía/póliza de seguros⟩

insure [ɪn'ʃʊr] *vt* -**sured**; -**suring** **1** UNDERWRITE : asegurar **2** ENSURE : asegurar, garantizar

insured [ɪn'ʃʊrd] *n* : asegurado *m*, -da *f*

insurer [ɪn'ʃʊrər] *n* : asegurador *m*, -dora *f*

insurgent[1] [ɪn'sɔrʤənt] *adj* : insurgente

insurgent[2] *n* : insurgente *mf*

insurmountable [ˌɪnsər'maʊntəbəl] *adj* : insuperable, insalvable — **insurmountably** [-bli] *adv*

insurrection [ˌɪnsə'rekʃən] *n* : insurrección *f*, levantamiento *m*, alzamiento *m*

intact [ɪn'tækt] *adj* : intacto

intake ['ɪnˌteɪk] *n* **1** OPENING : entrada *f*, toma *f* ⟨fuel intake : toma de combustible⟩ **2** : entrada *f* (de agua o aire), consumo *m* (de sustancias nutritivas) **3 intake of breath** : inhalación *f*

intangible [ɪn'tænʤəbəl] *adj* : intangible, impalpable — **intangibly** [-bli] *adv*

integer ['ɪntɪʤər] *n* : entero *m*

integral ['ɪntɪɡrəl] *adj* : integral, esencial

integrate ['ɪntəˌɡreɪt] *v* -**grated**; -**grating** *vt* **1** UNITE : integrar, unir **2** DESEGRE-

GATE : eliminar la segregación de — *vi* : integrarse

integration [ˌɪntəˈɡreɪʃən] *n* : integración *f*

integrity [ɪnˈtɛɡrəti] *n* : integridad *f*

intellect [ˈɪntəlˌɛkt] *n* : intelecto *m*, inteligencia *f*, capacidad *f* intelectual

intellectual¹ [ˌɪntəˈlɛktʃuəl] *adj* : intelectual — **intellectually** *adv*

intellectual² *n* : intelectual *mf*

intelligence [ɪnˈtɛləʤən/s] *n* **1** : inteligencia *f* **2** INFORMATION, NEWS : inteligencia *f*, información *f*, noticias *fpl*

intelligent [ɪnˈtɛləʤənt] *adj* : inteligente — **intelligently** *adv*

intelligentsia [ɪnˌtɛləˈʤɛnt/siə, -ˈɡɛn-] *ns & pl* : intelectualidad *f*

intelligible [ɪnˈtɛləʤəbəl] *adj* : inteligible, comprensible — **intelligibly** [-bli] *adv*

intemperance [ɪnˈtɛmpərənt/s] *n* : inmoderación *f*, intemperancia *f*

intemperate [ɪnˈtɛmpərət] *adj* : excesivo, inmoderado, desmedido

intend [ɪnˈtɛnd] *vt* **1** (*indicating goal or purpose*) : querer, tener la intención de ⟨I didn't intend to hurt you : no quería hacerte daño⟩ ⟨no insult was intended : no fue mi intención ofender⟩ ⟨it was intended as a warning : pretendía servir de advertencia⟩ ⟨she intended for him to come : su intención era que viniera⟩ ⟨I intended it as a joke : lo dije en broma⟩ ⟨a film intended to educate : una película tendiente a educar⟩ **2** MEAN, SIGNIFY : querer decir **3** PLAN : pensar, tener planeado, proyectar, proponerse ⟨what do you intend to do? : ¿qué piensas hacer?⟩ ⟨I intend to finish by Thursday : me propongo acabar para el jueves⟩ ⟨if all goes as intended : si todo va según lo planeado⟩ **4 to be intended for** : ser para, ir dirigido a (un público, etc.), estar destinado a (un fin), estar diseñado para (un uso)

intended [ɪnˈtɛndəd] *adj* **1** PLANNED : previsto, proyectado **2** INTENTIONAL : intencional, deliberado

intense [ɪnˈtɛnt/s] *adj* **1** EXTREME : intenso, extremo ⟨intense pain : dolor intenso⟩ **2** : profundo, intenso ⟨to my intense relief : para mi alivio profundo⟩ ⟨intense enthusiasm : entusiasmo ardiente⟩

intensely [ɪnˈtɛnt/sli] *adv* : sumamente, profundamente, intensamente

intensification [ɪnˌtɛnt/səfəˈkeɪʃən] *n* : intensificación *f*

intensifier [ɪnˈtɛnt/səˌfaɪər] *n* : intensificador *m* (en lingüística)

intensify [ɪnˈtɛnt/səˌfaɪ] *v* **-fied; -fying** *vt* **1** STRENGTHEN : intensificar, redoblar ⟨to intensify one's efforts : redoblar uno sus esfuerzos⟩ **2** SHARPEN : intensificar, agudizar (dolor, ansiedad) — *vi* : intensificarse, hacerse más intenso

intensity [ɪnˈtɛnt/səti] *n*, *pl* **-ties** : intensidad *f*

intensive [ɪnˈtɛnt/sɪv] *adj* : intensivo ⟨intensive care : cuidados intensivos⟩ — **intensively** *adv*

intent¹ [ɪnˈtɛnt] *adj* **1** FIXED : concentrado, fijo ⟨an intent stare : una mirada fija⟩ **2 intent on** *or* **intent upon** : resuelto a, atento a

intent² *n* **1** PURPOSE : intención *f*, propósito *m* **2 for all intents and purposes** : a todos los efectos, prácticamente

intention [ɪnˈtɛnʃən] *n* : intención *f*, propósito *m*

intentional [ɪnˈtɛnʃənəl] *adj* : intencional, deliberado

intentionally [ɪnˈtɛnʃənəli] *adv* : a propósito, adrede

intently [ɪnˈtɛntli] *adv* : atentamente, fijamente

inter [ɪnˈtər] *vt* **-terred; -terring** : enterrar, inhumar

inter- *pref* inter-

interact [ˌɪntərˈækt] *vi* : interactuar, actuar recíprocamente, relacionarse

interaction [ˌɪntərˈækʃən] *n* : interacción *f*, interrelación *f*

interactive [ˌɪntərˈæktɪv] *adj* : interactivo

interbreed [ˌɪntərˈbriːd] *v* **-bred** [-ˈbred]; **-breeding** *vt* : cruzar — *vi* : cruzarse

intercede [ˌɪntərˈsiːd] *vi* **-ceded; -ceding** : interceder

intercept [ˌɪntərˈsɛpt] *vt* : interceptar

interception [ˌɪntərˈsɛpʃən] *n* : intercepción *f*

intercession [ˌɪntərˈsɛʃən] *n* : intercesión *f*

interchange¹ [ˌɪntərˈtʃeɪnʤ] *vt* **-changed; -changing** : intercambiar

interchange² [ˈɪntərˌtʃeɪnʤ] *n* **1** EXCHANGE : intercambio *m*, cambio *m* **2** JUNCTION : empalme *m*, enlace *m* de carreteras

interchangeable [ˌɪntərˈtʃeɪnʤəbəl] *adj* : intercambiable

intercity [ˈɪntərˌsɪti] *adj* : interurbano

intercollegiate [ˌɪntərkəˈliːʤət, -ʤiət] *adj* : interuniversitario

intercom [ˈɪntərˌkɑm] *n* : interfono *m* *Spain*, interfón *m* *Mex*

interconnect [ˌɪntərkəˈnɛkt] *vt* **1** : conectar, interconectar (en tecnología) **2** RELATE : interrelacionar — *vi* **1** : conectar **2** : interrelacionarse

intercontinental [ˌɪntərˌkɑntənˈɛntəl] *adj* : intercontinental

intercourse [ˈɪntərˌkors] *n* **1** RELATIONS : relaciones *fpl*, trato *m* **2** COPULATION : acto *m* sexual, relaciones *fpl* sexuales, coito *m*

interdenominational [ˌɪntərdɪˌnɑmənˈeɪʃənəl] *adj* : interconfesional

interdepartmental [ˌɪntərdɪˌpɑrtˈmɛntəl, -ˌdi-] *adj* : interdepartamental

interdependence [ˌɪntərdɪˈpɛndənt/s] *n* : interdependencia *f*

interdependent [ˌɪntərdɪˈpɛndənt] *adj* : interdependiente

interdict [ˌɪntərˈdɪkt] *vt* **1** PROHIBIT : prohibir **2** : cortar (las líneas de comunicación o provisión del enemigo)

interdisciplinary [ˌɪntərˈdɪsəpləˌneri] *adj* : interdisciplinario

interest¹ [ˈɪntrəst, -təˌrɛst] *vt* : interesar

interest² n **1** SHARE, STAKE : interés m, participación f **2** BENEFIT : provecho m, beneficio m, interés m ⟨in the public interest : en el interés público⟩ **3** CHARGE : interés m, cargo m ⟨compound interest : interés compuesto⟩ ⟨interest rate : tasa de interés⟩ **4** CURIOSITY : interés m, curiosidad f ⟨to take an interest in : interesarse por⟩ ⟨to lose interest : perder interés⟩ **5** COLOR : color m, interés m ⟨places of local interest : lugares de color local⟩ **6** HOBBY : afición f

interested ['ɪntrəstəd, -tə,restəd] adj : interesado

interesting ['ɪntrəstɪŋ, -tə,restɪŋ] adj : interesante — **interestingly** adv

interface ['ɪntər,feɪs] n **1** : interfaz f, interfase f **2** : punto m de contacto (en la física, etc.)

interfere [,ɪntər'fɪr] vi **-fered; -fering 1** INTERPOSE : interponerse, hacer interferencia ⟨to interfere with a play : obstruir una jugada⟩ **2** MEDDLE : entrometerse, interferir, intervenir **3 to interfere with** DISRUPT : afectar (una actividad), interferir (la transmisión de una señal) **4 to interfere with** TOUCH : tocar ⟨someone interfered with my papers : alguien tocó mis papeles⟩

interference [,ɪntər'fɪrənts] n : interferencia f, intromisión f

intergalactic [,ɪntərɡə'læktɪk] adj : intergaláctico

intergovernmental [,ɪntər,ɡʌvər-'mɛntəl, -vərn-] adj : intergubernamental

interim¹ ['ɪntərəm] adj : interino, provisional

interim² n **1** : interín m, intervalo m **2 in the interim** : en el interín, mientras tanto

interior¹ [ɪn'tɪriər] adj : interior

interior² n : interior m

interject [,ɪntər'dʒɛkt] vt : interponer, agregar

interjection [,ɪntər'dʒɛkʃən] n **1** : interjección f (en lingüística) **2** EXCLAMATION : exclamación f **3** INTERRUPTION : interrupción f

interlace [,ɪntər'leɪs] vt **-laced; -lacing 1** INTERWEAVE : entrelazar **2** INTERSPERSE : intercalar

interlock [,ɪntər'lɑk] vt **1** UNITE : trabar, unir **2** ENGAGE : engranar — vi : entrelazarse, trabarse

interloper [,ɪntər'lo:pər] n **1** INTRUDER : intruso m, -sa f **2** MEDDLER : entrometido m, -da f

interlude ['ɪntər,lu:d] n **1** INTERVAL : intervalo m, intermedio m (en el teatro) **2** : interludio m (en música)

intermarriage [,ɪntər'mærɪdʒ] n **1** : matrimonio m mixto (entre miembros de distintas razas o religiones) **2** : matrimonio m entre miembros del mismo grupo

intermarry [,ɪntər'mæri] vi **-married; -marrying 1** : casarse (con miembros de otros grupos) **2** : casarse entre sí (con miembros del mismo grupo)

intermediary¹ [,ɪntər'mi:di,ɛri] adj : intermediario

intermediary² n, pl **-aries** : intermediario m, -ria f

intermediate¹ [,ɪntər'mi:diət] adj : intermedio

intermediate² n GO-BETWEEN : intermediario m, -ria f; mediador m, -dora f

interment [ɪn'tərmənt] n : entierro m

interminable [ɪn'tərmənəbəl] adj : interminable, constante — **interminably** [-bli] adv

intermingle [,ɪntər'mɪŋɡəl] vt **-mingled; -mingling** : entremezclar, mezclar — vi : entremezclarse

intermission [,ɪntər'mɪʃən] n : intermisión f, intervalo m, intermedio m

intermittent [,ɪntər'mɪtənt] adj : intermitente — **intermittently** adv

intermix [,ɪntər'mɪks] vt : entremezclar

intern¹ ['ɪn,tərn, ɪn'tərn] vt : confinar (durante la guerra) — vi : servir de interno, hacer las prácticas

intern² ['ɪn,tərn] n : interno m, -na f

internal [ɪn'tərnəl] adj : interno, interior ⟨internal bleeding : hemorragia interna⟩ ⟨internal affairs : asuntos interiores, asuntos domésticos⟩ — **internally** adv

international [,ɪntər'næʃənəl] adj : internacional — **internationally** adv

internationalize [,ɪntər'næʃənə,laɪz] vt **-ized; -izing** : internacionalizar

internecine [,ɪntər'nɛ,si:n, ɪn'tərnə,si:n] adj : intestino, interno

Internet ['ɪntər,nɛt] n : Internet mf

Internet café n : cibercafé m

Internet service provider → ISP

internist ['ɪn,tərnɪst] n : internista mf

internment [ɪ'tərnmənt] n : internamiento m

interpersonal [,ɪntər'pərsənəl] adj : interpersonal

interplay ['ɪntər,pleɪ] n : interacción f, juego m

interpolate [ɪn'tərpə,leɪt] vt **-lated; -lating** : interpolar

interpose [,ɪntər'po:z] v **-posed; -posing** vt : interponer, interrumpir con — vi : interponerse

interpret [ɪn'tərprət] vt : interpretar

interpretation [ɪn,tərprə'teɪʃən] n : interpretación f

interpretative [ɪn'tərprə,teɪtɪv] adj : interpretativo

interpreter [ɪn'tərprətər] n : intérprete mf

interpretive [ɪn'tərprətɪv] adj : interpretativo

interracial [,ɪntər'reɪʃəl] adj : interracial

interrelate [,ɪntəri'leɪt] v **-related; -relating** : interrelacionar

interrelationship [,ɪntəri'leɪʃən,ʃɪp] n : interrelación f

interrogate [ɪn'tɛrə,ɡeɪt] vt **-gated; -gating** : interrogar, someter a un interrogatorio

interrogation [ɪn,tɛrə'ɡeɪʃən] n : interrogatorio m, interrogación f

interrogative¹ [,ɪntə'rɑɡətɪv] adj : interrogativo

interrogative² n : interrogativo m

interrogator [ɪn'tɛrə,ɡeɪtər] n : interrogador m, -dora f

interrogatory [ˌɪntəˈrɑɡəˌtɔri] adj → **interrogative**[1]

interrupt [ˌɪntəˈrʌpt] v : interrumpir

interruption [ˌɪntəˈrʌpʃən] n : interrupción f

intersect [ˌɪntərˈsɛkt] vt : cruzar, cortar — vi : cruzarse (dícese de los caminos), intersecarse (dícese de las líneas o figuras), cortarse

intersection [ˌɪntərˈsɛkʃən] n : intersección f, cruce m

intersperse [ˌɪntərˈspɜrs] vt -**spersed**; -**spersing** : intercalar, entremezclar

interstate [ˌɪntərˈsteɪt] adj : interestatal

interstellar [ˌɪntərˈstɛlər] adj : interestelar

interstice [ɪnˈtɜrstəs] n, pl -**stices** [-stəˌsiːz, -stəsəz] : intersticio m

intertwine [ˌɪntərˈtwaɪn] vi -**twined**; -**twining** : entrelazarse

interval [ˈɪntərvəl] n : intervalo m

intervene [ˌɪntərˈviːn] vi -**vened**; -**vening** **1** ELAPSE : transcurrir, pasar ⟨the intervening years : los años intermedios⟩ **2** INTERCEDE : intervenir, interceder, mediar

intervention [ˌɪntərˈvɛnʃən] n : intervención f

interview[1] [ˈɪntərˌvjuː] vt : entrevistar — vi : hacer entrevistas

interview[2] n : entrevista f

interviewer [ˌɪntərˈvjuːər] n : entrevistador m, -dora f

interweave [ˌɪntərˈwiːv] v -**wove** [-ˈwoːv]; -**woven** [-ˈwoːvən]; -**weaving** vt : entretejer, entrelazar — vi INTERTWINE : entrelazarse, entretejerse

interwoven [ˌɪntərˈwoːvən] adj : entretejido

intestate [ɪnˈtɛsˌteɪt, -tət] adj : intestado

intestinal [ɪnˈtɛstənəl] adj : intestinal

intestine [ɪnˈtɛstən] n **1** : intestino m **2 small intestine** : intestino m delgado **3 large intestine** : intestino m grueso

intimacy [ˈɪntəməsi] n, pl -**cies 1** CLOSENESS : intimidad f **2** FAMILIARITY : familiaridad f

intimate[1] [ˈɪntəˌmeɪt] vt -**mated**; -**mating** : insinuar, dar a entender

intimate[2] [ˈɪntəmət] adj **1** CLOSE : íntimo, de confianza ⟨intimate friends : amigos íntimos⟩ **2** PRIVATE : íntimo, privado ⟨intimate clubs : clubes íntimos⟩ **3** INNERMOST, SECRET : íntimo, secreto ⟨intimate fantasies : fantasías secretas⟩

intimate[3] n : amigo m íntimo, amiga f íntima

intimidate [ɪnˈtɪməˌdeɪt] vt -**dated**; -**dating** : intimidar

intimidation [ɪnˌtɪməˈdeɪʃən] n : intimidación f

into [ˈɪnˌtuː] prep **1** (indicating motion) : en, a, contra, dentro de ⟨she got into bed : se metió en la cama⟩ ⟨to get into a plane : subir a un avión⟩ ⟨he crashed into the wall : chocó contra la pared⟩ ⟨looking into the sun : mirando al sol⟩ ⟨staring into space : mirando al vacío⟩ **2** (indicating state or condition) : a, en ⟨to burst into tears : echarse a llorar⟩ ⟨the water turned into ice : el agua se convir-

tió en hielo⟩ ⟨to translate into English : traducir al inglés⟩ **3** (indicating time) ⟨far into the night : hasta bien entrada la noche⟩ ⟨he's well into his eighties : tiene los ochenta bien cumplidos⟩ **4** (in mathematics) ⟨3 into 12 is 4 : 12 dividido por 3 es 4⟩ **5** fam (indicating interest or involvement) ⟨he's really into sports : le ha dado fuerte por los deportes⟩

intolerable [ɪnˈtɑlərəbəl] adj : intolerable — **intolerably** [-bli] adv

intolerance [ɪnˈtɑlərən(t)s] n : intolerancia f

intolerant [ɪnˈtɑlərənt] adj : intolerante

intonation [ˌɪntoˈneɪʃən] n : entonación f

intone [ɪnˈtoːn] vt -**toned**; -**toning** : entonar

intoxicant [ɪnˈtɑksɪkənt] n : bebida f alcohólica

intoxicate [ɪnˈtɑksəˌkeɪt] vt -**cated**; -**cating** : emborrachar, embriagar

intoxicated [ɪnˈtɑksəˌkeɪtəd] adj : borracho, embriagado

intoxicating [ɪnˈtɑksəˌkeɪtɪŋ] adj : embriagador

intoxication [ɪnˌtɑksəˈkeɪʃən] n : embriaguez f

intractable [ɪnˈtræktəbəl] adj : obstinado, intratable

intramural [ˌɪntrəˈmjurəl] adj : interno, dentro de la universidad

intransigence [ɪnˈtrænˌfsədʒən(t)s, -ˈtrænzə-] n : intransigencia f

intransigent [ɪnˈtrænˌfsədʒənt, -ˈtrænzə-] adj : intransigente

intransitive [ɪnˈtrænˌfsətɪv, -ˈtrænzə-] adj : intransitivo

intrauterine device [ˌɪntrəˈjuːtərən-] n : dispositivo m intrauterino, DIU m

intravenous [ˌɪntrəˈviːnəs] adj : intravenoso — **intravenously** adv

intrepid [ɪnˈtrɛpəd] adj : intrépido

intricacy [ˈɪntrɪkəsi] n, pl -**cies** : complejidad f, lo intrincado

intricate [ˈɪntrɪkət] adj : intrincado, complicado — **intricately** adv

intrigue[1] [ɪnˈtriːɡ] v -**trigued**; -**triguing** : intrigar

intrigue[2] [ˈɪnˌtriːɡ, ɪnˈtriːɡ] n : intriga f

intriguing [ɪnˈtriːɡɪŋ] adj : intrigante, fascinante

intrinsic [ɪnˈtrɪnzɪk, -ˈtrɪnˌsɪk] adj : intrínseco, esencial — **intrinsically** [-zɪkli, -sɪ-] adv

introduce [ˌɪntrəˈduːs, -ˈdjuːs] vt -**duced**; -**ducing 1** : presentar ⟨let me introduce my father : permítame presentar a mi padre⟩ ⟨to introduce oneself : presentarse⟩ **2** : introducir (algo nuevo), lanzar (un producto), presentar (una ley), proponer (una idea o un tema)

introduction [ˌɪntrəˈdʌkʃən] n : introducción f, presentación f

introductory [ˌɪntrəˈdʌktəri] adj : introductorio, preliminar, de introducción

introspection [ˌɪntrəˈspɛkʃən] n : introspección f

introspective [ˌɪntrəˈspɛktɪv] adj : introspectivo — **introspectively** adv

introvert [ˈɪntrəˌvərt] n : introvertido m, -da f

introverted [ˈɪntrəˌvərtəd] *adj* : introvertido

intrude [ɪnˈtruːd] *v* **-truded; -truding** *vi* **1** INTERFERE : inmiscuirse, entrometerse **2** DISTURB, INTERRUPT : molestar, estorbar, interrumpir — *vt* : introducir por fuerza

intruder [ɪnˈtruːdər] *n* : intruso *m*, -sa *f*

intrusion [ɪnˈtruːʒən] *n* : intrusión *f*

intrusive [ɪnˈtruːsɪv] *adj* : intruso

intuit [ɪnˈtuːɪt, -ˈtjuː-] *vt* : intuir

intuition [ˌɪntuˈɪʃən, -tjuː-] *n* : intuición *f*

intuitive [ɪnˈtuːəṭɪv, -ˈtjuː-] *adj* : intuitivo
— **intuitively** *adv*

inundate [ˈɪnənˌdeɪt] *vt* **-dated; -dating** : inundar

inundation [ˌɪnənˈdeɪʃən] *n* : inundación *f*

inure [ɪˈnʊr, -ˈnjʊr] *vt* **-ured; -uring** : acostumbrar, habituar

invade [ɪnˈveɪd] *vt* **-vaded; -vading** : invadir

invader [ɪnˈveɪdər] *n* : invasor *m*, -sora *f*

invalid¹ [ɪnˈvæləd] *adj* : inválido, nulo

invalid² [ˈɪnvələd] *adj* : inválido, discapacitado

invalid³ [ˈɪnvələd] *n* : inválido *m*, -da *f*

invalidate [ɪnˈvæləˌdeɪt] *vt* **-dated; -dating** : invalidar

invalidity [ˌɪnvəˈlɪdəṭi] *n*, *pl* **-ties** : invalidez *f*, falta de validez *f*

invaluable [ɪnˈvæljəbəl, -ˈvæljʊə-] *adj* : invalorable, inestimable, inapreciable

invariable [ɪnˈværiəbəl] *adj* : invariable, constante — **invariably** [-bli] *adv*

invasion [ɪnˈveɪʒən] *n* : invasión *f*

invasive [ɪnˈveɪsɪv] *adj* : invasivo

invective [ɪnˈvɛktɪv] *n* : invectiva *f*, improperio *m*

inveigh [ɪnˈveɪ] *vi* **to inveigh against** : arremeter contra, lanzar invectivas contra

inveigle [ɪnˈveɪgəl, -ˈviː-] *vt* **-gled; -gling** : engatusar, embaucar, persuadir con engaños

invent [ɪnˈvɛnt] *vt* : inventar

invention [ɪnˈvɛntʃən] *n* : invención *f*, invento *m*

inventive [ɪnˈvɛntɪv] *adj* : inventivo

inventiveness [ɪnˈvɛntɪvnəs] *n* : ingenio *m*, inventiva *f*

inventor [ɪnˈvɛntər] *n* : inventor *m*, -tora *f*

inventory¹ [ˈɪnvənˌtɔri] *vt* **-ried; -rying** : inventariar

inventory² *n*, *pl* **-ries** **1** LIST : inventario *m* **2** STOCK : existencias *fpl*

inverse¹ [ɪnˈvərs, ˈɪnˌvərs] *adj* : inverso — **inversely** *adv*

inverse² *n* : inverso *m*

inversion [ɪnˈvərʒən] *n* : inversión *f*

invert [ɪnˈvərt] *vt* : invertir

invertebrate¹ [ɪnˈvərtəbrət, -ˌbreɪt] *adj* : invertebrado

invertebrate² *n* : invertebrado *m*

invest [ɪnˈvɛst] *vt* **1** AUTHORIZE : investir, autorizar **2** CONFER : conferir **3** : invertir, dedicar ⟨he invested his savings in stocks : invirtió sus ahorros en acciones⟩ ⟨to invest one's time : dedicar uno su tiempo⟩

investigate [ɪnˈvɛstəˌgeɪt] *v* **-gated; -gating** : investigar

investigation [ɪnˌvɛstəˈgeɪʃən] *n* : investigación *f*, estudio *m*

investigative [ɪnˈvɛstəˌgeɪṭɪv] *adj* : investigador

investigator [ɪnˈvɛstəˌgeɪṭər] *n* : investigador *m*, -dora *f*

investiture [ɪnˈvɛstəˌtʃʊr, -tʃər] *n* : investidura *f*

investment [ɪnˈvɛstmənt] *n* : inversión *f*

investor [ɪnˈvɛstər] *n* : inversor *m*, -sora *f*; inversionista *mf*

inveterate [ɪnˈvɛṭərət] *adj* **1** DEEP-SEATED : inveterado, enraizado **2** HABITUAL : empedernido, incorregible

invidious [ɪnˈvɪdiəs] *adj* **1** OBNOXIOUS : repugnante, odioso **2** UNJUST : injusto — **invidiously** *adv*

invigorate [ɪnˈvɪgəˌreɪt] *vt* **-rated; -rating** : vigorizar, animar

invigorating [ɪnˈvɪgəˌreɪṭɪŋ] *adj* : vigorizante, estimulante

invincibility [ɪnˌvɪnsəˈbɪləṭi] *n* : invencibilidad *f*

invincible [ɪnˈvɪnsəbəl] *adj* : invencible — **invincibly** [-bli] *adv*

inviolable [ɪnˈvaɪələbəl] *adj* : inviolable

inviolate [ɪnˈvaɪələt] *adj* : inviolado, puro

invisibility [ɪnˌvɪzəˈbɪləṭi] *n* : invisibilidad *f*

invisible [ɪnˈvɪzəbəl] *adj* : invisible — **invisibly** [-bli] *adv*

invitation [ˌɪnvəˈteɪʃən] *n* : invitación *f*

invite [ɪnˈvaɪt] *vt* **-vited; -viting** **1** ATTRACT : atraer, tentar ⟨a book that invites interest : un libro que atrae el interés⟩ **2** PROVOKE : provocar, buscar ⟨to invite trouble : buscarse problemas⟩ **3** ASK : invitar ⟨we invited them for dinner : los invitamos a cenar⟩ **4** SOLICIT : solicitar, buscar (preguntas, comentarios, etc.)

inviting [ɪnˈvaɪṭɪŋ] *adj* : atractivo, atrayente

invocation [ˌɪnvəˈkeɪʃən] *n* : invocación *f*

invoice¹ [ˈɪnˌvɔɪs] *vt* **-voiced; -voicing** : facturar

invoice² *n* : factura *f*

invoke [ɪnˈvoːk] *vt* **-voked; -voking** **1** : invocar, apelar a ⟨she invoked our aid : apeló a nuestra ayuda⟩ **2** CITE : invocar, citar ⟨to invoke a precedent : invocar un precedente⟩ **3** CONJURE UP : hacer aparecer, invocar

involuntary [ɪnˈvɑlənˌtɛri] *adj* : involuntario — **involuntarily** [ɪnˌvɑlənˈtrɛli] *adv*

involve [ɪnˈvɑlv] *vt* **-volved; -volving** **1** ENGAGE : ocupar (con una tarea, etc.) **2** IMPLICATE : involucrar, enredar, implicar ⟨to be involved in a crime : estar involucrado en un crimen⟩ **3** CONCERN : concernir, afectar **4** CONNECT : conectar, relacionar **5** ENTAIL, INCLUDE : suponer, incluir, consistir en ⟨what does the job involve? : ¿en qué consiste el trabajo?⟩ **6 to be involved with someone** : tener una relación (amorosa) con alguien

involved [ɪnˈvɑlvd] *adj* **1** COMPLEX, INTRICATE : complicado, complejo **2** CONCERNED : interesado, afectado

involvement [ɪnˈvɑlvmənt] *n* **1** PARTICI-PATION : participación *f*, complicidad *f* **2** RELATIONSHIP : relación *f*

invulnerable [ɪnˈvʌlnərəbəl] *adj* : invulnerable

inward[1] [ˈɪnwərd] *or* **inwards** [-wərdz] *adv* : hacia adentro, hacia el interior

inward[2] *adj* INSIDE : interior, interno

inwardly [ˈɪnwərdli] *adv* **1** MENTALLY, SPIRITUALLY : por dentro **2** INTER-NALLY : internamente, interiormente **3** PRIVATELY : para sus adentros, para sí

iodine [ˈaɪəˌdaɪn, -dən] *n* : yodo *m*, tintura *f* de yodo

ion [ˈaɪən, ˈaɪˌɑn] *n* : ion *m*

ionic [aɪˈɑnɪk] *adj* : iónico

ionize [ˈaɪəˌnaɪz] *v* **ionized; ionizing** : ionizar

ionosphere [aɪˈɑnəˌsfɪr] *n* : ionosfera *f*

iota [aɪˈoːt̬ə] *n* : pizca *f*, ápice *m*

IOU [ˌaɪˌoˈjuː] *n* : pagaré *m*, vale *m*

IPA [ˌaɪˌpiːˈeɪ] *n* : *International Phonetic Alphabet* : AFI *m*

IQ [ˌaɪˈkjuː] *n* (*intelligence quotient*) : CI *m*, coeficiente *m* intelectual

Iranian [ɪˈreɪniən, -ˈræ-, -ˈrɑ-; aɪ-] *n* : iraní *mf* — **Iranian** *adj*

Iraqi [ɪˈrɑki] *n* : iraquí *mf* — **Iraqi** *adj*

irascibility [ɪˌræsəˈbɪlət̬i] *n* : irascibilidad *f*

irascible [ɪˈræsəbəl] *adj* : irascible

irate [aɪˈreɪt] *adj* : furioso, airado, iracundo — **irately** *adv*

ire [ˈaɪr] *n* : ira *f*, cólera *f*

iridescence [ˌɪrəˈdɛsənts] *n* : iridiscencia *f*

iridescent [ˌɪrəˈdɛsənt] *adj* : iridiscente

iridium [ɪˈrɪdiəm] *n* : iridio *m*

iris [ˈaɪrəs] *n*, *pl* **irises** *or* **irides** [ˈaɪrəˌdiːz, ˈɪr-] **1** : iris *m* (del ojo) **2** : lirio *m* (planta)

Irish[1] [ˈaɪrɪʃ] *adj* : irlandés

Irish[2] **1** : irlandés *m* (idioma) **2 the Irish** (*used with a plural verb*) : los irlandeses

Irishman [ˈaɪrɪʃmən] *n*, *pl* **-men** : irlandés *m*

Irishwoman [ˈaɪrɪʃˌwʊmən] *n*, *pl* **-women** : irlandesa *f*

irk [ˈərk] *vt* : fastidiar, irritar, preocupar

irksome [ˈərksəm] *adj* : irritante, fastidioso — **irksomely** *adv*

iron[1] [ˈaɪərn] *v* **1** : planchar **2 to iron out** : resolver

iron[2] *n* **1** : hierro *m*, fierro *m* ⟨a will of iron : una voluntad de hierro, una voluntad férrea⟩ **2** : plancha *f* (para planchar la ropa)

ironclad [ˈaɪərnˈklæd] *adj* **1** : acorazado, blindado **2** STRICT : riguroso, estricto

ironic [aɪˈrɑnɪk] *or* **ironical** [-nɪkəl] *adj* : irónico — **ironically** [-kli] *adv*

ironing [ˈaɪərnɪŋ] *n* **1** PRESSING : planchada *f* **2** : ropa *f* para planchar

ironing board *n* : tabla *f* (de planchar)

ironwork [ˈaɪərnˌwərk] *n* **1** : obra *f* de hierro **2 ironworks** *npl* : fundición *f*

irony [ˈaɪərni] *n*, *pl* **-nies** : ironía *f*

irradiate [ɪˈreɪdiˌeɪt] *vt* **-ated; -ating** : irradiar, radiar

irradiation [ɪˌreɪdiˈeɪʃən] *n* : irradiación *f*, radiación *f*

irrational [ɪˈræʃənəl] *adj* : irracional — **irrationally** *adv*

irrationality [ɪˌræʃəˈnælət̬i] *n*, *pl* **-ties** : irracionalidad *f*

irreconcilable [ɪˌrɛkənˈsaɪləbəl] *adj* : irreconciliable

irrecoverable [ˌɪrɪˈkʌvərəbəl] *adj* : irrecuperable — **irrecoverably** [-bli] *adv*

irredeemable [ˌɪrɪˈdiːməbəl] *adj* **1** : irredimible (dícese de un bono) **2** HOPELESS : irremediable, irreparable

irrefutable [ɪrɪˈfjuːt̬əbəl, ɪˈrɛfjə-] *adj* : irrefutable

irregular[1] [ɪˈrɛgjələr] *adj* : irregular — **irregularly** *adv*

irregular[2] *n* **1** : soldado *m* irregular **2 irregulars** *npl* : artículos *mpl* defectuosos

irregularity [ɪˌrɛgjəˈlærət̬i] *n*, *pl* **-ties** : irregularidad *f*

irrelevance [ɪˈrɛləvənts] *n* : irrelevancia *f*

irrelevant [ɪˈrɛləvənt] *adj* : irrelevante

irreligious [ˌɪrɪˈlɪdʒəs] *adj* : irreligioso

irreparable [ɪˈrɛpərəbəl] *adj* : irreparable

irreplaceable [ˌɪrɪˈpleɪsəbəl] *adj* : irreemplazable, insustituible

irrepressible [ˌɪrɪˈprɛsəbəl] *adj* : incontenible, incontrolable

irreproachable [ɪrɪˈproːtʃəbəl] *adj* : irreprochable, intachable

irresistible [ˌɪrɪˈzɪstəbəl] *adj* : irresistible — **irresistibly** [-bli] *adv*

irresolute [ɪˈrɛzəˌluːt] *adj* : irresoluto, indeciso

irresolutely [ɪˈrɛzəˌluːtli, -ˌrɛzəˈluːt-] *adv* : de manera indecisa

irresolution [ɪˌrɛzəˈluːʃən] *n* : irresolución *f*

irrespective of [ˌɪrɪˈspɛktɪvəv] *prep* : sin tomar en consideración, sin tener en cuenta

irresponsibility [ˌɪrɪˌspɑntsəˈbɪlət̬i] *n*, *pl* **-ties** : irresponsabilidad *f*, falta *f* de responsabilidad

irresponsible [ˌɪrɪˈspɑntsəbəl] *adj* : irresponsable — **irresponsibly** [-bli] *adv*

irretrievable [ˌɪrɪˈtriːvəbəl] *adj* IRRECOV-ERABLE : irrecuperable

irreverence [ɪˈrɛvərənts] *n* : irreverencia *f*, falta *f* de respeto

irreverent [ɪˈrɛvərənt] *adj* : irreverente, irrespetuoso

irreversible [ˌɪrɪˈvərsəbəl] *adj* : irreversible

irrevocable [ɪˈrɛvəkəbəl] *adj* : irrevocable — **irrevocably** [-bli] *adv*

irrigate [ˈɪrəˌgeɪt] *vt* **-gated; -gating** : irrigar, regar

irrigation [ˌɪrəˈgeɪʃən] *n* : irrigación *f*, riego *m*

irritability [ˌɪrət̬əˈbɪlət̬i] *n*, *pl* **-ties** : irritabilidad *f*

irritable [ˈɪrət̬əbəl] *adj* : irritable, colérico

irritably [ˈɪrət̬əbli] *adv* : con irritación

irritant[1] [ˈɪrət̬ənt] *adj* : irritante

irritant[2] *n* : agente *m* irritante

irritate [ˈɪrəˌteɪt] *vt* **-tated; -tating 1** AN-NOY : irritar, molestar **2** : irritar (en medicina)

irritating [ˈɪrəˌteɪt̬ɪŋ] *adj* : irritante

irritatingly [ˈɪrəˌteɪtɪŋli] *adv* : de modo irritante, fastidiosamente

irritation [ˌɪrəˈteɪʃən] *n* : irritación *f*

is → **be**

-ish [ˌɪʃ] *suf* ALMOST, APPROXIMATELY ⟨grayish : grisáceo⟩ ⟨she's fiftyish : tiene unos cincuenta años⟩

Islam [ɪsˈlɑm, ɪz-, -ˈlæm; ˈɪsˌlɑm, ˈɪz-, -ˌlæm] *n* : el Islam

Islamic [ɪsˈlɑmɪk, ɪz-, -ˈlæ-] *adj* : islámico

Islamism [ɪsˈlɑˌmɪzəm, ɪz-, -ˈlæ-; ˈɪzlə-] *n* : islamismo *m* — **Islamist** *n*

island [ˈaɪlənd] *n* : isla *f*

islander [ˈaɪləndər] *n* : isleño *m*, -ña *f*

isle [ˈaɪl] *n* : isla *f*, islote *m*

islet [ˈaɪlət] *n* : islote *m*

isn't [ˈɪzənt] *contraction of* **is not** → **be**

isolate [ˈaɪsəˌleɪt] *vt* **-lated; -lating** : aislar

isolated [ˈaɪsəˌleɪtəd] *adj* : aislado, solo

isolation [ˌaɪsəˈleɪʃən] *n* : aislamiento *m*

isometric [ˌaɪsəˈmetrɪk] *adj* : isométrico

isometrics [ˌaɪsəˈmetrɪks] *ns & pl* : isometría *f*

isosceles [aɪˈsɑsəˌliːz] *adj* : isósceles

isotope [ˈaɪsəˌtoːp] *n* : isótopo *m*

ISP [ˌaɪˌesˈpiː] *n* (*Internet service provider*) : PSI *m*, proveedor *m* de servicios de Internet

Israeli [ɪzˈreɪli] *n* : israelí *mf* — **Israeli** *adj*

issue¹ [ˈɪˌʃuː] *v* **-sued; -suing** *vi* 1 EMERGE : emerger, salir, fluir 2 DESCEND : descender (dícese de los padres o antepasados específicos) 3 EMANATE, RESULT : emanar, surgir, resultar — *vt* 1 EMIT : emitir 2 DISTRIBUTE : emitir, distribuir ⟨to issue a new stamp : emitir un sello nuevo⟩ 3 PUBLISH : publicar

issue² *n* 1 EMERGENCE, FLOW : emergencia *f*, flujo *m* 2 PROGENY : descendencia *f*, progenie *f* 3 OUTCOME, RESULT : desenlace *m*, resultado *m*, consecuencia *f* 4 MATTER, QUESTION : asunto *m*, cuestión *f* ⟨to avoid the issue : evitar el tema⟩ ⟨to make an issue of something : darle demasiada importancia a algo⟩ 5 PUBLICATION : publicación *f*, distribución *f*, emisión *f* 6 : número *m* (de un periódico o una revista)

isthmus [ˈɪsməs] *n* : istmo *m*

it [ˈɪt] *pron* 1 (*as subject; generally omitted*) : él, ella, ello ⟨it's a big building : es un edificio grande⟩ ⟨who was it? : ¿quién era?⟩ ⟨one more and that's it : uno más y se acabó⟩ 2 (*as indirect object*) : le ⟨I'll give it some water : voy a darle agua⟩ ⟨give it time : dale tiempo⟩ 3 (*as direct object*) : lo, la ⟨give it to me : dámelo⟩ ⟨I don't understand it : no lo entiendo⟩ ⟨stop it! : ¡basta!⟩ 4 (*as object of a preposition; generally omitted*) : él, ella, ello ⟨behind it : detrás, detrás de él⟩ 5 (*in impersonal constructions*) ⟨it's raining : está lloviendo⟩ ⟨what time is it? : ¿qué hora es?⟩ ⟨it's 8 o'clock : son las ocho⟩ ⟨it's hot/cold : hace calor/frío⟩ 6 (*as the implied subject or object of a verb*) ⟨it is necessary to study : es necesario estudiar⟩ ⟨it's good to see you : (me) da gusto verte⟩ ⟨it is known/said that . . . : se sabe/dice que . . .⟩ ⟨it would seem so : eso parece⟩ ⟨to give it all one's got : dar lo mejor de sí⟩

Italian [ɪˈtæliən, aɪ-] *n* 1 : italiano *m*, -na *f* 2 : italiano *m* (*idioma*) — **Italian** *adj*

italic¹ [ɪˈtælɪk, aɪ-] *adj* : en cursiva, en bastardilla

italic² *n* : cursiva *f*, bastardilla *f*

italicize [ɪˈtæləˌsaɪz, aɪ-] *vt* **-cized; -cizing** : poner en cursiva

itch¹ [ˈɪtʃ] *vi* 1 : picar ⟨her arm itched : le pica el brazo⟩ 2 : morirse ⟨they were itching to go outside : se morían por salir⟩ — *vt* : dar picazón, hacer picar

itch² *n* 1 ITCHING : picazón *f*, picor *m*, comezón *f* 2 RASH : sarpullido *m*, erupción *f* 3 DESIRE : ansia *f*, deseo *m*

itchiness [ˈɪtʃinəs] *n* ITCHING : picazón *f*, picor *m*, comezón *f*

itchy [ˈɪtʃi] *adj* **itchier; -est** : que pica, que da comezón

it'd [ˈɪtəd] *contraction of* **it had** *or* **it would** → **have, would**

item [ˈaɪtəm] *n* 1 OBJECT : artículo *m*, pieza *f* ⟨item of clothing : prenda de vestir⟩ 2 : punto *m* (en una agenda), número *m* (en el teatro), ítem *m* (en un documento) 3 **news item** : noticia *f*

itemization [ˌaɪtəməˈzeɪʃən] *n* : desglose *m*

itemize [ˈaɪtəˌmaɪz] *vt* **-ized; -izing** : detallar, enumerar, listar

itinerant [aɪˈtɪnərənt] *adj* : itinerante, ambulante

itinerary [aɪˈtɪnəˌreri] *n, pl* **-aries** : itinerario *m*

it'll [ˈɪtəl] *contraction of* **it shall** *or* **it will** → **shall, will**

its [ˈɪts] *adj* : su, sus ⟨its kennel : su perrera⟩ ⟨a city and its inhabitants : una ciudad y sus habitantes⟩

it's [ˈɪts] *contraction of* **it is** *or* **it has** → **be, have**

itself [ɪtˈsɛlf] *pron* 1 (*used reflexively*) : se ⟨the cat gave itself a bath : el gato se bañó⟩ 2 (*used for emphasis*) : (él) mismo, (ella) misma, sí (mismo), solo ⟨he is courtesy itself : es la misma cortesía⟩ ⟨in and of itself : por sí mismo⟩ ⟨it opened by itself : se abrió solo⟩

IUD [ˌaɪˌjuˈdiː] *n* intrauterine device : DIU *m*, dispositivo *m* intrauterino

I've [ˈaɪv] *contraction of* **I have** → **have**

ivory [ˈaɪvəri] *n, pl* **-ries** 1 : marfil *m* 2 : color *m* de marfil

ivy [ˈaɪvi] *n, pl* **ivies** 1 : hiedra *f*, yedra *f* 2 → **poison ivy**

J

j ['ʤeɪ] *n*, *pl* **j's** *or* **js** ['ʤeɪz] : décima letra del alfabeto inglés

jab¹ ['ʤæb] *v* **jabbed; jabbing** *vt* **1** PUNCTURE : clavar, pinchar **2** POKE : dar, golpear (con la punta de algo) ⟨he jabbed me in the ribs : me dio un codazo en las costillas⟩ — *vi* **to jab at** : dar, golpear

jab² *n* **1** PRICK : pinchazo *m* **2** POKE : golpe *m* abrupto

jabber ['ʤæbər] *v* : farfullar

jack¹ ['ʤæk] *vt* **to jack up 1** : levantar (con un gato) **2** INCREASE : subir, aumentar

jack² *n* **1** : gato *m*, cric *m* ⟨hydraulic jack : gato hidráulico⟩ **2** FLAG : pabellón *m* **3** SOCKET : enchufe *m* hembra **4** : jota *f*, valet *m* ⟨jack of hearts : jota de corazones⟩ **5 jacks** *npl* : cantillos *mpl*

jackal ['ʤækəl] *n* : chacal *m*

jackass ['ʤæk,æs] *n* : asno *m*, burro *m*

jacket ['ʤækət] *n* **1** : chaqueta *f* **2** COVER : sobrecubierta *f* (de un libro), carátula *f* (de un disco)

jackhammer ['ʤæk,hæmər] *n* : martillo *m* neumático

jack–in–the–box ['ʤækɪnðə,bɑks] *n* : caja *f* de sorpresa

jackknife¹ ['ʤæk,naɪf] *vi* **-knifed; -knifing** : doblarse como una navaja, plegarse

jackknife² *n* : navaja *f*

jack–of–all–trades *n* : persona *f* que sabe un poco de todo, persona *f* de muchos oficios

jack–o'–lantern ['ʤækə,læntərn] *n* : linterna *f* hecha de una calabaza

jackpot ['ʤæk,pɑt] *n* **1** : primer premio *m*, gordo *m* **2 to hit the jackpot** : sacarse la lotería, sacarse el gordo

jackrabbit ['ʤæk,ræbət] *n* : liebre *f* grande de Norteamérica

Jacuzzi [ʤə'ku:zi] *trademark* se usa para una bañera de hidromasaje

jade ['ʤeɪd] *n* : jade *m*

jaded ['ʤeɪdəd] *adj* **1** TIRED : agotado **2** BORED : hastiado

jagged ['ʤægəd] *adj* : dentado, mellado

jaguar ['ʤæg,wɑr, 'ʤægju,wɑr] *n* : jaguar *m*

jai alai ['haɪ,laɪ] *n* : jai alai *m*, pelota *f* vasca

jail¹ ['ʤeɪl] *vt* : encarcelar

jail² *n* : cárcel *f*

jailbreak ['ʤeɪl,breɪk] *n* : fuga *f*, huida *f* (de la cárcel)

jailer *or* **jailor** ['ʤeɪlər] *n* : carcelero *m*, -ra *f*

jalapeño [,hɑlə'peɪnjo, ,hæ-, -'pi:no] *n* : jalapeño *m*

jalopy [ʤə'lɑpi] *n*, *pl* **-lopies** : cacharro *m* *fam*, carro *m* destartalado

jalousie ['ʤæləsi] *n* : celosía *f*

jam¹ ['ʤæm] *v* **jammed; jamming** *vt* **1** CRAM : apiñar, embutir, atiborrar ⟨jammed with people : atestado de gente⟩ **2** STICK, THRUST : meter **3** BLOCK : atascar, atorar **4** : interferir (una señal, etc.) **5 to jam on the brakes** : frenar en seco — *vi* **1** : atascarse, atrancarse, bloquearse (dícese de un mecanismo) ⟨the copier has jammed : la fotocopiadora se ha bloqueado/atascado⟩ **2** PLAY *fam* : tocar

jam² *n* **1** *or* **traffic jam** : atasco *m*, embotellamiento *m* (de tráfico) **2** PREDICAMENT : lío *m*, aprieto *m*, apuro *m* **3** : mermelada *f* ⟨strawberry jam : mermelada de fresa⟩

Jamaican [ʤə'meɪkən] *n* : jamaiquino *m*, -na *f*; jamaicano *m*, -na *f* — **Jamaican** *adj*

jamb ['ʤæm] *n* : jamba *f*

jamboree [,ʤæmbə'ri:] *n* : fiesta *f* grande

jam–packed *adj* : repleto, hasta el tope (dícese de un recipiente), atestado (de gente)

jangle¹ ['ʤæŋgəl] *v* **-gled; -gling** *vi* : hacer un ruido metálico — *vt* **1** : hacer sonar **2 to jangle one's nerves** : irritar, crispar

jangle² *n* : ruido *m* metálico

janitor ['ʤænətər] *n* : portero *m*, -ra *f*; conserje *mf*

January ['ʤænju,ɛri] *n* : enero *m* ⟨they arrived on January 12th, they arrived on the 12th of January : llegaron el 12 de enero⟩

Japanese¹ [,ʤæpə'ni:z, -'ni:s] *adj* : japonés

Japanese² *n* **1** : japonés *m* (idioma) **2 the Japanese** (*used with a plural verb*) : los japoneses

jar¹ ['ʤɑr] *v* **jarred; jarring** *vi* **1** GRATE : chirriar **2** CLASH : desentonar **3** SHAKE : sacudirse **4 to jar on** : crispar, enervar — *vt* JOLT : sacudir

jar² *n* **1** GRATING : chirrido *m* **2** JOLT : vibración *f*, sacudida *f* **3** : tarro *m*, bote *m*, pote *m* ⟨a jar of honey : un tarro de miel⟩

jargon ['ʤɑrgən] *n* : jerga *f*

jasmine ['ʤæzmən] *n* : jazmín *m*

jasper ['ʤæspər] *n* : jaspe *m*

jaundice ['ʤɔndɪs] *n* : ictericia *f*

jaundiced ['ʤɔndɪst] *adj* **1** : ictérico **2** EMBITTERED, RESENTFUL : amargado, resentido, negativo ⟨with a jaundiced eye : con una actitud de cinismo⟩

jaunt ['ʤɔnt] *n* : excursión *f*, paseo *m*

jauntily ['ʤɔntəli] *adv* : animadamente

jauntiness ['ʤɔntinəs] *n* : animación *f*, vivacidad *f*

jaunty ['ʤɔnti] *adj* **jauntier; -est 1** SPRIGHTLY : animado, alegre **2** RAKISH : desenvuelto, desenfadado

Javanese [,ʤævə'ni:z, ,ʤɑ-, -'ni:s] *n* **1** : javanés *m* (idioma) **2** : javanés *m*, -nesa *f* — **Javanese** *adj*

javelin ['ʤævələn] *n* : jabalina *f*

jaw¹ ['ʤɔ] *vi* GAB : cotorrear *fam*, parlotear *fam*

jaw² *n* **1** : mandíbula *f*, quijada *f* **2** : mordaza *f* (de una herramienta) **3 the jaws of death** : las garras *f* de la muerte

jawbone ['dʒɔ,boːn] *n* : mandíbula *f*
jay ['dʒeɪ] *n* : arrendajo *m*, chara *f Mex*, azulejo *m Mex*
jaybird ['dʒeɪ,bərd] → jay
jaywalk ['dʒeɪ,wɔk] *vi* : cruzar la calle sin prudencia
jaywalker ['dʒeɪ,wɔkər] *n* : peatón *m* imprudente
jazz[1] ['dʒæz] *vt* **to jazz up** : animar, alegrar
jazz[2] *n* : jazz *m*
jazzy ['dʒæzi] *adj* **jazzier; -est 1** : con ritmo de jazz **2** FLASHY, SHOWY : llamativo, ostentoso
jealous ['dʒɛləs] *adj* : celoso, envidioso — **jealously** *adv*
jealousy ['dʒɛləsi] *n* : celos *mpl*, envidia *f*
jeans ['dʒiːnz] *npl* : jeans *mpl*; vaqueros *mpl*; tejanos *mpl*; pantalones *mpl* de mezclilla *Chile, Mex*
jeep ['dʒiːp] *n* : jeep *m* (vehículo militar)
Jeep *trademark* se usa para un camión pequeño
jeer[1] ['dʒɪr] *vi* **1** BOO : abuchear **2** SCOFF : mofarse, burlarse — *vt* RIDICULE : mofarse de, burlarse de
jeer[2] *n* **1** : abucheo *m* **2** TAUNT : mofa *f*, burla *f*
Jehovah [dʒɪ'hoːvə] *n* : Jehová *m*
jell ['dʒɛl] *vi* **1** SET : gelificarse, cuajar **2** FORM : cuajar, formarse (una idea, etc.)
Jell-O ['dʒɛ,loː] *trademark* se usa para gelatina con sabor a frutas, etc.
jelly *n*, *pl* **-lies 1** : jalea *f* **2** GELATIN : gelatina *f*
jellyfish ['dʒɛli,fɪʃ] *n* : medusa *f*
jeopardize ['dʒɛpər,daɪz] *vt* **-dized; -dizing** : arriesgar, poner en peligro
jeopardy ['dʒɛpərdi] *n* : peligro *m*, riesgo *m*
jerk[1] ['dʒərk] *vt* **1** JOLT : sacudir **2** TUG, YANK : darle un tirón a — *vi* JOLT : dar sacudidas ⟨the train lerked along : el tren iba moviéndose a sacudidas⟩
jerk[2] *n* **1** TUG : tirón *m*, jalón *m* **2** JOLT : sacudida *f* brusca **3** FOOL : estúpido *m*, -da *f*; idiota *mf*
jerkin ['dʒərkən] *n* : chaqueta *f* sin mangas, chaleco *m*
jerky[1] ['dʒərki] *adj* **jerkier; -est 1** : espasmódico (dícese de los movimientos) **2** CHOPPY : inconexo (dícese de la prosa) — **jerkily** [-kəli] *adv*
jerky[2] *n* : cecina *f*; tasajo *m*; charqui *m Chile, Peru*
jerry-built ['dʒɛri,bɪlt] *adj* : mal construido, chapucero
jersey ['dʒərzi] *n*, *pl* **-seys** : jersey *m*
jest[1] ['dʒɛst] *vi* : bromear
jest[2] *n* : broma *f*, chiste *m*
jester ['dʒɛstər] *n* : bufón *m*, -fona *f*
Jesuit ['dʒɛzuət] *n* : jesuita *m* — **Jesuit** *adj*
Jesus ['dʒiːzəs, -zəz] *n* **1** : Jesús *m* **2 Jesus Christ** : Jesucristo *m* **3 Jesus (Christ)!** *fam* : ¡por Dios!
jet[1] ['dʒɛt] *vt* **jetted; jetting** *vt* SPOUT : arrojar a chorros — *vi* **1** GUSH : salir a chorros, chorrear **2** FLY : viajar en avión, volar

jet[2] *n* **1** STREAM : chorro *m* **2** *or* **jet airplane** : avión *m* a reacción, reactor *m* **3** : azabache *m* (mineral)
jet—black *adj* : negro azabache
jet black *n* : negro *m* azabache
jet engine *n* : reactor *m*, motor *m* a reacción
jet lag *n* : desfase *m* (de) horario
jet-propelled *adj* : a reacción
jetsam ['dʒɛtsəm] *n* **in flotsam and jetsam** : restos *mpl*, desechos *mpl*
jettison ['dʒɛtəsən] *vt* **1** : echar al mar **2** DISCARD : desechar, deshacerse de
jetty ['dʒɛti] *n*, *pl* **-ties 1** PIER, WHARF : embarcadero *m*, muelle *m* **2** BREAKWATER : malecón *m*, rompeolas *m*
Jew ['dʒuː] *n* : judío *m*, -día *f*
jewel ['dʒuːəl] *n* **1** : joya *f*, alhaja *f* **2** GEM : piedra *f* preciosa, gema *f* **3** : rubí *m* (de un reloj) **4** TREASURE : joya *f*, tesoro *m*
jeweler *or* **jeweller** ['dʒuːələr] *n* : joyero *m*, -ra *f*
jewelry ['dʒuːəlri] *n* : joyas *fpl*, alhajas *fpl* ⟨jewelry store : joyería⟩ ⟨jewelry box : alhajero, joyero⟩
Jewish ['dʒuːɪʃ] *adj* : judío
jibe ['dʒaɪb] *vi* **jibed; jibing** AGREE : concordar
jicama ['hiːkəmə] *n* : jícama *f*
jiffy ['dʒɪfi] *n*, *pl* **-fies** : santiamén *m*, segundo *m*, momento *m*
jig[1] ['dʒɪg] *vi* **jigged; jigging** : bailar la giga
jig[2] *n* **1** : giga *f* **2 the jig is up** : se acabó la fiesta
jigger ['dʒɪgər] *n* : medida de 1 a 2 onzas (para licores)
jiggle[1] ['dʒɪgəl] *v* **-gled; -gling** *vt* : agitar o sacudir ligeramente — *vi* : agitarse, vibrar
jiggle[2] *n* : sacudida *f*, vibración *f*
jigsaw ['dʒɪg,sɔ] *n* **1** : sierra *f* de vaivén **2 jigsaw puzzle** : rompecabezas *m*
jihad [dʒɪ'hɑd] *n* : yihad *f*, jihad *mf*
jilt ['dʒɪlt] *vt* : dejar plantado, dar calabazas a
jimmy[1] ['dʒɪmi] *vt* **-mied; -mying** : forzar con una palanqueta
jimmy[2] *n*, *pl* **-mies** : palanqueta *f*
jingle[1] ['dʒɪŋgəl] *v* **-gled; -gling** *vi* : tintinear — *vt* : hacer sonar
jingle[2] *n* **1** TINKLE : tintineo *m*, retintín *m* **2** : canción *f* rimada
jingoism ['dʒɪŋgoˌɪzəm] *n* : jingoísmo *m*, patriotería *f*
jingoistic [ˌdʒɪŋgoˈɪstɪk] *or* **jingoist** ['dʒɪŋgoɪst] *adj* : jingoísta, patriotero
jinx[1] ['dʒɪŋks] *vt* : traer mala suerte a, salar *CoRi, Mex*
jinx[2] *n* **1** : cenizo *m*, -za *f* **2 to put a jinx on** : echarle el mal de ojo a
jitters ['dʒɪtərz] *npl* : nervios *mpl* ⟨he got the jitters : se puso nervioso⟩
jittery ['dʒɪtəri] *adj* : nervioso
Jivaro ['hiːvəˌroː] *n* : jíbaro *m*, -ra *f*
job ['dʒɑb] *n* **1** : trabajo *m* ⟨he did odd jobs for her : le hizo algunos trabajos⟩ **2** CHORE, TASK : tarea *f*, quehacer *m* **3** EMPLOYMENT : trabajo *m*, empleo *m*, puesto *m*

jobber ['dʒabər] *n* MIDDLEMAN : intermediario *m*, -ria *f*

jobless ['dʒabləs] *adj* : desempleado

jock ['dʒak] *n* : deportista *mf*, atleta *mf*

jockey¹ ['dʒaki] *v* **-eyed; -eying** *vt* 1 MANIPULATE : manipular 2 MANEUVER : maniobrar — *vi* **to jockey for position** : maniobrar para conseguir algo

jockey² *n, pl* **-eys** : jockey *mf*

jocose [dʒo'ko:s] *adj* : jocoso

jocular ['dʒakjulər] *adj* : jocoso — **jocularly** *adv*

jocularity [,dʒakju'lærəti] *n* : jocosidad *f*

jodhpurs ['dʒadpərz] *npl* : pantalones *mpl* de montar

jog¹ ['dʒag] *v* **jogged; jogging** *vt* 1 NUDGE : dar, empujar, codear 〈to jog one's memory : refrescar la memoria〉 — *vi* 1 RUN : correr despacio, trotar, hacer footing (como ejercicio) 2 TRUDGE : andar a trote corto

jog² *n* 1 PUSH, SHAKE : empujoncito *m*, sacudida *f* leve 2 TROT : trote *m* corto, footing *m* (en deportes) 3 TWIST : recodo *m*, vuelta *f*, curva *f*

jogger ['dʒagər] *n* : persona *f* que hace footing

jogging ['dʒagɪŋ] *n* : footing *m*, jogging *m*

john ['dʒan] *n fam* TOILET : inodoro *m*

join¹ ['dʒɔɪn] *vt* 1 CONNECT, LINK : unir, juntar 〈to join in marriage : unir en matrimonio〉 〈to join hands : tomarse de la mano〉 2 ADJOIN : lindar con, colindar con 3 MEET : reunirse con, encontrarse con 〈we joined them for lunch : nos reunimos con ellos para almorzar〉 〈may I join you? : ¿puedo sentarme aquí?〉 4 ACCOMPANY : acompañar 5 : hacerse socio de (una organización), afiliarse a (un partido), entrar en (una empresa) 〈to join the ranks of : sumarse a las filas de〉 — *vi* 1 UNITE : unirse 2 MERGE : empalmar (dícese de las carreteras), confluir (dícese de los ríos) 3 : hacerse socio, afiliarse, entrar 4 **to join in** PARTICIPATE : participar, tomar parte 5 **to join up** ENLIST : enrolarse, alistarse

join² *n* JUNCTURE : juntura *f*, unión *f*

joiner ['dʒɔɪnər] *n* 1 CARPENTER : carpintero *m*, -ra *f* 2 : persona *f* que se une a varios grupos

joint¹ ['dʒɔɪnt] *adj* : conjunto, colectivo, mutuo 〈a joint effort : un esfuerzo conjunto〉 〈a joint account : una cuenta conjunta〉 — **jointly** *adv*

joint² *n* 1 : articulación *f*, coyuntura *f* 〈out of joint : dislocado〉 2 ROAST : asado *m* 3 JUNCTURE : juntura *f*, unión *f* 4 DIVE : antro *m*, tasca *f* 5 *fam* : porro *m*

joist ['dʒɔɪst] *n* : viga *f*

joke¹ ['dʒo:k] *vi* **joked; joking** : bromear

joke² *n* 1 STORY : chiste *m* 2 PRANK : broma *f*

joker ['dʒo:kər] *n* 1 PRANKSTER : bromista *mf* 2 : comodín *m* (en los naipes)

jokingly ['dʒo:kɪŋli] *adv* : en broma

jollity ['dʒaləti] *n, pl* **-ties** MERRIMENT : alegría *f*, regocijo *m*

jolly ['dʒali] *adj* **jollier; -est** : alegre, jovial

jolt¹ ['dʒo:lt] *vi* JERK : dar tumbos, dar sacudidas — *vt* : sacudir

jolt² *n* 1 JERK : sacudida *f* brusca 2 SHOCK : golpe *m* (emocional)

jonquil ['dʒankwɪl] *n* : junquillo *m*

Jordanian [dʒɔr'deɪniən] *n* : jordano *m*, -na *f* — **Jordanian** *adj*

josh ['dʒaʃ] *vt* TEASE : tomarle el pelo (a alguien) — *vi* JOKE : bromear

jostle ['dʒasəl] *v* **-tled; -tling** *vi* 1 SHOVE : empujar, dar empellones 2 CONTEND : competir — *vt* 1 SHOVE : empujar 2 **to jostle one's way** : abrirse paso a empellones

jot¹ ['dʒat] *vt* **jotted; jotting** : anotar, apuntar 〈jot it down : apúntalo〉

jot² *n* BIT : ápice *m*, jota *f*, pizca *f*

jounce¹ ['dʒaʊns] *v* **jounced; jouncing** *vt* JOLT : sacudir — *vi* : dar tumbos, dar sacudidas

jounce² *n* JOLT : sacudida *f*, tumbo *m*

journal ['dʒərnəl] *n* 1 DIARY : diario *m* 2 PERIODICAL : revista *f*, publicación *f* periódica 3 NEWSPAPER : periódico *m*, diario *m*

journalism ['dʒərnəl,ɪzəm] *n* : periodismo *m*

journalist ['dʒərnəlɪst] *n* : periodista *mf*

journalistic [,dʒərnəl'ɪstɪk] *adj* : periodístico

journey¹ ['dʒərni] *vi* **-neyed; -neying** : viajar

journey² *n, pl* **-neys** : viaje *m*

journeyman ['dʒərnimən] *n, pl* **-men** [-mən, -,mɛn] : oficial *m*

joust¹ ['dʒaʊst] *vi* : justar

joust² *n* : justa *f*

jovial ['dʒo:viəl] *adj* : jovial — **jovially** *adv*

joviality [,dʒo:vi'æləti] *n* : jovialidad *f*

jowl ['dʒaʊl] *n* 1 JAW : mandíbula *f* 2 CHEEK : mejilla *f*, cachete *m*

joy ['dʒɔɪ] *n* 1 HAPPINESS : gozo *m*, alegría *f*, felicidad *f* 2 DELIGHT : placer *m*, deleite *m* 〈the child is a real joy : el niño es un verdadero placer〉

joyful ['dʒɔɪfəl] *adj* : gozoso, alegre, feliz — **joyfully** *adv*

joyless ['dʒɔɪləs] *adj* : sin alegría, triste

joyous ['dʒɔɪəs] *adj* : alegre, feliz, eufórico — **joyously** *adv*

joyousness ['dʒɔɪəsnəs] *n* : alegría *f*, felicidad *f*, euforia *f*

joyride ['dʒɔɪ,raɪd] *n* 1 : paseo *m* en coche a alta velocidad 2 : paseo *m* en un coche robado

joyriding ['dʒɔɪ,raɪdɪŋ] *n* **to go joyriding** 1 : pasear en coche a alta velocidad (por diversión) 2 : pasear en un coche robado

joystick ['dʒɔɪ,stɪk] *n* : joystick *m*

jubilant ['dʒu:bələnt] *adj* : jubiloso, alborozado — **jubilantly** *adv*

jubilation [,dʒu:bə'leɪʃən] *n* : júbilo *m*

jubilee ['dʒu:bə,li:] *n* 1 : quincuagésimo aniversario *m* 2 CELEBRATION : celebración *f*, festejos *mpl*

Judaic [dʒu'deɪɪk] *adj* : judaico

Judaism ['dʒu:də,ɪzəm, 'dʒu:dɪ-, 'dʒu:,deɪ-] *n* : judaísmo *m*

judge¹ ['ʤʌʤ] *vt* **judged; judging 1** AS-SESS : evaluar, juzgar **2** DEEM : juzgar, considerar **3** TRY : juzgar (ante el tribunal) **4 judging by** : a juzgar por ⟨judging by the results : a juzgar por los resultados⟩

judge² *n* **1** : juez *mf*, jueza *f* **2** : jurado *mf* (en una competencia) **3 to be a good judge of** : saber juzgar a, entender mucho de

judge's chambers → chamber

judgment *or* **judgement** ['ʤʌʤmənt] *n* **1** RULING : fallo *m*, sentencia *f* **2** OPINION : opinión *f* **3** DISCERNMENT : juicio *m*, discernimiento *m* ⟨against my better judgment, I agreed to go : aunque me pareció mala idea, consentí en ir⟩

judgmental [ˌʤʌʤˈmntəl] *adj* : crítico — **judgmentally** *adv*

judicature ['ʤuːdɪkəˌʧʊr] *n* : judicatura *f*

judicial [ʤuˈdɪʃəl] *adj* : judicial — **judicially** *adv*

judiciary¹ [ʤuˈdɪʃiˌri, -ˈdɪʃəri] *adj* : judicial

judiciary² *n* **1** JUDICATURE : judicatura *f* **2** : poder *m* judicial

judicious [ʤuˈdɪʃəs] *adj* SOUND, WISE : juicioso, sensato — **judiciously** *adv*

judo ['ʤuːdoː] *n* : judo *m*

jug ['ʤʌɡ] *n* **1** : jarra *f*, jarro *m*, cántaro *m* **2** JAIL : cárcel *f*, chirona *f fam*

juggernaut ['ʤʌɡərˌnɔt] *n* : gigante *m*, fuerza *f* irresistible ⟨a political juggernaut : un gigante político⟩

juggle ['ʤʌɡəl] *v* **-gled; -gling** *vt* **1** : hacer juegos malabares con **2** MANIPULATE : manipular, jugar con — *vi* : hacer juegos malabares

juggler ['ʤʌɡələr] *n* : malabarista *mf*

jugular ['ʤʌɡjʊlər] *adj* : yugular ⟨jugular vein : vena yugular⟩

juice ['ʤuːs] *n* **1** : jugo *m* (de carne, de frutas) *m*, zumo *m* (de frutas) **2** ELEC-TRICITY : electricidad *f*, luz *f*

juicer ['ʤuːsər] *n* : exprimidor *m*

juiciness ['ʤuːsinəs] *n* : jugosidad *f*

juicy ['ʤuːsi] *adj* **juicier; -est 1** SUCCU-LENT : jugoso, suculento **2** PROFITABLE : jugoso, lucrativo **3** RACY : picante

jukebox ['ʤuːkˌbɑks] *n* : rocola *f*, máquina *f* de discos

julep ['ʤuːləp] *n* : bebida *f* hecha con whisky americano y menta

July [ʤuˈlaɪ] *n* **1** : julio *m* ⟨they arrived on July 29th, they arrived on the 29th of July : llegaron el 29 de julio⟩ **2 the Fourth of July** INDEPENDENCE DAY : el 4 de julio (día festivo en los EEUU)

jumble¹ ['ʤʌmbəl] *vt* **-bled; -bling** : mezclar, revolver

jumble² *n* : revoltijo *m*, fárrago *m*, embrollo *m*

jumbo¹ ['ʤʌmˌboː] *adj* : gigante, enorme, de tamaño extra grande

jumbo² *n, pl* **-bos** : coloso *m*, cosa *f* de tamaño extra grande

jump¹ ['ʤʌmp] *vi* **1** LEAP : saltar, brincar **2** START : levantarse de un salto, sobresaltarse **3** MOVE, SHIFT : moverse, pasar ⟨to jump from job to job : pasar de un

empleo a otro⟩ **4** INCREASE, RISE : dar un salto, aumentarse de golpe, subir bruscamente **5** BUSTLE : animarse, ajetrearse **6 to jump at** : no dejar escapar (una oportunidad) **7 to jump in** : meterse (en una conversación, etc.) **8 to jump on** ATTACK, CRITICIZE : atacar, criticar **9 to jump on** SCOLD : regañar, reprender, reñir **10 to jump out at** POUNCE ON : abalanzarse sobre **11 to jump out at** : llamar la atención de ⟨it jumps out at you : salta a la vista⟩ **12 to jump to conclusions** : sacar conclusiones precipitadas — *vt* **1** : saltar ⟨to jump a fence : saltar una valla⟩ **2** SKIP : saltarse **3** ATTACK : atacar, asaltar **5 to jump the gun** : precipitarse

jump² *n* **1** LEAP : salto *m* **2** START : sobresalto *m*, respingo *m* **3** INCREASE : subida *f* brusca, aumento *m* **4** ADVANTAGE : ventaja *f* ⟨we got the jump on them : les llevamos la ventaja⟩

jumper ['ʤʌmpər] *n* **1** : saltador *m*, -dora *f* (en deportes) **2** : jumper *m*, vestido *m* sin mangas

jumper cables *npl* : cables *mpl* de arranque, cables *mpl* pasacorriente *Mex*

jump–start *vt* : arrancar haciendo puente

jumpy ['ʤʌmpi] *adj* **jumpier; -est** : asustadizo, nervioso

junction ['ʤʌŋkʃən] *n* **1** JOINING : unión *f* **2** : cruce *m* (de calles), empalme *m* (de un ferrocarril), confluencia *f* (de ríos)

juncture ['ʤʌŋkʧər] *n* **1** UNION : juntura *f*, unión *f* **2** MOMENT, POINT : coyuntura *f* ⟨at this juncture : en esta coyuntura, en este momento⟩

June ['ʤuːn] *n* : junio *m* ⟨they arrived on the 15th of June, they arrived on June 15th : llegaron el 15 de junio⟩

jungle ['ʤʌŋɡəl] *n* : jungla *f*, selva *f*

junior¹ ['ʤuːnjər] *adj* **1** YOUNGER : más joven ⟨John Smith, Junior : John Smith, hijo⟩ **2** SUBORDINATE : subordinado, subalterno

junior² *n* **1** : persona *f* de menor edad ⟨she's my junior : es menor que yo⟩ **2** SUBORDINATE : subalterno *m*, -na *f*; subordinado *m*, -da *f* **3** : estudiante *mf* de penúltimo año

junior high school *n* : primer ciclo *m* de la educación secundaria en los EEUU

juniper ['ʤuːnəpər] *n* : enebro *m*

junk¹ ['ʤʌŋk] *vt* : echar a la basura

junk² *n* **1** RUBBISH : desechos *mpl*, desperdicios *mpl* **2** STUFF : trastos *mpl fam*, cachivaches *mpl fam* **3 piece of junk** : cacharro *m*, porquería *f*

junk food *n* : comida *f* basura

junket ['ʤʌŋkət] *n* : viaje *m* (pagado con dinero público)

junkie ['ʤʌŋki] *n* : drogadicto *m*, -ta *f*

junk mail *n* : correo *m* basura, propaganda *f*

junta ['huːntə, 'ʤʌn-, 'hʌn-] *n* : junta *f* militar

Jupiter ['ʤuːpətər] *n* : Júpiter *m*

jurisdiction [ˌʤʊrəsˈdɪkʃən] *n* : jurisdicción *f* — **jurisdictional** [-ˈdɪkʃənəl] *adj*

jurisprudence [ˌʤʊrəsˈpruːdənts] *n* : jurisprudencia *f*

jurist ['dʒʊrɪst] n : jurista mf; magistrado m, -da f
juror ['dʒʊrər] n : jurado m, -da f
jury ['dʒʊri] n, pl **-ries** : jurado m
just¹ ['dʒʌst] adv 1 EXACTLY : justo, precisamente, exactamente ⟨it was just what she hoped for : fue exactamente lo que esperaba⟩ ⟨it is just what I need : es justo lo que necesito⟩ ⟨just as/when : justo cuando⟩ 2 POSSIBLY : posiblemente ⟨it just might work : tal vez resulte⟩ 3 BARELY : justo, apenas ⟨just in time : justo a tiempo⟩ ⟨I had just enough time : tenía el tiempo justo⟩ ⟨just over an hour : una hora larga, una hora y pico⟩ ⟨we just missed the plane : perdimos el avión por un pelo⟩ ⟨we just missed each other : no nos vimos por poco⟩ ⟨it's just around the corner : está a la vuelta de la esquina⟩ 4 ONLY : sólo, solamente, nada más ⟨just us : sólo nosotros⟩ ⟨just one more : sólo uno más⟩ ⟨she's just a child : es sólo una niña⟩ ⟨just for fun : sólo por diversión⟩ ⟨just a moment/minute, please : un momento, por favor⟩ ⟨I'm just kidding : (sólo) estoy bromeando⟩ ⟨she's not just my friend, she's my lawyer : además de ser mi amiga, es mi abogada⟩ 5 (used for emphasis) ⟨it's just horrible! : ¡qué horrible!⟩ ⟨I just don't understand it : simplemente no lo entiendo⟩ ⟨I just knew it! : ¡ya me lo sospechaba!⟩ ⟨just imagine! : ¡imagínate!⟩ ⟨just tell him how you feel! : ¿por qué no le dices lo que sientes?⟩ ⟨don't just stand there—do something! : no te quedes ahí parado—¡haz algo!⟩ 6 **to have just**

done something : acabar de hacer algo ⟨he just called : acaba de llamar⟩ 7 **just about** ALMOST : casi 8 **just about to** : al punto de 9 **just as . . . as** : tan . . . como ⟨just as good as : tan bueno como⟩ 10 **just as soon** RATHER : ⟨I'd just as soon stay home : prefiero quedarme en casa⟩ 11 **just as well (that)** : menos mal (que) 12 **just like that** : de repente 13 **just now** : hace un momento ⟨I saw him just now : acabo de verlo⟩ 14 **just now** RIGHT NOW : ahora mismo 15 **just so** PERFECT : perfecto 16 **just the thing** ⟨just the thing for you : justo lo que necesitas⟩ 17 **just yet** ⟨are you ready?—not just yet : ¿estás lista?—casi⟩ ⟨don't buy it just yet : no lo compres ahora mismo⟩
just² adj : justo — **justly** adv
justice ['dʒʌstɪs] n 1 : justicia f ⟨to do justice to : hacerle justicia a⟩ 2 JUDGE : juez mf, jueza f
justice of the peace n : juez mf de paz, jueza f de paz
justification [ˌdʒʌstəfəˈkeɪʃən] n : justificación f
justify ['dʒʌstəˌfaɪ] vt **-fied; -fying** : justificar — **justifiable** [ˌdʒʌstəˈfaɪəbəl] adj
jut ['dʒʌt] vi **jutted; jutting** : sobresalir
jute ['dʒuːt] n : yute m
juvenile¹ ['dʒuːvəˌnaɪl, -vənəl] adj 1 : juvenil ⟨juvenile delinquent : delincuente juvenil⟩ ⟨juvenile court : tribunal de menores⟩ 2 CHILDISH : infantil
juvenile² n : menor mf
juxtapose ['dʒʌkstəˌpoːz] vt **-posed; -posing** : yuxtaponer
juxtaposition [ˌdʒʌkstəpəˈzɪʃən] n : yuxtaposición f

K

k ['keɪ] n, pl **k's** or **ks** ['keɪz] : undécima letra del alfabeto inglés
kabob [kəˈbɑb] → **kebab**
kaiser ['kaɪzər] n : káiser m
kale ['keɪl] n : col f rizada
kaleidoscope [kəˈlaɪdəˌskoːp] n : calidoscopio m
kamikaze [ˌkɑmɪˈkɑzi] n : kamikaze m — **kamikaze** adj
kangaroo [ˌkæŋgəˈruː] n, pl **-roos** : canguro m
karaoke [ˌkæriˈoːki] n : karaoke m
karat ['kærət] n : quilate m
karate [kəˈrɑti] n : karate m
katydid ['keɪtɪˌdɪd] n : saltamontes m
kayak ['kaɪˌæk] n : kayac m, kayak m
kebab [kəˈbɑb] or **kebob** n : kebab m
keel¹ ['kiːl] vi **to keel over** : volcar (dícese de un barco), desplomarse (dícese de una persona)
keel² n : quilla f
keen ['kiːn] adj 1 SHARP : afilado, filoso ⟨a keen blade : una hoja afilada⟩ 2 PENETRATING : cortante, penetrante ⟨a keen

wind : un viento cortante⟩ 3 ENTHUSIASTIC : entusiasta 4 ACUTE : agudo, fino ⟨keen hearing : oído fino⟩ ⟨keen intelligence : inteligencia aguda⟩
keenly ['kiːnli] adv 1 ENTHUSIASTICALLY : con entusiasmo 2 INTENSELY : vivamente, profundamente ⟨keenly aware of : muy consciente de⟩
keenness ['kiːnnəs] n 1 SHARPNESS : lo afilado, lo filoso 2 ENTHUSIASM : entusiasmo m 3 ACUTENESS : agudeza f
keep¹ ['kiːp] v **kept** ['kept]; **keeping** vt 1 RETAIN : guardar, conservar, quedarse con ⟨do you want to keep these papers? : ¿quieres guardar estos papeles?⟩ ⟨he kept the money : se quedó con el dinero⟩ ⟨to keep one's cool : mantener la calma⟩ 2 : mantener ⟨keep me informed : mantenme informado⟩ ⟨she keeps herself fit : se mantiene en forma⟩ ⟨he kept his coat on : se quedó con el abrigo puesto⟩ ⟨to keep something a secret : mantener algo en secreto⟩ 3 DETAIN : retener, detener ⟨I won't keep you any longer : no

te entretengo más⟩ ⟨what kept you? : ¿por qué tardaste?⟩ **4** (*with a present participle*) ⟨don't keep her waiting : no la hagas esperar⟩ ⟨he kept the company going : mantuvo la compañía a flote⟩ **5** : cumplir (su palabra), acudir a (una cita) **6** PRESERVE : guardar ⟨to keep a secret : guardar un secreto⟩ ⟨he kept it to himself : no se lo contó a nadie⟩ **7** HIDE : ocultar ⟨he kept it from her : se lo ocultó, no se lo dijo⟩ **8** OBSERVE : observar (una fiesta) **9** STORE : guardar **10** RESERVE : guardar **11** GUARD : guardar, cuidar **12** : llevar, escribir (un diario, etc.) **13** SUPPORT : mantener (una familia) **14** RAISE : criar (animales) **15** : mantener (a un amante) **16 to keep after** (school) : hacer quedar después de clase **17 to keep back** : no dejar acercarse a **18 to keep back** : hacer repetir un año (a un estudiante) **19 to keep back** HIDE, REPRESS : ocultar, retener **20 to keep company** : hacerle compañía a **21 to keep company with** : andar en compañía de **22 to keep down** : mantener bajo ⟨to keep prices down : mantener los precios bajos⟩ **23 to keep down** : retener (en el estómago) **24 to keep in** : no dejar salir **25 to keep it down** : no hacer tanto ruido **26 to keep in** CONTAIN : contener **27 to keep off** : no dejar pisar, tocar, etc. ⟨keep the dog off the sofa : no dejes que el perro se suba al sofá⟩ **28 to keep off** : hacer evitar (un tema) **29 to keep weight off** ⟨he has kept the weight off : ha mantenido el peso (tras adelgazar)⟩ **30 to keep on** : mantener (a un empleado) en el puesto **31 to keep out** BLOCK : no dejar pasar **32 to keep up** CONTINUE : seguir con **33 to keep up** MAINTAIN : mantener **34 to keep up one's end of something** : cumplir (con) su parte de algo — *vi* **1** REMAIN, STAY : mantener ⟨to keep quiet : mantener silencio⟩ ⟨to keep still : estarse quieto⟩ ⟨to keep calm : mantener la calma⟩ ⟨she likes to keep busy : le gusta estar ocupada⟩ **2** : conservarse (dícese de los alimentos) ⟨the soup will keep for a week : la sopa se conserva una semana⟩ **3** or **to keep on** (*with a present participle*) CONTINUE : seguir, no dejar de ⟨keep going straight : sigue todo recto⟩ ⟨he keeps on pestering us : no deja de molestarnos⟩ **4 to keep after** NAG : estarle encima a ⟨he kept after me to quit smoking : me estaba encima para que deje de fumar⟩ **5 to keep at it** PERSIST : seguir dándole a ⟨ **6 to keep back** : no acercarse **7 to keep down** : no levantarse **8 to keep from** : abstenerse de ⟨I couldn't keep from laughing : no pude contener la risa⟩ **9 to keep off** : no pisar (el césped, etc.) **10 to keep off** AVOID : evitar (un tema) **11 to keep on** CONTINUE : seguir, continuar ⟨the rain kept on : seguía lloviendo⟩ **12 to keep out** (of): no entrar (en) ⟨the sign says "keep out" : el letrero dice "prohibido el paso"⟩ ⟨to keep out of an argument : no me-

terse en una discusión⟩ **13 to keep to** : no apartarse de (un camino, etc.), quedarse dentro de (una casa, etc.) **14 to keep to** : ceñirse a (las reglas, un tema, etc.) **15 to keep to oneself** : ser muy reservado **16 to keep up** CONTINUE : seguir, continuar ⟨the rain kept up : seguía lloviendo⟩ **17 to keep up** : mantenerse al tanto/corriente (de las noticias, etc.) **18 to keep up** (with) : seguir/mantener el ritmo (de) ⟨I can't keep up (with him) : no puedo seguir su ritmo, no puedo seguirle el ritmo⟩ ⟨to keep up with the Joneses : no ser menos que el vecino⟩ **19 to keep up with someone** : mantener contacto con alguien

keep² *n* **1** TOWER : torreón *m* (de un castillo), torre *f* del homenaje **2** SUSTENANCE : manutención *f*, sustento *m* **3 for keeps** : para siempre

keeper [ˈkiːpər] *n* **1** : guarda *mf* (en un zoológico); conservador *m*, -dora *f* (en un museo) **2** GAMEKEEPER : guardabosque *mf*

keeping [ˈkiːpɪŋ] *n* **1** CONFORMITY : conformidad *f*, acuerdo *m* ⟨in keeping with : de acuerdo con⟩ **2** CARE : cuidado *m* ⟨in the keeping of : al cuidado de⟩

keepsake [ˈkiːpˌseɪk] *n* : recuerdo *m*

keg [ˈkɛg] *n* : barril *m*

kelp [ˈkɛlp] *n* : alga *f* marina

ken [ˈkɛn] *n* **1** SIGHT : vista *f*, alcance *m* de la vista **2** UNDERSTANDING : comprensión *f*, alcance *m* del conocimiento ⟨it's beyond his ken : no lo puede entender⟩

kennel [ˈkɛnəl] *n* : caseta *f* para perros, perrera *f*

Kenyan [ˈkɛnjən, ˈkiːn-] *n* : keniano *m*, -na *f* — **Kenyan** *adj*

kept → **keep**

kerchief [ˈkərtʃəf, -ˌtʃiːf] *n* : pañuelo *m*

kernel [ˈkərnəl] *n* **1** : almendra *f* (de semillas y nueces) **2** : grano *m* (de cereales) **3** CORE : meollo *m* ⟨a kernel of truth : un fondo de verdad⟩

kerosene or **kerosine** [ˈkɛrəˌsiːn, ˌkɛrə'-] *n* : queroseno *m*, kerosén *m*, kerosene *m*

ketchup [ˈkɛtʃəp, ˈkæ-] *n* : salsa *f* catsup

kettle [ˈkɛtəl] *n* **1** : hervidor *m*, pava *f Arg, Bol, Chile* **2** → **teakettle**

kettledrum [ˈkɛtəlˌdrʌm] *n* : timbal *m*

key¹ [ˈkiː] *vt* **1** ATTUNE : adaptar, adecuar **2 to key up** : poner nervioso, inquietar

key² *adj* : clave, fundamental

key³ *n* **1** : llave *f* **2** SOLUTION : clave *f*, soluciones *fpl* **3** : tecla *f* (de un piano o una máquina) **4** : tono *m*, tonalidad *f* (en la música) **5** ISLET, REEF : cayo *m*, islote *m*

keyboard [ˈkiːˌbord] *n* : teclado *m*

keyhole [ˈkiːˌhoːl] *n* : bocallave *f*, ojo *m* (de una cerradura)

keynote¹ [ˈkiːˌnoːt] *vt* **-noted; -noting** **1** : establecer la tónica de (en música) **2** : pronunciar el discurso principal de

keynote² *n* **1** : tónica *f* (en música) **2** : idea *f* fundamental

keypad [ˈkiːˌpæd] *n* : teclado *m* numérico

key ring *n* : llavero *m*

keystroke ['ki:ˌstro:k] n : pulsación f (de tecla)
khaki ['kæki, 'kɑ-] n : caqui m
khan ['kɑn, 'kæn] n : kan m
kibbutz [kə'bʊts, -'bu:ts] n, pl **-butzim** [-ˌbʊt'si:m, -ˌbu:t-] : kibutz m
kibitz ['kɪbɪts] vi : dar consejos molestos
kibitzer ['kɪbɪtsər, kɪ'bɪt-] n : persona f que da consejos molestos
kick¹ ['kɪk] vi 1 : dar patadas (dícese de una persona), cocear (dícese de un animal) 2 PROTEST : patalear, protestar 3 RECOIL : dar un culatazo (dícese de un arma de fuego) 4 **to kick around** fam : andar dando vueltas (por), viajar (por) 5 **to kick back** fam : relajarse 6 **to kick in** fam : arrancar (dícese de un motor, etc.), hacer efecto (dícese de drogas), tener efecto (dícese de una ley) 7 **to kick off** BEGIN : empezar, iniciar 8 **to kick off** : hacer el saque inicial (en deportes) — vt 1 : patear, dar una patada (a alguien) ⟨to kick someone when they're down⟩ ⟨to kick someone when they're down : pegarle a alguien en el suelo⟩ 2 : dejar, perder (un vicio) 3 **to kick around** fam : considerar, barajar (ideas, etc.) 4 **to kick in** fam CONTRIBUTE : contribuir, poner 5 **to kick off** : empezar 6 **to kick oneself** fam : castigarse, culparse 7 **to kick out** EJECT : echar 8 **to kick up** : levantar (polvo, etc.) 9 **to kick up a fuss** fam : armar la bronca
kick² n 1 : patada f, puntapié m, coz f (de un animal) 2 RECOIL : culatazo m (de un arma de fuego) 3 : fuerza f ⟨a drink with a kick : una bebida fuerte⟩ 4 **to get a kick out of** : disfrutar de, deleitarse con
kicker ['kɪkər] n : pateador m, -dora f (en deportes)
kickoff ['kɪkˌɔf] n : saque m (inicial)
kid¹ ['kɪd] v **kidded; kidding** vt 1 FOOL : engañar 2 TEASE : tomarle el pelo (a alguien) 3 **to kid oneself** : hacerse ilusiones — vi JOKE : bromear ⟨I'm only kidding : lo digo en broma⟩
kid² n 1 : chivo m, -va f; cabrito m, -ta f 2 CHILD : chico m, -ca f; niño m, -ña f
kidder ['kɪdər] n : bromista mf
kiddingly ['kɪdɪŋli] adv : en broma
kidnap ['kɪdˌnæp] vt **-napped** or **-naped** [-ˌnæpt], **-napping** or **-naping** [-ˌnæpɪŋ] : secuestrar, raptar
kidnapper or **kidnaper** ['kɪdˌnæpər] n : secuestrador m, -dora f; raptor m, -tora f
kidnapping ['kɪdˌnæpɪŋ] n : secuestro m
kidney ['kɪdni] n, pl **-neys** : riñón m
kidney bean n : frijol m
kill¹ ['kɪl] vt 1 : matar 2 END : acabar con, poner fin a 3 **to kill off** : matar 4 **to kill time** : matar el tiempo
kill² n 1 KILLING : matanza f 2 PREY : presa f
killer ['kɪlər] n : asesino m, -na f
killer whale n : orca f
killjoy ['kɪlˌdʒɔɪ] n : aguafiestas mf
kiln ['kɪl, 'kɪln] n : horno m
kilo ['ki:ˌlo:] n, pl **-los** : kilo m
kilobyte ['kɪləˌbaɪt] n : kilobyte m

kilocycle ['kɪləˌsaɪkəl] n : kilociclo m
kilogram ['kɪləˌgræm, 'ki:-] n : kilogramo m
kilohertz ['kɪləˌhərts] n : kilohertzio m
kilometer [kɪ'lɑmətər, 'kɪləˌmi:-] n : kilómetro m
kilowatt ['kɪləˌwɑt] n : kilovatio m
kilt ['kɪlt] n : falda f escocesa
kilter ['kɪltər] n 1 ORDER : buen estado m 2 **out of kilter** : descompuesto, estropeado
kimono [kə'mo:no, -nə] n, pl **-nos** : kimono m, quimono m
kin ['kɪn] n : familiares mpl, parientes mpl
kind¹ ['kaɪnd] adj : amable, bondadoso, benévolo
kind² n 1 ESSENCE : esencia f ⟨a difference in degree, not in kind : una diferencia cuantitativa y no cualitativa⟩ 2 CATEGORY : especie f, género m 3 TYPE : clase f, tipo m, índole f ⟨they're two of a kind : son tal para cual⟩ ⟨of all kinds : de todo tipo⟩
kindergarten ['kɪndərˌgɑrtən, -dən] n : kinder m, kindergarten m, jardín m de infantes, jardín m de niños Mex
kindhearted [ˌkaɪnd'hɑrtəd] adj : bondadoso, de buen corazón
kindle ['kɪndəl] v **-dled; -dling** vt 1 IGNITE : encender 2 AROUSE : despertar, suscitar — vi : encenderse
kindliness ['kaɪndlinəs] n : bondad f
kindling ['kɪndlɪŋ, 'kɪndlən] n : astillas fpl, leña f
kindly¹ ['kaɪndli] adv 1 AMIABLY : amablemente, bondadosamente 2 COURTEOUSLY : cortésmente, con cortesía ⟨we kindly ask you not smoke : les rogamos que no fumen⟩ 3 PLEASE : por favor 4 **to take kindly to** : aceptar de buena gana
kindly² adj **kindlier; -est** : bondadoso, amable
kindness ['kaɪndnəs] n : bondad f
kind of adv SOMEWHAT : un tanto, algo
kindred¹ ['kɪndrəd] adj SIMILAR : similar, afín ⟨kindred spirits : almas gemelas⟩
kindred² n 1 FAMILY : familia f, parentela f 2 → kin
kinfolk ['kɪnˌfo:k] or **kinfolks** [-ˌfo:ks] npl → kin
king ['kɪŋ] n : rey m
kingdom ['kɪŋdəm] n : reino m
kingfisher ['kɪŋˌfɪʃər] n : martín m pescador
kingly ['kɪŋli] adj **kinglier; -est** : regio, real
king–size ['kɪŋˌsaɪz] or **king–sized** [-ˌsaɪzd] adj : de tamaño muy grande, extra largo (dícese de cigarrillos)
kink ['kɪŋk] n 1 : rizo m (en el pelo), vuelta f (en una cuerda) 2 CRAMP : calambre m ⟨to have a kink in the neck : tener tortícolis⟩
kinky ['kɪŋki] adj **kinkier; -est** : rizado (dícese del pelo), enroscado (dícese de una cuerda)
kinship ['kɪnˌʃɪp] n : parentesco m
kinsman ['kɪnzmən] n, pl **-men** [-mən, -ˌmɛn] : familiar m, pariente m

kinswoman [ˈkɪnzˌwʊmən] *n, pl* **-women** [-ˌwɪmən] : familiar *f*, pariente *f*

kiosk [ˈkiːˌɑsk] *n* : quiosco *m*

kipper [ˈkɪpər] *n* : arenque *m* ahumado

kiss¹ [ˈkɪs] *vt* : besar — *vi* : besarse

kiss² *n* : beso *m* ⟨to blow someone a kiss : tirarle un beso a alguien⟩

kit [ˈkɪt] *n* **1** SET : juego *m*, kit *m* **2** CASE : estuche *m*, caja *f* **3** first–aid kit : botiquín *m* **4** → tool kit **5** travel kit : neceser *m*

kitchen [ˈkɪtʃən] *n* : cocina *f*

kitchenette [ˌkɪtʃəˈnɛt] *n* : cocineta *f*

kite [ˈkaɪt] *n* : cometa *f*, papalote *m Mex* ⟨to fly a kite : hacer volar una cometa⟩

kith [ˈkɪθ] *n* : amigos *mpl* ⟨kith and kin : amigos y parientes⟩

kitten [ˈkɪtən] *n* : gatito *m*, -ta *f*

kitty [ˈkɪti] *n, pl* **-ties 1** FUND, POOL : bote *m*, fondo *m* común **2** CAT : gato *m*, gatito *m*

kitty–corner [ˈkɪtiˌkɔrnər] *or* **kitty–cornered** [-nərd] → **catercorner**

kiwi [ˈkiːˌwiː] *or* **kiwifruit** [ˈkiːˌwiːˌfruːt] *n* : kiwi *m*

Kleenex [ˈkliːˌnɛks] *trademark* se usa para un pañuelo de papel

kleptomania [ˌklɛptəˈmeɪniə] *n* : cleptomanía *f*

kleptomaniac [ˌklɛptəˈmeɪniˌæk] *n* : cleptómano *m*, -na *f*

klutz [ˈklʌts] *n* : torpe *mf*

knack [ˈnæk] *n* : maña *f*, facilidad *f* ⟨to have a knack for something : tener habilidad para algo⟩ ⟨to get the knack of something : agarrarle la onda a algo⟩

knapsack [ˈnæpˌsæk] *n* : mochila *f*, morral *m*

knave [ˈneɪv] *n* : bellaco *m*, pícaro *m*

knead [ˈniːd] *vt* **1** : amasar, sobar **2** MASSAGE : masajear

knee [ˈniː] *n* : rodilla *f*

kneecap [ˈniːˌkæp] *n* : rótula *f*

kneel [ˈniːl] *vi* **knelt** [ˈnɛlt] *or* **kneeled** [ˈniːld]; **kneeling** : arrodillarse, ponerse de rodillas

knell [ˈnɛl] *n* : doble *m*, toque *m* ⟨death knell : toque de difuntos⟩

knew → **know**

knickers [ˈnɪkərz] *npl* : pantalones *mpl* bombachos de media pierna

knickknack [ˈnɪkˌnæk] *n* : chuchería *f*, baratija *f*

knife¹ [ˈnaɪf] *vt* **knifed** [ˈnaɪft]; **knifing** : acuchillar, apuñalar

knife² *n, pl* **knives** [ˈnaɪvz] : cuchillo *m*

knight¹ [ˈnaɪt] *vt* : conceder el título de *Sir* a

knight² *n* **1** : caballero *m* ⟨knight errant : caballero andante⟩ **2** : caballo *m* (en ajedrez) **3** : uno que tiene el título de *Sir*

knighthood [ˈnaɪtˌhʊd] *n* **1** : caballería *f* **2** : título *m* de *Sir*

knightly [ˈnaɪtli] *adj* : caballeresco

knit¹ [ˈnɪt] *v* **knit** *or* **knitted** [ˈnɪt̬əd]; **knitting** *vt* **1** UNITE : unir, enlazar **2** : tejer ⟨to knit a sweater : tejer un suéter⟩ **3** to knit one's brows : fruncir el ceño — *vi* **1** : tejer **2** : soldarse (dícese de los huesos)

knit² *n* : prenda *f* tejida

knitter [ˈnɪt̬ər] *n* : tejedor *m*, -dora *f*

knitwear [ˈnɪtˌwær] *n* : ropa *f* de punto

knob [ˈnɑb] *n* **1** LUMP : bulto *m*, protuberancia *f* **2** HANDLE : perilla *f*, tirador *m*, botón *m*

knobbed [ˈnɑbd] *adj* **1** KNOTTY : nudoso **2** : que tiene perilla o botón

knobby [ˈnɑbi] *adj* **knobbier; -est 1** KNOTTY : nudoso **2 knobby knees** : rodillas *fpl* huesudas

knock¹ [ˈnɑk] *vt* **1** HIT, RAP : golpear, golpetear **2** : hacer chocar ⟨they knocked heads : se dieron en la cabeza⟩ **3** CRITICIZE : criticar **4 to knock around** *fam* BEAT : pegarle a **5 to knock back** *fam* DRINK : beberse, tomarse **6 to knock dead** *fam* STUN : dejar boquiabierto **7 to knock down** : derribar, echar abajo (una puerta, etc.), tirar al suelo (a una persona) **8 to knock off** *fam* KILL : asesinar, liquidar *fam* **9 to knock off** *fam* : quitar (puntos, etc.) ⟨he knocked 10% off the price : rebajó el precio un 10%⟩ **10 to knock off** *fam* RIP OFF : copiar (un diseño, etc.) ilegalmente **11 knock it off!** *fam* : ¡basta ya!, ¡déjala! **12 to knock out** : dejar sin sentido, dejar fuera de combate (en el boxeo) **13 to knock out** ELIMINATE : eliminar **14 to knock out** DESTROY : destruir (un edificio, etc.) ⟨the storm knocked out the power : la tormenta nos dejó sin luz⟩ **15 to knock oneself out** *fam* : matarse (trabajando, etc.) ⟨go ahead—knock yourself out! : ¡adelante!, ¡disfruta!⟩ **16 to knock over** OVERTURN : tirar, volcar **17 to knock over** *fam* ROB : robar **18 to knock up** *fam* : dejar embarazada — *vi* **1** RAP : dar un golpe, llamar (a la puerta) **2** COLLIDE : darse, chocar **3 to knock around in** *fam* : viajar por **4 to knock off** *fam* : salir del trabajo ⟨to knock off early : salir temprano⟩

knock² *n* : golpe *m*, llamada *f* (a la puerta), golpeteo *m* (de un motor)

knocker [ˈnɑkər] *n* : aldaba *f*, llamador *m*

knock–kneed [ˈnɑkˈniːd] *adj* : patizambo

knockout [ˈnɑkˌaʊt] *n* **1** : nocaut *m*, knockout *m* (en deportes) **2 to be a knockout** *fam* : estar bueno *fam*, ser muy guapo

knoll [ˈnoːl] *n* : loma *f*, otero *m*, montículo *m*

knot¹ [ˈnɑt] *v* **knotted; knotting** *vt* : anudar — *vi* : anudarse

knot² *n* **1** : nudo *m* (en cordel o madera), nódulo *m* (en los músculos) **2** CLUSTER : grupo *m* **3** : nudo *m* (unidad de velocidad)

knotty [ˈnɑti] *adj* **knottier; -est 1** GNARLED : nudoso **2** COMPLEX : espinoso, enredado, complejo

know [ˈnoː] *v* **knew** [ˈnuː, ˈnjuː]; **known** [ˈnoːn]; **knowing** *vt* **1** : saber ⟨to know French/the answer : sabe francés/la respuesta⟩ ⟨I might/should have known that . . . : debería haber sabido que . . .⟩ ⟨he made it known that . . . : hizo saber que . . .⟩ ⟨she let me know that . . . : me avisó que . . .⟩ ⟨to know something for a fact : constarse que algo es así⟩ **2** : conocer (a una persona, un lugar) ⟨do you know Julia? : ¿conoces a Julia?⟩ ⟨she knows the city well : conoce bien la ciudad⟩ ⟨he's better known as . . . : es más conocido por el nombre de . . .⟩ ⟨to be known for : conocerse por⟩ **3** RECOGNIZE : reconocer **4** DISCERN, DISTINGUISH : distinguir, discernir **5 before you know it** : antes de que te des cuenta **6 for all I know** : que yo sepa **7 God/heaven (only) knows** : quién sabe **8 if you know what I mean** : si me entiendes **9 not to know the first thing about** : no saber nada de, no tener ni idea de **10 to know how to do something** : saber hacer algo **11 to know something inside out** or **to know something like the back of your hand** : saberse algo al dedillo **12 to know what's best** : saber lo que es lo mejor — *vi* **1** : saber ⟨yes, I know : sí, lo sé⟩ ⟨how should I know? : ¿qué sé yo?⟩ **2 to know best** : saber lo que es lo mejor **3 to know better** ⟨you're old enough to know better : a tu edad no debes hacer eso⟩ ⟨she doesn't know any better : es demasiado joven/novata (etc.) para saber lo que hace⟩ ⟨you know better than to ask : ya deberías saber que es mejor no preguntar⟩ **4 you know** (*used for emphasis*) ⟨you know, we really have to go : bueno, ya es hora de irnos⟩ ⟨it's cold out, you know : hace frío, ¿eh?⟩ **5 you know** (*expressing uncertainty*) ⟨we're going to, you know, hang out : vamos a . . . pues nada, pasar el rato⟩ **6 you never know** : nunca se sabe

knowable ['noːəbəl] *adj* : conocible
know–how ['noː,hau] *n* EXPERTISE : pericia *f*

knowing ['noːɪŋ] *adj* **1** KNOWLEDGEABLE : informado ⟨a knowing look : una mirada de complicidad⟩ **2** ASTUTE : astuto **3** DELIBERATE : deliberado, intencional
knowingly ['noːɪŋli] *adv* **1** : con complicidad ⟨she smiled knowingly : sonrió con una mirada de complicidad⟩ **2** DELIBERATELY : a sabiendas, adrede, a propósito
know–it–all ['noːɪt,ɔl] *n* : sabelotodo *mf fam*
knowledge ['nɑlɪdʒ] *n* **1** AWARENESS : conocimiento *m* **2** LEARNING : conocimientos *mpl*, saber *m*
knowledgeable ['nɑlɪdʒəbəl] *adj* : informado, entendido, enterado
known ['noːn] *adj* : conocido, familiar
knuckle ['nʌkəl] *n* : nudillo *m*
KO[1] [,keɪˈoː, 'keɪ,oː] *vt* **KO'd; KO'ing** KNOCK OUT : noquear (en deportes)
KO[2] *n* KNOCKOUT : nocaut *m*, knockout *m* (en deportes)
koala [koˈwalə] *n* : koala *m*
Koran [kəˈran, -ˈræn] *n* **the Koran** : el Corán
Korean [kəˈriːən] *n* **1** : coreano *m*, -na *f* **2** : coreano *m* (idioma) — **Korean** *adj*
kosher ['koːʃər] *adj* : aprobado por la ley judía
kowtow [,kauˈtau, 'kau,tau] *vi* **to kowtow to** : humillarse ante, doblegarse ante
krypton ['krɪp,tɑn] *n* : criptón *m*
kudos ['kjuː,dɑs, 'kuː-, -,doːz] *n* : fama *f*, renombre *m*
kumquat ['kʌm,kwɑt] *n* : naranjita *f* china
Kurd ['kurd, 'kərd] *n* : kurdo *m*, -da *f*
Kurdish ['kurdɪʃ, 'kər-] *adj* : kurdo
Kuwaiti [kuˈweɪti] *n* : kuwaití *mf* — **Kuwaiti** *adj*

L

l ['ɛl] *n, pl* **l's** or **ls** ['ɛlz] : duodécima letra del alfabeto inglés
la ['lɑ] *n* : la *m* (en el canto)
lab ['læb] → **laboratory**
label[1] ['leɪbəl] *vt* **-beled** or **-belled; -beling** or **-belling 1** : etiquetar, poner etiqueta a **2** BRAND, CATEGORIZE : calificar, tildar, tachar ⟨they labeled him as a fraud : lo calificaron de farsante⟩
label[2] *n* **1** : etiqueta *f*, rótulo *m* **2** DESCRIPTION : calificación *f*, descripción *f* **3** BRAND : marca *f*
labial ['leɪbiəl] *adj* : labial
labor[1] ['leɪbər] *vi* **1** WORK : trabajar **2** STRUGGLE : avanzar penosamente (dícese de una persona), funcionar con dificultad (dícese de un motor) **3 to labor under a delusion** : hacerse ilusiones, tener una falsa impresión — *vt* BELABOR : insistir en, extenderse sobre
labor[2] *n* **1** EFFORT, WORK : trabajo *m*, esfuerzos *mpl* **2** : parto *m* ⟨to be in labor

: estar de parto⟩ **3** TASK : tarea *f*, labor *m* **4** WORKERS : mano *f* de obra
laboratory ['læbrə,tori, lə'bɔrə-] *n, pl* **-ries** : laboratorio *m*
Labor Day *n* : Día *m* del Trabajo
laborer ['leɪbərər] *n* : peón *m*; trabajador *m*, -dora *f*
laborious [lə'boriəs] *adj* : laborioso, difícil
laboriously [lə'boriəsli] *adv* : laboriosamente, trabajosamente
labor union → **union**
labyrinth ['læbə,rɪnθ] *n* : laberinto *m*
labyrinthine [,læbə'rɪnθən, -,θaɪn, -,θiːn] *adj* : laberíntico
lace[1] ['leɪs] *vt* **laced; lacing 1** TIE : acordonar, atar los cordones de **2** : adornar de encaje ⟨I laced the dress in white : adorné el vestido de encaje blanco⟩ **3** SPIKE : echar licor a
lace[2] *n* **1** : encaje *m* **2** SHOELACE : cordón *m* (de zapatos), agujeta *f* Mex
lacerate ['læsə,reɪt] *vt* **-ated; -ating** : lacerar

laceration [ˌlæsəˈreɪʃən] *n* : laceración *f*

lack[1] [ˈlæk] *vt* : carecer de, no tener ⟨she lacks patience : carece de paciencia⟩ — *vi* : faltar ⟨they lack for nothing : no les falta nada⟩

lack[2] *n* : falta *f*, carencia *f*

lackadaisical [ˌlækəˈdeɪzɪkəl] *adj* : apático, indiferente, lánguido — **lackadaisically** [-kli] *adv*

lackey [ˈlæki] *n, pl* **-eys** 1 FOOTMAN : lacayo *m* 2 TOADY : adulador *m*, -dora *f*

lackluster [ˈlækˌlʌstər] *adj* 1 DULL : sin brillo, apagado, deslustrado 2 MEDIOCRE : deslucido, mediocre

laconic [ləˈkɑnɪk] *adj* : lacónico — **laconically** [-nɪkli] *adv*

lacquer[1] [ˈlækər] *vt* : laquear, pintar con laca

lacquer[2] *n* : laca *f*

lacrosse [ləˈkrɔs] *n* : lacrosse *m*

lacy [ˈleɪsi] *adj* **lacier; -est** : de encaje, como de encaje

lad [ˈlæd] *n* : muchacho *m*, niño *m*

ladder [ˈlædər] *n* : escalera *f*

laden [ˈleɪdən] *adj* : cargado

ladle[1] [ˈleɪdəl] *vt* **-dled; -dling** : servir con cucharón

ladle[2] *n* : cucharón *m*, cazo *m*

lady [ˈleɪdi] *n, pl* **-dies** 1 : señora *f*, dama *f* 2 WOMAN : mujer *f*

ladybird [ˈleɪdiˌbərd] → **ladybug**

ladybug [ˈleɪdiˌbʌg] *n* : mariquita *f*

lag[1] [ˈlæg] *vi* **lagged; lagging to lag behind** 1 : quedarse atrás, quedarse rezagado, ir a la zaga ⟨she lagged behind the group⟩ : se quedó atrás (del grupo), iba a la zaga (del grupo)⟩ ⟨we lag behind other countries : quedamos rezagados con respecto a otros países, vamos a la zaga de otros países⟩ 2 : atrasarse, retrasarse (con respecto a un programa, etc.)

lag[2] *n* 1 DELAY : retraso *m*, demora *f* 2 INTERVAL : lapso *m*, intervalo *m*

lager [ˈlɑgər] *n* : cerveza *f* rubia

laggard[1] [ˈlægərd] *adj* : retardado, retrasado

laggard[2] *n* : rezagado *m*, -da *f*

lagoon [ləˈguːn] *n* : laguna *f*

laid → **lay**[1]

laid–back [ˈleɪdˈbæk] *adj* : tranquilo, relajado

lain *pp* → **lie**[1]

lair [ˈlær] *n* : guarida *f*, madriguera *f*

laissez–faire [ˌlɛˌseɪˈfær, ˌlɛˌzeɪ-] *n* : liberalismo *m* económico

laity [ˈleɪəti] *n* **the laity** : los laicos, el laicado

lake [ˈleɪk] *n* : lago *m*

lama [ˈlɑmə] *n* : lama *m*

lamb [ˈlæm] *n* 1 : cordero *m*, borrego *m* (animal) 2 : carne *f* de cordero

lambaste [læmˈbeɪst] *or* **lambast** [-ˈbæst] *vt* **-basted; -basting** 1 BEAT, THRASH : golpear, azotar, darle una paliza (a alguien) 2 CENSURE : arremeter contra, censurar

lame[1] [ˈleɪm] *vt* **lamed; laming** : lisiar, hacer cojo

lame[2] *adj* **lamer; lamest** 1 : cojo, renco, rengo 2 WEAK : pobre, débil, poco convincente ⟨a lame excuse : una excusa débil⟩

lame duck *n* : persona *f* sin poder ⟨a lame-duck President : un presidente saliente⟩

lamely [ˈleɪmli] *adv* : sin convicción

lameness [ˈleɪmnəs] *n* 1 : cojera *f*, renquera *f* 2 : falta *f* de convicción, debilidad *f*, pobreza *f* ⟨the lameness of her response : la pobreza de su respuesta⟩

lament[1] [ləˈmɛnt] *vt* 1 MOURN : llorar, llorar por 2 DEPLORE : lamentar, deplorar — *vi* : llorar

lament[2] *n* : lamento *m*

lamentable [ˈlæməntəbəl, ləˈmɛntə-] *adj* : lamentable, deplorable — **lamentably** [-bli] *adv*

lamentation [ˌlæmənˈteɪʃən] *n* : lamentación *f*, lamento *m*

laminate[1] [ˈlæməˌneɪt] *vt* **-nated; -nating** : laminar

laminate[2] [ˈlæmənət] *n* : laminado *m*

laminated [ˈlæməˌneɪtəd] *adj* : laminado

lamp [ˈlæmp] *n* : lámpara *f*

lampoon[1] [læmˈpuːn] *vt* : satirizar

lampoon[2] *n* : sátira *f*

lamppost [ˈlæmpˌpoːst] *n* : farol *m*, farola *f*

lamprey [ˈlæmpri] *n, pl* **-preys** : lamprea *f*

lampshade [ˈlæmpˌʃeɪd] *n* : pantalla *f* (de lámpara)

lance[1] [ˈlæn/s] *vt* **lanced; lancing** : sajar

lance[2] *n* : lanza *f*

lance corporal *n* : cabo *m* interino, soldado *m* de primera clase

land[1] [ˈlænd] *vt* 1 : desembarcar (pasajeros de un barco), hacer aterrizar (un avión) 2 CATCH : pescar, sacar (un pez) del agua 3 GAIN, SECURE : conseguir, ganar ⟨to land a job : conseguir empleo⟩ 4 DELIVER : dar, asestar ⟨he landed a punch : asestó un puñetazo⟩ — *vi* 1 : aterrizar, tomar tierra, atracar ⟨the plane just landed : el avión acaba de aterrizar⟩ ⟨the ship landed an hour ago : el barco atracó hace una hora⟩ 2 ALIGHT : posarse, aterrizar ⟨to land on one's feet : caer de pie⟩ 3 FALL : caer 4 END UP, WIND UP : ir a parar

land[2] *n* 1 GROUND : tierra *f* ⟨dry land : tierra firme⟩ 2 TERRAIN : terreno *m* 3 NATION : país *m*, nación *f* 4 DOMAIN : mundo *m*, dominio *m* ⟨the land of dreams : el mundo de los sueños⟩

landfill [ˈlændˌfɪl] *n* : vertedero *m* (de basuras)

landing [ˈlændɪŋ] *n* 1 : aterrizaje *m* (de aviones), desembarco *m* (de barcos) 2 : descanso *m*, descansillo *m* Spain (de una escalera)

landing field *n* : campo *m* de aterrizaje

landing pad *n* : plataforma *f* de aterrizaje

landing strip → **airstrip**

landlady [ˈlændˌleɪdi] *n, pl* **-dies** : casera *f*, dueña *f*, arrendadora *f*

landless [ˈlændləs] *adj* : sin tierra

landlocked [ˈlændˌlɑkt] *adj* : sin salida al mar

landlord [ˈlænd,lɔrd] n : dueño m, casero m, arrendador m

landlubber [ˈlænd,lʌbər] n : marinero m de agua dulce

landmark [ˈlænd,mɑrk] n 1 : señal f (geográfica), punto m de referencia 2 MILESTONE : hito m ⟨a landmark in our history : un hito en nuestra historia⟩ 3 MONUMENT : monumento m histórico

landowner [ˈlænd,oːnər] n : hacendado m, -da f; terrateniente mf

landscape¹ [ˈlænd,skeɪp] vt -scaped; -scaping : ajardinar

landscape² n : paisaje m

landscaper [ˈlænd,skeɪpər] n : paisajista mf

landscaping [ˈlænd,skeɪpɪŋ] n : paisajismo m

landslide [ˈlænd,slaɪd] n 1 : desprendimiento m de tierras, derrumbe m 2 **landslide victory** : victoria f arrolladora

landward [ˈlændwərd] adv : en dirección de la tierra, hacia tierra

lane [ˈleɪn] n 1 PATH, WAY : camino m, sendero m 2 : carril m (de una carretera)

language [ˈlæŋgwɪdʒ] n 1 : idioma m, lengua f ⟨the English language : el idioma inglés⟩ 2 : lenguaje m ⟨body language : lenguaje corporal⟩

languid [ˈlæŋgwɪd] adj : lánguido — **languidly** adv

languish [ˈlæŋgwɪʃ] vi 1 WEAKEN : languidecer, debilitarse 2 PINE : consumirse, suspirar (por) ⟨to languish for love : suspirar por el amor⟩ ⟨he languished in prison : estuvo pudriéndose en la cárcel⟩

languor [ˈlæŋgər] n : languidez f

languorous [ˈlæŋgərəs] adj : lánguido — **languorously** adv

lank [ˈlæŋk] adj 1 THIN : delgado, larguirucho fam 2 LIMP : lacio

lanky [ˈlæŋki] adj **lankier; -est** : delgado, larguirucho fam

lanolin [ˈlænəlɪn] n : lanolina f

lantern [ˈlæntərn] n : linterna f, farol m

Laotian [leɪˈoːʃən, ˈlaʊʃən] n : laosiano m, -na f — **Laotian** adj

lap¹ [ˈlæp] v **lapped; lapping** vt 1 FOLD : plegar, doblar 2 WRAP : envolver 3 : lamer, besar ⟨waves were lapping the shore : las olas lamían la orilla⟩ 4 **to lap up** : beber a lengüetadas (como un gato) — vi OVERLAP : traslaparse

lap² n 1 : falda f, regazo m (del cuerpo) 2 OVERLAP : traslapo m 3 : vuelta f (en deportes) 4 STAGE : etapa f (de un viaje)

lapdog [ˈlæp,dɔg] n : perro m faldero

lapel [ləˈpɛl] n : solapa f

lapp [ˈlæp] n : lapón m, -pona f — **Lapp** adj

lapse¹ [ˈlæps] vi **lapsed; lapsing** 1 FALL, SLIP : caer ⟨to lapse into bad habits : caer en malos hábitos⟩ ⟨to lapse into unconsciousness : perder el conocimiento⟩ ⟨to lapse into silence : quedarse callado⟩ 2 FADE : decaer, desvanecerse ⟨her dedication lapsed : su dedicación se desvaneció⟩ 3 CEASE : cancelarse, perderse 4 ELAPSE : transcurrir, pasar 5 EXPIRE : caducar

lapse² n 1 SLIP : lapsus m, desliz m, falla f ⟨a lapse of memory : una falla de memoria⟩ 2 INTERVAL : lapso m, intervalo m, período m 3 EXPIRATION : caducidad f

laptop¹ [ˈlæp,tɑp] adj : portátil, laptop

laptop² n : laptop m

larcenous [ˈlɑrsənəs] adj : de robo

larceny [ˈlɑrsəni] n, pl **-nies** : robo m, hurto m

larch [ˈlɑrtʃ] n : alerce m

lard [ˈlɑrd] n : manteca f de cerdo

larder [ˈlɑrdər] n : despensa f, alacena f

large [ˈlɑrdʒ] adj **larger; largest** 1 BIG : grande 2 COMPREHENSIVE : amplio, extenso 3 **by and large** : por lo general 4 **at large** : en general ⟨society at large : la sociedad en general⟩ 5 **at large** FREE : prófugo, suelto ⟨the criminal is still at large : el criminal permanece prófugo⟩ 6 **at large** : general, que habla/escribe (etc.) de diversos temas

largely [ˈlɑrdʒli] adv : en gran parte, en su mayoría

largeness [ˈlɑrdʒnəs] n : lo grande

largesse or **largess** [lɑrˈʒɛs, -ˈdʒɛs] n : generosidad f, largueza f

lariat [ˈlæriət] n : lazo m

lark [ˈlɑrk] n 1 FUN : diversión f ⟨what a lark! : ¡qué divertido!⟩ 2 : alondra f (pájaro)

larva [ˈlɑrvə] n, pl **-vae** [-,viː, -,vaɪ] : larva f — **larval** [-vəl] adj

laryngitis [,lærənˈdʒaɪtəs] n : laringitis f

larynx [ˈlærɪŋks] n, pl **-rynges** [ləˈrɪn,dʒiːz] or **-ynxes** [ˈlærɪŋksəz] : laringe f

lasagna [ləˈzɑnjə] n : lasaña f

lascivious [ləˈsɪviəs] adj : lascivo

lasciviousness [ləˈsɪviəsnəs] n : lascivia f, lujuria f

laser [ˈleɪzər] n : láser m

laser disc n : disco m láser

laser printer n : impresora f láser

lash¹ [ˈlæʃ] vt 1 WHIP : azotar 2 BIND : atar, amarrar

lash² n 1 WHIP : látigo m 2 STROKE : latigazo m 3 EYELASH : pestaña f

lass [ˈlæs] or **lassie** [ˈlæsi] n : muchacha f, chica f

lasso¹ [ˈlæ,soː, læˈsuː] vt : lazar

lasso² n, pl **-sos** or **-soes** : lazo m, reata f Mex

last¹ [ˈlæst] vi 1 CONTINUE : durar ⟨how long will it last? : ¿cuánto durará?⟩ 2 ENDURE : aguantar, durar 3 SURVIVE : durar, sobrevivir 4 SUFFICE : durar, bastar — vt 1 : durar ⟨it will last you a lifetime : te durará toda la vida⟩ 2 **to last out** : aguantar

last² adv 1 : en último lugar, al último ⟨we came in last : llegamos en último lugar⟩ 2 : por última vez, la última vez ⟨I saw him last in Bogota : lo vi por última vez en Bogotá⟩ 3 FINALLY : por último, en conclusión ⟨last but not least : por último, pero no por ello menos importante⟩

last³ adj 1 FINAL : último, final 2 PREVIOUS : pasado ⟨last year : el año pasado⟩

last[4] *n* **1** : el último, la última, lo último ⟨at last : por fin, al fin, finalmente⟩ **2** : horma *f* (de zapatero)

last–ditch ['læst'dɪtʃ] *adj* : desesperado, último

lasting ['læstɪŋ] *adj* : perdurable, duradero, estable

lastly ['læstli] *adv* : por último, finalmente

last–minute ['læst'mɪnət] *adj* : de última hora

latch[1] ['lætʃ] *vt* **1** : cerrar con picaporte **2 to latch on to** *or* **to latch onto** GRAB : agarrarse de **3 to latch on to** *or* **to latch onto** : pegarse a (alguien), abrazar (una costumbre, etc.)

latch[2] *n* : picaporte *m*, pestillo *m*, pasador *m*

late[1] ['leɪt] *adv* **later; latest 1** : tarde ⟨to arrive late : llegar tarde⟩ ⟨to sleep late : dormir hasta tarde⟩ ⟨I'm running late : voy a llegar tarde⟩ **2** : a última hora, a finales ⟨late in the evening : a últimas horas de la tarde⟩ ⟨late in the month : a finales del mes⟩ **3** RECENTLY : recién, últimamente ⟨as late as last year : todavía en el año pasado⟩ **4 of late → lately**

late[2] *adj* **later; latest 1** TARDY : tardío ⟨I'm sorry I'm late : perdón por llegar tarde⟩ ⟨I was two hours late : llegué dos horas tarde⟩ ⟨the plane was two hours late : el avión llegó con dos horas de retraso⟩ ⟨we had a late start : salimos tarde⟩ ⟨the train's late arrival/departure : el retraso en la llegada/salida del tren⟩ **2** : avanzado ⟨because of the late hour : a causa de la hora avanzada⟩ ⟨he's in his late thirties : tiene cerca de cuarenta años⟩ **3** DECEASED : difunto, fallecido **4** RECENT : reciente, último ⟨our last quarrel : nuestra última pelea⟩ **5 it's getting late** : se hace tarde **6 late in the day** : tarde ⟨it's a little late in the day for an apology : ya es un poco tarde para pedir disculpas⟩

latecomer ['leɪt,kʌmər] *n* : rezagado *m*, -da *f*

lately ['leɪtli] *adv* : recientemente, últimamente

lateness ['leɪtnəs] *n* **1** DELAY : retraso *m*, atraso *m*, tardanza *f* **2** : lo avanzado (de la hora)

latent ['leɪtənt] *adj* : latente — **latently** *adv*

later[1] ['leɪtər] *adv* **1** : más tarde, después ⟨she returned later : volvió más tarde⟩ ⟨later in the week : a finales de la semana⟩ **2 later on** : más tarde, después **3 no later than** : a más tardar **4 see you later!** : ¡hasta luego!

later[2] *adj* **1** : posterior, ulterior ⟨his later works : sus obras posteriores⟩ ⟨in her later years : en su madurez⟩ **2 at a later time/date** : más tarde, más adelante

lateral ['lætərəl] *adj* : lateral — **laterally** *adv*

latest[1] ['leɪtəst] *adj* : último

latest[2] *n* **1** : lo último **2 at the latest** : a más tardar

latex ['leɪ,tɛks] *n, pl* **-tices** ['leɪtə,si:z, 'lætə-] *or* **-texes** : látex *m*

lath ['læθ, 'læð] *n, pl* **laths** *or* **lath** : listón *m*

lathe ['leɪð] *n* : torno *m*

lather[1] ['læðər] *vt* : enjabonar — *vi* : espumar, hacer espuma

lather[2] *n* **1** : espuma *f* (de jabón) **2** : sudor *m* (de caballo) **3 to get into a lather** : ponerse histérico

Latin[1] *adj* : latino

Latin[2] *n* **1** : latín *m* (idioma) **2 → Latin American**

Latin–American ['lætənə'mrikən] *adj* : latinoamericano

Latin American *n* : latinoamericano *m*, -na *f*

latitude ['lætə,tu:d, -,tju:d] *n* : latitud *f*

latrine [lə'tri:n] *n* : letrina *f*

latte ['lɑ,teɪ] *n* : café *m* con leche

latter ['lætər] *adj* **1** SECOND : segundo **2** LAST : último **3 the latter** : éste, ésta, éstos *pl*, éstas *pl*

lattice ['lætəs] *n* : enrejado *m*, celosía *f*

Latvian ['lætvian] *n* : letón *m*, -tona *f* — **Latvian** *adj*

laud[1] ['lɔd] *vt* : alabar, loar

laud[2] *n* : alabanza *f*, loa *f*

laudable ['lɔdəbəl] *adj* : loable — **laudably** [-bli] *adv*

laugh[1] ['læf] *vi* : reír, reírse **2 to laugh at** : reírse de — *vt* **to laugh off** : tomar en/a broma

laugh[2] *n* **1** LAUGHTER : risa *f* **2** JOKE : chiste *m*, broma *f* ⟨he did it for a laugh : lo hizo en broma, lo hizo para divertirse⟩

laughable ['læfəbəl] *adj* : risible, de risa

laughingstock ['læfɪŋ,stɑk] *n* : hazmerreír *m*

laughter ['læftər] *n* : risa *f*, risas *fpl*

launch[1] ['lɔntʃ] *vt* **1** HURL : lanzar **2** : botar (un barco) **3** START : iniciar, empezar **4** : lanzar, abrir (un programa)

launch[2] *n* **1** : lancha *f* (bote) **2** LAUNCHING : lanzamiento *m*

launchpad ['lɔntʃ,pæd] *n* : plataforma *f* de lanzamiento

launder ['lɔndər] *vt* **1** : lavar y planchar (ropa) **2** : blanquear, lavar (dinero)

launderer ['lɔndərər] *n* : lavandero *m*, -ra *f*

laundress ['lɔndrəs] *n* : lavandera *f*

laundry ['lɔndri] *n, pl* **laundries 1** : ropa *f* sucia, ropa *f* para lavar ⟨to do the laundry : lavar la ropa⟩ **2** : lavandería *f* (servicio de lavar)

laureate ['lɔriət] *n* : laureado *m*, -da *f* ⟨poet laureate : poeta laureado⟩

laurel ['lɔrəl] *n* **1** : laurel *m* (planta) **2 laurels** *npl* : laureles *mpl* ⟨to rest on one's laurels : dormirse uno en sus laureles⟩

lava ['lɑvə, 'læ-] *n* : lava *f*

lavatory ['lævə,tori] *n, pl* **-ries** : baño *m*, cuarto *m* de baño

lavender ['lævəndər] *n* : lavanda *f*, espliego *m*

lavish[1] ['lævɪʃ] *vt* : prodigar (a), colmar (de)

lavish[2] *adj* **1** EXTRAVAGANT : pródigo, generoso, derrochador **2** ABUNDANT

: abundante **3** LUXURIOUS : lujoso, espléndido

lavishly ['lævɪʃli] *adv* : con generosidad, espléndidamente ⟨to live lavishly : vivir a lo grande⟩

lavishness ['lævɪʃnəs] *n* : generosidad *f*, esplendidez *f*

law ['lɔ] *n* **1** : ley *f* ⟨to break the law : violar la ley⟩ **2** : derecho *m* ⟨criminal law : derecho criminal⟩ ⟨to study law : estudiar derecho⟩ ⟨law school : facultad de Derecho⟩ **3** : abogacía *f* ⟨to practice law : ejercer la abogacía⟩ **4** PRINCIPLE : ley *f* ⟨the laws of physics : las leyes de la física⟩ **5** RULE : ley *f* (en religión, etc.) **6 the law** POLICE : policía *f* ⟨to be in trouble with the law : tener problemas con la ley⟩

law–abiding ['lɔə,baɪdɪŋ] *adj* : observante de la ley

lawbreaker ['lɔ,breɪkər] *n* : infractor *m*, -tora *f* de la ley

lawful ['lɔfəl] *adj* : legal, legítimo, lícito — **lawfully** *adv*

lawgiver ['lɔ,gɪvər] *n* : legislador *m*, -dora *f*

lawless ['lɔləs] *adj* : anárquico, ingobernable — **lawlessly** *adv*

lawlessness ['lɔləsnəs] *n* : anarquía *f*, desorden *m*

lawmaker ['lɔ,meɪkər] *n* : legislador *m*, -dora *f*

lawman ['lɔmən] *n, pl* **-men** [-mən, -,mɛn] : agente *m* del orden

lawn ['lɔn] *n* : césped *m*, pasto *m*

lawn mower *n* : cortadora *f* de césped

lawsuit ['lɔ,su:t] *n* : pleito *m*, litigio *m*, demanda *f*

lawyer ['lɔɪər, 'lɔjər] *n* : abogado *m*, -da *f*

lax ['læks] *adj* : laxo, relajado — **laxly** *adv*

laxative ['læksətɪv] *n* : laxante *m*

laxity ['læksəti] *n* : relajación *f*, descuido *m*, falta *f* de rigor

lay¹ ['leɪ] *v* **laid** ['leɪd]; **laying** *vt* **1** PLACE, PUT : poner, colocar ⟨she laid it on the table : lo puso en la mesa⟩ ⟨to lay a hand/finger on someone : ponerle a alguien la mano encima⟩ **2** INSTALL : poner, colocar (ladrillos, etc.), tender (vías, cables, etc.) ⟨to lay the foundation : poner los cimientos⟩ **3** PREPARE : preparar ⟨to lay a trap : tender una trampa⟩ ⟨the best-laid plans : los planes mejor trazados⟩ **4** BET : apostar **5** PLACE : poner (énfasis, etc.) ⟨to lay the blame on : echarle la culpa a⟩ **6 to lay aside/by** SAVE : guardar, ahorrar **10 to lay down** IMPOSE, ESTABLISH : imponer, establecer **11 to lay down** : dejar, deponer (armas) **12 to lay eggs** : poner huevos **13 to lay in** STOCK : comprar, proveerse de **14 to lay it on** (thick) : exagerar, cargar las tintas **15 to lay out** PRESENT : presentar, exponer ⟨he laid out his plan : presentó su proyecto⟩ **16 to lay off** : despedir (a un empleado) **17 to lay out** DESIGN : diseñar (el tra-

zado de) **18 to lay up** STORE : guardar, almacenar — *vi* **1 to lay into** ATTACK : arremeter contra **2 to lay off** : dejar (un vicio) **3 to lay off** : dejar en paz ⟨lay off him! : ¡déjalo en paz!⟩ ⟨lay off! : ¡basta ya!⟩ **4 to lay over** : hacer escala

lay² → **lie¹**

lay³ *adj* SECULAR : laico, lego

lay⁴ *n* **1** : disposición *f*, configuración *f* ⟨the lay of the land : la configuración del terreno⟩ **2** BALLAD : romance *m*, balada *f*

layer ['leɪər] *n* **1** : capa *f* (de pintura, etc.), estrato *m* (de roca) **2** : gallina *f* ponedora

layman ['leɪmən] *n, pl* **-men** [-mən, -,mɛn] **1** : laico *m*, lego *m*, seglar *mf* (en religión) **2** : profano *m*, -na *f*; lego *m*, -ga *f* ⟨in layman's terms : en lenguaje sencillo⟩

layoff ['leɪ,ɔf] *n* : despido *m*

layout ['leɪ,aʊt] *n* : disposición *f*, distribución *f* (de una casa, etc.), trazado *m* (de una ciudad)

layover ['leɪ,o:vər] *n* STOPOVER : escala *f*

layperson ['leɪ,pərsən] *n* **1** : laico *m*, -ca *f*; lego *m*, -ga *f*; seglar *mf* (en religión) **2** : profano *m*, -na *f*; lego *m*, -ga *f*

laywoman ['leɪ,wʊmən] *n, pl* **-women** [-,wɪmən] : laica *f*, lega *f*

laziness ['leɪzɪnəs] *n* : pereza *f*, flojera *f*

laze ['leɪz] *v* **lazed; lazing** *vi* or **to laze around** : holgazanear — *vt* **to laze away** ⟨she lazed away the afternoon : pasó la tarde holgazaneando⟩

lazy ['leɪzi] *adj* **lazier; -est** : perezoso, holgazán — **lazily** ['leɪzəli] *adv*

lazybones ['leɪzi,bo:nz] *n* : gandul *m*, -dula *f*

LCD [,ɛl,si:'di:] *n* (liquid *c*rystal *d*isplay) : LCD *m*, pantalla *f* de cristal líquido

leach ['li:tʃ] *vt* : filtrar

lead¹ ['li:d] *v* **led** ['lɛd]; **leading** *vt* **1** GUIDE : conducir, llevar, guiar **2** DIRECT : dirigir **3** HEAD : encabezar, ir al frente de **4** : llevar (una vida) **5 to lead on** : engañar — *vi* **1 to lead to** : conducir a, llevar a **2 to lead to** : dar a (dícese de una puerta) **3** : ir a la cabeza, ir en cabeza (en una competición, etc.) ⟨they're leading by 20 points : van ganando por 20 puntos, tienen 20 puntos de ventaja⟩ **4 to lead to** : resultar en, llevar a ⟨it only leads to trouble : sólo resulta en problemas⟩ **5 to lead up to** PRECEDE : preceder a **6 to lead up to** INTRODUCE : introducir

lead² *n* **1** : delantera *f*, primer lugar *m* ⟨to take the lead : tomar la delantera⟩ ⟨to be in the lead : ir a la cabeza, ir en cabeza⟩ ⟨to follow someone's lead : seguir el ejemplo de alguien⟩ **2 lead actor** : primer actor *m*, primera actriz *f* **3** or **lead guitarist** : guitarrista *mf* principal **4** or **lead role** : papel *m* principal **5** or **lead singer** : cantante *mf* principal **6** or **lead story** : artículo *m* principal **7** CLUE : pista *f* **8** : correa *f* (de un perro)

lead³ ['lɛd] *n* **1** : plomo *m* (metal) **2** : mina *f* (de lápiz) **3 lead poisoning** : saturnismo *m*

leaden ['lɛdən] *adj* **1** : plomizo ⟨a leaden sky : un cielo plomizo⟩ **2** HEAVY : pesado

leader ['liːdər] *n* : jefe *m*, -fa *f*; líder *mf*; dirigente *mf*; gobernante *mf*

leadership ['liːdər,ʃɪp] *n* : mando *m*, dirección *f*

leading ['liːdɪŋ] *adj* **1** IMPORTANT : principal, importante ⟨a leading expert : un destacado experto⟩ **2** FOREMOST : principal, más importante ⟨the leading cause of death : la principal causa de muerte⟩

leaf¹ ['liːf] *vi* **1** : echar hojas (dícese de un árbol) **2 to leaf through** : hojear (un libro)

leaf² *n, pl* **leaves** ['liːvz] **1** : hoja *f* (de plantas o libros) **2 to turn over a new leaf** : hacer borrón y cuenta nueva

leafless ['liːfləs] *adj* : sin hojas, pelado

leaflet ['liːflət] *n* : folleto *m*

leafy ['liːfi] *adj* **leafier; -est** : frondoso

league¹ ['liːg] *v* **leagued; leaguing** *vt* : aliar, unir — *vi* : aliarse, unirse

league² *n* **1** : legua *f* (medida de distancia) **2** ASSOCIATION : alianza *f*, sociedad *f*, liga *f*

leak¹ ['liːk] *vt* **1** : perder, dejar escapar (un líquido o un gas) **2** : filtrar (información) — *vi* **1** : gotear, escaparse, fugarse (dícese de un líquido o un gas) **2** : hacer agua (dícese de un bote) **3** : filtrarse, divulgarse (dícese de información)

leak² *n* **1** HOLE : agujero *m* (en recipientes), gotera *f* (en un tejado) **2** ESCAPE : fuga *f*, escape *m* **3** : filtración *f* (de información)

leakage ['liːkɪdʒ] *n* : escape *m*, fuga *f*

leaky ['liːki] *adj* **leakier; -est** : agujereado (dícese de un recipiente), que hace agua (dícese de un bote), con goteras (dícese de un tejado)

lean¹ ['liːn] *vi* **1** BEND : inclinarse, ladearse **2** RECLINE : reclinarse **3** RELY : apoyarse (en), depender (de) **4** INCLINE, TEND : inclinarse, tender — *vt* : apoyar

lean² *adj* **1** THIN : delgado, flaco **2** : sin grasa, magro (dícese de la carne)

leaning ['liːnɪŋ] *n* TENDENCY : inclinación *f*

leanness ['liːnnəs] *n* : delgadez *f*

lean-to ['liːn,tuː] *n* : cobertizo *m*

leap¹ ['liːp] *vi* **leaped** ['liːpt, 'lɛpt] *or* **leapt; leaping** : saltar, brincar

leap² *n* : salto *m*, brinco *m*

leap year *n* : año *m* bisiesto

learn ['lərn] *vt* **1** : aprender ⟨to learn to sing : aprender a cantar⟩ **2** MEMORIZE : aprender de memoria **3** DISCOVER : saber, enterarse de — *vi* **1** : aprender ⟨to learn from experience : aprender por experiencia⟩ **2** FIND OUT : enterarse, saber

learned ['lərnəd] *adj* : erudito

learner ['lərnər] *n* : principiante *mf*, estudiante *mf*

learning ['lərnɪŋ] *n* : erudición *f*, saber *m*

lease¹ ['liːs] *vt* **leased; leasing** : arrendar

lease² *n* : contrato *m* de arrendamiento

leash *n* : traílla *f*

least¹ ['liːst] *adv* : menos ⟨when least expected : cuando menos se espera⟩

least² *adj* (*superlative of* **little**) : menor, más mínimo

least³ *n* **1 at least** : al menos, por lo menos **2 the least** : lo menos ⟨it's the least I can do : es lo menos que puedo hacer⟩ ⟨it doesn't bother me in the least : no me molesta nada⟩ **3 to say the least** : por no decir más

leather ['lɛðər] *n* : cuero *m*

leathery ['lɛðəri] *adj* : curtido (dícese de la piel), correoso (dícese de la carne)

leave¹ ['liːv] *v* **left** ['lɛft]; **leaving** *vt* **1** DEPART : salir(se) de, ir(se) de ⟨she left the office/party : salió de la oficina/fiesta⟩ ⟨I left home after high school : me fui de casa después de terminar el colegio⟩ **2** : dejar ⟨we left her doing her work : la dejamos trabajando⟩ **3** : dejar (que alguien haga algo) ⟨leave the dishes for me : deja los trastes, los lavaré después⟩ ⟨we left all the arrangements to him : dejamos que él lo arreglara todo⟩ ⟨I'll leave it (up) to you (to decide) : te dejo a ti decidir⟩ ⟨leave it to me! : ¡yo me encargo!⟩ ⟨ leave it to her to arrive early : llegó temprano, como siempre⟩ **4** ABANDON : dejar (una a su familia, etc.) ⟨they left me to clean up : se fueron y me tocó a mí limpiar⟩ **5** QUIT, GIVE UP : dejar (un trabajo, etc.) **6** *or* **to leave behind** FORGET : dejar, olvidarse (en casa, etc.) **7** *or* **to leave behind** : dejar ⟨she left her home/family (behind) : dejó (atrás) su hogar/a su familia⟩ ⟨to leave the past behind : dejar atrás el pasado⟩ **8** DEPOSIT : dejar ⟨leave it on the table/with me : déjalo en la mesa/conmigo⟩ ⟨I left him at the airport : lo dejé en el aeropuerto⟩ ⟨to leave a message : dejar un mensaje⟩ **9** : dejar (en un estado) ⟨I left the lights on : dejé las luces encendidas⟩ ⟨he was left paralyzed : se quedó paralizado⟩ **10** ALLOW, RESERVE : dejar (espacio, etc.) **11** : dejar (una marca, etc.) **12** BEQUEATH : dejar, legar **13** : dejar ⟨he left (behind) a wife and child : dejó esposa y un hijo⟩ **14 to be left** : quedar ⟨it's all I have left : es todo lo que me queda⟩ **15 to be left over** : sobrar **16 to be/get left behind** : quedarse atrás **17 to leave off** : dejar de, parar de **18 to leave off/out** OMIT : omitir, excluir — *vi* : irse, salir, partir, marcharse ⟨she left yesterday morning : se fue ayer por la mañana⟩ ⟨they left for Paris : salieron para París⟩

leave² *n* **1** PERMISSION : permiso *m* ⟨by your leave : con su permiso⟩ **2** *or* **leave of absence** : permiso *m*, licencia *f* ⟨maternity leave : licencia por maternidad⟩ **3 to take one's leave** : despedirse

leaven ['lɛvən] *n* : levadura *f*

leaves → **leaf²**

leaving ['liːvɪŋ] *n* **1** : salida *f*, partida *f* **2 leavings** *npl* : restos *mpl*, sobras *fpl*

Lebanese [,lɛbə'niːz, -'niːs] *n* : libanés *m*, -nesa *f* — **Lebanese** *adj*

lecherous ['lɛtʃərəs] *adj* : lascivo, libidinoso — **lecherously** *adv*

lechery ['lɛtʃəri] *n* : lascivia *f*, lujuria *f*

lectern ['lɛktərn] *n* : atril *m*

lecture¹ [ˈlɛktʃər] v **-tured; -turing** vi : dar clase, dictar clase, dar una conferencia — vt SCOLD : sermonear, echar una reprimenda a, regañar

lecture² n 1 : conferencia f 2 REPRIMAND : reprimenda f

lecturer [ˈlɛktʃərər] n 1 SPEAKER : conferenciante mf 2 TEACHER : profesor m, -sora f

led → **lead**¹

LED [ˌɛl,i'di:] n (light-emitting diode) : LED m, led m

ledge [ˈlɛdʒ] n : repisa f (de una pared), antepecho m (de una ventana), saliente m (de una montaña)

ledger [ˈlɛdʒər] n : libro m mayor, libro m de contabilidad

lee¹ [ˈli:] adj : de sotavento

lee² n : sotavento m

leech [ˈli:tʃ] n : sanguijuela f

leek [ˈli:k] n : puerro m

leer¹ [ˈlɪr] vi : mirar con lascivia

leer² n : mirada f lasciva

leery [ˈlɪri] adj : receloso

lees [ˈli:z] npl : posos mpl, heces fpl

leeward¹ [ˈli:wərd, ˈlu:ərd] adj : de sotavento

leeward² n : sotavento m

leeway [ˈli:,weɪ] n 1 : libertad f, margen m

left¹ [ˈlɛft] adv : hacia la izquierda

left² → **leave**¹

left³ adj : izquierdo

left n : izquierda f ⟨on the left : a la izquierda⟩

left–hand [ˈlɛftˈhænd] adj 1 : de la izquierda 2 → **left–handed**

left–handed [ˈlɛftˈhændəd] adj 1 : zurdo (dícese de una persona) 2 : con doble sentido ⟨a left-handed compliment : un cumplido a medias⟩

leftist [ˈlɛftɪst] n : izquierdista mf — **leftist** adj

leftover [ˈlɛft,o:vər] adj : sobrante, que sobra

leftovers [ˈlɛft,o:vərz] npl : restos mpl, sobras fpl

left wing n the left wing : la izquierda

left–winger [ˈlɛftˈwɪŋər] n : izquierdista mf

leg [ˈlɛg] n 1 : pierna f (de una persona, de carne, de ropa), pata f (de un animal, de muebles) 2 STAGE : etapa f (de un viaje), vuelta f (de una carrera)

legacy [ˈlɛgəsi] n, pl **-cies** : legado m, herencia f

legal [ˈli:gəl] adj 1 : legal, jurídico ⟨legal advisor : asesor jurídico⟩ ⟨the legal profession : la abogacía⟩ 2 LAWFUL : legítimo, legal ⟨legal tender : moneda de curso legal⟩

legalistic [ˌli:gəˈlɪstɪk] adj : legalista

legality [li'gæləti] n, pl **-ties** : legalidad f

legalize [ˈli:gə,laɪz] vt **-ized; -izing** : legalizar

legally [ˈli:gəli] adv : legalmente

legate [ˈlɛgət] n : legado m

legation [lɪˈgeɪʃən] n : legación f

legend [ˈlɛdʒənd] n 1 STORY : leyenda f 2 INSCRIPTION : leyenda f, inscripción f 3

: signos mpl convencionales (en un mapa)

legendary [ˈlɛdʒən,dɛri] adj : legendario

legerdemain [ˌlɛdʒərdəˈmeɪn] → **sleight of hand**

leggings [ˈlɛgɪnz, ˈlɛgənz] npl : mallas fpl

legibility [ˌlɛdʒəˈbɪləti] n : legibilidad f

legible [ˈlɛdʒəbəl] adj : legible

legibly [ˈlɛdʒəbli] adv : de manera legible

legion [ˈli:dʒən] n : legión f

legionnaire [ˌli:dʒəˈnær] n : legionario m, -ria f

legislate [ˈlɛdʒəs,leɪt] vi **-lated; -lating** : legislar

legislation [ˌlɛdʒəsˈleɪʃən] n : legislación f

legislative [ˈlɛdʒəs,leɪtɪv] adj : legislativo, legislador

legislator [ˈlɛdʒəs,leɪtər] n : legislador m, -dora f

legislature [ˈlɛdʒəs,leɪtʃər] n : asamblea f legislativa

legitimacy [lɪˈdʒɪtəməsi] n : legitimidad f

legitimate [lɪˈdʒɪtəmət] adj 1 VALID : legítimo, válido, justificado 2 LAWFUL : legítimo, legal

legitimately [lɪˈdʒɪtəmətli] adv : legítimamente

legitimize [lɪˈdʒɪtə,maɪz] vt **-mized; -mizing** : legitimar, hacer legítimo

legume [ˈlɛ,gju:m, lɪˈgju:m] n : legumbre f

leisure [ˈli:ʒər, ˈlɛ-] n 1 : ocio m, tiempo m libre ⟨a life of leisure : una vida de ocio⟩ 2 to take one's leisure : reposar 3 at your leisure : cuando te venga bien, cuando tengas tiempo

leisurely [ˈli:ʒərli, ˈlɛ-] adj & adv : lento, sin prisas

lemming [ˈlɛmɪŋ] n : lemming m

lemon [ˈlɛmən] n : limón m

lemonade [ˌlɛməˈneɪd] n : limonada f

lemony [ˈlɛməni] adj : a limón

lend [ˈlɛnd] vt lent [ˈlɛnt]; lending 1 : prestar ⟨to lend money : prestar dinero⟩ 2 GIVE : dar ⟨it lends force to his criticism : da fuerza a su crítica⟩ ⟨to lend a hand to someone : echarle una mano a alguien⟩ 3 to lend oneself to : prestarse a

length [ˈlɛŋkθ] n 1 : longitud f, largo m ⟨10 feet in length : 10 pies de largo⟩ 2 DURATION : duración f 3 : trozo m (de madera), corte m (de tela) 4 to go to any lengths : hacer todo lo posible 5 at ~ : extensamente ⟨to speak at length : hablar largo y tendido⟩ 6 at ~ FINALLY : por fin

lengthen [ˈlɛŋkθən] vt 1 : alargar ⟨can they lengthen the dress? : ¿se puede alargar el vestido?⟩ 2 EXTEND, PROLONG : prolongar, extender — vi : alargarse, crecer ⟨the days are lengthening : los días están creciendo⟩

lengthways [ˈlɛŋkθ,weɪz] → **lengthwise**

lengthwise [ˈlɛŋkθ,waɪz] adv : a lo largo, longitudinalmente

lengthy [ˈlɛŋkθi] adj **lengthier; -est** 1 OVERLONG : largo y pesado 2 EXTENDED : prolongado, largo

leniency [ˈli:niəntsi] n, pl **-cies** : lenidad f, indulgencia f

lenient ['li:niənt] *adj* : indulgente, poco severo

leniently ['li:niəntli] *adv* : con lenidad, con indulgencia

lens ['lɛnz] *n* **1** : cristalino *m* (del ojo) **2** : lente *mf* (de un instrumento o una cámara) **3** → **contact lens**

lent → **lend**

Lent ['lɛnt] *n* : Cuaresma *f*

lentil ['lɛntəl] *n* : lenteja *f*

Leo ['li:o] *n* **1** : Leo *m* (signo o constelación) **2** : Leo *mf* (persona)

leopard ['lɛpərd] *n* : leopardo *m*

leotard ['li:ə,tɑrd] *n* : leotardo *m*, malla *f*

leper ['lɛpər] *n* : leproso *m*, -sa *f*

leprechaun ['lɛprə,kɑn] *n* : duende *m* (irlandés)

leprosy ['lɛprəsi] *n* : lepra *f* — **leprous** ['lɛprəs] *adj*

lesbian¹ ['lɛzbiən] *adj* : lesbiano

lesbian² *n* : lesbiana *f*

lesbianism ['lɛzbiə,nɪzəm] *n* : lesbianismo *m*

lesion ['li:ʒən] *n* : lesión *f*

less¹ ['lɛs] *adv* (*comparative of* **little¹**) : menos ⟨the less you know, the better : cuanto menos sepas, mejor⟩ ⟨less and less : cada vez menos⟩

less² *adj* (*comparative of* **little²**) : menos ⟨less than three : menos de tres⟩ ⟨less money : menos dinero⟩ ⟨nothing less than perfection : nada menos que la perfección⟩

less³ *pron* : menos ⟨I'm earning less : estoy ganando menos⟩

less⁴ *prep* : menos ⟨one month less two days : un mes menos dos días⟩

-less [ləs] *suf* : sin

lessee [lɛ'si:] *n* : arrendatario *m*, -ria *f*

lessen ['lɛsən] *vt* : disminuir, reducir — *vi* : disminuir, reducirse

lesser ['lɛsər] *adj* : menor ⟨to a lesser degree : en menor grado⟩

lesson ['lɛsən] *n* **1** CLASS : clase *f*, curso *m* **2** : lección *f* ⟨the lessons of history : las lecciones de la historia⟩

lessor ['lɛ,sɔr, lɛ'sɔr] *n* : arrendador *m*, -dora *f*

lest ['lɛst] *conj* : para (que) no ⟨lest we forget : para que no olvidemos⟩

let ['lɛt] *v* **let**; **letting** *vt* **1** ALLOW : dejar, permitir ⟨let me see it : déjame verlo⟩ ⟨let it chill : dejarlo enfriar⟩ ⟨let him in/out : déjalo entrar/salir⟩ **2** MAKE : hacer ⟨let me know : házmelo saber, avísame⟩ ⟨let them wait! : ¡que esperen!⟩ **3** RENT : alquilar **4** (*used in the first person plural imperative*) ⟨let's go! : ¡vamos!, ¡vámonos!⟩ ⟨let us pray : oremos⟩ **5 let alone** : ni mucho menos, (y) menos aún ⟨I can barely understand it, let alone explain it : apenas puedo entenderlo, ni mucho menos explicarlo⟩ **6 to let down** LOWER : bajar **7 to let down** DISAPPOINT : fallar ⟨to let someone down gently : suavizarle el golpe a alguien⟩ **8 to let go** RELEASE, FREE : soltar ⟨let me go! : ¡suéltame!⟩ **9 to let oneself go** : dejarse, abandonarse **10 to let in on** ⟨to let someone in on a secret : contarle un se-

creto a alguien⟩ **11 to let off** FORGIVE : perdonar ⟨they let him off the hook : lo dejaron ir sin castigo⟩ ⟨they let her off lightly : la dieron un leve castigo⟩ **12 to let off** : echar (vapor), hacer estallar (un petardo, etc.) **13 to let oneself in for** : exponerse a (críticas), buscarse (problemas) ⟨I didn't know what I was letting myself in for : no sabía en la que me estaba metiendo⟩ **14 to let out** REVEAL : revelar **15 to let out** : soltar (un grito, etc.) **16 to let out** : ensanchar (un vestido, etc.) — *vi* **1 to let go** RELAX : soltarse el pelo **2 to let go (of)** : soltar ⟨let go (of me)! : ¡suélta(me)!⟩ **3 to let on** REVEAL, SHOW : revelar, demostrar ⟨don't let on! : ¡no digas nada!⟩ ⟨he didn't let on that he knew : hizo como si no lo supiera⟩ **4 to let on** PRETEND, SEEM : fingir, aparentar **5 to let out** END : terminar ⟨school lets out in June : el año escolar termina en junio⟩ **6 to let up** ABATE : amainar, disminuir ⟨the pace never lets up : el ritmo nunca disminuye⟩ **7 to let up** STOP : parar **8 to let up on** : soltar (un freno, etc.), no ser tan duro con (alguien)

letdown ['lɛt,daʊn] *n* : chasco *m*, decepción *f*

lethal ['li:θəl] *adj* : letal — **lethally** *adv*

lethargic [lɪ'θɑrdʒɪk] *adj* : letárgico

lethargy ['lɛθərdʒi] *n* : letargo *m*

let's ['lɛts] *contraction of* **let us** → **let**

letter¹ ['lɛtər] *vt* : marcar con letras, inscribir letras en

letter² *n* **1** : letra *f* (del alfabeto) **2** : carta *f* ⟨a letter to my mother : una carta a mi madre⟩ **3 letters** *npl* ARTS : letras *fpl* **4 to the letter** : al pie de la letra

letter bomb *n* : carta *f* bomba

letterhead ['lɛtər,hɛd] *n* **1** : membrete *m* (de una carta) **2** : papel *m* con membrete

lettering ['lɛtərɪŋ] *n* : letra *f*

lettuce ['lɛtəs] *n* : lechuga *f*

letup ['lɛt,ʌp] *n* LULL : pausa *f*, respiro *m*

leukemia [lu:'ki:miə] *n* : leucemia *f*

levee ['lɛvi] *n* : dique *m*

level¹ ['lɛvəl] *v* **-eled** *or* **-elled**; **-eling** *or* **-elling** *vt* **1** *or* **to level off** FLATTEN : nivelar, aplanar **2** AIM : apuntar (una pistola), dirigir (una acusación) **3** RAZE : rasar, arrasar — *vi* **1 to level off/out** : estabilizarse (dícese de los precios, etc.), nivelarse (dícese de un avión), allanarse (dícese del paisaje) **2 to level with someone** : ser sincero con alguien

level² *adj* **1** EVEN : llano, plano, parejo **2** CALM : tranquilo ⟨to keep a level head : no perder la cabeza⟩

level³ *n* : nivel *m*

leveler ['lɛvələr] *n* : nivelador *m*, -dora *f*

levelheaded ['lɛvəl'hɛdəd] *adj* : sensato, equilibrado

levelly ['lɛvəli] *adv* CALMLY : con ecuanimidad *f*, con calma

levelness ['lɛvəlnəs] *n* : uniformidad *f*

lever ['lɛvər, 'li:-] *n* : palanca *f*

leverage ['lɛvərɪdʒ, 'li:-] *n* **1** : apalancamiento *m* (en física) **2** INFLUENCE : influencia *f*, palanca *f fam*

leviathan [lɪ'vaɪəθən] n : leviatán m, gigante m

levitate ['levə,teɪt] vi -tated; -tating : levitar — vt : hacer levitar

levity ['levəti] n : ligereza f, frivolidad f

levy¹ ['levi] vt levied; levying 1 IMPOSE : imponer, exigir, gravar (un impuesto) 2 COLLECT : recaudar (un impuesto)

levy² n, pl levies : impuesto m, gravamen m

lewd ['lu:d] adj : lascivo — **lewdly** adv

lewdness ['lu:dnəs] n : lascivia f

lexical ['lɛksɪkəl] adj : léxico

lexicographer [,lɛksə'kɑgrəfər] n : lexicógrafo m, -fa f

lexicographical [,lɛksəko'græfɪkəl] or **lexicographic** ['-'græfɪk] adj : lexicográfico

lexicography [,lɛksə'kɑgrəfi] n : lexicografía f

lexicon ['lɛksɪ,kɑn] n, pl -ica [-kə] or -icons : léxico m

liability [,laɪə'bɪləti] n, pl -ties 1 RESPONSIBILITY : responsabilidad f 2 SUSCEPTIBILITY : propensión f 3 DRAWBACK : desventaja f 4 liabilities npl DEBTS : deudas fpl, pasivo m

liable ['laɪəbəl] adj 1 RESPONSIBLE : responsable 2 SUSCEPTIBLE : propenso 3 PROBABLE : probable ⟨it's liable to happen : es probable que suceda⟩

liaison ['li:ə,zɑn, li'eɪ-] n 1 CONNECTION : enlace m, relación f 2 AFFAIR : amorío m, aventura f

liar ['laɪər] n : mentiroso m, -sa f; embustero m, -ra f

libel¹ ['laɪbəl] vt -beled or -belled; -beling or -belling : difamar, calumniar

libel² n : difamación f, calumnia f

libelous or **libellous** ['laɪbələs] adj : difamatorio, calumnioso, injurioso

liberal¹ ['lɪbrəl, 'lɪbərəl] adj 1 TOLERANT : liberal, tolerante 2 GENEROUS : generoso 3 ABUNDANT : abundante 4 **liberal arts** : humanidades fpl, artes fpl liberales

liberal² n : liberal mf

liberalism ['lɪbrə,lɪzəm, 'lɪbərə-] n : liberalismo m

liberality [,lɪbə'ræləti] n, pl -ties : liberalidad f, generosidad f

liberalize ['lɪbrə,laɪz, 'lɪbərə-] vt -ized; -izing : liberalizar

liberally ['lɪbrəli, 'lɪbərə-] adv 1 GENEROUSLY : generosamente 2 ABUNDANTLY : abundantemente 3 FREELY : libremente

liberate ['lɪbə,reɪt] vt -ated; -ating : liberar, libertar

liberation [,lɪbə'reɪʃən] n : liberación f

liberator ['lɪbə,reɪtər] n : libertador m, -dora f

Liberian [laɪ'bɪriən] n : liberiano m, -na f — **Liberian** adj

libertarian [,lɪbər'teriən] adj & n : libertario m, -ria f

libertine ['lɪbər,ti:n] n : libertino m, -na f

liberty ['lɪbərti] n, pl -ties 1 : libertad f 2 **to take the liberty of** : tomarse la libertad de 3 **to take liberties with** : tomarse confianzas con, tomarse libertades con

libido [lə'bi:do:, -'baɪ-] n, pl -dos : libido f — **libidinous** [lə'bɪdənəs] adj

Libra ['li:brə] n 1 : Libra m (signo o constelación) 2 : Libra mf (persona)

librarian [laɪ'breriən] n : bibliotecario m, -ria f

library ['laɪ,breri] n, pl -braries : biblioteca f

librettist [lɪ'bretɪst] n : libretista mf

libretto [lɪ'breto] n, pl -tos or -ti [-ti:] : libreto m

Libyan ['lɪbiən] n : libio m, -bia f — **Libyan** adj

lice → louse

license¹ ['laɪsənts] vt licensed; licensing : licenciar, autorizar, dar permiso a

license² or **licence** n 1 PERMISSION : licencia f, permiso m 2 PERMIT : licencia f, carnet m Spain ⟨driver's license : licencia de conducir⟩ 3 FREEDOM : libertad f 4 LICENTIOUSNESS : libertinaje m

licensed adj CERTIFIED : autorizado, certificado, licenciado ⟨a licensed physician : un médico certificado⟩ ⟨a licensed driver : un conductor con licencia⟩

license plate n : placa f de matrícula; chapa f Arg, Uru; patente f Arg, Chile, Uru

licentious [laɪ'sentʃəs] adj : licencioso, disoluto — **licentiously** adv

licentiousness [laɪ'sentʃəsnəs] n : libertinaje m

lichen ['laɪkən] n : liquen m

licit ['lɪsət] adj : lícito

lick¹ ['lɪk] vt 1 : lamer 2 BEAT : darle una paliza (a alguien)

lick² n 1 : lamida f, lengüetada f ⟨a lick of paint : una mano de pintura⟩ 2 BIT : pizca f, ápice m ⟨a lick and a promise : una lavada a la carrera⟩

licorice ['lɪkərɪʃ, -rəs] n : regaliz m, dulce m de regaliz

lid ['lɪd] n 1 COVER : tapa f 2 EYELID : párpado m

lie¹ ['laɪ] vi lay ['leɪ]; lain ['leɪn]; lying ['laɪɪŋ] 1 or **to lie down** : acostarse, echarse, tumbarse, tenderse ⟨I lay down on the bed : me acosté en la cama⟩ ⟨lie on your back : acuéstate boca arriba⟩ ⟨he was lying unconscious on the floor : estaba tendido en el suelo sin sentido⟩ ⟨to take something lying down : dejar pasar algo sin protestar⟩ 2 : estar, estar situado, encontrarse ⟨the book lay on the table : el libro estaba en la mesa⟩ ⟨the city lies to the south : la ciudad se encuentra al sur⟩ ⟨there were papers lying around : había papeles tirados por todos lados⟩ 3 CONSIST : consistir 4 **to lie ahead** AWAIT : estar por venir 5 **to lie around** RELAX : holgazanear 6 **to lie back** : reclinarse 7 **to lie down on the job** : no cumplir 8 **to lie in/with** : residir en ⟨the power lies in the people : el poder reside en el pueblo⟩ 9 **to lie low** : tratar de no llamar la atención

lie² vi lied; lying ['laɪɪŋ] : mentir

lie³ n 1 UNTRUTH : mentira f ⟨to tell lies : decir mentiras⟩ 2 POSITION : posición f

liege ['li:dʒ] n : señor m feudal

lien ['li:n, 'li:ən] *n* : derecho *m* de retención

lieu ['lu:] *n* **in lieu of** : en lugar de

lieutenant [lu:'tɛnənt] *n* : teniente *mf*

life ['laɪf] *n, pl* **lives** ['laɪvz] **1** : vida *f* ⟨plant life : la vida vegetal⟩ **2** EXISTENCE : vida *f* ⟨early/late in life : en la juventud/vejez⟩ ⟨later in life : a una edad más avanzada⟩ ⟨I've lived here my whole/entire life, I've lived here all my life : siempre he vivido aquí⟩ ⟨never in my life : (jamás) en la vida⟩ ⟨life of crime : vida delictiva⟩ ⟨way of life : estilo de vida⟩ **3** BIOGRAPHY : biografía *f*, vida *f* **4** DURATION : duración *f*, vida *f* **5** LIVELINESS : vivacidad *f*, animación *f* **6** *or* **life imprisonment** : cadena *f* perpetua **7 a matter of life and death** : una cuestión de vida o muerte **8 as big as life** : en carne y hueso **9 for dear life** : desesperadamente **10 for the life of me** : por nada del mundo **11 not on your life** : ni pensarlo **12 that's life** : así es la vida **13 the life of the party** : el alma de la fiesta **14 to bring back to life** : resucitar **15 to come to life** : animarse **16 to claim/take someone's life** : matar a alguien **17 to frighten/scare the life out of** : darle/pegarle un susto mortal a **18 to lose one's life** : perder la vida **19 to risk life and limb** : arriesgar la vida **20 to save someone's life** : salvarle la vida **21 to take one's own life** : suicidarse **22 true to life** : verosímil

lifeblood ['laɪf,blʌd] *n* : parte *f* vital, sustento *m*

lifeboat ['laɪf,bo:t] *n* : bote *m* salvavidas

life cycle *n* : ciclo *m* vital

life expectancy *n* : esperanza *f* de vida, expectativa *f* de vida, expectativas *fpl* de vida

lifeguard ['laɪf,gɑrd] *n* : socorrista *mf*; salvavidas *mf*; bañero *m*, -ra *f Arg, Uru*

life insurance *n* : seguro *m* de vida

life jacket *n* : chaleco *m* salvavidas

lifeless ['laɪfləs] *adj* : sin vida, muerto

lifelike ['laɪf,laɪk] *adj* : que parece vivo, natural, verosímil

lifeline ['laɪf,laɪn] *n* **1** : cuerda *f* de salvamento **2** : salvavidas *m*

lifelong ['laɪf'lɔŋ] *adj* : de toda la vida ⟨a lifelong friend : un amigo de toda la vida⟩

life preserver *n* : salvavidas *m*

lifesaver ['laɪf,seɪvər] *n* **1** : salvación *f* **2** → lifeguard

lifesaving ['laɪf,seɪvɪŋ] *n* : socorrismo *m*

life sentence *n* : cadena *f* perpetua

life-size ['laɪf'saɪz] *or* **life-sized** ['laɪf-'saɪzd] *adj* : de tamaño natural

lifespan ['laɪf,spæn] *n* : vida *f*

lifestyle ['laɪf,staɪl] *n* : estilo *m* de vida

lifetime ['laɪf,taɪm] *n* : vida *f*, curso *m* de la vida

lift¹ ['lɪft] *vt* **1** RAISE : levantar, alzar, subir **2** END : levantar ⟨to lift a ban : levantar una prohibición⟩ — *vi* **1** RISE : levantarse, alzarse **2** CLEAR UP : despejar ⟨the fog lifted : se disipó la niebla⟩

lift² *n* **1** LIFTING : levantamiento *m*, alzamiento *m* **2** BOOST : impulso *m*, estímulo *m* **3 to give someone a lift** : llevar en coche a alguien

liftoff ['lɪft,ɔf] *n* : despegue *m*

ligament ['lɪgəmənt] *n* : ligamento *m*

ligature ['lɪgə,tʃʊr, -tʃər] *n* : ligadura *f*

light¹ ['laɪt] *v* **lit** ['lɪt] *or* **lighted; lighting** *vt* **1** ILLUMINATE : iluminar, alumbrar **2** IGNITE : encender, prenderle fuego a — *vi* : encenderse, prender

light² *vi* **lighted** *or* **lit** ['lɪt]; **lighting** **1** LAND, SETTLE : posarse **2** DISMOUNT : bajarse, apearse

light³ ['laɪt] *adv* **1** LIGHTLY : suavemente, ligeramente **2 to travel light** : viajar con poco equipaje

light⁴ *adj* **1** LIGHTWEIGHT : ligero, liviano, poco pesado **2** EASY : fácil, ligero, liviano ⟨light reading : lectura fácil⟩ ⟨light work : trabajo liviano⟩ **3** GENTLE, MILD : fino, suave, leve ⟨a light breeze : una brisa suave⟩ ⟨a light rain : una lluvia fina⟩ **4** DELICATE : leve, ligero ⟨she wore light makeup : llevaba poco maquillaje⟩ **5** LOW : bajo ⟨light turnout : baja asistencia⟩ ⟨light trading : poco movimiento (en los mercados)⟩ ⟨traffic was light : había poco tráfico⟩ **6** MINOR, SUPERFICIAL : de poca importancia, superficial **7** BRIGHT : brillante (dícese de una luz), luminoso (dícese de una habitación) ⟨to be light out : ser de día⟩ ⟨to get light out : amanecer⟩ **8** PALE : claro (dícese de los colores), rubio (dícese del pelo) **9** *or* **lite** : light

light⁵ *n* **1** ILLUMINATION : luz *f* **2** DAYLIGHT : luz *f* del día **3** DAWN : amanecer *m*, madrugada *f* **4** LAMP : lámpara *f* ⟨to turn off the light : apagar la luz⟩ **5** ASPECT : aspecto *m* ⟨in a new light : con otros ojos⟩ ⟨to show in a good/bad light : dar una imagen positiva/negativa a⟩ ⟨in (the) light of : en vista de, a la luz de⟩ **6** MATCH : fósforo *m*, cerillo *m* **7 the light at the end of the tunnel** : la luz al final del túnel **8 the light of someone's life** : la niña de los ojos de alguien **9 to be out like a light** : dormirse como un tronco **10 to bring to light** : sacar a (la) luz **11 to cast/shed/throw light on** : arrojar luz sobre **12 to come to light** : salir a (la) luz **13 to see the light** : abrir los ojos

lightbulb ['laɪt,bʌlb] *n* : bombilla *f*; foco *m*; bombillo *m CA, Col, Ven*; bombita *f Arg, Uru*

lighten ['laɪtən] *vt* **1** ILLUMINATE : iluminar, dar más luz a **2** : aclararse (el pelo) **3** : aligerar (una carga, etc.) **4** RELIEVE : aliviar **5** GLADDEN : alegrar ⟨it lightened his heart : alegró su corazón⟩

lighter ['laɪtər] *n* : encendedor *m*

light-headed ['laɪt'hɛdəd] *adj* : mareado

lighthearted ['laɪt'hɑrtəd] *adj* : alegre, despreocupado, desenfadado — **lightheartedly** *adv*

lightheartedness ['laɪt'hɑrtədnəs] *n* : desenfado *m*, alegría *f*

lighthouse ['laɪt,haʊs] *n* : faro *m*

lighting ['laɪtɪŋ] n : iluminación f
lightly ['laɪtli] adv 1 GENTLY : suavemente 2 SLIGHTLY : ligeramente 3 FRIVOLOUSLY : a la ligera 4 to let off lightly : tratar con indulgencia
lightness ['laɪtnəs] n 1 BRIGHTNESS : luminosidad f, claridad f 2 GENTLENESS : ligereza f, suavidad f, delicadeza f 3 : ligereza f, liviandad f (de peso)
lightning ['laɪtnɪŋ] n : relámpago m, rayo m
lightning bug → firefly
lightproof ['laɪt,pru:f] adj : impenetrable por la luz, opaco
lightweight[1] ['laɪt,weɪt] adj : ligero, liviano, de poco peso
lightweight[2] n : peso m ligero (en deportes)
light–year ['laɪt,jɪr] n : año m luz
likable or **likeable** ['laɪkəbəl] adj : simpático, agradable
like[1] ['laɪk] v **liked; liking** vt 1 : gustarle (algo a uno) ⟨he likes rice : le gusta el arroz⟩ ⟨she doesn't like flowers : a ella no le gustan las flores⟩ ⟨I like you : me caes bien⟩ 2 WANT : querer, desear ⟨I'd like a hamburger : quiero una hamburguesa⟩ ⟨he would like more help : le gustaría tener más ayuda⟩ ⟨I'd like to come : quiero venir⟩ ⟨I'd like to think (that) . . . : quiero creer que . . .⟩ — vi : querer ⟨do as you like : haz lo que quieras⟩ ⟨if you like : si quieres, si te parece⟩ ⟨whenever you like : cuando quieras⟩
like[2] adj : parecido, semejante, similar
like[3] n 1 PREFERENCE : preferencia f, gusto m 2 the like : cosa f parecida, cosas fpl ⟨I've never seen the like : nunca he visto cosa parecida⟩
like[4] conj 1 AS IF : como si ⟨they looked at me like I was crazy : se me quedaron mirando como si estuviera loca⟩ 2 AS : como, igual que ⟨she doesn't love you like I do : ella no te quiere como yo⟩
like[5] prep 1 : como, parecido a ⟨she acts like my mother : se comporta como mi madre⟩ ⟨he looks like me : se parece a mí⟩ 2 : propio de, típico de ⟨that's just like her : eso es muy típico de ella⟩ 3 : como ⟨animals like cows : animales como vacas⟩ 4 like this, like that : así ⟨do it like that : hazlo así⟩
-like ['laɪk] suf 1 : como, parecido a ⟨cat-like : como un gato, parecido a un gato, felino⟩ 2 : propio de ⟨ladylike : propio de una dama⟩
likelihood ['laɪkli,hʊd] n : probabilidad f ⟨in all likelihood : con toda probabilidad⟩
likely[1] ['laɪkli] adv : probablemente ⟨most likely he's sick : lo más probable es que esté enfermo⟩ ⟨they're likely to come : es probable que vengan⟩
likely[2] adj **likelier; -est** 1 PROBABLE : probable ⟨to be likely to : ser muy probable que⟩ 2 SUITABLE : apropiado, adecuado 3 BELIEVABLE : verosímil, creíble 4 PROMISING : prometedor
liken ['laɪkən] vt : comparar

likeness ['laɪknəs] n 1 SIMILARITY : semejanza f, parecido m 2 PORTRAIT : retrato m
likewise ['laɪk,waɪz] adv 1 SIMILARLY : de la misma manera, asimismo 2 ALSO : también, además, asimismo
liking ['laɪkɪŋ] n 1 FONDNESS : afición f (por una cosa), simpatía f (por una persona) 2 TASTE : gusto m ⟨is it to your liking? : ¿te gusta?⟩ ⟨to take a liking to : tomarle el gusto a algo⟩
lilac ['laɪlək, -,læk, -,lɑk] n : lila f — **lilac** adj
lilt ['lɪlt] n : cadencia f, ritmo m alegre
lily ['lɪli] n, pl **lilies** 1 : lirio m, azucena f 2 lily of the valley : lirio m de los valles, muguete m
lily pad n : hoja f grande (de un nenúfar)
lima bean ['laɪmə] n : frijol m de media luna
limb ['lɪm] n 1 APPENDAGE : miembro m, extremidad f 2 BRANCH : rama f
limber[1] ['lɪmbər] vi or **to limber up** : calentarse, prepararse
limber[2] adj : ágil (dícese de las personas), flexible (dícese de los objetos)
limbo ['lɪm,bo:] n, pl **-bos** 1 : limbo m (en religión) 2 OBLIVION : olvido m ⟨the project is in limbo : el proyecto ha caído en el olvido⟩
lime ['laɪm] n 1 : cal f (óxido) 2 : lima f (fruta), limón m verde Mex
limelight ['laɪm,laɪt] n **to be in the limelight** : ser el centro de atención, estar en el candelero
limerick ['lɪmərɪk] n : poema m jocoso de cinco versos
limestone ['laɪm,sto:n] n : piedra f caliza, caliza f
limit[1] ['lɪmət] vt : limitar, restringir
limit[2] n 1 MAXIMUM : límite m, máximo m ⟨speed limit : límite de velocidad⟩ 2 **limits** npl : límites mpl, confines mpl ⟨city limits : límites de la ciudad⟩ 3 **that's the limit!** : ¡eso es el colmo!
limitation [,lɪmə'teɪʃən] n : limitación f, restricción f
limited ['lɪmətəd] adj : limitado, restringido
limitless ['lɪmətləs] adj : ilimitado, sin límites
limousine ['lɪmə,zi:n, ,lɪmə'-] n : limusina f
limp[1] ['lɪmp] vi : cojear
limp[2] adj 1 FLACCID : fláccido 2 LANK : lacio (dícese del pelo) 3 WEAK : débil ⟨to feel limp : sentirse desfallecer, sentirse sin fuerzas⟩
limp[3] n : cojera f
limpet ['lɪmpət] n : lapa f
limpid ['lɪmpəd] adj : límpido, claro
limply ['lɪmpli] adv : sin fuerzas
limpness ['lɪmpnəs] n : flaccidez f, debilidad f
limy ['laɪmi] adj : calizo
linden ['lɪndən] n : tilo m
line[1] ['laɪn] v **lined; lining** vt 1 : forrar, cubrir ⟨to line a dress : forrar un vestido⟩ ⟨to line the walls : cubrir las paredes⟩ 2 MARK : rayar, trazar líneas en 3

BORDER : bordear **4** *or* **to line up** ALIGN : alinear **5 to line up** : organizar — *vi* **to line up** : ponerse en fila, hacer cola

line² *n* **1** MARK : línea *f*, raya *f* ⟨straight line : (línea) recta⟩ ⟨dotted line : línea de puntos⟩ **2** BOUNDARY : línea *f*, límite *m* ⟨dividing line : línea divisoria⟩ ⟨property line : límite de la propiedad⟩ ⟨to draw the line : fijar límites⟩ ⟨to draw the line at something : no tolerar algo⟩ **3** ROW : fila *f*, hilera *f* **4** QUEUE : cola *f* ⟨to wait in line : hacer cola⟩ **5 lines** SILHOU-ETTE : líneas *fpl* **6** CORD, ROPE : cuerda *f* **7** → **pipeline** **8** WIRE : cable *m* ⟨power line : cable eléctrico⟩ **9** : línea *f* (de teléfono) ⟨the line is busy : está ocupado⟩ ⟨the boss is on the line : le llama el jefe⟩ **10** : línea *f* (de texto), verso *m* (de poesía) **11** NOTE : nota *f*, líneas *fpl* ⟨drop me a line : mándame unas líneas⟩ **12 lines** *npl* : diálogo *m* (de un actor) **13** COMMENT : comentario *m* **14** WRINKLE : línea *f*, arruga *f* (de la cara) **15** PATH : línea *f* ⟨line of fire : línea de fuego⟩ **16** SERVICE : línea *f* ⟨bus line : línea de autobuses⟩ **17** : línea *f*, cadena *f* ⟨production line : línea de producción⟩ **18** SERIES : serie *f* (de problemas, etc.) **19** LINEAGE : línea *f*, linaje *m* **20** MANNER : línea *f* ⟨line of inquiry : línea de investigación⟩ ⟨to take a firm line on : ponerse firme sobre⟩ **21** POSITION : línea *f* ⟨the party line : la línea del partido⟩ **22** OCCUPATION : ocupación *f*, rama *f*, especialidad *f* **23 lines** *npl* RANKS : líneas *fpl*, filas *fpl* ⟨behind enemy lines : tras las líneas enemigas⟩ **24** RANGE : línea *f* ⟨product line : línea de productos⟩ **25** AGREEMENT : conformidad *f* ⟨to be in line with : estar conforme con⟩ ⟨to fall into line : conformarse⟩ **26 along the line** ⟨somewhere along the line : en algún momento⟩ **27 along the lines of** : por el estilo de **28 down the line** : en el futuro **29 in line** ⟨he's in line for a promotion : lo consideran para un ascenso⟩ ⟨first/next in line to succeed the President : primero en la línea de sucesión a la presidencia⟩ **30 in line** ⟨to keep someone in line : mantener a alguien a raya⟩ **31 on the line** ENDAN-GERED : en peligro **32 out of line** DISRE-SPECTFUL : fuera de lugar (dícese de un comentario) ⟨you're out of line : te has pasado de la raya⟩ **33 to lay it on the line** : no andarse con rodeos **34 to read between the lines** : leer entre líneas

lineage [ˈlɪniɪdʒ] *n* : linaje *m*, abolengo *m*

lineal [ˈlɪniəl] *adj* : en línea directa

lineaments [ˈlɪniəmənts] *npl* : facciones *fpl* (de la cara), rasgos *mpl*

linear [ˈlɪniər] *adj* : lineal

lined [ˈlaɪnd] *adj* **1** : de rayas (dícese de papel, etc.) **2** WRINKLY : arrugado (dícese de la cara)

linen [ˈlɪnən] *n* **1** : lino *m* **2** *or* **bed linen** : ropa *f* de cama **3** *or* **table linen** : mantelería *f*

liner [ˈlaɪnər] *n* **1** LINING : forro *m* **2** SHIP : buque *m*, transatlántico *m*

lineup [ˈlaɪnˌəp] *n* **1** : fila *f* de sospechosos **2** : formación *f* (en deportes) **3** ALIGN-MENT : alineación *f*

linger [ˈlɪŋgər] *vi* **1** TARRY : quedarse, entretenerse, rezagarse **2** PERSIST : persistir, sobrevivir

lingerie [ˌlɑndʒəˈreɪ, ˌlænʒəˈriː] *n* : ropa *f* íntima femenina, lencería *f*

lingo [ˈlɪŋgo] *n, pl* **-goes 1** LANGUAGE : idioma *m* **2** JARGON : jerga *f*

linguist [ˈlɪŋgwɪst] *n* : lingüista *mf*

linguistic [lɪŋˈgwɪstɪk] *adj* : lingüístico

linguistics [lɪŋˈgwɪstɪks] *n* : lingüística *f*

liniment [ˈlɪnəmənt] *n* : linimento *m*

lining [ˈlaɪnɪŋ] *n* : forro *m*

link¹ [ˈlɪŋk] *vt* : unir, enlazar, conectar — *vi* **to link up** : unirse, conectar

link² *n* **1** : eslabón *m* (de una cadena) **2** BOND : conexión *f*, lazo *m*, vínculo *m* **3** HYPERLINK : enlace *m*, vínculo *m*

linkage [ˈlɪŋkɪdʒ] *n* : conexión *f*, unión *f*, enlace *m*

links [ˈlɪŋks] *n* : campo *m* de golf, cancha *f* de golf

linoleum [ləˈnoːliəm] *n* : linóleo *m*

lint [ˈlɪnt] *n* : pelusa *f*

lintel [ˈlɪntəl] *n* : dintel *m*

lion [ˈlaɪən] *n* : león *m*

lioness [ˈlaɪənɪs] *n* : leona *f*

lionize [ˈlaɪəˌnaɪz] *vt* **-ized; -izing** : tratar a una persona como muy importante

lip [ˈlɪp] *n* **1** : labio *m* **2** EDGE, RIM : pico *m* (de una jarra), borde *m* (de una taza)

lip–read [ˈlɪpˌriːd] *vi* : leer los labios

lipreading [ˈlɪpˌriːdɪŋ] *n* : lectura *f* de los labios

lipstick [ˈlɪpˌstɪk] *n* : lápiz *m* labial, barra *f* de labios

liquefy [ˈlɪkwəˌfaɪ] *v* **-fied; -fying** *vt* : licuar — *vi* : licuarse

liqueur [lɪˈkʊr, -ˈkər, -ˈkjʊr] *n* : licor *m*

liquid¹ [ˈlɪkwəd] *adj* : líquido

liquid² *n* : líquido *m*

liquidate [ˈlɪkwəˌdeɪt] *vt* **-dated; -dating** : liquidar

liquidation [ˌlɪkwəˈdeɪʃən] *n* : liquidación *f*

liquidity [lɪkˈwɪdəti] *n* : liquidez *f*

liquor [ˈlɪkər] *n* : alcohol *m*, bebidas *fpl* alcohólicas, licor *m*

lisp¹ [ˈlɪsp] *vi* : cecear

lisp² *n* : ceceo *m*

lissome [ˈlɪsəm] *adj* **1** FLEXIBLE : flexible **2** LITHE : ágil y grácil

list¹ [ˈlɪst] *vt* **1** ENUMERATE : hacer una lista de, enumerar **2** INCLUDE : poner en una lista, incluir — *vi* : escorar (dícese de un barco)

list² *n* : lista *f* ⟨he's first/last on the list : es el primero/último de la lista⟩

listen [ˈlɪsən] *vi* **1** : escuchar, oír **2 to listen to** HEED : escuchar, prestar atención a, hacer caso de (algo), hacerle caso (a alguien) **3 to listen to reason** : atender a razones

listener [ˈlɪsənər] *n* : oyente *mf*, persona *f* que sabe escuchar

listless [ˈlɪstləs] *adj* : lánguido, apático — **listlessly** *adv*

listlessness ['lɪstləsnəs] *n* : apatía *f*, languidez *f*, desgana *f*

lit ['lɪt] → **light**

litany ['lɪtəni] *n, pl* **-nies** : letanía *f*

liter ['liːtər] *n* : litro *m*

literacy ['lɪtərəsi] *n* : alfabetismo *m*

literal ['lɪtərəl] *adj* : literal — **literally** *adv*

literary ['lɪtəˌreri] *adj* : literario

literate ['lɪtərət] *adj* : alfabetizado

literature ['lɪtərəˌtʃur, -ˌtʃor] *n* : literatura *f*

lithe ['laɪð, 'laɪθ] *adj* : ágil y grácil

lithesome ['laɪðsəm, 'laɪθ-] → **lissome**

lithium ['lɪθiəm] *n* : litio *m*

lithograph ['lɪθəˌɡræf] *n* : litografía *f*

lithographer [lɪ'θɑɡrəfər, 'lɪθəˌɡræfər] *n* : litógrafo *m*, -fa *f*

lithography [lɪ'θɑɡrəfi] *n* : litografía *f*

lithosphere ['lɪθəˌsfɪr] *n* : litosfera *f*

Lithuanian [ˌlɪθə'weɪniən] *n* **1** : lituano *m* (idioma) **2** : lituano *m*, -na *f* — **Lithuanian** *adj*

litigant ['lɪtɪɡənt] *n* : litigante *mf*

litigate ['lɪtəˌɡeɪt] *vi* **-gated; -gating** : litigar

litigation [ˌlɪtə'ɡeɪʃən] *n* : litigio *m*

litmus ['lɪtməs] *n* : tornasol *m*

litmus paper *n* : papel *m* de tornasol

litmus test *n* : prueba *f* decisiva

litter[1] ['lɪtər] *vt* : tirar basura en, ensuciar — *vi* : tirar basura

litter[2] *n* **1** : camada *f*, cría *f* ⟨a litter of kittens : una cría de gatitos⟩ **2** STRETCHER : camilla *f* **3** RUBBISH : basura *f* **4** : arena *f* higiénica (para gatos)

little[1] ['lɪtəl] *adv* **less** ['lɛs]; **least** ['liːst] **1** : poco ⟨she sings very little : canta muy poco⟩ **2** little did I know that . . . : no tenía la menor idea de que . . . **3 as little as possible** : lo menos posible

little[2] *adj* **littler** *or* **less** ['lɛs] *or* **lesser** ['lɛsər]; **littlest** *or* **least** ['liːst] **1** SMALL : pequeño **2** : poco ⟨they speak little Spanish : hablan poco español⟩ ⟨little by little : poco a poco⟩ ⟨a little bit : un poco⟩ ⟨a little while : un ratito⟩ **3** TRIVIAL : sin importancia, trivial

little[3] *n* **1** : poco *m* ⟨little has changed : poco ha cambiado⟩ **2 a little** : un poco, algo ⟨it's a little surprising : es algo sorprendente⟩

Little Dipper → **dipper**

little person *n, pl* **little people 1** : persona *f* pequeña; enano *m*, -na *f* **2 the little people** : la gente común

liturgical [lə'tərdʒɪkəl] *adj* : litúrgico — **liturgically** [-kli] *adv*

liturgy ['lɪtərdʒi] *n, pl* **-gies** : liturgia *f*

livable ['lɪvəbəl] *adj* : habitable

live[1] ['lɪv] *v* **lived; living** *vi* **1** EXIST : vivir ⟨as long as I live : mientras viva⟩ ⟨to live from day to day : vivir al día⟩ ⟨long live the Queen/King! : ¡viva el rey/la reina!⟩ **2** : llevar una vida, vivir ⟨he lived simply : llevó una vida sencilla⟩ ⟨they lived happily ever after : vivieron felices (y comieron perdices)⟩ **3** SUBSIST : vivir, mantenerse ⟨to live within/beyond one's means : vivir dentro/fuera de sus posibilidades⟩ **4** RESIDE : vivir, residir ⟨where do you live? : ¿dónde vives?⟩ **5 live and**

let live : vive y deja vivir a los demás **6 to live down** ⟨they'll never let you live it down, you'll never live it down : nunca te dejarán olvidarlo⟩ **7 to live off** : vivir de (algo), vivir a costa de (alguien) **8 to live on** : vivir de (un sueldo, etc.), alimentarse de (comida) ⟨they live on less than a dollar a day : viven con menos de un dólar por día⟩ **9 to live on** PERSIST : permanecer **10 to live out one's life** : vivir toda su vida **11 to live through** SURVIVE : sobrevivir **12 to live together** : vivir juntos **13 to live up to** : estar a la altura de (las expectativas, etc.) **14 to live up to** : cumplir (su palabra, etc.) **15 to live with** : vivir con (alguien) **16 to live with** ACCEPT : aceptar — *vt* : llevar, vivir ⟨he lived a simple life : llevó una vida sencilla⟩ ⟨to live the good life : vivir la buena vida⟩

live[2] ['laɪv] *adj* **1** LIVING : vivo **2** BURNING : encendido ⟨a live coal : una brasa⟩ **3** : con corriente ⟨live wires : cables con corriente⟩ **4** : cargado, sin estallar ⟨a live bomb : una bomba sin estallar⟩ **5** CURRENT : de actualidad ⟨a live issue : un asunto de actualidad⟩ **6** : en vivo, en directo ⟨a live interview : una entrevista en vivo⟩

livelihood ['laɪvliˌhʊd] *n* : sustento *m*, vida *f*, medio *m* de vida

liveliness ['laɪvlinəs] *n* : animación *f*, vivacidad *f*

livelong ['lɪvˌlɔŋ] *adj* : entero, completo

lively ['laɪvli] *adj* **livelier; -est** : animado, vivaz, vivo, enérgico

liven ['laɪvən] *vt* : animar — *vi* : animarse

liver ['lɪvər] *n* : hígado *m*

livery ['lɪvəri] *n, pl* **-eries** : librea *f*

lives → **life**

livestock ['laɪvˌstɑk] *n* : ganado *m*

live wire *n* : persona *f* vivaz y muy activa

livid ['lɪvəd] *adj* **1** BLACK-AND-BLUE : amoratado **2** PALE : lívido **3** ENRAGED : furioso

living[1] ['lɪvɪŋ] *adj* : vivo

living[2] *n* **to make a living** : ganarse la vida

living room *n* : living *m*, sala *f* de estar

lizard ['lɪzərd] *n* : lagarto *m*

llama ['lɑmə, 'jɑ-] *n* : llama *f*

load[1] ['loːd] *vt* **1** : cargar, embarcar (vehículos, cargamento, etc.) **2** : embarcar (pasajeros) **3** : cargar (una pistola, etc.) **4** : cargar (un programa, etc.) **5** : cargar, sobrecargar ⟨she loaded (up) her plate with food : llenó el plato de comida⟩ **6 to load down with** BURDEN : cargar de ⟨to be loaded down with debt : estar agobiado por las deudas⟩ — *vi* **1** : cargar **2 to load up on** : pasarse con (la comida, etc.)

load[2] *n* **1** CARGO : carga *f* **2** WEIGHT : peso *m* **3** BURDEN : carga *f*, peso *m* **4 loads** *npl* : montón *m*, pila *f*, cantidad *f* ⟨loads of work : un montón de trabajo⟩

loaded ['loːdəd] *adj* **1** : cargado (dícese de una pistola, una cámara, etc.) **2** WEIGHTED : cargado ⟨loaded dice : dados cargados⟩ **3** : cargado (de connotaciones) ⟨a loaded question : una pregunta capciosa⟩ **4** RICH : muy rico **5** *fam* DRUNK : borracho, chupado *fam* **6** **to be loaded with** : estar repleto de

loaf[1] ['lo:f] *vi* : holgazanear, flojear, haraganear

loaf[2] *n, pl* **loaves** ['lo:vz] **1** : pan *m*, pan *m* de molde, barra *f* de pan **2** meat loaf : pan *m* de carne

loafer ['lo:fər] *n* : holgazán *m*, -zana *f*; haragán *m*, -gana *f*; vago *m*, -ga *f*

loan[1] ['lo:n] *vt* : prestar

loan[2] *n* : préstamo *m*, empréstito *m* (del banco)

loanword ['lo:n,wərd] *n* : préstamo *m*, barbarismo *m*

loath ['lo:θ, 'lo:ð] *adj* : poco dispuesto ⟨I am loath to say it : me resisto a decirlo⟩

loathe ['lo:ð] *vt* **loathed; loathing** : odiar, aborrecer

loathing ['lo:ðɪŋ] *n* : aversión *f*, odio *m*, aborrecimiento *m*

loathsome ['lo:θsəm, 'lo:ð-] *adj* : odioso, repugnante

lob[1] ['lab] *vt* **lobbed; lobbing** : hacerle un globo (a otro jugador)

lob[2] *n* : globo *m* (en deportes)

lobby[1] ['labi] *v* **-bied; -bying** *vt* : presionar, ejercer presión sobre — *vi* **to lobby for** : presionar para (lograr algo)

lobby[2] *n, pl* **-bies** **1** FOYER : vestíbulo *m* **2** LOBBYISTS : grupo *m* de presión, lobby *m*

lobbyist ['labiist] *n* : miembro *m* de un lobby

lobe ['lo:b] *n* : lóbulo *m*

lobed ['lo:bd] *adj* : lobulado

lobotomy [lə'baṭəmi, lo-] *n, pl* **-mies** : lobotomía *f*

lobster ['labstər] *n* : langosta *f*

local[1] ['lo:kəl] *adj* : local

local[2] *n* **1** : anestesia *f* local **2** **the locals** : los vecinos del lugar, los habitantes

locale [lo'kæl] *n* : lugar *m*, escenario *m*

locality [lo'kæləṭi] *n* : localidad *f*

localization [,lo:kələ'zeɪʃən] *n* POSITION : localización *f*

localize ['lo:kə,laɪz] *vt* **-ized; -izing** : localizar

locally ['lo:kəli] *adv* : en la localidad, en la zona

locate ['lo:,keɪt, lo'keɪt] *v* **-cated; -cating** *vt* **1** POSITION : situar, ubicar **2** FIND : localizar, ubicar — *vi* SETTLE : establecerse

location [lo'keɪʃən] *n* **1** POSITION : posición *f*, emplazamiento *m*, ubicación *f* **2** PLACE : lugar *m*, sitio *m*

loch ['lak] *n* : lago *m*

lock[1] ['lak] *vt* **1** FASTEN : cerrar (con llave) **2** CONFINE : encerrar ⟨they locked me in the room : me encerraron en la habitación⟩ **3** IMMOBILIZE : bloquear (una rueda) **4** **to lock away/up** : encerrar (a alguien), guardar (algo) bajo llave **5** **to lock out** : dejar fuera a, cerrar la puerta a ⟨I locked myself out : me quedé fuera (sin llaves)⟩ — *vi* **1** or **to lock up** : cerrar (con llave) **2** : cerrarse (dícese de una puerta) **3** : trabarse, bloquearse (dícese de una rueda)

4 **to lock horns** : chocar, pelearse **5** **to lock on/onto** TARGET : fijar (el blanco)

lock[2] *n* **1** : mechón *m* (de pelo) **2** FASTENER : cerradura *f*, cerrojo *m*, chapa *f* **3** : esclusa *f* (de un canal)

locker ['lakər] *n* : armario *m*, cajón *m* con llave, lócker *m*

locker room *n* : vestuario *m*; camarín *m* *Chile, Peru, Uru*

locket ['lakət] *n* : medallón *m*, guardapelo *m*, relicario *m*

lockjaw ['lak,jɔ] *n* : tétano *m*

lockout ['lak,aʊt] *n* : cierre *m* patronal

locksmith ['lak,smɪθ] *n* : cerrajero *m*, -ra *f*

lockup ['lak,ʌp] *n* JAIL : cárcel *f*

locomotion [,lo:kə'mo:ʃən] *n* : locomoción *f*

locomotive[1] [,lo:kə'mo:ṭɪv] *adj* : locomotor

locomotive[2] *n* : locomotora *f*

locust ['lo:kəst] *n* **1** : langosta *f*, chapulín *m* *CA, Mex* **2** CICADA : cigarra *f*, chicharra *f* **3** : acacia *f* blanca (árbol)

locution [lo'kju:ʃən] *n* : locución *f*

lode ['lo:d] *n* : veta *f*, vena *f*, filón *m*

lodestar ['lo:d,star] *n* : estrella *f* polar

lodestone ['lo:d,sto:n] *n* : piedra *f* imán

lodge[1] ['ladʒ] *v* **lodged; lodging** *vt* **1** HOUSE : hospedar, alojar **2** FILE : presentar ⟨to lodge a complaint : presentar una demanda⟩ — *vi* **1** : posarse, meterse ⟨the bullet lodged in the door : la bala se incrustó en la puerta⟩ **2** STAY : hospedarse, alojarse

lodge[2] *n* **1** : pabellón *m*, casa *f* de campo ⟨hunting lodge : refugio *m* de caza⟩ **2** : madriguera *f* (de un castor) **3** : logia *f* ⟨Masonic lodge : logia masónica⟩

lodger ['ladʒər] *n* : inquilino *m*, -na *f*; huésped *m*, -peda *f*

lodging ['ladʒɪŋ] *n* **1** : alojamiento *m* **2** **lodgings** *npl* ROOMS : habitaciones *fpl*

loft ['lɔft] *n* **1** ATTIC : desván *m*, ático *m*, buhardilla *f* **2** : piso *m* superior (de un depósito comercial) ⟨a converted loft : un depósito convertido en apartamentos⟩ **3** HAYLOFT : pajar *m* **4** : galería *f* ⟨choir loft : galería del coro⟩

loftily ['lɔftəli] *adv* : altaneramente, con altivez

loftiness ['lɔftinəs] *n* **1** NOBILITY : nobleza *f* **2** ARROGANCE : altanería *f*, arrogancia *f* **3** HEIGHT : altura *f*, elevación *f*

lofty ['lɔfti] *adj* **loftier; -est** **1** NOBLE : noble, elevado **2** HAUGHTY : altivo, arrogante, altanero **3** HIGH : majestuoso, elevado

log[1] ['lɔg, 'lag] *vi* **logged; logging** **1** : talar (árboles) **2** RECORD : registrar, anotar **3** **to log on** : entrar (al sistema) **4** **to log off** : salir (del sistema)

log[2] *n* **1** : tronco *m*, leño *m* **2** RECORD : diario *m*

logarithm ['lɔgə,rɪðəm, 'la-] *n* : logaritmo *m*

logger ['lɔgər, 'la-] *n* : leñador *m*, -dora *f*

loggerhead ['lɔgər,hd, 'la-] *n* **1** : tortuga *f* boba **2** **to be at loggerheads** : estar en pugna, estar en desacuerdo

logic ['laʤɪk] *n* : lógica *f* — **logical** ['laʤɪkəl] *adj* — **logically** [-kli] *adv*

logistic [lə'ʤɪstɪk, lo-] *adj* : logístico

logistics [lə'ʤɪstɪks, lo-] *ns & pl* : logística *f*

logo ['lo:,go:] *n, pl* **logos** [-,go:z] : logotipo *m*

loin ['lɔɪn] *n* **1** : lomo *m* ⟨pork loin : lomo de cerdo⟩ **2 loins** *npl* : lomos *mpl* ⟨to gird one's loins : prepararse para la lucha⟩

loincloth ['lɔɪn,klɔθ] *n* : taparrabos *m*

loiter ['lɔɪtər] *vi* : vagar, perder el tiempo

loll ['lal] *vi* **1** SLOUCH : repantigarse **2** IDLE : holgazanear, hacer el vago

lollipop *or* **lollypop** ['lali,pap] *n* : dulce *m* en palito, chupete *m Chile, Peru*, paleta *f CA, Mex*

Londoner ['lʌndənər] *n* : londinense *mf*

lone ['lo:n] *adj* **1** SOLITARY : solitario **2** ONLY : único

loneliness ['lo:nlinəs] *n* : soledad *f*

lonely ['lo:nli] *adj* **lonelier; -est** SOLITARY : solitario, aislado ⟨to feel lonely : sentirse muy solo⟩

loner ['lo:nər] *n* : solitario *m*, -ria *f*; recluso *m*, -sa *f*

lonesome ['lo:nsəm] *adj* : solo, solitario

long[1] ['lɔŋ] *vi* **1 to long for** : añorar, desear, anhelar **2 to long to** : anhelar, estar deseando ⟨they longed to see her : estaban deseando verla, tenían muchas ganas de verla⟩

long[2] *adv* **1** : mucho, mucho tiempo ⟨it didn't take long : no llevó mucho tiempo⟩ ⟨will it last long? : ¿va a durar mucho?⟩ ⟨will you be long? : ¿tardarás mucho?⟩ ⟨a (little) bit longer : un poco más (tiempo)⟩ ⟨I didn't have long enough to visit : no me alcanzó el tiempo para visitar⟩ **2 all day long** : todo el día **3 as/so long as** IF : mientras, con tal (de) que **4 as/so long as** SINCE : ya que **5 as/so long as** WHILE : mientras **6 before long** : antes de poco **7 long ago** : hace mucho tiempo **8 long before/after** : mucho antes/después **9 long gone** ⟨that building is long gone : ese edificio se desapareció hace mucho⟩ **10 long since** : hace mucho **11 no longer** *or* **(not) any longer** ⟨it's no longer needed : ya no hace falta⟩ ⟨I can't wait any longer : no puedo esperar más⟩ **12 so long!** : ¡hasta luego!, ¡adiós!

long[3] *adj* **longer** ['lɔŋgər]; **longest** ['lɔŋgəst] **1** (*indicating length*) : largo ⟨long hair : pelo largo⟩ ⟨the dress is too long : el vestido es demasiado largo⟩ ⟨the book is two hundred pages long : el libro tiene doscientas páginas⟩ ⟨a long way from : bastante lejos de⟩ **2** (*indicating time*) : largo, prolongado ⟨a long illness : una enfermedad prolongada⟩ ⟨a long walk : un paseo largo⟩ ⟨a long time ago : hace mucho (tiempo)⟩ ⟨I've known him for a long time : lo conozco desde hace mucho⟩ ⟨the drive is five hours long : el viaje dura cinco horas⟩ ⟨a long last : por fin⟩ ⟨in the long run : a la larga⟩ **3 to be long on** : estar cargado de

long[4] *n* **1 before long** : dentro de poco **2 the long and (the) short of it** : lo esencial, lo fundamental

long–distance ['lɔŋ'dɪstən/s] *adj* **1** : de larga distancia ⟨long-distance call : llamada de larga distancia, llamada interurbana⟩ ⟨long-distance trip : viaje de largo recorrido⟩ ⟨long-distance runner : fondista⟩ **2** : a larga distancia ⟨a long-distance romance : una relación a (larga) distancia⟩

longevity [lan'ʤɛvəṭi] *n* : longevidad *f*

long–haired ['lɔŋ'hærd] *adj* : melenudo

longhand ['lɔŋ,hænd] *n* : escritura *f* a mano, escritura *f* cursiva

long–haul ['lɔŋ'hɔl] *adj* : de larga distancia

longing ['lɔŋɪŋ] *n* : vivo deseo *m*, ansia *f*, anhelo *m*

longingly [lɔŋɪŋli] *adv* : ansiosamente, con ansia

longitude ['lanʤə,tu:d, -,tju:d] *n* : longitud *f*

longitudinal [,lanʤə'tu:dənəl, -'tju:-] *adj* : longitudinal — **longitudinally** *adv*

long jump *n* : salto *m* de longitud, salto *m* (en) largo

long–lived ['lɔŋ'lɪvd, -'laɪvd] *adj* : longevo

long–range ['lɔŋ'reɪndʒ] *adj* **1** : de largo alcance ⟨dícese de un avión, etc.⟩ **2** : a largo plazo ⟨dícese de un plan, etc.⟩

longshoreman ['lɔŋ'ʃormən] *n, pl* **-men** [-mən, -,mɛn] : estibador *m*, -dora *f*

longshorewoman ['lɔŋ'ʃor,wumən] *n, pl* **-women** [-,wɪmən] : cargadora *f*

long–standing ['lɔŋ'stændɪŋ] *adj* : de larga data

long–suffering ['lɔŋ'sʌfərɪŋ] *adj* : paciente, sufrido

long–term ['lɔŋ'tərm] *adj* : a largo plazo ⟨dícese de un plan, etc.⟩

long–winded [,lɔŋ'wɪndəd] *adj* : prolijo

look[1] ['luk] *vi* **1** : mirar ⟨to look out the window : mirar por la ventana⟩ ⟨to look ahead/back : mirar hacia adelante/atrás⟩ ⟨look around you : mira a tu alrededor⟩ ⟨look! there he is : ¡mira! ahí está⟩ **2** INVESTIGATE : buscar, mirar ⟨look in the closet : busca en el clóset⟩ ⟨look before you leap : mira lo que haces⟩ **3** SEEM : parecer ⟨he looks happy : parece estar contento⟩ ⟨you look very nice! : ¡estás guapísima!⟩ ⟨she looked (to be) about forty : parecía tener alrededor de cuarenta años⟩ **4** (*used to warn, express anger, etc.*) ⟨look, it's not going to work : mira, no va a funcionar⟩ ⟨now look what you've done! : ¡mira lo que has hecho!⟩ ⟨(now) look here! : ¡oye!⟩ **5** FACE, POINT : dar a **6 to look after** TAKE CARE OF : cuidar, cuidar de (personas o animales), encargarse de (una empresa, etc.) **7 to look ahead** : mirar hacia el futuro **8 to look around** EXPLORE : mirar, echar un vistazo a **9 to look around for** : buscar **10 to look as if/though** : parecer que ⟨it looks as if it will rain : parece que va a llover⟩ **11 to look at** : mirar **12 to look at** CONSIDER : considerar **13**

to look at EXAMINE : examinar **14** to look at FACE : estar frente a, enfrentarse a (problemas, etc.) **15** to look back : mirar hacia el pasado **16** to look down on : despreciar, menospreciar **17** to look for EXPECT : esperar **18** to look for SEEK : buscar **19** to look forward to ANTICIPATE : estar ansioso de (hacer algo), estar ansioso de que llegue(n) (una fecha, etc.) **20** to look in on : ir a ver (a alguien) **21** to look into INVESTIGATE : investigar **22** to look like : parecer, parecerse ⟨it looks like a large bird : parece un pájaro grande⟩ ⟨it looks like (it will) rain : parece que va a llover⟩ ⟨I look like my mother : me parezco a mi madre⟩ **23** to look on WATCH : mirar **24** to look on CONSIDER : considerar ⟨I look on her as a friend : la considero una amiga⟩ ⟨he looked on his accomplishments with pride : sus logros lo llenaba de orgullo⟩ **25** to look out : tener cuidado **26** to look out for WATCH for : estar alerta por **27** to look out for PROTECT : mirar por ⟨she only looks out for number one : sólo piensa en sí misma⟩ **28** to look the other way : hacer la vista gorda **29** to look through : hojear (una revista, etc.) **30** to look to ... for ... ⟨to look to someone for something : recurrir a alguien para hacer algo⟩ ⟨they looked to history for an answer : buscaron la solución en la historia⟩ **31** to look up IMPROVE : mejorar **32** to look up to ADMIRE : respetar, admirar — vt **1** : mirar ⟨look what I found! : ¡mira lo que encontré!⟩ **2** HOPE, EXPECT : esperar ⟨we look to have a good year, we're looking to have a good year : esperamos tener un buen año⟩ **3** to look over/through EXAMINE : revisar **4** to look up : buscar (en un diccionario, etc.) **5** to look up CALL, VISIT : llamar, visitar

look² n **1** GLANCE : mirada f ⟨to take a look at : mirar⟩ **2** EXPRESSION : cara f ⟨a look of disapproval : una cara de desaprobación⟩ **3** ASPECT : aspecto m, apariencia f, aire m **4** looks npl : belleza f

looker ['lʊkər] n to be a looker : ser guapísimo

looking ['lʊkɪŋ] adj used in combination : de aspecto ⟨nice-looking : (de aspecto) atractivo⟩

lookout ['lʊk,aʊt] n **1** : centinela mf, vigía mf **2** to be on the lookout for : estar al acecho de, andar a la caza de

loom¹ ['lu:m] vi **1** : aparecer, surgir ⟨the city loomed up in the distance : la ciudad surgió en la distancia⟩ **2** MENACE, APPROACH : amenazar, ser inminente **3** to loom large : cobrar mucha importancia

loom² n : telar m

loon ['lu:n] n : somorgujo m, somormujo m

loony or **looney** ['lu:ni] adj loonier; -est : loco, chiflado m

loop¹ ['lu:p] vt **1** : hacer lazadas con **2** to loop around : pasar alrededor de — vi **1** : rizar el rizo (dícese de un avión) **2** : serpentear (dícese de una carretera)

loop² n **1** : lazada f (en hilo o cuerda) **2** BEND : curva f **3** CIRCUIT : circuito m cerrado **4** : rizo m (en la aviación) ⟨to loop the loop : rizar el rizo⟩

loophole ['lu:p,ho:l] n : escapatoria f, pretexto m

loose¹ ['lu:s] vt loosed; loosing **1** RELEASE : poner en libertad, soltar **2** UNTIE : deshacer, desatar **3** DISCHARGE, UNLEASH : descargar, desatar

loose² → loosely

loose³ adj looser; -est **1** INSECURE : flojo, suelto, poco seguro ⟨a loose tooth : un diente flojo⟩ **2** ROOMY : suelto, holgado ⟨loose clothing : ropa holgada⟩ **3** OPEN : suelto, abierto ⟨loose soil : suelo suelto⟩ ⟨a loose weave : una tejida abierta⟩ **4** FREE : suelto ⟨to break loose : soltarse⟩ ⟨to let loose : soltar⟩ ⟨loose sheets of paper : papeles sueltos⟩ ⟨loose change : dinero suelto⟩ **5** SLACK : flojo, flexible ⟨a loose translation : una traducción aproximada⟩

loosely ['lu:sli] adv **1** : sin apretar **2** ROUGHLY : aproximadamente, más o menos

loose-leaf ['lu:s'li:f] adj : de hojas sueltas

loosen ['lu:sən] vt **1** : aflojar **2** to loosen up RELAX : relajar — vi **1** : aflojarse **2** to loosen up RELAX : relajarse

looseness ['lu:snəs] n **1** : holgura f (de ropa) **2** IMPRECISION : imprecisión f

loot¹ ['lu:t] vt : saquear, robar

loot² n : botín m

looter ['lu:tər] n : saqueador m, -dora f

lop ['lɑp] vt lopped; lopping : cortar, podar

lope¹ ['lo:p] vi loped; loping : correr a paso largo

lope² n : paso m largo

lopsided ['lɑp,saɪdəd] adj **1** CROOKED : torcido, chueco, ladeado **2** ASYMMETRICAL : asimétrico

loquacious [lo'kweɪʃəs] adj : locuaz

lord ['lɔrd] n **1** : señor m, noble m **2** : lord m (en la Gran Bretaña) **3** the Lord : el Señor **4** (good) Lord! : ¡Dios mío!

lordly ['lɔrdli] adj lordlier; -est HAUGHTY : arrogante, altanero

lordship ['lɔrd,ʃɪp] n : señoría f

Lord's Supper n : Eucaristía f

lore ['lɔr] n : saber m popular, tradición f

lose ['lu:z] v lost ['lɔst]; losing ['lu:zɪŋ] vt **1** MISLAY : perder ⟨I lost my umbrella : perdí mi paraguas⟩ **2** : perder (un partido, etc.) **3** (to fail to keep) : perder ⟨to lose blood : perder sangre⟩ ⟨to lose one's appetite : perder el apetito⟩ ⟨to lose track of the time : perder la noción del tiempo⟩ ⟨to have nothing to lose : no tener nada que perder⟩ ⟨to lose sight of : perder de vista⟩ **4** : perder (dinero) **5** (to be deprived of) : perder ⟨they lost everything : lo perdieron todo⟩ ⟨we lost power : se cortó la luz⟩ ⟨to lose one's voice : quedarse afónico⟩ ⟨she lost her husband : perdió a su esposo⟩ ⟨we're sorry to lose you! : ¡qué pena que te vayas!⟩ **6** (to gradually have less of) : perder (peso, interés, etc.) **7** : perder (valor) **8** WASTE : perder ⟨there's no time to lose : no hay tiempo que perder⟩ **9** : perder (la calma, el control, etc.) ⟨to lose one's temper : perder los estribos, enojarse, enfadarse⟩ ⟨to lose one's nerve : perder el valor⟩ **10** : costar, hacer perder (the errors lost him his job : los errores le costaron su empleo⟩ **11** : atrasar ⟨my watch loses 5 minutes a day : mi reloj se atrasa 5 minutos por día⟩ **12** CONFUSE : confundir **13** GET RID OF : deshacerse de **14** GET AWAY FROM : deshacerse de **15** to lose oneself : perderse, ensimismarse **16** to lose one's way : perderse — *vi* : perder ⟨we lost to the other team : perdimos contra el otro equipo⟩

loser [ˈluːzər] *n* : perdedor *m*, -dora *f*

loss [ˈlɔs] *n* **1** LOSING : pérdida *f* ⟨loss of memory : pérdida de memoria⟩ ⟨to sell at a loss : vender con pérdida⟩ ⟨to cut one's losses : reducir las pérdidas (económicas)⟩ ⟨to be at a loss to : no saber cómo⟩ ⟨to be at a loss for words : no saber qué decir⟩ **2** DEFEAT : derrota *f*, juego *m* perdido **3** losses *npl* DEATHS : muertos *mpl*

lost [ˈlɔst] *adj* **1** : perdido ⟨a lost cause : una causa perdida⟩ ⟨lost in thought : absorto⟩ **2** to get lost : perderse **3** to make up for lost time : recuperar el tiempo perdido

lot [ˈlɑt] *n* **1** DRAWING : sorteo *m* ⟨by lot : por sorteo⟩ **2** SHARE : parte *f*, porción *f* **3** FATE : suerte *f* **4** LAND, PLOT : terreno *m*, solar *m*, lote *m*, parcela *f* ⟨parking lot : estacionamiento⟩ **5** a lot : mucho ⟨I liked it a lot : me gustó mucho⟩ ⟨she doesn't travel a lot : no viaja mucho⟩ **6** a lot *or* lots : mucho ⟨a lot better : mucho mejor⟩ ⟨thanks a lot : muchas gracias⟩ ⟨there's lots to do : hay mucho que hacer⟩ **7** a lot of *or* lots of : mucho, un montón de, bastante ⟨lots of books : un montón de libros, muchos libros⟩ ⟨a lot of people : mucha gente⟩

loth [ˈloːθ, ˈloːð] → **loath**

lotion [ˈloːʃən] *n* : loción *f*

lottery [ˈlɑtəri] *n*, *pl* **-teries** : lotería *f*

lotus [ˈloːtəs] *n* : loto *m*

loud[1] [ˈlaʊd] *adv* : alto, fuerte ⟨out loud : en voz alta⟩

loud[2] *adj* **1** : alto, fuerte ⟨a loud voice : una voz alta⟩ **2** NOISY : ruidoso ⟨a loud party : una fiesta ruidosa⟩ **3** FLASHY : llamativo, chillón

loudly [ˈlaʊdli] *adv* : alto, fuerte, en voz alta

loudmouth [ˈlaʊdˌmaʊθ] *n* : bocón *m*, -cona *f*

loudness [ˈlaʊdnəs] *n* : volumen *m*, fuerza *f* (del ruido)

loudspeaker [ˈlaʊdˌspiːkər] *n* : altavoz *m*, altoparlante *m*

lounge[1] [ˈlaʊndʒ] *vi* **lounged; lounging** : holgazanear, gandulear

lounge[2] *n* : salón *m*, sala *f* de estar

louse [ˈlaʊs] *n*, *pl* **lice** [ˈlaɪs] : piojo *m*

lousy [ˈlaʊzi] *adj* **lousier; -est 1** : piojoso, lleno de piojos **2** BAD : pésimo, muy malo

lout [ˈlaʊt] *n* : bruto *m*, patán *m*

louver *or* **louvre** [ˈluːvər] *n* : persiana *f*, listón *m* de persiana

lovable [ˈlʌvəbəl] *adj* : adorable, amoroso, encantador

love[1] [ˈlʌv] *v* **loved; loving** *vt* **1** : querer, amar ⟨I love you : te quiero⟩ **2** ENJOY : encantarle a alguien, ser (muy) aficionado a, gustarle mucho a uno (algo) ⟨she loves flowers : le encantan las flores⟩ ⟨he loves golf : es muy aficionado al golf⟩ ⟨I'd love to go with you : me gustaría mucho acompañarte⟩ — *vi* : querer, amar

love[2] *n* **1** : amor *m*, cariño *m* ⟨to be in love with : estar enamorado de⟩ ⟨to fall in love with : enamorarse de⟩ ⟨to fall out of love with : dejar de querer a⟩ ⟨love affair : aventura⟩ ⟨love life : vida amorosa⟩ **2** ENTHUSIASM, INTEREST : amor *m*, afición *f*, gusto *m* ⟨love of music : afición a la música⟩ **3** BELOVED : amor *m*; amado *m*, -da *f*; enamorado *m*, -da *f* ⟨yes, my love : sí, mi amor⟩ **4** REGARDS : recuerdos *mpl* ⟨Love, Brian : cariños, Brian⟩ **5** love at first sight : amor a primera vista **6** no/little love lost ⟨there is no love lost between them : no se pueden ver⟩ **7** not for love or money : por nada del mundo **8** to make love : hacer el amor

loveless [ˈlʌvləs] *adj* : sin amor

loveliness [ˈlʌvlinəs] *n* : belleza *f*, hermosura *f*

lovelorn [ˈlʌvˌlɔrn] *adj* : herido de amor, perdidamente enamorado

lovely [ˈlʌvli] *adj* **lovelier; -est** : hermoso, bello, lindo, precioso

lover [ˈlʌvər] *n* : amante *mf* (de personas); aficionado *m*, -da *f* (a alguna actividad)

loving [ˈlʌvɪŋ] *adj* : amoroso, cariñoso

lovingly [ˈlʌvɪŋli] *adv* : cariñosamente

low[1] [ˈloː] *vi* : mugir

low[2] *adv* : bajo, profundo ⟨to aim low : apuntar bajo⟩ ⟨to lie low : mantenerse escondido⟩ ⟨to turn the lights down low : bajar las luces⟩

low[3] *adj* **lower** [ˈloːər], **lowest 1** : bajo ⟨a low building : un edificio bajo⟩ ⟨a low bow : una profunda reverencia⟩ **2** : bajo ⟨low temperatures/speeds : bajas temperaturas/velocidades⟩ ⟨low-calorie/low-fat : bajo en calorías/grasas⟩ **3** SHALLOW : bajo, poco profundo **4** WEAK, GENTLE : flojo (dícese del viento), tenue (dícese de la luz) ⟨over low heat : a fuego lento⟩ **5** SOFT : bajo, suave ⟨in a low voice : en voz baja⟩ **6** DEEP : grave, profundo (dícese de la voz, etc.) **7** HUMBLE : humilde, modesto **8** DEPRESSED : deprimido, bajo de moral **9** INFERIOR : bajo, inferior **10** UNFAVORABLE : malo ⟨she has a low opinion of him : tiene un mal concepto de él⟩ **11** LOW-CUT : escotado **12** to be low on : tener poco de, estar escaso de ⟨we're low on gas : nos queda muy poca gasolina⟩

low[4] *n* **1** : punto *m* bajo ⟨to reach an all-time low : estar más bajo que nunca⟩ **2**

or **low gear** : primera velocidad *f* **3** : mugido *m* (de una vaca)

lowbrow ['loː̣ˌbraʊ] *n* : persona *f* inculta

low-class ['loːˈklæs] *adj* → **lower-class**

low-cut ['loːˈkʌt] *adj* : escotado

lower¹ ['loːər] *vt* **1** DROP : bajar ⟨to lower one's voice : bajar la voz⟩ **2** : arriar, bajar ⟨to lower the flag : arriar la bandera⟩ **3** REDUCE : reducir, bajar **4 to lower oneself** : rebajarse

lower² ['loːər] *adj* : inferior, más bajo, de abajo

lowercase¹ [ˌloːərˈkeɪs] *adj* : minúsculo

lowercase² *n* **in lowercase** : en minúsculas

lower-class [ˌloːərˈklæs] *adj* : de clase baja

lower class *n* : clase *f* baja

low-key ['loːˈkiː] *adj* : informal, sin ceremonias

lowland ['loːlənd, -ˌlænd] *n* : tierras *fpl* bajas

lowliness ['loːlinəs] *n* : humildad *f*, bajeza *f*

lowly ['loːli] *adj* **lowlier; -est** : humilde, modesto

loyal ['lɔɪəl] *adj* : leal, fiel — **loyally** *adv*

loyalist ['lɔɪəlɪst] *n* : partidario *m*, -ria *f* del régimen

loyalty ['lɔɪəlti] *n*, *pl* **-ties** : lealtad *f*, fidelidad *f*

loyalty card *n* : tarjeta *f* de cliente

lozenge ['lɑzəndʒ] *n* : pastilla *f*

LSD [ˌɛlˌɛsˈdiː] *n* : LSD *m*

lubricant ['luːbrɪkənt] *n* : lubricante *m*

lubricate ['luːbrɪˌkeɪt] *vt* **-cated; -cating** : lubricar — **lubrication** [ˌluːbrɪˈkeɪʃən] *n*

lucid ['luːsəd] *adj* : lúcido, claro — **lucidly** *adv*

lucidity [luːˈsɪdəti] *n* : lucidez *f*

luck ['lʌk] *n* **1** : suerte *f* ⟨hard luck : mala suerte⟩ **2 as luck would have it** : quiso la suerte que **3 good luck!** : ¡(buena) suerte! **4 the luck of the draw** ⟨to depend on the luck of the draw : ser cuestión de suerte⟩ **5 to be down on one's luck** : estar de mala racha **6 to be in luck** : estar de suerte **7 to be out of luck** : no estar de suerte **8 to have bad luck** : tener mala suerte **9 to press/push one's luck** : desafiar a la suerte **10 to try one's luck** : probar suerte **11 with any luck** : con un poco de suerte

luckily ['lʌkəli] *adv* : afortunadamente, por suerte

luckless ['lʌkləs] *adj* : desafortunado

lucky ['lʌki] *adj* **luckier; -est 1** : afortunado, que tiene suerte ⟨a lucky woman : una mujer afortunada⟩ **2** FORTUITOUS : fortuito, de suerte **3** OPPORTUNE : oportuno **4** : de (la) suerte ⟨lucky number : número de la suerte⟩

lucrative ['luːkrətɪv] *adj* : lucrativo, provechoso — **lucratively** *adv*

ludicrous ['luːdəkrəs] *adj* : ridículo, absurdo — **ludicrously** *adv*

ludicrousness ['luːdəkrəsnəs] *n* : ridiculez *f*, absurdo *m*

lug ['lʌg] *vt* **lugged; lugging** : arrastrar, transportar con dificultad

luggage ['lʌgɪdʒ] *n* : equipaje *m*

lugubrious [luˈguːbriəs] *adj* : lúgubre — **lugubriously** *adv*

lukewarm ['luːkˈwɔrm] *adj* **1** TEPID : tibio **2** HALFHEARTED : poco entusiasta

lull¹ ['lʌl] *vt* **1** CALM, SOOTHE : calmar, sosegar **2 to lull to sleep** : arrullar, adormecer

lull² *n* : calma *f*, pausa *f*

lullaby ['lʌləˌbaɪ] *n*, *pl* **-bies** : canción *f* de cuna, arrullo *m*, nana *f*

lumbago [ˌlʌmˈbeɪgo] *n* : lumbago *m*

lumbar ['lʌmbər, -ˌbɑr] *adj* : lumbar

lumber¹ ['lʌmbər] *vt* : aserrar (madera) — *vi* : moverse pesadamente

lumber² *n* : madera *f*

lumberjack ['lʌmbərˌdʒæk] *n* : leñador *m*, -dora *f*

lumberyard ['lʌmbərˌjɑrd] *n* : almacén *m* de maderas

luminary ['luːməˌneri] *n*, *pl* **-naries** : lumbrera *f*, luminaria *f*

luminescence [ˌluːməˈnɛsənts] *n* : luminiscencia *f* — **luminescent** [-ˈnɛs-ənt] *adj*

luminosity [ˌluːməˈnɑsəti] *n*, *pl* **-ties** : luminosidad *f*

luminous ['luːmənəs] *adj* : luminoso — **luminously** *adv*

lump¹ ['lʌmp] *vt or* **to lump together** : juntar, agrupar, amontonar — *vi* CLUMP : agruparse, aglutinarse

lump² *n* **1** GLOB : grumo *m* **2** PIECE : pedazo *m*, trozo *m*, terrón *m* ⟨a lump of coal : un trozo de carbón⟩ ⟨a lump of sugar : un terrón de azúcar⟩ **3** SWELLING : bulto *m*, hinchazón *f*, protuberancia *f* **4 to have a lump in one's throat** : tener un nudo en la garganta

lump sum *n* : cantidad *f* global, pago *m* único

lumpy ['lʌmpi] *adj* **lumpier; -est 1** : lleno de grumos (dícese de una salsa) **2** UNEVEN : desigual, disparejo

lunacy ['luːnəsi] *n*, *pl* **-cies** : locura *f*

lunar ['luːnər] *adj* : lunar

lunatic¹ ['luːnəˌtɪk] *adj sometimes offensive* : lunático, loco

lunatic² *n sometimes offensive* : loco *m*, -ca *f*

lunch¹ ['lʌntʃ] *vi* : almorzar, comer

lunch² *n* : almuerzo *m*, comida *f*, lonche *m Mex*

luncheon ['lʌntʃən] *n* **1** : comida *f*, almuerzo *m* **2 luncheon meat** : fiambres *fpl*

lunchroom ['lʌntʃˌruːm, -ˌrʊm] *n* : merendero *m*, cafetería *f*

lunchtime ['lʌntʃˌtaɪm] *n* : hora *f* del almuerzo

lung ['lʌŋ] *n* : pulmón *m*

lunge¹ ['lʌndʒ] *vi* **lunged; lunging 1** THRUST : atacar (en la esgrima) **2 to lunge forward** : arremeter, lanzarse

lunge² *n* **1** : arremetida *f*, embestida *f* **2** : estocada *f* (en la esgrima)

lurch¹ ['lərtʃ] *vi* **1** PITCH : cabecear, dar bandazos, dar sacudidas **2** STAGGER : tambalearse

lurch² n **1** : sacudida f, bandazo m (de un vehículo) **2** : tambaleo m (de una persona)

lure¹ ['lʊr] vt **lured; luring** : atraer

lure² n **1** ATTRACTION : atractivo m **2** ENTICEMENT : señuelo m, aliciente m **3** BAIT : cebo m artificial (en la pesca)

lurid ['lʊrəd] adj **1** GRUESOME : espeluznante, horripilante **2** SENSATIONAL : sensacionalista, chocante **3** GAUDY : chillón

lurk ['lərk] vi : estar al acecho

luscious ['lʌʃəs] adj **1** DELICIOUS : delicioso, exquisito **2** SEDUCTIVE : seductor, cautivador

lush ['lʌʃ] adj **1** LUXURIANT : exuberante, lozano **2** LUXURIOUS : suntuoso, lujoso — **lushness** ['lʌʃnəs] n

lust¹ ['lʌst] vi **to lust after** : desear (a una persona), codiciar (riquezas, etc.)

lust² n **1** LASCIVIOUSNESS : lujuria f, lascivia f **2** CRAVING : deseo m, ansia f, anhelo m

luster or **lustre** ['lʌstər] n **1** GLOSS, SHEEN : lustre m, brillo m **2** SPLENDOR : lustre m, esplendor m

lusterless ['lʌstərləs] adj : deslustrado, sin brillo

lustful ['lʌstfəl] adj : lujurioso, lascivo, lleno de deseo

lustrous ['lʌstrəs] adj : brillante, brilloso, lustroso

lusty ['lʌsti] adj **lustier; -est** : fuerte, robusto, vigoroso — **lustily** ['lʌstəli] adv

lute ['luːt] n : laúd m

luxuriance [ˌlʌgˈʒʊriənts, ˌlʌkˈʃʊr-] n : lozanía f, exuberancia f

luxuriant [ˌlʌgˈʒʊriənt, ˌlʌkˈʃʊr-] adj **1** : exuberante, lozano (dícese de las plantas) **2** : abundante y hermoso (dícese del pelo) — **luxuriantly** adv

luxuriate [ˌlʌgˈʒʊriˌeɪt, ˌlʌkˈʃʊr-] vi **-ated; -ating 1** : disfrutar **2 to luxuriate in** : deleitarse con

luxurious [ˌlʌgˈʒʊriəs, ˌlʌkˈʃʊr-] adj : lujoso, suntuoso — **luxuriously** adv

luxury ['lʌkʃəri, 'lʌgʒə-] n, pl **-ries** : lujo m

-ly [li] suf : -mente ⟨frequently : frecuentemente⟩

lye ['laɪ] n : lejía f

lying → lie¹, lie²

lymph ['lɪmpf] n : linfa f

lymphatic [lɪmˈfætɪk] adj : linfático

lynch ['lɪntʃ] vt : linchar

lynx ['lɪŋks] n, pl **lynx** or **lynxes** : lince m

lyre ['laɪr] n : lira f

lyric¹ ['lɪrɪk] adj : lírico

lyric² n **1** : poema m lírico **2 lyrics** npl : letra f (de una canción)

lyrical ['lɪrɪkəl] adj : lírico, elocuente

lyricist ['lɪrɪsɪst] n : letrista mf

M

m ['ɛm] n, pl **m's** or **ms** ['ɛmz] : decimotercera letra del alfabeto inglés

ma'am ['mæm] → **madam**

macabre [məˈkab, -ˈkabər, -ˈkabrə] adj : macabro

macadam [məˈkædəm] n : macadán m

macaroni [ˌmækəˈroːni] n : macarrones mpl

macaroon [ˌmækəˈruːn] n : macarrón m, mostachón m

macaw [məˈkɔ] n : guacamayo m

mace ['meɪs] n **1** : maza f (arma o símbolo) **2** : macis f (especia)

machete [məˈʃɛti] n : machete m

machination [ˌmækəˈneɪʃən, ˌmæʃə-] n : maquinación f, intriga f

machine¹ [məˈʃiːn] vt **-chined; -chining** : trabajar a máquina

machine² n **1** : máquina f ⟨machine shop : taller de máquinas⟩ ⟨machine language : lenguaje de la máquina⟩ **2** : aparato m, maquinaria f (en política)

machine gun n : ametralladora f

machinery [məˈʃiːnəri] n, pl **-eries 1** : maquinaria f **2** WORKS : mecanismo m

machinist [məˈʃiːnɪst] n : maquinista mf

machismo [məˈtʃizmoː] n : machismo m, masculinidad f

macho ['matʃoː] adj : machote, macho

mackerel ['mækərəl] n, pl **-el** or **-els** : caballa f

mad ['mæd] adj **madder; maddest 1** INSANE : loco, demente **2** RABID : rabioso **3** FOOLISH : tonto, insensato **4** ANGRY : enojado, furioso **5** CRAZY : loco ⟨I'm mad about you : estoy loco por ti⟩

Madagascan [ˌmædəˈgæskən] n : malgache mf — **Madagascan** adj

madam ['mædəm] n, pl **mesdames** [meɪˈdam, -ˈdæm] : señora f

madcap¹ ['mæd,kæp] adj ZANY : alocado, disparatado

madcap² n : alocado m, -da f

madden ['mædən] vt : enloquecer, enfurecer

maddening ['mædənɪŋ] adj : enloquecedor, exasperante ⟨I find it maddening : me saca de quicio⟩

made → make¹

made-to-measure adj : hecho a la medida

made-up adj **1** : maquillado **2** INVENTED : inventado

madhouse ['mæd,haʊs] n : manicomio m ⟨the office was a madhouse : la oficina parecía una casa de locos⟩

madly ['mædli] adv : como un loco, locamente

madman ['mæd,mæn, -mən] n, pl **-men** [-mən, -mɛn] : loco m, demente m

madness ['mædnəs] n : locura f, demencia f

madwoman ['mæd,wʊmən] *n, pl* **-women**
[-,wɪmən] : loca *f*, demente *f*

maelstrom ['meɪlstrəm] *n* : remolino *m*,
vorágine *f*

maestro ['maɪ,stro:] *n, pl* **-stros** *or* **-stri**
[-,stri:] : maestro *m*

Mafia ['mafiə] *n* : Mafia *f*

mafioso [,mafi'o:so] *n* : mafioso *m*, -sa *f*

magazine [,mægə,zi:n] *n* **1** STOREHOUSE
: almacén *m*, polvorín *m* (de explosivos)
2 PERIODICAL : revista *f* **3** : cargador *m*
(de un arma de fuego)

magenta [mə'dʒɛntə] *n* : magenta *f*, color
m magenta

maggot ['mægət] *n* : gusano *m*

Magi ['meɪ,dʒaɪ, 'mæ-] *npl* **the Magi** : los
Reyes Magos

magic[1] ['mædʒɪk] *or* **magical** ['mædʒɪkəl]
adj : mágico

magic[2] *n* : magia *f*

magically ['mædʒɪkli] *adv* : mágicamente
⟨they magically appeared : aparecieron
como por arte de magia⟩

magician [mə'dʒɪʃən] *n* **1** SORCERER
: mago *m*, -ga *f* **2** CONJURER : prestidigitador *m*, -dora *f*; mago *m*, -ga *f*

magistrate ['mædʒə,streɪt] *n* : magistrado
m, -da *f*

magma ['mægmə] *n* : magma *m*

magnanimity [,mægnə'nɪməti] *n, pl* **-ties**
: magnanimidad *f*

magnanimous [mæg'nænəməs] *adj*
: magnánimo, generoso — **magnani-
mously** *adv*

magnate ['mæg,neɪt, -nət] *n* : magnate *mf*

magnesium [mæg'ni:ziəm, -ʒəm] *n*
: magnesio *m*

magnet ['mægnət] *n* : imán *m*

magnetic [mæg'nɛtɪk] *adj* : magnético —
magnetically [-tɪkli] *adv*

magnetic field *n* : campo *m* magnético

magnetism ['mægnə,tɪzəm] *n* : magnetismo *m*

magnetize ['mægnə,taɪz] *vt* **-tized; -tizing**
1 : magnetizar, imantar **2** ATTRACT
: magnetizar, atraer

magnification [,mægnəfə'keɪʃən] *n*
: aumento *m*, ampliación *f*

magnificence [mæg'nɪfəsəns] *n* : magnificencia *f*

magnificent [mæg'nɪfəsənt] *adj* : magnífico — **magnificently** *adv*

magnify ['mægnə,faɪ] *vt* **-fied; -fying 1**
ENLARGE : ampliar **2** EXAGGERATE
: magnificar, exagerar

magnifying glass *n* : lupa *f*

magnitude ['mægnə,tu:d, -,tju:d] *n* **1**
GREATNESS : magnitud *f*, grandeza *f* **2**
QUANTITY : cantidad *f* **3** IMPORTANCE
: magnitud *f*, envergadura *f*

magnolia [mæg'no:ljə] *n* : magnolia *f*
(flor), magnolio *m* (árbol)

magpie ['mæg,paɪ] *n* : urraca *f*

maguey [mə'geɪ] *n* : maguey *m*

mahogany [mə'hagəni] *n, pl* **-nies** : caoba
f

maid ['meɪd] *n* **1** MAIDEN : doncella *f* **2** *or*
maidservant ['meɪd,sərvənt] : sirvienta *f*,
muchacha *f*, mucama *f*, criada *f*

maiden[1] ['meɪdən] *adj* **1** UNMARRIED
: soltera **2** FIRST : primero ⟨maiden
voyage : primera travesía⟩

maiden[2] *n* : doncella *f*

maiden name *n* : nombre *m* de soltera

mail[1] ['meɪl] *vt* : enviar por correo, echar
al correo

mail[2] *n* **1** : correo *m* ⟨airmail : correo
aéreo⟩ **2** : malla *f* ⟨coat of mail : cota
de malla⟩

mailbox ['meɪl,baks] *n* : buzón *m*

mailing list *n* : lista *f* de correo(s), lista *f*
de direcciones

mailman ['meɪl,mæn, -mən] *n, pl* **-men**
[-mən, -,mn] : cartero *m*

mail order *n* : venta *f* por correo

maim ['meɪm] *vt* : mutilar, desfigurar,
lisiar

main[1] ['meɪn] *adj* : principal, central ⟨the
main office : la oficina central⟩ ⟨main
course : plato principal/fuerte⟩ ⟨main
road : carretera principal⟩

main[2] *n* **1** HIGH SEAS : alta mar *f* **2**
: tubería *f* principal (de agua o gas),
cable *m* principal (de un circuito) **3 with
might and main** : con todas sus fuerzas

mainframe ['meɪn,freɪm] *n* : mainframe
m, computadora *f* central

mainland ['meɪn,lænd, -lənd] *n* : continente *m*

mainly ['meɪnli] *adv* **1** PRINCIPALLY
: principalmente, en primer lugar **2**
MOSTLY : principalmente, en la mayor
parte

mainstay ['meɪn,steɪ] *n* : pilar *m*, sostén *m*
principal

mainstream[1] ['meɪn,stri:m] *adj* : dominante, corriente, convencional

mainstream[2] *n* : corriente *f* principal

maintain [meɪn'teɪn] *vt* **1** SERVICE : dar
mantenimiento a (una máquina) **2** PRE-
SERVE : mantener, conservar ⟨to maintain silence : guardar silencio⟩ **3** SUP-
PORT : mantener, sostener **4** ASSERT
: mantener, sostener, afirmar

maintenance ['meɪntənəns] *n* : mantenimiento *m*

maize ['meɪz] *n* : maíz *m*

majestic [mə'dʒɛstɪk] *adj* : majestuoso —
majestically [-tɪkli] *adv*

majesty ['mædʒəsti] *n, pl* **-ties 1** : majestad *f* ⟨Your Majesty : su Majestad⟩ **2**
SPLENDOR : majestuosidad *f*, esplendor
m

major[1] ['meɪdʒər] *vi* **-jored; -joring** : especializarse

major[2] *adj* **1** GREATER : mayor **2** NOTE-
WORTHY : mayor, notable **3** SERIOUS
: grave **4** : mayor (en la música)

major[3] *n* **1** : mayor *mf*, comandante *mf*
(en las fuerzas armadas) **2** : especialidad
f (universitaria)

Majorcan [mə'dʒɔrkən, mə-, -'jɔr-] *n* : mallorquín *m*, -quina *f* — **Majorcan** *adj*

major general *n* : general *mf* de división

majority [mə'dʒɔrəti] *n, pl* **-ties 1** ADULT-
HOOD : mayoría *f* de edad **2** : mayoría
f, mayor parte *f* ⟨the vast majority : la
inmensa mayoría⟩

make¹ ['meɪk] v **made** ['meɪd]; **making** vt
1 CREATE, PRODUCE : hacer, fabricar
(máquinas, etc.), promulgar (leyes) ⟨she
made a dress : hizo un vestido⟩ ⟨to make
a fire : hacer un fuego⟩ ⟨to make a
movie : hacer una película⟩ ⟨the milk is
made into cheese : con la leche se hace
queso⟩ ⟨to be made from : hacerse de⟩
⟨made (out) of stone : hecho de piedra⟩
2 CAUSE, PRODUCE : hacer (ruido, etc.)
⟨to make trouble : hacer problemas⟩ ⟨to
make a mistake : cometer un error⟩ ⟨to
make room for : hacer lugar para⟩ **3** AR-
RANGE : hacer (planes, etc.) ⟨to make an
appointment : hacer/pedir/concertar
una cita, pedir hora⟩ **4** PREPARE : hacer
(una cama, etc.), preparar (una comida,
etc.) **5** RENDER : hacer, poner ⟨it makes
him nervous : lo pone nervioso⟩ ⟨it
made me happy : me hizo feliz, me ale-
gró⟩ ⟨it made me sad : me dio pena⟩ ⟨it
made her famous : la hizo famosa⟩ **6**
: hacer, convertir en ⟨it'll make a man of
you : te hará hombre⟩ ⟨to make a fool of
: dejar en ridículo⟩ ⟨to make a big deal
of : hacer un problema por⟩ ⟨to make a
mess of things : hacer la pata⟩ ⟨wait—
make that a cheeseburger : o mejor,
dame una hamburguesa con queso⟩ **7**
BE, BECOME : ser ⟨you'll make a fine
doctor : serás una médica buenísima⟩ **8**
EQUAL : ser ⟨two plus two makes four
: dos y dos son cuatro⟩ ⟨that makes two
of us! : ¡ya somos dos!⟩ **9** SCORE : hacer,
marcar **10** PERFORM : hacer ⟨to make a
gesture : hacer un gesto⟩ ⟨to make a
speech : pronunciar un discurso⟩ **11**
: no perder (un vuelo, etc.), cumplir con
(una fecha de entrega) **12** REACH : llegar a (un lugar, etc.) ⟨they made the finals : llegaron a las finales⟩ **13** ATTEND
: asistir a **14** COMPEL : hacer, forzar,
obligar **15** EARN : hacer (dinero, amigos)
⟨to make a living : ganarse la vida⟩
16 to make do (with something)
: arreglárselas (con algo) **17 to make
into** : convertir en **18 to make it** SUC-
CEED : tener éxito en la vida **19 to make
it** SURVIVE : vivir, sobrevivir **20 to make
it** : llegar ⟨we made it home safely : llegamos bien a casa⟩ ⟨I'm glad you could
make it! : ¡me alegro de que hayas po-
dido venir!⟩ **21 to make it up to someone** ⟨I'll make it up to you : te lo com-
pensaré⟩ **22 to make of** : pensar de ⟨I
don't know what to make of him/it : no
sé qué pensar de él/ello⟩ ⟨I can't make
anything of it : no lo entiendo⟩ **23 to
make or break** : ser el éxito o la ruina de
24 to make out DISCERN : distinguir **25
to make out** : comprender, entender (a
alguien) **26 to make out** WRITE : hacer
(una lista, etc.) ⟨to make a check out to
: extender un cheque a nombre de⟩ **27
to make out** PORTRAY : pintar, hacer parecer **28 to make over** : transformar,
maquillar (a alguien), redecorar (una
habitación) **29 to make someone's day**
: alegrarle el día a alguien **30 to make
up** INVENT : inventar **31 to make up**

PREPARE : preparar **32 to make up**
FORM : formar, constituir **33 to make
up** : compensar (tiempo) **34 to make up
one's mind** : decidirse — vi **1** HEAD : ir,
dirigirse ⟨we made for home : nos fuimos a casa⟩ **2 to make away with** : escaparse con **3 to make do** : arreglárselas **4
to make for** HEAD FOR : dirigirse a **5 to
make for** PROMOTE : contribuir a **6 to
make good** REPAY : pagar **7 to make
good** SUCCEED : tener éxito **8 to make
off** : salir corriendo **9 to make off with**
: escaparse con **10 to make out** fam : besuquearse ⟨to make out with someone
: besar y acariciar a alguien⟩ **11 to make
up for** : compensar

make² n BRAND : marca f

make–believe¹ [ˌmeɪkbəˈliːv] adj : imaginario

make–believe² n : fantasía f, invención f
⟨a world of make-believe : un mundo de
ensueño⟩

make out vt **1** WRITE : hacer (un cheque).
2 DISCERN : distinguir, divisar **3** UNDER-
STAND : comprender, entender — vi **1**
: arreglárselas ⟨how did you make out?
: ¿qué tal te fue?⟩

makeover ['meɪkˌoːvər] n **1** : cambio m
de imagen **2** REMODELING : reformas
fpl, remodelación f

maker ['meɪkər] n : fabricante mf

makeshift ['meɪkˌʃɪft] adj : provisional,
improvisado

makeup ['meɪkˌʌp] n **1** COMPOSITION
: composición f **2** CHARACTER : carácter
m, temperamento m **3** COSMETICS : maquillaje m

make up vt **1** INVENT : inventar **2** : recuperar ⟨she made up the time : recuperó
las horas perdidas⟩ — vi RECONCILE
: hacer las paces, reconciliarse

making ['meɪkɪŋ] n **1** : creación f, producción f ⟨in the making : en ciernes⟩
2 to have the makings of : tener madera
de (dícese de personas), tener los ingredientes para

maladjusted [ˌmæləˈdʒʌstəd] adj : inadaptado

maladjustment [ˌmæləˈdʒʌstmənt] n
: desajuste m

malady ['mælədi] n, pl **-dies** : dolencia f,
enfermedad f, mal m

malaise [məˈleɪz, mæ-] n : malestar m

malaria [məˈleriə] n : malaria f, paludismo
m

Malawian [məˈlɑwiən] n : malauiano m,
-na f — **Malawian** adj

Malay [məˈleɪ, 'meɪˌleɪ] n **1** or **Malayan**
[məˈleɪən, meɪ-; 'meɪˌleɪən] : malayo m,
-ya f **2** : malayo m (idioma) — **Malay** or
Malayan adj

Malaysian [məˈleɪʒən, -ʃən] n : malasio
m, -sia f; malaisio m, -sia f — **Malaysian**
adj

male¹ ['meɪl] adj **1** : macho **2** MASCULINE
: masculino

male² n **1** : macho m (de animales o plantas), varón m (de personas)

malefactor ['mæləˌfæktər] n : malhechor
m, -chora f

maleness [ˈmeɪlnəs] n : masculinidad f

malevolence [məˈlɛvələn/ts] n : malevolencia f

malevolent [məˈlɛvələnt] adj : malévolo

malformation [ˌmælfɔrˈmeɪʃən] n : malformación f

malformed [mælˈfɔrmd] adj : mal formado, deforme

malfunction¹ [mælˈfʌŋkʃən] vi : funcionar mal

malfunction² n : mal funcionamiento m

malice [ˈmælɪs] n 1 : malicia f, malevolencia f 2 **with malice aforethought** : con premeditación

malicious [məˈlɪʃəs] adj : malicioso, malévolo — **maliciously** adv

malign¹ [məˈlaɪn] vt : calumniar, difamar

malign² adj : maligno

malignancy [məˈlɪɡnən/si] n, pl **-cies** : malignidad f

malignant [məˈlɪɡnənt] adj : maligno

malinger [məˈlɪŋɡər] vi : fingirse enfermo

malingerer [məˈlɪŋɡərər] n : uno que se finge enfermo

mall [ˈmɔl] n 1 PROMENADE : alameda f, paseo m (arbolado) 2 : centro m comercial ⟨shopping mall : galería comercial⟩

mallard [ˈmælərd] n, pl **-lard** or **-lards** : pato m real, ánade mf real

malleable [ˈmæliəbəl] adj : maleable

mallet [ˈmælət] n : mazo m

malnourished [mælˈnərɪʃt] adj : desnutrido, malnutrido

malnutrition [ˌmælnuˈtrɪʃən, -njʊ-] n : desnutrición f, malnutrición f

malodorous [mælˈoːdərəs] adj : maloliente

malpractice [ˌmælˈpræktəs] n : mala práctica f, negligencia f

malt [ˈmɔlt] n : malta f

maltreat [mælˈtriːt] vt : maltratar

mama or **mamma** [ˈmɑmə] n : mamá f

mambo [ˈmɑmbo] n : mambo m

mammal [ˈmæməl] n : mamífero m

mammalian [məˈmeɪliən, mæ-] adj : mamífero

mammary [ˈmæməri] adj 1 : mamario 2 **mammary gland** : glándula mamaria

mammogram [ˈmæməˌɡræm] n : mamografía f

mammoth¹ [ˈmæməθ] adj : colosal, gigantesco

mammoth² n : mamut m

man¹ [ˈmæn] vt **manned; manning** : tripular (un barco o avión), encargarse de (un servicio)

man² n, pl **men** [ˈmɛn] 1 PERSON : hombre m, persona f ⟨the man in the street : el hombre de la calle⟩ ⟨to a man : todos sin excepción⟩ ⟨every man for himself : sálvese quien pueda⟩ ⟨to be one's own man : ser independiente⟩ 2 MALE : hombre m 3 MANKIND : humanidad f 4 HUSBAND, BOYFRIEND : marido m, novio m 5 **men** npl : trabajadores mpl (de una empresa), soldados mpl (en el ejército) 6 **hey, man** fam : hola amigo

manacles [ˈmænɪkəlz] npl HANDCUFFS : esposas fpl

manage [ˈmænɪdʒ] v **-aged; -aging** vt 1 HANDLE : controlar, manejar 2 DIRECT : administrar, dirigir ⟨to manage one's life : organizar uno su vida⟩ 3 CONTRIVE : lograr, ingeniárselas para ⟨I managed to do it : pude hacerlo⟩ — vi COPE : arreglárselas

manageable [ˈmænɪdʒəbəl] adj : manejable

management [ˈmænɪdʒmənt] n 1 DIRECTION : administración f, gestión f, dirección f 2 HANDLING : manejo m 3 MANAGERS : dirección f, gerencia f

manager [ˈmænɪdʒər] n : director m, -tora f; gerente mf; administrador m, -dora f

managerial [ˌmænəˈdʒɪriəl] adj : directivo, gerencial

managing director n : director m gerente, directora f gerente

manatee [ˈmænəˌtiː] n : manatí m

mandarin [ˈmændərən] n 1 : mandarín m 2 or **mandarin orange** : mandarina f

mandate [ˈmænˌdeɪt] n : mandato m

mandatory [ˈmændəˌtori] adj : obligatorio

mandible [ˈmændəbəl] n : mandíbula f

mandolin [ˌmændəˈlɪn, ˈmændələn] n : mandolina f

mane [ˈmeɪn] n : crin f (de un caballo), melena f (de un león o una persona)

maneuver¹ [məˈnuːvər, -ˈnjuː-] vt 1 PLACE, POSITION : maniobrar, posicionar, colocar 2 MANIPULATE : manipular, maniobrar ⟨to maniobrar

maneuver² n : maniobra f

manfully [ˈmænfəli] adv : valientemente

manganese [ˈmæŋɡəˌniːz, -ˌniːs] n : manganeso m

mange [ˈmeɪndʒ] n : sarna f

manger [ˈmeɪndʒər] n : pesebre m

mangle [ˈmæŋɡəl] vt **-gled; -gling** 1 CRUSH, DESTROY : aplastar, despedazar, destrozar 2 MUTILATE : mutilar ⟨to mangle a text : mutilar un texto⟩

mango [ˈmæŋˌɡoː] n, pl **-goes** : mango m

mangrove [ˈmæŋˌɡroːv, ˈmæn-] n : mangle m

mangy [ˈmeɪndʒi] adj **mangier; -est** 1 : sarnoso 2 SHABBY : gastado

manhandle [ˈmænˌhændəl] vt **-dled; -dling** : maltratar, tratar con poco cuidado

manhole [ˈmænˌhoːl] n : boca f de alcantarilla

manhood [ˈmænˌhʊd] n 1 : madurez f (de un hombre) 2 COURAGE, MANLINESS : hombría f, valor m 3 MEN : hombres mpl

manhunt [ˈmænˌhʌnt] n : búsqueda f (de un criminal)

mania [ˈmeɪniə, -njə] n : manía f

maniac [ˈmeɪniˌæk] n : maníaco m, -ca f; maniático m, -ca f

maniacal [məˈnaɪəkəl] adj fam : maníaco, maniaco

manic [ˈmænɪk] adj : maníaco, maniaco

manicure¹ [ˈmænəˌkjʊr] vt **-cured; -curing** 1 : hacer la manicura a 2 TRIM : recortar

manicure² n : manicura f

manicurist ['mænə,kjʊrɪst] *n* : manicuro *m*, -ra *f*

manifest[1] ['mænə,fɛst] *vt* : manifestar

manifest[2] *adj* : manifiesto, patente — **manifestly** *adv*

manifestation [,mænəfə'steɪʃən] *n* : manifestación *f*

manifesto [,mænə'fɛs,to:] *n, pl* **-tos** or **-toes** : manifiesto *m*

manifold[1] ['mænə,fo:ld] *adj* : diverso, variado

manifold[2] *n* : colector *m* (de escape)

manioc ['mæni,ɑk] *n* : mandioca *f*, yuca *f*

manipulate [mə'nɪpjə,leɪt] *vt* **-lated; -lating** : manipular

manipulation [mə,nɪpjə'leɪʃən] *n* : manipulación *f*

manipulative [mə'nɪpjə,leɪtɪv, -lətɪv] *adj* : manipulador

manipulator [mə'nɪpjə,leɪtər] *n* : manipulador *m*, -dora *f*

mankind ['mæn'kaɪnd, -,kaɪnd] *n* : género *m* humano, humanidad *f*

manliness ['mænlinəs] *n* : hombría *f*, masculinidad *f*

manly ['mænli] *adj* **manlier; -est** : varonil, viril

man–made ['mæn'meɪd] *adj* : artificial ⟨man-made fabrics : telas sintéticas⟩

manna ['mænə] *n* : maná *m*

mannequin ['mænɪkən] *n* **1** DUMMY : maniquí *m* **2** MODEL : modelo *mf*

manner ['mænər] *n* **1** KIND, SORT : tipo *m*, clase *f* **2** WAY : manera *f*, modo *m* **3** STYLE : estilo *m* (artístico) **4 manners** *npl* CUSTOMS : costumbres *fpl* ⟨Victorian manners : costumbres victorianas⟩ **5 manners** *npl* ETIQUETTE : modales *mpl*, educación *f*, etiqueta *f* ⟨good manners : buenos modales⟩

mannered ['mænərd] *adj* **1** AFFECTED, ARTIFICIAL : amanerado, afectado **2 well–mannered** : educado, cortés **3** → **ill–mannered**

mannerism ['mænə,rɪzəm] *n* : peculiaridad *f*, gesto *m* particular

mannish ['mænɪʃ] *adj* : masculino, hombruno

man–of–war [,mænə'wɔr, -əv'wɔr] *n, pl* **men–of–war** [,mɛn-] WARSHIP : buque *m* de guerra

manor ['mænər] *n* **1** : casa *f* solariega, casa *f* señorial **2** ESTATE : señorío *m*

manpower ['mæn,paʊər] *n* : personal *m*, mano *f* de obra

mansion ['mænʃən] *n* : mansión *f*

manslaughter ['mæn,slɔtər] *n* : homicidio *m* sin premeditación

mantel ['mæntəl] *n* : repisa *f* de chimenea

mantelpiece ['mæntəl,pi:s] → **mantel**

mantis ['mæntəs] *n, pl* **-tises** or **-tes** ['mæn,ti:z] : mantis *f* religiosa

mantle ['mæntəl] *n* : manto *m*

manual[1] ['mænjʊəl] *adj* : manual — **manually** *adv*

manual[2] *n* : manual *m*

manufacture[1] ['mænjə'fækʧər] *vt* **-tured; -turing** : fabricar, manufacturar, confeccionar (ropa), elaborar (comestibles)

manufacture[2] *n* : manufactura *f*, fabricación *f*, confección *f* (de ropa), elaboración *f* (de comestibles)

manufacturer [,mænjə'fækʧərər] *n* : fabricante *m*; manufacturero *m*, -ra *f*

manure [mə'nʊr, -'njʊr] *n* : estiércol *m*

manuscript ['mænjə,skrɪpt] *n* : manuscrito *m*

many[1] ['mɛni] *adj* **more** ['mor]; **most** ['mo:st] **1** : muchos ⟨for many years : durante muchos años⟩ ⟨many years ago : hace muchos años⟩ ⟨so/too many ideas : tantas/demasiadas ideas⟩ ⟨I don't have that many employees : no tengo tantos empleados⟩ ⟨a good/great many people : muchísima gente⟩ ⟨one of her many interests : uno de sus muchos intereses⟩ **2 as many** ⟨I have as many books as she does : tengo tantos libros como ella⟩ ⟨take as many books as you want : llévate cuantos libros quieras⟩ ⟨we saw three plays in as many days : vimos tres obras en el mismo número de días⟩ **3 how many** : cuántos, cuántas ⟨how many people were there? : ¿cuánta gente había?⟩

many[2] *pron* **1** : muchos ⟨many of them : muchos de ellos⟩ ⟨many of the novels : muchas de las novelas⟩ ⟨some stayed, but many left : algunos se quedaron, pero muchos se fueron⟩ ⟨I don't have that many : no tengo tantos⟩ **2 as many as** ⟨I have as many as she does : tengo tantos como ella⟩ ⟨as many as a hundred people : hasta cien personas⟩ ⟨take as many as you want : llévate cuantos quieras⟩ **3 many a/an** ⟨many a time : muchas veces⟩ **4 the many** : la mayoría

map[1] ['mæp] *vt* **mapped; mapping 1** : trazar el mapa de **2** PLAN : planear, proyectar ⟨to map out a program : planear un programa⟩

map[2] *n* : mapa *m*

maple ['meɪpəl] *n* : arce *m*

mar ['mɑr] *vt* **marred; marring 1** SPOIL : estropear, echar a perder **2** DEFACE : desfigurar

maraca [mə'rɑkə] *n* : maraca *f*

maraschino [,mærə'ski:no:, -'ʃi:-] *n, pl* **-nos** : cereza *f* al marrasquino

marathon ['mærə,θɑn] *n* **1** RACE : maratón *m* **2** CONTEST : competencia *f* de resistencia

maraud [mə'rɔd] *vi* : merodear

marauder [mə'rɔdər] *n* : merodeador *m*, -dora *f*

marble ['mɑrbəl] *n* **1** : mármol *m* **2** : canica *f*, bolita *f* ⟨to play marbles : jugar a las canicas⟩

march[1] ['mɑrʧ] *vi* **1** : marchar, desfilar ⟨they marched past the grandstand : desfilaron ante la tribuna⟩ **2** : caminar con resolución ⟨she marched right up to him : se le acercó sin vacilación⟩

march[2] *n* **1** MARCHING : marcha *f* **2** PASSAGE : paso *m* (del tiempo) **3** PROGRESS : avance *m*, progreso *m* **4** : marcha *f* (en música)

March ['mɑrʧ] *n* : marzo *m* ⟨they arrived on the 13th of March, they arrived on March 13th : llegaron el trece de marzo⟩

marchioness ['mɑrʃənɪs] *n* : marquesa *f*

Mardi Gras ['mɑrdi,grɑ] *n* : martes *m* de Carnaval

mare ['mær] *n* : yegua *f*

margarine ['mɑrdʒərən] *n* : margarina *f*

margarita [,mɑrgə'ri:tə] *n* : margarita *f* (cóctel)

margin ['mɑrdʒən] *n* : margen *m*

marginal ['mɑrdʒənəl] *adj* 1 : marginal 2 MINIMAL : mínimo — **marginally** *adv*

marginalization [,mɑrdʒənələ'zeɪʃən] *n* : marginación *f*

mariachi [,mɑri'ɑtʃi, ,mæ-] *n* 1 *or* **mariachi band** : mariachi *m* (grupo) 2 *or* **mariachi musician** : mariachi *m* (músico) 3 **mariachi music** : mariachi *m*, música *f* de mariachi

marigold ['mærə,goːld] *n* : maravilla *f*, caléndula *f*

marijuana *or* **marihuana** [,mærə'hwɑnə] *n* : marihuana *f*

marimba [mə'rɪmbə] *n* : marimba *f*

marina [mə'ri:nə] *n* : puerto *m* deportivo

marinade [,mærə'nɑd] *n* : adobo *m*, marinada *f*

marinate ['mærə,neɪt] *vt* **-nated; -nating** : marinar

marine[1] [mə'ri:n] *adj* 1 : marino ⟨marine life : vida marina⟩ 2 NAUTICAL : náutico, marítimo 3 : de la infantería de marina

marine[2] *n* : soldado *m* de marina

mariner ['mærɪnər] *n* : marinero *m*, marino *m*

marionette [,mæriə'nɛt] *n* : marioneta *f*, títere *m*

marital ['mærətəl] *adj* 1 : matrimonial 2 **marital status** : estado *m* civil

maritime ['mærə,taɪm] *adj* : marítimo

marjoram ['mɑrdʒərəm] *n* : mejorana *f*

mark[1] ['mɑrk] *vt* 1 : marcar 2 MAR : dejar marca en 3 CHARACTERIZE : caracterizar 4 SIGNAL : señalar, marcar 5 GRADE : corregir (exámenes, etc.) 6 **mark my words!** : ¡acuérdate de lo que te digo! 7 **to mark down** : rebajar 8 **to mark off** : demarcar, delimitar 9 **to mark up** : anotar (un manuscrito, etc.) 10 **to mark up** : aumentar el precio de

mark[2] *n* 1 TARGET : blanco *m* ⟨to miss the mark, to be wide of the mark : no dar en el blanco⟩ 2 : marca *f*, señal *f* ⟨put a mark where you left off : pon una señal donde terminaste⟩ 3 INDICATION : señal *f*, indicio *m* ⟨a mark of respect : una señal de respeto⟩ 4 GRADE : nota *f* 5 LEVEL : nivel *m* ⟨to reach the halfway mark : llegar al ecuador⟩ ⟨we've topped the one million dollar mark : hemos superado el millón de dólares⟩ 6 IMPRINT : huella *f*, marca *f* 7 BLEMISH : marca *f*, imperfección *f* 8 **on your mark(s), get set, go!** : en sus marcas, listos, ¡ya!; en sus marcas, listos, ¡fuera! *Mex*; preparados, listos, ¡ya! *Spain* 9 **to fall short of the mark** : quedarse corto 10 **to make/leave one's mark** : dejar su impronta 11 **to miss the mark** ERR, FAIL : errar, fracasar

marked ['mɑrkt] *adj* : marcado, notable — **markedly** ['mɑrkədli] *adv*

marker ['mɑrkər] *n* : marcador *m*

market[1] ['mɑrkət] *vt* : poner en venta, comercializar

market[2] *n* 1 MARKETPLACE : mercado *m* ⟨the open market : el mercado libre⟩ 2 DEMAND : demanda *f*, mercado *m* 3 STORE : tienda *f* 4 → **stock market**

marketable ['mɑrkətəbəl] *adj* : vendible

marketing ['mɑrkətɪŋ] *n* : mercadotecnia *f*, mercadeo *m*

marketplace ['mɑrkət,pleɪs] *n* : mercado *m*

market research *n* : estudio *m* de mercado

marking *n* 1 : corrección *f* (de exámenes, etc.) 2 : marca *f*, señal *f* 3 : pinta *f*, mancha *f* (de un animal) 4 **to have all the markings of** : tener madera de (dícese de personas), tener los ingredientes para

marksman ['mɑrksmən] *n*, *pl* **-men** [-mən, -,mɛn] : tirador *m*

marksmanship ['mɑrksmən,ʃɪp] *n* : puntería *f*

markswoman ['mɑrks,wʊmən] *n*, *pl* **-women** [-,wɪmən] : tiradora *f*

marmalade ['mɑrmə,leɪd] *n* : mermelada *f*

marmoset ['mɑrmə,sɛt] *n* : tití *m*

marmot ['mɑrmət] *n* : marmota *f*

maroon[1] [mə'ru:n] *vt* : abandonar, aislar

maroon[2] *n* : rojo *m* oscuro, granate *m*

marquee [mɑr'ki:] *n* : marquesina *f*

marquess ['mɑrkwɪs] *or* **marquis** ['mɑrkwɪs, mɑr'ki:] *n*, *pl* **-quesses** *or* **-quises** [-'ki:z, -'ki:zəz] *or* **-quis** [-'ki:, -'ki:z] : marqués *m*

marquise [mɑr'ki:z] → **marchioness**

marriage ['mærɪdʒ] *n* 1 : matrimonio *m* 2 WEDDING : casamiento *m*, boda *f*

marriageable ['mærɪdʒəbəl] *adj* **of marriageable age** : de edad de casarse

marriage certificate *n* : certificado *m* de matrimonio, acta *f* de matrimonio

married ['mærid] *adj* 1 : casado 2 **to get married** : casarse

marrow ['mæro] *n* : médula *f*, tuétano *m*

marry ['mæri] *vt* **-ried; -rying** 1 : casar ⟨the priest married them : el cura los casó⟩ 2 : casarse con ⟨she married John : se casó con John⟩

Mars ['mɑrz] *n* : Marte *m*

marsh ['mɑrʃ] *n* 1 : pantano *m* 2 **salt marsh** : marisma *f*

marshal[1] ['mɑrʃəl] *vt* **-shaled** *or* **-shalled; -shaling** *or* **-shalling** 1 : poner en orden, reunir 2 USHER : conducir

marshal[2] *n* 1 : maestro *m* de ceremonias 2 : mariscal *m* (en el ejército); jefe *m*, -fa *f* (de la policía, de los bomberos, etc.)

marshmallow ['mɑrʃ,mɛloː, -,mæloː] *n* : malvavisco *m*

marshy ['mɑrʃi] *adj* **marshier; -est** : pantanoso

marsupial [mɑr'su:piəl] *n* : marsupial *m*

mart ['mɑrt] *n* MARKET : mercado *m*

marten ['mɑrtən] *n*, *pl* **-ten** *or* **-tens** : marta *f*

martial ['mɑrʃəl] *adj* : marcial ⟨martial arts : artes marciales⟩ ⟨martial law : ley marcial⟩

Martian ['mɑrʃən] n : marciano m, -na f — **Martian** adj

martin ['mɑrtən] n 1 SWALLOW : golondrina f 2 SWIFT : vencejo m

martyr[1] ['mɑrtər] vt : martirizar

martyr[2] n : mártir mf

martyrdom ['mɑrtərdəm] n : martirio m

marvel[1] ['mɑrvəl] vi **-veled** or **-velled**; **-veling** or **-velling** : maravillarse

marvel[2] n : maravilla f

marvelous ['mɑrvələs] or **marvellous** adj : maravilloso — **marvelously** adv

Marxism ['mɑrk,sɪzəm] n : marxismo m

Marxist[1] ['mɑrksɪst] adj : marxista

Marxist[2] n : marxista mf

marzipan ['mɑrtsə,pæn, 'mɑrzə,pæn] n : mazapán m

mascara [mæs'kærə] n : rímel m, rimel m

mascot ['mæs,kɑt, -kət] n : mascota f

masculine ['mæskjələn] adj : masculino

masculinity [,mæskjə'lɪnəʈi] n : masculinidad f

mash[1] ['mæʃ] vt 1 ; hacer puré de (papas, etc.) 2 CRUSH : aplastar, majar

mash[2] n 1 FEED : afrecho m 2 : malta f (para hacer bebidas alcohólicas) 3 PASTE, PULP : papilla f, pasta f

mask[1] ['mæsk] vt 1 CONCEAL, DISGUISE : enmascarar, ocultar 2 COVER : cubrir, tapar

mask[2] n 1 : máscara f, careta f, mascarilla f (de un cirujano o dentista) 2 or **facial mask** : mascarilla f (facial)

masochism ['mæsə,kɪzəm, 'mæzə-] n : masoquismo m

masochist ['mæsə,kɪst, 'mæzə-] n : masoquista mf

masochistic [,mæsə'kɪstɪk, ,mæzə-] adj : masoquista

mason ['meɪsən] n 1 BRICKLAYER : albañil mf 2 or **stonemason** ['sto:n,-] : mampostero m, cantero m 3 Mason → **freemason**

Masonic [mə'sɑnɪk] adj : masónico

masonry ['meɪsənri] n, pl **-ries** 1 BRICKLAYING : albañilería f 2 or **stonemasonry** ['sto:n,-] : mampostería f

masquerade[1] [,mæskə'reɪd] vi **-aded**; **-ading** 1 : disfrazarse (de), hacerse pasar (por) : asistir a una mascarada

masquerade[2] n 1 : mascarada f, baile m de disfraces 2 FACADE : farsa f, fachada f

mass[1] ['mæs] vi : concentrarse, juntarse en masa — vt : concentrar

mass[2] n 1 : masa f ⟨atomic mass : masa atómica⟩ 2 BULK : mole f, volumen m 3 MULTITUDE : cantidad f, montón m (de cosas), multitud f (de gente) 4 **the masses** : las masas, el pueblo, el populacho

Mass ['mæs] n : misa f

massacre[1] ['mæsɪkər] vt **-cred**; **-cring** : masacrar

massacre[2] n : masacre f

massage[1] [mə'sɑ:ʒ, -'sɑʤ] vt **-saged**; **-saging** : masajear

massage[2] n : masaje m

masseur [mæ'sər] n : masajista m

masseuse [mæ'søz, -'su:z] n : masajista f

massive ['mæsɪv] adj 1 BULKY : voluminoso, macizo 2 HUGE : masivo, enorme — **massively** adv

mass media npl : medios mpl de comunicación masiva, medios mpl de comunicación de masas

mass-produce vt : producir en masa, fabricar en serie

mass production n : producción f en masa, fabricación f en serie

mass transit n : transporte m público

mast ['mæst] n : mástil m, palo m

master[1] ['mæstər] vt 1 SUBDUE : dominar 2 : llegar a dominar ⟨she mastered French : llegó a dominar el francés⟩

master[2] n 1 TEACHER : maestro m, profesor m 2 EXPERT : experto m, -ta f; maestro m, -tra f 3 : amo m (de animales o esclavos), señor m (de la casa) 4 **master's degree** : maestría f

masterful ['mæstərfəl] adj 1 IMPERIOUS : autoritario, imperioso, dominante 2 SKILLFUL : magistral — **masterfully** adv

masterly ['mæstərli] adj : magistral

mastermind[1] ['mæstər,maɪnd] n : cerebro m, artífice mf

mastermind[2] vt : ser el cerebro de, planear, organizar

masterpiece ['mæstər,pi:s] n : obra f maestra

masterwork ['mæstər,wərk] → **masterpiece**

mastery ['mæstəri] n 1 DOMINION : dominio m, autoridad f 2 SUPERIORITY : superioridad f 3 EXPERTISE : maestría f

masticate ['mæstə,keɪt] v **-cated**; **-cating** : masticar

mastiff ['mæstɪf] n : mastín m

mastodon ['mæstə,dɑn] n : mastodonte m

masturbate ['mæstər,beɪt] v **-bated**; **-bating** vi : masturbarse

masturbation [,mæstər'beɪʃən] n : masturbación f

mat[1] ['mæt] v **matted**; **matting** vt TANGLE : enmarañar — vi : enmarañarse

mat[2] n 1 : estera f 2 TANGLE : maraña f 3 PAD : colchoneta f (de gimnasia) 4 or **matt** or **matte** ['mæt] FRAME : marco m (de cartón)

mat[3] → **matte**

matador ['mætə,dɔr] n : matador m

match[1] ['mæʧ] vt 1 PIT : enfrentar, oponer 2 EQUAL, FIT : igualar, corresponder a, coincidir con 3 : combinar con, hacer juego con ⟨her shoes match her dress : sus zapatos hacen juego con su vestido⟩ — vi 1 CORRESPOND : concordar, coincidir 2 : hacer juego ⟨with a tie to match : con una corbata que hace juego⟩

match[2] n 1 EQUAL : igual mf ⟨he's no match for her : no puede competir con ella⟩ 2 FIGHT, GAME : partido m, combate m (en boxeo) 3 MARRIAGE : matrimonio m, casamiento m 4 : fósforo m, cerilla f, cerillo m (in various countries) ⟨he lit a match : encendió un fósforo⟩ 5 **to be a good match** : hacer buena pareja (dícese de las personas), hacer juego (dícese de la ropa)

matchbox ['mætʃ,bɑks] *n* : caja *f* de cerillas

matchless ['mætʃləs] *adj* : sin igual, sin par

matchmaker ['mætʃ,meɪkər] *n* : casamentero *m*, -ra *f*

mate¹ ['meɪt] *v* **mated; mating** *vi* **1** FIT : encajar **2** PAIR : emparejarse **3** (*relating to animals*) : aparearse, copular — *vt* : aparear, acoplar (animales)

mate² *n* **1** COMPANION : compañero *m*, -ra *f*; camarada *mf* **2** : macho *m*, hembra *f* (de animales) **3** : oficial *mf* (de un barco) ⟨first mate : primer oficial⟩ **4** : compañero *m*, -ra *f*; pareja *f* (de un zapato, etc.)

maté ['mɑ,teɪ] *n* : yerba *f*, mate *m*

material¹ [mə'tɪriəl] *adj* **1** PHYSICAL : material, físico ⟨the material world : el mundo material⟩ ⟨material needs : necesidades materiales⟩ **2** IMPORTANT : importante, esencial **3 material evidence** : prueba *f* sustancial

material² *n* **1** : material *m* **2** CLOTH : tejido *m*, tela *f*

materialism [mə'tɪriə,lɪzəm] *n* : materialismo *m*

materialist [mə'tɪriəlɪst] *n* : materialista *mf*

materialistic [mə,tɪriə'lɪstɪk] *adj* : materialista

materialize [mə'tɪriə,laɪz] *v* **-ized; -izing** *vt* : materializar, hacer aparecer — *vi* : materializarse, aparecer

maternal [mə'tərnəl] *adj* MOTHERLY : maternal — **maternally** *adv*

maternity¹ [mə'tərnəti] *adj* : de maternidad ⟨maternity clothes : ropa de futura mamá⟩ ⟨maternity leave : licencia por maternidad⟩

maternity² *n, pl* **-ties** : maternidad *f*

math ['mæθ] → **mathematics**

mathematical [,mæθə'mætɪkəl] *adj* : matemático — **mathematically** *adv*

mathematician [,mæθəmə'tɪʃən] *n* : matemático *m*, -ca *f*

mathematics [,mæθə'mætɪks] *ns & pl* : matemáticas *fpl*, matemática *f*

matinee *or* **matinée** [,mætən'eɪ] *n* : matiné *f*

matriarch ['meɪtri,ɑrk] *n* : matriarca *f*

matriarchy ['meɪtri,ɑrki] *n, pl* **-chies** : matriarcado *m*

matriculate [mə'trɪkjə,leɪt] *v* **-lated; -lating** *vt* : matricular — *vi* : matricularse

matriculation [mə,trɪkjə'leɪʃən] *n* : matrícula *f*, matriculación *f*

matrimony ['mætrə,moni] *n* : matrimonio *m* — **matrimonial** [,mætrə'moniəl] *adj*

matrix ['meɪtrɪks] *n, pl* **-trices** ['meɪtrə,siːz, 'mæ-] *or* **-trixes** ['meɪtrɪksəz] : matriz *f*

matron ['meɪtrən] *n* : matrona *f*

matronly ['meɪtrənli] *adj* : de matrona, matronal

matte ['mæt] *adj* : mate, de acabado mate

matter¹ ['mætər] *vi* : importar ⟨it doesn't matter : no importa⟩

matter² *n* **1** QUESTION : asunto *m*, cuestión *f* ⟨a matter of taste/opinion/time : una cuestión de gusto/opiniones/tiempo⟩ **2** SUBSTANCE : materia *f*, sustancia *f* **3 matters** *npl* CIRCUMSTANCES : situación *f*, cosas *fpl* ⟨to make matters worse : para colmo de males⟩ **4 as a matter of course** : automáticamente **5 as a matter of fact** : en efecto, en realidad **6 for that matter** : de hecho **7 no matter how much** : por mucho que **8 the fact/truth of the matter** : la verdad **9 to be no laughing matter** : no ser motivo de risa **10 to be the matter** : pasar ⟨what's the matter? : ¿qué pasa?⟩

matter–of–fact ['mætərəv'fækt] *adj* : práctico, realista

mattress ['mætrəs] *n* : colchón *m*

mature¹ [mə'tʊr, -'tjʊr, -'tʃʊr] *vi* **-tured; -turing 1** : madurar **2** : vencer ⟨when does the loan mature? : ¿cuándo vence el préstamo?⟩

mature² *adj* **maturer; -est 1** : maduro **2** DUE : vencido

maturity [mə'tʊrəti, -'tjʊr-, -'tʃʊr-] *n* : madurez *f*

maudlin ['mɔdlɪn] *adj* : sensiblero

maul¹ ['mɔl] *vt* **1** BEAT : golpear, pegar **2** MANGLE : mutilar **3** MANHANDLE : maltratar

maul² *n* MALLET : mazo *m*

Mauritanian [,mɔrə'teɪniən] *n* : mauritano *m*, -na *f* — **Mauritanian** *adj*

mausoleum [,mɔsə'liːəm, ,mɔzə-] *n, pl* **-leums** *or* **-lea** [-'liːə] : mausoleo *m*

mauve ['moːv, 'mɔv] *n* : malva *m*

maven *or* **mavin** ['meɪvən] *n* EXPERT : experto *m*, -ta *f*

maverick ['mævrɪk, 'mævə-] *n* **1** : ternero *m* sin marcar **2** NONCONFORMIST : inconformista *mf*, disidente *mf*

maw ['mɔ] *n* : fauces *fpl*

mawkish ['mɔkɪʃ] *adj* : sensiblero

maxim ['mæksəm] *n* : máxima *f*

maximize ['mæksə,maɪz] *vt* **-mized; -mizing** : maximizar, llevar al máximo

maximum¹ ['mæksəməm] *adj* : máximo

maximum² *n, pl* **-ma** ['mæksəmə] *or* **-mums** : máximo *m*

may ['meɪ] *v aux, past* **might** ['maɪt] *pres s & pl* **may 1** (*expressing permission*) : poder ⟨you may go : puedes ir⟩ ⟨if I may : si me lo permites⟩ **2** (*expressing possibility or probability*) : poder ⟨you may be right : puede que tengas razón⟩ ⟨it may happen occasionally : puede pasar de vez en cuando⟩ ⟨be that as it may : sea como sea⟩ **3** (*expressing desires, intentions, or contingencies*) ⟨may the best man win : que gane el mejor⟩ ⟨I laugh that I may not weep : me río para no llorar⟩ ⟨come what may : pase lo que pase⟩

May ['meɪ] *n* : mayo *m* ⟨they arrived on the 20th of May, they arrived on May 20th : llegaron el 20 de mayo⟩

Maya ['maɪə] *or* **Mayan** ['maɪən] *n* : maya *mf* — **Maya** *or* **Mayan** *adj*

maybe ['meɪbi] *adv* PERHAPS : quizás, tal vez

mayfly ['meɪˌflaɪ] *n, pl* **-flies** : efímera *f*
mayhem ['meɪˌhɛm, 'meɪəm] *n* **1** MUTILATION : mutilación *f* **2** DEVASTATION : estragos *mpl*
mayonnaise ['meɪəˌneɪz] *n* : mayonesa *f*
mayor ['meɪər, 'mɛr] *n* : alcalde *m*, -desa *f*
mayoral ['meɪərəl, 'mɛrəl] *adj* : de alcalde
maze ['meɪz] *n* : laberinto *m*
me ['mi:] *pron* **1** *me* ⟨she called me : me llamó⟩ ⟨give it to me : dámelo⟩ **2** (*after a preposition*) : mí ⟨for me : para mí⟩ ⟨with me : conmigo⟩ **3** (*after conjunctions and verbs*) : yo ⟨it's me : soy yo⟩ ⟨as big as me : tan grande como yo⟩ **4** (*emphatic use*) : yo ⟨me, too! : ¡yo también!⟩ ⟨who, me? : ¿quién, yo?⟩
meadow ['mɛdo:] *n* : prado *m*, pradera *f*
meadowland ['mɛdoˌlænd] *n* : pradera *f*
meadowlark ['mɛdoˌlɑrk] *n* : pájaro *m* cantor con el pecho amarillo
meager *or* **meagre** ['mi:gər] *adj* **1** THIN : magro, flaco **2** POOR, SCANTY : exiguo, escaso, pobre
meagerly ['mi:gərli] *adv* : pobremente
meagerness ['mi:gərnəs] *n* : escasez *f*, pobreza *f*
meal ['mi:l] *n* **1** : comida *f* ⟨a hearty meal : una comida sustanciosa⟩ **2** : harina *f* (de maíz, etc.)
mealtime ['mi:lˌtaɪm] *n* : hora *f* de comer
mean[1] ['mi:n] *vt* **meant** ['mɛnt]; **meaning 1** INTEND : querer, pensar, tener la intención de ⟨I didn't mean to do it : lo hice sin querer⟩ ⟨what do you mean to do? : ¿qué piensas hacer?⟩ ⟨I don't mean you any harm : no quiero hacerte daño⟩ ⟨she meant for him to come : su intención era que viniera⟩ **2** : querer decir ⟨what do you mean? : ¿qué quieres decir?⟩ ⟨if you know what I mean : si me entiendes⟩ ⟨I meant it : lo dije en serio⟩ ⟨she meant it as a compliment : lo dijo como un cumplido⟩ **3** SIGNIFY : querer decir, significar ⟨what does that mean? : ¿qué quiere decir eso?⟩ ⟨that means nothing to me : no significa nada para mí⟩ ⟨that means trouble : eso supone problemas⟩ **4** : importar ⟨health means everything : lo que más importa es la salud⟩ ⟨she means the world to me : ella es muy importante para mí⟩ **5 to mean well** : tener buenas intenciones
mean[2] *adj* **1** HUMBLE : humilde **2** NEGLIGIBLE : despreciable ⟨it's no mean feat : no es poca cosa⟩ **3** STINGY : mezquino, tacaño **4** CRUEL : malo, cruel ⟨to be mean to someone : tratar mal a alguien⟩ **5** AVERAGE, MEDIAN : medio
mean[3] *n* **1** MIDPOINT : término *m* medio **2** AVERAGE : promedio *m*, media *f* aritmética **3 means** *npl* WAY : medio *m*, manera *f*, vía *f* **4 means** *npl* RESOURCES : medios *mpl*, recursos *mpl* **5 by all means** : por supuesto, cómo no **6 by means of** : por medio de **7 by no means** : de ninguna manera, de ningún modo
meander [mi'ændər] *vi* **-dered; -dering 1** WIND : serpentear **2** WANDER : vagar, andar sin rumbo fijo

meaning ['mi:nɪŋ] *n* **1** : significado *m*, sentido *m* ⟨double meaning : doble sentido⟩ **2** INTENT : intención *f*, propósito *m*
meaningful ['mi:nɪŋfəl] *adj* : significativo — **meaningfully** *adv*
meaningless ['mi:nɪŋləs] *adj* : sin sentido
meanness ['mi:nnəs] *n* **1** CRUELTY : crueldad *f*, mezquindad *f* **2** STINGINESS : tacañería *f*
meantime[1] ['mi:nˌtaɪm] *adv* → **meanwhile**[1]
meantime[2] *n* **1** : ínterin *m* **2 in the meantime** : entretanto, mientras tanto
meanwhile[1] ['mi:nˌʰwaɪl] *adv* : entretanto, mientras tanto
meanwhile[2] *n* → **meantime**[2]
measles ['mi:zəlz] *ns & pl* : sarampión *m*
measly ['mi:zli] *adj* **measlier; -est** : miserable, mezquino
measurable ['mɛʒərəbəl, 'meɪ-] *adj* : mensurable — **measurably** [-bli] *adv*
measure[1] ['mɛʒər, 'meɪ-] *v* **-sured; -suring** : medir ⟨he measured the table : midió la mesa⟩ ⟨it measures 15 feet tall : mide 15 pies de altura⟩
measure[2] *n* **1** AMOUNT : medida *f*, cantidad *f* ⟨in large measure : en gran medida⟩ ⟨a full measure : una cantidad exacta⟩ ⟨a measure of proficiency : una cierta competencia⟩ ⟨for good measure : de ñapa, por añadidura⟩ **2** DIMENSIONS, SIZE : medida *f*, tamaño *m* **3** RULER : regla *f* ⟨tape measure : cinta métrica⟩ **4** MEASUREMENT : medida *f* ⟨cubic measure : medida de capacidad⟩ **5** MEASURING : medición *f* **6 measures** *npl* : medidas *fpl* ⟨security measures : medidas de seguridad⟩
measureless ['mɛʒərləs, 'meɪ-] *adj* : inmensurable
measurement ['mɛʒərmənt, 'meɪ-] *n* **1** MEASURING : medición *f* **2** DIMENSION : medida *f*
measure up *vi* **to measure up to** : estar a la altura de
meat ['mi:t] *n* **1** FOOD : comida *f* **2** : carne *f* ⟨meat and fish : carne y pescado⟩ **3** SUBSTANCE : sustancia *f*, esencia *f* ⟨the meat of the story : la sustancia del cuento⟩
meatball ['mi:tˌbɔl] *n* : albóndiga *f*
meaty ['mi:ti] *adj* **meatier; -est** : con mucha carne, carnoso
mechanic [mɪ'kænɪk] *n* : mecánico *m*, -ca *f*
mechanical [mɪ'kænɪkəl] *adj* : mecánico — **mechanically** *adv*
mechanics [mɪ'kænɪks] *ns & pl* **1** : mecánica *f* ⟨fluid mechanics : la mecánica de fluidos⟩ **2** MECHANISMS : mecanismos *mpl*, aspectos *mpl* prácticos
mechanism ['mɛkəˌnɪzəm] *n* : mecanismo *m*
mechanization [ˌmɛkənə'zeɪʃən] *n* : mecanización *f*
mechanize ['mɛkəˌnaɪz] *vt* **-nized; -nizing** : mecanizar

medal ['mɛdəl] *n* : medalla *f*, condecoración *f*

medalist ['mɛdəlɪst] *or* **medallist** *n* : medallista *mf*

medallion [mə'dæljən] *n* : medallón *m*

meddle ['mɛdəl] *vi* **-dled; -dling** : meterse, entrometerse

meddler ['mɛdələr] *n* : entrometido *m*, -da *f*

meddlesome ['mɛdəlsəm] *adj* : entrometido

media ['mi:diə] *npl* : medios *mpl* de comunicación ⟨social media : redes/medios sociales⟩

median¹ ['mi:diən] *adj* : medio

median² *n* : valor *m* medio

mediate ['mi:di,eɪt] *vi* **-ated; -ating** : mediar

mediation [,mi:di'eɪʃən] *n* : mediación *f*

mediator ['mi:di,eɪtər] *n* : mediador *m*, -dora *f*

medical ['mɛdɪkəl] *adj* : médico

medicate ['mɛdə,keɪt] *vt* **-cated; -cating** : medicar ⟨medicated powder : polvos medicinales⟩

medication [,mɛdə'keɪʃən] *n* **1** TREATMENT : tratamiento *m*, medicación *f* **2** MEDICINE : medicamento *m* ⟨to be on medication : estar medicado⟩

medicinal [mə'dɪsənəl] *adj* : medicinal

medicine ['mɛdəsən] *n* **1** MEDICATION : medicina *f*, medicamento *m* **2** : medicina *f* ⟨he's studying medicine : estudia medicina⟩

medicine man *n* : hechicero *m*

medieval *or* **mediaeval** [mɪ'di:vəl, ,mi:-, ,m-, -di'i:vəl] *adj* : medieval

mediocre [,mi:di'o:kər] *adj* : mediocre

mediocrity [,mi:di'akrəti] *n*, *pl* **-ties** : mediocridad *f*

meditate ['mɛdə,teɪt] *vi* **-tated; -tating** : meditar

meditation [,mɛdə'teɪʃən] *n* : meditación *f*

meditative ['mɛdə,teɪtɪv] *adj* : meditabundo

Mediterranean [,mɛdətə'reɪniən] *adj* : mediterráneo

medium¹ ['mi:diəm] *adj* : mediano ⟨of medium height : de estatura mediana/regular⟩ ⟨medium-sized : de tamaño mediano⟩

medium² *n*, *pl* **-diums** *or* **-dia** ['mi:diə] **1** MEAN : punto *m* medio, término *m* medio ⟨happy medium : justo medio⟩ **2** MEANS : medio *m* **3** SUBSTANCE : medio *m*, sustancia *f* ⟨a viscous medium : un medio viscoso⟩ **4** : medio *m* de comunicación **5** : medio *m* (artístico) **6** *pl* **mediums** : médium *mf* (persona)

medley ['mɛdli] *n*, *pl* **-leys** : popurrí *m* (de canciones)

meek ['mi:k] *adj* **1** LONG-SUFFERING : paciente, sufrido **2** SUBMISSIVE : sumiso, dócil, manso

meekly ['mi:kli] *adv* : dócilmente

meekness ['mi:knəs] *n* : mansedumbre *f*, docilidad *f*

meet¹ ['mi:t] *v* **met** ['mɛt]; **meeting** *vt* **1** ENCOUNTER : encontrarse con ⟨he met me at the park : nos encontramos en el parque⟩ **2** JOIN : unirse con **3** CONFRONT : enfrentarse a **4** ENCOUNTER : encontrar **5** SATISFY : satisfacer, cumplir con ⟨to meet costs : cubrir los gastos⟩ **6** REACH : alcanzar (una meta, etc.) **7** MATCH : igualar **8** : conocer ⟨I met his sister : conocí a su hermana⟩ **9 to meet someone halfway** : llegar a un arreglo con alguien **10 to meet someone's eyes/gaze** : mirarlo a la cara a alguien — *vi* **1** : encontrarse ⟨I hope we meet again : espero que nos volvamos a encontrar⟩ **2** ASSEMBLE : reunirse, congregarse **3** COMPETE, BATTLE : enfrentarse **4** : conocerse **5** JOIN : unirse **6** : encontrarse (dícese de los ojos) **7** : cerrarse (dícese de una chaqueta, etc.), tocar (dícese de dos extremos) **8 to meet up** : encontrarse **9 to meet with** : reunirse con **10 to meet with** RECEIVE : ser recibido con

meet² *n* : encuentro *m*

meeting ['mi:tɪŋ] *n* **1** : reunión *f* ⟨to open the meeting : abrir la sesión⟩ **2** ENCOUNTER : encuentro *m* **3** : entrevista *f* (formal)

meetinghouse ['mi:tɪŋ,haʊs] *n* : iglesia *f* (de ciertas confesiones protestantes)

megabyte ['mɛgə,baɪt] *n* : megabyte *m*

megahertz ['mɛgə,hərts, -,hrts] *n* : megahercio *m*

megaphone ['mɛgə,fo:n] *n* : megáfono *m*

megaton ['mɛgə,tʌn] *n* : megatón *m*

megawatt ['mɛgə,wat] *n* : megavatio *m*

melancholy¹ ['mɛlən,kali] *adj* : melancólico, triste, sombrío

melancholy² *n*, *pl* **-cholies** : melancolía *f*

melanoma [,mɛlə'no:mə] *n*, *pl* **-mas** : melanoma *m*

meld ['mɛld] *vt* : fusionar, unir — *vi* : fusionarse, unirse

melee ['meɪ,leɪ, meɪ'leɪ] *n* BRAWL : reyerta *f*, riña *f*, pelea *f*

meliorate ['mi:ljə,reɪt, 'mi:liə-] → **ameliorate**

mellow¹ ['mɛlo:] *vt* : suavizar, endulzar — *vi* : suavizarse, endulzarse

mellow² *adj* **1** RIPE : maduro **2** MILD : apacible ⟨a mellow character : un carácter apacible⟩ ⟨mellow wines : vinos añejos⟩ **3** : suave, dulce ⟨mellow colors : colores suaves⟩ ⟨mellow tones : tonos dulces⟩

mellowness ['mɛlonəs] *n* : suavidad *f*, dulzura *f*

melodic [mə'ladɪk] *adj* : melódico — **melodically** [-dɪkli] *adv*

melodious [mə'lo:diəs] *adj* : melodioso — **melodiously** *adv*

melodiousness [mə'lo:diəsnəs] *n* : calidad *f* de melódico

melodrama ['mɛlə,dramə, -,dræ-] *n* : melodrama *m*

melodramatic [,mɛlədrə'mætɪk] *adj* : melodramático — **melodramatically** [-tɪkli] *adv*

melody ['mɛlədi] *n*, *pl* **-dies** : melodía *f*, tonada *f*

melon ['mɛlən] *n* : melón *m*

melt ['mɛlt] *vt* **1** : derretir, disolver **2**
SOFTEN : ablandar ⟨it melted his heart
: ablandó su corazón⟩ **3 to melt down**
: fundir — *vi* **1** : derretirse, disolverse **2**
SOFTEN : ablandarse **3** DISAPPEAR : desvanecerse, esfumarse ⟨the clouds melted
away : las nubes se desvanecieron⟩

melting point *n* : punto *m* de fusión

member ['mɛmbər] *n* **1** LIMB : miembro
m **2** : miembro *m* (de un grupo); socio
m, -cia *f* (de un club) **3** PART : miembro
m, parte *f*

membership ['mɛmbər,ʃɪp] *n* **1** : membresía *f* ⟨application for membership
: solicitud de entrada⟩ **2** MEMBERS
: membresía *f*, miembros *mpl*, socios *mpl*

membrane ['mɛm,breɪn] *n* : membrana *f*
— **membranous** ['mɛmbrə-nəs] *adj*

memento [mɪ'mɛn,to:] *n*, *pl* -**tos** *or* -**toes**
: recuerdo *m*

memo ['mɛmo:] *n*, *pl* **memos** : memorándum *m*

memoirs ['mɛm,wɑrz] *npl* : memorias *fpl*,
autobiografía *f*

memorabilia [,mɛmərə'bɪliə, -'bɪljə] *npl* **1**
: objetos *mpl* de interés histórico **2** ME-
MENTOS : recuerdos *mpl*

memorable ['mɛmərəbəl] *adj* : memorable, notable — **memorably** [-bli] *adv*

memorandum [,mɛmə'rændəm] *n*, *pl*
-**dums** *or* -**da** [-də] : memorándum *m*

memorial[1] [mə'moriəl] *adj* : conmemorativo

memorial[2] *n* : monumento *m* conmemorativo

Memorial Day *n* : el último lunes de mayo
(observado en Estados Unidos como día
feriado para conmemorar a los caídos en
guerra)

memorialize [mə'moriə,laɪz] *vt* -**ized**;
-**izing** COMMEMORATE : conmemorar

memorization [,mɛmərə'zeɪʃən] *n* : memorización *f*

memorize ['mɛmə,raɪz] *vt* -**rized**; -**rizing**
: memorizar, aprender de memoria

memory ['mɛmri, 'mɛmə-] *n*, *pl* -**ries**
1 : memoria *f* ⟨he has a good memory
: tiene buena memoria⟩ **2** RECOLLEC-
TION : recuerdo *m* **3** COMMEMORA-
TION : memoria *f*, conmemoración *f*

men → **man**[2]

menace[1] ['mɛnəs] *vt* -**aced**; -**acing** **1**
THREATEN : amenazar **2** ENDANGER
: poner en peligro

menace[2] *n* : amenaza *f*

menacing ['mɛnəsɪŋ] *adj* : amenazador,
amenazante

menagerie [mə'næʤəri, -'næʒəri] *n* : colección *f* de animales salvajes

mend[1] ['mɛnd] *vt* **1** CORRECT : enmendar, corregir ⟨to mend one's ways : en-
mendarse⟩ **2** REPAIR : remendar, arreglar, reparar — *vi* HEAL : curarse

mend[2] *n* : remiendo *m*

mendicant ['mɛndɪkənt] *n* BEGGAR : mendigo *m*, -ga *f*

menhaden ['mɛn'heɪdən, mən-] *ns & pl*
: pez *m* de la misma familia que los
arenques

menial[1] ['mi:niəl] *adj* : servil, bajo

menial[2] *n* : sirviente *m*, -ta *f*

meningitis [,mɛnən'ʤaɪtəs] *n*, *pl* -**gitides**
[-'ʤɪtə,di:z] : meningitis *f*

menopausal [,mɛnə'pɔzəl] *adj* : menopáusico

menopause ['mɛnə,pɔz] *n* : menopausia *f*

menorah [mə'norə] *n* : candelabro *m*
(usado en los oficios religiosos judíos)

men's room *n* : servicios *mpl* de caballeros

menstrual ['mɛnstrəl] *adj* : menstrual

menstruate ['mɛnstru,eɪt] *vi* -**ated**; -**ating**
: menstruar

menstruation [,mɛnstru'eɪʃən] *n* : menstruación *f*

menswear ['mɛnz,wær] *n* : ropa *f* de caballero

-ment [mənt] *suf* : -miento ⟨entertainment
: entretenimiento⟩

mental ['mɛntəl] *adj* : mental ⟨mental
hospital : hospital psiquiátrico⟩ ⟨mental
block : bloqueo mental⟩ — **mentally** *adv*

mentality [mɛn'tæləti] *n*, *pl* -**ties** : mentalidad *f*

mental retardation [,ri:,tɑr'deɪʃən] *n sometimes offensive* : retraso *m* mental

menthol ['mɛn,θɔl, -,θo:l] *n* : mentol *m* —
mentholated [,mɛnθə,leɪtəd] *adj*

mention[1] ['mɛnʃən] *vt* : mencionar,
mentar, referirse a ⟨don't mention it!
: ¡de nada!, ¡no hay de qué!⟩

mention[2] *n* : mención *f*

mentor ['mɛn,tɔr, 'mɛntər] *n* : mentor *m*

menu ['mɛn,ju:] *n* **1** : menú *m*, carta *f* (en
un restaurante) **2** : menú *m* (en
informática)

meow[1] [mi'aʊ] *vi* : maullar

meow[2] *n* : maullido *m*, miau *m*

mercantile ['mərkən,ti:l, -,taɪl] *adj*
: mercantil

mercenary[1] ['mərsənɛ,ri] *adj* : mercenario

mercenary[2] *n*, *pl* -**naries** : mercenario *m*,
-ria *f*

merchandise ['mərtʃən,daɪz, -,daɪs] *n*
: mercancía *f*, mercadería *f*

merchandiser ['mərtʃən,daɪzər] *n* : comerciante *mf*; vendedor *m*, -dora *f*

merchant ['mərtʃənt] *n* : comerciante *mf*

merchant marine *n* : marina *f* mercante

merciful ['mərsɪfəl] *adj* : misericordioso,
clemente

mercifully ['mərsɪfli] *adv* **1** : con misericordia, con compasión **2** FORTUNATELY
: afortunadamente

merciless ['mərsɪləs] *adj* : despiadado —
mercilessly *adv*

mercurial [,mər'kjʊriəl] *adj* TEMPERA-
MENTAL : temperamental, volátil

mercury ['mərkjəri] *n*, *pl* -**ries** : mercurio *m*

Mercury *n* : Mercurio *m*

mercy ['mərsi] *n*, *pl* -**cies** **1** CLEMENCY
: misericordia *f*, clemencia *f* **2** BLESSING
: bendición *f*

mere ['mɪr] *adj, superlative* **merest** : mero,
simple

merely ['mɪrli] *adv* : solamente, simplemente

merengue [mə'rɛŋ,geɪ] *n* : merengue *m*
(música o baile)

merge ['mərdʒ] v **merged; merging** vi : unirse, fusionarse (dícese de las compañías), confluir (dícese de los ríos, las calles, etc.) — vt : unir, fusionar, combinar

merger ['mərdʒər] n : unión f, fusión f

meridian [mə'rɪdiən] n : meridiano m

meringue [mə'ræn] n : merengue m

merit[1] ['mɛrət] vt : merecer, ser digno de

merit[2] n : mérito m, valor m

meritorious [,mɛrə'toriəs] adj : meritorio

mermaid ['mər,meɪd] n : sirena f

merriment ['mɛrimənt] n : alegría f, júbilo m, regocijo m

merry ['mɛri] adj **merrier; -est** : alegre — **merrily** ['mɛrəli] adv

merry–go–round ['mɛrigo,raʊnd] n : carrusel m, tiovivo m

merrymaker ['mɛri,meɪkər] n : juerguista mf

merrymaking ['mɛri,meɪkɪŋ] n : juerga f

mesa ['meɪsə] n : mesa f

mesdames → madam, Mrs.

mesh[1] ['mɛʃ] vi **1** ENGAGE : engranar (dícese de las piezas mecánicas) **2** TANGLE : enredarse **3** COORDINATE : coordinarse, combinar

mesh[2] n **1** : malla f ⟨wire mesh : malla metálica⟩ **2** NETWORK : red f **3** MESHING : engranaje m ⟨in mesh : engranado⟩

mesmerize ['mɛzmə,raɪz] vt **-ized; -izing 1** HYPNOTIZE : hipnotizar **2** FASCINATE : cautivar, embelesar, fascinar

mess[1] ['mɛs] vt **1 to mess up** DISARRANGE : desordenar, desarreglar **2 to mess up** BUNGLE : echar a perder — vi **1 to mess around** HANG OUT : pasar el rato, entretenerse **2 to mess around** : tener líos (amorosos) **3 to mess (around) with** : tocar, jugar con ⟨don't mess with my things! : ¡no toques mis cosas!⟩ **4 to mess with** PROVOKE : meterse con

mess[2] n **1** : rancho m (para soldados, etc.) **2** DISORDER : desorden m ⟨your room is a mess : tienes el cuarto hecho un desastre⟩ **3** CONFUSION, TURMOIL : confusión f, embrollo m, lío m fam

message ['mɛsɪdʒ] n : mensaje m, recado m

messenger ['mɛsəndʒər] n : mensajero m, -ra f

Messiah [mə'saɪə] n : Mesías m

Messrs. → Mr.

messy ['mɛsi] adj **messier; -est** UNTIDY : desordenado, sucio — **messily** adv

mestizo [mɛ'sti:zo] n, **-za** f; ladino m, -na f CA, Mex — **mestizo** adj

met → meet

metabolic [,mɛtə'bɑlɪk] adj : metabólico

metabolism [mə'tæbə,lɪzəm] n : metabolismo m

metabolize [mə'tæbə,laɪz] vt **-lized; -lizing** : metabolizar

metal ['mɛtəl] n : metal m

metallic [mə'tælɪk] adj : metálico

metallurgical [,mɛtəl'ərdʒɪkəl] adj : metalúrgico

metallurgy ['mɛtəl,ərdʒi] n : metalurgia f

metalwork ['mɛtəl,wərk] n : objeto m de metal

metalworker ['mɛtəl,wərkər] n : metalúrgico m, -ca f

metalworking ['mɛtəl,wərkɪŋ] n : metalistería f

metamorphosis [,mɛtə'mɔrfəsɪs] n, pl **-phoses** [-,si:z] : metamorfosis f

metaphor ['mɛtə,for, -fər] n : metáfora f

metaphoric [,mɛtə'fɔrɪk] or **metaphorical** [-ɪkəl] adj : metafórico

metaphysical [,mɛtə'fɪzəkəl] adj : metafísico

metaphysics [,mɛtə'fɪzɪks] n : metafísica f

mete ['mi:t] vt **meted; meting** ALLOT : repartir, distribuir ⟨to mete out punishment : imponer castigos⟩

meteor ['mi:tiər, -ti:,ɔr] n : meteoro m

meteoric [,mi:ti'ɔrɪk] adj : meteórico

meteorite ['mi:tiə,raɪt] n : meteorito m

meteorologic [,mi:ti,ɔrə'lɑdʒɪk] or **meteorological** [-'lɑdʒɪkəl] adj : meteorológico

meteorologist [,mi:tiə'rɑlədʒɪst] n : meteorólogo m, -ga f

meteorology [,mi:tiə'rɑlədʒi] n : meteorología f

meter ['mi:tər] n **1** : metro m ⟨it measures 2 meters : mide 2 metros⟩ **2** : contador m, medidor m (de electricidad, etc.) ⟨parking meter : parquímetro⟩ **3** : metro m (en literatura o música)

methane ['mɛ,θeɪn] n : metano m

method ['mɛθəd] n : método m

methodical [mə'θɑdɪkəl] adj : metódico — **methodically** adv

Methodist ['mɛθədɪst] n : metodista mf — **Methodist** adj

methodology [,mɛθə'dɑlədʒi] n, pl **-gies** : metodología f

meticulous [mə'tɪkjələs] adj : meticuloso — **meticulously** adv

meticulousness [mə'tɪkjələsnəs] n : meticulosidad f

metric ['mɛtrɪk] or **metrical** [-trɪkəl] adj : métrico

metric system n : sistema m métrico

metro ['mɛtro] n SUBWAY : metro m; subterráneo m Arg, Uru

metronome ['mɛtrə,no:m] n : metrónomo m

metropolis [mə'trɑpələs] n : metrópoli f, metrópolis f

metropolitan [,mɛtrə'pɑlətən] adj : metropolitano

mettle ['mɛtəl] n : temple m, valor m ⟨on one's mettle : dispuesto a mostrar su valía⟩

Mexican ['mɛksɪkən] n : mexicano m, -na f — **Mexican** adj

mezzanine ['mɛzə,ni:n, ,mɛzə'ni:n] n **1** : entrepiso m **2** : primer piso m (de un teatro)

mi ['mi:] n : mi m (en el canto)

miasma [maɪ'æzmə] n : miasma m

mica ['maɪkə] n : mica f

mice → mouse

micro ['maɪkro] adj : muy pequeño, microscópico

micro- *pref* : micro-

microbe ['maɪ,kro:b] *n* : microbio *m*

microbiology [,maɪkrobaɪ'aləʤi] *n* : microbiología *f*

microchip ['maɪkro,ʧɪp] *n* : microchip *m*

microcomputer ['maɪkrokəm,pju:ʧər] *n* : microcomputadora *f*

microcosm ['maɪkro,kɑzəm] *n* : microcosmos *m*

microfilm ['maɪkro,fɪlm] *n* : microfilm *m*

micrometer ['maɪkro,mi:ʧər] *n* : micrómetro *m*

microorganism [,maɪkro'ɔrgə,nɪzəm] *n* : microorganismo *m*, microbio *m*

microphone ['maɪkrə,fo:n] *n* : micrófono *m*

microprocessor [,maɪkro'prɑ'sɛsər] *n* : microprocesador *m*

microscope ['maɪkrə,sko:p] *n* : microscopio *m*

microscopic [,maɪkrə'skɑpɪk] *adj* : microscópico

microwave ['maɪkrə,weɪv] *n* **1** : microonda *f* **2** *or* **microwave oven** : microondas *m*

mid ['mɪd] *adj* : medio ⟨mid morning : a media mañana⟩ ⟨in mid-August : a mediados de agosto⟩ ⟨in mid ocean : en alta mar⟩

midair ['mɪd'ær] *n* **in ~** : en el aire ⟨to catch in midair : agarrar al vuelo⟩

midday ['mɪd'deɪ] *n* NOON : mediodía *m*

middle¹ ['mɪdəl] *adj* **1** CENTRAL : medio, del medio, de en medio **2** INTERMEDIATE : intermedio, mediano ⟨middle age : la mediana edad⟩

middle² *n* **1** CENTER : medio *m*, centro *m* ⟨fold it down the middle : dóblalo por la mitad⟩ **2 in the middle of** : en medio de (un espacio), a mitad de (una actividad) ⟨in the middle of the month : a mediados del mes⟩

Middle Ages *npl* : Edad *f* Media

middle–class *adj* : de clase media

middle class *n* : clase *f* media

middleman ['mɪdəl,mæn] *n*, *pl* **-men** [-mən, -,mɛn] : intermediario *m*, -ria *f*

middle school *n* : colegio *m* para niños de 10 a 14 años

middling ['mɪdlɪŋ, -lən] *adj* **1** MEDIUM, MIDDLE : mediano **2** MEDIOCRE : mediocre, regular

midfielder ['mɪd,fi:ldər] *n* : mediocampista *mf*

midge ['mɪʤ] *n* : mosca *f* pequeña

midget ['mɪʤət] *n* **1** : enano *m*, -na *f* (persona) **2** : cosa *f* diminuta

midland ['mɪdlənd, -,lænd] *n* : región *f* central (de un país)

midnight ['mɪd,naɪt] *n* : medianoche *f*

midpoint ['mɪd,pɔɪnt] *n* : punto *m* medio, término *m* medio

midriff ['mɪd,rɪf] *n* : diafragma *m*

midshipman ['mɪd,ʃɪpmən, ,mɪd'ʃɪp-] *n*, *pl* **-men** [-mən, -,mɛn] : guardiamarina *m*

midst¹ ['mɪdst] *n* : medio *m* ⟨in our midst : entre nosotros⟩ ⟨in the midst of : en medio de⟩

midst² *prep* : entre

midstream ['mɪd'stri:m, -,stri:m] *n* : medio *m* de la corriente ⟨in the midstream of his career : en medio de su carrera⟩

midsummer ['mɪd'sʌmər, -,sʌ-] *n* : pleno verano *m*

midtown ['mɪd,taʊn] *n* : centro *m* (de una ciudad)

midway ['mɪd,weɪ] *adv* HALFWAY : a mitad de camino

midweek ['mɪd,wi:k] *n* : medio *m* de la semana ⟨in midweek : a media semana⟩

midwife ['mɪd,waɪf] *n*, *pl* **-wives** [-,waɪvz] : partera *f*, comadrona *f*

midwinter ['mɪd'wɪntər, -,wɪn-] *n* : pleno invierno *m*

midyear ['mɪd,jɪr] *n* : medio *m* del año ⟨at midyear : a mediados del año⟩

mien ['mi:n] *n* : aspecto *m*, porte *m*, semblante *m*

miff ['mɪf] *vt* : ofender

might¹ ['maɪt] (*used to express permission or possibility or as a polite alternative to* **may**) → **may** ⟨it might be true : podría ser verdad⟩ ⟨might I speak with Sarah? : ¿se puede hablar con Sarah?⟩

might² *n* : fuerza *f*, poder *m*

mightily ['maɪtəli] *adv* : con mucha fuerza, poderosamente

mighty¹ ['maɪti] *adv* VERY : muy ⟨mighty good : muy bueno, buenísimo⟩

mighty² *adj* **mightier; -est 1** POWERFUL : poderoso, potente **2** GREAT : grande, imponente

migraine ['maɪ,greɪn] *n* : jaqueca *f*, migraña *f*

migrant ['maɪgrənt] *n* : trabajador *m*, -dora *f* ambulante

migrate ['maɪ,greɪt] *vi* **-grated; -grating** : emigrar, migrar

migration [maɪ'greɪʃən] *n* : migración *f*

migratory ['maɪgrə,tori] *adj* : migratorio

mike ['maɪk] *n fam* → **microphone**

mild ['maɪld] *adj* **1** GENTLE : apacible, suave ⟨a mild disposition : un temperamento suave⟩ **2** LIGHT : leve, ligero ⟨a mild punishment : un castigo leve, un castigo poco severo⟩ **3** TEMPERATE : templado (dícese del clima) — **mildly** *adv*

mildew¹ ['mɪl,du:, -,dju:] *vi* : enmohecerse

mildew² *n* : moho *m*

mildness ['maɪldnəs] *n* : suavidad *f*

mile ['maɪl] *n* : milla *f*

mileage ['maɪlɪʤ] *n* **1** ALLOWANCE : viáticos *mpl* (pagados por milla recorrida) **2** : distancia *f* recorrida (en millas), kilometraje *m*

milestone ['maɪl,sto:n] *n* LANDMARK : hito *m*, jalón *m* ⟨a milestone in his life : un hito en su vida⟩

milieu [mi:l'ju:, -'jə] *n*, *pl* **-lieus** *or* **-lieux** [-'ju:z, -'jə] SURROUNDINGS : entorno *m*, medio *m*, ambiente *m*

militancy ['mɪlətən/si] *n*, *pl* **-cies** : militancia *f*

militant¹ ['mɪlətənt] *adj* : militante, combativo

militant² *n* : militante *mf*

militarism ['mɪlətə,rɪzəm] *n* : militarismo *m*

militaristic [ˌmɪlətəˈrɪstɪk] *adj* : militarista

militarize [ˈmɪlətəˌraɪz] *vt* **-rized; -rizing** : militarizar

military¹ [ˈmɪləˌteri] *adj* : militar

military² *n* **the military** : las fuerzas armadas

militia [məˈlɪʃə] *n* : milicia *f*

milk¹ [ˈmɪlk] *vt* **1** : ordeñar (una vaca, etc.) **2** EXPLOIT : explotar

milk² *n* **1** : leche *f* **2** : leche *f* (de una planta)

milk chocolate *n* : chocolate *m* con leche

milkman [ˈmɪlkˌmæn, -mən] *n, pl* **-men** [-mən, -ˌmɛn] : lechero *m*

milk of magnesia *n* : leche *f* de magnesia

milk shake *n* : batido *m*, licuado *m*

milkweed [ˈmɪlkˌwiːd] *n* : algodoncillo *m*

milky [ˈmɪlki] *adj* **milkier; -est** : lechoso

Milky Way *n* : Vía *f* Láctea

mill¹ [ˈmɪl] *vt* : moler (granos), acordonar (monedas) — *vi* **to mill about/around** : arremolinarse

mill² *n* **1** : molino *m* (para moler granos) **2** FACTORY : fábrica *f* ⟨textile mill : fábrica textil⟩ **3** GRINDER : molinillo *m*

millennium [məˈlɛniəm] *n, pl* **-nia** [-niə] *or* **-niums** : milenio *m*

miller [ˈmɪlər] *n* : molinero *m*, -ra *f*

millet [ˈmɪlət] *n* : mijo *m*

milligram [ˈmɪləˌgræm] *n* : miligramo *m*

milliliter [ˈmɪləˌliːtər] *n* : mililitro *m*

millimeter [ˈmɪləˌmiːtər] *n* : milímetro *m*

milliner [ˈmɪlənər] *n* : sombrerero *m*, -ra *f* (de señoras)

millinery [ˈmɪləˌnɛri] *n* : sombreros *mpl* de señora

million¹ [ˈmɪljən] *adj* **a million** : un millón de

million² *n, pl* **millions** *or* **million** : millón *m*

millionaire [ˌmɪljəˈnær, ˈmɪljəˌnær] *n* : millonario *m*, -ria *f*

millionth¹ [ˈmɪljənθ] *adj* : millonésimo

millionth² *n* : millonésimo *m*

millipede [ˈmɪləˌpiːd] *n* : milpiés *m*

millstone [ˈmɪlˌstoːn] *n* : rueda *f* de molino, muela *f*

mime¹ [ˈmaɪm] *v* **mimed; miming** *vt* MIMIC : imitar, remedar — *vi* PANTOMIME : hacer la mímica

mime² *n* **1** : mimo *mf* **2** PANTOMIME : pantomima *f*

mimeograph [ˈmɪmiəˌgræf] *n* : mimeógrafo *m*

mimic¹ [ˈmɪmɪk] *vt* **-icked; -icking** : imitar, remedar

mimic² *n* : imitador *m*, -dora *f*

mimicry [ˈmɪmɪkri] *n, pl* **-ries** : mímica *f*, imitación *f*

minaret [ˌmɪnəˈrɛt] *n* : alminar *m*, minarete *m*

mince [ˈmɪnts] *v* **minced; mincing** *vt* **1** CHOP : picar, moler (carne) **2** **not to mince one's words** : no tener un pelos en la lengua — *vi* : caminar de manera afectada

mincemeat [ˈmɪntsˌmiːt] *n* : mezcla *f* de fruta picada, sebo, y especias

mind¹ [ˈmaɪnd] *vt* **1** TEND : cuidar, atender ⟨mind the children : cuida a los niños⟩ **2** OBEY : obedecer **3** : preocuparse por, sentirse molestado por ⟨I don't mind his jokes : sus bromas no me molestan⟩ ⟨if you don't mind my saying so : si me permites⟩ ⟨never mind him : no le hagas caso⟩ **4** : tener cuidado con ⟨mind the ladder! : ¡cuidado con la escalera!⟩ **5 never mind** LET ALONE : ni mucho menos, (y) menos aún ⟨I can barely understand it, never mind explain it : apenas puedo entenderlo, ni mucho menos explicarlo⟩ — *vi* **1** OBEY : obedecer **2** CARE : importarle a uno ⟨I don't mind : no me importa, me es igual⟩ **3 never mind** : no importa, no se preocupe

mind² *n* **1** : mente *f* ⟨the mind and the body : la mente y el cuerpo⟩ ⟨it's all in your mind : es pura imaginación tuya⟩ ⟨what's on your mind? : ¿qué te preocupa?⟩ **2** INTENTION : intención *f*, propósito *m* **3** : razón *f* ⟨he's out of his mind : está loco⟩ **4** OPINION : opinión *f* ⟨in/to my mind : a mi parecer⟩ **5** INTELLECT : mente *f* ⟨she has a brilliant mind : tiene una mente brillante⟩ **6** ATTENTION : atención *f* ⟨pay him no mind : no le hagas caso⟩ **7 at/in the back of one's mind** : en el fondo **8 great minds think alike** : los genios pensamos igual **9 state of mind** : estado *m* de ánimo **10 to be of one mind** *or* **to be of the same mind** : estar de acuerdo **11 to be of two minds about** : estar indeciso sobre **12 to blow someone's mind** *fam* : maravillar a alguien **13 to call/bring to mind** : recordar, traer a la memoria **14 to change one's mind** : cambiar de opinión **15 to change someone's mind** : hacerle a alguien cambiar de opinión **16 to come/leap/spring to mind** : ocurrírsele a alguien **17 to cross someone's mind** : pasársele a alguien por la cabeza **18 to give someone a piece of one's mind** : cantarle las cuarentas a alguien **19 to have a good mind to** *or* **to have half a mind to** : tener ganas de (regañar a alguien, etc.) **20 to have a mind of one's own** : ser independiente **21 to have in mind** : tener (algo, a alguien) en mente, tener pensado (hacer algo) ⟨what did you have in mind? : ¿qué tenías en mente?⟩ **22 to have one's mind set on** : estar empeñado en **23 to keep an open mind** : mantener la mente abierta **24 to keep/bear in mind** : tener en cuenta **25 to keep one's mind on** : concentrarse en **26 to lose one's mind** : perder la razón **27 to make up one's mind** : decidirse **28 to put/set one's mind to** : poner empeño en **29 to put someone in mind of something** : recordarle algo a alguien **30 to speak one's mind** : hablar sin rodeos **31 to take a load/weight off one's mind** : quitarse un peso de encima

minded [ˈmaɪndəd] *adj* **1** (*used in combination*) ⟨narrow-minded : de mentalidad cerrada⟩ ⟨health-minded : preocupado por la salud⟩ **2** INCLINED : inclinado

mindful ['maɪndfəl] *adj* AWARE : consciente — **mindfully** *adv*

mindless ['maɪndləs] *adj* 1 SENSELESS : estúpido, sin sentido ⟨mindless violence : violencia sin sentido⟩ 2 HEEDLESS : inconsciente

mindlessly ['maɪndləsli] *adv* 1 SENSELESSLY : sin sentido 2 HEEDLESSLY : inconscientemente

mine¹ ['maɪn] *vt* **mined; mining** 1 : extraer (oro, etc.) 2 : minar (con artefactos explosivos)

mine² *n* : mina *f* ⟨gold mine : mina de oro⟩

mine³ *pron* : mío ⟨that one's mine : ése es el mío, ésa es la mía⟩ ⟨some friends of mine : unos amigos míos⟩

minefield ['maɪn,fi:ld] *n* : campo *m* de minas

miner ['maɪnər] *n* : minero *m*, -ra *f*

mineral ['mɪnərəl] *n* : mineral *m* — **mineral** *adj*

mineralogy [,mɪnə'rɑlədʒi, -'ræ-] *n* : mineralogía *f*

mine shaft → **shaft**

mingle ['mɪŋgəl] *v* **-gled; -gling** *vt* MIX : mezclar — *vi* 1 MIX : mezclarse 2 CIRCULATE : circular

mini- *pref* : mini-

miniature¹ ['mɪniə,tʃʊr, 'mɪni,tʃʊr, -tʃər] *adj* : en miniatura, diminuto

miniature² *n* : miniatura *f*

minibus ['mɪni,bʌs] *n* : microbús *m*; pesera *f Mex*; buseta *f Col, CoRi, Ecua, Ven*

minicomputer ['mɪnikəm,pju:tər] *n* : minicomputadora *f*

minimal ['mɪnəməl] *adj* : mínimo

minimally ['mɪnəməli] *adv* : en grado mínimo

minimize ['mɪnə,maɪz] *vt* **-mized; -mizing** : minimizar

minimum¹ ['mɪnəməm] *adj* : mínimo

minimum² *n, pl* **-ma** ['mɪnəmə] *or* **-mums** : mínimo *m*

mining ['maɪnɪŋ] *n* : minería *f*

miniseries ['mɪni,sɪri:z] *n* : miniserie *f*

miniskirt ['mɪni,skərt] *n* : minifalda *f*

minister¹ ['mɪnəstər] *vi* **to minister to** : cuidar (de), atender a

minister² *n* 1 : pastor *m*, -tora *f* (de una iglesia) 2 : ministro *m*, -tra *f* (en política)

ministerial [,mɪnə'stɪriəl] *adj* : ministerial

ministry ['mɪnəstri] *n, pl* **-tries** 1 : ministerio *m* (en política) 2 : sacerdocio *m* (en el catolicismo), clerecía *f* (en el protestantismo)

minivan ['mɪni,væn] *n* : minivan *f*

mink ['mɪŋk] *n, pl* **mink** *or* **minks** : visón *m*

minnow ['mɪno:] *n, pl* **-nows** : pececillo *m* de agua dulce

minor¹ ['maɪnər] *adj* : menor

minor² *n* 1 : menor *mf* (de edad) 2 : asignatura *f* secundaria (de estudios)

minority [mə'nɔrəti, maɪ-] *n, pl* **-ties** : minoría *f*

minstrel ['mɪnstrəl] *n* : juglar *m*, trovador *m* (en el medioevo)

mint¹ ['mɪnt] *vt* : acuñar

mint² *adj* : sin usar ⟨in mint condition : como nuevo⟩

mint³ *n* 1 : menta *f* ⟨mint tea : té de menta⟩ 2 : pastilla *f* de menta 3 : casa *f* de la moneda ⟨the U.S. Mint : la casa de la moneda de los EE.UU.⟩ 4 FORTUNE : dineral *m*, fortuna *f*

minuet [,mɪnju'ɛt] *n* : minué *m*

minus¹ ['maɪnəs] *n* 1 : cantidad *f* negativa 2 **minus sign** : signo *m* de menos

minus² *prep* 1 : menos ⟨four minus two : cuatro menos dos⟩ 2 WITHOUT : sin ⟨minus his hat : sin su sombrero⟩

minuscule *or* **miniscule** ['mɪnəs,kju:l, mɪ'nʌs-] *adj* : minúsculo

minute¹ [maɪ'nu:t, mɪ-, -'nju:t] *adj* **minuter; -est** 1 TINY : diminuto, minúsculo 2 DETAILED : minucioso

minute² ['mɪnət] *n* 1 : minuto *m* 2 MOMENT : momento *m* ⟨at any minute : en cualquier momento⟩ 3 **minutes** *npl* : actas *fpl* (de una reunión) 4 **at the last minute** : a último momento, a última hora 5 **hang/hold on a minute** *or* **wait a minute** : espera un momento 6 **just a minute** : un momento 7 **this minute** : ahora mismo, inmediatamente

minute hand *n* : minutero *m*

minutely [maɪ'nu:tli, mɪ-, -'nju:t-] *adv* : minuciosamente

miracle ['mɪrɪkəl] *n* : milagro *m*

miraculous [mə'rækjələs] *adj* : milagroso — **miraculously** *adv*

mirage [mɪ'rɑʒ, *chiefly Brit* 'mɪr,ɑʒ] *n* : espejismo *m*

mire¹ ['maɪr] *vi* **mired; miring** : atascarse

mire² *n* 1 MUD : barro *m*, lodo *m* 2 : atolladero *m* ⟨stuck in a mire of debt : agobiado por la deuda⟩

mirror¹ ['mɪrər] *vt* : reflejar

mirror² *n* : espejo *m*

mirth ['mərθ] *n* : alegría *f*, regocijo *m*

mirthful ['mərθfəl] *adj* : alegre, regocijado

misadventure [,mɪsəd'ventʃər] *n* : malaventura *f*, desventura *f*

misanthrope ['mɪsən,θro:p] *n* : misántropo *m*, -pa *f*

misanthropic [,mɪsən'θrɑpɪk] *adj* : misantrópico

misanthropy [mɪ'sænθrəpi] *n* : misantropía *f*

misapprehend [,mɪs,æprə'hend] *vt* : entender mal

misapprehension [,mɪs,æprə'hentʃən] *n* : malentendido *m*

misappropriate [,mɪsə'pro:pri,eɪt] *vt* **-ated; -ating** : malversar

misappropriation [,mɪsə,pro:pri'eɪʃən] *n* : malversación *f*

misbegotten [,mɪsbi'gɑtən] *adj* 1 ILLEGITIMATE : ilegítimo 2 : mal concebido ⟨misbegotten laws : leyes mal concebidas⟩

misbehave [,mɪsbi'heɪv] *vi* **-haved; -having** : portarse mal

misbehavior [,mɪsbi'heɪvjər] *n* : mala conducta *f*

miscalculate [mɪs'kælkjə,leɪt] *v* **-lated; -lating** : calcular mal

miscalculation [mɪsˌkælkjə'leɪʃən] *n* : error *m* de cálculo, mal cálculo *m*

miscarriage [ˌmɪs'kærɪdʒ, 'mɪsˌkærɪdʒ] *n* 1 : aborto *m* 2 FAILURE : fracaso *m*, malogro *m* ⟨a miscarriage of justice : una injusticia, un error judicial⟩

miscarry [ˌmɪs'kæri, 'mɪsˌkæri] *vi* -ried; -rying 1 ABORT : abortar 2 FAIL : malograrse, fracasar

miscellaneous [ˌmɪsə'leɪniəs] *adj* : misceláneo

miscellany ['mɪsəˌleɪni] *n, pl* -nies : miscelánea *f*

mischance [mɪs'tʃænts] *n* : desgracia *f*, infortunio *m*, mala suerte *f*

mischief ['mɪstʃəf] *n* : diabluras *fpl*, travesuras *fpl*

mischievous ['mɪstʃəvəs] *adj* : travieso, pícaro

mischievously ['mɪstʃəvəsli] *adv* : de manera traviesa

misconception [ˌmɪskən'sɛpʃən] *n* : concepto *m* erróneo, idea *f* falsa

misconduct [mɪs'kɑndəkt] *n* : mala conducta *f*

misconstrue [ˌmɪskən'stru:] *vt* -strued; -struing : malinterpretar

misdeed [mɪs'di:d] *n* : fechoría *f*

misdemeanor [ˌmɪsdɪ'mi:nər] *n* : delito *m* menor

miser ['maɪzər] *n* : avaro *m*, -ra *f*; tacaño *m*, -ña *f*

miserable ['mɪzərəbəl] *adj* 1 UNHAPPY : triste, desdichado 2 WRETCHED : miserable, desgraciado ⟨a miserable hut : una choza miserable⟩ 3 UNPLEASANT : desagradable, malo ⟨miserable weather : tiempo malísimo⟩ 4 CONTEMPTIBLE : despreciable, mísero ⟨for a miserable $10 : por unos míseros diez dólares⟩

miserably ['mɪzərəbli] *adv* 1 SADLY : tristemente 2 WRETCHEDLY : miserablemente, lamentablemente 3 UNFORTUNATELY : desgraciadamente

miserly ['maɪzərli] *adj* : avaro, tacaño

misery ['mɪzəri] *n, pl* -eries : miseria *f*, sufrimiento *m*

misfire [mɪs'faɪr] *vi* -fired; -firing : fallar

misfit ['mɪsˌfɪt] *n* : inadaptado *m*, -da *f*

misfortune [mɪs'fɔrtʃən] *n* : desgracia *f*, desventura *f*, infortunio *m*

misgiving [mɪs'ɡɪvɪŋ] *n* : duda *f*, recelo *m*

misguided [mɪs'ɡaɪdəd] *adj* : desacertado, equivocado, mal informado

mishap ['mɪsˌhæp] *n* : contratiempo *m*, percance *m*, accidente *m*

misinform [ˌmɪsɪn'fɔrm] *vt* : informar mal

misinterpret [ˌmɪsɪn'tərprət] *vt* : malinterpretar

misinterpretation [ˌmɪsɪnˌtərprə'teɪ-ʃən] *n* : mala interpretación *f*, malentendido *m*

misjudge [mɪs'dʒʌdʒ] *vt* -judged; -judging : juzgar mal

mislay [mɪs'leɪ] *vt* -laid [-'leɪd] -laying : extraviar, perder

mislead [mɪs'li:d] *vt* -led [-'lɛd] -leading : engañar

misleading [mɪs'li:dɪŋ] *adj* : engañoso

mismanage [mɪs'mænɪdʒ] *vt* -aged; -aging : administrar mal

mismanagement [mɪs'mænɪdʒmənt] *n* : mala administración *f*

misnomer [mɪs'no:mər] *n* : nombre *m* inapropiado

misogynist [mɪ'sɑdʒənɪst] *n* : misógino *m*

misogyny [mə'sɑdʒəni] *n* : misoginia *f*

misplace [mɪs'pleɪs] *vt* -placed; -placing : extraviar, perder

misprint ['mɪsˌprɪnt, mɪs'-] *n* : errata *f*, error *m* de imprenta

mispronounce [ˌmɪsprə'naʊnts] *vt* -nounced; -nouncing : pronunciar mal

mispronunciation [ˌmɪsprəˌnʌntsi'eɪʃən] *n* : pronunciación *f* incorrecta

misquote [mɪs'kwo:t] *vt* -quoted; -quoting : citar incorrectamente

misread [mɪs'ri:d] *vt* -read [-'rɛd] -reading 1 : leer mal ⟨she misread the sentence : leyó mal la frase⟩ 2 MISUNDERSTAND : malinterpretar ⟨they misread his intention : malinterpretaron su intención⟩

misrepresent [ˌmɪsˌrprɪ'zɛnt] *vt* : distorsionar, falsear, tergiversar

miss¹ ['mɪs] *vt* 1 : errar, faltar ⟨to miss the target : no dar en el blanco⟩ 2 : no encontrar, perder ⟨they missed each other : no se encontraron⟩ ⟨I missed the plane : perdí el avión⟩ 3 : echar de menos, extrañar ⟨we miss him a lot : lo echamos mucho de menos⟩ 4 OVERLOOK : pasar por alto ⟨to miss the point : no entender algo⟩ ⟨you can't miss it : no puedes dejar de verlo⟩ 5 : no enterarse de (una noticia), no oír (palabras habladas) 6 : perderse (una oportunidad, etc.) 7 PASS UP : pasar por alto 8 : faltar a (una reunión, etc.) 9 AVOID : evitar ⟨they just missed hitting the tree : por muy poco chocan contra el árbol⟩ 10 OMIT : saltarse ⟨he missed breakfast : se saltó el desayuno⟩ 11 to be missing : faltarle (algo a uno) ⟨he's missing two teeth : le faltan dos dientes⟩ 12 to miss out on : perderse (una oportunidad, etc.)

miss² *n* 1 : fallo *m* (de un tiro, etc.) 2 FAILURE : fracaso *m* 3 : señorita *f* ⟨Miss Jones called us : nos llamó la señorita Jones⟩ ⟨excuse me, miss : perdone, señorita⟩

misshapen [mɪ'ʃeɪpən] *adj* : deforme

missile ['mɪsəl] *n* 1 : misil *m* ⟨guided missile : misil guiado⟩ 2 PROJECTILE : proyectil *m*

missing ['mɪsɪŋ] *adj* 1 ABSENT : ausente ⟨who's missing? : ¿quién falta?⟩ 2 LOST : perdido, desaparecido ⟨missing persons : los desaparecidos⟩

mission ['mɪʃən] *n* 1 : misión *f* (mandada por una iglesia) 2 DELEGATION : misión *f*, delegación *f*, embajada *f* 3 TASK : misión *f*

missionary¹ ['mɪʃəˌnɛri] *adj* : misionero

missionary² *n, pl* -aries : misionero *m*, -ra *f*

missive ['mɪsɪv] *n* : misiva *f*

misspell [mɪs'spɛl] *vt* : escribir mal

misspelling [mɪsˈspelɪŋ] *n* : falta *f* de ortografía

misstep [ˈmɪsˌstep] *n* : traspié *m*, tropezón *m*

mist [ˈmɪst] *n* 1 HAZE : neblina *f*, niebla *f* 2 SPRAY : rocío *m*

mistake¹ [mɪˈsteɪk] *vt* **-took** [-ˈstʊk]; **-taken** [-ˈsteɪkən] *vt* 1 MISINTERPRET : malinterpretar 2 CONFUSE : confundir ‹he mistook her for Clara : la confundió con Clara›

mistake² *n* 1 MISUNDERSTANDING : malentendido *m*, confusión *f* 2 ERROR : error *m* ‹I made a mistake : me equivoqué, cometí un error›

mistaken [mɪˈsteɪkən] *adj* WRONG : equivocado — **mistakenly** *adv*

mister [ˈmɪstər] *n* : señor *m* ‹watch out, mister : cuidado, señor›

mistiness [ˈmɪstinəs] *n* : nebulosidad *f*

mistletoe [ˈmɪsəlˌtoː] *n* : muérdago *m*

mistreat [mɪsˈtriːt] *vt* : maltratar

mistreatment [mɪsˈtriːtmənt] *n* : maltrato *m*, abuso *m*

mistress [ˈmɪstrəs] *n* 1 : dueña *f*, señora *f* (de una casa) 2 LOVER : amante *f*

mistrust¹ [mɪsˈtrʌst] *vt* : desconfiar de

mistrust² *n* : desconfianza *f*

mistrustful [mɪsˈtrʌstfəl] *adj* : desconfiado

misty [ˈmɪsti] *adj* **mistier; -est** 1 : neblinoso, nebuloso 2 TEARFUL : lloroso

misunderstand [ˌmɪsˌʌndərˈstænd] *vt* **-stood** [-ˈstʊd]; **-standing** 1 : entender mal 2 MISINTERPRET : malinterpretar ‹don't misunderstand me : no me malinterpretes›

misunderstanding [ˌmɪsˌʌndərˈstændɪŋ] *n* 1 MISINTERPRETATION : malentendido *m* 2 DISAGREEMENT, QUARREL : disputa *f*, discusión *f*

misuse¹ [mɪsˈjuːz] *vt* **-used; -using** 1 : emplear mal 2 ABUSE, MISTREAT : abusar de, maltratar

misuse² [mɪsˈjuːs] *n* 1 : mal empleo *m*, mal uso *m* 2 WASTE : derroche *m*, despilfarro *m* 3 ABUSE : abuso *m*

mite [ˈmaɪt] *n* 1 : ácaro *m* 2 BIT : poco *m* ‹a mite tired : un poquito cansado›

miter *or* **mitre** [ˈmaɪtər] *n* 1 : mitra *f* (de un obispo) 2 *or* **miter joint** : inglete *m*

mitigate [ˈmɪtəˌgeɪt] *vt* **-gated; -gating** : mitigar, aliviar

mitigation [ˌmɪtəˈgeɪʃən] *n* : mitigación *f*, alivio *m*

mitosis [maɪˈtoːsɪs] *n, pl* **-toses** [-ˌsiːz] : mitosis *f*

mitt [ˈmɪt] *n* 1 : manopla *f*, guante *m* (de béisbol) 2 HAND : mano *f*, manaza *f*

mitten [ˈmɪtən] *n* : manopla *f*

mix¹ [ˈmɪks] *vt* 1 COMBINE : mezclar 2 STIR : remover, revolver 3 **to mix up** CONFUSE : confundir 4 **to mix up** COMBINE : mezclar — *vi* : mezclarse

mix² *n* : mezcla *f*

mixed *adj* : mezclado, variado

mixed–up *adj* 1 CONFUSED, TROUBLED : confundido, con problemas 2 CONFUSING : confuso

mixer [ˈmɪksər] *n* 1 : batidora *f* (de la cocina) 2 **cement mixer** : hormigonera *f*

mixture [ˈmɪkstʃər] *n* : mezcla *f*

mix–up [ˈmɪksˌʌp] *n* CONFUSION : confusión *f*, lío *m fam*

mnemonic [nɪˈmɑnɪk] *adj* : mnemónico

moan¹ [ˈmoːn] *vi* : gemir

moan² *n* : gemido *m*

moat [ˈmoːt] *n* : foso *m*

mob¹ [ˈmɑb] *vt* **mobbed; mobbing** 1 ATTACK : atacar en masa 2 HOUND : acosar, rodear

mob² *n* 1 THRONG : multitud *f*, turba *f*, muchedumbre *f* 2 GANG : pandilla *f*

mobile¹ [ˈmoːbəl, -ˌbiːl, -ˌbaɪl] *adj* : móvil ‹mobile home : caravana, casa rodante›

mobile² [ˈmoːˌbiːl] *n* : móvil *m*

mobility [moːˈbɪləti] *n* : movilidad *f*

mobilize [ˈmoːbəˌlaɪz] *vt* **-lized; -lizing** : movilizar

moccasin [ˈmɑkəsən] *n* 1 : mocasín *m* 2 *or* **water moccasin** : serpiente *f* venenosa de Norteamérica

mocha [ˈmoːkə] *n* 1 : mezcla *f* de café y chocolate 2 : color *m* chocolate

mock¹ [ˈmɑk, ˈmɔk] *vt* 1 RIDICULE : burlarse de, mofarse de 2 MIMIC : imitar, remedar (de manera burlona)

mock² *adj* 1 SIMULATED : simulado 2 PHONY : falso

mockery [ˈmɑkəri, ˈmɔ-] *n, pl* **-eries** 1 JEER, TAUNT : burla *f*, mofa *f* ‹to make a mockery of : burlarse de› 2 FAKE : imitación *f* (burlona)

mockingbird [ˈmɑkɪŋˌbərd, ˈmɔ-] *n* : sinsonte *m*

mode [ˈmoːd] *n* 1 FORM : modo *m*, forma *f* 2 MANNER : modo *m*, manera *f*, estilo *m* 3 FASHION : moda *f*

model¹ [ˈmɑdəl] *v* **-eled** *or* **-elled; -eling** *or* **-elling** *vt* SHAPE : modelar — *vi* : trabajar de modelo

model² *adj* 1 EXEMPLARY : modelo, ejemplar ‹a model student : un estudiante modelo› 2 MINIATURE : en miniatura

model³ *n* 1 PATTERN : modelo *m* 2 MINIATURE : modelo *m*, miniatura *f* 3 EXAMPLE : modelo *m*, ejemplo *m* 4 MANNEQUIN : modelo *mf* 5 DESIGN : modelo *m* ‹the ' 97 model : el modelo ' 97›

modem [ˈmoːdəm, -ˌdem] *n* : módem *m*

moderate¹ [ˈmɑdəˌreɪt] *v* **-ated; -ating** *vt* : moderar, temperar — *vi* 1 CALM : moderarse, calmarse 2 : fungir como moderador (en un debate, etc.)

moderate² [ˈmɑdərət] *adj* : moderado

moderate³ [ˈmɑdərət] *n* : moderado *m*, -da *f*

moderately [ˈmɑdərətli] *adv* 1 : con moderación 2 FAIRLY : medianamente

moderation [ˌmɑdəˈreɪʃən] *n* : moderación *f*

moderator [ˈmɑdəˌreɪtər] *n* : moderador *m*, -dora *f*

modern [ˈmɑdərn] *adj* : moderno

modernism [ˈmɑdərˌnɪzəm] *n* : modernismo *m*

modernist [ˈmɑdərnɪst] *n* : modernista *mf* — **modernist** *adj*

modernity [mə'dərnəṭi] *n* : modernidad *f*

modernization [ˌmadərnə'zeɪʃən] *n* : modernización *f*

modernize ['madər,naɪz] *v* **-ized; -izing** *vt* : modernizar — *vi* : modernizarse

modest ['madəst] *adj* **1** HUMBLE : modesto **2** DEMURE : recatado, pudoroso **3** MODERATE : modesto, moderado — **modestly** *adv*

modesty ['madəsti] *n* : modestia *f*

modicum ['madɪkəm] *n* : mínimo *m*, pizca *f*

modification [ˌmadəfə'keɪʃən] *n* : modificación *f*

modifier ['madə,faɪər] *n* : modificante *m*, modificador *m*

modify ['madə,faɪ] *vt* **-fied; -fying** : modificar, calificar (en gramática)

modish ['moːdɪʃ] *adj* STYLISH : a la moda, de moda

modular ['madʒələr] *adj* : modular

modulate ['madʒə,leɪt] *vt* **-lated; -lating** : modular

modulation [ˌmadʒə'leɪʃən] *n* : modulación *f*

module ['madʒuːl] *n* : módulo *m*

mogul ['moːgəl] *n* : magnate *mf*; potentado *m*, -da *f*

moist ['mɔɪst] *adj* : húmedo

moisten ['mɔɪsən] *vt* : humedecer

moistness ['mɔɪstnəs] *n* : humedad *f*

moisture ['mɔɪstʃər] *n* : humedad *f*

moisturize ['mɔɪstʃə,raɪz] *vt* **-ized; -izing** : humedecer (el aire), hidratar (la piel)

moisturizer ['mɔɪstʃə,raɪzər] *n* : crema *f* hidratante, crema *f* humectante

molar ['moːlər] *n* : muela *f*, molar *m*

molasses [mə'læsəz] *n* : melaza *f*

mold[1] ['moːld] *vt* : moldear, formar (carácter, etc.) — *vi* : enmohecerse ⟨the bread will mold : el pan se enmohecerá⟩

mold[2] *n* **1** FORM : molde *m* ⟨to break the mold : romper el molde⟩ **2** FUNGUS : moho *m*

molder ['moːldər] *vi* CRUMBLE : desmoronarse

molding ['moːldɪŋ] *n* : moldura *f* (en arquitectura)

moldy ['moːldi] *adj* **moldier; -est** : mohoso

mole ['moːl] *n* **1** : lunar *m* (en la piel) **2** : topo *m* (animal)

molecule ['malɪ,kjuːl] *n* : molécula *f* — **molecular** [mə'lɛkjələr] *adj*

molehill ['moːl,hɪl] *n* to make a mountain out of a molehill : ahogarse en un vaso de agua

molest [mə'lɛst] *vt* **1** ANNOY, DISTURB : molestar **2** : abusar (sexualmente)

mollify ['malə,faɪ] *vt* **-fied; -fying** : apaciguar, aplacar

mollusk *or* **mollusc** ['maləsk] *n* : molusco *m*

mollycoddle ['mali,kadəl] *vt* **-dled; -dling** PAMPER : consentir, mimar

molt ['moːlt] *vi* : mudar, hacer la muda

molten ['moːltən] *adj* : fundido

mom ['mam, 'mʌm] *n* : mamá *f*

moment ['moːmənt] *n* **1** INSTANT : momento *m* ⟨one moment, please : un momento, por favor⟩ **2** TIME : momento *m* ⟨from that moment : desde entonces⟩ **3** **at any moment** : de un momento a otro **4** **at the moment** : de momento, actualmente **5** **for the moment** : de momento, por el momento **6** **the moment of truth** : la hora de la verdad

momentarily [ˌmoːmən'tɛrəli] *adv* **1** : momentáneamente **2** SOON : dentro de poco, pronto

momentary ['moːmən,tɛri] *adj* : momentáneo

momentous [moː'mɛntəs] *adj* : de suma importancia, fatídico

momentum [moː'mɛntəm] *n*, *pl* **-ta** [-tə] *or* **-tums** **1** : momento *m* (en física) **2** IMPETUS : ímpetu *m*, impulso *m*

mommy ['mami, 'mʌ-] *n* : mami *f*

monarch ['ma,nark, -nərk] *n* : monarca *mf*

monarchist ['ma,narkɪst, -nər-] *n* : monárquico *m*, -ca *f*

monarchy ['ma,narki, -nər-] *n*, *pl* **-chies** : monarquía *f*

monastery ['manə,steri] *n*, *pl* **-teries** : monasterio *m*

monastic [mə'næstɪk] *adj* : monástico — **monastically** [-tɪkli] *adv*

Monday ['mʌn,deɪ, -di] *n* : lunes *m* ⟨today is Monday : hoy es lunes⟩ ⟨(on) Monday : el lunes⟩ ⟨(on) Mondays : los lunes⟩ ⟨last Monday : el lunes pasado⟩ ⟨next Monday : el lunes que viene⟩ ⟨every other Monday : cada dos lunes⟩ ⟨Monday afternoon/morning : lunes por la tarde/mañana⟩

monetary ['manə,teri, 'mʌnə-] *adj* : monetario

money ['mʌni] *n*, *pl* **-eys** *or* **-ies** ['mʌniz] **1** : dinero *m*, plata *f* ⟨to make/lose money : ganar/perder dinero⟩ **2 monies** *npl* : sumas *fpl* de dinero **3 for my money** : en mi opinión, para mí **4 money talks** : poderoso caballero es don Dinero **5 on the money** : exacto, correcto

money changer [-'tʃeɪndʒər] *n* : cambista *mf* (de dinero)

moneyed ['mʌnid] *adj* : adinerado

moneylender ['mʌni,lɛndər] *n* : prestamista *mf*

money order *n* : giro *m* postal

Mongol ['maŋgəl, -goːl] → **Mongolian**

Mongolian [maŋ'goːliən, maŋ-] *n* : mongol *m*, -gola *f* — **Mongolian** *adj*

mongoose ['maŋ,guːs, 'maŋ-] *n*, *pl* **-gooses** : mangosta *f*

mongrel ['maŋgrəl, 'mʌŋ-] *n* **1** : perro *m* mestizo, perro *m* corriente *Mex* **2** HYBRID : híbrido *m*

monitor[1] ['manəṭər] *vt* : controlar, monitorear

monitor[2] *n* **1** : ayudante *mf* (en una escuela) **2** : monitor *m* (de una computadora, etc.)

monk ['mʌŋk] *n* : monje *m*

monkey[1] ['mʌŋki] *vi* **-keyed; -keying 1 to monkey around** : hacer payasadas, payasear **2 to monkey with** : juguetear con

monkey[2] *n*, *pl* **-keys** : mono *m*, -na *f*

monkeyshines [ˈmʌŋkiˌʃaɪnz] *npl* PRANKS : picardías *fpl*, travesuras *fpl*

monkey wrench *n* → **wrench**[2]

monocle [ˈmɑnɪkəl] *n* : monóculo *m*

monogamous [məˈnɑgəməs] *adj* : monógamo

monogamy [məˈnɑgəmi] *n* : monogamia *f*

monogram[1] [ˈmɑnəˌgræm] *vt* **-grammed; -gramming** : marcar con monograma ⟨monogrammed towels : toallas con monograma⟩

monogram[2] *n* : monograma *m*

monograph [ˈmɑnəˌgræf] *n* : monografía *f*

monolingual [ˌmɑnəˈlɪŋgwəl] *adj* : monolingüe

monolith [ˈmɑnəˌlɪθ] *n* : monolito *m*

monolithic [ˌmɑnəˈlɪθɪk] *adj* : monolítico

monologue [ˈmɑnəˌlɔg] *n* : monólogo *m*

monopolize [məˈnɑpəˌlaɪz] *vt* **-lized; -lizing** : monopolizar

monopoly [məˈnɑpəli] *n, pl* **-lies** : monopolio *m*

monosyllabic [ˌmɑnəsəˈlæbɪk] *adj* : monosilábico

monosyllable [ˈmɑnoˌsɪləbəl] *n* : monosílabo *m*

monotheism [ˈmɑnoθiˌɪzəm] *n* : monoteísmo *m* — **monotheist** *n*

monotheistic [ˌmɑnoθiˈɪstɪk] *adj* : monoteísta

monotone [ˈmɑnəˌtoːn] *n* : voz *f* monótona

monotonous [məˈnɑtənəs] *adj* : monótono — **monotonously** *adv*

monotony [məˈnɑtəni] *n* : monotonía *f*, uniformidad *f*

monsignor [mɑnˈsiːnjər] *n* : monseñor *m*

monsoon [mɑnˈsuːn] *n* : monzón *m*

monster [ˈmɑnstər] *n* : monstruo *m*

monstrosity [mɑnˈstrɑsəti] *n, pl* **-ties** : monstruosidad *f*

monstrous [ˈmɑnstrəs] *adj* : monstruoso — **monstrously** *adv*

montage [mɑnˈtɑʒ] *n* : montaje *m*

month [ˈmʌnθ] *n* : mes *m*

monthly[1] [ˈmʌnθli] *adv* : mensualmente

monthly[2] *adj* : mensual

monthly[3] *n, pl* **-lies** : publicación *f* mensual

monument [ˈmɑnjəmənt] *n* : monumento *m*

monumental [ˌmɑnjəˈmentəl] *adj* : monumental — **monumentally** *adv*

moo[1] [ˈmuː] *vi* : mugir

moo[2] *n* : mugido *m*

mood [ˈmuːd] *n* : humor *m* ⟨to be in a good mood : estar de buen humor⟩ ⟨to be in the mood for : tener ganas de⟩ ⟨to be in no mood for : no estar para⟩

moodiness [ˈmuːdinəs] *n* **1** SADNESS : melancolía *f*, tristeza *f* **2** : cambios *mpl* de humor, carácter *m* temperamental

moody [ˈmuːdi] *adj* **moodier; -est 1** GLOOMY : melancólico, deprimido **2** TEMPERAMENTAL : temperamental, de humor variable

moon [ˈmuːn] *n* : luna *f*

moonbeam [ˈmuːnˌbiːm] *n* : rayo *m* de luna

moonlight[1] [ˈmuːnˌlaɪt] *vi* : estar pluriempleado

moonlight[2] *n* : claro *m* de luna, luz *f* de la luna

moonlit [ˈmuːnˌlɪt] *adj* : iluminado por la luna ⟨a moonlit night : una noche de luna⟩

moonshine [ˈmuːnˌʃaɪn] *n* **1** MOONLIGHT : luz *f* de la luna **2** NONSENSE : disparates *mpl*, tonterías *fpl* **3** : whisky *m* destilado ilegalmente

moor[1] [ˈmʊr, ˈmɔr] *vt* : amarrar

moor[2] *n* : páramo *m*

Moor [ˈmʊr] *n* : moro *m*, -ra *f*

mooring [ˈmʊrɪŋ, ˈmɔr-] *n* DOCK : atracadero *m*

Moorish [ˈmʊrɪʃ] *adj* : moro

moose [ˈmuːs] *n* : alce *m* (norteamericano)

moot [ˈmuːt] *adj* DEBATABLE : discutible

mop[1] [ˈmɑp] *v* **mopped; mopping** *vt* **1** : trapear **2** to mop up : limpiar (un líquido) **3** to mop up FINISH : terminar, acabar — *vi* **1** : trapear el suelo **2** to mop up FINISH : terminar, acabar

mop[2] *n* : trapeador *m*

mope [ˈmoːp] *vi* **moped; moping** : andar deprimido, quedar abatido

moped [ˈmoːˌped] *n* : ciclomotor *m*

moraine [məˈreɪn] *n* : morena *f*

moral[1] [ˈmɔrəl] *adj* : moral ⟨moral judgment : juicio moral⟩ ⟨moral support : apoyo moral⟩ — **morally** *adv*

moral[2] *n* **1** : moraleja *f* (de un cuento, etc.) **2 morals** *npl* : moral *f*, moralidad *f*

morale [məˈræl] *n* : moral *f*

moralist [ˈmɔrəlɪst] *n* : moralista *mf*

moralistic [ˌmɔrəˈlɪstɪk] *adj* : moralista

morality [məˈræləti] *n, pl* **-ties** : moralidad *f*

morass [məˈræs] *n* **1** SWAMP : ciénaga *f*, pantano *m* **2** CONFUSION, MESS : lío *m* *fam*, embrollo *m*

moratorium [ˌmɔrəˈtoriəm] *n, pl* **-riums** or **-ria** [-iə] : moratoria *f*

moray [ˈmɔrˌeɪ, məˈreɪ] *n* : morena *f*

morbid [ˈmɔrbɪd] *adj* **1** : mórbido, morboso (en medicina) **2** GRUESOME : morboso, horripilante

morbidity [mɔrˈbɪdəti] *n, pl* **-ties** : morbosidad *f*

more[1] [ˈmor] *adv* **1** : más ⟨what more can I say? : ¿qué más puedo decir?⟩ ⟨you need to exercise more : debes hacer más ejercicio⟩ ⟨more important : más importante⟩ ⟨once more : una vez más⟩ ⟨more and more difficult : cada vez más difícil⟩ **2 more or less** : más o menos **3 more than** VERY : muy, bastante ⟨I'm more than happy to help you : te ayudo encantado⟩ **4 more than a little** ⟨I was more than a little surprised : me sorprendió bastante⟩

more[2] *adj* : más ⟨nothing more than that : nada más que eso⟩ ⟨more than a hundred : más de cien⟩ ⟨more work : más trabajo⟩

more[3] *n* : más *m* ⟨the more you eat, the more you want : cuanto más comes, tanto más quieres⟩

more[4] *pron* **1** : más 〈more were found : se encontraron más〉 〈I don't want any more : no quiero más〉 〈it costs more : cuesta más〉 〈no more, no less : ni más ni menos〉 〈more and more of them : un número cada vez mayor de ellos〉 〈and what's more : y lo que es más〉 〈we see more of each other now : ahora nos vemos más〉 **2 more of** : más bien 〈it's more of a maroon than a red : es más bien granate que rojo〉

morello [məˈrɛlo] *n* : guinda *f*

moreover [morˈoːvər] *adv* : además

mores [ˈmɔrˌeɪz, -ˌiːz] *npl* CUSTOMS : costumbres *fpl*, tradiciones *fpl*

morgue [ˈmɔrg] *n* : morgue *f*

moribund [ˈmɔrəˌbʌnd] *adj* : moribundo

Mormon [ˈmɔrmən] *n* : mormón *m*, -mona *f* — **Mormon** *adj*

morn [ˈmɔrn] → **morning**

morning [ˈmɔrnɪŋ] *n* : mañana *f* 〈good morning! : ¡buenos días!〉

morning sickness *n* : náuseas *fpl* matutinas (del embarazo)

Moroccan [məˈrɑkən] *n* : marroquí *mf* — **Moroccan** *adj*

moron [ˈmɔrˌɑn] *n* **1** *often offensive* : retrasado *m*, -da *f* mental **2** DUNCE : estúpido *m*, -da *f*; tonto *m*, -ta *f*

morose [məˈroːs] *adj* : hosco, sombrío — **morosely** *adv*

moroseness [məˈroːsnəs] *n* : malhumor *m*

morphine [ˈmɔrˌfiːn] *n* : morfina *f*

morphology [mɔrˈfɑləʤi] *n, pl* **-gies** : morfología *f*

morrow [ˈmɑro] *n* : día *m* siguiente

Morse code [ˈmɔrs] *n* : código *m* morse

morsel [ˈmɔrsəl] *n* **1** BITE : bocado *m* **2** FRAGMENT : pedazo *m*

mortadella [ˌmɔrtəˈdɛlə] *n* : mortadela *f*

mortal[1] [ˈmɔrtəl] *adj* : mortal 〈mortal blow : golpe mortal〉 〈mortal fear : miedo mortal〉 — **mortally** *adv*

mortal[2] *n* : mortal *mf*

mortality [mɔrˈtæləti] *n* : mortalidad *f*

mortar [ˈmɔrtər] *n* **1** : mortero *m*, molcajete *m* *Mex* 〈mortar and pestle : mortero y maja〉 **2** : mortero *m* 〈mortar shell : granada de mortero〉 **3** CEMENT : mortero *m*, argamasa *f*

mortarboard [ˈmɔrtərˌbord] *n* : bonete *m*, birrete *m*

mortgage[1] [ˈmɔrgɪʤ] *vt* **-gaged; -gaging** : hipotecar

mortgage[2] *n* : hipoteca *f*

mortification [ˌmɔrtəfəˈkeɪʃən] *n* **1** : mortificación *f* **2** HUMILIATION : humillación *f*, vergüenza *f*

mortify [ˈmɔrtəˌfaɪ] *vt* **-fied; -fying** **1** : mortificar (en religión) **2** HUMILIATE : humillar, avergonzar

mortuary [ˈmɔrtʃəˌweri] *n, pl* **-aries** FUNERAL HOME : funeraria *f*

mosaic [moˈzeɪɪk] *n* : mosaico *m*

Moslem [ˈmɑzləm] → **Muslim**

mosque [ˈmɑsk] *n* : mezquita *f*

mosquito [məˈskiːto] *n, pl* **-toes** : mosquito *m*, zancudo *m*

moss [ˈmɔs] *n* : musgo *m*

mossy [ˈmɔsi] *adj* **mossier; -est** : musgoso

most[1] [ˈmoːst] *adv* : más 〈the most interesting book : el libro más interesante〉 〈most certainly : con toda seguridad〉 〈most often : más a menudo〉

most[2] *adj* **1** : la mayoría de, la mayor parte de 〈most people : la mayoría de la gente〉 **2** GREATEST : más (dícese de los números), mayor (dícese de las cantidades) 〈the most ability : la mayor capacidad〉

most[3] *n* : más *m*, máximo *m* 〈the most I can do : lo más que puedo hacer〉 〈he did the most : hizo más que nadie〉 〈three weeks at (the) most : tres semanas como máximo〉 〈to make the most of something : sacar el mejor provecho/partido posible de algo〉

most[4] *pron* : la mayoría, la mayor parte 〈most will go : la mayoría irá〉 〈most of : la mayoría de〉 〈most of the time : la mayor parte del tiempo〉

mostly [ˈmoːstli] *adv* MAINLY : en su mayor parte, principalmente

mote [ˈmoːt] *n* SPECK : mota *f*

motel [moˈtɛl] *n* : motel *m*

moth [ˈmɔθ] *n* : palomilla *f*, polilla *f*

mothball [ˈmɔθˌbɔl] *n* : bola *f* de naftalina

mother[1] [ˈmʌðər] *vt* **1** BEAR : dar a luz a **2** PROTECT : cuidar de, proteger

mother[2] *n* : madre *f*

motherhood [ˈmʌðərˌhʊd] *n* : maternidad *f*

mother-in-law [ˈmʌðərɪnˌlɔ] *n, pl* **mothers-in-law** : suegra *f*

motherland [ˈmʌðərˌlænd] *n* : patria *f*

motherly [ˈmʌðərli] *adj* : maternal

mother-of-pearl [ˌmʌðərəvˈpərl] *n* : nácar *m*, madreperla *f*

mother-to-be *n* : futura madre *f*

mother tongue *n* : lengua *f* materna

motif [moˈtiːf] *n* : motivo *m*

motion[1] [ˈmoːʃən] *vt* : hacerle señas (a alguien) 〈she motioned us to come in : nos hizo señas para que entráramos〉

motion[2] *n* **1** MOVEMENT : movimiento *m* 〈to set in motion : poner en marcha〉 **2** PROPOSAL : moción *f* 〈to second a motion : apoyar una moción〉

motionless [ˈmoːʃənləs] *adj* : inmóvil, quieto

motion picture *n* MOVIE : película *f*

motivate [ˈmoːtəˌveɪt] *vt* **-vated; -vating** : motivar, mover, inducir

motivation [ˌmoːtəˈveɪʃən] *n* : motivación *f*

motive[1] [ˈmoːtɪv] *adj* : motor 〈motive power : fuerza motriz〉

motive[2] *n* : motivo *m*, móvil *m*

motley [ˈmɑtli] *adj* : abigarrado, variopinto

motor[1] [ˈmoːtər] *vi* : viajar en coche

motor[2] *n* : motor *m*

motorbike [ˈmoːtərˌbaɪk] *n* : motocicleta *f* (pequeña), moto *f*

motorboat [ˈmoːtərˌboːt] *n* : bote *m* a motor, lancha *f* motora

motorcar [ˈmoːtərˌkɑr] *n* : automóvil *m*

motorcycle ['mo:t̬ər,saɪkəl] *n* : motocicleta *f*

motorcycling ['mo:t̬ər,saɪklɪŋ] *n* : motociclismo *m*

motorcyclist ['mo:t̬ər,saɪklɪst] *n* : motociclista *mf*

motorist ['mo:t̬ərɪst] *n* : automovilista *mf*, motorista *mf*

motorized ['mo:t̬əraɪzd] *adj* : motorizado

motor racing *n* : carreras *fpl* de coches

motor vehicle → **vehicle**

mottled ['mɑt̬əld] *adj* : manchado, moteado ⟨mottled skin : piel manchada⟩ ⟨a mottled surface : una superficie moteada⟩

motto ['mɑt̬o:] *n, pl* **-toes** : lema *m*

mould ['mo:ld] → **mold**

mound ['maʊnd] *n* **1** PILE : montón *m* **2** KNOLL : montículo *m* **3** burial mound : túmulo *m*

mount¹ ['maʊnt] *vt* **1** : montar a (un caballo), montar en (una bicicleta), subir a **2** : montar (artillería, etc.) — *vi* INCREASE : aumentar

mount² *n* **1** SUPPORT : soporte *m* **2** HORSE : caballería *f*, montura *f* **3** MOUNTAIN : monte *m*, montaña *f*

mountain ['maʊnt̬ən] *n* **1** : montaña *f* **2** to make a mountain out of a molehill → **molehill**

mountain bike *n* : bicicleta *f* de montaña

mountaineer [,maʊntən'ɪr] *n* : alpinista *mf*; montañero *m*, -ra *f*

mountaineering [,maʊntən'ɪrɪŋ] *n* : montañismo *m*, alpinismo *m*

mountainous ['maʊntənəs] *adj* : montañoso

mountaintop ['maʊntən,tɑp] *n* : cima *f*, cumbre *f*

mourn ['morn] *vt* : llorar (por), lamentar ⟨to mourn the death of : llorar la muerte de⟩ — *vi* : llorar, estar de luto

mourner ['mornər] *n* : doliente *mf*

mournful ['mornfəl] *adj* **1** SORROWFUL : lloroso, plañidero, triste **2** GLOOMY : deprimente — **mournfully** *adv*

mourning ['mornɪŋ] *n* : duelo *m*, luto *m*

mouse ['maʊs] *n, pl* **mice** ['maɪs] **1** : ratón *m*, -tona *f* **2** : ratón *m* (de una computadora)

mouse pad *n* : alfombrilla *f* de/para ratón, almohadilla *f* de/para ratón

mousetrap ['maʊs,træp] *n* : ratonera *f*

mousse ['mu:s] *n* : mousse *mf*

moustache ['mʌ,stæʃ, mə'stæʃ] → **mustache**

mouth¹ ['maʊð] *vt* **1** : decir con poca sinceridad, repetir sin comprensión **2** : articular en silencio ⟨she mouthed the words : formó las palabras con los labios⟩

mouth² ['maʊθ] *n* : boca *f* (de una persona o un animal), entrada *f* (de un túnel), desembocadura *f* (de un río)

mouthed ['maʊðd, 'maʊθt] *adj* used in combination : de boca ⟨a large-mouthed jar : un tarro de boca grande⟩

mouthful ['maʊθ,fʊl] *n* : bocado *m* (de comida), bocanada *f* (de líquido o humo)

mouth organ *n* → **harmonica**

mouthpiece ['maʊθ,pi:s] *n* : boquilla *f* (de un instrumento musical)

mouth-to-mouth resuscitation *or* **mouth-to-mouth** *n* : respiración *f* boca a boca, el boca a boca

mouthwash ['maʊθ,wɔʃ, -,wɑʃ] *n* : enjuague *m* bucal

mouth-watering ['maʊθ,wɔt̬ərɪŋ, -,wɑ-] *n* : delicioso

movable ['mu:vəbəl] *or* **moveable** *adj* : movible, móvil

move¹ ['mu:v] *v* **moved; moving** *vi* **1** GO : ir ⟨to move closer : acercarse⟩ ⟨to move forward/back : echarse (hacia) adelante/atrás⟩ **2** RELOCATE : mudarse, trasladarse **3** STIR : moverse ⟨don't move! : ¡no te muevas!⟩ **4** ACT : actuar **5** to move aside : hacerse a un lado **6** to move along PROCEED : circular **7** to move away LEAVE : marcharse **8** to move away STEP BACK : apartarse **9** to move heaven and earth : hacer todo lo posible **10** to move in : mudarse (a un lugar) ⟨to move in with someone : irse a vivir con alguien⟩ **11** to move on LEAVE : marcharse **12** to move on CONTINUE : pasar **13** to move out : mudarse (de un lugar) **14** to move over : hacer sitio **15** to move up : subir — *vt* **1** : mover ⟨he kept moving his feet : no dejaba de mover los pies⟩ ⟨move it forward/back : muévalo hacia adelante/atrás⟩ ⟨move it over there : ponlo allí⟩ **2** RELOCATE : trasladar **3** INDUCE, PERSUADE : inducir, persuadir, mover **4** TOUCH : conmover ⟨it moved him to tears : lo hizo llorar⟩ **5** PROPOSE : proponer **6** to move along : dispersar, hacer circular **7** to move up : adelantar (una fecha)

move² *n* **1** MOVEMENT : movimiento *m* **2** RELOCATION : mudanza *f* (de casa), traslado *m* **3** STEP : paso *m* ⟨a good move : un paso acertado⟩

movement ['mu:vmənt] *n* : movimiento *m*

mover ['mu:vər] *n* : persona *f* que hace mudanzas

movie ['mu:vi] *n* **1** : película *f* **2** movies *npl* : cine *m*

movie theater *n* : cine *m*

moving ['mu:vɪŋ] *adj* **1** : en movimiento ⟨a moving target : un blanco móvil⟩ **2** TOUCHING : conmovedor, emocionante

mow¹ ['mo:] *vt* **mowed; mowed** *or* **mown** ['mo:n]; **mowing** **1** : cortar (la hierba) **2** mow down SHOOT : acribillar

mow² ['maʊ] *n* : pajar *m*

mower ['mo:ər] → **lawn mower**

MP3 [,ɛm,pi:'θri:] *n* : MP3 *m*

Mr. ['mɪstər] *n, pl* **Messrs.** ['mɛsərz] : señor *m*

Mrs. ['mɪsəz, -səs, *esp South* 'mɪzəz, -zəs] *n, pl* **Mesdames** [meɪ'dɑm, -'dæm] : señora *f*

Ms. ['mɪz] *n* : señora *f*, señorita *f*

much¹ ['mʌtʃ] *adv* **more** ['mor]; **most** ['mo:st] **1** : mucho ⟨I'm much happier : estoy mucho más contenta⟩ ⟨she talks as much as I do : habla tanto como yo⟩ ⟨do you travel much? : ¿viajas mucho?⟩ ⟨I like it very much : me gusta mucho⟩

⟨thank you very much : muchas gracias⟩ **2** VERY : muy ⟨he's not much good at golf : no es muy bueno para el golf⟩ **3** NEARLY : casi ⟨the town looks much the same : el pueblo no ha cambiado mucho, el pueblo es casi igual que antes⟩ **4** LONG : mucho ⟨not much before noon : poco antes del mediodía⟩ **5 as much** : lo mismo ⟨she'd do as much for me : haría lo mismo para mí⟩ ⟨I thought as much : ya me lo imaginaba⟩ **6 as much as** : tanto como **7 as much as** NEARLY : casi **8 much as** ALTHOUGH : aunque **9 very much** (*used for emphasis*) ENTIRELY, UNQUESTIONABLY : totalmente, indudablemente

much² *adj* **more; most** : mucho ⟨there isn't much difference : no hay mucha diferencia⟩ ⟨he doesn't know much French : no sabe mucho francés⟩ ⟨she wasn't much help : no nos ayudó mucho⟩ ⟨was there much food? : ¿había mucha comida?⟩ ⟨we spent so much money : gastamos tanto dinero⟩ ⟨too much time : demasiado tiempo⟩ ⟨it was all too much for him : no podía con todo⟩

much³ *pron* **1** : mucho ⟨I don't need much : no necesito mucho⟩ ⟨there was food, but not much : había comida, pero poca cantidad⟩ ⟨I don't see much of them : no los veo mucho⟩ ⟨it doesn't amount to much : no es gran cosa⟩ ⟨much of the time : una buena parte del tiempo⟩ ⟨too much : demasiado⟩ **2 as much as** : tanto como **3 not much of a** ⟨he's not much of a cook : no cocina muy bien⟩ ⟨it wasn't much of a vacation : mis vacaciones no fueron nada especial⟩ **4 not much on** ⟨she's not much on studying : no estudia mucho⟩ ⟨he's not much on looks : no es muy guapo⟩

mucilage ['mju:səlɪʤ] *n* : mucílago *m*

muck ['mʌk] *n* **1** MANURE : estiércol *m* **2** DIRT, FILTH : mugre *f*, suciedad *f* **3** MIRE, MUD : barro *m*, fango *m*, lodo *m*

mucous ['mju:kəs] *adj* : mucoso ⟨mucous membrane : membrana mucosa⟩

mucus ['mju:kəs] *n* : mucosidad *f*

mud ['mʌd] *n* : barro *m*, fango *m*, lodo *m*

muddle¹ ['mʌdəl] *v* **-dled; -dling** *vt* **1** CONFUSE : confundir (a alguien) **2** *or* **to muddle up** MIX UP : confundir ⟨I always get them muddled up in my mind : siempre los confundo⟩ — *vi* : andar confundido ⟨to muddle through : arreglárselas⟩

muddle² *n* : confusión *f*, embrollo *m*, lío *m*

muddleheaded [ˌmʌdəl'hɛdəd, 'mʌdəlˌ-] *adj* CONFUSED : confuso, despistado

muddy¹ ['mʌdi] *vt* **-died; -dying** : llenar de barro

muddy² *adj* **muddier; -est** : barroso, fangoso, lodoso, enlodado ⟨you're all muddy : estás cubierto de barro⟩

mudguard ['mʌdˌgɑrd] *n* : guardabarros *m*

muff¹ ['mʌf] *vt* BUNGLE : echar a perder, fallar (un tiro, etc.)

muff² *n* : manguito *m*

muffin ['mʌfən] *n* : magdalena *f*

muffle ['mʌfəl] *vt* **-fled; -fling 1** ENVELOP : cubrir, tapar **2** DEADEN : amortiguar (un sonido)

muffler ['mʌflər] *n* **1** SCARF : bufanda *f* **2** : silenciador *m*; mofle *m* CA, Mex (de un automóvil)

mug¹ ['mʌg] *v* **mugged; mugging** *vi* **1** : posar (con afectación), hacer muecas ⟨mugging for the camera : haciendo muecas para la cámara⟩ — *vt* ASSAULT : asaltar, atracar

mug² *n* CUP : tazón *m*

mugger ['mʌgər] *n* : atracador *m*, -dora *f*

mugginess ['mʌginəs] *n* : bochorno *m*

mugging ['mʌgɪŋ] *n* : atraco *m*

muggy ['mʌgi] *adj* **muggier; -est** : bochornoso

mulatto [muˈlɑto, -ˈlæ-] *n, pl* **-toes** *or* **-tos** : mulato *m*, -ta *f*

mulberry ['mʌlˌbɛri] *n, pl* **-ries** : morera *f* (árbol), mora *f* (fruta)

mulch¹ ['mʌlʧ] *vt* : cubrir con pajote

mulch² *n* : pajote *m*

mule ['mju:l] *n* **1** : mula *f* **2** : obstinado *m*, -da *f*; terco *m*, -ca *f*

mulish ['mju:lɪʃ] *adj* : obstinado, terco

mull ['mʌl] *vt* **to mull over** : reflexionar sobre

mullet ['mʌlət] *n, pl* **-let** *or* **-lets** : mújol *m*

multi- [ˌmʌlti-, ˌmʌltaɪ-] *pref* : multi-

multicolored [ˌmʌlti'kʌlərd, ˌmʌltaɪ-] *adj* : multicolor, abigarrado

multicultural [ˌmʌlti'kʌlʧərəl, ˌmʌltaɪ-] *adj* : multicultural — **multiculturalism** [ˌmʌlti'kʌlʧərəˌlɪzəm] *n*

multidisciplinary [ˌmʌlti'dɪsəpləˌnɛri] *adj* : multidisciplinario

multifaceted [ˌmʌlti'fæsətəd, ˌmʌltaɪ-] *adj* : multifacético

multifamily [ˌmʌlti'fæmli, ˌmʌltaɪ-] *adj* : multifamiliar

multifarious [ˌmʌltə'færiəs] *adj* DIVERSE : diverso, variado

multilateral [ˌmʌlti'lætərəl, ˌmʌltaɪ-] *adj* : multilateral

multimedia [ˌmʌlti'mi:diə, ˌmʌltaɪ-] *adj* : multimedia

multimillionaire [ˌmʌltiˌmɪljə'nær, ˌmʌltaɪ-, -'mɪljəˌnær] *adj* : multimillonario

multinational [ˌmʌlti'næʃənəl, ˌmʌltaɪ-] *adj* : multinacional

multiple¹ ['mʌltəpəl] *adj* : múltiple

multiple² *n* : múltiplo *m*

multiple sclerosis [skləˈroːsɪs] *n* : esclerosis *f* múltiple

multiplex ['mʌltəˌplɛks] *n* : multicine *m*

multiplication [ˌmʌltəpləˈkeɪʃən] *n* : multiplicación *f*

multiplicity [ˌmʌltəˈplɪsəti] *n, pl* **-ties** : multiplicidad *f*

multiply ['mʌltəˌplaɪ] *v* **-plied; -plying** *vt* : multiplicar — *vi* : multiplicarse

multipurpose [ˌmʌlti'pərpəs, ˌmʌltaɪ-] *adj* : multiuso

multistory [ˌmʌlti'stori, ˌmʌltaɪ-] *adj* : de varias plantas, de varios pisos

multitude ['mʌltəˌtuːd, -ˌtjuːd] *n* **1** CROWD : multitud *f*, muchedumbre *f* **2** HOST

: multitud *f*, gran cantidad *f* ⟨a multitude of ideas : numerosas ideas⟩

multivitamin [ˌmʌltiˈvaɪtəmən, ˌmʌltaɪ-] *adj* : multivitamínico

mum[1] [ˈmʌm] *adj* SILENT : callado

mum[2] *n* → **chrysanthemum**

mumble[1] [ˈmʌmbəl] *v* **-bled; -bling** *vt* : mascullar, musitar — *vi* : mascullar, hablar entre dientes, murmurar

mumble[2] *n* **to speak in a mumble** : hablar entre dientes

mumbo jumbo [ˌmʌmboˈdʒʌmbo] *n* : jerigonza *f*

mummy [ˈmʌmi] *n, pl* **-mies** : momia *f*

mumps [ˈmʌmps] *ns & pl* : paperas *fpl*

munch [ˈmʌntʃ] *v* : mascar, masticar

mundane [ˌmʌnˈdeɪn, ˈmʌn-] *adj* **1** EARTHLY, WORLDLY : mundano, terrenal **2** COMMONPLACE : rutinario, ordinario

municipal [mjuˈnisəpəl] *adj* : municipal

municipality [mjuˌnisəˈpæləti] *n, pl* **-ties** : municipio *m*

munitions [mjuˈnifənz] *npl* : municiones *fpl*

mural[1] [ˈmjurəl] *adj* : mural

mural[2] [ˈmjurəlist] *n* : mural *m*

murder[1] [ˈmərdər] *vt* : asesinar, matar — *vi* : matar

murder[2] *n* : asesinato *m*, homicidio *m*

murderer [ˈmərdərər] *n* : asesino *m*, -na *f*; homicida *mf*

murderess [ˈmərdərəs] *n* : asesina *f*, homicida *f*

murderous [ˈmərdərəs] *adj* : asesino, homicida

murk [ˈmərk] *n* DARKNESS : oscuridad *f*, tinieblas *fpl*

murkiness [ˈmərkinəs] *n* : oscuridad *f*, tenebrosidad *f*

murky [ˈmərki] *adj* **murkier; -est** : oscuro, tenebroso

murmur[1] [ˈmərmər] *vi* **1** DRONE : murmurar **2** GRUMBLE : refunfuñar, regañar, rezongar — *vt* MUMBLE : murmurar

murmur[2] *n* **1** COMPLAINT : queja *f* **2** DRONE : murmullo *m*, rumor *m*

muscle[1] [ˈmʌsəl] *vi* **-cled; -cling** : meterse ⟨to muscle in on : meterse por la fuerza en, entrometerse en⟩

muscle[2] *n* **1** : músculo *m* **2** STRENGTH : fuerza *f*

muscular [ˈmʌskjələr] *adj* **1** : muscular ⟨muscular tissue : tejido muscular⟩ **2** BRAWNY : musculoso

muscular dystrophy *n* : distrofia *f* muscular

musculature [ˈmʌskjələˌtʃur, -ˌtʃər] *n* : musculatura *f*

muse[1] [ˈmjuːz] *vi* **mused; musing** PONDER, REFLECT : cavilar, meditar, reflexionar

muse[2] *n* : musa *f*

museum [mjuˈziːəm] *n* : museo *m*

mush [ˈmʌʃ] *n* **1** : gachas *fpl* (de maíz) **2** SENTIMENTALITY : sensiblería *f*

mushroom[1] [ˈmʌʃˌruːm, -ˌrum] *vi* GROW, MULTIPLY : crecer rápidamente, multiplicarse

mushroom[2] *n* : hongo *m*, champiñón *m*, seta *f*, callampa *f Chile*

mushy [ˈmʌʃi] *adj* **mushier; -est 1** SOFT : blando **2** MAWKISH : sensiblero

music [ˈmjuːzik] *n* : música *f*

musical[1] [ˈmjuːzikəl] *adj* : musical, de música ⟨musical instrument : instrumento musical⟩ — **musically** *adv*

musical[2] *n* : comedia *f* musical

music box *n* : cajita *f* de música

musician [mjuˈzifən] *n* : músico *m*, -ca *f*

musk [ˈmʌsk] *n* : almizcle *m*

musket [ˈmʌskət] *n* : mosquete *m*

musketeer [ˌmʌskəˈtir] *n* : mosquetero *m*

muskrat [ˈmʌskˌræt] *n, pl* **-rat** *or* **-rats** : rata *f* almizclera

Muslim[1] [ˈmʌzləm, ˈmus-, ˈmuz-] *adj* : musulmán

Muslim[2] *n* : musulmán *m*, -mana *f*

muslin [ˈmʌzlən] *n* : muselina *f*

muss[1] [ˈmʌs] *vt* : desordenar, despeinar (el pelo)

muss[2] *n* : desorden *m*

mussel [ˈmʌsəl] *n* : mejillón *m*

must[1] [ˈmʌst] *v aux* **1** (*expressing obligation or necessity*) : deber, tener que ⟨you must stop : debes parar⟩ ⟨we must obey : tenemos que obedecer⟩ **2** (*expressing probability*) : deber (de), haber de ⟨you must be tired : debes de estar cansado⟩ ⟨it must be late : ha de ser tarde⟩

must[2] *n* **1** : necesidad *f* ⟨exercise is a must : el ejercicio es imprescindible⟩ **2** : mosto *m*

mustache [ˈmʌˌstæʃ, mʌˈstæʃ] *n* : bigote *m*, bigotes *mpl*

mustang [ˈmʌˌstæŋ] *n* : caballo *m* mesteño

mustard [ˈmʌstərd] *n* : mostaza *f*

muster[1] [ˈmʌstər] *vt* **1** ASSEMBLE : reunir **2 to muster up** : armarse de, cobrar (valor, fuerzas, etc.)

muster[2] *n* **1** INSPECTION : revista *f* (de tropas) ⟨it didn't pass muster : no resistió un examen minucioso⟩ **2** COLLECTION : colección *f*

mustiness [ˈmʌstinəs] *n* : lo mohoso

musty [ˈmʌsti] *adj* **mustier; -est** : mohoso, que huele a moho, que huele a encerrado

mutant[1] [ˈmjuːtənt] *adj* : mutante

mutant[2] *n* : mutante *m*

mutate [ˈmjuːˌteɪt] *vi* **-tated; -tating 1** : mutar (genéticamente) **2** CHANGE : transformarse

mutation [mjuˈteɪfən] *n* : mutación *f* (genética)

mute[1] [ˈmjuːt] *vt* **muted; muting** MUFFLE : amortiguar, ponerle sordina a (un instrumento musical)

mute[2] *adj* **muter; mutest** : mudo — **mutely** *adv*

mute[3] *n* **1** *sometimes offensive* : mudo *m*, -da *f* (persona) **2** : sordina *f* (para un instrumento musical)

muted *adj* **1** : apagado (dícese de colores, la voz, etc.), sordo (dícese de sonidos) **2** RESTRAINED, WEAK : contenido, débil

mutilate [ˈmjuːtəˌleɪt] *vt* **-lated; -lating** : mutilar

mutilation [ˌmjuːtəˈleɪfən] *n* : mutilación *f*

mutineer [ˌmjuːtənˈɪr] *n* : amotinado *m*, -da *f*
mutinous [ˈmjuːtənəs] *adj* : amotinado
mutiny¹ [ˈmjuːtəni] *vi* -**nied**; -**nying** : amotinarse
mutiny² *n, pl* -**nies** : amotinamiento *m*, motín *m*
mutt [ˈmʌt] *n* MONGREL : perro *m* mestizo, perro *m* corriente *Mex*
mutter [ˈmʌtər] *vi* **1** MUMBLE : mascullar, hablar entre dientes, murmurar **2** GRUMBLE : refunfuñar, regañar, rezongar
mutton [ˈmʌtən] *n* : carne *f* de carnero
mutual [ˈmjuːtʃʊəl] *adj* **1** : mutuo ⟨mutual respect : respeto mutuo⟩ **2** COMMON : común ⟨a mutual friend : un amigo común⟩
mutually [ˈmjuːtʃʊəli, -tʃəli] *adv* **1** : mutuamente ⟨mutually beneficial : mutuamente beneficioso⟩ **2** JOINTLY : conjuntamente
muzzle¹ [ˈmʌzəl] *vt* -**zled**; -**zling** : ponerle un bozal a (un animal), amordazar
muzzle² *n* **1** SNOUT : hocico *m* **2** : bozal *m* (para un perro, etc.) **3** : boca *f* (de un arma de fuego)
my¹ [ˈmaɪ] *adj* : mi ⟨my parents : mis padres⟩
my² *interj* : ¡caramba!, ¡Dios mío!
myopia [maɪˈoːpiə] *n* : miopía *f*

myopic [maɪˈoːpɪk, -ˈɑ-] *adj* : miope
myriad¹ [ˈmɪriəd] *adj* INNUMERABLE : innumerable
myriad² *n* : miríada *f*
myrrh [ˈmər] *n* : mirra *f*
myrtle [ˈmərtəl] *n* : mirto *m*, arrayán *m*
myself [maɪˈsɛlf] *pron* **1** (*used reflexively*) : me ⟨I washed myself : me lavé⟩ **2** (*used for emphasis*) : yo mismo, yo misma ⟨I did it myself : lo hice yo mismo⟩
mysterious [mɪˈstɪriəs] *adj* : misterioso — **mysteriously** *adv*
mysteriousness [mɪˈstɪriəsnəs] *n* : lo misterioso
mystery [ˈmɪstəri] *n, pl* -**teries** : misterio *m*
mystic¹ [ˈmɪstɪk] *adj* : místico
mystic² *n* : místico *m*, -ca *f*
mystical [ˈmɪstɪkəl] *adj* : místico — **mystically** *adv*
mysticism [ˈmɪstəˌsɪzəm] *n* : misticismo *m*
mystify [ˈmɪstəˌfaɪ] *vt* -**fied**; -**fying** : dejar perplejo, confundir
mystique [mɪˈstiːk] *n* : aura *f* de misterio
myth [ˈmɪθ] *n* : mito *m*
mythic [ˈmɪθɪk] *adj* : mítico
mythical [ˈmɪθɪkəl] *adj* : mítico
mythological [ˌmɪθəˈlɑdʒɪkəl] *adj* : mitológico
mythology [mɪˈθɑlədʒi] *n, pl* -**gies** : mitología *f*

N

n [ˈɛn] *n, pl* **n's** *or* **ns** [ˈɛnz] : decimocuarta letra del alfabeto inglés
nab [ˈnæb] *vt* **nabbed**; **nabbing** : prender, pillar *fam*, pescar *fam*
nadir [ˈneɪdər, ˈneɪˌdɪr] *n* : nadir *m*, punto *m* más bajo
nag¹ [ˈnæg] *v* **nagged**; **nagging** *vi* **1** COMPLAIN : quejarse, rezongar **2 to nag at** HASSLE : molestar, darle (la) lata (a alguien) — *vt* **1** PESTER : molestar, fastidiar **2** SCOLD : regañar, estarle encima a *fam*
nag² *n* **1** GRUMBLER : gruñón *m*, -ñona *f* **2** HORSE : jamelgo *m*
nail¹ [ˈneɪl] *vt* : clavar, sujetar con clavos
nail² *n* **1** FINGERNAIL : uña *f* ⟨nail file : lima de uñas⟩ ⟨nail polish : laca de uñas⟩ **2** : clavo *m* ⟨to hit the nail on the head : dar en el clavo⟩
naive *or* **naïve** [nɑˈiːv] *adj* **naiver**; -**est 1** INGENUOUS : ingenuo, cándido **2** GULLIBLE : crédulo
naively [nɑˈiːvli] *adv* : ingenuamente
naïveté [ˌnɑˌiːvəˈteɪ, nɑˈiːvəˌ-] *n* : ingenuidad *f*
naked [ˈneɪkəd] *adj* **1** UNCLOTHED : desnudo **2** UNCOVERED : desenvainado (dícese de una espada), pelado (dícese de los árboles), expuesto al aire (dícese de una llama) **3** OBVIOUS, PLAIN : manifiesto, puro, desnudo ⟨the naked truth

: la pura verdad⟩ **4 to the naked eye** : a simple vista
nakedly [ˈneɪkədli] *adv* : manifiestamente
nakedness [ˈneɪkədnəs] *n* : desnudez *f*
name¹ [ˈneɪm] *vt* **named**; **naming 1** CALL : llamar, bautizar, ponerle nombre a ⟨they named the baby after his father : le pusieron al niño el nombre de su padre⟩ **2** MENTION : mentar, mencionar, dar el nombre de ⟨they have named a suspect : han dado el nombre de un sospechoso⟩ **3** APPOINT : nombrar **4 to name a price** : fijar un precio
name² *adj* PROMINENT : de renombre, de prestigio
name³ *n* **1** : nombre *m* ⟨what is your name? : ¿cómo se llama?⟩ ⟨my name is Ted : me llamo Ted⟩ ⟨first name : nombre de pila⟩ ⟨middle name : segundo nombre⟩ ⟨last name : apellido⟩ ⟨full name : nombre completo, nombre y apellido(s)⟩ ⟨she wasn't mentioned by name : no dieron su nombre⟩ **2** EPITHET : epíteto *m* ⟨to call somebody names : insultar a alguien⟩ **3** REPUTATION : fama *f*, reputación *f* ⟨to make a name for oneself : darse a conocer, hacerse famoso⟩ ⟨to have a good name : tener buena fama⟩ **5 in all/everything but name** : a todos los efectos **6 in name only** : sólo de nombre **7 in the name of** : en nom-

bre de **8 to drop names** : mencionar a gente importante

name–brand [ˈneɪmˌbrænd] *adj* : de marca conocida

name brand *n* : marca *f* conocida

nameless [ˈneɪmləs] *adj* **1** ANONYMOUS : anónimo **2** INDESCRIBABLE : indecible, indescriptible

namelessly [ˈneɪmləsli] *adv* : anónimamente

namely [ˈneɪmli] *adv* : a saber

namesake [ˈneɪmˌseɪk] *n* : tocayo *m*, -ya *f*; homónimo *m*, -ma *f*

Namibian [nəˈmɪbiən] *n* : namibio *m*, -bia *f* — **Namibian** *adj*

nanny [ˈnæni] *n, pl* **nannies** : niñera *f*; nana *f CA, Col, Mex, Ven*

nap¹ [ˈnæp] *vi* **napped; napping 1** : dormir, dormir la siesta **2 to be caught napping** : estar desprevenido

nap² *n* **1** SLEEP : siesta *f* ⟨to take a nap : echarse una siesta⟩ **2** FUZZ, PILE : pelo *m*, pelusa *f* (de telas)

nape [ˈneɪp, ˈnæp] *n* : nuca *f*, cerviz *f*, cogote *m*

naphtha [ˈnæfθə] *n* : nafta *f*

napkin [ˈnæpkən] *n* : servilleta *f*

narcissism [ˈnɑrsəˌsɪzəm] *n* : narcisismo *m*

narcissist [ˈnɑrsəsɪst] *n* : narcisista *mf*

narcissistic [ˌnɑrsəˈsɪstɪk] *adj* : narcisista

narcissus [nɑrˈsɪsəs] *n, pl* **-cissus** *or* **-cissuses** *or* **-cissi** [-ˈsɪˌsaɪ, -ˌsiː] : narciso *m*

narcotic¹ [nɑrˈkɑtɪk] *adj* : narcótico

narcotic² *n* : narcótico *m*, estupefaciente *m*

narrate [ˈnærˌeɪt] *vt* **-rated; -rating** : narrar, relatar

narration [næˈreɪʃən] *n* : narración *f*

narrative¹ [ˈnærətɪv] *adj* : narrativo

narrative² *n* : narración *f*, narrativa *f*, relato *m*

narrator [ˈnærˌeɪtər] *n* : narrador *m*, -dora *f*

narrow¹ [ˈnærˌoː] *vi* : estrecharse, angostarse ⟨the river narrowed : el río se estrechó⟩ — *vt* **1** : estrechar, angostar **2** LIMIT : restringir, limitar ⟨to narrow the search : limitar la búsqueda⟩

narrow² *adj* **1** : estrecho, angosto **2** LIMITED : estricto, limitado ⟨in the narrowest sense of the word : en el sentido más estricto de la palabra⟩ **3 to have a narrow escape** : escapar por un pelo

narrowly [ˈnæroli] *adv* **1** BARELY : por poco **2** CLOSELY : de cerca

narrow–minded [ˌnæroˈmaɪndəd] *adj* : de miras estrechas

narrowness [ˈnæronəs] *n* : estrechez *f*

narrows [ˈnæroːz] *npl* STRAIT : estrecho *m*

nasal [ˈneɪzəl] *adj* : nasal

nasally [ˈneɪzəli] *adv* **1** : por la nariz **2** : con voz nasal

nastily [ˈnæstɪli] *adv* : con maldad, cruelmente

nastiness [ˈnæstinəs] *n* : porquería *f*

nasty [ˈnæsti] *adj* **nastier; -est 1** FILTHY : sucio, mugriento **2** OBSCENE : obsceno

3 MEAN, SPITEFUL : malo, malicioso **4** UNPLEASANT : desagradable, feo **5** REPUGNANT : asqueroso, repugnante ⟨a nasty smell : un olor asqueroso⟩

natal [ˈneɪtəl] *adj* : natal

nation [ˈneɪʃən] *n* : nación *f*

national¹ [ˈnæʃənəl] *adj* : nacional

national² *n* : ciudadano *m*, -na *f*; nacional *mf*

national anthem *n* : himno *m* nacional

nationalism [ˈnæʃənəˌlɪzəm] *n* : nacionalismo *m*

nationalist¹ [ˈnæʃənəlɪst] *adj* : nacionalista

nationalist² *n* : nacionalista *mf*

nationalistic [ˌnæʃənəˈlɪstɪk] *adj* : nacionalista

nationality [ˌnæʃəˈnæləti] *n, pl* **-ties** : nacionalidad *f*

nationalization [ˌnæʃənələˈzeɪʃən] *n* : nacionalización *f*

nationalize [ˈnæʃənəˌlaɪz] *vt* **-ized; -izing** : nacionalizar

nationally [ˈnæʃənəli] *adv* : a escala nacional, a nivel nacional

national park *n* : parque *m* nacional

nationwide [ˈneɪʃənˌwaɪd] *adj* : en toda la nación, por todo el país

native¹ [ˈneɪtɪv] *adj* **1** INNATE : innato **2** : natal ⟨her native city : su ciudad natal⟩ ⟨native speaker : hablante nativo/nativa⟩ ⟨native language : lengua materna⟩ **3** INDIGENOUS : indígena, autóctono

native² *n* **1** ABORIGINE : nativo *m*, -va *f*; indígena *mf* **2** : natural *m* ⟨he's a native of Mexico : es natural de México⟩

Native American *n* : nativo *m* americano, nativa *f* americana; indígena *m* (americano), indígena *f* (americana) — **Native American** *adj*

nativity [nəˈtɪvəti, neɪ-] *n, pl* **-ties 1** BIRTH : navidad *f* **2 the Nativity** : la Natividad, la Navidad

natty [ˈnæti] *adj* **nattier; -est** : elegante, garboso

natural¹ [ˈnæʧərəl] *adj* **1** : natural, de la naturaleza ⟨natural woodlands : bosques naturales⟩ ⟨natural childbirth : parto natural⟩ **2** INNATE : innato, natural **3** UNAFFECTED : natural, sin afectación **4** LIFELIKE : natural, vivo

natural² *n* **to be a natural** : tener un talento innato (para algo)

natural gas *n* : gas *m* natural

natural history *n* : historia *f* natural

naturalism [ˈnæʧərəˌlɪzəm] *n* : naturalismo *m*

naturalist [ˈnæʧərəlɪst] *n* : naturalista *mf* — **naturalist** *adj*

naturalistic [ˌnæʧərəˈlɪstɪk] *adj* : naturalista

naturalization [ˌnæʧərələˈzeɪʃən] *n* : naturalización *f*

naturalize [ˈnæʧərəˌlaɪz] *vt* **-ized; -izing** : naturalizar

naturally [ˈnæʧərəli] *adv* **1** INHERENTLY : naturalmente, intrínsecamente **2** UNAFFECTEDLY : de manera natural **3** OF COURSE : por supuesto, naturalmente

naturalness [ˈnætʃərəlnəs] n : naturalidad f

natural science n : ciencias fpl naturales

nature [ˈneɪtʃər] n 1 : naturaleza f ⟨the laws of nature : las leyes de la naturaleza⟩ 2 KIND, SORT : índole f, clase f ⟨things of this nature : cosas de esta índole⟩ 3 DISPOSITION : carácter m, natural m, naturaleza f ⟨it is his nature to be friendly : es de natural simpático⟩ ⟨human nature : la naturaleza humana⟩

naught [ˈnɔt] n 1 : nada f ⟨to come to naught : reducirse a nada, fracasar⟩ 2 ZERO : cero m

naughtily [ˈnɔtəli] adv : traviesamente, con malicia

naughtiness [ˈnɔtinəs] n : mala conducta f, travesuras fpl, malicia f

naughty [ˈnɔti] adj naughtier; -est 1 MISCHIEVOUS : travieso, pícaro 2 RISQUÉ : picante, subido de tono

nausea [ˈnɔziə, ˈnɔʃə] n 1 SICKNESS : náuseas fpl 2 DISGUST : asco m

nauseate [ˈnɔziˌeɪt, -ʒi-, -si-, -ʃi-] vt -ated; -ating 1 SICKEN : darle náuseas (a alguien) 2 DISGUST : asquear, darle asco (a alguien)

nauseating adj : nauseabundo, repugnante

nauseatingly [ˈnɔziˌeɪtiŋli, -ʒi-, -si-, -ʃi-] adv : hasta el punto de dar asco ⟨nauseatingly sweet : tan dulce que da asco⟩

nauseous [ˈnɔʃəs, -ziəs] adj 1 SICK : mareado, con náuseas 2 SICKENING : nauseabundo

nautical [ˈnɔtɪkəl] adj : náutico

nautilus [ˈnɔtələs] n, pl -luses or -li [-ˌlaɪ, -ˌli:] : nautilo m

Navajo [ˈnævəˌhoː, ˈnɑ-] n : navajo m, -ja f — **Navajo** adj

naval [ˈneɪvəl] adj : naval

nave [ˈneɪv] n : nave f

navel [ˈneɪvəl] n : ombligo m

navigability [ˌnævɪgəˈbɪləti] n : navegabilidad f

navigable [ˈnævɪgəbəl] adj : navegable

navigate [ˈnævəˌgeɪt] v -gated; -gating vi : navegar — vt 1 STEER : gobernar (un barco), pilotar (un avión) 2 : navegar por (un río, etc.)

navigation [ˌnævəˈgeɪʃən] n : navegación f

navigator [ˈnævəˌgeɪtər] n : navegante mf

navy [ˈneɪvi] n, pl -vies 1 FLEET : flota f 2 : marina f de guerra, armada f ⟨the United States Navy : la armada de los Estados Unidos⟩ 3 or navy blue : azul m marino

nay[1] [ˈneɪ] adv : no

nay[2] n : no m, voto m en contra

Nazi [ˈnɑtsi, ˈnæt-] n : nazi mf

Nazism [ˈnɑtˌsɪzəm, ˈnæt-] or **Naziism** [ˈnɑtsiˌɪzəm, ˈnæt-] n : nazismo m

Neanderthal [niˈændərˌθɔl, -ˌtɔl] n 1 or **Neanderthal man** : Neandertal m, hombre m de Neandertal 2 fam : neandertal m

near[1] [ˈnɪr] vt 1 : acercarse a ⟨the ship is nearing port : el barco se está acercando al puerto⟩ 2 : estar a punto de ⟨she is

nearing graduation : está a punto de graduarse⟩

near[2] adv 1 CLOSE : cerca ⟨my family lives quite near : mi familia vive muy cerca⟩ ⟨the day of the wedding was drawing near : se acercaba el día de la boda⟩ 2 NEARLY : casi ⟨near perfect/impossible : casi perfecto/imposible⟩ 3 (as) near as I can tell/figure : según parece, por lo visto 4 nowhere near → nowhere[1]

near[3] adj 1 CLOSE : cercano, próximo ⟨the nearest pharmacy : la farmacia más cercana/próxima⟩ ⟨in the near future : en un/el futuro próximo/cercano⟩ 2 CLOSER : más cercano, más próximo ⟨the near side/end : el lado/extremo más cercano/próximo, el lado/extremo de acá⟩ 3 (close to or similar to being) ⟨they had a near win : perdieron por poco⟩ ⟨a near miracle : casi un milagro⟩ ⟨the nearest thing to : lo más parecido a⟩ 4 : cercano (dícese de un pariente) 5 : cercano (de grado, etc.) ⟨his nearest rival : su más cercano rival⟩ 6 near and dear ⟨my nearest and dearest friend : mi amigo más íntimo⟩ 7 to the nearest ⟨it's rounded to the nearest dollar : se redondea al dólar más cercano⟩

near[4] prep : cerca de ⟨near the store : cerca de la tienda⟩ ⟨she lives near here : vive cerca de aquí, vive aquí cerca⟩ ⟨it was near midnight : era casi medianoche⟩ ⟨near the end : casi al final⟩ ⟨near death : al borde de la muerte⟩ ⟨to go near someone/something : acercarse a alguien/algo⟩

nearby[1] [nɪrˈbaɪ, ˈnɪrˌbaɪ] adv : cerca

nearby[2] adj : cercano

nearly [ˈnɪrli] adv 1 ALMOST : casi ⟨nearly asleep : casi dormido⟩ 2 not nearly : ni con mucho, ni mucho menos ⟨it was not nearly so bad as I had expected : no fue ni con mucho tan malo como esperaba⟩

nearness [ˈnɪrnəs] n : proximidad f

nearsighted [ˈnɪrˌsaɪtəd] adj : miope, corto de vista

nearsightedly [ˈnɪrˌsaɪtədli] adv : con miopía

nearsightedness [ˈnɪrˌsaɪtədnəs] n : miopía f

neat [ˈniːt] adj 1 CLEAN, ORDERLY : ordenado, pulcro, limpio 2 UNDILUTED : solo, sin diluir 3 SIMPLE, TASTEFUL : sencillo y de buen gusto 4 CLEVER : hábil, ingenioso ⟨a neat trick : un truco ingenioso⟩ 5 GREAT, TERRIFIC : genial, estupendo

neaten [ˈniːtən] vt : arreglar, ordenar, poner en orden — vi to neaten up : poner las cosas en orden

neatly [ˈniːtli] adv 1 TIDILY : ordenadamente 2 CLEVERLY : ingeniosamente

neatness [ˈniːtnəs] n : pulcritud f, limpieza f, orden m

nebula [ˈnɛbjələ] n, pl -lae [-ˌliː, -ˌlaɪ] : nebulosa f

nebulous [ˈnɛbjələs] adj : nebuloso, vago

necessarily [ˌnɛsəˈserəli] adv : necesariamente, forzosamente

necessary[1] ['nɛsəˌsɛri] *adj* **1** INEVITABLE : inevitable **2** COMPULSORY : necesario, obligatorio **3** ESSENTIAL : imprescindible, preciso, necesario

necessary[2] *n, pl* **-saries** : lo esencial, lo necesario

necessitate [nɪ'sɛsəˌteɪt] *vt* **-tated; -tating** : necesitar, requerir

necessity [nɪ'sɛsəti] *n, pl* **-ties** **1** NEED : necesidad *f* **2** REQUIREMENT : requisito *m* indispensable **3** POVERTY : indigencia *f*, necesidad *f* **4** INEVITABILITY : inevitabilidad *f*

neck[1] ['nɛk] *vi* : besuquearse

neck[2] *n* **1** : cuello *m* (de una persona), pescuezo *m* (de un animal) **2** COLLAR : cuello *m* **3** : cuello *m* (de una botella), mástil *m* (de una guitarra)

necklace ['nɛkləs] *n* : collar *m*

neckline ['nɛkˌlaɪn] *n* : escote *m*

necktie ['nɛkˌtaɪ] *n* : corbata *f*

nectar ['nɛktər] *n* : néctar *m*

nectarine [ˌnɛktə'riːn] *n* : nectarina *f*

née *or* **nee** ['neɪ] *adj* : de soltera ⟨Mrs. Smith, née Whitman : la señora Smith, de soltera Whitman⟩

need[1] ['niːd] *vt* **1** : necesitar ⟨I need your help : necesito tu ayuda⟩ ⟨I need money : me falta dinero⟩ **2** REQUIRE : requerir, exigir ⟨that job needs patience : ese trabajo exige paciencia⟩ **3 to need to** : tener que ⟨he needs to study : tiene que estudiar⟩ ⟨they need to be scolded : hay que reprenderlos⟩ — *v aux* **1** MUST : tener que, deber ⟨need you shout? : ¿tienes que gritar?⟩ **2 to be needed** : hacer falta ⟨you needn't worry : no hace falta que te preocupes, no hay por qué preocuparse⟩

need[2] *n* **1** NECESSITY : necesidad *f* ⟨in case of need : en caso de necesidad⟩ **2** LACK : falta *f* ⟨the need for better training : la falta de mejor capacitación⟩ ⟨to be in need : necesitar⟩ **3** POVERTY : necesidad *f*, indigencia *f* **4 needs** *npl* : requisitos *mpl*, carencias *fpl*

needful ['niːdfəl] *adj* : necesario

needle[1] ['niːdəl] *vt* **-dled; -dling** : pinchar

needle[2] *n* **1** : aguja *f* ⟨to thread a needle : enhebrar una aguja⟩ ⟨knitting needle : aguja de tejer⟩ **2** POINTER : aguja *f*, indicador *m*

needlepoint ['niːdəlˌpɔɪnt] *n* **1** LACE : encaje *m* de mano **2** EMBROIDERY : bordado *m*

needless ['niːdləs] *adj* : innecesario

needlessly ['niːdləsli] *adv* : sin ninguna necesidad, innecesariamente

needlework ['niːdəlˌwərk] *n* : bordado *m*

needn't ['niːdənt] *contraction of* **need not** → **need**

needy[1] ['niːdi] *adj* **needier; -est** : necesitado

needy[2] **the needy** : los necesitados *mpl*

nefarious [nɪ'færiəs] *adj* : nefario, nefando, infame

negate [nɪ'geɪt] *vt* **-gated; -gating** **1** DENY : negar **2** NULLIFY : invalidar, anular

negation [nɪ'geɪʃən] *n* : negación *f*

negative[1] ['nɛgətɪv] *adj* : negativo

negative[2] *n* **1** : negación *f* (en lingüística) **2** : negativa *f* ⟨to answer in the negative : contestar con una negativa⟩ **3** : término *m* negativo (en matemáticas) **4** : negativo *m*, imagen *f* en negativo (en fotografía)

negatively ['nɛgətɪvli] *adv* : negativamente

neglect[1] [nɪ'glɛkt] *vt* **1** : desatender, descuidar ⟨to neglect one's health : descuidar la salud⟩ **2** : no cumplir con, faltar a ⟨to neglect one's obligations : faltar uno a sus obligaciones⟩ ⟨he neglected to tell me : omitió decírmelo⟩

neglect[2] *n* **1** : negligencia *f*, descuido *m*, incumplimiento *m* ⟨through neglect : por negligencia⟩ ⟨neglect of duty : incumplimiento del deber⟩ **2 in a state of neglect** : abandonado, descuidado

neglected [nɪ'glɛktəd] *adj* : abandonado, descuidado

neglectful [nɪ'glɛktfəl] *adj* : descuidado *m*

negligee [ˌnɛglə'ʒeɪ] *n* : negligé *m*

negligence ['nɛglɪdʒənts] *n* : descuido *m*, negligencia *f*

negligent ['nɛglɪdʒənt] *adj* : negligente, descuidado — **negligently** *adv*

negligible ['nɛglɪdʒəbəl] *adj* : insignificante, despreciable

negotiable [nɪ'goːʃəbəl, -ʃiə-] *adj* : negociable

negotiate [nɪ'goːʃiˌeɪt] *v* **-ated; -ating** *vi* : negociar — *vt* **1** : negociar, gestionar ⟨to negotiate a treaty : negociar un trato⟩ **2** : salvar, franquear ⟨they negotiated the obstacles : salvaron los obstáculos⟩ ⟨to negotiate a turn : tomar una curva⟩

negotiation [nɪˌgoːʃi'eɪʃən, -siˈeɪ-] *n* : negociación *f*

negotiator [nɪ'goːʃiˌeɪtər, -siˌeɪ-] *n* : negociador *m*, -dora *f*

Negro ['niːˌgroː] *n, pl* **-groes** *sometimes offensive* : negro *m*, -gra *f*

neigh[1] ['neɪ] *vi* : relinchar

neigh[2] *n* : relincho *m*

neighbor[1] ['neɪbər] *vt* : ser vecino de, estar junto a ⟨her house neighbors mine : su casa está junto a la mía⟩ — *vi* : estar cercano, lindar, colindar ⟨her land neighbors on mine : sus tierras lindan con las mías⟩

neighbor[2] *n* **1** : vecino *m*, -na *f* **2 love thy neighbor** : ama a tu prójimo

neighborhood ['neɪbərˌhʊd] *n* **1** : barrio *m*, vecindad *f*, vecindario *m* **2 in the neighborhood of** : alrededor de, cerca de

neighboring ['neɪbərɪŋ] *adj* : vecino

neighborly ['neɪbərli] *adv* : amable, de buena vecindad

neither[1] ['niːðər, 'naɪ-] *adj* : ninguno (de los dos)

neither[2] *conj* **1** : ni ⟨neither asleep nor awake : ni dormido ni despierto⟩ **2** NOR : ni (tampoco) ⟨I'm not asleep—neither am I : no estoy dormido—ni yo tampoco⟩

neither[3] *pron* : ninguno ⟨which do you want? neither : ¿cuál quieres? ninguno⟩ ⟨neither of the two sisters : ninguna de las dos hermanas⟩

nemesis ['nɛməsɪs] *n, pl* **-eses** [-,si:z] **1** RIVAL : rival *mf* **2** RETRIBUTION : justo castigo *m*

neologism [ni'ɑlə,dʒɪzəm] *n* : neologismo *m*

neon[1] ['ni:,ɑn] *adj* : de neón ⟨neon sign : letrero de neón⟩

neon[2] *n* : neón *m*

neophyte ['ni:ə,faɪt] *n* : neófito *m*, -ta *f*

Nepali [nə'pɔli, -'pɑ-, -'pæ-] *n* : nepalés *m*, -lesa *f* — **Nepali** *adj*

nephew ['nɛ,fju:, *chiefly Brit* 'nɛ,vju:] *n* : sobrino *m*

nepotism ['nɛpə,tɪzəm] *n* : nepotismo *m*

Neptune ['nɛp,tu:n, -,tju:n] *n* : Neptuno *m*

nerd ['nərd] *n* : ganso *m*, -sa *f*

nerve ['nərv] *n* **1** : nervio *m* **2** COURAGE : coraje *m*, valor *m*, fuerza *f* de la voluntad ⟨to lose one's nerve : perder el valor⟩ **3** AUDACITY, GALL : atrevimiento *m*, descaro *m* ⟨of all the nerve!, some/what nerve! : ¡qué descaro!⟩ ⟨you have a lot of nerve! : ¡qué cara tienes!⟩ **4 nerves** *npl* : nervios *mpl* ⟨to be a bag/bundle of nerves : ser un manojo de nervios⟩ ⟨to calm one's nerves : calmarse (los nervios)⟩ ⟨to get on someone's nerves : crisparle los nervios a alguien⟩ ⟨to have a (bad) case of nerves : estar nerviosísimo⟩ ⟨to have nerves of steel : tener nervios de acero⟩ ⟨to have one's nerves on edge : tener los nervios de punta⟩ ⟨a war of nerves : una guerra de nervios⟩ **5 to hit/strike/touch a nerve** : poner el dedo en la llaga

nerve–racking *or* **nerve-wracking** ['nərv-,rækɪŋ] *adj* : estresante, desesperante, angustioso

nervous ['nərvəs] *adj* **1** : nervioso ⟨the nervous system : el sistema nervioso⟩ **2** EXCITABLE : nervioso ⟨to get nervous : excitarse, ponerse nervioso⟩ **3** FEARFUL : miedoso, temeroso

nervous breakdown *n* → **breakdown**

nervously ['nərvəsli] *adv* : nerviosamente

nervousness ['nərvəsnəs] *n* : nerviosismo *m*, nerviosidad *f*, ansiedad *f*

nervy ['nərvi] *adj* **nervier; -est 1** COURAGEOUS : valiente **2** IMPUDENT : atrevido, descarado, fresco *fam* **3** NERVOUS : nervioso

nest[1] ['nɛst] *vi* : anidar

nest[2] *n* **1** : nido *m* (de un ave), avispero *m* (de una avispa), madriguera *f* (de un animal) **2** REFUGE : nido *m*, refugio *m* **3** SET : juego *m* ⟨a nest of tables : un juego de mesitas⟩

nestle ['nɛsəl] *vi* **-tled; -tling** : acurrucarse, arrimarse cómodamente

net[1] ['nɛt] *vt* **netted; netting 1** CATCH : pescar, atrapar con una red **2** CLEAR : ganar neto ⟨they netted $ 50 00 : ganaron $ 50 00 netos⟩ **3** YIELD : producir

net[2] *adj* : neto ⟨net weight : peso neto⟩ ⟨net gain : ganancia neta⟩

net[3] *n* : red *f*, malla *f*

nether ['nɛðər] *adj* **1** : inferior, más bajo **2 the nether regions** : el infierno

nettle[1] ['nɛtəl] *vt* **-tled; -tling** : irritar, provocar, molestar

nettle[2] *n* : ortiga *f*

network ['nɛt,wərk] *n* **1** SYSTEM : red *f* ⟨social network : red social⟩ **2** CHAIN : cadena *f* (de tiendas, etc.)

neural ['nʊrəl, 'njʊr-] *adj* : neural

neuralgia [nʊ'rældʒə, njʊ-] *n* : neuralgia *f*

neuritis [nʊ'raɪtəs, njʊ-] *n, pl* **-ritides** [-'rɪtə,di:z] *or* **-ritises** : neuritis *f*

neurological [,nʊrə'lɑdʒɪkəl, ,njʊr-] *or* **neurologic** [,nʊrə'lɑdʒɪk, ,njʊr-] *adj* : neurológico

neurologist [nʊ'rɑlədʒɪst, njʊ-] *n* : neurólogo *m*, -ga *f*

neurology [nʊ'rɑlədʒi, njʊ-] *n* : neurología *f*

neurosis [nʊ'ro:sɪs, njʊ-] *n, pl* **-roses** [-,si:z] : neurosis *f*

neurotic[1] [nʊ'rɑtɪk, njʊ-] *adj* : neurótico

neurotic[2] *n* : neurótico *m*, -ca *f*

neuter[1] ['nu:tər, 'nju:-] *vt* : castrar

neuter[2] *adj* : neutro

neutral[1] ['nu:trəl, 'nju:-] *adj* **1** IMPARTIAL : neutral, imparcial ⟨to remain neutral : permanecer neutral⟩ **2** : neutro ⟨a neutral color : un color neutro⟩ **3** : neutro (en la química o la electricidad)

neutral[2] *n* : punto *m* muerto (de un automóvil)

neutrality [nu:'trælət̬i:, nju:-] *n* : neutralidad *f*

neutralization [,nu:trələ'zeɪʃən, ,nju:-] *n* : neutralización *f*

neutralize ['nu:trə,laɪz, 'nju:-] *vt* **-ized; -izing** : neutralizar

neutron ['nu:,trɑn, 'nju:-] *n* : neutrón *m*

never ['nɛvər] *adv* **1** : nunca, jamás ⟨he never studies : nunca estudia⟩ **2 never again** : nunca más, nunca jamás **3 never mind** : no importa

never–ending ['nɛvər'ɛndɪŋ] *adj* ENDLESS : interminable, inacabable, sin fin

nevermore [,nɛvər'mor] *adv* : nunca más

nevertheless [,nɛvərðə'lɛs] *adv* : sin embargo, no obstante

new ['nu:, 'nju:] *adj* **1** : nuevo ⟨a new dress : un vestido nuevo⟩ **2** RECENT : nuevo, reciente ⟨what's new? : ¿qué hay de nuevo?⟩ ⟨a new arrival : un recién llegado⟩ **3** DIFFERENT : nuevo, distinto ⟨this problem is new : este problema es distinto⟩ ⟨new ideas : ideas nuevas⟩ **4 like new** : como nuevo

newborn ['nu:,born, 'nju:-] *adj* : recién nacido

newcomer ['nu:,kʌmər, 'nju:-] *n* : recién llegado *m*, recién llegada *f*

newfangled ['nu:'fæŋgəld, 'nju:-] *adj* : novedoso

newfound ['nu:'faʊnd, 'nju:-] *adj* : recién descubierto

newly ['nu:li, 'nju:-] *adv* : recién, recientemente

newlywed ['nu:li,wɛd, 'nju:-] *n* : recién casado *m*, -da *f*

new moon *n* : luna *f* nueva

newness ['nu:nəs, 'nju:-] *n* : novedad *f*

news ['nu:z, 'nju:z] *n* **1** INFORMATION
: noticias *fpl* ⟨good/bad news : buenas/
malas noticias⟩ ⟨to break the news to
someone : darle la noticia a alguien⟩
⟨further news : más noticias⟩ ⟨that's
news to me! : ¡(es la) primera noticia
(que tengo)!⟩ ⟨no news is good news
: (el) que no haya noticias es (una) buena
noticia⟩ **2** : noticias *fpl* ⟨local/interna-
tional news : noticias locales/internacio-
nales⟩ ⟨to be in the news : salir en las
noticias⟩ **3** NEWSCAST : noticias *fpl*, noticiero *m*, informativo *m*, noticiario *m*
⟨the nightly news : el noticiero noc-
turno⟩ ⟨I saw it on the news : lo vi en las
noticias⟩

newscast ['nu:z‚kæst, 'nju:z-] *n* : noticiero *m*, informativo *m*, noticiario *m*

newscaster ['nu:z‚kæstər, 'nju:z-] *n*
: presentador *m*, -dora *f*; locutor *m*, -tora
f

newsgroup ['nu:z‚gru:p, 'nju:z-] *n* : grupo
m de noticias

newsletter ['nu:z‚lɛtər, 'nju:z-] *n* : boletín
m informativo

newsman ['nu:zmən, 'nju:z-, -‚mæn] *n, pl*
-men [-mən, -‚mɛn] : periodista *m*, reportero *m*

newspaper ['nu:z‚peɪpər, 'nju:z-] *n* **1**
: periódico *m*, diario *m* ⟨newspaper articles : artículos periodísticos⟩ ⟨newspa-
per reporter : periodista⟩ **2** : papel *m* de
periódico

newspaperman ['nu:z‚peɪpər‚mæn, 'nju:z-]
n, pl **-men** [-mən, -‚mɛn] **1** REPORTER
: periodista *m*, reportero *m* **2** : dueño *m*
de un periódico

newsprint ['nu:z‚prɪnt, 'nju:z-] *n* : papel *m*
de prensa

newsstand ['nu:z‚stænd, 'nju:z-] *n*
: quiosco *m*, puesto *m* de periódicos

newswoman ['nu:z‚wʊmən, 'nju:z-] *n, pl*
-women [-‚wɪmən] : periodista *f*, reportera *f*

newsworthy ['nu:z‚wərði, 'nju:z-] *adj*
: de interés periodístico

newsy ['nu:zi, 'nju:-] *adj* **newsier; -est**
: lleno de noticias

newt ['nu:t, 'nju:t] *n* : tritón *m*

New Testament *n* : Nuevo Testamento *m*

New Year *n* : Año *m* Nuevo

New Year's Day *n* : día *m* del Año Nuevo

New Year's Eve *n* : noche *f* de Fin de Año,
Nochevieja *f*

New Yorker [nu:'jɔrkər, nju:-] *n* : neoyor-
quino *m*, -na *f*

New Zealander [nu:'zi:ləndər, nju:-] *n*
: neozelandés *m*, -desa *f*

next¹ ['nɛkst] *adv* **1** AFTERWARD : después, luego ⟨what will you do next?
: ¿qué harás después?⟩ **2** NOW : después,
ahora, entonces ⟨next I will sing a song
: ahora voy a cantar una canción⟩ **3** : la
próxima vez ⟨when next we meet : la
próxima vez que nos encontremos⟩

next² *adj* **1** ADJACENT : contiguo, de al
lado **2** COMING : que viene, próximo
⟨next Friday : el viernes que viene⟩ **3**

FOLLOWING : siguiente ⟨the next year
: el año siguiente⟩

next–door ['nɛkst'dor] *adj* : de al lado

next–of–kin *n, pl* **next–of–kin** : familiar
m más cercano, pariente *m* más cercano

next to¹ *adv* ALMOST : casi, prácticamente
⟨next to impossible : casi imposible⟩

next to² *prep* : junto a, al lado de

nexus ['nɛksəs] *n* : nexo *m*

nib ['nɪb] *n* : plumilla *f*

nibble¹ ['nɪbəl] *v* **-bled; -bling** *vt* : pellizcar, mordisquear, picar — *vi* : picar

nibble² *n* : mordisco *m*

Nicaraguan [‚nɪkə'rɑgwən] *n* : nicaragüense *mf* — **Nicaraguan** *adj*

nice ['naɪs] *adj* **nicer; nicest** **1** REFINED
: pulido, refinado **2** SUBTLE : fino, sutil
3 PLEASING : agradable, bueno, lindo
⟨nice weather : buen tiempo⟩ **4** RE-
SPECTABLE : bueno, decente **5** **nice and**
: bien, muy ⟨nice and hot : bien caliente⟩
⟨nice and slow : despacito⟩

nicely ['naɪsli] *adv* **1** KINDLY : amablemente **2** POLITELY : con buenos modales
3 ATTRACTIVELY : de buen gusto

niceness ['naɪsnəs] *n* : simpatía *f*, amabilidad *f*

nicety ['naɪsəti] *n, pl* **-ties** **1** DETAIL, SUB-
TLETY : sutileza *f*, detalle *m* **2** **niceties**
npl : lujos *mpl*, detalles *mpl*

niche ['nɪtʃ] *n* **1** RECESS : nicho *m*, hornacina *f* **2** : nicho *m*, hueco *m* ⟨to make a
niche for oneself : hacerse un hueco,
encontrarse una buena posición⟩

nick¹ ['nɪk] *vt* : cortar, hacer una muesca
en

nick² *n* **1** CUT : corte *m*, muesca *f* **2** **in the
nick of time** : en el momento crítico,
justo a tiempo

nickel ['nɪkəl] *n* **1** : níquel *m* **2** : moneda
f de cinco centavos

nickname¹ ['nɪk‚neɪm] *vt* **-named; -nam-
ing** : apodar

nickname² *n* : apodo *m*, mote *m*, sobrenombre *m*

nicotine ['nɪkə‚ti:n] *n* : nicotina *f*

niece ['ni:s] *n* : sobrina *f*

Nigerian [naɪ'dʒɪriən] *n* : nigeriano *m*, -na
f — **Nigerian** *adj*

niggardly ['nɪɡərdli] *adj* : mezquino, tacaño

niggling ['nɪɡəlɪŋ] *adj* **1** PETTY : insignificante **2** PERSISTENT : constante, persistente ⟨a niggling doubt : una duda
constante⟩

nigh¹ ['naɪ] *adv* **1** NEARLY : casi **2** **to draw
nigh** : acercarse, avecinarse

nigh² *adj* : cercano, próximo

night¹ ['naɪt] *adj* : nocturno, de la noche
⟨the night sky : el cielo nocturno⟩ ⟨night
shift : turno de la noche⟩

night² *n* **1** EVENING : noche *f* ⟨at night
: de noche⟩ ⟨last night : anoche⟩ ⟨to-
morrow night : mañana por la noche⟩ **2**
DARKNESS : noche *f*, oscuridad *f* ⟨night
fell : cayó la noche⟩

nightclothes ['naɪt‚klo:ðz, -‚klo:z] *npl*
: ropa *f* de dormir

nightclub ['naɪt‚klʌb] *n* : cabaret *m*; club
m nocturno; boliche *m Arg, Uru*

night crawler [ˈnaɪtˌkrɔlər] *n* EARTH-WORM : lombriz *f* (de tierra)

nightdress [ˈnaɪtˌdrɛs] → **nightgown**

nightfall [ˈnaɪtˌfɔl] *n* : anochecer *m*

nightgown [ˈnaɪtˌgaʊn] *n* : camisón *m* (de noche)

nightie [ˈnaɪti] *n* : camisón *m* corto (de noche)

nightingale [ˈnaɪtənˌgeɪl, ˈnaɪtɪŋ-] *n* : ruiseñor *m*

nightlife [ˈnaɪtˌlaɪf] *n* : vida *f* nocturna

nightly[1] [ˈnaɪtli] *adv* : cada noche, todas las noches

nightly[2] *adj* : de todas las noches

nightmare [ˈnaɪtˌmær] *n* : pesadilla *f*

nightmarish [ˈnaɪtˌmærɪʃ] *adj* : de pesadilla

night owl *n* : noctámbulo *m*, -la *f*

night school *n* : escuela *f* nocturna, clases *fpl* nocturnas

nightshade [ˈnaɪtˌʃeɪd] *n* : hierba *f* mora

nightshirt [ˈnaɪtˌʃərt] *n* : camisa *f* de dormir

nightstick [ˈnaɪtˌstɪk] *n* : porra *f*

night table *or* **nightstand** [ˈnaɪtˌstænd] *n* : mesita *f*, mesilla *f* Spain (de noche)

nighttime [ˈnaɪtˌtaɪm] *n* : noche *f*

nihilism [ˈnaɪəˌlɪzəm] *n* : nihilismo *m*

nil [ˈnɪl] *n* : nada *f*, cero *m*

nimble [ˈnɪmbəl] *adj* **nimbler; -blest 1** AGILE : ágil **2** CLEVER : hábil, ingenioso

nimbleness [ˈnɪmbəlnəs] *n* : agilidad *f*

nimbly [ˈnɪmbli] *adv* : con agilidad, ágilmente

nincompoop [ˈnɪŋkəmˌpuːp, ˈnɪŋ-] *n* FOOL : tonto *m*, -ta *f*; bobo *m*, -ba *f*

nine[1] [ˈnaɪn] *adj* **1** : nueve ⟨he's nine (years old) : tiene nueve años⟩ **2 nine times out of ten** : casi siempre

nine[2] *n* : nueve *m* ⟨the nine of hearts : el nueve de corazones⟩

nine[3] *pron* : nueve ⟨it's nine (o'clock) : son las nueve⟩ ⟨there are nine of us : somos nueve⟩

nine hundred[1] *adj* : novecientos

nine hundred[2] *n* : novecientos *m*

ninepins [ˈnaɪnˌpɪnz] *n* : bolos *mpl*

nineteen[1] [naɪnˈtiːn] *adj & pron* : diecinueve

nineteen[2] *n* : diecinueve *m*

nineteenth[1] [naɪnˈtiːnθ] *adj* : decimonoveno, decimonono ⟨the nineteenth century : el siglo diecinueve⟩

nineteenth[2] *n* **1** : decimonoveno *m*, -na *f*; decimonono *m*, -na *f* (en una serie) **2** : diecinueveavo *m*, diecinueveava parte *f*

ninetieth[1] [ˈnaɪntɪə] *adj* : nonagésimo

ninetieth[2] *n* **1** : nonagésimo *m*, -ma *f* (en una serie) **2** : noventavo *m*, noventava parte *f*

ninety[1] [ˈnaɪnti] *adj & pron* : noventa

ninety[2] *n, pl* **-ties** : noventa *m*

ninny [ˈnɪni] *n, pl* **ninnies** FOOL : tonto *m*, -ta *f*; bobo *m*, -ba *f*

ninth[1] [ˈnaɪnθ] *adv* : en noveno lugar

ninth[2] *adj* : noveno

ninth[3] *n* **1** : noveno *m*, -na *f* (en una serie) **2** (on) the ninth of June : el nueve de junio⟩ **2** : noveno *m*, novena parte *f*

nip[1] [ˈnɪp] *vt* **nipped; nipping 1** PINCH : pellizcar **2** BITE : morder, mordisquear **3 to nip in the bud** : cortar de raíz

nip[2] *n* **1** TANG : sabor *m* fuerte **2** PINCH : pellizco *m* **3** NIBBLE : mordisco *m* **4** SWALLOW : trago *m*, traguito *m* **5 there's a nip in the air** : hace fresco

nipple [ˈnɪpəl] *n* : pezón *m* (de una mujer), tetilla *f* (de un hombre)

nippy [ˈnɪpi] *adj* **nippier; -est 1** SHARP : fuerte, picante **2** CHILLY : frío ⟨it's nippy today : hoy hace frío⟩

nit [ˈnɪt] *n* : liendre *f*

nitrate [ˈnaɪˌtreɪt] *n* : nitrato *m*

nitric acid [ˈnaɪtrɪk] *n* : ácido *m* nítrico

nitrogen [ˈnaɪtrədʒən] *n* : nitrógeno *m*

nitroglycerin *or* **nitroglycerine** [ˌnaɪtroʊˈglɪsərən] *n* : nitroglicerina *f*

nitwit [ˈnɪtˌwɪt] *n* : zonzo *m*, -za *f*; bobo *m*, -ba *f*

no[1] [ˈnoː] *adv* : no ⟨are you leaving?—no : ¿te vas?—no⟩ ⟨no less than : no menos de⟩ ⟨to say no : decir que no⟩ ⟨like it or no : quieras o no quieras⟩

no[2] *adj* **1** : ninguno ⟨it's no trouble : no es ningún problema⟩ ⟨she has no money : no tiene dinero⟩ ⟨with little or no experience : con poca o ninguna experiencia⟩ ⟨the sign says "no smoking" : el letrero dice "no fumar"⟩ ⟨there's no arguing with him : no se puede discutir con él⟩ **2** (*indicating a small amount*) ⟨we'll be there in no time : enseguida llegamos⟩ **3** (*expressing that someone or something is not the kind of person or thing being described*) ⟨that's no liar : no es mentiroso⟩ ⟨that's no excuse : eso no es ninguna excusa⟩

no[3] *n, pl* **noes** *or* **nos** [ˈnoːz] **1** DENIAL : no *m* ⟨I won't take no for an answer : no aceptaré un no por respuesta⟩ **2** : voto *f* en contra ⟨the noes have it : se ha rechazado la moción⟩

nobility [noˈbɪləti] *n* : nobleza *f*

noble[1] [ˈnoːbəl] *adj* **nobler; -blest 1** ILLUSTRIOUS : noble, glorioso **2** ARISTOCRATIC : noble **3** STATELY : majestuoso, magnífico **4** LOFTY : noble, elevado ⟨noble sentiments : sentimientos elevados⟩

noble[2] *n* : noble *mf*, aristócrata *mf*

nobleman [ˈnoːbəlmən] *n, pl* **-men** [-mən, -ˌmɛn] : noble *m*, aristócrata *m*

nobleness [ˈnoːbəlnəs] *n* : nobleza *f*

noblewoman [ˈnoːbəlˌwʊmən] *n, pl* **-women** [-ˌwɪmən] : noble *f*, aristócrata *f*

nobly [ˈnoːbli] *adv* : noblemente

nobody[1] [ˈnoːbədi, -ˌbɑdi] *n, pl* **-bodies** : don nadie *m* ⟨he's a mere nobody : es un don nadie⟩

nobody[2] *pron* : nadie

nocturnal [nɑkˈtərnəl] *adj* : nocturno *m*

nocturne [ˈnɑkˌtərn] *n* : nocturno *m*

nod[1] [ˈnɑd] *v* **nodded; nodding** *vi* **1** : saludar con la cabeza, asentir con la cabeza **2 to nod off** : dormirse, quedarse dormido — *vt* : inclinar (la cabeza) ⟨to nod one's head in agreement : asentir con la cabeza⟩

nod² *n* : saludo *m* con la cabeza, señal *m* con la cabeza, señal *m* de asentimiento

node ['no:d] *n* : nudo *m* (de una planta)

nodule ['nɑˌdʒu:l] *n* : nódulo *m*

noel [no'ɛl] *n* **1** CAROL : villancico *m* de Navidad **2 Noel** CHRISTMAS : Navidad *f*

noes → no³

noise *n* : ruido *m*

noiseless ['nɔɪzləs] *adj* : silencioso, sin ruido

noiselessly ['nɔɪzləsli] *adv* : silenciosamente

noisemaker ['nɔɪzˌmeɪkər] *n* : matraca *f*

noisiness ['nɔɪzinəs] *n* : ruido *m*

noisy ['nɔɪzi] *adj* **noisier; -est** : ruidoso — **noisily** ['nɔɪzəli] *adv*

nomad¹ ['no:ˌmæd] → **nomadic**

nomad² *n* : nómada *mf*

nomadic [no'mædɪk] *adj* : nómada

nomenclature ['no:mənˌkleɪtʃər] *n* : nomenclatura *f*

nominal ['nɑmənəl] *adj* **1** : nominal ⟨the nominal head of his party : el jefe nominal de su partido⟩ **2** TRIFLING : insignificante

nominally ['nɑmənəli] *adv* : sólo de nombre, nominalmente

nominate ['nɑməˌneɪt] *vt* **-nated; -nating 1** PROPOSE : proponer (como candidato), nominar **2** APPOINT : nombrar

nomination [ˌnɑmə'neɪʃən] *n* **1** PROPOSAL : propuesta *f*, postulación *f* **2** APPOINTMENT : nombramiento *m*

nominative¹ ['nɑmənəˌtɪv] *adj* : nominativo

nominative² *n or* **nominative case** : nominativo *m*

nominee [ˌnɑmə'ni:] *n* : candidato *m*, -ta *f*

non- [ˌnɑn] *pref* : no ⟨non-smoker : no fumador⟩

nonaddictive [ˌnɑnə'dɪktɪv] *adj* : que no crea dependencia

nonalcoholic [ˌnɑnˌælkə'hɑlɪk] *adj* : sin alcohol, no alcohólico

nonaligned [ˌnɑnə'laɪnd] *adj* : no alineado

nonbeliever [ˌnɑnbə'li:vər] *n* : no creyente *mf*

nonbreakable [ˌnɑn'breɪkəbəl] *adj* : irrompible

nonce ['nɑnts] *n* **for the nonce** : por el momento

nonchalance [ˌnɑnʃə'lɑnts] *n* : indiferencia *f*, despreocupación *f*

nonchalant [ˌnɑnʃə'lɑnt] *adj* : indiferente, despreocupado, impasible

nonchalantly [ˌnɑnʃə'lɑntli] *adv* : con aire despreocupado, con indiferencia

noncombatant [ˌnɑnkəm'bætənt, -'kɑmbə-] *n* : no combatiente *mf*

noncommissioned officer [ˌnɑnkə'mɪʃənd] *n* : suboficial *mf*

noncommittal [ˌnɑnkə'mɪtəl] *adj* : evasivo, que no se compromete

nonconductor [ˌnɑnkən'dʌktər] *n* : aislante *m*

nonconformist [ˌnɑnkən'fɔrmɪst] *n* : inconformista *mf*, inconforme *mf*

nonconformity [ˌnɑnkən'fɔrməti] *n* : inconformidad *f*, no conformidad *f*

noncontagious [ˌnɑnkən'teɪdʒəs] *adj* : no contagioso

nondenominational [ˌnɑndɪˌnɑmə'neɪʃənəl] *adj* : no sectario

nondescript [ˌnɑndɪ'skrɪpt] *adj* : anodino, soso

nondiscriminatory [ˌnɑndɪ'skrɪmənəˌtori] *adj* : no discriminatorio

nondrinker [ˌnɑn'drɪŋkər] *n* : abstemio *m*, -mia *f*

none¹ ['nʌn] *adv* : de ninguna manera, de ningún modo, nada ⟨he was none too happy : no se sintió nada contento⟩ ⟨I'm none the worse for it : no estoy peor por ello⟩ ⟨none too soon : a buena hora⟩

none² *pron* **1** (*not one*) : ninguno ⟨there's none left : no queda ninguno/ninguna⟩ ⟨none of the cities : ninguna de las ciudades⟩ ⟨do you have any ideas? none whatsoever : ¿se te ocurre algo? no, nada⟩ **2** (*no amount or part*) : nada, ninguna parte ⟨there's none left : no queda nada⟩ ⟨none of it makes any sense : no tiene ningún sentido⟩ ⟨it's none of your business : no es asunto tuyo⟩ **3 to have none of** : no permitir, no aceptar **4 ~ but** : sólo, solamente **5 none other than** : ni más ni menos que **6 second to none** : insuperable

nonentity [ˌnɑn'entəti] *n, pl* **-ties** : persona *f* insignificante, nulidad *f*

nonessential [ˌnɑnɪ'sentʃəl] *adj* : secundario, no esencial

nonessentials [ˌnɑnɪ'sentʃəlz] *npl* : cosas *fpl* secundarias, cosas *fpl* accesorias

nonexistence [ˌnɑnɪg'zɪstənts] *n* : inexistencia *f*

nonexistent [ˌnɑnɪg'zɪstənt] *adj* : inexistente

nonfat [ˌnɑn'fæt] *adj* : sin grasa

nonfattening [ˌnɑn'fætənɪŋ] *adj* : que no engorda

nonfiction [ˌnɑn'fɪkʃən] *n* : no ficción *f*

nonflammable [ˌnɑn'flæməbəl] *adj* : no inflamable

nonintervention [ˌnɑnˌɪntər'ventʃən] *n* : no intervención *f*

nonmalignant [ˌnɑnmə'lɪgnənt] *adj* : no maligno, benigno

nonnegotiable [ˌnɑnnɪ'go:ʃəbəl, -ʃiə-] *adj* : no negociable

nonpareil¹ [ˌnɑnpə'rɛl] *adj* : sin parangón, sin par

nonpareil² *n* : persona *f* sin igual, cosa *f* sin par

nonpartisan [ˌnɑn'pɑrtəzən, -sən] *adj* : imparcial

nonpaying [ˌnɑn'peɪɪŋ] *adj* : que no paga

nonpayment [ˌnɑn'peɪmənt] *n* : impago *m*, falta *f* de pago

nonperson [ˌnɑn'pərsən] *n* : persona *f* sin derechos

nonplus [ˌnɑn'plʌs] *vt* **-plussed; -plussing** : confundir, desconcertar, dejar perplejo

nonprescription [ˌnɑnprɪ'skrɪpʃən] *adj* : disponible sin receta del médico

nonproductive [ˌnɑnprəˈdʌktɪv] *adj* : improductivo

nonprofit [ˌnɑnˈprɑfət] *adj* : sin fines lucrativos

nonproliferation [ˌnɑnprəˌlɪfəˈreɪʃən] *adj* : no proliferación

nonresident [ˌnɑnˈrɛzədənt, -ˌdɛnt] *n* : no residente *mf*

nonscheduled [ˌnɑnˈskɛˌdʒuːld] *adj* : no programado, no regular

nonsectarian [ˌnɑnˌsɛkˈtæriən] *adj* : no sectario

nonsense [ˈnɑnˌsɛns, ˈnɑntsənts] *n* : tonterías *fpl*, disparates *mpl*

nonsensical [nɑnˈsɛntsɪkəl] *adj* ABSURD : absurdo, disparatado — **nonsensically** [-kli] *adv*

nonsmoker [ˌnɑnˈsmoːkər] *n* : no fumador *m*, -dora *f*; persona *f* que no fuma

nonstandard [ˌnɑnˈstændərd] *adj* : no regular, no estándar

nonstick [ˌnɑnˈstɪk] *adj* : antiadherente

nonstop¹ [ˌnɑnˈstɑp] *adv* : sin parar ⟨he talked nonstop : habló sin parar⟩

nonstop² *adj* : directo, sin escalas ⟨nonstop flight : vuelo directo⟩

nonsupport [ˌnɑnsəˈpɔrt] *n* : falta *f* de manutención

nontaxable [ˌnɑnˈtæksəbəl] *adj* : exento de impuestos

nontoxic [ˌnɑnˈtɑksɪk] *adj* : no tóxico

nontransferable [ˌnɑnˌtrænsˈfərəbəl] *adj* : intransferible

nonviolence [ˌnɑnˈvaɪlənts, -ˈvaɪə-] *n* : no violencia *f*

nonviolent [ˌnɑnˈvaɪlənt, -ˈvaɪə-] *adj* : pacífico, no violento

noodle [ˈnuːdəl] *n* : fideo *m*, tallarín *m*

nook [ˈnʊk] *n* : rincón *m*, recoveco *m*, escondrijo *m* ⟨in every nook and cranny : en todos los rincones⟩

noon [ˈnuːn] *n* : mediodía *m*

noonday [ˈnuːnˌdeɪ] *n* : mediodía *m* ⟨the noonday sun : el sol de mediodía⟩

no one *pron* NOBODY : nadie

noontime [ˈnuːnˌtaɪm] *n* : mediodía *m*

noose [ˈnuːs] *n* 1 LASSO : lazo *m*, cuerda *f* (con un nudo corredizo) 2 **hangman's noose** : soga *f*

nor [ˈnɔr] *conj* : ni ⟨neither good nor bad : ni bueno ni malo⟩ ⟨nor I! : ¡ni yo tampoco!⟩

Nordic [ˈnɔrdɪk] *adj* : nórdico

norm [ˈnɔrm] *n* 1 STANDARD : norma *f*, modelo *m* 2 CUSTOM, RULE : regla *f* general, lo normal

normal [ˈnɔrməl] *adj* : normal — **normally** *adv*

normalcy [ˈnɔrməlsi] *n* : normalidad *f*

normality [nɔrˈmæləti] *n* : normalidad *f*

normalization [ˌnɔrmələˈzeɪʃən] *n* : normalización *f*, regularización *f*

normalize [ˈnɔrməˌlaɪz] *vt* : normalizar

Norse [ˈnɔrs] *adj* : nórdico

north¹ [ˈnɔrθ] *adv* : al norte

north² *adj* : norte, del norte ⟨the north coast : la costa del norte⟩

north³ *n* 1 : norte *m* 2 **the North** : el Norte *m*

North American *n* : norteamericano *m*, -na *f* — **North American** *adj*

northbound¹ [ˈnɔrθˌbaʊnd] *adv* : con rumbo al norte

northbound² *adj* : que va hacia el norte

northeast¹ [nɔrθˈiːst] *adv* : hacia el nordeste

northeast² *adj* : nordeste, del nordeste

northeast³ *n* : nordeste *m*, noreste *m*

northeasterly¹ [nɔrθˈiːstərli] *adv* : hacia el nordeste

northeasterly² *adj* : nordeste, del nordeste

northeastern [nɔrθˈiːstərn] *adj* : nordeste, del nordeste

northerly¹ [ˈnɔrðərli] *adv* : hacia el norte

northerly² *adj* : del norte ⟨a northerly wind : un viento del norte⟩

northern [ˈnɔrðərn] *adj* : norte, norteño, septentrional

Northerner [ˈnɔrðərnər] *n* : norteño *m*, -ña *f*

northern lights → aurora borealis

North Pole : Polo *m* Norte

North Star *n* : estrella *f* polar

northward [ˈnɔrθwərd] *adv & adj* : hacia el norte

northwest¹ [nɔrθˈwɛst] *adv* : hacia el noroeste

northwest² *adj* : del noroeste

northwest³ *n* : noroeste *m*

northwesterly¹ [nɔrθˈwɛstərli] *adv* : hacia el noroeste

northwesterly² *adj* : del noroeste

northwestern [nɔrθˈwɛstərn] *adj* : noroeste, del noroeste

Norwegian [nɔrˈwiːdʒən] *n* 1 : noruego *m*, -ga *f* 2 : noruego *m* (idioma) — **Norwegian** *adj*

nose¹ [ˈnoːz] *v* **nosed; nosing** *vt* 1 SMELL : olfatear 2 : empujar con el hocico ⟨the dog nosed open the bag : el perro abrió el saco con el hocico⟩ 3 EDGE, MOVE : mover poco a poco — *vi* 1 PRY : entrometerse, meter las narices 2 EDGE : avanzar poco a poco

nose² *n* 1 : nariz *f* (de una persona), hocico *m* (de un animal) ⟨to blow one's nose : sonarse las narices⟩ 2 SMELL : olfato *m*, sentido *m* del olfato 3 FRONT : parte *f* delantera, nariz *f* (de un avión), proa *f* (de un barco) 4 **to be right on the nose** : dar en el clavo 5 **to follow one's nose** : dejarse guiar por el instinto 6 **to look down one's nose at someone** : mirar a alguien por encima del hombro 7 **to pay through the nose** : pagar un ojo de la cara 8 **to poke/stick one's nose in** : meter las narices en 9 **to turn up one's nose at** : hacerle ascos a 10 **to win by a nose** : ganar por un pelo 11 **under one's nose** : delante de las narices

nosebleed [ˈnoːzˌbliːd] *n* : hemorragia *f* nasal

nosed [ˈnoːzd] *adj* : de nariz ⟨big-nosed : de nariz grande, narigón⟩

nosedive [ˈnoːzˌdaɪv] *n* 1 : descenso *m* en picada (de un avión) 2 : caída *f* súbita (de precios, etc.)

nose–dive ['noːz,daɪv] *vi* : descender en picada, caer en picada

nostalgia [nɑ'stældʒə, nə-] *n* : nostalgia *f*

nostalgic [nɑ'stældʒɪk, nə-] *adj* : nostálgico

nostril ['nɑstrəl] *n* : ventana *f* de la nariz

nostrum ['nɑstrəm] *n* : panacea *f*

nosy *or* **nosey** ['noːzi] *adj* **nosier; -est** : entrometido

not ['nɑt] *adv* **1** (*used to form a negative*) : no ⟨she is not tired : no está cansada⟩ ⟨not many came : no vinieron muchos⟩ ⟨not to say something would be wrong : no decir nada sería injusto⟩ ⟨not at all : en absoluto⟩ ⟨not a chance : de ninguna manera⟩ ⟨not only . . . but also . . . : no sólo . . . sino también . . .⟩ **2** (*used to replace a negative clause*) : no ⟨are we going or not? : ¿vamos a ir o no?⟩ ⟨of course not! : ¡claro que no!⟩ ⟨I hope/think not : espero/creo que no⟩ ⟨believe it or not : aunque no lo creas⟩ **3** : menos de ⟨not six inches away : a menos de seis pulgadas⟩ ⟨not all of us agree : no todos estamos de acuerdo⟩

notable¹ ['noːtəbəl] *adj* **1** NOTEWORTHY : notable, de notar **2** DISTINGUISHED, PROMINENT : distinguido, destacado

notable² *n* : persona *f* importante, personaje *m*

notably ['noːtəbli] *adv* : notablemente, particularmente

notarize ['noːtə,raɪz] *vt* **-rized; -rizing** : autenticar, autorizar

notary ['noːtəri] *or* **notary public** *n, pl* **notaries** *or* **notaries public** *or* **notary publics** : notario *m*, -ria *f*; escribano *m*, -na *f*

notation [noˈteɪʃən] *n* **1** NOTE : anotación *f*, nota *f* **2** : notación *f* ⟨musical notation : notación musical⟩

notch¹ ['nɑtʃ] *vt* : hacer una muesca en, cortar

notch² *n* : muesca *f*, corte *m*

note¹ ['noːt] *vt* **noted; noting 1** NOTICE : notar, observar, tomar nota de **2** RECORD : anotar, apuntar

note² *n* **1** : nota *f* (musical) **2** COMMENT : nota *f*, comentario *m* **3** ANNOTATION : nota *f*, apunte *m* ⟨to take notes : tomar notas/apuntes⟩ ⟨to compare notes : cambiar impresiones⟩ ⟨I'll make a note of it : lo apuntaré⟩ **4** LETTER : nota *f*, cartita *f* ⟨to leave a note : dejar una nota⟩ **5** PROMINENCE : prestigio *m* ⟨a musician of note : un músico destacado⟩ **6** ATTENTION : atención *f* ⟨to take note of : tomar nota de, prestar atención a⟩ **7** TOUCH : nota *f*, dejo *m* **8 on a high note** : con una nota de optimismo

notebook ['noːt,bʊk] *n* **1** : libreta *f*, cuaderno *m* **2** : notebook *m* (computadora)

noted ['noːtəd] *adj* EMINENT : renombrado, eminente, celebrado

notepad ['noːt,pæd] *n* : bloc *m* de notas

notepaper ['noːt,peɪpər] *n* : papel *m* de escribir

noteworthy ['noːt,wərði] *adj* : notable, de notar, de interés

nothing¹ ['nʌθɪŋ] *adv* **1** : de ninguna manera ⟨nothing daunted, we carried on : sin amilanarnos, seguimos adelante⟩ **2**

nothing like : no . . . en nada ⟨he's nothing like his brother : no se parece en nada a su hermano⟩

nothing² *n* **1** NOTHINGNESS : nada *f* **2** ZERO : cero *m* **3** : persona *f* de poca importancia, cero *m* **4** TRIFLE : nimiedad *f*

nothing³ *pron* : nada ⟨there's nothing better : no hay nada mejor⟩ ⟨there's nothing like . . . : no hay nada como . . .⟩ ⟨there's nothing to it : es facilísimo⟩ ⟨nothing else : nada más⟩ ⟨nothing but : solamente⟩ ⟨they're nothing but trouble : no traen más que problemas⟩ ⟨they mean nothing to me : ellos me son indiferentes⟩ ⟨I got it for nothing : me lo dieron gratis⟩ ⟨it was all for nothing : todo fue en vano⟩ ⟨are you hurt? it's nothing : ¿te hiciste daño? no es nada⟩ ⟨he's nothing if not polite : es muy cortés⟩

nothingness ['nʌθɪŋnəs] *n* **1** VOID : vacío *m*, nada *f* **2** NONEXISTENCE : inexistencia *f* **3** TRIFLE : nimiedad *f*

notice¹ ['noːtɪs] *vt* **-ticed; -ticing** : notar, observar, advertir, darse cuenta de

notice² *n* **1** NOTIFICATION : aviso *m*, notificación *f* ⟨at/on short notice, at a moment's notice : con poca antelación⟩ ⟨until further notice : hasta nuevo aviso⟩ ⟨without notice : sin previo aviso⟩ ⟨to give notice : presentar la renuncia⟩ **2** ATTENTION : atención *f* ⟨to take notice of : prestar atención a⟩ ⟨to make someone sit up and take notice : hacer que alguien preste atención⟩

noticeable ['noːtɪsəbəl] *adj* : evidente, perceptible — **noticeably** [-bli] *adv*

notification [,noːtəfə'keɪʃən] *n* : notificación *f*, aviso *m*

notify ['noːtə,faɪ] *vt* **-fied; -fying** : notificar, avisar

notion ['noːʃən] *n* **1** IDEA : idea *f*, noción *f* **2** WHIM : capricho *m*, antojo *m* **3 notions** *npl* : artículos *mpl* de mercería

notoriety [,noːtə'raɪəti] *n* : mala fama *f*, notoriedad *f*

notorious [noˈtoːriəs] *adj* : de mala fama, célebre, bien conocido

notwithstanding¹ [,nɑtwɪθ'stændɪŋ, -wɪð-] *adv* NEVERTHELESS : no obstante, sin embargo

notwithstanding² *conj* : a pesar de que

notwithstanding³ *prep* : a pesar de, no obstante

nougat ['nuːgət] *n* : turrón *m*

nought ['nɔt, 'nɑt] → **naught**

noun ['naʊn] *n* : nombre *m*, sustantivo *m*

nourish ['nərɪʃ] *vt* **1** FEED : alimentar, nutrir, sustentar **2** FOSTER : fomentar, alentar

nourishing ['nərɪʃɪŋ] *adj* : alimenticio, nutritivo

nourishment ['nərɪʃmənt] *n* : nutrición *f*, alimento *m*, sustento *m*

novel¹ ['nɑvəl] *adj* : original, novedoso

novel² *n* : novela *f*

novelist ['nɑvəlɪst] *n* : novelista *mf*

novelty ['nɑvəlti] *n, pl* **-ties** 1 : novedad *f* 2 **novelties** *npl* TRINKETS : baratijas *fpl*, chucherías *fpl*

November [no'vɛmbər] *n* : noviembre *m* ⟨they arrived on the 18th of November, they arrived on November 18th : llegaron el 18 de noviembre⟩

novena [no'vi:nə] *n* : novena *f*

novice ['nɑvɪs] *n* : novato *m*, -ta *f*; principiante *mf*; novicio *m*, -cia *f*

novocaine ['no:və,keɪn] *n* : novocaína *f*

now[1] ['naʊ] *adv* 1 PRESENTLY : ahora, ya, actualmente ⟨from now on : de ahora en adelante⟩ ⟨for now : por ahora⟩ ⟨for several months now : desde hace varios meses⟩ ⟨between now and . . ., from now until . . . : de aquí a . . .⟩ ⟨long before now : ya hace tiempo⟩ ⟨now or never : ahora o nunca⟩ 2 SOON : dentro de poco, pronto ⟨any day now : cualquier día de estos⟩ ⟨they'll be here any minute now : estarán por caer⟩ 3 : ahora, como están las cosas ⟨do you believe me now? : ¿ahora me crees?⟩ 4 IMMEDIATELY : ahora (mismo), inmediatamente ⟨do it right now! : ¡hazlo ahora mismo!⟩ 5 THEN : ya, entonces ⟨now they were ready : ya estaban listos⟩ 6 (*used to introduce a statement, a question, a command, or a transition*) ⟨now hear this! : ¡presten atención!⟩ ⟨now what do you think of that? : ¿qué piensas de eso?⟩ 7 **now and then** : de vez en cuando 8 **now, now** : vamos, vamos

now[2] *n* (*indicating the present time*) ⟨until now : hasta ahora⟩ ⟨by now : ya⟩ ⟨ten years from now : dentro de 10 años⟩

now[3] *conj* **now that** : ahora que, ya que

nowadays ['naʊə,deɪz] *adv* : hoy en día, actualmente, en la actualidad

nowhere[1] ['no:,ʰwer] *adv* 1 : en ninguna parte, a ningún lado ⟨nowhere to be found : en ninguna parte, por ningún lado⟩ ⟨you're going nowhere : no estás yendo a ningún lado, no estás yendo a ninguna parte⟩ 2 **nowhere near** : ni con mucho, nada cerca ⟨it's nowhere near here : no está nada cerca de aquí⟩ ⟨it's nowhere near finished : no está terminado ni mucho menos⟩

nowhere[2] *n* 1 : ninguna parte *f* 2 **out of nowhere** : de la nada

noxious ['nɑkʃəs] *adj* : nocivo, dañino, tóxico

nozzle ['nɑzəl] *n* : boca *f*, boquilla *f*

nth ['ɛnθ] *adj* 1 : enésimo ⟨for the nth time : por enésima vez⟩ 2 **to the nth degree** EXTREMELY : al máximo, sumamente

nuance ['nu:,ɑnts, 'nju:-] *n* : matiz *m*

nub ['nʌb] *n* 1 KNOB, LUMP : protuberancia *f*, nudo *m* 2 GIST : quid *m*, meollo *m*

nuclear ['nu:kliər, 'nju:-] *adj* : nuclear

nucleus ['nu:kliəs, 'nju:-] *n, pl* **-clei** [-kli,aɪ] : núcleo *m*

nude[1] ['nu:d, 'nju:d] *adj* **nuder; nudest** : desnudo

nude[2] *n* : desnudo *m*

nudge[1] ['nʌdʒ] *vt* **nudged; nudging** : darle con el codo (a alguien)

nudge[2] *n* : toque *m* que se da con el codo

nudism ['nu:,dɪzəm, 'nju:-] *n* : nudismo *m*

nudist ['nu:dɪst, 'nju:-] *n* : nudista *mf*

nudity ['nu:dəti, 'nju:-] *n* : desnudez *f*

nugget ['nʌgət] *n* : pepita *f*

nuisance ['nu:sənts, 'nju:-] *n* 1 BOTHER : fastidio *m*, molestia *f*, lata *f* 2 PEST : pesado *m*, -da *f fam*

nuke[1] ['nu:k, 'nju:k] *vt* **nuked; nuking** *fam* 1 : atacar con armas nucleares 2 : cocinar en el microondas

nuke[2] *n fam* : arma *m* nuclear

null ['nʌl] *adj* : nulo ⟨null and void : nulo y sin efecto⟩

nullify ['nʌlə,faɪ] *vt* **-fied; -fying** : invalidar, anular

nullity ['nələti] *n, pl* **-ties** : nulidad *f*

numb[1] ['nʌm] *vt* : entumecer, adormecer

numb[2] *adj* : entumecido, dormido ⟨numb with fear : paralizado de miedo⟩

number[1] ['nʌmbər] *vt* 1 COUNT, INCLUDE : contar, incluir 2 : numerar ⟨number the pages : numera las páginas⟩ 3 TOTAL : ascender a, sumar

number[2] *n* 1 : número *m* ⟨in round numbers : en números redondos⟩ 2 *or* **telephone number** *or* **phone number** : número *m* (de teléfono) 3 **a number of** : varios, unos pocos, unos cuantos 4 **any number of** : una cantidad de 5 **to look out for number one** : pensar ante todo en el propio interés

numberless ['nʌmbərləs] *adj* : innumerable, sin número

numbness ['nʌmnəs] *n* : entumecimiento *m*

numeral ['nu:mərəl, 'nju:-] *n* : número *m* ⟨Roman numeral : número romano⟩

numerator ['nu:mə,reɪtər, 'nju:-] *n* : numerador *m*

numeric [nʊ'mɛrɪk, nju-] *adj* : numérico

numerical [nʊ'mɛrɪkəl, nju-] *adj* : numérico — **numerically** [-kli] *adv*

numerous ['nu:mərəs, 'nju:-] *adj* : numeroso

numismatics [,nu:məz'mætɪks, ,nju:-] *n* : numismática *f*

numskull ['nʌm,skʌl] *n* : tonto *m*, -ta *f*; mentecato *m*, -ta *f*; zoquete *m fam*

nun ['nʌn] *n* : monja *f*

nuptial ['nʌpʃəl] *adj* : nupcial

nuptials ['nʌpʃəlz] *npl* WEDDING : nupcias *fpl*, boda *f*

nurse[1] ['nərs] *vt* **nursed; nursing** 1 SUCKLE : amamantar 2 : cuidar (de), atender ⟨to nurse the sick : cuidar a los enfermos⟩ ⟨to nurse a cold : curarse de un resfriado⟩

nurse[2] *n* 1 : enfermero *m*, -ra *f* 2 → **nursemaid**

nursemaid ['nərs,meɪd] *n* : niñera *f*

nursery ['nərsəri] *n, pl* **-eries** 1 *or* **day nursery** : guardería *f* 2 : vivero *m* (de plantas)

nursery rhyme *n* : canción *f* infantil

nursery school *n* : parvulario *m*

nursing ['nərsɪŋ] *n* : profesión *f* de enfermero

nursing home *n* : hogar *m* de ancianos, clínica *f* de reposo

nurture[1] ['nərtʃər] *vt* -tured; -turing 1 FEED, NOURISH : nutrir, alimentar 2 EDUCATE : criar, educar 3 FOSTER : alimentar, fomentar

nurture[2] *n* 1 UPBRINGING : crianza *f*, educación *f* 2 FOOD : alimento *m*

nut ['nʌt] *n* 1 : nuez *f* 2 : tuerca *f* ⟨nuts and bolts : tuercas y tornillos⟩ 3 LUNATIC : loco *m*, -ca *f*; chiflado *m*, -da *f fam* 4 ENTHUSIAST : fanático *m*, -ca *f*; entusiasta *mf*

nutcracker ['nʌt,krækər] *n* : cascanueces *m*

nuthatch ['nʌt,hætʃ] *n* : trepador *m*

nutmeg ['nʌt,mɛg] *n* : nuez *f* moscada

nutria ['nuːtriə, 'njuː-] *n* : nutria *f*

nutrient ['nuːtriənt, 'njuː-] *n* : nutriente *m*, alimento *m* nutritivo

nutriment ['nuːtrəmənt, 'njuː-] *n* : nutrimento *m*

nutrition [nʊ'trɪʃən, njʊ-] *n* : nutrición *f*

nutritional [nʊ'trɪʃənəl, njʊ-] *adj* : alimenticio

nutritionist [nʊ'trɪʃənɪst, njʊ-] *n* : nutricionista *mf*

nutritious [nʊ'trɪʃəs, njʊ-] *adj* : nutritivo, alimenticio

nuts ['nʌts] *adj* 1 FANATICAL : fanático 2 CRAZY : loco, chiflado *fam*

nutshell ['nʌt,ʃɛl] *n* 1 : cáscara *f* de nuez 2 **in a nutshell** : en pocas palabras

nutty ['nʌti] *adj* nuttier; -est : loco, chiflado *fam*

nuzzle ['nʌzəl] *v* -zled; -zling *vi* NESTLE : acurrucarse, arrimarse — *vt* : acariciar con el hocico

nylon ['nai,lan] *n* 1 : nilón *m* 2 **nylons** *npl* : medias *fpl* de nilón

nymph ['nɪmpf] *n* : ninfa *f*

O

o ['oː] *n*, *pl* **o's** *or* **os** ['oːz] 1 : decimoquinta letra del alfabeto inglés 2 ZERO : cero *m*

O ['oː] → **oh**

oaf ['oːf] *n* : zoquete *m*; bruto *m*, -ta *f*

oafish ['oːfɪʃ] *adj* : torpe, lerdo

oak ['oːk] *n*, *pl* **oaks** *or* **oak** : roble *m*

oaken ['oːkən] *adj* : de roble

oar ['or] *n* : remo *m*

oarlock ['or,lak] *n* : tolete *m*

oasis [oʊ'eɪsɪs] *n*, *pl* **oases** [-,siːz] : oasis *m*

oat ['oːt] *n* : avena *f*

oath ['oːθ] *n*, *pl* **oaths** ['oːðz, 'oːθs] 1 : juramento *m* ⟨to take an oath : prestar juramento⟩ 2 SWEARWORD : mala palabra *f*, palabrota *f*

oatmeal ['oːt,miːl] *n* : avena *f* ⟨instant oatmeal : avena instantánea⟩

obdurate ['abdʊrət, -djʊ-] *adj* : inflexible, firme, obstinado

obedience [o'biːdiənts] *n* : obediencia *f*

obedient [o'biːdiənt] *adj* : obediente — **obediently** *adv*

obelisk ['abə,lɪsk] *n* : obelisco *m*

obese [o'biːs] *adj* : obeso

obesity [o'biːsəti] *n* : obesidad *f*

obey [o'beɪ] *v* **obeyed; obeying** : obedecer ⟨to obey the law : cumplir la ley⟩

obfuscate ['abfə,skeɪt] *vt* -cated; -cating : ofuscar, confundir

obituary [ə'bɪtʃu,ɛri] *n*, *pl* -aries : obituario *m*, necrológica *f*

object[1] [əb'dʒɛkt] *vt* : objetar — *vi* : oponerse, poner reparos, hacer objeciones

object[2] ['abdʒɪkt] *n* 1 : objeto *m* 2 OBJECTIVE, PURPOSE : objetivo *m*, propósito *m* 3 : complemento *m* (en gramática)

objection [əb'dʒɛkʃən] *n* : objeción *f*

objectionable [əb'dʒɛkʃənəbəl] *adj* : ofensivo, indeseable — **objectionably** [-bli] *adv*

objective[1] [əb'dʒɛktɪv] *adj* 1 IMPARTIAL : objetivo, imparcial 2 : de complemento, directo (en gramática)

objective[2] *n* 1 : objetivo *m* 2 *or* **objective case** : acusativo *m*

objectively [əb'dʒɛktɪvli] *adv* : objetivamente

objectivity [,ab,dʒɛk'tɪvəti] *n*, *pl* -ties : objetividad *f*

objector [əb'dʒɛktər] *n* : objetor *m*, -tora *f* ⟨conscientious objector : objetor de conciencia⟩

obligate ['ablə,geɪt] *vt* -gated; -gating : obligar

obligation [,ablə'geɪʃən] *n* : obligación *f*

obligatory [ə'blɪgə,tori] *adj* : obligatorio

oblige [ə'blaɪdʒ] *vt* **obliged; obliging** 1 COMPEL : obligar 2 : hacerle un favor (a alguien), complacer ⟨to oblige a friend : hacerle un favor a un amigo⟩ 3 **to be much obliged** : estar muy agradecido

obliging [ə'blaɪdʒɪŋ] *adj* : servicial, complaciente — **obligingly** *adv*

oblique [o'bliːk] *adj* 1 SLANTING : oblicuo 2 INDIRECT : indirecto — **obliquely** *adv*

obliterate [ə'blɪtə,reɪt] *vt* -ated; -ating 1 ERASE : obliterar, borrar 2 DESTROY : destruir, eliminar

obliteration [ə,blɪtə'reɪʃən] *n* : obliteración *f*

oblivion [ə'blɪviən] *n* : olvido *m*

oblivious [ə'blɪviəs] *adj* : inconsciente — **obliviously** *adv*

oblong[1] ['a,blɔŋ] *adj* : oblongo

oblong[2] *n* : figura *f* oblonga, rectángulo *m*

obnoxious [ab'nakʃəs, əb-] *adj* : repugnante, odioso — **obnoxiously** *adv*

oboe ['oː,boː] *n* : oboe *m*

oboist ['o,boɪst] *n* : oboe *mf*

obscene [ab'siːn, əb-] *adj* : obsceno, indecente — **obscenely** *adv*

obscenity [əb'sɛnəti, əb-] *n, pl* **-ties** : obscenidad *f*

obscure¹ [ab'skjur, əb-] *vt* **-scured; -scuring 1** CLOUD, DIM : oscurecer, nublar **2** HIDE : ocultar

obscure² *adj* **1** DIM : oscuro **2** REMOTE, SECLUDED : recóndito **3** VAGUE : oscuro, confuso, vago **4** UNKNOWN : desconocido ⟨an obscure poet : un poeta desconocido⟩ — **obscurely** *adv*

obscurity [ab'skjurəti, əb-] *n, pl* **-ties** : oscuridad *f*

obsequious [əb'si:kwiəs] *adj* : servil, excesivamente atento

observable [əb'zərvəbəl] *adj* : observable, perceptible

observance [əb'zərvən̂ts] *n* **1** FULFILLMENT : observancia *f*, cumplimiento *m* **2** PRACTICE : práctica *f*

observant [əb'zərvənt] *adj* : observador

observation [ˌɑbsərˈveɪʃən, -zər-] *n* : observación *f*

observatory [əb'zərvəˌtori] *n, pl* **-ries** : observatorio *m*

observe [əb'zərv] *v* **-served; -serving** *vt* **1** OBEY : observar, obedecer **2** CELEBRATE : celebrar, guardar (una práctica religiosa) **3** WATCH : observar, mirar **4** REMARK : observar, comentar — *vi* LOOK : mirar

observer [əb'zərvər] *n* : observador *m*, -dora *f*

obsess [əb'sɛs] *vt* : obsesionar

obsession [ab'sɛʃən, əb-] *n* : obsesión *f*

obsessive [ab'sɛsɪv, əb-] *adj* : obsesivo — **obsessively** *adv*

obsolescence [ˌɑbsəˈlɛsən̂ts] *n* : obsolescencia *f*

obsolescent [ˌɑbsəˈlɛsənt] *adj* : obsolescente ⟨to become obsolescent : caer en desuso⟩

obsolete [ˌɑbsəˈli:t, ˈɑbsəˌ-] *adj* : obsoleto, anticuado

obstacle [ˈɑbstɪkəl] *n* : obstáculo *m*, impedimento *m*

obstetric [əb'stɛtrɪk] *or* **obstetrical** [-trɪkəl] *adj* : obstétrico

obstetrician [ˌɑbstəˈtrɪʃən] *n* : obstetra *mf*; tocólogo *m*, -ga *f*

obstetrics [əb'stɛtrɪks] *ns & pl* : obstetricia *f*, tocología *f*

obstinacy [ˈɑbstənəsi] *n, pl* **-cies** : obstinación *f*, terquedad *f*

obstinate [ˈɑbstənət] *adj* : obstinado, terco — **obstinately** *adv*

obstreperous [əb'strɛpərəs] *adj* **1** CLAMOROUS : ruidoso, clamoroso **2** UNRULY : rebelde, indisciplinado

obstruct [əb'strʌkt] *vt* : obstruir, bloquear

obstruction [əb'strʌkʃən] *n* : obstrucción *f*, bloqueo *m*

obstructive [əb'strʌktɪv] *adj* : obstructor

obtain [əb'teɪn] *vt* : obtener, conseguir — *vi* PREVAIL : imperar, prevalecer

obtainable [əb'teɪnəbəl] *adj* : obtenible, asequible

obtrusive [əb'truːsɪv] *adj* **1** IMPERTINENT, MEDDLESOME : impertinente, entrometido **2** PROTRUDING : prominente

obtuse [ɑb'tuːs, əb-, -ˈtjuːs] *adj* : obtuso, torpe

obtuse angle *n* : ángulo obtuso

obvious [ˈɑbviəs] *adj* : obvio, evidente, manifiesto

obviously [ˈɑbviəsli] *adv* **1** CLEARLY : obviamente, evidentemente **2** OF COURSE : claro, por supuesto

occasion¹ [əˈkeɪʒən] *vt* : ocasionar, causar

occasion² *n* **1** OPPORTUNITY : oportunidad *f*, ocasión *f* **2** CAUSE : motivo *m*, razón *f* **3** INSTANCE : ocasión *f* **4** EVENT : ocasión *f*, acontecimiento *m* **5** on ~ : de vez en cuando, ocasionalmente

occasional [əˈkeɪʒənəl] *adj* : ocasional

occasionally [əˈkeɪʒənəli] *adv* : de vez en cuando, ocasionalmente

occult¹ [əˈkʌlt, ˈɑˌkʌlt] *adj* **1** HIDDEN, SECRET : oculto, secreto **2** ARCANE : arcano, esotérico

occult² *n* **the occult** : las ciencias ocultas

occupancy [ˈɑkjəpən̂tsi] *n, pl* **-cies** : ocupación *f*, habitación *f*

occupant [ˈɑkjəpənt] *n* : ocupante *mf*

occupation [ˌɑkjəˈpeɪʃən] *n* : ocupación *f*, profesión *f*, oficio *m*

occupational [ˌɑkjəˈpeɪʃənəl] *adj* : ocupacional

occupier [ˈɑkjəˌpaɪər] *n* : ocupante *mf*

occupy [ˈɑkjəˌpaɪ] *vt* **-pied; -pying** : ocupar

occur [əˈkər] *vi* **occurred; occurring 1** EXIST : encontrarse, existir **2** HAPPEN : ocurrir, acontecer, suceder, tener lugar **3** : ocurrirse ⟨it occurred to him that . . . : se le ocurrió que . . .⟩

occurrence [əˈkərən̂ts] *n* : acontecimiento *m*, suceso *m*, ocurrencia *f*

ocean [ˈoːʃən] *n* : océano *m*

oceanic [ˌoːʃiˈænɪk] *adj* : oceánico

oceanography [ˌoːʃəˈnɑgrəfi] *n* : oceanografía *f* — **oceanographic** *adj*

ocelot [ˈɑsəˌlɑt, ˈoː-] *n* : ocelote *m*

ocher *or* **ochre** [ˈoːkər] *n* : ocre *m*

o'clock [əˈklɑk] *adv* (*used in telling time*) ⟨it's ten o'clock : son las diez⟩ ⟨at six o'clock : a las seis⟩

octagon [ˈɑktəˌgɑn] *n* : octágono *m*

octagonal [ɑk'tægənəl] *adj* : octagonal

octave [ˈɑktɪv] *n* : octava *f*

October [ɑk'toːbər] *n* : octubre *m* ⟨they arrived on the 13th of October, they arrived on October 13th : llegaron el 13 de octubre⟩

octopus [ˈɑktəˌpus, -pəs] *n, pl* **-puses** *or* **-pi** [-ˌpaɪ] : pulpo *m*

ocular [ˈɑkjələr] *adj* : ocular

oculist [ˈɑkjəlɪst] *n* **1** OPHTHALMOLOGIST : oftalmólogo *m*, -ga *f*; oculista *mf* **2** OPTOMETRIST : optometrista *mf*

odd [ˈɑd] *adj* **1** : sin pareja, suelto ⟨an odd sock : un calcetín sin pareja⟩ **2** UNEVEN : impar ⟨odd numbers : números impares⟩ **3** : y pico, y tantos ⟨forty-odd years ago : hace cuarenta y pico años⟩ **4** : alguno, uno que otro ⟨odd jobs : algunos trabajos⟩ **5** STRANGE : extraño, raro

oddball [ˈɑdˌbɔl] *n* : excéntrico *m*, -ca *f*; persona *f* rara

oddity ['ɑdəʈi] *n, pl* **-ties** : rareza *f*, cosa *f* rara

oddly ['ɑdli] *adv* : de manera extraña

oddness ['ɑdnəs] *n* : rareza *f*, excentricidad *f*

odds ['ɑdz] *npl* **1** CHANCES : probabilidades *fpl* ⟨against all odds : contra viento y marea⟩ **2** : puntos *mpl* de ventaja (de una apuesta) **3 to be at odds** : estar en desacuerdo

odds and ends *npl* : costillas *fpl*, cosas *fpl* sueltas, cachivaches *mpl*

ode ['o:d] *n* : oda *f*

odious ['o:diəs] *adj* : odioso — **odiously** *adv*

odometer [o'dɑmətər] *n* : cuentakilómetros *m*, odómetro *m*

odor ['o:dər] *n* : olor *m*

odorless ['o:dərləs] *adj* : inodoro, sin olor

odyssey ['ɑdəsi] *n, pl* **-seys** : odisea *f*

o'er ['or] → **over**

of ['ʌv, 'əv] *prep* **1** FROM : de ⟨a man of the city : un hombre de la ciudad⟩ **2** (*indicating a quality or characteristic*) : de ⟨a woman of great ability : una mujer de gran capacidad⟩ ⟨a boy of twelve : un niño de doce años⟩ ⟨her husband of 30 years : su marido, con quien lleva 30 años de casada⟩ **3** (*describing behavior*) : de parte de (alguien) ⟨that was very nice of you : fue muy amable de tu parte⟩ **4** (*indicating cause*) : de ⟨he died of the flu : murió de la gripe⟩ **5** BY : de ⟨the works of Shakespeare : las obras de Shakespeare⟩ **6** (*indicating contents, material, or quantity*) : de ⟨a house of wood : una casa de madera⟩ ⟨a glass of water : un vaso de agua⟩ ⟨thousands of people : miles de personas⟩ **7** (*indicating belonging or connection*) : de ⟨the front of the house : el frente de la casa⟩ ⟨a friend of mine : un amigo mío⟩ ⟨the President of the United States : el presidente de los Estados Unidos⟩ ⟨the best of intentions : las mejores intenciones⟩ **8** (*indicating belonging to a group*) : de ⟨one of my friends : uno de mis amigos⟩ ⟨the four of us went : fuimos los cuatro⟩ ⟨two of which : dos de los/las cuales⟩ **9** ABOUT : sobre, de ⟨tales of the West : los cuentos del Oeste⟩ **10** (*indicating a particular example*) : de ⟨the city of Caracas : la ciudad de Caracas⟩ **11** FOR : por, a ⟨love of country : amor por la patria⟩ **12** (*indicating time or date*) ⟨five minutes of ten : las diez menos cinco⟩ ⟨the eighth of April : el ocho de abril⟩

off¹ ['ɔf] *adv* **1** (*indicating change of position or state*) ⟨to march off : marcharse⟩ ⟨he dozed off : se puso a dormir⟩ **2** (*indicating distance in space or time*) ⟨some miles off : a varias millas⟩ ⟨the holiday is three weeks off : faltan tres semanas para la fiesta⟩ **3** (*indicating removal*) ⟨the knob came off : se le cayó el pomo⟩ ⟨he took off his coat : se quitó el abrigo⟩ **4** (*indicating termination*) ⟨shut the television off : apaga la televisión⟩ ⟨to finish off : terminar, acabar⟩ **5** (*indicating suspension of work*) ⟨to take a day off : to-

marse un día de descanso⟩ **6 off and on** : de vez en cuando

off² *adj* **1** FARTHER : más remoto, distante ⟨the off side of the building : el lado distante del edificio⟩ **2** STARTED : empezado ⟨to be off on a spree : irse de juerga⟩ **3** OUT : apagado ⟨the light is off : la luz está apagada⟩ **4** CANCELED : cancelado, suspendido **5** INCORRECT : erróneo, incorrecto **6** REMOTE : remoto, lejano ⟨an off chance : una posibilidad remota⟩ **7** FREE : libre ⟨I'm off today : hoy estoy libre⟩ **8** SPOILED : estropeado, cortado **9 to be well off** : vivir con desahogo, tener bastante dinero

off³ *prep* **1** (*indicating physical separation*) : de ⟨she took it off the table : lo tomó de la mesa⟩ ⟨a shop off the main street : una tienda al lado de la calle principal⟩ **2** : a la costa de, a expensas de ⟨he lives off his sister : vive a expensas de su hermana⟩ **3** (*indicating the suspension of an activity*) ⟨to be off duty : estar libre⟩ ⟨he's off liquor : ha dejado el alcohol⟩ **4** BELOW : por debajo de ⟨he's off his game : está por debajo de su juego normal⟩

offal ['ɔfəl] *n* **1** RUBBISH, WASTE : desechos *mpl*, desperdicios *mpl* **2** VISCERA : vísceras *fpl*, asaduras *fpl*

off-balance ['ɔf'bæləns] *adj* : desequilibrado

off-color ['ɔf'kʌlər] *adj* : subido de tono, pícaro, picante

offend [ə'fɛnd] *vt* **1** VIOLATE : violar, atentar contra **2** HURT : ofender ⟨to be easily offended : ser muy susceptible⟩

offender [ə'fɛndər] *n* : delincuente *mf*; infractor *m*, -tora *f*

offense *or* **offence** [ə'fɛns, 'ɔ,fɛns] *n* **1** INSULT : ofensa *f*, injuria *f*, agravio *m* ⟨to take offense : ofenderse⟩ **2** ASSAULT : ataque *m* **3** ofensiva *f* (en deportes) **4** CRIME, INFRACTION : infracción *f*, delito *m*

offensive¹ [ə'fɛntsɪv, 'ɔ,fɛnt-] *adj* : ofensivo — **offensively** *adv*

offensive² *n* : ofensiva *f*

offer¹ ['ɔfər] *vt* **1** : ofrecer ⟨they offered him the job : le ofrecieron el puesto⟩ **2** PROPOSE : proponer, sugerir **3** SHOW : ofrecer, mostrar ⟨to offer resistance : ofrecer resistencia⟩

offer² *n* : oferta *f*, ofrecimiento *m*, propuesta *f*

offering ['ɔfərɪŋ] *n* : ofrenda *f*

offhand¹ ['ɔf'hænd] *adv* : sin preparación, sin pensarlo

offhand² *adj* **1** IMPROMPTU : improvisado **2** ABRUPT : brusco

office ['ɔfəs] *n* **1** : cargo *m* ⟨to run for office : presentarse como candidato⟩ **2** : oficina *f*, despacho *m*, gabinete *m* (en la casa)

officeholder ['ɔfəs,ho:ldər] *n* : titular *mf*

office hours *n* : horas *fpl* de oficina

officer ['ɔfəsər] *n* **1** → **police officer 2** OFFICIAL : oficial *mf*; funcionario *m*, -ria *f*; director *m*, -tora *f* (en una empresa) **3** COMMISSIONED OFFICER : oficial *mf*

office worker *n* : oficinista *mf*

official¹ [ə'fɪʃəl] *adj* : oficial — **officially** *adv*

official² *n* : funcionario *m*, -ria *f*; oficial *mf*

officiate [ə'fɪʃiˌeɪt] *v* **-ated; -ating** *vi* **1** : arbitrar (en deportes) **2 to officiate at** : oficiar, celebrar — *vt* : arbitrar

officious [ə'fɪʃəs] *adj* : oficioso

offing ['ɔfɪŋ] *n* **in the offing** : en perspectiva

off-key ['ɔf'ki:] *adj* : desafinado

off-line ['ɔf'laɪn] *adj* : fuera de línea

off-peak ['ɔf'pi:k] *adj* : fuera de las horas pico

off-putting ['ɔfˌpʊtɪŋ] *adj* : desagradable, repelente

offset ['ɔfˌsɛt] *vt* **-set; -setting** : compensar

offshoot ['ɔfˌʃu:t] *n* **1** OUTGROWTH : producto *m*, resultado *m* **2** BRANCH, SHOOT : retoño *m*, rama *f*, vástago *m* (de una planta)

offshore¹ ['ɔf'ʃor] *adv* : a una distancia de la costa

offshore² *adj* **1** : de (la) tierra ⟨an offshore wind : un viento que sopla de tierra⟩ **2** : (de) costa afuera, cercano a la costa ⟨an offshore island : una isla costera⟩

offside ['ɔf'saɪd] *adj* : fuera de juego (en deportes)

offspring ['ɔfˌsprɪŋ] *ns* & *pl* **1** YOUNG : crías *fpl* (de los animales) **2** PROGENY : prole *f*, progenie *f*

off-white ['ɔf'hwaɪt] *adj* : blancuzco

often ['ɔfən, 'ɔftən] *adv* : muchas veces, a menudo, seguido

oftentimes ['ɔfənˌtaɪmz, 'ɔftən-] *or* **ofttimes** ['ɔft,taɪmz] → **often**

ogle ['oːgəl] *vt* **ogled; ogling** : comerse con los ojos, quedarse mirando a

ogre ['oːgər] *n* : ogro *m*

oh ['oː] *interj* : ¡oh!, ¡ah!, ¡ay! ⟨oh, of course : ah, por supuesto⟩ ⟨oh no! : ¡ay no!⟩ ⟨oh really? : ¿de veras?⟩

ohm ['oːm] *n* : ohm *m*, ohmio *m*

oil¹ ['ɔɪl] *vt* : lubricar, engrasar, aceitar

oil² *n* **1** : aceite *m* **2** PETROLEUM : petróleo *m* **3** *or* **oil painting** : óleo *m*, pintura *f* al óleo **4** *or* **oil paint(s)** : óleo *m*

oilcan ['ɔɪlˌkæn] *n* : aceitera *f*

oilcloth ['ɔɪlˌklɔθ] *n* : hule *m*

oiliness ['ɔɪlinəs] *n* : lo aceitoso

oil rig → **rig²**

oilskin ['ɔɪlˌskɪn] *n* **1** : hule *m* **2 oilskins** *npl* : impermeable *m*

oil slick *n* : marea *f* negra

oil well *n* : pozo *m* petrolero

oily ['ɔɪli] *adj* **oilier; -est** : aceitoso, grasiento, grasoso ⟨oily fingers : dedos grasientos⟩

ointment ['ɔɪntmənt] *n* : ungüento *m*, pomada *f*

OK¹ ['oː'keɪ] *vt* OK'd *or* **OK'd** *or* **okayed** [ˌoː'keɪd]; **OK'ing** *or* **okaying** APPROVE, AUTHORIZE : dar el visto bueno a, autorizar, aprobar

OK² *or* **okay** [ˌoː'keɪ] *adv* **1** WELL : bien **2** YES : sí, por supuesto

OK³ *adj* : bien ⟨he's OK : está bien⟩ ⟨it's OK with me : estoy de acuerdo⟩

OK⁴ *n* : autorización *f*, visto *m* bueno

okra ['oːkrə, *South also* -kri] *n* : quingombó *m*

old ['oːld] *adj* **1** ANCIENT : antiguo ⟨old civilizations : antiguas civilizaciones⟩ **2** FAMILIAR : viejo ⟨old friends : viejos amigos⟩ ⟨the same old story : la misma historia de siempre⟩ **3** (*indicating a certain age*) ⟨how old is he? : ¿cuántos años tiene?⟩ ⟨he's ten years old : tiene diez años (de edad)⟩ ⟨he's a year older than I am : es un año mayor que yo⟩ ⟨she's my older sister : es mi hermana mayor⟩ ⟨our oldest daughter : nuestra hija mayor⟩ **4** AGED : viejo, anciano ⟨an old woman : una anciana⟩ **5** FORMER : antiguo ⟨her old neighborhood : su antiguo barrio⟩ **6** WORN-OUT : viejo, gastado **7 any old** *fam* : cualquier

old² *n* **1 the old** : los viejos, los ancianos **2 in the days of old** : antaño, en los tiempos antiguos

old age *n* : vejez *f*

olden ['oːldən] *adj* : de antaño, de antigüedad

old-fashioned ['oːld'fæʃənd] *adj* : anticuado, pasado de moda

old maid *n offensive* SPINSTER : solterona *f*

Old Testament *n* : Antiguo Testamento *m*

old-time ['oːld'taɪm] *adj* : antiguo

old-timer ['oːld'taɪmər] *n* **1** VETERAN : veterano *m*, -na *f* **2** *or* **oldster** : anciano *m*, -na *f*

old-world ['oːld'wərld] *adj* : pintoresco (de antaño)

oleander ['oːliˌændər] *n* : adelfa *f*

oleomargarine [ˌoːlio'mardʒərən] → **margarine**

olfactory [ɑl'fæktəri, ol-] *adj* : olfativo

olive ['ɑlɪv, -ləv] *n* **1** : aceituna *f*, oliva *f* (fruta) **2** : olivo *m* (árbol) **3** *or* **olive green** : color *m* aceituna, verde *m* oliva

olive oil *n* : aceite *m* de oliva

Olmec ['ɑlˌmɛk, 'oːl-] *n* : olmeca *mf* — **Olmec** *adj*

Olympiad [ə'lɪmpiˌæd, oː-] *n* : olimpiada *f*

Olympic [ə'lɪmpɪk, oː-] *adj* : olímpico

Olympic Games *npl* : Juegos *mpl* Olímpicos

Olympics [ə'lɪmpɪks, oː-] *npl* : olimpiadas *fpl*

Omani [oː'mɑni, -'mæ-] *n* : omaní *mf* — **Omani** *adj*

ombudsman ['ɑmˌbudzmən, ɑm-'budz-] *n, pl* **-men** [-mən, -ˌmɛn] : ombudsman *m*

omelet *or* **omelette** ['ɑmlət, 'ɑmə-] *n* : omelette *mf*, tortilla *f* (de huevo)

omen ['oːmən] *n* : presagio *m*, augurio *m*, agüero *m*

ominous ['ɑmənəs] *adj* : ominoso, agorero, de mal agüero

ominously ['ɑmənəsli] *adv* : de manera amenazadora

omission [oː'mɪʃən] *n* : omisión *f*

omit [o'mɪt] *vt* **omitted; omitting 1** LEAVE OUT : omitir, excluir **2** NEGLECT : omitir ⟨they omitted to tell us : omitieron decírnoslo⟩

omnipotence [am'nɪpətənts] *n* : omnipotencia *f* — **omnipotent** [am-'nɪpətənt] *adj*

omnipresence [ˌamnɪ'prezənts] *n* : omnipresencia *f*

omnipresent [ˌamnɪ'prezənt] *adj* : omnipresente

omniscient [am'nɪʃənt] *adj* : omnisciente

omnivorous [am'nɪvərəs] *adj* **1** : omnívoro **2** AVID : ávido, voraz

on¹ [ɑn, ɔn] *adv* **1** (*indicating contact with a surface*) ⟨put the top on : pon la tapa⟩ ⟨he has a hat on : lleva un sombrero puesto⟩ **2** (*indicating forward movement*) ⟨from that moment on : a partir de ese momento⟩ ⟨farther on : más adelante⟩ **3** (*indicating operation or an operating position*) ⟨turn the light on : prende la luz⟩

on² *adj* **1** (*being in operation*) ⟨the radio is on : el radio está prendido⟩ **2** (*taking place*) ⟨the game is on : el juego ha comenzado⟩ **3 to be on to** : estar enterado de

on³ *prep* **1** (*indicating location or position*) : en, sobre, encima de ⟨on the table : en/ sobre la mesa, encima de la mesa⟩ ⟨shadows on the wall : sombras en la pared⟩ ⟨on foot/horseback : a pie/caballo⟩ ⟨on one's hands and knees : a gatas⟩ ⟨she kissed him on the cheek : lo besó en la mejilla⟩ ⟨on page 102 : en la página 102⟩ ⟨on a Web site : en un sitio web⟩ **2** BY, BESIDE : junto a, al lado de ⟨a house on the lake : una casa junto al lago⟩ **3** AT, TO : a ⟨it's on the right : está a la derecha⟩ **4** ABOARD, IN : en, a ⟨on the plane : en el avión⟩ ⟨he got on the train : subió al tren⟩ **5** (*indicating time*) ⟨she worked on Saturdays : trabajaba los sábados⟩ ⟨every hour on the hour : cada hora en punto⟩ **6** (*indicating means or agency*) : por ⟨he cut himself on a tin can : se cortó con una lata⟩ ⟨to talk on the telephone : hablar por teléfono⟩ **7** (*indicating source*) : de ⟨to live on a salary : vivir de un sueldo⟩ ⟨it runs on diesel : funciona con diesel⟩ ⟨based on fact : basado en hechos reales⟩ **8** ACCORDING TO : de, según ⟨on good authority : de buena fuente⟩ **9** (*indicating a state or process*) : en ⟨on fire : en llamas⟩ ⟨on the increase : en aumento⟩ ⟨on sale : rebajado⟩ **10** (*indicating connection or membership*) : en ⟨on a committee : en una comisión⟩ **11** (*indicating an activity*) ⟨on vacation : de vacaciones⟩ ⟨on a diet : a dieta⟩ **12** ABOUT, CONCERNING : sobre ⟨a book on insects : un libro sobre insectos⟩ ⟨reflect on that : reflexiona sobre eso⟩ **13** : tomando ⟨to be on medication : tomar medicamentos⟩ ⟨to be on drugs : drogarse⟩ **14 on it** *fam* ⟨don't worry—I'm on it : no te preocupes, yo me encargo de eso⟩ **15 on one** : encima ⟨I don't have it on me : no

lo llevo/tengo encima⟩ **16 on someone** : por cuenta de alguien ⟨drinks are on the house : invita la casa⟩

once¹ ['wʌnts] *adv* **1** : una vez ⟨once a month : una vez al mes⟩ ⟨once and for all : de una vez por todas⟩ ⟨once in a while : de vez en cuando⟩ ⟨once or twice : alguna que otra vez⟩ ⟨for once : por una vez⟩ **2** EVER : alguna vez **3** FORMERLY : antes, anteriormente

once² *adj* FORMER : antiguo

once³ *n* **1** : una vez **2 (all) at ~** : de una vez, de un golpe, de un tirón **3 at ~** : SIMULTANEOUSLY : al mismo tiempo, simultáneamente **4 at ~** : IMMEDIATELY : inmediatamente, en seguida

once⁴ *conj* : una vez que, tan pronto como

once–over [ˌwʌnts'o:vər, 'wʌnts̩-] *n* **to give someone the once–over** : echarle un vistazo a alguien

oncoming ['ɑn̩kʌmɪŋ, 'ɔn-] *adj* : que viene

one¹ ['wʌn] *adj* **1** (*being a single unit*) : un, una ⟨he only wants one apple : sólo quiere una manzana⟩ **2** (*being a particular one*) : un, una ⟨he arrived early one morning : llegó temprano una mañana⟩ **3** (*being the same*) : mismo, misma ⟨they're all members of one team : todos son miembros del mismo equipo⟩ ⟨one and the same thing : la misma cosa⟩ **4** SOME : alguno, alguna; un, una ⟨I'll see you again one day : algún día te veré otra vez⟩ ⟨at one time or another : en una u otra ocasión⟩

one² *n* **1** : uno *m* (número) **2** (*indicating the first of a set or series*) ⟨from day one : desde el primer momento⟩ **3** (*indicating a single person or thing*) ⟨the one (girl) on the right : la de la derecha⟩ ⟨he has the one but needs the other : tiene uno pero necesita el otro⟩

one³ *pron* **1** : uno ⟨it's one (o'clock) : es la una⟩ ⟨one of his friends : una de sus amigas⟩ ⟨one never knows : uno nunca sabe, nunca se sabe⟩ ⟨to cut one's finger : cortarse el dedo⟩ **2 one and all** : todos, todo el mundo **3 one another** : el uno al otro, se ⟨they loved one another : se amaban⟩ **4 that one** : aquél, aquella **5 which one?** : ¿cuál?

one–handed [ˌwʌn'hændəd] *adj* & *adv* : con una sola mano

one–on–one [wʌnɔn'wʌn, -ɑn-] *adj* : uno a uno — **one–on–one** *adv*

onerous ['ɑnərəs, 'o:nə-] *adj* : oneroso, gravoso

oneself [ˌwʌn'sɛlf] *pron* **1** (*used reflexively or for emphasis*) : se, sí mismo, uno mismo ⟨to control oneself : controlarse⟩ ⟨to talk to oneself : hablarse a sí mismo⟩ ⟨to do it oneself : hacérselo uno mismo⟩ **2 by ~** : solo

one–sided ['wʌn'saɪdəd] *adj* **1** : de un solo lado **2** LOPSIDED : asimétrico **3** BIASED : parcial, tendencioso **4** UNILATERAL : unilateral

onetime ['wʌn̩taɪm] *adj* FORMER : antiguo

one—way [ˈwʌnˈweɪ] *adj* **1** : de sentido único, de una sola dirección ⟨a one-way street : una calle de sentido único⟩ **2** : de ida, sencillo ⟨a one-way ticket : un boleto de ida⟩

one—way mirror *n* : espejo *m* polarizado

ongoing [ˈɑnˌgoːɪŋ] *adj* **1** CONTINUING : en curso, corriente **2** DEVELOPING : en desarrollo

onion [ˈʌnjən] *n* : cebolla *f*

online [ˈɔnˌlaɪn, ˈɑn-] *adj* : en línea

onlooker [ˈɔnˌlʊkər, ˈɑn-] *n* : espectador *m*, -dora *f*, circunstante *mf*

only¹ [ˈoːnli] *adv* **1** MERELY : sólo, solamente, nomás ⟨for only two dollars : por tan sólo dos dólares⟩ ⟨only once : sólo una vez, no más de una vez⟩ ⟨I only did it to help : lo hice por ayudar nomás⟩ **2** SOLELY : únicamente, sólo, solamente ⟨only he knows it : solamente él lo sabe⟩ ⟨only because you asked me to : sólo porque tú me lo pediste⟩ **3** ASSUMING : sólo, solamente ⟨I'll go only if he goes with me : iré sólo si él me acompaña⟩ **4** (*indicating a result*) ⟨it will only cause him problems : no hará más que crearle problemas⟩ **5** (*used for emphasis*) ⟨I only hope it will work! : ¡espero que resulte!⟩ **6** (*indicating that something was recent*) ⟨it seems like only yesterday : parece que fue ayer⟩ **7 if only** : ojalá, por lo menos ⟨if only it were true! : ¡ojalá sea cierto!⟩ ⟨if he could only dance : si por lo menos pudiera bailar⟩ **8 not only . . . but also . . .** : no sólo . . . sino también **9 only just** BARELY : apenas ⟨we've only just begun : acabamos de empezar⟩ ⟨I only just missed the flight : perdí el vuelo por un pelo⟩

only² *adj* : único ⟨an only child : un hijo único⟩ ⟨the only chance : la única oportunidad⟩

only³ *conj* BUT : pero ⟨I would go, only I'm sick : iría, pero estoy enfermo⟩

onset [ˈɑnˌsɛt] *n* : comienzo *m*, llegada *f*

onslaught [ˈɑnˌslɔt, ˈɔn-] *n* : arremetida *f*, embestida *f*, embate *m*

onto [ˈɑnˌtuː, ˈɔn-] *prep* **1** : sobre **2** (*indicating knowledge or awareness*) ⟨the police are onto them : la policía anda tras ellos⟩ ⟨I think you're onto something : creo que has dado con algo interesante/importante⟩ ⟨the scientists were onto something big : los científicos estaban a punto de descubrir algo importante⟩

onus [ˈoːnəs] *n* : responsabilidad *f*, carga *f*

onward¹ [ˈɑnwərd, ˈɔn-] *or* **onwards** *adv* FORWARD : adelante, hacia adelante

onward² *adj* : hacia adelante

onyx [ˈɑnɪks] *n* : ónix *m*

oops [ˈʊps, ˈwʊps] *interj* : ¡huy! ⟨oops! I goofed : ¡huy! me equivoqué⟩

ooze¹ [ˈuːz] *v* **oozed; oozing** *vi* : rezumar — *vt* **1** : rezumar **2** EXUDE : irradiar, rebosar ⟨to ooze confidence : irradiar confianza⟩

ooze² *n* SLIME : cieno *m*, limo *m*

opacity [oˈpæsəti] *n, pl* **-ties** : opacidad *f*

opal [ˈoːpəl] *n* : ópalo *m*

opaque [oˈpeɪk] *adj* **1** : opaco **2** UN-CLEAR : poco claro

open¹ [ˈoːpən] *vt* **1** : abrir ⟨open the door : abre la puerta⟩ ⟨open your books : abran sus libros⟩ **2** UNCOVER : abrir, destapar (una botella, etc.) **3** UNFOLD : abrir, desplegar **4** CLEAR : abrir (un camino, etc.) **5** INAUGURATE : abrir (una tienda), inaugurar (una exposición, etc.) **6** INITIATE : iniciar, entablar, abrir ⟨to open the meeting : abrir la sesión⟩ ⟨to open a discussion : entablar un debate⟩ ⟨to open a document : abrir un documento⟩ **7 to open fire (on)** : abrir fuego (sobre) **8 to open up** : abrir — *vi* **1** : abrirse **2** BEGIN : empezar, comenzar **3 to open onto** : dar a **4 to open up** : abrirse **5 to open up** : abrir (dícese de una empresa, etc.)

open² *adj* **1** : abierto ⟨an open window : una ventana abierta⟩ **2** FRANK : abierto, franco, directo ⟨to be open with : ser sincero/franco con⟩ **3** UNCOV-ERED : abierto, descubierto ⟨an open box : una caja abierta⟩ **4** EXTENDED : abierto, extendido ⟨with open arms : con los brazos abiertos⟩ **5** UNRE-STRICTED : libre, abierto ⟨in the open air : al aire libre⟩ ⟨open to the public : abierto al público⟩ ⟨open admission : entrada libre⟩ ⟨an open letter : una carta abierta⟩ **6** : abierto (dícese de una tienda, etc.) **7** UNDECIDED : pendiente, por decidir, sin resolver ⟨an open question : una cuestión pendiente⟩ **8** AVAIL-ABLE : vacante, libre ⟨the job is open : el puesto está vacante⟩ **9** EXPOSED, VUL-NERABLE : expuesto, vulnerable ⟨he has left himself open to criticism : se ha expuesto a las críticas⟩ ⟨to be open to abuse : prestarse al abuso⟩ ⟨to be open to doubt/question : ser discutible⟩

open³ *n* **in the open 1** OUTDOORS : al aire libre **2** KNOWN : conocido, sacado a la luz

open—air [ˈoːpənˌær] *adj* OUTDOOR : al aire libre

open—and—shut [ˈoːpənəndˈʃʌt] *adj* : claro, evidente ⟨an open-and-shut case : un caso muy claro⟩

opener [ˈoːpənər] *n* : destapador *m*, abre-latas *m*, abridor *m*

openhanded [ˌoːpənˈhændəd] *adj* : generoso, liberal

open—heart [ˈoːpənˈhɑrt] *adj* : de corazón abierto

openhearted [ˌoːpənˈhɑrtəd] *adj* **1** FRANK : franco, sincero **2** : generoso, de gran corazón

opening [ˈoːpənɪŋ] *n* **1** BEGINNING : comienzo *m*, principio *m*, apertura *f* **2** AP-ERTURE : abertura *f*, brecha *f*, claro *m* (en el bosque) **3** OPPORTUNITY : oportunidad *f*

openly [ˈoːpənli] *adv* **1** FRANKLY : abiertamente, francamente **2** PUBLICLY : públicamente, claramente

open—minded [ˌoːpənˈmaɪndəd] *adj* : sin prejuicios, de actitud abierta

open–mouthed [ˌoːpənˈmauðd, -ˈmauθt] *adj* : boquiabierto

openness [ˈoːpənnəs] *n* : franqueza *f*

opera [ˈɑprə, ˈɑpərə] *n* **1** : ópera *f* **2** → **opus**

opera glasses *npl* : gemelos *mpl* de teatro

operate [ˈɑpəˌreɪt] *v* **-ated; -ating** *vi* **1** ACT, FUNCTION : operar, funcionar, actuar **2 to operate on (someone)** : operar a (alguien) — *vt* **1** WORK : operar, manejar, hacer funcionar (una máquina) **2** MANAGE : manejar, administrar (un negocio)

operatic [ˌɑpəˈrætɪk] *adj* : operístico

operating room *n* : quirófano *m*

operation [ˌɑpəˈreɪʃən] *n* **1** FUNCTIONING : funcionamiento *m* **2** USE : uso *m*, manejo *m* (de máquinas) **3** SURGERY : operación *f*, intervención *f* quirúrgica

operational [ˌɑpəˈreɪʃənəl] *adj* : operacional, de operación

operative [ˈɑpərətɪv, -ˌreɪ-] *adj* **1** OPERATING : vigente, en vigor **2** WORKING : operativo **3** SURGICAL : quirúrgico

operator [ˈɑpəˌreɪtər] *n* : operador *m*, -dora *f*

operetta [ˌɑpəˈretə] *n* : opereta *f*

ophthalmologist [ˌɑf‚θælˈmɑləʤɪst, -θəˈmɑ-] *n* : oftalmólogo *m*, -ga *f*

ophthalmology [ˌɑf‚θælˈmɑləʤi, -θəˈmɑ-] *n* : oftalmología *f*

opiate [ˈoːpiət, -piˌeɪt] *n* : opiato *m*

opine [oˈpaɪn] *v* : opinar

opinion [əˈpɪnjən] *n* : opinión *f*

opinionated [əˈpɪnjəˌneɪtəd] *adj* : testarudo, dogmático

opinion poll *n* SURVEY : sondeo *m*, encuesta *f* de opinión

opium [ˈoːpiəm] *n* : opio *m*

opossum [əˈpɑsəm] *n* : zarigüeya *f*, opossum *m*

opponent [əˈponənt] *n* : oponente *mf*; opositor *m*, -tora *f*; contrincante *mf* (en deportes)

opportune [ˌɑpərˈtuːn, -ˈtjuːn] *adj* : oportuno — **opportunely** *adv*

opportunism [ˌɑpərˈtuːˌnɪzəm, -ˈtjuː-] *n* : oportunismo *m*

opportunist [ˌɑpərˈtuːnɪst, -ˈtjuː-] *n* : oportunista *mf*

opportunistic [ˌɑpərtuːˈnɪstɪk, -tjuː-] *adj* : oportunista

opportunity [ˌɑpərˈtuːnəti, -ˈtjuː-] *n, pl* **-ties** : oportunidad *f*, ocasión *f*, chance *m*, posibilidades *fpl*

oppose [əˈpoːz] *vt* **-posed; -posing 1** : ir en contra de, oponerse a ⟨good opposes evil : el bien se opone al mal⟩ **2** COMBAT : luchar contra, combatir, resistir

opposite¹ [ˈɑpəzət] *adv* : enfrente

opposite² *adj* **1** FACING : de enfrente ⟨the opposite side : el lado de enfrente⟩ **2** CONTRARY : opuesto, contrario ⟨in opposite directions : en direcciones contrarias⟩ ⟨the opposite sex : el sexo opuesto, el otro sexo⟩

opposite³ *n* : lo contrario, lo opuesto

opposite⁴ *prep* : enfrente de, frente a

opposition [ˌɑpəˈzɪʃən] *n* : oposición *f*, resistencia *f* **2 in opposition to** AGAINST : en contra de

oppress [əˈpres] *vt* **1** PERSECUTE : oprimir, perseguir **2** BURDEN : oprimir, agobiar

oppression [əˈpreʃən] *n* : opresión *f*

oppressive [əˈpresɪv] *adj* **1** HARSH : opresivo, severo **2** STIFLING : agobiante, sofocante ⟨oppressive heat : calor sofocante⟩

oppressor [əˈpresər] *n* : opresor *m*, -sora *f*

opprobrium [əˈproːbriəm] *n* : oprobio *m*

opt [ˈɑpt] *vi* **1** : optar **2 to opt for** : optar por **3 to opt in** : decidir participar **4 to opt into** : decidir participar en **5 to opt out (of)** : decidir no participar (en)

optic [ˈɑptɪk] *or* **optical** [-tɪkəl] *adj* : óptico

optical disk *n* : disco *m* óptico

optician [ɑpˈtɪʃən] *n* : óptico *m*, -ca *f*

optics [ˈɑptɪks] *npl* : óptica *f*

optimal [ˈɑptəməl] *adj* : óptimo

optimism [ˈɑptəˌmɪzəm] *n* : optimismo *m*

optimist [ˈɑptəmɪst] *n* : optimista *mf*

optimistic [ˌɑptəˈmɪstɪk] *adj* : optimista

optimistically [ˌɑptəˈmɪstɪkli] *adv* : con optimismo, positivamente

optimum¹ [ˈɑptəməm] *adj* → **optimal**

optimum² *n, pl* **-ma** [ˈɑptəmə] : lo óptimo, lo ideal

option [ˈɑpʃən] *n* : opción *f* ⟨she has no option : no tiene más remedio⟩

optional [ˈɑpʃənəl] *adj* : facultativo, optativo

optometrist [ɑpˈtɑmətrɪst] *n* : optometrista *mf*

optometry [ɑpˈtɑmətri] *n* : optometría *f*

opulence [ˈɑpjələnts] *n* : opulencia *f*

opulent [ˈɑpjələnt] *adj* : opulento

opus [ˈoːpəs] *n, pl* **opera** [ˈoːpərə, ˈɑpə-] : opus *m*, obra *f* (de música)

or [ˈɔr] *conj* **1** (*indicating an alternative*) : o u *before words beginning with o or ho* ⟨coffee or tea : café o té⟩ ⟨one day or another : un día u otro⟩ **2** (*following a negative*) : ni ⟨he didn't have his keys or his wallet : no llevaba ni sus llaves ni su billetera⟩

oracle [ˈɔrəkəl] *n* : oráculo *m*

oral [ˈorəl] *adj* : oral — **orally** *adv*

orange [ˈɔrɪnʤ] *n* **1** : naranja *f*, china *f* *PRi* (fruto) **2** : naranja *m* (color), color *m* de china *PRi*

orangeade [ˌɔrɪnʤˈeɪd] *n* : naranjada *f*

orangutan [əˈrænəˌtæn, -ˈrænɡə-, -ˌtæn] *n* : orangután *m*

oration [əˈreɪʃən] *n* : oración *f*, discurso *m*

orator [ˈɔrətər] *n* : orador *m*, -dora *f*

oratorio [ˌɔrəˈtoriˌoː] *n, pl* **-rios** : oratorio *m*

oratory [ˈɔrəˌtori] *n, pl* **-ries** : oratoria *f*

orb [ˈɔrb] *n* : orbe *m*

orbit¹ [ˈɔrbət] *vt* **1** CIRCLE : girar alrededor de, orbitar **2** : poner en órbita (un satélite, etc.) — *vi* : orbitar

orbit² *n* : órbita *f*

orbital [ˈɔrbətəl] *adj* : orbital

orca [ˈɔrkə] *n* : orca *f*

orchard [ˈɔrtʃərd] *n* : huerto *m*

orchestra [ˈɔrkəstrə] *n* : orquesta *f*

orchestral [ɔrˈkestrəl] *adj* : orquestal

orchestrate ['ɔrkə,streɪt] vt **-trated; -trating 1** : orquestar, instrumentar (en música) **2** ORGANIZE : arreglar, organizar

orchestration [,ɔrkə'streɪʃən] n : orquestación f

orchid ['ɔrkɪd] n : orquídea f

ordain [ɔr'deɪn] vt **1** : ordenar (en religión) **2** DECREE : decretar, ordenar

ordeal [ɔr'di:l, 'ɔr,di:l] n : prueba f dura, experiencia f terrible

order[1] ['ɔrdər] vt **1** ORGANIZE : arreglar, ordenar, poner en orden **2** COMMAND : ordenar, mandar **3** REQUEST : pedir, encargar ⟨to order a meal : pedir algo de comer⟩ — vi : hacer un pedido

order[2] n **1** : orden f ⟨a religious order : una orden religiosa⟩ **2** COMMAND : orden f, mandato m ⟨to give an order : dar una orden⟩ ⟨to give the order to do something : dar orden de hacer algo⟩ ⟨by order of : por orden de⟩ **3** REQUEST : orden f, pedido m ⟨purchase order : orden de compra⟩ ⟨to place/take an order : hacer/tomar un pedido⟩ ⟨to be on order : estar pedido⟩ **4** SERVING : porción f, ración f ⟨an order of fries : una porción de papas fritas⟩ **5** ARRANGEMENT : orden m ⟨in chronological order : por orden cronológico⟩ ⟨out of order : desordenado⟩ ⟨everything seems to be in order : parece que todo está en orden⟩ **6** DISCIPLINE : orden m ⟨law and order : el orden público⟩ ⟨to keep order : mantener el orden⟩ **7 in order for** : para que ⟨in order for this to work : para que esto funcione⟩ **8 in order that** : para que ⟨in order that others might live : para que otros puedan vivir⟩ **9 in order to** : para **10 in (working) order** : funcionando **11 out of order** BROKEN : descompuesto, averiado **12 orders** npl or **holy orders** : órdenes fpl sagradas

orderliness ['ɔrdərlinəs] n : orden m

orderly[1] ['ɔrdərli] adj **1** METHODICAL : ordenado, metódico **2** PEACEFUL : pacífico, disciplinado

orderly[2] n, pl **-lies 1** : ordenanza m (en el ejército) **2** : camillero m (en un hospital)

ordinal ['ɔrdənəl] n or **ordinal number** : ordinal m, número m ordinal

ordinance ['ɔrdənəns] n : ordenanza f, reglamento m

ordinarily [,ɔrdən'erəli] adv : ordinariamente, por lo general

ordinary ['ɔrdən,eri] adj **1** NORMAL, USUAL : normal, usual **2** AVERAGE : común y corriente, normal **3** MEDIOCRE : mediocre, ordinario

ordination [,ɔrdən'eɪʃən] n : ordenación f

ordnance ['ɔrdnəns] n : artillería f

ore ['ɔr] n : mineral m (metálico), mena f

oregano [ə'regə,no:] n : orégano m

organ ['ɔrgən] n **1** : órgano m (instrumento) **2** : órgano m (del cuerpo) **3** PERIODICAL : publicación f periódica, órgano m

organic [ɔr'gænɪk] adj : orgánico — **organically** adv

organism ['ɔrgə,nɪzəm] n : organismo m

organist ['ɔrgənɪst] n : organista mf

organization [,ɔrgənə'zeɪʃən] n **1** ORGANIZING : organización f **2** BODY : organización f, organismo m

organizational [,ɔrgənə'zeɪʃənəl] adj : organizativo

organize ['ɔrgə,naɪz] vt **-nized; -nizing** : organizar, arreglar, poner en orden

organizer ['ɔrgə,naɪzər] n : organizador m, -dora f

orgasm ['ɔr,gæzəm] n : orgasmo m

orgy ['ɔrdʒi] n, pl **-gies** : orgía f

orient ['ori,ent] vt : orientar

Orient n **the Orient** : el Oriente

oriental [,ori'entəl] adj : del Oriente, oriental

Oriental n : oriental mf

orientation [,oriən'teɪʃən] n : orientación f

orifice ['ɔrəfəs] n : orificio m

origin ['ɔrədʒən] n **1** ANCESTRY : origen m, ascendencia f **2** SOURCE : origen m, raíz f, fuente f

original[1] [ə'rɪdʒənəl] adj : original

original[2] n : original m

originality [ə,rɪdʒə'næləti] n : originalidad f

originally [ə'rɪdʒənəli] adv **1** AT FIRST : al principio, originariamente **2** CREATIVELY : originalmente, con originalidad

originate [ə'rɪdʒə,neɪt] v **-nated; -nating** vt : originar, iniciar, crear — vi **1** BEGIN : originarse, empezar **2** COME : provenir, proceder, derivarse

originator [ə'rɪdʒə,neɪtər] n : creador m, -dora f; inventor m, -tora f

oriole ['ori,o:l, -əl] n : oropéndola f

ornament[1] ['ɔrnəmənt] vt : adornar, decorar, ornamentar

ornament[2] n : ornamento m, adorno m, decoración f

ornamental [,ɔrnə'məntəl] adj : ornamental, de adorno, decorativo

ornamentation [,ɔrnəmən'teɪʃən, -mən-] n : ornamentación f

ornate [ɔr'neɪt] adj : elaborado, recargado

ornery ['ɔrnəri, 'ɑrnəri] adj **ornerier; -est** : de mal genio, malhumorado

ornithologist [,ɔrnə'θɑlədʒɪst] n : ornitólogo m, -ga f

ornithology [,ɔrnə'θɑlədʒi] n, pl **-gies** : ornitología f

orphan[1] ['ɔrfən] vt : dejar huérfano

orphan[2] n : huérfano m, -na f

orphanage ['ɔrfənɪdʒ] n : orfelinato m, orfanato m

orthodontics [,ɔrθə'dɑntɪks] n : ortodoncia f

orthodontist [,ɔrθə'dɑntɪst] n : ortodoncista mf

orthodox ['ɔrθə,dɑks] adj : ortodoxo

orthodoxy ['ɔrθə,dɑksi] n, pl **-doxies** : ortodoxia f

orthographic [,ɔrθə'græfɪk] adj : ortográfico

orthography [ɔr'θɑgrəfi] n, pl **-phies** SPELLING : ortografía f

orthopedic [,ɔrθə'pi:dɪk] adj : ortopédico

orthopedics [ˌɔrθəˈpiːdɪks] *ns & pl* : ortopedia *f*

orthopedist [ˌɔrθəˈpiːdɪst] *n* : ortopedista *mf*

oscillate [ˈɑsəˌleɪt] *vi* -lated; -lating : oscilar

oscillation [ˌɑsəˈleɪʃən] *n* : oscilación *f*

osmosis [ɑzˈmoːsɪs, ɑs-] *n* : ósmosis *f*, osmosis *f*

osprey [ˈɑspri, -ˌpreɪ] *n* : pigargo *m*

ostensible [ɑˈstɛnsəbəl] *adj* APPARENT : aparente, ostensible — **ostensibly** [-bli] *adv*

ostentation [ˌɑstənˈteɪʃən] *n* : ostentación *f*, boato *m*

ostentatious [ˌɑstənˈteɪʃəs] *adj* : ostentoso — **ostentatiously** *adv*

osteopath [ˈɑstiəˌpæθ] *n* : osteópata *f*

osteopathy [ˌɑstiˈɑpəθi] *n* : osteopatía *f*

osteoporosis [ˌɑstioʊpəˈroːsɪs] *n, pl* -roses [-ˌsiːz] : osteoporosis *f*

ostracism [ˈɑstrəˌsɪzəm] *n* : ostracismo *m*

ostracize [ˈɑstrəˌsaɪz] *vt* -cized; -cizing : condenar al ostracismo, marginar, aislar

ostrich [ˈɑstrɪtʃ, ˈɔs-] *n* : avestruz *m*

other[1] [ˈʌðər] *adv* **other than** : aparte de, fuera de

other[2] *adj* **1** : otro ⟨the other boys : los otros muchachos⟩ ⟨smarter than other people : más inteligente que los demás⟩ ⟨on the other hand : por otra parte, por otro lado⟩ **2 every other** : cada dos ⟨every other day : cada dos días⟩

other[3] *pron* **1** : otro ⟨one in front of the other : uno tras otro⟩ ⟨either one or the other : uno u otro⟩ ⟨myself and three others : yo y tres otros/más⟩ ⟨this class and three others : esta clase y tres otras/más⟩ ⟨from one extreme to the other : de un extremo al otro⟩ ⟨somewhere or other : en alguna parte⟩ ⟨somehow or other : de alguna manera⟩ **2 the others** : los otros, los demás ⟨this class and the others : esta clase y las otras⟩

otherwise[1] [ˈʌðərˌwaɪz] *adv* **1** DIFFERENTLY : de otro modo, de manera distinta ⟨he could not act otherwise : no pudo actuar de manera distinta⟩ **2** : eso aparte, por lo demás ⟨I'm dizzy, but otherwise I'm fine : estoy mareado pero, por lo demás, estoy bien⟩ **3** OR ELSE : de lo contrario, si no ⟨do what I tell you, otherwise you'll be sorry : haz lo que te digo, de lo contrario, te arrepentirás⟩

otherwise[2] *adj* : diferente, distinto ⟨the facts are otherwise : la realidad es diferente⟩

otitis [oʊˈtaɪtəs] *n* : otitis *f*

otter [ˈɑtər] *n* : nutria *f*

Ottoman [ˈɑtəmən] *n* **1** : otomano *m*, -na *f* **2** : otomana *f* (mueble) — **Ottoman** *adj*

ouch [ˈaʊtʃ] *interj* : ¡ay!, ¡huy!

ought [ˈɔt] *v aux* : deber ⟨you ought to take care of yourself : deberías cuidarte⟩

oughtn't [ˈɔtənt] *contraction of* ought not → **ought**

ounce [ˈaʊnts] *n* : onza *f*

our [ˈɑr, ˈaʊr] *adj* : nuestro

ours [ˈɑrz, ˈaʊrz] *pron* : nuestro ⟨a cousin of ours : un primo nuestro, una prima nuestra⟩

ourselves [ɑrˈsɛlvz, aʊr-] *pron* **1** (*used reflexively*) : nos, nosotros, nosotras ⟨we amused ourselves : nos divertimos⟩ ⟨we were always thinking of ourselves : siempre pensábamos en nosotros⟩ **2** (*used for emphasis*) : nosotros mismos, nosotras mismas ⟨we did it ourselves : lo hicimos nosotros mismos⟩

oust [ˈaʊst] *vt* : desbancar, expulsar

ouster [ˈaʊstər] *n* : expulsión *f* (de un país, etc.), destitución *f* (de un puesto)

out[1] [ˈaʊt] *vi* : revelarse, hacerse conocido

out[2] *adv* **1** (*indicating direction or movement*) OUTSIDE : para afuera ⟨she opened the door and looked out : abrió la puerta y miró para afuera⟩ ⟨he went out to the garden : salió al jardín⟩ ⟨she took the dog out : sacó al perro⟩ **2** (*indicating location*) OUTSIDE : fuera, afuera ⟨out in the garden : afuera en el jardín⟩ ⟨it's sunny out : hace sol⟩ ⟨your shirt is hanging out : tienes la camisa afuera⟩ **3** (*indicating outward movement*) ⟨they flew out yesterday : salieron ayer en avión⟩ ⟨out to sea : mar adentro⟩ **4** (*indicating distance*) ⟨they live out in the country : viven en el campo⟩ **5** (*indicating omission*) ⟨you left out a comma : omitiste una coma⟩ ⟨count me out : no cuentes conmigo⟩ **6** (*indicating removal, loss, or incorrect placement*) ⟨they voted him out : no lo reeligieron⟩ ⟨his hair is falling out : se le está cayendo el pelo⟩ ⟨she threw out her shoulder : se lastimó el hombro⟩ **7** (*indicating drawing from a group*) ⟨she picked out a shirt : escogió una camisa⟩ **8** (*indicating a location away from home or work*) : fuera, afuera ⟨to eat out : comer afuera⟩ ⟨he asked her out : la invitó a salir⟩ **9** (*indicating loss of control or possession*) ⟨they let the secret out : sacaron el secreto a la luz⟩ **10** (*indicating ending or stopping*) ⟨his money ran out : se le acabó el dinero⟩ ⟨to turn out the light : apagar la luz⟩ **11** (*indicating completion*) ⟨to fill out a form : rellenar un formulario⟩ **12** ALOUD : en voz alta, en alto ⟨to cry out : gritar⟩ **13** UNCONSCIOUS : inconsciente **14** : abiertamente homosexual **15** → **out-of-bounds** **16 to be out for** : estar buscando (venganza, etc.) **17 to be out to** : querer (vengarse, etc.) ⟨he's out to get me : me la tiene jurada⟩

out[3] *adj* **1** EXTERNAL : externo, exterior **2** OUTLYING : alejado, distante ⟨the out islands : las islas distantes⟩ **3** ABSENT **4** UNFASHIONABLE : fuera de moda **5** EXTINGUISHED : apagado **6 to be out and about** : estar andando por ahí

out[4] *prep* **1** (*used to indicate an outward movement*) : por ⟨I looked out the window : miré por la ventana⟩ ⟨she ran out the door : corrió por la puerta⟩ **2** → **out of**

out-and-out [ˈaʊtənˈaʊt] *adj* UTTER : redomado, absoluto

outback [ˈaʊtˌbæk] *n* **the outback** : el interior (de Australia)

outboard motor [ˈaʊtˌbord] *n* : motor *m* fuera de borde

outbound [ˈaʊtˌbaʊnd] *adj* : que sale, de salida

out-box [ˈaʊtˌbɑks] *n* : bandeja *f* de salida

outbreak [ˈaʊtˌbreɪk] *n* : brote *m* (de una enfermedad), comienzo *m* (de guerra), ola *f* (de violencia), erupción *f* (de granos)

outbuilding [ˈaʊtˌbɪldɪŋ] *n* : edificio *m* anexo

outburst [ˈaʊtˌbərst] *n* : arranque *m*, arrebato *m*

outcast [ˈaʊtˌkæst] *n* : marginado *m*, -da *f*; paria *mf*

outcome [ˈaʊtˌkʌm] *n* : resultado *m*, desenlace *m*, consecuencia *f*

outcry [ˈaʊtˌkraɪ] *n*, *pl* **-cries** : clamor *m*, protesta *f*

outdated [ˌaʊtˈdeɪtəd] *adj* : anticuado, fuera de moda

outdistance [ˌaʊtˈdɪstənts] *vt* **-tanced; -tancing** : aventajar, dejar atrás

outdo [ˌaʊtˈduː] *vt* **-did** [-ˈdɪd]; **-done** [-ˈdʌn]; **-doing; -does** [-ˈdʌz] : superar

outdoor [ˈaʊtˈdor] *adj* : al aire libre ⟨outdoor sports : deportes al aire libre⟩ ⟨outdoor clothing : ropa de calle⟩

outdoors[1] [ˈaʊtˈdorz] *adv* : afuera, al aire libre

outdoors[2] *n* : aire *m* libre

outer [ˈaʊtər] *adj* **1** : exterior, externo **2 outer space** : espacio *m* exterior

outermost [ˈaʊtərˌmost] *adj* : más remoto, más exterior, extremo

outfield [ˈaʊtˌfiːld] *n* **the outfield** : los jardines

outfielder [ˈaʊtˌfiːldər] *n* : jardinero *m*, -ra *f*

outfit[1] [ˈaʊtˌfɪt] *vt* **-fitted; -fitting** EQUIP : equipar

outfit[2] *n* **1** EQUIPMENT : equipo *m* **2** COSTUME, ENSEMBLE : traje *m*, conjunto *m* **3** GROUP : conjunto *m*

outgo [ˈaʊtˌgoː] *n*, *pl* **outgoes** : gasto *m*

outgoing [ˈaʊtˌgoːɪŋ] *adj* **1** OUTBOUND : que sale **2** DEPARTING : saliente ⟨an outgoing president : un presidente saliente⟩ **3** EXTROVERTED : extrovertido, expansivo

outgrow [ˌaʊtˈgroː] *vt* **-grew** [-ˈgruː]; **-grown** [-ˈgroːn]; **-growing 1** : crecer más que ⟨that tree outgrew all the others : ese árbol creció más que todos los otros⟩ **2 to outgrow one's clothes** : quedarle pequeña la ropa a uno

outgrowth [ˈaʊtˌgroːθ] *n* **1** OFFSHOOT : brote *m*, vástago *m* (de una planta) **2** CONSEQUENCE : consecuencia *f*, producto *m*, resultado *m*

outing [ˈaʊtɪŋ] *n* : excursión *f*

outlandish [aʊtˈlændɪʃ] *adj* : descabellado, muy extraño

outlast [ˌaʊtˈlæst] *vt* : durar más que

outlaw[1] [ˈaʊtˌlɔ] *vt* : hacerse ilegal, declarar fuera de la ley, prohibir

outlaw[2] *n* : bandido *m*, -da *f*; bandolero *m*, -ra *f*; forajido *m*, -da *f*

outlay [ˈaʊtˌleɪ] *n* : gasto *m*, desembolso *m*

outlet [ˈaʊtˌlet, -lət] *n* **1** EXIT : salida *f*, escape *m* ⟨electrical outlet : toma de corriente⟩ **2** RELIEF : desahogo *m* **3** MARKET : mercado *m*, salida *f*

outline[1] [ˈaʊtˌlaɪn] *vt* **-lined; -lining 1** SKETCH : diseñar, esbozar, bosquejar **2** DEFINE, EXPLAIN : perfilar, delinear, explicar ⟨she outlined our responsibilities : delineó nuestras responsabilidades⟩

outline[2] *n* **1** PROFILE : perfil *m*, silueta *f*, contorno *m* **2** SKETCH : bosquejo *m*, boceto *m* **3** SUMMARY : esquema *m*, resumen *m*, sinopsis *m* ⟨an outline of world history : un esquema de la historia mundial⟩

outlive [ˌaʊtˈlɪv] *vt* **-lived; -living** : sobrevivir a

outlook [ˈaʊtˌlʊk] *n* **1** VIEW : vista *f*, panorama *f* **2** POINT OF VIEW : punto *m* de vista **3** PROSPECTS : perspectivas *fpl*

outlying [ˈaʊtˌlaɪŋ] *adj* : alejado, distante, remoto ⟨the outlying areas : las afueras⟩

outmoded [ˌaʊtˈmoːdəd] *adj* : pasado de moda, anticuado

outnumber [ˌaʊtˈnʌmbər] *vt* : superar en número a, ser más numeroso de

out of *prep* **1** (*indicating direction or movement from within*) : de, por ⟨we ran out of the house : salimos corriendo de la casa⟩ ⟨to look out of the window : mirar por la ventana⟩ **2** (*being beyond the limits of*) ⟨out of control : fuera de control⟩ ⟨to be out of sight : desaparecer de vista⟩ **3** OF : de ⟨one out of four : uno de cada cuatro⟩ **4** (*indicating absence or loss*) : sin ⟨out of money : sin dinero⟩ ⟨we're out of matches : nos hemos quedado sin fósforos⟩ **5** BECAUSE OF : por ⟨out of curiosity : por curiosidad⟩ **6** FROM : de ⟨made out of plastic : hecho de plástico⟩

out-of-bounds [ˌaʊtəvˈbaʊndz] *adj* : fuera de juego

out-of-date [ˌaʊtəvˈdeɪt] *adj* : anticuado, obsoleto, pasado de moda

out-of-door [ˌaʊtəvˈdor] *or* **out-of-doors** [-ˈdorz] → **outdoor**

out-of-doors *n* → **outdoors**[2]

out-of-the-way [ˌaʊtəvðəˈweɪ] *adj* : alejado, distante, remoto

outpatient [ˈaʊtˌpeɪʃənt] *n* : paciente *m* externo, paciente *f* externa

outpost [ˈaʊtˌpoːst] *n* : puesto *m* avanzado

output[1] [ˈaʊtˌpʊt] *vt* **-putted** *or* **-put; -putting** : producir

output[2] *n* : producción *f* (de una fábrica), rendimiento *m* (de una máquina), productividad *f* (de una persona)

outrage[1] [ˈaʊtˌreɪdʒ] *vt* **-raged; -raging 1** INSULT : ultrajar, injuriar **2** INFURIATE : indignar, enfurecer

outrage[2] *n* **1** ATROCITY : atropello *m*, atrocidad *f*, atentado *m* **2** SCANDAL : escándalo *m* **3** ANGER : ira *f*, furia *f*

outrageous [ˌaʊˈreɪʤəs] *adj* 1 SCANDAL-OUS : escandaloso, ofensivo, atroz 2 UN-CONVENTIONAL : poco convencional, extravagante 3 EXORBITANT : exorbitante, excesivo (dícese de los precios, etc.)

outright¹ [ˌaʊtˈraɪt] *adv* 1 COMPLETELY : por completo, totalmente (to sell outright : vender por completo) (he refused it outright : lo rechazó rotundamente) 2 DIRECTLY : directamente, sin reserva 3 INSTANTLY : al instante, en el acto

outright² [ˈaʊtˌraɪt] *adj* 1 COMPLETE : completo, absoluto, categórico (an outright lie : una mentira absoluta) 2 : sin reservas (an outright gift : un regalo sin reservas)

outset [ˈaʊtˌsɛt] *n* : comienzo *m*, principio *m*

outshine [ˌaʊtˈʃaɪn] *vt* **-shone** [-ˈʃoːn, -ˈʃɑn] *or* **-shined; -shining** : eclipsar

outside¹ [ˌaʊtˈsaɪd, ˈaʊt-] *adv* : fuera, afuera

outside² *adj* 1 : exterior, externo (the outside edge : el borde exterior) (outside influences : influencias externas) 2 REMOTE : remoto (an outside chance : una posibilidad remota)

outside³ *n* 1 EXTERIOR : parte *f* de afuera, exterior *m* 2 MOST : máximo *m* (three weeks at the outside : tres semanas como máximo) 3 **from the outside** : desde afuera, desde fuera

outside⁴ *prep* : fuera de, afuera de (outside my window : fuera de mi ventana) (outside regular hours : fuera del horario normal) (outside the law : afuera de la ley)

outside of *prep* 1 → outside⁴ 2 → besides²

outsider [ˌaʊtˈsaɪdər] *n* : forastero *m*, -ra *f*

outsize [ˈaʊtˌsaɪz] *also* **outsized** [ˈaʊtˌsaɪzd] *adj* : enorme

outskirts [ˈaʊtˌskərts] *npl* : afueras *fpl*, alrededores *mpl*

outsmart [ˌaʊtˈsmɑrt] → outwit

outsource [ˈaʊtˌsors] *vt* : externalizar

outsourcing [ˈaʊtˌsorsɪŋ] *n* : externalización *f*

outspoken [ˌaʊtˈspoːkən] *adj* : franco, directo

outstanding [ˌaʊtˈstændɪŋ] *adj* 1 UNPAID : pendiente 2 NOTABLE : destacado, notable, excepcional, sobresaliente

outstandingly [ˌaʊtˈstændɪŋli] *adv* : excepcionalmente

outstretched [ˌaʊtˈstrɛʧt] *adj* : extendido

outstrip [ˌaʊtˈstrɪp] *vt* **-stripped** *or* **-stript** [-ˈstrɪpt]; **-stripping** 1 : aventajar, dejar atrás (he outstripped the other runners : aventajó a los otros corredores) 2 SUR-PASS : aventajar, sobrepasar

outward¹ [ˈaʊtwərd] *or* **outwards** [-wərdz] *adv* : hacia afuera, hacia el exterior

outward² *adj* 1 : hacia afuera (an outward flow : un flujo hacia afuera) 2 : externo (outward beauty : belleza externa)

outwardly [ˈaʊtwərdli] *adv* 1 EXTER-NALLY : exteriormente 2 APPARENTLY : aparentemente (outwardly friendly : aparentemente simpático)

outweigh [ˌaʊtˈweɪ] *vt* 1 : pesar más que 2 : ser mayor que (the benefit outweighs the risk : el beneficio es mayor que el riesgo)

outwit [ˌaʊtˈwɪt] *vt* **-witted; -witting** : ser más listo que

ova → ovum

oval¹ [ˈoːvəl] *adj* : ovalado, oval

oval² *n* : óvalo *m*

ovarian [oˈværiən] *adj* : ovárico

ovary [ˈoːvəri] *n, pl* **-ries** : ovario *m*

ovation [oˈveɪʃən] *n* : ovación *f*

oven [ˈʌvən] *n* : horno *m*

over¹ [ˈoːvər] *adv* 1 (*indicating movement across*) (he flew over to London : voló a Londres) (come on over! : ¡ven acá!) (we crossed over to the other side : cruzamos al otro lado) 2 (*indicating movement from an upright position*) (to fall over : caerse) (to push someone over : tirar a alguien al suelo) 3 (*indicating reversal of position*) (to turn/flip something over : darle la vuelta a algo, voltear algo) (roll over, please : date la vuelta, por favor) 4 (*indicating an additional amount*) (the show ran 10 minutes over : el espectáculo terminó 10 minutos tarde) (there's a lot of food left over : sobra/queda mucha comida) (women 65 and over : mujeres de 65 años en adelante) (parties of six or over : grupos de seis o más) 5 (*indicating a later time*) (to sleep over : quedarse a dormir) (some money to tide him over : un poco de dinero para sacarlo del apuro) 6 (*indicating covering*) (the sky clouded over : se nubló) 7 THOROUGHLY : bien (read it over : léelo bien) 8 ABOVE, OVER-HEAD : por encima 9 (*indicating repetition*) (over and over : una y otra vez) (to start over : volver a empezar) (twice over : dos veces) (many times over : muchas veces) 10 **all over** EVERY-WHERE : por todas partes 11 **over (and done) with** (I want to get this over (and done) with : quiero quitarme esto de encima) 12 **over and out** (*in radio transmissions*) : cambio y corto/fuera, corto y cambio

over² *adj* 1 HIGHER, UPPER : superior 2 REMAINING : sobrante, que sobra 3 ENDED : terminado, acabado (the work is over : el trabajo está terminado)

over³ *prep* 1 ABOVE : encima de, arriba de, sobre (over the fireplace : encima de la chimenea) (the hawk flew over the hills : el halcón voló sobre los cerros) 2 : más de (over $50 : más de $50) 3 ALONG : por, sobre (to glide over the ice : deslizarse sobre el hielo) 4 (*indicating motion through a place or thing*) (they showed me over the house : me mostraron la casa) 5 ACROSS : por encima de, sobre (he jumped over the ditch : saltó por encima de la zanja) (we crossed over the border : cruzamos la frontera) 6 BEYOND : más allá de (just over that hill : un poco más allá de esa colina) 7

OFF : por ⟨she fell over the side of the boat : se cayó por la borda del barco⟩ **8** (*indicating direction*) : por ⟨it's over here somewhere : está por acá⟩ ⟨look over there! : ¡mira allí!⟩ **9** UPON : sobre ⟨a cape over my shoulders : una capa sobre los hombros⟩ ⟨she hit him over the head : le dio en la cabeza⟩ **10** ON : por ⟨to speak over the phone : hablar por teléfono⟩ ⟨over the radio : por la radio⟩ **11** DURING : en, durante ⟨over the past 25 years : durante los últimos 25 años⟩ **12** PAST, THROUGH : terminado con ⟨we're over the worst of it : hemos pasado lo peor⟩ **13** BECAUSE OF : por ⟨they fought over the money : se pelearon por el dinero⟩ ⟨to laugh over something : reírse por algo⟩ **14** CONCERNING : sobre **15** (*indicating comparison*) ⟨to be an improvement over : ser mejor que⟩ ⟨to choose one thing over another : elegir una cosa en lugar de otra⟩ ⟨to have an advantage over : tener una ventaja sobre⟩ **16** DESPITE : a pesar de (objeciones, etc.) **17** (*indicating omission*) ⟨to skip over something : saltarse algo⟩ **18** (*referring to power or authority*) : por encima de, sobre ⟨those over you : los que están por encima de ti⟩ ⟨to have control over : tener control sobre⟩ **19** all over ⟨there was water all over the floor : había agua por todo el suelo⟩ ⟨all over the place : por todas partes⟩ **20** over and above : además de

over- *pref* : demasiado, excesivamente

overabundance [ˌoːvərˈbʌndənts] *n* : superabundancia *f*

overabundant [ˌoːvərˈbʌndənt] *adj* : superabundante

overactive [ˌoːvərˈæktɪv] *adj* : hiperactivo

overall [ˌoːvərˈɔl] *adj* : total, global, de conjunto

overalls [ˈoːvərˌɔlz] *npl* : overol *m*

overawe [ˌoːvərˈɔ] *vt* **-awed; -awing** : intimidar, impresionar

overbearing [ˌoːvərˈbærɪŋ] *adj* : dominante, imperioso, prepotente

overblown [ˌoːvərˈbloːn] *adj* **1** INFLATED : inflado, exagerado **2** BOMBASTIC : grandilocuente, rimbombante

overboard [ˈoːvərˌbord] *adv* : por la borda, al agua

overburden [ˌoːvərˈbərdən] *vt* : sobrecargar, agobiar

overcast [ˈoːvərˌkæst] *adj* CLOUDY : nublado

overcharge [ˌoːvərˈtʃɑrdʒ] *vt* **-charged; -charging** : cobrarle de más (a alguien)

overcoat [ˈoːvərˌkoːt] *n* : abrigo *m*

overcome [ˌoːvərˈkʌm] *v* **-came** [-ˈkeɪm]; **-come; -coming** *vt* **1** CONQUER : vencer, derrotar, superar **2** OVERWHELM : abrumar, agobiar — *vi* : vencer

overconfidence [ˌoːvərˈkɑnfədənts] *n* : exceso *m* de confianza

overconfident [ˌoːvərˈkɑnfədənt] *adj* : demasiado confiado

overcook [ˌoːvərˈkʊk] *vt* : recocer, cocer demasiado

overcrowded [ˌoːvərˈkraʊdəd] *adj* **1** PACKED : abarrotado, atestado de gente **2** OVERPOPULATED : superpoblado

overcrowding [ˌoːvərˈkraʊdɪŋ] *n* **1** : hacinamiento *m*, masificación *f* Spain **2** OVERPOPULATION : superpoblación *f*

overdo [ˌoːvərˈduː] *vt* **-did** [-ˈdɪd]; **-done** [-ˈdʌn]; **-doing; -does** [-ˈdʌz] **1** : hacer demasiado **2** EXAGGERATE : exagerar **3** OVERCOOK : recocer

overdose [ˈoːvərˌdoːs] *n* : sobredosis *f*

overdraft [ˈoːvərˌdræft] *n* : sobregiro *m*, descubierto *m*

overdraw [ˌoːvərˈdrɔ] *vt* **-drew** [-ˈdruː]; **-drawn** [-ˈdrɔn]; **-drawing 1** : sobregirar ⟨my account is overdrawn : tengo la cuenta en descubierto⟩ **2** EXAGGERATE : exagerar

overdue [ˌoːvərˈduː] *adj* **1** UNPAID : vencido y sin pagar **2** TARDY : de retraso, tardío

overeat [ˌoːvərˈiːt] *vi* **-ate** [-ˈeɪt]; **-eaten** [-ˈiːtən]; **-eating** : comer demasiado

overelaborate [ˌoːvərɪˈlæbərət] *adj* : recargado

overestimate [ˌoːvərˈɛstəˌmeɪt] *vt* **-mated; -mating** : sobreestimar

overexcited [ˌoːvərɪkˈsaɪtəd] *adj* : sobreexcitado

overexpose [ˌoːvərɪkˈspoːz] *vt* **-posed; -posing** : sobreexponer

overfeed [ˌoːvərˈfiːd] *vt* **-fed** [-ˈfɛd]; **-feeding** : sobrealimentar

overflow¹ [ˌoːvərˈfloː] *vt* **1** : desbordar **2** INUNDATE : inundar — *vi* : desbordarse, rebosar

overflow² [ˈoːvərˌfloː] *n* **1** : derrame *m*, desbordamiento *m* (de un río) **2** SURPLUS : exceso *m*, excedente *m*

overfly [ˌoːvərˈflaɪ] *vt* **-flew** [-ˈfluː]; **-flown** [-ˈfloːn]; **-flying** : sobrevolar

overgrown [ˌoːvərˈgroːn] *adj* **1** : cubierto ⟨overgrown with weeds : cubierto de malas hierbas⟩ **2** : demasiado grande

overhand¹ [ˈoːvərˌhænd] *adv* : por encima de la cabeza

overhand² *adj* : por lo alto (tirada)

overhang¹ [ˌoːvərˈhæŋ] *v* **-hung** [-ˈhʌŋ]; **-hanging** *vt* **1** : sobresalir por encima de **2** THREATEN : amenazar — *vi* : sobresalir

overhang² [ˈoːvərˌhæŋ] *n* : saliente *mf*

overhaul [ˌoːvərˈhɔl] *vt* **1** : revisar ⟨to overhaul an engine : revisar un motor⟩ **2** OVERTAKE : adelantar

overhead¹ [ˌoːvərˈhɛd] *adv* : por encima, arriba, por lo alto

overhead² [ˈoːvərˌhɛd] *adj* : de arriba

overhead³ [ˈoːvərˌhɛd] *n* : gastos *mpl* generales

overhear [ˌoːvərˈhɪr] *vt* **-heard** [-ˈhərd]; **-hearing** : oír por casualidad

overheat [ˌoːvərˈhiːt] *vt* : recalentar, sobrecalentar, calentar demasiado

overjoyed [ˌoːvərˈdʒɔɪd] *adj* : rebosante de alegría

overkill [ˈoːvərˌkɪl] *n* : exceso *m*, excedente *m*

overland¹ [ˈoːvərˌlænd, -lənd] *adv* : por tierra

overland[2] *adj* : terrestre, por tierra
overlap[1] [ˌoːvərˈlæp] *v* **-lapped; -lapping**
vt : traslapar — *vi* : traslaparse, solaparse
overlap[2] [ˈoːvərˌlæp] *n* : traslapo *m*
overlay[1] [ˌoːvərˈlei] *vt* **-laid** [-ˈleid]; **-laying**
: recubrir, revestir
overlay[2] [ˈoːvərˌlei] *n* : revestimiento *m*
overload [ˌoːvərˈloːd] *vt* : sobrecargar
overlong [ˌoːvərˈlɔŋ] *adj* : excesivamente
largo, largo y pesado
overlook [ˌoːvərˈlʊk] *vt* **1** INSPECT : inspeccionar, revisar **2** : tener vista a, dar a
⟨a house overlooking the valley : una
casa que tiene vista al valle⟩ **3** MISS : pasar por alto **4** EXCUSE : dejar pasar, disculpar
overly [ˈoːvərli] *adv* : demasiado
overnight[1] [ˌoːvərˈnait] *adv* **1** : por la noche, durante la noche **2** : de la noche a
la mañana ⟨we can't do it overnight : no
podemos hacerlo de la noche a la
mañana⟩
overnight[2] [ˈoːvərˌnait] *adj* **1** : de noche
⟨an overnight stay : una estancia de una
noche⟩ ⟨an overnight bag : una bolsa de
viaje⟩ **2** SUDDEN : repentino
overpass [ˈoːvərˌpæs] *n* : paso *m* elevado,
paso *m* a desnivel *Mex*
overpopulated [ˌoːvərˈpɑpjəˌleitəd] *adj*
: superpoblado, sobrepoblado
overpopulation [ˌoːvərˌpɑpjəˈleiʃən] *n*
: superpoblación *f*, sobrepoblación *f*
overpower [ˌoːvərˈpaʊər] *vt* **1** CONQUER,
SUBDUE : vencer, superar **2** OVER-
WHELM : abrumar, agobiar ⟨overpow-
ered by the heat : sofocado por el calor⟩
overpraise [ˌoːvərˈpreiz] *vt* **-praised;**
-praising : adular
overprotective [ˌoːvərprəˈtɛktɪv] *adj* : sobreprotector
overrate [ˌoːvərˈreit] *vt* **-rated; -rating**
: sobrevalorar, sobrevaluar
overreact [ˌoːvəriˈækt] *vi* : reaccionar de
forma exagerada
override [ˌoːvərˈraid] *vt* **-rode** [-ˈroːd]; **-rid-
den** [-ˈridən]; **-riding** **1** : predominar sobre, contar más que ⟨hunger overrode
our manners : el hambre predominó sobre los modales⟩ **2** ANNUL : anular, invalidar ⟨to override a veto : anular un
veto⟩
overripe [ˌoːvərˈraip] *adj* : pasado
overrule [ˌoːvərˈruːl] *vt* **-ruled; -ruling**
: anular (una decisión), desautorizar
(una persona), denegar (un pedido)
overrun [ˌoːvərˈrʌn] *v* **-ran** [-ˈræn]; **-run-
ning** *vt* **1** INVADE : invadir **2** INFEST
: infestar, plagar **3** EXCEED : exceder,
rebasar — *vi* : rebasar el tiempo previsto
overseas[1] [ˌoːvərˈsiːz] *adv* : en el extranjero ⟨to travel overseas : viajar al extran-
jero⟩
overseas[2] [ˈoːvərˌsiːz] *adj* : extranjero, exterior
oversee [ˌoːvərˈsiː] *vt* **-saw** [-ˈsɔ]; **-seen**
[-ˈsiːn]; **-seeing** SUPERVISE : supervisar
overseer [ˈoːvərˌsiːər] *n* : supervisor *m*,
-sora *f*; capataz *mf*
oversell [ˌoːvərˈsɛl] *vt* : sobrevender

overshadow [ˌoːvərˈʃædoː] *vt* **1** DARKEN
: oscurecer, ensombrecer **2** ECLIPSE,
OUTSHINE : eclipsar
overshoe [ˈoːvərˌʃuː] *n* : chanclo *m*
overshoot [ˌoːvərˈʃuːt] *vt* **-shot** [-ˈʃɑt];
-shooting : pasarse de ⟨to overshoot the
mark : pasarse de la raya⟩
oversight [ˈoːvərˌsait] *n* : descuido *m*,
inadvertencia *f*
oversleep [ˌoːvərˈsliːp] *vi* **-slept** [-ˈslɛpt];
-sleeping : no despertarse a tiempo,
quedarse dormido
overspread [ˌoːvərˈsprɛd] *vt* **-spread;**
-spreading : extenderse sobre
overstaffed [ˌoːvərˈstæft] *adj* : con exceso
de personal
overstate [ˌoːvərˈsteit] *vt* **-stated; -stating**
EXAGGERATE : exagerar
overstatement [ˌoːvərˈsteitmənt] *n* : exageración *f*
overstep [ˌoːvərˈstɛp] *vt* **-stepped; -step-
ping** EXCEED : sobrepasar, traspasar,
exceder
overt [oːˈvərt, ˈoːˌvərt] *adj* : evidente, manifiesto, patente
overtake [ˌoːvərˈteik] *vt* **-took** [-ˈtʊk];
-taken [-ˈteikən]; **-taking** : pasar, adelantar, rebasar *Mex*
overthrow[1] [ˌoːvərˈθroː] *vt* **-threw** [-ˈθruː]
: **-thrown** [-ˈθroːn]; **-throwing** **1** OVER-
TURN : dar la vuelta a, volcar **2** DEFEAT,
TOPPLE : derrocar, derribar, deponer
overthrow[2] [ˈoːvərˌθroː] *n* : derrocamiento *m*, caída *f*
overtime [ˈoːvərˌtaim] *n* **1** : horas *fpl* extras (de trabajo) **2** : prórroga *f*; alargue
m *Arg, Chile, Uru* (en deportes)
overtly [oːˈvərtli, ˈoːˌvərt-] *adv* OPENLY
: abiertamente
overtone [ˈoːvərˌtoːn] *n* **1** : armónico *m*
(en música) **2** HINT, SUGGESTION : tinte
m, insinuación *f*
overture [ˈoːvərˌtʃʊr, -tʃər] *n* **1** PROPOSAL
: propuesta *f* **2** : obertura *f* (en música)
overturn [ˌoːvərˈtərn] *vt* **1** UPSET : dar
la vuelta a, volcar **2** NULLIFY : anular,
invalidar — *vi* TURN OVER : volcar, dar
un vuelco
overuse [ˌoːvərˈjuːz] *vt* **-used; -using**
: abusar de
overview [ˈoːvərˌvjuː] *n* : resumen *m*,
visión *f* general
overweening [ˌoːvərˈwiːnɪŋ] *adj* **1** ARRO-
GANT : arrogante, soberbio **2** IMMODER-
ATE : desmesurado
overweight [ˌoːvərˈweit] *adj* : demasiado
gordo, demasiado pesado
overwhelm [ˌoːvərˈhwɛlm] *vt* **1** CRUSH,
DEFEAT : aplastar, arrollar **2** SUBMERGE
: inundar, sumergir **3** OVERPOWER
: abrumar, agobiar ⟨overwhelmed by
remorse : abrumado de remordimiento⟩
overwhelming [ˌoːvərˈhwɛlmɪŋ] *adj* **1**
CRUSHING : abrumador, apabullante **2**
SWEEPING : arrollador, aplastante ⟨an
overwhelming majority : una mayoría
aplastante⟩
overwork [ˌoːvərˈwərk] *vt* **1** : hacer trabajar demasiado **2** OVERUSE : abusar de —
vi : trabajar demasiado

overwrought [ˌoːvərˈrɔt] *adj* : alterado, sobreexcitado

ovoid [ˈoːˌvɔɪd] *or* **ovoidal** [oˈvoɪdəl] *adj* : ovoide

ovulate [ˈɑvjəˌleɪt, ˈoː-] *vi* **-lated; -lating** : ovular

ovulation [ˌɑvjəˈleɪʃən, ˌoː-] *n* : ovulación *f*

ovum [ˈoːvəm] *n, pl* **ova** [-və] : óvulo *m*

ow [ˈaʊ] *interj* : ¡ay!; ¡huy!, ¡uy!

owe [ˈoː] *vt* **owed; owing** : deber ⟨you owe me $ 10 : me debes $ 10⟩ ⟨he owes his wealth to his father : le debe su riqueza a su padre⟩

owing to *prep* : debido a

owl [ˈaʊl] *n* : búho *m*, lechuza *f*, tecolote *m Mex*

own¹ [ˈoːn] *vt* **1** POSSESS : poseer, tener, ser dueño de **2** ADMIT : reconocer, admitir — *vi* **to own up** : reconocer (algo), admitir (algo)

own² *adj* : propio, personal, particular ⟨his own car : su propio coche⟩

own³ *pron* **1** (*used with a possessive*) ⟨the book is his own : el libro es suyo, el libro escribió él⟩ ⟨money of your own : tu/ su propio dinero⟩ ⟨I want an apartment to call my own : quiero un apartamento para mí solo⟩ ⟨she has a style all her own : tiene un estilo muy particular⟩ ⟨to each his own : cada uno a lo suyo⟩ **2 on one's own** : solo ⟨we did it on our own : lo hicimos solos⟩ ⟨they left her on her own : la dejaron sola⟩

owner [ˈoːnər] *n* : dueño *m*, -ña *f*; propietario *m*, -ria *f*

ownership [ˈoːnərˌʃɪp] *n* : propiedad *f*

ox [ˈɑks] *n, pl* **oxen** [ˈɑksən] : buey *m*

oxidation [ˌɑksəˈdeɪʃən] *n* : oxidación *f*

oxide [ˈɑkˌsaɪd] *n* : óxido *m*

oxidize [ˈɑksəˌdaɪz] *vt* **-dized; -dizing** : oxidar

oxygen [ˈɑksɪʤən] *n* : oxígeno *m*

oxygenate [ˈɑksɪʤəˌneɪt] *vt* **-nated; -nating** : oxigenar

oyster [ˈɔɪstər] *n* : ostra *f*, ostión *m Mex*

ozone [ˈoːˌzoːn] *n* : ozono *m* ⟨ozone layer : capa de ozono⟩

P

p [ˈpiː] *n, pl* **p's** *or* **ps** [ˈpiːz] : decimosexta letra del alfabeto inglés

PA [ˌpiːˈeɪ] *n* (*public address system*) : altavoces *mpl*, altoparlantes *mpl*

pace¹ [ˈpeɪs] *v* **paced; pacing** *vi* : caminar, ir y venir — *vt* **1** : caminar por ⟨she paced the floor : caminaba de un lado a otro del cuarto⟩ **2 to pace a runner** : marcarle el ritmo a un corredor

pace² *n* **1** STEP : paso *m* **2** RATE : paso *m*, ritmo *m* ⟨to set the pace : marcar el paso, marcar la pauta⟩

pacemaker [ˈpeɪsˌmeɪkər] *n* : marcapasos *m*

pacific [pəˈsɪfɪk] *adj* : pacífico

pacifier [ˈpæsəˌfaɪər] *n* : chupete *m*, chupón *m*, mamila *f Mex*

pacifism [ˈpæsəˌfɪzəm] *n* : pacifismo *m*

pacifist [ˈpæsəfɪst] *n* : pacifista *mf*

pacify [ˈpæsəˌfaɪ] *vt* **-fied; -fying 1** SOOTHE : apaciguar, pacificar **2** : pacificar (un país, una región, etc.) — **pacification** *n*

pack¹ [ˈpæk] *vt* **1** PACKAGE : empaquetar, embalar, envasar **2** : empacar, meter (en una maleta) ⟨to pack one's bags : hacer las maletas⟩ **3** FILL : llenar, abarrotar ⟨a packed theater : un teatro abarrotado⟩ **4** TAMP : apisonar (tierra), compactar (nieve) ⟨firmly packed brown sugar : azúcar morena bien compacta⟩ **5 to pack in** LEAVE : dejar **6 to pack in/ into** : meter en ⟨they packed us all into one room : nos metieron a todos en una sala⟩ ⟨to pack them in : atraer una multitud⟩ **7 to pack it in** *fam* QUIT, STOP : parar **8 to pack off** SEND : mandar **9 to pack up** : recoger, guardar (para lle-

var) — *vi or* **to pack up** : empacar, hacer las maletas

pack² *n* **1** BUNDLE : bulto *m*, fardo *m* **2** BACKPACK : mochila *f* **3** PACKAGE : paquete *m*, cajetilla *f* (de cigarrillos, etc.) **4** : manada *f* (de lobos, etc.), jauría *f* (de perros) ⟨a pack of thieves : una pandilla de ladrones⟩ **5** : baraja *f* (de naipes)

package¹ [ˈpækɪʤ] *vt* **-aged; -aging** : empaquetar, embalar

package² *n* : paquete *m*, bulto *m*

packaging [ˈpækɪʤɪŋ] *n* **1** : embalaje *m* **2** WRAPPING : envoltorio *m*

packer [ˈpækər] *n* : empacador *m*, -dora *f*

packet [ˈpækət] *n* : paquete *m*

packing [ˈpækɪŋ] *n* : embalaje *m*

pact [ˈpækt] *n* : pacto *m*, acuerdo *m*

pad¹ [ˈpæd] *vt* **padded; padding 1** FILL, STUFF : rellenar, acolchar (una silla, una pared) **2** : meter paja en, rellenar ⟨to pad a speech : rellenar un discurso⟩

pad² *n* **1** CUSHION : almohadilla *f* ⟨a shoulder pad : una hombrera⟩ **2** TABLET : bloc *m* (de papel) **3** → **lily pad 4** → **ink pad 5** → **launchpad 6** → **landing pad**

padding [ˈpædɪŋ] *n* **1** FILLING : relleno *m* **2** : paja *f* (en un discurso, etc.)

paddle¹ [ˈpædəl] *v* **-dled; -dling** *vt* **1** : hacer avanzar (una canoa) con canalete **2** HIT : azotar, darle nalgadas a (con una pala o paleta) — *vi* **1** : remar (en una canoa) **2** SPLASH : chapotear, mojarse los pies

paddle² *n* **1** : canalete *m*, zagual *m* (de una canoa, etc.) **2** : pala *f*, paleta *f* (en deportes)

paddock [ˈpædək] *n* **1** PASTURE : potrero *m* **2** : paddock *m*, cercado *m* (en un hipódromo)

paddy ['pædi] *n, pl* **-dies** : arrozal *m*

padlock¹ ['pæd,lɑk] *vt* : cerrar con candado

padlock² *n* : candado *m*

paella [pɑ'elə, -'eljə, -'eɪə] *n* : paella *f*

pagan¹ ['peɪgən] *adj* : pagano

pagan² *n* : pagano *m*, -na *f*

paganism ['peɪgən,ɪzəm] *n* : paganismo *m*

page¹ ['peɪdʒ] *vt* **paged; paging** : llamar por altavoz

page² *n* **1** BELLHOP : botones *m* **2** : página *f* (de un libro, etc.) ⟨page six : la página seis⟩

pageant ['pædʒənt] *n* **1** SPECTACLE : espectáculo *m* **2** PROCESSION : desfile *m*

pageantry ['pædʒəntri] *n* : pompa *f*, fausto *m*

pager ['peɪdʒər] *n* BEEPER : buscapersonas *m*

pagoda [pə'goːdə] *n* : pagoda *f*

paid → **pay**

pail ['peɪl] *n* : balde *m*, cubo *m*, cubeta *f* Mex

pailful ['peɪl,fʊl] *n* : balde *m*, cubo *m*, cubeta *f* Mex

pain¹ ['peɪn] *vt* : doler

pain² *n* **1** PENALTY : pena *f* ⟨under pain of death : so pena de muerte⟩ **2** SUFFERING : dolor *m*, malestar *m*, pena *f* (mental) **3 pains** *npl* EFFORT : esmero *m*, esfuerzo *m* ⟨to take pains : esmerarse⟩ **4** ANNOYANCE : molestia *f*, fastidio *m* ⟨he's a pain in the neck : es un pesado⟩

painful ['peɪnfəl] *adj* : doloroso — **painfully** *adv*

painkiller ['peɪn,kɪlər] *n* : analgésico *m*

painless ['peɪnləs] *adj* : indoloro, sin dolor

painlessly ['peɪnləsli] *adv* : sin dolor

painstaking ['peɪn,steɪkɪŋ] *adj* : esmerado, cuidadoso, meticuloso — **painstakingly** *adv*

paint¹ ['peɪnt] *vt* : pintar

paint² *n* : pintura *f*

paintbrush ['peɪnt,brʌʃ] *n* : pincel *m* (de un artista), brocha *f* (para pintar casas, etc.)

painter ['peɪntər] *n* : pintor *m*, -tora *f*

painting ['peɪntɪŋ] *n* : pintura *f*

pair¹ ['pær] *vt* : emparejar, poner en parejas — *vi* : emparejarse

pair² *n* : par *m* (de objetos), pareja *f* (de personas o animales) ⟨a pair of scissors : unas tijeras⟩

pajamas [pə'dʒɑməz, -'dʒæ-] *npl* : pijama *m*, piyama *mf*

Pakistani [,pækɪ'stæni, ,pɑkɪ'stɑni] *n* : paquistaní *mf* — **Pakistani** *adj*

pal ['pæl] *n* : amigo *m*, -ga *f*; compinche *mf* fam; chamo *m*, -ma *f* Ven fam; cuate *m*, -ta *f* Mex

palace ['pæləs] *n* : palacio *m*

palatable ['pælətəbəl] *adj* : sabroso

palate ['pælət] *n* **1** : paladar *m* (de la boca) **2** TASTE : paladar *m*, gusto *m*

palatial [pə'leɪʃəl] *adj* : suntuoso, espléndido

palaver [pə'lævər, -'lɑ-] *n* : palabrería *f*

pale¹ ['peɪl] *v* **paled; paling** *vi* : palidecer — *vt* : hacer pálido

pale² *adj* **paler; palest 1** : pálido ⟨to turn pale : palidecer, ponerse pálido⟩ **2** : claro (dícese de los colores)

paleness ['peɪlnəs] *n* : palidez *f*

paleontologist [,peɪliˌɑn'tɑlədʒɪst] *n* : leontólogo *m*, -ga *f*

paleontology [,peɪliˌɑn'tɑlədʒi] *n* : paleontología *f*

Palestinian [,pælə'stɪniən] *n* : palestino *m*, -na *f* — **Palestinian** *adj*

palette ['pælət] *n* : paleta *f* (para mezclar pigmentos)

palisade [,pælə'seɪd] *n* **1** FENCE : empalizada *f*, estacada *f* **2** CLIFFS : acantilado *m*

pall¹ ['pɔl] *vi* : perder su sabor, dejar de gustar

pall² *n* **1** : paño *m* funerario (sobre un ataúd) **2** COVER : cortina *f* (de humo, etc.) **3 to cast a pall over** : ensombrecer

pallbearer ['pɔl,berər] *n* : portador *m*, -dora *f* del féretro

pallet ['pælət] *n* **1** BED : camastro *m* **2** PLATFORM : plataforma *f* de carga

palliative ['pæliˌeɪtɪv, 'pæljətɪv] *adj* : paliativo ⟨palliative care : cuidados paliativos⟩

pallid ['pæləd] *adj* : pálido

pallor ['pælər] *n* : palidez *f*

palm¹ ['pɑm, 'pɑlm] *vt* **1** CONCEAL : escamotear (un naipe, etc.) **2 to palm off** : encajar, endilgar *fam* ⟨he palmed it off on me : me lo endilgó⟩

palm² *n* **1** *or* **palm tree** : palmera *f* **2** : palma *f* (de la mano)

palmistry ['pɑməstri, 'pɑlmə-] *n* : quiromancia *f*

Palm Sunday *n* : Domingo *m* de Ramos

palomino [,pælə'miːˌnoː] *n, pl* **-nos** : caballo *m* de color dorado

palpable ['pælpəbəl] *adj* : palpable — **palpably** [-bli] *adv*

palpitate ['pælpəˌteɪt] *vi* **-tated; -tating** : palpitar

palpitation [,pælpə'teɪʃən] *n* : palpitación *f*

palsy ['pɔlzi] *n, pl* **-sies 1** : parálisis *f* **2** → **cerebral palsy**

paltry ['pɔltri] *adj* **paltrier; -est** : mísero, mezquino, insignificante ⟨a paltry excuse : una mala excusa⟩

pampas ['pæmpəz, 'pɑmpəs] *npl* : pampa *f*

pamper ['pæmpər] *vt* : mimar, consentir, chiquear *Mex*

pamphlet ['pæmpflət] *n* : panfleto *m*, folleto *m*

pan¹ ['pæn] *vt* **panned; panning** CRITICIZE : poner por los suelos — *vi* **1 to pan for gold** : cribar el oro con batea, lavar oro **2 to pan out** : resultar, salir

pan² *n* **1** : cacerola *f*, cazuela *f* **2 frying pan** : sartén *mf*, freidera *f* Mex

pan- *pref* : pan- ⟨panacea : panacea⟩

panacea [,pænə'siːə] *n* : panacea *f*

Panamanian [,pænə'meɪniən] *n* : panameño *m*, -ña *f* — **Panamanian** *adj*

pancake ['pæn,keɪk] *n* : panqueque *m*

pancreas ['pæŋkriəs, 'pæn-] n : páncreas m

panda ['pændə] n : panda mf

pandemonium [,pændə'mo:niəm] n : pandemonio m, pandemónium m

pander ['pændər] vi **to pander to** : satisfacer, complacer (a alguien) ⟨to pander to popular taste : satisfacer el gusto popular⟩

pane ['pein] n : cristal m, vidrio m

panel¹ ['pænəl] vt **-eled** or **-elled; -eling** or **-elling** : adornar con paneles

panel² n 1 : lista f de nombres (de un jurado, etc.) 2 GROUP : grupo m, panel m (de discusión), jurado m (de un concurso, etc.) 3 : panel m (de una pared, etc.) 4 : tablero m ⟨control panel : tablero de control⟩

paneling ['pænəliŋ] n : paneles mpl

pang ['pæŋ] n : puntada f, punzada f

panhandler ['pæn,hændlər] n : mendigo m, -ga f

panic¹ ['pænik] v **-icked; -icking** vt : llenar de pánico — vi : ser presa de pánico

panic² n : pánico m

panicky ['pæniki] adj : presa del pánico

panic–stricken adj : presa del pánico ⟨to be panic-stricken : ser presa del pánico⟩

panorama [,pænə'ræmə, -'rɑ-] n : panorama m

panoramic [,pænə'ræmik, -'rɑ-] adj : panorámico

pansy ['pænzi] n, pl **-sies** : pensamiento m

pant¹ ['pænt] vi : jadear, resoplar

pant² adj : del pantalón

pant³ n : jadeo m, resoplo m

pantaloons [,pæntə'lu:nz] → **pants**

pantheon ['pænθi,ɑn, -ən] n : panteón m

panther ['pænθər] n : pantera f

panties ['pæntiz] npl : calzones mpl; pantaletas fpl Mex, Ven; bombacha f Arg, Uru; panties mfpl CA, Car; bragas fpl Spain

pantomime¹ ['pæntə,maim] v **-mimed; -miming** vt : representar mediante la pantomima — vi : hacer la mímica

pantomime² n : pantomima f

pantry ['pæntri] n, pl **-tries** : despensa f

pants ['pænts] npl 1 TROUSERS : pantalón m, pantalones mpl 2 : panties

pantsuit ['pænt,su:t] n : traje m pantalón

panty hose ['pænti] ns & pl : medias fpl, panties mfpl Spain, pantimedias fpl Mex

pap ['pæp] n : papilla f (para bebés, etc.)

papa ['pɑpə] n : papá m

papal ['peipəl] adj : papal

papaya [pə'paiə] n : papaya f (fruta)

paper¹ ['peipər] vt WALLPAPER : empapelar

paper² adj : del papel

paper³ n 1 : papel m ⟨a piece of paper : un papel⟩ 2 DOCUMENT : papel m, documento m 3 NEWSPAPER : periódico m, diario m 4 ESSAY : ensayo m

paperback ['peipər,bæk] n : libro m en rústica

paper clip n : clip m, sujetapapeles m

paperweight ['peipər,weit] n : pisapapeles m

paperwork ['peipər,wərk] n : papeleo m

papery ['peipəri] adj : parecido al papel

papier–mâché [,peipərmə'ʃei, ,pæ,pjer-mæ'ʃei] n : papel m maché

papoose [pæ'pu:s, pə-] n : niño m, -ña f de los indios norteamericanos

paprika [pə'pri:kə, pæ-] n : pimentón m, paprika f

Pap smear ['pæp-] n : Papanicolau m

papyrus [pə'pairəs] n, pl **-ruses** or **-ri** [-ri, -,rai] : papiro m

par ['pɑr] n 1 VALUE : valor m (nominal), par f ⟨below par : debajo de la par⟩ 2 EQUALITY : igualdad f ⟨to be on a par with : estar al mismo nivel que⟩ 3 : par m (en golf)

parable ['pærəbəl] n : parábola f

parabola [pə'ræbələ] n : parábola f (en matemáticas)

parachute¹ ['pærə,ʃu:t] vi **-chuted; -chuting** : lanzarse en paracaídas

parachute² n : paracaídas m

parachutist ['pærə,ʃu:tist] n : paracaidista mf

parade¹ [pə'reid] vi **-raded; -rading** 1 MARCH : desfilar 2 SHOW OFF : pavonearse, lucirse

parade² n 1 PROCESSION : desfile m 2 DISPLAY : alarde m

paradigm ['pærə,daim] n : paradigma m

paradise ['pærə,dais, -,daiz] n : paraíso m

paradox ['pærə,dɑks] n : paradoja f

paradoxical [,pærə'dɑksikəl] adj : paradójico — **paradoxically** adv

paraffin ['pærəfən] n : parafina f

paragliding ['pærə,glaidiŋ] n : parapente m

paragon ['pærə,gɑn, -gən] n : dechado m

paragraph¹ ['pærə,græf] vt : dividir en párrafos

paragraph² n : párrafo m, acápite m

Paraguayan [,pærə'gwaiən, -'gwei-] n : paraguayo m, -ya f — **Paraguayan** adj

parakeet ['pærə,ki:t] n : periquito m

paralegal [,pærə'li:gəl] n : asistente mf de abogado

parallel¹ ['pærə,lɛl, -ləl] vt 1 MATCH, RESEMBLE : ser paralelo a, ser análogo a, corresponder con 2 : extenderse en línea paralela con ⟨the road parallels the river : el camino se extiende a lo largo del río⟩

parallel² adj : paralelo

parallel³ n 1 : línea f paralela, superficie f paralela 2 : paralelo m (en geografía) 3 SIMILARITY : paralelismo m, semejanza f

parallelogram [,pærə'lɛlə,græm] n : paralelogramo m

paralysis [pə'ræləsis] n, pl **-yses** [-,si:z] : parálisis f

paralyze ['pærə,laiz] vt **-lyzed; -lyzing** : paralizar

paramedic [,pærə'mɛdik] n : paramédico m, -ca f

parameter [pə'ræmətər] n : parámetro m

paramount ['pærə,maunt] adj : supremo ⟨of paramount importance : de suma importancia⟩

paranoia [ˌpærə'nɔɪə] n : paranoia f
paranoid ['pærəˌnɔɪd] adj : paranoico
paranormal [ˌpærə'nɔrməl] adj : para-normal
parapet ['pærəpət, -ˌpet] n : parapeto m
paraphernalia [ˌpærəfə'neɪljə, -fər-] ns & pl : parafernalia f
paraphrase¹ ['pærəˌfreɪz] vt **-phrased; -phrasing** : parafrasear
paraphrase² n : paráfrasis f
paraplegic¹ [ˌpærə'pli:dʒɪk] adj : para-pléjico
paraplegic² n : parapléjico m, -ca f
parasite ['pærəˌsaɪt] n : parásito m
parasitic [ˌpærə'sɪtɪk] adj : parasitario
parasol ['pærəˌsɔl] n : sombrilla f, quitasol m, parasol m
paratrooper ['pærəˌtru:pər] n : paracai-dista mf (militar)
parboil ['parˌbɔɪl] vt : sancochar, cocer a medias
parcel¹ ['parsəl] vt **-celed** or **-celled; -cel-ing** or **-celling** or **to parcel out** : repartir, parcelar (tierras)
parcel² n 1 LOT : parcela f, lote m 2 PACKAGE : paquete m, bulto m
parch ['partʃ] vt : resecar
parched adj 1 DRY : muy seco, quemado 2 THIRSTY : seco
parchment ['partʃmənt] n : pergamino m
pardon¹ ['pardən] vt 1 FORGIVE : perdo-nar, disculpar ⟨pardon me! : ¡perdone!, ¡disculpe la molestia!⟩ 2 REPRIEVE : indultar (a un delincuente)
pardon² n 1 FORGIVENESS : perdón m 2 REPRIEVE : indulto m
pardonable ['pardənəbəl] adj : perdona-ble
pare ['pær] vt **pared; paring** 1 PEEL : pe-lar 2 TRIM : recortar 3 REDUCE : redu-cir ⟨he pared it (down) to 50 pages : lo redujo a 50 páginas⟩
parent ['pærənt] n 1 : madre f, padre m 2 **parents** npl : padres mpl
parentage ['pærəntɪdʒ] n : linaje m, abo-lengo m, origen m
parental [pə'rɛntəl] adj : de los padres
parenthesis [pə'rɛnθəsɪs] n, pl **-theses** [-ˌsi:z] : paréntesis m
parenthetic [ˌpærən'θɛtɪk] or **parentheti-cal** [-tɪkəl] adj : parentético — **paren-thetically** [-tɪkli] adv
parenthood ['pærəntˌhʊd] n : paternidad f
parfait [par'feɪ] n : postre m elaborado con frutas y helado
pariah [pə'raɪə] n : paria mf
parish ['pærɪʃ] n : parroquia f
parishioner [pə'rɪʃənər] n : feligrés m, -gresa f
parity ['pærəti] n, pl **-ties** : paridad f
park¹ ['park] vt : estacionar, parquear, aparcar Spain — vi : estacionarse, par-quearse, aparcar Spain
park² n : parque m
parka ['parkə] n : parka f
parking ['parkɪŋ] n : estacionamiento m, aparcamiento m Spain
parking lot n : estacionamiento m, par-king m, aparcamiento m Spain (lugar)
parking meter n : parquímetro m

parking ticket n : multa f (de parquímetro o por estacionarse mal)
parkway ['parkˌweɪ] n : carretera f ajar-dinada, bulevar m
parley¹ ['parli] vi : parlamentar, negociar
parley² n, pl **-leys** : negociación f, parla-mento m
parliament ['parləmənt, 'parljə-] n : parla-mento m
parliamentary [ˌparlə'mɛntəri, ˌparljə-] adj : parlamentario
parlor ['parlər] n 1 : sala f, salón m (en una casa) 2 : salón m ⟨beauty parlor : salón de belleza⟩ 3 **funeral parlor** : funeraria f
parochial [pə'ro:kiəl] adj 1 : parroquial 2 PROVINCIAL : pueblerino, de miras estre-chas
parody¹ ['pærədi] vt **-died; -dying** : paro-diar
parody² n, pl **-dies** : parodia f
parole [pə'ro:l] n : libertad f condicional
paroxysm ['pærəkˌsɪzəm, pə'rak-] n : pa-roxismo m
parquet ['parˌkeɪ, par'keɪ] n : parquet m, parqué m
parrakeet → **parakeet**
parrot ['pærət] n : loro m, papagayo m
parry¹ ['pæri] v **-ried; -rying** vi : parar un golpe — vt EVADE : esquivar (una pre-gunta, etc.)
parry² n, pl **-ries** : parada f
parsimonious [ˌparsə'mo:niəs] adj : ta-caño, mezquino
parsley ['parsli] n : perejil m
parsnip ['parsnɪp] n : chirivía f
parson ['parsən] n : pastor m, -tora f; clé-rigo m
parsonage ['parsənɪdʒ] n : rectoría f, casa f del párroco
part¹ ['part] vi 1 SEPARATE : separarse, despedirse ⟨we should part as friends : debemos separarnos amistosamente⟩ 2 OPEN : abrirse ⟨the curtains parted : las cortinas se abrieron⟩ 3 **to part with** : deshacerse de — vt 1 SEPARATE : separ-ar 2 **to part one's hair** : hacerse la raya, peinarse con raya
part² n 1 SECTION, SEGMENT : parte f, sección f ⟨for the better part of a year : durante casi un año⟩ ⟨in the latter part of the century : hacia finales de siglo⟩ ⟨the western part of the state : la parte oeste del estado⟩ ⟨the best/worst part is that . . . : lo mejor/peor es que . . .⟩ 2 PIECE : pieza f (de una máquina, etc.) 3 ROLE : papel m (en teatro, etc.) ⟨to play a part : hacer un papel⟩ ⟨to look the part : tener el aspecto para el papel⟩ 4 ROLE, INFLUENCE : papel m ⟨to play a part : ju-gar un papel⟩ ⟨to want no part of/in : no querer tener nada que ver con⟩ 5 : raya f (del pelo) 6 **for my/his (etc.) part** : por mi/su (etc.) parte 7 **for the most part** MOSTLY : en su mayoría, en su mayor parte 8 **for the most part** USUALLY : en general 9 **in part** : en parte 10 **in these parts** : por aquí 11 **on the part of** : de/por parte de 12 **to take part (in)** : tomar parte (en), participar (en)

partake [pɑr'teɪk, pər-] *vi* **-took** [-'tʊk]; **-taken** [-'teɪkən]; **-taking 1 to partake of** CONSUME : comer, beber, tomar **2 to partake in** : participar en (una actividad, etc.)

partial ['pɑrʃəl] *adj* **1** BIASED : parcial, tendencioso **2** INCOMPLETE : parcial, incompleto **3 to be partial to** : ser aficionado a

partiality [ˌpɑrʃi'æləti] *n, pl* **-ties** : parcialidad *f*

partially ['pɑrʃəli] *adv* : parcialmente

participant [pər'tɪsəpənt, pɑr-] *n* : participante *mf*

participate [pər'tɪsəˌpeɪt, pɑr-] *vi* **-pated; -pating** : participar

participation [pərˌtɪsə'peɪʃən, pɑr-] *n* : participación *f*

participle ['pɑrtəˌsɪpəl] *n* : participio *m*

particle ['pɑrtɪkəl] *n* : partícula *f*

particular[1] [pɑr'tɪkjələr] *adj* **1** SPECIFIC : particular, en particular ⟨this particular person : esta persona en particular⟩ **2** SPECIAL : particular, especial ⟨with particular emphasis : con un énfasis especial⟩ **3** FUSSY : exigente, maniático ⟨to be very particular : ser muy especial⟩ ⟨I'm not particular : me da igual⟩

particular[2] *n* **1** DETAIL : detalle *m*, sentido *m* **in particular** : en particular, en especial

particularly [pɑr'tɪkjələrli] *adv* **1** ESPECIALLY : particularmente, especialmente **2** SPECIFICALLY : específicamente, en especial

partisan ['pɑrtəzən, -sən] *n* **1** ADHERENT : partidario *m*, -ria *f* **2** GUERRILLA : partisano *m*, -na *f*; guerrillero *m*, -ra *f*

partition[1] ['pɑrtɪʃən, pɑr-] *vt* : dividir ⟨to partition off (a room) : dividir (una habitación) con un tabique⟩

partition[2] *n* **1** DISTRIBUTION : partición *f*, división *f*, reparto *m* **2** DIVIDER : tabique *m*, mampara *f*, biombo *m*

partly ['pɑrtli] *adv* : en parte, parcialmente

partner ['pɑrtnər] *n* **1** COMPANION : compañero *m*, -ra *f* **2** : pareja *f* (en un juego, etc.) ⟨dancing partner : pareja de baile⟩ **3** MATE : pareja *f*; compañero *m*, -ra *f* ⟨(marital) partner : cónyuge⟩ **4** : socio *m*, -cia *f*; asociado *m*, -da *f* ⟨business/ senior partner : socio comercial/mayoritario⟩

partnership ['pɑrtnərˌʃɪp] *n* **1** ASSOCIATION : asociación *f*, compañerismo *m* **2** : sociedad *f* (de negociantes) ⟨to form a partnership : asociarse⟩

part of speech : categoría *f* gramatical

partridge ['pɑrtrɪdʒ] *n, pl* **-tridge** or **-tridges** : perdiz *f*

part-time[1] ['pɑrt'taɪm] *adv* : medio tiempo, a tiempo parcial

part-time[2] *adj* : de medio tiempo, a tiempo parcial

party ['pɑrti] *n, pl* **-ties 1** : partido *m* (político) **2** PARTICIPANT : parte *f*, participante *mf* **3** GROUP : grupo *m* (de personas) **4** GATHERING : fiesta *f* ⟨to throw a party : dar una fiesta⟩

parvenu ['pɑrvəˌnu:, -ˌnju:] *n* : advenedizo *m*, -za *f*

pass[1] ['pæs] *vi* **1** : pasar, cruzarse ⟨a plane passed overhead : pasó un avión⟩ ⟨we passed in the hallway : nos cruzamos en el pasillo⟩ **2** CEASE : pasarse ⟨the pain passed : se pasó el dolor⟩ **3** ELAPSE : pasar, transcurrir **4** PROCEED : pasar ⟨let me pass : déjame pasar⟩ **5** HAPPEN : pasar, ocurrir **6** : pasar, aprobar (en un examen) **7** *or* **to pass down** : pasar ⟨the throne passed to his son : el trono pasó a su hijo⟩ **8 to pass as** : pasar por **9 to pass away/on** DIE : fallecer, morir **10 to pass by** : pasar **11 to pass out** FAINT : desmayarse — *vt* **1** : pasar por (un lugar) **2** OVERTAKE : pasar, adelantar **3** SPEND : pasar (tiempo) **4** HAND : pasar ⟨pass me the salt : pásame la sal⟩ **5** : aprobar (un examen) **6** : aprobar (a un estudiante) **7** APPROVE : aprobar (una ley) **8 to let pass** OVERLOOK, IGNORE : pasar por alto, dejar pasar **9 to pass by** : escapársele a (alguien) ⟨don't let life pass you by : no dejes que la vida se te pase⟩ **10 to pass off as** : hacer pasar por ⟨to pass oneself off as : hacerse pasar por⟩ **11 to pass on** TRANSMIT, RELAY : pasar **12 to pass over** SKIP, OMIT : pasar por alto **13 to pass up** DECLINE : dejar pasar **14 to pass the time** : pasar el rato

pass[2] *n* **1** CROSSING, GAP : paso *m*, desfiladero *m*, puerto *m* ⟨mountain pass : puerto de montaña⟩ **2** PERMIT : pase *m*, permiso *m* **3** : pase *m* (en deportes) **4** SITUATION : situación *f* (difícil) ⟨how did we come to such a pass? : ¿cómo llegamos a tal extremo?⟩

passable ['pæsəbəl] *adj* **1** ADEQUATE : adecuado, pasable **2** : transitable (dícese de un camino, etc.)

passably ['pæsəbli] *adv* : pasablemente

passage ['pæsɪdʒ] *n* **1** PASSING : paso *m* ⟨the passage of time : el paso del tiempo⟩ **2** PASSAGEWAY : pasillo *m* (dentro de un edificio), pasaje *m* (entre edificios) **3** VOYAGE : travesía *f* (por el mar), viaje *m* ⟨to grant safe passage : dar un salvoconducto⟩ **4** SECTION : pasaje *m* (en música o literatura) **5** APPROVAL : aprobación *f* (de un proyecto de ley, etc.)

passageway ['pæsɪdʒˌweɪ] *n* : pasillo *m*, pasadizo *m*, corredor *m*

passbook ['pæsˌbʊk] *n* BANKBOOK : libreta *f* de ahorros

passé [pæ'seɪ] *adj* : pasado de moda

passenger ['pæsəndʒər] *n* : pasajero *m*, -ra *f*

passerby [ˌpæsər'baɪ, 'pæsərˌ-] *n, pl* **passersby** : transeúnte *mf*

passing[1] *adj* **1** : que pasa ⟨he saw a passing train : vio un tren que pasaba⟩ ⟨with each passing day/year : con cada día/año que pasa⟩ **2** TRANSIENT : pasajero **3** CURSORY : somero ⟨to make a passing reference to : referirse de pasada a⟩ **4** SLIGHT, SUPERFICIAL : ligero (dícese de un parecido), superficial (dícese de un conocimiento, un interés, etc.) **5** SATIS-

FACTORY : satisfactorio ⟨to get a passing grade : aprobar (en un examen, etc.)⟩

passing² ['pæsɪŋ] *n* **1** DEATH : fallecimiento *m* **2** PASSAGE, MOVEMENT : paso *m* (del tiempo, etc.) **3** PASSAGE, APPROVAL : aprobación *f* **4 in passing** : de pasada

passion ['pæʃən] *n* : pasión *f*, ardor *m*

passionate ['pæʃənət] *adj* **1** IRASCIBLE : irascible, iracundo **2** ARDENT : apasionado, ardiente, ferviente, fogoso

passionately ['pæʃənətli] *adv* : apasionadamente, fervientemente, con pasión

passive¹ ['pæsɪv] *adj* : pasivo — **passively** *adv*

passive² *n* : voz *f* pasiva (en gramática)

Passover ['pæs,o:vər] *n* : Pascua *f* (en el judaísmo)

passport ['pæs,port] *n* : pasaporte *m*

password ['pæs,wərd] *n* : contraseña *f*

past¹ ['pæst] *adv* : por delante ⟨he drove past : pasamos en coche⟩

past² *adj* **1** AGO : hace ⟨10 years past : hace 10 años⟩ **2** LAST : último ⟨the past few months : los últimos meses⟩ **3** BYGONE : pasado ⟨in past times : en tiempos pasados⟩ **4** : pasado (en gramática)

past³ *n* : pasado *m*

past⁴ *prep* **1** BY : por, por delante de ⟨he ran past the house : pasó por la casa corriendo⟩ **2** BEYOND : más allá de ⟨just past the corner : un poco más allá de la esquina⟩ ⟨we went past the exit : pasamos la salida⟩ **3** AFTER : después de ⟨past noon : después del mediodía⟩ ⟨half past two : las dos y media⟩

pasta ['pɑstə, 'pæs-] *n* : pasta *f*

paste¹ ['peɪst] *vt* **pasted; pasting** : pegar (con engrudo)

paste² *n* **1** : pasta *f* ⟨tomato paste : pasta de tomate⟩ **2** : engrudo *m* (para pegar)

pasteboard ['peɪst,bord] *n* : cartón *m*, cartulina *f*

pastel [pæ'stel] *n* : pastel *m* — **pastel** *adj*

pasteurization [,pæstʃərə'zeɪʃən, ,pæstjə-] *n* : pasteurización *f*

pasteurize ['pæs,tʃəraɪz, 'pæstjə-] *vt* **-ized; -izing** : pasteurizar

pastime ['pæs,taɪm] *n* : pasatiempo *m*

pastor ['pæstər] *n* : pastor *m*, -tora *f*

pastoral ['pæstərəl] *adj* : pastoral

past participle *n* : participio *m* pasado

pastry ['peɪstri] *n, pl* **-ries 1** DOUGH : pasta *f*, masa *f* **2 pastries** *npl* : pasteles *mpl*

pasture¹ ['pæstʃər] *v* **-tured; -turing** *vi* GRAZE : pacer, pastar — *vt* : apacentar, pastar

pasture² *n* : pastizal *m*, potrero *m*, pasto *m*

pasty ['peɪsti] *adj* **pastier; -est 1** : pastoso (en consistencia) **2** PALLID : pálido

pat¹ ['pæt] *vt* **patted; patting** : dar palmaditas a, tocar

pat² *adv* : de memoria ⟨to have down pat : saberse de memoria⟩

pat³ *adj* **1** APT : apto, apropiado **2** GLIB : fácil **3** UNYIELDING : firme ⟨to stand pat : mantenerse firme⟩

pat⁴ *n* **1** TAP : golpecito *m*, palmadita *f* ⟨a pat on the back : una palmadita en la espalda⟩ **2** CARESS : caricia *f* **3** : porción *f* ⟨a pat of butter : una porción de mantequilla⟩

patch¹ ['pætʃ] *vt* **1** MEND, REPAIR : remendar, parchar, ponerle un parche a **2 to patch together** IMPROVISE : confeccionar, improvisar **3 to patch up** : arreglar ⟨they patched things up : hicieron las paces⟩

patch² *n* **1** : parche *m*, remiendo *m* (para la ropa) ⟨eye patch : parche para el ojo⟩ **2** PIECE : mancha *f*, trozo *m* ⟨a patch of sky : un trozo de cielo⟩ **3** PLOT : parcela *f*, terreno *m* ⟨cabbage patch : parcela de repollos⟩ **4** : período *m* ⟨to go through a bad/rough patch : pasar una mala racha⟩ **5** : parche *m* (para el software)

patchwork ['pætʃ,wərk] *n* : labor *f* de retazos

patchy ['pætʃi] *adj* **patchier; -est 1** IRREGULAR : irregular, desigual **2** INCOMPLETE : parcial, incompleto

pâté [pɑ'teɪ, pæ-] *n* : paté *m*

patent¹ ['pætənt] *vt* : patentar

patent² ['pætənt, 'peɪt-] *adj* **1** OBVIOUS : patente, evidente **2** ['pæt-] PATENTED : patentado

patent³ ['pætənt] *n* : patente *f*

patent leather *n* : charol *m*

patently ['pætəntli] *adv* : patentemente, evidentemente

paternal [pə'tərnəl] *adj* **1** FATHERLY : paternal **2** : paterno ⟨paternal grandfather : abuelo paterno⟩

paternity [pə'tərnəti] *n* : paternidad *f* ⟨paternity leave : licencia por paternidad⟩

path ['pæθ, 'pɑθ] *n* **1** TRACK, TRAIL : camino *m*, sendero *m*, senda *f* **2** COURSE, ROUTE : recorrido *m*, trayecto *m*, trayectoria *f*

pathetic [pə'θetɪk] *adj* : patético — **pathetically** [-tɪkli] *adv*

pathological [,pæθə'lɑdʒɪkəl] *adj* : patológico

pathologist [pə'θɑlədʒɪst] *n* : patólogo *m*, -ga *f*

pathology [pə'θɑlədʒi] *n, pl* **-gies** : patología *f*

pathos ['peɪ,θɑs, 'pæ-, -,θɔs] *n* : patetismo *m*

pathway ['pæθ,weɪ] *n* : camino *m*, sendero *m*, senda *f*, vereda *f*

patience ['peɪʃəns] *n* : paciencia *f*

patient¹ ['peɪʃənt] *adj* : paciente — **patiently** *adv*

patient² *n* : paciente *mf*

patina [pə'ti:nə, 'pætənə] *n* : pátina *f*

patio ['pæti,o:] *n, pl* **-tios** : patio *m*

patriarch ['peɪtri,ɑrk] *n* : patriarca *m*

patriarchy ['peɪtri,ɑrki] *n, pl* **-chies** : patriarcado *m*

patrimony ['pætrə,mo:ni] *n, pl* **-nies** : patrimonio *m*

patriot ['peɪtriət] *n* : patriota *mf*

patriotic [,peɪtri'ɑtɪk] *adj* : patriótico — **patriotically** *adv*

patriotism ['peɪtriə,tɪzəm] *n* : patriotismo *m*

patrol[1] [pə'tro:l] v **-trolled; -trolling** : patrullar

patrol[2] n : patrulla f

patrol car n : patrulla f, patrullero m (automóvil)

patrolman [pə'tro:lmən] n, pl **-men** [-mən, -ˌmɛn] : policía mf, guardia mf

patron ['peɪtrən] n **1** SPONSOR : patrocinador m, -dora f **2** CUSTOMER : cliente m, -ta f **3** or **patron saint** : patrono m, -na f

patronage ['peɪtrənɪdʒ, 'pæ-] n **1** SPONSORSHIP : patrocinio m **2** CLIENTELE : clientela f **3** : influencia f (política)

patronize ['peɪtrəˌnaɪz, 'pæ-] vt **-ized; -izing 1** SPONSOR : patrocinar **2** : ser cliente de (un negocio) **3** : tratar con condescendencia

patronizing adj : condescendiente

patter[1] ['pætər] vi TAP : golpetear, tamborilear (dícese de la lluvia)

patter[2] n **1** TAPPING : golpeteo m, tamborileo m (de la lluvia), correteo m (de pies) **2** CHATTER : palabrería f, parloteo m fam

pattern[1] ['pætərn] vt **1** BASE : basar (en un modelo) **2 to pattern after** : hacer imitación de

pattern[2] n **1** MODEL : modelo m, patrón m (de costura) **2** DESIGN : diseño m, dibujo m, estampado m (de tela) **3** NORM, STANDARD : pauta f, norma f, patrón m

patty ['pæti] n, pl **-ties** : porción f de carne picada (u otro alimento) en forma de ruedita ⟨a hamburger patty : una hamburguesa⟩ ⟨a turkey patty : una hamburguesa de pavo⟩

paucity ['pɔsəti] n : escasez f

paunch ['pɔntʃ] n : panza f, barriga f

pauper ['pɔpər] n : pobre mf, indigente mf

pause[1] ['pɔz] vi **paused; pausing** : hacer una pausa, pararse (brevemente)

pause[2] n : pausa f

pave ['peɪv] vt **paved; paving** : pavimentar ⟨to pave with stones : empedrar⟩

pavement ['peɪvmənt] n : pavimento m, empedrado m

pavilion [pə'vɪljən] n : pabellón m

paving ['peɪvɪŋ] → **pavement**

paw[1] ['pɔ] vt : tocar, manosear, sobar

paw[2] n : pata f, garra f, zarpa f

pawn[1] ['pɔn] vt : empeñar, prendar

pawn[2] n **1** PLEDGE, SECURITY : prenda f **2** PAWNING : empeño m **3** : peón m (en ajedrez)

pawnbroker ['pɔnˌbro:kər] n : prestamista mf

pawnshop ['pɔnˌʃɑp] n : casa f de empeños, monte m de piedad

pay[1] ['peɪ] v **paid** ['peɪd]; **paying** vt **1** : pagar ⟨she paid the bill/rent : pagó la cuenta/renta⟩ ⟨he paid $ 200 for the bike : pagó $ 200 por la bici⟩ ⟨they paid her to mow the lawn : la pagaron para cortar el pasto⟩ **2 to pay attention** : poner atención, prestar atención, hacer caso **3 to pay a visit** : hacer una visita **4 to pay back** : pagar (un préstamo), devolver (dinero) ⟨she paid them back : les

devolvió el dinero⟩ ⟨I'll pay you back for what you did! : ¡me las pagarás!⟩ **5 to pay off** SETTLE : saldar, cancelar (una deuda, etc.) **6 to pay one's respects** : presentar uno sus respetos — vi **1** : pagar ⟨to pay in cash : pagar en efectivo⟩ ⟨the job pays well : el trabajo está bien pagado⟩ **2** : valer la pena ⟨crime doesn't pay : no hay crimen sin castigo⟩ **3 to pay for** : pagar ⟨he paid for our dinner : nos pagó la comida⟩ ⟨she paid dearly for her mistakes : pagó caro sus errores⟩ ⟨you'll pay for this! : ¡me las pagarás!⟩ **4 to pay one's (own) way** ⟨she paid her way through college : se pagó los estudios⟩ ⟨he paid his own way at dinner : pagó su parte de la cena⟩ **5 to pay up** : pagar

pay[2] n : paga f

payable ['peɪəbəl] adj DUE : pagadero

paycheck ['peɪˌtʃɛk] n : sueldo m, cheque m del sueldo

payday ['peɪˌdeɪ] n : día m de pago/paga

payee [peɪ'i:] n : beneficiario m, -ria f (de un cheque, etc.)

payer ['peɪər] n : pagador m, -dora f

payment ['peɪmənt] n **1** : pago m **2** INSTALLMENT : plazo m, cuota f **3** REWARD : recompensa f

payoff ['peɪˌɔf] n **1** REWARD : recompensa f **2** PROFIT : ganancia f **3** BRIBE : soborno m

pay phone n : teléfono m público

payroll ['peɪˌro:l] n : nómina f

PC [ˌpi:'si:] n, pl **PCs** or **PC's** : PC mf, computadora f personal

PDA [ˌpi:ˌdi:'eɪ] n, pl **PDAs** or **PDA's** (personal digital assistant) : PDA m

pea ['pi:] n : chícharo m, guisante m, arveja f

peace ['pi:s] n **1** : paz f ⟨peace treaty : tratado de paz⟩ ⟨peace and tranquillity : paz y tranquilidad⟩ **2** ORDER : orden m (público)

peaceable ['pi:səbəl] adj : pacífico — **peaceably** [-bli] adv

peaceful ['pi:sfəl] adj **1** PEACEABLE : pacífico **2** CALM, QUIET : tranquilo, sosegado — **peacefully** adv

peacemaker ['pi:sˌmeɪkər] n : conciliador m, -dora f; mediador m, -dora f

peacetime ['pi:sˌtaɪm] n : tiempos mpl de paz

peach ['pi:tʃ] n : durazno m, melocotón m

peacock ['pi:ˌkɑk] n : pavo m real

peak[1] ['pi:k] vi : alcanzar su nivel máximo

peak[2] adj : máximo

peak[3] n **1** POINT : punta f **2** CREST, SUMMIT : cima f, cumbre f **3** APEX : cúspide f, apogeo m, nivel m máximo

peaked ['pi:kəd] adj SICKLY : pálido

peal[1] ['pi:l] vi : repicar

peal[2] n : repique m, tañido m (de campanada) ⟨peals of laughter : carcajadas⟩

peanut ['pi:ˌnʌt] n : maní m, cacahuate m Mex, cacahuete m Spain

peanut butter n : mantequilla/crema f de maní, manteca f de maní Arg, crema/ mantequilla f de cacahuate Mex, mantequilla/crema f de cacahuete Spain

pear ['pær] *n* : pera *f*

pearl ['pərl] *n* : perla *f*

pearly ['pərli] *adj* **pearlier; -est** : nacarado

peasant ['pɛzənt] *n* : campesino *m*, -na *f*

peat ['pi:t] *n* : turba *f*

pebble ['pɛbəl] *n* : guijarro *m*, piedrecita *f*, piedrita *f*

pecan [pɪ'kɑn, -'kæn, 'pi:,kæn] *n* : pacana *f*, nuez *f Mex*

peccary ['pɛkəri] *n*, *pl* **-ries** : pécari *m*, pecarí *m*

peck¹ ['pɛk] *vt* : picar, picotear

peck² *n* **1** : medida *f* de áridos equivalente a 8. 81 0 litros **2** : picotazo *m* (de un pájaro) ⟨a peck on the cheek : un besito en la mejilla⟩

pectoral ['pɛktərəl] *adj* : pectoral

peculiar [pɪ'kju:ljər] *adj* **1** DISTINCTIVE : propio, peculiar, característico ⟨peculiar to this area : propio de esta zona⟩ **2** STRANGE : extraño, raro — **peculiarly** *adv*

peculiarity [pɪ,kju:li'jærəti, -,kju:li'ær-] *n*, *pl* **-ties** **1** DISTINCTIVENESS : peculiaridad *f* **2** ODDITY, QUIRK : rareza *f*, idiosincrasia *f*, excentricidad *f*

pecuniary [pɪ'kju:ni,ɛri] *adj* : pecuniario

pedagogical [,pɛdə'gɑdʒɪkəl, -'go:-] *or* **pedagogic** [,pɛdə'gɑdʒɪk, -'go:-] *adj* : pedagógico

pedagogy ['pɛdə,go:dʒi, -,gɑ-] *n* : pedagogía *f*

pedal¹ ['pɛdəl] *v* **-aled** *or* **-alled; -aling** *or* **-alling** *vi* : pedalear — *vt* : darle a los pedales de

pedal² *n* : pedal *m*

pedant ['pɛdənt] *n* : pedante *mf*

pedantic [pɪ'dæntɪk] *adj* : pedante

pedantry ['pɛdəntri] *n*, *pl* **-ries** : pedantería *f*

peddle ['pɛdəl] *vt* **-dled; -dling** : vender (en las calles)

peddler ['pɛdlər] *n* : vendedor *m*, -dora *f* ambulante; mercachifle *m*

pedestal ['pɛdəstəl] *n* : pedestal *m*

pedestrian¹ [pə'dɛstriən] *adj* **1** COMMONPLACE : pedestre, ordinario **2** : de peatón, peatonal ⟨pedestrian crossing : paso de peatones⟩

pedestrian² *n* : peatón *m*, -tona *f*

pediatric [,pi:di'ætrɪk] *adj* : pediátrico

pediatrician [,pi:diə'trɪʃən] *n* : pediatra *mf*

pediatrics [,pi:di'ætrɪks] *ns & pl* : pediatría *f*

pedigree ['pɛdə,gri:] *n* **1** FAMILY TREE : árbol *m* genealógico **2** LINEAGE : pedigrí *m* (de un animal), linaje *m* (de una persona)

pee¹ ['pi:] *vi fam* URINATE : hacer pipí *fam*

pee² *n fam* : pipí *m fam* ⟨to take a pee : hacer pipí⟩

peek¹ ['pi:k] *vi* **1** PEEP : espiar, mirar furtivamente **2** GLANCE : echar un vistazo

peek² *n* **1** : miradita *f* (furtiva) **2** GLANCE : vistazo *m*, ojeada *f*

peel¹ ['pi:l] *vt* **1** : pelar (fruta, etc.) **2** *or* **to peel away** : quitar — *vi* : pelarse (dícese

de la piel), desconcharse (dícese de la pintura)

peel² *n* : cáscara *f*

peeler ['pi:lər] *n* : pelador *m*, pelapapas *mpl*

peep¹ ['pi:p] *vi* **1** PEEK : espiar, mirar furtivamente **2** CHEEP : piar **3 to peep out** SHOW : asomarse

peep² *n* **1** CHEEP : pío *m* (de un pajarito) **2** GLANCE : vistazo *m*, ojeada *f*

peer¹ ['pɪr] *vi* : mirar detenidamente, mirar con atención

peer² *n* **1** EQUAL : par *m*, igual *mf* ⟨peer group : grupo paritario⟩ **2** NOBLE : noble *mf*

peerage ['pɪrɪdʒ] *n* : nobleza *f*

peerless ['pɪrləs] *adj* : sin par, incomparable

peeve¹ ['pi:v] *vt* **peeved; peeving** : fastidiar, irritar, molestar

peeve² *n* : queja *f*

peevish ['pi:vɪʃ] *adj* : quejoso, fastidioso — **peevishly** *adv*

peevishness ['pi:vɪʃnəs] *n* : irritabilidad *f*

peg¹ ['pɛg] *vt* **pegged; pegging 1** PLUG : tapar (con una clavija) **2** FASTEN, FIX : sujetar (con estaquillas) **3 to peg out** MARK : marcar (con estaquillas)

peg² *n* : estaquilla *f* (para clavar), clavija *f* (para tapar)

pejorative [pɪ'dʒɔrətɪv] *adj* : peyorativo — **pejoratively** *adv*

pelican ['pɛlɪkən] *n* : pelícano *m*

pellagra [pə'lægrə, -'leɪ-] *n* : pelagra *f*

pellet ['pɛlət] *n* **1** BALL : bolita *f* ⟨food pellet : bolita de comida⟩ **2** SHOT : perdigón *m*

pell—mell ['pɛl'mɛl] *adv* : desordenadamente, atropelladamente

pelt¹ ['pɛlt] *vt* **1** THROW : lanzar, tirar (algo a alguien) **2 to pelt with stones** : apedrear — *vi* **1** BEAT : golpear con fuerza ⟨the rain was pelting down : llovía a cántaros⟩ **2** : ir a todo correr

pelt² *n* : piel *f*, pellejo *m*

pelvic ['pɛlvɪk] *adj* : pélvico

pelvis ['pɛlvɪs] *n*, *pl* **-vises** *or* **-ves** ['pɛl,vi:z] : pelvis *f*

pen¹ ['pɛn] *vt* **penned; penning 1** *or* **pen in** : encerrar (animales) **2** WRITE : escribir

pen² *n* **1** CORRAL : corral *m*, redil *m* (para ovejas) **2** : pluma *f* ⟨fountain pen : pluma fuente⟩ ⟨ballpoint pen : bolígrafo⟩

penal ['pi:nəl] *adj* : penal

penalize ['pi:nə,laɪz, 'pɛn-] *vt* **-ized; -izing** : penalizar, sancionar, penar

penalty ['pɛnəlti] *n*, *pl* **-ties 1** PUNISHMENT : pena *f*, castigo *m* **2** DISADVANTAGE : desventaja *f*, castigo *m*, penalty *m* (en deportes) **3** FINE : multa *f*

penance ['pɛnənts] *n* : penitencia *f*

pence → **penny**

penchant ['pɛntʃənt] *n* : inclinación *f*, afición *f*

pencil¹ ['pɛntsəl] *vt* **-ciled** *or* **-cilled; -ciling** *or* **-cilling** : escribir con lápiz, dibujar con lápiz

pencil² *n* : lápiz *m*

pencil case *n* : estuche *m* (para lápices)
pencil sharpener *n* : sacapuntas *m*
pencil skirt *n* : falda *f* de tubo
pendant [ˈpɛndənt] *n* : colgante *m*
pending¹ [ˈpɛndɪŋ] *adj* : pendiente
pending² *prep* **1** DURING : durante **2** AWAITING : en espera de
pendulum [ˈpɛndʒələm, -djuləm] *n* : péndulo *m*
penetrate [ˈpɛnəˌtreɪt] *vt* **-trated; -trating** : penetrar
penetrating [ˈpɛnəˌtreɪtɪŋ] *adj* : penetrante, cortante
penetration [ˌpɛnəˈtreɪʃən] *n* : penetración *f*
penguin [ˈpɛŋgwɪn, ˈpɛn-] *n* : pingüino *m*
penicillin [ˌpɛnəˈsɪlən] *n* : penicilina *f*
peninsula [pəˈnɪnsələ, -ˈnɪntʃələ] *n* : península *f*
penis [ˈpiːnəs] *n, pl* **-nes** [-ˌniːz] *or* **-nises** : pene *m*
penitence [ˈpɛnətənts] *n* : arrepentimiento *m*, penitencia *f*
penitent¹ [ˈpɛnətənt] *adj* : arrepentido, penitente
penitent² *n* : penitente *mf*
penitentiary [ˌpɛnəˈtɛntʃəri] *n, pl* **-ries** : penitenciaría *f*, prisión *f*, presidio *m*
penknife [ˈpɛnˌnaɪf] *n* : navaja *f*
penmanship [ˈpɛnmənˌʃɪp] *n* : escritura *f*, caligrafía *f*
pen name *n* : seudónimo *m*
pennant [ˈpɛnənt] *n* : gallardete *m* (de un barco), banderín *m*
penniless [ˈpɛnɪləs] *adj* : sin un centavo
penny [ˈpɛni] *n, pl* **-nies** *or* **pence** [ˈpɛnts] **1** : penique *m* (del Reino Unido) **2** *pl* **-nies** CENT : centavo *m* (de los Estados Unidos)
pen pal *n* : amigo *m*, -ga *f* por correspondencia
pension¹ [ˈpɛntʃən] *vt or* **to pension off** : jubilar
pension² [ˈpɛntʃən] *n* : pensión *f*, jubilación *f*
pensioner [ˈpɛntʃənər] *n* : pensionista *mf*
pensive [ˈpɛntsɪv] *adj* : pensativo, meditabundo — **pensively** *adv*
pentagon [ˈpɛntəˌgɑn] *n* : pentágono *m*
pentagonal [pɛnˈtægənəl] *adj* : pentagonal
penthouse [ˈpɛntˌhaʊs] *n* : ático *m*, penthouse *m*
pent–up [ˈpɛntˈʌp] *adj* : encerrado ⟨pent-up feelings : emociones reprimidas⟩
penultimate [pɪˈnʌltəmət] *adj* : penúltimo
penury [ˈpɛnjəri] *n* : penuria *f*, miseria *f*
peon [ˈpiːˌɑn, -ən] *n, pl* **-ons** *or* **-ones** [peɪˈoːniːz] : peón *m*
peony [ˈpiːəni] *n, pl* **-nies** : peonía *f*
people¹ [ˈpiːpəl] *v* **-pled; -pling** : poblar
people² *ns & pl* **1 people** *npl* : gente *f*, personas *fpl* ⟨people like him : él le cae bien a la gente⟩ ⟨many people : mucha gente, muchas personas⟩ **2** *pl* **peoples** : pueblo *m* ⟨the Cuban people : el pueblo cubano⟩
pep¹ [ˈpɛp] *vt* **pepped; pepping** *or* **to pep up** : animar
pep² *n* : energía *f*, vigor *m*

pepper¹ [ˈpɛpər] *vt* **1** : añadir pimienta a **2** RIDDLE : acribillar (a balazos) **3** SPRINKLE : salpicar ⟨peppered with quotations : salpicado de citas⟩
pepper² *n* **1** : pimienta *f* (condimento) **2** : pimiento *m*, pimentón *m* (fruta) **3** → **chili**
peppermint [ˈpɛpərˌmɪnt] *n* : menta *f*
pepper shaker → **shaker**
peppery [ˈpɛpəri] *adj* : picante
peppy [ˈpɛpi] *adj* **peppier; -est** : lleno de energía, vivaz
pep rally *n* : reunión *f* (para animar a un equipo antes de un partido)
pep talk *n* : plática *f*, charla *f* (para animar a un equipo, etc.) ⟨to give someone a pep talk : animar a alguien⟩
peptic [ˈpɛptɪk] *adj* **peptic ulcer** : úlcera *f* estomacal
per [ˈpər] *prep* **1** : por ⟨miles per hour : millas por hora⟩ **2** ACCORDING TO : según ⟨per his specifications : según sus especificaciones⟩
per annum [pərˈænəm] *adv* : al año, por año
percale [ˌpərˈkeɪl, ˈpər-; ˌpərˈkæl] *n* : percal *m*
per capita [pərˈkæpɪtə] *adv & adj* : per cápita
perceive [pərˈsiːv] *vt* **-ceived; -ceiving 1** REALIZE : percatarse de, concientizarse de, darse cuenta de **2** NOTE : percibir, notar
percent¹ [pərˈsɛnt] *adv* : por ciento
percent² *n, pl* **-cent** *or* **-cents 1** : por ciento ⟨10 percent of the population : el 10 por ciento de la población⟩ **2** → **percentage**
percentage [pərˈsɛntɪdʒ] *n* : porcentaje *m*
perceptible [pərˈsɛptəbəl] *adj* : perceptible — **perceptibly** [-bli] *adv*
perception [pərˈsɛpʃən] *n* **1** : percepción *f* ⟨color perception : la percepción de los colores⟩ **2** INSIGHT : perspicacia *f* **3** IDEA : idea *f*, imagen *f*
perceptive [pərˈsɛptɪv] *adj* : perspicaz
perceptively [pərˈsɛptɪvli] *adv* : con perspicacia
perch¹ [ˈpərtʃ] *vi* **1** ROOST : posarse **2** SIT : sentarse (en un sitio elevado) — *vt* PLACE : posar, colocar
perch² *n* **1** ROOST : percha *f* (para los pájaros) **2** *pl* **perch** *or* **perches** : perca *f* (pez)
percolate [ˈpərkəˌleɪt] *vi* **-lated; -lating** : colarse, filtrarse ⟨percolated coffee : café filtrado⟩
percolator [ˈpərkəˌleɪtər] *n* : cafetera *f* de filtro
percussion [pərˈkʌʃən] *n* **1** STRIKING : percusión *f* **2** *or* **percussion instruments** : instrumentos *mpl* de percusión
peremptory [pəˈrɛmptəri] *adj* : perentorio
perennial¹ [pəˈrɛniəl] *adj* **1** : perenne, vivaz ⟨perennial flowers : flores perennes⟩ **2** RECURRENT : perenne, continuo ⟨a perennial problem : un problema eterno⟩
perennial² *n* : planta *f* perenne, planta *f* vivaz

perfect[1] [pər'fɛkt] *vt* : perfeccionar

perfect[2] ['pərfɪkt] *adj* : perfecto — **perfectly** *adv*

perfection [pər'fɛkʃən] *n* : perfección *f*

perfectionism [pər'fɛkʃə,nɪzəm] *n* : perfeccionismo *m*

perfectionist [pər'fɛkʃənɪst] *n* : perfeccionista *mf*

perfidious [pər'fɪdiəs] *adj* : pérfido

perforate ['pərfə,reɪt] *vt* -**rated**; -**rating** : perforar

perforation [,pərfə'reɪʃən] *n* : perforación *f*

perform [pər'fɔrm] *vt* 1 CARRY OUT : realizar, hacer, desempeñar 2 PRESENT : representar, dar (una obra teatral, etc.) — *vi* 1 : actuar (en una obra teatral), cantar (en una ópera, etc.), tocar (en un concierto, etc.), bailar (en un ballet, etc.) 2 : funcionar

performance [pər'fɔrmənts] *n* 1 EXECUTION : ejecución *f*, realización *f*, desempeño *m*, rendimiento *m* 2 INTERPRETATION : interpretación *f* ⟨his performance of Hamlet : su interpretación de Hamlet⟩ 3 PRESENTATION : representación *f* (de una obra teatral), función *f*

performer [pər'fɔrmər] *n* : artista *mf*; actor *m*, -triz *f*; intérprete *mf* (de música)

perfume[1] [pər'fju:m, 'pər,-] *vt* -**fumed**; -**fuming** : perfumar

perfume[2] ['pər,fju:m, pər'-] *n* : perfume *m*

perfunctory [pər'fʌŋktəri] *adj* : mecánico, superficial, somero

perhaps [pər'hæps] *adv* : tal vez, quizá, quizás, a lo mejor ⟨perhaps so/not : tal vez sí/no⟩ ⟨perhaps he didn't know : quizá(s) no lo sabía⟩ ⟨perhaps I'm wrong : a lo mejor me equivoco⟩ ⟨perhaps I can go tomorrow : quizá(s) pueda ir mañana⟩

peril ['pɛrəl] *n* : peligro

perilous ['pɛrələs] *adj* : peligroso — **perilously** *adv*

perimeter [pə'rɪmətər] *n* : perímetro *m*

period ['pɪriəd] *n* 1 : punto *m* (en puntuación) 2 : período *m* ⟨a two-hour period : un período de dos horas⟩ 3 STAGE : época *f* (histórica), fase *f*, etapa *f* 4 MENSTRUATION : período *m*, regla *f* ⟨to have one's period : tener el período, tener la regla⟩ 5 : hora *f* (de clase)

periodic [,pɪri'ɑdɪk] *or* **periodical** [-dɪkəl] *adj* : periódico — **periodically** [-dɪkli] *adv*

periodical [,pɪri'ɑdɪkəl] *n* : publicación *f* periódica, revista *f*

peripheral [pə'rɪfərəl] *adj* : periférico

periphery [pə'rɪfəri] *n, pl* -**eries** : periferia *f*

periscope ['pɛrə,sko:p] *n* : periscopio *m*

perish ['pɛrɪʃ] *vi* DIE : perecer, morirse

perishable[1] ['pɛrɪʃəbəl] *adj* : perecedero

perishable[2] *n* : producto *m* perecedero

perjure ['pərdʒər] *vt* -**jured**; -**juring** *used in law* to perjure oneself : perjurar, perjurarse

perjury ['pərdʒəri] *n* : perjurio *m*

perk[1] ['pərk] *vt* 1 : levantar (las orejas, etc.) 2 *or* to perk up FRESHEN : arreglar — *vi* to perk up : animarse, reanimarse

perk[2] *n* : extra *m*

perky ['pərki] *adj* **perkier**; -**est** : animado, alegre, lleno de vida

perm ['pərm] *n* : permanente *f*

permanence ['pərmənənts] *n* : permanencia *f*

permanent[1] ['pərmənənt] *adj* : permanente — **permanently** *adv*

permanent[2] *n* : permanente *f*

permeability [,pərmiə'bɪləti] *n* : permeabilidad *f*

permeable ['pərmiəbəl] *adj* : permeable

permeate ['pərmi,eɪt] *v* -**ated**; -**ating** *vt* 1 PENETRATE : penetrar, impregnar 2 PERVADE : penetrar, difundirse por — *vi* : penetrar

permissible [pər'mɪsəbəl] *adj* : permisible, lícito

permission [pər'mɪʃən] *n* : permiso *m*

permissive [pər'mɪsɪv] *adj* : permisivo

permissiveness [pər'mɪsɪvnəs] *n* : permisividad *f*

permit[1] [pər'mɪt] *vt* -**mitted**; -**mitting** : permitir, dejar ⟨weather permitting : si el tiempo lo permite⟩

permit[2] ['pər,mɪt, pər'-] *n* : permiso *m*, licencia *f*

permutation [,pərmju'teɪʃən] *n* : permutación *f*

pernicious [pər'nɪʃəs] *adj* : pernicioso

peroxide [pə'rɑk,saɪd] *n* 1 : peróxido *m* 2 → hydrogen peroxide

perpendicular[1] [,pərpən'dɪkjələr] *adj* 1 VERTICAL : vertical 2 : perpendicular ⟨perpendicular lines : líneas perpendiculares⟩ — **perpendicularly** *adv*

perpendicular[2] *n* : perpendicular *f*

perpetrate ['pərpə,treɪt] *vt* -**trated**; -**trating** : perpetrar, cometer (un delito)

perpetrator ['pərpə,treɪtər] *n* : autor *m*, -tora *f* (de un delito)

perpetual [pər'pɛtʃuəl] *adj* 1 EVERLASTING : perpetuo, eterno 2 CONTINUAL : perpetuo, continuo, constante

perpetually [pər'pɛtʃuəli, -tʃəli] *adv* : para siempre, eternamente

perpetuate [pər'pɛtʃu,eɪt] *vt* -**ated**; -**ating** : perpetuar

perpetuity [,pərpə'tu:əti, -'tju:-] *n, pl* -**ties** : perpetuidad *f*

perplex [pər'plɛks] *vt* : dejar perplejo, confundir

perplexed [pər'plɛkst] *adj* : perplejo

perplexity [pər'plɛksəti] *n, pl* -**ties** : perplejidad *f*, confusión *f*

per se [pər'seɪ] *adv* : per se, de por sí, en sí

persecute ['pərsɪ,kju:t] *vt* -**cuted**; -**cuting** : perseguir

persecution [,pərsɪ'kju:ʃən] *n* : persecución *f*

persecutor ['pərsɪ,kju:tər] *n* : perseguidor *m*, -dora *f*

perseverance [,pərsə'vɪrənts] *n* : perseverancia *f*

persevere [,pərsə'vɪr] *vi* -**vered**; -**vering** : perseverar

Persian ['pərʒən] *n* 1 : persa *mf* 2 : persa *m* (idioma) — **Persian** *adj*

persist [pər'sɪst] *vi* : persistir

persistence [pər'sɪstənts] n 1 CONTINUATION : persistencia f 2 TENACITY : perseverancia f, tenacidad f

persistent [pər'sɪstənt] adj : persistente — **persistently** adv

person ['pərsən] n 1 pl **people** or **persons** HUMAN, INDIVIDUAL : persona f, individuo m, ser m humano 2 : persona f (en gramática) 3 **in person** : en persona

personable ['pərsənəbəl] adj : agradable

personage ['pərsənɪdʒ] n : personaje m

personal ['pərsənəl] adj 1 OWN, PRIVATE : personal, particular, privado ⟨for personal reasons : por razones personales⟩ 2 : en persona ⟨to make a personal appearance : presentarse en persona, hacerse acto de presencia⟩ 3 : íntimo, personal ⟨personal hygiene : higiene personal⟩ 4 INDISCREET, PRYING : indiscreto, personal

personal assistant n : secretario m, -ria f personal

personal computer n : computadora f personal, ordenador m personal Spain

personality [ˌpərsən'ælətɪ] n, pl **-ties** 1 DISPOSITION : personalidad f, temperamento m 2 CELEBRITY : personalidad f, personaje m, celebridad f

personalize ['pərsənəˌlaɪz] vt **-ized; -izing** : personalizar

personally ['pərsənəlɪ] adv 1 : personalmente, en persona ⟨I'll do it personally : lo haré personalmente⟩ 2 : como persona ⟨personally she's very amiable : como persona es muy amable⟩ 3 : personalmente ⟨personally, I don't believe it : yo, personalmente, no me lo creo⟩

personification [pərˌsɑnəfə'keɪʃən] n : personificación f

personify [pər'sɑnəˌfaɪ] vt **-fied; -fying** : personificar

personnel [ˌpərsən'ɛl] n : personal m

perspective [pər'spɛktɪv] n : perspectiva f

perspicacious [ˌpərspɪ'keɪʃəs] adj : perspicaz

perspicacity [ˌpərspɪ'kæsətɪ] n : clarividencia f, perspicacia f

perspiration [ˌpərspə'reɪʃən] n : transpiración f, sudor m

perspire [pər'spaɪr] vi **-spired; -spiring** : transpirar, sudar

persuade [pər'sweɪd] vt **-suaded; -suading** : persuadir, convencer

persuasion [pər'sweɪʒən] n : persuasión f

persuasive [pər'sweɪsɪv, -zɪv] adj : persuasivo — **persuasively** adv

persuasiveness [pər'sweɪsɪvnəs, -zɪv-] n : persuasión f

pert ['pərt] adj 1 SAUCY : descarado, impertinente 2 JAUNTY : alegre, animado ⟨a pert little hat : un sombrero coqueto⟩

pertain [pər'teɪn] vi 1 BELONG : pertenecer (a) 2 RELATE : estar relacionado (con)

pertinence ['pərtənənts] n : pertinencia f

pertinent ['pərtənənt] adj : pertinente

perturb [pər'tərb] vt : perturbar

perusal [pə'ruːzəl] n : lectura f cuidadosa

peruse [pə'ruːz] vt **-rused; -rusing** 1 READ : leer con cuidado 2 SCAN : recorrer con la vista ⟨he perused the newspaper : echó un vistazo al periódico⟩

Peruvian [pə'ruːviən] n : peruano m, -na f — **Peruvian** adj

pervade [pər'veɪd] vt **-vaded; -vading** : penetrar, difundirse por

pervasive [pər'veɪsɪv, -zɪv] adj : penetrante

perverse [pər'vərs] adj 1 CORRUPT : perverso, corrompido 2 STUBBORN : obstinado, porfiado, terco (sin razón) — **perversely** adv

perversion [pər'vərʒən] n : perversión f

perversity [pər'vərsətɪ] n, pl **-ties** 1 CORRUPTION : corrupción f 2 STUBBORNNESS : obstinación f, terquedad f

pervert[1] [pər'vərt] vt 1 DISTORT : pervertir, distorsionar 2 CORRUPT : pervertir, corromper

pervert[2] ['pər,vərt] n : pervertido m, -da f

peseta [pə'seɪtə] n : peseta f

pesky ['pɛski] adj : molestoso, molesto

peso ['peɪˌsoː] n, pl **-sos** : peso m

pessimism ['pɛsəˌmɪzəm] n : pesimismo m

pessimist ['pɛsəmɪst] n : pesimista mf

pessimistic [ˌpɛsə'mɪstɪk] adj : pesimista

pest ['pɛst] n 1 NUISANCE : peste f; latoso m, -sa f fam ⟨to be a pest : dar (la) lata⟩ 2 : insecto m nocivo, animal m nocivo ⟨the squirrels were pests : las ardillas eran una plaga⟩

pester ['pɛstər] vt **-tered; -tering** : molestar, fastidiar

pesticide ['pɛstəˌsaɪd] n : pesticida m

pestilence ['pɛstələnts] n : pestilencia f, peste f

pestle ['pɛsəl, 'pɛstəl] n : mano f de mortero, mazo m, maja f

pet[1] ['pɛt] vt **petted; petting** : acariciar

pet[2] n 1 : animal m doméstico, mascota f ⟨pet store : tienda de mascotas⟩ ⟨pet food : alimento para mascotas⟩ 2 FAVORITE : favorito m, -ta f

pet[3] adj : preferido, favorito ⟨her pet theory : su teoría preferida⟩ ⟨his pet project : su proyecto favorito⟩ ⟨pet name : apodo (cariñoso)⟩

petal ['pɛtəl] n : pétalo m

peter ['piːtər] vi **to peter out** : agotarse, apagarse, disminuir (poco a poco)

petite [pə'tiːt] adj : pequeña, menuda, chiquita

petition[1] [pə'tɪʃən] vt : peticionar

petition[2] n : petición f

petitioner [pə'tɪʃənər] n : peticionario m, -ria f

petrify ['pɛtrəˌfaɪ] vt **-fied; -fying** : petrificar

petroleum [pə'troːliəm] n : petróleo m

petroleum jelly n : vaselina f

petticoat ['pɛtiˌkoːt] n : enagua f, fondo m Mex

pettiness ['pɛtinəs] n 1 INSIGNIFICANCE : insignificancia f 2 MEANNESS : mezquindad f

petty ['pɛti] adj **pettier; -est** 1 MINOR : menor ⟨petty cash : dinero para gastos menores⟩ **2** INSIGNIFICANT : insignificante, trivial, nimio **3** MEAN : mezquino

petty officer *n* : suboficial *mf*

petulance ['pɛtʃələnʦ] *n* : irritabilidad *f*, mal genio *m*

petulant ['pɛtʃələnt] *adj* : irritable, de mal genio

petunia [pɪ'tuːnjə, -'tjuː-] *n* : petunia *f*

pew ['pjuː] *n* : banco *m* (de iglesia)

pewter ['pjuːtər] *n* : peltre *m*

pH [ˌpiː'eɪtʃ] *n* : pH *m*

phallic ['fælɪk] *adj* : fálico

phallus ['fæləs] *n, pl* **-li** ['fæˌlaɪ] *or* **-luses** : falo *m*

phantasy ['fæntəsi] → **fantasy**

phantom ['fæntəm] *n* : fantasma *m*

pharaoh ['fɛrˌoː, 'feɪˌroː] *n* : faraón *m*

pharmaceutical [ˌfɑrmə'suːtɪkəl] *adj* : farmacéutico

pharmacist ['fɑrməsɪst] *n* : farmacéutico *m*, -ca *f*

pharmacology [ˌfɑrmə'kɑləʤi] *n* : farmacología *f*

pharmacy ['fɑrməsi] *n, pl* **-cies** : farmacia *f*

pharynx ['færɪŋks] *n, pl* **pharynges** [fə'rɪnˌʤiːz] : faringe *f*

phase¹ ['feɪz] *vt* **phased; phasing 1** SYNCHRONIZE : sincronizar, poner en fase **2** STAGGER : escalonar **3 to phase in** : introducir progresivamente **4 to phase out** : retirar progresivamente, dejar de producir

phase² *n* **1** : fase *f* (de la luna, etc.) **2** STAGE : fase *f*, etapa *f*

pheasant ['fɛzənt] *n, pl* **-ant** *or* **-ants** : faisán *m*

phenomenal [fɪ'nɑmənəl] *adj* : extraordinario, excepcional

phenomenon [fɪ'nɑməˌnɑn, -nən] *n, pl* **-na** [-nə] *or* **-nons 1** : fenómeno *m* **2** *pl* **-nons** PRODIGY : fenómeno *m*, prodigio *m*

phew ['fjuː] *interj* : ¡uf!

philanthropic [ˌfɪlən'θrɑpɪk] *adj* : filantrópico

philanthropist [fə'lænˌθrəpɪst] *n* : filántropo *m*, -pa *f*

philanthropy [fə'lænˌθrəpi] *n, pl* **-pies** : filantropía *f*

philately [fə'lætəli] *n* : filatelia *f*

philharmonic [ˌfɪlər'mɑnɪk] *n* : filarmónica *f*

philosopher [fə'lɑsəfər] *n* : filósofo *m*, -fa *f*

philosophic [ˌfɪlə'sɑfɪk] *or* **philosophical** [-fɪkəl] *adj* : filosófico — **philosophically** [-kli] *adv*

philosophize [fə'lɑsəˌfaɪz] *vi* **-phized; -phizing** : filosofar

philosophy [fə'lɑsəfi] *n, pl* **-phies** : filosofía *f*

phlegm ['flɛm] *n* : flema *f*

phlegmatic [flɛg'mætɪk] *adj* : flemático

phlox ['flɑks] *n, pl* **phlox** *or* **phloxes** : polemonio *m*

phobia ['foːbiə] *n* : fobia *f*

phoenix ['fiːnɪks] *n* : fénix *m*

phone¹ ['foːn] → **telephone¹**

phone² → **telephone²**

phone book *n* : guía *f* telefónica

phone call → **call²**

phone card *n* : tarjeta *f* telefónica

phoneme ['foːˌniːm] *n* : fonema *m*

phone number → **number²**

phonetic [fə'nɛtɪk] *adj* : fonético

phonetics [fə'nɛtɪks] *n* : fonética *f*

phonics ['fɑnɪks] *n* : método *m* fonético de aprender a leer

phony¹ *or* **phoney** ['foːni] *adj* **phonier; -est** : falso

phony² *or* **phoney** *n, pl* **-nies** : farsante *mf*; charlatán *m*, -tana *f*

phosphate ['fɑsˌfeɪt] *n* : fosfato *m*

phosphorescence [ˌfɑsfə'rɛsənʦ] *n* : fosforescencia *f*

phosphorescent [ˌfɑsfə'rɛsənt] *adj* : fosforescente — **phosphorescently** *adv*

phosphorus ['fɑsfərəs] *n* : fósforo *m*

photo ['foːˌtoː] *n, pl* **-tos** : foto *f*

photocopier ['foːˌtoːˌkɑpiər] *n* : fotocopiadora *f*

photocopy¹ ['foːˌtoːˌkɑpi] *vt* **-copied; -copying** : fotocopiar

photocopy² *n, pl* **-copies** : fotocopia *f*

photoelectric [ˌfoːˌtoːi'lɛktrɪk] *adj* : fotoeléctrico

photogenic [ˌfoːtə'ʤɛnɪk] *adj* : fotogénico

photograph¹ ['foːtəˌgræf] *vt* : fotografiar

photograph² *n* : fotografía *f*, foto *f* ⟨to take a photograph of : tomarle una fotografía a, tomar una fotografía de⟩

photographer [fə'tɑgrəfər] *n* : fotógrafo *m*, -fa *f*

photographic [ˌfoːtə'græfɪk] *adj* : fotográfico — **photographically** [-fɪkli] *adv*

photography [fə'tɑgrəfi] *n* : fotografía *f*

photojournalist [ˌfoːtoː'ʤərnəlɪst] *n* : reportero *m* gráfico, reportera *f* gráfica

photosynthesis [ˌfoːtoː'sɪnθəsɪs] *n* : fotosíntesis *f*

phrasal verb *n* : verbo *m* con partícula(s)

phrase¹ ['freɪz] *vt* **phrased; phrasing** : expresar

phrase² *n* : frase *f*, locución *f* ⟨to coin a phrase : para decirlo así⟩

phrase book *n* : guía *f* de conversación

phylum ['faɪləm] *n, pl* **-la** [-lə] : phylum *m*

phys ed ['fɪz'ɛd] *n fam* → **physical education**

physical¹ ['fɪzɪkəl] *adj* **1** : físico ⟨physical laws : leyes físicas⟩ **2** MATERIAL : material, físico **3** BODILY : físico, corpóreo — **physically** [-kli] *adv*

physical² *n* CHECKUP : chequeo *m*, reconocimiento *m* médico

physical education *n* : educación *f* física

physical therapist *n* : fisioterapeuta *mf*

physical therapy *n* : fisioterapia *f*

physician [fə'zɪʃən] *n* : médico *m*, -ca *f*

physicist ['fɪzəsɪst] *n* : físico *m*, -ca *f*

physics ['fɪzɪks] *ns & pl* : física *f*

physiognomy [ˌfɪzi'ɑgnəmi] *n, pl* **-mies** : fisonomía *f*

physiological [ˌfɪziə'lɑʤɪkəl] *or* **physiologic** [-ʤɪk] *adj* : fisiológico

physiologist [ˌfɪzi'ɑləʤɪst] *n* : fisiólogo *m*, -ga *f*

physiology [ˌfɪziˈɑlədʒi] n : fisiología f
physique [fəˈziːk] n : físico m
pi [ˈpaɪ] n, pl **pis** [ˈpaɪz] : pi f
pianist [piˈænɪst, ˈpiːənɪst] n : pianista mf
piano [piˈænoː] n, pl **-anos** : piano m
piazza [piˈæzə, -ˈatsə] n, pl **-zas** or **-ze** [-ˈɑtˌseɪ] : plaza f
picador [ˈpɪkəˌdɔr] n : picador m, -dora f
picaresque [ˌpɪkəˈrɛsk, ˌpiː-] adj : picaresco
picayune [ˌpɪkiˈjuːn] adj : trivial, nimio, insignificante
piccolo [ˈpɪkəˌloː] n, pl **-los** : flautín m
pick¹ [ˈpɪk] vt **1** SELECT : escoger, elegir ⟨pick a card : elige una carta⟩ **2** : quitar, sacar (poco a poco) ⟨to pick meat off the bones : quitar pedazos de carne de los huesos⟩ **3** : recoger, arrancar (frutas, flores, etc.) **4** PROVOKE : provocar ⟨to pick a fight : buscar pelea⟩ **5** : hurgarse (la nariz), escarbarse (los dientes) **6 to pick a lock** : forzar una cerradura **7 to pick out** CHOOSE : escoger **8 to pick out** IDENTIFY : identificar, distinguir **9 to pick someone's pocket** : robarle a alguien la cartera (etc.) del bolsillo **10 to pick up** LIFT : levantar **11 to pick up** TIDY : ordenar (una habitación, etc.), recoger (juguetes, etc.) **12 to pick up** FETCH : (ir a) recoger **13 to pick up** LOAD : recoger (pasajeros), cargar **14 to pick up** BUY, GET : comprar, conseguir **15 to pick up** LEARN : aprender (un idioma, etc.), adquirir (una costumbre) **16 to pick up** RESUME : continuar **17 to pick up** DETECT : captar (una señal) **18 to pick up speed** : detectar **19 to pick up speed** : ganar velocidad **20 to pick up the pace** : ir/trabajar (etc.) más rápido **21 to pick up the tab/bill/check** : cargar con la cuenta — vi **1** NIBBLE : picar, picotear **2 to pick and choose** : ser exigente **3 to pick at** : tocar, rascarse (una herida, etc.) **4 to pick on** TEASE : mofarse de, atormentar **5 to pick up** IMPROVE : mejorar **6 to pick up** : levantarse (dícese del viento), acelerarse (dícese de un ritmo, etc.) **7 to pick up** ANSWER : contestar (el teléfono) **8 to pick up** TIDY : ordenar ⟨pick up after yourself : ordena lo que has desordenado⟩ **9 to pick up** RESUME : continuar ⟨let's pick up where we left off : retomemos donde lo dejamos⟩ **10 to pick up on** : darse cuenta de
pick² n **1** CHOICE : selección f **2** BEST : lo mejor ⟨the pick of the crop : la crema y nata⟩ **3** → **pickax** **4** : púa f (para una guitarra, etc.)
pickax [ˈpɪkˌæks] n : pico m, zapapico m, piqueta f
pickerel [ˈpɪkərəl] n, pl **-el** or **-els** : lucio m pequeño
picket¹ [ˈpɪkət] v : piquetear
picket² n **1** STAKE : estaca f **2** STRIKER : huelguista mf, integrante mf de un piquete
picketer [ˈpɪkətər] n : piquete nm
pickle¹ [ˈpɪkəl] vt **-led; -ling** : encurtir, escabechar

pickle² n **1** BRINE : escabeche m **2** GHERKIN : pepinillo m (encurtido) **3** JAM, TROUBLE : lío m, apuro m
pickpocket [ˈpɪkˌpɑkət] n : carterista mf
pickup [ˈpɪkˌəp] n **1** IMPROVEMENT : mejora f **2** or **pickup truck** : camioneta f
picky [ˈpɪki] adj : quisquilloso, melindroso, mañoso ⟨he's a picky eater : es muy quisquilloso para comer⟩
picnic¹ [ˈpɪkˌnɪk] vi **-nicked; -nicking** : ir de picnic
picnic² n : picnic m
pictorial [pɪkˈtoriəl] adj : pictórico
picture¹ [ˈpɪktʃər] vt **-tured; -turing** **1** DEPICT : representar **2** IMAGINE : imaginarse ⟨can you picture it? : ¿te lo puedes imaginar?⟩
picture² n **1** : cuadro m (pintado o dibujado), ilustración f, fotografía f **2** DESCRIPTION : descripción f **3** IMAGE : imagen f ⟨he's the picture of his father : es la viva imagen de su padre⟩ **4** MOVIE : película f **5** IMAGE : imagen f (de una pantalla) **6** : idea f ⟨now I get the picture : ahora lo entiendo⟩ **7** : situación f ⟨the economic picture : la situación económica⟩ ⟨marriage never entered the picture : nunca pensaron en casarse⟩ ⟨her old boyfriend is back in the picture : ha vuelto a salir con su antiguo novio⟩ **8** → **big picture**
picturesque [ˌpɪktʃəˈrɛsk] adj : pintoresco
pie [ˈpaɪ] n : pastel m (con fruta o carne), empanada f (con carne)
piece¹ [ˈpiːs] vt **pieced; piecing** **1** PATCH : parchar, arreglar **2 to piece together** : construir pieza por pieza
piece² n **1** FRAGMENT : pedazo m ⟨to rip/tear something to pieces : hacer pedazos algo, romper algo en pedazos⟩ ⟨to fall to pieces : hacerse pedazos⟩ ⟨in pieces : en pedazos⟩ ⟨in one piece : intacto⟩ **2** SEGMENT : pedazo m, trozo m (de pan, carne, cordel, etc.) **3** COMPONENT : pieza f ⟨a three-piece suit : un traje de tres piezas⟩ **4** UNIT : pieza f ⟨a piece of fruit : una (pieza de) fruta⟩ ⟨a piece of clothing : una prenda⟩ ⟨a piece of paper : un papel⟩ **5** (indicating an instance of something) ⟨a piece of advice : un consejo⟩ ⟨a piece of news : una noticia⟩ ⟨a nice piece of work : un buen trabajo⟩ **6** WORK : obra f, pieza f (de música, arte) **7** (in board games) : ficha f, pieza f, figura f (en ajedrez) **8** ARTICLE : artículo m **9** COIN : moneda f, pieza f **10** fam GUN : pistola f **11** fam DISTANCE : trecho m **12 in one piece** SAFE : sano y salvo **13 to fall/go to pieces** : venirse abajo **14 to give someone a piece of one's mind** : cantarle las cuarenta a alguien ⟨she was thrilled to pieces : estaba contentísima⟩ ⟨he loves her to pieces : la quiere muchísimo⟩
piecemeal¹ [ˈpiːsˌmiːl] adv : poco a poco, por partes

piecemeal² *adj* : hecho poco a poco, poco sistemático

piecework ['pi:s,wərk] *n* : trabajo *m* a destajo

pied ['paɪd] *adj* : pío

pier ['pɪr] *n* **1** : pila *f* (de un puente) **2** WHARF : muelle *m*, atracadero *m*, embarcadero *m* **3** PILLAR : pilar *m*

pierce ['pɪrs] *vt* **pierced; piercing 1** PENETRATE : atravesar, traspasar, penetrar (en) ⟨the bullet pierced his leg : la bala le atravesó la pierna⟩ ⟨to pierce one's heart : traspasarle el corazón a uno⟩ **2** PERFORATE : perforar, agujerear (las orejas, etc.) **3 to pierce the silence** : desgarrar el silencio

piety ['paɪəti] *n, pl* **-eties** : piedad *f*

pig ['pɪg] *n* **1** HOG, SWINE : cerdo *m*, -da *f*; puerco *m*, -ca *f* **2** SLOB : persona *f* desaliñada; cerdo *m*, -da *f* **3** GLUTTON : glotón *m*, -tona *f* **4** *or* **pig iron** : lingote *m* de hierro

pigeon ['pɪʤən] *n* : paloma *f*

pigeonhole ['pɪʤən,ho:l] *n* : casilla *f*

piggish ['pɪgɪʃ] *adj* **1** GREEDY : glotón **2** DIRTY : cochino, sucio

piggyback ['pɪgi,bæk] *adv & adj* : a cuestas

piggy bank *n* : alcancía *f*

pigheaded ['pɪg,hɛdəd] *adj* : terco, obstinado

piglet ['pɪglət] *n* : cochinillo *m*; lechón *m*, -chona *f*

pigment ['pɪgmənt] *n* : pigmento *m*

pigmentation [,pɪgmən'teɪʃən] *n* : pigmentación *f*

pigmy → pygmy

pig out *vi* **to pig out (on)** : darse un atracón (de)

pigpen ['pɪg,pɛn] *n* : chiquero *m*, pocilga *f*

pigsty ['pɪg,staɪ] **→ pigpen**

pigtail ['pɪg,teɪl] *n* : coleta *f*, trenza *f*

pike ['paɪk] *n, pl* **pike** *or* **pikes 1** : lucio *m* (pez) **2** LANCE : pica *f* **3 → turnpike**

pile¹ ['paɪl] *v* **piled; piling** *vt* : amontonar, apilar — *vi* **to pile up** : amontonarse, acumularse

pile² *n* **1** STAKE : pilote *m* **2** HEAP : montón *m*, pila *f* **3** NAP : pelo *m* (de telas)

pileup ['paɪl,ʌp] *n* : choque *m* en cadena

piles ['paɪlz] *npl* HEMORRHOIDS : hemorroides *fpl*, almorranas *fpl*

pilfer ['pɪlfər] *vt* : robar (cosas pequeñas), ratear

pilgrim ['pɪlgrəm] *n* : peregrino *m*, -na *f*

pilgrimage ['pɪlgrəmɪʤ] *n* : peregrinación *f*

pill ['pɪl] *n* : pastilla *f*, píldora *f* ⟨to be on the pill, to be on birth control pills : tomar la píldora (anticonceptiva)⟩

pillage¹ ['pɪlɪʤ] *vt* **-laged; -laging** : saquear

pillage² *n* : saqueo *m*

pillar ['pɪlər] *n* : pilar *m*, columna *f*

pillory ['pɪləri] *n, pl* **-ries** : picota *f*

pillow ['pɪ,lo:] *n* : almohada *f*

pillowcase ['pɪ,lo:,keɪs] *n* : funda *f*

pilot¹ ['paɪlət] *vt* : pilotar, pilotear

pilot² *n* : piloto *mf*

pilot light *n* : piloto *m*

pimento [pə'mɛn,to:] **→ pimiento**

pimiento [pə'mɛn,to:, -'mjɛn-] *n, pl* **-tos** : pimiento *m* morrón

pimp ['pɪmp] *n* : proxeneta *m*

pimple ['pɪmpəl] *n* : grano *m*

pimply ['pɪmpəli] *adj* **pimplier; -est** : cubierto de granos

pin¹ ['pɪn] *vt* **pinned; pinning 1** FASTEN : prender, sujetar (con alfileres) **2** HOLD, IMMOBILIZE : inmovilizar, sujetar **3 to pin one's hopes on** : poner sus esperanzas en **4 to pin down** : identificar, determinar, definir

pin² *n* **1** : alfiler *m* ⟨safety pin : alfiler de gancho⟩ ⟨a bobby pin : una horquilla⟩ **2** BROOCH : alfiler *m*, broche *m*, prendedor *m* **3 → bowling pin**

pinafore ['pɪnə,for] *n* : delantal *m*

piñata [pin'jɑtə] *n* : piñata *f*

pinball ['pɪn,bɔl] *n* : pinball *m*

pincer ['pɪnsər] *n* **1** CLAW : pinza *f* (de una langosta, etc.) **2 pincers** *npl* : pinzas *fpl*, tenazas *fpl*, tenaza *f*

pinch¹ ['pɪnʧ] *vt* **1** : pellizcar ⟨she pinched my cheek : me pellizcó el cachete⟩ **2** STEAL : robar — *vi* : apretar ⟨my shoes pinch : me aprietan los zapatos⟩

pinch² *n* **1** EMERGENCY : emergencia *f* ⟨in a pinch : en caso necesario⟩ **2** PAIN : dolor *m*, tormento *m* **3** SQUEEZE : pellizco *m* (con los dedos) **4** BIT : pizca *f*, pellizco *m* ⟨a pinch of cinnamon : una pizca de canela⟩

pinch hitter *n* **1** SUBSTITUTE : sustituto *m*, -ta *f* **2** : bateador *m* emergente (en beisbol)

pincushion ['pɪn,kuʃən] *n* : acerico *m*, alfiletero *m*

pine¹ ['paɪn] *vi* **pined; pining 1 to pine away** : languidecer, consumirse **2 to pine for** : añorar, suspirar por

pine² *n* **1** : pino *m* (árbol) **2** : madera *f* de pino

pineapple ['paɪn,æpəl] *n* : piña *f*, ananá *f*, ananás *m*

ping ['pɪŋ] *n* : sonido *m* metálico

Ping-Pong ['pɪŋ,pɑŋ, -,pɔŋ] *trademark* — se usa para tenis de mesa

pinion¹ ['pɪnjən] *vt* : sujetar los brazos de, inmovilizar

pinion² *n* : piñón *m*

pink¹ ['pɪŋk] *adj* : rosa, rosado

pink² *n* **1** : clavelito *m* (flor) **2** : rosa *m*, rosado *m* (color) **3 to be in the pink** : estar en plena forma, rebosar de salud

pinkeye ['pɪŋk,aɪ] *n* : conjuntivitis *f* aguda

pinkie *or* **pinky** ['pɪŋki] *n* : meñique *m*

pinkish ['pɪŋkɪʃ] *adj* : rosáceo

pinnacle ['pɪnɪkəl] *n* **1** : pináculo *m* (de un edificio) **2** PEAK : cima *f*, cumbre *f* (de una montaña) **3** ACME : pináculo *m*, cúspide *f*, apogeo *m*

pinpoint ['pɪn,pɔɪnt] *vt* : precisar, localizar con precisión

pint ['paɪnt] *n* : pinta *f*

pinto ['pɪn,to:] *n, pl* **pintos** : caballo *m* pinto

pinworm ['pɪn,wərm] n : oxiuro m
pioneer¹ [,paɪə'nɪr] vt : promover, iniciar, introducir
pioneer² n : pionero m, -ra f
pious ['paɪəs] adj **1** DEVOUT : piadoso, devoto **2** SANCTIMONIOUS : beato, santurrón — **piously** ['paɪəsli] adv
pip ['pɪp] n : pepita f
pipe¹ ['paɪp] v **piped**; **piping** vi : hablar en voz chillona — vt **1** PLAY : tocar (el caramillo o la flauta) **2** : conducir por tuberías ⟨to pipe water : transportar el agua por tubería⟩
pipe² n **1** : caramillo m (instrumento musical) **2** BAGPIPE : gaita f **3** : tubo m, caño m ⟨gas pipes : tubería de gas⟩ **4** : pipa f (para fumar)
pipe dream n : quimera f, sueño m imposible
pipeline ['paɪp,laɪn] n **1** : conducto m, oleoducto m (para petróleo), gasoducto m (para gas) **2** CONDUIT : vía f (de información, etc.)
piper ['paɪpər] n : músico m, -ca f que toca el caramillo o la gaita
piping¹ ['paɪpɪŋ] n **1** : música f del caramillo o de la gaita **2** TRIM : cordoncillo m, ribete m con cordón
piping hot adj : muy caliente
piquant ['pi:kənt, 'pɪkwənt] adj **1** SPICY : picante **2** INTRIGUING : intrigante, estimulante
pique¹ ['pi:k] vt **piqued**; **piquing** **1** IRRITATE : picar, irritar **2** AROUSE : despertar (la curiosidad, etc.)
pique² n : pique m, resentimiento m
piracy ['paɪrəsi] n, pl **-cies** : piratería f
piranha ['pi'rɑnə, -'rɑnjə, -'rænjə] n : piraña f
pirate¹ ['paɪrət] n : pirata mf
pirate² vt **-rated**; **-rating** : piratear (software, etc.)
pirouette [,pɪrə'wɛt] n : pirueta f
pis → pi
Pisces ['paɪ,si:z, 'pɪ-, 'pɪs,keɪs] n **1** : Piscis m (signo o constelación) **2** : Piscis mf (persona)
piss¹ ['pɪs] vi usu vulgar : mear usu vulgar — vt fam **to piss off** ANGER : enojar, enfadar
piss² n usu vulgar **1** URINE : meados mpl, usu vulgar; pipí m fam; pis m fam **2 to take a piss** : mear usu vulgar, hacer pipí/pis fam
pistachio [pə'stæ,ʃi,o:, -'stɑ-] n, pl **-chios** : pistacho m
pistil ['pɪstəl] n : pistilo m
pistol ['pɪstəl] n : pistola f
piston ['pɪstən] n : pistón m, émbolo m
pit¹ ['pɪt] v **pitted**; **pitting** vt **1** : marcar de hoyos, picar (una superficie) **2** : deshuesar (una fruta) **3 to pit against** : enfrentar a, oponer a — vi : quedar marcado
pit² n **1** HOLE : fosa f, hoyo m ⟨a bottomless pit : un pozo sin fondo⟩ **2** MINE : mina f **3** : foso m (orchestra pit : foso orquestal) **4** POCKMARK : marca f (en la cara), cicatriz f (de viruela) **5** STONE : hueso m, pepa f (de una fruta) **6 pit of the stomach** : boca f del estómago

pita ['pi:tə] or **pita bread** n : pita f; pan m pita; pan m árabe Arg, Ven, Uru
pitch¹ ['pɪtʃ] vt **1** SET UP : montar, armar (una tienda) **2** THROW : lanzar, arrojar **3** ADJUST, SET : dar el tono de (un discurso, un instrumento musical) — vi **1** or **to pitch forward** FALL : caerse **2** LURCH : cabecear (dícese de un barco o un avión), dar bandazos **3 to pitch in** : arrimar el hombro
pitch² n **1** LURCHING : cabezada f, cabeceo m (de un barco o un avión) **2** SLOPE : (grado de) inclinación f, pendiente f **3** : tono m (en música) ⟨perfect pitch : oído absoluto⟩ **4** THROW : lanzamiento m **5** DEGREE : grado m, nivel m, punto m ⟨the excitement reached a high pitch : la excitación llegó a un punto culminante⟩ **6** or **sales pitch** : presentación f (de un vendedor) **7** TAR : pez f, brea f
pitch–black ['pɪtʃ'blæk] adj : muy oscuro, oscuro como boca de lobo fam
pitcher ['pɪtʃər] n **1** JUG : jarra f, jarro m, cántaro m, pichel m **2** : lanzador m, -dora f (en béisbol, etc.)
pitchfork ['pɪtʃ,fork] n : horquilla f, horca f
piteous ['pɪtiəs] adj : lastimoso, lastimero — **piteously** adv
pitfall ['pɪt,fɔl] n **1** : peligro m (poco obvio), dificultad f
pith ['pɪθ] n **1** : médula f (de una planta) **2** CORE : meollo m, entraña f
pithy ['pɪθi] adj **pithier**; **-est** : conciso y sustancioso ⟨pithy comments : comentarios sucintos⟩
pitiable ['pɪtiəbəl] → **pitiful**
pitiful ['pɪtɪfəl] adj **1** LAMENTABLE : lastimero, lastimoso, lamentable **2** CONTEMPTIBLE : despreciable, lamentable — **pitifully** [-fli] adv
pitiless ['pɪtɪləs] adj : despiadado — **pitilessly** adv
pittance ['pɪtənts] n : miseria f
pituitary [pə'tu:ə,teri, -'tju:-] adj : pituitario
pity¹ ['pɪti] vt **pitied**; **pitying** : compadecer, compadecerse de
pity² n, pl **pities** **1** COMPASSION : compasión f, piedad f **2** SHAME : lástima f, pena f ⟨what a pity! : ¡qué lástima!⟩
pivot¹ ['pɪvət] vi **1** : girar sobre un eje **2 to pivot on** : girar sobre, depender de
pivot² n : pivote m
pivotal ['pɪvətəl] adj : fundamental, central
pixie or **pixy** ['pɪksi] n, pl **pixies** : elfo m, hada f
pizza ['pi:tsə] n : pizza f
pizzazz or **pizazz** [pə'zæz] n **1** GLAMOR : encanto m **2** VITALITY : animación f, vitalidad f
pizzeria [,pi:tsə'ri:ə] n : pizzería f
placard ['plækərd, -,kɑrd] n POSTER : cartel m, póster m, afiche m
placate ['pleɪ,keɪt, 'plæ-] vt **-cated**; **-cating** : aplacar, apaciguar
place¹ ['pleɪs] vt **placed**; **placing** **1** PUT, SET : poner, colocar ⟨she carefully placed the book on the table : colocó el

libro con cuidado sobre la mesa⟩ **2** SITU-
ATE : sitio m, llano m, planicie f
place : estar bien situado⟩ ⟨to place in
a job : colocar en un trabajo⟩ **3** IDEN-
TIFY, RECALL : identificar, ubicar, recordar ⟨I can't place him : no lo ubico⟩ **4 to**
place an order : hacer un pedido
place² n **1** SPACE : sitio m, lugar m
⟨there's no place to sit : no hay sitio para
sentarse⟩ **2** LOCATION : lugar m, sitio m,
parte f ⟨place of work : lugar de trabajo⟩
⟨faraway places : lugares remotos⟩ ⟨all
over the place : por todas partes⟩ **3**
HOME : casa f ⟨our summer place : nuestra casa de verano⟩ **4** POSITION, SPOT
: lugar m, sitio m ⟨everything in its place
: todo en su lugar⟩ ⟨to hold in place : su-
jetar⟩ ⟨I got distracted and lost my place
: me distraje y ya no sé por donde iba⟩ **5**
SEAT, SPOT : asiento m, sitio m ⟨she
changed places with him : le cambió el
asiento⟩ ⟨would you hold/save my
place? : ¿me guardas el asiento?⟩ **6** or
place setting : cubierto m **7** RANK : lugar m, puesto m ⟨he took first place
: ganó el primer lugar⟩ **8** JOB : puesto m
9 ROLE : lugar m, papel m ⟨to trade
places with someone : cambiarse por alguien, cambiarle el lugar a alguien⟩ ⟨put
yourself in my place : ponte en mi lugar⟩
⟨she put him in his place : lo puso en su
lugar⟩ **10** : lugar m ⟨the ones/tens place
: el lugar de las unidades/decenas⟩ ⟨a
decimal place : un decimal⟩ **11 in place**
: en marcha ⟨to put a plan/system in
place : poner en marcha un plan/sis-
tema⟩ **12 in place of** : en lugar de **13 in**
the first place : para empezar **14 in the**
first/second place : en primer/segundo
lugar **15 out of place** : fuera de lugar **16**
to go places : tener éxito, llegar lejos **17**
to take place : tener lugar **18 to take**
the place of : sustituir a
placebo [plə'si:₁bo:] n, pl **-bos** : placebo m
place mat n : individual m, mantel m individual
placement ['pleɪsmənt] n : colocación f
placenta [plə'sɛntə] n, pl **-tas** or **-tae** [-ti,
-₁taɪ] : placenta f
placid ['plæsəd] adj : plácido, tranquilo —
placidly adv
plagiarism ['pleɪdʒə₁rɪzəm] n : plagio m
plagiarist ['pleɪdʒərɪst] n : plagiario m, -ria
f
plagiarize ['pleɪdʒə₁raɪz] vt **-rized; -rizing**
: plagiar
plague¹ ['pleɪg] vt **plagued; plaguing 1**
AFFLICT : plagar, afligir ⟨plagued with
problems : plagado de problemas⟩ **2**
DISTRESS : acosar, atormentar ⟨plagued
by doubts : acosado por dudas⟩
plague² n **1** : plaga f (de insectos, etc.) **2**
: peste f (en medicina)
plaid¹ ['plæd] adj : escocés, de cuadros ⟨a
plaid skirt : una falda escocesa⟩
plaid² n TARTAN : tela f escocesa, tartán m
plain¹ ['pleɪn] adj **1** SIMPLE, UNADORNED
: liso, sencillo, sin adornos **2** CLEAR
: claro ⟨in plain language : en palabras
claras⟩ ⟨to make something plain : dejar

algo (en) claro⟩ **3** FRANK : franco, puro
⟨the plain truth : la pura verdad⟩ **4**
HOMELY : ordinario, poco atractivo **5 in**
plain sight : a la vista de todos
plain² n : llanura f, llano m, planicie f
plainclothes ['pleɪn'klo:z, -'klo:ðz] adj
: de civil; de paisano; de particular Arg,
Uru (dícese de un policía, etc.)
plainly ['pleɪnli] adv **1** CLEARLY : claramente **2** FRANKLY : francamente, con
franqueza **3** SIMPLY : sencillamente
plaintiff ['pleɪntɪf] n : demandante mf
plaintive ['pleɪntɪv] adj MOURNFUL : lastimero, plañidero
plait¹ ['pleɪt, 'plæt] vt **1** PLEAT : plisar **2**
BRAID : trenzar
plait² n **1** PLEAT : pliegue m **2** BRAID
: trenza f
plan¹ ['plæn] v **planned; planning** vt **1**
: planear, proyectar, planificar ⟨to plan a
trip : planear un viaje⟩ ⟨to plan a city
: planificar una ciudad⟩ **2** INTEND : tener planeado, proyectar — vi : hacer planes
plan² n **1** DIAGRAM : plano m, esquema m
2 SCHEME : plan m, proyecto m, programa m ⟨to draw up a plan : elaborar
un proyecto⟩
plane¹ ['pleɪn] vt **planed; planing** : cepillar (madera)
plane² adj : plano
plane³ n **1** : plano m (en matemáticas,
etc.) **2** LEVEL : nivel m **3** : cepillo m (de
carpintero) **4** → **airplane**
planet ['plænət] n : planeta f
planetarium [₁plænə'tɛriəm] n, pl **-iums**
or **-ia** [-iə] : planetario m
planetary ['plænə₁tɛri] adj : planetario
plank ['plæŋk] n **1** BOARD : tablón m, tabla f **2** : artículo m, punto m (de una
plataforma política)
plankton ['plæŋktən] n : plancton m
planner ['plænər] n : planificador m,
-dora f ⟨wedding planner : organizador
de bodas⟩ ⟨financial planner : asesor fi-
nanciero⟩
plant¹ ['plænt] vt **1** : plantar, sembrar (semillas) ⟨planted with flowers : plantado
de flores⟩ **2** PLACE : plantar, colocar ⟨to
plant an idea : inculcar una idea⟩
plant² n **1** : planta f ⟨leafy plants : plantas
frondosas⟩ **2** FACTORY : planta f, fábrica
f ⟨hydroelectric plant : planta hidroeléc-
trica⟩ **3** MACHINERY : maquinaria f,
equipo m
plantain ['plæntən] n **1** : llantén m (mala
hierba) **2** : plátano m, plátano m macho
Mex (fruta)
plantation [plæn'teɪʃən] n : plantación f,
hacienda f ⟨a coffee plantation : un cafe-
tal⟩
planter ['plæntər] n **1** : hacendado m, -da
f (de una hacienda) **2** FLOWERPOT
: tiesto m, maceta f
plaque ['plæk] n **1** TABLET : placa f **2**
: placa f (dental)
plasma ['plæzmə] n : plasma m
plaster¹ ['plæstər] vt **1** : enyesar, revocar
(con yeso) **2** COVER : cubrir, llenar ⟨a

wall plastered with notices : una pared cubierta de avisos⟩

plaster² *n* **1** : yeso *m*, revoque *m* (para paredes, etc.) **2** : escayola *f*, yeso *m* (en medicina) **3 plaster of Paris** [ˈpærɪs] : yeso *m* mate

plastered ['plæstərd] *adj* INTOXICATED : colocado

plastic¹ ['plæstɪk] *adj* **1** : de plástico **2** PLIABLE : plástico, flexible

plastic² *n* : plástico *m*

plasticity [plæˈstɪsəʈi] *n, pl* **-ties** : plasticidad *f*

plastic surgery *n* : cirugía *f* plástica

plastic wrap *n* : papel *m* film

plate¹ ['pleɪt] *vt* **plated; plating** : chapar (en metal)

plate² *n* **1** PLAQUE, SHEET : placa *f* ⟨a steel plate : una placa de acero⟩ **2** UTENSILS : vajilla *f* (de metal) ⟨silver plate : vajilla de plata⟩ **3** DISH : plato *m* **4** DENTURES : dentadura *f* postiza **5** ILLUSTRATION : lámina *f* (en un libro) **6 license plate** : matrícula *f*, placa *f* de matrícula

plateau [plæˈtoː] *n, pl* **-teaus** or **-teaux** [-ˈtoːz] : meseta *f*

platform ['plætˌfɔrm] *n* **1** STAGE : plataforma *f*, estrado *m*, tribuna *f* **2** : andén *m* (de una estación de ferrocarril) **3 political platform** : plataforma *f* política, programa *m* electoral

plating ['pleɪʈɪŋ] *n* **1** : enchapado *m* **2 silver plating** : plateado *m*

platinum ['plæʈənəm] *n* : platino *m*

platitude ['plæʈəˌtuːd, -ˌtjuːd] *n* : lugar *m* común, perogrullada *f*

platonic [pləˈtɑnɪk] *adj* : platónico

platoon [pləˈtuːn] *n* : sección *f* (en el ejército)

platter ['plæʈər] *n* : fuente *f*

platypus ['plæʈɪpəs, -ˌpʊs] *n, pl* **platypuses** or **platypi** [-ˌpaɪ, -ˌpiː] : ornitorrinco *m*

plausibility [ˌplɔzəˈbɪləʈi] *n, pl* **-ties** : credibilidad *f*, verosimilitud *f*

plausible ['plɔzəbəl] *adj* : creíble, convincente, verosímil — **plausibly** [-bli] *adv*

play¹ ['pleɪ] *vi* **1** : jugar ⟨the children were playing in the yard : los niños jugaban en el jardín⟩ ⟨she plays on the basketball team : juega con el equipo de baloncesto⟩ ⟨he plays for the Red Sox : juega para los Red Sox⟩ ⟨we play for fun : jugamos por diversión⟩ ⟨they're playing against the Yankees : juegan contra los Yanquis⟩ ⟨it's your turn to play : te toca a ti jugar⟩ ⟨to play with a doll : jugar con una muñeca⟩ ⟨to play with an idea : darle vueltas a una idea⟩ **2** or **to play around** FIDDLE, TOY : jugar, juguetear ⟨don't play (around) with your food : no juegues con la comida⟩ **3** or **to play around** JOKE : bromear, hacer el tonto ⟨I was only playing (around) : sólo estaba bromeando⟩ **4** : tocar ⟨to play in a band : tocar en un grupo⟩ **5** : sonar (en la radio, etc.) **6** : actuar (en una obra de teatro) **7** SHOW ⟨what's playing at the movies/theatre? : ¿qué dan/ponen en el cine?⟩ **8** BEHAVE ⟨to play fair/dirty : jugar limpio/sucio⟩ ⟨to play by the rules : respetar las reglas⟩ **9** ACT : hacerse ⟨to play dumb/dead : hacerse el tonto/muerto⟩ **10 to play along (with someone)** : seguirle la corriente a alguien, hacerle el juego a alguien **11 to play around** : perder el tiempo ⟨he plays around instead of working : pierde el tiempo en vez de trabajar⟩ **12 to play around** : tener líos (amorosos) **13 to play for time** STALL : tratar de ganar tiempo **14 to play hard to get** : hacerse (de) rogar **15 to play into** SUPPORT : dar crédito a **16 to play into the hands of** : dárselo en bandeja a **17 to play off** COMPLEMENT : complementar **18 to play on** EXPLOIT : explotar, aprovecharse de **19 to play out** DEVELOP, UNFOLD : desarrollarse, desenvolverse — *vt* **1** : jugar (un deporte, etc.), jugar a (un juego), jugar contra (un contrincante) ⟨he wouldn't play her at chess : no quiso jugar (al) ajedrez con ella⟩ ⟨the Yankees are playing the Red Sox : los Yanquis juegan contra los Red Sox⟩ ⟨he plays shortstop : juega de/como torpedero⟩ ⟨to play house : jugar a las casitas, jugar a papás y mamás⟩ **2** : tirar (una carta), mover (una pieza), tirar/patear (etc.) (una pelota) ⟨to play a shot : tirar un tiro⟩ **3** : tocar (música o un instrumento), tocar en (un lugar) **4** : poner (un DVD, etc.), poner/pasar (una canción en la radio, etc.) ⟨he plays his music too loud : pone la música demasiado alta/fuerte⟩ **5** SHOW : dar, poner (una película) **6** : jugar a (la lotería, etc.) **7** PERFORM : interpretar, hacer el papel de (un carácter), representar (una obra de teatro) ⟨she plays the lead : hace el papel principal⟩ **8** CARRY OUT : jugar, desempeñar ⟨she played an important role in the negotiations : jugó un papel importante en las negociaciones⟩ **9** ACT : hacerse ⟨to play the fool : hacerse el tonto⟩ **10** BEHAVE ⟨to play it cool : (actuar) como si nada⟩ ⟨to play it safe : ir a la segura, ir a lo seguro⟩ **11** MANIPULATE : manipular ⟨to play someone for a fool : engañar a alguien⟩ **12** : hacer, gastar ⟨he played a joke on her : le hizo/gastó una broma⟩ ⟨to play a dirty trick on : garle una mala pasada a⟩ **13 to play back** : poner (una grabación) **14 to play down** : minimizar **15 to play God** : jugar a ser Dios **16 to play out** : realizar, vivir (un sueño, etc.) ⟨this scene plays itself out every day : esta situación ocurre cada día⟩ **17 to play up** EMPHASIZE : resaltar

play² *n* **1** GAME, RECREATION : juego *m* ⟨children at play : niños jugando⟩ ⟨a play on words : un juego de palabras⟩ **2** ACTION : juego *m* ⟨rain held up play for an hour : el partido tuvo una hora de retraso por lluvia⟩ ⟨the ball is in play : la pelota está en juego⟩ ⟨to bring into play : poner en juego⟩ **3** DRAMA : obra *f* de teatro, pieza *f* (de teatro) ⟨to put on a play : presentar/representar una obra⟩ **4**

MOVEMENT : juego *m* (de la luz, una brisa, etc.) **5** **SLACK** : juego *m* ⟨there's not enough play in the wheel : la rueda no da lo suficiente⟩

playacting [ˈpleɪˌæktɪŋ] *n* : actuación *f*, teatro *m*

playboy [ˈpleɪˌbɔɪ] *n* : playboy *m*

player [ˈpleɪər] *n* **1** : jugador *m*, -dora *f* (en un juego) **2** **ACTOR** : actor *m*, actriz *f* **3** **MUSICIAN** : músico *m*, -ca *f* **4** : reproductor *m* (de DVD, etc.)

playful [ˈpleɪfəl] *adj* **1** **FROLICSOME** : juguetón **2** **JOCULAR** : jocoso — **playfully** *adv*

playfulness [ˈpleɪfəlnəs] *n* : lo juguetón, jocosidad *f*, alegría *f*

playground [ˈpleɪˌɡraʊnd] *n* : patio *m* de recreo, jardín *m* para jugar

playgroup [ˈpleɪˌɡruːp] *n* : grupo *m* de recreo para niños

playhouse [ˈpleɪˌhaʊs] *n* **1** **THEATER** : teatro *m* **2** : casita *f* de juguete

playing card *n* : naipe *m*, carta *f*

playing field *n* : campo *m* de juego

playmate [ˈpleɪˌmeɪt] *n* : compañero *m*, -ra *f* de juego

play–off [ˈpleɪˌɔf] *n* : desempate *m*

playpen [ˈpleɪˌpɛn] *n* : corral *m* (para niños)

playroom [ˈpleɪˌruːm] *n* : cuarto *m* de juegos

plaything [ˈpleɪˌθɪŋ] *n* : juguete *m*

playtime [ˈpleɪˌtaɪm] *n* : hora *f* de recreo

playwright [ˈpleɪˌraɪt] *n* : dramaturgo *m*, -ga *f*

plaza [ˈplæzə, ˈplɑ–] *n* **1** **SQUARE** : plaza *f* **2 shopping plaza** **MALL** : centro *m* comercial

plea [ˈpliː] *n* **1** : acto *m* de declararse ⟨he entered a plea of guilty : se declaró culpable⟩ **2** **APPEAL** : ruego *m*, súplica *f*

plead [ˈpliːd] *v* **pleaded** *or* **pled** [ˈplɛd]; **pleading** *vi* **1** : declararse (culpable o inocente) **2 to plead for** : suplicar, implorar **3 to plead with** : implorarle, suplicarle (a alguien) — *vt* **1** : alegar, pretextar ⟨he pleaded illness : pretextó la enfermedad⟩ **2 to plead a case** : defender un caso

pleasant [ˈplɛzənt] *adj* : agradable, grato, bueno — **pleasantly** *adv*

pleasantness [ˈplɛzəntnəs] *n* : lo agradable, amenidad *f*

pleasantries [ˈplɛzəntriz] *npl* : cumplidos *mpl*, cortesías *fpl* ⟨to exchange pleasantries : intercambiar cumplidos⟩

please¹ [ˈpliːz] *v* **pleased; pleasing** *vt* **1** **GRATIFY** : complacer ⟨please yourself! : ¡cómo quieras!⟩ **2** **SATISFY** : contentar, satisfacer — *vi* **1** **SATISFY** : complacer, agradar ⟨anxious to please : deseoso de complacer⟩ **2** **LIKE** : querer ⟨do as you please : haz lo que quieras, haz lo que te parezca⟩

please² *adv* : por favor

pleased [ˈpliːzd] *adj* : contento, satisfecho, alegre ⟨to be pleased about/with : estar contento por/con⟩ ⟨pleased to meet you! : ¡mucho gusto!⟩

pleasing [ˈpliːzɪŋ] *adj* : agradable — **pleasingly** *adv*

pleasurable [ˈplɛʒərəbəl] *adj* **PLEASANT** : agradable

pleasure [ˈplɛʒər] *n* **1** **WISH** : deseo *m*, voluntad *f* ⟨at your pleasure : cuando guste⟩ **2** **ENJOYMENT** : placer *m*, disfrute *m*, goce *m* ⟨with pleasure : con mucho gusto⟩ **3** : placer *m*, gusto *m* ⟨it's a pleasure to be here : me da gusto estar aquí⟩ ⟨the pleasures of reading : los placeres de leer⟩

pleat¹ [ˈpliːt] *vt* : plisar

pleat² *n* : pliegue *m*

plebeian [plɪˈbiən] *adj* : ordinario, plebeyo

pledge¹ [ˈplɛdʒ] *vt* **pledged; pledging** **1** **PAWN** : empeñar, prendar **2** **PROMISE** : prometer, jurar

pledge² *n* **1** **SECURITY** : garantía *f*, prenda *f* **2** **PROMISE** : promesa *f*

plenteous [ˈplɛntiəs] *adj* : copioso, abundante

plentiful [ˈplɛntɪfəl] *adj* : abundante — **plentifully** [-fli] *adv*

plenty [ˈplɛnti] *n* : abundancia *f* ⟨plenty of time : tiempo de sobra⟩ ⟨plenty of visitors : muchos visitantes⟩

plethora [ˈplɛθərə] *n* : plétora *f*

pleurisy [ˈplʊrəsi] *n* : pleuresía *f*

pliable [ˈplaɪəbəl] *adj* : flexible, maleable

pliant [ˈplaɪənt] → **pliable**

pliers [ˈplaɪərz] *npl* : alicates *mpl*, pinzas *fpl*

plight [ˈplaɪt] *n* : situación *f* difícil, apuro *m*

plod [ˈplɑd] *vi* **plodded; plodding** **1** **TRUDGE** : caminar pesadamente y lentamente **2** **DRUDGE** : trabajar laboriosamente

plonk → **plunk**

plot¹ [ˈplɑt] *v* **plotted; plotting** *vt* **1** **DEVISE** : tramar **2 to plot out** : trazar, determinar (una posición, etc.) — *vi* **CONSPIRE** : conspirar

plot² *n* **1** **LOT** : terreno *m*, parcela *f*, lote *m* **2** **STORY** : argumento *m* (en el teatro), trama *f* (en un libro, etc.) **3** **CONSPIRACY, INTRIGUE** : complot *m*, intriga *f*

plotter [ˈplɑtər] *n* : conspirador *m*, -dora *f*; intrigante *mf*

plow¹ *or* **plough** [ˈplaʊ] *vt* **1** : arar (la tierra) **2 to plow the seas** : surcar los mares

plow² *or* **plough** *n* **1** : arado *m* **2** → **snow-plow**

plowshare [ˈplaʊˌʃɛr] *n* : reja *f* del arado

ploy [ˈplɔɪ] *n* : estratagema *f*, maniobra *f*

pluck¹ [ˈplʌk] *vt* **1** **PICK** : arrancar **2** : desplumar (un pollo, etc.) — *vi* **to pluck at** : tirar de

pluck² *n* **1** **TUG** : tirón *m* **2** **COURAGE, SPIRIT** : valor *m*, ánimo *m*

plucky [ˈplʌki] *adj* **pluckier; -est** : valiente, animoso

plug¹ [ˈplʌɡ] *vt* **plugged; plugging** **1** **BLOCK** : tapar **2** **PROMOTE** : hacerle publicidad a, promocionar **3 to plug in** : enchufar

plug² n **1** STOPPER : tapón m **2** : enchufe m (eléctrico) **3** ADVERTISEMENT : publicidad f, propaganda f

plum ['plʌm] n **1** : ciruela f (fruta) **2** : color m ciruela **3** PRIZE : premio m, algo muy atractivo

plumage ['plu:mɪʤ] n : plumaje m

plumb¹ ['plʌm] vt **1** : aplomar ⟨to plumb a wall : aplomar una pared⟩ **2** SOUND : sondear, sondar

plumb² adv VERTICALLY : a plomo, verticalmente **2** EXACTLY : justo, exactamente **3** COMPLETELY : completamente, absolutamente ⟨plumb crazy : loco de remate⟩

plumb³ adj : a plomo

plumb⁴ n or plumb line : plomada f

plumber ['plʌmər] n : plomero m, -ra f; fontanero m, -ra f

plumbing ['plʌmɪŋ] n **1** : plomería f, fontanería f (trabajo del plomero) **2** PIPES : cañería f, tubería f

plume ['plu:m] n **1** FEATHER : pluma f **2** TUFT : penacho m (en un sombrero, etc.)

plumed ['plu:md] adj : con plumas ⟨white-plumed birds : aves de plumaje blanco⟩

plummet ['plʌmət] vi : caer en picada, desplomarse

plump¹ ['plʌmp] vi or to plump down : dejarse caer (pesadamente)

plump² adv **1** STRAIGHT : a plomo **2** DIRECTLY : directamente, sin rodeos ⟨he ran plump into the door : dio de cara con la puerta⟩

plump³ adj : llenito fam, regordete fam, rechoncho fam

plumpness ['plʌmpnəs] n : gordura f

plunder¹ ['plʌndər] vi : saquear, robar

plunder² n : botín m

plunderer ['plʌndərər] n : saqueador m, -dora f

plunge¹ ['plʌnʤ] v plunged; plunging vt **1** IMMERSE : sumergir **2** THRUST : hundir, clavar — vi **1** DIVE : zambullirse (en el agua) **2** : meterse precipitadamente o violentamente ⟨they plunged into war : se enfrascaron en una guerra⟩ ⟨he plunged into depression : cayó en la depresión⟩ **3** DESCEND : descender en picada ⟨the road plunges dizzily : la calle desciende vertiginosamente⟩

plunge² n **1** DIVE : zambullida f **2** DROP : descenso m abrupto ⟨the plunge in prices : el desplome de los precios⟩

plunger ['plʌnʤər] n : desatorador m, desatascador m Spain, destapacaños m Mex, bomba f (destapacaños) Mex, sopapa f Arg

plunk ['plʌŋk] or plonk ['plɑŋk] vt **1** : dejar caer **2** to plunk down : gastar (dinero) — vi to plunk down : dejarse caer

pluperfect [,plu:'pərfɪkt] n : pluscuamperfecto m

plural¹ ['plʊrəl] adj : plural

plural² n : plural m

plurality [plʊ'ræləṭi] n, pl -ties : pluralidad f

pluralize ['plʊrə,laɪz] vt -ized; -izing : pluralizar

plus¹ ['plʌs] adj **1** POSITIVE : positivo ⟨a plus factor : un factor positivo⟩ **2** (indicating a quantity in addition) : a grade of C plus : una calificación entre C y B⟩ ⟨a salary of $30,000 plus : un sueldo de más de $30,000⟩

plus² n **1** or plus sign : más m, signo m de más **2** ADVANTAGE : ventaja f

plus³ prep : más (en matemáticas)

plus⁴ conj : y

plush¹ ['plʌʃ] adj **1** : afelpado **2** LUXURIOUS : lujoso

plush² n : felpa f, peluche m

plushy ['plʌʃi] adj plushier; -est : lujoso

Pluto ['plu:to:] n : Plutón m

plutocracy [plu:'tɑkrəsi] n, pl -cies : plutocracia f

plutonium [plu:'to:niəm] n : plutonio m

ply ['plaɪ] v plied; plying vt **1** USE, WIELD : manejar ⟨to ply an ax : manejar un hacha⟩ **2** PRACTICE : ejercer ⟨to ply a trade : ejercer un oficio⟩ **3** to ply with questions : acosar con preguntas

ply² n, pl plies **1** LAYER : chapa f (de madera), capa f (de papel) **2** STRAND : cabo m (de hilo, etc.)

plywood ['plaɪ,wʊd] n : contrachapado m

PMS [,pi:,ɛm'ɛs] → premenstrual syndrome

pneumatic [nʊ'mæṭɪk, njʊ-] adj : neumático

pneumonia [nʊ'mo:njə, njʊ-] n : pulmonía f, neumonía f

poach ['po:ʧ] vt **1** : cocer a fuego lento ⟨to poach an egg : escalfar un huevo⟩ **2** to poach game : cazar ilegalmente — vi : cazar ilegalmente

poacher ['po:ʧər] n : cazador m furtivo, cazadora f furtiva

P.O. Box n (Post Office Box) : apartado m postal, casilla f de correos Arg

pock ['pɑk] n **1** PUSTULE : pústula f **2** → pockmark

pocket¹ ['pɑkət] vt **1** : meterse en el bolsillo ⟨he pocketed the pen : se metió la pluma en el bolsillo⟩ **2** STEAL : embolsarse

pocket² n **1** : bolsillo m, bolsa f Mex ⟨a coat pocket : el bolsillo de un abrigo⟩ ⟨air pockets : bolsas/baches de aire⟩ **2** CENTER : foco m, centro m ⟨a pocket of resistance : un foco de resistencia⟩

pocketbook ['pɑkət,bʊk] n **1** PURSE : cartera f, bolso m, bolsa f Mex **2** MEANS : recursos mpl

pocketknife ['pɑkət,naɪf] n, pl -knives : navaja f

pocket money n : dinero m de bolsillo

pocket–size ['pɑkət'saɪz] adj : de bolsillo

pockmark ['pɑk,mɑrk] n : cicatriz f de viruela, viruela f

pod ['pɑd] n : vaina f ⟨pea pod : vaina de guisantes⟩

podcast ['pɑd,kæst] n : podcast m

podiatrist [pə'daɪətrɪst, po-] n : podólogo m, -ga f

podiatry [pə'daɪətri, po-] n : podología f, podiatría f

podium ['po:diəm] *n, pl* **-diums** *or* **-dia** [-diə] : podio *m*, estrado *m*, tarima *f*

poem ['po:əm] *n* : poema *m*, poesía *f*

poet ['po:ət] *n* : poeta *mf*

poetess ['po:ətəs] *n* : poetisa *f*

poetic [po'ɛtɪk] *or* **poetical** [-tɪkəl] *adj* : poético

poetry ['po:ətri] *n* : poesía *f*

pogrom ['po:grəm, pə'grɑm, 'pɑgrəm] *n* : pogrom *m*

poignancy ['pɔɪnjəntsi] *n, pl* **-cies** : lo conmovedor

poignant ['pɔɪnjənt] *adj* **1** PAINFUL : penoso, doloroso ⟨poignant grief : profundo dolor⟩ **2** TOUCHING : conmovedor, emocionante

poinsettia [pɔɪn'sɛtiə, -'sɛtə] *n* : flor *f* de Nochebuena

point¹ ['pɔɪnt] *vt* **1** : apuntar (una pistola, etc.), señalar con (el dedo) **2** DIRECT : encaminar ⟨can you point me towards the highway? : ¿me puedes indicar cómo llegar a la carretera?⟩ **3** INDICATE : señalar, indicar ⟨to point the way : señalar el camino⟩ **4** SHARPEN : afilar (la punta de) **5 to point out** : señalar, indicar — *vi* **1** : señalar (con el dedo) **2** : apuntar ⟨the needle points north : la aguja apunta hacia el norte⟩ **3** : apuntar (en una pantalla, etc.) ⟨to point and click : apuntar y hacer clic⟩ **4 to point at/to** : señalar (con el dedo) **5 to point to** REFERENCE : señalar **6 to point to/toward** INDICATE : señalar, indicar

point² *n* **1** ITEM : punto *m* ⟨the main points : los puntos principales⟩ **2** : argumento *m*, observación *f* ⟨what's your point? : ¿qué quieres decir?⟩ ⟨that's a good point : es cierto⟩ ⟨I see what you're saying : entiendo⟩ ⟨to have a point : tener razón⟩ ⟨to make a point : hacer una observación⟩ ⟨to get one's point across : hacerse entender⟩ **3 the point** (*indicating the chief idea or meaning*) ⟨to get to the point : ir al grano⟩ ⟨to be beside the point : no venir al caso⟩ ⟨to stick to the point : no salirse del tema⟩ **4** PURPOSE : fin *m*, propósito *m* ⟨there's no point to it : no vale la pena, no sirve para nada⟩ ⟨to make a point of doing something : proponerse hacer algo⟩ **5** QUALITY : cualidad *f* ⟨her good points : sus buenas cualidades⟩ ⟨it's not his strong point : no es su (punto) fuerte⟩ **6** PLACE : punto *m*, lugar *m* ⟨points of interest : puntos interesantes⟩ **7** : punto *m* (en una escala) ⟨boiling point : punto de ebullición⟩ **8** MOMENT : momento *m*, coyuntura *f* ⟨at this point : en este momento⟩ **9** TIP : punta *f* **10** HEADLAND : punta *f*, cabo *m* **11** PERIOD : punto *m* (marca de puntuación) **12** UNIT : punto *m* ⟨he scored 15 points : ganó 15 puntos⟩ ⟨shares fell 10 points : las acciones bajaron 10 enteros⟩ **13 → decimal point 14 compass points** : puntos *mpl* cardinales **15 sore point** : asunto *m* delicado

point–blank¹ ['pɔɪnt'blæŋk] *adv* **1** : a quemarropa ⟨to shoot point-blank : disparar a quemarropa⟩ **2** BLUNTLY, DI-RECTLY : a bocajarro, sin rodeos, francamente

point–blank² *adj* **1** : a quemarropa ⟨point-blank shots : disparos a quemarropa⟩ **2** BLUNT, DIRECT : directo, franco

pointed ['pɔɪntəd] *adj* **1** POINTY : puntiagudo **2** PERTINENT : atinado **3** CONSPICUOUS : marcado, manifiesto

pointedly ['pɔɪntədli] *adv* : intencionadamente, directamente

pointer ['pɔɪntər] *n* **1** STICK : puntero *m* (para maestros, etc.) **2** INDICATOR, NEEDLE : indicador *m*, aguja *f* **3** : perro *m* de muestra **4** HINT, TIP : consejo *m*

pointless ['pɔɪntləs] *adj* : inútil, ocioso, vano ⟨it's pointless to continue : no tiene sentido continuar⟩

point of view *n* : perspectiva *f*, punto *m* de vista

pointy ['pɔɪnti] *adj* : puntiagudo

poise¹ ['pɔɪz] *vt* **poised; poising** BALANCE : equilibrar, balancear

poise² *n* : aplomo *m*, compostura *f*

poison¹ ['pɔɪzən] *vt* **1** : envenenar, intoxicar **2** CORRUPT : corromper

poison² *n* : veneno *m*

poisoning *n* : envenenamiento *m*

poison ivy *n* : hiedra *f* venenosa

poisonous ['pɔɪzənəs] *adj* : venenoso, tóxico, ponzoñoso

poke¹ ['po:k] *v* **poked; poking** *vt* **1** JAB : golpear (con la punta de algo), dar ⟨he poked me with his finger : me dio con el dedo⟩ **2** THRUST : introducir, asomar ⟨I poked my head out the window : asomé la cabeza por la ventana⟩ — *vi* **1 to poke around** RUMMAGE : hurgar **2 to poke along** DAWDLE : demorarse, entretenerse **3 to poke out of** : asomar por, sobresalir por

poke² *n* : golpe *m* abrupto (con la punta de algo)

poker ['po:kər] *n* **1** : atizador *m* (para el fuego) **2** : póker *m*, poker *m* (juego de naipes)

poky ['po:ki] *adj fam* **1** SLOW : lento **2** TINY : diminuto

polar ['po:lər] *adj* : polar

polar bear *n* : oso *m* blanco

Polaris [po'lærɪs, -'lɑr-] → North Star

polarize ['po:lə,raɪz] *vt* **-ized; -izing** : polarizar

Polaroid ['po:lə,rɔɪd] *trademark* se usa para una cámara que produce fotos reveladas o para las fotos así producidas

pole ['po:l] *n* **1** : palo *m*, poste *m*, vara *f* ⟨telephone pole : poste de teléfonos⟩ **2** : polo *m* ⟨the South Pole : el Polo Sur⟩ **3** : polo *m* (eléctrico o magnético)

Pole ['po:l] *n* : polaco *m*, -ca *f*

polecat ['po:l,kæt] *n, pl* **polecats** *or* **polecat 1** : turón *m* (de Europa) **2** SKUNK : mofeta *f*, zorrillo *m*

polemical [pə'lɛmɪkəl] *adj* : polémico

polemics [pə'lɛmɪks] *ns & pl* : polémica *f*

polestar ['po:l,stɑr] → North Star

pole vault *n* : salto *m* con/de pértiga, salto *m* con/de garrocha

police[1] [pə'li:s] vt **-liced; -licing** : mantener el orden en ⟨to police the streets : patrullar las calles⟩

police[2] ns & pl **1** : policía f (organización) **2** POLICE OFFICERS : policías mfpl

police car n : patrulla f, patrullero m

police force n : fuerza f policial, cuerpo m policial

policeman [pə'li:smən] n, pl **-men** [-mən, -ˌmɛn] : policía m

police officer n : policía mf, agente mf de policía

police station n : comisaría f

policewoman [pə'li:sˌwʊmən] n, pl **-women** [-ˌwɪmən] : policía f, mujer f policía

policy ['pɑləsi] n, pl **-cies** **1** : política f ⟨foreign policy : política exterior⟩ **2** or **insurance policy** : póliza f de seguros, seguro m

polio[1] ['po:liˌo:] adj : de polio ⟨polio vaccine : vacuna contra la polio⟩

polio[2] n → **poliomyelitis**

poliomyelitis [ˌpo:liˌo:ˌmaɪə'laɪtəs] n : poliomielitis f, polio f

polish[1] ['pɑlɪʃ] vt **1** : pulir, lustrar, sacar brillo a ⟨to polish one's nails : pintarse las uñas⟩ **2** REFINE : pulir, perfeccionar **3 to polish off** : despacharse (comida)

polish[2] n **1** LUSTER : brillo m, lustre m **2** REFINEMENT : refinamiento m **3** : betún m (para zapatos), cera f (para suelos y muebles), esmalte m (para las uñas)

Polish[1] ['po:lɪʃ] adj : polaco

Polish[2] n : polaco m (idioma)

polite [pə'laɪt] adj **politer; -est** : cortés, correcto, educado

politely [pə'laɪtli] adv : cortésmente, correctamente, con buenos modales

politeness [pə'laɪtnəs] n : cortesía f

politic ['pɑləˌtɪk] adj : diplomático, prudente

political [pə'lɪtɪkəl] adj : político — **politically** [-tɪkli] adv

politically correct adj : políticamente correcto

politician [ˌpɑlə'tɪʃən] n : político m, -ca f

politics ['pɑləˌtɪks] ns & pl : política f

polka ['po:lkə, 'po:kə] n : polka f

polka dot ['po:kəˌdɑt] n : lunar m (en un diseño)

poll[1] ['po:l] vt **1** : obtener (votos) ⟨she polled over 1000 votes : obtuvo más de 1000 votos⟩ **2** CANVASS : encuestar, sondear — vi : obtener votos

poll[2] n **1** SURVEY : encuesta f, sondeo m **2 polls** npl : urnas fpl ⟨to go to the polls : acudir a las urnas, ir a votar⟩

pollen ['pɑlən] n : polen m

pollinate ['pɑləˌneɪt] vt **-nated; -nating** : polinizar

pollination [ˌpɑlə'neɪʃən] n : polinización f

polling place n : centro m de votación

pollster ['po:lstər] n : encuestador m, -dora f

pollutant [pə'lu:tənt] n : contaminante m

pollute [pə'lu:t] vt **-luted; -luting** : contaminar

pollution [pə'lu:ʃən] n : contaminación f

pollywog or **polliwog** ['pɑliˌwɑg] n TADPOLE : renacuajo m

polo ['po:ˌlo:] n **1** : polo m (deporte) **2** or **polo shirt** : polo m

poltergeist ['po:ltərˌgaɪst] n : fantasma m travieso

polyester ['pɑliˌɛstər, ˌpɑli'-] n : poliéster m

polygamist [pə'lɪgəmɪst] n : polígamo m, -ma f

polygamous [pə'lɪgəməs] adj : polígamo

polygamy [pə'lɪgəmi] n : poligamia f

polygon ['pɑliˌgɑn] n : polígono m — **polygonal** [pə'lɪgənəl] adj

polymer ['pɑləmər] n : polímero m

Polynesian [ˌpɑlə'ni:ʒən, -ʃən] n : polinesio m, -sia f — **Polynesian** adj

polytheism ['pɑliˌθiˌɪzəm] n : politeísmo m

polyunsaturated [ˌpɑliˌʌn'sætʃəˌreɪtəd] adj : poliinsaturado

pomegranate ['pɑməˌgrænət, 'pɑmˌgrænət] n : granada f (fruta)

pommel[1] ['pʌməl] vt → **pummel**

pommel[2] ['pʌməl, 'pɑ-] n **1** : pomo m (de una espada) **2** : perilla f (de una silla de montar)

pomp ['pɑmp] n **1** SPLENDOR : pompa f, esplendor m **2** OSTENTATION : boato m, ostentación f

pom–pom ['pɑmˌpɑm] n : borla f, pompón m

pomposity [pɑm'pɑsəti] n, pl **-ties** : pomposidad f

pompous ['pɑmpəs] adj : pomposo — **pompously** adv

poncho ['pɑnˌtʃo:] n, pl **-chos** : poncho m

pond ['pɑnd] n : charca f (natural), estanque m (artificial)

ponder ['pɑndər] vt : reflexionar, considerar — vi **to ponder over** : reflexionar sobre, sopesar

ponderous ['pɑndərəs] adj : pesado

pontiff ['pɑntɪf] n POPE : pontífice m

pontificate [pɑn'tɪfəˌkeɪt] vi **-cated; -cating** : pontificar

pontoon [pɑn'tu:n] n : pontón m

pony ['po:ni] n, pl **-nies** : poni m, poney m, jaca f

ponytail ['po:niˌteɪl] n : cola f de caballo, coleta f

poodle ['pu:dəl] n : caniche m

pool[1] ['pu:l] vt : mancomunar (recursos), hacer un fondo común de (dinero) — vi : encharcarse

pool[2] n **1** : charca f ⟨a swimming pool : una piscina⟩ **2** PUDDLE : charco m **3** RESERVE, SUPPLY : fondo m común (de recursos), reserva f **4** : billar m (juego)

poop[1] ['pu:p] vi fam : hacerse caca — vt **to poop one's pants/diaper (etc.)** : hacerse caca

poop[2] n fam : caca f

poor ['pʊr, 'por] adj **1** : pobre ⟨poor people : los pobres⟩ **2** SCANTY : pobre, escaso ⟨poor attendance : baja asistencia⟩ **3** UNFORTUNATE : pobre ⟨poor thing! : ¡pobrecito!⟩ **4** BAD : malo ⟨to be in poor health : estar mal de salud⟩

poorly ['pʊrli, 'por-] adv : mal

pop¹ [ˈpɑp] v **popped; popping** vi 1 BURST : reventarse, estallar 2 : saltar (dícese de un corcho) 3 : ir, venir, o aparecer abruptamente ⟨he popped into the house : se metió en la casa⟩ ⟨a menu pops up : aparece un menú⟩ 4 **to pop out** PROTRUDE : salirse, saltarse ⟨my eyes popped out of my head : se me saltaban los ojos⟩ 5 **to pop the question** fam : proponerle matrimonio a alguien — vt 1 BURST : reventar 2 : sacar o meter abruptamente ⟨he popped it into his mouth : se lo metió en la boca⟩ ⟨she popped her head out the window : sacó la cabeza por la ventana⟩

pop² adj : popular ⟨pop music : música popular⟩ ⟨pop star : estrella de música popular⟩

pop³ n 1 : estallido m pequeño (de un globo, etc.) 2 SODA : refresco m, gaseosa f

popcorn [ˈpɑpˌkɔrn] n : palomitas fpl (de maíz)

pope [ˈpoːp] n : papa m ⟨Pope John : el Papa Juan⟩

poplar [ˈpɑplər] n : álamo m

poplin [ˈpɑplɪn] n : popelín m, popelina f

poppy [ˈpɑpi] n, pl **-pies** : amapola f

Popsicle [ˈpɑpˌsɪkəl] trademark se usa para una paleta helada

populace [ˈpɑpjələs] n 1 MASSES : pueblo m 2 POPULATION : población f

popular [ˈpɑpjələr] adj 1 : popular ⟨the popular vote : el voto popular⟩ 2 COMMON : generalizado, común ⟨popular beliefs : creencias generalizadas⟩ 3 : popular, de gran popularidad ⟨a popular singer : un cantante popular⟩

popularity [ˌpɑpjəˈlærəti] n : popularidad f

popularize [ˈpɑpjələˌraɪz] vt **-ized; -izing** : popularizar

popularly [ˈpɑpjələrli] adv : popularmente, vulgarmente

populate [ˈpɑpjəˌleɪt] vt **-lated; -lating** : poblar

population [ˌpɑpjəˈleɪʃən] n : población f

populist [ˈpɑpjəlɪst] n : populista mf — **populist** adj

populous [ˈpɑpjələs] adj : populoso

pop–up [ˈpɑpˌʌp] n : ventana f emergente (de una página web)

porcelain [ˈpɔrsələn] n : porcelana f

porch [ˈpɔrtʃ] n : porche m

porcupine [ˈpɔrkjəˌpaɪn] n : puerco m espín

pore¹ [ˈpor] vi **pored; poring** 1 GAZE : mirar (con atención) 2 **to pore over** : leer detenidamente, estudiar

pore² n : poro m

pork [ˈpork] n : carne f de cerdo, carne f de puerco ⟨pork chop : chuleta de cerdo⟩

pornographic [ˌpɔrnəˈgræfɪk] adj : pornográfico

pornography [pɔrˈnɑgrəfi] n : pornografía f

porous [ˈporəs] adj : poroso

porpoise [ˈpɔrpəs] n 1 : marsopa f 2 DOLPHIN : delfín m

porridge [ˈpɔrɪdʒ] n : sopa f espesa de harina, gachas fpl

port¹ [ˈport] adj : de babor ⟨on the port side : a babor⟩

port² n 1 HARBOR : puerto m 2 ORIFICE : orificio m (de una válvula, etc.) 3 : puerto m (de una computadora) 4 PORTHOLE : portilla f 5 **or port side** : babor m (de un barco) 6 : oporto m (vino)

portable [ˈportəbəl] adj : portátil

portal [ˈportəl] n : portal m

portend [porˈtend] vt : presagiar, augurar

portent [ˈporˌtent] n : presagio m, augurio m

portentous [porˈtentəs] adj : profético, que presagia

porter [ˈportər] n : maletero m, mozo m (de estación)

portfolio [portˈfoːliˌo] n, pl **-lios** 1 FOLDER : cartera f (para llevar papeles), carpeta f 2 : cartera f (diplomática) 3 **investment portfolio** : cartera de inversiones

porthole [ˈportˌhoːl] n : portilla f (de un barco), ventanilla f (de un avión)

portico [ˈportɪˌko] n, pl **-coes** or **-cos** : pórtico m

portion¹ [ˈporʃən] vt DISTRIBUTE : repartir

portion² n PART, SHARE : porción f, parte f

portly [ˈportli] adj **portlier; -est** : corpulento

portrait [ˈportrət, -ˌtreɪt] n : retrato m

portray [porˈtreɪ] vt 1 DEPICT : representar, retratar 2 DESCRIBE : describir 3 PLAY : interpretar (un personaje)

portrayal [porˈtreɪəl] n 1 REPRESENTATION : representación f 2 PORTRAIT : retrato m

Portuguese¹ [ˌportʃəˈgiːz, -ˈgiːs] adj : portugués

Portuguese² n 1 : portugués m (idioma) 2 **the Portuguese** (used with a plural verb) : los portugueses

pose¹ [ˈpoːz] v **posed; posing** vt PRESENT : plantear (una pregunta, etc.), representar (una amenaza) — vi 1 : posar (para una foto, etc.) 2 **to pose as** : hacerse pasar por

pose² n 1 : pose f ⟨to strike a pose : asumir una pose⟩ 2 PRETENSE : pose f, afectación f

posh [ˈpɑʃ] adj : elegante, de lujo

position¹ [pəˈzɪʃən] vt : colocar, situar, ubicar

position² n 1 LOCATION : posición f, ubicación f 2 : posición f, postura f (del cuerpo) 3 OPINION, STANCE : posición f, postura f, planteamiento m 4 STATUS : posición f (en una jerarquía) 5 JOB : puesto m 6 : posición f (en un equipo) 7 SITUATION : situación f ⟨to be in no position to do something : no estar en condiciones de hacer algo⟩

positive [ˈpɑzəˌtɪv] adj 1 DEFINITE : incuestionable, inequívoco ⟨positive evidence : pruebas irrefutables⟩ 2 CONFIDENT : seguro 3 : positivo (en gramática, matemáticas, y física) 4 AFFIRMATIVE

: positivo, afirmativo ⟨a positive response : una respuesta positiva⟩

positively [ˈpazətivli] adv 1 FAVORABLY : favorablemente 2 OPTIMISTICALLY : positivamente 3 DEFINITELY : definitivamente, en forma concluyente 4 (used for emphasis) : realmente, verdaderamente ⟨it's positively awful! : ¡es verdaderamente malo!⟩

posse [ˈpasi] n 1 : partida f, patrulla f 2 fam GANG, ENTOURAGE : grupo m de amigos/seguidores (etc.) 3 fam GROUP : grupo m

possess [pəˈzɛs] vt 1 HAVE, OWN : poseer, tener 2 SEIZE : apoderarse de ⟨he was possessed by fear : el miedo se apoderó de él⟩

possession [pəˈzɛʃən] n 1 POSSESSING : posesión f 2 posesión f (por un demonio, etc.) 3 **possessions** npl PROPERTY : bienes mpl, propiedad f

possessive[1] [pəˈzɛsiv] adj 1 : posesivo (en gramática) 2 JEALOUS : posesivo, celoso

possessive[2] n or **possessive case** : posesivo m

possessor [pəˈzɛsər] n : poseedor m, -dora f

possibility [ˌpasəˈbiləti] n, pl **-ties** : posibilidad f

possible [ˈpasəbəl] adj : posible ⟨as soon as possible : lo antes posible⟩ ⟨as much as possible : lo más posible⟩ ⟨if possible : si es posible⟩

possibly [ˈpasəbli] adv 1 CONCEIVABLY : posiblemente ⟨it can't possibly be true! : ¡no puede ser!⟩ ⟨I can't possibly do that : me es imposible, no puedo hacerlo de ninguna manera⟩ 2 PERHAPS : quizás, posiblemente

possum [ˈpasəm] → opossum

post[1] [ˈpoːst] vt 1 MAIL : echar al correo, mandar por correo 2 ANNOUNCE : anunciar ⟨they've posted the grades : han anunciado las notas⟩ 3 AFFIX : fijar, poner (noticias, etc.) 4 STATION : apostar 5 **to keep (someone) posted** : tener al corriente (a alguien)

post[2] n 1 POLE : poste m, palo m 2 STATION : puesto m 3 CAMP : puesto m (militar) 4 JOB, POSITION : puesto m, empleo m, cargo m

post- [poːst] pref : pos-, post- ⟨postpone : posponer⟩ ⟨postgraduate : postgraduado⟩

postage [ˈpoːstidʒ] n : franqueo m

postage stamp → stamp[2]

postal [ˈpoːstəl] adj : postal

postcard [ˈpoːstˌkard] n : postal f, tarjeta f postal

postdate [ˌpoːstˈdeit] vt **-dated; -dating** : posfechar

poster [ˈpoːstər] n : póster m, cartel m, afiche m

posterior[1] [paˈstiriər, po-] adj : posterior

posterior[2] n BUTTOCKS : trasero m, nalgas fpl, asentaderas fpl

posterity [paˈstɛrəti] n : posteridad f

postgraduate[1] [ˌpoːstˈgrædʒuət] adj : de postgrado

postgraduate[2] n : postgraduado m, -da f

posthaste [ˈpoːstˈheist] adv : a toda prisa

posthumous [ˈpastʃəməs] adj : póstumo — **posthumously** adv

Post-it [ˈpoːstˌit] trademark se usa para un papelito con borde adhesivo

postman [ˈpoːstmən, -ˌmæn] n, pl **-men** [-mən, -ˌmɛn] → mailman

postmark[1] [ˈpoːstˌmark] vt : matasellar

postmark[2] n : matasellos m

postmaster [ˈpoːstˌmæstər] n : administrador m, -dora f de correos

postmodern [ˌpoːstˈmadərn] adj : posmoderno

postmortem [ˌpoːstˈmortəm] n : autopsia f

postnatal [ˌpoːstˈneitəl] adj : postnatal

postnatal depression → postpartum depression

post office n : correo m, oficina f de correos

post office box → P.O. Box

postoperative [ˌpoːstˈapərətiv, -ˌrei-] adj : posoperatorio

postpaid [ˌpoːstˈpeid] adv : con franqueo pagado

postpartum depression [ˌpoːstˈpartəm-] n : depresión f posparto

postpone [ˌpoːstˈpoːn] vt **-poned; -poning** : postergar, aplazar, posponer

postponement [ˌpoːstˈpoːnmənt] n : postergación f, aplazamiento m

postscript [ˈpoːstˌskript] n : postdata f, posdata f

postulate [ˈpastʃəˌleit] vt **-lated; -lating** : postular

posture[1] [ˈpastʃər] vi **-tured; -turing** : posar, asumir una pose

posture[2] n : postura f

postwar [ˈpoːstˈwor] adj : de (la) posguerra

posy [ˈpoːzi] n, pl **-sies** 1 FLOWER : flor f 2 BOUQUET : ramo m, ramillete m

pot[1] [ˈpat] vt **potted; potting** : plantar (en una maceta)

pot[2] n 1 : olla f (de cocina) 2 **pots and pans** : cacharros mpl 3 **to go to pot** : echarse a perder

potable [ˈpoːtəbəl] adj : potable

potash [ˈpatˌæʃ] n : potasa f

potassium [pəˈtæsiəm] n : potasio m

potato [pəˈteitoː] n, pl **-toes** : papa f, patata f Spain

potato chips npl : papas fpl fritas (de bolsa)

potbellied [ˈpatˌbelid] adj : panzón, barrigón fam

potbelly [ˈpatˌbeli] n : panza f, barriga f

potency [ˈpoːtənsi] n, pl **-cies** 1 POWER : fuerza f, potencia f 2 EFFECTIVENESS : eficacia f

potent [ˈpoːtənt] adj 1 POWERFUL : potente, poderoso 2 EFFECTIVE : eficaz ⟨a potent medicine : una medicina bien fuerte⟩

potential[1] [pəˈtɛnʃəl] adj : potencial, posible

potential[2] n 1 : potencial m ⟨growth potential : potencial de crecimiento⟩ ⟨a child with potential : un niño que promete⟩ **2** : potencial *m* (eléctrico) — **potentially** *adv*

potful ['pɑt,fʊl] *n* : contenido *m* de una olla ⟨a potful of water : una olla de agua⟩

pothole ['pɑt,hoːl] *n* : bache *m*

potion ['poːʃən] *n* : brebaje *m*, poción *f*

potluck ['pɑt,lʌk] *n* **to take potluck** : tomar lo que haya

potpourri [,poːpʊ'riː] *n* : popurrí *m*

potshot ['pɑt,ʃɑt] *n* **1** : tiro *m* al azar ⟨to take potshots at : disparar al azar a⟩ **2** CRITICISM : crítica *f* (hecha al azar)

potter¹ ['pɑtər] *n* : alfarero *m*, -ra *f*

potter² → **putter**

pottery ['pɑtəri] *n*, *pl* **-teries** : cerámica *f*

potty ['pɑti] *n fam* **1** : bacinica *f* (para niños) **2 to go potty** : hacer pipí, hacer popó

pouch ['paʊtʃ] *n* **1** BAG : bolsa *f* pequeña **2** : bolsa *f* (de un animal)

poultice ['poːltəs] *n* : emplasto *m*, cataplasma *f*

poultry ['poːltri] *n* : aves *fpl* de corral

pounce ['paʊnts] *vi* **pounced; pouncing** : abalanzarse

pound¹ ['paʊnd] *vt* **1** CRUSH : machacar, machucar, majar **2** BEAT : golpear, machacar ⟨she pounded the lessons into them : les machacaba las lecciones⟩ ⟨he pounded home his point : les hizo entender su razonamiento⟩ — *vi* **1** BEAT : palpitar ⟨dícese del corazón⟩ **2** RESOUND : retumbar, resonar **3** : andar con paso pesado ⟨we pounded through the mud : caminamos pesadamente por el barro⟩

pound² *n* **1** : libra *f* (unidad de peso) **2** : libra *f* (unidad monetaria) **3 dog pound** : perrera *f*

pour ['por] *vt* **1** : echar, verter, servir (bebidas) ⟨pour it into a pot : viértalo en una olla⟩ **2** : proveer con abundancia ⟨they poured money into it : le invirtieron mucho dinero⟩ **3 to pour out** : dar salida a ⟨he poured out his feelings to her : se desahogó con ella⟩ — *vi* **1** FLOW : manar, fluir, salir ⟨blood was pouring from the wound : la sangre le manaba de la herida⟩ ⟨people poured out of the subway : la gente salía del metro a raudales⟩ ⟨the orders came pouring in : había un aluvión de pedidos⟩ **2 it's pouring (outside)** : está lloviendo a cántaros

pout¹ ['paʊt] *vi* : hacer pucheros

pout² *n* : puchero *m*

poverty ['pɑvərti] *n* : pobreza *f*, indigencia *f*

poverty–stricken *adj* : necesitado, paupérrimo

powder¹ ['paʊdər] *vt* **1** : empolvar ⟨to powder one's face : empolvarse la cara⟩ **2** PULVERIZE : pulverizar

powder² *n* : polvo *m*, polvos *mpl*

powdery ['paʊdəri] *adj* : polvoriento, como polvo

power¹ ['paʊər] *vt* : impulsar, propulsar

power² *n* **1** CONTROL, AUTHORITY : poder *m*, autoridad *f* ⟨executive powers : poderes ejecutivos⟩ ⟨power struggle : lucha por el poder⟩ ⟨to have power

over somebody : tener poder sobre alguien⟩ ⟨to come to power : llegar al poder⟩ ⟨to be in power : estar en el poder⟩ **2** ABILITY : capacidad *f*, poder *m* ⟨the power of speech : el habla⟩ ⟨I'll do everything in my power : haré todo lo que pueda⟩ ⟨it's not within my power : no está en mis manos⟩ **3** : potencia *f* (política) ⟨foreign powers : potencias extranjeras⟩ **4** STRENGTH : fuerza *f*, poder *m* ⟨the power of love : la fuerza del amor⟩ **5** : potencia *f* (en física y matemáticas) **6** : electricidad *f*, luz *f* ⟨power failure : corte de luz, corte de energía eléctrica, apagón⟩

powerboat ['paʊər,boːt] *n* **1** → **motorboat 2** → **speedboat**

powerful ['paʊərfəl] *adj* : poderoso, potente — **powerfully** *adv*

powerhouse ['paʊər,haʊs] *n* : persona *f* dinámica

powerless ['paʊərləs] *adj* : impotente

powerlessness ['paʊərləsnəs] *n* : impotencia *f*

power plant *n* : central *f* eléctrica

powwow ['paʊ,waʊ] *n* : conferencia *f*

pox ['pɑks] *n*, *pl* **pox** *or* **poxes 1** CHICKEN POX : varicela *f* **2** SYPHILIS : sífilis *f*

PR ['piː'ɑr] → **public relations**

practicable ['præktɪkəbəl] *adj* : practicable, viable, factible

practical ['præktɪkəl] *adj* : práctico

practicality [,præktɪ'kæləti] *n*, *pl* **-ties** : factibilidad *f*, viabilidad *f*

practical joke *n* : broma *f* (pesada)

practically ['præktɪkli] *adv* **1** : de manera práctica **2** ALMOST : casi, prácticamente

practice¹ *or* **practise** ['præktəs] *vt* **-ticed** *or* **-tised; -ticing** *or* **-tising 1** : practicar, ensayar, entrenar ⟨he practiced his German on us : practicó el alemán con nosotros⟩ ⟨to practice politeness : practicar la cortesía⟩ **2** : ejercer ⟨to practice medicine : ejercer la medicina⟩

practice² *n* **1** USE : práctica *f* ⟨to put into practice : poner en práctica⟩ **2** CUSTOM : costumbre *f* ⟨it's a common practice here : por aquí se acostumbra hacerlo⟩ **3** TRAINING : práctica *f* ⟨she's out of practice : le falta práctica⟩ ⟨practice makes perfect : la práctica hace al maestro⟩ **4** : ejercicio *m* (de una profesión)

practitioner [præk'tɪʃənər] *n* **1** : profesional *mf* **2 general practitioner** : médico *m*, -ca *f*

pragmatic [præg'mætɪk] *adj* : pragmático — **pragmatically** *adv*

pragmatism ['prægmə,tɪzəm] *n* : pragmatismo

prairie ['preri] *n* : pradera *f*, llanura *f*

praise¹ ['preɪz] *vt* **praised; praising** : elogiar, alabar ⟨to praise God : alabar a Dios⟩

praise² *n* : elogio *m*, alabanza *f*

praiseworthy ['preɪz,wərði] *adj* : digno de alabanza, loable

prance¹ ['prænts] *vi* **pranced; prancing 1** : hacer cabriolas, cabriolar ⟨a prancing horse : un caballo haciendo cabriolas⟩ **2** SWAGGER : pavonearse

prance² *n* : cabriola *f*

prank ['præŋk] *n* : broma *f*, travesura *f*

prankster ['præŋkstər] *n* : bromista *mf*

prattle¹ ['prætəl] *vt* -tled; -tling : parlotear *fam*, cotorrear *fam*, balbucear (como un niño)

prattle² *n* : parloteo *m fam*, cotorreo *m fam*, cháchara *f fam*

prawn ['prɔn] *n* : langostino *m*, camarón *m*, gamba *f*

pray ['preɪ] *vt* ENTREAT : rogar, suplicar — *vi* : rezar

prayer ['prɛr] *n* 1 : plegaria *f*, oración *f* ⟨to say one's prayers : orar, rezar⟩ ⟨the Lord's Prayer : el Padrenuestro⟩ 2 PRAYING : rezo *m*, oración *f* ⟨to kneel in prayer : arrodillarse para rezar⟩

praying mantis → mantis

pre- [ˌpri] *pref* 1 : antes de 2 : con antelación

preach ['pritʃ] *vi* : predicar — *vt* ADVOCATE : abogar por ⟨to preach cooperation : promover la cooperación⟩

preacher ['pritʃər] *n* 1 : predicador *m*, -dora *f* 2 MINISTER : pastor *m*, -tora *f*

preamble ['priˌæmbəl] *n* : preámbulo *m*

prearrange [ˌpriəˈreɪndʒ] *vt* -ranged; -ranging : arreglar de antemano

precarious [prɪˈkæriəs] *adj* : precario — **precariously** *adv*

precariousness [prɪˈkæriəsnəs] *n* : precariedad *f*

precaution [prɪˈkɔʃən] *n* : precaución *f*

precautionary [prɪˈkɔʃəˌnɛri] *adj* : preventivo, cautelar, precautorio

precede [prɪˈsiːd] *v* -ceded; -ceding : preceder a

precedence ['prɛsədənts, prɪˈsiːdənts] *n* : precedencia *f*

precedent ['prɛsədənt] *n* : precedente *m*

precept ['priˌsɛpt] *n* : precepto *m*

precinct ['priˌsɪŋkt] *n* 1 DISTRICT : distrito *m* (policial, electoral, etc.) 2 **precincts** *npl* PREMISES : recinto *m*, predio *m*, límites *mpl* (de una ciudad)

precious ['prɛʃəs] *adj* 1 : precioso ⟨precious gems : piedras preciosas⟩ 2 DEAR : querido 3 AFFECTED : afectado

precipice ['prɛsəpəs] *n* : precipicio *m*

precipitate [prɪˈsɪpəˌteɪt] *v* -tated; -tating *vt* 1 HASTEN, PROVOKE : precipitar, provocar 2 HURL : arrojar 3 : precipitar (en química) — *vi* : precipitarse (en química), condensarse (en meteorología)

precipitation [prɪˌsɪpəˈteɪʃən] *n* 1 HASTE : precipitación *f*, prisa *f* 2 : precipitaciones *fpl* (en meteorología)

precipitous [prɪˈsɪpətəs] *adj* 1 HASTY, RASH : precipitado 2 STEEP : escarpado, empinado ⟨a precipitous drop : una caída vertiginosa⟩

précis [preɪˈsiː] *n, pl* **précis** [-ˈsiːz] : resumen *m*

precise [prɪˈsaɪs] *adj* 1 DEFINITE : preciso, explícito 2 EXACT : exacto, preciso ⟨precise calculations : cálculos precisos⟩ — **precisely** *adv*

preciseness [prɪˈsaɪsnəs] *n* : precisión *f*, exactitud *f*

precision [prɪˈsɪʒən] *n* : precisión *f*

preclude [prɪˈkluːd] *vt* -cluded; -cluding : evitar, impedir, excluir (una posibilidad, etc.)

precocious [prɪˈkoːʃəs] *adj* : precoz — **precociously** *adv*

precocity [prɪˈkɑsəti] *n* : precocidad *f*

preconceived [ˌpriːkənˈsiːvd] *adj* : preconcebido

preconception [ˌpriːkənˈspʃən] *n* : idea *f* preconcebida

precondition [ˌpriːkənˈdɪʃən] *n* : precondición *f*, condición *f* previa

precook [ˌpriːˈkʊk] *vt* : precocinar

precursor [prɪˈkɜrsər] *n* : precursor *m*, -sora *f*

predator ['prɛdətər] *n* : depredador *m*, -dora *f*

predatory ['prɛdəˌtɔri] *adj* : depredador

predecessor ['prɛdəˌsɛsər, ˈpriː-] *n* : antecesor *m*, -sora *f*; predecesor *m*, -sora *f*

predestination [prɪˌdɛstəˈneɪʃən] *n* : predestinación *f*

predestine [prɪˈdɛstən] *vt* -tined; -tining : predestinar

predetermine [ˌpriːdɪˈtɜrmən] *vt* -mined; -mining : predeterminar

predicament [prɪˈdɪkəmənt] *n* : apuro *m*, aprieto *m*

predicate¹ ['prɛdəˌkeɪt] *vt* -cated; -cating 1 AFFIRM : afirmar, aseverar 2 **to be predicated on** : estar basado en

predicate² ['prɛdɪkət] *n* : predicado *m*

predict [prɪˈdɪkt] *vt* : pronosticar, predecir

predictable [prɪˈdɪktəbəl] *adj* : previsible — **predictably** [-bli] *adv*

prediction [prɪˈdɪkʃən] *n* : pronóstico *m*, predicción *f*

predilection [ˌprɛdəlˈɛkʃən, ˌpriː-] *n* : predilección *f*

predispose [ˌpriːdɪˈspoːz] *vt* -posed; -posing : predisponer

predisposition [ˌpriːˌdɪspəˈzɪʃən] *n* : predisposición *f*

predominance [prɪˈdɑmənənts] *n* : predominio *m*

predominant [prɪˈdɑmənənt] *adj* : predominante — **predominantly** *adv*

predominate [prɪˈdɑməˌneɪt] *vi* -nated; -nating 1 : predominar (en cantidad) 2 PREVAIL : prevalecer

preeminence [prɪˈɛmənənts] *n* : preeminencia *f*

preeminent [prɪˈɛmənənt] *adj* : preeminente

preeminently [prɪˈɛmənəntli] *adv* : especialmente

preempt [prɪˈɛmpt] *vt* 1 APPROPRIATE : apoderarse de, apropiarse de 2 : reemplazar (un programa de televisión, etc.) 3 FORESTALL : adelantarse a (un ataque, etc.)

preemptive [prɪˈɛmptɪv] *adj* : preventivo

preen ['priːn] *vt* : arreglarse (el pelo, las plumas, etc.)

prefabricated [ˌpriːˈfæbrəˌkeɪtəd] *adj* : prefabricado

preface ['prɛfəs] *n* : prefacio *m*, prólogo *m*

prefatory ['prɛfəˌtɔri] *adj* : preliminar

prefect ['priːˌfɛkt] *n* 1 : prefecto *m* (oficial) 2 : monitor *m*, -tora *f* (estudiante)
prefer [priˈfər] *vt* -ferred; -ferring 1 : preferir ⟨I prefer coffee : prefiero café⟩ 2 to prefer charges against : presentar cargos contra
preferable ['prɛfərəbəl] *adj* : preferible
preferably ['prɛfərəbli] *adv* : preferentemente, de preferencia
preference ['prɛfrəns, 'prɛfər-] *n* : preferencia *f*, gusto *m*
preferential [ˌprɛfəˈrɛntʃəl] *adj* : preferencial, preferente
prefigure [priˈfɪɡjər] *vt* -ured; -uring FORESHADOW : prefigurar, anunciar
prefix ['priːˌfɪks] *n* : prefijo *m*
pregnancy ['prɛɡnənsi] *n*, *pl* -cies : embarazo *m*, preñez *f*
pregnant ['prɛɡnənt] *adj* 1 : embarazada (dícese de una mujer), preñada (dícese de un animal) 2 MEANINGFUL : significativo
preheat [ˌpriːˈhiːt] *vt* : precalentar
prehensile [priˈhɛnsəl, -ˈhɛnˌsaɪl] *adj* : prensil
prehistoric [ˌpriːhɪsˈtɔrɪk] *or* **prehistorical** [-ɪkəl] *adj* : prehistórico
prejudge [ˌpriːˈdʒʌdʒ] *vt* -judged; -judging : prejuzgar
prejudice[1] ['prɛdʒədəs] *vt* -diced; -dicing 1 DAMAGE : perjudicar 2 BIAS : predisponer, influir en
prejudice[2] *n* 1 DAMAGE : perjuicio *m* (en derecho) 2 BIAS : prejuicio *m*
prelate ['prɛlət] *n* : prelado *m*
preliminary[1] [priˈlɪməˌnɛri] *adj* : preliminar
preliminary[2] *n*, *pl* -naries 1 : preámbulo *m*, preludio *m* 2 preliminaries *npl* : preliminares *mpl*
prelude ['prɛˌljuːd, 'prɛlˌjuːd; 'preɪˌljuːd, 'priː-] *n* : preludio *m*
premarital [ˌpriːˈmærətəl] *adj* : prematrimonial
premature [ˌpriːməˈtʊr, -ˈtjʊr, -ˈtʃʊr] *adj* : prematuro — **prematurely** *adv*
premeditate [priˈmɛdəˌteɪt] *vt* -tated; -tating : premeditar
premeditation [priˌmɛdəˈteɪʃən] *n* : premeditación *f*
premenstrual [priˈmɛnstruəl] *adj* : premenstrual
premenstrual syndrome *n* : síndrome *m* premenstrual, SPM *m*
premier[1] [priˈmɪr, -ˈmjɪr; 'priːmiər] *adj* : principal
premier[2] *n* PRIME MINISTER : primer ministro *m*, primera ministra *f*
premiere[1] [priˈmjɛr, -ˈmɪr] *vt* -miered; -miering : estrenar
premiere[2] *n* : estreno *m*
premise ['prɛmɪs] *n* 1 : premisa *f* ⟨the premise of his arguments : la premisa de sus argumentos⟩ 2 premises *npl* : recinto *m*, local *m*
premium ['priːmiəm] *n* 1 BONUS : prima *f* 2 SURCHARGE : recargo *m* ⟨to sell at a premium : vender (algo) muy caro⟩ 3 insurance premium : prima *f* (de seguros) 4 to set a premium on : darle un gran valor (a algo)
premonition [ˌpriːməˈnɪʃən, ˌprɛmə-] *n* : presentimiento *m*, premonición *f*
prenatal [ˌpriːˈneɪtəl] *adj* : prenatal
preoccupation [priˌɑkjəˈpeɪʃən] *n* : preocupación *f*
preoccupied [priˈɑkjəˌpaɪd] *adj* : abstraído, ensimismado, preocupado
preoccupy [priˈɑkjəˌpaɪ] *vt* -pied; -pying : preocupar
preparation [ˌprɛpəˈreɪʃən] *n* 1 PREPARING : preparación *f* 2 MIXTURE : preparado *m* ⟨a preparation for burns : un preparado para quemaduras⟩ 3 preparations *npl* ARRANGEMENTS : preparativos *mpl*
preparatory [priˈpærəˌtori] *adj* : preparatorio
preparatory school → prep school
prepare [priˈpær] *v* -pared; -paring *vt* : preparar — *vi* : prepararse
prepay [ˌpriːˈpeɪ] *vt* -paid; -paying : pagar por adelantado
preponderance [priˈpɑndərəns] *n* : preponderancia *f*
preponderant [priˈpɑndərənt] *adj* : preponderante — **preponderantly** *adv*
preposition [ˌprɛpəˈzɪʃən] *n* : preposición *f*
prepositional [ˌprɛpəˈzɪʃənəl] *adj* : preposicional
prepossessing [ˌpriːpəˈzɛsɪŋ] *adj* : atractivo, agradable
preposterous [priˈpɑstərəs] *adj* : absurdo, ridículo
prep school ['prɛp-] *n* : escuela *f* secundaria privada
prerecorded [ˌpriːrɪˈkɔrdəd] *adj* : pregrabado
prerequisite[1] [priˈrɛkwəzət] *adj* : necesario, esencial
prerequisite[2] *n* : condición *f* necesario, requisito *m* previo
prerogative [priˈrɑɡətɪv] *n* : prerrogativa *f*
presage ['prɛsɪdʒ, priˈseɪdʒ] *vt* -saged; -saging : presagiar
preschool [ˌpriːˈskuːl] *adj* : preescolar
preschooler ['priːˌskuːlər] *n* : párvulo *m*, -la *f*; estudiante *mf* de preescolar
prescient ['prɛʃənt] *adj* : profético
prescribe [priˈskraɪb] *vt* -scribed; -scribing 1 ORDAIN : prescribir, ordenar 2 : recetar (medicinas, etc.)
prescription [priˈskrɪpʃən] *n* : receta *f*
presence ['prɛzənts] *n* : presencia *f*
presence of mind *n* : aplomo *m*
present[1] [priˈzɛnt] *vt* 1 INTRODUCE : presentar ⟨to present oneself : presentarse⟩ 2 : presentar (una obra de teatro, etc.) 3 GIVE : entregar (un regalo, etc.), regalar, obsequiar 4 SHOW : presentar, ofrecer ⟨it presents a lovely view : ofrece una vista muy linda⟩
present[2] ['prɛzənt] *adj* 1 : actual ⟨present conditions : condiciones actuales⟩ 2 : presente ⟨all the students were present : todos los estudiantes estaban presentes⟩

present³ [ˈprɛzənt] n **1** GIFT : regalo m, obsequio m **2** : presente m ⟨at present : en este momento⟩ **3** or **present tense** : presente m

presentable [priˈzɛntəbəl] adj : presentable

presentation [ˌpriːzɛnˈteɪʃən, ˌprɛzən-] n : presentación f ⟨presentation ceremony : ceremonia de entrega⟩

present–day [ˈprɛzəntˈdeɪ] adj : actual, de hoy en día

presenter [priˈzɛntər] n : presentador m, -dora f

presentiment [priˈzɛntəmənt] n : presentimiento m, premonición f

presently [ˈprɛzəntli] adv **1** SOON : pronto, dentro de poco **2** NOW : actualmente, ahora

present participle n : participio m presente, participio m activo

preservation [ˌprɛzərˈveɪʃən] n : conservación f, preservación f

preservative [priˈzərvətɪv] n : conservante m

preserve¹ [priˈzərv] vt **-served; -serving** **1** PROTECT : proteger, preservar **2** : conservar (los alimentos, etc.) **3** MAINTAIN : conservar, mantener

preserve² n **1** or **preserves** npl : conserva f ⟨peach preserves : duraznos en conserva⟩ **2** : coto m ⟨game preserve : coto de caza⟩

preside [priˈzaɪd] vi **-sided; -siding** **1 to preside over** : presidir ⟨he presided over the meeting : presidió la reunión⟩ **2 to preside over** : supervisar ⟨she presides over the department : dirige el departamento⟩

presidency [ˈprɛzədənsi] n, pl **-cies** : presidencia f

president [ˈprɛzədənt] n : presidente m, -ta f

presidential [ˌprɛzəˈdɛntʃəl] adj : presidencial

press¹ [ˈprɛs] vt **1** PUSH : apretar (un botón, etc.) **2** SQUEEZE : apretar, prensar (frutas, flores, etc.) **3** IRON : planchar (ropa) **4** URGE : instar, apremiar ⟨he pressed me to come : insistió en que viniera⟩ **5** STRESS : recalcar ⟨to press the point/issue : insistir⟩ **6** IMPOSE : imponer **7 to press charges against** : demandar a **8 to press the flesh** fam : estrechar manos — vi **1** PUSH : apretar ⟨press hard : aprieta con fuerza⟩ **2** CROWD : apiñarse **3** : abrirse paso ⟨I pressed through the crowd : me abrí paso entre el gentío⟩ **4** URGE : presionar **5 to press ahead/on/forward** : seguir adelante **6 to press for** DEMAND : exigir, presionar para

press² n **1** CROWD : multitud f **2** : imprenta f, prensa f ⟨to go to press : entrar en prensa⟩ **3** URGENCY : urgencia f, prisa f **4** PRINTER, PUBLISHER : imprenta f, editorial f **5 the press** : la prensa ⟨freedom of the press : libertad de prensa⟩

press conference n : conferencia f de prensa, rueda f de prensa

pressing [ˈprɛsɪŋ] adj URGENT : urgente

press release n : boletín m de prensa

pressure¹ [ˈprɛʃər] vt **-sured; -suring** : presionar, apremiar

pressure² n **1** : presión f ⟨to be under pressure : estar bajo presión⟩ **2** → **blood pressure**

pressure cooker n : olla f a presión

pressure group n : grupo m de presión

pressurize [ˈprɛʃəˌraɪz] vt **-ized; -izing** : presurizar

prestige [prɛˈstiːʒ, -ˈstiːdʒ] n : prestigio m

prestigious [prɛˈstɪdʒəs] adj : prestigioso

presto [ˈprɛsˌtoː] adv : de pronto

presumably [priˈzuːməbli] adv : es de suponer, supuestamente ⟨presumably, he's guilty : supone que es culpable⟩

presume [priˈzuːm] vt **-sumed; -suming** **1** ASSUME, SUPPOSE : suponer, asumir, presumir **2 to presume to** : atreverse a, osar

presumption [priˈzʌmpʃən] n **1** AUDACITY : atrevimiento m, osadía f **2** ASSUMPTION : presunción f, suposición f

presumptuous [priˈzʌmptʃuəs] adj : descarado, atrevido

presuppose [ˌpriːsəˈpoːz] vt **-posed; -posing** : presuponer

pretend [priˈtɛnd] vt **1** CLAIM : pretender ⟨I won't pretend to understand it : no voy a pretender comprenderlo⟩ **2** FEIGN : fingir, simular ⟨to pretend to do something : fingir hacer algo⟩ ⟨he pretended everything was fine : fingía que todo estaba bien⟩ ⟨she pretended not to hear me : hacía como si no me oyera⟩ — vi : fingir

pretender [priˈtɛndər] n : pretendiente mf (al trono, etc.)

pretense or **pretence** [ˈpriːˌtɛns, priˈtɛns] n **1** CLAIM : afirmación f (falsa), pretensión f **2** FEIGNING : fingimiento m, simulación f ⟨to make a pretense of doing something : fingir hacer algo⟩ ⟨a pretense of order : una apariencia de orden⟩ **3** PRETEXT : pretexto m ⟨under false pretenses : con pretextos falsos, de manera fraudulenta⟩

pretension [priˈtɛnʃən] n **1** CLAIM : pretensión f, afirmación f **2** ASPIRATION : aspiración f, ambición f **3** PRETENTIOUSNESS : pretensiones fpl, presunción f

pretentious [priˈtɛntʃəs] adj : pretencioso

pretentiousness [priˈtɛntʃəsnəs] n : presunción f, pretensiones fpl

preterit [ˈprɛtərət] nm : pretérito m

pretext [ˈpriːˌtɛkst] n : pretexto m, excusa f

prettily [ˈprɪtəli] adv : atractivamente

prettiness [ˈprɪtinəs] n : lindeza f

pretty¹ [ˈprɪti] adv : bastante, bien ⟨it's pretty obvious : está bien claro⟩ ⟨it's pretty much the same : es más o menos igual⟩

pretty² adj **prettier; -est** : bonito, lindo, guapo ⟨a pretty girl : una muchacha guapa⟩ ⟨what a pretty dress! : ¡qué vestido más lindo!⟩

pretzel ['prɛtsəl] n : galleta f salada (en forma de nudo)
prevail [pri'veɪl] vi 1 TRIUMPH : prevalecer 2 PREDOMINATE : predominar 3 to
prevail upon : persuadir, convencer ⟨I prevailed upon her to sing : la convencí para que cantara⟩
prevailing [pri'veɪlɪŋ] adj : imperante, prevaleciente
prevalence ['prɛvələnts] n : preponderancia f, predominio m
prevalent ['prɛvələnt] adj 1 COMMON : común y corriente, general 2 WIDESPREAD : extendido
prevaricate [pri'værə,keɪt] vi -cated; -cating LIE : mentir
prevarication [pri,værə'keɪʃən] n : mentira f
prevent [pri'vɛnt] vt 1 AVOID : prevenir, evitar ⟨steps to prevent war : medidas para evitar la guerra⟩ 2 HINDER : impedir
preventable [pri'vɛntəbəl] adj : evitable
preventative [pri'vɛntətɪv] → **preventive**
prevention [pri'vɛntʃən] n : prevención f
preventive [pri'vɛntɪv] adj : preventivo
preview ['pri:,vju] n : preestreno m
previous ['pri:viəs] adj : previo, anterior ⟨previous knowledge : conocimientos previos⟩ ⟨the previous day : el día anterior⟩ ⟨in the previous year : en el año pasado⟩
previously ['pri:viəsli] adv : antes
prewar [,pri:'wɔr] adj : de antes de la guerra
prey [preɪ] n, pl **preys** : presa f
prey on vt 1 : cazar, alimentarse de ⟨it preys on fish : se alimenta de peces⟩ 2 to
prey on one's mind : hacer presa en alguien, atormentar a alguien
price[1] ['praɪs] vt **priced; pricing** : poner un precio a ⟨to be reasonably/competitively priced : tener precios razonables/competitivos⟩
price[2] n 1 : precio m ⟨to pay the price for something : pagar el precio de algo⟩ ⟨price tag : etiqueta de precio⟩ ⟨price range : gama de precios⟩ ⟨to go up/down in price : subir/bajar de precio⟩ ⟨price cut : rebaja en el precio⟩ 2 at any price : a toda costa
priceless ['praɪsləs] adj : inestimable, inapreciable
pricey ['praɪsi] adj : caro
prick[1] ['prɪk] vt 1 : pinchar 2 to prick up one's ears : levantar las orejas — vi : pinchar
prick[2] n 1 STAB : pinchazo m ⟨a prick of conscience : un remordimiento⟩ 2 → **pricker**
pricker ['prɪkər] n THORN : espina f
prickle[1] ['prɪkəl] vi -**led; -ling** : sentir un cosquilleo, tener un hormigueo
prickle[2] n 1 : espina f (de una planta) 2 TINGLE : cosquilleo m, hormigueo m
prickly ['prɪkəli] adj 1 THORNY : espinoso 2 : que pica ⟨a prickly sensation : un hormigueo⟩
prickly pear n 1 : nopal m, tuna f (planta) 2 : tuna f, higo m chumbo (fruta)

pride[1] ['praɪd] vt **prided; priding** : estar orgulloso de ⟨to pride oneself on : preciarse de, enorgullecerse de⟩
pride[2] n : orgullo m
priest ['pri:st] n : sacerdote m, cura m
priestess ['pri:stɪs] n : sacerdotisa f
priesthood ['pri:st,hʊd] n : sacerdocio m
priestly ['pri:stli] adj : sacerdotal
prig ['prɪg] n : mojigato m, -ta f; gazmoño m, -ña f
prim ['prɪm] adj **primmer; primmest** 1 PRISSY : remilgado 2 PRUDISH : mojigato, gazmoño
prima ballerina ['pri:mə-] n : prima bailarina f
prima donna [,pri:mə'dɑnə, ,pri:-] n : divo m, diva f
primarily [praɪ'mɛrəli] adv : principalmente, fundamentalmente
primary[1] ['praɪ,mɛri, 'praɪməri] adj 1 FIRST : primario 2 PRINCIPAL : principal 3 BASIC : fundamental
primary[2] n, pl -**ries** : elección f primaria
primary color n : color m primario
primary school → **elementary school**
primate n 1 ['praɪ,meɪt, -mət] : primado m (obispo) 2 [-,meɪt] : primate m (animal)
prime[1] ['praɪm] vt **primed; priming** 1 : cebar ⟨to prime a pump : cebar una bomba⟩ 2 PREPARE : preparar (una superficie para pintar) 3 COACH : preparar (a un testigo, etc.)
prime[2] adj 1 CHIEF, MAIN : principal, primero 2 EXCELLENT : de primera (categoría), excelente
prime[3] n the prime of one's life : la flor de la vida
prime minister n : primer ministro m, primera ministra f
prime number n : número m primo
primer[1] ['prɪmər] n 1 READER : cartilla f 2 MANUAL : manual m
primer[2] ['praɪmər] n 1 : cebo m (para explosivos) 2 : base f (de pintura)
prime time n : horas fpl de mayor audiencia
primeval [praɪ'mi:vəl] adj : primitivo, primigenio
primitive ['prɪmətɪv] adj : primitivo
primly ['prɪmli] adv : mojigatamente
primness ['prɪmnəs] n : mojigatería f, gazmoñería f
primordial [praɪ'mɔrdiəl] adj : primordial, fundamental
primp ['prɪmp] vi : arreglarse, acicalarse
primrose ['prɪm,ro:z] n : primavera f, prímula f
prince ['prɪnts] n : príncipe m
princely ['prɪntsli] adj : principesco
princess ['prɪntsəs, 'prɪn,sɛs] n : princesa f
principal[1] ['prɪntsəpəl] adj : principal — **principally** adv
principal[2] n 1 PROTAGONIST : protagonista mf 2 : director m, -tora f (de una escuela) 3 CAPITAL : principal m, capital m (en finanzas)
principality [,prɪntsə'pæləti] n, pl -**ties** : principado m

principle ['prɪntʃəpəl] n   1 : principio m ⟨it's against my principles : va en contra de mis principios⟩ ⟨it's a matter of principle : es una cuestión de principios⟩   2 **as a matter of principle** : por principio   3 **in principle** : en principio   4 **on principle** : por principio

print¹ ['prɪnt] vt   1 : imprimir (libros, etc.)   2 : publicar   3 : estampar (tela)   4 **to print out** : imprimir — vi : escribir con letra de molde/imprenta

print² n   1 IMPRESSION : marca f, huella f, impresión f   2 : texto m impreso ⟨to be out of print : estar agotado⟩   3 LETTERING : letra f   4 ENGRAVING : grabado m   5 : copia f (en fotografía)   6 : estampado m (de tela)

printer ['prɪntər] n   1 : impresor m, -sora f (persona)   2 : impresora f (máquina)

printing ['prɪntɪŋ] n   1 : impresión f (acto) ⟨the third printing : la tercera tirada⟩   2 : imprenta f (profesión)   3 LETTERING : letras fpl de molde

printing press n : prensa f

print out vt : imprimir (de una computadora)

printout ['prɪnt,aʊt] n : copia f impresa (de una computadora)

prior¹ ['praɪər] adj   1 : previo ⟨prior engagement/commitment : compromiso previo⟩ ⟨without prior notice : sin previo aviso⟩   2 **prior to** : antes de

prior² n : prior m

prioress ['praɪərəs] n : priora f

priority [praɪ'ɔrəti] n, pl -ties : prioridad f

priory ['praɪəri] n, pl -ries : priorato m

prism ['prɪzəm] n : prisma m

prison ['prɪzən] n : prisión f, cárcel f ⟨he's in prison : está preso, está en la cárcel⟩ ⟨they put him in prison : lo encarcelaron, lo metieron en la cárcel⟩ ⟨a prison sentence : una pena de prisión⟩ ⟨she was sentenced to ten years in prison : fue condenada a diez años de prisión⟩

prisoner ['prɪzənər] n : preso m, -sa f; recluso m, -sa f ⟨prisoner of war : prisionero de guerra⟩

prison warden → warden

prissy ['prɪsi] adj **prissier; -est** : remilgado, melindroso

pristine ['prɪsˌtiːn, prɪs'-] adj : puro, prístino

privacy ['praɪvəsi] n, pl -cies : privacidad f

private¹ ['praɪvət] adj   1 PERSONAL : privado, particular ⟨private property : propiedad privada⟩   2 INDEPENDENT : privado, independiente ⟨private studies : estudios privados⟩   3 SECRET : secreto   4 SECLUDED : aislado, privado   5 SHY : reservado — **privately** adv

private² n : soldado m raso

private detective → private investigator

private enterprise → free enterprise

private eye fam → private investigator

private investigator n : investigador m privado, investigadora f privada, detective m privado, detective f privada

private school n : escuela f privada

privation [praɪ'veɪʃən] n : privación f

privatize ['praɪvəˌtaɪz] vt **-ized; -izing** : privatizar

privilege ['prɪvlɪdʒ, 'prɪvə-] n : privilegio m

privileged ['prɪvlɪdʒd, 'prɪvə-] adj : privilegiado

privy¹ ['prɪvi] adj **to be privy to** : estar enterado de

privy² n, pl **privies** : excusado m, retrete m (exterior)

prize¹ ['praɪz] vt **prized; prizing** : valorar, apreciar

prize² adj   1 : premiado ⟨a prize stallion : un semental premiado⟩   2 OUTSTANDING : de primera, excepcional

prize³ n   1 AWARD : premio m ⟨third prize : el tercer premio⟩   2 : joya f, tesoro m ⟨he's a real prize : es un tesoro⟩

prizefighter ['praɪzˌfaɪtər] n : boxeador m, -dora f profesional

prizewinner ['praɪzˌwɪnər] n : premiado m, -da f

prizewinning ['praɪzˌwɪnɪŋ] adj : premiado, galardonado

pro¹ ['proː] adv : a favor

pro² adj → **professional¹**

pro³ n   1 : pro m ⟨the pros and cons : los pros y los contras⟩   2 → **professional²**

pro- pref : pro-

probability [ˌprɑbə'bɪləti] n, pl -ties : probabilidad f

probable ['prɑbəbəl] adj : probable — **probably** [-bli] adv

probate¹ ['proːˌbeɪt] vt **-bated; -bating** : autenticar (un testamento)

probate² n : autenticación f (de un testamento)

probation [proː'beɪʃən] n   1 : período m de prueba (para un empleado, etc.)   2 : libertad f condicional (para un preso) ⟨to put someone on probation : dejar/poner a alguien en libertad condicional⟩

probationary [proː'beɪʃəˌnɛri] adj : de prueba

probe¹ ['proːb] vt **probed; probing**   1 : sondar (en medicina y tecnología)   2 INVESTIGATE : investigar, sondear

probe² n   1 : sonda f (en medicina, etc.) ⟨space probe : sonda espacial⟩   2 INVESTIGATION : investigación f, sondeo m

probity ['proːbəti] n : probidad f

problem¹ ['prɑbləm] adj : difícil

problem² n : problema m

problematic [ˌprɑblə'mætɪk] or **problematical** [-tɪkəl] adj : problemático

proboscis [prə'bɑsɪs] n, pl -cises also -cides [-səˌdiːz] : trompa f, probóscide f

procedural [prə'siːdʒərəl] adj : de procedimiento

procedure [prə'siːdʒər] n : procedimiento m ⟨administrative procedures : trámites administrativos⟩

proceed [proː'siːd] vi   1 : proceder ⟨to proceed to do something : proceder a hacer algo⟩   2 CONTINUE : continuar, proseguir, seguir ⟨he proceeded to the next phase : pasó a la segunda fase⟩   3 ADVANCE : avanzar ⟨as the conference proceeded : mientras seguía avanzando la conferencia⟩ ⟨the road proceeds south : la calle sigue hacia el sur⟩

proceeding [proˈsiːdɪŋ] *n* **1** PROCEDURE : procedimiento *m* **2 proceedings** *npl* EVENTS : acontecimientos *mpl* **3 proceedings** *npl* MINUTES : actas *fpl* (de una reunión, etc.)

proceeds [ˈproːˌsiːdz] *npl* : ganancias *fpl*

process¹ [ˈprɑˌsɛs, ˈproː-] *vt* : procesar, tratar

process² *n, pl* **-cesses** [ˈprɑˌsɛsəz, ˈproː-, -ˌsɑsəz, -səˌsiːz] **1** : proceso *m* ⟨the process of elimination : el proceso de eliminación⟩ **2** METHOD : proceso *m*, método *m* ⟨manufacturing processes : procesos industriales⟩ **3** : acción *f* judicial ⟨due process of law : el debido proceso (de la ley)⟩ **4** SUMMONS : citación *f* **5** PROJECTION : protuberancia *f* (anatómica) **6 in the process of** : en vías de ⟨in the process of repair : en reparaciones⟩

processing *n* : procesamiento *m* (en informática)

procession [prəˈsɛʃən] *n* : procesión *f*, desfile *m* ⟨a funeral procession : un cortejo fúnebre⟩

processional [prəˈsɛʃənəl] *n* : himno *m* para una procesión

processor [ˈprɑˌsɛsər, ˈproː-, -səsər] *n* **1** : procesador *m* (de una computadora) **2 food processor** : procesador *m* de alimentos

proclaim [proˈkleɪm] *vt* : proclamar

proclamation [ˌprɑkləˈmeɪʃən] *n* : proclamación *f*

proclivity [proˈklɪvəti] *n, pl* **-ties** : proclividad *f*

procrastinate [prəˈkræstəˌneɪt] *vi* **-nated; -nating** : demorar, aplazar las responsabilidades

procrastination [prəˌkræstəˈneɪʃən] *n* : aplazamiento *m*, demora *f*, dilación *f*

procreate [ˈproːkriˌeɪt] *vi* **-ated; -ating** : procrear

procreation [ˌproːkriˈeɪʃən] *n* : procreación *f*

proctor¹ [ˈprɑktər] *vt* : supervisar (un examen)

proctor² *n* : supervisor *m*, -sora *f* (de un examen)

procure [prəˈkjʊr] *vt* **-cured; -curing** **1** OBTAIN : procurar, obtener **2** BRING ABOUT : provocar, lograr, conseguir

procurement [prəˈkjʊrmənt] *n* : obtención *f*

prod¹ [ˈprɑd] *vt* **prodded; prodding** **1** JAB, POKE : pinchar, golpear (con la punta de algo) **2** GOAD : incitar, estimular

prod² *n* **1** JAB, POKE : golpe *m* (con la punta de algo), pinchazo *m* **2** STIMULUS : estímulo *m* **3 cattle prod** : picana *f*, aguijón *m*

prodigal¹ [ˈprɑdɪɡəl] *adj* SPENDTHRIFT : pródigo, despilfarrador, derrochador

prodigal² *n* : pródigo *m*, -ga *f*; derrochador *m*, -dora *f*

prodigious [prəˈdɪdʒəs] *adj* **1** MARVELOUS : prodigioso, maravilloso **2** HUGE : enorme, vasto ⟨prodigious sums : muchísimo dinero⟩ — **prodigiously** *adv*

prodigy [ˈprɑdədʒi] *n, pl* **-gies** : prodigio *m* ⟨child prodigy : niño prodigio⟩

produce¹ [prəˈduːs, -ˈdjuːs] *vt* **-duced; -ducing** **1** EXHIBIT : presentar, mostrar **2** YIELD : producir **3** CAUSE : producir, causar **4** CREATE : producir ⟨to produce a poem : escribir un poema⟩ **5** : poner en escena (una obra de teatro), producir (una película)

produce² [ˈprɑˌduːs, ˈproː-, -ˌdjuːs] *n* : productos *mpl* agrícolas

producer [prəˈduːsər, -ˈdjuː-] *n* : productor *m*, -tora *f*

product [ˈprɑˌdʌkt] *n* : producto *m*

production [prəˈdʌkʃən] *n* : producción *f*

productive [prəˈdʌktɪv] *adj* : productivo

productivity [ˌproːˌdʌkˈtɪvəti, ˌprɑ-] *n* : productividad *f*

profane¹ [proˈfeɪn] *vt* **-faned; -faning** : profanar

profane² *adj* **1** SECULAR : profano **2** IRREVERENT : irreverente

profanity [proˈfænəti] *n, pl* **-ties** **1** IRREVERENCE : irreverencia *f*, impiedad *f* **2** : blasfemias *fpl*, obscenidades *fpl* ⟨don't use profanity : no digas blasfemias⟩

profess [prəˈfɛs] *vt* **1** DECLARE : declarar, manifestar **2** CLAIM : pretender **3** : profesar (una religión, etc.)

professedly [prəˈfɛsədli] *adv* **1** OPENLY : declaradamente **2** ALLEGEDLY : supuestamente

profession [prəˈfɛʃən] *n* : profesión *f*

professional¹ [prəˈfɛʃənəl] *adj* : profesional — **professionally** *adv*

professional² *n* : profesional *mf*

professionalism [prəˈfɛʃənəˌlizəm] *n* : profesionalismo *m*

professor [prəˈfɛsər] *n* : profesor *m* (universitario), profesora *f* (universitaria); catedrático *m*, -ca *f*

professorship [prəˈfɛsərˌʃɪp] *n* : cátedra *f*

proffer [ˈprɑfər] *vt* **-fered; -fering** : ofrecer, dar

proficiency [prəˈfɪʃəntsi] *n* : competencia *f*, capacidad *f*

proficient [prəˈfɪʃənt] *adj* : competente, experto — **proficiently** *adv*

profile [ˈproːˌfaɪl] *n* : perfil *m* ⟨a portrait in profile : un retrato de perfil⟩ ⟨to keep a low profile : no llamar la atención, hacerse pasar desapercibido⟩

profit¹ [ˈprɑfət] *vi* : sacar provecho (de), beneficiarse (de)

profit² *n* **1** ADVANTAGE : provecho *m*, partido *m*, beneficio *m* **2** GAIN : beneficio *m*, utilidad *f*, ganancia *f* ⟨to make a profit : sacar beneficios⟩

profitability [ˌprɑfətəˈbɪləti] *n* : rentabilidad *f*

profitable [ˈprɑfətəbəl] *adj* : rentable, lucrativo — **profitably** [-bli] *adv*

profitless [ˈprɑfətləs] *adj* : infructuoso, inútil

profligate [ˈprɑflɪɡət, -ˌɡeɪt] *adj* **1** DISSOLUTE : disoluto, licencioso **2** SPENDTHRIFT : despilfarrador, derrochador, pródigo

profound [prəˈfaʊnd] *adj* : profundo

profoundly [prə'faʊndli] *adv* : profundamente, en profundidad

profundity [prə'fʌndəti] *n, pl* **-ties** : profundidad *f*

profuse [prə'fju:s] *adj* **1** COPIOUS : profuso, copioso **2** LAVISH : pródigo — **profusely** *adv*

profusion [prə'fju:ʒən] *n* : abundancia *f*, profusión *f*

progenitor [pro'ʤenətər] *n* : progenitor *m*, -tora *f*

progeny ['prɑʤəni] *n, pl* **-nies** : progenie *f*

progesterone [pro'ʤɛstə,ro:n] *n* : progesterona *f*

prognosis [prɑg'no:sɪs] *n, pl* **-noses** [-,si:z] : pronóstico *m* (médico)

program[1] ['pro:,græm, -grəm] *vt* **-grammed** *or* **-gramed; -gramming** *or* **-graming** : programar

program[2] *n* : programa *m*

programmable ['pro:,græməbəl] *adj* : programable

programmer ['pro:,græmər] *n* : programador *m*, -dora *f*

programming ['pro:,græmɪŋ] *n* : programación *f*

progress[1] [prə'grɛs] *vi* **1** PROCEED : progresar, adelantar **2** IMPROVE : mejorar

progress[2] ['prɑgrəs, -,grɛs] *n* **1** ADVANCE : progreso *m*, adelanto *m*, avance *m* ⟨to make progress : hacer progresos⟩ **2** BETTERMENT : mejora *f*, mejoramiento *m*

progression [prə'grɛʃən] *n* **1** ADVANCE : avance *m* **2** SEQUENCE : desarrollo *m* (de eventos)

progressive [prə'grɛsɪv] *adj* **1** : progresista ⟨a progressive society : una sociedad progresista⟩ **2** : progresivo ⟨a progressive disease : una enfermedad progresiva⟩ **3** *or* **Progressive** : progresista (en política) **4** : progresivo (en gramática)

progressively [prə'grɛsɪvli] *adv* : progresivamente, poco a poco

prohibit [pro'hɪbət] *vt* : prohibir

prohibition [,pro:ə'bɪʃən, ,pro:hə-] *n* : prohibición *f*

prohibitive [pro'hɪbətɪv] *adj* : prohibitivo

project[1] [prə'ʤɛkt] *vt* **1** PLAN : proyectar, planear **2** : proyectar (imágenes, misiles, etc.) — *vi* PROTRUDE : sobresalir, salir

project[2] ['prɑ,ʤɛkt, -ʤɪkt] *n* : proyecto *m*, trabajo *m* (de un estudiante) ⟨research project : proyecto de investigación⟩

projectile [prə'ʤɛktəl, -,taɪl] *n* : proyectil *m*

projection [prə'ʤɛkʃən] *n* **1** PLAN : plan *m*, proyección *f* **2** : proyección *f* (de imágenes, misiles, etc.) **3** PROTRUSION : saliente *m*

projectionist [prə'ʤɛkʃənɪst] *n* : proyeccionista *mf*; operador *m*, -dora *f*

projector [prə'ʤɛktər] *n* : proyector *m*

proletarian[1] [,pro:lə'tɛriən] *adj* : proletario

proletarian[2] *n* : proletario *m*, -ria *f*

proletariat [,pro:lə'tɛriət] *n* : proletariado *m*

proliferate [prə'lɪfə,reɪt] *vi* **-ated; -ating** : proliferar

proliferation [prə,lɪfə'reɪʃən] *n* : proliferación *f*

prolific [prə'lɪfɪk] *adj* : prolífico

prologue ['pro:,lɔg] *n* : prólogo *m*

prolong [prə'lɔŋ] *vt* : prolongar

prolongation [,pro:,lɔŋ'geɪʃən] *n* : prolongación *f*

prom ['prɑm] *n* : baile *m* formal (de un colegio)

promenade[1] [,prɑmə'neɪd, -'nɑd] *vi* **-naded; -nading** : pasear, pasearse, dar un paseo

promenade[2] *n* : paseo *m*

prominence ['prɑmənənts] *n* **1** PROJECTION : prominencia *f* **2** EMINENCE : eminencia *f*, prestigio *m*

prominent ['prɑmənənt] *adj* **1** OUTSTANDING : prominente, destacado **2** PROJECTING : prominente, saliente

prominently ['prɑmənəntli] *adv* : destacadamente, prominentemente

promiscuity [,prɑmɪs'kju:əti] *n, pl* **-ties** : promiscuidad *f*

promiscuous [prə'mɪskjuəs] *adj* : promiscuo — **promiscuously** *adv*

promise[1] ['prɑməs] *v* **-ised; -ising** : prometer

promise[2] *n* **1** : promesa *f* ⟨he kept his promise : cumplió su promesa⟩ **2 to show promise** : prometer

promising ['prɑməsɪŋ] *adj* : prometedor

promissory ['prɑmə,sori] *adj* : que promete ⟨a promissory note : un pagaré⟩

promontory ['prɑmən,tori] *n, pl* **-ries** : promontorio *m*

promote [prə'mo:t] *vt* **-moted; -moting 1** : ascender (a un alumno o un empleado) **2** ADVERTISE : promocionar, hacerle publicidad a **3** FURTHER : promover, fomentar

promoter [prə'mo:tər] *n* : promotor *m*, -tora *f*; empresario *m*, -ria *f* (en deportes)

promotion [prə'mo:ʃən] *n* **1** : ascenso *m* (de un alumno o un empleado) **2** FURTHERING : promoción *f*, fomento *m* **3** ADVERTISING : publicidad *f*, propaganda *f*

promotional [prə'mo:ʃənəl] *adj* : promocional

prompt[1] ['prɑmpt] *vt* **1** INDUCE : provocar (una cosa), inducir (a una persona) ⟨curiosity prompted me to ask you : la curiosidad me indujo a preguntarle⟩ **2** : apuntar (a un actor, etc.)

prompt[2] *adj* : pronto, rápido ⟨prompt payment : pago puntual⟩

prompter ['prɑmptər] *n* : apuntador *m*, -dora *f* (en teatro)

promptly ['prɑmptli] *adv* : inmediatamente, rápidamente

promptness ['prɑmptnəs] *n* : prontitud *f*, rapidez *f*

promulgate ['prɑməl,geɪt] *vt* **-gated; -gating** : promulgar

prone ['pro:n] *adj* **1** LIABLE : propenso, proclive ⟨accident-prone : propenso a los accidentes⟩ **2** : boca abajo, decúbito prono ⟨in a prone position : en decúbito prono⟩

prong [ˈprɔŋ] n : punta f, diente m

pronoun [ˈproːˌnaʊn] n : pronombre m

pronounce [prəˈnaʊnts] vt **-nounced; -nouncing 1** : pronunciar ⟨how do you pronounce your name? : ¿cómo se pronuncia su nombre?⟩ **3** DECLARE : declarar **3 to pronounce sentence** : dictar sentencia, pronunciar un fallo

pronounced [prəˈnaʊntst] adj MARKED : pronunciado, marcado

pronouncement [prəˈnaʊntsmənt] n : declaración f

pronunciation [prəˌnʌntsiˈeɪʃən] n : pronunciación f

proof¹ [ˈpruːf] adj : a prueba ⟨proof against tampering : a prueba de manipulación⟩

proof² n : prueba f

proofread [ˈpruːˌriːd] v **-read; -reading** vt : corregir — vi : corregir pruebas

proofreader [ˈpruːˌriːdər] n : corrector m, -tora f (de pruebas)

prop¹ [ˈprɑp] vt **propped; propping 1 to prop against** : apoyar contra **2 to prop up** SUPPORT : apoyar, apuntalar, sostener **3 to prop up** SUSTAIN : alentar (a alguien), darle ánimo (a alguien)

prop² n **1** SUPPORT : puntal m, apoyo m, soporte m **2** : accesorio m (en teatro)

propaganda [ˌprɑpəˈɡændə, ˌproː-] n : propaganda f

propagandize [ˌprɑpəˈɡænˌdaɪz, ˌproː-] v **-dized; -dizing** vt : someter a propaganda — vi : hacer propaganda

propagate [ˈprɑpəˌɡeɪt] v **-gated; -gating** vi : propagarse — vt : propagar

propagation [ˌprɑpəˈɡeɪʃən] n : propagación f

propane [ˈproːˌpeɪn] n : propano m

propel [prəˈpɛl] vt **-pelled; -pelling** : impulsar, propulsar, impeler

propellant or **propellent** [prəˈpɛlənt] n : propulsor m

propeller [prəˈpɛlər] n : hélice f

propensity [prəˈpɛntsəti] n, pl **-ties** : propensión f, tendencia f, inclinación f

proper [ˈprɑpər] adj **1** RIGHT, SUITABLE : apropiado, adecuado **2** : propio, mismo ⟨the city proper : la propia ciudad⟩ **3** CORRECT : correcto **4** GENTEEL : fino, refinado, cortés **5** OWN, SPECIAL : propio — **properly** adv

proper noun or **proper name** n : nombre m propio

property [ˈprɑpərti] n, pl **-ties 1** CHARACTERISTIC : característica f, propiedad f **2** POSSESSIONS : propiedad f **3** BUILDING : inmueble m **4** LAND, LOT : terreno m, lote m, parcela f **5** PROP : accesorio m (en teatro)

prophecy [ˈprɑfəsi] n, pl **-cies** : profecía f, vaticinio m

prophesy [ˈprɑfəˌsaɪ] v **-sied; -sying** vt **1** FORETELL : profetizar (como profeta) **2** PREDICT : profetizar, predecir, vaticinar — vi : hacer profecías

prophet [ˈprɑfət] n : profeta m

prophetic [prəˈfɛtɪk] or **prophetical** [-ˌtɪkəl] adj : profético — **prophetically** [-ˌtɪkli] adv

propitiate [proˈpɪʃiˌeɪt] vt **-ated; -ating** : propiciar

propitious [prəˈpɪʃəs] adj : propicio

proponent [prəˈpoːnənt] n : defensor m, -sora f; partidario m, -ria f

proportion¹ [prəˈporʃən] vt : proporcionar ⟨well-proportioned : de buenas proporciones⟩

proportion² n **1** RATIO : proporción f **2** SYMMETRY : proporción f, simetría f ⟨out of proportion : desproporcionado⟩ ⟨to keep things in proportion : no exagerar⟩ ⟨you're blowing things out of proportion : estás exagerando⟩ **3** PART, SHARE : parte f **4 proportions** npl SIZE : dimensiones fpl

proportional [prəˈporʃənəl] adj : proporcional — **proportionally** adv

proportionate [prəˈporʃənət] adj : proporcional — **proportionately** adv

proposal [prəˈpoːzəl] n **1** PROPOSITION : propuesta f, proposición f ⟨marriage proposal : propuesta de matrimonio⟩ **2** PLAN : proyecto m, propuesta f

propose [prəˈpoːz] v **-posed; -posing** vi : proponer matrimonio — vt **1** INTEND : pensar, proponerse **2** SUGGEST : proponer

proposition [ˌprɑpəˈzɪʃən] n **1** PROPOSAL : proposición f, propuesta f **2** STATEMENT : proposición f

propound [prəˈpaʊnd] vt : proponer, exponer

proprietary [prəˈpraɪəˌteri] adj : propietario, patentado

proprietor [prəˈpraɪətər] n : propietario m, -ria f

propriety [prəˈpraɪəti] n, pl **-eties 1** DECORUM : decencia f, decoro m **2 proprieties** npl CONVENTIONS : convenciones fpl, cánones mpl sociales

propulsion [prəˈpʌlʃən] n : propulsión f

prosaic [proˈzeɪk] adj : prosaico

proscribe [proˈskraɪb] vt **-scribed; -scribing** : proscribir

prose [ˈproːz] n : prosa f

prosecute [ˈprɑsɪˌkjuːt] vt **-cuted; -cuting 1** CARRY OUT : llevar a cabo **2** : procesar, enjuiciar ⟨prosecuted for fraud : procesado por fraude⟩

prosecution [ˌprɑsɪˈkjuːʃən] n **1** : procesamiento m ⟨the prosecution of forgers : el procesamiento de falsificadores⟩ **2** PROSECUTORS : acusación f ⟨witness for the prosecution : testigo de cargo⟩

prosecutor [ˈprɑsɪˌkjuːtər] n : acusador m, -dora f; fiscal mf

prospect¹ [ˈprɑˌspɛkt] vi : prospectar (el terreno) ⟨to prospect for gold : buscar oro⟩

prospect² n **1** VISTA : vista f, panorama m **2** OPPORTUNITY : posibilidad f, perspectiva f ⟨he has few prospects for employment : tiene pocas posibilidades/perspectivas de empleo⟩ **3** POSSIBILITY : posibilidad f ⟨the prospect of going to war : la posibilidad de entrar en guerra⟩

4 CANDIDATE : candidato *m*, -ta *f* **5 in prospect** : en perspectiva

prospective [prə'spɛktɪv, 'prɑˌspɛk-] *adj* **1** EXPECTANT : futuro ⟨prospective mother : futura madre⟩ **2** POTENTIAL : potencial, posible ⟨prospective employee : posible empleado⟩

prospector [prə'spɛktər, prɑ'spɛk-] *n* : prospector *m*, -tora *f*; explorador *m*, -dora *f*

prospectus [prə'spɛktəs] *n* : prospecto *m*

prosper ['prɑspər] *vi* : prosperar

prosperity [prɑ'spɛrəṭi] *n* : prosperidad *f*

prosperous ['prɑspərəs] *adj* : próspero

prostate ['prɑˌsteɪt] *n* : próstata *f*

prosthesis [prɑs'θiːsɪs, 'prɑsθə-] *n, pl* **-theses** [-ˌsiːz] : prótesis *f*

prostitute¹ ['prɑstəˌtuːt, -ˌtjuːt] *vt* **-tuted; -tuting 1** : prostituir **2 to prostitute oneself** : prostituirse

prostitute² *n* : prostituto *m*, -ta *f*

prostitution [ˌprɑstə'tuːʃən, -'tjuː-] *n* : prostitución *f*

prostrate¹ ['prɑˌstreɪt] *vt* **-trated; -trating 1** : postrar **2 to prostrate oneself** : postrarse

prostrate² *adj* : postrado

prostration [prɑ'streɪʃən] *n* : postración *f*

protagonist [pro'tægənɪst] *n* : protagonista *mf*

protect [prə'tɛkt] *vt* : proteger

protection [prə'tɛkʃən] *n* : protección *f*

protective [prə'tɛktɪv] *adj* : protector

protector [prə'tɛktər] *n* **1** : protector *m*, -tora *f* (persona) **2** GUARD : protector *m* (aparato)

protectorate [prə'tɛktərət] *n* : protectorado *m*

protégé ['proːṭəˌʒeɪ] *n* : protegido *m*, -da *f*

protein ['proːˌtiːn] *n* : proteína *f*

protest¹ [pro'tɛst, prə-] *vt* **1** ASSERT : afirmar, declarar **2** : protestar ⟨they protested the decision : protestaron (por) la decisión⟩ — *vi* **to protest against** : protestar contra

protest² ['proːˌtɛst] *n* **1** DEMONSTRATION : manifestación *f* (de protesta) ⟨a public protest : una manifestación pública⟩ **2** COMPLAINT : queja *f*, protesta *f*

Protestant ['prɑṭəstənt] *n* : protestante *mf*

Protestantism ['prɑṭəstənˌtɪzəm] *n* : protestantismo *m*

protester [pro'tɛstər, prə-] *n* : manifestante *mf*

protocol ['proːṭəˌkɔl] *n* : protocolo *m*

proton ['proːˌtɑn] *n* : protón *m*

protoplasm ['proːṭəˌplæzəm] *n* : protoplasma *m*

prototype ['proːṭəˌtaɪp] *n* : prototipo *m*

protract [pro'trækt] *vt* : prolongar

protractor [pro'træktər] *n* : transportador *m* (instrumento)

protrude [pro'truːd] *vi* **-truded; -truding** : salir, sobresalir

protrusion [pro'truːʒən] *n* : protuberancia *f*, saliente *m*

protuberance [pro'tuːbərənts, -'tjuː-] *n* : protuberancia *f*

proud ['praʊd] *adj* **1** HAUGHTY : altanero, orgulloso, arrogante **2** : orgulloso ⟨she was proud of her work : estaba orgullosa de su trabajo⟩ ⟨too proud to beg : demasiado orgulloso para rogar⟩ **3** GLORIOUS : glorioso — **proudly** *adv*

provable ['pruːvəbəl] *adj* : comprobable

prove ['pruːv] *v* **proved; proved** *or* **proven** ['pruːvən]; **proving** *vt* **1** TEST : probar **2** DEMONSTRATE : probar, demostrar ⟨this proves her guilt, this proves that she is guilty : esto prueba/demuestra que es culpable⟩ ⟨you've already proven your point : ya sé que tienes razón⟩ **3** (*show someone/something to be*) ⟨can you prove him wrong? : ¿puedes demostrar que está equivocado?⟩ ⟨evidence that proves her guilty : pruebas que demuestran que es culpable⟩ ⟨it has been proven effective : se ha demostrado ser eficaz⟩ — *vi* **1** : resultar ⟨it proved effective : resultó eficaz⟩ **2 to prove oneself** : demostrar sus cualidades

Provençal [ˌproːvɑn'sɑl, ˌprɑvən-] *n* **1** : provenzal *mf* **2** : provenzal *m* (idioma) — **Provençal** *adj*

proverb ['prɑˌvərb] *n* : proverbio *m*, refrán *m*

proverbial [prə'vərbiəl] *adj* : proverbial

provide [prə'vaɪd] *v* **-vided; -viding** *vt* **1** STIPULATE : estipular **2 to provide with** : proveer de, proporcionar — *vi* **1** : proveer ⟨the Lord will provide : el Señor proveerá⟩ **2 to provide for** SUPPORT : mantener **3 to provide for** ANTICIPATE : hacer previsiones para, prever

provided [prə'vaɪdəd] *or* **provided that** *conj* : con tal (de) que, siempre que

providence ['prɑvədənts] *n* **1** PRUDENCE : previsión *f*, prudencia *f* **2** *or* **Providence** : providencia *f* ⟨divine providence : la Divina Providencia⟩ **3 Providence** GOD : Providencia *f*

provident ['prɑvədənt] *adj* **1** PRUDENT : previsor, prudente **2** FRUGAL : frugal, ahorrativo

providential [ˌprɑvə'dɛntʃəl] *adj* : providencial

provider [prə'vaɪdər] *n* **1** PURVEYOR : proveedor *m*, -dora *f* **2** BREADWINNER : sostén *m* (económico)

providing that → provided

province ['prɑvɪnts] *n* **1** : provincia *f* (de un país) ⟨to live in the provinces : vivir en las provincias⟩ **2** FIELD, SPHERE : campo *m*, competencia *f* ⟨it's not in my province : no es de mi competencia⟩

provincial [prə'vɪntʃəl] *adj* **1** : provincial ⟨provincial government : gobierno provincial⟩ **2** : provinciano, pueblerino ⟨a provincial mentality : una mentalidad provinciana⟩

provision¹ [prə'vɪʒən] *vt* : aprovisionar, abastecer

provision² *n* **1** PROVIDING : provisión *f*, suministro *m* **2** STIPULATION : condición *f*, salvedad *f*, estipulación *f* **3 provisions** *npl* : despensa *f*, víveres *mpl*, provisiones *fpl*

provisional [prə'vɪʒənəl] *adj* : provisional, provisorio — **provisionally** *adv*

proviso [prə'vaɪ,zo:] *n*, *pl* **-sos** *or* **-soes** : condición *f*, salvedad *f*, estipulación *f*

provocation [,prɑvə'keɪʃən] *n* : provocación *f*

provocative [prə'vakətɪv] *adj* **1** INCITING : provocador **2** SUGGESTIVE : provocativo, insinuante **3** INTRIGUING : que hace pensar

provoke [prə'vo:k] *vt* **-voked; -voking** : provocar

prow ['praʊ] *n* : proa *f*

prowess ['praʊəs] *n* **1** VALOR : valor *m*, valentía *f* **2** SKILL : habilidad *f*, destreza *f*

prowl ['praʊl] *vi* : merodear, rondar — *vt* : rondar por

prowler ['praʊlər] *n* : merodeador *m*, -dora *f*

proximity [prɑk'sɪməti] *n* : proximidad *f*

proxy ['praksi] *n*, *pl* **proxies 1** : poder *m* (de actuar en nombre de alguien) ⟨by proxy : por poder⟩ **2** AGENT : apoderado *m*, -da *f*; representante *mf*

prude ['pru:d] *n* : mojigato *m*, -ta *f*; gazmoño *m*, -ña *f*

prudence ['pru:dənts] *n* **1** SHREWDNESS : prudencia *f*, sagacidad *f* **2** CAUTION : prudencia *f*, cautela *f* **3** THRIFT : frugalidad *f*

prudent ['pru:dənt] *adj* **1** SHREWD : prudente, sagaz **2** CAUTIOUS, FARSIGHTED : prudente, previsor, precavido **3** THRIFTY : frugal, ahorrativo — **prudently** *adv*

prudery ['pru:dəri] *n*, *pl* **-eries** : mojigatería *f*, gazmoñería *f*

prudish ['pru:dɪʃ] *adj* : mojigato, gazmoño

prune[1] ['pru:n] *vt* **pruned; pruning** : podar (arbustos, etc.), acortar (un texto), recortar (gastos, etc.)

prune[2] *n* : ciruela *f* pasa

prurient ['prʊriənt] *adj* : lascivo

pry ['praɪ] *v* **pried; prying** *vi* : curiosear, huronear ⟨to pry into other people's business : meterse uno en lo que no le importa⟩ — *vt* *or* **to pry open** : abrir (con una palanca), apalancar

psalm ['sɑm, 'sɑlm] *n* : salmo *m*

pseudonym ['su:də,nɪm] *n* : seudónimo *m*

psoriasis [sə'raɪəsɪs] *n* : soriasis *f*, psoriasis *f*

psyche ['saɪki] *n* : psique *f*, psiquis *f*

psychedelic[1] [,saɪkə'dɛlɪk] *adj* psicodélico

psychedelic[2] *n* : droga *f* psicodélica

psychiatric [,saɪki'ætrɪk] *adj* : psiquiátrico, siquiátrico

psychiatrist [sə'kaɪətrɪst, saɪ-] *n* : psiquiatra *mf*, siquiatra *mf*

psychiatry [sə'kaɪətri, saɪ-] *n* : psiquiatría *f*, siquiatría *f*

psychic[1] ['saɪkɪk] *adj* **1** : psíquico, síquico (en psicología) **2** CLAIRVOYANT : clarividente

psychic[2] *n* : vidente *mf*, clarividente *mf*

psychoanalysis [,saɪkoə'næləsɪs] *n*, *pl* **-yses** : psicoanálisis *m*, sicoanálisis *m*

psychoanalyst [,saɪko'ænəlɪst] *n* : psicoanalista *mf*, sicoanalista *mf*

psychoanalytic [,saɪkoˌænəl'ɪtɪk] *adj* : psicoanalítico, sicoanalítico

psychoanalyze [,saɪko'ænəˌlaɪz] *vt* **-lyzed; -lyzing** : psicoanalizar, sicoanalizar

psychological [,saɪkə'lɑʤɪkəl] *adj* : psicológico, sicológico — **psychologically** *adv*

psychologist [saɪ'kɑləʤɪst] *n* : psicólogo *m*, -ga *f*; sicólogo *m*, -ga *f*

psychology [saɪ'kɑləʤi] *n*, *pl* **-gies** : psicología *f*, sicología *f*

psychopath ['saɪkə,pæθ] *n* : psicópata *mf*, sicópata *mf*

psychopathic [,saɪkə'pæθɪk] *adj* : psicopático, sicopático

psychosis [saɪ'ko:sɪs] *n*, *pl* **-choses** [-'ko:,si:z] : psicosis *f*, sicosis *f*

psychosomatic [,saɪkosə'mætɪk] *adj* : psicosomático, sicosomático

psychotherapist [,saɪko'θɛrəpɪst] *n* : psicoterapeuta *mf*, sicoterapeuta *mf*

psychotherapy [,saɪko'θɛrəpi] *n*, *pl* **-pies** : psicoterapia *f*, sicoterapia *f*

psychotic[1] [saɪ'kɑtɪk] *adj* : psicótico, sicótico

psychotic[2] *n* : psicótico *m*, -ca *f*; sicótico *m*, -ca *f*

pub ['pʌb] *n* : cervecería *f*, taberna *m*, bar *m*

puberty ['pju:bərti] *n* : pubertad *f*

pubic ['pju:bɪk] *adj* : pubiano, púbico

public[1] ['pʌblɪk] *adj* **1** : público ⟨public opinion : opinión pública⟩ ⟨a public figure : un personaje público⟩ **2 to go public** : salir a la bolsa, comenzar/empezar a cotizar en (la) bolsa (dícese de una empresa) **3 to go public with** REVEAL : revelar — **publicly** *adv*

public[2] *n* : público *m*

publication [,pʌblə'keɪʃən] *n* : publicación *f*

publicist ['pʌbləsɪst] *n* : publicista *mf*

publicity [pə'blɪsəti] *n* : publicidad *f*

publicize ['pʌblə,saɪz] *vt* **-cized; -cizing** : publicitar

public relations *npl* : relaciones *fpl* públicas

public school *n* : escuela *f* pública

public-spirited *adj* : de espíritu cívico

public transit *n* : transporte *m* público

publish ['pʌblɪʃ] *vt* : publicar

publisher ['pʌblɪʃər] *n* : casa *f* editorial (compañía); editor *m*, -tora *f* (persona)

publishing ['pʌblɪʃɪŋ] *n* : industria *f* editorial

pucker[1] ['pʌkər] *vt* : fruncir, arrugar — *vi* : arrugarse

pucker[2] *n* : arruga *f*, fruncido *m*

pudding ['pʊdɪŋ] *n* : budín *m*, pudín *m*

puddle ['pʌdəl] *n* : charco *m*

pudgy ['pʌʤi] *adj* **pudgier; -est** : regordete *fam*, rechoncho *fam*, gordinflón *fam*

puerile ['pjʊrəl] *adj* : pueril

Puerto Rican[1] [,pwertə'ri:kən, ,portə-] : puertorriqueño

Puerto Rican[2] n : puertorriqueño m, -ña f

puff[1] ['pʌf] vi **1** BLOW : soplar **2** PANT : resoplar, jadear **3 to puff up** SWELL : hincharse — vt **1** BLOW : soplar ⟨to puff smoke : echar humo⟩ **2** INFLATE : inflar, hinchar ⟨to puff out one's cheeks : inflar las mejillas⟩

puff[2] n **1** GUST : soplo m, ráfaga f, bocanada f (de humo) **2** DRAW : chupada f (a un cigarrillo) **3** SWELLING : hinchazón f **4 cream puff** : pastelito m de crema **5 powder puff** : borla f

puff pastry n : hojaldre m

puffy ['pʌfi] adj **puffier; -est 1** SWOLLEN : hinchado, inflado **2** SPONGY : esponjoso, suave

pug ['pʌg] n **1** : doguillo m (perro) **2 or pug nose** : nariz f achatada

pugnacious [ˌpʌg'neɪʃəs] adj : pugnaz, agresivo

pug-nosed ['pʌg'noːzd] adj : de nariz chata

puke ['pjuːk] vi **puked; puking** fam : vomitar, devolver

pull[1] ['pʊl, 'pʌl] vt **1** DRAW, TUG : tirar de, jalar **2** EXTRACT : sacar, extraer ⟨to pull teeth : sacar muelas⟩ ⟨to pull a gun on someone : amenazar a alguien con una pistola⟩ **3** TEAR : desgarrarse (un músculo, etc.) **4** DO : hacer (una broma, un turno, etc.) ⟨to pull a heist : dar un golpe⟩ ⟨to pull an all-nighter : trasnochar (estudiando, etc.)⟩ **5 to pull a fast one on** DECEIVE : engañar, jugarle una mala pasada a **6 to pull apart** SEPARATE, TEAR : separar, hacer pedazos **7 to pull aside** : llevar aparte, llevar a un lado **8 to pull down** : bajar, echar abajo, derribar (un edificio) **9 to pull in** ATTRACT : atraer (clientes, etc.) ⟨to pull in votes : conseguir votos⟩ **10 to pull off** REMOVE : sacar, quitar **11 to pull off** ACHIEVE : conseguir, lograr **12 to pull oneself together** : calmarse, tranquilizarse **13 to pull out** EXTRACT : sacar, arrancar **14 to pull out** RECALL, WITHDRAW : retirar **15 to pull over** : parar ⟨he was pulled over for speeding : lo pararon por exceso de velocidad⟩ **16 to pull through** SUSTAIN : sacar adelante **17 to pull up** RAISE : levantar, subir **18 to pull up** STOP : parar (un vehículo) — vi **1** DRAW, TUG : tirar, jalar **2** (indicating movement of a vehicle in a specific direction) : ⟨he pulled off the highway : salió de la carretera⟩ ⟨they pulled in front of us : se nos metieron delante⟩ ⟨to pull to a stop : pararse⟩ **3 to pull ahead** : tomar la delantera **4 to pull at** : tirar, dar tirones de **5 to pull away** : alejarse **6 to pull back** : echarse atrás **7 to pull for** : apoyar a, alentar **8 to pull out** : tirar de, jalar **9 to pull on** DON : ponerse **10 to pull out** LEAVE : salir, arrancar (en un vehículo) **11 to pull out** WITHDRAW : retirarse **12 to pull over** : hacerse a un lado (en un vehículo) **13 to pull through** SURVIVE, ENDURE : sobrevivir, salir adelante **14 to pull together** COOPERATE : trabajar juntos, cooperar **15 to pull up** STOP : parar (en un vehículo)

pull[2] n **1** TUG : tirón m, jalón m ⟨he gave it a pull : le dio un tirón⟩ **2** ATTRACTION : atracción f, fuerza f ⟨the pull of gravity : la fuerza de la gravedad⟩ **3** INFLUENCE : influencia f **4** HANDLE : tirador m (de un cajón, etc.) **5 bell pull** : cuerda f

pullet ['pʊlət] n : polla f, gallina f (joven)

pulley ['pʊli] n, pl **-leys** : polea f

pullover ['pʊlˌoːvər] n : suéter m

pulmonary ['pʊlməˌneri, 'pʌl-] adj : pulmonar

pulp ['pʌlp] n **1** : pulpa f (de una fruta, etc.) **2** MASH : papilla f, pasta f ⟨wood pulp : pasta de papel, pulpa de papel⟩ ⟨to beat to a pulp : hacer papilla a alguien⟩ **3** : pulpa f (de los dientes)

pulpit ['pʊlˌpɪt] n : púlpito m

pulsate ['pʌlˌseɪt] vi **-sated; -sating 1** BEAT : latir, palpitar **2** VIBRATE : vibrar

pulsation [ˌpʌl'seɪʃən] n : pulsación f

pulse ['pʌls] n : pulso m

pulverize ['pʌlvəˌraɪz] vt **-ized; -izing** : pulverizar

puma ['puːmə, 'pjuː-] n : puma m; león m, leona f (in various countries)

pumice ['pʌməs] n : piedra f pómez

pummel ['pʌməl] vt **-meled; -meling** : aporrear, apalear

pump[1] ['pʌmp] vt **1** : bombear ⟨to pump water : bombear agua⟩ ⟨to pump (up) a tire : inflar una llanta⟩ **2** : mover (una manivela, un pedal, etc.) de arriba abajo ⟨to pump someone's hand : darle un fuerte apretón de manos a alguien⟩ **3 to pump iron** : hacer pesas **4 to pump out** : sacar, vaciar (con una bomba) **5 to pump out** CHURN OUT : producir (en masa) — vi : bombear

pump[2] n **1** : bomba f ⟨water pump : bomba de agua⟩ **2** SHOE : zapato m de tacón

pumpernickel ['pʌmpərˌnɪkəl] n : pan m negro de centeno

pumpkin ['pʌmpkɪn, 'pʌŋkən] n : calabaza f, zapallo m Arg, Chile, Peru, Uru

pun[1] ['pʌn] vi **punned; punning** : hacer juegos de palabras

pun[2] n : juego m de palabras, albur m Mex

punch[1] ['pʌntʃ] vt **1** HIT : darle un puñetazo (a alguien), golpear ⟨she punched him in the nose : le dio un puñetazo en la nariz⟩ **2** PERFORATE : perforar (papel, etc.), picar (un boleto)

punch[2] n **1** : perforadora f ⟨paper punch : perforadora de papel⟩ **2** BLOW : golpe m, puñetazo m **3** : ponche m ⟨fruit punch : ponche de frutas⟩

punch line n : remate m

punctilious [pəŋk'tɪliəs] adj : puntilloso

punctual ['pʌŋktʃuəl] adj : puntual

punctuality [ˌpʌŋktʃu'æləti] n : puntualidad f

punctually ['pʌŋktʃuəli] adv : puntualmente, a tiempo

punctuate ['pʌŋktʃuˌeɪt] vt **-ated; -ating** : puntuar

punctuation [ˌpʌŋktʃu'eɪʃən] n : puntuación f

punctuation mark *n* : signo *m* de puntuación

puncture[1] ['pʌŋktʃər] *vt* **-tured; -turing** : pinchar, punzar, perforar, ponchar *Mex*

puncture[2] *n* : pinchazo *m*, ponchadura *f* *Mex*

pundit ['pʌndɪt] *n* : experto *m*, -ta *f*

pungency ['pʌndʒənsi] *n* : acritud *f*, acrimonia *f*

pungent ['pʌndʒənt] *adj* : acre

punish ['pʌnɪʃ] *vt* : castigar

punishable ['pʌnɪʃəbəl] *adj* : punible

punishment ['pʌnɪʃmənt] *n* : castigo *m*

punitive ['pju:nətɪv] *adj* : punitivo

punk[1] ['pʌŋk] *adj* : punk

punk[2] *n* **1** *or* **punk rock** : punk *m* (música) **2** *or* **punk rocker** : punk *mf* **3** HOODLUM : matón *m*, maleante *mf*

punt[1] ['pʌnt] *vt* : impulsar (un barco) con una pértiga — *vi* : despejar (en deportes)

punt[2] *n* **1** : batea *f* (barco) **2** : patada *f* de despeje (en deportes)

puny ['pju:ni] *adj* **punier; -est** : enclenque, endeble

pup ['pʌp] *n* : cachorro *m*, -rra *f* (de un perro); cría *f* (de otros animales)

pupa ['pju:pə] *n*, *pl* **-pae** [-pi:, -ˌpaɪ] *or* **-pas** : crisálida *f*, pupa *f*

pupil ['pju:pəl] *n* **1** : alumno *m*, -na *f* (de colegio) **2** : pupila *f* (del ojo)

puppet ['pʌpət] *n* : títere *m*, marioneta *f*

puppeteer [ˌpʌpə'tɪr] *n* : titiritero *m*, -ra *f*

puppy ['pʌpi] *n*, *pl* **-pies** : cachorro *m*, -rra *f*

purchase[1] ['pərtʃəs] *vt* **-chased; -chasing** : comprar — **purchaser** *n*

purchase[2] *n* **1** PURCHASING : compra *f*, adquisición *f* **2** : compra *f* ⟨last-minute purchases : compras de última hora⟩ **3** GRIP : agarre *m*, asidero *m* ⟨she got a firm purchase on the wheel : se agarró bien del volante⟩

purchase order *n* : orden *f* de compra

pure ['pjur] *adj* **purer; purest** : puro

purebred ['pjurˌbred] *adj* : de pura raza

puree[1] [pju'reɪ, -'ri:] *vt* **-reed; -reeing** : hacer un puré con

puree[2] *n* : puré *m*

purely ['pjurli] *adv* **1** WHOLLY : puramente, completamente ⟨purely by chance : por pura casualidad⟩ **2** SIMPLY : sencillamente, meramente

purgative ['pərgətɪv] *n* : purgante *m*

purgatory ['pərgəˌtori] *n*, *pl* **-ries** : purgatorio *m*

purge[1] ['pərdʒ] *vt* **purged; purging** : purgar

purge[2] *n* : purga *f*

purification [ˌpjurəfə'keɪʃən] *n* : purificación *f*

purifier ['pjurəˌfaɪər] *n* : purificador *m*

purify ['pjurəˌfaɪ] *vt* **-fied; -fying** : purificar

puritan ['pjurətən] *n* : puritano *m*, -na *f* — **puritan** *adj*

puritanical [ˌpjurə'tænɪkəl] *adj* : puritano

purity ['pjurəti] *n* : pureza *f*

purl[1] ['pərl] *v* : tejer al revés, tejer del revés

purl[2] *n* : punto *m* del revés

purloin [pər'lɔɪn, 'pərˌlɔɪn] *vt* : hurtar, robar

purple ['pərpəl] *n* : morado *m*, color *m* púrpura

purport [pər'port] *vt* : pretender ⟨to purport to be : pretender ser⟩

purpose ['pərpəs] *n* **1** INTENTION : propósito *m*, intención *f* ⟨on purpose : a propósito, adrede⟩ ⟨for a purpose : por una razón⟩ ⟨for all practical purposes : a efectos prácticos⟩ **2** FUNCTION : función *f* ⟨to serve a purpose : servir de algo⟩ **3** RESOLUTION : resolución *f*, determinación *f* ⟨to have a sense of purpose : tener un norte en la vida⟩

purposeful ['pərpəsfəl] *adj* : determinado, decidido, resuelto

purposefully ['pərpəsfəli] *adv* : decididamente, resueltamente

purposely ['pərpəsli] *adv* : intencionadamente, a propósito, adrede

purr[1] ['pər] *vi* : ronronear

purr[2] *n* : ronroneo *m*

purse[1] ['pərs] *vt* **pursed; pursing** : fruncir ⟨to purse one's lips : fruncir la boca⟩

purse[2] *n* **1** HANDBAG : cartera *f*, bolsa *f*, bolsa *f Mex* ⟨a change purse : un monedero⟩ **2** FUNDS : fondos *mpl* **3** PRIZE : premio *m*

purser ['pərsər] *n* : sobrecargo *mf*

pursue [pər'su:] *vt* **-sued; -suing 1** CHASE : perseguir **2** SEEK : buscar, tratar de encontrar ⟨to pursue pleasure : buscar el placer⟩ **3** FOLLOW : seguir ⟨the road pursues a northerly course : el camino sigue hacia al norte⟩ **4** : dedicarse a ⟨to pursue a hobby : dedicarse a un pasatiempo⟩

pursuer [pər'su:ər] *n* : perseguidor *m*, -dora *f*

pursuit [pər'su:t] *n* **1** CHASE : persecución *f* **2** SEARCH : búsqueda *f*, busca *f* **3** ACTIVITY : actividad *f*, pasatiempo *m*

purveyor [pər'veɪər] *n* : proveedor *m*, -dora *f*

pus ['pʌs] *n* : pus *m*

push[1] ['pʊʃ] *vt* **1** : empujar ⟨he pushed the chair back/forward : empujó la silla hacia atrás/adelante⟩ ⟨she pushed him aside : lo apartó (de un empujón)⟩ **2** PRESS : apretar, pulsar (un botón, etc.) **3** PRESSURE, URGE : presionar ⟨to push someone to do something : presionar a alguien a hacer algo⟩ ⟨to push someone too hard : exigir demasiado de alguien⟩ **4** STRESS : recalcar ⟨to push the point/issue : insistir⟩ **5** PROVOKE, PESTER : provocar, fastidiar ⟨don't push him too far : no lo provoques⟩ **6** FORCE : hacer cambiar ⟨to push prices up/down : hacer subir/bajar los precios⟩ **7** PROMOTE : promocionar **8** : pasar (drogas) **9** APPROACH : rayar, rozar (una edad, un número, un límite) **10 to push around** BULLY : intimidar, mangonear **11 to push back** : aplazar, postergar (una fecha) **12 to push it (too far)** : pasarse **13 to push through** : conseguir que se apruebe **14 to push one's luck** : tentar a la suerte **15 to push over** : echar abajo, tirar al suelo — *vi* **1** : empujar **2** INSIST : insistir, presionar **3 to push ahead/forward/on** : seguir adelante **4 to push for** DEMAND : exigir, presionar para **5 to push off** LEAVE : marcharse, irse, largarse *fam*

push² *n* **1** SHOVE : empujón *m* **2** DRIVE : empuje *m*, energía *f*, dinamismo *m* **3** EFFORT : esfuerzo *m*

push–button ['pʊʃˌbʌtən] *adj* : de botones

pusher ['pʊʃər] *n* : camello *m fam*

push-up ['pʊʃˌʌp] *n* : flexión *f*

pushy ['pʊʃi] *adj* **pushier; -est** : mandón, prepotente

pussy ['pʊsi] *n, pl* **pussies** : gatito *m*, -ta *f*; minino *m*, -na *f*

pussy willow *n* : sauce *m* blanco

pustule ['pʌsˌtʃuːl] *n* : pústula *f*

put ['pʊt] *v* **put; putting** *vt* **1** PLACE : poner, colocar ⟨put it on the table : ponlo en la mesa⟩ ⟨put the car in the garage : guarda el auto en el garaje⟩ ⟨she put her arms around me : me abrazó⟩ **2** INSERT : meter ⟨to poner (en cierto estado) ⟨it put her in a good mood : la puso de buen humor⟩ ⟨to put into effect : poner en práctica⟩ **4** IMPOSE : imponer ⟨they put a tax on it : lo gravaron con un impuesto⟩ **5** SUBJECT : someter, poner ⟨to put to the test : poner a prueba⟩ ⟨to put to death : ejecutar⟩ **6** EXPRESS : expresar, decir ⟨he put it simply : lo dijo sencillamente⟩ **7** APPLY : aplicar ⟨to put one's mind to something : proponerse hacer algo⟩ **8** SET : poner ⟨I put him to work : lo puse a trabajar⟩ **9** ATTACH : dar ⟨to put a high value on : dar gran valor a⟩ **10** PRESENT : presentar, exponer ⟨to put a question to someone : hacerle una pregunta a alguien⟩ **11 to put across/over** : comunicar (un mensaje, etc.) **12 to put oneself across/over as** : dar la impresión de ser **13 to put aside** : dejar a un lado **14 to put aside** RESERVE : guardar, reservar **15 to put at** : calcular en ⟨they put the number of deaths at 3,000 : calculan en 3000 la cifra de muertos⟩ **16 to put away** SAVE : guardar **17 to put back/away** : volver a su sitio **18 to put before** : presentar a **19 to put behind one** : olvidar ⟨to put the past behind you : olvidar el pasado⟩ **20 to put down** DEPOSIT : dejar (en el suelo, etc.) **21 to put down** SUPPRESS : aplastar, suprimir **22 to put down** *fam* DISPARAGE : menospreciar **23 to put down** ATTRIBUTE : atribuir ⟨she put it down to luck : lo atribuyó a la suerte⟩ **24 to put down** : dejar (un depósito) **25 to put down** WRITE DOWN : escribir, apuntar **26 to put down** INSTALL, LAY : poner, colocar **27 to put down** EUTHANIZE : sacrificar **28 to put forth/forward** PROPOSE : proponer, presentar **29 to put in** INVEST : dedicar (tiempo), invertir (dinero) ⟨to put in a lot of effort : esforzarse mucho⟩ **30 to put in** DO : hacer, trabajar (horas extras, etc.) ⟨to put in one's time : cumplir su condena⟩ **31 to**

put in PRESENT : presentar, hacer (una oferta, etc.) **32 to put in** INSTALL : instalar **33 to put in** MAKE : hacer (una llamada, etc.) ⟨to put in an appearance : hacer acto de presencia⟩ **34 to put in** INTERJECT : hacer (un comentario) **35 to put in a good word for** RECOMMEND, PRAISE : recomendar, hablar bien de **36 to put into** INVEST : dedicar (tiempo) a, invertir (dinero) en ⟨to put effort into something : esforzarse en algo⟩ ⟨to put thought into something : pensar algo⟩ **37 to put off** DEFER : aplazar, posponer **38 to put off** STALL, DISTRACT : hacer esperar, distraer **39 to put off** DISSUADE, DISCOURAGE : disuadir, desalentar ⟨it put him off his food : le quitó las ganas de comer⟩ **40 to put on** DON : ponerse (ropa, etc.) **41 to put on** ASSUME : afectar, adoptar ⟨to put on a brave face : ponerle buena cara a algo/alguien⟩ **42 to put on** ADD, INCREASE : añadir, aumentar ⟨to put on weight : engordar, ganar peso⟩ **43 to put on** PRODUCE : presentar (una obra de teatro, etc.) **44 to put on** TURN ON, START : encender (luces, etc.), poner (música) ⟨to put the water on (to boil) : poner el agua a calentar⟩ **45 to put money (etc.) on** : apostar dinero (etc.) por **46 to put on** : poner en (una lista, un menú, etc.) **47 to put on** : poner a (régimen, etc.), recetarle (medicina) a **48 to put on (the phone)** ⟨put Dad on (the phone) : pásame a papá⟩ **49 to put someone on** *fam* TEASE : tomarle el pelo a alguien **50 to put out** : apagar (llamas, luces, etc.) **51 to put out** BOTHER, INCONVENIENCE : molestar, incomodar **52 to put out** : sacar (la basura, etc.) **53 to put out** DISPLAY : disponer **54 to put out** EXTEND : extender, tender (la mano) **55 to put out** PRODUCE : producir ⟨to put out RELEASE, ISSUE : sacar (un álbum, etc.), publicar (un estudio, etc.), emitir (un aviso, etc.) ⟨to put word out that . . . : hacer correr la voz que . . .⟩ **57 to put something/one over on** TRICK : engañar **58 to put through** : pasar (una llamada) **59 to put through** : hacer pasar (dificultades, etc.) ⟨she put us through hell : nos hizo pasar las de Caín⟩ **60 to put someone through college** : pagarle los estudios a alguien **61 to put together** COMBINE : reunir, juntar **62 to put together** PREPARE : preparar, hacer **63 to put together** ASSEMBLE : armar, montar **64 to put up** RAISE : subir, levantar (la mano, etc.), izar (una bandera) ⟨to put up one's hair : recoger el pelo⟩ **65 to put up** PRESERVE : hacer conserva de **66 to put up** LODGE : alojar **67 to put up** BUILD, ERECT, ASSEMBLE : construir, levantar, montar **68 to put up** HANG : poner, colgar **69 to put up** : oponer ⟨to put up a fight/struggle : oponer resistencia⟩ ⟨to put up a fuss : armar un lío⟩ **70 to put up** OFFER UP : ofrecer ⟨to put up for sale : poner a la venta⟩ ⟨to put up for adoption : dar en adopción⟩ **71 to put**

up PRESENT : presentar (argumentos), hacer (una propuesta) **72 to put up** PROVIDE : poner (dinero), ofrecer (una recompensa) **73 to put someone up to something** : incitar a alguien a algo, animar a alguien a hacer algo — *vi* **1 to put forth** : echar, extender **2 to put in for** REQUEST : solicitar (una promoción, etc.) **3 to put to sea** : hacerse a la mar **4 to put up with** : aguantar, soportar

putrefy [ˈpjuːtrəˌfaɪ] *v* **-fied; -fying** *vt* : pudrir — *vi* : pudrirse

putrid [ˈpjuːtrɪd] *adj* : putrefacto, pútrido

putter¹ [ˈpʌtər] *vi* **or to putter around** : entretenerse

putty¹ [ˈpʌti] *vt* **-tied; -tying** : poner masilla en

putty² *n, pl* **-ties** : masilla *f*

puzzle¹ [ˈpʌzəl] *vt* **-zled; -zling 1** CONFUSE : confundir, dejar perplejo **2 to puzzle out** : dar vueltas a, tratar de resolver

puzzle² *n* **1** : rompecabezas *m* ⟨a crossword puzzle : un crucigrama⟩ **2** MYSTERY : misterio *m*, enigma *m*

puzzlement [ˈpʌzəlmənt] *n* : desconcierto *m*, perplejidad *f*

puzzling *adj* : desconcertante

pygmy [ˈpɪɡmi] *adj* : enano, pigmeo

Pygmy *n, pl* **-mies** : pigmeo *m*, -mea *f*

pylon [ˈpaɪˌlɑn, -lən] *n* **1** : torre *f* de conducta eléctrica **2** : pilón *m* (de un puente)

pyramid [ˈpɪrəˌmɪd] *n* : pirámide *f*

pyre [ˈpaɪr] *n* : pira *f*

pyromania [ˌpaɪroˈmeɪniə] *n* : piromanía *f*

pyromaniac [ˌpaɪroˈmeɪniˌæk] *n* : pirómano *m*, -na *f*

pyrotechnics [ˌpaɪroˈtɛknɪks] *npl* **1** FIREWORKS : fuegos *mpl* artificiales **2** DISPLAY, SHOW : espectáculo *m*, muestra *f* de virtuosismo ⟨computer pyrotechnics : efectos especiales hechos por computadora⟩ — **pyrotechnic** *adj*

Pyrrhic [ˈpɪrɪk] *adj* : pírrico

python [ˈpaɪˌθɑn, -θən] *n* : pitón *f*, serpiente *f* pitón

Q

q [ˈkjuː] *n, pl* **q's** *or* **qs** [ˈkjuːz] : decimoséptima letra del alfabeto inglés

Q–tips [ˈkjuːˌtɪps] *trademark* se usa para hisopos

quack¹ [ˈkwæk] *vi* : graznar

quack² *n* **1** : graznido *m* (de pato) **2** CHARLATAN : curandero *m*, -ra *f*; matasanos *m fam*

quad [ˈkwɑd] → **quadrangle** 1

quadrangle [ˈkwɑˌdræŋɡəl] *n* **1** COURTYARD : patio *m* interior (de una universidad, etc.) **2** → **quadrilateral**

quadrant [ˈkwɑdrənt] *n* : cuadrante *m*

quadrilateral [ˌkwɑdrəˈlætərəl] *n* : cuadrilátero *m*

quadruple¹ [kwɑˈdruːpəl, -ˈdrʌ-; ˈkwɑdrə-] *v* **-pled; -pling** *vt* : cuadruplicar — *vi* : cuadruplicarse

quadruple² *adj* : cuádruple

quadruplet [kwɑˈdruːplət, -ˈdrʌ-; ˈkwɑdrə-] *n* : cuatrillizo *m*, -za *f*

quagmire [ˈkwæɡˌmaɪr, ˈkwɑɡ-] *n* **1** : lodazal *m*, barrizal *m* **2** PREDICAMENT : atolladero *m*

quail¹ [ˈkweɪl] *n, pl* **quail** *or* **quails** : codorniz *f*

quaint [ˈkweɪnt] *adj* **1** ODD : extraño, curioso **2** PICTURESQUE : pintoresco — **quaintly** *adv*

quake¹ [ˈkweɪk] *vi* **quaked; quaking** : temblar

quake² *n* : temblor *m*, terremoto *m*

Quaker [ˈkweɪkər] *n* : cuáquero *m*, -ra *f* — **Quaker** *adj*

qualification [ˌkwɑləfəˈkeɪʃən] *n* **1** LIMITATION, RESERVATION : reserva *f*, limitación *f* ⟨without qualification : sin reservas⟩ **2** REQUIREMENT : requisito *m* **3** **qualifications** *npl* ABILITY : aptitud *f*, capacidad *f*

qualified [ˈkwɑləˌfaɪd] *adj* **1** : capacitado, habilitado ⟨to be qualified to : ser capacitado para⟩ ⟨she's qualified for the job : cumple los requisitos para el puesto⟩ **2** LIMITED : limitado

qualifier [ˈkwɑləˌfaɪər] *n* **1** : clasificador *m*, -da *f* (en deportes) **2** : calificativo *m* (en gramática)

qualify [ˈkwɑləˌfaɪ] *v* **-fied; -fying** *vt* **1** : matizar ⟨to qualify a statement : matizar una declaración⟩ **2** : calificar (en gramática) **3** : habilitar, capacitar ⟨the certificate qualified her to teach : el certificado la habilitó para enseñar⟩ — *vi* **1** : obtener el título, recibirse ⟨to qualify as an engineer : recibirse de ingeniero⟩ **2** : tener derecho ⟨to qualify for assistance : tener derecho a recibir ayuda⟩ **3** : clasificarse (en deportes)

qualitative [ˈkwɑləˌteɪtɪv] *adj* : cualitativo

quality [ˈkwɑləti] *n, pl* **-ties 1** NATURE : carácter *m* **2** ATTRIBUTE : cualidad *f* **3** GRADE : calidad *f* ⟨of good quality : de buena calidad⟩

qualm [ˈkwɑm, ˈkwɑlm, ˈkwɔm] *n* **1** MISGIVING : duda *f*, aprensión *f* **2** RESERVATION, SCRUPLE : escrúpulo *m*, reparo *m*

quandary [ˈkwɑndri] *n, pl* **-ries** : dilema *m*

quantify [ˈkwɑntəˌfaɪ] *vt* **-fied; -fying** : cuantificar

quantitative [ˈkwɑntəˌteɪtɪv] *adj* : cuantitativo

quantity [ˈkwɑntəti] *n, pl* **-ties** : cantidad *f*

quantum¹ [ˈkwɑntəm] *n* : cuanto *m* (en física)

quantum² *adj* : cuántico ⟨quantum theory : teoría cuántica⟩

quarantine[1] [ˈkwɔrənˌtiːn] vt **-tined; -tining** : poner en cuarentena

quarantine[2] n : cuarentena f

quarrel[1] [ˈkwɔrəl] vi **-reled** or **-relled; -reling** or **-relling** : pelearse, reñir, discutir

quarrel[2] n : pelea f, riña f, disputa f

quarrelsome [ˈkwɔrəlsəm] adj : pendenciero, discutidor

quarry[1] [ˈkwɔri] vt **quarried; quarrying 1** EXTRACT : extraer (mármol, etc.) **2** EXCAVATE : excavar (un cerro, etc.)

quarry[2] n, pl **quarries 1** : cantera f **2** PREY : presa f

quart [ˈkwɔrt] n : cuarto m de galón

quarter[1] [ˈkwɔrtər] vt **1** : dividir en cuatro partes **2** LODGE : alojar, acuartelar (tropas)

quarter[2] adj : cuarto ⟨a quarter hour/mile : un cuarto de hora/milla⟩

quarter[3] n **1** : cuarto m, cuarta parte f ⟨a foot and a quarter : un pie y cuarto⟩ ⟨a quarter after three : las tres y cuarto⟩ **2** : moneda f de 25 centavos, cuarto m de dólar **3** DISTRICT : barrio m ⟨business quarter : barrio comercial⟩ **4** PLACE : parte f ⟨from all quarters : de todas partes⟩ ⟨at close quarters : de muy cerca⟩ **5** MERCY : clemencia f, cuartel m ⟨to give no quarter : no dar cuartel⟩ **6 quarters** npl LODGING : alojamiento m, cuartel m (militar)

quarterback [ˈkwɔrtərˌbæk] n : mariscal m de campo

quarterfinal [ˌkwɔrtərˈfaɪnəl] n : cuarto m de final

quarterly[1] [ˈkwɔrtərli] adv : cada tres meses, trimestralmente

quarterly[2] adj : trimestral

quarterly[3] n, pl **-lies** : publicación f trimestral

quartermaster [ˈkwɔrtərˌmæstər] n : intendente m

quarter note n : negra f (en música)

quartet [kwɔrˈtet] n : cuarteto m

quartz [ˈkwɔrts] n : cuarzo m

quash [ˈkwɑʃ, ˈkwɔʃ] vt **1** ANNUL : anular **2** QUELL : sofocar, aplastar

quasi- [ˈkweɪˌzaɪ, ˈkwɑziˌ] pref : cuasi-

quaver[1] [ˈkweɪvər] vi **1** SHAKE : temblar ⟨her voice was quavering : le temblaba la voz⟩ **2** TRILL : trinar

quaver[2] n : temblor m (de la voz)

quay [ˈkiː, ˈkeɪ, ˈkweɪ] n : muelle m

queasiness [ˈkwiːzinəs] n : mareo m, náusea f

queasy [ˈkwiːzi] adj **queasier; -est** : mareado

quebracho [keɪˈbrɑtʃoː, kɪ-] or **quebracho tree** n : quebracho m

queen [ˈkwiːn] n : reina f

queenly [ˈkwiːnli] adj **queenlier; -est** : de reina, regio

queer[1] [ˈkwɪr] adj **1** : extraño, raro, curioso **2** usu offensive : homosexual — **queerly** adv

queer[2] n usu offensive : homosexual mf

quell [ˈkwɛl] vt : aplastar, sofocar

quench [ˈkwɛntʃ] vt **1** EXTINGUISH : apagar, sofocar **2** SATISFY : saciar, satisfacer (la sed)

query[1] [ˈkwɪri, ˈkwɛr-] vt **-ried; -rying 1** ASK : preguntar, interrogar ⟨to query someone about something : preguntarle a alguien sobre algo⟩ **2** QUESTION, CHALLENGE : cuestionar

query[2] n, pl **-ries 1** QUESTION : pregunta f **2** DOUBT : duda f

quesadilla [ˌkeɪsəˈdiːə] n : quesadilla f

quest [ˈkwɛst] v : buscar

quest[2] n : búsqueda f

question[1] [ˈkwɛstʃən] vt **1** ASK : preguntar **2** DOUBT : poner en duda, cuestionar **3** INTERROGATE : interrogar — vi INQUIRE : inquirir, preguntar

question[2] n **1** QUERY : pregunta f ⟨to ask a question : hacer una pregunta⟩ **2** ISSUE : cuestión f, asunto m, problema f **3** POSSIBILITY : posibilidad f ⟨it's out of the question : es absolutamente imposible⟩ **4** DOUBT : duda f ⟨without question : sin duda⟩ ⟨to call into question : poner en duda⟩ ⟨there's no question about it : no cabe duda⟩ **5 in question** : en cuestión ⟨the book in question : el libro en cuestión⟩

questionable [ˈkwɛstʃənəbəl] adj : cuestionable

questioner [ˈkwɛstʃənər] n : interrogador m, -dora f

questioning[1] [ˈkwɛstʃənɪŋ] adj : inquisitivo

questioning[2] n INTERROGATION : interrogatorio m, interrogación f

question mark n : signo m de interrogación

questionnaire [ˌkwɛstʃəˈnær] n : cuestionario m

quetzal [kɛtˈsɑl] n, pl **-zals** or **-zales** [-ˈsɑles] : quetzal m

queue[1] [ˈkjuː] vi **queued; quiuing** or **queueing** : hacer cola

queue[2] n LINE : cola f, fila f

quibble[1] [ˈkwɪbəl] vi **-bled; -bling** : quejarse por nimiedades ⟨to quibble about : quejarse por⟩ ⟨to quibble over : discutir sobre⟩

quibble[2] n : queja f (menor)

quiche [ˈkiːʃ] n : quiche f (pastel)

quick[1] [ˈkwɪk] adv : rápidamente

quick[2] adj **1** RAPID : rápido ⟨make it quick : date prisa⟩ ⟨a quick fix : una solución rápida⟩ ⟨she was quick to criticize us : se apresuró a criticarnos⟩ **2** ALERT, CLEVER : listo, vivo, agudo ⟨to have a quick wit/mind : ser muy agudo⟩ **3 a quick temper** : un genio vivo

quick[3] n **1** FLESH : carne f viva **2 to cut someone to the quick** : herir a alguien en lo más vivo

quicken [ˈkwɪkən] vt **1** REVIVE : resucitar **2** AROUSE : estimular, despertar **3** HASTEN : acelerar (el paso, etc.)

quickly [ˈkwɪkli] adv : rápidamente, rápido

quickness [ˈkwɪknəs] n : rapidez f

quicksand [ˈkwɪkˌsænd] n : arena f movediza

quick-tempered [ˈkwɪkˈtempərd] adj : de genio vivo

quick-witted [ˈkwɪkˈwɪtəd] adj : agudo

quid [ˈkwɪd] *n fam* POUND : libra *f* (unidad monetaria)
quiet¹ [ˈkwaɪət] *vt* 1 SILENCE : hacer callar, acallar 2 CALM : calmar, tranquilizar — *vi* **to quiet down** : calmarse, tranquilizarse
quiet² *adv* : silenciosamente
quiet³ *adj* 1 : silencioso ⟨a quiet voice : una voz baja⟩ 2 CALM : tranquilo ⟨a quiet life : una vida tranquila⟩ 3 : callado ⟨be quiet! : ¡cállate!⟩ ⟨to keep quiet about : no decir nada de⟩ 4 MILD : sosegado, suave ⟨a quiet disposition : un temperamento sosegado⟩ 5 UNOBTRUSIVE : discreto 6 SECLUDED : aislado ⟨a quiet nook : un rincón aislado⟩ — **quietly** *adv*
quiet⁴ *n* 1 CALM : calma *f*, tranquilidad *f* 2 SILENCE : silencio *m*
quietness [ˈkwaɪətnəs] *n* : suavidad *f* (de la voz, etc.), quietud *f* (de un lugar, etc.)
quietude [ˈkwaɪə,tuːd, -ˌtjuːd] *n* : quietud *f*, reposo *m*
quill [ˈkwɪl] *n* 1 : púa *f* (de un puerco espín) 2 : pluma *f* (de ave para escribir)
quilt¹ [ˈkwɪlt] *vt* : acolchar
quilt² *n* : colcha *f*, edredón *m*
quince [ˈkwɪnts] *n* : membrillo *m*
quinine [ˈkwaɪˌnaɪn] *n* : quinina *f*
quintessence [kwɪnˈtɛsənts] *n* : quintaesencia *f*
quintessential [ˌkwɪntəˈsɛtʃəl] *adj* : arquetípico
quintet [kwɪnˈtɛt] *n* : quinteto *m*
quintuple [kwɪnˈtuːpəl, -ˈtjuː-, -ˈtʌ-, ˈkwɪntə-] *adj* : quíntuplo
quintuplet [kwɪnˈtʌplət, -ˈtuː-, -ˈtjuː-, ˈkwɪntə-] *n* : quintillizo *m*, -za *f*
quip¹ [ˈkwɪp] *vi* **quipped; quipping** : bromear
quip² *n* : ocurrencia *f*, salida *f*
quirk [ˈkwərk] *n* : peculiaridad *f*, rareza *f* ⟨a quirk of fate : un capricho del destino⟩
quirky [ˈkwərki] *adj* **quirkier; -est** : peculiar, raro
quit [ˈkwɪt] *v* **quit; quitting** *vt* : dejar, abandonar ⟨to quit smoking : dejar de fumar⟩ ⟨quit complaining! : ¡deja de quejarte!⟩ ⟨quit it! : ¡basta ya!⟩ — *vi* 1 STOP : parar 2 RESIGN : dimitir, renunciar

quite [ˈkwaɪt] *adv* 1 VERY : muy, bastante ⟨quite near : bastante cerca⟩ ⟨quite ill : muy enfermo⟩ 2 COMPLETELY : completamente, totalmente ⟨I'm not quite sure : no estoy del todo seguro⟩ 3 EXACTLY : exactamente ⟨there's nothing quite like Paris : no hay como París⟩ 4 (*used as an intensifier*) ⟨that's quite enough! : ¡basta ya!⟩ ⟨that's quite all right : no fue nada⟩ ⟨I haven't seen her in quite a while : hace bastante tiempo que no la veo⟩ ⟨quite a few things : muchas cosas⟩ ⟨quite a lot/bit of money : bastante dinero⟩ ⟨quite a surprise : una gran sorpresa⟩ ⟨quite an experience : toda una experiencia⟩
quits [ˈkwɪts] *adj* **to call it quits** : quedar en paz
quitter [ˈkwɪtər] *n* : derrotista *mf*
quiver¹ [ˈkwɪvər] *vi* : temblar, estremecerse, vibrar
quiver² *n* 1 : carcaj *m*, aljaba *f* (para flechas) 2 TREMBLING : temblor *m*, estremecimiento *m*
quixotic [kwɪkˈsɑtɪk] *adj* : quijotesco
quiz¹ [ˈkwɪz] *vt* **quizzed; quizzing** 1 QUESTION : interrogar 2 TEST : hacerle una prueba a, examinar
quiz² *n, pl* **quizzes** : examen *m* corto, prueba *f*
quizzical [ˈkwɪzɪkəl] *adj* CURIOUS : curioso, interrogativo
quorum [ˈkwɔrəm] *n* : quórum *m*
quota [ˈkwoːtə] *n* : cuota *f*, cupo *m*
quotable [ˈkwoːtəbəl] *adj* : citable
quotation [kwoːˈteɪʃən] *n* 1 CITATION : cita *f* 2 ESTIMATE : presupuesto *m*, estimación *f* 3 PRICE : cotización *f*
quotation marks *npl* : comillas *fpl*
quote¹ [ˈkwoːt] *vt* **quoted; quoting** 1 CITE : citar (un pasaje, a un autor, etc.) ⟨don't quote me on that : no lo repitas⟩ ⟨he said, (and I) quote, . . . : dijo textualmente : . . .⟩ 2 VALUE : cotizar (en finanzas)
quote² *n* 1 → quotation 2 **quotes** *npl* → quotation marks 3 ESTIMATE : presupuesto *m*
quotient [ˈkwoːʃənt] *n* : cociente *m*
quotidian [kwoːˈtɪdiən] *adj* : cotidiano

R

r [ˈɑr] *n, pl* **r's** *or* **rs** [ˈɑrz] : decimoctava letra del alfabeto inglés
rabbi [ˈræˌbaɪ] *n* : rabino *m*, -na *f*
rabbit [ˈræbət] *n, pl* **-bit** *or* **-bits** : conejo *m*, -ja *f*
rabble [ˈræbəl] *n* 1 MASSES : populacho *m* 2 RIFFRAFF : chusma *f*, gentuza *f*
rabid [ˈræbɪd] *adj* 1 : rabioso, afectado con la rabia 2 FURIOUS : furioso 3 FANATIC : fanático
rabies [ˈreɪbiːz] *ns & pl* : rabia *f*

raccoon [ræˈkuːn] *n, pl* **-coon** *or* **-coons** : mapache *m*
race¹ [ˈreɪs] *vi* **raced; racing** 1 : correr, competir (en una carrera) 2 RUSH : ir a toda prisa, ir corriendo
race² *n* 1 CURRENT : corriente *f* (de agua) 2 : carrera *f* ⟨dog race : carrera de perros⟩ ⟨the presidential race : la carrera presidencial⟩ 3 : raza *f* ⟨all races and creeds : todas las razas y religiones⟩ ⟨the human race : el género humano⟩

race car n : carro/auto/coche m de carreras

race course n : pista f (de carreras)

racehorse ['reɪs,hors] n : caballo m de carreras

racer ['reɪsər] n : corredor m, -dora f

racetrack ['reɪs,træk] n : pista f (de carreras)

racial ['reɪʃəl] adj : racial ⟨racial discrimination : discriminación racial⟩ — **racially** adv

racing ['reɪsɪŋ] n : carreras fpl

racing shell → **shell²**

racism ['reɪ,sɪzəm] n : racismo m

racist ['reɪsɪst] n : racista mf

rack¹ ['ræk] vt 1 : atormentar ⟨racked with pain : atormentado por el dolor⟩ **2 to rack one's brains** : devanarse los sesos

rack² n SHELF, STAND : estante m ⟨a luggage/roof rack : un portaequipajes, una baca⟩ ⟨a coatrack : un perchero, una percha⟩

racket ['rækət] n 1 or **racquet** : raqueta f (en deportes) **2** DIN : estruendo m, bulla f, jaleo m fam **3** SWINDLE : estafa f, timo m fam

racketeer [,rækə'tɪr] n : estafador m, -dora f

racy ['reɪsi] adj **racier; -est** : subido de tono, picante

radar ['reɪ,dar] n : radar m

radial ['reɪdiəl] adj : radial

radiance ['reɪdiəns] n : resplandor m

radiant ['reɪdiənt] adj : radiante — **radiantly** adv

radiate ['reɪdi,eɪt] v **-ated; -ating** vt : irradiar (calor), emitir (luz) ⟨to radiate happiness : rebosar de alegría⟩ — vi 1 : irradiar **2 or to radiate out** SPREAD : extenderse, salir (de un centro)

radiation [,reɪdi'eɪʃən] n : radiación f

radiator ['reɪdi,eɪtər] n : radiador m

radical¹ ['rædɪkəl] adj : radical — **radically** [-kli] adv

radical² n : radical mf

radicalism ['rædɪkə,lɪzəm] n : radicalismo m

radii → **radius**

radio¹ ['reɪdi,oː] v : llamar por radio, transmitir por radio

radio² n, pl **-dios** : radio m (aparato), radio f (emisora, radiodifusión)

radioactive ['reɪdi'æktɪv] adj : radiactivo, radioactivo

radioactivity [,reɪdio,æk'tɪvəti] n, pl **-ties** : radiactividad f, radioactividad f

radio-controlled adj : teledirigido

radiologist [,reɪdi'alədʒɪst] n : radiólogo m, -ga f

radiology [,reɪdi'alədʒi] n : radiología f

radio station n : emisora f

radish ['rædɪʃ] n : rábano m

radium ['reɪdiəm] n : radio m

radius ['reɪdiəs] n, pl **radii** [-di,aɪ] : radio m

radon ['reɪ,dan] n : radón m

raffle¹ ['ræfəl] vt **-fled; -fling** : rifar, sortear

raffle² n : rifa f, sorteo m

raft ['ræft] n 1 : balsa f ⟨rubber rafts : balsas de goma⟩ **2** LOT, SLEW : montón m

rafter ['ræftər] n : par m, viga f

rafting ['ræftɪŋ] n : rafting m

rag ['ræg] n 1 CLOTH : trapo m ⟨rag doll : muñeca de trapo⟩ **2 rags** npl TATTERS : harapos mpl, andrajos mpl

ragamuffin ['rægə,mʌfən] n : pilluelo m, -la f

rage¹ ['reɪdʒ] vi **raged; raging** 1 : estar furioso, rabiar ⟨to rage against : clamar contra⟩ **2** : seguir de manera violenta ⟨the wind was raging : el viento bramaba⟩ ⟨the debate raged on : el debate continuaba desenfrenado⟩

rage² n 1 ANGER : furia f, ira f, cólera f ⟨to fly into a rage : enfurecerse⟩ **2** FAD : moda f, furor m

ragged ['rægəd] adj 1 UNEVEN : irregular, desigual **2** TORN : hecho jirones **3** TATTERED : andrajoso, harapiento

ragtime ['ræg,taɪm] n : ragtime m

raid¹ ['reɪd] vt 1 : invadir, hacer una incursión en ⟨raided by enemy troops : invadido por tropas enemigas⟩ **2** : asaltar, atracar ⟨the gang raided the warehouse : la pandilla asaltó el almacén⟩ **3** : allanar, hacer una redada ⟨police raided the house : la policía allanó la vivienda⟩

raid² n 1 : invasión f (militar) **2** : asalto m (por delincuentes) **3** : redada f, batida f, allanamiento m (por la policía)

raider ['reɪdər] n 1 ATTACKER : asaltante mf; invasor m, -sora f **2 corporate raider** : tiburón m

rail¹ ['reɪl] vi **1 to rail against** REVILE : denostar contra **2 to rail at** SCOLD : regañar, reprender

rail² n 1 BAR : barra f, barrera f **2** HANDRAIL : pasamanos m, barandilla f **3** TRACK : riel m (para ferrocarriles) **4** RAILROAD : ferrocarril m

railing ['reɪlɪŋ] n 1 : baranda f (de un balcón, etc.) **2** RAILS : verja f

raillery ['reɪləri] n, pl **-leries** : bromas fpl

railroad ['reɪl,roːd] n : ferrocarril m

railroad tie → **tie²**

railroad track → **track²**

railway ['reɪl,weɪ] n → **railroad**

raiment ['reɪmənt] n : vestiduras fpl

rain¹ ['reɪn] vi 1 : llover ⟨it's raining : está lloviendo⟩ **2 to rain down** : llover ⟨insults rained down on him : le llovieron los insultos⟩

rain² n : lluvia f

rainbow ['reɪn,boː] n : arco m iris

raincoat ['reɪn,koːt] n : impermeable m

raindrop ['reɪn,drap] n : gota f de lluvia

rainfall ['reɪn,fɔl] n : lluvia f, precipitación f

rain forest n : bosque m tropical

rainstorm ['reɪn,stɔrm] n : temporal m (de lluvia)

rainwater ['reɪn,wɔtər] n : agua f de lluvia

rainy ['reɪni] adj **rainier; -est** : lluvioso

raise¹ ['reɪz] vt **raised; -ing** 1 LIFT : levantar, subir, alzar ⟨to raise someone's spirits : levantarle el ánimo a alguien⟩ **2** ERECT : levantar, erigir **3** COLLECT : recaudar ⟨to raise money : recaudar dinero⟩ 4 REAR : criar ⟨she raised her two children : crió a sus dos niños⟩ 5 GROW : cultivar 6 INCREASE : aumentar, subir ⟨to raise one's voice : levantar la voz⟩ 7 PROMOTE : ascender 8 PROVOKE : provocar ⟨it raised a laugh : provocó una risa⟩ 9 BRING UP : sacar (temas, objeciones, etc.)

raise² n : aumento m

raisin ['reɪzən] n : pasa f

raja or **rajah** ['rɑdʒə, -dʒɑ, -ʒɑ] n : rajá m

rake¹ ['reɪk] v **raked; raking** vt 1 : rastrillar ⟨to rake (up) leaves : rastrillar las hojas⟩ 2 SWEEP : barrer ⟨raked with gunfire : barrido con balas⟩ 3 to rake it in : hacer mucho dinero — vi to rake through : revolver, hurgar en

rake² n 1 : rastrillo m 2 LIBERTINE : libertino m, -na f; calavera m

rakish ['reɪkɪʃ] adj 1 JAUNTY : desenvuelto, desenfadado 2 DISSOLUTE : libertino, disoluto

rally¹ ['ræli] v **-lied; -lying** vi 1 MEET, GATHER : reunirse, congregarse 2 RECOVER : recuperarse 3 to rally against : unirse en contra de 4 to rally around : juntarse para apoyar (algo/a alguien) 5 to rally for/behind : unirse a favor de — vt 1 ASSEMBLE : reunir (tropas, etc.) 2 RECOVER : recobrar (la fuerza, el ánimo, etc.)

rally² n, pl **-lies** : reunión f, mitin m, manifestación f

ram¹ ['ræm] v **rammed; ramming** vt 1 DRIVE : hincar, clavar ⟨he rammed it into the ground : lo hincó en la tierra⟩ 2 SMASH : estrellar, embestir — vi COLLIDE : chocar (contra), estrellarse

ram² n 1 : carnero m (animal) 2 **battering ram** : ariete m

RAM ['ræm] n : RAM f, memoria f de acceso aleatorio

Ramadan ['rɑmə,dɑn] n : Ramadán m

ramble¹ ['ræmbəl] vi **-bled; -bling** 1 WANDER : pasear, deambular 2 to ramble on : divagar, perder el hilo 3 SPREAD : trepar (dícese de una planta)

ramble² n : paseo m, excursión f

rambler ['ræmblər] n 1 WALKER : excursionista mf 2 ROSE : rosa f trepadora

rambling ['ræmblɪŋ] adj 1 : laberíntico 2 DISJOINTED : inconexo, incoherente

rambunctious [ræm'bʌŋkʃəs] adj UNRULY : alborotado

ramification [,ræməfə'keɪʃən] n : ramificación f

ramp ['ræmp] n : rampa f

rampage¹ ['ræm,peɪdʒ, ,ræm'peɪdʒ] vi **-paged; -paging** : andar arrasando todo, correr destrozando

rampage² ['ræm,peɪdʒ] n : alboroto m, frenesí m (de violencia)

rampant ['ræmpənt] adj : desenfrenado

rampart ['ræm,pɑrt] n : terraplén m, muralla f

ramrod ['ræm,rɑd] n : baqueta f

ramshackle ['ræm,ʃækəl] adj : destartalado

ran → **run**

ranch¹ ['ræntʃ] vi : trabajar en una hacienda f — vt : criar (ganado)

ranch² n 1 : hacienda f, rancho m, finca f ganadera 2 or **ranch house** : casa f (en una hacienda) 3 or **ranch house** : casa f de una sola planta

ranch dressing n : aderezo m a base de leche de manteca, mayonesa, y hierbas

rancher ['ræntʃər] n : estanciero m, -ra f; ranchero m, -ra f

rancid ['rænsɪd] adj : rancio

rancor ['ræŋkər] n : rencor m — **rancorous** ['ræŋkərəs] adj

random ['rændəm] adj 1 : fortuito, aleatorio 2 at ~ : al azar — **randomly** adv

random–access memory n : memoria f de acceso aleatorio, RAM f

rang → **ring**

range¹ ['reɪndʒ] v **ranged; ranging** vt ARRANGE : alinear, ordenar, arreglar — vi 1 ROAM : deambular 2 EXTEND : extenderse ⟨the results range widely : los resultados se extienden mucho⟩ 3 VARY : variar ⟨discounts range from 20% to 40% : los descuentos varían entre 20% y 40%⟩

range² n 1 ROW : fila f, hilera f ⟨a mountain range : una cordillera⟩ 2 GRASSLAND : pradera f, pampa f 3 STOVE : cocina f 4 VARIETY : variedad f, gama f 5 SPHERE : ámbito m, esfera f, campo m 6 REACH : registro m (de la voz), alcance m (de un arma de fuego) ⟨out of range : fuera del alcance⟩ ⟨at close range : de cerca⟩ 7 **shooting range** : campo m de tiro

ranger ['reɪndʒər] n or **forest ranger** : guardabosque mf

rangy ['reɪndʒi] adj **rangier; -est** : alto y delgado

rank¹ ['ræŋk] vt 1 RANGE : alinear, ordenar, poner en fila 2 CLASSIFY : clasificar — vi 1 to rank above : ser superior a 2 to rank among : encontrarse entre, figurar entre

rank² adj 1 SMELLY : fétido, maloliente 2 OUTRIGHT : completo, absoluto ⟨a rank injustice : una injusticia manifiesta⟩

rank³ n 1 LINE, ROW : fila f ⟨to close ranks : cerrar filas⟩ 2 GRADE, POSITION : grado m, rango m (militar) ⟨to pull rank : abusar de su autoridad⟩ 3 CLASS : categoría f, clase f 4 **ranks** npl : soldados mpl rasos

rank and file n 1 RANKS : soldados mpl rasos 2 : bases fpl (de un partido, etc.)

rankle ['ræŋkəl] v **-kled; -kling** vi : doler — vt : irritar, herir

ransack ['ræn,sæk] vt : revolver, desvalijar, registrar de arriba abajo

ransom¹ ['ræntsəm] vt : rescatar, pagar un rescate por

ransom² n : rescate m

rant ['rænt] vi or **to rant and rave** : despotricar, desvariar

rap¹ ['ræp] v **rapped; rapping** vt 1 KNOCK : golpetear, dar un golpe en 2 CRITICIZE : criticar — vi 1 CHAT : charlar, cotorrear fam 2 KNOCK : dar un golpe

rap² n **1** BLOW, KNOCK : golpe m, golpecito m **2** CHAT : charla f **3** or **rap music** : rap m **4 to take the rap** : pagar el pato fam

rapacious [rə'peɪʃəs] adj GREEDY : avaricioso, codicioso

rape¹ ['reɪp] vt **raped; raping** : violar

rape² n **1** : colza f (planta) **2** : violación f (de una persona)

rapid ['ræpɪd] adj : rápido — **rapidly** adv

rapidity [rə'pɪdəti] n : rapidez f

rapids ['ræpɪdz] npl : rápidos mpl

rapier ['reɪpɪər] n : estoque m

rapist ['reɪpɪst] n : violador m, -dora f

rapper ['ræpər] n : cantante mf de rap; rapero m, -ra f

rapport [ræ'por] n : relación f armoniosa, entendimiento m

rapprochement [,ræ,pro:ʃ'mɑnt] n : acercamiento m, aproximación f

rapt ['ræpt] adj : absorto, embelesado

rapture ['ræptʃər] n : éxtasis m

rapturous ['ræptʃərəs] adj : extasiado, embelesado

rare ['rær] adj **rarer; rarest 1** FINE : excelente, excepcional ⟨a rare talent : un talento excepcional⟩ **2** UNCOMMON : raro, poco común **3** : poco cocido (dícese de la carne)

rarefy ['ræri,faɪ] vt **-fied; -fying** : enrarecer

rarely ['rærli] adv SELDOM : pocas veces, rara vez

raring ['rærən, -ɪŋ] adj : lleno de entusiasmo, con muchas ganas

rarity ['ræriti] n, pl **-ties** : rareza f

rascal ['ræskəl] n : pillo m, -lla f; pícaro m, -ra f

rash¹ ['ræʃ] adj : imprudente, precipitado — **rashly** adv

rash² n : sarpullido m, erupción f

rashness ['ræʃnəs] n : precipitación f

rasp¹ ['ræsp] vt SCRAPE : raspar **2** : decir en voz áspera — vi : hacer un ruido áspero

rasp² n : escofina f

raspberry ['ræz,bɛri] n, pl **-ries** : frambuesa f

rat ['ræt] n : rata f

ratchet ['rætʃət] n : trinquete m

rate¹ ['reɪt] vt **rated; rating 1** CONSIDER, REGARD : considerar, estimar **2** DESERVE : merecer

rate² n **1** SPEED, PACE : velocidad f, ritmo m ⟨at this rate : a este paso⟩ **2** : índice m, tasa f ⟨birth rate : índice de natalidad⟩ ⟨interest rate : tasa de interés⟩ **3** CHARGE, PRICE : precio m, tarifa f **4 at any rate** ANYWAY : de todos modos **5 at any rate** AT LEAST : al menos, por lo menos

rather ['ræðər, 'rʌ-, 'rɑ-] adv **1** (indicating preference) ⟨she would rather stay : preferiría quedarse⟩ ⟨I'd rather not : mejor que no⟩ **2** (indicating preciseness) ⟨my father, or rather, my stepfather : mi padre, o mejor dicho mi padrastro⟩ **3** INSTEAD : sino que, más que, al contrario ⟨I'm not pleased; rather, I'm disappointed : no estoy satisfecho, sino desilu-

sionado⟩ **4** SOMEWHAT : algo, un tanto ⟨rather strange : un poco extraño⟩ **5** QUITE : bastante ⟨rather difficult : bastante difícil⟩ **6** ~ **than** INSTEAD OF : en vez de

ratification [,rætəfə'keɪʃən] n : ratificación f

ratify ['rætə,faɪ] vt **-fied; -fying** : ratificar

rating ['reɪtɪŋ] n **1** STANDING : clasificación f, posición f **2 ratings** npl : índice m de audiencia

ratio ['reɪʃo] n, pl **-tios** : proporción f, relación f

ration¹ ['ræʃən, 'reɪʃən] vt : racionar

ration² n **1** : ración f **2 rations** npl PROVISIONS : víveres mpl

rational ['ræʃənəl] adj **1** : racional **2** REASONABLE : razonable, racional — **rationally** adv — **rationality** [,ræʃə'næləti] n

rationale [,ræʃə'næl] n **1** EXPLANATION : explicación f **2** BASIS : base f, razones fpl

rationalize ['ræʃənə,laɪz] vt **-ized; -izing** : racionalizar — **rationalization** [,ræʃənələ'zeɪʃən] n

rat race n : competencia f laboral (excesiva)

rattle¹ ['rætəl] v **-tled; -tling** vi **1** CLATTER : traquetear, hacer ruido **2 to rattle on** CHATTER : parlotear fam — vt **1** : hacer sonar, agitar ⟨the wind rattled the door : el viento sacudió la puerta⟩ **2** DISCONCERT, WORRY : desconcertar, poner nervioso **3 to rattle off** : despachar, recitar, decir de corrido

rattle² n **1** CLATTER : traqueteo m, ruido m **2** : sonajero m (para bebés) **3** : cascabel m (de una culebra)

rattler ['rætələr] → **rattlesnake**

rattlesnake ['rætəl,sneɪk] n : serpiente f de cascabel

ratty ['ræti] adj **rattier; -est** : raído, andrajoso

raucous ['rɔkəs] adj **1** HOARSE : ronco **2** BOISTEROUS : escandaloso, bullicioso — **raucously** adv

ravage¹ ['rævɪdʒ] vt **-aged; -aging** : devastar, arrasar, hacer estragos

ravage² n : destrozo m, destrucción f ⟨the ravages of war : los estragos de la guerra⟩

rave ['reɪv] vi **raved; raving 1** : delirar, desvariar **2 to rave about** : hablar con entusiasmo sobre, entusiasmarse por

ravel ['rævəl] v **-eled** or **-elled; -eling** or **-elling** vt UNRAVEL : desenredar, desenmarañar — vi FRAY : deshilacharse

raven ['reɪvən] n : cuervo m

ravenous ['rævənəs] adj : hambriento, voraz — **ravenously** adv

ravine [rə'vi:n] n : barranco m, quebrada f

ravings ['reɪvɪŋz] npl : desvaríos mpl, delirios mpl

ravioli [,rævi'o:li] ns & pl : raviolis mpl, ravioles mpl

ravish ['rævɪʃ] vt **1** PLUNDER : saquear **2** ENCHANT : embelesar, cautivar, encantar

ravishing ['rævɪʃɪŋ] adj : deslumbrante, impresionante (dícese de la belleza, etc.)

raw ['rɔ] *adj* **rawer; rawest** **1** : crudo ⟨raw meat : carne cruda⟩ **2** UNTREATED : sin tratar, sin refinar, puro ⟨raw data : datos en bruto⟩ ⟨raw materials : materias primas⟩ **3** INEXPERIENCED : novato, inexperto **4** SORE, CHAFED : en carne viva **5** : frío y húmedo ⟨a raw day : un día crudo⟩ **6** UNFAIR : injusto ⟨a raw deal : un trato injusto, una injusticia⟩

rawhide ['rɔ,haɪd] *n* : cuero *m* sin curtir

ray ['reɪ] *n* **1** : rayo *m* (de la luz, etc.) ⟨a ray of hope : un resquicio de esperanza⟩ **2** : raya *f* (pez)

rayon ['reɪ,ɑn] *n* : rayón *m*

raze ['reɪz] *vt* **razed; razing** : arrasar, demoler

razor ['reɪzər] *n* **1** *or* **straight razor** : navaja *f* (de afeitar) **2** *or* **safety razor** : maquinilla *f* de afeitar, rastrillo *m* Mex **3** *or* **electric razor** SHAVER : afeitadora *f*, rasuradora *f* **4** *or* **razor blade** : hoja *f* de afeitar, cuchilla *f* de afeitar

re [,ri:] *n* : re *m* (en el canto)

re- [,ri:] *pref* : re-

reach ['ri:tʃ] *vt* **1** EXTEND : extender, alargar ⟨to reach out one's hand : extender la mano⟩ **2** : alcanzar ⟨I couldn't reach the apple : no pude alcanzar la manzana⟩ **3** : llegar a/hasta ⟨the shadow reached the wall : la sombra llegó hasta la pared⟩ **4** CONTACT : contactar, ponerse en contacto con — *vi* **1** *or* **to reach out** : extender la mano **2** STRETCH : extenderse **3 to reach for** : tratar de agarrar

reach² *n* : alcance *m*, extensión *f* ⟨within reach : a mi/tu (etc.) alcance⟩ ⟨within reach of : al alcance de⟩ ⟨out of reach : fuera de mi/tu (etc.) alcance⟩

react [ri'ækt] *vi* : reaccionar

reaction [ri'ækʃən] *n* : reacción *f*

reactionary¹ [ri'ækʃə,neri] *adj* : reaccionario

reactionary² *n, pl* **-ries** : reaccionario *m*, -ria *f*

reactivate [ri'æktə,veɪt] *vt* **-vated; -vating** : reactivar — **reactivation** *n*

reactor [ri'æktər] *n* : reactor *m* ⟨nuclear reactor : reactor nuclear⟩

read¹ ['ri:d] *v* **read** ['red]; **reading** *vt* **1** : leer ⟨to read a story : leer un cuento⟩ **2** INTERPRET : interpretar ⟨it can be read two ways : se puede interpretar de dos maneras⟩ **3** : decir, poner ⟨the sign read "No smoking" : el letrero decía "No Fumar"⟩ **4** : marcar ⟨the thermometer reads 70° : el termómetro marca 70°⟩ **5 to read aloud/out** : leer en voz alta **6 to read between the lines** : leer entre las líneas **7 to read into something** : buscarle el significado a algo ⟨don't read too much into it : no le des demasiada importancia⟩ **8 to read through/over** : leer (del principio al fin) **9 to read up on** : documentarse sobre — *vi* **1** : leer ⟨he can read : sabe leer⟩ **2** SAY : decir ⟨the list reads as follows : la lista dice lo siguiente⟩

read² *n* **to be a good read** : ser una lectura amena

readable ['ri:dəbəl] *adj* : legible

reader ['ri:dər] *n* : lector *m*, -tora *f*

readership ['ri:dər,ʃɪp] *n* : lectores *mpl*

readily ['redəli] *adv* **1** WILLINGLY : de buena gana, con gusto **2** EASILY : fácilmente, con facilidad

readiness ['redinəs] *n* **1** WILLINGNESS : buena disposición *f* **2 to be in readiness** : estar preparado

reading ['ri:dɪŋ] *n* : lectura *f*

readjust [,ri:ə'dʒʌst] *vt* : reajustar — *vi* : volverse a adaptar

readjustment [,ri:ə'dʒʌstmənt] *n* : reajuste *m*

readout ['ri:d,aʊt] *n* : lectura *f* (en informática)

ready¹ ['redi] *vt* **readied; readying** : preparar

ready² *adj* **readier; -est** **1** PREPARED : listo, preparado ⟨they'll be ready soon : enseguida están listos⟩ ⟨to be ready to : estar listo para⟩ ⟨to make ready : prepararse⟩ **2** WILLING : dispuesto ⟨ready and willing : dispuesto a todo⟩ **3** : a punto de ⟨ready to cry : a punto de llorar⟩ **4** AVAILABLE : disponible ⟨ready cash/money : efectivo⟩ **5** QUICK : vivo, agudo ⟨a ready wit : un ingenio agudo⟩

ready-made ['redi'meɪd] *adj* : preparado, confeccionado

reaffirm [,ri:ə'fərm] *vt* : reafirmar

real¹ ['ri:l] *adv fam* VERY : muy ⟨we had a real good time : lo pasamos muy bien⟩

real² *adj* **1** : inmobiliario ⟨real property : bien inmueble, bien raíz⟩ **2** GENUINE : auténtico, genuino **3** ACTUAL, TRUE : real, verdadero ⟨a real friend : un verdadero amigo⟩ **4 for real** SERIOUSLY : de veras, de verdad **5 for real** GENUINE, TRUE : auténtico, verdadero **6 for real** SINCERE : sincero ⟨is that guy for real? : ¿nos está tomando el pelo?⟩ **7 get real!** *fam* : ¡no te engañes! **8 to keep it real** *fam* : ser sincero, no darse aires

real estate *n* : propiedad *f* inmobiliaria, bienes *mpl* raíces

real estate agent *n* : agente *m* inmobiliario, agente *f* inmobiliaria

realign [,ri:ə'laɪn] *vt* : realinear — **realignment** [,ri:ə'laɪnmənt] *n*

realism ['ri:ə,lɪzəm] *n* : realismo *m*

realist ['ri:əlɪst] *n* : realista *mf*

realistic [,ri:ə'lɪstɪk] *adj* : realista

realistically [,ri:ə'lɪstɪkli] *adv* : de manera realista

reality [ri'æləti] *n, pl* **-ties** : realidad *f*

reality TV *or* **reality television** *n* : telerrealidad *f*

realizable [,ri:ə'laɪzəbəl] *adj* : realizable, asequible

realization [,ri:ələ'zeɪʃən] *n* : realización *f*

realize ['ri:ə,laɪz] *vt* **-ized; -izing** **1** UNDERSTAND : darse cuenta de, saber **2** FULFILL : realizar (sueños, etc.) ⟨my worst fears were realized : mis mayores temores se hicieron realidad⟩ **3** ACCOMPLISH : realizar, llevar a cabo **4** EARN : obtener, realizar

really ['rɪli, 'rɪ-] *adv* **1** ACTUALLY : de verdad, en realidad ⟨really good : buenísimo⟩ **2** TRULY : verdaderamente, realmente ⟨I really don't care : la verdad es que no me importa⟩ **3** FRANKLY : francamente, en serio

realm ['rɛlm] *n* **1** KINGDOM : reino *m* **2** SPHERE : esfera *f*, campo *m*

Realtor ['riːltər, -ˌtor] *service mark* se usa para un agente inmobiliario autorizado

ream ['riːm] *n* **1** : resma *f* (de papel) **2** **reams** *npl* LOADS : montones *mpl*

reap ['riːp] *v* : cosechar

reaper ['riːpər] *n* **1** : cosechador *m*, -dora *f* (persona) ⟨the Grim Reaper : la muerte⟩ **2** : cosechadora *f* (máquina)

reappear [ˌriːə'pɪr] *vi* : reaparecer

reappearance [ˌriːə'pɪrəns] *n* : reaparición *f*

rear[1] ['rɪr] *vt* **1** LIFT, RAISE : levantar **2** BREED, BRING UP : criar — *vi* **or to rear up** : encabritarse

rear[2] *adj* : trasero, posterior, de atrás

rear[3] *n* **1** BACK : parte *f* de atrás ⟨to bring up the rear : cerrar la marcha⟩ **2 or rear end** : trasero *m*

rear admiral *n* : contraalmirante *mf*

rearrange [ˌriːə'reɪndʒ] *vt* **-ranged; -ranging** : colocar de otra manera, volver a arreglar, reorganizar

rearview mirror ['rɪrˌvjuː-] *n* : retrovisor *m*

reason[1] ['riːzən] *vt* THINK : pensar — *vi* : razonar ⟨I can't reason with her : no puedo razonar con ella⟩ — **reasoned** ['riːzənd] *adj*

reason[2] *n* **1** CAUSE, GROUND : razón *f*, motivo *m* ⟨the reason for his trip : el motivo de su viaje⟩ ⟨for this reason : por esta razón, por lo cual⟩ ⟨for no (good) reason : sin razón⟩ ⟨he's the champion for a reason : por algo es el campeón⟩ ⟨the reason why : la razón por la cual, el porqué⟩ ⟨to have reason to : tener motivos para⟩ **2** SENSE : razón *f* ⟨to listen to reason, to see reason : avenirse a razones⟩ ⟨to stand to reason : ser lógico⟩ ⟨within reason : dentro de lo razonable⟩

reasonable ['riːzənəbəl] *adj* **1** SENSIBLE : razonable **2** INEXPENSIVE : barato, económico

reasonably ['riːzənəbli] *adv* **1** SENSIBLY : razonablemente **2** FAIRLY : bastante

reasoning ['riːzənɪŋ] *n* : razonamiento *m*, raciocinio *m*, argumentos *mpl*

reassess [ˌriːə'sɛs] *vt* : revaluar, reconsiderar

reassurance [ˌriːə'ʃurəns] *n* : consuelo *m*, palabras *fpl* alentadoras

reassure [ˌriːə'ʃur] *vt* **-sured; -suring** : tranquilizar

reassuring [ˌriːə'ʃurɪŋ] *adj* : tranquilizador

reawaken [ˌriːə'weɪkən] *vt* : volver a despertar, reavivar

rebate ['riːˌbeɪt] *n* : reembolso *m*, devolución *f*

rebel[1] ['rɪˌbɛl] *vi* **-belled; -belling** : rebelarse, sublevarse

rebel[2] ['rɛbəl] *adj* : rebelde

rebel[3] ['rɛbəl] *n* : rebelde *mf*

rebellion [rɪ'bɛljən] *n* : rebelión *f*

rebellious [rɪ'bɛljəs] *adj* : rebelde

rebelliousness [rɪ'bɛljəsnəs] *n* : rebeldía *f*

rebirth [ˌriː'bərθ] *n* : renacimiento *m*

reboot [riː'buːt] *vt* : reiniciar (una computadora)

reborn [riː'born] *adj* **to be reborn** : renacer

rebound[1] ['riːˌbaund, rɪ'baund] *vi* : rebotar

rebound[2] ['riːˌbaund] *n* : rebote *m*

rebuff[1] [rɪ'bʌf] *vt* : desairar, rechazar

rebuff[2] *n* : desaire *m*, rechazo *m*

rebuild [ˌriː'bɪld] *vt* **-built** [-'bɪlt]; **-building** : reconstruir

rebuke[1] [rɪ'bjuːk] *vt* **-buked; -buking** : reprender, regañar

rebuke[2] *n* : reprimenda *f*, reproche *m*

rebut [rɪ'bʌt] *vt* **-butted; -butting** : rebatir, refutar

rebuttal [rɪ'bʌtəl] *n* : refutación *f*

recalcitrant [rɪ'kælsətrənt] *adj* : recalcitrante

recall[1] [rɪ'kɔl] *vt* **1** : llamar, retirar ⟨recalled to active duty : llamado al servicio activo⟩ **2** REMEMBER : recordar, acordarse de **3** REVOKE : revocar

recall[2] [rɪ'kɔl, 'riːˌkɔl] *n* **1** : retirada *f* (de personas o mercancías) **2** MEMORY : memoria *f* ⟨to have total recall : poder recordar todo⟩

recant [rɪ'kænt] *vt* : retractarse de — *vi* : retractarse, renegar

recap[1] ['riːˌkæp] *v* **-capped; -capping** *fam* → **recapitulate**

recap[2] ['riːˌkæp] *n* SUMMARY : resumen *m*

recapitulate [ˌriːkə'pɪtʃəˌleɪt] *v* **-lated; -lating** : resumir, recapitular

recapture [ˌriː'kæptʃər] *vt* **-tured; -turing** **1** : volver a capturar **2** REGAIN : recuperar

recast [riː'kæst] *vt* **-cast; -casting** **1** : cambiar el reparto de (una película, etc.), cambiarle el papel a (un actor) **2** REWRITE : refundir

recede [rɪ'siːd] *vi* **-ceded; -ceding** **1** WITHDRAW : retirarse, retroceder **2** FADE : desvanecerse, alejarse **3** SLANT : inclinarse **4 to have a receding hairline** : tener entradas

receipt [rɪ'siːt] *n* **1** : recibo *m*, boleta *f*, ticket *m* **2 receipts** *npl* : ingresos *mpl*, entradas *fpl*

receivable [rɪ'siːvəbəl] *adj* **accounts receivable** : cuentas por cobrar

receive [rɪ'siːv] *vt* **-ceived; -ceiving** **1** GET : recibir (una carta, un golpe, etc.) **2** WELCOME : acoger, recibir ⟨to receive guests : tener invitados⟩ **3** : recibir, captar (señales de radio)

receiver [rɪ'siːvər] *n* **1** : receptor *m*, -tora *f* (en futbol americano) **2** : receptor *m* (de radio o televisión) **3 or telephone receiver** : auricular *m*

recent ['riːsənt] *adj* : reciente — **recently** *adv*

receptacle [rɪ'sɛptɪkəl] *n* : receptáculo *m*, recipiente *m*

reception [rɪ'sɛpʃən] *n* : recepción *f* ⟨reception desk : recepción⟩ ⟨reception area : vestíbulo⟩

receptionist [rɪ'sɛpʃənɪst] *n* : recepcionista *mf*

receptive [rɪ'sɛptɪv] *adj* : receptivo — **receptivity** [ˌriːˌsɛp'tɪvət̬i] *n*

receptiveness [rɪ'sɛptɪvnəs] *n* : receptividad *f*

recess¹ ['riːˌsɛs, rɪ'sɛs] *vt* ADJOURN : suspender, levantar

recess² *n* **1** ALCOVE : hueco *m*, nicho *m* **2** BREAK : receso *m*, descanso *m*, recreo *m* (en el colegio)

recessed ['riːˌsɛst, rɪ'sɛst] *adj* : empotrado

recession [rɪ'sɛʃən] *n* : recesión *f*, depresión *f* económica

recessive [rɪ'sɛsɪv] *adj* : recesivo

recharge [ˌriː'tʃɑrdʒ] *vt* **-charged; -charging** : recargar

rechargeable [ˌriː'tʃɑrdʒəbəl] *adj* : recargable

recidivism [rɪ'sɪdəˌvɪzəm] *n* : reincidencia *f*

recidivist [rɪ'sɪdəvɪst] *n* : reincidente *mf* — **recidivist** *adj*

recipe ['rɛsəˌpi] *n* : receta *f*

recipient [rɪ'sɪpiənt] *n* : recipiente *mf*

reciprocal [rɪ'sɪprəkəl] *adj* : recíproco

reciprocate [rɪ'sɪprəˌkeɪt] *vi* **-cated; -cating** : reciprocar

reciprocity [ˌrɛsə'prɑsət̬i] *n*, *pl* **-ties** : reciprocidad *f*

recital [rɪ'saɪt̬əl] *n* **1** PERFORMANCE : recital *m* **2** ENUMERATION : relato *m*, enumeración *f*

recitation [ˌrɛsə'teɪʃən] *n* : recitación *f*

recite [rɪ'saɪt] *vt* **-cited; -citing** **1** : recitar (un poema, etc.) **2** LIST : enumerar

reckless ['rɛkləs] *adj* : imprudente, temerario — **recklessly** *adv*

recklessness ['rɛkləsnəs] *n* : imprudencia *f*, temeridad *f*

reckon ['rɛkən] *vt* **1** *fam* THINK, SUPPOSE : creer ⟨I reckon so : creo que sí⟩ **2** CALCULATE : calcular, contar **3** CONSIDER : considerar **4 to reckon on/with** : contar con **5 to reckon with** : enfrentarse a ⟨they'll have me to reckon with : se las verán conmigo⟩ ⟨to be a force to be reckoned with : ser algo/alguien de temer⟩

reckoning ['rɛkənɪŋ] *n* **1** CALCULATION : cálculo *m* **2** SETTLEMENT : ajuste *m* de cuentas ⟨day of reckoning : día del juicio final⟩

reclaim [rɪ'kleɪm] *vt* **1** : ganar (tierra) ⟨to reclaim marshy land : sanear las tierras pantanosas⟩ **2** RECOVER : recobrar, reciclar ⟨to reclaim old tires : reciclar llantas desechadas⟩ **3** REGAIN : reclamar, recuperar ⟨to reclaim one's rights : reclamar uno sus derechos⟩

recline [rɪ'klaɪn] *vi* **-clined; -clining** **1** LEAN : reclinarse **2** REPOSE : recostarse

reclining [rɪ'klaɪnɪŋ] *adj* : reclinable

recluse ['rɛˌkluːs, rɪ'kluːs] *n* : solitario *m*, -ria *f*

recognition [ˌrɛkɪg'nɪʃən] *n* : reconocimiento *m*

recognizable ['rɛkəgˌnaɪzəbəl] *adj* : reconocible

recognize ['rɛkɪgˌnaɪz] *vt* **-nized; -nizing** : reconocer

recoil¹ [rɪ'kɔɪl] *vi* : retroceder, dar un culatazo

recoil² ['riːˌkɔɪl, rɪ'-] *n* : retroceso *m*, culatazo *m*

recollect [ˌrɛkə'lɛkt] *v* : recordar

recollection [ˌrɛkə'lɛkʃən] *n* : recuerdo *m*

recommend [ˌrɛkə'mɛnd] *vt* **1** : recomendar **2** ADVISE, COUNSEL : aconsejar, recomendar

recommendation [ˌrɛkəmən'deɪʃən] *n* : recomendación *f*

recompense¹ ['rɛkəmˌpɛnts] *vt* **-pensed; -pensing** : indemnizar, recompensar

recompense² *n* : indemnización *f*, compensación *f*

reconcile ['rɛkənˌsaɪl] *v* **-ciled; -ciling** *vt* **1** : reconciliar (personas), conciliar (ideas, etc.) **2 to reconcile oneself to** : resignarse a — *vi* MAKE UP : reconciliarse, hacer las paces

reconciliation [ˌrɛkənˌsɪli'eɪʃən] *n* : reconciliación *f* (con personas), conciliación *f* (con ideas, etc.)

recondition [ˌriːkən'dɪʃən] *vt* : reacondicionar

reconnaissance [rɪ'kɑnəzənts, -sənts] *n* : reconocimiento *m*

reconnoiter *or* **reconnoitre** [ˌriːkə'nɔɪt̬ər, ˌrɛkə-] *vt* **-tered** *or* **-tred; -tering** *or* **-tring** *vt* : reconocer — *vi* : hacer un reconocimiento

reconquer [ˌriː'kɑŋkər] *vt* : reconquistar

reconquest [ˌriː'kɑn̩ˌkwɛst, -'kɑŋ-] *n* : reconquista *f*

reconsider [ˌriːkən'sɪdər] *vt* : reconsiderar, repensar

reconsideration [ˌriːkənˌsɪdə'reɪʃən] *n* : reconsideración *f*

reconstruct [ˌriːkən'strʌkt] *vt* : reconstruir

reconstruction [ˌriːkən'strʌkʃən] *n* : reconstrucción *f*

reconstructive [ˌriːkən'strʌktɪv] *adj* : reconstructivo

record¹ [rɪ'kɔrd] *vt* **1** WRITE DOWN : anotar, apuntar **2** REGISTER : registrar, hacer constar **3** INDICATE : marcar (una temperatura, etc.) **4** : grabar (audio o video)

record² ['rɛkərd] *adj* : récord

record³ ['rɛkərd] *n* **1** DOCUMENT : registro *m*, documento *m* oficial **2** HISTORY : historial *m* ⟨a good academic record : un buen historial académico⟩ ⟨criminal record : antecedentes penales⟩ **3** : récord *m* ⟨the world record : el récord mundial⟩ **4** : disco *m* (de música, etc.) **5 for the record** : que conste **6 off the record** : extraoficialmente **7 on record** ⟨he is on record as saying . . . : dijo públicamente que . . .⟩ **8 on record** : registrado ⟨the highest on record : el más alto registrado⟩ **9 on the record** : oficial-

mente **10 to set the record straight**
: poner las cosas en su lugar
recorder [rɪ'kordər] n **1** : flauta f dulce
(instrumento de viento) **2 tape recorder**
: grabadora f
recording [rɪ'kordɪŋ] n : grabación f
record player n : tocadiscos m
recount[1] [rɪ'kaʊnt] vt **1** NARRATE : narrar, relatar **2** : volver a contar (votos,
etc.)
recount[2] [ˈriː,kaʊnt, ˌriː'-] n : recuento m
recoup [rɪ'kuːp] vt : recuperar, recobrar
recourse [ˈriː,kors, rɪ'-] n : recurso m ⟨to
have recourse to : recurrir a⟩
recover [rɪ'kʌvər] vt **1** REGAIN : recobrar, recuperar **2** : rescatar (algo robado o perdido) **3** RECOUP : recuperar
— vi RECUPERATE : recuperarse
recovery [rɪ'kʌvəri] n, pl **-eries** : recuperación f
re-create [ˌriːkri'eɪt] vt **-ated; -ating** : recrear — **re-creation** [ˌriːkri'eɪʃən] n
recreation [ˌrɛkri'eɪʃən] n : recreo m,
esparcimiento m, diversión f
recreational [ˌrɛkri'eɪʃənəl] adj : recreativo, de recreo
recreational vehicle n : vehículo m de recreo
recrimination [rɪˌkrɪmə'neɪʃən] n : recriminación f
recruit[1] [rɪ'kruːt] vt : reclutar
recruit[2] n : recluta mf
recruitment [rɪ'kruːtmənt] n : reclutamiento m, alistamiento m
rectal [ˈrɛktəl] adj : rectal
rectangle [ˈrɛk,tæŋɡəl] n : rectángulo m
rectangular [rɛk'tæŋɡjələr] adj : rectangular
rectify [ˈrɛktə,faɪ] vt **-fied; -fying** : rectificar — **rectification** [ˌrɛktəfə'keɪʃən] n
rectitude [ˈrɛktə,tuːd, -,tjuːd] n : rectitud f
rector [ˈrɛktər] n : rector m, -tora f
rectory [ˈrɛktəri] n, pl **-ries** : rectoría f
rectum [ˈrɛktəm] n, pl **-tums** or **-ta** [-tə]
: recto m
recuperate [rɪ'kuːpə,reɪt, -'kjuː-] v **-ated;
-ating** vt : recuperar — vi : recuperarse,
restablecerse
recuperation [rɪˌkuːpə'reɪʃən, -ˌkjuː-] n
: recuperación f
recur [rɪ'kər] vi **-curred; -curring** : volver
a ocurrir, volver a producirse, repetirse
recurrence [rɪ'kərənts] n : repetición f,
reaparición f
recurrent [rɪ'kərənt] adj : recurrente, que
se repite
recyclable [riˈsaɪkələbəl] adj : reciclable
recycle [riˈsaɪkəl] vt **-cled; -cling** : reciclar
recycling [riˈsaɪkəlɪŋ] n : reciclaje m
red[1] [ˈrɛd] adj **1** : rojo, colorado ⟨to be
red in the face : ponerse colorado⟩ ⟨to
have red hair : ser pelirrojo⟩ **2** COMMU-
NIST : rojo, comunista
red[2] n **1** : rojo m, colorado m **2 Red**
COMMUNIST : comunista mf
red blood cell n : glóbulo m rojo
red-blooded [ˈrɛd'blʌdəd] adj : vigoroso
redden [ˈrɛdən] vt : enrojecer — vi BLUSH
: enrojecerse, ruborizarse

reddish [ˈrɛdɪʃ] adj : rojizo
redecorate [ˌriː'dɛkə,reɪt] vt **-rated; -rat-
ing** : renovar, pintar de nuevo
redeem [rɪ'diːm] vt **1** RESCUE, SAVE
: rescatar, salvar **2** : desempeñar ⟨she
redeemed it from the pawnshop : lo des-
empeñó de la casa de empeños⟩ **3**
: redimir (en religión) **4** : canjear, vender
⟨to redeem coupons : canjear cupones⟩
redeemer [rɪ'diːmər] n : redentor m, -tora f
redeeming [rɪ'diːmɪŋ] adj : positivo ⟨re-
deeming qualities : cualidades positivas⟩
redefine [ˌriːdɪ'faɪn] vt : redefinir
redemption [rɪ'dɛmpʃən] n : redención f
redesign [ˌriːdɪ'zaɪn] vt : rediseñar
red-eye [ˈrɛd,aɪ] or **red-eye flight** n
: vuelo m nocturno
red-haired [ˈrɛd'hærd] adj : pelirrojo
red-handed [ˈrɛd'hændəd] adv : in fraganti
redhead [ˈrɛd,hɛd] n : pelirrojo m, -ja f
redheaded [ˈrɛd,hɛdəd] → **red-haired**
red herring n : trampa f (para distraer la
atención)
red-hot [ˈrɛd'hɑt] adj **1** : al rojo vivo,
candente **2** CURRENT : de candente actualidad **3** POPULAR : de gran popularidad
redirect [ˌriːdə'rɛkt, -daɪ-] vt : desviar
(tráfico, dinero, etc.)
rediscover [ˌriːdɪ'skʌvər] vt : redescubrir
redistribute [ˌriːdɪ'strɪ,bjuːt] vt **-uted;
-uting** : redistribuir
red-letter day [ˈrɛd'lɛtər-] n : día m
memorable
redness [ˈrɛdnəs] n : rojez f
redo [ˌriː'duː] vt **-did** [-'dɪd]; **-done** [-'dʌn]
-doing 1 : hacer de nuevo **2** → **redecorate**
redolence [ˈrɛdələnts] n : fragancia f
redolent [ˈrɛdələnt] adj **1** FRAGRANT
: fragante, oloroso **2** SUGGESTIVE : evocador
redouble [rɪ'dʌbəl] vt **-bled; -bling** : redoblar, intensificar (esfuerzos, etc.)
redress [rɪ'drɛs] vt : reparar, remediar,
enmendar
red snapper n : pargo m, huachinango m
Mex
red tape n : papeleo m
reduce [rɪ'duːs, -'djuːs] v **-duced; -ducing**
vt **1** LESSEN : reducir, disminuir, rebajar
(precios) **2** DEMOTE : bajar de categoría,
degradar **3** : dejar reducir (un líquido) **4
to be reduced to** : quedar reducido a
(escombros, etc.) **5 to be reduced to**
: verse rebajado/forzado a **6 to reduce
someone to tears** : hacer llorar a
alguien — vi SLIM : adelgazar
reduction [rɪ'dʌkʃən] n : reducción f, rebaja f
redundancy [rɪ'dʌndəntsi] n, pl **-cies 1**
: superfluidad f **2** REPETITION : redundancia f
redundant [rɪ'dʌndənt] adj : superfluo,
redundante
redwood [ˈrɛd,wʊd] n : secoya f
reed [ˈriːd] n **1** : caña f, carrizo m, junco
m **2** : lengüeta f (para instrumentos de
viento)

reef ['ri:f] *n* : arrecife *m*, escollo *m*

reek[1] ['ri:k] *vi* : apestar

reek[2] *n* : hedor *m*

reel[1] ['ri:l] *vt* **1 to reel in** : enrollar, sacar (un pez) del agua **2 to reel off** : recitar de un tirón — *vi* **1** SPIN, WHIRL : girar, dar vueltas **2** STAGGER : tambalearse

reel[2] *n* **1** : carrete *m* (de película, etc.) ⟨fishing reel : carrete de pesca⟩ **2** : baile *m* escocés **3** STAGGER : tambaleo *m*

reelect [,ri:ɪ'lɛkt] *vt* : reelegir

reenact [,ri:ɪ'nækt] *vt* : representar de nuevo, reconstruir

reenter [,ri:'ɛntər] *vt* : volver a entrar

reestablish [,ri:ɪ'stæblɪʃ] *vt* : restablecer — **reestablishment** [,ri:ɪ'stæblɪʃmənt] *n*

reevaluate [,ri:ɪ'vælju,eɪt] *vt* -ated; -ating : revaluar

reevaluation [,ri:ɪ,vælju'eɪʃən] *n* : revaluación *f*

reexamine [,ri:ɪg'zæmən, -g-] *vt* -ined; -ining : volver a examinar, reexaminar

ref → referee[2]

refer [rɪ'fər] *v* -ferred; -ferring *vt* DIRECT, SEND : remitir, enviar ⟨to refer a patient to a specialist : enviar a un paciente a un especialista⟩ — *vi* **to refer to** MENTION : referirse a, aludir a

referee[1] [,rɛfə'ri:] *vt* -eed; -eeing : arbitrar

referee[2] *n* : árbitro *m*, -tra *f*; réferi *mf*

reference ['rɛfrəns, 'rɛfə-] *n* **1** ALLUSION : referencia *f*, alusión *f* ⟨to make reference to : hacer referencia a⟩ **2** CONSULTATION : consulta *f* ⟨for future reference : para futuras consultas⟩ **3** *or* **reference book** : libro *m* de consulta **4** TESTIMONIAL : informe *m*, referencia *f*, recomendación *f* **5 in/with reference to** : con referencia a

referendum [,rɛfə'rɛndəm] *n*, *pl* **-da** [-də] *or* **-dums** : referéndum *m*

refill[1] [,ri:'fɪl] *vt* : rellenar

refill[2] ['ri:,fɪl] *n* : recambio *m*

refinance [,ri:'faɪ,næns] *vt* -nanced; -nancing : refinanciar

refine [rɪ'faɪn] *vt* -fined; -fining **1** : refinar (azúcar, petróleo, etc.) **2** PERFECT : perfeccionar, pulir

refined [rɪ'faɪnd] *adj* **1** : refinado (dícese del azúcar, etc.) **2** CULTURED : culto, educado, refinado

refinement [rɪ'faɪnmənt] *n* : refinamiento *m*, fineza *f*, finura *f*

refinery [rɪ'faɪnəri] *n*, *pl* **-eries** : refinería *f*

reflect [rɪ'flɛkt] *vt* **1** : reflejar **2 to be reflected in** : reflejarse en **3 to reflect that** : pensar que, considerar que — *vi* **1** : reflejarse **2 to reflect on** : reflexionar sobre **3 to reflect badly on** : desacreditar, dejar mal parado

reflection [rɪ'flɛkʃən] *n* **1** : reflexión *f*, reflejo *m* (de la luz, de imágenes, etc.) **2** THOUGHT : reflexión *f*, meditación *f*

reflective [rɪ'flɛktɪv] *adj* **1** THOUGHTFUL : reflexivo, pensativo **2** : reflectante (en física)

reflector [rɪ'flɛktər] *n* : reflector *m*

reflex ['ri:,flɛks] *n* : reflejo *m*

reflexive [rɪ'flɛksɪv] *adj* : reflexivo ⟨a reflexive verb : un verbo reflexivo⟩

reform[1] [rɪ'fɔrm] *vt* : reformar — *vi* : reformarse

reform[2] *n* : reforma *f*

reformation [,rɛfər'meɪʃən] *n* : reforma *f* ⟨the Reformation : la Reforma⟩

reform school *n* : reformatorio *m*

reformer [rɪ'fɔrmər] *n* : reformador *m*, -dora *f*

refract [rɪ'frækt] *vt* : refractar — *vi* : refractarse

refraction [rɪ'frækʃən] *n* : refracción *f*

refrain[1] [rɪ'freɪn] *vi* **to refrain from** : abstenerse de

refrain[2] *n* : estribillo *m* (en música)

refresh [rɪ'frɛʃ] *vt* : refrescar ⟨to refresh one's memory : refrescar la memoria a uno⟩

refreshing [rɪ'frɛʃɪŋ] *adj* : refrescante ⟨a refreshing sleep : un sueño reparador⟩

refreshment [rɪ'frɛʃmənt] *n* **1** : refresco *m* **2 refreshments** *npl* : refrigerio *m*

refried ['ri:,fraɪd] *adj* : refrito

refrigerate [rɪ'frɪdʒə,reɪt] *vt* -ated; -ating : refrigerar

refrigeration [rɪ,frɪdʒə'reɪʃən] *n* : refrigeración *f*

refrigerator [rɪ'frɪdʒə,reɪtər] *n* : refrigerador *m*, -dora *f*; nevera *f*

refuel [ri:'fju:əl] *v* -eled *or* -elled; -eling *or* -elling *vi* : repostar — *vt* : llenar de combustible

refuge ['rɛ,fju:dʒ] *n* : refugio *m*

refugee [,rɛfju'dʒi:] *n* : refugiado *m*, -da *f*

refund[1] [rɪ'fʌnd, 'ri:,fʌnd] *vt* : reembolsar, devolver

refund[2] ['ri:,fʌnd] *n* : reembolso *m*, devolución *f*

refundable [rɪ'fʌndəbəl] *adj* : reembolsable

refurbish [rɪ'fərbɪʃ] *vt* : renovar, restaurar

refusal [rɪ'fju:zəl] *n* : negativa *f*, rechazo *m*, denegación *f* (de una petición)

refuse[1] [rɪ'fju:z] *vt* -fused; -fusing **1** REJECT : rechazar, rehusar **2** DENY : negar, rehusar, denegar ⟨to refuse permission : negar el permiso⟩ **3 to refuse to** : negarse a

refuse[2] ['rɛ,fju:s, -,fju:z] *n* : basura *f*, desechos *mpl*, desperdicios *mpl*

refutation [,rɛfju'teɪʃən] *n* : refutación *f*

refute [rɪ'fju:t] *vt* -futed; -futing **1** DENY : desmentir, negar **2** DISPROVE : refutar, rebatir

regain [ri:'geɪn] *vt* **1** RECOVER : recuperar, recobrar **2** REACH : alcanzar ⟨to regain the shore : llegar a la tierra⟩

regal ['ri:gəl] *adj* : real, regio

regale [rɪ'geɪl] *vt* -galed; -galing **1** ENTERTAIN : agasajar, entretener **2** AMUSE, DELIGHT : deleitar, divertir

regalia [rɪ'geɪljə] *n* : ropaje *m*, vestiduras *fpl*, adornos *mpl*

regard[1] [rɪ'gard] *vt* **1** OBSERVE : observar, mirar ⟨she regarded me with suspicion : me miró con recelo⟩ **2** HEED : tener en cuenta, hacer caso de **3** CONSIDER : considerar ⟨I regard her as a friend : la con-

sidero una amiga⟩ **4** RESPECT : respetar
⟨highly regarded : muy estimado⟩ **5 as
regards** : en cuanto a, en lo que se refiere a
regard² *n* **1** CONSIDERATION : consideración *f* ⟨with no regard for : sin ninguna
consideración por⟩ **2** ESTEEM : respeto
m, estima *f* ⟨to hold someone in high regard : tener a alguien en gran estima⟩ **3**
PARTICULAR : aspecto *m*, sentido *m* ⟨in
this regard : en este sentido⟩ **4 regards**
npl : saludos *mpl*, recuerdos *mpl* **5 with
regard to** : con relación a, con respecto
a
regarding [rɪ'ɡɑrdɪŋ] *prep* : con respecto
a, en cuanto a
regardless [rɪ'ɡɑrdləs] *adv* : a pesar de
todo
regardless of *prep* : a pesar de, sin tener
en cuenta ⟨regardless of our mistakes : a
pesar de nuestros errores⟩ ⟨regardless of
age : sin tener en cuenta la edad⟩
regatta [rɪ'ɡɑtə] *n* : regata *f*
regency ['riːdʒəntsi] *n, pl* **-cies** : regencia *f*
regenerate [rɪ'dʒɛnə,reɪt] *v* **-ated; -ating** *vt*
: regenerar — *vi* : regenerarse
regeneration [rɪ,dʒɛnə'reɪʃən] *n* : regeneración *f*
regent ['riːdʒənt] *n* **1** RULER : regente *mf*
2 : miembro *m* de la junta directiva (de
una universidad, etc.)
reggae ['rɛ,ɡeɪ, 'reɪ-] *n* : reggae *m*
regime [reɪ'ʒiːm, rɪ-] *n* : régimen *m*
regimen ['rɛdʒəmən] *n* : régimen *m*
regiment¹ ['rɛdʒə,mɛnt] *vt* : reglamentar
regiment² ['rɛdʒəmənt] *n* : regimiento *m*
region ['riːdʒən] *n* **1** : región *f* **2 in the
region of** : alrededor de
regional ['riːdʒənəl] *adj* : regional — **re-
gionally** *adv*
register¹ ['rɛdʒəstər] *vt* **1** RECORD : registrar, inscribir, matricular (un vehículo) **2** INDICATE : marcar (temperatura, medidas, etc.) **3** SHOW : manifestar,
acusar ⟨to register surprise : acusar sor-
presa⟩ **4** : certificar (correo) — *vi* EN-
ROLL : matricularse ⟨to register to vote : inscribirse para
votar⟩
register² *n* : registro *m*
registrar ['rɛdʒə,strɑr] *n* : registrador *m*,
-dora *f* oficial
registration [,rɛdʒə'streɪʃən] *n* **1** REGIS-
TERING : inscripción *f*, matriculación *f*,
registro *m* **2 or registration number**
: matrícula *f*, número *m* de matrícula
registry ['rɛdʒəstri] *n, pl* **-tries** : registro *m*
regress [rɪ'ɡrɛs] *vi* : retroceder
regression [rɪ'ɡrɛʃən] *n* : retroceso *m*, regresión *f*
regressive [rɪ'ɡrɛsɪv] *adj* : regresivo
regret¹ [rɪ'ɡrɛt] *vt* **-gretted; -gretting**
: arrepentirse de, lamentar ⟨he regrets
nothing : no se arrepiente de nada⟩ ⟨I
regret to tell you : lamento decirle⟩
regret² *n* **1** REMORSE : arrepentimiento
m, remordimiento *m* **2** SADNESS : pesar *m*, dolor *m* **3 regrets** *npl* : excusas
fpl ⟨to send one's regrets : excusarse⟩
regretful [rɪ'ɡrɛtfəl] *adj* : arrepentido, pesaroso

regretfully [rɪ'ɡrɛtfəli] *adv* : con pesar
regrettable [rɪ'ɡrɛtəbəl] *adj* : lamentable
— **regrettably** [-bli] *adv*
regroup [rɪ'ɡruːp] *vi* **1** : reagruparse **2**
: tomarse un respiro (para prepararse,
etc.)
regular¹ ['rɛɡjələr] *adj* **1** NORMAL : normal ⟨regular-sized⟩ : de tamaño nor-
mal⟩ ⟨at the regular time : a la hora de
siempre⟩ **2** ORDINARY : normal **3** : regular ⟨a regular pace/pattern : un ritmo/
dibujo regular⟩ ⟨on a regular basis : regularmente, con regularidad⟩ **4** : habitual ⟨a regular customer : un cliente ha-
bitual⟩ **5** : regular (en gramática) **6**
REAL : verdadero
regular² *n* : cliente *mf* habitual
regularity [,rɛɡjə'lærəti] *n, pl* **-ties** : regularidad *f*
regularly ['rɛɡjələrli] *adv* : regularmente,
con regularidad
regulate ['rɛɡjə,leɪt] *vt* **-lated; -lating** : regular
regulation [,rɛɡjə'leɪʃən] *n* **1** REGULAT-
ING : regulación *f* **2** RULE : regla *f*, reglamento *m*, norma *f* ⟨safety regulations
: reglas de seguridad⟩
regulator ['rɛɡjə,leɪtər] *n* **1** : regulador *m*
(mecanismo) **2** : persona *f* que regula
regulatory ['rɛɡjələ,tori] *adj* : regulador
regurgitate [rɪ'ɡərdʒə,teɪt] *v* **-tated; -tat-
ing** : regurgitar, vomitar
rehab ['riː,hæb] → **rehabilitate, rehabilitation**
rehabilitate [,riːhə'bɪlə,teɪt, ,riːə-] *vt*
-tated; -tating : rehabilitar
rehabilitation [,riːhə,bɪlə'teɪʃən, ,riːə-] *n*
: rehabilitación *f*
rehearsal [rɪ'hərsəl] *n* : ensayo *m*
rehearse [rɪ'hərs] *v* **-hearsed; -hearsing**
: ensayar
reheat [,riː'hiːt] *vt* : recalentar
reign¹ [reɪn] *vi* **1** RULE : reinar **2** PRE-
VAIL : reinar, predominar ⟨the reigning
champion : el actual campeón⟩
reign² *n* : reinado *m*
reimburse [,riːəm'bərs] *vt* **-bursed; -burs-
ing** : reembolsar
reimbursement [,riːəm'bərsmənt] *n* : reembolso *m*
rein¹ ['reɪn] *vt* : refrenar (un caballo)
rein² *n* **1** : rienda *f* ⟨to give free rein to
: dar rienda suelta⟩ **2** CHECK : control
m ⟨to keep a tight rein on : llevar un
estricto control de⟩
reincarnation [,riːɪn,kɑr'neɪʃən] *n* : reencarnación *f*
reindeer ['reɪn,dɪr] *n* : reno *m*
reinforce [,riːən'fors] *vt* **-forced; -forcing**
: reforzar
reinforcement [,riːən'forsmənt] *n* : refuerzo *m*
reinstall [,riːɪn'stɔl] *vt* **-stalled; -stalling**
: reinstalar
reinstate [,riːən'steɪt] *vt* **-stated; -stating**
1 : reintegrar, restituir (una persona) **2**
RESTORE : restablecer (un servicio, etc.)
reinstatement [,riːən'steɪtmənt] *n* : reintegración *f*, restitución *f*, restablecimiento
m

reintegrate [ri'ıntə,greıt] vt **-ated; -ating** : reintegrar — **reintegration** [ri,ıntə'greıʃən] n

reintroduce [ri,ıntrə'du:s, -'dju:s] vt **-duced; -ducing** : reintroducir (un animal, una política, etc.)

reiterate [ri'ıtə,reıt] vt **-ated; -ating** : reiterar, repetir

reiteration [ri,ıtə'reıʃən] n : reiteración f, repetición f

reject[1] [rı'dʒɛkt] vt : rechazar

reject[2] ['ri:,dʒɛkt] n : desecho m (cosa), persona f rechazada

rejection [rı'dʒɛkʃən] n : rechazo m

rejoice [rı'dʒɔıs] vi **-joiced; -joicing** : alegrarse, regocijarse

rejoin [,ri:'dʒɔın] vt 1 : reincorporarse a, reintegrarse a ⟨he rejoined the firm : se reincorporó a la firma⟩ 2 [rı'-] REPLY, RETORT : replicar

rejoinder [rı'dʒɔındər] n : réplica f

rejuvenate [rı'dʒu:və,neıt] vt **-nated; -nating** : rejuvenecer

rejuvenation [rı,dʒu:və'neıʃən] n : rejuvenecimiento m

rekindle [,ri:'kındəl] vt **-dled; -dling** : reavivar

relapse[1] [rı'læps] vi **-lapsed; -lapsing** : recaer, volver a caer

relapse[2] ['ri:,læps, rı'læps] n : recaída f

relate [rı'leıt] v **-lated; -lating** vt 1 TELL : relatar, contar 2 ASSOCIATE : relacionar, asociar ⟨to relate crime to poverty : relacionar la delincuencia con la pobreza⟩ — vi 1 INTERACT : relacionarse (con), llevarse bien (con) 2 **relating to** : relacionado con 3 **to be related (to)** : estar relacionado (con) 4 **to relate to** UNDERSTAND : identificarse con, simpatizar con

related [rı'leıtəd] adj : emparentado ⟨to be related to : ser pariente de⟩

relation [rı'leıʃən] n 1 NARRATION : relato m, narración f 2 RELATIVE : pariente mf, familiar mf 3 RELATIONSHIP : relación f ⟨in relation to : en relación con, con relación a⟩ ⟨to have/bear no relation to : no tener nada que ver con⟩ 4 **relations** npl : relaciones fpl ⟨public relations : relaciones públicas⟩

relationship [rı'leıʃən,ʃıp] n 1 CONNECTION : relación f 2 KINSHIP : parentesco m

relative[1] ['relətıv] adj 1 : relativo 2 **relative to** CONCERNING : con relación a 3 **relative to** : en comparación a — **relatively** adv

relative[2] n : pariente mf, familiar mf

relativism ['relətı,vızəm] n : relativismo m

relativity [,relə'tıvət̬i] n, pl **-ties** : relatividad f

relaunch [ri'lɔntʃ] v : relanzar

relax [rı'læks] vt : relajar, aflojar — vi : relajarse

relaxation [,ri:,læk'seıʃən] n 1 RELAXING : relajación f 2 DIVERSION : esparcimiento m, distracción f

relaxing [rı'læksıŋ] adj : relajante

relay[1] ['ri:,leı, rı'leı] vt **-layed; -laying** : transmitir

relay[2] ['ri:,leı] n 1 : relevo m 2 or **relay race** : carrera de relevos

release[1] [rı'li:s] vt **-leased; -leasing** 1 FREE : liberar, poner en libertad 2 LOOSEN : soltar, aflojar ⟨to release the brake : soltar el freno⟩ 3 GIVE OFF : despedir, emitir 4 DIVULGE : divulgar 5 RELINQUISH : renunciar a, ceder 6 ISSUE : publicar (un libro), estrenar (una película), sacar (un disco)

release[2] n 1 LIBERATION : liberación f, puesta f en libertad 2 RELINQUISHING : cesión f (de propiedad, etc.) 3 ISSUE : estreno m (de una película), puesta f en venta (de un disco), publicación f (de un libro) 4 ESCAPE : escape m, fuga f (de un gas)

relegate ['relə,geıt] vt **-gated; -gating** : relegar

relent [rı'lent] vi : ablandarse, ceder

relentless [rı'lentləs] adj : implacable, sin tregua

relentlessly [rı'lentləsli] adv : implacablemente

relevance ['reləvənts] n : pertinencia f, relación f

relevant ['reləvənt] adj : pertinente — **relevantly** adv

reliability [rı,laıə'bıləti] n, pl **-ties** 1 : fiabilidad f, seguridad f (de una cosa) 2 : formalidad f, seriedad f (de una persona)

reliable [rı'laıəbəl] adj : confiable, fiable, fidedigno, seguro

reliably [rı'laıəbli] adv : sin fallar ⟨to be reliably informed : saber (algo) de fuentes fidedignas⟩

reliance [rı'laıənts] n 1 DEPENDENCE : dependencia f 2 CONFIDENCE : confianza f

reliant [rı'laıənt] adj : dependiente

relic ['relık] n 1 : reliquia f 2 VESTIGE : vestigio m

relief [rı'li:f] n 1 : alivio m, desahogo m ⟨what a relief! : ¡qué alivio!⟩ ⟨pain relief : alivio del dolor⟩ 2 AID, WELFARE : ayuda f (benéfica), asistencia f social 3 : relieve m ⟨relief map : mapa en relieve⟩ 4 REPLACEMENT : relevo m

relieve [rı'li:v] vt **-lieved; -lieving** 1 ALLEVIATE : aliviar, mitigar ⟨to feel relieved : sentirse aliviado⟩ 2 FREE : liberar 3 EXEMPT : eximir 4 REPLACE : relevar (a un centinela, etc.) 5 BREAK : romper ⟨to relieve the monotony : romper la monotonía⟩ 6 **to relieve someone of** : relevar a alguien de (su cargo, etc.)

religion [rı'lıdʒən] n : religión f

religious [rı'lıdʒəs] adj : religioso — **religiously** adv

relinquish [rı'lıŋkwıʃ, -'lın-] vt 1 GIVE UP : renunciar a, abandonar 2 RELEASE : soltar

relish[1] ['relıʃ] vt : saborear (comida), disfrutar con (un reto, etc.) ⟨I don't relish the idea : no me entusiasma la idea⟩

relish² n **1** ENJOYMENT : gusto m, deleite m **2** : salsa f de pepinillos en vinagre

relive [ˌriːˈlɪv] vt -lived; -living : revivir

reload [ˌriːˈloːd] vt : recargar

relocate [ˌriːˈloːˌkeɪt, ˌriːloˈkeɪt] v -cated; -cating vt : reubicar, trasladar — vi : trasladarse

relocation [ˌriːloˈkeɪʃən] n : reubicación f, traslado m

reluctance [rɪˈlʌktənts] n : renuencia f, reticencia f, desgana f

reluctant [rɪˈlʌktənt] adj : renuente, reacio, reticente

reluctantly [rɪˈlʌktəntli] adv : a regañadientes

rely [rɪˈlaɪ] vi -lied; -lying **1** DEPEND : depender (de), contar (con) **2** TRUST : confiar (en)

remain [rɪˈmeɪn] vi **1** : quedar ⟨very little remains : queda muy poco⟩ ⟨the remaining 10 minutes : los 10 minutos que quedan⟩ **2** STAY : quedarse, permanecer **3** CONTINUE : seguir, continuar ⟨to remain the same : seguir siendo igual⟩ **4 to remain to** : quedar por ⟨to remain to be done : quedar por hacer⟩ ⟨it remains to be seen : está por ver⟩

remainder [rɪˈmeɪndər] n : resto m, remanente m

remains [rɪˈmeɪnz] npl : restos mpl ⟨mortal remains : restos mortales⟩

remake¹ [rɪˈmeɪk] vt -made; -making **1** TRANSFORM : rehacer **2** : hacer una nueva versión de (una película, etc.)

remake² [ˈriːˌmeɪk] n : nueva versión f

remand [rɪˈmænd] vt **1** : devolver (un juicio) a otro tribunal **2 to remand someone into custody** : dictarle a alguien la prisión preventiva

remark¹ [rɪˈmɑrk] vt **1** NOTICE : observar **2** SAY : comentar, observar — vi **to remark on** : hacer observaciones sobre

remark² n : comentario m, observación f

remarkable [rɪˈmɑrkəbəl] adj : extraordinario, notable — **remarkably** [-bli] adv

remarry [ˌriːˈmæri] v -ried; -rying vi : volver a casarse — vt : volver a casarse con

rematch [ˈriːˌmætʃ] n : revancha f

remedial [rɪˈmiːdiəl] adj : correctivo ⟨remedial classes : clases para alumnos atrasados⟩

remedy¹ [ˈrɛmədi] vt -died; -dying : remediar

remedy² n, pl -dies : remedio m, medicamento m

remember [rɪˈmɛmbər] vt **1** RECOLLECT : acordarse de, recordar **2** : no olvidar ⟨remember my words : no olvides mis palabras⟩ ⟨to remember to : acordarse de⟩ **3** : dar saludos, dar recuerdos ⟨remember me to her : dale saludos de mi parte⟩ **4** COMMEMORATE : recordar, conmemorar

remembrance [rɪˈmɛmbrənts] n **1** RECOLLECTION : recuerdo m ⟨in remembrance of : en conmemoración de⟩ **2** MEMENTO : recuerdo m

remind [rɪˈmaɪnd] vt : recordar ⟨remind me to do it : recuérdame que lo haga⟩

⟨she reminds me of Clara : me recuerda de Clara⟩

reminder [rɪˈmaɪndər] n : recuerdo m

reminisce [ˌrɛməˈnɪs] vi -nisced; -niscing : rememorar los viejos tiempos

reminiscence [ˌrɛməˈnɪsənts] n : recuerdo m, reminiscencia f

reminiscent [ˌrɛməˈnɪsənt] adj **1** NOSTALGIC : nostálgico **2** SUGGESTIVE : evocador, que recuerda — **reminiscently** adv

remiss [rɪˈmɪs] adj : negligente, descuidado, remiso

remission [rɪˈmɪʃən] n : remisión f

remit [rɪˈmɪt] vt -mitted; -mitting **1** PARDON : perdonar **2** SEND : remitir, enviar (dinero)

remittance [rɪˈmɪtənts] n : remesa f

remnant [ˈrɛmnənt] n : restos mpl, vestigio m

remodel [rɪˈmɑdəl] vt -eled or -elled; -eling or -elling : remodelar, reformar

remonstrate [rɪˈmɑnˌstreɪt] vi -strated; -strating : protestar ⟨to remonstrate with someone : quejarse a alguien⟩

remorse [rɪˈmɔrs] n : remordimiento m

remorseful [rɪˈmɔrsfəl] adj : arrepentido, lleno de remordimiento

remorseless [rɪˈmɔrsləs] adj **1** PITILESS : despiadado **2** RELENTLESS : implacable

remote¹ [rɪˈmoːt] adj remoter; -est **1** FAR-OFF : lejano, remoto ⟨remote countries : países remotos⟩ ⟨in the remote past : en el pasado lejano⟩ **2** SECLUDED : recóndito **3** : a distancia, remoto **4** SLIGHT : remoto **5** ALOOF : distante

remote² or **remote control** n : control m remoto

remote–controlled adj : teledirigido

remotely [rɪˈmoːtli] adv **1** SLIGHTLY : remotamente **2** DISTANTLY : en un lugar remoto, muy lejos

remoteness [rɪˈmoːtnəs] n : lejanía f

removable [rɪˈmuːvəbəl] adj : removible

removal [rɪˈmuːvəl] n : separación f, extracción f, supresión f (en algo escrito), eliminación f (de problemas, etc.)

remove [rɪˈmuːv] v -moved; -moving **1** : quitar, quitarse ⟨remove the lid : quite la tapa⟩ ⟨to remove one's hat : quitarse el sombrero⟩ **2** EXTRACT : sacar, extraer ⟨to remove the contents of : sacar el contenido de⟩ **3** ELIMINATE : eliminar, disipar

remover [rɪˈmuːvər] n **1 nail polish remover** : quitaesmalte m **2 stain remover** : quitamanchas m

remunerate [rɪˈmjuːnəˌreɪt] vt -ated; -ating : remunerar

remuneration [rɪˌmjuːnəˈreɪʃən] n : remuneración f

renaissance [ˌrɛnəˈsɑnts, -ˈzɑnts; ˈrɛnəˌ-] n : renacimiento m ⟨the Renaissance : el Renacimiento⟩

renal [ˈriːnəl] adj : renal

rename [ˌriːˈneɪm] vt -named; -naming : ponerle un nombre nuevo a

rend [ˈrɛnd] vt rent [ˈrɛnt]; rending : desgarrar

render ['rɛndər] vt **1** : derretir (manteca, etc.) **2** GIVE : prestar, dar ⟨to render aid : prestar ayuda⟩ **3** MAKE : hacer, volver, dejar ⟨it rendered him helpless : lo dejó incapacitado⟩ **4** TRANSLATE : traducir, verter ⟨to render into English : traducir al inglés⟩

rendezvous ['rɑndɪˌvu:, -deɪ-] ns & pl : encuentro m, cita f

rendition [rɛn'dɪʃən] n : interpretación f

renegade ['rɛnɪˌgeɪd] n : renegado m, -da f

renege [rɪ'nɪg, -'nɛg] vi **-neged; -neging to renege on** : no cumplir (una promesa, etc.)

renew [rɪ'nu:, -'nju:] vt **1** REVIVE : renovar (esperanzas, etc.) **2** RESUME : reanudar **3** EXTEND : renovar ⟨to renew a subscription : renovar una suscripción⟩

renewable [rɪ'nu:əbəl, -'nju:-] adj : renovable

renewal [rɪ'nu:əl, -'nju:-] n : renovación f

renounce [rɪ'naʊnts] vt **-nounced; -nouncing** : renunciar a

renovate ['rɛnəˌveɪt] vt **-vated; -vating** : restaurar, renovar

renovation [ˌrɛnə'veɪʃən] n : restauración f, renovación f

renown [rɪ'naʊn] n : renombre m, fama f, celebridad f

renowned [rɪ'naʊnd] adj : renombrado, célebre, famoso

rent¹ ['rɛnt] vt : rentar, alquilar

rent² n **1** : renta f, alquiler m ⟨for rent : se alquila⟩ **2** RIP : rasgadura f

rental¹ ['rɛntəl] adj RENT : de alquiler

rental² n : alquiler m

renter ['rɛntər] n : arrendatario m, -ria f

renunciation [rɪˌnʌntsi'eɪʃən] n : renuncia f

reopen [ˌri:'o:pən] vt : volver a abrir

reorganization [ˌri:ˌɔrgənə'zeɪʃən] n : reorganización f

reorganize [ˌri:'ɔrgənˌaɪz] vt **-nized; -nizing** : reorganizar

rep ['rɛp] n REPRESENTATIVE : representante mf

repair¹ [rɪ'pær] vt : reparar, arreglar, refaccionar

repair² n **1** : reparación f, arreglo m **2** CONDITION : estado m ⟨in bad repair : en mal estado⟩

repairman [rɪ'pærˌmæn, -mən] n, pl **-men** [-mən, -ˌmɛn] : mecánico m, técnico m

reparation [ˌrɛpə'reɪʃən] n **1** AMENDS : reparación f **2 reparations** npl COMPENSATION : indemnización f

repartee [ˌrɛpər'ti:, -ˌpɑr-, 'rɛpˌteɪ] n : intercambio m de réplicas ingeniosas

repast [rɪ'pæst, 'ri:ˌpæst] n : comida f

repatriate [rɪ'peɪtriˌeɪt] vt **-ated; -ating** : repatriar

repay [rɪ'peɪ] vt **-paid; -paying 1** : pagar (una deuda), devolver (dinero) **2** : pagar (un favor)

repayment [rɪ'peɪmənt] n : pago m

repeal¹ [rɪ'pi:l] vt : abrogar, revocar

repeal² n : abrogación f, revocación f

repeat¹ [rɪ'pi:t] vt : repetir

repeat² n : repetición f

repeatedly [rɪ'pi:tədli] adv : repetidamente, repetidas veces

repel [rɪ'pɛl] vt **-pelled; -pelling 1** REPULSE : repeler (un enemigo, etc.) **2** RESIST : repeler **3** REJECT : rechazar, repeler **4** DISGUST : repugnar, darle asco (a alguien)

repellent or **repellant** [rɪ'pɛlənt] n : repelente m

repent [rɪ'pɛnt] vi : arrepentirse

repentance [rɪ'pɛntənts] n : arrepentimiento m

repentant [rɪ'pɛntənt] adj : arrepentido

repercussion [ˌri:pər'kʌʃən, ˌrɛpər-] n : repercusión f

repertoire ['rɛpərˌtwɑr] n : repertorio m

repertory ['rɛpərˌtori] n, pl **-ries** : repertorio m

repetition [ˌrɛpə'tɪʃən] n : repetición f

repetitious [ˌrɛpə'tɪʃəs] adj : repetitivo, reiterativo — **repetitiously** adv

repetitive [rɪ'pɛtətɪv] adj : repetitivo, reiterativo

repetitive stress or **repetitive strain** n : esfuerzo m repetitivo ⟨repetitive stress injury : lesión por esfuerzo repetitivo⟩

rephrase [rɪ'freɪz] vt **-phrased; -phrasing** REWORD : expresar de otra forma

replace [rɪ'pleɪs] vt **-placed; -placing 1** : volver a poner (en un lugar) **2** SUBSTITUTE : reemplazar, sustituir **3** : reponer ⟨to replace the worn carpet : reponer la alfombra raída⟩

replaceable [rɪ'pleɪsəbəl] adj : reemplazable

replacement [rɪ'pleɪsmənt] n **1** SUBSTITUTION : reemplazo m, sustitución f **2** SUBSTITUTE : sustituto m, -ta f; suplente mf (persona) **3 replacement part** : repuesto m, pieza f de recambio

replay¹ [rɪ'pleɪ] vt **1** : volver a poner (un video, etc.) **2** : volver a jugar (un partido)

replay² ['ri:ˌpleɪ] n : repetición f

replenish [rɪ'plɛnɪʃ] vt : rellenar, llenar de nuevo

replenishment [rɪ'plɛnɪʃmənt] n : reabastecimiento m

replete [rɪ'pli:t] adj : repleto, lleno

replica ['rɛplɪkə] n : réplica f, reproducción f

replicate ['rɛpləˌkeɪt] v **-cated; -cating** vt : duplicar, repetir — vi : duplicarse

replication [ˌrɛplə'keɪʃən] n **1** REPRODUCTION : reproducción f **2** REPETITION : repetición f **3** : replicación f (celular)

reply¹ [rɪ'plaɪ] vi **-plied; -plying** : contestar, responder

reply² n, pl **-plies** : respuesta f, contestación f

report¹ [rɪ'port] vt **1** : informar sobre (una noticia, etc.) **2** ANNOUNCE : anunciar **3** : decir, afirmar ⟨35% reported having voted : el 35% dijo haber votado⟩ **4** : dar parte de, reportar (un accidente, etc.), denunciar (un delito) — vi **1** : informar ⟨to report on : informar sobre⟩ **2 to report back** : volver (a la base, etc.) **3 to report back** : dar parte a un jefe) **4 to report for duty** : presentarse, reportarse **5 to report to some-one** : reportar a alguien

report[2] *n* **1** ACCOUNT : informe *m*, reportaje *m* (en un periódico, etc.) **2** RUMOR : rumor *m* **3** BANG : estallido *m* (de un arma de fuego)

report card *n* : boletín *m* de calificaciones, boletín *m* de notas, boleta *f* de calificaciones *Mex*

reportedly [rɪ'pɔrtədli] *adv* : según se dice, según se informa

reporter [rɪ'pɔrtər] *n* : periodista *mf*; reportero *m*, -ra *f*

repose[1] [rɪ'poːz] *vi* **-posed; -posing** : reposar, descansar

repose[2] *n* **1** : reposo *m*, descanso *m* **2** CALM : calma *f*, tranquilidad *f*

repository [rɪ'pɑzə,tori] *n*, *pl* **-ries** : depósito *m*

repossess [,ri:pə'zes] *vt* : recuperar, recobrar la posesión de

reprehensible [,repri'hentsəbəl] *adj* : reprensible — **reprehensibly** [-bli] *adv*

represent [,repri'zent] *vt* **1** SYMBOLIZE, EXEMPLIFY : representar **2** CONSTITUTE : representar **3** : representar (a un cliente, etc.), ser un representante de (una compañía, etc.) **4** PORTRAY : presentar ⟨he represents himself as a friend : se presenta como amigo⟩

representation [,repri,zen'teɪʃən, -zən-] *n* : representación *f*

representative[1] [,repri'zentətiv] *adj* : representativo

representative[2] *n* **1** : representante *mf* **2** : diputado *m*, -da *f* (en la política)

repress [rɪ'pres] *vt* : reprimir

repression [rɪ'preʃən] *n* : represión *f*

repressive [rɪ'presɪv] *adj* : represivo

reprieve[1] [rɪ'pri:v] *vt* **-prieved; -prieving** : indultar

reprieve[2] *n* : indulto *m*

reprimand[1] ['reprə,mænd] *vt* : reprender

reprimand[2] *n* : reprimenda *f*

reprint[1] [rɪ'print] *vt* : reimprimir

reprint[2] ['ri:,print, rɪ'print] *n* : reedición *f*

reprisal [rɪ'praizəl] *n* : represalia *f*

reproach[1] [rɪ'pro:tʃ] *vt* : reprochar

reproach[2] *n* **1** DISGRACE : deshonra *f* **2** REBUKE : reproche *m*, recriminación *f*

reproachful [rɪ'pro:tʃfəl] *adj* : de reproche

reproduce [,ri:prə'du:s, -'dju:s] *v* **-duced; -ducing** *vt* : reproducir — *vi* BREED : reproducirse

reproduction [,ri:prə'dʌkʃən] *n* : reproducción *f*

reproductive [,ri:prə'dʌktiv] *adj* : reproductor

reproof [rɪ'pru:f] *n* : reprobación *f*, reprimenda *f*, reproche *m*

reprove [rɪ'pru:v] *vt* **-proved; -proving** : reprender, censurar

reptile ['rep,tail] *n* : reptil *m*

reptilian ['rep,tiliən] *n* : reptil

republic [rɪ'pʌblɪk] *n* : república *f*

republican[1] [rɪ'pʌblɪkən] *adj* : republicano

republican[2] *n* : republicano *m*, -na *f* — **Republicanism** [rɪ'pʌblɪkə,nizəm] *n*

repudiate [rɪ'pju:di,eɪt] *vt* **-ated; -ating 1** REJECT : rechazar **2** DISOWN : repudiar, renegar de

repudiation [rɪ,pju:di'eɪʃən] *n* : rechazo *m*, repudio *m*

repugnance [rɪ'pʌgnənts] *n* : repugnancia *f*

repugnant [rɪ'pʌgnənt] *adj* : repugnante, asqueroso

repulse[1] [rɪ'pʌls] *vt* **-pulsed; -pulsing 1** REPEL : repeler **2** REBUFF : desairar, rechazar

repulse[2] *n* : rechazo *m*

repulsive [rɪ'pʌlsɪv] *adj* : repulsivo, repugnante, asqueroso — **repulsively** *adv*

reputable ['repjətəbəl] *adj* : acreditado, de buena reputación

reputation [,repjə'teɪʃən] *n* : reputación *f*, fama *f*

repute [rɪ'pju:t] *n* : reputación *f*, fama *f*

reputed [rɪ'pju:təd] *adj* : reputado, supuesto ⟨she's reputed to be the best : tiene fama de ser la mejor⟩

reputedly [rɪ'pju:tədli] *adv* : supuestamente, según se dice

request[1] [rɪ'kwest] *vt* : pedir, solicitar, rogar ⟨to request information : solicitar/pedir información⟩ ⟨as requested : conforme a lo solicitado⟩

request[2] *n* : petición *f*, solicitud *f*, pedido *m*

requiem ['rekwiəm, 'reɪ-] *n* : réquiem *m*

require [rɪ'kwair] *vt* **-quired; -quiring 1** CALL FOR, DEMAND : requerir, exigir ⟨if required : si se requiere⟩ ⟨to require that something be done : exigir que algo se haga⟩ **2** NEED : necesitar, requerir

requirement [rɪ'kwairmənt] *n* **1** NECESSITY : necesidad *f* **2** DEMAND : requisito *m*, demanda *f*

requisite[1] ['rekwəzɪt] *adj* : esencial, necesario

requisite[2] *n* : requisito *m*, necesidad *f*

requisition[1] [,rekwə'zɪʃən] *vt* : requisar

requisition[2] *n* : requisa *f*

reread [,ri:'ri:d] *vt* **-read** [-'red]; **-reading** : releer

reroute [,ri:'ru:t, -'raut] *vt* **-routed; -routing** : desviar

rerun[1] [rɪ'rʌn] *vt* **-ran; -run; -running** : reponer (un programa televisivo)

rerun[2] ['ri:,rʌn] *n* **1** : reposición *f* (de un programa televisivo) **2** REPEAT : repetición *f*

resale ['ri:,seɪl, ,ri:'seɪl] *n* : reventa *f*

reschedule [ri:'ske,dʒu:l, -dʒəl, *esp Brit* -'ʃedju:l] *vt* **-duled; -duling** : cambiar la hora/fecha de (una cita, etc.)

rescind [rɪ'sɪnd] *vt* **1** CANCEL : rescindir, cancelar **2** REPEAL : abrogar, revocar

rescue[1] ['res,kju:] *vt* **-cued; -cuing** : rescatar, salvar

rescue[2] *n* : rescate *m*

rescuer ['res,kju:ər] *n* : salvador *m*, -dora *f*

research[1] [rɪ'sərtʃ, 'ri:,sərtʃ] *v* : investigar

research[2] *n* : investigación *f*

researcher [rɪ'sərtʃər, 'ri:,-] *n* : investigador *m*, -dora *f*

resell [ri'sɛl] **-sold** [-'so:ld]; **-selling** vt : revender

resemblance [ri'zɛmblənts] n : semejanza f, parecido m

resemble [ri'zɛmbəl] vt **-sembled; -sembling** : parecerse a, asemejarse a

resent [ri'zɛnt] vt : molestarse por (algo), ofenderse por (algo), guardarle rencor a (alguien)

resentful [ri'zɛntfəl] adj : resentido, rencoroso — **resentfully** adv

resentment [ri'zɛntmənt] n : resentimiento m

reservation [,rɛzər'veɪʃən] n 1 : reservación f, reserva f ⟨to make a reservation : hacer una reservación⟩ 2 DOUBT, MISGIVING : reserva f, duda f ⟨without reservations : sin reservas⟩ 3 : reserva f (de indios americanos)

reserve¹ [ri'zərv] vt **-served; -serving** : reservar

reserve² n 1 STOCK : reserva f ⟨to keep in reserve : guardar en reserva⟩ 2 RESTRAINT : reserva f, moderación f 3 **reserves** npl : reservas fpl (militares)

reserved [ri'zərvd] adj : reservado

reservoir ['rɛzər,vwɑr, -,vwɔr, -,vɔr] n : embalse m

reset [,ri:'sɛt] vt **-set; -setting** : poner en hora (un reloj), poner a cero (un temporizador), reiniciar (una computadora), borrar (una contraseña)

reside [ri'zaɪd] vi **-sided; -siding** 1 DWELL : residir 2 LIE : radicar, residir ⟨the power resides in the presidency : el poder radica en la presidencia⟩

residence ['rɛzədənts] n : residencia f

resident¹ ['rɛzədənt] adj : residente

resident² n : residente mf

residential [,rɛzə'dɛntʃəl] adj : residencial

residual [ri'zɪdʒuəl] adj : residual

residue ['rɛzə,du:, -,dju:] n : residuo m, resto m

resign [ri'zaɪn] vt 1 QUIT : dimitir, renunciar 2 **to resign oneself** : aguantarse, resignarse

resignation [,rɛzɪg'neɪʃən] n : resignación f

resilience [ri'zɪljənts] n 1 : capacidad f de recuperación, adaptabilidad f 2 ELASTICITY : elasticidad f

resiliency [ri'zɪljəntsi] → **resilience**

resilient [ri'zɪljənt] adj 1 STRONG : resistente, fuerte 2 ELASTIC : elástico

resin ['rɛzən] n : resina f

resist [ri'zɪst] vt 1 : resistir (el calor, la tentación, etc.) 2 OPPOSE : oponerse a — vi 1 OPPOSE : resistir 2 : resistirse ⟨I couldn't resist : no me pude resistir⟩

resistance [ri'zɪstənts] n : resistencia f

resistant [ri'zɪstənt] adj : resistente

resolute ['rɛzə,lu:t] adj : firme, resuelto, decidido

resolutely ['rɛzə,lu:tli, ,rɛzə'-] adv : resueltamente, firmemente

resolution [,rɛzə'lu:ʃən] n 1 SOLUTION : solución f 2 RESOLVE : resolución f, determinación f 3 DECISION : propósito m, decisión f ⟨New Year's resolutions : propósitos para el Año Nuevo⟩ 4 MOTION, PROPOSAL : moción f, resolución f (legislativa)

resolve¹ [ri'zɑlv] vt **-solved; -solving** 1 SOLVE : resolver, solucionar 2 DECIDE : resolver ⟨she resolved to get more sleep : resolvió dormir más⟩

resolve² n : resolución f, determinación f

resonance ['rɛzənənts] n : resonancia f

resonant ['rɛzənənt] adj : resonante

resort¹ [ri'zɔrt] vi **to resort to** : recurrir a ⟨to resort to force : recurrir a la fuerza⟩

resort² n 1 RECOURSE : recurso m ⟨as a last resort : como último recurso⟩ 2 HANGOUT : lugar m popular, lugar m muy frecuentado 3 : lugar m de vacaciones ⟨tourist resort : centro turístico⟩

resound [ri'zaʊnd] vi : retumbar, resonar

resounding [ri'zaʊndɪŋ] adj 1 RESONANT : resonante 2 ABSOLUTE, CATEGORICAL : rotundo, tremendo ⟨a resounding success : un éxito rotundo⟩

resource ['ri:,sɔrs, ri'sɔrs] n 1 RESOURCEFULNESS : ingenio m, recursos mpl 2 **resources** npl : recursos mpl ⟨natural resources : recursos naturales⟩ 3 **resources** npl MEANS : recursos mpl, medios mpl, fondos mpl

resourceful [ri'sɔrsfəl, -'zɔrs-] adj : ingenioso

resourcefulness [ri'sɔrsfəlnəs, -'zɔrs-] n : ingenio m, recursos mpl, inventiva f

respect¹ [ri'spɛkt] vt : respetar, estimar

respect² n 1 REFERENCE : relación f, respecto m ⟨with respect to : en lo que respecta a⟩ 2 ESTEEM : respeto m 3 DETAIL, PARTICULAR : respeto m, sentido m, respecto m ⟨in some respects : en algunos aspectos⟩ ⟨in this/that respect : en este/ese sentido⟩ 4 **respects** npl : respetos mpl ⟨to pay one's respects : presentar uno sus respetos⟩

respectability [ri,spɛktə'bɪləti] n : respetabilidad f

respectable [ri'spɛktəbəl] adj 1 PROPER : respetable, decente 2 CONSIDERABLE : considerable, respetable ⟨a respectable amount : una cantidad respetable⟩ — **respectably** [-bli] adv

respectful [ri'spɛktfəl] adj : respetuoso — **respectfully** adv

respectfulness [ri'spɛktfəlnəs] n : respetuosidad f

respective [ri'spɛktɪv] adj : respectivo ⟨their respective homes : sus casas respectivas⟩ — **respectively** adv

respiration [,rɛspə'reɪʃən] n : respiración f

respirator ['rɛspə,reɪtər] n : respirador m

respiratory ['rɛspərə,tori, ri'spairə-] adj : respiratorio

respite ['rɛspɪt, ri'spaɪt] n : respiro m, tregua f

resplendent [ri'splɛndənt] adj : resplandeciente — **resplendently** adv

respond [ri'spɑnd] vi 1 ANSWER : contestar, responder 2 REACT : responder, reaccionar ⟨to respond to treatment : responder al tratamiento⟩

response [ri'spɑnts] n : respuesta f

responsibility [rɪˌspɑnsəˈbɪləti] *n, pl* **-ties**
: responsabilidad *f*

responsible [rɪˈspɑnsəbəl] *adj* **1** : responsable **2 to be responsible for**
CAUSE : ser el/la responsable de (dícese de una persona), ser la causa de **3 to be responsible for** MANAGE : ser responsable de (algo), tener (a alguien) a su cargo **4 to be responsible to** : ser responsable ante **5 to hold someone responsible for** : hacer responsable a alguien de — **responsibly** [-bli] *adv*

responsive [rɪˈspɑnsɪv] *adj* **1** ANSWERING : que responde **2** SENSITIVE : sensible, receptivo

responsiveness [rɪˈspɑnsɪvnəs] *n* : receptividad *f*, sensibilidad *f*

rest[1] [ˈrɛst] *vi* **1** : descansar ⟨to rest comfortably : descansar cómodamente⟩ **2** STOP : pararse, detenerse **3** DEPEND : basarse (en), descansar (sobre), depender (de) ⟨the decision rests with her : la decisión pesa sobre ella⟩ **4 to rest easy** : quedarse tranquilo **5 to rest on** : apoyarse en, descansar sobre ⟨to rest on one's arm : apoyarse en el brazo⟩ — *vt* **1** RELAX : descansar **2** SUPPORT : apoyar **3 to rest one's eyes on** : fijar la mirada en

rest[2] *n* **1** RELAXATION : descanso *m*, reposo *m* ⟨to get some rest : descansar⟩ **2** BREAK : descanso *m* **3** SUPPORT : soporte *m*, apoyo *m* **4** : silencio *m* (en música) **5** REMAINDER : resto *m* ⟨the rest (of us/them) : los demás⟩ **6 to come to rest** : pararse

rest area → rest stop

restart [rɪˈstɑrt] *vt* **1** : volver a empezar **2** RESUME : reanudar **3** : volver a arrancar (un motor), reiniciar (una computadora) — *vi* **1** : reanudarse **2** : volver a arrancar

restate [ˌriːˈsteɪt] *vt* **-stated; -stating** : replantear (una pregunta, etc.), repetir

restatement [ˌriːˈsteɪtmənt] *n* : repetición *f*

restaurant [ˈrɛstəˌrɑnt, -rənt] *n* : restaurante *m*

restful [ˈrɛstfəl] *adj* **1** RELAXING : relajante **2** PEACEFUL : tranquilo, sosegado

rest home → nursing home

restitution [ˌrɛstəˈtuːʃən, -ˈtjuː-] *n* : restitución *f*

restive [ˈrɛstɪv] *adj* : inquieto, nervioso

restless [ˈrɛstləs] *adj* **1** FIDGETY : inquieto, agitado **2** IMPATIENT : impaciente **3** SLEEPLESS : desvelado ⟨a restless night : una noche en blanco⟩

restlessly [ˈrɛstləsli] *adv* : nerviosamente

restlessness [ˈrɛstləsnəs] *n* : inquietud *f*, agitación *f*

restoration [ˌrɛstəˈreɪʃən] *n* : restauración *f*, restablecimiento *m*

restore [rɪˈstor] *vt* **-stored; -storing** **1** RETURN, GIVE BACK : devolver, restituir **2** REESTABLISH : restablecer (el orden, etc.), recuperar (la confianza, la salud, etc.), restaurar (una monarquía, etc.) **3** REPAIR : restaurar

restrain [rɪˈstreɪn] *vt* **1** : refrenar, contener **2 to restrain oneself** : contenerse

restrained [rɪˈstreɪnd] *adj* : comedido, templado, contenido

restraint [rɪˈstreɪnt] *n* **1** RESTRICTION : restricción *f*, limitación *f*, control *m* **2** CONFINEMENT : encierro *m* **3** RESERVE : reserva *f*, control *m* de sí mismo

restrict [rɪˈstrɪkt] *vt* : restringir, limitar, constreñir

restricted [rɪˈstrɪktəd] *adj* **1** LIMITED : limitado, restringido **2** CLASSIFIED : secreto, confidencial

restriction [rɪˈstrɪkʃən] *n* : restricción *f*

restrictive [rɪˈstrɪktɪv] *adj* : restrictivo — **restrictively** *adv*

restroom [ˈrɛstˌruːm, -ˌrʊm] *n* : servicios *mpl*, baño *m*

restructure [ˌriːˈstrʌktʃər] *vt* **-tured; -turing** : reestructurar

rest stop *n* : área *f* de descanso (en una carretera)

result[1] [rɪˈzʌlt] *vi* : resultar ⟨to result in : resultar en, tener por resultado⟩ ⟨to result from : resultar de⟩

result[2] *n* : resultado *m*, consecuencia *f* ⟨as a result of : como consecuencia de⟩

resultant [rɪˈzʌltənt] *adj* : resultante

resume [rɪˈzuːm] *v* **-sumed; -suming** *vt* : reanudar — *vi* : reanudarse

résumé *or* **resume** *or* **resumé** [ˈrɛzəˌmeɪ, ˌrɛzəˈ-] *n* **1** SUMMARY : resumen *m* **2** CURRICULUM VITAE : currículum *m*, currículo *m*

resumption [rɪˈzʌmpʃən] *n* : reanudación *f*

resurface [ˌriːˈsərfəs] *v* **-faced; -facing** *vt* : pavimentar (una carretera) de nuevo — *vi* **1** : volver a salir a la superficie **2** REAPPEAR : resurgir, reaparecer

resurgence [rɪˈsərdʒənts] *n* : resurgimiento *m*

resurrect [ˌrɛzəˈrɛkt] *vt* : resucitar, desempolvar

resurrection [ˌrɛzəˈrɛkʃən] *n* : resurrección *f*

resuscitate [rɪˈsʌsəˌteɪt] *vt* **-tated; -tating** : resucitar, revivir

resuscitation [rɪˌsʌsəˈteɪʃən] *n* : reanimación *f*, resucitación *f*

retail[1] [ˈriːˌteɪl] *vt* : vender al por menor, vender al detalle

retail[2] *adv* : al por menor, al detalle

retail[3] *adj* : detallista, minorista ⟨retail price : precio de venta al público⟩

retail[4] *n* : venta *f* al detalle, venta *f* al por menor

retailer [ˈriːˌteɪlər] *n* : detallista *mf*, minorista *mf*

retain [rɪˈteɪn] *vt* : retener, conservar, guardar

retainer [rɪˈteɪnər] *n* **1** SERVANT : criado *m*, -da *f* **2** ADVANCE : anticipo *m*

retaliate [rɪˈtæliˌeɪt] *vi* **-ated; -ating** : responder, contraatacar, tomar represalias

retaliation [rɪˌtæliˈeɪʃən] *n* : represalia *f*, retaliación *f*

retard [rɪˈtɑrd] *vt* : retardar, retrasar

retardation → mental retardation

retarded [rɪˈtɑrdəd] *adj often offensive* : retrasado

retch [ˈretʃ] *vi* : hacer arcadas

retention [rɪˈtentʃən] *n* : retención *f*

retentive [rɪˈtentɪv] *adj* : retentivo

rethink [ˌriːˈθɪŋk] *vt* -thought; -thinking : reconsiderar, repensar

reticence [ˈretəsənts] *n* : reticencia *f*

reticent [ˈretəsənt] *adj* : reticente

retina [ˈretənə] *n, pl* -nas *or* -nae [-əni, -ən,aɪ] : retina *f*

retinue [ˈretən,uː, -,juː] *n* : séquito *m*, comitiva *f*, cortejo *m*

retire [rɪˈtaɪr] *vi* -tired; -tiring 1 RETREAT, WITHDRAW : retirarse, retraerse 2 : retirarse, jubilarse (de su trabajo) 3 : acostarse, irse a dormir

retiree [rɪˌtaɪˈriː] *n* : jubilado *m*, -da *f*

retirement [rɪˈtaɪrmənt] *n* : jubilación *f*

retiring [rɪˈtaɪrɪŋ] *adj* SHY : retraído

retort[1] [rɪˈtort] *vt* : replicar

retort[2] *n* : réplica *f*

retrace [ˌriːˈtreɪs] *vt* -traced; -tracing : volver sobre, desandar ⟨to retrace one's steps : volver uno sobre sus pasos⟩

retract [rɪˈtrækt] *vt* 1 TAKE BACK, WITHDRAW : retirar, retractarse de 2 : retraer (las garras) — *vi* : retractarse

retractable [rɪˈtræktəbəl] *adj* : retractable

retraction [rɪˈtrækʃən] *n* : retracción *f*, retractación *f*

retrain [rɪˈtreɪn] *vt* : reciclar, reconvertir

retreat[1] [rɪˈtriːt] *vi* : retirarse, batirse en retirada

retreat[2] *n* 1 : retirada *f* ⟨to beat a hasty retreat : salir huyendo⟩ 2 REFUGE : retiro *m* (espiritual), retiro *m*

retrial [ˌriːˈtraɪəl] *n* : nuevo juicio *m*

retribution [ˌretrəˈbjuːʃən] *n* : castigo *m*

retrieval [rɪˈtriːvəl] *n* : recuperación *f* ⟨beyond retrieval : irrecuperable⟩ ⟨data retrieval : recuperación de datos⟩

retrieve [rɪˈtriːv] *vt* -trieved; -trieving 1 RECOVER : recuperar 2 FETCH : ir a buscar, cobrar (la caza)

retriever [rɪˈtriːvər] *n* : perro *m* cobrador

retroactive [ˌretroˈæktɪv] *adj* : retroactivo — **retroactively** *adv*

retrograde [ˈretrəˌgreɪd] *adj* : retrógrado

retrospect [ˈretrəˌspekt] *n* in retrospect : mirando hacia atrás, retrospectivamente

retrospective [ˌretrəˈspektɪv] *adj* : retrospectivo

return[1] [rɪˈtərn] *vi* 1 : volver, regresar ⟨to return home : regresar a casa⟩ 2 REAPPEAR : reaparecer, resurgir 3 REVERT : volver (a un estado anterior) 4 : volver (a una actividad, un tema, etc.) 5 ANSWER : responder 6 : emitir (un veredicto) — *vt* 1 REPLACE, RESTORE : devolver, volver (a poner), restituir ⟨to return something to its place : volver a poner algo en su lugar⟩ 2 YIELD : producir, redituar, rendir 3 REPAY : devolver, corresponder a ⟨to return a compliment : devolver un cumplido⟩

return[2] *adj* : de vuelta

return[3] *n* 1 RETURNING : regreso *m*, vuelta *f*, retorno *m* 2 *or* tax return : declaración *f* de impuestos, declaración *f* de la renta 3 YIELD : rédito *m*, rendimiento *m*, ganancia *f* 4 returns *npl* DATA, RESULTS : resultados *mpl*, datos *mpl* 5 in return (for) : a cambio (de)

reunion [rɪˈjuːnjən] *n* : reunión *f*, reencuentro *m*

reunite [ˌriːjuˈnaɪt] *v* -nited; -niting *vt* : (volver a) reunir — *vi* : (volver a) reunirse

reusable [rɪˈjuːzəbəl] *adj* : reutilizable

reuse [rɪˈjuːz] *vt* -used; -using : reutilizar, usar de nuevo

rev[1] [ˈrev] *v* -revved; -revving *vt* 1 *or* rev up : acelerar (un motor) 2 to rev up : impulsar (la economía), acelerar (un proceso, etc.) — *vi* to rev up : prepararse

rev[2] *n* : revolución *f* (de un motor)

revamp [ˌriːˈvæmp] *vt* : renovar

reveal [rɪˈviːl] *vt* 1 DIVULGE : revelar, divulgar ⟨to reveal a secret : revelar un secreto⟩ 2 SHOW : manifestar, mostrar, dejar ver

revealing [rɪˈviːlɪŋ] *adj* : revelador

reveille [ˈrevəli] *n* : toque *m* de diana

revel[1] [ˈrevəl] *vi* -eled *or* -elled; -eling *or* -elling 1 CAROUSE : ir de juerga 2 to revel in : deleitarse en

revel[2] *n* : juerga *f*, parranda *f fam*

revelation [ˌrevəˈleɪʃən] *n* : revelación *f*

reveler *or* **reveller** [ˈrevələr] *n* : juerguista *mf*

revelry [ˈrevəlri] *n, pl* -ries : juerga *f*, parranda *f fam*, jarana *f fam*

revenge[1] [rɪˈvendʒ] *vt* -venged; -venging to revenge oneself on : vengarse de

revenge[2] *n* : venganza *f* ⟨to take (one's) revenge on : vengarse de⟩ ⟨in revenge for : como venganza por⟩

revenue [ˈrevəˌnuː, -ˌnjuː] *n* : ingresos *mpl*, rentas *fpl*

reverberate [rɪˈvərbəˌreɪt] *vi* -ated; -ating : reverberar

reverberation [rɪˌvərbəˈreɪʃən] *n* : reverberación *f*

revere [rɪˈvɪr] *vt* -vered; -vering : reverenciar, venerar

reverence [ˈrevərənts] *n* : reverencia *f*, veneración *f*

reverend [ˈrevərənd] *adj* : reverendo ⟨the Reverend John Chapin : el reverendo John Chapin⟩

reverent [ˈrevərənt] *adj* : reverente — **reverently** *adv*

reverie [ˈrevəri] *n, pl* -eries : ensueño *m*

reversal [rɪˈvərsəl] *n* 1 INVERSION : inversión *f* (del orden normal) 2 CHANGE : cambio *m* total 3 SETBACK : revés *m*, contratiempo *m*

reverse[1] [rɪˈvərs] *v* -versed; -versing *vt* 1 INVERT : invertir (el orden, los roles, etc.) 2 CHANGE : cambiar totalmente 3 UNDO : reparar (daño, etc.), revertir ⟨to reverse a trend : revertir una tendencia⟩ 4 ANNUL : revocar, revertir — *vi* : dar marcha atrás

reverse[2] *adj* 1 : inverso ⟨in reverse order : en orden inverso⟩ ⟨the reverse side : el reverso⟩ 2 OPPOSITE : contrario, opuesto

reverse[3] *n* 1 BACK : reverso *m*, dorso *m*, revés *m* 2 SETBACK : revés *m*, contratiempo *m* **3 the reverse** : lo contrario, lo opuesto **4** *or* **reverse gear** : marcha *f* atrás; reversa *f Col, Mex* ⟨to put a car in reverse : dar marcha atrás, dar reversa⟩

reversible [rɪ'vərsəbəl] *adj* : reversible

reversion [rɪ'vərʒən] *n* : reversión *f*, vuelta *f*

revert [rɪ'vərt] *vi* **1** : revertir (a un propietario) **2** : volver (a un estado anterior)

review¹ [rɪ'vju:] *vt* **1** REEXAMINE : volver a examinar, repasar (una lección) **2** CRITICIZE : reseñar, hacer una crítica de **3** EXAMINE : examinar, analizar ⟨to review one's life : examinar su vida⟩ **4 to review the troops** : pasar revista a las tropas

review² *n* **1** INSPECTION : revista *f* (de tropas) **2** ANALYSIS, OVERVIEW : resumen *m*, análisis *m* ⟨a review of current affairs : un análisis de las actualidades⟩ **3** CRITICISM : reseña *f*, crítica *f* (de un libro, etc.) **4** : repaso *m* (para un examen) **5** REVUE : revista *f* (musical)

reviewer [rɪ'vju:ər] *n* : crítico *m*, -ca *f*

revile [rɪ'vaɪl] *vt* **-viled; -viling** : injuriar, denostar

revise [rɪ'vaɪz] *vt* **-vised; -vising** : revisar, corregir, refundir ⟨to revise a dictionary : corregir un diccionario⟩

revision [rɪ'vɪʒən] *n* : revisión *f*

revitalize [ri:'vaɪtə̩laɪz] *vt* **-ized; -izing** : resucitar, revitalizar

revival [rɪ'vaɪvəl] *n* **1** : renacimiento *m* (de ideas — etc.), restablecimiento *m* (de costumbres, etc.), reactivación *f* (de la economía) **2** : reanimación *f*, resucitación *f* (en medicina) **3** *or* **revival meeting** : asamblea *f* evangelista

revive [rɪ'vaɪv] *v* **-vived; -viving** *vt* **1** REAWAKEN : reavivar, reanimar, reactivar (la economía), resucitar (a un paciente) **2** REESTABLISH : restablecer — *vi* **1** : renacer, reanimarse, reactivarse **2** COME TO : recobrar el sentido, volver en sí

revoke [rɪ'vo:k] *vt* **-voked; -voking** : revocar — **revocation** [̩revə'keɪʃən, rɪ̩vo:-] *n*

revolt [rɪ'vo:lt] *vi* **1** REBEL : rebelarse, sublevarse **2 to revolt at** : sentir repugnancia por — *vt* DISGUST : darle asco (a alguien), repugnar

revolt² *n* REBELLION : rebelión *f*, revuelta *f*, sublevación *f*

revolting [rɪ'vo:ltɪŋ] *adj* : asqueroso, repugnante

revolution [̩revə'lu:ʃən] *n* : revolución *f*

revolutionary¹ [̩revə'lu:ʃənə̩ri] *adj* : revolucionario

revolutionary² *n, pl* **-aries** : revolucionario *m*, -ria *f*

revolutionize [̩revə'lu:ʃən̩aɪz] *vt* **-ized; -izing** : cambiar radicalmente, revolucionar

revolve [rɪ'vɑlv] *v* **-volved; -volving** *vt* ROTATE : hacer girar — *vi* **1** ROTATE : girar ⟨to revolve around : girar alrededor de⟩ **2 to revolve in one's mind** : darle vueltas en la cabeza a alguien

revolver [rɪ'vɑlvər] *n* : revólver *m*

revolving [rɪ'vɑlvɪŋ] *adj* : giratorio ⟨revolving door : puerta giratoria⟩

revue [rɪ'vju:] *n* : revista *f* (musical)

revulsion [rɪ'vʌlʃən] *n* : repugnancia *f*

reward¹ [rɪ'wɔrd] *vt* : recompensar, premiar

reward² *n* : recompensa *f*

rewarding [rɪ'wɔrdɪŋ] *adj* **1** : gratificante **2** PROFITABLE : rentable

rewind [̩ri:'waɪnd] *vt* : rebobinar

reword [̩ri:'wərd] *vt* REPHRASE : expresar de otra forma

rewrite [̩ri:'raɪt] *vt* **-wrote; -written; -writing** : escribir de nuevo, volver a escribir

rhapsody ['ræpsədi] *n, pl* **-dies 1** : elogio *m* excesivo ⟨to go into rhapsodies over : extasiarse por⟩ **2** : rapsodia *f* (en música)

rhea ['ri:ə] *n* : ñandú *m*

rhetoric ['reṯərɪk] *n* : retórica *f*

rhetorical [rɪ'tɔrɪkəl] *adj* : retórico ⟨rhetorical question : pregunta retórica⟩

rheumatic [ru'mæṯɪk] *adj* : reumático

rheumatism ['ru:mə̩tɪzəm, 'rʊ-] *n* : reumatismo *m*

rhinestone ['raɪn̩sto:n] *n* : diamante *m* de imitación

rhino ['raɪ̩no:] *n, pl* **rhino** *or* **rhinos** → rhinoceros

rhinoceros [raɪ'nɑsərəs] *n, pl* **-eroses** *or* **-eros** *or* **-eri** [-̩raɪ] : rinoceronte *m*

rhododendron [̩ro:də'dendrən] *n* : rododendro *m*

rhombus ['rɑmbəs] *n, pl* **-buses** *or* **-bi** [-̩baɪ, -bi] : rombo *m*

rhubarb ['ru:̩bɑrb] *n* : ruibarbo *m*

rhyme¹ ['raɪm] *vi* **rhymed; rhyming** : rimar

rhyme² *n* **1** : rima *f* **2** VERSE : verso *m* (en rima)

rhythm ['rɪðəm] *n* : ritmo *m*

rhythmic ['rɪðmɪk] *or* **rhythmical** [-mɪkəl] *adj* : rítmico — **rhythmically** [-mɪkli] *adv*

rib¹ ['rɪb] *vt* **ribbed; ribbing 1** : hacer en canalé ⟨a ribbed sweater : un suéter en canalé⟩ **2** TEASE : tomarle el pelo (a alguien)

rib² *n* **1** : costilla *f* (de una persona o un animal) **2** : nervio *m* (de una bóveda o una hoja), varilla *f* (de un paraguas), canalé *m* (de una prenda tejida)

ribald ['rɪbəld] *adj* : escabroso, procaz

ribbon ['rɪbən] *n* **1** : cinta *f* **2 to tear to ribbons** : hacer jirones

rib cage *n* : caja *f* torácica

rice ['raɪs] *n* : arroz *m*

rich ['rɪtʃ] *adj* **1** WEALTHY : rico **2** SUMPTUOUS : suntuoso, lujoso **3** : pesado ⟨rich foods : comidas pesadas⟩ **4** ABUNDANT : abundante **5** : vivo, intenso ⟨rich colors : colores vivos⟩ **6** FERTILE : fértil, rico

riches ['rɪtʃəz] *npl* : riquezas *fpl*

richly ['rɪtʃli] *adv* **1** SUMPTUOUSLY : suntuosamente, ricamente **2** ABUNDANTLY : abundantemente **3 richly deserved** : bien merecido

richness ['rɪtʃnəs] *n* : riqueza *f*

rickets ['rɪkəts] n : raquitismo m

rickety ['rɪkəṭi] adj : desvencijado, destartalado

rickshaw ['rɪk,ʃɔ] n : rickshaw m

ricochet¹ ['rɪkə,ʃeɪ] vi **-cheted** [-,ʃeɪd] or **-chetted** [-,ʃɛṭəd]; **-cheting** [-,ʃeɪɪŋ] or **-chetting** [-,ʃɛṭɪŋ] : rebotar

ricochet² n : rebote m

rid ['rɪd] vt **rid; ridding** 1 FREE : librar ⟨to rid the city of thieves : librar la ciudad de ladrones⟩ 2 **to get rid of** or **to rid oneself of** : deshacerse de, desembarazarse de

riddance ['rɪdən̩ts] n : libramiento m ⟨good riddance! : ¡adiós y buen viaje!, ¡vete con viento fresco!⟩

riddle¹ ['rɪdəl] vt **-dled; -dling** : acribillar ⟨riddled with bullets : acribillado a balazos⟩ ⟨riddled with errors : lleno de errores⟩

riddle² n : acertijo m, adivinanza f

ride¹ ['raɪd] v **rode** ['roːd]; **ridden** ['rɪdən]; **riding** vt 1 : montar, ir, andar ⟨to ride a horse : montar a caballo⟩ ⟨to ride a bicycle : montar/andar en bicicleta⟩ ⟨to ride the bus/train : ir en autobús/tren⟩ 2 : recorrer ⟨he rode 5 miles : recorrió 5 millas⟩ ⟨we rode the trails : recorrimos los senderos⟩ 3 TEASE : burlarse de, ridiculizar 4 **to ride out** WEATHER : capear ⟨they rode out the storm : capearon el temporal⟩ 5 **to ride the waves** : surcar los mares — vi 1 : montar a caballo, cabalgar 2 TRAVEL : ir, viajar (en coche, en bicicleta, etc.) 3 RUN : andar, marchar ⟨the car rides well : el coche anda bien⟩ 4 **to be riding high** : estar encantado de la vida 5 **to be riding on** : depender de 6 **to be riding for a fall** : ir camino al desastre 7 **to let something ride** fam : dejar pasar algo 8 **to ride herd on** fam : vigilar 9 **to ride shotgun** fam : ir en el asiento del pasajero delantero 10 **to ride up** : subírsele (dícese de la ropa)

ride² n 1 : paseo m, vuelta f (en coche, en bicicleta, a caballo) ⟨to go for a ride : dar una vuelta⟩ ⟨to give someone a ride : llevar en coche a alguien⟩ 2 : aparato m, juego m (en un parque de diversiones)

rider ['raɪdər] n 1 : jinete mf ⟨the rider fell off his horse : el jinete se cayó de su caballo⟩ 2 CYCLIST : ciclista mf 3 MOTORCYCLIST : motociclista mf 4 CLAUSE : cláusula f añadida

ridge ['rɪʤ] n 1 CHAIN : cadena f (de montañas o cerros) 2 : caballete m (de un techo), cresta f (de una ola o una montaña), cordoncillo m (de tela)

ridicule¹ ['rɪdə,kjuːl] vt **-culed; -culing** : burlarse de, mofarse de, ridiculizar

ridicule² n : burlas fpl

ridiculous [rə'dɪkjələs] adj : ridículo, absurdo

ridiculously [rə'dɪkjələsli] adv : de forma ridícula

rife ['raɪf] adj : abundante, común ⟨to be rife with : estar plagado de⟩

riffraff ['rɪf,ræf] n : chusma f, gentuza f

rifle¹ ['raɪfəl] v **-fled; -fling** vt RANSACK : desvalijar, saquear — vi **to rifle through** : revolver

rifle² n : rifle m, fusil m

rift ['rɪft] n 1 FISSURE : grieta f, fisura f 2 BREAK : ruptura f (entre personas), división f (dentro de un grupo)

rig¹ ['rɪg] vt **rigged; rigging** 1 : aparejar (un barco) 2 EQUIP : equipar 3 FIX : amañar (una elección, etc.) 4 to rig CONSTRUCT : construir, erigir 5 **to rig oneself out as** : vestirse de

rig² n 1 : aparejo m (de un barco) 2 or **oil rig** : torre f de perforación, plataforma f petrolífera

rigamarole → rigmarole

rigging ['rɪgɪŋ, -gən] n : jarcia f, aparejo m

right¹ ['raɪt] vt 1 FIX, RESTORE : reparar 2 STRAIGHTEN : enderezar

right² adv 1 PRECISELY : justo ⟨right here : aquí mismo⟩ ⟨right on time : a la hora exacta⟩ 2 DIRECTLY, STRAIGHT : derecho, directamente ⟨to go right home : ir derecho a casa⟩ ⟨come right this way : pase por aquí⟩ 3 CORRECTLY : correctamente ⟨to guess right : acertar⟩ 4 WELL : bien ⟨to eat right : comer bien⟩ ⟨nothing is going right : nada está saliendo bien⟩ 5 IMMEDIATELY : inmediatamente ⟨right after class : inmediatamente después de la clase⟩ ⟨I'll be right with you : enseguida lo atiendo⟩ 6 COMPLETELY : completamente ⟨to feel right at home : sentirse completamente cómodo⟩ ⟨right from the start : desde el principio⟩ 7 : a la derecha ⟨to turn right : girar a la derecha⟩ 8 **~ away** : enseguida 9 **~ now** IMMEDIATELY : ahora mismo 10 **~ now** PRESENTLY : en este momento

right³ adj 1 MORAL : justo ⟨to be right : ser justo⟩ ⟨to do the right thing : hacer lo correcto⟩ ⟨you were right to forgive him : hiciste bien en perdonarlo⟩ 2 CORRECT : correcto ⟨the right answer : la respuesta correcta⟩ ⟨you're right : tienes razón⟩ ⟨you know him, right? : lo conoces, ¿verdad?⟩ ⟨that's right : así es⟩ 3 APPROPRIATE : apropiado, adecuado ⟨the right man for the job : el hombre indicado para el trabajo⟩ ⟨the right moment : el momento oportuno⟩ ⟨if the price is right : si está bien de precio⟩ 4 (used for emphasis) : bien, bueno ⟨the price is right : bien, bueno —let's go : bueno, vamos⟩ 5 (used ironically) ⟨it's true! yeah, right : ¡es verdad! sí, claro⟩ 6 : derecho ⟨the right hand : la mano derecha⟩ 7 : bien ⟨I don't feel right : no me siento bien⟩ ⟨he's not in his right mind : no está bien de la cabeza⟩ 8 **right side** : derecho m ⟨right side up : con el derecho para arriba⟩ ⟨right side out : del/al derecho⟩

right⁴ n 1 GOOD : bien m ⟨you did right : hiciste bien⟩ ⟨to know right from wrong : saber la diferencia entre el bien y el mal⟩ 2 : derecha f ⟨on the right : a la derecha⟩ 3 : derecho m ⟨to have a right to : tener derecho a⟩ ⟨the right to vote : el derecho a votar⟩ ⟨women's rights : los derechos de la mujer⟩ **4 rights** *npl* : derechos *mpl* ⟨television rights : derechos televisivos⟩ **5 to take/ make a right** : girar a la derecha ⟨take the next right : gire en la próxima a la derecha⟩ **6 the Right** : la derecha (en la política)

right angle *n* : ángulo *m* recto

righteous ['raɪtʃəs] *adj* : recto, honrado — **righteously** *adv*

righteousness ['raɪtʃəsnəs] *n* : rectitud *f*, honradez *f*

rightful ['raɪtfəl] *adj* **1** JUST : justo **2** LAWFUL : legítimo — **rightfully** *adv*

right–hand ['raɪt'hænd] *adj* **1** : situado a la derecha **2** RIGHT–HANDED : para la mano derecha, con la mano derecha **3 right–hand man** : brazo *m* derecho

right–handed ['raɪt'hændəd] *adj* **1** : diestro ⟨a right–handed pitcher : un lanzador diestro⟩ **2** : para la mano derecha, con la mano derecha **3** CLOCKWISE : en la dirección de las manecillas del reloj

rightist ['raɪtɪst] *n* : derechista *mf* — **rightist** *adj*

rightly ['raɪtli] *adv* **1** JUSTLY : justamente, con razón **2** PROPERLY : debidamente, apropiadamente **3** CORRECTLY : correctamente

right–of–way ['raɪtə'weɪ, -əv-] *n, pl* **rights–of–way** **1** : preferencia, (del tráfico) **2** ACCESS : derecho *m* de paso

right triangle *n* : triángulo *m* rectángulo

rightward ['raɪtwərd] *adj* : a la derecha, hacia la derecha

right–wing ['raɪt'wɪŋ] *adj* : derechista

right wing *n* **the right wing** : la derecha

right–winger ['raɪt'wɪŋər] *n* : derechista *mf*

rigid ['rɪdʒɪd] *adj* : rígido — **rigidly** *adv*

rigidity [rɪ'dʒɪdəti] *n, pl* **-ties** : rigidez *f*

rigmarole ['rɪgmə,ro:l, 'rɪgə-] *n* **1** NONSENSE : galimatías *m*, disparates *mpl* **2** PROCEDURES : trámites *mpl*

rigor ['rɪgər] *n* : rigor *m*

rigor mortis [,rɪgər'mɔrtəs] *n* : rigidez *f* cadavérica

rigorous ['rɪgərəs] *adj* : riguroso — **rigorously** *adv*

rile ['raɪl] *vt* **riled; riling** : irritar

rill ['rɪl] *n* : riachuelo *m*

rim ['rɪm] *n* **1** EDGE : borde *m* **2** : llanta *f*, rin *m* *Col, Mex* (de una rueda) **3** FRAME : montura *f* (de anteojos)

rime ['raɪm] *n* : escarcha *f*

rind ['raɪnd] *n* : corteza *f*

ring¹ ['rɪŋ] *v* **rang** ['ræŋ]; **rung** ['rʌŋ]; **ringing** *vi* **1** : sonar ⟨the doorbell rang : sonó el timbre⟩ ⟨to ring for : llamar⟩ **2** RESOUND : resonar **3** SEEM : parecer ⟨to ring true : parecer cierto⟩ **4 to ring out** : sonar, oírse — *vt* **1** : tocar, hacer sonar (un timbre, una alarma, etc.) ⟨the name rings a bell : el nombre me suena⟩ **2** SURROUND : cercar, rodear **3 to ring up** : cobrar (compras) **4 to ring in the New Year** : recibir el Año Nuevo

ring² *n* **1** : anillo *m*, sortija *f* ⟨wedding ring : anillo de matrimonio⟩ **2** BAND : aro *m*, anillo *m* ⟨key ring : llavero⟩ **3** CIRCLE : círculo *m* **4** ARENA : arena *f*, ruedo *m* ⟨a boxing ring : un cuadrilátero, un ring⟩ **5** GANG : banda *f* (de ladrones, etc.) **6** SOUND : timbre *m*, sonido *m* **7** CALL : llamada *f* (por teléfono)

ringer ['rɪŋər] *n* **to be a dead ringer for** : ser un vivo retrato de

ringing ['rɪŋɪŋ] *adj* **1** : de timbre, de campana (dícese de un sonido) **2** LOUD : sonoro **3** RESOUNDING : categórico

ringleader ['rɪŋ,li:dər] *n* : cabecilla *mf*

ringlet ['rɪŋlət] *n* : sortija *f*, rizo *m*

ringtone ['rɪŋ,to:n] *n* : tono *m* de llamada

ringworm ['rɪŋ,wɔrm] *n* : tiña *f*

rink ['rɪŋk] *n* : pista *f* ⟨skating rink : pista de patinaje⟩

rinse¹ ['rɪnts] *vt* **rinsed; rinsing** : enjuagar ⟨to rinse out one's mouth : enjuagarse la boca⟩

rinse² *n* : enjuague *m*

riot¹ ['raɪət] *vi* : amotinarse

riot² *n* : motín *m*, tumulto *m*, alboroto *m*

rioter ['raɪətər] *n* : alborotador *m*, -dora *f*

riotous ['raɪətəs] *adj* **1** UNRULY, WILD : desenfrenado, alborotado **2** ABUNDANT : abundante

rip¹ ['rɪp] *v* **ripped; ripping** *vt* **1** : rasgar, arrancar, desgarrar **2 to rip apart** : destruir **3 to rip up** : hacer pedazos — *vi* : rasgarse, desgarrarse

rip² *n* : rasgón *m*, desgarrón *m*

ripe ['raɪp] *adj* **riper; ripest** **1** MATURE : maduro ⟨ripe fruit : fruta madura⟩ **2** READY : listo, preparado

ripen ['raɪpən] *v* : madurar

ripeness ['raɪpnəs] *n* : madurez *f*

rip–off ['rɪp,ɔf] *n* **1** THEFT : robo *m* **2** SWINDLE : estafa *f*, timo *m* *fam* **3** COPY : copia *f* (plagiada)

rip off *vt* **1** : rasgar, arrancar, desgarrar **2** SWINDLE *fam* : estafar, timar

ripple¹ ['rɪpəl] *v* **-pled; -pling** *vi* : rizarse, ondear, ondular — *vt* : rizar

ripple² *n* : onda *f*, ondulación *f*

rise¹ ['raɪz] *vi* **rose** ['ro:z]; **risen** ['rɪzən]; **rising** **1** GET UP : levantarse ⟨to rise to one's feet : ponerse de pie⟩ **2** : elevarse, alzarse ⟨the mountains rose to the west : las montañas se elevaron al oeste⟩ **3** : salir (dícese del sol y de la luna) **4** : subir (dícese de las aguas, del humo, etc.) ⟨the river rose : las aguas del río subieron de nivel⟩ ⟨let the dough rise : dejar subir la masa⟩ ⟨my spirits rose : me animé⟩ **5** INCREASE : aumentar, subir **6** ORIGINATE : nacer, proceder **7 to rise in rank** : ascender **8 to rise to the occasion** : estar a la altura de las circunstancias **9 to rise up** REBEL : sublevarse, rebelarse

rise² *n* **1** ASCENT : ascensión *f*, subida *f* **2** ORIGIN : origen *m* **3** ELEVATION : elevación *f* **4** INCREASE : subida *f*, aumento *m*, alzamiento *m* ⟨on the rise : en alza, en ascenso⟩ **5** SLOPE : pendiente *f*, cuesta *f* **6 to get a rise out of** PROVOKE : provocar, fastidiar **7 to give rise to** CAUSE : causar, dar origen a

riser ['raɪzər] n 1 : contrahuella f (de una escalera) 2 **early riser** : madrugador m, -dora f 3 **late riser** : dormilón m, -lona f

risk¹ ['rɪsk] vt : arriesgar, arriesgarse ⟨to risk one's life : arriesgar la vida⟩ ⟨to risk losing : arriesgarse a perder⟩ ⟨I won't risk it : no me arriesgo⟩

risk² n : riesgo m, peligro m ⟨at risk : en peligro⟩ ⟨at your own risk : por su cuenta y riesgo⟩ ⟨to take a risk : arriesgarse⟩ ⟨to run the risk of : arriesgarse a, correr el riesgo de⟩ ⟨at the risk of : a riesgo de⟩

risky ['rɪski] adj **riskier; -est** : arriesgado, peligroso, riesgoso

risqué [rɪ'skeɪ] adj : escabroso, picante, subido de tono

rite ['raɪt] n : rito m

ritual¹ ['rɪtʃuəl] adj : ritual — **ritually** adv

ritual² n : ritual m

rival¹ ['raɪvəl] vt **-valed** or **-valled; -valing** or **-valling** : rivalizar con, competir con

rival² adj : competidor, rival

rival³ n : rival mf; competidor m, -dora f

rivalry ['raɪvəlri] n, pl **-ries** : rivalidad f

river ['rɪvər] n : río m

riverbank ['rɪvər,bæŋk] n : ribera f, orilla f

riverbed ['rɪvər,bɛd] n : cauce m, lecho m

riverside ['rɪvər,saɪd] n : ribera f, orilla f

rivet¹ ['rɪvət] vt 1 : remachar 2 FIX : fijar (los ojos, etc.) 3 FASCINATE : fascinar, cautivar

rivet² n : remache m

riveting ['rɪvətɪŋ] adj : fascinante

rivulet ['rɪvjələt] n : arroyo m, riachuelo m ⟨rivulets of sweat : gotas de sudor⟩

roach ['roːtʃ] → cockroach

road ['roːd] n 1 : carretera f, calle f, camino m ⟨road map : mapa de rutas⟩ ⟨road rage : agresividad al volante⟩ ⟨road safety : seguridad vial⟩ ⟨road trip : viaje en coche (de larga distancia)⟩ ⟨to hit the road : ponerse en marcha⟩ ⟨I've been on the road since six : llevo viajando desde las seis⟩ 2 PATH : camino m, sendero m, vía f ⟨on the road to a solution : en vías de una solución⟩

roadblock ['roːd,blɑk] n : control m

roadrunner ['roːd,rʌnər] n : correcaminos m

roadside ['roːd,saɪd] n : borde m de la carretera

road sign n : señal f de tráfico, señal f de tránsito

roadway ['roːd,weɪ] n : carretera f, calzada f

roadwork ['roːd,wərk] n : obras fpl (viales)

roam ['roːm] vi : vagar, deambular, errar — vt : vagar por

roar¹ ['ror] vi : rugir, bramar ⟨to roar with laughter : reírse a carcajadas⟩ — vt : decir a gritos

roar² n 1 : rugido m, bramido m (de un animal) 2 DIN : clamor m (de gente), fragor m (del trueno), estruendo m (del tráfico, etc.)

roaring ['rorɪŋ] adj 1 THUNDEROUS : estruendoso, atronador 2 ACTIVE, STRONG : vivo (dícese de un fuego), caudaloso (dícese de un río), pujante (dícese de la economía) ⟨a roaring success : un gran éxito⟩

roast¹ ['roːst] vt : asar (carne, papas), tostar (café, nueces) — vi : asarse

roast² adj 1 : asado ⟨roast chicken : pollo asado⟩ 2 **roast beef** : rosbif m

roast³ n : asado m

roaster ['roːstər] n 1 : asador m (para carne), tostador m (para café) 2 : pollo m (para asar)

rob ['rɑb] v **robbed; robbing** vt 1 STEAL : robar 2 DEPRIVE : privar, quitar — vi : robar

robber ['rɑbər] n : ladrón m, -drona f

robbery ['rɑbəri] n, pl **-beries** : robo m

robe¹ ['roːb] vt **robed; robing** : vestirse

robe² n 1 : toga f (de magistrados, etc.), sotana f (de eclesiásticos) ⟨robe of office : traje de ceremonias⟩ 2 BATHROBE : bata f

robin ['rɑbən] n : petirrojo m

robot ['roː,bɑt, -bət] n : robot m — **robotic** [roː'bɑtɪk] adj

robotics [roː'bɑtɪks] ns & pl : robótica f

robust [roː'bʌst, 'roː,bʌst] adj : robusto, fuerte — **robustly** adv

robustness [roː'bʌstnəs, 'roː,bʌst-] n : robustez f, lozanía f

rock¹ ['rɑk] vt 1 : acunar (a un niño), mecer (una cuna) 2 SHAKE : sacudir 3 SHOCK : sacudir, conmocionar — vi SWAY : mecerse, balancearse

rock² n 1 : roca f (sustancia) ⟨rock climbing : escalada en roca⟩ 2 STONE : piedra f 3 ROCKING : balanceo m 4 or **rock music** : rock m, música f rock ⟨a rock band : una banda de rock⟩ 5 **on the rocks** : con hielo 6 **to be on the rocks** : andar mal

rock and roll n : rock and roll m

rock bottom n **to hit/reach rock bottom** : tocar fondo

rocker ['rɑkər] n 1 : balancín m 2 or **rocking chair** : mecedora f, balancín m 3 **to be off one's rocker** : estar chiflado, estar loco

rocket¹ ['rɑkət] vi : dispararse, subir rápidamente

rocket² n : cohete m

rocking horse n : caballito m (de balancín)

rock salt n : sal f gema

rocky ['rɑki] adj **rockier; -est** 1 : rocoso, pedregoso 2 UNSTEADY : inestable

rod ['rɑd] n 1 BAR : barra f, varilla f, vara f (de madera) ⟨a fishing rod : una caña (de pescar)⟩ 2 : medida f de longitud equivalente a 5.03 metros (5 yardas)

rode → ride¹

rodent ['roːdənt] n : roedor m

rodeo ['roːdi,oː, roː'deɪ,oː] n, pl **-deos** : rodeo m

roe ['roː] n : hueva f

rogue ['roːg] n SCOUNDREL : pícaro m, -ra f; pillo m, -lla f

roguish ['roːgɪʃ] adj : pícaro, travieso

role ['roːl] n : papel m, función f, rol m

role model n : modelo m de conducta

roll[1] [ˈroːl] *vi* **1** : rodar (dícese de una pelota, etc.) **2** SLIP : resbalar **3** : ir (en un vehículo) ⟨to roll to a stop : detenerse poco a poco⟩ ⟨to roll up : llegar⟩ **4** SWAY : balancearse **5** : tronar (dícese del trueno), redoblar (dícese de un tambor) **6** FILM : rodar **7** *or* **to get rolling** : ponerse en marcha **8** *or* **to roll over** : darse la vuelta ⟨to roll (over) onto one's back/ stomach : ponerse boca arriba/abajo⟩ **9** *or* **to roll over** OVERTURN : volcarse **10** *or* **to roll up** CURL : enrollarse ⟨he rolled up into a ball : se hizo una bola⟩ **11** **to be rolling in it** : tener ricachón **12 to roll around** THRASH : revolcarse **13 to roll around** : llegar (dícese de una fecha, etc.) **14 to roll by/past** : pasar — *vt* **1** : hacer rodar (una pelota, etc.) ⟨to roll the dice : echar los dados⟩ ⟨to roll one's eyes : poner los ojos en blanco⟩ **2** *fam* : hacer volcar ⟨he rolled his car : se volcó (en su auto)⟩ **3** : liar (un cigarrillo) **4** *or* **to roll up** : enrollar ⟨to roll something (up) into a ball : hacer una bola de algo⟩ **5** *or* **to roll out** FLATTEN : estirar (masa), laminar (metales) **6 to roll back** : rebajar (precios) **7 to roll back** : revertir (cambios, etc.) ⟨to roll back the clock : volver atrás⟩ **8 to roll down/up** : bajar/ subir (una ventanilla, etc.) **9 to roll out** : lanzar (un producto) **10 to roll the cameras** : rodar **11 to roll up one's sleeves** : arremangarse

roll[2] *n* **1** LIST : lista *f* ⟨to call the roll : pasar lista⟩ ⟨to have on the roll : tener inscrito⟩ **2** BUN : panecito *m*, bolillo *m Mex* **3** : rollo *m* (de papel, de tela, etc.) ⟨a roll of film : un carrete⟩ ⟨a roll of bills : un fajo⟩ **4** : redoble *m* (de tambores), retumbo *m* (del trueno, etc.) **5** ROLLING, SWAYING : balanceo *m*

roller [ˈroːlər] *n* **1** : rodillo *m* **2** CURLER : rulo *m*

Rollerblade [ˈroːlərˌbleɪd] *trademark* se usa para patines en línea

roller coaster [ˈroːlərˌkoːstər] *n* : montaña *f* rusa

roller–skate [ˈroːlərˌskeɪt] *vi* **-skated; -skating** : patinar (sobre ruedas)

roller skate *n* : patín *m* (de ruedas)

rollicking [ˈrɑlɪkɪŋ] *adj* : animado, alegre

rolling [ˈroːlɪŋ] *adj* : ondulante

rolling pin *n* : rodillo *m*

ROM [ˈrɑm] *n* : ROM *f*

Roman[1] [ˈroːmən] *n* : romano *m*

Roman[2] *n* : romano *m*, -na *f*

Roman Catholic *n* : católico *m*, -ca *f* — **Roman Catholic** *adj*

Roman Catholicism *n* : catolicismo *m*

romance[1] [roˈmænts, ˈroːˌmænts] *vi* **-manced; -mancing** FANTASIZE : fantasear

romance[2] *n* **1** : romance *m*, novela *f* de caballerías **2** : novela *f* de amor, novela *f* romántica **3** AFFAIR : romance *m*, amorío *m*

Romanian [ruˈmeɪniən, ro-] *n* **1** : rumano *m*, -na *f* **2** : rumano *m* (idioma) — **Romanian** *adj*

Roman numeral *n* : número *m* romano

romantic [roˈmæntɪk] *adj* : romántico — **romantic** *n* — **romantically** [-tɪkli] *adv*

romanticism [roˈmæntəˌsɪzəm] *n* : romanticismo *m*

romp[1] [ˈrɑmp] *vi* FROLIC : retozar, juguetear

romp[2] *n* : retozo *m*

roof[1] [ˈruːf, ˈrʊf] *vt* : techar

roof[2] *n, pl* **roofs** [ˈruːfs, ˈrʊfs; ˈruːvz, ˈrʊvz] **1** : techo *m*, tejado *m*, techado *m* **2 roof of the mouth** : paladar *m*

roofing [ˈruːfɪŋ, ˈrʊfɪŋ] *n* : techumbre *f*

roof rack *n* : portaequipajes *m*

rooftop [ˈruːfˌtɑp, ˈrʊf-] *n* ROOF : tejado *m*

rook[1] [ˈrʊk] *vt* CHEAT : defraudar, estafar, timar

rook[2] *n* **1** : grajo *m* (ave) **2** : torre *f* (en ajedrez)

rookie [ˈrʊki] *n* : novato *m*, -ta *f*

room[1] [ˈruːm, ˈrʊm] *vi* LODGE : alojarse, hospedarse

room[2] *n* **1** SPACE : espacio *m*, sitio *m*, lugar *m* ⟨to make room for : hacer lugar para⟩ **2** : cuarto *m*, habitación *f* (en una casa), sala *f* (para reuniones, etc.) **3** BEDROOM : dormitorio *m*, habitación *f*, pieza *f* **4** (*indicating possibility or opportunity*) ⟨room for improvement : posibilidad de mejorar⟩ ⟨there's no room for error : no hay lugar para errores⟩

room divider → **divider**

roomer [ˈruːmər, ˈrʊmər] *n* : inquilino *m*, -na *f*

rooming house *n* : pensión *f*

roommate [ˈruːmˌmeɪt, ˈrʊm-] *n* : compañero *m*, -ra *f* de cuarto

room service *n* : servicio *m* de habitaciones, servicio *m* a la habitación

roomy [ˈruːmi, ˈrʊmi] *adj* **roomier; -est 1** SPACIOUS : espacioso, amplio **2** LOOSE : suelto, holgado ⟨a roomy blouse : una blusa holgada⟩

roost[1] [ˈruːst] *vi* : posarse, dormir (en una percha)

roost[2] *n* : percha *f*

rooster [ˈruːstər, ˈrʊs-] *n* : gallo *m*

root[1] [ˈruːt, ˈrʊt] *vi* **1** : arraigar (en botánica) **2** : hozar (dícese de los cerdos) ⟨to root around in : hurgar en⟩ **3 to be rooted in** : estar basado en, tener su origen en **4 to be rooted to** : no poder moverse de (su silla, etc.) **5 to root for** : apoyar a, alentar — *vt* **to root out** : desarraigar (plantas), extirpar (problemas, etc.)

root[2] *n* **1** : raíz *f* (de una planta) **2** ORIGIN : origen *m*, raíz *f* **3** CORE : centro *m*, núcleo *m* ⟨to get to the root of the matter : ir al centro del asunto⟩ **4 to put down roots** SETTLE : afincarse **5 to take root** : arraigar, enraizar, echar raíces

root beer *n* : refresco *m* hecho de raíces e hierbas

rootless [ˈruːtləs, ˈrʊt-] *adj* : desarraigado

rope[1] [ˈroːp] *vt* **roped; roping 1** TIE : amarrar, atar **2** LASSO : lazar **3 to rope in/ into** ⟨they roped me into driving : me agarraron para manejar⟩ ⟨I didn't want to go, but I was roped in : no quería ir, pero me arrastraron⟩ **4 to rope off** : acordonar

rope² n : soga f, cuerda f

rosary ['ro:zəri] n, pl **-ries** : rosario m

rose¹ → **rise¹**

rose² ['ro:z] adj : rosa, color de rosa

rose³ n **1** : rosal m (planta), rosa f (flor) **2** : rosa m (color)

rosé [ro:zeɪ] n : vino m rosado

rosebush ['ro:zˌbʊʃ] n : rosal m

rosemary ['ro:zˌmɛri] n, pl **-maries** : romero m

rosette [ro:ˈzɛt] n : escarapela f (hecho de cintas), roseta f (en arquitectura)

Rosh Hashanah [ˌrɑʃhɑˈʃɑnə, ˌro:ʃ-] n : el Año Nuevo judío

rosin ['rɑzən] n : colofonia f

roster ['rɑstər] n : lista f

rostrum ['rɑstrəm] n, pl **-trums** or **-tra** [-trə] : tribuna f, estrado m

rosy ['ro:zi] adj **rosier; -est 1** : sonrosado, de color rosa **2** PROMISING : prometedor

rot¹ ['rɑt] v **rotted; rotting** vi : pudrirse, descomponerse — vt : pudrir, descomponer

rot² n : putrefacción f, descomposición f, podredumbre f

rotary¹ ['ro:təri] adj : rotativo, rotatorio

rotary² n, pl **-ries 1** : máquina f rotativa **2** TRAFFIC CIRCLE : rotonda f, glorieta f

rotate ['ro:ˌteɪt] v **-tated; -tating** vi REVOLVE : girar, rotar — vt **1** TURN : hacer girar, darle vueltas a **2** ALTERNATE : alternar

rotation [ro:ˈteɪʃən] n : rotación f

rote [ro:t] n **to learn by rote** : aprender de memoria

rotisserie [ro:ˈtɪsəri, -ˈtɪsəri] n SPIT : asador m

rotor ['ro:tər] n : rotor m

rotten ['rɑtən] adj **1** PUTRID : podrido, putrefacto **2** CORRUPT : corrompido **3** BAD : malo ⟨a rotten day : un día malísimo⟩

rottenness ['rɑtənnəs] n : podredumbre f

rotund [ro:ˈtʌnd] adj **1** ROUNDED : redondeado **2** PLUMP : regordete fam, llenito fam

rotunda [ro:ˈtʌndə] n : rotonda f

rouge ['ru:ʒ, 'ru:dʒ] n : colorete m

rough¹ ['rʌf] vt **1** ROUGHEN : poner áspero **2 to rough out** SKETCH : esbozar, bosquejar **3 to rough up** BEAT : darle una paliza (a alguien) **4 to rough it** : vivir sin comodidades

rough² adj **1** COARSE : áspero, basto **2** UNEVEN : desigual, escabroso, accidentado (dícese del terreno) **3** : agitado (dícese del mar), tempestuoso (dícese del tiempo), violento (dícese del viento) **4** VIOLENT : violento, brutal ⟨a rough neighborhood : un barrio peligroso⟩ **5** DIFFICULT : duro, difícil **6** CRUDE : rudo, tosco, burdo ⟨a rough cottage : una casita tosca⟩ ⟨a rough draft : un borrador⟩ ⟨a rough sketch : un bosquejo⟩ **7** APPROXIMATE : aproximado ⟨a rough idea : una idea aproximada⟩

rough³ n **1 the rough** : el rough (en golf) **2 in the rough** : en borrador

roughage ['rʌfɪdʒ] n : fibra f (dietética)

roughen ['rʌfən] vt : poner áspero — vi : ponerse áspero

roughly ['rʌfli] adv **1** : bruscamente ⟨to treat roughly : maltratar⟩ **2** CRUDELY : burdamente **3** APPROXIMATELY : aproximadamente, más o menos

roughneck ['rʌfˌnɛk] n : matón m

roughness ['rʌfnəs] n : rudeza f, aspereza f

roulette [ru:ˈlɛt] n : ruleta f

round¹ ['raʊnd] vt **1** TURN : doblar ⟨to round the corner : dar la vuelta a la esquina⟩ **2** : redondear ⟨she rounded the edges : redondeó los bordes⟩ **3 to round off** : redondear (un número) **4 to round off/out** COMPLETE : rematar, terminar **5 to round up** GATHER : reunir (a personas), rodear (ganado), hacer una redada de (delincuentes) ⟨to round up suspects : detener a los sospechosos⟩ **6 to round up/down** : redondear (un número) por exceso/defecto

round² adv → **around¹**

round³ adj **1** CIRCULAR, SPHERICAL : redondo ⟨a round table/face : una mesa/cara redonda⟩ **2** CYLINDRICAL : circular, cilíndrico **3** CURVED : redondeado ⟨round shoulders : espaldas cargadas⟩ **4** : redondo ⟨round number : número m redondo **5 round trip** : viaje m de ida y vuelta

round⁴ n **1** CIRCLE : círculo m ⟨cucumber rounds : rodajas de pepino⟩ **2** SERIES : serie f, sucesión f ⟨a round of talks : una ronda de negociaciones⟩ **3** : asalto m (en boxeo), recorrido m (en golf), vuelta f (en varios juegos) **4** : salva f (de aplausos) **5** : ronda f (de bebidas) **6** or **round of ammunition** : disparo m, cartucho m **7 rounds** npl : recorridos mpl (de un cartero), rondas fpl (de un vigilante), visitas fpl (de un médico) ⟨to make the rounds : hacer visitas⟩

round⁵ prep → **around²**

roundabout ['raʊndəˌbaʊt] adj : indirecto ⟨to speak in a roundabout way : hablar con rodeos⟩

roundly ['raʊndli] adv **1** THOROUGHLY : completamente **2** BLUNTLY : francamente, rotundamente **3** VIGOROUSLY : con vigor

roundness ['raʊndnəs] n : redondez f

round–shouldered ['raʊndˌʃo:ldərd] adj : cargado de hombros

round–trip ['raʊndˌtrɪp] adj : de ida y vuelta

roundup ['raʊndˌʌp] n **1** : rodeo m (de animales), redada f (de delincuentes, etc.) **2** SUMMARY : resumen m

roundworm ['raʊndˌwərm] n : lombriz f intestinal

rouse ['raʊz] vt **roused; rousing 1** AWAKE : despertar **2** EXCITE : excitar ⟨it roused him to fury : lo enfureció⟩

rout¹ ['raʊt] vt **1** DEFEAT : derrotar, aplastar **2 to rout out** : hacer salir

rout² n **1** DISPERSAL : desbandada f, dispersión f **2** DEFEAT : derrota f aplastante

route¹ ['ru:t, 'raʊt] vt **routed; routing** : dirigir, enviar, encaminar

route² n : camino m, ruta f, recorrido m

router ['raʊtər] n : router m (en informática)

routine¹ [ru:'ti:n] adj : rutinario — **routinely** adv

routine² n : rutina f

rove ['ro:v] v **roved; roving** vi : vagar, errar — vt : errar por

rover ['ro:vər] n 1 : vagabundo m, -da f 2 : explorador m (robot)

row¹ ['ro:] vt 1 : avanzar a remo ⟨to row a boat : remar⟩ 2 : llevar a remo ⟨he rowed me to shore : me llevó hasta la orilla⟩ — vi : remar

row² ['raʊ] n 1 : paseo m en barca ⟨to go for a row : salir a remar⟩ 2 LINE, RANK : fila f, hilera f 3 SERIES : serie f ⟨three days in a row : tres días seguidos⟩ 4 RACKET : estruendo m, bulla f 5 QUARREL : pelea f, riña f

rowboat ['ro:,bo:t] n : bote m de remos

rowdiness ['raʊdinəs] n : bulla f

rowdy¹ ['raʊdi] adj **rowdier; -est** : escandaloso, alborotador

rowdy² n, pl **-dies** : alborotador m, -dora f

rower ['ro:ər] n : remero m, -ra f

row house n : casa f adosada

royal¹ ['rɔɪəl] adj : real — **royally** adv

royal² n : persona f de linaje real, miembro de la familia real

royalist ['rɔɪəlɪst] n : realista mf — **royalism** ['rɔɪə,lɪzəm] n

royalty ['rɔɪəlti] n, pl **-ties** 1 : realeza f (posición) 2 : miembros mpl de la familia real 3 **royalties** npl : derechos mpl de autor

rub¹ ['rʌb] v **rubbed; rubbing** vt 1 : frotar, restregar, friccionar ⟨to rub one's hands together : frotarse las manos⟩ ⟨rub the lotion into your skin : frote la loción en la piel⟩ 2 CHAFE : rozar 3 POLISH : frotar, pulir 4 SCRUB : fregar 5 **to rub elbows with** : codearse con 6 **to rub off on** ⟨the ink rubbed off on my fingers : se me mancharon los dedos de tinta⟩ ⟨his enthusiasm rubbed off on me : me contagió con su entusiasmo⟩ 7 **to rub someone the wrong way** fam : crispar a alguien 8 **to rub something in (someone's face)** fam : restregarle (en la cara) algo a alguien ⟨you don't have to rub it in : no tienes que restregármelo⟩ — vi **to rub against** : rozar

rub² n 1 RUBBING : fricción f, friega f 2 **the rub** : el problema

rubber ['rʌbər] n 1 : goma f, caucho m, hule m Mex 2 **rubbers** npl OVERSHOES : chanclos mpl

rubber band n : goma f (elástica), gomita f

rubber-stamp ['rʌbər'stæmp] vt 1 APPROVE : aprobar, autorizar 2 STAMP : sellar

rubber stamp n : sello m (de goma)

rubbery ['rʌbəri] adj : gomoso

rubbish ['rʌbɪʃ] n : basura f, desechos mpl, desperdicios mpl

rubble ['rʌbəl] n : escombros mpl, ripio m

rubella [ru:'bɛlə] n : rubéola f

ruble ['ru:bəl] n : rublo m

ruby ['ru:bi] n, pl **-bies** 1 : rubí m (gema) 2 : color m de rubí

rucksack ['rʌk,sæk, 'rʊk-] n BACKPACK : mochila f

ruckus ['rʌkəs] n COMMOTION : alboroto m, bullicio m

rudder ['rʌdər] n : timón m

ruddy ['rʌdi] adj **ruddier; -est** : rubicundo (dícese del rostro, etc.), sanguíneo (dícese de la complexión)

rude ['ru:d] adj **ruder; rudest** 1 CRUDE : tosco, rústico 2 IMPOLITE : grosero, descortés, maleducado 3 ABRUPT : brusco ⟨a rude awakening : una sorpresa desagradable⟩

rudely ['ru:dli] adv : groseramente

rudeness ['ru:dnəs] n 1 IMPOLITENESS : grosería f, descortesía f, falta f de educación 2 ROUGHNESS : tosquedad f 3 SUDDENNESS : brusquedad f

rudiment ['ru:dəmənt] n : rudimento m, noción f básica ⟨the rudiments of Spanish : los rudimentos del español⟩

rudimentary [,ru:də'mɛntəri] adj : rudimentario, básico

rue ['ru:] vt **rued; ruing** : lamentar, arrepentirse de

rueful ['ru:fəl] adj 1 PITIFUL : lastimoso 2 REGRETFUL : arrepentido, pesaroso

ruffian ['rʌfiən] n : matón m

ruffle¹ ['rʌfəl] vt **-fled; -fling** 1 AGITATE : agitar, rizar (agua) 2 RUMPLE : arrugar (ropa), despeinar (pelo) 3 ERECT : erizar (plumas) 4 VEX : alterar, irritar, perturbar 5 : fruncir volantes en (tela)

ruffle² n FLOUNCE : volante m

ruffly ['rʌfəli] adj : con volantes

rug ['rʌg] n : alfombra f, tapete m

rugby ['rʌgbi] n : rugby m

rugged ['rʌgəd] adj 1 ROUGH, UNEVEN : accidentado, escabroso ⟨rugged mountains : montañas accidentadas⟩ 2 HARSH : duro, severo 3 ROBUST, STURDY : robusto, fuerte

ruin¹ ['ru:ən] vt 1 DESTROY : destruir, arruinar 2 BANKRUPT : arruinar, hacer quebrar

ruin² n 1 : ruina f ⟨to fall into ruin : caer en ruinas⟩ 2 : ruina f, perdición f ⟨to be the ruin of : ser la perdición de⟩ 3 **ruins** npl : ruinas fpl, restos mpl ⟨the ruins of the ancient temple : las ruinas del templo antiguo⟩

ruinous ['ru:ənəs] adj : ruinoso

rule¹ ['ru:l] v **ruled; ruling** vt 1 CONTROL, GOVERN : gobernar (un país), controlar (las emociones) 2 DECIDE : decidir, fallar ⟨the judge ruled that . . . : el juez falló que . . .⟩ 3 DRAW : trazar con una regla 4 **to rule out** EXCLUDE : descartar — vi 1 GOVERN : gobernar, reinar 2 PREVAIL : prevalecer, imperar 3 **to rule against** : fallar en contra de 4 **to rule in favor of** : fallar a favor de 5 **to rule on** : fallar en

rule² n 1 REGULATION : regla f, norma f ⟨to follow/break the rules : seguir/violar las reglas⟩ ⟨to be against the rules : ir en

contra de las reglas⟩ **2** CUSTOM, HABIT
: regla *f* general ⟨as a rule : por lo gene-
ral⟩ **3** GOVERNMENT : gobierno *m*, dominio *m* ⟨to be under the rule of : estar
bajo el dominio de⟩ **4** RULER : regla *f*
(para medir)

ruler [¹ruːlər] *n* **1** LEADER, SOVEREIGN
: gobernante *m*; soberano *m*, -na *f* **2**
: regla *f* (para medir)

ruling [¹ruːlɪŋ] *n* : resolución *f*, fallo *m*

rum [¹rʌm] *n* : ron *m*

Rumanian [ruˈmeɪniən] → **Romanian**

rumba [¹rʌmbə, ¹rʊm-, ¹ruːm-] *n* : rumba *f*

rumble[1] [¹rʌmbəl] *vi* **-bled; -bling** : retumbar, hacer ruidos (dícese del estómago)

rumble[2] *n* : estruendo *m*, ruido *m* sordo,
retumbo *m*

ruminant[1] [¹ruːmənənt] *adj* : rumiante

ruminant[2] *n* : rumiante *m*

ruminate [¹ruːməˌneɪt] *vi* **-nated; -nating**
1 : rumiar (en zoología) **2** REFLECT : reflexionar, rumiar

rummage [¹rʌmɪdʒ] *vi* **-maged; -maging**
: hurgar ⟨to rummage (around) in, to
rummage through : hurgar en⟩

rummage sale *n* : venta *f* de beneficencia
(de objetos de segunda mano)

rummy [¹rʌmi] *n* : rummy *m* (juego de
naipes)

rumor[1] [¹ruːmər] *vt* : rumorear ⟨it is rumored that . . . : se rumorea que . . .⟩, se
dice que . . .⟩ ⟨her rumored resignation
: su rumoreada dimisión⟩

rumor[2] [¹ruːmər] *n* : rumor *m*

rump [¹rʌmp] *n* **1** : ancas *fpl*, grupa *f* (de
un animal) **2** : cadera *f* ⟨rump steak : filete de cadera⟩

rumple [¹rʌmpəl] *vt* **-pled; -pling** : arrugar
(ropa, etc.), despeinar (pelo)

run[1] [¹rʌn] *v* **ran** [¹ræn]; **run; running** *vi*
1 : correr ⟨she ran to catch the bus
: corrió para alcanzar el autobús⟩ ⟨run
and fetch the doctor : corre a buscar al
médico⟩ ⟨he ran to the store : salió
rápido a la tienda⟩ ⟨to run after some-
one/something : correr tras alguien/
algo⟩ **2** : circular, correr ⟨the train runs
between Detroit and Chicago : el tren
circula entre Detroit y Chicago⟩ ⟨to run
on time : ser puntual⟩ **3** FUNCTION
: funcionar, ir ⟨the engine runs on gasoline : el motor funciona con gasolina⟩
⟨with the motor running : con el motor
en marcha⟩ ⟨to run smoothly : ir bien⟩
4 FLOW : correr, ir **5** LAST : durar ⟨the
movie runs for two hours : la película
dura dos horas⟩ ⟨the contract runs for
three years : el contrato es válido por
tres años⟩ **6** : desteñir, despintar (dícese
de los colores) **7** EXTEND : correr, extenderse ⟨the path runs along the lake : el
sendero bordea el lago⟩ **8** TRAVEL,
SPREAD : correr, extenderse **9** to run
away : salir corriendo ⟨to run away from
: fugarse de⟩ ⟨to run away from home
: escaparse de casa⟩ **10** to run down
: agotarse, gastarse (dícese de pilas, etc.)
11 to run for office : postularse, presentarse (como candidato) **12** to run out
: acabarse ⟨time is running out : se acaba

el tiempo⟩ ⟨I ran out of money : se me
acabó el dinero⟩ **13** to run over OVER-
FLOW : rebosar — *vt* **1** : correr ⟨to run
10 miles : correr 10 millas⟩ ⟨to run
errands : hacer los mandados⟩ ⟨to run
out of town : hacer salir del pueblo⟩ **2**
PASS : pasar ⟨she ran her fingers through
her hair : se pasó la mano por el pelo⟩ **3**
DRIVE : llevar (en coche) **4** OPERATE
: hacer funcionar (un motor, etc.) **5**
PERFORM : realizar (un análisis, etc.) **6**
: echar ⟨to run water over : echarle agua
a⟩ ⟨to run the water/faucet : abrir la
llave (del agua)⟩ **7** MANAGE : dirigir,
llevar (un negocio, etc.) **8** EXTEND : tender (un cable, etc.) **9** to run across : encontrarse con **10** to run a risk : correr
un riesgo **11** to run down USE UP : gastar, agotar **12** to run down/over : atropellar **13** to run into : encontrar **14** to
run off PRINT : tirar, sacar **15** to run
through : repasar, ensayar **16** to run up
: incurrir en **17** to run up against : tropezar con

run[2] *n* **1** : carrera *f* ⟨at a run : a la carrera, corriendo⟩ ⟨to go for a run : ir a
correr⟩ ⟨to make a run for it : huir co-
rriendo⟩ ⟨to be on the run : estar fugi-
tivo⟩ **2** TRIP : vuelta *f*, paseo *m* (en coche), viaje *m* (en avión) **3** SERIES : serie
f ⟨a run of disappointments : una serie
de desilusiones⟩ ⟨in the long run : a la
larga⟩ ⟨in the short run : a corto plazo⟩
4 DEMAND : gran demanda *f* ⟨a run on
the banks : una corrida bancaria⟩ **5**
(*used for theatrical productions and films*)
⟨to have a long run : mantenerse mucho
tiempo en la cartelera⟩ **6** TYPE : tipo *m*
⟨the average run of students : el tipo más
común de estudiante⟩ **7** : carrera *f* (en
béisbol) **8** : carrera *f* (en una media) **9**
to have the run of : tener libre acceso de
(una casa, etc.) **10** ski run : pista *f* (de
esquí)

runaway[1] [¹rʌnəˌweɪ] *adj* **1** FUGITIVE
: fugitivo **2** UNCONTROLLABLE : incontrolable, fuera de control ⟨runaway inflation : inflación desenfrenada⟩ ⟨a runaway success : un éxito aplastante⟩

runaway[2] *n* : fugitivo *m*, -va *f*

rundown [¹rʌnˌdaʊn] *n* SUMMARY : resumen *m*

run-down [¹rʌnˌdaʊn] *adj* **1** DILAPI-
DATED : ruinoso, destartalado **2** SICKLY,
TIRED : cansado, débil

rung[1] *pp* → **ring**[1]

rung[2] [¹rʌŋ] *n* : peldaño *m*, escalón *m*

run-in [¹rʌnˌɪn] *n* : disputa *f*, altercado *m*

runner [¹rʌnər] *n* **1** RACER : corredor *m*,
-dora *f* **2** MESSENGER : mensajero *m*, -ra
f **3** TRACK : riel *m* (de un cajón, etc.) **4**
: patín *m* (de un trineo), cuchilla *f* (de un
patín) **5** : estolón *m* (planta)

runner-up [ˌrʌnərˈʌp] *n*, *pl* **runners-up**
: subcampeón *m*, -peona *f*

running [¹rʌnɪŋ] *adj* **1** FLOWING : corriente ⟨running water : agua corriente⟩
2 CONTINUOUS : continuo ⟨a running
battle : una lucha continua⟩ **3** CONSEC-

UTIVE : seguido ⟨six days running : por seis días seguidos⟩

runny [ˈrʌni] *adj* **runnier; -est 1** WATERY : caldoso **2 to have a runny nose** : moquear

run-of-the-mill [ˌrʌnəvðəˈmɪl] *adj* : normal y corriente, común

runt [ˈrʌnt] *n* : animal *m* pequeño ⟨the runt of the litter : el más pequeño de la camada⟩

runway [ˈrʌnˌweɪ] *n* : pista *f* de aterrizaje

rupee [ruˈpiː, ˈruˌ-] *n* : rupia *f*

rupture¹ [ˈrʌpfər] *v* **-tured; -turing** *vt* **1** BREAK, BURST : romper, reventar **2** : causar una hernia en — *vi* : reventarse

rupture² *n* **1** BREAK : ruptura *f* **2** HERNIA : hernia *f*

rural [ˈrʊrəl] *adj* : rural, campestre

ruse [ˈruːs, ˈruːz] *n* : treta *f*, ardid *m*, estratagema *f*

rush¹ [ˈrʌʃ] *vi* **1** : correr, ir de prisa ⟨to rush around : correr de un lado a otro⟩ ⟨to rush off/in/out : irse/entrar/salir corriendo⟩ ⟨let's not rush into it : no nos precipitemos⟩ **2** FLOW : correr con fuerza — *vt* **1** HURRY : apresurar, apurar ⟨don't rush me : no me apures⟩ ⟨to rush something : hacer algo apresuradamente⟩ ⟨she rushed me into making a decision : me hizo tomar una decisión apresurada⟩ **2** : llevar o enviar urgentemente ⟨he was rushed to the hospital : fue trasladado de urgencia al hospital⟩ **3** ATTACK : abalanzarse sobre, asaltar

rush² *adj* : urgente

rush³ *n* **1** HASTE : prisa *f*, apuro *m* ⟨there's no rush : no hay ninguna prisa⟩ ⟨to be in a rush : tener prisa, estar/ir apurado⟩ **2** SURGE : ráfaga *f* (de aire), torrente *m* (de aguas), avalancha *f* (de gente) **3** DEMAND : demanda *f* ⟨a rush on sugar : una gran demanda para el azúcar⟩ **4** : carga *f* (en futbol americano) **5** : junco *m* (planta)

rush hour *n* : hora *f* pico

russet [ˈrʌsət] *n* : color *m* rojizo

Russian [ˈrʌʃən] *n* **1** : ruso *m*, -sa *f* **2** : ruso *m* (idioma) — **Russian** *adj*

rust¹ [ˈrʌst] *vi* : oxidarse — *vt* : oxidar

rust² *n* **1** : herrumbre *f*, orín *m*, óxido *m* (en los metales) **2** : roya *f* (en las plantas)

rustic¹ [ˈrʌstɪk] *adj* : rústico, campestre

rustic² *n* : rústico *m*, -ca *f*; campesino *m*, -na *f*

rustle¹ [ˈrʌsəl] *v* **rustled; rustling** *vt* **1** : hacer susurrar, hacer crujir ⟨to rustle a newspaper : hacer crujir un periódico⟩ **2** STEAL : robar (ganado) **3 to rustle up** : improvisar (una comida), conseguir (información, etc.) — *vi* : susurrar, crujir

rustle² *n* : murmullo *m*, susurro *m*, crujido *m*

rustler [ˈrʌsələr] *n* : ladrón *m*, -drona *f* de ganado

rustproof [ˈrʌstˌpruːf] *adj* : inoxidable

rusty [ˈrʌsti] *adj* **rustier; -est** : oxidado, herrumbroso

rut [ˈrʌt] *n* **1** GROOVE, TRACK : rodada *f*, surco *m* **2 to be in a rut** : ser esclavo de la rutina

ruthless [ˈruːθləs] *adj* : despiadado, cruel — **ruthlessly** *adv*

ruthlessness [ˈruːθləsnəs] *n* : crueldad *f*, falta *f* de piedad

RV [ˌɑrˈviː] → **recreational vehicle**

Rwandan [rʊˈandən] *n* : ruandés *m*, -desa *f* — **Rwandan** *adj*

rye [ˈraɪ] *n* **1** : centeno *m* **2** *or* **rye bread** : pan *m* de centeno **3** *or* **rye whiskey** : whisky *m* de centeno

S

s [ˈɛs] *n, pl* **s's** *or* **ss** [ˈɛsəz] : decimonovena letra del alfabeto inglés

Sabbath [ˈsæbəθ] *n* **1** : sábado *m* (en el judaísmo) **2** : domingo *m* (en el cristianismo)

sabbatical [səˈbætɪkəl] *n* : sabático *f*

saber [ˈseɪbər] *n* : sable *m*

sable [ˈseɪbəl] *n* **1** BLACK : negro *m* **2** : marta *f* cebellina (animal)

sabotage¹ [ˈsæbəˌtɑʒ] *vt* **-taged; -taging** : sabotear

sabotage² *n* : sabotaje *m*

saboteur [ˌsæbəˈtər] *n* : saboteador *m*, -dora *f*

sac [ˈsæk] *n* : saco *m* (anatómico)

saccharin [ˈsækərən] *n* : sacarina *f*

saccharine [ˈsækərən, -ˌriːn, -ˌraɪn] *adj* : meloso, empalagoso

sachet [sæˈʃeɪ] *n* : bolsita *f* (perfumada)

sack¹ [ˈsæk] *n* **1** FIRE : echar (del trabajo), despedir **2** PLUNDER : saquear

sack² *n* BAG : saco *m*

sacrament [ˈsækrəmənt] *n* : sacramento *m*

sacramental [ˌsækrəˈmɛntəl] *adj* : sacramental

sacred [ˈseɪkrəd] *adj* **1** RELIGIOUS : sagrado, sacro ⟨sacred texts : textos sagrados⟩ **2** HOLY : sagrado **3 sacred to** : consagrado a

sacrifice¹ [ˈsækrəˌfaɪs] *vt* **-ficed; -ficing 1** : sacrificar **2 to sacrifice oneself** : sacrificarse

sacrifice² *n* : sacrificio *m*

sacrilege [ˈsækrəlɪʤ] *n* : sacrilegio *m*

sacrilegious [ˌsækrəˈlɪʤəs, -ˈliː-] *adj* : sacrílego

sacrosanct [ˈsækroˌsæŋkt] *adj* : sacrosanto

sad [ˈsæd] *adj* **sadder; saddest** : triste — **sadly** *adv*

sadden [ˈsædən] *vt* : entristecer

saddle¹ [ˈsædəl] *vt* **-dled; -dling 1** : ensillar **2 to saddle someone with some-**

thing : cargar a alguien con algo, endilgarle algo a alguien

saddle² n : silla f (de montar)

saddlebag ['sædəl,bæg] n : alforja f

sadism ['seɪ,dɪzəm, 'sæ-] n : sadismo m

sadist ['seɪdɪst, 'sæd-] n : sádico m, -ca f

sadistic [sə'dɪstɪk] adj : sádico — **sadistically** [-tɪkli] adv

sadness ['sædnəs] n : tristeza f

safari [sə'fɑri, -'fær-] n : safari m

safe¹ ['seɪf] adj **safer; safest** **1** UNHARMED : ileso ⟨safe and sound : sano y salvo⟩ **2** SECURE, PROTECTED : seguro **3** : seguro (dícese de vehículos, actividades, etc.) ⟨have a safe trip! : ¡(que tengas un) buen viaje!⟩ **4** : seguro (dícese de medicamentos, etc.) ⟨safe to eat/drink : comestible/potable⟩ **5** PROTECTIVE : seguro ⟨a safe place : un lugar seguro⟩ ⟨at a safe distance : a una distancia prudencial⟩ **6** : seguro (dícese de inversiones, etc.) **7** CAREFUL : prudente ⟨a safe driver : un conductor responsable⟩ **8 (it's) better (to be) safe than sorry** : más vale prevenir que curar **9 it's safe to say that . . .** or **it's a safe bet that . . .** : se puede decir, sin temor a equivocarse, que . . . **10 to be on the safe side** : para mayor seguridad **11 to play it safe** : ir a la segura

safe² n : caja f fuerte

safe–conduct ['seɪf'kɑn,dʌkt] n : salvoconducto m

safe–deposit box n : caja f de seguridad

safeguard¹ ['seɪf,gɑrd] vt : salvaguardar, proteger

safeguard² n : salvaguarda f, protección f

safekeeping ['seɪf'kiːpɪŋ] n : custodia f, protección f ⟨to put into safekeeping : poner en buen recaudo⟩

safely ['seɪfli] adv **1** UNHARMED : sin incidentes, sin novedades ⟨they landed safely : aterrizaron sin novedades⟩ **2** SECURELY : con toda seguridad, sin peligro **3** : sin temor a equivocarse ⟨one can safely say that . . . : se puede decir, sin temor a equivocarse, que . . .⟩

safety ['seɪfti] n, pl **-ties** : seguridad f

safety belt n : cinturón m de seguridad

safety net n **1** : red f de seguridad **2** : protección f

safety pin n : alfiler m de gancho, alfiler m de seguridad, imperdible m Spain

safety razor → razor

saffron ['sæfrən] n : azafrán m

sag¹ ['sæg] vi **sagged; sagging 1** DROOP, SINK : combarse, hundirse, inclinarse **2** : colgar, caer ⟨his jowls sagged : le colgaban las mejillas⟩ **3** FLAG : flaquear, decaer ⟨his spirits sagged : se le flaqueó el ánimo⟩

sag² n : comba f

saga ['sɑgə, 'sæ-] n : saga f

sagacious [sə'geɪʃəs] adj : sagaz

sage¹ ['seɪʤ] adj **sager; sagest** : sabio — **sagely** adv

sage² n **1** : sabio m, -bia f **2** : salvia f (planta)

sagebrush ['seɪʤ,brʌʃ] n : artemisa f

Sagittarius [,sæʤə'teriəs] n **1** : Sagitario m (signo o constelación) **2** : Sagitario mf (persona)

said → say

sail¹ ['seɪl] vi **1** : navegar (en un barco) **2** : ir/marchar (etc.) fácilmente ⟨we sailed right in : entramos sin ningún problema⟩ ⟨she sailed through the exam : aprobó/pasó el examen sin problemas⟩ — vt **1** : gobernar (un barco) **2 to sail the seas** : cruzar los mares

sail² n **1** : vela f (de un barco) **2** : viaje m en velero ⟨to go for a sail : salir a navegar⟩

sailboat ['seɪl,boːt] n : velero m, barco m de vela

sailfish ['seɪl,fɪʃ] n : pez m vela

sailing ['seɪlɪŋ] n **1** : navegación f (de un barco de vela) **2** : vela f (deporte)

sailing ship n : barco m de vela

sailor ['seɪlər] n : marinero m

saint ['seɪnt, before a name ,seɪnt or sənt] n : santo m, -ta f ⟨Saint Francis : San Francisco⟩ ⟨Saint Rose : Santa Rosa⟩

saintliness ['seɪntlinəs] n : santidad f

saintly ['seɪntli] adj **saintlier; -est** : santo

sake ['seɪk] n **1** BENEFIT : bien m ⟨for the children's sake : por el bien de los niños⟩ **2** (indicating an end or a purpose) ⟨art for art's sake : el arte por el arte⟩ ⟨let's say, for argument's sake, that he's wrong : pongamos que está equivocado⟩ **3 for goodness' sake!** : ¡por (el amor de) Dios!

salable or **saleable** ['seɪləbəl] adj : vendible

salacious [sə'leɪʃəs] adj : salaz — **salaciously** adv

salad ['sæləd] n : ensalada f

salad dressing → dressing

salamander ['sælə,mændər] n : salamandra f

salami [sə'lɑmi] n : salami m

salary ['sæləri] n, pl **-ries** : sueldo m

sale ['seɪl] n **1** SELLING : venta f **2** : liquidación f, rebajas fpl ⟨on sale : de rebaja⟩ **3 sales** npl : ventas fpl ⟨to work in sales : trabajar en ventas⟩

salesman ['seɪlzmən] n, pl **-men** [-mən, -,mɛn] **1** : vendedor m, dependiente m (en una tienda) **2 traveling salesman** : viajante m, representante m

salesperson ['seɪlz,pərsən] n : vendedor m, -dora f; dependiente m, -ta f (en una tienda)

sales pitch → pitch²

saleswoman ['seɪlz,wʊmən] n, pl **-women** [-,wɪmən] **1** : vendedora f, dependienta f (en una tienda) **2 traveling saleswoman** : viajante f, representante f

salient ['seɪljənt] adj : saliente, sobresaliente

saline ['seɪ,liːn, -,laɪn] adj : salino

salinity [,seɪ'lɪnəti, sə-] n : salinidad f

saliva [sə'laɪvə] n : saliva f

salivary ['sælə,veri] adj : salival ⟨salivary gland : glándula salival⟩

salivate ['sælə,veɪt] vi **-vated; -vating** : salivar

sallow ['sælo:] adj : amarillento

sally[1] ['sæli] *vi* **-lied; -lying** SET OUT : salir, hacer una salida

sally[2] *n, pl* **-lies 1** : salida *f* (militar), misión *f* **2** QUIP : salida *f*, ocurrencia *f*

salmon ['sæmən] *n & pl* **1** : salmón *m* (pez) **2** : color *m* salmón

salon [sə'lɑn, 'sæˌlɑn, sæ'lɔ̃] *n* : salón *m* ⟨beauty salon : salón de belleza⟩

saloon [sə'lu:n] *n* **1** HALL : salón *m* (en un barco) **2** BARROOM : bar *m*

salsa ['sɔlsə, 'sɑl-] *n* : salsa *f* mexicana, salsa *f* picante

salt[1] ['sɔlt] *vt* : salar, echarle sal a

salt[2] *adj* : salado

salt[3] *n* : sal *f*

saltiness ['sɔltinəs] *adj* : lo salado, salinidad *f*

salt shaker → shaker

saltwater ['sɔltˌwɔtər, -ˌwɑ-] *adj* : de agua salada

salty ['sɔlti] *adj* **saltier; -est** : salado

salubrious [sə'lu:briəs] *adj* : salubre

salutary ['sæljəˌteri] *adj* : saludable, salubre

salutation [ˌsæljə'teɪʃən] *n* : saludo *m*, salutación *f*

salute[1] [sə'lu:t] *v* **-luted; -luting** *vt* **1** : saludar (con gestos o ceremonias) **2** ACCLAIM : reconocer, aclamar — *vi* : hacer un saludo

salute[2] *n* **1** : saludo *m* (gesto), salva *f* (de cañonazos) **2** TRIBUTE : reconocimiento *m*, homenaje *m*

Salvadoran [ˌsælvə'dorən] **→ El Salvadoran**

salvage[1] ['sælvɪdʒ] *vt* **-vaged; -vaging** : salvar, rescatar

salvage[2] *n* **1** SALVAGING : salvamento *m*, rescate *m* **2** : objetos *mpl* salvados

salvation [sæl'veɪʃən] *n* : salvación *f*

salve[1] ['sæv, 'sɑv] *vt* **salved; salving** : calmar, apaciguar ⟨to salve one's conscience : aliviarse la conciencia⟩

salve[2] *n* : ungüento *m*

salvo ['sælˌvo:] *n, pl* **-vos** *or* **-voes** : salva *f*

samba ['sæmbə, 'sɑ-] *n* : samba *f*

same[1] ['seɪm] *adj* **1** : mismo ⟨he and I are from the same town : él y yo somos del mismo pueblo⟩ ⟨the same exact day, the exact/very same day : el mismísimo día⟩ ⟨they're one and the same person : son la misma persona⟩ **2** ALIKE, IDENTICAL : igual ⟨I have the same shirt : tengo una camisa igual a la tuya⟩ ⟨they're spelled the same way : se escriben igual⟩ **3** (*indicating repetition*) : mismo ⟨the same thing happened yesterday : ayer pasó lo mismo⟩ **4** (*indicating a shared characteristic*) : mismo ⟨they're the same age : tienen la misma edad⟩ ⟨she has the same eyes as her father : tiene los mismos ojos de su padre⟩ **5 the same old** ⟨it's always the same old thing : siempre pasa lo mismo⟩ ⟨the same old story : la misma historia de siempre⟩ **6 the same thing** ⟨it amounts to the same thing : viene a ser lo mismo⟩

same[2] *pron* **1 the same** : lo mismo ⟨it's all the same to me : me da lo mismo, me da igual⟩ ⟨the same to you! : ¡igualmente!⟩ ⟨the same goes for you : también va por ti⟩ ⟨you should do the same : deberías hacer lo mismo⟩ ⟨they're one and the same : son la misma persona/cosa⟩ ⟨I could say the same : podría decir lo mismo⟩ **2 the same** : igual ⟨the two cars are the same : los dos coches son iguales⟩ **3 the same** : igual (que antes) ⟨things are still the same : las cosas siguen igual⟩ ⟨he was never quite the same again : ya no era el mismo de antes⟩ **4 all/just the same** : de todos modos **5 same here** *fam* : yo también, a mí también

sameness ['seɪmnəs] *n* **1** SIMILARITY : identidad *f*, semejanza *f* **2** MONOTONY : monotonía *f*

sample[1] ['sæmpəl] *vt* **-pled; -pling** : probar

sample[2] *n* : muestra *f*, prueba *f*

sampler ['sæmplər] *n* **1** : dechado *m* (de bordado) **2** COLLECTION : colección *f* **3** ASSORTMENT : surtido *m*

sanatorium [ˌsænə'toriəm] *n, pl* **-riums** *or* **-ria** [-iə] : sanatorio *m*

sanctify ['sæŋktəˌfaɪ] *vt* **-fied; -fying** : santificar

sanctimonious [ˌsæŋktə'moːniəs] *adj* : beato, santurrón

sanction[1] ['sæŋkʃən] *vt* : sancionar, aprobar

sanction[2] *n* **1** AUTHORIZATION : sanción *f*, autorización *f* **2 sanctions** *npl* : sanciones *fpl* ⟨to impose sanctions on : imponer sanciones a⟩

sanctity ['sæŋktəti] *n, pl* **-ties** : santidad *f*

sanctuary ['sæŋktʃuˌeri] *n, pl* **-aries 1** : presbiterio *m* (en una iglesia) **2** REFUGE : refugio *m*, asilo *m*

sand[1] ['sænd] *vt* : lijar (madera)

sand[2] *n* : arena *f*

sandal ['sændəl] *n* : sandalia *f*

sandalwood ['sændəlˌwʊd] *n* : sándalo *m*

sandbank ['sændˌbæŋk] *n* : banco *m* de arena

sandbar ['sændˌbɑr] *n* : banco *m* de arena

sandbox ['sændˌbɑks] *n* : cajón *m* de arena

sand castle *n* : castillo *m* de arena

sand dune *n* **→ dune**

sandpaper ['sændˌpeɪpər] *n* : papel *m* de lija

sandstone ['sændˌstoːn] *n* : arenisca *f*

sandstorm ['sændˌstɔrm] *n* : tormenta *f* de arena

sandwich[1] ['sændˌwɪtʃ] *vt* : intercalar, encajonar, meter (entre dos cosas)

sandwich[2] *n* : sandwich *m*, emparedado *m*, bocadillo *m* Spain

sandy ['sændi] *adj* **sandier; -est** : arenoso

sane ['seɪn] *adj* **saner; sanest 1** : cuerdo **2** SENSIBLE : sensato, razonable

sang → sing

sangria [ˌsæŋ'griːə, ˌsæn-] *n* : sangría *f*

sanguine ['sæŋgwən] *adj* **1** RUDDY : sanguíneo, rubicundo **2** HOPEFUL : optimista

sanitarium [ˌsænə'teriəm] *n, pl* **-iums** *or* **-ia** [-iə] **→ sanatorium**

sanitary [ˈsænəteri] adj **1** : sanitario ⟨sanitary measures : medidas sanitarias⟩ **2** HYGIENIC : higiénico ⟨**3 sanitary napkin** : compresa f, paño m higiénico

sanitation [ˌsænəˈteɪʃən] n : sanidad f

sanitize [ˈsænəˌtaɪz] vt **-tized; -tizing 1** : desinfectar **2** EXPURGATE : expurgar

sanity [ˈsænəti] n : cordura f, razón f ⟨to lose one's sanity : perder el juicio⟩

sank → sink

Santa Claus [ˈsæntəˌklɔz] n : Papá Noel, San Nicolás

sap[1] [ˈsæp] vt **sapped; sapping 1** UNDERMINE : socavar **2** WEAKEN : minar, debilitar

sap[2] n **1** : savia f (de una planta) **2** SUCKER : inocentón m, -tona f

sapling [ˈsæplɪŋ] n : árbol m joven

sapphire [ˈsæˌfaɪr] n : zafiro m

Saran Wrap [səˈræn-] trademark se usa para papel film

sarcasm [ˈsɑrˌkæzəm] n : sarcasmo m

sarcastic [sɑrˈkæstɪk] adj : sarcástico — **sarcastically** [-tɪkli] adv

sarcophagus [sɑrˈkɑfəgəs] n, pl **-gi** [-ˌgaɪ, -ˌdʒaɪ] : sarcófago m

sardine [sɑrˈdiːn] n : sardina f

sardonic [sɑrˈdɑnɪk] adj : sardónico — **sardonically** [-nɪkli] adv

sari [ˈsɑri] n : sari m

sarsaparilla [ˌsæspəˈrɪlə, ˌsɑrs-] n : zarzaparrilla f

sash [ˈsæʃ] n **1** : faja f (de un vestido), fajín m (de un uniforme) **2** pl **sash** : marco m (de una ventana)

sassafras [ˈsæsəˌfræs] n : sasafrás m

sassy [ˈsæsi] adj **sassier; -est 1** fam IMPERTINENT : fresco, descarado, impertinente **2** STYLISH : moderno, llamativo **3** VIVACIOUS : vivaz

sat → sit

Satan [ˈseɪtən] n : Satanás m, Satán m

satanic [səˈtænɪk, seɪ-] adj : satánico — **satanically** [-nɪkli] adv

satchel [ˈsætʃəl] n : cartera f, saco m

sate [ˈseɪt] vt **sated; sating** : saciar

satellite [ˈsætəˌlaɪt] n : satélite m ⟨spy satellite : satélite espía⟩

satellite dish n : antena m parabólica

satiate [ˈseɪʃiˌeɪt] vt **-ated; -ating** : saciar, hartar

satin [ˈsætən] n : raso m, satín m, satén m

satire [ˈsæˌtaɪr] n : sátira f

satiric [səˈtɪrɪk] or **satirical** [-ɪkəl] adj : satírico

satirize [ˈsætəˌraɪz] vt **-rized; -rizing** : satirizar

satisfaction [ˌsætəsˈfækʃən] n : satisfacción f

satisfactory [ˌsætəsˈfæktəri] adj : satisfactorio, bueno — **satisfactorily** [-rəli] adv

satisfy [ˈsætəsˌfaɪ] v **-fied; -fying** vt **1** PLEASE : satisfacer, contentar **2** CONVINCE : convencer **3** FULFILL : satisfacer, cumplir con, llenar **4** SETTLE : pagar, saldar (una cuenta) — vi SUFFICE : bastar

satisfying [ˈsætəsˌfaɪɪŋ] adj : satisfactorio

saturate [ˈsætʃəˌreɪt] vt **-rated; -rating 1** SOAK : empapar **2** FILL : saturar

saturation [ˌsætʃəˈreɪʃən] n : saturación f

Saturday [ˈsætərˌdeɪ, -di] n : sábado m ⟨today is Saturday : hoy es sábado⟩ ⟨(on) Saturday : el sábado⟩ ⟨(on) Saturdays : los sábados⟩ ⟨last Saturday : el sábado pasado⟩ ⟨next Saturday : el sábado que viene⟩ ⟨every other Saturday : cada dos sábados⟩ ⟨Saturday afternoon/morning : sábado por la tarde/mañana⟩

Saturn [ˈsætərn] n : Saturno m

satyr [ˈseɪtər, ˈsæ-] n : sátiro m

sauce [ˈsɔs] n : salsa f

saucepan [ˈsɔsˌpæn] n : cacerola f, cazo m, cazuela f

saucer [ˈsɔsər] n : platillo m

sauciness [ˈsɔsinəs] n : descaro m, frescura f

saucy [ˈsɔsi] adj **saucier; -est** IMPUDENT : descarado, fresco fam — **saucily** adv

Saudi [ˈsaʊdi, ˈsɔ-] → **Saudi Arabian**

Saudi Arabian n : saudita mf, saudí mf — **Saudi Arabian** adj

sauna [ˈsɔnə, ˈsaʊnə] n : sauna mf

saunter [ˈsɔntər, ˈsɑn-] vi : pasear, pasearse

sausage [ˈsɔsɪdʒ] n : salchicha f, embutido m

sauté [sɔˈteɪ, so:-] vt **-téed** or **-téd; -téing** : saltear, sofreír

savage[1] [ˈsævɪdʒ] adj **1** offensive PRIMITIVE : salvaje **2** : salvaje, feroz — **savagely** adv

savage[2] n **1** offensive : salvaje mf **2** BEAST, BRUTE : salvaje mf

savagery [ˈsævɪdʒri, -dʒəri] n, pl **-ries 1** FEROCITY : ferocidad f **2** ATROCITY : salvajada f, atrocidad f, crueldad f ⟨the savageries of war : las atrocidades de la guerra⟩

savanna [səˈvænə] n : sabana f

save[1] [ˈseɪv] v **saved; saving** vt **1** RESCUE : salvar, rescatar ⟨she saved him from drowning : lo salvó de morir ahogado⟩ ⟨you really saved my bacon/hide/neck/skin! : ¡me salvaste el pellejo!⟩ **2** PRESERVE : salvar, preservar, conservar ⟨he hopes to save his job : espera salvar su trabajo⟩ **3** KEEP : guardar, ahorrar (dinero), almacenar (alimentos) ⟨to save one's strength : guardarse las fuerzas⟩ **4** : guardar (en informática) **5** ECONOMIZE : ahorrar (tiempo, espacio, combustible, etc.) **6** SPARE : ahorrar ⟨you saved me a trip : me ahorraste el viaje⟩ **7 to save someone's life** : salvarle la vida a alguien **8 to save the day** : salvar la situación — vi : ahorrar ⟨to save for the future : ahorrar para el futuro⟩ ⟨you'll save on insurance : ahorrarás dinero en tu seguro⟩

save[2] prep EXCEPT : salvo, excepto, menos

savings [ˈseɪvɪŋz] n : ahorros mpl

savings account n : cuenta f de ahorro(s)

savings bank n : caja f de ahorros

savior [ˈseɪvjər] n **1** : salvador m, -dora f **2 the Savior** : el Salvador m

savor[1] [ˈseɪvər] vt : saborear

savor[2] n : sabor m

savory ['seɪvəri] *adj* : sabroso
saw[1] → **see**
saw[2] ['sɔ] *vt* **sawed; sawed** *or* **sawn** ['sɔn]; **sawing** : serrar, cortar (con sierra)
saw[3] *n* : sierra *f*
sawdust ['sɔˌdʌst] *n* : aserrín *m*, serrín *m*
sawhorse ['sɔˌhɔrs] *n* : caballete *m*, burro *m* (en carpintería)
sawmill ['sɔˌmɪl] *n* : aserradero *m*
sax ['sæks] *n* : saxo *m fam* (instrumento)
saxophone ['sæksəˌfoːn] *n* : saxofón *m* — **saxophonist** ['sɔˌhɔrs] : ['sæksəˌfoːnɪst] *n*
say[1] ['seɪ] *v* **said** ['sed]; **saying; says** ['sez] *vt* **1** EXPRESS, UTTER : decir, expresar ⟨to say yes/no : decir que sí/no⟩ ⟨to say again : repetir⟩ ⟨to say one's prayers : rezar⟩ ⟨she didn't say a word : no dijo ni una palabra⟩ **2** INDICATE : marcar (dícese de un reloj), poner (dícese de un letrero, etc.) **3** EXPRESS, REVEAL : decir, revelar ⟨her face says it all : su cara lo dice todo⟩ **4** OPINE : decir ⟨so they say : eso dicen⟩ **5** KNOW : decir, saber ⟨it's hard to say why : es difícil decir por qué⟩ **6** COMMAND : decir, mandar ⟨what she says goes : lo que ella dice va a misa⟩ ⟨do as I say : haz lo que te digo⟩ ⟨whatever you say : lo que tú digas⟩ **7** PRONOUNCE : decir, pronunciar **8** SUPPOSE : suponer, decir **9 if I say so myself** : modestia aparte **10 no sooner said than done** : dicho y hecho **11 that goes without saying** : ni que decir tiene **12 that is to say** : es decir **13 that said, . . .** : dicho esto, . . . **14 to say the least** : y me quedo corto **15 when all is said and done** : al fin y al cabo **16 you can say that again!** *fam* : ¡y tanto! **17 you said it!** : ¡de acuerdo! — *vi* **1** : decir ⟨I couldn't say : no podría decirte⟩ **2 I'll say!** : ¡y tanto! **3 you don't say!** : ¡no me digas!
say[2] *n, pl* **says** ['seɪz] : voz *f*, opinión *f* ⟨to have no say : no tener ni voz ni voto⟩ ⟨to have one's say : dar uno su opinión⟩
saying ['seɪɪŋ] *n* : dicho *m*, refrán *m*
scab ['skæb] *n* **1** : costra *f*, postilla *f* (en una herida) **2** STRIKEBREAKER : rompehuelgas *mf*, esquirol *mf*
scabbard ['skæbərd] *n* : vaina *f* (de una espada), funda *f* (de un puñal, etc.)
scabby ['skæbi] *adj* **scabbier; -est** : lleno de costras
scaffold ['skæfəld, -ˌfoːld] *n* **1** *or* **scaffolding** : andamio *m* (para obreros, etc.) **2** : patíbulo *m*, cadalso *m* (para ejecuciones)
scald ['skɔld] *vt* **1** BURN : escaldar **2** HEAT : calentar (hasta el punto de ebullición)
scale[1] ['skeɪl] *v* **scaled; scaling** *vt* **1** : escamar (un pescado) **2** CLIMB : escalar (un muro, etc.) **3 to scale down** : reducir — *vi* WEIGH : pesar ⟨he scaled in at 200 pounds : pesó 200 libras⟩
scale[2] *n* **1** *or* **scales** *npl* : balanza *f*, báscula *f* (para pesar), baremo *m* ⟨bathroom scale : báscula de baño⟩ ⟨kitchen scale : balanza de cocina⟩ ⟨to tip the

scales in one's favor : inclinar la balanza a su favor⟩ **2** : escama *f* (de un pez, etc.)
3 EXTENT : escala *f*, proporción *f* ⟨on a worldwide scale : a escala mundial⟩ ⟨large-scale production : producción a gran escala⟩ **4** RANGE : escala *f* ⟨wage scale : escala salarial⟩ **5** : escala *f* (en cartografía, etc.) ⟨to draw to scale : dibujar a escala⟩ **6** : escala *f* (en música)
scallion ['skæljən] *n* : cebollino *m*, cebolleta *f*
scallop ['skɑləp, 'skæ-] *n* **1** : vieira *f* (molusco) **2** : festón *m* (decoración)
scalp[1] ['skælp] *vt* **1** : arrancar la cabellera a **2** : revender (ilegalmente)
scalp[2] *n* : cuero *m* cabelludo
scalpel ['skælpəl] *n* : bisturí *m*, escalpelo *m*
scalper ['skælpər] *n* : revendedor *m*, -dora *f* (de entradas)
scaly ['skeɪli] *adj* **scalier; -est** : escamoso
scam ['skæm] *n* : estafa *f*, timo *m fam*, chanchullo *m fam*
scamp ['skæmp] *n* : bribón *m*, -bona *f*; granuja *mf*; travieso *m*, -sa *f*
scamper ['skæmpər] *vi* : corretear
scan[1] ['skæn] *vt* **scanned; scanning 1** : escandir (versos) **2** SCRUTINIZE : escudriñar, escrutar ⟨to scan the horizon : escudriñar el horizonte⟩ **3** PERUSE : echarle un vistazo a (un periódico, etc.) **4** EXPLORE : explorar (con radar), hacer un escáner de (en ecografía) **5** : escanear (una imagen)
scan[2] *n* **1** : ecografía *f*, examen *m* ultrasónico, escáner *m* (en medicina) **2** : imagen *f* escaneada (en una computadora)
scandal ['skændəl] *n* **1** DISGRACE, OUTRAGE : escándalo *m* **2** GOSSIP : habladurías *fpl*, chismes *mpl*
scandalize ['skændəˌlaɪz] *vt* **-ized; -izing** : escandalizar
scandalous ['skændələs] *adj* : de escándalo
Scandinavian[1] [ˌskændəˈneɪviən] *adj* : escandinavo
Scandinavian[2] *n* : escandinavo *m*, -va *f*
scanner ['skænər] *n* : escáner *m*, scanner *m*
scant ['skænt] *adj* : escaso
scanty ['skænti] *adj* **scantier; -est** : exiguo, escaso ⟨a scanty meal : una comida insuficiente⟩ — **scantily** [-təli] *adv*
scapegoat ['skeɪpˌgoːt] *n* : chivo *m* expiatorio, cabeza *f* de turco
scapula ['skæpjələ] *n, pl* **-lae** [-ˌliː, -ˌlaɪ] *or* **-las** → **shoulder blade**
scar[1] ['skɑr] *vt* **scarred; scarring** : dejar una cicatriz en — *vi* : cicatrizar
scar[2] *n* : cicatriz *f*, marca *f*
scarab ['skærəb] *n* : escarabajo *m*
scarce ['skɛrs] *adj* **scarcer; -est** : escaso
scarcely ['skɛrsli] *adv* **1** BARELY : apenas **2** : ni mucho menos, ni nada que se le parezca ⟨he's scarcely an expert : ciertamente no es experto⟩
scarcity ['skɛrsəti] *n, pl* **-ties** : escasez *f*
scare[1] ['skɛr] *vt* **scared; scaring 1** : asustar, espantar **2 to scare away/off** : ahuyentar

scare[2] *n* **1** FRIGHT : susto *m*, sobresalto *m* **2** ALARM : pánico *m*

scarecrow ['skɛr,kroː] *n* : espantapájaros *m*, espantajo *m*

scared ['skɛrd] *n* : asustado ⟨to be scared stiff, to be scared to death : estar muerto de miedo⟩ ⟨I'm scared of snakes : las culebras me dan miedo⟩

scarf ['skɑrf] *n, pl* **scarves** ['skɑrvz] *or* **scarfs 1** MUFFLER : bufanda *f* **2** KERCHIEF : pañuelo *m*

scarlet ['skɑrlət] *n* : escarlata *f* — **scarlet** *adj*

scarlet fever *n* : escarlatina *f*

scary ['skɛri] *adj* **scarier; -est** : espantoso, pavoroso

scathing ['skeɪðɪŋ] *adj* : mordaz, cáustico

scatter ['skæt̬ər] *vt* : esparcir, desparramar — *vi* DISPERSE : dispersarse

scatterbrained ['skæt̬ər,breɪnd] *adj* : atolondrado, despistado, alocado

scavenge ['skævəndʒ] *v* **-venged; -venging** *vt* : rescatar (de la basura); pepenar *CA, Mex* — *vi* : rebuscar, hurgar en la basura ⟨to scavenge for food : andar buscando comida⟩

scavenger ['skævəndʒər] *n* **1** : persona *f* que rebusca en las basuras; pepenador *m*, -dora *f CA, Mex* **2** : carroñero *m*, -ra *f* (animal)

scenario [sə'næriˌoː, -'nɑr-] *n, pl* **-ios 1** PLOT : argumento *m* (en teatro), guión *m* (en cine) **2** SITUATION : situación *f* hipotética ⟨in the worst-case scenario : en el peor de los casos⟩

scene ['siːn] *n* **1** : escena *f* (en una obra de teatro) **2** SCENERY : decorado *m* (en el teatro) ⟨behind the scenes : entre bastidores⟩ **3** VIEW : escena *f* **4** LOCALE, LOCATION : escena *f*, escenario *m* ⟨the scene where the movie was filmed : el lugar donde la película se filmó⟩ ⟨the scene of the crime : la escena del crimen⟩ ⟨police are on/at the scene : los policías están en el lugar⟩ **5** COMMOTION, FUSS : escándalo *m*, escena *f* ⟨to make a scene : armar un escándalo⟩ **6** **to set the scene** : describir el escenario (de un cuento, etc.) **7** **to set the scene for** : crear un ambiente propicio para

scenery ['siːnəri] *n, pl* **-eries 1** : decorado *m* (en el teatro) **2** LANDSCAPE : paisaje *m*

scenic ['siːnɪk] *adj* : pintoresco

scent[1] ['sɛnt] *vt* **1** SMELL : oler, olfatear **2** PERFUME : perfumar **3** SENSE : sentir, percibir

scent[2] *n* **1** ODOR : olor *m*, aroma *m* **2** : olfato *m* ⟨a dog with a keen scent : un perro con un buen olfato⟩ **3** PERFUME : perfume *m*

scented ['sɛnt̬əd] *adj* : perfumado

scepter ['sɛptər] *n* : cetro *m*

sceptic ['skɛptɪk] → **skeptic**

schedule ['skɛˌdʒuːl, -dʒəl, *esp Brit* 'ʃɛdˌjuːl] *vt* **-uled; -uling** : planear, programar

schedule[2] *n* **1** PLAN : programa *m*, plan *m* ⟨on schedule : según lo previsto⟩

⟨behind schedule : atrasado, con retraso⟩ **2** TIMETABLE : horario *m*

schematic[1] [skɪ'mæt̬ɪk] *adj* : esquemático

schematic[2] *n* : plano *m*, esquema *m*

scheme[1] ['skiːm] *vi* **schemed; scheming** : intrigar, conspirar

scheme[2] *n* **1** PLAN : plan *m*, proyecto *m* **2** PLOT, TRICK : intriga *f*, ardid *m* **3** FRAMEWORK : esquema *m* ⟨a color scheme : una combinación de colores⟩

schemer ['skiːmər] *n* : intrigante *mf*

schism ['sɪzəm, 'skɪ-] *n* : cisma *m*

schizophrenia [ˌskɪtsə'friːniə, ˌskɪzə-, -'frɛ-] *n* : esquizofrenia *f*

schizophrenic [ˌskɪtsə'frɛnɪk, ˌskɪzə-] *n* : esquizofrénico *m*, -ca *f* — **schizophrenic** *adj*

scholar ['skɑlər] *n* **1** STUDENT : escolar *mf*; alumno *m*, -na *f* **2** EXPERT : especialista *mf*

scholarly ['skɑlərli] *adj* : erudito

scholarship ['skɑlərˌʃɪp] *n* **1** LEARNING : erudición *f* **2** GRANT : beca *f*

scholastic [skə'læstɪk] *adj* : académico

school[1] ['skuːl] *vt* : instruir, enseñar

school[2] *n* **1** : escuela *f*, colegio *m* (institución) ⟨to go to school : ir a la escuela⟩ ⟨school district : distrito escolar⟩ ⟨law/medical school : facultad de derecho/medicina⟩ **2** : estudiantes y profesores (de una escuela) **3** : escuela *f* (en pintura, etc.) ⟨the Flemish school : la escuela flamenca⟩ **4** **school of fish** : banco *m*, cardumen *m*

schoolbook ['skuːlˌbʊk] *n* : libro *m* de texto

schoolboy ['skuːlˌbɔɪ] *n* : escolar *m*, colegial *m*

schoolchild ['skuːlˌtʃaɪld] *n* : colegial *m*, -giala *f*; escolar *mf*

schoolgirl ['skuːlˌɡərl] *n* : escolar *f*, colegiala *f*

schoolhouse ['skuːlˌhaʊs] *n* : escuela *f*

schooling ['skuːlɪŋ] *n* : educación *f* escolar

schoolmate ['skuːlˌmeɪt] *n* : compañero *m*, -ra *f* de escuela

schoolroom ['skuːlˌruːm, -ˌrʊm] → **classroom**

schoolteacher ['skuːlˌtiːtʃər] *n* : maestro *m*, -tra *f*; profesor *m*, -sora *f*

schoolwork ['skuːlˌwərk] *n* : trabajo *m* escolar

schooner ['skuːnər] *n* : goleta *f*

science ['saɪənts] *n* : ciencia *f*

science fiction *n* : ciencia ficción *f*

scientific [ˌsaɪən'tɪfɪk] *adj* : científico — **scientifically** [-fɪkli] *adv*

scientist ['saɪəntɪst] *n* : científico *m*, -ca *f*

sci-fi ['saɪˈfaɪ] *fam* → **science fiction**

scintillating ['sɪntəˌleɪt̬ɪŋ] *adj* : chispeante, brillante

scissors ['sɪzərz] *npl* : tijeras *fpl*

sclerosis [skləˈroːsəs] *n, pl* **-roses** : esclerosis *f*

scoff ['skɑf] *vi* **to scoff at** : burlarse de, mofarse de

scold ['skoːld] *vt* : regañar, reprender, reñir

scoop[1] ['sku:p] vt **1** : sacar (con pala o cucharón) **2 to scoop out** HOLLOW : vaciar, ahuecar

scoop[2] n **1** : pala f (para harina, etc.), cucharón m (para helado, etc.) **2** : bola f (de helado), cucharada f

scoot ['sku:t] vi : ir rápidamente ⟨she scooted around the corner : volvió la esquina a toda prisa⟩

scooter ['sku:t̬ər] n : patineta f, monopatín m, patinete m

scope ['sko:p] n **1** RANGE : alcance m, ámbito m, extensión f **2** OPPORTUNITY : posibilidades fpl, libertad f

scorch ['skɔrtʃ] vt : chamuscar, quemar — vi : chamuscarse, quemarse

score[1] ['skor] v **scored; scoring** vt **1** RECORD : anotar **2** MARK, SCRATCH : marcar, rayar **3** : marcar, meter (en deportes) **4** GAIN : ganar, apuntarse **5** GRADE : calificar (exámenes, etc.) **6** : instrumentar, orquestar (música) — vi **1** : marcar (en deportes) **2** : obtener una puntuación (en un examen)

score[2] n, pl **scores 1** or pl **score** TWENTY : veintena f **2** LINE, SCRATCH : línea f, marca f **3** : resultado m (en deportes) ⟨what's the score? : ¿cómo va el marcador?⟩ ⟨to keep score : anotar los tantos⟩ **4** GRADE, POINTS : calificación f (en un examen), puntuación f (en un concurso) **5** ACCOUNT : cuenta f ⟨to settle a score : ajustar una cuenta⟩ ⟨on that score : a ese respecto⟩ **6** : partitura f (musical)

scoreboard ['skor,bord] n : marcador m, tanteador m, pizarra f

scorer ['skorər] n : anotador m, -dora f; goleador m, -dora f (de fútbol, etc.) ⟨the team's top scorer : el máximo anotador del equipo⟩

scorn[1] ['skɔrn] vt : despreciar, menospreciar, desdeñar

scorn[2] n : desprecio m, menosprecio m, desdén m

scornful ['skɔrnfəl] adj : desdeñoso, despreciativo — **scornfully** adv

Scorpio ['skɔrpi,o:] n **1** : Escorpio m, Escorpión m (signo o constelación) **2** : Escorpio mf, Escorpión mf (persona)

scorpion ['skɔrpiən] n : alacrán m, escorpión m

Scot ['skɑt] n : escocés m, -cesa f

Scotch[1] ['skɑtʃ] adj → **Scottish**[1]

Scotch[2] npl **the Scotch** (used with a plural verb) : los escoceses

Scotch[3] trademark se usa para un tipo de cinta adhesiva

scot-free ['skɑt'fri:] adj **to get off scot-free** : salir impune, quedar sin castigo

Scots ['skɑts] n : escocés m (idioma)

Scottish[1] ['skɑtʃ] adj : escocés

Scottish[2] n → **Scots**

scoundrel ['skaʊndrəl] n : sinvergüenza mf; bellaco m, -ca f

scour ['skaʊər] vt **1** EXAMINE, SEARCH : registrar (un área), revisar (documentos, etc.) **2** SCRUB : fregar, restregar

scourge[1] ['skɜrdʒ] vt **scourged; scourging** : azotar

scourge[2] n : azote m

scout[1] ['skaʊt] vi **1** RECONNOITER : reconocer **2 to scout around for** : explorar en busca de

scout[2] n **1** : explorador m, -dora f **2** or **talent scout** : cazatalentos mf

scowl[1] ['skaʊl] vi : fruncir el ceño

scowl[2] n : ceño m fruncido

scrabble ['skræbəl] vi **scrabbled; -bling** : escarbar/hurgar (etc.) frenéticamente ⟨they scrabbled in the dirt : escarbaban en el suelo⟩ ⟨she scrabbled around in her handbag : hurgaba en el bolso⟩ ⟨he scrabbled at the rock : intentó agarrarse a la roca⟩

scram ['skræm] vi **scrammed; scramming** : largarse

scramble[1] ['skræmbəl] v **scrambled; -bling** vi **1** : trepar, gatear (apresuradamente) ⟨he scrambled over the fence : se trepó a la cerca con rapidez⟩ **2** : hacer/ir (etc.) frenéticamente ⟨we scrambled for cover : corrimos a ponernos a cubierto⟩ **3** STRUGGLE : pelearse (por) ⟨they scrambled for seats : se pelearon por los asientos⟩ — vt **1** JUMBLE : mezclar **2** ENCODE, ENCRYPT : codificar, cifrar, encriptar **3 to scramble eggs** : hacer huevos revueltos

scramble[2] n : rebatiña f, pelea f

scrambled eggs npl : huevos mpl revueltos

scrap[1] ['skræp] v **scrapped; scrapping** vt DISCARD : desechar — vi FIGHT : pelearse

scrap[2] n **1** FRAGMENT : pedazo m, trozo m ⟨a scrap of paper : un pedacito de papel, un papelito⟩ ⟨scraps of fabric : retazos⟩ **2** FIGHT : pelea f **3** or **scrap metal** : chatarra f **4 scraps** npl LEFTOVERS : restos mpl, sobras fpl

scrapbook ['skræp,bʊk] n : álbum m de recortes

scrape[1] ['skreɪp] v **scraped; scraping** vt **1** GRAZE, SCRATCH : rozar, rascar ⟨to scrape one's knee : rasparse la rodilla⟩ **2** CLEAN : raspar ⟨to scrape carrots : raspar zanahorias⟩ **3 to scrape off** : raspar (pintura, etc.) **4 to scrape up/together** : juntar, reunir poco a poco — vi **1** RUB : rozar **2 to scrape by/along** : arreglárselas, ir tirando **3 to scrape by/through** ⟨he just barely scraped by on the exam : aprobó el examen por los pelos⟩

scrape[2] n **1** SCRAPING : raspadura f **2** SCRATCH : rasguño m **3** PREDICAMENT : apuro m, aprieto m

scraping ['skreɪpɪŋ] n SHAVING : raspadura f

scrap paper n : papel para borrador, papel usado

scratch[1] ['skrætʃ] vt **1** : rascarse (la cabeza, etc.) ⟨to scratch an itch : rascarse⟩ **2** : arañar, rasguñar (con las uñas, etc.) **3** MARK : rayar, marcar **4 to scratch out** : tachar — vi **1** : rascarse **2** : arañar **3** : rayar **4 to scratch at** : arañar, rasguñar (una puerta, etc.)

scratch[2] n **1** : rasguño m, arañazo m (en la piel) **2** MARK : raya f, rayón m (en un mueble, etc.) **3** : sonido *m* rasposo ⟨I heard a scratch at the door : oí como que raspaban a la puerta⟩ **4 from ~** ⟨to start from scratch : empezar desde cero⟩ ⟨I made the cake from scratch : el pastel lo hice yo⟩ **5 to be up to scratch** : dar la talla

scratchy [ˈskrætʃi] *adj* **scratchier; -est** : áspero, que pica ⟨a scratchy sweater : un suéter que pica⟩

scrawl¹ [ˈskrɔl] *v* : garabatear

scrawl² *n* : garabato *m*

scrawny [ˈskrɔni] *adj* **scrawnier; -est** : flaco, escuálido

scream¹ [ˈskriːm] *vi* : chillar, gritar

scream² *n* : chillido *m*, grito *m*

screech¹ [ˈskriːtʃ] *vi* : chillar (dícese de las personas o de los animales), chirriar (dícese de los frenos, etc.)

screech² *n* **1** : chillido *m*, grito *m* (de una persona o un animal) **2** : chirrido *m* (de frenos, etc.)

screen¹ [ˈskriːn] *vt* **1** SHIELD : proteger **2** CONCEAL : tapar, ocultar **3** TEST : someter (a un paciente) a pruebas preventivas o de detección ⟨to screen for drugs/cancer : someter a una prueba de detección (de drogas/cáncer) **4** INSPECT : revisar (equipaje, etc.) **5** SELECT : seleccionar (candidatos, etc.), filtrar (llamadas, etc.) **6** SIEVE : cribar **7** : emitir (un programa de televisión), proyectar (una película)

screen² *n* **1** PARTITION : biombo *m*, pantalla *f* **2** SIEVE : criba *f* **3** : pantalla *f* (de un televisor, una computadora, etc.) **4** MOVIES : cine *m* **5** *or* **window screen** : ventana *f* de tela metálica

screening [ˈskriːnɪŋ] *n* **1** : proyección *f* (de una película), emisión *f* (de un programa de televisión) **2** TESTING : acto *m* de hacer pruebas médicas (preventivas o de drogas) **3** INSPECTION : control *m* (de pasajeros, equipaje), selección *f* (de candidatos)

screenplay [ˈskriːnˌpleɪ] *n* SCRIPT : guión *m*

screen saver *n* : protector *m* de pantalla, salvapantallas *m*

screw¹ [ˈskruː] *vt* **1** : atornillar (un tornillo) **2** : atornillar, sujetar (con tornillos) **3** : enroscar (una tapa) **4** *or* **to screw over** *fam* CHEAT, DECEIVE : estafar, engañar **5 to screw someone out of something** *fam* : quitarle algo a alguien (injustamente) — *vi* **1 to screw around** *fam* TOY : jugar, juguetear **2 to screw around** *fam* : perder el tiempo **3 to screw around** *fam* : tener líos (amorosos) **4 to screw in** : atornillarse **5 to screw up** *fam* : meter la pata

screw² *n* **1** : tornillo *m* (para fijar algo) **2** TWIST : vuelta *f* **3** PROPELLER : hélice *f*

screwdriver [ˈskruːˌdraɪvər] *n* : destornillador *m*, desarmador *m* Mex

scribble¹ [ˈskrɪbəl] *v* **-bled; -bling** : garabatear

scribble² *n* : garabato *m*

scribe [ˈskraɪb] *n* : escriba *m*

scrimmage [ˈskrɪmɪdʒ] *n* : escaramuza *f*

scrimp [ˈskrɪmp] *vi* **1 to scrimp on** : escatimar **2 to scrimp and save** : hacer economías

script [ˈskrɪpt] *n* **1** HANDWRITING : letra *f*, escritura *f* **2** : guión *m* (de una película, etc.)

scriptural [ˈskrɪptʃərəl] *adj* : bíblico

scripture [ˈskrɪptʃər] *n* **1** : escritos *mpl* sagrados (de una religión) **2 the Scriptures** *npl* : las Sagradas Escrituras

scriptwriter [ˈskrɪptˌraɪtər] *n* : guionista *mf*, libretista *mf*

scroll¹ [ˈskroːl] *n* **1** : rollo *m* (de pergamino, etc.) **2** : voluta *f* (adorno en arquitectura)

scroll² *vi* : desplazarse (en informática) — *vt* : desplazar (en informática)

scrotum [ˈskroːtəm] *n, pl* **scrota** [-tə] *or* **scrotums** : escroto *m*

scrounge [ˈskraʊndʒ] *v* **scrounged; scrounging** *vt* **1** BUM, SPONGE : gorrear *fam*, sablear *fam* (dinero) **2** *or* **to scrounge up** : conseguir, encontrar — *vi* **1 to scrounge off** : vivir a costa de **2 to scrounge around for** : buscar

scrounger [ˈskraʊndʒər] *n* : gorrón *m*, -rrona *f*

scrub¹ [ˈskrʌb] *vt* **scrubbed; scrubbing** : restregar, fregar

scrub² *n* **1** THICKET, UNDERBRUSH : maleza *f*, matorral *m*, matorrales *mpl* **2** SCRUBBING : fregado *m*, restregadura *f*

scrubby [ˈskrʌbi] *adj* **scrubbier; -est** **1** STUNTED : achaparrado **2** : cubierto de maleza

scruff [ˈskrʌf] *n* **by the scruff of the neck** : por el cogote, por el pescuezo

scruffy [ˈskrʌfi] *adj* **scruffier; -est** : dejado, desaliñado

scrumptious [ˈskrʌmpʃəs] *adj* : delicioso, muy rico

scruple [ˈskruːpəl] *n* : escrúpulo *m*

scrupulous [ˈskruːpjələs] *adj* : escrupuloso — **scrupulously** *adv*

scrutinize [ˈskruːtənˌaɪz] *vt* **-nized; -nizing** : escrutar, escudriñar

scrutiny [ˈskruːtəni] *n, pl* **-nies** : escrutinio *m*, inspección *f*

scuba [ˈskuːbə] *n* **1** *or* **scuba gear** : equipo *m* de submarinismo **2 scuba diver** : submarinista *mf* **3 scuba diving** : submarinismo *m*

scuff [ˈskʌf] *vt* : rayar, raspar ⟨to scuff one's feet : arrastrar los pies⟩

scuffle¹ [ˈskʌfəl] *vi* **-fled; -fling** **1** TUSSLE : pelearse **2** SHUFFLE : caminar arrastrando los pies

scuffle² *n* **1** TUSSLE : refriega *f*, pelea *f* **2** SHUFFLE : arrastre *m* de los pies

sculpt [ˈskʌlpt] *v* : esculpir

sculptor [ˈskʌlptər] *n* : escultor *m*, -tora *f*

sculptural [ˈskʌlptʃərəl] *adj* : escultórico

sculpture¹ [ˈskʌlptʃər] *vt* **-tured; -turing** : esculpir

sculpture² *n* : escultura *f*

scum [ˈskʌm] *n* **1** FROTH : espuma *f*, nata *f* **2** : verdín *m* (encima de un líquido)

scurrilous [ˈskərələs] *adj* : difamatorio, calumnioso, injurioso

scurry [ˈskəri] *vi* **-ried; -rying** : corretear

scurvy ['skərvi] n : escorbuto m
scuttle[1] ['skʌtəl] v **-tled; -tling** vt : hundir (un barco) — vi SCAMPER : corretear
scuttle[2] n : cubo m (para carbón)
scythe ['saɪð] n : guadaña f
sea[1] ['si:] adj : del mar
sea[2] n **1** : mar mf ⟨the Black Sea : el Mar Negro⟩ ⟨on the high seas : en alta mar⟩ ⟨heavy seas : mar gruesa, mar agitada⟩ **2** MASS : mar m, multitud f ⟨a sea of faces : un mar de rostros⟩
sea bass n : lubina f
seabed ['si:,bed] n : fondo m del mar
seabird ['si:,bərd] n : ave f marina
seaboard ['si:,bord] n : litoral m
seacoast ['si:,ko:st] n : costa f, litoral m
seafarer ['si:,færər] n : marinero m
seafaring[1] ['si:,færɪŋ] adj : marinero
seafaring[2] n : navegación f
seafood ['si:,fu:d] n : mariscos mpl
seafront ['si:,frʌnt] n : paseo m marítimo ⟨a restaurant on the seafront : un restaurante frente al mar⟩
seagull ['si:,gʌl] n : gaviota f
sea horse ['si:,hors] n : hipocampo m, caballito m de mar
seal[1] ['si:l] vt **1** CLOSE : sellar, cerrar ⟨to seal a letter : cerrar una carta⟩ ⟨to seal an agreement : sellar un acuerdo⟩ **2 to seal off** : acordonar, cerrar **3 to seal up** : tapar, rellenar (una grieta, etc.)
seal[2] n **1** : foca f (animal) **2** : sello m ⟨seal of approval : sello de aprobación⟩ **3** CLOSURE : cierre m, precinto m
sea level n : nivel m del mar
sea lion n : león m marino
sealskin ['si:l,skɪn] n : piel f de foca
seam[1] ['si:m] vt **1** STITCH : unir con costuras **2** MARK : marcar
seam[2] n **1** STITCHING : costura f **2** LODE, VEIN : veta f, filón m
seaman ['si:mən] n, pl **-men** [-mən, -,mɛn] **1** SAILOR : marinero m **2** : marino m (en la armada)
seamless ['si:mləs] adj **1** : sin costuras, de una pieza **2** : perfecto ⟨a seamless transition : una transición fluida⟩
seamstress ['si:mˌstrəs] n : costurera f
seamy ['si:mi] adj **seamier; -est** : sórdido
séance ['seɪˌɑnts] n : sesión f de espiritismo
seaplane ['si:,pleɪn] n : hidroavión m
seaport ['si:,port] n : puerto m marítimo
sear ['sɪr] vt **1** PARCH, WITHER : secar, resecar **2** SCORCH : chamuscar, quemar
search[1] ['sərtʃ] vt : registrar (un edificio, un área), cachear (a una persona), buscar en — vi **to search for** : buscar
search[2] n **1** : búsqueda f, registro m (de un edificio, etc.), cacheo m (de una persona) **2 in search of** : en busca de
search engine n : buscador m
searching ['sərtʃɪŋ] adj : inquisitivo, penetrante
searchlight ['sərtʃ,laɪt] n : reflector m
seashell ['si:,ʃɛl] n : concha f (marina)
seashore ['si:,ʃor] n : orilla f del mar
seasick ['si:,sɪk] adj : mareado ⟨to get seasick : marearse⟩
seasickness ['si:,sɪknəs] n : mareo m

seaside → **seacoast**
season[1] ['si:zən] vt **1** FLAVOR, SPICE : sazonar, condimentar **2** CURE : curar, secar (madera)
season[2] n **1** : estación f (del año) **2** : temporada f ⟨baseball season : la temporada de beisbol⟩ ⟨the holiday season : las fiestas⟩ ⟨in season : en temporada⟩ ⟨out of season : fuera de temporada⟩ **3** HEAT, ESTRUS : celo m
seasonable ['si:zənəbəl] adj **1** : propio de la estación (dícese del tiempo, de las temperaturas, etc.) **2** TIMELY : oportuno
seasonal ['si:zənəl] adj : estacional — **seasonally** adv
seasoned ['si:zənd] adj **1** SPICED : condimentado, sazonado **2** EXPERIENCED : veterano ⟨a seasoned veteran : un veterano avezado⟩ **3** : curado, seco ⟨seasoned wood : madera curada/seca⟩
seasoning ['si:zənɪŋ] n : condimento m, sazón f
season ticket n : abono m
seat[1] ['si:t] vt **1** SIT : sentar ⟨please be seated : siéntense, por favor⟩ **2** HOLD : tener cabida para ⟨the stadium seats 40,000 : el estadio tiene 40,000 asientos⟩
seat[2] n **1** : asiento m, plaza f (en un vehículo) ⟨take a seat : tome asiento⟩ **2** : asiento m (de una silla) **3** BOTTOM : fondillos mpl (de la ropa), trasero m (del cuerpo) **4** : sede f (de un gobierno, del poder, etc.), centro m (de enseñanza, etc.)
seat belt n : cinturón m de seguridad
seating ['si:tɪŋ] n **1** : asientos mpl ⟨is there enough seating for everyone? : ¿hay asientos para todos?⟩ ⟨seating capacity : aforo⟩ ⟨the seating plan/arrangement for the wedding reception : el plano de mesas para el banquete de bodas⟩ **2** SITTING : turno m
sea urchin n : erizo m de mar
seawall ['si:,wɑl] n : rompeolas m, dique m marítimo
seawater ['si:,wɔtər, -,wɑ-] n : agua f de mar
seaweed ['si:,wi:d] n : alga f marina
seaworthy ['si:,wərði] adj : en condiciones de navegar
secede [sɪ'si:d] vi **-ceded; -ceding** : separarse (de una nación, etc.)
seclude [sɪ'klu:d] vt **-cluded; -cluding** : aislar
seclusion [sɪ'klu:ʒən] n : aislamiento m
second[1] ['sɛkənd] vt : secundar, apoyar (una moción)
second[2] or **secondly** ['sɛkəndli] adv : en segundo lugar
second[3] adj **1** : segundo ⟨her second husband : su segundo marido⟩ ⟨the second house on the left : la segunda casa a la izquierda⟩ ⟨he took second place : ganó el segundo lugar⟩ **2** : otro ⟨a second chance/time : otra oportunidad/vez⟩ **3 every second** EVERY OTHER : cada dos ⟨every second month : cada dos meses⟩

second⁴ n 1 : segundo m, -da f (en una serie) ⟨the second of July : el dos de julio⟩ 2 : segundo m, ayudante m (en deportes) 3 MOMENT : segundo m, momento m 4 or **second base** : segunda base f 5 or **second gear** : segunda f (de un automóvil) 6 **seconds** npl : segunda ración f ⟨to have seconds : repetir⟩ ⟨who wants seconds? : ¿quién quiere más?⟩

secondary ['sɛkən,dri] adj : secundario

secondary school n : escuela f de enseñanza secundaria

second–class ['sɛkənd'klæs] adj : de segunda clase/categoría, mediocre

secondhand ['sɛkənd'hænd] adj : de segunda mano

second lieutenant n : alférez mf, subteniente m

second-rate ['sɛkənd'reɪt] adj : mediocre, de segunda categoría

second thought n 1 : duda f ⟨later he had second thoughts about going : luego le entró la duda sobre si ir o no⟩ ⟨don't give it a second thought : no tiene importancia, no te preocupes⟩ 2 **on second thought** : pensándolo bien 3 **without a second thought** : sin pensarlo dos veces

secrecy ['si:krəsi] n, pl **-cies** : secreto m

secret¹ ['si:krət] adj 1 : secreto ⟨to keep a secret : guardar un secreto⟩ ⟨to make no secret of something : no ocultar/esconder algo⟩ ⟨in secret : en secreto⟩ 2 → **secretive** — **secretly** adv

secret² n : secreto m

secretarial [,sɛkrə'triəl] adj : de secretario, de oficina

secretariat [,sɛkrə'triət] n : secretaría f, secretariado m

secretary ['sɛkrə,tri] n, pl **-taries** 1 : secretario m, -ria f (en una oficina, etc.) 2 : ministro m, -tra f; secretario m, -ria f ⟨Secretary of State : Secretario de Estado⟩

secrete [sɪ'kri:t] vt **-creted; -creting** 1 : secretar, segregar (en fisiología) 2 HIDE : ocultar

secretion [sɪ'kri:ʃən] n : secreción f

secretive ['si:krətɪv, sɪ'kri:tɪv] adj : reservado, callado, secreto

sect ['sɛkt] n : secta f

sectarian [sɛk'triən] adj : sectario

section¹ ['sɛkʃən] vt 1 : dividir 2 **to section off** : separar

section² n : sección f, parte f (de un mueble, etc.), sector m (de la población), barrio m (de una ciudad)

sectional ['sɛkʃənəl] adj 1 : en sección, en corte ⟨a sectional diagram : un gráfico en corte⟩ 2 FACTIONAL : de grupo, entre facciones 3 : modular ⟨sectional furniture : muebles modulares⟩

sector ['sɛktər] n : sector m

secular ['sɛkjələr] adj 1 : secular, laico ⟨secular life : la vida secular⟩ 2 : seglar (dícese de los sacerdotes, etc.)

secure¹ [sɪ'kjʊr] vt **-cured; -curing** 1 FASTEN : asegurar (una puerta, etc.), sujetar 2 GET : conseguir

secure² adj **securer; -est** : seguro — **securely** adv

security [sɪ'kjʊrəti] n, pl **-ties** 1 SAFETY : seguridad f 2 GUARANTEE : garantía f 3 **securities** npl : valores mpl

security guard n : guardia mf de seguridad, guarda mf de seguridad

sedan [sɪ'dæn] n 1 or **sedan chair** : silla f de manos 2 : sedán m (automóvil)

sedate¹ [sɪ'deɪt] vt **-dated; -dating** : sedar

sedate² adj : sosegado — **sedately** adv

sedation [sɪ'deɪʃən] n : sedación f

sedative¹ ['sɛdətɪv] adj : sedante

sedative² n : sedante m, calmante m

sedentary ['sɛdən,teri] adj : sedentario

sedge ['sɛdʒ] n : juncia f

sediment ['sɛdəmənt] n : sedimento m (geológico), poso m (en un líquido) — **sedimentary** [,sɛdə'mɛntəri] adj — **sedimentation** [,sɛdəmən'teɪʃən] n

sedition [sɪ'dɪʃən] n : sedición f

seditious [sɪ'dɪʃəs] adj : sedicioso

seduce [sɪ'du:s, -'dju:s] vt **-duced; -ducing** : seducir

seduction [sɪ'dʌkʃən] n : seducción f

seductive [sɪ'dʌktɪv] adj : seductor, seductivo

seducer [sɪ'du:sər, -'dju:-] n : seductor m, -tora f

see¹ ['si:] v **saw** ['sɔ]; **seen** ['si:n]; **seeing** vt 1 : ver ⟨I saw a dog : vi un perro⟩ ⟨see you later! : ¡hasta luego!⟩ ⟨I'll believe it when I see it : hasta que no lo vea, no lo creo⟩ ⟨so I see : ya veo⟩ ⟨did you see the game? : ¿viste el partido?⟩ ⟨see below : ver más abajo, véase más abajo⟩ 2 ASCERTAIN : ver ⟨see who's at the door : ve a abrir (la puerta)⟩ ⟨let's wait and see what happens : esperemos a ver qué pasa⟩ 3 READ : leer 4 EXPERIENCE : ver, conocer 5 UNDERSTAND : ver, entender 6 CONSIDER : ver ⟨as I see it : a mi entender⟩ 7 IMAGINE : imaginar 8 FORESEE : ver 9 ENSURE : asegurarse ⟨see that it's correct : asegúrese de que sea correcto⟩ 10 MEET, VISIT : ver 11 CONSULT : ver 12 ACCOMPANY : acompañar ⟨to see someone to the door : acompañar a alguien a la puerta⟩ 13 **to be seeing someone** : salir con alguien 14 **to see in someone** ⟨what does she see in him? : ¿qué le ve?⟩ 15 **to see off** : despedir, despedirse de 16 **to see out/through** COMPLETE : terminar 17 **to see through** HELP : sacar adelante — vi 1 ⟨seeing is believing : ver para creer⟩ 2 UNDERSTAND : entender, ver ⟨now I see! : ¡ya entiendo!⟩ 3 ASCERTAIN : ver ⟨can I go? we'll see : ¿puedo ir? vamos a ver⟩ ⟨you'll see : ya verás⟩ 4 CONSIDER : ver ⟨let's see : vamos a ver⟩ 5 **see here!** : ¡oye!, ¡mira! 6 **to see about** : ocuparse de (algo) 7 **we'll see about that** : ya veremos. 8 **to see after/to** : ocuparse de 9 **to see through** : calar (a alguien)

see² n : sede f ⟨the Holy See : la Santa Sede⟩

seed¹ ['si:d] vt 1 SOW : sembrar 2 : quitarle las semillas a

seed² n, pl **seed** or **seeds** 1 : semilla f, pepita f (de una fruta) 2 SOURCE : germen m, semilla f

seedless ['si:dləs] *adj* : sin semillas

seedling ['si:dlɪŋ] *n* : plantón *m*

seedpod ['si:d,pad] → **pod**

seedy ['si:di] *adj* **seedier; -est 1** : lleno de semillas **2** SHABBY : raído (dícese de la ropa) **3** RUN-DOWN : ruinoso (dícese de los edificios, etc.), sórdido

Seeing Eye *trademark* se usa para un perro guía

seek ['si:k] *v* **sought** ['sɔt]; **seeking** *vt* **1** : buscar ⟨to seek an answer : buscar una solución⟩ **2** REQUEST : solicitar, pedir **3 to seek to** : tratar de, intentar de — *vi* SEARCH : buscar

seem ['si:m] *vi* : parecer

seeming ['si:mɪŋ] *adj* : aparente, ostensible

seemingly ['si:mɪŋli] *adv* : aparentemente, según parece

seemly ['si:mli] *adj* **seemlier; -est** : apropiado, decoroso

seep ['si:p] *vi* : filtrarse

seer ['si:ər] *n* : vidente *mf*, clarividente *mf*

seesaw[1] ['si:,sɔ] *vi* **1** : jugar en un subibaja **2** VACILLATE : vacilar, oscilar

seesaw[2] *n* : balancín *m*, subibaja *m*

seethe ['si:ð] *vi* **seethed; seething 1** : bullir, hervir **2 to seethe with anger** : rabiar, estar furioso

segment ['sɛgmənt] *n* : segmento *m*

segmented ['sɛg,mɛntəd, sɛg'mɛn-] *adj* : segmentado

segregate ['sɛgrɪ,geɪt] *vt* **-gated; -gating** : segregar

segregation [,sɛgrɪ'geɪʃən] *n* : segregación *f*

seismic ['saɪzmɪk, 'saɪs-] *adj* : sísmico

seismograph ['saɪzmə,græf, 'saɪs-] *n* : sismógrafo *m*

seize ['si:z] *v* **seized; seizing** *vt* **1** CAPTURE : capturar, tomar, apoderarse de **2** ARREST : detener **3** CLUTCH, GRAB : agarrar, coger, aprovechar (una oportunidad) **4 to be seized with** : estar sobrecogido por — *vi or* **to seize up** : agarrotarse

seizure ['si:ʒər] *n* **1** CAPTURE : toma *f*, captura *f* **2** ARREST : detención *f* **3** : ataque *m* ⟨an epileptic seizure : un ataque epiléptico⟩

seldom ['sɛldəm] *adv* : pocas veces, rara vez, casi nunca

select[1] [sə'lɛkt] *vt* : escoger, elegir, seleccionar (a un candidato, etc.)

select[2] *adj* : selecto

selection [sə'lɛkʃən] *n* : selección *f*, elección *f*

selective [sə'lɛktɪv] *adj* : selectivo

selenium [sə'li:niəm] *n* : selenio *m*

self ['sɛlf] *n, pl* **selves** ['sɛlvz] **1** : ser *m*, persona *f* ⟨the self : el yo⟩ ⟨with his whole self : con todo su ser⟩ ⟨her own self : su propia persona⟩ ⟨his better self : su lado bueno⟩ **2** SIDE : lado (de la personalidad)

self- [,sɛlf] *pref* : auto-

self–addressed [,sɛlfə'drst] *adj* : con la dirección del remitente ⟨include a self-addressed envelope : incluya un sobre con su nombre y dirección⟩

self–appointed [,sɛlfə'pɔɪntəd] *adj* : autoproclamado, autonombrado

self–assurance [,sɛlfə'ʃʊrənts] *n* : seguridad *f* en sí mismo

self–assured [,sɛlfə'ʃʊrd] *adj* : seguro de sí mismo

self–centered [,sɛlf'sɛntərd] *adj* : egocéntrico

self–confidence [,sɛlf'kanfədənts] *n* : confianza *f* en sí mismo

self–confident [,sɛlf'kanfədənt] *adj* : seguro de sí mismo

self–conscious [,sɛlf'kantʃəs] *adj* : cohibido, tímido

self–consciously [,sɛlf'kantʃəsli] *adv* : de manera cohibida

self–consciousness [,sɛlf'kantʃəsnəs] *n* : vergüenza *f*, timidez *f*

self–contained [,sɛlfkən'teɪnd] *adj* **1** INDEPENDENT : independiente **2** RESERVED : reservado

self–control [,sɛlfkən'tro:l] *n* : autocontrol *m*, control *m* de sí mismo

self–defense [,sɛlfdɪ'fɛnts] *n* : defensa *f* propia, defensa *f* personal ⟨to act in self-defense : actuar en defensa propia⟩ ⟨self-defense class : clase de defensa personal⟩

self–denial [,sɛlfdɪ'naɪəl] *n* : abnegación *f*

self–destructive [,sɛlfdɪ'strʌktɪv] *adj* : autodestructivo — **self–destruction** *n*

self–determination [,sɛlfdɪ,tərmə'neɪʃən] *n* : autodeterminación *f*

self–discipline [,sɛlf'dɪsəplən] *n* : autodisciplina *f*

self–employed [,sɛlfɪm'plɔɪd] *adj* : que trabaja por cuenta propia, autónomo

self–esteem [,sɛlfɪ'sti:m] *n* : autoestima *f*, amor *m* propio

self–evident [,sɛlf'ɛvədənt] *adj* : evidente, manifiesto

self–explanatory [,sɛlfɪk'splænə,tori] *adj* : fácil de entender, evidente

self–expression [,sɛlfɪk'sprʃən] *n* : expresión *f* personal

self–government [,sɛlf'gʌvərmənt, -vərn-] *n* : autogobierno *m*

self–help [,sɛlf'hɛlp] *n* : autoayuda *f*

self–important [,sɛlfɪm'pɔrtənt] *adj* **1** VAIN : vanidoso, presumido **2** ARROGANT : arrogante

self–indulgent [,sɛlfɪn'dʌldʒənt] *adj* : que se permite excesos

self–inflicted [,sɛlfɪn'flɪktəd] *adj* : autoinfligido

self–interest [,sɛlf'ɪntrəst, -tə,rst] *n* : interés *m* personal

selfish ['sɛlfɪʃ] *adj* : egoísta

selfishly ['sɛlfɪʃli] *adv* : de manera egoísta

selfishness ['sɛlfɪʃnəs] *n* : egoísmo *m*

selfless ['sɛlfləs] *adj* UNSELFISH : desinteresado

self–made [,sɛlf'meɪd] *adj* : próspero gracias a sus propios esfuerzos

self–pity [,sɛlf'pɪti] *n, pl* **-ties** : autocompasión *f*

self–portrait [,sɛlf'pɔrtrət] *n* : autorretrato *m*

self–proclaimed [ˌsɛlfproˈkleɪmd] *adj*
: autoproclamado

self–propelled [ˌsɛlfproˈpɛld] *adj* : autopropulsado

self–reliance [ˌsɛlfrɪˈlaɪənts] *n* : independencia *f*, autosuficiencia *f*

self–respect [ˌsɛlfrɪˈspɛkt] *n* : autoestima
f, amor *m* propio

self–restraint [ˌsɛlfrɪˈstreɪnt] *n* : autocontrol *m*, moderación *f*

self–righteous [ˌsɛlfˈraɪtʃəs] *adj* : santurrón, moralista

self–sacrifice [ˌsɛlfˈsækrəˌfaɪs] *n* : abnegación *f*

self–sacrificing [ˌsɛlfˈsækrəˌfaɪsɪŋ] *adj*
: abnegado

selfsame [ˈsɛlfˌseɪm] *adj* : mismo

self–satisfaction [ˌsɛlfˌsætəsˈfækʃən] *n*
: suficiencia *f*

self–satisfied [ˌsɛlfˈsætəsˌfaɪd] *adj* : ufano
fam

self–seeking [ˌsɛlfˈsiːkɪŋ] *adj* : interesado

self–service [ˌsɛlfˈsɜrvɪs] *adj* **1** : de autoservicio **2 self–service restaurant** : autoservicio *m*

self–sufficiency [ˌsɛlfsəˈfɪʃəntsi] *n* : autosuficiencia *f*

self–sufficient [ˌsɛlfsəˈfɪʃənt] *adj* : autosuficiente

self–taught [ˌsɛlfˈtɔt] *adj* : autodidacta

sell [ˈsɛl] *v* **sold** [ˈsoːld]; **selling** *vt* **1**
: vender ⟨to sell someone something, to
sell something to someone : venderle
algo a alguien⟩ **2 to sell at a loss** : vender con pérdidas **3 to sell off** : liquidar
4 to sell on ⟨can you sell them on the
project? : ¿puedes convencerles de los
méritos del proyecto?⟩ ⟨she's not sold
on the idea : la idea no la convence⟩ **5 to
sell out** BETRAY : vender, traicionar a **6
to sell short** UNDERESTIMATE : subestimar, menospreciar — *vi* **1** : venderse
⟨this car sells well : este coche se vende
bien⟩ **2 to sell out** : agotarse (dícese de
entradas, etc.) **3 to sell out** : venderse
(dícese de un músico, etc.)

seller [ˈsɛlər] *n* : vendedor *m*, -dora *f*

selves → self

semantic [sɪˈmæntɪk] *adj* : semántico

semantics [sɪˈmæntɪks] *ns & pl* : semántica *f*

semaphore [ˈsɛməˌfor] *n* : semáforo *m*

semblance [ˈsɛmblənts] *n* : apariencia *f*

semen [ˈsiːmən] *n* : semen *m*

semester [səˈmɛstər] *n* : semestre *m*

semi- [ˌsɛmi, ˈsɛmaɪ] *pref* : semi-

semiannual [ˌsɛmiˈænjʊəl, ˈsɛmaɪ-] *adj*
: semestral

semicircle [ˈsɛmiˌsərkəl, ˈsɛˌmaɪ-] *n* : semicírculo *m*

semicolon [ˈsɛmiˌkoːlən, ˈsɛˌmaɪ-] *n*
: punto y coma *m*

semiconductor [ˈsɛmikənˌdʌktər, ˈsɛˌmaɪ-]
n : semiconductor *m*

semifinal [ˈsɛmiˌfaɪnəl, ˈsɛˌmaɪ-] *n* : semifinal *f*

semimonthly [ˈsɛmiˌmʌnθli, ˈsɛˌmaɪ-] *adj*
: bimensual, quincenal

seminar [ˈsɛməˌnɑr] *n* : seminario *m*

seminary [ˈsɛməˌnɛri] *n, pl* **-naries** : seminario *m*

semiprecious [ˌsɛmiˈprɛʃəs, ˈsɛˌmaɪ-] *adj*
: semiprecioso

Semite [ˈsɛˌmaɪt] *n* : semita *mf* — **Semitic**
[səˈmɪtɪk] *adj*

semolina [ˌsɛməˈliːnə] *n* : sémola *f*

senate [ˈsɛnət] *n* : senado *m*

senator [ˈsɛnətər] *n* : senador *m*, -dora *f*

send [ˈsɛnd] *vt* **sent** [ˈsɛnt]; **sending 1**
: mandar, enviar ⟨to send a letter : mandar una carta⟩ ⟨to send word : avisar,
mandar decir⟩ ⟨he was sent to prison : lo
mandaron a la cárcel, lo encarcelaron⟩
2 PROPEL : mandar, lanzar ⟨he sent it
into left field : lo mandó al jardín
izquierdo⟩ ⟨it sent a shiver down my
spine : me dio un escalofrío⟩ ⟨to send up
dust : levantar polvo⟩ **3 to send away
for** : pedir (por correo) **4 to send back**
RETURN : devolver, mandar de vuelta **5
to send for** SUMMON : mandar llamar **6
to send for** REQUEST : pedir (ayuda, re-
fuerzos, etc.) **7 to send in** SUBMIT : enviar, mandar, presentar **8 to send in**
: enviar, mandar (tropas, etc.) **9 to send
into a rage** : poner furioso **10 to send
off** : mandar, enviar (por correo, etc.) **11
to send on** : enviar por adelantado **12 to
send out** : enviar, mandar (invitaciones,
etc.) **13 to send out** EMIT : emitir

sender [ˈsɛndər] *n* : remitente *mf* (de una
carta, etc.)

send–off [ˈsɛndˌɔf] *n* FAREWELL : despedida *f*

Senegalese [ˌsɛnəɡəˈliːz, -ˈliːs] *n* : senegalés *m*, -lesa *f* — **Senegalese** *adj*

senile [ˈsiːˌnaɪl] *adj* : senil

senility [sɪˈnɪləti] *n* : senilidad *f*

senior¹ [ˈsiːnjər] *adj* **1** ELDER : mayor
⟨John Doe, Senior : John Doe, padre⟩ **2**
: superior (en rango), más antiguo (en
años de servicio) ⟨a senior official : un
alto oficial⟩

senior² *n* **1** : superior *m* (en rango) **2 to
be someone's senior** : ser mayor que
alguien ⟨she's two years my senior : me
lleva dos años⟩

senior citizen *n* : persona *f* de la tercera
edad

seniority [ˌsiːˈnjorəti] *n* : antigüedad *f* (en
años de servicio)

sensation [sɛnˈseɪʃən] *n* : sensación *f*

sensational [sɛnˈseɪʃənəl] *adj* : que causa
sensación ⟨sensational stories : historias
sensacionalistas⟩

sensationalism [sɛnˈseɪʃənəˌlɪzəm] *n*
: sensacionalismo *m*

sensationalist [sɛnˈseɪʃənəlɪst] *or* **sensa-
tionalistic** [sɛnˌseɪʃənəˈlɪstɪk] *adj* : sensacionalista

sense¹ [ˈsɛnts] *vt* **sensed; sensing** : sentir
⟨he sensed danger : se dio cuenta del pe-
ligro⟩

sense² *n* **1** MEANING : sentido *m*, significado *m* **2** : sentido *m* ⟨the sense of smell
: el sentido del olfato⟩ **3** : sentido *m*
⟨sense of humor : sentido del humor⟩
⟨sense of duty : sentido del deber⟩
⟨sense of direction : sentido de la orien-

tación⟩ 4 FEELING : sensación *f* ⟨a huge sense of relief : un gran alivio⟩ ⟨his sense of accomplishment : su satisfacción (por haber logrado algo)⟩ 5 WISDOM : sensatez *f*, tino *m* ⟨he had the (good) sense to leave : tuvo la sensatez de retirarse⟩ ⟨common sense : sentido común⟩ ⟨to come to one's senses : entrar en razón⟩ ⟨there's no sense in arguing : no tiene sentido discutir⟩ 6 **to make sense** : tener sentido 7 **to make sense of** : entender

senseless ['sɛntsləs] *adj* 1 MEANINGLESS : sin sentido, sin razón 2 UNCONSCIOUS : inconsciente

senselessly ['sɛntsləsli] *adv* : sin sentido

sensibility [ˌsɛntsə'bɪləti] *n, pl* **-ties** : sensibilidad *f*

sensible ['sɛntsəbəl] *adj* 1 PERCEPTIBLE : sensible, perceptible 2 AWARE : consciente 3 REASONABLE : sensato ⟨a sensible man : un hombre sensato⟩ ⟨sensible shoes : zapatos prácticos⟩ — **sensibly** [-bli] *adv*

sensibleness ['sɛntsəbəlnəs] *n* : sensatez *f*, solidez *f*

sensitive ['sɛntsətɪv] *adj* 1 : sensible, delicado ⟨sensitive skin : piel sensible⟩ 2 TOUCHY : susceptible, sensible ⟨to be sensitive to criticism : ser susceptible a las críticas⟩ ⟨to be sensitive about something : tener complejo por algo, preocuparse mucho por algo⟩ 3 AWARE : sensibilizado ⟨sensitive to something : sensibilizado sobre/con algo, sensibilizado frente a algo⟩ 4 : de mucha sensibilidad (dícese de un artista, una interpretación, etc.) 5 DELICATE : delicado 6 CONTROVERSIAL : controvertido 7 CONFIDENTIAL : confidencial

sensitiveness ['sɛntsətɪvnəs] → **sensitivity**

sensitivity [ˌsɛntsə'tɪvəti] *n, pl* **-ties** : sensibilidad *f*

sensitize ['sɛntsə,taɪz] *vt* **-tized; -tizing** : sensibilizar

sensor ['sɛn,sɔr, 'sɛntsər] *n* : sensor *m*

sensory ['sɛntsəri] *adj* : sensorial

sensual ['sɛntʃuəl] *adj* : sensual — **sensually** *adv*

sensuality [ˌsɛntʃə'wæləti] *n, pl* **-ties** : sensualidad *f*

sensuous ['sɛntʃuəs] *adj* : sensual

sent → send

sentence[1] ['sɛntəns, -ənz] *vt* **-tenced; -tencing** : sentenciar

sentence[2] *n* 1 JUDGMENT : sentencia *f* 2 : oración *f*, frase *f* (en gramática)

sentient ['sɛntʃənt, -ʃiənt] *adj* : sensitivo, sensible

sentiment ['sɛntəmənt] *n* 1 BELIEF : opinión *f* 2 FEELING : sentimiento *m* 3 → **sentimentality**

sentimental [ˌsɛntə'mɛntəl] *adj* : sentimental

sentimentality [ˌsɛntə,mɛn'tæləti] *n, pl* **-ties** : sentimentalismo *m*, sensiblería *f*

sentinel ['sɛntənəl] *n* : centinela *mf*, guardia *mf*

sentry ['sɛntri] *n, pl* **-tries** : centinela *mf*

separate[1] ['sɛpə,reɪt] *v* **-rated; -rating** *vt* 1 DETACH, SEVER : separar 2 DISTINGUISH : diferenciar, distinguir — *vi* PART : separarse

separate[2] ['sɛprət, 'sɛpə-] *adj* 1 INDIVIDUAL : separado, aparte ⟨a separate state : un estado separado⟩ ⟨in a separate envelope : en un sobre aparte⟩ 2 DISTINCT : distinto

separately ['sɛprətli, 'sɛpə-] *adv* : por separado, separadamente, aparte

separation [ˌsɛpə'reɪʃən] *n* : separación *f*

sepia ['si:piə] *n* : color *m* sepia

September [sɛp'tɛmbər] *n* : septiembre *m*, setiembre *m* ⟨they arrived on the 30th of September, they arrived on September 30th : llegaron el 30 de septiembre⟩

septic ['sɛptɪk] *adj* : séptico ⟨septic tank : fosa séptica⟩

sepulchre ['sɛpəlkər] *n* : sepulcro *m*

sequel ['si:kwəl] *n* 1 CONSEQUENCE : secuela *f*, consecuencia *f* 2 : continuación *f* (de una película, etc.)

sequence ['si:kwənts] *n* 1 SERIES : serie *f*, sucesión *f*, secuencia *f* (matemática o música) 2 ORDER : orden *m*

sequester [sɪ'kwɛstər] *vt* : aislar

sequin ['si:kwən] *n* : lentejuela *f*

sequoia [sɪ'kwɔɪə] *n* : secoya *f*, secuoya *f*

sera → serum

Serb ['sərb] *or* **Serbian** ['sərbiən] *n* 1 : serbio *m*, -bia *f* 2 : serbio *m* (idioma) — **Serb** *or* **Serbian** *adj*

Serbo–Croatian [ˌsərbokro'eɪʃən] *n* : serbocroata *m* (idioma) — **Serbo–Croatian** *adj*

serenade[1] [ˌsɛrə'neɪd] *vt* **-naded; -nading** : darle una serenata (a alguien)

serenade[2] *n* : serenata *f*

serene [sə'ri:n] *adj* : sereno — **serenely** *adv*

serendipity [ˌsɛrən'dɪpəti] *n* : suerte *f*, fortuna *f* (de descubrir algo bueno por pura casualidad)

serenity [sə'rɛnəti] *n* : serenidad *f*

serf ['sərf] *n* : siervo *m*, -va *f*

serge ['sərdʒ] *n* : sarga *f*

sergeant ['sɑrdʒənt] *n* : sargento *mf*

serial[1] ['sɪriəl] *adj* : seriado

serial[2] *n* : serie *f*, serial *m* (de radio o televisión), publicación *f* por entregas

serially ['sɪriəli] *adv* : en serie

serial number *n* : número *m* de serie

series ['sɪr,i:z] *n, pl* **series** : serie *f*, sucesión *f*

serious ['sɪriəs] *adj* 1 SOBER : serio 2 DEDICATED, EARNEST : serio, dedicado ⟨to be serious about something : tomar algo en serio⟩ 3 GRAVE : serio, grave ⟨serious problems : problemas graves⟩

seriously ['sɪriəsli] *adv* 1 EARNESTLY : seriamente, con seriedad, en serio ⟨to take seriously : tomar an serio⟩ 2 SEVERELY : gravemente ⟨seriously ill : gravemente enfermo⟩

seriousness ['sɪriəsnəs] *n* : seriedad *f*, gravedad *f*

sermon ['sərmən] *n* : sermón *m*

serpent ['sərpənt] *n* : serpiente *f*

serrated [səˈreɪtəd, ˈsɛrˌeɪtəd] *adj* : dentado, serrado

serum [ˈsɪrəm] *n, pl* **serums** *or* **sera** [ˈsɪrə] : suero *m*

servant [ˈsərvənt] *n* : criado *m*, -da *f*; sirviente *m*, -ta *f*

serve [ˈsərv] *v* **served; serving** *vi* 1 : servir ⟨to serve in the navy : servir en la armada⟩ ⟨to serve on a jury : ser miembro de un jurado⟩ 2 DO, FUNCTION : servir ⟨to serve as : servir de, servir como⟩ 3 : sacar (en deportes) — *vt* 1 : servir ⟨to serve God : servir a Dios⟩ 2 HELP : servir ⟨it serves no purpose : no sirve para nada⟩ ⟨it serves you right : te lo mereces⟩ 3 : servir (comida o bebida) ⟨dinner is served : la cena está servida⟩ 4 SUPPLY : abastecer 5 CARRY OUT : cumplir, hacer ⟨to serve time : servir una pena⟩ 6 to serve a summons : entregar una citación

server [ˈsərvər] *n* 1 : camarero *m*, -ra *f*; mesero *m*, -ra *f* (en un restaurante) 2 *or* **serving dish** : fuente *f* (para servir comida) 3 : servidor *m* (en informática)

service¹ [ˈsərvəs] *vt* **-viced; -vicing** 1 MAINTAIN : darle mantenimiento a (una máquina), revisar 2 REPAIR : arreglar, reparar

service² *n* 1 HELP, USE : servicio *m* ⟨to do someone a service : hacerle un servicio a alguien⟩ ⟨at your service : a sus órdenes⟩ ⟨to be out of service : no funcionar⟩ 2 CEREMONY : oficio *m* (religioso) 3 DEPARTMENT, SYSTEM : servicio *m* ⟨social services : servicios sociales⟩ ⟨train service : servicio de trenes⟩ 4 SET : juego *m*, servicio *m* ⟨tea service : juego de té⟩ 5 MAINTENANCE : mantenimiento *m*, revisión *f*, servicio *m* 6 : servicio *m* (en un restaurante, etc.) ⟨customer service : atención al cliente⟩ 7 : saque *m* (en deportes) 8 armed services : fuerzas *fpl* armadas

serviceable [ˈsərvəsəbəl] *adj* 1 USEFUL : útil 2 DURABLE : duradero

service charge *n* : servicio *m*

serviceman [ˈsərvəsˌmæn, -mən] *n, pl* **-men** [-mən, -ˌmɛn] : militar *m*

service station → **gas station**

servicewoman [ˈsərvəsˌwʊmən] *n, pl* **-women** [-ˌwɪmən] : militar *f*

servile [ˈsərvəl, -ˌvaɪl] *adj* : servil

servility [sərˈvɪləti] *n* : servilismo *m*

serving [ˈsərvɪŋ] *n* HELPING : porción *f*, ración *f*

servitude [ˈsərvəˌtuːd, -ˌtjuːd] *n* : servidumbre *f*

sesame [ˈsɛsəmi] *n* : ajonjolí *m*, sésamo *m*

session [ˈsɛʃən] *n* : sesión *f*

set¹ [ˈsɛt] *v* **set; setting; sets** *vt* 1 *or* **to set down** PLACE : poner, colocar ⟨set the books (down) on the table : pon los libros en la mesa⟩ 2 INSTALL : poner, colocar (ladrillos, etc.) 3 MOUNT : engarzar, montar (un diamante, etc.) 4 ESTABLISH : fijar (una fecha, un precio, etc.), establecer (reglas, una récord, etc.) ⟨to set (oneself) a goal : fijarse una meta⟩ ⟨to set a precedent : sentar precedente⟩ ⟨to set a good/bad example : dar buen/mal ejemplo⟩ 5 PREPARE : tender (una trampa), poner (un freno de mano, etc.) ⟨to set the table : poner la mesa⟩ 6 ADJUST : poner (un reloj, etc.) 7 (*indicating the causing of a certain condition*) : poner ⟨to set fire to : prenderle fuego a⟩ ⟨she set it free : lo soltó⟩ 8 MAKE, START : poner, hacer ⟨I set them working : los puse a trabajar⟩ ⟨it set me (to) thinking : me hizo pensar⟩ ⟨to set something in motion : poner algo en marcha⟩ 9 : ambientar ⟨the book is set in Chicago : el libro está ambientado en Chicago⟩ 10 : componer (un hueso roto, etc.) 11 : tensar (la mandíbula, la boca, etc.) 12 : marcar (el pelo) 13 : componer (texto) 14 to set about BEGIN : comenzar 15 to set aside RESERVE : reservar, dejar de lado 16 to set back DELAY : retrasar, atrasar 17 to set off PROVOKE : provocar 18 to set off EXPLODE : hacer estallar (una bomba, etc.) 19 to set out INTEND : proponerse 20 to set up ASSEMBLE : montar, armar 21 to set up ERECT : levantar, erigir 22 to set up ESTABLISH : establecer, fundar, montar (un negocio) 23 to set up CAUSE : armar ⟨they set up a clamor : armaron un alboroto⟩ — *vi* 1 SOLIDIFY : fraguar (dícese del cemento, etc.), cuajar (dícese de la gelatina, etc.) 2 : ponerse (dícese del sol o de la luna) 3 to set in BEGIN : comenzar, empezar 4 to set off/forth : salir 5 to set out : salir (de viaje)

set² *adj* 1 ESTABLISHED, FIXED : fijo, establecido 2 RIGID : inflexible ⟨to be set in one's ways : tener costumbres muy arraigadas⟩ 3 READY : listo, preparado

set³ *n* 1 COLLECTION : juego *m* ⟨a set of dishes : un juego de platos, una vajilla⟩ ⟨a tool set : una caja de herramientas⟩ 2 *or* **stage set** : decorado *m* (en el teatro), plató *m* (en el cine) 3 APPARATUS : aparato *m* ⟨a television set : un televisor⟩ 4 : conjunto *m* (en matemáticas)

setback [ˈsɛtˌbæk] *n* : revés *m*, contratiempo *m*

settee [sɛˈtiː] *n* : sofá *m*

setter [ˈsɛtər] *n* 1 : setter *mf* ⟨Irish setter : setter irlandés⟩ 2 (*one that establishes*) ⟨record setter : persona que establece un récord⟩ ⟨style setter : persona que inicia una moda⟩

setting [ˈsɛtɪŋ] *n* 1 : posición *f*, ajuste *m* (de un control) 2 : montura *f* (de una gema) 3 SCENE : escenario *m* (de una novela, etc.) 4 SURROUNDINGS : ambiente *m*, entorno *m*, marco *m*

settle [ˈsɛtəl] *v* **settled; settling** *vi* 1 ALIGHT, LAND : posarse (dícese de las aves, una mirada, etc.), depositarse (dícese del polvo) 2 SINK : asentarse (dícese de los edificios) 3 : acomodarse ⟨he settled into the chair : se arrellanó en la silla⟩ 4 : resolver una disputa ⟨they settled out of court : resolvieron extrajudicialmente su disputa⟩ 5 DECIDE : decidir (un asunto) ⟨that settles it : ya está decidido⟩ 6 : instalarse (en una casa), establecerse (en una ciudad o región) **7 to settle down** : calmarse, tranquilizarse ⟨settle down! : ¡tranquilízate!, ¡cálmate!⟩ **8 to settle down** : sentar cabeza, hacerse sensato ⟨to marry and settle down : casarse y sentar cabeza⟩ **9 to settle for** : conformarse con **10 to settle in** : instalarse (en una casa, etc.), adaptarse (a un trabajo, etc.) **11 to settle up** : arreglar las cuentas — *vt* **1** ARRANGE, DECIDE : fijar, decidir, acordar (planes, etc.) **2** RESOLVE : resolver, solucionar ⟨to settle an argument : resolver una discusión⟩ **3** PAY : pagar ⟨to settle an account : saldar una cuenta⟩ **4** CALM : calmar (los nervios), asentar (el estómago) **5** : acomodar, poner ⟨he settled the baby into its crib : puso al bebé en su cuna⟩ **6** COLONIZE : colonizar **7 to settle oneself** : acomodarse, hacerse cómodo

settlement [ˈsɛtəlmənt] *n* **1** PAYMENT : pago *m*, liquidación *f* **2** COLONY : asentamiento *m* **3** RESOLUTION : acuerdo *m*

settler [ˈsɛtələr] *n* : poblador *m*, -dora *f*; colono *m*, -na *f*

setup [ˈsɛtˌʌp] *n* **1** ASSEMBLY : montaje *m*, ensamblaje *m* **2** ARRANGEMENT : disposición *f* **3** PREPARATION : preparación *f* **4** TRAP, TRICK : encerrona *f*

seven[1] [ˈsɛvən] *adj* : siete ⟨he's seven (years old) : tiene siete años⟩

seven[2] *n* : siete *m* ⟨the seven of hearts : el siete de corazones⟩

seven[3] *pron* : siete ⟨there are seven of us : somos siete⟩ ⟨it's seven (o'clock) : son las siete⟩

seven hundred[1] *adj & pron* : setecientos

seven hundred[2] *n* : setecientos *m*

seventeen[1] [ˌsɛvənˈtiːn] *adj & pron* : diecisiete

seventeen[2] *n* : diecisiete *m*

seventeenth[1] [ˌsɛvənˈtiːnθ] *adj* : decimoséptimo

seventeenth[2] *n* **1** : decimoséptimo *m*, -ma *f* (en una serie) **2** : diecisieteavo *m*, diecisieteava parte *f*

seventh[1] [ˈsɛvənθ] *adv* : en séptimo lugar

seventh[2] *adj* : séptimo

seventh[3] *n* **1** : séptimo *m*, -ma *f* (en una serie) **2** : séptimo *m*, séptima parte *f*

seventieth[1] [ˈsɛvəntiəθ] *adj* : septuagésimo

seventieth[2] *n* **1** : septuagésimo *m*, -ma *f* (en una serie) **2** : setentavo *m*, setentava parte *f*, septuagésima parte *f*

seventy[1] [ˈsɛvənti] *adj & pron* : setenta

seventy[2] *n, pl* **-ties** : setenta *m*

sever [ˈsɛvər] *vt* **-ered; -ering** : cortar, romper

several[1] [ˈsɛvrəl, ˈsɛvə-] *adj* **1** DISTINCT : distinto **2** SOME : varios ⟨several weeks : varias semanas⟩

several[2] *pron* : varios ⟨several of the novels : varias de las novelas⟩

severance [ˈsɛvrənts, ˈsɛvə-] *n* **1** : ruptura *f* (de relaciones, etc.) **2 severance pay** : indemnización *f* (por despido)

severe [səˈvɪr] *adj* **severer; -est 1** STRICT : severo **2** AUSTERE : sobrio, austero **3**

SERIOUS : grave ⟨a severe wound : una herida grave⟩ ⟨severe aches : dolores fuertes⟩ **4** DIFFICULT : duro, difícil — **severely** *adv*

severity [səˈvrəti] *n* **1** HARSHNESS : severidad *f* **2** AUSTERITY : sobriedad *f*, austeridad *f* **3** SERIOUSNESS : gravedad *f* (de una herida, etc.)

sew [ˈsoː] *v* **sewed; sewn** [ˈsoːn] *or* **sewed; sewing** : coser

sewage [ˈsuːɪdʒ] *n* : aguas *fpl* negras, aguas *fpl* residuales

sewer[1] [ˈsoːər] *n* : uno que cose

sewer[2] [ˈsuːər] *n* : alcantarilla *f*, cloaca *f*

sewing [ˈsoːɪŋ] *n* : costura *f*

sewing machine *n* : máquina *f* de coser

sex [ˈsɛks] *n* **1** : sexo *m* ⟨the opposite sex : el sexo opuesto⟩ **2** COPULATION : relaciones *fpl* sexuales ⟨sex education : educación sexual⟩

sexism [ˈsɛkˌsɪzəm] *n* : sexismo *m*

sexist[1] [ˈsɛksɪst] *adj* : sexista

sexist[2] *n* : sexista *mf*

sextant [ˈsɛkstənt] *n* : sextante *m*

sextet [sɛkˈstɛt] *n* : sexteto *m*

sexton [ˈsɛkstən] *n* : sacristán *m*

sexual [ˈsɛkʃʊəl] *adj* : sexual ⟨sexual intercourse : relaciones sexuales⟩ ⟨sexual discrimination/harassment : discriminación/acoso sexual⟩ — **sexually** *adv*

sexuality [ˌsɛkʃuˈæləti] *n* : sexualidad *f*

sexy [ˈsɛksi] *adj* **sexier; -est** : sexy

sh *or* **ssh** *or* **sssh** [ʃ, *often prolonged*] *interj* : chis!, chist!

shabbily [ˈʃæbəli] *adv* **1** : pobremente ⟨shabbily dressed : pobremente vestido⟩ **2** UNFAIRLY : mal, injustamente

shabbiness [ˈʃæbinəs] *n* **1** : lo gastado (de ropa, etc.) **2** : lo mal vestido (de personas) **3** UNFAIRNESS : injusticia *f*

shabby [ˈʃæbi] *adj* **shabbier; -est 1** : gastado (dícese de la ropa, etc.) **2** : mal vestido (dícese de las personas) **3** UNFAIR : malo, injusto ⟨shabby treatment : mal trato⟩

shack [ˈʃæk] *n* : choza *f*, rancho *m*

shackle[1] [ˈʃækəl] *v* **-led; -ling** : ponerle grilletes (a alguien)

shackle[2] *n* : grillete *m*

shad [ˈʃæd] *n* : sábalo *m*

shade[1] [ˈʃeɪd] *v* **shaded; shading** *vt* **1** SHELTER : proteger (del sol o de la luz) **2** *or* **to shade in** : matizar los colores de — *vi* : convertirse gradualmente ⟨his irritation shaded into rage : su irritación iba convirtiéndose en furia⟩

shade[2] *n* **1** : sombra *f* ⟨to give shade : dar sombra⟩ **2** : tono *m* (de un color) **3** NUANCE : matiz *m* **4** : pantalla *f* (de una lámpara), persiana *f* (de una ventana)

shadow[1] [ˈʃædoː] *vt* **1** DARKEN : ensombrecer **2** TRAIL : seguir de cerca, seguirle la pista (a alguien)

shadow[2] *n* **1** : sombra *f* **2** DARKNESS : oscuridad *f* **3** TRACE : sombra *f*, atisbo *m*, indicio *m* ⟨without a shadow of a doubt : sin sombra de duda, sin lugar a dudas⟩ **4 to cast a shadow over** : ensombrecer

shadowy ['ʃædowi] *adj* **1** INDISTINCT : vago, indistinto **2** DARK : oscuro

shady ['ʃeidi] *adj* **shadier; -est** **1** : sombreado (dícese de un lugar), que da sombra (dícese de un árbol) **2** DISREPUTABLE : sospechoso (dícese de una persona), turbio (dícese de un negocio, etc.)

shaft ['ʃæft] *n* **1** : asta *f* (de una lanza), astil *m* (de una flecha), mango *m* (de una herramienta) **2** *or* **mine shaft** : pozo *m*

shaggy ['ʃægi] *adj* **shaggier; -est** **1** HAIRY : peludo (a shaggy dog : un perro peludo) **2** UNKEMPT : enmarañado, despeinado (dícese del pelo, de las barbas, etc.)

shake¹ ['ʃeik] *v* **shook** ['ʃuk]; **shaken** ['ʃeikən]; **shaking** *vt* **1** : sacudir, agitar, hacer temblar (he shook his head : negó con la cabeza) **2** WEAKEN : debilitar, hacer flaquear (it shook her faith : debilitó su confianza) **3** UPSET : afectar, alterar **4 to shake hands with someone** : darle/estrecharle la mano a alguien **5 to shake off** : deshacer **6 to shake up** : reestructurar, reorganizar — *vi* : temblar, sacudirse (to shake with fear : temblar de miedo)

shake² *n* : sacudida *f*, apretón *m* (de manos)

shaker ['ʃeikər] *n* **1 salt shaker** : salero *m* **2 pepper shaker** : pimentero *m* **3 cocktail shaker** : coctelera *f*

shake–up ['ʃeik,ʌp] *n* : reorganización *f*

shakily ['ʃeikəli] *adv* : temblorosamente

shaky ['ʃeiki] *adj* **shakier; -est** **1** SHAKING : tembloroso **2** UNSTABLE : poco firme, inestable **3** PRECARIOUS : precario, incierto **4** QUESTIONABLE : dudoso, cuestionable (shaky arguments : argumentos discutibles)

shale ['ʃeil] *n* : esquisto *m*

shall ['ʃæl] *v aux, past* **should** ['ʃud] *present & pl* **shall** **1** (*used formally to express a command*) (you shall do as I say : harás lo que te digo) (there shall be no talking during the test : se prohíbe hablar durante el examen) **2** (*used formally to request an opinion*) (shall I call a taxi? : ¿quiere que llame un taxi?) **3** (*used formally to express futurity*) (we shall see : ya veremos) (when shall we expect you? : ¿cuándo te podemos esperar?) (I shall not mention it, I shan't mention it : no lo mencionaré) **4** (*used formally to express determination*) (you shall have the money : tendrás el dinero)

shallow ['ʃælo] *adj* **1** : poco profundo (dícese del agua, etc.) **2** SUPERFICIAL : superficial

shallows ['ʃælo:z] *npl* : bajío *m*, bajos *mpl*

sham¹ ['ʃæm] *v* **shammed; shamming** : fingir

sham² *adj* : falso, fingido

sham³ *n* **1** FAKE, PRETENSE : farsa *f*, simulación *f*, imitación *f* **2** FAKER : impostor *m*, -tora *f*; farsante *mf*

shamble ['ʃæmbəl] *vi* **-bled; -bling** : caminar arrastrando los pies

shambles ['ʃæmbəlz] *ns & pl* : caos *m*, desorden *m*, confusión *f*

shame¹ ['ʃeim] *vt* **shamed; shaming** **1** : avergonzar (he was shamed by their words : sus palabras le dieron vergüenza) **2** DISGRACE : deshonrar

shame² *n* **1** : vergüenza *f* (to have no shame : no tener vergüenza) **2** DISGRACE : vergüenza *f*, deshonra *f* **3** PITY : lástima *f*, pena *f* (what a shame! : ¡qué pena!)

shamefaced ['ʃeim,feist] *adj* : avergonzado

shameful ['ʃeimfəl] *adj* : vergonzoso — **shamefully** *adv*

shameless ['ʃeimləs] *adj* : descarado, desvergonzado — **shamelessly** *adv*

shampoo¹ [ʃæm'pu:] *vt* : lavar (el pelo)

shampoo² *n, pl* **-poos** : champú *m*

shamrock ['ʃæm,rɑk] *n* : trébol *m*

shank ['ʃæŋk] *n* : parte *f* baja de la pierna

shan't ['ʃænt] *contraction of* **shall not** → **shall**

shanty ['ʃænti] *n, pl* **-ties** : choza *f*, rancho *m*

shantytown ['ʃænti,taun] *n* : barriada *f*, cinturón *m* de miseria, ciudad *f* perdida *Mex*, villa *f* miseria *Arg*, villa *f* de emergencia *Arg*, pueblo *m* joven *Peru*, población *f* callampa *Chile*, barrio *m* de invasión *Col*, barrio *m* de chabolas *Spain*

shape¹ ['ʃeip] *v* **shaped; shaping** *vt* **1** : dar forma a, modelar (arcilla, etc.), tallar (madera, piedra), formar (carácter) (to be shaped like : tener forma de) **2** DETERMINE : decidir, determinar — *vi or* **to shape up** : tomar forma

shape² *n* **1** : forma *f*, figura *f* (in the shape of a circle : en forma de círculo) (to take shape : tomar forma) **2** CONDITION : estado *m*, condiciones *fpl*, forma *f* (física) (to be in good shape : estar en forma) (to be in bad shape : no estar en forma) (to get in shape : ponerse en forma)

-shaped [,ʃeipt] *suf* : en forma de

shapeless ['ʃeipləs] *adj* : informe

shapely ['ʃeipli] *adj* **shapelier; -est** : curvilíneo, bien proporcionado

shard ['ʃɑrd] *n* : fragmento *m*, casco *m* (de cerámica, etc.)

share¹ ['ʃer] *v* **shared; sharing** *vt* **1** APPORTION : dividir, repartir **2** : compartir (they share a room : comparten una habitación) — *vi* : compartir

share² *n* **1** PORTION : parte *f*, porción *f* (one's fair share : lo que le corresponde a uno) **2** : acción *f* (en una compañía) (to hold shares : tener acciones)

sharecropper ['ʃer,krɑpər] *n* : aparcero *m*, -ra *f*

shareholder ['ʃer,ho:ldər] *n* : accionista *mf*

shark ['ʃɑrk] *n* : tiburón *m*

sharp¹ ['ʃɑrp] *adv* : en punto (at two o'clock sharp : a las dos en punto)

sharp² *adj* **1** : afilado, filoso (a sharp knife : un cuchillo afilado) **2** PENETRATING : cortante, fuerte **3** CLEVER : agudo, listo, perspicaz **4** ACUTE : agudo

⟨sharp eyesight : vista aguda⟩ 5 HARSH, SEVERE : duro, severo, agudo ⟨a sharp rebuke : una reprimenda mordaz⟩ ⟨to have a sharp tongue : tener una lengua afilada⟩ 6 STRONG : fuerte ⟨sharp cheese : queso fuerte⟩ 7 ABRUPT : brusco, repentino 8 DISTINCT : nítido, definido ⟨a sharp image : una imagen bien definida⟩ 9 ANGULAR : angulos (dícese de la cara) 10 : sostenido (en música)

sharp³ n : sostenido m (en música)

sharpen ['ʃɑrpən] vt : afilar, aguzar ⟨to sharpen a pencil : sacarle punta a un lápiz⟩ ⟨to sharpen one's wits : aguzar el ingenio⟩

sharpener ['ʃɑrpənər] n : afilador m (para cuchillos, etc.), sacapuntas m (para lápices)

sharply ['ʃɑrpli] adv 1 ABRUPTLY : bruscamente 2 DISTINCTLY : claramente, marcadamente

sharpness ['ʃɑrpnəs] n 1 : lo afilado (de un cuchillo, etc.) 2 ACUTENESS : agudeza f (de los sentidos o de la mente) 3 INTENSITY : intensidad f, agudeza f (de dolores, etc.) 4 HARSHNESS : dureza f, severidad f 5 ABRUPTNESS : brusquedad f 6 CLARITY : nitidez f

sharpshooter ['ʃɑrp,ʃuːtər] n : tirador m, -dora f de primera

shatter ['ʃætər] vt 1 : hacer añicos ⟨to shatter the silence : romper el silencio⟩ 2 to be shattered by : quedar destrozado por — vi : hacerse añicos, romperse en pedazos

shave¹ ['ʃeɪv] v shaved; shaved or shaven ['ʃeɪvən]; shaving vt 1 : afeitar, rasurar ⟨she shaved her legs : se rasuró las piernas⟩ ⟨they shaved (off) his beard : le afeitaron la barba⟩ 2 SLICE : cortar (en pedazos finos) — vi : afeitarse, rasurarse

shave² n : afeitada f, rasurada f

shaver ['ʃeɪvər] n : afeitadora f, máquina f de afeitar, rasuradora f

shaving ['ʃeɪvɪŋ] n : viruta f ⟨wood shavings : virutas de madera⟩

shaving cream n : crema f de afeitar

shawl ['ʃɔl] n : chal m, mantón m, rebozo m

she ['ʃiː] pron : ella

sheaf ['ʃiːf] n, pl **sheaves** ['ʃiːvz] : gavilla f (de cereales), haz m (de flechas), fajo m (de papeles)

shear ['ʃɪr] vt **sheared**; **sheared** or **shorn** ['ʃɔrn]; **shearing** 1 : esquilar, trasquilar ⟨to shear sheep : trasquilar ovejas⟩ 2 CUT : cortar (el pelo, etc.)

shears ['ʃɪrz] npl : tijeras fpl (grandes)

sheath ['ʃiːθ] n, pl **sheaths** ['ʃiːðz, 'ʃiːθs] : funda f, vaina f

sheathe ['ʃiːð] vt **sheathed**; **sheathing** : envainar, enfundar

shed¹ ['ʃɛd] vt **shed**; **shedding** 1 : derramar (sangre o lágrimas) 2 EMIT : emitir (luz) ⟨to shed light on : aclarar⟩ 3 DISCARD : mudar (la piel, etc.) ⟨to shed one's clothes : quitarse una ropa⟩

shed² n : cobertizo m

she'd ['ʃiːd] contraction of **she had** or **she would** → **have, would**

sheen ['ʃiːn] n : brillo m, lustre m

sheep ['ʃiːp] ns & pl : oveja f

sheepdog ['ʃiːp,dɔɡ] n : perro m pastor

sheepfold ['ʃiːp,foːld] n : redil m

sheepish ['ʃiːpɪʃ] adj : avergonzado

sheepskin ['ʃiːp,skɪn] n : piel f de oveja, piel f de borrego

sheer¹ ['ʃɪr] adv 1 COMPLETELY : completamente, totalmente 2 VERTICALLY : verticalmente

sheer² adj 1 TRANSPARENT : vaporoso, transparente 2 ABSOLUTE, UTTER : puro ⟨by sheer luck : por pura suerte⟩ 3 STEEP : escarpado, vertical

sheet ['ʃiːt] n 1 or **bedsheet** ['bɛd-,ʃiːt] : sábana f 2 : hoja f (de papel) 3 : capa f (de hielo, etc.) 4 : lámina f, placa f (de vidrio, metal, etc.), plancha f (de metal, madera, etc.) ⟨baking sheet : placa de horno⟩

sheikh or **sheik** ['ʃiːk, 'ʃeɪk] n : jeque m

shelf ['ʃɛlf] n, pl **shelves** ['ʃɛlvz] 1 : estante m, anaquel m (en una pared) 2 : banco m, arrecife m (en geología) ⟨continental shelf : plataforma continental⟩

shell¹ ['ʃɛl] vt 1 : pelar (nueces, etc.) 2 BOMBARD : bombardear

shell² n 1 SEASHELL : concha f 2 : cáscara f (de huevos, nueces, etc.), vaina f (de chícharos, etc.), caparazón m (de crustáceos, tortugas, etc.) 3 : cartucho m, casquillo m ⟨a .45 caliber shell : un cartucho calibre .45⟩ 4 or **racing shell** : bote m (para hacer regatas de remos)

she'll ['ʃiːl, 'ʃɪl] contraction of **she shall** or **she will** → **shall, will**

shellac¹ [ʃə'læk] vt -lacked; -lacking 1 : laquear (madera, etc.) 2 DEFEAT : darle una paliza (a alguien), derrotar

shellac² n : laca f

shellfish ['ʃɛl,fɪʃ] n : marisco m

shelter¹ ['ʃɛltər] vt 1 PROTECT : proteger, abrigar 2 HARBOR : dar refugio a, albergar

shelter² n : refugio m, abrigo m ⟨to take shelter : refugiarse⟩

shelve ['ʃɛlv] vt **shelved**; **shelving** 1 : poner en estantes 2 DEFER : dar carpetazo a

shenanigans [ʃə'nænɪɡənz] npl 1 TRICKERY : artimañas fpl 2 MISCHIEF : travesuras fpl

shepherd¹ ['ʃɛpərd] vt 1 : cuidar (ovejas, etc.) 2 GUIDE : conducir, guiar

shepherd² n : pastor m

shepherdess ['ʃɛpərdəs] n : pastora f

sherbet ['ʃərbət] or **sherbert** [-bərt] n : sorbete m; nieve f Cuba, Mex, PRi

sheriff ['ʃɛrɪf] n : sheriff mf

sherry ['ʃɛri] n, pl -ries : jerez m

she's ['ʃiːz] contraction of **she is** or **she has** → **be, have**

shield¹ ['ʃiːld] vt 1 PROTECT : proteger 2 CONCEAL : ocultar ⟨to shield one's eyes : taparse los ojos⟩

shield² n 1 : escudo m (armadura) 2 PROTECTION : protección f, blindaje m (de un cable) shier, shiest → shy

shift¹ ['ʃɪft] vt 1 CHANGE : cambiar ⟨to shift gears : cambiar de velocidad⟩ 2 MOVE : mover 3 TRANSFER : transferir ⟨to shift the blame : echarle la culpa (a otro)⟩ — vi 1 CHANGE : cambiar 2 MOVE : moverse 3 to shift for oneself : arreglárselas solo

shift² n 1 CHANGE, TRANSFER : cambio m ⟨a shift in priorities : un cambio de prioridades⟩ 2 : turno m ⟨night shift : turno de noche⟩ 3 DRESS : vestido m (suelto) 4 → gearshift

shiftless ['ʃɪftləs] adj : perezoso, vago, holgazán

shifty ['ʃɪfti] adj shiftier; -est : taimado, artero ⟨a shifty look : una mirada huidiza⟩

shilling ['ʃɪlɪŋ] n : chelín m

shimmer ['ʃɪmər] vi GLIMMER : brillar con luz trémula

shin¹ ['ʃɪn] vi shinned; shinning : trepar, subir ⟨she shinned up the pole : subió al poste⟩

shin² n : espinilla f, canilla f

shine¹ ['ʃaɪn] v shone ['ʃoːn] or shined; shining vi 1 : brillar, relucir ⟨the stars were shining : las estrellas brillaban⟩ 2 EXCEL : brillar, lucirse — vt 1 : alumbrar ⟨he shined the flashlight on it : lo alumbró con la linterna⟩ 2 POLISH : sacarle brillo a, lustrar

shine² n : brillo m, lustre m

shingle¹ ['ʃɪŋgəl] vt -gled; -gling : techar

shingle² n : tablilla f (para techar)

shingles ['ʃɪŋgəlz] npl : herpes m

shinny ['ʃɪni] vi -nied; -nying → shin¹

shiny ['ʃaɪni] adj shinier; -est : brillante

ship¹ ['ʃɪp] vt shipped; shipping 1 LOAD : embarcar (en un barco) 2 SEND : transportar (en barco), enviar ⟨to ship by air : enviar por avión⟩

ship² n 1 : barco m, buque m 2 → spaceship

shipboard ['ʃɪp,bord] n on ~ : a bordo

shipbuilder ['ʃɪp,bɪldər] n : constructor m, -tora f naval

shipment ['ʃɪpmənt] n 1 SHIPPING : transporte m, embarque m 2 : envío m, remesa f ⟨a shipment of medicine : un envío de medicina⟩

shipper ['ʃɪpər] n : exportador m, -dora f

shipping ['ʃɪpɪŋ] n 1 SHIPS : barcos mpl, embarcaciones fpl 2 TRANSPORTATION : transporte m (de mercancías)

shipshape ['ʃɪp,ʃeɪp] adj : ordenado

shipwreck¹ ['ʃɪp,rɛk] vt to be shipwrecked : naufragar

shipwreck² n : naufragio m

shipyard ['ʃɪp,jard] n : astillero m

shirk ['ʃərk] vt : eludir, rehuir ⟨to shirk one's responsibilities : esquivar uno sus responsabilidades⟩

shirt ['ʃərt] n : camisa f

shiver¹ ['ʃɪvər] vi 1 : tiritar (de frío) 2 TREMBLE : estremecerse, temblar

shiver² n : escalofrío m, estremecimiento m

shoal ['ʃoːl] n : banco m, bajío m

shock¹ ['ʃɑk] vt 1 UPSET : conmover, conmocionar 2 STARTLE : asustar, sobresaltar 3 SCANDALIZE : escandalizar 4 : darle una descarga eléctrica a

shock² n 1 COLLISION, JOLT : choque m, sacudida f 2 UPSET : shock m, choque m, golpe m (emocional) ⟨she's in for a shock : se va a llevar un shock⟩ ⟨it came as a shock to me : me sorprendió/afectó mucho⟩ 3 : shock m, choque m (en medicina) ⟨to be in shock : estar en estado de shock⟩ 4 or electric shock : descarga f eléctrica, calambre m 5 SHEAVES : gavillas fpl 6 shock of hair : mata f de pelo

shock absorber n : amortiguador m

shocker ['ʃɑkər] n : bomba f, bombazo m

shocking ['ʃɑkɪŋ] adj 1 : chocante 2 shocking pink : rosa m estridente

shoddy ['ʃɑdi] adj shoddier; -est : de mala calidad ⟨a shoddy piece of work : un trabajo chapucero⟩

shoe¹ ['ʃuː] vt shod ['ʃɑd]; shoeing : herrar (un caballo)

shoe² n 1 : zapato m ⟨the shoe industry : la industria del calzado⟩ 2 HORSESHOE : herradura f 3 brake shoe : zapata f

shoehorn ['ʃuː,hɔrn] n : calzador m

shoelace ['ʃuː,leɪs] n : cordón m (de zapatos)

shoemaker ['ʃuː,meɪkər] n : zapatero m, -ra f

shoe polish n : betún m, grasa f Mex

shoeshine ['ʃuː,ʃaɪn] n : acto m de limpiar o lustrar los zapatos ⟨shoeshine boy/girl : limpiabotas, lustrabotas, bolero/bolera⟩

shoe store n : zapatería f

shone → shine

shoo ['ʃuː] vt to shoo away/off/out (etc.) : espantar, mandar a otra parte

shook → shake

shoot¹ ['ʃuːt] v shot ['ʃɑt]; shooting vt 1 : disparar, tirar ⟨to shoot a bullet/pistol : disparar una bala/pistola⟩ 2 : pegarle un tiro a, darle un balazo a, balacear, balear ⟨he shot her : le pegó un tiro⟩ ⟨to shoot oneself : pegarse un tiro⟩ ⟨to shoot and kill, to shoot dead/down : matar a balazos⟩ 3 THROW : lanzar (una pelota, una mirada, etc.) 4 SCORE : anotar ⟨to shoot a basket : encestar⟩ 5 PLAY : jugar (a los dados, etc.) 6 PHOTOGRAPH : fotografiar 7 FILM : filmar 8 to shoot down : derribar (un avión) 9 to shoot down DEFEAT : echar por tierra 10 to shoot oneself in the foot fam : crearse problemas — vi 1 : disparar ⟨to shoot with an arma de fuego⟩ 2 DART : ir rápidamente ⟨it shot past : pasó como una bala⟩ 3 : disparar (en deportes) 4 to shoot for : poner como objetivo ⟨let's shoot for Monday : intentémoslo para el lunes⟩ 5 to shoot up : pincharse, inyectarse 6 to shoot up INCREASE : dispararse

shoot² n : brote m, retoño m, vástago m

shooting ['ʃuːtɪŋ] n : baleo m, tiroteo m ⟨shooting death : asesinato (con arma de fuego)⟩

shooting star n : estrella f fugaz

shoot–out [ˈʃuːtˌaʊt] *n* : balacera *f*, baleo *m*, tiroteo *m*

shop¹ [ˈʃɑp] *vi* **shopped; shopping** : hacer compras ⟨to go shopping : ir de compras⟩

shop² *n* **1** WORKSHOP : taller *m* **2** STORE : tienda *f*

shopkeeper [ˈʃɑpˌkiːpər] *n* : tendero *m*, -ra *f*

shoplift [ˈʃɑpˌlɪft] *vi* : hurtar mercancía (de una tienda) — *vt* : hurtar (de una tienda)

shoplifter [ˈʃɑpˌlɪftər] *n* : ladrón *m*, -drona *f* (que roba en una tienda)

shopper [ˈʃɑpər] *n* : comprador *m*, -dora *f*

shopping bag *n* : bolsa *f* (para las compras)

shopping center *or* **shopping plaza** *n* : centro *m* comercial

shopping mall *n* : centro *m* comercial

shop window *n* : vitrina *f*, escaparate *m*, aparador *m*

shore¹ [ˈʃor] *vt* **shored; shoring** : apuntalar ⟨they shored up the wall : apuntalaron la pared⟩

shore² *n* **1** : orilla *f* (del mar, etc.) **2** PROP : puntal *m*

shoreline [ˈʃorˌlaɪn] *n* : orilla *f*

shorn → **shear**

short¹ [ˈʃort] *v* → **short–circuit**

short² *adv* **1** ABRUPTLY : repentinamente, súbitamente ⟨the car stopped short : el carro se paró en seco⟩ ⟨the sight of it brought me up short : lo que vi me hizo parar en seco⟩ **2 to be running short** ⟨the food is running short, we're running short on food : se nos está acabando la comida⟩ **3 to cut short** : interrumpir **4 to fall short** : no alcanzar, quedarse corto ⟨to fall short of expectations : no estar a la altura de las expectativas⟩ **5 to stop short of doing something** : no llegar a hacer algo

short³ *adj* **1** : corto (de medida), bajo (de estatura) ⟨a short distance away : a poca distancia⟩ **2** BRIEF : corto ⟨short and sweet : corto y bueno⟩ ⟨a short time ago : hace poco⟩ ⟨a short delay : una pequeña demora⟩ ⟨on short notice : con poca antelación⟩ **3** ABBREVIATED : abreviado ⟨to be short for : ser una forma breve de⟩ **4** CURT : brusco, cortante, seco **5** : corto (de dinero, etc.) ⟨I'm one dollar short : me falta un dólar⟩ ⟨to be short on/of time : andar corto de tiempo⟩ ⟨to be short of breath : quedarse sin aliento⟩ **6 nothing short of** : nada menos que, ni más ni menos que

short⁴ *n* **1 shorts** *npl* : shorts *mpl*, pantalones *mpl* cortos **2** → **short circuit** **3** : cortometraje *m* (en el cine) **4 for short** : para abreviar **5 in short** : en resumen

shortage [ˈʃortɪdʒ] *n* : falta *f*, escasez *f*, carencia *f*

shortbread [ˈʃortˌbrɛd] *n* : galleta *f* dulce de mantequilla, harina, y azúcar

shortcake [ˈʃortˌkeɪk] *n* : tarta *f* de fruta

shortchange [ˈʃortˈtʃeɪndʒ] *vt* **-changed; -changing** : darle mal el cambio (a alguien)

short–circuit *vt* : provocar un cortocircuito en — *vi* **1** : provocar un cortocircuito **2** : hacer cortocircuito ⟨the lamp short-circuited : la lámpara hizo cortocircuito⟩

short circuit *n* : cortocircuito *m*, corto *m* (eléctrico)

shortcoming [ˈʃortˌkʌmɪŋ] *n* : defecto *m*

shortcut [ˈʃortˌkʌt] *n* **1** : atajo *m* ⟨to take a shortcut : cortar camino⟩ **2** : alternativa *f* fácil, método *m* rápido

shorten [ˈʃortən] *vt* : acortar — *vi* : acortarse

shortfall [ˈʃortˌfol] *n* : déficit *m*

shorthand [ˈʃortˌhænd] *n* : taquigrafía *f*

short list *n* : lista *f* de candidatos finales

short–lived [ˈʃortˈlɪvd, -ˈlaɪvd] *adj* : efímero

shortly [ˈʃortli] *adv* **1** BRIEFLY : brevemente ⟨to put it shortly : para decirlo en pocas palabras⟩ **2** SOON : dentro de poco

shortness [ˈʃortnəs] *n* **1** : lo corto ⟨shortness of stature : estatura baja⟩ **2** BREVITY : brevedad *f* **3** CURTNESS : brusquedad *f* **4** SHORTAGE : falta *f*, escasez *f*, carencia *f*

shortsighted [ˈʃortˌsaɪtəd] → **nearsighted**

short–sleeved [ˈʃortˌsliːvd] *adj* : de manga corta

short–staffed [ˈʃortˌstæft] *adj* **to be short-staffed** : faltarle personal a

shortstop [ˈʃortˌstɑp] *n* : torpedero *m*, -ra *f*; parador *m*, -dora *f* en corto *Car, Mex, Ven*

short story *n* : cuento *m*

short–tempered [ˈʃortˌtɛmpərd] *adj* : de mal genio

short–term [ˈʃortˌtɔrm] *adj* : a corto plazo

shorty [ˈʃorti] *n* : enano *m*, -na *f*; petiso *m*, -sa *f* (persona)

shot [ˈʃɑt] *n* **1** : disparo *m*, tiro *m* ⟨to fire a shot : disparar⟩ **2** PELLETS : perdigones *mpl* **3** : tiro *m* (en deportes) **4** ATTEMPT : intento *m*, tentativa *f* ⟨to have/take a shot at : hacer un intento por⟩ **5** CHANCE : posibilidad *f*, chance *m* ⟨we have a shot at winning : tenemos posibilidades de ganar⟩ ⟨a long shot : una posibilidad remota⟩ **6** PHOTOGRAPH : foto *f* **7** INJECTION : inyección *f* **8** : trago *m* (de licor) **9** MARKSMAN : tirador *m*, -dora *f* ⟨a good/poor shot : un buen/mal tirador⟩

shotgun [ˈʃɑtˌɡʌn] *n* : escopeta *f*

shot put *n* : lanzamiento *m* de bala

should [ˈʃʊd] *v aux past of* **shall 1** (*expressing a condition*) ⟨if he should die : si muriera⟩ ⟨if they should call, tell me : si llaman, dímelo⟩ **2** (*indicating what is proper, required, or desirable*) ⟨they should be punished : deberían ser castigados⟩ ⟨what time should we meet? : ¿a qué hora nos encontramos?⟩ **3** (*indicating a preferred thing that did not happen*) ⟨I should have realized : tendría que haberme dado cuenta⟩ ⟨he shouldn't have said it : no debería haberlo dicho⟩ **4** (*expressing polite thanks*) ⟨you shouldn't have gone to all that trouble! : ¡no debarías haberte molestado tanto!⟩ **5** (*expressing a wish*) ⟨you should have seen her face! : ¡tendrías que haber visto la cara que puso!⟩ **6** (*requesting an opinion*) ⟨what should I do? : ¿qué hago?⟩ **7** (*expressing a feeling about someone's words or behavior*) ⟨(it's) funny you should say that—I was just thinking the same thing : ¡qué casualidad! estaba pensando lo mismo⟩ **8** (*emphasizing a belief, thought, or hope*) ⟨I should hope so/not! : ¡faltaría más!⟩ **9** (*expressing probability*) ⟨they should arrive soon : deben (de) llegar pronto⟩ ⟨why should he lie? : ¿porqué ha de mentir?⟩

shoulder[1] [ˈʃoːldər] *vt* **1** JOSTLE : empujar (con el hombro) **2** : ponerse al hombro (una mochila, etc.) **3** : cargar con (la responsabilidad, etc.)

shoulder[2] *n* **1** : hombro *m* ⟨to shrug one's shoulders : encogerse los hombros⟩ **2** : arcén *m*; banquina *f Arg, Uru*; berma *f Chile, Col, Ecua, Peru* (de una carretera)

shoulder bag *n* HANDBAG : cartera *f*, bolso *m*, bolsa *f Mex* (con correa)

shoulder blade *n* : omóplato *m*, omoplato *m*, escápula *f*

shoulder-length *n* : hasta los hombros

shoulder strap *n* : tirante *m*

shouldn't [ˈʃʊdənt] *contraction of* **should not → should**

shout[1] [ˈʃaʊt] *v* : gritar, vocear

shout[2] *n* : grito *m*

shove[1] [ˈʃʌv] *v* **shoved**; **shoving** : empujar bruscamente

shove[2] *n* : empujón *m*, empellón *m*

shovel[1] [ˈʃʌvəl] *vt* -**veled** *or* -**velled**; -**veling** *or* -**velling** **1** : mover con (una) pala ⟨they shoveled the dirt out : sacaron la tierra con palas⟩ **2** DIG : cavar (con una pala)

shovel[2] *n* : pala *f*

show[1] [ˈʃoː] *v* **showed**; **shown** [ˈʃoːn] *or* **showed**; **showing** *vt* **1** PRESENT, DISPLAY : mostrar, enseñar ⟨I showed him the photo : le mostré la foto⟩ **2** REVEAL : demostrar, manifestar, revelar ⟨he showed himself to be a coward : se reveló como cobarde⟩ ⟨to show signs of : dar muestras/señales/indicios de⟩ ⟨to show one's feelings : demostrar uno sus emociones⟩ **3** TEACH : enseñar ⟨show me how to do it : enséñame cómo hacerlo⟩ ⟨to show someone who's boss : demostrarle a alguien quién manda⟩ ⟨I'll show him! : ¡ya lo verá!⟩ **4** PROVE : demostrar, probar ⟨it just goes to show that . . . : esto demuestra que . . .⟩ **5** DEPICT : representar ⟨the photo shows children playing : la foto es de unos niños jugando⟩ **6** DISPLAY, READ : marcar **7** INDICATE : indicar **8** CONDUCT, LEAD : llevar, conducir ⟨to show someone the way : conducir a alguien⟩ ⟨to show someone out : acompañar a alguien a la puerta⟩ ⟨they showed us around their house : nos mostraron su casa⟩ **9** : proyectar (una película), dar

(un programa de televisión) **10 to show off** : lucirse con **11 to show off** ACCENTUATE : hacer resaltar **12 to show up** EMBARRASS : hacer quedar mal — *vi* **1** : notarse, verse ⟨the stain doesn't show : la mancha no se ve⟩ **2** APPEAR : aparecer, dejarse ver **3 to show off** : lucirse

show[2] *n* **1** : demostración *f* ⟨a show of force/strength : una demostración de fuerza⟩ **2** EXHIBITION : exposición *f*, exhibición *f* ⟨flower show : exposición de flores⟩ ⟨to be on show : estar expuesto⟩ **3** : espectáculo *m* (teatral), programa *m* (de televisión, etc.) ⟨to go to a show : ir al teatro⟩ **4** APPEARANCE : apariencia *f* ⟨she put on a show of sympathy : fingió compasión⟩ ⟨his friendliness was all show : su simpatía era puro teatro⟩ **5 to run the show** : ser el/la que manda

show business *n* : mundo *m* del espectáculo

showcase [ˈʃoːˌkeɪs] *n* : vitrina *f*

showdown [ˈʃoːˌdaʊn] *n* : confrontación *f* (decisiva)

shower[1] [ˈʃaʊər] *vt* **1** SPRAY : regar, mojar **2** HEAP : colmar ⟨they showered him with gifts : lo colmaron de regalos, le llovieron los regalos⟩ — *vi* **1** BATHE : ducharse, darse una ducha **2** RAIN : llover

shower[2] *n* **1** : chaparrón *m*, chubasco *m* ⟨a chance of showers : una posibilidad de chaparrones⟩ **2** : ducha *f* ⟨to take a shower : ducharse⟩ **3** PARTY : fiesta *f* ⟨a bridal shower : una despedida de soltera⟩

shower cap *n* : gorro *m* de ducha

showing [ˈʃoɪŋ] *n* : exposición *f*

show-off [ˈʃoʊˌɔf] *n* : fanfarrón *m*, -rrona *f*

show off *vt* : hacer alarde de, ostentar — *vi* : lucirse

showroom [ˈʃoʊˌruːm, -ˌrʊm] *n* : sala *f* de exposición

show up *vi* APPEAR : aparecer — *vt* EXPOSE : revelar

showy [ˈʃoːi] *adj* **showier**; -**est** : llamativo, ostentoso — **showily** *adv*

shrank → shrink

shrapnel [ˈʃræpnəl] *ns & pl* : metralla *f*

shred[1] [ˈʃred] *vt* **shredded**; **shredding** : hacer trizas, desmenuzar (con las manos), triturar (con una máquina) ⟨to shred vegetables : cortar verduras en tiras⟩

shred[2] *n* **1** STRIP : tira *f*, jirón *m* (de tela) ⟨to tear to shreds : hacer trizas⟩ **2** BIT : pizca *f* ⟨not a shred of evidence : ni la más mínima prueba⟩ ⟨not a shred of truth : ni pizca de verdad⟩

shredder *n* : trituradora *f* ⟨paper shredder : trituradora de papel⟩

shrew [ˈʃruː] *n* **1** : musaraña *f* (animal) **2** : mujer *f* regañona

shrewd [ˈʃruːd] *adj* : astuto, inteligente, sagaz — **shrewdly** *adv*

shrewdness [ˈʃruːdnəs] *n* : astucia *f*

shriek[1] [ˈʃriːk] *vi* : chillar, gritar

shriek[2] *n* : chillido *m*, alarido *m*, grito *m*

shrill [ˈʃrɪl] *adj* : agudo, estridente

shrilly ['ʃrɪli] *adv* : agudamente

shrimp ['ʃrɪmp] *n* **1** : camarón *m*; langostino *m*; gamba *f* *Arg, Uru, Spain* **2** : enano *m*, -na *f*; petiso *m*, -sa *f* (persona)

shrine ['ʃraɪn] *n* **1** TOMB : sepulcro *m* (de un santo) **2** SANCTUARY : lugar *m* sagrado, santuario *m*

shrink ['ʃrɪŋk] *vi* **shrank** ['ʃræŋk] *or* **shrunk** ['ʃrʌŋk]; **shrunk** *or* **shrunken** ['ʃrʌŋkən]; **shrinking 1** RECOIL : retroceder ⟨he shrank back : se echó para atrás⟩ **2** : encogerse (dícese de la ropa) **3 to shrink from** AVOID : eludir

shrinkage ['ʃrɪŋkɪdʒ] *n* : encogimiento *m* (de ropa, etc.), contracción *f*, reducción *f*

shrivel ['ʃrɪvəl] *vi* **-veled** *or* **-velled; -veling** *or* **-velling** : arrugarse, marchitarse

shroud[1] ['ʃraʊd] *vt* : envolver

shroud[2] *n* **1** : sudario *m*, mortaja *f* **2** VEIL : velo *m* ⟨wrapped in a shroud of mystery : envuelto en un aura de misterio⟩

shrub ['ʃrʌb] *n* : arbusto *m*, mata *f*

shrubbery ['ʃrʌbəri] *n, pl* **-beries** : arbustos *mpl*, matas *fpl*

shrug ['ʃrʌg] *vi* **shrugged; shrugging** : encogerse de hombros — *vt* **to shrug off** DISMISS : hacer caso omiso de

shrunk → **shrink**

shuck ['ʃʌk] *vt* : pelar (mazorcas, etc.), abrir (almejas, etc.)

shudder[1] ['ʃʌdər] *vi* : estremecerse

shudder[2] *n* : estremecimiento *m*, escalofrío *m*

shuffle[1] ['ʃʌfəl] *v* **-fled; -fling** *vt* MIX : mezclar, revolver, barajar (naipes) — *vi* : caminar arrastrando los pies

shuffle[2] *n* **1** : acto *m* de revolver ⟨each player gets a shuffle : a cada jugador le toca barajar⟩ **2** JUMBLE : revoltijo *m* **3** : el arrastrar los pies

shun ['ʃʌn] *vi* **shunned; shunning** : evitar, esquivar, eludir

shunt ['ʃʌnt] *vt* : desviar, cambiar de vía (un tren)

shut ['ʃʌt] *v* **shut; shutting** *vt* **1** CLOSE : cerrar (una puerta, los ojos, un libro, etc.) ⟨shut the lid : tápalo⟩ **2 to shut away/in** : encerrar **3 to shut down** CLOSE : cerrar (un negocio, etc.) **4 to shut down** TURN OFF : apagar **5 to shut off** TURN OFF : cortar (la electricidad), apagar (las luces, etc.) **6 to shut off** ISOLATE : aislar **7 to shut out** EXCLUDE : excluir, dejar fuera a (personas), no dejar que entre (luz, ruido, etc.) **8 to shut up** CLOSE : cerrar **9 to shut up** CONFINE : encerrar **10 to shut up** *fam* SILENCE : callar — *vi* **11 to shut down** : cerrar, cerrar sus puertas (dícese de una empresa) **12 to shut up** *fam* : callarse ⟨shut up! : ¡cállate (la boca)!⟩

shut-in ['ʃʌt,ɪn] *n* : inválido *m*, -da *f* (que no puede salir de casa)

shutter ['ʃʌtər] *n* **1** : contraventana *f*, postigo *m* (de una ventana o puerta) **2** : obturador *m* (de una cámara)

shuttle[1] ['ʃʌtəl] *v* **-tled; -tling** *vt* : transportar ⟨she shuttled him back and forth : lo llevaba de acá para allá⟩ — *vi* : ir y venir

shuttle[2] *n* **1** : lanzadera *f* (para tejer) **2** : vehículo *m* que hace recorridos cortos **3** → **space shuttle**

shuttlecock ['ʃʌtəl,kak] *n* : volante *m*

shy[1] ['ʃaɪ] *vi* **shied; shying** : retroceder, asustarse

shy[2] *adj* **shier** *or* **shyer** ['ʃaɪər]; **shiest** *or* **shyest** ['ʃaɪəst] **1** TIMID : tímido **2** WARY : cauteloso ⟨he's not shy about asking : no vacila en preguntar⟩ **3** SHORT : corto (de dinero, etc.) ⟨I'm two dollars shy : me faltan dos dólares⟩

shyly ['ʃaɪli] *adv* : tímidamente

shyness ['ʃaɪnəs] *n* : timidez *f*

Siamese[1] [,saɪə'miːz, -'miːs] *adj* : siamés ⟨Siamese twins : hermanos siameses⟩

Siamese[2] *n* **1** : siamés *m*, -mesa *f* **2** : siamés *m* (idioma) **3** *or* **Siamese cat** : gato *m* siamés

sibling ['sɪblɪŋ] *n* : hermano *m*, hermana *f*

Sicilian [sə'sɪljən] *n* : siciliano *m*, -na *f* — **Sicilian** *adj*

sick ['sɪk] *adj* **1** : enfermo ⟨the baby is sick : el bebé está enfermo⟩ **2** NAUSEOUS : mareado, con náuseas ⟨to get sick : vomitar⟩ **3** : para uso de enfermos ⟨sick day : día de permiso (por enfermedad)⟩ **4 to be sick (and tired) of** : estar harto de, estar hasta la coronilla de

sickbed ['sɪk,bed] *n* : lecho *m* de enfermo

sicken ['sɪkən] *vt* **1** : poner enfermo **2** REVOLT : darle asco a (alguien) — *vi* : enfermar(se), caer enfermo

sickening ['sɪkənɪŋ] *adj* : asqueroso, repugnante, nauseabundo

sickle ['sɪkəl] *n* : hoz *f*

sick leave *n* : baja *f* por enfermedad

sickly ['sɪkli] *adj* **sicklier; -est 1** : enfermizo **2** → **sickening**

sickness ['sɪknəs] *n* **1** : enfermedad *f* **2** NAUSEA : náuseas *fpl*

side[1] ['saɪd] *n* **1** : lado *m* (de un lago, una cama, una frontera, etc.) ⟨by the side of the road : al lado de la calle⟩ ⟨the far side : el otro lado⟩ ⟨on the left-hand side : a mano izquierda⟩ ⟨on both sides : a ambos lados⟩ ⟨on either side : a cada lado⟩ ⟨from side to side : de un lado a otro⟩ ⟨side by side : uno al lado del otro⟩ ⟨they attacked from all sides : atacaron desde todos los frentes⟩ ⟨there are mountains on all sides : todo alrededor hay montañas⟩ **2** : lado *m*, cara *f* (de una moneda, una caja, etc.) ⟨this side up : este lado hacia arriba⟩ **3** : falda *f* (de una montaña) **4** : lado *m*, costado *m* (de una persona), ijada *f* (de un animal) **5** *or* **side dish** : guarnición *f*, acompañamiento *m* ⟨with a side of fries : con papas fritas (como guarnición)⟩ **6** : lado *m*, parte *f* ⟨he's on my side : está de mi parte⟩ ⟨to take sides : tomar partido⟩ ⟨to listen to both sides (of the story) : escuchar las dos campanas⟩ **7** : aspecto *m* ⟨to look on the bright side : ver el aspecto positivo⟩ **8 on the side** SEPARATELY : aparte **9 on the side** : como segundo trabajo **10 on the side** ⟨a lover on the side : un/una amante (de una persona casada)⟩

side² v **sided; siding** vt : instalar revestimiento exterior en — vi **1 to side against** : ponerse en contra de **2 to side with** : ponerse de parte de

sideboard ['saɪd,bord] n : aparador m

sideburns ['saɪd,bərnz] npl : patillas fpl

sided ['saɪdəd] adj : que tiene lados ⟨one-sided : de un lado⟩

side effect n : efecto m secundario

sideline ['saɪd,laɪn] n **1** : línea f de banda (en deportes) **2** : actividad f suplementaria (en negocios) **3 to be on the sidelines** : estar al margen

sidelong ['saɪd,lɔŋ] adj : de reojo, de soslayo

sideshow ['saɪd,ʃo:] n : espectáculo m secundario, atracción f secundaria

sidestep ['saɪd,stɛp] v **-stepped; -stepping** vi : dar un paso hacia un lado — vt AVOID : esquivar, eludir

side street n : calle f lateral

sidetrack ['saɪd,træk] vt : desviar (una conversación, etc.), distraer (a una persona)

sidewalk ['saɪd,wɔk] n : acera f; vereda f; andén m CA, Col; banqueta f Mex

sideways¹ ['saɪd,weɪz] adv **1** : hacia un lado ⟨it leaned sideways : se inclinaba hacia un lado⟩ **2** : de lado, de costado ⟨lie sideways : acuéstese de costado⟩

sideways² adj : hacia un lado ⟨a sideways glance : una mirada de reojo⟩

siding ['saɪdɪŋ] n : revestimiento m exterior (de un edificio)

sidle ['saɪdəl] vi **-dled; -dling** : moverse furtivamente

siege ['si:ʤ, 'si:ʒ] n : sitio m ⟨to be under siege : estar sitiado⟩

siesta [si:'ɛstə] n : siesta f

sieve ['sɪv] n : tamiz m, cedazo m, criba f (en mineralogía)

sift ['sɪft] vt **1** : tamizar, cerner ⟨sift the flour : tamice la harina⟩ **2** or **to sift through** : examinar cuidadosamente, pasar por el tamiz

sifter ['sɪftər] n : tamiz m, cedazo m

sigh¹ ['saɪ] vi : suspirar

sigh² n : suspiro m '

sight¹ ['saɪt] vt : ver (a una persona), divisar (la tierra, un barco)

sight² n **1** EYESIGHT : vista f (facultad) **2** VIEW : vista f ⟨out of sight : fuera de vista⟩ ⟨to come into sight : aparecer⟩ ⟨in plain sight : a plena vista⟩ **3** : algo visto ⟨it's a familiar sight : se ve con frecuencia⟩ ⟨she's a sight for sore eyes : da gusto verla⟩ **4** : lugar m de interés (para turistas, etc.) **5** : mira f (de un rifle, etc.) **6** GLIMPSE : mirada f breve ⟨at first sight : a primera vista⟩ ⟨I know him by sight : lo conozco de vista⟩ ⟨I caught sight of her : la divisé, alcancé a verla⟩ ⟨to lose sight of : perder de vista⟩ ⟨he faints at the sight of blood : cuando ve sangre se desmaya⟩ ⟨to shoot on sight : disparar sin previo aviso⟩

sighting ['saɪtɪŋ] n : avistamiento m

sightless ['saɪtləs] adj : invidente, ciego

sightseeing ['saɪt,si:ɪŋ] n : acto m de visitar los lugares de interés ⟨to go sightseeing : hacer turismo⟩ ⟨sightseeing tour : excursión, tour⟩

sightseer ['saɪt,si:ər] n : turista mf

sign¹ ['saɪn] vt **1** : firmar ⟨to sign a check : firmar un cheque⟩ **2** or **to sign on/up** HIRE : contratar (a un empleado), fichar (a un jugador) **3 to sign in/out** : registrar la entrada/salida de — vi **1** : hacer una seña ⟨she signed for him to stop : le hizo una seña para que se parara⟩ **2** : comunicarse por señas **3 to sign for** : firmar el recibo de **4 to sign in/out** : firmar el registro (al entrar/salir), registrar la entrada/salida **5 to sign off** : despedirse (en una carta, etc.) **6 to sign off (on)** APPROVE : dar el visto bueno a **7 to sign up** : inscribirse, matricularse

sign² n **1** SYMBOL : símbolo m, signo m ⟨minus sign : signo de menos⟩ ⟨sign of the zodiac : signo del zodíaco⟩ **2** GESTURE : seña f, señal f, gesto m **3** : letrero m, cartel m ⟨neon sign : letrero de neón⟩ **4** TRACE : señal f, indicio m

signage ['saɪnɪʤ] n : señalización f

signal¹ ['sɪgnəl] vt **-naled** or **-nalled; -naling** or **-nalling 1** : hacerle señas (a alguien) ⟨she signaled me to leave : me hizo señas para que saliera⟩ **2** INDICATE : señalar, indicar — vi : hacer señas, comunicar por señas

signal² adj NOTABLE : señalado, notable

signal³ n : señal f

signatory ['sɪgnə,tori] n, pl **-ries** : firmante mf; signatario m, -ria f

signature ['sɪgnə,tʃur] n : firma f

signer ['saɪnər] n : firmante mf

signet ['sɪgnət] n : sello m

significance [sɪg'nɪfɪkənts] n **1** MEANING : significado m **2** IMPORTANCE : importancia f

significant [sɪg'nɪfɪkənt] adj **1** IMPORTANT : importante **2** MEANINGFUL : significativo — **significantly** adv

signify ['sɪgnə,faɪ] vt **-fied; -fying 1** : indicar ⟨he signified his desire for more : haciendo señas indicó que quería más⟩ **2** MEAN : significar

sign language n : lenguaje m por señas

signpost ['saɪn,po:st] n : poste m indicador

silence¹ ['saɪlənts] vt **-lenced; -lencing** : silenciar, acallar

silence² n : silencio m

silencer ['saɪlənsər] n : silenciador m

silent ['saɪlənt] adj **1** : callado ⟨to remain silent : quedarse callado, guardar silencio⟩ **2** QUIET, STILL : silencioso **3** MUTE : mudo ⟨a silent letter : una letra muda⟩

silently ['saɪləntli] adv : silenciosamente, calladamente

silhouette¹ [,sɪlə'wɛt] vt **-etted; -etting** : destacar la silueta de ⟨it was silhouetted against the sky : se perfilaba contra el cielo⟩

silhouette² n : silueta f

silica ['sɪlɪkə] n : sílice f

silicon ['sɪlɪkən, -ˌkɑn] n : silicio m ⟨silicon chip : chip de silicio⟩

silk ['sɪlk] n : seda f

silk–cotton tree n : ceiba f

silken ['sɪlkən] adj 1 : de seda ⟨a silken veil : un velo de seda⟩ 2 SILKY : sedoso ⟨silken hair : cabellos sedosos⟩

silkworm ['sɪlkˌwərm] n : gusano m de seda

silky ['sɪlki] adj silkier; -est : sedoso

sill ['sɪl] n : alféizar m (de una ventana), umbral m (de una puerta)

silliness ['sɪlinəs] n : tontería f, estupidez f

silly ['sɪli] adj sillier; -est : tonto, estúpido, ridículo

silo ['saɪˌlo:] n, pl **silos** : silo m

silt ['sɪlt] n : cieno m

silver[1] ['sɪlvər] adj 1 : de plata ⟨a silver spoon : una cuchara de plata⟩ 2 → silvery

silver[2] n 1 : plata f 2 COINS : monedas fpl 3 → silverware 4 : color m plata

silver–plated ['sɪlvərˈpleɪtəd] adj : plateado

silversmith ['sɪlvərˌsmɪθ] n : orfebre mf

silverware ['sɪlvərˌwær] n 1 : artículos mpl de plata, platería f 2 FLATWARE : cubertería f

silvery ['sɪlvəri] adj : plateado

similar ['sɪmələr] adj : similar, parecido, semejante

similarity [ˌsɪməˈlærəti] n, pl **-ties** : semejanza f, parecido m

similarly ['sɪmələrli] adv : de manera similar

simile ['sɪməˌli:] n : símil m

simmer ['sɪmər] v : hervir a fuego lento

simper[1] ['sɪmpər] vi : sonreír como un tonto

simper[2] n : sonrisa f tonta

simple ['sɪmpəl] adj simpler; simplest 1 INNOCENT : inocente 2 PLAIN : sencillo, simple 3 EASY : simple, sencillo, fácil 4 STRAIGHTFORWARD : puro, simple ⟨the simple truth : la pura verdad⟩ 5 NAIVE : ingenuo, simple

simpleminded [ˌsɪmpəlˈmaɪndəd] adj : simple (dícese de una persona)

simpleton ['sɪmpəltən] n : bobo m, -ba f; tonto m, -ta f

simplicity [sɪmˈplɪsəti] n : simplicidad f, sencillez f

simplification [ˌsɪmpləfəˈkeɪʃən] n : simplificación f

simplify ['sɪmpləˌfaɪ] vt -fied; -fying : simplificar

simplistic [sɪmˈplɪsətɪk] n : simplista

simply ['sɪmpli] adv 1 PLAINLY : sencillamente 2 SOLELY : simplemente, sólo 3 REALLY : absolutamente

simulate ['sɪmjəˌleɪt] vt -lated; -lating : simular

simulation [ˌsɪmjəˈleɪʃən] n : simulación f

simultaneous [ˌsaɪməlˈteɪniəs] adj : simultáneo — **simultaneously** adv

sin[1] ['sɪn] vi sinned; sinning : pecar

sin[2] n : pecado m

since[1] ['sɪnts] adv 1 : desde entonces ⟨they've been friends ever since : desde entonces han sido amigos⟩ ⟨she's since become mayor : más tarde se hizo alcalde⟩ 2 AGO : hace ⟨he's long since dead : murió hace mucho⟩

since[2] conj 1 : desde que ⟨since he was born : desde que nació⟩ 2 INASMUCH AS : ya que, puesto que, dado que

since[3] prep : desde

sincere [sɪnˈsɪr] adj -cerer; -est : sincero — **sincerely** adv

sincerity [sɪnˈserəti] n : sinceridad f

sinew ['sɪnjuː, 'sɪnˌnuː] n 1 TENDON : tendón m, nervio m (en la carne) 2 POWER : fuerza f

sinewy ['sɪnjui, 'sɪnui] adj 1 STRINGY : fibroso 2 STRONG, WIRY : fuerte, nervudo

sinful ['sɪnfəl] adj : pecador (dícese de las personas), pecaminoso

sing ['sɪŋ] v sang ['sæŋ] or sung ['sʌŋ]; sung; singing : cantar

singe ['sɪndʒ] vt singed; singeing : chamuscar, quemar

singer ['sɪŋər] n : cantante mf

singer–songwriter ['sɪŋərˈsɔŋˌraɪtər] n : cantautor m, -tora f

single[1] ['sɪŋɡəl] vt -gled; -gling or to single out 1 SELECT : escoger 2 DISTINGUISH : señalar

single[2] adj 1 UNMARRIED : soltero ⟨a single parent : un padre soltero, una madre soltera⟩ 2 SOLE : solo ⟨a single survivor : un solo sobreviviente⟩ ⟨every single one : cada uno, todos⟩

single[3] n 1 : soltero m, -ra f ⟨for married couples and singles : para los matrimonios y los solteros⟩ 2 or single room : habitación f individual 3 DOLLAR : billete m de un dólar

single file[1] adv : en fila india

single file[2] n in single file : en fila india

single–handed ['sɪŋɡəlˈhændəd] adj : sin ayuda, solo

single–minded ['sɪŋɡəlˈmaɪndəd] adj : resuelto

singly ['sɪŋɡli] adv : individualmente, uno por uno

singular[1] ['sɪŋɡjələr] adj 1 : singular (en gramática) 2 OUTSTANDING : singular, sobresaliente 3 STRANGE : singular, extraño

singular[2] n : singular m

singularity [ˌsɪŋɡjəˈlærəti] n, pl **-ties** : singularidad f

singularly ['sɪŋɡjələrli] adv : singularmente

sinister ['sɪnəstər] adj : siniestro

sink[1] ['sɪŋk] v sank ['sæŋk] or sunk ['sʌŋk]; sunk; sinking vi 1 : hundirse (dícese de un barco, etc.) ⟨his foot sank into the mud : su pie se hundió en el barro⟩ 2 DROP, FALL : descender, caer ⟨to sink into a chair : dejarse caer en una silla⟩ ⟨her heart sank : se le cayó el alma a los pies⟩ ⟨I had the sinking feeling that . . . : tenía un mal presentimiento de que . . .⟩ 3 DECREASE : bajar ⟨the company's stock sank : las acciones de la compañía cayeron en picada⟩ ⟨his voice sank to a whisper : su voz se redujo a un susurro⟩ **4** FOUNDER : hundirse, irse a pique (dícese de una compañía, etc.) **5** STOOP : rebajarse ⟨to sink so/that low : caer tan bajo⟩ **6 to sink in** : hacer mella — *vt* **1** : hundir (un barco, etc.) **2** EXCAVATE : excavar (un pozo para minar), perforar (un pozo de agua) **3** PLUNGE, STICK : clavar, hincar **4** INVEST : invertir (fondos) **5** : meter (en deportes) ⟨to sink a basket : encestar⟩

sink² *n* **1** *or* **kitchen sink** : fregadero *m*; lavaplatos *m Chile, Col, Mex* **2** *or* **bathroom sink** : lavabo *m*, lavamanos *m* **3** WEIGHT : plomo *m*, plomada *f*

sinker ['sɪŋkər] *n* WEIGHT : plomada *f*, plomo *m*

sinner ['sɪnər] *n* : pecador *m*, -dora *f*

sinuous ['sɪnjuəs] *adj* : sinuoso — **sinuously** *adv*

sinus ['saɪnəs] *n* : seno *m*

sip¹ ['sɪp] *v* **sipped; sipping** *vt* : sorber — *vi* : beber a sorbos

sip² *n* : sorbo *m*

siphon¹ ['saɪfən] *vt* : sacar con sifón

siphon² *n* : sifón *m*

sir ['sər] *n* **1** *(in titles)* : sir *m* **2** *(as a form of address)* : señor *m* ⟨Dear Sir : Muy señor mío⟩ ⟨yes sir! : ¡sí, señor!⟩

sire¹ ['saɪr] *vt* **sired; siring** : engendrar, ser el padre de

sire² *n* : padre *m*

siren ['saɪrən] *n* : sirena *f*

sirloin ['sər,lɔɪn] *n* : solomillo *m*

sirup → syrup

sissy ['sɪsi] *n*, *pl* **-sies** : mariquita *f fam*

sister ['sɪstər] *n* **1** : hermana *f* **2 Sister** : hermana *f*, Sor *f* ⟨Sister Mary : Sor María⟩

sisterhood ['sɪstər,hʊd] *n* **1** : condición *f* de ser hermana **2** : sociedad *f* de mujeres

sister-in-law ['sɪstərɪn,lɔ] *n*, *pl* **sisters-in-law** : cuñada *f*

sisterly ['sɪstərli] *adj* : de hermana

sit ['sɪt] *v* **sat** ['sæt]; **sitting** *vi* **1** : sentarse ⟨he sat down : se sentó⟩ ⟨he sat (down) in the chair : se sentó en la silla⟩ **2** : estar sentado ⟨she was sitting in the chair : estaba sentada en la silla⟩ ⟨they sat across from me : estaban sentados frente a mí⟩ **3** ROOST : posarse **4** : sesionar ⟨the legislature is sitting : la legislatura está en sesión⟩ **5** POSE : posar (para un retrato) **6** LIE, REST : estar (ubicado) ⟨the house sits on a hill : la casa está en una colina⟩ ⟨it was sitting right in front of me : lo tenía delante de las narices⟩ **7 to sit around** : relajarse, no hacer nada **8 to sit back** : relajarse **9 to sit in for** : sustituir a **10 to sit in on** : asistir a (como observador) **11 to sit on** : darle largas a (algo) **12 to sit out** ENDURE : aguantar **13 to sit out** : no participar en ⟨I'll sit this one out : no voy a bailar/ jugar (etc.) esta vez⟩ **14 to sit through** : aguantar (un discurso, etc.) **15 to sit tight** : esperar **16 to sit up** : incorporarse **17 to sit up** : quedarse levantado ⟨we sat up talking : nos quedamos ha-

blando hasta muy tarde⟩ — *vt* SEAT : sentar, colocar ⟨I sat him on the sofa : lo senté en el sofá⟩

sitcom ['sɪt,kɑm] → **situation comedy**

site ['saɪt] *n* **1** : sitio *m*, lugar *m* (en general), emplazamiento *m*, ubicación *f* (de un edificio, etc.) ⟨construction/building site : obra⟩ **2** SCENE : lugar *m*, escena *f* (de un accidente, etc.), escenario *m* (de una batalla) **3 → Web site**

sitter ['sɪtər] → **baby-sitter**

sitting ['sɪtɪŋ] *n* **1** : turno *m* (de cena, etc.) **2** : sesión *f*

sitting room → living room

situate ['sɪtʃu,eɪt] *vt* **-ated; -ating** **1** ESTABLISH, LOCATE : situar, ubicar **2** PLACE : poner, colocar

situated ['sɪtʃu,eɪtəd] *adj* LOCATED : ubicado, situado

situation [,sɪtʃu'eɪʃən] *n* **1** LOCATION : ubicación *f*, emplazamiento *m* **2** CIRCUMSTANCES : situación *f* **3** JOB : empleo *m*

situation comedy *n* : comedia *f* de situación

six¹ ['sɪks] *adj* : seis ⟨she's six (years old) : tiene seis años⟩

six² *n* : seis *m* ⟨the six of hearts : el seis de corazones⟩

six³ *pron* : seis ⟨there are six of us : somos seis⟩ ⟨it's six (o'clock) : son las seis⟩

six-gun ['sɪks,gʌn] *n* : revólver *m* (con seis cámaras)

six hundred¹ *adj & pron* : seiscientos

six hundred² *n* : seiscientos *m*

six-shooter ['sɪks,ʃuːtər] → **six-gun**

sixteen¹ [sɪks'tiːn] *adj & pron* : dieciséis

sixteen² *n* : dieciséis *m*

sixteenth¹ [sɪks'tiːnθ] *adj* : decimosexto

sixteenth² *n* **1** : decimosexto *m*, -ta *f* (en una serie) **2** : dieciseisavo *m*, dieciseisava parte *f*

sixth¹ ['sɪksθ, 'sɪks] *adv* : en sexto lugar

sixth² *adj* : sexto

sixth³ *n* **1** : sexto *m*, -ta *f* (en una serie) **2** : sexto *m*, sexta parte *f*

sixtieth¹ ['sɪkstiəθ] *adj* : sexagésimo

sixtieth² *n* **1** : sexagésimo *m*, -ma *f* (en una serie) **2** : sesentavo *m*, sesentava parte *f*

sixty¹ ['sɪksti] *adj & pron* : sesenta

sixty² *n*, *pl* **-ties** : sesenta *m*

sizable *or* **sizeable** ['saɪzəbəl] *adj* : considerable

size¹ ['saɪz] *vt* **sized; sizing** **1** : clasificar según el tamaño **2 to size up** : evaluar, apreciar

size² *n* **1** DIMENSIONS : tamaño *m*, talla *f* (de ropa), número *m* (de zapatos) **2** MAGNITUDE : magnitud *f*

sized ['saɪzd] *adj used in combination* : de tamaño ⟨large-sized : (de tamaño) grande⟩

sizzle ['sɪzəl] *vi* **-zled; -zling** : chisporrotear

skate¹ ['skeɪt] *vi* **skated; skating** : patinar

skate² *n* **1** : patín *m* ⟨roller skate : patín de ruedas⟩ **2** : raya *f* (pez)

skateboard [ˈskeɪtˌbord] n : monopatín m, patineta f, skateboard m

skateboarding [ˈskeɪtˌbordɪŋ] n : monopatinaje m, skateboarding m

skater [ˈskeɪtər] n : patinador m, -dora f

skating [ˈskeɪtɪŋ] n : patinaje m

skating rink n : pista f de patinaje

skein [ˈskeɪn] n : madeja f

skeletal [ˈskɛlətəl] adj 1 : óseo (en anatomía) 2 EMACIATED : esquelético

skeleton [ˈskɛlətən] n 1 : esqueleto m (anatómico) 2 FRAMEWORK : armazón mf

skeleton key n : llave f maestra

skeptic [ˈskɛptɪk] n : escéptico m, -ca f

skeptical [ˈskɛptɪkəl] adj : escéptico

skepticism [ˈskɛptəˌsɪzəm] n : escepticismo m

sketch¹ [ˈskɛtʃ] vt : bosquejar — vi : hacer bosquejos

sketch² n 1 DRAWING, OUTLINE : esbozo m, bosquejo m 2 ESSAY : ensayo m

sketchy [ˈskɛtʃi] adj sketchier; -est : incompleto, poco detallado

skewer¹ [ˈskjuːər] vt : ensartar (carne, etc.)

skewer² n : brocheta f, broqueta f

ski¹ [ˈskiː] vi skied; skiing : esquiar

ski² n, pl skis : esquí m

ski boot n : bota f de esquiar

skid¹ [ˈskɪd] vi skidded; skidding : derrapar, patinar

skid² n : derrape m, patinazo m

skier [ˈskiːər] n : esquiador m, -dora f

skiing [ˈskiːɪŋ] n : esquí m

ski jump n : trampolín m (de esquí)

ski lift n : telesquí m, telesilla f

skill [ˈskɪl] n 1 DEXTERITY : habilidad f, destreza f 2 CAPABILITY : capacidad f, arte m, técnica f ⟨organizational skills : la capacidad para organizar⟩

skilled [ˈskɪld] adj : hábil, experto

skillet [ˈskɪlət] n : sartén mf

skillful [ˈskɪlfəl] adj : hábil, diestro

skillfully [ˈskɪlfəli] adv : con habilidad, con destreza

skim¹ [ˈskɪm] v skimmed; skimming vt 1 : espumar (sopa, etc.), quitar (grasa, etc.) ⟨I skimmed the broth to remove the fat, I skimmed the fat off/from the broth : le quité la grasa al caldo⟩ 2 : echarle un vistazo a (un libro, etc.) 3 : pasar rozando (una superficie) 4 or to skim off : embolsarse (dinero) — vi to skim through/over : echarle un vistazo a (un libro, etc.)

skim² adj : descremado ⟨skim milk : leche descremada⟩

ski mask n : pasamontañas m

skimp [ˈskɪmp] vi to skimp on : escatimar

skimpy [ˈskɪmpi] adj skimpier; -est : exiguo, escaso, raquítico

skin¹ [ˈskɪn] vt skinned; skinning : despellejar, desollar

skin² n 1 : piel f, cutis m (de la cara) ⟨dark skin : piel morena⟩ 2 RIND : piel f

skin–deep [ˈskɪnˈdiːp] adj : superficial

skin diving n : buceo m, submarinismo m

skinflint [ˈskɪnˌflɪnt] n : tacaño m, -ña f

skinhead [ˈskɪnˌhɛd] n : cabeza mf rapada

skinned [ˈskɪnd] adj used in combination : de piel ⟨tough-skinned : de piel dura⟩

skinny [ˈskɪni] adj skinnier; -est : flaco

skip¹ [ˈskɪp] v skipped; skipping vi : ir dando brincos — vt : saltarse

skip² n : brinco m, salto m

skipper [ˈskɪpər] n : capitán m, -tana f

ski pole n : bastón m (de esquí)

skirmish¹ [ˈskərmɪʃ] vi : escaramuzar

skirmish² n : escaramuza f, refriega f

skirt¹ [ˈskərt] vt 1 BORDER : bordear 2 EVADE : evadir, esquivar

skirt² n : falda f, pollera f

skit [ˈskɪt] n : sketch m (teatral)

skittish [ˈskɪtɪʃ] adj : asustadizo, nervioso

skulk [ˈskʌlk] vi : merodear

skull [ˈskʌl] n 1 : cráneo m, calavera f 2 **skull and crossbones** : calavera f (bandera pirata)

skullcap [ˈskʌlˌkæp] n : casquete m

skunk [ˈskʌŋk] n : zorrillo m, mofeta f

sky [ˈskaɪ] n, pl skies : cielo m

skylark [ˈskaɪˌlɑrk] n : alondra f

skylight [ˈskaɪˌlaɪt] n : claraboya f, tragaluz m

skyline [ˈskaɪˌlaɪn] n : horizonte m

skyrocket [ˈskaɪˌrɑkət] vi : dispararse

skyscraper [ˈskaɪˌskreɪpər] n : rascacielos m

slab [ˈslæb] n : losa f (de piedra), tabla f (de madera), pedazo m grueso (de pan, etc.)

slack¹ [ˈslæk] adj 1 CARELESS : descuidado, negligente 2 LOOSE : flojo 3 SLOW : de poco movimiento

slack² n 1 : parte f floja ⟨to take up the slack : tensar (una cuerda, etc.)⟩ 2 **slacks** npl : pantalones mpl

slacken [ˈslækən] vt : aflojar — vi : aflojarse

slacker [ˈslækər] n : vago m, -ga f; holgazán m, -zana f

slackness [ˈslæknəs] n 1 LOOSENESS : soltura f 2 LAXITY : laxitud f

slag [ˈslæg] n : escoria f

slain → slay

slake [ˈsleɪk] vt slaked; slaking : saciar (la sed), satisfacer (la curiosidad)

slam¹ [ˈslæm] v slammed; slamming vt 1 : cerrar de golpe ⟨he slammed the door : dio un portazo⟩ 2 : tirar o dejar caer de golpe ⟨he slammed down the book : dejó caer el libro de un golpe⟩ — vi 1 : cerrarse de golpe 2 **to slam into** : chocar contra

slam² n : golpe m, portazo m (de una puerta)

slam dunk n : clavada f, mate m, donqueo m

slander¹ [ˈslændər] vt : calumniar, difamar

slander² n : calumnia f, difamación f

slanderous [ˈslændərəs] adj ; difamatorio, calumnioso

slang [ˈslæŋ] n : argot m, jerga f

slant¹ [ˈslænt] vi : inclinarse, ladearse.— vt 1 SLOPE : inclinar 2 ANGLE : sesgar, orientar, dirigir ⟨a story slanted towards youth : un artículo dirigido a los jóvenes⟩

slant² *n* **1** INCLINE : inclinación *f* **2** PERSPECTIVE : perspectiva *f*, enfoque *m*

slap¹ ['slæp] *vt* **slapped; slapping 1** : bofetear, cachetear ⟨she slapped him in/across the face, she slapped his face : le dio una bofetada⟩ ⟨to slap someone on the back : darle una palmada a alguien en la espalda⟩ **2** : golpear (dícese de las olas, etc.) **3** : tirar (con fuerza) ⟨she slapped the book (down) on the desk : tiró el libro en el escritorio⟩ **4** : poner (rápidamente) ⟨he slapped some butter on the bread : le puso mantequilla al pan⟩ ⟨she slapped some paint on it : le dio una pasada rápida de pintura⟩ **5 to slap around** : darle palizas a **6 to slap together** : preparar de prisa **7 to slap with** : ponerle (una multa, etc.) a

slap² *n* **1** : bofetada *f*, cachetada *f*, palmada *f* **2 slap in the face** INSULT : bofetada *f*

slapdash ['slæp,dæʃ] *adj* : chapucero

slapstick ['slæp,stɪk] *n* : payasadas *fpl*, bufonadas *fpl*

slash¹ ['slæʃ] *vt* **1** GASH : cortar, hacer un tajo en **2** REDUCE : reducir, rebajar (precios)

slash² *n* **1** : tajo *m*, corte *m* **2 or forward slash** : diagonal *f*, barra *f* (oblicua)

slat ['slæt] *n* : tablilla *f*, listón *m*

slate ['sleɪt] *n* **1** : pizarra *f* ⟨a slate roof : un techo de pizarra⟩ **2** : lista *f* de candidatos (políticos)

slaughter¹ ['slɔtər] *vt* **1** BUTCHER : matar (animales) **2** MASSACRE : masacrar (personas)

slaughter² *n* **1** : matanza *f* (de animales) **2** MASSACRE : masacre *f*, carnicería *f*

slaughterhouse ['slɔtər,haʊs] *n* : matadero *m*

Slav ['slav, 'slæv] *n* : eslavo *m*, -va *f*

slave¹ ['sleɪv] *vi* **slaved; slaving** : trabajar como un burro

slave² *n* : esclavo *m*, -va *f*

slaver ['slævər, 'sleɪ-] *vi* : babear

slavery ['sleɪvəri] *n* : esclavitud *f*

Slavic ['slɑvɪk, 'slæ-] *adj* : eslavo

slavish ['sleɪvɪʃ] *adj* **1** SERVILE : servil **2** IMITATIVE : poco original

slay ['sleɪ] *vt* **slew** ['slu:]; **slain** ['sleɪn]; **slaying** : asesinar, matar

slayer ['sleɪər] *n* : asesino *m*, -na *f*

sleazy ['sli:zi] *adj* **sleazier; -est 1** SHODDY : chapucero, de mala calidad **2** DILAPIDATED : ruinoso **3** DISREPUTABLE : de mala fama

sled¹ ['slɛd] *v* **sledded; sledding** *vi* : ir en trineo — *vt* : transportar en trineo

sled² *n* : trineo *m*

sledge ['slɛdʒ] *n* **1** : trineo *m* (grande) **2** → sledgehammer

sledgehammer ['slɛdʒ,hæmər] *n* : almádena *f*, combo *m* Chile, Peru

sleek¹ ['sli:k] *vt* SLICK : alisar

sleek² *adj* : liso y brillante

sleep¹ ['sli:p] *vi* **slept** ['slɛpt]; **sleeping 1** : dormir **2 to sleep in** : levantarse tarde

3 to sleep together : acostarse, tener relaciones **4 to sleep with** : acostarse con

sleep² *n* **1** : sueño *m* **2** : legañas *fpl* (en los ojos) **3 to go to sleep** : dormirse

sleeper ['sli:pər] *n* **1** : durmiente *mf* ⟨to be a light sleeper : tener el sueño ligero⟩ **2 or sleeping car** : coche *m* cama, coche *m* dormitorio

sleepily ['sli:pəli] *adv* : de manera somnolienta

sleepiness ['sli:pinəs] *n* : somnolencia *f*

sleeping bag *n* : saco *m* de dormir

sleeping pill *n* : pastilla *f* para dormir

sleepless ['sli:pləs] *adj* : sin dormir, desvelado ⟨to have a sleepless night : pasar la noche en blanco⟩

sleepwalk ['sli:p,wɔk] *vi* : caminar dormido

sleepwalker ['sli:p,wɔkər] *n* : sonámbulo *m*, -la *f*

sleepwalking ['sli:p,wɔkɪŋ] *n* : sonambulismo *m*

sleepy ['sli:pi] *adj* **sleepier; -est 1** DROWSY : somnoliento, soñoliento ⟨to be sleepy : tener sueño⟩ **2** LETHARGIC : aletargado, letárgico

sleet¹ ['sli:t] *vi* **to be sleeting** : caer aguanieve

sleet² *n* : aguanieve *f*

sleeve ['sli:v] *n* : manga *f* (de una camisa, etc.)

sleeveless ['sli:vləs] *adj* : sin mangas

sleigh¹ ['sleɪ] *vi* : ir en trineo

sleigh² *n* : trineo *m* (tirado por caballos)

sleight of hand [,slaɪtəv'hænd] : prestidigitación *f*, juegos *mpl* de manos

slender ['slɛndər] *adj* **1** SLIM : esbelto, delgado **2** SCANTY : exiguo, escaso ⟨a slender hope : una esperanza lejana⟩

sleuth ['slu:θ] *n* : detective *mf*, sabueso *m*

slew → slay

slice¹ ['slaɪs] *vt* **sliced; slicing** : cortar

slice² *n* : rebanada *f*, tajada *f*, lonja *f* (de carne, etc.), rodaja *f* (de una verdura, fruta, etc.), trozo *m* (de pastel, etc.)

slicer ['slaɪsər] *n* : cortadora *f* (de fiambres, etc.), rebanadora *f* (de pan)

slick¹ ['slɪk] *vt* : alisar

slick² *adj* **1** SLIPPERY : resbaladizo, resbaloso **2** CRAFTY : astuto, taimado

slicker ['slɪkər] *n* : impermeable *m*

slide¹ ['slaɪd] *v* **slid** ['slɪd]; **sliding** ['slaɪdɪŋ] *vi* **1** SLIP : resbalar **2** GLIDE : deslizarse **3** DECLINE : bajar ⟨to let things slide : dejar pasar las cosas⟩ — *vt* : correr, deslizar

slide² *n* **1** SLIDING : deslizamiento *m* **2** SLIP : resbalón *m* **3** : tobogán *m* (para niños) **4** TRANSPARENCY : diapositiva *f* (fotográfica) **5** DECLINE : descenso *m*

slier, sliest → sly

slight¹ ['slaɪt] *vt* : desairar, despreciar

slight² *adj* **1** SLENDER : esbelto, delgado **2** FLIMSY : endeble **3** TRIFLING : leve, insignificante ⟨a slight pain : un leve dolor⟩ **4** SMALL : pequeño, ligero ⟨not in the slightest : en absoluto⟩

slight³ *n* SNUB : desaire *m*

slightly ['slaɪtli] *adv* : ligeramente, un poco

slim¹ ['slɪm] *v* **slimmed; slimming** : adelgazar

slim² *adj* **slimmer; slimmest** 1 SLENDER : esbelto, delgado 2 SCANTY : exiguo, escaso

slime ['slaɪm] *n* 1 : baba *f* (secretada por un animal) 2 MUD, SILT : fango *m*, cieno *m*

slimy ['slaɪmi] *adj* **slimier; -est** : viscoso

sling¹ ['slɪŋ] *v* **slung** ['slʌŋ]; **slinging** 1 THROW : lanzar, tirar 2 HANG : colgar

sling² *n* 1 : honda *f* (arma) 2 : cabestrillo *m* ⟨my arm is in a sling : llevo el brazo en cabestrillo⟩

slingshot ['slɪŋˌʃɑt] *n* : tiragomas *m*, resortera *f* Mex

slink ['slɪŋk] *vi* **slunk** ['slʌŋk]; **slinking** : caminar furtivamente

slip¹ ['slɪp] *v* **slipped; slipping** *vi* 1 STEAL : ir sigilosamente ⟨to slip away : escabullirse⟩ ⟨to slip out the door : escaparse por la puerta⟩ ⟨an error slipped through : se deslizó un error⟩ 2 SLIDE : resbalarse, deslizarse ⟨he slipped and fell : se resbaló y se cayó⟩ 3 FALL, LAPSE : caer ⟨she slipped into a coma : cayó en coma⟩ 4 WORSEN, DECLINE : empeorar, bajar ⟨I must be slipping : voy perdiendo facultades⟩ 5 to let slip : dejar escapar 6 to slip off *or* to slip out of TAKE OFF : quitarse (una prenda) 7 to slip on/into PUT ON : ponerse (una prenda) 8 to slip through one's fingers : escaparse de las manos 9 to slip up : meter la pata — *vt* 1 PUT : meter, poner 2 PASS : pasar ⟨she slipped me a note : me pasó una nota⟩ 3 ESCAPE : escaparse de 4 to slip one's mind : olvidársele a uno

slip² *n* 1 PIER : atracadero *m* 2 MISHAP : percance *m*, contratiempo *m* 3 MISTAKE : error *m*, desliz *m* ⟨a slip of the tongue : un lapsus⟩ 4 PETTICOAT : enagua *f* 5 : injerto *m*, esqueje *m* (de una planta) 6 RECEIPT, TICKET : recibo *m*, boleta *f*, ticket *m* 7 slip of paper : papelito *m* 8 to give someone the slip : dar esquinazo a alguien

slipknot ['slɪpˌnɑt] *n* : nudo *m* corredizo

slipper ['slɪpər] *n* : zapatilla *f*, pantufla *f*

slipperiness ['slɪpərinəs] *n* 1 : lo resbaloso, lo resbaladizo 2 CRAFTINESS : astucia *f*

slippery ['slɪpəri] *adj* **slipperier; -est** 1 : resbaloso, resbaladizo ⟨a slippery road : un camino resbaloso⟩ 2 TRICKY : artero, astuto, taimado 3 ELUSIVE : huidizo, escurridizo

slipshod ['slɪpˌʃɑd] *adj* : descuidado, chapucero

slipup *n* ERROR : patinazo *m*

slip up *vi* : equivocarse

slit¹ ['slɪt] *vt* **slit; slitting** : cortar, abrir por lo largo

slit² *n* 1 OPENING : abertura *f*, rendija *f* 2 CUT : corte *m*, raja *f*, tajo *m*

slither ['slɪðər] *vi* : deslizarse

sliver ['slɪvər] *n* : astilla *f*

slob ['slɑb] *n* : persona *f* desaliñada ⟨what a slob! : ¡qué cerdo!⟩

slobber¹ ['slɑbər] *vi* : babear

slobber² *n* : baba *f*

slog ['slɑg] *vi* : trabajar duro

slog² *n* : trabajo *m* largo y arduo

slogan ['sloˌgən] *n* : lema *m*, eslogan *m*

sloop ['slu:p] *n* : balandra *f*

slop¹ ['slɑp] *v* **slopped; slopping** *vt* : derramar — *vi* : derramarse

slop² *n* : bazofia *f*

slope¹ ['slo:p] *vi* **sloped; sloping** : inclinarse ⟨the road slopes upward : el camino sube (en pendiente)⟩

slope² *n* : inclinación *f*, pendiente *f*, declive *m*

sloppiness ['slɑpinəs] *n* : falta *f* de cuidado (en el trabajo, etc.), desaliño *m* (de aspecto)

sloppy ['slɑpi] *adj* **sloppier; -est** 1 : que chorrea ⟨a sloppy kiss : un beso baboso⟩ 2 : descuidado (en el trabajo, etc.), desaliñado (de aspecto)

slot ['slɑt] *n* 1 : ranura *f* 2 *or* **time slot** : espacio *m* (de un programa de televisión, etc.)

sloth ['slɔθ, 'slo:θ] *n* 1 LAZINESS : pereza *f* 2 : perezoso *m* (animal)

slot machine *n* : tragamonedas *mf*, tragaperras *mf* Spain

slotted spoon ['slɑtəd-] *n* : espumadera *f*

slouch¹ ['slaʊtʃ] *vi* : andar con los hombros caídos, repantigarse (en un sillón)

slouch² *n* 1 SLUMPING : mala postura *f* 2 BUNGLER, IDLER : haragán *m*, -gana *f*; inepto *m*, -ta *f* ⟨to be no slouch : no quedarse atrás⟩

slough¹ ['slʌf] *vt* : mudar de (piel)

slough² ['slu:, 'slaʊ] *n* SWAMP : ciénaga *f*

Slovak ['slo:ˌvɑk, -ˌvæk] *or* **Slovakian** [slo:'vɑkiən, -'væ-] *n* : eslovaco *m*, -ca *f* — **Slovak** *or* **Slovakian** *adj*

Slovene ['slo:ˌvi:n] *or* **Slovenian** [slo:-'vi:niən] *n* : esloveno *m*, -na *f* — **Slovene** *or* **Slovenian** *adj*

slovenliness ['slʌvənlinəs, 'slʌv-] *adj* : falta *f* de cuidado (en el trabajo, etc.), desaliño *m* (de aspecto)

slovenly ['slʌvənli, 'slʌv-] *adj* : descuidado (en el trabajo, etc.), desaliñado (de aspecto)

slow¹ ['slo:] *vt* : retrasar, reducir la marcha de — *vi* : ir más despacio

slow² *adv* : despacio, lentamente

slow³ *adj* 1 : lento ⟨a slow process : un proceso lento⟩ 2 : atrasado ⟨my watch is slow : mi reloj está atrasado, mi reloj se atrasa⟩ 3 SLUGGISH : lento, poco activo 4 STUPID : lento, torpe, corto de alcances

slowly ['slo:li] *adv* : lentamente, despacio

slow motion *n* : cámara *f* lenta ⟨in slow motion : a cámara lenta⟩

slowness ['slo:nəs] *n* : lentitud *f*, torpeza *f*

slow-witted ['slo:'wɪtəd] *adj* : limitado, lento, lerdo

sludge ['slʌdʒ] *n* : aguas *fpl* negras, aguas *fpl* residuales

slug¹ ['slʌg] *vt* **slugged; slugging** : pegarle un porrazo (a alguien)

slug² *n* **1** : babosa *f* (molusco) **2** BULLET : bala *f* **3** TOKEN : ficha *f* **4** BLOW : porrazo *m*, puñetazo *m*

sluggish ['slʌgɪʃ] *adj* : aletargado, lento

sluice¹ ['slu:s] *vt* **sluiced; sluicing** : lavar en agua corriente

sluice² *n* : canal *m*

slum ['slʌm] *n* : barriada *f*, barrio *m* bajo

slumber¹ ['slʌmbər] *vi* : dormir

slumber² *n* : sueño *m*

slump¹ ['slʌmp] *vi* **1** DECLINE, DROP : disminuir, bajar **2** SLOUCH : encorvarse, dejarse caer (en una silla, etc.)

slump² *n* : bajón *m*, declive *m* (económico)

slung → sling

slunk → slink

slur¹ ['slər] *vt* **slurred; slurring** : ligar (notas musicales), tragarse (las palabras)

slur² *n* **1** : ligado *m* (en música), mala pronunciación *f* (de las palabras) **2** ASPERSION : calumnia *f*, difamación *f*

slurp¹ ['slərp] *vi* : beber o comer haciendo ruido — *vt* : sorber ruidosamente

slurp² *n* : sorbo *m* (ruidoso)

slush ['slʌʃ] *n* : nieve *f* medio derretida

slut ['slʌt] *n offensive* : fulana *f*, ramera *f*

sly ['slaɪ] *adj* **slier** ['slaɪər], **sliest** ['slaɪəst] **1** CUNNING : astuto, taimado **2** UNDERHANDED : solapado — **slyly** *adv*

slyness ['slaɪnəs] *n* : astucia *f*

smack¹ ['smæk] *vi* **to smack of** : oler a, saber a — *vt* **1** KISS : besar, plantarle un beso (a alguien) **2** SLAP : pegarle una bofetada (a alguien) **3** **to smack one's lips** : relamerse

smack² *adv* : justo, exactamente ⟨smack in the face : en plena cara⟩

smack³ *n* **1** TASTE, TRACE : sabor *m*, indicio *m* **2** : chasquido *m* (de los labios) **3** SLAP : bofetada *f* **4** KISS : beso *m*

small ['smɔl] *adj* **1** : pequeño, chico ⟨a small house : una casa pequeña⟩ ⟨small change : monedas de poco valor⟩ **2** TRIVIAL : pequeño, insignificante

smallness ['smɔlnəs] *n* : pequeñez *f*

smallpox ['smɔl,pɑks] *n* : viruela *f*

small talk *n* **to make small talk** : hablar de cosas sin importancia

smart¹ ['smɑrt] *vi* **1** STING : escocer, picar, arder **2** HURT : dolerse, resentirse ⟨to smart under a rejection : dolerse ante un rechazo⟩

smart² *adj* **1** BRIGHT : listo, vivo, inteligente **2** STYLISH : elegante — **smartly** *adv*

smart³ *n* **1** PAIN : escozor *m*, dolor *m* **2** **smarts** *npl* : inteligencia *f*

smarten up ['smɑrtən,ʌp] *vt* : atildar, arreglar — *vi* : atildarse, arreglarse

smartness ['smɑrtnəs] *n* **1** INTELLIGENCE : inteligencia *f* **2** ELEGANCE : elegancia *f*

smash¹ ['smæʃ] *vt* **1** BREAK : romper, quebrar, hacer pedazos **2** WRECK : destrozar, arruinar **3** CRASH : estrellar, chocar — *vi* **1** SHATTER : hacerse pedazos, hacerse añicos **2** COLLIDE, CRASH : estrellarse, chocar ⟨to smash against/into something : chocar contra algo⟩

smash² *n* **1** BLOW : golpe *m* **2** COLLISION : choque *m* **3** BANG, CRASH : estrépito *m* **4** HIT, SUCCESS : exitazo *m*

smattering ['smætərɪŋ] *n* **1** : nociones *fpl* ⟨she has a smattering of programming : tiene nociones de programación⟩ **2** : un poco, unos cuantos ⟨a smattering of spectators : unos cuantos espectadores⟩

smear¹ ['smɪr] *vt* **1** DAUB : embadurnar, untar (mantequilla, etc.) **2** SMUDGE : emborronar **3** SLANDER : calumniar, difamar

smear² *n* **1** SMUDGE : mancha *f* **2** SLANDER : calumnia *f*

smell¹ ['smɛl] *v* **smelled** *or* **smelt** ['smɛlt]; **smelling** *vt* : oler, olfatear ⟨to smell danger : olfatear el peligro⟩ — *vi* : oler ⟨to smell good : oler bien⟩

smell² *n* **1** : olfato *m*, sentido *m* del olfato **2** ODOR : olor *m*

smelly ['smɛli] *adj* **smellier; -est** : maloliente

smelt¹ ['smɛlt] *vt* : fundir

smelt² *n*, *pl* **smelt** *or* **smelts** : eperlano *m* (pez)

smidgen ['smɪdʒən] *or* **smidge** ['smɪdʒ] *or* **smidgeon** ['smɪdʒən] *n* BIT : poquito *m*

smile¹ ['smaɪl] *vi* **smiled; smiling** : sonreír

smile² *n* : sonrisa *f*

smirk¹ ['smərk] *vi* : sonreír con suficiencia

smirk² *n* : sonrisa *f* satisfecha

smite ['smaɪt] *vt* **smote** ['smoːt]; **smitten** ['smɪtən] *or* **smote; smiting 1** STRIKE : golpear **2** AFFLICT : afligir

smith ['smɪθ] *n* : herrero *m*, -ra *f*

smithereens [ˌsmɪðə'riːnz] *npl* : añicos *mpl*

smithy ['smɪθi] *n*, *pl* **smithies** : herrería *f*

smock ['smɑk] *n* : bata *f*, blusón *m*

smog ['smɑg, 'smɔg] *n* : smog *m*

smoke¹ ['smoːk] *v* **smoked; smoking** *vi* **1** : echar humo, humear ⟨a smoking chimney : una chimenea que echa humo⟩ **2** : fumar ⟨I don't smoke : no fumo⟩ — *vt* : ahumar (carne, etc.)

smoke² *n* : humo *m*

smoked ['smoːkt] *adj* : ahumado

smoke detector [dɪ'tɛktər] *n* : detector *m* de humo

smoker ['smoːkər] *n* : fumador *m*, -dora *f*

smokescreen ['smoːkˌskriːn] *n* : cortina *f* de humo

smoke signal *n* : señal *f* de humo

smokestack ['smoːkˌstæk] *n* : chimenea *f*

smoky ['smoːki] *adj* **smokier; -est 1** SMOKING : humeante **2** : a humo ⟨a smoky flavor : un sabor a humo⟩ **3** : lleno de humo ⟨a smoky room : un cuarto lleno de humo⟩

smolder ['smoːldər] *vi* **1** : arder sin llama **2** : arder (en el corazón) ⟨his anger smoldered : su rabia ardía⟩

smooch ['smuːtʃ] *vi* : besuquearse

smooth¹ ['smuːð] *vt* **1** : alisar ⟨she smoothed (down/back) her hair : alisó el pelo⟩ ⟨he smoothed (out) the tablecloth : alisó los pliegues del mantel⟩ **2** SPREAD : extender ⟨smooth the cream on/onto over your skin : extienda la crema sobre la piel⟩ **3 to smooth away/over** RE-MOVE : allanar (dificultades, etc.) ⟨to smooth things over : limar asperezas⟩ **4 to smooth the way** for *or* **to smooth a path for** : allanarle el camino a

smooth² *adj* **1** : liso (dícese de una superficie) ⟨smooth skin : piel lisa⟩ **2** : suave (dícese de un movimiento) ⟨a smooth landing : un aterrizaje suave⟩ **3** : sin grumos ⟨a smooth sauce : una salsa sin grumos⟩ **4** : fluido ⟨smooth writing : escritura fluida⟩

smoothly ['smuːðli] *adv* **1** GENTLY, SOFTLY : suavemente **2** EASILY : con facilidad, sin problemas

smoothness ['smuːðnəs] *n* : suavidad *f*

smother ['smʌðər] *vt* **1** SUFFOCATE : ahogar, sofocar **2** COVER : cubrir **3** SUPPRESS : contener — *vi* : asfixiarse

smudge¹ ['smʌdʒ] *v* **smudged; smudging** *vt* : emborronar — *vi* : correrse

smudge² *n* : mancha *f*, borrón *m*

smug ['smʌg] *adj* **smugger; smuggest** : suficiente, pagado de sí mismo

smuggle ['smʌgəl] *vt* **-gled; -gling** : contrabandear, pasar de contrabando

smuggler ['smʌgələr] *n* : contrabandista *mf*

smuggling ['smʌgəlɪŋ] *n* : contrabando *m* (acto)

smugly ['smʌgli] *adv* : con suficiencia

smut ['smʌt] *n* **1** SOOT : tizne *m*, hollín *m* **2** OBSCENITY : obscenidad *f*, inmundicia *f*

smutty ['smʌti] *adj* **smuttier; -est 1** SOOTY : tiznado **2** OBSCENE : obsceno, indecente

snack ['snæk] *n* : refrigerio *m*, bocado *m*, tentempié *m* *fam* ⟨an afternoon snack : una merienda⟩

snack bar *n* : cafetería *f*

snag¹ ['snæg] *v* **snagged; snagging** *vt* : enganchar — *vi* : engancharse

snag² *n* : problema *m*, inconveniente *m*

snail ['sneɪl] *n* : caracol *m*

snake ['sneɪk] *n* : culebra *f*, serpiente *f*

snakebite ['sneɪk,baɪt] *n* : mordedura *f* de serpiente

snap¹ ['snæp] *v* **snapped; snapping** *vi* **1** BREAK : romperse, quebrarse (haciendo un chasquido) ⟨the branch snapped : la rama se rompió⟩ **2** : intentar morder (dícese de un perro, etc.) **3** : hablar con severidad ⟨he snapped at me! : ¡me gritó!⟩ **4** : moverse de un golpe ⟨the trap snapped shut : la trampa se cerró de golpe⟩ ⟨the branch snapped back : la rama se volvió de golpe⟩ ⟨the pieces snap together : las piezas se encajan⟩ **5 to snap out of** *fam* : salir de (la depresión, el ensueño, etc.) ⟨snap out of it! : ¡anímate!, ¡espabílate!⟩ **6 to snap to it** *fam* : moverse, apurarse — *vt* **1** BREAK : partir (en dos), quebrar **2** : hacer (algo) de un golpe ⟨she snapped it open : lo abrió de golpe⟩ **3** RETORT : decir bruscamente **4** CLICK : chasquear ⟨to snap one's fingers : chasquear los dedos⟩ **5 to snap up** : no dejar escapar

snap² *n* **1** CLICK, CRACK : chasquido *m* **2** FASTENER : broche *m* **3** CINCH : cosa *f* fácil ⟨it's a snap : es facilísimo⟩

snapdragon ['snæp,drægən] *n* : dragón *m* (flor)

snapper ['snæpər] → red snapper

snappy ['snæpi] *adj* **snappier; -est 1** FAST : rápido ⟨make it snappy! : ¡date prisa!⟩ **2** LIVELY : vivaz **3** CHILLY : frío **4** STYLISH : elegante

snapshot ['snæp,ʃɑt] *n* : instantánea *f*

snare¹ ['snær] *vt* **snared; snaring** : atrapar

snare² *n* : trampa *f*, red *f*

snare drum *n* : tambor *m* con bordón

snarl¹ ['snɑrl] *vi* **1** TANGLE : enmarañar, enredar **2** GROWL : gruñir

snarl² *n* **1** TANGLE : enredo *m*, maraña *f* **2** GROWL : gruñido *m*

snatch¹ ['snætʃ] *vt* : arrebatar

snatch² *n* : fragmento *m*

sneak¹ ['sniːk] *vi* : ir a hurtadillas ⟨to sneak in/out : entrar/salir a escondidas⟩ ⟨to sneak away : escabullirse⟩ — *vt* : hacer furtivamente ⟨to sneak a look : mirar con disimulo⟩ ⟨he sneaked a smoke : fumó un cigarrillo a escondidas⟩

sneak² *n* : soplón *m*, -plona *f*

sneaker ['sniːkərz] *npl* : tenis *m*, zapatilla *f* ⟨a pair of sneakers : un par de tenis/zapatillas⟩

sneaky ['sniːki] *adj* **sneakier; -est** : solapado

sneer¹ ['snɪr] *vi* : sonreír con desprecio

sneer² *n* : sonrisa *f* de desprecio

sneeze¹ ['sniːz] *vi* **sneezed; sneezing** : estornudar

sneeze² *n* : estornudo *m*

snicker¹ ['snɪkər] *vi* : reírse (disimuladamente)

snicker² *n* : risita *f*

snide ['snaɪd] *adj* : sarcástico

sniff¹ ['snɪf] *vi* **1** SMELL : oler, husmear (dícese de los animales) **2 to sniff at** : despreciar, desdeñar — *vt* **1** SMELL : oler **2 to sniff out** : olerse, husmear

sniff² *n* **1** SNIFFING : aspiración *f* por la nariz **2** SMELL : olor *m*

sniffle ['snɪfəl] *vi* **-fled; -fling** : respirar con la nariz congestionada

sniffles ['snɪfəlz] *npl* : resfriado *m*

snigger¹ ['snɪgər] → snicker¹

snigger² → snicker²

snip¹ ['snɪp] *vt* **snipped; snipping** : cortar (con tijeras)

snip² *n* : tijeretada *f*, recorte *m*

snipe¹ ['snaɪp] *vi* **sniped; sniping** : disparar

snipe² *n*, *pl* **snipes** *or* **snipe** : agachadiza *f*

sniper ['snaɪpər] *n* : francotirador *m*, -dora *f*

snippet ['snɪpət] *n* : fragmento *m* (de un texto, etc.)

snitch¹ ['snɪtʃ] *v* *fam* *vi* : cantar (a la policía, etc.) ⟨to snitch on someone : acusar/delatar a alguien⟩ — *vt* STEAL : robar

snitch² *n* *fam* : chivato *m*, -ta *f*

snivel ['snɪvəl] vi -veled or -velled; -veling or -velling 1 → snuffle 2 WHINE : lloriquear

snob ['snɑb] n : esnob mf, snob mf

snobbery ['snɑbəri] n, pl -beries : esnobismo m

snobbish ['snɑbɪʃ] adj : esnob, snob

snobbishness ['snɑbɪʃnəs] n : esnobismo m

snoop¹ ['snu:p] vi : husmear, curiosear

snoop² n : fisgón m, -gona f

snooty ['snu:ti] adj snootier; -est fam HAUGHTY : esnob, snob, altanero, altivo

snooze¹ ['snu:z] vi snoozed; snoozing : dormitar

snooze² n : siestecita f, siestita f

snore¹ ['snor] vi snored; snoring : roncar

snore² n : ronquido m

snorkel¹ ['snorkəl] vi : bucear con esnórquel

snorkel² n : esnórquel m, snorkel m, tubo m respiratorio/respirador

snort¹ ['snɔrt] vi : bufar, resoplar

snort² n : bufido m, resoplo m

snot ['snɑt] n : mocos mpl

snotty ['snɑti] adj snottier; -est 1 → snooty 2 : lleno de mocos

snout ['snaʊt] n : hocico m, morro m

snow¹ ['sno:] vi : nevar ⟨I'm snowed in : estoy aislado por la nieve⟩ 2 to be snowed under : estar inundado

snow² n : nieve f

snowball¹ ['sno:,bɔl] vi : aumentar, agravarse (rápidamente)

snowball² n : bola f de nieve

snowboard ['sno:,bord] n : snowboard m

snowboarding ['sno:,bordɪŋ] n : snowboard m (deporte)

snowcapped ['sno:,kæpt] adj : nevado

snowdrift ['sno:,drɪft] n : ventisquero m

snowdrop ['sno:,drɑp] n : campanilla f blanca

snowfall ['sno:,fɔl] n : nevada f

snowflake ['sno:,fleɪk] n : copo m de nieve

snowman ['sno:,mæn] n, pl -men [-mən, -,mɛn] : muñeco m de nieve

snowplow ['sno:,plaʊ] n : quitanieves m

snowshoe ['sno:,ʃu:] n : raqueta f (para nieve)

snowstorm ['sno:,stɔrm] n : tormenta f de nieve, ventisca f

snow-white adj : blanco como la nieve

snowy ['sno:i] adj snowier; -est : nevoso ⟨a snowy road : un camino nevado⟩

snub¹ ['snʌb] vt snubbed; snubbing : desairar

snub² n : desaire m

snub-nosed ['snʌb,no:zd] adj : de nariz respingada

snuff¹ ['snʌf] vt 1 : apagar (una vela) 2 : sorber (algo) por la nariz

snuff² n : rapé m

snuffle ['snʌfəl] vi -fled; -fling : respirar con la nariz congestionada

snug ['snʌg] adj snugger; snuggest 1 COMFORTABLE : cómodo 2 TIGHT : ajustado, ceñido ⟨snug pants : pantalones ajustados⟩

snuggle ['snʌgəl] vi -gled; -gling : acurrucarse ⟨to snuggle up to someone : arrimársele a alguien⟩

snugly ['snʌgli] adv 1 COMFORTABLY : cómodamente 2 : de manera ajustada ⟨the shirt fits snugly : la camisa queda ajustada⟩

so¹ ['so:] adv 1 (indicating a stated or suggested degree) : tan, tanto ⟨he'd never been so happy : nunca había estado tan contento⟩ ⟨she was so tired that she almost fell asleep : estaba tan cansada que casi se durmió⟩ ⟨would you be so kind as to help me? : ¿tendría la amabilidad de ayudarme? ⟨it's not so much a science as an art : no es tanto una ciencia como un arte⟩ ⟨all the more so because : tanto más cuanto que⟩ ⟨never more so than : nunca más que⟩ 2 VERY : tan, tanto ⟨it's so much fun : es tan divertido⟩ ⟨I'm so glad to meet you : me alegro tanto de conocerte⟩ ⟨he loves her so : la quiere tanto⟩ ⟨not so long ago : no hace mucho tiempo⟩ ⟨thank you so much : muchísimas gracias⟩ 3 ALSO : también ⟨so do I : yo también⟩ 4 THUS : así, de esta manera ⟨and so it began : y así empezó⟩ ⟨it so happened that . . . : resultó que . . .⟩ 5 (used for emphasis) fam ⟨it's so not fair : es totalmente injusto⟩ ⟨I so wanted to go : tenía tantas ganas de ir⟩ 6 CONSEQUENTLY : por lo tanto 7 and so forth/on : etcétera 8 so much for (indicating that something has ended) ⟨so much for that idea : hasta ahí llegó esa idea⟩ 9 so much so (that) : tanto es así que 10 without so much as : sin siquiera

so² adj : cierto, verdad ⟨it's not so : no es cierto, no es verdad⟩ ⟨is that so? : ¿ah, sí?⟩

so³ conj 1 THEREFORE : así que ⟨he didn't answer, so I called again : no contestó, así que lo llamé otra vez⟩ 2 or so that : para que, así que, de manera que ⟨move over so I can sit down : córrete para que pueda sentarme⟩ ⟨we left early so that we would arrive on time : salimos temprano para llegar a tiempo⟩ 3 so what? : ¿y qué?

so⁴ pron 1 (referring to something indicated or suggested) ⟨do you think so? : ¿tú crees?⟩ ⟨so it would seem : eso/así parece⟩ ⟨I told her so : se lo dije⟩ ⟨he's ready, or he says : según dice, está listo⟩ ⟨do it like so : hazlo así⟩ ⟨so be it : así sea⟩ ⟨if so : si es así⟩ ⟨I'm afraid so : me temo que sí⟩ 2 or so : más o menos ⟨a week or so : una semana, más o menos⟩

soak¹ ['so:k] vi : estar en remojo — vt 1 : poner en remojo 2 DRENCH : empapar 3 to soak up ABSORB : absorber

soak² n : remojo m

so-and-so n : fulano m, -na f

soap¹ ['so:p] vt : enjabonar

soap² n 1 : jabón m 2 → soap opera

soap opera n : culebrón m, telenovela f

soapsuds ['so:p,sʌdz] → suds

soapy ['so:pi] *adj* **soapier; -est** : jabonoso ⟨a soapy taste : un gusto a jabón⟩ ⟨a soapy texture : una textura de jabón⟩

soar ['sor] *vi* **1** FLY : volar **2** RISE : remontar el vuelo (dícese de las aves) ⟨her hopes soared : su esperanza renació⟩ ⟨prices are soaring : los precios están subiendo vertiginosamente⟩

sob[1] ['sab] *vi* **sobbed; sobbing** : sollozar

sob[2] *n* : sollozo *m*

sober[1] ['so:bər] *adj* **1** : sobrio ⟨he's not sober enough to drive : está demasiado borracho para manejar⟩ **2** SERIOUS : serio

sober[2] *vi* **1** SADDEN : entristecer **2 to sober up** : pasársele la borrachera

soberly ['so:bərli] *adv* **1** : sobriamente **2** SERIOUSLY : seriamente

sobriety [sə'braɪəti, so-] *n* **1** : sobriedad *f* ⟨sobriety test : prueba de alcoholemia⟩ **2** SERIOUSNESS : seriedad *f*

so-called ['so:'kɔld] *adj* : supuesto, presunto ⟨the so-called experts : los expertos, así llamados⟩

soccer ['sakər] *n* : futbol *m*, fútbol *m*

sociability [,so:ʃə'bɪləti] *n* : sociabilidad *f*

sociable ['so:ʃəbəl] *adj* : sociable

social[1] ['so:ʃəl] *adj* : social — **socially** *adv*

social[2] *n* : reunión *f* social

socialism ['so:ʃə,lɪzəm] *n* : socialismo *m*

socialist[1] ['so:ʃəlɪst] *adj* : socialista

socialist[2] *n* : socialista *mf*

socialize ['so:ʃə,laɪz] *v* **-ized; -izing** *vt* **1** NATIONALIZE : nacionalizar **2** : socializar (en psicología) — *vi* : alternar, circular ⟨to socialize with friends : alternar con amigos⟩

social security *n* : seguridad *f* social

social work *n* : asistencia *f* social

social worker *n* : asistente *m*, -ta *f* social

society [sə'saɪəti] *n*, *pl* **-eties 1** COMPANIONSHIP : compañía *f* **2** : sociedad *f* ⟨a democratic society : una sociedad democrática⟩ ⟨high society : alta sociedad⟩ **3** ASSOCIATION : sociedad *f*, asociación *f*

socioeconomic [,so:sio,i:kə'namɪk, -,ekə-] *adj* : socioeconómico

sociological [,so:siə'ladʒɪkəl] *adj* : sociológico

sociologist [,so:si'alədʒɪst] *n* : sociólogo *m*, -ga *f*

sociology [,so:si'alədʒi] *n* : sociología *f*

sock[1] ['sak] *vt* : pegar, golpear, darle un puñetazo a

sock[2] *n* **1** *pl* **socks** *or* **sox** ['saks] : calcetín *m*, media *f* ⟨shoes and socks : zapatos y calcetines⟩ **2** *pl* **socks** ['saks] PUNCH : puñetazo *m*

socket ['sakət] *n* **1** *or* **electric socket** : enchufe *m*, toma *f* de corriente **2** : glena *f* (de una articulación) ⟨shoulder socket : glena del hombro⟩ **3** **eye socket** : órbita *f*, cuenca *f*

sod[1] ['sad] *vt* **sodded; sodding** : cubrir de césped

sod[2] *n* TURF : césped *m*, tepe *m*

soda ['so:də] *n* **1** *or* **soda water** : soda *f* **2** *or* **soda pop** : gaseosa *f*; refresco *m*; fresco *m*; soda *f* CA, Car **3** *or* **ice-cream soda** : refresco *m* con helado

sodden ['sadən] *adj* SOGGY : empapado

sodium ['so:diəm] *n* : sodio *m*

sodium bicarbonate *n* : bicarbonato *m* de soda

sodium chloride → salt

sofa ['so:fə] *n* : sofá *m*

soft ['sɔft] *adj* **1** : blando ⟨a soft pillow : una almohada blanda⟩ **2** SMOOTH : suave (dícese de las texturas, de los sonidos, etc.) **3** NONALCOHOLIC : no alcohólico ⟨a soft drink : un refresco⟩

softball ['sɔft,bɔl] *n* : softbol *m*

soft-boiled ['sɔft'bɔɪld] *adj* : pasado por agua

soften ['sɔfən] *vt* : ablandar (algo sólido), suavizar (la piel, un golpe, etc.), amortiguar (un impacto) — *vi* : ablandarse, suavizarse

softener ['sɔfənər] *n* : suavizante *m*

softly ['sɔftli] *adv* : suavemente ⟨she spoke softly : habló en voz baja⟩

softness ['sɔftnəs] *n* **1** : blandura *f*, lo blando (de una almohada, de la mantequilla, etc.) **2** SMOOTHNESS : suavidad *f*

soft-spoken ['sɔft'spo:kən] *adj* : de voz suave

software ['sɔft,wær] *n* : software *m*

soggy ['sagi] *adj* **soggier; -est** : empapado

soil[1] ['sɔɪl] *vt* : ensuciar — *vi* : ensuciarse

soil[2] *n* **1** DIRTINESS : suciedad *f* **2** DIRT, EARTH : suelo *m*, tierra *f* **3** COUNTRY : patria *f* ⟨her native soil : su tierra natal⟩

sojourn[1] ['so:,dʒərn, so:'dʒərn] *vi* : pasar una temporada

sojourn[2] *n* : estadía *f*, estancia *f*, permanencia *f*

sol ['so:l] *n* : sol *m* (en el canto)

solace ['saləs] *n* : consuelo *m*

solar ['so:lər] *adj* : solar ⟨the solar system : el sistema solar⟩ ⟨solar energy/power : energía solar⟩

sold → sell

solder[1] ['sadər, 'sɔ-] *vt* : soldar

solder[2] *n* : soldadura *f*

soldier[1] ['so:ldʒər] *vi* : servir como soldado

soldier[2] *n* : soldado *mf*

sole[1] ['so:l] *adj* : único

sole[2] *n* **1** : suela *f* (de un zapato) **2** : lenguado *m* (pez)

solely ['so:li] *adv* : únicamente, sólo

solemn ['saləm] *adj* : solemne, serio — **solemnly** *adv*

solemnity [sə'lɛmnəti] *n*, *pl* **-ties** : solemnidad *f*

sol-fa [,so:l'fa] *n* : solfeo *m*

solicit [sə'lɪsət] *vt* : solicitar

solicitous [sə'lɪsətəs] *adj* : solícito

solicitude [sə'lɪsə,tu:d, -,tju:d] *n* : solicitud *f*

solid[1] ['saləd] *adj* **1** : macizo ⟨a solid rubber ball : una bola maciza de caucho⟩ **2** CUBIC : tridimensional **3** COMPACT : compacto, denso **4** STURDY : sólido **5** CONTINUOUS : seguido, continuo ⟨two solid hours : dos horas seguidas⟩ ⟨a solid line : una línea continua⟩ **6** UNANIMOUS : unánime **7** DEPENDABLE : serio, fiable

8 PURE : macizo, puro ⟨solid gold : oro macizo⟩
solid² n : sólido m
solidarity [ˌsɑlə'dærəti] n : solidaridad f
solidify [sə'lɪdəˌfaɪ] v -fied; -fying vt : solidificar — vi : solidificarse
solidity [sə'lɪdəti] n, pl -ties : solidez f
solidly ['sɑlədli] adv 1 : sólidamente 2 UNANIMOUSLY : unánimemente
soliloquy [sə'lɪləkwi] n, pl -quies : soliloquio m
solitaire ['sɑləˌtɛr] n : solitario m
solitary ['sɑləˌtɛri] adj 1 ALONE : solitario 2 SECLUDED : apartado, retirado 3 SINGLE : solo
solitude ['sɑləˌtuːd, -ˌtjuːd] n : soledad f
solo¹ ['soʊˌloː] vi : volar en solitario (dícese de un piloto)
solo² adv & adj : en solitario, a solas
solo³ n, pl solos : solo m
soloist ['soʊloɪst] n : solista mf
solstice ['sɑlstəs] n : solsticio m
soluble ['sɑljəbəl] adj : soluble
solution [sə'luːʃən] n : solución f
solve ['sɑlv] vt solved; solving : resolver, solucionar
solvency ['sɑlvəntsi] n : solvencia f
solvent ['sɑlvənt] n : solvente m
somber ['sɑmbər] adj 1 DARK : sombrío, oscuro ⟨somber colors : colores oscuros⟩ 2 GRAVE : sombrío, serio 3 MELANCHOLY : sombrío, lúgubre
sombrero [səm'brɛrˌoː] n, pl -ros : sombrero m (mexicano)
some¹ adv 1 : unos, unas ⟨some 80 people came, 80-some people came : unas 80 personas vinieron⟩ 2 : un poco ⟨he helped me some fam : me ayudó un poco⟩ ⟨I need to work on it some more : necesito pulirlo un poco más⟩
some² [ˈsʌm] adj 1 : un, algún ⟨some lady stopped me : una mujer me detuvo⟩ ⟨some distant galaxy : alguna galaxia lejana⟩ ⟨there must be some mistake : debe de haber algún error⟩ 2 : algo de, un poco de ⟨he drank some water : tomó (un poco de) agua⟩ 3 : unos ⟨do you want some apples? : ¿quieres unas manzanas?⟩ ⟨some years ago : hace varios años⟩ 4 fam (expressing approval) ⟨that was some game! : ¡vaya partido!⟩ 5 fam (expressing disapproval) ⟨you've got some nerve! : ¡qué cara tienes!⟩ ⟨some friend he is! : ¡qué clase de amigo!⟩
some³ pron 1 : algunos ⟨some went, others stayed : algunos se fueron, otros se quedaron⟩ ⟨some of my friends : algunos de mis amigos⟩ ⟨some of the movies : algunas de las películas⟩ 2 : un poco, algo ⟨there's some left : queda un poco⟩ ⟨some of the cake : parte del pastel⟩ ⟨I have gum; do you want some? : tengo chicle, ¿quieres?⟩
somebody ['sʌmbədi, -ˌbɑdi] pron : alguien
someday ['sʌmˌdeɪ] adv : algún día
somehow ['sʌmˌhaʊ] adv 1 : de alguna manera, de algún modo ⟨I'll do it somehow : lo haré de alguna manera⟩ 2 : por

alguna razón ⟨somehow I don't trust her : por alguna razón no me fío de ella⟩
someone ['sʌmˌwʌn] pron : alguien
someplace ['sʌmˌpleɪs] → somewhere
somersault¹ ['sʌmərˌsɔlt] vi : dar volteretas, dar un salto mortal
somersault² n : voltereta f, salto m mortal
something ['sʌmθɪn] pron : algo ⟨I want something else : quiero otra cosa⟩ ⟨she's writing a novel or something : está escribiendo una novela o no sé qué⟩
sometime ['sʌmˌtaɪm] adv : algún día, en algún momento ⟨sometime next month : durante el mes que viene⟩
sometimes ['sʌmˌtaɪmz] adv : a veces, algunas veces, de vez en cuando
somewhat ['sʌmˌhwʌt, -ˌhwɑt] adv : algo, un tanto
somewhere ['sʌmˌhwɛr] adv 1 (indicating location) : en algún lugar ⟨it must be somewhere else : estará en otra parte⟩ 2 (indicating destination) : a algún lugar ⟨she went somewhere else : fue a otra parte⟩ 3 APPROXIMATELY : alrededor de ⟨somewhere around a thousand dollars : alrededor de mil dólares⟩ ⟨he's somewhere in his thirties : tiene unos treinta años, tiene treinta y tantos/pico⟩
son ['sʌn] n : hijo m
sonar ['soʊˌnɑr] n : sonar m
sonata [sə'nɑtə] n : sonata f
song ['sɔn] n : canción f, canto m (de un pájaro)
songbird ['sɔnˌbərd] n : pájaro m cantor
songbook ['sɔnˌbʊk] n : cancionero m
songwriter ['sɔnˌraɪtər] n : compositor m, -tora f
sonic ['sɑnɪk] adj 1 : sónico 2 sonic boom : estampido m sónico
son-in-law ['sʌnɪnˌlɔ] n, pl sons-in-law : yerno m, hijo m político
sonnet ['sɑnət] n : soneto m
son of a bitch n, pl sons of bitches sometimes offensive : hijo m de puta sometimes offensive
sonorous ['sɑnərəs, sə'norəs] adj : sonoro
soon ['suːn] adv 1 : pronto, dentro de poco ⟨he'll arrive soon : llegará pronto⟩ 2 QUICKLY : pronto ⟨as soon as possible : lo más pronto posible⟩ ⟨the sooner the better : cuanto antes mejor⟩ 3 : de buena gana ⟨I'd sooner walk : prefiero caminar⟩
soot ['sʊt, 'suːt, 'sʌt] n : hollín m, tizne m
soothe ['suːð] vt soothed; soothing 1 CALM : calmar, tranquilizar 2 RELIEVE : aliviar
soothsayer ['suːθˌseɪər] n : adivino m, -na f
sooty ['sʊti, 'suː-, 'sʌ-] adj sootier; -est : cubierto de hollín, tiznado
sop¹ ['sɑp] vt sopped; sopping 1 DIP : mojar 2 SOAK : empapar 3 to sop up : rebañar, absorber
sop² n 1 CONCESSION : concesión f 2 BRIBE : soborno m
sophisticated [sə'fɪstəˌkeɪtəd] adj 1 : sofisticado 2 COMPLEX : complejo
sophistication [səˌfɪstə'keɪʃən] n 1 COMPLEXITY : complejidad f 2 : sofisticación f

sophomore ['saf,mor, 'safə,mor] *n* : estudiante *mf* de segundo año

sophistry ['safəstri] *n* : sofistería *f*

soporific [,sapə'rıfık, ,so:-] *adj* : soporífero

soprano [sə'præ,no:] *n, pl* **-nos** : soprano *mf*

sorbet [,sor'beı] *n* : sorbete *m*

sorcerer ['sorsərər] *n* : hechicero *m*, brujo *m*, mago *m*

sorceress ['sorsərəs] *n* : hechicera *f*, bruja *f*, maga *f*

sorcery ['sorsəri] *n* : hechicería *f*, brujería *f*

sordid ['sordıd] *adj* : sórdido

sore[1] ['sor] *adj* **sorer; sorest** **1** PAINFUL : dolorido, doloroso ⟨I have a sore throat : me duele la garganta⟩ **2** ACUTE, SEVERE : extremo, grande ⟨in sore straits : en grandes apuros⟩ **3** ANGRY : enojado, enfadado

sore[2] *n* : llaga *f*

sorely ['sorli] *adv* : muchísimo ⟨it was sorely needed : se necesitaba urgentemente⟩ ⟨she was sorely missed : la echaban mucho de menos⟩

soreness ['sornəs] *n* : dolor *m*

sorghum ['sorgəm] *n* : sorgo *m*

sorority [sə'rorəti] *n, pl* **-ties** : hermandad *f* (de estudiantes femeninas)

sorrel ['sorəl] *n* **1** : alazán *m* (color o animal) **2** : acedera *f* (hierba)

sorrow ['sar,o:] *n* : pesar *m*, dolor *m*, pena *f*

sorrowful ['sarəfəl] *adj* : triste, afligido, apenado

sorrowfully ['sarəfəli] *adv* : con tristeza

sorry ['sari] *adj* **sorrier; -est** **1** PITIFUL : lastimero, lastimoso ⟨to be a sorry sight : tener un aspecto lamentable/horrible⟩ **2 to be sorry** : sentir, lamentar ⟨I'm sorry : lo siento⟩ ⟨I'm sorry to have to tell you that . . . : siento tener que decirte que . . .⟩ ⟨I'm sorry, but I disagree : lo siento, pero no estoy de acuerdo⟩ ⟨I'm sorry to disturb you : siento molestarlo⟩ **3 to feel sorry for** : compadecer ⟨I feel sorry for him : me da pena⟩ ⟨to feel sorry for oneself : lamentarse de su suerte⟩

sort[1] ['sort] *vt* **1** : dividir en grupos **2** CLASSIFY : clasificar **3 to sort out** ORGANIZE : poner en orden **4 to sort out** RESOLVE : resolver

sort[2] *n* **1** KIND : tipo *m*, clase *f* ⟨a sort of writer : una especie de escritor⟩ ⟨all sorts of : todo tipo de⟩ **2** NATURE : índole *f* **3 of the sort** ⟨I said nothing of the sort : no dije nada semejante⟩ **4 of sorts** *or* **a sort** ⟨he's a poet of sorts : es poeta, si se le puede llamar así⟩ **5 out of sorts** : de mal humor **6 sort of** : más o menos **7 sort of a** : una especie de

sortie ['sor,ti:, sor'ti:] *n* : salida *f*

SOS [,ɛs,o:'ɛs] *n* : SOS *m*

so–so ['so:'so:] *adj & adv* : así así, de modo regular

soufflé [su:'fleı] *n* : suflé *m*

sought → **seek**

soul ['so:l] *n* **1** SPIRIT : alma *f* **2** ESSENCE : esencia *f* **3** PERSON : persona *f*, alma *f*

soulful ['so:lfəl] *adj* : conmovedor, lleno de emoción

sound[1] ['saʊnd] *vt* **1** : sondar (en navegación) **2** *or* **to sound out** PROBE : sondear **3** : hacer sonar, tocar (una trompeta, etc.) — *vi* **1** : sonar ⟨the alarm sounded : la alarma sonó⟩ **2** SEEM : parecer

sound[2] *adj* **1** HEALTHY : sano ⟨safe and sound : sano y salvo⟩ ⟨of sound mind and body : en pleno uso de sus facultades⟩ **2** FIRM, SOLID : sólido **3** SENSIBLE : lógico, sensato **4** DEEP : profundo ⟨a sound sleep : un sueño profundo⟩

sound[3] *adv* : profundamente ⟨sound asleep : profundamente dormido⟩

sound[4] *n* **1** : sonido *m* ⟨the speed of sound : la velocidad del sonido⟩ **2** NOISE : sonido *m*, ruido *m* ⟨I heard a sound : oí un sonido⟩ **3** CHANNEL : brazo *m* de mar, canal *m* (ancho)

soundless ['saʊndləs] *adj* : sordo

soundlessly ['saʊndləsli] *adv* : silenciosamente

soundly ['saʊndli] *adv* **1** SOLIDLY : sólidamente **2** SENSIBLY : lógicamente, sensatamente **3** DEEPLY : profundamente ⟨sleeping soundly : durmiendo profundamente⟩

soundness ['saʊndnəs] *n* **1** SOLIDITY : solidez *f* **2** SENSIBLENESS : sensatez *f*, solidez *f*

soundproof ['saʊnd,pru:f] *adj* : insonorizado

sound system *n* : equipo *m* de sonido

soundtrack ['saʊnd,træk] *n* : banda *f* sonora

sound wave *n* : onda *f* sonora

soup ['su:p] *n* : sopa *f*

sour[1] ['saʊər] *vi* : agriarse, cortarse (dícese de la leche) — *vt* : agriar, cortar (leche)

sour[2] *adj* **1** ACID : agrio, ácido (dícese de la fruta, etc.), cortado (dícese de la leche) **2** DISAGREEABLE : desagradable, agrio

source ['sors] *n* : fuente *f*, origen *m*, nacimiento *m* (de un río)

sourness ['saʊərnəs] *n* : acidez *f*

soursop ['saʊər,sap] *n* : guanábana *f*

south[1] ['saʊθ] *adv* : al sur, hacia el sur ⟨the window looks south : la ventana mira al sur⟩ ⟨she continued south : continuó hacia el sur⟩

south[2] *adj* : sur, del sur ⟨the south entrance : la entrada sur⟩ ⟨South America : Sudamérica, América del Sur⟩

south[3] *n* : sur *m*

South African *n* : sudafricano *m*, -na *f* — **South African** *adj*

South American[1] *adj* : sudamericano, suramericano

South American[2] *n* : sudamericano *m*, -na *f*; suramericano *m*, -na *f*

southbound ['saʊθ,baʊnd] *adj* : con rumbo al sur

southeast[1] [saʊ'θi:st] *adj* : sureste, sudeste, del sureste

southeast[2] *n* : sureste *m*, sudeste *m*

southeasterly [sau̇ˈθiːstərli] *adv & adj* **1** : del sureste (dícese del viento) **2** : hacia el sureste

southeastern [sau̇ˈθiːstərn] *adj* → **southeast¹**

southerly [ˈsʌðərli] *adv & adj* : del sur

southern [ˈsʌðərn] *adj* : sur, sureño, meridional, austral ⟨a southern city : una ciudad del sur del país, una ciudad meridional⟩ ⟨the southern side : el lado sur⟩

Southerner [ˈsʌðərnər] *n* : sureño *m*, -ña *f*

South Pole : Polo *m* Sur

southward [ˈsau̇θwərd] *or* **southwards** [-wərdz] *adv & adj* : hacia el sur

southwest¹ [sau̇θˈwest, *as a nautical term often* sau̇ˈwest] *adj* : suroeste, sudoeste, del suroeste

southwest² *n* : suroeste *m*, sudoeste *m*

southwesterly [sau̇θˈwestərli] *adv & adj* **1** : del suroeste (dícese del viento) **2** : hacia el suroeste

southwestern [sau̇θˈwestərn] *adj* → **southwest¹**

souvenir [ˌsuːvəˈnɪr, ˈsuːvəˌ-] *n* : recuerdo *m*, souvenir *m*

sovereign¹ [ˈsavərən] *adj* : soberano

sovereign² *n* **1** : soberano *m*, -na *f* (monarca) **2** : soberano *m* (moneda)

sovereignty [ˈsavərənti] *n*, *pl* **-ties** : soberanía *f*

Soviet [ˈsoːviˌɛt, ˈsa-, -viət] *adj* : soviético

sow¹ [ˈsoː] *vt* **sowed**; **sown** [ˈsoːn] *or* **sowed**; **sowing** **1** PLANT : sembrar **2** SCATTER : esparcir

sow² [ˈsau̇] *n* : cerda *f*

sox → **sock**

soy [ˈsɔɪ] *n* : soya *f*, soja *f*

soybean [ˈsɔɪˌbiːn] *n* : soya *f*, soja *f*

spa [ˈspɑ] *n* : balneario *m*

space¹ [ˈspeɪs] *vt* **spaced**; **spacing** : espaciar

space² *n* **1** PERIOD : espacio *m*, lapso *m*, período *m* **2** ROOM : espacio *m*, sitio *m*, lugar *m* ⟨is there space for me? : ¿hay sitio para mí?⟩ **3** : espacio *m* ⟨blank space : espacio en blanco⟩ **4** : espacio *m* (en física) **5** PLACE : plaza *f*, sitio *m* ⟨to reserve space : reservar plazas⟩ ⟨parking space : sitio para estacionarse⟩

spacecraft [ˈspeɪsˌkræft] *n* : nave *f* espacial

spaceflight [ˈspeɪsˌflaɪt] *n* : vuelo *m* espacial

spaceman [ˈspeɪsmən, -ˌmæn] *n*, *pl* **-men** [-mən, -ˌmɛn] : astronauta *m*, cosmonauta *m*

spaceship [ˈspeɪsˌʃɪp] *n* : nave *f* espacial

space shuttle *n* : transbordador *m* espacial

space station *n* : estación *f* espacial

space suit *n* : traje *m* espacial

spacious [ˈspeɪʃəs] *adj* : espacioso, amplio

spade¹ [ˈspeɪd] *v* **spaded**; **spading** *vt* : palear — *vi* : usar una pala

spade² *n* **1** SHOVEL : pala *f* **2** : pica *f* (naipe)

spaghetti [spəˈgɛti] *n* : espagueti *m*, espaguetis *mpl*, spaghetti *mpl*

spam¹ [ˈspæm] *vt* **spammed**; **spamming** : enviarle spam a

spam² *n* : spam *m*, correo *m* electrónico no solicitado

Spam *trademark* se usa para un tipo de carne enlatada

span¹ [ˈspæn] *vt* **spanned**; **spanning** : abarcar (un período de tiempo), extenderse sobre (un espacio)

span² *n* **1** : lapso *m*, espacio *m* (de tiempo) ⟨life span : duración de la vida⟩ **2** : luz *f* (entre dos soportes)

spangle [ˈspæŋgəl] *n* : lentejuela *f*

Spaniard [ˈspænjərd] *n* : español *m*, -ñola *f*

spaniel [ˈspænjəl] *n* : spaniel *m*

Spanish¹ [ˈspænɪʃ] *adj* : español

Spanish² *n* **1** : español *m* (idioma) **2 the Spanish** (*used with a plural verb*) : los españoles

spank [ˈspæŋk] *vt* : darle nalgadas (a alguien)

spar¹ [ˈspɑr] *vi* **sparred**; **sparring** : entrenarse (en boxeo)

spar² *n* : palo *m*, verga *f* (de un barco)

spare¹ [ˈspær] *vt* **spared**; **sparing** **1** : perdonar ⟨to spare someone's life : perdonarle la vida a alguien⟩ ⟨to spare someone's feelings : no herir los sentimientos de alguien⟩ ⟨the fire spared their house : su casa se salvó del fuego⟩ **2** SAVE : ahorrar, evitar ⟨he spared us the trouble/embarrassment : nos ahorró la molestia/vergüenza⟩ ⟨spare me the details : ahórrate los detalles⟩ ⟨she was spared (from) punishment : se libró del castigo⟩ **3** : prescindir de ⟨I can't spare her : no puedo prescindir de ella⟩ ⟨I can't spare the time : no me da el tiempo⟩ ⟨can you spare a dollar? : ¿me das un dólar?⟩ ⟨can you spare a minute? : ¿tienes un momento?⟩ **4** STINT : escatimar ⟨they spared no expense : no repararon en gastos⟩ **5 to spare** : de sobra

spare² *adj* **sparer**; **sparest** **1** : de repuesto, de recambio ⟨spare tire : llanta de repuesto⟩ **2** EXCESS, EXTRA : de más, de sobra, libre ⟨spare time : tiempo libre⟩ ⟨spare room : cuarto de huéspedes⟩ **3** LEAN : delgado

spare³ *n or* **spare part** : repuesto *m*, recambio *m*

sparing [ˈspærɪŋ] *adj* : parco, económico — **sparingly** *adv*

spark¹ [ˈspɑrk] *vi* : chispear, echar chispas — *vt* PROVOKE : despertar, provocar ⟨to spark interest : despertar interés⟩

spark² *n* **1** : chispa *f* ⟨to throw off sparks : echar chispas⟩ **2** GLIMMER, TRACE : destello *m*, pizca *f*

sparkle¹ [ˈspɑrkəl] *vi* **-kled**; **-kling** **1** FLASH, SHINE : destellar, centellear, brillar **2** : estar muy animado (dícese de una conversación, etc.)

sparkle² *n* : destello *m*, centelleo *m*

sparkler [ˈspɑrklər] *n* : luz *f* de bengala

spark plug *n* : bujía *f*

sparrow [ˈspæroː] *n* : gorrión *m*

sparse [ˈspɑrs] *adj* **sparser**; **sparsest** : escaso — **sparsely** *adv*

spasm ['spæzəm] *n* **1** : espasmo *m* (muscular) **2** BURST, FIT : arrebato *m*

spasmodic [spæz'mɑdɪk] *adj* **1** : espasmódico **2** SPORADIC : irregular, esporádico — **spasmodically** [-dɪkli] *adv*

spastic ['spæstɪk] *adj* : espástico

spat¹ → **spit¹**

spat² ['spæt] *n* : discusión *f*, disputa *f*, pelea *f*

spate ['speɪt] *n* : avalancha *f*, torrente *m*

spatial ['speɪʃəl] *adj* : espacial

spatter¹ ['spætər] *v* : salpicar

spatter² *n* : salpicadura *f*

spatula ['spæʧələ] *n* : espátula *f*, paleta *f* (para servir)

spawn¹ ['spɔn] *vi* : desovar — *vt* GENERATE : generar, producir

spawn² *n* : hueva *f*

spay ['speɪ] *vt* : esterilizar (una perra, etc.)

speak ['spi:k] *v* **spoke** ['spo:k]; **spoken** ['spo:kən]; **speaking** *vi* **1** TALK : hablar ⟨to speak to/with someone : hablar con alguien⟩ ⟨who's speaking? : ¿de parte de quien?⟩ ⟨so to speak : por así decirlo⟩ ⟨generally speaking : por lo general, generalmente⟩ ⟨they're not speaking (to each other) : no se hablan⟩ ⟨she spoke at the conference : habló en el congreso⟩ ⟨she spoke well of you : habló bien de ti⟩ **2 to be spoken for** : estar reservado (dícese de un asiento, etc.), estar comprometido (dícese de una persona) **3 to speak for** : hablar en nombre de ⟨speak for yourself! : ¡habla por ti mismo!⟩ **4 to speak of** SIGNIFICANT : significante, que merece comentario ⟨there's been no progress to speak of : no han avanzado nada⟩ **5 to speak of** MENTION : mencionar ⟨(and) speaking of which . . . : a propósito . . .⟩ **6 to speak out** : hablar claramente **7 to speak out against** : denunciar **8 to speak up** : hablar en voz alta **9 to speak up for** : defender — *vt* **1** SAY : decir ⟨she spoke her mind : habló con franqueza⟩ **2** : hablar (un idioma)

speaker ['spi:kər] *n* **1** : hablante *mf* ⟨a native speaker : un hablante nativo⟩ **2** : orador *m*, -dora *f* ⟨the keynote speaker : el orador principal⟩ **3** LOUDSPEAKER : altavoz *m*, altoparlante *m*

spear¹ ['spɪr] *vt* : atravesar con una lanza

spear² *n* : lanza *f*

spearhead¹ ['spɪr,hɛd] *vt* : encabezar

spearhead² *n* : punta *f* de lanza

spearmint ['spɪrmɪnt] *n* : menta *f* verde

special ['spɛʃəl] *adj* : especial ⟨nothing special : nada en especial, nada en particular⟩ — **specially** *adv*

special delivery *n* : correo *m* urgente

special effects *npl* : efectos *mpl* especiales

specialist ['spɛʃəlɪst] *n* : especialista *mf*

specialization [ˌspɛʃələ'zeɪʃən] *n* : especialización *f*

specialize ['spɛʃəˌlaɪz] *vi* **-ized; -izing** : especializarse

specialty ['spɛʃəlti] *n*, *pl* **-ties** : especialidad *f*

species ['spi:ˌʃi:z, -ˌsi:z] *ns & pl* : especie *f*

specific [spɪ'sɪfɪk] *adj* : específico, determinado — **specifically** [-fɪkli] *adv*

specification [ˌspɛsəfə'keɪʃən] *n* : especificación *f*

specify ['spɛsəˌfaɪ] *vt* **-fied; -fying** : especificar

specimen ['spɛsəmən] *n* **1** SAMPLE : espécimen *m*, muestra *f* **2** EXAMPLE : espécimen *m*, ejemplar *m*

speck ['spɛk] *n* **1** SPOT : manchita *f* **2** BIT, TRACE : mota *f*, pizca *f*, ápice *m*

speckled ['spɛkəld] *adj* : moteado

spectacle ['spɛktɪkəl] *n* **1** : espectáculo *m* **2 spectacles** *npl* GLASSES : lentes *fpl*, gafas *fpl*, anteojos *mpl*, espejuelos *mpl*

spectacular [spɛk'tækjələr] *adj* : espectacular

spectator ['spɛkˌteɪtər] *n* : espectador *m*, -dora *f*

specter *or* **spectre** ['spɛktər] *n* : espectro *m*, fantasma *m*

spectrum ['spɛktrəm] *n*, *pl* **spectra** [-trə] *or* **spectrums** **1** : espectro *m* (de colores, etc.) **2** RANGE : gama *f*, abanico *m*

speculate ['spɛkjəˌleɪt] *vi* **-lated; -lating** **1** : especular (en finanzas) **2** WONDER : preguntarse, hacer conjeturas

speculation [ˌspɛkjə'leɪʃən] *n* : especulación *f*

speculative ['spɛkjəˌleɪtɪv] *adj* : especulativo

speculator ['spɛkjəˌleɪtər] *n* : especulador *m*, -dora *f*

speech ['spi:ʧ] *n* **1** : habla *f*, modo *m* de hablar, expresión *f* **2** ADDRESS : discurso *m*

speechless ['spi:ʧləs] *adj* : enmudecido, estupefacto

speed¹ ['spi:d] *v* **sped** ['spɛd] *or* **speeded**; **speeding** *vi* **1** : ir a toda velocidad, correr a toda prisa ⟨he sped off : se fue a toda velocidad⟩ **2** : conducir a exceso de velocidad — *vt* **to speed up** : acelerar

speed² *n* **1** SWIFTNESS : rapidez *f* **2** VELOCITY : velocidad *f*

speedboat ['spi:d,bo:t] *n* : lancha *f* motora (rápida), deslizador *m*

speed bump *n* : badén *m*

speeding ['spi:dɪŋ] *n* : exceso *m* de velocidad ⟨he was stopped/ticketed for speeding : lo pararon/multaron por exceso de velocidad⟩

speed limit *n* : velocidad *f* máxima, límite *m* de velocidad

speedometer [spɪ'dɑmətər] *n* : velocímetro *m*

speedup ['spi:d,ʌp] *n* : aceleración *f*

speedy ['spi:di] *adj* **speedier; -est** : rápido — **speedily** [-dəli] *adv*

spell¹ ['spɛl] *vt* **1** : escribir, deletrear (verbalmente) ⟨how do you spell it? : ¿cómo se escribe?, ¿cómo se deletrea?⟩ **2** MEAN : significar ⟨that could spell trouble : eso puede significar problemas⟩ **3** RELIEVE : relevar **4 to spell out** EXPLAIN : explicar en detalle — *vi* : escribir correctamente, deletrear (verbalmente)

spell² *n* **1** TURN : turno *m* **2** PERIOD, TIME : período *m* (de tiempo) ⟨a dry

spell : un período de sequía ⟨a cold spell : una ola de frío⟩ 3 : condición *f* pasajera ⟨a fainting spell : un desmayo⟩ ⟨a dizzy spell : un mareo⟩ 4 ENCHANTMENT : encanto *m*, hechizo *m*, maleficio *m*

spellbinding ['spɛl,baɪndɪŋ] *adj* : hipnotizador

spellbound ['spɛl,baʊnd] *adj* : embelesado

spell–checker ['spɛl,tʃɛkər] *n* : corrector *m* ortográfico

speller ['spɛlər] *n* : persona *f* que escribe ⟨she's a good speller : tiene buena ortografía⟩

spelling ['spɛlɪŋ] *n* : ortografía *f*

spend ['spɛnd] *vt* **spent** ['spɛnt]; **spending 1** : gastar (dinero, etc.) **2** PASS : pasar (el tiempo) ⟨to spend time on : dedicar tiempo a⟩

spendthrift ['spɛnd,θrɪft] *n* : derrochador *m*, -dora *f*; despilfarrador *m*, -dora *f*

sperm ['spərm] *n*, *pl* **sperm** *or* **sperms** : esperma *mf*

sperm whale : cachalote *m*

spew ['spju:] *vi* : salir a chorros — *vt* : vomitar, arrojar (lava, etc.)

sphere ['sfɪr] *n* : esfera *f*

spherical ['sfɪrɪkəl, 'sfɛr-] *adj* : esférico

sphinx ['sfɪŋks] *n* : esfinge *f*

spice¹ ['spaɪs] *vt* **spiced**; **spicing 1** SEASON : condimentar, sazonar **2** *or* **to spice up** : salpimentar, hacer más interesante

spice² *n* **1** : especia *f* **2** FLAVOR, INTEREST : sabor *m* ⟨the spice of life : la sal de la vida⟩

spick–and–span ['spɪkənd'spæn] *adj* : limpio y ordenado

spiciness ['spaɪsinəs] *n* : picante *m*, lo picante

spicy ['spaɪsi] *adj* **spicier**; **-est 1** SPICED : condimentado, sazonado **2** HOT : picante **3** RACY : picante

spider ['spaɪdər] *n* : araña *f*

spiderweb ['spaɪdər,wɛb] *n* : telaraña *f*, tela *f* de araña

spiel ['spi:l] *n* : rollo *m*, perorata *f*

spigot ['spɪgət, -kət] *n* : llave *f*; grifo *m*; canilla *f* Arg, Uru

spike¹ ['spaɪk] *vt* **spiked**; **spiking 1** FASTEN : clavar (con clavos grandes) **2** PIERCE : atravesar **3** : añadir alcohol a ⟨he spiked her drink with rum : le puso ron a la bebida⟩

spike² *n* **1** : clavo *m* grande **2** CLEAT : clavo *m* **3** : remache *m* (en voleibol) **4** PEAK : pico *m*

spill¹ ['spɪl] *vt* **1** SHED : derramar, verter ⟨to spill blood : derrame sangre⟩ **2** DIVULGE : revelar, divulgar — *vi* : derramarse

spill² *n* **1** SPILLING : derrame *m*, vertido *m* ⟨oil spill : derrame de petróleo⟩ **2** FALL : caída *f*

spin¹ ['spɪn] *v* **spun** ['spʌn]; **spinning** *vi* **1** : hilar **2** TURN : girar ⟨the car spun out of control : el auto giró fuera de control⟩ ⟨he spun around to look at me : se dio la vuelta para mirarme⟩ **3** REEL : dar vuel-

tas ⟨my head is spinning : la cabeza me está dando vueltas⟩ — *vt* **1** : hilar (hilo, etc.) **2** : tejer ⟨to spin a web : tejer una telaraña⟩ **3** TWIRL : hacer girar **4** : darle un sesgo positivo a (en política) **5 to spin a yarn/tale** : contar un cuento **6 to spin one's wheels** *fam* STAGNATE : estancarse

spin² *n* : vuelta *f*, giro *m* ⟨to go for a spin : dar una vuelta (en coche)⟩

spinach ['spɪnɪtʃ] *n* : espinacas *fpl*, espinaca *f*

spinal ['spaɪnəl] *adj* : espinal

spinal column *n* BACKBONE : columna *f* vertebral

spinal cord *n* : médula *f* espinal

spindle ['spɪndəl] *n* **1** : huso *m* (para hilar) **2** : eje *m* (de un mecanismo)

spindly ['spɪndli] *adj* : larguirucho *fam*, largo y débil (dícese de una planta)

spin doctor *n* : portavoz *mf*

spine ['spaɪn] *n* **1** BACKBONE : columna *f* vertebral, espina *f* dorsal **2** QUILL : púa *f* (de un animal) **3** THORN : espina *f* **4** : lomo *m* (de un libro)

spineless ['spaɪnləs] *adj* **1** : sin púas, sin espinas **2** INVERTEBRATE : invertebrado **3** WEAK : débil (de carácter)

spinster ['spɪnstər] *n* : soltera *f*

spiny ['spaɪni] *adj* **spinier**; **-est** : con púas (dícese de los animales), espinoso (dícese de las plantas)

spiral¹ ['spaɪrəl] *vi* **-raled** *or* **-ralled**; **-raling** *or* **-ralling** : ir en espiral

spiral² *adj* : espiral, en espiral ⟨a spiral staircase : una escalera de caracol⟩

spiral³ *n* : espiral *f*

spire ['spaɪr] *n* : aguja *f*

spirit¹ ['spɪrət] *vt* **to spirit away** : hacer desaparecer

spirit² *n* **1** : espíritu *m* ⟨body and spirit : cuerpo y espíritu⟩ **2** GHOST : espíritu *m*, fantasma *m* **3** MOOD : espíritu *m*, humor *m* ⟨in the spirit of friendship : en el espíritu de amistad⟩ ⟨to be in good spirits : estar de buen humor⟩ **4** ENTHUSIASM, VIVACITY : espíritu *m*, ánimo *m*, brío *m* **5 spirits** *npl* : licores *mpl*

spirited ['spɪrətəd] *adj* : animado, enérgico

spiritless ['spɪrətləs] *adj* : desanimado

spiritual¹ ['spɪrɪtʃʊəl, -tʃəl] *adj* : espiritual — **spiritually** *adv*

spiritual² *n* : espiritual *m* (canción)

spiritualism ['spɪrɪtʃʊə,lɪzəm, -tʃə-] *n* : espiritismo *m*

spiritualist ['spɪrɪtʃʊəlɪst, -tʃə-] *n* : médium *mf*, espiritista *mf*

spirituality [,spɪrɪtʃʊ'æləti] *n*, *pl* **-ties** : espiritualidad *f*

spit¹ ['spɪt] *v* **spit** *or* **spat** ['spæt]; **spitting** : escupir

spit² *n* **1** SALIVA : saliva *f* **2** ROTISSERIE : asador *m* **3** POINT : lengua *f* (de tierra)

spite¹ ['spaɪt] *vt* **spited**; **spiting** : fastidiar, molestar

spite² *n* **1** : despecho *m*, rencor *m* **2 in spite of** : a pesar de (que), pese a (que)

spiteful ['spaɪtfəl] *adj* : malicioso, rencoroso

spitting image *n* **to be the spitting image of** : ser el vivo retrato de

spittle ['spɪtəl] *n* : saliva *f*

splash¹ ['splæʃ] *vt* : salpicar — *vi* 1 : salpicar 2 **to splash around** : chapotear

splash² *n* 1 SPLASHING : salpicadura *f* 2 SQUIRT : chorrito *m* 3 SPOT : mancha *f*

splatter ['splætər] → **spatter**

splay ['spleɪ] *vt* : extender (hacia afuera) ⟨to splay one's fingers : abrir los dedos⟩ — *vi* : extenderse (hacia afuera)

spleen ['spliːn] *n* 1 : bazo *m* (órgano) 2 ANGER, SPITE : ira *f*, rencor *m*

splendid ['splɛndəd] *adj* : espléndido — **splendidly** *adv*

splendor ['splɛndər] *n* : esplendor *m*

splice¹ ['splaɪs] *vt* **spliced; splicing** : empalmar, unir

splice² *n* : empalme *m*, unión *f*

splint ['splɪnt] *n* : tablilla *f*

splinter¹ ['splɪntər] *vt* : astillar — *vi* : astillarse

splinter² *n* : astilla *f*

split ['splɪt] *v* **split; splitting** *vt* 1 CLEAVE : partir, hender ⟨to split wood : partir madera⟩ 2 BURST : romper, rajar ⟨to split open : abrir⟩ 3 DIVIDE, SHARE : dividir, repartir — *vi* 1 : partirse (dícese de la madera, etc.) 2 BURST, CRACK : romperse, rajarse 3 *or* **to split up** : dividirse

split² *n* 1 CRACK : rajadura *f* 2 TEAR : rotura *f* 3 DIVISION : división *f*, escisión *f*

splurge¹ ['splərdʒ] *v* **splurged; splurging** *vt* : derrochar — *vi* : derrochar dinero

splurge² *n* : derroche *m*

splutter ['splʌtər] *vi* 1 : balbucear (dícese de una persona) 2 SPUTTER : petardear (dícese de un motor)

spoil¹ ['spɔɪl] *vt* 1 PILLAGE : saquear 2 RUIN : estropear, arruinar 3 PAMPER : consentir, mimar — *vi* : estropearse, echarse a perder

spoil² *n* PLUNDER : botín *m*

spoiled ['spɔɪld, 'spɔɪlt] *adj* 1 : estropeado, cortado (dícese de la comida) 2 PAMPERED : consentido

spoilsport ['spɔɪl,sport] *n* : aguafiestas *mf*

spoke¹ → **speak**

spoke² ['spoːk] *n* : rayo *m* (de una rueda)

spoken → **speak**

spokesman ['spoːksmən] *n*, *pl* **-men** [-mən, -,mɛn] : portavoz *mf*; vocero *m*, -ra *f*

spokesperson ['spoːks,pərsən] *n* : portavoz *mf*; vocero *m*, -ra *f*

spokeswoman ['spoːks,wʊmən] *n*, *pl* **-women** [-,wɪmən] : portavoz *f*, vocera *f*

sponge¹ ['spʌndʒ] *vt* **sponged; sponging** 1 : limpiar con una esponja 2 BUM, SCROUNGE : gorrear *fam*, gorronear *fam* (dinero) — *vi* **to sponge off someone** : vivir a costa de alguien

sponge² *n* : esponja *f*

sponge cake *n* : bizcocho *m*

sponger ['spʌndʒər] *n* : gorrero *m*, -ra *f* *fam*; vividor *m*, -dora *f*; sanguijuela *f*; arrimado *m*, -da *f* *Mex fam*

spongy ['spʌndʒi] *adj* **spongier; -est** : esponjoso

sponsor¹ ['spɑntsər] *vt* : patrocinar, auspiciar, apadrinar (a una persona)

sponsor² *n* : patrocinador *m*, -dora *f*; padrino *m*, madrina *f*

sponsorship ['spɑntsər,ʃɪp] *n* : patrocinio *m*

spontaneity [,spɑntə'niːəti, -'neɪ-] *n* : espontaneidad *f*

spontaneous [spɑn'teɪniəs] *adj* : espontáneo — **spontaneously** *adv*

spoof ['spuːf] *n* : burla *f*, parodia *f*

spook¹ ['spuːk] *vt* : asustar

spook² *n* : fantasma *m*, espíritu *m*, espectro *m*

spooky ['spuːki] *adj* **spookier; -est** : que da miedo, espeluznante

spool ['spuːl] *n* : carrete *m*, bobina *f*

spoon¹ ['spuːn] *vt* : comer, servir, o echar con cuchara

spoon² *n* : cuchara *f*

spoonful ['spuːn,fʊl] *n* : cucharada *f* ⟨by the spoonful : a cucharadas⟩

spoor ['spʊr, 'spor] *n* : rastro *m*, pista *f*

sporadic [spə'rædɪk] *adj* : esporádico — **sporadically** [-dɪkli] *adv*

spore ['spor] *n* : espora *f*

sport¹ ['sport] *vi* FROLIC : retozar, juguetear — *vt* SHOW OFF : lucir, ostentar

sport² *n* 1 : deporte *m* ⟨outdoor sports : deportes al aire libre⟩ 2 JEST : broma *f* 3 **to be a good sport** : tener espíritu deportivo

sporting ['sportɪŋ] *adj* : deportivo ⟨a sporting chance : buenas posibilidades⟩

sports car *n* : carro *m* sport, auto *m* sport, coche *m* deportivo

sports center *n* : centro *m* deportivo

sportsman ['sportsmən] *n*, *pl* **-men** [-mən, -,mɛn] : deportista *m*

sportsmanship ['sportsmən,ʃɪp] *n* : espíritu *m* deportivo, deportividad *f* *Spain*

sportswear ['sports,wær] *n* : ropa *f* deportiva

sportswoman ['sports,wʊmən] *n*, *pl* **-women** [-,wɪmən] : deportista *f*

sport–utility vehicle *n* → **SUV**

sporty ['sporti] *adj* **sportier; -est** : deportivo

spot¹ ['spɑt] *v* **spotted; spotting** *vt* 1 STAIN : manchar 2 RECOGNIZE, SEE : ver, reconocer ⟨to spot an error : descubrir un error⟩ — *vi* : mancharse

spot² *adj* : hecho al azar ⟨a spot check : un vistazo, un control aleatorio⟩

spot³ *n* 1 STAIN : mancha *f* 2 DOT : punto *m* 3 PIMPLE : grano *m* ⟨to break out in spots : salirle granos a alguien⟩ 4 PREDICAMENT : apuro *m*, aprieto *m*, lío *m* ⟨in a tight spot : en apuros⟩ 5 PLACE : lugar *m*, sitio *m* ⟨to be on the spot : estar en el lugar⟩

spotless ['spɑtləs] *adj* : impecable, inmaculado — **spotlessly** *adv*

spotlight¹ ['spɑt,laɪt] *vt* **-lighted** *or* **-lit** [-,lɪt]; **-lighting** 1 LIGHT : iluminar (con un reflector) 2 HIGHLIGHT : destacar, poner en relieve

spotlight² *n* 1 : reflector *m*, foco *m* 2 **to be in the spotlight** : ser el centro de atención

spotty ['spɑṭi] *adj* **spottier; -est** : irregular, desigual

spouse ['spaʊs] *n* : cónyuge *mf*

spout¹ ['spaʊt] *vt* **1** : lanzar chorros de **2** DECLAIM : declamar — *vi* : salir a chorros

spout² *n* **1** : pico *m* (de una jarra, etc.) **2** STREAM : chorro *m*

sprain¹ ['spreɪn] *vt* : sufrir un esguince en

sprain² *n* : esguince *m*, torcedura *f*

sprawl¹ ['sprɔl] *vi* **1** LIE : tumbarse, echarse, despatarrarse **2** EXTEND : extenderse

sprawl² *n* **1** : postura *f* despatarrada **2** SPREAD : expansión *f*, expansión *f*

spray¹ ['spreɪ] *vt* : rociar (una superficie), pulverizar (un líquido)

spray² *n* **1** BOUQUET : ramillete *m* **2** MIST : rocío *m* **3** ATOMIZER : atomizador *m*, pulverizador *m*

spray gun *n* : pistola *f*

spread¹ ['spred] *v* **spread; spreading** *vt* **1** *or* **to spread out** : desplegar, extender **2** SCATTER, STREW : esparcir **3** SMEAR : untar (mantequilla, etc.) **4** DISSEMINATE : difundir, sembrar, propagar — *vi* **1** : difundirse, correr, propagarse **2** EXTEND : extenderse

spread² *n* **1** EXTENSION : extensión *f*, difusión *f* (de noticias, etc.), propagación *f* (de enfermedades, etc.) **2** : colcha *f* (para una cama), mantel *m* (para una mesa) **3** PASTE : pasta *f* ⟨cheese spread : pasta de queso⟩

spreadsheet ['spred,ʃiːt] *n* : hoja *f* de cálculo

spree ['spriː] *n* **1** : acción *f* desenfrenada ⟨to go on a shopping spree : comprar como loco⟩ **2** BINGE : parranda *f*, juerga *f* ⟨on a spree : de parranda, de juerga⟩

sprig ['sprɪg] *n* : ramita *f*, ramito *m*

sprightly ['spraɪtli] *adj* **sprightlier; -est** : vivo, animado ⟨with a sprightly step : con paso ligero⟩

spring¹ ['sprɪŋ] *v* **sprang** ['spræŋ] *or* **sprung** ['sprʌŋ]; **sprung; springing** *vi* **1** LEAP : saltar **2** : mover rápidamente ⟨the lid sprang shut : la tapa se cerró de un golpe⟩ ⟨he sprang to his feet : se paró de un salto⟩ **3 to spring up** : brotar (dícese de las plantas), surgir **4 to spring from** : surgir de — *vt* **1** RELEASE : soltar (de repente) ⟨to spring the news on someone : sorprender a alguien con las noticias⟩ ⟨to spring a trap : hacer saltar una trampa⟩ **2** ACTIVATE : accionar (un mecanismo) **3 to spring a leak** : hacer agua

spring² *n* **1** SOURCE : fuente *f*, origen *m* **2** : manantial *m*, fuente *f* ⟨hot spring : fuente termal⟩ **3** : primavera *f* ⟨spring and summer : la primavera y el verano⟩ **4** : resorte *m*, muelle *m* (de metal, etc.) **5** LEAP : salto *m*, brinco *m* **6** RESILIENCE : elasticidad *f*

springboard ['sprɪŋ,bord] *n* : trampolín *m*

spring cleaning *n* : limpieza *f* a fondo

springtime ['sprɪŋ,taɪm] *n* : primavera *f*

springy ['sprɪŋi] *adj* **springier; -est 1** RESILIENT : elástico **2** LIVELY : enérgico

sprinkle¹ ['sprɪŋkəl] *vt* **-kled; -kling** : rociar (con agua), espolvorear (con azúcar, etc.), salpicar

sprinkle² *n* : llovizna *f*

sprinkler ['sprɪŋkələr] *n* : rociador *m*, aspersor *m*

sprint¹ ['sprɪnt] *vi* : echar la carrera, esprintar (en deportes)

sprint² *n* : esprint *m* (en deportes)

sprinter ['sprɪntər] *n* : esprínter *mf*

sprite ['spraɪt] *n* : hada *f*, elfo *m*

sprocket ['sprɑkət] *n* : diente *m* (de una rueda dentada)

sprout¹ ['spraʊt] *vi* : brotar

sprout² *n* : brote *m*, retoño *m*, vástago *m*

spruce¹ ['spruːs] *v* **spruced; sprucing** *vt* : arreglar — *vi or* **to spruce up** : arreglarse, acicalarse

spruce² *adj* **sprucer; sprucest** : pulcro, arreglado

spruce³ *n* : picea *f* (árbol)

spry ['spraɪ] *adj* **sprier** *or* **spryer** ['spraɪər]; **spriest** *or* **spryest** ['spraɪəst] : ágil, activo

spun → spin

spunk ['spʌŋk] *n* : valor *m*, coraje *m*, agallas *fpl fam*

spunky ['spʌŋki] *adj* **spunkier; -est** : animoso, corajudo

spur¹ ['spər] *vt* **spurred; spurring** *or* **to spur on** : espolear (un caballo), motivar (a una persona, etc.)

spur² *n* **1** : espuela *f*, acicate *m* **2** STIMULUS : acicate *m* **3** : espolón *m* (de un gallo) **4** : ramal *m* (de una línea de ferrocarril)

spurious ['spjʊriəs] *adj* : espurio

spurn ['spərn] *vt* : desdeñar, rechazar

spurt¹ ['spərt] *vt* SQUIRT : lanzar un chorro de — *vi* SPOUT : salir a chorros

spurt² *n* **1** : actividad *f* repentina ⟨a spurt of energy : una explosión de energía⟩ ⟨to do in spurts : hacer por rachas⟩ **2** JET : chorro *m* (de agua, etc.)

sputter¹ ['spʌtər] *vi* **1** JABBER : farfullar **2** : petardear (dícese de un motor)

sputter² *n* : petardeo *m* (de un motor)

spy¹ ['spaɪ] *v* **spied; spying** *vt* SEE : ver, divisar — *vi* : espiar ⟨to spy on someone : espiar a alguien⟩

spy² *n* : espía *mf*

squab ['skwɑb] *n, pl* **squabs** *or* **squab** : pichón *m*

squabble¹ ['skwɑbəl] *vi* **-bled; -bling** : reñir, pelearse, discutir

squabble² *n* : riña *f*, pelea *f*, discusión *f*

squad ['skwɑd] *n* : pelotón *m* (militar), brigada *f* (de policías), cuadrilla *f* (de obreros, etc.)

squadron ['skwɑdrən] *n* : escuadrón *m* (de militares), escuadrilla *f* (de aviones), escuadra *f* (de naves)

squalid ['skwɑlɪd] *adj* : miserable

squall ['skwɔl] *n* **1** : aguacero *m* tormentoso, chubasco *m* tormentoso **2 snow squall** : torménta *f* de nieve

squalor ['skwɑlər] *n* : miseria *f*

squander ['skwɑndər] *vt* : derrochar (dinero, etc.), desaprovechar (una oportu-

square¹ ['skwær] *vt* **squared; squaring 1** : cuadrar **2** : elevar al cuadrado (en matemáticas) **3** CONFORM : conciliar (con), ajustar (con) **4** SETTLE : saldar (una cuenta) ⟨I squared it with him : lo arreglé con él⟩

square² *adj* **squarer; -est 1** : cuadrado ⟨a square house : una casa cuadrada⟩ **2** : a escuadra, en ángulo recto (en carpintería, etc.) ⟨cuadrado (en matemáticas) ⟨a square mile : una milla cuadrada⟩ **4** HONEST : justo ⟨a square deal : un buen acuerdo⟩ ⟨fair and square : en buena lid⟩

square³ *n* **1** : escuadra *f* (instrumento) **2** : cuadrado *m*, cuadro *m* ⟨to fold into squares : plegar en cuadrados⟩ **3** : plaza *f* (de una ciudad) **4** : cuadrado *m* (en matemáticas)

squarely ['skwærli] *adv* **1** EXACTLY : exactamente, directamente, justo **2** HONESTLY : honradamente, justamente

square root *n* : raíz *f* cuadrada

squash¹ ['skwɑʃ, 'skwɔʃ] *vt* **1** CRUSH : aplastar **2** SUPPRESS : acallar (protestas), sofocar (una rebelión)

squash² *n* **1** *pl* **squashes** *or* **squash** : calabaza *f* (vegetal) **2** *or* **squash racquets** : squash *m* (deporte)

squat¹ ['skwɑt] *vi* **squatted; squatting 1** CROUCH : agacharse, ponerse en cuclillas **2** : ocupar un lugar sin derecho

squat² *adj* **squatter; squattest** : bajo y ancho, rechoncho *fam* (dícese de una persona)

squat³ *n* **1** : posición *f* en cuclillas, flexión *f* (en deportes) **2** : ocupación *f* ilegal (de un lugar)

squatter ['skwɑt̬ər] *n* : okupa *mf*

squawk¹ ['skwɔk] *vi* : graznar (dícese de las aves), chillar

squawk² *n* : graznido *m* (de un ave), chillido *m*

squeak¹ ['skwi:k] *vi* : chillar (dícese de un animal), chirriar (dícese de un objeto)

squeak² *n* : chillido *m*, chirrido *m*

squeaky ['skwi:ki] *adj* **squeakier; -est** : chirriante ⟨a squeaky voice : una voz chillona⟩

squeal¹ ['skwi:l] *vi* **1** : chillar (dícese de las personas o los animales), chirriar (dícese de los frenos, etc.) **2** PROTEST : quejarse **3** *fam* SNITCH : cantar (a la policía, etc.) ⟨to squeal on someone : acusar/delatar a alguien⟩

squeal² *n* **1** : chillido *m* (de una persona o un animal) **2** SCREECH : chirrido *m* (de frenos, etc.)

squeamish ['skwi:mɪʃ] *adj* : impresionable, sensible ⟨he's squeamish about cockroaches : las cucarachas le dan asco⟩

squeeze¹ ['skwi:z] *vt* **squeezed; squeezing 1** PRESS : apretar, exprimir (naranjas, etc.) **2** EXTRACT : extraer (jugo, etc.) **3** : meter

squeeze² *n* : apretón *m*

squelch ['skwɛltʃ] *vt* : aplastar (una rebelión, etc.)

squid ['skwɪd] *n, pl* **squid** *or* **squids** : calamar *m*

squint¹ ['skwɪnt] *vi* : mirar con los ojos entornados

squint² *adj or* **squint–eyed** ['skwɪnt̬ˌaɪd] : bizco

squint³ *n* : estrabismo *m*

squire ['skwaɪr] *n* : hacendado *m*, -da *f*; terrateniente *mf*

squirm ['skwərm] *vi* : retorcerse

squirrel ['skwərəl] *n* : ardilla *f*

squirt¹ ['skwərt] *vt* : lanzar un chorro de — *vi* SPURT : salir a chorros

squirt² *n* : chorrito *m*

stab¹ ['stæb] *vt* **stabbed; stabbing 1** KNIFE : acuchillar, apuñalar **2** STICK : clavar (con una aguja, etc.), golpear (con el dedo, etc.)

stab² *n* **1** : puñalada *f*, cuchillada *f* **2** JAB : pinchazo *m* (con una aguja, etc.), golpe *m* (con un dedo, etc.) **3** to take a stab at : intentar

stability [stə'bɪlət̬i] *n, pl* **-ties** : estabilidad *f*

stabilize ['steɪbəˌlaɪz] *v* **-lized; -lizing** *vt* : estabilizar — *vi* : estabilizarse — **stabilization** *n* — **stabilizer** *n*

stable¹ ['steɪbəl] *vt* **-bled; -bling** : poner (ganado) en un establo, poner (caballos) en una caballeriza

stable² *adj* **stabler; -blest 1** FIXED, STEADY : fijo, sólido, estable **2** LASTING : estable, perdurable ⟨a stable government : un gobierno estable⟩ **3** : estacionario (en medicina), equilibrado (en psicología)

stable³ *n* : establo *m* (para ganado), caballeriza *f* o cuadra *f* (para caballos)

staccato [stə'kɑt̬o:] *adj* : staccato

stack¹ ['stæk] *vt* **1** PILE : amontonar, apilar **2** COVER : cubrir, llenar ⟨he stacked the table with books : cubrió la mesa de libros⟩

stack² *n* **1** PILE : montón *m*, pila *f* **2** SMOKESTACK : chimenea *f*

stadium ['steɪdiəm] *n, pl* **-dia** [-diə] *or* **-diums** : estadio *m*

staff¹ ['stæf] *vt* : proveer de personal

staff² *n, pl* **staffs** ['stæfs, 'stævz] *or* **staves** ['stævz, 'steɪvz] **1** : bastón *m* (de mando), báculo *m* (de obispo) **2** *pl* **staffs** PERSONNEL : personal *m* **3** *or* **stave** : pentagrama *m* (en música)

stag¹ ['stæg] *adv* : solo, sin pareja ⟨to go stag : ir solo⟩

stag² *adj* : sólo para hombres

stag³ *n, pl* **stags** *or* **stag** : ciervo *m*, venado *m*

stage¹ ['steɪdʒ] *vt* **staged; staging** : poner en escena (una obra de teatro)

stage² *n* **1** PLATFORM : estrado *m*, tablado *m*, escenario *m* (de un teatro) **2** PHASE, STEP : fase *f*, etapa *f* ⟨stage of development : fase de desarrollo⟩ ⟨in stages : por etapas⟩ **3 the stage** : el teatro *m*

stagecoach ['steɪdʒˌkoːtʃ] *n* : diligencia *f*

stage fright n : miedo m escénico, pánico m escénico

stage set → set³

stagger¹ ['stægər] vi TOTTER : tambalearse — vt **1** ALTERNATE : alternar, escalonar (turnos de trabajo) **2** : hacer tambalear ⟨to be staggered by : quedarse estupefacto por⟩

stagger² n : tambaleo m

staggering ['stægərɪŋ] adj : asombroso

stagnant ['stægnənt] adj : estancado

stagnate ['stæg,neɪt] vi -nated; -nating : estancarse

stagnation [stæg'neɪʃən] n : estancamiento m

staid ['steɪd] adj : serio, sobrio

stain¹ ['steɪn] vt **1** DISCOLOR : manchar **2** DYE : teñir (madera, etc.) **3** SULLY : manchar, empañar

stain² n **1** SPOT : mancha f **2** DYE : tinte m, tintura f **3** BLEMISH : mancha f, mácula f

stained glass n : vidrio m de color ⟨stained-glass window : vidriera, vitral⟩

stainless ['steɪnləs] adj : sin mancha ⟨stainless steel : acero inoxidable⟩

stair ['stær] n **1** STEP : escalón m, peldaño m **2** stairs npl : escalera f, escaleras fpl

staircase ['stær,keɪs] n : escalera f, escaleras fpl

stairway ['stær,weɪ] n : escalera f, escaleras fpl

stairwell ['stær,wɛl] n : caja f, hueco m (de la escalera)

stake¹ ['steɪk] vt staked; staking **1** : estacar, marcar (con estacas (una propiedad) **2** BET : jugarse, apostar **3** to stake a claim to : reclamar, reivindicar

stake² n **1** POST : estaca f **2** BET : apuesta f ⟨to be at stake : estar en juego⟩ **3** INTEREST, SHARE : interés m, participación f

stalactite [stə'læk,taɪt] n : estalactita f

stalagmite [stə'læg,maɪt] n : estalagmita f

stale ['steɪl] adj staler; stalest : viejo ⟨stale bread : pan duro⟩ ⟨stale news : viejas noticias⟩

stalemate ['steɪl,meɪt] n : punto m muerto, impasse m

stalk¹ ['stɔk] vt : acechar — vi : caminar rígidamente (por orgullo, ira, etc.)

stalk² n : tallo m (de una planta)

stall¹ ['stɔl] vt **1** : parar (un motor) **2** DELAY : entretener (a una persona), demorar — vi **1** : pararse (dícese de un motor) **2** DELAY : demorar, andar con rodeos ⟨to stall for time : tratar de ganar tiempo⟩

stall² n **1** : compartimiento m (de un establo) **2** : puesto m (en un mercado, etc.)

stallion ['stæljən] n : caballo m semental

stalwart ['stɔlwərt] adj **1** STRONG : fuerte ⟨a stalwart supporter : un firme partidario⟩ **2** BRAVE : valiente, valeroso

stamen ['steɪmən] n : estambre m

stamina ['stæmənə] n : resistencia f

stammer¹ ['stæmər] vi : tartamudear, titubear

stammer² n : tartamudeo m, titubeo m

stamp¹ ['stæmp] vt **1** : pisotear (con los pies) ⟨to stamp one's feet : patear, dar una patada⟩ **2** IMPRESS, IMPRINT : sellar (una factura, etc.), acuñar (monedas) **3** : franquear, ponerle estampillas a (correo) **4 to stamp out** : aplastar, sofocar, erradicar

stamp² n **1** : sello m (para documentos, etc.) **2** DIE : cuño m (para monedas) **3** or **postage stamp** : sello m, estampilla f, timbre m CA, Mex

stampede¹ [stæm'piːd] vi -peded; -peding : salir en estampida

stampede² n : estampida f

stance ['stæns] n : postura f

stanch ['stɔntʃ, 'stæntʃ] vt : detener, estancar (un líquido)

stand¹ ['stænd] v stood ['stʊd]; standing vi **1** : estar de pie, estar parado ⟨I was standing on the corner : estaba parada en la esquina⟩ ⟨to stand still : estarse quieto⟩ ⟨to stand in line : hacer cola⟩ ⟨to stand around waiting/watching : quedarse esperando/mirando (sin hacer nada)⟩ **2** MOVE : ponerse, pararse ⟨stand beside me : ponte a mi lado⟩ ⟨stand aside/back! : ¡apártate!⟩ **3** or **to stand up** : levantarse, pararse, ponerse de pie ⟨she stood up and left : se paró y se fue⟩ ⟨to stand up straight : ponerse derecho⟩ **4** (indicating a specified position or location) ⟨they stand third in the country : ocupan el tercer lugar en el país⟩ **5** (referring to an opinion) ⟨how does he stand on the matter? : ¿cuál es su postura respecto al asunto?⟩ **6** : estar ⟨the house stands on a hill : la casa está en una colina⟩ ⟨I won't stand in your way : no te lo voy a impedir⟩ **7** REMAIN : estar ⟨the machines are standing idle : las máquinas están paradas⟩ ⟨as things stand : tal (y) como están las cosas⟩ **8** CONTINUE : seguir ⟨the order still stands : el mandato sigue vigente⟩ **9** MEASURE : medir ⟨he stands six feet two (inches tall) : mide seis pies y dos pulgadas⟩ **10 to stand by** : estar listo, estar disponible **11 to stand by** SUPPORT : apoyar **12 to stand by** HONOR : cumplir con (una promesa, etc.) **13 to stand down** : bajar las armas (dícese de un soldado), retirarse (dícese de un ejército) **14 to stand firm** : mantenerse firme **15 to stand for** SIGNIFY, REPRESENT : significar, representar **16 to stand for** ALLOW : permitir **17 to stand guard** : hacer la guardia **18 to stand in (for)** : sustituir (a) **19 to stand on end** : ponerse de punta, pararse (dícese de los pelos) **20 to stand out** : resaltar **21 to stand out** EXCEL : destacarse **22 to stand up for** DEFEND : defender **23 to stand up to** WITHSTAND : resistir **24 to stand up to** CONFRONT : hacerle frente a — vt **1** PLACE, SET : poner, colocar ⟨he stood them in a row : los colocó en hilera⟩ **2** TOLERATE : aguantar, soportar ⟨he can't stand her : no la puede tragar⟩ **3** WITHSTAND : resistir **4** USE : beneficiarse de ⟨you could stand a nap : una siesta te vendría bien⟩ **5 to**

stand someone up : dejar plantado a alguien

stand² n **1** RESISTANCE : resistencia f ⟨to make a stand against : resistir a⟩ **2** BOOTH, STALL : stand m, puesto m, quiosco m (para vender periódicos, etc.) **3** BASE : pie m, base f **4** : grupo m (de árboles, etc.) **5** POSITION : posición f, postura f **6** stands npl GRANDSTAND : tribuna f

standard¹ ['stændərd] adj **1** ESTABLISHED : estándar, oficial ⟨standard measures : medidas oficiales⟩ ⟨standard English : el inglés estándar⟩ **2** NORMAL : normal, estándar, común **3** CLASSIC : estándar, clásico ⟨a standard work : una obra clásica⟩

standard² n **1** BANNER : estandarte m **2** CRITERION : criterio m **3** RULE : estándar m, norma f, regla f **4** LEVEL : nivel m ⟨standard of living : nivel de vida⟩ **5** SUPPORT : poste m, soporte m

standard–bearer ['stændərd,bærər] n : abanderado m, -da f

standardization [,stændərdə'zeɪʃən] n : estandarización f

standardize ['stændər,daɪz] vt -ized; -izing : estandarizar

standard time n : hora f oficial

standby ['stænd,baɪ] n **1** BACKUP ⟨we bought another as a standby : compramos otro de reserva/emergencia⟩ **2 to be on standby** : estar a la espera de órdenes, etc. ⟨the passengers who are on standby : los pasajeros que están en la lista de espera⟩

stand by vt : atenerse a, cumplir con (una promesa, etc.) — vi **1** : mantenerse aparte ⟨to stand by and do nothing : mirar sin hacer nada⟩ **2** : estar preparado, estar listo (para un anuncio, un ataque, etc.)

stand for vt **1** REPRESENT : significar **2** PERMIT, TOLERATE : permitir, tolerar

stand–in ['stænd,ɪn] n : doble m, sustituto m, -ta f

standing¹ ['stændɪŋ] adj **1** : de pie, parado ⟨in a standing position : en posición parada, (en posición) de pie⟩ **2** STAGNANT : estancado **3** ACTIVE : en pie (dícese de una oferta, etc.), fijo (dícese de un pedido) **4** PERMANENT : permanente

standing² n **1** POSITION, RANK : posición f **2** DURATION : duración f

stand out vi **1** : destacar(se) ⟨she stands out from the rest : se destaca entre los otros⟩ **2 to stand out against** RESIST : oponerse a

standpoint ['stænd,pɔɪnt] n : punto m de vista

standstill ['stænd,stɪl] n **1** STOP : detención f, paro m ⟨to come to a standstill : pararse⟩ **2** DEADLOCK : punto m muerto, impasse m

stand up vt : dejar plantado ⟨he stood me up again : otra vez me dejó plantado⟩ — vi **1** ENDURE : durar, resistir **2 to stand up for** : defender **3 to stand up to** : hacerle frente (a alguien)

stank → **stink**

stanza ['stænzə] n : estrofa f

staple¹ ['steɪpəl] vt -pled; -pling : engrapar, grapar

staple² adj : principal, básico ⟨a staple food : un alimento básico⟩

staple³ n **1** : producto m principal, producto m de primera necesidad **2** : grapa f, broche m Arg (para engrapar papeles)

stapler ['steɪplər] n : engrapadora f, grapadora f

star¹ ['star] v **starred; starring** vt **1** : marcar con una estrella o un asterisco **2** FEATURE : estar protagonizado por — vi : tener el papel principal ⟨to star in : protagonizar⟩

star² n **1** : estrella f (en astronomía) **2** : estrella f (medalla, etc.), asterisco m (símbolo) **3** CELEBRITY : estrella f ⟨rock/movie star : estrella de rock/cine⟩ ⟨the star of the movie : el protagonista de la película⟩ ⟨our star player : la estrella de nuestro equipo⟩

starboard ['starbərd] n : estribor m

starch¹ ['startʃ] vt : almidonar

starch² n : almidón m, fécula f (comida)

starchy ['startʃi] adj **starchier; -est** : lleno de almidón

stardom ['stardəm] n : estrellato m

stare¹ ['stær] vi **stared; staring** : mirar fijamente

stare² n : mirada f fija

starfish ['star,fɪʃ] n : estrella f de mar

stark¹ ['stark] adv : completamente ⟨stark raving mad : loco de remate⟩ ⟨stark naked : completamente desnudo⟩

stark² adj **1** ABSOLUTE : absoluto **2** BARREN, DESOLATE : desolado, desierto **3** BARE : desnudo **4** HARSH : severo, duro

starlight ['star,laɪt] n : luz f de las estrellas

starling ['starlɪŋ] n : estornino m

starry ['stari] adj **starrier; -est** : estrellado

start¹ ['start] vi **1** JUMP : sobresaltarse, dar un respingo **2** BEGIN : empezar, comenzar ⟨let's get started : empecemos⟩ ⟨she started (off/out) by thanking us : empezó por agradecernos⟩ ⟨he started (off/out) as a receptionist : empezó como recepcionista⟩ ⟨young couples who are just starting off/out : parejas jóvenes que acaban de casarse⟩ **3 to start off/out** SET OUT : salir (de viaje, etc.) **4 or to start off/out start up** : arrancar (dícese de un motor, etc.) **5 to start from scratch** : empezar desde cero **6 to start in** : empezar ⟨after a break he started in again : tras un descanso empezó otra vez⟩ **7 to start over** : volver a empezar, empezar de nuevo — vt **1** BEGIN : empezar, comenzar, iniciar ⟨I started cleaning, I started to clean : empecé a limpiar⟩ ⟨she started (off/out) her speech with a joke : empezó su discurso con una broma⟩ **2** CAUSE : empezar (una discusión, etc.), provocar (un incendio, etc.), causar **3** SET : hacer, poner ⟨her questions started me thinking : sus preguntas me hicieron pensar⟩ ⟨I started them working : los puse a trabajar⟩ ⟨he started us (off) with some questions : para empezar nos hizo unas preguntas⟩ **4** ESTABLISH : fundar, montar, establecer ⟨to start (up) a business : montar un negocio⟩ **5** : arrancar, poner en marcha, encender ⟨to start (up) the car : arrancar el auto/carro/coche⟩ **6 to start a family** : tener hijos **7 to start over** : volver a empezar, empezar de nuevo

start² n **1** JUMP : sobresalto m, respingo m **2** BEGINNING : principio m, comienzo m ⟨to get an early start : salir temprano⟩

starter ['stɑrtər] n **1** : participante mf (en una carrera, etc.); jugador m titular, jugadora f titular (en beisbol, etc.) **2** APPETIZER : entremés m, aperitivo m **3 or starter motor** : motor m de arranque

starting point n : punto m de partida

startle ['stɑrt̬əl] vt **-tled; -tling** : asustar, sobresaltar

start-up ['stɑrt̬ʌp] adj : de puesta en marcha

starvation [stɑr'veɪʃən] n : inanición f, hambre f

starve ['stɑrv] v **starved; starving** vi **1** : morirse de hambre ⟨starving children : niños hambrientos/famélicos⟩ **2 to be starved/starving** ⟨fam⟩ ⟨I'm starved/starving! : ¡me muero de hambre!⟩ **3 to be starved/starving for** or **to be starved of** : estar hambriento/sediento de (atención, cariño, etc.) — vt : privar de comida

stash ['stæʃ] vt : esconder, guardar (en un lugar secreto)

stat ['stæt] → **statistic**

state¹ ['steɪt] vt **stated; stating 1** REPORT : puntualizar, exponer (los hechos, etc.) ⟨state your name : diga su nombre⟩ **2** ESTABLISH, FIX : establecer, fijar

state² n **1** CONDITION : estado m, condición f ⟨a liquid state : un estado líquido⟩ ⟨state of mind : estado de ánimo⟩ ⟨in a bad state : en malas condiciones⟩ **2** NATION : estado m, nación f **3** : estado m (dentro de un país) ⟨the States : los Estados Unidos⟩

stateliness ['steɪtlinəs] n : majestuosidad f

stately ['steɪtli] adj **statelier; -est** : majestuoso

statement ['steɪtmənt] n **1** DECLARATION : declaración f, afirmación f **2 or bank statement** : estado m de cuenta

stateroom ['steɪt̬ru:m, -ˌrʊm] n : camarote m

statesman ['steɪtsmən] n, pl **-men** [-mən, -ˌmen] : estadista mf

static¹ ['stæt̬ɪk] adj : estático

static² n : estática f, interferencia f

station¹ ['steɪʃən] vt : apostar, estacionar

station² n **1** : estación f (de trenes, etc.) **2** RANK, STANDING : condición f (social) **3** : canal m (de televisión), estación f o emisora f (de radio) **4** → **police station** **5** → **fire station**

stationary ['steɪʃəˌneri] adj **1** IMMOBILE : estacionario, inmovible **2** UNCHANGING : inmutable, inalterable

stationery ['steɪʃəˌneri] n : papel y sobres (para correspondencia) ⟨stationery store : papelería⟩

station wagon n : camioneta f ranchera, camioneta f guayín Mex

statistic [stə'tɪstɪk] n : estadística f ⟨according to statistics : según las estadísticas⟩

statistical [stə'tɪstɪkəl] adj : estadístico

statistician [ˌstæt̬ə'stɪʃən] n : estadístico m, -ca f

statue ['stætʃu:] n : estatua f

statuesque [ˌstætʃu'ɛsk] adj : escultural

statuette [ˌstætʃu'ɛt] n : estatuilla f

stature ['stætʃər] n **1** HEIGHT : estatura f, talla f **2** PRESTIGE : talla f, prestigio m

status ['steɪt̬əs, 'stæ-] n : condición f, situación f, estatus m (social) ⟨marital status : estado civil⟩

status quo [-'kwo:] n : statu quo m

status symbol n : símbolo m de estatus

statute ['stætʃu:t] n : ley f, estatuto m

statutory ['stætʃəˌtori] adj : estatutario

staunch ['stɔntʃ] adj : acérrimo, incondicional, leal ⟨a staunch supporter : un partidario incondicional⟩ — **staunchly** adv

stave ['steɪv] vt **staved** or **stove** ['sto:v]; **staving 1 to stave in** : romper **2 to stave off** : evitar (un ataque), prevenir (un problema)

staves → **staff**

stay¹ ['steɪ] vi **1** REMAIN : quedarse, permanecer ⟨she stayed after class : se quedó después de clase⟩ ⟨stay out of my room! : ¡no entres a/en mi cuarto!⟩ ⟨stay off the grass : no pisar el césped⟩ ⟨he stayed in the city : permaneció en la ciudad⟩ **2** CONTINUE : seguir, quedarse ⟨it stayed cloudy : seguía nublado⟩ ⟨to stay awake : mantenerse despierto⟩ ⟨stay in touch! : ¡mantente en contacto!⟩ ⟨they stayed friends : siguieron siendo amigos⟩ **3** LODGE : hospedarse, alojarse (en un hotel, etc.) **4 to stay away from** : no acercarse a (una persona, un lugar) ⟨I stay away from coffee : no puedo tomar café⟩ **5 to stay in** : quedarse en casa **6 to stay off** AVOID : evitar (un tema, etc.) ⟨stay off drugs : no volver a tomar drogas⟩ **7 to stay on** : permanecer, quedarse (en un trabajo, etc.) **8 to stay out** : quedarse fuera **9 to stay out of** : no meterse en (problemas, una discusión, etc.) **10 to stay over** : quedarse a dormir **11 to stay up (late)** : quedarse levantado (hasta tarde) — vt **1** HALT : detener, suspender (una ejecución, etc.) **2 to stay the course** : aguantar hasta el final

stay² n **1** SOJOURN : estadía f, estancia f, permanencia f **2** SUSPENSION : suspensión f (de una sentencia) **3** SUPPORT : soporte m

stead ['stɛd] n **1** : lugar m ⟨she went in his stead : fue en su lugar⟩ **2 to stand (someone) in good stead** : ser muy útil a, servir de mucho a

steadfast ['stɛdˌfæst] adj : firme, resuelto ⟨a steadfast friend : un fiel amigo⟩ ⟨a steadfast refusal : una negativa categórica⟩

steadily ['stɛdəli] *adv* **1** CONSTANTLY : continuamente, sin parar **2** FIRMLY : con firmeza **3** FIXEDLY : fijamente

steady[1] ['stɛdi] *v* **steadied; steadying** *vt* : sujetar ⟨she steadied herself : recobró el equilibrio⟩ — *vi* : estabilizarse

steady[2] *adj* **steadier; -est 1** FIRM, SURE : seguro, firme ⟨to have a steady hand : tener buen pulso⟩ **2** FIXED, REGULAR : fijo ⟨a steady income : ingresos fijos⟩ **3** CALM : tranquilo, ecuánime ⟨she has steady nerves : es imperturbable⟩ **4** DEPENDABLE : responsable, fiable **5** CONSTANT : constante

steak ['steɪk] *n* : bistec *m*; filete *m*; churrasco *m*; bife *m* Arg, Chile, Uru

steal ['sti:l] *v* **stole** ['sto:l]; **stolen** ['sto:lən]; **stealing** *vt* : robar, hurtar — *vi* **1** : robar, hurtar **2** : ir sigilosamente ⟨to steal away : escabullirse⟩

stealth ['stɛlθ] *n* : sigilo *m*

stealthily ['stɛlθəli] *adv* : furtivamente

stealthy ['stɛlθi] *adj* **stealthier; -est** : furtivo, sigiloso

steam[1] ['sti:m] *vi* **1** : echar vapor ⟨to steam away/along (etc.) : moverse echando vapor⟩ **2 to steam up** : empañarse — *vt* **1** : cocer al vapor (en cocina) **2 to steam open** : abrir con vapor **3 to steam up** : empañar

steam[2] *n* **1** : vapor *m* **2 to let off steam** : desahogarse

steamboat ['sti:m,bo:t] → **steamship**

steamed *adj* **1** : cocido al vapor **2** IRATE : furioso

steam engine *n* : motor *m* de vapor

steamer ['sti:mər] *n* **1** → **steamship 2** : vaporera, olla vaporera (en cocina) **3** : almeja *f* de Nueva Inglaterra

steaming *adj* **1 or steaming hot** : muy caliente **2 or steaming mad** : furioso

steamroller ['sti:m,ro:lər] *n* : apisonadora *f*

steamship ['sti:m,ʃɪp] *n* : vapor *m*, barco *m* de vapor

steamy ['sti:mi] *adj* **steamier; -est 1** : lleno de vapor **2** EROTIC : erótico ⟨a steamy romance : un tórrido romance⟩

steed ['sti:d] *n* : corcel *m*

steel[1] ['sti:l] *vt* **to steel oneself** : armarse de valor

steel[2] *adj* : de acero

steel[3] *n* : acero *m*

steely ['sti:li] *adj* **steelier; -est** : como acero ⟨a steely gaze : una mirada fría⟩ ⟨steely determination : determinación férrea⟩

steep[1] ['sti:p] *vt* : remojar, dejar (té, etc.) en infusión

steep[2] *adj* **1** : empinado, escarpado ⟨a steep cliff : un precipicio escarpado⟩ **2** CONSIDERABLE : considerable, marcado **3** EXCESSIVE : excesivo ⟨steep prices : precios muy altos⟩

steeple ['sti:pəl] *n* : aguja *f*, campanario *m*

steeplechase ['sti:pəl,tʃeɪs] *n* : carrera *f* de obstáculos

steeply ['sti:pli] *adv* : abruptamente

steer[1] ['stɪr] *vt* **1** : manejar, conducir (un automóvil), gobernar (un barco) **2** GUIDE : dirigir, guiar — *vi* **to steer clear of** : evitar (algo, a alguien)

steer[2] *n* : buey *m*

steering ['stɪrɪŋ] *n* : dirección *f*

steering wheel → **wheel**

stein ['staɪn] *n* : jarra *f* (para cerveza)

stellar ['stɛlər] *adj* : estelar

stem[1] ['stɛm] *v* **stemmed; stemming** *vt* : detener, contener, parar ⟨to stem the tide : detener el curso⟩ — *vi* **to stem from** : provenir de, ser el resultado de

stem[2] *n* : tallo *m* (de una planta)

stem cell *n* : célula *f* madre

stench ['stɛntʃ] *n* : hedor *m*, mal olor *m*

stencil[1] ['stɛnsəl] *vt* **-ciled** *or* **-cilled; -ciling** *or* **-cilling** : marcar utilizando una plantilla

stencil[2] *n* : plantilla *f* (para marcar)

stenographer [stə'nɑɡrəfər] *n* : taquígrafo *m*, -fa *f*

stenographic [,stɛnə'ɡræfɪk] *adj* : taquigráfico

stenography [stə'nɑɡrəfi] *n* : taquigrafía *f*

step[1] ['stɛp] *v* **stepped; stepping** *vi* **1** : dar un paso ⟨step this way, please : pase por aquí, por favor⟩ ⟨step aside : apártate⟩ ⟨step forward/back : dar un paso (hacia) adelante/atrás⟩ ⟨he stepped outside : salió⟩ ⟨step right up! : ¡acérquense!⟩ **2 to step back** : distanciarse **3 to step down** RESIGN : renunciar **4 to step in** INTERVENE : intervenir **5 to step on** : pisar **6 to step out** *fam* : salir **7 to step up** INCREASE : aumentar **8 to step up** *fam* : mejorarse, esforzarse más — *vt* **1 to step up** INCREASE : aumentar **2 to step up** *fam* IMPROVE : mejorar

step[2] *n* **1** : paso *m* ⟨to take a step : dar un paso⟩ **2** : paso *m* (distancia) ⟨a few steps away : a unos pasos⟩ **3** : paso *m* (sonido) **4** FOOTPRINT : huella *f* **5** STAIR : escalón *m*, peldaño *m* **6** RUNG : escalón *m*, travesaño *m* **7** RANK, DEGREE : peldaño *m*, escalón *m* ⟨a step up : un ascenso⟩ **8** MEASURE, MOVE : medida *f*, paso *m* ⟨to take steps : tomar medidas⟩ **9** STAGE : paso *m* ⟨step by step : paso a paso⟩ **10** STRIDE : paso *m* ⟨with a quick step : con paso rápido⟩ **11 to be a/one step ahead of** : llevarle ventaja a **12 to be in step** : llevar el paso **13 to watch one's step** : mirar uno donde camina **14 to watch one's step** BEWARE : andarse con cuidado

stepbrother ['stɛp,brʌðər] *n* : hermanastro *m*

stepchild ['stɛp,tʃaɪld] *n* : hijastro *m*, -tra *f*; entenado *m*, -da *f* Mex

stepdaughter ['stɛp,dɔtər] *n* : hijastra *f*

stepfather ['stɛp,fɑðər, -,fɑ-] *n* : padrastro *m*

stepladder ['stɛp,lædər] *n* : escalera *f* de tijera

stepmother ['stɛp,mʌðər] *n* : madrastra *f*

steppe ['stɛp] *n* : estepa *f*

stepping–stone ['stɛpɪŋ,sto:n] *n* : **1** : piedra *f* (para cruzar un arroyo, etc.) **2** : trampolín *m* (al éxito)

stepsister ['stɛp,sɪstər] n : hermanastra f

stepson ['stɛp,sʌn] n : hijastro m

step up vt INCREASE : aumentar

stereo[1] ['steri,o:, 'stɪr-] adj : estéreo

stereo[2] n, pl **stereos** : estéreo m

stereophonic [,sterio'fɑnɪk, ,stɪr-] adj : estereofónico

stereotype[1] ['sterio,taɪp, 'stɪr-] vt **-typed; -typing** : estereotipar

stereotype[2] n : estereotipo m

sterile ['sterəl] adj : estéril

sterility [stə'rɪləti] n : esterilidad f

sterilization [,sterələ'zeɪʃən] n : esterilización f

sterilize ['sterə,laɪz] vt **-ized; -izing** : esterilizar

sterling ['stərlɪŋ] adj 1 : de ley ⟨sterling silver : plata de ley⟩ 2 EXCELLENT : excelente

stern[1] ['stərn] adj : severo, adusto — **sternly** adv

stern[2] n : popa f

sternness ['stərnnəs] n : severidad f

sternum ['stərnəm] n, pl **sternums** or **sterna** [-nə] : esternón m

steroid ['stɪr,ɔɪd, 'ster-] n, pl **steroids** : esteroide m

stethoscope ['steθə,sko:p] n : estetoscopio m

stevedore ['sti:və,dor] n : estibador m, -dora f

stew[1] ['stu:, 'stju:] vt : estofar, guisar — vi 1 : cocer (dícese de la carne, etc.) 2 FRET : preocuparse

stew[2] n 1 : estofado m, guiso m 2 **to be in a stew** : estar agitado

steward ['stu:ərd, 'stju:-] n 1 MANAGER : administrador m 2 : auxiliar m de vuelo (en un avión), camarero m (en un barco)

stewardess ['stu:ərdəs, 'stju:-] n 1 MANAGER : administradora f 2 : camarera f (en un barco) 3 : auxiliar f de vuelo, azafata f, aeromoza f (en un avión)

stick[1] ['stɪk] v **stuck** ['stʌk]; **sticking** vt 1 STAB : clavar 2 ATTACH : pegar 3 PUT : poner, meter ⟨she stuck the letter under the door : metió la carta por debajo de la puerta⟩ ⟨stick 'em up! : ¡manos arriba!, ¡arriba las manos!⟩ 4 **to stick it to** : darle duro a 5 **to stick out** : sacar (la lengua, etc.), extender (la mano) 6 **to stick out** ENDURE : aguantar en 7 **to stick someone with** : endilgarle (una responsabilidad) a alguien, dejar a alguien solo con (una persona) — vi 1 ADHERE : pegarse, adherirse 2 JAM : atascarse ⟨the door sticks : la puerta se atasca⟩ ⟨the song stuck in my head/mind : la canción se me grabó en la cabeza/mente⟩ 3 **to stick around** : quedarse 4 **to stick by** : no abandonar 5 **to stick out** PROJECT : sobresalir (de una superficie), asomar (por detrás o debajo de algo) 6 **to stick out** STAND OUT : resaltar 7 **to stick to** : no abandonar, no desviarse de ⟨stick to your guns : manténgase firme⟩ ⟨to stick to the rules : atenerse a las reglas⟩ ⟨to stick to one's word : cumplir uno con su palabra⟩ 8 **to stick up** : estar parado (dícese del pelo, etc.), sobresalir (de una superficie) 9 **to stick up for** : defender 10 **to stick with** : serle fiel a (una persona), seguir con (una cosa) ⟨I'll stick with what I know : prefiero lo conocido⟩

stick[2] n 1 BRANCH, TWIG : ramita f 2 : palo m, vara f ⟨a walking stick : un bastón⟩

sticker ['stɪkər] n : etiqueta f adhesiva

stick-in-the-mud n : aguafiestas mf

stickler ['stɪklər] n : persona f exigente ⟨to be a stickler for : insistir mucho en⟩

sticky ['stɪki] adj **stickier; -est** 1 ADHESIVE : pegajoso, adhesivo 2 MUGGY : bochornoso 3 DIFFICULT : difícil

stiff ['stɪf] adj 1 RIGID : rígido, tieso ⟨a stiff dough : una masa firme⟩ 2 : agarrotado, entumecido ⟨stiff muscles : músculos entumecidos⟩ 3 STILTED : acartonado, poco natural 4 STRONG : fuerte (dícese del viento, etc.) 5 DIFFICULT, SEVERE : severo, difícil, duro

stiffen ['stɪfən] vt 1 STRENGTHEN : fortalecer, reforzar (tela, etc.) 2 : hacer más duro (un castigo, etc.) — vi 1 HARDEN : endurecerse 2 : entumecerse (dícese de los músculos)

stiffly ['stɪfli] adv 1 RIGIDLY : rígidamente 2 COLDLY : con frialdad

stiffness ['stɪfnəs] n 1 RIGIDITY : rigidez f 2 COLDNESS : frialdad f 3 SEVERITY : severidad f

stifle ['staɪfəl] vt **-fled; -fling** SMOTHER, SUPPRESS : sofocar, reprimir, contener ⟨to stifle a yawn : reprimir un bostezo⟩

stifling ['staɪfəlɪŋ] adj : sofocante

stigma ['stɪgmə] n, pl **stigmata** [stɪg'mɑtə, 'stɪgmətə] or **stigmas** : estigma m

stigmatize ['stɪgmə,taɪz] vt **-tized; -tizing** : estigmatizar

stile ['staɪl] n : escalones mpl para cruzar un cerco

stiletto [stə'lɛˌto:] n, pl **-tos** or **-toes** : estilete m

still[1] ['stɪl] vt CALM : pacificar, apaciguar — vi : pacificarse, apaciguarse

still[2] adv 1 QUIETLY : quieto ⟨sit still! : ¡quédate quieto!⟩ 2 : de todos modos, aún, todavía ⟨she still lives there : aún vive allí⟩ ⟨it's still the same : sigue siendo lo mismo⟩ 3 IN ANY CASE : de todos modos, aún así ⟨he still has doubts : aún así le quedan dudas⟩ ⟨I still prefer that you stay : de todos modos prefiero que te quedes⟩

still[3] adj 1 MOTIONLESS : quieto, inmóvil 2 SILENT : callado

still[4] n 1 SILENCE : quietud f, calma f 2 : alambique m (para destilar alcohol)

stillborn ['stɪl,bɔrn] adj : nacido muerto

still life n : naturaleza f muerta, bodegón m

stillness ['stɪlnəs] n : calma f, silencio m

stilt ['stɪlt] n : zanco m

stilted ['stɪltəd] adj : afectado, poco natural

stimulant ['stɪmjələnt] n : estimulante m — **stimulant** adj stimulate ['stɪmjə,leɪt] vt -lated; -lating : estimular

stimulation [,stɪmjə'leɪʃən] n 1 STIMULATING : estimulación f 2 STIMULUS : estímulo m

stimulus ['stɪmjələs] n, pl -li [-,laɪ] 1 : estímulo m 2 INCENTIVE : acicate m

sting¹ ['stɪŋ] v stung ['stʌŋ]; stinging vt 1 : picar ⟨a bee stung him : le picó una abeja⟩ 2 HURT : hacer escocer (físicamente), herir (emocionalmente) — vi 1 : picar (dícese de las abejas, etc.) 2 SMART : escocer, arder

sting² n : picadura f (herida), escozor m (sensación)

stinger ['stɪŋər] n : aguijón m (de una abeja, etc.)

stinginess ['stɪndʒinəs] n : tacañería f

stingy ['stɪndʒi] adj stingier; -est 1 MISERLY : tacaño, avaro 2 PALTRY : mezquino, mísero

stink¹ ['stɪŋk] vi stank ['stæŋk] or stunk ['stʌŋk]; stunk; stinking : apestar, oler mal

stink² n : hedor m, mal olor m, peste f

stint¹ ['stɪnt] vt : escatimar ⟨to stint oneself : privarse de⟩ — vi to stint on : escatimar

stint² n : período m

stipend ['staɪ,pɛnd, -pənd] n : estipendio m

stipulate ['stɪpjə,leɪt] vt -lated; -lating : estipular

stipulation [,stɪpjə'leɪʃən] n : estipulación f

stir¹ ['stər] v stirred; stirring vt 1 AGITATE : mover, agitar 2 MIX : revolver, remover 3 INCITE : incitar, impulsar, motivar 4 or to stir up AROUSE : despertar (memorias, etc.), provocar (ira, etc.) — vi : moverse, agitarse

stir² n 1 MOTION : movimiento m 2 COMMOTION : revuelo m

stirrup ['stərəp, 'stɪr-] n : estribo m

stitch¹ ['stɪtʃ] vt : coser, bordar (para decorar) — vi : coser

stitch² n 1 : puntada f 2 TWINGE : punzada f, puntada f

stock¹ ['stɑk] vt : surtir, abastecer, vender — vi to stock up : abastecerse

stock² n 1 SUPPLY : reserva f, existencias fpl (en comercio) ⟨to be out of stock : estar agotadas las existencias⟩ 2 SECURITIES : acciones fpl, valores mpl 3 LIVESTOCK : ganado m 4 ANCESTRY : linaje m, estirpe f 5 BROTH : caldo m 6 to take stock (of) : evaluar

stockade [stɑ'keɪd] n : estacada f

stockbroker ['stɑk,broːkər] n : corredor m, -dora f de bolsa

stock exchange : bolsa f

stockholder ['stɑk,hoːldər] n : accionista mf

stocking ['stɑkɪŋ] n : media f ⟨a pair of stockings : unas medias⟩

stock market n : mercado m de valores, bolsa f de valores

stockpile¹ ['stɑk,paɪl] vt -piled; -piling : acumular, almacenar

stockpile² n : reservas fpl

stocky ['stɑki] adj stockier; -est : robusto, fornido

stockyard ['stɑk,jɑrd] n : corral m

stodgy ['stɑdʒi] adj stodgier; -est 1 DULL : aburrido, pesado 2 OLD-FASHIONED : anticuado

stoic¹ ['stoːɪk] or stoical [-ɪkəl] adj : estoico — stoically [-ɪkli] adv

stoic² n : estoico m, -ca f

stoicism ['stoːə,sɪzəm] n : estoicismo m

stoke ['stoːk] vt stoked; stoking : atizar (un fuego), echarle carbón a (un horno)

stole¹ → steal

stole² ['stoːl] n : estola f

stolen → steal

stolid ['stɑlɪd] adj : impasible, imperturbable — stolidly adv

stomach¹ ['stʌmɪk] vt : aguantar, soportar

stomach² n 1 : estómago m 2 BELLY : vientre m, barriga f, panza f 3 DESIRE : ganas fpl ⟨he had no stomach for a fight : no quería pelea⟩

stomachache ['stʌmɪk,eɪk] n : dolor m de estómago

stomp ['stɑmp, 'stɔmp] vt : pisotear — vi : pisar fuerte

stone¹ ['stoːn] vt stoned; stoning : apedrear, lapidar

stone² n 1 : piedra f 2 PIT : hueso m, pepa f (de una fruta)

Stone Age n : Edad f de Piedra

stoned ['stoːnd] adj fam : drogado

stonemason → mason

stonemasonry → masonry

stony ['stoːni] adj stonier; -est 1 ROCKY : pedregoso 2 UNFEELING : insensible, frío ⟨a stony stare : una mirada glacial⟩

stood → stand

stool ['stuːl] n 1 SEAT : taburete m, banco m 2 FOOTSTOOL : escabel m 3 FECES : deposición f de heces

stoop¹ ['stuːp] vi 1 CROUCH : agacharse 2 to stoop to : rebajarse a

stoop² n 1 : espaldas fpl encorvadas ⟨to have a stoop : ser encorvado⟩ 2 : entrada f (de una casa)

stop¹ ['stɑp] v stopped; stopping vt 1 or to stop up PLUG : tapar 2 PREVENT : impedir, evitar ⟨she stopped me from leaving : me impidió que saliera⟩ 3 HALT : parar, detener ⟨I was stopped by the police : me paró un policía⟩ ⟨he stopped the car : paró el carro⟩ 4 CEASE, QUIT : dejar de ⟨he stopped talking : dejó de hablar⟩ ⟨stop it! : ¡basta!⟩ 5 END : terminar (una pelea, etc.), detener (una hemorragia) ⟨we must stop the violence : tenemos que poner fin a la violencia⟩ 6 to stop (payment on) a check : dar orden de no pago (a un cheque) — vi 1 HALT : detenerse, parar ⟨she stopped to watch : se detuvo a mirar⟩ ⟨we stopped for gas : paramos a por gasolina⟩ ⟨he stopped dead : paró en seco⟩ ⟨stop! who goes there? : ¡alto! ¿quién va?⟩ 2 : detenerse, parar ⟨let's stop and take a break : paremos para descansar⟩ ⟨to stop to consider something : detenerse a pensar en algo⟩ 3 : pararse (dícese de un motor, etc.) ⟨his heart stopped : se le paró el corazón⟩ 4

CEASE, END : cesar, terminar ⟨the rain won't stop : no deja de llover⟩ **5** STAY : quedarse ⟨I can't stop for long : no puedo quedarme mucho tiempo⟩ **6 to stop by/in** : pasar a ver, visitar **7 to stop off** : hacer una parada **8 to stop over** : parar, quedarse **9 to stop over** : hacer escala (dícese de un avión)

stop² n **1** STOPPER : tapón m **2** HALT : parada f, alto m ⟨to come to a stop : pararse, detenerse⟩ ⟨to put a stop to : poner fin a⟩ **3** : parada f ⟨bus stop : parada de autobús⟩

stopgap ['stɑp,gæp] n : arreglo m provisorio

stoplight ['stɑp,laɪt] n : semáforo m

stopover ['stɑp,o:vər] n LAYOVER : escala f

stoppage ['stɑpɪdʒ] n : acto m de parar ⟨a work stoppage : un paro⟩

stopper ['stɑpər] n : tapón m

stopwatch ['stɑp,wɑtʃ] n : cronómetro m

storage ['stɔrɪdʒ] n : almacenamiento m, almacenaje m

storage battery n : acumulador m

store¹ ['stɔr] vt **stored; storing** : guardar, almacenar

store² n **1** RESERVE, SUPPLY : reserva f **2** SHOP : tienda f ⟨grocery store : tienda de comestibles⟩

storehouse ['stɔr,haʊs] n : almacén m, depósito m

storekeeper ['stɔr,ki:pər] n : tendero m, -ra f

storeroom ['stɔr,ru:m, -,rʊm] n : almacén m, depósito m

stork ['stɔrk] n : cigüeña f

storm¹ ['stɔrm] vi **1** : llover o nevar tormentosamente **2** RAGE : ponerse furioso, vociferar **3 to storm out** : salir echando pestes — vt ATTACK : asaltar

storm² n **1** : tormenta f, tempestad f **2** UPROAR : alboroto m, revuelo m, escándalo m ⟨a storm of abuse : un torrente de abusos⟩

stormy ['stɔrmi] adj **stormier; -est** : tormentoso — **stormily** adv

story ['stɔri] n, pl **stories 1** NARRATIVE, TALE : cuento m, relato m ⟨a bedtime story : un cuento para dormir⟩ **2** ACCOUNT : historia f, relato m ⟨it's a long story : es largo de contar⟩ ⟨to make a long story short : en pocas palabras⟩ **3** ARTICLE : artículo m **4** TALE, LIE : cuento m, mentira f **5** INFORMATION : información f ⟨what's his story? : ¿qué me puedes contar de él?⟩ ⟨the story behind the changes : la razón de los cambios⟩ **6** : piso m, planta f (de un edificio) ⟨first story : planta baja⟩

stout ['staʊt] adj **1** FIRM, RESOLUTE : firme, resuelto **2** STURDY : fuerte, robusto, sólido **3** FAT : corpulento, gordo

stoutness ['staʊtnəs] n **1** FIRMNESS : firmeza f **2** STURDINESS : fuerza f, robustez f, solidez f **3** FATNESS : corpulencia f, gordura f

stove¹ ['sto:v] n : cocina f (para cocinar), estufa f (para calentar)

stove² → **stave¹**

stow ['sto:] vt **1** STORE : poner, meter, guardar **2** LOAD : cargar — vi **to stow away** : viajar de polizón

stowaway ['sto:ə,weɪ] n : polizón m

straddle ['strædəl] vt **-dled; -dling** : sentarse a horcajadas sobre

straggle ['strægəl] vi **-gled; -gling** : rezagarse, quedarse atrás

straggler ['stræglər] n : rezagado m, -da f

straight¹ ['streɪt] adv **1** : derecho, directamente ⟨go straight, then turn right : sigue derecho, luego gira a la derecha⟩ **2** HONESTLY : honestamente ⟨to go straight : enmendarse⟩ **3** CLEARLY : con claridad **4** FRANKLY : francamente, con franqueza

straight² adj **1** : recto (dícese de las líneas, etc.), derecho (dícese de algo vertical), lacio (dícese del pelo) **2** HONEST, JUST : honesto, justo **3** NEAT, ORDERLY : arreglado, ordenado **4** : solo (dícese de una bebida alcohólica)

straightaway [,streɪtə'weɪ] adv : inmediatamente

straighten ['streɪtən] vt **1** or **to straighten out** : enderezar, poner derecho **2 to straighten out/up** NEATEN : arreglar, ordenar ⟨he straightened up the house : arregló la casa⟩ ⟨I straightened out my papers : ordené los papeles⟩ **3 to straighten out** FIX : arreglar, resolver (problemas, etc.), poner (la vida) en orden **4 to straighten out** : enderezar, meter en vereda (a un niño rebelde, etc.) **5 to straighten out** ENLIGHTEN : aclararle las dudas (a alguien) — vi **1 to straighten up** : ponerse derecho **2 to straighten up/out** IMPROVE : enderezarse

straightforward [streɪt'fɔrwərd] adj **1** FRANK : franco, sincero **2** CLEAR, PRECISE : puro, simple, claro

straight razor → **razor**

strain¹ ['streɪn] vt **1** EXERT : forzar (la vista, la voz) ⟨to strain oneself : hacer un gran esfuerzo⟩ **2** FILTER : colar, filtrar **3** INJURE : lastimarse, hacerse daño en ⟨to strain a muscle : sufrir un esguince⟩ — vi **to strain to do something** : esforzarse por hacer algo

strain² n **1** LINEAGE : linaje m, abolengo m **2** STREAK, TRACE : veta f **3** VARIETY : tipo m, variedad f **4** STRESS : tensión f, presión f **5** SPRAIN : esguince m, torcedura f (del tobillo, etc.) **6 strains** npl TUNE : melodía f, acordes mpl, compases fpl

strained ['streɪnd] adj **1** FORCED : forzado **2** ANXIOUS : preocupado **3** TIRED : cansado **4** TENSE : tenso

strainer ['streɪnər] n : colador m

strait ['streɪt] n **1** : estrecho m **2 straits** npl DISTRESS : aprietos mpl, apuros mpl ⟨in dire straits : en serios aprietos⟩

straitened ['streɪtənd] adj **in straitened circumstances** : en apuros económicos

straitjacket ['streɪt,dʒækət] n : camisa f de fuerza

strand¹ ['strænd] *vt* **1** : varar **2 to be left stranded** : quedar(se) varado, quedar colgado ⟨they left me stranded : me dejaron abandonado⟩

strand² *n* **1** : hebra *f* (de hilo, etc.) ⟨a strand of hair : un pelo⟩ **2** BEACH : playa *f*

strange ['streɪndʒ] *adj* **stranger; -est 1** QUEER, UNUSUAL : extraño, raro **2** UNFAMILIAR : desconocido, nuevo

strangely ['streɪndʒli] *adv* ODDLY : de manera extraña ⟨to behave strangely : portarse de una manera rara⟩ ⟨strangely, he didn't call : curiosamente, no llamó⟩

strangeness ['streɪndʒnəs] *n* **1** ODDNESS : rareza *f* **2** UNFAMILIARITY : lo desconocido

stranger ['streɪndʒər] *n* : desconocido *m*, -da *f*; extraño *m*, -ña *f*

strangle ['stræŋgəl] *vt* **-gled; -gling** : estrangular

strangler ['stræŋglər] *n* : estrangulador *m*, -dora *f*

strangulation [ˌstræŋgjə'leɪʃən] *n* : estrangulamiento *m*

strap¹ ['stræp] *vt* **strapped; strapping 1** FASTEN : sujetar con una correa **2** FLOG : azotar (con una correa)

strap² *n* **1** : correa *f* **2 shoulder strap** : tirante *m*

strapless ['stræpləs] *n* : sin tirantes

strapping ['stræpɪŋ] *adj* : robusto, fornido

stratagem ['stræt̬ədʒəm, -ˌdʒɛm] *n* : estratagema *f*, artimaña *f*

strategic [strə'ti:dʒɪk] *adj* : estratégico

strategist ['stræt̬ədʒɪst] *n* : estratega *mf*

strategy ['stræt̬ədʒi] *n, pl* **-gies** : estrategia *f*

stratified ['stræt̬əˌfaɪd] *adj* : estratificado

stratosphere ['stræt̬əˌsfɪr] *n* : estratosfera *f*

stratospheric [ˌstræt̬ə'sfɪrɪk, -'sfɛr-] *adj* : estratosférico

stratum ['streɪt̬əm, 'stræ-] *n, pl* **strata** [-t̬ə] : estrato *m*, capa *f*

straw *n* ['strɔ] **1** : paja *f* ⟨the last straw : el colmo⟩ **2 or drinking straw** : pajita *f*, popote *m Mex*

strawberry ['strɔˌbɛri] *n, pl* **-ries** : fresa *f*

stray¹ ['streɪ] *vi* **1** WANDER : alejarse, extraviarse ⟨the cattle strayed away : el ganado se descarrió⟩ **2** DIGRESS : desviarse, divagar

stray² *adj* : perdido, callejero (dícese de un perro o un gato), descarriado (dícese del ganado)

stray³ *n* : animal *m* perdido, animal *m* callejero

streak¹ ['stri:k] *vt* : hacer rayas en ⟨blue streaked with grey : azul veteado con gris⟩ — *vi* : ir como una flecha

streak² *n* **1** : raya *f*, veta *f* (en mármol, queso, etc.), mechón *m* (en el pelo) **2** : rayo *m* (de luz) **3** TRACE : veta *f* **4** : racha *f* ⟨a streak of luck : una racha de suerte⟩

stream¹ ['stri:m] *vi* : correr, salir a chorros ⟨tears streamed from his eyes : las lágrimas brotaban de sus ojos⟩ — *vt* : derramar, dejar correr ⟨to stream blood : derramar sangre⟩

stream² *n* **1** BROOK : arroyo *m*, riachuelo *m* **2** RIVER : río *m* **3** FLOW : corriente *f*, chorro *m* **4** SERIES : serie *f*, sarta *f*

streamer ['stri:mər] *n* **1** PENNANT : banderín *m* **2** RIBBON : serpentina *f* (de papel), cinta *f* (de tela)

streamline ['stri:mˌlaɪn] *vt* : racionalizar (un proceso, etc.)

streamlined ['stri:mˌlaɪnd] *adj* **1** : aerodinámico (dícese de los automóviles, etc.) **2** EFFICIENT : eficiente, racionalizado

street ['stri:t] *n* : calle *f*

streetcar ['stri:tˌkɑr] *n* : tranvía *m*

streetlight ['stri:tˌlaɪt] *or* **streetlamp** ['stri:tˌlæmp] *n* : farol *m*, farola *f*

strength ['strɛŋkθ] *n* **1** : fuerza *f* ⟨with all her strength : con toda(s) su(s) fuerza(s)⟩ ⟨to save one's strength : reservar uno sus energías⟩ **2** POWER : poder *m*, fuerza *f* ⟨economic/military strength : poder económico/militar⟩ ⟨there is strength in numbers : la unión hace la fuerza⟩ **3** FORTITUDE : fortaleza *f* ⟨strength of character : fortaleza/fuerza de carácter⟩ **4** SOLIDITY, TOUGHNESS : solidez *f*, resistencia *f*, dureza *f* (de un material) **5** INTENSITY : intensidad *f* (de emociones, etc.), fuerza *f* (del viento, etc.), lo fuerte (de un sabor, etc.) **6** CONCENTRATION : concentración *f* ⟨full strength : sin diluir⟩ **7** POTENCY : potencia *f* (de un medicamento) ⟨full/maximum strength : máxima potencia⟩ **8** : fuerte *m*, punto *m* fuerte ⟨strengths and weaknesses : virtudes y defectos⟩ **9** NUMBER : número *m*, complemento *m* ⟨in full strength : en gran número⟩

strengthen ['strɛŋkθən] *vt* **1** : fortalecer (los músculos, el espíritu, etc.) **2** REINFORCE : reforzar **3** INTENSIFY : intensificar, redoblar (esfuerzos, etc.) — *vi* **1** : fortalecerse, hacerse más fuerte **2** INTENSIFY : intensificarse

strenuous ['strɛnjuəs] *adj* **1** VIGOROUS : vigoroso, enérgico **2** ARDUOUS : duro, riguroso

strenuously ['strɛnjuəsli] *adv* : vigorosamente, duro

stress¹ ['strɛs] *vt* **1** : someter a tensión (física) **2** EMPHASIZE : enfatizar, recalcar **3 to stress out** : estresar

stress² *n* **1** : tensión *f* (en un material) **2** EMPHASIS : énfasis *m*, acento *m* (en lingüística) **3** TENSION : tensión *f* (nerviosa), estrés *m*

stressful ['strɛsfəl] *adj* : estresante

stretch¹ ['strɛtʃ] *vt* **1** : estirar (un suéter, un cable, etc.), extender (un lienzo, etc.), desplegar (alas) ⟨to stretch one's legs : estirar las piernas, caminar⟩ **2 to stretch the truth** : forzar la verdad, exagerar — *vi* **1** *or* **to stretch out** : estirarse **2** REACH : extenderse **3 to stretch back (in time)**: remontarse

stretch² *n* **1** STRETCHING : extensión *f*, estiramiento *m* (de músculos) **2**

ELASTICITY : elasticidad *f* 3 EXPANSE : tramo *m*, trecho *m* ⟨the home stretch : la recta final⟩ 4 PERIOD : período *m* (de tiempo)

stretcher ['stretʃər] *n* : camilla *f*

strew ['stru:] *vt* **strewed; strewed** *or* **strewn** ['stru:n]; **strewing** 1 SCATTER : esparcir (semillas, etc.), desparramar (papeles, etc.) 2 to strew with : cubrir de

stricken ['strɪkən] *adj* **stricken with** : aquejado de (una enfermedad), afligido por (tristeza, etc.)

strict ['strɪkt] *adj* : estricto — **strictly** *adv*

strictness ['strɪktnəs] *n* : severidad *f*, lo estricto

stricture ['strɪktʃər] *n* : crítica *f*, censura *f*

stride[1] ['straɪd] *vi* **strode** ['stro:d]; **stridden** ['strɪdən]; **striding** : ir dando trancos, ir dando zancadas

stride[2] *n* : tranco *m*, zancada *f*

strident ['straɪdənt] *adj* : estridente

strife ['straɪf] *n* : conflictos *mpl*, disensión *f*

strike[1] ['straɪk] *v* **struck** ['strʌk]; **striking** *vt* 1 HIT : golpear, pegarle (a una persona) ⟨the bullet struck him in the leg : la bala lo alcanzó en la pierna⟩ 2 HIT : chocar contra, dar contra ⟨the car struck a tree : el carro chocó contra un árbol⟩ 3 DELETE : suprimir, tachar 4 COIN, MINT : acuñar (monedas) 5 : dar (la hora) 6 AFFLICT : sobrevenir ⟨he was stricken with a fever : le sobrevino una fiebre⟩ 7 IMPRESS : impresionar, parecer ⟨her voice struck me : su voz me impresionó⟩ ⟨it struck him as funny : le pareció chistoso⟩ 8 : ocurrírsele a ⟨it struck me that . . . : se me ocurrió que . . .⟩ 9 : encender (un fósforo) 10 FIND : descubrir (oro, petróleo) 11 ADOPT : adoptar (una pose, etc.) 12 : tocar (en música) 13 REACH : llegar a, alcanzar (un acuerdo, etc.) 14 to strike a blow : pegar un golpe 15 to strike down : fulminar 16 to strike out : tachar (palabras, etc.) 17 to strike up : entablar (una conversación, una amistad), empezar a tocar (una canción) — *vi* 1 HIT : golpear ⟨to strike against : chocar contra⟩ 2 ATTACK : atacar 3 : declararse en huelga 4 to strike back : devolverle el golpe a 5 to strike out : poncharse (en beisbol) ⟨to strike out with FAIL : fracasar 7 to strike out at ATTACK : arremeter contra 8 to strike out for : emprender el camino hacia 9 to strike out on one's own : emprender algo solo

strike[2] *n* 1 BLOW : golpe *m* 2 : huelga *f*, paro *m* ⟨to be on strike : estar en huelga⟩ 3 ATTACK : ataque *m*

strikebreaker ['straɪk,breɪkər] *n* : rompehuelgas *mf*, esquirol *mf*

strike out *vi* 1 HEAD : salir (para) 2 : ser ponchado (en béisbol) ⟨the batter struck out : poncharon al bateador⟩

striker ['straɪkər] *n* : huelguista *mf*

strike up *vt* START : entablar, empezar

striking ['straɪkɪŋ] *adj* : notable, sorprendente, llamativo ⟨a striking beauty : una belleza imponente⟩ — **strikingly** *adv*

string[1] ['strɪŋ] *vt* **strung** ['strʌŋ]; **stringing** 1 THREAD : ensartar ⟨to string beads : ensartar cuentas⟩ 2 HANG : colgar (con un cordel)

string[2] *n* 1 : cordel *m*, cuerda *f* 2 SERIES : serie *f*, sarta *f* (de insultos, etc.) 3 strings *npl* : cuerdas *fpl* (en música) 4 strings *npl* : influencias *fpl* ⟨to pull strings : utilizar sus influencias⟩ 5 strings *npl* : compromisos *mpl* ⟨with no strings attached : sin compromiso(s)⟩

string bean *n* : judía *f*, ejote *m Mex*

stringent ['strɪndʒənt] *adj* : estricto, severo

stringy ['strɪŋi] *adj* **stringier; -est** : fibroso

strip[1] ['strɪp] *v* **stripped; stripping** *vt* : quitar (ropa, pintura, etc.), desnudar, despojar — *vi* UNDRESS : desnudarse

strip[2] *n* : tira *f* ⟨a strip of land : una faja⟩

stripe[1] ['straɪp] *vt* **striped** ['straɪpt]; **striping** : marcar con rayas o listas

stripe[2] *n* 1 : raya *f*, lista *f* 2 BAND : franja *f*

striped ['straɪpt, 'straɪpəd] *adj* : a rayas, de rayas, rayado, listado

strive ['straɪv] *vi* **strove** ['stro:v]; **striven** ['strɪvən] *or* **strived; striving** 1 to strive for : luchar por lograr 2 to strive to : esforzarse por

strode → stride

stroke[1] ['stro:k] *vt* **stroked; stroking** : acariciar

stroke[2] *n* 1 : apoplejía *f*, derrame *m* cerebral (en medicina) 2 : pincelada *f*, trazo *m* (en el arte) 3 : estilo *m* (de nadar) 4 : movimiento *m*, batir *m* (de alas), brazada *f* (al nadar), remada *f* (al remar) 5 CARESS : caricia *f* 6 : golpe *m* (en beisbol, etc.) 7 ACT : golpe *m* ⟨in one stroke : de un golpe⟩ ⟨a stroke of genius/inspiration : una genialidad/inspiración⟩ 8 : golpe *m* ⟨a stroke of luck : un golpe de suerte⟩ 9 : campanada *f* (de un reloj)

stroll[1] ['stro:l] *vi* : pasear, pasearse, dar un paseo

stroll[2] *n* : paseo *m*

stroller ['stro:lər] *n* : cochecito *m* (para niños)

strong ['strɔŋ] *adj* 1 : fuerte ⟨strong arms : brazos fuertes⟩ ⟨strong winds : vientos fuertes⟩ ⟨a strong odor : un olor fuerte⟩ ⟨strong coffee/medicine : café/medicina fuerte⟩ ⟨strong language : lenguaje fuerte⟩ ⟨a strong candidate/leader : un candidato/líder fuerte⟩ ⟨strong opposition : fuerte oposición⟩ ⟨of strong character : de carácter fuerte⟩ ⟨his strong point : su (punto) fuerte⟩ 2 DURABLE : resistente, fuerte 3 HEALTHY : sano 4 NOTICEABLE : marcado 5 FIRM : firme (dícese de convicciones, etc.) 6 PERSUASIVE : poderoso, convincente 7 CONCENTRATED : concentrado (dícese de detergente, etc.) 8 : con mucho aumento (dícese de lentes) 9 (*with numbers*) ⟨an organization five hundred people strong : una organización de quinientas personas⟩

strongbox ['strɔŋ,bɑks] *n* : caja *f* fuerte

stronghold ['strɔŋ,ho:ld] *n* : fortaleza *f*, fuerte *m*, bastión *m* ⟨a cultural stronghold : un baluarte de la cultura⟩

strongly ['strɔŋli] *adv* **1** POWERFULLY : fuerte, con fuerza **2** STURDILY : fuertemente, sólidamente **3** INTENSELY : intensamente, profundamente ⟨to feel strongly about something : tener ideas muy claras sobre algo⟩ ⟨to feel/believe strongly that . . . : estar totalmente convencido de que . . ., tener la convicción de que . . .⟩ ⟨I am strongly tempted : me siento muy tentada⟩ **4** WHOLEHEARTEDLY : totalmente ⟨I strongly agree : estoy totalmente de acuerdo⟩ ⟨I strongly disagree : estoy totalmente en desacuerdo⟩ **5** EMPHATICALLY : enérgicamente ⟨to criticize strongly : criticar duramente⟩ ⟨a strongly worded letter : una carta muy dura⟩ ⟨I strongly advise that you see a doctor : le recomiendo encarecidamente que vaya a un médico⟩ **6 to smell/taste strongly of** : oler/saber fuertemente a

struck → **strike**¹

structural ['strʌktʃərəl] *adj* : estructural

structure¹ ['strʌktʃər] *vt* **-tured; -turing** : estructurar

structure² *n* **1** BUILDING : construcción *f* **2** ARRANGEMENT, FRAMEWORK : estructura *f*

struggle¹ ['strʌgəl] *vi* **-gled; -gling 1** CONTEND : forcejear (físicamente), luchar, contender **2** : hacer con dificultad ⟨she struggled forward : avanzó con dificultad⟩

struggle² *n* : lucha *f*, pelea *f* (física)

strum ['strʌm] *vt* **strummed; strumming** : rasguear

strung → **string**¹

strut¹ ['strʌt] *vi* **strutted; strutting** : pavonearse

strut² *n* **1** : pavoneo *m* ⟨he walked with a strut : se pavoneaba⟩ **2** : puntal *m* (en construcción, etc.)

stub¹ ['stʌb] *vt* **stubbed; stubbing 1 to stub one's toe** : darse en el dedo (del pie) **2 to stub out** : apagarse

stub² *n* : colilla *f* (de un cigarrillo), cabo *m* (de un lápiz, etc.), talón *m* (de un cheque)

stubble ['stʌbəl] *n* **1** : rastrojo *m* (de plantas) **2** BEARD : barba *f*

stubborn ['stʌbərn] *adj* **1** OBSTINATE : terco, obstinado, empecinado **2** PERSISTENT : pertinaz, persistente — **stubbornly** *adv*

stubbornness ['stʌbərnnəs] *n* **1** OBSTINACY : terquedad *f*, obstinación *f* **2** PERSISTENCE : persistencia *f*

stubby ['stʌbi] *adj* **stubbier; -est** : corto y grueso ⟨stubby fingers : dedos regordetes⟩

stucco ['stʌko:] *n, pl* **stuccos** *or* **stuccoes** : estuco *m*

stuck → **stick**¹

stuck-up ['stʌk'ʌp] *adj* : engreído, creído *fam*

stud¹ ['stʌd] *vt* **studded; studding** : tachonar, salpicar

stud² *n* **1** *or* **stud horse** : semental *m* **2** : montante *m* (en construcción) **3** HOBNAIL : tachuela *f*, tachón *m*

student ['stu:dənt, 'stju:-] *n* : estudiante *mf*; alumno *m*, -na *f* (de un colegio)

studied ['stʌdid] *adj* : intencionado, premeditado

studio ['stu:di,o:, 'stju:-] *n, pl* **studios** : estudio *m*

studious ['stu:diəs, 'stju:-] *adj* : estudioso — **studiously** *adv*

study¹ ['stʌdi] *v* **studied; studying 1** : estudiar **2** EXAMINE : examinar, estudiar

study² *n, pl* **studies 1** STUDYING : estudio *m* **2** OFFICE : estudio *m*, gabinete *m* (en una casa) **3** RESEARCH : investigación *f*, estudio *m*

stuff¹ ['stʌf] *vt* : rellenar, llenar, atiborrar ⟨a stuffed toy : un juguete de peluche⟩

stuff² *n* **1** POSSESSIONS : cosas *fpl* ⟨my stuff : mis cosas⟩ **2** SUPPLIES, EQUIPMENT : cosas *fpl* ⟨baby stuff : cosas para bebés⟩ **3** *fam* : cosa *f*, cosas *fpl* ⟨some sticky stuff : una cosa pegajosa⟩ ⟨this stuff really works! : ¡esto funciona de maravilla!⟩ ⟨they're giving away free stuff : están regalando cosas⟩ ⟨and stuff (like that) : y cosas por el estilo⟩ **4** (*referring to something heard, read, etc.*) *fam* ⟨this is fascinating stuff : esto es fascinante⟩ ⟨the stuff he said isn't true : lo que dijo no es verdad⟩ **5** (*referring to behavior*) *fam* : cosas *fpl* ⟨she does stuff to bug me : hace cosas para fastidiarme⟩ ⟨how can he get away with that stuff? : ¿cómo es que siempre se sale con la suya?⟩ **6** ESSENCE : esencia *f* **7 to know your stuff** : ser experto

stuffing ['stʌfɪŋ] *n* : relleno *m*

stuffy ['stʌfi] *adj* **stuffier; -est 1** CLOSE : viciado, cargado ⟨a stuffy room : una sala mal ventilada⟩ ⟨stuffy weather : tiempo bochornoso⟩ **2** : tapado (dícese de la nariz) **3** STODGY : pesado, aburrido

stumble¹ ['stʌmbəl] *vi* **-bled; -bling 1** TRIP : tropezar, dar un traspié **2** FLOUNDER : quedarse sin saber qué hacer o decir **3 to stumble across** *or* **to stumble upon** : dar con, tropezar con

stumble² *n* : tropezón *m*, traspié *m*

stumbling block *n* : obstáculo *m*

stump¹ ['stʌmp] *vt* : dejar perplejo ⟨to be stumped : no tener respuesta⟩

stump² *n* **1** : muñón *m* (de un brazo o una pierna) **2** *or* **tree stump** : cepa *f*, tocón *m* **3** STUB : cabo *m*

stun ['stʌn] *vt* **stunned; stunning 1** : aturdir (con un golpe) **2** ASTONISH, SHOCK : dejar estupefacto, dejar atónito, aturdir

stung → **sting**¹

stunk → **stink**¹

stunning ['stʌnɪŋ] *adj* **1** ASTONISHING : asombroso, pasmoso, increíble **2** STRIKING : imponente, impresionante (dícese de la belleza)

stunt¹ ['stʌnt] *vt* : atrofiar

stunt² *n* : proeza *f* (acrobática)

stupefy ['stu:pə,faɪ, 'stju:-] *vt* **-fied; -fying 1** : aturdir, atontar (con drogas, etc.) **2** AMAZE : dejar estupefacto, dejar atónito

stupendous [stu'pɛndəs, stju-] *adj* 1 MARVELOUS : estupendo, maravilloso 2 TREMENDOUS : tremendo — **stupendously** *adv*

stupid ['stu:pəd, 'stju:-] *adj* 1 IDIOTIC, SILLY : tonto, bobo, estúpido 2 DULL, OBTUSE : lento, torpe, lerdo

stupidity [stu'pɪdət̬i, stju-] *n* : tontería *f*, estupidez *f*

stupidly ['stu:pədli, stju:-] *adv* 1 IDIOTICALLY : estúpidamente, tontamente 2 DENSELY : torpemente

stupor ['stu:pər, 'stju:-] *n* : estupor *m*

sturdily ['stərdəli] *adv* : sólidamente

sturdiness ['stərdinəs] *n* : solidez *f* (de muebles, etc.), robustez *f* (de una persona)

sturdy ['stərdi] *adj* **sturdier; -est** : fuerte, robusto, sólido

sturgeon ['stərdʒən] *n* : esturión *m*

stutter¹ ['stʌt̬ər] *vi* : tartamudear

stutter² *n* STAMMER : tartamudeo *m*

sty ['staɪ] *n* 1 *pl* **sties** PIGPEN : chiquero *m*, pocilga *f* 2 *or* **stye** *pl* **sties** *or* **styes** : orzuelo *m* (en el ojo)

style¹ ['staɪl] *vt* **styled; styling** 1 NAME : llamar 2 : peinar (pelo), diseñar (vestidos, etc.) ⟨carefully styled prose : prosa escrita con gran esmero⟩

style² *n* 1 : estilo *m* ⟨that's just his style : él es así⟩ ⟨to live in style : vivir a lo grande⟩ 2 FASHION : moda *f*

stylish ['staɪlɪʃ] *adj* : de moda, elegante, chic

stylishly ['staɪlɪʃli] *adv* : con estilo

stylishness ['staɪlɪʃnəs] *n* : estilo *m*

stylist ['staɪlɪst] *n* : estilista *mf*

stylize ['staɪ‚laɪz, 'staɪə-] *vt* : estilizar

stylus ['staɪləs] *n*, *pl* **styli** ['staɪ‚laɪ] 1 PEN : estilo *m* 2 NEEDLE : aguja *f* (de un tocadiscos)

stymie ['staɪmi] *vt* **-mied; -mieing** : obstaculizar

suave ['swɑv] *adj* : fino, urbano

sub¹ ['sʌb] *vi* **subbed; subbing** → **substitute¹**

sub² *n* 1 → **substitute²** 2 → **submarine²**

sub- [‚sʌb] *pref* : sub-

subcommittee ['sʌbkə‚mɪt̬i] *n* : subcomité *m*

subconscious¹ [‚səb'kɑntʃəs] *adj* : subconsciente — **subconsciously** *adv*

subconscious² *n* : subconsciente *m*

subcontract [‚sʌb'kɑn‚trækt] *n* : subcontratar

subcontractor [‚sʌb'kɑn‚træktər] *n* : subcontratista *mf*

subculture ['sʌb‚kʌltʃər] *n* : subcultura *f*

subdivide [‚sʌbdə‚vaɪd, 'sʌbdə‚vaɪd] *vt* **-vided; -viding** : subdividir

subdivision ['sʌbdə‚vɪʒən] *n* : subdivisión *f*

subdue [səb'du:, -'dju:] *vt* **-dued; -duing** 1 OVERCOME : sojuzgar (a un enemigo), vencer, superar 2 CONTROL : dominar 3 SOFTEN : suavizar, atenuar (luz, etc.), moderar (lenguaje)

subgroup ['sʌb‚gru:p] *n* : subgrupo *m*

subhead ['sʌb‚hɛd] *or* **subheading** [-‚hɛdɪŋ] *n* : subtítulo *m*

subhuman [‚sʌb'hju:mən, -'ju:-] *adj* : infrahumano

subject¹ [səb'dʒɛkt] *vt* 1 CONTROL, DOMINATE : controlar, dominar 2 : someter ⟨they subjected him to pressure : lo sometieron a presiones⟩

subject² ['sʌbdʒɪkt] *adj* 1 : subyugado, sometido ⟨a subject nation : una nación subyugada⟩ 2 PRONE : sujeto, propenso ⟨subject to colds : sujeto a resfriarse⟩ 3 **subject to** : sujeto a ⟨subject to congressional approval : sujeto a la aprobación del congreso⟩

subject³ ['sʌbdʒɪkt] *n* 1 : súbdito *m*, -ta *f* (de un gobierno) 2 *or* **subject matter** TOPIC : tema *m* 3 : sujeto *m* (en gramática)

subjection [səb'dʒɛkʃən] *n* : sometimiento *m*

subjective [səb'dʒɛktɪv] *adj* : subjetivo — **subjectively** *adv*

subjectivity [‚sʌb‚dʒɛk'tɪvət̬i] *n* : subjetividad *f*

subjugate ['sʌbdʒɪ‚geɪt] *vt* **-gated; -gating** : subyugar, someter, sojuzgar

subjunctive [səb'dʒʌŋktɪv] *n* : subjuntivo *m* — **subjunctive** *adj*

sublet ['sʌb‚lɛt] *vt* **-let; -letting** : subarrendar

sublimate ['sʌblə‚meɪt] *vt* **-mated; -mating** : sublimar — **sublimation** [‚sʌblə'meɪʃən] *n*

sublime [sə'blaɪm] *adj* : sublime

sublimely [sə'blaɪmli] *adv* 1 : de manera sublime 2 UTTERLY : absolutamente, completamente

submarine¹ ['sʌbmə‚ri:n, ‚sʌbmə'-] *adj* : submarino

submarine² *n* : submarino *m*

submachine gun [‚sʌbmə'ʃi:n-] *n* : metralleta *f*

submerge [səb'mərdʒ] *v* **-merged; -merging** *vt* : sumergir — *vi* : sumergirse

submission [səb'mɪʃən] *n* 1 YIELDING : sumisión *f* 2 PRESENTATION : presentación *f*

submissive [səb'mɪsɪv] *adj* : sumiso, dócil

submissiveness [səb'mɪsɪvnəs] *n* : sumisión *f*

submit [səb'mɪt] *v* **-mitted; -mitting** *vi* YIELD : rendirse ⟨to submit to : someterse a⟩ — *vt* PRESENT : presentar

subnormal [‚sʌb'nɔrməl] *adj* : por debajo de lo normal

subordinate¹ [sə'bɔrdən‚eɪt] *vt* **-nated; -nating** : subordinar

subordinate² [sə'bɔrdənət] *adj* : subordinado ⟨a subordinate clause : una oración subordinada⟩

subordinate³ *n* : subordinado *m*, -da *f*; subalterno *m*, -na *f*

subordination [sə‚bɔrdən'eɪʃən] *n* : subordinación *f*

subpoena¹ [sə'pi:nə] *vt* **-naed; -naing** : citar

subpoena² *n* : citación *f*, citatorio *m*

subscribe [səb'skraɪb] *vi* **-scribed; -scribing** 1 : suscribirse (a una revista, etc.) 2

to subscribe to : suscribir (una opinión, etc.), estar de acuerdo con

subscriber [səb'skraɪbər] *n* : suscriptor *m*, -tora *f* (de una revista, etc.); abonado *m*, -da *f* (de un servicio)

subscription [səb'skrɪpʃən] *n* : suscripción *f*

subsection ['sʌb,sɛkʃən] *n* : inciso *m* (de un artículo, etc.)

subsequent ['sʌbsɪkwənt, -sə,kwɛnt] *adj* : subsiguiente ⟨subsequent to : posterior a⟩

subsequently ['sʌb,sɪkwɛntli, -kwənt-] *adv* : posteriormente

subservient [səb'sərviənt] *adj* : servil

subside [səb'saɪd] *vi* **-sided; -siding** 1 SINK : hundirse, descender 2 ABATE : calmarse (dícese de las emociones), amainar (dícese del viento, etc.)

subsidiary¹ [səb'sɪdi,ɛri] *adj* : secundario

subsidiary² *n, pl* **-ries** : filial *f*, subsidiaria *f*

subsidize ['sʌbsə,daɪz] *vt* **-dized; -dizing** : subvencionar, subsidiar

subsidy ['sʌbsədi] *n, pl* **-dies** : subvención *f*, subsidio *m*

subsist [səb'sɪst] *vi* : subsistir, mantenerse, vivir

subsistence [səb'sɪstənts] *n* : subsistencia *f*

substance ['sʌbstənts] *n* 1 ESSENCE : sustancia *f*, esencia *f* ⟨a substance : una sustancia tóxica⟩ 3 WEALTH : riqueza *f* ⟨a woman of substance : una mujer acaudalada⟩

substandard [,sʌb'stændərd] *adj* : inferior, deficiente

substantial [səb'stæntʃəl] *adj* 1 ABUNDANT : sustancioso ⟨a substantial meal : una comida sustanciosa⟩ 2 CONSIDERABLE : considerable, apreciable 3 SOLID, STURDY : sólido

substantially [səb'stæntʃəli] *adv* : considerablemente

substantiate [səb'stæntʃi,eɪt] *vt* **-ated; -ating** : confirmar, probar, justificar

substitute¹ ['sʌbstə,tu:t, -,tju:t] *v* **-tuted; -tuting** *vt* : sustituir — *vi* **to substitute for** : sustituir

substitute² *n* 1 : sustituto *m*, -ta *f*; suplente *mf* (persona) 2 : sucedáneo *m* ⟨sugar substitute : sucedáneo de azúcar⟩

substitute teacher *n* : profesor *m*, -sora *f* suplente

substitution [,sʌbstə'tu:ʃən, -'tju:-] *n* : sustitución *f*

subterfuge ['sʌbtər,fju:dʒ] *n* : subterfugio *m*

subterranean [,sʌbtə'reɪniən] *adj* : subterráneo

subtitle ['sʌb,taɪtəl] *n* : subtítulo *m*

subtle ['sʌtəl] *adj* **subtler; subtlest** 1 DELICATE, ELUSIVE : sutil, delicado 2 CLEVER : sutil, ingenioso

subtlety ['sʌtəlti] *n, pl* **-ties** : sutileza *f*

subtly ['sʌtəli] *adv* : sutilmente

subtotal ['sʌb,to:təl] *n* : subtotal *m*

subtract [səb'trækt] *vt* : restar, sustraer

subtraction [səb'trækʃən] *n* : resta *f*, sustracción *f*

suburb ['sʌ,bərb] *n* : municipio *m* periférico, suburbio *m*

suburban [sə'bərbən] *adj* : de las afueras (de una ciudad), suburbano

suburbia [sə'bərbiə] *n* : municipios *mpl* periféricos, suburbios *mpl*

subversion [səb'vərʒən] *n* : subversión *f*

subversive [səb'vərsɪv] *adj* : subversivo

subvert [səb'vərt] *vt* : subvertir

subway ['sʌb,weɪ] *n* : metro *m*; subterráneo *m* Arg, Uru

succeed [sək'si:d] *vt* FOLLOW : suceder a — *vi* 1 : tener éxito (dícese de las personas), dar resultado (dícese de los planes, etc.) ⟨she succeeded in finishing : logró terminar⟩ ⟨to succeed in life : triunfar en la vida⟩ 2 : subir, acceder ⟨to succeed to the throne : subir/acceder al trono⟩ — *vt* 1 : suceder a (algo) 2 : suceder a (alguien)

success [sək'sɛs] *n* : éxito *m*

successful [sək'sɛsfəl] *adj* : exitoso, logrado — **successfully** *adv*

succession [sək'sɛʃən] *n* : sucesión *f* ⟨in succession : sucesivamente⟩

successive [sək'sɛsɪv] *adj* : sucesivo, consecutivo — **successively** *adv*

successor [sək'sɛsər] *n* : sucesor *m*, -sora *f*

succinct [sək'sɪŋkt, sə'sɪŋkt] *adj* : sucinto — **succinctly** *adv*

succor¹ ['sʌkər] *vt* : socorrer

succor² *n* : socorro *m*

succotash ['sʌkə,tæʃ] *n* : guiso *m* de maíz y frijoles

succulent¹ ['sʌkjələnt] *adj* : suculento, jugoso

succulent² *n* : suculenta *f* (planta)

succumb [sə'kʌm] *vi* : sucumbir

such¹ ['sʌtʃ] *adv* (*used for emphasis*) : tan ⟨she's such a nice person! : ¡es tan amable!⟩ ⟨it's been such a long time! : ¡(hace) tanto tiempo!⟩ ⟨it's such a long trip : es un viaje tan largo, es un viaje larguísimo⟩ ⟨such tall buildings! : ¡qué edificios más grandes!⟩ ⟨he's not in such good shape : anda un poco mal⟩ 2 (*indicating degree*) : tan ⟨I've never seen such a large cat! : ¡nunca he visto un gato tan grande como ése!⟩ 3 **such as** : como ⟨animals such as cows and sheep : animales como vacas y ovejas⟩

such² *adj* 1 : tal ⟨there's no such thing : no existe tal cosa⟩ ⟨there's no such person here : no hay nadie aquí con ese nombre⟩ ⟨in such cases : en tales casos⟩ ⟨to such a degree : hasta tal punto⟩ 2 (*indicating degree*) : tal . . . que, tanto . . . que ⟨where are you off to in such a rush? : ¿adónde vas con tanta prisa?⟩ ⟨I'm such a fool! : ¡qué tonto soy!⟩ 3 **such that** : tal . . . que, tanto . . . que ⟨her excitement was such that . . . : tal/tanto era su entusiasmo que . . .⟩

such³ *pron* 1 : tal ⟨such was the result : tal fue el resultado⟩ ⟨he's a child, and acts as such : es un niño, y se porta como tal⟩ 2 : algo o alguien semejante ⟨books, papers and such : libros, papeles y cosas por el estilo⟩

such-and-such *adj* : tal, cual ⟨at such-and-such (a) time : a tal tiempo⟩

suck [ˈsʌk] *vi* **1** : chupar **2** : aspirar (dícese de las máquinas) **3** SUCKLE : mamar **4** *fam* : apestar, ser una lata ⟨this sucks : qué lata⟩ **5** *fam* : ser malísimo ⟨I suck at sports : soy malísimo en los deportes⟩ **6** to suck on : chupar **7** to suck up to : dar coba a — *vt* **1** : sorber (bebidas), chupar (dulces, etc.) **2** PULL, DRAG : arrastrar **3** *or* to suck up ABSORB : absorber **4** to suck in : meter (la panza), aspirar (aire) **5** to be/get sucked in : dejarse engañar **6** to be/get sucked into : verse envuelto en (un asunto)

sucker [ˈsʌkər] *n* **1** : ventosa *f* (de un insecto, etc.) **2** : chupón *m* (de una planta) **3** → **lollipop** **4** FOOL : tonto *m*, -ta *f*; idiota *mf*

suckle [ˈsʌkəl] *v* **-led; -ling** *vt* : amamantar — *vi* : mamar

suckling [ˈsʌklɪŋ] *n* : lactante *mf*

sucrose [ˈsuːˌkroːs, -ˌkroːz] *n* : sacarosa *f*

suction [ˈsʌkʃən] *n* : succión *f*

Sudanese¹ [ˌsuːdənˈiːz, -ˈiːs] *adj* : sudanés

Sudanese² *n* the Sudanese (*used with a plural verb*) : los sudaneses

sudden [ˈsʌdən] *adj* **1** : repentino, súbito ⟨all of a sudden : de pronto, de repente⟩ **2** UNEXPECTED : inesperado, improvisto **3** ABRUPT, HASTY : precipitado, brusco

suddenly [ˈsʌdənli] *adv* **1** : de repente, de pronto **2** ABRUPTLY : bruscamente

suddenness [ˈsʌdənnəs] *n* **1** : lo repentino **2** ABRUPTNESS : brusquedad *f* **3** HASTE : lo precipitado

suds [ˈsʌdz] *npl* : espuma *f* (de jabón)

sue [ˈsuː] *v* **sued; suing** *vt* : demandar — *vi* to sue for : demandar por (daños, etc.)

suede [ˈsweɪd] *n* : ante *m*, gamuza *f*

suet [ˈsuːət] *n* : sebo *m*

suffer [ˈsʌfər] *vi* : sufrir — *vt* **1** : sufrir, padecer (dolores, etc.) **2** PERMIT : permitir, dejar

sufferer [ˈsʌfərər] *n* : persona que padece (una enfermedad, etc.)

suffering [ˈsʌfərɪŋ] *n* : sufrimiento *m*

suffice [səˈfaɪs] *vi* **-ficed; -ficing** : ser suficiente, bastar

sufficient [səˈfɪʃənt] *adj* : suficiente

sufficiently [səˈfɪʃəntli] *adv* : (lo) suficientemente, bastante

suffix [ˈsʌˌfɪks] *n* : sufijo *m*

suffocate [ˈsʌfəˌkeɪt] *v* **-cated; -cating** *vt* : asfixiar, ahogar — *vi* : asfixiarse, ahogarse

suffocation [ˌsʌfəˈkeɪʃən] *n* : asfixia *f*, ahogo *m*

suffrage [ˈsʌfrɪdʒ] *n* : sufragio *m*, derecho *m* al voto

suffuse [səˈfjuːz] *vt* **-fused; -fusing** : impregnar (de olores, etc.), bañar (de luz), teñir (de colores), llenar (de emociones)

sugar¹ [ˈʃʊgər] *vt* : azucarar

sugar² *n* : azúcar *mf*

sugarcane [ˈʃʊgərˌkeɪn] *n* : caña *f* de azúcar

sugary [ˈʃʊgəri] *adj* **1** : azucarado ⟨sugary desserts : postres azucarados⟩ **2** SACCHARINE : empalagoso

suggest [səgˈdʒest, sə-] *vt* **1** PROPOSE : sugerir **2** IMPLY : indicar, dar a entender

suggestible [səgˈdʒestəbəl, sə-] *adj* : influenciable

suggestion [səgˈdʒestʃən, sə-] *n* **1** PROPOSAL : sugerencia *f* **2** INDICATION : indicio *m* **3** INSINUATION : insinuación *f*

suggestive [səgˈdʒestɪv, sə-] *adj* : insinuante — **suggestively** *adv*

suicidal [ˌsuːəˈsaɪdəl] *adj* : suicida

suicide [ˈsuːəˌsaɪd] *n* **1** : suicidio *m* (acto) **2** : suicida *mf* (persona)

suit¹ [ˈsuːt] *vt* **1** ADAPT : adaptar **2** BEFIT : convenir a, ser apropiado a **3** BECOME : favorecer, quedarle bien (a alguien) ⟨the dress suits you : el vestido te queda bien⟩ **4** PLEASE : agradecer, satisfacer, convenirle bien (a alguien) ⟨does Friday suit you? : ¿le conviene el viernes?⟩ ⟨suit yourself! : ¡como quieras!⟩

suit² *n* **1** LAWSUIT : pleito *m*, litigio *m* **2** : traje *m* (ropa) **3** : palo *m* (de naipes)

suitability [ˌsuːtəˈbɪləti] *n* : idoneidad *f*, lo apropiado

suitable [ˈsuːtəbəl] *adj* : apropiado, idóneo — **suitably** [-bli] *adv*

suitcase [ˈsuːtˌkeɪs] *n* : maleta *f*, valija *f*, petaca *f* Mex

suite [ˈswiːt, *for 2 also* ˈsuːt] *n* **1** : suite *f* (de habitaciones) **2** SET : juego *m* (de muebles)

suitor [ˈsuːtər] *n* : pretendiente *m*

sulfur [ˈsʌlfər] *n* : azufre *m*

sulfuric acid [ˌsʌlˈfjʊrɪk] *adj* : ácido *m* sulfúrico

sulk¹ [ˈsʌlk] *vi* : estar de mal humor, enfurruñarse *fam*

sulk² *n* : mal humor *m*

sulky [ˈsʌlki] *adj* **sulkier; -est** : malhumorado, taimado *Chile*

sullen [ˈsʌlən] *adj* **1** MOROSE : hosco, taciturno **2** DREARY : sombrío, deprimente

sullenly [ˈsʌlənli] *adv* **1** MOROSELY : hoscamente **2** GLOOMILY : sombríamente

sully [ˈsʌli] *vt* **sullied; sullying** : manchar, empañar

sultan [ˈsʌltən] *n* : sultán *m*

sultry [ˈsʌltri] *adj* **sultrier; -est 1** : bochornoso ⟨sultry weather : tiempo sofocante, tiempo bochornoso⟩ **2** SENSUAL : sensual, seductor

sum¹ [ˈsʌm] *v* **summed; summing 1** : sumar (números) **2** → **sum up**

sum² *n* **1** AMOUNT : suma *f*, cantidad *f* **2** TOTAL : suma *f*, total *f* **3** : suma *f*, adición *f* (en matemáticas)

sumac [ˈʃuːˌmæk, ˈsuː-] *n* : zumaque *m*

summarize [ˈsʌməˌraɪz] *v* **-rized; -rizing** : resumir, compendiar

summary¹ [ˈsʌməri] *adj* **1** CONCISE : breve, conciso **2** IMMEDIATE : inmediato ⟨a summary dismissal : un despido inmediato⟩ — **summarily** *adv*

summary² *n, pl* **-ries** : resumen *m*, compendio *m*

summation [sə'meɪʃən] *n* : resumen *m*

summer ['sʌmər] *n* : verano *m*

summertime ['sʌmər,taɪm] *n* : verano *m*, estío *m*

summery ['sʌməri] *adj* : veraniego

summit ['sʌmət] *n* **1** : cumbre *f*, cima *f* (de una montaña) **2** *or* **summit conference** : cumbre *f*

summon ['sʌmən] *vt* **1** CALL : convocar (una reunión, etc.), llamar (a una persona) **2** : citar (en derecho) **3 to summon up** : armarse de (valor, etc.) ⟨to summon up one's strength : reunir fuerzas⟩

summons ['sʌmənz] *n, pl* **summonses 1** SUBPOENA : citación *f*, citatorio *m* Mex **2** CALL : llamada *f*, llamamiento *m*

sumptuous ['sʌmptʃʊəs] *adj* : suntuoso — **sumptuously** *adv*

sum up *vt* **1** SUMMARIZE : resumir **2** EVALUATE : evaluar — *vi* : recapitular

sun¹ ['sʌn] *vt* **sunned; sunning 1** : poner al sol **2 to sun oneself** : asolearse, tomar el sol

sun² *n* : sol *m* **2** SUNSHINE : luz *f* del sol

sunbathe ['sʌn,beɪð] *vi* **-bathed; -bathing** : asolearse, tomar el sol

sunbeam ['sʌn,biːm] *n* : rayo *m* de sol

sunblock ['sʌn,blɑk] *n* : filtro *m* solar

sunburn¹ ['sʌn,bərn] *vi* **-burned** [-,bərnd] *or* **-burnt** [-,bərnt]; **-burning** : quemarse por el sol

sunburn² ['sʌn,bərn] *n* : quemadura *f* de sol

sundae ['sʌn,deɪ, -di] *n* : postre *m* de helado (con jarabe, crema batida, etc.)

Sunday ['sʌn,deɪ, -di] *n* : domingo *m* ⟨today is Sunday : hoy es domingo⟩ ⟨(on) Sunday : el domingo⟩ ⟨(on) Sundays : los domingos⟩ ⟨last Sunday : el domingo pasado⟩ ⟨next Sunday : el domingo que viene⟩ ⟨every other Sunday : cada dos domingos⟩ ⟨Sunday afternoon/morning : domingo por la tarde/mañana⟩

sundial ['sʌn,daɪl] *n* : reloj *m* de sol

sundown ['sʌn,daʊn] → **sunset**

sundries ['sʌndriz] *npl* : artículos *mpl* diversos

sundry ['sʌndri] *adj* : varios, diversos

sunflower ['sʌn,flaʊər] *n* : girasol *m*, mirasol *m*

sung → **sing**

sunglasses ['sʌn,glæsəz] *npl* : gafas *fpl* de sol, lentes *mpl* de sol

sunk → **sink¹**

sunken ['sʌŋkən] *adj* : hundido

sunlight ['sʌn,laɪt] *n* : sol *m*, luz *f* del sol

Sunni ['sʊni] *n* : sunita *mf*

sunny ['sʌni] *adj* **sunnier; -est** : soleado

sunrise ['sʌn,raɪz] *n* : salida *f* del sol

sunroof ['sʌn,ruf] *n* : techo *m* corredizo

sunscreen ['sʌn,skriːn] *n* : filtro *m* solar

sunset ['sʌn,sɛt] *n* : puesta *f* del sol

sunshine ['sʌn,ʃaɪn] *n* : sol *m*, luz *f* del sol

sunspot ['sʌn,spɑt] *n* : mancha *f* solar

sunstroke ['sʌn,stroːk] *n* : insolación *f*

suntan ['sʌn,tæn] *n* : bronceado *m* ⟨suntan lotion : bronceador⟩

suntanned ['sʌn,tænd] *adj* : bronceado

sup ['sʌp] *vi* **supped; supping** : cenar

super ['suːpər] *adj* : súper ⟨super! : ¡fantástico!⟩

super- [,suːpər] *pref* : super-

superb [sʊ'pərb] *adj* : magnífico, espléndido — **superbly** *adv*

supercilious [,suːpər'sɪliəs] *adj* : altivo, altanero, desdeñoso

supercomputer ['suːpərkəm,pjuːtər] *n* : supercomputadora *f*

superficial [,suːpər'fɪʃəl] *adj* : superficial — **superficially** *adv* — **superficiality** *n*

superfluous [sʊ'pərfluəs] *adj* : superfluo — **superfluity** *n*

superhighway ['suːpər,haɪ,weɪ, ,suːpər'-] *n* : autopista *f*

superhuman [,suːpər'hjuːmən] *adj* **1** SUPERNATURAL : sobrenatural **2** HERCULEAN : sobrehumano

superimpose [,suːpərɪm'poːz] *vt* **-posed; -posing** : superponer, sobreponer

superintend [,suːpərɪn'tɛnd] *vt* : supervisar

superintendent [,suːpərɪn'tɛndənt] *n* : portero *m*, -ra *f* (de un edificio); director *m*, -tora *f* (de una escuela, etc.); superintendente *mf* (de policía)

superior¹ [sʊ'pɪriər] *adj* **1** BETTER : superior **2** HAUGHTY : altivo, altanero

superior² *n* : superior *m*

superiority [sʊ,pɪri'ɔrəti] *n, pl* **-ties** : superioridad *f*

superlative¹ [sʊ'pərlətɪv] *adj* **1** : superlativo (en gramática) **2** SUPREME : supremo **3** EXCELLENT : excelente, excepcional

superlative² *n* : superlativo *m*

supermarket ['suːpər,mɑrkət] *n* : supermercado *m*

supernatural [,suːpər'nætʃərəl] *adj* : sobrenatural

supernaturally [,suːpər'nætʃərəli] *adv* : de manera sobrenatural

superpower ['suːpər,paʊər] *n* : superpotencia *f*

supersede [,suːpər'siːd] *vt* **-seded; -seding** : suplantar, reemplazar, sustituir

supersonic [,suːpər'sɑnɪk] *adj* : supersónico

superstar ['suːpər,stɑr] *n* : superestrella *f*

superstition [,suːpər'stɪʃən] *n* : superstición *f*

superstitious [,suːpər'stɪʃəs] *adj* : supersticioso

superstore ['suːpər,stɔr] *n* : hipermercado *m*

superstructure ['suːpər,strʌkt[ər] *n* : superestructura *f*

supervise ['suːpər,vaɪz] *vt* **-vised; -vising** : supervisar, dirigir

supervision [,suːpər'vɪʒən] *n* : supervisión *f*, dirección *f*

supervisor ['suːpər,vaɪzər] *n* : supervisor *m*, -sora *f*

supervisory [,suːpər'vaɪzəri] *adj* : de supervisor

supine [sʊ'paɪn] *adj* **1** : en decúbito supino, en decúbito dorsal **2** ABJECT, INDIFFERENT : indiferente, apático

supper ['sʌpər] n : cena f, comida f

supplant [sə'plænt] vt : suplantar

supple ['sʌpəl] adj suppler; supplest : flexible

supplement¹ ['sʌplə,mɛnt] vt : complementar, completar

supplement² ['sʌpləmənt] n 1 : complemento m ⟨dietary supplement : complemento alimenticio⟩ 2 : suplemento m (de un libro o periódico)

supplementary [,sʌplə'mɛntəri] adj : suplementario

supplicate ['sʌpli,keit] v -cated; -cating vi : rezar — vt : suplicar

supplier [sə'plaiər] n : proveedor m, -dora f; abastecedor m, -dora f

supply¹ [sə'plai] vt -plied; -plying : suministrar, proveer de, proporcionar

supply² n, pl -plies 1 PROVISION : provisión f, suministro m ⟨supply and demand : la oferta y la demanda⟩ 2 STOCK : reserva f, existencias fpl (de un negocio) 3 **supplies** npl PROVISIONS : provisiones fpl, víveres mpl, despensa f

support¹ [sə'port] vt 1 BACK : apoyar, respaldar 2 MAINTAIN : mantener, sostener, sustentar 3 PROP UP : sostener, apoyar, apuntalar, soportar

support² n 1 : apoyo m (moral), ayuda f (económica) 2 PROP : soporte m, apoyo m

supporter [sə'portər] n : partidario m, -ria f

supportive [sə'portɪv] adj : que apoya ⟨his family is very supportive : su familia lo apoya mucho⟩

suppose [sə'po:z] vt -posed; -posing 1 ASSUME : suponer, imaginarse ⟨(let's) suppose that . . . : supongamos que . . .⟩ 2 BELIEVE : suponer, creer ⟨I suppose so/not : supongo que sí/no⟩ 3 (used in polite requests) ⟨I don't suppose you could help me? : ¿tú no podrías ayudarme?⟩ 4 to be supposed to (indicating expectation or intention) ⟨he's supposed to arrive today : se supone que llegue hoy⟩ ⟨it was supposed to be a surprise : se suponía que iba a ser una sorpresa⟩ ⟨what's that supposed to mean? : ¿qué quieres decir con eso?⟩ 5 to be supposed to (indicating obligation or permission) ⟨I'm supposed to study : (se supone que) tengo que estudiar⟩ ⟨you're not supposed to go : no deberías ir⟩ 6 to be supposed to (indicating what others say) ⟨she's supposed to be the best : dicen que es la mejor⟩

supposed [sə'po:zd, -'po:zəd] adj : supuesto — **supposedly** [sə'po:zədli] adv

supposition [,sʌpə'zɪʃən] n : suposición f

suppository [sə'pazə,tori] n, pl -ries : supositorio m

suppress [sə'prɛs] vt 1 SUBDUE : sofocar, suprimir, reprimir (una rebelión, etc.) 2 : suprimir, ocultar (información) 3 REPRESS : reprimir, contener ⟨to suppress a yawn : reprimir un bostezo⟩

suppression [sə'prɛʃən] n 1 SUBDUING : represión f 2 : supresión f (de informa-

ción) 3 REPRESSION : represión f, inhibición f

supremacy [su'prɛməsi] n, pl -cies : supremacía f

supreme [su'pri:m] adj : supremo

Supreme Being n : Ser m Supremo

supremely [su'pri:mli] adv : totalmente, sumamente

surcharge ['sər,tʃardʒ] n : recargo m

sure¹ ['ʃur] adv 1 ALL RIGHT : por supuesto, claro 2 (used as an intensifier) ⟨it sure is hot! : ¡hace tanto calor!⟩ ⟨she sure is pretty! : ¡qué linda es!⟩

sure² adj surer; -est 1 : seguro ⟨a sure sign : una clara señal⟩ ⟨a sure method : un método seguro⟩ ⟨it's a sure thing that . . . : seguro que . . .⟩ 2 for sure ⟨to know for sure : saber a ciencia cierta, saber con certeza⟩ ⟨for sure! : ¡ya lo creo!⟩ ⟨that's for sure : eso es seguro⟩ 3 to be sure ⟨to be sure (about/of something) : estar seguro (de algo)⟩ ⟨to be sure that . . . : estar seguro de que . . .⟩ ⟨to be sure of oneself : estar seguro de sí mismo⟩ ⟨I'm not sure why : no sé por qué⟩ ⟨be sure to call! : ¡no dejes de llamar!⟩ 4 to make sure ⟨he made sure (that) the door was locked : se aseguró de que la puerta estaba cerrada con llave⟩ ⟨make sure to call! : ¡no dejes de llamar!⟩ ⟨make sure it doesn't happen again : que no vuelva a pasar⟩

surely ['ʃurli] adv 1 CERTAINLY : seguramente 2 (used as an intensifier) ⟨you surely don't mean that! : ¡no me digas que estás hablando en serio!⟩

sureness ['ʃurnəs] n : certeza f, seguridad f

surety ['ʃurəti] n, pl -ties : fianza f, garantía f

surf¹ ['sərf] vi : hacer surf — vt : navegar ⟨to surf the Web : navegar por/en la web⟩

surf² n 1 WAVES : oleaje m 2 FOAM : espuma f

surface¹ ['sərfəs] v -faced; -facing vi : salir a la superficie — vt : revestir (una carretera)

surface² n 1 : superficie f 2 on the surface : en apariencia

surfboard ['sərf,bord] n : tabla f de surf, tabla f de surfing

surfeit ['sərfət] n : exceso m

surfer ['sərfər] n : surfista mf ⟨Internet surfers : internautas⟩

surfing ['sərfɪŋ] n : surf m, surfing m

surge¹ ['sərdʒ] vi surged; surging 1 : hincharse (dícese del mar), levantarse (dícese de las olas) 2 SWARM : salir en tropel (dícese de la gente, etc.)

surge² n 1 : oleaje m (del mar), oleada f (de gente) 2 FLUSH : arranque m, arrebato m (de ira, etc.) 3 INCREASE : aumento m (súbito)

surgeon ['sərdʒən] n : cirujano m, -na f

surgery ['sərdʒəri] n, pl -geries : cirugía f

surgical ['sərdʒɪkəl] adj : quirúrgico — **surgically** [-kli] adv

surly ['sərli] adj surlier; -est : hosco, arisco

surmise[1] [sər'maɪz] vt **-mised; -mising** : conjeturar, suponer, concluir

surmise[2] n : conjetura f

surmount [sər'maʊnt] vt **1** OVERCOME : superar, vencer, salvar **2** CLIMB : escalar **3** CAP, TOP : coronar

surname ['sər,neɪm] n : apellido m

surpass [sər'pæs] vt : superar, exceder, rebasar, sobrepasar

surplus ['sər,pləs] n : excedente m, sobrante m, superávit m (de dinero)

surprise[1] ['sə,praɪz, sər-] vt **-prised; -prising** : sorprender

surprise[2] n : sorpresa f ⟨to take by surprise : sorprender⟩

surprising [sə'praɪzɪŋ, sər-] adj : sorprendente — **surprisingly** adv

surreal [sə'ri:l] adj : surrealista

surrealism [sə'ri:ə,lɪzəm] n : surrealismo m

surrealist [sə'ri:əlɪst] n : surrealista mf

surrealistic [sə,ri:ə'lɪstɪk] adj : surrealista

surrender[1] [sə'rendər] vt **1** : entregar, rendir **2 to surrender oneself** : entregarse — vi : rendirse

surrender[2] n : rendición m (de una ciudad, etc.), entrega f (de posesiones)

surreptitious [,sərəp'tɪʃəs] adj : subrepticio — **surreptitiously** adv

surrogate ['sərəgət, -,geɪt] n **1** : sustituto m **2 or surrogate mother** : madre f de alquiler

surround [sə'raʊnd] vt : rodear

surroundings [sə'raʊndɪŋz] npl : ambiente m, entorno m

surveillance [sər'veɪlənts, -'veɪljənts, -'veɪənts] n : vigilancia f

survey[1] [sər'veɪ] vt **-veyed; -veying 1** : medir (un terreno) **2** EXAMINE : inspeccionar, examinar, revisar **3** POLL : hacer una encuesta de, sondear

survey[2] ['sər,veɪ] n, pl **-veys 1** INSPECTION : inspección f, revisión f **2** : medición f (de un terreno) **3** POLL : encuesta f, sondeo m

surveyor [sər'veɪər] n : agrimensor m, -sora f

survival [sər'vaɪvəl] n : supervivencia f, sobrevivencia f

survive [sər'vaɪv] v **-vived; -viving** vi : sobrevivir — vt OUTLIVE : sobrevivir a

survivor [sər'vaɪvər] n : superviviente mf, sobreviviente mf

susceptibility [sə,septə'bɪləti] n, pl **-ties** : vulnerabilidad f, propensión f (a enfermedades, etc.)

susceptible [sə'septəbəl] adj **1** VULNERABLE : vulnerable, sensible ⟨susceptible to flattery : sensible a halagos⟩ **2** PRONE : propenso ⟨susceptible to colds : propenso a resfriarse⟩

suspect[1] [sə'spekt] vt **1** DISTRUST : dudar de **2** : sospechar (algo), sospechar de (una persona) **3** IMAGINE, THINK : imaginarse, creer

suspect[2] ['sʌs,pekt, sə'spekt] adj : sospechoso, dudoso, cuestionable

suspect[3] ['sʌs,pekt] n : sospechoso m, -sa f

suspend [sə'spend] vt : suspender

suspenders [sə'spendərz] npl : tirantes mpl

suspense [sə'spents] n : incertidumbre f, suspenso m (en una película, etc.)

suspenseful [sə'spentsfəl] adj : de suspenso

suspension [sə'spentʃən] n : suspensión f

suspension bridge n : puente m colgante

suspicion [sə'spɪʃən] n **1** : sospecha f **2** TRACE : pizca f, atisbo m

suspicious [sə'spɪʃəs] adj **1** QUESTIONABLE : sospechoso, dudoso **2** DISTRUSTFUL : suspicaz, desconfiado

suspiciously [sə'spɪʃəsli] adv : de modo sospechoso, con recelo

sustain [sə'steɪn] vt **1** NOURISH : sustentar **2** PROLONG : sostener **3** SUFFER : sufrir **4** SUPPORT, UPHOLD : apoyar, respaldar, sostener

sustainable [sə'steɪnəbəl] adj : sostenible

sustenance ['sʌstənənts] n **1** NOURISHMENT : sustento m **2** SUPPORT : sostén m

suture ['su:tʃər] n : sutura f

SUV [,es,ju:'vi:] n : SUV m, vehículo m deportivo utilitario

svelte ['sfelt] adj : esbelto

swab[1] ['swɑb] vt **swabbed; swabbing 1** CLEAN : lavar, limpiar **2** : aplicar a (con hisopo)

swab[2] n **or cotton swab** : hisopo m, bastoncillo m, cotonete m Mex

swaddle ['swɑdəl] vt **-dled; -dling** ['swɑdəlɪŋ] : envolver (en pañales)

swagger[1] ['swæɡər] vi : pavonearse

swagger[2] n : pavoneo m

swallow[1] ['swɑlo] vt **1** : tragar (comida, etc.) **2** ENGULF : tragarse, envolver **3** REPRESS : tragarse (insultos, etc.) — vi : tragar

swallow[2] n **1** : golondrina f (pájaro) **2** GULP : trago m

swam → **swim**[1]

swamp[1] ['swɑmp] vt : inundar ⟨to swamp with : inundar de⟩

swamp[2] n : pantano m, ciénaga f

swampy ['swɑmpi] adj **swampier; -est** : pantanoso, cenagoso

swan ['swɑn] n : cisne f

swap[1] ['swɑp] vt **swapped; swapping** : cambiar, intercambiar ⟨to swap places : cambiarse de sitio⟩

swap[2] n : cambio m, intercambio m

swarm[1] ['swɔrm] vi : enjambrar

swarm[2] n : enjambre m

swarthy ['swɔrði, -θi] adj **swarthier; -est** : moreno

swashbuckling ['swɑʃ,bʌklɪŋ] adj : de aventurero

swastika ['swɑstɪskə] n : esvástica f

swat[1] ['swɑt] vt **swatted; swatting** : aplastar (un insecto), darle una palmada (a alguien)

swat[2] n : palmada f (con la mano), golpe m (con un objeto)

swatch ['swɑtʃ] n : muestra f

swath ['swɑθ, 'swɔθ] **or swathe** ['swɑð, 'swɔð, 'sweɪð] n : franja f (de grano segado)

swathe ['swɑð, 'swɔð, 'sweɪð] vt **swathed; swathing** : envolver

swatter ['swɑt̬ər] → **flyswatter**

sway[1] ['sweɪ] vi : balancearse, mecerse — vt INFLUENCE : influir en, convencer

sway[2] n **1** SWINGING : balanceo m **2** INFLUENCE : influjo m

swear ['swær] v **swore** ['swor]; **sworn** ['sworn]; **swearing** vi **1** VOW : jurar ⟨I could have sworn it was true : habría jurado que era verdad⟩ **2** CURSE : decir palabrotas — vt **1** : jurar ⟨I couldn't swear to it : no me atrevería a jurarlo⟩ **2 to swear in** : juramentar (a un testigo), investir (a un oficial)

swearword ['swær,wərd] n : mala palabra f, palabrota f

sweat[1] ['swɛt] vi **sweat** or **sweated; sweating 1** PERSPIRE : sudar, transpirar **2** OOZE : rezumar **3 to sweat over** : sudar la gota gorda por

sweat[2] n : sudor m, transpiración f

sweater ['swɛt̬ər] n : suéter m, buzo m Uru

sweatpants ['swɛt,pænts] n : pantalón m de ejercicio, jogging m Arg, pants m Mex

sweatshirt ['swɛt,ʃərt] n : sudadera f; buzo m Arg, Col; polerón m Chile (camisa)

sweatsuit ['swɛt,su:t] n : sudadera f; buzo m Chile, Peru; jogging m Arg; pants m Mex; chándal m Spain (traje)

sweaty ['swɛt̬i] adj **sweatier; -est** : sudoroso, sudado, transpirado

Swede ['swi:d] n : sueco m, -ca f

Swedish[1] ['swi:dɪʃ] adj : sueco

Swedish[2] n **1** : sueco m (idioma) **2 the Swedish** (used with a plural verb) : los suecos

sweep[1] ['swi:p] v **swept** ['swɛpt]; **sweeping** vt **1** : barrer (el suelo, etc.), limpiar (la suciedad, etc.) ⟨he swept the books aside : apartó los libros de un manotazo⟩ **2** or **to sweep through** : extenderse por (dícese del fuego, etc.), azotar (dícese de una tormenta) ⟨a craze that's sweeping the nation : una moda que está haciendo furor en todo el país⟩ **3** DRAG : barrer, arrastrar **4** : recorrer ⟨her gaze swept the class : recorrió la clase con la mirada⟩ **5** SEARCH : peinar **6** : ir (dramáticamente) ⟨she swept into the room : entró a lo grande en la habitación⟩ **7** DEFEAT : barrer con (un rival, etc.) **8** : barrer en, arrasar en (elecciones, etc.) ⟨the team swept the series : el equipo barrió en la serie⟩ **9 to sweep aside** DISMISS : desechar **10 to sweep up** : recoger — vi **1** : barrer, limpiar **2** : extenderse (en una curva), describir una curva ⟨the sun swept across the sky : el sol describía una curva en el cielo⟩ **3 to sweep up** : barrer

sweep[2] n **1** : barrido m, barrida f (con una escoba) **2** : movimiento m circular **3** SCOPE : alcance m

sweeper ['swi:pər] n : barrendero m, -ra f

sweeping ['swi:pɪŋ] adj **1** WIDE : amplio (dícese de un movimiento) **2** EXTENSIVE : extenso, radical **3** INDISCRIMINATE : indiscriminado, demasiado general **4** OVERWHELMING : arrollador, aplastante

sweepstakes ['swi:p,steɪks] ns & pl **1** : carrera f (en que el ganador se lleva el premio entero) **2** LOTTERY : lotería f

sweet[1] ['swi:t] adj **1** : dulce ⟨sweet desserts : postres dulces⟩ **2** FRESH : fresco **3** : sin sal (dícese de la mantequilla, etc.) **4** PLEASANT : dulce, agradable **5** DEAR : querido

sweet[2] n : dulce m

sweet–and–sour adj : agridulce

sweeten ['swi:tən] vt : endulzar

sweetener ['swi:tənər] n : endulzante m

sweetheart ['swi:t,hɑrt] n : novio m, -via f ⟨thanks, sweetheart : gracias, cariño⟩

sweetly ['swi:tli] adv : dulcemente

sweetness ['swi:tnəs] n : dulzura f

sweet potato n : batata f, boniato m

swell[1] ['swɛl] vi **swelled; swelled** or **swollen** ['swo:lən, 'swʌl-]; **swelling 1** or **to swell up** : hincharse ⟨her ankle swelled : se le hinchó el tobillo⟩ **2** or **to swell out** : inflarse, hincharse (dícese de las velas, etc.) **3** INCREASE : aumentar, crecer

swell[2] n **1** : oleaje m (del mar) **2** → **swelling**

swelling ['swɛlɪŋ] n : hinchazón f

swelter ['swɛltər] vi : sofocarse de calor

swept → **sweep**

swerve[1] ['swərv] vi **swerved; swerving** : virar bruscamente

swerve[2] n : viraje m brusco

swift[1] ['swɪft] adj **1** FAST : rápido, veloz **2** SUDDEN : repentino, súbito — **swiftly** adv

swift[2] n : vencejo m (pájaro)

swiftness ['swɪftnəs] n : rapidez f, velocidad f

swig[1] ['swɪg] vi **swigged; swigging** : tomar a tragos, beber a tragos

swig[2] n : trago m

swill[1] ['swɪl] vt : chupar, beber a tragos grandes

swill[2] n **1** SLOP : bazofia f **2** GARBAGE : basura f

swim[1] ['swɪm] vi **swam** ['swæm]; **swum** ['swʌm]; **swimming 1** : nadar **2** FLOAT : flotar **3** REEL : dar vueltas ⟨his head was swimming : la cabeza le daba vueltas⟩

swim[2] n : baño m, chapuzón m ⟨to go for a swim : ir a nadar⟩

swimmer ['swɪmər] n : nadador m, -dora f

swimming ['swɪmɪŋ] n : natación f ⟨to go swimming : ir a nadar⟩

swimming pool n : piscina f

swimming trunks n : traje m de baño; malla f de baño Arg, Uru; bañador m Spain (de hombre)

swimsuit ['swɪm,su:t] n : traje m de baño; malla f de baño Arg, Uru; bañador m Spain

swindle[1] ['swɪndəl] vt **-dled; -dling** : estafar, timar

swindle[2] n : estafa f, timo m fam

swindler ['swɪndlər] n : estafador m, -dora f; timador m, -dora f

swine ['swaɪn] *ns & pl* : cerdo *m*, -da *f*
swing[1] ['swɪŋ] *v* swung ['swʌŋ]; **swinging**
vt 1 : describir una curva con ⟨she
swung the ax at the tree : le dio al árbol
con el hacha⟩ ⟨he swung himself (up)
into the truck : se subió al camión⟩ 2
: balancear (los brazos, etc.), hacer oscilar 3 SUSPEND : colgar 4 MANAGE
: arreglar ⟨he'll come if he can swing it
: vendrá si puede arreglarlo⟩ ⟨I can't
swing a new car : no me alcanza para
comprar un auto nuevo⟩ — *vi* 1 SWAY
: balancearse (dícese de los brazos, etc.),
oscilar (dícese de un objeto), columpiarse, mecerse (en un columpio) 2
SWIVEL : girar (en un pivote) ⟨the door
swung shut : la puerta se cerró⟩ 3
CHANGE : virar, cambiar (dícese de las
opiniones, etc.) 4 : intentar darle algo/
alguien ⟨he swung at me : intentó pe-
garme⟩ ⟨she swung (at the ball) but
missed : bateó pero no conectó⟩ 5 **to
swing by** *fam* : pasar (por) ⟨I'll swing by
later : pasaré a verte luego⟩ ⟨he'll swing
by the store on his way home : pasará
por la tienda de camino a casa⟩ 6 **to
swing into action** : entrar en acción
swing[2] *n* 1 SWINGING : vaivén *m*, balanceo *m* 2 CHANGE, SHIFT : viraje *m*, movimiento *m* 3 : columpio *m* (para niños)
4 **to take a swing at someone** : intentar
pegarle a alguien
swipe[1] ['swaɪp] *vt* **swiped; swiping** 1
STRIKE : dar, pegar (con un movimiento
amplio) 2 WIPE : limpiar 3 STEAL : birlar
fam, robar
swipe[2] *n* BLOW : golpe *m*
swirl[1] ['swərl] *vi* : arremolinarse
swirl[2] *n* 1 EDDY : remolino *m* 2 SPIRAL
: espiral *f*
swish[1] ['swɪʃ] *vt* : mover (produciendo un
sonido) ⟨she swished her skirt : movía la
falda⟩ — *vi* : moverse (produciendo un
sonido) ⟨the cars swished by : se oían
pasar los coches⟩
swish[2] *n* : silbido *m* (de un látigo, etc.),
susurro *m* (de agua), crujido *m* (de ropa,
etc.)
Swiss[1] ['swɪs] *adj* : suizo
Swiss[2] *n* **the Swiss** (*used with a plural
verb*) : los suizos
swiss chard *n* : acelga *f*
switch[1] ['swɪtʃ] *vt* 1 LASH, WHIP : azotar 2
CHANGE : cambiar de 3 EXCHANGE
: intercambiar 4 **to switch on** : encender,
prender 5 **to switch off** : apagar — *vi* 1
: moverse de un lado al otro 2 CHANGE
: cambiar 3 SWAP : intercambiarse
switch[2] *n* 1 WHIP : vara *f* 2 CHANGE,
SHIFT : cambio *m* 3 : interruptor *m*,
llave *f* (de la luz, etc.)
switchblade ['swɪtʃ,bleɪd] *n* : navaja *f* de
muelle
switchboard ['swɪtʃ,bord] *n* : conmutador
m, centralita *f*
swivel[1] ['swɪvəl] *vi* **-veled** *or* **-velled; -vel-
ing** *or* **-velling** : girar (sobre un pivote)
swivel[2] *n* : base *f* giratoria
swollen *pp* → **swell**[1]

swoon[1] ['swuːn] *vi* : desvanecerse, desmayarse
swoon[2] *n* : desvanecimiento *m*, desmayo
m
swoop[1] ['swuːp] *vi* : abatirse (dícese de las
aves), descender en picada (dícese de un
avión)
swoop[2] *n* : descenso *m* en picada
sword ['sord] *n* : espada *f*
swordfish ['sord,fɪʃ] *n* : pez *m* espada
swore, sworn → **swear**
swum *pp* → **swim**[1]
swung → **swing**[1]
sycamore ['sɪkə,mor] *n* : sicomoro *m*
sycophant ['sɪkəfənt, -,fænt] *n* : adulador
m, -dora *f*
syllabic [sə'læbɪk] *adj* : silábico
syllable ['sɪləbəl] *n* : sílaba *f*
syllabus ['sɪləbəs] *n, pl* **-bi** [-,baɪ] *or*
-buses : programa *m* (de estudios)
symbol ['sɪmbəl] *n* : símbolo *m*
symbolic [sɪm'bɑlɪk] *adj* : simbólico —
symbolically [-kli] *adv*
symbolism ['sɪmbə,lɪzəm] *n* : simbolismo
m
symbolize ['sɪmbə,laɪz] *vt* **-ized; -izing**
: simbolizar
symmetrical [sə'mɛtrɪkəl] *or* **symmetric**
[-trɪk] *adj* : simétrico — **symmetrically**
[-trɪkli] *adv*
symmetry ['sɪmətri] *n, pl* **-tries** : simetría
f
sympathetic [,sɪmpə'θɛtɪk] *adj* 1 PLEAS-
ING : agradable 2 RECEPTIVE : receptivo, favorable 3 COMPASSIONATE,
UNDERSTANDING : comprensivo, compasivo
sympathetically [,sɪmpə'θɛtɪkli] *adv* : con
compasión, con comprensión
sympathize ['sɪmpə,θaɪz] *vi* **-thized; -thiz-
ing** : compadecer ⟨I sympathize with
you : te compadezco⟩
sympathizer ['sɪmpə,θaɪzər] *n* : simpatizante *mf*
sympathy ['sɪmpəθi] *n, pl* **-thies** 1 COM-
PASSION : compasión *f* 2 UNDERSTAND-
ING : comprensión *f* 3 AGREEMENT : solidaridad *f* ⟨in sympathy with : de
acuerdo con⟩ 4 CONDOLENCES : pésame
m, condolencias *fpl*
symphonic [sɪm'fɑnɪk] *adj* : sinfónico
symphony ['sɪmfəni] *n, pl* **-nies** 1
: sinfonía *f* 2 *or* **symphony orchestra**
: orquesta *f* sinfónica
symposium [sɪm'poːziəm] *n, pl* **-sia** [-ziə]
or **-siums** : simposio *m*
symptom ['sɪmptəm] *n* : síntoma *m*
symptomatic [,sɪmptə'mætɪk] *adj* : sintomático
synagogue ['sɪnə,gɑg, -,gɔg] *n* : sinagoga
f
sync ['sɪŋk] *n* : sincronización *f* ⟨in sync
: sincronizado⟩
synchronize ['sɪŋkrə,naɪz, 'sɪn-] *v* **-nized;
-nizing** *vi* : estar sincronizado — *vt*
: sincronizar
syncopate ['sɪŋkə,peɪt, 'sɪn-] *vt* **-pated;
-pating** : sincopar
syncopation [,sɪŋkə'peɪʃən, ,sɪn-] *n*
: síncopa *f*

syndicate¹ [ˈsɪndəˌkeɪt] *vi* **-cated; -cating** : formar una asociación

syndicate² [ˈsɪndɪkət] *n* : asociación *f*, agrupación *f*

syndrome [ˈsɪnˌdroːm] *n* : síndrome *m*

synonym [ˈsɪnəˌnɪm] *n* : sinónimo *m*

synonymous [səˈnɑnəməs] *adj* : sinónimo *m*

synopsis [səˈnɑpsɪs] *n, pl* **-opses** [-ˌsiːz] : sinopsis *f*

syntactic [sɪnˈtæktɪk] *adj* : sintáctico

syntax [ˈsɪnˌtæks] *n* : sintaxis *f*

synthesis [ˈsɪnθəsɪs] *n, pl* **-theses** [-ˌsiːz] : síntesis *f*

synthesize [ˈsɪnθəˌsaɪz] *vt* **-sized; -sizing** : sintetizar

synthesizer [ˈsɪnθəˌsaɪzər] *n* : sintetizador *m*

synthetic¹ [sɪnˈθɪk] *adj* : sintético, artificial — **synthetically** [-ˌtɪkli] *adv*

synthetic² *n* : producto *m* sintético

syphilis [ˈsɪfələs] *n* : sífilis *f*

Syrian [ˈsɪriən] *n* : sirio *m*, -ria *f* — **Syrian** *adj*

syringe [səˈrɪndʒ, ˈsɪrɪndʒ] *n* : jeringa *f*, jeringuilla *f*

syrup [ˈsərəp, ˈsɪrəp] *n* : jarabe *m*, almíbar *m* (de azúcar y agua)

system [ˈsɪstəm] *n* **1** METHOD : sistema *m*, método *m* **2** APPARATUS : sistema *m*, instalación *f*, aparato *m* ⟨electrical system : instalación eléctrica⟩ ⟨digestive system : aparato digestivo⟩ **3** BODY : organismo *m*, cuerpo *m* ⟨diseases that affect the whole system : enfermedades que afectan el organismo entero⟩ **4** NETWORK : red *f*

systematic [ˌsɪstəˈmætɪk] *adj* : sistemático — **systematically** [-ˌtɪkli] *adv*

systematize [ˈsɪstəməˌtaɪz] *vt* **-tized; -tizing** : sistematizar

systemic [sɪsˈtɛmɪk] *adj* : sistémico

systems analyst *n* : analista *mf* de sistemas (en informática)

T

t [ˈtiː] *n, pl* **t's** *or* **ts** [ˈtiːz] : vigésima letra del alfabeto inglés

tab [ˈtæb] *n* **1** FLAP, TAG : lengüeta *f* (de un sobre, una caja, etc.), etiqueta *f* (de ropa) **2** → **tabulator 3** BILL, CHECK : cuenta *f* **4 to keep tabs on** : tener bajo vigilancia

tabby [ˈtæbi] *n, pl* **-bies 1** *or* **tabby cat** : gato *m* atigrado **2** : gata *f*

tabernacle [ˈtæbərˌnækəl] *n* : tabernáculo *m*

table [ˈteɪbəl] *n* **1** : mesa *f* ⟨a table for two : una mesa para dos⟩ ⟨table lamp : lámpara de mesa⟩ **2** LIST : tabla *f* ⟨multiplication table : tabla de multiplicar⟩ **3 table of contents** : índice *m* de materias

tableau [tæˈbloː, ˈtæˌ-] *n, pl* **-leaux** [-ˈbloːz, -ˌbloːz] : retablo *m*, cuadro *m* vivo (en teatro)

tablecloth [ˈteɪbəlˌklɔθ] *n* : mantel *m*

tablespoon [ˈteɪbəlˌspuːn] *n* **1** : cuchara *f* (de mesa) **2** → **tablespoonful**

tablespoonful [ˈteɪbəlˌspuːnˌful] *n* : cucharada *f*

tablet [ˈtæblət] *n* **1** PLAQUE : placa *f* **2** PAD : bloc *m* (de papel) **3** PILL : tableta *f*, pastilla *f*, píldora *f* **4** : tableta *f*, tablet *f* (computadora)

table tennis *n* : tenis *m* de mesa

tableware [ˈteɪbəlˌwær] *n* : vajillas *fpl*, cubiertos *mpl* (de mesa)

tabloid [ˈtæˌblɔɪd] *n* : tabloide *m*

taboo¹ [təˈbuː, tæ-] *adj* : tabú

taboo² *n* : tabú *m*

tabular [ˈtæbjələr] *adj* : tabular

tabulate [ˈtæbjəˌleɪt] *vt* **-lated; -lating** : tabular

tabulator [ˈtæbjəˌleɪtər] *n* : tabulador *m*

tacit [ˈtæsɪt] *adj* : tácito, implícito — **tacitly** *adv*

taciturn [ˈtæsɪˌtərn] *adj* : taciturno

tack¹ [ˈtæk] *vt* **1** : sujetar con tachuelas **2 to tack on** ADD : añadir, agregar

tack² *n* **1** : tachuela *f* **2** COURSE : rumbo *m* ⟨to change tack : cambiar de rumbo⟩

tackle¹ [ˈtækəl] *v* **-led; -ling 1** : taclear (en futbol americano) **2** CONFRONT : abordar, enfrentar, emprender (un problema, un trabajo, etc.)

tackle² *n* **1** EQUIPMENT, GEAR : equipo *m*, aparejo *m* ⟨fishing tackle : aparejo *m* (de un buque)⟩ **3** : tacleada *f* (en futbol americano)

tacky [ˈtæki] *adj* **tackier; -est 1** STICKY : pegajoso **2** CHEAP, GAUDY : de mal gusto, naco *Mex*

taco [ˈtɑko] *n, pl* **tacos** : taco *m*

tact [ˈtækt] *n* : tacto *m*, delicadeza *f*, discreción *f*

tactful [ˈtæktfəl] *adj* : discreto, diplomático, de mucho tacto

tactfully [ˈtæktfəli] *adv* : discretamente, con mucho tacto

tactic [ˈtæktɪk] *n* : táctica *f*

tactical [ˈtæktɪkəl] *adj* : táctico, estratégico

tactics [ˈtæktɪks] *ns & pl* : táctica *f*, estrategia *f*

tactile [ˈtæktəl, -ˌtaɪl] *adj* : táctil

tactless [ˈtæktləs] *adj* : indiscreto, poco delicado

tactlessly [ˈtæktləsli] *adv* : rudamente, sin tacto

tadpole [ˈtædˌpoːl] *n* : renacuajo *m*

taffeta [ˈtæfətə] *n* : tafetán *m*; tafeta *f Arg, Mex, Uru*

taffy [ˈtæfi] *n, pl* **-fies** : caramelo *m* de melaza, chicloso *m Mex*

tag¹ [ˈtæg] *v* **tagged; tagging** *vt* **1** LABEL : etiquetar **2** TAIL : seguir de cerca **3**

TOUCH : tocar (en varios juegos) — *vi* **to tag along** : pegarse, acompañar

tag[2] *n* **1** LABEL : etiqueta *f* **2** SAYING : dicho *m*, refrán *m*

tail[1] ['teɪl] *vt* FOLLOW : seguir de cerca, pegarse

tail[2] *n* **1** : cola *f*, rabo *m* (de un animal) **2** : cola *f*, parte *f* posterior ⟨a comet's tail : la cola de un cometa⟩ **3 tails** *npl* : cruz *f* (de una moneda) ⟨heads or tails : cara o cruz⟩ **4 tails** *npl* → tailcoat

tailcoat ['teɪl,koːt] *n* : frac *m*

tailed ['teɪld] *adj* **1** : que tiene cola **2** (*used in combination*) : de cola ⟨long-tailed : de cola larga⟩

tail end *n* : final *m*, últimos momentos *mpl* (de un espectáculo, etc.), cola *f* (de un grupo, etc.)

tailgate[1] ['teɪl,geɪt] *vi* **-gated; -gating** : seguir a un vehículo demasiado de cerca

tailgate[2] *n* : puerta *f* trasera (de un vehículo)

taillight ['teɪl,laɪt] *n* : luz *f* trasera (de un vehículo), calavera *f* Mex

tailor[1] ['teɪlər] *vt* **1** ADAPT : adaptar, ajustar (ropa) **2** ADAPT : adaptar, ajustar

tailor[2] *n* : sastre *m*, -tra *f*

tailor–made *adj* : hecho a la medida

tailpipe ['teɪl,paɪp] *n* : tubo *m* de escape

tailspin ['teɪl,spɪn] *n* : barrena *f*

taint[1] ['teɪnt] *vt* : contaminar, corromper

taint[2] *n* : corrupción *f*, impureza *f*

take[1] ['teɪk] *v* **took** ['tʊk]; **taken** ['teɪkən]; **taking** *vt* **1** GRASP : tomar, agarrar ⟨to take by the hand : tomar de la mano⟩ ⟨to take the bull by the horns : tomar al toro por los cuernos⟩ **2** BRING, CARRY : llevar, sacar, cargar ⟨take them with you : llévalos contigo⟩ ⟨take this note to your teacher : lleva esta nota a tu maestro⟩ ⟨I took her to school : la llevé a la escuela⟩ ⟨to take him aside : lo llevé aparte⟩ **3** REMOVE, EXTRACT : sacar, extraer ⟨take a beer from the fridge : saca una cerveza de la nevera⟩ ⟨to take blood : sacar sangre⟩ **4** CATCH : tomar, agarrar ⟨taken by surprise : tomado por sorpresa⟩ **5** CAPTURE, SEIZE : tomar ⟨to take someone prisoner : hacer/tomar a alguien prisionero⟩ ⟨to take someone hostage : tomar a alguien como rehén⟩ ⟨to take control of : tomar el control de⟩ **6** CAPTIVATE : encantar, fascinar **7** REMOVE, STEAL : llevarse ⟨someone took the painting : alguien se llevó la pintura⟩ ⟨he took it from her : se lo quitó⟩ ⟨to take someone's life : quitarle la vida a alguien⟩ **8** (*indicating selection*) ⟨I'll take the fish : dame el pescado⟩ ⟨I'll take it : me lo llevo⟩ ⟨take your pick : escoge el que quieras⟩ ⟨do you take cream in your coffee? : ¿le pones crema al café?⟩ **9** NEED, REQUIRE : tomar, requerir ⟨it will take a month to complete : llevará un mes terminarlo⟩ ⟨these things take time : estas cosas toman tiempo⟩ ⟨will it take long? : ¿tardará mucho (tiempo)?⟩ ⟨what size do you take? : ¿qué talla usas?⟩ ⟨it takes diesel : usa diesel⟩ **10**

BORROW : tomar (una frase, etc.) ⟨to take one's inspiration from : inspirarse en⟩ **11** OCCUPY : ocupar ⟨to take a seat : tomar asiento⟩ ⟨this seat is taken : este asiento está ocupado⟩ ⟨to take the place of : ocupar el lugar de⟩ **12** INGEST : tomar, ingerir ⟨to take two pills : tome dos píldoras⟩ ⟨to take drugs : drogarse⟩ **13** : tomar, coger (un tren, un autobús, etc.) **14** TRAVEL : tomar (un camino) **15** BEAR, ENDURE : soportar, aguantar (dolores, etc.), resistir (el frío, etc.) ⟨I can't take it anymore : no puedo más⟩ ⟨she can't take a joke : no sabe aguantar una broma⟩ ⟨to take something well/badly : llevar algo bien/mal⟩ **16** ACCEPT : aceptar (un cheque, un cliente, un trabajo, etc.), seguir (consejos), cargar con (la culpa, la responsabilidad) ⟨take it or leave it : tómalo o déjalo⟩ ⟨take it from me : hazme caso⟩ **17** ADOPT : adoptar (una perspectiva, etc.) **18** INTERPRET : tomar, interpretar ⟨don't take it the wrong way : no te lo tomes a mal, no me malinterpretes⟩ **19** FEEL : sentir ⟨to take offense : ofenderse⟩ ⟨to take pride in : sentirse orgulloso de⟩ **20** SUPPOSE : suponer ⟨I take it that . . . : supongo que . .⟩ **21** CONSIDER : mirar (como ejemplo) **22** (*indicating an action or an undertaking*) ⟨to take a walk : dar un paseo⟩ ⟨to take a class : tomar una clase⟩ ⟨to take a picture : sacar una foto⟩ ⟨to take a right/left : girar a la derecha/izquierda⟩ **23** MEASURE, RECORD : tomar ⟨to take someone's temperature : tomarle la temperatura a alguien⟩ ⟨to take notes : tomar apuntes⟩ **24** EXACT ⟨to take a toll on : afectar⟩ ⟨to take revenge : vengarse⟩ **25** WIN : ganar **26 to be taken sick/ill** : caer enfermo **27 to take aback** : sorprender, desconcertar **28 to take a lot out of someone** : agotar a alguien **29 to take apart** : desmontar **30 to take away** REMOVE : quitar **31 take it away!** : ¡adelante!, ¡vamos! (dícese a un cantante, etc.) **32 to take back** : retirar (palabras, etc.) **33 to take back** RETURN : devolver **34 to take back** RECLAIM : llevarse **35 to take back** : aceptar la devolución de (mercancía), dejar regresar (a un amante) **36 to take down** NOTE : tomar nota de **37 to take down** DISASSEMBLE : desmontar **38 to take down** REMOVE : quitar **39 to take down** LOWER : bajar **40 to take for** : tomar por **41 to take in** : recoger (a un perro, etc.) **42 to take in** : detener, llevar a la comisaría **43 to take in** : hacer (dinero) **44 to take in** : tomarle a, achicar (un vestido, etc.) **45 to take in** INCLUDE : incluir, abarcar **46 to take in** ATTEND, VISIT : ir a (una película, etc.), visitar (un museo, etc.) **47 to take in** GRASP, UNDERSTAND : captar, entender **48 to take in** DECEIVE : engañar **49 to take it upon oneself (to do something)** : encargarse (de hacer algo) **50 to take note/notice of** : notar, prestarle atención a **51 to take off** REMOVE : quitar ⟨take off your hat : quítate el sombrero⟩ ⟨take your hands off me!⟩ : ¡quítame las manos de encima!⟩ **52 to take off** : tomar (el día, etc.) libre **53 to take someone off (of)** : hacerle a alguien dejar (un proyecto, etc.) **54 to take on** TACKLE : abordar, enfrentar (problemas, etc.) **55 to take on** or **to take on** UNDERTAKE : encargarse de, emprender (una tarea), asumir (una responsabilidad) **56 to take on** ACCEPT : tomar (como un cliente, etc.) **57 to take on** CONTRACT : contratar (trabajadores) **58 to take on** ASSUME : adoptar, asumir, adquirir ⟨the neighborhood took on a dingy look : el barrio asumió una apariencia deprimente⟩ **59 to take out** REMOVE, WITHDRAW, EXTRACT : sacar ⟨take the trash out : saca la basura⟩ ⟨they took her tonsils out : la operaron de las amígdalas⟩ **60 to take out** OBTAIN : sacar **61 to take out** : sacar (libros, etc.) **62 to take out** : llevar (a cenar, etc.), sacar (a pasear, etc.) **63 to take out** DESTROY : eliminar **64 to take it out on someone** : desquitarse con alguien, agarrársela con alguien **65 to take over** SEIZE : apoderarse de **66 to take over** : hacerse cargo de (una compañía, etc.), asumir (una responsabilidad) **67 to take over** RELIEVE : sustituir, relevar **68 to take place** HAPPEN : tener lugar, suceder, ocurrir **69 to take shape/form** : tomar forma **70 to take something to something** : ⟨he took an axe to the tree : empezó a cortar el árbol con un hacha⟩ **71 to take up** LIFT : levantar **72 to take up** SHORTEN : acortar (una falda, etc.) **73 to take up** BEGIN : empezar, dedicarse a (un pasatiempo, etc.) **74 to take up** OCCUPY : ocupar (espacio), llevar (tiempo) **75 to take up** PURSUE : volver a (una cuestión, un asunto) **76 to take up** CONTINUE : seguir con **77 to take someone up on** : aceptar la invitación (etc.) a alguien — *vi* **1** : agarrar (dícese de un tinte), prender (dícese de una vacuna) **2 to take after** : parecerse a, salir a **3 to take away from** : restarle valor/atractivo (etc.) a **4 to take off** : despegar (dícese de un avión, etc.) **5 to take off** *fam* LEAVE : irse **6 to take over** : asumir el mando **7 to take to** : aficionarse a (un pasatiempo), adaptarse a (una situación), tomarle simpatía a (alguien) ⟨he doesn't take kindly to criticism : no le gusta nada que lo critiquen⟩ **8 to take to** START : empezar a, acostumbrarse a (hacer algo)

take² *n* **1** PROCEEDS : recaudación *f*, ingresos *mpl*, ganancias *fpl* **2** : toma *f* (de un rodaje o una grabación)
takeoff ['teɪkˌɔf] *n* **1** PARODY : parodia *f* **2** : despegue *m* (de un avión o cohete)
takeout ['teɪkˌaʊt] *n* : comida *f* para llevar
takeover ['teɪkˌoːvər] *n* : toma *f* (de poder o de control), adquisición *f* (de una empresa por otra)
taker ['teɪkər] *n* : persona *f* interesada ⟨available to all takers : disponible a cuantos estén interesados⟩

takings ['teɪkɪŋz] *n* EARNINGS : recaudación *f*
talc ['tælk] *n* : talco *m*
talcum powder ['tælkəm] *n* : talco *m*, polvos *mpl* de talco
tale ['teɪl] *n* **1** ANECDOTE, STORY : cuento *m*, relato *m*, anécdota *f* **2** FALSEHOOD : cuento *m*, mentira *f*
talent ['tælənt] *n* : talento *m*, don *m*
talented ['tæləntəd] *adj* : talentoso
talent scout → scout²
talisman ['tælɪsmən, -lɪz-] *n*, *pl* **-mans** : talismán *m*
talk¹ ['tɔk] *vi* **1** : hablar ⟨he talks for hours : se pasa horas hablando⟩ **2** CHAT : charlar, platicar **3 to talk about/of** : hablar de **4 to talk back** : contestar (de manera impertinente) **5 to talk down to** : hablarle en tono condescendiente a — *vt* **1** SPEAK : hablar ⟨to talk French : hablar francés⟩ ⟨to talk business : hablar de negocios⟩ **2 to talk into** ⟨I talked him into coming : lo convencí de que viniera⟩ **3 to talk out of** ⟨she talked me out of it : me convenció de que no lo hiciera⟩ **4 to talk over** DISCUSS : hablar de, discutir
talk² *n* **1** CONVERSATION : charla *f*, plática *f*, conversación *f* **2** GOSSIP, RUMOR : chisme *m*, rumores *mpl* **3** SPEECH : charla *f*
talkative ['tɔkətɪv] *adj* : locuaz, parlanchín, charlatán
talker ['tɔkər] *n* : conversador *m*, -dora *f*; hablador *m*, -dora *f*
talk show *n* : programa *m* de entrevistas
tall ['tɔl] *adj* : alto ⟨how tall is he? : ¿cuánto mide?⟩
tallow ['tæloː] *n* : sebo *m*
tall tale *adj* : cuento *m* chino
tally¹ ['tæli] *v* **-lied**; **-lying** *vt* RECKON : contar, hacer una cuenta de — *vi* MATCH : concordar, corresponder, cuadrar
tally² *n*, *pl* **-lies** : cuenta *f* ⟨to keep a tally : llevar la cuenta⟩
talon ['tælən] *n* : garra *f* (de un ave de rapiña)
tamale [tə'mɑli] *n* : tamal *m*
tamarind ['tæmərənd] *n* : tamarindo *m*
tambourine [ˌtæmbə'riːn] *n* : pandero *m*, pandereta *f*
tame¹ ['teɪm] *vt* **tamed**; **taming** : domar, amansar, domesticar
tame² *adj* **tamer**; **-est** **1** DOMESTICATED : domesticado, manso **2** DOCILE : manso, dócil **3** DULL : aburrido, soso
tamely ['teɪmli] *adv* : mansamente, dócilmente
tamer ['teɪmər] *n* : domador *m*, -dora *f*
tamp ['tæmp] *vt* : apisonar
tamper ['tæmpər] *vi* **to tamper with** : adulterar (una sustancia), forzar (un sello, una cerradura), falsear (documentos), manipular (una máquina)
tampon ['tæmˌpɑn] *n* : tampón *m*
tan¹ ['tæn] *v* **tanned**; **tanning** *vt* **1** : curtir (pieles) **2** : broncear — *vi* : broncearse
tan² *n* **1** SUNTAN : bronceado *m* ⟨to get a tan : broncearse⟩ **2** : color *m* canela, color *m* café con leche

tandem¹ ['tændəm] *adv or* **in tandem** : en tándem

tandem² *n* : tándem *m* (bicicleta)

tang ['tæŋ] *n* : sabor *m* fuerte

tangent ['tændʒənt] *n* : tangente *f* ⟨to go off on a tangent : irse por la tangente⟩

tangerine ['tændʒə,ri:n, ,tændʒə'-] *n* : mandarina *f*

tangible ['tændʒəbəl] *adj* : tangible, palpable — **tangibly** [-bli] *adv*

tangle¹ ['tæŋgəl] *v* **-gled; -gling** *vt* : enredar, enmarañar — *vi* : enredarse

tangle² *n* : enredo *m*, maraña *f*

tango¹ ['tæŋ,go:] *vi* : bailar el tango

tango² *n, pl* **-gos** : tango *m*

tangy ['tæŋi] *adj* **tangier; -est** : que tiene un sabor fuerte

tank ['tæŋk] *n* : tanque *m*; depósito *m*; bomba *f* *Spain, Ven* ⟨fuel tank : depósito de combustibles⟩

tankard ['tæŋkərd] *n* : jarra *f*

tanker ['tæŋkər] *n* : buque *m* cisterna, camión *m* cisterna, avión *m* cisterna ⟨an oil tanker : un petrolero⟩

tanner ['tænər] *n* : curtidor *m*, -dora *f*

tannery ['tænəri] *n, pl* **-neries** : curtiduría *f*, tenería *f*

tannin ['tænən] *n* : tanino *m*

tantalize ['tæntə,laɪz] *vt* **-lized; -lizing** : tentar, atormentar (con algo inasequible)

tantalizing ['tæntə,laɪzɪŋ] *adj* : tentador, seductor

tantamount ['tæntə,maʊnt] *adj* : equivalente

tantrum ['tæntrəm] *n* : rabieta *f*, berrinche *m* ⟨to throw a tantrum : hacer un berrinche⟩

tap¹ ['tæp] *vt* **tapped; tapping** 1 : ponerle una espita a, sacar líquido de (un barril, un tanque, etc.) 2 : intervenir, pinchar *fam* (un teléfono) 3 PAT, TOUCH : tocar, golpear ligeramente ⟨he tapped me on the shoulder : me tocó en el hombro⟩

tap² *n* 1 FAUCET : llave *f*, grifo *m* ⟨beer on tap : cerveza de barril⟩ 2 : extracción *f* (de líquido) ⟨a spinal tap : una punción lumbar⟩ 3 PAT, TOUCH : golpecito *m*, toque *m*

tape¹ ['teɪp] *vt* **taped; taping** 1 : sujetar o arreglar con cinta adhesiva 2 RECORD : grabar (en cinta)

tape² *n* 1 : cinta *f* (adhesiva, magnética, etc.) 2 → **tape measure**

tape measure *n* : cinta *f* métrica

taper¹ ['teɪpər] *vi* 1 : estrecharse gradualmente ⟨its tail tapers towards the tip : su cola va estrechándose hacia la punta⟩ 2 *or* **to taper off** : disminuir gradualmente

taper² *n* 1 CANDLE : vela *f* larga y delgada 2 TAPERING : estrechamiento *m* gradual

tape recorder *n* : grabadora *f*, grabador *m* (de cinta)

tapestry ['tæpəstri] *n, pl* **-tries** : tapiz *m*

tapeworm ['teɪp,wərm] *n* : solitaria *f*, tenia *f*

tapioca [,tæpi'o:kə] *n* : tapioca *f*

tapir ['teɪpər] *n* : tapir *m*

tar¹ ['tɑr] *vt* **tarred; tarring** : alquitranar

tar² *n* : alquitrán *m*, brea *f*, chapopote *m* *Mex*

tarantula [tə'ræntʃələ, -'ræntələ] *n* : tarántula *f*

tardiness ['tɑrdinəs] *n* : tardanza *f*, retraso *m*

tardy ['tɑrdi] *adj* **tardier; -est** LATE : tardío, de retraso

target¹ ['tɑrgət] *vt* : fijar como objetivo, dirigir, destinar

target² *n* 1 : blanco *m* ⟨target practice : tiro al blanco⟩ 2 GOAL, OBJECTIVE : meta *f*, objetivo *m*

tariff ['tærɪf] *n* DUTY : tarifa *f*, arancel *m*

tarmac ['tɑr,mæk] *n* : pista *f* (de un aeropuerto)

Tarmac ['tɑr,mæk] *trademark* (se usa para un tipo de pavimento)

tarnish¹ ['tɑrnɪʃ] *vt* 1 DULL : deslustrar 2 SULLY : empañar, manchar (una reputación, etc.) — *vi* : deslustrarse

tarnish² *n* : deslustre *m*

taro ['tɑro, 'ter-] *n* : taro *m*, malanga *f*

tarpaulin [tɑr'pɔlən, 'tɑrpə-] *n* : lona *f* (impermeable)

tarragon ['tærə,gɑn, -gən] *n* : estragón *m*

tarry¹ ['tæri] *vi* **-ried; -rying** : demorarse, entretenerse

tarry² ['tɑri] *adj* 1 : parecido al alquitrán 2 : cubierto de alquitrán

tart¹ ['tɑrt] *adj* 1 SOUR : ácido, agrio 2 CAUSTIC : mordaz, acrimonioso — **tartly** *adv*

tart² *n* : tartaleta *f*

tartan ['tɑrtən] *n* : tartán *m*

tartar ['tɑrtər] *n* 1 : tártaro *m* ⟨tartar sauce : salsa tártara⟩ 2 : sarro *m* (dental)

tartness ['tɑrtnəs] *n* 1 SOURNESS : acidez *f* 2 ACRIMONY, SHARPNESS : mordacidad *f*, acrimonia *f*, acritud *f*

task ['tæsk] *n* : tarea *f*, trabajo *m*

taskmaster ['tæsk,mæstər] *n* **to be a hard taskmaster** : ser exigente, ser muy estricto

tassel ['tæsəl] *n* : borla *f*

taste¹ ['teɪst] *v* **tasted; tasting** *vt* : probar (alimentos), degustar, catar (vinos) ⟨taste this soup : prueba esta sopa⟩ — *vi* : saber ⟨this tastes good : esto sabe bueno⟩

taste² *n* 1 SAMPLE : prueba *f*, bocado *m* (de comida), trago *m* (de bebidas) 2 FLAVOR : gusto *m*, sabor *m* 3 : gusto *m* ⟨she has good taste : tiene buen gusto⟩ ⟨in bad taste : de mal gusto⟩

taste bud *n* : papila *f* gustativa

tasteful ['teɪstfəl] *adj* : de buen gusto

tastefully ['teɪstfəli] *adv* : con buen gusto

tasteless ['teɪstləs] *adj* 1 FLAVORLESS : sin sabor, soso, insípido 2 : de mal gusto ⟨a tasteless joke : un chiste de mal gusto⟩

taster ['teɪstər] *n* : degustador *m*, -dora *f*; catador *m*, -dora *f* (de vinos)

tastiness ['teɪstinəs] *n* : lo sabroso

tasty ['teɪsti] *adj* **tastier; -est** : sabroso, gustoso

tatter ['tætər] *n* 1 SHRED : tira *f*, jirón *m* (de tela) 2 **tatters** *npl* : andrajos *mpl*, harapos *mpl* ⟨to be in tatters : estar por los suelos⟩

tattered [ˈtætərd] *adj* : andrajoso, en jirones

tattle [ˈtætəl] *vi* **-tled; -tling 1** CHATTER : parlotear *fam*, cotorrear *fam* **2 to tattle on someone** : acusar a alguien

tattletale [ˈtætəlˌteɪl] *n* : soplón *m*, -plona *f fam*

tattoo¹ [tæˈtuː] *vt* : tatuar

tattoo² *n* : tatuaje *m* ⟨to get a tattoo : tatuarse⟩

tatty [ˈtæti] *adj* **tattier; -est** SHABBY, WORN : gastado

taught → **teach**

taunt¹ [ˈtɔnt] *vt* MOCK : mofarse de, burlarse de

taunt² *n* : mofa *f*, burla *f*

Taurus [ˈtɔrəs] *n* **1** : Tauro *m* (signo o constelación) **2** : Tauro *mf* (persona)

taut [ˈtɔt] *adj* : tirante, tenso — **tautly** *adv*

tautness [ˈtɔtnəs] *n* : tirantez *f*, tensión *f*

tavern [ˈtævərn] *n* : taberna *f*

tawdry [ˈtɔdri] *adj* **tawdrier; -est** : chabacano, vulgar

tawny [ˈtɔni] *adj* **tawnier; -est** : leonado

tax¹ [ˈtæks] *vt* **1** : gravar, cobrar un impuesto sobre **2** CHARGE : acusar ⟨they taxed him with neglect : fue acusado de incumplimiento⟩ **3 to tax someone's strength** : ponerle a prueba las fuerzas (a alguien)

tax² *n* **1** : impuesto *m*, tributo *m* ⟨tax collector : recaudador de impuestos⟩ ⟨tax evasion : evasión de impuestos⟩ **2** BURDEN : carga *f*

taxable [ˈtæksəbəl] *adj* : sujeto a un impuesto

taxation [tækˈseɪʃən] *n* : impuestos *mpl*

tax–exempt [ˈtæksɪgˈzɛmpt, -ɛg-] *adj* : libre de impuestos

taxi¹ [ˈtæksi] *vi* **taxied; taxiing** *or* **taxying; taxis** *or* **taxies** : ir en taxi **2** : rodar sobre la pista de aterrizaje (dícese de un avión)

taxi² *n, pl* **taxis** : taxi *m*, libre *m Mex*

taxicab [ˈtæksiˌkæb] *n* → **taxi²**

taxidermist [ˈtæksəˌdərmɪst] *n* : taxidermista *f*

taxidermy [ˈtæksəˌdərmi] *n* : taxidermia *f*

taxi driver *n* : taxista *mf*

taxpayer [ˈtæksˌpeɪər] *n* : contribuyente *mf*, causante *mf Mex*

tax return → **return³**

TB [ˌtiˈbiː] → **tuberculosis**

tea [ˈtiː] *n* **1** : té *m* (planta y bebida) **2** : merienda *f*, té *m* (comida)

tea bag *n* : bolsita *f* de té

teach [ˈtiːtʃ] *v* **taught** [ˈtɔt]; **teaching** *vt* : enseñar, dar clases de ⟨she teaches math : da clases de matemáticas⟩ ⟨she taught me everything I know : me enseñó todo lo que sé⟩ — *vi* : enseñar, dar clases

teacher [ˈtiːtʃər] *n* : maestro *m*, -tra *f* (de enseñanza primaria); profesor *m*, -sora *f* (de enseñanza secundaria)

teaching [ˈtiːtʃɪŋ] *n* : enseñanza *f*

teacup [ˈtiːˌkʌp] *n* : taza *f* para té

teak [ˈtiːk] *n* : teca *f*

teakettle [ˈtiːˌkɛtəl] *n* : tetera *f*

teal [ˈtiːl] *n, pl* **teal** *or* **teals 1** : cerceta *f* (pato) **2** *or* **teal blue** : azul *m* verdoso oscuro

team¹ [ˈtiːm] *vi or* **to team up 1** : formar un equipo (en deportes) **2** COLLABORATE : asociarse, juntarse, unirse

team² *adj* : de equipo

team³ *n* **1** : tiro *m* (de caballos), yunta *f* (de bueyes o mulas) **2** : equipo *m* (en deportes, etc.)

teammate [ˈtiːmˌmeɪt] *n* : compañero *m*, -ra *f* de equipo

teamster [ˈtiːmstər] *n* : camionero *m*, -ra *f*

teamwork [ˈtiːmˌwərk] *n* : trabajo *m* en equipo, cooperación *f*

teapot [ˈtiːˌpat] *n* : tetera *f*

tear¹ [ˈtær] *v* **tore** [ˈtor]; **torn** [ˈtorn]; **tearing** *vt* **1** RIP : desgarrar, romper, rasgar (tela) ⟨to tear to pieces : hacer pedazos⟩ ⟨to tear apart : desgarrar⟩ **2** *or* **to tear apart** DIVIDE : dividir **3** REMOVE : arrancar ⟨torn from his family : arrancado de su familia⟩ **4 to tear down** : derribar **5 to tear off** : arrancar (un pedazo, etc.) **6 to tear out** : arrancar (una página, etc.) **7 to tear up** : hacer pedazos — *vi* **1** RIP : desgarrarse, romperse **2** RUSH : ir a gran velocidad ⟨she went tearing down the street : se fue como rayo por la calle⟩ **3 to tear into** ATTACK : arremeter contra

tear² *n* : desgarradura *f*, rotura *f*, desgarro *m* (muscular)

tear³ [ˈtɪr] *n* : lágrima *f*

teardrop [ˈtɪrˌdrap] *n* → **tear³**

tearful [ˈtɪrfəl] *adj* : lloroso, triste — **tearfully** *adv*

tear gas *n* : gas *m* lacrimógeno

tearoom [ˈtiːˌruːm, -ˌrum] *n* : salón *m* de té, confitería *f*

tease¹ [ˈtiːz] *vt* **teased; teasing 1** MOCK : burlarse de, mofarse de **2** ANNOY : irritar, fastidiar

tease² *n* **1** TEASING : burla *f*, mofa *f* **2** : bromista *mf*; guasón *m*, -sona *f*

teaspoon [ˈtiːˌspuːn] *n* **1** : cucharita *f* **2** → **teaspoonful**

teaspoonful [ˈtiːˌspuːnˌful] *n, pl* **-spoonfuls** [-ˌfulz] *or* **-spoonsful** [-ˌspuːnzˌful] : cucharadita *f*

teat [ˈtiːt] *n* : tetilla *f*

technical [ˈtɛknɪkəl] *adj* : técnico — **technically** [-kli] *adv*

technicality [ˌtɛknəˈkæləti] *n, pl* **-ties** : detalle *m* técnico

technician [tɛkˈnɪʃən] *n* : técnico *m*, -ca *f*

technique [tɛkˈniːk] *n* : técnica *f*

technological [ˌtɛknəˈladʒɪkəl] *adj* : tecnológico

technology [tɛkˈnalədʒi] *n, pl* **-gies** : tecnología *f*

teddy bear [ˈtɛdi] *n* : oso *m* de peluche

tedious [ˈtiːdiəs] *adj* : aburrido, pesado, monótono — **tediously** *adv*

tediousness [ˈtiːdiəsnəs] *n* : lo aburrido, lo pesado

tedium [ˈtiːdiəm] *n* : tedio *m*, pesadez *f*

tee [ˈtiː] *n* : tee *m* (en golf)

teem [ˈtiːm] *vi* **to teem with** : estar repleto de, estar lleno de

teenage ['tiːnˌeɪdʒ] *or* **teenaged** [-ˌeɪdʒd] *adj* : adolescente, de adolescencia

teenager ['tiːnˌeɪdʒər] *n* : adolescente *mf*

teens ['tiːnz] *npl* : adolescencia *f*

teepee → **tepee**

teeter[1] ['tiːt̬ər] *vi* : balancearse, tambalearse

teeter[2] *n or* **teeter–totter** ['tiːt̬ər-ˌtɑt̬ər] → **seesaw**

teeth → **tooth**

teethe ['tiːð] *vi* **teethed; teething** : formársele a uno los dientes 〈the baby's teething : le están saliendo los dientes al niño〉

teetotal ['tiːˈtoːt̬əl] *adj* : abstemio

teetotaler ['tiːˈtoːt̬ələr] *n* : abstemio *m*, -mia *f*

Teflon ['tɛˌflɑn] *trademark* se usa para un revestimiento antiadherente

telecast[1] ['tɛləˌkæst] *vt* **-cast; -casting** : televisar, transmitir por televisión

telecast[2] *n* : transmisión *f* por televisión

telecommunication [ˌtɛləkəˌmjuːnəˈkeɪʃən] *n* : telecomunicación *f*

teleconference ['tɛliˌkɑnfrənts, -fərənts] *n* : teleconferencia *f*

telegram ['tɛləˌgræm] *n* : telegrama *m*

telegraph[1] ['tɛləˌgræf] *v* : telegrafiar

telegraph[2] *n* : telégrafo *m*

telemarketing [ˌtɛləˈmɑrkət̬ɪŋ] *n* : telemárketing *m*

telepathic [ˌtɛləˈpæθɪk] *adj* : telepático — **telepathically** [-θɪkli] *adv*

telepathy [təˈlɛpəθi] *n* : telepatía *f*

telephone[1] ['tɛləˌfoːn] *v* **-phoned; -phoning** *vt* : llamar por teléfono a, telefonear — *vi* : telefonear

telephone[2] *n* : teléfono *m*

telephone book → **phone book**

telephone call → **call**[2]

telephone directory → **phone book**

telephone exchange → **exchange**[2]

telephone number → **number**[2]

telephone receiver → **receiver**

telescope[1] ['tɛləˌskoːp] *vi* **-scoped; -scoping** : plegarse (como un telescopio)

telescope[2] *n* : telescopio *m*

telescopic [ˌtɛləˈskɑpɪk] *adj* : telescópico

televise ['tɛləˌvaɪz] *vt* **-vised; -vising** : televisar

television ['tɛləˌvɪʒən] *n* : televisión *f*

tell ['tɛl] *v* **told** ['toːld]; **telling** *vt* 1 : decir, contar 〈he told us the story : nos contó la historia〉 〈he told us what happened : nos contó qué pasó〉 〈she told me the news : me dio la noticia〉 〈tell me all about it : cuéntamelo todo〉 〈tell her that . . . : dile que . . .〉 〈tell her hello for me : dale saludos de mi parte〉 2 INFORM : decir 〈tell me when they get here : dime cuando lleguen〉 〈I won't tell anyone : no se lo diré a nadie〉 〈I'm telling Mom! : ¡se lo voy a decir a mamá!〉 3 INSTRUCT : decir 〈do what I tell you : haz lo que te digo〉 〈they told her to wait : le dijeron que esperara〉 4 RELATE : contar 〈to tell a story : contar una historia〉 〈to tell a lie : decir una mentira〉 5 DISCERN : discernir, notar 〈I can't tell the difference : no noto la diferencia〉 〈I

could tell that she was lying : me di cuenta de que estaba mintiendo〉 6 : indicar, señalar 〈the evidence tells us that . . . : las pruebas nos indican que . . .〉 7 **all told** : en total 8 **don't tell me** : no me digas 9 **I'll tell you what** (*introducing a suggestion*) : hagamos así 10 **I told you so** : te lo dije 11 **to tell apart** : distinguir 12 **to tell it like it is** *fam* : contar/decir las cosas como son 13 **to tell off** *fam* : regañar 14 **to tell (you) the truth** : a decir verdad 15 **you're telling me!** : ¡a mí me lo vas a decir! — *vi* 1 SAY : decir 〈I won't tell : no voy a decírselo a nadie〉 2 KNOW : saber 〈you never can tell : nunca se sabe〉 〈as far as I can tell : según parece〉 3 SHOW : notarse, hacerse sentir 〈the strain is beginning to tell : la tensión se empieza a notar〉 4 **to tell on** : denunciar

teller ['tɛlər] *n* 1 NARRATOR : narrador *m*, -dora *f* 2 *or* **bank teller** : cajero *m*, -ra *f*

telltale ['tɛlˌteɪl] *adj* : revelador

temerity [təˈmɛrət̬i] *n, pl* **-ties** : temeridad *f*

temp[1] ['tɛmp] *n* : empleado *m*, -da *f* temporal

temp[2] *vi* : hacer trabajo temporal

temper[1] ['tɛmpər] *vt* 1 MODERATE : moderar, temperar 2 ANNEAL : templar (acero, etc.)

temper[2] *n* 1 DISPOSITION : carácter *m*, genio *m* 2 HARDNESS : temple *m*, dureza *f* (de un metal) 3 COMPOSURE : calma *f*, serenidad *f* 〈to lose one's temper : perder los estribos〉 4 RAGE : furia *f* 〈to fly into a temper : ponerse furioso〉

temperament ['tɛmpərmənt, -prə-, -pərə-] *n* : temperamento *m*

temperamental [ˌtɛmpərˈmɛnt̬əl, -prə-, -pərə-] *adj* : temperamental

temperance ['tɛmprənts] *n* : templanza *f*, temperancia *f*

temperate ['tɛmpərət] *adj* : templado (dícese del clima, etc.), moderado

temperature ['tɛmpərˌtʃur, -prə-, -pərə-, -ˌtʃər] *n* 1 : temperatura *f* 2 FEVER : calentura *f*, fiebre *f*

tempest ['tɛmpəst] *n* 1 : tempestad *f* 2 **a tempest in a teapot** : una tormenta en un vaso de agua

tempestuous [tɛmˈpɛstʃuəs] *adj* : tempestuoso

template ['tɛmplət] *n* : plantilla *f*

temple ['tɛmpəl] *n* 1 : templo *m* (en religión) 2 : sien *f* (en anatomía)

tempo ['tɛmˌpoː] *n, pl* **-pi** [-ˌpiː] *or* **-pos** : ritmo *m*, tempo *m* (en música)

temporal ['tɛmpərəl] *adj* : temporal

temporarily [ˌtɛmpəˈrɛrəli] *adv* : temporalmente, provisionalmente

temporary ['tɛmpəˌrɛri] *adj* : temporal, provisional, provisorio

tempt ['tɛmpt] *vt* : tentar

temptation [tɛmpˈteɪʃən] *n* : tentación *f*

tempter ['tɛmptər] *n* : tentador *m*

temptress ['tɛmptrəs] *n* : tentadora *f*

ten[1] ['tɛn] *adj* : diez 〈she's ten (years old) : tiene diez años〉

ten² *n* **1** : diez *m* (número) ⟨the ten of hearts : el diez de corazones⟩ **2** : decena *f* ⟨tens of thousands : decenas de millares⟩

ten³ *pron* : diez ⟨there are ten of us : somos diez⟩ ⟨it's ten (o'clock) : son las diez⟩

tenable ['tɛnəbəl] *adj* : sostenible, defendible

tenacious [tə'neɪʃəs] *adj* : tenaz — **tenaciously** [tə'neɪʃəsli] *adv*

tenacity [tə'næsəti] *n* : tenacidad *f*

tenancy ['tɛnənʦi] *n, pl* **-cies** : tenencia *f*, inquilinato *m* (de un inmueble)

tenant ['tɛnənt] *n* : inquilino *m*, -na *f*; arrendatario *m*, -ria *f*

tend ['tɛnd] *vt* : atender, cuidar (de), ocuparse de — *vi* : tender ⟨it tends to benefit the consumer : tiende a beneficiar al consumidor⟩

tendency ['tɛndənʦi] *n, pl* **-cies** : tendencia *f*, proclividad *f*, inclinación *f*

tender¹ ['tɛndər] *vt* : entregar, presentar ⟨I tendered my resignation : presenté mi renuncia⟩

tender² *adj* **1** : tierno, blando ⟨tender steak : bistec tierno⟩ **2** AFFECTIONATE, LOVING : tierno, cariñoso, afectuoso **3** DELICATE : tierno, sensible, delicado

tender³ *n* **1** OFFER : propuesta *f*, oferta *f* (en negocios) **2** legal tender : moneda *f* de curso legal

tenderize ['tɛndə,raɪz] *vt* **-ized; -izing** : ablandar (carnes)

tenderloin ['tɛndr,lɔɪn] *n* : lomo *f* (de res o de puerco)

tenderly ['tɛndərli] *adv* : tiernamente, con ternura

tenderness ['tɛndərnəs] *n* : ternura *f*

tendon ['tɛndən] *n* : tendón *m*

tendril ['tɛndrɪl] *n* : zarcillo *m*

tenement ['tɛnəmənt] *n* : casa *f* de vecindad

tenet ['tɛnət] *n* : principio *m*

tennis ['tɛnəs] *n* : tenis *m* ⟨tennis ball/court/match/racket : pelota/cancha/partido/raqueta de tenis⟩ ⟨tennis player : tenista⟩

tenor ['tɛnər] *n* **1** PURPORT : tenor *m*, significado *m* **2** : tenor *m* (en música)

tenpins ['tɛn,pɪnz] *npl* : bolos *mpl*, boliche *m*

tense¹ ['tɛnʦ] *vt* **tensed; tensing** *vt* : tensar — *vi* : tensarse, ponerse tenso

tense² *adj* **tenser; tensest 1** TAUT : tenso, tirante **2** NERVOUS : tenso, nervioso

tense³ *n* : tiempo *m* (de un verbo)

tensely ['tɛnʦli] *adv* : tensamente

tenseness ['tɛnʦnəs] → **tension**

tension ['tɛnʃən] *n* **1** TAUTNESS : tensión *f*, tirantez *f* **2** STRESS : tensión *f*, nerviosismo *m*, estrés *m*

tent ['tɛnt] *n* : tienda *f* de campaña

tentacle ['tɛntɪkəl] *n* : tentáculo *m*

tentative ['tɛntəʧɪv] *adj* **1** HESITANT : indeciso, vacilante **2** PROVISIONAL : sujeto a cambios, provisional

tentatively ['tɛntəʧɪvli] *adv* : provisionalmente

tenth¹ ['tɛnθ] *adv* : en décimo lugar

tenth² *adj* : décimo

tenth³ *n* **1** : décimo *m*, -ma *f* (en una serie) **2** : décimo *m*, décima parte *f*

tenuous ['tɛnjuəs] *adj* : tenue, débil ⟨tenuous reasons : razones poco convincentes⟩

tenuously ['tɛnjuəsli] *adv* : ligeramente, débilmente

tenure ['tɛnjər] *n* : tenencia *f* (de un cargo o una propiedad), titularidad *f* (de un puesto académico)

tepee ['ti:,pi:] *n* : tipi *m*

tepid ['tɛpɪd] *adj* : tibio

tequila [tə'ki:lə] *n* : tequila *m*

term¹ ['tərm] *vt* : calificar de, llamar, nombrar

term² *n* **1** PERIOD : término *m*, plazo *m*, período *m* **2** : término *m* (en matemáticas) **3** WORD : término *m*, vocablo *m* ⟨a term of endearment : un apelativo cariñoso⟩ ⟨medical terms : términos médicos⟩ **4** terms *npl* CONDITIONS : términos *mpl*, condiciones *fpl* **5** terms *npl* RELATIONS : relaciones *fpl* ⟨to be on good terms with : tener buenas relaciones con⟩ **6** in terms of : con respecto a, en cuanto a **7** to come to terms with : aceptar

terminal¹ ['tərmənəl] *adj* : terminal

terminal² *n* **1** : terminal *m*, polo *m* (en electricidad) **2** : terminal *m* (de una computadora) **3** STATION : terminal *f*, estación *f* (de transporte público)

terminate ['tərmə,neɪt] *v* **-nated; -nating** *vi* : terminar(se), concluirse — *vt* : terminar, poner fin a

termination [,tərmə'neɪʃən] *n* : cese *m*, terminación *f*

terminology [,tərmə'nɑlədʒi] *n, pl* **-gies** : terminología *f*

terminus ['tərmənəs] *n, pl* **-ni** [-,naɪ] *or* **-nuses 1** END : término *m*, fin *m* **2** : terminal *f* (de transporte público)

termite ['tər,maɪt] *n* : termita *f*

tern ['tərn] *n* : golondrina *f* de mar

terrace¹ ['tɛrəs] *vt* **-raced; -racing** : formar en terrazas, disponer en bancales

terrace² *n* **1** PATIO : terraza *f*, patio *m* **2** : terraplén *m*, terraza *f*, bancal *m* (en agricultura)

terra–cotta [,tɛrə'kɑtə] *n* : terracota *f*

terrain [tə'reɪn] *n* : terreno *m*

terrapin ['tɛrəpɪn] *n* : galápago *m* norteamericano

terrestrial [tə'rɛstriəl] *adj* : terrestre

terrible ['tɛrəbəl] *adj* : atroz, horrible, terrible

terribly ['tɛrəbli] *adv* **1** BADLY : muy mal **2** EXTREMELY : terriblemente, extremadamente

terrier ['tɛriər] *n* : terrier *mf*

terrific [tə'rɪfɪk] *adj* **1** FRIGHTFUL : aterrador **2** EXTRAORDINARY : extraordinario, excepcional **3** EXCELLENT : excelente, estupendo

terrify ['tɛrə,faɪ] *vt* **-fied; -fying** : aterrorizar, aterrar, espantar

terrifying ['tɛrə,faɪɪŋ] *adj* : espantoso, aterrador

territory ['tɛrə,tori] *n, pl* **-ries** : territorio *m* — **territorial** [,tɛrə'toriəl] *adj*

terror ['tɛrər] *n* : terror *m*

terrorism ['tɛrər,ɪzəm] *n* : terrorismo *m*

terrorist[1] ['tɛrərɪst] *adj* : terrorista

terrorist[2] *n* : terrorista *mf*

terrorize ['tɛrər,aɪz] *vt* **-ized; -izing** : aterrorizar

terry ['tɛri] *n, pl* **-ries** *or* **terry cloth** : (tela de) toalla *f*

terse ['tɜrs] *adj* **terser; tersest** : lacónico, conciso, seco — **tersely** *adv*

tertiary ['tɜr,ʃeri] *adj* : terciario

test[1] ['tɛst] *vt* **1** : examinar (estudiantes, etc.), evaluar (conocimientos, etc.) **2** : hacerle un análisis a, hacerle una prueba a, someter a pruebas ⟨to test someone for drugs/cancer : hacerle a alguien pruebas de drogas/cáncer⟩ **3** : analizar ⟨to test soil for lead : analizar tierra para detectar la presencia de plomo⟩ **4** : probar, experimentar (productos, etc.) **5** CHALLENGE, TRY : poner a prueba ⟨you're testing my patience : estás poniendo a prueba mi paciencia⟩ — *vi* : hacer pruebas

test[2] *n* : prueba *f*, examen *m*, test *m* ⟨to put to the test : poner a prueba⟩

testament ['tɛstəmənt] *n* **1** WILL : testamento *m* **2** : Testamento *m* (en la Biblia) ⟨the Old Testament : el Antiguo Testamento⟩

tester ['tɛstər] *n* **1** : probador *m*, -dora *f*; verificador *m*, -dora *f* (persona) **2** : verificador *m* (aparato)

testicle ['tɛstɪkəl] *n* : testículo *m*

testify ['tɛstə,faɪ] *v* **-fied; -fying** *vi* : testificar, atestar, testimoniar — *vt* : testificar

testimonial [,tɛstə'moniəl] *n* **1** REFERENCE : recomendación *f* **2** TRIBUTE : homenaje *m*, tributo *m*

testimony ['tɛstə,moni] *n, pl* **-nies** : testimonio *m*, declaración *f*

test tube *n* : probeta *f*, tubo *m* de ensayo

testy ['tɛsti] *adj* **testier; -est** : irritable

tetanus ['tɛtənəs] *n* : tétano *m*, tétanos *m*

tête-à-tête [,tɛtə'tɛt, ,teɪtə'teɪt] *n* : conversación *f* en privado

tether[1] ['tɛðər] *vt* : atar (con una cuerda), amarrar

tether[2] *n* : atadura *f*, cadena *f*, correa *f*

text[1] ['tɛkst] *n* **1** : texto *m* **2** TOPIC : tema *m* **3** → **textbook** **4** *or* **text message** : mensaje *m* de texto, SMS *m*

text[2] *vt* : enviar un mensaje de texto — *vt* : enviarle un mensaje de texto a

textbook ['tɛkst,bʊk] *n* : libro *m* de texto

texting ['tɛkstɪŋ] *or* **text messaging** *n* : mensajería *f* de texto

textile ['tɛk,staɪl, 'tɛkstəl] *n* : textil *m*, tela *f* ⟨the textile industry : la industria textil⟩

textual ['tɛkstʃuəl] *adj* : textual

texture ['tɛkstʃər] *n* : textura *f*

Thai ['taɪ] *n* **1** : tailandés *m*, -desa *f* **2** : tailandés *m* (idioma) — **Thai** *adj*

than[1] ['ðæn] *conj* : que, de ⟨it's worth more than that : vale más que eso⟩

⟨more than you think : más de lo que piensas⟩

than[2] *prep* : que, de ⟨you're better than he is : eres mejor que él⟩ ⟨more than once : más de una vez⟩

thank ['θæŋk] *vt* : agradecer, darle (las) gracias (a alguien) ⟨thank you! : ¡gracias!⟩ ⟨I thanked her for the present : le di las gracias por el regalo⟩ ⟨I thank you for your help : le agradezco su ayuda⟩

thankful ['θæŋkfəl] *adj* : agradecido

thankfully ['θæŋkfəli] *adv* **1** GRATEFULLY : con agradecimiento **2** FORTUNATELY : afortunadamente, por suerte ⟨thankfully, it's over : se acabó, gracias a Dios⟩

thankfulness ['θæŋkfəlnəs] *n* : agradecimiento *m*, gratitud *f*

thankless ['θæŋkləs] *adj* : ingrato ⟨a thankless task : un trabajo ingrato⟩

thanks ['θæŋks] *npl* **1** : agradecimiento *m* **2 thanks!** : ¡gracias!

Thanksgiving [θæŋks'gɪvɪŋ, 'θæŋks,-] *n* : el día de Acción de Gracias (fiesta estadounidense)

that[1] ['ðæt] *adv in negative constructions* : tan ⟨it's not that expensive : no es tan caro⟩ ⟨not that much : no tanto⟩

that[2] *adj, pl* **those** : ese, esa, aquel, aquella ⟨do you see those children? : ¿ves a aquellos niños?⟩

that[3] *conj & pron* : que ⟨he said that he was afraid : dijo que tenía miedo⟩ ⟨the book that he wrote : el libro que escribió⟩

that[4] *pron, pl* **those** ['ðo:z] **1** : ese/ése, esa/ésa, eso ⟨that's my father : ese es mi padre⟩ ⟨those are the ones he likes : esos/ésos son los que le gustan⟩ ⟨what's that? : ¿qué es eso?⟩ ⟨why did you do that? : ¿por qué hiciste eso?⟩ ⟨that's impossible : (eso) es imposible⟩ ⟨is that so? : ¿de veras?, ¿ah, sí?⟩ ⟨after that : después, luego⟩ **2 those** *pl (referring to a group of people)* ⟨those who came : los que vinieron⟩ ⟨there are those who say . . . : hay quien dice . . .⟩ **3** *(referring to more distant objects or times)* : aquel/aquél, aquella/aquélla, aquello ⟨those are maples and these are elms : aquellos/aquéllos son arces y estos/éstos son olmos⟩ ⟨that came to an end : aquello se acabó⟩ **4 at that** ALSO, MOREOVER : además **5 at that** THEREUPON : al decir/oír (etc.) eso **6 at that** : sin decir más ⟨let's leave it at that : dejémoslo ahí⟩ **7 for all that** : a pesar de ello **8 that is (to say)** : o sea, es decir **9 that's it** ⟨that's it—it's finished : ya está (terminado)⟩ ⟨that's it—I'm leaving! : ¡se acabó! ¡me voy!⟩ ⟨do it like this—that's it! : hazlo así—¡eso es!⟩

thatch[1] ['θætʃ] *vt* : cubrir o techar con paja, hojas, etc.

thatch[2] *n* : paja *f*, hojas *fpl* (para techos)

thaw[1] ['θɔ] *vt* : descongelar — *vi* : derretirse (dícese de la nieve), descongelarse (dícese de los alimentos)

thaw[2] *n* : deshielo *m*

the[1] [ðə, *before vowel sounds usu* ði:] *adv* **1** *(used to indicate comparison)* ⟨the sooner the better : cuanto más pronto, mejor⟩ ⟨she likes this one the best : éste es el que más le gusta⟩ **2** (*used as a conjunction*) : cuanto ⟨the more I learn, the less I understand : cuanto más aprendo, menos entiendo⟩

the² *art* : el, la, los, las, lo ⟨the gloves : los guantes⟩ ⟨the girl : la chica⟩ ⟨the winter : el invierno⟩ ⟨the worst part : lo peor⟩ ⟨forty cookies to the box : cuarenta galletas por caja⟩ ⟨today is the ninth : hoy es nueve⟩ ⟨the 18th of august : el 18 de agosto⟩ ⟨William the Conqueror : Guillermo el Conquistador⟩ ⟨the French : los franceses⟩ ⟨the Smiths : los Smith⟩ ⟨the Mississippi River : el río Mississippi⟩ ⟨the English language : la lengua inglesa, el idioma inglés⟩

theater *or* **theatre** [ˈθiːəţər] *n* **1** : teatro *m* (edificio) **2** DRAMA : teatro *m*, drama *m*

theatrical [θiˈætrɪkəl] *adj* : teatral, dramático

thee [ˈðiː] *pron* : te, ti

theft [ˈθɛft] *n* : robo *m*, hurto *m*

their [ˈðɛr] *adj* : su ⟨their friends : sus amigos⟩

theirs [ˈðɛrz] *pron* : (el) suyo, (la) suya, (los) suyos, (las) suyas ⟨they came for theirs : vinieron por el suyo⟩ ⟨theirs is bigger : la suya es más grande, la de ellos es más grande⟩ ⟨a brother of theirs : un hermano suyo, un hermano de ellos⟩

them [ˈðɛm] *pron* **1** (*as a direct object*) : los ⟨*Spain sometimes* les, las ⟨I know them : los conozco⟩ **2** (*as indirect object*) : les, se ⟨I sent them a letter : les mandé una carta⟩ ⟨give it to them : dáselo (a ellos)⟩ **3** (*as object of a preposition*) : ellos, ellas ⟨go with them : ve con ellos⟩ **4** (*for emphasis*) : ellos, ellas ⟨I wasn't expecting them : no los esperaba a ellos⟩

thematic [θiˈmæţɪk] *adj* : temático

theme [ˈθiːm] *n* **1** SUBJECT, TOPIC : tema *m* **2** COMPOSITION : composición *f*, trabajo *m* (escrito) **3** : tema *m* (en música)

theme park *n* : parque *m* temático

themselves [ðəmˈsɛlvz, ðɛm-] *pron* **1** (*as a reflexive*) : se, sí ⟨they enjoyed themselves : se divirtieron⟩ ⟨they divided it among themselves : lo repartieron entre sí, se lo repartieron⟩ **2** (*for emphasis*) : ellos mismos, ellas mismas ⟨they built it themselves : ellas mismas lo construyeron⟩

then¹ [ˈðɛn] *adv* **1** : entonces, en ese tiempo ⟨I was sixteen then : tenía entonces dieciséis años⟩ ⟨by/since/until then : para/desde/hasta entonces⟩ **2** NEXT : después, luego ⟨we'll go to Toronto, then to Winnipeg : iremos a Toronto, y luego a Winnipeg⟩ **3** BESIDES, FURTHERMORE : además, aparte ⟨then there's the tax : y aparte está el impuesto⟩ **4** : entonces, en ese caso ⟨if you like music, then you should attend : si te gusta la música, entonces deberías asistir⟩ ⟨it's true, then? : ¿entonces es cierto?⟩ ⟨OK, then, I'll see you later : hasta luego, entonces⟩ ⟨you're sure? all

right, then : ¿estás seguro? bueno, está bien⟩ **5 then and there** : en el momento

then² *adj* : entonces ⟨the then governor of Georgia : el entonces gobernador de Georgia⟩

thence [ˈðɛns, ˈθɛnts] *adv* : de ahí, de ahí en adelante

theologian [ˌθiːəˈloːdʒən] *n* : teólogo *m*, -ga *f*

theological [ˌθiːəˈlɑdʒɪkəl] *adj* : teológico

theology [θiˈɑlədʒi] *n, pl* **-gies** : teología *f*

theorem [ˈθiːərəm, ˈθɪrəm] *n* : teorema *m*

theoretical [ˌθiːəˈrɛţɪkəl] *adj* : teórico — **theoretically** *adv*

theorist [ˈθiːərɪst] *n* : teórico *m*, -ca *f*

theorize [ˈθiːəˌraɪz] *vi* **-rized; -rizing** : teorizar

theory [ˈθiːəri, ˈθɪri] *n, pl* **-ries** : teoría *f*

therapeutic [ˌθɛrəˈpjuːţɪk] *adj* : terapéutico — **therapeutically** *adv*

therapist [ˈθɛrəpɪst] *n* : terapeuta *mf*

therapy [ˈθɛrəpi] *n, pl* **-pies** : terapia *f*

there¹ [ˈðɛr] *adv* **1** : allí, allá, ahí ⟨stand over there : párate ahí⟩ ⟨we can walk there : podemos ir a pie⟩ ⟨over there : por allí/allá⟩ ⟨out/in there : ahí fuera/dentro⟩ ⟨who's there? : ¿quién es?⟩ ⟨is Mom there? : ¿está mamá?⟩ ⟨there it is : ahí está⟩ ⟨there you are/go : aquí tienes, toma⟩ ⟨. . . and there you have it! : ¡ . . . y ya está!⟩ ⟨that clock there : ese reloj que ves allí⟩ ⟨you there! : ¡oye, tú!⟩ ⟨hello there! : ¡hola!⟩ **2** : ahí, en esto, en eso ⟨there is where we disagree : en eso es donde no estamos de acuerdo⟩ **3** THEN : entonces ⟨from there : de ahí, a partir de ese momento⟩ **4 to be out there** EXIST : existir **5 to have been there** (*referring to an experience*) ⟨I've been there myself : yo también he pasado por eso⟩

there² *pron* **1** (*introducing a sentence or clause*) ⟨there comes a time to decide : llega un momento en que uno tiene que decidir⟩ **2 there is/are** : hay ⟨there are many children here : aquí hay muchos niños⟩ ⟨are there a lot of errors? : ¿hay muchos errores?⟩ ⟨there's a good hotel downtown : hay un buen hotel en el centro⟩ ⟨there was no way to know : no había manera de saberlo⟩

thereabouts [ˌðɛrəˈbaʊts, ˈðɛrəˌ-] *or* **thereabout** [-ˈbaʊt, -ˌbaʊt] *adv or* **thereabouts** : por ahí, más o menos ⟨at five o'clock or thereabouts : por ahí de las cinco⟩

thereafter [ðɛrˈæftər] *adv* : después ⟨shortly thereafter : poco después⟩

thereby [ðɛrˈbaɪ, ˈðɛrˌbaɪ] *adv* : de tal modo, de esa manera, así

therefore [ˈðɛrˌfor] *adv* : por lo tanto, por consiguiente

therein [ðɛrˈɪn] *adv* **1** : allí adentro, ahí adentro ⟨the contents therein : lo que allí se contiene⟩ **2** : allí, en ese aspecto ⟨therein lies the problem : allí está el problema⟩

thereof [ðɛrˈʌv, -ˈɑv] *adv* : de eso, de ello

thereupon [ˈðɛrəˌpɑn, -ˌpɔn; ˌðɛrəˈpɑn, -ˈpɔn] *adv* : acto seguido, inmediatamente (después)

therewith [ðær'wɪθ, -'wɪθ] *adv* : con eso, con ello

thermal ['θərməl] *adj* **1** : térmico (en física) **2** HOT : termal

thermodynamics [,θərmodaɪ'næmɪks] *ns & pl* : termodinámica *f*

thermometer [θər'mɑmətər] *n* : termómetro *m*

thermos ['θərməs] *n* : termo *m*

thermostat ['θərmə,stæt] *n* : termostato *m*

thesaurus [θɪ'sɔrəs] *n, pl* **-sauri** [-'sɔr,aɪ] *or* **-sauruses** [-'sɔrəsəz] : diccionario *m* de sinónimos

these → **this**

thesis ['θi:sɪs] *n, pl* **theses** ['θi:,si:z] : tesis *f*

they ['ðeɪ] *pron* : ellos, ellas ⟨they are here : están aquí⟩ ⟨they don't know : ellos no saben⟩

they'd ['ðeɪd] *contraction of* **they had** *or* **they would** → **have, would**

they'll ['ðeɪl, 'ðel] *contraction of* **they shall** *or* **they will** → **shall, will**

they're ['ðr] *contraction of* **they are** → **be**

they've ['ðeɪv] *contraction of* **they have** → **have**

thiamine ['θaɪəmɪn, -,mi:n] *n* : tiamina *f*

thick¹ ['θɪk] *adj* **1** : grueso ⟨a thick plank : una tabla gruesa⟩ **2** : espeso, denso ⟨thick syrup : jarabe espeso⟩ — **thickly** *adv*

thick² *n* **1 in the thick of** : en medio de ⟨in the thick of the battle : en lo más reñido de la batalla⟩ **2 through thick and thin** : a las duras y a las maduras

thicken ['θɪkən] *vt* : espesar (un líquido) — *vi* : espesarse

thickener ['θɪkənər] *n* : espesante *m*

thicket ['θɪkət] *n* : matorral *m*, maleza *f*, espesura *f*

thickness ['θɪknəs] *n* : grosor *m*, grueso *m*, espesor *m*

thickset ['θɪk'sɛt] *adj* STOCKY : robusto, fornido

thick–skinned ['θɪk'skɪnd] *adj* : poco sensible, que no se ofende fácilmente

thief ['θi:f] *n, pl* **thieves** ['θi:vz] : ladrón *m*, -drona *f*

thieve ['θi:v] *v* **thieved; thieving** : hurtar, robar

thievery ['θi:vəri] *n* : hurto *m*, robo *m*, latrocinio *m*

thigh ['θaɪ] *n* : muslo *m*

thighbone ['θaɪ,bo:n] *n* : fémur *m*

thimble ['θɪmbəl] *n* : dedal *m*

thin¹ ['θɪn] *v* **thinned; thinning** *vt* : hacer menos denso, diluir, aguar (un líquido), enrarecer (un gas) — *vi* : diluirse, aguarse (dícese de un líquido), enrarecerse (dícese de un gas)

thin² *adj* **thinner; thinnest 1** LEAN, SLIM : delgado, esbelto, flaco **2** SPARSE : ralo, escaso ⟨a thin beard : una barba rala⟩ **3** WATERY : claro, aguado, diluido **4** FINE : delgado, fino ⟨thin slices : rebanadas finas⟩

thing ['θɪŋ] *n* **1** MATTER, FACT, IDEA : cosa *f* ⟨don't talk about those things : no hables de esas cosas⟩ ⟨how are things? : ¿cómo van las cosas?⟩ ⟨the main thing : lo principal⟩ ⟨the thing is . . . : el caso es que . . .⟩ ⟨to think things over : pensarlo (bien)⟩ ⟨for one thing, . . . : para empezar, . . .⟩ ⟨I said no such thing! : ¡no dije tal/semejante cosa!⟩ **2** ACT, EVENT : cosa *f* ⟨the flood was a terrible thing : la inundación fue una cosa terrible⟩ ⟨it's a good thing that . . . : menos mal que . . .⟩ ⟨to do the right thing : hacer lo correcto⟩ **3** OBJECT : cosa *f* ⟨don't forget your things : no olvides tus cosas⟩ ⟨baby things : cosas para bebés⟩ ⟨there's no such thing : no existe (tal cosa)⟩ ⟨I can't see a thing : no puedo ver nada⟩ ⟨I have just the thing for you : tengo justo lo que necesitas⟩ **4 as things stand** : tal como están las cosas **5 a thing or two** : unas cuantas cosas **6 first/last thing** : a primera/última hora ⟨I'll do it first thing tomorrow : lo haré mañana a primera hora⟩ **7 it's (just) one of those things** : son cosas de la vida **8 of all things** ⟨he's learning jousting, of all things! : ¡está aprendiendo a justar! ¿te lo imaginas?⟩ **9 to have another thing coming** : estar muy equivocado

thingamajig ['θɪŋəmə,dʒɪg] *or* **thingamabob** ['θɪŋəmə,bɑb] *n fam* : cosa *f*, vaina *f fam*, chisme *m Spain fam*

think ['θɪŋk] *v* **thought** ['θɔt]; **thinking** *vt* **1** PLAN : pensar, creer ⟨he thinks (that) he'll return early : piensa regresar temprano⟩ ⟨I think (that) I'll call her : creo que la llamaré⟩ **2** BELIEVE : creer, opinar ⟨I think (that) I can go : creo que puedo ir⟩ ⟨I think so : creo que sí⟩ ⟨I don't think so : creo que no⟩ ⟨what do you think? : ¿qué opinas?⟩ ⟨who does she think she is? : ¿quién se cree?⟩ **3** PONDER : pensar ⟨"how odd," he thought : qué raro—pensó⟩ ⟨what were you thinking? : ¿en qué pensabas?⟩ **4** REMEMBER : acordarse de ⟨I didn't think to ask : no se me ocurrió preguntar⟩ **5 to think better of** : cambiar de idea **6 to think nothing of** ⟨she thinks nothing of running 10 miles : correr 10 millas no le parece nada extraño⟩ ⟨think nothing of it : de nada, no hay de qué⟩ **7 to think out/through** : pensar bien, estudiar **8 to think over** CONSIDER : pensar **9 to think up** : idear, inventar ⟨we've thought up a plan : se nos ha ocurrido un plan⟩ — *vi* **1** : pensar ⟨let me think : déjame pensar⟩ **2 to think about/of** : pensar en ⟨I was just thinking about/of you when you called : pensaba en ti justo cuando llamaste⟩ **3 to think about/of** WEIGH : pensar (en) ⟨think about it : piénsalo⟩ ⟨I'm thinking about/of buying it : estoy pensando en comprarlo⟩ **4 to think about/of** : pensar en ⟨think about/of your family! : ¡piensa en tu familia!⟩ **5 to think about/of** : pensar de ⟨what did you think about/of the book? : ¿qué pensaste del libro?, ¿qué te pareció el libro?⟩ **6 to think again** : pensar dos veces **7 to think ahead** : ser previsor **8 to think aloud**

: pensar en voz alta **9 to think back** : recordar **10 to think of** REMEMBER : acordarse de **11 to think of** : idear, inventar ⟨we'll think of something : algo se nos ocurrirá⟩ **12 to think poorly of** : pensar mal de **13 to think twice** : pensárselo dos veces **14 to think well of** : tener buena opinión de

think² *n* **1 to have a think about** : pensar **2 to have another think coming** : estar muy equivocado

thinker [ˈθɪŋkər] *n* : pensador *m*, -dora *f*

thinly [ˈθɪnli] *adv* **1** LIGHTLY : ligeramente **2** SPARSELY : escasamente ⟨thinly populated : poco poblado⟩ **3** BARELY : apenas

thinness [ˈθɪnnəs] *n* : delgadez *f*

thin–skinned [ˈθɪnˈskɪnd] *adj* : susceptible, muy sensible

third¹ [ˈθərd] *or* **thirdly** [-li] *adv* : en tercer lugar ⟨she came in third : llegó en tercer lugar⟩

third² *adj* : tercero ⟨the third day : el tercer día⟩

third³ *n* **1** : tercero *m*, -ra *f* (en una serie) ⟨the third of June : el tres de junio⟩ **2** : tercero *m*, tercera parte *f* **3** *or* **third base** : tercera base *f* **4** *or* **third gear** : tercera *f*

third world *n sometimes offensive* **the Third World** : el Tercer Mundo *m*

thirst¹ [ˈθərst] *vi* **1** : tener sed **2 to thirst for** DESIRE : tener sed de, estar sediento de

thirst² *n* : sed *f*

thirsty [ˈθərsti] *adj* **thirstier; -est** : sediento, que tiene sed ⟨I'm thirsty : tengo sed⟩

thirteen¹ [ˌθərˈtiːn] *adj & pron* : trece

thirteen² *n* : trece *m*

thirteenth¹ [ˌθərˈtiːnθ] *adj* : décimo tercero

thirteenth² *n* **1** : decimotercero *m*, -ra *f* (en una serie) **2** : treceavo *m*, treceava parte *f*

thirtieth¹ [ˈθərtɪəθ] *adj* : trigésimo

thirtieth² *n* **1** : trigésimo *m*, -ma *f* (en una serie) **2** : treintavo *m*, treintava parte *f*

thirty¹ [ˈθərti] *adj & pron* : treinta

thirty² *n, pl* **thirties** : treinta *m*

this¹ [ˈðɪs] *adv* : así, a tal punto ⟨this big : así de grande⟩

this² *adj, pl* **these** [ˈðiːz] : este ⟨these things : estas cosas⟩ ⟨read this book : lee este libro⟩

this³ *pron, pl* **these** : este/éste, esta/ésta, esto ⟨what's this? : ¿qué es esto?⟩ ⟨this wasn't here yesterday : esto no estaba aquí ayer⟩ ⟨this is for you : esto es para ti⟩ ⟨those magazines and these : aquellas revistas y estas/éstas⟩ ⟨these aren't the files I need : estos/éstos no son los archivos que necesito⟩

thistle [ˈθɪsəl] *n* : cardo *m*

thong [ˈθɔŋ] *n* **1** STRAP : correa *f*, tira *f* **2** FLIP-FLOP : chancla *f*, chancleta *f*

thorax [ˈθorˌæks] *n, pl* **-raxes** *or* **-races** [ˈθorəˌsiːz] : tórax *m*

thorn [ˈθorn] *n* : espina *f*

thorny [ˈθorni] *adj* **thornier; -est** : espinoso

thorough [ˈθəroː] *adj* **1** CONSCIENTIOUS : concienzudo, meticuloso **2** COMPLETE : absoluto, completo — **thoroughly** *adv*

thoroughbred [ˈθəroˌbrɛd] *adj* : de pura sangre (dícese de un caballo)

Thoroughbred *n or* **Thoroughbred horse** : pura sangre *mf*

thoroughfare [ˈθəroˌfær] *n* : vía *f* pública, carretera *f*

thoroughness [ˈθəronəs] *n* : esmero *m*, meticulosidad *f*

those → **that**

thou [ˈðaʊ] *pron* : tú

though¹ [ˈðoː] *adv* **1** HOWEVER, NEVERTHELESS : sin embargo, no obstante **2 as ~** : como si ⟨as though nothing had happened : como si nada hubiera pasado⟩

though² *conj* : aunque, a pesar de ⟨though it was raining, we went out : salimos a pesar de la lluvia⟩

thought¹ → **think**

thought² [ˈθɔt] *n* **1** THINKING : pensamiento *m*, ideas *fpl* ⟨Western thought : el pensamiento occidental⟩ **2** COGITATION : pensamiento *m*, reflexión *f*, raciocinio *m* **3** IDEA : idea *f*, ocurrencia *f* ⟨it was just a thought : fue sólo una idea⟩

thoughtful [ˈθɔtfəl] *adj* **1** PENSIVE : pensativo, meditabundo **2** CONSIDERATE : considerado, atento, cortés — **thoughtfully** *adv*

thoughtfulness [ˈθɔtfəlnəs] *n* : consideración *f*, atención *f*, cortesía *f*

thoughtless [ˈθɔtləs] *adj* **1** CARELESS : descuidado, negligente **2** INCONSIDERATE : desconsiderado — **thoughtlessly** *adv*

thoughtlessness *n* **1** CARELESSNESS : descuido *m*, irreflexión *f*, imprevisión *f* **2** : falta *f* de consideración

thousand¹ [ˈθaʊzənd] *adj & pron* : mil

thousand² *n, pl* **-sands** *or* **-sand** : mil *m*

thousandth¹ [ˈθaʊzənθ] *adj* : milésimo

thousandth² *n* **1** : milésimo *m*, -ma *f* (en una serie) **2** : milésimo *m*, milésima parte *f*

thrash [ˈθræʃ] *vt* **1** → **thresh 2** BEAT : golpear, azotar, darle una paliza (a alguien) **3** FLAIL : sacudir, agitar bruscamente

thread¹ [ˈθrɛd] *vt* **1** : enhilar, enhebrar (una aguja) **2** STRING : ensartar (cuentas en un hilo) **3 to thread one's way** : abrirse paso

thread² *n* **1** : hilo *m*, hebra *f* ⟨needle and thread : aguja e hilo⟩ ⟨the thread of an argument : el hilo de un debate⟩ **2** : rosca *f*, filete *m* (de un tornillo)

threadbare [ˈθrɛdˌbær] *adj* **1** SHABBY, WORN : raído, gastado **2** TRITE : trillado, tópico, manido

threat [ˈθrɛt] *n* : amenaza *f*

threaten [ˈθrɛtən] *v* : amenazar

threatening [ˈθrɛtənɪŋ] *adj* : amenazador — **threateningly** *adv*

three¹ [ˈθriː] *adj* : tres ⟨he's three (years old) : tiene tres años⟩

three² *n* : tres *m* ⟨the three of hearts : el tres de corazones⟩

three³ *pron* : tres ⟨there are three of us : somos tres⟩ ⟨it's three (o'clock) : son las tres⟩

3–D [ˈθriːˈdiː] *adj* → three–dimensional

three–dimensional [ˈθriːdəˈmɛntʃ∫ənəl] *adj* : tridimensional

threefold [ˈθriːˌfoːld] *adj* TRIPLE : triple

three hundred¹ *adj & pron* : trescientos

three hundred² *n* : trescientos *m*

three–piece suit *n* : terno *m*, tresillo *m*

threescore [ˈθriːˈskor] *adj* SIXTY : sesenta

thresh [ˈθrɛʃ] *vt* : trillar (grano)

thresher [ˈθrɛʃər] *n* : trilladora *f*

threshold [ˈθrɛʃˌhoːld, -ˌoːld] *n* : umbral *m*

threw → throw¹

thrice [ˈθraɪs] *adv* : tres veces

thrift [ˈθrɪft] *n* : economía *f*, frugalidad *f*

thriftless [ˈθrɪftləs] *adj* : despilfarrador, manirroto

thrifty [ˈθrɪfti] *adj* **thriftier; -est** : económico, frugal — **thriftily** [ˈθrɪftəli] *adv*

thrill¹ [ˈθrɪl] *vt* : emocionar — *vi* **to thrill to** : dejarse conmover por, estremecerse con

thrill² *n* : emoción *f*

thriller [ˈθrɪlər] *n* **1** : evento *m* emocionante **2** : obra *f* de suspenso

thrilling [ˈθrɪlɪŋ] *adj* : emocionante, excitante

thrive [ˈθraɪv] *vi* **throve** [ˈθroːv] *or* **thrived; thriven** [ˈθrɪvən] **1** FLOURISH : florecer, crecer abundantemente **2** PROSPER : prosperar

throat [ˈθroːt] *n* : garganta *f*

throaty [ˈθroːti] *adj* **throatier; -est** : ronco (dícese de la voz)

throb¹ [ˈθrɑb] *vi* **throbbed; throbbing** : palpitar, latir (dícese del corazón), vibrar (dícese de un motor, etc.)

throb² *n* : palpitación *f*, latido *m*, vibración *f*

throe [ˈθroː] *n* **1** PAIN, SPASM : espasmo *m*, dolor *m* ⟨the throes of childbirth : los dolores de parto⟩ **2 throes** *npl* : lucha *f* larga y ardua ⟨in the throes of : en el medio de⟩

thrombosis [θrɑmˈboːsəs] *n* : trombosis *f*

throne [ˈθroːn] *n* : trono *m*

throng¹ [ˈθrɔŋ] *vt* CROWD : atestar, atiborrar, llenar — *vi* : aglomerarse, amontonarse

throng² *n* : muchedumbre *f*, gentío *m*, multitud *f*

throttle¹ [ˈθrɑtəl] *vt* **-tled; -tling 1** STRANGLE : estrangular, ahogar **2 to throttle down** : desacelerar (un motor)

throttle² *n* **1** : válvula *f* reguladora **2 at full throttle** : a toda máquina

through¹ [ˈθruː] *adv* **1** : a través, de un lado a otro ⟨let them through : déjenlos pasar⟩ **2** : de principio a fin ⟨she read the book through : leyó el libro de principio a fin⟩ **3** COMPLETELY : completamente ⟨soaked through : completamente empapado⟩

through² *adj* **1** DIRECT : directo ⟨a through train : un tren directo⟩ **2** FINISHED : terminado, acabado ⟨we're through : hemos terminado⟩

through³ *prep* **1** : a través de, por ⟨through the door : por la puerta⟩ ⟨a road through the woods : un camino que atraviesa el bosque⟩ **2** BETWEEN : entre ⟨a path through the trees : un sendero entre los árboles⟩ **3** BECAUSE OF : a causa de, como consecuencia de **4** DURING : por, durante ⟨through the night : durante la noche⟩ **5** : a, hasta ⟨from Monday through Friday : de lunes a viernes⟩ **6** (*indicating completion*) ⟨she's been through a lot : ha pasado muchas dificultades⟩ ⟨we're through the worst of it : hemos pasado lo peor⟩ **7** VIA : a través de, por ⟨I got the job through her cousin : conseguí el trabajo a través de su primo⟩

throughout¹ [θruːˈaʊt] *adv* **1** EVERYWHERE : por todas partes **2** THROUGH : desde el principio hasta el fin de (algo)

throughout² *prep* **1** : en todas partes de, a través de ⟨throughout the United States : en todo Estados Unidos⟩ **2** : de principio a fin de, durante ⟨throughout the winter : durante todo el invierno⟩

throve → thrive

throw¹ [ˈθroː] *v* **threw** [ˈθruː]; **thrown** [ˈθroːn]; **throwing 1** TOSS : tirar; lanzar; echar; arrojar; aventar *Col, Mex* ⟨to throw a ball : tirar una pelota⟩ **2** : desmontar (a un jinete) **3** CAST : proyectar ⟨it threw a long shadow : proyectó una sombra larga⟩ **4 to throw a party** : dar una fiesta **5 to throw in** : dar de ñapa **6 to throw into confusion** : desconcertar **7 to throw away/out** DISCARD : botar, tirar (a la basura) **8 to throw out** REJECT : rechazar **9 to throw out** EJECT : echar **10 to throw up** VOMIT : vomitar, devolver (comida, etc.) — *vi* **to throw up** VOMIT : vomitar, devolver

throw² *n* TOSS : tiro *m*, tirada *f*, lanzamiento *m*, lance *m* (de dados)

thrower [ˈθroːər] *n* : lanzador *m*, -dora *f*

thrush [ˈθrʌʃ] *n* : tordo *m*, zorzal *m*

thrust¹ [ˈθrʌst] *vt* **thrust; thrusting 1** SHOVE : empujar bruscamente **2** PLUNGE, STAB : apuñalar, clavar ⟨he thrust a dagger into her heart : la apuñaló en el corazón⟩ **3 to thrust one's way** : abrirse paso **4 to thrust upon** : imponer a

thrust² *n* **1** PUSH, SHOVE : empujón *m*, empellón *m* **2** LUNGE : estocada *f* (en esgrima) **3** IMPETUS : ímpetu *m*, impulso *m*, propulsión *f* (de un motor)

thud¹ [ˈθʌd] *vi* **thudded; thudding** : producir un ruido sordo

thud² *n* : ruido *m* sordo (que produce un objeto al caer)

thug [ˈθʌg] *n* : matón *m*

thumb¹ [ˈθʌm] *vt* : hojear (con el pulgar)

thumb² *n* : pulgar *m*, dedo *m* pulgar

thumbnail [ˈθʌmˌneɪl] *n* : uña *f* del pulgar

thumbtack [ˈθʌmˌtæk] *n* : tachuela *f*, chinche *f*

thump[1] [ˈθʌmp] vt POUND : golpear, aporrear — vi : latir con vehemencia (dícese del corazón)

thump[2] n THUD : ruido m sordo

thunder[1] [ˈθʌndər] vi 1 : tronar ⟨it rained and thundered all night : llovió y tronó durante la noche⟩ 2 BOOM : retumbar, bramar, resonar — vt ROAR, SHOUT : decir a gritos, vociferar

thunder[2] n : truenos mpl

thunderbolt [ˈθʌndərˌboːlt] n : rayo m

thunderclap [ˈθʌndərˌklæp] n : trueno m

thunderous [ˈθʌndərəs] adj : atronador, ensordecedor, estruendoso

thundershower [ˈθʌndərˌʃauər] n : lluvia f con truenos y relámpagos

thunderstorm [ˈθʌndərˌstɔrm] n : tormenta f con truenos y relámpagos

thunderstruck [ˈθʌndərˌstrʌk] adj : atónito

Thursday [ˈθərzˌdeɪ, -di] n : jueves m ⟨today is Thursday : hoy es jueves⟩ ⟨(on) Thursday : el jueves⟩ ⟨(on) Thursdays : los jueves⟩ ⟨last Thursday : el jueves pasado⟩ ⟨next Thursday : el jueves que viene⟩ ⟨every other Thursday : cada dos jueves⟩ ⟨Thursday afternoon/morning : jueves por la tarde/mañana⟩

thus [ˈðʌs] adv 1 : así, de esta manera 2 SO : hasta (cierto punto) ⟨the weather's been nice thus far : hasta ahora ha hecho buen tiempo⟩ 3 HENCE : por consiguiente, por lo tanto

thwart [ˈθwɔrt] vt : frustrar

thy [ˈðaɪ] adj : tu

thyme [ˈtaɪm, ˈθaɪm] n : tomillo m

thyroid [ˈθaɪˌrɔɪd] n or **thyroid gland** : tiroides mf, glándula f tiroidea ⟨thyroid hormone : hormona tiroidea⟩

thyself [ðaɪˈsɛlf] pron : ti, ti mismo

ti [ˈtiː] n : si m (en el canto)

tiara [tiˈæro, -ˈɑr-] n : diadema f

Tibetan [təˈbɛtən] n 1 : tibetano m, -na f 2 : tibetano m (idioma) — **Tibetan** adj

tibia [ˈtɪbiə] n, pl -**iae** [-biˌiː] : tibia f

tic [ˈtɪk] n : tic m

tick[1] [ˈtɪk] vi 1 : hacer tictac 2 OPERATE, RUN : operar, andar (dícese de un mecanismo) ⟨what makes him tick? : ¿qué es lo que lo mueve?⟩ — vt or **to tick off** CHECK : marcar

tick[2] n 1 : tictac m (de un reloj) 2 CHECK : marca f 3 : garrapata f (insecto)

ticket[1] [ˈtɪkət] vt LABEL : etiquetar

ticket[2] n 1 : boleto m, boleta f, entrada f (de un espectáculo), pasaje m (de avión, tren, etc.) 2 SLATE : lista f de candidatos

ticket collector n : revisor m, -sora f

ticket office n : taquilla f

tickle[1] [ˈtɪkəl] v -**led**; -**ling** vt 1 AMUSE : divertir, hacerle gracia (a alguien) 2 : hacerle cosquillas (a alguien) ⟨don't tickle me! : ¡no me hagas cosquillas!⟩ — vi : picar

tickle[2] n : cosquilleo m, cosquillas fpl, picor m (en la garganta)

ticklish [ˈtɪkəlɪʃ] adj 1 : cosquilloso (dícese de una persona) 2 DELICATE, TRICKY : delicado, peliagudo

tick–tock n : tictac m

tidal [ˈtaɪdəl] adj : de marea, relativo a la marea

tidal wave n : maremoto m

tidbit [ˈtɪdˌbɪt] n 1 BITE, SNACK : bocado m, golosina f 2 : dato m o noticia f interesante ⟨useful tidbits of information : informaciones útiles⟩

tide[1] [ˈtaɪd] vt **tided**; **tiding** or **to tide over** : proveer lo necesario para aguantar una dificultad ⟨this money will tide you over until you find work : este dinero te mantendrá hasta que encuentres empleo⟩

tide[2] n 1 : marea f 2 CURRENT : corriente f (de eventos, opiniones, etc.)

tidily [ˈtaɪdəli] adv : ordenadamente

tidiness [ˈtaɪdinəs] n : aseo m, limpieza f, orden m

tidings [ˈtaɪdɪŋz] npl : nuevas fpl

tidy[1] [ˈtaɪdi] v -**died**; -**dying** vt : asear, limpiar, poner en orden — vi **to tidy up** : poner las cosas en orden

tidy[2] adj **tidier**; -**est** 1 CLEAN, NEAT : limpio, aseado, en orden 2 SUBSTANTIAL : grande, considerable ⟨a tidy sum : una suma considerable⟩

tie[1] [ˈtaɪ] v **tied**; **tying** or **tieing** vt 1 : atar, amarrar ⟨to tie a knot : atar un nudo⟩ ⟨to tie one's shoelaces : atarse los cordones⟩ 2 BIND, UNITE : ligar, atar 3 : empatar ⟨they tied the score : empataron el marcador⟩ 4 **to be fit to be tied** : estar hecho una furia 5 **to tie down/up** : atar 6 **to tie in with** : relacionar con 7 **to tie up** : ocupar (a alguien), inmovilizar (dinero), atascar (tráfico) — vi 1 : empatar ⟨the two teams were tied : los dos equipos empataron⟩ 2 **to tie in with** : relacionarse con

tie[2] n 1 : ligadura f, cuerda f, cordón m (para atar algo) 2 BOND, LINK : atadura f, ligadura f, vínculo m, lazo m ⟨family ties : lazos familiares⟩ 3 or **railroad tie** : traviesa f 4 DRAW : empate m (en deportes) 5 NECKTIE : corbata f

tiebreaker [ˈtaɪˌbreɪkər] n : desempate m

tier [ˈtɪr] n : hilera f, escalón m

tiff [ˈtɪf] n : disgusto m, disputa f

tiger [ˈtaɪgər] n : tigre m

tight[1] [ˈtaɪt] adv TIGHTLY : bien, fuerte ⟨shut it tight : ciérralo bien⟩

tight[2] adj 1 : bien cerrado, hermético ⟨a tight seal : un cierre hermético⟩ 2 STRICT : estricto, severo 3 TAUT : tirante, tenso 4 SNUG : apretado, ajustado, ceñido ⟨a tight dress : un vestido ceñido⟩ 5 DIFFICULT : ⟨to be in a tight spot : estar en un aprieto⟩ 6 STINGY : apretado, avaro, agarrado fam 7 CLOSE : reñido ⟨a tight game : un juego reñido⟩ 8 SCARCE : escaso ⟨money is tight : escasea el dinero⟩

tighten [ˈtaɪtən] vt : tensar (una cuerda, etc.), apretar (un nudo, un tornillo, etc.), apretarse (el cinturón), reforzar (las reglas)

tightfisted [ˈtaɪtˈfɪstəd] adj STINGY : apretado, avaro, agarrado fam

tightly [ˈtaɪtli] adv : bien, fuerte

tightness ['taɪtnəs] *n* : lo apretado, lo tenso, tensión *f*

tightrope ['taɪt‚ro:p] *n* : cuerda *f* floja

tights ['taɪts] *npl* : leotardo *m*, malla *f*

tightwad ['taɪt‚wɑd] *n* : avaro *m*, -ra *f*; tacaño *m*, -ña *f*

tigress ['taɪgrəs] *n* : tigresa *f*

tilde ['tɪldə] *n* : tilde *mf*

tile[1] ['taɪl] *vt* **tiled; tiling** : embaldosar (un piso), revestir de azulejos (una pared), tejar (un techo)

tile[2] *n* **1** *or* **floor tile** : losa *f*, baldosa *f*, mosaico *m Mex* (de un piso) **2** : azulejo *m* (de una pared) **3** : teja *f* (de un techo)

till[1] ['tɪl] *vt* : cultivar, labrar

till[2] *n* : caja *f*, caja *f* registradora

till[3] *prep & conj → until*

tiller ['tɪlər] *n* **1** : cultivador *m*, -dora *f* (de la tierra) **2** : caña *f* del timón (de un barco)

tilt[1] ['tɪlt] *vt* : ladear, inclinar — *vi* : ladearse, inclinarse

tilt[2] *n* **1** SLANT : inclinación *f* **2 at full tilt** : a toda velocidad

timber ['tɪmbər] *n* **1** : madera *f* (para construcción) **2** BEAM : viga *f*

timberland ['tɪmbər‚lænd] *n* : bosque *m* maderero

timbre ['tæmbər, 'tɪm-] *n* : timbre *m*

time[1] ['taɪm] *vt* **timed; timing 1** SCHEDULE : fijar la hora de, calcular el momento oportuno para **2** CLOCK : cronometrar, medir el tiempo de (una competencia, etc.)

time[2] *n* **1** : tiempo *m* ⟨the passing of time : el paso del tiempo⟩ ⟨she doesn't have time : no tiene tiempo⟩ **2** MOMENT : tiempo *m*, momento *m* ⟨this is not the time to bring it up : no es el momento de sacar el tema⟩ ⟨it can wait until another time : podemos dejarlo para otro momento⟩ ⟨since that time : desde entonces⟩ **3** : vez *f* ⟨he called you three times : te llamó tres veces⟩ ⟨three times greater : tres veces mayor⟩ ⟨this time : esta vez⟩ ⟨one more time : una vez más⟩ **4** AGE : tiempo *m*, era *f* ⟨in your grandparents' time : en el tiempo de tus abuelos⟩ ⟨it was before your time : fue antes de que nacieras⟩ **5** TEMPO : tiempo *m*, ritmo *m* (en música) **6** : hora *f* (del día), época *f* (del año) ⟨what time is it? : ¿qué hora es?⟩ ⟨do you have the time? : ¿tienes hora?⟩ ⟨it's time for dinner : es hora de comer⟩ ⟨at the usual time : a la hora acostumbrada⟩ ⟨during work time : en horas de trabajo⟩ ⟨local time : hora local⟩ ⟨arrival/departure time : hora de llegada/salida⟩ **7** WHILE : tiempo *m*, rato *m* ⟨a short/long time ago : hace poco/mucho tiempo⟩ ⟨for (quite) some time now : desde hace mucho tiempo⟩ ⟨he watched us the whole/entire time : nos miraba (durante) todo el tiempo⟩ **8** EXPERIENCE : rato *m*, experiencia *f* ⟨we had a nice time together : pasamos juntos un rato agradable⟩ ⟨to have a rough time : pasarlo mal⟩ ⟨have a good time! : ¡que se diviertan!⟩ **9 against time** : contra el reloj **10 ahead of one's time**

⟨she was ahead of her time : se adelantó a su época⟩ **11 ahead of time** ⟨I prepared it ahead of time : lo preparé con antelación⟩ ⟨she handed it in ahead of time : lo entregó antes de tiempo⟩ ⟨he showed up ahead of time : apareció antes de la hora⟩ **12 all in good time** : todo a su debido tiempo **13 all the time** ALWAYS, OFTEN : todo el tiempo **14 all the time** THROUGHOUT : (durante) todo el tiempo **15 at all times** : siempre, en todo momento **16 (at) any time** : en cualquier momento **17 at a time** SIMULTANEOUSLY : al mismo tiempo, a la vez ⟨one at a time : uno por uno, de a uno⟩ ⟨two at a time : de dos en dos⟩ ⟨one thing at a time : una cosa por vez⟩ ⟨one step at a time : paso por paso⟩ **18 at a time** : sin parar ⟨he read for hours at a time : pasaba horas enteras leyendo⟩ ⟨she disappears for months at a time : desaparece por meses⟩ **19 at no time** : en ningún momento **20 at the same time** CONVERSELY : al mismo tiempo **21 at the same time** SIMULTANEOUSLY : al mismo tiempo, a la vez **22 at times** SOMETIMES : a veces **23 behind the times** OUTDATED : anticuado **24 each and every time** : cada vez **25 each/every time** : cada vez **26 for a time** : (por) un tiempo **27 for the time being** : por el momento, de momento **28 from time to time** OCCASIONALLY : de vez en cuando **29 in good time** : con tiempo **30 in no time** : enseguida, en un santiamén **31 in time** PUNCTUALLY : a tiempo **32 in time** EVENTUALLY : con el tiempo **33 it's about time** : ya es hora, ya va siendo hora ⟨it was about time (that) you got here : ya era hora de que llegaras⟩ **34 most of the time** : la mayor parte del tiempo **35 on time** : a tiempo **36 over time** : con el paso del tiempo **37 after time** : una y otra vez **38 time flies** : el tiempo pasa volando **39 time marches on** : el tiempo pasa **40 time off** : tiempo *m* libre, vacaciones *fpl* **41 to buy time** : ganar tiempo **42 to give someone a hard time** : mortificar a alguien **43 to have time on one's hands** : sobrarle el tiempo a uno **44 to keep time** : marcar la hora (dícese de un reloj) **45 to keep time** : seguir/marcar el ritmo (en música) **46 to lose time** : atrasar (dícese de un reloj) **47 to make good time** : ir adelantado (en un viaje, etc.) **48 to make time for** : encontrar tiempo para **49 to pass the time** : pasar el rato **50 to serve/do time** : cumplir una condena **51 to take one's time** : tomarse tiempo ⟨take your time : tómate todo el tiempo que necesites⟩ ⟨you sure took your time! : tardaste mucho⟩ **52 to take the time to** : tomar el tiempo para/de **53 to take time** : tomar tiempo, tomarse tiempo ⟨these things take time : estas cosas toman tiempo⟩ ⟨take all the time you need : tómate todo el tiempo que necesites⟩ **54 to waste time** : perder el tiempo

time bomb *n* : bomba *f* de tiempo, bomba *f* de relojería *Spain*

timekeeper ['taɪm,kiːpər] *n* : cronometrador *m*, -dora *f*

timeless ['taɪmləs] *adj* : eterno

time limit *n* : plazo *m*

timely ['taɪmli] *adj* **timelier; -est** : oportuno

timepiece ['taɪm,piːs] *n* : reloj *m*

timer ['taɪmər] *n* : temporizador *m*, cronómetro *m*

times ['taɪmz] *prep* : por ⟨3 times 4 is 12 : 3 por 4 son 12⟩

timeshare ['taɪm,ʃer] *n* : multipropiedad *f*, tiempo *m* compartido

time slot → **slot**

timetable ['taɪm,teɪbəl] *n* : horario *m*

time zone *n* : huso *m* horario

timid ['tɪmɪd] *adj* : tímido — **timidly** *adv*

timidity [tə'mɪdəti] *n* : timidez *f*

timorous ['tɪmərəs] *adj* : timorato, miedoso

timpani ['tɪmpəni] *npl* : timbales *mpl*

tin ['tɪn] *n* **1** : estaño *m* (elemento), hojalata *f* (metal) **2** CAN, BOX : lata *f*, bote *m*, envase *m*

tincture ['tɪŋktʃər] *n* : tintura *f*

tinder ['tɪndər] *n* : yesca *f*

tine ['taɪn] *n* : diente *m* (de un tenedor, etc.)

tinfoil ['tɪn,fɔɪl] *n* : papel *m* (de) aluminio

tinge¹ ['tɪndʒ] *vt* **tinged; tingeing** *or* **tinging** ['tɪndʒɪŋ] TINT : matizar, teñir ligeramente

tinge² *n* **1** TINT : matiz *m*, tinte *m* sutil **2** TOUCH : dejo *m*, sensación *f* ligera

tingle¹ ['tɪŋgəl] *vi* **-gled; -gling** : sentir (un) hormigueo, sentir (un) cosquilleo

tingle² *n* : hormigueo *m*, cosquilleo *m*

tinker ['tɪŋkər] *vi* **to tinker with** : arreglar con pequeños ajustes, toquetear (con intento de arreglar)

tinkle¹ ['tɪŋkəl] *vi* **-kled; -kling** : tintinear

tinkle² *n* : tintineo *m*

tinplate ['tɪn'pleɪt] *n* : hojalata *f*

tinsel ['tɪntsəl] *n* : oropel *m*

tint¹ ['tɪnt] *vt* : teñir, colorear

tint² *n* : tinte *m*

tiny ['taɪni] *adj* **tinier; -est** : diminuto, minúsculo

tip¹ ['tɪp] *v* **tipped; tipping** *vt* **1** *or* **to tip over** : volcar, voltear, hacer caer **2** TILT : ladear, inclinar ⟨to tip one's hat : saludar con el sombrero⟩ **3** TAP : tocar, golpear ligeramente **4** : darle una propina (a un mesero, etc.) ⟨I tipped him $5 : le di $5 de propina⟩ **5** : adornar o cubrir la punta de ⟨wings tipped in red : alas que tienen las puntas rojas⟩ **6 to tip off** : avisar a, dar información a (la policía, etc.) — *vi* **1** TILT : ladearse, inclinarse **2 to tip over** : volcarse, caerse

tip² *n* **1** END, POINT : punta *f*, extremo *m* ⟨on the tip of one's tongue : en la punta de la lengua⟩ **2** GRATUITY : propina *f* **3** ADVICE, INFORMATION : consejo *m*, información *f* (confidencial)

tip-off ['tɪp,ɔf] *n* **1** SIGN : indicación *f*, señal *f* **2** TIP : información *f* (confidencial)

tipple ['tɪpəl] *vi* **-pled; -pling** : tomarse unas copas

tipsy ['tɪpsi] *adj* **tipsier; -est** : achispado

tiptoe¹ ['tɪp,toː] *vi* **-toed; -toeing** : caminar de puntillas

tiptoe² *adv* : de puntillas

tiptoe³ *n* : punta *f* del pie

tip–top¹ ['tɪp'tɑp, -,tɑp] *adj* EXCELLENT : excelente

tip–top² *n* SUMMIT : cumbre *f*, cima *f*

tirade ['taɪ,reɪd] *n* : diatriba *f*

tire¹ ['taɪr] *v* **tired; tiring** *vt* : cansar — *vi* : cansarse

tire² *n* : llanta *f*, neumático *m*, goma *f*

tired ['taɪrd] *adj* : cansado ⟨to get tired : cansarse⟩

tiredness *n* : cansancio *m*

tireless ['taɪrləs] *adj* : incansable, infatigable — **tirelessly** *adv*

tiresome ['taɪrsəm] *adj* : fastidioso, pesado, tedioso — **tiresomely** *adv*

tissue ['tɪ,ʃuː] *n* **1** : pañuelo *m* de papel **2** : tejido *m* ⟨lung tissue : tejido pulmonar⟩

tissue paper *n* : papel *m* de seda

titanic [taɪ'tænɪk, tə-] *adj* GIGANTIC : titánico, gigantesco

titanium [taɪ'teɪniəm, tə-] *n* : titanio *m*

titillate ['tɪtəl,eɪt] *vt* **-lated; -lating** : excitar, estimular placenteramente

title¹ ['taɪtəl] *vt* **-tled; -tling** : titular, intitular

title² *n* : título *m*

titter¹ ['tɪtər] *vi* GIGGLE : reírse tontamente

titter² *n* : risita *f*, risa *f* tonta

titular ['tɪtʃələr] *adj* : titular

tizzy ['tɪzi] *n, pl* **tizzies** : estado *m* agitado o nervioso ⟨I'm all in a tizzy : estoy todo alterado⟩

TNT [,tiː,ɛn'tiː] *n* : TNT *m*

to¹ ['tuː] *adv* **1** : a un estado consciente ⟨to come to : volver en sí⟩ **2 to and fro** : de aquí para allá, de un lado para otro

to² *prep* **1** (*indicating a place or activity*) : a ⟨to go to the doctor : ir al médico⟩ ⟨I'm going to John's : voy a casa de John⟩ ⟨we went to lunch : fuimos a almorzar⟩ **2** TOWARD : a, hacia ⟨two miles to the south : dos millas hacia el sur⟩ ⟨to the right : a la derecha⟩ ⟨she ran to her mother : corrió a su mamá⟩ **3** UP TO : hasta, a ⟨to a degree : hasta cierto grado⟩ ⟨from head to toe : de pies a cabeza⟩ ⟨the water was up to my waist : el agua me llegaba a la cintura⟩ **4** (*in expressions of time*) ⟨it's quarter to seven : son las siete menos cuarto⟩ **5** UNTIL : a, hasta ⟨from May to December : de mayo a diciembre⟩ **6** (*indicating belonging or association*) : de, con ⟨the key to the lock : la llave del candado⟩ ⟨he's married to my sister : está casado con mi hermana⟩ **7** (*indicating recipient*) : a ⟨I gave it to the boss : se lo di a la jefa⟩ ⟨she spoke to his parents : habló con sus padres⟩ ⟨listen to me : escúchame⟩ **8** (*indicating response or result*) : a ⟨dancing to the rhythm : bailando al compás⟩ ⟨to my surprise : para mi sorpresa⟩ ⟨the answer to your question : la respuesta a su pregunta) **9** (*indicating comparison or proportion*) : a ⟨it's similar to mine : es parecido al mío⟩ ⟨they won 4 to 2 : ganaron 4 a 2⟩ **10** (*indicating agreement or conformity*) : a, de acuerdo con ⟨made to order : hecho a la orden⟩ ⟨to my knowledge : a mi saber⟩ **11** (*indicating opinion or viewpoint*) : a, para ⟨it's agreeable to all of us : nos parece bien a todos⟩ ⟨it seemed odd to us : nos pareció raro⟩ ⟨it's news to me : no lo sabía⟩ ⟨it means nothing to him : para él no significa nada⟩ **12** (*indicating inclusion*) : en cada, por ⟨twenty to the box : veinte por caja⟩ **13** (*indicating joining or touching*) : a ⟨he tied it to a tree : lo ató a un árbol⟩ ⟨apply salve to the wound : póngale ungüento a la herida⟩ **14** (*used to form the infinitive*) : to ⟨to understand : entender⟩ ⟨to go away : irse⟩ ⟨I didn't mean to (do it) : lo hice sin querer⟩ **15** (all) to oneself : para sí sólo

toad ['to:d] *n* : sapo *m*

toadstool ['to:d,stu:l] *n* : hongo *m* (no comestible)

toady ['to:di] *n, pl* **toadies** : adulador *m*, -dora *f*

toast[1] ['to:st] *vt* **1** : tostar (pan) **2** : brindar por ⟨to toast the victors : brindar por los vencedores⟩ **3** WARM : calentar ⟨to toast oneself : calentarse⟩

toast[2] *n* **1** : pan *m* tostado, tostadas *fpl* **2** : brindis *m* ⟨to propose a toast : proponer un brindis⟩

toaster ['to:stər] *n* : tostador *m*

tobacco [tə'bæko:] *n, pl* -cos : tabaco *m*

toboggan[1] [tə'bɑgən] *vi* : deslizarse en tobogán

toboggan[2] *n* : tobogán *m*

today[1] [tə'deɪ] *adv* **1** : hoy ⟨she arrives today : hoy llega⟩ **2** NOWADAYS : hoy en día

today[2] *n* : hoy *m* ⟨today is a holiday : hoy es día de fiesta⟩

toddle ['tɑdəl] *vi* **-dled; -dling** : hacer pinitos, hacer pinitos

toddler ['tɑdələr] *n* : niño *m* pequeño, niña *f* pequeña (que comienza a caminar)

to-do [tə'du:] *n, pl* **to-dos** [-'du:z] FUSS : lío *m*, alboroto *m*

toe[1] ['to:] *vt* **toed; toeing** to toe the line : acatar la disciplina

toe[2] *n* : dedo *m* del pie

TOEFL ['to:fəl] *trademark* se usa para un examen que evalúa el dominio del inglés de personas que estudian este idioma como lengua extranjera

toenail ['to:,neɪl] *n* : uña *f* del pie

toffee or **toffy** ['tɔfi, 'tɑ-] *n, pl* **toffees** or **toffies** : caramelo *m* elaborado con azúcar y mantequilla

toga ['to:gə] *n* : toga *f*

together [tə'gɛðər] *adv* **1** : juntamente, juntos (el uno con el otro) ⟨Susan and Sarah work together : Susan y Sarah trabajan juntas⟩ **2** ~ with : junto con

togetherness [tə'gɛðərnəs] *n* : unión *f*, compañerismo *m*

togs ['tɑgz, 'tɔgz] *npl* : ropa *f*

toil[1] ['tɔɪl] *vi* : trabajar arduamente

toil[2] *n* : trabajo *m* arduo

toilet ['tɔɪlət] *n* **1** : arreglo *m* personal **2** BATHROOM : (cuarto de) baño *m*, servicios *mpl* (públicos), sanitario *m* Col, Mex, Ven **3** : inodoro *m* ⟨to flush the toilet : jalar la cadena⟩

toilet paper *n* : papel *m* higiénico

toiletries ['tɔɪlətriz] *npl* : artículos *mpl* de tocador

token[1] ['to:kən] *adj* : simbólico

token[2] *n* **1** PROOF, SIGN : prueba *f*, muestra *f*, señal *m* **2** SYMBOL : símbolo *m* **3** SOUVENIR : recuerdo *m* **4** : ficha *f* (para transporte público, etc.) **5 by the same token** : del mismo modo

told → **tell**

tolerable ['tɑlərəbəl] *adj* : tolerable — **tolerably** [-bli] *adv*

tolerance ['tɑlərənts] *n* : tolerancia *f*

tolerant ['tɑlərənt] *adj* : tolerante — **tolerantly** *adv*

tolerate ['tɑlə,reɪt] *vt* **-ated; -ating** **1** ACCEPT : tolerar, aceptar **2** BEAR, ENDURE : tolerar, aguantar, soportar

toleration [,tɑlə'reɪʃən] *n* : tolerancia *f*

toll[1] ['to:l] *vt* : tañer, sonar (una campana) — *vi* : sonar, doblar (dícese de las campanas)

toll[2] *n* **1** : peaje *m* (de una carretera, un puente, etc.) **2** CASUALTIES : pérdida *f*, número *m* de víctimas **3** TOLLING : tañido *m* (de campanas)

tollbooth ['to:l,bu:θ] *n* : caseta *f* de peaje; caseta *f* de cobro CA, Mex

toll-free ['to:l'fri:] *adj* : gratuito

tollgate ['to:l,geɪt] *n* : barrera *f* de peaje

tomahawk ['tɑmə,hɔk] *n* : hacha *f* de guerra (de los indígenas norteamericanos)

tomato [tə'meɪto, -'mɑ-] *n, pl* **-toes** : tomate *m*

tomb ['tu:m] *n* : sepulcro *m*, tumba *f*

tomboy ['tɑm,bɔɪ] *n* : marimacho *mf*; niña *f* que se porta como muchacho

tombstone ['tu:m,sto:n] *n* : lápida *f*

tomcat ['tɑm,kæt] *n* : gato *m* (macho)

tome ['to:m] *n* : tomo *m*

tomorrow[1] [tə'mɑro] *adv* : mañana

tomorrow[2] *n* : mañana *m*

tom-tom ['tɑm,tɑm] *n* : tam-tam *m*

ton ['tən] *n* : tonelada *f*

tone[1] ['to:n] *vt* **toned; toning** **1** or **to tone down** : atenuar, suavizar, moderar **2** or **to tone up** STRENGTHEN : tonificar, vigorizar

tone[2] *n* : tono *m* ⟨in a friendly tone : en tono amistoso⟩ ⟨a grayish tone : un tono grisáceo⟩

tongs ['tɑŋz, 'tɔŋz] *npl* : tenazas *fpl*

tongue ['tʌŋ] *n* **1** : lengua *f* **2** LANGUAGE : lengua *f*, idioma *m*

tongue-tied ['tʌŋ,taɪd] *adj* **to get tongue-tied** : trabársele la lengua a uno

tongue-twister ['tʌŋ,twɪstər] *n* : trabalenguas *m*

tonic[1] ['tɑnɪk] *adj* : tónico

tonic² *n* **1** : tónico *m* **2** *or* **tonic water** : tónica *f*

tonight¹ [təˈnaɪt] *adv* : esta noche

tonight² *n* : esta noche *f*

tonnage [ˈtʌnɪdʒ] *n* : tonelaje *m*

tonsil [ˈtɑntsəl] *n* : amígdala *f*, angina *f* Mex

tonsillitis [ˌtɑntsəˈlaɪtəs] *n* : amigdalitis *f*, anginas *fpl* Mex

too [ˈtuː] *adv* **1** ALSO : también **2** EXCESSIVELY : demasiado ⟨it's too hot in here : aquí hace demasiado calor⟩

took → **take¹**

tool¹ [ˈtuːl] *vt* **1** : fabricar, confeccionar (con herramientas) **2** EQUIP : instalar maquinaria en (una fábrica)

tool² *n* : herramienta *f*

toolbar [ˈtuːlˌbɑr] *n* : barra *f* de herramientas

toolbox [ˈtuːlˌbɑks] *n* : caja *f* de herramientas

tool kit *n* : juego *m* de herramientas

toot¹ [ˈtuːt] *vt* : sonar (un claxon o un pito)

toot² *n* : pitido *m*, bocinazo *m* (de un claxon)

tooth [ˈtuːθ] *n*, *pl* **teeth** [ˈtiːθ] **1** : diente *m* **2** like pulling teeth : casi imposible **3** long in the tooth : viejo **4** to grit one's teeth : apretar los dientes, aguantarse **5** to have a sweet tooth : ser goloso, gustarle mucho los dulces a uno **6** to lie through one's teeth : mentir descaradamente **7** tooth and nail : a ultranza, a capa y espada **8** to set someone's teeth on edge : crispar/erizar a alguien **9** to sink one's teeth into : clavar los dientes en **10** to sink/get one's teeth into : hincarle el diente a (una actividad, etc.)

toothache [ˈtuːθˌeɪk] *n* : dolor *m* de muelas

toothbrush [ˈtuːθˌbrʌʃ] *n* : cepillo *m* de dientes

toothed [ˈtuːθt] *adj* **1** : dentado **2** (*used in combination*) : de dientes ⟨bucktoothed : de dientes salientes⟩

toothless [ˈtuːθləs] *adj* : desdentado

toothpaste [ˈtuːθˌpeɪst] *n* : pasta *f* de dientes, crema *f* dental, dentífrico *m*

toothpick [ˈtuːθˌpɪk] *n* : palillo *m* (de dientes), mondadientes *m*

top¹ [ˈtɑp] *vt* **topped; topping** **1** COVER : cubrir, coronar **2** SURPASS : sobrepasar, superar **3** CLEAR : pasar por encima de **4** : encabezar (una lista, etc.) ⟨to top the charts : ser el número uno en las listas de éxitos⟩ **5** to top off END : terminar ⟨to top it all off : para colmo⟩ **6** to top off : llenar hasta arriba (un depósito, un vaso, etc.)

top² *adj* : superior ⟨the top shelf : la repisa superior⟩ ⟨one of the top lawyers : uno de los mejores abogados⟩

top³ *n* **1** : parte *f* superior, cumbre *f*, cima *f* (de un monte, etc.) ⟨to climb to the top : subir a la cumbre⟩ ⟨from top to bottom : de arriba abajo⟩ **2** COVER : tapa *f*, cubierta *f* **3** : trompo *m* (juguete) **4** at the top of one's lungs/voice : a voz en grito/cuello, a grito pelado **5** on top of : encima de **6** on top of BESIDES

: además de **7** on top of the world : muy alegre **8** over the top : exagerado **9** to be on top of CONTROL : controlar, tener controlado **10** to be/stay on top of : estar/mantenerse al día en (las noticias, etc.) **11** to come out on top : salir ganando

topaz [ˈtoʊˌpæz] *n* : topacio *m*

topcoat [ˈtɑpˌkoːt] *n* : sobretodo *m*, abrigo *m*

top hat *n* : sombrero *m* de copa

topic [ˈtɑpɪk] *n* : tema *m*, tópico *m*

topical [ˈtɑpɪkəl] *adj* : de interés actual

topless [ˈtɑpləs] *adj* : sin camisa

topmost [ˈtɑpˌmoːst] *adj* : más alto

top–notch [ˈtɑpˈnɑtʃ] *adj* : de lo mejor, de primera categoría

topographic [ˌtɑpəˈɡræfɪk] *or* **topographical** [-fɪkəl] *adj* : topográfico

topography [təˈpɑɡrəfi] *n*, *pl* **-phies** : topografía *f*

topple [ˈtɑpəl] *v* **-pled; -pling** *vi* : caerse, venirse abajo — *vt* : volcar, derrocar (un gobierno, etc.)

top secret *adj* : ultrasecreto

topsoil [ˈtɑpˌsɔɪl] *n* : capa *f* superior del suelo

topsy-turvy [ˌtɑpsiˈtərvi] *adv* & *adj* : patas arriba, al revés

torch [ˈtɔrtʃ] *n* : antorcha *f*

tore → **tear¹**

torment¹ [tɔrˈmɛnt, ˈtɔrˌ-] *vt* : atormentar, torturar, martirizar

torment² [ˈtɔrˌmɛnt] *n* : tormento *m*, suplicio *m*, martirio *m*

tormentor [tɔrˈmɛntər] *n* : atormentador *m*, -dora *f*

torn *pp* → **tear¹**

tornado [tɔrˈneɪdo] *n*, *pl* **-does** *or* **-dos** : tornado *m*

torpedo¹ [tɔrˈpiːdo] *vt* : torpedear

torpedo² *n*, *pl* **-does** : torpedo *m*

torpid [ˈtɔrpɪd] *adj* **1** SLUGGISH : aletargado **2** APATHETIC : apático

torpor [ˈtɔrpər] *n* : letargo *m*, apatía *f*

torrent [ˈtɔrənt] *n* : torrente *m*

torrential [təˈrɛntʃəl, tə-] *adj* : torrencial

torrid [ˈtɔrɪd] *adj* : tórrido

torso [ˈtɔrˌso] *n*, *pl* **-sos** *or* **-si** [-ˌsi] : torso *m*

tortilla [tɔrˈtiːjə] *n* : tortilla *f* (de maíz)

tortoise [ˈtɔrtəs] *n* : tortuga *f* (terrestre)

tortoiseshell [ˈtɔrtəsˌʃɛl] *n* : carey *m*, concha *f*

tortuous [ˈtɔrtʃuəs] *adj* : tortuoso

torture¹ [ˈtɔrtʃər] *vt* **-tured; -turing** : torturar, atormentar

torture² *n* : tortura *f*, tormento *m* ⟨it was sheer torture! : ¡fue un verdadero suplicio!⟩

torturer [ˈtɔrtʃərər] *n* : torturador *m*, -dora *f*

toss¹ [ˈtɔs, ˈtɑs] *vt* **1** AGITATE, SHAKE : sacudir, agitar ⟨to toss a salad : mezclar una ensalada⟩ **2** THROW : tirar, echar, lanzar ⟨to toss a coin : echarlo a cara o cruz⟩ **3** to toss away/out DISCARD : botar, tirar (a la basura) **4** to toss back *fam* : tomarse **5** to toss off : escribir (rápidamente) **6** to toss out REJECT : re-

chazar **7 to toss out** EJECT : echar — *vi*
: sacudirse ⟨to toss and turn : dar vueltas⟩

toss² *n* THROW : lanzamiento *m*, tiro *m*,
tirada *f*, lance *m* (de dados, etc.)

toss-up [ˈtɔsˌʌp] *n* : posibilidad *f* igual
⟨it's a toss-up : quizá sí, quizá no⟩

tot [ˈtɑt] *n* : pequeño *m*, -ña *f*

total¹ [ˈtoːtəl] *vt* **-taled** *or* **-talled; -taling** *or*
-talling 1 *or* **to total up** ASCENDER a, sumar,
totalizar **2** AMOUNT TO : ascender a, llegar a **3** *fam* WRECK : destrozar (un automóvil)

total² *adj* : total, completo, absoluto —
totally *adv*

total³ *n* : total *m*

totalitarian [toːˌtæləˈteriən] *adj* : totalitario

totalitarianism [toːˌtæləˈteriəˌnɪzəm] *n*
: totalitarismo *m*

totality [toːˈtæləti] *n, pl* **-ties** : totalidad *f*

tote [ˈtoːt] *vt* **toted; toting** : cargar, llevar

totem [ˈtoːtəm] *n* : tótem *m*

totter [ˈtɑtər] *vi* : tambalearse

touch¹ [ˈtʌtʃ] *vt* **1** FEEL, HANDLE : tocar,
tentar **2** AFFECT, MOVE : conmover,
afectar, tocar ⟨his gesture touched our
hearts : su gesto nos tocó el corazón⟩ —
to touch up : retocar — *vi* **1** : tocar ⟨do
not touch : no tocar⟩ **2** : tocarse ⟨our
hands touched : nuestras manos se tocaron⟩ **3 to touch down** : aterrizar **4 to
touch on** : tocar (un tema)

touch² *n* **1** : tacto *m* (sentido) **2** DETAIL
: toque *m*, detalle *m* ⟨a touch of color/
humor : un toque de color/humor⟩ ⟨the
finishing touches : los toques finales⟩ **3**
BIT : pizca *f*, gota *f*, poco *m* **4** ABILITY
: habilidad *f* ⟨to lose one's touch : perder
la habilidad⟩ **5** CONTACT : contacto,
comunicación *f* ⟨to keep/stay in touch
: mantenerse en contacto⟩ ⟨to lose touch
: perder el contacto⟩ **6 out of touch**
: desconectado (de la realidad, etc.)

touch-and-go *adj* : poco seguro, poco
cierto ⟨it was touch-and-go for a while
: no sabíamos qué pasaría⟩

touchdown [ˈtʌtʃˌdaʊn] *n* : touchdown *m*
(en futbol americano)

touching [ˈtʌtʃɪŋ] *adj* MOVING : conmovedor

touchline [ˈtʌtʃˌlaɪn] *n* : banda *f*, línea *f* de
banda (en fútbol)

touchstone [ˈtʌtʃˌstoːn] *n* : piedra *f* de toque

touch-up [ˈtʌtʃˌʌp] *n* : retoque *m*

touchy [ˈtʌtʃi] *adj* **touchier; -est 1** : sensible,
susceptible (dícese de una persona)
2 : delicado ⟨a touchy subject : un tema
delicado⟩

tough¹ [ˈtʌf] *adj* **1** STRONG : fuerte, resistente (dícese de materiales) **2** LEATHERY
: correoso ⟨a tough steak : un bistec
duro⟩ **3** HARDY : fuerte, robusto (dícese
de una persona) **4** STRICT : severo, exigente **5** DIFFICULT : difícil **6** STUBBORN
: terco, obstinado

tough² *n* : matón *m*, persona *f* ruda y
brusca

toughen [ˈtʌfən] *vt* : fortalecer, endurecer
— *vi* : endurecerse, hacerse más fuerte

toughness [ˈtʌfnəs] *n* : dureza *f*

toupee [tuːˈpeɪ] *n* : peluquín *m*, bisoñé *m*

tour¹ [ˈtʊr] *vi* : tomar una excursión, viajar
— *vt* : recorrer, hacer una gira por

tour² *n* **1** : gira *f*, tour *m*, excursión *f* **2**
tour of duty : período *m* de servicio

tourism [ˈtʊrˌɪzəm] *n* : turismo *m*

tourist [ˈtʊrɪst, ˈtʊr-] *n* : turista *mf*

tournament [ˈtɜrnəmənt, ˈtʊr-] *n* : torneo
m

tourniquet [ˈtɜrnɪkət, ˈtʊr-] *n* : torniquete
m

tousle [ˈtaʊzəl] *vt* **-sled; -sling** : desarreglar, despeinar (el cabello)

tout [ˈtaʊt] *vt* : promocionar, elogiar (con
exageración)

tow¹ [ˈtoː] *vt* : remolcar

tow² *n* : remolque *m*

toward [ˈtord, təˈword] *or* **towards** [ˈtordz,
təˈwordz] *prep* **1** (*indicating direction*)
: hacia, rumbo a ⟨heading toward town
: dirigiéndose rumbo al pueblo⟩ ⟨efforts
towards peace : esfuerzos hacia la paz⟩
2 (*indicating time*) : alrededor de ⟨toward midnight : alrededor de la medianoche⟩ **3** REGARDING : hacia, con respecto a ⟨his attitude toward life : su
actitud hacia la vida⟩ **4** FOR : para,
como pago parcial de (una compra o
deuda)

towel [ˈtaʊəl] *n* **1** : toalla *f* **2 to throw in
the towel** : tirar la toalla

tower¹ [ˈtaʊər] *vi* **to tower over** : descollar
sobre, elevarse sobre, dominar

tower² *n* : torre *f*

towering [ˈtaʊərɪŋ] *adj* : altísimo, imponente

town [ˈtaʊn] *n* : pueblo *m*, ciudad *f* (pequeña)

town hall *n* : ayuntamiento *m*

township [ˈtaʊnˌʃɪp] *n* : municipio *m*

tow truck [ˈtoːˌtrʌk] *n* : grúa *f*

toxic [ˈtaksɪk] *adj* : tóxico

toxicity [takˈsɪsəti] *n, pl* **-ties** : toxicidad *f*

toxin [ˈtaksɪn] *n* : toxina *f*

toy¹ [ˈtɔɪ] *vi* : juguetear, jugar

toy² *adj* : de juguete ⟨a toy rifle : un rifle
de juguete⟩

toy³ *n* : juguete *m*

trace¹ [ˈtreɪs] *vt* **traced; tracing 1** : calcar
(un dibujo, etc.) **2** OUTLINE : delinear,
trazar (planes, etc.) **3** TRACK : describir
(un curso, una historia) **4** FIND : localizar, ubicar

trace² *n* **1** SIGN, TRACK : huella *f*, rastro
m, indicio *m*, vestigio *m* ⟨he disappeared
without a trace : desapareció sin dejar
rastro⟩ **2** BIT, HINT : pizca *f*, ápice *m*,
dejo *m*

trachea [ˈtreɪkiə] *n, pl* **-cheae** [-kiˌiː]
: tráquea *f*

tracing paper *n* : papel *m* de calcar

track¹ [ˈtræk] *vt* **1** TRAIL : seguir la pista
de, rastrear **2** : dejar huellas de ⟨he
tracked mud all over : dejó huellas de
lodo por todas partes⟩ **3 to track down**
: localizar

track² n 1 : rastro m, huella f (de animales), pista f (de personas) 2 PATH : pista f, sendero m, camino m 3 or railroad track : vía f (férrea) 4 → racetrack 5 : oruga f (de un tanque, etc.) 6 : atletismo m (deporte) 7 **the wrong side of the tracks** : los barrios bajos 8 **to be on the right/wrong track** : ir bien/mal encaminado, ir por buen/mal camino 9 **to be on track** : ir bien encaminado 10 **to cover one's tracks** : no dejar rastros 11 **to get back on track** : volver a encarrilarse 12 **to get/go off track** : desviarse del tema/plan (etc.) 13 **to keep track of** : llevar la cuenta de 14 **to lose track of** : perder la cuenta de ⟨I lost track of the time : no me di cuenta de la hora⟩ 15 **to throw someone off the track** : despistar a alguien

track–and–field ['trækənd'fi:ld] adj : de pista y campo

tracksuit ['træk,su:t] n : sudadera f; buzo m Chile, Peru; jogging m Arg; pants m Mex; chándal m Spain (traje)

tract ['trækt] n 1 AREA : terreno m, extensión f, área f 2 : tracto m ⟨digestive tract : tracto digestivo⟩ 3 PAMPHLET : panfleto m, folleto m

traction ['trækʃən] n : tracción f

tractor ['træktər] n 1 : tractor m (vehículo agrícola) 2 TRUCK : camión m (con remolque)

trade¹ ['treɪd] v traded; trading vi 1 : comerciar, negociar 2 EXCHANGE : hacer un cambio 3 **to trade on** : explotar — vt 1 EXCHANGE : cambiar, intercambiar, canjear ⟨we traded seats : nos cambiamos de asiento⟩ ⟨I'll trade (you) a cookie for a chocolate : te cambio una galleta por un chocolate⟩ 2 **to trade in** : entregar en/como parte de pago

trade² n 1 OCCUPATION : oficio m, profesión f, ocupación f ⟨a carpenter by trade : carpintero de oficio⟩ 2 COMMERCE : comercio m, industria f ⟨free trade : libre comercio⟩ ⟨the book trade : la industria del libro⟩ 3 EXCHANGE : intercambio m, canje m

trade–in ['treɪd,ɪn] n : artículo m que se canjea por otro

trademark ['treɪd,mɑrk] n 1 : marca f ⟨registered trademark : marca registrada⟩ 2 : sello m característico (de un grupo, una persona, etc.)

trader ['treɪdər] n : negociante mf, tratante mf, comerciante mf

tradesman ['treɪdzmən] n, pl -men [-mən, -,men] 1 CRAFTSMAN : artesano m, -na f 2 SHOPKEEPER : tendero m, -ra f; comerciante mf

tradition [trə'dɪʃən] n : tradición f

traditional [trə'dɪʃənəl] adj : tradicional — **traditionally** adv

traffic¹ ['træfɪk] vi trafficked; trafficking : traficar (con)

traffic² n 1 COMMERCE : tráfico m, comercio m ⟨the drug traffic : el narcotráfico⟩ 2 : tráfico m, tránsito m, circulación f (de vehículos, etc.)

traffic circle n : rotonda f, glorieta f

traffic jam → jam²

trafficker ['træfɪkər] n : traficante mf

traffic light n : semáforo m, luz f (de tránsito)

tragedy ['trædʒədi] n, pl -dies : tragedia f

tragic ['trædʒɪk] adj : trágico — **tragically** adv

trail¹ ['treɪl] v 1 DRAG : arrastrarse 2 LAG : quedarse atrás, retrasarse 3 **to trail away** or **to trail off** : disminuir, menguar, desvanecerse — vt 1 DRAG : arrastrar 2 PURSUE : perseguir, seguir la pista de

trail² n 1 TRACK : rastro m, huella f, pista f ⟨a trail of blood : un rastro de sangre⟩ 2 : cola f, estela f (de un meteoro) 3 PATH : sendero m, camino m, vereda f

trailer ['treɪlər] n 1 : remolque m, tráiler m (de un camión) 2 : caravana f (vivienda ambulante)

train¹ ['treɪn] vt 1 : adiestrar, entrenar (atletas), capacitar (trabajadores), amaestrar (animales) 2 POINT : apuntar (un arma, etc.) — vi : entrenar(se) (físicamente), prepararse (profesionalmente) ⟨she's training at the gym : se está entrenando en el gimnasio⟩

train² n 1 : cola f (de un vestido) 2 RETINUE : cortejo m, séquito m 3 SERIES : serie f (de eventos) 4 : tren m ⟨passenger train : tren de pasajeros⟩ 5 : tren m (mecanismo) ⟨drive train : tren motriz⟩ 6 **train of thought** : hilo m de razonamiento

trainee [treɪ'ni:] n : aprendiz m, -diza f

trainer ['treɪnər] n : entrenador m, -dora f

training ['treɪnɪŋ] n : adiestramiento m, entrenamiento m (físico), capacitación f (de trabajadores)

traipse ['treɪps] vi traipsed; traipsing : andar de un lado para otro, vagar

trait ['treɪt] n : rasgo m, característica f

traitor ['treɪtər] n : traidor m, -dora f

traitorous ['treɪtərəs] adj : traidor

trajectory [trə'dʒɛktəri] n, pl -ries : trayectoria f

tramp¹ ['træmp] vi : caminar (a paso pesado) — vt : deambular por, vagar por ⟨to tramp the streets : vagar por las calles⟩

tramp² n 1 VAGRANT : vagabundo m, -da f 2 HIKE : caminata f

trample ['træmpəl] vt -pled; -pling : pisotear, hollar

trampoline [,træmpə'li:n, 'træmpə,-] n : trampolín m, cama f elástica

trance ['trænts] n : trance m

tranquil ['træŋkwəl] adj : calmo, tranquilo, sereno — **tranquilly** adv

tranquilize ['træŋkwə,laɪz] vt -ized; -izing : tranquilizar

tranquilizer ['træŋkwə,laɪzər] n : tranquilizante m

tranquillity or **tranquility** [træŋ'kwɪləti] n : sosiego m, tranquilidad f

transact [træn'zækt] vt : negociar, gestionar, hacer (negocios)

transaction [træn'zækʃən] n 1 : transacción f, negocio m, operación f 2 **transactions** npl RECORDS : actas fpl

transatlantic [ˌtrænsətˈlæntɪk, ˌtrænz-] *adj* : transatlántico

transcend [trænˈsɛnd] *vt* : trascender, sobrepasar

transcendent [trænˈsɛndənt] *adj* : trascendente — **transcendence** [trænˈsɛndənts] *n*

transcendental [ˌtrænsɛnˈdɛntəl, -sən-] *adj* : trascendental ⟨transcendental meditation : meditación trascendental⟩

transcribe [trænˈskraɪb] *vt* -**scribed**; -**scribing** : transcribir

transcript [ˈtrænˌskrɪpt] *n* : copia *f* oficial

transcription [trænˈskrɪpʃən] *n* : transcripción *f*

transfer¹ [trænsˈfər, ˈtrænsˌfər] *v* -**ferred**; -**ferring** *vt* **1** : trasladar (a una persona), transferir (fondos) **2** : transferir, traspasar, ceder (propiedad) **3** PRINT : imprimir (un diseño) — *vi* **1** MOVE : trasladarse, cambiarse **2** CHANGE : transbordar, cambiar (de un transporte a otro) ⟨he transfers at E Street : hace transbordo en la calle E⟩

transfer² [ˈtrænsˌfər] *n* **1** TRANSFERRING : transferencia *f* (de fondos, de propiedad, etc.), traslado *m* (de una persona) **2** DECAL : calcomanía *f* **3** : boleto *m* (para cambiar de un avión, etc., a otro)

transferable [trænsˈfərəbəl] *adj* : transferible

transference [trænsˈfərənts] *n* : transferencia *f*

transfigure [trænsˈfɪgjər] *vt* -**ured**; -**uring** : transfigurar, transformar

transfix [trænsˈfɪks] *vt* **1** PIERCE : traspasar, atravesar **2** IMMOBILIZE : paralizar

transform [trænsˈfɔrm] *vt* : transformar

transformation [ˌtrænsfərˈmeɪʃən] *n* : transformación *f*

transformer [trænsˈfɔrmər] *n* : transformador *m*

transfusion [trænsˈfjuːʒən] *n* : transfusión *f*

transgress [trænsˈgrɛs, trænz-] *vt* : transgredir, infringir — **transgression** [trænsˈgrɛʃən, trænz-] *n* — **transgressor** [trænsˈgrɛsər, trænz-] *n*

transient¹ [ˈtrænʃənt, ˈtrænsiənt] *adj* : pasajero, transitorio — **transiently** *adv*

transient² *n* : transeúnte *mf*

transistor [trænˈzɪstər, -ˈsɪs-] *n* : transistor *m*

transit [ˈtrænsɪt, ˈtrænzɪt] *n* **1** PASSAGE : pasaje *m*, tránsito *m* ⟨in transit : en tránsito⟩ **2** TRANSPORTATION : transporte *m* (público)

transition [trænˈsɪʃən, -ˈzɪʃ-] *n* : transición *f*

transitional [trænˈsɪʃənəl, -ˈzɪʃ-] *adj* : de transición

transitive [ˈtrænsətɪv, ˈtrænzə-] *adj* : transitivo

transitory [ˈtrænsəˌtori, ˈtrænzə-] *adj* : transitorio

translatable [trænsˈleɪtəbəl, trænz-] *adj* : traducible

translate [trænsˈleɪt, trænz-; ˈtrænsˌ-, ˈtrænzˌ-] *vt* -**lated**; -**lating** : traducir

translation [trænsˈleɪʃən, trænz-] *n* : traducción *f*

translator [trænsˈleɪtər, trænz-; ˈtrænsˌ-, ˈtrænzˌ-] *n* : traductor *m*, -tora *f*

translucent [trænsˈluːsənt, trænz-] *adj* : translúcido

transmissible [trænsˈmɪsəbəl, trænz-] *adj* : transmisible

transmission [trænsˈmɪʃən, trænz-] *n* : transmisión *f*

transmit [trænsˈmɪt, trænz-] *vt* -**mitted**; -**mitting** : transmitir

transmitter [trænsˈmɪtər, trænz-; ˈtrænsˌ-, ˈtrænzˌ-] *n* : transmisor *m*, emisor *m*

transom [ˈtrænsəm] *n* : montante *m* (de una puerta), travesaño *m* (de una ventana)

transparency [trænsˈpærəntsi] *n, pl* -**cies** : transparencia *f*

transparent [trænsˈpærənt] *adj* **1** : transparente, traslúcido ⟨a transparent fabric : una tela transparente⟩ **2** OBVIOUS : transparente, obvio, claro — **transparently** *adv*

transpiration [ˌtrænspəˈreɪʃən] *n* : transpiración *f*

transpire [trænsˈpaɪr] *vi* -**spired**; -**spiring** **1** : transpirar (en biología y botánica) **2** TURN OUT : resultar **3** HAPPEN : suceder, ocurrir, tener lugar

transplant¹ [trænsˈplænt] *vt* : trasplantar

transplant² [ˈtrænsˌplænt] *n* : trasplante *m*

transport¹ [trænsˈport, ˈtrænsˌ-] *vt* **1** CARRY : transportar, acarrear **2** ENRAPTURE : transportar

transport² [ˈtrænsˌport] *n* **1** TRANSPORTATION : transporte *m*, transportación *f* **2** RAPTURE : éxtasis *m* **3** *or* **transport ship** : buque *m* de transporte (de personal militar)

transportation [ˌtrænspərˈteɪʃən] *n* : transporte *m*, transportación *f*

transpose [trænsˈpoːz] *vt* -**posed**; -**posing** : trasponer, trasladar, transportar (una composición musical)

transsexual [trænsˈsɛkʃuəl] *n* : transexual *mf* — **transsexual** *adj*

transverse [trænsˈvərs, trænz-] *adj* : transversal, transverso, oblicuo — **transversely** *adv*

transvestite [trænsˈvɛstaɪt, trænz-] *n* : travesti *mf*, travestí *mf* — **transvestite** *adj*

trap¹ [ˈtræp] *vt* **trapped; trapping** : atrapar, apresar (en una trampa)

trap² *n* : trampa *f* ⟨to set a trap : tender una trampa⟩

trapdoor [ˈtræpˈdor] *n* : trampilla *f*

trapeze [træˈpiːz] *n* : trapecio *m*

trapezoid [ˈtræpəˌzɔɪd] *n* : trapezoide *m*, trapecio *m*

trapper [ˈtræpər] *n* : trampero *m*, -ra *f*; cazador *m*, -dora *f* (que usa trampas)

trappings [ˈtræpɪŋz] *npl* **1** : arreos *mpl*, jaeces *mpl* (de un caballo) **2** ADORNMENTS : adornos *mpl*, pompa *f*

trash [ˈtræʃ] *n* : basura *f*

trash can → garbage can

trashy ['træʃi] *adj* : de pacotilla

trauma ['trɔmə, 'trau-] *n* : trauma *m*

traumatic [trə'mætɪk, trɔ-, trau-] *adj* : traumático

travel[1] ['trævəl] *vi* **-eled** *or* **-elled; -eling** *or* **-elling** **1** JOURNEY : viajar **2** GO, MOVE : desplazarse, moverse, ir ⟨the waves travel at uniform speed : las ondas se desplazan a una velocidad uniforme⟩

travel[2] *n or* **travels** *npl* : viajes *mpl*

travel agency *n* : agencia *f* de viajes

travel agent *n* : agente *mf* de viajes

traveler *or* **traveller** ['trævələr] *n* : viajero *m*, -ra *f*

traveler's check *or* **traveller's check** *n* : cheque *m* de viajero

traverse [trə'vərs, træ'vərs, 'trævərs] *vt* **-versed; -versing** CROSS : atravesar, extenderse a través de, cruzar

travesty ['trævəsti] *n, pl* **-ties** : parodia *f*

trawl[1] ['trɔl] *vi* : pescar con red de arrastre, rastrear

trawl[2] *n or* **trawl net** : red *f* de arrastre

trawler ['trɔlər] *n* : barco *m* de pesca (utilizado para rastrear)

tray ['treɪ] *n* : bandeja *f*, charola *f Bol, Mex, Peru*

treacherous ['trɛtʃərəs] *adj* **1** TRAITOROUS : traicionero, traidor **2** DANGEROUS : peligroso

treacherously ['trɛtʃərəsli] *adv* : a traición

treachery ['trɛtʃəri] *n, pl* **-eries** : traición *f*

tread[1] ['trɛd] *v* **trod** ['trɑd]; **trodden** ['trɑdən] *or* **trod; treading** *vt* TRAMPLE : pisotear, hollar — *vi* **1** WALK : caminar, andar **2 to tread on** : pisar

tread[2] *n* **1** STEP : paso *m*, andar *m*, **2** : banda *f* de rodadura (de un neumático, etc.) **3** : escalón *m* (de una escalera)

treadle ['trɛdəl] *n* : pedal *m* (de una máquina)

treadmill ['trɛd,mɪl] *n* **1** : rueda *f* de andar **2** ROUTINE : rutina *f*

treason ['tri:zən] *n* : traición *f* (a la patria, etc.)

treasure[1] ['trɛʒər, 'treɪ-] *vt* **-sured; -suring** : apreciar, valorar

treasure[2] *n* : tesoro *m*

treasurer ['trɛʒərər, 'treɪ-] *n* : tesorero *m*, -ra *f*

treasury ['trɛʒəri, 'treɪ-] *n, pl* **-suries** : tesorería *f*, tesoro *m*

treat[1] ['tri:t] *vt* **1** DEAL WITH : tratar (un asunto) ⟨the article treats of poverty : el artículo trata de la pobreza⟩ **2** HANDLE : tratar (a una persona), manejar (un objeto) ⟨to treat something as a joke : tomar(se) algo a broma⟩ **3** INVITE : invitar, convidar ⟨he treated me to a meal : me invitó a comer⟩ **4** : tratar, atender (en medicina) **5** PROCESS : tratar ⟨to treat sewage : tratar las aguas negras⟩ — **treatable** ['tri:təbəl] *adj*

treat[2] *n* : gusto *m*, placer *m* ⟨it was a treat to see you : fue un placer verte⟩ ⟨it's my treat : yo invito⟩

treatise ['tri:tɪs] *n* : tratado *m*, estudio *m*

treatment ['tri:tmənt] *n* : trato *m*, tratamiento *m* (médico)

treaty ['tri:ti] *n, pl* **-ties** : tratado *m*, convenio *m*

treble[1] ['trɛbəl] *vt* **-bled; -bling** : triplicar

treble[2] *adj* **1** → **triple 2** : de tiple, soprano (en música) **3 treble clef** : clave *f* de sol

treble[3] *n* : tiple *m*, parte *f* de soprano

tree ['tri:] *n* : árbol *m*

treeless ['tri:ləs] *adj* : carente de árboles

tree–lined ['tri:,laɪnd] *adj* : bordeado de árboles

tree stump → **stump**[2]

trek[1] ['trɛk] *vi* **trekked; trekking** : hacer un viaje largo y difícil

trek[2] *n* : viaje *m* largo y difícil

trellis ['trɛlɪs] *n* : enrejado *m*, celosía *f*

tremble ['trɛmbəl] *vi* **-bled; -bling** : temblar

tremendous [trɪ'mɛndəs] *adj* : tremendo — **tremendously** *adv*

tremor ['trɛmər] *n* : temblor *m*

tremulous ['trɛmjələs] *adj* : trémulo, tembloroso

trench ['trɛntʃ] *n* **1** DITCH : zanja *f* **2** : trinchera *f* (militar)

trenchant ['trɛntʃənt] *adj* : cortante, mordaz

trend[1] ['trɛnd] *vi* : tender, inclinarse

trend[2] *n* **1** TENDENCY : tendencia *f* **2** FASHION : moda *f*

trendy ['trɛndi] *adj* **trendier; -est** : de moda

trepidation [,trɛpə'deɪʃən] *n* : inquietud *f*, ansiedad *f*

trespass[1] ['trɛspəs, -,pæs] *vi* **1** SIN : pecar, transgredir **2** : entrar ilegalmente (en propiedad ajena)

trespass[2] *n* **1** SIN : pecado *m*, transgresión *f* ⟨forgive us our trespasses : perdónanos nuestras deudas⟩ **2** : entrada *f* ilegal (en propiedad ajena)

tress ['trɛs] *n* : mechón *m*

trestle ['trɛsəl] *n* **1** : caballete *m* (armazón) **2** *or* **trestle bridge** : puente *m* de caballete

tri- ['traɪ] *pref* : tri-

triad ['traɪ,æd] *n* : tríada *f*

trial[1] ['traɪəl] *adj* : de prueba ⟨trial period : período de prueba⟩

trial[2] *n* **1** : juicio *m*, proceso *m* ⟨to stand trial : ser sometido a juicio⟩ **2** AFFLICTION : aflicción *f*, tribulación *f* **3** TEST : prueba *f*, ensayo *m* ⟨by trial and error : por ensayo y error⟩

triangle ['traɪ,æŋgəl] *n* : triángulo *m*

triangular [traɪ'æŋgələr] *adj* : triangular

tribal ['traɪbəl] *adj* : tribal

tribe ['traɪb] *n* : tribu *f*

tribesman ['traɪbzmən] *n, pl* **-men** [-mən, -,mɛn] : miembro *m* de una tribu

tribulation [,trɪbjə'leɪʃən] *n* : tribulación *f*

tribunal [traɪ'bju:nəl, trɪ-] *n* : tribunal *m*, corte *f*

tributary ['trɪbjə,tɛri] *n, pl* **-taries** : afluente *m*

tribute ['trɪb,ju:t] *n* : tributo *m*

trick[1] ['trɪk] *vt* : engañar, embaucar

trick[2] *n* **1** RUSE : trampa *f*, treta *f*, artimaña *f* **2** PRANK : broma *f* ⟨we played a trick on her : le gastamos una broma⟩ **3**

: truco *m* ⟨magic tricks : trucos de magia⟩ ⟨the trick is to wait five minutes : el truco está en esperar cinco minutos⟩ **4** MANNERISM : peculiaridad *f*, manía *f* **5** : baza *f* (en juegos de naipes)

trickery ['trɪkəri] *n* : engaños *mpl*, trampas *fpl*

trickle¹ ['trɪkəl] *vi* **-led; -ling** : gotear, chorrear

trickle² *n* : goteo *m*, hilo *m*

trickster ['trɪkstər] *n* : estafador *m*, -dora *f*; embaucador *m*, -dora *f*

tricky ['trɪki] *adj* **trickier; -est 1** SLY : astuto, taimado **2** DIFFICULT : delicado, peliagudo, difícil

tricolor ['traɪ,kʌlər] *adj* : tricolor

tricycle ['traɪsəkəl, -,sɪkəl] *n* : triciclo *m*

trident ['traɪdənt] *n* : tridente *m*

triennial [traɪ'ɛniəl] *adj* : trienal

trifle¹ ['traɪfəl] *vi* **-fled; -fling** : jugar, juguetear

trifle² *n* : nimiedad *f*, insignificancia *f*

trifling ['traɪflɪŋ] *adj* : trivial, insignificante

trigger¹ ['trɪgər] *vt* : causar, provocar

trigger² *n* : gatillo *m*

trigonometry [,trɪgə'nɑmətri] *n* : trigonometría *f*

trill¹ ['trɪl] *vi* QUAVER : trinar, gorjear — *vt* : vibrar ⟨to trill the *r* : vibrar la *r*⟩

trill² *n* **1** QUAVER : trino *m*, gorjeo *m* **2** : vibración *f* (en fonética)

trillion ['trɪljən] *n* : billón *m*

trilogy ['trɪlədʒi] *n, pl* **-gies** : trilogía *f*

trim¹ ['trɪm] *vt* **trimmed; trimming 1** DECORATE : adornar, decorar **2** CUT : recortar **3** REDUCE : recortar, reducir ⟨to trim the excess : recortar el exceso⟩

trim² *adj* **trimmer; trimmest 1** SLIM : esbelto **2** NEAT : limpio y arreglado, bien cuidado

trim³ *n* **1** CONDITION : condición *f*, estado *m* ⟨to keep in trim : mantenerse en buena forma⟩ **2** CUT : recorte *m* **3** TRIMMING : adornos *mpl*

trimester [,traɪ'mɛstər] *n* : trimestre *m*

trimming ['trɪmɪŋ] *n* : adornos *mpl*, accesorios *mpl*

Trinity ['trɪnəti] *n* : Trinidad *f*

trinket ['trɪŋkət] *n* : chuchería *f*, baratija *f*

trio ['tri:,oː] *n, pl* **trios** : trío *m*

trip¹ ['trɪp] *v* **tripped; tripping** *vi* **1** : caminar (a paso ligero) **2** STUMBLE : tropezar **3** **to trip up** ERR : equivocarse, cometer un error — *vt* **1** : hacerle una zancadilla (a alguien) ⟨you tripped me on purpose! : ¡me hiciste la zancadilla a propósito!⟩ **2** ACTIVATE : activar (un mecanismo) **3** **to trip up** : hacer equivocar (a alguien)

trip² *n* **1** JOURNEY : viaje *m* ⟨to take a trip : hacer un viaje⟩ **2** STUMBLE : tropiezo *m*, traspié *m*

tripartite [traɪ'pɑr,taɪt] *adj* : tripartito

tripe ['traɪp] *n* **1** : mondongo *m*, callos *mpl*, pancita *f Mex* **2** TRASH : porquería *f*

triple¹ ['trɪpəl] *vt* **-pled; -pling** : triplicar

triple² *adj* : triple

triple³ *n* : triple *m*

triplet ['trɪplət] *n* **1** : terceto *m* (en poesía, música, etc.) **2** : trillizo *m*, -za *f* (persona)

triplicate ['trɪplɪkət] *n* : triplicado *m*

tripod ['traɪ,pɑd] *n* : trípode *m*

trite ['traɪt] *adj* **triter; tritest** : trillado, tópico, manido

triumph¹ ['traɪəmpf] *vi* : triunfar

triumph² *n* : triunfo *m*

triumphal [traɪ'ʌmpfəl] *adj* : triunfal

triumphant [traɪ'ʌmpfənt] *adj* : triunfante, triunfal — **triumphantly** *adv*

triumvirate [traɪ'ʌmvərət] *n* : triunvirato *m*

trivet ['trɪvət] *n* : salvamanteles *m*

trivia ['trɪviə] *ns & pl* : trivialidades *fpl*, nimiedades *fpl*

trivial ['trɪviəl] *adj* : trivial, intrascendente, insignificante

triviality [,trɪvi'æləti] *n, pl* **-ties** : trivialidad *f*

trod, trodden → tread¹

troll ['tro:l] *n* : duende *m* o gigante *m* de cuentos folklóricos

trolley ['trɑli] *n, pl* **-leys** : tranvía *m*

trombone [trɑm'bo:n] *n* : trombón *m*

trombonist [trɑm'bo:nɪst] *n* : trombón *m*

troop¹ ['tru:p] *vi* : desfilar, ir en tropel

troop² *n* **1** : escuadrón *m* (de caballería) **2** GROUP : grupo *m*, banda *f* (de personas) **3** **troops** *npl* SOLDIERS : tropas *fpl*, soldados *mpl*

trooper ['tru:pər] *n* **1** : soldado *m* (de caballería) **2** : policía *m* montado **3** : policía *m* (estatal)

trophy ['tro:fi] *n, pl* **-phies** : trofeo *m*

tropic¹ ['trɑpɪk] *or* **tropical** [-pɪkəl] *adj* : tropical

tropic² *n* **1** : trópico *m* ⟨tropic of Cancer : trópico de Cáncer⟩ **2** **the tropics** : el trópico

trot¹ ['trɑt] *vi* **trotted; trotting** : trotar

trot² *n* : trote *m*

troubadour ['tru:bə,dɔr] *n* : trovador *m*, -dora *f*

trouble¹ ['trʌbəl] *v* **-bled; -bling** *vt* **1** DISTURB, WORRY : molestar, perturbar, inquietar **2** AFFLICT : afligir, afectar — *vi* : molestarse, hacer un esfuerzo ⟨they didn't trouble to come : no se molestaron en venir⟩

trouble² *n* **1** PROBLEMS : problemas *mpl*, dificultades *fpl* ⟨to be in trouble : estar en un aprieto⟩ ⟨heart trouble : problemas de corazón⟩ **2** EFFORT : molestia *f*, esfuerzo *m* ⟨to take the trouble : tomarse la molestia⟩ ⟨it's not worth the trouble : no vale la pena⟩

troublemaker ['trʌbəl,meɪkər] *n* : agitador *m*, -dora *f*; alborotador *m*, -dora *f*

troubleshooter ['trʌbəl,ʃu:tər] *n* : persona *f* que resuelve problemas

troublesome ['trʌbəlsəm] *adj* : problemático, dificultoso — **troublesomely** *adv*

trough ['trɔf] *n, pl* **troughs** ['trɔfs, 'trɔvz] **1** : comedero *m*, bebedero *m* (de animales) **2** CHANNEL, HOLLOW : depresión *f* (en el suelo), seno *m* (de olas)

trounce ['traʊɲʃs] *vt* **trounced; trouncing 1** THRASH : apalear, darle una paliza (a alguien) **2** DEFEAT : derrotar contundentemente

troupe ['tru:p] *n* : troupe *f*

trouser ['traʊzər] *adj* : del pantalón

trousers ['traʊzərz] *npl* : pantalón *m*, pantalones *mpl*

trousseau ['tru:ˌso:, tru'so:] *n* : ajuar *m*

trout ['traʊt] *ns & pl* : trucha *f*

trowel ['traʊəl] *n* **1** : llana *f*, paleta *f* (de albañil) **2** : desplantador *m* (de jardinero)

truant ['tru:ənt] *n* : alumno *m*, -na *f* que falta a clase sin permiso

truce ['tru:s] *n* : tregua *f*, armisticio *m*

truck¹ ['trʌk] *vt* : transportar en camión

truck² *n* **1** : camión *m* (vehículo automóvil), carro *m* (manual) ⟨truck driver : camionero⟩ **2** *or* hand truck : carretilla *f*, carro *m* (para llevar cajones, etc.) **3** DEALINGS : tratos *mpl* ⟨to have no truck with : no tener nada que ver con⟩

trucker ['trʌkər] *n* : camionero *m*, -ra *f*

truculent ['trʌkjələnt] *adj* : agresivo, beligerante

trudge ['trʌʤ] *vi* **trudged; trudging** : caminar a paso pesado

true¹ ['tru:] *vt* **trued; trueing** : aplomar (algo vertical), nivelar (algo horizontal), centrar (una rueda)

true² *adv* **1** TRUTHFULLY : lealmente, sinceramente **2** ACCURATELY : exactamente, certeramente

true³ *adj* **truer; truest 1** LOYAL : fiel, leal **2** : cierto, verdadero, verídico ⟨it's true : es cierto, es la verdad⟩ ⟨a true story : una historia verídica⟩ **3** GENUINE : auténtico, genuino — **truly** *adv*

true–blue ['tru:'blu:] *adj* LOYAL : leal, fiel

truffle ['trʌfəl] *n* : trufa *f*

truism ['tru:ˌɪzəm] *n* : perogrullada *f*, verdad *f* obvia

trump¹ ['trʌmp] *vt* : matar (en juegos de naipes)

trump² *n* : triunfo *m* (en juegos de naipes)

trumped–up ['trʌmpt'ʌp] *adj* : inventado, fabricado ⟨trumped-up charges : falsas acusaciones⟩

trumpet¹ ['trʌmpət] *vi* **1** : sonar una trompeta **2** : berrear, bramar (dícese de un animal) — *vt* : proclamar a los cuatro vientos

trumpet² *n* : trompeta *f*

trumpeter ['trʌmpətər] *n* : trompetista *mf*

truncate ['trʌŋˌkeɪt, 'trʌn-] *vt* **-cated; -cating** : truncar

trundle ['trʌndəl] *v* **-dled; -dling** *vi* : rodar lentamente — *vt* : hacer rodar, empujar lentamente

trunk ['trʌŋk] *n* **1** : tronco *m* (de un árbol o del cuerpo) **2** : trompa *f* (de un elefante) **3** CHEST : baúl *m* **4** : maletero *m*, baúl *m* (*in various countries*), cajuela *f* *Mex* (de un auto) **5** trunks *npl* → swimming trunks

truss¹ ['trʌs] *vt* : atar (con fuerza)

truss² *n* **1** FRAMEWORK : armazón *m* (de una estructura) **2** : braguero *m* (en medicina)

trust¹ ['trʌst] *vi* : confiar, esperar ⟨to trust in God : confiar en Dios⟩ — *vt* **1** ENTRUST : confiar, encomendar **2** : confiar en, tenerle confianza a ⟨I trust you : te tengo confianza⟩

trust² *n* **1** CONFIDENCE : confianza *f* **2** HOPE : esperanza *f*, fe *f* **3** CREDIT : crédito *m* ⟨to sell on trust : fiar⟩ **4** : fideicomiso *m* ⟨to hold in trust : guardar en fideicomiso⟩ **5** : trust *m* (consorcio empresarial) **6** CUSTODY : responsabilidad *f*, custodia *f*

trustee [ˌtrʌs'ti:] *n* : fideicomisario *m*, -ria *f*; fiduciario *m*, -ria *f*

trustful ['trʌstfəl] *adj* : confiado — **trustfully** *adv*

trustworthiness ['trʌst,wərðinəs] *n* : integridad *f*, honradez *f*

trustworthy ['trʌst,wərði] *adj* : digno de confianza, confiable

trusty ['trʌsti] *adj* **trustier; -est** : fiel, confiable

truth ['tru:θ] *n, pl* **truths** ['tru:ðz, 'tru:θs] : verdad *f*

truthful ['tru:θfəl] *adj* : sincero, veraz — **truthfully** *adv*

truthfulness ['tru:θfəlnəs] *n* : sinceridad *f*, veracidad *f*

try¹ ['traɪ] *v* **tried; trying** *vt* **1** : enjuiciar, juzgar, procesar ⟨he was tried for murder : fue procesado por homicidio⟩ **2** : probar ⟨did you try the salad? : ¿probaste la ensalada?⟩ **3** TEST : tentar, poner a prueba ⟨to try one's patience : tentarle la paciencia a uno⟩ **4** ATTEMPT : tratar de, tratar ⟨to try on : probarse (ropa) **6** to try out : poner a prueba — *vi* **1** : tratar, intentar **2** to try out (for) : presentarse a una prueba (para)

try² *n, pl* **tries** : intento *m*, tentativa *f*

tryout ['traɪ,aʊt] *n* : prueba *f*

tsar ['zɑr, 'tsɑr, 'sɑr] → **czar**

T–shirt ['ti:,ʃərt] *n* : camiseta *f*

tub ['tʌb] *n* **1** CASK : cuba *f*, barril *m*, tonel *m* **2** CONTAINER : envase *m* (de plástico, etc.) ⟨a tub of margarine : un envase de margarina⟩ **3** BATHTUB : tina *f* (de baño), bañera *f*

tuba ['tu:bə, 'tju:-] *n* : tuba *f*

tube ['tu:b, 'tju:b] *n* **1** PIPE : tubo *m* **2** : tubo *m* (de dentífrico, etc.) **3** *or* inner tube : cámara *f* **4** : tubo *m* (de un aparato electrónico) **5** : trompa *f* (en anatomía)

tubeless ['tu:bləs, 'tju:b-] *adj* : sin cámara (dícese de una llanta)

tuber ['tu:bər, 'tju:-] *n* : tubérculo *m*

tubercular [tʊ'bərkjələr, tjʊ-] → **tuberculous**

tuberculosis [tʊˌbərkjə'lo:sɪs, tjʊ-] *n, pl* **-loses** [-ˌsi:z] : tuberculosis *f*

tuberculous [tʊ'bərkjələs, tjʊ-] *adj* : tuberculoso

tuberous ['tu:bərəs, 'tju:-] *adj* : tuberoso

tubing ['tu:bɪŋ, 'tju:-] *n* : tubería *f*

tubular ['tu:bjələr, 'tju:-] *adj* : tubular

tuck¹ ['tʌk] vt **1** PLACE, PUT : meter, colocar ⟨tuck in your shirt : métete la camisa⟩ **2** : guardar, esconder ⟨to tuck away one's money : guardar uno bien su dinero⟩ **3** or **to tuck in** COVER : arropar (a un niño en la cama)

tuck² n : pliegue m, alforza f

Tuesday ['tu:z,deɪ, 'tju:z,-di] n : martes m ⟨today is Tuesday : hoy es martes⟩ ⟨(on) Tuesday : el martes⟩ ⟨(on) Tuesdays : los martes⟩ ⟨last Tuesday : el martes pasado⟩ ⟨next Tuesday : el martes que viene⟩ ⟨every other Tuesday : cada martes⟩ ⟨Tuesday afternoon/morning : martes por la tarde/mañana⟩

tuft ['tʌft] n : penacho m (de plumas), copete m (de pelo)

tug¹ ['tʌg] v **tugged; tugging** vi : tirar, jalar, dar un tirón — vt : jalar, arrastrar, remolcar (con un barco)

tug² n **1** : tirón m, jalón m **2** → tugboat

tugboat ['tʌg,boːt] n : remolcador m

tug–of–war ['tʌgǝv'wɔr] n, pl **tugs–of–war 1** : juego m de tirar de la cuerda **2** : lucha f

tuition [tu'ɪʃǝn] n or **tuition fees** : tasas fpl de matrícula, colegiatura f Mex

tulip ['tu:lɪp, 'tju:-] n : tulipán m

tulle ['tu:l] n : tul m

tumble¹ ['tʌmbǝl] v **-bled; -bling** vi **1** : dar volteretas (en acrobacia) **2** FALL : caerse, venirse abajo — vt **1** TOPPLE : volcar **2** TOSS : hacer girar

tumble² n : voltereta f, caída f

tumbledown ['tʌmbǝl'daʊn] adj : en ruinas

tumbler ['tʌmblǝr] n **1** ACROBAT : acróbata mf, saltimbanqui mf **2** GLASS : vaso m (de mesa) **3** : clavija f (de una cerradura)

tummy ['tʌmi] n, pl **-mies** BELLY : panza f, vientre m

tumor ['tu:mǝr, 'tju:-] n : tumor m

tumult ['tu:,mʌlt, 'tju:-] n : tumulto m, alboroto m

tumultuous [tu'mʌltʃʊǝs, tju:-] adj : tumultuoso

tuna ['tu:nǝ, 'tju:-] n, pl **-na** or **-nas** : atún m

tundra ['tʌndrǝ] n : tundra f

tune¹ ['tu:n, 'tju:n] v **tuned; tuning** vt **1** ADJUST : ajustar, hacer más preciso, afinar (un motor) **2** : afinar (un instrumento musical) **3** : sintonizar (un radio o televisor) — vi **to tune in** : sintonizar (con una emisora)

tune² n **1** MELODY : tonada f, canción f, melodía f **2 in tune** : afinado (dícese de un instrumento o de la voz), sintonizado, en sintonía

tuneful ['tu:nfǝl, 'tju:n-] adj : armonioso, melódico

tuner ['tu:nǝr, 'tju:-] n : afinador m, -dora f (de instrumentos); sintonizador m (de un radio o un televisor)

tune–up ['tu:n,ʌp] n : afinado m, afinación f, puesta f a punto

tungsten ['tʌŋkstǝn] n : tungsteno m

tunic ['tu:nɪk, 'tju:-] n : túnica f

tuning fork n : diapasón m

Tunisian [tu'ni:ʒǝn, tju:'nɪziǝn] n : tunecino m, -na f — **Tunisian** adj

tunnel¹ ['tʌnǝl] vi **-neled** or **-nelled; -neling** or **-nelling** : hacer un túnel

tunnel² n : túnel m

turban ['tǝrbǝn] n : turbante m

turbid ['tǝrbɪd] adj : turbio

turbine ['tǝrbǝn, -,baɪn] n : turbina f

turbulence ['tǝrbjǝlǝns] n : turbulencia f

turbulent ['tǝrbjǝlǝnt] adj : turbulento — **turbulently** adv

tureen [tǝ'ri:n, tju-] n : sopera f

turf ['tǝrf] n SOD : tepe m

turgid ['tǝrdʒɪd] adj **1** SWOLLEN : turgente **2** : ampuloso, hinchado ⟨turgid style : estilo ampuloso⟩

Turk ['tǝrk] n : turco m, -ca f

turkey ['tǝrki] n, pl **-keys** : pavo m

Turkish¹ ['tǝrkɪʃ] adj : turco

Turkish² n : turco m (idioma)

turmoil ['tǝr,mɔɪl] n : agitación f, desorden m, confusión f

turn¹ ['tǝrn] vt **1** : girar, voltear, volver ⟨to turn one's head : voltear la cabeza⟩ ⟨she turned her chair toward the fire : giró su asiento hacia la hoguera⟩ **2** ROTATE, SPIN : darle vuelta(s) a, hacer girar ⟨turn the handle : dale vuelta a la manivela⟩ **3** FLIP : darle vuelta a, dar vuelta, voltear ⟨to turn the page : darle vuelta a la página/hoja, voltear/pasar la hoja/página⟩ ⟨to turn face up/down : volver boca arriba/abajo⟩ **4** SET : poner (un termostato, etc.) **5** SPRAIN, WRENCH : torcer, dislocar **6** DIRECT : dirigir (los esfuerzos, la atención, etc.) ⟨to turn one's mind/thoughts to : ponerse a pensar en⟩ **7** UPSET : revolver (el estómago) **8** TRANSFORM : convertir ⟨to turn water into wine : convertir el agua en vino⟩ **9** SHAPE : tornear (en carpintería) **10 to turn against** : poner a (alguien) en contra de **11 to turn a profit** : obtener ganancias/beneficios **12 to turn around** SPIN : hacer girar **13 to turn around** FLIP : dar la vuelta a, dar vuelta, voltear **14 to turn away** : no dejar/permitir entrar **15 to turn back** : hacer volver **16 to turn down** REFUSE, REJECT : rehusar, rechazar ⟨they turned down our invitation : rehusaron nuestra invitación⟩ **17 to turn down** LOWER : bajar (el volumen) **18 to turn in** : entregar ⟨to turn in one's work : entregar uno su trabajo⟩ ⟨they turned in the suspect : entregaron al sospechoso⟩ **19 to turn off/out** : apagar (la luz, la radio, etc.) **20 to turn on** : prender (la luz, etc.), encender (un motor, etc.) **21 to turn on** : interesarle a, excitar (sexualmente) **22 to turn on to** : despertarle el interés por **23 to turn out** EVICT, EXPEL : expulsar, echar, desalojar **24 to turn out** PRODUCE : producir **25 to turn over** TRANSFER : entregar, transferir (un cargo, una responsabilidad) **26 to turn over** FLIP : voltear, darle la vuelta a ⟨turn the pancake over : voltea el panqueque⟩ **27 to turn over** CONSIDER : considerar ⟨I kept turning the problem over in my mind : el problema

me estaba dando vueltas en la cabeza⟩
28 to turn up : subir (el volumen) — *vi*
1 ROTATE, SPIN : girar, dar vueltas **2** : girar, doblar, dar una vuelta (en un vehículo) ⟨turn left : gira/dobla a la izquierda⟩ ⟨to turn around : dar la media vuelta⟩ ⟨turn onto Main : toma la calle Main⟩ **3** : volverse, darse la vuelta, voltearse ⟨to turn towards : volverse hacia⟩ ⟨I turned (around) and left : di media vuelta y me fui⟩ **4** BECOME : hacerse, volverse, ponerse ⟨it got cold (out) : (el tiempo) se volvió frío⟩ ⟨she turned red : se puso colorado, se sonrojó⟩ ⟨he turned 80 : cumplió los 80⟩ **5** CHANGE : cambiar (dícese de la marea, etc.) **6** SOUR : agriarse, cortarse (dícese de la leche) **7 to turn against** : volverse en contra de **8 to turn away** : volverse (de espaldas), darse la vuelta, voltearse **9 to turn back** RETURN : volverse **10 to turn in** : acostarse, irse a la cama **11 to turn into** : convertirse en **12 to turn off** : salir (de una carretera), desviarse de ⟨turn off at/onto Main : toma (la calle) Main⟩ ⟨turn off (of) First onto Main : sal de First tomando Main⟩ **13 to turn on** ATTACK : atacar (inesperadamente) **14 to turn out** : concurrir, presentarse ⟨many turned out to vote : muchos concurrieron a votar⟩ **15 to turn out** PROVE, RESULT : resultar **16 to turn** : darse (la) vuelta (dícese de una persona, etc.), volcarse (dícese de un vehículo) **17 to turn over** START : arrancar **18 to turn to** : recurrir a ⟨they have no one to turn to : no tienen quien les ayude⟩ ⟨to turn to violence : recurrir a la violencia⟩ **19 to turn up** APPEAR : aparecer, presentarse **20 to turn up** HAPPEN : ocurrir, suceder (inesperadamente)

turn² *n* **1** : vuelta *f*, giro *m* ⟨give it a turn : dale vuelta⟩ ⟨a sudden turn : una vuelta repentina⟩ **2** CHANGE : cambio *m* ⟨to take a turn for the better/worse : mejorar/empeorar⟩ ⟨turn of events : giro de los acontecimientos⟩ **3** INTERSECTION : bocacalle *f* ⟨we took a wrong turn : nos equivocamos de calle/salida (etc.), dimos una vuelta equivocada⟩ **4** CURVE : curva *f* (en un camino) **5** : turno *m* ⟨they're awaiting their turn : están esperando su turno⟩ ⟨whose turn is it? : ¿a quién le toca?⟩ ⟨to take turns : turnarse⟩ **6 at every turn** : a cada paso **7 in turn** : sucesivamente **8 in turn** LIKEWISE : a su vez **9 one good turn deserves another** : favor por favor se paga **10 out of turn** : fuera de lugar **11 the turn of the century** : el final del siglo
turnaround [ˈtərnəˌraʊnd] *n* PROCESSING : procesamiento *m*
turncoat [ˈtərnˌkoːt] *n* : traidor *m*, -dora *f*
turning point *n* : momento *m* decisivo
turnip [ˈtərnəp] *n* : nabo *m*
turnout [ˈtərnˌaʊt] *n* : concurrencia *f*
turnover [ˈtərnˌoːvər] *n* **1** : empanada *f* (salada o dulce) **2** : volumen *m* (de ventas) **3** : rotación *f* (de personal) ⟨a high turnover : un alto nivel de rotación⟩

turnpike [ˈtərnˌpaɪk] *n* : carretera *f* de peaje
turnstile [ˈtərnˌstaɪl] *n* : torniquete *m* (de acceso)
turntable [ˈtərnˌteɪbəl] *n* : tornamesa *mf*
turpentine [ˈtərpənˌtaɪn] *n* : aguarrás *m*, trementina *f*
turquoise [ˈtərˌkɔɪz, -ˌkwɔɪz] *n* : turquesa *f*
turret [ˈtərət] *n* **1** TOWER : torre *f* pequeña **2** : torreta *f* (de un tanque, un avión, etc.)
turtle [ˈtərtəl] *n* : tortuga *f* (marina)
turtledove [ˈtərtəlˌdʌv] *n* : tórtola *f*
turtleneck [ˈtərtəlˌnɛk] *n* : cuello *m* de tortuga, cuello *m* alto
tusk [ˈtʌsk] *n* : colmillo *m*
tussle¹ [ˈtʌsəl] *vi* **-sled; -sling** SCUFFLE : pelearse, reñir
tussle² *n* : riña *f*, pelea *f*
tutelage [ˈtuːtəlɪdʒ, ˈtjuː-] *n* : tutela *f*
tutor¹ [ˈtuːtər, ˈtjuː-] *vt* : darle clases particulares (a alguien)
tutor² *n* : tutor *m*, -tora *f*; maestro *m*, -tra *f* (particular)
tutorial [ˌtuːˈtɔriəl, tjuː-] *n* **1** : tutorial *m* **2** : clase *f* (individual o con un pequeño grupo de estudiantes)
tuxedo [ˌtəkˈsiːˌdoː] *n*, *pl* **-dos** *or* **-does** : esmoquin *m*, smoking *m* (traje)
TV [ˌtiːˈviː, ˈtiːˌviː] → **television**
twain [ˈtweɪn] *n* : dos *m*
twang¹ [ˈtwæŋ] *vt* : pulsar la cuerda de (una guitarra) — *vi* : hablar en tono nasal
twang² *n* **1** : tañido *m* (de una cuerda de guitarra) **2** : tono nasal (de voz)
tweak¹ [ˈtwiːk] *vt* : pellizcar
tweak² *n* : pellizco *m*
tweed [ˈtwiːd] *n* : tweed *m*
tweet¹ [ˈtwiːt] *vi* : piar
tweet² *n* : gorjeo *m*, pío *m*
tweezers [ˈtwiːzərz] *npl* : pinzas *fpl*
twelfth¹ [ˈtwɛlfθ] *adj* : duodécimo
twelfth² *n* **1** : duodécimo *m*, -ma *f* (en una serie) **2** : doceavo *m*, doceava parte *f*
twelve¹ [ˈtwɛlv] *adj & pron* : doce
twelve² *n* : doce *m*
twentieth¹ [ˈtwʌntiəθ, ˈtwɛn-] *adj* : vigésimo
twentieth² *n* **1** : vigésimo *m*, -ma *f* (en una serie) **2** : veinteavo *m*, veinteava parte *f*
twenty¹ [ˈtwʌnti, ˈtwɛn-] *adj & pron* : veinte
twenty² *n*, *pl* **-ties** : veinte *m*
twice [ˈtwaɪs] *adv* : dos veces ⟨twice a day : dos veces al día⟩ ⟨it costs twice as much : cuesta el doble⟩
twig [ˈtwɪg] *n* : ramita *f*
twilight [ˈtwaɪˌlaɪt] *n* : crepúsculo *m*
twill [ˈtwɪl] *n* : sarga *f*, tela *f* cruzada
twin¹ [ˈtwɪn] *adj* **1** : gemelo, mellizo **2** : doble, gemelo ⟨twin city : ciudad hermana⟩ ⟨twin-engine plane : avión bimotor⟩
twin² *n* : gemelo *m*, -la *f*; mellizo *m*, -za *f*
twin bed *n* : cama *f* individual
twine¹ [ˈtwaɪn] *v* **twined; twining** *vt* : entrelazar, entrecruzar — *vi* : enroscarse (alrededor de algo)

twine² *n* : cordel *m*, cuerda *f*, mecate *m* CA, Mex, Ven

twinge¹ ['twɪndʒ] *vi* **twinged; twinging** *or* **twingeing** : sentir punzadas

twinge² *n* : punzada *f*, dolor *m* agudo

twinkle¹ ['twɪŋkəl] *vi* **-kled; -kling** 1 : centellear, titilar (dícese de las estrellas o de la luz) 2 : chispear, brillar (dícese de los ojos)

twinkle² *n* : centelleo *m* (de las estrellas), brillo *m* (de los ojos)

twirl¹ ['twərl] *vt* : girar, darle vueltas a — *vi* : girar, dar vueltas (rápidamente)

twirl² *n* : giro *m*, vuelta *f*

twist¹ ['twɪst] *vt* 1 : torcer, retorcer ⟨twisted my arm : me torció el brazo⟩ 2 DISTORT : tergiversar — *vi* : retorcerse, enroscarse, serpentear (dícese de un río, un camino, etc.)

twist² *n* 1 BEND : vuelta *f*, recodo *m* (en el camino, el río, etc.) 2 TURN : giro *m* ⟨give it a twist : hazlo girar⟩ 3 SPIRAL : espiral *f* ⟨a twist of lemon : una rodajita de limón⟩ 4 : giro *m* inesperado (de eventos, etc.)

twisted ['twɪstəd] *adj* : retorcido ⟨a twisted mind : una mente retorcida⟩

twister ['twɪstər] *n* 1 → **tornado** 2 → **waterspout**

twitch¹ ['twɪtʃ] *vi* : moverse nerviosamente, contraerse espasmódicamente (dícese de un músculo)

twitch² *n* : espasmo *m*, sacudida *f* ⟨a nervous twitch : un tic nervioso⟩

twitter¹ ['twɪtər] *vi* CHIRP : gorjear, cantar (dícese de los pájaros)

twitter² *n* : gorjeo *m*

two¹ ['tu:] *adj* : dos ⟨she's two (years old) : tiene dos años⟩

two² *n, pl* **twos** : dos *m* ⟨the two of hearts : el dos de corazones⟩

two³ *pron* : dos ⟨there are two of us : somos dos⟩ ⟨it's two (o'clock) : son las dos⟩

two–faced ['tu:'feɪst] *adj* : hipócrita

twofold¹ ['tu:'fo:ld] *adv* : al doble

twofold² ['tu:'fo:ld] *adj* : doble

two hundred¹ *adj & pron* : doscientos

two hundred² *n* : doscientos *m*

two–piece ['tu:'pi:s] *adj* : de dos piezas

twosome ['tu:səm] *n* COUPLE : pareja *f*

two–tone ['tu:'to:n] *adj* : bicolor

two–way *adj* 1 : de doble sentido, de doble dirección (dícese de una calle) 2 MUTUAL : mutuo 3 : bidireccional

two–way mirror → **one–way mirror**

tycoon [taɪ'ku:n] *n* : magnate *mf*

tying → **tie¹**

type¹ ['taɪp] *v* **typed; typing** *vt* 1 TYPEWRITE : escribir a máquina, pasar (un texto) a máquina 2 CATEGORIZE : categorizar, identificar — *vi* : escribir a máquina

type² *n* 1 KIND : tipo *m*, clase *f*, categoría *f* 2 : tipo *m* (de imprenta) ⟨italic type : bastardilla, cursiva⟩

typeface ['taɪp,feɪs] *n* : tipo *m* de imprenta

typewrite ['taɪp,raɪt] *v* **-wrote; -written** : escribir a máquina

typewriter ['taɪp,raɪtər] *n* : máquina *f* de escribir

typhoid¹ ['taɪ,fɔɪd, taɪ'-] *adj* : relativo al tifus o a la tifoidea

typhoid² *n or* **typhoid fever** : tifoidea *f*

typhoon [taɪ'fu:n] *n* : tifón *m*

typhus ['taɪfəs] *n* : tifus *m*

typical ['tɪpɪkəl] *adj* : típico, característico — **typically** *adv*

typify ['tɪpə,faɪ] *vt* **-fied; -fying** : ser típico o representativo de (un grupo, una clase, etc.)

typing ['taɪpɪŋ] *n* : mecanografía *f*

typist ['taɪpɪst] *n* : mecanógrafo *m*, -fa *f*

typographer [taɪ'pɑgrəfər] *n* : tipógrafo *m*, -fa *f*

typographic [,taɪpə'græfɪk] *or* **typographical** [-fɪkəl] *adj* : tipográfico — **typographically** [-fɪkli] *adv*

typography [taɪ'pɑgrəfi] *n* : tipografía *f*

tyrannical [tə'rænɪkəl, taɪ-] *adj* : tiránico — **tyrannically** [-nɪkli] *adv*

tyrannize ['tɪrə,naɪz] *vt* **-nized; -nizing** : tiranizar

tyranny ['tɪrəni] *n, pl* **-nies** : tiranía *f*

tyrant ['taɪrənt] *n* : tirano *m*, -na *f*

Tyrolean [tə'ro:liən, taɪ-] *adj* : tirolés

tzar ['zɑr, 'tsɑr, 'sɑr] → **czar**

U

u ['ju:] *n, pl* **u's** *or* **us** ['ju:z] : vigésima primera letra del alfabeto inglés

ubiquitous [ju:'bɪkwəṭəs] *adj* : ubicuo, omnipresente

udder ['ʌdər] *n* : ubre *f*

UFO [ju:,ɛf'o:, 'ju:,fo:] *n, pl* **UFO's** *or* **UFOs** (*u*nidentified *f*lying *o*bject) : ovni *m*, OVNI *m*

Ugandan [ju:'gændən, -'gɑn-; u:'gɑn-] *n* : ugandés *m*, -desa *f* — **Ugandan** *adj*

ugliness ['ʌglinəs] *n* : fealdad *f*

ugly ['ʌgli] *adj* **uglier; -est** 1 UNATTRACTIVE : feo 2 DISAGREEABLE : desagradable, feo ⟨ugly weather : tiempo feo⟩ ⟨to have an ugly temper : tener mal genio⟩

Ukrainian [ju:'kreɪniən, -'kraɪ-] *n* 1 : ucraniano *m*, -na *f* 2 : ucraniano *m* (idioma) — **Ukrainian** *adj*

ukulele [ju:kə'leɪli] *n* : ukelele *m*

ulcer ['ʌlsər] *n* : úlcera *f* (interna), llaga *f* (externa)

ulcerate ['ʌlsə,reɪt] *vi* **-ated; -ating** : ulcerarse

ulcerous ['ʌlsərəs] *adj* : ulceroso

ulna ['ʌlnə] *n* : cúbito *m*

ulterior [,ʌl'tɪriər] *adj* : oculto ⟨ulterior motive : motivo oculto, segunda intención⟩

ultimate [ˈʌltəmət] *adj* **1** FINAL : último, final **2** SUPREME : supremo, máximo **3** FUNDAMENTAL : fundamental, esencial

ultimately [ˈʌltəmətli] *adv* **1** FINALLY : por último, finalmente **2** EVENTUALLY : a la larga, con el tiempo

ultimatum [ˌʌltəˈmeɪtəm, -ˈmɑ-] *n, pl* **-tums** *or* **-ta** [- t̬ə] : ultimátum *m*

ultra- [ˌʌltrə] *pref* : ultra-, super-

ultrasonic [ˌʌltrəˈsɑnɪk] *adj* : ultrasónico

ultrasound [ˈʌltrəˌsaʊnd] *n* **1** : ultrasonido *m* **2** : ecografía *f* (técnica o imagen)

ultraviolet [ˌʌltrəˈvaɪələt] *adj* : ultravioleta

umbilical cord [ˌʌmˈbɪlɪkəl] *n* : cordón *m* umbilical

umbrage [ˈʌmbrɪʤ] *n* **to take umbrage at** : ofenderse por

umbrella [ˌʌmˈbrɛlə] *n* **1** : paraguas *m* **2 beach umbrella** : sombrilla *f*

umpire¹ [ˈʌmˌpaɪr] *v* **-pired; -piring** : arbitrar

umpire² *n* : árbitro *m*, -tra *f*

umpteen [ˌʌmpˈtiːn] *adj* : miles de, un millón de

umpteenth [ˌʌmpˈtiːnθ] *adj* : enésimo ⟨for the umpteenth time : por enésima vez⟩

un- [ˌʌn] *pref* : in-, im-, ir-, i-, des-, poco, no ⟨uncertain : incierto⟩ ⟨unforeseeable : imprevisible⟩ ⟨unreasonable : irrazonable⟩ ⟨unlimited : ilimitado⟩ ⟨unfavorable : desfavorable⟩ ⟨uncommon : poco común⟩ ⟨unresolved : no resuelto⟩ ⟨to uncurl : desenrollar⟩

unable [ˌʌnˈeɪbəl] *adj* : incapaz ⟨to be unable to : no poder⟩

unabridged [ˌʌnəˈbrɪʤd] *adj* : íntegro

unacceptable [ˌʌnɪkˈsɛptəbəl] *adj* : inaceptable

unaccompanied [ˌʌnəˈkʌmpənid] *adj* : solo, sin acompañamiento (en música)

unaccountable [ˌʌnəˈkaʊntəbəl] *adj* : inexplicable, incomprensible — **unaccountably** [-bli] *adv*

unaccustomed [ˌʌnəˈkʌstəmd] *adj* **1** UNUSUAL : desacostumbrado, inusual **2** UNUSED : inhabituado ⟨unaccustomed to noise : inhabituado al ruido⟩

unacquainted [ˌʌnəˈkweɪntəd] *adj* **to be unacquainted with** : desconocer, ignorar

unadorned [ˌʌnəˈdɔrnd] *adj* : sin adornos, puro y simple

unadulterated [ˌʌnəˈdʌltəˌreɪt̬əd] *adj* **1** PURE : puro ⟨unadulterated food : comida pura⟩ **2** ABSOLUTE : completo, absoluto

unaffected [ˌʌnəˈfɛktəd] *adj* **1** : no afectado, indiferente **2** NATURAL : sin afectación, natural

unaffectedly [ˌʌnəˈfɛktədli] *adv* : de manera natural

unafraid [ˌʌnəˈfreɪd] *adj* : sin miedo

unaided [ˌʌnˈeɪdəd] *adj* : sin ayuda, solo

unalterable [ˌʌnˈɔltərəbəl] *adj* : inalterable

unambiguous [ˌʌnæmˈbɪgjuəs] *adj* : inequívoco

unanimity [ˌjuːnəˈnɪmət̬i] *n* : unanimidad *f*

unanimous [juˈnænəməs] *adj* : unánime — **unanimously** *adv*

unannounced [ˌʌnəˈnaʊnst] *adj* : sin dar aviso

unanswerable [ˌʌnˈænsərəbəl] *adj* **1** : incontestable **2** IRREFUTABLE : irrefutable, irrebatible

unanswered [ˌʌnˈænsərd] *adj* : sin contestar

unappealing [ˌʌnəˈpiːlɪŋ] *adj* : desagradable

unarmed [ˌʌnˈɑrmd] *adj* : sin armas, desarmado

unashamed [ˌʌnəˈʃeɪmd] *adj* : sin vergüenza ⟨he's unashamed of his patriotism : no tiene reparos en demostrar su patriotismo⟩

unassailable [ˌʌnəˈseɪləbəl] *adj* IRREFUTABLE : irrefutable, irrebatible

unassisted [ˌʌnəˈsɪst̬əd] *adj* : sin ayuda

unassuming [ˌʌnəˈsuːmɪŋ] *adj* : modesto, sin pretensiones

unattached [ˌʌnəˈtæʧt] *adj* **1** LOOSE : suelto **2** INDEPENDENT : independiente **3** : solo (ni casado ni prometido)

unattainable [ˌʌnəˈteɪnəbəl] *adj* : inalcanzable, inasequible

unattended [ˌʌnəˈtɛndəd] *adj* : desatendido

unattractive [ˌʌnəˈtræktɪv] *adj* : poco atractivo

unauthorized [ˌʌnˈɔθəˌraɪzd] *adj* : sin autorización, no autorizado

unavailable [ˌʌnəˈveɪləbəl] *adj* : no disponible

unavoidable [ˌʌnəˈvɔɪdəbəl] *adj* : inevitable, ineludible — **unavoidably** *adv*

unaware¹ [ˌʌnəˈwær] *adv* → **unawares**

unaware² *adj* : inconsciente

unawares [ˌʌnəˈwærz] *adv* **1** : por sorpresa ⟨to catch someone unawares : agarrar a alguien desprevenido⟩ **2** UNINTENTIONALLY : inconscientemente, inadvertidamente

unbalance [ˌʌnˈbæləns] *vt* : desequilibrar

unbalanced [ˌʌnˈbælənst] *adj* : desequilibrado

unbearable [ˌʌnˈbærəbəl] *adj* : insoportable, inaguantable — **unbearably** [-bli] *adv*

unbeatable [ˌʌnˈbiːt̬əbəl] *adj* : insuperable

unbeaten [ˌʌnˈbiːt̬ən] *adj* : invicto

unbecoming [ˌʌnbiˈkʌmɪŋ] *adj* **1** UNSEEMLY : impropio, indecoroso **2** UNFLATTERING : poco favorecedor

unbeknownst [ˌʌbiˈnoʊnst] *adj* **unbeknownst to** : sin el conocimiento de

unbelievable [ˌʌbiˈliːvəbəl] *adj* : increíble — **unbelievably** [-bli] *adv*

unbend [ˌʌnˈbend] *vi* **-bent** [-ˈbent]; **-bending** RELAX : relajarse

unbending [ˌʌnˈbendɪŋ] *adj* : inflexible

unbiased [ˌʌnˈbaɪəst] *adj* : imparcial, objetivo

unblock [ˌʌnˈblɑk] *vt* : desatascar, destapar (cañería, etc.)

unbolt [ˌʌnˈboʊlt] *vt* : abrir el cerrojo de, descorrer el pestillo de

unborn [ˌʌnˈbɔrn] *adj* : aún no nacido, que va a nacer

unbosom [ˌʌnˈbuzəm, -ˈbuː-] vt : revelar, divulgar

unbreakable [ˌʌnˈbreɪkəbəl] adj : irrompible

unbreathable [ˌʌˈbriːðəbəl] adj : irrespirable

unbridled [ˌʌnˈbraɪdəld] adj : desenfrenado

unbroken [ˌʌnˈbroːkən] adj 1 INTACT : intacto, sano 2 CONTINUOUS : continuo, ininterrumpido

unbuckle [ˌʌnˈbʌkəl] vt -led; -ling : desabrochar

unburden [ˌʌnˈbərdən] vt 1 UNLOAD : descargar 2 to unburden oneself : desahogarse

unbutton [ˌʌnˈbʌtən] vt : desabrochar, desabotonar

uncalled–for [ˌʌnˈkɔːldˌfɔr] adj : inapropiado, innecesario

uncanny [ənˈkæni] adj uncannier; -est 1 STRANGE : extraño 2 EXTRAORDINARY : raro, extraordinario — **uncannily** [-ˈkænəli] adv

uncaring [ˌʌnˈkærɪŋ] adj : indiferente

unceasing [ˌʌnˈsiːsɪŋ] adj : incesante, continuo — **unceasingly** adv

unceremonious [ˌʌnˌserəˈmoːniəs] adj 1 INFORMAL : sin ceremonia, sin pompa 2 ABRUPT : abrupto, brusco — **unceremoniously** adv

uncertain [ˌʌnˈsərtən] adj 1 INDEFINITE : indeterminado 2 UNSURE : incierto, dudoso 3 CHANGEABLE : inestable, variable ⟨uncertain weather : tiempo inestable⟩ 4 HESITANT : indeciso 5 VAGUE : poco claro

uncertainly [ˌʌnˈsərtənli] adv : dudosamente, con desconfianza

uncertainty [ˌʌnˈsərtənti] n, pl -ties : duda f, incertidumbre f

unchain [ˌʌnˈtʃeɪn] vt : desencadenar

unchangeable [ˌʌnˈtʃeɪndʒəbəl] adj : inalterable, inmutable

unchanged [ˌʌnˈtʃeɪndʒd] adj : sin cambiar

unchanging [ˌʌnˈtʃeɪndʒɪŋ] adj : inalterable, inmutable, firme

uncharacteristic [ˌʌnˌkærɪktəˈrɪstɪk] adj : inusual, desacostumbrado

uncharged [ˌʌnˈtʃɑrdʒd] adj : sin carga (eléctrica)

uncharitable [ˌʌnˈtʃærətəbəl] adj : poco caritativo

unchecked [ˌʌnˈtʃɛkt] adj : sin freno, sin obsáculos

uncivilized [ˌʌnˈsɪvəˌlaɪzd] adj 1 BARBAROUS : incivilizado, bárbaro 2 WILD : salvaje

uncle [ˈʌŋkəl] n : tío m

unclean [ˌʌnˈkliːn] adj 1 IMPURE : impuro 2 DIRTY : sucio

unclear [ˌʌnˈklɪr] adj : confuso, borroso, poco claro

Uncle Sam [ˈsæm] n : el Tío Sam

unclog [ˌʌnˈklɑg] vt -clogged; -clogging : desatascar, destapar

unclothed [ˌʌnˈkloːðd] adj : desnudo

uncluttered [ˌʌnˈklʌtərd] adj : despejado (dícese de una habitación, etc.)

uncoil [ˌʌnˈkɔɪl] vi : desenroscarse — vt : desenroscar

uncomfortable [ˌʌnˈkʌmpfərtəbəl] adj 1 : incómodo (dícese de una silla, etc.) 2 UNEASY : inquieto, incómodo — **uncomfortably** adv

uncommitted [ˌʌnkəˈmɪtəd] adj : sin compromisos

uncommon [ˌʌnˈkamən] adj 1 UNUSUAL : raro, poco común 2 REMARKABLE : excepcional, extraordinario

uncommonly [ˌʌnˈkamənli] adv : extraordinariamente

uncommunicative [ˌʌnkəˈmjuːnɪˌkeɪtɪv, -kətɪv] adj : poco comunicativo

uncomplaining [ˌʌnkəmˈpleɪnɪŋ] adj : que no se queja

uncomplicated [ˌʌˈkampləˌkeɪtəd] adj : sencillo ⟨he's an uncomplicated person : no es una persona complicada⟩

uncompromising [ˌʌnˈkamprəˌmaɪzɪŋ] adj : inflexible, intransigente

unconcerned [ˌʌnkənˈsərnd] adj : indiferente — **unconcernedly** [-ˈsərnədli] adv

unconditional [ˌʌnkənˈdɪʃənəl] adj : incondicional — **unconditionally** adv

unconnected [ˌʌnkəˈnɛktəd] adj 1 UNRELATED : no relacionado, sin conexión 2 DISCONNECTED : desconectado

unconscious[1] [ˌʌnˈkanʃəs] adj : inconsciente — **unconsciously** adv

unconscious[2] n : inconsciente m

unconsciousness [ˌʌnˈkanʃəsnəs] n : inconsciencia f

unconstitutional [ˌʌnˌkanʲstəˈtuːʃənəl, -ˈtjuː-] adj : inconstitucional — **unconstitutionality** n

uncontrollable [ˌʌnkənˈtroːləbəl] adj : incontrolable, incontenible — **uncontrollably** [-bli] adv

uncontrolled [ˌʌnkənˈtroːld] adj : incontrolado

unconventional [ˌʌnkənˈvɛntʃənəl] adj : poco convencional

unconvinced [ˌʌnkənˈvɪntst] adj : no convencido, escéptico

unconvincing [ˌʌnkənˈvɪntsɪŋ] adj : poco convincente

uncoordinated [ˌʌnkoˈɔrdənˌeɪtəd] adj 1 : no coordinado 2 CLUMSY : torpe

uncork [ˌʌnˈkɔrk] vt : descorchar

uncorroborated [ˌʌnkəˈrabəˌreɪtəd] adj : no corroborado

uncountable [ˌʌnˈkauntəbəl] adj : no contable

uncouple [ˌʌnˈkʌpəl] vt : desenganchar

uncouth [ˌʌnˈkuːθ] adj CRUDE, ROUGH : grosero, rudo

uncover [ˌʌnˈkʌvər] vt 1 : destapar (un objeto), dejar al descubierto 2 EXPOSE, REVEAL : descubrir, revelar, exponer

uncultivated [ˌʌnˈkʌltəˌveɪtəd] adj : inculto

uncultured [ˌʌnˈkʌltʃərd] adj : inculto

uncurl [ˌʌnˈkərl] vt UNROLL : desenrollar — vi : desenrollarse

uncut [ˌʌnˈkʌt] adj 1 : sin cortar ⟨uncut grass : hierba sin cortar⟩ 2 : sin tallar, en bruto ⟨an uncut diamond : un diamante en bruto〉 **3** UNABRIDGED : completo, íntegro

undamaged [ˌʌn'dæmɪʤd] *adj* : intacto, no dañado

undaunted [ˌʌn'dɔntəd] *adj* : impávido

undecided [ˌʌndɪ'saɪdəd] *adj* **1** IRRESOLUTE : indeciso, irresoluto **2** UNRESOLVED : pendiente, no resuelto

undefeated [ˌʌndɪ'fiːtəd] *adj* : invicto

undefined [ˌʌndɪ'faɪnd] *adj* : indefinido

undemanding [ˌʌndɪ'mændɪŋ] *adj* : que exige poco

undeniable [ˌʌndɪ'naɪəbəl] *adj* : innegable — **undeniably** [-bli] *adv*

under[1] ['ʌndər] *adv* **1** LESS : menos 〈$10 or under : $10 o menos〉 **2** UNDERWATER : debajo del agua **3** : bajo los efectos de la anestesia

under[2] *adj* **1** LOWER : (más) bajo, inferior **2** SUBORDINATE : inferior **3** : insuficiente 〈an under dose of medicine : una dosis insuficiente de medicina〉

under[3] *prep* **1** BELOW, BENEATH : debajo de, abajo de 〈under the table : abajo de la mesa〉〈we walked under the arch : pasamos por debajo del arco〉〈under the sun : bajo el sol〉 **2** : menos de 〈in under 20 minutes : en menos de 20 minutos〉 **3** : bajo (un nombre, una categoría, etc.) **4** (*indicating rank or authority*) : bajo 〈under the command of : bajo las órdenes de〉 **6** SUBJECT TO : bajo 〈under suspicion : bajo sospecha〉〈he's under stress : está estresado, sufre de estrés〉〈under the influence of alcohol : bajo los efectos del alcohol〉〈under the circumstances : dadas las circunstancias〉〈I was under the impression that . . . : tenía la impresión de que . . .〉 **7** : en (una condición) 〈under arrest : detenido〉〈under construction : en construcción〉〈it's under discussion : se está discutiendo〉 **8** ACCORDING TO : según, de acuerdo con, conforme a 〈under the present laws : según las leyes actuales〉

under- [ˌʌndər] *pref* **1** : sub-, abajo 〈underside : parte de abajo〉〈underlying : subyacente〉 **2** : sub-, insuficientemente 〈underdeveloped : subdesarrollado〉〈underestimate : subestimar〉

underage [ˌʌndər'eɪʤ] *adj* : menor de edad

underarm[1] ['ʌndər,ɑrm] *adj* : de axila, para las axilas 〈underarm deodorant : desodorante〉

underarm[2] ['ʌndər,ɑrm] *n* ARMPIT : axila *f*, sobaco *m*

underbrush ['ʌndər,brʌʃ] *n* : maleza *f*

undercarriage ['ʌndər,kærɪʤ] *n* **1** CHASSIS : chassis *m*, armazón *m* **2** : tren *f* de aterrizaje (de un avión)

undercharge [ˌʌndər'ʧɑrʤ] *vt* : cobrarle de menos a

underclass ['ʌndər,klæs] *n* : clases *fpl* marginadas

underclothes ['ʌndər,kloz, -ˌkloːðz] → **underwear**

underclothing ['ʌndər,kloːðɪŋ] → **underwear**

undercoat ['ʌndər,koːt] *n* : primera capa *f* (de pintura)

undercooked [ˌʌndər'kʊkt] *adj* : medio crudo

undercover [ˌʌndər'kʌvər] *adj* : secreto, clandestino

undercurrent ['ʌndər,kərənt] *n* **1** : corriente *f* submarina **2** UNDERTONE : corriente *f* oculta, trasfondo *m*

undercut [ˌʌndər'kʌt] *vt* **-cut; -cutting** : vender más barato que

underdeveloped [ˌʌndərdɪ'veləpt] *adj* : subdesarrollado, atrasado

underdevelopment [ˌʌndərdɪ'veləpmənt] *n* : subdesarrollo *m*

underdog ['ʌndər,dɔg] *n* : persona *f* que tiene menos posibilidades

underdone [ˌʌndər'dʌn] *adj* RARE : poco cocido

underestimate [ˌʌndər'ɛstəˌmeɪt] *vt* **-mated; -mating** : subestimar, menospreciar

underexpose [ˌʌndərɪk'spoːz] *vt* : subexponer (en fotografía)

underexposure [ˌʌndərɪk'spoːʒər] *vt* : subexposición *f*

underfoot [ˌʌndər'fʊt] *adv* **1** : bajo los pies 〈to trample underfoot : pisotear〉 **2 to be underfoot** : estorbar 〈they're always underfoot : están siempre estorbando〉

undergarment ['ʌndər,ɡɑrmənt] *n* : prenda *f* íntima

undergo [ˌʌndər'goː] *vt* **-went** [-'wɛnt]; **-gone** [-'ɡɔn]; **-going** : sufrir, experimentar 〈to undergo an operation : someterse a una intervención quirúrgica〉

undergraduate [ˌʌndər'ɡræʤuət] *n* : estudiante *m* universitario, estudiante *f* universitaria

underground[1] [ˌʌndər'ɡraʊnd] *adv* **1** : bajo tierra **2** SECRETLY : clandestinamente, en secreto 〈to go underground : pasar a la clandestinidad〉

underground[2] ['ʌndər,ɡraʊnd] *adj* **1** SUBTERRANEAN : subterráneo **2** SECRET : secreto, clandestino

underground[3] ['ʌndər,ɡraʊnd] *n* : movimiento *m* o grupo *m* clandestino

undergrowth ['ʌndər,ɡroːθ] *n* : maleza *f*, broza *f*

underhand[1] ['ʌndər,hænd] *adv* **1** SECRETLY : de manera clandestina **2 or underhanded** : sin levantar el brazo por encima del hombro (en deportes)

underhand[2] *adj* **1** SLY : solapado **2** : por debajo del hombro (en deportes)

underhanded [ˌʌndər'hændəd] *adj* **1** SLY : solapado **2** SHADY : turbio, poco limpio

underlie [ˌʌndər'laɪ] *vt* **-lay; -lain; -lying** : subyacer en/a

underline ['ʌndər,laɪn] *vt* **-lined; -lining** **1** : subrayar **2** EMPHASIZE : subrayar, acentuar, hacer hincapié en

underling ['ʌndər,lɪŋ] *n* : subordinado *m*, -da *f*; inferior *mf*

underlying [ˌʌndər'laɪɪŋ] *adj* **1** : subyacente 〈the underlying rock : la roca subyacente〉 **2** FUNDAMENTAL : fundamental, esencial

undermine [ˌʌndər'maɪn] vt **-mined; -mining** 1 : socavar (una estructura, etc.) 2 SAP, WEAKEN : minar, debilitar

underneath[1] [ˌʌndər'niːθ] adv : debajo, abajo ⟨the part underneath : la parte de abajo⟩

underneath[2] prep : debajo de, abajo de

undernourished [ˌʌndər'nərɪʃt] adj : desnutrido

underpaid [ˌʌndər'peɪd] adj : mal pagado

underpants ['ʌndər,pænts] npl : calzoncillos mpl, calzones mpl

underpass ['ʌndər,pæs] n : paso m a desnivel

underprivileged [ˌʌndər'prɪvlɪdʒd] adj : desfavorecido

underrate [ˌʌndər'reɪt] vt **-rated; -rating** : subestimar, menospreciar

underscore [ˌʌndər,skor] vt **-scored; -scoring → underline**

undersea[1] [ˌʌndər'siː] or **underseas** [-'siːz] adv : bajo la superficie del mar

undersea[2] adj : submarino

undersecretary [ˌʌndər'sɛkrə,tɛri] n, pl **-ries** : subsecretario m, -ria f

undersell [ˌʌndər'sɛl] vt **-sold; -selling** : vender más barato que

undeserved [ˌʌndɪ'zərvd] adj : inmerecido

undershirt ['ʌndər,ʃərt] n : camiseta f

undershorts ['ʌndər,ʃorts] npl : calzoncillos mpl

underside ['ʌndər,saɪd, ˌʌndər'saɪd] n : parte f de abajo

undersigned ['ʌndər,saɪnd] n the undersigned : el abajo firmante, la abajo firmante, los abajo firmantes, las abajo firmantes

undersized [ˌʌndər'saɪzd] adj : más pequeño de lo normal

understand [ˌʌndər'stænd] v **-stood** [-'stʊd]; **-standing** vt 1 COMPREHEND : comprender, entender ⟨I don't understand it : no lo entiendo⟩ ⟨that's understood : eso se comprende⟩ ⟨to make oneself understood : hacerse entender⟩ 2 BELIEVE : entender ⟨to give someone to understand : dar a alguien a entender⟩ 3 INFER : tener entendido ⟨I understand that she's leaving : tengo entendido que se va⟩ — vi : comprender, entender

understandable [ˌʌndər'stændəbəl] adj : comprensible

understanding[1] [ˌʌndər'stændɪŋ] adj : comprensivo, compasivo

understanding[2] n 1 GRASP : comprensión f, entendimiento m 2 SYMPATHY : comprensión f (mutua) 3 INTERPRETATION : interpretación f ⟨it's my understanding that . . . : tengo la impresión de que . . ., tengo entendido que . . .⟩ 4 AGREEMENT : acuerdo m, arreglo m

understate [ˌʌndər'steɪt] vt **-stated; -stating** : minimizar, subestimar

understatement [ˌʌndər'steɪtmənt] n : atenuación f ⟨that's an understatement : decir sólo eso es quedarse corto⟩

understudy ['ʌndər,stʌdi] n, pl **-dies** : sobresaliente mf, suplente mf (en el teatro)

undertake [ˌʌndər'teɪk] vt **-took** [-'tʊk]; **-taken** [-'teɪkən]; **-taking** 1 : emprender (una tarea), asumir (una responsabilidad) 2 PROMISE : comprometerse (a hacer algo)

undertaker ['ʌndər,teɪkər] n : director m, -tora f de funeraria

undertaking ['ʌndər,teɪkɪŋ, ˌʌndər'-] n 1 ENTERPRISE, TASK : empresa f, tarea f 2 PLEDGE : promesa f, garantía f

undertone ['ʌndər,toːn] n 1 : voz f baja ⟨to speak in an undertone : hablar en voz baja⟩ 2 HINT, UNDERCURRENT : trasfondo m, matiz m

undertow ['ʌndər,toː] n : resaca f

undervalue [ˌʌndər'væl,juː] vt **-ued; -uing** : menospreciar, subestimar

underwater[1] [ˌʌndər'wɔtər, -'wɑ-] adv : debajo (del agua)

underwater[2] adj : submarino

under way [ˌʌndər'weɪ] adv : en marcha, en camino ⟨to get under way : ponerse en marcha⟩

underwear ['ʌndər,wær] n : ropa f interior, ropa f íntima

underworld ['ʌndər,wərld] n 1 HELL : infierno m 2 the underworld CRIMINALS : la hampa, los bajos fondos

underwrite ['ʌndər,raɪt, ˌʌndər'-] vt **-wrote** [-,roːt, -'roːt]; **-written** [-,rɪtən, -'rɪtən]; **-writing** 1 INSURE : asegurar 2 FINANCE : financiar 3 BACK, ENDORSE : suscribir, respaldar

underwriter ['ʌndər,raɪtər, ˌʌndər'-] n INSURER : asegurador m, -dora f

undeserving [ˌʌndɪ'zərvɪŋ] adj : indigno

undesirable[1] [ˌʌndɪ'zaɪrəbəl] adj : deseseable

undesirable[2] n : indeseable mf

undeveloped [ˌʌndɪ'vɛləpt] adj : sin desarrollar, sin revelar (dícese de una película)

undies ['ʌndiːz] → **underwear**

undignified [ˌʌn'dɪgnəfaɪd] adj : indecoroso

undiluted [ˌʌndaɪ'luːtəd, -də-] adj : sin diluir, concentrado

undisciplined [ˌʌn'dɪsəplənd] adj : indisciplinado

undiscovered [ˌʌndɪ'skʌvərd] adj : no descubierto

undisputed [ˌʌndɪ'spjuːtəd] adj : indiscutible

undisturbed [ˌʌndɪ'stərbd] adj : tranquilo (dícese de una persona), sin tocar (dícese de un objeto)

undivided [ˌʌndɪ'vaɪdəd] adj : íntegro, completo

undo [ˌʌn'duː] vt **-did** [-'dɪd]; **-done** [-'dʌn]; **-doing** 1 UNFASTEN : desabrochar, desatar, abrir 2 ANNUL : anular 3 REVERSE : deshacer, reparar (daños, etc.) 4 RUIN : arruinar, destruir

undoing [ˌʌn'duːɪŋ] n : ruina f, perdición f

undoubted [ˌʌn'daʊtəd] adj : cierto, indudable — **undoubtedly** adv

undress [ˌʌn'drɛs] vt : desvestir, desabrigar, desnudar — vi : desvestirse, desnudarse

undue [ˌʌnˈduː, -ˈdjuː] *adj* : excesivo, indebido — **unduly** *adv*

undulate [ˈʌndʒəˌleɪt] *vi* **-lated; -lating** : ondular

undulation [ˌʌndʒəˈleɪʃən] *n* : ondulación *f*

undying [ˌʌnˈdaɪɪŋ] *adj* : perpetuo, imperecedero

unearth [ˌʌnˈərθ] *vt* **1** EXHUME : desenterrar, exhumar **2** DISCOVER : descubrir

unearthly [ˌʌnˈərθli] *adj* **unearthlier; -est** : sobrenatural, de otro mundo

unease [ˌʌnˈiːz] *n* : inquietud *f*

uneasily [ˌʌnˈiːzəli] *adv* : inquietamente, con inquietud

uneasiness [ˌʌnˈiːzinəs] *n* : inquietud *f*

uneasy [ˌʌnˈiːzi] *adj* **uneasier; -est** **1** AWKWARD : incómodo **2** WORRIED : preocupado, inquieto **3** RESTLESS : inquieto, agitado

uneducated [ˌʌnˈɛdʒəˌkeɪtəd] *adj* : inculto, sin educación

unemotional [ˌʌniˈmoːʃənəl] *adj* **1** COLD : frío, indiferente **2** IMPARTIAL : imparcial, objetivo

unemployed [ˌʌnɪmˈplɔɪd] *adj* : desempleado

unemployment [ˌʌnɪmˈplɔɪmənt] *n* : desempleo *m*

unending [ˌʌnˈɛndɪŋ] *adj* ENDLESS : interminable, inacabable, sin fin

unenthusiastic [ˌʌnɪnˌθuːziˈæstɪk, -ɛn-, -ˌθjuː-] *adj* : poco entusiasta, tibio

unenviable [ˌʌnˈɛnviəbəl] *adj* : nada envidiable

unequal [ˌʌnˈiːkwəl] *adj* **1** : desigual **2** INADEQUATE : incapaz, incompetente ⟨to be unequal to a task : no estar a la altura de una tarea⟩

unequaled *or* **unequalled** [ˌʌnˈiːkwəld] *adj* : sin igual

unequivocal [ˌʌnɪˈkwɪvəkəl] *adj* : inequívoco, claro — **unequivocally** *adv*

unerring [ˌʌnˈɛrɪŋ, -ˈər-] *adj* : infalible

unethical [ˌʌnˈɛθɪkəl] *adj* : poco ético

uneven [ˌʌnˈiːvən] *adj* **1** ODD : impar (dícese de un número) **2** : desigual, disparejo, desnivelado (dícese de una superficie) ⟨uneven terrain : terreno accidentado⟩ **3** IRREGULAR : irregular, desigual, disparejo **4** UNEQUAL : desigual — **unevenly** [ˌʌnˈiːvənli] *adv*

unevenness [ˌʌnˈiːvənnəs] *n* **1** : lo desigual, lo desnivelado (de una superficie) **2** IRREGULARITY : irregularidad *f* **3** : lo desigual (de una contienda, etc.)

uneventful [ˌʌnɪˈvɛntfəl] *adj* : sin incidentes, tranquilo

unexpected [ˌʌnɪkˈspɛktəd] *adj* : imprevisto, inesperado — **unexpectedly** *adv*

unexplored [ˌʌnɪkˈsplord] *adj* : inexplorado

unfailing [ˌʌnˈfeɪlɪŋ] *adj* **1** CONSTANT : constante **2** INEXHAUSTIBLE : inagotable **3** SURE : a toda prueba, indefectible

unfair [ˌʌnˈfær] *adj* : injusto — **unfairly** *adv*

unfairness [ˌʌnˈfærnəs] *n* : injusticia *f*

unfaithful [ˌʌnˈfeɪθfəl] *adj* : desleal, infiel — **unfaithfully** *adv*

unfaithfulness [ˌʌnˈfeɪθfəlnəs] *n* : infidelidad *f*, deslealtad *f*

unfamiliar [ˌʌnfəˈmɪljər] *adj* **1** STRANGE : desconocido, extraño ⟨an unfamiliar place : un lugar nuevo⟩ **2 to be unfamiliar with** : no estar familiarizado con, desconocer

unfamiliarity [ˌʌnfəˌmiliˈæræti] *n* : falta *f* de familiaridad

unfashionable [ˌʌnˈfæʃənəbəl] *adj* : fuera de moda

unfasten [ˌʌnˈfæsən] *vt* : desabrochar, desatar (una cuerda, etc.), abrir (una puerta)

unfavorable [ˌʌnˈfeɪvərəbəl] *adj* : desfavorable, mal — **unfavorably** [-bli] *adv*

unfeeling [ˌʌnˈfiːlɪŋ] *adj* : insensible — **unfeelingly** *adv*

unfinished [ˌʌnˈfɪnɪʃd] *adj* : inacabado, incompleto

unfit [ˌʌnˈfɪt] *adj* **1** UNSUITABLE : inadecuado, impropio **2** UNSUITED : no apto, incapaz **3** : incapacitado (físicamente) ⟨to be unfit : no estar en forma⟩

unflagging [ˌʌnˈflægɪŋ] *adj* : inagotable

unflappable [ˌʌnˈflæpəbəl] *adj* : imperturbable

unflattering [ˌʌnˈflætərɪŋ] *adj* : poco favorecedor

unfold [ˌʌnˈfoːld] *vt* **1** EXPAND : desplegar, desdoblar, extender ⟨to unfold a map : desplegar un mapa⟩ **2** DISCLOSE, REVEAL : revelar, exponer (un plan, etc.) — *vi* **1** DEVELOP : desarrollarse, desenvolverse ⟨the story unfolded : el cuento se desarrollaba⟩ **2** EXPAND : extenderse, desplegarse

unforeseeable [ˌʌnforˈsiːəbəl] *adj* : imprevisible

unforeseen [ˌʌnforˈsiːn] *adj* : imprevisto

unforgettable [ˌʌnfərˈgɛtəbəl] *adj* : inolvidable, memorable — **unforgettably** [-bli] *adv*

unforgivable [ˌʌnfərˈgɪvəbəl] *adj* : imperdonable

unfortunate[1] [ˌʌnˈfortʃənət] *adj* **1** UNLUCKY : desgraciado, infortunado, desafortunado ⟨how unfortunate! : ¡qué mala suerte!⟩ **2** INAPPROPRIATE : inoportuno ⟨an unfortunate comment : un comentario poco feliz⟩

unfortunate[2] *n* : desgraciado *m*, -da *f*

unfortunately [ˌʌnˈfortʃənətli] *adv* : desafortunadamente

unfounded [ˌʌnˈfaʊndəd] *adj* : infundado

unfreeze [ˌʌnˈfriːz] *v* **-froze** [-ˈfroːz]; **-frozen** [-ˈfroːzən]; **-freezing** *vt* : descongelar — *vi* : descongelarse

unfriendliness [ˌʌnˈfrɛndlinəs] *n* : hostilidad *f*, antipatía *f*

unfriendly [ˌʌnˈfrɛndli] *adj* **unfriendlier; -est** : poco amistoso, hostil

unfulfilled [ˌʌnfulˈfɪld] *adj* **1** UNSATISFIED : insatisfecho **2** : no realizado

unfurl [ˌʌnˈfərl] *vt* : desplegar, desdoblar — *vi* : desplegarse

unfurnished [ˌʌnˈfərnɪʃt] *adj* : desamueblado

ungainly [ˌʌnˈgeɪnli] *adj* : desgarbado

ungodly [ˌʌnˈgɑdli, -ˈgad-] *adj* **1** IMPIOUS : impío **2** OUTRAGEOUS : atroz, terrible ⟨at an ungodly hour : a una hora intempestiva⟩

ungovernable [ˌʌnˈgʌvərnəbəl] *adj* : ingobernable

ungracious [ˌʌnˈgreɪʃəs] *adj* : descortés

ungrateful [ˌʌnˈgreɪtfəl] *adj* : desagradecido, ingrato — **ungratefully** *adv*

ungratefulness [ˌʌnˈgreɪtfəlnəs] *n* : ingratitud *f*

unguarded [ˌʌnˈgardəd] *adj* **1** CARELESS : irreflexivo, desprevenido **2** UNPROTECTED : sin vigilancia, no vigilado

unhappily [ˌʌnˈhæpəli] *adv* **1** SADLY : tristemente **2** UNFORTUNATELY : desafortunadamente, lamentablemente

unhappiness [ˌʌnˈhæpinəs] *n* : infelicidad *f*, tristeza *f*, desdicha *f*

unhappy [ˌʌnˈhæpi] *adj* **unhappier; -est** **1** UNFORTUNATE : desafortunado, desventurado **2** MISERABLE, SAD : infeliz, triste, desdichado **3** INOPPORTUNE : inoportuno, poco feliz

unharmed [ˌʌnˈharmd] *adj* : salvo, ileso

unhealthy [ˌʌnˈhelθi] *adj* **unhealthier; -est** **1** UNWHOLESOME : insalubre, malsano, nocivo a la salud ⟨an unhealthy climate : un clima insalubre⟩ **2** SICKLY : de mala salud, enfermizo

unheard–of [ˌʌnˈhərdəv] *adj* : sin precedente, inaudito, insólito

unhelpful [ˌʌnˈhelpfəl] *adj* : poco servicial (dícese de personas), inútil (dícese de consejos, etc.)

unhinge [ˌʌnˈhɪndʒ] *vt* **-hinged; -hinging** **1** : desquiciar (una puerta, etc.) **2** DISRUPT, UNSETTLE : trastornar, perturbar

unhitch [ˌʌnˈhɪtʃ] *vt* : desenganchar

unholy [ˌʌnˈhoːli] *adj* **unholier; -est** **1** : profano, impío **2** UNGODLY : atroz, terrible

unhook [ˌʌnˈhʊk] *vt* **1** : desenganchar, descolgar (de algo) **2** UNDO : desabrochar

unhurried [ˌʌnˈhərid] *adj* : lento, sin prisas

unhurt [ˌʌnˈhərt] *adj* : ileso

unhygienic [ˌʌnhaɪˈdʒɛnɪk, -ˈdʒiː-; -ˌhaɪdʒiˈɛnɪk] *adj* : antihigiénico

unicorn [ˈjuːnəˌkɔrn] *n* : unicornio *m*

unidentified [ˌʌnaɪˈdɛntəˌfaɪd] *adj* : no identificado ⟨unidentified flying object : objeto volador no identificado⟩

unification [ˌjuːnəfəˈkeɪʃən] *n* : unificación *f*

uniform¹ [ˈjuːnəˌfɔrm] *adj* : uniforme, homogéneo, constante — **uniformly** *adv*

uniform² *n* : uniforme *m*

uniformed [ˈjuːnəˌfɔrmd] *adj* : uniformado

uniformity [ˌjuːnəˈfɔrməti] *n*, *pl* **-ties** : uniformidad *f*

unify [ˈjuːnəˌfaɪ] *vt* **-fied; -fying** : unificar, unir

unilateral [ˌjuːnəˈlætərəl] *adj* : unilateral — **unilaterally** *adv*

unimaginable [ˌʌnɪˈmædʒənəbəl] *adj* : inimaginable, inconcebible

unimaginative [ˌʌnɪˈmædʒənəˌtɪv, -əˌneɪtɪv] *adj* : poco imaginativo

unimportant [ˌʌnɪmˈpɔrtənt] *adj* : intrascendente, insignificante, sin importancia

unimpressive [ˌʌnɪmˈprɛsɪv] *adj* : mediocre

uninformed [ˌʌnɪnˈfɔrmd] *adj* : no enterado

uninhabitable [ˌʌnɪnˈhæbətəbəl] *adj* : inhabitable

uninhabited [ˌʌnɪnˈhæbətəd] *adj* : deshabitado, desierto, despoblado

uninhibited [ˌʌnɪnˈhɪbətəd] *adj* : desenfadado, desinhibido, sin reservas

uninjured [ˌʌnɪnˈdʒərd] *adj* : ileso

unintelligent [ˌʌnɪnˈtɛlədʒənt] *adj* : poco inteligente

unintelligible [ˌʌnɪnˈtɛlədʒəbəl] *adj* : ininteligible, incomprensible

unintentional [ˌʌnɪnˈtɛnʃənəl] *adj* : no deliberado, involuntario

unintentionally [ˌʌnɪnˈtɛnʃənəli] *adv* : involuntariamente, sin querer

uninterested [ˌʌnˈɪntəˌrɛstəd, -trəstəd] *adj* : indiferente

uninteresting [ˌʌnˈɪntəˌrɛstɪŋ, -trəstɪŋ] *adj* : poco interesante, sin interés

uninterrupted [ˌʌnˌɪntəˈrʌptəd] *adj* : ininterrumpido, continuo

uninvited [ˌʌnɪnˈvaɪtəd] *adj* : no invitado ⟨she showed up uninvited : vino sin que nadie la invitara⟩

uninviting [ˌʌnɪnˈvaɪtɪŋ] *adj* : poco acogedor (dícese de una casa, etc.), poco atractivo

union [ˈjuːnjən] *n* **1** : unión *f* **2** *or* **labor union** : sindicato *m*, gremio *m*

unionism [ˈjuːnjəˌnɪzəm] *n* : sindicalismo *m* — **unionist** [ˈjuːnjənɪst] *n*

unionize [ˈjuːnjəˌnaɪz] *v* **-ized; -izing** *vt* : sindicalizar, sindicar — *vi* : sindicalizarse

unique [juˈniːk] *adj* **1** SOLE : único, solo **2** UNUSUAL : extraordinario

uniquely [juˈniːkli] *adv* **1** EXCLUSIVELY : exclusivamente **2** EXCEPTIONALLY : excepcionalmente

uniqueness [juˈniːknəs] *n* : singularidad *f*

unison [ˈjuːnəsən, -zən] *n* **1** : unísono *m* (en música) **2** CONCORD : acuerdo *m*, armonía *f*, concordia *f* **3 in —** SIMULTANEOUSLY : simultáneamente, al unísono

unit [ˈjuːnɪt] *n* **1** : unidad *f* **2** : módulo *m* (de un mobiliario)

unitary [ˈjuːnəˌtɛri] *adj* : unitario

unite [juˈnaɪt] *v* **united; uniting** *vt* : unir, juntar, combinar — *vi* : unirse, juntarse

unity [ˈjuːnəti] *n*, *pl* **-ties** **1** UNION : unidad *f*, unión *f* **2** HARMONY : armonía *f*, acuerdo *m*

universal [ˌjuːnəˈvərsəl] *adj* **1** GENERAL : general, universal ⟨a universal rule : una regla universal⟩ **2** WORLDWIDE : universal, mundial — **universality** *n* — **universally** *adv*

universe [ˈjuːnəˌvərs] *n* : universo *m*

university [ˌjuːnəˈvərsəti] *n*, *pl* **-ties** : universidad *f*

unjust [ˌʌnˈdʒʌst] *adj* : injusto — **unjustly** *adv*

unjustifiable [ˌʌnˈʤʌstəˈfaɪəbəl] *adj* : injustificable — **unjustifiably** *adv*

unjustified [ˌʌnˈʤʌstəˌfaɪd] *adj* : injustificado

unkempt [ˌʌnˈkɛmpt] *adj* : descuidado, desaliñado, despeinado (dícese del pelo)

unkind [ˌʌnˈkaɪnd] *adj* : poco amable, cruel — **unkindly** *adv*

unkindness [ˌʌnˈkaɪndnəs] *n* : crueldad *f*, falta *f* de amabilidad

unknowing [ˌʌnˈnoːɪŋ] *adj* : inconsciente, ignorante — **unknowingly** *adv*

unknown [ˌʌnˈnoːn] *adj* : desconocido

unlawful [ˌʌnˈlɔfəl] *adj* : ilícito, ilegal — **unlawfully** *adv*

unleaded [ˌʌnˈlɛdəd] *adj* : sin plomo

unleash [ˌʌnˈliːʃ] *vt* : soltar, desatar

unless [ənˈlɛs] *conj* : a menos que, salvo que, a no ser que

unlike¹ [ˌʌnˈlaɪk] *adj* **1** DIFFERENT : diferente, distinto **2** UNEQUAL : desigual

unlike² *prep* **1** : diferente de, distinto de ⟨unlike the others : distinto a los demás⟩ **2** : a diferencia de ⟨unlike her sister, she is shy : a diferencia de su hermana, es tímida⟩

unlikelihood [ˌʌnˈlaɪkliˌhʊd] *n* : improbabilidad *f*

unlikely [ˌʌnˈlaɪkli] *adj* **unlikelier; -est 1** IMPROBABLE : improbable, poco probable **2** UNPROMISING : poco prometedor

unlimited [ˌʌnˈlɪmətəd] *adj* : ilimitado

unlisted [ˌʌnˈlɪstəd] *adj* : que no aparece en la guía telefónica

unload [ˌʌnˈloːd] *vt* **1** REMOVE : descargar, desembarcar (mercancías o pasajeros) **2** : descargar (un avión, un camión, etc.) **3** DUMP : deshacerse de — *vi* : descargar (dícese de un camión, etc.)

unlock [ˌʌnˈlɑk] *vt* **1** : abrir (con llave) **2** DISCLOSE, REVEAL : revelar

unluckily [ˌʌnˈlʌkəli] *adv* : desgraciadamente

unlucky [ˌʌnˈlʌki] *adj* **unluckier; -est 1** : de mala suerte, desgraciado, desafortunado ⟨an unlucky year : un año de mala suerte⟩ **2** INAUSPICIOUS : desfavorable, poco propicio **3** REGRETTABLE : lamentable

unmanageable [ˌʌnˈmænɪʤəbəl] *adj* : difícil de controlar, poco manejable, ingobernable

unmanned [ˌʌnˈmænd] *adj* : no tripulado, sin tripulación

unmarried [ˌʌnˈmærid] *adj* : soltero

unmask [ˌʌnˈmæsk] *vt* EXPOSE : desenmascarar

unmerciful [ˌʌnˈmərsɪfəl] *adj* MERCILESS : despiadado — **unmercifully** *adv*

unmistakable [ˌʌnmɪˈsteɪkəbəl] *adj* : evidente, inconfundible, obvio — **unmistakably** [-bli] *adv*

unmotivated [ˌʌnˈmoːtəˌveɪtəd] *adj* : inmotivado

unmoved [ˌʌnˈmuːvd] *adj* : impasible ⟨to be unmoved by : permanecer impasible ante⟩

unnatural [ˌʌnˈnæʧərəl] *adj* **1** ABNORMAL, UNUSUAL : anormal, poco natural, poco normal **2** AFFECTED : afectado, forzado ⟨an unnatural smile : una sonrisa forzada⟩ **3** PERVERSE : perverso, antinatural

unnecessary [ˌʌnˈnɛsəˌsɛri] *adj* : innecesario — **unnecessarily** [-ˌnɛsəˈsɛrəli] *adv*

unnerve [ˌʌnˈnərv] *vt* **-nerved; -nerving** : turbar, desconcertar, poner nervioso

unnoticed [ˌʌnˈnoːtəst] *adj* : inadvertido ⟨to go unnoticed : pasar inadvertido⟩

unobjectionable [ˌʌnəbˈʤɛkʃənəbəl] *adj* : inobjetable

unobstructed [ˌʌnəbˈstrʌktəd] *adj* : libre, despejado

unobtainable [ˌʌnəbˈteɪnəbəl] *adj* : inasequible

unobtrusive [ˌʌnəbˈstruːsɪv] *adj* : discreto

unoccupied [ˌʌnˈɑkjəˌpaɪd] *adj* **1** IDLE : desempleado, desocupado **2** EMPTY : desocupado, libre, deshabitado

unofficial [ˌʌnəˈfɪʃəl] *adj* : extraoficial, no oficial, oficioso

unopened [ˌʌnˈoːpənd] *adj* : sin abrir

unorganized [ˌʌnˈɔrgəˌnaɪzd] *adj* : desorganizado

unorthodox [ˌʌnˈɔrθəˌdɑks] *adj* : poco ortodoxo, poco convencional

unpack [ˌʌnˈpæk] *vt* : desempacar — *vi* : desempacar, deshacer las maletas

unpaid [ˌʌnˈpeɪd] *adj* : no remunerado, no retribuido ⟨an unpaid bill : una cuenta pendiente⟩

unparalleled [ˌʌnˈpærəˌlɛld] *adj* : sin igual

unpatriotic [ˌʌnˌpeɪtriˈɑtɪk] *adj* : antipatriótico

unpayable [ˌʌnˈpeɪəbəl] *adj* : impagable

unpleasant [ˌʌnˈplɛzənt] *adj* : desagradable — **unpleasantly** *adv*

unplug [ˌʌnˈplʌg] *vt* **-plugged; -plugging 1** UNCLOG : destapar, desatascar **2** DISCONNECT : desconectar, desenchufar

unpolished [ˌʌnˈpɑlɪʃt] *adj* IMPERFECT : poco pulido

unpopular [ˌʌnˈpɑpjələr] *adj* : impopular, poco popular

unprecedented [ˌʌnˈprɛsəˌdɛntəd] *adj* : sin precedentes, inaudito, nuevo

unpredictable [ˌʌnprɪˈdɪktəbəl] *adj* : impredecible

unprejudiced [ˌʌnˈprɛʤədəst] *adj* : imparcial, objetivo

unprepared [ˌʌnprɪˈpærd] *adj* : no preparado ⟨an unprepared speech : un discurso improvisado⟩

unpretentious [ˌʌnprɪˈtɛntʃəs] *adj* : modesto, sin pretensiones

unprincipled [ˌʌnˈprɪntsəpəld] *adj* : sin principios, carente de escrúpulos

unproductive [ˌʌnprəˈdʌktɪv] *adj* : improductivo

unprofessional [ˌʌnprəˈfɛʃənəl] *adj* : poco profesional

unprofitable [ˌʌnˈprɑfətəbəl] *adj* : no rentable, poco provechoso

unpromising [ˌʌnˈprɑməsɪŋ] *adj* : poco prometedor

unprotected [ˌʌnprəˈtɛktəd] *adj* : sin protección, desprotegido

unproven [ˌʌn'pruːvən] *adj* : no demostrado

unprovoked [ˌʌnprə'voːkt] *adj* : no provocado

unpublished [ˌʌn'pʌblɪʃt] *adj* : inédito

unpunished [ˌʌn'pʌnɪʃt] *adj* : impune ⟨to go unpunished : escapar sin castigo⟩

unqualified [ˌʌn'kwɑləˌfaɪd] *adj* **1** : no calificado, sin título **2** COMPLETE : completo, absoluto ⟨an unqualified denial : una negación incondicional⟩

unquestionable [ˌʌn'kwɛstʃənəbəl] *adj* : incuestionable, indudable, indiscutible — **unquestionably** [-bli] *adv*

unquestioning [ˌʌn'kwɛstʃənɪŋ] *adj* : incondicional, absoluto, ciego

unravel [ˌʌn'rævəl] *v* **-eled** *or* **-elled**; **-eling** *or* **-elling** *vt* **1** DISENTANGLE : desenmarañar, desenredar **2** SOLVE : aclarar, desenmarañar, desentrañar — *vi* : deshacerse

unreachable [ˌʌn'riːtʃəbəl] *adj* : inalcanzable

unreadable [ˌʌn'riːdəbəl] *adj* **1** ILLEGIBLE : ilegible **2** : difícil de leer

unreal [ˌʌn'riːl] *adj* : irreal

unrealistic [ˌʌnriːə'lɪstɪk] *adj* : poco realista

unreasonable [ˌʌn'riːzənəbəl] *adj* **1** IRRATIONAL : poco razonable, irrazonable, irracional **2** EXCESSIVE : excesivo ⟨unreasonable prices : precios excesivos⟩

unreasonably [ˌʌn'riːzənəbli] *adv* **1** IRRATIONALLY : irrazonablemente, de manera irrazonable **2** EXCESSIVELY : excesivamente

unrecognizable [ˌʌn'rɛkəgˌnaɪzəbəl] *adj* : irreconocible

unrefined [ˌʌnri'faɪnd] *adj* **1** : no refinado, sin refinar (dícese del azúcar, de la harina, etc.) **2** : poco refinado, inculto (dícese de una persona)

unrelated [ˌʌnri'leɪtəd] *adj* : no relacionado, inconexo

unrelenting [ˌʌnri'lɛntɪŋ] *adj* **1** STERN : severo, inexorable **2** CONSTANT, RELENTLESS : constante, implacable

unreliable [ˌʌnri'laɪəbəl] *adj* : que no es de fiar, de poca confianza, inestable (dícese del tiempo)

unrepeatable [ˌʌnri'piːtəbəl] *adj* : irrepetible

unrepentant [ˌʌnri'pɛntənt] *adj* : impenitente

unrepresentative [ˌʌnˌrɛprɪ'zɛntətɪv] *adj* : poco representativo

unrequited [ˌʌnri'kwaɪtəd] *adj* : no correspondido

unreserved [ˌʌnri'zərvd] *adv* **1** UNLIMITED : sin reservas **2** : sin reservar

unresolved [ˌʌnri'zɑlvd] *adj* : pendiente, no resuelto

unresponsive [ˌʌnri'spɑnsɪv] *adj* **1** : indiferente **2** : insensible, inconsciente (en medicina)

unrest [ˌʌn'rɛst] *n* : inquietud *f*, malestar *m* ⟨political unrest : disturbios políticos⟩

unrestrained [ˌʌnri'streɪnd] *adj* : desenfrenado, incontrolado

unrestricted [ˌʌnri'strɪktəd] *adj* : sin restricción ⟨unrestricted access : libre acceso⟩

unrewarding [ˌʌnri'wɔrdɪŋ] *adj* THANKLESS : ingrato

unripe [ˌʌn'raɪp] *adj* : inmaduro, verde

unrivaled *or* **unrivalled** [ˌʌn'raɪvəld] *adj* : incomparable

unroll [ˌʌn'roːl] *vt* : desenrollar — *vi* : desenrollarse

unruffled [ˌʌn'rʌfəld] *adj* **1** SERENE : sereno, tranquilo **2** SMOOTH : tranquilo, liso ⟨unruffled waters : aguas tranquilas⟩

unruliness [ˌʌn'ruːlinəs] *n* : indisciplina *f*

unruly [ˌʌn'ruːli] *adj* : indisciplinado, díscolo, rebelde

unsafe [ˌʌn'seɪf] *adj* : inseguro

unsaid [ˌʌn'sɛd] *adj* : sin decir ⟨to leave unsaid : quedar por decir⟩

unsalted [ˌʌn'sɒltəd] *adj* : sin sal

unsanitary [ˌʌn'sænəˌteri] *adj* : antihigiénico

unsatisfactory [ˌʌnˌsætəs'fæktəri] *adj* : insatisfactorio

unsatisfied [ˌʌn'sætəsˌfaɪd] *adj* : insatisfecho

unsavory [ˌʌn'seɪvəri] *adj* : desagradable

unscathed [ˌʌn'skeɪðd] *adj* UNHARMED : ileso

unscheduled [ˌʌn'skɛˌdʒuːld] *adj* : no programado, imprevisto

unscientific [ˌʌnˌsaɪən'tɪfɪk] *adj* : poco científico

unscramble [ˌʌn'skræmbəl] *vt* : descifrar, descodificar (una señal, etc.)

unscrew [ˌʌn'skruː] *vt* **1** : quitar (una tapa, etc.) **2** : destornillar

unscrupulous [ˌʌn'skruː'pjələs] *adj* : inescrupuloso, sin escrúpulos — **unscrupulously** *adv*

unseal [ˌʌn'siːl] *vt* : abrir, quitarle el sello a

unseasonable [ˌʌn'siːzənəbəl] *adj* **1** : extemporáneo ⟨unseasonable rain : lluvia extemporánea⟩ **2** UNTIMELY : extemporáneo, inoportuno

unseat [ˌʌn'siːt] *vt* : derribar, derrocar

unseemly [ˌʌn'siːmli] *adj* **unseemlier; -est** **1** INDECOROUS : indecoroso **2** INAPPROPRIATE : impropio, inapropiado

unseen [ˌʌn'siːn] *adj* **1** UNNOTICED : inadvertido **2** INVISIBLE : oculto, invisible

unselfish [ˌʌn'sɛlfɪʃ] *adj* : generoso, desinteresado — **unselfishly** *adv*

unselfishness [ˌʌn'sɛlfɪʃnəs] *n* : generosidad *f*, desinterés *m*

unsentimental [ˌʌnˌsɛntə'mɛntəl] *adj* : poco sentimental

unsettle [ˌʌn'sɛtəl] *vt* **-tled; -tling** DISTURB : trastornar, alterar, perturbar

unsettled [ˌʌn'sɛtəld] *adj* **1** CHANGEABLE : inestable, variable ⟨unsettled weather : tiempo inestable⟩ **2** DISTURBED : agitado, inquieto ⟨unsettled waters : aguas agitadas⟩ **3** UNDECIDED : pendiente (dícese de un asunto), indeciso (dícese de una persona) **4** UNPAID : sin saldar, pendiente **5** UNINHABITED : despoblado, no colonizado

unsettling [ˌʌn'sɛtəlɪŋ] *adj* : inquietante

unshakable [ˌʌn'ʃeɪkəbəl] *adj* : inquebrantable

unshaped [ˌʌn'ʃeɪpt] *adj* : sin forma, informe

unshaven [ˌʌn'ʃeɪvən] *adj* : sin afeitar, sin rasurar

unsheathe [ˌʌn'ʃiːð] *vt* : desenvainar

unsightly [ˌʌn'saɪtli] *adj* UGLY : feo, de aspecto malo

unsigned [ˌʌn'saɪnd] *adj* : sin firmar

unskilled [ˌʌn'skɪld] *adj* : no calificado

unsmiling [ˌʌn'smaɪlɪŋ] *adj* : de aspecto serio

unsnap [ˌʌn'snæp] *vt* -**snapped**; -**snapping** : desabrochar

unsociable [ˌʌn'soːʃəbəl] *adj* : poco sociable

unsolicited [ˌʌnsə'lɪsətəd] *adj* : no solicitado

unsolved [ˌʌn'sɑlvd] *adj* : no resuelto, sin resolver

unsophisticated [ˌʌnsə'fɪstəˌkeɪtəd] *adj* 1 NAIVE : ingenuo, de poco mundo 2 SIMPLE : simple, poco sofisticado, rudimentario

unsound [ˌʌn'saʊnd] *adj* 1 UNHEALTHY : enfermizo, de mala salud 2 : poco sólido, defectuoso (dícese de una estructura, etc.) 3 INVALID : inválido, erróneo 4 **of unsound mind** : mentalmente incapacitado

unspeakable [ˌʌn'spiːkəbəl] *adj* 1 INDESCRIBABLE : indecible, inexpresable, incalificable 2 HEINOUS : atroz, nefando, abominable — **unspeakably** [-bli] *adv*

unspecified [ˌʌn'spɛsəˌfaɪd] *adj* : indeterminado, sin especificar

unspoiled [ˌʌn'spɔɪld] *adj* 1 : conservado, sin estropear (dícese de un lugar) 2 : que no está mimado (dícese de un niño)

unspoken [ˌʌn'spoːkən] *adj* TACIT : tácito

unstable [ˌʌn'steɪbəl] *adj* 1 CHANGEABLE : variable, inestable, cambiable ⟨an unstable pulse : un pulso irregular⟩ 2 UNSTEADY : inestable, poco sólido (dícese de una estructura)

unsteadily [ˌʌn'stɛdəli] *adv* : de modo inestable

unsteadiness [ˌʌn'stɛdinəs] *n* : inestabilidad *f*, inseguridad *f*

unsteady [ˌʌn'stɛdi] *adj* 1 UNSTABLE : inestable, variable 2 SHAKY : tembloroso

unstoppable [ˌʌn'stɑpəbəl] *adj* : irrefrenable, incontenible

unsubstantiated [ˌʌnsəb'stæntʃiˌeɪtəd] *adj* : no corroborado, no demostrado

unsuccessful [ˌʌnsək'sɛsfəl] *adj* : fracasado, infructuoso

unsuitable [ˌʌn'suːtəbəl] *adj* : inadecuado, impropio, inapropiado ⟨an unsuitable time : una hora inconveniente⟩

unsuited [ˌʌn'suːtəd] *adj* : inadecuado, inepto

unsung [ˌʌn'sʌŋ] *adj* : olvidado

unsure [ˌʌn'ʃʊr] *adj* : incierto, dudoso

unsurpassed [ˌʌnsər'pæst] *adj* : sin par, sin igual

unsuspecting [ˌʌnsə'spɛktɪŋ] *adj* : desprevenido, desapercibido, confiado

unsweetened [ˌʌn'swiːtənd] *adj* : sin endulzar

unsympathetic [ˌʌnˌsɪmpə'θɛtɪk] *adj* : poco comprensivo, indiferente

untamed [ˌʌn'teɪmd] *adj* : indómito, agreste

untangle [ˌʌn'tæŋgəl] *vt* -**gled**; -**gling** : desenmarañar, desenredar

untapped [ˌʌn'tæpt] *adj* : sin explotar

untenable [ˌʌn'tɛnəbəl] *adj* : insostenible

unthinkable [ˌʌn'θɪŋkəbəl] *adj* : inconcebible, impensable

unthinking [ˌʌn'θɪŋkɪŋ] *adj* : irreflexivo, inconsciente — **unthinkingly** *adv*

untidiness [ˌʌn'taɪdinəs] *n* : desarreglo *m*

untidy [ˌʌn'taɪdi] *adj* 1 SLOVENLY : desaliñado 2 DISORDERLY : desordenado, desarreglado — **untidily** *adv*

untie [ˌʌn'taɪ] *vt* -**tied**; -**tying** *or* -**tieing** : desatar, deshacer

until[1] [ˌʌn'tɪl] *prep* : hasta ⟨until now : hasta ahora⟩

until[2] *conj* : hasta que ⟨until they left : hasta que salieron⟩ ⟨don't answer until you're sure : no contestes hasta que (no) estés seguro⟩

untimely [ˌʌn'taɪmli] *adj* 1 PREMATURE : prematuro ⟨an untimely death : una muerte prematura⟩ 2 INOPPORTUNE : inoportuno, intempestivo

untold [ˌʌn'toːld] *adj* 1 : nunca dicho ⟨the untold secret : el secreto sin contar⟩ 2 INCALCULABLE : incalculable, indecible

untouchable [ˌʌn'tʌtʃəbəl] *adj* : intocable

untouched [ˌʌn'tʌtʃt] *adj* 1 INTACT : intacto, sin tocar, sin probar (dícese de la comida) 2 UNAFFECTED : insensible, indiferente

untoward [ˌʌn'tɔrd, -'toːərd, -tə-'wɔrd] *adj* 1 : indecoroso, impropio (dícese del comportamiento) 2 ADVERSE, UNFORTUNATE : desafortunado, adverso ⟨untoward effects : efectos perjudiciales⟩ 3 UNSEEMLY : indecoroso

untrained [ˌʌn'treɪnd] *adj* : inexperto, no capacitado

untreated [ˌʌn'triːtəd] *adj* : no tratado (dícese de una enfermedad, etc.), sin tratar (dícese de un material)

untroubled [ˌʌn'trʌbəld] *adj* : tranquilo ⟨to be untroubled by : no estar afectado por⟩

untrue [ˌʌn'truː] *adj* 1 UNFAITHFUL : infiel 2 FALSE : falso

untrustworthy [ˌʌn'trʌstˌwərði] *adj* : de poca confianza (dícese de una persona), no fidedigno (dícese de la información)

untruth [ˌʌn'truːθ, 'ʌnˌ-] *n* : mentira *f*, falsedad *f*

untruthful [ˌʌn'truːθfəl] *adj* : mentiroso, falso

unusable [ˌʌn'juːzəbəl] *adj* : inútil, inservible

unused [ˌʌn'juːzd, *in sense 1 usually* -'juːst] *adj* 1 UNACCUSTOMED : inhabituado 2 NEW : nuevo 3 IDLE : no utilizado (dícese de la tierra) 4 REMAINING : restante ⟨the unused portion : la porción restante⟩

unusual [ˌʌnˈjuːʒʊəl] *adj* : inusual, poco común, raro

unusually [ˌʌnˈjuːʒʊəli, -ˈjuːʒəli] *adv* : excepcionalmente, extraordinariamente, fuera de lo común

unveil [ˌʌnˈveɪld] *vt* **1** REVEAL : revelar **2** : develar, descubrir (una estatua, etc.)

unwanted [ˌʌnˈwɑntəd] *adj* : superfluo, de sobre

unwarranted [ˌʌnˈwɔrəntəd] *adj* : injustificado

unwary [ˌʌnˈwæri] *adj* : incauto

unwashed [ˌʌnˈwɔʃt, -ˈwɑʃt] *adj* : sin lavar, sucio

unwavering [ˌʌnˈweɪvərɪŋ] *adj* : firme, inquebrantable ⟨an unwavering gaze : una mirada fija⟩

unwed [ˌʌnˈwɛd] *adj* : soltero

unwelcome [ˌʌnˈwɛlkəm] *adj* : importuno, molesto

unwell [ˌʌnˈwɛl] *adj* : enfermo, mal

unwholesome [ˌʌnˈhoːlsəm] *adj* **1** UNHEALTHY : malsano, insalubre **2** PERNICIOUS : pernicioso **3** LOATHSOME : repugnante, muy desagradable

unwieldy [ˌʌnˈwiːldi] *adj* CUMBERSOME : difícil de manejar, torpe y pesado

unwilling [ˌʌnˈwɪlɪŋ] *adj* : poco dispuesto ⟨to be unwilling to : no estar dispuesto a⟩

unwillingly [ˌʌnˈwɪlɪŋli] *adv* : a regañadientes, de mala gana

unwillingness [ˌʌnˈwɪlɪŋnəs] *n* : desgana *f*, renuncia *f*

unwind [ˌʌnˈwaɪnd] *v* -**wound** [-ˈwaʊnd]; -**winding** *vt* UNROLL : desenrollar — *vi* **1** : desenrollarse **2** RELAX : relajarse

unwise [ˌʌnˈwaɪz] *adj* : imprudente, desacertado, poco aconsejable

unwisely [ˌʌnˈwaɪzli] *adv* : imprudentemente

unwitting [ˌʌnˈwɪtɪŋ] *adj* **1** UNAWARE : inconsciente **2** INADVERTENT : involuntario, inadvertido ⟨an unwitting mistake : un error inadvertido⟩ — **unwittingly** *adv*

unworkable [ˌʌnˈwərkəbəl] *adj* : impracticable

unworthiness [ˌʌnˈwərðinəs] *n* : falta *f* de valía

unworthy [ˌʌnˈwərði] *adj* **1** UNDESERVING : indigno ⟨to be unworthy of : no ser digno de⟩ **2** UNMERITED : inmerecido

unwrap [ˌʌnˈræp] *vt* -**wrapped**; -**wrapping** : desenvolver, deshacer

unwritten [ˌʌnˈrɪtən] *adj* : no escrito

unyielding [ˌʌnˈjiːldɪŋ] *adj* : firme, inflexible, rígido

unzip [ˌʌnˈzɪp] *vt* -**zipped**; -**zipping** : abrir el cierre de

up¹ [ˈʌp] *v* **upped** [ˈʌpt]; **upping**; **ups** *vt* INCREASE : aumentar, subir ⟨they upped the prices : aumentaron los precios⟩ — *vi* **to up and** : agarrar y *fam* ⟨she up and left : agarró y se fue⟩

up² *adv* **1** ABOVE : arriba, en lo alto ⟨up in the mountains : arriba en las montañas⟩ ⟨put it up on the shelf : ponlo en el estante⟩ ⟨we keep it up in the attic : lo guardamos arriba en el desván⟩ ⟨what's going on up there? : ¿qué pasa allí arriba?⟩ **2** UPWARDS : hacia arriba ⟨push it up : empújalo hacia arriba⟩ ⟨pull up your pants : súbete los pantalones⟩ ⟨the sun came up : el sol salió⟩ ⟨prices went up : los precios subieron⟩ ⟨she called up to me : me llamó desde abajo⟩ ⟨he looked up at the sky : miró al cielo⟩ **3** (*indicating an upright position*) ⟨to sit up : ponerse derecho⟩ **4** (*indicating a waking state*) ⟨they got up late : se levantaron tarde⟩ ⟨I stayed up all night : pasé toda la noche sin dormir⟩ **5** (*indicating a usable state*) ⟨we set up the equipment : instalamos el equipo⟩ **6** (*indicating closure*) ⟨I sealed up the package : precinté el paquete⟩ **7** (*indicating activity or excitement*) ⟨they stirred up the crowd : incitaron a la muchedumbre⟩ **8** (*indicating greater or higher volume or intensity*) ⟨to speak up : hablar más fuerte⟩ ⟨to speed up : acelerar⟩ **9** (*indicating a northerly direction*) ⟨the climate up north : el clima del norte⟩ ⟨I'm going up to Canada : voy para Canadá⟩ ⟨come up and see us! : ¡ven a visitarnos!⟩ **10** (*indicating the appearance or existence of something*) ⟨the book turned up : el libro apareció⟩ **11** (*indicating consideration*) ⟨she brought the matter up : mencionó el asunto⟩ **12** COMPLETELY : completamente ⟨eat it up : cómetelo todo⟩ **13** : en pedazos ⟨he tore it up : lo rompió en pedazos⟩ **14** (*indicating approaching and stopping*) ⟨the car pulled up to the curb : el carro paró al borde de la acera⟩ ⟨he walked up to her : se le acercó⟩ **15** (*indicating advancement or progress*) ⟨we moved up to the front of the line : nos pusimos al principio de la fila⟩ ⟨she has moved up in the company : ha ascendido en la compañía⟩ ⟨to grow up : hacerse mayor⟩ **16** (*indicating greater importance in a series, etc.*) ⟨it's pretty far/high up on my list : es muy importante para mí⟩ **17** (*indicating an even score*) ⟨the game was 10 up : empataron a 10⟩ **18 to be one up on someone** : tener ventaja sobre alguien **19 up and down** : de arriba abajo

up³ *adj* **1** (*above the horizon*) ⟨the sun is up : ha salido el sol⟩ **2** (*above a surface*) ⟨the tulips are up : los tulipanes han salido⟩ **3** (*in a high or higher position*) ⟨it's up on the top shelf : está en el estante de arriba⟩ ⟨it's further up : está más arriba⟩ ⟨I'm up here : estoy aquí arriba⟩ **4** (*in a forward place or position*) ⟨we were up near the stage : estábamos cerca del escenario⟩ ⟨the table was up against the wall : la mesa estaba contra la pared⟩ **5** (*above a normal or former level*) ⟨prices are up : los precios han aumentado⟩ ⟨the river is up : las aguas están altas⟩ **6** (*equal to a given level*) ⟨it wasn't up to our expectations : no estuvo a la altura de lo que esperábamos⟩ ⟨I've had it up to here with your nonsense! : ¡estoy hasta las narices de tus tonterías!⟩ **7**

: despierto, levantado ⟨up all night : despierto toda la noche⟩ **8** BUILT : construido ⟨the house is up : la casa está construida⟩ **9** OPEN : abierto ⟨the windows are up : las ventanas están abiertas⟩ **10** *(moving or going upward)* ⟨the up staircase : la escalera para subir⟩ **11** ABREAST : enterado, al día, al corriente ⟨to be up on the news : estar al corriente de las noticias⟩ **12** PREPARED : preparado ⟨we were up for the test : estuvimos preparados para el examen⟩ **13** CAPABLE : capaz ⟨she's up to the task : es capaz de hacerlo⟩ **14** FUNCTIONING : funcionando ⟨the system is back up, the system is up and running again : el sistema ha vuelto a funcionar⟩ **15** AHEAD : ganando ⟨they're up (by) ten points : van ganando por diez puntos⟩ **16** FINISHED : terminado, acabado ⟨time is up : se ha terminado el tiempo permitido⟩ **17 to be up** : pasar ⟨what's up? : ¿qué pasa?⟩ **18 to be up and about** : estar levantado **19 to be up against** : enfrentarse a **20 to be up to something** : estar tramando algo

up⁴ *prep* **1** *(to, toward, or at a higher point of)* ⟨he went up the stairs : subió la escalera⟩ **2** *(to or toward the source of)* ⟨to go up the river : ir río arriba⟩ **3** ALONG : a lo largo, por ⟨up the coast : a lo largo de la costa⟩ ⟨just up the way : un poco más adelante⟩ ⟨up and down the city : por toda la ciudad⟩

up–and–coming *adj* : prometedor

upbraid [ˌʌpˈbreɪd] *vt* : reprender, regañar

upbringing [ˈʌpˌbrɪŋɪŋ] *n* : crianza *f*, educación *f*

upcoming [ˌʌpˈkʌmɪŋ] *adj* : próximo

update¹ [ˌʌpˈdeɪt] *vt* **-dated; -dating** : poner al día, poner al corriente, actualizar

update² [ˈʌpˌdeɪt] *n* : actualización *f*, puesta *f* al día

upend [ˌʌpˈend] *vt* **1** : poner vertical **2** OVERTURN : volcar

upgrade¹ [ˌʌpˈɡreɪd, ˌʌpˈ-] *vt* **-graded; -grading 1** PROMOTE : ascender **2** IMPROVE : mejorar

upgrade² [ˈʌpˌɡreɪd] *n* **1** SLOPE : cuesta *f*, pendiente *f* **2** RISE : aumento *m* de categoría (de un puesto), ascenso *m* (de un empleado) **3** IMPROVEMENT : mejoramiento *m*

upheaval [ˌʌpˈhiːvəl] *n* **1** : levantamiento *m* (en geología) **2** DISTURBANCE, UPSET : trastorno *m*, agitación *f*, conmoción *f*

uphill¹ [ˌʌpˈhɪl] *adv* : cuesta arriba

uphill² [ˈʌpˌhɪl] *adj* **1** ASCENDING : en subida **2** DIFFICULT : difícil, arduo

uphold [ˌʌpˈhoːld] *vt* **-held; -holding 1** SUPPORT : sostener, apoyar, mantener **2** RAISE : levantar **3** CONFIRM : confirmar (una decisión judicial)

upholster [ˌʌpˈhoːlstər] *vt* : tapizar

upholsterer [ˌʌpˈhoːlstərər] *n* : tapicero *m*, -ra *f*

upholstery [ˌʌpˈhoːlstəri] *n, pl* **-steries** : tapicería *f*

upkeep [ˈʌpˌkiːp] *n* : mantenimiento *m*

upland [ˈʌplənd, -ˌlænd] *n* : altiplanicie *f*, altiplano *m*

uplift¹ [ˌʌpˈlɪft] *vt* **1** RAISE : elevar, levantar **2** ELEVATE : elevar, animar (el espíritu, la mente, etc.)

uplift² [ˈʌpˌlɪft] *n* : elevación *f*

uplifting [ˈʌpˌlɪftɪŋ] *adj* : inspirador

upload [ˌʌpˈloːd, ˈʌpˌloːd] *vt* : cargar, subir (un archivo, etc.)

upon [əˈpɑn, əˈpʌn] *prep* : en, sobre ⟨upon the desk : sobre el escritorio⟩ ⟨upon leaving : al salir⟩ ⟨questions upon questions : pregunta tras pregunta⟩

upper¹ [ˈʌpər] *adj* **1** HIGHER : superior **2** : alto (en geografía) ⟨the upper Mississippi : el alto Mississippi⟩

upper² *n* : parte *f* superior (del calzado, etc.)

uppercase¹ [ˌʌpərˈkeɪs] *adj* : mayúsculo

uppercase² *n* **in uppercase** : en mayúsculas

upper–class [ˌʌpərˈklæs] *adj* : de clase alta

upper class *n* : clase *f* alta

upper hand *n* : ventaja *f*, dominio *m*

uppermost [ˈʌpərˌmoːst] *adj* : más alto ⟨it was uppermost in his mind : era lo que más le preocupaba⟩

upright¹ [ˈʌpˌraɪt] *adj* **1** VERTICAL : vertical **2** ERECT : erguido, derecho **3** JUST : recto, honesto, justo

upright² *n* : montante *m*, poste *m*, soporte *m*

uprising [ˈʌpˌraɪzɪŋ] *n* : insurrección *f*, revuelta *f*, alzamiento *m*

uproar [ˈʌpˌror] *n* COMMOTION : alboroto *m*, jaleo *m*, escándalo *m*

uproarious [ˌʌpˈroriəs] *adj* **1** CLAMOROUS : estrepitoso, clamoroso **2** HILARIOUS : muy divertido, hilarante — **uproariously** *adv*

uproot [ˌʌpˈruːt, -ˈrut] *vt* : desarraigar

upset¹ [ˌʌpˈset] *vt* **-set; -setting 1** OVERTURN : volcar **2** SPILL : derramar **3** DISTURB : perturbar, disgustar, inquietar, alterar **4** SICKEN : sentar mal a ⟨it upsets my stomach : me sienta mal al estómago⟩ **5** DISRUPT : trastornar, desbaratar (planes, etc.) **6** DEFEAT : derrotar (en deportes)

upset² *adj* **1** DISPLEASED, DISTRESSED : disgustado, alterado **2 to have an upset stomach** : estar mal del estómago, estar descompuesto (de estómago)

upset³ [ˈʌpˌset] *n* **1** OVERTURNING : vuelco *m* **2** DISRUPTION : trastorno *m* (de planes, etc.) **3** DEFEAT : derrota *f* (en deportes)

upshot [ˈʌpˌʃɑt] *n* : resultado *m* final

upside–down [ˌʌpˌsaɪdˈdaʊn] *adj* : al revés

upside down [ˌʌpˌsaɪdˈdaʊn] *adv* **1** : al revés **2** : en confusión, en desorden

upstairs¹ [ˌʌpˈstærz] *adv* : arriba, en el piso superior

upstairs² [ˈʌpˌstærz, ˌʌpˈ-] *adj* : de arriba

upstairs³ [ˈʌpˌstærz, ˌʌpˈ-] *ns & pl* : piso *m* de arriba, planta *f* de arriba

upstanding [ˌʌpˈstændɪŋ, ˈʌpˌ-] *adj* HONEST, UPRIGHT : honesto, íntegro, recto

upstart [ˈʌpˌstɑrt] *n* : advenedizo *m*, -za *f*

upstream [ˈʌpˈstriːm] *adv* : río arriba

upsurge [ˈʌpˌsərdʒ] *n* : aumento *m* apreciable

upswing [ˈʌpˌswɪŋ] *n* : alza *f*, mejora *f* notable ⟨to be on the upswing : estar mejorándose⟩

uptight [ˌʌpˈtaɪt] *adj* : tenso, nervioso

up to *prep* **1** : hasta ⟨up to a year : hasta un año⟩ ⟨in mud up to my ankles : en barro hasta los tobillos⟩ **2 to be up to** : estar a la altura de ⟨I'm not up to going : no estoy en condiciones de ir⟩ **3 to be up to** : depender de ⟨it's up to the director : depende del director⟩

up–to–date [ˌʌptəˈdeɪt] *adj* **1** CURRENT : corriente, al día ⟨to keep up-to-date : mantenerse al corriente⟩ **2** MODERN : moderno

uptown [ˈʌpˈtaʊn] *adv* : hacia la parte alta de la ciudad, hacia el distrito residencial

upturn [ˈʌpˌtərn] *n* : mejora *f*, auge *m* (económico)

upward¹ [ˈʌpwərd] *or* **upwards** [-wərdz] *adv* **1** : hacia arriba **2** ~ **of** : más de

upward² *adj* : ascendente, hacia arriba

upwind [ˈʌpˈwɪnd] *adv & adj* : contra el viento

uranium [jʊˈreɪniəm] *n* : uranio *m*

Uranus [jʊˈreɪnəs, ˈjʊrənəs] *n* : Urano *m*

urban [ˈərbən] *adj* : urbano

urbane [ˌərˈbeɪn] *adj* : urbano, cortés

urchin [ˈərtʃən] *n* **1** SCAMP : granuja *mf*; pillo *m*, -lla *f* **2 sea urchin** : erizo *m* de mar

urethra [jʊˈriːθrə] *n, pl* **-thras** *or* **-thrae** [-ˌθriː] : uretra *f*

urge¹ [ˈərdʒ] *vt* **urged; urging 1** PRESS : instar, apremiar, insistir ⟨we urged him to come : insistimos en que viniera⟩ **2** ADVOCATE : recomendar, abogar por **3 to urge on** : animar, alentar

urge² *n* : impulso *m*, ganas *fpl*, compulsión *f*

urgency [ˈərdʒənsi] *n, pl* **-cies** : urgencia *f*

urgent [ˈərdʒənt] *adj* **1** PRESSING : urgente, apremiante **2** INSISTENT : insistente **3 to be urgent** : urgir

urgently [ˈərdʒəntli] *adv* : urgentemente

urinal [ˈjʊrənəl, *esp Brit* jʊˈraɪnəl] *n* : orinal *m*

urinary [ˈjʊrəˌnɛri] *adj* : urinario

urinate [ˈjʊrəˌneɪt] *vi* **-nated; -nating** : orinar

urination [ˌjʊrəˈneɪʃən] *n* : orinación *f*

urine [ˈjʊrən] *n* : orina *f*

urn [ˈərn] *n* **1** VASE : urna *f* **2** : recipiente *m* (para servir café, etc.)

Uruguayan [ˌʊrəˈgwaɪən, ˌjʊr-, -ˈgweɪ-] *n* : uruguayo *m*, -ya *f* — **Uruguayan** *adj*

us [ˈʌs] *pron* **1** (*as direct object*) : nos ⟨they were visiting us : nos visitaban⟩ **2** (*as indirect object*) : nos ⟨he gave us a present : nos dio un regalo⟩ **3** (*as object of preposition*) : nosotros, nosotras ⟨stay with us : quédese con nosotros⟩ ⟨both of us : nosotros dos⟩ ⟨all/some of us : to-

dos/algunos de nosotros⟩ **4** (*for emphasis*) : nosotros, nosotras ⟨it's us! : ¡somos nosotros!⟩

usable [ˈjuːzəbəl] *adj* : utilizable

usage [ˈjuːsɪdʒ, -zɪdʒ] *n* **1** HABIT : costumbre *f*, hábito *m* **2** USE : uso *m*

use¹ [ˈjuːz] *v* **used** [ˈjuːzd, *in phrase "used to" usually* ˈjuːstuː]; **using** *vt* **1** EMPLOY, UTILIZE : usar, utilizar, emplear ⟨can I use your phone? : ¿puedo usar tu teléfono?⟩ ⟨they use traditional methods : utilizan métodos tradicionales⟩ ⟨use your head! : ¡usa la cabeza!⟩ ⟨use a contractor : contratarás a un contratista⟩ ⟨use this to clean it : usa esto para limpiarlo, límpialo con esto⟩ ⟨he uses it as an office : lo usa de/como oficina⟩ ⟨she used the money for college : usó el dinero para pagar la matrícula (universitaria)⟩ **2** CONSUME : consumir (electricidad, etc.), tomar (drogas, etc.) **3** EXPLOIT : usar, utilizar ⟨he used his friends to get ahead : usó a sus amigos para mejorar su posición⟩ **4** TREAT : tratar ⟨they used the horse cruelly : maltrataron al caballo⟩ **5** STAND : beneficiarse de ⟨you could use a nap : una siesta te vendría bien⟩ **6 to use up** : agotar, consumir, gastar — *vi* (*used in the past with* **to** *to indicate a former fact or state*) : soler, acostumbrar ⟨winters used to be colder : los inviernos solían ser más fríos, los inviernos eran más fríos⟩ ⟨she used to dance : acostumbraba bailar⟩

use² [ˈjuːs] *n* **1** : uso *m*, empleo *m*, utilización *f* ⟨ready for use : listo para usar⟩ ⟨the use of seat belts : el uso de los cinturones de seguridad⟩ ⟨to wear down from/with use : desgastarse por el uso⟩ **2** USEFULNESS : utilidad *f* ⟨to be of use : ser útil⟩ ⟨to be of no use : no servir (para nada)⟩ ⟨it's no use! : ¡es inútil!⟩ **3** : uso *m* ⟨a tool with many uses : una herramienta con muchos usos⟩ ⟨to find a use for : encontrar uso a⟩ **4** : uso *m* ⟨to have the use of : poder usar, tener acceso a⟩ ⟨for member use only : para uso exclusivo de los socios⟩ **5** : uso *m* (de las piernas, etc.) **6 to be in use** : usarse, estar en uso ⟨dícese de máquinas, palabras, etc.⟩ ⟨the room is in use : la sala está ocupada⟩ **7 to fall out of use** : caer en desuso **8 to have no use for** : no necesitar ⟨she has no use for poetry : a ella no le gusta la poesía⟩ **9 to make use of** : servirse de, aprovechar **10 to put to (good) use** : hacer (buen) uso de

used [ˈjuːzd] *adj* **1** SECONDHAND : usado, de segunda mano ⟨used cars : coches usados⟩ **2** ACCUSTOMED : acostumbrado ⟨used to the heat : acostumbrado al calor⟩

useful [ˈjuːsfəl] *adj* : útil, práctico — **usefully** *adv*

usefulness [ˈjuːsfəlnəs] *n* : utilidad *f*

useless [ˈjuːsləs] *adj* : inútil — **uselessly** *adv*

uselessness [ˈjuːsləsnəs] *n* : inutilidad *f*

user [ˈjuːzər] *n* : usuario *m*, -ria *f*

user–friendly *adj* : fácil de usar

user name *n* : nombre *m* de usuario

usher[1] ['ʌʃər] *vt* **1** ESCORT : acompañar, conducir **2 to usher in** : hacer pasar (a alguien) ⟨to usher in a new era : anunciar una nueva época⟩

usher[2] *n* : acomodador *m*, -dora *f*

usherette [ˌʌʃə'rɛt] *n* : acomodadora *f*

usual ['juːʒəl] *adj* **1** NORMAL : usual, normal **2** CUSTOMARY : acostumbrado, habitual, de costumbre **3** ORDINARY : ordinario, típico

usually ['juːʒuəli, 'juːʒəli] *adv* : usualmente, normalmente

usurp [juˈsərp, -'zərp] *vt* : usurpar

usurper [juˈsərpər, -'zər-] *n* : usurpador *m*, -dora *f*

usury ['juːʒəri] *n* : usura *f*

utensil [juˈtɛntsəl] *n* **1** : utensilio *m* (de cocina) **2** IMPLEMENT : implemento *m*, útil *m* (de labranza, etc.)

uterine ['juːtəˌraɪn, -rən] *adj* : uterino

uterus ['juːtərəs] *n, pl* **uteri** [-ˌraɪ] : útero *m*, matriz *f*

utilitarian [juˌtɪlə'tɛriən] *adj* : utilitario

utility [juˈtɪləti] *n, pl* **-ties** **1** USEFULNESS : utilidad *f* **2 public utility** : empresa *f* de servicio público

utilization [ˌjuːtələ'zeɪʃən] *n* : utilización *f*

utilize ['juːtəˌlaɪz] *vt* **-lized; -lizing** : utilizar, hacer uso de

utmost[1] ['ʌtˌmoːst] *adj* **1** FARTHEST : extremo, más lejano **2** GREATEST : sumo, mayor ⟨of the utmost importance : de suma importancia⟩

utmost[2] *n* : lo más posible ⟨to the utmost : al máximo⟩

utopia [juˈtoːpiə] *n* : utopía *f*

utopian [juˈtoːpiən] *adj* : utópico

utter[1] ['ʌtər] *vt* : decir, articular, pronunciar (palabras)

utter[2] *adj* : absoluto — **utterly** *adv*

utterance ['ʌtərənts] *n* : declaración *f*, articulación *f*

U-turn ['juːˌtərn] *n* **1** : giro *m* en U, vuelta *f* en U, cambio *m* de sentido **2** *fam* ABOUT-FACE, REVERSAL : giro *m* de 180 grados

uvula ['juːvjələ] *n* : campanilla *f*

V

v ['viː] *n, pl* **v's** *or* **vs** ['viːz] : vigésima segunda letra del alfabeto inglés

vacancy ['veɪkəntsi] *n, pl* **-cies** **1** EMPTINESS : vacío *m*, vacuidad *f* **2** : vacante *f*, puesto *m* vacante ⟨to fill a vacancy : ocupar un puesto⟩ **3** : habitación *f* libre (en un hotel) ⟨no vacancies : completo⟩

vacant ['veɪkənt] *adj* **1** EMPTY : libre, desocupado (dícese de los edificios, etc.) **2** : vacante (dícese de los puestos) **3** BLANK : vacío, ausente ⟨a vacant stare : una mirada ausente⟩

vacate ['veɪˌkeɪt] *vt* **-cated; -cating** : desalojar, desocupar

vacation[1] [veɪˈkeɪʃən, və-] *vi* : pasar las vacaciones, vacacionar *Mex*

vacation[2] *n* : vacaciones *fpl* ⟨to be on vacation : estar de vacaciones⟩

vacationer [veɪˈkeɪʃənər, və-] *n* : turista *mf*, veraneante *mf*, vacacionista *mf CA*, *Mex*

vaccinate ['væksəˌneɪt] *vt* **-nated; -nating** : vacunar

vaccination [ˌvæksə'neɪʃən] *n* : vacunación *f*

vaccine [væk'siːn, 'væk-] *n* : vacuna *f*

vacillate ['væsəˌleɪt] *vi* **-lated; -lating** **1** HESITATE : vacilar **2** SWAY : oscilar

vacillation [ˌvæsə'leɪʃən] *n* : indecisión *f*, vacilación *f*

vacuous ['vækjuəs] *adj* **1** EMPTY : vacío **2** INANE : vacuo, necio, estúpido

vacuousness ['vækjuəsnəs] *n* : vacuidad *f*

vacuum[1] ['vækˌkjuːm, -kjəm] *vt* : limpiar con aspiradora, pasar la aspiradora por

vacuum[2] *n, pl* **vacuums** *or* **vacua** ['vækjuə] : vacío *m*

vacuum cleaner *n* : aspiradora *f*

vagabond[1] ['vægəˌbɑnd] *adj* : vagabundo

vagabond[2] *n* : vagabundo *m*, -da *f*

vagary ['veɪgəri, və'geri] *n, pl* **-ries** : capricho *m*

vagina [və'dʒaɪnə] *n, pl* **-nae** [-ˌniː, -ˌnaɪ] *or* **-nas** : vagina *f*

vagrancy ['veɪgrəntsi] *n, pl* **-cies** : vagancia *f*

vagrant[1] ['veɪgrənt] *adj* : vagabundo

vagrant[2] *n* : vagabundo *m*, -da *f*

vague ['veɪg] *adj* **vaguer; vaguest** **1** IMPRECISE : vago, impreciso ⟨a vague feeling : una sensación indefinida⟩ ⟨I haven't the vaguest idea : no tengo la más remota idea⟩ **2** UNCLEAR : borroso, poco claro ⟨a vague outline : un perfil indistinto⟩ **3** ABSENTMINDED : distraído

vaguely ['veɪgli] *adv* : vagamente, de manera imprecisa

vagueness ['veɪgnəs] *n* : vaguedad *f*, imprecisión *f*

vain ['veɪn] *adj* **1** WORTHLESS : vano **2** FUTILE : vano, inútil ⟨in vain : en vano⟩ **3** CONCEITED : vanidoso, presumido

vainly ['veɪnli] *adv* : en vano, vanamente, inútilmente

valance ['vælənts, 'veɪ-] *n* **1** FLOUNCE : volante *m* (de una cama, etc.) **2** : galería *f* de cortina (sobre una ventana)

vale ['veɪl] *n* : valle *m*

valedictorian [ˌvælədɪk'toriən] *n* : estudiante *mf* que pronuncia el discurso de despedida en ceremonia de graduación

valedictory [ˌvælə'dɪktəri] *adj* : de despedida

valentine ['vælənˌtaɪn] *n* : tarjeta *f* que se manda el Día de los Enamorados (el 14 de febrero)

Valentine's Day *n* : Día *m* de los Enamorados

valet ['væˌleɪ, væˈleɪ, 'vælət] *n* : ayuda *m* de cámara

valiant ['væljənt] *adj* : valiente, valeroso

valiantly ['væljəntli] *adv* : con valor, valientemente

valid ['væləd] *adj* : válido

validate ['vælə,deɪt] *vt* -dated; -dating : validar, dar validez a

validity [və'lɪdəti, væ-] *n* : validez *f*

valise [və'liːs] *n* : maleta *f* (de mano)

Valium ['væliəm, 'væljəm] *trademark* se usa para una droga que reduce la ansiedad y el estrés

valley ['væli] *n, pl* -leys : valle *m*

valor ['vælər] *n* : valor *m*, valentía *f*

valuable¹ ['væljuəbəl, 'væljəbəl] *adj* 1 EXPENSIVE : valioso, de valor 2 WORTHWHILE : valioso, apreciable

valuable² *n* : objeto *m* de valor

valuation [ˌvælju'eɪʃən] *n* 1 APPRAISAL : valoración *f*, tasación *f* 2 VALUE : valuación *f*

value¹ ['væl,juː] *vt* -ued; -uing 1 APPRAISE : valorar, avaluar, tasar 2 APPRECIATE : valorar, apreciar

value² *n* 1 : valor *m* ⟨of little value : de poco valor⟩ ⟨to be a good value : estar bien de precio, tener buen precio⟩ ⟨at face value : en su sentido literal⟩ 2 **values** *npl* : valores *mpl* (morales), principios *mpl*

valueless ['væljuːləs] *adj* : sin valor

valve ['vælv] *n* : válvula *f*

vampire ['væm,paɪr] *n* 1 : vampiro *m* 2 *or* **vampire bat** : vampiro *m*

van¹ ['væn] → **vanguard**

van² *n* : furgoneta *f*, camioneta *f*

vandal ['vændəl] *n* : vándalo *m*

vandalism ['vændəl,ɪzəm] *n* : vandalismo *m*

vandalize ['vændəl,aɪz] *vt* : destrozar, destruir, estropear

vane ['veɪn] *n or* **weather vane** : veleta *f*

vanguard ['væn,gɑrd] *n* : vanguardia *f*

vanilla [və'nɪlə, -'nɛ-] *n* : vainilla *f*

vanish ['vænɪʃ] *vi* : desaparecer, disiparse, desvanecerse

vanity ['vænəti] *n, pl* -ties 1 : vanidad *f* 2 *or* **vanity table** : tocador *m*

vanquish ['væŋkwɪʃ, 'væn-] *vt* : vencer, conquistar

vantage point ['væntɪʤ] *n* : posición *f* ventajosa

vapid ['væpəd, 'veɪ-] *adj* : insípido, insulso

vapor ['veɪpər] *n* : vapor *m*

vaporize ['veɪpə,raɪz] *v* -rized; -rizing *vt* : vaporizar — *vi* : vaporizarse, evaporarse

vaporizer ['veɪpə,raɪzər] *n* : vaporizador *m*

variability [ˌvɛriə'bɪləti] *n, pl* -ties : variabilidad *f*

variable¹ ['vɛriəbəl] *adj* : variable ⟨variable cloudiness : nubosidad variable⟩

variable² *n* : variable *f*, factor *m*

variance ['vɛriənts] *n* 1 DISCREPANCY : varianza *f*, discrepancia *f* 2 DISAGREEMENT : desacuerdo *m* ⟨at variance with : en desacuerdo con⟩

variant¹ ['vɛriənt] *adj* : variante, divergente

variant² *n* : variante *f*

variation [ˌvɛri'eɪʃən] *n* : variación *f*, diferencias *fpl*

varicose ['værə,koːs] *adj* : varicoso

varicose veins *npl* : varices *fpl*, várices *fpl*

varied ['vɛrid] *adj* : variado, dispar, diferente

variegated ['vɛriə,geɪtd] *adj* : abigarrado, multicolor

variety [və'raɪəti] *n, pl* -ties 1 DIVERSITY : diversidad *f*, variedad *f* 2 ASSORTMENT : surtido *m* ⟨for a variety of reasons : por diversas razones⟩ 3 SORT : clase *f* 4 BREED : variedad *f* (de plantas)

various ['vɛriəs] *adj* : varios, diversos

varnish¹ ['vɑrnɪʃ] *vt* : barnizar

varnish² *n* : barniz *f*

varsity ['vɑrsəti] *n, pl* -ties : equipo *m* universitario

vary ['vɛri] *v* **varied; varying** *vt* : variar, diversificar — *vi* 1 CHANGE : variar, cambiar 2 DEVIATE : desviarse

vascular ['væskjələr] *adj* : vascular

vase ['veɪs, 'veɪz, 'vaz] *n* : jarrón *m*, florero *m*

Vaseline ['væsə,liːn, ˌvæsə'liːn] *trademark* se usa para vaselina

vassal ['væsəl] *n* : vasallo *m*, -lla *f*

vast ['væst] *adj* : inmenso, enorme, vasto

vastly ['væstli] *adv* : enormemente

vastness ['væstnəs] *n* : vastedad *f*, inmensidad *f*

vat ['væt] *n* : cuba *f*, tina *f*

vaudeville ['vɑdvəl, -ˌvɪl; 'vɔdə,vɪl] *n* : vodevil *m*

vault¹ ['vɔlt] *vi* LEAP : saltar

vault² *n* 1 JUMP : salto *m* ⟨pole vault : salto de pértiga, salto con garrocha⟩ 2 DOME : bóveda *f* 3 : bodega *f* (para vino), bóveda *f* de seguridad (de un banco) 4 CRYPT : cripta *f*

vaulted ['vɔltəd] *adj* : abovedado

vaunted ['vɔntəd] *adj* : cacareado, alardeado ⟨a much vaunted wine : un vino muy alardeado⟩

VCR [ˌviˌsiˈɑr] *n* : video *m*, videocasetera *f*

veal ['viːl] *n* : ternera *f*, carne *f* de ternera

veer ['vɪr] *vi* : virar (dícese de un barco), girar (dícese de un coche), torcer (dícese de un camino)

vegan ['viːgən] *n* : vegetariano *m* estricto, vegetariana *f* estricta

vegetable¹ ['vɛʤtəbəl, 'vɛʤətə-] *adj* : vegetal

vegetable² *n* 1 : vegetal *m* ⟨the vegetable kingdom : el reino vegetal⟩ 2 : verdura *f*, hortaliza *f* (para comer)

vegetarian [ˌvɛʤə'tɛriən] *n* : vegetariano *mf* — **vegetarian** *adj* — **vegetarianism** *n*

vegetate ['vɛʤə,teɪt] *vi* -tated; -tating : vegetar

vegetation [ˌvɛʤə'teɪʃən] *n* : vegetación *f*

vegetative ['vɛʤə,teɪtɪv] *adj* : vegetativo

veggie ['vɛʤi] *n fam* VEGETABLE : verdura *f*, hortaliza *f* (para comer)

vehemence ['viːəmənts] *n* : intensidad *f*, vehemencia *f*

vehement ['viːəmənt] *adj* : intenso, vehemente

vehemently ['viːəməntli] *adv* : vehementemente, con vehemencia

vehicle ['viːəkəl, 'viːˌhɪkəl] *n* **1** *or* **motor vehicle** : vehículo *m* **2** MEDIUM : vehículo *m*, medio *m*

vehicular [vɪ'hɪkjələr, və-] *adj* : vehicular ⟨vehicular homicide : muerte por atropello⟩

veil¹ ['veɪl] *vt* **1** CONCEAL : velar, disimular **2** : cubrir con un velo ⟨to veil one's face : cubrirse con un velo⟩

veil² *n* : velo *m* ⟨bridal veil : velo de novia⟩

vein ['veɪn] *n* **1** : vena *f* (en anatomía, botánica, etc.) **2** LODE : veta *f*, vena *f*, filón *m* **3** STYLE : vena *f* ⟨in a humorous vein : en vena humorística⟩

veined ['veɪnd] *adj* : veteado (dícese del queso, de los minerales, etc.)

Velcro ['vɛlˌkroː] *trademark* se usa para un tipo de cierre de nilón

velocity [və'lɑːsəti] *n, pl* **-ties** : velocidad *f*

velour [və'lʊr] *or* **velours** [-'lʊrz] *n* : velour *m*

velvet¹ ['vɛlvət] *adj* **1** : de terciopelo **2** → **velvety**

velvet² *n* : terciopelo *m*

velvety ['vɛlvəti] *adj* : aterciopelado

venal ['viːnəl] *adj* : venal

vend ['vɛnd] *vt* : vender

vendetta [vɛn'dɛtə] *n* : vendetta *f*

vending machine *n* : máquina *f* expendedora

vendor ['vɛndər] *n* : vendedor *m*, -dora *f*; puestero *m*, -ra *f*

veneer *n* **1** : enchapado *m*, chapa *f* **2** APPEARANCE : apariencia *f*, barniz *m* ⟨a veneer of culture : un barniz de cultura⟩

venerable ['vɛnərəbəl] *adj* : venerable

venerate ['vɛnəˌreɪt] *vt* **-ated; -ating** : venerar

veneration [ˌvɛnə'reɪʃən] *n* : veneración *f*

venereal disease [və'nɪriəl] *n* : enfermedad *f* venérea

venetian blind [və'niːʃən] *n* : persiana *f* (de lamas)

Venezuelan [ˌvɛnə'zweɪlən, -zʊ'eɪ-] *n* : venezolano *m*, -na *f* — **Venezuelan** *adj*

vengeance ['vɛndʒənts] *n* : venganza *f* ⟨to take vengeance on : vengarse de⟩

vengeful ['vɛndʒfəl] *adj* : vengativo

venial ['viːniəl] *adj* : venial ⟨a venial sin : un pecado venial⟩

venison ['vɛnəsən, -zən] *n* : venado *m*, carne *f* de venado

venom ['vɛnəm] *n* **1** : veneno *m* **2** MALICE : veneno *m*, malevolencia *f*

venomous ['vɛnəməs] *adj* : venenoso

vent¹ ['vɛnt] *vt* : desahogar, dar salida a ⟨to vent one's feelings : desahogarse⟩

vent² *n* **1** OPENING : abertura *f* (de escape), orificio *m* **2** *or* **air vent** : respiradero *m*, rejilla *f* de ventilación **3** OUTLET : desahogo *m* ⟨to give vent to one's anger : desahogar la ira⟩

ventilate ['vɛntəl̩ˌeɪt] *vt* **-lated; -lating** : ventilar

ventilation [ˌvɛntəl̩'eɪʃən] *n* : ventilación *f*

ventilator ['vɛntəl̩ˌeɪtər] *n* : ventilador *m*

ventricle ['vɛntrɪkəl] *n* : ventrículo *m*

ventriloquism [vɛn'trɪləˌkwɪzəm] *n* : ventriloquia *f*

ventriloquist [vɛn'trɪləˌkwɪst] *n* : ventrílocuo *m*, -cua *f*

venture¹ ['vɛntʃər] *v* **-tured; -turing** *vt* **1** RISK : arriesgar **2** OFFER : aventurar ⟨to venture an opinion : aventurar una opinión⟩ — *vi* : arriesgarse, atreverse, aventurarse

venture² *n* **1** UNDERTAKING : empresa *f* **2** GAMBLE, RISK : aventura *f*, riesgo *m*

venturesome ['vɛntʃərsəm] *adj* **1** ADVENTUROUS : audaz, atrevido **2** RISKY : arriesgado

venue ['vɛnˌjuː] *n* **1** PLACE : lugar *m* **2** : jurisdicción *f* (en derecho)

Venus ['viːnəs] *n* : Venus *m*

veracity [və'ræsəti] *n, pl* **-ties** : veracidad *f*

veranda *or* **verandah** [və'rændə] *n* : terraza *f*, veranda *f*

verb ['vərb] *n* : verbo *m*

verbal ['vərbəl] *adj* : verbal

verbalize ['vərbəˌlaɪz] *vt* **-ized; -izing** : expresar con palabras, verbalizar

verbally ['vərbəli] *adv* : verbalmente, de palabra

verbatim¹ [vər'beɪtəm] *adv* : palabra por palabra, textualmente

verbatim² *adj* : literal, textual

verbose [vər'boːs] *adj* : verboso, prolijo

verdant ['vərdənt] *adj* : verde, verdeante

verdict ['vərdɪkt] *n* **1** : veredicto *m* (de un jurado) **2** JUDGMENT, OPINION : juicio *m*, opinión *f*

verge¹ ['vərdʒ] *vi* **verged; verging** : estar al borde, rayar ⟨it verges on madness : raya en la locura⟩

verge² *n* **1** EDGE : borde *m* **2 to be on the verge of** : estar a pique de, estar al borde de, estar a punto de

verification [ˌvɛrəfə'keɪʃən] *n* : verificación *f*

verify ['vɛrəˌfaɪ] *vt* **-fied; -fying** : verificar, comprobar, confirmar

veritable ['vɛrətəbəl] *adj* : verdadero — **veritably** [-bli] *adv*

vermicelli [ˌvərmə'tʃɛli, -'sɛli] *n* : fideos *mpl* finos

vermin ['vərmən] *ns & pl* : alimañas *fpl*, bichos *mpl*, sabandijas *fpl*

vermouth [vər'muːθ] *n* : vermut *m*

vernacular¹ [vər'nækjələr] *adj* : vernáculo

vernacular² *n* : lengua *f* vernácula

vernal ['vərnəl] *adj* : vernal

versatile ['vərsətəl] *adj* : versátil

versatility [ˌvərsə'tɪləti] *n* : versatilidad *f*

verse ['vərs] *n* **1** LINE, STANZA : verso *m*, estrofa *f* **2** POETRY : poesía *f* **3** : versículo *m* (en la Biblia)

versed ['vərst] *adj* : versado ⟨to be well versed in : ser muy versado en⟩

version ['vərʒən] *n* : versión *f*

versus ['vərsəs] *prep* : versus

vertebra ['vərtəbrə] *n, pl* **-brae** [-ˌbreɪ, -ˌbriː] *or* **-bras** : vértebra *f*

vertebrate[1] [ˈvərtəbrət, -ˌbreɪt] adj : vertebrado

vertebrate[2] n : vertebrado m

vertex [ˈvərˌtɛks] n, pl **vertices** [ˈvərtəˌsiːz] 1 : vértice m (en matemáticas y anatomía) 2 SUMMIT, TOP : ápice m, cumbre f, cima f

vertical[1] [ˈvərtɪkəl] adj : vertical — **vertically** adv

vertical[2] n : vertical f

vertigo [ˈvərtɪˌgoː] n, pl **-goes** or **-gos** : vértigo m

verve [ˈvərv] n : brío m

very[1] [ˈvɛri] adv 1 EXTREMELY : muy, sumamente ⟨very few : muy pocos⟩ ⟨very much : mucho⟩ ⟨I am very sorry : lo siento mucho⟩ 2 (used for emphasis) ⟨at the very least : por lo menos, como mínimo⟩ ⟨the very same dress : el mismo vestido⟩ ⟨a room of my very own : mi propio cuarto⟩ ⟨on the very next day : al día siguiente⟩

very[2] adj **verier; -est** 1 EXACT, PRECISE : mismo, exacto ⟨at that very moment : en ese mismo momento⟩ ⟨it's the very thing : es justo lo que hacía falta⟩ 2 BARE, MERE : solo, mero ⟨the very thought of it : sólo pensarlo⟩ 3 EXTREME : extremo, de todo ⟨at the very top : arriba de todo⟩

vesicle [ˈvɛsɪkəl] n : vesícula f

vespers [ˈvɛspərz] npl : vísperas fpl

vessel [ˈvɛsəl] n 1 CONTAINER : vasija f, recipiente m 2 BOAT, CRAFT : nave f, barco m, buque m 3 : vaso m ⟨blood vessel : vaso sanguíneo⟩

vest[1] [ˈvɛst] vt 1 CONFER : conferir ⟨to vest authority in : conferirle la autoridad a⟩ 2 CLOTHE : vestir

vest[2] n 1 : chaleco m 2 UNDERSHIRT : camiseta f

vestibule [ˈvɛstəˌbjuːl] n : vestíbulo m

vestige [ˈvɛstɪdʒ] n : vestigio m, rastro m

vestments [ˈvɛstmənts] npl : vestiduras fpl

vestry [ˈvɛstri] n, pl **-tries** : sacristía f

vet [ˈvɛt] n 1 → **veterinarian** 2 → **veteran**[2]

veteran[1] [ˈvɛtərən, ˈvɛtrən] adj : veterano

veteran[2] n : veterano m, -na f

Veterans Day n : día m del Armisticio (celebrado el 11 de noviembre en los Estados Unidos)

veterinarian [ˌvɛtərəˈnɛriən, ˌvɛtrə-] n : veterinario m, -ria f

veterinary [ˈvɛtərəˌnɛri] adj : veterinario

veto[1] [ˈviːˌtoː] vt 1 FORBID : prohibir 2 : vetar ⟨to veto a bill : vetar un proyecto de ley⟩

veto[2] n, pl **-toes** 1 : veto m ⟨the power of veto : el derecho de veto⟩ 2 BAN : veto m, prohibición f

vex [ˈvɛks] vt : contrariar, molestar, irritar

vexation [vɛkˈseɪʃən] n : contrariedad f, irritación f

via [ˈvaɪə, ˈviːə] prep : por, vía

viability [ˌvaɪəˈbɪləti] n : viabilidad f

viable [ˈvaɪəbəl] adj : viable

viaduct [ˈvaɪəˌdʌkt] n : viaducto m

vial [ˈvaɪəl] n : frasco m

vibrant [ˈvaɪbrənt] adj 1 LIVELY : vibrante, animado, dinámico 2 BRIGHT : fuerte, vivo (dícese de los colores)

vibrate [ˈvaɪˌbreɪt] vi **-brated; -brating** 1 OSCILLATE : vibrar, oscilar 2 THRILL : bullir ⟨to vibrate with excitement : bullir de emoción⟩

vibration [vaɪˈbreɪʃən] n : vibración f

vibrator [ˈvaɪˌbreɪtər] n : vibrador m

vicar [ˈvɪkər] n : vicario m, -ria f

vicarious [vaɪˈkæriəs, vɪ-] adj : indirecto — **vicariously** adv

vice [ˈvaɪs] n : vicio m

vice- [ˈvaɪs] pref : vice-

vice admiral n : vicealmirante mf

vice president n : vicepresidente m, -ta f

viceroy [ˈvaɪsˌrɔɪ] n : virrey m, -rreina f

vice versa [ˌvaɪsiˈvərsə, ˌvaɪsˈvər-] adv : viceversa

vicinity [vəˈsɪnəti] n, pl **-ties** 1 NEIGHBORHOOD : vecindad f, inmediaciones fpl 2 NEARNESS : proximidad f

vicious [ˈvɪʃəs] adj 1 DEPRAVED : depravado, malo 2 SAVAGE : malo, fiero, salvaje ⟨a vicious dog : un perro feroz⟩ 3 MALICIOUS : malicioso

vicious circle n : círculo m vicioso

viciously [ˈvɪʃəsli] adv : con saña, brutalmente

viciousness [ˈvɪʃəsnəs] n : brutalidad f, ferocidad f (de un animal), malevolencia f (de un comentario, etc.)

vicissitude [vəˈsɪsəˌtuːd, vaɪ-, -ˌtjuːd] n : vicisitud f

victim [ˈvɪktəm] n : víctima f

victimize [ˈvɪktəˌmaɪz] vt **-mized; -mizing** : tomar como víctima; perseguir; victimizar Arg, Mex

victor [ˈvɪktər] n : vencedor m, -dora f

Victorian [vɪkˈtoːriən] adj : victoriano

victorious [vɪkˈtoːriəs] adj : victorioso — **victoriously** adv

victory [ˈvɪktəri] n, pl **-ries** : victoria f, triunfo m

video[1] [ˈvɪdiˌoː] adj : de video ⟨video recording : grabación de video⟩

video[2] n : video m

video camera n : videocámara f

videocassette [ˌvɪdioʊkəˈsɛt] n : videocasete m, videocassette m

videocassette recorder → **VCR**

video game n : videojuego m, juego m de video

video recorder → **VCR**

videotape[1] [ˈvɪdioˌteɪp] vt **-taped; -taping** : grabar en video, videograbar

videotape[2] n : videocinta f

vie [ˈvaɪ] vi **vied; vying** [ˈvaɪɪŋ] : competir, rivalizar

Vietnamese [viˌɛtnəˈmiːz, -ˈmiːs] n 1 : vietnamita mf 2 : vietnamita m (idioma) — **Vietnamese** adj

view[1] [ˈvjuː] vt 1 OBSERVE : mirar, ver, observar 2 CONSIDER : considerar, contemplar

view[2] n 1 SIGHT : vista f ⟨to come into view : aparecer⟩ 2 ATTITUDE, OPINION : opinión f, parecer m, actitud f ⟨in my view : en mi opinión⟩ 3 SCENE : vista f, panorama f 4 INTENTION : idea f, vista f

⟨with a view to : con vistas a, con la idea de⟩ **5 in view of** : dado que, en vista de (que)

viewer [ˈvjuːər] *n* : televidente *mf*; telespectador *m*, -dora *f* ⟨the show was watched by millions of viewers : el programa fue visto por millones de televidentes⟩

viewfinder [ˈvjuːˌfaɪndər] *n* : visor *m*

viewpoint [ˈvjuːˌpɔɪnt] *n* : punto *m* de vista

vigil [ˈvɪʤəl] *n* **1** : vigilia *f*, vela *f* **2 to keep vigil** : velar

vigilance [ˈvɪʤələnts] *n* : vigilancia *f*

vigilant [ˈvɪʤələnt] *adj* : vigilante

vigilante [ˌvɪʤəˈlænˌtiː] *n* : integrante *mf* de un comité de vigilancia (que actúa como policía)

vigilantly [ˈvɪʤələntli] *adv* : con vigilancia

vigor [ˈvɪgər] *n* : vigor *m*, energía *f*, fuerza *f*

vigorous [ˈvɪgərəs] *adj* : vigoroso, enérgico — **vigorously** *adv*

Viking [ˈvaɪkɪŋ] *n* : vikingo *m*, -ga *f*

vile [ˈvaɪl] *adj* **viler; vilest** **1** WICKED : vil, infame **2** REVOLTING : asqueroso, repugnante **3** TERRIBLE : horrible, atroz ⟨vile weather : tiempo horrible⟩ ⟨to be in a vile mood : estar de un humor de perros⟩

vileness [ˈvaɪlnəs] *n* : vileza *f*

vilify [ˈvɪləˌfaɪ] *vt* **-fied; -fying** : vilipendiar, denigrar, difamar

villa [ˈvɪlə] *n* : casa *f* de campo, quinta *f*

village [ˈvɪlɪʤ] *n* : pueblo *m* (grande), aldea *f* (pequeña)

villager [ˈvɪlɪʤər] *n* : vecino *m*, -na *f* (de un pueblo); aldeano *m*, -na *f* (de una aldea)

villain [ˈvɪlən] *n* : villano *m*, -na *f*; malo *m*, -la *f* (en ficción, películas, etc.)

villainess [ˈvɪlənəs, -nəs] *n* : villana *f*

villainous [ˈvɪlənəs] *adj* : infame, malvado

villainy [ˈvɪləni] *n, pl* **-lainies** : vileza *f*, maldad *f*

vim [ˈvɪm] *n* : brío *m*, vigor *m*, energía *f*

vinaigrette [ˌvɪnɪˈgrɛt] *n* : vinagreta *f*

vindicate [ˈvɪndəˌkeɪt] *vt* **-cated; -cating** **1** EXONERATE : vindicar, disculpar **2** JUSTIFY : justificar

vindication [ˌvɪndəˈkeɪʃən] *n* : vindicación *f*, justificación *f*

vindictive [vɪnˈdɪktɪv] *adj* : vengativo

vine [ˈvaɪn] *n* **1** GRAPEVINE : vid *f*, parra *f* **2** : planta *f* trepadora, enredadera *f*

vinegar [ˈvɪnɪgər] *n* : vinagre *m*

vinegary [ˈvɪnɪgəri] *adj* : avinagrado

vineyard [ˈvɪnjərd] *n* : viña *f*, viñedo *m*

vintage¹ [ˈvɪntɪʤ] *adj* **1** : añejo (dícese de un vino) **2** CLASSIC : clásico, de época

vintage² *n* **1** : cosecha *f* ⟨the 1947 vintage : la cosecha de 1947⟩ **2** ERA : época *f*, era *f* ⟨slang of recent vintage : argot de la época reciente⟩

vinyl [ˈvaɪnəl] *n* : vinilo *m*

viola [viːˈoːlə] *n* : viola *f*

violate [ˈvaɪəˌleɪt] *vt* **-lated; -lating** **1** BREAK : infringir, violar, quebrantar ⟨to violate the rules : violar las reglas⟩ **2** RAPE : violar **3** DESECRATE : profanar

violation [ˌvaɪəˈleɪʃən] *n* **1** : violación *f*, infracción *f* (de una ley) **2** DESECRATION : profanación *f*

violator [ˈvaɪəˌleɪtər] *n* : infractor *m*, -tora *f*

violence [ˈvaɪlənts, ˈvaɪə-] *n* : violencia *f*

violent [ˈvaɪlənt, ˈvaɪə-] *adj* : violento

violently [ˈvaɪləntli, ˈvaɪə-] *adv* : violentamente, con violencia

violet [ˈvaɪlət, ˈvaɪə-] *n* : violeta *f*

violin [ˌvaɪəˈlɪn] *n* : violín *m*

violinist [ˌvaɪəˈlɪnɪst] *n* : violinista *mf*

violoncello [ˌvaɪələnˈʧɛloː, ˌviː-] → **cello**

VIP [ˌviːˌaɪˈpiː] *n, pl* **VIPs** [-ˈpiːz] : VIP *mf*, persona *f* de categoría

viper [ˈvaɪpər] *n* : víbora *f*

viral [ˈvaɪrəl] *adj* : viral, vírico ⟨viral pneumonia : pulmonía viral⟩

virgin¹ [ˈvərʤən] *adj* **1** CHASTE : virginal ⟨the virgin birth : el alumbramiento virginal⟩ **2** : virgen, intacto ⟨a virgin forest : una selva virgen⟩ ⟨virgin wool : lana virgen⟩

virgin² *n* : virgen *mf*

virginal [ˈvərʤənəl] *adj* : virginal

virginity [vərˈʤɪnəti] *n* : virginidad *f*

Virgo [ˈvərˌgoː, ˈvɪr-] *n* **1** : Virgo *m* (signo o constelación) **2** : Virgo *mf* (persona)

virile [ˈvɪrəl, -ˌraɪl] *adj* : viril, varonil

virility [vəˈrɪləti] *n* : virilidad *f*

virtual [ˈvərʧuəl] *adj* : virtual ⟨a virtual dictator : un virtual dictador⟩ ⟨virtual reality : realidad virtual⟩

virtually [ˈvərʧuəli, ˈvərʧəli] *adv* : en realidad, de hecho, casi

virtue [ˈvərˌʧuː] *n* **1** : virtud *f* **2 by virtue of** : en virtud de, debido a

virtuosity [ˌvərʧuˈɑsəti] *n, pl* **-ties** : virtuosismo *m*

virtuoso [ˌvərʧuˈoːsoː, -zoː] *n, pl* **-sos** *or* **-si** [-ˌsiː, -ˌziː] : virtuoso *m*, -sa *f*

virtuous [ˈvərʧuəs] *adj* : virtuoso, bueno — **virtuously** *adv*

virulence [ˈvɪrələnts, ˈvɪrjə-] *n* : virulencia *f*

virulent [ˈvɪrələnt, ˈvɪrjə-] *adj* : virulento

virus [ˈvaɪrəs] *n* : virus *m*

visa [ˈviːzə, -sə] *n* : visa *f*

vis-à-vis [ˌviːzəˈviː, -sə-] *prep* : con relación a, con respecto a

viscera [ˈvɪsərə] *npl* : vísceras *fpl*

visceral [ˈvɪsərəl] *adj* : visceral

viscosity [vɪsˈkɑsəti] *n, pl* **-ties** : viscosidad *f*

viscous [ˈvɪskəs] *adj* : viscoso

vise [ˈvaɪs] *n* : torno *m* de banco, tornillo *m* de banco

visibility [ˌvɪzəˈbɪləti] *n, pl* **-ties** : visibilidad *f*

visible [ˈvɪzəbəl] *adj* **1** : visible ⟨the visible stars : las estrellas visibles⟩ **2** OBVIOUS : evidente, patente

visibly [ˈvɪzəbli] *adv* : visiblemente

vision [ˈvɪʒən] *n* **1** EYESIGHT : vista *f*, visión *f* **2** APPARITION : visión *f*, aparición *f* **3** FORESIGHT : visión *f* (del futuro), previsión *f* **4** IMAGE : imagen *f* ⟨she had visions of a disaster : se imaginaba un desastre⟩

visionary[1] [ˈvɪʒəˌnɛri] *adj* **1** FARSIGHTED : visionario, con visión de futuro **2** UTOPIAN : utópico, poco realista

visionary[2] *n, pl* **-ries** : visionario *m*, -ria *f*

visit[1] [ˈvɪzət] *vt* **1** : visitar, ir a ver **2** AFFLICT : azotar, afligir ⟨visited by troubles : afligido con problemas⟩ — *vi* : hacer (una) visita ⟨visiting hours : horas de visita⟩

visit[2] *n* : visita *f*

visitor [ˈvɪzətər] *n* : visitante *mf* (a una ciudad, etc.), visita *f* (a una casa)

visor [ˈvaɪzər] *n* : visera *f*

vista [ˈvɪstə] *n* : vista *f*

visual [ˈvɪʒuəl] *adj* : visual ⟨the visual arts : las artes visuales⟩ — **visually** *adv*

visualize [ˈvɪʒuəˌlaɪz] *vt* **-ized; -izing** : visualizar, imaginarse, hacerse una idea de — **visualization** [ˌvɪʒəwələˈzeɪʃən] *n*

vital [ˈvaɪt̬əl] *adj* **1** : vital ⟨vital organs : órganos vitales⟩ **2** CRUCIAL : esencial, crucial, decisivo ⟨of vital importance : de suma importancia⟩ **3** LIVELY : enérgico, lleno de vida, vital

vitality [vaɪˈtæləti] *n, pl* **-ties** : vitalidad *f*, energía *f*

vitally [ˈvaɪt̬əli] *adv* : sumamente

vital statistics *npl* : estadísticas *fpl* demográficas

vitamin [ˈvaɪt̬əmən] *n* : vitamina *f* ⟨vitamin deficiency : carencia vitamínica⟩

vitriol [ˈvɪtriəl] *n* : vitriolo *m*

vitriolic [ˌvɪtriˈɑlɪk] *adj* : mordaz, virulento

vivacious [vəˈveɪʃəs, vaɪ-] *adj* : vivaz, animado, lleno de vida

vivaciously [vəˈveɪʃəsli, vaɪ-] *adv* : con vivacidad, animadamente

vivacity [vəˈvæsət̬i, vaɪ-] *n* : vivacidad *f*

vivid [ˈvɪvəd] *adj* **1** LIVELY : lleno de vitalidad **2** BRILLIANT : vivo, intenso ⟨vivid colors : colores vivos⟩ **3** INTENSE, SHARP : vívido, gráfico ⟨a vivid dream : un sueño vívido⟩

vividly [ˈvɪvədli] *adv* **1** BRIGHTLY : con colores vivos **2** SHARPLY : vívidamente

vividness [ˈvɪvədnəs] *n* **1** BRIGHTNESS : intensidad *f*, viveza *f* **2** SHARPNESS : lo gráfico, nitidez *f*

vivisection [ˌvɪvəˈsɛkʃən, ˈvɪvə-] *n* : vivisección *f*

vixen [ˈvɪksən] *n* : zorra *f*, raposa *f*

V-neck [ˈviːˌnɛk] *n* **1** : escote *m* en V, cuello *m* en V **2** : camisa *f* (etc.) con escote/cuello en V

vocabulary [voˈkæbjəˌleri] *n, pl* **-laries 1** : vocabulario *m* **2** LEXICON : léxico *m*

vocal [ˈvoːkəl] *adj* **1** : vocal **2** LOUD, OUTSPOKEN : ruidoso, muy franco

vocal cords *npl* : cuerdas *fpl* vocales

vocalist [ˈvoːkəlɪst] *n* : cantante *mf*, vocalista *mf*

vocalize [ˈvoːkəˌlaɪz] *vt* **-ized; -izing** : vocalizar

vocation [voˈkeɪʃən] *n* : vocación *f* ⟨to have a vocation for : tener vocación de⟩

vocational [voˈkeɪʃənəl] *adj* : profesional ⟨vocational guidance : orientación profesional⟩

vociferous [voˈsɪfərəs] *adj* : ruidoso, vociferante

vodka [ˈvɑdkə] *n* : vodka *m*

vogue [ˈvoːg] *n* : moda *f*, boga *f* ⟨to be in vogue : estar de moda, estar en boga⟩

voice[1] [ˈvɔɪs] *vt* **voiced; voicing** : expresar

voice[2] *n* **1** : voz *f* ⟨in a low voice : en voz baja⟩ ⟨a high/deep voice : una voz aguda/profunda⟩ ⟨to raise/lower one's voice : hablar más alto/bajo⟩ ⟨to lose one's voice : quedarse sin voz⟩ ⟨his voice is changing : le está cambiando la voz⟩ ⟨to have a good (singing) voice : tener una buena voz, cantar bien⟩ **2** WISH, OPINION : voz *f* ⟨the voice of the people : la voz del pueblo⟩ **3** SAY, INFLUENCE : voz *f* ⟨to have no voice : no tener voz, no tener ni voz ni voto⟩ **4** : voz *f* (en gramática) **5 to make one's voice heard** : hacerse oír

voice box → larynx

voiced [ˈvɔɪst] *adj* : sonoro

voice mail *n* : correo *m* de voz, buzón *m* de voz

void[1] [ˈvɔɪd] *vt* : anular, invalidar ⟨to void a contract : anular un contrato⟩

void[2] *adj* **1** EMPTY : vacío, desprovisto ⟨void of content : desprovisto de contenido⟩ **2** INVALID : inválido, nulo

void[3] *n* : vacío *m*

volatile [ˈvɑlət̬əl] *adj* : volátil, inestable

volatility [ˌvɑləˈtɪlət̬i] *n* : volatilidad *f*, inestabilidad *f*

volcanic [vɑlˈkænɪk] *adj* : volcánico

volcano [vɑlˈkeɪˌnoː] *n, pl* **-noes** *or* **-nos** : volcán *m*

vole [ˈvoːl] *n* : campañol *m*

volition [voˈlɪʃən] *n* : volición *f*, voluntad *f* ⟨of one's own volition : por voluntad propia⟩

volley [ˈvɑli] *n, pl* **-leys 1** : descarga *f* (de tiros) **2** : torrente *m*, lluvia *f* (de insultos, etc.) **3** : salva *f* (de aplausos) **4** : volea *f* (en deportes)

volleyball [ˈvɑliˌbɔl] *n* : voleibol *m*; volibol *m* Car, Hond, Mex

volt [ˈvoːlt] *n* : voltio *m*

voltage [ˈvoːltɪdʒ] *n* : voltaje *m*

voluble [ˈvɑljəbəl] *adj* : locuaz

volume [ˈvɑljəm, -ˌjuːm] *n* **1** BOOK : volumen *m*, tomo *m* **2** SPACE : capacidad *f*, volumen *m* (en física) **3** AMOUNT : cantidad *f*, volumen *m* **4** LOUDNESS : volumen *m*

voluminous [vəˈluːmənəs] *adj* : voluminoso

voluntary [ˈvɑlənˌteri] *adj* : voluntario — **voluntarily** [ˌvɑlənˈterəli] *adv*

volunteer[1] [ˌvɑlənˈtɪr] *vt* : ofrecer, dar ⟨to volunteer one's assistance : ofrecer la ayuda⟩ — *vi* : ofrecerse, alistarse como voluntario

volunteer[2] *n* : voluntario *m*, -ria *f*

voluptuous [vəˈlʌptʃuəs] *adj* : voluptuoso

voluptuousness [vəˈlʌptʃuəsnəs] *n* : voluptuosidad *f*

vomit[1] [ˈvɑmət] *v* : vomitar

vomit[2] *n* : vómito *m*

voodoo [ˈvuːˌduː] *n, pl* **voodoos** : vudú *m*

voracious [vɔˈreɪʃəs, və-] *adj* : voraz

voraciously [vɔˈreɪʃəsli, və-] *adv* : vorazmente, con voracidad

voracity [vɔˈræsəti, və-] *n* : voracidad *f*

vortex [ˈvɔrˌtɛks] *n, pl* **vortices** [ˈvɔrtəˌsiːz] : vórtice *m*

vote[1] [ˈvoːt] *v* **voted; voting** *vi* **1** : votar ⟨to vote Democratic/Republican : votar por los demócratas/republicanos⟩ **2 to vote against** : votar en contra de **3 to vote for** : votar, votar a favor de (una propuesta, etc.), votar por (un candidato) **4 to vote on** : someter a votación, votar sobre — *vt* **1** : votar **2 to vote down** : rechazar **3 to vote in** : elegir **4 to vote out** : no reelegir

vote[2] *n* **1** : voto *m* **2 SUFFRAGE** : sufragio *m*, derecho *m* al voto

voter [ˈvoːtər] *n* : votante *mf*

voting [ˈvoːtɪŋ] *n* : votación *f*

vouch [ˈvaʊtʃ] *vi* **to vouch for** : garantizar (algo), responder de (algo), responder por (alguien)

voucher [ˈvaʊtʃər] *n* **1 RECEIPT** : comprobante *m* **2** : vale *m* ⟨travel voucher : vale de viajar⟩

vow[1] [ˈvaʊ] *vt* : jurar, prometer, hacer voto de

vow[2] *n* : promesa *f*, voto *m* (en la religión) ⟨a vow of poverty : un voto de pobreza⟩

vowel [ˈvaʊəl] *n* : vocal *m*

voyage[1] [ˈvɔɪdʒ] *vi* **-aged; -aging** : viajar

voyage[2] *n* : viaje *m*

voyager [ˈvɔɪdʒər] *n* : viajero *m*, -ra *f*

voyeur [vwaˈjər, vɔɪˈər] *n* : mirón *m*, -rona *f*

vulgar [ˈvʌlgər] *adj* **1 COMMON** : ordinario, populachero, del vulgo **2 COARSE, CRUDE** : grosero, de mal gusto, majadero *Mex* **3 INDECENT** : indecente, colorado (dícese de un chiste, etc.)

vulgarity [ˌvʌlˈgærəti] *n, pl* **-ties** : grosería *f*, vulgaridad *f*

vulgarly [ˈvʌlgərli] *adv* : vulgarmente, groseramente

vulnerability [ˌvʌlnərəˈbɪləti] *n, pl* **-ties** : vulnerabilidad *f*

vulnerable [ˈvʌlnərəbəl] *adj* : vulnerable

vulture [ˈvʌltʃər] *n* : buitre *m*; zopilote *m CA, Mex*

vying → **vie**

W

w [ˈdʌbəlˌjuː] *n, pl* **w's** *or* **ws** [-ˌjuːz] : vigésima tercera letra del alfabeto inglés

wad[1] [ˈwɑd] *vt* **wadded; wadding 1** : hacer un taco con, formar en una masa **2 STUFF** : rellenar

wad[2] *n* : taco *m* (de papel), bola *f* (de algodón, etc.), fajo *m* (de billetes)

waddle[1] [ˈwɑdəl] *vi* **-dled; -dling** : andar como un pato

waddle[2] *n* : andar *m* de pato

wade [ˈweɪd] *v* **waded; wading** *vi* **1** : caminar por el agua **2 to wade through** : leer (algo) con dificultad — *vt* *or* **to wade across** : vadear

wading bird *n* : zancuda *f*, ave *f* zancuda

wafer [ˈweɪfər] *n* : barquillo *m*, galleta *f* de barquillo

waffle[1] [ˈwɑfəl] *vi* **waffled; waffling VACILLATE** : vacilar

waffle[2] *n* **1** : wafle *m* **2 waffle iron** : waflera *f*

waft [ˈwɑft, ˈwæft] *vt* : llevar por el aire — *vi* : flotar

wag[1] [ˈwæg] *v* **wagged; wagging** *vt* : menear — *vi* : menearse, moverse

wag[2] *n* **1** : meneo *m* (de la cola) **2 JOKER, WIT** : bromista *mf*

wage[1] [ˈweɪdʒ] *vt* **waging** : hacer, librar ⟨to wage war : hacer la guerra⟩

wage[2] *n* *or* **wages** *npl* : sueldo *m*, salario *m* ⟨minimum wage : salario mínimo⟩

wage earner → **earner**

wager[1] [ˈweɪdʒər] *v* : apostar

wager[2] *n* : apuesta *f*

waggish [ˈwægɪʃ] *adj* : burlón, bromista (dícese de una persona), chistoso (dícese de un comentario)

waggle [ˈwægəl] *vt* **-gled; -gling** : menear, mover (de un lado a otro)

wagon [ˈwægən] *n* **1** : carro *m* (tirado por caballos) **2 CART** : carrito *m* **3** → **station wagon**

waif [ˈweɪf] *n* : niño *m* abandonado, animal *m* sin hogar

wail[1] [ˈweɪl] *vi* : gemir, lamentarse

wail[2] *n* : gemido *m*, lamento *m*

wainscot [ˈweɪnskət, -ˌskɑt, -ˌskoːt] *or* **wainscoting** [-skətɪŋ, -ˌskɑ-, -ˌskoː-] *n* : revestimiento *m* de paneles de madera

waist [ˈweɪst] *n* : cintura *f* (del cuerpo humano o de ropa), talle *m* (de ropa)

waistband [ˈweɪstˌbænd] *n* : cinturilla *f*

waistline [ˈweɪstˌlaɪn] → **waist**

wait[1] [ˈweɪt] *vi* **1** : esperar ⟨wait and see! : ¡espera y verás!⟩ ⟨I can't wait : me muero de ganas⟩ **2 to wait for** : esperar ⟨what are you waiting for? : ¿a qué esperas?⟩ **3 to wait on** : servir **4 to wait up (for someone)** : quedarse despierto esperando (a alguien) — *vt* **1 AWAIT** : esperar ⟨wait your turn : espera a que te toque⟩ ⟨wait a minute : espere un momento⟩ **2 SERVE** : servir, atender ⟨to wait tables : servir (a la mesa)⟩ **3 to wait out** : esperar hasta que pase

wait[2] *n* **1** : espera *f* **2 to lie in wait** : estar al acecho

waiter [ˈweɪtər] *n* : mesero *m*, camarero *m*, mozo *m Arg, Chile, Col, Peru*

waiting list *n* : lista *f* de espera

waiting room *n* : sala *f* de espera

waitress [ˈweɪtrəs] *n* : mesera *f*, camarera *f*, moza *f Arg, Chile, Col, Peru*

waive [ˈweɪv] *vt* **waived; waiving** : renunciar a ⟨to waive one's rights : renunciar a sus derechos⟩ ⟨to waive the rules : no aplicar las reglas⟩

waiver ['weɪvər] n : renuncia f

wake¹ ['weɪk] v **woke** ['woːk]; **woken** ['woːkən] or **waked**; **waking** vi or **to wake up** : despertar(se) ⟨he woke at noon : se despertó al mediodía⟩ ⟨wake up! : ¡despiértate!⟩ — vt : despertar

wake² n 1 VIGIL : velatorio m, velorio m (de un difunto) 2 TRAIL : estela f (de un barco, un huracán, etc.) 3 AFTERMATH : consecuencias fpl ⟨in the wake of : tras, como consecuencia de⟩

wakeful ['weɪkfəl] adj 1 SLEEPLESS : desvelado 2 VIGILANT : alerta, vigilante

wakefulness ['weɪkfəlnəs] n : vigilia f

waken ['weɪkən] → awake

walk¹ ['wɔk] vi 1 : caminar, andar, pasear ⟨you're walking too fast : estás caminando demasiado rápido⟩ ⟨to walk around the city : pasearse por la ciudad⟩ 2 : in andando, ir a pie ⟨we had to walk home : tuvimos que ir a casa a pie⟩ 3 : recibir una base por bolas (dícese de un bateador) 4 **to walk away** LEAVE : irse 5 **to walk away** : salir ileso (de un accidente, etc.) 6 **to walk away from** ABANDON : abandonar, retirarse de (negociaciones, etc.), rechazar (un acuerdo, etc.) 7 **to walk away with** : ganar fácilmente (un premio, etc.) 8 **to walk in** on INTERRUPT, SURPRISE : interrumpir, sorprender 9 **to walk off** LEAVE : irse 10 **to walk off with** : llevarse 11 **to walk out** LEAVE : irse 12 **to walk out** STRIKE : declararse en huelga 13 **to walk out** on : abandonar — vt 1 : recorrer, caminar ⟨she walked two miles : caminó dos millas⟩ 2 ACCOMPANY : acompañar 3 : sacar a pasear (a un perro) 4 : darle una base por bolas (a un bateador) 5 **to walk off** : caminar para aliviar (un calambre, etc.)

walk² n 1 : paseo m, caminata f ⟨to go for a walk : ir a caminar, dar un paseo⟩ 2 PATH : camino m 3 GAIT : andar m 4 : marcha f (en beisbol) 5 **walk of life** : esfera f, condición f

walker ['wɔkər] n 1 : paseante mf 2 HIKER : excursionista mf 3 : andador m (aparato)

walking n : (el) caminar, (el) andar ⟨walking is good exercise : (el) caminar es buen ejercicio⟩

walking stick n : bastón m

walkout ['wɔkˌaʊt] n STRIKE : huelga f

walk out vi 1 STRIKE : declararse en huelga 2 LEAVE : salir, irse 3 **to walk out on** : abandonar, dejar

walkway ['wɔkˌweɪ] n 1 SIDEWALK : acera f 2 PATH : sendero m 3 PASSAGEWAY : pasadizo m

wall¹ ['wɔl] vt 1 **to wall in** : cercar con una pared o un muro, tapiar, amurallar 2 **to wall off** : separar con una pared o un muro 3 **to wall up** : tapiar, condenar (una ventana, etc.)

wall² n 1 : pared f 2 : muro m, barda f Mex ⟨the walls of the city : las murallas de la ciudad⟩ 3 BARRIER : barrera f ⟨a

wall of mountains : una barrera de montañas⟩ 4 : pared f (en anatomía) 5 **to drive someone up the wall** fam : volver loco a alguien

walled ['wɔld] adj : amurallado

wallet ['wɑlət] n : billetera f, cartera f

wallflower ['wɔlˌflaʊər] n 1 : alhelí m (flor) 2 **to be a wallflower** : comer pavo

wallop¹ ['wɑləp] vt 1 TROUNCE : darle una paliza a (alguien) 2 SOCK : pegar fuerte

wallop² n : golpe m fuerte, golpazo m

wallow ['wɑˌloː] vi 1 : revolcarse ⟨to wallow in the mud : revolcarse en el lodo⟩ 2 DELIGHT : deleitarse ⟨to wallow in luxury : nadar en lujos⟩

wallpaper¹ ['wɔlˌpeɪpər] vt : empapelar

wallpaper² n : papel m pintado

wall-to-wall adj 1 FILLED : lleno ⟨it was wall-to-wall (with) people : estaba repleto de gente⟩ 2 **wall-to-wall carpeting** : alfombra f (de pared a pared); moquette f Arg, Uru; moqueta f Spain

walnut ['wɔlˌnʌt] n 1 : nuez f (fruta) 2 : nogal m (árbol y madera)

walrus ['wɔlrəs, 'wɑl-] n, pl **-rus** or **-ruses** : morsa f

waltz¹ ['wɔlts] vi 1 : bailar el vals 2 BREEZE : pasar con ligereza ⟨to waltz in : entrar tan campante⟩

waltz² n : vals m

wan ['wɑn] adj **wanner; wannest** 1 PALLID : pálido 2 DIM : tenue ⟨wan light : luz tenue⟩ 3 LANGUID : lánguido ⟨a wan smile : una sonrisa lánguida⟩ — **wanly** adv

wand ['wɑnd] n : varita f (mágica)

wander ['wɑndər] vi 1 RAMBLE : deambular, vagar, vagabundear 2 STRAY : alejarse, desviarse, divagar ⟨she let her mind wander : dejó vagar la imaginación⟩ — vt : recorrer ⟨to wander the streets : vagar por las calles⟩

wanderer ['wɑndərər] n : vagabundo m, -da f; viajero m, -ra f

wanderlust ['wɑndərˌlʌst] n : pasión f por viajar

wane¹ ['weɪn] vi **waned; waning** 1 : menguar (dícese de la luna) 2 DECLINE : disminuir, decaer, menguar

wane² n **on the wane** : decayendo, en decadencia

wangle ['wæŋgəl] vt **-gled; -gling** FINAGLE : arreglárselas para conseguir

wannabe ['wɑnəˌbiː] n : aspirante mf (a algo); imitador m, -dora f (de alguien)

want¹ ['wɑnt, 'wɔnt] vt 1 LACK : faltar 2 REQUIRE : requerir, necesitar 3 DESIRE : querer, desear

want² n 1 LACK : falta f 2 DESTITUTION : indigencia f, miseria f 3 DESIRE, NEED : deseo m, necesidad f

wanting ['wɑntɪŋ, 'wɔn-] adj 1 ABSENT : ausente 2 DEFICIENT : deficiente ⟨he's wanting in common sense : le falta sentido común⟩

wanton ['wɑntən, 'wɔn-] adj 1 LEWD, LUSTFUL : lascivo, lujurioso, licencioso 2 INHUMANE, MERCILESS : despiadado ⟨wanton cruelty : crueldad despiadada⟩

wapiti [ˈwɑpəṭi] *n*, *pl* **-ti** *or* **-tis** ELK : uapití *m*, wapití *m*

war¹ [ˈwɔr] *adj* **warred; warring** : combatir, batallar, hacer la guerra

war² *n* : guerra *f* ⟨to go to war : entrar en guerra⟩ ⟨to be at war : estar en guerra⟩

warble¹ [ˈwɔrbəl] *vi* **-bled; -bling** : gorjear, trinar

warble² *n* : trino *m*, gorjeo *m*

warbler [ˈwɔrblər] *n* : curruca *f*

ward¹ [ˈwɔrd] *vt* **to ward off** : desviar, protegerse contra

ward² *n* **1** : sala *f* (de un hospital, etc.) ⟨maternity ward : sala de maternidad⟩ **2** : distrito *m* electoral o administrativo (de una ciudad) **3** : pupilo *m*, -la *f* (de un tutor, etc.)

warden [ˈwɔrdən] *n* **1** KEEPER : guarda *mf*; guardián *m*, -diana *f* ⟨game warden : guardabosque⟩ **2** *or* **prison warden** : alcaide *m*

wardrobe [ˈwɔrdˌroːb] *n* **1** CLOSET : armario *m* **2** CLOTHES : vestuario *m*, guardarropa *f*

ware [ˈwær] *n* **1** POTTERY : cerámica *f* **2** **wares** *npl* GOODS : mercancía *f*, mercadería *f*

warehouse [ˈwærˌhaʊs] *n* : depósito *m*, almacén *m*, bodega *f* *Chile, Col, Mex*

warfare [ˈwɔrˌfær] *n* **1** WAR : guerra *f* **2** STRUGGLE : lucha *f* ⟨the warfare against drugs : la lucha contra las drogas⟩

warhead [ˈwɔrˌhɛd] *n* : ojiva *f*, cabeza *f* (de un misil)

warily [ˈwærəli] *adv* : cautelosamente, con cautela

wariness [ˈwærinəs] *n* : cautela *f*

warlike [ˈwɔrˌlaɪk] *adj* : belicoso, guerrero

warm¹ [ˈwɔrm] *vt* **1** HEAT : calentar, recalentar **2 to warm one's heart** : reconfortar a uno, alegrar el corazón **3 to warm up** : calentar (los músculos, un automóvil, etc.) — *vi* **1** : calentarse **2 to warm to** : tomarle simpatía (a alguien), entusiasmarse con (algo)

warm² *adj* **1** LUKEWARM : tibio, templado **2** : caliente, cálido, caluroso ⟨a warm wind : un viento cálido⟩ ⟨a warm day : un día caluroso, un día de calor⟩ ⟨warm hands : manos calientes⟩ **3** : caliente, que abriga ⟨warm clothes : ropa de abrigo⟩ ⟨I feel warm : tengo calor⟩ **4** CARING, CORDIAL : cariñoso, cordial **5** : cálido (dícese de colores) **6** FRESH : fresco, reciente ⟨a warm trail : un rastro reciente⟩ **7** *(used for riddles)* : caliente

warm–blooded [ˈwɔrmˈblʌdəd] *adj* : de sangre caliente

warmhearted [ˈwɔrmˈhɑrṭəd] *adj* : cariñoso

warmly [ˈwɔrmli] *adv* **1** AFFECTIONATELY : calurosamente, afectuosamente **2 to dress warmly** : abrigarse

warmonger [ˈwɔrˌmɑŋgər, -ˌmʌŋ-] *n* : belicista *mf*

warmth [ˈwɔrmpθ] *n* **1** : calor *m* **2** AFFECTION : cariño *m*, afecto *m* **3** ENTHUSIASM : ardor *m*, entusiasmo *m*

warm–up [ˈwɔrmˌʌp] *n* : calentamiento *m*

warn [ˈwɔrn] *vt* **1** CAUTION : advertir, alertar **2** INFORM : avisar, informar

warning [ˈwɔrnɪŋ] *n* **1** ADVICE : advertencia *f*, aviso *m* **2** ALERT : alerta *f*, alarma *f*

warp¹ [ˈwɔrp] *vt* **1** : alabear, combar **2** PERVERT : pervertir, deformar — *vi* : pandearse, alabearse, combarse

warp² *n* **1** : urdimbre *f* ⟨the warp and the weft : la urdimbre y la trama⟩ **2** : alabeo *m* (en la madera, etc.)

warrant¹ [ˈwɔrənt] *vt* **1** ASSURE : asegurar, garantizar **2** GUARANTEE : garantizar **3** JUSTIFY, MERIT : justificar, merecer

warrant² *n* **1** AUTHORIZATION : autorización *f*, permiso *m* ⟨an arrest warrant : una orden de detención⟩ **2** JUSTIFICATION : justificación *f*

warranty [ˈwɔrənti, ˌwɔrənˈtiː] *n*, *pl* **-ties** : garantía *f*

warren [ˈwɔrən] *n* : madriguera *f* (de conejos)

warrior [ˈwɔriər] *n* : guerrero *m*, -ra *f*

warship [ˈwɔrˌʃɪp] *n* : buque *m* de guerra

wart [ˈwɔrt] *n* : verruga *f*

wartime [ˈwɔrˌtaɪm] *n* : tiempo *m* de guerra

wary [ˈwæri] *adj* **warier; -est** : cauteloso, receloso ⟨to be wary of : desconfiar de⟩

was → **be**

wash¹ [ˈwɑʃ, ˈwɔʃ] *vt* **1** CLEAN : lavar(se), limpiar, fregar ⟨to wash the dishes : lavar los platos⟩ ⟨to wash one's hands : lavarse las manos⟩ **2** DRENCH : mojar **3** LAP : bañar ⟨waves were washing the shore : las olas bañaban la orilla⟩ **4** CARRY, DRAG : arrastrar ⟨they were washed out to sea : fueron arrastrados por el mar⟩ **5 to be/get washed out** : cancelarse por lluvia **6 to wash away** : llevarse (un puente, etc.) **7 to wash down** : lavar (paredes, etc.) **8 to wash down** : tragarse (con agua, etc.) **9 to wash off** : lavar **10 to wash off** : quitar (la suciedad, etc.) **11 to wash out** : lavar (un recipiente, etc.) **12 to wash out** : destruir, inundar (una carretera, etc.) **13 to wash out** : quitar (una mancha, etc.) — *vi* **1** : lavar(se) ⟨I'll wash, you dry : yo lavo y tú secas⟩ ⟨wash before dinner : lávate antes de cenar⟩ ⟨the dress washes well : el vestido se lava bien⟩ **2 to wash over** : bañar ⟨relief washed over me : sentí un gran alivio⟩ **3 to wash off/out** : quitarse **4 to wash up** BATHE : lavarse **5 to wash up/ashore** : ser arrojado por el mar

wash² *n* **1** : lavado *m* ⟨to give something a wash : lavar algo⟩ **2** LAUNDRY : artículos *mpl* para lavar, ropa *f* sucia **3** : estela *f* (de un barco)

washable [ˈwɑʃəbəl, ˈwɔ-] *adj* : lavable

washboard [ˈwɑʃˌbord, ˈwɔʃ-] *n* : tabla *f* de lavar

washbowl [ˈwɑʃˌboːl, ˈwɔʃ-] *n* : lavabo *m*, lavamanos *m*

washcloth [ˈwɑʃˌklɔθ, ˈwɔʃ-] *n* : toallita *f* (para lavarse)

washed–out [ˈwɑʃtˈaʊt, ˈwɔʃt-] *adj* **1** : desvaído (dícese de colores) **2** EXHAUSTED : agotado, desanimado

washed–up [ˈwɔʃtˈʌp, ˈwaʃt-] *adj* : acabado (dícese de una persona), fracasado (dícese de un negocio, etc.)

washer [ˈwɔʃər, ˈwɑ-] *n* **1** → **washing machine 2** : arandela *f* (de una llave, etc.)

washing [ˈwɔʃɪŋ, ˈwɑ-] *n* WASH : ropa *f* para lavar

washing machine *n* : máquina *f* de lavar, lavadora *f*

washout [ˈwɔʃˌaʊt, ˈwaʃ-] *n* **1** : erosión *f* (de la tierra) **2** FAILURE : fracaso *m* ⟨she's a washout : es un desastre⟩

washroom [ˈwɔʃˌruːm, ˈwaʃ-, -ˌrʊm] *n* : servicios *mpl* (públicos); baño *m*; sanitario *m* Col, Mex, Ven

wasn't [ˈwazənt] *contraction of* was not → be

wasp [ˈwasp] *n* : avispa *f*

waspish [ˈwaspɪʃ] *adj* **1** IRRITABLE : irritable, irascible **2** CAUSTIC : cáustico, mordaz

waste¹ [ˈweɪst] *v* **wasted; wasting** *vt* **1** DEVASTATE : arrasar, arruinar, devastar **2** SQUANDER : desperdiciar, despilfarrar, malgastar ⟨to waste time : perder tiempo⟩ — *vi or* **to waste away** : consumirse, chuparse

waste² *adj* **1** BARREN : yermo, baldío **2** DISCARDED : de desecho **3** EXCESS : sobrante

waste³ *n* **1** → **wasteland 2** MISUSE : derroche *m*, desperdicio *m*, despilfarro *m* ⟨a waste of time : una pérdida de tiempo⟩ **3** RUBBISH : basura *f*, desechos *mpl*, desperdicios *mpl* **4** EXCREMENT : excremento *m*

wastebasket [ˈweɪstˌbæskət] *or* **wastepaper basket** *n* : cesto *m* (de basura), papelera *f*, zafacón *m* Car

wasteful [ˈweɪstfəl] *adj* : despilfarrador, derrochador, pródigo

wastefulness [ˈweɪstfələs] *n* : derroche *m*, despilfarro *m*

wasteland [ˈweɪstˌlænd, -lənd] *n* : baldío *m*, yermo *m*, desierto *m*

wastepaper [ˈweɪstˌpeɪpər] *n* : papel *m* de desecho

wastepaper basket → **wastebasket**

watch¹ [ˈwatʃ] *vt* **1** OBSERVE : mirar, observar ⟨to watch television : mirar/ver la televisión⟩ ⟨watch this! : ¡mira!⟩ **2** MONITOR : vigilar **3** *or* **to watch over** : vigilar, cuidar (a niños, etc.) ⟨would you watch my things? : ¿me puedes cuidar/vigilar las cosas?⟩ **4** : tener cuidado de, vigilar ⟨watch what you do : ten cuidado con lo que haces⟩ ⟨I have to watch my cholesterol : tengo que vigilar el colesterol⟩ — *vi* **1** OBSERVE : mirar, ver, observar **2** **to watch for** AWAIT : esperar, quedar a la espera de **3** **to watch out** : tener cuidado ⟨watch out! : ¡ten cuidado!, ¡ojo!⟩

watch² *n* **1** : guardia *f* ⟨to be on watch, to stand watch : estar de guardia⟩ **2** SURVEILLANCE : vigilancia *f* **3** LOOKOUT : guardia *mf*, centinela *f*, vigía *mf* **4** TIMEPIECE : reloj *m* **5** **to keep watch on/over** : vigilar, cuidar

watchdog [ˈwatʃˌdɔg] *n* : perro *m* guardián

watcher [ˈwatʃər] *n* : observador *m*, -dora *f*

watchful [ˈwatʃfəl] *adj* : alerta, vigilante, atento

watchfulness [ˈwatʃfələs] *n* : vigilancia *f*

watchmaker [ˈwatʃˌmeɪkər] *n* : relojero *m*, -ra *f*

watchmaking [ˈwatʃˌmeɪkɪŋ] *n* : relojería *f* (actividad)

watchman [ˈwatʃmən] *n, pl* **-men** [-mən, -ˌmɛn] : vigilante *m*, guarda *m*

watchtower [ˈwatʃˌtaʊər] *n* : atalaya *f*

watchword [ˈwatʃˌwərd] *n* **1** PASSWORD : contraseña *f* **2** SLOGAN : lema *m*, eslogan *m*

water¹ [ˈwɔtər, ˈwɑ-] *vt* **1** : regar (el jardín, etc.) **2** **to water down** DILUTE : diluir, aguar — *vi* : lagrimear (dícese de los ojos), hacérsele agua la boca a uno ⟨my mouth is watering : se me hace agua la boca⟩

water² *n* **1** : agua *f* ⟨drinking water : agua potable⟩ ⟨running water : agua corriente⟩ **2 waters** *npl* : aguas *fpl* **3** **not to hold water** : hacer agua por todos lados **4** **to pass water** : orinar

water buffalo *n* : búfalo *m* de agua

watercolor [ˈwɔtərˌkʌlər, ˈwɑ-] *n* : acuarela *f*

watercourse [ˈwɔtərˌkɔrs, ˈwɑ-] *n* : curso *m* de agua

watercress [ˈwɔtərˌkrɛs, ˈwɑ-] *n* : berro *m*

waterfall [ˈwɔtərˌfɔl, ˈwɑ-] *n* : cascada *f*, salto *m* de agua, catarata *f*

waterfowl [ˈwɔtərˌfaʊl, ˈwɑ-] *n* : ave *f* acuática

waterfront [ˈwɔtərˌfrʌnt, ˈwɑ-] *n* **1** : tierra *f* que bordea un río, un lago, o un mar **2** WHARF : muelle *m*

water heater *n* : calentador *m* de agua, bóiler *m* Mex

watering can *n* : regadera *f*

water lily *n* : nenúfar *m*

waterlogged [ˈwɔtərˌlɔgd, ˈwɔtərˌlɑgd] *adj* : lleno de agua, empapado, inundado (dícese del suelo)

watermark [ˈwɔtərˌmɑrk, ˈwɑ-] *n* **1** : marca *f* del nivel de agua **2** : filigrana *f* (en el papel)

watermelon [ˈwɔtərˌmɛlən, ˈwɑ-] *n* : sandía *f*

water moccasin → **moccasin**

waterpower [ˈwɔtərˌpaʊər, ˈwɑ-] *n* : energía *f* hidráulica

waterproof¹ [ˈwɔtərˌpruːf, ˈwɑ-] *vt* : hacer impermeable, impermeabilizar

waterproof² *adj* : impermeable, a prueba de agua

waterproofing *n* : impermeabilizante *nm* (sustancia química)

water repellent *n* : impermeabilizante *nm*

water–resistant *or* **water–repellent** *adj* : hidrófugo, impermeabilizado

watershed [ˈwɔtərˌʃed, ˈwɑ-] *n* **1** : línea *f* divisoria de aguas **2** BASIN : cuenca *f* (de un río)

waterskiing [ˈwɔtərˌskiːɪŋ, ˈwɑ-] *n* : esquí *m* acuático

waterspout [ˈwɔtərˌspaʊt, ˈwɑ-] *n* WHIRLWIND : tromba *f* marina

watertight ['wɔtər,taɪt, 'wɑ-] *adj* **1**
: hermético **2** IRREFUTABLE : irrebatible, irrefutable ⟨a watertight contract
: un contrato sin lagunas⟩
waterwheel ['wɔtər,ʰwiːl, 'wɑ-] *n* : noria *f*
waterway ['wɔtər,weɪ, 'wɑ-] *n* : vía *f* navegable
waterworks ['wɔtər,wərks, 'wɑ-] *npl*
: central *f* de abastecimiento de agua
watery ['wɔtəri, 'wɑ-] *adj* **1** : acuoso,
como agua **2** : aguado, diluido ⟨watery
soup : sopa aguada⟩ **3** : lloroso ⟨watery
eyes : ojos llorosos⟩ **4** WASHED-OUT
: desvaído ⟨dícese de colores⟩
watt ['wɑt] *n* : vatio *m*
wattage ['wɑtɪdʒ] *n* : vataje *m*
wave¹ ['weɪv] *v* **waved; waving** *vi* **1** : saludar con la mano, hacer señas con la
mano ⟨she waved at him : lo saludó con
la mano⟩ **2** FLUTTER, SHAKE : ondear,
agitarse **3** UNDULATE : ondular — *vt* **1**
SHAKE : agitar **2** BRANDISH : blandir **3**
CURL : ondular, marcar (el pelo) **4** SIG-
NAL : hacerle señas a (con la mano) ⟨he
waved farewell : se despidió con la
mano⟩
wave² *n* **1** : ola *f* (de agua) **2** CURL : onda
f (en el pelo) **3** : onda *f* (en física) **4**
SURGE : oleada *f* ⟨a wave of enthusiasm
: una oleada de entusiasmo⟩ **5** GESTURE
: señal *f* con la mano, saludo *m* con la
mano
wavelength ['weɪv,lɛŋkθ] *n* : longitud *f* de
onda
waver ['weɪvər] *vi* **1** VACILLATE : vacilar,
fluctuar **2** FLICKER : parpadear, titilar,
oscilar **3** FALTER : flaquear, tambalearse
wavy ['weɪvi] *adj* **wavier; -est** : ondulado
wax¹ ['wæks] *vi* **1** : crecer (dícese de la
luna) **2** BECOME : volverse, ponerse ⟨to
wax indignant : indignarse⟩ — *vt* : encerar
wax² *n* **1** BEESWAX : cera *f* de abejas **2**
: cera *f* ⟨floor wax : cera para el piso⟩ **3**
or **earwax** ['ɪr,wæks] : cerilla *f*, cerumen
m
waxen ['wæksən] *adj* : de cera
waxy ['wæksi] *adj* **waxier; -est** : ceroso
way ['weɪ] *n* **1** PATH, ROAD : camino *m*,
vía *f* ⟨they live across the way : viven en-
frente⟩ **2** ROUTE : camino *m*, ruta *f* ⟨to
go the wrong way : equivocarse de ca-
mino⟩ ⟨to lose one's way : perderse⟩ ⟨do
you know the way? : ¿sabes el camino?⟩
⟨can you tell me the way to . . .? : ¿me
puedes indicar cómo llegar a . . .?⟩ ⟨I'm
on my way : estoy de camino⟩ ⟨we
should be on our way : tenemos que
irnos⟩ ⟨on the way back : en el camino
de regreso/vuelta⟩ ⟨the only way in/out
: la única entrada/salida⟩ **3** : línea *f* de
conducta, camino *m* ⟨he chose the easy
way : optó por el camino fácil⟩ **4** MAN-
NER, MEANS : manera *f*, modo *m*, forma
f ⟨in the same way : del mismo modo,
igualmente⟩ ⟨in no way : de ninguna ma-
nera⟩ ⟨to my way of thinking : a mi
modo de ver⟩ ⟨the way she spends
money, you would think she was rich!
: gasta dinero como si fuera rica⟩ ⟨their

way of life : su modo de vida⟩ **5** (*indicating a wish*) ⟨have it your way : como tú
quieras⟩ ⟨to get one's own way : salirse
uno con la suya⟩ **6** (*indicating progress*)
⟨we inched on our way forward : avanza-
mos poco a poco⟩ ⟨to talk one's way out
of something : librarse de algo (en-
gatusándole a alguien)⟩ **7** (*indicating a
condition or situation*) ⟨he's in a bad
way : está muy mal de salud⟩ ⟨that's just
the way things are : así son las cosas⟩ **8**
(*indicating one of two alternatives*) ⟨ei-
ther way : de cualquier manera⟩ ⟨you
can't have it both ways : tienes que ele-
gir⟩ **9** (*indicating a portion*) ⟨we split it
three ways : lo dividimos en tres⟩ **10**
RESPECT : aspecto *m*, sentido *m* ⟨in a
way, it was a relief : en cierto modo fue
un alivio⟩ ⟨in every way : en todo⟩ **11**
CUSTOM : costumbre *f* ⟨to change/mend
one's ways : dejar las malas costumbres,
enmendarse⟩ ⟨to be set in one's ways
: ser inflexible⟩ **12** PASSAGE : camino *m*
⟨to be/get in the way : estar/meterse en
el camino⟩ ⟨get it out of the way!
: ¡quítalo de en medio!⟩ ⟨to make way
for, to clear the way for : abrirle paso a⟩
13 DISTANCE : distancia *f* ⟨to come a
long way : hacer grandes progresos⟩ ⟨he
talked the whole way home : habló durante todo el camino a casa⟩ ⟨she ran all
the way there : corrió hasta allí⟩ ⟨it
stretches all the way along the beach : se
extiende a lo largo de la playa⟩ ⟨we went
all the way up : subimos hasta arriba⟩
⟨we sat all the way at the back : nos sen-
tamos al fondo⟩ ⟨you came all this way
just to see me? : ¿viniste desde tan lejos
sólo para verme?⟩ **14** DIRECTION : dirección *f* ⟨come this way : venga por
aquí⟩ ⟨this way and that : de un lado a
otro⟩ ⟨which way did he go? : ¿por
dónde fue?⟩ **15** **all the way** COM-
PLETELY : completamente **16** **all the
way** CONTINUOUSLY : en todo momento
⟨he was with us all the way : nos apoyó
en todo momento⟩ ⟨all the way through
the concert : durante todo el concierto⟩
17 **by the way** : a propósito, por cierto
18 **by way of** VIA : vía, pasando por **19**
by way of *or* **in the way of** : a modo
de, a manera de **20** **every step of the
way** : en todo momento **21** **no way** : de
ninguna manera, ni hablar **22** **out of the
way** REMOTE : remoto, recóndito **23** **out
of the way** FINISHED : acabado ⟨to get a
task out of the way : quitar una tarea de
en medio⟩ **24** **the other way (around)**
: al revés **25** **there are no two ways
about it** : no cabe la menor duda **26** **to
give way** COLLAPSE : romperse, hundirse, ceder **27** **to give way to** : ceder a
28 **to go out of one's way (to)** : tomarse
muchas molestias (para), desvivirse
(por) **29** **to go someone's way** : salirle
bien a alguien **30** **to have a way of** : soler, tender a ⟨things have a way of working out : las cosas suelen arreglarse so-
las⟩ ⟨she has a way of exaggerating
: tiende a exagerar las cosas⟩ **31** **to have**

a way with : saber como tratar a (los niños, los animales, etc.) ⟨to have a way with words : tener facilidad de palabra⟩ **32** → **under way** **33 way to go!** *fam* : ¡bien hecho!

wayfarer ['weɪˌfærər] *n* : caminante *mf*

waylay ['weɪˌleɪ] *vt* **-laid** [-ˌleɪd]; **-laying** ACCOST : abordar

wayside ['weɪˌsaɪd] *n* : borde *m* del camino

wayward ['weɪwərd] *adj* **1** UNRULY : díscolo, rebelde **2** UNTOWARD : adverso

we ['wiː] *pron* : nosotros, nosotras

weak ['wiːk] *adj* **1** : débil ⟨weak arms/ eyes : brazos/ojos débiles⟩ ⟨a weak leader/character : un líder/carácter débil⟩ ⟨a weak drug/signal/economy : una droga/señal/economía débil⟩ **2** GENTLE : flojo (dícese de un golpe), leve (dícese de un viento) **3** : flojo (dícese de un estudiante, etc.) **4** : flojo (dícese de una pieza, etc.) **5** : débil, flojo, endeble (dícese de un argumento, una excusa, etc.) ⟨a weak attempt : un intento tímido⟩ **6** DILUTED : aguado, diluido ⟨weak tea : té poco cargado⟩ **7** FAINT : tenue (dícese de los colores, las luces, los sonidos, etc.) **8** : poco pronunciado (dícese de la barbilla) **9** : regular (en gramática)

weaken ['wiːkən] *vt* : debilitar — *vi* : debilitarse, flaquear

weakling ['wiːklɪŋ] *n* : alfeñique *m fam*; debilucho *m*, -cha *f*

weakly[1] ['wiːkli] *adv* : débilmente

weakly[2] *adj* **weaklier; -est** : débil, enclenque

weakness ['wiːknəs] *n* **1** FEEBLENESS : debilidad *f* **2** FAULT, FLAW : flaqueza *f*, punto *m* débil

wealth ['welθ] *n* **1** RICHES : riqueza *f* **2** PROFUSION : abundancia *f*, profusión *f*

wealthy ['welθi] *adj* **wealthier; -est** : rico, acaudalado, adinerado

wean ['wiːn] *vt* **1** : destetar (a los niños o las crías) **2 to wean someone away from** : quitarle a alguien la costumbre de

weapon ['wepən] *n* : arma *f* ⟨biological/ chemical weapon : arma biológica/química⟩ ⟨weapon of mass destruction : arma de destrucción masiva⟩

weaponless ['wepənləs] *adj* : desarmado

weaponry ['wepənri] *n* : armamento *m*

wear[1] ['wær] *v* **wore** ['wor]; **worn** ['worn]; **wearing** *vt* **1** : llevar (ropa, un reloj, etc.), calzar (zapatos) ⟨to wear a smile : sonreír⟩ **2** *or* **to wear away** : gastar, desgastar, erosionar (rocas, etc.) ⟨the carpet was badly worn : la alfombra estaba muy gastada⟩ **3** : hacer (por el uso) ⟨he wore a hole in his pants : se le hizo un agujero en los pantalones⟩ **4** **to wear down** DRAIN : agotar **5 to wear down** : convencer por cansancio **6 to wear on** IRRITATE : molestar, irritar **7 to wear one's heart on one's sleeve** : no ocultar uno sus sentimientos **8 to wear out** : gastar ⟨he wore out his shoes : gastó sus zapatos⟩ **9 to wear out** EX-

HAUST : agotar, fatigar ⟨to wear oneself out : agotarse⟩ **10 to wear through** : gastar (completamente) ⟨he wore through his shoes : se le hizo agujeros en los zapatos⟩ — *vi* **1** LAST : durar **2** **to wear on** : avanzar

wear away : desgastarse **3 to wear off** DIMINISH, VANISH : disminuir, desaparecer ⟨the drug wears off in a few hours : los efectos de la droga desaparecen después de unas horas⟩ **4 to wear on** CONTINUE, DRAG : continuar, alargarse **5 to wear out** : gastarse **6 to wear the pants** : llevar los pantalones **7 to wear thin** : gastarse (dícese de tela, etc.) **8 to wear thin** : agotarse (dícese de la paciencia, etc.), perder la gracia (dícese de un chiste)

wear[2] *n* **1** USE : uso *m* ⟨for everyday wear : para todos los días⟩ **2** CLOTHING : ropa *f* ⟨children's wear : ropa de niños⟩ **3** DETERIORATION : desgaste *m* ⟨to be the worse for wear : estar deteriorado⟩

wearable ['wærəbəl] *adj* : que puede ponerse (dícese de una prenda)

wear and tear *n* : desgaste *m*

weariness ['wɪrinəs] *n* : fatiga *f*, cansancio *m*

wearisome ['wɪrisəm] *adj* : aburrido, pesado, cansado

weary[1] ['wɪri] *v* **-ried; -rying** *vt* **1** TIRE : cansar, fatigar **2** BORE : hastiar, aburrir — *vi* : cansarse

weary[2] *adj* **wearier; -est** **1** TIRED : cansado **2** FED UP : harto **3** BORED : aburrido

weasel ['wiːzəl] *n* : comadreja *f*

weather[1] ['weðər] *vt* **1** WEAR : erosionar, desgastar **2** ENDURE : aguantar, sobrellevar, capear ⟨to weather the storm : capear el temporal⟩

weather[2] *n* **1** : tiempo *m* ⟨good/bad weather : buen/mal tiempo⟩ ⟨weather permitting : si hace buen tiempo⟩ ⟨weather forecast : pronóstico del tiempo, parte meteorológico⟩ **2 to be under the weather** : estar enfermo, no estar muy bien

weather–beaten ['weðərˌbiːtən] *adj* : curtido

weatherman ['weðərˌmæn] *n, pl* **-men** [-mən, -ˌmen] METEOROLOGIST : meteorólogo *m*, -ga *f*

weatherproof ['weðərˌpruːf] *adj* : que resiste a la intemperie, impermeable

weather vane → **vane**

weave[1] ['wiːv] *v* **wove** ['woːv] *or* **weaved**; **woven** ['woːvən] *or* **weaved**; **weaving** *vt* **1** : tejer (tela) **2** INTERLACE : entretejer, entrelazar **3 to weave one's way through** : abrirse camino por — *vi* **1** : tejer **2** WIND : serpentear, zigzaguear

weave[2] *n* : tejido *m*, trama *f*

weaver ['wiːvər] *n* : tejedor *m*, -dora *f*

web[1] ['web] *vt* **webbed; webbing** : cubrir o proveer con una red

web[2] *n* **1** COBWEB, SPIDERWEB : telaraña *f*, tela *f* de araña **2** ENTANGLEMENT, SNARE : red *f*, enredo *m* ⟨a web of intrigue : una red de intriga⟩ **3** : membrana *f* interdigital (de aves) **4** NET-

WORK : red *f* ⟨a web of highways : una red de carreteras⟩ **5 the Web** : la web

webbed [ˈwɛbd] *adj* : palmeado ⟨webbed feet : patas palmeadas⟩

Web browser → **browser**

webcam [ˈwɛbˌkæm] *n* : webcam *f*

Webmaster [ˈwɛbˌmæstər] *n* : webmaster *mf*

Web page *n* : página *f* web

Web site *n* : sitio *m* web

wed [ˈwɛd] *vt* **wedded; wedding 1** MARRY : casarse con **2** UNITE : ligar, unir

we'd [ˈwiːd] *contraction of* **we had, we should,** *or* **we would** → **have, should, would**

wedding [ˈwɛdɪŋ] *n* : boda *f*, casamiento *m* ⟨wedding dress : traje de novia⟩ ⟨wedding ring : anillo de boda⟩

wedge¹ [ˈwɛdʒ] *vt* **wedged; wedging 1** : apretar (con una cuña) ⟨to wedge open : mantener abierto con una cuña⟩ **2** CRAM : meter, embutir

wedge² *n* **1** : cuña *f* **2** PIECE : porción *f*, trozo *m*

wedlock [ˈwɛdˌlɑk] → **marriage**

Wednesday [ˈwɛnzˌdeɪ, -di] *n* : miércoles *m* ⟨today is Wednesday : hoy es miércoles⟩ ⟨(on) Wednesday : el miércoles⟩ ⟨(on) Wednesdays : los miércoles⟩ ⟨last Wednesday : el miércoles pasado⟩ ⟨next Wednesday : el miércoles que viene⟩ ⟨every other Wednesday : cada dos miércoles⟩ ⟨Wednesday afternoon/morning : miércoles por la tarde/mañana⟩

wee [ˈwiː] *adj* **1** : pequeño, minúsculo **2 the wee hours** → **hour**

weed¹ [ˈwiːd] *vt* **1** : desherbar **2 to weed out** : eliminar, quitar

weed² *n* : mala hierba *f*

weed killer *n* : herbicida *m*

weedy [ˈwiːdi] *adj* **weedier; -est 1** : cubierto de malas hierbas **2** LANKY, SKINNY : flaco, larguirucho *fam*

week [ˈwiːk] *n* : semana *f* ⟨last week : la semana pasada⟩ ⟨next week : la semana que viene⟩

weekday [ˈwiːkˌdeɪ] *n* : día *m* laborable

weekend [ˈwiːkˌɛnd] *n* : fin *m* de semana

weekly¹ [ˈwiːkli] *adv* : semanalmente

weekly² *adj* : semanal

weekly³ *n, pl* **-lies** : semanario *m*

weep [ˈwiːp] *v* **wept** [ˈwɛpt]; **weeping** : llorar

weeping willow *n* : sauce *m* llorón

weepy [ˈwiːpi] *adj* **weepier; -est** : lloroso, triste

weevil [ˈwiːvəl] *n* : gorgojo *m*

weft [ˈwɛft] *n* : trama *f*

weigh [ˈweɪ] *vt* **1** : pesar **2** CONSIDER : considerar, sopesar **3 to weigh anchor** : levar anclas **4 to weigh down** : sobrecargar (con una carga), abrumar (por preocupaciones, etc.) **5 to weigh up** : hacerse una idea de — *vi* **1** : pesar ⟨it weighs 10 pounds : pesa 10 libras⟩ **2** COUNT : tener importancia, contar ⟨to weigh for/against : favorecer/perjudicar⟩ **3 to weigh in** : intervenir **4 to weigh on one's mind** : preocuparle a uno

weight¹ [ˈweɪt] *vt or* **to weight down 1** : poner peso en, sujetar con un peso **2** BURDEN : cargar, oprimir

weight² *n* **1** HEAVINESS : peso *m* ⟨to lose weight : bajar de peso, adelgazar⟩ **2** : peso *m* ⟨weights and measures : pesos y medidas⟩ **3** : pesa *f* ⟨to lift weights : levantar pesas⟩ **4** SINKER : plomo *m*, plomada *f* **5** BURDEN : peso *m*, carga *f* ⟨to take a weight off one's mind : quitarle un peso de encima a uno⟩ **6** IMPORTANCE : peso *m* **7** INFLUENCE : influencia *f*, autoridad *f* ⟨to throw one's weight around : hacer sentir su influencia⟩ **8 to pull one's weight** : poner uno de su parte

weightless [ˈweɪtləs] *adj* : ingrávido

weight lifting *n* : halterofilia *f*, levantamiento *m* de pesas

weighty [ˈweɪti] *adj* **weightier; -est 1** HEAVY : pesado **2** IMPORTANT : importante, de peso

weir [ˈwɛr, ˈwɪr] *n* : dique *m*

weird [ˈwɪrd] *adj* **1** MYSTERIOUS : misterioso **2** STRANGE : extraño, raro — **weirdly** *adv*

weirdo [ˈwɪrˌdoː] *n, pl* **weirdos** : bicho *m* raro

welcome¹ [ˈwɛlkəm] *vt* **-comed; -coming** : darle la bienvenida a, recibir

welcome² *adj* : bienvenido ⟨to make someone welcome : acoger bien a alguien⟩ ⟨you're welcome! : ¡de nada!, ¡no hay de qué!⟩

welcome³ *n* : bienvenida *f*, recibimiento *m*, acogida *f*

weld¹ [ˈwɛld] *v* : soldar

weld² *n* : soldadura *f*

welder [ˈwɛldər] *n* : soldador *m*, -dora *f*

welfare [ˈwɛlˌfær] *n* **1** WELL-BEING : bienestar *m* **2** : asistencia *f* social

well¹ [ˈwɛl] *vi or* **to well up** : brotar, manar

well² *adv* **better** [ˈbɛtər]; **best** [ˈbɛst] **1** RIGHTLY : bien, correctamente **2** SATISFACTORILY : bien ⟨to turn out well : resultar/salir bien⟩ ⟨well done! : ¡muy bien!⟩ **3** SKILLFULLY : bien ⟨she sings well : canta bien⟩ **4** (*indicating benevolence*) : bien ⟨to speak well of : hablar bien de⟩ ⟨to wish someone well : desearle lo mejor a alguien⟩ ⟨he means well : tiene buenas intenciones⟩ **5** COMPLETELY : completamente ⟨well-hidden : completamente escondido⟩ **6** : bien ⟨I knew him well : lo conocía bien⟩ **7** CONSIDERABLY, FAR : muy, bastante ⟨well ahead : muy adelante⟩ ⟨well before the deadline : bastante antes de la fecha⟩ **8** CERTAINLY : bien ⟨you know very well that . . . : sabes muy bien que . . .⟩ ⟨he can well afford it : bien puede permitírselo⟩ **9** LIKELY : bien ⟨it could/may/might well be true : bien puede/podría/pudiera ser verdad⟩ **10** (*used for emphasis*) ⟨one might well ask if . . . : uno podría preguntarse si . . .⟩ ⟨I couldn't very well refuse! : ¿cómo iba a decir que no?⟩ **11 as well** ALSO : también **12 as well** (*indicating advisability*) ⟨we may/might as well get started : más vale que empecemos⟩ **13 as well** (*indicating equiva-*

lence) ⟨I might as well have stayed home : bien podría haberme quedado en casa⟩ **14 → as well as 15 well and truly :** completamente

well³ *adj* **1** SATISFACTORY : bien ⟨all is well : todo está bien⟩ **2** DESIRABLE : conveniente ⟨it would be well if you left : sería conveniente que te fueras⟩ **3** HEALTHY : bien, sano **4** it's just as well : menos mal

well⁴ *n* **1** : pozo *m* (de agua, petróleo, gas, etc.), aljibe *m* (de agua) **2** SOURCE : fuente *f* ⟨a well of information : una fuente de información⟩ **3 → stairwell**

well⁵ *interj* **1** (*used to introduce a remark*) : bueno **2** (*used to express surprise*) : ¡vaya!

we'll [ˈwiːl, wɪl] *contraction of* **we shall** *or* **we will → shall, will**

well–balanced [ˈwɛlˈbælənst] *adj* : equilibrado

well–behaved [ˈwɛlbɪˈheɪvd] *adj* : (bien) educado, que se porta bien

well–being [ˈwɛlˈbiːɪŋ] *n* : bienestar *m*

well–bred [ˈwɛlˈbrɛd] *adj* : fino, (bien) educado

well–built [ˈwɛlˈbɪlt] *adj* : fornido

well–defined [ˌwɛldɪˈfaɪnd] *adj* : bien definido

well–done [ˈwɛlˈdʌn] *adj* **1** : bien hecho ⟨well-done! : ¡bravo!⟩ **2** : bien cocido

well–dressed [ˈwɛlˈdrɛst] *adj* : bien vestido

well–founded [ˈwɛlˈfaʊndəd] *adj* : bien fundado

well–informed [ˈwɛlɪnˈfɔrmd] *adj* : bien informado

well–kept [ˈwɛlˈkɛpt] *adj* : bien cuidado

well–known [ˈwɛlˈnoːn] *adj* : famoso, bien conocido

well–made [ˈwɛlˈmeɪd] *adj* : sólido

well–mannered [ˈwɛlˈmænərd] *adj* : (bien) educado, de buenos modales

well–meaning [ˈwɛlˈmiːnɪŋ] *adj* : bienintencionado, que tiene buenas intenciones

well–nigh [ˈwɛlˈnaɪ] *adv* : casi ⟨well-nigh impossible : casi imposible⟩

well–off [ˈwɛlˈɔf] **1 → well–to–do 2** FORTUNATE : afortunado

well–read [ˈwɛlˈrɛd] *adj* : culto

well–rounded [ˈwɛlˈraʊndəd] *adj* : completo, equilibrado

well–to–do [ˌwɛltəˈduː] *adj* : próspero, adinerado, rico

well–wisher [ˈwɛlˈwɪʃər] *n* ⟨a group of well-wishers gathered to say goodbye to him : un grupo de amigos/admiradores (etc.) se congregó para despedirlo⟩

well–worn [ˈwɛlˈworn] *adj* : muy gastado

Welsh [ˈwɛlʃ] *n* **1** : galés *m*, galesa *f* **2** : galés *m* (idioma) — **Welsh** *adj*

Welshman [ˈwɛlʃmən] *n, pl* **-men** [-mən, -ˌmɛn] : galés *m*

Welshwoman [ˈwɛlʃˌwʊmən] *n, pl* **-women** [-ˌwɪmən] : galesa *f*

welt [ˈwɛlt] *n* : verdugón *m*

welter [ˈwɛltər] *n* : fárrago *m*, revoltijo *m* ⟨a welter of data : un fárrago de datos⟩

wend [ˈwɛnd] *vi* **to wend one's way** : ponerse en camino, encaminar sus pasos

went → go¹

wept → weep

were → be

we're [ˈwɪr, wər, ˈwiːər] *contraction of* **we are → be**

weren't [ˈwərənt] *contraction of* **were not → be**

werewolf [ˈwɪrˌwʊlf, ˈwɛr-, ˈwər-, -, ˈwʌlf] *n, pl* **-wolves** [-ˌwʊlvz, -ˌwʌlvz] : hombre *m* lobo

west¹ [ˈwɛst] *adv* : al oeste

west² *adj* : oeste, del oeste, occidental ⟨west winds : vientos del oeste⟩

west³ *n* **1** : oeste *m* **2 the West** : el Oeste, el Occidente

westbound [ˈwɛstˌbaʊnd] *adj* : que va hacia el oeste

westerly [ˈwɛstərli] *adv & adj* : del oeste

western¹ [ˈwɛstərn] *adj* **1** : Occidental, del Oeste **2** : occidental, oeste

western² *n* : western *m*

Westerner [ˈwɛstərnər] *n* : habitante *mf* del oeste

West Indian *n* : antillano *m*, -na *f* — **West Indian** *adj*

westward [ˈwɛstwərd] *adv & adj* : hacia el oeste

wet¹ [ˈwɛt] *vt* **wet** *or* **wetted; wetting** : mojar, humedecer

wet² *adj* **wetter; wettest 1** : mojado, húmedo ⟨wet clothes : ropa mojada⟩ ⟨wet paint : pintura fresca⟩ **2** RAINY : lluvioso

wet³ *n* **1** MOISTURE : humedad *f* **2** RAIN : lluvia *f*

wet blanket *n* : aguafiestas *mf*

wet nurse *n* : nodriza *f*

wet suit *n* : traje *m* de neopreno, traje *m* de buzo

we've [ˈwiːv] (*contraction of* **we have**) **→ have**

whack¹ [ˈhwæk] *vt* : golpear (fuertemente), aporrear

whack² *n* **1** : golpe *m* fuerte, porrazo *m* **2** ATTEMPT : intento *m*, tentativa *f*

whale¹ [ˈhweɪl] *vi* **whaled; whaling** : cazar ballenas

whale² *n, pl* **whales** *or* **whale** : ballena *f*

whaleboat [ˈhweɪlˌboːt] *n* : ballenero *m*

whalebone [ˈhweɪlˌboːn] *n* : barba *f* de ballena

whaler [ˈhweɪlər] *n* **1** : ballenero *m*, -ra *f* **2 → whaleboat**

wham [ˈhwæm] *interj* : zas!

wharf [ˈhworf] *n, pl* **wharves** [ˈhworvz] : muelle *m*, embarcadero *m*

what¹ [ˈhwɑt, ˈhwʌt] *adv* **1** HOW : cómo, qué, cuánto ⟨what does it matter? : ¿qué importa?⟩ **2 what with** : entre ⟨what with one thing and another : entre una cosa y otra⟩ **3 so what?** : ¿y qué?

what² *adj* **1** (*used in questions*) : qué ⟨what more do you want? : ¿qué más quieres?⟩ ⟨what color is it? : ¿de qué color es?⟩ **2** (*used in exclamations*) : qué ⟨what an idea! : ¡qué idea!⟩ **3** ANY, WHATEVER : cualquier ⟨give what help you can : da cualquier contribución que puedas⟩

what³ *pron* **1** (*used in direct questions*) : qué ⟨what happened? : ¿qué pasó?⟩ ⟨what does it cost? : ¿cuánto cuesta?⟩ ⟨what does this mean? : ¿que significa esto?⟩ ⟨what's it called? : ¿cómo se llama?⟩ ⟨what's the problem? : ¿cuál es el problema?⟩ ⟨what (did you say)? : ¿qué?, ¿cómo?⟩ ⟨what else did she say? : ¿qué más dijo?⟩ **2** : lo que, qué ⟨tell me what happened : dime qué pasó⟩ ⟨I don't know what to do : no sé qué hacer⟩ ⟨do what I tell you : haz lo que te digo⟩ ⟨guess what! : ¿sabes qué?⟩ **3 and/or what have you** : y no sé qué, y cosas por el estilo **4 what about** ⟨we're all going together—what about Kenny? : vamos todos juntos—¿y Kenny?⟩ ⟨what about if . . .? : ¿qué te parece si . . .?⟩ **5 what for** WHY : por qué ⟨what did you do that for? : ¿por qué hiciste eso?⟩ **6 what if** : y si ⟨what if he knows? : ¿y si lo sabe?⟩ **7 what's more** : además **8 what's up?** *fam* : ¿qué pasa? **9 what's up?** (*used as a greeting*) *fam* : ¿qué hay?, ¿qué tal? **10 what's with . . .?** *fam* : ¿a qué viene/vienen . . .?

whatever¹ [*h*wɑt'ɛvər, ˌ*h*wʌt-] *adj* **1** ANY : cualquier, cualquier . . . que ⟨whatever way you prefer : de cualquier manera que prefiera, como prefiera⟩ **2** (*in negative constructions*) ⟨there's no chance whatever : no hay ninguna posibilidad⟩ ⟨nothing whatever : nada en absoluto⟩

whatever² *pron* ANYTHING : (todo) lo que ⟨I'll do whatever I want : haré lo que quiera⟩ **2** (*no matter what*) whatever it may be : sea lo que sea⟩ ⟨whatever happens : pase lo que pase⟩ **3** WHAT : qué ⟨whatever do you mean? : ¿qué quieres decir?⟩

whatnot [*h*wɑt'nɑt, *h*wʌt-] *pron* : y qué sé yo ⟨diamonds, pearls, and whatnot : diamantes, perlas, y qué sé yo⟩

what's-his-name [*h*wɑtsəz'neɪm, *h*wʌt-] *n* : fulano *m*

what's-her-name [*h*wɑtsər'neɪm, *h*wʌt-] *n* : fulana *f*

whatsoever¹ [ˌ*h*wɑtso'ɛvər, ˌ*h*wʌt-] *adj* → **whatever¹**

whatsoever² *pron* → **whatever²**

wheat [*h*wi:t] *n* : trigo *m*

wheaten [*h*wi:tən] *adj* : de trigo

wheedle [*h*wi:dəl] *vt* **-dled; -dling** CAJOLE : engatusar ⟨to wheedle something out of someone : sonsacarle algo a alguien⟩

wheel¹ [*h*wi:l] *vt* : empujar (una bicicleta, etc.), mover (algo sobre ruedas) — *vi* **1** ROTATE : girar, rotar **2 to wheel around** TURN : darse la vuelta

wheel² *n* **1** : rueda *f* **2 or steering wheel** : volante *m* (de automóviles, etc.), timón *m* (de barcos o aviones) **3 wheels** *npl* : maquinaria *f*, fuerza *f* impulsora ⟨the wheels of government : la maquinaria del gobierno⟩

wheelbarrow [*h*wi:l‚bær‚o:] *n* : carretilla *f*

wheelchair [*h*wi:l‚fær] *n* : silla *f* de ruedas

wheeze¹ [*h*wi:z] *vi* **wheezed; wheezing** : resollar, respirar con dificultad

wheeze² *n* : resuello *m*

whelp¹ [*h*wɛlp] *vi* : parir

whelp² *n* : cachorro *m*, -rra *f*

when¹ [*h*wɛn] *adv* : cuándo ⟨when will you return? : ¿cuándo volverás?⟩ ⟨he asked me when I would be home : me preguntó cuándo estaría en casa⟩ ⟨say when : di basta/cuándo⟩

when² *conj* **1** (*referring to a particular time*) : cuando, en que ⟨when you are ready : cuando estés listo⟩ ⟨the days when I clean the house : los días en que limpio la casa⟩ **2** IF : cuando, si ⟨how can I go when I have no money? : ¿cómo voy a ir si no tengo dinero?⟩ **3** ALTHOUGH : cuando ⟨you said it was big when actually it's small : dijiste que era grande cuando en realidad es pequeño⟩

when³ *pron* : cuándo ⟨since when are you the boss? : ¿desde cuándo eres el jefe?⟩

whence [*h*wɛns] *adv* : de donde

whenever¹ [*h*wɛn'ɛvər] *adv* **1** : cuando sea ⟨tomorrow or whenever : mañana o cuando sea⟩ **2** (*in questions*) : cuándo

whenever² *conj* **1** : siempre que, cada vez que ⟨whenever I go, I'm disappointed : siempre que voy, quedo desilusionado⟩ **2** WHEN : cuando ⟨whenever you like : cuando quieras⟩

where¹ [*h*wɛr] *adv* : dónde, adónde ⟨where is he? : ¿dónde está?⟩ ⟨where did they go? : ¿adónde fueron?⟩

where² *conj* : donde, adonde ⟨she knows where the house is : sabe dónde está la casa⟩ ⟨she goes where she likes : va adonde quiera⟩

where³ *pron* : donde ⟨Chicago is where I live : Chicago es donde vivo⟩

whereabouts¹ [*h*wɛrə‚baʊts] *adv* : dónde, por dónde ⟨whereabouts is the house? : ¿dónde está la casa?⟩

whereabouts² *ns & pl* : paradero *m*

whereas [*h*wɛr'æz] *conj* **1** : considerando que (usado en documentos legales) **2** : mientras que ⟨I like the white one whereas she prefers the black : me gusta el blanco mientras que ella prefiere el negro⟩

whereby [*h*wɛr'baɪ] *adv* : por lo cual

wherefore [*h*wɛr‚for] *adv* : por qué

wherein [*h*wɛr'ɪn] *adv* : en el cual, en el que

whereof [*h*wɛr'ʌv, -ɑv] *conj* : de lo cual

whereupon [*h*wɛrə‚pɑn, -‚pɔn] *conj* : con lo cual, después de lo cual

wherever¹ [*h*wɛr'ɛvər] *adv* **1** WHERE : dónde, adónde **2** : en cualquier parte ⟨or wherever : o donde sea⟩

wherever² *conj* : dondequiera que, donde sea ⟨wherever you go : dondequiera que vayas⟩

wherewithal [*h*wɛrwɪ‚ðɔl, -‚θɔl] *n* : medios *mpl*, recursos *mpl*

whet [*h*wɛt] *vt* **whetted; whetting 1** SHARPEN : afilar **2** STIMULATE : estimular ⟨to whet the appetite : estimular el apetito⟩

whether [ˈʰwɛðər] *conj* **1** : si ⟨I don't know whether it is finished : no sé si está acabado⟩ ⟨we doubt whether he'll show up : dudamos que aparezca⟩ **2** (*used in comparisons*) ⟨whether I like it or not : tanto si quiero como si no⟩ ⟨whether he comes or he doesn't : venga o no⟩

whetstone [ˈʰwɛtˌstoːn] *n* : piedra *f* de afilar

whey [ˈʰweɪ] *n* : suero *m* (de la leche)

which¹ [ˈʰwɪtʃ] *adj* : qué, cuál ⟨which tie do you prefer? : ¿cuál corbata prefieres?⟩ ⟨which ones? : ¿cuáles?⟩ ⟨tell me which house is yours : dime qué casa es la tuya⟩

which² *pron* **1** : cuál ⟨which is the right answer? : ¿cuál es la respuesta correcta?⟩ **2** : que, el cual, la cual, los cuales, las cuales ⟨the cup which broke : la taza que se quebró⟩ ⟨the houses, which are made of brick . . . : las casas, la cuales son de ladrillo . . .⟩

whichever¹ [ʰwɪtʃˈevər] *adj* : el (la) que, cualquiera que ⟨whichever book you like : cualquier libro que te guste⟩

whichever² *pron* : el que, la que, cualquiera que ⟨take whichever you want : toma el que quieras⟩ ⟨whichever I choose : cualquiera que elija⟩

whiff¹ [ˈʰwɪf] *v* PUFF : soplar

whiff² *n* **1** PUFF : soplo *m*, ráfaga *f* **2** SNIFF : olor *m* **3** HINT : dejo *m*, pizca *f*

while¹ [ˈʰwaɪl] *vt* **whiled; whiling** : pasar ⟨to while away the time : matar el tiempo⟩

while² *n* **1** TIME : rato *m*, tiempo *m* ⟨after a while : después de un rato⟩ ⟨in a while : dentro de poco⟩ **2 to be worth one's while** : valer la pena

while³ *conj* **1** : mientras ⟨whistle while you work : silba mientras trabajas⟩ **2** WHEREAS : mientras que **3** ALTHOUGH : aunque ⟨while it's very good, it's not perfect : aunque es muy bueno, no es perfecto⟩

whim [ˈʰwɪm] *n* : capricho *m*, antojo *m*

whimper¹ [ˈʰwɪmpər] *vi* : lloriquear, gimotear

whimper² *n* : quejido *m*

whimsical [ˈʰwɪmzɪkəl] *adj* **1** CAPRICIOUS : caprichoso, fantasioso **2** ERRATIC : errático — **whimsically** *adv*

whine¹ [ˈʰwaɪn] *vi* **whined; whining** **1** : lloriquear, gimotear, gemir **2** COMPLAIN : quejarse

whine² *n* : quejido *m*, gemido *m*

whiner [ˈʰwaɪnər] *n* : llorón *m*, -rona *f*

whiny [ˈʰwaɪni] *adj* **whinier; -est** : ñoño

whinny¹ [ˈʰwɪni] *vi* **-nied; -nying** : relinchar

whinny² *n, pl* **-nies** : relincho *m*

whip¹ [ˈʰwɪp] *v* **whipped; whipping** *vt* **1** SNATCH : arrebatar ⟨she whipped the cloth off the table : arrebató el mantel de la mesa⟩ **2** LASH : azotar **3** MOVE, STIR : agitar (con fuerza) **4** FLING : lanzar, tirar (rápidamente) **5** *fam* DEFEAT : vencer, derrotar **6** INCITE : incitar, despertar, provocar ⟨to whip up enthusiasm : despertar el entusiasmo⟩ ⟨to whip

up a controversy : provocar una polémica⟩ ⟨he whipped the crowd into a frenzy : enardeció a la multitud⟩ **7** BEAT : batir (huevos, crema, etc.) **8 to whip into shape** *fam* : poner en forma **9 to whip out** *fam* : sacar (rápidamente) **10 to whip up** *fam* PREPARE : improvisar, preparar (rápidamente) — *vi* **1** FLAP : agitarse **2** RACE : ir rápidamente ⟨I whipped through my chores : hice las tareas volando⟩ ⟨to whip past/by : pasar como una bala⟩

whip² *n* **1** : látigo *m*, azote *m*, fusta *f* (de jinete) **2** : miembro *m* de un cuerpo legislativo encargado de disciplina

whiplash [ˈʰwɪpˌlæʃ] *n or* **whiplash injury** : traumatismo *m* cervical

whippet [ˈʰwɪpət] *n* : galgo *m* pequeño, galgo *m* inglés

whir¹ [ˈʰwər] *vi* **whirred; whirring** : zumbar

whir² *n* : zumbido *m*

whirl¹ [ˈʰwərl] *vi* **1** SPIN : dar vueltas, girar ⟨my head is whirling : la cabeza me está dando vueltas⟩ **2 to whirl about** : arremolinarse, moverse rápidamente

whirl² *n* **1** SPIN : giro *m*, vuelta *f*, remolino *m* (dícese del polvo, etc.) **2** BUSTLE : bullicio *m*, torbellino *m* (de actividad, etc.) **3 to give it a whirl** : intentar hacer, probar

whirlpool [ˈʰwərlˌpuːl] *n* **1** : vorágine *f*, remolino *m* **2 or whirlpool bath** : bañera *f* de hidromasaje

whirlwind¹ [ˈʰwərlˌwɪnd] *n* : remolino *m*, torbellino *m*, tromba *f*

whirlwind² *adj* : muy rápido

whisk¹ [ˈʰwɪsk] *vt* **1** : llevar ⟨she whisked the children off to bed : llevó a los niños a la cama⟩ **2** : batir ⟨to whisk eggs : batir huevos⟩ **3 to whisk away** *or* **to whisk off** : sacudir

whisk² *n* **1** WHISKING : sacudida *f* (movimiento) **2** : batidor *m* (para batir huevos, etc.)

whisk broom *n* : escobilla *f*

whisker [ˈʰwɪskər] *n* **1** : pelo *m* (de la barba o el bigote) **2 whiskers** *npl* : bigotes *mpl* (de animales)

whiskey *or* **whisky** [ˈʰwɪski] *n, pl* **-keys** *or* **-kies** : whisky *m*

whisper¹ [ˈʰwɪspər] *vi* : cuchichear, susurrar — *vt* : decir en voz baja, susurrar

whisper² *n* **1** WHISPERING : susurro *m*, cuchicheo *m* **2** RUMOR : rumor *m* **3** TRACE : dejo *m*, pizca *f*

whistle¹ [ˈʰwɪsəl] *v* **-tled; -tling** *vi* : silbar, chiflar, pitar (dícese de un tren, etc.) — *vt* : silbar ⟨to whistle a tune : silbar una melodía⟩

whistle² *n* **1** WHISTLING : chiflido *m*, silbido *m* **2** : silbato *m*, pito *m* (instrumento)

whit [ˈʰwɪt] *n* BIT : ápice *m*, pizca *f*

white¹ [ˈʰwaɪt] *adj* **whiter; whitest** : blanco

white² *n* **1** : blanco *m* (color) **2** : clara *f* (de huevos) **3** : blanco *m* (del ojo) **4 or white person** : blanco *m*, -ca *f*

white blood cell *n* : glóbulo *m* blanco

white chocolate *n* : chocolate *m* blanco

white–collar [ˈʰwaɪtˈkɑlər] *adj* **1** : de oficina **2 white–collar worker** : oficinista
mf

whitefish [ˈʰwaɪtˌfɪʃ] *n* : pescado *m* blanco

white–hot *adj* : candente

white lie *n* : mentira *f* piadosa

whiten [ˈʰwaɪtən] *vt* : blanquear — *vi* : ponerse blanco

whitener [ˈʰwaɪtənər] *n* : blanqueador *m*

whiteness [ˈʰwaɪtnəs] *n* : blancura *f*

white–tailed deer [ˈʰwaɪtˈteɪld] *n* : ciervo
f de Virginia

whitewash[1] [ˈʰwaɪtˌwɔʃ] *vt* **1** : enjalbegar,
blanquear ⟨to whitewash a fence : enjalbegar una valla⟩ **2** CONCEAL : encubrir
(un escándalo, etc.)

whitewash[2] *n* **1** : jalbegue *m*, lechada *f* **2**
COVER-UP : encubrimiento *m*

whither [ˈʰwɪðər] *adv* : adónde

whittle [ˈʰwɪtəl] *vt* **-tled; -tling 1** : tallar
(madera) **2 to whittle down** : reducir,
recortar ⟨to whittle down expenses : reducir los gastos⟩

whiz[1] *or* **whizz** [ˈʰwɪz] *vi* **whizzed; whiz-
zing 1** BUZZ : zumbar **2 to whiz by**
: pasar muy rápido, pasar volando

whiz[2] *or* **whizz** *n, pl* **whizzes 1** BUZZ
: zumbido *m* **2 to be a whiz** : ser un
prodigio, ser muy hábil

whiz kid *or* **whizz kid** *n* : prodigio *m*,
genio *m*

who [ˈhuː] *pron* **1** (*used in direct and indirect questions*) : quién ⟨who is that?
: ¿quién es ése?⟩ ⟨who did it? : ¿quién lo
hizo?⟩ ⟨we know who they are : sabemos quiénes son⟩ **2** (*used in relative
clauses*) : que, quien ⟨the lady who lives
there : la señora que vive allí⟩ ⟨for those
who wait : para los que esperan, para
quienes esperan⟩

whodunit [huːˈdʌnɪt] *n* : novela *f* policíaca

whoever [huːˈevər] *pron* **1** : quienquiera
que, quien ⟨whoever did it : quienquiera
que lo hizo⟩ ⟨give it to whoever you
want : dalo a quien quieras⟩ **2** (*used in
questions*) : quién ⟨whoever could that
be? : ¿quién podría ser?⟩

whole[1] [ˈhoːl] *adj* **1** UNHURT : ileso **2** IN-
TACT : intacto, sano **3** ENTIRE : entero,
íntegro ⟨the whole island : toda la isla⟩
⟨whole milk : leche entera⟩ **4 a whole
lot** : muchísimo

whole[2] *n* **1** : todo *m* **2 as a whole** : en
conjunto **3 on the whole** : en general

wholehearted [ˈhoːlˈhɑrtəd] *adj* : sin reservas, incondicional — **wholeheartedly**
adv

whole note *n* : semibreve *f*, redonda *f*

whole number *n* : entero *m*

wholesale[1] [ˈhoːlˌseɪl] *v* **-saled; -saling** *vt*
: vender al por mayor — *vi* : venderse al
por mayor

wholesale[2] *adv* : al por mayor

wholesale[3] *adj* **1** : al por mayor ⟨whole-
sale grocer : tendero al por mayor⟩ **2**
TOTAL : total, absoluto ⟨wholesale
slaughter : matanza sistemática⟩

wholesale[4] *n* : mayoreo *m*

wholesaler [ˈhoːlˌseɪlər] *n* : mayorista *mf*

wholesome [ˈhoːlsəm] *adj* **1** : sano
⟨wholesome advice : consejo sano⟩ **2**
HEALTHY : sano, saludable

whole wheat *adj* : de trigo integral ⟨whole
wheat bread : pan integral⟩

wholly [ˈhoːli] *adv* **1** COMPLETELY : completamente **2** SOLELY : exclusivamente,
únicamente

whom [ˈhuːm] *pron* **1** (*used in direct questions*) : a quién ⟨whom did you choose?
: ¿a quién elegiste?⟩ **2** (*used in indirect
questions*) : de quién, con quién, en
quién ⟨I don't know whom to consult
: no sé con quién consultar⟩ **3** (*used in
relative clauses*) : que, a quien ⟨the lawyer whom I recommended to you : el
abogado que te recomendé⟩

whomever [huːmˈevər] *pron* WHOEVER
: quienquiera, quien ⟨marry whomever
you please : cásate con quien quieras⟩

whoop[1] [ˈʰwuːp, ˈʰwʊp] *vi* : gritar, chillar

whoop[2] *n* : grito *m*

whooping cough *n* : tos *f* ferina

whopper [ˈʰwɑpər] *n* **1** : cosa *f* enorme **2**
LIE : mentira *f* colosal

whopping [ˈʰwɑpɪŋ] *adj* : enorme

whore [ˈhor] *n* : puta *f* offensive, ramera *f*

whorl [ˈʰworl, ˈʰwərl] *n* : espiral *f*, línea *f*
(de una huella digital)

whose[1] [ˈhuːz] *adj* **1** (*used in questions*)
: de quién ⟨whose truck is that? : ¿de
quién es ese camión?⟩ **2** (*used in relative
clauses*) : cuyo ⟨the person whose work
is finished : la persona cuyo trabajo está
terminado⟩

whose[2] *pron* : de quién ⟨tell me whose it
was : dime de quién era⟩

why[1] [ˈʰwaɪ] *adv* : por qué ⟨why did you
do it? : ¿por qué lo hizo?⟩

why[2] *n, pl* **whys** REASON : porqué *m*,
razón *f*

why[3] *conj* : por qué ⟨I know why he left
: yo sé por qué salió⟩ ⟨there's no reason
why it should exist : no hay razón para
que exista⟩

why[4] *interj* (*used to express surprise*)
: ¡vaya!, ¡mira!

wick [ˈwɪk] *n* : mecha *f*

wicked [ˈwɪkəd] *adj* **1** EVIL : malo, malvado **2** MISCHIEVOUS : travieso, pícaro
⟨a wicked grin : una sonrisa traviesa⟩ **3**
TERRIBLE : terrible, horrible ⟨a wicked
storm : una tormenta horrible⟩

wickedly [ˈwɪkədli] *adv* : con maldad

wickedness [ˈwɪkədnəs] *n* : maldad *f*

wicker[1] [ˈwɪkər] *adj* : de mimbre

wicker[2] *n* **1** : mimbre *m*, **2** → **wickerwork**

wickerwork [ˈwɪkərˌwərk] *n* : artículos
mpl de mimbre

wicket [ˈwɪkət] *n* **1** WINDOW : ventanilla *f*
2 *or* **wicket gate** : postigo *m* **3** : aro *m*
(en croquet), palos *mpl* (en críquet)

wide[1] [ˈwaɪd] *adv* **wider; widest 1** WIDELY
: por todas partes ⟨to travel far and wide
: viajar por todas partes⟩ **2** COMPLETELY
: completamente, totalmente ⟨wide open
: abierto de par en par⟩ ⟨**3 wide apart**
: muy separados

wide[2] *adj* **wider; widest 1** VAST : vasto,
extensivo ⟨a wide area : una área exten-

siva⟩ **2** : ancho ⟨three meters wide : tres metros de ancho⟩ **3** BROAD : ancho, amplio **4** *or* **wide-open** : muy abierto **5 wide of the mark** : desviado, lejos del blanco

wide-awake ['waɪdə'weɪk] *adj* : (completamente) despierto

wide-eyed ['waɪd'aɪd] *adj* **1** : con los ojos muy abiertos **2** NAIVE : inocente, ingenuo

widely ['waɪdli] *adv* : extensivamente, por todas partes

widen ['waɪdən] *vt* : ampliar, ensanchar — *vi* : ampliarse, ensancharse

wide-ranging ['waɪd'reɪndʒɪŋ] *adj* EXTENSIVE, DIVERSE : amplio, diverso ⟨wide-ranging implications : implicaciones de gran alcance⟩ ⟨a wide-ranging discussion : una discusión que abarca muchos temas⟩

widescreen ['waɪd'skri:n] *adj* : de pantalla ancha

widespread ['waɪd'sprɛd] *adj* : extendido, extenso, difuso

widow¹ ['wɪ,do:] *vt* : dejar viuda ⟨to be widowed : enviudar⟩

widow² *n* : viuda *f*

widower ['wɪdowər] *n* : viudo *m*

width ['wɪdθ] *n* : ancho *m*, anchura *f*

wield ['wi:ld] *vt* **1** USE : usar, manejar ⟨to wield a broom : usar una escoba⟩ **2** EXERCISE : ejercer ⟨to wield influence : influir⟩

wiener ['wi:nər] → frankfurter

wife ['waɪf] *n, pl* **wives** ['waɪvz] : esposa *f*, mujer *f*

wifely ['waɪfli] *adj* : de esposa, conyugal

wig ['wɪg] *n* : peluca *f*

wiggle¹ ['wɪgəl] *v* **-gled; -gling** *vt* **1** : menear ⟨to wiggle one's hips : menear las caderas, menearse, contonearse⟩ **2** : mover (los dedos, etc.) — *vi* **1** : menearse, contonearse **2** SQUIRM, WRIGGLE : retorcerse

wiggle² *n* : meneo *m*, contoneo *m*

wiggly ['wɪgəli] *adj* **wigglier; -est 1** : que se menea **2** WAVY : ondulado

wigwag ['wɪg,wæg] *vi* **-wagged; -wagging** : comunicar por señales

wigwam ['wɪg,wɑm] *n* : wigwam *m*

wild¹ ['waɪld] *adv* **1** → **wildly 2 to run wild** : descontrolarse

wild² *adj* **1** : salvaje, silvestre, cimarrón ⟨wild horses : caballos salvajes⟩ ⟨wild rice : arroz silvestre⟩ **2** DESOLATE : yermo, agreste **3** UNRULY : desenfrenado **4** CRAZY : loco, fantástico ⟨wild ideas : ideas locas⟩ **5** BARBAROUS : salvaje, bárbaro **6** ERRATIC : errático ⟨a wild throw : un tiro errático⟩ **7** FRENETIC : frenético **8** : extravagante ⟨to take/make a wild guess : adivinar, hacer una conjetura (al azar)⟩ **9 to be wild about** : estar loco por

wild³ *n* → **wilderness**

wild boar *n* : jabalí *m*

wild card *n* **1** : factor *m* desconocido **2** : comodín *m* (carta) **3** *usu* **wildcard** : comodín *m* (símbolo)

wildcat ['waɪld,kæt] *n* **1** : gato *m* montés **2** BOBCAT : lince *m* rojo

wilderness ['wɪldərnəs] *n* : yermo *m*, desierto *m*

wildfire ['waɪld,faɪr] *n* **1** : fuego *m* descontrolado **2 to spread like wildfire** : propagarse como un reguero de pólvora

wildflower ['waɪld,flaʊər] *n* : flor *f* silvestre

wildfowl ['waɪld,faʊl] *n* : ave *f* de caza

wild goose chase *n fam* : misión *f* imposible o inútil ⟨it turned out to be a wild goose chase : resultó ser una pérdida de tiempo⟩

wildlife ['waɪld,laɪf] *n* : fauna *f*

wildly ['waɪldli] *adv* **1** FRANTICALLY : frenéticamente, como un loco **2** EXTREMELY : extremadamente ⟨wildly happy : loco de felicidad⟩

wile¹ ['waɪl] *vt* **wiled; wiling** LURE : atraer

wile² *n* : ardid *m*, artimaña *f*

will¹ ['wɪl] *v, past* **would** ['wʊd]; *pres sing & pl* **will** *vt* WISH : querer ⟨do what you will : haz lo que quieras⟩ — *v aux* **1** (*expressing willingness*) ⟨no one would take the job : nadie aceptaría el trabajo⟩ ⟨I won't do it : no lo haré⟩ **2** (*expressing habitual action*) ⟨he will get angry over nothing : se pone furioso por cualquier cosa⟩ **3** (*forming the future tense*) ⟨tomorrow we will go shopping : mañana iremos de compras⟩ **4** (*expressing capacity*) ⟨the couch will hold three people : en el sofá cabrán tres personas⟩ **5** (*expressing determination*) ⟨I will go despite them : iré a pesar de ellos⟩ **6** (*expressing probability*) ⟨that will be the mailman : eso ha de ser el cartero⟩ **7** (*expressing inevitability*) ⟨accidents will happen : los accidentes ocurrirán⟩ **8** (*expressing a command*) ⟨you will do as I say : harás lo que digo⟩

will² *vt* **1** ORDAIN : disponer, decretar ⟨if God wills it : si Dios lo dispone, si Dios quiere⟩ **2** : lograr a fuerza de voluntad ⟨they were willing him to succeed : estaban deseando que tuviera éxito⟩ **3** BEQUEATH : legar

will³ *n* **1** DESIRE : deseo *m*, voluntad *f* **2** VOLITION : voluntad *f* ⟨free will : libre albedrío⟩ **3** WILLPOWER : voluntad *f*, fuerza *f* de voluntad ⟨a will of iron : una voluntad férrea⟩ **4** : testamento *m* ⟨to make a will : hacer testamento⟩

willful *or* **wilful** ['wɪlfəl] *adj* **1** OBSTINATE : obstinado, terco **2** INTENTIONAL : intencionado, deliberado — **willfully** *adv*

willing ['wɪlɪŋ] *adj* **1** INCLINED, READY : listo, dispuesto **2** OBLIGING : servicial, complaciente

willingly ['wɪlɪŋli] *adv* : con gusto

willingness ['wɪlɪŋnəs] *n* : buena voluntad *f*

willow ['wɪ,lo:] *n* : sauce *m*

willowy ['wɪlowi] *adj* : esbelto

willpower ['wɪl,paʊər] *n* : voluntad *f*, fuerza *f* de voluntad

willy-nilly [,wɪli'nɪli] *adv fam* : de cualquier manera

wilt [ˈwɪlt] vi **1** : marchitarse (dícese de las flores) **2** LANGUISH : debilitarse, languidecer

wily [ˈwaɪli] adj **wilier; -est** : artero, astuto

wimp [ˈwɪmp] n **1** COWARD : gallina f, cobarde mf **2** WEAKLING : debilucho m, -cha f, alfeñique m

win¹ [ˈwɪn] v **won** [ˈwʌn]; **winning** vi : ganar — vt **1** : ganar, conseguir **2 to win over** : ganarse a **3 to win someone's heart** : conquistar a alguien

win² n : triunfo m, victoria f

wince¹ [ˈwɪnts] vi **winced; wincing** : estremecerse, hacer una mueca de dolor

wince² n : mueca f de dolor

winch [ˈwɪntʃ] n : torno m

wind¹ [ˈwɪnd] vt : dejar sin aliento ⟨to be winded : quedarse sin aliento⟩

wind² [ˈwaɪnd] v **wound** [ˈwaʊnd]; **winding** vi **1** MEANDER : serpentear **2 to wind down** END : acabarse poco a poco **3 to wind down** UNWIND : relajarse **4 to wind up** END : terminar, acabar ⟨the meeting will be winding up soon : la reunión va a terminar pronto⟩ **5 to wind up** END UP : acabar, terminar ⟨to wind up doing something : acabar/terminar haciendo algo, acabar/terminar por hacer algo⟩ — vt **1** COIL, ROLL : envolver, enrollar **2** TURN : hacer girar ⟨to wind (up) a clock : darle cuerda a un reloj⟩ **3 to wind up** END : terminar, concluir

wind³ [ˈwɪnd] n **1** : viento m ⟨against the wind : contra el viento⟩ **2** BREATH : aliento m **3** FLATULENCE : flatulencia f, ventosidad f **4 to get wind of** : enterarse de

wind⁴ [ˈwaɪnd] n **1** TURN : vuelta f **2** BEND : recodo m, curva f

windbreak [ˈwɪnd,breɪk] n : barrera f contra el viento, abrigadero m

windfall [ˈwɪnd,fɔl] n **1** : fruta f caída **2** : beneficio m imprevisto

wind instrument n : instrumento m de viento

windmill [ˈwɪnd,mɪl] n : molino m de viento

window [ˈwɪn,doː] n **1** : ventana f (de un edificio o una computadora), ventanilla f (de un vehículo o avión), vitrina f (de una tienda) **2 → windowpane**

window box n : jardinera f de ventana

windowpane [ˈwɪn,doː,peɪn] n : vidrio m

window screen → screen²

window-shop [ˈwɪndo,ʃɑp] vi **-shopped; -shopping** : mirar las vitrinas

windowsill [ˈwɪn,doː,sɪl] n : alféizar m de la ventana

windpipe [ˈwɪnd,paɪp] n : tráquea f

windshield [ˈwɪnd,ʃiːld] n **1** : parabrisas m **2 windshield wiper** : limpiaparabrisas m

windsurfing [ˈwɪnd,sərfɪŋ] n : windsurf m

windswept [ˈwɪnd,swɛpt] adj **1** : azotado por el viento **2** DISHEVELED : despeinado

windup [ˈwaɪnd,ʌp] n : conclusión f

windy [ˈwɪndi] adj **windier; -est 1** : ventoso ⟨it's windy : hace viento⟩ **2** VERBOSE : verboso, prolijo

wine¹ [ˈwaɪn] v **wined; wining** vi : beber vino — vt **to wine and dine** : agasajar

wine² n : vino m

wineglass [ˈwaɪn,glæs] n : copa f (de vino)

winery [ˈwaɪnəri] n, pl **-eries** : bodega f

wineskin [ˈwaɪn,skɪn] n : odre m, bota f

wine tasting n : degustación f de vinos

wing¹ [ˈwɪŋ] vi FLY : volar

wing² n **1** : ala f (de un ave o un avión) ⟨to take wing : levantar vuelo⟩ **2** : ala f (de un edificio) **3** FACTION : ala f ⟨the right wing of the party : el ala derecha del partido⟩ **4 wings** npl : bastidores mpl (de un teatro) ⟨to be waiting in the wings : estar esperando su momento⟩ **5 on the wing** : al vuelo, volando **6 under one's wing** : bajo el cargo de uno ⟨to take someone under one's wing : encargarse de alguien⟩

winged [ˈwɪŋd, ˈwɪŋəd] adj : alado

wink¹ [ˈwɪŋk] vi **1** : guiñar el ojo **2** BLINK : pestañear, parpadear **3** FLICKER : parpadear, titilar

wink² n **1** : guiño m (del ojo) **2** NAP : siesta f ⟨not to sleep a wink : no pegar el ojo⟩

winner [ˈwɪnər] n : ganador m, -dora f

winning [ˈwɪnɪŋ] adj **1** VICTORIOUS : ganador **2** CHARMING : encantador

winnings [ˈwɪnɪŋz] npl : ganancias fpl

winnow [ˈwɪ,noː] vt : aventar (el grano, etc.)

winsome [ˈwɪnsəm] adj CHARMING : encantador

winter¹ [ˈwɪntər] adj : invernal, de invierno

winter² n : invierno m

wintertime [ˈwɪntər,taɪm] n : invierno m

wintry [ˈwɪntri] adj **wintrier; -est 1** WINTER : invernal, de invierno **2** COLD : frío ⟨she gave us a wintry greeting : nos saludó fríamente⟩

wipe¹ [ˈwaɪp] v **wiped; wiping** vt **1** or **to wipe off** : limpiar, pasarle un trapo a ⟨to wipe one's feet : limpiarse los pies⟩ ⟨to wipe dry : secar⟩ **2** or **to wipe off** REMOVE : limpiar, quitar **3** or **to wipe clean** ERASE : borrar (un disco, etc.) **4 to wipe away** REMOVE : limpiar (suciedad), secar (lágrimas), borrar (una memoria) **5 to wipe down** : pasarle un trapo a **6 to wipe out** ANNIHILATE : aniquilar, destruir **7 to wipe up** : limpiar, secar (líquido, etc.) — vi **to wipe out** fam FALL : caerse (violentamente)

wipe² n : pasada f (con un trapo, etc.)

wire¹ [ˈwaɪr] vt **wired; wiring 1** : instalar el cableado en (una casa, etc.) **2** BIND : atar con alambre **3** TELEGRAPH : telegrafiar, mandarle un telegrama a (alguien)

wire² n **1** : alambre m ⟨barbed wire : alambre de púas⟩ **2** : cable m (eléctrico o telefónico) **3** TELEGRAM : telegrama m, cable m

wireless [ˈwaɪrləs] adj : inalámbrico ⟨a wireless microphone : un micrófono inalámbrico⟩ ⟨wireless Internet access : acceso inalámbrico a Internet⟩

wiretap[1] ['waɪr,tæp] *vt* TAP : intervenir, pinchar *fam* (un teléfono)

wiretap[2] *n* TAP : micrófono *m* oculto (para la intervención telefónica)

wiretapping ['waɪr,tæpɪŋ] *n* : intervención *f* telefónica

wiring ['waɪrɪŋ] *n* : cableado *m*

wiry ['waɪri] *adj* **wirier; -est 1** : hirsuto, tieso (dícese del pelo) **2** : esbelto y musculoso (dícese del cuerpo)

wisdom ['wɪzdəm] *n* **1** KNOWLEDGE : sabiduría *f* **2** JUDGMENT, SENSE : sensatez *f*

wisdom tooth *n* : muela *f* de juicio

wise[1] ['waɪz] *adj* **wiser; wisest 1** LEARNED : sabio **2** SENSIBLE : sabio, sensato, prudente **3** KNOWLEDGEABLE : entendido, enterado ⟨they're wise to his tricks : conocen muy bien sus mañas⟩

wise[2] *n* : manera *f*, modo *m* ⟨in no wise : de ninguna manera⟩

wisecrack ['waɪz,kræk] *n* : broma *f*, chiste *m*

wisely ['waɪzli] *adv* : sabiamente, sensatamente

wish[1] ['wɪʃ] *vt* **1** : pedir (como deseo) ⟨I wish I were rich : ojalá fuera rica⟩ ⟨I wish I'd known : ojalá lo hubiera sabido⟩ ⟨I wish you'd be quiet! : ¿quieres callarte?⟩ **2** WANT : desear, querer ⟨I wish to be alone : quiero estar sólo⟩ **3** : desear ⟨they wished me well : me desearon lo mejor⟩ ⟨I wish you luck : te deseo suerte⟩ ⟨I wish you a Happy New Year! : ¡que tengas un feliz Año Nuevo!⟩ — *vi* **1** : pedir un deseo ⟨to wish upon a star : pedir un deseo a una estrella⟩ **2** : querer ⟨as you wish : como quiera⟩ **3 to wish for** : pedir (como deseo)

wish[2] *n* **1** : deseo *m* ⟨to grant a wish : conceder un deseo⟩ **2 wishes** *npl* : saludos *mpl*, recuerdos *mpl* ⟨to send best wishes : mandar muchos recuerdos⟩

wishbone ['wɪʃ,boːn] *n* : espoleta *f*

wishful ['wɪʃfəl] *adj* **1** HOPEFUL : deseoso, lleno de esperanza **2 wishful thinking** : ilusiones *fpl*

wishy-washy ['wɪʃi,wɔʃi, -,wɑʃi] *adj* : insípido, soso

wisp ['wɪsp] *n* **1** BUNCH : manojo *m* (de paja) **2** STRAND : mechón *m* (de pelo) **3** : voluta *f* (de humo)

wispy ['wɪspi] *adj* **wispier; -est** : tenue, ralo (dícese del pelo)

wisteria [wɪs'tɪriə] *n* : glicinia *f*

wistful ['wɪstfəl] *adj* : anhelante, melancólico — **wistfully** *adv*

wistfulness ['wɪstfəlnəs] *n* : añoranza *f*, melancolía *f*

wit ['wɪt] *n* **1** INTELLIGENCE : inteligencia *f* **2** CLEVERNESS : ingenio *m*, gracia *f*, agudeza *f* **3** HUMOR : humorismo *m* **4** JOKER : chistoso *m*, -sa *f* **5 wits** *npl* : razón *f*, buen juicio *m* ⟨scared out of one's wits : muerto de miedo⟩ ⟨to be at one's wits' end : estar desesperado⟩

witch ['wɪtʃ] *n* : bruja *f*

witchcraft ['wɪtʃ,kræft] *n* : brujería *f*, hechicería *f*

witch doctor *n* : hechicero *m*, -ra *f*

witchery ['wɪtʃəri] *n, pl* **-eries 1** → witchcraft **2** CHARM : encanto *m*

witch-hunt ['wɪtʃ,hʌnt] *n* : caza *f* de brujas

with ['wɪð, 'wɪθ] *prep* **1** : con ⟨I'm going with you : voy contigo⟩ ⟨coffee with milk : café con leche⟩ **2** AGAINST : con ⟨to argue with someone : discutir con alguien⟩ **3** (*used in descriptions*) : con, de ⟨the girl with red hair : la muchacha de pelo rojo⟩ **4** (*indicating manner, means, or cause*) : con ⟨to cut with a knife : cortar con un cuchillo⟩ ⟨fix it with tape : arréglalo con cinta⟩ ⟨with luck : con suerte⟩ ⟨trembling with fear : temblando de miedo⟩ **5** DESPITE : a pesar de, aún con ⟨even with all his work, the business failed : a pesar de todo su trabajo, el negocio fracasó⟩ **6** REGARDING : con respecto a, con ⟨the trouble with your plan : el problema con su plan⟩ **7** ACCORDING TO : según ⟨it varies with the season : varía según la estación⟩ **8** (*indicating support or understanding*) : con ⟨I'm with you all the way : estoy contigo hasta el final⟩

withdraw [wɪð'drɔ, wɪθ-] *v* **-drew** [-'druː]; **-drawn** [-'drɔn]; **-drawing** *vt* **1** REMOVE : retirar, apartar, sacar (dinero) **2** RETRACT : retractarse de — *vi* : retirarse, recluirse (de la sociedad)

withdrawal [wɪð'drɔəl, wɪθ-] *n* **1** : retirada *f*, retiro *m* (de fondos, etc.), retraimiento *m* (social) **2** RETRACTION : retractación *f* **3 withdrawal symptoms** : síndrome *m* de abstinencia

withdrawn [wɪð'drɔn, wɪθ-] *adj* : retraído, reservado, introvertido

wither ['wɪðər] *vt* : marchitar, agostar — *vi* **1** WILT : marchitarse **2** WEAKEN : decaer, debilitarse

withhold [wɪθ'hoːld, wɪð-] *vt* **-held** [-'hld]; **-holding** : retener (fondos), aplazar (una decisión), negar (permiso, etc.)

within[1] [wɪð'ɪn, wɪθ-] *adv* : dentro

within[2] *prep* **1** : dentro de ⟨within the limits : dentro de los límites⟩ ⟨within sight of : a la vista de⟩ **2** (*in expressions of distance*) : a menos de ⟨within 10 miles of the ocean : a menos de 10 millas del mar⟩ **3** (*in expressions of time*) : dentro de ⟨within an hour : dentro de una hora⟩ ⟨within a month of her birthday : a poco menos de un mes de su cumpleaños⟩

without[1] [wɪð'aʊt, wɪθ-] *adv* **1** OUTSIDE : fuera **2 to do without** : pasar sin algo

without[2] *prep* **1** OUTSIDE : fuera de **2** : sin ⟨without fear : sin temor⟩ ⟨he left without his briefcase : se fue sin su portafolios⟩

withstand [wɪθ'stænd, wɪð-] *vt* **-stood** [-'stʊd]; **-standing 1** BEAR : aguantar, soportar **2** RESIST : resistir, resistirse a

witless ['wɪtləs] *adj* : estúpido, tonto

witness[1] ['wɪtnəs] *vt* **1** SEE : presenciar, ver, ser testigo de **2** : atestiguar (una firma, etc.) — *vi* TESTIFY : atestiguar, testimoniar

witness[2] *n* **1** TESTIMONY : testimonio *m* ⟨to bear witness : atestiguar, testimoniar⟩ 2 : testigo *mf* ⟨witness for the prosecution : testigo de cargo⟩

witness stand *n* : estrado *m*

witticism [ˈwɪtə‚sɪzəm] *n* : agudeza *f*, ocurrencia *f*

witty [ˈwɪti] *adj* **wittier; -est** : ingenioso, ocurrente, gracioso

wives → **wife**

wizard [ˈwɪzərd] *n* **1** SORCERER : mago *m*, brujo *m*, hechicero *m* **2** : genio *m* ⟨a math wizard : un genio en matemáticas⟩

wizened [ˈwɪzənd, ˈwiː-] *adj* : arrugado, marchito

wobble [ˈwɑbəl] *vi* **-bled; -bling** : bambolearse, tambalearse, temblar (dícese de la voz)

wobble[2] *n* : tambaleo *m*, bamboleo *m*

wobbly [ˈwɑbəli] *adj* **wobblier; -est** : que se tambalea, inestable

woe [ˈwoː] *n* **1** GRIEF, MISFORTUNE : desgracia *f*, infortunio *m*, aflicción *f* **2 woes** *npl* TROUBLES : penas *fpl*, males *mpl*

woeful [ˈwoːfəl] *adj* **1** SORROWFUL : afligido, apenado, triste **2** UNFORTUNATE : desgraciado, infortunado **3** DEPLORABLE : lamentable

woke, woken → **wake**[1]

wolf[1] [ˈwʊlf] *vt* **or to wolf down** : engullir

wolf[2] *n, pl* **wolves** [ˈwʊlvz] : lobo *m*, -ba *f*

wolfram [ˈwʊlfrəm] → **tungsten**

wolverine [‚wʊlvəˈriːn] *n* : glotón *m* (animal)

woman [ˈwʊmən] *n, pl* **women** [ˈwɪmən] : mujer *f*

womanhood [ˈwʊmən‚hʊd] *n* **1** : condición *f* de mujer **2** WOMEN : mujeres *fpl*

womanizer [ˈwʊmə‚naɪzər] *n* : picaflor *m*

womanly [ˈwʊmənli] *adj* : femenino

womb [ˈwuːm] *n* : útero *m*, matriz *f*

won → **win**

wonder[1] [ˈwʌndər] *vi* **1** SPECULATE : preguntarse, pensar ⟨to wonder about : preguntarse por⟩ **2** MARVEL : asombrarse, maravillarse — *vt* : preguntarse ⟨I wonder if/whether they're coming : me pregunto si vendrán⟩

wonder[2] *n* **1** MARVEL : maravilla *f*, milagro *m* ⟨to work wonders : hacer maravillas⟩ **2** AMAZEMENT : asombro *m*

wonderful [ˈwʌndərfəl] *adj* : maravilloso, estupendo

wonderfully [ˈwʌndərfəli] *adv* : maravillosamente, de maravilla

wonderland [ˈwʌndər‚lænd, -lənd] *n* : país *m* de las maravillas

wonderment [ˈwʌndərmənt] *n* : asombro *m*

wondrous [ˈwʌndrəs] → **wonderful**

wont[1] [ˈwɔnt, ˈwoːnt, ˈwʌnt] *adj* : acostumbrado, habituado

wont[2] *n* : hábito *m*, costumbre *f*

won't [ˈwoːnt] (*contraction of* **will not**) → **will**[1]

woo [ˈwuː] *vt* **1** COURT : cortejar **2** : buscar el apoyo de (clientes, votantes, etc.)

wood[1] [ˈwʊd] *adj* : de madera

wood[2] *n* **1 or woods** *npl* FOREST : bosque *m* **2** : madera *f* (materia) **3** FIREWOOD : leña *f*

woodchuck [ˈwʊd‚tʃʌk] *n* : marmota *f* de América

woodcut [ˈwʊd‚kʌt] *n* **1** : plancha *f* de madera (para imprimir imágenes) **2** : grabado *m* en madera

woodcutter [ˈwʊd‚kʌtər] *n* : leñador *m*, -dora *f*

wooded [ˈwʊdəd] *adj* : arbolado, boscoso

wooden [ˈwʊdən] *adj* **1** : de madera ⟨a wooden cross : una cruz de madera⟩ **2** STIFF : rígido, inexpresivo (dícese del estilo, de la cara, etc.)

woodland [ˈwʊdlənd, -‚lænd] *n* : bosque *m*

woodpecker [ˈwʊd‚pɛkər] *n* : pájaro *m* carpintero

woodshed [ˈwʊd‚ʃɛd] *n* : leñera *f*

woodsman [ˈwʊdzmən] *n, pl* **-men** [-mən, -‚mɛn] → **woodcutter**

woodwind [ˈwʊd‚wɪnd] *n* : instrumento *m* de viento de madera

woodwork [ˈwʊd‚wərk] *n* : carpintería *f*

woodworking [ˈwʊd‚wərkɪŋ] *n* : carpintería *f*

woody [ˈwʊdi] *adj* **woodier; -est 1** → **wooded 2** : leñoso ⟨woody plants : plantas leñosas⟩ **3** : leñoso (dícese de la textura), a madera (dícese del aroma, etc.)

woof[1] [ˈwʊf] → **weft**

wool [ˈwʊl] *n* : lana *f*

woolen[1] *or* **woollen** [ˈwʊlən] *adj* : de lana

woolen[2] *or* **woollen** *n* **1** : lana *f* (tela) **2 woolens** *npl* : prendas *fpl* de lana

woolly [ˈwʊli] *adj* **woollier; -est 1** : lanudo **2** CONFUSED : confuso, vago

woozy [ˈwuːzi] *adj* **woozier; -est** : mareado

word[1] [ˈwərd] *vt* : expresar, formular, redactar

word[2] *n* **1** : palabra *f*, vocablo *m*, voz *f* ⟨word for word : palabra por palabra⟩ ⟨words fail me : me quedo sin habla⟩ ⟨I can't understand a word she says : no entiendo ni una sola palabra de lo que dice⟩ **2** REMARK : palabra *f* ⟨by word of mouth : de palabra⟩ ⟨in a word : en una palabra⟩ ⟨in other words : en otras palabras⟩ ⟨in one's own words : en/con sus propias palabras⟩ ⟨in so many words : con esas palabras⟩ ⟨the last word : la última palabra⟩ ⟨to have a word with : hablar (dos palabras) con⟩ ⟨don't believe a word of it : no te creas ni una sola palabra⟩ ⟨don't say/breathe a word of this (to anyone) : de esto ni una palabra (a nadie)⟩ **3** COMMAND : orden *f* ⟨to give the word : dar la orden⟩ ⟨just say the word : no tienes más que decirlo⟩ **4** MESSAGE, NEWS : noticias *fpl* ⟨is there any word from her? : ¿hay noticias de ella?⟩ ⟨to send word : mandar un recado⟩ ⟨word has it that . . . : dicen que . . ., corre el rumor de que . . .⟩ **5** PROMISE : palabra *f* ⟨word of honor : palabra de honor⟩ ⟨to keep one's word : cumplir uno su palabra⟩ ⟨you have my word (on it) : te doy mi palabra⟩ ⟨take my word for it : te lo digo yo⟩ ⟨to take someone at his/her word : confiar en la palabra de alguien, fiarse de la palabra de alguien⟩ **6 words** *npl* QUARREL : palabra *f*, riña *f* ⟨to have words with : tener unas palabras con, reñir con⟩ **7 words** *npl* TEXT : letra *f* (de una canción, etc.) **8 from the word go** : desde el principio **9 to get a word in edgewise** : meter la cuchara **10 to have the last word** : tener/decir la última palabra **11 to put in a good word for someone** : recomendar a alguien **12 to put words into someone's mouth** : atribuirle a alguien algo que no dijo **13 to take the words out of someone's mouth** : quitarle las palabras de la boca a alguien **14 to waste words** : gastar saliva

wordiness ['wərdinəs] *n* : verbosidad *f*

wording ['wərdɪŋ] *n* : redacción *f*, lenguaje *m* (de un documento)

word processing *n* : procesamiento *m* de textos

word processor *n* : procesador *m* de textos

wordy ['wərdi] *adj* **wordier; -est** : verboso, prolijo

wore → **wear**¹

work¹ ['wərk] *v* **worked** ['wərkt] *or* **wrought** ['rɔt]; **working** *vi* **1** LABOR : trabajar ⟨to work hard : trabajar mucho/duro⟩ ⟨to work full-time : trabajar a tiempo completo⟩ ⟨to work part-time : trabajar a/de medio tiempo⟩ ⟨to work overtime : trabajar horas extras⟩ **2** FUNCTION : funcionar, servir **3 to work around** : esquivar (un problema, etc.) **4 to work at** : esforzarse para mejorar ⟨she's working at controlling her temper : está tratando de aprender a controlar su mal genio⟩ ⟨you'll have to work harder at it : tendrás que esforzarte más⟩ **5 to work loose** : soltarse, desprenderse **6 to work on** : trabajar en (un proyecto, etc.) ⟨to work on a cure : trabajar para encontrar una cura⟩ ⟨she's working on (controlling) her temper : está tratando de aprender a controlar su mal genio⟩ **7 to work out** TURN OUT : resultar, salir **8 to work out** SUCCEED : dar resultado, salir bien **9 to work out** EXERCISE : hacer ejercicio **10 to work up to** (*indicating a gradual increase*) ⟨to work up to full speed : ir cobrando velocidad poco a poco⟩ — *vt* **1** : trabajar ⟨to work long hours : trabajar muchas horas⟩ ⟨to work weekends : trabajar los fines de semana⟩ ⟨to work nights : trabajar de noche⟩ ⟨to work the night shift : hacer el turno de noche⟩ ⟨she works two jobs : tiene dos empleos⟩ **2** : trabajar, labrar (la tierra, etc.) **3** : hacer trabajar (a alguien) **4** OPERATE : trabajar, operar **5** : hacer/conseguir (etc.) con esfuerzo ⟨gradually work in the flour : incorpore la harina poco a poco⟩ ⟨to work one's way up : lograr subir por sus propios esfuerzos⟩ **6** EFFECT : efectuar, llevar a cabo, obrar (milagros) **7** MANIPULATE, SHAPE : trabajar, formar ⟨work the dough : trabaje la masa⟩ ⟨a beautifully wrought vase : un florero bellamente elaborado⟩ **8** HANDLE : manejar (a alguien) ⟨he knows how to work a crowd/room : sabe conquistar al público⟩ **9 to work off** : pagar trabajando **10 to work out** DEVELOP, PLAN : idear, planear, desarrollar **11 to work out** RESOLVE : solucionar, resolver ⟨to work out the answer : calcular la solución⟩ **12 to work over** : darle una paliza a **13 to work up** : estimular, excitar ⟨don't work yourself up : no te agites⟩ **14 to work up** PRODUCE : generar ⟨to work up the courage to : armarse de valor para⟩ ⟨to work up a sweat : empezar a sudar⟩

work² *adj* : laboral

work³ *n* **1** : trabajo *m* ⟨work to do : trabajo que hacer⟩ ⟨the quality of his work : la calidad de su trabajo⟩ ⟨to bring work home : llevar trabajo a casa⟩ **2** EMPLOYMENT : trabajo *m*, empleo *m* ⟨out of work : desempleado⟩ ⟨line of work : profesión⟩ **3** : trabajo *m* (lugar) ⟨to go to work : ir a trabajar⟩ ⟨to leave work : salir del trabajo⟩ ⟨she's at work : está en el trabajo⟩ **4** EFFORT : trabajo *m* **5** DEED : obra *f*, labor *f* ⟨works of charity : obras de caridad⟩ **6** : obra *f* (de arte o literatura) ⟨works *fpl* (de arte o literatura)⟩ **7** : obras *fpl* ⟨road work : obras viales⟩ **8** → **workmanship 9 works** *npl* FACTORY : fábrica *f* **10 works** *npl* MECHANISM : mecanismo *m* **11 the works** EVERYTHING : absolutamente todo *m* **12 at ~** WORKING : trabajando **13 at ~** INVOLVED : en juego **14 in the works** : en trámite **15 it's all in a day's work** : es el pan nuestro de cada día **16 to have one's work cut out for one** : tener mucho trabajo por delante **17 to make short work of** : hacer rápidamente

workable ['wərkəbəl] *adj* **1** : explotable (dícese de una mina, etc.) **2** FEASIBLE : factible, realizable

workaday ['wərkə,dei] *adj* : ordinario, banal

workaholic [,wərkə'hɔlɪk] *n* : adicto *m*, -ta *f* al trabajo

workbench ['wərk,bentʃ] *n* : mesa *f* de trabajo

workday ['wərk,dei] *n* **1** : jornada *f* laboral **2** WEEKDAY : día *m* hábil, día *m* laborable

worked up *adj* : agitado ⟨to get (all) worked up : agitarse⟩

worker ['wərkər] *n* : trabajador *m*, -dora *f*; obrero *m*, -ra *f*

workforce ['wərk,fors] *n* **1** STAFF : mano *f* de obra **2** : fuerza *f* de trabajo, fuerza *f* laboral

working ['wərkɪŋ] *adj* **1** : que trabaja ⟨working mothers : madres que trabajan⟩ ⟨the working class : la clase obrera⟩ **2** : de trabajo ⟨working hours : horas de trabajo⟩ **3** FUNCTIONING : que funciona, operativo **4** SUFFICIENT : suficiente ⟨working majority : una mayoría suficiente⟩ ⟨working knowledge : conocimientos básicos⟩

working–class ['wərkɪŋ'klæs] *adj* : obrero

workingman ['wərkɪŋ,mæn] *n, pl* **-men** [-mən, -,mɛn] : obrero *m*

workload ['wərk,lo:d] *n* : cantidad *f* de trabajo

workman ['wərkmən] *n, pl* **-men** [-mən, -,mɛn] **1 → workingman 2** ARTISAN : artesano *m*

workmanlike ['wərkmən,laik] *adj* : bien hecho, competente

workmanship ['wərkmən,ʃɪp] *n* **1** WORK : ejecución *f*, trabajo *m* **2** CRAFTSMANSHIP : artesanía *f*, destreza *f*

workout ['wərk,aut] *n* : ejercicios *mpl* físicos, entrenamiento *m*

workplace ['wərk,ples] *n* : lugar *m* de trabajo

workroom ['wərk,ru:m, -,rum] *n* : taller *m*

worksheet ['wərk,ʃi:t] *n* **1** : hoja *f* de ejercicios **2** : hoja *f* de cálculo (de impuestos, etc.)

workshop ['wərk,ʃap] *n* : taller *m* ⟨ceramics workshop : taller de cerámica⟩

workstation ['wərk,steɪʃən] *n* : estación *f* de trabajo (en informática)

world¹ ['wərld] *adj* : mundial, del mundo ⟨world championship : campeonato mundial⟩

world² *n* **1** : mundo *m* ⟨around the world : alrededor del mundo⟩ **2** : mundo *m* ⟨the industrialized world : el mundo industrializado⟩ **3** SOCIETY : mundo *m* ⟨the real world : la realidad⟩ **4** PEOPLE : mundo *m*, gente *f* ⟨to watch the world go by : ver pasar a la gente⟩ **5** REALM : mundo *m* ⟨the fashion world : el mundo de la moda⟩ **6** LIFE : mundo *m*, vida *f* ⟨his world fell apart : su mundo se derrumbó⟩ **7** PLANET : mundo *m*, planeta *f* **8 the world** EVERYTHING : todo *m* ⟨to mean the world to someone : ser todo para alguien⟩ **9 a world of** ⟨a world of difference : una diferencia enorme⟩ ⟨it'll do you a world of good : te hará la mar de bien⟩ **10 for all the world** *fam* EXACTLY : exactamente **11 (not) for the world** *fam* : por nada del mundo **12 in one's own world** *or* **in a world of one's own** *fam* : en su mundo **13 in the world** *fam* : del mundo ⟨the best in the world : el mejor del mundo⟩ ⟨what in the world . . .? : ¿qué diablos/demonios . . .?⟩ **14 out of this world** *fam* : increíble, fantástico **15 the (whole) world over** *fam* : por/en/de todo el mundo **16 to have all the time in the world** : tener todo el tiempo del mundo **17 to come/move up in the world** : prosperar, tener éxito **18 to think the world of someone** *fam* : tener a alguien en alta estima

world–famous *adj* : mundialmente famoso, de fama mundial

worldly ['wərldli] *adj* **worldlier; -est 1** : mundano ⟨worldly goods : bienes materiales⟩ **2** SOPHISTICATED : sofisticado, de mundo

worldwide¹ ['wərld'waid] *adv* : mundialmente, en todo el mundo

worldwide² *adj* : global, mundial

World Wide Web *n* : World Wide Web *f*, Red *f* (informática) mundial

worm¹ ['wərm] *vi* CRAWL : arrastrarse, deslizarse (como gusano) — *vt* **1** : desparasitar (un animal) **2 to worm one's way into** : introducirse en ⟨he wormed his way into her confidence : se ganó su confianza⟩ **3 to worm something out of someone** : sonsacarle algo a alguien

worm² *n* **1** : gusano *m*, lombriz *f* **2 worms** *npl* : lombrices *fpl* (parásitos)

worm–eaten ['wərm,i:tən] *adj* : carcomido

wormy ['wərmi] *adj* **wormier; -est** : infestado de gusanos

worn *pp → wear¹*

worn–out ['worn'aut] *adj* **1** USED : gastado, desgastado **2** TIRED : agotado

worried ['wərid] *adj* : inquieto, preocupado

worrier ['wəriər] *n* : persona *f* que se preocupa mucho

worrisome ['wərisəm] *adj* **1** DISTURBING : preocupante, inquietante **2** : que se preocupa mucho (dícese de una persona)

worry¹ ['wəri] *v* **-ried; -rying** *vt* : preocupar, inquietar — *vi* : preocuparse, inquietarse, angustiarse

worry² *n, pl* **-ries** : preocupación *f*, inquietud *f*, angustia *f*

worrying ['wəriɪŋ] *adj* DISTURBING : preocupante, inquietante

worse¹ ['wərs] *adv* (*comparative of* **bad** *or of* **ill**) : peor

worse² *adj* (*comparative of* **bad** *or of* **ill**) : peor ⟨from bad to worse : de mal en peor⟩ ⟨to get worse : empeorar⟩ ⟨to feel worse : sentirse peor⟩

worse³ *n* : estado *m* peor ⟨to take a turn for the worse : ponerse peor⟩ ⟨so much the worse : tanto peor⟩

worsen ['wərsən] *vt* : empeorar — *vi* : empeorar(se)

worship¹ ['wərʃəp] *v* **-shiped** *or* **-shipped; -shiping** *or* **-shipping** *vt* : adorar, venerar ⟨to worship God : adorar a Dios⟩ — *vi* : practicar una religión

worship² *n* : adoración *f*, culto *m*

worshiper *or* **worshipper** ['wərʃəpər] *n* : devoto *m*, -ta *f*; adorador *m*, -dora *f*

worst¹ ['wərst] *vt* DEFEAT : derrotar

worst² *adv* (*superlative of* **ill** *or of* **bad** *or* **badly**) : peor ⟨the worst dressed of all : el peor vestido de todos⟩

worst³ *adj* (*superlative of* **bad** *or of* **ill**) : peor ⟨the worst movie : la peor película⟩

worst⁴ *n* **the worst** : lo peor, el/la peor ⟨the worst is over : ya ha pasado lo peor⟩ ⟨if worst comes to worst : en el peor de los casos⟩

worst–case *adj* **a/the worst-case scenario** : el peor de los casos

worsted ['wʊstəd, 'wərstəd] *n* : estambre *m*

worth¹ ['wərθ] *n* **1** : valor *m* (monetario) ⟨ten dollars' worth of gas : diez dólares de gasolina⟩ **2** MERIT : valor *m*, mérito *m*, valía *f* ⟨an employee of great worth : un empleado de gran valía⟩

worth² *prep* **to be worth** : valer ⟨her holdings are worth a fortune : sus propiedades valen una fortuna⟩ ⟨it's not worth it : no vale la pena⟩

worthiness ['wərðinəs] *n* : mérito *m*

worthless ['wərθləs] *adj* **1** : sin valor ⟨worthless trinkets : chucherías sin valor⟩ **2** USELESS : inútil

worthwhile [wərθ'hwaɪl] *adj* : que vale la pena

worthy ['wərði] *adj* **worthier; -est 1** : digno ⟨worthy of promotion : digno de un ascenso⟩ **2** COMMENDABLE : meritorio, encomiable

would ['wʊd] (*past of* **will**) **1** (*expressing preference, desire, or willingness*) ⟨I would rather go alone than with her : preferiría ir sola que con ella⟩ ⟨I would like to help : me gustaría ayudar⟩ ⟨he would do anything for her : haría cualquier cosa por ella⟩ **2** (*expressing intent*) ⟨those who would ban certain books : aquellos que prohibirían ciertos libros⟩ **3** (*expressing habitual action*) ⟨he would often take his kids to the park : solía llevar a sus hijos al parque⟩ **4** (*expressing possibility or contingency*) ⟨I would go if I had the money : iría yo si tuviera el dinero⟩ ⟨I would if I could : lo haría si pudiera⟩ **5** (*offering or requesting advice*) ⟨if I were you, I would do it : yo en tu lugar lo haría⟩ ⟨what would you do? : ¿qué harías tú?⟩ **6** (*expressing probability*) ⟨she would have won if she hadn't tripped : habría ganado si no hubiera tropezado⟩ **7** (*expressing a request*) ⟨would you kindly help me with this? : ¿tendría la bondad de ayudarme con esto?⟩ ⟨would you mind waiting? : ¿le importaría esperar?⟩

would–be ['wʊd'bi:] *adj* : potencial ⟨a would-be celebrity : un aspirante a celebridad⟩

wouldn't ['wʊdənt] (*contraction of* **would not**) → **would**

wound¹ ['wu:nd] *vt* : herir

wound² *n* : herida *f*

wound³ ['waʊnd] → **wind²**

wove, woven → **weave¹**

wow ['waʊ] *interj* (*expressing surprise or pleasure*) : ¡guau!, ¡híjole! *Mex*, ¡hala! *Spain*

wrangle¹ ['ræŋgəl] *vi* **-gled; -gling** : discutir, reñir ⟨to wrangle over : discutir por⟩

wrangle² *n* : riña *f*, disputa *f*

wrap¹ ['ræp] *v* **wrapped; wrapping** *vt* **1** COVER : envolver, cubrir ⟨to wrap a package : envolver un paquete⟩ ⟨wrapped in mystery : envuelto en misterio⟩ **2** ENCIRCLE : rodear, ceñir ⟨to wrap one's arms around someone : estrechar a alguien⟩ **3 to wrap up** FINISH : darle fin a (algo) — *vi* **1** COIL : envolverse, enroscarse **2 to wrap up** DRESS : abrigarse ⟨wrap up warmly : abrígate bien⟩

wrap² *n* **1** WRAPPER : envoltura *f* **2** : prenda *f* que envuelve (como un chal, una bata, etc.)

wrapper ['ræpər] *n* : envoltura *f*, envoltorio *m*

wrapping ['ræpɪŋ] *n* : envoltura *f*, envoltorio *m*

wrath ['ræθ] *n* : ira *f*, cólera *f*

wrathful ['ræθfəl] *adj* : iracundo

wreak ['ri:k] *vt* : infligir, causar ⟨to wreak havoc : crear caos, causar estragos⟩

wreath ['ri:θ] *n, pl* **wreaths** ['ri:ðz, 'ri:θs] : corona *f* (de flores, etc.)

wreathe ['ri:ð] *vt* **wreathed; wreathing 1** ADORN : coronar (de flores, etc.) **2** ENVELOP : envolver ⟨wreathed in mist : envuelto en niebla⟩

wreck¹ ['rɛk] *vt* : destruir, arruinar, estrellar (un automóvil), naufragar (un barco)

wreck² *n* **1** WRECKAGE : restos *mpl* (de un buque naufragado, un avión siniestrado, etc.) **2** RUIN : ruina *f*, desastre *m* ⟨this place is a wreck! : ¡este lugar está hecho un desastre!⟩ ⟨to be a nervous wreck : tener los nervios destrozados⟩

wreckage ['rɛkɪdʒ] *n* : restos *mpl* (de un buque naufragado, un avión siniestrado, etc.), ruinas *fpl* (de un edificio)

wrecker ['rɛkər] *n* TOW TRUCK : grúa *f*

wren ['rɛn] *n* : chochín *m*

wrench¹ ['rɛntʃ] *vt* **1** PULL : arrancar (de un tirón) **2** SPRAIN, TWIST : torcerse (un tobillo, un músculo, etc.)

wrench² *n* **1** TUG : tirón *m*, jalón *m* **2** SPRAIN : torcedura *f* **3** *or* **monkey wrench** : llave *f* inglesa

wrest ['rɛst] *vt* : arrancar

wrestle¹ ['rɛsəl] *v* **-tled; -tling** *vi* **1** : luchar, practicar la lucha (en deportes) **2** STRUGGLE : luchar ⟨to wrestle with a dilemma : lidiar con un dilema⟩ — *vt* : luchar contra

wrestle² *n* STRUGGLE : lucha *f*

wrestler ['rɛsələr] *n* : luchador *m*, -dora *f*

wrestling ['rɛsəlɪŋ] *n* : lucha *f*

wretch ['rɛtʃ] *n* : infeliz *mf*; desgraciado *m*, -da *f*

wretched ['rɛtʃəd] *adj* **1** MISERABLE, UNHAPPY : desdichado, afligido ⟨I feel wretched : me siento muy mal⟩ **2** UNFORTUNATE : miserable, desgraciado, lastimoso ⟨wretched weather : tiempo espantoso⟩ **3** INFERIOR : inferior, malo

wretchedly ['rɛtʃədli] *adv* : miserablemente, lamentablemente

wriggle ['rɪgəl] *vi* **-gled; -gling** : retorcerse, menearse

wring ['rɪŋ] *vt* **wrung** ['rʌŋ]; **wringing 1** *or* **to wring out** : escurrir, exprimir (el lavado) **2** EXTRACT : arrancar, sacar (por la fuerza) **3** TWIST : torcer, retorcer **4 to wring someone's heart** : partirle el corazón a alguien

wringer ['rɪŋər] *n* : escurridor *m*

wrinkle¹ ['rɪŋkəl] *v* **-kled; -kling** *vt* : arrugar — *vi* : arrugarse

wrinkle² *n* : arruga *f*

wrinkly ['rɪŋkəli] *adj* **wrinklier; -est** : arrugado

wrist ['rɪst] *n* **1** : muñeca *f* (en anatomía) **2** *or* **wristband** ['rɪst-ˌbænd] CUFF : puño *m*

wristwatch ['rɪst,wɑtʃ] *n* : reloj *m* de pulsera

writ ['rɪt] *n* : orden *f* (judicial)

write ['raɪt] *v* **wrote** ['roːt]; **written** ['rɪtən]; **writing** *vi* **1** : escribir **2 to write back** : contestar **3 to write in** : escribir — *vt* **1** : escribir **2 to write back** : contestar **3 to write down** : apuntar, anotar **4 to write in** INSERT : escribir, insertar **5 to write into** : incluir (en un contrato, etc.) **6 to write off** : declarar siniestro total (en contabilidad) **7 to write off** DEDUCT : deducir, descontar (de los impuestos) **8 to write off** : dar por perdido ⟨he wrote it off as a failure : lo consideró un fracaso⟩ **9 to write out** : escribir **10 to write out** : hacer ⟨un cheque, una factura⟩ **11 to write someone out of** : eliminar a alguien de (un testamento, etc.) **12 to write up** : redactar **13 to write up** REPORT : ponerle una multa a (un conductor), darle una carta de amonestación a (un empleado)

write–off ['raɪt,ɔf] *n* **1** : cancelación *f* (de una deuda) **2** : siniestro *m* total, pérdida *f* total

writer ['raɪt̬ər] *n* : escritor *m*, -tora *f*

writhe ['raɪð] *vi* **writhed; writhing** : retorcerse

writing ['raɪt̬ɪŋ] *n* **1** : escritura *f* **2** HANDWRITING : letra *f* **3 writings** *npl* WORKS : escritos *mpl*, obra *f*

writing paper *n* : papel *m* de carta

wrong¹ ['rɔŋ] *vt* **wronged; wronging** : ofender, ser injusto con

wrong² *adv* : mal, incorrectamente

wrong³ *adj* **wronger** ['rɔŋər]; **wrongest** ['rɔŋəst] **1** EVIL, SINFUL : malo, injusto,

inmoral ⟨it's wrong to lie : mentir está mal⟩ ⟨I've done nothing wrong : no he hecho nada malo⟩ **2** IMPROPER, UNSUITABLE : inadecuado, inapropiado, malo ⟨you're asking the wrong guy : no soy la persona indicada para responder⟩ **3** INCORRECT : malo, equivocado, incorrecto, erróneo ⟨a wrong answer : una mala respuesta, una respuesta equivocada⟩ ⟨I dialed the wrong number : me equivoqué de número (al marcar)⟩ ⟨the clock is wrong : el reloj anda mal⟩ **4 to be wrong** : equivocarse, estar equivocado ⟨I could be wrong : puede que esté equivocado⟩

wrong⁴ *n* **1** INJUSTICE : injusticia *f*, mal *m* **2** OFFENSE : ofensa *f*, agravio *m* (en derecho) **3 to be in the wrong** : haber hecho mal, estar equivocado

wrongdoer ['rɔŋ,duːər] *n* : malhechor *m*, -chora *f*

wrongdoing ['rɔŋ,duːɪŋ] *n* : fechoría *f*, maldad *f*

wrongful ['rɔŋfəl] *adj* **1** UNJUST : injusto **2** UNLAWFUL : ilegal

wrongly ['rɔŋli] *adv* **1** : injustamente **2** INCORRECTLY : erróneamente, incorrectamente

wrote → **write**

wrought ['rɔt] *adj* **1** SHAPED : formado, forjado ⟨wrought iron : hierro forjado⟩ **2** *or* **wrought up** : agitado, excitado

wrung → **wring**

wry ['raɪ] *adj* **wrier** ['raɪər]; **wriest** ['raɪəst] **1** TWISTED : torcido ⟨a wry neck : un cuello torcido⟩ **2** : irónico, sardónico (dícese del humor)

X

x¹ *n, pl* **x's** *or* **xs** ['ɛksəz] **1** : vigésima cuarta letra del alfabeto inglés **2** : incógnita *f* (en matemáticas)

x² ['ks] *vt* **x–ed** ['ɛkst]; **x–ing** *or* **x'ing** ['ɛksɪŋ] DELETE : tachar

xenon ['ziː,nɑn, 'zɛ-] *n* : xenón *m*

xenophobe ['zɛnə,foːb, 'ziː-] *n* : xenófobo *m*, -ba *f*

xenophobia [,zɛnə'foːbiə, ,ziː-] *n* : xenofobia *f*

xenophobic [,zɛnə'foːbɪk, ,ziː-] *adj* : xenófobo

xerox ['zɪr,ɑks] *vt* : xerografiar

Xerox ['zɪr,ɑks] *trademark* se usa para una fotocopiadora

Xmas ['krɪsməs] *n* : Navidad *f*

x–ray ['ɛks,reɪ] *vt* : radiografiar

X ray ['ɛks,reɪ] *n* **1** : rayo *m* X **2** : radiografía *f* (imagen)

xylophone ['zaɪlə,foːn] *n* : xilófono *m*

Y

y ['waɪ] *n, pl* **y's** *or* **ys** ['waɪz] : vigésima quinta letra del alfabeto inglés

yacht¹ ['jɑt] *vi* : navegar (a vela), ir en yate ⟨to go yachting : irse a navegar⟩

yacht² *n* : yate *m*

yak ['jæk] *n* : yac *m*

yam ['jæm] *n* **1** : ñame *m* **2** SWEET POTATO : batata *f*, boniato *m*

yang ['jæŋ, 'jɑŋ] *n* : yang *m* ⟨(the) yin and yang : el yin y el yang⟩

yank¹ ['jæŋk] *vt* : tirar de, jalar, darle un tirón a

yank² *n* : tirón *m*

Yankee ['jæŋki] *n* : yanqui *mf*

yap¹ ['jæp] *vi* **yapped; yapping 1** BARK, YELP : ladrar, gañir **2** CHATTER : cotorrear *fam*, parlotear *fam*

yap² *n* : ladrido *m*, gañido *m*
yard ['jɑrd] *n* **1** : yarda *f* (medida) **2** SPAR : verga *f* (de un barco) **3** COURTYARD : patio *m* **4** : jardín *m* (de una casa) **5** : depósito *m* (de mercancías, etc.)
yardage ['jɑrdɪdʒ] *n* : medida *f* en yardas
yardarm ['jɑrd,ɑrm] *n* : penol *m*
yardstick ['jɑrd,stɪk] *n* **1** : vara *f* **2** CRITERION : criterio *m*, norma *f*
yarn ['jɑrn] *n* **1** : hilado *m* **2** TALE : historia *f*, cuento *m* ⟨to spin a yarn : inventar una historia⟩
yawn¹ ['jɔn] *vi* **1** : bostezar **2** OPEN : abrirse
yawn² *n* : bostezo *m*
ye ['ji:] *pron* : vosotros, vosotras
yea¹ ['jeɪ] *adv* YES : sí
yea² *n* : voto *m* a favor
yeah ['jɛə, 'jæə] *adv fam* YES : sí ⟨are you coming? yeah : ¿vienes? sí⟩ ⟨oh, yeah? : ¿ah, sí?⟩ ⟨it's true! yeah, right : ¡es verdad! sí, claro⟩
year ['jɪr] *n* **1** : año *m* ⟨last year : el año pasado⟩ ⟨he's ten years old : tiene diez años⟩ **2** : curso *m*, año *m* (escolar) **3** **years** *npl* AGES : siglos *mpl*, años *mpl* ⟨I haven't seen them in years : hace siglos que no los veo⟩
yearbook ['jɪr,bʊk] *n* : anuario *m*
year–end ['jɪr'ɛnd] *adj* : de fin de año
yearling ['jɪrlɪŋ, 'jɜrlən] *n* : animal *m* menor de dos años
yearly¹ ['jɪrli] *adv* : cada año, anualmente
yearly² *adj* : anual
yearn ['jɜrn] *vi* : anhelar, ansiar
yearning ['jɜrnɪŋ] *n* : anhelo *m*
yeast ['ji:st] *n* : levadura *f*
yell¹ ['jɛl] *vi* : gritar, chillar — *vt* : gritar
yell² *n* : grito *m*, alarido *m* ⟨to let out a yell : dar un grito⟩
yellow¹ ['jɛlo] *vi* : ponerse amarillo, volverse amarillo
yellow² *adj* **1** : amarillo **2** COWARDLY : cobarde
yellow³ *n* : amarillo *m*
yellow fever *n* : fiebre *f* amarilla
yellowish ['jɛloɪʃ] *adj* : amarillento
yellow jacket *n* : avispa *f* (con rayas amarillas)
yelp¹ ['jɛlp] *vi* : dar un gañido (dícese de un animal), dar un grito (dícese de una persona)
yelp² *n* : gañido *m* (de un animal), grito *m* (de una persona)
yen ['jɛn] *n* **1** DESIRE : deseo *m*, ganas *fpl* **2** : yen *m* (moneda japonesa)
yeoman ['jo:mən] *n, pl* **-men** [-mən, -mɛn] : suboficial *m* de marina
yes¹ ['jɛs] *adv* : sí ⟨to say yes : decir que sí⟩
yes² *n* : sí *m*
yesterday¹ ['jɛstər,deɪ, -di] *adv* : ayer
yesterday² *n* **1** : ayer *m* **2 the day before yesterday** : anteayer
yesteryear ['jɛstər,jɪr] *n* **of** ~ : de antaño
yet¹ ['jɛt] *adv* **1** BESIDES, EVEN : aún ⟨yet more problems : más problemas aún⟩ ⟨yet again : otra vez⟩ **2** SO FAR : aún, todavía ⟨not yet : todavía no⟩ ⟨as yet : hasta ahora, todavía⟩ **3** : ya ⟨has he come yet? : ¿ya ha venido?⟩ **4** EVENTU-

ALLY : todavía, algún día **5** NEVERTHELESS : sin embargo
yet² *conj* : pero
yew ['ju:] *n* : tejo *m*
Yiddish ['jɪdɪʃ] *n* : yídish *m*
yield¹ ['ji:ld] *vt* **1** SURRENDER : ceder ⟨to yield the right of way : ceder el paso⟩ **2** PRODUCE : producir, dar, rendir (en finanzas) — *vi* **1** GIVE : ceder ⟨to yield under pressure : ceder por la presión⟩ **2** GIVE IN, SURRENDER : ceder, rendirse, entregarse
yield² *n* : rendimiento *m*, rédito *m* (en finanzas)
yin ['jɪn] *n* : yin *m* ⟨(the) yin and yang : el yin y el yang⟩
yodel¹ ['jo:dəl] *vi* **-deled** *or* **-delled; -deling** *or* **-delling** : cantar al estilo tirolés
yodel² *n* : canción *f* al estilo tirolés
yoga ['jo:gə] *n* : yoga *m*
yogurt ['jo:gərt] *n* : yogur *m*, yogurt *m*
yoke¹ ['jo:k] *vt* **yoked; yoking** : uncir (animales)
yoke² *n* **1** : yugo *m* (para uncir animales) ⟨the yoke of oppression : el yugo de la opresión⟩ **2** TEAM : yunta *f* (de bueyes)
yokel ['jo:kəl] *n* : palurdo *m*, -da *f*
yolk ['jo:k] *n* : yema *f* (de un huevo)
Yom Kippur [,jo:mkɪ'pʊr, ,jɑm-, -'kɪpər] *n* : el Día *m* del Perdón, Yom Kippur
yon ['jɑn] → **yonder**
yonder¹ ['jɑndər] *adv* : allá ⟨over yonder : allá lejos⟩
yonder² *adj* : aquel ⟨yonder hill : aquella colina⟩
yore ['jo:r] *n* **in days of yore** : antaño
you ['ju:] *pron* **1** (*used as subject — familiar*) : tú; vos *in some Latin American countries*; ustedes *pl*; vosotros, vosotras *pl Spain* **2** (*used as subject — formal*) : usted, ustedes *pl* **3** (*used as indirect object — familiar*) : te, les *pl* (se *before lo, la, los, las*), os *pl Spain* ⟨he told it to you : te lo contó⟩ ⟨I gave them to (all of, both of) you : se los di⟩ **4** (*used as indirect object — formal*) : lo *Spain sometimes* : le, la; los *Spain sometimes* : les, las *pl* **5** (*used after a preposition — familiar*) : ti; vos *in some Latin American countries*; ustedes *pl*; vosotros, vosotras *pl Spain* **6** (*used after a preposition — formal*) : usted, ustedes *pl* **7** (*used as an impersonal subject*) ⟨you never know : nunca se sabe⟩ ⟨you have to be aware : hay que ser consciente⟩ ⟨you mustn't do that : eso no se hace⟩ **8 with you** (*familiar*) : contigo; con ustedes *pl*; con vosotros, con vosotras *pl Spain* **9 with you** (*formal*) : con usted, con ustedes *pl*
you'd ['ju:d, 'jʊd] (*contraction of* **you had** *or* **you would**) → **have, would**
you'll ['ju:l, 'jʊl] (*contraction of* **you shall** *or* **you will**) → **shall, will**
young¹ ['jʌŋ] *adj* **younger** ['jʌŋɡər]; **youngest** [-ɡəst] **1** : joven, pequeño, menor ⟨young people : los jóvenes⟩ ⟨my younger brother : mi hermano menor⟩ ⟨she is the youngest : es la más pequeña⟩ **2** FRESH, NEW : tierno (dícese de las ver-

duras), joven (dícese del vino) **3** YOUTH-
FUL : joven, juvenil
young² *npl* : jóvenes *mfpl* (de los humanos), crías *fpl* (de los animales)
youngster [ˈjʌŋkstər] *n* **1** YOUTH : joven
mf **2** CHILD : chico *m*, -ca *f*; niño *m*, -ña
f
your [ˈjʊr, ˈjoːr, jər] *adj* **1** (*familiar singular*) : tu ⟨your cat : tu gato⟩ ⟨your books
: tus libros⟩ ⟨wash your hands : lávate
las manos⟩ **2** (*familiar plural*) : su, vuestro *Spain* ⟨your car : su coche, el coche
de ustedes⟩ **3** (*formal*) : su ⟨your houses
: sus casas⟩ **4** (*impersonal*) : el, la, los, las
⟨on your left : a la izquierda⟩
you're [ˈjʊr, ˈjoːr, jər, ˈjuːər] (*contraction
of* you are) → **be**
yours [ˈjʊrz, ˈjoːrz] *pron* **1** (*belonging to
one person — familiar*) : (el) tuyo, (la)
tuya, (los) tuyos, (las) tuyas ⟨those are
mine; yours are there : ésas son mías; las
tuyas están allí⟩ ⟨is this one yours?
: ¿éste es tuyo?⟩ **2** (*belonging to more
than one person — familiar*) : (el) suyo,
(la) suya, (los) suyos, (las) suyas; (el)
vuestro, (la) vuestra, (los) vuestros, (las)
vuestras *Spain* ⟨your house and yours
: nuestra casa y la suya⟩ **3** (*formal*) : (el)
suyo, (la) suya, (los) suyos, (las) suyas
yourself [jərˈsɛlf] *pron, pl* **yourselves**
[-ˈsɪvz] **1** (*used reflexively — familiar*)
: te, se *pl*, os *pl Spain* ⟨wash yourself

: lávate⟩ ⟨you dressed yourselves : se vistieron, os vestisteis⟩ **2** (*used reflexively
— formal*) : se ⟨did you hurt yourself?
: ¿se hizo daño?⟩ ⟨you've gotten yourselves dirty : se ensuciaron⟩ **3** (*used for
emphasis*) : tú mismo, tú misma; usted
mismo, usted misma; ustedes mismos,
ustedes mismas *pl*; vosotros mismos, vosotras mismas *pl Spain* ⟨you did it yourselves? : ¿lo hicieron ustedes mismos?,
¿lo hicieron por sí solos?⟩
youth [ˈjuːθ] *n, pl* **youths** [ˈjuːðz, ˈjuːθs]
1 : juventud *f* ⟨in her youth : en su ju-
ventud⟩ **2** BOY : joven *m* **3** : jóvenes
mfpl, juventud *f* ⟨the youth of our city
: los jóvenes de nuestra ciudad⟩
youthful [ˈjuːθfəl] *adj* **1** : de juventud **2**
YOUNG **3** JUVENILE : juvenil
youthfulness [ˈjuːθfəlnəs] *n* : juventud *f*
youth hostel → **hostel**
you've [ˈjuːv] (*contraction of* you have) →
have
yowl¹ [ˈjaʊl] *vi* : aullar
yowl² *n* : aullido *m*
yo-yo [ˈjoːˌjoː] *n, pl* **-yos** : yoyo *m*, yoyó *m*
yucca [ˈjʌkə] *n* : yuca *f*
Yugoslavian [ˌjuːɡoˈslɑviən] *n* : yugoslavo
m, -va *f* — **Yugoslavian** *adj*
yule [ˈjuːl] *n* CHRISTMAS : Navidad *f*
yuletide [ˈjuːlˌtaɪd] *n* : Navidades *fpl*
yuppie [ˈjʌpi] *n* : yuppy *mf*

Z

z [ˈziː] *n, pl* **z's** *or* **zs** : vigésima sexta letra
del alfabeto inglés
zany¹ [ˈzeɪni] *adj* **zanier; -est** : alocado,
disparatado
zany² *n, pl* **-nies** : bufón *m*, -fona *f*
zap¹ [ˈzæp] *vt* **zapped; zapping 1** ELIMI-
NATE : eliminar **2** : enviar o transportar
rápidamente — *vi* : ir rápidamente
zap² *n* **1** ZEST : sabor *m*, sazón *f* **2** BLAST
: golpe *m* fuerte
zeal [ˈziːl] *n* : fervor *m*, celo *m*, entusiasmo
m
zealot [ˈzɛlət] *n* : fanático *m*, -ca *f*
zealous [ˈzɛləs] *adj* : celoso — **zealously**
adv
zebra [ˈziːbrə] *n* : cebra *f*
zebu [ˈziːˌbuː, -ˌbjuː] *n* : cebú *m*
zenith [ˈziːnəθ] *n* **1** : cenit *m* (en astronomía) **2** PEAK : apogeo *m*, cenit *m* ⟨at
the zenith of his career : en el apogeo de
su carrera⟩
zeppelin [ˈzɛplən, -pəlɪn] *n* : zepelín *m*
zero¹ [ˈziːro, ˈzɪro] *vi* **to zero in on** : apuntar hacia, centrarse en (un problema,
etc.)
zero² *adj* : cero, nulo ⟨zero degrees : cero
grados⟩ ⟨zero opportunities : oportunidades nulas⟩
zero³ *n, pl* **-ros** : cero *m* ⟨below zero
: bajo cero⟩

zest [ˈzɛst] *n* **1** GUSTO : entusiasmo *m*,
brío *m* **2** FLAVOR : sabor *m*, sazón *f*
zestful [ˈzɛstfəl] *adj* : brioso
zesty [ˈzɛsti] *adj* **zestier; -est 1** FLAVOR-
FUL : sabroso, gustoso, picante **2** LIVELY
: brioso
zigzag¹ [ˈzɪɡˌzæɡ] *vi* **-zagged; -zagging**
: zigzaguear
zigzag² *adv & adj* : en zigzag
zigzag³ *n* : zigzag *m*
Zimbabwean [zɪmˈbɑbwiən, -bweɪ-] *n*
: zimbabuense *mf* — **Zimbabwean** *adj*
zinc [ˈzɪŋk] *n* : cinc *m*, zinc *m*
zing [ˈzɪŋ] *n* **1** HISS, HUM : zumbido *m*,
silbido *m* **2** ENERGY : brío *m*
zinnia [ˈzɪniə, ˈziː-, -njə] *n* : zinnia *f*
Zionism [ˈzaɪəˌnɪzəm] *n* : sionismo *m*
Zionist [ˈzaɪənɪst] *n* : sionista *mf*
zip¹ [ˈzɪp] *v* **zipped; zipping** *vt or* **to zip
up** : cerrar el cierre de — *vi* **1** SPEED
: pasarse volando ⟨the day zipped by : el
día se pasó volando⟩ **2** HISS, HUM : silbar, zumbar
zip² *n* **1** ZING : zumbido *m*, silbido *m* **2**
ENERGY : brío *m*
zip code *n* : código *m* postal
zipper [ˈzɪpər] *n* : cierre *m*, cremallera *f*,
zíper *m CA, Mex*
zippy [ˈzɪpi] *adj* **zippier; -est** : brioso
zit [ˈzɪt] *n* : grano *m*
zodiac [ˈzoːdiˌæk] *n* : zodíaco *m*

zombie ['zɑmbi] *n* : zombi *mf*, zombie *mf*
zone¹ ['zo:n] *vt* **zóned; zoning** **1** : dividir en zonas **2** DESIGNATE : declarar ⟨to zone for business : declarar como zona comercial⟩
zone² *n* : zona *f*
zoo ['zu:] *n, pl* **zoos** : zoológico *m*, zoo *m*
zoological [ˌzo:ə'lɑʤɪkəl, ˌzu:ə-] *adj* : zoológico
zoologist [zo'ɑləʤɪst, zu:-] *n* : zoólogo *m*, -ga *f*
zoology [zo'ɑləʤi, zu:-] *n* : zoología *f*

zoom¹ ['zu:m] *vi* **1** : zumbar, ir volando ⟨to zoom past : pasar volando⟩ **2** CLIMB : elevarse ⟨the plane zoomed up : el avión se elevó⟩
zoom² *n* **1** : zumbido *m* ⟨the zoom of an engine : el zumbido de un motor⟩ **2** : subida *f* vertical (de un avión, etc.) **3** *or* **zoom lens** : zoom *m*
zucchini [zu'ki:ni] *n, pl* **-ni** *or* **-nis** : calabacín *m*, calabacita *f Mex*
Zulu ['zu:lu:] *n* **1** : zulú *mf* **2** : zulú *m* (idioma) — **Zulu** *adj*
zygote ['zaɪˌgo:t] *n* : zigoto *m*, cigoto *m*

Common Spanish Abbreviations

SPANISH ABBREVIATION AND EXPANSION		ENGLISH EQUIVALENT	
abr.	abril	Apr.	April
a/c	a cargo de	c/o	care of
A.C., a.C.	antes de Cristo	BC	before Christ
a. de J.C.	antes de Jesucristo	BC	before Christ
admón.	administración	—	administration
a/f	a favor	—	in favor
ago.	agosto	Aug.	August
a.m.	ante meridiem (de la mañana)	a.m., AM	ante meridiem (before noon)
Apdo.	apartado (de correos)	—	P.O. box
aprox.	aproximadamente	approx.	approximately
Aptdo.	apartado (de correos)	—	P.O. box
Arq.	arquitecto	arch.	architect
A.T.	Antiguo Testamento	O.T.	Old Testament
atte.	atentamente	—	sincerely
atto., atta.	atento, atenta	—	kind, courteous
av., avda.	avenida	Ave.	Avenue
a/v.	a vista	—	on receipt
ayte.	ayudante	asst.	assistant
BID	Banco Interamericano de Desarrollo	IDB	Interamerican Development Bank
Bº., Bº	banco, barrio	—	Bank, District
blvar.	bulevar	Blvd.	Boulevard
BM	Banco Mundial	—	World Bank
br.	bulevar	Blvd.	Boulevard
c/, C/	calle	St.	Street
C	centígrado, Celsius	C	centigrade, Celsius
C.	compañía	Co.	Company
CA	corriente alterna	AC	alternating current
cap.	capítulo	ch., chap.	chapter
Cap.	capitán	Capt.	Captain
c/c	cuenta corriente	—	current account, checking account
c.c.	centímetros cúbicos	cc, cu. cm	cubic centimeters
CC	corriente continua	DC	direct current
c/d	con descuento	—	with discount
Cd.	ciudad	—	city
CE	Comunidad Europea	EC	European Community
CEE	Comunidad Económica Europea	EEC	European Economic Community
cf.	compárese	cf.	compare
cg.	centigramo	cg	centigram
CGT	Confederación General de Trabajadores *or* del Trabajo	—	confederation of workers, union

CI	coeficiente intelectual *or* de inteligencia	**IQ**	intelligence quotient
Cía.	compañía	**Co.**	Company
cm.	centímetro	**cm**	centimeter
Cmte.	comandante	**Cmdr.**	Commander
Cnel.	coronel	**Col.**	Colonel
col.	columna	**col.**	column
Col. *Mex*	colonia	—	residential area
Com.	comandante	**Cmdr.**	Commander
comp.	compárese	**comp.**	compare
Cor.	coronel	**Col.**	Colonel
C.P.	código postal	—	zip code
CSF, c.s.f.	coste, seguro y flete	**c.i.f.**	cost, insurance, and freight
cta.	cuenta	**ac., acct.**	account
cte.	corriente	**cur.**	current
CTI	centro de tratamiento intensivo *Uru*	**ICU**	intensive care unit
c/u	cada uno, cada una	**ea.**	each
CV	caballo de vapor	**hp**	horsepower
D.	don	—	—
Da., D.ª	doña	—	—
dB	decibel, decibelio	**dB**	decibel
d.C.	después de Cristo	**AD**	anno Domini (in the year of our Lord)
dcha.	derecha	—	right
d. de J.C.	después de Jesucristo	**AD**	anno Domini (in the year of our Lord)
dep.	departamento	**dept.**	department
DF, D.F.	Distrito Federal	—	Federal District
dic.	diciembre	**Dec.**	December
dir.	director, directora	**dir.**	director
dir.	dirección	—	direction, address
DNI	*Arg, Spain* documento nacional de identidad	—	national identity card
Dña.	doña	—	—
dom., do.	domingo	**Sun.**	Sunday
dpto.	departamento	**dept.**	department
Dr.	doctor	**Dr.**	Doctor
Dra.	doctora	**Dr.**	Doctor
DSL	línea de abonado digital	**DSL**	digital subscriber line
dto.	descuento	—	discount
E, E.	Este, este	**E**	East, east
Ed.	editorial	—	publishing house
Ed., ed.	edición	**Ed., ed.**	edition
edif.	edificio	**Bldg.**	building
edo.	estado	**st.**	state
EEUU, EE.UU.	Estados Unidos	**US, U.S.**	United States
ej.	ejemplo	**e.g.**	example
E.M.	esclerosis múltiple	**MS**	multiple sclerosis
ene.	enero	**Jan.**	January
etc.	etcétera	**etc.**	et cetera
ext.	extensión	**ext.**	extension

F	Fahrenheit	**F**	Fahrenheit
f.a.b.	franco a bordo	**f.o.b.**	free on board
FAQ	pregunta(s) frecuente(s)	**FAQ**	frequently asked question(s)
FC	ferrocarril	**RR**	railroad
feb.	febrero	**Feb.**	February
FF AA, FF.AA.	Fuerzas Armadas	—	armed forces
FMI	Fondo Monetario Internacional	**IMF**	International Monetary Fund
g.	gramo	**g., gm, gr.**	gram
G	(talla) grande	**L**	large
GMT	tiempo medio de Greenwich, hora del meridiano de Greenwich	**GMT**	Greenwich Mean Time
G.P.	giro postal	**M.O.**	money order
gr.	gramo	**g., gm, gr.**	gram
Gral.	general	**Gen.**	General
h.	hora	**hr.**	hour
Hno(s).	hermano(s)	**Bro(s).**	Brother(s)
I + D, I & D, I y D	investigación y desarrollo	**R & D**	research and development
i.e.	esto es, es decir	**i.e.**	that is
incl.	inclusive	**incl.**	inclusive, inclusively, including
Ing.	ingeniero, ingeniera	**eng.**	engineer
IPC	índice de precios al consumo	**CPI**	consumer price index
IVA	impuesto al valor agregado	**VAT**	value-added tax
izq.	izquierda	**l.**	left
JJ.OO., JJ OO	Juegos Olímpicos	—	Olympics, Olympic Games
Jr.	Júnior	**Jr., Jun.**	Junior
juev.	jueves	**Thu., Thur., Thurs.**	Thursday
jul.	julio	**Jul.**	July
jun.	junio	**Jun.**	June
kg.	kilogramo	**kg**	kilogram
km.	kilómetro	**km**	kilometer
km/h	kilómetros por hora	**kph**	kilometers per hour
kv, kV	kilovatio	**kw, kW**	kilowatt
l.	litro	**l, lit.**	liter
Lic.	licenciado, licenciada	—	—
Ltda.	limitada	**Ltd.**	Limited
lun.	lunes	**Mon.**	Monday
m	masculino	**m**	masculine
m	metro	**m**	meter
m	minuto	**m**	minute
M	mediano, (talla) mediana	**M**	medium
mar.	marzo	**Mar.**	March
mart.	martes	**Tue., Tues.**	Tuesday

	mexicano, México	**Mex.**	Mexican, Mexico
	miligramo	**mg**	milligram
	miércoles	**Wed.**	Wednesday
	minuto	**min.**	minute
	mililitro	**ml**	milliliter
	milímetro	**mm**	millimeter
, M.N.,	moneda nacional	—	national currency
.n., m/n			
.ons.	monseñor	**Msgr.**	Monsignor
/tra.	maestra	—	teacher
Mtro.	maestro	—	teacher
N, N.	Norte, norte	**N, no.**	North, north
NIP	número de identificación personal	**PIN**	personal identification number
n/	nuestro	—	our
N. de (la) R.	nota de (la) redacción	**Ed.**	editor's note
NE	nordeste	**NE**	northeast
NN.UU.	Naciones Unidas	**UN**	United Nations
n.º	número	**no.**	number
NO	noroeste	**NW**	northwest
nov.	noviembre	**Nov.**	November
N.T.	Nuevo Testamento	**N.T.**	New Testament
ntra., ntro.	nuestra, nuestro	—	our
NU	Naciones Unidas	**UN**	United Nations
núm.	número	**no.**	number
NY	Nueva York, New York	**NY**	New York
O, O.	Oeste, oeste	**W**	West, west
oct.	octubre	**Oct.**	October
OEA, O.E.A.	Organización de Estados Americanos	**OAS**	Organization of American States
OMS	Organización Mundial de la Salud	**WHO**	World Health Organization
ONG	organización no gubernamental	**NGO**	non-governmental organization
ONU	Organización de las Naciones Unidas	**UN**	United Nations
OTAN	Organización del Tratado del Atlántico Norte	**NATO**	North Atlantic Treaty Organization
p.	página	**p.**	page
P	(talla) pequeña	**S**	small
P, P.	padre	**Fr.**	Father
pág(s).	página(s)	**p(p)., pg(s).**	page(s)
Pat.	patente	**pat.**	patent
PBI	producto bruto interno	**GDP**	gross domestic product
PCL	pantalla de cristal líquido	**LCD**	liquid crystal display
P.D.	post data	**P.S.**	postscript
p. ej.	por ejemplo	**e.g.**	for example
PIB	producto interno bruto, producto interior bruto	**GDP**	gross domestic product

PIN	número de identificación personal	**PIN**	personal identification number
p.m.	post meridiem (de la tarde)	**p.m., PM**	post meridiem (afternoon)
PNB	Producto Nacional Bruto	**GNP**	gross national product
pº	paseo	**Ave.**	Avenue
p.p.	porte pagado	**ppd.**	postpaid
PP, p.p.	por poder, por poderes	**p.p.**	by proxy
PR	Puerto Rico	**PR**	Puerto Rico
prom.	promedio	**av., avg.**	average
pto.	punto	**pt.**	point
ptas., pts.	pesetas	—	
PYME	Pequeña y Mediana Empresa	—	Small to Medium-Sized Business
Pza.	Plaza	**Sq.**	Square
q.e.p.d.	que en paz descanse	**R.I.P.**	(may he/she) rest in peace
R, R/	remite	—	sender
RAE	Real Academia Española	—	—
R & B	rhythm and blues, rhythm y blues	**R & B**	rhythm and blues
RCP	reanimación cardiopulmonar, resucitación cardiopulmonar	**CPR**	cardiopulmonary resuscitation
Rdo., Rda.	reverendo, reverenda	**Rev.**	Reverend
ref., ref.ª	referencia	**ref.**	reference
Rep.	República	**Rep.**	Republic
r.p.m.	revoluciones por minuto	**rpm**	revolutions per minute
Rte.	remite, remitente	—	sender
s.	siglo	**c., cent.**	century
s/	su, sus	—	his, her, your, their
S, S.	Sur, sur	**S, so.**	South, south
S.	san, santo	**St.**	Saint
Sr.	Sénior	**Sr.**	Senior
S.A.	Sociedad Anónima	**Inc.**	Incorporated (company)
sáb.	sábado	**Sat.**	Saturday
s/c	su cuenta	—	your account
SE	sudeste, sureste	**SE**	southeast
seg.	segundo, segundos	**sec.**	second, seconds
sep., sept.	septiembre	**Sept.**	September
s.e.u.o.	salvo error u omisión	—	errors and omissions excepted
Sgto.	sargento	**Sgt.**	Sergeant
S.L.	Sociedad Limitada	**Ltd.**	Limited (corporation)
S.M.	Su Majestad	**HM**	His Majesty, Her Majesty
s/n	sin número	—	no (street) number
s.n.m.	sobre el nivel de mar	**a.s.l.**	above sea level
SO	sudoeste/suroeste	**SW**	southwest

	se ruega contestación	**R.S.V.P.**	please reply
	siguientes	—	the following ones
.S.	Su Santidad	**H.H.**	His Holiness
	santa	**St.**	Saint
	santo	**St.**	Saint
	tonelada	**t., tn.**	ton
l	tasa anual efectiva	**APR**	annual percentage rate
	también	—	also
l., Tel.	teléfono	**tel.**	telephone
Tm.	tonelada métrica	**MT**	metric ton
Tn.	tonelada	**t., tn.**	ton
trad.	traducido, traductor, traducción	**tr., trans., transl.**	translated, translator, translation
UCI	unidad de cuidados intensivos	**ICU**	intensive care unit
UE	Unión Europea	**EU**	European Union
Univ.	universidad	**Univ., U.**	University
Urb.	urbanización	—	residential area
UTI	unidad de terapia intensiva, unidad de tratamiento intensivo *Chile*	**ICU**	intensive care unit
v	versus	**v., vs.**	versus
v	verso	**v:, vs.**	verse
v.	véase	**viz.**	see
Vda.	viuda	—	widow
v.g., v.gr.	verbigracia	**e.g.**	for example
vier., viern.	viernes	**Fri.**	Friday
V.M.	Vuestra Majestad	—	Your Majesty
VºBº, V.ºB.º	visto bueno	—	OK, approved
vol, vol.	volumen	**vol.**	volume
vra., vro.	vuestra, vuestro	—	your
www	world wide web, red mundial	**www**	World Wide Web

Abreviaturas comunes en inglés

ABREVIATURA INGLESA Y EXPANSIÓN		EQUIVALENTE ESPAÑOL	
AAA	American Automobile Association	—	—
AC	alternating current	CA	corriente alterna
AC	air-conditioning	—	aire acondicionado
ac., acct.	account	cta.	cuenta
AD	anno Domini (in the year of our Lord)	d.C., d. de J.C.	después de Cristo, después de Jesucristo
AK	Alaska	—	Alaska
aka	also known as	—	alias
AL, Ala.	Alabama	—	Alabama
Alas.	Alaska	—	Alaska
a.m., AM	ante meridiem (before noon)	a.m.	ante meridiem (de la mañana)
Am., Amer.	America, American	—	América, americano
amt.	amount	—	cantidad
anon.	anonymous	—	anónimo
ans.	answer	—	respuesta
Apr.	April	abr.	abril
approx.	approximately	aprox.	aproximadamente
APR	annual percentage rate	TAE	tasa anual efectiva
AR	Arkansas	—	Arkansas
arch.	architect	Arq.	arquitecto
Ariz.	Arizona	—	Arizona
Ark.	Arkansas	—	Arkansas
a.s.l.	above sea level	s.n.m.	sobre el nivel de mar
asst.	assistant	ayte.	ayudante
atty.	attorney	—	abogado, -da
Aug.	August	ago.	agosto
av.	average	prom.	promedio
Ave.	Avenue	av., avda.	avenida
avg.	average	prom.	promedio
AZ	Arizona	—	Arizona
BA	Bachelor of Arts	Lic.	Licenciado, -da en Filosofía y Letras
BA	Bachelor of Arts (degree)	—	Licenciatura en Filosofía y Letras
BC	before Christ	a.C., A.C., a. de J.C.	antes de Cristo, antes de Jesucristo
BCE	before the Christian Era, before the Common Era	—	antes de la era cristiana, antes de la era común
bet.	between	—	entre
Bldg.	Building	edif.	edificio
Blvd.	Boulevard	blvar., br.	bulevar
Br., Brit.	Britain, British	—	Gran Bretaña, británico
Bro(s).	Brother(s)	Hno(s).	hermano(s)
BS	Bachelor of Science	Lic.	Licenciado, -da en Ciencias
BS	Bachelor of Science (degree)	—	Licenciatura en Ciencias
c	carat	—	quilate

c	cent	—	centavo
c	centimeter	**cm.**	centímetro
c	century	**s.**	siglo
c	cup	—	taza
C	Celsius, centigrade	**C**	Celsius, centígrado
CA, Cal., Calif.	California	—	California
Can., Canad.	Canada, Canadian	—	Canadá, canadiense
cap.	capital	—	capital
cap.	capital	—	mayúscula
Capt.	Captain	**Cap.**	capitán
cc	cubic centimeters	**c.c.**	centímetros cúbicos
cent.	century	**s.**	siglo
CEO	chief executive officer	—	presidente, -ta (de una corporación)
cf.	compare	**cf.**	compárese
cg	centigram	**cg.**	centigramo
ch., chap.	chapter	**cap.**	capítulo
CIA	Central Intelligence Agency	—	—
cm	centimeter	**cm.**	centímetro
Cmdr.	Commander	**Com., Cmte.**	comandante
Co.	Company	**C., Cía.**	compañía
co.	county	—	condado
CO	Colorado	—	Colorado
c/o	care of	**a/c**	a cargo de
COD	cash on delivery, collect on delivery	—	(pago) contra reembolso
col.	column	**col.**	columna
Col., Colo.	Colorado	—	Colorado
comp.	compare	**comp.**	compárese
Conn.	Connecticut	—	Connecticut
Corp.	Corporation	—	corporación
CPI	consumer price index	**IPC**	índice de precios al consumo
CPR	cardiopulmonary resuscitation	**RCP**	reanimación cardiopulmonar, resucitación cardiopulmonar
ct.	cent	—	centavo
CT	Connecticut	—	Connecticut
cu. cm	cubic centimeters	**c.c.**	centímetros cúbicos
D.A.	district attorney	—	fiscal (del distrito)
dB	decibel	**dB**	decibel, decibelio
DC	District of Columbia	—	—
DC	direct current	**CC**	corriente continua
DDS	Doctor of Dental Surgery	—	doctor de cirugía dental
DE	Delaware	—	Delaware
Dec.	December	**dic.**	diciembre
Del.	Delaware	—	Delaware
dir.	director	**dir.**	director, directora
dir.	direction	**dir.**	dirección
DJ	disc jockey	—	disc jockey
dept.	department	**dep., dpto.**	departamento
DMD	Doctor of Dental Medicine	—	doctor de medicina dental
doz.	dozen	—	docena
Dr.	Doctor	**Dr., Dra.**	doctor, doctora

DSL	digital subscriber line	**DSL**	línea de abonado digital
DST	daylight saving time	—	—
DVM	Doctor of Veterinary Medicine	—	doctor de medicina veterinaria
E	East, east	**E, E.**	Este, este
ea.	each	**c/u**	cada uno, cada una
EC	European Community	**CE**	Comunidad Europea
EEC	European Economic Community	**CEE**	Comunidad Económica Europea
Ed., ed.	edition	**Ed., ed.**	edición
e.g.	for example	**v.g., v.gr., p.ej.**	verbigracia, por ejemplo
enc., encl.	enclosure	—	anexo
EMT	emergency medical technician	—	técnico, -ca en urgencias médicas
Eng.	England, English	—	Inglaterra, inglés
esp.	especially	—	especialmente
ER	emergency room	—	sala de urgencia(s), sala de emergencia(s)
EST	eastern standard time	—	—
etc.	et cetera	**etc.**	etcétera
ETA	estimated time of arrival	—	hora aproximada de llegada
EU	European Union	**UE**	Unión Europea
ex.	example	**ej.**	ejemplo
ext.	extension	**ext.**	extensión
f	false	—	falso
f	female	**f**	femenino
F	Fahrenheit	**F**	Fahrenheit
FAQ	frequently asked question(s)	**FAQ**	pregunta(s) frecuente(s)
FBI	Federal Bureau of Investigation	—	—
Feb.	February	**feb.**	febrero
fem.	feminine	—	femenino
FL, Fla.	Florida	—	Florida
f.o.b.	free on board	**f.a.b.**	franco a bordo
Fr.	Father	**P, P.**	padre
Fri.	Friday	**vier., viern.**	viernes
ft.	feet, foot	—	pie(s)
FYI	for your information	—	para su información
g	gram	**g., gr.**	gramo
Ga., GA	Georgia	—	Georgia
gal.	gallon	—	galón
GDP	gross domestic product	**PBI, PIB**	producto bruto interno, producto interno bruto, producto interior bruto
Gen.	General	**Gral.**	general
GMT	Greenwich Mean Time	**GMT**	tiempo medio de Greenwich, hora del meridiano de Greenwich
GNP	gross national product	**PNB**	producto nacional bruto
gm	gram	**g., gr.**	gramo
Gov.	Governor	—	gobernador, -dora

govt.	government	—	gobierno
gr.	gram	g., gr.	gramo
H.H.	His Holiness	SS, S.S.	Su Santidad
HI	Hawaii	—	Hawai, Hawaii
hp	horsepower	CV	caballo de vapor
hr.	hour	h.	hora
HM	His Majesty, Her Majesty	S.M.	Su Majestad
HS	high school	—	colegio secundario
ht.	height	—	altura
Ia., IA	Iowa	—	Iowa
ICU	intensive care unit	UCI, UTI, CTI *Uru*	unidad de cuidados intensivos, unidad de terapia intensiva, unidad de tratamiento intensivo *Chile*, centro de tratamiento intensivo *Uru*
ID	Idaho	—	Idaho
i.e.	that is	i.e.	esto es, es decir
IL, Ill.	Illinois	—	Illinois
IMF	International Monetary Fund	FMI	Fondo Monetario Internacional
in.	inch	—	pulgada
IN	Indiana	—	Indiana
Inc.	Incorporated (company)	S.A.	sociedad anónima
incl.	inclusive, inclusively, including	incl.	inclusive
Ind.	Indian, Indiana	—	indio (americano), india (americana); Indiana
IRS	Internal Revenue Service	—	Servicio de Rentas Internas
IQ	intelligence quotient	CI	coeficiente intelectual *or* de inteligencia
Jan.	January	ene.	enero
Jul.	July	jul.	julio
Jun.	June	jun.	junio
Jr., Jun.	Junior	Jr.	Júnior
Kan., Kans.	Kansas	—	Kansas
kg	kilogram	kg.	kilogramo
km	kilometer	km.	kilómetro
kph	kilometers per hour	km/h	kilómetros por hora
KS	Kansas	—	Kansas
kw, kW	kilowatt	kv, kV	kilovatio
Ky., KY	Kentucky	—	Kentucky
l	liter	l.	litro
l.	left	izq.	izquierda
L	large	G	(talla) grande
La., LA	Louisiana	—	Luisiana, Louisiana
lb.	pound	—	libra
LCD	liquid crystal display	PCL	pantalla de cristal líquido
lit.	liter	l.	litro
LOL	laugh out loud, laughing out loud	—	reírse a carcajadas, riendo a carcajadas
Ltd.	Limited (corporation)	S.L.	Sociedad Limitada
m	male	m	masculino
m	meter	m	metro
m	mile	—	milla

M	medium	M	mediano, talla med
MA	Massachusetts	—	Massachusetts
Maj.	Major	—	mayor
Mar.	March	mar.	marzo
masc.	masculine	—	masculino
Mass.	Massachusetts	—	Massachusetts
Md., MD	Maryland	—	Maryland
M.D.	Doctor of Medicine	—	doctor de medicin:
Me., ME	Maine	—	Maine
Mex.	Mexico	Méx.	México
Mex.	Mexican	—	mexicano
mg	milligram	mg.	miligramo
mi.	mile	—	milla
MI, Mich.	Michigan	—	Michigan
min.	minute	min	minuto
Minn.	Minnesota	—	Minnesota
Miss.	Mississippi	—	Mississippi, Misisi]
ml	milliliter	ml.	mililitro
mm	millimeter	mm.	milímetro
MN	Minnesota	—	Minnesota
mo.	month	—	mes
M.O.	money order	G.P.	giro postal
Mo., MO	Missouri	—	Missouri
Mon.	Monday	lun.	lunes
Mont.	Montana	—	Montana
mpg	miles per gallon	—	millas por galón
mph	miles per hour	—	millas por hora
MS	Mississippi	—	Mississippi, Misisi]
MS	multiple sclerosis	E.M.	esclerosis múltiple
Msgr.	Monsignor	Mons.	monseñor
Mt.	Mount, Mountain	—	monte, montaña
MT	Montana	—	Montana
MT	Mountain Time	—	Hora de la(s) Montaña(s)
Mtn.	Mountain	—	montaña
N	North, north	N, N.	Norte, norte
NASA	National Aeronautics and Space Administration	—	—
NATO	North Atlantic Treaty Organization	OTAN	Organización del Tratado del Atlá Norte
NC	North Carolina	—	Carolina del Nort North Carolina
ND, N. Dak.	North Dakota	—	Dakota del Norte North Dakota
NE	northeast	NE	nordeste
NE, Neb., Nebr.	Nebraska	—	Nebraska
Nev.	Nevada	—	Nevada
NGO	non-governmental organization	ONG	organización no gubernamental
NH	New Hampshire	—	Nueva Hampshir Nuevo Hampshi New Hampshire
NJ	New Jersey	—	Nueva Jersey, Ne Jersey
NM., N. Mex.	New Mexico	—	Nuevo México, N Mexico
no.	north	N, N.	norte
no.	number	n.°	número

November	**nov.**	noviembre
New Testament	**N.T.**	Nuevo Testamento
Nevada	—	Nevada
northwest	**NO**	noroeste
New York	**NY**	Nueva York, New York
Ohio	—	Ohio
Organization of American States	**OEA, O.E.A.**	Organización de Estados Americanos
October	**oct.**	octubre
Ohio	—	Ohio
Oklahoma	—	Oklahoma
Oregon	—	Oregon
Old Testament	**A.T.**	Antiguo Testamento
ounce, ounces	—	onza, onzas
page	**p., pág.**	página
Pennsylvania	—	Pennsylvania, Pensilvania
patent	**pat.**	patente
police department	—	departamento de policía
physical education	—	educación física
Pennsylvania	—	Pennsylvania, Pensilvania
page	**pág., p.**	página
pages	**págs.**	páginas
Doctor of Philosophy	—	doctor, -tora (en filosofía)
personal identification number	**PIN, NIP**	número de identificación personal
package	—	paquete
post meridiem (after noon)	**p.m.**	post meridiem (de la tarde)
post office	—	oficina de correos, correo
pages	**págs.**	páginas
by proxy	**PP, p.p.**	por poder, por poderes
postpaid	**p.p.**	porte pagado
Puerto Rico	**PR**	Puerto Rico
present	—	presente
president	—	presidente, -ta
professor	—	profesor, -sora
postscript	**P.D.**	postdata
public school	—	escuela pública
pint	—	pinta
point	**pto.**	punto
part-time, physical therapist, physical therapy	—	(de) medio tiempo, fisioterapeuta, fisioterapia
Parent-Teacher Association	—	—
Parent-Teacher Organization	—	—
quart	—	cuarto de galón
right	**dcha.**	derecha
rhythm and blues	**R & B**	rhythm and blues, rhythm y blues
research and development	**I + D, I & D, I y D**	investigación y desarrollo

R & R	rest and recreation, rest and recuperation, rest and relaxation	—	descanso y recreo, descanso y recuperación, descanso y relajación
rd.	road	c/, C/	calle
RDA	recommended daily allowance	—	consumo diario recomendado
recd.	received	—	recibido
ref.	reference	ref., ref. a	referencia
Rep.	Republic	Rep.	República
Rev.	Reverend	Rdo., Rda.	reverendo, reverenda
RI	Rhode Island	—	Rhode Island
R.I.P.	(may he/she) rest in peace	q.e.p.d.	que en paz descanse
rpm	revolutions per minute	r.p.m.	revoluciones por minuto
RR	railroad	FC	ferrocarril
R.S.V.P.	please reply (répondez s'il vous plaît)	S.R.C.	se ruega contestación
rt.	right	dcha.	derecha
Rte.	Route	—	ruta
S	small	P	(talla) pequeña
S	South, south	S, S.	Sur, sur
S.A.	South America	—	Sudamérica, América del Sur
Sat.	Saturday	sáb.	sábado
SC	South Carolina	—	Carolina del Sur, South Carolina
SD, S. Dak.	South Dakota	—	Dakota del Sur, South Dakota
SE	southeast	SE	sudeste, sureste
sec.	second, seconds	seg.	segundo, segundos
Sept.	September	sep., sept.	septiembre
Sgt.	Sergeant	Sgto.	sargento
so.	south	S, S.	sur
sq.	square	—	cuadrado
Sq.	Square	Pza.	Plaza
Sr.	Senior	Sr.	Sénior
Sr.	Sister (in religion)	—	sor
st.	state	—	estado
St.	Street	c/, C/	calle
St.	Saint	S.; Sto., Sta.	santo, santa
Sun.	Sunday	dom., do.	domingo
SW	southwest	SO	sudoeste, suroeste
t.	teaspoon	—	cucharadita
t.	ton	t, t.	tonelada
T, tb., tbsp.	tablespoon	—	cucharada (grande)
tel.	telephone	tel., Tel.	teléfono
Tenn.	Tennessee	—	Tennessee
Tex.	Texas	—	Texas
Thu., Thur., Thurs.	Thursday	juev.	jueves
TM	trademark	—	marca (de un producto)
tn.	ton	t, t.	tonelada
TN	Tennessee	—	Tennessee
tr., trans., transl.	translated, translator, translation	trad.	traducido, traductor, traducción

tsp.	teaspoon	—	cucharadita
Tue., Tues.	Tuesday	**mart.**	martes
TX	Texas	—	Texas
U.	University	**Univ.**	universidad
UN	United Nations	**NU,**	Naciones Unidas
		NN.UU.	
Univ.	University	**Univ.**	universidad
US	United States	**EEUU,**	Estados Unidos
		EE.UU.	
USA	United States of	**EEUU,**	Estados Unidos de
	America	**EE.UU.**	América
usu.	usually	—	usualmente
UT	Utah	—	Utah
v.	versus	**v**	versus
v.	verse	**v**	verso
Va., VA	Virginia	—	Virginia
VAT	value-added tax	**IVA**	impuesto al valor
			agregado
viz.	see	**v.**	véase
ver.	verse	**v**	verso
vol.	volume	**vol, vol.**	volumen
VP	vice president	—	vicepresidente, -ta
vs.	versus	**v**	versus
vs.	verse	**v**	verso
Vt., VT	Vermont	—	Vermont
W	West, west	**O, O.**	Oeste, oeste
WA, Wash.	Washington (state)	—	Washington
Wed.	Wednesday	**miérc.**	miércoles
WHO	World Health	**OMS**	Organización Mundial
	Organization		de la Salud
WI, Wis.,	Wisconsin	—	Wisconsin
Wisc.			
wt.	weight	—	peso
WV, W.	West Virginia	—	Virginia del Oeste,
Va.			West Virginia
www	World Wide Web	**www**	world wide web, red
			mundial
WY, Wyo.	Wyoming	—	Wyoming
yd.	yard	—	yarda
yr.	year	—	año

Spanish Numbers

Cardinal Numbers[1]

1	uno	28	veintiocho
2	dos	29	veintinueve
3	tres	30	treinta
4	cuatro	31	treinta y uno
5	cinco	40	cuarenta
6	seis	50	cincuenta
7	siete	60	sesenta
8	ocho	70	setenta
9	nueve	80	ochenta
10	diez	90	noventa
11	once	100	cien
12	doce	101	ciento uno
13	trece	200	doscientos
14	catorce	300	trescientos
15	quince	400	cuatrocientos
16	dieciséis	500	quinientos
17	diecisiete	600	seiscientos
18	dieciocho	700	setecientos
19	diecinueve	800	ochocientos
20	veinte	900	novecientos
21	veintiuno	1000	mil
22	veintidós	1001	mil uno
23	veintitrés	2000	dos mil
24	veinticuatro	100,000	cien mil
25	veinticinco	1,000,000	un millón
26	veintiséis	1,000,000,000	mil millones
27	veintisiete	1,000,000,000,000	un billón

[1]Most Spanish-speaking countries use either a decimal point (e.g., 38.25%) or a decimal comma (e.g., 38,25). In countries that use the decimal point, a different symbol (such as a comma, an apostrophe, or a space) is used as a thousands separator. Similarly, in countries where the decimal comma is preferred, a symbol other than a comma (such as a point, an apostrophe, or a space) is used to separate thousands.

Ordinal Numbers

1.º, 1.ª	primero, -ra[2]
2.º, 2.ª	segundo, -da
3.º, 3.ª	tercero, -ra[2]
4.º, 4.ª	cuarto, -ta
5.º, 5.ª	quinto, -ta
6.º, 6.ª	sexto, -ta
7.º, 7.ª	séptimo, -ma
8.º, 8.ª	octavo, -va
9.º, 9.ª	noveno, -na
10.º, 10.ª	décimo, -ma[3]
11.º, 11.ª	undécimo, -ma
12.º, 12.ª	duodécimo, -ma
13.º, 13.ª	decimotercero, -ra
14.º, 14.ª	decimocuarto, -ta
15.º, 15.ª	decimoquinto, -ta
16.º, 16.ª	decimosexto, -ta
17.º, 17.ª	decimoséptimo, -ma
18.º, 18.ª	decimoctavo, -va
19.º, 19.ª	decimonoveno, -na *or* decimonono, -na
20.º, 20.ª	vigésimo, -ma
21.º, 21.ª	vigésimoprimero, -ra[2]
30.º, 30.ª	trigésimo, -ma
40.º, 40.ª	cuadragésimo, -ma
50.º, 50.ª	quincuagésimo, -ma
60.º, 60.ª	sexagésimo, -ma
70.º, 70.ª	septuagésimo, -ma
80.º, 80.ª	octogésimo, -ma
90.º, 90.ª	nonagésimo, -ma
100.º, 100.ª	centésimo, -ma
1000.º, 1000.ª	milésimo, -ma
1,000,000.º, 1,000,000.ª	millonésimo, -ma
1,000,000,000.º, 1,000,000,000.ª	milmillonésimo, -ma

---

[2]The shortened forms of *primero* and *tercero* (which are *primer* and *tercer*, respectively) are abbreviated as *1.*er and *3.*er. Higher ordinals that end in these forms follow the same pattern (e.g., *vigésimoprimer → 21.*er).

[3]In informal Spanish speech and writing, higher ordinals are often replaced with their corresponding cardinal number: *el 35 aniversario de la compañía*, the company's 35th anniversary.

Números ingleses

Números cardinales

1	one	50	fifty
2	two	60	sixty
3	three	70	seventy
4	four	80	eighty
5	five	90	ninety
6	six	100	one hundred
7	seven	101	one hundred (and) one
8	eight	200	two hundred
9	nine	300	three hundred
10	ten	400	four hundred
11	eleven	500	five hundred
12	twelve	600	six hundred
13	thirteen	700	seven hundred
14	fourteen	800	eight hundred
15	fifteen	900	nine hundred
16	sixteen	1,000	one thousand
17	seventeen	1,001	one thousand (and) one
18	eighteen	2,000	two thousand
19	nineteen	10,000	ten thousand
20	twenty	100,000	one hundred thousand
21	twenty-one	1,000,000	one million
30	thirty	1,000,000,000	one billion
40	forty	1,000,000,000,000	one trillion

Números ordinales

1st	first	17th	seventeenth
2nd	second	18th	eighteenth
3rd	third	19th	nineteenth
4th	fourth	20th	twentieth
5th	fifth	21st	twenty-first
6th	sixth	30th	thirtieth
7th	seventh	40th	fortieth
8th	eighth	50th	fiftieth
9th	ninth	60th	sixtieth
10th	tenth	70th	seventieth
11th	eleventh	80th	eightieth
12th	twelfth	90th	ninetieth
13th	thirteenth	100th	hundredth
14th	fourteenth	1,000th	thousandth
15th	fifteenth	1,000,000th	millionth
16th	sixteenth	1,000,000,000th	billionth

Nations of the World
(Naciones del mundo)

Africa/África

Algeria	Argelia
Angola	Angola
Benin	Benin
Botswana	Botswana, Botsuana
Burkina Faso	Burkina Faso
Burundi	Burundi
Cameroon	Camerún
Cape Verde	Cabo Verde
Central African Republic	República Centroafricana
Chad	Chad
Comoros	Comores, Comoras
Congo, Democratic Republic of the	Congo, República Democrática del
Congo, Republic of the	Congo, República del
Djibouti	Yibuti, Djibouti
Egypt	Egipto
Equatorial Guinea	Guinea Ecuatorial
Eritrea	Eritrea
Ethiopia	Etiopía
Gabon	Gabón
Gambia	Gambia
Ghana	Ghana
Guinea	Guinea
Guinea-Bissau	Guinea-Bissau
Ivory Coast (Côte d'Ivoire)	Costa de Marfil
Kenya	Kenya, Kenia
Lesotho	Lesotho, Lesoto
Liberia	Liberia
Libya	Libia
Madagascar	Madagascar
Malawi	Malawi, Malaui
Mali	Malí
Mauritania	Mauritania
Mauritius	Mauricio
Morocco	Marruecos
Mozambique	Mozambique
Namibia	Namibia
Niger	Níger
Nigeria	Nigeria
Rwanda	Ruanda
São Tomé and Principe	Santo Tomé y Príncipe
Senegal	Senegal

Seychelles	Seychelles
Sierra Leone	Sierra Leona
Somalia	Somalia
South Africa, Republic of	Sudáfrica, República de
South Sudan	Sudán del Sur
Sudan	Sudán
Swaziland	Swazilandia, Suazilandia
Tanzania	Tanzania, Tanzanía
Togo	Togo
Tunisia	Túnez
Uganda	Uganda
Zambia	Zambia
Zimbabwe	Zimbabwe, Zimbabue

Antarctica/Antártida

No independent countries

Asia/Asia

Afghanistan	Afganistán
Armenia	Armenia
Azerbaijan	Azerbaiyán, Azerbaiján
Bahrain	Bahrein
Bangladesh	Bangladesh
Bhutan	Bután, Bhután
Brunei	Brunei
Cambodia	Camboya
China	China
East Timor (Timor-Leste)	Timor Oriental
Georgia	Georgia
India	India
Indonesia	Indonesia
Iran	Irán
Iraq	Iraq, Irak
Israel	Israel
Japan	Japón
Jordan	Jordania
Kazakhstan	Kazajistán, Kazajstán
Korea, North	Corea del Norte
Korea, South	Corea del Sur
Kuwait	Kuwait
Kyrgyzstan	Kirguizistán, Kirguistán
Laos	Laos
Lebanon	Líbano
Malaysia	Malasia
Maldives	Maldivas
Mongolia	Mongolia
Myanmar (Burma)	Myanmar (Birmania)
Nepal	Nepal
Oman	Omán

Pakistan	Pakistán, Paquistán
Philippines	Filipinas
Qatar	Qatar
Saudi Arabia	Arabia Saudí, Arabia Saudita
Singapore	Singapur
Sri Lanka	Sri Lanka
Syria	Siria
Taiwan	Taiwán, Taiwan
Tajikistan	Tayikistán
Thailand	Tailandia
Turkey	Turquía
Turkmenistan	Turkmenistán
United Arab Emirates	Emiratos Árabes Unidos
Uzbekistan	Uzbekistán
Vietnam	Vietnam
Yemen	Yemen

Europe/Europa

Albania	Albania
Andorra	Andorra
Austria	Austria
Belarus	Belarús
Belgium	Bélgica
Bosnia and Herzegovina	Bosnia-Herzegovina
Bulgaria	Bulgaria
Croatia	Croacia
Cyprus	Chipre
Czech Republic	República Checa
Denmark	Dinamarca
Estonia	Estonia
Finland	Finlandia
France	Francia
Germany	Alemania
Greece	Grecia
Hungary	Hungría
Iceland	Islandia
Ireland	Irlanda
Italy	Italia
Kosovo	Kosovo
Latvia	Letonia
Liechtenstein	Liechtenstein
Lithuania	Lituania
Luxembourg	Luxemburgo
Macedonia	Macedonia
Malta	Malta
Moldova	Moldova
Monaco	Mónaco
Montenegro	Montenegro

Netherlands	Países Bajos
Norway	Noruega
Poland	Polonia
Portugal	Portugal
Romania	Rumanía, Rumania
Russia	Rusia
San Marino	San Marino
Serbia	Serbia
Slovakia	Eslovaquia
Slovenia	Eslovenia
Spain	España
Sweden	Suecia
Switzerland	Suiza
Ukraine	Ucrania
United Kingdom	Reino Unido
Vatican City	Ciudad del Vaticano

North America/Norteamérica

Antigua and Barbuda	Antigua y Barbuda
Bahamas	Bahamas
Barbados	Barbados
Belize	Belice
Canada	Canadá
Costa Rica	Costa Rica
Cuba	Cuba
Dominica	Dominica
Dominican Republic	República Dominicana
El Salvador	El Salvador
Grenada	Granada
Guatemala	Guatemala
Haiti	Haití
Honduras	Honduras
Jamaica	Jamaica
Mexico	México, Méjico
Nicaragua	Nicaragua
Panama	Panamá
Saint Kitts and Nevis	San Cristóbal y Nieves, Saint Kitts y Nevis
Saint Lucia	Santa Lucía
Saint Vincent and the Grenadines	San Vicente y las Granadinas
Trinidad and Tobago	Trinidad y Tobago
United States of America	Estados Unidos de América

Oceania/Oceanía

Australia	Australia
Fiji	Fiji, Fiyi

Kiribati	Kiribati
Marshall Islands	Islas Marshall
Micronesia, Federated States of	Estados Federados de Micronesia
Nauru	Nauru
New Zealand	Nueva Zelanda, Nueva Zelandia
Palau	Palaos
Papua New Guinea	Papúa Nueva Guinea, Papua Nueva Guinea
Samoa	Samoa
Solomon Islands	Islas Salomón
Tonga	Tonga
Tuvalu	Tuvalu
Vanuatu	Vanuatu

South America/Sudamérica

Argentina	Argentina
Bolivia	Bolivia
Brazil	Brasil
Chile	Chile
Colombia	Colombia
Ecuador	Ecuador
Guyana	Guyana
Paraguay	Paraguay
Peru	Perú
Suriname	Surinam
Uruguay	Uruguay
Venezuela	Venezuela

Metric System : Conversions
(Sistema métrico : conversiones)

Length

unit	number of meters	approximate U.S. equivalents	
millimeter	0.001	0.039	inch
centimeter	0.01	0.39	inch
meter	1	39.37	inches
kilometer	1,000	0.62	mile

Longitud

unidad	número de metros	equivalentes aproximados de los EEUU	
milímetro	0.001	0.039	pulgada
centímetro	0.01	0.39	pulgada
metro	1	39.37	pulgadas
kilómetro	1000	0.62	milla

Area

unit	number of square meters	approximate U.S. equivalents	
square centimeter	0.0001	0.155	square inch
square meter	1	10.764	square feet
hectare	10,000	2.47	acres
square kilometer	1,000,000	0.3861	square mile

Superficie

unidad	número de metros cuadrados	equivalentes aproximados de los EEUU	
centímetro cuadrado	0.0001	0.155	pulgada cuadrada
metro cuadrado	1	10.764	pies cuadrados
hectárea	10 000	2.47	acres
kilómetro cuadrado	1 000 000	0.3861	milla cuadrada

Volume

unit	number of cubic meters	approximate U.S. equivalents	
cubic centimeter	0.000001	0.061	cubic inch
cubic meter	1	1.307	cubic yards

Volumen

unidad	número de metros cúbicos	equivalentes aproximados de los EEUU	
centímetro cúbico	0.000001	0.061	pulgada cúbica
metro cúbico	1	1.307	yardas cúbicas

Capacity

unit	number of liters	approximate U.S. equivalents		
		CUBIC	DRY	LIQUID
liter	1	61.02 cubic inches	0.908 quart	1.057 quarts

Capacidad

unidad	número de litros	equivalentes aproximados de los EEUU		
		CÚBICO	SECO	LÍQUIDO
litro	1	61.02 pulgadas cúbicas	0.908 cuarto de galón	1.057 cuartos de galón

Mass and Weight

unit	number of grams	approximate U.S. equivalents	
milligram	0.001	0.015	grain
centigram	0.01	0.154	grain
gram	1	0.035	ounce
kilogram	1,000	2.2046	pounds
metric ton	1,000,000	1.102	short tons

Masa y peso

unidad	número de gramos	equivalentes aproximados de los EEUU	
miligramo	0.001	0.015	grano
centigramo	0.01	0.154	grano
gramo	1	0.035	onza
kilogramo	1000	2.2046	libras
tonelada métrica	1 000 000	1.102	toneladas cortas